China

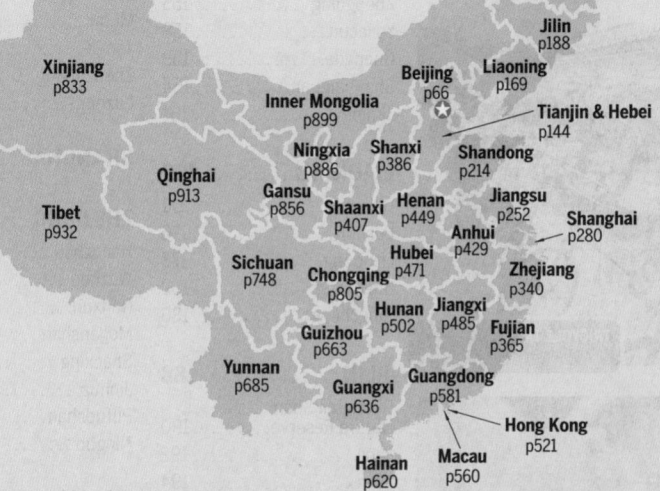

Heilongjiang
p199

Jilin
p188

Liaoning
p169

Beijing
p66

Tianjin & Hebei
p144

Xinjiang
p833

Inner Mongolia
p899

Ningxia
p886

Shanxi
p386

Shandong
p214

Qinghai
p913

Gansu
p856

Shaanxi
p407

Henan
p449

Jiangsu
p252

Shanghai
p280

Tibet
p932

Anhui
p429

Hubei
p471

Zhejiang
p340

Sichuan
p748

Chongqing
p805

Hunan
p502

Jiangxi
p485

Fujian
p365

Guizhou
p663

Yunnan
p685

Guangxi
p636

Guangdong
p581

Hong Kong
p521

Hainan
p620

Macau
p560

Damian Harper, Jade Bremner, Stuart Butler, Kate Chapman,
Piera Chen, Megan Eaves, Daisy Harper, Trent Holden, Tess
Humphrys, Stephen Lioy, Vesna Maric, Tom Masters, Bradley
Mayhew, Daniel McCrohan, Thomas O'Malley, Lorna Parkes,
Christopher Pitts, Tom Spurling, Phillip Tang

MARK READ/LONELY PLANET ©

TRICYCLE TAXIS

WANG SONG/SHUTTERSTOCK ©

STEAMED PORK DUMPLINGS P48

Contents

TERRACOTTA WARRIORS,
XI'AN P418

Contents

Right:
Tianzifang
(p297),
Shanghai

RALPH ROZEMA/SHUTTERSTOCK ©

WELCOME TO
China

 *A passion for Chinese martial arts saw me enrolling in a four-year degree in Chinese at university in London back in the 1990s. They were fun days, when travelling to China was testing but exciting in equal measure. Hotspots such as Pingyao were unheard of, and Shanghai's Pudong was a cocktail-free flatland. I could say it's the fantastic food, the awesome landscapes, the thrill of train travel, the delightful people or pitching up in a small town I've never been to before, and I wouldn't be lying. But it's the Chinese language I still love most of all.*

By Damian Harper, Writer

instagram @damian.harper

For more about our writers, see p1080

China

Karakoram Highway
The awe-inspiring road to Pakistan (p849)

Silk Road
Camels, deserts and vanished cities (p852)

Dunhuang
Silk Road oasis town (p877)

Jiuzhaigou National Park
Hiking in the beautiful wilds of Sìchuān (p798)

Mt Kailash
Deeply sacred mountain in west Tibet (p955)

Yushu
Adorable Tibetan town in high-up Qinghai (p927)

Tiger Leaping Gorge
Stunning Yunnan scenery (p722)

Longji Rice Terraces
Awe-inspiring views of layered rice fields (p642)

RUSSIA

KAZAKHSTAN

TASHKENT
BISHKEK
Yīníng
Ürümqi
KYRGYZSTAN
Kuqa
TAJIKISTAN
Kashgar
XĪNJIĀNG
PAKISTAN
Tashkurgan
Dūnhuáng
GĀNSŪ
Zhāngyè
Dégé
QĪNGHĂI
Qinghai Hu
Xīníng
Changtang Nature Preserve
Xiàhé
Mt Kailash (6714m)
Lake Manasarovar
TIBET
Siling-tso
Yushu
DELHI
Milam Glacier
Nam-tso
Ngui-chu
NEPAL
SÌCHUĀN
Mt Everest (8488m)
Lhasa
KATHMANDU
Thimphu Valley
THIMPHU
INDIA
BHUTAN
Zhōngdiàn (Shangri-la)
Shíbǎoshān
BANGLADESH
Xiàguān (Dàlì City)
Yangzi River
DHAKA
MYANMAR (BURMA)
Kūnmíng
YÚNNÁN
ELEVATION
NAY PYI TAW
Jìnghóng
Jìngzhēn
6000m
5000m
4000m
3000m
2000m
1000m
500m
0
20°N
THAILAND
LAOS
Bay of Bengal
85°E
90°E

MONGOLIA

RUSSIA

Yungang Caves
Breathtaking Buddhist statuary (p392)

Great Wall
Walking on the mother of all walls (p131)

Beijing's Hutong
Get lost down the capital's adorable lanes (p104)

Terracotta Warriors
Astonishing artistry from ancient China (p418)

Tai Shan
China's holiest Taoist mountain (p223)

Zhangjiajie
Spectacular sandstone panoramas (p510)

The Bund
Old-world meets new-world Shanghai (p281)

Huangshan
China's mountain of mists (p439)

Yangzi River Cruise
China's greatest river journey (p811)

Yangshuo
Gorgeous karst scenery (p645)

Hong Kong
Islands, hikes, dim sum (and a free press; p521)

Cycling Hainan
Wheel it around the tropical south (p627)

0 — 500 km
0 — 250 miles

N

Hēihé
Yīchūn
HĒILÓNGJIĀNG
Amur
45°N
140°E

Hǎilā'ěr
Buir Nuur
Qíqíhā'ěr

Hā'ěrbīn

Mǔdānjiāng

Chángchūn
Jílín
Yánjí
JÍLÍN
NORTH KOREA

ULAANBAATAR

Xilinhot

Sìpíng
Liáoyán

Shěnyáng
Ānshān

HÉBĚI
Jǐnzhōu
Dāndōng

Zhāngjiākǒu
Chéngdé
Qínhuángdǎo
PYONGYANG

Hohhot
Dàtóng
BĚIJĪNG
Tiānjīn
Dàlián
SEOUL
JAPAN

INNER MONGOLIA
Wūhǎi
SHĀNXĪ
Yāntái
SOUTH KOREA
35°N

Yínchuān
Tàiyuán
Shíjiāzhuāng
Jǐ'nán
Wéifāng
SHĀNDŌNG
125°E

Zhōngwèi
Píngyáo
Handan
Tài'ān
Qīngdǎo

NÍNGXIÀ
Chángzhì
Tài Shan (1532m)
Qūfù
Rìzhào

Lánzhōu
Hánchéng
Ānyáng
Jīning
Liányúngǎng

Bǎojī
Xī'ān
Yùnchéng
Kāifēng
Xúzhōu

Luòyáng
Zhèngzhōu

SHAANXI (SHÁNXĪ)
HÉNÁN
JIĀNGSŪ

Huáinán
Nánjīng
Wúxī
Shànghǎi

Nányáng
Héféi
Sūzhōu
30°N
130°E

Xiāngfán
ĀNHUĪ
Pǔtuóshān

HÚBĚI
Hángzhōu
Níngbō

Yíchāng
Wǔhàn
Jiǔjiāng
ZHÈJIĀNG
Wēnzhōu

Chéngdū
Zhāngjiājiè
EAST CHINA SEA

Lèshān
Chóngqìng
CHÓNGQÌNG
Changdé
Nánchāng

Fènghuáng
Chángshā
Píngxiāng
Nánpíng

Zūnyì
Píngxiāng
Jí'ān
Fúzhōu

GUÌZHŌU
Héngyáng
JIĀNGXĪ
TAIPEI

Guìyáng
HÚNÁN
FÚJIÀN

Ānshùn
Gànzhōu

Wēiníng
Guìlín
Zhāngzhōu
Xiàmén
TAIWAN

Liǔzhōu
Cháozhōu

GUǍNGDŌNG
Shàntóu

Wúzhōu
Guǎngzhōu

Chóngzuǒ
Nánníng
Hong Kong
SOUTH CHINA SEA

GUǍNGXĪ
Kāipíng
Macau
120°E

Zhànjiāng

HANOI
Zhànjiāng

Hǎikǒu

VIETNAM
HĂINÁN

China's Top Experiences

1 THE GREAT WALL

If there's one sight that exclusively belongs to China, it's the Great Wall. It may be most famously seen snaking into the hills outside Beijing, but get your hiking boots on and set your sights further afield to discover a trail of vestiges across the whole north of China, from the hardy Manchurian northeast to the Silk Road deserts of the northwest, and many points in between. p131

Above: The Great Wall at Badaling (p137)

ANDRIUS ALEKSANDRAVICIUS/GETTY IMAGES ©

Jiankou Great Wall

Beijing's most authentic section of Great Wall ruin is a sublime portrait of disintegrating brickwork and dilapidated watchtowers, overgrown with saplings and thrust into a splendid mountain panorama. p138

Right: Jiankou Great Wall

VIEW STOCK/GETTY IMAGES ©

STEFAN BRUDER/SHUTTERSTOCK ©

Jiayuguan Fort

With a stunning backdrop of snow-capped mountains, this mighty fortress stands firmly against the relentless desert winds of Gansu province, traditionally guarding the western entrance to China. Nearby relics of the Great Wall run to wind-scoured beacon platforms and Ming dynasty vestiges, slowly returning to the soil. p875

Above: Jiayuguan Fort

Tiger Mountain Great Wall

Climbing up a steep embankment by the Yalu River outside Dandong in Liaoning province, this length of superbly named Ming dynasty Great Wall is a top choice to flee the crowds, while putting you right on the border with North Korea. p178

Above: Tiger Moutain Great Wall

2 THE BIG OUTDOORS

You haven't really experienced China until you've had your socks well and truly blown off by one of its scenic marvels. This is a big, big country and the sheer landscape diversity can make it hard to know where to begin. So pick according to taste: there's everything from glistening rice terraces to emerald karst peaks, high-altitude glaciers or sand dunes taller than the Empire State Building.

Yangshuo

You've almost certainly seen Yangshuo's surreally beautiful karst peaks in dazzling magazine spreads – now see them with your own eyes. It's hard to exaggerate the beauty of these mossy-green limestone peaks: ride a bamboo raft along the river and grasp why this stunning landscape has inspired poets and painters for centuries. p645

Below: Karst peaks and the Li River around Guilin (p638), Yangshuo

WEERAPORN PUTTIWONGRAK/SHUTTERSTOCK ©

EASTFOOTAGE/SHUTTERSTOCK ©

APHOTOSTORY/SHUTTERSTOCK ©

Yuanyang Rice Terraces

Possessing an almost surreal allure and hewn from hills that range spectacularly off into the far beyond, these rice terraces are off-the-scale beautiful. Any time of the year will do, but winter sees the terraces flooded with water, catching the morning or late afternoon sun and turning the wow factor up high. p700 Above left: Yuanyang rice terraces

The Silk Road

The desertscapes and vanished Buddhist civilisations of northwest China lie along the Silk Road, where the land steadily merges with Central Asia. You may not be setting off on camelback from Xi'an, but some of China's most unmissable sights await, however you travel. p852 Above right: Dunhuang (p877), Gansu

3

DUMPLINGS, DUCK AND DIM SUM

With its unexpected flavours, ever-tempting aromas and endless surprises, China is a culinary adventure every time and in every sense. To help get you get your bearings: point your chopsticks west for zing, zest and spice, north for hearty, salty and more savoury tastes, east for fresh and ever-so lightly-seasoned seafood and due south for dim sum.Hey, they didn't film *Endless Summer II* here for nothing, dude.

Xiaolongbao

Shanghai's moreish bite-size snacks are quite simply once-bitten, for-ever smitten. They pack a serious amount of juicy flavour into small dimensions and serve as a meal in themselves, but be on the alert to jets of super-heated meat juice spurting all over the tablecloth. p55

Above left: Xiaolongbao

Chongqing Hotpot

Chongqing old-timers sit around town devouring this sweltering infusion in all weathers. For the nov-ice, hotpot is a volcanic wake-up call that requires gradual adjusting to. But once you have acquired the taste – and the cast-iron palate – there's no going back. p823

Top right: Chongqin hotpot

Peking Duck

You can Peking Duck up and down the land, but experts insist the best duck needs to be served within waddling distance of Beijing's Forbidden City, roasted in a brick oven with fruitwood and pre-pared with every attention to detail and maximisa-tion of flavour. p116

Above right: Peking Duck

4 RIVER & HARBOUR CRUISES

Getting waterborne gets you out of the fast lane to see China's panoramas unfurl in slow motion. It's a time to relax, ease into low gear and remind yourself of the slower sensations of travel, where getting from A to B is not as important as being somewhere right in between. Cruises range from the dazzlingly urban to jaw-dropping geological wonders.

Cruising up Victoria Harbour

It may be a brief voyage, but the cruise across Victoria Harbour permits unrivalled views of the steel and neon brilliance of Hong Kong's skyscrapers, set to a backdrop of hills. The Star Ferry has been transporting passengers from the Kowloon peninsula to Hong Kong island since the 19th century; for little more than a pittance, it's possibly the world's best value cruise. p534

Below: Star Ferry crossing Victoria Harbour

Yangzi River Cruise

Starting off as snowmelt way off in the Qinghai-Tibet plateau, the mighty Yangzi River – China's longest – goes through several name changes before it pours through the Three Gorges in between Chongqing and Yichang, themselves carved through the millennia by the river's inexorable flow. The gorges are a truly unique experience that should never be rushed. p811

Above left: Three Gorges, Yangzi River

Li River

Welcome to the hypnotising karst scenery of northeast Guangxi province, on a leisurely four-hour journey from Guilin to the beauty of the landscape around Yangshuo. p649

Above right: Cruise boat on the Li River

5 SACRED CHINA

From the esoteric mysteries of Tibetan Buddhism to the palpable magic of Taoist mountains and the harmonies of Confucian temples – not to forget the countless churches, mosques and shrines – China's sacred realm is where the supernatural and natural worlds converge. It's a domain of faith and mystery, where the stresses of modern life are replaced with worship and prayer.

Puning Temple, Chengde

Size up the colossal wooden effigy of the Goddess of Mercy in the Mahayana Hall, who dispenses limitless compassion upon the silent flow of worshippers at her outsize feet. p162
Top left: Puning Temple

Wudang Shan

A mountain infused with the spirits and legends of the Taoist martial arts, the birthplace of Taichi invites unhurried explorations of its mist-wreathed peaks, temples and vistas. p478
Above left: Wudang Shan

Labrang Monastery

Tap into the ineffable spiritual mystique of southern Gansu's primary place of pilgrimage for legions of Tibetans. Join them walking the kora or hike off into the hills and grasslands. p862
Above: Labrang Monastery

6 IMPERIAL GRANDEUR

Forbidden City

Home to two dynasties of emperors and their concubines, China's most imposing imperial residence sits at the heart of Beijing, a place of expansive courtyards, solemn halls and imposing magnificence. p70
Top left: Forbidden City

Summer Palace

An unbridled display of traditional Chinese aesthetics with all those crucial and charming ingredients: hills, bridges, pavilions and temples, with spectacular sunsets that turn the waters of Kunming Lake copper, gold and bronze. p99
Bottom left: Summer Palace

Xi'an City Walls

Most people are here for the Terracotta Warriors, but Xi'an's formidable Ming walls better define the city, making for a superb half-day out, either on foot, or on bicycle. p409

China's turbulent history is indivisible from the ascendency and inevitable decline of ancient dynasties – Mongolian, Manchurian and Han Chinese – which left an imposing trail of antiquity across the nation, from the breathtaking majesty of China's imperial palaces to the monumental architecture of its surviving city walls which rise up around some of the land's most notable former dynastic capitals

7 TRADITIONAL VILLAGE RHYTHMS

China isn't just gleaming skyscrapers and heaving flyovers, most of the land is a calm expanse of rural life. The tempo in China's ancient villages is as unhurried as the change of the seasons, which set the pace for a more relaxing take on the land. Traditional China can be found here too: in the architecture, the clothing, the dialects and of course, the food.

Xinye

Take yourself off to this gorgeous Zhejiang village to meditate on the rhythms of rural life. It's a charming place designed with an eye for traditional Chinese harmony, balance and aesthetics. p359
Below: Xinye

SILVIA CAMP/SHUTTERSTOCK ©

Pingyao
China's best-preserved walled town – by a long shot – has to be seen, especially come evening, when the red lanterns are hung out on the streets and alleys. p399
Above: Pingyao

Fujian Tulou
Each one a village in itself, the walled, fortress-like roundhouses of Fujian are an astonishing and imposing sight. Spend the night in one, to fully immerse yourself in their charms. p374
Right: Fujian Tulou

8 EXPLORE THE FARTHER REACHES

SILVIA CAMPI/SHUTTERSTOCK ©

TIAN YU MAO/EYEEM/GETTY IMAGES ©

ATOSAN/SHUTTERSTOCK ©

Head in the direction of the borderlands and a colourful patchwork of diverse cultures begins to appear, with distinctive languages, architecture, clothing, cuisine and customs. Pair this with the context of rural landscapes and local handicrafts and you've little reason to want to leave.

Shi Wei

Winter might be staggeringly cold at this village in Inner Mongolia (where the local Russians all grow up speaking Mandarin), but arrive in mid-summer for early sunup and horse-riding by the Russian border. p910

Tibet Borderlands

Central Tibet is hard to access, but the historic Tibetan provinces of Kham and Amdo are not, so consider exploring these regions (southwest Gansu, Qinghai, west Sichuan and north Yunnan provinces) instead, for Tibetan culture and heritage.
Above: Xiahe (p862), Gansu

Lijiang

Perhaps China's most famous community and rightly so, famed for its distinctive Naxi culture and outstanding scenery. If you needed it, it's yet another reason to come to Yunnan province. p714

9 URBAN EXTRAVAGANZA

Though Shanghai is most synonymous with cashed-up consumers thronging chic malls, fashionistas sipping drinks in snazzy cocktail bars and gastronomes joining the queue at the latest culinary sensation, this is a land that has urbanised at a dizzying rate across the board. Cityscapes are never far away in China and many are quite simply show-stopping.

DUKAI PHOTOGRAPHER/GETTY IMAGES ©

IAKOV KALININ/SHUTTERSTOCK ©

Beijing

China's capital and centre of political power is a riveting blend of ancient city and modern metropolis, with the delightful hutong and the imperial grandeur of the Forbidden City at its heart. p66
Top left: Beijing

Shanghai

Find out about the city that everyone – from architects to foodies, cocktail connoisseurs, urban travellers and interior designers – is talking about. p280
Above left: Shanghai

Hangzhou

One of China's most beautiful and relaxing urban settings, with the romantic West Lake – a serene vignette of willow-lined shores, pagodas, boats and scenic hills – pulling out all the stops. p342
Above: Hangzhou

10 HIKING INTO THE HILLS

Tiger Leaping Gorge

Yunnan province's best-known hike outside Lijiang is not for the faint-hearted, but it's an exciting, once-in-a-life-time journey into some of the most dramatic landscapes that China has to offer, alongside a major tributary of the Yangzi River. p722

Top left: Tiger Leaping Gorge

Ganden Kora

This stunning kora offers beautiful valley views, accompanied by unforgettable impressions of pilgrims and monks prostrating themselves and offering prayers at shrines along this sacred path in Tibet. p946

Bottom left: Ganden Kora

Langmusi

Tempting hikes radiate out in almost every direction from this charming monastic town straddling the Gansu-Sichuan border in the adventurous west of China. p869

Despite urban encroachment, it's never hard to hike away from it all. This is, after all, one of the world's largest nations with a huge topographical diversity that means there's always a hiking trail nearby, winding off into the valleys, climbing into the mountains or disappearing into forests of rippling bamboo.

PLAN YOUR TRIP

11 GROTTOES & CAVE SCULPTURE

China's Buddhist cave sculpture is a rich vein of cultural heritage that you cannot afford to miss. The artistry, technical skill, profound sacredness and sheer antiquity of each network of caves is jaw dropping, so give yourself enough time to do them justice.

Mogao Grottoes, Dunhuang

Dunhuang has a crop of fine sights – including colossal sand dunes and transfixing desertscapes – but the Mogao Caves are what all the fuss is about. The crème de la crème of China's astonishing Buddhist cave heritage, the statues here are ineffably sublime, entirely beautiful and worth the long trip to Dunhuang. p880
Below: Mogao Grottoes

MEIQIANBAO/SHUTTERSTOCK ©

Yungang Caves

The Yungang Caves house some of China's most astonishing statues, displaying pronounced artistic influences from as far away as Greece and Persia. p392
Above: Yungang Caves

Longmen Grottoes

A breath-taking display of Buddhist cave sculpture hewn from the limestone cliffs by the Yi River outside Luoyang in Henan province, dating from the late 5th century. p462
Right: Longmen Grottoes

12 CLIMATIC EXTREMES

SPACES IMAGES/GETTY IMAGES ©

JOONFEP/GETTY IMAGES ©

BULE SKY STUDIO/SHUTTERSTOCK ©

China has more than enough to satisfy thrill-seekers, crowd-avoiders or just the plain inquisitive. Whether you want to find yourself as far from the sea as is terrestrially possible or look up at the world's tallest mountain, China is a place of superlatives and extremes.

Everest Base Camp

Rise early for dramatic images onto the north face of the world's highest mountain in the morning sun. The nearby Rongphu Monastery is the highest in the world, making for dramatic images with the vast peak rising up in the background. p953
Above: Everest Base Camp

Turpan

China's hottest spot and the world's second lowest depression, where the thermostat has topped 48 degrees centigrade. Step from the air-conditioned chill of your taxi and feel the heat hit you like an express train. p841

Beihongcun

China's northernmost village is found in Heilongjiang province, where temperatures sink to unimaginable lows. The flipside is long summer days with only two hours of night, and the chance to see the northern lights. p213

Need to Know

For more information, see Survival Guide (p1011)

Currency
Yuán (元; ¥)

Language
Mandarin, Cantonese

Visas
While visas are needed for most visits to mainland China, visa-free transits of up to 144 hours are available in Beijing, Shanghai, Guangdong, Chengdu, Xi'an and other places.

Money
ATMs are plentiful in big cities and towns. Credit cards less widely used; always carry cash.

Mobile Phones
A mobile phone should be the first choice for calls, but ensure your mobile is unlocked for use in China if taking your own. SIM cards can be bought at the arrivals area at major airports.

Time
China Standard Time (GMT/UTC plus eight hours)

When to Go

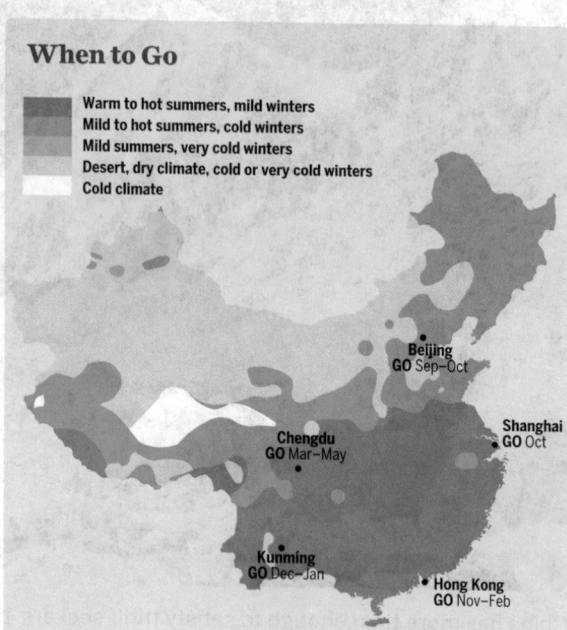

Warm to hot summers, mild winters
Mild to hot summers, cold winters
Mild summers, very cold winters
Desert, dry climate, cold or very cold winters
Cold climate

Beijing
GO Sep–Oct

Shanghai
GO Oct

Chengdu
GO Mar–May

Kunming
GO Dec–Jan

Hong Kong
GO Nov–Feb

High Season
(May–Aug)

➡ Prepare for downpours and crowds at traveller hotspots.

➡ Accommodation prices peak during the first week of the May holiday period.

Shoulder
(mid-Feb–Apr, Sep & Oct)

➡ Expect warmer days in spring and cooler days in autumn.

➡ In the north this is the optimal season, with fresh weather and clear skies.

➡ Accommodation prices peak in early-October holidays.

Low Season
(Nov–mid-Feb)

➡ Domestic tourism is at a low ebb, but things are busy and expensive for Chinese New Year.

➡ Weather is bitterly cold in the north and at altitude, and only warm in the far south.

Useful Websites

China blocks Facebook, WhatsApp, Instagram, Gmail and many other sites. Access them via roaming, or by subscribing to a VPN service.

Lonely Planet (www.lonely planet.com/china) Destination information, hotel bookings, traveller forum and more.

WeChat Messaging and social media app used by virtually all Chinese.

Sup China (https://supchina. com) Chinese news stories; home of the Chinese current affairs Sinica Podcast.

Microsoft Translator Excellent voice-activated translation app.

Pleco Chinese Dictionary Versatile dictionary app.

Air Pollution (http://aqicn.org/ city/shanghai/) Real-time Air Quality Index (AQI) for Shanghai and cities across China.

Important Numbers

Ambulance	☑120
Fire	☑119
Police	☑110
Country code (China/Hong Kong/ Macau)	☑86/ 852/ 853
International access code	☑00
Directory assistance	☑114

Exchange Rates

Australia	A$1	¥4.81
Canada	C$1	¥5.36
Euro zone	€1	¥7.82
Hong Kong	HK$1	¥0.90
Japan	¥100	¥6.61
New Zealand	NZ$1	¥4.47
UK	UK£1	¥8.84
US	US$1	¥7.11

For current exchange rates, see www.xe.com.

Daily Costs

Budget: Less than ¥200

➡ Dorm bed: ¥40–60

➡ Food markets, street food: ¥40

➡ Bike hire: ¥20

➡ Free museums

Midrange: ¥200–1000

➡ Double room in a midrange hotel: ¥200–600

➡ Lunch and dinner in a local restaurant: ¥80–100

➡ Drinks in a bar: ¥60

➡ Taxis: ¥60

Top end: More than ¥1000

➡ Double room in a top-end hotel: ¥600 and up

➡ Lunch and dinner in an excellent local or hotel restaurant: ¥300

➡ Shopping at top-end stores: ¥300

➡ Two Chinese opera tickets: ¥300

Opening Hours

China officially has a five-day working week; Saturday and Sunday are holidays.

Banks, offices and government departments 9am–5pm (or 6pm) Monday to Friday; may close for two hours in the afternoon. Many open Saturday, some Sunday.

Post offices Generally open daily (9am–5pm).

Restaurants Around 10.30am–11pm; some shut at 2pm and reopen at 5pm or 6pm.

Bars Open late afternoon, shut midnight or later.

Shops, department stores and shopping malls Daily 10am–10pm.

Arriving in China

Beijing Capital International Airport Airport Express (30 minutes) trains to city every 10 minutes. Taxis (45 minutes) cost ¥90 to ¥140.

Beijing Daxing International Airport The 'New Airport Line' (20 minutes) meets the Beijing subway (50 minutes into town). Taxis to the centre cost ¥200.

Pudong International Airport (Shanghai) Maglev trains (eight minutes) run every 20 minutes. Metro Line 2 (45 minutes) reaches Hongqiao Airport. Taxis (one hour) to central Shanghai cost ¥180.

Hong Kong International Airport Airport Express trains run every 10 minutes. Taxis to Kowloon/Central cost HK$270/370.

Getting Around

Despite being a vast country, it's straightforward to navigate around China by rail and bus.

Air Affordable and excellent for long distances; large range of routes but delays are common.

Train Very reasonably priced (except high-speed rail, which is still excellent value for money) and very efficient.

Bus Cheaper and slower than trains, but crucial for remote destinations.

Car China is too large with too many restrictions to make this a viable option.

For much more on **getting around**, see p1032

PLAN YOUR TRIP NEED TO KNOW

First Time China

For more information, see Survival Guide (p1011)

Checklist

➡ Check the validity of your passport

➡ Make any necessary bookings (for accommodation and travel)

➡ Secure visa and additional permits well in advance

➡ Organise travel insurance

➡ Work out your itinerary

➡ Inform your credit-/debit-card company and bank about the countries you'll be visiting

➡ Check to see if you can use your mobile phone

➡ Install a VPN on your phone and laptop

What to Pack

➡ Passport

➡ Credit card

➡ Phrasebook

➡ Money belt

➡ Electrical adaptor

➡ Medical kit

➡ Insect repellent

➡ Mobile-phone charger

➡ Sunscreen

➡ Sunhat and shades

➡ Waterproof clothing

➡ Torch

➡ Earplugs

Top Tips for Your Trip

➡ Be patient and understand that many things you may take for granted – orderly queues, international levels of English ability, personal space, etc – may not exist.

➡ Although they are not that user friendly, taking local buses instead of taxis could mean you're the only foreigner on board and a local could well strike up a conversation with you.

➡ Sightseeing on foot is an excellent way to get under the skin of Chinese cities and towns.

➡ Carrying a stash of toilet paper is crucial; be prepared to deal with squat toilets.

➡ Carry hand sanitiser as not all toilets in rural areas have taps for washing your hands.

➡ You will need your passport with you when you buy train and bus tickets and also for admission to certain museums and sights.

➡ Treat China as an adventure and learning curve, rather than purely as a holiday.

➡ Dining in street markets is a great way to eat out of your comfort zone and discover the full, flavoursome variety of Chinese cooking.

What to Wear

You can pretty much wear casual clothes throughout your entire journey in China, unless dining in a smart restaurant in Shanghai, Beijing or Hong Kong, when you may need to dress less casually. In general, trousers (pants) and shirts or T-shirts for guys, and dresses, skirts or trousers for women will serve you well nationwide. Shorts and short sleeves are generally fine in summer, but don long trousers and long sleeves in the evenings to keep mosquitoes at bay. A sunhat can be invaluable, as can sunglasses. A thin waterproof coat and sturdy shoes are a good idea for all-weather hiking and sightseeing. Winter is a different ball game up north and especially at altitude: you'll need several layers, thick shirts, jerseys, warm coats, jackets, gloves, socks and a hat.

Money

Cards Credit and debit cards, particularly Visa and Master-Card, are increasingly accepted in tourist towns and big cities, but always carry enough cash to tide you over for a couple of days.

ATMs 24-hour ATMs are available at Bank of China and ICBC branches.

Changing money You can change money at hotels, large branches of Bank of China, and international airports.

Mobile payment apps Chinese widely use the mobile payment apps WeChat Pay and Alipay, but their use is not straightforward for foreign travellers.

For more information, see p1021.

Bargaining

Haggling is standard procedure in markets, and to a lesser extent in local shops where prices are not clearly marked. There's no harm in coming in really low, especially in the tourist markets of Beijing and Shanghai, but remain polite at all times.

Tipping

Hotels Porters may expect a tip.

Restaurants Tipping is not expected, but a service charge might be levied at more expensive places.

Taxis Drivers do not expect tips.

Language

It is entirely possible to travel around China without hearing any English at all. Tourist-industry employees are more likely to speak English. In the big cities such as Shanghai, Beijing and Hong Kong, English is more widely spoken and understood, but generally only among educated Chinese or those who have frequent dealings with foreigners. In smaller towns and the countryside, English is often of little or no use.

① Please don't add any MSG.
不放味精和鸡精。 Bù fàng wèi jīng hé jī jīng.

Many Chinese dishes are enhanced with a sprinkle of MSG or 'chicken essence' (also MSG!). If you don't want it, it's fine to say so.

② Please bring a knife and fork.
请拿一副刀叉来。 Qǐng ná yī fù dāochā lái.

Don't be afraid to ask for cutlery at a restaurant if you haven't quite mastered the art of eating with chopsticks.

③ Can I get a discount (for the room)?
这（房间）能打折吗? Zhè (fángjiān) néng dǎzhé ma?

You can bargain for the price in many Chinese hotels. Discounts of 10% to 50% off the rack rate are the norm, available by simply asking at reception.

④ I'd like to hire a bicycle.
我想租一辆自行车。 Wǒ xiǎng zū yīliàng zìxíngchē.

Bikes are a great option for getting around Chinese cities and tourist sites. They can also be invaluable for exploring the countryside.

⑤ Can you write that in Pinyin for me?
请用拼音写。 Qǐng yòng Pīnyīn xiě.

If you can't read Chinese script, Pinyin (the official system for writing Mandarin in the Roman alphabet) is your next best option.

Etiquette

China is a pretty relaxed country regarding etiquette, but be aware of a few things:

Greetings and goodbyes Shake hands, but never kiss someone's cheek. Say 'nǐhǎo' for hello and 'zàijiàn' for goodbye.

Asking for help To ask for directions start with 'Qǐng wèn...' ('Can I ask...'); say 'Duìbuqǐ' ('Sorry') to apologise.

Religion Dress sensitively when visiting Buddhist (especially in Tibet) and Taoist temples, churches and mosques.

Eating and drinking Help fill your neighbour's plate at the dinner table. Toast the host and others at the table. Wait till toasting starts before drinking from your glass. Offer your cigarettes around if you smoke. Always offer to buy drinks in a bar, but never fight over the drink/food tab if someone else wants to pay (offer at least once).

Top: Le Shan Grand Buddha (p769), Sichuan

Bottom: Zhangjiajie National Forest Park (p510), Hunan

APHOTOSTORY/SHUTTERSTOCK ©

Month by Month

TOP EVENTS

Harbin Ice & Snow Festival, January to February

Monlam Great Prayer Festival, February or March

Spring Festival, January, February or March

Luoyang Peony Festival, April

Naadam, July

January

North China is in a deep freeze but the south is less bitter; preparations for the Lunar New Year get under way well in advance, arriving any time between late January and March.

✿ Spring Festival

The Lunar New Year is family focused, with dining on dumplings and gift-giving of *hóngbāo* (red envelopes stuffed with money). Most families feast together on New Year's Eve, then China goes on a big week-long holiday. Expect fireworks, parades, temple fairs and lots of colour.

◉ Harbin Ice & Snow Festival

Heilongjiang's good-looking capital Harbin is aglow with rainbow lights refracted through fanciful buildings and statues carved from blocks of ice. It's peak season and outrageously cold. (p204)

◉ Yuanyang Rice Terraces

The watery winter is the optimum season for the rice terraces' spectacular combination of liquid and light. Don't forget your camera, or your sense of wonder.

February

North China remains shockingly icy and dry, but things are slowly warming up in Hong Kong and Macau. The Lunar New Year could well be under way, but sort out any tickets well in advance.

✿ Monlam Great Prayer Festival

Held during two weeks from the third day of the Tibetan New Year and celebrated with spectacular processions (except in Lhasa or the Tibet Autonomous Region). Huge silk *thangka* (sacred art) are unveiled and, on the last day, a statue of the Maitreya Buddha is conveyed around.

✿ Lantern Festival

Held 15 days after the spring festival, this was traditionally a time when Chinese hung out highly decorated lanterns. Pingyao in Shanxi is an atmospheric place to soak it up (sometimes held as late as March).

March

China comes to life after a long winter, though it remains glacial at high altitudes. The mercury climbs in Hong Kong and abrasive dust storms billow into Beijing, scouring everything in their path. It's still low season.

◉ Fields of Yellow

Delve into south Chinese countryside to be bowled over by a landscape saturated in bright-yellow rapeseed. In some parts of China, such as lovely Wuyuan in Jiangxi province, it's a real tourist draw. In colder provinces like Qinghai, you can catch them in summer.

April

Most of China is warm and it's a good time to be on the road. The Chinese take several days off for the Qingming festival, a traditional date for honouring their ancestors and now an official holiday.

A Good Soaking

Flush away the dirt, demons and sorrows of the old year and bring in the fresh at the Dai New Year, with its water-splashing festival in Xishuangbanna. Taking an umbrella is pointless. (p745)

Luoyang Peony Festival

Wangcheng Park in Luoyang bursts into full-coloured bloom with its peony festival: pop a flower garland on your head and join in the floral fun. (p460)

Third Moon Fair

This Bai ethnic minority festival is another excellent reason to pitch up in the lovely north Yunnan town of Dali. It's a week of horse racing, singing and merrymaking from the 15th day of the third lunar month (usually April) to the 21st. (p706)

Formula 1 Chinese Grand Prix

Petrolheads and aficionados of speed, burnt rubber and hairpin bends flock to Shanghai for some serious motor racing at the track near Anting. Get your hotel room booked early – it's one of the most glamorous events on the Shanghai calendar (www.formula1.com).

May

Mountain regions, such as Sichuan's Jiuzhaigou National Park, are in full bloom. For the first four days of May, China is on holiday (Labour Day). Buddha's Birthday falls on

the 8th day of the fourth lunar month, usually in May.

Buddha's Birthday in Xiahe

A fascinating time to enjoy the Tibetan charms of Gansu province's Xiahe, when Buddhist monks make charitable handouts to beggars and the streets throng with pilgrims.

Circling the Mountain Festival

On Paoma Shan, Kangding's famous festival celebrates the birthday of Sakyamuni, the historical Buddha, with a magnificent display of horse racing, wrestling and a street fair. (p776)

Great Wall Marathon

Experience the true meaning of pain at this 20-year-old event. Not for the infirm or unfit. See www.great-wall-marathon.com for more details.

June

Most of China is hot and getting hotter. Once-frozen areas, such as Jilin's Heaven Lake, are accessible – and nature springs instantly to life. The great China peak tourist season is cranking up.

Festival of Aurora Borealis

The Northern Lights are sometimes visible during the Festival of Aurora Borealis in Mohe, the ultra-far north of China, not far from the Russian border. Even if you don't get to see the (elusive) multicoloured glow, the June midnight sun is a memorable experience. (p213)

Dragon Boat Festival

Head to Zhenyuan or the nearest large river and catch all the water-borne drama of dragon boat racers in this celebration of one of China's most famous poets. The Chinese traditionally eat zòngzi (triangular glutinous rice dumplings wrapped in reed leaves) on the day of the festival.

Dhama Festival

This three-day festival in Gyantse in Tibet kicks off on 20 June for horse racing, wrestling, archery, yak races and more.

Shangri-la Horse Racing Festival

In mid- to late June, the Yunnan town of Shangri-la (Zhongdian) lets go of the reins with this celebration of horse racing, coupled with singing, dancing and merriment on the southeastern fringes of Tibet.

Tagong Horse Festival

Celebrated on varying dates each year based on the Tibetan calendar, this festival on a hilltop overlooking Tagong's two monasteries and surrounding mountain peaks is a breathtaking display of Tibetan horsemanship.

July

Typhoons can wreak havoc with travel down south, lashing the Guangdong and Fujian coastlines. Plenty of rain sweeps across China: the 'plum rains' give Shanghai a big soaking, and the grasslands of Inner Mongolia and Qinghai turn green.

Top: Harbin Ice & Snow Festival (p204)

Bottom: Dragon Boat racing, Zhenyan

🎇 Torch Festival, Dali

Held on the 24th day of the sixth lunar month (usually July), this festival is held throughout Yunnan by the Bai and Yi minorities. Making for great photos, flaming torches are paraded at night through streets and fields, and go up outside shops around town. (p707)

☆ Naadam

Mongolian wrestling, horse racing, archery and more during the week-long Naadam festival on the grasslands of Inner Mongolia, when the grass is at its summer greenest.

🍷 Dalian International Beer Festival

Xinghai Sq in the Liaoning port city is steeped in the aroma of hops and ale, and strewn with beer tents in this 12-day celebration of more than 400 international and Chinese beers from a plethora of breweries. (p173)

August

The temperature gauge of Yangzi's 'three ovens' – Chongqing, Wuhan and Nanjing – gets set to blow. Rainstorms hit Beijing, which is at peak heat, as is Shanghai. So head uphill to Lushan, Moganshan, Huangshan or Guoliangcun.

☆ Litang Horse Festival

Occasionally cancelled in recent years (restrictions on travel may suddenly appear) or shrunk from one week to one day, this festival in West Sichuan is a breathtaking display of Tibetan horsemanship, archery and more.

🍷 Qingdao International Beer Festival

Slake that chronic summer thirst with a round of beers and devour a plate of mussels in Shandong's best-looking port town, a former German concession and home of the famous Tsingtao beer label. (p239)

September

Come to Beijing and stay put – September is part of the fleetingly lovely *tiāngāo qìshuǎng* ('the sky is high and the air is fresh') autumnal season, which is an event in itself. It's also a pleasant time to visit the rest of north China.

🏃 International Mount Tai Climbing Festival

Held annually since 1987, this festival at the sacred Taoist mountain of Tai Shan in Shandong draws hundreds of trail runners, mountain bikers, climbers and worshippers of all ages and abilities. (p227)

🍴 Mid-Autumn Festival

Also called the moon festival, it's celebrated by devouring daintily prepared moon cakes stuffed with bean paste, egg yolk, walnuts and more. With a full moon, it's a romantic occasion for lovers and a special time for families. Held on the 15th day of the eighth lunar month.

☉ International Qiantang River Tide Observing Festival

The most popular time to witness the surging river tides sweeping at up to 40km/h along the Qiantang River in Yanguan is during the mid-autumn festival, though you can catch the wall of water during the beginning and middle of every lunar month.

⭐🎎 Confucius' Birthday

Head to the Confucius Temple in Qufu for the 28 September birthday celebrations of axiom-quipping philosopher, sage and patriarch Confucius.

October

The first week of October can be hellish if you're on the road: the National Day holiday kicks off, so everywhere is swamped. Go mid-month instead, when everywhere is deserted. Weather across China is appealing: it's cooling down and leaves are turning golden, bronze and red.

🍴 Hairy Crabs in Shanghai

Now's the time to sample delicious hairy crabs in Shanghai; they are at their best – male and female crabs eaten together with shots of lukewarm Shaoxing rice wine – between October and December.

⭐🎎 Miao New Year

Load up with rice wine and get on down to Guizhou for the ethnic festivities in the very heart of the minority-rich southwest.

⭐🎎 Kurban Bairam (Gǔěrbāng Jié)

Catch the four-day festivities of the Muslim festival of sacrifice in communities across China; the festival is at its liveliest and most colourful in Kashgar.

November

Most of China is getting pretty cold as tourist numbers drop and holidaymakers begin to flock south for sun and the last pockets of warmth.

🗓 Surfing Hainan

The peak surfing season kicks off in Ri Yue Bay (Sun and Moon Bay) in Hainan, where the island's best surf rolls in. Hordes of Chinese flee the cold mainland for these warmer climes.

December

The lakes freeze over, Beijingers get their skates on, and shopping malls put up the Christmas tinsel. Don't expect a white one, though. Snow is a non-event in Beijing's dry winters.

🗓 Christmas Day

It's far from an official Chinese festival, but Christmas (圣诞节, Shèngdàn Jié) is an increasingly big deal on the commercial calendar. Shopping zones in larger cities come alive with decorations, and international hotels put on festive events.

⭐🎎 New Year's Eve

Chinese New Year being a family affair, the Western New Year (元旦, Yuándàn) is an excuse for young Chinese to have fun with friends. Expect lots of parties at venues in Shanghai and Beijing.

Itineraries

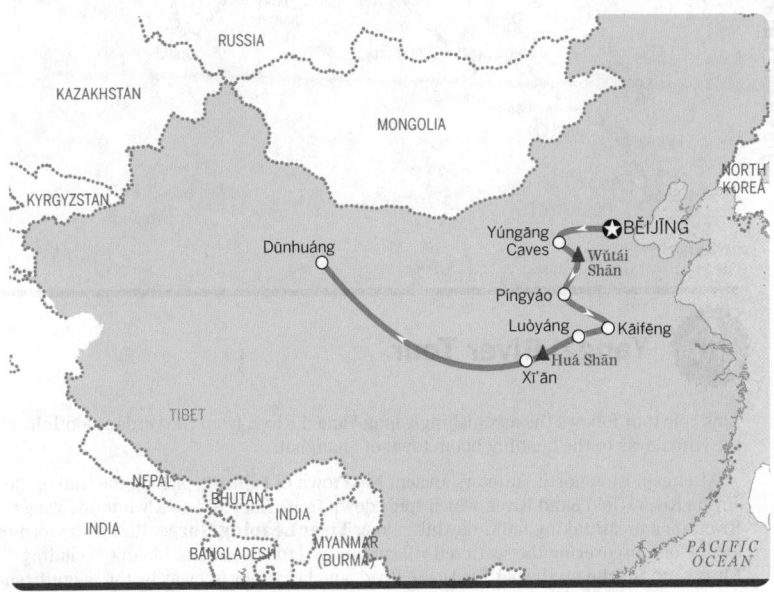

4 WEEKS Northern Tour

China's richest seam of historic antiquity runs through the rugged, dry north of the country. This route embraces all the north's signature sights, all the way from Beijing and the Great Wall via the Terracotta Warriors to the Silk Road of the distant northwest.

Beijing is fundamental to this tour and the north, so give yourself five days to explore the Forbidden City, size up the Great Wall, the Summer Palace and delve along the city's *hutong* (narrow alleyways). The splendour of the **Yungang Caves** outside the city of Datong should put you in a Buddhist mood, heightened by a few nights on monastic **Wutai Shan**. Make a three-day stopover in the ancient walled town of **Pingyao**, followed by the historic city of **Kaifeng** in Henan, once the traditional home of China's small community of Chinese Jews. Move on to **Luoyang** and the Buddhist spectacle of the Longmen Caves and the Shaolin Temple, also within reach. Four days' sightseeing in **Xi'an** brings you face to face with the Army of Terracotta Warriors and allows time for the Taoist mysteries of **Hua Shan**. Xi'an traditionally marked the start of the Silk Road, which you can follow through Gansu province all the way to the oasis town of **Dunhuang**, and beyond.

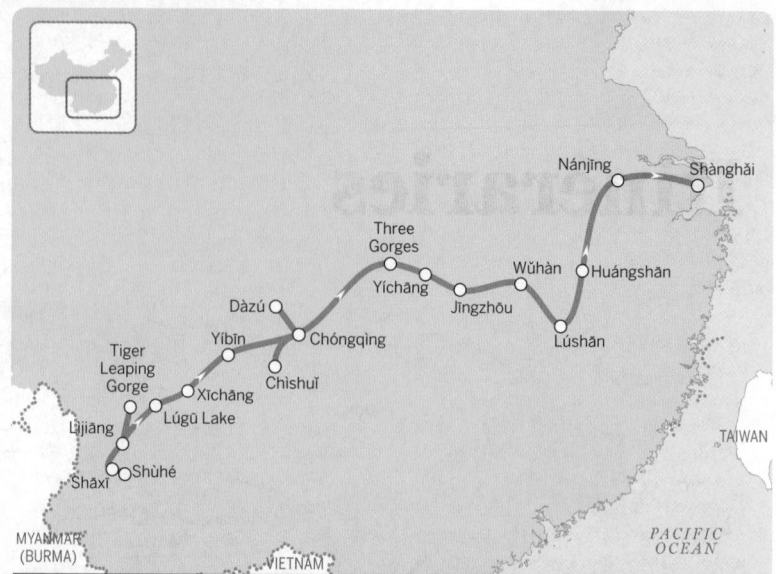

4 WEEKS Yangzi River Tour

This epic tour follows the astonishingly long Yangzi River, from the verdant foothills of the Himalayas to the bustling boom town of Shanghai.

After exploring north Yunnan's ancient Naxi town of **Lijiang**, pick up the trail of the Jinsha River (Gold Sand River, which spills down from Tibet and swells into the Yangzi River) on a breathtaking multi-day hike along **Tiger Leaping Gorge**. Rest your worn-out legs before discovering the scattered villages and old towns around Lijiang, including **Shaxi** and **Shuhe** on the old Tea Horse Road, and being blown away by the magnificent views of Yulong Xueshan. Also consider (warmer months only) a trip from Lijiang north-east towards west Sichuan and the gorgeous **Lugu Lake** on the provincial border, where you can spend several days unwinding by the lakeside. During the winter months this entire area is snowbound, so you may have to fly on from Lijiang. Daily minibuses do the long run from Lugu Lake to **Xichang** in Sichuan, from where you can reach **Yibin** and then **Chongqing**. Alternatively, return to Lijiang to fly to Chongqing, home of the spicy and searing Chongqing hotpot and gateway to the Three Gorges. Detour by bus to the stunning landscapes and natural beauty of **Chishui** on the Guizhou border to relax, unwind and explore the region before returning by bus to urban Chongqing. You'll need around three days in Chongqing for the sights in town and for a journey to the Buddhist Caves and religious carvings at **Dazu**. Then hop on a cruise vessel (or even a bus followed by a cruise) to **Yichang** in Hubei through the magnificent **Three Gorges**. Journey from Yichang to the Yangzi River city of **Wuhan** via the walled town of **Jingzhou**, where it's worth spending the night. After two days in Wuhan, jump on a bus to **Lushan** in Jiangxi province, from where you can head into the Yangzi River province of Anhui to clamber into the mists of **Huangshan**. Beyond lies the former capital city of Nanjing and its imposing city wall and Yangzi River setting, while a meander further east eventually deposits you in **Shanghai** via a delightful string of canal towns – Suzhou, Tongli, Luzhi and Zhujiajiao. Explore Shanghai and consider launching yourself into the **East–Southwest Rural Tour**.

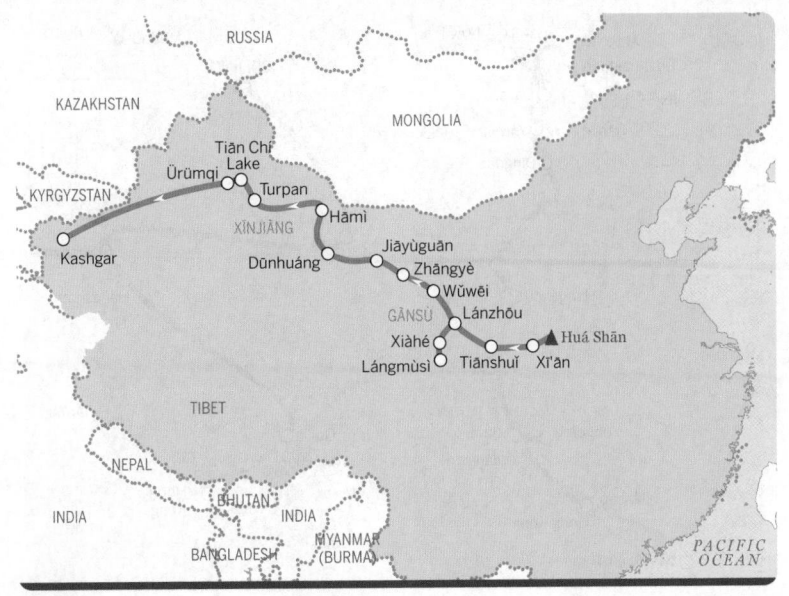

5 WEEKS Silk Road Tour

This breathtaking journey takes you from the must-see Terracotta Warriors, via the Buddhist heritage of Gansu, to the vast desert distances of Xinjiang and far-flung Kashgar.

From the southernmost extents of the Silk Road at **Xi'an**, discover one of imperial China's most iconic remains at the Army of Terracotta Warriors and, for a major workout, climb the precipitous Taoist mountain of **Hua Shan** – just don't look down. Back in Xi'an, explore the Muslim Quarter to feast on local Hui specialities – one of the culinary high points of China travel – and climb atop the imposing city walls. Hop aboard the train to **Lanzhou** but get off in southeast Gansu at **Tianshui** for the remarkable Buddhist grottoes at verdant Maiji Shan. From Lanzhou you have the option to disengage temporarily from the Silk Road to ramble along the fringes of the Tibetan world in the Buddhist monastic settlements of **Xiahe** and **Langmusi**. The Hexi Corridor draws you on to the ancient Great Wall outpost of **Jiayuguan**, via the Silk Road stopover town of **Wuwei** and the Great Buddha Temple with its oversized effigy of a reclining Sakyamuni in **Zhangye**. Stand on the wind-blasted ramparts of Jiayuguan Fort, the last major stronghold of imperial China, and tramp alongside westerly remnants of the Great Wall. The delightful oasis outpost of **Dunhuang** is one of China's tidiest and most pleasant towns, with the mighty sand dunes of the Singing Sands Mountains pushing up from the south, a scattered array of sights in the surrounding desert and some excellent food. The town is also the hopping-off point for China's splendid hoard of Buddhist art, the spellbinding Mogao Grottoes. From Dunhuang you can access the mighty northwestern Uyghur province of Xinjiang via the melon town of **Hami** before continuing to **Turpan** and **Ürümqi**. Consider also spending the night in a yurt or camping on the shores of mountainous **Tian Chi Lake**. Thread your way by rail through a string of Silk Road towns to the Central Asian outpost of **Kashgar**, or reach the distant Uyghur town via the Marco Polo–journeyed southern Silk Road along the cusp of the Taklamakan Desert. In Kashgar, hatch exciting plans to conquer the Karakoram Hwy or, in the other direction, work out how to get back into China proper.

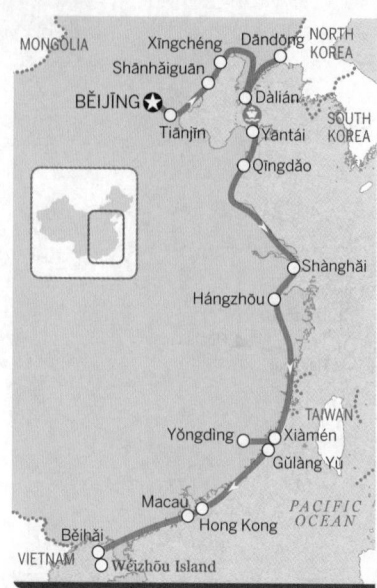

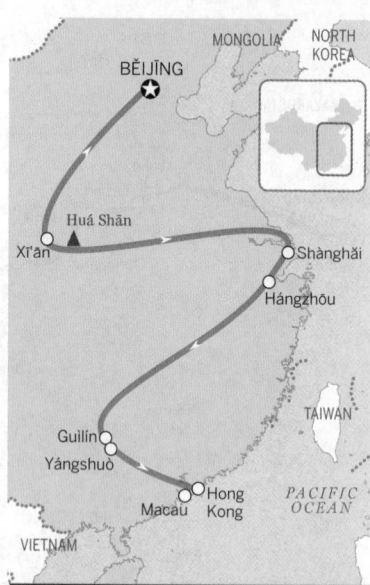

4 WEEKS Coastal China

This coastal tour journeys through China's largest collection of concession-era heritage as well as big-ticket port towns, all set to a sublime maritime backdrop.

From **Beijing**, zip to **Tianjin** en route to the Ming dynasty garrison town of **Shanhaiguan** on the edge of Manchuria. Beyond the ancient port town of **Xingcheng** and around the coast lies urbane **Dalian** and trips to the North Korean border at **Dandong**, or the ferry crossing to **Yantai** en route to a two-day sojourn around breezy **Qingdao**. Cashing in on dashing **Shanghai** is crucial – allow five to six days to tick off surrounding sights, including a trip to the cultured former southern Song dynasty capital of **Hangzhou**. Work your way south around the coast to **Xiamen** to capture some of the magic of **Gulang Yu**, using the port town as a base to explore the roundhouses around **Yongding**. Conclude the tour feasting on dim sum and getting in step with the rhythms of **Hong Kong** before surrendering to the Portuguese lilt of **Macau**, or go further along the coast to the sleepy port town of **Beihai** in Guangxi and bounce over the sea in a boat to the volcanic outpost of **Weizhou Island**.

2 WEEKS Big Ticket Tour

Tick off the top sights on this diverse tour that covers everything from antiquities to some of China's most awesome landscapes, capped with the modern and bustling allure of Hong Kong.

Give yourself four days for **Beijing**'s mandatory highlights before zipping by high-speed G-class train to **Xi'an** to inspect the Terracotta Warriors, walk around the city's formidable Ming dynasty walls and climb the granite peaks of Taoist **Hua Shan**. Then climb aboard the 10-hour overnight high-speed D-class sleeper to pulsating **Shanghai**. After three days of sightseeing, museum-going, shopping and sizing up the skyscrapers of Pudong, detour for a day to the former southern Song dynasty capital of **Hangzhou**, before flying from either Hangzhou or Shanghai to **Guilin** for some of China's most serene and timeless panoramas amid the breathtaking karst landscapes of **Yangshuo**. For a fitting and natural conclusion to your voyage, fly straight from Guilin to **Hong Kong**, or head by high-speed train first to Guangzhou and then by high-speed train to the former British territory. Squeeze in a day exploring **Macau** to add a Portuguese complexion to your voyage.

Top: Traffic in Hong Kong (p521)

Bottom: Riding the Karakoram Highway (p849)

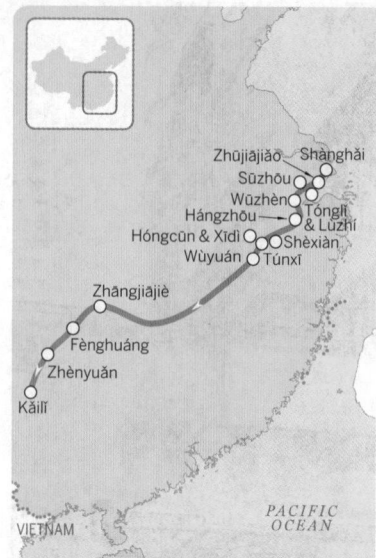

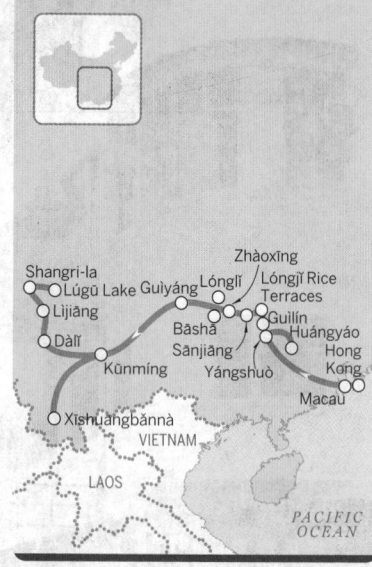

2 WEEKS East–Southwest Rural Tour

Flee the big cities and get rural on this tour that takes you through some of China's best-looking villages and water towns, as well as choice scenic areas and sublime panoramas.

From **Shanghai**, head to **Zhujiajiao** for its canalside charms, followed by the pretty water towns and villages of Jiangsu and north Zhejiang, including **Tongli**, **Luzhi** and **Wuzhen**. From either **Suzhou** or **Hangzhou**, bus it to **Tunxi** in Anhui province to spend several days exploring the delightful ancient Huizhou villages of **Hongcun**, **Xidi** in Yixian and **Shexian** and to scale gorgeous Huangshan. Hop on a bus again to cross the border to Jiangxi province for two or three days' fabulous hiking from village to village in the gorgeous rural landscape around **Wuyuan**. Take the bus to Nanchang and then a high-speed train to Changsha, the Hunan provincial capital, from where you can fly or take the train to the stunning karst panoramas of **Zhangjiajie**. Jump on a bus to the funky river town of **Fenghuang**, from where it's a hop, skip, and a bus-then-train jump via Huaihua into Guizhou and the scenic riverside town of **Zhenyuan**. Kaili and the rest of the province lies beyond.

3 WEEKS Southwest China

Embark on this tour of China's southwest for vibrant ethnic colour, overwhelmingly beautiful landscapes, an enticing array of ancient towns and villages, the fizz of Hong Kong and a profusion of hiking opportunities around the southwest borders.

Four days' wining and dining in **Hong Kong** and **Macau** should whet your appetite, before you head inland to **Guilin** and three days' immersion in the dreamy karst landscape of **Yangshuo**. Join a local tour from Yangshuo to delightful **Huangyao** before backtracking to Guilin and journeying north to the **Longji Rice Terraces** and the Wind and Rain bridges and ethnic hues of **Sanjiang**. Creep over the border to explore the villages of eastern Guizhou, including **Longli**, **Basha** and **Zhaoxing**, before continuing to **Guiyang** and on by train to the capital of Yunnan province, **Kunming**. Spend a few days in Kunming before penetrating north Yunnan to explore **Dali**, **Lijiang** and **Shangri-la**. Consider exploring the border area with Sichuan at the remote **Lugu Lake**, from where you can head into Sichuan. In the other direction, the fertile **Xishuangbanna** region lies in the deep south of the province.

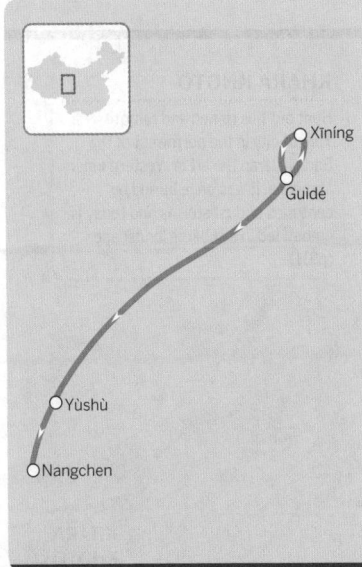

10 DAYS Qinghai: Xining to Nangchen

An epic journey through Qinghai, China's largest province and a region deeply coloured with Tibetan culture. This colossal, rough-and-ready adventure draws you through stunning landscapes.

Spend three days exploring **Xining**, the capital of Qinghai, visiting the Tibetan Culture and Medicine Museum and the Dongguan and Nanguan mosques at the heart of town. Take a bus to the charming, historic town of **Guide** on the crystal-clear waters of the Yellow River – spend time wandering around the ancient city wall and photographing the town's extraordinary and towering river-powered prayer wheel. Return by bus to Xining and buy a bus ticket to **Yushu**, high up at almost 3700m. The bus will actually climb higher than 4000m on its 12- to 16-hour journey, so pack a fleece and only do this trip in summer (it's too cold even in spring). Prepare for bus breakdowns and high altitude. Spend at least a couple of days in the lovely Tibetan town of **Yushu (Jyekundo)** before jumping on a bus through some delightful scenery to **Nangchen (Sharda)**, where monasteries and dramatic scenery await. Return to Yushu and fly back to Xining.

3 WEEKS Contours of Historic Tibet

An arduous undertaking at the best of times, Tibet is a land periodically inaccessible to international travellers. This tour immerses you deeply in culturally Tibetan areas of China that are far more accessible.

Only undertake this tour in the warmer summer months; other times can be dangerous. From **Lanzhou** in Gansu province, head southwest to spend a few days hiking around **Langmusi** and then take a bus to spend at least a night or two in **Xiahe**. Pass some awesome scenery by bus or taxi into Qinghai province via the town of **Tongren**. After exploring Tongren's monasteries, continue by bus to **Xining**, then either fly or take the overnight sleeper to **Chengdu** in Sichuan. Head by bus to **Kangding**, or fly to Kangding via Chengdu. From Kangding you can journey by bus west to the stupendous scenery around **Litang**, with some breathtaking hiking opportunities, or travel south by minivan to **Xiangcheng** and on to **Shangri-la** and the gorgeous Tibetan region of north Yunnan. From Shangri-la take a bus to high-altitude **Deqin**, enveloped in stunning mountain panoramas.

Off the Beaten Track

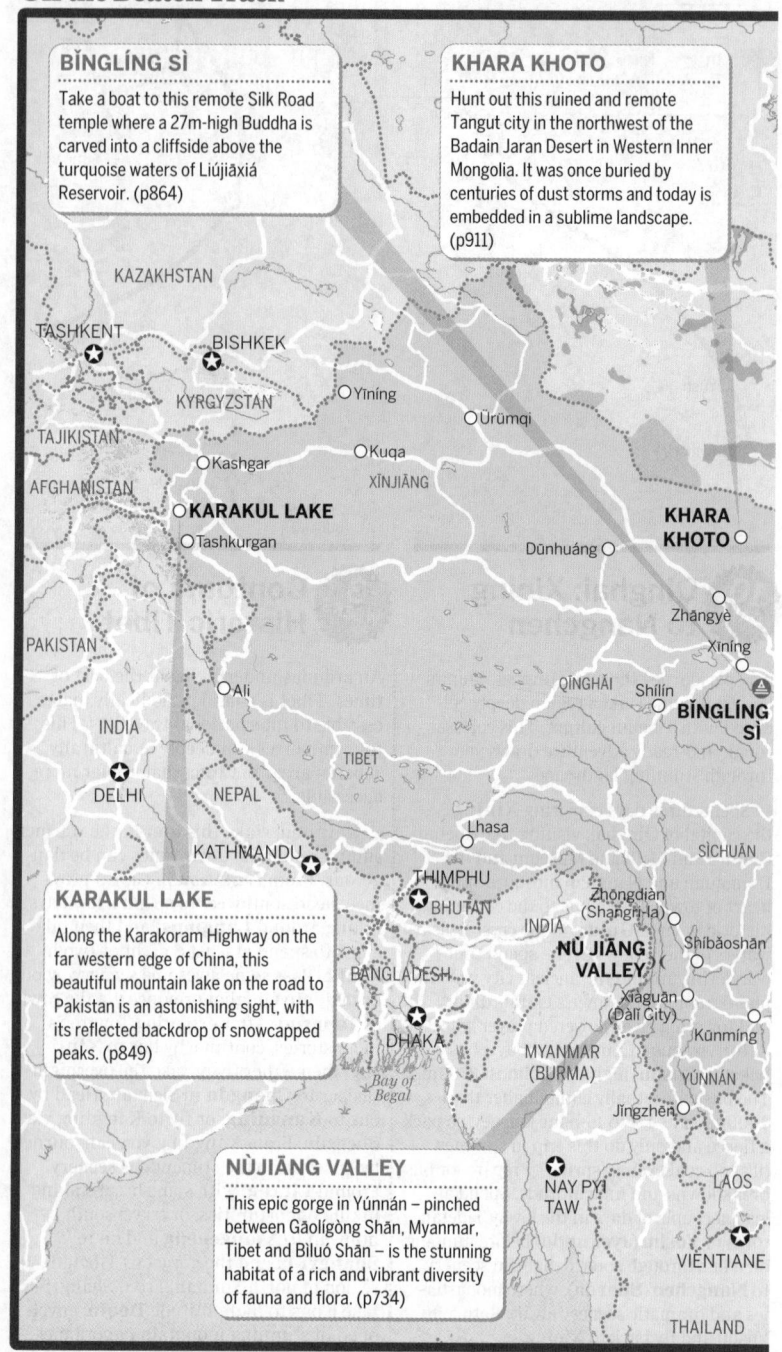

BĪNGLÍNG SÌ

Take a boat to this remote Silk Road temple where a 27m-high Buddha is carved into a cliffside above the turquoise waters of Liújiāxiá Reservoir. (p864)

KHARA KHOTO

Hunt out this ruined and remote Tangut city in the northwest of the Badain Jaran Desert in Western Inner Mongolia. It was once buried by centuries of dust storms and today is embedded in a sublime landscape. (p911)

KARAKUL LAKE

Along the Karakoram Highway on the far western edge of China, this beautiful mountain lake on the road to Pakistan is an astonishing sight, with its reflected backdrop of snowcapped peaks. (p849)

NÙJIĀNG VALLEY

This epic gorge in Yúnnán – pinched between Gāolígòng Shān, Myanmar, Tibet and Bìluó Shān – is the stunning habitat of a rich and vibrant diversity of fauna and flora. (p734)

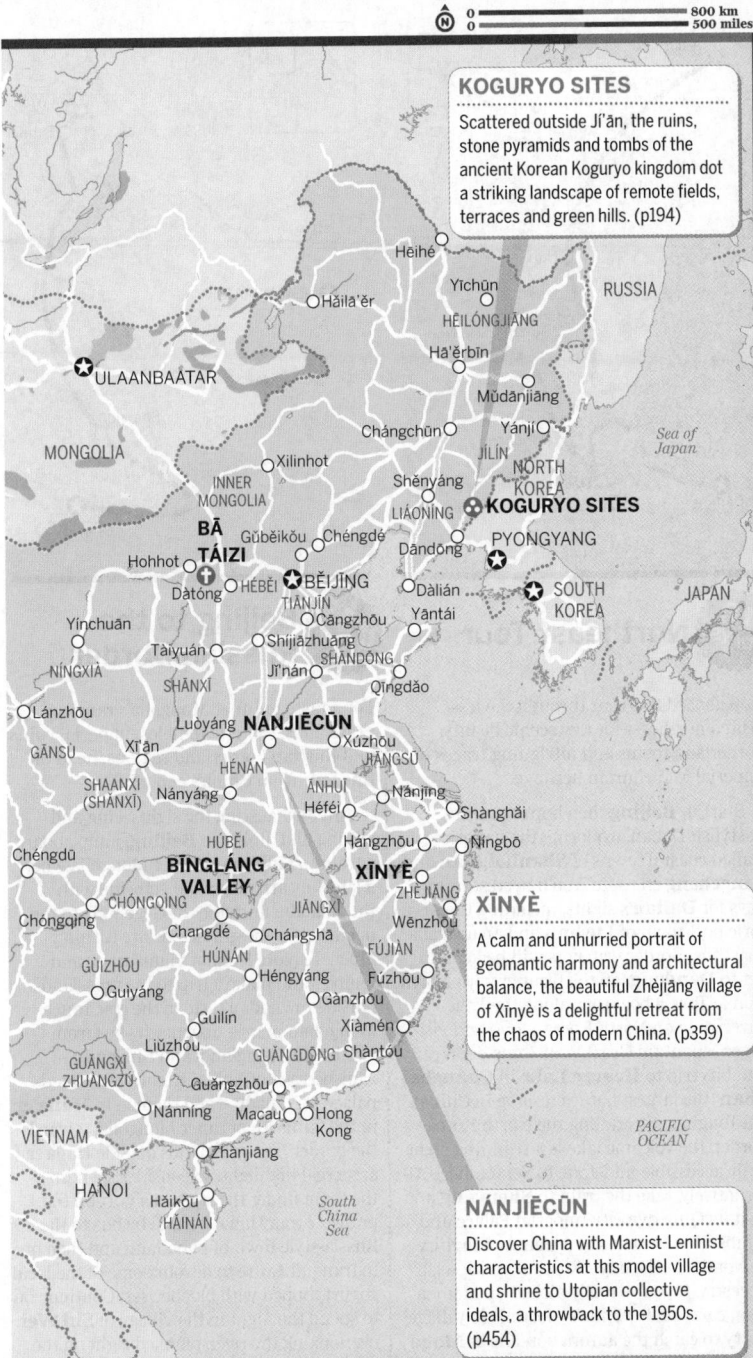

0 ——————— 800 km
0 ——————— 500 miles

KOGURYO SITES

Scattered outside Jí'ān, the ruins, stone pyramids and tombs of the ancient Korean Koguryo kingdom dot a striking landscape of remote fields, terraces and green hills. (p194)

XĪNYÈ

A calm and unhurried portrait of geomantic harmony and architectural balance, the beautiful Zhèjiāng village of Xīnyè is a delightful retreat from the chaos of modern China. (p359)

NÁNJIĒCŪN

Discover China with Marxist-Leninist characteristics at this model village and shrine to Utopian collective ideals, a throwback to the 1950s. (p454)

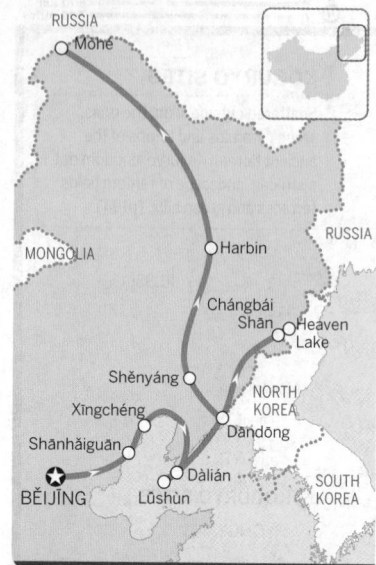

10 DAYS Northeast Tour

Hop aboard this tour through the less-visited northeast for raw scenic beauty, borderland towns and intriguing traces of imperial Manchurian heritage.

Start in **Beijing** then hop on a train to stylish Dalian, exploring the historic walled coastal towns of **Shanhaiguan** and **Xingcheng** en route. You'll need several days for **Dalian's** sights, including the historic port town of **Lushun** and an adorable coastline. Border watchers will be keen to get to **Dandong**, on the frontier with North Korea. Take a boat tour along the Yalu River, dine on North Korean food and visit Tiger Mountain Great Wall. Consider a rail and bus trip to **Heaven Lake** in **Changbai Shan** (the largest nature reserve in China) via Tonghua. Straddling the North Korea border, the volcanic lake is a stunning sight (only accessible mid-June to September). Alternatively, take the train to **Shenyang** and visit its Qing dynasty Imperial Palace and tombs. Hop on a bus or a train to **Harbin** to wonder at the city's Russian and Jewish ancestry. If you've really picked up momentum, carry on to China's 'North Pole Village' to try to catch the aurora borealis in **Mohe** or to bask in summer's midnight sun.

1 WEEK Beijing to the Russian Border

For a taste of Inner Mongolia's ranging grasslands, esoteric temples, imperial ruins and Russian borderland regions, head on this tour from China's capital.

After exhausting the sightseeing and wining and dining in **Beijing**, jump aboard a train to **Hohhot** in Inner Mongolia where a late-July arrival should coincide with the Naadam festivities at Gegentala to the north, when the grasslands are turning green. Explore Hohhot's lamaseries and temples and make a trip to the grasslands outside town for a taste of the epic Inner Mongolian prairie. Journey by bus from Hohhot to Zhenglanqi and **Shangdu** – vanished site of Kublai Khan's celebrated palace at Xanadu – and then on to **Haila'er** in the far north of Inner Mongolia, towards the border. The grasslands outside Haila'er are a real highlight, so consider spending the night under the stars in a yurt on the prairie. From Haila'er travel by bus to the Russia-style town of Labudalin and then on to tranquil **Enhe** to devour some of the local yogurt topped with blueberries. Continue on to spend the night in the village of **Shi Wei**, overlooking the river, plonked right on the Russian border. Winter is a no-no.

Plan Your Trip
Family Travel

Taking your kids to China can be challenging, eye-opening, fun and memorable. Sure you'll need to plan a bit, and at times be a super-patient parent, but you could also find yourself and your family on the journey of a lifetime.

Children Will Love...

Journeys

Star Ferry, Hong Kong (p534) Bundle the kids on the cross-harbour ferry for a dazzling, all-colour evening trip.

Hong Kong tram (p559) Grab seats at the front of the upper deck for a sightseeing tour of north Hong Kong island; tots under three go for free!

Xi'an City Walls (p409) Get the kids cycling around China's longest intact city wall.

The Great Outdoors

The Great Wall (p131) Best accessed from Beijing, it's a teenage kid's mandatory social-media pilgrimage and selfie spot.

Yangshuo (p646) Teenage kids will love cycling between the karst peaks and bamboo rafting along the Yulong River.

Hainan (p620) Tots will have a great time at the beaches and splashing about in the warm waters.

Excitement

The Plank Walk on Hua Shan (p421) Teenagers will get the ultimate white-knuckle buzz above a 2000m drop.

Shanghai World Financial Center (p304) Three observation decks and superfast elevators will wow little ones at this iconic skyscraper.

Harbin Ice & Snow Festival (p204) This fairytale wonderland of snow, ice and wintry fun in the deep-freeze of Heilongjiang is perfect for kids.

Keeping Costs Down

Trains

Request a child's ticket for kids between 1.2m and 1.5m tall (ticket prices for children are according to height rather than age). These are half the price of adult tickets for seats, and about 25% off for sleeper berths. Children under 1.2m travel for free but don't get their own seat or berth.

Tourist Sites

Kids can often get in for half price, or free if under 1.2 metres tall. It's always worth asking at the ticket office.

Dining

Choose Chinese restaurants over western-style ones. Dishes are typically large and designed for sharing, and staples like plain cooked rice only cost a few *yuan*.

Hotels

It's always worth enquiring about a family room (家庭房; *jiātíng fáng*), or failing that a suite (套房; *tàofáng*) where extra beds (加床; *jiā chuáng*) are permitted. And don't forget, always haggle for a discount in local hotels.

Parks

Parks in larger cities are either free or very cheap to enter. Ideal for family picnics and outdoor activities like kite-flying, some also have swimming facilities and fairground rides.

Shows

Beijing's Acrobatics Shows (p123) Daredevil feats of strength, agility and skill will captivate kids, and shows are short.

Symphony of Lights (p533) Little ones will gaze in wonder at the nightly light show painted across Hong Kong's iconic skyline.

Mickey's Storybook Express (p304) The character parade is a highlight of a trip to Shanghai Disney, and unlike the rides there are no queues.

Educational

Army of Terracotta Warriors (p418) Coming face to face with thousands of individually wrought soldiers from aeons ago will spark young imaginations.

Giant Panda Breeding Research Base (p752) Kids can learn all about giant pandas in Chengdu, and even feed them by hand.

Kite Flying (p245) Kids and kidults can take to the skies in Weifang, home of the International Kite Festival.

Region by Region

Shanghai Kids' big-ticket theme-park choices plus high-altitude observation decks, museums, delicious dumplings and much more.

Beijing The Great Wall is a mandatory stop, zipping across Beijing's frozen lakes in winter is fun for teens and tots, and guided tours will help Beijing's world-class historic sites to life.

Hong Kong The magic of the Star Ferry and the gravity-defying Peak Tram, Disneyland and dolphin watching, plus super parks and hiking trails.

Chengdu Watch your kids go wide-eyed at the pandas, especially the playful infants frolicking adorably with their human minders.

Hainan Island Surfing, swimming, China's best beaches and mountains of healthy tropical fruit. Resort hotels in Sanya have excellent facilities for kids of all ages.

Xi'an Young Indiana Joneses will relish all the archeological discoveries in China's ancient capital of Chang'an.

Yangshuo Family activities abound in the karst landscape of Yangshuo, from bamboo rafting and off-road cycling to cooking classes, hot-air ballooning and rock climbing.

Pingyao Little ones will enjoy exploring the crooked alleyways, delving into courtyard museums and walking atop the perimeter walls of this time-warped Qing dynasty town.

Yunnan The perfect province for an intrepid family adventure: biking between minority villages, visiting Dali and Lijiang, and checking out the rainforests of Xishuangbanna.

Qingdao Miles of sandy bathing beaches, fairy-tale Bavarian architecture, and bags (literally) of Qingdao beer to soothe harassed parents.

Harbin Kids can hit the slopes in summer at the world's biggest indoor ski centre. And when winter does arrive, ice and snow sculptures turn Harbin into a winter wonderland.

Good to Know

Look out for the 🖼 icon for family-friendly suggestions throughout this guide.

➡ Pack any medicines your kids may need as you may not be able to find them in China. Make sure vaccinations are up to date.

➡ Kids need to be prepared for squat toilets.

➡ Although improving, air pollution can be caustic in China; consider investing in face masks for your young ones.

➡ Your teenagers are going to need a VPN (virtual private network) on their smartphones to keep using Snapchat, Instagram or WhatsApp. Same applies to you. Download VPNs to devices before arriving in China.

➡ Flights are largely painless, but expect delays.

Dining Out

In big cities such as Shanghai, Beijing and Hong Kong you'll find lots of choice with kids' menus. In tourist towns and popular destinations, it's a similar story. Off the beaten path you'll have to dine as locals do and work through Chinese-language menus.

Snacking on the hoof: order up steaming ròujiāmó (cooked meat sandwich, usually pork), lamb kebabs, Hong Kong–style egg waffles or watermelons. Look out for street-side sellers of popcorn, cooked up old-school with a bang in a traditional flame-heated popcorn machine.

McDonalds and KFC are everywhere in towns and cities; Burger King was a rarity but is increasingly common. Dicos (德克士; Dekeshi) is a decent Chinese alternative with tasty rice lunch sets.

Picky eaters might be tempted by Chinese standbys like boiled dumplings (水饺; *shuǐjiǎo*) and egg-fried rice (蛋炒; *dàn chǎofàn*). Rice porridge (粥; *zhōu*) is plain, soothing and ideal for infants.

Open Spaces

Despite China's size there's often a surprising lack of free and accessible open space, and you often need to pay to access what you discover. Much land is used for agriculture and most national parks levy an admission fee, while city parks are often quite synthetic places, without lawns or grass.

Transport

Kids should love overnight train journeys. Long-distance bus journeys may be more fraught – limit their liquid intake as buses stop only rarely for the call of nature. Think about hiring a car or a taxi for the day to get to sights outside town. Prepare for seat-belt-free rear seats in taxis.

Crossing the Road

China's roads are chaotic, so exercise great care when crossing the road and keep a close eye on the very small ones.

Health

This will require a bit more planning than many destinations as China's disparities – altitude and climate as well as economic – can throw in some unexpected surprises.

Useful Resources

Lonely Planet Kids (lonelyplanetkids.com) Loads of activities and great family travel blog content.

First Words Mandarin (shop.lonelyplanet.com) An introduction to Mandarin for ages five to eight.

Time Out Beijing Family (http://www.timeout beijing.com/family) Up-to-date family events listings for Beijing and more. Shanghai has the same.

Kids' Corner

Say What?

Hello.	你好 *Nǐhǎo*
Goodbye.	再见 *Zàijiàn*
Thank you.	谢谢你 m *Xièxie nǐ*
My name is ...	我叫…… *Wǒ jiào...*

Did You Know? ℹ️

Giant pandas are born tiny, hairless and blind.

The largest dumpling ever made was 1.2m long and weighed 72kg!

Have You Tried?

Thousand-year egg It's aged for months until it turns dark brown.

Plan Your Trip
Eat & Drink Like a Local

Half of China travel revolves around food; so does half of Chinese life. The catalyst for enjoyment, meals are occasions for pleasure and entertainment, to clinch deals, strike up new friendships and rekindle old ones. Put China on a plate: all you need is a visa, a pair of chopsticks and an adventurous palate.

The Year in Food

China's vast size and climatic disparities means there's no shortage of interesting bites year-round, but there are some seasonal specialities for your diary:

Spring (March–May) The best season for bright-red *xiǎolóngxiā* (小龙虾) – spicy crayfish, sold in street-food markets. The Lantern Festival sees steaming bowls of *yuánxiāo* (元宵), a sweet dessert of soft balls made from glutinous rice flour. Bamboo shoots (笋; *sǔn*) spring up on the menu.

Summer (June–August) Watermelons, *hami* melons and grapes slake a national thirst. *Zòngzi* (粽子) – sweet parcels of glutinous rice wrapped in vine leaves – are devoured during the Dragon Boat Festival in June.

Autumn (September–October) October is a tip-top month to corner hairy crabs (大闸蟹; *dàzháxiè*) with your chopsticks in Shanghai. The land is awash with moon cakes for the eponymous festival in September. Lotus roots (藕; *ǒu*) are in season.

Winter (November–February) Street sellers roast up warming *tángchǎo lìzi* (糖炒栗子) – sweetened, roast chestnuts – and baked sweet potatoes (烤红薯; *kǎohóngshǔ*) steam from every street corner.

Food Experiences
Meals of a Lifetime

Taste of Dadong (p116) Sampler platters of perfect Peking duck and creative fare from a Beijing celebrity chef.

Yang's Fry Dumplings (p318) Shanghai's most famous place for *shēngjiān bāo* – soup-filled pork buns that taste divine.

Kam's Roast Goose (p545) Michelin-starred roast goose in Hong Kong's foodie heartland of Wan Chai.

Ultraviolet (p319) China's most conceptual dining experience – and the only restaurant in Shanghai with three Michelin stars.

Yúfúnán (p114) A deliciously stylish reimagining of the fiery fare of Hunan province – but in Beijing's *hutong* (narrow alleyways).

Cheap Treats

Niúròu miàn (牛肉面) Beef noodles, found across north China but especially in the northwest; cheap, filling, ubiquitous.

Yángròu pàomó (羊肉泡馍) Popular Muslim dish – warming servings of mutton broth and shredded flatbread – in Xi'an and Shaanxi and neighbouring provinces.

Yóutiáo (油条) Not unlike churros, these deep-fried dough sticks are breakfast fare, served up with a cup of warm soy milk (豆浆; *dòujiāng*). Found everywhere.

Ròujiāmó (肉夹馍) Shredded pork sandwiched between two halves of a flatbread, originally from Shanxi. Great for eating on the go.

Yángròu chuàn (羊肉串) Lamb kebabs, often – but not exclusively – cooked up by Muslim chefs across the land.

Jīdànzǎi (鸡蛋仔) Egg, flour and milk batter cooked between two griddles with semi-spherical cells (essentially an egg waffle). From Hong Kong, but now everywhere.

Jiānbǐng guǒzi (煎饼果子) Originally from Tianjin, but sold everywhere in Beijing. A kind of steaming crêpe with egg, fried dough sticks, diced scallions, chilli or bean sauce.

Málàtàng (麻辣烫) Spicy and numbing soup base into which are added skewers of *dòufu* (tofu), meat and veggies. Universal.

Dare to Try

Phoenix claws (凤爪; *fèngzhuǎ*) The extravagantly named and ever-popular steamed chicken's feet, served at dim sum restaurants.

Stinky dòufu (臭豆腐; *chòudòufu*) This form of fermented tofu has an aroma somewhere between unwashed socks and rotting vegetation. It's ubiquitous, but Shaoxing in Zhejiang province does the best.

Dog meat (狗肉; *gǒuròu*) Man's best friend, done to a turn. Popular down south and in the northeast.

Fertilised chicken egg (毛鸡蛋; *máojīdàn*) Shell out for this delicacy in Guangdong and down south.

Thousand-year old egg (松花蛋; *sōnghuā dàn*) Also known as *pídàn* (皮蛋), this preserved chicken, duck or quail egg stands the test of time.

Pig's ears (猪耳; *zhūěr*) China abounds with opportunities to truly pig out.

Sheep penis (羊鞭, *yáng biān*) Not everyone's cup of tea.

Scorpion or spider skewers Put Zhongshan Lu Market in Nanning on your itinerary.

Snake soup (蛇羹; *shégēng*) Cantonese delicacy.

Lamb offal Hardcore fans go for just offal (纯羊杂; *chún yángzá*), or you can order it with a steamed bun (馒头; *mántou*) or fried dough (油饼; *yóubǐng*) to soak up the soup.

PLAN YOUR TRIP EAT & DRINK LIKE A LOCAL

STREET FOOD

Snacking your way around China is a fine way to sample the different flavours of the land while on the move. Most towns have a street market or a night market (夜市; *yèshì*), a great place for good-value snacks and meals. You can either take it away or park yourself on a wobbly stool and grab a beer.

Street markets such as Kaifeng's boisterous night market abound with choices you may not find in restaurants. Vocal vendors will be forcing their tasty creations on you, but you can also see what other people are buying and what's being cooked up. All you have to do is join the queue and point.

Gelatinous sheep hooves (羊蹄; *yáng tí*) Ningxia province's answer to pork knuckle.

Cicada skewer (蝉串; *chánchuàn*) Crunchy.

Rabbit heads (兔头; *tùtóu*) Done to perfection in Chengdu, Sichuan province.

Real Chinese Food

Because the nation so skilfully exported its cuisine abroad, your very first impressions of China were probably via your taste buds. Chinatowns the world over teem with the aromas of Chinese cuisine, ferried overseas by China's versatile and hard-working cooks; Sundays often see diners flocking to them for 'yum cha' and feasts of dim sum. Chinese food is indeed a wholesome and succulent point of contact between an immigrant Chinese population and everyone else.

Despite the widening of overseas Chinese culinary horizons responding to the growth of Chinese tourism abroad and a wider diaspora of Chinese living in the West, what you see – and taste – abroad remains a wafer-thin slice of a very hefty and wholesome pie. Chinese cuisine in the West was traditionally lifted from the cookbook of an emigrant community that originated mainly from China's southern seaboard. In a similar vein, the sing-song melodies of Cantonese were the most familiar of China's languages in Chinatowns, even though the

MARK ANDREWS/ALAMY STOCK PHOTO ©

Top: Chef making noodles

Bottom: Steamed dumplings

dialect finds little traction in China beyond Hong Kong, Macau, Guangdong, parts of Guangxi and KTV parlours nationwide. You may be hard-pressed to avoid dim sum and *cha siu* in your local Chinatown, but finding more 'obscure' specialities from elsewhere in China may still be a challenge (albeit not as hard as it once was), though you will pay a hefty premium for the experience. Nothing beats coming to China, however, to dine on regional delicacies on home turf.

To get an idea of the size of its diverse menu, remember that China is not that much smaller than Europe. Just as Europe is a patchwork of different nation states, languages, cultural traditions and climates, China is also a smorgasbord of dialects, languages, ethnic minorities and extreme geographic and climatic differences, despite the common Han Chinese cultural glue.

The sheer size of the land, the strength of local culture, and differences in geography and altitude mean there's little in common between the cuisines of Xinjiang and Tibet, even though they are adjacent to each other. Following your nose (and palate) around China is one of the exciting ways to journey the land, so pack a sense of culinary adventure along with your travelling boots.

Local Specialities

China's diverse regional cooking styles have undergone a long process of evolution, influenced by climate, the distribution of crop and animal varieties, topography, proximity to the sea, the influence of neighbouring nations and cultures and the arrival of ingredients and flavours from overseas. It's almost impossible to know where to start breaking it all down, but naturally seafood is prevalent in coastal regions of China, while in the landlocked and mighty northwest there is a dependence on meat such as beef and lamb. In between those two poles is as varied a selection of regional cuisine as you could imagine.

Eight Schools of Cooking

Another crucial ingredient in the evolution of China's wide-ranging regional cuisines is history. The flight of the Song court south of the Yangzi River (Cháng Jiāng) from northern Jurchen invaders in the 12th century helped develop China's major regional cuisines. This process was further influenced by urbanisation, itself made possible by the commercialisation of agriculture and food distribution. This led to the emergence of the restaurant industry and the further consolidation of regional schools. Further impetus came from the merchants and bureaucrats who travelled the land, and from improved transport options such as the Grand Canal, which allowed for the shipping of ingredients and recipes between Beijing in the north and Hangzhou in the south.

Many Chinese regions lay claim to their own culinary conventions, which may overlap and cross-pollinate. The cooking traditions of China's ethnic minorities aside, Han cooking has traditionally been divided into eight schools (中华八大菜系; *zhōnghuá bādàcàixì*):

Chuān (川; Sichuan cuisine)

Huī (徽; Anhui cuisine)

Lǔ (鲁; Shandong cuisine)

Mǐn (闽; Fujian cuisine)

Sū (苏; Jiangsu cuisine)

Xiāng (湘; Hunan cuisine)

Yuè (粤; Cantonese/Guangdong cuisine)

Zhè (浙; Zhejiang cuisine)

Although each school is independent and well defined, it is possible to group these eight culinary traditions into northern, southern, western and eastern cooking.

A common philosophy lies at the heart of Chinese cooking, whatever the school. Most vegetables and fruits are yin foods, generally moist and soft, possessing a cooling effect while nurturing the feminine aspect. Yang foods – fried, spicy, or with red meat

TIPPING

Tipping is never done at cheap restaurants in mainland China. Smart, international restaurants will encourage tipping, but it is not obligatory and it's uncertain whether wait staff receive their tips at the end of the night.

Hotel restaurants automatically add a 15% service charge; some high-end restaurants may do the same.

– are warming and nourish the masculine side. Any meal should harmonise flavours and achieve a balance between cooling and warming foods.

Travel Your Taste Buds

China is such a gourmand's paradise, you won't know when to stop. In the north, fill up on a tasty dish of wontons (*húntún*) stuffed with juicy leeks and minced pork, or Mongolian hotpot (*Ménggǔ huǒguō*), a hearty brew of mutton, onions and cabbage.

Chefs from China's arid northwest might slide a bowl of noodles topped with sliced donkey meat (*lǘròu huáng miàn*) under your nose, or pop sizzling lamb kebabs (*kǎo yángròu*) between your fingers. Stop by Xi'an for warming servings of mutton broth and shredded flatbread (*yángròu pàomó*). A dish of Lanzhou hand-pulled noodles (*lā miàn*) is a meal in itself.

In case you're pining for something sweet, head to Shanghai for delicious honey-smoked carp (*mìzhī xūnyú*). Here you can also dine on more savoury helpings of steaming *xiǎolóngbāo* dumplings, which require considerable dexterity to consume without meat juices jetting to all compass points.

Cleanse your palate with a glass of heady Shaoxing yellow wine (*Shaoxing huángjiǔ*) or the more delicate flavours of Dragonwell

tea (*lóngjǐng chá*). It may not exactly give you wings, but a dose of Huangshan braised pigeon (*Huangshan dùngē*) will definitely give you the stamina to clamber up the misty inclines of Huangshan.

Some like it hot, and little comes hotter than the fiery flavours of Sichuan. Begin with mouth-numbing mapo tofu (*mápó dòufu*), followed by the celebrated spicy chicken with peanuts (*gōngbǎo jīdīng*). If smoke isn't now coming out of your ears, fish smothered in chilli (*shuǐzhǔ yú*) should have you breathing fire. Alternatively, test your mettle with a volcanic Chongqing hotpot.

In the south relax with morning dim sum in Guangzhou or a bowl of Cantonese snake soup (*shé gēng*) in one of the city's boisterous night markets. While in Macau taste the Macanese dish *porco à alentejana*, a mouthwatering casserole of pork and clams.

Northern Cooking

Northern Chinese cuisine ranges across a vast area that includes Beijing, Shandong, northeastern (Manchurian) and Shanxi cuisine, cooking up the most time-honoured and most central form of Chinese dining.

In this dry northern Chinese wheat belt, the accent falls on millet, sorghum, maize, barley and wheat rather than rice (the lush south takes care of that). At home in the harsh and hardy winter climate, northern cooking is rich, wholesome and rather salty. Filling breads – such as *mántou* (馒头) or *bǐng* (饼; flatbreads) – are steamed, baked or fried, while noodles may form the basis of any northern meal and filling dumplings (饺子; *jiǎozi*) are widely eaten – usually boiled, but also fried. You can always find rice if you want it!

Beijing was the principal capital through the Yuan, Ming and Qing dynasties, so imperial cooking is a chief characteristic of the northern school. Peking duck is Beijing's signature dish, served with typical northern ingredients – pancakes, spring onions and fermented bean paste. You can find it across China, but it's only true to form in the capital, roasted in ovens fired up with fruit-tree wood.

With China ruled from 1644 to 1911 by non-Han Manchurians, the influence of northeast cuisine (东北菜; *dōngběi cài*) has naturally permeated northern cooking, infusing it with rich and hearty stews, dense breads, preserved foods and dumplings.

PANIC MENU

Despite your best-laid plans, there are times when you'll find yourself hungry and in a random Chinese restaurant with no English menu. Never fear! Any chef worth his wok can whip up these cheap and tasty *jiācháng cài* (common family-style dishes):

➡ *Gōng bǎo jīdīng* (宫保鸡丁) Sichuan-style chicken and peanuts

➡ *Dàn chǎofàn* (蛋炒饭) Egg-fried rice

➡ *Xīhóngshì chǎo jīdàn* (西红柿炒鸡蛋) Tomato and egg stir-fry

➡ *Pāi huángguā* (拍黄瓜) Cold cucumber salad

➡ *Yúxiāng ròusī* (鱼香肉丝) Fragrant shredded pork

➡ *Tǔdòu sī* (土豆丝) Stir-fried potato

➡ *Gānbiān sìjìdòu* (干煸四季豆) Sichuan-style green beans

Fragrant shredded pork

Meat roasting is also more common in the north than in other parts of China. Meats in northern China are braised until falling from the bone, or slathered with spices and barbecued until smoky. Pungent garlic, chives and spring onions are used with abandon and also employed raw. Muslim Uyghur cuisine from the desert northwest is another principal cuisine, based around lamb, beef, chicken and breads and represented in restaurants across China.

The nomadic and carnivorous diet of the Mongolians also permeates northern cooking, most noticeably in the Mongolian hotpot and the Mongolian barbecue. Milk from nomadic herds of cattle, goats and horses has also crept into northern cuisine – as yogurts (*suānnǎi*), for example.

Southern Cooking

The southern Chinese – particularly the entrepreneurial and itinerant Cantonese – historically spearheaded successive waves of immigration overseas, leaving aromatic constellations of Chinatowns around the world. Consequently, much of the world most often associates this school of cooking with China.

Typified by Cantonese (粤菜; *yuècài*) cooking, southern cooking avoids the richness and saltiness of northern cooking to instead coax subtle aromas to the surface. The Cantonese believe good cooking does not need much flavouring and the *xiān* (natural freshness) of ingredients marks culinary perfection. A near-obsessive attention to freshness of ingredients in southern cuisine ensues.

The hallmark Cantonese dish is dim sum (点心; Mandarin: *diǎnxīn*). Yum cha (literally 'drink tea') – another name for dim sum dining – in Guangzhou and Hong Kong can be enjoyed on any day of the week. Dishes, often in steamers, are wheeled around on trolleys so you can see what's available to order. Well-known dim sum dishes include *guōtiē* (a kind of fried dumpling), *shāomài* (a kind of open pork dumpling), *chāshāobāo* (pork-filled bun) and *chūnjuǎn* (spring rolls).

Fujian (闽菜; *mǐncài*) cuisine is another important southern cooking style, with its emphasis on light flavours and, due to the

Hairy crabs, a Shanghai specialty

province's proximity to the East China Sea, seafood.

Hakka cuisine from the disparate and migratory Hakka folk (*Kèjiāzú*) is another feature of southern Chinese cooking, as is the food of Cháozhōu in eastern Guangdong.

Sparkling paddy fields glitter across the south – the humid climate, plentiful rainfall and well-irrigated land means that rice has been farmed here since the Chinese first populated the region during the Han dynasty (206 BC–AD 220). It's the staple of southern dishes.

Western Cooking

The cuisine of landlocked western China, a region heavily dappled with ethnic shades and contrasting cultures, welcomes the diner to the scarlet end of the culinary spectrum. The trademark ingredient here is the fiercely hot red chilli, a potent firecracker of flavour that floods dishes with an all-pervading spiciness. Aniseed, coriander, garlic and peppercorns are chucked in for good measure to add extra pungency and bite.

The trademark cuisine of the western school is fiery Sichuan (川菜; *chuāncài*) food, renowned for its eye-watering peppery aromas, and marked by the use of 'flower pepper' (*huājiāo*), a numbing, peppercorn-like herb that floods the mouth with an anaesthetising fragrance in a culinary effect termed *málà* (numb and hot). The delicious sour cabbage fish soup (酸菜鱼; *suāncàiyú*) features wholesome fish chunks in a spicy broth. The Chongqing hotpot is a force to be reckoned with, but must be approached with a stiff upper lip (and copious amounts of liquid refreshment). If you want a hotpot pitched between spicy and mild, select a *yuanyang* hotpot (*yuānyāng huǒguō*), a vessel divided yin-yang style into two different compartments for different soup bases. Sichuan restaurants are everywhere in China – swarming around train stations, squeezed away down food streets, or squished into street markets.

Dishes from Hunan (湘菜; *xiāngcài*) are similarly pungent, with a heavy reliance on chilli. Unlike Sichuan food, flower pepper is not employed and instead spicy flavours are often sharper, fiercer and more to the fore.

In the far west, Tibetan cuisine includes *tsampa* (porridge of roasted barley flour), *bö cha* (yak-butter tea), momos (dumplings filled with vegetables or yak meat), *thugpa* (noodles with meat), *thenthuk* (fried noodle squares) and *shemdre* (rice, potato and yak-meat curry).

Eastern Cooking

The eastern school of Chinese cuisine lies in a fertile region, slashed by waterways and canals, glistening with lakes, fringed by a long coastline and nourished by a subtropical climate. Generally more oily and sweeter than other Chinese schools, the eastern school revels in fish and seafood, reflecting its geographical proximity to major rivers and the sea. Fish is usually *qīngzhēng* (清蒸; steamed) but can be stir-fried, pan-fried or grilled. Hairy crabs (*dàzháxiè*) are a Shanghai speciality between October and December, devoured with soy, ginger and vinegar and downed with warm Shaoxing wine – the crab increases the body's yin (coldness), so yang (warmth) is added by imbibing lukewarm rice wine.

As with Cantonese food, freshness is a key ingredient in the cuisine, and sauces and seasonings are only employed to augment essential flavours. Stir-frying and steaming are also used, the latter with Shanghai's famous *xiǎolóngbāo* – steamer buns filled with nuggets of pork or crab swimming in a scalding meat broth. Learning how to devour these carefully without the meat juice squirting everywhere and scalding the roof of your mouth (or blinding your neighbour) requires dexterity.

Jiangsu (苏菜; *sūcài*) – one of the core regions of the eastern school – is famed as the 'Land of Fish and Rice', a tribute to its abundance of food and produce. A culture of epicurism and gastronomic enjoyment prevails here.

South of Jiangsu, Zhejiang (浙菜; *zhècài*) cuisine is another cornerstone of eastern cooking. With a lightness of flavour, Anhui (徽菜; *huīcài*) cuisine puts less emphasis on seafood. Braising and stewing of vegetables and wildlife from its mountainous habitats is a pronounced feature of this regional cuisine.

China's best soy sauce is also produced in the eastern provinces, and the technique of braising meat using soy sauce, sugar and spices was perfected here. Meat cooked in this manner takes on a dark mauve hue auspiciously described as 'red', a colour associated with good fortune.

How to Eat & Drink

When dining together the Chinese tend to eat in a communal fashion, with all dishes arriving on the table at roughly the same time and everyone sharing from each plate, rather than ordering their own dish. Tables often tend to be large and banquet style, to accommodate large numbers of diners. In this case, dishes may be laid on a lazy Susan, to be revolved. Diners will tend to fill the bowls of their neighbours or guests, out of courtesy.

Large Chinese restaurants are often bright and flooded with light, rather than concocting a darker, more subdued dining environment, though more romantic restaurants can be found.

Table Manners

Chinese meals are generally relaxed affairs with no strict rules of etiquette. Meals can commence in a Confucian vein before spiralling into total Taoist mayhem, fuelled by incessant toasts with *báijiǔ* (a white spirit) or beer.

Meals typically unfold with one person ordering on behalf of a group. When a group dines, a selection of dishes is ordered for everyone to share rather than individual diners ordering a dish just for themselves. It is common practice and not impolite (unless messy) to use your own chopsticks to serve yourself straight from each dish. Soup may appear midway through the meal, or at the end. Rice often arrives at the end of the meal; if you would like it earlier, just ask. Chinese diners will often slurp their noodles quite noisily, which is not considered impolite.

It is good form to fill your neighbours' tea cups or beer glasses when they are empty. To serve yourself tea or any other drink without serving others first is bad

---

DESSERTS & SWEETS

The Chinese do not generally eat dessert, but fruit – typically watermelon (*xīguā*) or oranges (*chéng*) – often concludes a meal. Ice cream can be ordered in some places, but in general sweet desserts (*tiánpǐn*) are consumed as snacks and are seldom available in restaurants.

form. Appreciation to the pourer is indicated by gently tapping the middle finger on the table.

When your teapot needs a refill, signal this to the waiter by simply taking the lid off the pot.

Don't insist on paying for the bill if someone else is tenaciously determined to pay – usually the person who invited you to dinner. By all means offer to pay, but then raise your hands in mock surrender when resistance is met. To pay for a meal when another person is determined to do so is to make them lose face.

Chinese toothpick etiquette is similar to that found in other Asian nations: one hand excavates with the toothpick, while the other hand shields the mouth.

When to Eat

Breakfast (早饭; *zǎofàn*) Gets going from around 6am and is generally light, simple and over and done with in a flash. Brekkie may simply be a bowl of rice porridge (粥; *zhōu*) or its watery relative, rice gruel (稀饭; *xīfàn*). Pickles, boiled eggs, steamed buns, fried peanuts and deep-fried dough sticks (油条; *yóutiáo*) are also popular, washed down with warm soy milk. Breakfast at your Chinese hotel often looks like this. Coffee can

be hard to find down the side streets, unless you can stumble across a cafe.

Lunch (午饭; *wǔfàn*) Usually eaten early, from around 11.30am, either self-cooked or a takeaway at home, or in a street-side restaurant. Lunch is taken pretty seriously, but can be rushed into a short break for harried white-collar staff in big cities. It won't ever be skipped, however. Some restaurants will close at around 2.30pm to take a break before reopening around 5pm.

Dinner (晚饭; *wǎnfàn*) The social meal of the day, when everyone stops work (下班; *xiàbān*) and gets together (聚一聚; *jùyijù*) to let their hair down or have some fun (热闹一下; *rènàoyixià*). Dinner kicks off around 6pm – slightly later than in the old communist days when everyone would typically down tools at 5pm and reach for their chopsticks. If you're dining out, it can go on to the early hours, but it's also not unusual for local restaurants to close their kitchens by 9pm, so check ahead and plan to eat earlier than you usually might.

Where to Eat

Chinese eateries come in every conceivable shape, size and type, from shabby, hole-in-the-wall noodle outfits with flimsy PVC furniture, blaring TV sets and well-worn plastic menus, to gilded, banquet-style

---

VEGETARIANISM

If you'd rather chew on a legume than a leg of lamb, it can be hard to find truly vegetarian dishes. China's history of famine and poverty means the consumption of meat has always been a sign of status, and is symbolic of health and wealth. Eating meat is also considered to enhance male virility, so vegetarian men raise eyebrows. Partly because of this, there is virtually no vegetarian movement in China, although Chinese people may forgo meat for Buddhist reasons. For the same reasons, they may avoid meat on certain days of the month but remain carnivorous at other times.

You will find that vegetables are often fried in animal-based oils. Vegetable soups are often made with chicken or beef stock, so simply choosing 'vegetable' items on the menu is ineffective. A dish that you are told does not contain meat may still mean it is riddled with tiny pieces of meat. In Beijing and Shanghai you will, however, find a generous crop of vegetarian restaurants to choose from, alongside outfits such as Element Fresh, which has a decent range of healthy vegetarian options.

Out of the large cities, your best bet may be to head to a sizeable active Buddhist temple or monastery, where Buddhist vegetarian restaurants are often open to the public. Buddhist vegetarian food typically consists of 'mock meat' dishes created from tofu, wheat gluten, potato and other vegetables. Some of the dishes are almost works of art, with vegetarian ingredients sculpted to look like spare ribs or fried chicken. Sometimes the chefs go to great lengths to create 'bones' from carrots and lotus roots.

If you want to say 'I am a vegetarian' in Chinese, the phrase to use is '*wǒ chī sù*' (我吃素).

Preparing dim sum

restaurants where elegant *cheongsam*-clad waitresses show you to your seat, straighten your chopsticks and bring you a warm hand towel and a gold-embossed wine list. In between are legions of very serviceable midrange restaurants serving cuisine from across China.

As dining in China is such a big, sociable and often ostentatious affair, many Chinese banqueting-style restaurants have huge round tables, 1000-candle-power electric lights and precious little sense of intimacy or romance. Over-attentive and ever-present staff may add to the discomfort for foreigners, but remember that they are trying their best.

Cāntīng (餐厅), **Cānguǎn** (餐馆), **Fànguǎn** (饭馆) or occasionally **Fàndiàn** (饭店; this term also used to mean a 'hotel') or **Jiǔdiàn** (酒店; also often means a 'hotel') Restaurants, serving pretty much everything, but often with a speciality, eg Chuāncài (川菜; Sichuan food), Yuècài (粤菜; Cantonese food) or Dōngběicài (东北菜; northeast food).

Miànguǎn (面馆) Noodle bar, serving all manner of noodles, either dry or in soup.

Jiǎoziguǎn (饺子馆) Serves dumplings, either boiled (水饺; *shuǐjiǎo*) or fried (煎饺; *jiānjiǎo*).

Shāokǎodiàn (烧烤店) Barbecue or grilled-meat restaurants.

Sùcàiguǎn (素菜馆) Vegetarian restaurant (often found in Buddhist temples).

Yèshì (夜市) Night market; most towns will have one. Point at what you want, grab a wobbly stool, tuck your elbows in and enjoy.

Kāfēiguǎn (咖啡馆) Cafe, serving coffee and usually baked goodies, too. Will normally have an English menu, but not always.

Xīcāntīng (西餐厅) Western restaurant.

Kuàicāntīng (快餐厅) Fast food.

Menu Decoder

Càidān (菜单) Menu. Very occasionally with English translations, usually just in Chinese.

Yīngwén càipǔ (英文菜谱) English menu. Next best thing is a trusty photo menu.

Tāng (汤) Soup. Usually served with the other dishes, rather than up front.

Ròu (肉) Meat (sometimes the word Hūn – 荤 – is used). Meat dishes will generally, but not always, be listed separately on the menu.

Shūcài or **Sùcài** (蔬菜; 素菜) Vegetables; generally a large amount of choice on any menu.

Tàocān (套餐) Set meal. Not a very common choice at all, unless it's a fast-food restaurant.

Tiánpǐn (甜品) Dessert, served at the end of the meal.

Értóng Càipǔ (儿童菜谱) Children's menu. Usually a selection of kids' dishes, sometimes served as a set. Rare.

Drinking

China's most popular drink is tea (茶; *chá*), consumed across the nation. When you sit down in a restaurant, you will often be presented with a cup.

The Chinese were the first to cultivate tea, and the art of brewing and drinking it has been popular since Tang times (AD 618–907). An old Chinese saying identifies tea as one of the seven basic necessities of life, along with firewood, oil, rice, salt, soy sauce and vinegar. Tea is to the Chinese what fine wine is to the French: a beloved beverage savoured for its fine aroma, distinctive flavour and pleasing aftertaste.

China has three main types of tea: green tea (绿茶; *lǜ chá)*, black tea (红茶; *hóng chá)* and *wūlóng* (乌龙茶; a semifermented tea, halfway between black and green tea). In addition there are other variations, including jasmine (茶水; *cháshuǐ)* and chrysanthemum (菊花茶; *júhuā chá)*. Some famous regional teas of China are Fujian's *tiě guānyīn, pú'ěrh* from Yunnan and Zhejiang's *lóngjǐng* tea. Eight-treasure tea (*bābǎo chá)* consists of rock sugar, dates, nuts and tea combined in a cup; it makes a delicious treat.

Alcohol in China

China drinks more beer than any other nation – almost twice as much as the US – though its huge population is to blame for that statistic. Per capita, the Chinese drink less than half of what their US counterparts consume. Most drinking is done with meals and is an important, if not crucial, part of many business deals.

Beer

If tea is the most popular drink in China, then beer (啤酒; *píjiǔ*) is surely second. Many towns and cities have their own brewery and label, though a remarkable feat of socialist standardisation ensures a striking similarity in flavour and strength. You can drink bathtubs of the stuff and still navigate a straight line. If you want your beer cold, ask for *liáng de* (凉的); if you want it truly arctic, call for *bīngzhèn de* (冰镇的).

The best-known beer is Tsingtao, made with Lao Shan mineral water, which lends it a sparkling quality. It was originally a German beer, since the town of Qingdao (formerly spelled 'Tsingtao') was once a German concession. The Chinese inherited the brewery, which dates to 1903, along with Bavarian brewing methods. Look out too for various forms of dark beer (黑啤; *hēipí*), brewed by Tsingtao and other breweries.

Several foreign beers are also brewed in China and there's a growing market for craft brews in the wealthier cities. If you crave variety, many of the bars we list should have a selection of foreign imported beers; prices will be high, however.

Spirits

The word 'wine' gets rather loosely translated – many Chinese 'wines' are in fact spirits. Maotai, a favourite of Chinese drinkers, is a very expensive spirit called *báijiǔ* made from sorghum (a type of millet) and used for toasts at banquets. The cheap alternative is Erguotou, distilled in Beijing but available all over China; look out for the Red Star (Hongxing) brand. *Báijiǔ* ranges across the alcohol spectrum, from milder forms to around 65% proof. Milder rice wine is intended mainly for cooking rather than drinking, but can be drunk warm like sake.

Whiskey, red wine and cocktails are largely status symbols and consumed as such.

Regions at a Glance

The high-altitude, far west of China, including Tibet, Qinghai and west Sichuan, gradually and fitfully steps down to level out as it nears the prosperous and well-irrigated canal-town provinces of Jiangsu and Zhejiang, and the dazzling metropolis of Shanghai in the east. The lion's share of scenic showstoppers and hiking territory resides in the mountainous interior of China, while in the mighty northwest, peaks and deserts meet in dramatic fashion. Minority culture is a speciality of the west and southwest, and of the remote border regions. Different cuisines range across the entire nation, from the hardy northeast to the warm jungles of the steamy southwest.

Beijing

History
Temples
Food

Beijing's imperial pedigree (and the Great Wall) assures it a rich vein of dynastic history, balanced by splendid seams of temple and *hutong* (narrow alleyway) architecture. Wining and dining is a further attraction, with the capital home to a resourceful restaurant scene.

p66

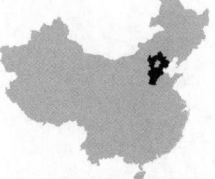

Tianjin & Hebei

History
Temples
Outdoors

Tianjin's spruced-up foreign concession streetscapes echo stylish Shanghai, and some standout pagodas and temples can be found in Hebei, where the rural side of China – peppered with rustic village getaways – comes to the fore.

p144

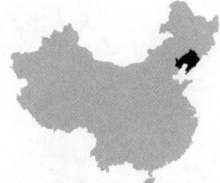

Liaoning

Festivals
History
Minority Culture

In history-rich Liaoning, imperial relics contend with the legacy of Russian and Japanese colonialism. The North Korean border at Dandong is a sobering contrast to the wild beer festival at Dalian.

p169

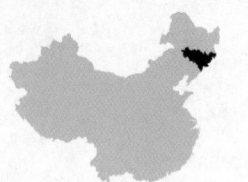

Jilin

Landscapes
Culture
Skiing

Boasting China's largest nature reserve, and a top ski destination, Jilin exerts a pull on the nature lover. On the trail of the exotic? Head to Ji'an for the ruins of the ancient Korean Koguryo empire.

p188

Heilongjiang

Festivals
Culture
Nature

Fire and ice are the highlights in this province where volcanic explosions have left one of China's most mesmerising landscapes, and the winter's bitter climate provides the raw materials for a spectacular ice-sculpture festival.

p199

Shandong

History
Mountains
Seaside

Shandong groans under the weight of its historical heavy hitters: Confucius' home and tomb at Qufu, and sacred Tai Shan. Then there's the home of Tsingtao beer, Qingdao, a breezy, laid-back, modern and sophisticated port city.

p214

Jiangsu

Canal Towns
Outdoors
History

Jiangsu's awash with cute-as-pie canal towns – all reachable as day trips from neighbouring Shanghai. The provincial capital, Nanjing, has history in spades, with its fabulous Ming wall and epic past as former national capital.

p252

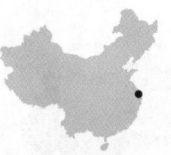

Shanghai

Architecture
Food
Urban Style

Shanghai exudes a unique style unlike anywhere else in China. There's plenty to do, from non-stop shopping and skyscraper-hopping to standout art, fantastic eats and touring the city's elegant art deco heritage.

p280

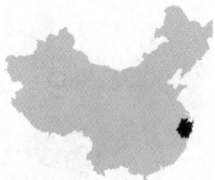

Zhejiang

Canal Towns
Outdoors
Islands

Hangzhou is one of China's most appealing cities, while traditional charm abounds in the canal town of Wuzhen. Further south, the gorgeous villages of Xinye and Zhuge, and the island of Putuoshan, are stunning pastoral escapes.

p340

Fujian

Architecture
History
Islands

Fujian is Hakka heartland and home to the intriguing *tǔlóu* – massive packed stone, wood and mud structures once housing hundreds of families. Gulang Yu, a tiny, hilly island off Xiamen, is decorated with crumbling colonial villas.

p365

Shanxi

History
Culture
Mountains

Repository to the superlative Buddhist grottoes at Yungang, Shanxi also brings you the beautiful Buddhist mountain, Wutai Shan; the intact walled city of Pingyao; the rebuilt city fortifications of Datong; and time-worn sections of the Great Wall.

p386

Shaanxi

Historic Sites
Museums
Mountains

Archaeological sites lie scattered across the plains surrounding Shaanxi's magnificent walled capital, Xi'an, where museums galore await. Blow off all that ancient dust with a trip to Hua Shan, one of China's five holy Taoist peaks.

p407

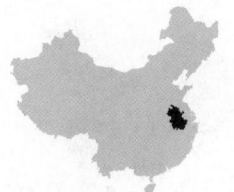

Anhui

Villages
Mountains
Outdoors

The charming World Heritage–listed Hui villages of Hongcun and Xidi are some of China's best-preserved settlements. But let's not forget that astonishing mountain, Huangshan, where soaring granite peaks and ethereal mists have inspired legions of poets and painters.

p429

Henan

History
Temples
Mountains

Henan's overture of dynastic antiquity is balanced by some excellent mountain escapes and the quirky allure of Nanjiecun, China's last Maoist collective. The province's *wǔshù* (martial arts) credentials come no better: the Shaolin Temple is here.

p449

Hubei

Scenic Wonders
History
Rivers

Slashed by the mighty Yangzi River, history-rich Hubei is one of the gateways to the Three Gorges, but Taoist martial artists may find themselves drawn to Wudang Shan, home of taichi and scenic views.

p471

Jiangxi

Scenery
Mountains
Ancient Villages

Communists herald it as the mythic starting point of the Long March, but it's the spectacular mountain scenery and hiking trails past preserved villages and terraced fields that should pop Jiangxi into your travel plans.

p485

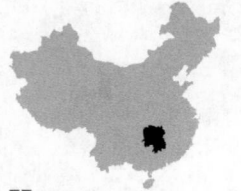

Hunan

Ancient Towns
Minority Villages
Mountains

Home to one of China's most enjoyable ancient towns, Fenghuang (beautifully illuminated come nightfall), as well as the sacred mountain of Heng Shan, the otherworldly peaks of Zhangjiajie, and secluded Miao and Dong villages.

p502

Hong Kong

Food
Shopping
Scenery

This culinary capital offers the best of China and beyond, while a seductive mix of vintage and cutting-edge fashion attracts armies of shoppers. Meanwhile, leafy mountains, shimmering waters, skyscrapers and tenements make an unlikely but poetic match.

p521

Macau

Food
Architecture
Casinos

Marrying flavours from five continents, Macanese cooking is as unique as the cityscape, where Taoist temples meet baroque churches on cobbled streets with Chinese names. It's also a billionaires playground where casino-resorts and other luxuries vie for space.

p560

Guangdong

Food
History
Architecture

A strong gastronomic culture offers travellers the chance to savour world-renowned Cantonese cuisine. Guangdong's seafaring temperament has brought the region diverse, exotic architectural styles, including the World Heritage–listed watchtowers of Kaiping.

p581

Hainan

Beaches
Cycling
Surfing

When it comes to golden-sand beaches and warm clear waters, this tropical island doesn't disappoint. An ideal cycling destination, Hainan attracts in-the-know adventurers with its good roads, balmy winters, varied landscape and surfing spots.

p620

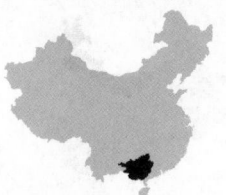

Guangxi

Scenery
Outdoors
Cycling

Famed for the dreamy karst landscapes of Yangshuo, Guangxi also offers lush green valleys, charming folksy villages and countless walking, cycling and rafting opportunities, as well as Weizhou Island, a short trip from sleepy Beihai.

p636

Guizhou

Festivals
Minority Villages
Waterfalls

With more folk festivals than anywhere else in China, you can celebrate here with locals year-round. Throw in an abundance of waterfalls for nature lovers, lovely Zhenyuan and countless wooden Dong and Miao minority villages.

p663

Yunnan

Ancient Towns
Mountains
Minority Villages

Yunnan has it all: towering Himalayan mountains, tropical jungle, sublime rice terraces and over half of China's minority groups, plus historic, little-visited villages such as Nuodeng and Heijing, gorgeous and ancient Lijiang, fantastic trekking and great food.

p685

Sichuan

Mountains
Scenery
Cuisine

Stay in central or southern Sichuan for steamy bamboo forests and Ming dynasty villages. Head north for stunning lakes and alpine scenery. Venture west for remote Tibetan grasslands and towering peaks. Spicy Sichuan cuisine is an abundant pleasure.

p748

Chongqing

Cuisine
Ancient Villages
River Trips

A unique city with a unique location, hilly Chongqing hugs cliffs overlooking the Yangzi, bursts with old-China energy, offers some fascinating day trips to historic villages and is home to Chongqing hotpot – the spiciest dish on the planet.

p805

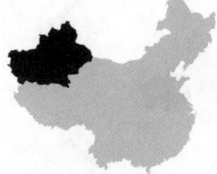

Xinjiang

History
Minority Culture
Nature

Bazaars, kebabs, camels and Uyghur culture are just a few of the things that hint at your arrival in Central Asia. Ancient Silk Road towns include Turpan, Kashgar and Hotan, while hikers gravitate to Kanas Lake and the Tian Shan range.

p833

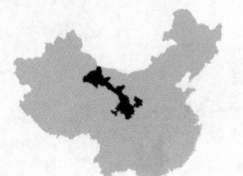

Gansu

Silk Road
Tibetan Culture
Buddhism

Gansu is about diversity: colourful Tibetan regions in the southwest, desert dunes in the northwest and a rich accumulation of Silk Road culture through the middle. Think deserts, mountains, Buddhist temples, camels, yaks, pilgrims and nomads.

p856

Ningxia

History
Minority Culture
Outdoor Activities

In the designated homeland of the Muslim Hui, visit the great tombs of the Xixia, nomadic rock art and the enormous Buddhas of Xumi Shan. For camel trekking or sliding down sand dunes, head for the Tengger Desert.

p886

Inner Mongolia

Remote Journeys
Food
Outdoor Activities

Ride a Mongolian horse alongside the Russian border, roam across verdant grasslands or sit down to a steaming Mongolian hotpot. Further-flung western Inner Mongolia is a stunning landscape of towering sand dunes, desert lakes and ancient ruins.

p899

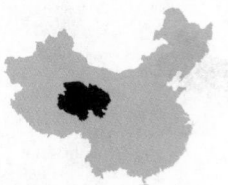

Qinghai

Monasteries
Scenery
Culture

A land of monasteries, sublime mountain and grassland vistas and Tibetan culture, vast and remote Qinghai – way up on the Tibetan plateau – is for those who like their travel rough. Don't expect a hot shower and a coffee every morning.

p913

Tibet

Monasteries
Scenery
Culture

The 'Roof of the World' is a stunningly beautiful high plateau of turquoise lakes, desert valleys and Himalayan peaks, dotted with monasteries, yaks and sacred Buddhist sites. Tight and ever-changing travel regulations can easily derail travel plans.

p932

On the Road

Heilongjiang p199

Jilin p188

Liaoning p169

Xinjiang p833

Inner Mongolia p899

Beijing p66

Tianjin & Hebei p144

Ningxia p886

Shanxi p386

Shandong p214

Qinghai p913

Gansu p856

Shaanxi p407

Henan p449

Jiangsu p252

Shanghai p280

Tibet p932

Anhui p429

Hubei p471

Zhejiang p340

Sichuan p748

Chongqing p805

Hunan p502

Jiangxi p485

Fujian p365

Guizhou p663

Yunnan p685

Guangxi p636

Guangdong p581

Hong Kong p521

Hainan p620

Macau p560

Beijing

🔊 010 / POP 21.54 MILLION

Best Places for Peking Duck

➡ Taste of Dadong (p116)

➡ Shèng Yǒng Xīng (p118)

➡ Duck de Chine (p111)

➡ Siji Minfu (p112)

➡ Jigzun Peking Duck (p117)

Best Places to Stay

➡ Orchid (p108)

➡ Rosewood Beijing (p110)

➡ Opposite House (p110)

➡ Côté Cour (p108)

➡ Mandarin Oriental Wangfujing (p108)

Why Go?

Ancient walled capital turned sprawling megacity, Beijing (Běijīng, 北京), remains the central stronghold of Chinese power. Ghosts of emperors past haunt the Forbidden City, tourists trail past Mao in his Tian'anmen Sq mausoleum, while the current crop of cadres run the show from their lakeside HQ at Zhongnanhai.

A uniquely micromanaged metropolis, Beijing today is the control room for the 'Chinese Dream' of great rejuvenation. Yet it's also China's richest repository of historic and cultural attractions. Multiple Unesco World Heritage Sites, temples, altars, palaces and socialist monuments jostle for space with skyscrapers, ring roads and mega-malls.

If that all sounds a bit overwhelming, you can still tune out amid historic *hutong* (alleyways), alongside willow-lined lakes, in divey music clubs and avant-garde art galleries, or out on the Great Wall, draped dreamily across Beijing's northern mountains.

When to Go
Beijing

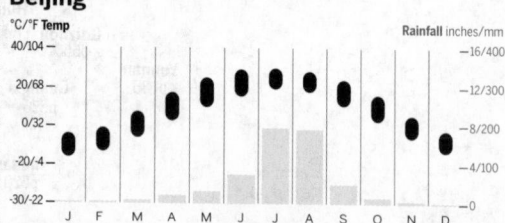

Late Apr – early Jun Fine weather and fewer tourists.	**Sep** The best month, before the October holiday hordes descend.	**Dec** From hot chestnuts to ice-skating, Beijing wears its winter coat well.

History

Although it seems it has presided over China since time immemorial, Beijing (literally, 'Northern Capital') – positioned outside the central heartland of Chinese civilisation – only emerged as a cultural and political force that would shape the destiny of China with the 13th-century Mongol occupation of China.

Chinese historical sources identify the earliest settlements from 1045 BC. In later centuries Beijing was successively occupied by foreign forces: it was established as an auxiliary capital under the Khitan, nomadic Mongolic people who formed China's Liao dynasty (AD 907–1125). Later the Jurchens, Tungusic people originally from the Siberian region, turned the city into their Jin dynasty capital (1115–1234), during which time it was enclosed within fortified walls, accessed by eight gates.

But in 1215 the army of the great Mongol warrior Genghis Khan razed Beijing, an event that was paradoxically to mark the city's transformation into a powerful national capital. Apart from the first 53 years of the Ming dynasty and 21 years of Nationalist rule in the 20th century, it has enjoyed this status to the present day.

The city came to be called Dàdū (大都; Great Capital), also assuming the Mongol name Khanbalik (the Khan's town). By 1279, under the rule of Kublai Khan, grandson of Genghis Khan, Dàdū was the capital of the largest empire the world has ever known.

The basic grid of present-day Beijing was laid during the Ming dynasty, and Emperor Yongle (r 1403–24) is credited with being the true architect of the modern city. Much of Beijing's grandest architecture, such as the Forbidden City and the iconic Hall of Prayer for Good Harvests in the Temple of Heaven Park, date from his reign.

The Manchus, who invaded China in the 17th century to establish the Qing dynasty, essentially preserved Beijing's form. In the last 120 years of the Qing dynasty, though, Beijing was subjected to power struggles, invasions and ensuing chaos. The list is long: Anglo-French troops, who in 1860 burnt the Old Summer Palace to the ground; the corrupt regime of Empress Dowager Cixi; the catastrophic Boxer Rebellion; the Japanese occupation of 1937; and the Nationalists. Each and every period left its indelible mark, although the shape and symmetry of Beijing was maintained.

Modern Beijing came of age when, in January 1949, the People's Liberation Army (PLA) entered the city. On 1 October of that year Mao Zedong proclaimed a 'People's Republic' from the Gate of Heavenly Peace to an audience of some 500,000 citizens.

Like the emperors before them, the communists significantly altered the face of Beijing. The *páilóu* (decorative archways) were destroyed and city blocks pulverised to widen major boulevards. The city's magnificent outer walls were levelled in the interests of traffic circulation. Soviet experts and technicians poured in, bringing their own Stalinesque touches.

The past three decades have finalised Beijing's century-long transformation from an ancient walled capital into a showpiece megacity, with towering skyscrapers, vast shopping malls and the world's second-largest subway system (behind Shanghai). In the process, Beijing has shed whole neighbourhoods of *hutong* alleyways and transformed (in some areas) beyond recognition.

And yet, a counter-narrative to Beijing's woeful record of heritage preservation is that once off-limits slices of the old capital are being restored and opened to the public for the first time. From unseen nooks of the Forbidden City to former temples and guildhalls, arguably there's more for the average tourist to see today than at any time in the past. Which, naturally, is all the more reason to put Beijing at the very top of your itinerary.

 Sights

Beijing is inseparable from the Forbidden City, the vast and secretive palace complex

---

ⓘ PRICES

Sleeping
The following price ranges represent a standard double room per night.
¥ less than ¥600
¥¥ ¥600–¥1200
¥¥¥ more than ¥1200

Eating
The following price ranges refer to the cost of a meal for one person.
¥ less than ¥70
¥¥ ¥70–170
¥¥¥ more than ¥170

Beijing Highlights

1 Forbidden City (p70) Exploring the secretive world of 24 emperors.

2 Temple of Heaven (p90) Communicating with the gods at China's most sacred imperial altar.

3 Summer Palace (p99) Walking the impossibly ornate Long Corridor, before clambering up Longevity Hill for the grand view.

4 798 Art District (p95) Gallery-hopping in Asia's finest contemporary-art cluster, set within a model communist factory complex.

5 Jingshan Park (p77) Clambering up to the Pavilion of Ten Thousands Springs for one of the finest views in China.

6 Lama Temple (p84) Gazing in wonder at the 18m-tall Buddha carved from a single trunk of Tibetan sandalwood.

7 Drum & Bell Towers (p81) Standing in the square that connects this mighty edifice to its compatriot the Bell Tower.

8 Tian'anmen Square (p75) Seeing the five-starred Red Flag raised or lowered by goose-stepping soldiers under the stony gaze of Mao Zedong (in portrait form).

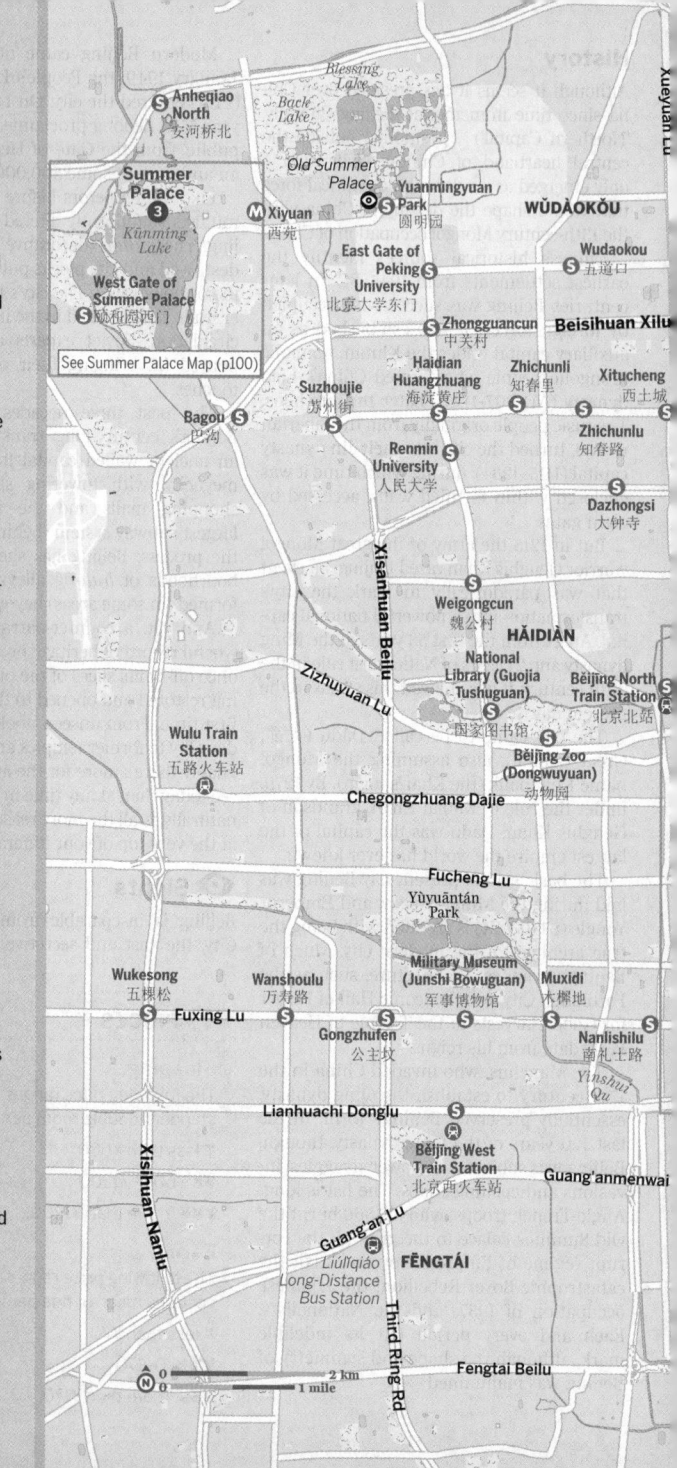

at the dead centre of a compass-perfect cityscape conceived by Ming emperor Yongle, the great builder. Remarkably, central Beijing retains its historic, low-slung layout, a fantastical masterwork of feng shui and divine order, where you'll find most of the major historic sights. For a grand overview, clamber up Jingshan Park (p77) and drink it all in.

◉ Forbidden City & Dongcheng Central

★**Forbidden City**　　　　HISTORIC SITE
(紫禁城, Zǐjìn Chéng; Map p74; ☑ 010 8500 7114; www.dpm.org.cn; Nov-Mar ¥40, Apr-Oct ¥60, Clock Exhibition Hall ¥10, Hall of Jewellery ¥10, audio guide ¥40; ◷ 8.30am-5pm Apr-Oct, to 4.30pm Nov-Mar, last entry 1hr prior to closing, closed Mon; Ⓢ Line 1 to Tian'anmen West, exit B, or Tian'anmen East, exit A) Enclosed by 3.5km of citadel walls at the very heart of Beijing, the Unescolisted Forbidden City is China's largest and best-preserved collection of ancient buildings – large enough to comfortably absorb the 16 million visitors it receives each year. Steeped in stultifying ritual, this otherworldly palace was the reclusive home to two dynasties of imperial rule, sharing 900-plus buildings with a retinue of eunuchs, servants and concubines, until the Republic overthrew the last Qing emperor in 1911.

The year 2020 marks the 600th anniversary of the Forbidden City, which the palace intends to celebrate by ensuring more of the complex is open for visitors than at any other time in its history as a tourist attraction. Which is a longer history than you might think – the Palace Museum (故宫博物馆, Gùgōng Bówùguǎn), as the Forbidden City is officially called, first opened in 1925, just one year after Puyi, the abdicated 'last emperor', was evicted from the Inner Court.

Built between 1406 and 1420 by the Ming emperor Yongle, the construction of the Forbidden City was a titanic undertaking, employing battalions of labourers and craftspeople. Pillars of precious *nanmu* wood were floated from the jungles of southwest China to the capital, while blocks of quarried stone were hauled to the palace in winter over ingenious ice roads. Once built, the Forbidden City was governed by a stultifying code of rules, protocol and superstition; 24 emperors of the Ming and Qing dynasties governed China from its closed-off world, often erratically and haphazardly, until revolution swept them all away just a century ago. Despite its age, most of the buildings you see are post-18th-century Qing dynasty constructions and renovations – fire was a constant hazard, hence the enormous brass water vats everywhere.

➡ **Entering the Forbidden City**

Through the Meridian Gate, you pass into a vast courtyard and cross the **Golden Stream** (金水, Jīn Shuǐ) – shaped to resemble a Tartar bow and spanned by five marble bridges – on your way to the magnificent **Gate of Supreme Harmony** (太和门, Tàihé Mén; Map p74; Forbidden City), beyond which the courtyard could hold an imperial audience of 100,000 people.

➡ **Mounting the Wall**

Since 2018 visitors have been permitted to climb the Forbidden City's Wall just inside and to the east of the **Meridian Gate** (午门, Wǔ Mén; Map p74; Forbidden City); follow it eastwards to the Corner Tower, and then north to the East Prosperity Gate. This route includes the **Gallery of Historic Architecture**, with exhibition spaces in the Corner Tower and the splendid East Prosperity Gate. In total, around three-quarters of the 3.4km wall wall can now be climbed: a fine way to leave the crowds behind and take awesome photographs.

➡ **First Side Galleries**

Before you pass through the Gate of Supreme Harmony to reach the Forbidden City's star attractions, veer off to the west of the huge courtyard to visit the **Hall of Martial Valour** (武英殿, Wǔyīng Diàn; Map p74; Forbidden City), where emperors would receive ministers. It houses a changing line-up of exhibitions. Just to the south is the **Furniture Gallery**, occupying an area known as

---

ⓘ **FORBIDDEN CITY TICKETS**

Tickets for the Forbidden City now need to be booked and paid for online, but there's a snag: at time of research the official ticketing website (https://gugong.ktmtech.cn) was in Chinese only. Although a single ticket booth remains open for foreign tourists, with daily visitor numbers capped at 80,000, you might be turned away if you arrive without a ticket. Many hotels and hostels can help you buy tickets in advance. You can also purchase tickets at Trip.com (www.trip.com), selecting either a morning or afternoon entry slot for the day of your choice. You will need your passport for entry.

the Southern Storehouses, which opened for the first time in 2018.

The **Hall of Literary Brilliance** (文化殿, Wénhuà Diàn; Map p74; Forbidden City) complex to the east of the Meridian Gate was formerly used as a residence by the crown prince. It was rebuilt in 1683 after being destroyed by fire. It, too, hosts a changing line-up of exhibitions throughout the year, but is sometimes closed between November and March.

➔ Three Great Halls

Raised on a three-tier marble terrace representing the Chinese character for king (王, *wáng*), are the **Three Great Halls** (三大殿, Sān Dàdiàn), the glorious heart of the Forbidden City. The **Hall of Supreme Harmony** (太和殿, Tàihé Diàn; Map p74; Forbidden City) is the most important and largest structure in the Forbidden City, and was once the tallest building in the capital. It was used for state occasions, such as the emperor's birthday, coronations and the nomination of military leaders. Inside the Hall of Supreme Harmony is a richly decorated **Dragon Throne** (龙椅, Lóngyǐ), from which the emperor would preside over trembling officials. The entire court had to touch the floor nine times with their foreheads (known as kowtowing) in the emperor's presence. At the back of the throne is a carved Xumishan, the Buddhist paradise, signifying the throne's supremacy. Today you can only view it from the outside, and it virtually requires a rugby scrum to do so.

Behind the Hall of Supreme Harmony is the **Hall of Central Harmony** (中和殿, Zhōnghé Diàn; Map p74; Forbidden City), which was used as the emperor's transit lounge. Here he would make last-minute preparations, rehearse speeches and receive ministers.

The third of the Great Halls is the **Hall of Preserving Harmony** (保和殿, Bǎohé Diàn; Map p74; Forbidden City), used for banquets and later for imperial examinations. The hall has no support pillars, and to its rear is a 250-tonne marble imperial carriageway carved with dragons and clouds, which was hauled into the city on an ingenious path of ice – they had to wait until winter to do so. The peripheral buildings surrounding the Three Great Halls were used for storing gold, silver, silks, carpets and other treasures, and now house museum exhibits.

➔ Lesser Central Halls

The basic configuration of the Three Great Halls is echoed by the next group of buildings, reached through the **Gate of Heavenly Purity** (乾清门, Qiánqīng Mén; Map p74; Forbidden City). Traditionally, this gate was the dividing line between the ceremonial outer court and the inner court to the north, where the emperors and their entourage actually lived and work. Smaller in scale, these buildings were more important in terms of real power, which in China traditionally lies at the back door.

The first structure is the **Palace of Heavenly Purity** (乾清宫, Qiánqīng Gōng; Map p74; Forbidden City; ▣), a residence of Ming and early Qing emperors, and later an audience hall for receiving foreign envoys and high officials.

Immediately behind it is the **Hall of Union** (交泰殿, Jiāotài Diàn; Map p74; Forbidden City), which contains a clepsydra – a water clock made in 1745 with five bronze vessels and a calibrated scale. You'll also find a mechanical clock built in 1797 and a collection of imperial jade seals on display. The **Palace of Earthly Tranquillity** (坤宁宫, Kūnníng Gōng; Map p74; Forbidden City) was the imperial couple's bridal chamber and the centre of operations for the palace harem.

➔ Imperial Garden

At the northern end of the Forbidden City is the **Imperial Garden** (御花园, Yù Huāyuán; Map p74; Forbidden City), a classical Chinese garden with 7000 sq metres of fine landscaping, including rockeries, walkways, pavilions and ancient, carbuncular cypresses. At its centre is the double-eaved **Hall of Imperial Peace**. Nearby, the **Lodge of Spiritual Cultivation** is where British tutor Sir Reginald Johnston gave English lessons to the abdicated 'last emperor' Puyi.

➔ Treasure Gallery

On the northeastern edge of the complex is what feels like a mini Forbidden City all of its own. This is the **Palace of Tranquil Longevity** (宁寿宫, Níng Shòu Gōng), built around 1771 for Qing Emperor Qianlong's retirement, though he never moved in. Today it holds the **Treasure Gallery** (珍宝馆, Zhēn Bǎo Guǎn; Map p74; Forbidden City; ¥10), one of the palace's most important collections of ornamental objects, which are crafted from gold, silver, jade, emeralds, pearls, and other gems and semi-precious stones.

The complex is entered from the south – not far from the unmissable **Gallery of Clocks** (钟表馆, Zhōngbiǎo Guǎn; Map p74; Forbidden City; ¥10; ⊙ 8.30am-4pm). Just inside the **entrance** (Map p74), you'll find a beautiful glazed **Nine Dragon Screen** (九龙壁, Jiǔlóng Bì; Map

Forbidden City

WALKING TOUR

After entering through the imperious Meridian Gate, resist the temptation to dive straight into the star attractions and veer west to see the **1 Hall of Martial Valour**, and the new Furniture Exhibition in the Southern Storehouses beside it.

Walk back to the central complex and head through the magnificent Gate of Supreme Harmony towards the Three Great Halls: first, the largest – the **2 Hall of Supreme Harmony** – followed by the **3 Hall of Middle Harmony** and the **4 Hall of Preserving Harmony**, behind which slopes the enormous Marble Imperial Carriageway.

Turn right here to visit the fascinating **5 Clock Exhibition Hall** before entering the **6 Complete Palace of Peace & Longevity**, a mini Forbidden City constructed along the eastern axis of the main complex. It includes the beautiful **7 Nine Dragon Screen** and, to the north, a series of halls, housing some excellent exhibitions and known collectively as the Treasure Gallery. Don't miss the **8 Pavilion of Cheerful Melodies**, a wonderful three-storey opera house.

Work your way to the far north of this section, then head west to the **9 Imperial Garden**, with its ancient cypress trees and pretty pavilions, before exiting via the garden's West Gate (behind the Thousand Year Pavilion) to explore the **10 Western Palaces**, an absorbing collection of courtyard homes where many of the emperors lived during their reign.

Exit this section at its southwest corner before turning back on yourself to walk north through the Gate of Heavenly Purity to see the three final Central Halls – the **11 Palace of Heavenly Purity**, the **12 Hall of Union** and the **13 Palace of Earthly Tranquillity** – before leaving via the North Gate.

Water Vats

More than 300 copper and brass water vats dot the palace complex. They were used for fighting fires and in winter were prevented from freezing over by using thick quilts.

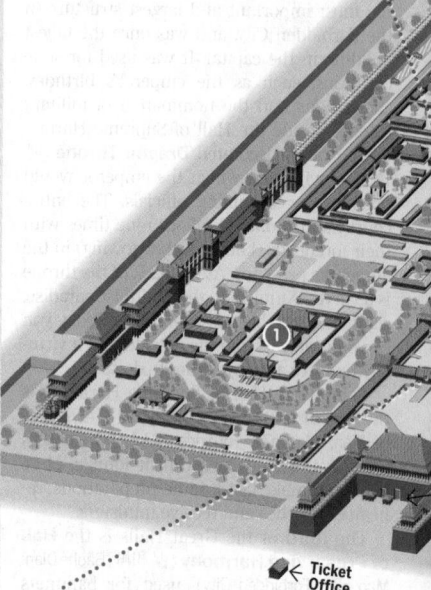

← Ticket Office

Guardian Lions

Pairs of lions guard important buildings. The male has a paw placed on a globe (representing the emperor's power over the world). The female has her paw on a baby lion (representing the emperor's fertility).

Kneeling Elephants
At the northern entrance of the Imperial Garden are two bronze elephants kneeling in an anatomically impossible fashion, which symbolise the power of the emperor; even elephants kowtowed before him.

Nine Dragon Screen
One of only three of its type left in China, this beautiful glazed dragon screen served to protect the Hall of Imperial Supremacy from evil spirits.

Forbidden City North Gate (exit only)

Thousand Year Pavilion

Marble Imperial Carriageway

Gate of Heavenly Purity

Gate of Supreme Harmony

Meridian Gate

Forbidden City East Gate (exit only)

The Treasure Gallery

NORTH →

Opera House
The largest of the Forbidden City's opera stages; look out for the trapdoors, which allowed supernatural characters to make dramatic entrances and exits during performances.

ENTRANCE/EXIT
You must enter through the south gate (Meridian Gate), but you can exit via south, north or east.

Dragon-Head Spouts
More than a thousand dragon-head spouts encircle the raised marble platforms at the centre of the Forbidden City. They were – and still are – part of the drainage system.

Roof Guardians
The imperial dragon is at the tail of the procession, which is led by a figure riding a phoenix followed by a number of mythical beasts. The more beasts, the more important the building.

Forbidden City

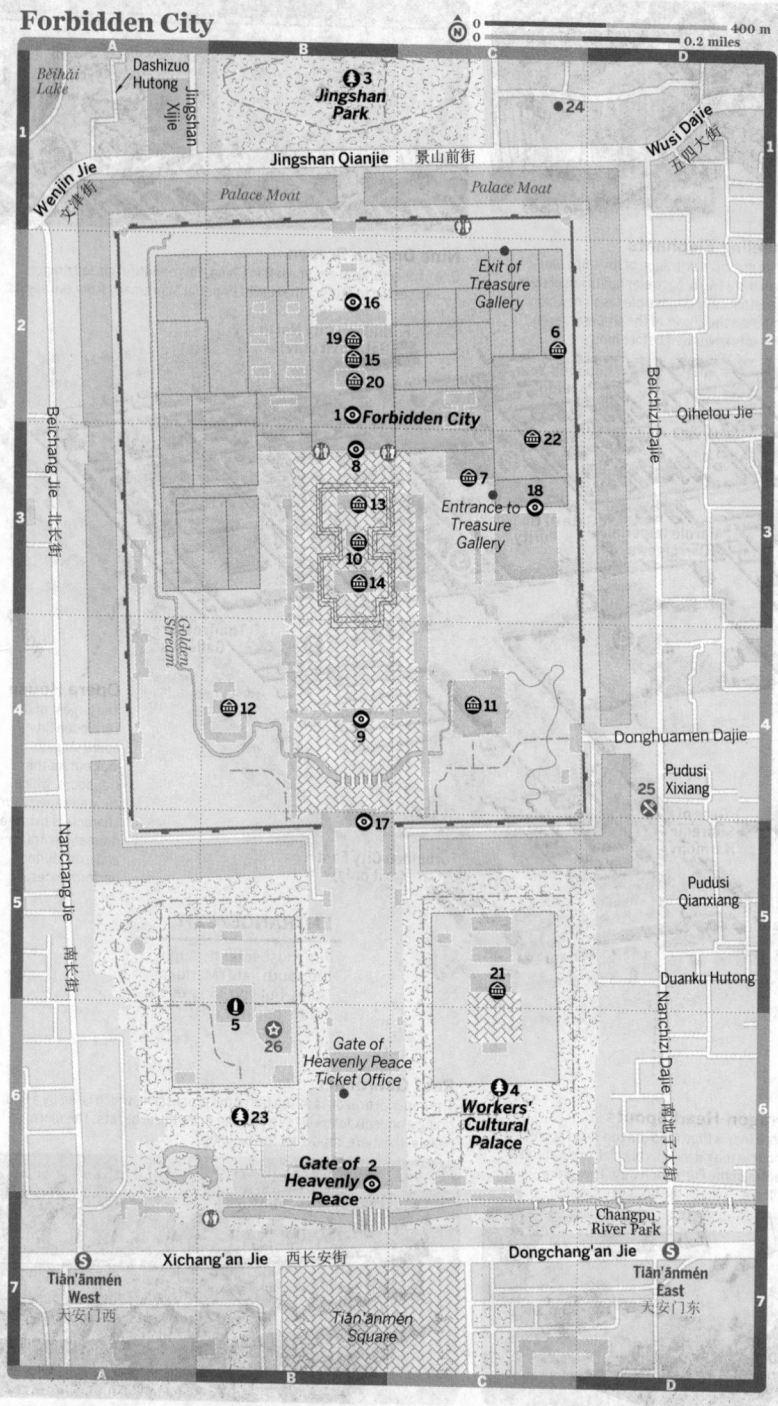

A B C D

N
0   400 m
0   0.2 miles

Běihǎi Lake

Dashizuo Hutong

Jingshan Xijie

🏛 3
Jingshan Park

● 24

Wenjin Jie 文津街

Jingshan Qianjie 景山前街

Wusi Dajie 五四大街

Palace Moat   *Palace Moat*

Beichizi Dajie

Qihelou Jie

Exit of Treasure Gallery

◎ 16

19 🏛
🏛 15
🏛 20

🏛 6

1 ◎ *Forbidden City*

🏛 22

◎ 8

🏛 7

🏛 13

◎ 18

Entrance to Treasure Gallery

🏛 10

🏛 14

Beichang Jie 北长街

Golden Stream

🏛 12

🏛 11

Donghuamen Dajie

◎ 9

Pudusi Xixiang

25 ✕

◎ 17

Nanchang Jie 南长街

Pudusi Qianxiang

Duanku Hutong

🏛 21

❶ 5

☆ 26

Gate of Heavenly Peace Ticket Office

❶ 4
Workers' Cultural Palace

❶ 23

Nanchizi Dajie 南池子大街

Gate of 2 Heavenly Peace ◎

Changpu River Park

Xichang'an Jie 西长安街

Dongchang'an Jie

Ⓢ
Tiān'ānmén West
天安门西

Ⓢ
Tiān'ānmén East
天安门东

Tiān'ānmén Square

Forbidden City

BEIJING SIGHTS

p74; Forbidden City; incl in through ticket), modelled after the one in Beihai Park.

From there you work your way north, exploring various halls and courtyards before exiting at the **northern end** (Map p74) of the Forbidden City. En route, seek out the **Pavilion of Cheerful Melodies** (畅音阁, Chàngyīn Gé; Map p74; Forbidden City), a three-storey wooden opera house that was the palace's largest theatre. Note the trapdoors that allowed actors to make dramatic stage entrances.

➡ **Western & Eastern Palaces**

A dozen smaller palace courtyards lie to the west and east of the three lesser central halls. It was in these self-contained abodes, like far grander versions of Beijing's *sìhéyuàn* mansions in the *hutong,* where most of the emperors and empresses actually lived. Many of the buildings, particularly those to the west, are decked out with imperial furniture.

➡ **Other Attractions**

Parts of the palace that were previously off limits are opening all the time. Due west of the **Gate of Heavenly Purity** is a collection of halls and gardens where the empresses and concubines of deceased emperors resided. Known as the **Palace of Compassion and Tranquillity,** it was used for storage for many decades after 1925 and today houses the **Sculpture Gallery,** which includes Buddhist statues, terracotta warriors, exquisite stone reliefs and more, from as far back as the Warring States period.

To the south is the **Garden of Compassion and Tranquillity,** where empress dowagers and imperial consorts worshipped the Buddha, entertained themselves and rested.

To the west is the **Palace of Longevity and Health,** built for Emperor Qianlong's mother.

★ **Gate of Heavenly Peace**　　HISTORIC SITE

(天安门, Tiān'ānmén; Map p74; Xichang'an Jie, 西长安街; ¥15, bag storage ¥3-6; ⊗8.30am-4.30pm, to 4pm Nov-Mar; ⑤Line 1 to Tian'anmen West, exit B, or Line 1 to Tian'anmen East, exit A) Instantly recognisable by its giant framed portrait of Mao, and guarded by two pairs of Ming dynasty stone lions, the double-eaved Gate of Heavenly Peace (literally 'Tian'anmen') is a potent national symbol. Formerly the largest of the four gates of the Imperial City Wall, it was from here that Mao proclaimed the founding of the People's Republic of China in 1949. Climb the gate for excellent views of Tian'anmen Sq. The **ticket office** (Map p74) is on the northwest side of the gate.

Mao's portrait – a 6m x 4.6m oil painting repainted annually – is a relatively recent permanent addition. During the 1950s, it was only hung on the gate for the May and 1 October celebrations. In the early years of the PRC, the gate and its vicinity also occasionally sported portraits of Sun Yatsen, Karl Marx, Vladimir Lenin and Joseph Stalin. Mao has been a constant fixture since 1975. Either side of the portrait are placards reading: 'Long Live the People's Republic of China' and 'Long Live the Unity of the People of the World'.

★ **Tian'anmen Square**　　SQUARE

(天安门广场, Tiān'ānmén Guǎngchǎng; Map p78; ⊗opens before dawn, closes at night; ⑤Line 1 to Tian'anmen West or Tian'anmen East, or Line 2 to Qianmen) **FREE** Flanked by triumphalist Soviet-style buildings, Tian'anmen Sq is an immense void of paved stone (440,000 sq metres, to be precise) at the symbolic centre of the Chinese universe. Watched over by Mao's portrait (and the eyes of hundreds of security personnel), it's an iconic if disquieting place for a stroll. Highlights on the square itself include the daily flag-raising (and lowering) ceremony, Mao's mausoleum and the Zhengyang Gate. Access is via the underpasses beside Tian'anmen East and Tian'anmen West subway stations (Line 1).

The rectangular arrangement of the square, echoing the layout of the Forbidden City, to some extent pays obeisance to traditional Chinese culture, but most of its ornaments and buildings are Soviet-inspired. Mao conceived the square to project the power of the Communist Party, and during the Cultural Revolution he reviewed parades of up to a million people here. The 'Tian'anmen Incident', in 1976, is the term given to the near-riot in the square that accompanied the death of Premier Zhou Enlai. Another million people jammed the square to pay their last respects to Mao in the same year. Most infamously, in 1989 the army forced prodemocracy demonstrators out of the square. Hundreds – possibly thousands – lost their lives in the surrounding streets, an event the Chinese government has spent the intervening decades removing from the national consciousness. Contrary to widespread belief, it is thought that few if any were killed in the square itself. The famous 'tank man' photo was taken not on the square but from a balcony of the Beijing Hotel on Chang'an Jie; now Beijing Hotel NUO (p108).

Early risers can watch the daily **flag-raising ceremony** at sunrise, performed by a troop of People's Liberation Army (PLA) soldiers marching at precisely 108 paces per minute, 75cm per pace. The soldiers emerge through the Gate of Heavenly Peace to goose-step impeccably across Dongchang'an Jie (the reverse ceremony is performed at sunset). In the centre of the square is the **Monument to the People's Heroes** (人民英雄纪念碑, Rénmín Yīngxióng Jìniànbēi), a 40m-tall obelisk emblazoned with calligraphy from Mao and Zhou Enlai, while behind it sits the Chairman Mao Memorial Hall, where Mao's body lies inside a glass coffin. At the foot of the square, the magnificent Zhengyang Gate can be climbed for superb views and an exhibition of historical photographs showing the area as it was at the beginning of the last century.

★Chairman Mao Memorial Hall
MAUSOLEUM

(毛主席纪念堂, Máo Zhǔxí Jìniàntáng; Map p78; Tian'anmen Sq; bag storage ¥10, electronics storage per device ¥10; ☉8am-noon Tue-Sun; Ⓢ Line 1 to Tian'anmen West or Tian'anmen East, or Line 2 to Qianmen) **FREE** One of Beijing's more surreal spectacles is the sight of Mao Zedong's embalmed corpse on public display within his mausoleum. The Soviet-inspired memorial hall was constructed just 10 months after Mao died in September 1976, and is a prominent landmark in the middle of Tian'anmen Sq. The Chairman is still revered across much of China, as evidenced by the snaking queues here; one or two are solemn-faced but many are in high spirits, treating it like any other stop on their Beijing tour.

Before you join the queue, all bags and cameras need to be deposited at the signposted storage area beside the National Museum of China east of the square; collect them before 2pm. And don't forget your passport – you won't be let into the hall without it.

National Museum of China
MUSEUM

(中国国家博物馆, Zhōngguó Guójiā Bówùguǎn; Map p78; http://en.chnmuseum.cn; 东长安街16号, 16 Dongchang'an Jie; audio guide ¥30; ☉9am-5pm Tue-Sun, last entry 4pm; Ⓢ Line 1 to Tian'anmen East, exit D) **FREE** Vast and energy-sapping, China's showpiece museum is housed in an immense 1950s Soviet-style building on the eastern side of Tian'anmen Sq, and claims to be the world's largest by display space. Dozens of galleries present a party-line portrayal of Chinese civilisation – you could lose hours in the **Ancient China** exhibition alone, with its priceless ceramics, calligraphy, jade and bronze pieces from prehistoric China through to the late Qing dynasty. Passport required.

Great Hall of the People
NOTABLE BUILDING

(人民大会堂, Rénmín Dàhuìtáng; Map p86; Xichang'an Jie, 西长安街; adult ¥30, bag deposit ¥2-5; ☉8.15am-4pm, hours vary; Ⓢ Line 1 to Qianmen, exit A, or Line 1 to Tian'anmen West, exit C) Monolithic and intimidating, the Stalinist Great Hall of the People (1959) houses the highest organ of state power, the National People's Congress (NPC). While few travellers go inside, it's worth the diversion to marvel at the 10,000-seat auditorium with a red star embedded in a galaxy of ceiling lights. The ticket office is on the south side of the building and bags must be checked.

★ **Jingshan Park**   PARK

(景山公园, Jǐngshān Gōngyuán; Map p74; Jingshan Qianjie, 景山前街; ¥2; ⏱ 6.30am-9pm, to 8pm Nov-Mar; Ⓢ Lines 6, 8 to Nanluoguxiang, exit A) Beijing's finest park is also one of the only hills in the inner city, a mound that was created from the loess (sediment) excavated to make the Forbidden City moat. Called Coal Hill by westerners during Legation days, Jingshan also serves as a feng shui shield, protecting the palace from evil spirits – or dust storms – from the north. Clamber to the top for a magnificent panorama of the capital and princely views over of the Forbidden City.

On the eastern side of the park, a locust tree stands in the place where the last of the Ming emperors, Chongzhen, hanged himself as rebels swarmed at the city walls. The original tree survived right up until the Cultural Revolution, some say, when it was uprooted. In the north of the park, the **Shouhuang Temple** (寿皇殿, Shòuhuáng Diàn; Map p78; Jingshan Park, 景山公园; ⏱ 9am-4pm; Ⓢ Line 6 to Nanluoguxiang, exit A) FREE, built in 1749 under the reign of Emperor Qianlong to honour his royal ancestors, opened in 2018 after four years of restoration.

Zhengyang Gate   HISTORIC SITE

(正阳门城楼, Zhèngyáng Mén Chénglóu; Map p78; Tian'anmen Sq; ¥20, audio guide ¥20; ⏱ 9am-4.30pm Tue-Sun, last entry 4pm; Ⓢ Line 2 to Qianmen, exit A) Qianmen (前门), or the Front Gate, consists of a pair of gate-like towers; the northernmost being the 40m-high Zhengyang Gate, which was also the largest of the nine gates of the Inner City Wall and the only gate proper that still stands, and the **Zhengyang Gate Arrow Tower**, just south of here. The gate can be climbed for fine views of the square and houses a museum charting the history and demise of Beijing's city fortifications.

★ **Workers' Cultural Palace**   PARK

(劳动人民文化宫, Láodòng Rénmín Wénhuà Gōng, Imperial Ancestral Temple; Map p74; ☐ 010 6512 2856; Dongchang'an Jie, 东长安街; park/Sacrificial Hall ¥2/15; ⏱ 6.30am-7.30pm; Ⓢ Line 1 to Tian'anmen East, exit A) One of Beijing's best-kept secrets – despite being next to the Gate of Heavenly Peace (p75) – the Workers' Cultural Palace was gifted to the masses by Mao in 1950 as a place of wholesome recreation. For several centuries prior, it was the most sacred temple in Beijing, where emperors would come to worship their ancestors. The cathedral-like **Sacrificial Hall** (太庙, Tài Miào;

¥15) is as magnificent as any imperial building in Beijing.

Zhongshan Park   PARK

(中山公园, Zhōngshān Gōngyuán; Map p74; 4 Zhonghua Lu, 中华路4号; adult ¥3, Spring Flower & Tulips Show ¥10; ⏱ 6am-9pm; ☐ 5, Ⓢ Line 1 to Tian'anmen West, exit B) Named after China's first president Sun Yatsen (alo called Sun Zhongshan), whose body was placed here briefly after his death, this lovely park, filled with flower displays and ancient cyprus trees, sits at the southwest corner of the Forbidden City facing the palace moat (you can rent pedal-boats here). The park used to be royal gardens containing the sacred **Altar of Land and Grain** (北京社稷坛, Shèjìtán), where the emperor offered sacrifices. The altar, a square open-air platform, is the centrepiece.

National Art Museum of China   MUSEUM

(中国美术馆, Zhōngguó Měishùguǎn; Map p78; www.namoc.org; 1 Wusi Dajie, 五四大街1号; ⏱ 9am-5pm Tue-Sun, last entry 4pm; Ⓢ Lines 6, 8 to National Art Museum, exit A) FREE Opened in 1963 with the personal endorsement of Mao Zedong, this gallery complex was conceived as the PRC's national nerve centre for artistic expression. In recent years the museum has shaken off its reputation for stodgy, state-supervised exhibitions by inviting galleries from abroad to exhibit, while at the same time revamping its own output, often in collaboration with Beijing's prestigious Central Academy of Fine Arts.

There are usually at least four exhibitions being staged at once. Check the website (in Chinese) to see what's on. You'll need your passport to enter.

Wangfujing Street   SHOPPING STREET

(王府井大街, Wángfǔjǐng Dàjiē; Map p78; Ⓢ Line 1 to Wangfujing, exit C2 or B) Monolithic shopping malls face each other across this prestigious avenue thronged with mostly out-of-town tourists. The late-20th-century Chinese architecture is looking worn out these days (despite some local tour companies who rather hopefully dub Wangfujing Street 'Beijing's Champs-Elysées'), but developments like WF Central (p124) are adding a welcome touch of glamour.

Shijia Hutong Museum   MUSEUM

(史家胡同博物馆, Shǐjiā Hútòng Bówùguǎn; Map p78; 24 Shijia Hutong, 史家胡同24号; ⏱ 9.30am-4.30pm Tue-Sun; Ⓢ Line 5 to Dengshikou) FREE Shijia Hutong has seen plenty of

Dongcheng Central

0 _____ 500 m
0 _____ 0.25 miles

Qiánhǎi Lake

Beihai North
北海北

Di'anmen Xidajie
地安门西大街
Can Altar

Gongjian Hutong

Di'anmenwai Dajie
地安门内大街

Di'anmen Dongdajie
地安门东大街

Nanluoguxiang
南锣鼓巷

地安门东大街

Nantluoguxiang
南锣鼓巷

Donghuangchenggen Beijie
东皇城根北街

Meishuguan Houjie

Zhangzizhong Lu

Dongsi Beidajie
东四北大街

Zhangzizhonglu
张自忠路

Dongsishitiao Lu

Dongsi Shitiao
东四十条

Mu Bus to
Mutianyu Great Wall

23

黄花门街
Huanghuamen Jie

Nianzi Hutong

Jingshan Table
Tennis Park
Jingshan Houjie

Sanyanjing Hutong
三眼井胡同

Shatanbei Jie

Beiheyan Dajie

30

Dongsi Liutiao
18

15

Qianliang Hutong

24
27

National Art Museum
中国美术馆

Jingshan Dongjie

Jingshan Xijie

Shouhuang Temple

25

Liangguochang
亮果厂

22

7

Dongsi Beixiaojie

Chaoyangmen Beidajie

State Administration
of Cultural Heritage

See Forbidden City Map (p74)

Jingshan Qianjie 景山前街
Palace Moat

Wusi Dajie

26

五四大街

17

Wangfujing Dajie 王府井大街

Chenguang Jie

Dongsi Xidajie
东四西大街

Dongsi Nandajie
东四

Dongsi
东四

Chaoyangmennei Dajie

Chaoyangmen
朝阳门

Chaoyangmen Nandajie
(Second Ring Rd)

Forbidden City

Baofang Hutong

Beichang Jie 北长街

Beichizi Dajie 北池子大

Qihelou Jie

Dengshikou Xijie

Dengshikou Xijie

Yanyue Hutong

演乐胡同
14

Neiwubu Jie

Shijia Hutong

9

32

5

Dafangjia Hutong

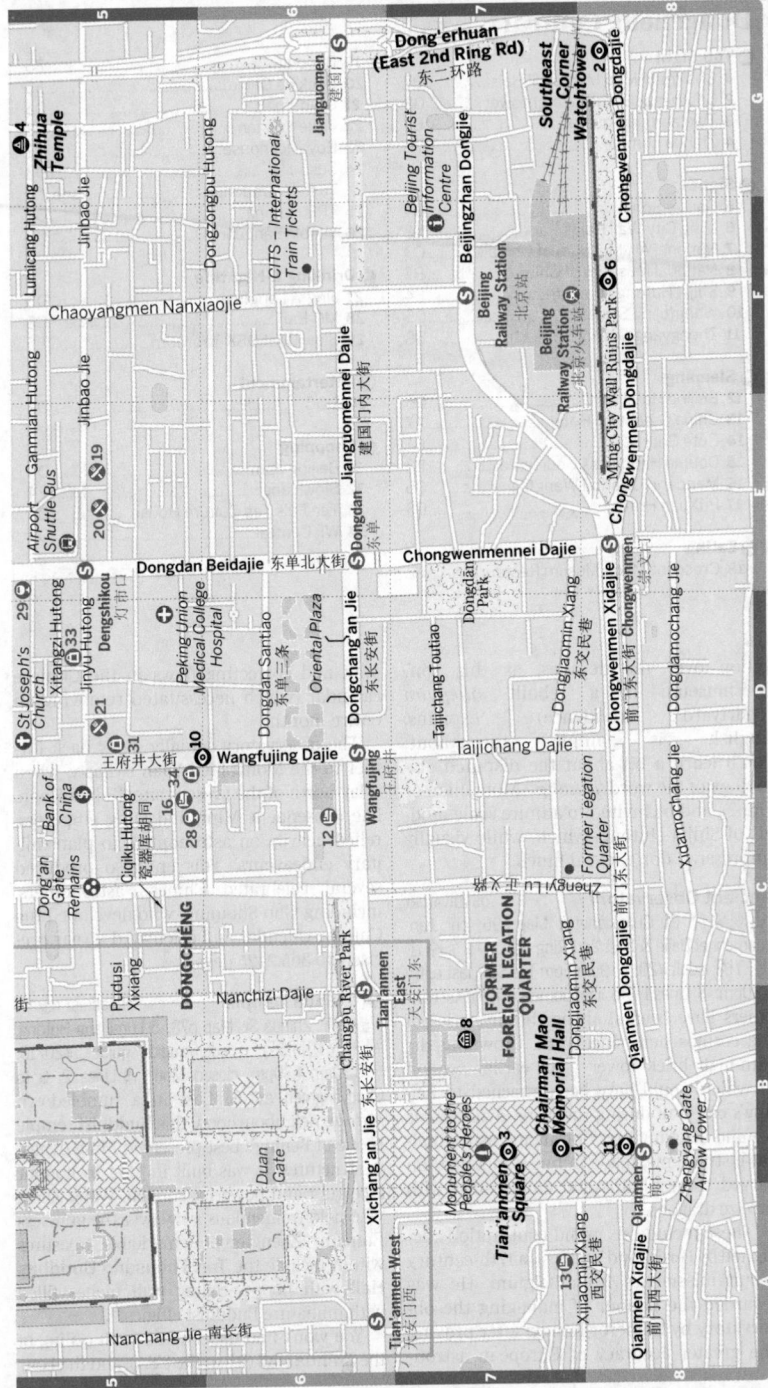

Dong'erhuan
(East 2nd Ring Rd)
东二环路

Southeast
Corner
Watchtower

Zhihua
Temple

Lumicang Hutong

Jinbao Jie

Jinbao Hutong

Dongzongbu Hutong

Jianguomen

CITS – International
Train Tickets

Beijing Tourist
Information
Centre

Beijingzhan Dongjie

Chongwenmen Dongdajie

Chaoyangmen Nanxiaojie

Ganmian Hutong

Jinbao Jie

Jianguomennei Dajie
建国门内大街

Beijing
Railway Station

Beijing
Railway Station
北京火车站

Beijing
Railway Station

Chongwenmen Dongdajie

Ming City Wall Ruins Park

Airport
Shuttle Bus

St Joseph's
Church

Xitangzi Hutong

Dengshikou

Jinyu Hutong

Dongdan Beidajie 东单北大街

Dongdan
东单

Chongwenmennei Dajie

Dongdan
Park

Chongwenmen Xidajie

Peking Union
Medical College
Hospital

Dongdan Santiao

Oriental Plaza

Dongchang'an Jie
东长安街

Taijichang Toutiao

Dongjiaomin Xiang
东交民巷

Chongwenmen Xidajie Chongwenmen
前门东大街

Dongdamochang Jie

Ciqiku Hutong
瓷器库胡同

Wangfujing Dajie
王府井大街

Taijichang Dajie

Wangfujing
王府井

Bank of
China

Dong'an
Gate Remains

DŌNGCHÉNG

Former Legation
Quarter

Zhengyi Lu 正义路

Dongjiaomin Xiang
东交民巷

Xidamochang Jie

Pudusi
Xixiang

Nanchizi Dajie

Changpu River Park

Tian'anmen
East
天安门东

FORMER
FOREIGN
LEGATION
QUARTER

Dongjiaomin Xiang
东交民巷

Qianmen Dongdajie 前门东大街

Duan
Gate

Xichang'an Jie 东长安街

Tian'anmen West
天安门西

Monument to the
People's Heroes

Chairman Mao
Memorial Hall

Tian'anmen
Square

Qianmen Xidajie
前门西大街

Qianmen
前门

Zhengyang Gate
Arrow Tower

Nanchang Jie 南长街

Xijiaomin Xiang
西交民巷

Qianmen Xidajie
前门西大街

Dongcheng Central

action over the decades, as this spiffy museum in a rebuilt *sìhéyuàn* (courtyard residence) explains. English is ample throughout; you'll learn a bit about the disputed etymology of the word *'hutong'* (Mongolian or Han?), and be invited to admire scale models of Shijia Hutong, which, while visually impressive, don't reveal much.

Ancient Observatory   OBSERVATORY
(古观象台, Gǔ Guānxiàngtái; Map p96; cnr Jianguomennei Dajie & East 2nd Ring Rd, 二环东路建国门桥; adult ¥20; ⊙9am-5pm Tue-Sun, last entry 4.30pm; Ⓢ Lines 1, 2 to Jianguomen, exit A) Astronomers have been studying the mysteries of the cosmos here since 1442. Crowning the 18m-high brick tower – an earlier version of which would have been attached to Beijing's city wall during the Ming dynasty – is a mind-boggling array of arcane astronomical instruments, made in brass, mounted on carved stone plinths and embellished with bronze dragons.

These include six grand contraptions designed by Ferdinand Verbiest, a 17th-century Jesuit missionary from Belgium. He was awarded the honour of managing the observatory by Emperor Kangxi after proving the greater accuracy of European astron-

omy, and correcting flaws in the Chinese calendar (which necessitated removing an entire month).

The observatory actually dates back further to the Mongol-led Yuan dynasty, when it lay north of the present site. Kublai Khan, like subsequent Ming and Qing emperors, relied heavily on astronomers to plan military endeavours. This era also produced several celebrated Chinese astronomers, including Guo Shoujing, who developed the Chinese calendar and calculated a year precisely to 365.2425 days.

★**Zhihua Temple**   BUDDHIST TEMPLE
(智化寺, Zhìhuà Sì; Map p78; 5 Lumicang Hutong, 禄米仓胡同5号; adult/audio guide ¥20/10; ⊙8.30am-4.30pm, closed Mon; Ⓢ Lines 2, 6 to Chaoyangmen, exit G) Lost in a tumbledown *hutong* neighbourhood, this Buddhist temple is one of Beijing's best-preserved Ming dynasty structures. It was built in 1444 to honour a corrupt and powerful eunuch, Wang Zhen, who held tremendous sway over the guileless Emperor Zhengtong. Remarkable treasures within include the **Ten Thousand Buddhas Hall** with floor-to-ceiling wall niches filled with miniature Buddhist effigies.

You won't find the coffered vault ceiling of the **Zhihua Hall** (it's in the USA), and the Four

Heavenly Kings have vanished from **Zhihua Gate**, but the **Scriptures Hall**, to the west of the central courtyard, encases a spectacular, eight-sided *zhuǎnlún zàng* (转轮藏), a rotating scriptures cabinet mounted on a marble base, crowned with animal carvings and a seated Buddha beneath a mandala fresco.

The **Ten Thousand Buddhas Hall** is at the far rear of the complex, dominated by a trio of wood-carved deities (a 20ft-tall Tathagata Buddha, flanked by Brahma and Indra). Unfortunately, visitors are no longer allowed to climb to the 2nd floor, which houses a seated Buddha.

Time your visit to coincide with a short musical performance, taking place in Zhihua Hall at 10am and 3pm daily. Performers use traditional Chinese instruments associated with Buddhist worship.

Following renovations in 2018, the temple has added several museum displays to its offerings, including notes on temple construction and restoration over the years, and an exhibit on 'jing' religious music.

Galaxy Soho   ARCHITECTURE

(银河Soho, Yínhé Soho; Map p78; Chaoyangmennei Dajie, 朝阳门内大街; ⑤Lines 2, 6 to Chaoyangmen, exit G) After the CCTV Tower and the Bird's Nest Stadium, Beijing's Galaxy Soho trumpeted itself as the capital's next modern architectural landmark when it opened in 2012. Zaha Hadid's creation looks astonishing in photographs, the retail and office complex writhing futuristically like a Star Wars city (never mind that the adjoining *hutong* housing was bulldozed for its development). But up close you'll see empty commercial units and poorly maintained public areas, and wonder where it all went wrong.

◉ Drum Tower & Dongcheng North

★ Drum Tower   HISTORIC SITE

(鼓楼, Gǔlóu; Map p82; Gulou Dongdajie, 鼓楼东大街; ¥20, Drum & Bell towers through ticket ¥30; ⊙9am-5pm, last entry 4.40pm; ⑤Line 8 to Shichahai, exit A2) Venerable bastions of timekeeping, the Drum Tower and its counterpart the Bell Tower were for centuries the tallest buildings in Beijing, lording it over the surrounding *hutong*. Up in the 46m-high tower, the great drums would beat to sound the curfew after nightfall in the Qing dynasty, and thereafter every two hours to coordinate the patrols of the city's nightwatch.

Originally built in 1272, the Drum Tower (and the Bell Tower to the north) are aligned on Beijing's central axis, at the heart of the former Mongol-led Yuan capital of Dàdū, as Beijing was then known. It was rebuilt by Emperor Yongle as part of his grand plan for Ming dynasty Beijing. Since then it has been destroyed and rebuilt several times (the current edition dates from around 1894).

In 1924, after Puyi (the 'Last Emperor') had been evicted from the Forbidden City, the timekeeping functions of the towers ceased. The Drum Tower became a library for a time, and the Bell Tower a cinema.

Accessed by a very steep stairway, the tower itself preserves the **Night Watchman's Drum** (更鼓, Gēnggǔ), the sole survivor of the original watch drums. A drumming troupe bashes out rhythms on a set of replica drums every hour from 9.30am, with the last performance at 4.45pm (and no lunchtime performance at 12.30pm).

The original drummers would have known exactly when to bash their instruments thanks to a water clock (clepsydra), a copy of which is on display in the tower.

Bell Tower   HISTORIC SITE

(钟楼, Zhōnglóu; Map p82; Gulou Dongdajie, 鼓楼东大街; ¥20, Drum & Bell towers through ticket ¥30; ⊙9am-5pm, last tickets 4.40pm; ⑤Line 8 to Shichahai, exit A2) The restrained, grey-stone

---

DON'T MISS

A thrilling discovery, the exquisite collection of treasures at the **Poly Art Museum** (保利艺术博物馆, Bǎolì Yìshù Bówùguǎn; Map p96; ☏010 6500 8117; 9th fl, Poly Plaza, 14 Dongzhimen Nandajie, 东直门南大街14号保利大厦9层; ¥20; ⊙9.30am-4.30pm, closed Sun; ⑤Line 2 to Dongsi Shitiao, exit D) is hidden halfway up an office building! China's state-owned Poly Group has funnelled a fraction of its mega-wealth into buying up Chinese antiquities from auctions overseas, displayed here on artfully lit plinths. There are ancient bronzes from the Shang and Zhou dynasties, vividly detailed Buddha statuary, and several of the 12 bronze zodiac animals plundered at the sacking of the Old Summer Palace (p107) in 1860 – Poly Group is still rounding up the rest.

Buy your tickets from the information counter in the lobby of the Poly Plaza building, then ride the lift to the 9th floor.

Drum Tower & Dongcheng North

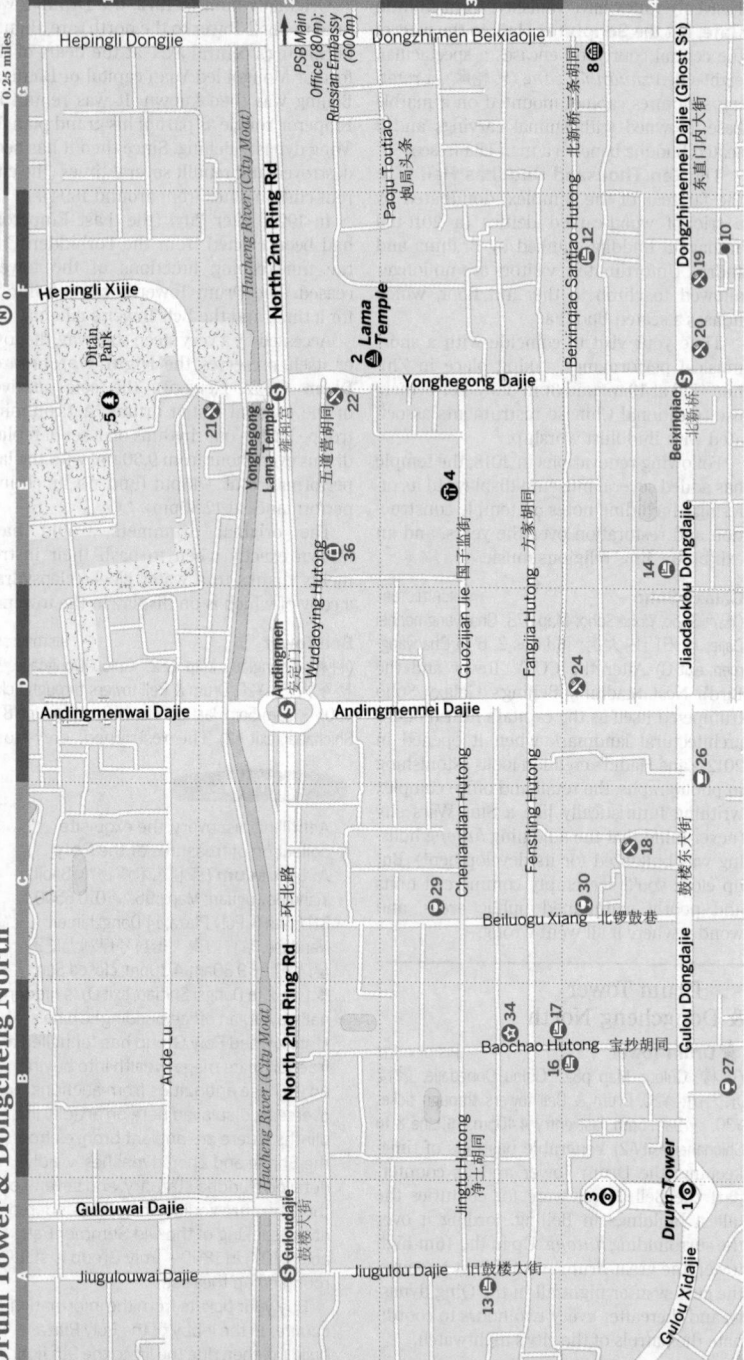

BEIJING

Map labels:
- Dongzhimen Nanxiaojie
- Dongsishitiao Lu
- Dongsishizhonglu 张自忠路
- Zhangzizhonglu
- Dongsi Beidajie
- Zhangzizhong Lu
- Jiaodaokou Nandajie 交道口南大街
- Dongcheng Disease Prevention & Control Centre
- Beibingmasi Hutong 北兵马司胡同
- Dongmianhua Hutong 东棉花胡同
- Chaodou Hutong 炒豆胡同
- Nanluoguxiang 南锣鼓巷
- Nanluogu Xiang
- Jingyang Hutong
- Doujiao Hutong
- Shichahai 什刹海
- Di'anmenwai Dajie
- Di'anmen Dongdajie 地安门东大街
- Qianhai Lake
- Beijing Tourist Information Centre

Drum Tower & Dongcheng North

◎ Top Sights
1 Drum Tower A4
2 Lama Temple F2

◎ Sights
3 Bell Tower A4
4 Confucius Temple & Imperial
   College E3
5 Ditan Park E1
6 Duan Qirui Former Government
   Building E6
7 Nanluogu Xiang C6
8 Overseas Chinese History
   Museum G4
9 Silver Ingot Bridge A5

⊕ Activities, Courses & Tours
B Electric Bike Tours .... (see 10)
10 Culture Yard F4
11 The Hutong F5

⊟ Sleeping
12 161 Lama Temple Courtyard
   Hotel F4
13 Beijing Drum Tower Youth
   Hostel A3
14 Grand Mercure Dongcheng E4
15 Happy Dragon Alley Hotel F6
16 Orchid B4
17 Orchid Private Residences B3

⊗ Eating
18 Dali Courtyard C4
   Furongji .... (see 16)
19 Ghost Street F4
20 Hú Dà F4
21 Jīn Dǐng Xuān E2
22 King's Joy E2
23 Mercante B5
   Toast .... (see 16)
24 Xiàn Lǎo Mǎn D4
25 Zhang Mama D5

⊖ Drinking & Nightlife
   Arch Bar .... (see 6)
26 Cafe Zarah D4
27 Dada B4
28 Great Leap Brewing #6 .... B5
29 Mai Bar C3
30 Nina C4
31 Nuoyan Wine Bar F5

⊕ Entertainment
32 East Shore Jazz Bar A5
33 Jiang Hu D5
34 Modernista B3
   Temple Bar .... (see 27)

⊜ Shopping
35 Plastered 8 .... C5
36 Plastered 8 Wudaoying E2
37 Three Stone Kite Shop A6
38 Yandai Xiejie A5

edifice of the Bell Tower (Zhonglou) is arguably even more charming than its resplendent other half, the Drum Tower (p81; Gulou), after which this area of Beijing is casually named. You can mount the steep steps to get a look at the giant copper bell, and peek out over the *hutong* from behind safety barriers.

Along with the Drum Tower, the Bell Tower was Beijing's official timekeeper throughout the Yuan, Ming and Qing dynasties, until 1924. The bell, claimed to weigh over 54 tonnes, was sounded in sequence together with the drums to mark the changes of the morning and night watches. Since 1990, the bell has been rung once a year on 31 December.

Buy your ticket for the Bell Tower at the Drum Tower.

★ **Lama Temple**   BUDDHIST TEMPLE
(雍和宫, Yōnghé Gōng; Map p82; www.yonghe gong.cn; 12 Yonghegong Dajie, 北新桥雍和宫大街12号; ¥25, audio guide ¥50; ⏱ 9am-4.30pm; Ⓢ Lines 2, 5 to Yonghegong-Lama Temple, exit C) Converted from a princely residence to a lamasery in the 18th century, the Lama Temple extends through a crescendo of ever more divine halls in a whirl of incense and prayer wheels to its astonishing finale, an 18m-high statue of Buddha carved from a single trunk of Tibetan sandalwood. Expect to spend at least an hour wandering the halls and courtyards, admiring the architecture, statues, wall-mounted mandalas and temple relics on show throughout.

The most revered Tibetan Buddhist temple outside Tibet, the Lama Temple was originally the royal residence of the prince who would become the Yongzheng emperor, hence the yellow roof tiles on its central halls. While it remains an active place of worship staffed by monks, the temple is today visited mostly by tourists.

Arranged on a north–south axis, the temple halls ascend in height and importance as you move through the complex. The **Hall of the Wheel of the Law** (Fǎlún Diàn), the fourth hall, contains a substantial bronze statue of a benign and smiling Tsongkhapa (1357–1419), founder of the Gelug school or Yellow Hat sect.

The fifth hall, the **Wanfu Pavilion** (Wànfú Gé), reveals an awe-inspiring, 18m-tall statue of the Maitreya Buddha in its Tibetan form, clothed in yellow satin and reputedly carved from a single trunk of Tibetan sandalwood. The statue was a gift from the seventh Dalai Lama to the Emperor Qianlong, and took three years to be transported from Lhasa to

the capital. A further 8m of the statue is concealed below ground.

The two rearmost side halls, **Jietai Lou** and **Banchan Lou**, are given over to changing displays of religious relics and treasures from the temple, served up with a tendentious account of China's relationship with Tibet and Tibetan Buddhism.

Confucius Temple & Imperial College   CONFUCIAN TEMPLE

(孔庙、国子监, Kǒng Miào & Guózǐjiàn; Map p82; 13 Guozijian Jie, 国子监街13号; ¥30, audio guide ¥30; ⏱ 8.30am-6pm Tue-Sun, to 5pm Nov-Apr, last entry 1hr before closing; Ⓢ Lines 2, 5 to Yonghegong-Lama Temple, exit C) An incense stick's toss away from the Lama Temple, China's second-largest Confucian temple is a haven of scholarly calm and contemplation. Come to wander between the towering stone stelae mounted on the backs of mythical *bìxì* (mythical, tortoise-like dragons) and inscribed with the achievements of scholars past. For centuries, China's sharpest minds would sit for imperial examinations on the Confucian classics at the connecting Guózǐjiàn, which was replaced by the Imperial University of Peking (what would become Peking University) in 1898.

At the rear of the Confucius Temple are the **Qianlong Stone Scriptures**, a stone 'forest' of 190 stelae recording the 13 Confucian classics in 630,000 Chinese characters. Next to the Confucius Temple, but within the same grounds, stands the **Imperial College**, where the emperor expounded the Confucian classics to an audience of thousands of kneeling students, professors and court officials – an annual rite. Built by the grandson of Kublai Khan in 1306, the former college was the supreme academy during the Yuan, Ming and Qing dynasties. The **Biyong Hall** (辟雍大殿, Pìyōng Dàdiàn) is a twin-roofed structure with yellow (royal) tiles surrounded by a moat and topped with a splendid gold knob. Inside the stupendous interior is housed a vermilion-and-gold lectern. The side pavilions feature several interesting museums on Confucianism, detailing the life of the Great Sage (551–479 BC) and the academy itself.

Some of Beijing's last remaining *páilóu* (decorative archways) survive on the street outside (Guozijian Jie).

Nánluógǔ Xiàng   STREET

(南锣鼓巷, South Gong & Drum Lane; Map p82; Nanluogu Xiang; Ⓢ Lines 6, 8 to Nanluoguxiang, exit E) Beijing's most touristy *hutong*, Nanluogu

EXPLORING THE HUTONG

One of the pleasures of Beijing is picking your way through the *hutong*, a dense matrix of grey-brick alleyways surviving in pockets within Beijing's old centre, and brimming with local life. A unique form of residential architecture, the *hutong* are Beijing's ever-diminishing heart and soul – visit before they're gone.

Around the Drum Tower

Bookended by the Drum Tower and the Lama Temple is Beijing's buzziest district of historic *hutong* alleyways, and the best area of the city for strolling. Gulou Dongdajie, the main east–west drag, divides an enticing grid of *hutong* to the north and south, including Nanluogu Xiang (p90), Beijing's most overhyped alley, which is easily avoided in favour of quieter, more authentic lanes.

Subway Take Line 8 to Shichahai.

Hutongs of Xisi

The Xisi area is one of Beijing's most authentic and least touristed *hutong* neighbourhoods, where views of the ancient White Dagoba Temple loom over tiled rooftops. Venture into the *hutong* north of Fuchengmen Inner St and around Xisi subway station and you'll discover a Beijing that time forgot. Men stroll about in Mao suits, holes-in-the-wall bake sesame sha-obing bread, and the soundtrack is authentically gruff Běijīnghua, the local dialect.

Subway Take Line 4 to Xisi or Line 2 to Fuchengmen.

Down in Dashilar

The gentrifying *hutong* district of Dashilar, southwest of Tian'anmen Sq, rewards the explorer with hip cafes, Republic-era architecture and mahjong dens. Delve into the alleys flowing west from Meishi Jie – like Yangmeizhu Xiejie, a former printing street once home to author Lu Xun. The history buffs at Beijing Postcards (p108) run local walking tours through what was Beijing's red-light district before 1949.

Subway Take Line 2 to Qianmen.

Xiang is a north–south strip of snack stalls, small food courts, souvenir shops and more people than you can possibly imagine crowding onto a single street. The main reason to visit is to delve into the quieter alleys that cross the main lane, fishbone-style, where you'll turn up a more compelling array of cafes, bars and restaurants between historic residences.

It wasn't too long ago that Nanluogu Xiang was a sleepy residential *hutong*. Even after bars started to open up in the early noughties, it remained a hip destination for those in the know. The alley was given a makeover in 2006, and another in 2016, and today is mostly snack vendors sating the daily hordes with everything from churros to bubble tea. Authentic it ain't, but a few creative businesses have endured, like iconic T-shirt brand Plastered 8 (p124), here since 2006.

**Overseas Chinese
History Museum** MUSEUM
(中国华侨历史博物馆, Zhōngguó Huáqiáo Lìshǐ Bówùguǎn; Map p82; ☑010 6409 3039; www.oc-museum.cn; Beixinqiao Santiao Dong Kou, 北新桥 三条东口; ☺9am-5pm Tue-Sun, last entry 4pm; Ⓢ Line 5 to Beixinqiao, exit B) **FREE** Charting the history of Chinese emigration from the era of the Silk Road to the present day, this is a terrific museum with full English captions throughout. Diorama-rich exhibits celebrate the plucky Chinese diaspora, from American gold-rush adventurers to the hugely influential Chinese communities in Southeast Asia. If you even have a passing interest in the subject, it's a must visit.

◎ Beihai Park & Xicheng North

★ **Beihai Park** PARK
(北海公园, Běihǎi Gōngyuán; Map p86; ☑010 6403 1102; 1 Wenjin Jie, 文津街1号; high/low season ¥10/5, through ticket ¥20/15; ☺6.30am-8.30pm, sights to 5pm; Ⓢ Line 6 to Beihai North) Beihai Park, inside the old Imperial City, looks much as it would have done in the 18th century when it served as Emperor Qianlong's private gardens. The Tibetan-style White Dagoba soars majestically over the lake (Beihai means 'northern sea'),

Beihai Park & Xicheng North

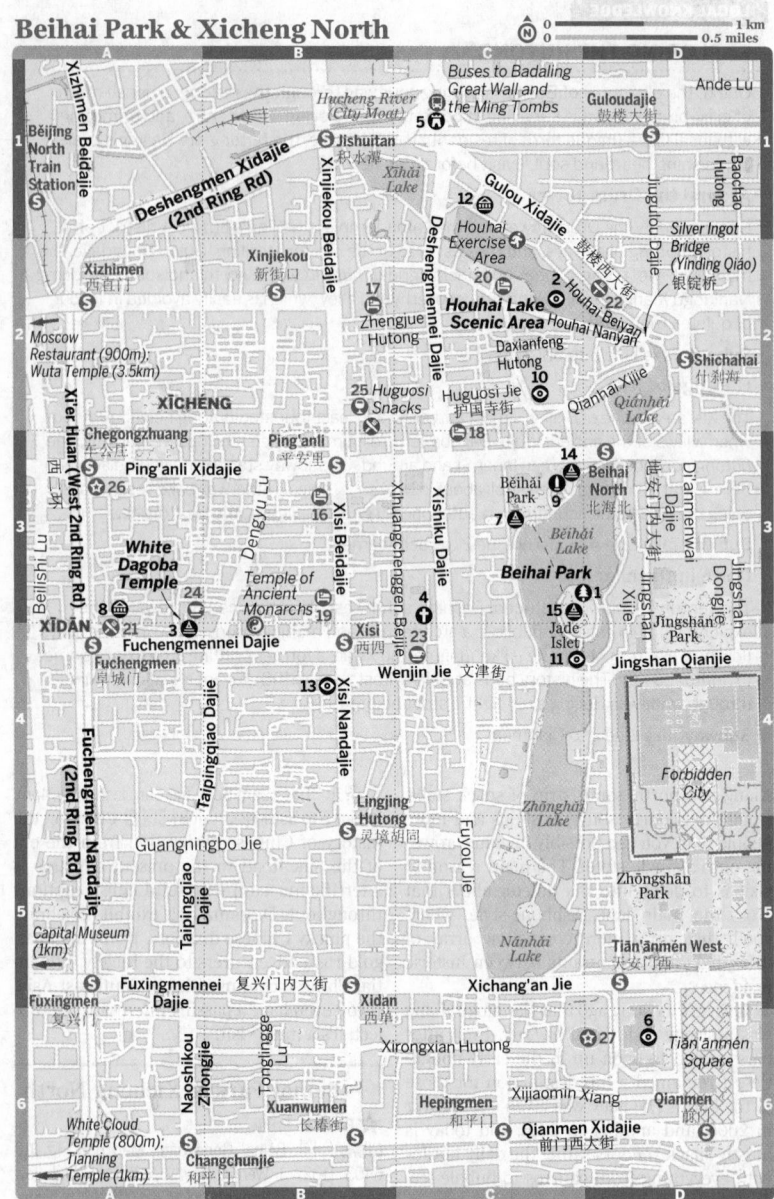

around which are found temples, pavilions, imperial stelae and other grand designs. A public park since 1925, Beihai now offers a window onto pastimes like *dìshū* (地书), where locals demonstrate their calligraphy skills using giant brushes and water.

Beihai has been a royal playground since the Jin dynasty (1115–1234), when Jade Islet was shaped from the earth scooped out to create the lake. Crowning the islet is the 36m-high Tibetan-style **White Dagoba** (白塔, Báitǎ; ¥30, not incl in through ticket for Beihai Park; ⏱9am-5pm), built in 1651 by the first

Beihai Park & Xicheng North

BEIJING SIGHTS

Qing emperor to honour a visit by the Dalai Lama. You can reach the islet by boat (¥5 to ¥15) or via bridges at the south and east gates. Entering via the south gate is the grand approach because you can climb up the steep southern approach through **Yong'an Temple** (永安寺, Yŏng'ān Sì; incl in through ticket for Beihai Park) to the top.

The north shore of Beihai has the most interesting buildings. **Jingxin Studio** (静心斋, Jìngxīn Zhāi) FREE, a 'garden within a garden', was a favourite retreat of Emperor Qianlong, who would sip tea, listen to the plucking of the *guqin* (Chinese zither) and enjoy the carp-filled pools and scenic views. **Western Elysium** (西天梵境, Xītiān Fánjìng; incl in through ticket for Beihai Park), with its centrepiece Míng-era hall (recently restored) made of unpainted cedar, was a lamasery during the Ming dynasty, and was later rebuilt by Emperor Qianlong. Nearby is the **Nine Dragon Screen** (九龙壁, Jiǔlóng Bì; incl in through ticket for Beihai Park), a 5m-high, 27m-long 'spirit wall' emblazoned with writhing dragons picked out in coloured glazed tiles. At the northeast corner of the lake, **Little Western Heaven** (小西天, Xiǎoxītiān; incl in through ticket for Beihai Park) is the largest square pavilion-style palace in China, built in secret as a gift for Emperor Qianlong's mother on her 80th birthday. Inside the cavernous hall is an enormous and rather garish diorama of Mt Sumeru.

This circular fortress known as **Round City** (团城, Tuán Chéng; ¥1; Ⓢ Line 4 to Xisi, exit C), just outside the south gate of Beihai, was the site of Kublai Khan's palace in the Yuan dynasty. All that survives are a few ancient cypress trees and a vast, ceremonial wine vessel made of green jade dating from 1265. It's on display in front of the **Hall of Divine Light** (Chéngguāng Diàn), where a 1.5m-tall statue of Sakyamuni, made from Burmese 'white jade', can be admired from afar.

★**Houhai Lake Scenic Area** LAKE
(什刹海, Shíchàhǎi; Map p86; ⬛; Ⓢ Line 8 to Shichahai, exit A1, or Line 6 to Beihai North, exit B) FREE A grand sweep of willow-lined waterways enclosed by invitingly maze-like *hutongs*, this trio of lakes is one of Beijing's best-loved outdoor spots, whether for strolling, fishing, pedal-boating, or ice-skating in winter. After dark, live-music bars skirting the shores of Qianhai (Front Lake) and Houhai (Back Lake) blare into life. Xihai (West Lake) is more idyllic. Several worthwhile sights can be found here, notably Prince Gong's Mansion (p88) and Song Qingling's Former Residence (p88).

The lakes date back to the Yuan dynasty and the canal system built by engineers to transport drinking water into the capital. Houhai once marked the northern terminus of the Grand Canal, and became a royal retreat during the Qing dynasty as Manchu nobles built their mansions around it, the most famous of which is Prince Gong's Mansion.

There are pedal-boat hire stations around the shoreline of Houhai and Qianhai; snacks and cold beers can be picked up at lakeside shops for an impromptu picnic afloat. Some of the best people-watching can be had at the **public exercise area** (新街口社区健身乐园, Xīnjiēkǒu Shèqū Jiànshēn Lèyuán; Map p86; Houhai Lake North Shore, 后海北沿; ⊙24h; Ⓢ Line 8 to Shichaihai, exit A2) FREE on the north shore of Houhai, especially in winter when hardy locals take an ice-dip in the water. Rickshaw drivers ply the shoreline hawking 'hutong tours', though few speak English.

When the lakes freeze over (usually from mid-December to early March), Qianhai becomes an enormous ice-skating rink, separated into two zones. The larger one is given over to ice-trikes and chair sleds (great fun for kids), while the smaller section is for skaters. Expect to pay ¥80 to get on to the ice.

Prince Gong's Mansion　　　GARDENS
(恭王府, Gōng Wángfǔ; Map p86; ⏱010 8328 8149; 17 Qianhai Xijie, 前海西街17号; ¥40, tours incl opera show & tea ceremony ¥70; ⊙8am-5pm Apr-Oct, 9am-4pm Nov-Mar; Ⓢ Line 6 to Beihai North, exit B) The sprawling residence of Prince Gong (1833–1898), half-brother of the Xianfeng emperor, is most notable for its marvellous gardens, which feature artificial hills, ponds, rocks that mimic mountain ranges, whimsical pavilions and even a Great Wall folly. The architectural highlights of this fantastical royal playground are the **Western-style Gate** (西洋门; Xīyáng mén), a marble portal built in the Jesuit style, and the **Grand Theatre House** (大戏楼; Dàxì Lóu), where tour groups (lots of them) are treated to short Peking opera performances.

Built in 1777 for Heshen, a corrupt Qing dynasty official doted on by Emperor Qianlong, the mansion didn't pass to Prince Gong until 1851. During the Second Opium War in 1860, successive Anglo-French victories sent the emperor and his inner court fleeing Beijing, leaving Prince Gong to sign the Treaty of Peking on his emperor's behalf, which ceded Kowloon to the British and allowed foreign ambassadors to install themselves permanently in Beijing. Prince Gong would later become the Prince Regent under Empress Cixi, and run the Qing dynasty's foreign ministry.

Song Qingling's Former Residence　　　MUSEUM
(宋庆龄故居, Sòng Qìnglíng Gùjū; Map p86; ⏱010 6402 3195; 46 Houhai Beiyan, 后海北沿46号; ¥20; ⊙9am-5.30pm Apr-Oct, to 4.30pm Nov-Mar; Ⓢ Line 2 to Jishuitan, exit B) Set in well-tended gardens on the north shore of Houhai Lake (p87), this is the mansion of Madam Song, venerated by the Chinese as the wife of Sun Yatsen, first president of the Republic of China. The buildings preserve her stylish living quarters, an 'ideal home' of 1970s China, while an attached museum takes visitors through the story of her astonishing life.

Deshengmen Arrow Tower　　　FORTRESS
(德胜门箭楼, Déshèngmén Jiànlóu; Map p86; 19 Xinjiekouwai Dajie, 新街口外大街19号; ¥20; ⊙9am-4pm Tue-Sun; Ⓢ Line 2, 8 to Guloudajie, exit A1) A monumental landmark along the 2nd Ring Rd is this surviving hulk of Beijing's dearly departed ramparts. A *jiànlóu* (arrow tower), it would have stood in front of the gate and walls itself, guarding the northern approach to the city. Today it's easy to forget that Beijing, situated on a flat, dusty plain, was once defined by its awe-inspiring, seemingly impregnable walls. Gazing up at mighty Deshengmen at least imparts a fleeting sense of that vanished majesty.

You can climb the the battlements if you buy a ticket for the **Beijing Ancient Coins Museum**. The tower itself houses a smart little exhibition of weaponry and old photographs between the square firing embrasures.

The original Ming dynasty tower was rebuilt in 1902 after it was destroyed by allied forces following the Boxer Rebellion. The current edifice is a 1951 rebuild.

On the north side of Deshengmen, public buses depart for the **Ming Tombs** (十三陵, Shísān Líng; Changchi Lu, Changping District, 昌平区昌赤路; per site ¥20-60, through ticket ¥100 Nov-Mar, ¥135 Apr-Oct; ⊙8am-5.30pm; 🚌872, Ⓢ Changping Line to Ming Tombs) and the Badaling (p137) section of Great Wall.

★ **White Dagoba Temple**　　　BUDDHIST TEMPLE
(妙应寺白塔, Miàoyīng Sì Báitǎ; Map p86; ⏱010 6616 0211; 171 Fuchengmennei Dajie, 阜成门内大街171号; adult ¥20; ⊙9am-5pm Tue-Sun; Ⓢ Line 2 to Fuchengmen, exit B, or Line 4 to Xisi, exit A) Originally built in 1271 under the reign of Kublai Khan, the serene Miaoying Temple slumbers beneath its astonishing 51m-high *dagoba*, the tallest in China. A glimpse of it rising imperiously above the surrounding *hutong* is one of

WORTH A TRIP

THE MING TOMBS

Cradled by Tianshou Mountain in Beijing's northern reaches are the tombs of 13 Ming dynasty emperors (十三陵, Shísān Líng), arranged according to *feng shui* across a lush valley once sealed off to the living by an 80km wall.

Despite not generally being considered a 'must-see' like the Great Wall or the Forbidden City, the Ming Tombs (p94) can be an incredibly rewarding place to visit on a quiet day in fine weather, beginning with a stroll along the **Spirit Way** between its solemn guard of stone beasts and officials, before exploring the first and largest of the tombs, the **Yong Ling**, boasting architecture that easily rivals the Forbidden City. At **Ding Ling** you can descend into the tomb itself, though the experience isn't as exciting as it sounds, being mostly empty and without ornament.

Aside from the **Zhao Ling**, the other 10 tombs are fenced off, and best viewed from afar when standing atop the burial mound citadels at each of the three accessible tombs. That said, the hillsides here would reward the intrepid hiker with incredible views of the tomb sites spread over 40 sq km of fields, orchards, rivers and scattered villages.

The most direct way to get there is on bus 872 (¥9, one hour, 7.10am to 7.10pm), which departs from the north side of Deshengmen Arrow Tower. It calls at the Spirit Way and Ding Ling, before terminating at Chang Ling. The last bus back is at 6pm.

the most emotive sights in Beijing. The *dagoba* was built on the site of an earlier temple by a Nepali architect, invited to Dadu (as Beijing was known) by the Khan to cement the new dynasty's relations with Tibet.

You can't enter the *dagoba* itself, but you can circumnavigate the base and explore the temple halls, the largest of which, the **Hall of the Great Enlightened One** (大觉宝殿, Dàjué Bǎodiàn), contains a display of Buddhist statuary. The **Hall of the Seven Buddhas** houses scale models presenting the Yuan dynasty cities of Dadu (Beijing), Shangdu ('Xanadu' of Coleridge's famous poem) and Zhongdu, another Yuan-era city between the other two.

The *hutong* to the north and east of the temple are some of the more atmospheric in the city, and are well worth a stroll after your visit.

Lu Xun Museum MUSEUM
(鲁迅博物馆, Lǔ Xùn Bówùguǎn; Map p86; ☏010 6616 4080; www.luxunmuseum.com.cn; 19 Gongmenkou Ertiao, 宫门口二条19号; ⊘9am-4pm Tue-Sun; ⑤Line 2 to Fuchengmen, exit B) **FREE** This modern, two-storey museum presents in great detail the life of Lu Xun (1881–1936), considered the greatest Chinese writer of the 20th century. Preserved here is his small courtyard home where he lived for three years from 1924, during which time he witnessed the student massacre of 18 March 1926, and wrote his famous essay *Rose Without a Flower*. Passport required for entry.

Wansong Laoren Pagoda PAGODA
(万松老人塔, Wàn Sōng Lǎorén Tǎ; Map p86; 43 Xisi Nandajie, 西四南大街43号; ⊘9am-9pm; ⑤Line 4 to Xisi, exit D) **FREE** Dating back to the Mongol Yuan dynasty but partially rebuilt in the 1980s, this nine-tiered brick pagoda sits in a lovely walled garden of pomegranate trees and grapevines, with a hotchpotch of historic *hutong* timber frames and stone carvings scattered about. A bookshop sells old postcards and pots of jasmine tea.

Cathedral of Our Saviour CATHEDRAL
(西什库天主堂, Xīshíkù Tiānzhǔtáng; Map p86; ☏010 6617 5198; 33 Xishiku Dajie, 西什库大街33号; ⊘5am-6pm; ⑤Line 4 to Xisi, exit B) Formerly known as Beitang, this Gothic church (c 1897) is Beijing's most exemplary, with a pair of 31m-high bell towers looking resplendent (read: gaudy) after a 2018 paint job. The church yard, where hawkers sell cherubic portraits of Jesus, has several notable Chinese-style buildings providing contrast to the European architecture. Notoriously, Beitang was the site of a bloody siege during the Boxer Rebellion in 1900, costing the lives of around 400 churchgoers. A tiny memorial stone in the east chapel records the dates.

Inscribed on the stone is 'Gesta Dei Per Francos', an oblique reference to the First Crusade (the Boxer Rebellion was an uprising against the spread of foreign ideas in China, especially Christianity). Beneath is recorded the dates of the siege, from 13 June to 16 August 1900. During this time, something like 10,000 Boxers surrounded the church,

HUTONG TODAY

From around 3200 in 1949, the number of intact *hutong* lanes was thought to have shrunk to 900 by 2012 as new office buildings, apartment blocks and the widening of roads prompted widespread demolition. More alarming is that in 2017 some sources put the number of *hutong* at just 300, with about half truncated or changed in part by construction.

which was protected by just 41 French and Italian marines. By digging tunnels and planting improvised mines, the Boxers killed hundreds inside the church, with many also dying of disease and starvation, but remarkably it was never taken. The number of Boxers killed is unrecorded, but was undoubtedly high (they believed they were impervious to bullets). The siege was eventually relieved by the arrival of Allied soldiers.

Capital Museum MUSEUM
(首都博物馆, Shǒudū Bówùguǎn; ☑010 6339 3339; www.capitalmuseum.org.cn; 16 Fuxingmen-wai Dajie, 复兴门外大街16号; ⊗9am-5pm Tue-Sun, last entry 4pm; ⑤Line 1 to Muxidi, exit C1) FREE It's a case of 'so near and yet so far' for Beijing's flagship museum, which, on architecture alone, promises so much. A neat timeline exhibit charts the history of Beijing from the Jin dynasty to the 20th century via artefacts and diorama rooms, while galleries of porcelain and Buddhist art are also nicely presented. Elsewhere, though, it's mostly style over substance, with an entire floor given over to poorly explained folk customs and a faux, recreated *hutong,* which pales next to the real thing.

You'll need your passport for entry. English is mostly limited to captions, so pick up an audio guide.

White Cloud Temple TAOIST TEMPLE
(白云观, Báiyún Guàn; ☑010 6346 3887; 9 Baiyun-guan Jie, 白云路白云观街9号; ¥10; ⊗8.30am-4.30pm May-early Oct, to 4pm early Oct-Apr; ⑤Line 1 to Muxidi, exit C1) White Cloud Temple is an active, vast and fascinating maze of halls, shrines and brightly painted immortals, tended by Taoist monks with their hair gathered into topknots. It was first established in 741, and was a particularly prestigious centre for Taoism during the Mongol Yuan dynasty, though most of the temple halls are fairly recent rebuilds.

Grab a free box of incense sticks at the entrance. These are to be lit (in multiples of three) at burners stationed outside the 19 halls, whose attendant deities ascend in order of rank up to the **Hall of the Three Pure Ones** (San Qing), a 2nd-floor shrine containing statues of Taoism's three holiest figures, regarded as the origin of all beings.

Head east from the subway exit, past the hulking Capital Museum (p90) then turn right on Baiyun Lu. After crossing the canal, take the second left (Baiyunguan Jie).

◉ Temple of Heaven Park & Dongcheng South

★ **Temple of Heaven Park** PARK
(天坛公园, Tiāntán Gōngyuán; Map p91; ☑010 6702 9917; Tiantan Donglu, 天坛东路; park/through ticket Apr-Oct ¥15/35, Nov-Mar ¥10/30, audio guide ¥40, deposit ¥50; ⊗park 6.30am-10pm, sights 8am-5.30pm Apr-Oct, park 6.30am-8pm, sights 8am-5pm Nov-Mar; ⑤Line 5 to Tiantandongmen, exit A) An oasis of methodical Confucian design, the 267-hectare Temple of Heaven Park is unique. It originally served as a vast stage for solemn rites performed by the emperor (the literal 'Son of Heaven'), who prayed here for good harvests at winter solstice and sought divine clearance and atonement. Since 1918 this private imperial domain has opened its gates to common folk, who still congregate daily to perform taichi, twirl on gymnastics bars and sing revolutionary songs en masse.

Don't expect to see worshippers at prayer; this is not so much a temple as a place of arcane, Confucian-inspired statecraft. The emperor, the Son of Heaven (天子, Tiānzǐ), visited the Temple of Heaven twice a year, with the more important ceremony performed at winter solstice. The royal entourage proceeded from the Forbidden City to the **Imperial Vault of Heaven** (皇穹宇, Huáng Qióng Yǔ) in silence, with commoners instructed to close all windows and remain indoors. The procession included elephant and horse chariots and long lines of lancers, nobles, officials and musicians. The imperial sedan chair was 12m long, 3m wide and employed 10 bearers.

Although there are four main entry points to the park (with the east and west gates most convenient for visitors; through tickets cannot be purchased after 4pm), the imperial approach was via **Zhaoheng Gate** (天坛南门, Tiāntán Nánmén) in the south leading directly to the **Round Altar** (圜丘, Yuán Qiū).

Temple of Heaven Park & Dongcheng South

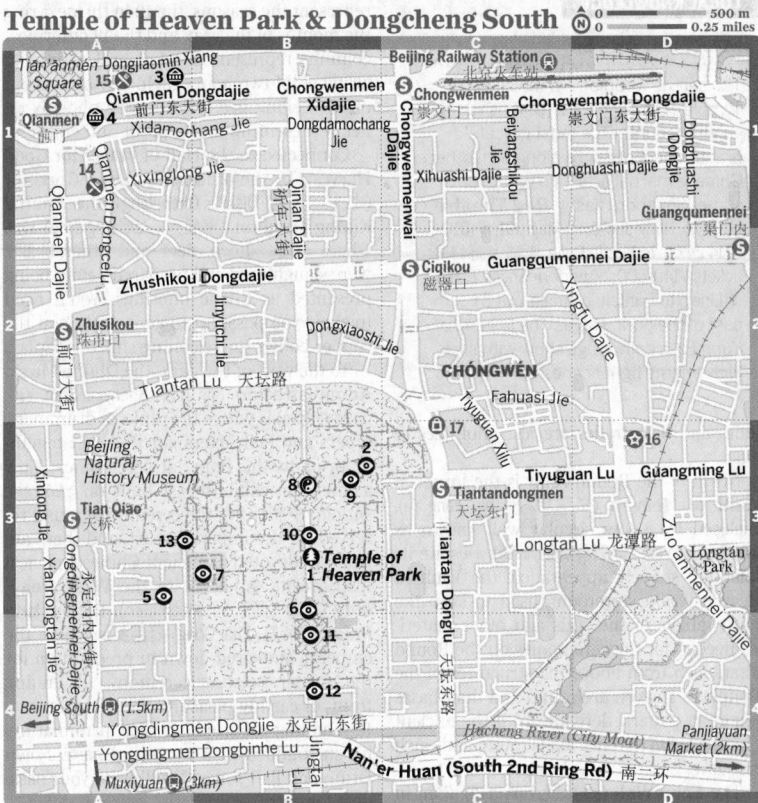

Temple of Heaven Park & Dongcheng South

On this open-air, raised dais the ceremonies to heaven took place, performed according to solemn protocol every winter solstice by the emperor himself.

Arranged in three tiers, the Round Altar revolves around the imperial number nine.

Odd numbers were considered sacrosanct in imperial China – nine (*jiǔ*) is the highest single-digit odd number and a homonym for long life. The altar is arranged in three tiers, with the top tier containing nine rings of stones, arranged in multiples of nine. The

MARTIAL ARTS

The serene woodland in the south of Temple of Heaven Park (p96) is where you'll encounter the most graceful practitioners of taichi, along with other Chinese martial arts – go early. For something more flashy, **Red Theatre** (红剧场, Hóng Jùchǎng; Map p91; ☑ 010 6714 2473; 44 Xingfu Dajie, 幸福大街44号; tickets ¥140-600; ☺ performances 7.30pm; Ⓢ Line 5 to Tiantandongmen, exit B), 1km east of the park, stages The Legend of Kung Fu, a daily stage show with slick, high-energy fight scenes.

stairs and balustrades are also multiples of nine.

North of the Round Altar is the **Imperial Vault of Heaven** (皇穹宇, Huáng Qióng Yǔ), enclosed by a low circular wall known as the **Echo Wall** (回音壁, Huíyīn Bì). Despite its splendid, shapely appearance, the Vault of Heaven was a storeroom, used to keep the spirit tablets of the gods and other materials needed for the ceremonies on the Round Altar. Seen from above the structures of the Temple of Heaven are round and their bases square, a pattern deriving from the ancient Chinese belief that heaven is round and earth is square.

The **Echo Wall** (回音壁, Huíyīn Bì), 65m in diameter, is so named for its unique acoustic properties. A quiet word or two spoken a few feet from the wall can be heard at the opposite point on the circle (although the din of other tourists chattering can drown it out!). Continuing on from the Imperial Vault of Heaven is the majestic, 360m-long **Red Stairway Bridge** (丹陛桥, Dānbì Qiáo; Imperial Walkway), an imperial thoroughfare leading to the marvellous centrepiece of the Temple of Heaven, the **Hall of Prayer for Good Harvests** (祈年殿, Qínián Diàn; ☺ 8am-5pm).

A much-photographed icon, the triple-eaved Hall of Prayer for Good Harvests is made entirely of wood without the use of nails, with the heavy roof supported by 28 wooden pillars. First built around 1420, it was burnt to cinders by a lightning strike in 1889. A faithful reproduction based on Ming architectural methods was erected the following year, with timber imported from the USA, since by that point China lacked trees big enough for the task. Rich in esoteric symbolism, the four largest central pillars

represent the seasons, the 12 in the next ring the months of the year, and the 12 outermost columns represent the day, broken into 12 'watches' of two hours each. Writhing about on the ceiling is a vivid dragon-phoenix relief, representing the emperor and empress.

Connected to the Hall of Prayer for Good Harvests by the ornamental **Long Corridor** (七十二长廊, Qīshí'èr Chángláng), the **Animal Killing Pavilion** (宰牲亭, Zǎishēng Tíng) was where oxen, sheep, deer and other beasts were slaughtered and prepared before being presented as divine offerings. You'll need to show you passport to get a look in at the copper boilers and cleaning sink on display.

To the west of the park, the **Divine Music Administration** (神乐署, Shényuè Shǔ; ¥10; ☺9am-4pm) is where the ranks of drummers, pipers and bellringers got their act together prior to the imperial ceremonies. Now a museum, exhibits cast light on *zhōnghé sháolè* (中和韶乐), the ceremonial music reserved for the imperial court, and there are galleries devoted to ancient Chinese musical instruments. Adjacent to the **West Heavenly Gate** (西天门, Xītiān Mén), the **Fasting Palace** (斋宫, Zhāi Gōng) 𝗙𝗥𝗘𝗘 is where the emperor hunkered down in preparation for the winter solstice ceremony, abstaining from all earthly pleasures for a day or two. Resembling a Forbidden City in miniature, it's surrounded by a moat and has its own Drum and Bell Tower. You'll need your passport for entry.

Since 1918 the Temple of Heaven has opened its gates to Beijing's *laobaoxing* (old 'hundred names' – literally common folk). Among the 4000 or so knotted cypresses, you'll see locals performing taichi, kung-fu routines, dancing, or assembling into impromptu choirs and orchestras to belt out the old revolutionary songs with gusto. The **exercise area** in the northeast of the park has some of Beijing's best people-watching, where you might catch sight of a septuagenarian twirling on gymnastics bars, and other feats of athleticism.

★ Southeast Corner Watchtower

WATCHTOWER

(东南角楼, Dōngnán Jiǎolóu; Map p78; 9 Chongwenmen Dondajie, 崇文门东大街9号; ¥10; ☺8am-5pm; Ⓢ Jianguomen or Chongwenmen) This immense fortress, part of the Ming City Wall Ruins Park (p93), guarded the southeast corner of Beijing's city walls. Built in 1439 but repaired numerous times over the centuries, the tower is skewered with a formidable grid of 144 archery embrasures to rain fire on would-be attackers. Visitors can mount the battlements and explore the tower itself, a magnificent maze of carpentry over multiple floors, including an exhibition of historic photographs.

From the ramparts, you can photograph the remains of the city wall as it flows west, while trainspotters can admire the rolling stock grinding in and out of Beijing Railway Station. Keep an eye out for graffiti scratched into the tower by American and Russian soldiers during the Boxer Rebellion in 1900. Allied forces overwhelmed the redoubt after a lengthy engagement (during which it was heavily damaged), en route to relieving the besieged Legation Quarter.

Ming City Wall Ruins Park WALLS
(明城墙遗址公园, Míng Chéngqiáng Yízhǐ Gōngyuán; Map p78; Chongwenmen Dongdajie, 崇文门东大街; ⊙24hr; SLines 2, 5 to Chongwenmen, exit F) FREE This wistful stretch of brick and stone is all that remains (besides a couple of other denuded nubs) of Beijing's once formidable city walls that girded the capital from the early Ming dynasty. The walls have been dismantled piecemeal since the 1950s, making way for the 2nd Ring Rd and Line 2 of the Beijing subway. A park at the wall's base makes for a pleasant stroll through the past.

In 1996 this scrap of wall, concealed by weeds and being used as a rear wall for buildings, was to be removed to make way for a hotel. When it was realised the remains were largely Ming in origin, it was instead preserved. The *Beijing Evening News* ran a 'donate bricks' campaign, asking residents to return original wall bricks that had been repurposed for other uses, to aid in the restoration. In total over 30,000 Ming and Qing bricks were received, and 2700 residents relocated.

The park also contains a restored signal house of the old Beijing–Fengtian Railway, which ran just outside the city walls here.

China Railway Museum – Zhengyang Gate MUSEUM
(中国铁道博物馆, Zhōngguó Tiědào Bówùguǎn; Map p91; ☑010 6705 1638; 2a Qianmen Dongdajie, 前门东大街2a号; ¥20; ⊙9am-5pm Tue-Sun; SLine 2 to Qianmen, exit B) In the old Qianmen Railway Station, which served Beijing from 1906 to 1959 (although only the clock tower is original), this museum offers a fairly uninspired retelling of the development of the capital and of China's railway system, with plenty of photos and models, but few English captions.

A lack of space means it doesn't have many actual trains, although you can clamber into the cab of a life-sized model of China's high-speed trains. Hardcore trainspotters should make tracks to its sister museum (p99) on the northeastern outskirts of Beijing, which is vast and filled to the brim with historic locos.

Qianmen Avenue STREET
(前门大街, Qiánmén Dàjiē; Map p94; SLine 2 to Qianmen, exit C) Running due south from Beijing's 'front gate', the mighty **Qianmen** (前门, Front Gate; Zhèngyáng Mén; Map p78; Tian'anmen Sq; ¥20, audio guide ¥20; ⊙9am-4pm Tue-Sun; SLine 2 to Qianmen, exit B or C), this street was once the main commercial thoroughfare through what was known as the 'Chinese City', where non-Manchu were permitted to reside during the Qing dynasty. Razed and rebuilt for the 2008 Olympics, it's character has now changed, with mock-period frontages housing international shopping brands, tour-group restaurants and a touristy tram ride.

At the northern end, 2019's Beijing Fun (p125) is a stylish shopping complex, which has at least attempted to preserve several handsome old buildings within its footprint.

⊙ Dashilar & Xicheng South

Dashilar Commercial Street AREA
(大栅栏商业街, Dàshìlàn Shāngyè Jiē; Map p94; Dazhalan Jie, 大栅栏街; SLine 2 to Qianmen, exit B or C) This centuries-old shopping street, although tarted up for tourists, retains several timeworn emporia selling silk (p125), cloth shoes (p125) and **traditional Chinese**

Dating back to the Liao dynasty (around 1120), the pagoda in the little-visited **Tianning Temple** (天宁寺; Tiānníng Sì; 3 Tianningsi Qianjie, 天宁寺前街3号; ⊙9am-4pm; SLine 7 to Daguanying, exit C) is reputedly the oldest structure in Beijing. The octagonal tower stands at a majestic 57.8m tall with 13 eaves, though much of its exterior statuary has crumbled away. Tianning Temple is a 25-minute schlep from the subway, so you might consider taking a taxi.

Dashilar & Xicheng South

medicine (同仁堂; ☑ 010 6303 1155; 24 Dashilan Jie, 大栅栏街24号; ☺ 8am-8pm). Once part of a vice-infested enclave of opera theatres, opium dens and bordellos west of Qianmen Dajie, it was put to the torch during the Boxer Rebellion in 1900, and subsequently rebuilt during the Republic of China.

Beijing Ancient Architecture Museum
MUSEUM

(北京古代建筑博物馆, Běijīng Gǔdài Jiànzhú Bówùguǎn; Map p94; ☑ 010 6304 5608; 21 Dongjing Lu, 东经路21号; ¥15, audio guide ¥10; ☺ 9am-4pm Tue-Sun; Ⓢ Line 8 to Tianqiao, exit D) On the site of the old Temple of Agriculture (先农坛, Xiānnóng Tán), you'll find this museum exploring traditional Chinese building techniques. Brush up on your *dǒugǒng* (brackets) and *sǔnmǎo* (joints), and get the lowdown on Beijing's courtyard houses as you explore the historic complex, centred on the magnificent Jupiter Hall (太岁殿, Tàisuì Diàn) with its fine restored ceiling.

Fayuan Temple
BUDDHIST TEMPLE

(法源寺, Fǎyuán Sì; Map p94; 7 Fayuansi Qianjie, 法源寺前街7号; adult ¥5; ☺ 8.30-4pm; Ⓢ Lines 4, 7 to Caishikou, exit D) Infused with an air of sleepy reverence, this working Buddhist temple is one of Beijing's most transportative. Perhaps it's the ancient Song dynasty pines, interspersed with thickets of lilacs, gingkos and crabapple trees from the time of Emperor Qianlong, or the way monks and local retirees outnumber tourists, but bustling Beijing feels aeons away. Originally built in the 7th century to honour soldiers killed in battle with Korean tribes, the current halls are 20th-century renovations.

That being said, the courtyards contain several ancient stelae and the halls dozens of handsome Buddhist relics in glass cases. Beijing's longest reclining Buddha at 7.4m lies supine in the rearmost hall (closed for renovations at time of research). And do seek out the Pilu Hall for its enormous stone lotus bulb engraved with '1000 leaves' of Buddha images and crowned with the Five Dhyani Buddhas.

You can be certain of seeing monks here, because Dayuan Temple also serves as as a Buddhist teaching academy, well furnished with precious religious texts stored within the Pavilion of Buddhist Sutras.

Niu Jie Mosque
MOSQUE

(牛街礼拜寺, Niú Jiē Lǐbài Sì; ☑ 010 6353 2564; 18 Niu Jie, 牛街18号; adult ¥10, Muslims free; ☺ 8am-5pm; Ⓢ Line 7 to Guang'anmennei, exit D) Dating from around the 10th century when Chinese first began converting to Islam, Beijing's oldest mosque appears more like a Chinese temple with Islamic characteristics. Dome and minarets are conspicuously absent, but it does have a fine prayer hall serving the local community of Hui Chinese Muslims, who also run the many halal butchers in the vicinity of Ox St (Niu Jie).

◉ Sanlitun & Chaoyang

★ 798 Art District
AREA

(798 艺术区, Qī Jiǔ Bā Yìshù Qū; cnr Jiuxianqiao Lu & 798 Lu, 酒仙桥路; ☺ galleries 10am-6pm, most closed Mon; ☐ 403, 909, Ⓢ Line 14 to Wangjing South, exit B1) Contemporary art meets communist history at this thrilling enclave of international galleries installed within China's model factory complex of the 1950s. Most of Beijing's best galleries are here, staging shows from the likes of Ai Weiwei and David Hockney in gorgeous Bauhaus workshops that once produced munitions and electronics. Toss into the mix oodles of street art, stylish cafes and restaurants, art shops, and an elevated walkway (D-Park; ☺ 8am-8pm) FREE offering views of astonishing industrial architecture, and you can easily spend a full day here.

The '718 Joint Factory', as 798 was originally known, was built with East German expertise in the 1950s, using materials imported from East Germany via the Trans-Siberian Railway all the way into the factory itself. Preservation orders have saved the old factory station, tracks and a steam loco, along with giant industrial chimneys, workers' dorms and, most importantly, the light-filled Bauhaus factories and workshops, now home to galleries like 798 Art Factory (798艺术工厂, 798 Yìshù Gōngchǎng; 4 Jiuxianqiao Lu, 酒仙桥路4号) FREE and BTAP (东京画廊, Dōngjīng Huàláng; www.tokyo-gallery.com; off 798 Lu, 798路; ☺ 10am-5.30pm Tue-Sat) FREE, where scarlet slogans praising Chairman Mao are still visible on the lofty ceilings.

The most famous gallery is UCCA (Ullens Center for Contemporary Art, 尤伦斯当代艺术中心, Yóulúnsī Dāngdài Yìshù Zhōngxīn; ☑ 010 5780 0200; www.ucca.org.cn/en; 4 Jiuxianqiao Lu, 酒仙桥路4号; ¥60-100; ☺ 10am-7pm), which usually hosts two or three big-ticket international exhibitions at a time. Faurschou Foundation (林冠艺术基金会, Línguān Yìshù Jījīnhuì; ☑ 010 5978 9316; www.faurschou.com; 2 Jiuxianquao Lu 酒仙桥路2号) FREE from Denmark and the Chinese-run M Woods Art Museum (木木美术馆, Mùmù Měishùguǎn; ☑ 010 8312 3450; www.mwoods.org; 2 Jiuxuanqiao Lu, 酒仙桥路2号; ¥80; ☺ 10.30am-7pm Tue-Sun) consistently stage thought-provoking exhibitions from the biggest names in art, both Chinese and international.

It's not all world class, of course; dozens of smaller galleries range from the edgy to

Sanlitun & Chaoyang

Shard Box Store (4km)
Kyrgyzstan Embassy (1km)
Indian Embassy (50m); Israeli Embassy (300m); South Korean Embassy (400m); US Embassy (400m); Japanese Embassy (500m)
Dos Kolegas (2km)

0   1 km
0   0.5 miles

Zuojiazhuang Xijie

Xindong Lu

Raffles Medical

40

Liangmaqiao
亮马桥

Liangmaqiao Lu

Xinyuan Nanlu

Liangma River

Xiangheyuan Lu

Dongzhimenwai Xiejie 东直门外斜街

Dongzhimenwai Xiaojie

53

48

43   49

Sanlitun Dongliujie

18   SĀNLǏTÚN EMBASSY AREA

Cháoyáng Park

Beijing Airport Express

Dongzhimen Transport Hub

Dongzhimen
东直门

Dongzhimenwai Dajie

38   39

Sanlitun Xiwujie

41

52

Agricultural Exhibition Center (Nongye Zhanlanguan)
农业展览馆

CHÁOYÁNG

30

Xinzhong Jie

Chunxiu Lu

23

Xindong Lu

Sanlitun Lu

44   47

Sanlitun Dongsijie

Dong'erhuan (East 2nd Ring Rd)
东二环

Dongzhong Jie

20

8

19

Sanlitun Beijie

10

Sanlitun Dongsanjie

Dongsanhuan Beilu (East 3rd Ring Rd)

Xingfucun Lu

12

Dongsi Shitiao
东四十条

4

Gongrentiyuchang Beilu

7

37

Tuanjiehu
团结湖

Nongzhanguan Nanlu

22

China DIY Travel (500m)

Gongrentiyuchang Xilu

工人体育场东路

Nansanlitun Lu

16

29

26

28   Workers' Stadium

15   31

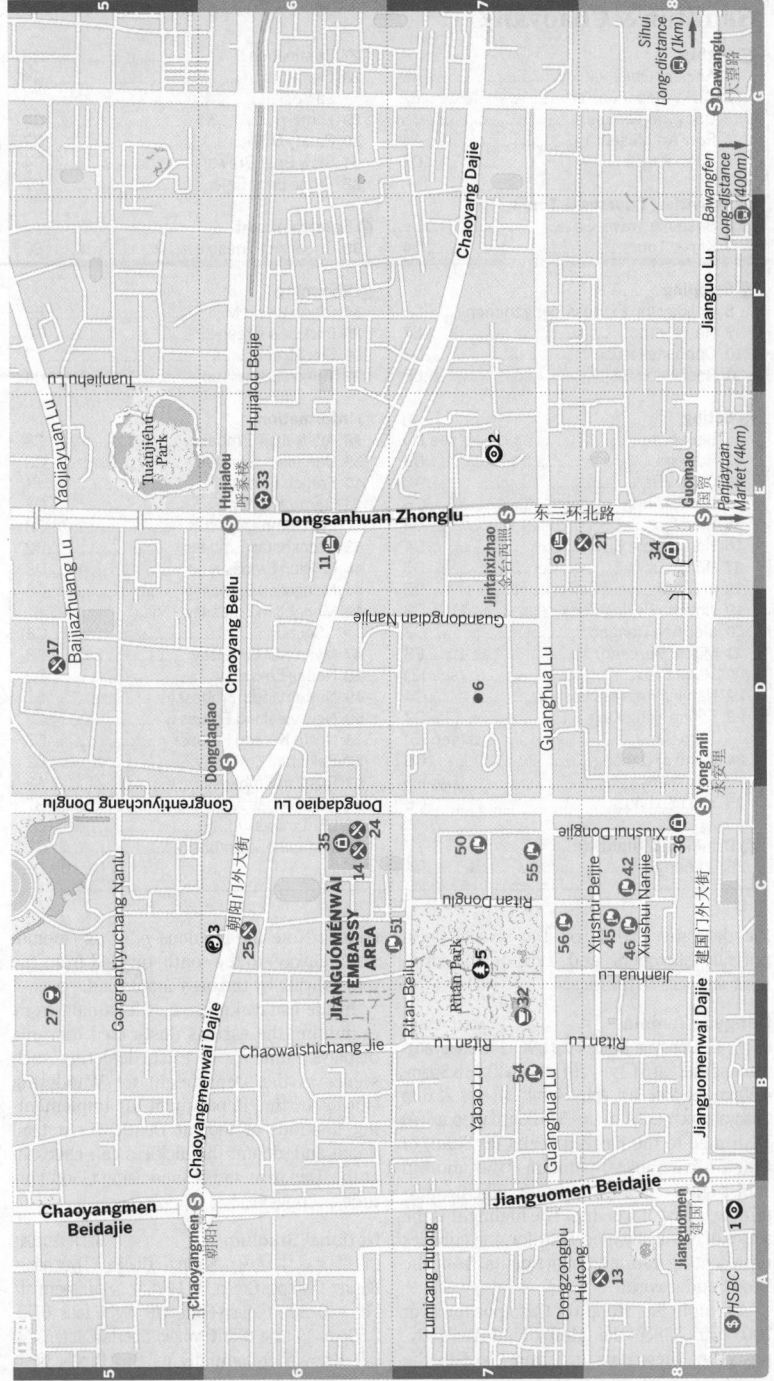

Sanlitun & Chaoyang

the derivative, while on the streets, local portrait sketchers and cartoonists hawk their services to tourists.

Dongyue Temple TAOIST TEMPLE
(东岳庙, Dōngyuè Miào; Map p96; 141 Chaoyangmenwai Dajie, 朝阳门外大街141号; ¥10; ⊗8.30am-4.30pm Tue-Sun, last entry 4pm; ⑤Lines 2, 6 to Chaoyangmen, exit A, or Line 6 to Dongdaqiao, exit A) Dedicated to the Eastern Peak (Tài Shān) of China's five Taoist mountains, this morbid Taoist shrine is an unsettling, albeit entertaining, place of worship. The highlight is the series of comically macabre diorama cubicles representing various 'departments' from the Taoist underworld.

A temple has stood on this spot for over 700 years since the Mongol-led Yuan dynasty, but these days it's almost lost in the sprawl. Note the fabulous *páifāng* (memorial archway) to the south, divided from the main shrine by the busy main road.

Inside you can muse on life's finalities by examining the various dust-caked diorama displays, some 72 in total, depicting such scenes as the 'Department for Wandering Ghosts' or the 'Department for Implementing 15 Kinds of Violent Death'. It's not all doom and gloom: the luckless can check in at the 'Department for Increasing Good Fortune & Longevity'.

National Stadium ARCHITECTURE
(北京国家体育场, Běijīng Guójiā Tǐyùchǎng; Beijing Olympic Green, 奥林匹克公园; normal/VIP ¥40/80; ⊗9am-6pm, VIP night tour 6.30-8.50pm; ⑤Line 8 to Olympic Sports Center, exit B2) Known colloquially as the Bird's Nest

(鸟巢, Niǎocháo), the spectacular showpiece of the 2008 Olympics Games was designed by Swiss firm Herzog & de Meuron in consultancy with Beijing artist Ai Weiwei. Most visitors are content to snap photos of the exterior, but sports fans might get a kick out of seeing the track where Usain Bolt broke the 100m world record.

Along with the adjacent **Water Cube** (国家游泳中心, Guójiā Yóuyǒng Zhōngxīn; www.water-cube.com/en; 11 Tianchen Lu, Olympic Park, 天辰东路11号; ¥30; ⏱9am-7pm, water park 10am-3pm; 🚇) and other venues, the National Stadium was part of a vast Olympic development on Beijing's central axis that necessitated the eviction of over one million people, according to reports at the time. Appropriately, the area can feel as lifeless as a post-apocalypse zombie flick, although the stadium will be pressed into service once again as the site of the opening and closing ceremonies of the 2022 Winter Olympics, becoming the only stadium to host both the summer and winter games.

Yuan Dynasty Walls Relics Park　　　PARK
(元大都城垣遗址公园, Yuán Dàdū Chéngyuán Yízhǐ Gōngyuán; 🚇Lines 8, 10 to Beituchang, or Line 10 to Xitucheng) FREE Back when Beijing was 'Dadu', capital of Kublai Khan's Yuan dynasty, the city was sheltered by an earthwork wall, the northern battlements of which are marked by this 9km-long strip of sculpted parkland. Remarkably, traces of the old earthworks endure. From Beitucheng (literally 'north earthen wall') subway station cross to the south side of the moat and head east; in a few moments you'll spot the original, misshapen mound, overgrown with trees.

Ritan Park　　　PARK
(日坛公园, Rìtán Gōngyuán; Map p96; 6 Ritan Beilu, 日坛北路6号; ⏱6am-9pm; 🚇Lines 1, 2 to Jianguomen, exit B) FREE Landscaped like an ornamental Chinese garden, Ritan Park provides peaceful respite for the embassy district's diplomats and worker bees. The historic highlight is the **Altar of the Sun** (rìtán), an open-air platform where emperors would perform rites and sacrifices.

During the Ming dynasty, Beijing had several such altars, the most famous being *Tiantan*, otherwise known as the Temple of Heaven Park (p90). The **Stone Boat** (石舫咖啡, Shífǎng Kāfēi; ☎010 6501 9986; beers & coffee from ¥20, cocktails from ¥40; ⏱10am-6pm; 🛜), beside an ornamental pond overhung with willows, is a lovely spot for a drink.

CCTV Headquarters　　　ARCHITECTURE
(央视大楼, Yāngshì Dàlóu; Map p96; 32 Dongsanhuan Zhonglu, 东三环中路32号; 🚇Line 10 to Jintaixizhao, exit C) Known locally as *dà kùchǎ* (大裤衩, Big Pants), the 234m-tall CCTV Tower is an architectural fantasy that appears to defy gravity. Designed by Rem Koolhaas and Ole Scheeren, the building has become an icon of the Beijing skyline since being completed in 2008 in time for the Olympics.

◎ Summer Palace & Haidian

★**Summer Palace**　　　HISTORIC SITE
(颐和园, Yíhé Yuán; Map p100; 19 Xinjian Gongmen, 新建宫门19号; Apr-Oct ¥30, through ticket ¥60, Nov-Mar ¥20, through ticket ¥50, audio guide ¥40; ⏱6.30am-6pm, sights 8.30am-5pm Apr-Oct, 7am-5pm, sights 9am-4pm Nov-Mar; 🚇Line 4 to Beigongmen or Xiyaun, 🚊Xijiao Line to West Gate of Summer Palace) A marvel of Chinese garden design and one of Beijing's must-see attractions, the Summer Palace was the royal retreat for emperors fleeing the suffocating summer torpor of the old imperial city and, most recently, it was the retirement playground of Empress Dowager Cixi. It merits an entire day's exploration, although a (high-paced) morning or afternoon exploring its waterways, pavilions, bridges and temples may suffice.

The domain had long been a royal garden before being considerably enlarged and embellished by Emperor Qianlong in the 18th century. He marshalled an army of labourers to deepen and expand **Kunming Lake** (昆明湖; Kunming Hú), originally a reservoir dug in the Yuan dynasty, and reputedly surveyed imperial navy drills from a hilltop perch.

Anglo-French troops vandalised the palace at the end of the Second Opium War in 1860. Empress Dowager Cixi launched into a refit

OFF THE BEATEN TRACK

Way out on the northeastern fringes of Beijing, the hangar-like **China Railway Museum** (中国铁道博物馆, Zhōngguó Tiědào Bówùguǎn; ☎010 6438 1317; north of 1 Jiuxianqiao Bei Lu, Chaoyang District, 朝阳区酒仙桥北路1号院北侧; ¥20; ⏱9am-4pm Tue-Sun) contains dozens of historic locos, including several souped-up carriages used by Mao and other senior cadres during the 1960s and '70s – trainspotters will be ecstatic. There are English captions. A taxi from the centre of town will cost around ¥60.

Summer Palace

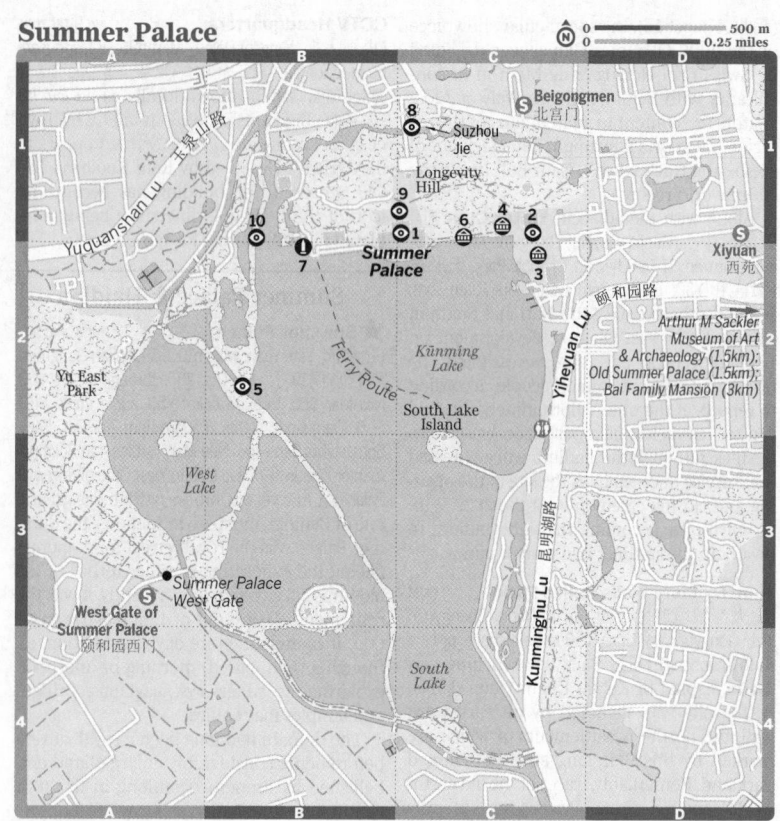

Summer Palace

in 1888 with money earmarked for a modern navy; the **marble boat** (清晏舫, Qīngyuàn Chuán) at the northern edge of the lake was her only nautical, albeit quite unsinkable, concession. Foreign troops, angered by the Boxer Rebellion, had another go at torching the Summer Palace in 1900, prompting further restoration work. By 1949 the palace had once more fallen into disrepair, eliciting a major overhaul.

Glittering Kunming Lake swallows up three-quarters of the park, overlooked by **Longevity Hill** (万寿山, Wànshòu Shān), itself crowned by the eight-tiered **Tower of Buddhist Incense** (佛香阁, Fóxiāng Gé), the most elaborate and expensive restoration project of Cixi's grand redesign. Arranged on a north–south axis, the tower rises up behind the **Hall of Dispelling Clouds** (排云殿, Páiyún Diàn), built by Emperor Qianlong for his mother on her 60th birthday. At the foot of Longevity Hill, hugging the north shore of the lake, is the **Long Corridor** (长廊, Cháng Láng), a canopied, 728m-long ornamental walkway. Thousands of artworks adorn every crossbeam, column and ceiling arch, depicting scenic views from around China, much-loved myths, Buddhist scenes and folk tales.

At the western end of the Long Corridor is Cixi's **Marble Boat** (清晏舫, Qīngyuàn Chuán), a place to entertain (and a common garden design motif), while at the eastern end are her living quarters, the **Hall of Joy and Longevity** (乐寿堂, Lèshòu Táng), which echoes the *sìhéyuàn* layout of traditional Beijing courtyards, and still contains dusty Qing-era furniture. Continue east to the three-storey **Grand Theatre** (大戏楼, Dàxìlóu; ¥10) where Cixi would enjoy her beloved Peking opera. Nearby, the **Hall of Benevolence and Longevity** (仁寿殿, Rénshòu Diàn) was where the empress dowager still pulled the government strings late into her official retirement. Glimpse the grand throne within; the rockery outside was designed to mimic the famous Lion Grove Garden in Suzhou. Note also the dragon and phoenix statues in the courtyard, the symbolic embodiment of emperor and empress. Here it's the phoenix that commands centre spot, a clear sign that a woman – Cixi – was running the show.

If time permits, try to do a circuit of the lake along the **West Causeway** (西堤, Xīdī). You can exit the palace via the West Gate, where you can pick up the Xijiao Line back to the city, or return along the east shore. Based on the famous Su Causeway in Hangzhou, and lined with willow and mulberry trees, the causeway kicks off northwest of the **Marble Boat** (清晏舫, Qīngyuàn Chuán). With its delightful moon hump, the **Jade Belt Bridge** (玉带桥, Yùdài Qiáo) dates from the reign of Emperor Qianlong and crosses the point where the Jade River enters the lake (when it flows).

At the base of the rear of Longevity Hill is **Suzhou Street** (苏州街, Sūzhōu Jiē), built to mimic the waterways and architecture of the famous Jiangsu canal town. Here is where emperors and their concubines would pretend to be common folk by 'shopping' for trinkets in the ersatz stores that lined the shore, with eunuchs acting as shopkeepers. Today it's full of actual souvenir shops, which, ironically, makes it rather authentic.

Old Summer Palace
HISTORIC SITE

(圆明园, Yuánmíng Yuán; ☏ 010 6261 6375; 28 Qinghua Xilu, 清华西路28号; adult ¥10, through ticket ¥25, map ¥6; ⏰ 7am-6pm Apr, Sep & Oct, to 5.30pm Nov-Mar, to 7pm May-Aug; ⑤ Line 4 to Yuanmingyuan, exit A) Shattered ruins are all that remain of the 'Garden of Perfection and Light,' once known as the 'Versailles of the East' for its profound beauty, even surpassing Cixi's 19th century reboot (p99). Jesuit-designed palaces and hundreds of Chinese, Tibetan and

Mongolian-style buildings ranged across 350 hectares of exquisitely landscaped gardens – all put to the torch by the British in 1860 (after a thorough looting by the French) at the close of the Second Opium War. What's left is now a public park.

The looting and destruction of the Old Summer Palace is an event forever inscribed in Chinese history books as a low point in China's humiliation by foreign powers. Lord Elgin, British High Commissioner to China in 1860, ordered the destruction in response to the torture and killing of British envoys attempting to negotiate under a flag of truce. Some 3500 troops systematically set the palace ablaze, the fire lasting three days.

The subdued marble ruins of the **Palace Buildings Scenic Area** (Xīyánglóu Jǐngqū) can be mulled over in the **Eternal Spring Garden** (Chángchūn Yuán) in the northeast of the park, near the east gate. There were once more than 10 buildings here, designed by Jesuits Giuseppe Castiglione and Michael Benoist. The buildings were only partially destroyed during the 1860 Anglo-French looting and the structures apparently remained usable for quite some time afterwards. However, the ruins were gradually picked over and carted away by local people all the way up to the 1970s.

The **Great Fountain Ruins** (Dàshuǐfǎ) are considered the best-preserved relics. Built in 1759, the main building was fronted by a lion-head fountain. Standing opposite is the **Guanshuifa**, five large stone screens embellished with European carvings of military flags, armour, swords and guns. The screens were discovered in the grounds of Peking University in the 1970s and later restored to their original positions. Just east of the Great Fountain Ruins stood a four-pillar archway, chunks of which remain.

★Wuta Temple
BUDDHIST TEMPLE

(五塔寺, Wǔtǎ Sì; ☏ 010 6218 9514; 24 Wutasi Cun, 五塔寺村24号; adult ¥20; ⏰ 9am-4pm Tue-Sun; ⑤ Line 4 to National Library, exit C) If any Beijing sight can vanquish the dreaded 'temple fatigue', it's Wǔtǎ Sì. This little-known gem is eminently worthy of a pilgrimage, not just for its remarkable design, which owes more to India than imperial China, but also for the magnificent scatter of ancient stonemasonry – statues, stelae, altars and thrones – salvaged from sights around Beijing and plonked here for posterity.

Built in 1473 for a visiting Indian lama, Zhenjue Temple (as it was actually called) was one of many temples lining the imperial waterway linking the capital with the northwest palaces. This one was a particular favourite of the Qing emperors – Qianlong threw two lavish birthday parties here for his mum, and had a similar pagoda built at the Azure Clouds Temple. But by the end of the dynasty, neglect, fire and general upheaval had seen off its six wooden halls, and so it became known for its remaining standout feature, the all-stone Wǔtǎ (Five Pagodas).

Inspired by the Mahabodhi Temple in India, the boxlike Wǔtǎ (or Diamond Throne Pagoda) is pockmarked on all four sides by hundreds of images of Buddha, each with unique *mudras* (hand gestures), above a band of elephants, deities and Buddhist symbols, with Sanskrit trimming the base. Among its crown of five stupas, the yellow glazed-tile roof was a later Qing dynasty embellishment, effectively a seal of approval for royal use.

In lieu of its long-lost temple halls, foundations of which can still be seen, the relatively empty grounds have been given over to the **Beijing Art Museum of Stone Carvings**, and are full of inspiring slabs of sculpture and stonework, many dating back to the Mongol Yuan dynasty and some as far back as the Eastern Han.

For more temple action, stroll west along the riverbank and you'll come to Wanshou Temple in 20 to 30 minutes.

Wanshou Temple   BUDDHIST TEMPLE

(万寿寺, Wànshòu Sì; 121 Wanshousi Lu, 万寿寺路 121号; adult ¥20; ⊙9am-4.30pm Tue-Sun; [S] Lines 4, 9 to National Library, exit A) This tranquil, little-visited temple was originally consecrated for the storage of Buddhist texts. Its name echoes the Summer Palace's Longevity Hill (Wanshou means 'longevity') and the imperial entourage would stop here to quaff tea en route to and from the palace. It was undergoing extensive renovation at time of research.

Great Bell Temple   BUDDHIST SITE

(大钟寺, Dàzhōng Sì; ☑010 8213 9050; 31a Beisanhuan Xilu, 北三环西路31a号; ¥30; ⊙9am-4.30pm Tue-Sun; [S] Line 13 to Dazhongsi, exit A) Despite being stranded along the North 3rd Ring Rd, this Qing-era temple is well worth a diversion to marvel at its centrepiece, the humongous Yongle Bell, cast in 1406 and almost 7m tall. The temple halls have been entirely given over to the fascinating and well-presented **Dazhongsi Ancient Bell Museum**, where you can admire up close the intricate inscriptions and artistry adorning hundreds of temple bells.

Military Museum of
the People's Revolution   MUSEUM

(军事博物馆, Junshi Bówùguǎn; http://eng.jb.mil. cn; 9 Fuxing Lu, 复兴路9号; ⊙9am-5pm Tue-Sun; [S] Lines 1, 9 to Military Museum, exit A) FREE Bristling with Cold War–era planes, guns and bombs, this cavernous museum shows China at its most hawkish. Expanded in 2018, many of the side exhibits were yet to open at time of research, but if they were anything like the former Hall of Agrarian Revolutionary War and the Hall of the War to Resist US Aggression and Aid Korea, then they will remain a tour de force of communist spin.

☞ Tours & Activities

Guided walks and tours are a great way to see beyond the state-sanctioned narrative to the deeper, more human stories, both complex and compelling, that make Beijing such a fascinating city. A little knowledge goes a long way!

★ Beijing Postcards   HISTORY

(Map p94; ☑156 1145 3992; www.bjpostcards.com; 97 Yangmeizhu Xiejie, Dashilar, 杨梅竹斜街97号;

STUDENT LIFE

A stroll through the historic campus of prestigious **Peking University** (北京大学, Běijīng Dàxué; http://english.pku.edu. cn; 5 Yiheyuan Lu, 颐和园路5号; [S] Line 4 to East Gate of Peking University, exit A) offers a window on to the student lives of China's brightest young minds. Be sure to stop in at the **Arthur M Sackler Museum of Art & Archaeology** (赛克勒考古与艺术博物馆, Sàikèlè Kǎogǔ Yǔ Yìshù Bówùguǎn; ⊙9am-4.30pm Tue-Sun) FREE near the west gate.

FRAGRANT HILLS PARK

A great swath of Beijing's Western Hills (Xīshān) was once an imperial pleasure resort, its acres of undulating pine-cypress forest peppered with temples, pavilions and lookouts dating from the Qing dynasty. Opened to the masses as a public park in 1956, **Fragrant Hills** (香山公园, Xiāng Shān Gōngyuán; 40 Maimai Jie, 买卖街40号; Apr-Oct ¥10, Nov-Mar ¥5; ⊙6am-6.30pm Apr-Oct, to 6pm Nov-Mar; 🚇Xijiao Line to Fragrant Hills) is busiest in autumn when the maples are ablaze. On reasonably clear days you can see Beijing's skyscrapers, 20km distant, from Incense-Burner Peak.

To most visitors, Fragrant Hills Park is a thigh-burning ascent up zigzag lanes and endless steps, passing imperial villas and temples, many of which, incredibly, served as summer homes to Beijing's foreign diplomatic community in the late 19th and early 20th centuries. Allow an hour from the main north entrance to **Incense-Burner Peak** (Xiānglú Fēng, 557m). From the top you get all-embracing views of the countryside, and you can leave the crowds behind by hiking further into the Western Hills.

Rather than making straight for the summit, you could start with a visit to the **Azure Clouds Temple** (碧云寺, Bìyún Sì; 40 Maimai Jie, Fragrant Hills Park, 买卖街40号香山公园; adult ¥10; ⊙9am-4.30pm; 🚇Xijiao Line to Fragrant Hills), just inside the park's main north entrance, with its five-towered pagoda and hall of 500 Buddhist luóhàn statues. Southwest of the temple is the enormous, Tibetan-style **Temple of Brilliance** (Zhāo Miào), under restoration at time of research, while nearby is Xiangshan's iconic **Glazed Tile Pagoda**. Both survived visits by foreign troops intent on sacking the area in 1860, and then in 1900.

Then you could take the **chairlift** (¥80 one way, 9am to 4pm) to the peak, saving your energy for a long amble downhill, past various of the park's '28 scenic spots' as selected by Emperor Qianlong in the 18th century, several of which were undergoing restoration at time of research.

There are restaurants, shops and snacks along Meichang Jie, the old paved approach to the north gate of the park.

One stop away on the Xijiao Line is the **Botanical Gardens** (北京植物园, Běijīng Zhíwùyuán; www.beijingbg.com; Xiangshan Nanlu, 香山南路; ¥5, through ticket ¥50; ⊙6am-8pm Apr-Oct, 7.30am-5pm Nov-Mar; 🚇Xijiao Line to Botanical Garden), where Puyi, China's last emperor, tended the gardens between 1960 and 1961 after 10 years of political re-education under the communists.

---

walks per person from ¥300; ⊙noon-6pm Wed-Sun; 🚇Line 2 to Qianmen, exit C) The capital's best purveyor of history tours in English, Beijing Postcards hosts a range of rigorously researched walks and talks led by Danish co-founder Lars. The weekly 'Crash Course to the Forbidden City' walk is a fine way to navigate the capital's confounding imperial waters. Check the website for schedules and booking.

Beijing by Foot TOURS
(www.beijingbyfoot.com; tours from ¥300) Perpetually in search of old Peking, American guide and teacher of modern Chinese history Jeremiah Jenne spins gripping yarns at Beijing's major sites. Get acquainted with Empress Cixi at the Summer Palace, meet Mao and the making of modern China at Tian'anmen and much more besides. Regularly scheduled tours can be booked on the website, or via The Hutong (p105). Private and custom tours available on request.

UnTour Food Tours FOOD
(https://untourfoodtours.com; per person US$70; ⊙7pm Mon, Tue, Fri & Sat) A belt-busting adventure for foodies, UnTour's 'Old Beijing Dinner Tour' is three hours of unbridled eating and drinking at locales scattered throughout the *hutong* of Dongcheng district. Each meal (and there are many, so pace yourself) comes with an informed introduction and all the beer and *báijiǔ* (clear liquor) you can drink.

Newman Tours TOURS
(https://newmantours.com; per person from ¥290, based on group of 4; 👶) Garnishing guided walks with iPads, props and fancy dress, Newman Tours are ideal for families and those who like their Beijing history served up with a side order of laughs and surprises. Popular tours include the 'History of China in 50 Objects' jaunt around the National Museum of China (p76) and an evening ghost tour at Houhai Lake (p87).

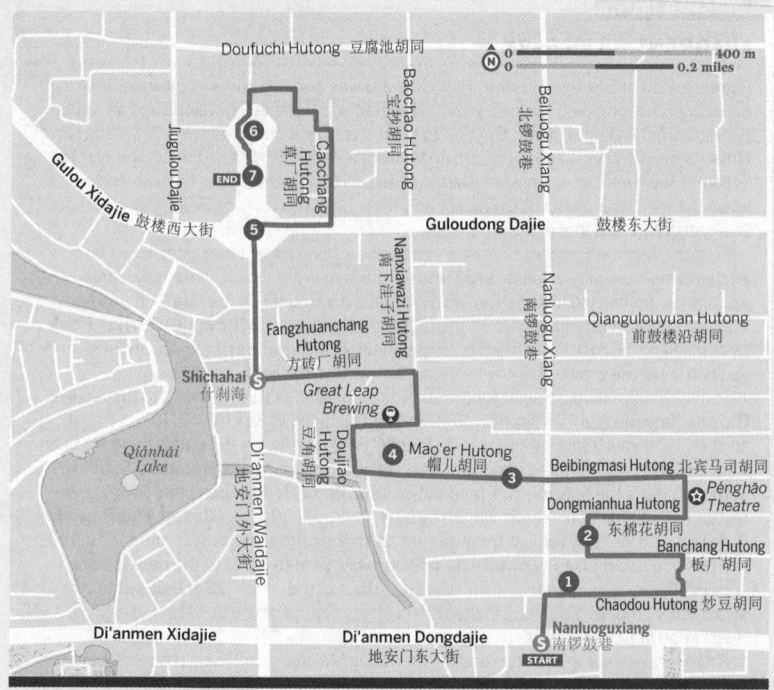

City Walk
Nanluogu Xiang Alleyway Ramble

START NANLUOGUXIANG SUBWAY STATION
END DRUM & BELL TOWERS
LENGTH 2KM; ONE HOUR

From exit E of Nanluoguxiang station, go north into the main alley then take the first right onto Chaodou Hutong (炒豆胡同). Starting at No 77, the next few courtyards once made up the **❶ former mansion of Seng Gelinqin**, a Qing dynasty general. Note the enormous *bǎogǔshí* (drum stones) at the entranceway to No 77, followed by more impressive gateways at Nos 75, 69, 67 and 63. After No 53, turn left into an unmarked alleyway and follow it north to Banchang Hutong (板厂胡同).

Heading left (west) to No 19, turn right through the unusual **❷ hallway gate** – a rare connecting passageway leads all the way to Dongmianhua Hutong (东棉花胡同). Turn right on to the *hutong*, then left along an unnamed alley signposted to Penghao Theatre, a small arthouse theatre with a lovely cafe and tree-shaded roof terrace.

Emerge onto Beibingmasi Hutong (北兵马司胡同) and cross Nanluogu Xiang into historic **❸ Mao'er Hutong** (帽儿胡同). Admire the grand old entranceways and if the gates are open, step into the charming courtyards at Nos 5 and 11. Further on, No 37 was the **❹ former home of Wan Rong**, who would later marry China's last emperor, Puyi.

Next, turn right on Doujiao Hutong (豆角胡同), winding your way past Great Leap Brewing #6, Beijing's first craft-beer bar, to Fangzhuanchang Hutong (方砖厂胡同), then Nanxiawazi Hutong (南下洼子胡同), and continue north to Gulou Dongjie (鼓楼东大街). Turn left here and then, just before you reach the imperious red **❺ Drum Tower** (p81), make a right into Caochang Hutong (草厂胡同). Continue along the lane, then bear left as the *hutong* turns right. Follow this wonderfully winding alley to the back of the **❻ Bell Tower** (p81), then walk around the tower and head south to the **❼ Drum & Bell Square**, a great spot for photos. If you've timed it just right, you can climb the Drum Tower to catch one of several daily drumming performances (the schedule is posted above the ticket office).

Newman Tours need to be booked privately in advance via email.

B Electric Bike Tours
TOURS

(Map p82; http://belectricbeijing.com; 10 Shiqie Hutong, 石雀胡同10号; per person ¥300; S Line 5 to Beixinqiao, exit C) Zip effortlessly around the Dongcheng sights on this three-hour e-scooter tour – ideal for sticky summer days when walking or cycling feels like too much effort. You'll pass the Drum & Bell towers, Houhai Lake and the Forbidden City, keeping mostly to *hutong* alleyways along the way. Twice-weekly group tours start and end at the Culture Yard; see website. Private tours can be arranged on request.

The Hutong
COOKING

(Map p82; 159 0104 6127; www.thehutong.com; 1 Jiudaowan Zhongxiang, 九道弯中巷1号; per member/nonmember ¥260/300; ⏰9.30am-10pm; S Line 5 to Beixinqiao, exit C) A smorgasbord of cooking classes covers everything from Chinese knife skills to *xiaolongbao* soup dumplings at this long-established cultural centre in a *hutong* courtyard. Tea lovers can embark on a highly caffeinated tour of the Maliandao Tea Market (p129), discovering China's most famous teas and tea regions.

Culture Yard
LANGUAGE

(天井越洋, Tiānjǐng Yuèyáng; Map p82; 010 8404 4166; www.cultureyard.net; 10 Shique Hutong, 石雀胡同10号; ⏰9am-9pm Mon-Thu, 10am-4pm Fri & Sat; S Line 5 to Beixinqiao, exit C) A little language goes a long way in China, so consider investing in a 'Survival Chinese' course at this *hutong* school as the prelude to your wider Middle Kingdom sojourns. Five days of lessons (¥1800, 20 hours), shared between classroom time and field trips to local markets and restaurants, will furnish you with a basic toolbox for bargaining, meeting and greeting, and getting around.

Black Sesame Kitchen
COOKING

(黑芝麻厨房, Hēi Zhīma Chúfáng; Map p74; 136 9147 4408; www.blacksesamekitchen.com; 28 Zhonglao Hutong, 中老胡同28号; ⏰cooking classes 11am Wed & Sun, dinner 7pm most nights; S Lines 6, 8 to Nanluoguxiang, exit A) Learn the ways of the wok, and get your dumpling-wrapping skills in order, at this long-established cooking school better known these days for its 10-course communal dinners (¥350 including wine and beer). The cooking classes (same price, no booze) take place on Wednesdays and Sundays at 11am – booking ahead is required.

HUTONG TOURS

To delve deeper into the daily life of the *hutong*, sign up for a half-day tour with Beijing by Foot (p103), The Hutong or Bespoke Travel Co..

Bespoke Travel Co
TOURS

(Map p96; 151 0167 9082; https://bespoketravelcompany.com; 7th fl, 10 Jintong Xilu, 金桐西路10号远洋光华国际AB座7层; S Line 10 to Jintaixizhao, exit B) This high-end travel concierge company with celebrity clientele offers creative day tours including a history-rich romp through the *hutong*, taking in the Drum Tower, a secret folk museum and the home of a champion trainer of fighting crickets. It also books tour guides and chauffeurs.

🛏 Sleeping

If you're able and willing to splurge, you'll get a lot for your money in Beijing compared to other world capitals. Pickings are more slender at the bottom end, especially since the government's bizarre 'bunk-bed ban' in 2018, but hunt around and you can still bag a bargain.

Check out Drum Tower & Dongcheng North or Beihai Park & Xicheng North for cheaper courtyard hotels and hostels with those rustic *hutong* vibes.

Forbidden City & Dongcheng Central

China Great Hall Hotel
HOTEL ¥¥

(人民大会堂宾馆, Rénmín Dàhuìtáng Bīnguǎn; Map p78; 010 6607 1188; www.chinagreathall hotel.com; 19 Xijiaomin Xiang, 西交民巷19号; Tian'anmen Sq viewing r ¥900; ✳ ❂ 🛜 🛁; S Line 2 to Qianmen, exit C, or Line 1 to Tian'anmen West, exit C) A little-known oddity, this building beside the Great Hall of the People (p80) was strictly cadres only until it opened as a hotel in 2012. Functionally, it's a stock Chinese business hotel, but the 'Square Viewing Room' category opens onto remarkable vistas of Tian'anmen Sq – you'll pinch yourself when you draw back the curtains.

Geographically, it's akin to staying in an annex of the Houses of Parliament, and it's quite simply the closest digs to Tian'anmen Sq without pitching a tent next to Mao's Mausoleum. Avoid the other room types – only the 'Square Viewing Room' is worthwhile. English is limited, and rooms are on

WALTER BIBIKOW/GETTY IMAGES ©

1. 798 Art District (p95)
An exciting enclave of international galleries in an old factory complex.

2. National Centre for the Performing Arts (p122)
Designed by Paul Andreu, this is a spectacular venue to watch a performance of opera or ballet.

3. Scooting the city (p105)
A scooter tour can be an ideal way to see the city on hot days.

4. Gate of Heavenly Peace, Tian'anmen Square (p75)
Mao proclaimed the founding of the People's Republic of China from here in 1949. Climb the gate for great views of the square..

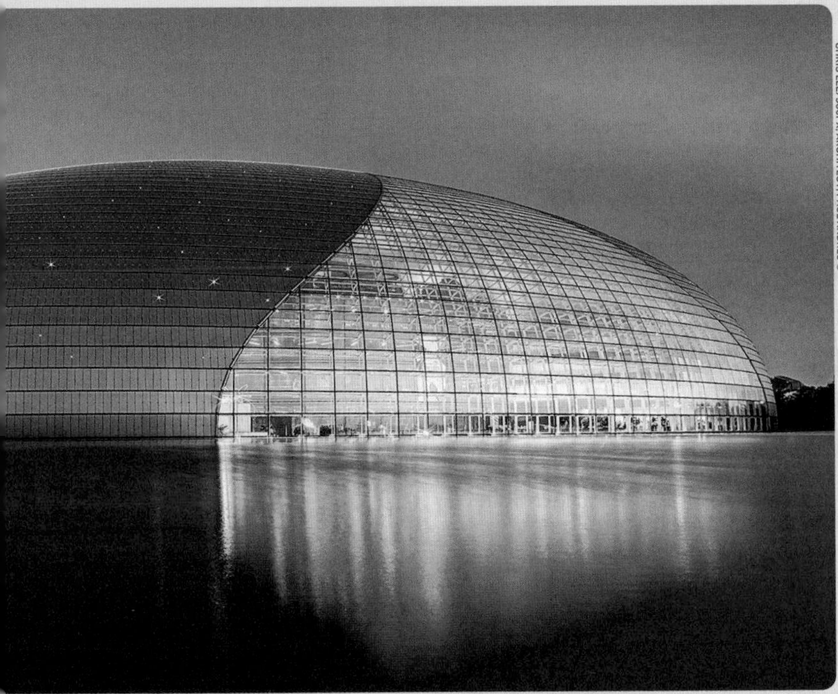

CHRIS LEE/500PX, ARCHITECT: PAUL ANDREU ©

MARIO GIL/SHUTTERSTOCK ©

3

MATT MUNRO/LONELY PLANET ©

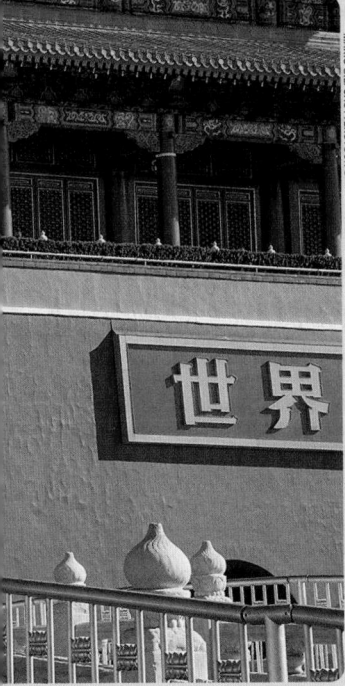

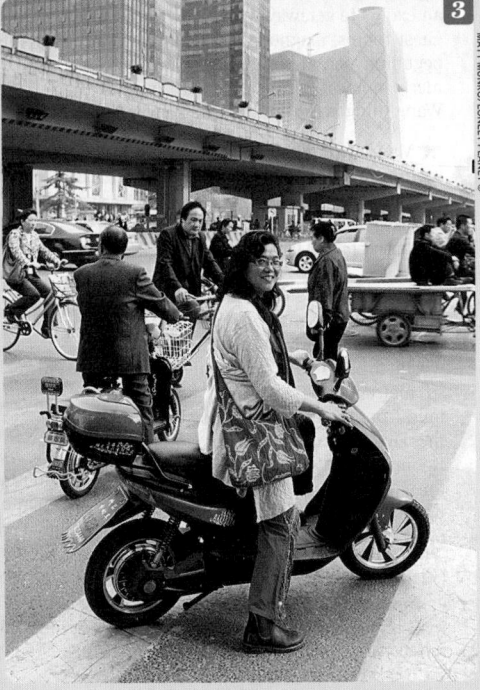

the small side. The pool and gym occupy a windowless basement area.

Happy Dragon Alley Hotel
HOSTEL ¥¥

(Map p82; ☑ 010 8400 2660; 78 Dongsi Jiutiao, 东四九条78号; r from ¥700; 🏶🛜; ⓢ Line 5 to Zhangzizhonglu, exit C) A former hostel turned mini-hotel (Beijing's bunk-bed ban strikes again), Happy Dragon gets plaudits for its friendly staff and authentic alleyway location. The subway is a couple of minutes away on foot.

Double Happiness Courtyard
HOTEL ¥¥¥

(北京阅微庄四合院宾馆, Běijīng Yuèwēi Zhuāng Sìhéyuàn Bīnguǎn; Map p78; ☑ 010 6400 7762; 37 Dongsi Sitiao, 东四四条37号; r from ¥1250; 🏶🛜; ⓢ Line 5, 6 to Dongsi, exit B) Service shines at this sprawling courtyard hotel on a lively *hutong*. Chinese-styled rooms are arranged on outdoor corridors, with hidden nooks to explore. It also has a bar, which is a rarity for a courtyard hotel.

★ Côté Cour
BOUTIQUE HOTEL ¥¥¥

(北京演乐酒店, Běijīng Yǎnyuè Jiǔdiàn; Map p78; ☑ 010 6523 9598; www.hotelcotecourbj.com; 70 Yanyue Hutong, 演乐胡同70号; r from ¥1400; 🏶@🛜; ⓢ Line 5 to Dengshikou, exit A, or Lines 5, 6 to Dongsi, exit C) One of Beijing's most charming courtyard hotels, Côté Cour makes for an exquisite getaway with its boutique-style guest rooms, magnolia-filled courtyard and beguiling period setting, on a *hutong* formerly home to imperial court musicians. Wangfujing is a 20-minute walk away.

★ Mandarin Oriental Wangfujing
LUXURY HOTEL ¥¥¥

(北京王府井文华东方酒店, Wángfǔjīng Wénhuá Dōngfāng Jiǔdiàn; Map p78; ☑ 010 8509 8888; www.mandarinoriental.com; WF Central, 269 Wangfujing Dajie, 王府井大街269号王府中环; r from ¥3600; ⊝🏶🛜; ⓢ Line 1 to Wangfujing, exit C2) Ten years in the making (the first MO burnt down in 2009), the Mandarin Oriental was worth the wait. Palatial rooms (at least 55 sq metres) have luxurious, fine-tuned details, from the ubertrendy 'bowl' bathtubs to the Dyson-branded hair dryers. 'Mandarin Rooms' frame a sensational panorama of the Forbidden City through floor-to-ceiling windows.

★ PuXuan Hotel
LUXURY HOTEL ¥¥¥

(璞瑄酒店, Púxuān Jiǔdiàn; Map p78; ☑ 010 5393 6688; https://thepuxuan.com; 1 Wangfujing Dajie, 王府井大街1号; r from ¥2900; ⊝🏶🛜; ⓢ Line 8 to National Art Museum, exit D2) Opened in 2019, the PuXuan (sister hotel to Shanghai's acclaimed Puli) is Beijing's most stylish sanctuary, made for grown-ups who demand the finer things in life. Rooms are a masterclass of taste and design – choose a west-facing Grand Deluxe for artfully framed views of Jingshan Park, a sea of *hutong* and a tantalising corner of the Forbidden City.

Beijing Hotel NUO
HOTEL ¥¥¥

(北京饭店诺金, Běijīng Fàndiàn Nuò Jīn; Map p78; ☑ 010 6526 3388; www.nuohotel.com; 33 Dongchang'an Jie, 东长安街33号; r from ¥1400; ⊝🏶@🛜≋; ⓢ Line 1 to Wangfujing, exit C1) Formerly the Grand Hotel du Pekin (c 1917), this debonair old dame celebrates the golden age of travel in its showpiece marble staircase, glittering chandeliers and polished 1920s dance floor in the Writer's Bar. Local operator NUO took over from Raffles in 2016, enhancing the food offerings but leaving the period features intact. Avoid the characterless newer wing at the rear.

It's easily confused with NUO's **sister hotel** (北京诺金酒店, Běijīng Nuò Jīn Jiǔdiàn; ☑ 010 5926 8888; 2A Jiangtai Lu, 将台路甲2号; d from ¥1240; 🅿🏶🛜≋; ⓢ Line 14 to Jiangtai, Exit A) near the 798 Art District, so the check the address carefully.

🛏 Drum Tower & Dongcheng North

Beijing Drum Tower Youth Hostel
HOSTEL ¥

(鼓韵青年旅舍, Gǔyùn Qīngnián Lǚshè; Map p82; ☑ 010 8401 6565; 51 Jiugulou Dajie, 旧鼓楼大街51号; dm/s/d & tw from ¥110/150/450; 🏶@🛜; ⓢ Lines 2, 8 to Guloudajie, exit G) A no-frills hostel with nifty, capsule-style singles and spacious twins and doubles. The subway is very close, and it's a short stroll to the area's lively *hutong* alleyways.

★ Orchid
COURTYARD HOTEL ¥¥

(兰花宾馆, Lánhuā Bīnguǎn; Map p82; ☑ 010 5799 0806; www.theorchidbeijing.com; 65 Baochao Hutong, 鼓楼东大街宝钞胡同65号; r ¥700-1400; 🏶🛜; ⓢ Lines 2, 8 to Guloudajie, exit F, or Line 8 to Shichahai, exit A2) A garden sanctuary in the *hutong*, the Orchid is Beijing's best-run boutique hotel, going the extra mile with memory-foam mattresses, mobile phones, marvellous breakfasts and a local area map for alleyway adventures. The cheapest rooms occupy wood-beamed Qing-era buildings that wrap around a cobbled courtyard, while premium digs have petite private gardens and roof terraces.

Food is an integral part of the Orchid experience, with homemade bread and sausages in the breakfasts and creative mezze-style fare served at in-house restaurant **Toast** (📋010 8404 4818; mains from ¥88; ⏰10am-2.30pm & 6-10pm Wed-Mon). A stylish event space hosts wine-fuelled dumpling-wrapping and Shaanxi-noodle-making classes.

Outside the hotel are **several larger rooms** (胡同公寓, Hútòng Gōngyù; 📋010 8404 8787; 66 Baochao Hutong, 宝钞胡同65号; residences ¥1000-1600) dispersed in thrillingly local nooks around the Drum and Bell Tower neighbourhood. These studios and maisonettes come with kitchenettes, but you can still breakfast at the hotel, never more than a stroll away.

161 Lama Temple Courtyard Hotel
HUTONG HOTEL ¥¥

(北京161酒店一雍和宫四合院店; Map p82; 📋010 8401 5027; www.161hotel.com; 46 Beixinqiao Santiao Hutong, 北新桥三条46号; r ¥750-900; ⑤Line 5 to Beixinqiao, exit B) Part of the local 161 chain, this *hutong* hotel has around a dozen compact rooms made to feel larger thanks to photo-murals of Beijing tourist attractions. Staff are courteous and speak English, and the location, between Ghost Street (p117) and the Lama Temple (p90), is ideal for alleyway explorers.

Grand Mercure Dongcheng
HOTEL ¥¥

(北京东方美爵酒店, Běijīng Dōngfāng Měijué Jiǔdiàn; Map p82; 📋010 8403 1188; www.grand-mercure.com; 101 Jiaodaokou Dongdajie, 交道口东街101号; r from ¥700; ❋📶; ⑤Line 5 to Beixinqiao, exit A) This chain hotel is a bargain considering the high-spec rooms with soft beds, flat-screen TVs and buffet breakfast. The location is handy too. Shell out a bit more for the executive floor and you get free evening cocktails and canapes. Mmm, canapes.

🛏 Beihai Park & Xicheng North

Pagoda Light
HOSTEL ¥

(宝塔灯, Bǎotǎ Dēng; Map p86; 📋010 6655 2188; 185 Fuchengmennei Dajie, 阜成门内大街185号; dm/d/tw ¥168/488/528; ❋📶; ⑤Line 2 to Fuchengmen, exit B, or Line 4 to Xisi, exit A) The owners here have transformed a dilapidated *hutong* pile into a stylish, light-filled hostel that blends boutique design with Chinese courtyard decor. The four- to six-person bunk-bed dorms are a better choice than the cramped 'tatami' rooms. Private rooms are

COURTYARD HOTELS

Staying in a courtyard hotel can be a wonderful way to get acquainted with local *hutong* life. These digs typically run to fewer than 10 small, Chinese-styled rooms, opening on to a central covered courtyard, which is often the setting for breakfast, so noise and privacy might be an issue. Another potential drawback can be lack of taxi access. Quality and service can vary dramatically, so do your research and shop around.

on the small side, but clean and modern. The White Dagoba Temple (p94) is next door.

Red Lantern House
HOSTEL ¥

(仿古园, Fǎnggǔ Yuán; Map p86; 📋010 8328 5771; www.redlanternhouse.com; 5 Zhengjue Hutong, 正觉胡同 5号; dm ¥110-115, s/d without bathroom ¥260/270, d/family with bathroom from ¥340/450; ❋@📶; ⑤Line 2 to Jishuitan, exit C) This old hostel in a gloomy but spacious covered courtyard has been here for years (and the beers are still only ¥5!). Chinese-style rooms encircle a sociable central hangout. All but a couple of rooms have shared bathrooms. The location is a great base for *hutong* explorations.

Siheju Courtyard Hotel
HOSTEL ¥

(四隅居四合院酒店, Sihéjū Sìhéyuàn Jiǔdiàn; Map p86; 📋010 6313 4585; www.sihejucourtyard.com; 12 Xisi Beiertiao, 西四北二条12号; dm ¥160, r from ¥600; ❋📶; ⑤Line 4 to Xisi, exit A) Tiny, Chinese-styled bedrooms open on to a central courtyard at this family-owned *hutong* hotel in an enticingly local part of Beijing. To find it, walk north on Xisi Beidajie from the subway exit; it's two alleyways up on the left.

★Shichahai Sandalwood Boutique Hotel
BOUTIQUE HOTEL ¥¥

(什刹海紫檀酒店, Shíchàhǎi Zǐtán Jiǔdiàn; Map p86; 📋010 8322 6686; www.sandalwoodboutique.com; 42 Xinghua Hutong, 兴华胡同42; r from ¥1100; ❋📶; ⑤Line 6 to Beihai North, exit A) Formerly the mansion of a Qing dynasty official, this *hutong* hotel has put a lot of effort into its ornamental Chinese styling, with wooden furniture, silk screens and four-poster beds. Most rooms open on to a central courtyard, which hosts regular cultural activities including calligraphy and dumpling-making.

Note that the cheapest rooms don't have windows.

Vue Hotel

BOUTIQUE HOTEL ¥¥

(花间堂酒店, Huājiāntáng Jiǔdiàn; Map p86; ☑010 5385 9000; 9 Yangfang Hutong, 羊房胡同9号; r from ¥1150; ※@; ⑤Line 6 to Beihai North, exit B) In its own private compound, this trendy lakeside sanctuary has 80 designer guest rooms tricked out with music players, capsule coffee machines and open-plan bathrooms – the more expensive digs boast hot tubs and balconies. Taxi access is tricky; it's a 1km walk through the *hutong* to the subway.

161 Beihai Courtyard Hotel

HOTEL ¥¥

(161北海四合院酒店, 161 Běihǎi Sìhéyuàn Jiǔdiàn; Map p86; ☑010 6612 8341; www.161hotel.com; 29 Xisi Beiqitiao, 西四北七条29号; r from ¥750; ※☎; ⑤Lines 4, 6 to Ping'anli, exit G) Managed by local courtyard-hotel specialists 161, this place is a safe bet if you're looking for a well-run *hutong* hotel in the area, with a smidge more style than most. Avoid the lowest category of rooms, which lack windows. Pay a bit more and you get a seating area and garden views.

The hotel is a 2km walk from Beihai, but very handy for the subway.

🛏 Sanlitun & Chaoyang

Holiday Inn Express Dongzhimen

HOTEL ¥¥

(智选假日酒店东直门, Zhìxuǎn Jiàrì Jiǔdiàn Dōngzhímén; Map p96; ☑010 6416 9999; www.holidayinnexpress.com.cn; 1 Chunxiu Lu, 春秀路1号; r incl breakfast from ¥650; ※☎☎; ⑤Line 2 to Dongsi Shitiao, exit B) Supremely comfy beds beckon at this affordable chain hotel with a dash more personality than most. Standing tall in a buzzy, expat-friendly neighbourhood of bars and eateries, it's a 1km walk from the subway.

★ Opposite House

DESIGN HOTEL ¥¥¥

(瑜舍, Yúshè; Map p96; ☑010 6417 6688; www.theoppositehouse.com; 11 Sanlitun Lu, 三里屯路11号; r from ¥1950; ☜※@☎☎; ⑤Line 10 to Tuanjiehu, exit A, or Agricultural Exhibition Center, exit D2) The haunt of celebs and media types, Sanlitun's trendiest hotel has 99 minimalist rooms, a stainless-steel pool, art installations in the vertigo-inducing lobby, and fabulous dining and drinking options. The location is right in the heart of things at Taikoo Li Sanlitun (p130).

★ Rosewood Beijing

LUXURY HOTEL ¥¥¥

(北京瑰丽酒店, Běijīng Guìlì Jiǔdiàn; Map p96; ☑010 6597 8888; www.rosewoodhotels.com/en/beijing; Jing Guang Centre, Dongsanhuan, 东三环呼家楼京广中心; r from ¥2000; ※☎☎; ⑤Line 10 to Jintaixizhao, exit A, or Lines 6, 10 to Hujialou, exit D) Beijing's most glamorous hotel, the Rosewood seduces with serene public spaces, innovative restaurants and guest rooms of designer furniture, arty curios, and floor-to-ceiling vistas of the iconic CCTV building. The isolated ring road location is a negative, but subway connections are good.

Hotel Jen

HOTEL ¥¥¥

(新国贸饭店, Xīn Guómào Fàndiàn; Map p96; ☑010 6505 2277; www.hoteljen.com/beijing; 1 Jianguomenwai Dajie, 建国门外大街1号; r from ¥1250; ☎; ⑤Lines 1, 10 to Guomao, exit E2) Targeted at millennial travellers, Jen has its own co-working space, a craft-beer brewpub and the biggest gym in the city. Rooms are spacious and comfy if a little characterless. Usefully, Jen connects below ground with the subway and the China World Mall.

🍴 Eating

From the regal (Peking duck) to the humble (*bàodǔ*, or boiled tripe with sesame sauce), Beijing food is hearty, rich and fortifying for when those wintry winds whip south from the Great Wall.

As capital, Beijing is a melting pot of regional Chinese cooking, where you can be eating wild Yunnan mushrooms one day and whole roasted Inner Mongolian lamb the next. Top quality international food is on the menu too, whether you crave authentic Japanese countertop ramen or just a good burger.

🍴 Forbidden City & Dongcheng Central

★ Crescent Moon Muslim Restaurant

XINJIANG ¥

(弯弯月亮, Wānwān Yuèliàng; Map p78; 16 Dongsi Liutiao Hutong, 东四六条胡同16号; mains from ¥38; ⊙11am-11pm; ※☎; ⑤Line 5 to Zhangzizhonglu, exit C) Mount your culinary camel and traverse the Silk Road sands to this singular Central Asian food fest. Grilled lamb doused in cumin and chilli, baked flatbreads, hearty stews and noodles are dished up by ethnic-minority Uyghurs from Xinjiang in the far west of China. You can also get Xinjiang tea, dark beer, wine and even homemade yoghurt.

Yuèbīn Fànguǎn

BEIJING ¥

(悦宾饭馆; Map p78; 43 Cuihua Hutong, off Wusi Dajie, 五四大街翠花胡同43号; mains ¥27-91; ⊙11am-2pm & 5-9pm; ⑤Line 8 to National Art Museum, exit D1) A marvellous, messy microcosm of Beijing at its most boisterous, this old-school canteen slings giant platters of traditional grub, which tastes more elegant than it looks! Everyone orders the *suànní zhǒuzi* (蒜泥肘子, pork shoulder in garlic and vinegar), and don't skip the *guōshāo yā* (锅烧鸭, crispy fried duck).

The menu is Chinese only, so you might also want to ask for *miànjīn pá báicài* (面筋扒白菜, braised cabbage with wheat gluten), *qīngchǎo xiārén* (清炒虾仁, stir-fried shrimp) and *wǔ sī tǒng* (五丝筒, chicken and vegetable egg rolls). Yuebin claims to be the first restaurant run as a private business in Beijing after the Cultural Revolution. Fun atmosphere and good food.

Grandma's
ZHEJIANG ¥

(外婆家, Wàipó Jiā; Map p78; ☑ 010 6527 5115; 6th fl, Beijing apm mall, 138 Wangfujing Dajie, 王府井大街138号apm6楼; mains ¥12-48; ⊗ 10am-2.30pm & 4-9pm; ⑤ Line 5 to Dengshikou) The good: delicious Hangzhou-style dishes are astonishing value at this popular chain restaurant. The bad: it's in Beijing's busiest shopping mall and the queues can be intolerable. Recommendations include 'Grandma's pork' (a Hangzhou braised pork-belly dish, otherwise called *Dōngpō ròu,* 东坡肉) and tea-flavoured chicken, cooked with Hángzhōu's famous *Lóngjǐng* green tea.

Little Yunnan
YUNNAN ¥¥

(小云南, Xiǎo Yúnnán; Map p78; ☑ 010 6401 9498; 28 Donghuangchenggen Beijie, 东皇城根北街28号; mains around ¥65; ⊗ 10am-10pm; ⑤ Line 8 to National Art Museum, exit A) Perhaps it's due to Yunnan's exotic culinary allusions to Southeast Asia, but this crossover cuisine has long been held dear by foreign foodies in China. Little Yunnan plays to the crowd with light, aromatic dishes, a wine list and a relaxed, *hutong*-chic vibe degrees closer to 'date night' than most local eateries.

Susu
VIETNAMESE ¥¥

(苏苏会, Sūsū Huì; Map p78; ☑ 010 8400 2699; www.susubeijing.com; 10 Qianliang Xixiang, 钱粮西巷10号; mains from ¥68; ⊗ 11.30am-10pm Tue-Sun; ✽ 🐾; ⑤ Lines 5, 6 to Dongsi, exit E) Dine on Vietnamese fare like fresh spring rolls and *phở* (beef noodle soup) at this well-loved *hutong* eatery with a tree-shaded courtyard. The signature La Vong fish is a DIY affair to share, consisting of turmeric-yellow fish fillets, fennel leaves, glass noodles and heaps of fresh herbs. Find Susu at the end of a tiny alleyway a short way east along Qianliang Hutong.

Cocktails recommended. Try 'The Quiet American', a mix of whisky, lemon, ginger and grapefruit bitters.

Chuan Ban
SICHUAN ¥¥

(川办, Chuān Bàn; Map p96; ☑ 010 6512 2277; 5 Gongyuan Xijie Toutiao, off Jianguomennei Dajie, 建国门内大街贡院西街头条5号; mains from ¥65; ⊗ 11am-2pm, 5-9pm; ⑤ Lines 1, 2 to Jianguomen, exit A) Every Chinese province has its own government office in Beijing, usually furnished with a hotel and restaurant for visiting cadres. With some exceptions, these tend to offer the most authentic regional eats in the capital. Chuan Ban is attached to the Sichuan provincial office here, serving up an encyclopedic spice-fest of delicacies guaranteed to delight acolytes of the mouth-numbing Sichuan peppercorn.

★ Dadong
PEKING DUCK ¥¥¥

(大董, Dàdǒng; Map p78; ☑ 010 8522 1111; 5th fl Jinbao Place, 88 Jinbao Jie, 金宝街88号金宝汇购物中心5层; Peking duck ¥298; ⊗ 11am-10pm; ✽ 🐾; ⑤ Line 5 to Dengshikou, exit C) Dadong could be the best meal of your trip or an occasion to forget, and it all comes down to expectation. Less Peking duck restaurant and more temple to contemporary Chinese fine dining, Dadong (real name Dong Zhenxiang) is one of mainland China's most celebrated chefs, as adept at riffing on Beijing classics as he is at making thorny sea cucumber taste like rare beef.

Nevertheless, a meal at Dadong can be a daunting experience for the first-time visitor. The ice-blue nightclub vibe doesn't help, and then you're handed the 120-page menu, with dish photos that look like abstract art pieces. To break it down, you'll want to get a duck (which is divine), and then build your supporting dishes around it (the soups, vegetable dishes and anything towards the back end of the menu are more affordable).

If you do fancy a splurge, this is the place, with no shortage of creative dishes starring king crab, lobster, Wagyu beef and other pricey cuts.

There are a dozen Dadong restaurants around town (and some in New York!); this branch is convenient for Wangfujing. To sample chef Dadong's cooking smarts on a budget, check out his hugely popular casual chain Taste of Dadong (p120).

★ Duck de Chine
PEKING DUCK ¥¥¥

(1949全鸭季, 1949 Quányājì; Map p78; ☑ 010 6521 2221; 98 Jinbao Jie, 金宝街98号; Peking duck ¥298; ◷11am-2.30pm & 5.30-10pm; 🛜; Ⓢ Line 5 to Dengshikou, exit C) Beijing's most re-fined destination for duck, where perfectly bronzed birds are announced to the dining room by the chiming of a gong. Maybe it's the 30-year-old jujube wood in the ovens, or the house-made duck sauce using medicinal herbs, but the duck here is as good as it gets.

Dining at Duck de Chine is an expensive treat, especially if you order from the attached Bollinger bar, but the lunchtime dim sum menu is great value for the quality.

★TRB Hutong   EUROPEAN ¥¥¥

(Map p78; ☏ 010 8400 2232; www.trb-cn.com; 23 Shatan Beijie, off Wusi Dajie, 五四大街沙滩北街23号; set menus ¥398-698; ◷11am-3pm & 5.30-11pm; ❉🛜; Ⓢ Lines 6, 8 to Nanluoguxiang, exit B, or Lines 5, 6 to Dongsi, exit E) Beijing's most fa-mous international fine-dining experience, TRB (Temple Restaurant Beijing) serves modern European dishes with a French twist – house-smoked salmon, lobster sal-ad, Wagyu beef – but the real delight is the setting: the exquisite, 250-year-old *Zhīzhù Sì* (智珠寺, Temple of Wisdom), a long-forgotten temple buried deep in the *hutong*. Service is pampering and the wine list is encyclopedic.

The temple grounds, illuminated at night and strewn with contemporary-art pieces, make for a delightful post-meal stroll. Art exhibitions and recitals are often staged within the temple's former prayer halls.

★Lost Heaven   YUNNAN ¥¥¥

(花马天堂, Huāmǎ Tiāntáng; Map p91; ☏ 010 8516 2698; 23 Qianmen Dongdajie, 前门东大街23号; dishes ¥68-200; ◷11am-2pm & 5.30-10.30pm; Ⓢ Line 2 to Qianmen, exit A) Set back in the corner of the parade ground on the old US Legation, Lost Heaven presents the dreamy flavours of exotic Yunnan province. Sour-spicy dishes – Dali chicken, Dai-style pork, black cod – are imbued with wild mountain herbs, mushrooms, Burmese tea leaves and Yunnan truffles. A lovely setting for a special occasion.

Siji Mínfú   PEKING DUCK ¥¥¥

(四季民福; Map p74; ☏ 010 6526 7369; 11 Nanchizi Dajie, 南池子大街11号; Peking duck whole/half ¥228/128; ◷10.30am-10.30pm; ❉🛜; Ⓢ Line 1 to Tian'anmen East, exit B) A relative newcomer to the Peking duck scene, this local chain boasts some of the best birds in town, and this branch in particular is a beauty, with a prize perch overlooking the

Forbidden City's moat. There is a catch, though: crowds. Summer weekends might be a four-hour wait. Come on a winter weekday, however, and you could breeze right in.

If the crowds thwart you, two more branches are within walking distance at 53 Donghuamen Dajie (due east) and 32 Deng-shikou Xijie (one block northeast).

✕ Drum Tower & Dongcheng North

★Zhang Mama   SICHUAN ¥

(张妈妈川味馆, Zhāng Māma Chuānwèiguǎn; Map p82; 76 Jiaodaokou Nandajie, 交道口南大街76号; mains ¥18-78; ◷11am-10pm; Ⓢ Line 5 to Beixinqiao, exit A) An absurdly affordable spice-fest, humble Zhang Mama is run by a multi-generational family of Sichuan ex-iles (including mama), all with mad wok skills. The signature is *xiāngguō* (香锅; ¥48 to ¥58), a humongous bowl of either chicken (香锅鸡, *xiāngguō jī*), shrimp (香锅虾, *xiāngguō xiā*) or pork ribs (香锅排骨, *xiāngguō páigǔ*) amid a witch's brew of veggies, whole spices and chillies. One bowl will do two to three diners.

Similarly abundant is the *huíguōròu* (回锅肉; ¥28), a smoky, 'twice-cooked' Sichuan pork rump sliced thinly and served with veggies, fried dough pieces and, yep, more chillies. Sichuan-style dandan noodles (担担面, *dàndàn miàn*; ¥8) are authentically dry, while classics like mapo tofu (麻婆豆腐, *mápó dòufu*; ¥16) are equally assured.

Zhang Mama is hugely popular, so expect to queue; a useful hack is to arrive between 9pm and 9.30pm. There are a few other lo-cations around town, including one a short walk north of Gulou subway station. No English menu.

Xiàn Lǎo Mǎn   DUMPLINGS ¥

(馅老满; Map p82; ☏ 010 6404 6944; 252 And-ingmennei Dajie, 安定门内大街252号; dumplings from ¥16; ◷11am-9.30pm; ❉; Ⓢ Line 2 to Anding-men, exit B) No wonder this locals' favourite is always packed – for boiled or fried *jiǎozi* (dumplings) that are as delicious as they are light on the wallet, you can't go wrong. Or-dering via a bilingual menu card is easy – just note that dumplings are sold by the *liǎng* (50g, about five dumplings), and for each fill-ing, it's a minimum order of two *liǎng*.

As well as dumplings, there's a huge se-lection of comforting *jiācháng cài* (typical home-cooked dishes) like kungpao chicken

(宫保鸡丁, *gōngbǎo jīdīng*), tofu (麻婆豆腐, *mápó dòufu*) and braised eggplant.

★ Jīn Dǐng Xuān
CANTONESE ¥¥

(金鼎轩; Map p82; ☑ 010 6429 6699; 77 Hepingli Xijie, 地坛南门和平里西街77号; dim sum ¥15-30, mains ¥30-100; ⊗24hr; Ⓢ Lines 2, 5 to Yonghegong-Lama Temple, exit A) Dripping in red neon and lanterns, this raucous Chinese restaurant by the south gate of Ditan Park is a magnificent monstrosity that never closes – even for Chinese New Year! Four bustling floors of great-value Southern Chinese, dim sum and family-style dishes are rarely less than heaving; expect to take a number and queue at busy periods. Great fun.

Furongji
DIM SUM ¥¥

(福荣记, *Fúróngjì*; Map p82; ☑ 010 5394 5228; www.theorchidbeijing.com/furongji; 63 Baochao Hutong, 宝钞胡同63号; dishes ¥18-58; ⊗11am-2pm & 5-11pm Tue-Sun; ⊛☏; Ⓢ Lines 2, 8 to Guloudajie, exit G) Feast on modern dim sum at this stylish *hutong* joint run by the Orchid (p112) boutique hotel next door. Everything on the tick-box menu is deliciously creative; the shrimp spring rolls have a wasabi kick, and the curry-filled sesame puffs are sinful perfection. Pair with a Hong Kong–style *yuenyang* (milk tea and coffee mix), Great Leap beer, or a cocktail in the 'secret' bar at the back.

Dali Courtyard
YUNNAN ¥¥

(大里院子, *Dàlǐ Yuànzi*; Map p82; ☑ 010 8404 1430; 67 Xiaojingchang Hutong, Gulou Dongdajie, 鼓楼东大街小经厂胡同67号; set menu ¥160; ⊗noon-2pm & 6-10pm; Ⓢ Line 2 to Andingmen, exit D, or Line 5 to Beixinqiao, exit A) Dali Courtyard has been serving the same set menu since 2006, and it still packs out nightly with (almost exclusively) foreign tourists. The secret, aside from the charming courtyard setting, is simplicity. No menu means no hassle – just course after course of play-it-safe Yunnan classics at ¥160 per person, starting with cold starters and ending with grilled fish.

Drinks cost extra, and are rather expensive.

King's Joy
VEGETARIAN ¥¥¥

(京兆尹, *Jīng Zhào Yǐn*; Map p82; ☑ 010 8404 9191; 2 Wudaoying Hutong, 五道营胡同2号; mains from ¥129; ⊗11am-10pm; ☏; Ⓢ Lines 2, 5 to Yonghegong-Lama Temple, exit D) Aspiring to the Chinese notion that good health starts in the stomach, this graceful vegetarian restaurant serves fine-dining renditions of the meat-free cuisine enjoyed by Buddhist monks. Zen-like dining rooms hum to the arpeggios of a

GHOST STREET

Overseas visitors tend to be flummoxed when they discover that Ghost Street (簋街, Gui Jie; Dongzhimennei Dajie, 东直门内大街), Beijing's most famous restaurant strip, specialises not in Peking duck or other local eats but mostly in Sichuan-style 'mala' (spicy and mouth-numbing) crayfish, or bowls of frog, fish or beef in hot chilli oil, gobbled up until dawn along with copious bottles of beer. **Hu Da** (胡大饭馆, *Hú Dà Fànguǎn*; Map p82; ☑ 010 6400 3188; 284 Dongzhimennei Dajie, 东直门内大街284号; per crayfish ¥5-15; ⊗10.30am-4am; ☏; Ⓢ Line 5 to Beixinqiao, exit C), with five restaurants along the 1.5km strip, is wildly popular for its crayfish, with huge queues every evening.

harpist, as dry ice wafts over flower displays. Your *qi* will rebalance itself in no time.

Mercante
ITALIAN ¥¥¥

(商贾意大利餐厅, *Shānggǔ Yìdàlì Cāntīng*; Map p82; ☑ 010 8402 5098; www.thegoodfood group.asia; 4 Fangzhuanchang Hutong, 方砖厂胡同4号; pasta from ¥78, mains around ¥160; ⊗6-10.30pm; ☏; Ⓢ Line 8 to Shichahai, exit A1) A shoebox of a trattoria teleported to a Beijing *hutong*, Mercante is a delightfully incongruous outpost of Italian cooking. The boss hails from Bologna, imparting earthy authenticity in the homemade pasta with duck ragu, imported cheese and cured meats, and the city's booziest tiramisu.

✕ Beihai Park & Xicheng North

★ Wang Pangzi Donkey Burger
HEBEI ¥

(王胖子驴肉火烧, *Wáng Pàngzi Lǘròu Huǒshāo*; Map p86; 76 Gulou Xidajie, 鼓楼西大街76号; donkey meat sandwiches ¥14; ⊗24hr; Ⓢ Line 8 to Shichahai, exit A2, or Lines 2, 8 to Gulou Dajie, exit G) Opened by the titular 'Fatty Wang' in 2004, Wang Pangzi is lauded by many as Beijing's best purveyor of donkey-meat snacks. The lip-smacking speciality here is *lǘròu huǒshāo* (驴肉火烧; ¥12/14), toasted pastry pockets stuffed with thinly sliced donkey and diced green peppers (the meat tastes somewhat like pastrami). Two per person, plus soup and salad dishes, is a feast for lunch.

The practice of eating donkey is said to have originated in the city of Baoding, 150km to the south. For years, traversing

TRY: SWEET TREATS

Resembling skewers of tiny toffee apples, *bīngtánghúlu* (冰糖葫芦) are a winter favourite eaten outdoors. The natural tartness of the Chinese hawthorn fruits used offsets the sweet candied shell.

Less sweet are Beijing's traditional desserts like those at **Huguosi Snacks** (护国寺小吃, Hùguósì Xiǎochī; Map p86; ☑010 6618 1705; 93 Huguosi Jie, 护国寺街93号; snacks from ¥3; ⏰5.30am-9pm; Ⓢ Line 4 to Pinganli, exit B). *Wāndòuhuáng* (豌豆黄) is a cake made from mashed split peas and sugar cooked to a fudge consistency, while *lǘdǎgǔn* (驴打滚), literally 'donkey rolls on the ground', is a glutinous rice roll dusted in brown soybean flour.

the intervening hills to the capital was done on four legs, until the railway came along in the early 20th century, putting a whole lot of donkeys out of a job...and into a cooking pot.

Royal Palace Crisp Beef Pies PIES ¥

(宫廷香酥牛肉饼, Gōngtíng Xiāng Sū Niúròu Bǐng; Map p86; 341 Fuchengmennei Dajie, 阜成门内大街341号; pastries ¥4.5; ⏰9am-7pm; Ⓢ Line 2 to Fuchengmen, exit B) This hole-in-the-wall bakes 'royal crispy beef pies', a Tang dynasty treat seldom found on Beijing's streets anymore. Filled with beef, leeks and the tingle of Sichuan peppercorns, you can watch them being made in the open kitchen as you line up. No English sign.

An essential foodie detour if visiting the White Dagoba Temple (p94).

Royal Icehouse SHANDONG ¥¥

(皇家冰窖小院, Huángjiā Bīngjiào Xiǎoyuàn; Map p78; ☑010 6401 1358; 5 Gongjian Wuxiang, Gongjian Hutong, 恭俭胡同5巷5号; Peking duck ¥198; ⏰11.30am-2pm & 5.30-9.30pm; Ⓢ Line 6 to Beihai North, exit B, or Lines 6, 8 to Nanluoguxiang, exit A) Serving imperial banquet fare like Peking duck, braised sea cucumber and sweetmeats like sugared crabapples, this intriguing restaurant was once a royal refrigerator, its arched stone cellars built to store oversized ice cubes cut from the lake at Beihai Park. Dining in the cellars themselves is discouraged (which is a shame as the main room lacks atmosphere), but you're free to explore.

★ Yúfúnán HUNAN ¥¥

(渔芙南, Southern Fish; Map p86; ☑010 8306 3022; 49 Gongmenkou Toutiao, 宫门口头条49号;

mains ¥58-117; ⏰11am-2pm & 5-9pm; 📶; Ⓢ Line 2 to Fuchengmen, exit B) One of the best modern Chinese dining experiences in the capital, Yufunan is an insanely stylish spice fest, serving the sweat-inducing fare of Hunan province in an all-white, modernist dining space squeezed between *hutong* homes. *Duo lajiao* – spicy, pickled chillies – dominate almost every dish, with salt, sour and spice levels all cranked up to 11. Enjoy!

There's no English menu, so here's a sample order for two to three diners: *léi làjiāo pídàn* (擂辣椒皮蛋, spicy green peppers and preserved eggs); *duò jiāo máo yùtou* (剁椒毛芋头, steamed taro with pickled chillies); *mìzhì lǔdàn páigǔ* (秘制卤蛋排骨, 'secret' pork ribs with quail eggs); and *zhǎng dòujiǎo qiézi* (长豆角茄子, eggplant with green beans). We could go on! Failing that, point at anything tasty your neighbours are tucking into.

Moscow Restaurant RUSSIAN ¥¥

(莫斯科餐厅, Mòsīkē Cāntīng; ☑010 6831 6758; 135 Xizhimenwai Dajie, 西直门外大街135号; mains from ¥100; ⏰11am-2pm & 5-9pm; 📶; Ⓢ Line 4 to Beijing Zoo, exit C2) In the early days of the PRC, a slap-up meal at 'Old Mo' was considered an exotic treat. Moscow Restaurant has been dishing up borscht to its Beijing comrades since 1954, and looks the part with its soaring ceilings, regal chandeliers and velvet-draped walls. The steak-heavy menu also features stroganoff, caviar, and vodka by the glass.

Temple of Heaven Park & Dongcheng South

Bianyifang Roast Duck PEKING DUCK ¥¥¥

(便宜坊烤鸭店, Biànyìfāng Kǎoyādiàn; Map p91; ☑010 6708 8680; 65-77 Xianyukou Jie, 鲜鱼口街65-77号; Peking duck ¥168-298; ⏰11am-9.30pm; 📶; Ⓢ Line 2 to Qianmen, exit B) The grandaddy of duck roasting, Bianyifang has been dishing up waterfowl since the early Ming dynasty. The restaurant's antique roasting method – using closed ovens rather than hanging over a fruitwood flame a la rival **Quanjude** (前门全聚德烤鸭店, Qiánmén Quánjùdé Kǎoyādiàn; Map p94; ☑010 6701 1379; 30 Qianmen Dajie, 前门大街30号; roast duck ¥258; ⏰11am-1.30pm & 4.30-8pm) – results in juicier meat with softer skin, which eaters stuff into hollow sesame rolls called *shaobing,* though pancakes and hoisin sauce are available.

Now a citywide chain, a branch of Bianyifang has stood here on Xianyukou (Fresh Fish Crossroads) since 1855...until bulldozers razed the area in the lead-up to the 2008 Olympics. In typical fashion, the neighbourhood was rebuilt from the ground up into a district of ersatz food streets, and Bianyifang received brand new digs.

Not content to rest on its Ming dynasty laurels, Bianyifang has patented a technique of flavour-infused duck (either 'flower' or 'vegetable'), which is more expensive that the standard fowl. Alternatively, the signature braised lamb breast (¥158) is a mighty tasty duck substitute.

✖ Dashilar & Xicheng South

Jùbǎoyuán   HOTPOT ¥
(聚宝源; ☎010 8354 4602; 5-2 Niu Jie, 牛街5-2号; mutton per portion from ¥46; ⊙11am-10pm; ⑤Line 7 to Guang'anmennei, exit D) A culinary mecca for hotpot-obsessed Hui Chinese, this is one of Beijing's most famous *shuan yangrou* (scalding mutton) eateries. Perennially packed, the faithful queue up to get their turn at the charcoal-burning pots, dunking hand-cut meat slices into a clear broth before coating liberally in sesame paste and consuming heartily. English menus are available on request.

Directly opposite the restaurant is **Shuru Hutong**, which is worth a stroll for its many halal butchers and snack vendors.

Suzuki Kitchen   JAPANESE ¥
(铃木食堂, Língmù Shítáng; Map p94; ☎010 6313 5409; http://suzukikitchen.com; 10-14 Yangmeizhu Xiejie, 杨梅竹斜街10-14号; mains from ¥45; ⊙11.30am-2.30pm & 5.30-9pm; ☏; ⑤Line 2 to Qianmen, exit C) Opened by a cultured crew of local Japanophiles, this enormously popular restaurant brings together refined, minimalist design, a beguiling *hutong* locale and neatly presented Japanese comfort food like curry, rice bowls, *udon* noodles, hamburger steaks, hotpots and salads. Book ahead.

Deyuan Roast Duck   PEKING DUCK ¥¥
(德缘烤鸭店, Déyuán Kǎoyā Diàn; Map p94; ☎010 6308 5371; 57 Dashilan Xijie, 大栅栏西街57号; Peking duck ¥168, dishes from ¥39; ⊙10am-2pm & 4.30-9pm; ☏☏; ⑤Line 2 to Qianmen, exit C) A great-value choice for Beijing's trinity of trad meats: Peking duck, roast mutton and donkey. The ducks (¥168) are cooked in hung ovens and carved theatrically at the front of the restaurant. Unlike Beijing's more distinguished duckeries, this is a spot to crack open a cold Yanjing beer or three, loosen your belt, and eat till you burst.

You can't miss the restaurant for its humongous painted *páilóu* facade. English picture menus available.

Quanjude Roast
Duck Hepingmen   PEKING DUCK ¥¥¥
(全聚德和平门店, Quánjùdé Hépíngmén Diàn; Map p94; ☎010 8319 3101; www.qmquanjude.com.cn; 14 Qianmen Xidajie, 前门西大街14号楼; roast duck ¥288; ⊙11am-1.30pm & 4.30-8.30pm; ☒☏; ⑤Line 2 to Hepingmen, exit C) Founded in 1864 by a poultry dealer named Yang Quanren, Quanjude is China's most famous destination for duck. This seven-floor emporium, its 41 dining rooms bedecked in communist-chic red and gold decor, is the flagship. The elegantly plated duck, while not the finest in town, hits the spot, and as a bonus you get a numbered certificate of authenticity for your bird.

The restaurant is geared to the tourist hordes (both domestic and foreign), which means booking is advised and service can be peremptory. It also caters for visiting VIPs in its many private rooms. Check out the photos of everyone from Fidel Castro to Zhang Yimou adorning the wall – proof that 'duck diplomacy' is a thing.

For the adventurous foodie, Quanjude offers some serious nose-to-tail eating. As part of a banquet, a series of dishes make use of every part of the duck, from the liver and heart to the webbed feet.

✖ Sanlitun & Chaoyang

Nanjing Impressions   JIANGSU ¥
(南京大牌档, Nánjīng Dàpáidàng; Map p96; ☎010 8405 9777; 4th fl, Shimao Shopping Centre, 13 Gongrentiyuchang Beilu, 工体北路13号世茂百货4层; dishes from ¥28; ⊙11am-2pm & 5-10pm; ⑤Line 10 to Tuanjiehu, exit A) A beacon of foodie fun in a dismal shopping mall, this is Nanjing's best-loved restaurant chain, recreat-

---

TRY: ZHAJIANG NOODLES

Beijing's native noodle dish, *zhájiàng miàn* (炸酱面) pairs thick, chewy wheat noodles with a dollop of rich pork sauce and side dishes of cucumber, radish, bean sprouts and soybeans, which are mixed into the noodles before eating. Beijingers swear the best *zhájiàng miàn* is always cooked at home, but failing that, Taste of Dadong does a delicious take on the dish.

LOCAL KNOWLEDGE

HOW TO EAT PEKING DUCK

Peking duck is typically carved tableside, so cameras at the ready! You'll be served a dish of duck skin and another with meat attached. Begin by eating shards of duck skin dipped in sugar. Next, hold a piece of duck in your chopsticks and use it to 'paint' sauce on to your pancake before assembling to taste. Traditionalists also stuff the juicy duck meat inside mini sesame buns called *shaobing* (烧饼).

ing with theatrical aplomb the *dàpáidàng* ('cooked food' markets) of southern China. All the tastes of the Yangtze River Delta are on show, from salted duck (served cold) to plump pork and chive potsticker dumplings, duck blood and vermicelli soup (delicious!), and even snails.

You can tick off your order via the paper menu, or saunter up to the various in-restaurant market stalls and point at what you fancy.

Meizhou Dongpo   SICHUAN ¥
(眉州东坡酒楼, Méizhōu Dōngpō Jiǔlóu; Map p96; ☑010 5968 3370; 7 Chunxiu Lu, 春秀路7号; mains from ¥37; ⏰6.30am-10pm; Ⓢ Line 2 to Dongsi Shitiao, exit B) Enjoy good-value Sichuan classics alive with the tongue tingle of *huājiāo* (Sichuan peppercorns) at this reliable chain restaurant, recognisable by its period-style facade.

⭐ **Taste of Dadong**   BEIJING ¥¥
(小大董, Xiǎo Dàdǒng; Map p96; ☑010 8563 0016; LG2-11, Parkview Green, 9 Dongdaqiao Lu, 东大桥路9号桥芳草地LG2-11; duck portion ¥118; ⏰11am-9.30pm; ❋ ⏰; Ⓢ Line 6 to Dongdaqiao, exit D2) This casual concept eatery from Beijing's duck maestro Dong Zhenxiang – of famed sister restaurant, Dadong (p115) – lets you enjoy a portion of his famous roast fowl without having to order the whole bird. The rest of the menu is also fantastic, offering playful takes on local dishes that are surprisingly affordable for the quality.

Dadong can't resist a bit of food theatre (a dusting of icing sugar on the sweet-and-sour ribs, candyfloss 'flowers'), but the basics, like the individual soups and stir-fries, are delectable. Don't miss his take on Beijing's famous noodle dish *zhájiàng miàn,* akin to a rustic bowl of pasta whipped up by a Milanese grandma.

This is the flagship, but more locations have popped up in shopping-mall food courts around town.

⭐ **Din Tai Fung**   SHANGHAI ¥¥
(鼎泰丰, Dǐng Tài Fēng; Map p96; ☑8562 6583; www.dintaifung.com.cn; LG2-20, Parkview Green, 9 Dongdaqiao Lu, 东大桥路9号桥芳草地LG2-20; 5/10 dumplings from ¥30/59; ⏰11.30am-9.30pm; Ⓢ Line 6 to Dongdaqiao, exit D2) Pleated with precision, the *xiǎolóngbāo* (Shanghai-style soup dumplings) at this acclaimed Taiwan chain taste as good as they look. Delicate pork, rich consommé and paper-thin pastry – perfection! Don't skimp on the starters either; they include tangy ribs and fried pork cutlet. Terrific value.

⭐ **In & Out**   YUNNAN ¥¥
(一坐一忘, Yī Zuò Yī Wàng; Map p96; ☑010 8454 0086; 1 Sanlitun Beixiaojie, 三里屯北小街1号; mains ¥42-178; ⏰11am-9.30pm; Ⓢ Line 2 to Agricultural Exhibition Centre, exit A) Take your taste buds on a dreamy sojourn southwest at Beijing's most stylish Yunnan restaurant. A sophisticated, industrial-chic space is the setting for aromatic favourites like 'Crossing the Bridge' noodles, tilapia fish with lemongrass, scrambled eggs with jasmine flowers, and sticky bamboo rice, all gorgeously presented and begging to be Instagrammed.

Moka Bros   INTERNATIONAL ¥¥
(Map p96; ☑010 5208 6079; http://mokabros.com/en; Nali Patio, 1st fl, 81 Sanlitun Lu, 那里花园一楼 三里屯北路81号; dishes around ¥70; ⏰8am-10pm; ❋ ⏰; Ⓢ Line 10 to Tuanjiehu, exit A) A Beijing original, Moka's hipster combo of brunch food, Edison bulb lighting and subway tile walls muralled by Plastered 8 (p128) has seen this mini-chain extend to Shanghai and Chengdu. Wraps, salads, power bowls and smoothies offer respite after a heavy night on the Peking duck. Equally adept at coffee and cake, Moka's 4pm to 8pm happy hour also makes it a decent place to start your night.

Bottega   ITALIAN ¥¥
(意库, Yì Kù; Map p96; ☑010 6416 1752; www.bottegacn.com; 2nd fl, Nali Patio, 81 Sanlitun Lu, 三里屯路81号那里花园2层; pizza ¥78-138; ⏰noon-midnight; ⏰; Ⓢ Line 10 to Tuanjiehu, exit A) A party restaurant with hipster decor and a menu of wood-fired pizza (a bit doughy), pasta, salads, meaty mains and cocktails. Bandana-toting chefs work like maniacs in the open kitchen, and food comes out at a zip. Music too loud for date night.

Biteapitta
MIDDLE EASTERN ¥¥

(吧嗒饼, Bāda Bǐng; Map p96; Unit 201, 2nd Fl, Tongli Bldg, 43 Sanlitunbei Lu; 三里屯北路43号同里花园201号; mains ¥40-100; ⏰11am-11.30pm, to midnight Fri & Sat; 📵; Ⓢ Line 10 to Tuanjiehu, exit A) Run by the same Israeli couple since 2004, this veteran Sanlitun eatery whips up loaded pita-bread sandwiches, thick-set hummus, crisp falafel, grilled-meat skewers and sensational baklava, all served with a side of order of bass thump from the neighbouring bars.

★ Taco Bar
MEXICAN ¥¥

(塔科酒吧, Tǎkē Jiǔbā; Map p96; www.tacobarchina.com; Lot 10, Courtyard 4, off Gongrentiyuchang Beilu, 北京机电院内4号院; 3 tacos ¥55-75; ⏰5pm-midnight Tue-Fri, noon-midnight Sat & Sun; 📵; Ⓢ Line 10 to Tuanjiehu, exit A or D) The king, nay the emperor of Chinese *taquerias*, Taco Bar packs out with punters feasting on fiendishly tasty Mexican street-style tacos like *al pastor* (pork belly) and *carne asada* (steak), slathered in homemade hot sauces. Opened by a Taiwanese-American (whose beloved Beijing mutt Rocky is muralled on the wall), it's a place to party, pouring killer cocktails heavy on the lime and tequila.

Home Plate BBQ
AMERICAN ¥¥

(本垒美式烤肉, Běnlěi Měishì Kǎoròu; Map p96; 📵010 6585 9200; www.homeplatebbq.com; Lot 10, Courtyard 4, off Gongrentiyuchang Beilu, 三里屯机电院10号; burgers from ¥50, mains ¥108-238; ⏰11am-2pm & 5-10pm Mon-Fri, to 11pm Fri & Sat; Ⓢ Line 10 to Tuanjiehu, exit A or D) Flying the flag for southern American barbecue in a decidedly duck-centric city, this Texas-owned restaurant-bar is all about slow-cooked meats, burgers and craft beer. A charcoal-wood smoker takes centre stage, loaded with fruit wood to cook bone-lickin' ribs, plates of barbecued pulled pork, smoky chicken, and beef brisket cooked for 12 hours. Expect to wait for a table on weekends.

Tienstiens
FRENCH ¥¥

(将将, Jiāng Jiāng; Map p96; 📵010 8587 8897; Lot 10, Courtyard 4, off Gongrentiyuchang Beilu, 工人体育场北路4号10号楼; cakes ¥48-58; ⏰8.30am-11pm; 📵; Ⓢ Line 10 to Tuanjiehu, exit A or D) What appears at ground level to be a petite bakery selling Parisian-grade baguettes and perfect *pâtisserie* is in fact a sophisticated, spacious rooftop cafe with French wines and cider, imported cheese platters, seven types of hot chocolate and a whole lot of *joie de vivre*.

Haidilao
HOTPOT ¥¥

(海底捞火锅, Hǎidǐlāo Huǒguō; Map p96; 📵010 6595 2982; Soho Mall Bldg 6, 8 Gongti Beilu, 工体北路8号三里屯SOHO6号商场; per person from ¥140; ⏰10am-7am; 📵📵; Ⓢ Line 10 to Tuanjiehu, exit D) China's best-loved chain of hotpot restaurants sells itself not just on the quality of the food but also on its remarkable service culture. Free drinks, snacks, shoe shines and even manicures are laid on while diners wait to be seated! Order the hand-pulled noodles for a tableside performance of warrior-level twirling.

Hóng Lú
BEIJING ¥¥

(红炉; Map p96; 📵010 6595 9872; 6 Nansanlitun Lu, 三里屯南路6号; mains from ¥39; ⏰11.30am-10pm; Ⓢ Line 10 to Tuanjiehu, exit D) Reworking old Beijing grub for modern palates, this stylish upstairs space knocks out classics like *zhájiàng* noodles, sweet-and-sour fish, and a half-serving of roast duck, all well priced and packed with flavour.

There's no English sign, but it's next door to Slow Boat Brewery (p126); look for the red door.

★ Jingzun Peking Duck
PEKING DUCK ¥¥

(京尊烤鸭店, Jīngzūn Kǎoyā Diàn; Map p96; 📵010 6417 4075; 6 Chunxiu Lu, 春秀路6号; mains ¥23-98; ⏰11am-10pm; Ⓢ Line 2 to Dongsi Shitiao, exit B) An unsung purveyor of Peking duck, Jingzun's bargain birds (¥138/79 for a whole/half) are every bite the equal of Beijing's more elite brands, unruly presentation aside. Lacquer-skinned and succulent, the ducks are roasted in a traditional *guàlú* (hung oven). For a few extra yuan it'll turn the carcass into an enormous duck soup (鸭汤, *yā tāng*) swimming with tofu and cabbage.

Yàn Lán Lóu
GANSU ¥¥

(燕兰楼; Map p96; 📵010 6599 1668; 4th fl, 12 Chaoyangmenwai Dajie, 朝阳门外大街12号昆泰商厦4层; lamb skewers ¥10; ⏰10.30am-9.30pm; Ⓢ Line 6 to Dongdaqiao, exit D) A temple to the pleasures of eating sheep, this restaurant celebrates the food of Gansu province, 1500km west. That means skewers of mutton dusted in cumin and chilli, and roasted over hot coals, delectably tender boiled lamb ribs, and other more offal-type cuts. The sheep-averse can try hand-pulled noodles in a beef broth (兰州牛肉拉面, *Lánzhōu niúròu lāmiàn*), as good as any in Beijing.

Fodder Factory
SICHUAN ¥¥

(草料厂, Cǎoliào Chǎng; 📵010 5601 4768; Qilingliu Beijie, 798 Art District, 七零六北一街

798艺术区; mains from ¥45; ⊘ 11am-2.30pm & 5-10pm; 🖥; 🔲 Line 14 to Wangjing South, exit B1) With China's overworked millennials pining for simpler times, it's no wonder nostalgia has become big business. Fodder Factory tugs at the heartstrings with its rotary dial telephones, boxy television sets and exercise-book menu – a nod, too, to 798's past life as an electronics factory. Well-executed whimsy aside, the spicy Sichuan and Hunan dishes here are the best in the area.

★ Najia Xiaoguan
CHINESE ¥¥

(那家小馆, Nàjiā Xiǎoguǎn; 🖥 010 5978 9999; 2 Jiuxianqiao Beilu, 798 Art District, 酒仙桥北路2号798艺术区; Peking duck ¥198; ⊘ 11am-9.30pm; 🖥; 🔲 Line 14 to Wangjing South, exit B1) With modern Chinese interiors fit for an emperor, this Manchu-inspired restaurant is a regal delight, serving imperial fare like Peking duck, braised sea cucumber and curiosities like DIY venison buns – in recognition of the game-hunting Qing dynasty from which the restaurant draws its thematic cues.

Shèng Yǒng Xīng
PEKING DUCK ¥¥¥

(晟永興烤鸭店, Shèng Yǒng Xīng Kǎoyā Diàn; Map p96; 🖥 010 6464 0968; 5 Xindong Lu, 新东路5号; Peking duck ¥398; ⊘ 11am-9.30pm; 🖥; 🔲 Line 10 to Agricultural Exhibition Center, exit D) This beautifully styled 2nd-floor dining room serves high-roller Peking duck, roasted over jujube wood at a higher temperature for a less oily bite. Upgrade to the ultra-fancy duck option (¥500) and you get bronze shards of duck skin crowned with caviar. Pair your bird with a huge range of flawlessly executed Chinese favourites, from spicy Sichuan stir-fries to crispy shrimp.

Migas Mercado
SPANISH ¥¥¥

(米家思, Mǐjiāsī; Map p96; 🖥 010 6500 7579; 7th fl, China World Mall, 1 Jianguomenwai Dajie, 建国门外大街1号国贸商城三期北区7层; paella ¥298; ⊘ 11.30am-1am; 🖥; 🔲 Line 1, 10 to Guomao, exit E2) A fun-loving, well-heeled CBD hangout, Spanish-run Migas serves sun-drenched fare like grilled octopus and Iberian pork on a fabulous terrace space facing the much-photographed CCTV Headquarters (p105). It's a gorgeous setting worth your time, even if you just stop by for evening cocktails.

🍴 Summer Palace & Haidian

Bai Family Mansion
CHINESE ¥¥¥

(白家大院, Bái Jiā Dàyuàn; 🖥 010 6265 8851; 15 Suzhou Jie, 苏州街15号; mains from ¥158; ⊘ 11am-

10pm; 🔲 Line 10 to Suzhoujie, exit A) Staff dressed as Qing dynasty nobles preside over this charming garden restaurant, serving 'official cuisine' – in other words, the emperor's leftovers. Qing royals were served hundreds of dishes at mealtimes, of which they would only eat a tiny proportion, the rest passing down through the ranks with not a crumb wasted. Several dishes on the menu were supposedly favourites of Cixi, the Empress Dowager.

🍷 Drinking & Nightlife

From celebrity bartenders to Beijing-born craft-beer brands, the drinks scene in Beijing has never been tipsier. Head to Sanlitun for pumping nightclubs, glam cocktail bars and sports pubs, or the Drum Tower neighbourhood for hidden *hutong* bars and speakeasies.

🍷 Forbidden City & Dongcheng Central

★ MO Bar
COCKTAIL BAR

(Map p78; 🖥 010 8509 8850; Mandarin Oriental Wangfujing, WF Central, 269 Wangfujing Jie, 北京王府井文华东方酒店王府井大街269号王府中环; ⊘ 5pm-1am Mon-Thu, to 2am Fri & Sat, 4pm-midnight Sun; 🖥; 🔲 Line 1 to Wangfujing, exit C2) Legendary bar Hope and Sesame from Guangzhou, voted one of Asia's best bars in 2019, crafted the molecular-style cocktail list at MO Bar, an uber-glam hangout in the Mandarin Oriental (p112). Arrive early to bag a terrace table for the chance to see the sun set behind the Forbidden City.

Jing-A Longfusi
CRAFT BEER

(京-A 隆福寺, Jīng-A lóngfú Sì; Map p78; 🖥 010 8400 1058; 38 Qianliang Hutong, 钱粮胡同38号; ⊘ 11am-midnight Sun-Thu, to 2am Fri & Sat; 🔲 Line 8 to National Art Museum, exit B, or Lines 5, 6 to Dongsi, exit A) Knock back Beijing-inspired craft beers at this hip taproom, which shares a gentrified *hutong* development with restaurants, shops, an art gallery and one of Beijing's many WeWork offices. The kitchen turns out tasty pizzas (go for the Yunnan mushroom) and other beer-friendly fodder.

Slow Boat DSK Taproom
CRAFT BEER

(悠航鲜啤灯市口店, Yōuháng Xiānpí Dēngshìkǒu Diàn; Map p78; www.slowboatbrewery.com; 157 Dongsi Nandajie, 东四南大街157号; beers from ¥40; ⊘ 11am-midnight, to 2am Fri & Sat; 🔲 Line 5 to Dengshikou, exit A) The good ship Slow Boat has dropped anchor in central Beijing,

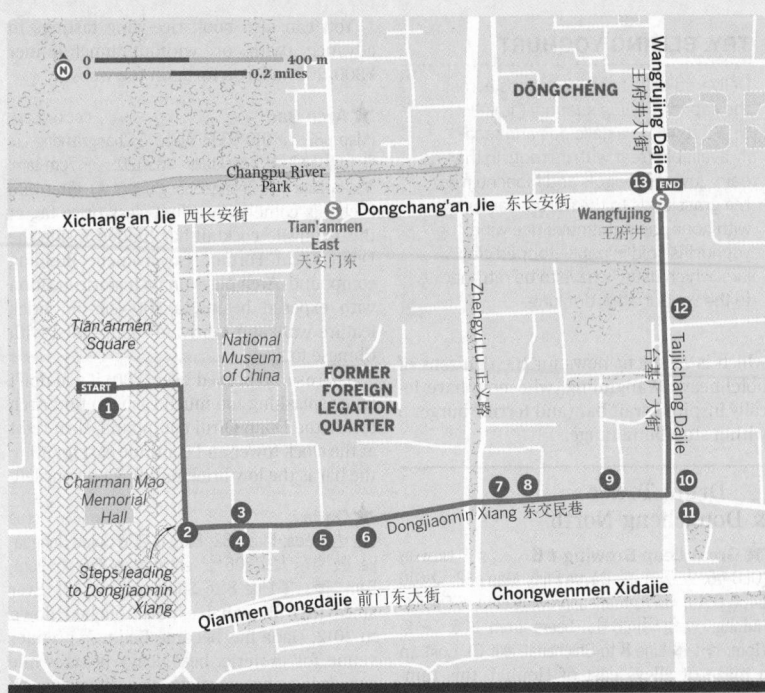

🚶 City Walk
Tian'anmen Square & Foreign Legation Quarter

START TIAN'ANMEN SQ
END WANGFUJING DAJIE
LENGTH 2KM; ONE HOUR

After the Second Opium War in 1860, one of Britain's treaty demands was for permanent diplomatic digs in Beijing, hence the Legation Quarter, a three-quarter square mile of inner city given over to foreign legations (embassies) in Beijing until WWII. Western-style banks, apartments, embassy gates and a church from that era survive to this day.

Exit **1 Tian'anmen Sq** (p75) and climb the steps into **2 Dongjiaomin Xiang** (东交民巷), the main drag through the quarter. The red-brick building on your left was the old **3 French Hospital**. Through an archway on your right stands the former **4 American Legation.**

A green roof rises above the wall at No 40, the former **5 Dutch Legation**. Further ahead on your right, you can't miss the collonaded facade of the First National City Bank of New York, now the **6 Beijing Police Museum**

(北京警察博物馆; 9am-4pm Tue-Sun, last entry 3.30pm; show passport for free entry).

Keep walking to the impressive domed building on the corner of Zhengyi Lu (正义路) and Dongjiaomin Xiang, the former **7 Yokohama Specie Bank**, built in 1910, and now home to the China Court Museum.

The low-slung building at No 19 is the former **8 French post office**, a few steps from the old **9 French Legation** at No 15, now the Ministry of Foreign Affairs.

The twin spires of the wonderfully Gothic **10 St Michael's Church** rise up at No 11, established in 1904. Directly across the road is the old **11 Belgian Legation**.

Turn left and head north along Taijichang Dajie. Hunt down the brick street sign in the northern wall of Taijichang Toutiao (台基厂头条), carved with the old name of the road, **12 Rue Hart**. Located at No 3 Rue Hart was the Austro-Hungarian Legation.

Reaching the end of Taijichang Dajie, across busy Dongchang'an Jie is the former Grand Hôtel de Pékin – now **13 Beijing Hotel NUO** (p108), a historic spot for a drink.

TRY: BEIJING YOGHURT

Delivered daily to corner shops across the capital, *Běijīng suānnǎi* (北京酸奶; ¥3 to ¥6) is a delicious and readily available treat with its roots in the dairy-loving Mongols and Manchu from the grasslands to the north. Flavoured with honey and glutinous rice wine, the yoghurt is sold in paper-topped clay jars, which usually have to be returned to the vendor after drinking.

which is excellent news for the denizens of hotel-heavy Wangfujing, who now have locally inspired craft bar (and terrific burgers) within stumbling range.

Drum Tower & Dongcheng North

★ Great Leap Brewing #6
BREWERY
(GLB #6, 大跃啤酒; Dàyuè Píjiǔ; Map p82; ☎ 010 6406 0510; www.greatleapbrewing.com; 6 Doujiao Hutong, 豆角胡同6号; beers from ¥25; ☉ 2-11pm; 🛱; ⑤ Line 8 to Shichahai, exit C) Lost in a maze of alleys east of Houhai, this tumbledown courtyard is where Beijing's craft-beer scene first burped into life back in the heady, pre-Xi days of 2010. The bar, with its lovely walled yard, remains Beijing's most atmospheric spot for a pint. Choose from a chalkboard list of locally inspired creations like Honey Ma Gold, with its Sichuan peppercorns and Shandong honey.

★ Nuoyan Wine Bar
WINE BAR
(糯言酒馆, Nuòyán Jiǔguǎn; Map p82; www.nuoyanricewine.cn; 7 Banqiao Nanxiang, 板桥南巷7号; per bottle ¥150-220; ☉ 5pm-midnight Mon-Thu, to 1.30am Fri, noon-1.30am Sat, to 12.30am Sun; 🛱; ⑤ Line 5 to Beixinqiao, exit C) Move aside, Merlot, it's *mǐjiǔ* time! Try something new at this rustic tavern specialising in Chinese wine made from glutinous rice (米酒, *mǐjiǔ*), a delicately sweet tipple the same potency as sherry. There's no English menu, but you'll be given a tot of several types (rose, plum, osmanthus, aged etc) from which to choose a bottle (380ml, ¥150 to ¥220).

Nuoyan is actually a brand of rice wine, founded in Beijing in 2014. Unlike traditional wine-making, the process of making rice wine is more akin to brewing beer. The bar is inside the People's Art Printing House compound (人民美术印刷厂, *rénmín měishù yìnshuā chǎng*), up in the northwest corner.

You can also book rice-wine tastings in advance (with or without lunch/dinner ¥300/200) using a form on the website.

★ Arch Bar
COCKTAIL BAR
(Map p82; ☎ 010 6333 6188; 3 Zhangzizhong Lu, 张自忠路3号; cocktails ¥85-120; ☉ 7pm-1am; 🛱; ⑤ Line 5 to Zhangzizhonglu, exit A) First-rate cocktails come with a first-class price tag at this exquisite cocktail bar hidden inside the Duan Qirui Former Government Building compound. Arch plays on its historic location with exposed beams, a 100-year-old brick feature wall, and a private room styled with Chinese folk art.

There's also bottled beer (¥30) if you don't fancy splashing too much cash. To find Arch inside the Duan Qirui compound, turn right at the clock tower and continue east for 50m; the bar is the low brick building on your left.

★ Dada
CLUB
(达达, Dádá; Map p82; Bldg B, 206 Gulou Dongdajie, 鼓楼东大街206号; entry from ¥50; ☉ 9pm-5am; 🛱; ⑤ Line 8 to Shichahai, exit A2) Ever since this Shanghai export touched down in 2012, Dada has become Beijing's premier venue for esoteric, bass-heavy beats, while remaining unpretentious and divey enough for the casual party-goer. By combining an imaginative line-up of DJs at weekends with a commitment to keeping entry at around ¥60, Dada gets the party vibe spot on.

On the floor above is rock-music dive **Temple Bar** (坛酒吧, Tán Jiǔbā; ☎ 134 2607 0554; ☉ 7pm-late); Beijing party animals tend to move from one to the other on any given night.

Nina
COCKTAIL BAR
(Map p82; ☎ 139 1111 0763; 66 Beiluogu Xiang, 北锣鼓巷66号; cocktails from ¥45; ☉ 6pm-2am Mon-Thu, to late Fri & Sat, noon-late Sun; 🛱; ⑤ Lines 2, 8 to Guloudajie, exit G) Set up for *aperitivo* with a bar list that boasts spritz, snacks and multiple variations on the Negroni cocktail, this charmingly simple *hutong* bar pulls in a hip crowd of Italian expats who gather at the wooden bar or smoke in the alley.

Mai Bar
BAR
(麦, Mài; Map p82; 40 Beiluogu Xiang, 北锣鼓巷40号; cocktails/beers from ¥50/30; ☉ 6pm-2am; ⑤ Lines 2, 8 to Guloudajie, exit G) An intimate affair, Mai Bar hides away in part of an old *hutong* courtyard, comprising a worn wooden bar, a scatter of candlelit tables and a narrow strip of outdoor seating. Cocktails are competently concocted by bow-tied bar-

tenders, and come with crunchy nibbles and hot towels. Or choose a craft bottled beer from the amply stocked fridge.

Cafe Zarah
CAFE

(Map p82; ☑ 010 8403 9807; www.cafezarah.com; 46 Gulou Dongdajie, 鼓楼东大街46号; breakfast from ¥65; ⊘ 9am-midnight Sun-Thu, to 2am Fri & Sat; ⛅🚻🐾; Ⓢ Line 5 to Beixinqiao, exit D) Ground zero for Gulou's laptop warriors, Zarah is a stylish *hutong* hangout adored for its charming staff, good coffee and welcomingly bookish atmosphere. By day the polished concrete space is all brainstorm meetings, bloggers and brunching mums; after dark it's cocktails and ambient electronic beats.

🍺 Beihai Park & Xicheng North

NBeer Pub
CRAFT BEER

(牛啤堂, Niú Pí Táng; Map p86; ☑ 010 8328 8823; www.nbcraftbrewing.com; Huguo Xintiandi, 85 Huguosi Lu, 护国寺路85号护国新天地一层; beer from ¥39; ⊘ 3pm-2am; ⛅; Ⓢ Lines 4, 6 to Ping'anli, exit B) The flagship bar of an all-Chinese craft brewer, NBeer is a Beijing original pouring sours, stouts and every style in between. If you only try one (good luck with that), make it the award-winning Beijing Gose Modern, a sour wheat beer brewed with coriander, salt and star anise. Bar nibbles include burgers, spicy Sichuan sausage and lamb-skewer pizza.

★ Bear Brew
CAFE

(熊煮咖啡, Xióng Zhǔ Kāfēi; Map p86; ☑ 176 1228 2405; 26 Baitasi Dongjiaodao, 白塔寺东夹道26号; coffee from ¥30; ⊘ 10am-8pm; ⛅; Ⓢ Line 4 to Xisi, exit A) Run by two affable, aproned Chinese bears (who speak excellent English), this gay-friendly *hutong* hangout pours a host of house creations like a 24-hour cold brew with coke, a 'dirty' (espresso shot dumped on iced milk) and the usual range of espresso and pour-over coffees. The rooftop terrace, with its poetry-inspiring views of the White Dagoba Temple (p94), is glorious on a sunny afternoon.

1901 Cafe
CAFE

(Map p86; ☑ 010 6616 0335; 101 Xi'anmen Dajie, 西安门大街101; coffee from ¥40; ⊘ 9am-midnight; ⛅; Ⓢ Line 4 to Xisi, exit C) This baroque-style, three-storey townhouse is a late-Qing gem that's barely changed inside or out since it was built in 1901, hence the name. It was donated to the Cathedral of Our Saviour (p95) nearby a few years later, and served as Beijing's centre for Catholic

Action until 1949. Today it's a whimsical cafe where you can while away hours at invitingly mismatched tables under wooden eaves.

Coffee, cakes and snacks are overpriced, admittedly, but there's nowhere quite like this left in Beijing.

Lotus Cafe & Bar
CAFE

(莲咖啡, Lián Kāfēi; Map p86; ☑ 010 6655 1588; 3rd fl, Pagoda Light Hostel, 185 Fuchengmennei Dajie, 阜成门内大街185号; ⊘ 10am-8pm; ⛅; Ⓢ Line 2 to Fuchengmen, exit B, or Line 4 to Xisi, exit A) At this popular rooftop cafe with seating indoors and out, your coffee, cake or sandwich is served with a side order of eye candy: the White Dagoba Temple (p94), lauding it over temple halls and surrounding *hutong*. With craft beer and wine available too, it's a super spot for sundowner drinks. Find it above the Pagoda Light (p113) hostel.

🍸 Dashilar & Xicheng South

★ Soloist Coffee Co
CAFE

(Map p94; www.soloistcoffee.com; 39 Yangmeizhu Xiejie, 杨梅竹斜街39号; coffee from ¥40; ⊘ noon-7pm; ⛅; Ⓢ Line 2 to Qianmen, exit B or C) Partway down a gentrifying *hutong* is this exquisite coffee roaster and cafe, born here as a pop-up during Beijing's annual Design Week, and now a small chain. Supposedly once a public bathhouse (the building is decades old), the cafe these days deals out liquid relief of the caffeinated kind, hawking a gourmet selection of coffee-based drinks, including cocktails like 'cold brew gin tonic'.

Berry Beans
CAFE

(Map p94; 7 Zhujia Hutong, 朱家胡同7号; coffee from ¥35; ⊘ 10am-10pm Tue-Sun, 1-9pm Mon; ⛅; Ⓢ Line 2 to Qianmen, exit C) Meticulously fussy coffee is the draw at this little *hutong* gem, part of a building that once offered more sybaritic pleasures (it was a Republic-era bordello, one of many in the neighbourhood).

> ### HOUHAI NIGHTLIFE
>
> Houhai (p87) is a raucous nightlife destination for local tourists, with strips of neon-lit bars stretching in all directions from Silver Ingot Bridge (银锭桥, Yínding Qiáo; 75 Yandai Xiejie, 烟袋斜街甲75号; Ⓢ Line 8 to Shichahai, exit A2). Expect live music, karaoke, dice-based drinking games, big-screen mobile-phone gaming, rudimentary cocktails and hearty drunkenness.

Contemplate that as you sip a hive-honey iced coffee (¥68): Ethiopian single origin poured over an orb of coffee ice, with a frozen tuile of honeycomb nesting on top.

🍷 Sanlitun & Chaoyang

La Social
BAR

(Map p96; ☎010 5208 6030; 3rd fl, Nali Patio, 81 Sanlitun Lu, 三里屯路81号D308 那里花园 3F; ⊙5.30pm-midnight Sun-Thu, to 3am Fri & Sat, closed Mon; Ⓢ Line 10 to Tuanjiehu, exit A) Day of the Dead meets Chairman Mao at this carnivalesque hotspot were revellers dance to Latin beats. Cocktails (from ¥60) are heavy-handed with the tequila, which you can soak up with Colombian *arepes* (grilled dough 'sandwiches' with various fillings).

Slow Boat Brewery
CRAFT BEER

(悠航鲜啤, Yōuháng Xiānpí; Map p96; ☎010 6592 5388; www.slowboatbrewery.com; 6 Nansanlitun Lu, 南三里屯路6号; beers ¥40-60; ⊙11am-2am; Ⓢ Line 10 to Tuanjiehu, exit D) Drop anchor at Slow Boat, one of Beijing's original American-run craft brewers, for three floors of busy, beery fun. At least a dozen beers are on tap at any time; Monkey's Fist IPA and Zombie Pirate Pale Ale are menu mainstays and good points of embarkation into the frothy seas ahead. Folks come here for the food as much as the drinks – Slow Boat burgers are nigh on the best in town, while a bucket o' fries, battered in ale and served with a tangy aioli, makes the perfect beer snack.

D Lounge
COCKTAIL BAR

(Map p96; www.dlounge.com.cn; Lot 10, Courtyard 4, off Gongrentiyuchang Beilu, 工体北路4号院; ⊙7pm-2am, to 3am Fri & Sat; Ⓢ Line 10 to Tuanjiehu, exit A or D) With its cathedral-like ceiling, low-slung chesterfield couches and sci-fi illuminated bar, D Lounge is the best-looking bar in Beijing, and draws a suitably sophisticated crowd. Stylish cocktails (from ¥80) include a range of signature gin and tonics.

Paddy O'Shea's
SPORTS BAR

(爱尔兰酒吧, Ài'érlán Jiǔbā; Map p96; ☎010 6415 6389; www.paddyosheasbeijing.com; 28 Dongzhimenwai Dajie, 东直门外大街28号; ⊙11.30am-2am; 🛜; Ⓢ Line 2 to Dongzhimen, exit C) For that crucial crunch match you simply can't miss while on hols, Paddy's is the place. Dealing in the happy union of beer and televised sports (on multiple screens), Beijing's best-loved Irish boozer is also HQ for various amateur sports clubs, and it can even whip up a beef-and-Guinness pie.

Lantern
CLUB

(灯笼俱乐部, Dēnglóng Jùlèbù; Map p96; Workers' Stadium West Gate, 工人体育场西门向北100米; entry ¥30-100; ⊙10am-6am Thu-Sun; Ⓢ Line 2 to Dongsi Shitiao, exit C) The best all-round underground club in Beijing, Lantern boasts an incredible sound system and an eclectic roster of DJs from China and abroad spinning proper techno, minimal and tech house. Boss and resident DJ Weng Weng is a stalwart of the scene, having played at some of Beijing's first parties in the late '90s.

Elements
CLUB

(Map p96; 58 Gongrentiyuchang Xilu, 工人体育场 西路58号; women free, men from ¥100; ⊙9pm-6am; Ⓢ Line 2 to Dongsi Shitiao, exit C) Put your hands in the air and touch the lasers at this cavernous club where 'World's Top 100 DJs' take to the decks on weekends. Like most Gongti nightspots, the main dance area includes rows of standing tables for waiter service, for which you're expected to buy a bottle of spirits if you want to party.

Destination
GAY & LESBIAN

(目的地, Mùdìdì; Map p96; 7 Gongrentiyuchang Xilu, 工体西路7号; ⊙9pm-late; Ⓢ Lines 2, 6 to Chaoyangmen, exit A) Beijing's best queer club really is a destination in itself, with multiple rooms, an outdoor bar, a restaurant and a program of LGBTIQ+-related cultural and arts events.

☆ Entertainment

The cultural capital of China, Beijing offers everything from death-defying acrobats to shoegazing Chinese indie bands. Peking opera (*jīngjù*) isn't as popular as in its Qing dynasty heyday, but you can still catch a performance at multiple venues around town.

Peking Opera & Performance

★National Centre
for the Performing Arts
CLASSICAL MUSIC

(国家大剧院, Guójiā Dàjùyuàn; Map p86; ☎010 6655 0000; www.chncpa.org/ens; 2 Xichang'an Jie, 西长安街2号; visit ¥40, tickets ¥100-880; ⊙theatre tour & box office 9am-4.30pm Tue-Sun; Ⓢ Line 1 to Tian'anmen West, exit C) Plonked in the middle of an artificial lake like an alien spaceship, the Paul Andreu–designed NCPA (aka 'The Egg') is a surreal yet spectacular venue at which to catch a performance of opera (western and Chinese), ballet and classical music. Online booking is in Chinese only, but local agent www.theatrebeijing.com

can deliver tickets to your hotel for a small commission.

Forbidden City Concert Hall CLASSICAL MUSIC
(中山公园音乐堂, Zhōngshān Gōngyuán Yīnyuè Táng; Map p74; ☑ 010 6559 8285; www.fcchbj.com; Zhongshan Park, 4 Zhonghua Lu, 中山公园内中华路4号; tickets ¥20-880; ⊙ performances 7.30pm; ⑤ Line 1 to Tian'anmen West, exit B) Considered one of the city's best venues for acoustics, the Forbidden City Concert Hall is the modern successor to an open-air stage built inside regal Zhongshan Park by the Japanese in 1942. It's a wonderfully romantic spot to savour a first-rate performance of classical or Chinese music, and you can often find seats for under ¥100.

Huguang Guild Hall PEKING OPERA
(湖广会馆, Húguǎng Huìguǎn; Map p94; ☑ 010 6351 8284; 3 Hufang Lu, 虎坊路3号; tickets ¥180-680, opera museum ¥10; ⊙ performances 6.30-7.30pm & 8-9pm, opera museum 9am-5.30pm; ⑤ Line 7 to Hufangqiao, exit C) The most atmospheric Peking opera house in town (it was undergoing refurbishment at time of research, so fingers crossed it stays that way...), Huguang Guild Hall was founded in 1807 and converted to a theatre a few decades later. Operas play out on an elaborate canopied stage enclosed by balconies. Local agent www.theatrebeijing. com can arrange tickets.

Mei Lanfang Grand Theatre CHINESE OPERA
(梅兰芳大戏院, Méi Lánfāng Dàxìyuàn; Map p86; ☑ 010 5833 1288; www.bjmlfdjy.cn; 32 Ping'anli Xidajie, 平安里西大街32号; tickets ¥100-300; ⊙ performances 7.30pm; ⑤ Lines 2, 6 to Chegongzhuang, exit C) Named after China's most famous practitioner of Peking opera, this modern theatre has around 1000 seats and is home turf for the prestigious China National Peking Opera Company, of which Mei Lanfang was the first president in 1955. Performances start at 7.30pm. The ticket office in the lobby opens between 9.30am and 8pm.

Liyuan Theatre PEKING OPERA
(梨园剧场, Líyuán Jùchǎng; Map p94; ☑ 010 6301 6688; Qianmen Jianguo Hotel, 175 Yong'an Lu, 前门建国饭店永安路175号; tickets ¥180-680; ⊙ performances 7.30pm; ⑤ Line 7 to Hufangqiao, exit C) This touristy theatre in the Qianmen Jianguo Hotel has nightly performances of Peking opera complete with English subtitles. The setting isn't traditional: it resembles a cinema auditorium (the stage facade is the only authentic touch), but it's an easy introduction to the art form, and shows only last

an hour. Use reputable agent www.theatre beijing.com for discounted tickets.

Chaoyang Theatre ACROBATICS
(朝阳剧场, Cháoyáng Jùchǎng; Map p96; ☑ 010 6507 2421; 36 Dongsanhuan Beilu, 东三环北路36号; ¥380-880; ⊙ performances 4pm, 5.30pm & 7pm; ⑤ Lines 6, 10 to Hujialou, exit C1) Beijing's premier acrobatic show is a rapid-fire fiesta of youthful acrobats, gymnasts, contortionists and daredevils, who between them pull off some heart-in-the-mouth stunts. The theatre itself has seen better days, and pulls in mostly tour groups. Tickets are often bookable through your hotel.

Live Music

DDC LIVE MUSIC
(黄昏黎明俱乐部, Huánghūn Líming Jùlèbù; Map p78; ☑ 010 6407 8969; https://site.douban. com/237627; 14 Shanlao Hutong, 山老胡同14号; tickets from ¥60; ⊙ 5pm-1am; ⑤ Lines 6, 8 to Nanluoguxiang, exit B, or Line 5 to Zhangzizhonglu, exit D) In a secluded *hutong*, Dusk Dawn Club is the place to catch small and mid-sized bands, from post-rock noise outfits to folk strummers, both Chinese and international. Established by a collective of local musicians, artists and curators, there are shows most evenings; check the website or Facebook for listings.

★ Jiang Hu LIVE MUSIC
(江湖酒吧, Jiāng Hú Jiǔbā; Map p82; 7 Dongmianhua Hutong, 东棉花胡同7号; live music ¥30-50; ⊙ 7pm-2am, closed Mon; ⑤ Lines 6, 8 to Nanluoguxiang, exit F) A hip *hutong* livehouse popular with local musicians, Jiang Hu stages folk, blues, jazz and open-mic shows most nights in its wood-beamed courtyard space. The owner, a trombone player, regularly joins in for a jam.

Modernista LIVE MUSIC
(Map p82; ☑ 136 9142 5744; www.facebook.com/ modernistabj; 44 Baochao Hutong, 宝钞胡同44号; ⊙ 6pm-2am; ⑤ Lines 2, 8 to Guloudajie, exit G) Local bands, cabaret, salsa dancing and life drawing are just some of the antics unfolding nightly at this arty, jazz-age-styled bar and performance space. A crescent of balcony tables overhangs the stage, a fun perch from which to sip a cocktail or absinthe and enjoy the show. Check the Facebook page for listings.

East Shore Jazz Bar JAZZ
(东岸爵士吧, Dōngàn Juéshì Ba; Map p82; ☑ 010 8403 2131; 2nd fl, 2 Qianhai Nanyan, Di'anmenwai Dajie, 什刹海南沿2号楼2层; beers/cocktails from ¥35/60; ⊙ 3pm-1am; ⑤ Line 8 to Shichahai, exit A1)

Rock star Cui Jian's saxophonist, whose quartet plays here, opened this dark and moody upstairs jazz den overlooking Qianhai Lake. It's the best place to hear local jazz cats showing off their chops, with live performances Wednesdays to Sundays (from 10pm).

Blue Note   JAZZ
(Map p91; ☑ box office 11am-9pm 170 0000 0288; www.bluenotebeijing.com; 23 Qianmen Dongdajie, 前门东大街23号; ⊘6-11.30pm; Ⓢ Line 2 to Qianmen, exit A) A classy, subterranean live-music venue staging high-profile international jazz, blues and fusion musicians. The historic Legation Quarter setting gives it the feel of a posh night out. Seating is at tables, with drinks and meal service.

🔒 Shopping

Modern mega-malls are the preserve of Wangfujing near the Forbidden City and out in Sanlitun. For time-honoured Chinese shops selling silk, ink stones, cloth shoes and medicines, head to Dashilar & Xicheng South. The Pearl Market (p130) by the Temple of Heaven is the best touristy souvenir market.

🔒 Forbidden City & Dongcheng Central

Slow Lane   GIFTS & SOUVENIRS
(细活裡, Xì Huó Lǐ; Map p78; ☑ 010 6522 7770; 13 Shijia Hutong, 史家胡同13号; ⊘10am-8pm Tue-Sun; Ⓢ Line 5 to Dengshikou, exit C) Such lovingly curated shelves! If only Beijing had more alleyway boutiques like this. Slow Lane tempts with Tibetan yak-wool blankets, ceramic teaware from Jingdezhen (China's pottery heartland), and traditional handicrafts and jewellery, ethically sourced from all corners of the Middle Kingdom. Sip complimentary tea as you browse.

Beijing apm   MALL
(新东安广场, Xīndōng'ān Guǎngchǎng; Map p78; www.beijingapm.cn; 138 Wangfujing Dajie, 王府井大街138号; ⊘9am-10pm; Ⓢ Line 5 to Dengshikou) Dominated at street level by its Apple store, this six-floor shopping mecca has the expected glut of fast fashion (Zara, H&M etc), cosmetics and electronics and a cinema complex. The choice of restaurants and cafes here is enormous, from posh Peking duck at **Taste of Dadong** (小大董, Xiǎo Dàdǒng; ☑010 8508 3960; 6th fl; Peking duck whole/half ¥199/109; ⊘11am-9.30pm; ☎) to Dunkin' Donuts.

WF Central   MALL
(王府中環, Wángfǔ Zhōnghuán; Map p78; www.wfcentral.cn; 269 Wangfujing Dajie, 王府井大街269号; ⊘10am-10pm; Ⓢ Line 1 to Wangfujing, exit C2) After decades of charmless development, this 2018 luxury shopping mall is at least trying to restore a little lost glamour to Wangfujing, once lined with princely mansions. All polished marble and wood tones, it encloses designer boutiques, a three-tiered Victoria's Secret and the exceedingly plush Mandarin Oriental (p112) hotel.

The western section of the mall has an attractive garden with brunch-style restaurants that offer outdoor seating.

Ten Fu's Tea Culture House   TEA
(天福茶文化馆, Tiānfú Chá Wénhuàguǎn; Map p78; ☑ 010 6527 5999; 3 Jinyu Hutong, 金鱼胡同3号; ⊘9am-10pm; Ⓢ Line 5 to Dengshikou, exit A) English-speaking sales staff are adept at parting tourists from their cash in exchange for high-grade teas from around China, sold loose by the *liǎng* (50g) or in various gift-box configurations. Ask to try before you buy. Fine teapots of Yixing clay range from ¥150 to thousands, or play it frugal with tea-infused biscuits (from ¥30).

🔒 Drum Tower & Dongcheng North

★ Plastered 8   CLOTHING
(创可贴8T恤, Chuàngkětiē Tìxù; Map p82; ☑ 010 6406 4872; www.plasteredtshirts.com; 61 Nanluogu Xiang, 南锣鼓巷61号; ⊘9.30am-10.30pm; Ⓢ Lines 6, 8 to Nanluoguxiang, exit E) A visual celebration of Beijing in all its chaotic glory, the T-shirts, hoodies, tote bags and gifts at this iconic streetwear shop make funky and desirable gifts. The boss – a long-term British expat and Chinese TV celebrity – works with Chinese artists in various media to create his always edgy designs.

To avoid the Nanluogu Xiang crowds, there's a newer branch of **Plastered 8** (创可贴, Chuàngkětiē; ☑ 010 6157 8517; 60 Wudaoying Hutong, 五道营胡同60号; T-shirts ¥168; ⊘10am-6pm; Ⓢ Lines 2, 6 to Lama Temple, exit C) at Wudaoying Hutong.

🔒 Beihai Park & Xicheng North

Yandai Xiejie   GIFTS & SOUVENIRS
(烟袋斜街; Map p82; Yandai Xiejie, off Di'anmenwai Dajie, 地安门内大街烟袋斜街; Ⓢ Line 8 to Shichahai, exit A2) So named for its yesteryear trade in pipes and the demon weed (that's

ning northeast from Houhai Lake towards
the Drum Tower. One or two older shops do
still sell the occasional pipe, but it's mostly
T-shirts, gifts, snacks and the like.

★ **Three Stone Kite Shop** ARTS & CRAFTS
(三石斋风筝, Sānshízhāi Fēngzhēng; Map p82;
☑ 010 8404 4505; www.cnkites.com; 25 Di'anmen
Xidajie, 地安门西大街甲25号; ⊙ 9am-8pm;
⑤ Lines 6, 8 to Nanluoguxiang, exit F) Home of
the last remaining traditional kite crafters in
Beijing, this cluttered little cave is piled high
with hand-painted *fēng zhēng* (kites) in the
shape of auspicious birds and beasts. Kites
in the ¥300 range (about 80cm wide) are a
suitable size for flying, while the miniature
kites make fine souvenirs.

Three Stone is a family business that
claims a kite-making lineage back several
generations to the Qing dynasty. The owner's
great-grandfather was supposedly a crafts-
man serving in the Forbidden City towards
the end of the dynasty, in charge of making
lanterns, fans and kites.

🛍 Dashilar & Xicheng South

Beijing Fun MALL
(北京坊, Běijīng Fāng; Map p94; 21 Langfang Toutiao, btwn Meishi Jie & Qianmen Dajie, 廊房头条21
号院; ⊙ 10am-10pm; 🛜; ⑤ Line 2 to Qianmen, exit
C) In a historic area marred by overzealous
redevelopment, the shiny new Beijing Fun
complex at least preserves several fine Qing-
era buildings within an open-air layout that
encompasses shops, restaurants, street art,
a vast Starbucks and a Muji Hotel (from the
Japanese lifestyle brand). It's a handy place to
relax and refuel after visiting Tian'anmen Sq.

★ **Caicifang Porcelain
Workshop** GIFTS & SOUVENIRS
(采瓷坊, Cǎi Cí Fāng; Map p94; ☑ 010 6313 5597;
www.caicifang.com; 35 Yangmeizhu Xiejie, 杨梅竹
斜街35号; ⊙ 10am-7pm; ⑤ Line 2 to Qianmen, exit
C) This charming boutique upcycles shards
of porcelain vases smashed during the Cultural Revolution into unique and desirable
jewellery, boxes, ornaments and art pieces.
You can pay ¥50 for a shard fridge magnet,
or a few hundred for a metal box inset with
the character for 'double happiness', a common decorative motif on blue-and-white
porcelain. English-speaking staff have a
wealth of porcelain-related knowledge.

125

BEIJING SHOPPING

A tenet of Mao's Cultural Revolution was
to smash the 'four olds' (old customs, culture,
habits and ideas), a campaign that began in
Beijing in 1966. Poor old porcelain never
stood a chance, sacrificed by households to
the rampaging Red Guards in the hope that
they would overlook smaller valuables like
jewellery, which were easier to squirrel away.

Ruifuxiang Silk CLOTHING
(瑞蚨祥丝绸店, Ruìfúxiáng Sīchóudiàn; Map
p94; ☑ 010 6303 5313; 5 Dashilan Jie, 大栅栏街
5号; ⊙ 9.30am-8pm; ⑤ Line 2 to Qianmen, exit B)
Squint at the historic facade of Ruifuxiang,
East China's esteemed silk-clothing merchants, trading here since 1893, and you
can almost imagine late Qing–era Dashilar
thronged with rickshaws, merchants and
well-to-do shoppers with their Manchu 'cue'
ponytails. You can still browse rolls of fine
Shandong silk, brocade and satin-silk, or
have a suit or dress made to measure.

Neiliansheng Shoe Shop SHOES
(内联升鞋店, Nèiliánshēng Xiédiàn; Map p94;
☑ 010 6301 4863; 34 Dashilan Jie, 大栅栏街34
号; ⊙ 9am-8.30pm; ⑤ Line 2 to Qianmen, exit B or
C) Treat your feet to a pair of hand-stitched
cloth shoes from this time-honoured Beijing
shop dating back to 1853. From the plain
slip-ons favoured by Beijing's senior citizens
to intricately patterned kicks, they start at
around ¥420.

Liulichang Culture Street ARTS & CRAFTS
(琉璃厂, Liúlíchǎng; Map p94; Liulichang Xijie, 琉
璃厂西街; ⊙ 9am-6pm; ⑤ Line 2 to Hepingmen,
exit D2) An avenue of art shops, antiques and
booksellers since the Qing dynasty, leafy Liulichang is a tourist favourite that's worth
delving into for its historic, albeit dressed-up
atmosphere and grand emporia selling calligraphy, paintings, curios and *wénfáng sì*

WORTH A TRIP

PANJIAYUAN MARKET

A curio hunter's heaven or an Everest of fakery? **Panjiayuan Market** (潘家园古玩市场, Pānjiāyuán Gǔwán Shìchǎng; 18 Huaweili, 华威里18号; ☉8.30am-6pm Mon-Fri, 4.30am-6pm Sat & Sun; ⑤Line 10 to Panjiayuan, exit B) is both, and marvellous fun to boot. Picking over the wares of some 4000 dealers, you won't chance upon that priceless *dòucǎi* stem cup, but you will find Mao busts, Little Red Books, coins, stamps and faded cigarette posters bobbing about in an endless sea of knock-off ceramics, cloisonné, Buddha icons and jade.

Other finds include calligraphy brushes and ink stones, silk paintings, replica Qing furniture, handicrafts from across China, and thread-your-own bead necklaces. Authenticity notwithstanding, you'll certainly pick up a memento, but make a few rounds to compare prices before forking out, and bargain heartily.

The market is at its biggest and best on weekends, starting well before dawn in the tradition of Qing dynasty *guǐ shì* (literally 'ghost markets'). Towards the beleaguered end of the dynasty, destitute nobles were forced to flog their family heirlooms and fineries, opting to do so under a face-saving veil of darkness. The present market was installed here in the early 1990s.

When you're all shopped out, look for El Padrino Club, a spiffy market cafe just inside the main entrance selling lattes, cake and bottles of craft beer.

From Panjiayuan subway station, head west for 200m to find the main entrance.

bǎo (文房四宝), the 'four treasures of study', namely brushes, ink, paper and inkstones.

Maliandao Tea Market
TEA

(马连道茶城, Mǎliándào Cháchéng; ☎010 6343 8550; 11 Maliandao Lu, 马连道路11号; ☉8.30am-5pm; ⑤Line 7 to Wanzi, exit D) Set up for wholesalers, Maliandao is a nondescript commercial district home to if not all the tea in China, then an awful lot of it. For leaf-hunters looking to venture beyond Beijing's favourite jasmine green tea, it can make for a fascinating, caffeine-fuelled excursion, but you'll probably need a Chinese speaker in tow. Alternatively, tour companies including The Hutong (p111) run tea-tasting excursions here.

Temple of Heaven Park & Dongcheng South

Hongqiao Pearl Market
GIFTS & SOUVENIRS

(红桥市场, Hóngqiáo Shìchǎng; Map p91; ☎010 6711 7429; 9 Tiantan Lu, 天坛路9号; ☉10am-7pm; ☎; ⑤Line 5 to Tiantandongmen, exit A2) Occupying a swish, purpose-built mall beside the Temple of Heaven's east gate, the Pearl Market is palpably less hectic than the more famous Silk Market (p130), while selling much the same tourist swag (fake designer handbags, cashmere scarves, mahjong sets etc). Though it feels comparatively posh and polished these days, you'll still need your haggling hat on. The namesake pearls are found on floors three to five.

Sanlitun & Chaoyang

★ Parkview Green
MALL

(芳草地, Fāngcǎodi; Map p96; ☎010 5690 7000; www.parkviewgreen.com; 9 Dongdaqiao Lu, 东大桥路9号; ☉10am-10pm; ☎; ⑤Line 6 to Dongdaqiao, exit A) In a city in thrall to the mall, this futuristic, ecofriendly pyramid stands out from the crowd. Hong Kong–owned Parkview Green is a fabulously ambitious, art-strewn wonderland enclosing designer boutiques from the likes of Stella McCartney and Sandro, a Tesla showroom, a cinema, and brilliant restaurants, including Italian fine-dining Opera Bombana and casual duck joint Taste of Dadong (p120).

Taikoo Li Sanlitun
MALL

(三里屯太古里; Map p96; 19 Sanlitun Lu, 三里屯路19号; ☉10am-10pm; ⑤Line 10 to Tuanjiehu, exit A) Beijing's premier destination for haute couture and urbane dining, Taikoo Li is where the fashionistas go to splash the cash. An open-air mall complex either side of Opposite House (p114) hotel, Taikoo Li North is the better-bred half, carrying luxe labels like Alexander McQueen, Canada Goose and Korea's Gentle Monster eyewear, while down south is Apple, Adidas and most of the restaurants, many with terrace seating.

Silk Street
CLOTHING

(秀水街, Xiùshuǐ Jiē; Map p96; 8 Xiushui Dongjie, 秀水东街8号; ☉9.30am-9pm; ⑤Line 1 to Yonganli, exit A1) A mandatory tour-group stop, this six-storey temple of retail contains acres of clothing, shoes, handbags and electronics – much of it counterfeit and of variable quality. It's worth remembering that, while fake can be fun, the ethics of purchasing are questionable. Mixed in with everything else are cashmere, silk scarves, souvenirs, toys, tailors and the unintentionally hilarious 'I <3 BJ' T-shirt. Haggle freely.

ℹ Information

MEDICAL SERVICES

As the national capital, Beijing has some of China's best medical facilities and services.

A consultation with a doctor in a private clinic will cost ¥600 and up, versus ¥20 to ¥50 in a state hospital.

Beijing United Family Hospital (和睦家医疗, Hémùjiā Yīliáo; ☑ 010 5927 7120, 24hr emergency hotline 4008 919191; http://beijing.ufh.com.cn; 2 Jiangtai Lu, 将台路2号; ⊙24hr; S Line 14 to Jiangtai, exit A or B) Beijing's premier international hospital is run to the highest global standards, with specialists in every department and prices to match. All medical and clerical staff speak English, with many doctors and physicians from Europe, the US and elsewhere.

Peking Union Medical College Hospital (PUMCH, 协和医院, Xiéhé Yīyuàn; Map p78; ☑ 010 6915 6699; www.pumch.cn; 1 Shuaifuyuan, 帅府园1号; ⊙24hr; S Lines 1, 5 to Dongdan, exit A) Enormous and well-regarded Chinese hospital offering a comprehensive range of facilities for inpatient and outpatient care. Head for International Medical Services (国际医疗部; Guójì Yīliáo Bù), a wing reserved for foreigners that has English-speaking staff.

Raffles Medical (莱佛士北京国际诊所, Láifúshì Běijīng Guójì Zhěnsuǒ; Map p96; ☑ 010 6462 9112, dental 010 6462 0333; www.rafflesmedicalgroup.com/beijing; Suite 105, Kunsha Bldg, 16 Xinyuan Nanli, 新源南里16号琨莎中心一座105室; ⊙8am-8pm; S Line 10 to Liangmaqiao, exit D) International health clinic and dental department with English-speaking staff.

MOBILE PHONES

Prepaid SIM cards can be purchased at the arrivals halls of Beijing's two airports. Otherwise you'll have to go in person to the China Mobile or China Unicom office nearest to your hotel, and take your passport with you. Alternatively, there are several companies online who can arrange SIM purchases and even deliver them to your Beijing hotel, for a higher fee.

MONEY

Fast becoming a cashless society, the vast majority of transactions in Beijing are made via smartphone. Cash is still accepted everywhere (for now!) with most ATMs accepting foreign cards and most large banks changing money.

Bank of China (中国银行; Zhōngguó Yínháng; Map p78; ☑ 010 6513 2214; 19 Dong'anmen Dajie, 东安门大街19号; ⊙8.30am-5.30pm) Just one of dozens of branches in Beijing with money-changing facilities.

HSBC (汇丰银行, Huìfēng Yínháng; Map p96; www.hsbc.com.cn; 1st fl, COFCO Plaza, 8 Jianguomennei Dajie, 建国门内大街8号北京中粮广场; ⊙9am-5pm Mon-Fri, 10am-6pm Sat) One of around eight branches in the capital, not including several stand-alone ATMs.

SCAMS

Teahouse invitations Refuse invitations to teahouses from sweet-talking girls around Tian'anmen Sq or Wangfujing Dajie – it's an expensive scam.

Taxis A common scam is where drivers claim your ¥100 note is fake, and hand it back. In fact, they've switched it. Some unlucky visitors have had their entire wallets emptied this way. If you suspect this has happened, photograph or take down the licence plate of the taxi and the details of the driver, which should be displayed over the front passenger seat.

Rickshaws Some of the riders at the North Gate of the Forbidden City are particularly unscrupulous. The cheap trip offered might end up costing you more.

SMOKING

While venues in Beijing are much more rigorous about enforcing the no-smoking law than in other parts of China, you might still encounter smokers in bars and local restaurants. A word to the staff can usually resolve the situation.

TICKETS & QUOTAS

Several major tourist sites, including the Forbidden City and sections of the Great Wall, have imposed daily quotas on visitor numbers. These sights and others have also begun experimenting with online-only ticket sales, so check with your hotel before heading out.

TOURIST INFORMATION

You'll find official Tourist Information Centres at **Capital Airport** (北京旅游咨询, Běijīng Lǚyóu Zīxún; ☑ 010 6459 8148; Terminal 3, Beijing Capital International Airport, 北京首都机场) and **Beijing Railway Station** (北京旅游咨询, Běijīng Lǚyóu Zīxún; Map p78; ☑ 010 6528 4848; 16 Laoqianju Hutong, 老钱局胡同16号; ⊙8.30am-6pm; S Line 2 to Beijing Railway Station, exit B), as well as major tourist sights and areas like **Houhai Lake** (北京旅游咨询, Běijīng Lǚyóu

BEIJING WITH CHILDREN

Historic Beihai Park (p85) has a large boating lake. The lakes at Houhai (p87) also provide pedal-boat action, and come winter they freeze over and become central Beijing's biggest playground. Rent ice skates, ice bikes and even ice bumper cars. Buy a handmade kite at Three Stone Kite Shop (p125) and head to one of the parks to join Beijing's legion of kite-flying enthusiasts. Teens will relish the adventure of visiting the Great Wall, especially at Mutianyu (p136) with its toboggan ride. Electric bicycle tours (p105) can also be great fun. Guided tours will help bring Beijing's major sights to life. The Beijing Ghost Tour, by Newman Tours (p103), is a hit with older kids.

Zīxún; Map p82; ☏ 010 6403 2726; 49 Di'anmen Xidajie, 地安门西大街49号; ⊙ 9am-5pm; Ⓢ Line 8 to Shichahai, exit B1). Most have free maps of Beijing. For an excellent map of the Drum Tower neighbourhood, the Orchid Hotel (p112) makes its own and are happy to give them to non-guests.

USEFUL WEBSITES

Time Out Beijing (www.timeoutbeijing. com) Comprehensive dining, art and nightlife coverage.

Beijinger (www.thebeijinger.com) Eating and entertainment listings, blog posts and forums.

Air Pollution (http://aqicn.org/city/beijing) Real-time Air Quality Index (AQI) for Beijing.

China History Podcast (https://www.teacup. media) The Ming and Qing dynasty podcasts are particularly useful for Beijing (episodes 31–41).

Lonely Planet (www.lonelyplanet.com/china/ beijing) Destination information, hotel bookings, traveller forum and more.

ⓘ Getting There & Away

AIR

Most international travellers will fly into Beijing. Average flight times include London 10 hours, New York 14 hours and Sydney 12 hours. Beijing's has two international airports: Beijing Capital International Airport (p1033) (PEK) and Beijing Daxing International Airport (p1033) (PKX). Beijing also has domestic flights to all major cities in China.

BUS

With the availability of cheap, high-speed rail travel all over the country, there's little need for travellers to use buses to move between cities, which

are far slower, less comfortable and more prone to accidents. The exception might be to nearby destinations such as Chengde and Datong, which are slightly faster to reach by bus than by train (though that will surely change in the future).

Useful Long-Distance Bus Routes

Sihui Long-Distance Bus Station (四惠长途汽 车站, Sìhuì Chángtú Qìchēzhàn; 68 Jianguo Lu, 建国路68号; Ⓢ Line 1 to Sihui, exit A)

Chengde 承德; ¥85, three hours, frequent (7.10am to 7.10pm)

Liuliqiao Long-Distance Bus Station (六里 桥长途站, Liùlǐqiáo Chángtúzhàn; ☏ 010 8383 1716; 201 Yuntong Xian, 运通201线; Ⓢ Line 9, 10 to Liuliqiao, exit C)

Datong 大同; ¥145, four hours, regular (7.10am to 6pm)

Shijiazhuang 石家庄; ¥100, three hours, frequent (8.20am to 3.40pm)

TRAIN

Most journeys between Beijing and other major cities use G-category bullet trains that zoom along at over 300kmh. Beijing has three major train stations for long-distance travel: Beijing, Beijing West and Beijing South. Beijing North was under renovation at time of research; it's set to re-open in 2020 with a new high-speed link out west to Zhangjiakou for the Winter Olympics in 2022.

There are international train routes to and from Mongolia, North Korea, Russia and Vietnam, which use slower trains, as well as trains to and from Hong Kong and Lhasa in Tibet.

Beijing Railway Station

The oldest and most central of Beijing's four main train stations, **Beijing Railway Station** (北 京站, Běijīng Zhàn; ☏ 010 5101 9999; 13 Maojji-awan Hutong, 毛家湾胡同甲13号; Ⓢ Line 2 to Beijing train station, exit C) serves high-speed services to northeast China, regular services to northeast, east and south China, and international trains to Russia, Mongolia, North Korea and Vietnam. Beijing Railway Station has its own subway stop on Line 2.

Useful destinations, train classes and fares include the following:

Dalian 大连; D-series, 2nd class ¥261, six hours (four per day)

Datong 大同; K-series, hard sleeper ¥101, six hours (12 per day)

Harbin 哈尔滨; D-series, soft seat ¥306 to ¥313, 7½ to 10 hours (four per day)

Jilin 吉林; D-series, 2nd class ¥285, nine hours (two per day)

Shanghai 上海; T-series, deluxe sleeper ¥919, hard sleeper ¥325, 14 hours (8.05pm)

Shanhaiguan 山海关; D-series, 2nd class ¥92, 2½ to three hours (11 per day)

Beijing West Railway Station

The gargantuan **Beijing West Railway Station** (北京西站; Běijīng Xī Zhàn; ☏ 010 5182 6253; 118 Lianhuachi Donglu, 莲花池东路118号; Ⓢ Line 9, 7 to Beijing West Railway Station) accommodates all trains heading west, southwest and northwest, as well as high-speed trains to Hong Kong, Guangzhou and other major destinations. The station has its own subway stop served by Line 7 and Line 9.

Changsha 长沙; G-series, 2nd class ¥649, 5½ to seven hours (15 per day)

Chengdu 成都; G-series, 2nd class ¥778, eight to 10 hours (four per day)

Chongqing 重庆; G-series, 2nd class ¥924, 11 hours (9.22am)

Guangzhou 广州; G and D-series, 2nd class ¥862, nine hours (10 per day)

Guilin 桂林; G-series, 2nd class ¥804, nine hours (8.34am, 9.05am)

Guiyang 贵阳; G-series, 2nd class ¥963, nine hours (five per day)

Hong Kong 香港; G-series, 2nd class ¥1077, nine hours (10am)

Kunming 昆明; G-series, 2nd class ¥1147, 11 hours (three per day)

Lanzhou 兰州; G-series, 2nd class ¥690, seven to nine hours (6.27am, 10.45am)

Lhasa (Tibet) 拉萨; Z-series, soft sleeper ¥1186, hard sleeper ¥763, 41 hours (8pm)

Nanchang 南昌; G-series, 2nd class ¥627, 6½ to eight hours (three per day)

Pingyao 平遥; G and D-series, 2nd class ¥225, four hours (four per day)

Shenzhen 深圳; D-series, 2nd class ¥756, 11 hours (four per day)

Urumqi 乌鲁木齐; Z-series, hard sleeper ¥575, 31 hours (10am)

Wuhan 武汉; G-series, 2nd class ¥520, four to six hours (20+ per day)

Xi'an 西安; G-series, 2nd class ¥515, 4½ to six hours (19 per day)

Xining 西宁; T-series, hard sleeper ¥377, 22 hours (1.05pm)

For Lhasa (拉萨; Lāsà) in Tibet (西藏; Xīzàng), the Z21 (hard seat/hard sleeper/soft sleeper ¥360/763/1186, 41 hours) leaves Beijing West Railway Station at 8pm, taking just under two days. In the return direction, the Z22 departs Lhasa at 3.50pm and arrives at Beijing West Railway Station at 8.28am.

Beijing South Railway Station

The ultramodern **Beijing South Railway Station** (北京南站; Běijīng Nánzhàn; 12 Chezhan Lu, Yongwai Dajie, 永外大街车站路12号; Ⓢ Line 4, 14 to Beijing South Railway Station), linked to the subway system on Line 4, operates high-speed

trains to destinations such as Shanghai, Tianjin, Hangzhou, Nanjing Qingdao and Harbin.

Fuzhou 福州; G-series, 2nd class ¥719, nine hours (five per day)

Hangzhou 杭州; G-series, 2nd-class ¥538, six hours (13 per day)

Huangshan 黄山; G-series, 2nd-class ¥548, six hours (10 per day)

Jinan 济南; G-series, 2nd-class ¥184, 1¾ hours (20+ per day)

Nanjing 南京; G-series, 2nd-class ¥443, four hours (20+ per day)

Qingdao 青岛; G-series, 2nd-class ¥314, five hours (16 per day)

Qufu 曲阜; G-series, 2nd-class ¥244, 2½ hours (16 per day)

Shanghai 上海虹桥; G-series, 2nd-class ¥553, 5½ hours (20+ per day)

Suzhou 苏州; G-series, 2nd-class ¥523, five hours (20 per day)

Tai'an 泰安; G-series, 2nd-class seat ¥214, two hours (18 per day)

Tianjin 天津; C-series, 1st/2nd-class ¥54/93, 30 minutes (frequent)

Beijing North Railway Station

Beijing North Railway Station (北京北站, Běijīng Běizhàn; ☏ 010 5186 6223; Xizhimen Beidajie, 西直门北大街; Ⓢ Lines 2, 4, 13 to Xizhimen, exit A1) was being renovated at time of research, and was due to reopen in 2020 as the terminus of the new high-speed Beijing–Zhangjiakou intercity railway being built for the 2022 Winter Olympic Games. It will also have a high-speed connection to Badaling Great Wall.

ⓘ Getting Around

TO/FROM BEIJING CAPITAL INTERNATIONAL AIRPORT

Closer to the city than Daxing, Beijing Capital (PEK, 北京首都国际机场; Běijīng Shǒudū Guójì Jīchǎng) is served by the **Airport Express** (机场快轨, Jīchǎng Kuàiguǐ; Map p96; 39 Dongzhi-

BEIJING GETTING AROUND

ⓘ TRAVEL CARD

Beijing's travel card (一卡通, yīkǎtōng; deposit ¥20) is an essential purchase – get one at any subway station or large bus station, and add as much cash as you think you'll need. It makes subway travel more convenient and gives you 50% off all bus rides, including those out to the Great Wall. You can recharge them at most (but not all) subway stations and bus-station ticket kiosks.

menwai Dajie, 东直门外大街39号; one way ¥25; Ⓢ Lines 2, 13 to Dongzhimen, exit B), which links terminals 2 and 3 to Beijing's subway system at Sanyuanqiao station (Line 10), Dongzhimen (Lines 2 and 13) and Beixinqiao (Line 5, due to open 2020). Trains operate from around 6am to 10.30pm. The Beijing subway runs until around 11pm.

The **airport shuttle bus** (机场巴士, Jīchǎng Bāshì; Beijing Capital International Airport, 北京首都机场; one way ¥20-30) has 16 routes into Beijing, the most useful for travellers being Line 7 that stops at Tian'anmen Sq and Line 13 that stops at Wangfujing. The buses run from 5am to midnight.

A taxi should cost ¥90 to ¥140 from the airport to the city centre including a ¥10 airport expressway toll. Bank on it taking 40 minutes to one hour to the centre of town. Ignore unofficial drivers who may approach you as you come out of arrivals. Have the name of your hotel written down in Chinese to show the driver, as very few speak English.

TO/FROM BEIJING DAXING INTERNATIONAL AIRPORT

Beijing's newest mega-airport, Daxing (PKX, 北京大兴国际机场; Běijīng Dàxīng Guójì Jīchǎng) opened in late 2019, with four runways and the world's second-largest terminal building.The **Daxing Airport Express** (¥35, 20 minutes) connects the airport with Caoqiao subway station (Line 10). Trains run from 6am to 10.30pm. From Caoqiao it's a further 50 minutes into the centre of town.

The **Beijing–Xiong'an high speed rail** connects Daxing Airport with Beijing West Railway Station (¥25-90, 30 minutes).

A taxi into town from Daxing airport (around ¥200) should take at least an hour.

BICYCLE

Cycling is the most enjoyable way of getting around Beijing, especially in summer. The city is as flat as a pancake and almost every road has a bike lane, even if cars and pedestrians invade them. The quiet, tree-lined *hutong* (alleys) are particularly conducive to cycling. Check to see if your accommodation offers bicycles for hire.

Shared Bikes

Like other major cities in China, Beijing has thousands of shared bikes, but at time of research these were tricky for non-Chinese to use. At minimum you'll need a smartphone with local SIM and a payment system like WeChat. You'll need to download the relevant app (most are in Chinese only) and complete the registration process, which involves submitting photos of your passport.

Note that you're not permitted to take shared bikes to the Forbidden City or Tian'anmen Sq – police posted on approach roads will turn you around.

BUS

Beijing's buses (公共汽车, *gōnggòng qìchē*) are plentiful, cheap (from ¥2 per journey; half price with a travel card) and reasonably straightforward to use for non-Chinese speakers, given that you can swipe your travel card for rides, announcements are in English and bus-stop signs are written in pinyin as well as Chinese characters. The main problem is that bus-stop timetables are only in Chinese.

RICKSHAW

Rickshaws (三轮车, *sānlúnchē*) come in two varieties: the pedal-powered kind specifically for tours around Houhai Lakes and the surrounding *hutong*, and the gas or battery-powered kind that hang around major tourist sights and nightlife spots, looking for fares. The latter are more expensive than taxis and should be considered a last resort. Agree a price up front before getting in.

SUBWAY

The world's busiest, the second-largest (behind Shanghai) and growing year on year, Beijing's subway system has well over 650km of lines burrowing through the municipality. Exceedingly foreigner-friendly, all signs, announcements, maps and ticket machines are in English. It's cheap by world standards too, with distance-based fares costing between ¥3 and ¥8.

TAXI

Taxis (出租车, *chūzūchē*) are everywhere, but good luck hailing one during rush hour, in rainstorms and between 8pm and 10pm – prime time for the post-dinner homeward rush.

Flagfall is ¥13, and lasts for 3km. After that it's ¥2.3 per kilometre. Rates increase slightly after 11pm.

Even in the capital it's rare for drivers to speak any English, so always have the name and address of your destination written down in Chinese characters.

DiDi Ride-Sharing

DiDi Chuxing (滴滴出行), China's ride-sharing app equivalent to Uber, has an English interface, which means non-Chinese speakers can get cheap rides all over the city. Although the ability to use private cars is limited and complex for foreign visitors, you can use the app to hail regular taxis and pay in cash according to the meter at the end of your journey.

The Great Wall

Best Great Wall Views

→ Zhengbei Tower at Jiankou (p138)

→ Crouching Tiger Mountain at Gubeikou (p140)

→ Tower 8 at Badaling (p137)

→ Tower 10 at Simatai (p143)

→ Nine-Eyed Tower at Jiankou (p138)

Best Places to Stay

→ Brickyard Retreat (p137)

→ Great Wall Box House (p142)

→ Guanlangu Hostel (p139)

→ Zaoxiang Yard (p140)

→ Commune by the Great Wall (p137)

Why Go?

Coiling its way through 23 degrees of longitude, the Great Wall (长城, Chángchéng) stands as an awe-inspiring monument to the grandeur of China's ancient history. With sections dating back 2000 years, the wall (or, more accurately, walls, because they belong to several different eras) wriggle haphazardly from their scattered Manchurian remains in Liaoning province to wind-scoured rubble in the Gobi desert and faint traces in the unforgiving sands of Xinjiang. Interspersed with natural defences (such as precipitous mountains), the Great Wall can be visited in 15 Chinese provinces, principalities and autonomous regions, but nowhere is better than Beijing for mounting your assault on this most iconic of bastions.

When to Go

Spring and autumn are the best times to hike unrestored Great Wall, although after summer the vegetation on the battlements in some areas can be too dense to pass.

Winters on the Wall are bracingly cold but refreshingly light on visitors.

Check the weather conditions carefully before embarking on a wild Great Wall hike.

The Great Wall

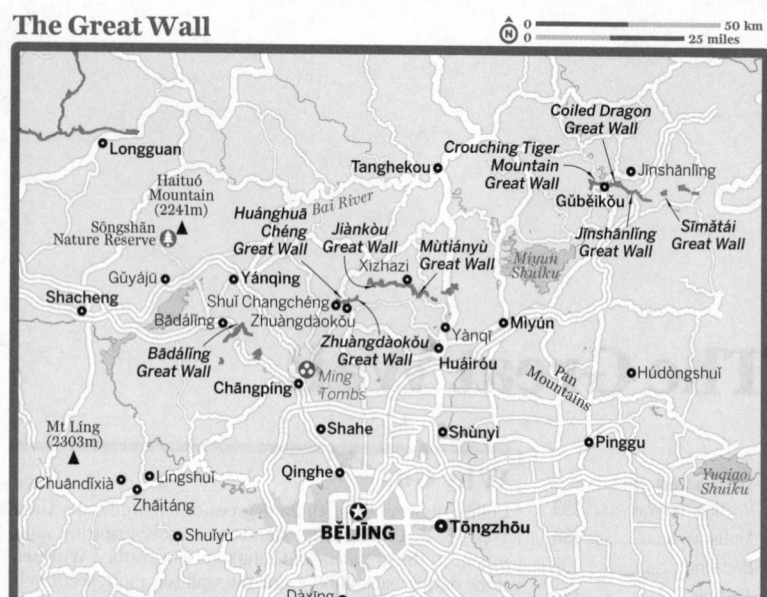

History

Official Chinese history likes to stress the unity of the Great Wall through the ages. In fact, there have been several disparate eras of Great Wall building throughout China's history. Work on the 'original' was begun during the Qin dynasty (221–207 BC), when China was unified for the first time under Emperor Qin Shi Huang. Hundreds of thousands of workers, many of them political prisoners, laboured for years to construct it.

After the fall of the Qin dynasty, work on the Wall continued during the Han dynasty (206 BC–AD 220). Little more was done until almost 1000 years later, during the Jin dynasty (1115–1234), when the impending threat of Genghis Khan spurred further construction.

The Wall's final and greatest incarnation, and the one most visitors see today, came during the Ming dynasty (1368–1644). The Ming built or rebuilt atop older stretches of wall to form an undulating, overlapping defensive barrier stretching from ocean to desert, shielding the northern reaches of their vast territory from the 'barbarians'– the Mongols, Manchu and other pastoral people. The absolute length, including every branch, tributary and intervening natural feature, of the Ming Great Wall has been put at about 8850km.

As a system of border defence, the Wall was garrisoned with troops (almost a million during the Ming Dynasty, or about 110 per kilometre) who resided in the watchtowers and could move rapidly between them to counter an invasion. As well as being a kind of elevated highway for transporting troops, horses and equipment, its beacon-tower system, using smoke signals generated by burning wolves' dung, quickly transmitted news of enemy movements back to the capital.

After the ascension of the Qing dynasty in 1644, there was less need for the new Manchu rulers to maintain a border defence that looked in part upon their own territories to the north. Although the Qing had some use for the Ming walls, and added a few of their own, the greatest era of wall building in the history of humankind had come to an end, and the battlements were eventually abandoned, their unprotected bricks and stone at the mercy of scavengers.

Ruin & Restoration

The Wall's decline accelerated during the war with Japan and then the civil war that preceded the founding of the new China in 1949. Compounding the problem was the fact that the communists didn't initially have much interest in the Wall. In fact, Mao Zedong encouraged people living near it to use it as a source of free building materials. It wasn't until 1984 that Mao's successor Deng Xiaoping ordered that the Wall be placed under government protection.

Classic postcard images of the Wall – clad flawlessly in bricks and coiling over distant peaks – do not accurately reflect the truth of the bastion today. The reality is that vast tracts of wall have been lost to the ravages of time and civilisation, and what remains exists in a state of precarious disrepair. For logistical reasons, the Great Wall was fashioned, chameleon-like, from whatever materials were to hand. Along China's arid northern plains this equated mostly to tamped earth. The strategically critical upland sections around Beijing, amounting to around 600km of the Ming Great Wall, were far sturdier, built from local granite and bricks, lined with watchtowers and often following the high ridgelines of mountains.

Restoration, beginning in the 1950s with Badaling, has tended to prioritise the wholesale rebuilding of short sections in order that they can be opened as tourist attractions. Basic repairs at various 'wild' tourist hotspots such as Jiankou have been ongoing for years, and typically involve stabilising the loose rubble with cement. At time of research, a new and welcome school of thought with regards to restoration was just starting to emerge – one that prioritises preserving and reinforcing the Wall in its present and picturesque state of ruin rather than attempting a less-than-authentic rebuild.

Visiting the Wall

Most first-time visitors head to the famous restored sections of Great Wall such as Badaling and Mutianyu. Those bitten by the Great Wall bug then graduate to more 'wild' hikes along ruined battlements at the likes of Jiankou, Gubeikou and Huanghua Cheng, potentially staying overnight for sunrise hikes. While most of these places can be visited by public transport, hiring a car and driver speeds things up considerably.

Tours run by hostels, or by specialist tour companies, are far preferable to those run by ordinary hotels or general Chinese travel companies, who often package pesky 'extras' like side trips to silk factories. The following reputable companies and associations run highly regarded trips to the Wall:

Beijing Hikers (p141) Varied and professionally run group hikes scheduled online two to three months in advance, and graded for difficulty.

China Hiking (☑ 156 5220 0950) Affordable hiking and camping trips run by a Chinese-Belgian couple.

Great Wall Hiking (www.greatwallhiking.com) Locally run hiking trips to various sections of Great Wall.

Wild Wall Experiences (p139) Expert-led dawn hikes and Great Wall field lectures at Jiankou – a must for Wall enthusiasts.

Bespoke Travel Co (p105) Drivers and guides for tailored Great Wall excursions.

Where to Visit the Wall

Here are just some of the many destinations where visitors can encounter the Great Wall of China, listed from east to west:

Shanhaiguan, Hebei
➡ Old Dragon Head (p166)
➡ First Pass Under Heaven (p166)
➡ Jiao Shan Great Wall (p164)
➡ Jiumenkou Great Wall (p166)

Tianjin
➡ Huangyaguan Great Wall (p147)

Beijing
➡ Simatai (p143)
➡ Jinshanling (p142)
➡ Gubeikou (p140)
➡ Mutianyu (p136)
➡ Jiankou (p138)
➡ Huanghua Cheng (p139)
➡ Badaling (p137)

Shanxi
➡ Zhenghongbao Canyon Great Wall (p393)
➡ Déshèngbǎo (p393)

Shaanxi
➡ Yulin Beacon Tower (p428)

Gansu
➡ Overhanging Great Wall (p876)
➡ Changchengxiang Great Wall (p872)
➡ First Beacon Platform of the Great Wall (p876)
➡ Jiayuguan Fort (p875)
➡ Jade Gate Pass (p883)

🛏 Sleeping & Eating

Although the vast majority of visitors do the Great Wall as a day trip, you'll find places to stay at pretty much every visitable part of Great Wall within range of Beijing, touristy or unrestored. Staying overnight allows you to see both sunrise and sunset from the

1. Mutianyu Great Wall (p136)

Mutianyu is the perfect introduction to the Great Wall, and, with features such as a toboggan ride down from the wall, is great for families.

2. Jinshanling Great Wall (p142)

One of the more remote sections of the Great Wall near Beijing, Jinshanling has some unusual features.

3. Gubeikou to Jinshanling (p141)

You can hike to Jinshanling from another section of the wall at Gubeikou. It will take about 6½ hours.

BJDLZX/GETTY IMAGES ©

LIANG ZHANG/500PX ©

GREAT WALL FACTS

Easternmost point of Ming Great Wall Dadong, Liaoning province, on the North Korean border

Westernmost point of Ming Great Wall Jiayuguan Fortress, Gansu province

Oldest surviving section State of Zhao Great Wall, Inner Mongolia (approx 300 BC)

Number of troops protecting the Ming Dynasty Great Wall 970,000

battlements and increases point-to-point hiking options considerably. Remember that many places close from November to March.

You can find official campsites close to the Great Wall at several sections, including Jinshanling and Huanghua Cheng 'Lakeside' Great Wall. Camping on the Wall itself is, strictly speaking, forbidden, but people do it. There are plenty of places to buy camping equipment in Beijing, including several discount Decathlon superstores.

The best advice for any Great Wall excursion is to take your own food and water with you. Ticketed Great Wall sections offer a basic spread of Chinese and western fast-food outlets, while at unrestored spots such as Jiankou you can often find farmer-style courtyards (农家院, *nóngjiāyuàn*) to eat at.

ⓘ Getting There & Away

You can access the Great Wall outside Beijing by road or rail. Official tourist buses connect directly with the ticketed sections at Badaling, Jinshanling and Simatai, while for Mutianyu there's the private **Mu Bus** (Map p82; www.beijingmubus.com; return trip ¥80) service.

At time of research, trains to Badaling and Gubeikou departed from the tiny **Huangtudian Train Station** (黄土店站, Huángtǔdiàn Zhàn; Huilongguan Zhen, 回龙观镇; Ⓢ Line 8, 13 to Huoying, exit G4) in northwest Beijing, but these services will likely revert to Beijing North Railway Station when it reopens in 2020 after extensive renovations.

Arranging a car and driver is generally the best way to visit unrestored sections like Jiankou and Huanghua Cheng.

The following car services offer tours from Beijing:

Miles Meng Car Service (www.beijingenglish driver.com; 137 1786 1403) Reliable, English-speaking driver service with a variety of decent

vehicles. Check the website for pricing by destination.

Bruce Beijing (www.beijingairportlayovertour.com/tours.html) Well-regarded local driver and guide for trips to the Great Wall and other jaunts.

Mr Sun (孙先生, Sūn Xiānsheng; 136 5109 3753) Only speaks Chinese but is reliable and can find other drivers if he's busy. Return trips to the Wall from ¥650.

Bespoke Travel Co (p105) Drivers and guides for tailor-made Great Wall excursions.

Mutianyu 慕田峪

Location 70km from Beijing

Price adult ¥45

Hours 7.30am to 6.30pm 16 March to 15 November, 8am to 5pm 16 November to 15 March

For the Great Wall newbie, Mutianyu (Mùtiányù) is the perfect introduction. Famed for its tightly woven chain of watchtowers and excellent views, it's easy to reach from the city, less crowded than Badaling, and is well set up for families, with a cable car, a chairlift and a toboggan ride. That said, with its gargantuan ticket hall, restaurant strip and irksome shuttle-bus system, Mutianyu is far from a 'wild' hike, and will only serve to whet the appetite of many to seek out more remote and rambling Great Wall adventures.

From the monolithic ticket office at Mutianyu, shuttle buses (¥15 return) ply the 3km up to the start of the **cable car** (缆车; Lǎn Chē; one way/return ¥100/120, kids ¥50/60), where there are also three or four stepped pathways leading up to the wall itself, plus a **chairlift** (索道, Suǒdào; 1-way ¥100, with toboggan ¥120), called a 'ropeway' on the signs here, and a **toboggan ride** (滑道, Huá Dào; 1-way ¥100, with chairlift ¥120), making Mutianyu ideal for those who can't manage too many steps, or have kids in tow.

🛏 Sleeping & Eating

There are some village guesthouses about 500m downhill from the Mutianyu entrance. All have English signage. Expect to pay anything from ¥200 to ¥400 for an en suite room.

Between the ticket office and the shuttle buses is a gauntlet of ever-expanding eateries and snack stalls, mainly of the fast-food variety – both Chinese and international. It might be preferable to grab a bite at one of the eateries closer to the Wall (after the shuttle bus); at any rate, the views are better.

★ **Brickyard Retreat** GUESTHOUSE ¥¥¥
(瓦厂, Wǎ Chǎng; ☑010 6162 6506; www.brickyard
atmutianyu.com; Beigou Village, Huairou District, 怀
柔区渤海镇北沟村; r incl breakfast ¥1570-5350;
❄☎) ◢ A 1960s glazed-tile factory renovated into an idyllic garden resort, Brickyard
has 25 stylish rooms with soaring skylight
views of the Great Wall. Rates include use
of a spa, and shuttle services to the Wall and
surrounding villages. Brickyard is in Beigou
village (北沟村, Běigōu Cūn), about 2km from
the Mutianyu Great Wall. Booking required.

ⓘ Getting There & Away

BUS

Mutianyu is fiddly to reach by public transport.
From Dongzhimen Transport Hub (东直门枢纽站,
Dōngzhímén Shūniǔ Zhàn; 39 Dongzhimenwai Dajie, 东直门外大街39号; Ⓢ Lines 2, 13 to Dongzhimen, exit B), you can take bus 916快 (快 is 'kuài',
or 'fast') to Huairou (¥12, 70 minutes, 6.30am to
7.30pm). Get off before the terminus, at Mingzhu
Guangchang (明珠广场) bus stop, or at either of
the next two stops at Qingchun Lu Beikou (青春路
北口) or Huairou Beidajie (怀柔北大街). You'll find
drivers waiting to take you the last 40 minutes up
to Mutianyu (¥60 to ¥80 one way). The last 916快
back to Beijing leaves Huairou at around 7pm.

The Mu Bus

Potentially a better bet than the public bus, this
private coach transfer aimed at foreigners has
an English-speaking guide on board for its two
daily departures from Dongsi Shitiao subway
station (Line 2) to Mutianyu Great Wall (7.40am
and noon, ¥80 return trip). Book online in advance at www.beijingmubus.com.

CAR & TAXI

The easiest and fastest way to get to Mutianyu
Great Wall. Expect to pay around ¥600 to ¥700 for
a return trip, with the price negotiated up front.

Badaling 八达岭

Location 70km from Beijing

Price ¥40 April to October, ¥35 November
to March

Hours summer 6.30am to 7pm, winter
7.30am to 6pm

Badaling (八达岭长城, Bādálíng Chángchéng;
Apr-Oct ¥40, Nov-Mar ¥35; ⊙6am-7pm Apr-Oct,
7am-6pm Nov-Mar; ☑877, ☒S2 from Huangtudian
Station), a strategic pass through a gorge in
the Jundu Mountains, is the easiest major
section of Great Wall to get to from Beijing,
and the busiest by far. Following Mao's proclamation that 'he who has not climbed the

Great Wall is not a true man', the crumbling
battlements at Badaling were rebuilt – the
first section to be restored – and it opened to
the masses in 1957.

Revitalised as a patriotic exemplar of the
PRC, the Badaling Great Wall is where Nixon,
Gorbachev, Thatcher and other heads of state
did their China diplomacy acts. Despite the
rampant crowds and commercialisation (it
feels like a tacky ski resort), Badaling remains
accessible, highly photogenic, authentically
steep and well equipped with tourist facilities
(restaurants, disabled access, cable cars etc). It
can be visited on a half-day trip from Beijing.

There are two ways to climb the Wall from
the ticket office; most visitors go north. An
hour's brisk uphill walk – or 10 minutes on
the **cable car** (缆车, Lǎn Chē; one way/return
¥100/140; ⊙8am-4.30pm) – will take you to
Watchtower 8 (北八楼, Běi Bā Lóu), Badaling's
highest point (1015m) marked with a stone
stele bearing Mao's macho Great Wall epithet.
The full Badaling 'loop' is just under 4km. You
can take the **toboggan ride** (¥80/100 one
way/return) down from Watchtower 4.

The south side is gentler and sees fewer visitors. A **cableway** (⊙one way/return ¥100/140)
funicular train climbs to a scenic viewpoint.

China Great Wall Museum MUSEUM
(中国长城博物馆, Zhōngguó Chángchéng Bówùguǎn; Badaling Great Wall, 八达岭长城; ⊙9am-4pm
Tue-Sun; ☑877) FREE This sizeable museum
blusters through a history of the Wall, from its
origins as an earthen embankment in the far-
off Qin dynasty (221–207 BC) to the Ming-era
battlements you see today. There are decent
English captions, and enthusiasts will appreciate the sections on warfare.

🛏 Sleeping & Eating

There are one or two lacklustre hotels in the
immediate vicinity, but with central Beijing
just over an hour away by bus (and soon to
be 20 minutes by high-speed train), there's
little reason to overnight.

You'll find a wide if uninspired choice
of fast food (KFC, Chinese noodle chains),
countless snack vendors and even a Starbucks along the main drags leading up to
the east and west entrances of the Wall.

Commune by the Great Wall DESIGN HOTEL ¥¥¥
(长城脚下的公社, Chángchéng Jiǎoxià de Gōngshè; ☑010 8118 1888; www.communebythegreat
wall.com; r from ¥1500; ❄@☎❄) Beside
the Shuǐguān Great Wall off the Badaling
Hwy, the Commune was heralded as an

architectural marvel when it opened in the early noughties. These days the dozen modernist villas, each designed by a different architect, are showing their age, and service standards have slipped since Kempinski hotel group parted ways with the project.

ⓘ Information

Ticket sales for Badaling are now online only, but until the official website (http://ticket. badaling.cn) can cater to foreigners, you can still purchase tickets on arrival. Be aware, though, of the daily visitor cap of 65,000 people. In high season, you might want to ask your hotel to help you pre-book (up to seven days in advance).

ⓘ Getting There & Away

BUS

The 877 leaves for Badaling (¥12, one to 1½ hours, 6am to 5pm) from the northern side of the Deshengmen Arrow Tower (Ⓢ Line 2 to Jishuitan, exit A). The last departure from Deshengmen is 12.30pm. Between November and March, the last bus back from Badaling is 4.30pm; it's 5pm at all other times.

CAR & TAXI

Expect to pay around ¥500 to ¥700 for a return trip, with the price agreed in advance.

TRAIN

The Badaling train used to depart from Beijing North Railway Station until the station closed for its Winter Olympics upgrade. It's slated to reopen

in 2020 as the terminus of the new high-speed Beijing–Zhangjiakou line. Badaling will get a brand new station, built 102m below ground (making it the 'deepest' high-speed station in the world), with the journey expected to take just 20 minutes.

Jiankou 箭扣

Location 100km from Beijing

Price free

Hours no official opening hours

One of the most photogenic and thrilling stretches of 'wild' Great Wall, Jiankou (Jiànkòu) rides the ridgelines like a brick roller coaster. White-knuckle sections like 'Upward Flying Eagle' and 'Heavenly Ladder' will make you marvel at just how they built the thing in the first place. Jiankou means 'arrow notch', named for a low pass along the ridge, and surely at least a passing reference to the weapon that proved so effective in the hands of the Mongols – the reason for the Ming Great Wall in the first place.

Accessible from Xizhazi village (西栅子村, Xīzhàzi Cūn) via the town of Huairou, and connected to Mutianyu Great Wall, you'll need a car and driver to get here, and someone to guide you up onto the wall. Be aware, too, of the dangers. The battlements are unstable, weather is changeable and you're a long way from help should you run into difficulties.

You can access the Wall from a number of points along the valley that twists around Xizhazhi village. Most visitors hike up through woodland paths to **Zhengbei Tower** (正北楼, Zhèngběi Lóu), the best lookout in the area. The Wall is too steep and dangerous to hike west from here, but the views are mind-blowing. Going the other way, you'll get to Mutianyu Great Wall in about two hours (mostly downhill), passing the **Ox Horn** (牛角边, Niú Jiǎo Biān; 90 minutes' walk to Mutianyu), which performs a sweeping, 180-degree U-turn on the hillside.

Another popular hike is to get on the wall further west, skipping the more dangerous sections like **Upward Flying Eagle** (鹰飞倒仰, Ying Fei Dao Yang). Hikers mount the wall near a section called the **Beijing Knot** (北京结, Běijīng Jié) where the Wall splits in two directions. From here you can hike northwards (with some hairy bits to circumvent along the way) to the **Nine-Eyed Tower** (九眼楼, Jiǔ Yǎn Lóu; 2½ hours), a scenic lookout so named for the nine windows in the watchtower, which offers sweeping views of Jiankou on a clear day.

JUST HOW GREAT IS IT?

The Chinese call the Great Wall the '10,000 Lǐ Wall' (万里长城, Wànlǐ Chángchéng). With one 'Lǐ' equivalent to around 500m, this would make the Wall around 5000km long; in fact, the character 万 (wàn), meaning 10,000, was often used to broadly indicate 'an awful lot'. The maths wasn't too far out, though. A 2009 report by China's State Administration for Cultural Heritage estimated the non-continuous length of the Ming dynasty Wall at 8851km. But the Ming dynasty was just one (albeit the most significant) of 13 dynasties to have contributed to the Wall over the course of history. A 2012 Chinese government survey calculated the total length of all fragments of the Great Wall that have ever stood, including sections that run parallel with others, and sections that have weathered away to nothing, to be 21,196km.

★ **Wild Wall Experiences**   HIKING
(www.wildwall.com; Jiankou Great Wall, 箭扣长城; per person US$625; ☺Mar-Jun) British 'wall nut' William Lindsay OBE and family have been running 'Wild Wall Weekends' from their Jiankou home for years. The tour includes city transfers, two nights' full board at 'The Barracks' (the remote and rustic countryside courtyard home of the Lindsays), and two or three guided Great Wall hikes at Jiankou that feature field lectures en route, covering military strategy, construction, architectural features and more.

Author of five books on the Great Wall, William Lindsay trekked some 2500km of the Ming Great Wall in the 1980s, the start of a decades-long obsession with the Wall.

🛏 Sleeping & Eating

Xizhazi village has several farmer-style courtyards (农家院, *nóngjiāyuàn*), some authentically traditional with heated 'kang' beds, musty blankets and framed portraits of Mao on the wall. Jiankou is a popular destination for hikers, so consider booking ahead at weekends in high season. Expect to pay ¥120 and up for a room with a bathroom. You can also tour the best of the Wall here with a stay at Wild Wall Experiences.

All the farmer-style courtyards offer hearty country cooking as well as rooms. You won't get an English menu, but you might get pictures.

Zhaoshi Shanju Farm House   GUESTHOUSE ¥
(赵氏山居, Zhàoshì Shānjū; ☎135 2054 9638, 010 6161 1762; Xizhazi village, Jiankou Great Wall, 箭扣长城西栅子村; r from ¥240; ※🛜) The last property in the valley (in Hamlet No 5 of Xizhazi village), this is a favourite for Chinese hikers. There is a large shaded terrace dining area with fine Great Wall views. Rooms are neat and clean, and sleep two to seven people on traditional 'kang'-style beds. Most have attached bathrooms. Accepts online bookings at www.trip.com.

Yáng Èr   GUESTHOUSE ¥
(杨二; ☎010 6161 1794, 136 9307 0117; Xizhazi village, Jiankou Great Wall, 箭扣长城西栅子村; r ¥200; ※🛜) This is one of the first *nóngjiāyuàn* (农家院, village guesthouses) you come to as you enter Hamlet No 1 of Xizhazi village. Simple rooms with private bathrooms are set around a vegetable-patch courtyard. Country cooking available (mains from ¥40). No English.

JIANKOU TOP TIPS

➡ Stay overnight in a Xizhazi village guesthouse to get an early start for your wall hiking.

➡ Check www.greatwallforum.com for GPS points, route maps and other tips if you plan on going without a guide.

Guanlangu Hostel   HOSTEL ¥¥
(☎010 6068 0116; Xizhazi village, Jiankou Great Wall, 箭扣长城西栅子村; r from ¥700) The poshest option at Jiankou, with comfortable, modern rooms that sleep up to five on long 'kang'-style beds. Can book via www.trip.com.

❶ Access Issues

At the time of research, access from Jiankou to Mutianyu had been blocked at Watchtower 20 of the Mutianyu section with a 2m-high wall. However, it was still possible to walk around the right side of the tower and rejoin the Great Wall past the obstruction.

The wall at Jiankou is officially closed when high-level government meetings take place at Beijing's APEC venue beside nearby Yanqi Lake, or during periods of heavy rain.

State media reported in 2019 that the Jiankou Great Wall had been earmarked for restoration.

❶ Getting There & Away

BUS

From Dongzhimen Transport Hub (p137), you can take bus 916快 (快 is 'kuài', or 'fast') to Huairou (¥13, 1½ hours, 6.30am to 7.30pm). Get off before the terminus, at Mingzhu Guangchang (明珠广场) bus stop, or either of the next two stops (Qingchun Lu Beikou 青春路北口 or Huairou Beidajie 怀柔北大街). You'll find drivers waiting for hikers, who will take you to Xizhazi village (西栅子村, Xīzhàzi Cūn) for about ¥150 one way (one hour).

CAR & TAXI

It costs around ¥700 to ¥900 for a return day trip from Beijing.

Huanghua Cheng   黄花城

Location 77km from Beijing

Price ¥45 (for 'Lakeside Great Wall')

Hours 8.30am to 5pm

The Great Wall plunges into two reservoirs in and around the village of Huanghua Cheng (Huánghuā Chéng). Most local tourists come for the 'Lakeside Great Wall', a sculpted section of restored battlements, pedal boats, 'cruises' and parkland.

The more rewarding unrestored Great Wall hiking, however, can be accessed at Huanghua Cheng village, 3km to the east of the 'Lakeside Great Wall', as well as at the village of Zhuangdaokou in between the two. Be aware that patrolling wardens in these parts are making the 'wild' Great Wall harder to access.

A handy access point for the unrestored Great Wall can be found behind the Tenglong Hotel, situated at the point where the Wall crosses the water at the southern tip of the Huanghuacheng Reservoir. You'll need to pay ¥10 to the boss of the restaurant to follow a path behind the hotel that climbs up up to a watchtower. The Great Wall here is steep, smooth and slippery, with stunning views from the top. Hiking west, you'll reach Zhuangdaokou village after 45 minutes; turn left off the Wall at its lowest point to access the village. You'll also need to pay a similar 'fee' in Zhuangdaokou – the trail to/from the Wall passes through private orchards.

Across the road from the Tenglong Hotel, there's a similar fiscal arrangement to climb the steep battlements above the reservoir, from where you can hike all the way to Jiankou in a couple of days.

🛏 Sleeping & Eating

Guesthouses in Huanghua Cheng and Zhuangdaokou charge from ¥150 for a room with a bathroom.

All guesthouses double as restaurants, many serving grilled rainbow trout (烤虹鳟鱼, *kǎo hóngzūn yú*).

Tenglong Hotel   GUESTHOUSE ¥
(滕龙饭店, Ténglóng Fàndiàn; ☎ 010 6165 1929; Ansi Lu, Huanghua Cheng Village, 黄花城安四路; r with bathroom ¥150; 🐾) One of a number of small guesthouses in Huanghua Cheng. Most are on the river side of the road, but this place, accessed via steps on your left just before the Wall, clings to the hill on the other side and offers fine views of the Wall. Rooms are basic but clean and sleep three to four people.

No English is spoken, but the restaurant, with terrace seating, has an English menu. Nonguests can access the Great Wall behind the hotel by paying a fee (¥10) to the owner.

Zaoxiang Yard   GUESTHOUSE ¥
(枣香庭院, Zǎoxiāng Tíngyuàn; ☎ 010 6165 2908, 135 2208 3605; 44 Zhuangdaokou Village; r from ¥150; 🐾) Modest but comfortable enough, this guesthouse is housed in a 70-year-old

courtyard building. Most of the rooms have private bathrooms, and the food is good (mains ¥30 to ¥80; English menu).

❶ Getting There & Away

BUS
From Dongzhimen Transport Hub (p137) take bus 916快 to Huairou (¥12, 80 minutes, 6.30am to 7.30pm). Get off at Nánhuáyuán Sānqū (南花园三区) bus stop, then walk straight ahead (crossing one road) until you get to the next bus stop, Nánhuáyuán Sìqū (南花园四区). From here take the H14 bound for Èr Dào Guān (二道关) and get off at Huanghua Cheng (¥8, one hour, until 6.30pm). It only runs about once an hour; taxi drivers hover by the bus stop offering a ride for around ¥120 one way. Returning from Huanghua Cheng, you can catch either the H14 or the H21, which passes the bus station in Huairou where the 916快 originates. The last 916快 from Huairou back to Beijing leaves at around 7pm.

CAR & TAXI
A car to Huanghua Cheng should cost between ¥700 and ¥900 return for a day trip from Beijing, negotiated in advance.

Gubeikou   古北口

Location 130km from Beijing

Price admission ¥45 through ticket (Great Wall and town), ¥20 town only

Once a vital, heavily guarded pass into Beijing from Northeast China, Gubeikou (Gŭběikǒu, meaning 'ancient north pass') offers a wealth of hiking options on unrestored stretches of the Great Wall, ranging from scenic day-long watchtower-hopping to more extreme, rubbly rambles.

The rapidly modernising settlement of Gubeikou, cleaved in two by the ridge that carries the Great Wall, contains a few old courtyard-style homes among the new builds – some, at Hexicun (河西村, literally 'West of River Village') have outhouses that look suspiciously like they were assembled with Great Wall bricks.

There are two main sections of Wall at Gubeikou, running east and west out of town. **Crouching Tiger Mountain** (卧虎山, Wò Hǔ Shān) rises up on the west side of the Chao River. You can hike along the wall for about 3km to 4km before turning back the way you came (there's no loop). The **Sister Towers** (姐妹楼, Jiěmèi Lóu) are two towers that sit unusually close together. There are some thrilling, steep sections, and fabulous views to the east.

HIKING THE GREAT WALL NEAR BEIJING

There are excellent hiking opportunities for would-be adventurers within range of Beijing, although at the time of research wardens posted at popular points were making it increasingly difficult for hikers to access parts of the 'wild' Great Wall. For the latest intelligence, check in with a reputable tour specialist such as **Beijing Hikers** (☏010 6432 2786; www.beijinghikers.com; per person ¥380-500).

Jiankou to Mutianyu

➡ 2½ hours (plus one-hour climb to the Wall)

Unrivalled for pure, untamed scenery, the Great Wall at Jiankou is tough to negotiate, but this mostly downhill stretch, which passes through the 180-degree U-turn known as the Ox Horn, is more easily navigated. Access the Wall from hamlet No 1 in Xizhaizi Village (西栅子村一队, Xīzhàizi Cūn Yīduì). Ideally you'll need someone to point you to the correct path, which climbs breathlessly up a steep forest trail to the **Zhengbei Tower** (正北楼, Zhèngbĕi Lóu). After admiring the stupendous views, head east along the Wall as it tapers gently downhill (the other direction is extremely dangerous), before arriving at the **Ox Horn** (牛角边, Niú Jiǎo Biān), a steep up and down (which can be skipped via a forest trail). Eventually you'll get to Mutianyu, passing around the right side of a tower where the way is blocked, and onwards to cable cars, toboggan rides and transport back to Beijing.

The Coiled Dragon Loop

➡ 2½ hours

This scenic but manageable hike starts and finishes in the town of Gubeikou and follows a curling stretch of the Wall known as the Coiled Dragon. From the Folk Customs Village (the southern half of Gubeikou), walk up to the newly reconstructed **Gubeikou Gate** (古北口关, Gǔbeikǒu Guǎn), but turn right up a dirt track just before the gateway. You should start seeing yellow-painted blobs left over from an old marathon that was run here: follow them. The first section of Wall you reach is a very rare stony stretch of **Northern Qi Dynasty Wall** (1500 years old). It soon joins up with the Ming dynasty bricked version, which you should continue to walk along (although at one stage, you need to follow yellow arrows down off the Wall to the left, before rejoining it later). Around 90 minutes after you set off, you should reach a big sweeping right-hand bend in the Wall (the coil), with three towers on top. The first and third of these towers are quite well preserved, with walls, windows and part of a roof (great for camping in). At the third tower (called **Jiangjun Tower**), turn left, skirting right around it, then walk down the steps before turning right at a point marked with a yellow 'X' (the marathon went straight on here). Follow this pathway all the way back to Gubeikou (30 minutes), turning right when you reach the road.

Gubeikou to Jinshanling

➡ 6½ hours

This day-long adventure takes in unrestored and restored Great Wall, as well as a 90-minute detour through the countryside. Bring plenty of food and water. Follow the first part of our Coiled Dragon Loop hike, but instead of leaving the Wall just after **Jiangjun Tower**, continue along the Wall for another hour until you reach the impressive **24-Window Tower** (there are only 15 windows left these days). Here, follow the yellow arrows off the Wall, to avoid a military zone up ahead, and walk down through the fields. Go through the park gate signposted 西门 and follow the path back up to the Wall, where you'll reach an archway to get up around the other side of the tower, then continue along the Wall to the restored section at Jinshanling. You'll have to buy a ticket from someone at **Xiliang Zhuandao Tower**, from where it's about 30 minutes to **Little Jinshan Tower** (for the path, or cable car, down to the entrance), or about 90 minutes to **East Tower with Five Holes** (for the path down off the Wall, from where it's a 30-minute walk to the bus back to Beijing).

Climbing east out of town is **Coiled Dragon Mountain** (蟠龙山, Pán Lóng Shān), a gentler ascent that eventually leads all the way to Jinshanling Great Wall (six hours, detouring around a restricted military zone en route). It's one of the most popular point-to-point hikes along the unrestored Great Wall, with notable towers including the **General Tower** (将军楼, Jiāngjūn Lóu; effectively the command HQ of the area during the Ming dynasty) and the **24 Window Tower** (二十四眼楼, Èrshísìyǎn Lóu; the loftiest en route, with six windows on each face, though only two faces remain).

🛏 Sleeping & Eating

You'll find dozens of *nóngjiāyuàn* (农家院, farmer-style courtyards) in the redeveloped southern half of the village (before the Gubeikou Tunnel), known as the **Folk Customs Village**. Expect to pay ¥150 to ¥300 for a room with a bathroom. All of them do food.

Great Wall Box House GUESTHOUSE ¥
(团园客栈, Tuán Yuán Kèzhàn; ☎ 010 8105 1123; http://en.greatwallbox.com; 18 Dongguan, Gubeikou Village, 古北口镇东关甲18号; d shared/private bathroom ¥585/950; dm mixed/female ¥190/230; ❄🛜) This hikers' hangout offers four doubles (two with private bathrooms) and dorms in a 100-year-old courtyard. An overgrown spur of the Great Wall runs along one side of the property. An on-site restaurant serves Chinese food and a few western dishes.

ℹ Getting There & Away

BUS

From Dongzhimen Transport Hub (p137), take bus 980快 to its terminus at Miyun bus station (密云区汽车站, Mìyúnqū qìchēzhàn; ¥17, 100 minutes, 6am to 8pm). Next, turn right (south) out of the bus station, cross the main road (京密路, Jingmi Lu) and turn right again (west) and walk for 250m to find the stop for local bus Mi 25, which runs to Gubeikou (¥11, 80 minutes). The last bus 25 back to Miyun leaves at 4.35pm. The last bus 980 back to Dongzhimen is at 6.30pm.

CAR & TAXI

Expect to pay ¥900 to ¥1200 for a day trip by car from Beijing.

TRAIN

New as of 2019, the 'S5' train ('S' denoting suburban) departs from the tiny Huangtudian Train

Station (p136) in northern Beijing, which is adjacent to Huoying subway station (Lines 8 and 13, exit G4), and terminates at **Gubeikou Station** (古北口站, Gǔběikǒu Zhàn). The journey takes two hours (¥10). There are two daily departures (6.50am and 2.27pm), and the train returns at 11.09am and 5.10pm.

Note that the origin station will likely change to Beijing North Railway Station once its renovation is completed in 2020. You can use your Beijing Travel Card to board the train.

Jinshanling 金山岭

Location 142km from Beijing

Price summer/winter ¥65/55

Hours 8am to 5pm

Mighty and imposing, the Jinshanling (Jīnshānlíng) section of Great Wall has been thoroughly restored, but it's distant enough from Beijing that it sees far fewer tourists than the likes of Mutianyu. The landscape here can be drier and starker than at, say, Jiankou, but it's arguably more powerful, and it leaves you in no doubt that this is remote territory. Jinshanling is the finish (or the start) of an adventurous 6½-hour hike from Gubeikou.

Jinshanling has some unusual features such as barrier walls (walls within the Wall), a particularly high density of watchtowers, thousands of bricks inscribed with maker's marks and the year 1578, and standout towers such as the **Storehouse Tower** (库房楼, Kùfáng Lóu) and the **Big Jinshan Tower** (大金山楼, Dà Jīnshān Lóu) with its upper storey and brick stairway.

In the **Small Pot Tower** (小虎楼, Xiǎohǔ Lóu), there is an elaborately carved Screen Wall depicting a mythical *qilin* (a unicorn-type beast).

Info boards in English at various points cover history and architecture. You can hike (in either direction) on the restored section of the Wall here and do as little or as much as you like, up to a total of about 6km. A **cable car** (缆车, Lǎn Chē; one way/return ¥40/80; ⏱8am-5pm Apr-Oct, to 4.30pm Nov-Mar) by the ticket office saves a trudge up to the battlements.

If you want to find some unrestored sections, keep marching west along the Wall, and you'll eventually get to Gubeikou (6½ hours), although you have to leave the Wall for an hour or so in order to circumvent the boundary of a military zone.

GUBEIKOU TOP TIPS

➡ The S5 train (new as of 2019) is a scenic and cheap way to visit the Great Wall at Gubeikou.

➡ Use Trip.com to book accommodation at Gubeikou in English.

🛏 Sleeping & Eating

There are a few guesthouses strung out along the road approaching the Wall, and a campsite close to the lower cable-car station (¥150, includes admission to Great Wall).

You'll find a few places to eat leading up to the main ticket office. Most shut down between November and March.

ⓘ Getting There & Away

BUS

Between 1 April and 15 November, direct buses (¥32, two hours) depart from Dongzhimen Transport Hub (p137) to the Jinshanling ticket office. There are two buses a day, departing at 7.40am and 8.20am, and returning to Beijing at 3.30pm and 4pm. If you can't find the bus, ask around for the Jīnshānlíng Chángchéng lǚyóu bānchē (金山岭长城旅游班车).

Otherwise, catch a bus headed to Luanping (滦平; ¥32, 90 minutes, 7.30am to 4pm) from outside Wangjing West subway station (Lines 13 and 15), which will drop you at the Jinshanling Service Area, from where it's a free (but infrequent) shuttle-bus ride or a 2km walk to the entrance.

CAR & TAXI

Arranging your own car and driver to Jinshanling should cost around ¥1000 to ¥1200 for a return day trip from Beijing.

TRAIN

You can ride the train to Gubeikou where you'll be able to find a driver to take you the last 40 minutes to Jinshanling.

Simatai　　　　司马台

Location 143km from Beijing

Price adult ¥40

Hours 8am to 6pm April to October, to 5.30pm November to March

Built during the reign of Ming emperor Hongwu, Simatai (Sīmǎtái) is the great mountain climber, famed for the precarious steepness of its battlements as they soar up the 'heavenly ladder' of the Yan Mountains. Heavily restored and reopened in 2014, its once rambling charm has been diluted by cash-ins like the faux-historic Gubei Water Town, although an admittedly nice feature is how part of the Wall is illuminated (and can be walked on) after dark.

There are some unusual features at Simatai, such as 'obstacle walls' or 'barrier walls' – walls within walls used for defending against enemies who had already scaled

GREAT WALL BY NIGHT

A short section of Simatai Great Wall is illuminated with lights inset into the battlements, and opens after dark (6pm to 10pm). At this time it's mandatory to use the cable car both ways, which bumps up the cost.

the battlements. Small cannons have been discovered in this area, as well as evidence of rocket-type weapons.

Gubei Water Town　　　　　　　　AREA

(古北水镇, Gǔběi Shuǐ Zhèn; www.wtown.com; ¥140, through ticket incl Simatai Great Wall ¥170; ◷9am-9pm) Cashing in on the magnificent Simatai Great Wall that overlooks it, this faux-historic village of waterways and old courtyards is a commercial venture built in 2014. There's not much to do here beyond wandering about, shopping and admiring the light show after dark.

🛏 Sleeping & Eating

Gubei Water Town has the full range of touristy hotels, from basic to boutique, as well as plenty of restaurants. But note that admission is extra on top of the Great Wall ticket.

ⓘ Access Issues

Since Simatai reopened in 2014, the hike west to Jinshanling has been sealed off. Also, the route east is shorter than it once was, as only 10 watchtowers were accessible at the time of research.

If you only want to visit the Wall and skip the ersatz Gubei Water Town, you need to reserve tickets in advance at www.wtown.com, which can then be paid for on entry.

ⓘ Getting There & Away

BUS

From Dongzhimen Transport Hub (p137), a tourist bus (¥48, two hours) leaves for Gubei Water Town four times a day: 8am, 9am, noon and 3.30pm, with an extra 2pm bus on weekends and holidays. Returning buses are at 1pm, 5pm and 9pm, with an extra bus at 7pm on weekends and holidays.

You can also take bus 980快 from Dongzhimen to Miyun Xidaqiao (¥15, one hour) and then change to Miyun Bus 51 to Gubei Water Town (¥31, two hours).

CAR & TAXI

Arranging your own car and driver to Simatai should cost around ¥1000 to ¥1200 for a return day trip from Beijing.

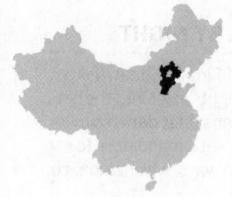

Tianjin & Hebei

POP 87.2 MILLION

Best Places to Eat

➜ Magic Room (p163)

➜ Shāguō Lǐ (p150)

➜ Dà Qīng Huā Jiǎozi (p163)

➜ Alley Dumplings (p166)

➜ Mix C Food Hall (p154)

Best Places to Stay

➜ Astor Hotel (p149)

➜ Liu Yue Capsule Hotel (p147)

➜ First Met Hostel (p163)

➜ Bǎilè Kèzhàn (p168)

➜ Xīngshuǐ Yuàn (p158)

Why Go?

Though you'll often be darting through it at 350km/h on one of China's phenomenal high-speed trains, Hebei (河北, Héběi) is in fact a slow-moving panorama of brown earth and fields of corn and wheat. Cosmopolitan Tianjin (天津) may put on a dazzling show, but the true charms of this region are its time-worn, earthy textures and its deep-rooted historical narrative.

Hebei offers the ideal chance to disengage from Beijing's modernity and frantic urban tempo and experience a more timeless China without having to travel too far. Wander through ancient settlements and walled towns, skirt the wild edges of the former Manchuria and journey to the majestic 18th-century summer retreat of the Qing emperors in Chengde.

There are temples to explore, rarely visited stretches of the Great Wall, and remote towns and villages whose ancient rhythms and rural seclusion make them the perfect retreats for those prepared to venture slightly off the beaten track.

When to Go
Tianjin

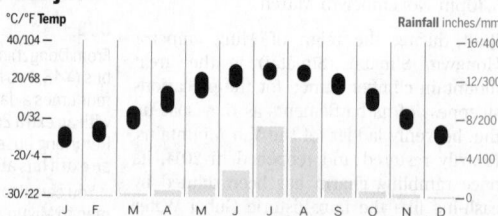

Jan & Feb It's bitterly cold, but Chinese New Year temple fairs in Zhengding will warm your spirits.

Apr & May Hebei starts to thaw after the big winter freeze. Comfortable temperatures.

Sep & Oct Autumn is Hebei's most pleasant season: not too hot, not too cold.

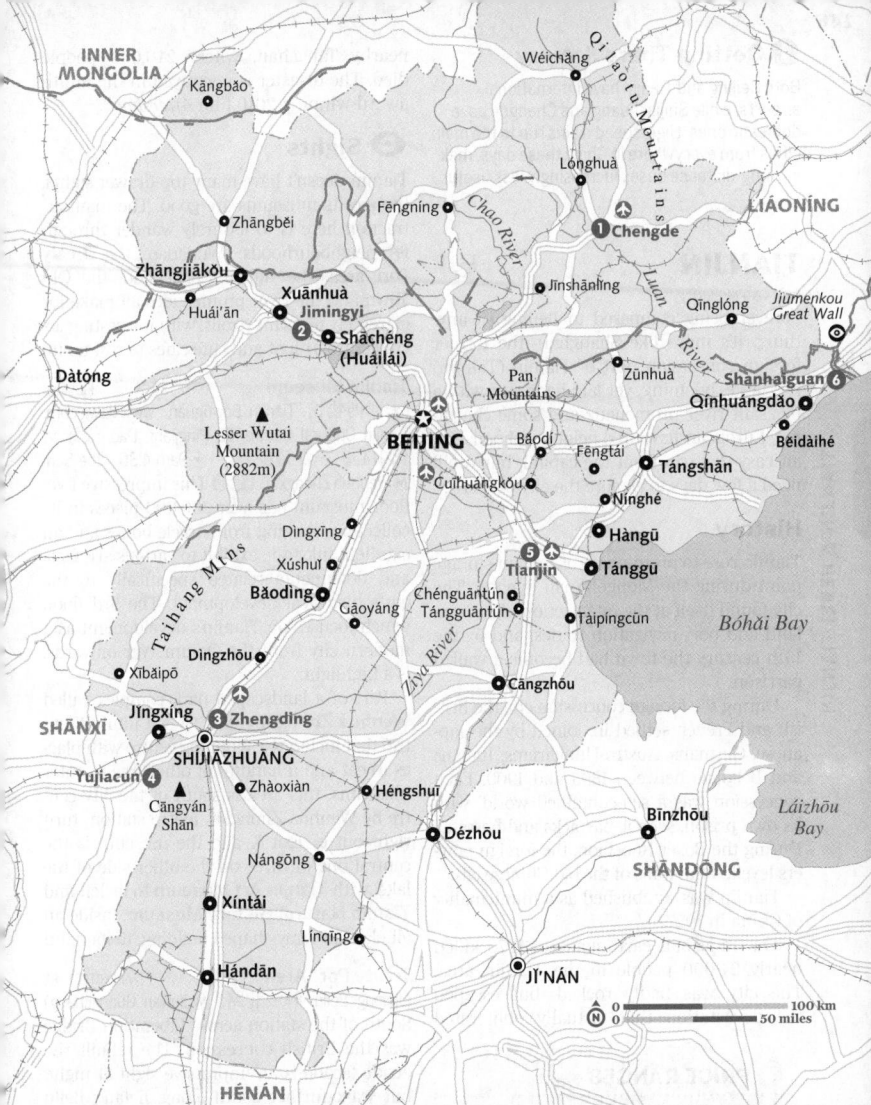

Tianjin & Hebei Highlights

① **Chengde** (p159) Visiting the staggering collection of imperial buildings at the Qing dynasty's summer resort.

② **Jimingyi** (p167) Venturing off the beaten track to this quiet, dusty, Yuan-dynasty walled town, before climbing its namesake mountain.

③ **Zhengding** (p155) Exploring the remarkable, 1500-year-old Longxing Temple, then seeking out Zhengding's four charming ancient pagodas.

④ **Yujiacun** (p158) Walking the cobbled streets of this little-known Ming dynasty 'stone village', before overnighting in a simple homestay.

⑤ **Tianjin** (p146) Enjoying the cultural riches (and modern comforts) of the former foreign concession port.

⑥ **Shanhaiguan** (p164) Hiking the crumbling, less-visited stretches of the Great Wall outside the Ming garrison town where the Wall famously meets the sea.

ℹ️ Getting There & Away

Both Beijing and Tianjin have international airports, while Shijiazhuang and Chengde have domestic ones. High-speed trains run to the main cities from everywhere in China these days, making long-distance buses increasingly less useful.

TIANJIN 天津

POP 12.5 MILLION

Forever being compared to Beijing (if anything, it's more like Shanghai), the former foreign concession port of Tianjin (Tiānjīn) is a large, booming, yet laid-back city, with a pleasant river promenade and some charming, European-flavoured neighbourhoods. It's an easy day trip from the capital, but you'll need a few days to explore the city properly.

History

Tianjin rose to prominence as a grain-storage point during the Mongol Yuan dynasty. The city found itself at the intersection of both inland and port navigation routes, and by the 15th century the town had become a walled garrison.

During the foreign concession era, the British and French settled in, joined by the Japanese, Germans, Austro-Hungarians, Italians and Belgians between 1895 and 1900. Each concession was a self-contained world, with its own prison, school, barracks and hospital. During the Boxer Rebellion, the foreign powers levelled the walls of the old Chinese city.

Tianjin was established as a municipality of China in 1927.

The Tangshan earthquake of 1976 killed nearly 24,000 people in the Tianjin area. The city was badly rocked, but escaped the devastation that virtually obliterated nearby Tangshan, where 240,000 people died. The disaster is portrayed in the multi-award-winning 2010 film *Aftershock*.

◉ Sights

Tianjin doesn't have many top-drawer sights, though its museums are good. The main attraction here is to leisurely wander through its neighbourhoods: Wudadao, the Treaty Port area, the Italian Concession, the Old Town and the river promenades all make for extremely pleasant strolls, with interesting architecture to spot and cute cafes to rest up in.

Tianjin Museum MUSEUM
(天津博物馆, Tiānjīn Bówùguǎn; www.tjbwg.com; Tianjin Cultural Centre, 62 Pingjiang Dao, 天津文化中心, 平江道62号; ⊙9am-4.30 Tue-Sun; Ⓜ Wenhua Zhongxin) FREE This impressive five-floor museum has over 200,000 pieces in its collection, ranging from oracle bones and an excellent inkstone exhibit to various artefacts and documents related specifically to the city's historical development. The 3rd floor, which focuses on Tianjin's development as a modern city from the Opium War onwards, is a highlight.

Part of a landscaped park complex called **Wénhuà Zhōngxīn** (文化中心, Cultural Centre) that includes a shopping centre with places to eat and a handful of other free-to-enter museums, this area is south of the city centre by Wenhua Zhongxin metro station; turn right out of Exit K and the museum is the central one of three on the other side of the lake, with **Tianjin Art Museum** to its left and **Tianjin Natural History Museum**, inside an all-glass stingray-shaped building, to its right.

Treaty Port Area ARCHITECTURE
(Jiefang Beilu, 解放北路; Ⓜ Jinwan Guangchang) South of the station across Liberation Bridge was the British concession. The rebuilt riverside facade is an impressive sight at night, but walk further south along Jiefang Beilu to see original, imposing, hundred-year-old European buildings, which once housed the city's international banks. Names are posted on plaques outside each building; many still house banks today. One building of particular note is the **former Qing dynasty post office** (109 Jiefang Beilu, 解放北路109号) FREE, which now has a historic stamp collection on display.

Minyuan Plaza STADIUM
(民园广场, Mínyuán Guǎngchǎng; 83 Chongqing Dao, 重庆道83号; Ⓜ Yingkoudao) The centrepiece of the Wudadao neighbourhood, Minyuan

Plaza was rebuilt in 2012 on the site of a 90-year-old stadium that was originally designed by former British Olympian Eric Liddell. It now functions as a giant park of sorts – you can still run laps if you want – with a visitors centre, two small museums (of limited interest), and a host of cafes and restaurants. It's particularly lively in the evening.

Guangdong Guild Hall HISTORIC BUILDING
(广东会馆, Guǎngdōng Huìguǎn; 31 Nanmenli Dajie, 南门里大街31号; ¥10; ◎ 9am-4pm Tue-Fri, to 2pm Sat & Sun; Ⓜ Gulou) This charming guildhall, built in 1907, is one of the few buildings of any genuine age in the Old Town. It's a lovely courtyard complex, centred on a beautiful, ornate, wooden theatre where Peking opera performances are held on Saturday and Sunday afternoons (2.30pm to 4pm; tickets from ¥40). Don't miss poking your head into the back courtyard, with its fading murals by the south entrance. The guildhall is directly opposite the southeast corner of the Drum Tower.

Folk Art Museum MUSEUM
(民俗博物馆, Mínsú Bówùguǎn; Beside Tianhou Temple; ◎ 9am-4pm Tue-Sun; Ⓜ Dongnanjiao) **FREE** You know all those souvenirs for sale on the Ancient Culture Street? Well, this collection of handicrafts is the real deal – historic clothing, paintings, ceramics and even an enormous abacus. As you walk north up Ancient Culture Street, the museum is off to your left, just before you reach Tianhou Temple. No English.

Tianhou Temple TEMPLE
(天后宫, Tiānhòu Gōng; Ancient Culture Street, 古文化街; ¥10; ◎ 8.30am-4.30pm Tue-Sun; Ⓜ Dongnanjiao) This busy temple, with its healthy mix of Taoist, Buddhist and Confucian deities, is dedicated to Tianhou (Empress of Heaven). Goddess of the sea and the protector of sailors, she is also popularly known as Mazu and Niangniang. The main hall is the Niangniang Palace, which features an effigy of Tianhou in a glass case, flanked by ferocious-looking weapons and attendant monsters.

Monastery of Deep Compassion BUDDHIST TEMPLE
(大悲禅院, Dàbēi Chányuàn; 40 Tianwei Lu, 天纬路40号; ¥5; ◎ 9am-6pm Apr-Oct, to 4pm Nov-Mar) Tianjin's most important Buddhist temple – signposted as 'Dabei Temple' on street signs – was built in three stages from 1436 to 1734. While most of the architecture has since been rebuilt, it's a very large and active place and an enthralling place to wander.

OLD TOWN

Originally enclosed by a wall on the west bank of the Hai River, Tianjin's reconstructed Old Town has two main tourist areas: the pedestrianised **Ancient Culture Street** (Guwenhua Jie, 古文化街; Ⓜ Dongnanjiao), which is packed with souvenirs and shoppers, and, less than 1km to the west, the rebuilt, pedestrianised area surrounding the **Drum Tower** (鼓楼, Gǔ Lóu; Chengxiang Zhonglu, 城厢中路; ◎ 9am-4pm Fri-Wed; Ⓜ Gulou) **FREE**, which was formerly the town centre.

Don't miss the huge, multi-armed statue of Guanyin – whose eyes seem to follow you around – standing in the Great Compassion Hall in a side courtyard. Admission includes three incense sticks; pick them up to the right of the Hall of Heavenly Kings.

The monastery is on the east side of the river.

Confucius Temple CONFUCIAN TEMPLE
(文庙, Wén Miào; 1 Dongmennei Dajie, 东门内大街1号; ¥25; ◎ 9am-4.30pm Tue-Sun; Ⓜ Dongnanjiao) Tianjin's quiet Confucius Temple is actually a two-for-one, with the provincial temple on the east side (dating from 1436) and the county temple on the west side (dating from 1734). Although almost everything has been rebuilt, the county side has some exhibits on the history and main tenets of Confucianism, all set to *qín* music playing beneath the cypress trees.

🎆 Festivals & Events

Great Wall Marathon SPORTS
(www.great-wall-marathon.com; ◎ May) This certifiably insane adventure marathon includes 5164 steps along the gorgeous (and very steep) Huángyáguān (黄崖关) stretch of the Great Wall, 150km from Tianjin. If you're not a glutton for punishment, no need to do the full thing: a half-marathon and 8.5km fun run are held on the same day.

🛏 Sleeping

Liu Yue Capsule Hotel HOSTEL ¥
(留阅胶囊酒店, Liú Yuè Jiāonáng Jiǔdiàn; ☑ 022 2712 6866; 48 Jiefang Beilu, 解放北路48号; s/d capsules ¥89/129, d ¥300; ✳ 🖥; Ⓜ Jinwan Guangchang) There's a friendly welcome from English-speaking staff at this unique hostel – also known as Books Hotel – located centrally on historic Jiefang Beilu. Housed in

Central Tianjin

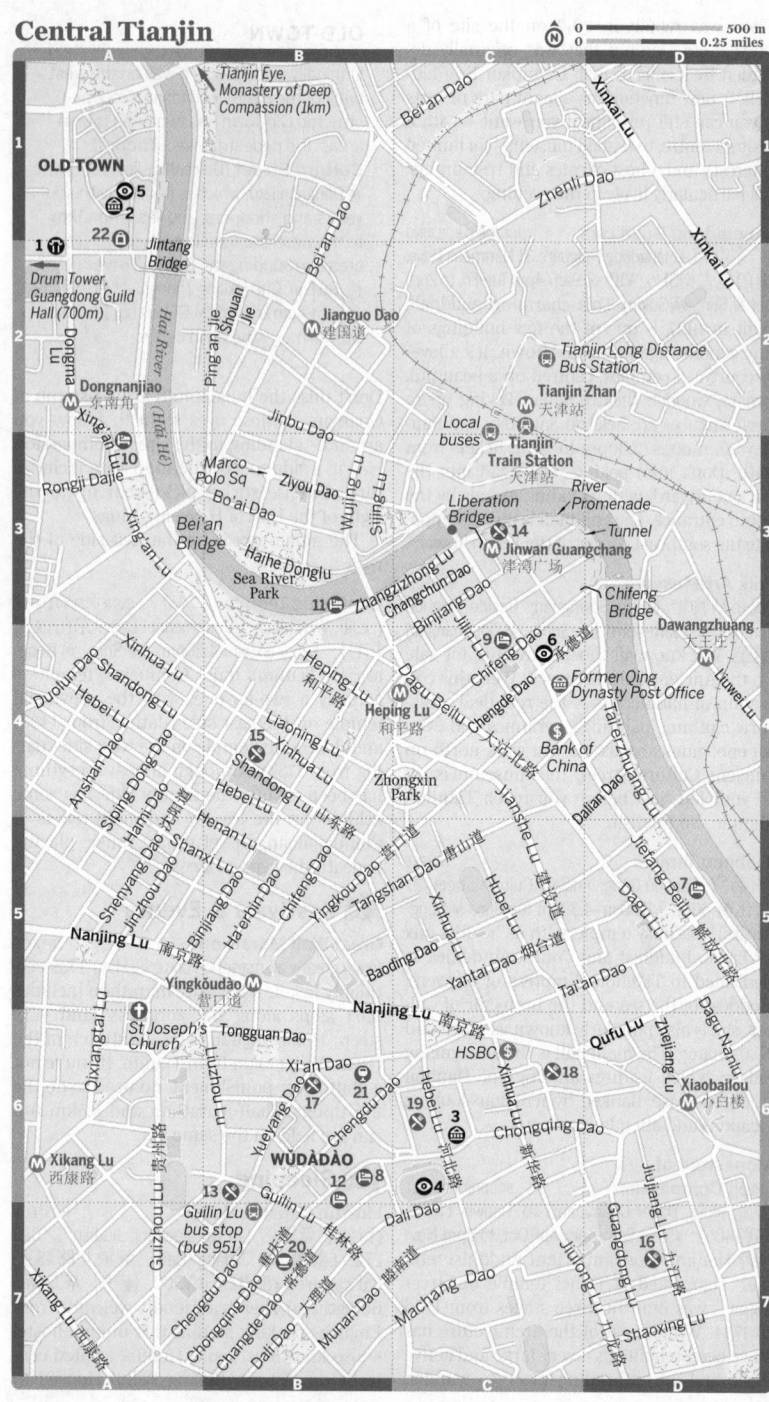

N

0 — 500 m
0 — 0.25 miles

OLD TOWN

Tianjin Eye,
Monastery of Deep
Compassion (1km)

Bei'an Dao

Zhenli Dao

Xinkai Lu

Xinkai Lu

5
2
1
22
Jintang
Bridge

Drum Tower,
Guangdong Guild
Hall (700m)

Dongma Lu

Hai River (Hǎi Hé)

Bei'an Dao

Jianguo Dao
建国道

Shouan Jie

Ping'an Jie

Tianjin Long Distance
Bus Station

Tianjin Zhan
天津站

Dongnanjiao
东南角

Xing'an Lu

Jinbu Dao

Local
buses

Tianjin
Train Station
天津站

Marco
Polo Sq

Ziyou Dao

Wujing Lu

Sijing Lu

Liberation
Bridge

River
Promenade

Rongji Dajie

10

Bo'ai Dao

Bei'an
Bridge

Haihe Donglu

Zhangzizhong Dao

Changchun Dao

Jinwan Guangchang
津湾广场

14

Tunnel

Sea River
Park

11

Binjiang Dao

Chifeng
Bridge

Dawangzhuang
大王庄

Xinhua Lu

Shandong Lu

Hebei Lu

Heping Lu
和平路

Dagu Beilu

Chifeng Dao

9

6

Chengde Dao

承德道

Former Qing
Dynasty Post Office

Liuwei Lu

Duolun Dao

Shandong Lu

Hebei Dao

Anshan Dao

Liaoning Lu

Xinhua Lu

15

Heping Lu
和平路

Dagu Beilu
大沽北路

Bank of
China

Dalian Dao

Hebei Lu

Henan Lu

Shanxi Lu

Jinzhou Dao

Hami Dao

Shenyang Dao

Siping Dong Dao

Zhongxin
Park

Jianshe Lu 建设道

Tai'erzhuang Lu

7

Jiefang Beilu
解放北路

Nanjing Lu 南京路

Binjiang Dao

Ha'erbin Dao

Chifeng Dao

Yingkou Dao 营口道

Tangshan Dao 唐山道

Xinhua Lu

Hubei Lu

Dagu Lu

Dagu Nanlu

Yingkǒudào
营口道

Baoding Dao

Yantai Dao 烟台道

Tai'an Dao

Qixiangtai Lu

St Joseph's
Church

Tongguan Dao

Nanjing Lu 南京路

Qufu Lu

Xikang Lu
西康路

Liuzhou Lu

Xi'an Dao

21
17

19

HSBC

18

Zhejiang Lu

Xiaobailou
小白楼

Yueyang Dao

Chengdu Dao

Hebei Lu

Xinhua Lu

3

Chongqing Dao

Guizhou Lu

Guilin Lu
bus stop
(bus 951)

13

12
8

Guilin Lu 桂林路

4

Dali Dao

新华路

Jiujiang Lu
九江路

16

Guangdong Lu

WǓDÀDÀO

20

Chengdu Dao

Chongqing Dao 重庆道

Changde Dao 常德道

Dali Dao 大理道

Munan Dao 睦南道

Machang Dao

Jiulong Lu 九龙路

Shaoxing Lu

Xikang Lu 西康路

Central Tianjin

an attractive concession-era brick building, Liu Yue has small capsule 'rooms' (singles are tiny, but doubles do at least have some standing space) and a handful of decadently decorated boutique doubles.

Jiànshě
HOSTEL ¥
(见舍, 青年旅舍, Qīngnián Lǔshě; ☑131 1616 5248; 101 Chongqing Dao, 重庆道101号; dm/d ¥62/142; ❀🛜; Ⓜ Yingkoudao) Secreted away at the end of an alleyway off Chongqing Dao, this simple but stylish hostel has spacious dorms and small private rooms with shared bathrooms, though one double (¥228) has its own bathroom. The bright, ground-floor lounge makes a pleasant hangout. Not much English spoken, and no English sign.

Three Brothers Youth Hostel
HOSTEL ¥
(戈萨国际青年旅舍, Gēsà Guójì Qīngniánlǔshè; ☑022 2723 9777; gesahostel@163.com; 141 Chongqing Dao, 庆道141号; dm/d ¥60/166; ❀@🛜; 🚍951 to Guilin Lu, Ⓜ Yingkoudao) Though it's lost some of its hostel vibe since turning its little cafe into a public restaurant (evenings only, no English menu), Three Brothers is still good value, and the staff, who speak some English, are very welcoming. Private rooms have bathrooms, and windows overlooking back gardens. Dorms are compact but clean, as are their shared bathrooms.

Orange Hotel
HOTEL ¥¥
(桔子酒店, Júzi Jiǔdiàn; ☑022 2734 8333; www. orangehotel.com.cn; 7 Xing'an Lu, 兴安路7号; r from ¥369, with river view from ¥438; ❀🛜; Ⓜ Dongnanjiao) This stylish boutique hotel has unfussy rooms, some of which have river views. Staff are welcoming, but don't speak English. Breakfast costs ¥38. Walk through the archway on Xing'an Lu then round the back of the building.

★ Astor Hotel
HOTEL ¥¥¥
(利顺德大饭店, Lìshùndé Dàfàndiàn; ☑022 5852 6888; 33 Tai'erzhuang Lu, 台儿庄路33号; d from ¥850; ❀❀@🛜; Ⓜ Xiaobailou) China's oldest foreign-run hotel, the Astor dates back to 1863, when it was opened by British missionary John Innocent. Although it's not as luxurious as some of the city's international chains, there's an undeniable character to the place that's hard to find elsewhere.

The new building has larger, more modern rooms with river views, but it's the old building you want with its creaking wooden floors, China's oldest lift (not still in use, though it is still operational) and four-poster beds in rooms with bags of character. Secreted away in the basement is the **Astor House Museum** (non-guests/guests ¥30/50; 11am to 8pm), which tells the story of the hotel and the city during the foreign concession era through old photos, maps and other artefacts.

St Regis Tianjin
HOTEL ¥¥¥
(天津瑞吉金融街酒店, Tiānjīn Ruìjí Jīnróngjiē Jiǔdiàn; ☑022 5830 9999; www.stregis.com/tianjin; 158 Zhangzizhong Lu, 张自忠路158号; r with city/ half-river/full-river view from ¥1100/1300/1500; ❀❀@🛜🏊; Ⓜ Heping Lu) The last word in luxury in Tianjin, the St Regis has a prime riverside location, with alfresco seating on the back terrace – perfect for enjoying its signature Lapsang Souchong Bloody Mary. The heated pool, spa treatments and personal butler service promise serious R & R, while the staff are well attuned to the expectations of international visitors.

✕ Eating

Shíjì Jiānbing Guǒzi
PANCAKES ¥
(时记煎饼果子; cnr Yueyang Lu & Changsha Lu, 岳阳路和长沙路的拐角; pancakes ¥7; ⊙5am-8pm;

WUDADAO

The area of Wudadao (五大道; Wǔdàdào; Five Great Avenues) is rich in the villas and pebble-dash former residences of the well-to-do of the early 20th century. It consists of five roads in the south of the city – Machang Dao, Changde Dao, Munan Dao, Dali Dao and Chengdu Dao – and the streetscapes have a European feel, lined with charming houses dating from the 1920s and before.

Dotted with tiny cafes, bars and boutiques, this is the most enjoyable part of the city for exploration on foot, even though overly zealous renovations have stripped some areas of their authentic charm.

Ⓜ Yingkoudao) On a lively crossroads lined with small restaurants, fruit stalls and snack shops, this typical hole-in-the-wall takeaway joint specialises in Tianjin's signature savoury pancake, *jiānbing guǒzi* (煎饼果子), often wrapped around a crispy fried cracker.

Ānhuī Bǎnmiàn Wáng   NOODLES ¥
(安徽板面王; cnr Guilin Lu & Yueyang Dao, 桂林路和岳阳道的拐角处; noodles ¥8-12; ⊙ 9.30am-10pm; Ⓜ Yingkoudao) On the periphery of gentrified Wudadao, this tiny, no-frills noodles joint is an English-free zone, but serves up delicious, filling bowls of noodles, washed down with ice-cold bottles of Harbin beer (¥5). The speciality is *bǎn miàn* (板面, hand-chopped noodles in a soup), but we particularly like the *rè gān miàn* (热干面, fried noodles with crunchy beansprouts and peanuts).

Shāguō Lǐ   CHINESE ¥¥
(砂锅李; ☑ 022 2326 0075; 46 Jiujiang Lu, 九江路46号; most dishes ¥36-98, noodles from ¥20; ⊙ 11am-2.30pm & 5-9pm; Ⓜ Xiaobailou) Despite having walls adorned with photos of television celebrities who've eaten here, this place remains refreshingly unpretentious, and locals still come for the speciality pork spare ribs in a sweet barbecue sauce – so tender they pull apart at the touch of a chopstick. The small portion (¥72) is easily enough for two people. Has an English menu.

YY Beer House   THAI ¥¥
(粤园泰餐厅, Yuèyuán Tàicāntīng; ☑ 022 2339 9634; 3 Aomen Lu, 澳门路3号; dishes ¥38-98, beers from ¥20; ⊙ 11am-11pm; Ⓜ Xiaobailou) Despite the name, this cosy, atmospheric place is actually a Thai restaurant with a wide range of flavourful dishes from the land of smiles. It does, however, also have an excellent range of imported beers, including some craft ales, and it's fine to just come for drinks. The English-speaking owner is super friendly and there's an English menu.

There's a **newer branch** (☑ 022 5835 2835; 1 Hunan Lu, 湖南路1号; ⊙ 11.30am-midnight; Ⓜ Yingkoudao) in Wudadao.

Gǒubùlǐ – Main Branch   DUMPLINGS ¥¥¥
(狗不理; 77 Shandong Lu, 山东路77号; dumplings ¥46, other dishes ¥50-150; ⊙ 8.30am-9pm; ☑; Ⓜ Heping Lu) Tianjin's most famous restaurant chain – sometimes called 'Go Believe' – is a mixed bag. While the trademark *xiǎo lóng bāo* (小笼包, steamed dumplings) are big, juicy and delicious, locals will also tell you they're overpriced (¥46 for eight). Nonetheless, it's been in business since 1858, they have vegetarian options and there's a picture menu with some English.

There are other outlets, including a **branch** (Zhangzi Zhonglu, 张自忠路; ⊙ 10.30am-2pm & 5-9pm; Ⓜ Jinwan Guangchang) opposite the train station.

🍷 Drinking & Nightlife

★ We Brewery   BAR
(www.webrewery.com; 4 Yi He Li, off Xi'an Dao, 西安道怡和里4号; beer from ¥35; ⊙ 5pm-midnight Sun-Thu, to 2am Fri & Sat; Ⓜ Yingkoudao) Leading the way in the Tianjin craft-beer scene, this hidden gem of a bar is tucked away down an alley off Xi'an Dao. Its English-speaking owner knows his stuff and is always happy to chat about China's emerging ale industry. Around half a dozen beers are brewed on-site. If you're having trouble choosing, go for the ¥50 three-beer sampler.

Rester Cafe   CAFE
(定格咖啡, Dìnggé Kāfēi; 177 Chongqing Dao, 重庆道177号; ⊙ 11.30am-10pm; ☎; Ⓜ Yingkoudao) One of a clutch of cafes on a quieter stretch of Chongqing Dao, this chic little place does quality coffee, healthy Italian lunches and evening cocktails and craft beers. The minimalist, cooled interior opens out onto a small 1st-floor balcony overlooking the street.

☆ Entertainment

★ Guandong Guild Hall
Peking Opera   CHINESE OPERA
(广东会馆京剧, Guǎngdōng Huìguǎn Jīngjù; 31 Nanmenli Dajie, Drum Tower, 鼓楼, 南门里大街

31号; ￥40-180; ⊘2.30pm Sat & Sun; Ⓜ Gulou)
Popular Peking opera performances are held every Saturday and Sunday afternoon at this fabulous 100-year-old wooden tea house-theatre inside the Guangdong Guild Hall (p147). Performances last for 90 minutes. Tea (from ￥30 per pot) is served throughout the show, but you'll need to bring your own snacks. Buy tickets on the door.

🔒 Shopping

If you're on the look out for Tiānjīn Nírén (天津泥人, traditional clay figurines), but don't have time to hunt down the specialist shop **Niren Zhang** (泥人张; ☑ 022 2337 4088; 1st fl, 202 Machang Dao, 河西区马场道202号; ⊘9am-5pm; 🚌871 or 870), you can also buy these famous clay figurines in the lobby of the main branch of the restaurant Goubuli.

ℹ Information

There are foreign-card friendly ATMs inside and outside the train station, and all over the city.

Bank of China (中国银行, Zhōngguó Yínháng; 80-82 Jiefang Beilu, 解放北路80-82号)

HSBC (汇丰银行, Huìfēng Yínháng; 75 Nanjing Lu, 南京路75号) There's an HSBC ATM inside the International Building.

Raffles Medical (莱佛士医疗, Láifúshì Yīliáo; ☑ 022 2352 0143; www.rafflesmedical.com/international; Tianjin Yanyuan International Hotel, Zijinshan Lu, 紫金山路天津燕园国际大酒店; ⊘9am-6pm Mon-Fri, to 1pm Sat; 🚌697) International-standard medical clinic with English-speaking staff and doctors.

ℹ Getting There & Away

AIR

Connected to the city's metro system, **Tianjin Binhai International Airport** (天津滨海国际机场, Tiānjīn Bīnhǎi Guójì Jīchǎng; ☑022 96777; Jichang Dadao, Dongli District, 东丽区机场大道) is just 15km east of the city centre and has flights to all major cities in China, plus numerous international destinations, including London, Singapore, Bangkok, Tokyo and Seoul.

BOAT

The nearest passenger port is the **Tianjin International Cruise Home Port** (天津国际邮轮母港, Tiānjīn Guójì Yóulún Mǔgǎng; ☑022 2560 5128; Guanhai Dao, Binhaixin District, 滨海新区观海道), 70km east of the city.

Sadly, ferries to Dalian in Liaoning province have been discontinued, usurped by high-speed trains. However, there are still twice-weekly ferries to Incheon (仁川, Rénchuān) in South Korea. They leave at 11am on Thursdays and Sundays and take around 25 hours. Tickets, which can be bought at the port on the day of travel, start from around ￥900. It's advisable to arrive at the port at least two hours before departure.

To reach the port from Tianjin, take metro Line 9 to Shimin Guangchang (市民广场) station, then bus 513 to the last stop (Dongjiang Youlun Mugang, 冻僵游轮母港; 40 minutes, 7am to 5pm). The last bus back from the port is at 6pm.

To reach the port from Beijing, take a high-speed train from Beijing South Station to Tanggu (塘沽, Tánggū; one hour, ￥66, half-hourly 6.07am to 9.39pm) then take bus 102.

ERIC LIDDELL

Olympic champion, rugby international and devout Christian, Scotsman Eric Liddell is best known as the subject of the 1981 Oscar-winning film *Chariots of Fire,* but few know about his connection to Tianjin. He was born here in 1902 before being educated in Scotland; he then embarked on a short but astonishing sporting career. He was capped seven times by the Scotland rugby union team and won gold in the 400m at the 1924 Paris Olympics. Famously, he pulled out of his favoured event – the 100m – because, as a Christian, he refused to run on a Sunday. A year later, he returned to Tianjin to follow his true passion as a Christian missionary, and he stayed in China until his death in 1945 in a Japanese internment camp in Shandong province.

While in Tianjin, he lived at 38 Cambridge Rd – now **Chongqing Dao** (李爱锐旧居, Lǐ Àiruì Jiùjū; 38 Chongqing Dao, 重庆道38号; Ⓜ Yingkoudao) – and he helped build the Minyuan Stadium, also in Cambridge Rd, in 1926. It's said that he based its design on Stamford Bridge (Chelsea Football Club's home ground and his favourite running track back in Britain). The stadium was demolished in 2012 before being reincarnated as Minyuan Plaza (p146). It still has a running track (you can run laps if you like), but the building itself is now a leisure and restaurant complex that's hugely popular with domestic tourists and locals, particularly in the evening.

YANGLIUQING ANCIENT TOWN

The old canal-side market town of Yangliuqing, 20km west of Tianjin, has been spruced up for tourists and is now home to an attractive collection of courtyards, temples, alleyways and squares, the centrepiece of which is the **Shi Family Residence** (石家大院, Shí Jiā Dàyuàn; 47 Yangliuqing Guyi Jie, 杨柳青估衣街47号; ¥25; ⏰9am-5pm Apr-Oct, to 4.30pm Nov-Mar). Built in 1875, this vast warren of courtyards and enclosed gardens formerly belonged to a prosperous merchant family and contains a theatre and 278 rooms, some of which are furnished.

The area immediately behind Shi Family Residence contains more courtyards and former temples, some of which can be entered free of charge, some of which are ticketed, and some of which are locked. A few of the buildings here are well-renovated originals, though much of this so-called 'Ancient Town' has been completely rebuilt from scratch. Nevertheless, it's pleasant to wander the streets, which are dotted with low-key shops and restaurants, and even the odd guesthouse. There are no residents living here, however, so the place does have an eerie ghost-town atmosphere.

The town runs alongside a diversion channel of the **Grand Canal** (p272), the world's longest canal (1794km), built in 1415; boat rides can be arranged along it.

While here, don't miss poking your head inside the **New Year Paintings Gallery** (年画张画馆, Niánhuà Zhāng Huàguǎn; 1 Guyi St, Yangliuqing Ancient Town, 杨柳青古镇估衣街1号; ⏰8am-5pm; 🚌824), a small art gallery that showcases, and sells, Yangliuqing's famous Chinese New Year block-print paintings, characterised by colourful childlike characters playing among auspicious new year symbols (fish, peaches and bats). You can pick up a beautiful scroll version for less than ¥200.

To get to Yangliuqing, take bus 824 (¥3, one hour) from Tianjin Train Station. Get off at the Yangliuqing Guzhen Shijia Dayuan (杨柳青古镇石家大院) bus stop, walk back over the river and take the first left. Shi Family Residence is soon on your right, and the New Year Paintings Gallery is about 100m beyond it. The last bus back to Tianjin is around 7.30pm.

BUS

Tianjin's most central **long distance bus station** (天津通莎客运站, Tiānjīn Tōngshā Kèyùnzhàn; Tianjin Train Station North Entrance, 天津站北广场), is at Tianjin Train Station's north entrance. However, thanks to the proliferation of high-speed train services, it serves an ever-decreasing number of destinations. Check train schedules before hopping on a bus – trains are usually faster, safer, more comfortable and cheaper.

Airport shuttle bus ¥15, 40 minutes, half-hourly (6am to 6pm)

Beijing (Sihui bus station) ¥38, 3½ hours, three daily (1.30pm, 3.30pm and 4.30pm)

Cangzhou ¥40, three hours, four daily (8am, 12.50pm, 1.10pm and 2pm)

Chengde ¥123 and ¥140, five hours, two daily (8am and 3pm)

Datong ¥162, seven hours, one daily (3pm)

Qingdao ¥182, eight hours, one daily (8.30am)

TRAIN

Tianjin has four main train stations: Tianjin, Tianjin North, Tianjin South and Tianjin West, all of which are connected to the metro system. Most trains leave from the centrally located Tianjin Train Station, though it's not uncommon for similar routes to also run from the South and West stations.

Bullet trains between here and Beijing make day trips extremely feasible. There's no need to prebook (except on holidays and Sunday evenings); just turn up and buy a ticket on the next available train. You'll rarely have to wait more than an hour. The last train to Beijing is at 10.39pm. The last train back to Tianjin leaves Beijing at 10.43pm.

Services from **Tianjin Train Station** (天津站, Tiānjīn Zhàn) include the following:

Beijing South C-class bullet 2nd-class seat ¥55, 30 minutes, every 10 minutes (5.50am to 10.39pm)

Chengde K-class hard seat/sleeper ¥51/97, six hours, two daily (1.19pm and 1.57pm)

Shanghai K/T/Z-class hard seat/sleeper ¥164/281, four daily at 10.51pm (14 hours), 11.18pm (16½ hours), 12.43am (17 hours) and 1.21am (11½ hours)

Shanhaiguan K/Z-class hard seat/sleeper ¥44/90, 3½ to four hours, 30 daily (5.10am to 9.24pm)

Xi'an K-class hard seat/sleeper ¥169/289, 19 hours, four daily (12.02pm, 2.33pm, 7.27pm and 1.45am)

Xi'an T-class hard seat/sleeper ¥164/281, 15½ hours, one daily (2.04pm)

Services from **Tianjin South Train Station** (南站, Nánzhàn) include the following:

Hangzhou East G-class bullet 2nd-class seat ¥494, five to 5½ hours, five daily (7.51am, 10.30am, 11.33am, 1.23pm and 4.41pm)

Jinan South G-class bullet 2nd-class seat ¥130, one to 1½ hours, 30 daily (7.33am to 9.44pm)

Qingdao (or Qingdao North or West) G-class bullet 2nd-class seat ¥280, three to 4½ hours, seven daily (8.01am to 5.57pm)

Shanghai Hongqiao G-class bullet 2nd-class seat ¥509, four to five hours, 10 daily (7.56am to 6.45pm)

Services from **Tianjin West Train Station** (西站, Xīzhàn) include the following:

Shanhaiguan G-class bullet 2nd-class seat ¥132, 1½ to two hours, 25 daily (9.02am to 6.36pm)

Shijiazhuang G-class bullet 2nd-class seat ¥123, 1½ to two hours, 24 daily (5.42am to 7.49pm)

Wuhan G-class bullet 2nd-class seat ¥525, five to six hours, six daily (10.58am, 1.04pm, 1.53pm, 2.09pm, 2.56pm and 3.10pm)

Xi'an North G-class bullet 2nd-class seat ¥520, six to 6½ hours, four daily (8.05am, 9.35am, 11,22am and 4.05pm)

❶ Getting Around

Taxi flagfall is ¥8 for the first 3km, then ¥2.50 to ¥3 per kilometre thereafter; there's also a ¥1 oil surcharge per trip.

TO/FROM THE AIRPORT

Metro line 2 runs from the city centre all the way to the airport (¥4, 30 minutes, 6am to 10.45pm).

An **airport shuttle bus** (机场巴士; jīchǎng bāshì; ¥15, 40 minutes, every 30 minutes, 6am to 6pm) leaves from the long distance bus station, at the north exit of Tianjin Train Station.

Taxis to the airport cost around ¥60.

PUBLIC TRANSPORT

Tianjin's ever-expanding **metro** (地铁; dìtiě; tickets ¥2-5) – six lines and counting – links the main train stations and the airport to the rest of the city, and runs from around 6am to 10.30pm. Ticket machines have bilingual instructions.

Local **buses** (¥2; exact change needed) run from around 5am to 11pm.

To catch a local bus after arriving at Tianjin Train Station, come out of the train station's South Exit 1 (南1出口, nán yī chūkǒu) and you'll emerge from beneath the train station's small **bus station** (公交车站, Gōngjiāo chēzhàn).

To get to Wudadao from Tianjin Train Station, take bus 951 and get off at **Guilin Lu** (Chengdu Dao, 成都道) (桂林路) bus stop.

HEBEI 河北

POP 74.7 MILLION

Though you'll often be darting through it at 350km/h on one of China's phenomenal high-speed trains, Hebei is a slow-moving panorama of brown earth and fields of corn and wheat. Cosmopolitan Tianjin may put on a dazzling show, but the true charms of this region are its time-worn, earthy textures and its deep-rooted historical narrative.

Shijiazhuang 石家庄

☑ 0311 / POP 2.2 MILLION

There's little to love about Shijiazhuang (Shíjiāzhuāng), Hebei's provincial capital. It's heavily polluted, has few tourist sights, and doesn't allow foreigners to stay at the vast majority of its hotels. It is, however, a regional transport hub, so makes a convenient base from which to explore gems such as Zhengding and Yujiacun.

❂ Sights

Hebei Museum MUSEUM
(河北博物院, Héběi Bówùyuàn; Fanxi Lu, 范西路; ⊙9am-5pm Tue-Sun, last entry 4pm; Ⓜ Bowuyuan) **FREE** Wandering the cavernous halls of this museum's two buildings will take you deep into the multilayered realms of Chinese history, with most exhibits focusing on archaeological excavations that date as far back as the Shang dynasty (1600–1046 BC). As fascinating as the trove of funeral figurines, jade burial suits and bronze vessels is, however, the real star is the Quyang Stone Carvings collection, which features masterful ancient statuary – mostly Buddhist – carved from Hebei's Quyuan marble. Bring your passport for entry.

🛏 Sleeping & Eating

Shijiazhuang only has a handful of hotels that are allowed to take foreigners, and none is cheap. Note in particular that a successful online booking does not necessarily mean you'll actually be able to stay.

Nan Xiaojie is a good spot to look for a meal, with a variety of small restaurants, some outdoor seating and a couple of bars. There are some decent mall food courts.

Yitel Lerthai Centre HOTEL ¥¥
(和颐酒店, Héyí Jiǔdiàn; ☑0311 6805 6666; www.wtphotels.com; 39 Zhongshan Donglu, 中山东路39号; tw/d from ¥339/349; ❈ 🛜; Ⓜ Beiguo Shangcheng) Also known as Ease Hotel, Yitel is a modern, well-run hotel tower with attractive

Shijiazhuang

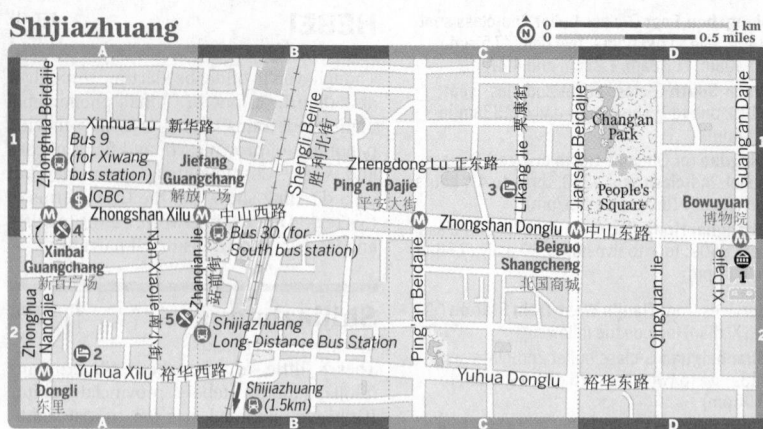

Shijiazhuang

◉ Sights
1 Hebei Museum D2

◉ Sleeping
2 Holiday Inn A2
3 Yitel Lerthai Centre C1

◉ Eating
4 Mix C Food Hall A1
5 Yáng Mázĭ Dà Bĭng A2

dark-wood furnishings and plenty of space. The location is good too: behind shopping-and-eating hotspot Lerthai Centre.

Holiday Inn
HOTEL ¥¥¥

(萬象天成假日酒店, Wànxiàng Tiānchéng Jiàrì Jiǔdiàn; ☑ 0311 6779 9999; www.ihg.com/holiday inn; 15 Yuhua Xilu, 裕华西路15号; r from ¥500; ☀✳ 🛰 🌐; Ⓜ Dongli) This jazzy four-star hotel has slick, modern rooms with glass-walled bathrooms that have rain showers and deep-soaker tubs. There's a top-floor gym and pool and some staff speak English.

Yáng Mázĭ Dà Bĭng
HEBEI ¥

(杨麻子大饼; 12 Zhanqian Jie, 站前街12号; dà bĭng ¥10-15, most other dishes ¥10-40; ☺ 10am-2pm & 5-9pm; Ⓜ Jiefang Guangchang) This no-frills canteen-like restaurant specialises in dà bĭng (大饼; plate-sized, golden-fried, pastry twirls with a variety of both savoury and sweet fillings), ideally washed down with a bowl of millet porridge (金瓜小米粥, jīnguā xiǎomĭ zhōu). Fillings include beef (牛肉, niúròu), pork and spring onion (猪肉大葱, zhūròu dàcōng), red bean paste (豆沙, dòu shā) and walnut (核桃, hé táo).

Mix C Food Hall
FOOD HALL ¥

(万象城, Wànxiàng Chéng; Zhongshan Xilu, 中山西路; meals ¥20-50; ☺ 10am-10pm; Ⓜ Xinbai Guangchang) There are restaurants and cafes dotted throughout Mix C, the city's snazziest shopping mall, but head up to the 6th floor to find the best-value offerings, inside a small Hong Kong–style food court called Skyland Discovery. You'll find dim sum, noodles, roast duck and more, and with English labelling and dishes on display it's a cinch to order what you want.

ⓘ Information

ICBC (中国工商银行, Zhōngguó Gōngshāng Yín-háng; Zhongshan Xilu, 中山西路) One of numerous banks with ATMs along the city's main drag.

ⓘ Getting There & Away

AIR

Shijiazhuang's airport is 40km northeast of town, and has flights to all major cities in China.

The airport bus (机场巴士; jīchǎng bāshì; ¥20, one hour, 5am to 9pm) leaves every 30 minutes from outside Jin Yuan Grand Hotel on Zhonghua Beidajie.

BUS

As elsewhere in China, long-distance bus services are on the decline due to the rise of high-speed trains. Services that still leave from Shijiazhuang's **long-distance bus station** (石家庄客运总站, Shijiāzhuāng Kèyùn Zǒngzhàn; Zhanqian Jie, 站前街) include the following:

Beijing ¥92, four hours, four daily (10am, noon, 2.20pm and 4.30pm)

Chengde ¥157, seven hours, three daily (9.30am, 11.30am and 2.30pm)

Ji'nan ¥112, four hours, two daily (8.50am and 10.30am)

Bus services to Zhengding and Zhaozhou Bridge depart from **South Bus Station** (石家庄南焦客运站, Shíjiāzhuāng Nánjiāo Kèyùnzhàn; ☏ 0311 8657 3806; Yuxiang Jie, 裕翔街), 6km southeast of the centre; to get there from central Shijiazhuang, take an east-bound **bus 30** (Zhongshan Xilu, 中山西路) from any bus stop along Zhongshan Xilu or Zhongshan Donglu.

Services to Cangyan Mountain and Yujiacun depart from the **Xiwang Bus Station** (西王客运站, Xīwáng Kèyùnzhàn; Xinhua Lu, 新华路), 6km west of town. Get there on **bus 9** (Zhonghua Beidajie, 中华北大街), which runs up Zhonghua Nandajie from the train station and then west on Xinhua Lu.

TRAIN

There's no need to book for short-hop high-speed services, including to Beijing; just turn up at the station and buy a ticket.

Shijiazhuang Train Station (石家庄火车站, Shíjiāzhuāng huǒchēzhàn; Zhonghuanan Dajie, 中华南大街) is about 3km south of the central former train station (老火车站; lǎo huǒchēzhàn), linked to the centre by the metro (tickets ¥2 to ¥6). A few trains also stop at or depart from **Shijiazhuang North Train Station** (石家庄北站, Shíjiāzhuāng Běizhàn; Taihua Jie, 泰华街), 4km north of the centre.

Services from Shijiazhuang Train Station include the following:

Beijing West G-class bullet 2nd-class seat ¥129, 1½ hours, 90 daily (6.03am to 10.22pm)

Beijing West K/Z/T-class hard-seat ¥44, 2½ to 3½ hours, 24 daily (7.23am to 8.38pm)

Chengde K-class hard-sleeper ¥133, two overnight trains, (10 hours) and 7.40pm (11 hours)

Datong K-class hard-sleeper ¥152, one overnight train, 8.45pm (10 hours)

Ji'nan D-class bullet 2nd-class seat ¥119, 2½ hours, seven daily (7.32am to 4.35pm)

Ji'nan East G-class bullet 2nd-class seat ¥112, two hours, eight daily (7.20am to 6.35pm)

Luoyang Longmen G-class bullet 2nd-class seat ¥252, 2½ to three hours, 19 daily (8.21am to 6.42pm)

Shanghai Z-class hard-sleeper ¥269, two overnight trains, (12 hours) and 10.52pm (13 hours), both from Shijiazhuang North

Shanghai Hongqiao G-class bullet 2nd-class seat ¥624, seven hours, four daily (8.38am, 10.40am, 2.16pm and 3.49pm)

Shanhaiguan G-class bullet 2nd-class seat ¥255, 3½ to four hours, nine daily (7.10am to 3.40pm)

Tianjin West G-class bullet 2nd-class seat ¥123, two hours, 26 daily (7.10am to 9.54pm)

Xi'an North G-class bullet 2nd-class seat ¥409, 3½ to 4½ hours, 28 daily (7.41am to 8.04pm)

Wuhan G-class bullet 2nd-class seat ¥415, four hours, 40 daily (7.53am to 7.56pm)

Wuhan Z-class hard-sleeper ¥215, eight hours, three overnight trains (11.01pm, 11.40pm and 11.54pm)

ℹ Getting Around

Shijiazhuang's fledgling **metro** (tickets ¥2 to ¥6) has stations all along Zhongshan Xilu and Zhongshan Donglu, the city's main drag, and runs out to the main train station.

Taxis are ¥8 at flagfall.

Zhengding 正定

☑ 0311 / POP 159,000

Its streets littered with temple remains, the part-walled town of Zhengding (Zhèngdìng) is an appetising – albeit incomplete – slice of

---

WORTH A TRIP

ZHAOZHOU BRIDGE

China's oldest bridge still standing, **Zhaozhou Bridge** (赵州桥, Zhàozhōu Qiáo; Zhaoxian County; ¥40) has spanned the Jiao River (Jiāo Hé) for 1400 years. As the world's first segmental arch bridge (ie its arch is a segment of a circle, as opposed to a complete semicircle), it predates other bridges of its type throughout the world by 800 years. In fine condition, and part of a riverside park, it is 50.82m long and 9.6m wide, with a span of 37m.

Twenty-two stone posts are topped with carvings of dragons and mythical creatures, with the centre slab featuring a magnificent tāotiè (an offspring of a dragon).

The bridge is in Zhaoxian County, about 40km southeast of Shijiazhuang and 2km south of Zhaoxian town. To get here from Shijiazhuang, head to the south bus station (p154), then take a bus to Zhaoxian (赵县, Zhàoxiàn; ¥13, one hour, frequent). Get off at Shí Tǎ (石塔), a beautifully carved, slim-line **stone pagoda** built in AD 1038, and now standing in the middle of a roundabout. Turn right at the pagoda (if coming from the direction the bus was moving) to walk the final 2km to the bridge, or else take dinky local bus 2 (¥2). The last bus back to Shijiazhuang swings past Shí Tǎ soon after 6pm.

CANGZHOU'S IRON LION

Standing proud in a long-forgotten corner of southeast Hebei, **Cangzhou's Iron Lion** (沧州铁狮子, Cāngzhōu Tiě Shīzi; County Rd 283, Cangxian, Cangzhou, 沧州沧县283县道; ¥30) is the oldest and largest cast-iron sculpture in China. Cast way back in AD 953, it weighs in at around 40 tonnes and stands almost 6m tall but, unsurprisingly for a creature that is more than 1000 years old, it is but a shadow of its former self.

The lion lost its tail in the 17th century; its snout and belly were damaged in a storm 200 years later; and the bronze statue of the Bodhisattva Manjusri, which once sat on top of the lotus flower on its back, was stolen centuries ago.

Despite today being almost 100km from the coast, in ancient times Cangzhou was a large seaport, which suffered from flooding and tsunamis. The Iron Lion was built to protect the city from sea spirits, and was known back then as Zhen Hai Hou (镇海吼), the Roaring Sea Calmer.

The site used to be the centre point of ancient Cangzhou, a walled settlement established in the far-off Han Dynasty (206 BC–AD 220). Incredibly, part of the **ancient city wall**, thought to have been built at the beginning of the Han Dynasty – so more than 2200 years ago – can still be seen a short distance from here.

For many years now the Iron Lion has cut a rather lonely figure, standing in an otherwise-empty courtyard surrounded by farmland, 15km from the modern city of Cangzhou. But things are about to change. The site was closed when we were last here and was in the final stages of being developed into the **Cangzhou Iron Lion Scenic Area** (沧州铁狮子景区, Cāngzhōu Tiě Shīzi Jǐngqū), a landscaped tourist park due to open at the end of 2019, and which will include the Iron Lion itself, plus a small temple with a slim, six-storey pagoda, another abandoned temple, called the **Iron Money Warehouse** (铁钱库; Tiě Qián Kù) and a new **museum**. Expect a price hike in the admission fee, and in the meantime keep your fingers crossed that the new development doesn't strip the site of its charming historical authenticity.

The remains of the ancient city wall will be outside the ticketed scenic area, 1.5km away. To reach it, walk up the country lane beside the new museum and cross the river. The earthen wall here is still around 5m tall, and you can walk along it in places. It once stretched for almost 10km around the city.

You can make a day trip to the Iron Lion from either Beijing or Tianjin. High-speed trains to Cangzhou West Station (沧州西站; Cāngzhōu Xī Zhàn) run roughly half-hourly from Beijing South Train Station (¥95, one hour, last train back 10.30pm) and roughly hourly from Tianjin South Train Station (¥50, 45 minutes, last train back 9.30pm). From Cangzhou West Station, take bus 16 to Cangzhou's main train station (火车站; huǒchēzhàn; ¥2, 40 minutes), then bus 901 (¥3, 40 minutes). Tell the driver you want tiě shīzi (tee-air shur-zuh) and he'll show you where to get off. Then follow the signposted lane beside the bus stop and very soon you'll see the pagoda then the Iron Lion on your right, with the Iron Money Warehouse and the new museum on your left.

The last 901 bus back to Cangzhou swings past here just after 6pm.

old China. From atop Zhengding's South Gate and its reconstructed city walls, you can see the silhouettes of four distinct pagodas jutting above the sleepy town. Affectionately known as the town of 'nine buildings, four pagodas, eight great temples and 24 golden archways', Zhengding has tragically lost many of its standout buildings and archways (Pingyao, it isn't), but enough remains to lend the place an air of faded grandeur. And in Longxing Temple, Zhengding can lay claim to having one of the finest temples in northern China. Zhengding is an easy day trip from Shijiazhuang.

◉ Sights

Start your temple tour at Longxing Temple. After visiting, turn right on Zhongshan Donglu (中山东路) and walk about 500m to reach Tianning Temple (on your right). From here, continue along the same road, then at the crossroads turn left down Yanzhou Nandajie (燕赵南大街) to reach Kaiyuan Temple (on your right). From here, continue another 500m south down Yanzhou Nandajie, past the huge **Yang He Gate**, built from scratch in 2017, then turn left down Linji Lu to reach Linji Temple. Walking further south on Yanzhou South St, you'll soon reach Guanghui Temple (on your left) and, finally, South Gate.

★ Longxing Temple
BUDDHIST TEMPLE

(隆兴寺, Lóngxīng Sì; Zhongshan Donglu, 中山东路; ¥50) Considering its age – almost 1500 years old – we think this is one of the most impressive temples in northern China. It's certainly Zhengding's star attraction. Popularly known as Dafo Temple (大佛寺, Dàfó Sì), or 'Great Buddha Temple', the complex contains an astonishing array of Buddhist statuary, housed in some stunning temple halls. Dating way back to AD 586, the temple has been much restored and stands divided from its spirit wall by Zhongshan Donglu.

The time-worn bridge out the front constitutes a handsome historical prelude. You are greeted in the first hall by the jovial Milefo (the laughing Buddha). The four Heavenly Kings flanking him in pairs are disconcertingly vast.

Beyond the ruined **Hall of Sakyamuni's Six Teachers** is the **Manichaean Hall** (摩尼殿, Móní Diàn), an astonishingly voluminous hall flagged in smoothed stone, with amazing carpentry overhead, a huge gilded statue of Sakyamuni and faded Ming frescoes detailing Buddhist tales. At the rear of the hall is a distinctly male statue of the goddess Guanyin, seated in a lithe pose with one foot resting on her/his thigh (a posture known as *lalitásana*) and surrounded by *luóhàn* (disciples freed from the cycle of rebirth).

The **Buddhist Altar** behind houses an unusual, bronze, Ming-dynasty two-faced Buddha, gazing north and south. Signs say 'no touching' but it's evident that its fingers and thumb have been smoothed by legions of worshippers. There are two halls behind the Buddhist Altar. On the left is the **Revolving Library Pavilion** (转轮藏阁, Zhuānlúnzàng Gé), which contains a highly unusual revolving, octagonal, wooden bookcase for the storing of *sutras,* and some stele on the back of snarling *bìxì* (a mythical, tortoise-like dragon). Opposite stands the **Pavilion of Kindness**, containing a fabulous, 7.4m-high statue of Maitreya (the future Buddha), one hand aloft.

The immense **Pavilion of Great Benevolence** (大悲阁, Dàbēi Gé) contains Longxing Temple's real drawcard: a 21.3m-tall, bronze colossus of Guanyin. Cast in AD 971 and sporting a third eye, the effigy is wonderful, standing on a magnificently carved base from the Northern Song. Examine the carvings, which include myriad characters and musicians, including Buddhist angels (apsaras).

Circumambulated by worshippers, the **Hall of Vairocana** at the rear of the complex contains a four-faced Buddha (the Buddha of four directions), crowned with another four-faced Buddha, upon which is supported a further set. The entire statue and its base contain 1072 statues of Buddha in all.

The **gardens** right at the back contain scattered temple remains, including some very old stele and a triple-arched stone *páilou* (decorative archway), dating from 1591.

Tianning Temple
BUDDHIST TEMPLE

(天宁寺, Tiānníng Sì; Zhongshan Donglu, 中山东路) **FREE** The remains of this temple contain the 41m-high Tang dynasty **Lofty Pagoda** (凌霄塔, Língxiāo Tǎ), also called the Wooden Pagoda (木塔, Mùtǎ). Originally dating from AD 779, the pagoda was restored in 1045, but is still in fine condition. The entrance is flanked by two beautifully expressive stone lions.

Kaiyuan Temple
BUDDHIST TEMPLE

(开元寺, Kāiyuán Sì; Yanzhao Nandajie, 燕赵南大街; ¥10) This temple dates from AD 540 but was destroyed in 1966, the first year of the Cultural Revolution. Little remains apart from a bell tower and the dirt-brown **Xumí Pagoda** (须弥塔; Xūmí Tǎ), a well-preserved, nine-eaved structure (dating from AD 636) topped with a spire. Its arched doors and carved stone doorway are particularly attractive, as are the carved figures on the base. You can enter a shrine at the bottom of the pagoda, but you can't climb up.

Linji Temple
BUDDHIST SITE

(临济寺, Línjì Sì; Linji Lu, 临济路) **FREE** This active monastery is notable for its tall, elegant, carved-brick **Chengling Pagoda** (澄灵塔, Chénglíng Tǎ; also called the Green Pagoda), topped with an elaborate lotus plinth plus ball and spire. In the Tang dynasty, the temple was home to one of Chan (Zen) Buddhism's most eccentric and important teachers, Linji Yixuan, who penned the now-famous words, 'If you meet the Buddha on the road, kill him!'

Guanghui Temple
BUDDHIST TEMPLE

(广惠寺, Guǎnghuì Sì; Yanzhao Nandajie, 燕赵南大街) **FREE** Nothing remains of this temple except **Hua Pagoda** (华塔; Huá Tǎ), dating from around AD 800. It's an unusual, Indian-style pagoda decorated with lions, elephants, sea creatures and *púsà* (Bodhisattvas, who are those worthy of nirvana who remain on earth to help others attain enlightenment). This is also the only one of Zhengding's four famous pagodas that you're allowed to climb (¥15).

Zhengding City Wall (South Gate)   GATE

(正定城墙 （南门), Zhèngdìng Chéngqiáng (Nán Mén); Yanzhao Nandajie, 燕赵南大街) **FREE** Up until about five years ago, all that remained of Zhengding's 24km-long, 6th-century city wall were sporadic stretches of tall earthen mounds, but now it seems the plan is to rebuild the whole thing. At the southern end of Yanzhao Nandajie, the enormous Chang Le Gate (长乐门, Cháng Lè Mén), commonly called South Gate (南门, Nán Mén), has been completely rebuilt.; you can climb up onto it and walk along for a while in either direction.

🛏 Sleeping & Eating

Most hotels do not accept foreign guests, but given Zhending's proximity to Shijiazhuang there is no need to spend the night here.

There are plenty of noodle and dumpling places along Zhongshan East Rd and Yanzhao South St (past Kaiyuan Temple). Expect to pay about ¥10 for a bowlful. Look out for *shǒu gǎn miàn* (手擀面), a local hand-pulled noodle dish with pork, spinach and beans.

You'll also find *lǘ ròu huǒshāo* (驴肉火烧; donkey-meat pastry pockets), a Hebei speciality.

❶ Getting There & Away

Zhengding is an easy day trip from Shijiazhuang. Take bus 177 (¥3, one hour, 6.50am to 7pm) from the main road outside South Bus Station (p154), and get off at Taiping Zhuang (太平庄, Tàipíng Zhuāng) bus stop. Cross the road then take bus 143 (¥2) four stops to Longxing Jiayuan (隆兴家园, Lóngxīng Jiāyuán). Walk back the way you came for a short distance then turn right to reach Longxing Temple.

From Longxing Temple, you can then walk to all the other temples before catching bus 177 back to Zhengding from behind South Gate.

❶ Getting Around

Zhengding is not huge and walking is easy as sights are largely clustered together.

A short taxi ride costs ¥5; three-wheel motorcycle rides are slightly cheaper.

Yujiacun   于家村

POP 1600

Hidden in the hills near the Hebei–Shanxi border is the peaceful little settlement of Yu-jiacun (Yújiācūn). Nearly everything, from the houses to furniture inside, was originally made of stone – hence its nickname, Stone Village (石头村; Shítou Cūn).

As such, Yujiacun is remarkably well preserved: bumpy little lanes lead past traditional Ming- and Qing-dynasty courtyard homes, old opera stages and tiny temples.

◉ Sights

Yujiacun is bisected by a small village road, where the bus will drop you off. Most of the historic buildings, including all the sights listed here, are to the left of the road. The ticket office (which was closed indefinitely at the time of research, so entrance was free – previously it had been ¥30) and Xingshui Yuan guesthouse are to the right of the road.

There is a number of historic buildings worth hunting down, including the **Guanyin Pavilion** (观音阁; Guānyīn Gé) and **Zhenwu Temple** (真武庙; Zhēnwǔ Miào). Some of the sights are padlocked, so can only be viewed from the outside, but just wandering the time-worn cobbled alleys is rewarding.

Qingliang Pavilion   HISTORIC BUILDING

(清凉阁, Qīngliáng Gé) Completed in 1581, this three-storey pavilion was supposedly the work of one thoroughly crazed individual – Yu Xichun, who wanted to be able to see Beijing from the top. It was, according to legend, built entirely at night, over a 16-year period, without the help of any other villagers.

Yu Ancestral Hall   TEMPLE

(于氏宗祠, Yúshì Zōngcí) Yujiacun is a model Chinese clan village, where 95% of the inhabitants all share the same surname of Yu (于). One of the village's more unusual sights is the town ancestral hall, where you'll find the 24-generation family tree, reaching back over 500 years. There are five tapestries, one for the descendants of each of the original Yu sons who founded the village.

🛏 Sleeping

Xīngshuǐ Yuàn   GUESTHOUSE ¥

(兴水院; ☎0311 8237 6517, 134 7311 0485; Yú-jiācūn, 于家村; r per person ¥30) One of a handful of *nóng jiā lè* (农家乐; village guesthouses) in Yujiacun, this typically simple courtyard guesthouse has rooms in an old stone building, although the main house itself is a white-tiled renovation. No English is spoken, but you'll get a friendly welcome. As with all village guesthouses, meals are also available, but the menu is in Chinese only.

Dishes cost from ¥15 to ¥30 and include *dòu miàn hé le* (豆面饸饹; bean noodles – a local speciality), *nóngjiā dòufu* (农家豆腐; village-style tofu), *chǎo bènjīdàn* (炒笨鸡蛋; fried free-range eggs) and *nóngjiā zhūtóu ròu* (农家猪头肉, village-style pig's head meat).

ℹ Getting There & Away

From Shijiazhuang's Xiwang Bus Station (p155), take one of the frequent buses to the small town of Jingxing (井陉; Jǐngxíng; ¥12, one hour, 6.30am to 6.30pm), from where you can catch a bus to Yujia-cun (¥7, one hour, hourly 8am to 5pm).

Tell the ticket seller and the driver that you want to go to Yujiacun (also known as Shitou Cun; 石头村, Shítou Cūn) to ensure that you get dropped off by the place where the Yujiacun buses leave from.

Note that the last bus back from Yujiacun leaves at 4.20pm – all the more reason to stay the night.

Chengde 承德

📋 0314 / POP 457,000

Built on the banks of the Wulie River and surrounded by forested hills, Chengde (Chéngdé) is a small, pleasant city that just happens to have an extraordinary history.

This was the summer playground of the emperors of the Qing dynasty; beginning with Emperor Kangxi, the Qing Court would flee here to escape the torpid summer heat of the Forbidden City (and occasionally also the threat of foreign armies), as well as to be closer to the hunting grounds of their northern homelands.

The Bìshǔ Shānzhuāng (Fleeing-the-Heat Mountain Villa) is a grand imperial palace and the walled enclosure it lies within houses China's largest regal gardens. Beyond the grounds is a remarkable collection of politically chosen temples, built to host dignitaries such as the sixth Panchen Lama. The Imperial Villa, the gardens and the eight temples are all, quite rightly, Unesco-protected.

History

In 1703, when an expedition passed through the Chengde valley, Emperor Kangxi was so enamoured with the surroundings that he had a hunting lodge built, which gradually grew into the summer resort. Jehol (or Rèhé, 热河, Warm River; named after a hot spring here) – as Chengde was then known – grew in importance and the Qing court began to spend more time here, sometimes up to several months a year, with some 10,000 people accompanying the emperor on his seven-day expedition from Beijing.

The emperors also convened in Jehol with the border tribes – undoubtedly more at ease here than in Beijing – who posed the greatest threats to the Qing frontiers: the Mongols, Tibetans, Uyghurs and, eventually, the Europeans. The resort reached its peak under Emperor Qianlong (1735–96), who commissioned many of the outlying temples to rawe visiting leaders.

Emperor Xianfeng died here in 1861, permanently warping Chengde's feng shui and tipping the Imperial Villa towards long-term decline.

⊙ Sights

You can buy a combined ticket (summer/winter ¥260/190) for the four main attractions: Bìshǔ Shānzhuāng, Puning Temple, Putuozongcheng Temple and the group of three Hammer Rock sights (Hammer Rock, Pule Temple and Anyuan Temple). It's good for three days, but you can only enter each sight once.

★ Bìshǔ Shānzhuāng HISTORIC SITE

(避暑山庄, Bìshǔ Shānzhuāng; Lizhengmen Dajie, 丽正门大街; summer/winter ¥130/90, or combined ¥260 ticket; ⊙7am-5.30pm Apr-Oct, 8am-4.30pm Nov-Oct) The imperial summer resort is composed of a main palace complex with vast, parklike gardens, all enclosed by a handsome 10km-long wall. The entrance price is steep (as it is with all the main sights in Chengde), and it gets packed with tourists here in summer, but the splendid gardens provide ample opportunity to take a quiet walk away from the crowds.

A huge spirit wall shields the resort entrance at Lizhengmen Dajie. Through Lizheng Gate (丽正门, Lìzhèng Mén), the Main Palace (正宫, Zhèng Gōng) is a series of nine courtyards and five elegant, unpainted halls, with a rusticity complemented by towering pine trees. The wings in each courtyard have various exhibitions (porcelain, clothing, weaponry), and most of the halls are decked out in period furnishings.

The first hall is the refreshingly cool Hall of Simplicity and Sincerity, built of an aromatic cedar called *nánmù*, and displaying a carved throne draped in yellow silk. Other prominent halls include the emperor's study (Study of Four Knowledges) and living quarters (Hall of Refreshing Mists and Waves). On the left-hand side of the latter is the imperial bedroom. Two residential areas branch

Chengde

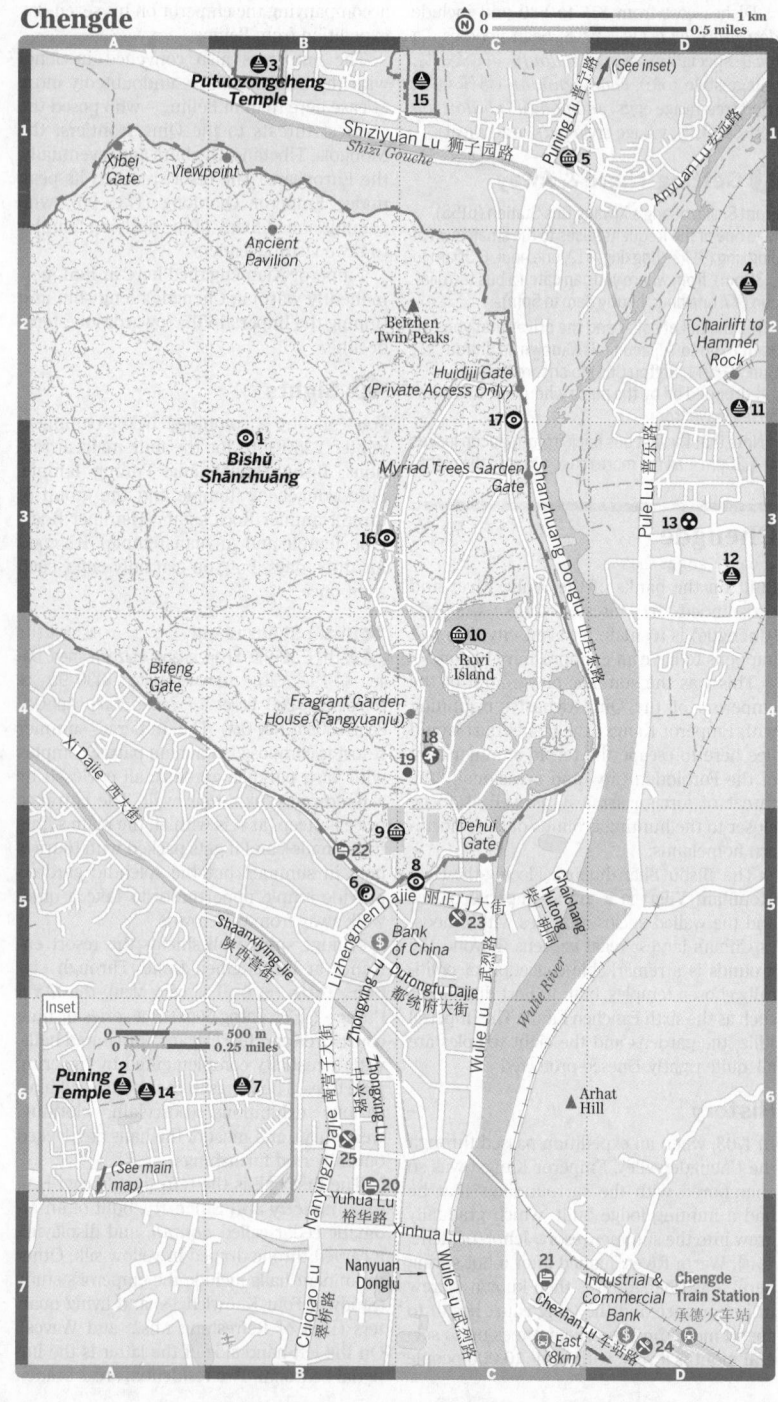

Chengde

out from here: the empress dowager's **Pine Crane Palace** (松鹤斋; Sōnghè Zhāi) to the east, and the smaller **Western Apartments**, where the concubines (including a young Cixi) resided.

Exiting the Main Palace brings you to the gardens and forested hunting grounds, with landscapes borrowed from famous southern scenic areas in Hangzhou, Suzhou and Jiaxing, as well as the Mongolian grasslands.

The double-storey **Misty Rain Tower** (烟雨楼, Yānyǔ Lóu), on the northwestern side of the main lake, served as an imperial study. Further north is the **Wenjin Pavilion** (文津阁, Wénjīn Gé), built in 1773. Don't miss the wonderfully elegant 250-year-old **Yongyousi Pagoda** (永佑寺塔, Yǒngyòusì Tǎ), which soars above the fragments of its vanished temple in the northeast of the complex.

Most of the compound is taken up by lakes, hills, forests and plains. There are magnificent views of some of the outlying temples from the northern wall.

Just beyond the Main Palace is the starting point for **bus tours of the gardens** (环山车, huánshān chē; per person ¥50). Further on you'll find a place for **boat rentals** (出租小船, Chūzū Xiǎochuán; Bìshǔ Shānzhuāng; boat hire per hour ¥60-90, deposit ¥300).

Almost all of the forested section is closed from November to May because of fire hazard in the dry months, but you can still wander around the rest of the park.

Tourists can exit by any of the gates, but entry tickets are only available for purchase at Lizheng Gate.

Guandi Temple   TAOIST TEMPLE
(关帝庙, Guāndì Miào; 18 Lizhengmen Dajie, 丽正门大街18号; ◎8am-6pm Apr-Oct, to 5pm Nov-Oct) **FREE** The heavily restored Guandi Temple was first built during the reign of Yongzheng, in 1732. For years the temple housed residents but is again home to a band of Taoist monks, garbed in distinctive jackets and trousers, their long hair twisted into topknots. Note the original 300-year-old beamwork in the ceiling of the final hall.

Chengde Museum   MUSEUM
(承德博物馆, Chéngdé Bówùguǎn; Puning Lu, 普宁路) This new, ultra-modern, strikingly good-looking museum wasn't quite finished at the time of research, but will be opening very soon and is set to showcase around 10,000 cultural relics in a multimedia complex.

◎ Eight Outer Temples

Skirting the northern and eastern walls of Bìshǔ Shānzhuāng, the Eight Outer Temples (外八庙; *wài bā miào*) were, unusually, designed for diplomatic rather than spiritual reasons. Some were based on actual Tibetan Buddhist monasteries, but the emphasis was on appearance: smaller temple buildings are sometimes solid, and the Tibetan facades (with painted windows) are often fronts for traditional Chinese temple interiors. The surviving temples and monasteries were all built between 1713 and 1780; the prominence given to Tibetan Buddhism was as much for the Mongols (fervent Lamaists) as the Tibetan leaders.

Three of these temples are currently closed to the public (and have been for a long time): **Puren Temple** (普仁寺, Pǔrén Sì), **Pushan Temple** (溥善寺, Pǔshàn Sì) and

Guanyuan Temple (广缘寺, Guǎngyuán Sì; off Puning Lu, 普宁路).

★Puning Temple BUDDHIST TEMPLE

(普宁寺, Pǔníng Sì; Puning Lu, 普宁路; Apr-Oct ¥80, Nov-Mar ¥60, or combined ¥260 ticket; ☺8am-5.30pm Apr-Oct, 8.30am-5pm Nov-Mar) With its squeaking prayer wheels and devotional intonations of its monks, this is Chengde's only active Buddhist temple. It was built in 1755 in anticipation of Qianlong's victory over the western Mongol tribes in Xinjiang. Supposedly modelled on the earliest Tibetan Buddhist monastery (Samye), the first half of the temple is distinctly Chinese, with Tibetan buildings at the rear.

Enter the temple grounds to a stele pavilion with inscriptions by the Qianlong emperor in Chinese, Manchu, Mongol and Tibetan. The halls behind are arranged in typical Buddhist fashion, with the **Hall of Heavenly Kings** (天王殿; Tiānwáng Diàn) and beyond, the **Mahavira Hall** (大雄宝殿; Dàxióng Bǎodiàn), where three images of the Buddhas of the three generations are arrayed. Some very steep steps rise up behind (the temple is arranged on a hillside) leading to a gate tower, which you can climb.

On the terrace at the top of the steps is the dwarfing **Mahayana Hall**. On either side are stupas and square, block-like Tibetan-style buildings, decorated with attractive water spouts. Some buildings have been converted to shops, while others are solid, serving a purely decorative purpose.

The mind-bogglingly vast gilded **statue of Guanyin** (the Buddhist Goddess of Mercy) towers within the Mahayana Hall. The effigy is astounding: over 22m high, it's the tallest of its kind in the world and radiates a powerful sense of divinity. Hewn from five different kinds of wood (pine, cypress, fir, elm and linden), Guanyin has 42 arms, with each palm bearing an eye and each hand holding instruments, skulls, lotuses and other Buddhist devices. Tibetan touches include the pair of hands in front of the goddess, below the two clasped in prayer, the right one of which holds a sceptre-like *dorje* (*vajra* in Sanskrit), a masculine symbol, and the left a *dril bu* (bell), a female symbol. On Guanyin's head sits the Teacher Longevity Buddha. To the right of the goddess stands a huge male guardian and disciple called Shàncái, opposite his female equivalent, Lóngnǚ (Dragon Girl). Unlike Guanyin, they are both coated in ancient and dusty pigments. On the wall on either side are hundreds of small effigies of Buddha.

Occasionally, tourists are allowed to climb up to the 1st-floor gallery for a closer inspection of Guanyin.

Housed within the grounds, on the east side, is the **Puyou Temple** (普佑寺, Pǔyòu Sì; ☺8am-6pm). It is dilapidated and missing its main hall, but it has a plentiful contingent of merry gilded *luóhàn* (Buddhists who have achieved nirvana) in the side wings, although a fire in 1964 incinerated many of their confrères. (The ticket price includes admission to Puyou Temple.)

Puning Temple has a number of friendly lamas who manage their domain, so be quiet and respectful at all times.

Take bus 6 (¥1) from in front of Mountain Villa Hotel.

★Putuozongcheng Temple BUDDHIST TEMPLE

(普陀宗乘之庙, Pǔtuózōngchéng Zhīmiào; Shiziyuan Lu, 狮子园路; Apr-Oct ¥80, Nov-Mar ¥60, or combined ¥260 ticket; ☺8am-5pm Apr-Oct, 8.30am-5pm Nov-Mar) Also known as Potala (布达拉, Bùdálā), Chengde's largest temple is a not-so-small replica of Lhasa's Potala Palace and houses the nebulous presence of Avalokiteshvara (Guanyin). A marvellous sight on a clear day, the temple's red walls stand out against its mountain backdrop. Enter to a huge stele pavilion, followed by a large triple archway topped with five small stupas in red, green, yellow, white and black.

Fronted by a collection of prayer wheels and flags, the **Red Palace** contains most of the main shrines and halls. Look out for the marvellous sandalwood pagodas in the front hall. Both are 19m tall and contain 2160 effigies of the Amitabha Buddha.

Among the many exhibits on view are displays of Tibetan Buddhist objects and instruments, including a *kapala* bowl, made from the skull of a young girl. The main hall is located at the very top, surrounded by several small pavilions and panoramic views.

The admission ticket includes the neighbouring Temple of Sumeru, Happiness and Longevity.

Bus 118 (¥1) goes here from in front of Mountain Villa Hotel.

Temple of Sumeru, Happiness & Longevity BUDDHIST TEMPLE

(须弥福寿之庙, Xūmífúshòu Zhīmiào; Shiziyuan Lu, 狮子园路; Apr-Oct ¥80, Nov-Mar ¥60, or combined ¥260 ticket; ☺8am-5pm Apr-Oct, from 8.30am Nov-Mar) This huge temple was built in honour of the sixth Panchen Lama, who stayed here in 1781. Incorporating Tibetan and Chinese architectural elements, it's an imitation of the Panchen's home monastery Tashilhunpo in Shigatse, Tibet. Note the eight huge, glinting dragons (each said to weigh over 1000kg) that adorn the roof of the main hall. The admission price includes entry to the neighbouring Putuozongcheng Temple.

Bus 118 (¥1) goes here from in front of Mountain Villa Hotel.

Pule Temple
BUDDHIST TEMPLE

(普乐寺, Pǔlè Sì; Pule Lu, 普乐路; Anyuan Temple & Hammer Rock ticket ¥50, combined ticket ¥260; ⊗8am-5pm Apr-Oct, 8.30am-4.30pm Nov-Mar) This peaceful temple was built in 1776 for the visits of minority envoys from the west (Kazakhs and Uyghurs among them). At the rear of the temple is the unusual **Round Pavilion**, modelled on the Hall of Prayer for Good Harvests at Beijing's Temple of Heaven Park. Inside is an enormous wooden mandala – a geometric representation of the Buddhist universe.

Admission also includes entry to **Hammer Rock** (磐锤峰; Qìngchuí Fēng) and **Anyuan Temple** (安远庙, Ānyuǎn Miào). It's a 60-minute walk to the club-shaped rock, which is visible for miles around and said to resemble a kind of musical hammer. It's a pleasant hike offering commanding views of the area. If you don't fancy walking, there's also a **chairlift** (索道, suǒ dào; one way/return ¥50/80; ⊗7.30am-5.30pm).

Bus 10 (¥1) from the Mountain Villa Hotel will drop you at Anyuan Miao (安远庙) bus stop, near the approach road to Hammer Rock.

🛏 Sleeping

First Met Hostel
HOSTEL ¥

(初见客栈, Chūjiàn Kèzhàn; ☑186 3148 1357; 2nd fl, No 4 Bldg, Yuhua Zonghe Market, Yuhua Lu, 裕华路裕华综合市场4号楼2楼; dm ¥40-60, s ¥78; ⊛🛜) The best budget digs in Chengde, this makeshift hostel has a pleasant setting on the roof of a low building, sharing the space with a pergola, a small garden and a few other apartments. The friendly owner speaks some English, rooms come with a toast-and-coffee breakfast, and there's bike rental (¥10), laundry (¥10) and a low-key bar (beer/cocktails from ¥5/20).

To find it, enter the 'market' courtyard, then take the exterior stairs up to your left.

Huilong Hotel
HOTEL ¥¥

(会龙酒店, Huìlóng Jiǔdiàn; ☑0314 252 8119; Huilong Plaza, Xinjuzhai, Chezhan Lu, 车站路新居

宅会龙大厦; d/tr from ¥288/388; ⊛🛜) This hulking old-timer, a short walk from the train station, has had a refurb and now has really rather decent midrange rooms with attractive decor, a modern finish and plenty of space – the triples are enormous.

Qǐ Wàng Lóu
HOTEL ¥¥¥

(绮望楼; ☑0314 218 2288; www.qiwanglou.com; 1 Bifengmen Donglu, 碧峰门东路1号; r incl breakfast from ¥1599; ⊛⊛🛜) If you fancy a splurge, this delightful hotel boasts a serene setting alongside the Imperial Villa's walls, accentuated by lovely courtyard gardens. It's far and away the most tasteful hotel in town, with museum-quality reproduced Chinese masterpieces hanging in all the rooms. Nicer rooms have balconies.

🍴 Eating

Magic Room
INTERNATIONAL ¥¥

(魔法厨房西餐厅, Mófǎ Chúfáng Xī Cāntīng; Sushunfu Lu, 肃顺府路; dishes ¥25-80; ⊗10.30am-9pm) The witch's forest lair theme is fun, but it's the food that's truly charmed – a mix of western comforts (steak, chips, salads, pasta and top-notch handmade pizzas) and Eastern treats (the Taiwanese braised-pork rice meal is delicious). Throw into the brew some fresh-fruit smoothies, oh-so-wicked desserts and an English menu, and hey presto! You have yourself a magic little restaurant.

Dà Qīng Huā Jiǎozi
DUMPLINGS ¥¥

(大清花饺子; Lizhengmen Dajie, 丽正门大街; most dishes ¥20-60; ⊗10.30am-9.30pm) The finest dumpling house in Chengde, this excellent establishment has a big choice of juicy *jiǎozi* (dumplings; ¥18 to ¥32 per serving). Choose boiled (水饺, *shuǐ jiǎo*) or steamed (蒸饺, *zhēng jiǎo*), then pick your filling: pork and cabbage (猪肉白菜, *zhūròu báicài*), egg and chives (韭菜鸡蛋, *jiǔcài jīdàn*) or shrimp with egg and horned melon (角瓜鸡蛋虾仁, *jiǎoguā jīdàn xiārén*).

There are plenty of other dishes besides dumplings, and although there's no English here, the menu does have photos. There's another **branch** (241 Chezhan Lu, 车站路241号) by the train station.

ℹ Information

Bank of China (中国银行, Zhōngguó Yínháng; 4 Dutongfu Dajie, 都统府大街4号) Also on Lizhengmen Dajie; has 24-hour ATMs.

Industrial & Commercial Bank (ICBC, 工商银行, Gōngshāng Yínháng; Chezhan Lu, 车站路) Has a 24-hour ATM.

ⓘ Getting There & Away

AIR

Chengde Puning Airport (承德普宁机场, Chéngdé Pǔníng Jīchǎng), 20km northeast of town, opened in 2017 and flies to destinations such as Xi'an, Shanghai, Guangzhou and Shijiazhuang.

Airport buses (¥10, 45 minutes) leave from outside Bìshǔ Shānzhuāng's main entrance and make a stop at Wuyun Qiao (五云桥) bus stop on Wulie Lu, and opposite the train station.

BUS

Buses for Chengde leave Beijing every 40 minutes from Liuliqiao bus station (六里桥长途车站, Liùlìqiáo Chángtú Chēzhàn; ¥85, 3½ hours, 5.40am to 6.50pm). Most stop at Chengde's East Bus Station before terminating at the train station. From Chengde, they leave every half-hour for Beijing (¥85, 3½ hours, 6am to 6pm) from the train station square.

Services from Chengde's **East Bus Station** (汽车东站, qìchē dōngzhàn; G101 Yingbin Lu, 101国道迎宾路), 8km south of town, include the following:

Beijing ¥85, 3½ hours, half-hourly (6.20am to 6pm)

Qinhuangdao (for Shanhaiguan) ¥100, three hours, nine daily (7am, 8am, 9am, 10.40am, noon, 1pm, 2.20pm, 3.40pm and 5pm)

Tianjin ¥120, four hours, two daily (8.50am and 2pm)

TRAIN

Chengde Train Station (承德火车站, Chéngdé Huǒchē Zhàn; Chezhan Lu, 车站路) only accommodates regular slow-train services, while the new **Chengde South Train Station** (承德南站, Chéngdé Nán Zhàn) is for high-speed trains. It is part of the new Beijing to Shenyang high-speed line, although at the time of writing the Chengde to Beijing section had yet to begin operating. When it does, you'll be able to do the journey in just one hour.

Until the high-speed trains to Beijing start up, the two fastest daytime trains from to Chengde leave Beijing at 7.56am (hard seat ¥41, 4½ hours) and 11.41am (hard seat ¥36, 5½ hours). Return services leave Chengde Train Station at 7.49am (¥41, five hours, to Beijing East), 1.13pm (¥41, five hours, to Beijing East) and 7.18pm (¥41, 4½ hours).

Other services from Chengde Train Station include the following:

Shijiazhuang Hard sleeper ¥133, 11 hours, two overnight services (8.04pm and 9.02pm)

Services from Chengde South Train Station include the following:

Shenyang G-class bullet 2nd-class seat ¥243, 2½ to three hours, four daily (9.48am, 11.59am, 1.53pm and 5.49pm)

Shenyang North G-class bullet 2nd-class seat ¥244, 2½ to three hours, three daily (11am, 11.29am and 2.35pm)

ⓘ Getting Around

Local buses cost either ¥1 or ¥2 per trip.

Buses 13, 24, 29 and 67 link the East Bus Station with the train station; bus 29 carries on to Bìshǔ Shānzhuāng. Buses 5, 15 and 28 also connect the train station to Bìshǔ Shānzhuāng.

Bus 67 goes from Chengde South Train to Chengde Train Station, via the East Bus Station.

A taxi from the train station to Bìshǔ Shānzhuāng should cost around ¥10, from the bus station around ¥25, and from the South Train Station around ¥35.

Shanhaiguan 山海关

☑ 0335 / POP 140,000

The drowsy walled town of Shanhaiguan (Shānhǎiguān) is the fabled point where the Great Wall snakes out of the hills to meet the sea.

The area holds real interest for Wall enthusiasts: in addition to its claim as the eastern end of the Ming Wall (in fact, the Hushan Great Wall, beside the North Korean border, is 380km further east), there's an excellent museum and plenty of opportunity to explore large stretches of wild, unrestored Wall, climbing up and over the rugged, scrubland hills.

Bear in mind, however, that the old walled town itself feels a bit soulless. With fewer residents than before and no discernible economy apart from tourism, what's left is something that feels a little like a theme park, but without the rides. However, things do get more interesting (and authentic) the further off the main drag you explore.

⊙ Sights

★ **Jiao Shan Great Wall** WALLS (角山, Jiǎo Shān; ¥40; ⊙24hr) Although a heavily restored section of the Great Wall, Jiao Shan (角山, Jiǎo Shān) nevertheless offers an excellent opportunity to hike up the Wall's first high peak – a telling vantage point over the narrow tongue of land below and one-time invasion route for northern armies. It's a steep 30-minute clamber from the base, or else use the old chairlift (索道; suǒdào, one way/return ¥15/20).

To leave behind the crowds, continue beyond the chairlift station to **Qixian Monastery** (栖贤寺, Qīxián Sì) or even further

Shanhaiguan

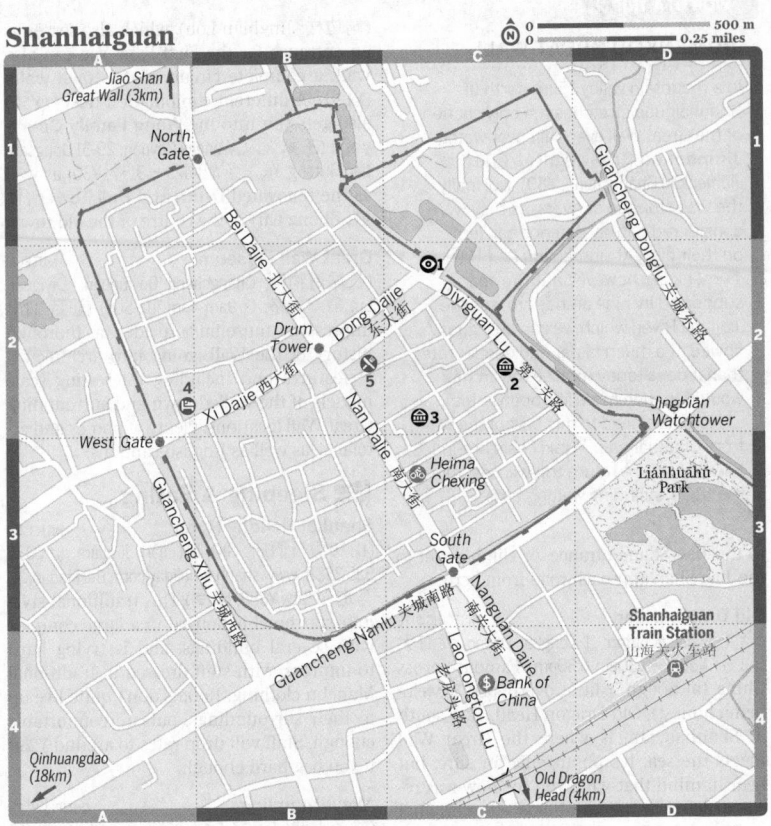

TIANJIN & HEBEI SHANHAIGUAN

to **Sweet Nectar Pavilion** (甘露亭, Gānlù Tíng). Better yet, climb up onto the closed section (accessed from paths on the side) and you'll be able to follow the crumbling Wall all the way up past several peaks. Explorers won't be able to resist – but use caution and don't go it alone.

You can get here on tourist bus 5 from Shanhaiguan train station (high season only) or hail a taxi (¥20 flat rate), but it's an easy 3km walk (or cycle) north of town; just follow the road straight on from Shanhaiguan's North Gate.

More fun than that, though, is to approach Jiao Shan on an original, overgrown stretch of Great Wall, which still creeps its way through farmland from Shanhaiguan to Jiao Shan. Most of its Ming brickwork has long since been pillaged, but there's still a scattering of bricks, including a couple of half-collapsed watchtowers. To take this route, walk straight on from North Gate then take the first right, along the main road, until

you reach the Wall (you can't miss it). Turn left up a pathway by the wall and walk under the iron footbridge before clambering up onto the Wall by the footbridge. You can walk on this earthen Wall all the way to Jiao Shan (it takes about an hour; you'll need to walk across a small restored section over the highway at one point). Just before you reach Jiao Shan, there's a final footbridge that may be closed off. Either ignore the sign and cross the bridge anyway, before clambering down

WORTH A TRIP

JIUMENKOU GREAT WALL

In a mountain valley 15km north of Shanhaiguan stretches the only section of the Great Wall ever built over water, **Jiumenkou Great Wall** (九门口长城, Jiǔménkǒu Chángchéng; ¥80). Normally the Wall stopped at rivers, as they were considered natural defence barriers on their own. At Jiumenkou (九门口, Jiǔménkǒu), however, a 100m span supported by nine arches crosses the Jiujiang River, which we can only guess flowed at a much faster and deeper rate than it does today (or else the arches would function more like open gates).

No buses head to this part of the Wall from Shanhaiguan. A taxi costs around ¥40 one way. A return trip will cost more like ¥100, including waiting time.

to the Jiao Shan entrance, or climb down to the Jiao Shan approach road from here.

Old Dragon Head　　　HISTORIC SITE
(老龙头, Lǎolóngtóu; 1 Longhai Dadao, 龙海大道1号; ¥50; ⊙7.30am-6.30pm) Famous across China (although a little overhyped if we're being honest), Old Dragon Head, 4km south of Shanhaiguan, is where the Great Wall meets the sea. It's photogenic for sure, but bear in mind that what you see now was re-constructed in the late 1980s – the original wall crumbled away long ago. Bus 25 (¥2) goes here from Shanhaiguan's South Gate.

To walk along the **beach** for free, and bag the famous wall-meets-sea photo, you can by-pass the ticketed area altogether; take the first left ahead of where the bus drops you off, and follow the road for around 300m, eventually walking through the Great Wall itself via a narrow traffic tunnel that pops you out beside the beach. The beach is a decent strip of sand, though you'll have to try to ignore the huge shipping port that looms large in the distance.

First Pass Under Heaven　　HISTORIC SITE
(天下第一关, Tiānxià Dìyī Guān; Dong Dajie, 东大街; ¥40; ⊙7am-5.30pm) The Great Wall's main gate as it snaked down the mountains towards the sea, the First Pass served as Shan-haiguan's east gate and principal watchtower. Two storeys tall, with double eaves and 68 arrow-slit windows, it's a towering 13.7m high, with an enceinte extending east.

The ¥40 ticket allows you to walk along the wall, south to the **Jingbian Watchtower**

(靖边楼; Jìngbiān Lóu), which also serves as an entrance for the First Pass. You can also walk a complete circuit of the **town walls** (¥120). A different combination ticket (¥50) also gets you into the **Wang Family Court-yard** (王家大院, Wángjiā Dàyuàn; 29-31 Dongsan-tiao Hutong, 东三条胡同29—31号; ¥30) as well as the renovated **Drum and Bell Tower** (钟鼓; Zhōng Gǔ) in the centre of the old town.

Great Wall Museum　　　MUSEUM
(长城博物馆, Chángchéng Bówùguǎn; Diyiguan Lu, 第一关路; ⊙9am-4pm Tue-Sun) **FREE** This impressive museum provides a thorough history of the Wall, going into architectur-al features and including interesting scale models of the walled town and surrounding Great Wall locations. Plenty of photos and ar-tefacts, as well as English captions.

🛌 Sleeping & Eating

Shanhai Holiday Hotel　　　HOTEL ¥¥
(山海假日酒店, Shānhǎi Jiàrì Jiǔdiàn; ☎0335 535 2888; www.shanhai-holiday.com; Bei Madao, 北马道; d & tw ¥388; ❄🔌) This traditional-style four-star hotel is housed in a large complex with several buildings, and is trying hard to impress, with staff dressed in traditional Manchu clothing. Rooms don't quite live up to their surroundings, but are comfortable enough. Staff will drop rates to around ¥250 if you beg hard enough.

Alley Dumplings　　　DUMPLINGS ¥
(二条小巷饺子馆, Èrtiáo Xiǎoxiàng Jiǎoziguǎn; 15 Ertiao Xiaoxiang, off Nan Dajie, 南大街二条小巷15号; dumplings per serving ¥12, other dishes ¥18-25; ⊙8am-7pm) Housed in a 200-year-old build-ing, this endearing family-home restaurant, run by a welcoming elderly couple, offers de-licious dumplings (饺子, jiǎozi) with three choices of fillings: pork and cabbage (白菜猪肉, báicài zhūròu), pork and chives (韭菜猪肉, jiǔcài zhūròu) and egg and chives (韭菜鸡蛋, jiǔcài jīdàn). You can have your dumplings boiled (水饺, shuǐ jiǎo) or, better still, pan-fried (煎饺, jiān jiǎo).

ℹ️ Information

Bank of China (中国银行, Zhōngguó Yínháng; Lao Longtou Lu, 龙头路; ⊙8.30am-5.30pm) Foreign-exchange facility and ATM.

ℹ️ Getting There & Away

BUS

There's no long-distance bus station in Shanhai-guan. Qinhuangdao's bus station (秦皇岛汽车

站, Qínhuángdǎo qìchēzhàn), where the nearest long-distance buses arrive, is diagonally opposite its train station.

To get to Shanhaiguan from Qinhuangdao's bus station, turn right out of the bus station, bear right and, from the bus stop on your left, take bus 33 to Shanhaiguan's South Gate (南门, Nán Mén; ¥2, 30 minutes).

Buses from Qinhuangdao's increasingly quiet bus station include the following:

Beijing (Bǎwángfén) ¥105, 3½ hours, one daily (9am)

Beijing Capital Airport ¥140, four hours, five daily (5am, 7am, 9am, noon and 2pm)

Chengde ¥100, three hours, eight daily (7am, 9am, 10.40am, noon, 1pm, 2.20pm, 3.40pm and 5pm)

TRAIN

An increasing number of high-speed trains use Shanhaiguan Train Station, meaning there's less need than before to use Qinhuangdao (秦皇岛) Train Station, although there are still more trains running in and out of the latter. To reach Shanhaiguan from Qinhuangdao's train station, walk directly straight ahead and pick up bus 33 from the bus stop on your left. A taxi from Shanhaiguan to Qinhuangdao's train station should cost approximately ¥50.

Services from **Shanhaiguan Train Station** (山海关火车站, Shānhǎiguān Huǒchēzhàn) include the following:

Beijing T/K-class hard seat ¥47, four to six hours, seven daily (5.59am to 2.59pm)

Beijing D-class bullet 2nd-class seat ¥93, 2½ hours, 11 daily (9.40am to 8.17pm)

Beijing South G-class bullet 2nd-class seat ¥183, two hours, eight daily (10.54am to 9.09pm)

Dalian T-class hard-sleeper ¥152, 9½ hours, one daily overnighter (8.40pm)

Dalian North D-class bullet 2nd-class seat ¥169, 3½ hours, four daily (9.53am, 12.33pm, 5.37pm and 6.44pm)

Dalian North G-class bullet 2nd-class seat ¥218, three hours, eight daily (6.13am to 7.06pm)

Shenyang North G-class bullet 2nd-class seat ¥114, 2½ hours, 17 daily (11.17am to 8.14pm)

Tianjin T/K/Z-class hard seat ¥45, three to five hours, 40 daily (24 hours)

Tianjin West G-class bullet 2nd-class seat ¥132, 1½ hours, 30 daily (9.34am to 9.09pm)

ⓘ Getting Around

Consider hiring a bike from **Heima Chexing** (黑马车行, Hēimǎ Chēxíng; 12-1 Nan Dajie, 南大街 12-1号; per day ¥10, deposit ¥100; ⏰7am-6pm) to get out to some of the nearby sights, or just to potter about the old town. Don't forget to ask for a bike lock (车锁, chē suǒ).

Jimingyi 鸡鸣驿

☑ 0313 / POP 1000

The sleepy hamlet of Jimingyi (Jīmíngyì) is a delightful surprise to find amid the scruffy northern Hebei countryside. This walled town, established during the Yuan dynasty (1206–1368), is China's oldest surviving post station, a historic reminder of a system that endured for 2000 years and enabled the officials in the Forbidden City to keep in touch with their far-flung counterparts around China. Whipped by dust storms in the spring and with archaic, fading Mao-era slogans still visible on walls, Jimingyi sees few visitors and feels much further from the gleaming capital than the 140km distance would suggest.

During the Ming and Qing dynasties, Jimingyi had considerably more bustle and wealth, as evidenced by its numerous surviving temples and towering town walls. Many of its courtyard houses remain, though in dilapidated condition.

⊙ Sights

Meandering along the warren of Jimingyi's baked-mud walls and courtyard houses takes you past ancient stages and scattered temples, some of which contain Ming and Qing murals (not all are in good condition). Admission to the village costs ¥40; you get a free (Chinese) map with your ticket.

It's possible to visit Jimingyi as a day trip from Beijing, but spending the night allows you time to enjoy the slower pace of rural life, and gives you the chance to climb the mountain in the cool of the early morning or evening.

Jiming Mountain BUDDHIST TEMPLE
(鸡鸣山, Jīmíng Shān; ¥60) Dominating the skyline to the northwest of the town, Jimingyi's namesake mountain means Cock's Crow Mountain, and is topped by the largest and oldest temple in the area, the **Temple of Eternal Tranquillity** (永宁寺, Yǒngníng Sì). It's still an active monastery and a large and lively festival is held here on the 15th day of the fourth lunar month (usually April or May).

It's a wonderful climb to the top – the views are outstanding – but the approach road is round the back of the mountain, on the Xia Huayuan (下花园, Xià Huāyuán) side, making it a long hike from Jimingyi. Expect to take at least three hours to summit it from the walled town. Alternatively, take a taxi (¥20 to ¥30) to a point roughly halfway up the mountain

TIANJIN & HEBEI JIMINGYI

(which is as far as cars can go), then walk the last bit (about 45 minutes).

Jimingyi City Walls
HISTORIC SITE

(城墙, Chéng Qiáng) Ascend the **East Gate** or **West Gate** and circle the walls for fine views of the town, the surrounding fields and Jiming Mountain, standing formidably to the northwest.

God of Wealth Temple
TAOIST TEMPLE

(财神庙, Cáishén Miào; Yicheng Yijie, near West Gate, 西门驿城一街) Pop into this tiny edifice to pray for fabulous riches or to check out the marvellous Ming mural, uncovered in 2012. It depicts an ancient bank (票号, *piàohào*); if you look closely you'll also see five foreigners and a *qílín* (麒麟; a mythical Chinese animal) in the lower left-hand corner, on their way to China to do business.

Taishan Temple
TAOIST TEMPLE

(泰山行宫, Tàishān Xínggōng; Near the East Gate) This temple is dedicated to Bixia, the goddess of Tai Shan. The paintings here, Jimingyi's largest collection of Ming murals, depict the life of the goddess. They were whitewashed – some say for protection – during the Cultural Revolution. A professor from Qinghua University helped to uncover them; you can still see streaks of white in places.

🛏 Sleeping & Eating

Sleeping options are limited to simple *kè zhàn* (客栈; guesthouses), with most either on or just off Yicheng Yijie (驿城一街), the road running between the East Gate (东门, Dōng Mén) and West Gate (西门, Xī Mén). Expect to pay around ¥100 for a room.

Village guesthouses all double up as restaurants, with simple home-cooked meals. Bear in mind that they eat donkey meat (驴肉; *lǘròu*) in these parts.

Bǎilè Kèzhàn
GUESTHOUSE ¥

(百乐客栈; ☑ 137 8533 9336; Yicheng Yijie, 驿城一街; d/tr ¥100/120; ❈ 🐾) There are quite a few guesthouses in Jimingyi these days, but this one, close to the West Gate, is still our favourite. It's nothing flash, and no English is spoken, but the family who run it are friendly, and each of the rooms now has its own small private bathroom. Note, the sign

for the guesthouse is written in traditional Chinese characters (百樂客棧).

❶ Getting There & Away

TRAIN

Jimingyi can be reached from the fast-developing mining town of **Xia Huayuan** (下花园, Xià Huāyuán), 4km away. The easiest way to Xia Huayuan is to hop on a train from Beijing Main (¥23.50, 2½ hours, 7.14am) or Beijing West (¥21.50, three hours, 10.24am, 2.53pm and 3.30pm). Same-day tickets can be bought easily at the stations. Once at Xia Huayuan, turn right out of the train station and either walk to Jimingyi (3km) or flag down one of the very frequent small buses that run to Shacheng (沙城, Shāchéng), via Jimingyi (¥3).

Trains back to Beijing from Xia Huayuan leave at 8.06am (four hours; Beijing Main), 11.45am (2½ hours; Beijing West) and 4.33pm (three hours; Beijing West).

Note, the Beijing to Zhangjiakou high-speed train line, due to open in 2020, will stop at the new **Xia Huayuan North Station** (下花园北站, Xià Huāyuán Běizhàn) and will use Beijing North Train Station, which is beside Xizhimen subway station. This new station is further away still from Jimingyi, but presumably local buses will link it either to Jimingyi, or at least to the old train station or Shacheng.

BUS

Taking a bus from Beijing offers more flexibility than the train, though it's a bit more of a pain. First, head to Zhuxinzhuang metro station at the end of Line 8. Come out of Exit B2, cross the main road and turn left. Then walk about 200m to find bus 899, which terminates at Xia Huayuan (¥24, with travel card ¥16, 2¼ hours). Buses leave every hour on the half hour from 5.30am to 5.30pm.

There are no buses from the bus station in Xia Huayuan to Jimingyi, so it's best to get to the train station and catch the Shacheng bus from there. Local bus 5 goes to the train station, but it's very infrequent. It's only a 1.5km walk, though; turn left out of the bus station and walk all the way along Xiyuan Lu (西苑路). Turn left at the end, onto Gonglu Jie (公路街), then take the second right (still Gonglu Jie) and the train station is soon on your right.

A taxi from Xia Huayuan to Jimingyi is around ¥30.

Return buses from Xia Huayuan to Beijing leave on the hour every hour. The last one is at 5pm.

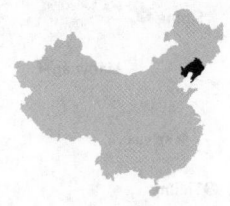

Liaoning

POP 43.8 MILLION

Best Places to Eat

➡ Meijin Hotpot (p184)

➡ Tiāntiān Yúgǎng (p174)

➡ Grandma's Home (p184)

Best Places to Stay

➡ Aloft Dalian (p173)

➡ UniLoft Hostel (p173)

➡ North Yorker Hotel (p183)

Why Go?

Liaoning (辽宁, Liáoníng) may be the smallest province in Dongbei, but it's a little marvel, with a long, winding coastline and some fine historical cities.

Hanging out over the Yellow Sea is Dalian, an attractive and relatively cosmopolitan former port turned resort city. Russian and Japanese forces clashed near here at Lushun in the early 20th century, but these days the warmer months see an influx of international tourists (many from Russian and Japan) for a rocking beer festival, affordable luxury hotels and perhaps China's finest stretch of golden-sand beaches.

In Dandong, regional tensions of recent history are causing some spine-tingling at the border with North Korea. The Yalu River here brings you within glimpsing distance of the hermit kingdom from a boat deck or halfway across a bridge. Nearby, ancient history buffs can get their Great Wall fix away from the crowds further west.

When to Go
Dalian

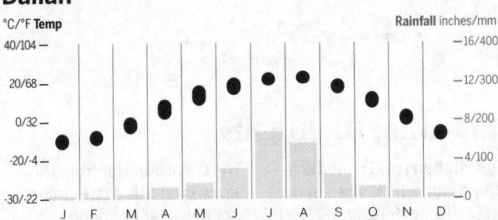

May & Jun Catch deals on a seaside hotel.	**Jun & Jul** Enjoy fresh cherries, mulberries and blueberries at roadside stands everywhere.	**Jul & Aug** Have fun at the Dalian International Beer Festival.

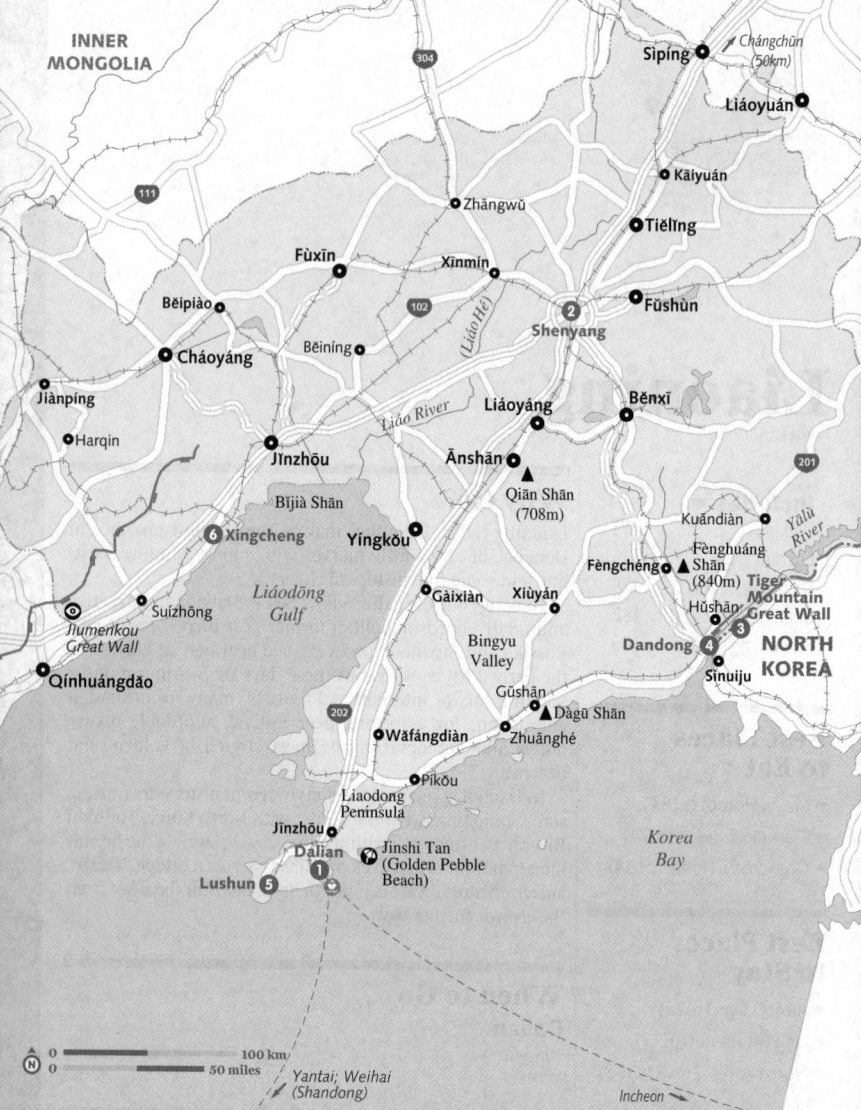

Liaoning Highlights

1 **Dalian** (p171) Catching the summertime vibes in the glitzy 'Hong Kong of the North'.

2 **Tomb of Huang Taiji** (p182) Discovering the tomb of the Qing dynasty founder in Shenyang's mini Forbidden City.

3 **Tiger Mountain Great Wall** (p178) Scrambling along the Great Wall, far from the crowds, at this easternmost section near Dandong.

4 **Dandong** (p178) Peering into North Korea from a speedboat at the Yālù River, and experiencing the mix of Korean and Chinese culture.

5 **Lushun** (p176) Wandering the old battlefields, graves and prison of Lushun, fought over by rival Japanese and Russian Empires.

6 **Xingcheng** (p186) Marvelling at the sight of a Ming walled city by a golden-sand beach.

History

The region formerly known as Manchuria, including the provinces of Liaoning, Jilin and Heilongjiang, plus parts of Inner Mongolia, is now called Dongbei (the Northeast).

The Manchurian warlords of this northern territory established the Qing dynasty, which ruled China from 1644 to 1911. From the late 1800s to the end of WWII, when western powers were busy carving up pieces of China for themselves, Manchuria was occupied alternately by the Russians and the Japanese.

Today there is a push to transform the flagging steel industry carried over from the 1950s into a tech hub. Despite the province's recent revival, a number of Communist Party officials were sanctioned for exaggerating the strength of Liaoning's economy by up to 20%.

Language

Nearly everyone in Liaoning speaks standard Mandarin, albeit with a distinct accent. In Dandong and areas close to the North Korean border, it's common to hear Korean spoken.

ⓘ Getting There & Around

Shenyang and Dalian have domestic and international airports. Dandong has an airport with infrequent domestic flights.

Boats connect Dalian with Shandong province and South Korea.

Buses are a slower alternative to high-speed trains but can outpace regular trains.

Rail lines criss-cross the region. Fast D and G trains link Shenyang with cities south to Dalian and Dandong; north to Harbin and Qiqiha'er; and east to Changchun, Jilin City and Yanji.

Dalian 大连

☑ 0411 / POP 6.97 MILLION

Surrounded by the Yellow Sea, Dalian (Dàlián) is one of China's most cosmopolitan cities. Its temperate climate, clean air and early-20th-century architecture alone attract the attention of international travellers from the region. But the second-tier city's tree-lined streets and impressive, swimmable seaside beaches, flanked by an undulating walkway, combine to create a seductive effect on China-hardened travellers and first-time visitors on three-day visa-free stopovers.

With a decent bar and seafood scene – and status as a Special Economic Zone to attract foreign investment – Dalian is a fine place to soak up a few days. But after lazing on the beaches and strolling along the southwest coastline, pay a visit to the historic port town of Lushun. The old battlefields and cemeteries offer a rare first-hand glimpse into some of the north's most turbulent days.

⦿ Sights

Fisherman's Wharf   VILLAGE

(渔人码头, Yúrén Mǎtóu; 66 Binhai Donglu, 滨海东路66号) FREE One of the wonders of modern China is its ability to rework certain western aesthetics into a recognisable, and eerily satisfying, contemporary kitsch. Fishermen's Wharf is a seaside community built in the style of an American east-coast village from the early 20th century. An afternoon in a wine shop, snapping photos of your surreal pan-cultural existence, can make your holiday. Take time to check out the perfect replica of the 1853 **German Bremen Port Lighthouse**, built with bricks from razed local villages.

Jinshi Tan   BEACH

(金石滩, Golden Pebble Beach) FREE The coast around Jinshi Tan, 50km northeast of the city, has been turned into a domestic tourism mecca with a number of theme parks and rock formations commanding inflated entrance fees. The long pebbly beach itself is free and quite pretty, set in a wide bay with distant headlands. For those who prefer their water chlorinated, there's a beautiful new public **swimming pool** (¥5, open 6am to 8pm) beside the sand.

To get here take the light rail, known by the locals as Line 3 (轻轨三号线, Qīngguǐ Sānhàoxiàn), from the depot on the east side of Victory Sq, behind the Dalian Train Station (¥8, 50 minutes) to its terminus 'Jin Shi Tan'. The ticket machine is in Chinese only, but just select the most expensive ticket, then the number of tickets and insert your money.

From the beach station it's a 10-minute walk to the beach, or catch a hop-on/hop-off

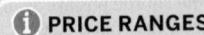

ⓘ PRICE RANGES

Sleeping

¥ Less than ¥250

¥¥ ¥250–450

¥¥¥ More than ¥450

Eating

¥ Less than ¥40

¥¥ ¥40–80

¥¥¥ More than ¥80

Dalian

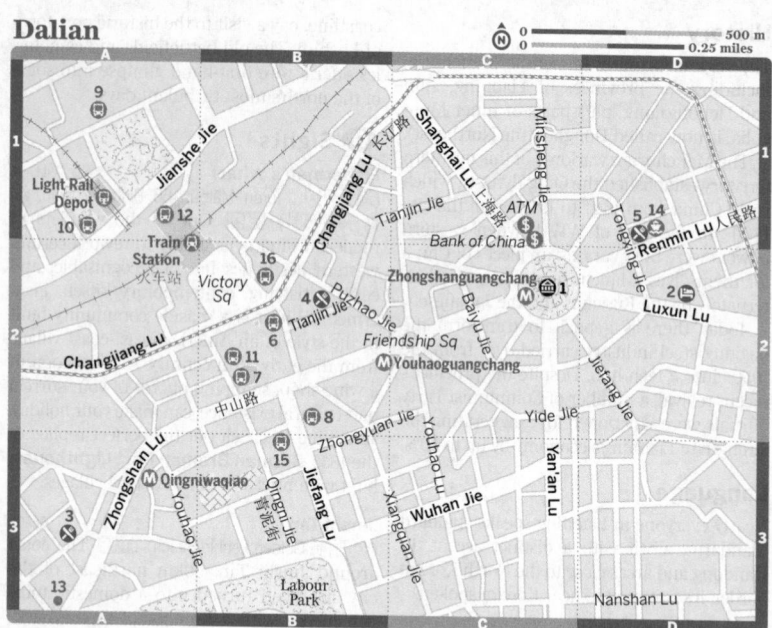

Dalian

⊙ Sights

🛏 Sleeping

🍴 Eating

ⓘ Transport

tourist shuttle bus (¥20), which winds round the coast first before dropping you off at the beach. Tickets for the shuttle bus are available from the visitor centre (open 8.30am to 5pm), to the right of the train station as you exit, which sometimes has English-speaking staff if you need help.

Fujiazhuang Beach BEACH
(傅家庄海滩, Fùjiāzhuāng Hǎitān) **FREE** At the height of summer, you'll see bathers 20 deep at this pretty pebble beach, which often features in crazy crowds in China photos. It's not always like that though – even in spring you can enjoy clean, clear water and plenty of space in the adjacent park. Junks float just offshore in a deep bay, small broken islands dot the horizon, and loads of families come here for no other reason than to have fun.

Bus 5 leaves from Jiefang Lu (¥1, 20 to 30 minutes) and drops you off across from the beach.

Xinghai Square SQUARE
(星海广场, Xīnghǎi Guǎngchǎng) **FREE** This square, which sports some gaudy architecture, is the site of Dalian's popular beer festival, and is a good place to people-watch, fly a kite or just stroll about. Nearby is a small beach and amusement park.

From the train station, take tram 201 (¥2; to its west terminus) or faster metro Line 2

(¥1; stop Xi'an, 西安路), then tram 202 (¥2) three stops. Last return tram is at 11pm. A taxi is about ¥20.

Zhongshan Square   SQUARE
(中山广场, Zhōngshān Guǎngchǎng) This is Dalian's hub, a 223m-wide square with 10 lanes radiating out from a central roundabout designed by the Russians in 1889. With the exception of the Dalian Financial Building, all the other grand structures hail from the early 20th century when Dalian was under the control of the Japanese. Styles range from art deco to French Renaissance.

The **Dàlián Bīnguǎn**, a dignified hotel built in 1914 and called then the Dalian Yamato Hotel, appeared in the movie *The Last Emperor*.

🛏 Sleeping

Reservations are highly recommended in the summer months, when prices may increase by 50%. The area around the train station's north exit has a number of budget hotels, but it's a noisy, frenetic place. Touts will find you if you do need a room: rates start at ¥100 a night. Better, quieter options are a few blocks southeast of the station. Luxury hotels near the port offer decent rates online.

★ UniLoft Hostel   HOSTEL ¥
(大连联合庭院青旅酒店, Dàlián Liánhé Tíngyuàn Qīnglǚ Jiǔdiàn; ☑ 0411 8369 7877; 17-1 Yinghua Jie, 英华街17-1号; dm ¥39-49, d with/without bathroom ¥149/129; 🅿 ⊕ ❄ @ 🛜) Arguably the best hostel between Harbin and Beijing, UniLoft has open-plan rooms and the feel of a hip office co-op, with statement pieces and a quiet buzz in the air. You could probably meet a budding Chinese entrepreneur or uni student lounging in the partitioned dorm beds and cosy doubles, or tapping on a laptop in the friendly in-house cafe.

UniLoft is behind a raised car park. A taxi from the train station is ¥10; alternatively, you can catch a free shuttle bus from Qingniwa Qiao downtown.

Tian Tian YHA
International Youth Hostel   HOSTEL ¥
(天天國際青年旅舍, Tiāntiān Guójì Qīngnián Lǚshě; ☑ 0411 8444 2458; 235 Huabei Jie, Shahekou, 沙河口華北街235號; dm/d from ¥49/89) This reliable hostel on the western edge of Dalian is popular with long-stay locals for its spotless dorm rooms and welcoming reception. The neighbourhood is pretty quiet, but it's near a subway station and the staff speak excellent English.

★ Amazing Koala
Boutique Hotel   BOUTIQUE HOTEL ¥¥
(Shénqí Kǎo Lā Jīngpǐn Jiǔdiàn; ☑ 138 4267 6224; www.amazingkoalachina.com; 102 Binhai Middle Road, Fujiazhuang, 福建省濱海中路102號; r from ¥700) Over on Fujiazhuang Beach is one of the rarer hotels for the region. The Amazing Koala is a large contemporary structure set back in dense foliage near the sea. There are six sleek rooms of varying size and formation, all furnished with impeccable taste and style. There's a fine western restaurant and hot tubs in every room.

Staff are intuitive and unobtrusively helpful. Pick-ups can be arranged.

Ibis Dalian Zhongshan Square   HOTEL ¥¥
(宜必思大連中山廣場酒店, Yíbìsī Dàlián Zhōngshān Guǎngchǎng Jiǔdiàn; ☑ 0411 3986 5555; www.ibishotel.com.cn; 49 Wuwu Lu, 中山区五五路49号; d & tw ¥229; ❄ @) This business hotel is in a fantastic location surrounded by restaurants and markets, yet only a five-minute walk from parks and quiet tree-lined streets. Bus 710 connects the hotel to the train station and southwestern coast. Rooms are clean and modern and the English-speaking staff are fairly attentive. For best rates book online.

It's just off Sanba Sq. A taxi from the train station costs ¥12.

★ Aloft Dalian   HOTEL ¥¥¥
(大连雅乐轩酒店, Dàlián Yǎlèxuān Jiǔdiàn; ☑ 0411 3907 1111; www.alofthotels.com/dalian; 18-1 Luxun Lu, 鲁迅路18-1号; r ¥1720-2220; ❄ @ 🛜) This could be the place to splurge during your dalliance with Dalian. Within walking distance of the train station, this Marriott-branded, hip hotel is surrounded by interesting shops and excellent restaurants. The rooms themselves are spacious, with bright colour schemes and good views down to the city street. The in-house restaurant and lounge area are good too. Discounts are widely available online.

BEER MANIA

For 12 days every July into August, Dalian stages the **Dalian International Beer Festival** (¥20, opening day ¥30; ⊙ Jul-Aug), resembling Munich's Oktoberfest. Beer companies from across China and around the world set up tents at the vast Xinghai Sq, near the coast, and locals and visitors (usually about 300,000) flock to sample the brews, gorge on snacks from around China, listen to live music and generally have a good time.

SOUTHWEST COASTLINE

Dalian's southwest coastline is the city's most alluring natural destination. Dramatic headlands, deep bays and sandy beaches are the obvious attractions, but there are also parks, lighthouses and quaint villages, and the longest continuous boardwalk (reportedly at 20.9km) in the world joining them all.

Start your exploration either by taking the tram from downtown to **Xinghai Square** (p172), or a bus to **Fujiazhuang Beach.** The massive square looking out to sea, which sports some gaudy architecture, is the site of Dalian's popular beer festival (p173), and is a good place to people-watch, fly a kite, or just stroll about. Nearby is a small beach and amusement park.

Fujiazhuang (p172) is a popular beach set in a deep bay. Junks float just offshore, small broken islands dot the horizon, and loads of families come here for no other reason than to have fun. Bus 5 leaves from Jiefang Lu (¥1, 20 to 30 minutes) and drops you off across from the beach.

A very pleasant boardwalk (it's really a wooden walkway built alongside the main coastal road) joins Fujiazhuang and Xinghai Sq. Continue on the same walkway another 8km to the square at Laohutan. Statue fanatics who want to see a huge work of tigers in motion can pay the steep entrance fee of over ¥200 for this glitzy theme park, which is hard to recommend because of its use of performing dolphins and seals, a practice that some view as cruel. At Laohutan you can catch bus 30 (¥1) to Sanba or Zhongshan Sq in central Dalian. You can also do the coastal route via taxi.

Head on from Laohutan to **Fisherman's Wharf** (p171), a seaside community in the style of an early-20th-century American east-coast village. The village makes a great backdrop for photos, has a row of pleasant coffee and wine shops, and features a perfect replica of the 1853 German Bremen Port Lighthouse, built with bricks from razed local villages.

✕ Eating

Small restaurants can be found on the roads leading off Friendship Sq and Zhongshan Sq. Friendship Sq has numerous malls with food courts on the higher floors. The food court in the nearby underground mall in Victory Sq has good food too (dishes ¥15 to ¥25), with international options. The plaza outside the train station is lined with fruit vendors and shops.

Tianjin Jie Night Market MARKET¥
(夜市, Yèshì; ⊙7pm-late) Stretching several blocks along Tianjin Jie from the train station to a giant incense-bowl sculpture, this outdoor market, open during the evenings, offers outdoor venues to eat barbecued seafood and other snacks with a beer. There's also a smaller (but better) market around Sanba Sq near the Carrefour Supermarket with outdoor barbecue stalls and seating, in addition to an abundance of fruit stands.

Brooklyn Bar & Restaurant PIZZA¥¥
(布鲁克林酒吧和餐廳; Bùlǔkè Lín Jiǔbā Hé Cāntīng; 184 Bulao Jie, Xigang, Wanda Huafu, 西崗區布劳街184號萬達華孚第; mains ¥60-100; ⊙4.30pm-midnight Tue-Fri, 11am-2pm & 4.30pm-midnight Sat & Sun) Down-to-earth Wayne set up this slice of American hospitality inspired by his visits abroad. Strong, tall cocktails support a menu spanning pizza (amazing dough!), huge burgers and colourful salads. Upstairs is popular with groups of young Chinese so it can get rowdy; downstairs is more intimate, where patrons sip beers, eat up and nod their head to the spirit of New York

Locomotive Guild Roast Duck PEKING DUCK¥¥¥
(火车头果木烤鸭, Huǒchētóu Guǒmù Kǎoyā; ☑0411 8597 6666; 17 Luxun Lu, 鲁迅路17号; duck ¥197, mains ¥30-80; ⊙11am-2pm & 5-9pm) We're not sure what locomotives have to do with duck, but the birds here are roasted in a wood-fired oven to delicate crispness before being deftly sliced and presented to your table. Live seafood is also available for those who prefer fish over fowl. Picture menu available.

Tiāntiān Yúgǎng SEAFOOD¥¥¥
(天天鱼港; 10 Renmin Lu, 人民路10号; dishes ¥25-100; ⊙11am-10pm) Choose your meal from the near museum-level variety of aquatic creatures at this upmarket seafood restaurant. Most dishes are set out in refrigerated displays making this a rare easy seafood-eating experience in China.

🍷 Drinking & Nightlife

Dalian has the most happening bar and club scene of any city in the northeast. Most of the action is on Wuwu Lu, which runs off Sanba Sq.

ℹ️ Information

There are ATMs all around town. Zhongshan Sq has a number of large bank branches including a **Bank of China** (中国银行, Zhōngguó Yínháng; 9 Zhongshan Sq), where you can change currency.

The 72-Hour Visa-Free Transit policy allows passport holders of many countries a stopover in Dalian without arranging a visa before arrival. This includes most European countries, the USA, Canada, Brazil, Mexico, Australia and Japan. You must have an onward ticket to a third country (ie not the country you arrived from). Inform your airline at check-in and seek the '72-hour Visa-Free Transit' counter on arrival. Check the website well before flying (http://english.gov.cn/services/visitchina).

ℹ️ Getting There & Away

AIR

Dalian International Airport (大连周水子国际机场) is 12km from the city centre and well connected to most cities in China and the region. Tickets can be purchased at the **Civil Aviation Administration of China** (CAAC, 中国民航, Zhōngguó Mínháng; ☑ 0411 8361 2888; Zhongshan Lu) or any of the travel offices nearby. In addition to the domestic destinations listed here, there are also flights to Khabarovsk, Vladivostok, Hong Kong and Tokyo. Dalian Jinzhouwan Airport is built on an artificial island and is being phased in as the main airport.

Beijing ¥700, one to 1½ hours

Harbin ¥900, 1½ hours

BOAT

There are several daily boats to Yantai (¥200 to ¥680, five to eight hours) and Weihai (¥210 to ¥700, seven to eight hours) in Shandong. Buy tickets at the passenger ferry terminal in the northeast of Dalian or from one of the many counters in front of the train station. To the ferry terminal, take **bus 13** (cnr Shengli Guangchang & Zhongshan Lu; ¥1) from the southeast corner of Shengli Guangchang and Zhongshan Lu near the train station.

BUS

Long-distance buses leave from various points around the train station. It can be tricky to find the correct ticket booths, and they do occasionally move. Destination include the following:

Dandong (丹东) ¥105, four hours, nine daily (6.20am to 2.30pm). Buses leave from stand No 2 on Shengli Guangchang just south of Changjiang Lu.

Lushun (旅顺) ¥7, 1½ hours, every 20 minutes. Buses leave from the back of the train station, across the square.

Shenyang (沈阳) ¥100, five hours, every two hours. Buses depart from south of Victory Sq.

Zhuanghe (庄河) ¥45, 2½ hours, frequent. Buses (Jianshe Jie) leave from in front of the ticket office on Jianshe Jie, the first street behind the train station. Onward connections to Bingyu Valley are regular.

TRAIN

Buy your ticket as early as possible. Most high-speed D and G trains leave from the north station. Get a bus (¥5, regular, 30 minutes) there from behind the light-rail station. At the main train station, the attendant at ticket window 1 speaks English. Destinations include the following:

Beijing hard seat/sleeper ¥143/290, 11 to 15 hours

Beijing (D/G train) ¥266/466, 6½/five hours

Changchun (G train) ¥304, three hours

Harbin (G train) ¥404, 3½ to 4½ hours

Shenyang (G train) ¥174, 1½ to two hours

ℹ️ Getting Around

TO/FROM THE AIRPORT

A shuttle bus (¥5) runs to the train station; bus 701 (¥1; no change given) does also, continuing to Zhongshan Sq. A taxi to/from the city centre costs about ¥40.

BUS

Buses (¥1) are plentiful and stops have English signboards explaining the route. There's a **tourist bus** (¥10, hourly, 8.30am to 4.30pm) in front of the train station in summer. It does a hop-on, hop-off loop of the city and the southwestern coast. From the train station, bus 710 passes Sanba Sq, while bus 701 passes Zhongshan Sq.

For buses to UniLoft Hostel, head to **Qingniwa Qiao Bus Stop** (青泥洼桥).

ℹ️ BORDER CROSSING: DALIAN TO SOUTH KOREA

The Korean-run **Da-in Ferry** (☑ Dalian 0411 8270 5082, Incheon 032 891 7100, Seoul 822 3218 6500; www.dainferry.co.kr; 17th fl, 68 Renmin Lu, 人民路68号, 宏誉商业大厦17楼) to Incheon in South Korea departs from Dalian on Monday, Wednesday and Friday at 4.30pm (¥980 to ¥1900, 16 hours).

Greater Dalian

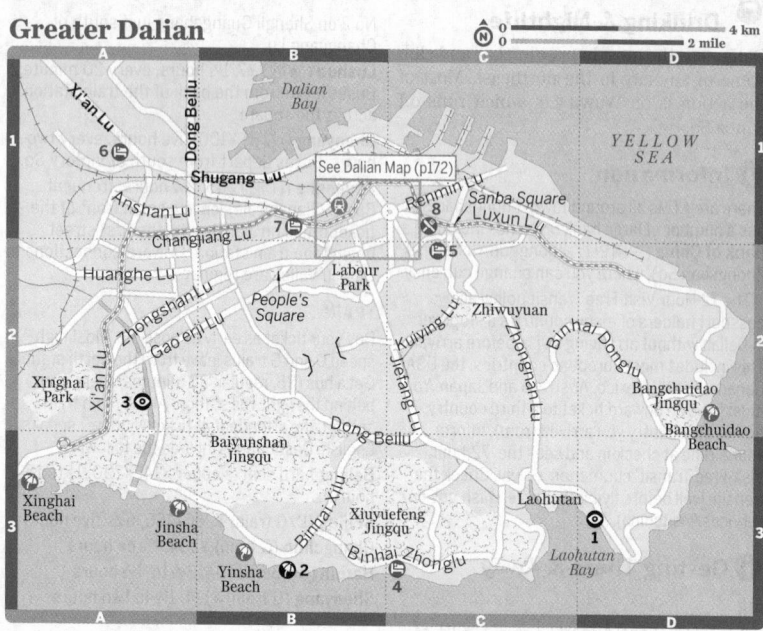

Dalian Bay

YELLOW SEA

See Dalian Map (p172)

Greater Dalian

⊙ **Sights**
1 Fisherman's Wharf D3
2 Fujiazhuang Beach B3
3 Xinghai Square A2

🛏 **Sleeping**
4 Amazing Koala Boutique Hotel C3
5 Ibis Dalian Zhongshan Square C2
6 Tian Tian YHA International
    Youth Hostel A1
7 UniLoft Hostel B1

✖ **Eating**
8 Locomotive Guild Roast Duck C1

METRO

Dalian has a modern, efficient subway metro system with two main lines running north–south and east–west. The most useful route for a visitor runs from Zhongshan Sq to the train station, which is actually an easily walkable distance.

TAXI

Fares start at ¥10; most trips are less than ¥20.

TRAM

Dalian has a slow but stylish tram with two lines: the 201 (¥2) and the 202 (¥1). The 201 runs past the train station on Changjiang Lu, while the 202 runs out to the ocean and Xinghai Sq (you must take the 201 or the faster metro first and transfer).

Lushun 旅顺

☏ 0411 / POP 324,800

With its excellent port and strategic location on the northeast coast, Lushun (Lǚshùn; formerly Port Arthur) was the focal point of both Russian and Japanese expansion in the late 19th and early 20th centuries. The bloody Russo-Japanese War (1904–05) finally saw the area fall under Japanese colonial rule, which would continue for the next 40 years.

Lushun is worth a visit during any trip to Dalian. Most sites are related to military history, but there's an excellent museum on Liaoning, as well as a number of scenic lookouts and parks. The extensive development here is mostly residential.

⊙ Sights

★**Lushun Prison** HISTORIC SITE
(旅顺日俄监狱旧址博物馆, Lǚshùn Rì'é Jiānyù Jiùzhǐ Bówùguǎn; ⊙9am-4.30pm Tue-Sun, last entry 3.30pm) **FREE** Most visitors to Lushun head straight for the notorious prison that, from 1902 to 1945, housed more than 450,000 war prisoners captured by the Russians, then the Japanese. Visitors are escorted on the half-hour by Chinese-speaking guides through a series of carefully preserved red-brick buildings. Sombre displays, including an

unearthed wooden-barrel coffin containing an executed inmate, and torture devices accompanied by graphic descriptions, paint a picture of a working early-20th-century jail.

English captions illuminate the plight of prisoners, surveillance strategies, work camps and more.

Bus 3 (¥1, 15 minutes) from opposite the bus station terminates outside the prison.

Lushun Museum MUSEUM
(旅顺博物馆, Lûshùn Bówùguǎn; ⊙9am-4pm Tue-Sun) FREE The history of Liaoning province is covered in this stylish old museum in two early 20th century buildings. Among the thousands of artefacts on display are ancient bronzes, coins and paintings, as well as several mummies and a quirky chopstick collection. The English captions are good.

The area around the museum has a number of other old buildings from the Japanese colonial era and is a great spot for photographs, especially in spring.

Take bus 4 or bus 33 (¥1) from outside the bus terminal to the Liening Jie stop (列宁街) and walk 450m east.

Baiyu Shan HISTORIC SITE
(白玉山; ¥40) Head to the top of this hill opposite the bus station for panoramic views out to the bay and across the ever-expanding city. The phallic-shaped monument is **Baiyu Shan Ta** (白玉山塔), a pagoda erected by the Japanese in 1909 after they took Lushun.

Climb to the top up the stairs (made in the USA) for ¥10.

Soviet Martyrs Cemetery CEMETERY
(苏军烈士陵园, Sūjūn Lièshì Língyuán; ⊙8.30am-4.30pm) FREE The largest cemetery in China for foreign-born nationals honours Soviet soldiers who died in the liberation of northeast China at the end of WWII, as well as pilots killed during the Korean War. Designed by Soviet advisers, the cemetery is heavy with communist-era iconography. A giant rifle-holding soldier guards the front, while inside are memorials to the sacrifice of Soviet soldiers and rows of neatly tended gravestones.

Bus 11 (¥1, about 25 minutes) passes here from outside the bus terminal.

Lushun Railway Station HISTORIC BUILDING
(旅顺火车站, Lûshùn Huǒchēzhàn) FREE Built in 1903 during Russia's brief control of the area, this handsome station was rebuilt in 2005 following the original design. It's worth a visit en route to other sights.

Bus 18 (¥1, about 20 minutes) passes here from outside the bus terminal.

🛏 Sleeping

Most people make a day trip of the area from Dalian, which has much better and more plentiful accommodation options. If you do get stuck, there are budget options opposite Lushun bus station, and a chain hotel at the end of the road south.

FREE TRADE AMONG COMMUNIST ALLIES

It's no exaggeration to say that without China, the North Korean regime would not survive. China has been trading with the Democratic People's Republic of Korea (DPRK) since the 1950s and is now the country's largest trading partner. Almost half of all DPRK imports come directly from China, and China is the largest provider of humanitarian assistance to the Hermit Kingdom. That China supports its neighbour for its own geopolitical reasons is no surprise – that it does so for economic reasons probably is. The honeymoon may be over, as tensions have grown ever since China signed UN sanctions against North Korea's nuclear testing. However, put simply, Chinese leaders in the northern provinces still insist they need market reforms across the border if they are to see their own long-term development plans fully realised.

Dandong is the hub of Sino–North Korean trade, and a free-trade zone between the two countries has been established in North Korea's northeastern cities of Rajin and Sonbong. The area is now known as Rason and is also a warm-water port. Another area where the two nations have made progress is in expanding working visas. In 2013 some 93,300 North Koreans were granted visas for employment in China, which translated to a 17% increase from 2012. However, Beijing has been cracking down on illegal North Korean migration in the wake of a number of high-profile escape attempts, while in 2019, a number of North Korean workers were repatriated suddenly by Pyongyang. As a result, Dandong remains closely watched by political observers in the region.

ⓘ Getting There & Around

Buses to Lushun (¥7, 1½ hours) leave every 20 minutes from a stop across the square at the back of the Dalian Train Station. Buy your ticket from the booth before lining up. Buses run back and forth between Lushun and Dalian from early morning to evening.

Most of Lushun's sights are easily visited via local buses (¥1), which leave from across the road outside Lushun bus station.

As soon as you exit the bus station at Lushun, taxis will cry out for your business. A few hours touring the sights will cost ¥150 (excluding ¥10 car-parking fees at some sights). If the driver doesn't have one, pick up a bilingual English-Chinese map at the station newsstand to help you negotiate. It is also possible to just flag down taxis as needed. Resist any attempts by taxi drivers to steer you towards sights with admission of ¥100 upwards: they are overpriced and underwhelming.

Dandong　　丹东

☑ 0415 / POP 866,000

Dandong (Dāndōng) is an oddly charming border town that enjoys a prominent position across the Yalu River (Yālù Jiāng) from its imperious neighbour, the Democratic People's Republic of Korea (DPRK). Laid out in a handy grid format, the town is more than a gateway to North Korea (Cháoxiǎn). Sure, it handles more than 50% of the DPRK's imports/exports and its increasing wealth means that there are now flashy malls stocking luxury brands and even a fast rail connection, but travellers will enjoy easy access to sections of the Great Wall and some fascinating military history.

For most visitors to Dandong, this is as close as they will get to the DPRK. While you can't see much, the contrast between Dandong's lively, built-up riverfront and the desolate stretch of land on the other side of the Yalu River speaks volumes about the dire state of the North Korean economy and the restrictions under which its people live.

⊙ Sights

Dandong is relatively compact and easy to walk around. The river is about 800m southeast of the train station straight down Shiwei Lu (and parallel streets), while the main shopping district is just east of the station. Korea Street is parallel to the river a few blocks north.

★ **Tiger Mountain Great Wall**　　WALLS
(虎山长城, Hǔshān Chángchéng; ¥60, museum ¥10; ⊙ 8am-5pm) The Tiger Mountain stretch of the Great Wall, about 20km northeast of Dandong, is an excellent location to get your wall fix, far from the madding crowds. Running up a steep embankment beside the Yalu River, this restored remnant of the Ming dynasty makes a perfect day trip combined with a speedboat ride along the North Korean border. The Wall ends at a small **museum** with a few weapons, vases and wartime dioramas (buy your ticket at the main entrance).

From here two routes loop back to the entrance. Buses to the Wall (¥6.50, 40 minutes)

WORTH A TRIP

BINGYU VALLEY

If you can't travel south to Guilin, **Bingyu Valley** (冰峪沟, Bīngyù Gōu; ¥168) offers a taste of what you're missing. About 250km northeast of Dalian, the valley has tree-covered limestone cliffs set alongside a river. From the entrance, a boat takes you along a brief stretch of the river, where rock formations rise steeply along the banks, before depositing you at a dock. From there, hire a little boat or bamboo raft and paddle around the shallow waters.

You can also follow short trails along the river and up to lookouts. Tame amusements clamour for attention, but it's worth pressing on.

In summer, day tours run from the train-station area in Dalian, leaving at 7.30am and returning around 8pm. Buy your ticket (¥258 including transport, lunch and admission fees) the day before from the tourism vans across from the light-rail depot in the back train-station area. Your hotel should be able to get you discounted rates.

The park is increasingly popular with tour groups, who come for the zip lines, amusement-park rides and even jet-skiing. Given the rather small area that you can explore, it can be tough to find any tranquillity in this otherwise lovely environment.

If on your own, it's best to drive en route to Dandong, but otherwise you can take one of many buses to Bingyu Gou from Dalian (¥43, two hours, 6am to 4pm) via Zhuanghe. Accommodation is available within the park, but is overpriced for what you get.

Dandong

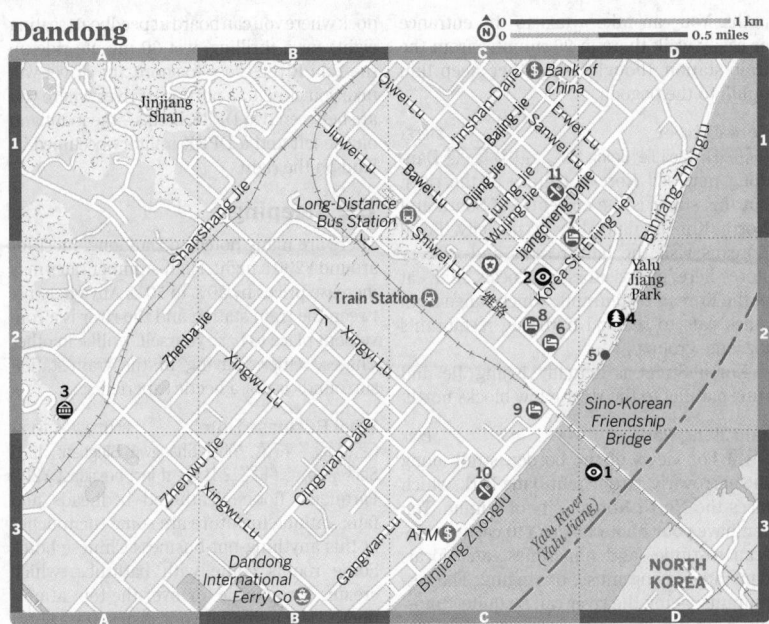

Dandong

◉ Sights

1 Broken Bridge	D3
2 Korea Street	C2
3 Museum to Commemorate US Aggression	A2
4 Yalu Jiang Park	D2

◑ Activities, Courses & Tours

5 Boat Cruises	D2

◉ Sleeping

6 Hilton Garden Inn	C2
7 Life's Business Hotel	C1
8 Yihai Business Hotel	C2
9 Zhong Lian Hotel	C2

◉ Eating

10 Sōngtāoyuán Fàndiàn	C3
11 Toudao Wonton	C1

run about every hour from Dandong's long-distance bus station. A taxi from town will cost ¥35 and you can usually flag a share taxi back for ¥10.

Broken Bridge BRIDGE
(鸭绿江断桥, Yālùjiāng Duànqiáo; 58 Binjiang Zhonglu, 滨江中路58号; ¥30; ⊙8am-5pm, last entry 4.30pm) A pile of mangled steel is an unlikely tourist attraction, but this aftermath of the Korean War is a symbolic reminder of a conflict which has shaped the region. There were two bridges crossing the Yalu River near Dandong, but in 1950 American troops 'accidentally' bombed the original steel-span bridge between North Korea and China. The North Koreans dismantled the bridge less than halfway across the river, leaving a row of support columns.

You can wander along the remaining section of the shrapnel-scarred bridge and get a good toss of a ball of the North Korean shoreline and an amusement park largely in disrepair, left behind by history.

The **Sino–Korean Friendship Bridge**, the official border crossing between China and North Korea, is next to the old one, and trains and trucks rumble across it on a regular basis.

Jinjiang Pagoda PAGODA
(锦江塔, Jǐnjiāng Tǎ) **FREE** The highest point for kilometres, this pagoda sits atop Jǐnjiāng Shān in the park of the same name. The views across to North Korea are unparalleled and the park itself (a former military zone) is a well-tended expanse of forested slopes, with a pretty pond and walking

paths. You can take a taxi to the entrance or easily walk there in 20 minutes from the train station, though it's another steep 1km uphill to the pagoda.

Korea Street
STREET

(高丽街, Gāolí Jiē; Erjing Jie, 二经街) FREE Dandong may sell Korean culture at the river, but this street is the epicentre of South and North Korean daily life in the city. Local Koreans visit the hairdressers and grocery stores here, and visitors and locals alike eat at the Korean restaurants, which range from quick eats to seafood barbecue restaurants for large groups.

Korea Street is actually Erjing Jie and runs parallel to the river a few blocks north.

Yalu Jiang Park
PARK

FREE For views of the border, stroll along the narrow riverfront Yalu Jiang Park, which faces the North Korean city of Sinuiju. You can have your photo taken (¥10 each) in Korean costumes and sometimes catch locals dancing, playing music or singing. The restaurants facing the river can be quite atmospheric at sunset.

Museum to Commemorate US Aggression
MUSEUM

(抗美援朝纪念馆, Kàngměi Yuáncháo Jìniànguǎn; ☑ 0415 215 0510; www.kmycjng.com; 68 Shanshang Jie, 山上街68号; ⊙9am-4pm Tue-Sun) FREE With everything from statistics to shells, this comprehensive museum offers Chinese and North Korean perspectives on the war with the US-led UN forces (1950–53) – they take the view that they won it. There are good English captions here, which offer a thought-provoking alternative view to the west's. The adjacent North Korean War Memorial Column was built 53m high, symbolising the year the Korean War ended. A taxi to the museum costs ¥12 from downtown.

Tours

Boat Cruises
BOATING

(观光船, Guānguāng Chuán; boat/speedboat ¥60/120; ⊙7am-6pm) To get close to North Korea, take a 30- to 40-minute boat cruise from the tour-boat piers on either side of the border bridges. You have to wait for boats to fill up with passengers (on average 30 minutes), but the pace allows you to take more in than on the smaller, splashy speedboats.

Speedboat Tours
BOATING

(快艇码头, Kuàitíng Mǎtóu; per speedboat ¥180) About 23km northeast of Dandong is a small dock where you can board a speedboat (seating eight) for a thrilling, wet 30-minute ride up the Yalu River. Close to shore, the driver will take you close to a portion of river where you are between two DPRK banks – the mainland on the left and a DPRK military-occupied island on the right.

Sleeping

There are many hotels in Dandong, most for around ¥200 a night. High-summer rates may increase prices by 30% to 50%. Anywhere between the train station and the river is a convenient place to base yourself. Unlike in other Chinese cities, staying in the train-station surrounds is not a hectic experience.

Yihai Business Hotel
BOUTIQUE HOTEL ¥¥

(艺海商务宾馆, Yìhǎi Shāngwù Bīnguǎn; 12-11 Shiwei Lu, 十纬路12-11号; d incl breakfast ¥218) Parquetry floors, leathered bedheads and faux-antique furniture are some of the touches at this anything-but-business Chinese hotel. Some rooms come with bathtubs, which creates a romantic, or over-the-top, atmosphere, depending on your tastes. It's a short walk to the river or train station.

Hilton Garden Inn
BUSINESS HOTEL ¥¥

(丹东希尔顿花园酒店, Dāndōng Xī'ěrdùn Huāyuán Jiǔdiàn; ☑ 0415 397 8888; 30 Shiwei Lu, 30世偉路; r ¥450-790) A very short walk from the train station, and set inside a small shopping mall, you can find an excellent example of the lower-tier Hilton brand. Rooms are stylish and spacious for the price, with large desk pods and new frosted-glass bathrooms. The breakfast hall next to reception doubles as a casual breakout area for North Korean businessmen.

Life's Business Hotel
BUSINESS HOTEL ¥¥

(莱弗仕商务快捷酒店, Láifúshì Shāngwù Kuàijié Jiǔdiàn; ☑ 0415 213 9555; 29 Liuwei Lu, 六纬路29号; r ¥168-318; ❈@⏚) Life's is a smart business hotel popular with North Korean businessmen and within walking distance of the riverfront, restaurants and a Tesco supermarket. Rooms are tidy and comfortable, with the ones on higher floors affording river views. Cheaper rooms have no windows.

Zhong Lian Hotel
HOTEL ¥¥¥

(中联大酒店, Zhōng Lián Dà Jiǔdiàn; ☑ 0415 233 3333; www.zlhotel.com; 62 Binjiang Zhonglu, 滨江中路62号; d/tw incl breakfast ¥478/598; ❈@⏚) Directly across from the Broken Bridge is this solid option with large rooms, an even larger marble lobby and English-speaking

VISITING THE HERMIT KINGDOM

Most tours to the Democratic People's Republic of Korea start with a flight from Beijing or Shenyang into Pyongyang, but Jilin and Liaoning offer a more interesting alternative launching pad. You can visit the Special Economic Zone of Rason from Yanji in Jilin province or consider taking a train from Dandong all the way to Pyongyang. The following tour agencies organise visas and offer trips designed for westerners. Check the websites for costs and itineraries. Note that some travel restrictions apply to American tourists (who must fly in) and Japanese tourists.

Explore North Korea (www.explorenorthkorea.com) Dandong-based agency.

Koryo Tours (Map p102; ☑ 010 6416 7544; www.koryogroup.com; 27 Beisanlitun Nan, 北三里屯南27号; Ⓢ Line 2 to Dongsi Shitiao, exit C, or Line 10 to Tuanjiehu, exit A) Large, long-running Beijing-based agency.

Young Pioneer Tours (www.youngpioneertours.com) Offers alternative itineraries into Rason, Namyang, Hoeryong city and Onsong county.

---

staff. The pricier rooms offer great views of the bridge and river. Discounts available.

✕ Eating

On summer nights, barbecue smoke drifts over Dandong as street corners become impromptu restaurants serving fresh seafood and bottles of Yalu River beer. One of the best places for barbecue is in the tents on the corner of Bawei Lu and Qijing Jie. More conventional restaurants, including a range of Korean, hotpot and DIY barbecue places, line the riverfront on either side of the bridges, as well as Korea Street parallel to the river a few blocks north.

Toudao Wonton CHINESE ¥
(头道美味馄饨馆, Tóudào Měiwèi Húntún Guǎn; ☑ 0415 212 2500; 37-12 Jiangcheng Dajie, cnr Liuwei Lu, 江城大街12号, 六纬路的路口; mains ¥9-25; ☺ 6am-11pm) Locals come to this nothing-fancy place for the good, homemade pork-filled wontons (馄饨, húntún) in soup and lěng miàn (冷面, cold noodle soup with meat and shredded vegetables) from the picture board. There are side dishes on display too, such as shíbǎn huángguā (pickled cucumber).

It is opposite a Tesco supermarket.

Sōngtāoyuán Fàndiàn NORTH KOREAN ¥¥
(松涛园饭店; 5 Binjiang Zhonglu, 滨江中路5号; dishes ¥18-108; ☺ 11am-3pm & 5-10pm) Known locally as 'North Korean Restaurant', this on-again-off-again enterprise near the Broken Bridge is a surreal dining experience serving up dog meat and typical Korean fare. The waitresses sing folk songs and attend dutifully, with the aid of a picture menu. It's directly beside SPR Coffee and certainly isn't for everyone.

Be aware that this restaurant may have affiliations with the government of the DPRK.

♟ Drinking & Nightlife

Drinking with a Korean meal is common practice. Korean beers and the potent spirit soju are popular choices in any of the restaurants in and around Korea Street, where there are also a few nondescript bars, which close before midnight.

ⓘ Information

Bank of China (中国银行, Zhōngguó Yínháng; 60 Jinshan Dajie, 锦山大街60号) has ATMs and will change currency. Another ATM is closer to the river at 77-1 Binjiang Zhonglu.

Public Security Bureau (PSB, 公安局; Gōng'ānjú; ☑ 0415 210 3138; 15 Jiangcheng Dajie, 15江城大街)

ⓘ Getting There & Away

Dandong airport has infrequent flights to a few cities in China; most travellers arrive by bus or train.

BUS

The **long-distance bus station** (cnr Shiwei Lu & Jinshan Dajie) is near the train station. Destinations include the following:

Dalian ¥105, 3½ hours, 15 daily (5.30am to 2.30pm)

Ji'an ¥87, seven hours, one daily (8.30am)

Shenyang ¥87, three hours, every 30 minutes (5.40am to 6.30pm)

Tonghua ¥84, seven hours, two daily (6.30am and 8.50am)

TRAIN

The train station is in the centre of town. A lofty Mao statue greets arriving passengers. There are much slower versions of the following trains,

BORDER CROSSING: DANDONG TO SOUTH KOREA

Dandong International Ferry Co (丹东国际航运有限公司, Dāndōng Guójì Hángyùn Yǒuxiàn Gōngsī; ☑ 0411 315 2666; www.dandongferry.co.kr; cnr Xingwu Lu & Gangwan Lu, 興武路和港灣路一角; ☺ 8am-5pm) runs a boat to Incheon in South Korea on Tuesday and Thursday at 6pm and Sunday at 4pm (¥1110 to ¥1810, 16 hours). Buy tickets at the company's office on Xingwu Lu. A bus to the ferry terminal leaves two hours before departure (¥20) on the respective departure days from the train station.

but the cost saving is minimal. The attendant at ticket window 1 speaks English. Destinations include the following:

Dalian (D/G) ¥109, two to 2½ hours, 10 daily
Shenyang (D/G) ¥51, 1½ hours, every 30 minutes

Shenyang　沈阳
♫ 024 / POP 6.25 MILLION

Shenyang (Shěnyáng) is a provincial capital on the rise. Its sleek metro hums beneath wide boulevards and contemporary glass monoliths, while an underrated Imperial Palace and tomb complex – sadly overlooked by all bar the history buffs – lies at either end of its park-lined urban centre.

Liaoning's largest city also has a proudly cosmopolitan dining scene (think Korean and Hui Muslim for starters) and a post-industrial wealth and sensibility befitting the more established cities further south. Easily accessible from Beijing and beyond, Shenyang also offers shopping, museums and a stroll around Zhongshan Lu, a picturesque neighbourhood with well-preserved early-20th-century architecture, another pleasant Dongbei surprise.

History

Shenyang's roots go back to 300 BC, when it was known as Hou City. By the 11th century it was a Mongol trading centre, before reaching its historical high point in the 17th century when it was the capital of the Manchzzu empire. With the Manchu conquest of Beijing in 1644, Shenyang became a secondary capital under the Manchu name of Mukden, and a centre of the ginseng trade.

Throughout its history Shenyang has often changed hands, dominated by warlords, the Japanese (1931), the Russians (1945), the Kuomintang (1946) and finally the Chinese Communist Party (CCP; 1948).

◉ Sights

★**Shenyang Imperial Palace** HISTORIC SITE (沈阳故宫, Shěnyáng Gùgōng; 171 Shenyang Lu, 沈阳路171号; ¥60; ☺ 8.30am-5.30pm, from 1pm Mon, last entry 4.45pm) This impressive palace complex resembles a small-scale Forbidden City. Constructed between 1625 and 1636 by Manchu emperor Nurhachi (1559–1626) and his son, Huang Taiji, the palace served as the residence of the Qing dynasty rulers until 1644. The central courtyard buildings include ornate ceremonial halls and imperial living quarters, including a royal baby cradle. In all, there are 114 buildings, not all of which are open to the public.

Zhong Jie metro station (exit B) is a few minutes north.

★**Tomb of Huang Taiji** HISTORIC SITE (北陵, Běilíng; 12 Taishan Lu, 泰山路12号; ¥50; ☺ 7am-6pm) One of Shenyang's highlights is this extensive tomb complex, the burial place of Huang Taiji (1592–1643), founder of the Qing dynasty. The tomb's animal statues lead up to the central mound known as the Luminous Tomb (Zhāo Líng). In many ways a better-preserved complex than Shenyang's Imperial Palace, the tomb site is worth a few hours examining the dozens of buildings with their traditional architecture and ornamentation.

The Tomb of Huang Taiji sits a few kilometres north of town inside expansive **Beiling Park** (北陵公园, Běilíng Gōngyuán; ♿) FREE.

Liaoning Provincial Museum MUSEUM (辽宁省博物馆, Liáoníng Shěng Bówùguǎn; SE cnr Government Sq; ☺ 9am-noon & 1-5pm Tue-Sun, last entry 3.30pm) FREE Three floors of exhibits highlight the region's art and history, from prehistoric times through the late Qing dynasty. English explanations accompany most displays.

🛏 Sleeping

Vienna International Hotel HOTEL ¥¥ (维也纳国际酒店, Wéiyěnà Guójì Jiǔdiàn; ☑ 024 8360 8888; 58 Minzu Beijie, 民族北街58号; d & tw ¥348-438, ste ¥538) Neat little Vienna's old-world charm – and perhaps comfortable beds and hot showers – keeps it marginally above the midrange competition, but it has

Shenyang

Shenyang

◎ Top Sights
1 Shenyang Imperial Palace.....................D2

◎ Sights
2 Liaoning Provincial Museum................C2

🛏 Sleeping
3 Liaoning Hotel...A3
4 North Yorker Hotel................................A3
5 Vienna International Hotel....................A3

🍴 Eating
6 Carrefour Supermarket.........................C1
7 Korea Town..A2
8 Laobian Dumplings.................................D2
9 Meijin Hotpot...A3

10 View & World Vegetarian
     Restaurant..B3

🍷 Drinking & Nightlife
11 Lenore's...B3
12 Stroller's..B3

🛍 Shopping
13 Taiyuan Jie..A3
14 Zhong Jie..D2

ℹ Information
15 French Consulate...................................B3
    South Korean Consulate..............(see 15)
    US Consulate...................................(see 15)

seen better days. It's tucked down a small road 150m east of the Main Train Station. Smart, clean and bright rooms paired with good service make this a good option. Discounts of 40% with ¥198 membership.

North Yorker Hotel   APARTMENT ¥¥¥
(北约客维景国际大酒店; Běiyuē Kè Wéi Jǐng Guójì Dà Jiǔdiàn; ☏ 024 8930 5555; www.northyorkhotel. com; 35 Tongze Beijie, 35同澤北街; r from ¥600, 1-/2-bed apt from ¥800/1000) The North Yorker's genuinely spacious, well-appointed hotel rooms and self-contained apartments are a pleasure to stay in, especially for families.

Liaoning Hotel   HOTEL ¥¥¥
(辽宁宾馆, Liáoníng Bīnguǎn; ☏ 024 2383 9104; www.liaoninghotel.com; 97 Zhongshan Lu, 中山路 97号; r incl breakfast from ¥458; ❋@🛜) Even if you don't stay here, it's worth stopping for a beer in the outdoor patio at Shenyang's most atmospheric older hotel. The interior and the smoky, red-themed rooms may be fading a little, but the floodlit building still has a presence opposite Mao's statue on busy Zhongshan Sq. The Chairman himself stayed here and it retains many of its period details.

THE 'MUKDEN INCIDENT'

By 1931 Japan was looking for a pretext to occupy Manchuria. The Japanese army took matters into its own hands by staging an explosion on the night of 18 September at a tiny section of a Japanese-owned railway outside Mukden, the present-day city of Shenyang. Almost immediately, the Japanese attacked a nearby Chinese army garrison and then occupied Shenyang the following night. Within five months, they controlled all of Manchuria and ruled the region until the end of WWII.

✕ Eating

Both the North and Main Train Stations are cheap-restaurant zones. You'll also find lots of reasonably priced restaurants around the Imperial Palace. Most have picture menus. For a kimchi fix head to **Korea Town** (西塔; Xītǎ; Xita Jie, 西塔街). There are supermarkets at the base of most malls, and a **Carrefour Supermarket** (家乐福, Jiālèfú; 39 Beizhan Yilu, 北站一路39号; ⊙8.30am-9.30pm) is beside the long-distance bus station.

Grandma's Home   CHINESE ¥¥
(☎024 2436 3389; 10 Xiao Donglu, 10肖东路; mains ¥20-80; ⊙11am-9pm Mon-Sun) This popular chain restaurant serves fresh, brightly coloured fare from Southern China – Hangzhou in particular – to a young local crowd who appreciate prompt service and a bit of buzz with their crispy duck.

★ Meijin Hotpot   HOTPOT ¥¥
(美津火锅, Měijīn Huǒguō; cnr Taiyuan Jie & Bei Sanma Lu, 太原街北三马路的路口; ingredients ¥3-22; ⊙10.30am-2am) This popular hotpot chain teems with the energy of dozens of diners chowing down on everything from veggies to meat and noodles. Friendly staff can help explain ingredients on the incredibly diverse English menu.

Laobian Dumplings   DUMPLINGS ¥¥
(老边饺子馆, Lǎobiān Jiǎoziguǎn; 2nd fl, 208 Zhong Jie Lu, 中街路208号2楼; dumplings ¥16-60; ⊙10am-10pm; ❀🔊✎) Open since 2019, Shenyang's most famous restaurant is a 2nd-floor dumpling house with efficient staff who toss around picture menus featuring hundreds of flavours of boiled, steamed and fried treasures. Plenty of vegetarian options.

The restaurant is on the 2nd floor of the Laobian Hotel, just across from the B1 exit of Zhong Jie metro station.

View & World Vegetarian Restaurant   VEGETARIAN ¥¥
(宽巷子素菜馆, Kuān Xiàngzi Sùcàiguǎn; ☎024 2284 8678; 202 Shiyi Wei Lu, 十一纬路202号; dishes ¥12-168; ⊙10am-10.30pm; ✎) Located on one of Shenyang's busy eating streets, there's neither MSG nor meat at this long-standing institution known more for its food than its service. Mock mutton, fish and beef appear alongside more traditional tofu and pulse dishes.

🍷 Drinking & Nightlife

There are bars ranging from glossy to homey on Zhongshan Lu east of Zhongshan Sq. Join the loud crowds in Korea Town on Xita Jie for some cheap and potent *soju*.

Lenore's   BAR
(丽纳尔斯咖啡馆和酒吧, Lìnà'ěrsī Kāfēiguǎn Hé Jiǔbā; ☎024 2285 7983; 60 Beiwu Malu, 北五马路60号; drinks ¥28-48; ⊙11am-midnight; 🔊) Lenore's is the passion project of Michael, the charismatic owner who dons a signature cowboy hat and warmly greets Shenyang's cool young things. The outdoor section with a glass floor is a great place to sit with friends over good cocktails, wine, local and imported beers, or decent coffee. Avoid the food; stay for the dancing.

Stroller's   BAR
(流浪者餐厅, Liúlàngzhě Cāntīng; ☎024 2287 6677; 36 Beiwu Jing Jie, 北五经街36号; drinks from ¥25, food ¥40-170; ⊙11.30am-2am; 🔊) This long-running atmospheric pub is especially popular with expats and has a decent imported beer selection and the usual pub grub. Take Exit B of Nan Shichang Station, cross the road and head up the side street for 150m.

🔒 Shopping

Zhong Jie   SHOPPING STREET
(中街, Zhōng Jiē) This street, near the Imperial Palace, is a popular pedestrianised shopping zone. It stretches across both sides of Chaoyang Jie. Expect glossy malls with all manner of shops (local and international) and restaurants.

Taiyuan Jie   SHOPPING STREET
(太原街步行街, Tàiyuán Jiē Bùxíng Jiē) Near the Main Train Station is Taiyuan Jie, one of Shenyang's major shopping streets, with

department stores and an extensive underground shopping street (mostly small clothing boutiques).

❶ Information

ATMs can be found all over the city and around Zhongshan Sq.

The Bank of China has ATMs and currency exchange at **Government Sq** (253 Shifu Dalu, 市府路253號) and **Zhonghua Lu** (中国银行, Zhōngguó Yínháng; 96 Zhonghua Lu, 中化路96号).

There's also a **Public Security Bureau** (PSB, 公安局, Gōng'ānjú; 📞 024 2253 4850; Zhongshan Guangchang, 中山广场) visa office opposite the entrance of the Tomb of Huang Taiji.

❶ Getting There & Away

AIR

Shenyang Taoxian International Airport keeps growing its destinations, with flights to South Korea, Japan, Thailand, Australia, Germany and Russia as well as Beijing (¥500, 1½ hours) and Shanghai (¥1000, two hours).

BUS

The **South Long-Distance Bus Station** (沈阳长途客运南站, Shěnyáng Chángtú Kèyùn Nánzhàn) is adjacent to the Main Train Station from the east exit. The **North Long-Distance Express Bus Station** (沈阳快速客运站, Shěnyáng Kuàisù Kèyùn Zhàn; 120 Huigong Jie, 惠工街120号) is south of Beizhan Lu, about a five-minute walk from the North Train Station and next to the Carrefour Supermarket. Schedules are available at the information counter as you walk in. You are much better off taking a train to Beijing. Buses service the following destinations from the north bus station unless stated otherwise:

Beijing ¥140, eight hours, 9am (south station at 2pm)

Changchun ¥66, 3½ hours, at least hourly (7am to 5pm)

Dalian ¥94, 4½ hours, every 1½ hours (9am to 4.30pm)

Dandong ¥76, 3½ hours, every 30 minutes (7am to 7pm)

Harbin ¥129, 6½ hours, six daily (8am to 3.30pm)

Xingcheng ¥77, 4½ hours, two daily (8.50am and 3.40pm)

TRAIN

Shenyang's major train stations are the **North Train Station** (沈阳北站; Shěnyáng Běi Zhàn) and **Main Train Station** (沈阳站; Shěnyáng Zhàn; also known by the old 'South Station' name Shěnyáng Nánzhàn). Many trains arrive at one station, stop briefly, then travel to the next. It may be different when departing – always confirm which station you need. Buy sleeper or G/D train tickets (to Beijing or Shanghai) as far in advance as possible. Bus 262 runs between the North and Main Train Stations, or take the metro.

Destinations from the Main Train Station include the following:

Baihe (for Changbai Shan) Hard/soft sleeper ¥203/27488, 13 to 14 hours, three daily (9.11am, 6.39pm and 7.45pm)

Beijing (D/G train) ¥206/295, five/four hours, frequent

Dalian (D, G train) ¥174, two hours

Dandong (D, G train) ¥70, 1½ hours, frequent

Harbin (D, G train) ¥247, two to three hours

Xingcheng Hard seat ¥54, four to five hours

Destinations from the North Train Station include the following:

Beijing (D/G train) ¥206/295, five/four hours, frequent

Beijing Hard seat/sleeper ¥112/239, six to 10 hours

Changchun (G train) ¥143, 1½ hours

Dalian (North) (D, G train) ¥176, two hours

Dandong (D, G train) ¥70, 1½ hours, four daily

Harbin (West) (D/G train) ¥166/245, three/2½ hours

❶ Getting Around

TO/FROM THE AIRPORT

The airport is 25km south of the city. **Shuttle buses** (cnr Zhonghua Lu & Heping Dajie, 中化路和平大街的路口; ¥17) leave from an alley just before the intersection of Zhonghua Lu and Heping Dajie, and from the Shenyang South Long-Distance Bus Station (p185), or Shenyang North Long-Distance Express Bus Station. Taxis cost ¥80.

Most travellers won't venture south of the river, but if you do, the modern Line 2 tram is a leisurely way to travel between the airport and the Olympic Centre.

BUS

Buses are cheap, frequent and cover the city, but the metro is easier to navigate.

METRO

With only two lines (Line 1 running east–west and Line 2 running north–south) and one connecting station, the clean and relaxed Shenyang Metro system is easy to figure out. There are stops at both the north and main train stations as well as the Tomb of Huang Taiji and Zhong Jie (for the Imperial Palace). The average ride costs ¥2 to ¥4. Stations have public toilets.

TAXI

Taxi flagfall starts at ¥9.

Xingcheng 兴城

📋 0429 / POP 560,000

Xingcheng (兴城, Xīngchéng) makes for a historian's dream beach holiday. Local travellers are waking up to its potential – a booming swimwear industry has put it on the fashion map – but few foreigners have caught on to the unkempt charm of this Ming dynasty city replete with its entire outer wall.

Adding to the contrast, Xingcheng also has the oldest surviving temple in all of northeastern China and some of the best seafood north of Beijing.

⊙ Sights

★ Xingcheng Old City   HISTORIC SITE

(兴城古城, Xīngchéng Gǔ Chéng; ⏱ 24hr, sights 8am-5pm) This walled city dates back to 1430 and is the principal reason to visit Xingcheng. Under renovation, it's nonetheless an atmospheric place to spend a few hours, perhaps between dips in the sea.

In addition to the **City Walls** (城墙, Chéngqiáng; ¥25; ⏱ 8am-5pm), the **Drum Tower** (钟鼓楼, Zhōng Gǔlóu; ¥20; ⏱ 8am-5pm), which sits slap in the middle of the Old City with 360-degree views, and the **watchtower**, on the southeastern corner of the city, are all intact. You can do a complete circuit of the walls in around an hour.

The Old City is home to around 3000 people, with shops for daily life. Also inside the Old City is the **Gao House** (将军府, Jiāngjūn Fǔ; ¥10; ⏱ 8am-5pm), the former residence of General Gao Rulian, who is one of Xingcheng's most famous sons. The impressive and well maintained **Confucius Temple** (文庙, Wénmiào; ¥35; ⏱ 8am-5pm), built in 1430, is reputedly the oldest temple in northeastern China.

You can enter the Old City by any of four gates, but the easiest one to find is the **South Gate** (南门; Nánmén), which is just off Xinghai Nan Jie Duan at a large intersection. There are signs in English and Chinese pointing the way and maps at each gate. If you plan on seeing everything, buy the ¥100 pass that grants admission to every paid sight within the walled town.

Xingcheng Beach   BEACH

(海滨浴场, Hǎibīn Yùchǎng) FREE Xingcheng's beach is clean and calm and provides a welcome respite for travellers on the history trail. Manicured, sandy paths lead from a stack of seafood vendors to a boardwalk and pagoda hanging over the gently swirling sea.

Bus 1 (¥1) travels from the bus station through Xinghai Lu to the beach (9km from the city centre) in about 30 minutes. A taxi to the area costs ¥15 to ¥20.

🛏 Sleeping & Eating

Cheap hotels immediately around the train station won't accept foreigners. The beach is a good place to stay in summer with many of the larger hotels accepting foreigners. Note that rooms in ordinary beach hotels go for hundreds a night during the peak season. When it's cold, you're better off staying closer to the train station and its nearby restaurants.

Seafood is big here. At beachfront restaurants you can pick your crustacean or fish from the tanks. Prices vary according to the season, so ask before eating. Most beach hotels have restaurants with picture menus and fair prices.

The busy street leading from the South Gate to the main Xinghai Nanjie is lined with stalls serving noodles, barbecued meats and vegetables. In winter most restaurants not attached to hotels stay closed.

Xingcheng Mingyang Homestay   B&B

(📱 0186 4293 4898; 588 Diaoyutai Village; r ¥100-120) Cheap and cheerful enough for the price, this homestay is run by a quiet local family who present neat, airy rooms (extra blankets are a must outside summer), and provide helpful maps and a laundry service.

Haiyi Holiday Hotel   HOTEL ¥¥

(海逸假日酒店, Hǎiyì Jiàrì Jiǔdiàn; 📱 0429 541 0000; 21 Haibin Lu, 海滨路21号; r & cabins ¥350-400; ❄@) Haiyi is a little tired, and a bit chilly in winter, but the cute cabins clustered under leafy trees are idyllic in summer and the restaurant draws customers from around town. The standard rooms are not such good value. To get here, turn left when you hit the beach strip and walk 300m.

Sichuan Mala Noodles   SICHUAN ¥

(四川麻辣面, Sìchuān Málà Miàn; 📱 0429 3915 583; 93 Xinghai Nanjie, 兴海南街93号; mains ¥7-12; ⏱ 11am-9pm Mon-Sun) Amid flashing KTV signs on Xinghai Nanjie, you can discover very good Sichuan style *málà miàn* (a spicy and numbing noodle soup) on offer. The photo board looks like there are lots of options, but it's just variations of meat or seafood. They make their own dumplings too.

Happy Family Mall   FOOD HALL ¥

(大家庭, Dàjiātíng; cnr Xinghai Nanjie & Yan Hui Lu, 兴海南街和延辉路的路口; dishes from ¥10;

⊙9am-9pm; ❋) For respite from the busy intersection near the South Gate, head to the food court on the 5th floor of the Happy Family Mall where you'll find delicious handmade *bāozi* (steamed buns) and other Chinese staples.

🛈 Getting There & Away

Xingcheng is a frequent stop on the Beijing–Harbin line, though buses from Beijing may be quicker. Note that buses and trains from Xingcheng go to the main station in the nearby city of Jinzhou; there are buses (¥5, 30 minutes) to the south station out the front.

BUS

Xingcheng's bus station (兴城市客运站; Xīngchéngshì Kèyùn Zhàn) is just to the left of the train station. Destinations include the following:

Beijing ¥127, five hours, one daily (9am)

Dalian ¥124, five hours, one daily (9.30am)

Jinzhou Slow/fast bus ¥19/21, two/1½ hours, every 30 minutes (6.30am to 3.50pm)

Shenyang ¥72, 3½ hours, five daily

TRAIN

Destinations include the following:

Beijing Seat/sleeper ¥75/142, six to seven hours, two daily (5.21am and 1.32pm)

Jinzhou Seat ¥13, one hour, regular

Shanhaiguan Seat ¥19, 1½ hours, regular

Shenyang Seat ¥47, four to five hours, regular

🛈 Getting Around

Useful bus 1 (¥1) runs from the train and bus stations, along Xinghai Nanjie near Xingcheng Old City South Gate, terminating at Xingcheng Beach in 35 minutes.

A taxi from the train station to the beach costs ¥15 to ¥20.

You can catch a **ferry** (round trip ¥90) to Juhua Island. Ferries depart the northern end of Xingcheng Beach at 8.30am, 10am, 11.30am, 2pm, 3pm and 4pm. Return trips are at 1pm, 2.30pm, 3.30pm and 5pm. Frequency drops outside of summer. A trip with a Chinese-speaking guide and local transport costs ¥175.

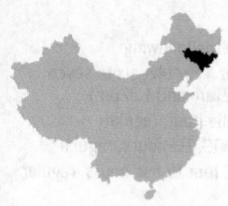

Jilin

POP 27.3 MILLION

Best Places to Eat

→ Quánzhōu Bànfàn Guǎn (p193)

→ San Qian Li Cold Noodles (p193)

→ Sānyú Zhúyuàn (p197)

→ Dong Teng (p197)

Best Places to Stay

→ Songyuan Hotel (p197)

→ Woodland Youth Hostel (p191)

Why Go?

While Jilin (吉林, Jílín) may not make typical China itineraries, there is cause for inspiration beyond the province's well-known rustbelt. For nature lovers, Jilin is an increasingly popular ski destination and boasts China's largest nature reserve at Changbai Shan – the journey to Baihe from Yanji is one of Dongbei's most bucolic. Inside the reserve, Heaven Lake, a stunning, deep-blue volcanic crater lake, is one of China's most mesmerising natural wonders.

Culture buffs also have grounds for inspiration. From the Japanese architecture of Changchun, once the capital of Manchukuo and the headquarters of the puppet emperor Puyi, travellers can move east to the ruins of an ancient Korean kingdom known as Koguryo. In fact, much of the far-eastern region comprises the little-known Korean Autonomous Prefecture, home to more than one million ethnic Koreans. Kimchi and cold noodles dominate the menu here and there's an easy acceptance of outsiders.

When to Go
Changchun

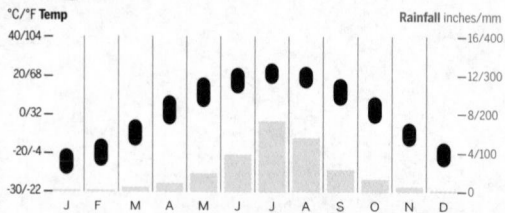

Jun–Sep Ideal hiking weather and visibility for visits to Changbai Shan.

Jul & Aug Fields in bloom around the Korean Autonomous Prefecture.

Nov–Mar Ski season at Beidahu Ski Resort.

Jilin Highlights

① Beidahu Ski Resort
(p194) Going off-piste in
preparation for China's
Winter Olympics in 2022.

**② Changbai Shan Nature
Reserve** (p190) Immersing
yourself in the birch forests
and waterfalls of China's
largest nature reserve before

peering into the stunning
blue waters at Heaven Lake.

③ Koguryo Kingdom
(p194) Donning your history
hat and exploring the
mysterious remains of this
ancient kingdom in present-
day Ji'an, a charming town

across the Yalu River from
North Korea.

**④ Imperial Palace of
the Manchu State** (p195)
Witnessing the remarkable
story of 'The Last Emperor',
the puppet Puyi, at his
beautifully restored palace in
Changchun.

History

Korean kings once ruled parts of Jilin, and
the discovery of important relics from the
ancient Koguryo kingdom (37 BC–AD 668)
in the small southeastern city of Ji'an has resulted in the area being designated a World
Heritage Site by Unesco.

The Japanese occupation of Manchuria
in the early 1930s pushed Jilin to the world's

centre stage. Changchun became the capital
of what the Japanese called Manchukuo, with
Puyi (the last emperor of the Qing dynasty)
given the role of figurehead of the puppet
government. In 1944 the Russians wrested
control of Jilin from the Japanese and, after stripping the area of its industrial base,
handed the region back to Chinese control.
For the next several years Jilin would pay a
heavy price as one of the front lines in the

> ### ⓘ PRICE RANGES
>
> **Sleeping**
>
> ¥ Less than ¥200
>
> ¥¥ ¥200–400
>
> ¥¥¥ More than ¥400
>
> **Eating**
>
> ¥ Less than ¥40
>
> ¥¥ ¥40–90
>
> ¥¥¥ More than ¥90

civil war between the Kuomintang and the Chinese Communist Party (CCP).

Climate

Jilin is bitterly cold during its long winter, with heavy snow, freezing winds and temperatures as low as -20°C (32° F). In contrast, summer is pleasantly warm, especially along the coastal east, but short. Rainfall is moderate.

ⓘ Getting There & Around

The airport at Changbai Shan has connections to Changchun and other major Chinese cities.

The rail and bus network connects all major cities and towns. High-speed D and G trains link Changchun with cities south to Shenyang, Dalian and Dandong; north to Harbin and Qiqiha'er; and east to Changchun, Jilin City and Yanji.

Jilin is a small province with excellent transport links, where an easy loop offers an authentically diverse China experience.

Changbai Shan Nature Reserve 长白山

Dominating the eastern fringes of Jilin, the 2100-sq-km Changbai Shan (Chángbái Shān, Ever-White Mountains), which also straddles the China–North Korea border, has long captured the imagination of the Chinese. It could be the thick green forest running to the horizon, or perhaps spellbinding Heaven Lake, where the evil *guaiwu* creature is said to lurk just beneath the surface. The reality of the lake is just as mystical, especially in summer when its frozen cover cracks to reveal an icy blue set inside an ocean-sized volcanic crater.

Koreans refer to the area as Mt Paekdu, or Paekdusan. North Korea claims that Kim Jong-il was born here (although he's believed to have entered the world in Khabarovsk, Russia).

Though you can visit most of the year, the best time to see the crater (and be assured the roads are open) is from June to early September.

About 15km from the local airport, **Wanda Changbai Shan International Resort** (万达长白山国际度假区, Wàndá Chángbái Shān Guójì Dùjià Qū; ☑ 0400 098 7666; 455 Baiyun Lu, 白云路455号) has 20 runs over two mountains with some decent hiking in summer. The ski runs are unlikely to challenge more experienced alpinists, but the set-up is world class and the crowds are often far smaller than you might expect.

The gateway town for the northern slope is Baihe and for the western slope it is Songjianghe; accommodation is widely available at both. It is possible to take buses or trains here from Changchung, Yanji, Tonghua and Shenyang.

Changbai Shan Airport, halfway between the reserve and Songjianghe, has flights to/from Shanghai, Changchun and Beijing.

Baihe 白河

☑ 0433

Erdao Baihe (二道白河), generally known as just Baihe, is a burgeoning 'tourist town' that sports the finest views of Changbai Shan from its location on the northern slope (北坡, *běi pō*). It's by far the best place to base yourself for excursions into the mountains, though there's not much to do other than rest and recharge.

ⓞ Sights

Changbai Waterfall WATERFALL
(长白瀑布, Chángbái Pùbù) From the bus stop, walk up to a small **hot spring** where you can soak your feet or buy delicious boiled eggs (cooked in the spring). Past that a 1km trail leads to the viewpoint for the magnificent 68m Changbai Waterfall.

If the 3.5km-long boardwalk running through birch forests from the falls to the Green Deep Pool area is open, it's worth the walk.

Green Deep Pool LAKE
(绿渊潭, Lǜ Yuān Tán) This large, aptly named pool of water, fed by Changbai Waterfall, is 450m ahead of the Small Heaven Lake (p195). The beautiful milky-green pool is great for photos, but not for swimming in.

Cross the bus parking lot and head up the stairs to reach it. Buses run from the waterfall down to the main junction and the Underground Forest.

Heaven Lake
LAKE

(天池, Tiān Chí) The jewel of the area, this heavenly blue lake seems impossibly elevated by a ring of 16 mountainous peaks. The dormant crater lake, 13km in circumference, was formed around AD 969. A fixed route takes you around part of the crater lip with panoramic views of its glorious mirrored surface, at such an altitude (2194m) that it feels other-worldly. Legend has it that the lake is home to a large, but shy, beastie with the magical power to blur any photo taken of him.

Small Heaven Lake
LAKE

(小天池, Xiǎo Tiān Chí) Grab a bus from the Changbai Waterfall to Small Heaven Lake. Nowhere near the size or majesty of the main crater lake, this is instead a placid lake (or large pond) worth circling. You could venture off into the surrounding forests for a short hike, but don't get lost and be careful not to cross into North Korea! A boardwalk takes you along a fissure stream to the Green Deep Pool.

Underground Forest
FOREST

(地下森林, Dìxià Sēnlín) Lying between the park entrance and transport junction, this verdant woodland area, also known as the Dell Forest (谷底森林, Gǔdǐ Sēnlín), has a 3km boardwalk through the woods to the forest base and back. Allow at least 1½ hours for the walk. Buses run from here back to the junction and north gate.

🛏 Sleeping & Eating

On your arrival at the train or bus station, touts for cheap guesthouses will likely approach. Many of these guesthouses can be found in the small lanes around town. Private rooms without bathroom go for ¥40 to ¥100. The more expensive rooms sometimes have their own computer.

There are small restaurants in all areas of Baihe, many of the Korean persuasion. Overpriced snacks are also sold inside the park on the northern slope, but there are no large restaurants, so it pays to bring your own supplies.

There are also overpriced restaurants inside the reserve.

Woodland Youth Hostel
HOSTEL ¥

(望松国际青年旅舍, Wàngsōng Guójì Qīngnián Lǚshě; ☑ 0433 571 0800; cbs800@126.com; Wenhua Lu, 文化路; dm/tw ¥45/100; ❀❅@☎) In an outer neighbourhood, the friendly Woodland is the pick of the admittedly limited budget offerings around Changbaishan. It has same-sex dorms, clean twins and the usual hostel amenities such as a restaurant (dishes from ¥18 to ¥88), laundry, wi-fi and travel information. The hostel runs its own return shuttle to the north and western slopes (¥30 and ¥70 respectively).

To get here from the train or bus station, take a taxi (¥8) or ask about free daytime pick-up.

★ Yiran International Holiday Service Apartment
APARTMENT ¥¥

(☑ +86 18844 357916; 5 Kangjing Dansha, Cuihu Lu, Erdao Baihe, 二道白河镇翠湖路康景大厦5号; apt ¥220-360) Yiran is a well-maintained apartment belonging to Jeremy, a friendly and professional host who will put your travelling party quickly at ease. The double-storey interior can sleep four adults and a couple of kids. Tours can be arranged, including a free sweep of the town's dining scene.

ℹ Information

The **Bank of China** (中国银行, Zhōngguó Yínháng; Baishan Jie, 白山街) is on the main street in Baihe towards the end of town. It has an ATM.

ℹ Getting There & Away

Public transport for the northern slope only goes as far as Baihe.

Buses leave from the long-distance bus station (kèyènzhàn). From the train station head to the main road; the station is across and to the left. Destinations include the following:

Changchun ¥133, 6½ hours, two daily (6.10am and 5pm)

Songjianghe ¥11, two hours, 9.10am, three daily (9.10am, 12.30pm and 2pm)

Yanji ¥53, 3½ hours, five daily

Trains from Baihe include the following:

Shenyang Hard/soft sleeper ¥203/288, 12½ hours, three daily (9.11am, 6.39pm and 7.45pm)

Songjianghe Seat ¥13, two hours, four daily

Tonghua Hard seat/sleeper ¥42/178, five to six hours, four daily

ℹ Getting Around

From Baihe train or bus station, a tourist bus (¥45) will drop you off at the flashy main entrance of the northern slope where you buy tickets (¥125) before proceeding to queue for a tourist shuttle (¥85) to the main transport junction/parking lot. From here you can catch a vehicle for the final 16km trek to Heaven Lake, or a shuttle to the Changbai Waterfall and other sights. Unlimited park bus rides are all included in the park's obligatory ¥85 tourist-shuttle fee, but the Heaven Lake vehicle is another ¥80 return.

From the Woodland Youth Hostel, you can take the hostel's own return shuttle (¥30; departs 8am and returns 4.30pm) to the northern slope entrance.

A taxi from the train station into town costs ¥10. Taxi rides within town districts cost ¥5.

Taxis charge ¥60 to ¥70 (per car) for the one-way trip from Baihe to the northern slope entrance. Returning, it's usually easy to share a taxi back (¥20 per person), but not if you leave after 5.30pm.

Songjianghe 松江河

📞 0439

Changbai Shan's western slope (西坡, xī pō) in the summer is covered in blankets of flowers and the approach is populated with picturesque hardwood forests. The gateway town, Songjianghe (Sōngjiānghé), is sometimes ignored by visitors who base themselves in Baihe, 40km northwest.

As in the north, it can be super popular with local tourists most of the year, but the set-up is a little fancier.

Filled with dramatic rock formations, the 70km-long, 200m-wide and 100m-deep **Changbai Shan Canyon** (长白山大峡谷, Chángbái Shān Dàxiágǔ) really deserves more fame, but it's tough to measure up against Heaven Lake. There's an easy 40-minute route along a boardwalk that follows the canyon rim through the forest.

Songjianghe offers midrange accommodation similar to Baihe, while closer to the reserve you'll find some decent resorts, with high-end eating and drinking venues, fitted with wood, glass and stone decor.

From Songjianghe there are buses and trains to Tonghua and Shenyang. Changbai Shan Airport, halfway between the reserve and Songjianghe, has flights to/from Shanghai (¥1000, 2½ hours), Changchun (¥1000, 45 minutes) and Beijing (¥1900, two hours).

Woodland Youth Hostel (p191) in Baihe has a return shuttle to the western slope for ¥70 (1½ hours). Taxis also run the route for ¥200 one way. Transport within the reserve costs ¥85.

Yanji 延吉

📞 0433 / POP 432,000

Yanji (Yánjí) is the capital of China's Korean Autonomous Prefecture, but there isn't much of interest here other than the aspects of Korean culture still apparent in the food, street signs and language on the street. The Han Chinese influence is kicking in, however, so don't expect Little Seoul.

Yanji's well-regarded university and a sprawling high school fuel a cool, young cafe vibe, while Yanji's air quality is equally fresh, with locals claiming it is cleaner than Hainan's.

Yanji is also a launching point for tours into Rason in North Korea.

◉ Sights

The Bu'erhatong River (布尔哈通河, Bù'ěrhātōng Hé) that bisects the city has pleasant parks and walkways running alongside that are worth strolling on. By night the colourfully lit bridges attract young people coming to hang out.

★ **Mao'er Mountain** MOUNTAIN
(帽儿山, Mào'ér Shān) **FREE** The clear favourite of Yanji families, especially on weekends, this relatively small mountaintop is dotted with young people lounging in the woods in tents or hammocks (¥40 to buy, or ¥10 per day) or walking the 60- to 90-minute return loop to the peak. The whole way is boardwalked, and the locals in all-white outfits and high heels reflect what an easy ascent it is, though the last section is quite steep.

The views of Yanji are the best around, and the air is as fresh as locals claim of the city, though not crystal clear.

🛏 Sleeping

The best area to stay is within a few blocks of the commercial district – along Guangming Lu near the corner with Renmin Lu – though it can be noisy. Towards the river are quieter options, and the north bus station is within walking distance. There are a few budget hotels around the scruffy train station. Isolated Yanji West train station has nothing built-up nearby.

Motel 268 HOTEL ¥
(📞 0433 511 6777; 633 Renmin Lu, 人民路633号时代广场; d & tw ¥165) New management have kept up the pace at this busy small hotel in the heart of the commercial district,

surrounded by Yanji's few malls and plenty of good restaurants. For early risers, the compact, clean rooms make a good choice for nearby places to eat and the north bus station. A taxi from the train station is just a couple yuan above minimum fare.

Yanbian Dazong Hotel HOTEL ¥¥
(延边大宇酒店, Yánbiān Dàyǔ Jiǔdiàn; 3118 Juzi Jie, 鉅子街3118號; d ¥450-650) This ostentatious hotel is a lot of fun for the kitsch hunters who have made it to Yanji and are happy to while away some time among heavy oil paintings, a faux-German brewery, and cavernous lobby and sitting rooms that appear to expect a military parade at any moment.

It's an excellent place to stretch out from a long bus ride and loiter at the Chinese buffet breakfast.

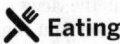 Eating

Head to Guangming Lu near the corner of Renmin Lu for a busy pedestrian street with plenty of restaurants and a street market. Excellent Korean food can be easily found in the surrounding streets and alleys for blocks around. Plenty of cool Korean-run coffee shops line Aidan Lu near the corner of Juzi Lu or Renmin Lu, around the north bus station (客运北站, *kèyùn běi zhàn*), with decent western food and wi-fi.

Rotti Bunn CAFE ¥
(2nd fl, 696 Aidan Lu, 爱丹路696号益华广场2楼; coffee ¥18-26; ⊙9am-midnight; ❋❒❂) Yanji is home to many Korean cafes that seem to open and close like DIY blogs, but Rotti Bunn has made it through the early years thanks to its well-designed communal spaces, mezzanines and closed-off rooms, which make for a comfy place to spend hours writing postcards, social-media posts or memoirs on the free-use Macs or wi-fi.

You'll need as much time to get through the bucket-sized, sweet Korean desserts.

Quánzhōu Bànfàn Guǎn KOREAN ¥
(全州拌饭馆; 142 Shenhua Jie, 参花街142号; mains ¥28-46; ⊙24hr; ⓅΒ❂) A large, restaurant well regarded for its excellent options – mainly *jiàngtāng* (酱汤; a bubbling pot of pork and potatoes in a miso broth) or *bànfàn* (拌饭, *bibimbap*; rice, vegetables and eggs served in a clay pot). Sit at tables or on a heated-floor booth, with good service either way. Off Renmin Lu, west riverside. Picture menu.

San Qian Li Cold Noodles KOREAN ¥
(三千里冷面部, Sānqiānlǐ Lěng Miànbù; 56 Xinhua Jie, 新华街56号; cold noodles ¥18-22; ⊙9am-8pm) One of the best places to slurp down a Yanji Korean speciality, *lěng miàn* (冷面; cold noodles). Order and almost immediately a large bowl of chewy bean thread noodles is served in a cold beef broth that is addictively savoury and sweet with a fresh topping of shredded cucumber and cabbage.

🍷 Drinking & Nightlife

Najia Coffee BAR
(那家咖啡, Nàjiā Kāfēi; ☑0433 256 1859; 2nd fl, 696 Aidan Lu, 爱丹路696号益华广场2楼; ⊙9am-midnight) A trendy cafe with a smoky bar side, Najia is an impressive, large space with huge curved windows and a mezzanine, great for watching the well dressed sip imported beers, or the blinking of traffic and neon outside.

❶ Information

ATMs are all over the city, including a 24-hour ATM at the **Industrial & Commercial Bank of China** (ICBC; 中国工商银行, Zhōnguó Gōngshāng Yínháng) three blocks up from the train station at the corner of Changbaishan Xilu and Zhanqian Jie.

❶ Getting There & Away

The Yanji train station and Yanji long-distance bus station are south of the river, while the commercial district and north bus station are near each other north.

Buses to Changchun (¥116, 5½ hours, hourly, 6am to 5pm) leave from in front of the train station or north bus station.

The **Yanji long-distance bus station** (延吉公路客运总站, Yánjí Gōnglù Kèyùn Zǒngzhàn; 2319 Changbaishan Xilu, 长白山西路2319号) serves the following destinations:

Erdao Baihe ¥45, four hours, six daily (6.40am to 2.30pm)

Hunchun ¥30, two hours, every 30 minutes (7am to 3.50pm)

Mudanjiang ¥74, 4½ hours, four daily (6.30am, 9.50am, 12.10pm and 4.30pm)

Yanji's **north bus station** (延吉客运北站, Yánjí Kèyùn Běi Zhàn; 743 Aidan Lu, 爱丹路743号; ⊙5.30am-6.30pm) serves the following destination:

Mudanjiang ¥74, five hours, four daily (6.50am, 10.20am, 12.40pm and 4.50pm)

Train services include the following:

Changchun Hard seat/sleeper ¥70/129, eight to nine hours, five daily

ℹ Getting Around

Shared taxis outside Yanji West train station will take you to Yanji train station or commercial district for ¥10 per passenger. Bus 4 (¥1) also runs to Yanji train station. Taxi fares start at ¥5; most rides around the commercial district cost less than ¥10.

Bus 60 (¥1) links the train station, commercial district and two bus stations.

Ji'an 集安

✔ 0435 / POP 245,000

For Korean history buffs – or anyone interested in ancient dynasties – Ji'an (Jí'ān) is a must-visit small town. Wrapped around by the Yalu River, it was once part of the Koguryo (高句丽, Gāogōulì) kingdom, a Korean dynasty that ruled areas of northern China and the Korean peninsula from 37 BC to AD 668. Ji'an's extensive Koguryo pyramids, ruins and tombs resulted in Unesco designating it a World Heritage Site in 2004. Archaeologists have unearthed remains of three cities plus some 40 tombs around Ji'an and the town of Huanren (in Liaoning province).

Modern-day Ji'an has transformed itself into one of northern China's more pleasant towns, with well-tended parks, leafy streets and a renovated riverfront area where you can gaze across to North Korea. Add in the town's mountain backdrop, excellent Korean food, friendly locals and scenic train or bus rides getting here, and it's a great little stopover on a loop through Dongbei.

BEIDAIHU SKI RESORT

Since it hosted the 2007 Asian Winter Games, **Beidahu Ski Resort** (Běidàhú Huáxuěchǎng, 北大湖滑雪场; www.beidahuski.com) has established itself as one of China's premier ski resorts. The resort has runs on two mountains ranging from beginner to advanced. Beidahu has expanded gradually with new runs and the opening of China's second Club Med resort. For more on skiing in Beidahu, including tour, transport and accommodation information, see China Ski Tours (www.chinaskitours.com).

The resort is in a tiny village 53km south of Jilin City, which has its own fast-train station, making it one of the more accessible ski spots in the region.

◉ Sights

★ Wandu Mountain City RUINS

(丸都山城, Wándū Shānchéng; Shancheng Lu, 山城路; ¥30) Wandu Mountain City is an inspiring site of ancient civilisation where visitors can walk freely, often alone in nature, among rock pyramids, reassembled artifices and giant stone cairns. Erected after the destruction of Wandu, this vast cemetery for the city's noblemen is so far unaffected by mass tourism. The sight of the massive rock piles in fields of Spanish needle (*Bidens pilosa*) is probably the most photogenic in all Ji'an.

First built in AD 3, this city became capital of the Koguryo kingdom in 209, after the fall of the first capital, Guonei city (on the site of present-day Ji'an). There's little left of the original buildings, but scrambling about the terraces and taking in the views is a highlight of travel to the region. You can sense why the Korean kingdom decided to establish the capital here.

Wandu is a 6.5km drive west of the train station.

Cemetery of Noblemen at Yushan TOMB

(禹山贵族墓地, Yǔshān Guìzú Mùdì; ¥30) Scattered about a small gated park lie the stone crypts of various Koguryo-kingdom noblemen. You can enter and explore Tomb No 5 (wait for the guide) via a creepy descent underground. As your eyes adjust to the light in the chilly stone chamber, look for paintings of dragons, white tigers, black tortoises and lotus flowers on the walls and ceilings.

Ji'an Museum MUSEUM

(集安博物馆, Jí'ān Bówùguǎn; Jianshe Jie, 建设街; ¥30; ⊙8.30am-4pm) The sleek museum sports a brown stone base and a glass top with sails that open up like leaves. It features a small display of artefacts from the Koguryo era with good English captions. A lovely park with stone fountains, landscaped gardens, cobbled walkways, lotus ponds and statues is located just next to the museum.

Riverside Plaza WATERFRONT

FREE This lively modern waterfront park features riverside decks where you can view North Korea across the Yalu River. You can also take a boat ride along the river (¥50, 40 minutes). The park is stretched out along Yanjiang Lu, south of the main Shengli Lu.

Haotaiwang Stele TOMB

(好太王碑, Hǎotàiwáng Bēi; ¥30) Inscribed with 1775 Chinese characters, the Haotaiwang

Stele, a 6m-tall stone slab that dates from AD 415, records the accomplishments of Koguryo king Tan De (374–412), known as Haotaiwang. The surface is blackened from a botched restoration effort when it was rediscovered in 1877: to remove the moss covering the surface, locals smeared it with cow dung and set it alight. Tan De's tomb (labelled 'Taiwang Tomb') is on the same site.

Jiangjunfen   TOMB

(将军坟, General's Tomb; ¥30) One of the largest pyramid-like structures in the region, the 12m-tall Jiangjunfen was built during the 4th century for a Koguryo ruler. The nearby smaller tomb is the resting place of a family member. The site is set among the hills 4km northeast of town.

🛏 Sleeping & Eating

There are a dozen guesthouses with very basic rooms for ¥60 to ¥80 and a couple of better business-hotel options that are more likely to accept foreigners for ¥180 to ¥220 on Shengli Lu (outside the bus station) and on Yanjiang Lu (outside the train station). Chinese chain-hotel options are at the northern, river-park end of Liming Jie.

Head to the markets east and west of Liming Jie for fruit, dumplings, bread and barbecue. Tuanjie Lu (the parallel road north of Shengli Lu) is home to Chinese greasy spoons, while Liming Jie offers a number of hotpot and barbecue spots. Jianshe Lu near Shengli Lu has several clean Chinese fast-food joints.

ℹ Information

Bank of China (中国银行, Zhōngguó Yínháng; 336 Shengli Lu, 胜利路336号) Located at the corner of Shengli Lu and Li Ming Jie; 24-hour ATM.

ℹ Getting There & Away

The main routes to Ji'an (not to be confused with the identically pronounced 吉安 in distant Jiangxi province) are via Tonghua and Baihe (the gateway to Changbai Shan) to the north, and Shenyang and Dandong in Liaoning province to the west and south. If you're travelling to Baihe by bus, you'll need to change in Tonghua.

Trains are less useful, but there are three per day to Tonghua (¥8.50, 2½ hours) at 6.04am, 10.58am and 4.20pm.

Shengli Lu runs east–west through town, with the **long-distance bus station** (集安市客运总站, Jí'ānshì Kèyùnzǒng Zhàn; 1028 Shengli Lu,

1028胜利路) at the west end. The **train station** (Yanjiang Lu) is 2.9km east, where Shengli Lu changes name to Yanjiang Lu.

Bus services include the following destinations:

Changchun ¥140, 5½ hours, three daily (5.30am, 6.25am and 2.50pm)

Dandong ¥95 to ¥104, six hours, two daily (7.30am and 9.20am)

Erdao Baihe (via Tonghua) ¥98, six hours, two daily (7.30am and 1.35pm)

Shenyang ¥96 to ¥125, six hours, three daily (6.20am, 11.20am and 2.55pm)

Tonghua ¥35, two hours, hourly (5am to 5pm)

After a number of delays, a new border crossing opened in Ji'an in 2019; as ever, entering North Korea as a non-Chinese traveller is only possible as past of an authorised group tour.

Changchun   长春

📞 0431 / POP 7.8 MILLION

Changchun (Chángchūn) is a large, sprawling industrial city with a friendly, youthful pulse and a colourful history at its core. The Japanese capital of Manchukuo between 1933 and 1945, Changchun is perhaps best known as the former home of Puyi, China's last emperor; a recently renovated museum is a fascinating glimpse into a remarkable modern history. The city was also the centre of the Chinese film industry in the 1950s and '60s, but now rides on the smell of automobile dollars. Its crossroad position, linking three provinces on the high-speed railway, makes Changchun a useful stop-off en route to places like Changbai Shan and Harbin.

🔍 Sights

⭐ Imperial Palace
of the Manchu State   MUSEUM

(Puppet Emperor's Palace, 伪满皇宫博物院, Wěimǎn Huánggōng Bówùyuàn; 5 Guangfu Beilu, 光复北路5号; ¥80; ⊙8.30am-4.50pm, last entry 40min before close; Ⓢ Line 4 to Weihuanggong) Recently renovated to an impeccable standard, this is the former residence of Puyi, the Qing dynasty's final emperor, famously depicted in Bernardo Bertolucci's film *The Last Emperor* (1987). His study, bedrooms, temple, his wife's quarters and opium den, as well as his concubine's rooms, are all on show, but it's the exhibition on his extraordinary life, told in part with a fantastic collection of photos, that is most enthralling. An English audio guide is well worth the extra ¥40.

JILIN CHANGCHUN

Changchun

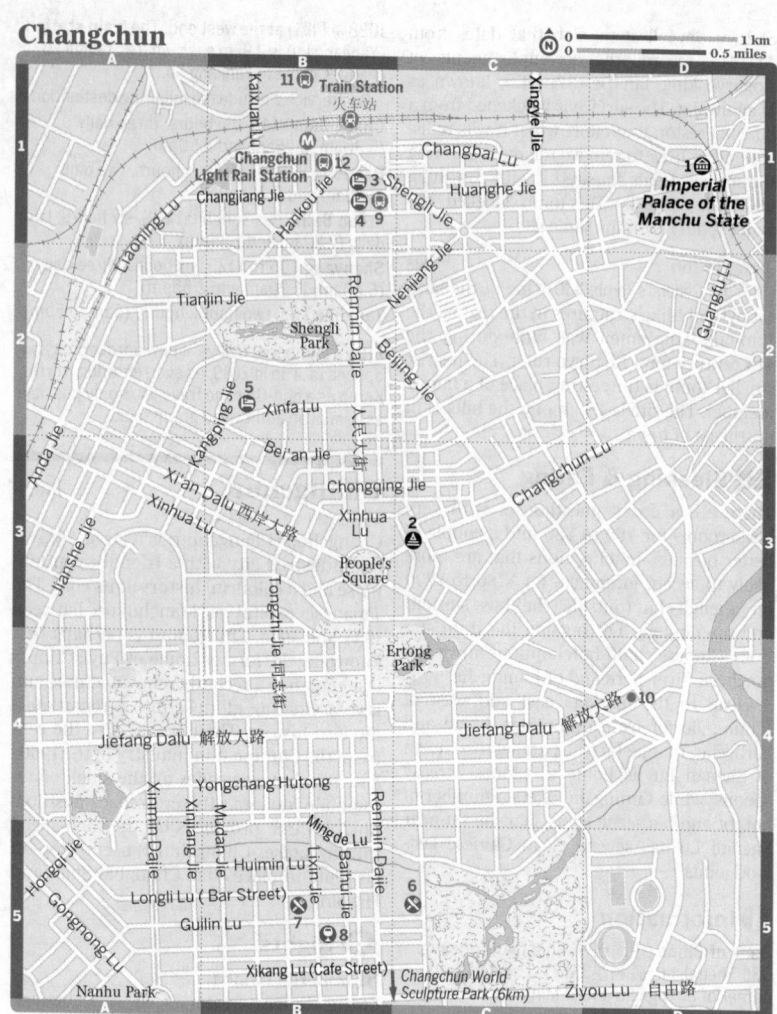

★ Changchun World Sculpture Park

SCULPTURE

(长春世界雕塑公园, Chángchūn Sìjiè Diāodù Gōngyuán; Renmin Dajie, 人民大街; ¥30, shuttle vehicles per person ¥10; ⊙8am-5pm, to 4pm winter; 🚌66, S Line 1 to Weixingguangchang) Nature and art blend stylishly on the edge of Changchun in this peaceful, tree-lined parkland dotted with mostly surrealist sculptures. The 90-hectare space is relatively under-visited; the huge stone and brass pieces peeking through the foliage take around two hours to circle. Entrance to the museum costs another ¥30, but is worth it for the impressive African pieces in particular. A taxi from People's Sq will cost about ¥30.

Banruo Temple

BUDDHIST SITE

(般若寺, Bānruò Sì; 137 Changchun Lu, 长春路137 号; ⊙9am-4pm; 🚌281, 256, S Line 1 to Renmin Guangchang) FREE Built in 1931, Banruo is a very active and engaging temple, acting as a spiritual meeting place for local Buddhists, and pilgrims both devout and curious. Its back alleys brim with merchants peddling all manner of charms, statues, shrines and incense to the faithful; beggars gather outside the entrance on Changchun Lu.

Changchun

🛏 Sleeping

Changchun is well stocked with sleeping options, particularly around the train station and long-distance bus station, which sit at the northern end of the city, where budget rooms start at about ¥150. If you plan on more than just overnighting in Changchun, however, the leafier southern end is by far a more pleasant neighbourhood to stay in.

Regent Hotel　　　　　　　　　HOTEL ¥
(丽晶饭店, Lìjīng Fàndiàn; ☑0431 8117 0888; www.ljfdvip.com; 6 Renmin Dajie, 人民大街6号; r from ¥190; ⓟ❋◉☏) This oval block is a just a few hundred metres south of the station and a step up in quality from the budget chains, while only costing marginally more. They certainly overdid it on the marble in the lobby, but the rooms are pleasant enough, and come with extras like complimentary fruit. The breakfast buffet, mostly Chinese, is bountiful.

★ **Chunyi Hotel**　　　　　　　　HOTEL ¥¥
(春谊宾馆; Chūnyì Bīnguǎn; ☑0431 8209 6888; 80 Renmin Dajie, 人民路80号; d & tw from ¥250; ⓟ❋◉☏) The Chunyi is a classic early-20th-century Chinese hotel with a hint of historical glamour. Lit up on a busy intersection on Renmin Dajie, its marble staircase ascends from a gaudy, Party-approved lobby. Period furniture and photographs remind guests of Changchun's once-booming film industry and the many foreign dignitaries who have graced the halls since it opened in 1909.

The brown, contemporary rooms are very comfortable, and have huge bathrooms and dressing areas.

Songyuan Hotel　　　　　　　HOTEL ¥¥¥
(松苑宾馆, Sōngyuàn Bīnguǎn; ☑0431 8272 7001; 1169 Xinfa Lu, 新发路1169号; d & tw ¥478-998; ❋◉☏) Nestled within its own park grounds, about 8km from downtown, the Songyuan was a former army commander's residence. Today its heritage buildings host tourists in slightly stained, yet clean and well-decorated rooms. The on-site restaurant serves overpriced Chinese fare, but the included breakfast is delicious.

A taxi from the train station costs ¥7.

🍴 Eating

The area surrounding Tongzhi Jie between Longli Lu and Ziyou Lu is very popular and packed with inexpensive restaurants, music and clothing shops. Tree-lined Xikang Lu (west of Tongzhi Jie) is now an unofficial cafe street. Guilin Lu (east from Tongzhi Jie) is lined with cheap eateries and street-food stalls.

★ **Dong Teng**　　　　　　　　　DONGBEI ¥
(社会主义新农村, Shèhuì Zhǔyì Xīn Nóngcūn; ☑0431 8566 6600; 50-7 Yueyang Jie, 岳阳街50-7号; mains from ¥28; ⊙noon-9.30pm; ⓢLine 1 to Dongzhiwuyuan) Climb the rickety wooden staircase to this Communist-themed, folk restaurant where the Dongbei beer and food flow freely courtesy of waitresses in Red-Guard regalia. The low-lit, private, non-smoking rooms feel like dens for hosting counter-surveillance meetings. There's even a spicy fish dish named 'Cultural Revolution' (文化大革命, Wénhuà Dàgémìng), but otherwise expect the more proletarian northern Chinese fare.

Dongbei food is notoriously meaty, but vegetarians won't go wrong with an order of 'big harvest' (大丰收; dà fēngshōu) – a basket of raw veggies, salad, tofu sheets and dipping sauces. Picture menu available.

Sānyú Zhúyuàn　　　　　　　SICHUAN ¥¥
(三俞竹苑; ☑0431 8802 8127; 2222 Tongzhi Jie, 同志街2222号; mains ¥32-88; ⊙10am-10pm; ❋☏🍽) At this upmarket chain, the decoration starts with the lovely faux-antique

interior and continues with fistfuls of chilli adorning every platter – meat, seafood, even frog. In true Sichuan style, mildly spicy can translate to very spicy. The picture English menu also contains lots of veggie and non-spicy options.

🍷 Drinking & Nightlife

⭐ LR Lounge Bar
COCKTAIL BAR

(左右酒吧, Zuǒyòu Jiǔbā; ☑ 0431 8868 7688; Longli Hutong, 30m west of Baihui Jie, 隆礼路胡同与百汇街交汇西行30米; cocktails from ¥45; ⊙ 6pm-2am; 🛜) Live acoustic music on weekends draws a crowd to Changchun's best small cocktail bar where bow-tied bartenders shake and pour for an eclectic mix of the young and groovy. Look for a large industrial door 30m west of the intersection.

ℹ️ Information

There are 24-hour ATMs all over town.

ℹ️ Getting There & Away

AIR

Changchun Longjia International Airport (长春龙嘉国际机场, Chángchūn Lóngjiā Guójì Jīchǎng) has daily flights to major cities, including Beijing (¥500, two hours) and Shanghai (¥800, 2½ hours), and also Changbai Shan (¥500, one hour).

BUS

The **long-distance bus station** (长途汽车站, Chángtú Qìchēzhàn; 226 Renmin Dajie, 人民大街226号) is two blocks south of the train station behind the Regent Hotel (p197). Buses to Harbin leave from the **North Bus Station** (客运北站, Kèyùn Běi Zhàn; 2088 Tiebei Er Lu, 铁北二路2088号) to the north of the train station, partially under construction at the time of writing. Facing the station, head left and take the underpass just past the 24-hour KFC (not to be confused with the non-24-hour KFC to the right of the train station, or the two across the street). Bus services include the following:

Harbin ¥76, 3½ hours, 8.30am, three daily (8.30am, 10am and noon)

Shenyang ¥83, 4½ hours, two daily (10am and 2pm)

Yanji ¥116, five hours, hourly (7am to 5pm)

TRAIN

Avoid getting tickets for Changchun's west station (xī zhàn), 13km out of town. Instead use Changchun's **main train station** (长春火车站, Chángchūn Huǒchē Zhàn), which serves the following destinations:

Beijing (D/G trains) Seat ¥266, seven hours, eight daily

Beijing Hard seat/sleeper ¥141/267, eight to 16½ hours, nine daily

Harbin (D/G trains) Seat ¥74 to ¥119, one to 1½ hours, hourly

Shenyang (D/G trains) Seat ¥92 to ¥145, 1½ to two hours, 33 daily

ℹ️ Getting Around

TO/FROM THE AIRPORT

The airport is 35km east of the city centre. Shuttle buses to the airport (¥20, 50 minutes, every 30 minutes from 6am to 7pm) leave from the **Civil Aviation Administration of China** (CAAC, 中国民航, Zhōngguó Mínháng; ☑ 0431 8298 8888; 480 Jiefang Dalu, 解放大路480号) on the east side of town. Taxi fares to the airport are ¥100 to ¥120 for the 40-minute trip.

BUS

Buses heading south leave from the **train station bus stop** outside the south exit. Bus 6 follows Renmin Dajie all the way to the south part of town. Buses 62 and 362 run to the Chongqing Lu and Tongzhi Jie shopping districts.

METRO

The Changchun Metro connects Changchun Railway Station with the Imperial Palace (p195). Like most Chinese underground lines, it's fast, clean and efficient. Take Line 4, which starts just north of the train station two stops to Weihuanggang (¥2). Line 1 goes south from the train station along Renmin Dajie. Dongzhiwuyuan is a useful stop to get close to the bars and eateries around Tongzhi Jie. Get off at Renminguangchang for Banruo Temple (p196).

The Changchun Light Rail (长春轻轨; Chángchūn Qīngguǐ; 6.30am to 9pm) is only useful for getting to **Jingyuetan National Forest Park** (净月潭国家森林公园; Jìngyuètán Guójiā Sēnlín Gōngyuán; ¥30; ⊙ 8.30am-5.30pm; light rail Line 3 to Jingyue Gongyuan). The station is just west of the train station square.

TAXI

Taxi fares start at ¥5.

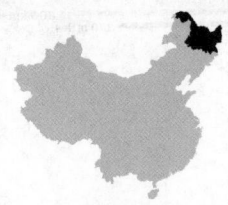

Heilongjiang

POP 38.4 MILLION

Best Places to Eat

➡ Wángmáolú Dòufu Měishí Diàn (p212)

➡ Laochujia (p206)

Best Places to Stay

➡ Harbin Longmen Capsule Hotel (p204)

➡ Kazy International Youth Hostel (p204)

Why Go?

Unfurling up to Russia in the north, Heilongjiang (黑龙江, Hēilóngjiāng), meaning 'Black Dragon River', is one of China's most beautifully rugged provinces. Forests, lakes, mountains and the dormant volcanoes of Wudalian Chi beckon well beyond the capital Harbin (Hā'ěrbīn), an architecturally diverse city with a distinctly cosmopolitan feel.

Of course, it gets cold – sub-Arctic cold – in China's northernmost province, but Harbin is a winter playground, hosting a world-renowned ice-sculpture festival and a brand-new indoor ski centre. The province also boasts some of China's most established ski slopes, which are increasingly popular as the country prepares for the Winter Olympics in 2022.

From Mohe, China's most northerly city, you can access the remote Beijicun and Beihongcun for bragging rights to say you have stood at the very top of the Middle Kingdom.

When to Go
Harbin

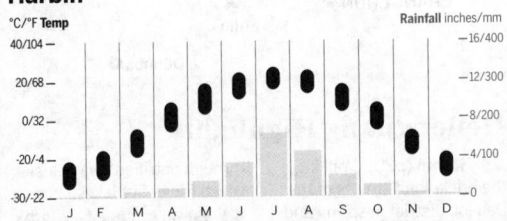

Jan Harbin hosts the Ice & Snow Festival.

Apr The Siberian cranes take flight.

Dec–Mar Ski season at Yabuli and Wudalian Chi.

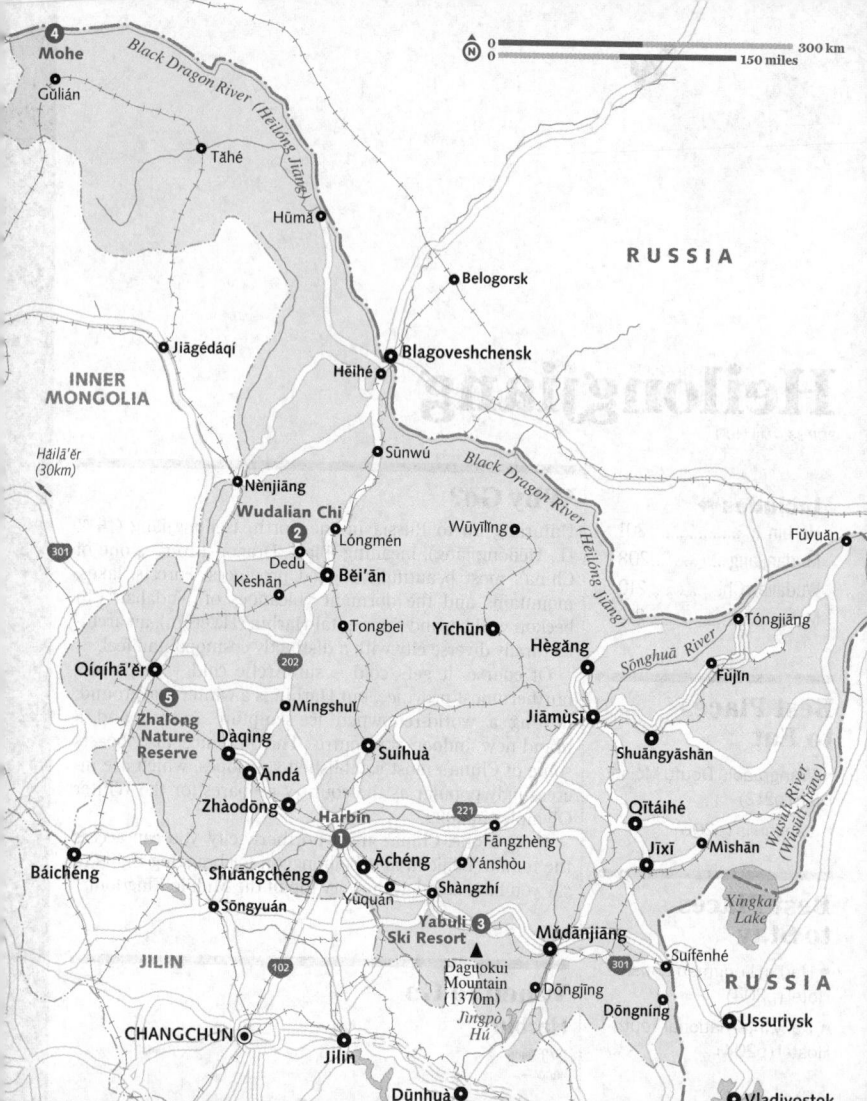

Heilongjiang Highlights

1 Harbin (p201) Walking the brick-lined streets of the Daoliqu district in spring and braving the winter chill for the world-famous Ice & Snow Festival.

2 Wudalian Chi (p210) Hiking to the top of a dormant volcano's crater mouth and through petrified lava fields, which fringe five lakes.

3 Yabuli Ski Resort (p210) Shredding the slopes at China's premier ski resort as the 2020 Winter Olympics draw near.

4 Mohe (p212) Exploring China's northernmost village, where every day feels like Christmas, while hoping to catch the elusive but spectacular aurora borealis.

5 Zhalong Nature Reserve (p212) Encountering Siberian cranes and other rare birds en route through northern China.

History

Heilongjiang forms the northernmost part of Dongbei, the region formerly known as Manchuria. Its proximity to Russia has long meant strong historical and trade links with its northern neighbour. In the mid-19th century, Russia annexed parts of Heilongjiang, while in 1897 Russian workers arrived to build a railway line linking Vladivostok with Harbin. By the 1920s well over 100,000 Russians resided in Harbin alone.

Heilongjiang was occupied by the Japanese between 1931 and 1945. After the Chinese Communist Party (CCP) took power in 1949, relations with Russia grew steadily frostier, culminating in a brief border war in 1969. Sino-Russian ties have much improved in recent years and the two sides finally settled on the border in July 2008, after 40-odd years of negotiation.

In 2016 China relaxed its one-child policy further in Heilongjiang, allowing overseas returnees to have up to three children in this ageing province.

Climate

The region experiences long, freezing winters, with temperatures dropping below -30°C. Short summers are warm and humid, especially in the south and east. Temperatures in the mid- to high 30°Cs are possible and afternoon showers are common.

ℹ Getting There & Around

Harbin is the logistical hub for the region and has extensive links with the rest of China. High-speed D and G trains link Harbin with the southern train hubs of Shenyang and Changchun, with Qiqiha'er to the north and with Mudanjiang to the west. If you're headed for Inner Mongolia, direct trains run from Harbin to the cities of Haila'er and Manzhouli.

Buses are often a quicker way of getting around than the slow local trains.

Harbin 哈尔滨

📞 0451 / POP 5.6 MILLION

Home to the wondrous Harbin Ice & Snow Festival (p204), and the world's largest indoor ski facility, the capital of Heilongjiang (Hā'ěrbīn), located on the Songhua River, is a stylish city and a highlight of any trip through Dongbei.

Cars (and even bicycles) are barred from the timeworn cobbles of Zhongyang Dajie, the main drag of the city's historic quarter, where the densest cluster of Harbin's old buildings can be found.

The city's sights are as varied as the architectural styles on the old street. Temples, churches and synagogues coexist, while deep in the southern suburbs a former Japanese germ-warfare base is a sobering reminder of less harmonious times.

Harbin's Russian and Jewish heritage is best explored during summer wanderings under blue skies, but winter is when Harbin really heats up, as travellers rug up to visit a neon-clad, subzero theme park created entirely from ice.

⊙ Sights

At its peak in the 1920s and '30s, Harbin was home to 120,000 Russians and roughly 50 synagogues and churches.

Although much has since been lost to development (and the Red Guards in the 1960s), the legacy of concession-era Harbin can be still be felt, particularly along the cobbles of **Zhongyang Dajie** (中央大街, Central Street, Walking Street) **FREE**. A pedestrian-only zone bustling with day-trippers, the avenue and parts of its surrounding streets are lined with former department stores, restaurants and cinemas dating back to the early 20th century. Some are imposing, others distinctly dilapidated, but the mix of architectural styles, from art nouveau to eclecticism and baroque, is fascinating.

The two streets running parallel to the east, **Shangzhi Dajie** and **Zhaolin Jie**, are also home to a dwindling number of old buildings, including the magnificent Church of St Sophia (p203). To the west, **Tongjiang Jie** reveals two former synagogues and the **Turkish Mosque**.

ℹ PRICE RANGES

Sleeping
Prices are for a double room.

¥ Less than ¥150

¥¥ ¥150–300

¥¥¥ More than ¥300

Eating
Price ranges are for meals, per person.

¥ Less than ¥30

¥¥ ¥30–80

¥¥¥ More than ¥80

Harbin

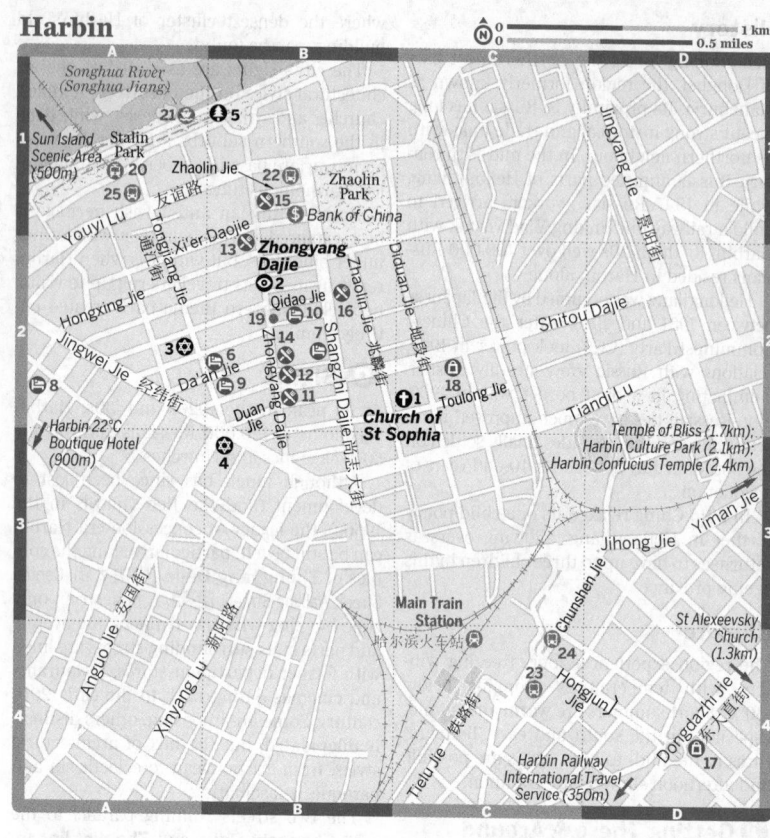

Harbin

◎ Top Sights

◎ Sights

🛏 Sleeping

✖ Eating

🍷 Drinking & Nightlife

☆ Entertainment

🛍 Shopping

ℹ Information

ℹ Transport

Further afield, **Hongjun Jie**, heading south from the train station, and parts of **Dongdazhi Jie** are home to several faded old structures including a handful of places of worship and former consulates. **Guogeli Dajie**, running south from Dongdazhi Jie to **St Alexeevsky Church** (士课街教堂, Shì Kè Jiē Jiàotáng; 211 Shike Jie, 士课街211号) **FREE**, is another former Russian thoroughfare with pockets of surviving heritage.

Two temples and a former church are within walking distance of each other in the Nangang district, connected by the less sacrosanct (but fun) Harbin Culture Park. The **Temple of Bliss** (极乐寺, Jílè Sì; 9 Dongdazhi Jie, 东大直街9号; ¥10; ⊙8am-5pm; 🚌53) sits off a pedestrian-only street reachable by bus 53 (¥1) or taxi (¥12) from the Zhongyang Dajie area 5km away. **Harbin Confucius Temple** (哈尔滨文庙, Hā'ěrbīn Wénmiào; 25 Wenmiao Jie, 文庙街; ⊙8.30am-3.30pm, closed Wed; 🚌53) **FREE** is a 15-minute walk east along Wenmiao Jie, or you can cut through **Harbin Culture Park** (哈尔滨文化公园, Hā'ěrbīn Wénhuà Gōngyuán; 208 Nantong Dajie, 南通大街208号; ¥5, rides from ¥30; ⊙8.30am-5pm; 🚌53), and seek out the **Holy Dormition Church** en route, now a park attraction.

★ **Harbin Ice & Snow World**   AMUSEMENT PARK
(冰雪大世界, Bīngxuě Dàshìjiè; Bingxue Dashijie Yuanqu, 冰雪大世界园区; adult/child under 1.4m ¥330/200; ⊙9am-9.30pm winter only; 🚌47) The signature venue for Harbin's winter-long Ice & Snow Festival is the main reason that both domestic and international travellers chase the cold weather here in huge numbers every year. It's a photogenic and fun-filled wonderland of iconic ice-sculpture, ice mazes, ice bikes, snow sports and snow slides. Live concerts and an ever-changing theme ensure an unpredictability that attracts return visitors. Like most major attractions in China, it's much better to visit during weekdays.

★ **Church of St Sophia**   CHURCH
(圣索菲亚教堂, Shèng Suǒfēiyà Jiàotáng; 88 Toulong Jie, cnr Zhaolin Jie, 透笼街88号; ¥20; ⊙8.30am-5pm) The red-brick Russian Orthodox Church of St Sophia, with its distinctive green onion dome and roosting pigeons, is Harbin's most famous landmark. Built in 1907 and expanded in 1932, it was the largest Orthodox church in the Far East and the centre of spiritual life for 100,000 Russian settlers. After surviving the Cultural Revolution it was used as a warehouse for a department store. Declared a protected landmark in the 1990s, the church was under renovation at the time of print due to damage caused by the resident pigeons; it is not known when it might reopen.

Japanese Germ Warfare Experimental Base   MUSEUM
(侵华日军第731部队遗址, Qīnhuá Rìjūn Dì 731 Bùduì Yízhǐ; Xinjiang Dajie, 新疆大街; ⊙9-11am & 1-3.30pm Tue-Sun) **FREE** This museum is set in the notorious Japanese Germ Warfare Experimental Base (Division 731). Between 1939 and 1945, prisoners of war and civilians were frozen alive, subjected to vivisection or infected with bubonic plague, syphilis and other virulent diseases. Three to four thousand people died here in the most gruesome fashion. The museum includes photos, sculptures and exhibits of the equipment used by the Japanese. There are extensive English captions and an audio guide is available for ¥15.

The base is in the south of Harbin and takes over an hour to reach by bus. From the small **bus station** (通江湿地公交枢纽站, Tōngjiāng Shīdì Gōngjiāo Shūniǔ Zhàn) at the north end of Tongjiang Jie (通江街), catch bus 348 (¥2). Get off at the temporary stop called Yiliu'er Zhong (一六二中). From there it's a 700m walk northeast to the base. If you get lost, just ask the locals the way to qīsānyī (731). Note that Chinese people can be, understandably, uncomfortable talking about this museum.

Sun Island Scenic Area   PARK
(太阳岛公园, Tàiyángdǎo Gōngyuán; cable car single/return ¥50/80; ⊙cable car 8.30am-5pm) Across the water from **Stalin Park** (斯大林公园, Sīdàlín Gōngyuán) **FREE** is Sun Island, a 38-sq-km recreational zone with landscaped gardens, a 'water world', a 'Russian-style' town, and various small galleries and museums. It's a pleasant place to have a picnic, walk or cycle (¥60 per hour) in summer, though as usual you need to pay extra to get into many areas (most people find these too kitsch and not worth the money).

During the Ice & Snow Festival (p204), Sun Island hosts a spectacular snow sculpture display (called the **Harbin International Snow Sculpture Art Expo**; ¥240), which is worth seeing. Distinct from the Harbin Ice & Snow World (p203) (3km away), but no less ambitious, the building-sized sculptures here are carved of snow, not ice. A short walk from the cable-car station, most visitors come here during the day then head to the Ice & Snow World come nightfall.

Ferries (return ¥10) to Sun Island depart from several docks northwest of the Flood Control Monument in Stalin Park in warmer months. During winter when the waters are frozen, catch the nearby **cable car** (one way/return ¥50/80; ⊙ 7am-8pm), or walk across.

Harbin Main Synagogue SYNAGOGUE
(哈尔滨犹太会堂, Hā'ěrbīn Yóutài Huìtáng; 82 Tongjiang Jie, 通江街82号) **FREE** The beautiful old Main Synagogue, built in 1909, has been refurbished as a concert venue (p206). You can buy tickets on-site to a variety of musical performances, including opera, usually starting around 7pm on most nights. The former Jewish Middle School shares the same compound.

Harbin New Synagogue SYNAGOGUE
(哈尔滨犹太新会堂, Hā'ěrbīn Yóutài Xīnhuìtáng; ☑ 0451 8763 0882; 162 Jingwei Jie, 经纬街162号; ¥25; ⊙ 8.30am-5pm) This synagogue was built in 1921 by the city's Jewish community, the vast majority of whom had emigrated from Russia. Beautifully restored and converted into a museum in 2004, the 2nd and 3rd floors present a fascinating exhibition (with detailed English captions) on the history and rich cultural life of Harbin's Jews. An American guide can be arranged with at least a day's notice.

Huangshan Jewish Cemetery CEMETERY
(皇山公墓, Huángshān Gōngmù; off G101 Hwy, G101I哈同高速) Located in the far eastern suburbs of Harbin, this is the largest Jewish cemetery in East Asia. There are more than 600 graves here, all well maintained. A taxi here takes around 45 minutes and costs about ¥100.

JEWISH HARBIN

The Jewish influence on Harbin was surprisingly long lasting; the last original Jewish resident of the city died in 1985. In the 1920s Harbin was home to some 20,000 Jews, the largest Jewish community in the Far East at the time. **Tongjiang Jie** was the centre of Jewish life in the city until the end of WWII, and is still home to two former synagogues (one a museum, the other a concert hall), and the **Jewish Middle School** (犹太中学, Yóutài Zhōngxué; Tongjiang Jie, 通江街), now a private music academy.

 ## Activities

Harbin Indoor Ski Resort SKIING
(哈尔滨万达娱雪乐园, Hā'ěrbīn Wàndá Yú Xuě Lèyuán; ☑ 0451 5556 6666; Shimao Dadao, 世茂大道, 2hr ¥288; ⊙ 9.30am-9.30pm; ☐ 47) The world's largest indoor ski area (at the time of writing), looming high above Harbin Wanda City like a poorly parked spaceship, is a remarkable place to get your snow-sport fix. Plus the snow falls from the ceiling, so it feels pretty much like the real thing!

Festivals & Events

★ **Harbin Ice & Snow Festival** ICE SCULPTURE
(冰雪节, Bīngxuě Jié, Harbin International Ice & Snow Sculpture Festival; ☑ 0451 8625 0068; day/evening ticket ¥135/330; ⊙ 11am-9.30pm) Every winter from early December to late February (officially the festival opens 5 January), Harbin dons a fur-lined, technicolour dreamcoat of ice, snow and neon and gets down, Narnia style – no matter that it's mind-numbingly cold and the sun vanishes by mid-afternoon.

Sleeping

By far the best place to stay is within a few blocks of Zhongyang Dajie (p201) in the city's historic quarter. If you need to catch an early train, hotels surrounding the hectic station can be handy (renovations were near complete at the time of writing). Prices are higher on weekends and significantly so in winter for the Ice & Snow Festival.

★ **Kazy International Youth Hostel** HOSTEL ¥
(卡兹国际青年旅舍, Kǎzī Guójì Qīngnián Lǚshě; ☑ 0451 8469 7113; kazyzcl@126.com; 27 Tongjiang Jie, 通将街27号; dm/s/tw without bathroom ¥40/60/80, d/tw ¥180/120; ☎; ☐ 13) Kazy is the best hostel for miles, and is rightfully popular year-round. English-speaking staff front a cosy reception-bar and can help with excursions in and around Harbin. The private rooms have internal stairs, high ceilings and clean bathrooms. The eight-bed dorms have firm beds and good-quality linen. Cute trinkets, maps, books and snacks are sold in the lobby library.

It's on leafy Tongjiang Jie, but is set back from the road so the traffic noise is minimised. A taxi from Harbin station is ¥14.

★ **Harbin Longmen Capsule Hotel** HOSTEL ¥
(哈尔滨龍門膠囊酒店; ☑ 0451 4512 5886; 61 Shiyi Jie, 經緯街61; capsule from ¥100) This

THE GREAT CATS

As with many of the world's powerful wild creatures, size did not give the Amur (Siberian) tiger much of an advantage during the 20th century. The largest feline in the world, topping 300kg for males and capable of taking down a brown bear in a fair fight, was no match for the poachers, wars, revolutions, railway construction and economic development in its traditional territory in Russia, China and Korea. These days it's believed that fewer than 500 of the great cats still prowl the wilds of Russia, with a fraction of these settling in Heilongjiang and Jilin provinces in China, and fewer still in neighbouring North Korea.

It's a dismal figure, and in 1986 the Chinese government set about boosting numbers by establishing the world's largest tiger breeding centre in Harbin. The majority of tigers are still in captivity, which makes any wild sighting a cause for celebration. In early 2019, a family of tigers was filmed in Jilin province in the Hunchun area, further evidence that the cats are expanding their range south – back into traditional Chinese territory.

In 2020 a 14,600-sq-km national park will be established, bridging the Jilin and Heilongjiang borders – and dedicated to tiger preservation. It's the clearest evidence yet that the Amur might yet have a future in China.

new capsule hotel in a central location is a beauty. The pods are spotless and blistering white, while the common areas have a youthful, comic-book feel. Staff are really helpful, though don't speak much English.

7 Days Inn HOTEL ¥
(7天连锁酒店, 7 Tiān Liánsuǒ Jiǔdiàn; ☑ 0451 5882 5888; 55 Tongjiang Jie, 通江街55号; s & d from ¥175; @ 🛜) While the yellow-and-blue paint job on a historic Harbin building is a little hard to appreciate, there's nothing wrong with the location of this popular chain hotel. All the rooms are identical, but ask for one with a view of the Main Synagogue on leafy Tongjiang Jie. Staff are a little curt but you can buy ice creams in the lobby.

Harbin 22°C
Boutique Hotel BOUTIQUE HOTEL ¥¥
(哈尔滨22度精品主题酒店; ☑ 0451 5101 9922; 19th fl B, Yuanda Bldg, Daoli, 远大商务公寓B座19层; d from ¥350) Just south of central Harbin is this unusual boutique hotel hidden inside the lower section of a commercial building. The designer rooms are very stylish for the price, with big beds and desk spaces, polished floorboards and quality linen. You won't get all-star treatment – staff are almost invisible – but facilities, including pool, gym and gorgeous breakfast buffet, ensure a luxurious experience.

Europa Hotel HOTEL ¥¥
(欧罗巴宾馆, Ōuluóbā Bīnguǎn, Russia Europa Hotel, Europaer Hotel; ☑ 0451 8929 3333; www.russia europahotel.com; 10 Xishidao Jie, 中央大街西十道街10号; tw & d from ¥220; ❀🛜) The Europa is housed in a renovated Russian building close to the St Sophia church (p203). The

price is good for the location – around the corner from Zhongyang Dajie – while rooms are clean, cramped and functional. It's worth paying a little extra for a suite (from ¥320).

✖ Eating

Local eateries specialise in Dongbei (northeast) food: hearty dishes designed to fortify against the cold. Boiled dumplings (煎饺, jiānjiǎo) are ubiquitous and cheap; guōbāoròu (锅包肉) is a famous local dish of sticky-sweet battered pork; while 'three treasures' (地三鲜, dì sān xiān) is a moreish plate of fried potato, peppers and aubergine in a garlicky sauce. Questionably Russian restaurants selling beet-red borsch and steaks abound in Harbin's touristy districts.

★ Old Chang's Spring Rolls CHINESE ¥
(老昌春饼, Lǎo Chāng Chūnbǐng; ☑ 0451 8468 5000; 180 Zhongyang Dajie, 中央大街180号; dishes ¥12-38; ⏱ 10.30am-9pm) Hungry foodies line up for Lao Chang's famous chūnbǐng, northern Chinese specialities, that are essentially DIY spring rolls. Descend the stairs to order a set of wheat roll skins (¥2 per roll), and insist on the crispy duck with sides of eggs and veggies, and then fold, tuck and gorge.

★ Orient King of
Eastern Dumplings DUMPLINGS ¥
(东方饺子王, Dōngfāng Jiǎozi Wáng; 81 Zhongyang Dajie, 中央大街81号; dumpling plates ¥13-38; ⏱ 10.30am-9.30pm; 🛜🍴) This busy main street chain dumpling house is the pick of the three options in Harbin (if it's full, head down the road to number 51). The handmade jiǎozi (饺子, stuffed dumplings) are

HARBIN CHEAP EATS

It's hard to stop eating in Harbin. In any season, the streets off Zhongyang Dajie are abuzz with open-air food stalls (and beer gardens in summer), where you can slug a Hāpí (the famous Harbin beer), while munching on squid on a stick, garlic oysters, *yángròu chuàn* (lamb skewers), roasted sweet potatoes and more.

Shops and stalls along Zhongyang Dajie hawk scarlet-skinned Russian sausages (ready to eat), Russian chocolate, bread and creamy ice-lollies branded to Harbin's **Modern Hotel** (马迭尔宾馆, Mǎdié'ěr Bīnguǎn; ☑ 0451 8488 4000; www.madieer.cn; 89 Zhongyang Dajie, 中央大街89号; r incl breakfast from ¥980; ※@☞☒). In winter, everyone gnaws *bīngtánghúlu* (冰糖葫芦): frozen, candied fruit skewers.

Tongjiang Jie, towards the river end, is lined with small restaurants and hotpot joints that are less touristy (and consequently cheaper) than those on Zhongyang Dajie.

soft and delicious; you can't go wrong with pork and cabbage, or prawn and cucumber. There are also plenty of tasty veggie side dishes and draught beer. Picture menu available.

Bomele 1931 Cafe
BAKERY ¥

(芭米莉咖啡, Bā Mǐ Lì Kāfēi; ☑ 0451 8768 0788; 45 Zhongyang Dajie, 中央大街45号; coffee from ¥20; ⊙ 8am-10pm; ☞) The 2nd-floor terrace overlooking Zhongyang Dajie is the main reason to swing by this friendly Chinese bakery. Downstairs is a self-serve takeaway where cakes and smoothies are created with precision. You can eat more substantial meals upstairs, plus there's free wi-fi and strong coffee.

Suxin Shidu Vegetarian
VEGETARIAN ¥

(素心食度素食餐厅, Sùxīn Shídù Sùshí Cāntīng; ☑ 0451 8469 9934; 8 Qidao Jie, 七道街8号; buffet ¥20; ⊙ 11.30am-1.30pm & 5-6.30pm; ☑) Elderly locals and wayward travellers line up for this health-conscious, meat-free buffet of filling dishes. All the usual pulse and tofu dishes are on offer, but try the more interesting blends of yams, cauliflower and verdant green vegetables cooked without onion or garlic as per Buddhist dietary traditions. You can also self-serve a variety of congee and mugs of sweetened soy milk.

Lóngjiāng Xiǎochī Jiē
FOOD HALL ¥

(龙江小吃街, Longjiang Snack St; Zhongyang Dajie, 中央大街; dishes ¥8-18; ⊙ 9am-6pm; ❄) This underground, mall-style food court is part of a large shopping mall and is well stocked with a variety of Chinese, Asian and western food outlets. In winter it makes a good refuge from the cold. You'll need to purchase a card (¥10) from the pay station then top it up with cash before you order.

Lǎochújiā
CHINESE ¥¥

(老厨家; ☑ 0451 8647 5018; 118 Wenzheng Jie, 118 文正傑; mains ¥18-68; ⊙ 11am-9pm) The 'Old Chef's House', 2km southeast of Zhongyang Dajie, is an excellent place to sample northeastern cuisine. There can be queues on weekends for good reason: succulent, well-priced hotpots and spicy side dishes in a faux-period setting. Service is attentive and friendly to foreigners.

Russia Coffee & Food
RUSSIAN ¥¥

(露西亚咖啡西餐厅, Lùxīyà Kāfēi Xī Cāntīng; 57 Xitoujiao, 西头到街57号; dishes ¥25-82; ⊙ 10am-midnight) Also known as Cafe Russia, this antique-filled cafe is replete with leather-backed dining chairs, a cavernous fireplace and a grandfather clock. You can peruse the extensive collection of photographs and oil paintings depicting Harbin's heyday, with one of many varieties of tea or coffee in hand. If hungry, you can graze on *pirozhki* (savoury pies), but the food is pretty much an afterthought. It's 20m east off Zhongyang Dajie along Xitoujiao.

🍷 Drinking & Nightlife

★ Carl Damo Bar
BAR

(卡尔大漠酒吧, Kǎ'ěr Dàmò Jiǔbā; ☑ 0451 8464 1258; 160 Zhongyang Dajie, 中央大街160号; cocktails from ¥35; ⊙ 2pm-2am) Look for the neon-lit guitar at the entrance, leave your itinerary on Zhongyang Dajie and enter the world of Carl Damo, Harbin's hippest conceptual artist and photographer. His basement bar, packed with dimly lit eye candy, is a tribute to his playful vision. Homemade music videos run on loop to a kind of Americana-indie soundtrack, on undulating volume, depending on the bar staff's whimsical mood.

☆ Entertainment

Main Synagogue Concert Hall
CONCERT VENUE

(哈尔滨犹太会堂, Yóutài Jiùhuìtáng; 82 Tongjiang Jie, 通江街82号) Harbin's Main Synagogue, dating back to 1909, is now a delightfully intimate, well-priced concert venue for classical music performances, with four shows per week (7pm, ¥20 to ¥100, one hour). The ticket office, a star-shaped window around the north side of the synagogue, opens daily at 2pm. Seating is on the old wooden pews; even the cheapest tickets are decent.

🔒 Shopping

Shops along Zhongyang Dajie (and all over the city) flog Russian knick-knacks like *matryoshki* alongside vodka, cigarettes and children's toys. Big-brand western clothing chains now occupy several of the heritage buildings.

Locals prefer to head to Dongdazhi Jie for their shopping needs, as well as the subterranean **Hongbo Century Square** (红博世纪广场, Hóngbó Shìjì Guǎngchǎng; Dongdazhi Jie, 东大直街; ⊙6.30am-5pm), and **Toulong Shopping City** (透笼国际商品城, Tòulóng Guójì Shāngpǐn Chéng; 58 Shitou Dajie, 石头道街58号; ⊙9am-6pm) for 11 floors of bargains.

ℹ️ Information

ATMs are all over town. Most large hotels will also change money.

Bank of China (中国银行, Zhōngguó Yínháng; Xi'er Daojie, 西二道街; ⊙8.30am-5.30pm) Has a 24-hour ATM and will cash travellers cheques and a wide range of foreign currencies. It's easy to spot on a side road as you walk up Zhongyang Dajie.

Many midrange and top-end hotels have travel services that book tickets and arrange tours throughout the province.

Harbin Modern Travel Company (哈尔滨马迭尔旅行社, Hā'ěrbīn Mǎdié'ěr Lǚxíngshè; 2nd fl, Modern Hotel, 89 Zhongyang Dajie, 中央大街89号) Offers one- and two-day ski trips to Yabuli (p210) and can handle flight tickets to Mohe and other regions.

ℹ️ Getting There & Away

AIR

Harbin Taiping International Airport (HRB, 哈尔滨太平国际机场, Hā'ěrbīn Tàipíng Guójì Jīchǎng) has flights to Russia, Japan, South Korea, Taiwan, Singapore, Malaysia and the US, as well as lots of domestic routes, including the following:

Beijing ¥900, two hours
Dalian ¥800, 1½ hours
Mohe ¥1200, 1¾ hours

BUS

The main **long-distance bus station** (长途客运站, Chángtú Kèyùn Zhàn) is a block southwest of the train station. Destinations include the following:

Changchun ¥44, four hours, six daily (10am, noon, 1pm, 1.30pm, 3pm and 4pm).
Mudanjiang ¥94, 4½ hours, hourly (6.30am to 6pm).
Qiqiha'er ¥78, 3½ hours, hourly (7am to 6pm).
Wudalian Chi ¥88 to ¥125, five to six hours, five daily (9am, 11.30am, noon, 1.30pm and 2.45pm). The noon bus goes to the scenic area while the others stop at Wudalian Chi City, a ¥40 taxi ride from the scenic area.

TRAIN

Harbin is a major rail transport hub with routes throughout the northeast and beyond. At the time of writing, Harbin's main **railway station** (哈尔滨站, Hā'ěrbīn Zhàn; 1 Tielu Jie, 铁路街1号) was being rebuilt (due to be completed in 2020), and so in the meantime, fewer services are stopping here, with **Harbin West Station** (西站; Xīzhàn), 10km from town, picking up the slack. A taxi will cost ¥30 to ¥40.

A new high-speed line between Beijing and Shenyang should shorten journey times significantly between Harbin and the capital. Destinations include the following:

Beijing Hard seat/sleeper ¥159/293, 10 to 16 hours, eight daily
Beijing (D/G train) Seat ¥307/542, seven to eight hours, six daily
Changchun (D/G train) Seat ¥74/119, one to 1½ hours, regular
Mohe Hard/soft sleeper ¥148/294, 13 to 15 hours, two daily (6pm and 7pm)
Mudanjiang Hard seat/sleeper ¥52/106, five to six hours, regular
Shenyang Seat ¥166/247, 2½ hours, regular

ℹ️ VISAS

The 72-Hour Visa-Free Transit policy allows passport-holders of many countries a stopover in Harbin without arranging a visa before arrival. This includes most European countries, the USA, Canada, Brazil, Mexico, Australia and Japan. You must have an onward ticket to a third country (ie not the country you arrived from). Inform your airline at check-in and seek the '72-Hour Visa-Free Transit' counter on arrival. Check the website well before flying: http://english.gov.cn/services/visitchina.

ⓘ BORDER CROSSING: GETTING TO RUSSIA

Trains no longer depart from Harbin East Train Station to Vladivostok. Trains do run as far as Suifenhe, however, from where you can make an onward connection to Vladivostok. There are now direct flights from Harbin to Vladivostok.

Travellers on the Trans-Siberian Railway to or from Moscow can start or finish in Harbin (six days). Contact the **Harbin Railway International Travel Service** (哈尔滨铁道国际旅行社, Hǎ'ěrbīn Tiědào Guójì Lǔxíngshè; ☑0451 5361 6718; www.ancn.net; 41 Xidazhijie, 西大直街41号; ⊙9am-5pm) for information on travelling through to Russia.

ⓘ Getting Around

TO/FROM THE AIRPORT

Harbin's airport (p207) is 46km from the city centre. From the airport, **shuttle bus route 1** (¥20) terminates at the Civil Aviation Building (99 Zhongshan Lu; around 6km southeast of the main train station), stopping near the train station on route (¥20). To the airport, shuttles leave every 30 minutes from the Civil Aviation Building from 5.30am to 6.30pm.

A taxi (¥100 to ¥125) takes 45 minutes to an hour. Drivers may ask you to change to another taxi for the final kilometre to save paying the airport expressway return toll.

BOAT

Ferries (p204) cross the Songhua River to Sun Island Park (¥10 return).

BUS

Buses 47 and 13 run from a **bus stop** outside the train station to Tongjiang Jie, one block west of Zhongyang Dajie, Harbin's famous historic street; bus 47 continues on to the Harbin Ice & Snow World and the Indoor Ski Resort. Large-scale station renovations mean bus stops are being shifted around periodically.

Catch buses to Harbin Grand Theatre (tourist bus 3) from the **Flood Control Monument Bus Stop** (防洪纪念塔公交首末站, Fánghóng Jìniàn Tǎ Gōngjiāo Shǒu Mò Zhàn; Youyi Lu, 友谊路), and from across the street for St Alexeevsky Church (bus 8).

METRO

Harbin's metro is currently of little use to tourists, but Line 2 (due to open in late 2020) will connect the train station with Zhongyang Dajie in Harbin's historic centre, continuing northwards to Zhaolin Park and on to Sun Island and Harbin North Station.

TAXI

Taxi flagfall is ¥8.

Mudanjiang 牡丹江

☑0453 / POP 809,000

The new fast train has arrived in Mudanjiang (Mǔdānjiāng), an attractive, small city in the east of the province, with a healthy agricultural swagger. The town is an ideal departure point for trips to Jingpo Lake and the Underground Forest, two of the region's most mesmerising natural features. Taiping Jie is the main drag in town and runs directly south of (opposite) the train station.

🛏 Sleeping & Eating

The train-station area has a number of good hotels. For budget accommodation head right as you exit the station; just past the station square on Guanghua Jie runs a row of guesthouses. There are at least half a dozen to choose from, all offering similar prices and decent digs: dorm beds go for ¥40, rooms with shared/private bathroom for around ¥50/100. A massive Holiday Inn sits incongruously north of the city.

Home Inn HOTEL ¥¥
(如家快捷酒店, Rújiā Kuàijié Jiǔdiàn; ☑0453 6911 1188; 651 Guanghua Jie, 光花街651号; r ¥139-189; ❀❀@❀) The Home Inn, among other chain hotels near the train station, will do a roaring trade on the back of the new fast service. This one boasts enthusiastic reception staff and spotless rooms. Showers are surpisingly strong. The top-floor 'nonsmoking' rooms are only slightly less, er, smoky.

Sunny Date International Hotel HOTEL ¥¥¥
(禧禄达国际酒店, Xǐlùdá Guójì Jiǔdiàn; ☑0453 687 8888; 8 Dongyitiao Lu, 东一条路8号; d & tw ¥328-498; ❀❀) The Sunny Date is the most glamorous hotel in Mudanjiang. Built in 2011, it has a faux-yesteryear vibe, including a chandelier-lined lobby fit for the imperialists. Some rooms come equipped with a mahjong table, but all rooms are top-notch with comfy beds, wi-fi and clean bathrooms. The gigantic attached bathhouse is equally opulent. Insist on a discount.

Shuānglóng Jiǎozi Wáng DUMPLINGS ¥
(双龙饺子王; cnr Qixing Jie & Taiping Jie, 七星街和太平街的一角; dumplings ¥13-38; ⊙9am-

9pm) Some of the juiciest *jiǎozi* (stuffed dumplings) this side of Jingpo Lake are served at this Dongbei classic. As you turn left off Taiping Jie, the restaurant is the big glass building with the red signboard on the right. It has an English sign out the front and a partial picture menu inside to help you order.

ℹ Information

There's a **Bank of China** (中国银行; Zhōngguó Yínháng) with a 24-hour ATM three blocks south of the train station along Taiping Jie.

ℹ Getting There & Away

BUS

Long-distance buses sometimes drop you off near the train station and depart from a long-distance station (客车站, *kè chēzhàn*) a few kilometres away on Xi'an Jie. A taxi to the station costs ¥7. Destinations include the following:

Dongjing Cheng ¥18, 1¼ hours, half-hourly

Harbin ¥100, 4½ hours, hourly (5.30am to 6pm)

Yanji ¥72, five hours, three daily (6.30am, 11.30am and 2pm)

TRAIN

Mudanjiang has rail connections to the following:

Harbin (D train) ¥72, 1½ hours, frequent services

Suifenhe Seat ¥19 to ¥22, one to two hours, 12 daily

Yanji Hard seat/sleeper ¥22/61, 6½ hours, one daily (4.24pm)

Jingpo Lake 镜泊湖

Part of a national park complex, the UNESCO-listed Jingpo Lake (Jìngpò Hú, Mirror Lake), 110km south of Mudanjiang, reflects the region's geological richness.

It was formed on the bend of the Mudan River 5000 years ago by the falling lava of five volcanic explosions, but these days Chinese day trippers come to snap the ultimate upside-down image of the surrounding forest hovering on the water's surface.

Whether paddling or picnicking by the lakeside, you can easily spend a couple of days at Jingpo Lake (two-day admission ¥80). It is a pleasant spot if you hike along to escape the summer crowds. Shuttle buses (¥12 per trip) run to various sights, and ferries (¥100, 1½ hours) make leisurely tours of the lake.

◉ Sights

Diaoshuilou Waterfall WATERFALL

(吊水楼瀑布, Diàoshuǐlóu Pùbù) FREE This waterfall boasts a 12m drop and 300m span. During the rainy season (June to September), when Diaoshuilou is in full throttle, it's a spectacular raging beauty, but during spring and autumn it's little more than a drizzle.

You can walk to the waterfall from the north-gate entrance in about five minutes. Just stay on the main road and follow the English signs.

Underground Forest FOREST

(地下森林, Dìxià Sēnlín; ¥55, internal shuttle bus ¥30) Despite its name, the Underground Forest isn't below the earth; instead it has grown within volcano craters that erupted some 10,000 years ago, giving the appearance of trees sinking into the earth. Hiking around the thick pine forest and several of the 10 craters takes about an hour.

The forest is 50km from Jingpo Lake. Some day tours include it in their itinerary. Otherwise, you have to take a bus from the north gate of Jingpo (¥40 return, one hour), which is doable but very tight if you only have a day at the lake.

🛏 Sleeping & Eating

It's pleasant to spend the night in the park and enjoy the lake when the crowds return to their hotels in Mudanjiang.

There are a few places to eat standard Chinese fare and snacks around the lake and ferry dock. For a day trip, you're better off bringing your own food for quality and cost.

Jìngpò Hú Shānzhuāng Jiǔdiàn HOTEL ¥¥¥

(镜泊湖山庄酒店; ☏ 0453 627 0039, 139 0483 9459; Jingpo Lake; r ¥500-580; ❄ @) This hotel sits just back from the water at the first lakeside drop-off point for the shuttle buses. Rooms are very modern, some with lake views, and the hotel's restaurant has decent food (if a little overpriced). Discounts can knock prices down if you choose a room without a view.

ℹ Getting There & Around

The easiest way to get to Jingpo Lake is on the one-day tours that leave from the train station in Mudanjiang from 6.30am to 7.30am. Tours cost ¥250 and include transport and admission, but no guide. Transport to the Diaoshuilou Waterfall and Underground Forest are an extra ¥50 and

SKIING IN CHINA

In the lead-up to hosting the 2022 Winter Olympics, China is riding the winter sports boom faster than a downhill skier in an attempt to better the country's modest 16th place in the 2018 Winter Olympics in Pyeongchang, South Korea.

From 20,000 visits to the slopes in 1996, numbers grew to around 15 million by 2012. In 2016 the government revealed plans to invest more than ¥1 trillion in snow sports infrastructure. There are now over 20 large resorts across the country in areas as diverse as Jilin, Heilongjiang, Yunnan and Hebei provinces.

Building slopes and resorts has been easy; maintaining them while a ski culture develops has not. The costs remain relatively high and, compared to nearby Japan, the weather is often far more challenging (ie cold!). To beat the elements, the world's largest indoor ski slope, the stunning Harbin Indoor Ski Resort (p204), opened in 2018. A year later, another colossal indoor ski resort was created in Shandong province in China's east, and the nation's first foreign ski school landed in the northwest.

In China's north, the largest resorts are Jilin's **Beidahu Ski Resort** (北大湖滑雪场, Běidàhú Huáxuěchǎng; www.beidahuski.com) and Heilongjiang's **Yabuli Ski Resort** (亚布力滑雪中心, Yàbùlì Huáxuě Zhōngxīn; www.yabuliski.com) 200km southeast of Harbin. Yabuli was China's first destination ski resort, and remains the training centre for the Chinese Olympic ski team. The resort has expanded to cover two mountains and now has a good division of advanced, intermediate and beginner runs, as well as a lodge that can reasonably cater to western guests.

At Changbai Shan on the China–North Korean border sits the impressive Wanda Changbai Shan International Resort (p194), where you'll find 20 runs on two mountains as well as a luxury alpine village offering hotels, restaurants and private condos. Top-notch hotels in the area include the Sheraton and Westin chain of hotels. They offer guest pick-ups from the train station or airport, located only 15km away.

Lift tickets in the north average around ¥500 per day on weekends, and a little less on weekdays. Clothing and equipment rental comes to another ¥140.

¥80 respectively, including waiting but not admission. Call 139 4533 1797 or book at a booth in front of the train station.

If you want to come here under your own steam, you can get a direct bus from the Mudanjiang bus station (¥25, 2½ hours, 1.30pm and 2.30pm) or train station (¥25, two hours, 7.30am). If you want an earlier start from Mudanjiang, first go to Dongjing Cheng (东京城; ¥15, 1½ hours, frequent) then change to a minibus (¥10, 40 to 60 minutes) to the lake. In the late afternoon you can try to get a seat on one of the tour buses directly back to Mudanjiang from the lake (¥30) or head back again via Dongjing Cheng.

The ticket centre for the lake is at the North Gate (Běimén). From here walk about five minutes to a car park for shuttle buses to the lake and ferry dock (get a ticket to the stop 'Jìngpò Shānzhuāng'; 镜泊山庄) and other sights (¥12 per ride). Diaoshuilou Waterfall is just behind this car park.

Wudalian Chi   五大连池

📞 0456

Basalt rivers, azure lakes and tree-sprouting volcanos await those hardy enough to head north from Harbin (or south from Russia) to the Lost World of Wudalian Chi (Wǔdàlián Chí). There's not much to do other than breathe in the heady vistas; luckily there aren't many quite like these.

The last time the volcanoes erupted was in 1720, when the lava flow blocked the nearby North River (Běi Hé), forming the series of five interconnected lakes that give the area its name. Wudalian Chi is about 250km northwest of Harbin and, in addition to the volcanic landscape, is home to mineral springs that draw busloads of Chinese and Russian tourists to slurp the allegedly curative waters. So many Russians roll up that the town's street signs are in both Chinese and Russian.

It's only really viable to visit Wudalian Chi between May and October because of the cold and wind the rest of the year.

☉ Sights

For a loop taking in lakes, volcanoes and caves, most people hire a taxi (¥180). If your time is short, just visit Laohei Shan and you will get most of what the area has to offer, as the other sites tend to be repeats of the hardened lava landscape on a smaller scale.

★**Laohei Shan**   VOLCANO
(老黑山; ¥80 plus compulsory shuttle fee ¥25; ⏱7.30am-7pm May-Oct) Laohei Shan is the humble zenith of a prehistoric landscape washed clean by hardened lava where ghost-like trees snake up from dormant craters, and brilliant blues shimmer off a cloud-strewn lake. It's also user-friendly, with mostly easy walking apart from the mainly uphill 1km stair climb to the summit of Laohei Shan itself, one of the area's 14 volcanoes. Do a circuit of the windy crater lip for panoramic views of the lakes and other volcanoes dotting the landscape.

Taxis drop you at the ticket booth, from where park shuttle buses take you to a large car park. To the left is the trail up the mountain. Returning down the same path, this time take the right path from the drop-off, along a boardwalk to the aptly named **Shi Hai** (石海, Stone Sea), a magnificent lava field.

Back in the car park smaller green shuttle buses take you to **Huoshao Shan** (火烧山) and the end of the road at another collection of weirdly shaped lava stones. This stretch is one of Wudalian Chi's most enchanting, with lava-rock rivers, birch forests, grassy fields, ponds around Third Lake and more wide stretches of lava fields.

There are only two (expensive) shops, so bring water and snacks.

Longmen 'Stone Village'   NATURAL FEATURE
(龙门石寨, Lóngmén Shízhài; ¥50; ⏱7am-6pm May-Oct) The residents of 'Stone Village' are in fact immobile orbs of rock-hard lava arranged by nature around a forest of white-and-black birch trees. It's eerily cool to march the network of boardwalks and wave an imaginary wand across your fantastical world.

That said, if you're visiting Wudalian Chi's other volcanic sites, especially Laohei Shan, you could easily skip this more distant (but very similar) site without missing much.

Third Lake   LAKE
(三池, Sān Chí; boat tour ¥80) The Third Lake is the biggest lake of the five that give rise to the region's name. Here you can feel the wind whip through your hair on a zippy 40-minute boat ride across the still water. Or just inspect the hardened lava edges along a series of dirt tracks and wooden platforms. Like much of the area, it's best visited in spring.

Wenbo Lake   VOLCANO
(温泊湖, Wēnbó Hú; ¥50; ⏱7.30am-5.30pm) A long boardwalk takes visitors through a lava field dotted with ponds and informative interpretive boards explaining lava-related phenomenon such as fissures and, of course, the field itself. The boardwalk ends at a small dock where you transfer to a boat for a slow putter down a reed-lined river. Your taxi will arrange to pick you up from where the boat docks.

🛏 Sleeping

Yaoquan Lu, the main east–west drag in Wudalian Chi, has a dozen or more hotels open from May to October. Newer hotels are about 500m up the road from the bus station.

Some travellers base themselves in Wudalian Chi City (五大连池市), a larger town 20km away where most buses drop you off from Harbin. Close to the bus station there are hotels and restaurants. However, it's worth basing yourself in Wudalian Chi itself.

Liu Jie   HOSTEL ¥
(刘姐, Liú Jiě; ☎158 4687 3866; dm ¥50; 🖥) A friendly teacher has converted a few apartments on the outskirts of town into comfortable dorms. There are only a few shops and restaurants nearby, but it's a perfectly fine base. Bus station pick-up/drop-off can be arranged, as well as a tour of local sights, but try to avoid the expensive restaurant at the end of the tour.

Liu Jie speaks barely any English but is willing to use translation and chat apps to communicate.

Quanshan New Holiday Inn   HOTEL ¥¥
(新泉山假日酒店, Xīnquánshān Jiàrì Jiǔdiàn; ☎0456 722 6999; Yaoquan Donglu, 药泉东路; d & tw incl breakfast ¥298-698; 🌀@🖥) Unrelated to the western Holiday Inn chain, this Chinese-run hotel is 500m up the road from the bus station just off the main road. Modern rooms are fitted with plush carpets and large comfy beds. The cheaper rooms are windowless but just as comfortable. Discounts are generous outside summer.

🍴 Eating

There are eateries on Guotu Jie, the street parallel to Yaoquan Lu near the Quanshan New Holiday Inn, or at the intersection of Yaoquan and Shilong Lu. Plenty of greasy-spoon choices (dishes ¥8 to ¥48) largely serve the same five types of local fish the area is famous for. You can also get cheap *jiǎozi*, noodles and barbecue. Several grocery stores sell fruit and imported snacks.

★ **Wángmáolǘ Dòufu**
Měishí Diàn CHINESE ¥¥
(王毛驴豆腐美食店; off Guotu Jie, 國土街; dishes ¥22-58; ⊙ 11am-9.30pm) Tofu ice cream, tofu salad, tofu burgers! This is soybean heaven, but even meat lovers will enjoy the soft delicacy at this incredible specialist restaurant. If you can't decide, take your pick from the picture menu on the wall. It's located off Guotu Jie, the street parallel to the main drag where the Quanshan New Holiday Inn hotel (p211) is located.

ℹ Information

There is an **ICBC** (工商银行; Gōngshāng Yínháng) ATM accepting foreign cards in Wudalian Chi on Guotu Jie, but it's worth bringing extra cash just in case.

ℹ Getting There & Around

Both Wudalian Chi and Wudalian Chi City have bus stations. Direct buses run from Harbin (¥100, six hours, four daily at 9am, 11.30am, 1.30pm and 2.45pm). The 1.30pm bus terminates at Wudalian Chi (making it the best choice for most visitors) while the other two terminate at the city proper of Wudalian Chi City, further from the sights. A taxi the rest of the way to the 'tourist zone' costs ¥40.

Buses leave for Harbin from Wudalian Chi (¥100, six hours, 5.40am and 8.10am) and Wudalian Chi City (6.50am and 9.30am). There are also buses to Heihe and Bei'an (1½ hours), the nearest train station, which has connections on to Harbin (seats ¥29 to ¥51, five to seven hours).

Taxis make the trip from the bus station to the hotel area for ¥10.

Mohe 漠河

📞 0457 / POP 81,200

A popular, if not always reliable, viewing spot for the aurora borealis, Mohe (Mòhé) is a modest town backed by Siberian pine forests and craggy mountain ranges. Its mushy bogs turn lush in summer, but much of the year Mohe is dipped in snow. In this region it is also possible to see dwindling settlements of northern Indigenous communities, such as the Daur, Ewenki, Hezhen and Oroqen.

Mohe is one of China's most intriguing outliers, sharing not just a border with Russia but architecture as well. In 1985 the town burned to the ground in a raging forest fire and when it came time to rebuild, Mohe decided to redo the main streets in an imperial-era Russian style with spired domes, pillared entrances and facades with rows of narrow windows.

CRANE COUNTRY

Northeastern China is home to several nature reserves established to protect endangered species of wild cranes. **Zhalong Nature Reserve** (扎龙自然保护区, Zhālóng Zìrán Bǎohùqū; ¥75; ⊙ 8am-5.30pm) near Qiqiha'er is the most accessible and most visited of these sanctuaries. The reserve is home to some 260 bird species, including several types of rare cranes. Four of the species that migrate here are on the endangered list: the extremely rare red-crowned crane, the white-naped crane, the Siberian crane and the hooded crane.

The reserve comprises some 2100 sq km of wetlands that are on a bird migration path extending from the Russian Arctic down into Southeast Asia. Hundreds of birds arrive in April and May, rear their young from June to August and depart in September and October. Unfortunately, a significant percentage of the birds you can see live are in captivity and are periodically released so that visitors can take photos.

The best time to visit Zhalong is in spring. In summer the mosquitoes can be more plentiful than the birds – take repellent! To get here, head to Qiqiha'er and board bus 306 (¥20, 45 minutes, half-hourly) from Darunfa (大润发). Birds are released at 9.30am, 11am, 2pm and 3.30pm.

The **Xianghai National Nature Reserve** (向海, Xiànghǎi Guójiā Zìrán Bǎohùqū), 310km west of Changchun in Jilin province, is on the migration path for Siberian cranes, and red-crowned, white-naped and demoiselle cranes breed here. More than 160 bird species, including several of these cranes, have been identified at the **Horqin National Nature Reserve** (科尔沁, Kē'ěrqìn Guójiā Zìrán Bǎohùqū), which borders Xianghai in Inner Mongolia. The **Momoge National Nature Reserve** (莫莫格, Mòmògé Guójiā Zìrán Bǎohùqū) in northern Jilin province is also an important wetlands area and bird breeding site.

For more information about China's crane population and these nature reserves, contact the International Crane Foundation (www.savingcranes.org).

Head 25km north from here to find Beihongcun, China's northernmost point.

Sights

Beihongcun
VILLAGE

(北红村) Walk astride the Russian border in this quaint Chinese village 100km from Beijicun, where wandering souls are welcomed with a glancing smile. No tourist tack around here – and usually no tourists, but you will find reindeer roaming freely in winter, and nowhere to go but back south. While there's not much beyond wooden houses and swaths of farmland, it is a quiet, idyllic spot and lays claim to being China's real northernmost village.

From Beihongcun, you can push across to **Heilong Jiang Diyi Wan** (黑龙江第一弯), the first bend in the river. The 800-plus steps to the viewing point are well worth the gorgeous panorama of the amazing horseshoe bend.

Beijicun
VILLAGE

(北极村, North Pole Village; ¥60) Further north from Mohe (roughly 50km) is Beijicun, a sprawling village and recreation area on the banks of the Heilong Jiang, separating China and Russia. The area is fast expanding with new hotels and resorts under construction.

Festivals & Events

Festival of Aurora Borealis
CULTURAL

(北极光节, Běijíguāng Jié; late Jun) The area around Mohe is best known for its midnight sun, visible for as long as 22 hours during this annual festival. Oddly, this is one of the few times you can see the Northern Lights, according to locals. Later in the summer, when there are more hours of darkness, the lights don't appear.

The odds of seeing the aurora are fairly slim, with the last period of high activity in 2017, and the next likely in 2023.

Sleeping & Eating

The best place to base yourself is at Beijicun for easy access to sights and getting

help with getting around. In Mohe there is a number of cheap guesthouses down the alleys off Fanrong Xiang, which is off Zhenxing Jie (the main street).

For cheap restaurants head to the alleys off Fanrong Xiang. Fresh produce isn't cheap in winter – blueberry products aside – as everything has to be imported from warmer provinces.

Mohe Time Travel Youth Hostel
HOSTEL ¥

(2 Guangang Jie, 2广岗街; dm/d from ¥60/100) A serviceable hostel in a local neighbourhood. The yellow-painted rooms at street level are well kept and very warm in winter. The friendly owners don't speak English, but will happily accommodate you as best they can.

Jinguan Renjia Farm Stay
FARMSTAY ¥¥

(金冠人家农庄; ☏139 0457 2910; Tongjiang Jie; d ¥180) This excellent farmstay in a handy part of Beiji village has been constructed with guests in mind. The friendly local family proudly welcomes guests to pristine wood-panelled rooms and a homey living area. The surrounding countryside is within easy reach from a number of walking paths leading from the back door.

Getting There & Around

China Southern has one direct flight a day from Harbin to Mohe (¥1800, 1¾ hours). Trains from Harbin (hard/soft sleeper ¥288/449, 5.55pm and 6.57pm) take 13 or 15 hours to reach the northern town. Heading back, trains leave at 2.30pm and 7.50pm and take 16 hours.

Mohe's train station is about 2km from the centre of town and it costs ¥12 to get here by taxi. To/from the airport, taxis charge ¥20. Buses for Beijicun (¥30, 1½ to two hours, 8.40am, 2.20pm and 6pm) leave from Mohe's bus station at the corner of Zhenxing Jie and Zhonghua Jie. Return buses from Beijicun depart at 10am and 2pm.

A good way to visit the area is to hire a private car or taxi for two days. Expect to pay around ¥350 per day; you can start your trip from Mohe and do all the sights listed in a loop back.

Shandong

POP 99.4 MILLION

Best Places to Eat

➡ Shawn Tren's (p240)

➡ Wù Yuán (p241)

➡ No 9 Courtyard (p249)

➡ Xiǎngfǔ Ròudīng Shuǐjiǎo (p248)

➡ Beer Street (p241)

Best Places to Stay

➡ Kaiyue Hostel (p239)

➡ Gucun Inn (p220)

➡ Qufu International Youth Hostel (p231)

➡ MG Hotel (p239)

➡ Shān Yǔ Hǎi (p218)

➡ Taishan International Youth Hostel (p221)

Why Go?

Steeped in natural and supernatural allure, the Shandong (山东, Shāndōng) peninsula on China's northeastern coast is the stuff of legends. Its captivating landscape – a fertile flood plain fed by rivers and underground springs, capped by granite peaks and framed in wild coastline – can't help but inspire wonder.

A lumpy-headed boy named Confucius was born here and grew up to develop a philosophy of virtue and ethics that would reach far beyond his lectures under an apricot tree. Three centuries later China's first emperor, Qin Shi Huang, would climb Tai Shan, Shandong's highest peak, to proclaim a unified empire in 219 BC.

But Shandong is more than the sum of its historical parts. The energetic buzz in seaside Qingdao ranks the city among the best places to live in China. This is Shandong's real draw: you can climb mountains, feast on fine seafood, quaff beer and still find time to hit the beach.

When to Go
Qingdao

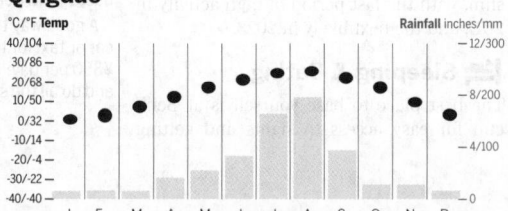

Jun–Aug Cool sea breezes and the beer festival make summer the time to explore Qingdao.	Sep & Oct Sacred Tai Shan is gloriously shrouded in mist for just part (not all) of the day.	Dec & Jan Dress warmly and ascend Shandong's frosted peaks in the dry winter.

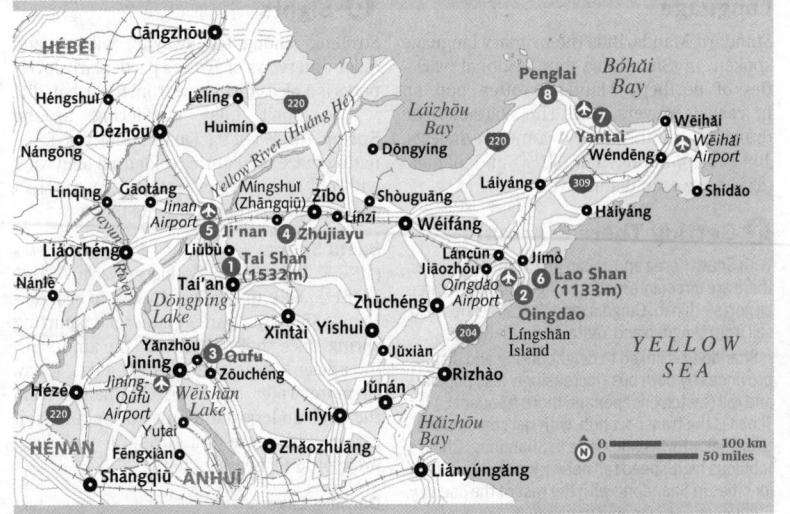

Shandong Highlights

❶ Tai Shan (p223)
Climbing the slopes of this sacred Taoist mountain, where stones speak the wisdom of millennia and views range in all directions.

❷ Qingdao (p234) Chilling by the sea with a pitcher (or plastic bag) of China's most famous brew.

❸ Qufu (p228) Perusing the ancient home town of

local boy and philosophical heavyweight Confucius.

❹ Zhujiayu (p220) Overnighting in this charming, rural Ming-dynasty village.

❺ Ji'nan (p216) Strolling among the swaying willows, quiet waterways and ancient residential alleyways of the city famously built on top of 72 artesian springs.

❻ Lao Shan (p244)
Forging uphill in search of Taoist secrets and magnificent views.

❼ Yantai (p246) Feeling the ocean breeze on your cheeks as you explore the history of this prosperous port city.

❽ Penglai Pavilion (p251) Discovering the legends of immortals, pirates and mirages.

History

Shandong's tumultuous history is tied to the capricious temperament of the Yellow River, which crosses the peninsula before emptying into the Bo Sea. The 'Mother River' nurtured Chinese civilisation, but when unhinged left death, disease and rebellion in its wake. In 1898, after a long period of floods followed by economic depression and unrest, the river again devastated the Shandong plain.

Europeans had also arrived. After two German missionaries died in a peasant uprising in western Shandong in 1897, Germany seized Qingdao, Britain forced a lease of Weihai, and soon six other nations scrambled for concessions. These acts, coupled with widespread famine, emboldened a band of superstitious nationalists, and in the closing years of the 19th century the Boxers rose out

of Shandong, armed with magical spells and broadswords to lead a rebellion against the eight-nation alliance of Austria-Hungary, France, Germany, Italy, Japan, Russia, the UK and the USA. After foreign powers violently seized Beijing in 1900, the Empress Cixi effectively surrendered and Boxer and other resistance leaders were executed. The Qing dynasty would soon collapse.

It was not until Japan's surrender in WWII that Shandong emerged from decades of war and recovered its cities. In 1955 engineers began an ambitious 50-year flood-control program, and 1959 marked Shandong's last catastrophic flood, though now China's economic boom threatens to suck the Yellow River dry.

Today Ji'nan, the provincial capital, and the prospering coastal cities of Yantai and Weihai, all play a supporting role to Qingdao, the province's headliner.

Language

Standard Mandarin is the primary language spoken in Shandong, but regional varieties of northern Mandarin often pop up in casual conversation. The characteristic drawls of the three most common dialects, Jìlǔ (冀鲁), Zhōngyuán (中原) and Jiāoliáo (胶辽), are each distinctive.

ℹ️ Getting There & Around

With South Korea and Japan just across the water, there are direct international flights through three airports – Ji'nan, Qingdao and Yantai. Ferries also sail from Qingdao and Yantai to South Korea.

Shandong is linked to neighbouring and distant provinces by both bus (increasingly less popular) and rail (faster, cheaper and more frequent). Ji'nan is the transport hub, with rail connections to all major towns and cities in Shandong. China's fabulous high-speed rail network now links all major cities in Shandong with the rest of the country.

With rail connecting all the big towns, cities and drawcard sights, getting around Shandong by train is straightforward, with buses playing second fiddle, but the roads are useful for opening up the smaller corners of the province.

Ji'nan   济南

📞 0531 / POP 4.7 MILLION

Ji'nan (Jǐ'nán) is more than just another provincial capital. On its surface the city is, like many others in China, a fast-developing metropolis, but beneath the urban sprawl are 72 artesian springs, which gently roil in azure pools and flow steadily into beautiful Daming Lake.

ℹ️ PRICE RANGES

Sleeping

The following price ranges refer to a double room with private shower or bathroom.

¥ less than ¥200

¥¥ ¥200–400

¥¥¥ more than ¥400

Eating

The following price ranges refer to a meal for one:

¥ less than ¥30

¥¥ ¥30–60

¥¥¥ more than ¥60

👁️ Sights

Strolling among the swaying willows and quiet waterways of Ji'nan's particularly lovely parks is a pleasant escape from the urban din.

Also don't miss wandering around **Spring Alley** (泉巷, Quán Xiàng), a fascinating maze of historic residential alleyways with old spring-water wells on some street corners still used by residents today.

Baotou Spring   PARK

(趵突泉, Bàotū Quán; 1 Baotuquan Nanlu, 趵突泉南路1号; ¥40; ⊙7am-7pm Apr-Oct, to 6pm Nov-Mar; 🚇K51) This park's namesake 'spurting spring' once shot metres into the air, inspiring ancient poets and painters alike. Today, as more water has been channelled from the city's underground limestone aquifers, it arrives with more of a gurgle. Ji'nan's local brew proudly bears its name.

Daming Lake   LAKE

(大明湖, Dàmíng Hú; ⊙5am-10pm) **FREE** All the water from Ji'nan's springs eventually flows into Daming Lake, set within the largest park in the city, with boat rides, paddle boats, temples, bridges and little islands to explore. In summer lotuses bloom in pink and white. The park has been a scenic site since the Tang dynasty, inspiring everyone from Marco Polo to Deng Xiaoping to wax lyrical about its beauty.

Five Dragon Pool Park   PARK

(五龙潭公园, Wǔlóngtán Gōngyuán; 18 Kuangshi Jie, 筐市街18号; ¥5; ⊙7am-7pm Apr-Oct, to 6pm Nov-Mar; 🚇5,101) These waters swirl up from the deepest depths of all the springs in the city to fill blue-green pools teeming with lucky carp. The park is a serene study of local life, where elders paint calligraphy on the steps and kids chase the goldfish.

Huancheng Park   PARK

(环城公园, Huánchéng Gōngyuán; 2 Nanmen Jie; ⊙24hr) **FREE** This park on the Hucheng River is built around **Black Tiger Spring** (黑虎泉, Hēihǔ Quán), which empties into the old city moat through three stone tiger heads. It gets its name from the sound of the roaring water as it rushed over a tiger-shaped stone, that's long gone but immortalised in Ming dynasty poetry. Locals still draw water from the springs here with buckets on ropes. The park is particularly popular in the early evening, when many of its features are lit up.

Ji'nan Museum   MUSEUM

(济南市博物馆, Jǐ'nán Shì Bówùguǎn; 📞0531 8295 9204; www.jnmuseum.com; 30 Jing Shiyilu,

Ji'nan

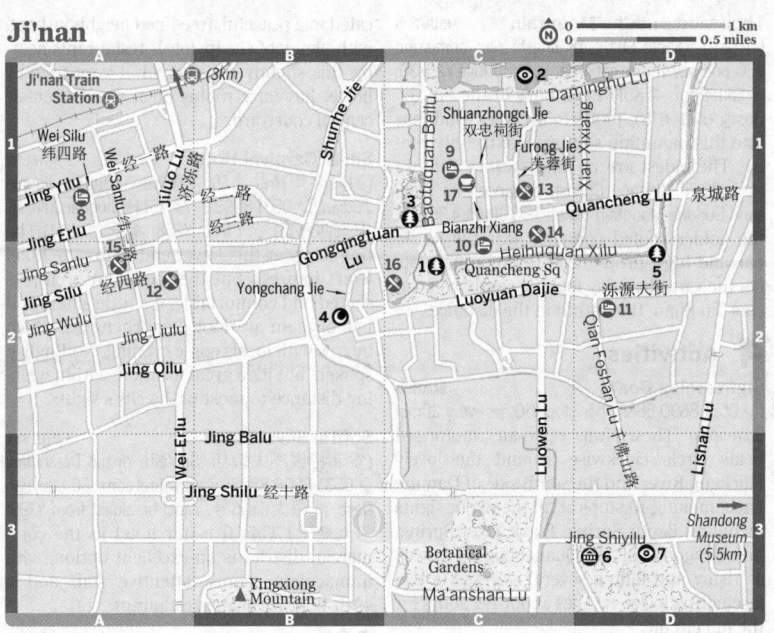

Ji'nan

◉ Sights

1 Baotu Spring	C2
2 Daming Lake	C1
3 Five Dragon Pool Park	C1
4 Great Southern Mosque	B2
5 Huancheng Park	D2
6 Ji'nan Museum	D3
7 Thousand Buddha Mountain	D3

⊜ Sleeping

8 Dengba International Youth Hostel	A1
9 Shān Yǔ Hǎi	C1
10 Silver Carnival Hotel	C2
11 Sofitel Silver Plaza	D2

⊗ Eating

12 Daguan Gardens	A2
13 Furong Jie	C1
Lǎopáifāng	(see 12)
14 Parc66 restaurants	C1
15 Ronghui Jinan Old Commercial Port	A2
16 Yīnhǔchí Jiē	C2

⊜ Drinking & Nightlife

17 Sonder Coffee	C1

经十一路30号; audio tour ¥10; ⊙9am-4.30pm Tue-Sun; 🚍K51) FREE North of Thousand Buddha Mountain's main entrance, the Ji'nan Museum has a small, distinctive collection that includes paintings, calligraphy, ceramics, Buddhist figures from the Tang dynasty and a delightful boat carved from a walnut shell.

Great Southern Mosque   MOSQUE
(清真南大寺, Qīngzhēn Nán Dà Sì; 47 Yongchang Jie; 🚍K50, 101) FREE Ji'nan's oldest mosque has stood in one form or another in the centre of town since 1295. Cover arms and remove hats before entering. A lively Hui (Muslim Chinese) neighbourhood is to the north.

Shandong Museum   MUSEUM
(山东博物馆, Shāndōng Bówùguǎn; 🕿 0531 8505 8201; www.sdmuseum.com; 11899 Jingshi Lu, 经十路11899号; ⊙9am-4pm Tue-Sun; 🚍18, 119, 115, 202, K139) FREE The enormous provincial museum, 7km east of the city centre, surveys local culture from the mesolithic age to the present. Its collection began as one of the first organised museums in China in 1904. On display are oracle bones, Qi and Lu kingdom pottery, Han tomb murals and clothing worn by the Kong clan (Confucius' descendants). Take any one of numerous buses along Jingshi Lu to Shěng Bówùguǎn (省博物馆) bus stop.

Thousand Buddha Mountain MOUNTAIN
(千佛山, Qiānfó Shān; 18 Jingshi Yilu; admission ¥30, one way/return cable car ¥20/30, luge ¥25/30; ⏰5am-9pm; 🚌K51) Beginning in the Sui dynasty (581–618), pious folk carved Buddhas into this mountain southeast of the city centre. The oldest are at **Xinguochan Temple** (兴国禅寺, Xīngguó Chánsì; entrance with Thousand Buddha Mountain ticket; ⏰7.30am-4.30pm), the golden-roofed complex near the **cable car** and **luge** drop-off on the mountaintop. On the rare clear day looking south, you can spot Tai Shan, the anthill in the distance.

🏃 Activities

Sightseeing Boats BOATING
(☎0531 8690 5886; per stop ¥10; ⏰every 20min 9am-5pm) These fun, open-air, motorised boats circle clockwise around the lovely Hucheng River and the south side of Daming Lake, making 10 stops at all the major sights including Baotu Spring, Black Tiger Spring, Five Dragon Pool and Quancheng Sq, as well as rising and falling several storeys via two fascinating locks. It takes about 1½ hours for the full circuit.

🛏 Sleeping

Ji'nan has a fair mix of accommodation to suit all budgets, although, as is often the case in China, the cheapest lodgings often don't accept foreigners.

Shān Yǔ Hǎi GUESTHOUSE¥
(山与海, Mountain & Sea Culture Hotel; ☎156 9231 2592, 0531 8118 7171; 1 Xiyundouyu Jie, off Shuanzhongci Jie, 双忠祠街西熨斗隅街1号; r from ¥160; ❀🖅) Hidden down a fascinating maze of historic residential alleyways – known collectively as Spring Alley (泉巷, Quán Xiàng) – this welcoming guesthouse with English-speaking staff is housed in a restyled old church building. The simple but spacious rooms have high ceilings and are off a central covered courtyard.

Walk north up Bianzhi Xiang (鞭指巷), then turn left at the end, down Shuanzhongci Jie (双忠祠街), and it's on your left at the entrance to tiny Xiyundouyu Jie (西熨斗隅街). No English sign, but on hotel-booking websites it's sometimes known as Mountain & Sea Culture Hotel.

Dengba International Youth Hostel HOSTEL¥
(登巴国际青年旅舍, Dēngbā Guójì Qīngnián Lǚshě; 7 Weisi Lu, 纬四路7号; dm from ¥40, d with shared/private bathroom from ¥80/125; ❀🖅) Lo-

cated in a peaceful, tree-lined neighbourhood with plenty of cheap, locals restaurants nearby, this slightly run-down but very friendly hostel has tatty rooms off a small open-air central courtyard.

Silver Carnival Hotel HOTEL¥¥
(银海嘉华精品酒店, Yínhǎi Jiāhuá Jīngpǐn Jiǔdiàn; ☎0531 8098 8777; 151 Heihuquan Xilu, 黑虎泉西路151号; r from ¥258; ❀🖅; 🚌K51) The tiny lobby at this lower-end midrange hotel won't impress, but the rooms are well presented and comfortable, if a little small, and half of them overlook Quancheng Sq, which buzzes with locals come evening. No English spoken, but it's a great location, within walking distance to most of the city's sights.

Sofitel Silver Plaza HOTEL¥¥¥
(索菲特银座大饭店, Suǒfēitè Yínzuò Dàfàndiàn; ☎0531 8606 8888; www.sofitel.com; 66 Luoyuan Dajie, 泺源大街66号; r incl breakfast from ¥799; ❀🖅@🏊) This five-star hotel in the commercial district is an excellent option, with immaculate rooms, attentive staff and a 49th-floor revolving restaurant.

🍴 Eating

Ji'nan is a famed centre of Lǔ (Shandong) cuisine, characterised by bold flavours brought out by cooking over a high heat with plenty of oil and spices. Most of the best eating is found in the city's streets and alleys.

Off Quancheng Lu's shopping strip, **Furong Jie** (芙蓉街; snacks from ¥10; ⏰9.30am-11pm) is a pedestrian alley crammed with restaurants and food stalls. Alternatively, for something more upmarket head to **Ronghui Jinan Old Commercial Port** (融汇济南老商埠, Rónghuì Jǐnán Lǎo Shāngbù; Jingsi Lu, 经四路; ⏰9am-10pm).

Lǎopáifāng SHANDONG¥
(老牌坊; ☎0531 8605 4567; 2 Daguan Yuan, 大观园2号; dishes ¥28-98; ⏰11am-3pm & 4.30-9pm) Just inside the low-key food street called **Daguan Gardens** (大观园, Dàguān Yuán; Jing Silu, 经四路; snacks from ¥10), this is a decent place for a refined take on Lǔ (Shandong) cuisine. Order the unpretentious classics like sweet and spicy cabbage with glass noodles (¥22) or lamb (braised or sautéed, from ¥19), accompanied with sesame cakes (¥2) – not rice. Chinese menu with pictures.

Yínhǔchí Jiē STREET FOOD¥
(饮虎池街; Yínhǔchí Jiē, 饮虎池街; snacks from ¥10) Evenings used to be smoky on Yinhuchi Jie in the Hui district near the Great

Southern Mosque, with hawkers fanning the flames of charcoal grills lining the street, roasting up all manner of *shāokǎo* (barbecue skewers). Sadly coal-fired barbecues have been banned – too polluting apparently (though cars seem to be OK!) – but small restaurants do the same job on indoor electric barbecues.

Tables spill out onto the pavements, so you can still eat your skewers on the street, and the food is still delicious. Not much English is spoken round here, but you can't go wrong if you just order some *yángròu chuàn* (羊肉串, lamb skewers) and a cold bottle of Tsingtao.

Parc66 restaurants   SHOPPING MALL ¥¥
(恒隆广场, Hénglóng Guǎngchǎng; 6th fl, Parc66 Shopping Mall, 188 Quancheng Lu, 泉城路188号; ⓣ10am-10pm) If you're struggling with Chinese-only menus, head to the 6th floor of this modern shopping mall, which is packed with restaurants (Cantonese, Japanese, Xinjiang, barbecue, noodles) and snack stalls, many of which have English menus. The other floors are also dotted with restaurants.

🍷 Drinking & Nightlife

There are one or two bars in the rebuilt enclave Ronghui Jinan Old Commercial Port (融汇济南老商埠, Rónghuì Jǐnán Lǎo Shāngbù).

Sonder Coffee   CAFE
(宿道咖啡, Sùdào Kāfēi; 23 Bianzhi Xiang, 鞭指巷23号; coffee from ¥25; ⓣ9am-8pm) Perfect for a pick-me-up on your aimless wanders around the lovely lanes of Quán Xiàng (泉巷, Spring Alley), this super-cool, super-tiny coffee shop serves espresso-machine and pour-over brews using beans mostly from Yunnan province.

❶ Information

ATMs are all over town.
Bank of China (中国银行, Zhōngguó Yínháng; 22 Luoyuan Dajie, 泺源大街22号; ⓣ9am-5pm Mon-Fri) Currency exchange and 24-hour ATMs accepting foreign cards.
Shandong Provincial Qianfo Shan Hospital International Clinic (千佛山医院国际医疗部, Qiānfó Shān Yīyuàn Guójì Yīliáo Bù; ☏0531 8926 8017, 0531 8926 8018; www.sdhospital.com.cn; Building 3, 2nd fl, Jingshi Lu, 经十路, 3座2楼; ⓣ8-11am & 2-5.30pm Mon-Fri) The international clinic is on the 2nd floor of Building 3. English spoken. Take bus K51 from the train station or the city centre and get off at the Qiān Fóshān Yīyuàn (千佛山医院) stop.

❶ Getting There & Away

AIR
Jinan Yaoqiang International Airport (济南遥墙国际机场, Jǐnán Yáoqiáng Guójì Jīchǎng; ☏0531 8208 6666; Jichang Lu, Yaoqiang, 济南市历城区遥墙镇机场路) is around 40km from the centre and has daily flights to all major Chinese cities, as well as flights to one or two international destinations such as Seoul, Bangkok and Singapore.

BUS
High-speed rail travel is slowly crippling China's long-distance bus industry, but there are still some services from Ji'nan.

The city's most convenient station is the **main long-distance bus station** (长途总汽车站, Chángtú Zǒng Qìchē Zhàn; ☏0531 8594 1472; 131 Jiluo Lu; ⛎K84), about 3km north of the train station, though buses to destinations within the province also leave from the **Jinan Guangcheng Bus station** (济南广城汽车站, Jǐnán Guǎngchéng Qìchēzhàn; ☏8830 3030; 22 Chezhan Jie, 车站街22号) directly across from the train station.

Buses departing from the main long-distance bus station include the following:
Beijing ¥122, 7½ hours, one daily (11.20am)
Qingdao ¥109, 4½ hours, two daily (9.40am and 1pm)
Qufu ¥45, two hours, hourly (6.50am to 5.30pm)
Shanghai ¥266, 12 hours, one daily (6pm)
Tai Shan ¥29, two hours, every 45 minutes (6.40am to 6pm)
Tiānjīn ¥124, 4½ hours, one daily (2.20pm)
Yantai ¥150, 5½ hours, three daily (9am, 12.50pm and 3pm)

TRAIN
Ji'nan is a major hub in the east China rail system and has several busy train stations. The main, central train station, **Jinan Train Station** (济南站; Jǐnán Zhàn), has high-speed and regular trains. The vast majority of high-speed trains, though, use **Jinan West Train Station** (济南西站, Jǐnán Xīzhàn; Dajinzhuang Lu, 大金庄路; ⛎K156).

At Jinan Train Station, if you're in a hurry and need to buy tickets, use the shorter queue in the far right-hand corner of the ticket office, which is reserved for military personal and other VIPs, but which will also sell tickets to foreigners. Staff rarely speak English, so come prepared. Same-day tickets are easy to come by for high-speed services to destinations within Shandong. For longer overnight services it's a good idea to buy your ticket a day or two in advance.

High-speed trains (1st-/2nd-class seat) departing from **Jinan Train Station** include the following:
Beijing South ¥330/195, two hours, 15 daily (7.13am to 7.59pm)

Qingdao ¥194/120, two to three hours, 35 daily (5.53am to 8.11pm)

Qufu East ¥100/60, 40 minutes, 13 daily (7.23am to 9.45pm)

Weifang ¥104/65, 1½ hours, 60 daily (7.07am to 8.27pm)

Yantai ¥264/165, 3½ to four hours, nine daily (7.14am to 7.14pm)

Regular trains (seat/hard sleeper) include the following:

Beijing ¥72/129, six hours, two daily (9.31am and 11.05pm)

Tai Shan ¥13/59, one hour, 33 daily (5.31am to 11.56pm)

High-speed trains (1st-/2nd-class seat) from **Jinan West Train Station** include the following:

Beijing South ¥315/185, two hours, 70 daily (7.45am to 10.16pm)

Qufu East ¥100/60, 40 minutes, 30 daily (6.43am to 9.20pm)

Shanghai Hongqiao ¥674/399, four hours, 50 daily (8.41am to 7.59pm)

Tai'an (for Tai Shan) ¥45/25, 17 minutes, 30 daily (6.43am to 8.48pm)

🛈 Getting Around

TO/FROM THE AIRPORT

Airport shuttle buses (¥20) run from the bus station opposite the train station (hourly, 5am to 8pm), and from outside Yuquan Simpson Hotel (玉泉森信大酒店, Yùquán Sēnxìn Dàjiǔdiàn; hourly, 6am to 7pm).

PUBLIC TRANSPORT

The useful bus K51 (¥2) runs from Jinan Train Station, past Baotu Spring and Quancheng Square, and on to Thousand Buddha Mountain and the hospital.

Bus K84 (¥2) goes from the train station to the main long-distance bus station.

Bus K156 (¥2, 45 minutes) goes from Jinan Train Station to Jinan West Train Station.

TAXI

Taxis cost ¥8 for the first 3km then ¥1.75 (slightly more at night) per kilometre thereafter.

Zhujiayu 朱家峪

✔ 0531 / POP 200

Eighty kilometres east of Ji'nan is one of Shandong's oldest hamlets. Most of the stone buildings in Zhujiayu (Zhūjiāyù) date back to the Ming and Qing dynasties. Many have been spruced up in recent years to serve as movie and soap-opera sets, but much of the village's historical authenticity

has been preserved and strolling the stone-paved streets is still a journey back in time.

Zhujiayu and its bucolic panoramas of rolling hills can be explored in an easy day trip from Ji'nan, though staying overnight in a homestay is a treat. Admission to the village is ¥40. Signboards outside the notable buildings have information on them written in English.

Follow the Ming-dynasty, **double-track ancient road** (双轨古道, *shuāngguǐ gǔdào*) to the Qing-dynasty **Wenchang Pavilion** (文昌阁, Wénchāng Gé), an arched gate topped by a single-roofed shrine where teachers would take new pupils to make offerings to Confucius before their first lesson. On your left is **Shanyin Primary School** (山阴小学, Shānyīn Xiǎoxué). It closed as a school in the 1990s, but its halls and courtyards now house exhibits on local life.

Walk on to see the many ancestral temples, including the **Zhu Family Ancestral Hall** (朱氏家祠, Zhūshì Jiācí), the numerous packed mudbrick homesteads, and the quaint, arched *shíqiáo* (stone bridges). Near the top of village, the intriguing double bridge, known as the **Kangxi Overpass** (康熙立交桥, Kāngxī Lìjiāo Qiáo), is one of the earliest examples in the world of such a traffic structure and dates from 1671. A further 30-minute climb past the last drystone walls of the village will take you to the gleaming white **Kuixing Pavilion** (魁星楼, Kuíxīng Lóu), crowning the hill overlooking the village.

To really appreciate the charms of the village, it's best to stay here overnight. There are plenty of homestay options; look for flags posting '农家乐' (*nóngjiālè*) or '住宿' (*zhùsù*). **Gucun Inn** (古村酒家, Gǔcūn Jiǔjiā; ✆ 0531 8380 8135; r ¥150; 🖥) has clean, simple, spacious rooms in a courtyard house with chickens roaming the yard. The friendly Zhang family running the place also cook up delicious meals (dishes ¥10 to ¥40). It's at the top of the village; walk under the Kangxi Overpass and take the low road at the split, following the bend to the left.

Numerous villagers have turned their homes into makeshift restaurants (often these are homestays too). You won't find any English menus. Dishes to look for include *làjiāo chǎo ròu* (辣椒炒肉, pork fried with mild green chillies), *tǔdòu sī* (土豆丝, light-fried potato shreds) and *fēngwèi qiézi* (风味茄子, braised aubergine). Mop up your sauce with big fluffy *mántou* (馒头, steamed buns), which are often preferred to rice here.

To get here from Ji'nan, catch bus K301 (¥9, 1½ hours, 7am to 6.30pm) from the Qiān Fóshān (千佛山) bus stop on Jing Shi-lu, and get off at the terminus stop, Jìshī Xuéyuàn (技师学院). From there take bus 9 two stops to Zhūjiāyù (朱家峪), from where its a straight, 20-minute, 2km-walk to the village. If you manage to find a lift up to the village from the main road, the going rate is ¥5. Returning, the last bus 9 leaves at around 6pm (6.30pm in summer).

Tai'an 泰安

☑ 0538 / POP 1.7 MILLION

The gateway to Tai Shan's sacred slopes is the town of Tai'an (Tài'ān), which has had a tourist industry in full swing since before the Ming dynasty. In the 17th century, historian Zhang Dai described package tours that included choice of lodging (enormous inns with more than 20 kitchens and hundreds of servants, opera performers and courtesans), a post-summit congratulatory banquet, plus an optional sedan-chair upgrade (climbing tax not included).

⦿ Sights

★ Dai Temple TAOIST TEMPLE

(岱庙, Dài Miào; Daimiao Beijie, 岱庙北街; ¥20 or free entrance with Tai Shan ticket; ⊙ 8am-6pm summer, to 5pm winter) This magnificent Taoist temple complex is where all Tai'an roads lead, being the traditional first stop on the pilgrimage route up Tai Shan. The grounds, enclosed within mighty walls, are an impressive example of Song-dynasty (960–1127) temple construction with features of an imperial palace, though other structures stood here 1000 years before that.

Many visitors enter from the north through **Hou Zai gate** (后载门, Hòu Zài Mén) (which you can climb for views of Tai Shan), but entering from the south through **Zheng-yang gate** (正阳门, Zhèngyáng Mén; Dongyue Dajie, 东岳大街) allows you to follow the traditional passage through the main temple and up Hongmen Lu to the start of Tai Shan's Central Route ascent.

From the south end, two lions watch cars pass by on Dongyue Dajie, flanking the splendid *páifāng* (ornamental arch). Beyond this and the Zhengyang gate is the **Yaocan Pavilion** (遥参亭, Yáocān Tíng; ⊙ 6.30am-6pm).

Between the buildings, the courtyards are filled with prized examples of poetry and imperial records. Fossilised-looking *bìxì* (the mythical tortoise son of the dragon), dating from the 12th century onwards, carry stelae on their backs documenting everything from the civil exam process to emperors' birthdays. The Han Emperor Wudi himself is said to have planted some of the massive, twisting trees in the **Cypress Tree Pavilion** 2100 years ago.

The main hall is the colossal **Hall of Heavenly Blessing** (天贶殿, Tiānkuàng Diàn), which dates from AD 1009, and whose dark interior houses an exquisite, 62m-long Song-dynasty mural depicting a journey undertaken by Emperor Zhenzong as the Lord of Tai Shan, the god of longevity to whom the entire complex is dedicated.

Rock Valley Scripture LANDMARK

(经石峪, Jīngshí Yù) Located along the first part of the climb up Tai Shan, this massive inscription of a Buddhist text on the rock face was once hidden behind a waterfall.

🛏 Sleeping

Since you will need at least a full day to explore the mountain, spending the night in Tai'an or at the summit is advised. It's cheaper and more comfortable to sleep in Tai'an, and there's far more choice, although staying on the mountain naturally has its own appeal.

Taishan International Youth Hostel HOSTEL ¥

(泰山国际青年旅舍, Tàishān Guójì Qīngnián Lǚshè; ☑ 0538 628 5196; 65 Tongtian Jie, 通天街 65号; dm ¥45-65, r from ¥138; ✳ @ 🛜; 🚍 1, 4, 7, 8, 17) This large youth hostel has clean, spacious rooms with pine furnishings and nice firm beds. Staff are very helpful and the location is ideal. Free laundry and a chilled-out ground-floor common area, where you can get beers, cocktails and fresh coffee, add to the experience. Look for the pair of arches just off Tongtian Jie.

Yuzuo Hotel HOTEL ¥¥

(御座宾馆, Yùzuò Bīnguǎn; ☑ 0538 826 9999; www.yuzuo.cn; 50 Daimiao Beilu, 岱庙北路50号; r incl breakfast from ¥390; ✳ 🛜; 🚍 4, 6) This attractive hotel beside Dai Temple's north gate, and within the temple's outer walls, was purposely kept to two storeys out of respect for its revered neighbour. Rooms are dotted around the grounds in stand-alone villas. The deluxe ones are decked out imperial style; cheaper rooms are rather ordinary, but very comfortable nonetheless. Not much English spoken, but what a location.

Tai'an

SHANDONG TAI'AN

Home Inn Plus   HOTEL ¥¥

(如家精选, Rújiā Jīngxuǎn; ☑ 0538 822 5888; 26 Red Gate Rd, 红门路26号; r from ¥398; ✳ ⊛ ⊗; ☐ K3) This midrange branch of the budget chain Home Inn has slick, modern rooms and a handy location close to Tai Shan's main entrance. Breakfast costs ¥25 per person.

Shānxī Huìguǎn   BOUTIQUE HOTEL ¥¥¥

(山西会馆; ☑ 134 4265 4515; 89 Hongmen Lu, 红门路89号; dm ¥40, r from ¥500; ✳ ⊗; ☐ K3, K37) The excellent former Hongmen International Youth Hostel – housed within the charming courtyards of an old guild hall once attached to Guandi Temple – was being renovated by new owners at the time of research, but it promises to still be a magical place to stay. Private rooms with modern interiors will go for around ¥500 and a large dorm will have beds for around ¥40.

🍴 Eating

There is a couple of fairly lively street-food markets in Tai'an. The **night market** (夜市, Yèshì; Naihe Donglu, 奈河东路; snacks from ¥10; ⏱5.30pm-11pm), which stretches along the Nai River's east bank, is mostly clothing and souvenirs, but there are plenty of snack stalls and small restaurants too. On the other side of Dai Temple, you'll find *mántóu* (馒头, steamed buns), various meats on skewers, fried chicken and more at the low-key **Dai Bei Market** (贷北市场, Dàibĕi Shìchăng; Daimiao Beijie, 岱庙北街).

Jiānbing Guŏzi   PANCAKES ¥
(煎饼果子; Yunzhou Jie, off Dongyua Dajie, 东岳大街云舟街; ¥5; ⏱5.30am-7pm) You find *jiānbing* (savoury pancakes sprinkled with chives, coriander, spring onion and a light chilli sauce) all over northern China, but Tai Shan folk are particularly proud of theirs, which they wrap around *yóu tiáo* (油条, fried dough sticks). Mrs Li fires up her pancake griddle from 5.30am and serves *jiānbing* all day.

Lĭjì Miànguăn   NOODLES ¥
(李记面馆; Yunzhou Jie, off Dongyua Dajie, 东岳大街云舟街; noodles ¥8-15; ⏱7am-10pm) This no-frills noodle shack is one of numerous noodle joints on and around the non-signposted lane Yunzhou Jie (云舟街), out the back of Tai Shan International Youth Hostel. As with all of them, there's no English menu, but tasty offerings include *hóngshāo niúròu miàn* (红烧牛肉面, braised beef noodles), *dāo xiāo miàn* (刀削面, knife-sliced noodles with pork) and *chăo miàn* (炒面, vegetable fried noodles).

Beijing Daoxiangcun   SNACKS ¥
(稻香村, Dàoxiāngcūn; 90 Qingnian Lu, 青年路90号; around ¥3 per piece; ⏱9am-9pm) Beijing's most famous brand of sweetmeat pastries, Daoxiangcun offers ideal rucksack fillers for your hike up Tai Shan. The flaky pastries have candied fruit fillings and are sold in biscuit-sized pieces (you'll get four or five for around ¥10) that you can mix and match.

ℹ️ Information

Bank of China (中国银行, Zhōngguó Yínháng; 116 Tongtian Jie, 通天街116号; ⏱8.30am-4.30pm) Currency exchange and 24-hour ATM that accepts foreign cards.

Central Hospital (中心医院, Zhōngxīn Yīyuàn; ☎822 4161; 29 Longtan Lu, 龙潭路29号) Limited English.

ℹ️ Getting There & Away

Whether by road or track, most routes pass through Ji'nan, 80km north.

It's easy to buy same-day train and bus tickets from the stations themselves, as long as you come armed with a few Chinese phrases.

BUS

Tai'an Bus Station (泰安汽车总站, Tài'ān Qìchē Zŏngzhàn; ☎0538 218 8777; cnr Tài'shān Dalu & Longtan Lu, 泰安大路龙潭路的路口) is a short walk south of Tai Shan Train Station. Destinations include the following:

Ji'nan ¥28, 1½ hours, every 40 minutes (6am to 6pm)

Qingdao ¥128, 5½ hours, two daily (8.40am and 2.30pm)

Qufu ¥23, 1½ hours, six daily (7.50am, 10.10am, 11.30am, 1.50pm, 4.40pm and 5.30pm)

Weihai ¥145, seven hours, one daily (7.20am)

TRAIN

Two train stations service this region. **Tai Shan Train Station** (泰山火车站, Tàishān Huŏchē Zhàn; ☎0538 688 7358; cnr Dongyue Dajie & Longtan Lu, 东岳大街龙潭路的路口) is more central, but high-speed trains use **Tai'an Train Station** (高铁泰安站, Gāotiĕ Tài'ān Zhàn; also known as *Gāotiĕ Zhàn*, 高铁站; High-Speed Train Station Xingaotiezhan Lu, 新高铁站路), 9km west of the town centre. Local bus 68 connects the two stations.

Tai Shan   泰山

☑0538

The most climbed mountain on earth, and the most revered of China's five sacred Taoist peaks, Unesco-protected **Tai Shan** (泰山, Tài Shān; www.taishangeopark.com; ¥115) is one-third of Shandong's claim to having '*yī shān, yī shuĭ, yī shèngrén*' (一山一水一圣人, 'one mountain, one water, one saint'); the water being the Yellow River and the saint being Confucius. You may have to share it with the masses – its supernatural allure attracts the Chinese in droves – but a pilgrimage hike to Tai Shan's summit is a unique experience few people forget.

Qin Shi Huang, the first emperor, chose the summit of Tai Shan to proclaim the unified kingdom of China in 219 BC. And from its heights Confucius uttered the dictum: 'The world is small'. You too can climb up and say: 'I'm knackered.'

Pilgrims – young, old and very old – still make their way up the steps as a symbol of their devotion to Taoist and Buddhist

Tai Shan

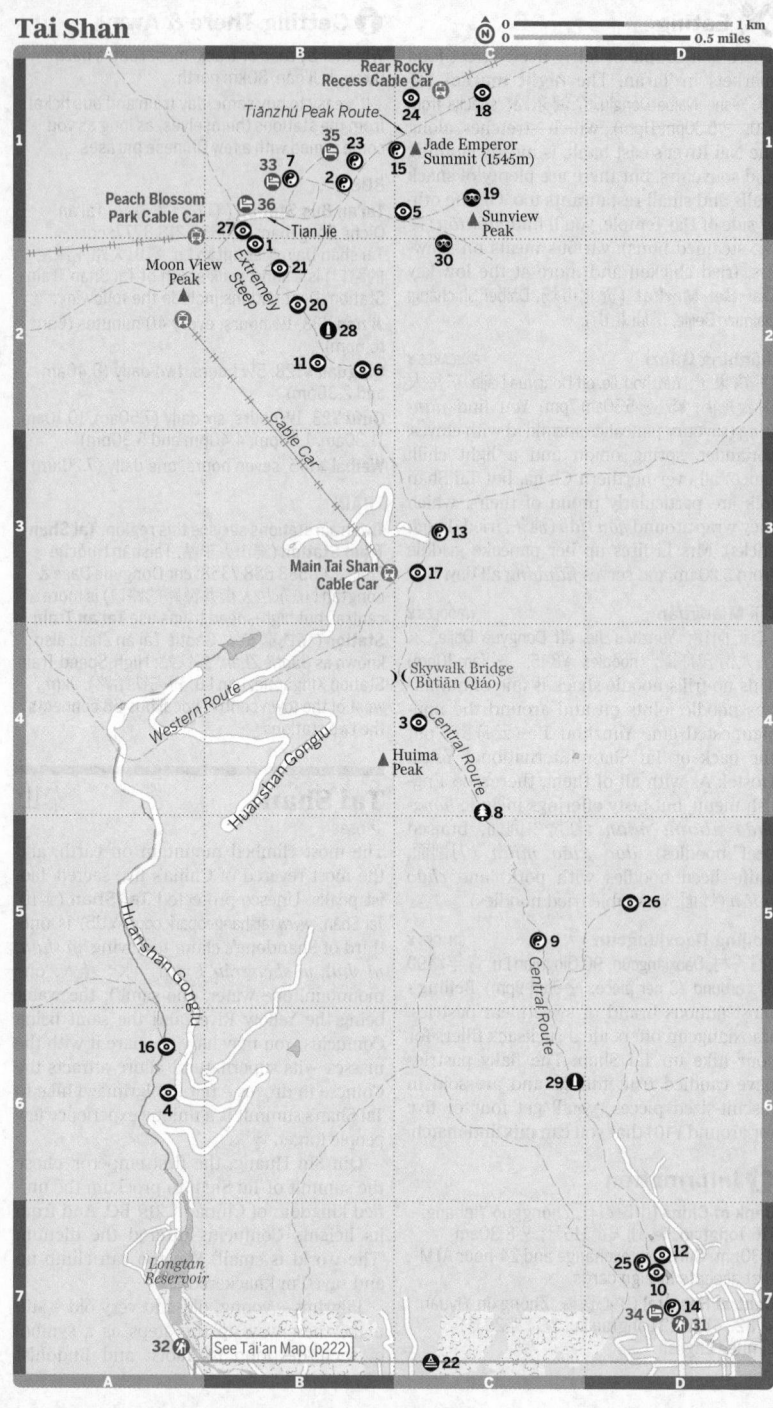

SHANDONG

0 — 1 km
0 — 0.5 miles

Rear Rocky Recess Cable Car 24

Tiānzhú Peak Route

Jade Emperor Summit (1545m)

Peach Blossom Park Cable Car 36

Tian Jie

Moon View Peak

Extremely Steep

Sunview Peak 19

30

28

11

6

Cable Car

13

Main Tai Shan Cable Car 17

Skywalk Bridge (Bùtiān Qiáo)

Western Route

Huima Peak

Central Route

Huanshan Gonglu

8

26

9

Huanshan Gonglu

16

4

Central Route

29

Longtan Reservoir

25 12
10
34 14
31

32

See Tai'an Map (p222)

22

Tai Shan

SHANDONG TAI SHAN

teachings. It is said that if you climb Tai Shan, you will live to see 100.

Beyond Qin Shi Huang, 71 other emperors and countless figures also paid this mountain their respects. To follow in their footsteps, there are four routes up to the highest peak (1532m) that can be done on foot: **Central Route**, historically the Emperor's Route, winds 8.9km from Dai Temple to the summit and gains 1400m in elevation; **Peach Blossom Park Route** climbs 13km on the west side; and the least travelled 5.4km **Tianzhu Peak Route** goes up the back of the mountain from the east. **Western Route** follows the 14km shuttle-bus route and converges with the Central Route at the halfway point (Midway Gate to Heaven), from where it's another 3.5km steep steps to the summit.

If this sounds like too much for your knees, there are alternatives: cover the Western Route by bus to Midway Gate to Heaven and then take the cable car to South Gate to Heaven near the summit. Reverse the journey or nab a bus to get back down.

Sights on the mountain close around 5pm. Weather can change suddenly and the summit gets very bitter, windy and wet, so bring warm layers and rain gear. Comfortable trainers are the best footwear: you don't want to be dragging heavyweight boots all the way to the top, and all the trails are laid with concrete steps in any case. You can buy brightly coloured rain ponchos and, at the top, rent overcoats (¥30).

As with all Chinese mountain hikes, viewing the sunrise is considered an integral part of the experience. You can either do a night hike (with torches – this is very popular) or, easier, stay overnight at one of the summit guesthouses to greet the first rays of dawn.

Climbing Tai Shan

The **entrance ticket** for Tai Shan costs ¥115 and is good for three days. It also grants you entrance to Dai Temple, which otherwise costs ¥20. Queues at the main **Central Route ticket office** (售票处, Shòupiào Chù; ☑ 0538 806 6077; ¥115; ☉ 24hr), part way up the mountain beside Wanxian Tower, can be long and very slow. You can save yourself a lot of queuing time by buying your Tai Shan ticket at Dai Temple.

If you're taking a shuttle bus up the Western Route, you'll have to buy your Tai Shan ticket with your bus ticket (¥30 one way). If you walk the Western Route you often don't have to buy the Tai Shan ticket because there is no one there to check tickets.

⚑ Central Route

The Central Route has been the main route up the mountain since the 3rd century BC, and over the past two millennia a bewildering number of bridges, trees, rivers, gullies, inscriptions, caves, pavilions and temples have become famous sites in their own right. As with all the routes, it's well paved so you won't need sherpas, climbing ropes, crampons or oxygen, but don't underestimate the challenge of its 7000 knee-wrenching steps. If you're fit you can easily climb up in four hours and down in three, but most people take more like six hours to get to the top.

Tai Shan also functions as an outdoor museum of antiquities. Two of the most prized are Rock Valley Scripture (p221), in the first part of the climb, a massive inscription of a Buddhist text that was once hidden behind a waterfall, and **North Prayer Rock** (拱北石; Gǒngběi Shí), a huge boulder pointing skyward and a site of imperial sacrifices to heaven, at the summit.

Purists begin with a south–north perambulation through Dai Temple, 1.7km south of the actual ascent, in accordance with imperial tradition, but there is no shame in starting at the bus stop by **Guandi Temple** (关帝庙, Guāndì Miào), the first of many dedicated to the Taoist protector of peace, and one that houses a charming old theatre stage dating from 1671. Passing **First Gate of Heaven** (一天门, Yītiān Mén) marks the start of the incline, though the ticket office (p225) is still a way further at **Wanxian Tower** (万仙楼, Wàn Xiān Lóu). The **Red Gate Palace** (红门宫, Hóng Mén Gōng) is the first of a series of temples dedicated to Bixia – the Heavenly Jade Maiden – daughter of the god of Tai Shan.

Consider taking a detour into the **Geoheritage Scenic Area** (地质园区, Dìzhí Yuánqū) for a look at unusual radial rock formations that mesmerised Confucius himself. Back on the main path is the **Doumu Hall** (斗母宫, Dǒumǔ Gōng), dedicated to the Taoist Mother of the Big Dipper, first constructed in 1542 under the name 'Dragon Spring Nunnery'. Continue through the tunnel of cypresses known as **Cypress Cave** (柏洞; Bó Dòng) to **Baulking Horse Ridge** (迥马嶺, Huímǎ Lǐng), which marks the point where Emperor Zhenzong had to dismount and continue by litter because his horse refused to go further.

The **Midway Gate to Heaven** (中天门, Zhōng Tiān Mén) marks the point where shuttle buses arrive from Tianwai Village and where some hikers, seeing the mountain steps disappearing into the clouds, make a run for the cable car. Don't give up! Rest your legs, visit the small and smoky **God of Wealth Temple** (财神庙, Cáishén Miào) to seek inspiration and strength, and stock up on calorific snacks.

If you decide to make a float for the summit, the **main cable car** (空中索道, Kōngzhōng Suǒdào; one way/return ¥100/200; ⏰7.30am-6.30pm 16 Apr-15 Oct, 8.30am-5pm 16

Oct-15 Apr) is a 15-minute ride to **Moon View Peak** (月观峰, Yuèguān Fēng) at the South Gate to Heaven. Be warned: peak-season and weekend queues can take two hours. Also, the cable car stops when there is any risk of lightning.

If you continue on foot you'll come next to **Cloud Step Bridge** (云步桥; Yúnbù Qiáo), once a modest wooden bridge spanning a torrent of waterfalls, and the withered and wiry **Wudafu Pine** (五大夫松, Wǔdàfū Sōng), under which Emperor Qin Shi Huang, overtaken by a violent storm, sought shelter. Across the valley, each character carved in the **Ten-Thousand Zhang Tablet** (万丈碑, Wànzhàng Bēi), dated 1748, measures 1m across.

You'll pass **Opposing Pines Pavilion** (对松亭, Duìsōng Tíng) and then finally reach the arduous **Path of 18 Bends** (十八盘, Shíbāpán), a 400m extremely steep ascent to the mountain's false summit. If you have the energy, see if you can spot the small shrine dedicated to the Lord of Tai Shan's grandmother along the way. There is an alternative route to the Azure Clouds Temple here via another steep, narrow staircase to the right. If you continue on the main route, at the top is the **Archway to Immortality** (升仙坊, Shēngxiān Fāng), once believed to bestow immortality on those dedicated enough to reach it.

The final short but very steep stretch takes you to the **South Gate to Heaven** (南天门, Nán Tián Mén), the third celestial gate, which marks the beginning of the summit area. Bear right up some steps onto Tian Jie (天街), the main strip, and pass through the gate to reach the sublimely perched **Azure Clouds Temple** (碧霞祠, Bìxiá Cí; ⏰8am-5.15pm) **FREE**, dedicated to Bixia.

You have to climb higher to get to the **Confucius Temple** (孔庙, Kǒng Miào), where statues of Confucius, Mencius, Zengzi and other Confucian luminaries are venerated. The Taoist **Qingdi Palace** (青帝宫, Qīngdì Gōng) is right before the fog- and cloud-swathed **Jade Emperor Temple** (玉皇顶, Yùhuáng Dǐng), which stands at the summit, the highest point of the Tai Shan plateau.

The main sunrise vantage point is the **North Pointing Rock** (拱北石, Gǒngběi Shí); if you're lucky, visibility extends over 200km to the coast.

At the summit, you can see another (far quieter) side of the mountain by descending via the Tianzhu Peak or Peach Blossom Park Route.

Western Route

The most popular way to descend is by bus via the Western Route. These buses are also very handy for night hikes up to catch the sunrise; they zip every 20 minutes (less frequently at night) between **Tianwai Village** (one way ¥30; ⏱6am-6pm & midnight-2am peak, 7am-6pm off-peak) and **Midway Gate to Heaven**, not stopping in between.

Walking the route is not so pleasant as the poorly marked footpath is closed off in parts, and often intercepts or coincides with the road, but it rewards you with a variety of scenic orchards and pools, and you can usually get away without paying the Tai Shan entrance fee if you walk this route. At the mountain's base, **Pervading Light Temple** (普照寺, Pǔzhào Sì; ¥5; ⏱8am-5.30pm) is a serene Buddhist temple dating from the Southern and Northern dynasties (420–589). The main attraction is **Black Dragon Pool** (黑龙潭, Hēilóng Tán), just below **Longevity Bridge** (长寿桥, Chángshòu Qiáo).

Tianzhu Peak Route

The less-travelled route through the **Tianzhu Peak Scenic Area** (天烛峰景区; Tiānzhú Fēng Jǐngqū) offers a rare chance to experience Tai Shan without the crowds. It's largely ancient pine forest, ruins and peaks back there, so consider combining it with the Central Route for an entirely different view.

If you ascend this way, get an early start to the trailhead, which is 15km by bus 19 (¥2) from Tai Shan's Tianwai Village or Hongmen bus stops. The challenging climb itself can take five hours.

It's 5.4km from the trailhead to the short **Rear Rocky Recess Cable Car** (后石坞索道, Hòu Shíwù suǒdào; ☑0538 833 0765; one way ¥20; ⏱8.30am-5pm Apr-Oct, closed Nov-Mar), which takes you from the back of the mountain to the **North Gate to Heaven** (北天门, Běi Tiānmén) and views of Tianzhu Peak.

Peach Blossom Park Route

This route to the summit passes through a scenic valley of striking geological formations and trees that explode with colour in early spring and autumn. It makes for an especially pleasant descent.

Near the South Gate to Heaven, take **Peach Blossom Park cable car** (桃花源索道, Táohuā Yuán suǒdào; ☑0853 833 0763; one way ¥100; ⏱6.30am-5.30pm) down to Peach Blossom Valley. From the cable car drop-off it is another 9km on foot or by shuttle bus (one way ¥30; departs when full 6am to 6pm and midnight to 2am) to reach the park exit and bus 16 back into town.

Festivals & Events

International Mount Tai Climbing Festival SPORTS
(泰山国际登山节, Tàishān Guójì Dēngshān Jié; ⏱Sep) Trail runners and stair steppers converge to race up the Central Route for this festival every September.

Sleeping & Eating

Sleeping on the mountain is atmospheric for sure, and essential if you want to view the sunrise, but it is more expensive and rooms are simpler than in Tai'an. Rates can triple during national holidays, but during slack periods you can bargain for discounts. Outside national holidays, there's generally no need to book.

Those on a tight budget can join the legions of Chinese students who sleep under the stars at the top of the mountain. At the summit, you can rent thick, full-length winter coats (¥20) to wrap yourself in, as well as simple camping mats (¥10). If it's raining (or freezing) some restaurants at the summit will let you sleep on their floors for ¥10 or ¥20.

The Central Route is dotted with stalls and restaurants, with clusters at the cable cars, but there's nowhere to buy food on the other routes, so come prepared. Prices rise as you do; expect to pay double the usual at the summit. Hawkers line the path to the summit (on the Central Route only), selling fruit, drinks and snacks that similarly increase in price with altitude. Alternatively, stock up in town before you climb.

Cloud Nest Hotel HOTEL ¥¥
(云巢宾馆, Yúncháo Bīnguǎn; ☑0538 806 6666; r ¥400-600, with shared bathroom ¥200; ❈❂❀) Sadly the rooms aren't as grand as the attractive courtyard entrance suggests, and the shared bathrooms don't have showers, but the rooms with private bathrooms are decent enough, albeit rather small. Some English spoken. Close to the Peach Blossom Park cable car.

Xiānjū Bīnguǎn HOTEL ¥¥
(仙居宾馆, ☑0538 652 2888; 5 Tian Jie, 天街5号; r¥300-500; ❈❀) Up the steps slightly and to your left as you begin walking up to Tian Jie, this deceptively large hotel has en suite rooms that are small but comfortable enough, and

a buffet restaurant. The older rooms at the back are cheapest and the best value.

Shenqi Hotel
HOTEL ¥¥¥

(神憩宾馆, Shénqì Bīnguǎn; ☑ 0538 822 3866; 18 Tian Jie, 天街18号; r ¥600-900, with mountain views from ¥1800; ❀❷) This old-timer is the only hotel on the actual summit, with prices reflecting that. The priciest mountain-view standard rooms are very pleasant and are pretty much the pick of the mountain crop. The restaurant does a lunchtime buffet (¥88 per head) and an evening menu (dishes ¥40 to ¥60).

❶ Getting There & Away

Local buses (¥2) connect Tai Shan Train Station (p223) with access points to the mountain, mostly from 6.30am to 7.30pm during peak season and to 5.30pm otherwise. Some buses, such as K3, run until 11pm in peak season.

Note, the bus stop closest to the main entrance of the mountain's Central Route is **Hongmen Bus Stop** (红门车站, Hóngmén chēzhàn; Hongmen Lu, 红门路). The bus stop closest to the Western Route entrance is **Tianwai Village Bus Stop** (天外村车站, Tiānwài Cūn chēzhàn).

Bus K3 Links Central Route's Hongmen entrance with the Western Route's Tianwai Village entrance.

Buses 4, 6 and 39 Link Tai Shan train station with Dai Temple.

Bus 6 Links Tai'an Bus Station with Dai Temple, via Tai Shan Train Station.

Bus 16 Connects to Peach Blossom Valley.

Bus 19 Runs from Tianwai Village to the Tianzhu Peak trailhead via the main Hongmen entrance.

Bus 68 Runs from Tai Shan Train Station to Tai'an Train Station (known as Gāotiě Tài'ān Zhàn, 高铁泰安站).

Taxis cost ¥7 for the first 3km and ¥1.50 (slightly more at night) per kilometre thereafter. It costs ¥12 from the Tai Shan Train Station or ¥26 from the Tai'an Train Station to the Central Route trailhead (红门, Hóng mén – Red Gate).

❶ Getting Around

Frequent shuttle buses (¥30) run up and down the mountain all day between Tianwai Village and Midway Gate to Heaven. Cable cars (p226) reach the summit area from Midway Gate to Heaven, Peach Blossom Park and Rear Rocky Recess.

Qufu
曲阜

☑ 0537 / POP 60,000

The home town of the great sage Confucius and his descendants, the Kong clan, Qufu (Qūfù) is a testament to the importance of Confucian thought in imperial China and to this day. The town is one of Shandong's top sights, and is a mandatory stop for anyone keen to see how revered the social philosopher remains.

Viewing the main sights in and around the city walls of ancient Qufu, a Unesco World Heritage Site, will take a full day.

⊙ Sights

The principal sights – Confucius Temple, Confucius Mansion and Confucius Forest – are known collectively as 'Sān Kǒng' (三孔, 'Three Kongs'). The **main ticket office** (孔庙售票处, Kǒng Miào shòupiàochù) is on Shendao Lu just outside the Confucius Temple's entrance. You can buy admission to the individual sights, but the **combination ticket** (¥140 per person) grants access to all Three Kongs.

From November to March, admission to individual sights is ¥10 cheaper (the combined ticket stays the same) and sights close about a half hour earlier.

Confucius Temple
CONFUCIAN TEMPLE

(孔庙, Kǒng Miào; Nanmadao Xijie, 南马道西街; incl in combination ticket, or ¥90; ⊙8am-5.10pm) Like shrines to Confucius throughout China and Asia, this is more museum than altar. The heart of the complex is the huge yellow-eaved **Dacheng Hall** (大成殿, Dàchéng Diàn), which in its present form dates from 1724. Craftspeople carved the 10 dragon-coiled columns so expertly that they were covered with red silk when Emperor Qianlong visited, lest he feel that the Forbidden City's Hall of Supreme Harmony paled in comparison. Inside is a huge statue of Confucius resplendent on a throne.

Above him are the characters 萬世師表 (wànshì shībiǎo), meaning 'model teacher for all ages'.

The temple has nine courtyards arranged on a central axis. China's largest imperial building complex after the Forbidden City began as Confucius' three-room house, but after his death in 478 BC the Duke of the Lu (鲁, Lǔ) state consecrated his simple abode as a temple. Everything in it, including his clothing, books, musical instruments and a carriage, was perfectly preserved. The house was rebuilt for the first time in AD 153, kicking off a series of expansions and renovations in subsequent centuries. By 1012 it had four courtyards and over 300 rooms. An imperial-palace-style wall was added. After a fire in 1499, it was rebuilt to its present scale.

Qufu

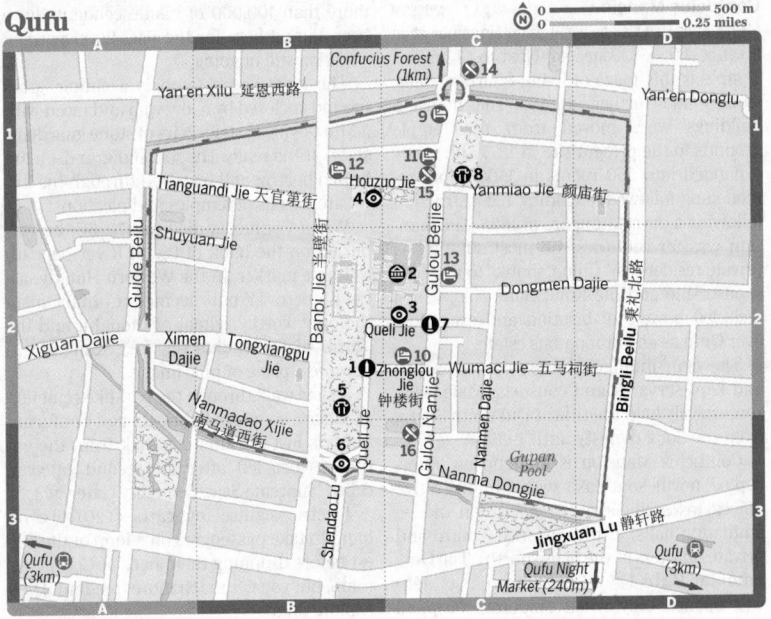

Over 1000 stelae documenting imperial gifts and sacrifices from the Han dynasty onwards, as well as treasured examples of calligraphy and stone reliefs, are preserved on the grounds. Look for a *bìxì* bearing the **Cheng Hua stele** (成化碑, Chénghuà bēi), dedicated by the Ming emperor in 1468, which praises Confucius in a particularly bold, formal hand. The characters are so perfect that copies were used to teach penmanship. The **Shengji Hall** (圣迹殿, Shèngjī Diàn) houses 120 famed Tang-dynasty paintings depicting Confucius' life immortalised as carvings.

Halfway through the complex rises the triple-eaved **Great Pavilion of the Constellation of Scholars** (奎文阁, Kuíwén Gé), an imposing Song-dynasty wooden structure. A series of gates and colossal, twin-eaved stele pavilions lead to the **Apricot Altar** (杏坛, Xìng Tán), which marks the spot where Confucius taught his students under an apricot tree.

South of **Chongsheng Hall** (崇圣祠, Chóngshèng Cí), which was once the site of the original family temple, the **Lu Wall** (鲁壁, Lǔ Bì) stands where Confucius' ninth-generation descendant hid Confucius' writings in the walls of his house during Emperor Qin Shi Huang's book-burning campaign around 213 BC. The texts were uncovered during an attempt to raze the grounds in 154 BC, spurring new schools of Confucian scholarship and long debates over what Confucius really said.

Confucius Mansion
MUSEUM

(孔府, Kǒng Fǔ; Queli Jie, 阙里街; incl in combination ticket, or ¥60; ☺ 8.10am-5pm) Next to Confucius Temple is this maze of living quarters, halls, studies and further studies. The mansion buildings were moved from the temple grounds to the present site in 1377 and vastly expanded into 560 rooms in 1503. More remodelling followed, including reconstruction following a devastating fire in 1885. The mansion was for centuries the most sumptuous private residence in China, thanks to imperial sponsorship and the Kong clan's rule, which included powers of taxation and execution, over Qufu as an autonomous estate.

The clan indulged in 180-course meals, and kept servants and consorts. Male heirs successively held the title of Duke Yan Sheng from the Song dynasty until 1935.

Confucius Mansion is built on an 'interrupted' north–south axis with administrative offices (taxes, edicts, rites, registration and examination halls) at the entrance (south) and private quarters at the back (north). The **Ceremonial Gate** (重光门, Chóngguāng Mén) was opened only when emperors dropped in. The central path passes a series of halls, including the **Great Hall** (大堂, Dà Táng) and **Nèizhái Gate** (内宅门, Nèizhái Mén), which separated the private and public parts of the residence and was guarded at all times.

The large '*shòu*' character (壽, longevity) presented in traditional Chinese script within the single-eaved **Upper Front Chamber** (前上房, Qián Shàng Fáng) north of Nèizhái Gate was a gift from Qing Empress Cixi. The Duke lived in the two-storey **Front Chamber** (前堂楼, Qián Táng Lóu).

Just east of Nèizhái Gate is the **Tower of Refuge** (奎楼, Kuí Lóu), not open to visitors, where the Kong clan could gather if the peasants turned nasty. It has an iron-lined ceiling on the ground floor and a staircase that could be yanked up.

There's a pleasant fruit-tree garden at the north end of the complex; you can then leave via the north gate (exit only).

Confucius Forest
CEMETERY

(孔林, Kǒng Lín; Lindao Lu, 林道路; incl in combination ticket, or ¥40; ☺ 8am-5.20pm) About 1km north of the walled town on Lindao Lu is the peaceful Confucius Forest, a cemetery of pine and cypress covering 200 hectares and bounded by a 10km-long wall, which was built on top of the foundations of the Zhou-dynasty wall that encircled the ancient capital city of the Lu State. Confucius and more than 100,000 of his descendants have been buried here for the past 2000 years, a tradition still ongoing.

The great sage's tomb is a simple grass mound enclosed by a low wall and faced with a Ming-dynasty stele. Pairs of stone guardians stand at the ready. His son and grandson are buried nearby, and scattered through the forest are dozens of temples and pavilions.

When Confucius died in 479 BC, he was buried on the bank of the Si River beneath a simple marker. In the Western Han dynasty, Emperor Wudi deemed Confucianism the only worthy school of thought, and the **Tomb of Confucius** (孔子墓, Kǒngzǐ Mù) became a place of pilgrimage.

A slow walk through the parklike cemetery can take a couple of hours, though Confucius' tomb is just a 10-minute walk from the entrance (turn left after the second gateway, called 'Supreme Sage Cemetery Gateway').

Electric sightseeing carts (¥20) are on hand to take passengers on a loop of the forest before dropping them back at Confucius' tomb, but you get much more freedom if you explore on foot.

The forest is a 15-minute walk from the old town, or take bus 1 (¥1) from Gulou Beijie, or a pedicab (¥10).

Confucius Cave
PARK

(夫子洞, Fūzǐ Dòng; Ni Shan, 尼山; ¥50; ☺ 8.10am-5pm) About 30km southeast of Qufu, this cave on Ni Mountain (尼山, Ní Shān) is where, according to legend, a frighteningly ugly Confucius was born, abandoned and cared for by a tiger and an eagle, before his mother realised he was sent from heaven and decided to care for him. The gravitas is a bit hokey, but the sight offers a chance for some fresh air. Bus 30 (¥1) goes to Ni Shan from Qufu Bus Station. A taxi is about ¥40.

Drum Tower
TOWER

(鼓楼, Gǔ Lóu; Gulou Beijie, 鼓楼北街) Qufu's Drum Tower stands at the centre of the old walled town at the point where Gulou Dajie – named after the Bell Tower – divides into its northern and southern sections.

Bell Tower
TOWER

(钟楼, Zhōnglóu; Zhonglou Jie, 钟楼街) The small and charming brick bell tower stands astride the road at the centre of town, to the east of the Confucius Temple.

Yan Temple
CONFUCIAN TEMPLE

(颜庙, Yán Miào; Yanmiao Jie, 颜庙街; ¥50; ☺ 8.10am-4.40pm; 🚌 1, 3) This tranquil temple

LOCAL KNOWLEDGE

CONFUCIUS SAYS: 'FREE TICKETS!'

As part of a drive to improve worldwide understanding of Confucian culture, foreign tourists are given a free ticket to the 'Three Kongs' (Confucius Temple, Confucius Mansion and Confucius Forest) if they can recite five Confucian quotations from the famous book of his teachings, *The Analects*. So, if you're willing to put in the effort, you could save yourself ¥140.

Here are five relatively short quotes you could use:

➡ *yǒu jiào wú lèi* (有教无类; education is for all)

➡ *guò yóu bù jí* (过犹不及; going too far is as bad as falling short)

➡ *dào bùtóng, bù xiāng wéi móu* (道不同, 不相为谋; to go separate ways)

➡ *jūnzǐ bù qì* (君子不器; the noble are not mere utensils)

➡ *dé bù gū, bì yǒu lín* (德不孤, 必有邻; virtue brings you neighbours, not loneliness)

If you want to try, go to the Confucius Temple ticket office and say: '*wǒ yào bèi lún yǔ*' (我要背论语; 'I'd like to recite from The Analects').

---

northeast of Confucius Mansion is dedicated to Confucius' beloved disciple Yan Hui, whose death at age 32 caused the understated Confucius 'excessive grief'. The main structure, **Fusheng Hall** (复圣殿, Fùshèng Diàn), has a magnificent ceiling decorated with a dragon head motif. Outside a *bìxì* (mythical tortoise-like dragon) carries a stele that posthumously granted Yan the title of Duke of Yanguo (in both Han and Mongol script) in AD 1331.

✸✸ Festivals & Events

Every morning at 8am, following a recitation, a costumed procession raucously walks up Shendao Lu from Jingxian Lu to the main gate to officially open the city.

Confucius Temple holds two major festivals a year: **Tomb Sweeping Day** (usually 5 April; celebrations may last all weekend) and the **Sage's Birthday** (28 September), both involving elaborate, costumed ceremonies. The city also comes alive with craftspeople, healers, acrobats and peddlers during annual fairs in the spring and autumn.

🛏 Sleeping

⭐ **Qufu International Youth Hostel**　　　　　HOSTEL ¥

(曲阜国际青年旅舍, Qūfù Guójì Qīngnián Lǚshè; ☑ 0537 441 8989; Gulou Beijie, 鼓楼北街北首路西; dm/tw ¥45/158; ❋ 🛜) This welcoming hostel at the north end of Gulou Beijie has particularly clean rooms and very comfortable beds. The twin rooms are better value than the doubles as they are much larger, but the same price. The dorms are quite cramped, but some have their own bathrooms. Helpful

staff speak some English, and the attached cafe-bar-restaurant is a nice hangout.

Shàngfǔ Běiyuàn Mínsù Jiǔdiàn　　　HOTEL ¥

(上府北院民宿酒店; ☑ 0537 775 1515; Houzuo Jie, 后作街西首; d/tw from ¥128/158; ❋ 🛜) This new hotel is good value, with clean, bright, modern rooms going for just over ¥100 after discounts. The linen is fresh, and the beds are large and comfortably firm. No English spoken, though.

Jinjiang Inn Select　　　　　　　　HOTEL ¥¥

(锦江之星, Jǐnjiāng Zhīxīng; ☑ 0537 505 5666; 1 Gulou Beijie, 鼓楼北街1号; r incl breakfast from ¥289; ❋ 🛜) This elegant branch of the dependable Jinjiang Inn brood has a calming lobby area leading to smart rooms, some of which look out over the small, central, bamboo courtyard.

Zi Yue Man Ju Hotel　　　　　　　　HOTEL ¥¥

(子曰漫居酒店, Zǐyuē Mànjū Jiǔdiàn; ☑ 0537 441 6666; 8 Gulou Beijie, 鼓楼北街8号; d/tw incl breakfast from ¥320/350; ❋ 🛜) Smack-bang in the middle of the old town, this attractive, traditional-style but brand-new hotel has large, bright, modern rooms with comfy beds and friendly staff.

Queli Hotel　　　　　　　　　　　　HOTEL ¥¥

(阙里宾舍, Quèlǐ Bīnshè; ☑ 0537 486 6400; 15 Zhonglou Jie, 钟楼街15号; r incl breakfast from ¥380; ❋ 🛜) This 30-year-old traditional-style hotel is the fanciest place to stay inside the old-town walls. Staff are courteous and friendly and some speak English, while rooms are stylish, albeit with very small bathrooms. Some ground-floor rooms have private courtyards, but can be musty in summer; 1st-floor rooms are fresher. There are some temple-view rooms too, but they cost a bit more.

🍴 Eating & Drinking

The local speciality is Confucius Cuisine (孔家菜, kǒng jiā cài – literally, Kong-family cuisine), which, despite its name, is the furthest thing from home cooking because it developed as a result of all the imperial-style banquets the family threw. Few restaurants serving Confucius Cuisine have English menus. One that does is the restaurant at Queli Hotel (p231).

There are a few low-key bars dotted around the streets of the walled town, including a couple intriguingly built into the southern wall (both left and right of the South Gate).

Zi Yue Man Ju Restaurant CHINESE ¥¥
(子曰漫居酒店餐厅, Zǐyuē Mànjū Jiǔdiàn Cāntīng; 8 Gulou Beijie, 鼓楼北街8号; most dishes ¥20-60; ⊙9am-9pm) This clean, modern restaurant attached to Zi Yue Man Ju Hotel does ordinary Chinese fried dishes and noodles, as well as Confucius Cuisine. Staff are welcoming, but there's no English here. Confucius Cuisine dishes to look for include yīpǐn dòufu (一品豆腐, stuffed tofu, ¥48) and shénxiān yāzi (神仙鸭子, fragrant, crispy, steamed-duck soup, ¥88), aka 'fairy duck'.

Late-night barbecue stalls STREET FOOD ¥
(烧烤夜市, Shāokǎo Yèshì; Yan'en Donglu, 延恩东路; skewers ¥1 to ¥2; ⊙6pm-3am) Street-side vendors are banned from Qufu these days, so the barbecue crew now set up their smoky grills just off the road in this large car park immediately northeast of the walled town's north gate. Barbecue skewers are the order of the day (veggie/meat ¥1/2), and they're all on display; just point and choose.

Zhèngzōng Tiānjīn Xiǎolóngbāo DUMPLINGS ¥
(正宗天津小笼包; Gulou Nanjie, 鼓楼南街; per basket ¥7; ⊙6am-8pm) Ideal for breakfast, the xiǎo lóng bāo (小笼包, steamed dumplings) at this tiny place come with various fillings including pork and onion (鲜肉, xiān ròu), pork and mushroom (香菇肉, xiānggū ròu), egg and chives (韭菜鸡蛋, jiǔcài jīdàn), and carrot and egg (胡萝卜鸡蛋, húluóbo jīdàn). A warming bowl of xiǎomǐ zhōu (小米粥, millet porridge) or dòu jiāng (豆浆, soy milk) make a perfect accompaniment.

Qufu Night Market MARKET ¥
(曲阜夜市, Qūfù Yèshì; Sports Park on Hongdao Lu, 弘道路体育公园; snacks/dishes from ¥5/10; ⊙around 6pm-11pm) The busy, aromatic night market is a short walk south of the south-east corner of the old-town wall, and cooks up lamb kebabs, noodles, húntún (wontons), tofu and many other dishes and street snacks. Bus 1 goes here from Gulou Beijie; get off at tǐyù gōngyuán (体育公园) stop.

Qing Lu Tea Restaurant INTERNATIONAL ¥¥
(青旅茶餐厅, Qīnglǚ Chá Cāntīng; Gulou Beijie, 鼓楼北街; most dishes ¥15-45, pizza ¥68-98; ⊙8am-midnight) One of the few places in town with an English menu, this friendly cafe-bar-restaurant attached to the town's excellent youth hostel does a mix of western (pizza, pasta, salads, sandwiches) and Chinese (noodles, dumplings, rice meals) food. Also good for a morning coffee, or an evening beer over a game of pool.

ℹ️ Information

ATMs accepting foreign cards are along and around Gulou Beijie.

Bank of China (中国银行, Zhōngguó Yínháng; 96 Dongmen Dajie, 东门大街96号; ⊙8.30am-4.30pm) Foreign exchange and ATM.

People's No 2 Hospital (第二人民医院, Dì'èr Rénmín Yīyuàn; ☑0537 448 8120; 7 Gulou Beijie, 鼓楼北街7号) Small local hospital next to the Qufu International Youth Hostel.

ℹ️ Getting There & Away

AIR
Jining Qufu Airport (济宁曲阜机场, Jìníng Qūfù Jīchǎng) is 80km southwest of Qufu's old town and connects to a handful of major cities including Beijing and Shanghai.

BUS
Qufu Bus Station (曲阜汽车站, Qūfù Qìchēzhàn; ☑0537 441 2554; Yulong Lu & Yulan Lu, 裕隆路与玉兰路) is 3km west of the city walls. Destinations include the following:

Ji'nan ¥45, three hours, hourly (6.40am to 5pm)

Qingdao ¥125, five hours, two daily (8.30am and 2pm)

Tai Shan ¥23, 1½ hours, six daily (9.10am, 10.30am, 12.10pm, 3.10pm, 4.30pm and 5.40pm)

TRAIN
For most destinations, trains are the best way to reach Qufu. High-speed trains use the **East Train Station** (曲阜东站, Qūfù Dōng Zhàn; ☑0537 442 1571; Kongzi Dadao, 孔子大道), 10km southeast of the walled city. **Qufu Train Station** (曲阜火车站, Qūfù Huǒchēzhàn; ☑0537 442 1571; Dianlan Lu, 电缆路) is closest to the walled city (3km east), but only regular trains stop there.

CONFUCIUS: THE FIRST TEACHER

An idealist born into a world of violent upheaval, Confucius (551–479 BC) spent his life trying to stabilise society according to traditional ideals. By his own measure he failed, but over time he became one of the most influential thinkers the world has known. Confucius' ideals remain at the core of values in East Asia today and still exercise massive power over Chinese thinking.

Confucius was born Kong Qiu (孔丘), earning the honorific Kongfuzi (孔夫子), literally 'Master Kong', after becoming a teacher. His family was poor but of noble rank, and eventually he became an official in his home state of Lǔ (鲁). At the age of 50 he put a plan into action to reform government that included routing corruption. This resulted in his exile, and he spent 13 years travelling from state to state, hoping to find a ruler who would put his ideas into practice. Eventually he returned to his home town of Qufu and spent the remainder of his life expounding the wisdom of the Six Classics (*The Book of Changes, Songs, Rites, History, Music* and the *Spring and Autumn Annals*). Taking on students from varied backgrounds, he believed that everyone, not just aristocracy, had a right to knowledge. This ideal became one of his greatest legacies.

Confucius' teachings were compiled by his disciples in *The Analects* (论语, Lúnyǔ), a collection of 497 aphorisms. Though he claimed to be merely transmitting the ideals of an ancient golden age, Confucius was in fact China's first humanist philosopher, upholding morality (humaneness, righteousness and virtue) and self-cultivation as the basis for social order. 'What you do not wish for yourself,' he said, 'do not do to others.'

High-speed trains (1st-/2nd-class seat) departing from East Train Station include the following:

Beijing South ¥409/244, 2½ hours, 24 daily (8.07am to 9.09pm)

Ji'nan West ¥100/60, 30 to 45 minutes, 40 daily (7.15am to 10.22pm)

Nanjing South ¥379/224, two hours, 20 daily (7.48am to 7.27pm)

Qingdao ¥244/179, 3½ hours, five daily (7.20am, 8.28am, 12.05pm, 4.42pm and 6.29pm)

Shanghai Hongqiao ¥584/344, 3½ hours, 15 daily (7.52am to 7.27pm)

Tai'an (for Tai Shan) ¥55/30, 20 minutes, 25 daily (7.20am to 10.10pm)

Tianjin West or South ¥334/199, two hours, 16 daily (8.07am to 8.46pm)

Yantai ¥444/275, two daily at 7.15am (4½ hours) and 4.15pm (five hours)

Yantai South ¥438/271, four to five hours, four daily (7.34am, 8.17am, 9.59am and 1.35pm)

Regular trains departing from Qufu Train Station include the following:

Ji'nan Hard/soft seat ¥29/45, 2½ hours, three daily (8.09am, 12.17pm and 7.12pm)

Tai Shan Hard/soft seat ¥19/25, 1½ to two hours, four daily (8.09am, 12.17pm, 4.22pm and 7.12pm)

ⓘ Getting Around

There are no direct buses from the airport to the old town of Qufu, so you will need to transfer to a bus or taxi at the bus station in Jining (济宁, Jǐníng), about 50km away. Flying into the provincial capital Ji'nan (济南, Jǐnán) is probably more convenient.

Local buses cost ¥1 per trip.

Bus K01 Connects Qufu Bus Station with the East Train Station, via Confucius Temple's south gate.

Bus K03 Connects Qufu Bus Station and Qufu Train Station, via Confucius Temple's south gate.

Bus 10 Goes from Qufu Bus Station to the Drum Tower and People's No 2 Hospital, via Confucius Temple's south gate.

Bus 1 Goes from the Drum Tower north to Confucius Forest and south to the night market.

A taxi to the walled town is about ¥40 from East Train Station and about ¥20 from Qufu Bus Station.

Ubiquitous pedicabs (¥5 to ¥10 within the walls; ¥10 to ¥20 outside the walls) are a pleasant way to get around, but be sure to negotiate the fare very clearly before your ride. Most places, however, can be walked to easily. If you care about animal welfare, give the horse-drawn carts a miss.

Zoucheng 邹城

☑ 0537 / POP 1.15 MILLION

Twenty-three kilometres south of Qufu is Zoucheng (Zōuchéng), where the revered Confucian scholar Mencius (孟子, Mèngzǐ; c 372–289 BC) was born. Like Confucius, Mencius was raised by a single mother and grew up to travel the country trying to reform government. His belief that humanity is by nature good formed the core of all his teachings, including his call to overthrow self-serving rulers. Not surprisingly, his criticism made him unpopular with those in power, but a thousand years after his death Mencius' work was elevated a step below Confucius'.

Zoucheng today is a pretty quiet town, with fewer tourist hassles than Qufu. A combined ticket (summer/winter ¥40/30) get you access to both Mencius Temple and Mencius Family Mansion, which are next to each other. In winter, they both close at 4pm.

It's fun to explore the myriad courtyards and gardens at **Mencius Family Mansion** (孟府, Mèng Fǔ; Miaoqian Lu, 庙前路; incl Mencius Temple ¥40; ⏱ 8.20am-5pm), which among other things exhibits the family's living quarters, including teacups and bedding left by Mencius' 74th-generation descendant, who lived here into the 1940s.

A portrait of ancient China and tranquillity, the **Mencius Temple** (孟庙, Mèng Miào) originally dates from the Song dynasty; it bears the marks of past anti-Confucian mood swings, though restoration is always ongoing. With few visitors around, you can sit in the shade of ancient gnarled cypresses, absorbing the serene surroundings. The twin-roofed **Hall of the Second Sage** (亚圣殿, Yàshèng Diàn) looms in the centre of the grounds, a small shrine next to it dedicated to Mencius' mother, the 'model for all mothers'.

The **Zoucheng Museum** (邹城博物馆, Zōuchéng Bówùguǎn; 56 Shunhe Lu, 顺和路56号; ⏱ 9am-11am & 2-4pm Tue-Sun) FREE on Shunhe Lu displays a collection of items relating to Zoucheng through history. Note the very long lunch break.

There are few sleeping options here for foreigners, but this is an easy day trip from Qufu. There's a handful of small restaurants selling noodles and the like on the walk between the museum and the two main sights. The rhythm of Zoucheng is Confucian in nature, so nightlife and drinking are done in rather low-key fashion.

Zoucheng is any easy bus ride from Qufu. Bus C609 (¥3, 40 minutes, 6.30am to 6.30pm) departs frequently from Qufu Bus Station. Get off at the museum bus stop (博物馆, Bówùguǎn), then walk ahead to the river (but don't cross it). To your left is the museum (50m). To your right are the temple and mansion (200m).

A new sky train (轻轨, *qīng guǐ*) that will link Zoucheng to Qufu's East Train Station was under construction at the time of research.

Qingdao

📞 0532 / POP 5.9 MILLION

Combining fresh sea air and dashing good looks, Qingdao (青岛, Qīngdǎo; sometimes spelled Tsingtao) – the name means 'Green Island' – is a rare Chinese city that has managed to preserve some of its past while angling a dazzling modern face to the future. Its blend of concession-era and modern architecture puts China's standard white-tile and blue-glass developments to shame. The winding cobbled streets, historic German architecture and red-capped hillside villas are captivating and there's much to enjoy in the city's diverse food scene, headlined by the ubiquitous home-town beer Tsingtao. Meanwhile, the seaside aspect keeps the town cooler than the inland swelter zones during summer, and slightly warmer in winter.

History

Before catching the acquisitive eye of Kaiser Wilhelm II, Qingdao was a harbour and fishing village known for producing delicious sea salt. Its excellent strategic location was not lost on the Ming dynasty, which built a defensive battery – nor on the Germans, who wrested it from them in 1897. China signed a 99-year concession, and it was during the next decade that the future Tsingtao Brewery was opened, electric lighting installed, missions and a university established, and the railway to Ji'nan built.

In 1914 Japan seized control with a bombing assault on the city. When the Treaty of Versailles strengthened Japan's occupation in 1919, student demonstrations erupted in Beijing and spread across the country in what became known as the May 4th Movement. After a period of domestic control, the Japanese took over again in 1938 and held on until the end of WWII.

In peacetime Qingdao became one of China's major ports and a flourishing centre of trade and manufacturing (home to both domestic and international brands). The port town hosted the sailing events of the 2008 Olympic Games and seems to hold a permanent spot on the list of China's most liveable cities (despite the larger-than-life green tide of algal blooms that infest Qingdao's waters in summer).

⊙ Sights

Shinan District (市南区, Shìnán Qū) is where you'll spend most of your time. Shinan's sights are squeezed into two main areas: Old Town (the former concession area), with the train and bus stations, historic architecture and budget accommodation, and Badaguan (八大关, Bādàguān), a serene residential area of parks, spas and old villas. At the time of research, much of Old Town (around the Zhufu Lu area) was being prepared for a massive facelift. Depending on how soon you visit it will either resemble a building site, or look beautiful.

East of Shandong Lu rises the modern city, with the central business district (CBD) to the north and retail and dining in an area called Dongbu (东部, Dōngbù), closer to the water to the south. Further east is the developing Lao Shan district (崂山区, Láoshān Qū), anchored by the Municipal Museum, Grand Theatre and International Beer City (site of Qingdao's famous annual International Beer Festival).

Huilan Pavilion   NOTABLE BUILDING
(回澜阁, Huílán Gé; 12 Taiping Lu, 太平路12号; ⊙8.30am-4pm; Ⓜ Qingdao Railway Station) FREE Lit up at night, this graceful pavilion decorates the end of Zhan Bridge poking into Qingdao Bay. If it looks familiar, that's because it's on every Tsingtao beer label.

Little Qingdao   LIGHTHOUSE, ISLAND
(小青岛, Xiǎo Qīngdǎo; 26 Qinyu Lu, 琴屿路26号; ¥10; ⊙6am-8pm; Ⓑ6, 26, 202, 231, 304, Ⓜ Hall of the People) In the shape of a *qín* (a stringed instrument) jutting into Qingdao Bay, this former island – which lends its name to the city – was connected to the mainland in the 1940s. The Germans built the white lighthouse in 1900 on the leafy promontory. It is an excellent spot for watching the city come to life in the morning; entry is free from 6am to 7.30am and from 6.30pm to 8pm.

Chinese Navy Museum   MUSEUM
(中国海军博物馆, Zhōngguó Hǎijūn Bówùguǎn; Ⓙ0532 8286 6784; www.hjbwg.com; 8 Caiyang Lu, 菜阳路8号; entrance ¥30, incl submarine entrance ¥100; ⊙9am-5pm; Ⓑ26, 202, 501, Ⓜ Hall of the People) Beside the entrance to Little Qingdao lighthouse, this museum's main attractions are the rusty submarine and destroyer anchored in the harbour, for which you need to buy the ¥100 ticket. The ¥30 ticket will get you into the complex, allowing to see all the other boats and naval equipment on show, as well as displays on Chinese naval history.

Protestant Church   CHURCH
(基督教堂, Jīdū Jiàotáng; 15 Jiangsu Lu, 江苏路15号; ¥10; ⊙8.30am-5.30pm; Ⓑ1, 221, 367, Ⓜ Hall of the People) On a street of German buildings, this copper-capped beauty was designed by Curt Rothkegel and built in 1908. The interior is simple and Lutheran in its sparseness, apart from some carvings on the pillar cornices. You can climb up to inspect the clock mechanism (from Bockenem, dated 1909).

Governor's House Museum   MUSEUM
(青岛德国总督楼旧址博物馆, Qīngdǎo Déguó Zǒngdū Lóu Jiùzhǐ Bówùguǎn; Ⓙ0532 8286 8838; 26 Longshan Lu, 龙山路26号; summer/winter ¥20/13, multilingual audio tour ¥20; ⊙8.30am-5.30pm; Ⓑ1, 221, Ⓜ Hall of the People) This museum is one of Qingdao's best examples of concession-era architecture – the former German governor's residence constructed in the style of a German palace. The building's interior is characteristic of Jugendstil, the German arm of art nouveau, with some German and Chinese furnishings of the era. It was built in 1903 at a cost of 2,450,000 taels of silver by an indulgent governor, whom Kaiser Wilhelm II immediately sacked when he saw the bill.

In 1957 Chairman Mao stayed here with his wife and kids on holiday. So did defence minister Lin Biao, who would later attempt to assassinate Mao.

Qingdao City Art Museum   MUSEUM
(青岛市美术馆, Qīngdǎo Shì Měishùguǎn; Ⓙ0532 8288 8886; http://qdmsg.sdgw.com; 7 Daxue Lu, 大学路7号; ⊙9am-4.30pm; Ⓑ1, 25, 221, 367, Ⓜ Hall of the People) FREE Contemporary works are on display in this compact museum housed in its own architectural masterpiece, a 1930s structure reflecting an eclectic mix of architectural styles from deco to Byzantine, Islamic and imperial Chinese.

St Michael's Cathedral   CHURCH
(天主教堂, Tiānzhǔ Jiàotáng; Ⓙ0532 8286 5960; 15 Zhejiang Lu, 浙江路15号; ¥10; ⊙8.30am-5pm Mon-Sat, from 10am Sun; Ⓑ1, 221, 367, Ⓜ Qingdao Railway Station) Up a hill off Zhongshan Lu looms this grand Gothic- and Roman-style edifice. Completed in 1934, the church spires were supposed to be clock towers, but Chancellor Hitler cut funding of overseas projects and the plans were scrapped. The church was badly damaged during the Cultural Revolution and the crosses capping its twin spires were torn off. Devout locals buried

Qingdao

Map of Qingdao showing the following labelled areas and features:

Districts and areas: SHIBEI DISTRICT, SHÌ'NÁN DISTRICT, TAIDONG, OLD TOWN, BĀDÀGUĀN

Parks and landmarks: Jiaozhou Bay, Qingdaoshan Park, Signal Hill Park, Guanhaishan Park, Zhongshan Park, Hall of the People, Lu Xun Park, Huiquan Bay, Qingdao Bay, Fushan Bay, Taipingjiao Park, Huiquan Square, Zhongshan Square, Tsingtao Beer Museum, Train Station, Qingdao Railway Station, Zhan Bridge

Off-map references:
- Qingdao Cruise Terminal (500m)
- Long-Distance (2.3km)
- Ninghai Lu →
- Culture Street (200m)
- Golden Sand Beach (15km)
- Mix C mall (850m)
- Shangri-La Hotel (850m)
- Shilaoren Beach (13km)
- Lao Shan (27km)
- Huàshí Lóu (300m)
- No 2 Bathing Beach (500m)
- No 3 Bathing Beach (300m)

Qingdao

the crosses for safe keeping. In 2005 workers uncovered them while repairing pipes in the hills, and they have since been restored.

Tianhou Temple TEMPLE
(天后宫, Tiānhòu Gōng; 19 Taiping Lu, 太平路19号; ⊙8am-6pm; ☐25, Ⓜ Hall of the People) **FREE** This small restored temple dedicated to Tiānhòu (天后), the patron of seafarers, has stood by the shore since 1467. The main hall contains a colourful statue of the goddess, flanked by fearsome guardians. There is also **Dragon King Hall** (龙王殿, Lóngwáng Diàn), where a splayed pig lies before the ruler of oceans and king of the rains, and a shrine to the God of Wealth. A temple fair is held here annually during the Spring Festival.

★Tsingtao Beer Museum BREWERY
(青岛啤酒博物馆, Qīngdǎo Píjiǔ Bówùguǎn; ☑0532 8383 3437; www.tsingtaomuseum.com; 56-1 Dengzhou Lu, 登州路56-1号; admission ¥60-90, English guide per group ¥150; ⊙8.30am-6pm; ☐2, 205) For a self-serving introduction to China's iconic beer, head to the original and still-operating brewery. On view are old photos, preserved brewery equipment and statistics, and there are also a few fascinating glimpses of the modern factory line. The aroma of hops is everywhere. And you get

to sample brews along the way (how much depends on which ticket you buy).

If you want to keep drinking, Tsingtao IPA and *yuan jiang* are both on tap in **1903 Cafe** (8am to 6pm), the brewery's own little pub, located by the ticket office.

To get here, take bus 2 or 205 from Zhongshan Lu and get off at Tai Dong bus stop. Tai Dong will have its own metro station soon too.

Qingdao Municipal Museum MUSEUM
(青岛市博物馆, Qīngdǎo Shì Bówùguǎn; ☑0532 8889 6286; www.qingdaomuseum.com; 51 Meiling Donglu, 梅岭东路51号; ⊙9am-4.30pm Tue-Sun; ☐230, 321, Ⓜ Miaoling Rd) **FREE** This massive collection of relics anchors the budding cultural zone in Lao Shan district. It has the usual broad span of exhibits expected in a big-city museum, ranging from the prehistoric to the industrial age. Collections of folk-art woodcuts and intriguing coins pressed with Kyrgyz script stand out. From Miaoling Rd metro station, walk south down Shenzhen Lu and take the first left.

Huashi Lou NOTABLE BUILDING
(花石楼, Huāshí Lóu; ☑0532 8387 2168; 18 Huanghai Lu, 黄海路18号; ¥8.50; ⊙8.30am-5.30pm; ☐26, 231, 604, Ⓜ Taipingjiao Park) This granite and marble villa built in 1930 was first the home of a Russian aristocrat, and

later the German governor's hunting lodge. It is also known as the 'Chiang Kaishek Building', as the generalissimo secretly stayed here in 1947. While most of the rooms are closed, you can clamber up two narrow stairwells to the turret for a great view.

It's at the east end of No 2 Bathing Beach at the southern tip of Zijingguan Lu in Badaguan district.

🏊 Beaches

Qingdao has very pleasant beaches, though they are sometimes afflicted in summer with outrageous blue-green algae blooms and litter. Chinese beach culture is low-key, with men sporting the skimpy swimwear and women covering up from the sun. Swimming season (June to September) means hordes of sun-seekers fighting for towel space on weekends. Shark nets, lifeguards, lifeboat patrols and medical stations are on hand.

There are a number of ways to enjoy the water without jumping in. If you give in to touts, 30-minute rides around the bay go for around ¥60. Or stroll the Binhai boardwalk (滨海步行道, Bīnhǎi bùxíngdào), which stretches almost unbroken for an incredible 40km along the city's shoreline.

No 6 Bathing Beach
BEACH

(第六海水浴场, Dì Liù Hǎishuǐ Yùchǎng; 🚌 25, 202, Ⓜ Qingdao Railway Station) This is the closest beach to the Old Town, and a great spot come early evening, when the buildings around the bay are illuminated. No 6 Bathing Beach is a short strip of sand and tide pools, next to Zhan Bridge, the pier that reaches into the bay. At the tip of the pier, the eight-sided Huilan Pavilion (p235) is a graceful sight, though it's often packed to the rafters.

Shilaoren Beach
BEACH

(石老人海水浴场, Shílǎorén Hǎishuǐ Yùchǎng; 🚌 301, Ⓜ Shilaoren Beach) On the far eastern side of town in Lao Shan district, and now with its own metro station, this 2.5km-long strip of clean sand is Qingdao's largest and has the highest waves in town (decent for bodyboarding); it can be very quiet in the morning too. The 'Old Stone Man' from which the beach gets its name is the rocky outcrop to the east.

Golden Sand Beach
BEACH

(金沙滩, Jīnshā Tān; 🚌 2, 🚌 7) For wide-open spaces of sand, sea and sky, there's Golden Sand Beach on the western peninsula of Huangdao district (团岛区, Huángdǎo Qū). An undersea tunnel linking Huangdao and the district of Shinan (市南, Shìnán) puts it within easy reach of Old Town. Take tunnel bus 7 (隧道7; ¥2, 30 minutes) from Jiaozhou Lu or the train station and get off at the second stop after the tunnel; from here, walk back, then turn right. A taxi costs around ¥70 including toll.

QINGDAO'S PARKS

Many parks that carry entrance tickets, including Little Fish Hill (p238) by No 1 Bathing Beach and Signal Hill Park (p238) in Old Town, are free to enter for around an hour before and after the official opening times.

Zhongshan Park (中山公园, Zhōngshān Gōngyuán; ⊙ 24hr; 🚌 25, 26, Ⓜ Zhongshan Pk) Within central Qingdao, Zhongshan Park is a vast 69 hectares of lakes, gardens and walking paths; it's an amusement park for kids and also the venue of lively festivals in the spring and summer. In the park's northeast rises **Taiping Hill** (太平山, Tàipíng Shān) with a **cable car** (one way/return ¥70/120; ⊙ 8.30am-5.30pm) to the **TV Tower** (电视塔, Diànshì Tǎ; 📞 0532 8361 2286; admission ¥100) at the top. Also within the park is Qingdao's largest temple, **Zhanshan Temple** (湛山寺, Zhànshān Sì; ¥10; ⊙ 8am-4pm), an active Buddhist sanctuary.

When you get off the cable car at the temple, look for a round concrete dome on the right. This is the entrance to a bunker, which the Germans used as a wine cellar, and today houses a wine bar.

Little Fish Hill (小鱼山公园, Xiǎoyúshān Gōngyuán; 📞 0532 8286 5645; 24 Fushanzhi Lu, 福山支路24号; ¥10; ⊙ 6am-8pm; Ⓜ Huaquan Sq) This sweet little park is near No 1 Bathing Beach. Admission is free after 6.30pm.

Signal Hill Park (信号山, Xìnhào Shān; 16 Longshan Lu, 龙山路16号; park entrance/viewing platform ¥5/10; ⊙ 6am-8.30pm; Ⓜ Hall of the People) This park above Qingdao's Old Town is free to enter from 6am to 7.30am and from 6pm to 8.30pm.

No 3 Bathing Beach BEACH

(第三海水浴场, Dì Sān Hǎishuǐ Yùchǎng; 🚌 26, 202, Ⓜ Taipingjiao Park) On the eastern side of Taiping Cape in Badaguan is this cove with dedicated swim lanes, paddle boats and gentle waves. Very close to Taipingjiao Park metro station.

No 1 Bathing Beach BEACH

(第一海水浴场, Dì Yī Hǎishuǐ Yùchǎng; 🚌 304, Ⓜ Huiquan Sq) South of the tree-lined area known as Badaguan (八大关, Bādàguān), No 1 Bathing Beach is a very popular spot, perhaps for its snack stalls and children's toy selection, but more likely for its muscle beach.

No 2 Bathing Beach BEACH

(第二海水浴场, Dì Èr Hǎishuǐ Yùchǎng; 🚌 214, Ⓜ Taipingjiao Park) Once reserved only for the likes of Mao and other state leaders, this sheltered cove just east of Badaguan has calm waters good for a swim. It's a short walk from Taipingjiao Park metro station.

🎇 Festivals & Events

⭐ International Beer Festival BEER

(9am-3pm ¥10, 3-10.30pm ¥20; ⊘ Aug) The city's premier party draws more than three million tipplers every August. It's not just Tsingtao on the menu, so expect a galaxy of international and domestic brands.

International Sailing Week SPORTS

(www.qdsailing.org; ⊘ Aug/Sep) Watch (or join) the regattas and windsurfing by the Olympic Sailing Center every August/September.

Cherry Blossom Festival CULTURAL

(Zhongshan Park, 中山公园; ⊘ Apr) The cherry blossoms explode with colour in Zhongshan Park around April, bringing splashes of colour to Qingdao's oldest and largest park.

🛌 Sleeping

Old Town in particular is packed with cheap youth hostels but, like many of the city's budget hotels, most of them do not accept foreigners. (The ones we've reviewed all do.) The CBD and Dongbu have the top-end international chains but a lot less soul. Rates increase by as much as 30% in July and August, when sun-seekers fill the beaches.

Mijiā Qīngnián Lǚshě HOSTEL ¥

(米家青年旅舍, 📞 155 5323 0890; 40 Hunan Lu, 湖南路40号; dm ¥38-80, r ¥120-240; ❋ 🛜; Ⓜ Qingdao Railway Station) This whole hostel is in the basement of a large building so there are no windows whatsoever, but it's clean,

modern and brightly lit, and staff are welcoming despite speaking no English. The dorms are self-contained 'capsules' and are tiny, as are the cheapest private rooms. The ¥210 and ¥240 rooms are larger, have bathrooms and can sleep four people.

⭐ Kaiyue Hostel HOSTEL ¥

(凯越国际青年旅馆, Kǎiyuè Guójì Qīngnián Lǚguǎn; 📞 0532 8284 5450; kaiyuehostel@126.com; 31 Jining Lu, 济宁路31号; dm ¥55-75, r from ¥270; ❋ @ 🛜; Ⓜ Qingdao Railway Station) This spacious, sociable, friendly and helpful hostel in a historic church at the junction of Sifang Lu and Jining Lu has a lively congregation. They come to worship in the slick ground-floor bar and restaurant, Jinns' Café (8am to 1am), which serves western food (mains ¥30 to ¥90) including great pizza and desserts. Rooms are pricy for a hostel, but very smart.

MG Hotel HOTEL ¥¥

(民国酒店, Mínguó Jiǔdiàn; 📞 0532 8288 6616; 31 Zhongshan Lu, 中山路31号; d/tw incl breakfast from ¥310/420; ❋ 🛜; Ⓜ Qingdao Railway Station) This sharp and sassy new hotel, close to the beach, has helpful, English-speaking staff and modern rooms that are comfortable despite being small. The cheapest doubles are Japanese-style *tatami* rooms with mattresses on the floor and low-level furniture to match. Other rooms have standard beds and more space.

Wheat Youth Hostel HOTEL ¥¥

(麦子青年旅社, Màizi Qīngnián Lǚshè; 📞 0532 8285 2121; 35 Hebei Lu, 河北路35号; dm ¥50-70, r from ¥328; ❋ @ 🛜; Ⓜ Qingdao Railway Station) This lovely Old Town hostel is in a beautiful, restored *pícháiyuàn,* the courtyard apartments of 1920s Qingdao, and within a 10-minute walk of the train station. Rooms are spotless with nostalgic details and creaky hardwood floors, and the communal courtyard spaces make pleasant hang-outs.

Villa Inn BOUTIQUE HOTEL ¥¥¥

(美墅假期酒店, Měishù Jiàqī Jiǔdiàn; 📞 0532 8387 8025, 189 53295010; villainn@163.com; 21 Tianlin Huayuan, off Donghai Xilu, 东海西路2号天林花园21号楼乙; r ¥400-2000, breakfast ¥50; ❋ 🛜; 🚌 312, 317, Ⓜ Yan'an 3rd Rd) In a quiet enclave of oceanside villas, this modern, wonderfully located 15-room hotel is a great choice for seaside seekers. You'll have to stump up at least ¥1000 for a sea view, but even without one No 3 Beach is just steps away, and the popular ocean promenade right outside makes for pleasant evening strolls.

It's a short walk from Yan'an 3rd Rd metro station; come out out of Exit C, walk back on yourself, turn left at the crossroads, then right at the end (onto Donghai Xilu), first left into Aomen Rd, then right into the enclave (天林花园).

Oceanwide Elite Hotel
HOTEL ¥¥¥

(泛海名人酒店, Fànhǎi Míngrén Jiǔdiàn; ☑0532 8299 6699; www.oweh.com; 29 Taiping Lu, 太平路29号; d incl breakfast with city/sea view from ¥670/770; ❈@◈; ☒220, 312, 321, ⓜHall of the People) This dignified five-storey hotel benefits from a superb seafront location overlooking Zhan Bridge and Qingdao Bay. Little touches like complimentary snacks put it leagues ahead of its neighbours.

Shangri-La Hotel
HOTEL ¥¥¥

(香格里拉大酒店; ☑0532 8388 3838; www. shangri-la.com/qingdao/shangrila; 9 Xianggang Zhong-lu, 香港中路9号; d incl breakfast from ¥1100; ❀❈◈☒; ⓜMay 4th Sq) The Shangri-La brand is a reliable symbol of excellence throughout China, and particularly so in this outstanding hotel. We could point to the stylish and comfortable rooms, the dazzling 25m swimming pool or the panoply of fine-dining choices and we would be right on the money. But it's the staff that make this place a clear cut above its top-end rivals.

✕ Eating

Qingdao's kitchens have no problem satisfying all tastes. Seafood is king, naturally, though ordering it without being able to speak Chinese can be daunting.

Mix C food court
FOOD COURT ¥

(万象城, Wànxiàng Chéng; Shandong Lu; dishes ¥15-40; ❸10am-10pm; ⓜMay 4th Sq) Do as the locals do and escape the heat by taking the metro out to the city's most dazzling shopping mall where a 5th-floor food court is waiting to wow you with flavours from across China – Shanghai dumplings, Chongqing noodles, Hong Kong roast duck... Dishes are clearly priced and displayed, so are easy to order.

Top-up a purchasing card (refundable deposit ¥10) with as much as you think you'll need, then hand it over as you order. You'll get any outstanding balance back when you return the card.

Pichaiyuan Food Street
STREET FOOD ¥

(劈柴院, Pīcháiyuàn; Zhongshan Lu, 中山路; snacks from ¥5; ❸6am-10pm; ☒2, 228, ⓜQingdao Railway Station) Off Zhongshan Lu, an archway with a plaster motif '1902' leads to a vast warren of street-food stalls that buzz with hungry tourists looking for seafood skewers, pig's trotters, dumplings and more. It's especially lively come evening.

Huangdao Market
STREET FOOD ¥

(黄岛路市场, Huángdǎo Lù Shìchǎng; Huángdǎo Lù, 黄岛路; dishes from ¥10; ❸7am-late; ☒228, 231, ⓜQingdao Railway Station) In the heart of Old Town, this long-standing, often frenetic street market is chock-a-block with vendors selling everything from squirming seafood, fried chicken and pancakes to fruit and soy milk. It's all cheap, so just stop when something catches your fancy. Come evening, sit-down curbside joints (look for a '加功' – jiā gōng – sign) will prepare whatever seafood you bring them for ¥5.

Wángjiě Shāokǎo
GRILL ¥

(王姐烧烤; 113 Zhongshan Lu, 中山路113号; skewers ¥3.50-8; ❸10am-9pm; ⓜQingdao Railway Station) Qingdao's kebabs are legendary and these are among the best, so give them your palate's undivided attention. Join the throng outside this street-side stand gorging on lamb (羊肉, yángròu; ¥4), cuttlefish (鱿鱼, yóuyú, ¥8) and chicken hearts (鸡心, jīxīn; ¥3.5), and toss your spent skewers in the bucket. There's a sit-down restaurant around the corner.

★ Shawn Tren's
SHANDONG ¥¥

(香椿, Xiāngchūn; ☑185 6276 1819; 216 Zhongshan Lu, 中山路216号; most dishes ¥20-40, seafood ¥35-90; ❸10.30am-2pm & 5-9.30pm; ◈) Housed in a former electrical office building dating from 1909, this super little restaurant, with big-window street views, knocks out delicious but affordable Shandong cuisine from its small open kitchen. There's a good selection of noodles, and the English menu makes ordering Qingdao's famous seafood much easier than at other places.

Jiāngníng Huìguǎn
SHANDONG ¥¥

(江宁会馆; Pichaiyuan Food Street, 劈柴院内; skewers ¥5-15, dishes ¥20-80; ❸9.30am-9pm; ⓜQingdao Railway Station) The drama stage inside Jiangning Assembly Hall has been a long-time draw for renowned performers in Qingdao, and they still perform for diners here. Lunchtime shows (noon to 1pm) are Peking opera, while evening (6.30pm to 7.30pm) is cabaret-type singing. The buffet-style food is easy to order, and diners get ¥5 cups of green tea with unlimited refills from metre-long dragon-spout teapots.

The hall is hidden down the second alley on your right after you enter Pichaiyuan Food Street from Zhongshan Lu.

Chun He Lou
SHANDONG ¥¥

(春和楼, Chūn Hé Lóu; ☑ 0532 8282 4346; 146-150 Zhongshan Lu, 中山路146-150号; dumplings per serving ¥20-48, other dishes ¥16-78; ⊙10am-10pm; 🚍 2, 228, Ⓜ Qingdao Railway Station) In the old quarter of town, this Lǔ (Shandong) cuisine institution was founded in 1891 and is known for its delicious dumplings. Choose either *shuǐ jiǎo* (水饺, boiled dumplings) or *zhēng jiǎo* (蒸饺, steamed dumplings). Fillings include *ròu sān xiān* (肉三鲜, pork, dried shrimp and mushroom; ¥30), *xiā rén* (虾仁, fresh shrimp with chives; ¥48) and *báicài dà bāo* (白菜大包, pork with cabbage; ¥20).

Wù Yuán
CAFE, INTERNATIONAL ¥¥¥

(雾缘; ☑ 0532 8768 1577; Zhan Shan 3rd Rd, 湛山三路; coffee from ¥36, salads ¥42-78, mains ¥118-138; ⊙9am-midnight; ❄🛜; Ⓜ Taipingjiao Pk or Yan'er 3rd Rd) This upmarket cafe-restaurant isn't quite on No 3 Beach, but it sure is close. The coffee is excellent, as is the western food (sirloin steaks, lamb chops, salads and soups), and there are sea views from the 1st floor, though it also has a large ground-floor terrace.

🍷 Drinking & Nightlife

The first stop for committed tipplers should be the many drinking holes along **Beer Street** (啤酒街, Píjiǔ Jiē; Dengzhou Lu, 登州路; 🚍 2, 205, 221, 301) where you can sample the delicious dark, unfiltered *yuánjiāng* (原浆啤酒; pint ¥15), which is hard to find elsewhere.

Jinns' Café in Kaiyue Hostel (p239) is a cafe-restaurant by day, but transforms into buzzing bar by night, with free-to-use pool table and table football.

Liángyǒu Shūfāng
CAFE

(良友书坊; 5 Anhui Lu, 安徽路5号; coffee from ¥28, dishes ¥28-75; ⊙9.30am-9.30pm; 🛜; Ⓜ Qingdao Railway Station) Hidden up in the rafters on the 4th floor of the former Jiaozhou Post Office (c1901), this cafe-cum-bookshop is a serene place to take a break from the summer sunshine. The coffee's good and there's a decent selection of western food (soups, salads, pasta, sandwiches). Has a ground-floor cafe too, but it's cosier up top.

LOCAL SEAFOOD

For the staple local seafood, stick to the streets. The **Taidong** neighbourhood between Taidong Yilu (台东一路) and Taidong Balu (台东八路) in Shibei district (市北区) north of Old Town is packed with restaurants, street markets and carts. Take bus 2, 222 or 217. For the quintessential Qingdao meal, buy a *jīn* of clams – in local-speak *gálá* (蛤蜊; from ¥18) – and take it to a street-side stall with '加功' (*jiā gōng*) on its sign. They'll cook up your catch for ¥5, and pour you a plastic bag of fresh Tsingtao beer for ¥8 more (decanting it into a glass is tricky, but pints and pitchers are also available if you want to be fancy).

K+ Kāfēi
CAFE

(K+ 咖啡; Feicheng Lu, 肥城路; coffee from ¥25; ⊙8.30am-10pm; Ⓜ Qingdao Railway Station) On a lovely perch overlooking the square in front of St Michael's Cathedral, and with benches outside that catch the breeze, this tiny, retro, European-style cafe does good coffee (espresso and drip) and also makes a pleasant spot for an evening Tsingtao.

Qīngdǎo Píjiǔ
BAR

(青岛啤酒; Anhui Lu, 安徽路; beer ¥10-15; ⊙9.30am-10pm; Ⓜ Qingdao Railway Station) Order your Tsingtao beer in a plastic bag with a straw from this typical hole-in-the-wall beer shop, and take it down to the beach to sip at sunset.

Hey John Coffee
CAFE

(海角咖啡, Hǎijiǎo Kāfēi; No 1 Bathing Beach, 第一海水浴场; coffee from ¥22; ⊙10am-6pm; Ⓜ Huiquan Sq) Up on the boardwalk, and with shaded terrace seating, this is the only cafe overlooking No 1 Bathing Beach that does proper coffee.

Spark Café & Brewery
BREWERY

(咖啡酿酒厂, Kāfēi Niàngjiǔ Chǎng; ☑ 0532 8578 2296; 35 Donghai Xilu, May 4th Sq, 东海西路35号, 五四广场; ⊙11am-10pm, food until 8.30pm; Ⓜ May 4th Sq) Grab a seat on a long wooden bench in this crowded watering hole on the east edge of the Municipal Government Square. There's all manner of drinks – beer (including the house 'dark' and 'light' microbrews at ¥35 a pint), cocktails, coffee, tea and milkshakes. Sister restaurant The Diner

MADE IN TSINGTAO

The beer of choice in Chinese restaurants around the world, Tsingtao is one of China's oldest and most respected brands. Established in 1903 by a joint German–British corporation, the Germania-Brauerei began as a microbrewery of sorts using spring water from nearby Lao Shan to brew a Pilsener Light and Munich Dark for homesick German troops. In 1914 the Japanese occupied Qingdao and confiscated the plant, rechristening it Dai Nippon and increasing production to sell under the Tsingtao, Asahi and Kirin labels. In 1945 the Chinese took over and gave the brewery its current name. At first, only China's elite could afford to drink it, but advertisements touting Tsingtao as a health drink boosted its appeal, and in 2014 the world drank more than 181 million kegs of the golden brew.

brings over burgers, pizza and sausage platters (mains ¥40 to ¥100).

☆ Entertainment

Qingdao Grand Theatre THEATRE
(青岛大剧院, Qīngdǎo Dàjùyuàn; ✆0352 8066 5555; www.qingdaograndtheatre.com; 5 Yunling Lu, 云岭路5号; tickets from ¥50; 🚌230, 321, Ⓜ Shilaoren Beach) Housed in a striking modern structure, the city's grand performing-arts centre puts on world-class theatre, opera, music, dance and comedy on its three stages. It's 1km east of Shilaoren Beach metro station; come out of Exit A2, walk straight along Xianggang East Rd and it's soon on your left.

Zhōngguó Diànyǐngyuàn CINEMA
(中国电影院; 97 Zhongshan Lu, 中山路97号; tickets ¥30; ⊗first/last showing 10am/9pm; Ⓜ Qingdao Railway Station) This historic 1930s cinema is much cheaper than the larger ones inside the city's modern shopping malls and at least one of its three screens usually shows a Hollywood blockbuster in English.

🛍 Shopping

Culture Street ANTIQUES
(文化路, Wénhuà Lù; Changle Lu, 长乐路; ⊗8am-4pm) 'Antiques' and handicrafts are sold on the street in front of a tidy row of concession architecture north of Old Town. The most vendors come out on Saturday and Sunday.

Take bus 2 to from Zhongshan Lu to Tai Dong (台东) bus stop, then walk back 100m.

Mix C MALL
(万象城, Wànxiàng Chéng; Shandong Luu, 山东路; ⊗10am-10pm; Ⓜ May 4th Sq) The city's snazziest shopping mall has all your retail cravings covered, plus an ice rink, a cinema, an indoor theme park and a rooftop garden. Right beside May 4th Sq metro station.

Jimolu Market MALL
(即墨路小商品市场, Jímòlù Xiǎoshàngpǐn Shìchǎng; 45 Liaocheng Lu, 聊城路45号; ⊗9am-5.30pm) A four-storey bargain bonanza north of Old Town, with pearls, clothing, shoes, backpacks, jade, wigs – all for the haggling.

ℹ Information

Skip the travel agencies and consult with one of the city's youth hostels for travel advice.

Useful websites include That's Qingdao (www.thatsqingdao.com), with listings and news clips, and Red Star (www.myredstar.com), an online entertainment guide and monthly magazine available in hostels, bars and foreign restaurants.

ATMs are easy to find in Qingdao.

Bank of China (中国银行, Zhōngguó Yínháng; 68 Zhongshan Lu, 中山路68号; ⊗9am-5pm Mon-Sat) is on Zhongshan Lu at Feicheng Lu in Old Town. Also in the tower at the intersection of **Fuzhou Nanlu and Xianggang Zhonglu** (59 Xianggang Zhonglu, 香港中路59号; ⊗8.30am-5pm) in the CBD. Branches have currency exchange and 24-hour ATMs.

ℹ Getting There & Away

A handy ticket office sells air, train and ferry tickets to the ground floor of the **Xin Tianqiao Hotel** (青岛新天桥宾馆售票处, Qīngdǎo Xīn Tiānqiáo Bīnguǎn Shòupiàochù; ✆air & boat 0532 8612 0222, train & bus 0532 8612 0111; 47 Feicheng Lu, 肥城路47号; usual commission ¥5; ⊗7.30am-9pm), near the train station, though no English is spoken. Otherwise hostels can help.

AIR

Qingdao's **Liuting International Airport** (青岛流亭国际机场, Qīngdǎo Liútíng Guójì Jīchǎng; ✆booking & flight status 0532 8471 5139, hotline 96567; www.qdairport.com; Minhang Lu, Chengyang District, 城阳区民航路; 🚌701, 702, 703) is 30km north of the city. There are flights to most large cities in China. International flights include daily flights to Seoul and Tokyo.

BUS

Check train schedules before you hop on a long-distance bus; they are usually faster, cheaper and more frequent.

Among Qingdao's many bus stations, the **long-distance bus station** (青岛长途汽车站, Qīngdǎo Chángtú Qìchēzhàn; ☑ 0532 8375 4240; 2 Wenzhou Lu) in the Sifang district (四方区, Sìfāng Qū), north of the Old Town, best serves most travellers. A limited number of buses also depart for provincial destinations, including Yantai (¥84, four hours, hourly, 6am to 5.30pm), directly across from the train station.

Daily direct buses from the long-distance bus station include the following:

Beijing Seat/sleeper ¥228/258, 11 hours, two daily (1pm and 3.10pm)

Qufu ¥134, six hours, two daily (6.50am and 2.30pm)

Tai'an ¥128, six hours, two daily (7am and 12.30pm)

Tianjin ¥177, eight to nine hours, one daily (8am)

Weihai ¥100, four hours, five daily (noon, 2pm, 3.20pm, 5pm and 7.30pm)

Yantai ¥83, four hours, roughly hourly (7.20am to 5.20pm)

TRAIN

Qingdao has numerous train stations. The oldest, most central and most attractive is the 120-year-old **Qingdao Train Station** (青岛火车站, Qīngdǎo Huǒchē Zhàn; ☑ 0532 9510 5175; 2 Tai'an Lu, 泰安路2号), but high-speed trains often use **Qingdao North Train Station** (青岛北站, Qīngdǎo Běizhàn; Cangtai Lu, 沧台路; Ⓜ Qingdao North Railway Station). Both are connected to the metro system.

It's easy to buy tickets at the train stations on the day of travel, unless you're buying sleeper tickets to far-off destinations, or travelling during national holidays. Most local people buy their tickets online these days, which means queues aren't too long. There will be little if any English spoken, though; your hotel or hostel may also be able to help.

Bullet trains (1st-/2nd-class seat) from Qingdao Train Station include the following:

Beijing South ¥524/314, 4½ to five hours, nine daily (6.55am to 5.06pm)

Ji'nan ¥194/120, two to three hours, 30 daily (5.30am to 7.43pm)

Qufu East ¥296/179, 3½ hours, eight daily (6.17am to 6.39am)

Shanghai ¥877/527, seven hours, one daily (4.22pm)

Shanghai Hongqiao ¥948/572, seven hours, two daily (7am and 9.07am)

Tai'an (for Tai Shan) ¥242/149, three to 3½ hours, eight daily (6.25am to 6.39pm)

Weifang ¥90/55, one hour, 40 daily (6.17am to 8.16pm)

Yantai South ¥100/62, 1½ to two hours, four daily (8.03am, 1.06pm, 5.22pm and 6pm)

Regular trains (seat/hard sleeper) from Qingdao Train Station include the following:

Ji'nan ¥55/101, five to six hours, four daily (6.01am, 11.01am, 4.37pm and 5.40pm)

Tai Shan ¥69/123, five to 6½ hours, six daily (6.01am, 11.01am, 1.44pm, 2.03pm, 4.37pm and 4.58pm)

Xi'an ¥190/323, two daily at 11.01am (23½ hours) and 1.44pm (17½ hours)

Bullet trains (1st-/2nd-class seat) from Qingdao North Train Station include the following:

Beijing South ¥550/336, three to 4½ hours, five daily (7.53am, 8.30pm, 12.55pm, 1.12pm and 7.20pm)

Shanghai Hongqiao ¥872/524, seven hours, one daily (1.57pm)

Xi'an North ¥645/1035, nine hours, three daily (6.29am, 10.35am and 2.03pm)

Yantai South ¥92/57, 1½ hours, 10 daily (7am to 3.22pm)

ⓘ BORDER CROSSINGS: QINGDAO TO JAPAN & SOUTH KOREA

International boats cross the Yellow Sea to South Korea from **Qingdao Cruise Terminal** (青岛母港, Qīngdǎo Mǔgǎng; Youlungang Rd, 邮轮港路), about 1km north of Old Town.

Weidong Ferry Company (威东航运, Wēidōng Hángyùn; ☑ 0532 8280 3574; www.weidong.com; ground fl of Cruise Terminal, 青岛母港; tickets from ¥780) operates boats to Incheon (仁川; 16½ hours, Monday, Wednesday and Friday, check in at 2.30pm, depart at 5.30pm, from here as well as from Yantai. The cheapest tickets (¥780) are for bunks in a large 50-person dorm. Private four-person rooms cost ¥920 per person.

Boats are almost never sold out so buying tickets on the day of departure at the cruise terminal is the norm; tickets go on sale from 1.30pm. For peace of mind you might want to call ahead just to check the boat you intend to take hasn't been booked out by a huge tour party. Some staff speak English. Alternatively, you can buy tickets at some ticket offices in the city, like the one at Xin Tianqiao Hotel (p242).

To get to the cruise terminal, take bus 217 (¥1) from the train station, and get off at Da Gang (大港) bus stop, or simply walk from Old Town: 400m north up Guanxian Rd (冠县路), then left down Youlungang Rd (邮轮港路).

❶ Getting Around

TO/FROM THE AIRPORT

Bright-blue airport shuttle buses (¥20, 80 minutes, 4.15am to 9.40pm) follow three routes through town. The handiest if you're staying in the Old Town is the 702 (also just 2 on some bus stops), which starts at the train station and stops along Zhongshan Lu. The 703 starts at the Grand Regency Hotel, on Xianggang Zhonglu, 10km east of the Old Town, and the 701 starts at the Fu Xin Hotel on Minjiang Lu, just east of Zhongshan Park. There's also an airport shuttle from North Train Station (¥10, 35 minutes, 8.40am to 6pm).

A taxi from the Old Town is at least ¥100. A metro line connecting the city with the airport is under construction.

BUS

Most city buses cost ¥1 or ¥2 (exact change needed), but onboard conductors issue tickets for further destinations.

A huge number of local buses leave from various bus stops outside Qingdao Train Station, which also has a metro station.

To get to the long-distance bus station (p243), take bus 325 (¥1, 30 minutes) from the train station, or along Zhongshan Lu, and get off at Qingdao Liushiliu Zhong (青岛六十六中) bus stop, then walk back 100m and turn left.

METRO

Qingdao's fledgling metro system (four lines and counting) links Qingdao Train Station with sights along the south coast, including Zhongshan Park and some of the beaches. It also serves the CBD, Qingdao North Train Station, and the northern section of Lao Shan. Dahedong, Lao Shan's main south gate, is also due to get its own metro station soon.

Tickets cost ¥2 to ¥8, and trains run from around 6am to 10.30pm.

TAXI

Flagfall is ¥10 for the first 3km and then ¥2.20 per kilometre thereafter.

Lao Shan 崂山

📞 0532

A quick ride 28km east from Qingdao, an arresting jumble of sun-bleached granite and hidden freshwater springs rises over the sea. It's easy to understand why Lao Shan (Láo Shān) has attracted spiritual pilgrims throughout the centuries. These days it's a great place to escape the city and recharge.

In his quest for immortality, Emperor Qin Shi Huang ascended these slopes (with the help of a litter party of course), and in the 5th century Buddhist pilgrim Faxian landed here returning from India with a complete set of Buddhist scriptures. Lao Shan has its share of religious sites, but it is most steeped in Taoist tradition. Adepts of the Quanzhen sect, founded near Yantai in the 12th century, cultivated themselves in hermitages scattered all over the mountain.

Paths wind past ancient temples (and ruins), bubbling springs trickling into azure pools, and inscriptions left by Chinese poets (and German alpinists).

❂ Sights & Activities

You almost need a degree in logistics to get your head around the ticketing system for Lao Shan. Some areas of the mountain have their own separate admission ticket, but there are also two-day joint-area tickets (summer/winter ¥130/100) and three-day all-area tickets (summer/winter ¥180/120). Then there are tickets for shuttle buses (¥60) and cable cars (from ¥35 one way). Try to be clear about where you want to go when buying your ticket.

There are several official scenic areas within the park, some of which are included on the same ticket. There are three main entrances:

Dahedong On the west side of the park, this is the closest to Qingdao, and the most popular gateway to the mountain.

Yangkou On the far eastern side, this is also very popular but takes longer to reach.

Beijiushui This lies between the two, if travelling around the northern edge of the park; Beijiushui is quieter, and easy to reach, but its trails aren't connected up to the other scenic areas.

Dahedong is the main gateway to the park and the start of the picturesque hike to Jufeng, the highest peak. You can access Taiqing Palace from either Dahedong or Yangkou. For the most part, routes are paved but there are plenty of opportunities to go off piste (look for red flags tied to branches marking trails).

Beijiushui Scenic Area CANYON

(北九水景区, Běijiǔshuǐ Jǐngqū; Jan-Mar ¥40, Apr-Dec ¥65; Ⓜ Beijiushui) This canyon area at the north end of Lao Shan is mostly flat and takes a couple of hours to traverse. The path winds alongside and across clear, blue streams before reaching **Chaoyin Waterfall** (潮音瀑, Cháoyīn Pù). The ticket office outside the metro station is 8km from the trailhead. There's a shuttle bus (¥30 return) to the trailhead, but it's much cheaper to take local bus 639 (¥1 one way) from opposite the metro station. You can buy your park entrance ticket when you get off the bus.

Jufeng
MOUNTAIN
(巨峰, Jùfēng; Jan-Mar ¥90, Apr-Dec ¥120) Most easily reached from the Dahedong (大河东, Dàhédòng) entrance to the park, this peak – the name literally means 'Huge Peak' – is Lao Shan's highest point at 1133m above sea level. If you take the **cable car** (巨峰索道, Jùfēng Suǒdào; one way/return ¥40/80) part way up the mountain, it's another four hours up steps past temples and a spring to the stone terrace at the peak and awe-inspiring views of mountains, sky and sea. It's a tremendous walk, but load up with water on a hot day.

Taiqing Palace
TAOIST TEMPLE
(太清宫, Tàiqīng Gōng; ¥27, plus ¥130 park entrance; ⊙ closes 5.30pm) Accessible from either the Dahedong entrance or the Yangkou entrance, Lao Shan's oldest and grandest temple was established by the first Song emperor around AD 960 to perform Taoist rites to protect the souls of the dead. Taoist devotees in blue and white still live here, and many credit their good health to drinking from the **Spring of the Immortals** (神水泉, Shénshuǐ Quán), which feeds into the grounds. The massive ancient gingko, cedar and cypress trees also apparently benefit your health.

Yangkou Scenic Area
MOUNTAIN
(仰口景区, Yǎngkǒu Jǐngqū; Jan-Mar ¥100, Apr-Dec ¥130) You can ascend this scenic area by foot or **cable car** (仰口景区索道, Yǎngkǒu Jǐngqū Suǒdào; one way/return ¥35/60) past wind- and water-carved granite. There's a 30m scramble in total darkness up a crevice to the top of **Looking for Heaven Cave** (觅天洞, Mìtiān Dòng) and then upwards still for bright views to the sea. The hike up takes about three hours. Your ticket includes entrance to three areas of the park (Yangkou, Taiqing and Huayan) and is good for two days.

🛏 Sleeping & Eating

There are numerous sleeping options right outside the Yangkou entrance, and a few on the approach to Dahedong (though they aren't very close). Rooms are much more expensive than staying in Qingdao though, so unless you bag a particularly nice place it's probably not worth staying out here, especially once the metro reaches Dahedong in 2020.

There are several restaurants outside the Yangkou entrance, but none immediately outside either Dahedong or Beijiushui, and very few inside the park (other than snack shops selling instant noodles).

ℹ Getting There & Away

Getting from Qingdao's Old Town to each of the main entrances using public transport is straightforward. Note that Dahedong metro station is due to open in 2020.

Dahedong Bus 304 or 301 (¥4, 90 minutes) from Qingdao Train Station, or metro to Shilaoren station (¥4, 20 minutes) then bus 104 or 310 (¥2, 20 minutes).

Yangkou Metro to Beijiushui station (¥6, 45 minutes), then bus 383 (¥2, 45 minutes).

Beijiushui Metro to Beijiushui station (¥6, 45 minutes), then bus 639 (¥1, 5 minutes) to the entrance proper.

Most buses back to Qingdao run until just before 8pm.

Note that tourist bus 5 (旅游5) links Beijiushui metro station and Dahedong (¥2, 45 minutes), but is only hourly.

The bus stop outside Beijiushui station is called Da Lao (大崂).

ℹ Getting Around

Private cars and taxis aren't allowed within park boundaries, but shuttle buses (unlimited rides ¥60) at each gate cover the routes. Local buses (¥1 to ¥2) skirt the fringes of the park, though none links Dahedong with Yangkou along the southeastern coastal stretch.

Most of your travel within the park will be on foot, although a cable car runs part way up Jufeng, and there is another cable car that ascends the Yangkou Scenic Area.

Weifang
潍坊

📞 0536 / POP 2 MILLION

Breezy Weifang (Wéifāng), birthplace of kites, offers unusual diversions for an easy day trip from Qingdao. The city was also the site of the Weixian Internment Camp, run by the Japanese during WWII to keep British, American, Australian and Canadian citizens, as well citizens of other nationalities, confined until the Japanese surrender in 1945, when it was liberated by a US rescue team.

In late April every year, delegations from 30 countries fly in for two days of **kite competitions** (潍坊国际风筝节; www.wfyilin.com; ⊙ late Apr), races, demos and general revelry in the giant open field on Fuyan Shan (浮烟山, Fúyān Shān), 16km southwest of the city.

It's a total field day for kite fanatics and the sky's the limit.

The riverside **Kite Museum** (潍坊风筝博物馆, Wéifāng Fēngzheng Bówùguǎn; ☑0536 825 1752; 66 Xingzheng Jie, 行政街66号; ◷9am-4.30pm Tue-Sun) FREE tells the story of kites – from the first one, a bamboo magpie fashioned in Weifang 2400 years ago by Lu Ban (he's the winged figure in front of the museum), to their use in warfare, meteorology, hunting, cartography and eventually the study of electricity. Kites of various styles, including some of the smallest and largest in the world, constructed by mostly master makers, are also on display. And you can buy them in the 1st-floor shop. The only disappointment is that there aren't any genuinely old kites on display. To get here from the train station, take bus 2 (¥2) four stops to Fēngzheng Guǎngchǎng (风筝广场) bus stop. Or it's a 2km walk; cross the square outside the station, turn right, left, then right down Jiankeng Xijie (健康西街). After crossing the river turn left and follow the river to the museum.

Shihu Yuan Museum (十笏园博物馆, Shíhù Yuán Bówùguǎn; 345 Hujia Paifang Jie, off Dongfeng Xijie, 东风西街胡家牌坊街345号; ¥30; ◷8.30am-5pm) is a Ming-dynasty courtyard home that belonged to Ding Shanbao, a Jiangsu merchant who at one time owned half the town. In 1885 he restored the property as his private residence and put the focus on its garden, considered a masterpiece of Suzhou-style design with an unusually compact arrangement of the requisite pond, bridge, pavilion and surrounding rockery. To get here from the train station, take bus 3 (¥2) four stops to Dōngfēng Jiē Xiàngyáng Lù Lùkǒu (东风街向阳路路口) bus stop, or it's a 2km walk; cross the square in front of the train station, turn left, then right along Xiangyang Jie (向阳路) for about 800m. Turn right onto Dongfeng Xijie (东风西街) and the museum is on your left behind the newly constructed old-style buildings.

Weifang is a large city and finding somewhere to eat is not difficult. There are places to eat and drink along the river, north of the Kite Museum, and in the reconstructed old-style lanes around Shihu Yuan Museum.

There are more than 50 high-speed trains a day from Qingdao (2nd-class seat ¥52 to ¥55, one to 1½ hours) and a similar amount from Ji'nan (2nd-class seat ¥65, 1½ to two hours). Buy your ticket to Weifang station (潍坊站, Wéifāng Zhàn), rather than the less central Weifang North station (潍坊北, Wéifāng Běi).

Yantai 烟台

☑0535 / POP 2.2 MILLION

The sleepy portside town of Yantai (Yāntái) has managed to court foreign investment in its high-tech industry while building itself into a popular beach resort with a distinctive treaty port history. A tunnel connects the older, tourist-friendly district of Zhifu (芝罘, Zhīfú) with the booming Laishan (莱山, Láishān) district to the southeast. For now, this is still a place where you can take things easy. And with Penglai Pavilion not far away, the town makes for a relaxing two-day sojourn.

History

Starting life as a defence outpost and fishing village, Yantai's name literally means 'Smoke Terrace': wolf-dung fires were lit on the headlands during the Ming dynasty to warn villagers of Japanese marauders. Yantai was thrust under the international spotlight in the late 19th century when the Qing government, reeling from defeat in the Opium War, signed over the city to the British and French, who established a treaty port here, when it was known as Chefoo (Zhifu). The rest of the eight-nation alliance followed with outposts, which remained until the province was captured by the Japanese in WWII. After the war, China kept Yantai's ports (ice-free in winter) open for foreign trade.

MAKING COPIES

For millennia, everything from imperial decrees to poetry, religious scriptures and maps were preserved by carving them into stone. This was done either as an inscription (yin-style) or a relief (yang-style). Copies were made by applying ink to the stone and pressing rice paper onto it, or by tamping a damp sheet of paper into the crevices and allowing it to dry, before patting ink onto the paper's surface. Over time, even stone would wear and the clearest, best-made prints became works of art themselves. Unfortunately, this prompted unscrupulous collectors to damage carvings to ensure they had the very best copy. These are some of the gouges and scratches you see in many of the most prized tablets and stelae.

◉ Sights

Sadly, the charming old-town street, Chaoyang Jie, and the lanes fanning off it, were closed at the time of research as part of a large renovation project, and some of our favourite restaurants, bars and hostels had been shut down and/or demolished. Quite how the area will emerge post-renovation is anyone's guess, but fingers crossed that the treaty-port heritage architecture remains unscathed.

There is still some pleasant strolling to be done along Binhai Beilu, a wide seaside promenade that's a popular evening hangout for kite-flying, karaoke-singing locals. Another buzzing early evening spot is the multi-level square in front of **Yantai Grand Theatre** (烟台大剧院, Yāntái Dà Jùyuàn; Nan Dajie, 南大街), where impromptu singing performances strike out among the badminton players, taichi practitoners and children on scooters.

Yantai Folk Custom Museum　　MUSEUM
(烟台民俗博物馆, Yāntái Mínsú Bówùguǎn; 257 Nan Dajie, 南大街257号; ◉9am-5pm Tue-Sun May-Oct, to 4.30pm Tue-Sun Nov-Apr; ▣43, 46) FREE It's really the architecture that's the big draw at this museum, housed in an amazing guild hall built between 1884 and 1906 by arrivals from Fujian (福建, Fújiàn). In the centre of the courtyard is a spectacularly intricate, decorated gate. Supported by 22 pillars, it's adorned with hundreds of carved and painted figures, phoenixes and other beasties, depicting classic folk tales including *The Eight Immortals Crossing the Sea*.

Yantai Hill Park　　PARK
(烟台山公园, Yāntáishān Gōngyuán; Chaoyang Jie, 朝阳街; park entrance free, lighthouse ¥10; ◉5am-5.30pm) FREE This quaint park of stone paths, leafy gardens and ocean vistas is also a museum of western treaty port architecture. Wolf-dung fires burned continuously along the smoke terrace above, beginning in the 14th-century reign of Emperor Hongwu. Stroll by the former **American Consulate Building**, which retains some original interior features and contains an exhibit on Yantai's port days. Nearby, the former **Yantai Union Church** dates from 1875. The former **British Consulate** overlooks the bay with its annexe surrounded by an overgrown English garden.

Laishan Beach　　BEACH
(莱山海水浴场, Láishān Hǎishuǐ Yùchǎng; ▣17) This vast expanse of golden sand in the developing district 11km east of the old town attracts clam diggers and sunbathers alike. Get off at the Huanghai City Flower Garden (黄海城市花园) stop.

No 1 Beach　　BEACH
(第一海水浴场, Dìyī Hǎishuǐ Yùchǎng; Binhai Beilu, 滨海北路; ▣17) One of Yantai's two main beaches, No 1 Beach is a long stretch of soft sand in a calm bay.

No 2 Beach　　BEACH
(第二海水浴场, Dì'èr Hǎishuǐ Yùchǎng; Binhai Zhonglu, 滨海中路; ▣17) About 3km east of the old town, No 2 Beach is rocky in parts but surrounded by lively tide pools.

Yantai Museum　　MUSEUM
(烟台市博物馆, Yāntái Shì Bówùguǎn; ☏0535 623 2976; 61 Nan Dajie, 南大街61号; ◉9am-5pm Tue-Sun May-Oct, to 4.30pm Tue-Sun Nov-Apr; ▣43, 46) FREE The sparkling museum traces the historical development of the Jiaodong peninsula, where Yantai currently stands, from the prehistoric age and successive kingdoms to the present day. There's a display on the 'Shell Mound' culture (a glimpse at a Neolithic civilisation's rubbish) and a wonderful collection of rare porcelain. There are reasonable English descriptions.

Changyu Wine Culture Museum　　MUSEUM
(张裕酒文化博物馆, Zhāngyù Jiǔwénhuà Bówùguǎn; 56 Dama Lu, 大马路56号; incl tasting ¥80; ◉8am-4.30pm) The Changyu Wine Culture Museum introduces the history of China's oldest and largest western-style winery, which produces grape wines as well as brandy and a Chinese 'health liquor'. Cheong Fatt-Tze, dubbed China's Rockfeller, founded the winery in 1894, after overhearing at a party at the French consulate that Yantai's climate might suit vineyards. Tastings of Changyu's (so-so but improving) wines are in the atmospheric, old wine cellar.

🛌 Sleeping

Most low-budget hotels do not accept foreign guests.

Hi Inn　　HOTEL ¥
(海友酒店, Hǎiyǒu Jiǔdiàn; ☏0535 215 0088; 79 Nan Dajie, 南大街79号; s/d from ¥99/169; ❋🛜) Rooms are tiny at this budget chain hotel, but they're very clean and tidy, and come with TV, kettle and a small desk. This is also one of the few cheapies that's happy to accept foreigners. The pool table in the lobby area is a nice little bonus.

Yantai

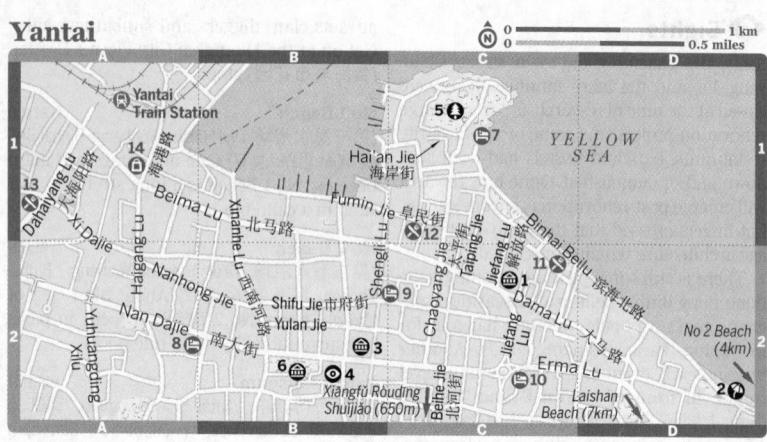

Yantai

◎ Sights

Pacific Hotel   HOTEL ¥

(太平洋大酒店, Tàipíngyáng Dàjiǔdiàn; ☑ 0535 658 8866; www.pacifichotel.com.cn; 74 Shifu Jie, 市府街74号; r from ¥90; ❄🛜) This hulking old-timer needs a serious facelift, but its rooms (and their windows) are enormous, it's dirt cheap and it welcomes foreigners, so we mustn't grumble. The cheapest rooms are quite tattered so bump yourself up to the next category (¥120) for less worn furniture and smarter bathrooms.

Shandong Machinery Hotel   HOTEL ¥¥

(山东机械大厦, Shāndōng Jīxiè Dàshà; ☑ 0535 622 4561; 162 Jiefang Lu, 解放路162号; d from ¥260; ❄🛜) With a ground-floor coffee shop and an international ticketing office on the premises, staff here know how to cater to non-Mandarin-speaking guests. The Asian-decor rooms have nicer details (wooden soaking tubs) than the western ones, but are all way nicer than the building's exterior suggests. Staff are congenial. Some rooms have distant sea views. Breakfast costs ¥20.

Golden Gulf Hotel   HOTEL ¥¥¥

(金海湾酒店, Jīnhǎiwān Jiǔdiàn; ☑ 0535 663 6999; 34 Hai'an Lu, 海安路34号; d incl breakfast from ¥700; ❄🛜) This impressive top-end hotel has a superb location, overlooking the sea and backing onto the park. Rooms are bright and well maintained, staff are pleasant, and the 1st-floor 'Sunshine Garden' catches a lovely sea breeze.

🍴 Eating

As well as the places to eat dotted around town, a good variety of restaurants, plus one or two cafes, can also be found in the luxury **Joy City** (大悦城, Dàyuè Chéng; 150 Beima Lu, 北马路150号; ⏲10am-10pm) shopping mall.

Xiāngfǔ Ròudǐng Shuǐjiǎo   DUMPLINGS ¥

(乡府肉丁水饺; ☑155 0545 3700; 75 Fulai Lijie, 福来里街75号; dumplings ¥20-40; ⏲8am-2pm & 4.30-9pm; 🚌6) At the south end of Fulai Lijie, this tiny restaurant draws foodies from afar with its speciality dumplings (水饺,shuǐjiǎo); the ones stuffed with tender *bàyú* (鲅鱼; ¥40 per *jīn*, more than enough for two), a locally caught mackerel, are delicious. A half portion (*bàn fēnr*) is plenty for solo diners. There are other dishes too, with a photo menu on the wall.

To get here, turn right off Nan Dajie onto Beihe Jie (北河街) and just keep walking. Beihe Jie becomes Fulai Lijie and the restaurant is eventually on your left, in a friendly neighbourhood with lots of low-key shops and restaurants.

Rùn Xuān Měishí Jiē   STREET FOOD ¥
(润轩美食街; cnr Xida Jie & Dahaiyang Lu, 西大街和大海阳路拐角处; snacks from ¥10; ⊙8am-10pm) A small pedestrianised 'food street' lined with street-food stalls and noodles joints.

No 9 Courtyard   BARBECUE ¥¥
(9号院, Jiǔ Hào Yuàn; Binhai Beilu; skewers ¥3-15, dishes ¥30-70; ⊙10.30am-1pm & 5.30pm-midnight) Set back from the promenade, but still with a view of the sea, this place comes alive in the evening when the barbecue is wheeled out, and punters sit in the courtyard enjoying grilled skewers (lamb chunks, chicken wings, tofu), pints of craft beer (¥25) or just plain old bottles of Tsingtao (¥12).

Róngxiáng Hǎixiān   SEAFOOD ¥¥
(荣祥海鲜; ☑155 0663 3177; 25-1 Fumin Jie, 阜民街25-1号; mains from ¥35; ⊙11am-9pm) At this perpetually packed local institution, the seafood is crawling/swimming/blinking at one end of the room where you put in your order. Everything is priced, even the veggies; you just point at what you want, and they'll go off and cook it.

🍷 Drinking & Nightlife

One or two drinking spots can be found on or near the promenade of Binhai Beilu.

ℹ️ Information

Bank of China (中国银行, Zhōngguó Yínháng; 166 Jiefang Lu, 解放路166号; ⊙9am-5pm Mon-Sat) ATM accepts all cards; changes money.

Yantai Shan Hospital (烟台山医院, Yāntái Shān Yīyuàn; ☑0535 660 2001; 91 Jiefang Lu, 解放路91号) Chinese-speaking only.

ℹ️ Getting There & Away

AIR
Yantai Penglai International Airport (烟台蓬莱国际机场, Yāntái Pénglái Guójì Jīchǎng; Yingbin Balu, 迎宾八路) serves both Yantai and Penglai and is around 43km northwest of Yantai. Book tickets online at www.english.ctrip.com.

There are flights to all major Chinese cities plus a few to South Korea.

BUS
From the **long-distance bus station** (汽车总站, Qìchē Zǒng Zhàn; ☑0535 666 6111; Xi Dajie, 西大街) there are buses to numerous destinations, including the following:

Beijing ¥258, 11 hours, at least one daily (7.20pm)

Ji'nan ¥150, 5½ hours, four daily (8am, 10am, 1.15pm and 4.10pm)

Penglai ¥28, 1½ hours, frequently (5.30am to 6pm)

Qingdao ¥84, four hours, hourly (5am to 5pm)

Weihai ¥30, one hour, every 45 minutes (6am to 6pm)

Yantai Penglai International Airport ¥20, one hour, half-hourly (4.30am to 8.30pm)

DALIAN–YANTAI TUNNEL

Two decades in the making, the blueprints are almost done for China's next epic infrastructure project: a ¥220 billion tunnel 100ft under the bottom of the Bo Sea that will trace Yantai's coastline before curving north to Dalian in Liaoning province.

At 123km long, the Dalian–Yantai tunnel will be longer than the two previous record-holders combined – the Seikan Tunnel (between Honshu and Hokkaido in Japan) and the 'Chunnel' (between Britain and France). More importantly, it will cut a seven-hour boat ride or a 1400km road trip down to a 40-minute high-speed-train ride or a quick drive, linking China's north and south like never before.

The tunnel will actually be three – one channel each for cars, trains and maintenance – plus many more vertical ventilation pipes bored through the ocean floor. Building it will rely on engineering that hasn't been tested before, and critics point out that the tunnel could disturb two active fault lines. Architects counter with the argument that it will all be accounted for in the plans. The tunnel was originally slated to open before 2020, but the go-ahead for construction has still yet to be met with final approval, and once started it will take an estimated 10 years to complete.

BORDER CROSSINGS: SOUTH KOREA

Boats depart three times a week from Yantai Harbour International Passenger Terminal (p250) for both Incheon (仁川, Rénchuān) and Pyeongtaek (平泽, Píngzé) in South Korea.

Boats are rarely sold out so tickets can be usually be bought on the day of departure from the terminal building's ticket office (to your right as you approach the terminal). Boats depart for Incheon (17 hours, check-in 3.30pm, departure 6pm) on Monday, Wednesday and Friday. Bunks in four-bunk and two-bunk dorms cost ¥600 and ¥700 per person respectively. VIP double rooms are ¥1588. Boats to Pyeongtaek (from ¥950, check-in 3.30pm, departure 6pm, 14½ hours) run on Tuesday, Thursday and Sunday.

Note that the relevant ticket counters are only open on the day of departure for the destination in question, but you can buy them in advance. Some English is spoken (though not much).

TRAIN

Trains departing from **Yantai Train Station** (火车站, Huǒchē Zhàn; ☑ 0535 9510 5175; Beima Lu, 北马路) include the following:

Beijing K-class soft/hard-sleeper ¥349/223, 15 hours, one daily (10.33pm)

Beijing South G-class bullet 1st/2nd-class seat ¥361, six hours, two daily (6.43am and 2.18pm)

Ji'nan K-class seat/hard-sleeper ¥75/133, seven hours, three daily (3.32pm, 6.33pm and 10.48pm)

Ji'nan G/D-class bullet 2nd-class seat ¥165, four hours, 10 daily (6.43am to 5.43pm)

Qingdao D/C-class bullet 1st/2nd-class seat ¥106/66, two hours, two daily (2.55pm and 3.57pm)

Qufu East G-class bullet 1st/2nd-class ¥336/226, 4½ hours, three daily (9.10am, 10.10am and 5.43pm)

Tai'an (for Tai Shan) G-class bullet 1st/2nd-class ¥312/194, 4½ hours, two daily (9.10am and 5.43pm)

Tai Shan K-class seat/hard-sleeper ¥81/144, 8½ hours, two daily (9.30am and 10.48pm)

High-speed trains from **Yantai South Train Station** (烟台南站, Yāntái Nán Zhàn), also known as 'Gāotiě Zhàn' (高铁站; high-speed train station), include the following:

Beijing South G-class bullet 2nd-class seat ¥357-375, five to six hours, three daily (9.44am, 1.08pm and 3.21pm)

Ji'nan G/D-class bullet 2nd-class seat ¥162, three to four hours, 13 daily (8.04am to 6.15pm)

Qingdao D/C-class bullet 1st/2nd-class seat ¥100/62, two hours, four daily (10.26am, 2.07pm, 5.01pm and 8.51pm)

Qingdao North D/C-class bullet 1st/2nd-class seat ¥92/57, 1½ hours, 10 daily (7.42am to 8.47pm)

Getting Around

TO/FROM THE AIRPORT

Airport shuttle buses (机场巴士, Jīchǎng Bāshì; ☑ 0535 629 9146; ¥20) leave half-hourly from the long-distance bus station between 4.30am and 8.30pm and take around one hour.

BOAT

It's very easy to purchase same-day tickets for ferries to Dalian (大连, Dàlián; seat ¥190, bed ¥210 to ¥890, seven hours, six daily, 9am to 10.30pm) at the **Yantai Harbour International Passenger Terminal** (烟台港国际客运站, Yāntáigǎng Guójì Kèyùnzhàn; ☑ 0535 660 7314, 0535 650 6666; www.bohaiferry.com; 155 Beima Lu, 北马路155号; ☉ 8.30-11.30am & 1.30-4.30pm), from ticket offices east of the train station or inside the exit area of the long-distance bus station, which have more extended hours. There's also at least one boat a day (sometimes two or three) to Lushun (旅顺, Lǚshùn; tickets from ¥160, 6½ hours).

BUS

Bus 17 (¥1) conveniently runs along Yantai's coastline, from the train station and on past all the main beaches that are worth jumping off for. Bus 6 runs along Beima Lu from the old town to the **Beima Lu Bus Station** (北马路汽车站, Běimǎ Lù Qìchē Zhàn; ☑ 0535 665 8714; cnr Beima Lu & Qingnian Lu, 北马路青年路的路口).

If you're catching a high-speed train from Yantai South Station, take **shuttle bus No 1** (高铁巴士1号线, gāotiě bāshì yī hào xiàn; ¥1, 40 minutes) from Yantai Train Station, or **shuttle bus No 2** (高铁巴士2号线, gāotiě bāshì èr hào xiàn; ¥1, 35 minutes) from Nan Dajie.

TAXI

Taxi flagfall is ¥8 for the first 6km and ¥1.80 (slightly more at night) per kilometre thereafter. It's about a ¥70 ride to the airport.

Penglai　　蓬莱

☑ 0535 / POP 450,000

The city of Penglai (Pénglái) has long been connected with the Taoist legend of the Eight Immortals Crossing the Sea. Though the exact location of the legendary land of Penglai, where the Four Immortals were said to live, is disputed, Penglai City in Shandong (about 75km northwest of Yantai) enjoys an understandable connection to the legend, especially thanks to the 1000-year-old Penglai Pavilion, which sits on a mountain overlooking the Bo Sea.

◎ Sights

Beside Penglai Pavilion, but outside its ticketed scenic area, is a stretch of quiet, sandy **beaches** that are perfect for a paddle. To get there, turn left out of the Penglai Pavilion scenic area, then left down Zhonglou Beilu (钟楼北路).

Penglai Pavilion   HISTORIC SITE
(蓬莱阁, Pénglái Gé; ¥120; ⊙ 7am-5pm; 🚍 4, 5 or 7)
About 75km northwest of Yantai, perched on a bluff overlooking the waves, the 1000-year-old Penglai Pavilion is closely entwined with Chinese mythology and the Taoist legend of the Eight Immortals Crossing the Sea. The entrance to the ticketed scenic area is at the south end, and the route up to the pavilion passes the grounds of an ancient naval base and a series of temples. The pavilion itself is unassuming as its restored exterior is rather similar to surrounding structures.

Inside is a collection of prized inscriptions left by famous visitors since the Song dynasty, and a beautiful modern rendering of the Eight Immortals by Zhou Jinyun. There are many versions of the story, but in this one the immortals, who came from different walks of life, shared drinks at the pavilion before crossing the Bo Sea using unique superpowers.

Close to the pavilion, and still within the ticketed scenic area, you can zip across the bay by **cable car** (索道, suǒ dào; one way/return ¥30/50; ⊙ 8am-5.10pm) for cliffside walks overlooking the Bo and Yellow Seas. The park also contains **museums** (open 7.30am to 5.30pm) dedicated to ancient shipbuilding, regional relics and Qi Jiguang, a local-born Ming-dynasty general who battled pirates.

If you arrive after a heavy rain, keep an eye out for mirages at sea that have appeared every few years. Long ago, this earned Penglai a reputation as a gateway to immortal lands and compelled Emperor Qin Shi Huang to send ships in search of islands of immortality further east.

🛏 Sleeping & Eating

There are many hotels in Penglai city, but few accept foreigners, so most travellers visit as a day trip from Yantai.

The road leading down to the beach, Zhonglou Beilu, is lined with restaurants.

Xī'ān Xǐchángcháng Miànguǎn   NOODLES ¥
(西安喜常常面馆; Zhonglou Beilu, 钟楼北路; noodles ¥12-28; ⊙ 6am-10pm) On the right as you walk towards the beach, just past Joy Plaza, this unassuming Shaanxi noodles joint is easily the best of the numerous restaurants on this stretch of Zhonglou Beilu. There are many types of noodles, but the house-speciality *yóupō làròu miàn* (油泼辣肉面, slightly spicy, flat noodles with beansprouts, spinach leaves and succulent chunks of cured pork; ¥16) is not to be missed.

❶ Getting There & Away

Penglai is an easy day trip by bus from Yantai (¥28, 1½ hours, frequent from 5.30am to 6pm), with the last bus returning at 6.30pm. Buses from Yantai terminate at Penglai's **New Bus Station** (新车站, Xīn Chē Zhàn; Zhonglou Nanlu, 钟楼南路), 3km south of the entrance to the pavilion's scenic area.

To get to Penglai Pavilion from the bus station, you can walk (turn right out of the bus station and you'll soon pick up the signs), take local buses 4, 5 or 7 (one way ¥1 to ¥2) to Qichezhan Beimen (汽车站北门) bus stop, or take the special shuttle buses (return ¥5) provided by a tourist company who will also sell you cost-price tickets to the pavilion at the bus station.

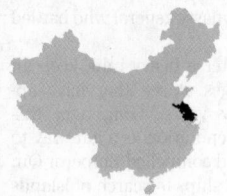

Jiangsu

POP 80.1 MILLION

Best Places to Eat

➜ Tóng Dé Xīng (p271)

➜ Yǎba Shēngjiān (p271)

➜ Aladdin (p262)

➜ Gūsū Cài Guǎn (p272)

Best Places to Stay

➜ Little Days Folk House (p271)

➜ Blue Gate Youth Hostel (p271)

➜ Yihe Mansions (p261)

➜ Garden Hotel (p271)

Why Go?

A zip – and an entire world – away from Shanghai, well-irrigated Jiangsu (江苏, Jiāngsū) spills over with as much charm and history as the waters that flow through its shimmering canals. The province, which owed its historical wealth to silk and salt production, boasts the Grand Canal as well as elaborate waterways that thread through this Yangzi River (Cháng Jiāng) region. It's known throughout China for its cute canal towns, enchanting gardens and sophisticated opera and folk arts.

Tourists descend on Suzhou all four seasons of the year, but kick-start your day early, go slightly off the main streets, and you'll see the old-world charm and have the place to yourself. In the lovely provincial capital and university town of Nanjing there's a lot that remains relatively undiscovered by outsiders: Ming-dynasty heritage, leafy boulevards, superb museums and some fantastic restaurants.

When to Go
Nanjing

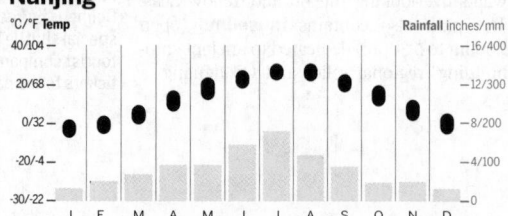

Mar & Apr Best time to visit the gardens when flowers bloom in early spring.

Oct Mist-shrouded vistas of gardens and canals in autumn.

Dec Snow-covered views of the pretty canal towns in winter.

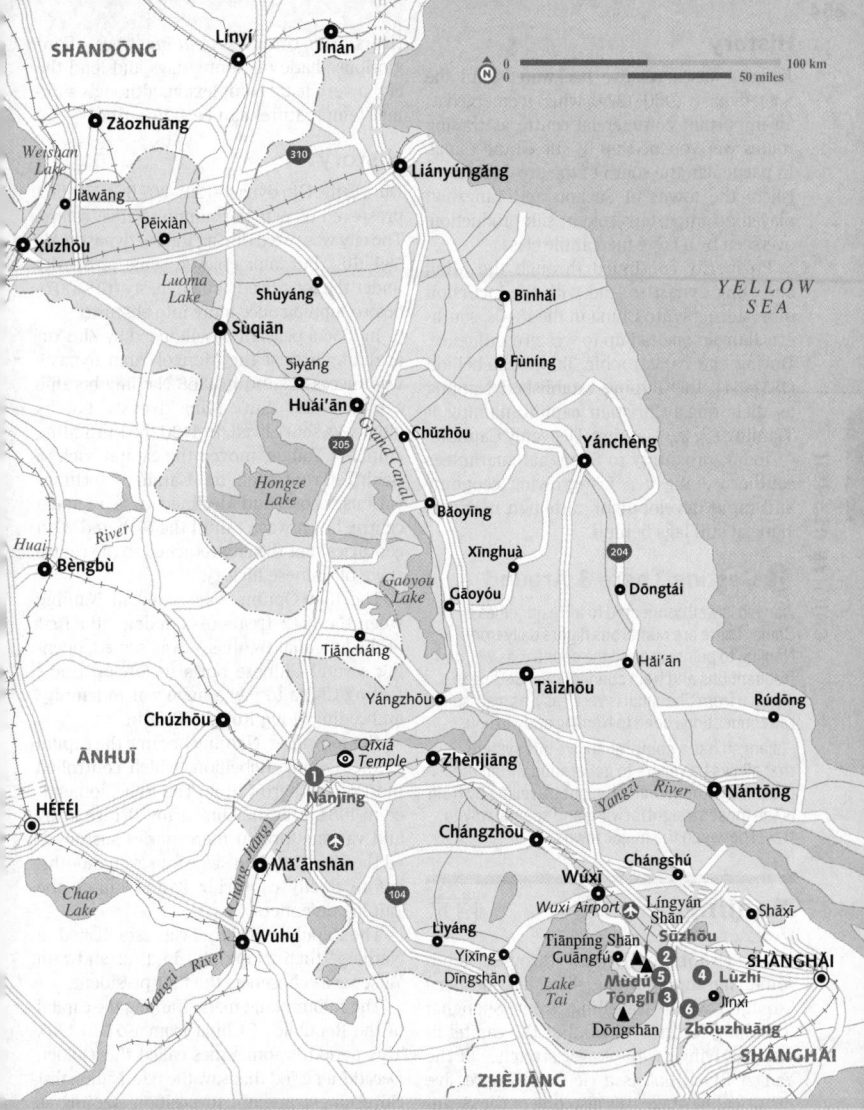

Jiangsu Highlights

1 **Nanjing** (p254) Admiring Nanjing Museum's splendid collection, climbing the sturdy brickwork of the City Walls and exploring Zijin Mountain.

2 **Suzhou** (p265) Feasting your eyes on the modern architecture of Suzhou Museum, being charmed by traditional gardens and strolling along delightful Pingjiang Lu.

3 **Tongli** (p276) Losing yourself in the water town's alleys and canals, stopping at small museums and enjoying the atmosphere.

4 **Luzhi** (p278) Relaxing at a charming canalside restaurant in this popular water town.

5 **Mudu** (p275) Taking a day trip to visit ancient residences and a hilltop temple.

6 **Zhouzhuang** (p277) Ticking off the delightful bridges and residences of this good-looking canalside settlement.

History

Jiangsu was a relative backwater until the Song dynasty (960–1279), when it emerged as an important commercial centre as trading routes were opened up by the Grand Canal. In particular, the south of the province flourished: the towns of Suzhou and Yangzhou played an important role in silk production, overseen by a large mercantile class.

Prosperity continued through the Ming and Qing dynasties, and with the incursion of westerners into China in the 1840s, southern Jiangsu opened up to western influence. During the catastrophic Taiping Rebellion (1851–64), the Taiping established Nanjing as their quasi-Christian capital, naming it Tianjing (天京, Tiānjīng, Heavenly Capital).

Today, proximity to Shanghai guarantees southern Jiangsu a fast-growing economy and rapid development, although northern Jiangsu still lags behind.

ⓘ Getting There & Around

Jiangsu is well connected to all major cities in China. There are numerous flights daily from Nanjing to points around the country, as well as frequent bus and train connections. Getting to Jiangsu from Shanghai is very easy, as high-speed rail connections head to Nanjing and Suzhou.

Jiangsu has a comprehensive bus system that allows travellers to get around the province without difficulty, but travelling by train is the most straightforward and speedy way to travel between the major towns.

Nanjing   南京

▸ 025 / POP 8.3 MILLION

Many visitors only pass through handsome Nanjing (Nánjīng; literally 'Southern Capital') when travelling from Shanghai to Beijing (or vice versa), but the capital of Jiangsu, lying on the lower stretches of the Yangzi River, boasts a rich and impressive historical heritage. It's also one of the cleanest and best-looking cities in China.

The major attractions are the echoes of the city's brief, former glory as the nation's capital during its Ming-dynasty apogee and then as the capital of the Republic of China. A magnificent city wall still encloses most of Nanjing, and elegant republican-era buildings dot the centre.

The famous university town's atmosphere is both cultured and relaxed, with wide, tree-lined boulevards and excellent museums, in a fine landscape of lakes, forested parks and rivers. The countless *wutong* trees afford glorious shade on sunny days and lend the city a very leafy complexion, although summer temperatures can be suffocating.

History

During the Qin dynasty (221–207 BC), Nanjing prospered as a major administrative centre. The city was razed during the Sui dynasty (AD 589–618), but later enjoyed some prosperity under the long-lived Tang dynasty (618–907), before slipping once more into obscurity.

In 1356 a peasant rebellion led by Zhu Yuanzhang against the Mongol Yuan dynasty was successful and in 1368 Nanjing became capital under Zhu's Ming dynasty, but its glory was short-lived. In 1420 the third Ming emperor, Yongle, moved the capital back to Beijing. From then on Nanjing's fortunes variously rose and declined as a regional centre, but it wasn't until the 19th and 20th centuries that the city returned to the centre stage of Chinese history.

The first Opium War ended in Nanjing when the 1842 Treaty of Nanking – the first of the 'unequal treaties' – was signed, opening several Chinese ports to foreign trade, forcing China to pay a huge war indemnity, and ceding Hong Kong to Britain.

Not long after, Nanjing became the capital of the Taiping Rebellion, which controlled most of southern China. The Rebellion ended in 1864 after the Qing army, British army and various foreign mercenaries surrounded the city. They laid siege for seven months, before finally capturing it and killing the Taiping defenders.

The Republic of China was established in Nanjing (then 'Nanking') in 1912 and Sun Yatsen was chosen as the first president.

The Kuomintang made Nanjing the capital of the Republic of China from 1927 to 1937. This period is sometimes called the 'Golden Decade', a period that saw the new Nationalist Government attempt to position Nanjing as a modern capital through economic growth and some major construction projects, including the Sun Yatsen Mausoleum.

The capital was shifted inland to Chongqing as Japanese troops advanced in 1937. When the troops reached Nanjing, they massacred 200,000 to 300,000 civilians in six horrific weeks, known as the 'Rape of Nanking'. Lingering at the edge of living memory, the invasion still looms large in the identity of the city today.

THE RAPE OF NANJING

In 1937, with the Chinese army comparatively weak and underfunded and the Japanese army on the horizon, the invasion and occupation of Nanjing (or Nanking, as it was known then) appeared imminent. As it packed up and fled, the Chinese government encouraged the people of Nanjing to stay and the city gates were locked, trapping more than half a million citizens inside.

What followed in Nanjing was six weeks of brutality to an extent unwitnessed in modern warfare. According to journalists and historians such as Iris Chang and Joshua Fogel, between 200,000 and 300,000 Chinese civilians were killed, either in group massacres or individual murders, during Japan's occupation of the city. Within the first month at least 20,000 women between the ages of 11 and 76 were raped. Women who attempted to refuse or children who interfered were often bayoneted or shot.

As well as stories of survival, the atrocities are documented in the **Memorial Hall of the Nanjing Massacre** (南京大屠杀纪念馆, Nánjīng Dàtúshā Jìniànguǎn; 418 Shuiximen Dajie, 水西门大街418号; ⊙8.30am-4.30pm Tue-Sun; M Yunjin Lu) **FREE**, in the city's southwestern suburbs. Exhibits include pictures of actual executions and a gruesome viewing hall built over a mass grave of massacre victims. At times it feels overwhelming, but visitors will begin to fathom the link between the massacre and the identity of the city.

JIANGSU NANJING

◉ Sights

The majority of Nanjing's sights fall within the boundaries of the old city walls. To the south, near Zhonghua Gate, the Laomendong area is home to a selection of boutique cafes and bookshops. It's popular in the evenings, when the trees are prettily lit. Fūzǐ Miào, where you'll find the Confucian Temple and Imperial Exams museum, is also popular for an evening stroll.

Xinjiekou is the city's buzzing central business district, home to malls, food courts and a massive subway interchange.

Peaceful Xuanwu Park is in the north, where you'll also find the city's most prestigious universities and student-dive-bar street, Shanghai Jie.

Just east of Zhongshan Gate, Zijin Mountain comprises more than 100 historical attractions and three show-stopping sights: ancient Ming Xiaoling Tomb, Sun Yatsen Mausoleum and Linggu Temple.

◉ East Nanjing

Presidential Palace HISTORIC BUILDING
(总统府, Zǒngtǒng Fǔ; 292 Changjiang Lu, 长江路292号; ¥40; ⊙8.30am-6pm Mar–mid-Oct, to 5pm mid-Oct–Feb; M Daxinggong, exit 5) After the Taiping took over Nanjing, they built the **Mansion of the Heavenly King** (天王府, Tiānwáng Fǔ) on the foundations of a former Ming-dynasty palace. This magnificent palace did not survive the fall of the Taiping, but there is a reconstruction and a classical Ming garden, now known as the Presidential Palace. Other buildings on the site were used briefly as presidential offices by Sun Yatsen's government in 1912 and by the Kuomintang from 1927 to 1949.

Ming Palace Ruins PARK
(明故宫, Míng Gùgōng; 311 Zhongshan Donglu, 中山东路311号; ⊙7.30am-9.30pm; M Minggugong) **FREE** Built by Zhu Yuanzhang in the 14th century, the imperial palace was reportedly a magnificent structure that served as a template for Beijing's Forbidden City. The ruins are part of pleasant **Wuchaomen Park** (午朝门公园, Wǔcháomén Gōngyuán) **FREE**, which is frequented by badminton-playing and ballroom-dancing locals as well as saxophonists and other musicians who practise in the resonant tunnels at the southern end of the park.

★**Nanjing Museum** MUSEUM
(南京博物院, Nánjīng Bówùyuàn; www.njmuseum.com; 321 Zhongshan Donglu, 中山东路321号; ⊙9am-noon Mon, to 5pm Tue-Sun; M Minggugong, exit 1) **FREE** This fabulous museum has three dramatically modern exhibition blocks alongside a traditional, temple-style hall. Exhibits range from 20th-century brush-and-ink paintings to ancient calligraphy (including sutra scrolls from Dunhuang) and a magnificent Han-dynasty jade burial suit.

Don't miss the **Gallery of the Republican Period**, a kitschy underground recreation of Nanjing in its 1930s heyday, complete with working cafes, post office and (stationary) steam engine. The adjoining **Digital Gallery** has a handful of interactive exhibits suitable for kids. Bring your passport.

Nanjing

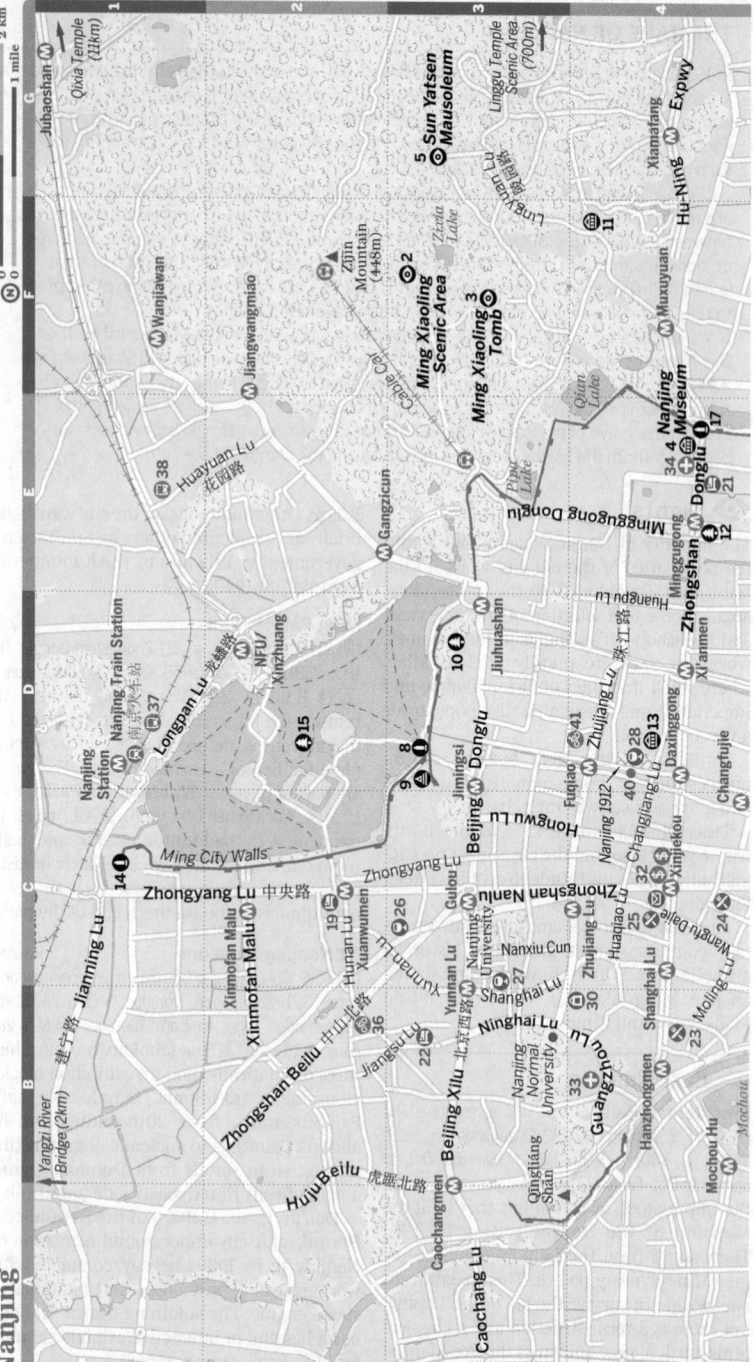

Qixia Temple (11km)

Jubaoshan

2 km
1 mile

Yangzi River Bridge (2km)

Jianning Lu 建宁路

Nanjing Station

Nanjing Train Station 南京火车站

Longpan Lu 龙蟠路

Huayuan Lu 花园路

Wanjiawan

Jiangwangmiao

Gangzicun

Cuiping Creek

Zijin Mountain (448m)

Ming Xiaoling Scenic Area

Ming Xiaoling Tomb 3

2

Zixia Lake

5 Sun Yatsen Mausoleum

Linggu Lu 灵谷路

Linggu Temple Scenic Area (700m)

Xiamafang

Hu-Ning Expwy

11

Qian Lake

Piqi Lake

4 Nanjing Museum 17

34 4

Donglu 21

12

Minggugong Donglu

Zhongshan

Xi'anmen

Muxuyuan

Xinzhuang

NFU

15

10

Jiuhuashan

8

9

Jimingsi

Beijing Donglu

Dongzhu Lu

Hongwu Lu

Huangpu Lu

Fuqiao

41

Nanjing 1912

40

28

Zhujiang Lu 珠江路

13

Daxinggong

Changfujie

14

Zhongyang Lu 中央路

Xinmofan Malu

Xinmofan Malu

Hunan Lu

Xuanwumen

Zhongyang Lu

19

26

Gulou

Nanjing University

Yunnan Lu

27

Shanghai Lu

Nanxiu Cun

Zhongshan Nanlu

Zhujiang Lu

Huaqiao

30

32

25

Xinjiekou

Shanghai Lu

Changjiang Lu

Moling Lu

24

Wangfu Dajie

23

Zhongshan Beilu 中山北路

36

Jiangsu Lu

22

Beijing Xilu 北京西路

Ninghai Lu

Nanjing Normal University

33

Guangzhou Lu

Hanzhongmen

Mochou Hu

Mochou

Huju Beilu 虎踞北路

Caochangmen

Qingliang Shan

Caochang Lu

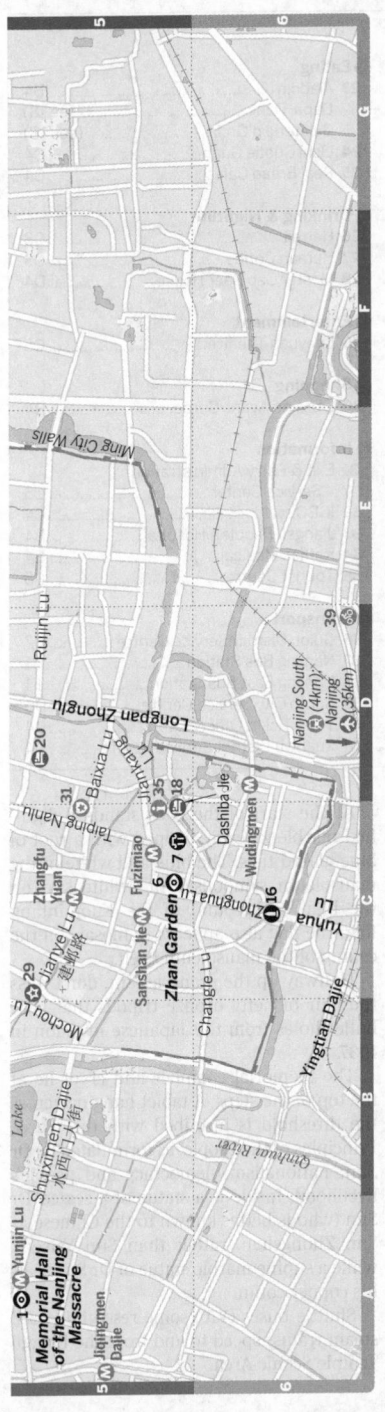

Zijin Mountain

Heavily forested Zijin Mountain (紫金山, Zǐ-jīn Shān) is one of the coolest escapes from the steamy summer heat and is home to scores of historical attractions. It's named 'Purple-Gold Mountain' for the raw-copper hue of the trees at dusk.

Expect crowds: start early and give yourself a full day to explore it properly. A combo ticket for Ming Xiaoling Tomb and Linggu Temple Scenic Area is valid for two days and costs ¥100.

Meiling Palace
HISTORIC BUILDING

(美龄宫, Měilíng Gōng; ¥30; ⊙7.30am-5.30pm; MMuxuyuan) Named by *Life* magazine in 1937 as 'the most powerful woman in the world', Song Meiling (aka 'Madame Chiang') was the First Lady of the Republic of China (1948–1975). An accomplished politician and painter, Meiling was actively involved in politics for much of her life, acting as English translator and adviser for her husband, Chiang Kaishek.

The complete furnishings, English explanations and unique focus on an extraordinary woman make this museum a particularly special find in China.

★ Ming Xiaoling Scenic Area
TOMB

(明孝陵风景区, Míng Xiàolíng Fēngjǐngqū; ⊙6am-6pm; ☑Y3, MMuxuyuan) FREE This scenic area on Zijin Mountain has loads of opportunities for rambling, but the main attraction is **Ming Xiaoling Tomb** (明孝陵, Míng Xiàolíng; ¥70), the magnificent mausoleum of Zhu Yuanzhang (1328–1398), the founding emperor of the Ming dynasty (also known as the Hongwu Emperor), and the only Ming emperor buried outside Beijing.

A tree-lined pathway winds around pavilions and picnic grounds and ends at scenic Zixia Lake, ideal for strolling.

The mausoleum begins with a 618m 'spirit path', lined with stone statues of lions, camels, elephants and horses that drive away evil spirits and guard the tomb. Among them lurk two mythical animals: a *xiè zhì*, which has a mane and a single horn on its head, and a *qílín*, which has a scaly body, a cow's tail, a deer's hooves and one horn.

Follow the path (and the crowds) past halls and a temple and you'll come to the grand stone frontage of the tomb. The uphill tunnel leads to a retaining wall for a huge earth tumulus (called the **Soul Tower**; 明楼,

JIANGSU NANJING

Nanjing

Mínglóu), beneath which is the unexcavated tomb vault of the emperor. On the wall are inscribed the characters '此山明太祖之墓' ('This hill is the tomb of the first Ming emperor').

From Muxuyuan metro station (Line 2), it's a 1.6km walk uphill. Tour bus Y3 from the city centre also takes you here.

★ **Sun Yatsen Mausoleum** MEMORIAL
(中山陵, Zhōngshān Líng; ⊙8.30am-5pm Tue-Sun; ⊟9, 34, Y1, Y2, Y3, Ⓜ Xiamafang) **FREE** An astonishing sight at the top of an enormous stone stairway (a breathless 392 steps), Sun Yatsen's tomb is a mandatory stop for most visitors. Reverentially referred to as *guófù* (国父, Father of the Nation), Dr Sun is esteemed by both communists and Kuomintang. He died in Beijing in 1925, and had wished to be buried in Nanjing, no doubt with far less pomp than the Ming-style tomb his successors fashioned for him. Within a year of his death, however, construction of this mausoleum began.

Admission is ticketed; bring your passport to collect a free ticket.

At the start of the path stands a dignified marble gateway, capped with a roof of blue-glazed tiles. The blue and white of the mausoleum symbolises the white sun on the blue background of the Kuomintang flag; the flag also appears in mosaic on the ceiling of the mausoleum itself.

Halfway up the grand ascent, don't miss the pair of hefty bronze tripods that bear bullet holes from the Japanese invasion in 1937.

The memorial chamber and crypt lie at the top of the steps. A tablet hanging across the threshold is inscribed with the 'Three Principles of the People', as formulated by Dr Sun: nationalism, democracy and people's livelihood. Inside is a statue of a seated Dr Sun (who is better known to the Chinese as Sun Zhongshan, rather than Sun Yatsen), while a supine marble statue of Dr Sun seals his copper coffin.

Shuttle buses (¥10, some resembling red steam trains) speed to and from the Linggu Temple Scenic Area.

★**Linggu Temple**
Scenic Area   BUDDHIST TEMPLE
(灵谷寺风景区, Línggǔ Sì Fēngjǐng Qū; ¥35; ⏰7am-5.30pm; 🚌Y2, Y3, Ⓜ Zhonglingjie, then bus 202) This expansive temple complex contains one of the most historic buildings in Nanjing – the **Beamless Hall** (无梁殿, Wúliáng Diàn), built in 1381 entirely out of brick and stone and containing no beam supports. Buildings during the Ming dynasty were normally constructed of wood, but timber shortages meant that builders had to rely on brick. The structure has a vaulted ceiling and a large stone platform where Buddhist statues once sat.

A road runs on both sides of the hall: head to the right for the **Dàbiàn Juétáng** (大遍觉堂) memorial hall, dedicated to Xuan Zang (the Buddhist monk who travelled to India and brought back the Buddhist scriptures). Inside the memorial hall is a statue of the travelling monk, brush aloft, with a cabinet housing a golden model of a pagoda with part of Xuan Zang's skull within it. To his left is a model wooden pagoda, also within a cabinet.

Uphill to the rear of the temple is the colourful **Linggu Pagoda** (灵谷塔, Línggǔ Tǎ). This nine-storey, 60m-high, octagonal pagoda was finished in 1933 under the direction of a US architect to remember those who died during the Kuomintang revolution. A vegetarian restaurant can be found nearby.

To get to the scenic area, take the metro to Zhonglingjie station, then catch bus 202 (¥2, five minutes, every 15 minutes) from Linggu Si Jie, a short walk west of metro Exit 5a, past the shopping centre. Open-sided shuttle buses regularly connect the area to the Sun Yatsen Mausoleum.

◉ **South Nanjing**

★**Zhan Garden**   GARDENS
(詹园, Zhān Yuán; 128 Zhan Yuan Lu, 瞻园路128号; ¥30; ⏰8.30am-5.30pm; Ⓜ Sanshanjie) If you don't have time to get to Suzhou, visit this delightful Ming-dynasty garden complex that once housed Taiping officials. The on-site **Taiping History Museum** (太平天国历史博物馆, Tàipíng Tiānguó Lìshǐ Bówùguǎn) is included with your ticket, but it's the garden itself that's the real draw. With willows, acers, magnolias, bamboo, potted bonsai pines and a lovely lawn, the garden is also decorated with courtyards, pools, corridors and rockeries.

Fūzǐ Miào   CONFUCIAN TEMPLE
(夫子庙; Gongyuan Jie, 贡院街; ¥30; ⏰9am-10pm; Ⓜ Fuzimiao, exit 2) In the south of the city in a smartened-up pedestrian zone full of restaurants, the Confucian temple Fūzǐ Miào has been a centre of Confucian study for more than 1500 years. What you see today, however, are newly restored, late-Qing-dynasty structures or wholly new buildings reconstructed in traditional style. The area surrounding the temple is a popular place for a stroll, particularly at night, when the streets are attractively lit up and the atmosphere is at its most festive.

JIANGSU NANJING

MING CITY WALLS

Unlike the lost city walls of Beijing and Shanghai, an impressive two-thirds of Nanjing's fabulous city wall is still in place today. Measuring more than 25km, Nanjing's imposing, five-storey Ming bastion is the longest city wall ever built.

Built between 1366 and 1393, by more than one million labourers, the layout of the wall is unusual for its time; rather than taking a square format, the wall zigzags around Nanjing's hills and rivers, accommodating the landscape. Averaging 12m high and 7m wide at the top, the fortification was built of bricks supplied from five Chinese provinces. Each brick was stamped with the place it came from, the overseer's name and rank, the brick-maker's name and sometimes the date. This was to ensure that brick-makers were held accountable for poorly made bricks. Many of these stamps are still intact today.

Some of the original 13 heavily fortified Ming city gates remain, including **Zhongshan Gate** (中山门, Zhōngshān Mén; Ⓜ Minggugong) in the east and the restored **Zhonghua Gate** (¥50; ⏰10am-9pm Mon-Thu, to 10pm Fri) in the south. You can climb onto the masonry for exploration at several points for long walks and fantastic views of town.

One of the best spots for starting or ending a treetop stroll is **Shence Gate** (神策门, Shéncè Mén; ¥30; ⏰8.30am-5pm; Ⓜ Nanjing Station), a short walk northwest of Xuanwu Lake. From Shence, you can walk all the way to Taiping Gate (5.2km) or hop off at Xuanwu Gate (2km) or Jiefang Gate (3.5km; p260) for a jaunt in **Xuanwu Lake Park** (玄武湖公园).

LIBRAIRIE AVANT-GARDE

Housed in a disused car park under Wutaishan Stadium, this astonishingly vast indie **bookshop** (先锋书店, Xiānfēng Shūdiàn; ☑ 8371 1455; 173 Guangzhou Lu, 广州路173号; ☺ 10am-9pm Mon-Thu, to 10pm Fri-Sun; Ⓜ Shanghai Lu) has very few foreign-language books, but the left-field ambience, chill cafe and miles of books make it a Nanjing cultural landmark, loved by students and literati alike.

Tour boats (游船, *yóuchuán*) leave from the dock across from the temple itself for 30-minute day (¥60) and evening (¥80) trips along the Qinhuai River (秦淮河, Qínhuái Hé) between 9am and 10pm.

Jiangnan Imperial Examination Hall
MUSEUM

(江南贡院历史陈列馆, Jiāngnán Gòngyuàn Lìshǐ Chénlièguǎn; 1 Jinling Lu, 金陵路1号; combined ticket ¥50; ☺ 9am-10pm; Ⓜ Fuzimiao, exit 2) The north section (北馆; ¥40) of this extensive subterranean museum, marked by the stunning reflection pool on Gongyuan Jie, has contemporary displays on imperial China's civil-service examinations and their modern-day equivalent, the *gāokǎo* (national college entrance examinations). Above ground, don't miss the reconstructions of the buildings where scholars once spent months – or years – in tiny booths preparing for the exacting examinations.

Across the street, the much-smaller **South Hall** (南馆; ¥25) has some old photographs and ceramic artefacts on display.

⊙ North Nanjing

Jiuhuashan Park
PARK

(九华山公园, Jiǔhuáshān Gōngyuán; Beijing Donglu, 北京东路; ☺ 8am-8pm; Ⓜ Jiuhuashan, exit 1) **FREE** This underrated park, just south of Xuanwu Lake, has a peaceful world-away feel and a delightful array of statues dotted around its leafy hills. The park is also home to a Buddhist temple and **Sanzang (Tripitaka) Pagoda**, which is said to contain a fragment of skull belonging to Xuan Zang, the monk of *Journey to the West* fame.

Jiming Temple
BUDDHIST TEMPLE

(鸡鸣寺, Jīmíng Sì; Jimingsi Lu, 鸡鸣寺路; ¥10; ☺ 7.30am-5.15pm; Ⓜ Jimingsi, exit 5) The most active temple in Nanjing, Jiming Temple was first built in AD 527 during the Three Kingdoms period and has been rebuilt many times since.

Enter the base of seven-storey-tall Yaoshifo Pagoda (药师佛塔, Yàoshīfó Tǎ) to see the spectacle of hundreds of small, gold Buddha figures in cabinets before heading into the on-site restaurant for a good-value vegetarian meal with a handy picture menu and excellent views towards the city's Ming walls.

At the time of writing, renovations had closed off the rear walkway to the **city wall** (¥30, 8am to 4pm), but it is only a short 150m-walk from the back of the temple to **Jiefang Gate** (解放门, Jiěfàng Mén; ¥30; ☺ 8.30am-5pm).

Xuanwu Lake Park
PARK

(玄武湖公园, Xuánwǔhú Gōngyuán; ☺ 6am-8pm; Ⓜ Xuanwumen, Nanjing Station) **FREE** The glassy lake in this lovely, verdant 530-hectare park – backing onto the towering city wall – is studded with five interconnected isles scattered with bonsai gardens, camphor and cherry-blossom trees, temples and bamboo groves. It's a lovely escape from Nanjing's urban expanses, while the entire lake circuit is a whopping (and enjoyable) 9.5km jaunt. There are also boat rides (¥120 to ¥140 per hour) and miniature train rides (¥20; 8.30am to 4.45pm).

Yangzi River Bridge
BRIDGE

(南京长江大桥, Nánjīng Chángjiāng Dàqiáo; incl Bridge Park ¥15; ☐ 67, Ⓜ Shangyuanmen) Opened in 1968, the Yangzi River Bridge is one of the longest bridges in China – a double-decker with a 4.5km-long road on top and a train line below. The odds are that you'll probably cross the bridge if you take a train from the north. Your ticket includes lift access to the viewing platforms, where you can admire the stirring socialist-realist sculptures and city views from up high.

✲ Festivals & Events

Qinhuai Lantern Festival
CULTURAL

(秦淮灯会, Qínhuái Dēnghuì; ☺ Jan/Feb) Held towards the end of Chinese New Year, this lantern festival is the biggest of its kind in China. People gather at Fūzǐ Miào, Zhonghua Gate and a handful of other locations around the city to admire extravagant lighting displays and to fly lanterns, a festival tradition that dates back to the Song dynasty.

★ **Nanjing International Plum Blossom Festival** CULTURAL
(梅花节, Méihuā Jié; ☉Feb-Mar) Held yearly from the last Saturday of February to mid-March, this festival takes place on Plum Blossom Hill near the Ming Xiaoling Tomb when the mountain explodes into pink and white blossoms. It's a gorgeous sight.

🛏 Sleeping

Most of Nanjing's accommodation is mid-range to top end in price and it can be hard to score a bargain. Most hotels, and particularly hostels, are geared towards domestic tourists, making English-speaking staff a rarity. Translation apps can help bridge the divide if you need assistance booking air and train tickets.

Fuzimiao Hostel HOSTEL ¥
(夫子庙国际青年旅舍, Fūzǐmiào Guóji Qīngniánlǚshě; ☎8662 5133; 68-3 Pingjiangfu Jie, 平江府路68-3号; dm ¥70, r ¥220-300; ❄🛜; Ⓜ Line 3 to Fuzimiao, exit 2) Fuzimiao Hostel is in a near-unbeatable location, close to the metro and just a minute's walk from Fūzǐ Miào. While dorms are basic and rooms can be scruffy around the edges, the rooftop beer garden is spectacular. Proximity to the canal makes mosquito repellent a good idea if you're sitting out after dusk.

Mork House HOSTEL ¥
(陌客青年旅舍, Mòkè Qīngniánlǚshě; ☎8435 3119; 402 New World Plaza, 85 Changfu Jie, 常府街85号新大都广场甲幢402; dm with/without bathroom ¥130/100; Ⓜ Line 3 to Changfu Jie) Mork House is a popular hostel burrowed into the 4th floor of a nondescript shopping mall. It's well run and well kept. Bunks are stacked three high, with decent privacy curtains and roomy lockers, although some overflow beds in the common area are considerably less private. Fairy lights, card games and beanbags dominate the common room.

The entrance is around the back of Changfu Jie; take lift 1 up to reception.

Orange Hotel HOTEL ¥¥
(桔子酒店, Júzi Jiǔdiàn; ☎025 6608 1122; www.orangehotel.com.cn; 532-1 Zhongshan Donglu, 中山东路532-1号; r ¥260-370; ❄@🛜; Ⓜ Minggugong) In a handy location opposite the museum, the Donghuamen branch of Orange Hotel has spick-and-span rooms with daily cleaning. Line 2 of the metro and the Ming Palace Ruins are just a hop, skip and jump away.

Lake View Xuanwu Hotel HOTEL ¥¥
(玄武饭店, Xuánwǔ Fàndiàn; ☎8681 1111; www.lakeviewxuanwuhotel.com; 193 Zhongyang Lu, 中央路193号; r from ¥600; P🅿❄🛜🏊; Ⓜ Line 1 to Xuanwu, exit 1) Conveniently situated next to Xuanwu Lake Park and the metro, this four-star hotel offers comfortable rooms and pleasant, if slightly outdated, decor. Some rooms have excellent views out over the lake (although the windows could be cleaner).

★ **Yihe Mansions** HISTORIC HOTEL ¥¥¥
(颐和公馆, Yíhé Gōngguǎn; ☎8486 8888; info@yihemansions.com; 3 Jiangsu Lu, 江苏路3号; r ¥3600; Ⓜ Yunnan Lu) Situated in Nanjing's former legation quarters, Yihe Mansions is a collection of magnificently restored former embassies and homes of military generals. Rooms are generous in size, with Nanjing-era dark-wood interiors and luxurious linens. You may hear the occasional rumble from the antique plumbing, but the enormous marble bathrooms are in excellent nick. Online discounts of up to 70% are not uncommon.

🍴 Eating

Nanjing abounds with fantastic. For street food, snacking zones and loads of restaurants, the main eating quarters include the Fūzǐ Miào area, Shiziqiao (狮子桥) off Hunan Lu, and Fengfu Lu (丰富路) south of Xinjiekou, where you can find snack stands and small eateries. Slick restaurants can be found towards the centre, in the large malls around Xinjiekou, and dotted around town.

ℹ PRICE RANGES

Eating

The following price ranges refer to the cost of a main course.

¥ less than ¥30

¥¥ ¥30–70

¥¥¥ more than ¥70

Sleeping

The following price ranges refer to the cost of a double room with private bathroom or shower room.

¥ less than ¥280

¥¥ ¥280–800

¥¥¥ more than ¥800

JIANGSU NANJING

★ **Lǐshì Guōtiē Guǎn** DUMPLINGS ¥

(李氏锅贴馆; ☏ 136 0158 2717; 25 Shigu Lu, 石鼓路25号; noodle soups ¥15-22; ⏰ 7am-9pm; ❄ 🀚; Ⓜ Xinjiekou, exit 15) This restaurant is popular for its juicy and totally delicious beef 'potsticker' dumplings (牛肉锅贴, *niúròu guōtiē*). These golden, crispy wonders are easy on the wallet (¥10 for five) if not the waistline. Order and pay inside and collect the dumplings from the front.

There's no English menu but there are pictures around, so pointing is always an option.

Gelateria d'Orcia GELATO ¥

(奥尔怡雪糕, Àoěrqià Xuěgāo; 29 Dashiba Jie, 大石坝街29号; ⏰ 10am-9pm; 🀚; Ⓜ Line 3 to Fuzimiao, exit 2) A small cafe serving up yummy Italian-style gelato, made on-site. Friendly, English-speaking service. The salted caramel flavour is especially delicious. One scoop in a tub is ¥17, while a decent cappuccino is ¥18.

Real Bread Cafe BAKERY ¥

(☏ 177 1433 0275; 47-5 Guan Jia Qiao, 管家桥47-5号; pastries ¥16-28; ⏰ 7.30am-9pm Mon-Fri, from 8am Sat & Sun; ❄ 🀚; Ⓜ Xinjiekou, exit 20) The best bakery in Nanjing, Real Bread Cafe serves its sandwiches in suitably crusty bread and its coffee (¥25) delightfully strong. Delicate and crispy pastries steal the show, from sugar-topped cruffins to Insta-worthy croissants with flavours such as strawberry milkshake or black-pepper parmesan.

Dàpái Dàng JIANGSU ¥

(大牌档, Nanjing Impressions; ☏ 6821 6777; 48 Dashiba Jie, 大石坝45号; dishes from ¥32; ⏰ 11am-11pm; Ⓜ Line 3 to Fuzimiao, exit 2) Equal parts hectic and fun, Dàpái Dàng is decorated like a Qing-dynasty eatery, complete with waiters scurrying around in period garb and lanterns hanging overhead. There's a handy English menu for ordering Nanjing specialities such as *yánshuǐyā* (salted duck), pork sticky-rice and mouth-watering duck dumplings.

The restaurant has numerous branches, all of which can get packed at mealtimes. If you arrive during a busy period, ask for a ticket and wait for your number to be called. There's another handy branch on the 5th floor of Friendship Plaza (Area C; Xinjiekou, Exit 21).

Aladdin XINJIANG ¥¥

(阿拉丁, Ālādīng; ☏ 8589 1799; 43 Luolang Xiang, 罗廊巷43号; mains ¥48; ⏰ 11am-9.30pm) This boisterous, two-level Xinjiang restaurant has a sizeable lamb-packed menu that runs that gamut from kebabs (¥5 each) and fried-bread-and-lamb (¥48) to roasted lamb shank (¥189) or whole lamb (¥1680). Other tasty dishes include *náng*-oven chicken wings (¥78), spicy dumpling soup (¥28) and fresh yoghurt (¥10). Don't miss the Sinkiang black beer (¥15).

🍷 Drinking & Nightlife

western-style drinking holes, sports bars and specialist beer bars congregate along Shanghai Lu.

Nanjing 1912, a large and attractively housed quadrant of neon-lit bars and cafes on the corner of Taiping Beilu and Changjiang Lu, is interesting for a stroll, but few of the bars are of much interest; you can find a branch of Starbucks here and other chain names.

Master Gao Beer House MICROBREWERY

(高大师啤酒屋, Gāodàshī Píjiǔwū; ☏ 8452 0589; www.mastergaobeer.com; 8 Chángjiāng Hòu Jie, Nanjing 1912, 长江后街8号南京1912街区; ⏰ 6pm-2am; 🀚; Ⓜ Line 3 to Daxinggong, exit 5) Founded by China's 'father of craft beer', Gao Yan, this micropub was the first of its kind when it opened in 2008. The beer house has 15 fresh brews on tap, including Master Gao's flagship 'Baby IPA' and 'Jasmine T-Lager' as well as a decent selection of bottled beers.

★ **Hermit** COCKTAIL BAR

(☏ 181 1615 7747; 49-1 Qingyun Alley, 青云巷49号-1; cocktails/dishes from ¥65/45; ⏰ 6pm-1am; 🀚; Ⓜ Line 1 to Gulou, exit 4a) Hermit offers two playfully sophisticated bars in one. Start downstairs at the science-themed beer bar, before heading up the candlelit stairway to an intimate whisky-and-cocktail bar. Up here you'll find artfully presented cocktails (try the Tyrant, served in a wolf's head goblet, or the Pirgot, served in a golden pineapple), an extensive whisky menu and tasty sharing plates.

Menus aren't in English but staff can help with recommendations.

Human Coffee CRAFT BEER

(20-1 Nanxiu Cun, 南秀村20-1号; ⏰ 10.30am-2am; 🀚; Ⓜ Yunnan Lu) Cafe by day, craft-beer bar by night, this trendy place tucked down a little road off Shanghai Lu is popular with students from nearby Nanjing University. Owner Max is friendly and speaks good English, while the cold, imported bottled beers are a welcome relief on a hot summer's evening.

QIXIA MOUNTAIN

Founded by the Buddhist monk Ming Sengshao during the Southern Qi dynasty, **Qixia Temple** (栖霞寺, Qīxiá Sì; ☑ 8576 6979; 88 Qixia Jie, 栖霞街88号; Jan-Sep ¥25, Oct-Dec ¥40; ⏱ 7am-5.30pm; 🚌 207) on Qīxiá Mountain (栖霞山, Qīxiá Shān), 22km northeast of Nanjing, is one of China's largest Buddhist seminaries. Relics believed to be part of Gautama Buddha's skull were unveiled and interred here. The mountain's maple trees are a major draw in spring when the hills are splashed in crimson and bronze.

The two main halls are the **Maitreya Hall**, with a statue of the Maitreya Buddha sitting cross-legged at the entrance; and the **Vairocana Hall**, housing a 5m-tall statue of the Vairocana Buddha.

Behind Qixia Temple is the **Thousand Buddha Cliff** (千佛岩, Qiānfó Yán). Several grottoes housing stone statues are carved into the hillside, the earliest of which dates as far back as the Qi dynasty (AD 479–502); others are from the Tang, Song, Yuan and Ming dynasties. There is also a small stone pagoda, **Sheli Pagoda** (舍利塔, Shèlì Tǎ), which was built in AD 601 and rebuilt during the late Tang period. The upper part has engraved sutras and carvings of Buddha; around the base, each of the pagoda's eight sides depicts tales from the life of Sakyamuni.

Continue northwards to admire lovely views in the **scenic area** behind the temple. The steep path meanders via an array of pavilions and rocky outcrops: it's serene, so consider bringing lunch and spending time here.

Get to the temple from Nanjing by public bus (南上, Nán Shàng; ¥3, one hour) from a stop by Nanjing Train Station. The bus stop is on a dusty highway, 500m south of the entrance.

☆ Entertainment

★ **Lanyuan Theatre**   CHINESE OPERA
(兰苑剧场, Lányuàn Jùchǎng; ☑ 84469284; 4 Chaotiangong, 朝天宫4号; M Shanghai Lu) Kūnqǔ, an extant form of Chinese opera originating from Jiangsu, is staged at this intimate theatre every Saturday evening at 7.15pm. The English subtitles retain the feeling and poetry of the original text, making the performances some of the most absorbing you'll find in China. Ticket prices vary by performance but generally cost from ¥50 up to ¥150.

🛍 Shopping

The pedestrian area around Fūzǐ Miào has souvenirs, clothing and shoes for sale, while the shopping malls around Xinjiekou station are excellent for finding everything under one roof.

ℹ Information

The *Nanjinger* (www.thenanjinger.com) is a handy expat listings magazine, available at restaurants and bars.

MEDICAL SERVICES

For on-the-ground help navigating Nanjing's hospitals, use WeChat to contact HospitalAid, a not-for-profit service that aims to assist foreigners with translation, bookings and hospital recommendations.

Raffles Medical (莱佛士医疗, Láifúshì Yīliáo; ☑ 8480 2842; www.rafflesmedicalgroup.com/international-clinics; 319 Zhongshan Donglu, 中山东路319号; ⏱ 9am-6pm Mon-Fri, to noon Sat; M Minggugong) Expat clinic on the ground floor of the Grand Metropark Hotel. Consultations from ¥1475.

MONEY

Most bank ATMs are open 24 hours and take international cards. The **ICBC** (中国工商银行, Zhōngguó Gōngshāng Yínháng; 3 Zhongshan Donglu, 中山东路3号; ⏱ 9am-5pm Mon-Sat; M Xinjiekou, exit 7) near Xinjiekou station also changes major currency and travellers cheques.

PUBLIC SECURITY BUREAU

Exit & Entry Administration Service Center (公安局出入境办证服务中心, Gōng'ānjú Chūrùjìng Bànzhèng Fúwù Zhōngxīn; ☑ 8442 0004; 173 Baixia Lu, 白下路173号; ⏱ 9am-5pm Mon-Sat, 9am-noon & 2pm-5pm Sun; M Line 3 to Fuzimiao, exit 1) For visa extensions.

TOURIST INFORMATION

Tourist Centre (夫子庙景区旅客中心, Fūzǐ Miào Jǐngqū Lǚkè Zhōngxīn; 80 Pingjiangfu Lu, 平江府路80号; ⏱ 9am-9pm; 🔊; M Line 3 to Fuzimiao, exit 2) Helpful tourist information centre at the east entrance of the Fūzǐ Miào (p259) pedestrian street. Has maps, free wi-fi, power points, toilets and a medical station. There are also water dispensers for topping up your bottle, free of charge.

ⓘ Getting There & Away

AIR

Nanjing Lukou International Airport (南京禄口国际机场, Nánjīng Lùkǒu Guójì Jīchǎng; Ⓜ Lukou International Airport) has regular air connections to all major Chinese cities.

BUS

Of Nanjing's two long-distance bus stations, **Nanjing Bus Station** (南京汽车客运站, Nánjīng Qìchē Kèyùnzhàn), is the larger and more convenient. It is at Nanjing Station (north square) and serves the following destinations:

Hefei ¥62, 2½ hours, three daily (11.10am, 2.10pm and 4.20pm)

Shanghai ¥75 to ¥100, four to five hours, three daily (9am, 2.30pm and 4.40pm)

Suzhou ¥70 to ¥78, 2½ hours, three daily (7.40am, 10am and 2pm)

Wuxi ¥62, two hours, three daily (10am, 1pm and 2pm)

Buses to **Yangzhou** (¥45, 1½ hours, every 20 minutes, 7.10am to 7pm) depart from the **East Bus Station** (南京长途汽车东站, Nánjīng Chángtú Qìchē Dōngzhàn).

Bus 2 from Xinjiekou goes to the East Bus Station. A taxi from town will cost ¥25 to ¥30 to either station.

TRAIN

Nanjing is a major stop on the Beijing–Shanghai train line. Heading eastward, the line to Shanghai connects with Changzhou, Wuxi and Suzhou.

Many G and D trains depart or terminate at Nanjing South, so check when you buy your ticket. G trains to Beijing all depart from Nanjing South Train Station.

Trains from **Nanjing Train Station** (南京站, Nánjīng Zhàn; Ⓜ Nanjing Railway Station) in the north of town include the following:

Huangshan (Tunxi) Hard/soft sleeper ¥108/159, six to eight hours, four daily

Shanghai G train (main train station, and Hongqiao), 2nd/1st class ¥140/220, 1½ to two hours, regular departures

Suzhou G train, 2nd/1st class ¥100/165, one to 1½ hours, regular departures

Xi'an Overnight Z train, hard/soft sleeper ¥280/420, 12 hours, six per day

Xi'an East G train, 2nd/1st class ¥540/877, six hours, regular departures

Zhengzhou G train, 2nd/1st class ¥318/520, 3½ hours, regular departures

Trains leaving from **Nanjing South Train Station** (南京南站, Nánjīng Nán Zhàn; Ⓜ Nanjing South Railway Station) include the following:

Beijing South G train, 2nd/1st class ¥444/749, 3½ to five hours, regular departures

Hangzhou East G train, 2nd/1st class ¥118/198, 1½ to three hours, regular departures

Shanghai G train, 2nd/1st class ¥140/220, two hours, regular departures

Suzhou G train, 2nd/1st class ¥100/160, 1½ hours, regular departures

Try to get tickets ahead of time via your hotel, online or at the **train ticket office** (火车票售票处, Huǒchēpiào Shòupiàochù; 35 Taiping Beilu, 太平北路35号; ⊙8-11am & noon-5pm).

ⓘ Getting Around

TO/FROM THE AIRPORT

The S1 Airport Line express metro link (¥7 to ¥10, 35 minutes, first/last time 6am/10.40pm) connects directly to the airport from Nanjing South train station, itself on Lines 1 and 3. Airport buses (¥20, 90 minutes, every 20 minutes, 6am to 11.30pm) also run from Lukou Airport along two different routes: Line 1 (East) goes to Nanjing Station; Line 2 (West) goes to Nanjing South and Zhonghua Gate. Most hotels have regular shuttle buses to and from the airport too. A taxi to the airport will cost around ¥140 to ¥150.

BICYCLE

You can get a card to use the city's orange bikes at the District Service Centres in **Gulou** (鼓楼区行政服务中心, Gǔlóu Qū Xíngzhèng Fúwù Zhōngxīn; 84 Shanxi Lu, 山西路84号; ⊙9am-noon & 1.30pm-5.30pm Mon-Fri, 9am-11.30am & 2pm-4pm Sat; 🚇3 to Fuzuolu) and **Xuanwu** (玄武区行政服务中心, Xuánwǔ Qū Xíngzhèng Fúwù Zhōngxīn; 455 Zhujiang Lu, 珠江路455号; ⊙9am-noon & 2-5.30pm; Ⓜ Fuqiao). Take your passport and expect to pay a ¥300 deposit. (Snap a photo of the bikes before you go to the office if your Chinese skills are limited.)

Simply swipe the card to hire an orange bike. Rental is free for the first two hours, the third hour is ¥1 and then it's ¥3 per hour thereafter.

Annoyingly, to get your deposit back, you must return the card on the city's fringe, at the **South City Service Centre** (大明客服中心, Dàmíng lù kèzhōngxīn; 19 Yingtian Dajie, 应天大街19号; ⊙9am-noon & 12.30-5.30pm) or the **City Service Hall** (市政服务大厅, Shìzhèngwù dàtīng; 265 Jiangdong Zhonglu, 江东中路265号; ⊙9am-noon & 12.30-5.30pm; Ⓜ Olympic Sports Centre East).

BUS

Many local maps contain bus routes. Normal buses cost ¥1 to ¥2 and tourist buses cost ¥2.

There are tourist bus routes that visit many of the sights:

Bus Y1 Goes from Nanjing Train Station, past the Presidential Palace and Ming Palace Ruins to the Sun Yatsen Mausoleum.

Bus Y2 Starts in the south at the Martyrs' Cemetery (烈士墓地, Lièshì Mùdì), passes Fūzǐ Miào and terminates halfway up Zijin Mountain.

Bus Y3 Passes by Nanjing Train Station en route to the Ming Xiaoling Tomb and Linggu Temple.

Two handy hop-on, hop-off **sightseeing buses** (南京观光巴士, Nánjīng Guānguāng Bāshì; ☑ 8321 1706; ¥30; ☉ half-hourly 9am-5pm) can also get you to the top attractions. Tickets are valid for 24 hours and routes run clockwise. A third route runs between Xinjiekou and Fūzǐ Miào from 7pm to 9pm.

A stored value transport card (jīnlíngtōng, 金陵通) is available for a deposit of ¥30 with a minimum top-up credit of ¥50. The card can be used on buses, the metro and taxis.

METRO

Nanjing has a very efficient, rapidly expanding metro system that cuts through the city centre and runs out to the suburbs. Line No 1 runs north to south and links both train stations. Line No 2 goes east from Jingtianlu to Youfangqiao in the west. Line 10 connects Andemen to Yushan Lu, while the S1 Line runs to the airport from Nanjing South Railway Station. The S8 Line runs north of the Chang Jiang. Tickets are ¥2 to ¥5 and trains generally run between around 6am and 10pm or 11pm.

TAXI

Taxi flagfall is ¥11 and about ¥2 for each kilometre thereafter. Trips to most destinations in the city are ¥11 to ¥22. Taxis are easy to flag down outside of peak hours.

Suzhou 苏州

☑ 0512 / POP 8.13 MILLION

Historically, Suzhou (Sūzhōu) was synonymous with high culture and elegance, and generations of artists, scholars, writers and high society in China were drawn by its exquisite art forms and the delicate beauty of its gardens. Like all modern Chinese towns, Suzhou has unfortunately endured much destruction of its heritage and its replacement with largely arbitrary chunks of modern architecture.

The city does still have enough pockets of charm to warrant two to three days' exploration on foot. And the gardens, Suzhou's main attraction, are a symphonic combination of rocks, water, trees and pavilions that reflects the Chinese appreciation of balance and harmony. Adding to the charm are some excellent museums, surviving canal scenes and pagodas. The gardens in particular can get busy, so avoid visiting at the weekend or during public holidays, if possible.

History

Dating back some 2500 years, Suzhou is one of the oldest towns in the Yangzi Basin. With the completion of the Grand Canal during the Sui dynasty (AD 589–618), Suzhou began to flourish as a centre of shipping and grain storage, bustling with merchants and artisans.

By the 14th century Suzhou had become China's leading silk-producing city. The town's winning image as a 'Garden City' or a 'Venice of the East' came from its medieval blend of woodblock guilds and embroidery societies, whitewashed housing, cobbled streets, tree-lined avenues and canals. Local women were considered the most beautiful in China, largely thanks to the mellifluous local accent, and the city was home to a variety of rich merchants and bookish scholars, many of whom established the garden residences that the city is known for today.

In 1860 Taiping troops took the town without a blow and in 1896 Suzhou was opened to foreign trade, with Japanese and other international concessions. Since 1949 much of the historic city, including its city walls, has vanished. A conscious beautification of the city has set the tone for the last decade or so, and areas such as Pingjiang Lu and Shantang Jie suggest the Suzhou of old.

⊙ Sights

While most of Suzhou's canals have been sealed and paved into roads, the surviving canals along Pingjiang Lu and Shantang Jie are picturesque areas to wander. Both areas are popular with tourists and the traditional whitewashed buildings are now home to boutiques and galleries, silk shops and snack stalls: visit on a weekday and be sure to step off the main streets for a quieter pace.

A short metro ride east of the old town, Suzhou Industrial Park (SIP) is home to the city's shining skyscrapers and expat bars. Jinji Lake is SIP's unmissable drawcard, whether you're enjoying the view from a nearby bar, boating across the lake or traversing a lakeside trail.

Bao'en Temple BUDDHIST TEMPLE
(报恩寺, Bào'ēn Sì; 1918 Renmin Lu, 人民路1918号; ☉8.30am-4pm; Ⓜ Line 4 to Beisita, exit 4) FREE The oldest Buddhist temple in Suzhou, Bao'en Temple dates back 1700 years and its current reincarnation goes back to the 17th century. The temple's star attraction is 76m-tall **North Temple Pagoda** (北寺塔, Běisì Tǎ), one of the tallest pagodas in China.

Suzhou

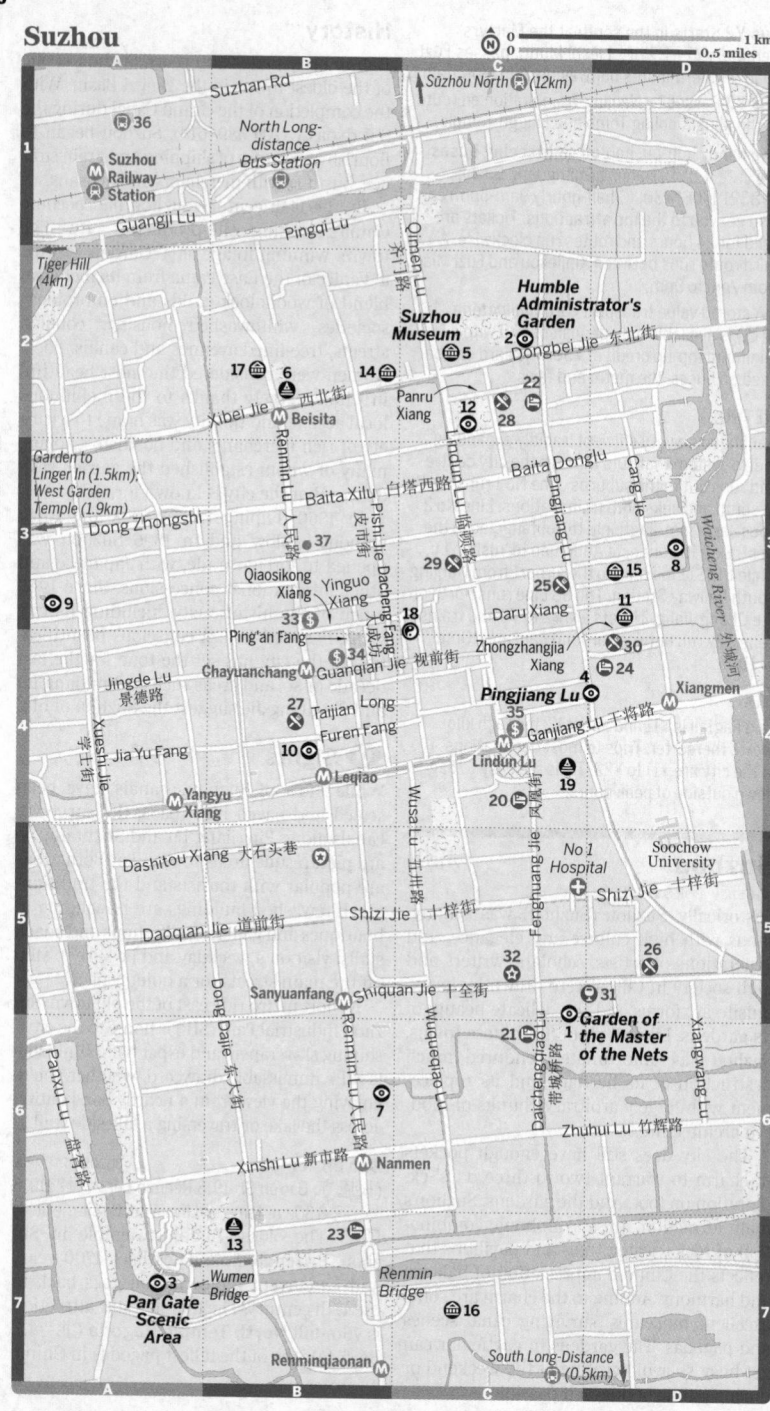

JIANGSU

0 ——————— 1 km
0 ——————— 0.5 miles

Suzhan Rd

Sùzhōu North (12km)

North Long-distance Bus Station

🚇 36

Suzhou Railway Station

Guangji Lu

Pingqi Lu

Qimen Lu 齐门路

Tiger Hill (4km)

Humble Administrator's Garden

Suzhou Museum

⊙ 2 Dongbei Jie 东北街

⊙ 5

17 🏛 6 西北街 14 22

Panru Xiang 12 28

Xibei Jie 🏛 Beisita

Garden to Linger In (1.5km); West Garden Temple (1.9km)

Baita Xilu 白塔西路

Baita Donglu

Pingjiang Lu

Cang Jie

Waicheng River 外城河

Dong Zhongshi

Renmin Lu 人民路

Pishi Jie Dacheng Fang 皮市街 大成坊

37

29 🏛 15 ⊙ 8

25 🏛 11

Qiaosikong Xiang
Yinguo Xiang

Daru Xiang

33 18 🏛

Ping'an Fang 34

Zhongzhangjia Xiang 30

Chayuanchang 🚇 Guanqian Jie 观前街 24

Jingde Lu 景德路

Pingjiang Lu 4

27 Taijian Long 35

Xueshi Jie 学士街

Jia Yu Fang

Furen Fang

Ganjiang Lu 干将路 Xiangmen

10 19

🚇 Leqiao Lindun Lu

Yangyu Xiang

20

Dashitou Xiang 大石头巷

Wusa Lu 五卅路

No 1 Hospital

Soochow University

Daoqian Jie 道前街

Shizi Jie 十梓街

Shizi Jie 十梓街

Fenghuang Jie 凤凰街

32

26

Dong Daijie 东大街

Sanyuanfang 🚇 Shiquan Jie 十全街

Wuquebiao Lu

31

Panxu Lu 盘胥路

Garden of the Master of the Nets 1

21

7

Daichengqiao Lu 带城桥路

Xinshi Lu 新市路 🚇 Nanmen

Zhuhui Lu 竹辉路

Xiangwang Lu

13

23 🏛

Wumen Bridge

Renmin Bridge

Pan Gate Scenic Area ⊙ 3

16 🏛

Renminqiaonan 🚇

South Long-Distance (0.5km)

Suzhou

The shady garden at the back of the complex has a small teahouse overlooking a peaceful pond and rocky paths frequented by exercising monks each morning.

★ Humble Administrator's Garden
GARDENS
(拙政园, Zhuōzhèng Yuán; 178 Dongbei Jie, 东北街178号; high/low season ¥90/70, audio guide ¥30; ⏱7.30am-5pm Nov-Feb, to 5.30pm Mar-Oct) The largest of Suzhou's gardens, the Humble Administrator's Garden is often considered to be the most impressive, but its fame draws in constant crowds, which are part of the experience. First built in 1509, this 5.2-hectare garden is clustered with water features, a museum, a teahouse, zigzagging bridges, bamboo groves and lotus ponds, along with at least 10 pavilions with poetic names such as 'Listening to the Sound of Rain' and 'Celestial Spring'. Bring your passport.

★ Suzhou Museum
MUSEUM
(苏州博物馆, Sūzhōu Bówùguǎn; www.szmuseum.com; 204 Dongbei Jie, 东北街204号; audio guide ¥40; ⏱9am-5pm Tue-Sun, last entry 4pm; 🚌Y5) **FREE** This stunning museum, one of only two in mainland China designed by IM Pei, is a modern interpretation of Suzhou architecture, with its confluence of water, courtyards and a distinctive grey-and-white motif. Although the impressive architecture steals the show, the collection contains a fascinating array of jade, ceramics and textiles, mostly labelled with informative English captions.

★ Pingjiang Lu
STREET
(平江路, Píngjiāng Lù; Ⓜ Lindun Rd or Xiangmen) On the eastern side of the city, this canalside road has whitewashed local houses sitting comfortably side by side with teahouses and trendy cafes selling overpriced beverages. Duck down some of the side streets that jut out from the main path for a glimpse at local life. It's a lovely place for a stroll, particularly in the early morning or on weekday evenings.

Lion Grove Garden
GARDENS
(狮子林, Shīzi Lín; 23 Yuanlin Lu, 园林路23号; high/low season ¥40/30; ⏱7.30am-5.30pm Mar-mid-Oct, to 5pm mid-Oct-Feb) Constructed in 1342 by the Buddhist monk Tianru to commemorate his master, who lived on Lion Cliff on Zhejiang's Tianmu Mountain, this garden's curiously

shaped rocks were meant to resemble lions, protectors of the Buddhist faith.

Couple's Garden
GARDENS

(耦园, Ŏu Yuán; 6 Xiaoxinqiao Xiang, 小新桥巷6号; high/low season ¥25/20; ⏱ 9.30am-4.30pm; M Xiangmen) The tranquil Couple's Garden is off the main tourist route and sees slightly fewer visitors than the other gardens, and its pond, courtyards and garden features are quite lovely. The entrance is 100m east of the ticket office.

Kunqu Opera Museum
MUSEUM

(昆曲博物馆, Kūnqǔ Bówùguǎn; ☎ 512 6727 3334; www.kunopera.com.cn; 14 Zhongzhangjia Xiang, 中张家巷14号; ⏱ 9am-4pm; M Xiamen) FREE Down a narrow lane, this small museum is dedicated to *kūnqǔ*, the opera style of the region. The beautiful old theatre houses a stage, musical instruments, costumes and photos of famous performers.

Twin Pagodas
BUDDHIST PAGODA

(双塔, Shuāng Tǎ; Dinghuisi Xiang, 定慧寺巷; ¥8; ⏱ 8am-4.30pm; M Line 1 to Lindun Rd, exit 2) Beautifully enhanced by flowering magnolias in spring, this delightful courtyard and former temple contains a pair of sublime pagodas, which don't often come in twos. It's one of the more relaxing, peaceful and composed parts of town, so come here for a break.

★ Garden of the Master of the Nets
GARDENS

(网师园, Wǎngshī Yuán; high/low season ¥40/30; ⏱ 7.30am-5.30pm mid-Apr–mid-Oct, to 5pm mid-Oct–mid-Apr; ☐ 55, 529, M Line 1 to Lindun Rd, exit 2) Off Shiquan Jie, this pocket-sized garden is considered one of Suzhou's best preserved. Laid out in the 12th century, it went to seed and was later restored in the 18th century as part of the home of a retired official turned fisherman (hence the name). In the 1920s, the famous painter Zhang Daqian and his brother Zhang Shanzi lived here with their pet tiger.

A striking feature of the garden is the use of space: the labyrinth of courtyards, with windows framing other parts of the garden, is ingeniously designed to give the illusion of a much larger area.

Temple of Mystery
TAOIST TEMPLE

(玄妙观, Xuánmiào Guàn; Guanqian Jie, 观前街; ¥10; ⏱ 7.30am-5pm May-Sep, to 4.30pm Oct-Apr; M Line 4 to Chayuanchang) Lashed by electronic music from the shops alongside, the Taoist Temple of Mystery stands in what was once Suzhou's old bazaar, a rowdy entertainment

district with travelling performers, acrobats and actors. The temple dates from 1181 and is one of the few surviving examples of Song architecture in Suzhou.

Blue Wave Pavilion
GARDENS

(沧浪亭, Cānglàng Tíng; 3 Canglang Ting Jie, 沧浪亭街3号; high/low season ¥20/15; ⏱ 7.30am-5pm mid-Oct–Apr, to 5.30pm Apr–mid-Oct; M Line 4 to Sanyuanfang, exit 2) Originally the home of a prince, the oldest garden in Suzhou was first built in the 11th century, and has been repeatedly rebuilt since. Instead of attracting hordes of tourists, the wild, overgrown garden around the Blue Wave Pavilion is one of those where the locals actually go to chill and enjoy a leisurely stroll.

Garden of Harmony
GARDENS

(怡园, Yí Yuán; 1265 Renmin Lu, 人民路1265号; ¥15; ⏱ 7.30am-5pm; M Line 1 to Leqiao, exit 8) One of the lesser-visited gardens around Suzhou is the charmingly small Qing-dynasty Garden of Harmony, which has assimilated many features of older gardens and delicately blended them into a style of its own.

★ Pan Gate Scenic Area
LANDMARK

(盘门, Pán Mén; 1 Dong Dajie, 东大街1号; Pan Gate only ¥40; ⏱ 7.30am-5.30pm Mar-Nov, 8.30am-5pm Dec-Feb; ☐ Y2) This quiet part of Suzhou is lovely, with a section of the city wall straddling the outer moat in the southwest corner of the city. Dating from 1355, the gate backs onto a delightful scenic area, dotted with great halls, bell towers, bridges, pavilions, lake, temple and the crumbling **Ruiguang Pagoda** (瑞光塔, Ruiguāng Tǎ; Dong Dajie, 东大街; ¥6), constructed in 1004.

Garden of Cultivation
GARDENS

(艺圃, Yì Pǔ; 5 Wenhao Long, 文衙弄5号; ¥10; ⏱ 7.30am-4pm Mar-Oct, to 4.30pm Nov-Feb; M Shi-lu) This small but perfectly formed garden is often overlooked by visitors who are drawn to Suzhou's larger and more famous gardens. Its simple layout makes use of rockeries, water features and covered corridors, while some of the living quarters are decorated with furniture, creating an intimate atmosphere.

The garden's hidden location means it largely remains free of the crowds that dominate other gardens, making it and the surrounding streets a wonderful place to appreciate the serenity that was once an essential feature of all Suzhou's gardens. Find it by following the arrows and name ('艺圃') daubed in bold red characters on the whitewashed walls of surrounding streets.

Shantang Jie
STREET

(山塘街, Shāntáng Jiē; Ⓜ Line 2 to Shantang Jie) **FREE** This picturesque canalside street has been in use for more than a thousand years, having been built in the Tang dynasty (around 825–826) to transport Suzhou's upper classes to Tiger Hill for leisurely outings. Nowadays it is pedestrianised and makes for a wonderful way to stroll or boat to Tiger Hill. Shantang Jie is very similar in feeling to Pingjiang Lu (p267), with whitewashed buildings backing directly onto the canal and quaint lantern-decorated bridges.

★ Tiger Hill
PARK

(虎丘山, Hǔqiū Shān; ☑ 0512 6723 2305; Huqiu Lu, 虎丘路; high/low season ¥80/60; ⏱ 7.30am-5.30pm May-Sep, to 5pm Oct-Apr; 🚌 Y1) In the far northwest of town, Tiger Hill is a major drawcard for Chinese tourists, and the beacon that draws them is the leaning **Cloud Rock Pagoda** (云岩塔, Yúnyán Tǎ) atop the hill. The octagonal seven-storey pagoda was built in the 10th century entirely of brick, an innovation in Chinese architecture at the time. It began tilting over 400 years ago, and today the highest point is displaced more than 2m from its original position.

The hill itself is artificial and is the final resting place of He Lu, founding father of Suzhou. He Lu died in the 6th century BC and myths have coalesced around him – he is said to have been buried with a collection of 3000 swords and be guarded by a white tiger (hence the name of the hill). He Lu was also a patron of Sun Tzu, the military advisor and author of *The Art of War* – you'll find a shrine dedicated to him in the northwest corner of the complex.

Take a break at **Clouds Melted in Tea Fragrance**, a working tea plantation hidden away on the northern hillside, where you can sip fresh tea in serene, wooded surrounds.

Tourist bus Y1 from Suzhou station goes to the north gate. Otherwise it's a pleasant 3km walk or 20-minute boat ride (¥50, every 25 minutes) along the canal from Shantang Jie.

Garden to Linger In
GARDENS

(留园, Liú Yuán; 79 Liuyuan Lu, 留园路79号; high/low season ¥55/45; ⏱ 7.30am-5.30pm mid-Mar–Oct, to 5pm Nov–mid-Mar; 🚌 Y1) One of the largest gardens in Suzhou, this 3-hectare plot was originally built in the Ming dynasty by a doctor as a relaxing place for his recovering patients. It's easy to see why the patients took to it: the winding corridors are inlaid

CLASSICAL GARDENS

With more than 60 classical gardens in Suzhou, it can be difficult to choose which to visit. None of the gardens were designed for tour groups, so don't expect too much Zen-like tranquillity. Famous gardens such as Humble Administrator's Garden (p267) have iconic views and architecture, but less-well-known gardens, such as the Garden of Cultivation or Garden of Harmony, are generally quieter and have the best atmospheres.

Gardens and museums stop selling tickets 30 minutes before closing, and are best visited early in the mornings before crowds arrive.

with calligraphy from celebrated masters, their windows and doorways opening onto unusually shaped rockeries, ponds and dense clusters of bamboo.

Hanshan Temple
BUDDHIST TEMPLE

(寒山寺, Hánshān Sì; Hanshan Si Nong 24, 寒山寺弄24号; ¥20; ⏱ 8am-4.15pm; 🚌 Y1, Ⓜ Line 1 to Xihuan Lu) Literally meaning 'Cold Mountain Temple' and founded around AD 500, Hanshan is famous in China thanks to a Tang-dynasty (618–907) poem that is taught at schools all over the mainland. The poem, by Zhang Ji, is inscribed on an enormous 16m-tall stelae behind the Great Bell Tower.

The Great Bell Tower was closed at the time of writing but it houses an 8.6m-high bell, reputed to be the largest Buddhist bell in the world. Every New Year's Eve, thousands of local people gather to ring the bell 108 times. Legend has it that the average person endures 108 kinds of annoyances per year and that listening to the bell tolling will bring good luck and happiness for the following year.

The temple is west of Suzhou's old town, about 1500m from Xihuan Lu metro station. An entrance ticket gives access to both Hanshan Temple and the Great Bell Tower area (8am to 4.30pm), which are actually in two separate compounds. You need to exit one to enter the other – be sure to keep your ticket on hand.

Jinji Lake
LAKE

(金鸡湖, Jīnjī Hú; Ⓜ Line 1) Jinji Lake lies at the very heart of Suzhou's Industrial Park neighbourhood, home to many of the city's

SILK, GLORIOUS SILK

Since the 13th century, Suzhou has been synonymous with silk production and weaving. Today the city has more silk shops and boutiques than you can shake a stick at. Quality and prices vary but offerings are similar from shop to shop.

Here are our best picks for getting to know the history of silk in Suzhou, seeing how the smooth stuff is made and appreciating its use in intricate Su embroidery.

Suzhou Silk Museum (苏州丝绸博物馆, Sūzhōu Sīchóu Bówùguǎn; 2001 Renmin Lu, 人民路2001号; ⊙9am-5pm Tue-Sun; M Line 4 to Beisita) The Suzhou Silk Museum houses fascinating exhibitions detailing the history of Suzhou's 4000-year-old silk industry. Exhibits include a section on silk-weaving techniques and silk fashion through the dynasties, while you can also see functioning looms and staff at work on, say, a large brocade.

Bring your passport.

Suzhou No 1 Silk Factory (苏州市第一丝厂, Sūzhōu Shì Dì Yī Sī Chǎng; ☎0512 6561 3733; 94 Nanmen Lu, 南门路94号; ⊙8am-5pm; M Line 4 to Renminqiao South) This museum and working silk factory was established as a state-owned silk factory in 1926. The highlight of the museum is seeing its massive, 80-year-old silk-spinning machines in action, weaving together impossibly thin threads of silk (eight cocoons are needed to make a single usable thread). If you're lucky, there'll also be live silkworms on display.

The second half of the museum is dedicated to selling silk products – prices are relatively high but, refreshingly, there is no pressure to buy.

The area south of the factory is was once part of the Japanese Concession, granted in an 1896 treaty. Several old red-brick buildings are still standing, most prominent of which is the former **Japanese Consulate**, recognisable by its grand, columned entranceway.

Suzhou Arts and Crafts Museum (苏州工艺美术博物馆, Sūzhōu Gōngyì Měishù Bówùguǎn; 88 Xibei Jie, 西北街88号; ¥5; ⊙9am-5pm) Housed in a historic building, this small museum boasts an impressive range of modern handicrafts created by skilled Suzhou artists. Its nearly 1000-piece collection showcases local talent in embroidery, wood and stone carving, and furniture-making. It has good English signage.

There are certainly a few unexpected gems in this museum. Keep an eye out for the double-sided portrait of Prince Charles and Princess Diana, noting that double-sided embroidery is a particularly complex art.

Suzhou Fan Museum (苏扇博物馆, Sū Shàn Bówùguǎn; 16 Wei Daoguan Qian, 卫道观前16号; ⊙9am-4.30pm Tue-Sun) The antique fans on display here demonstrate the skillful painting and embroidery of the art form. Many of the silk fans feature a cat motif; rat-catching cats, known as 'silkworm cats', were an essential part of Suzhou's silk industry.

---

young professionals and expats. At 7.4 sq km, Jinji is China's largest inner-city lake and is surrounded by pretty riverside parks, hip shopping centres and high-end hotels and restaurants.

You can take to the water on a sightseeing boat to **Ligongdi Pier** (¥30 one way) or **Peach Blossom Island** (桃花岛, Táohuā Dǎo; Jinji Hu Jingqu Nei, 金鸡湖景区内; ¥50; ⊙9.30am-5.30pm; 📷; M Line 1, Culture & Expo Centre) from the **Moon Harbour boat terminal** (金鸡湖游览, Jīnjī Hú Yóulǎn; Moon Harbour, 月光码头; M Line 1, Culture & Expo Centre), on the lake's northern edge. Another wonderful way to experience Jinji is by walking the 14km circular fitness trail, a pedestrian-only series of paths and bridges that skirt the lake's perimeter. En route, you'll take in views of one of China's prettiest purpose-built, modern neighbourhoods, a testament to thoughtful planned urban development.

🚩 Tours

Evening boat tours wind their way around the outer canal leaving nightly from 6pm to 8.30pm (¥180, 55 minutes, half-hourly). The trips, usually with *píngtán* (singing and storytelling art form sung in the Suzhou dialect) performance on board, are a great way to experience old Suzhou, passing Pan Gate and heading up to Chang Gate (in the west of the city wall). Remember to bring insect repellent as the mosquitoes are tenacious. Tickets can be bought at the Tourist Boat Wharf near Xu Gate.

✦✦✦ Festivals & Events

Dragon Boat Festival SAILING
(端午节, Duānwǔ Jié; ⏱ Jun) Each year on China's traditional Dragon Boat Day (on the 5th day of the 5th lunar month), Suzhou hosts one of the country's largest Dragon Boat Festivals on Jinji Lake. Boat teams from around China compete in strongly contested races on the water.

🛏 Sleeping

Hotels in Suzhou are not cheap, but there's no shortage of choice. Prices can rise across the board at weekends, when rooms can be harder to book, so try to visit from Sunday to Thursday if possible.

Suzhou Mingtown Youth Hostel HOSTEL ¥
(苏州明堂青年旅舍, Sūzhōu Míngtáng Qīngnián Lǚshè; ☎ 6581 6869; 28 Pingjiang Lu, 平江路28号; 6-bed dm ¥60-80, d ¥170-300; ❄ 🖥; Ⓜ Line 1 to Xiangmen or Lindun Rd) This well-run youth hostel has a fantastic location on Pingjiang Lu and charming rooms and dorms decorated with dark wooden 'antique' furniture. Rooms are not very well soundproofed, but there are laundry facilities and a pleasant common area. Staff speak some English and can help with travel tips around town.

★ Blue Gate Youth Hostel HOSTEL ¥
(蓝色大门青年旅舍, Lánsè Dàmén Qīngnián-lǚshè; ☎ 5111 1680; 259 Fenghuang Jie, 凤凰街259号; dm ¥40-60, d ¥150-220; 🖥; Ⓜ Line 1 to Lindun Rd, exit 2) The teensy common area has a reasonably priced beer (from ¥10) and an easy atmosphere for getting to know your fellow travellers. Rooms are basic and dorm mattresses are thin, but the location is great and the helpful manager speaks excellent English. Watch your head on the stairs.

★ Little Days Folk House BOUTIQUE HOTEL ¥¥
(小日子生活馆, Xiǎo Rìzi Shēnghuó Guǎn; ☎ 0512 5121 5120; www.facebook.com/littledays01; 4 Xinzao Bridge Xiatang, 新造桥下塘4号; d ¥480-830; ❄ 🖥) The most peaceful way to experience Pingjiang Lu: Little Days is a delightful family-run boutique hotel and cafe right on the canal. The five rooms are thoughtfully put together, with deep baths and comfortable beds. A tastefully presented Chinese-style breakfast is included.

Pace HOTEL ¥¥
(沛喜酒店, Pèixǐ Jiǔdiàn; ☎ 6687 6288; 347 Renmin Lu, 人民路347号; d ¥280-320, tr ¥360-390; ❄ 🖥; Ⓜ Line 4 to Nanmen) Pace isn't fancy but it does have clean, bright rooms with private bathrooms and large comfortable beds. Genuinely helpful staff, a decent buffet breakfast, free use of washing machines and dryers, and a convenient location by Nanmen station seal the deal.

Garden Hotel HOTEL ¥¥¥
(苏州南园宾馆, Sūzhōu Nányuán Bīnguǎn; ☎ 0512 6778 6778; www.gardenhotelsuzhou.com; 99 Daichengqiao Lu, 带城桥路99号; r from ¥1200; ❄ 🖥) Within huge, green grounds, the very popular five-star Garden Hotel has elegant, spacious and attractively decorated rooms. Washed over with mandolin music, the lobby is a picture of calm. It's often possible to get a room here for under ¥800.

🍴 Eating

In reflection of its busy and year-round tourist traffic, Suzhou has some excellent restaurants, both Chinese and international, dotted all over the town. Xueshi Jie (学士街) has a good selection of local eateries, from street-side Xinjiang barbecue to popular restaurants that serve mountains of red crayfish (龙虾, lóngxiā) by the jīn (斤, 500g).

Yī Rán Táng VEGETARIAN ¥
(一然堂; ☎ 135 1163 9196; 5 Zhangjiaqiaobang, 张家桥浜5号; buffet ¥10; ⏱ 11.30am-1pm & 5.30-7pm Mon-Fri, 11.30am-1pm Sat & Sun; 🍴) Come to this friendly Buddhist restaurant for a modest-yet-filling vegetarian buffet that, at ¥10, will barely make a dent in your wallet. Etiquette dictates that you eat everything that you put on your plate and clear your own dishes. To get here from Pingjiang Lu, take Zhuzhang Alley (邾长巷), go left at the public toilets and then left at Zhangjiaqiaobang.

Yǎba Shēngjiān DUMPLINGS ¥
(哑巴生煎; 12 Lindun Lu, 临顿路12号; 8 dumplings ¥16, soup ¥10; ⏱ 6am-7.30pm) With great clouds of steam rising from the kitchen, this local icon has been flogging noodles since 1943, but its handmade shēngjiān bāo (生煎包, pan-fried dumplings), stuffed with juicy pork, are outstanding and flavour-packed. During lunch hours expect to queue for 30 minutes just to order! Protocol: place your order, line up at the windows to pick up your food (soup left, dumplings right), snag a table and enjoy.

★ Tóng Dé Xīng NOODLES ¥
(同得兴; 6 Jia Yu Fang, 嘉馀坊6号; soup noodles with pork belly ¥23; ⏱ 7am-1pm; ❄; Ⓜ Line 1 to Leqiao, exit 8) This institution has been serving

up classic Suzhou-style soup noodles for 200 years. The delicious broth, which is made fresh each night from herbs, spices and a variety of animal bones, is the key component – come early, as once the broth runs out the restaurant stops serving. Do as locals do and slurp it out of the side of the bowl.

Try the signature *fēngzhèn* noodles served in white broth (白汤面底), with a huge hunk of soft, fatty pork belly (白焖肉). Order just inside the entrance.

Pinvon
TEAHOUSE ¥

(品芳, Pǐnfāng; 94 Pingjiang Lu, 平江路94号; small dishes from ¥10; ⊙9am-8pm) Often busy, this seriously cute little teahouse is perched beside one of Suzhou's most popular canalside streets, serving up excellent dumplings and delicate little morsels on small plates. The tearooms upstairs are more atmospheric. There are all sorts of bites, from spare-rib soup (¥28) to crab *dàtāngbāo* (大汤包, large soup dumpling; ¥25). Order by ticking what you want on a paper menu.

Gūsū Cài Guǎn
CHINESE ¥¥

(姑苏菜馆; 88 Caohu Xuxiang, Pingjiang Lu, 平江路曹胡徐巷88号; dishes ¥30-130; ⊙4.30-10pm) This small restaurant has a lovely setting overlooking the canal that runs alongside Pingjiang Lu (p267), right next to a picturesque stone bridge and a traditional teahouse. The restaurant serves up traditional Suzhounese dishes designed for sharing, including sweet and sour squirrelfish (松鼠鳜鱼, *sōngshǔ guìyú*) and fish caught in nearby Tai Lake.

Sera Nera
ITALIAN ¥¥

(40-1 Wuya Chang, 吴衙场40-1号; dishes/beer from ¥48/20; ⊙11am-2pm & 5-9pm; ❖ 🛜; Ⓜ Line 4 to Lindun Rd, exit 2) This romantic Italian restaurant is tucked down a canalside lane that runs parallel to Shiquan Jie. Run by an entirely Chinese team, headed up by the friendly Blaze, its pizzas are handmade fresh in an on-site pizza oven, while pasta dishes are served authentically al dente. It also offers reasonably priced European wines and beers, including bottled beer from Italy.

Wúmén Rénjiā
JIANGSU ¥¥¥

(吴门人家; ☎0512 6728 8041; 30 Panru Xiang, 潘儒巷30号; dishes ¥30-320; ⊙6.30-9.30am, 11am-3pm & 5-8.30pm; 🛜) Close to the Lion Grove Garden (p267), this restaurant attracts a mix of locals and visitors for its subtly flavoured Suzhou cooking. The menu takes inspiration from what Qing-dynasty emperor Qianlong allegedly ate during his famous visit to Suzhou in 1751.

Try the ever-popular squirrelfish or Empress Cixi's alleged favourite – cherry-braised pork loin, which is slow-cooked for seven or eight hours and might be the softest, most tender pork you'll try in China. Evening reservations are essential.

Drinking & Nightlife

Nightlife in the old town means strolling the streets, eating rather than drinking. There are, however, cafe-bars scattered along Pingjiang Lu, and Shiquan Jie – a former centre of student nightlife in down-

---

GRAND CANAL

The world's longest canal, the Grand Canal (大运河, Dàyùnhé) once meandered for almost 1800km from Beijing to Hangzhou, and is a striking example of China's engineering prowess. Sections of the canal have been silted up for centuries and today perhaps half of it remains seasonally navigable.

The Grand Canal's construction spanned many centuries. The first 85km were completed in 495 BC, but the mammoth task of linking the Yellow River (Huáng Hé) and the Yangzi River (Cháng Jiāng) was undertaken between AD 605 and 609 by a massive conscripted labour force during Sui times. It was developed again during the Yuan dynasty (1271–1368). The canal enabled the government to capitalise on the growing wealth of the Yellow River Basin and to ship supplies from south to north.

In Suzhou, one of the best ways to view the canal is around **Precious Belt Bridge Park**. To get there, take bus 529 to the corner of Taihu Donglu and Dangui Lu (太湖东路丹桂路) and walk across the plaza. The modern bridge (跨河景观桥, *Kuà Hé Jǐngguān Qiáo*) at the end of the plaza crosses the Grand Canal, where you're likely to see cargo boats that continue to ferry the ancient trade route. Across this bridge is the park; from here, it's a 10-minute walk through pleasant gardens to reach the ancient **Precious Belt Bridge** (宝带桥, Bǎodài Qiáo; 🚍529), which boasts 53 arches, and was once a Tang-dynasty construction, although the current bridge actually dates from the Ming.

town Suzhou – still houses one or two lively bars. The biggest concentration of bars and nightclubs is in the Ligongdi area of Suzhou Industrial Park, 9km east of the old town (a taxi from the old town will cost ¥25 to ¥30).

★**Locke Pub** PUB
(⌕186 6229 1372; Suzhou Culture and Expo Plaza iStation Shopping Centre D-10, 1 Guangfeng St, 苏州观枫1号文博官场负一层iStation D-10商铺; ⏱5pm-2am Tue-Sun; 🛜; Ⓜ Culture & Expo Centre, exit 2) Locke Pub is a key part of Suzhou's social and cultural scene, as much a community social space as a pub. As well as serving imported bottled beers, wine and cocktails, Locke hosts regular events and is a great place to meet locals.

★**Birdland** BAR
(飞度精酿啤酒餐吧, Fēidù Jīng Niàng Píjiǔ Cān Ba; ⌕0512 6723 9839; www.facebook.com/birdlandsuzhou; Block 2, Phase 4, Ligongdi, 李公堤4期2幢 (李公堤国际青年旅社一楼); drinks from ¥50; ⏱11am-1.30am Sat & Sun, from 4.30pm Mon-Fri) Friendly staff speak excellent English and there is an ever-changing selection of 15 well-kept, local brews on tap. There are also tasty burgers, pizza and potato wedges on the menu. On the ground floor of Ligongdi International Youth Hostel.

Flamingo Hops Brewery BREWERY
(火烈鸟精酿, Huǒlièniǎo Jīngniàng; ⌕6515 1800; 459 Shiquan Jie, 十全街459号; beers from ¥38; ⏱10.30am-midnight; 🛜) Flamingo bar opened its doors in 2018, when friendly co-owner Zhendong threw in his career as a painter to pursue his love of brewing. There are five fresh beers on tap and the osthmanthus ale is delicious.

Camel Sports Bar SPORTS BAR
(⌕0512 6547 9759; www.facebook.com/suzhoucamelsportsbar; B1 188 Xinghai Jie, 星海街188号恒宇广场一期地下一层108室; ⏱10am-late; 🛜; Ⓜ Line 1 to Xinghai Sq, exit 3) This casual basement pub in the Suzhou Industrial Park area shows international sports events, does western-style food and stocks a range of international beers and wines.

Hemingway Lounge & Terrace BAR
(⌕051262988851;www.facebook.com/Hemingway Suzhou; Ligongdi Phase 2, 2nd fl, Bldg A4, 1912 Bar St, 李公堤二期A4栋2楼 (李公堤1912酒吧街); ⏱8pm-late Tue-Sun) A long-standing expat hangout with a pleasant outdoor terrace

open in summer. This place is especially busy at weekends when live music and DJs entertain partygoers until the early hours. Salsa on Wednesdays also draws a crowd.

☆ Entertainment

Nightly music performances are held at the Garden of the Master of the Nets (p268) from April to November. Tickets are ¥100; don't expect anything too authentic and do expect to stand.

Kunqu Opera Museum CHINESE OPERA
(昆曲博物馆, Kūnqǔ Bówùguǎn; 14 Zhongzhangjia Xiang, 中张家巷14号; tickets ¥50) This place puts on performances of *kūnqǔ* (regional opera style) at 2pm on Sundays. Buy tickets by the theatre door on the day; arrive early as seats tend to fill up by 1.45pm. No English captions.

Pingtan Teahouse LIVE PERFORMANCE
(平弹茶馆, Píngtán Cháguǎn; ⌕136 0620 0502; 2nd fl, 626 Shiquan Jie, 十全街626号2楼; ⏱8-10pm) *Píngtán* enthusiasts gather here to keep the traditions alive. The music usually starts at 8pm. Order some tea (unlimited serves ¥200), and pick songs (¥50 to ¥100, some lyrics have English translations) for the master to play.

🛍 Shopping

Suzhou-style embroidery, calligraphy, paintings, sandalwood fans, writing brushes and silk underclothes are for sale nearly everywhere. Pingjiang Lu has a particularly wide selection of worthy souvenirs and gifts.

ℹ Information

Bank of China (中国银行, Zhōngguó Yínháng; 1450 Renmin Lu, 人民路1450号; ⏱8.30am-4.30pm) Exchanges currency and has 24-hour ATMs that take most international cards.

Industrial & Commercial Bank of China (工商银行, Gōngshāng Yínháng; 678 Heji Sq, 和基广场678号; ⏱8.10am-4.50pm Mon-Sat) Currency exchange and 24-hour ATMs.

Public Security Bureau (PSB, 公安局, Gōng'ānjú; ⌕0512 6522 5661, ext 20593; 1109 Renmin Lu, 人民路1109号) Can help with emergencies and visa problems. The visa office (出入境办证窗口, chūrùjìng bànzhèng chuāngkǒu) is about 200m down the lane at 17 Dashitou Xiang (大石头巷17号).

Sing Health Medical (新宁诊所, Xīnníng Zhěn-suǒ; ⌕6767 1655; www.singhealth.asia; 198 Xinghai Jie, 星海街198号; ⏱8.30am-9.30pm

Mon-Fri, 9am-6pm Sat & Sun; 🚇; Ⓜ Line 1 to Xinghai Sq, exit 2) Medical and dental clinic that is popular with expats. Has English- and German-speaking doctors. Consultations from ¥385.

ⓘ Getting There & Away

AIR

Suzhou's nearest airport is Wuxi, but Shanghai has cheaper and more frequent flights. Buses leave Suzhou North Long-distance Bus Station frequently between 6am and 5.30pm for Hong-qiao Airport (¥53) and Pudong International Airport (¥84) in Shanghai.

BUS

Suzhou has three long-distance bus stations and the two listed here are the most useful. Tickets can be bought at the stations or online with help from some hotels.

The principal station is the **North Long-distance Bus Station** (汽车北站, Qìchē Běizhàn; 29 Xihui Lu, 西汇路29号) at the northern end of Renmin Lu, a 1.5km walk east of the train station. Destinations include the following:

Hangzhou ¥74, three hours, regular departures (7.05am to 7pm)

Nanjing ¥60 to ¥76, three hours, four daily (9.25am, 1.25pm, 2.15pm and 6pm); the 6pm service only runs Monday to Friday

Tongli ¥9, 50 minutes, regular departures (7.05am to 4.25pm)

Zhouzhuang ¥17, 1¼ hours, every 40 minutes (7am to 6.10pm)

The **South Long-distance Bus Station** (汽车南门站客运站, Qìchē Nánmén Zhàn Kèyùn Zhàn; 601 Nanhuan Donglu, 南环东路601号) has buses to the following destinations:

Hangzhou ¥54 to ¥74, three hours, regular departures (7.35am to 7pm)

Nanjing ¥60 to ¥76, three hours, three departures (8.35am to 5.30pm Monday to Friday, to 2.30pm Saturday and Sunday)

Shanghai ¥31 to ¥100, two hours, regular departures (5.40am to 11.30pm)

Beside the train station, **North Square Bus Station** (苏州北广场汽车站, Sūzhōu Běiguǎng-chǎng Qìchēzhàn) is where you can catch bus 5 to Luzhi (¥3, one hour, every 15 minutes, 5.10am to 8.30pm). The bus station is the one nearest the North Square train ticket office.

TRAIN

Suzhou is on the Nanjing–Shanghai express G line and has a number of stations. The most useful are the central Suzhou Train Station (苏州站, Sūzhōu Zhàn) and Suzhou North Train Station (苏州北站, Sūzhōu Běizhàn), 12km north of the city centre. Book train tickets on the 2nd floor of the **Lianhe ticket centre** (火车票代售处,

Huǒchēpiào Dàishòu Chù; 📞 0512 6520 6681; 1606 Renmin Lu, 人民路1606号; ⊙ 8-11.30am & noon-6pm) or online at www.trip.com.

Trains for Beijing South (1st/2nd class ¥884/524, from five hours, 22 daily) depart from the Suzhou North Train Station (book ahead).

Trains departing from both stations include the following:

Nanjing 1st/2nd class ¥165/100, 49 minutes to 1¾ hours, frequent

Shanghai 1st/2nd class ¥65/35, 30 to 56 minutes, frequent

Wuxi 1st/2nd class ¥30/10, 10 to 30 minutes, frequent

ⓘ Getting Around

BICYCLE

Suzhou has a plethora of bike-rental schemes that are only available to citizens. At the time of writing, some hostels and hotels were trying to find ways for guests to borrow bikes.

BUS

Convenient tourist buses visit all sights and cost ¥3, passing by the train station. Look out for the Chinese character 游 in front of the bus number (and on the bus stops) – this identifies tourist bus services.

Bus 游1 Stops at Suzhou Museum, the Garden to Linger In and Tiger Hill.

Bus 游2 Travels from Tiger Hill, Pan Gate and along Shiquan Jie.

Bus 游4 Runs the length of Renmin Lu and terminates at Lingyan Mountain.

Bus 游5 Loops around the perimeter of the old town, stopping at Suzhou Museum and Pan Gate.

METRO

Suzhou metro Line 1 runs along Ganjiang Lu, connecting Mudu in the southwest with Zhong-nan Jie station in the east and running through stations Xinghai Sq, Culture & Expo Centre and Times Sq, in the Suzhou Industrial Park. Line 2 runs north–southeast from Qihi to Sangtiandao via Suzhou North Train Station, Suzhou Train Station and Shantang St. Line 4 runs north–south from Longdaobang before branching off at Hongquang to head to either Tongli or Muli.

Lines 3 and 5 were under construction at the time of writing.

TAXI

Fares start at ¥13 and drivers generally use their meters. A trip from Guanqian Jie to Suzhou Train Station should cost around ¥16 to ¥22. From Suzhou North Train Station to downtown, the fare is around ¥50 to ¥60. Pedicabs hover around the tourist areas and can be persistent (¥5 to ¥10 for short rides is standard).

Mudu 木渎

📞 0512 / POP 86,000

Dating from the Ming dynasty, the canal town of Mudu (Mùdú) was once the haunt of wealthy officials, intellectuals and artists, and even the Qing Emperor Qianlong visited six times. Today the village has become an extension of Suzhou as the city develops outwards. While it's not as picturesque as other canal towns, it's easy to reach from Suzhou (the metro runs here) and offers a glimpse of traditional Jiangsu canal-town heritage architecture in its bridges, ancient residences and gardens.

⊙ Sights

The village is free if you merely want to soak up the atmosphere. Entrance fees are for the top sights alone; however, they contain most of Mudu's character and history. A through ticket to all the sights is ¥78.

Mudu's best-known sight is the Ming-dynasty **Yan Family Garden** (严家花园, Yánjiā Huāyuán; cnr Shantang Jie & Mingqing Jie, 山塘街明清街的路口; ¥40; ⊙ 8.30am-4.30pm Nov-Mar, to 5pm Apr-Oct; Ⓜ Mudu) in the northwest corner of the village. The garden, with its rockeries and meandering lake, is divided into five sections, each designed to evoke a season.

Next along Shantang Jie is **Mingyue Temple** (明月古寺, Míngyuè Gǔsì; ⊙ 8.30am-4.30pm Nov-Mar, to 5pm Apr-Oct;) FREE, which dates back to the 10th century but has been largely reconstructed since the Cultural Revolution. The 1000-arm, four-faced Guanyin statue is worth a look – notice the ruler she holds in one of her lower hands, among other Buddhist ritual objects.

Hongyin Mountain Villa (虹饮山房, Hóngyǐn Shānfáng; Shantang Jie, 山塘街; ¥40; ⊙ 8.30am-4.30pm Nov-Mar, to 5pm Apr-Oct) has an opera stage, exhibits and an imperial pier where Emperor Qianlong docked his boat. The stage in the centre hall is impressive; honoured guests were seated in front and the galleries along the sides of the hall were for women. The emperor was a frequent visitor and you can see his uncomfortable-looking imperial chair and plastic displays of imperial feasts.

In the middle of Shantang Jie, the **Ancient Pine Garden** (古松园, Gǔsōngyuán; ¥20; ⊙ 8.30am-4.30pm Nov-Mar, to 5pm Apr-Oct) is an attractive courtyard complex; its carved beams depict officials, hats, phoenixes, flowers and other designs.

Around Suzhou

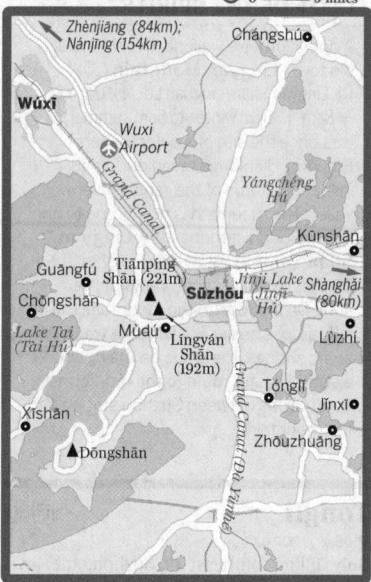

Bangyan Mansion (榜眼府第, Bǎngyǎn Fǔdì; Xiatang Jie, 下塘街; ¥10; ⊙ 8.30am-4.30pm Nov-Mar, to 5pm Apr-Oct) often serves as a movie set, and it's easy to see why, with its rich collection of antique furniture and intricate carvings of stone and wood. The attractive complex was home to 19th-century writer and politician Feng Guifen, who earned the prestigious second place (*bǎngyǎn*) in the imperial examinations of his year.

A short 10- to 15-minute **boat ride**, departing from Bangyan Mansion and Yan Family Garden, costs ¥30 per person (¥120 per boat minimum charge). Buy your ticket at any of the main sights.

🛏 Sleeping & Eating

Mudu doesn't cater well to those who want to spend the night and most people choose to spend the night in nearby Suzhou.

There's no shortage of places to eat along the canalside Shangtang Jie.

ℹ Getting There & Away

From Suzhou, jump aboard metro Line 1 to Mudu station then take exit 1 and hop on bus 2, 38 or 622 (all ¥1), 4km (four stops) away from the old town (木渎古镇站, Mùdú Gǔzhèn zhàn). Alternatively, a taxi from Mudu station to the old town will cost ¥15.

CLIFF OF THE SPIRITS

A one-kilometre walk north of Mudu's old town, **Lingyan Mountain** (灵岩山, Língyán Shān; Lingtian Lu, 灵田路; ¥2; ⊙8am-4.30pm winter, to 5pm summer) was once the site of a palace where Emperor Qianlong stayed during his inspection tours of the Yangzi River valley. The mountain is now home to an active Buddhist monastery, **Lingyan Shan Temple** (灵岩山寺, Língyán Shān Sì) that has panoramic views of the area. On the way up the mountain, the left ramp is busier but will take you past some shrines; the steps on the right take a slightly faster route to the top. Tourist bus Y4 runs between Suzhou station and the mountain.

Tongli 同里

☑ 0512 / POP 62,000

Only 18km southeast of Suzhou, the lovely water town of Tongli (Tónglǐ) has an old town with buildings that have mostly kept their traditional facades, with prim whitewashed walls, black tiled roofs and willow-shaded canal views. To fully appreciate Tongli's charm, stay the night, explore the cobbled backstreets, or visit on a weekday as the languorous tempo is frequently shredded by marauding tour groups on weekends.

Admission to the village (¥100) includes access to all the sights and is valid for two days. Get the ticket stamped at the gate if you intend to return. You can pick up a free map at the **tourist centre** (☑400 698 2990; ⊙7.30am-5.15pm).

◉ Sights

Gēnglè Táng　　HISTORIC BUILDING
(耕乐堂; ⊙9am-5.30pm) This elegant Ming-dynasty estate in the west of town has 41 beautifully restored halls that have been redecorated with paintings, calligraphy and elaborate tree-root carvings.

Pearl Pagoda　　PAGODA
(珍珠塔, Zhēnzhū Tǎ; ⊙9am-5.30pm) In the north of town, quiet Pearl Pagoda dates from the Qing dynasty and contains a spacious residential complex decorated with Qing-era antiques, an ancestral hall, a garden and an opera stage. It gets its name from a tiny model pagoda draped in pearls.

Tuisi Garden　　GARDENS
(退思园, Tuìsī Yuán; ⊙9am-5.30pm) This beautiful 19th-century garden in the east of the old town delightfully translates as the 'Withdraw and Reflect Garden', so named because it was the retirement home of a demoted Qing government official. The 'Tower of Fanning Delight' served as the living quarters, while the garden itself is a meditative portrait of a shimmering pond, rockeries and pavilions.

☞ Tours

Slow-moving six-person boats (¥90 per boat for 25 minutes) ply the waters of Tongli's canal system between 7.30am and 5.30pm.

English-speaking tours (¥160 per group, 1½ hours) can be arranged from the south ticket office.

🛏 Sleeping

If your lodgings are inside the old town, you'll need to pay the admission fee to access them if you arrive before 6pm. After 6pm, admission is free and the next day you'll only need a ticket if you wish to enter any of the sights.

Guesthouses can be hard to spot – look for small chalkboard signs around Huichuan Bridge and the north end of Fuguan Jie. Rooms are basic and start at about ¥120.

A couple of minutes outside the north gate, **Begonia Flowers Guesthouse** (海棠花开清水客栈, Hǎitánghuā Kāi Qīngshuǐ Kèzhàn; ☑137 7603 4000; sz129@hotmail.com; 79 Dongxi Jie, 东溪街79号; r ¥180-460; ✿❋❈) has clean, bright rooms with private bathrooms. Make sure you get the code for the door when you check in.

Taimuting Hotel (泰睦庭人文酒店, Tàimùtíng Rénwén Jiǔdiàn; ☑0512 6333 2333; 138 Xintian Jie, 新填街138号; r incl breakfast ¥1000-2600; ❋❈) has seven Zen-themed luxury suites above its own cosy teahouse in the old town.

🍴 Eating & Drinking

Restaurants are everywhere, but food prices here are relatively high. Some local dishes to try include *méigāncài shāoròu* (梅干菜烧肉, stewed meat with dried vegetables), *yínyú chǎodàn* (银鱼炒蛋, silver-fish omelette) and *zhuàngyuántí* (状元蹄, stewed pig's leg). Don't expect to eat late: many of the canalside restaurants close before 8pm if business is slow.

On the west side of town, **Xishan Vegetarian Restaurant** (喜善素食馆, Xǐshàn Sùshí Guǎn; ☑158 6259 8611; 129 Shangyuan Jie, 上元街129号; dishes ¥38-108; ⊙11am-8pm; ❈☑) serves flavoursome meals that draw on Chinese and Japanese Buddhist cooking methods. The simple set menu (¥68) comprises three small dishes, soup and rice.

There is a neon-lit bar street along the canal just outside the south gate. Drinks aren't cheap but live music is likely.

ℹ️ Getting There & Away

From Suzhou, you can get to Tongli by bus or metro.

Tongli metro station is on Line 4 (¥6, 50 minutes). From there, it's 3km to the old town: take bus 725 (¥1, 10 minutes, every 25 minutes) west on Ganquan Donglu (甘泉东路) for four stops.

Buses from Suzhou North Square Bus Station (p274; ¥9, 50 minutes, hourly) are convenient if you are coming by train from Shanghai (¥38, 30 minutes, frequent).

Buses running from **Tongli Long-distance Bus Station** (同里汽车站), 1.2km east of the old town, include the following:

Hangzhou North Station ¥67, three hours, four daily

Shanghai ¥78, 1½ hours, hourly; direct to Hongqiao and Pudong airports

Zhouzhuang Local bus 758; ¥7, 30 minutes, frequent departures

---

Zhouzhuang 周庄

📞 0512 / POP 33,000

The 900-year-old water village of Zhouzhuang (Zhōuzhuāng) is the best-known canal town in Jiangsu. Located some 30km southeast of Suzhou, it is very popular with tour groups, thanks to Chen Yifei, the late renowned Chinese painter whose works of the once-idyllic village are its claim to fame.

The town still has plenty of old-world charm, with its wide green canals, traditional architecture, delightful stone bridges and tall willow trees. Get up early or take an evening stroll, before the crowds arrive or when they begin to thin out.

◎ Sights & Activities

Admission to Zhouzhuang is ¥100 (access is free after 8pm); make sure you get your photo digitally added to the ticket at purchase, as this entitles you to a three-day pass.

The best way to view Zhouzhuang's bridges is by coasting under them on a 20-minute boat ride. There are a handful of different routes (¥150 per boat; 8am to 6.30pm) including an evening service (¥180 per boat; 6.30pm to 8pm). Many of the boaters are also

excellent singers. Make sure you negotiate the price first: ¥10 is the going rate for one song.

Shen's House HISTORIC BUILDING
(沈厅, Shěntīng; 85 Nanshi Jie, 南市街85号; ⊗8am-8pm) Near Fu'an Bridge, this residence of the Shen clan is a lavish piece of Qing-style architecture boasting three halls and more than 100 rooms. The first section (in front of the ticketed area) is particularly interesting, as it has a water gate and a wharf where the family moored their private boats. You can picture the compound entirely daubed in Maoist graffiti c 1969 (note the crudely smashed carvings above the doors).

Most tour groups skip the **2nd floor** (走马楼; ¥30; ⊗8.30am-4.00pm), possibly because of the steep staircase, but rooms up here are furnished and you can get a bird's-eye view of the hall.

Zhang's House HISTORIC BUILDING
(张厅, Zhāngtīng; 38 Beishi Jie, 北市街38号; ⊗8am-7pm) To the south of the Twin Bridges, this beautiful 60-room, three-hall structure was built in the Ming era and bought by the Zhang clan in early Qing times as their residence. There's an opera stage to keep the ladies entertained (they were not supposed to leave home or seek entertainment outside). Also note the chairs after the reception hall. Unmarried women could only sit on those with a hollow seatback, symbolising that they had nobody to rely on!

Don't overlook the garden, where boats could drift straight up to the house to its own little wharf. Trek back to the road via the 'side lane', a narrow 47m-long servants' hall that ends at the back of a souvenir shop.

ℹ️ TICKET WARNING

When buying a bus ticket from Suzhou to Zhouzhuang, you will likely be encouraged to purchase a package ticket (¥160) that covers the bus fare, and admission to the old town and the **Mystery of Life Museum** (生命奥秘馆, Shēngmìng Aomì Guǎn), a ghoulish exhibition of dissected people and animals that we only wish we could unsee.

You'll save money by purchasing only the bus ticket (¥17) and then buying the town ticket (¥100) in Zhouzhuang.

Twin Bridges BRIDGE

Zhouzhuang's most iconic bridges are this Ming-dynasty pair (双桥, Shuāngqiáo) gracing the intersection of two waterways in the heart of town.

Quanfu Temple BUDDHIST TEMPLE

(全福讲寺, Quánfú Jiǎngsì; ⊙8.30am-5.30pm) The amber-hued 'Full Fortune' temple was originally founded during the Song dynasty, but has been repeatedly rebuilt. The structure you see today is an incarnation from 1995, when a handful of halls and gardens were added to the mix.

Temple of the God of Wealth TEMPLE

(财神居, Cáishén Jū; ¥20; ⊙8am-5.30pm) Across Quanfu Bridge and 400m east of the old town, the Temple of the God of Wealth is housed in the former residence of Shen Wansan, Zhouzhuang's 14th-century 'local boy made good'. The temple includes a small museum on Wansan's life and entry is through a series of fun coin-shaped arches.

🛏 Sleeping & Eating

There are a handful of guesthouses in town that charge around ¥130 for a basic room. At the time of writing, no hostels were able to accept foreigners.

In a traditional white-walled residence right outside the southwest exit, **Show Year** (Sù Nián Huáijiù Jiǔdiàn, 素年怀旧酒店; ☑3680 7432; 6 Tongxiuli, 通秀里6号; d ¥340-520; ❄ 🛜) is a boutique hotel with industrial-concrete and cheerful, vintage vibes. Some rooms have a shared courtyard and all have private bathrooms. Chinese-style breakfast is included.

Restaurants serving tender wansan pork (steamed or braised hock) are at almost every corner. Avoid paying for the local $ā\ pó$ tea (old woman's tea), which can be extortionately priced.

For a cafe with a twist, cute **Momicafe** (☑5720 2307; Xianyuannong, 蚬园弄; ⊙10am-10pm) allows you to purchase a postcard and request a date (potentially years in the future) for it to be mailed. International postage rates are reasonable, the coffee is half-decent, and there's a good selection of pretty stationery on offer.

☆ Entertainment

The **ancient kūnqǔ stage** (昆曲古戏台, Kūnqǔ Gǔ Xìtái; 108 Beishi Jie, 北市街108号; ⊙10.30am-3.10pm Mon, Wed, Fri & Sun, 10.45am & 12.45pm Thu) **FREE** holds open-air performances every other day. While the quality won't blow your socks off, the costumes are merry and the actors enthusiastic. Don't worry about arriving for the beginning of a show or staying for the duration. Live music borders on karaoke here. If anything's playing, you will hear it before you see it.

ℹ Information

Zhouzhuang Visitor Centre (周庄游客中心, Zhōuzhuāng Yóukè Zhōngxīn; ☑0512 5721 1655; Quanfu Lu, 全福路; ⊙24hr) In front of the entrance archway. A little English is spoken here and staff are relatively helpful. Has maps.

ℹ Getting There & Away

Buses from Suzhou North Long-distance Bus Station (¥17, 1¼ hours, every 40 minutes, 7am to 6.10pm) terminate at a visitor centre 1.5km north of Zhouzhuang old town. From the visitor centre, head southeast (towards the pagoda) till you see the bridge on Yunhai Lu. Cross the bridge and continue south until you reach the archway that marks Quangong Lu. Walk one block along Quangong Lu and you'll see the bigger arch that marks the entrance to the village on your right. The walk takes about 15 minutes; a taxi should cost no more than ¥10.

Returning to Suzhou, buses (first/last bus 7am/6.05pm) do not leave from the visitor centre. You will need to catch a taxi (¥12, 15 minutes) or bus 261 (¥1, 30 minutes, every 25 minutes, 7.45am to 6.35pm) from the Quangong Lu memorial arch 3.5km north to Zhouzhuang New Passenger Station (新客站, Xīn Kèzhàn). Buses also run from here to Shanghai Long-distance Bus Station (¥32, 2½ hours, four daily).

To get to Tongli, local bus 758 (¥2, 25 minutes, every 30 minutes, 6.30am to 6pm) runs from Jiāngzé (江泽) bus station, a 10-minute walk east of the old town.

Luzhi 角直

☑0512 / POP 200,000

A lovely day trip only 25km east of Suzhou, the charming and petite canal town of Luzhi (Lùzhí) has a lovely assortment of streets, alleys and centuries-old humpbacked bridges to explore.

You will only need to buy a ticket (¥78) if you wish to enter any of the sights (8am to 5pm), all of which can be safely missed. If you're visiting in a group, a leisurely 20- or 40-minute boat ride (¥150 or ¥240) is much better value. Rides depart from the tourist centre.

Tacked onto the old town's east, **Luzhi Cultural Park** (角直文化园, Lùzhí Wénhuà

Yuán) FREE is a huge, faux-Ming-dynasty complex. Admission is free and the exhibition halls, ponds, pavilions and opera stage make it an interesting place to amble.

Most people head back to Suzhou after a few hours of sightseeing. Stay the night, however, and you'll find that evenings are relaxed and tranquil (if a little dark).

Down a whitewashed alley in the old town, **Yinxian Courtyard Inn** (文化主题客栈, Wénhuà Zhǔtí Kèzhàn; ☑137 7602 6159; 1 Rimaochang, 日茂场1号; d ¥160-200; ❋⑤) has simple rooms, all with private bathrooms. The two-level guesthouse is arranged around a leafy courtyard and charmingly cluttered calligraphy workshop. The alley is the first right off Dongfuxiatang Jie (东市下塘街), opposite a wooden cafe.

Just west of the old town, the **Ramada Suzhou Luzhi** (☑0512 8098 1777; 18 Fucheng Beilu, 甫澄北路18号; d¥650-800; ❂❋⑤◪) is a very comfortable option, though not at the budget end.

Luzhi is chock-full of traditional restaurants and smart cafes, perfect for enjoying a beer or coffee near the canal. Restaurant specialities include river clams, shrimps, pork hock and boiled, soft-textured water caltrop (菱角, língjiǎo; like a water chestnut), which you will see served up everywhere.

For super-fresh street food, **Yángjiànmíng Shāobǐng** (杨建明烧饼; ☑183 5608 0306; Zhengyuan Lu, 正源路; flatbread ¥4; ⊙10am-9pm) serves tasty northern-style flat-bread, cooked in a traditional oven – expect a small, chatty wait while the bread cooks, even if you don't speak Chinese.

ℹ Getting There & Away

Getting to Luzhi from Suzhou is easy: take bus 5 from Suzhou North Square Bus Station (¥3, one hour, every 15 minutes, 5.10am to 8.30pm) or Xinhai Sq (¥3, 45 minutes) to Xiaoshi Lu (晓市路). When you get off, continue along Xiaoshi Lu, turning left at the intersection. The old town entrance is 100m along on the right.

The last bus back to Suzhou leaves at 8pm.

LUZHI'S LÙDUĀN

The 6m-tall statue guarding the entrance to Luzhi's old town may resemble a one-horned *qílín* (scaly mythical creature with deer's hooves) but is actually of a *lùduān*, an auspicious truth-seeking beast that can travel 9000km in a single day. *Lùduān* always know when a lie is told and can compel people to speak the truth. Telling the two mythological creatures apart is easy – *lùduān* have claws, while *qílín* have hooves.

Luzhi and the word *lùduān* are spelled with the same first character, 甪, which is also the shape that the town's river makes on a map if you squint.

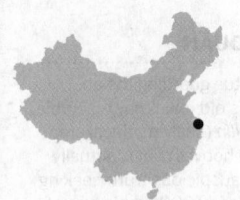

Shanghai

♪ 021 / POP 26.32 MILLION

Best Places to Eat

➡ Yang's Fry Dumplings (p318)

➡ El Willy (p320)

➡ Din Tai Fung (p324)

➡ Lost Heaven (p322)

Best Places to Stay

➡ Fairmont Peace Hotel (p316)

➡ Mandarin Oriental Pudong (p318)

➡ Kevin's Old House (p317)

➡ Waterhouse at South Bund (p316)

➡ Urbn (p317)

Why Go?

You can't see the Great Wall from space, but you'd have a job missing Shanghai (上海, Shànghǎi). One of the country's largest and most vibrant cities, Shanghai somehow typifies modern China while being unlike anywhere else in the land. Shanghai is real China, but – rather like Hong Kong or Macau – just not the China you had in mind.

This is a city of action and few places in the world evoke so much history, excess, glamour, mystique and exotic promise in name alone. It best serves as an epilogue to your China experience: submit to its charms after you've had your fill of dusty imperial palaces and bumpy 10-hour bus rides. From fancy dining, shopping and skyscraper-hopping to bullet-fast Maglev trains and glamorous cocktails – enjoy Shanghai.

When to Go
Shanghai

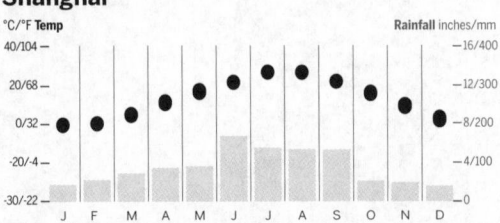

Feb or Mar Visit Yùyuán Gardens for the lantern festival, two weeks after Chinese New Year.	Apr & May March is chilly and 1 May is chaos, but otherwise spring is ideal.	Late Sep–Oct The optimal season: neither too hot nor too rainy.

History

Over just a few centuries, Shanghai transformed from an insignificant walled town south of the mouth of the Yangzi River to China's leading and wealthiest metropolis. A dizzying swirl of opium, trade, foreign control, vice, glamour, glitz, rebellion, restoration and money, Shanghai's story is a rags-to-riches saga of decadence, exploitation and, ultimately, achievement.

As the gateway to the Yangzi River (Chang Jiang), Shanghai (the name means 'by the sea') has long been an ideal trading port. However, although it supported as many as 50,000 residents by the late 17th century, it wasn't until after the British opened their concession here in 1842 that modern Shanghai really came into being.

The British were soon followed by the French and Americans, and by 1853 Shanghai had overtaken all other Chinese ports. Built on the trade of opium, silk and tea, the city also lured the world's big banks, which erected palaces on the Bund. Shanghai also became a byword for exploitation and vice; its countless opium dens, gambling joints and brothels managed by gangs were at the heart of Shanghai life. Guarding it all were the American, French and Italian marines, British Tommies and Japanese bluejackets.

After Chiang Kaishek's coup against the communists in 1927, the Kuomintang cooperated with the foreign police and the Shanghai gangs, and with Chinese and foreign factory owners, to suppress labour unrest. Exploited in workhouse conditions, crippled by hunger and poverty, sold into slavery, and excluded from the high life and the parks created by the foreigners, the poor of Shanghai formed the Chinese Communist Party (CCP) here in 1921 and, after numerous setbacks, became the new governors of the city in 1949.

The communists eradicated the slums, rehabilitated the city's hundreds of thousands of opium addicts, and eliminated child and slave labour. These were staggering achievements. Shanghai then became a factory town and political hotbed, and was the power base of the influential Gang of Four during the Cultural Revolution.

Shanghai's announcement of plans to develop Pudong, on the eastern side of the Huangpu River, came in 1990. Since then the city's burgeoning economy, leadership and intrinsic self-confidence have put it miles ahead of other Chinese cities. Its bright lights and opportunities have branded Shanghai a mecca for Chinese (and foreign) economic migrants. In 2010, 3600 people were squeezed into every square kilometre, compared with 2588 per sq km in 2000, and by 2014 the city's population had leaped to a staggering 24 million. Over nine million migrants have made Shanghai home, colouring the local complexion with a jumble of dialects, outlooks, lifestyles and cuisines.

The task of the Chinese leadership now demands a more pressing focus on balancing the economy away from its export and high-investment model, rooting out corruption, attempting to tame the rampant property market (as apartment prices put home ownership beyond the reach of most) and narrowing the chasm dividing low-wage earners from the wealthy elites. In recent years, the issue of migrant workers' rights in Shanghai and other cities became paramount, as workers sought to bring their rights (education for their children and access to health care) closer to native Shanghainese. Meanwhile Shanghai reached record-breaking levels of atmospheric pollutants, and in 2018 it superseded the capital on smog levels. Authorities have set targets to make serious reductions.

Language

Outside hotels, English is not widely spoken, and even less so outside the city. You'll be able to get by in tourist areas, but it's useful to learn a few basic phrases. Some restaurants may not have an English menu. You'll find yourself surrounded by written Chinese wherever you travel, so the Pleco app (www.pleco.com) or phrasebook is useful, or you can always call **Shanghai Call Centre** (☏ 021 962 288) for on the spot translations.

◉ Sights

◉ The Bund & People's Square

★**The Bund**   ARCHITECTURE
(外滩, Wàitān; Map p286; 3 East Zhongshan No 1 Rd, 3中山东一路; Ⓜ East Nanjing Rd) Symbolic of concession-era Shanghai, the Bund was the city's Wall Street, a place of feverish trading and fortunes made and lost. Originally a towpath for dragging barges of rice, the Bund (an Anglo-Indian term for the embankment of a muddy waterfront) was gradually transformed into a grandiose sweep of the most powerful banks and trading houses in Shanghai. The optimal activity here is to simply stroll, contrasting the bones of the past with the futuristic geometry of Pudong's skyline.

Shanghai Highlights

❶ The Bund
(p281) Strolling along Shanghai's famous promenade with Mainland China's most iconic concession-era district as a backdrop.

❷ Shanghai Tower
(p303) Gazing down on the Shanghai cityscape from the 118th-floor (632m) observation of China's tallest building.

❸ Yuyuan Gardens
(p292) Seeking out a quiet corner among the ponds, trees, bridges, pavilions and harmonic compositions within one of the country's best traditional gardens.

❹ Jade Buddha Temple (p300)
Witnesses a continual stream of worshippers at this iconic, century-old Buddhist temple.

❺ Shanghai Museum (p285)
Browsing everything from ancient bronzes and gorgeous Qing-dynasty ceramic masterpieces to the wonders of the natural world.

❻ M50 (p300)
Perusing cutting-edge contemporary art, photography and collaborative works in spaces repurposed from former factories and cotton mills.

The majority of the art deco and neoclassical buildings here were built in the early 20th century and presented an imposing – if strikingly un-Chinese – view for those nosing by boat into the busy port city. Today it has emerged as a designer retail and restaurant zone, and the city's most exclusive boutiques, restaurants and hotels see the Bund as the only place to be. Evening visits are rewarded by electric views of Pudong and the illuminated grandeur of the Bund. Other options include taking a boat tour on the Huangpu River or relaxing at some fabulous bars and restaurants. Huangpu Park, at the north end of the promenade, features the modest **Bund History Museum** (外滩历史纪念馆, Wàitān Lìshǐ Jìniànguǎn; ⊙9am-4pm Mon-Fri) FREE, which contains a collection of old photographs and maps.

Get here early for the intriguing sight of the morning exercises.

★**Shanghai History Museum** MUSEUM
(上海市历史博物馆, Shànghǎi Shì Lìshǐ Bówùguǎn; Map p286; ☑021 6323 2504; 325 Nanjing West Rd, 南京西路325号; ⊙9am-5pm Tue-Sun, last entry 4pm; Ⓜ People's Square) FREE Originally opened as the Shanghai Race Club in 1934, and having undergone several incarnations since, this iconic building now houses the Shanghai History Museum. Opened in 2018, the museum covers the city's history over three floors, spanning the Shanghai area's political, social, economic and cultural evolution from 4000 BC to the founding of the People's Republic of China in 1949. You're bound to gain some insight, political propaganda notwithstanding.

The well-chosen displays on the 2nd floor showcase the Shanghai Majiabang (approximately dated to the 4th or 5th century BC),

Songze and Liangzhu periods and beyond. Particularly insightful is the documentation of the ways in which geology influenced the area's early development – the relationship between land and water was skillfully managed by inhabitants to make it the thriving trade city that it later became. The 3rd and 4th floors focus on the colonial strivings for Shanghai – specifically the 19th-century period of British, French and US dominance – and the way that the Opium Wars influenced the commerce, trade and wealth of the city and devastated its population.

Expect archaeological findings, interactive digital displays, maps, dioramas, and recreations of Shanghai street scenes. Count on spending a couple of hours here; you can finish by having food or drink at **Roof 325** (屋顶325, Wūdǐng 325; ☑021 6327 0767; www.roof325.com; 2-course set lunch ¥138, à la carte meals ¥450-1500; ⊙10.30am-11.30pm) on the 5th floor.

★**Rockbund Art Museum** MUSEUM
(RAM, 上海外滩美术馆, Shànghǎi Wàitān Měishùguǎn; Map p286; www.rockbundartmuseum.org; 20 Huqiu Rd, 虎丘路20号; adult/child ¥50/20; ⊙10am-6pm Tue-Sun; Ⓜ East Nanjing Rd) Housed in the magnificent former Royal Asiatic Society building (1932) – once Shanghai's first museum – this world-class gallery behind the Bund focuses on contemporary Chinese and international art, with rotating exhibits year-round and no permanent collection. One of the city's top modern-art venues, the building's interior and exterior are both sublime. Check out the unique art deco eight-sided *bāguà* (trigram) windows at the front, a fetching synthesis of western modernist styling and traditional Chinese design.

The interior is all textbook deco lines and curves, including the fine staircase. Head to the rooftop terrace for excellent views, despite the hulking form of the Peninsula Hotel blocking out much of Lujiazui. Admission includes a free coffee from the top-floor cafe.

★**Shanghai Urban Planning Exhibition Hall** MUSEUM
(上海城市规划展示馆, Shànghǎi Chéngshì Guīhuà Zhǎnshìguǎn; Map p286; 100 Renmin Ave, entrance on Middle Xizang Rd, 人民大道100号西藏中路入口; adult/child ¥30/15; ⊙9am-5pm Tue-Sun, last entry 4pm; Ⓜ People's Square) Set over five levels, this modern museum covers Shanghai's urban planning history, tracing its development from swampy fishing village to modern-day megacity. Its mix of photography, models and interactive multimedia displays

---

ⓘ **PRICE RANGES**

Sleeping

The following price ranges represent the price per night for a double room.

¥ Less than ¥500

¥¥ ¥500–1300

¥¥¥ More than ¥1300

Eating

Price ranges for a meal for one person:

¥ less than ¥80

¥¥ ¥80–180

¥¥¥ more than ¥180

SHANGHAI SIGHTS

ⓘ TOP TIPS

➡ The Shanghai metro is fast, efficient, cheap, punctual and extensive.

➡ Taxis are widespread and great value for short hops.

➡ For budget accommodation, stick to Puxi, not Pudong.

➡ If you only have a few days, see the Bund, People's Square, the French Concession and Jing'an, with a foray to Pudong.

➡ Download a translation app to your phone and store the useful Shanghai Call Centre number for quick on-the-spot translations.

➡ Download a metro map app for quick reference and route planning around the city.

➡ Download a VPN before you arrive in China in order to access blocked websites (Facebook, Twitter, Google, Instagram etc).

---

keeps things entertaining. The 1st floor covers the city's rise, including the establishment of the international settlement, and profiles its colonial architecture and *shíkùmén* (stone gate) housing. The most popular feature is on the 3rd floor – a visually stunning model showing a detailed layout of the megalopolis-to-be, plus an impressive Virtual World 3D wrap-around tour.

The 4th floor is a bit more niche, covering themes of transport and sustainability, but all is well presented. There's a small cafe on the 5th floor overlooking People's Park. Audio guides are ¥20, but exhibits are generally well captioned. The 2nd floor shows temporary exhibits.

Upon exiting you'll find yourself in 'Old Shanghai Street', a recreation of 1930s Shanghai, complete with vintage cars, historical photographs and a cobblestone walkway that leads to a modern underground shopping plaza.

★ **Shanghai Museum**　　　　MUSEUM
(上海博物馆, Shànghǎi Bówùguǎn; Map p286; www.shanghaimuseum.net; 201 People's Ave, 201人民大道; ⊙9am-5pm Tue-Sun, last entry 4pm; ⑪; Ⓜ People's Square) **FREE** This must-see museum escorts you through the craft of millennia and the pages of Chinese history. It's home to one of the most impressive collections in the land: take your pick from the archaic green patinas of the Ancient Chinese Bronzes Gallery through to the silent solemnity of the Ancient Chinese Sculpture Gallery and from the exquisite beauty of the ceramics in the Zande Lou Gallery to the measured and timeless flourishes captured in the Chinese Calligraphy Gallery.

Chinese painting, seals, jade, Ming and Qing furniture, coins and ethnic costumes are also on offer, intelligently displayed in well-lit galleries. The building itself is designed to resemble the shape of an ancient Chinese *dǐng* (three-legged cooking vessel). The excellent museum shop sells postcards, a rich array of books, and faithful replicas of the museum's ceramics and other pieces.

The audio guide is well worth the ¥40 (deposit ¥400 or your passport). Expect to spend half, if not most of, a day here.

Former British Consulate　HISTORIC BUILDING
(英国驻上海总领事馆, Yīngguó Zhù Shànghǎi Zǒng Lǐngshìguǎn; Map p286; 33 East Zhongshan No 1 Rd, 33中山東路1号; Ⓜ East Nanjing Rd) The original British Consulate was one of the first foreign buildings to go up in Shanghai in 1852, though it was destroyed in a fire and replaced with the current structure in 1873. Now renovated, it is used as a financiers' club and restaurant, **No 1 Waitanyuan** (外滩源一号, Wàitān Yuán Yī Hào; ☏ 021 5308 9803; platter for 2 people ¥320; ⊙high tea 2-5pm), which serves high tea. Also within the grounds are the former Consul's Residence (1884) – now a flagship Patek Philippe store – and several century-old magnolia trees.

Hongkong & Shanghai Bank Building　HISTORIC BUILDING
(HSBC Building, 汇丰大厦; Map p286; 12 East Zhongshan No 1 Rd, 中山东一路12号; Ⓜ East Nanjing Rd) Adjacent to the Custom House (p288), the Hongkong & Shanghai Bank Building was constructed in 1923. The bank was first established in Hong Kong in 1864 and in Shanghai in 1865 to finance trade, and soon became one of the richest in Shanghai, arranging the indemnity paid after the Boxer Rebellion. The magnificent mosaic ceiling inside the entrance was plastered over until its restoration in 1997 and is therefore well preserved.

The Bund & People's Square

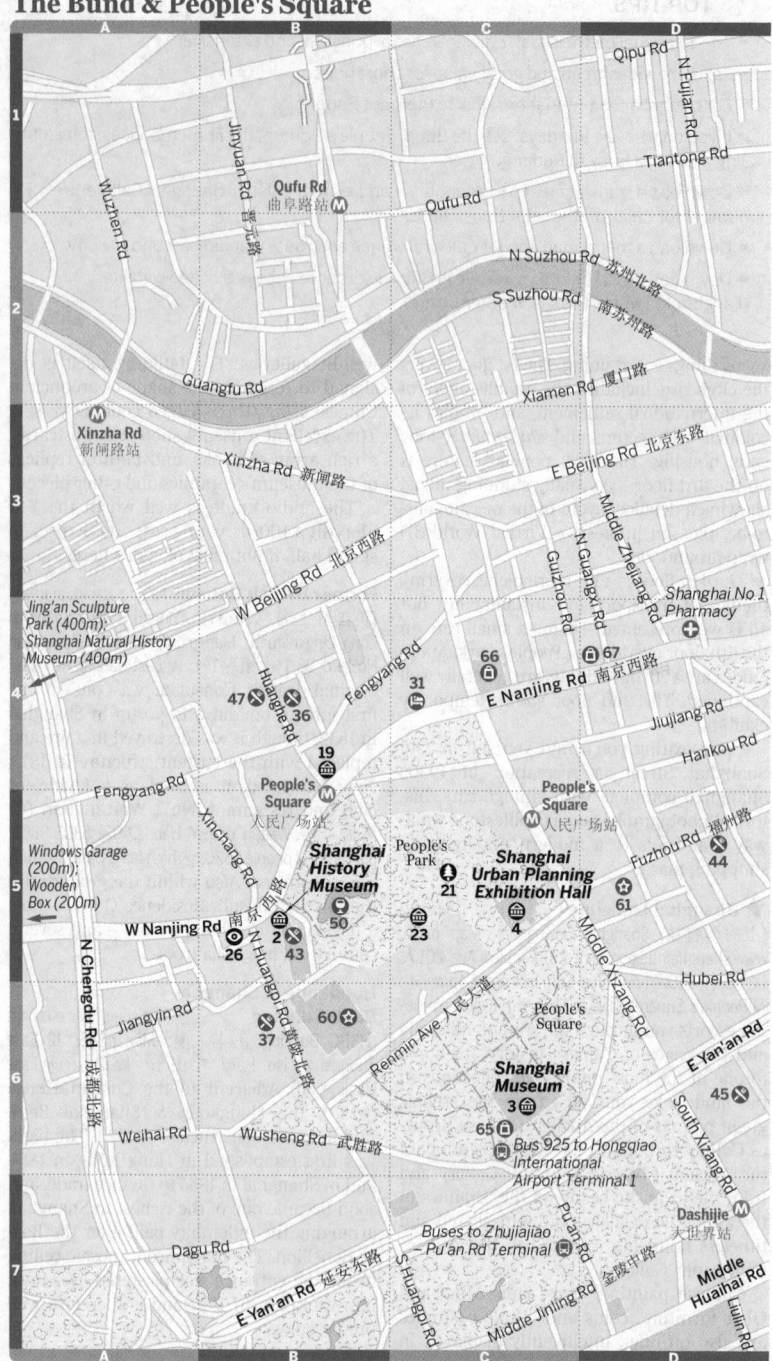

SHANGHAI

Qipu Rd

N Fujian Rd

Tiantong Rd

Jinyuan Rd 晋元路

Wuzhen Rd

Qufu Rd
曲阜路站 Ⓜ Qufu Rd

N Suzhou Rd 苏州北路

S Suzhou Rd 南苏州路

Guangfu Rd

Xiamen Rd 厦门路

Xinzha Rd
Ⓜ 新闸路站

Xinzha Rd 新闸路

E Beijing Rd 北京东路

W Beijing Rd 北京西路

Middle Zhejiang Rd

N Guangxi Rd

Guizhou Rd

**Shanghai No 1
Pharmacy**

Jing'an Sculpture
Park (400m);
Shanghai Natural History
Museum (400m)

Fengyang Rd

66 Ⓢ

Ⓐ 67

E Nanjing Rd 南京西路

31 🏛

47 ⊗   36 ⊗

Huangpi Rd

Jiujiang Rd

Hankou Rd

19 🏛

**People's
Square**
人民广场站 Ⓜ

**People's
Square**
Ⓜ 人民广场站

Fuzhou Rd 福州路

44 🍴

Fengyang Rd

Xinchang Rd

**Shanghai
History
Museum**

People's
Park

21 ⓘ

**Shanghai
Urban Planning
Exhibition Hall**

61 ⊛

Windows Garage
(200m);
Wooden
Box (200m)

W Nanjing Rd 南京西路

26 ⊙

2 🏛
43 ⊗

N Huangpi Rd

50 🏛

23 🏛

4 🏛

Middle Xizang Rd

Hubei Rd

N Chengdu Rd 成都北路

Jiangyin Rd

37 ⊗

60 ⊛

Renmin Ave 人民大道

People's
Square

E Yan'an Rd

Weihai Rd

Wusheng Rd 武胜路

**Shanghai
Museum**

3 🏛

65 Ⓢ

45 🍴

South Xizang Rd

Buses to Zhujiajiao
– Pu'an Rd Terminal

Ⓢ Bus 925 to Hongqiao
International
Airport Terminal 1

Pu'an Rd

Dashijie
Ⓜ 大世界站

Dagu Rd

E Yan'an Rd 延安东路

S Huangpi Rd

Middle Jinling Rd

金陵中路

**Middle
Huaihai Rd**

Luijin Rd

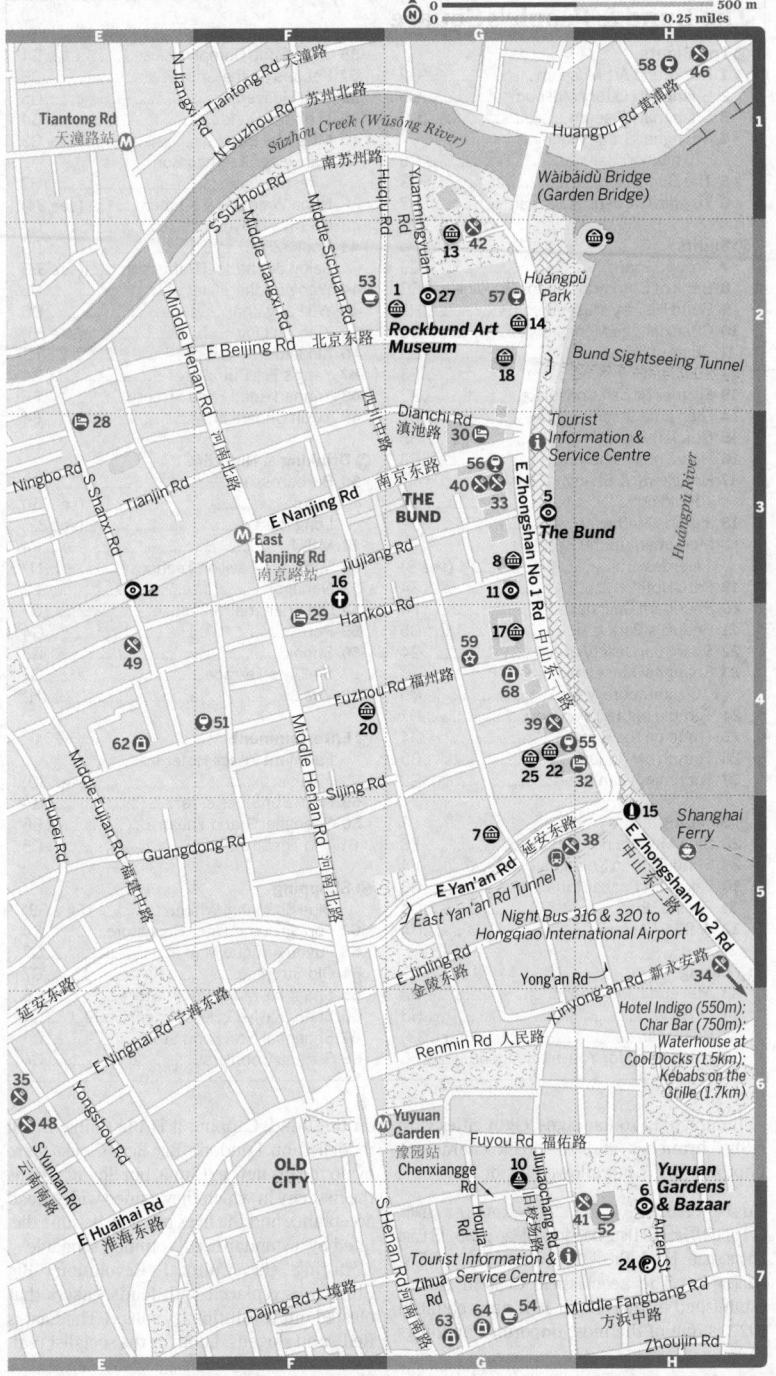

SHANGHAI

58
46
Huangpu Rd 黄浦路
N Jiangxi Rd
Tiantong Rd 天潼路
N Suzhou Rd 苏州北路
Tiantong Rd
天潼路站
Suzhou Creek (Wùsōng River)
南苏州路
Wàibáidù Bridge
(Garden Bridge)
Yuanmingyuan Rd
Middle Sichuan Rd
Middle Jiangxi Rd
Huqiu Rd
S Suzhou Rd
13 42
9
53 1
27 57
Huángpǔ Park
Rockbund Art Museum
14
E Beijing Rd 北京东路
18
Middle Henan Rd 河南北路
28
Dianchi Rd 滇池路
30
Tourist Information & Service Centre
Ningbo Rd
S Shanxi Rd
Tianjin Rd
E Nanjing Rd 南京东路
THE BUND
56
40
33
5
The Bund
E Zhongshan No 1 Rd
East Nanjing Rd 南京路站
Jiujiang Rd
8
Huángpǔ River
12
16
Hankou Rd
11
17
中山东一路
29
59
68
62
51
Fuzhou Rd 福州路
20
39
Middle Henan Rd 河南北路
Sijing Rd
25 22 55
32
Middle Fujian Rd 福建中路
Guangdong Rd
7
15
Shanghai Ferry
38
E Yan'an Rd 延安东路
E Zhongshan No 2 Rd
Hubei Rd
E Yan'an Rd Tunnel
East Yan'an Rd Tunnel
Night Bus 316 & 320 to Hongqiao International Airport
E Jinling Rd 金陵东路
Yong'an Rd
Xinyong'an Rd 新永安路
34
中山东二路
Hotel Indigo (550m);
Char Bar (750m);
Waterhouse at Cool Docks (1.5km);
Kebabs on the Grille (1.7km)
Renmin Rd 人民路
35
48
S Yunnan Rd 云南南路
Yongshou Rd
E Ninghai Rd 宁海东路
E Huaihai Rd 淮海东路
延安东路
Yuyuan Garden
豫园站
Chenxiangge Rd
Fuyou Rd 福佑路
OLD CITY
10
Jiujiachang Rd 旧校场路
Yuyuan Gardens & Bazaar
6
S Henan Rd 河南南路
Houjia Rd
41
52
Anren St
24
Tourist Information & Service Centre
Zihua Rd
Middle Fangbang Rd 方浜中路
Daijing Rd 大境路
63
64
54
Zhoujin Rd

The Bund & People's Square

It depicts 12 zodiac signs, eight cities with HSBC branches and 16 Greek characters. Photography is not allowed inside.

Custom House NOTABLE BUILDING
(自订的房子, Zì Dìng De Fángzi; Map p286; 13 East Zhongshan No 1 Rd, 中山东一路13号; M East Nanjing Rd) The neoclassical Custom House, established at this site in 1857 and rebuilt in 1927, is one of the most important buildings on the Bund. Capping it is Big Ching, a bell modelled on London's Big Ben. Clocks were by no means new to China, but Shanghai was the first city in which they gained widespread acceptance and the lives of many became dictated by a standardised, common schedule.

During the Cultural Revolution, Big Ching was replaced with loudspeakers that blasted out revolutionary songs ('The East is Red') and slogans. Look for the socialist realism plaque outside its front door, depicting scenes from the 'liberation' of Shanghai.

Yuanmingyuan Road
AREA

(圆明园路, Yuánmíngyuán Lù; Map p286; Ⓜ East Nanjing Rd) Like a smaller, more condensed version of the Bund, the pedestrianised, cobblestone Yuanmingyuan Rd is lined with a mishmash of colonial architecture. Running parallel with the Bund, just one block back, the road features some fine examples of renovated red-brick and stone buildings dating from the 1900s. Look for the art deco YWCA building (No 133) and Chinese Baptist Publication building (No 209), the ornate 1907 red-brick Panama Legation building (No 97) and the 1927 neoclassical Lyceum building.

AroundSpace
GALLERY

(周围艺术画廊, Zhōuwéi Yìshù Huàláng; Map p286; www.aroundspace.gallery; 33 Middle Sichuan Rd, 四川中路33号; ⏱10.30am-6pm Tue-Sun; Ⓜ East Nanjing Rd) FREE Housed in a beautiful 1932 art deco building, that – like several other galleries in the area – was formerly a Chinese bank, AroundSpace is an elegant art gallery. Several exhibitions are hosted concurrently, with a focus on emerging and established contemporary artists from China.

Get in touch with owner Ming Ming to arrange free art tours in the area.

PearlLam Galleries
GALLERY

(珍珠林画廊, Zhēnzhū Lín Huàláng; Map p286; www.pearllam.com; 181 Middle Jiangxi Rd, 江西中路181号; ⏱10.30am-7pm; Ⓜ East Nanjing Rd) FREE The Shanghai branch of this Hong Kong contemporary gallery is set within an old bank building dating from 1936. With a mix of Chinese and international abstract artists, it's definitely worth popping in to see what's showing. There's also another exhibition space in the somewhat creepy basement. It's part of the Art on the Bund gallery precinct.

Glen Line Steamship Co.
HISTORIC BUILDING

(葛兰线轮船公司, Gé Lán Xiàn Lúnchuán Gōngsī; Map p286; 28 East Zhongshan No 1 Rd, 中山东一路28号; Ⓜ East Nanjing Rd) This elegant 1922 neoclassical building served as the office of a British shipping company before being occupied by the Japanese during WWII and serving as an interim German consulate (directly opposite the British embassy at No 27). Following the war it was briefly the US consulate before becoming the headquarters for Shanghai People's radio station during the Cultural Revolution. Today it's the office for Shanghai Clearing House.

Bank of Communications Building
HISTORIC BUILDING

(中国银行通信大楼, Zhōngguó Yínháng Tōngxìn Dàlóu; Map p286; 14 East Zhongshan No 1 Rd, 中山东一路14号; Ⓜ East Nanjing Rd) With the Bund offering a showcase of the world's great architecture styles, representing art deco is the Bank of Communications Building with its classic geometric facade dating from 1948.

Jardine Matheson
HISTORIC BUILDING

(怡和洋行, Yí Hé Yángháng; Map p286; 27 East Zhongshan No 1 Rd, 中山东一路27号; Ⓜ East Nanjing Rd) Standing at No 27 on the Bund is the former headquarters of early opium traders Jardine Matheson, which went on to become one of the most powerful trading houses in Hong Kong and Shanghai. Also known as EWO, it was the first foreign company to erect a building on the Bund in 1851. It later invested in China's earliest railways and cotton mills, and even operated a popular brewery. The current building replaced the original and was completed in 1922 in British Renaissance style.

In 1941 the British Embassy occupied the top floor, facing the German Embassy across the road in the Glen Line building, at No 28. Jardine Matheson now holds the House of Roosevelt, which is quite possibly China's largest wine cellar and bar.

Park Hotel
HISTORIC BUILDING

(国际饭店, Guójì Fàndiàn; Map p286; www.thepark hotelshanghai.com; 170 West Nanjing Rd, 南京西路170号; Ⓜ People's Square) Designed by Hungarian architect Ladislaus Hudec and erected as a bank in 1934, the Park Hotel was Shanghai's tallest building until the 1980s, when shoulder-padded architects first started squinting hopefully in the direction of Pudong. Back in the days when building height had a different meaning, it was said your hat would fall off if you looked at the roof.

Peruse the foyer for its art deco overture. A short walk east along Nanjing Rd is the **Pacific Hotel** (金门大酒店, Jīnmén Dàjiǔdiàn; ☏021 5352 9898; http://pacific.jinjianghotels. com; 108 West Nanjing Rd, 南京西路108号; d from ¥1000; ❄🛜), formerly the China United Apartment Building, also equipped with some lovely lobby details.

Gutzlaff Signal Tower
TOWER

(外滩信号台, Wàitān Xìnhào Tái; Map p286; 1 East Zhongshan No 2 Rd, 中山东二路1号; ⏱10am-5pm; Ⓜ East Nanjing Rd) This signal tower was built in 1907 to replace the wooden original as well as to serve as a meteorological relay station

The Bund

ARCHITECTURAL HIGHLIGHTS

The best way to get acquainted with Shanghai is to take a stroll along the Bund.

This illustration shows the main sights along the Bund's central stretch, beginning near the intersection with East Nanjing Rd. The Bund is 1km long and walking it should take around an hour.

Head to the area south of the Hongkong & Shanghai Bank Building to find the biggest selection of drinking and dining destinations.

Hongkong & Shanghai Bank Building (1923)

Head into this massive bank to marvel at the beautiful mosaic ceiling, featuring the 12 zodiac signs and the world's (former) eight centres of finance.

Custom House (1927)

One of the most important buildings on the Bund, Custom House was capped by the largest clock face in Asia and 'Big Ching', a bell modelled on London's Big Ben.

Former Bank of Communications (1947)

Bund Public Service Centre (2010)

TOP TIP

The promenade is open around the clock, but it's at its best in the early morning, when locals are out practising taichi, or in the early evening, when both sides of the river are lit up and the majesty of the waterfront is at its grandest.

North China Daily News Building (1924)

Known as the 'Old Lady of the Bund'. The *News* ran from 1864 to 1951 as the main English-language newspaper in China. Look for the paper's motto above the central windows.

Fairmont Peace Hotel (1929)

Originally built as the Cathay Hotel, this art deco masterpiece was *the* place to stay in Shanghai and the crown jewel in Victor Sassoon's real-estate empire.

Russo-Chinese Bank Building (1902)

Former Bank of Taiwan (1927)

Former Chartered Bank Building (1923)

Reopened in 2004 as the upmarket entertainment complex Bund 18; the building's top-floor Bar Rouge is one of the Bund's premier late-night destinations.

Former Palace Hotel (1906)

Now known as the Swatch Art Peace Hotel (an artists' residence and gallery, with a top-floor restaurant and bar), this building was completed in 1908 and hosted Sun Yatsen's victory celebration in 1911 following his election as the first president of the Republic of China.

Bank of China (1942)

This unusual building was originally commissioned to be the tallest building in Shanghai but, probably because of Victor Sassoon's influence, wound up being 1m shorter than its neighbour.

for the tireless Shanghai Jesuits. In the early 1950s it was commandeered as a river-boat police station, and in 1995 the entire edifice was shunted 22.4m to its present location.

People's Park
PARK

(人民公园, Rénmín Gōngyuán; Map p286; ⊙6am-6pm, to 7pm Jul-Sep; M People's Square) Occupying the site of the colonial racetrack (which became a holding camp during WWII), People's Park is the city centre's green refuge. It's home to the Shanghai Museum of Contemporary Art, the Shanghai History Museum (p284), pond-side bar Barbarossa (p327) and a small children's fairground, and is overlooked by the towering form of **Tomorrow Square** (明天广场, Míngtiān Guǎngchǎng; 399 West Nanjing Rd, 南京西路399号), and the art deco classic Park Hotel (p289).

From noon on Sundays (and some Saturdays) it's the site of the Shanghai marriage market.

If you're in Shanghai in June, join the photographers ringing the gorgeous pink lotuses that flower in the pond.

Shanghai Museum of Contemporary Art
MUSEUM

(上海当代艺术馆, Shànghǎi Dāngdài Yìshùguǎn, MOCA Shanghai; Map p286; www.mocashanghai.org; People's Park, 人民公园; adult/student ¥80/40; ⊙10am-6pm; M People's Square) Non-profit MOCA Shanghai has an all-glass home to maximise natural sunlight (when it cuts through the clouds), a tip-top location in People's Park and a fresh approach to exhibiting contemporary artwork. Exhibits are temporary only; check the website to see what's on – the shows can be underwhelming, so choose carefully. On the top floor is a light-filled restaurant and bar with a terrace; there's a ¥20 discount for ticket holders.

Shanghai Gallery of Art
GALLERY

(外滩三号沪申画廊, Wàitān Sānhào Hùshēn Huàláng; Map p286; www.shanghaigalleryofart.com; 3rd fl, Three on the Bund, 3 East Zhongshan No1 Rd, 中山东一路三号三楼; ⊙10am-7pm; M East Nanjing Rd) **FREE** Take the lift up to the 3rd floor of **Three on the Bund** (外滩三号, Wàitān Sān Hào; Map p286; www.threeonthebund.com; 3 East Zhongshan No 1 Rd, 中山东一路3号; M East Nanjing Rd) to this neat, minimalist art gallery showcasing current highbrow and conceptual Chinese art. It's all bare concrete pillars, ventilation ducts and acres of wall space; there are a couple of divans on which you can sit and admire the works on view.

Monument to the People's Heroes
MONUMENT

(人民英雄纪念碑, Rénmín Yīngxióng Jìniànbēi; Map p286; M East Nanjing Rd) Up from Huangpu Park, this anachronistic monument stands above the Bund History Museum (p284). Its socialist realism friezes depict the postwar triumphs of communism in Shanghai. Come here early in the morning for excellent photo ops as locals perform taichi to the backdrop of Pudong's skyline.

East Nanjing Road
AREA

(南京东路, Nánjīng Dōnglù; Map p286; M East Nanjing Rd) Linking the Bund with People's Square is East Nanjing Rd, once known as Nanking Rd. The first department stores in China opened here in the 1920s, when the modern machine age – with its new products, automobiles, art deco styling and newfangled ideas – was ushered in. A glowing forest of neon at night, it's no longer the cream of Shanghai shopping, but its pedestrian strip remains one of the most famous and crowded streets in China.

Shanghai's reputation as the country's most fashionable city was forged in part here, through the new styles and trends introduced in department stores such as the Sun Sun (1926), today the Shanghai No 1 Food Store (p332), and the Sun Company (1936), now the **Shanghai No 1 Department Store** (上海市第一百货商店, Shànghǎi Shì Dìyī Bǎihuò Shāngdiàn; Map p286; 800 East Nanjing Rd, 南京东路800号; ⊙9.30am-10pm; M People's Square, East Nanjing Rd). Today shops such as the vast Apple Store dominate the shopping landscape. Small 'train' tourist buses (¥5) roll from one pedestrianised end to the other.

◉ Shanghai Old City

★ Yuyuan Gardens & Bazaar
GARDENS, BAZAAR

(豫园、豫园商城, Yùyuán & Yùyuán Shāngchéng; Map p286; Anren St, 安仁街; high/low season ¥40/30; ⊙8.30am-5.15pm, last entry 4.45pm; M Yuyuan Garden) With its shaded alcoves, glittering pools churning with fish, plus pavilions, pines sprouting wistfully from rockeries, and roving packs of Japanese tourists, the **Yuyuan Gardens** is one of Shanghai's premier sights, but becomes overpoweringly crowded at weekends. The spring and summer blossoms bring a fragrant, floral aspect to the gardens, especially the luxurious petals of its *Magnolia grandiflora,* Shanghai's flower. Other trees include the luohan pine, bristling with thick

SHANGHAI IN TWO DAYS

Day One

Follow the sweep of architectural pomp along the **Bund** before walking along the riverside promenade to view the **Pudong** skyline across the river. Art lovers can enjoy the **Rockbund Art Museum**, while architecture fans enjoy the highlights of **Yuanmingyuan Road**. Head west along East Nanjing Rd past shoppers to **People's Square**.

Immerse yourself in the collection of the **Shanghai Museum** before weighing up the **Shanghai Urban Planning Exhibition Hall** or discovering a pocket of greenery in **People's Park**. For views, shoot up in the lift to the lobby of the JW Marriott on the 38th floor of **Tomorrow Square**.

Hop on the metro (or a sightseeing bus) from People's Square to Lujiazui to wander round the walkway in front of the **Oriental Pearl TV Tower**. Select between the observation towers of the **Shanghai Tower**, **Jinmao Tower** and the **Shanghai World Financial Center**, or settle for evening cocktails at **Flair**.

Day Two

Peruse the architecture and boutiques of **Xintiandi** before watching artists at work at the **Shanghai Arts & Crafts Museum** or taking a seat to watch locals relaxing in French-designed **Fuxing Park**.

Disappear among **Tianzifang**'s warren of lanes, then boutique window-shop around Tianzifang, take your hat off to the collection in the **Propaganda Poster Art Centre**, and hunt down contemporary art at **Leo Gallery**.

needles, plus willows, gingkos, cherry trees and magnificent dawn redwoods.

The Pan family, rich Ming dynasty officials, founded these gardens, that took 18 years (1559–77) to be nurtured into existence before bombardment during the Opium War in 1842. The gardens took another trashing during French reprisals for attacks on their nearby concession during the Taiping Rebellion. Restored, they are a fine example of Ming garden design.

Next to the garden entrance is the Mid-Lake Pavilion Teahouse (p327), once part of the gardens and now one of the most famous teahouses in China.

The adjacent bazaar may be tacky, but it's good for a browse if you can handle the push and pull of the crowds. The nearby Taoist Temple of the Town God is also worth visiting. Just outside the bazaar is Old Street (p333), known more prosaically as Middle Fangbang Rd, a busy street lined with curio shops and teahouses.

Chenxiangge Monastery   BUDDHIST TEMPLE
(沉香阁, Chénxiāng Gé; Map p286; 29 Chenxiangge Rd, 沉香阁路29号; ¥12; ⊙7am-5pm; Ⓜ Yuyuan Garden) Sheltering a community of dark-brown-clothed monks from the Chenhai (Sea of Dust) – what Buddhists call the mortal world, but which could equally refer to Shanghai's murky atmosphere – this lovely yellow-walled temple is a tranquil refuge. At

the temple rear, the **Guanyin Tower** guides you upstairs to a glittering effigy of the male-looking goddess Guanyin, within a resplendent gilded cabinet.

Carved from *chénxiāng* wood (Chinese eaglewood) and seated in *lalitasana* posture, head tilted and with one arm resting on her leg, this version is a modern copy; the original disappeared during the Cultural Revolution.

At the front, the **Hall of Heavenly Kings** (天王殿, Tiānwáng Diàn) envelops four gilded Heavenly Kings (each belonging to a different compass point) and a slightly androgynous form of Maitreya. Muttered prayers and chanted hymns fill the **Great Treasure Hall** (大雄宝殿, Dàxióng Bǎodiàn), where a statue of Sakyamuni (Buddha) is flanked by two rows of nine *luóhàn* (arhats).

Temple of the Town God   TAOIST TEMPLE
(城隍庙, Chénghuáng Miào; Map p286; Yùyuán Bazaar, off Middle Fangbang Rd, 方浜中路豫园商城; ¥12; ⊙8.30am-4.30pm; Ⓜ Yuyuan Garden) Chinese towns traditionally had a Taoist temple of the town god, but many fell victim to periodic upheaval. Originally dating from the early 15th century, this particular temple was badly damaged during the Cultural Revolution and later restored. Note the fine carvings on the roof as you enter the main hall, which is dedicated to Huo Guang, a Han dynasty general, flanked by rows of effigies representing both martial and civil virtues.

French Concession

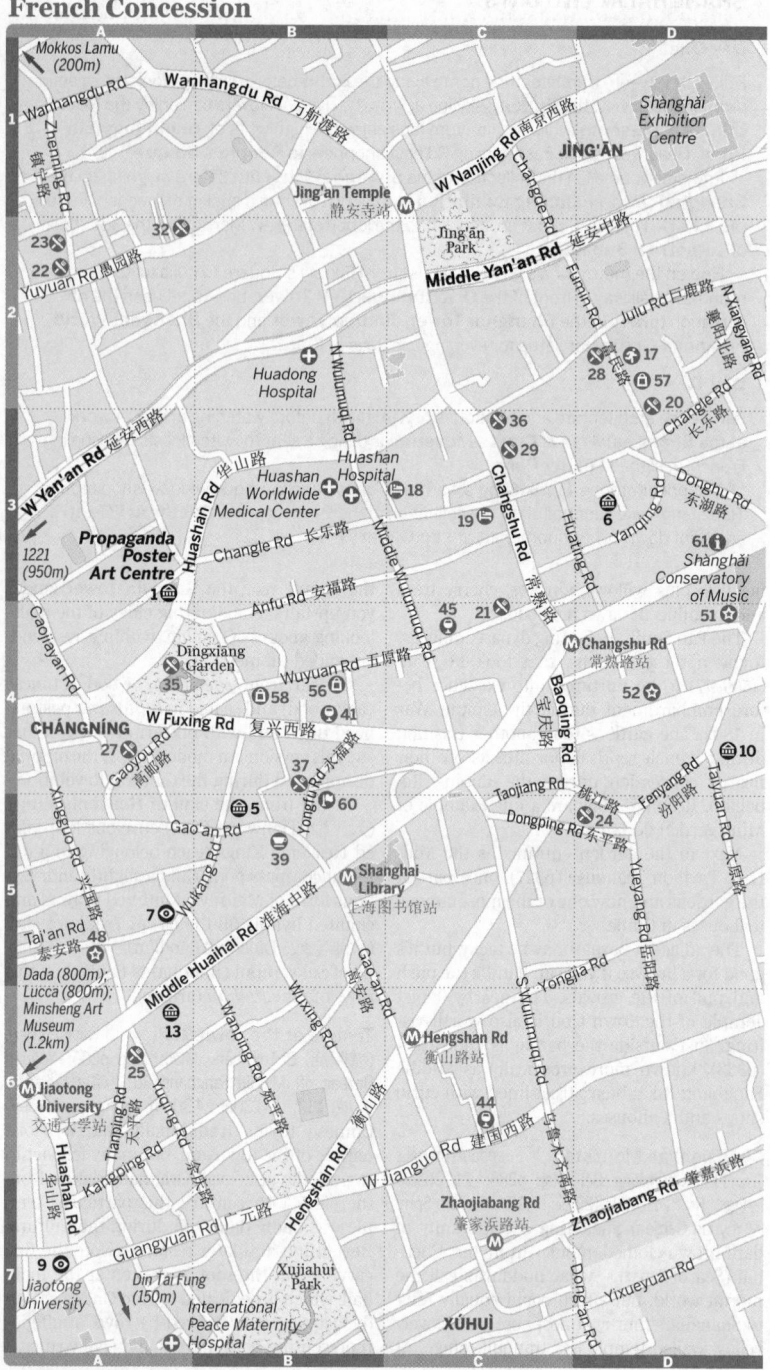

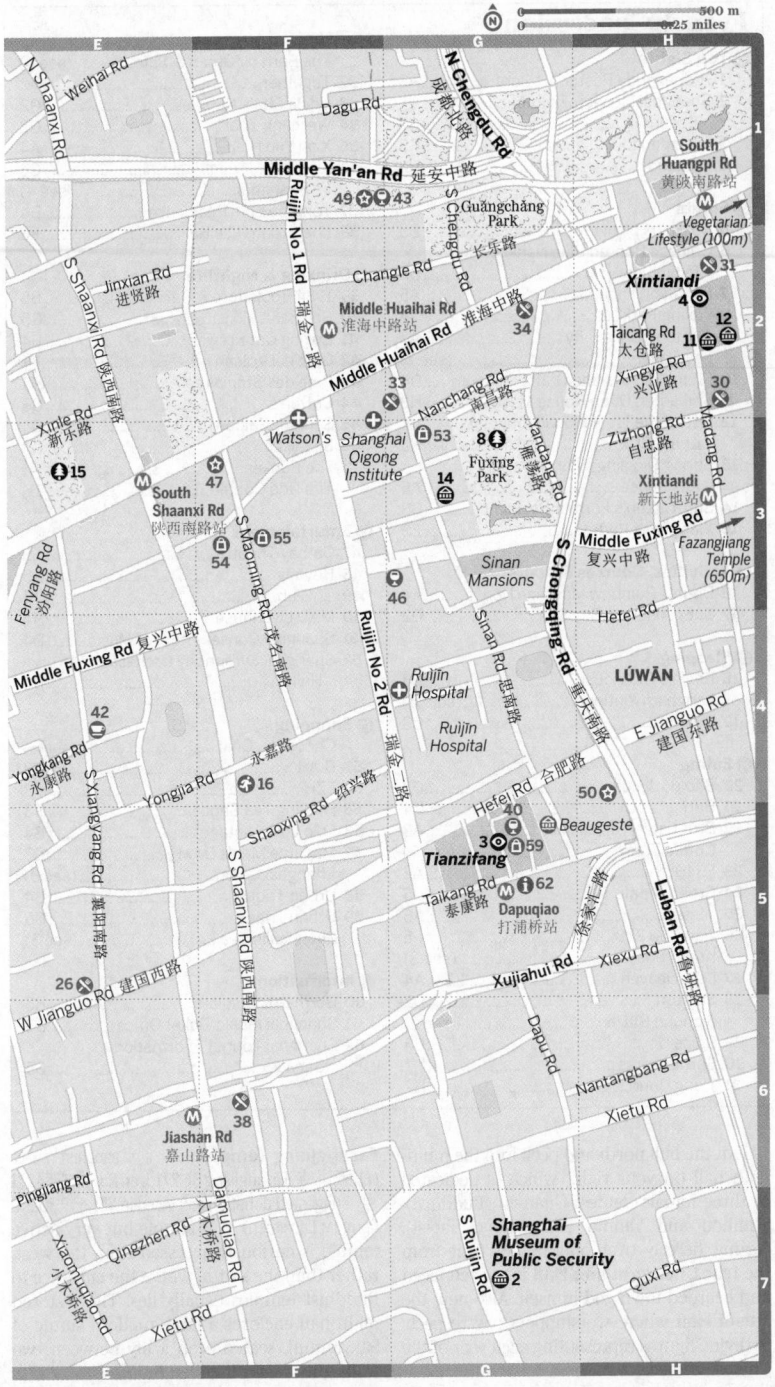

500 m
0.25 miles

SHANGHAI

Middle Yan'an Rd 延安中路

N Chengdu Rd 成都北路

Dagu Rd

South Huangpi Rd 黄陂南路站

Vegetarian Lifestyle (100m)

49 43

Guǎngchǎng Park

S Chengdu Rd 长乐路

Changle Rd

Xintiandi

4
31
12

Middle Huaihai Rd 淮海中路

N Shaanxi Rd

Weihai Rd

Jinxian Rd 进贤路

S Shaanxi Rd 陕西南路

Ruijin No 1 Rd 瑞金一路

34

Taicang Rd 太仓路

11

Xingye Rd 兴业路

30

Middle Huaihai Rd 淮海中路站

33

Nanchang Rd 南昌路

Zizhong Rd 自忠路

Watson's

Shanghai Qigong Institute

53

8

Yandang Rd 雁荡路

Madang Rd 马当路

Xintiandi 新天地站

15

Xinle Rd 新乐路

47

14

Fùxīng Park

Middle Fuxing Rd 复兴中路

Fazangjiang Temple (650m)

South Shaanxi Rd 陕西南路站

S Maoming Rd 茂名南路

54

55

Sinan Mansions

Hefei Rd

LÚWĀN

Fenyang Rd 汾阳路

Middle Fuxing Rd 复兴中路

46

Sinan Rd 思南路

S Chongqing Rd 重庆南路

42

Yongkang Rd 永康路

S Xiangyang Rd 襄阳南路

Yongjia Rd 永嘉路

Ruìjīn Hospital

Ruìjīn Hospital

Hefei Rd 合肥路

E Jianguo Rd 建国东路

50

16

Shaoxing Rd 绍兴路

Ruijin No 2 Rd 瑞金二路

S Shaanxi Rd 陕西南路

Hefei Rd 合肥路

40

Beaugeste

Luban Rd 鲁班路

3
59

Tianzifang

26

W Jianguo Rd 建国西路

Taikang Rd 泰康路

62

Dapuqiao 打浦桥

Xiexu Rd

38

Jiashan Rd 嘉山路站

Damuqiao Rd 大木桥路

Xujiahui Rd

Dapu Rd

Nantangbang Rd

Pingjiang Rd

Xietu Rd

Xiaomuqiao Rd 小木桥路

Qingzhen Rd

Xietu Rd

S Ruijin Rd 瑞金南路

Shanghai Museum of Public Security
2

Quxi Rd

French Concession

Exit the hall north and peek into the multi-faith hall on your right, which is dedicated to three female deities: Guanyin (Buddhist), Tianhou and Yanmu Niangniang (Taoist). Gazing fiercely over offerings of fruit from the rear **Chengghuang Hall** is the red-faced and bearded town god himself. Also note the **Taisui Hall** where worshippers pay respects to divine figures representing each year of the Chinese zodiac.

Fazangjiang Temple   BUDDHIST TEMPLE
(法藏讲寺, Fǎzàngjiǎng Sì; 271 Ji'an Rd, 吉安路271号; suggested donation incl incense ¥5; ⏰ 7.30am-4pm; M Laoximen) This simple but very active temple is curiously accessed from the west, rather than the south, where the entrance to Buddhist temples usually lies. The restored main hall encloses a large modern statue of Sakyamuni, seated atop a lily between two walls glinting with gilded *luóhàn*.

Other lesser halls shelter a trinity of golden Buddhist effigies and there's a small shrine to the Buddhist god of the underworld, Dizang Wang. A handy vegetarian restaurant (open 9am to 9pm) is right next door for karmic sustenance.

⊙ French Concession

★Shanghai Museum of
Public Security   MUSEUM

(上海公安博物馆, Shànghǎi Gōng'ān Bówùguǎn; Map p294; ☑021 6472 0256; 518 South Ruijin Rd, 瑞金南路518号; ⊙9am-4.30pm Mon-Sat, last entry 4pm; MDapuqiao) FREE This offbeat and macabre museum details over three floors how the Chinese authorities keep control. Display cases depict the illicit activities local cops have encountered, the equipment police use to aid their work and the punishments given for such crimes. On display are tasers, lots of guns (one concealed in a violin case), seized gambling tables, restraining equipment, and a model-scale replica of the room in which war criminals were hung, among other eye-opening displays.

There's also a full-sized seized amphetamine lab. Meanwhile, there are cabinets with police uniforms from throughout the decades, plus the drones used for surveillance and iconic vintage police cars from the mid-20th century. There's even a stuffed police dog. You need your passport to enter. Exhibition description boards are in Chinese only (bring a translation app).

★Propaganda Poster Art Centre   GALLERY

(宣传画年画艺术中心, Xuānchuánhuà Niánhuà Yìshù Zhōngxīn; Map p294; ☑021 6211 1845; www.shanghaipropagandaart.com; Bldg B/4, President Mansion, 868 Huashan Rd, 华山路868号B-0C室; ¥25; ⊙10am-5pm Tue-Sun; MShanghai Library) Design junkies and history buffs will love this vast collection of original posters from 1950s, '60s and '70s China, stored in the basement of a residential block. Many were produced in the golden age of Maoist poster production and are awash with iconic emblems of communism: red tractors, bumper harvests, muscled peasants and lantern-jawed proletarians. The exhibition rounds off with a collection of cigarette posters from the 1920s. There's also a shop selling collector's items including original and replica posters and postcards.

Once you find the main entrance, a guard will pop a small business card with a map on it into your hands and point the way. Head around the back of the apartment blocks to Building B (or 4) and take the lift or stairs to the basement.

★Tianzifang   AREA

(田子坊, Tiánzǐfáng; Map p294; Taikang Rd, 泰康路; MDapuqiao) Tianzifang and Xintiandi (p297) are based on a similar idea – an entertainment complex housed within a warren of lòngtáng (弄堂, alleyways). Unlike Xintiandi, families actually reside in Tianzifang and have done so for decades, meaning there's a genuine charm, vibrancy and community. You do need to wade through the souvenir stalls to get to the good stuff, but this network of design studios, cafes, bars and boutiques is the perfect antidote to Shanghai's oversized malls and intimidating skyscrapers.

There are three main north–south lanes (Nos 210, 248 and 274) criss-crossed by irregular east–west alleyways, which makes exploration slightly disorienting and fun. The real activity is shopping, and the creative independent start-ups make for some interesting finds, from vintage spectacle frames at **Shanghai Code** (上海密码, Shànghǎi Mìmǎ; No 9, Lane 274, 274弄9号田子坊; ⊙1-9pm) and crafted kid's clothes at **Chouchou Chic** (喆缤豆小童生活馆, Zhébīndòu Xiǎotóng Shēnghuó Guǎn; www.chouchouchic.com; No 5, Lane 248, 248弄5号; ⊙10am-9.30pm) to hand-wrapped pǔ'ěr teas from Zhenchalin (p333). Elsewhere, a band of cool cafes, restaurants and bars, such as **Kommune** (公社, Gōngshè; ☑021 6466 2416; www.kommune.me; The Yard, No 7, Lane 210, 210弄7号田子坊; meals from ¥78; ⊙9am-midnight; 🖘) and **Bell Bar** (www.bellbar.cn; back door No 11, Lane 248, 248弄11号后门田子坊; ⊙10am-2am; 🖘), can sort out meals and drinks and help take the weight off your feet. Tianzifang can get hugely popular during weekends and holidays, when security may limit access to the lanes. The best time to visit is weekdays, preferably early in the morning or later in the evening. There's a **tourist information** (⊙9am-4pm) centre at the entrance to Lane 210.

★Xintiandi   AREA

(新天地, Xīntiāndì; Map p294; www.xintiandi.com; 2 blocks btwn Taicang, Zizhong, Madang & South Huangpi Rds, 太仓路与马当路路口; MSouth Huangpi Rd, Xintiandi) With its own namesake metro station, Xintiandi has been a Shanghai icon for over a decade. An upmarket entertainment and shopping complex modelled on traditional alleyway (lòngtáng) homes, this was the first development in the city to prove that historical architecture makes big commercial sense. Elsewhere that might sound like a no-brainer, but in 21st-century China, where bulldozers are always on standby, it came as quite a revelation.

Well-heeled shoppers and alfresco diners keep things lively until late, and if you're looking for a memorable meal or to browse through some of Shanghai's more fashionable boutiques, you're in the right spot. The heart of the complex, divided into a pedestrianised north and south block, consists of largely rebuilt traditional *shíkùmén* houses, brought bang up to date with a stylish modern spin. But while the layout suggests a flavour of yesteryear, you should not expect much in the cultural realm. Xintiandi doesn't deliver any of the lived-in charms of Tianzifang (p297) or the creaking, rickety simplicity of Shanghai Old City. Beyond two worthwhile sights – the Shikumen Open House Museum and the Site of the 1st National Congress of the CCP (中共一大会址纪念馆, Zhōnggòng Yīdàhuìzhǐ Jìniànguǎn; Map p294; North Block, 76 Xingye Rd, 兴业路76号; ☉9am-4pm Tue-Sun) FREE – it's best for strolling the prettified alleyways and enjoying a summer evening over drinks or a meal.

Shanghai Arts and Crafts Museum MUSEUM
(上海工艺美术博物馆, Shànghǎi Gōngyì Měishù Bówùguǎn; Map p294; ☑021 6115 7072; 79 Fenyang Rd, 汾阳路79路; ¥8; ☉9am-5pm, last entry 4pm; Ⓜ Changshu Rd) Repositioned as a museum, this arts and crafts institute displays traditional crafts such as needlepoint embroidery, paper cutting, lacquer work, jade cutting and lantern making. Watch traditional crafts being executed live by craftspeople and admire the wonderful exhibits, from jade to ivory to inkstones and beyond. The 1905 building itself is a highlight, once serving as the residence for Chen Yi, Shanghai's first mayor after the founding of the Chinese Communist Party.

After exploring the lovely garden, head up the steps to a host of splendid ivory and boxwood carvings on the 1st floor, where divine (Guanyin) and semidivine (Mao Zedong) beings are displayed; also look out for the exquisite ivory spider hanging from a web. Further displays include opera costumes and Shanghai dough modelling.

Xiangyang Park PARK
(襄阳公园; Xiāngyáng Gōngyuán; Map p294; 1008 Huaihai Middle Rd, near Xiangyang Rd, 淮海中路1008号近襄阳路; Ⓜ South Shaanxi Rd) FREE This small, French-inspired park features a central avenue lined with statuesque plane trees. Come evening, this walkway regularly transforms into a stage for lively dancing locals. Leafy trees, colourful flowerbeds and well-trimmed hedges fill the rest of the space, making for a scenic stroll away from the busy, neighbouring shopping highway. A short breather here will leave you feeling calm and recharged.

Beaugeste GALLERY
(比极影像, Bǐjí Yǐngxiàng; Map p294; ☑021 6466 9012; www.beaugeste-gallery.com; Tianzifang, 5th fl, No 5, Lane 210, Taikang Rd, 泰康路210弄5号520室田子坊; ☉10am-6pm Sat & Sun; Ⓜ Dapuqiao) FREE One of Shanghai's top galleries, this small space is concealed high above the street-level crowds. Curator Jean Loh captures humanistic themes in contemporary Chinese photography, and his wide range of contacts and excellent eye ensure exhibits are always both moving and thought provoking. Note that during the week the gallery is open by appointment only.

Ba Jin's Former Residence HISTORIC BUILDING
(巴金故居, Bājīn Gùjū; Map p294; 113 Wukang Rd, 武康路113号; ☉10am-4.30pm Tue-Sun; Ⓜ Shanghai Library) FREE This charming little pebble-dash residence with a delightful garden is where the acclaimed author Ba Jin (1904–2005) lived from 1955 to the mid-1990s. Ba was the author of dozens of novels and short stories (including *Random Thoughts* and *Family,* which later influenced Norwegian playwright Henrik Ibsen). His house today contains a collection of old photos, books and manuscripts.

Many of his works were published during the peak of his career in the 1930s. Like many intellectuals, he was persecuted mercilessly during the Cultural Revolution, during which time his wife died after being denied medical treatment. A fingerprint is needed for entry.

Shikumen Open House Museum MUSEUM
(石库门屋里厢, Shíkùmén Wūlǐxiāng; Map p294; Xintiandi North Block, Bldg 25, 太仓路181弄25号楼新天地北里; adult/child ¥20/10; ☉10am-10pm; Ⓜ South Huangpi Rd, Xintiandi) This two-floor exhibition invites you into a typical *shíkùmén* (stone-gate house) household, decked out with period furniture. The ground-floor arrangement contains a courtyard, entrance hall, bedroom, study and lounge. There's a small kitchen to the rear and natural illumination spills down from *tiānjǐng* (light wells) above. The small, north-facing wedge-shaped *tíngzǐjiān* (pavilion) room on the landing, almost at the top of the stairs between the 1st and 2nd floors, was a common feature of *shíkùmén,* and was often rented out.

CONTEMPORARY & MODERN ART

Notable contemporary Shanghainese artists working across a large spectrum of styles include Pujie, with his colourful pop-art depictions of Shanghai, video-installation artists Shi Yong and Hu Jieming, and Hangzhou-born Sun Liang. Wu Yiming creates calmer, more impressionistic works, while Ding Yi is a significant abstract artist whose works employ a repetitive use of crosses. Also look out for works by graphic-design artist Guan Chun, and the diverse works of Chen Hangfeng and Yang Yongliang, which draw inspiration from the techniques and imagery of traditional Chinese painting.

The main bedrooms are all on the 2nd floor, linked together by doors, and there is an exhibition room displaying artworks depicting daily life in those days.

Fuxing Park
PARK

(复兴公园, Fùxīng Gōngyuán; Map p294; ⊙6am-6pm; M South Huangpi Rd, Xintiandi) This leafy spot with a large lawn, laid out by the French in 1909 and used by the Japanese as a parade ground in the late 1930s, remains one of the city's more enticing parks. There is always plenty to see here: the park is a refuge for the elderly and a practising field for itinerant musicians, chess players, people walking backwards and slow-moving taichi types.

Heavily shaded by big-leafed *wutong* trees, it's a choice place to take a seat and escape the summer sun; there's even a popular kids' playground. Impassive to the laughter of children, the huge stony-faced busts of Karl Marx and Friedrich Engels gaze out from a seemingly redundant epoch, and nobody seems to notice. The park stays open later during the summer months.

Sun Yatsen's
Former Residence
HISTORIC BUILDING

(孙中山故居, Sūn Zhōngshān Gùjū; Map p294; ☑021 6385 8283; 7 Xiangshan Rd, 香山路7号; adult ¥20, child, student & senior ¥10; ⊙9am-4.30pm Tue-Sun; M South Shaanxi Rd, Xintiandi) Sun Zhongshan predictably receives the full-on hagiographic treatment at this shrine to China's *guófù* (国父, father of the nation). A capacious exhibition hall next door has more than 150 cultural items on exhibit exalting his memory and serves as a full-on prelude to his pebble-dash 'Spanish-style' home. There's a free audio guide if you leave your driving licence or passport for a deposit.

Once you get to his house proper – where he lived on what was rue Moliere from 1918 to 1924 – you need to pop transparent shower caps over your shoes to protect the threadbare carpets. Don't forget to catch the lovely garden, where a *Magnolia grandiflora* flowers deliciously in summer.

Soong Qingling's
Former Residence
HISTORIC BUILDING

(宋庆龄故居, Sòng Qìnglíng Gùjū; Map p294; ☑021 6474 7183; www.shsoong-chingling.com; 1843 Middle Huaihai Rd, 淮海中路1843号; adult/child ¥20/10; ⊙9am-4.30pm; M Jiaotong University) Built in the 1920s by a Greek shipping magnate, this quiet building became home to Soong Qingling, wife of Dr Sun Yatsen, from 1948 to 1963. Size up two of her black limousines (one a gift from Stalin) in the garage and pad about the house, conjuring up sensations of yesteryear from its period furnishings. The highlight is the gorgeous garden, with tall magnolias and camphor trees towering over a delightful lawn, where Song entertained guests with conversation and tea.

A few personal belongings are also on display in the house, including autographed books from American journalists Edgar Snow and Agnes Smedley, and a collection of old photographs depicting the Soong sisters and various heads of state.

Leo Gallery
GALLERY

(狮语画廊, Shīyǔ Huàláng; Map p294; ☑021 5465 8785; www.leogallery.com.cn; 376 Wukang Rd, 武康路376号; ⊙11am-7pm Tue-Sun; M Shanghai Library, Jiaotong University) FREE Spread across two buildings in the charming Ferguson Lane complex (武康庭, Wǔkāng Tíng; www.ferguson-lane.com.cn; 378 Wukang Rd, 武康路378号), the Leo Gallery focuses on works by young Chinese artists.

Chinese Printed Blue Nankeen
Exhibition Hall
MUSEUM

(中国蓝印花布馆, Zhōngguó Lán Yìnhuābù Guǎn; Map p294; ☑021 5403 7947; No 24, Lane 637, Changle Rd, 长乐路637弄24号; ⊙9am-5.30pm; M Changshu Rd) FREE Head down the lane and through courtyards until you see blue cloth drying in the yard. Originally produced in Jiangsu, Zhejiang and Guizhou provinces, this blue-and-white cotton fabric

SHANGHAI SIGHTS

(sometimes called blue calico) is similar to batik, and is coloured using a starch-resist method and indigo dye bath. This museum and shop display and sell items made by hand, from the cloth right down to the buttons.

Started by Japanese artist Kubo Mase, it has been in business for decades, takes pride in quality and does not give discounts. Wind through the alleys to find it. Local residents will point you in the right direction if you show them the Chinese address.

◉ Jing'an

★ Jade Buddha Temple   BUDDHIST TEMPLE
(玉佛寺, Yùfó Sì; Map p303; cnr Anyuan & Jiangning Rds, 安远路和江宁路街口; ¥20; ⊙8am-4.30pm; Ⓜ Changshou Rd) One of Shanghai's few active Buddhist monasteries, this temple was built between 1918 and 1928. The highlight is a transcendent Buddha crafted from pure jade, one of five shipped back to China by the monk Hui Gen at the turn of the 20th century. It's a popular stopover for tour buses, so be prepared for crowds. During the Lunar New Year (usually February), the temple is very busy, as some 20,000 Chinese Buddhists throng to pray for prosperity.

The first temple on your immediate left upon entering is the **Hall of Heavenly Kings**, holding the statues of the Four Heavenly Kings who look upon the four cardinal points. Directly opposite is the twin-eaved **Grand Hall**, the temple's most significant building, where worshippers pray to the past, present and future Buddhas. Also within the Grand Hall are splendidly carved *luóhàn* (arhats), lashed to the walls with wires, and a copper-coloured statue of Guanyin at the rear. Passing through the Grand Hall you'll reach a gated tranquil courtyard, where stairs lead up to the **Jade Buddha Hall**. The absolute centrepiece of the temple is the 1.9m-high pale-green jade Buddha, seated upstairs and carved from one piece. Photographs are not permitted. Further into the complex is the **Reclining Budda Hall**, which contains a small reclining white jade Buddha from Burma that's displayed in a glass cabinet. The **Mahavira Hall** was renovated and reopened in 2019; it was raised by a metre and now stands at 18.2m tall and weighs in at 1000 tonnes.

To get here, take either Changshou metro station exit 5 and walk along Anyuan Rd, or get off at Jiangning Rd metro and walk south along Jiangning Rd. There's a vegetarian restaurant (p324) within the temple complex.

★ M50   ARTS CENTRE
(M50创意产业集聚区, M50 Chuàngyì Chǎnyè Jíjùqū; Map p303; 50 Moganshan Rd, 莫干山路50号; Ⓜ Jiangning Rd) FREE Shanghai may be known for its glitz and glamour, but it's got an edgy subculture too. The industrial M50 art complex is one prime example, where galleries have set up in disused factories and cotton mills, utilising the vast space to showcase emerging and established contemporary artists. There's a lot to see, so plan to spend half a day poking around the site.

The most established galleries here include ShanghART (p302) with a big, dramatic space showcasing the work of some of the dozens of artists it represents. The forward-thinking, provocative and downright entertaining island6 (p302) focuses on collaborative works created in a studio behind the gallery. Budding photographers should absolutely pop into **DN Club** (当年, Dāngnián; ☑021 6276 9657; Room 107, Bldg 17, M50创意产业17号楼107室; 3hr course ¥880; ⊙10am-6pm Tue-Sun), with its classes using vintage SLRs and a dark room for developing prints.

Most galleries are open from 10am to 6pm, with the majority closed Mondays.

★ Jing'an Temple   BUDDHIST TEMPLE
(静安寺, Jìng'ān Sì; Map p301; 1686-1688 West Nanjing Rd, 南京西路1686-1688号; ¥50; ⊙7.30am-5pm; Ⓜ Jing'an Temple) With the original temple dating back to AD 1216, the much-restored Jing'an Temple was here well before all the audacious skyscrapers and glitzy shopping malls. Today it stands like a shimmering mirage in defiance of West Nanjing Rd's soaring modern architecture: a sacred portal to the Buddhist world that partially, at least, underpins this metropolis of 24 million souls.

While the tinkle of wind chimes and burning of incense can't compete with the blaring horns outside, the temple still emits an air of reverence.

Constructed largely of Burmese teak, the temple has some impressive statues, including a massive 8.8m-high, 15-tonne silver Buddha in the main **Mahavira Hall** with 46 pillars; a 3.87m-high Burmese white-jade Sakyamuni in the side halls; and a five-tonne Guanyin statue in the **Guanyin Hall**, carved from a 1000-year-old camphor tree. It still rattles away to the sounds of construction, while in the bunker beneath the main hall is an unfinished space housing 18 glittering *luóhàn* and little else. The complex has been designed to incorporate shops and restaurants around its perimeter – including a fan-

West Nanjing Rd & Jing'an

West Nanjing Rd & Jing'an

tastic vegetarian restaurant (p324) – which stretches around the block, and the metro runs right underneath. The ¥50 admission charge is steep, however, for such a modest and thoroughly modern place of worship.

Khi Vehdu, who ran Jing'an Temple in the 1930s, was one of the most remarkable figures of the time. The nearly 2m-tall abbot had a large following as well as seven concubines, each of whom had a house and a car. During the Cultural Revolution, the temple was stripped of its Buddhist statues and transformed into a plastics factory before burning to the ground in 1972.

Good times to visit include the Festival of Bathing Buddha (on the eighth day of the fourth lunar month) and at the full moon.

★ **Shanghai Natural History Museum**   MUSEUM
(上海自然博物馆, Shànghǎi Zìrán Bówùguǎn; ☏ 021 6862 2000; www.snhm.org.cn; 510 West Beijing Rd, 北京西路510号; adult/teen/child ¥30/12/free; ◷ 9am-5.15pm Tue-Sun; Ⓜ Shanghai Natural History Museum) It's not quite on the same scale as Washington, DC's Smithsonian, but this sleek space is nevertheless as comprehensive as it is entertaining and informative. The museum is packed with displays of taxidermied animals, dinosaurs and cool interactive features. Its architecture is also a highlight, with a striking design that is beautifully integrated into its art-filled Jing'an Sculpture Park setting.

Spread over five levels, life-size creatures are the focal point throughout, with taxidermied (mostly realistic) animals, birds and reptiles, and models of soaring marine animals hanging spectacularly from the top floor. Exhibitions span diverse ecologies, humankind and geology, the treasures of earth and the way of evolution.

Dinosaur fossils are well represented (including the indigenous Yunnanese 'Lufeng lizard'); these are interspersed with impressive life-like mechanical dinosaurs that move and roar.

The building's exterior spirals like a nautilus shell topped by a curved lawn embankment, Chinese-inspired water garden and vertical garden wall. Within, the main architectural feature is a 30m-high glass atrium, with a conical molecular-shaped glass 'cell wall' that floods the building with natural light. Symbolic of the living organisms within, its transparent core holds a tranquil courtyard garden with a pond full of plants, trickling waterfalls and rocky outcrops.

★ **island6**   GALLERY
(六岛, Liù Dǎo; Map p303; ☏ 021 6227 7856; www.island6.org; 2nd fl, Bldg 6, 50 Moganshan Rd, 莫干山路50号6号楼; ◷ 10am-6pm; Ⓜ Jiangning Rd) One of the M50 art precinct's (p300) most creative, thought-provoking, interactive and engaging galleries is island6. Artist Liu Dao showcases his work and that of a collective of painters, writers and multimedia artists

who present pieces with moving LED lights, 2D wall hangings with integrated video, and countless retro and iconic graphics with futuristic features.

Jing'an Sculpture Park   SCULPTURE, GARDEN
(静安雕塑公园, Jìng'ān Diāosù Gōngyuán; 128 Shimen No 2 Rd, 石门二路128号; ◷ 6am-8.30pm; Ⓜ West Nanjing Rd, Shanghai Natural History Museum) FREE The attractive Jing'an Sculpture Park contains a mix of permanent and temporary pieces created by mainly international artists. The sculptures are carefully scattered, making it a wonderful place to stroll and browse the abstract, thought-provoking works, dabbled with absurdity and humour. You'll find everything from red metal trees and metal cows grazing on the grass to a pyramid of cellos and ostriches with their heads buried in the ground. In April the blossoming cherry trees are an attractive sight.

The impressive Shanghai Natural History Museum is also located here.

Shanghai Exhibition Centre   ARCHITECTURE
(上海展览中心, Shànghǎi Zhǎnlǎn Zhōngxīn; Map p301; 1000 Middle Yan'an Rd, 延安中路1000号; Ⓜ Jing'an Temple) FREE The hulking monolith of the Shanghai Exhibition Centre was built in 1955 as the Sino-Soviet Friendship Mansion – a friendship that soon turned sour and even regressed to the brink of war in the 1960s. The Stalinist-style architecture is based on St Petersberg's Admiralty Building, with neoclassical columns and a skeletal spire topped by a communist red star. The best view of it is from Yan'an Rd, where it's fronted by a stirring bronze socialist-realist monument and red-star stained-glass windows.

The site of the Exhibition Centre was originally the gardens of Jewish millionaire Silas Hardoon. You're allowed to wander its grounds and photograph the buildings. Architecture lovers will appreciate its monumentality and bold, unsubtle Bolshevik strokes. There was a time when Pudong was set to look like this.

ShanghART   GALLERY
(香格纳画廊, Xiānggénà Huàláng; Map p303; ☏ 021 6359 3923; www.shanghartgallery.com; Bldg 16 & 18, 50 Moganshan Rd, M50创意产业16, 18号楼; ◷ 10am-6pm Tue-Thu, 10.30am-6.30pm Fri-Sun; Ⓜ Jiangning Rd) FREE An original M50 gallery (p300) and one of Shanghai's first contemporary art spaces, ShanghART is still going strong 20 years on.

Shanghai Railway Station

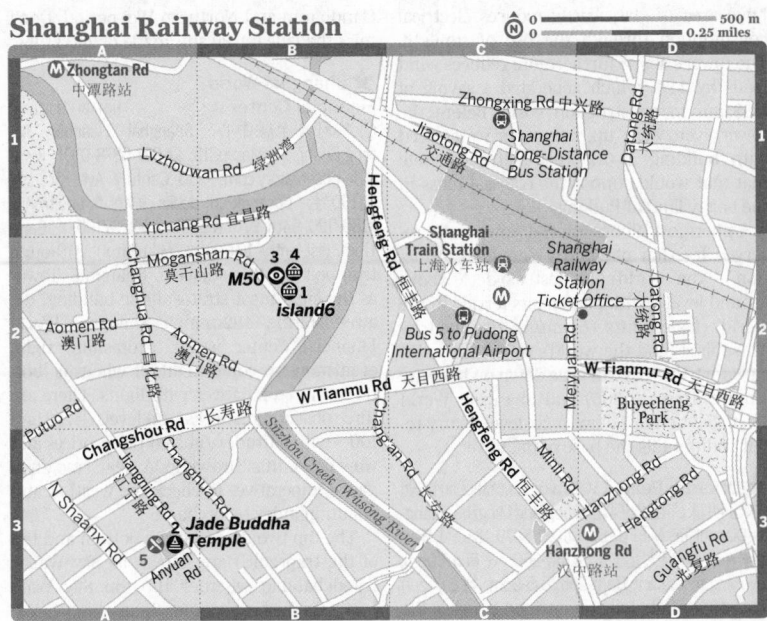

Shanghai Railway Station

**Former Residence
of Mao Zedong** HISTORIC BUILDING
(毛泽东旧居, Máo Zédōng Jiùjū; Map p301; ☏ 021
6272 3656; No 5-9, 120 North Maoming Rd, 茂名北
路120弄5-9号; ◷ 9-11.30am & 1-4.30pm Tue-Sun;
Ⓜ West Nanjing Rd) FREE The Great Helmsman
Mao Zedong lived here in the latter half of
1924 with his second wife, Yang Kaihui, and
their two children, Anying and Anqing. The
residence acts as a celebration of China's national hero with old photos and newspaper
clippings on display, but for many foreigners,
the real highlight is the building itself.

It's a beautiful example of *shíkùmén*
(stone-gate house) architecture. The displays
are all in Chinese; bring a translator or app
when you visit.

◎ Pudong

★**Shanghai Tower** NOTABLE BUILDING
(上海中心大厦, Shànghǎi Zhōngxīn Dàshà; Map
p313; www.shanghaitower.com.cn; cnr Middle Yin-
cheng & Huayuanshiqiao Rds; ¥180; ◷ 8.30am-
9.30pm, last entry 8.30pm; Ⓜ Lujiazui) China's
tallest building dramatically twists skywards
from its footing in Lujiazui. The 121-storey,
632m-tall, Gensler-designed Shanghai Tower
topped out in August 2013 and opened in
mid-2016. The spiral-shaped tower houses
office space, entertainment venues, shops, a
conference centre, a luxury hotel and 'sky lobbies'. The gently corkscrewing form – its nine
interior cylindrical units wrapped in two glass
skins – is the world's second-tallest building at
the time of writing. The observation deck on
the 118th floor is the world's highest.

The twist is introduced by the outer skin
of glass that swivels through 120 degrees
as it rises, while atrium 'sky gardens' in the
vertical spaces sandwiched between the two
layers of glass open up a large volume of the
tower to public use. The tower is sustainably
designed: as well as providing insulation, the

huge area of glass vastly reduces electrical consumption through the use of sunlight. The tower's shape furthermore reduces wind loads by 24%, which generated a saving of US$58m in construction costs. Before the tower even went up, engineers were faced with building a 61,000-cu-metre concrete mat that would support its colossal mass in the boggy land of Pudong.

Uppermost floors of the tower are reserved for that obligatory Shanghai attraction – the world's highest skydeck above ground level – with passengers ferried in the world's fastest lifts (64km/h), designed by Mitsubishi (and the world's tallest single-lift elevator). Visitors can gaze down on both the Jinmao Tower (p306) and Shanghai World Financial Center below. A six-level luxury retail podium fills the base of the tower.

★ **Oriental Pearl TV Tower** NOTABLE BUILDING
(东方明珠广播电视塔, Dōngfāng Míngzhū Guǎngbō Diànshì Tǎ; Map p313; ☑ 021 5879 1888; 1 Century Ave, 世纪大道1号; ¥160-260; ⊙ 8am-10pm, revolving restaurant 11am-2pm & 5-9pm; Ⓜ Lujiazui) This 468m-tall globe-on-a-tripod tower is the most iconic contemporary building in the city, and its image is omnipresent around town – from postcards to figurines and T-shirts. The highlight at this retro futurist Deng Xiaoping–era building is the **Transparent Observatory** (259m), where you can peer way down through the glass-bottomed walkway. To start your tour, take the lift to the 263m-high **Sightseeing Floor** for 360-degree views across to the Bund and its heritage buildings.

Other features of the tower include a revolving restaurant at 267m, a Space Capsule Sightseeing floor, a 5D cinema and an indoor roller coaster – all of which are good options if you have kids in tow.

★ **Aurora Museum** MUSEUM
(震旦博物馆, Zhèn Dàn Bówùguǎn; Map p313; ☑ 021 5840 8899; www.auroramuseum.cn; Aurora Bldg, 99 Fucheng Rd, 富城路99号震旦大厦; ¥60; ⊙ 10am-5pm Tue-Sun, to 9pm Fri, last entry 1hr before closing; Ⓜ Lujiazui) Designed by renowned Japanese architect Ando Tadao, the Aurora Museum is set over six floors of the Aurora building and houses a stunning collection of Chinese treasures. Artefacts and antiquities on display include pottery from the Han dynasty; jade dating from the Neolithic to the Qing dynasty; blue-and-white porcelain spanning the Yuan, Ming and Qing dynasties; and Buddhist sculptures from the

Gandharan and Northern Wei period. Don't miss the jade burial suit made of 2903 tiles.

★ **Shanghai World Financial Center** NOTABLE BUILDING
(上海环球金融中心, Shànghǎi Huánqiú Jīnróng Zhōngxīn; Map p313; ☑ 021 5878 0101; www.swfc-observatory.com; 100 Century Ave, 世纪大道100号; observation decks 94th fl adult/child ¥180/120, 94th, 97th & 100th fl ¥220/160; ⊙ 8am-11pm, last entry 10.30pm; Ⓜ Lujiazui) Although trumped by the adjacent Shanghai Tower as the city's most stratospheric building, the awe-inspiring 492m-high Shanghai World Financial Center is an astonishing sight, even more so come nightfall when its 'bottle opener' top dances with lights. There are three observation decks – on levels 94, 97 and 100 – with altitude-adjusted ticket prices and wow-factor lifts thrown in. A clear, smog-free day is imperative, so check the weather and pollution index beforehand.

The top two decks (at the bottom and top of the trapezoid) are known as Sky Walks. It's debatable whether the top Sky Walk (474m) is the best spot for Shang-high views, though. The hexagonal space is bright and futuristic, and some of the floor is transparent glass, but the lack of a 360-degree sweep – windows only face west or east – detracts somewhat. But you get to look down on the top of the Jinmao Tower (p306), which might be worth the ticket price alone.

Access to the observation deck is on the west side of the building off Dongtai Rd; access to the Park Hyatt is on the south side of the building. If you want to make a meal (or a cocktail) of it, or if lines are long, you can sashay into the Park Hyatt's restaurant/bar 100 Century Avenue on the 91st floor instead.

★ **Shanghai Disneyland** AMUSEMENT PARK
(上海迪士尼乐园, Shànghǎi Díshìní Lèyuán; ☑ 021 31580000; www.shanghaidisneyresort.com; Shanghai Disney Resort, Pudong; adult/child 1-1.4m from ¥575/431; ⊙ 8.30am-10pm; Ⓜ Disney Resort) Disney has magicked-up a spectacular theme park in Shanghai, offering a subtly Chinese take on Mickey and Co. Six themed areas encircle Disney's biggest-ever Enchanted Storybook Castle, with attractions including a TRON roller coaster joining high-tech reboots of old favourites like Pirates of the Caribbean. With an estimated 350 million people living less than three hours away, expect long queues for rides – arrive before 9am if you plan to do it all in a day.

MATTEO COLOMBO/GETTY IMAGES ©

Essential China

Cuisine »

Hiking »

Temples »

Festivals »

Above Jokhang Temple (p937), Tibet

Cuisine

To the Chinese, food is life. Dining is the cherished high point of the daily social calendar and often the one occasion to stop work and fully relax. The only problem is knowing where to begin: the sheer variety on offer can have your head spinning and your tummy quivering.

Noodles

Marco Polo may have nicked the recipe to make spaghetti (so they say), but he didn't quite get the flavouring right. Noodles range across an exciting spectrum of tastes, from the mouth-numbing *dàndan miàn* (spicy noodles) through to the super-salty *zhájiàng miàn* (fried sauce noodles).

Dim Sum

Dim sum is steamed up across China, but like the Cantonese dialect it's best left to the masters of the south to get it right. Hong Kong, Macau and Guangzhou should be your first stops – they set the dim sum benchmark.

Dumplings

Set your compass north and northeast for the best *jiǎozi* (northern-style boiled dumplings) – leek, pork, lamb, duck, egg, prawn or crabmeat wrapped in an envelope of dough. If you like them crispy, get *guōtiē* (fried). Shanghai's interpretation is *xiǎolóngbāo* – scrummy and steamed.

Peking Duck

Purists insist you must be in Beijing for true Peking duck roasted to an amber hue over fruit-tree wood. You might as well take their advice as that's where you'll find the best Peking-duck restaurants.

Hotpot

An all-weather meal, hotpot is ideal for banishing the bitter cold of a northern winter, while in steaming Chongqing, old folk devour the spiciest variety in the height of summer.

1. Roast duck preparation 2. Noodles in Hong Kong
3. Dim sum 4. Dumplings

BONCHAN/SHUTTERSTOCK ©

DUKAI PHOTOGRAPHER/GETTY IMAGES ©

ANDREW MURRAY/GETTY IMAGES ©

1. Tiger Leaping Gorge (p722) 2. View of Hong Kong from Kowloon Peak 3. Trek from Ganden to Samye 4. Yellow Mountain, Huangshan (p439)

PRIMEIMAGES/GETTY IMAGES ©

2

Hiking

If you're keen to escape the cities into the great outdoors, China's dramatic variety of landscapes is the perfect backdrop for bracing walks – whether island-hopping in Hong Kong, exploring the foothills of the Himalayas, or trekking through gorges in Yunnan province.

Tiger Leaping Gorge, Yunnan

The mother of all southwest China's treks, this magnificently named Yunnan route is at its most picturesque in early summer. It's not a walk in the park, so plan ahead and give yourself enough time.

Hong Kong's Outlying Islands & New Territories

A whopping 70% of Hong Kong is hiking territory, so fling off your Gucci loafers, lace up your hiking boots and go from island to island or make a break for the New Territories, where fantastic hiking trails await.

Ganden to Samye, Tibet

You'll need four to five days for this glorious high-altitude hike connecting two of Tibet's most splendid monasteries. The landscape is beautiful, but the trek requires both physical and mental preparation (plus a Tibet travel permit).

Huangshan, Anhui

Sooner or later you'll have to hike uphill, and where better than on China's most beautiful mountain. The steps may be punishing, but just focus on the scenery – even if the fabled mists are nowhere to be seen, the views are simply breathtaking.

Yangshuo, Guangxi

Yangshuo's karst topography is truly astonishing. Base yourself in town, give yourself three or four days, and walk your socks off (or hire a bike). Adventurous types can even try rock climbing.

4

TOM SALYER/ALAMY STOCK PHOTO ©

1. Performer at Confucius Temple (p228) 2. Jokhang Temple (p937) 3. Temple of Heaven (p90) 4. Prayer wheels, Labrang Monastery (p862)

VLADIMIR ZHOGA/SHUTTERSTOCK ©

Temples

Divided between Buddhist, Taoist and Confucian faiths, China's temples are places of introspection, peace and absolution. Find them on mountain peaks, in caves, on side streets, hanging from cliffsides or occupying the epicentre of towns, from Tibet to Beijing and beyond.

Temple of Heaven, Beijing

It's not really a temple, but let's not quibble. Beijing's Temple of Heaven was where Ming and Qing emperors communicated with the gods, encapsulating the Confucian desire for symmetry and order, and harmony between heaven and earth.

Puning Temple, Chengde

On a clear day this temple stands out sharply against the hills around Chengde, while in the Mahayana Hall towers the colossal statue of Guanyin, a 22m-high, multiarmed embodiment of Buddhist benevolence – perhaps China's most astonishing effigy.

Confucius Temple, Qufu

This is China's largest and most important Confucius temple. The Shandong sage has had an immeasurable influence on the Chinese persona through the millennia – visit the town where it began and try to put his teachings in perspective.

Labrang Monastery, Xiahe

Rustling up a Tibet travel permit can be a hassle, so pop down instead to this gargantuan Tibetan monastery in the scenic southwest corner of Gansu. Its aura of devotion is amplified by the nonstop influx of Tibetan pilgrims and worshippers.

Jokhang Temple, Lhasa

Tibet's holiest place of worship, the Jokhang Temple in Lhasa is a place of pilgrimage for every Tibetan Buddhist at least once in their lifetime.

Monks carrying the *thangka* up the hill, Monlam Festival (p31), Xiahe

Festivals

China is a nation of hard workers and entrepreneurs, but considerable energy is reserved for its festivals and celebrations. Festivals can be religious, fun-filled, commemorative or seasonal. Locals don their best clothes and get seriously sociable. Join in and be part of the party.

Dragon Boat Festival

Commemorating the death of the celebrated 3rd-century-BC poet and statesman Qu Yuan, dramatic dragon boat races can be seen in May or June churning up the waterways in Shanghai, Hong Kong, Tianjin and other cities.

Ice & Snow Festival, Harbin

The arctic temperatures may knock the wind from your lungs, but in January the frost-bitten capital of Heilongjiang province twinkles with an iridescent collection of carved ice sculptures.

Third Moon Fair, Dali

One of China's many ethnic minority festivals, usually held in April, this Bai fair commemorates the appearance of Guanyin, the Bodhisattva of Mercy, to the people of the Nanzhao kingdom.

Spring Festival

China's most commercially driven and full-on celebration takes the entire nation by storm at midnight on the first day of the first lunar month. The fuse is lit on a nationwide arsenal of fireworks.

Monlam (Great Prayer) Festival, Xiahe

The highlight of this Buddhist festival (in February or March), celebrated across Tibet, is easiest to witness in the monastic town of Xiahe, where a host of activities include the unfurling of a huge *thangka* (sacred painting) on the hillside.

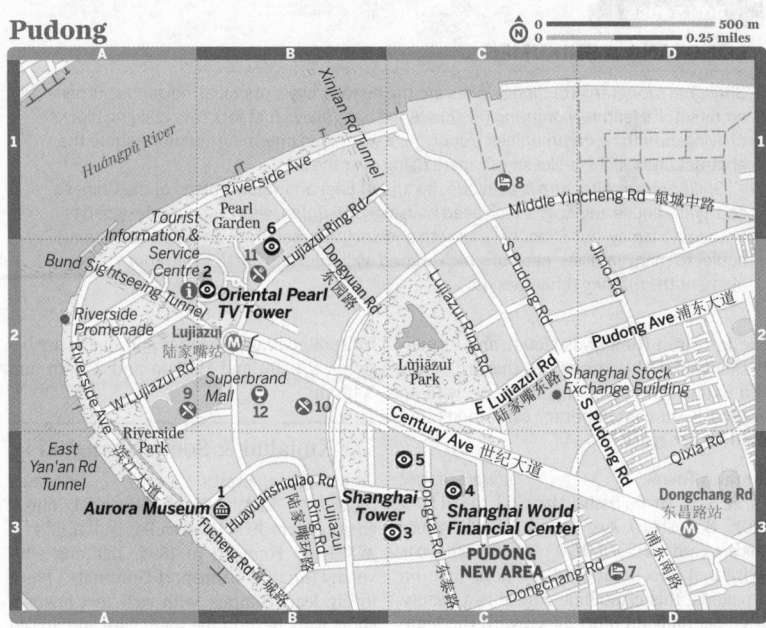

Pudong

China Art Museum   MUSEUM
(中华艺术宫, Zhōnghuá Yìshùgōng; 205 Shangnan Rd, 上南路205号; ⊙10am-6pm Tue-Sun, last entry 5pm; ⓜChina Art Museum) **FREE** Set on the former site of the World Expo China Pavilion, this 160,000-sq-metre, five-floor, modern-art museum hosts some excellent international exhibitions, and the inverted red pyramid building is a modern icon of Shanghai. On the downside, the permanent Chinese art collection is prosaic with lots of propaganda, there's a lack of information, and the layout

is quite confusing. Any captions that do exist are clumsily translated.

If you need a snack or drink stop, there is a Jamaica Blue cafe and a Starbucks on-site. Otherwise, across the road is the River Mall – although aside from Sichuan Folk (p325), the choice there is pretty limited.

Himalayas Museum   MUSEUM
(喜玛拉雅美术馆, Xǐmǎlāyǎ Měishùguǎn; www. himalayasart.cn; Himalayas Center, 1188 Fangdian Rd, 芳甸路1188弄1号喜玛拉雅中心; ⊙10am-6pm Tue-Sun; ⓜHuamu Rd) **FREE** In the eye-catching Himalayas Center (attached to

LONGTANG & SHIKUMEN

Shanghai's *lòngtáng* (or *lǐlòng*) lanes are the historic city's principal indigenous urban architectural feature. *Lòngtáng* (弄堂) are the back alleys that form the building blocks of living, breathing communities, supplying a warm and charming counterpoint to the abstract and machine-like skyscrapers rising over the city.

Shíkùmén architecture is a unique mixture of East and West, a blend of the Chinese courtyard house and English terraced housing. *Shíkùmén* were originally designed to house one family, but Shanghai's growth and socialist reorientation led to them being sublet to many families, each of which shared a kitchen and outside bathroom to complement the *mǎtǒng* (chamber pot).

the Jumeirah Himalayas Hotel), and formerly the Zendai Museum of Art, this art gallery is a fixture on the Pudong art scene, with an emphasis on contemporary exhibitions in a modern art space.

Jinmao Tower   NOTABLE BUILDING
(金茂大厦, Jīnmào Dàshà; Map p313; ☑ 021 5047 5101; 88 Century Ave, 世纪大道88号; adult/student/child ¥130/100/70; ⊙ 8.30am-10pm; Ⓜ Lujiazui) Resembling an art deco take on a pagoda, this crystalline edifice is a beauty. It's essentially an office block with the high-altitude **Grand Hyatt** (金茂君悦大酒店, Jīnmào Jūnyuè Dàjiǔdiàn; ☑ 021 5049 1234; www.hyatt.com; d ¥1500-2200; ❈ @ ⚹ ☀) renting space from the 53rd to 87th floors. You can zip up in the lifts to the 88th-floor **observation deck**, accessed from the separate podium building to the side of the main tower (aim for clear days at dusk for both day and night views).

Alternatively, sample the same view through the fizz of a gin and tonic at **Cloud 9** (九重天酒廊, Jiǔchóngtiān Jiǔláng; ☑ 021 5047 8838; http://shanghai.grand.hyatt.com; 87th fl, 世纪大道88号87楼; ⊙ 5pm-1am Mon-Fri, 2pm-2am Sat & Sun) on the 87th floor of the Grand Hyatt (accessed on the south side of the building), and photograph the hotel's astonishing barrel-vaulted atrium.

Shanghai Ocean Aquarium   AQUARIUM
(上海海洋水族馆, Shànghǎi Hǎiyáng Shuǐzúguǎn; Map p313; ☑ 021 5877 9988; www.sh-soa.com; 1388 Lujiazui Ring Rd, 陆家嘴环路1388号; adult/child ¥160/110; ⊙ 9am-6pm, last tickets 5.30pm; Ⓜ Lujiazui) Education meets entertainment in this slick and intelligently designed aquarium that children will love. Join them on a tour through the aquatic environments from the Yangzi River to Australia and South America, and from the frigid ecosystems of the Antarctic to the flourishing marine life of coral reefs. The 155m-long underwater clear viewing tunnel has gobsmacking views. Feeding times

for spotted seals, penguins and sharks are between 9.45am and 11.10am and 2.15pm and 3.40pm.

◉ Xujiahui & South Shanghai

Jiaotong University   UNIVERSITY
(交通大学, Jiāotōng Dàxué; Map p294; http://en.sjtu.edu.cn; 1954 Huashan Rd, 华山路1954号; Ⓜ Xujiahui) Founded in 1896, Jiaotong University (literally 'Transport University') has a lovely, leafy campus, with well-kept lawns a short walk beyond the main gate and an old library building (图书馆, *túshūguǎn*). Climb to the 3rd floor of the library for a **museum** detailing the university's history, complete with English captions. It's a great place to go if the sun's out – make like a student and collapse with a book on the grass among the magnolias.

◉ West Shanghai

★ **Qībǎo**   VILLAGE
(七宝; www.goqibao.com; 2 Minzhu Rd, Minhang, 闵行区民主路2号; high/low season ¥60/45; ⊙ sights 8.30am-4.30pm; Ⓜ Qibao) If you tire of Shanghai's incessant quest for modernity, this tiny town is only a hop, skip and metro ride away. An ancient settlement that prospered during the Ming and Qing dynasties, it is littered with traditional historic architecture, threaded by small, busy alleyways and cut by a picturesque canal. If you can somehow blot out the crowds, Qibao brings you the flavours of old China. When you exit the station, head down Minzhu Rd and follow the signs to the Old Street.

There are nine official sights included in the through ticket, though you can also skip the ticket and just pay ¥7 to ¥15 per sight as you go. The best of the bunch include the **Cotton Textile Mill**, the **Shadow Puppet Museum** (performances from 1pm to 3pm Wednesday and Sunday) and **Zhou's Minia-**

ture Carving House. Half-hour boat rides along the canal slowly ferry passengers from Number One Bridge to Dongtangtan (东塘滩, Dōngtángtān) and back. Also worth ferreting out is the **Catholic Church** (天主教堂, Tiānzhǔ Jiàotáng; 50 Nanjie, 南街50号), adjacent to a convent off Qibao Nanjie, south of the canal.

Wander along Bei Dajie north of the canal for souvenirs. South of the canal, Nan Dajie is full of snacks and small eateries, such as No 14, which sells sweet *tāngyuán* dumplings, and No 19, which is a rarely seen traditional teahouse.

Minsheng Art Museum MUSEUM
(民生现代美术馆, Mínshēng Xiàndài Měishùguǎn; ☑021 6282 8729; www.minshengart.com; 570 West Huaihai Rd, 淮海西路570号; ⊙10am-6pm Tue-Sun; Ⓜ Hongqiao Rd) Although sponsored mainly by the Minsheng Bank, this edgy art space also counts the Tate, Centre Pompidou, MoMA and Guggenheim among its partners, so it should come as no surprise that the exhibits (about three per year) are generally excellent. Adding to its street cred is artistic director Zhou Tiehai, one of Shanghai's best-known artists.

🏃 Activities & Tours

⭐**Double Rainbow Massage House** MASSAGE
(双彩虹保健按摩厅, Shuāng Cǎihóng Bǎojiàn Ànmó Tīng; Map p294; ☑021 6473 4000; 45 Yongjia Rd, 永嘉路45号; 45/60/90min ¥72/108/144; ⊙noon-midnight; Ⓜ South Shaanxi Rd) Perhaps Shanghai's best neighbourhood massage parlour, where the shared rooms have little ambience but the facilities are spotless and the prices are unbeatable. Choose your preference of soft, medium or hard, and the visually impaired masseuses here will work out your knots in no time and seek out those little-visited pressure points. Try the traditional massage and herbal foot bath.

⭐**Yu Massage** MASSAGE
(愉庭按摩, Yú Tíng Ànmó; ☑021 6266 9233; www.yumassage.cn; 484 Xikang Rd, 西康路484号; 1hr from ¥180; ⊙10am-12.30am; Ⓜ Changping Rd) Excellent unisex spa in tune with western sensibilities, and with relaxing rooms. Competitively priced massages include traditional Chinese full-body massages, oil foot massages and hot-stone massages. For something more unusual, try the mild buttock conditioning massage (women only).

Subconscious Day Spa MASSAGE
(桑格水疗会所, Sāngkē Shuǐliáo Huìsuǒ; Map p294; ☑021 6415 0636; www.subconsciousdayspa.com; 183 Fumin Rd, 富民路183号; 60/90min ¥240/360; ⊙10am-midnight; Ⓜ Changshu Rd, Jing'an Temple) The scent of lemongrass fills the air as you enter this serene, ecofriendly spa, which uses locally sourced materials, organic oils and non-toxic plants. A veritable centre for mind-body rejuvenation, Subconscious is on the pricier side, offering an array of traditional massages, from *tuīná* (traditional) and hotstone to Thai, as well as eight-person yoga classes and beauty treatments.

UnTour Shanghai FOOD & DRINK
(www.untourfoodtours.com; per person from ¥450) See a whole new side to Shanghai Old City on a night market food tour. Gregarious and knowledgeable guides introduce you to the city's vibrant scene through a walk around neighbourhood alleys famous for their street food. There are also dumpling tours, where you get a cooking class, breakfast street eats, and private tours.

The night markets food tour stops at sizzling stalls and neon-lit restaurants, giving you the chance to sample everything from chilli-oil-soaked crayfish to deep-fried water snake (butchered right there on the roadside), all washed down with beer and *báijiǔ* (a face-numbing spirit). It's a fantastic way to learn about the diverse flavours and cooking styles within China.

🎊 Festivals & Events

⭐**Shanghai Pride** LGBT
(www.shpride.com; ⊙Jun) While there isn't a parade, the city's annual celebration of the LGBTIQ+ community takes place in venues around town with film screenings, art events and educational activities, plus a rainbow bike ride and other social activities. The first-ever pride in China took place in Shanghai in 2009 at Cotton's bar.

Lantern Festival CULTURAL
(元宵节, Yuánxiāo Jié; ⊙Feb) The Lantern Festival falls on the 15th day of the first lunar month (15 February 2022, 5 Feruary 2023). Families make *yuán xiāo* (also called *tāng yuán;* delicious dumplings of glutinous rice with a variety of sweet fillings) and sometimes hang paper lanterns. It's a colourful time to visit Yuyuan Gardens.

Shanghai Biennale
ART

(www.shanghaibiennale.org/en; 200 Huayuangang Rd, 花园港路200号) Running since 1996, this contemporary art fair takes over Shanghai's Power Station of Art every other year. The themes change for each event; previous ones include 'Urban Creation' and the 'Spirit of Shanghai'.

🛏 Sleeping

🛏 The Bund & People's Square

Blue Mountain Bund
HOSTEL ¥

(蓝山国际青年旅舍, Lánshān Guójì Qīngnián Lǚshè; Map p286; ☎ 021 3366 1561; www.bm hostel.com; 6th fl, 350 South Shanxi Rd, 山西路350 号6楼; dm from ¥90, d with bathroom ¥250-380, without bathroom ¥190; 🌀@🛜; Ⓜ East Nanjing Rd) Sitting on top of a building block shared with other budget hotels, this hostel gets kudos for its central location. The prized rooms are the deluxe doubles with loft bed and spacious outdoor balconies. Ordinary doubles also get city views, but cheaper rooms have no window. Dorms are smallish but perfectly fine. There's a decent bar with pool table and a colossal rooftop terrace.

Prices are slightly higher on weekends and in August. Staff are friendly and there's a self-service laundry.

Bund Garden Shanghai
HERITAGE HOTEL ¥¥

(外滩花园酒店, Wàitān Huāyuán Jiǔdiàn; Map p286; ☎ 021 6329 8800; 200 Hankou Rd, 汉口路200号; r from ¥1125; 🌀🛜; Ⓜ East Nanjing Rd) Set in a beautiful colonial villa dating from the 1930s, the Bund Garden retains its distinct classic British feel with red-brick Gothic features, chimneys and a beautiful wooden staircase. With only nine rooms, the standard here is more dated B&B than luxury hotel,

but all rooms are large, with fireplaces, and are decorated in period style.

Leading off the lobby is a suitably posh dining room, and a large garden enclosed by heritage buildings, including the charming **Holy Trinity Church** (圣三一教堂, Shèng Sānyī Jiàotáng; Map p286; 219 Jiujiang Rd, 九江路219号; Ⓜ East Nanjing Rd). Rates include breakfast.

★ Fairmont Peace Hotel
HISTORIC HOTEL ¥¥¥

(费尔蒙和平饭店, Fèi'ěrméng Hépíng Fàndiàn; Map p286; ☎ 021 6321 6888; www.fairmont.com; 20 East Nanjing Rd, 南京东路20号; d ¥2500-4000; 🌀🌀🛜🅿; Ⓜ East Nanjing Rd) If anywhere in town fully conveys swish 1930s Shanghai, it's the old Cathay, rising imperiously from the Bund. One of the city's most iconic hotels, the Fairmont Peace is cast in the warm, subdued tints of a bygone era. Expect all the luxuries of a top-class establishment, with rooms decked out in art deco elegance, from light fixtures down to coffee tables.

Standard rooms come without a view, deluxe rooms with a street view and suites with the coveted river view. Note that wi-fi and broadband access cost an extra ¥100 per day for guests.

The hotel is also home to a luxury spa, two upmarket restaurants and several bars and cafes. Even if you're not staying here, it's worth popping in to admire the magnificent lobby (1929), or taking in an evening show at the jazz bar (p331).

🛏 Shanghai Old City

★ Waterhouse at South Bund
BOUTIQUE HOTEL ¥¥¥

(水舍时尚设计酒店, Shuǐshè Shíshàng Shèjì Jiǔdiàn; ☎ 021 6080 2988; 1-3 Maojiayuan Rd, Lane 479, South Zhongshan Rd, 中山南路479弄毛家园路1-3号; d ¥1300-2800; 🌀🛜; Ⓜ Xiaonanmen)

LOCAL KNOWLEDGE

IDENTITY & THE SHANGHAI DIALECT

Older Shanghainese are highly conscious of the disappearance of the Shanghai dialect (Shànghǎihuà), which is under assault from the increased promotion of the Mandarin (Pǔtōnghuà) dialect and the flood of immigrant tongues. It's a deeply tribal element of Shanghai culture and heritage, so the vanishing of the dialect equals a loss of identity. Fewer and fewer young Shanghainese and children are now able to speak the pure form of the dialect, or can understand it only and prefer to speak Mandarin. Youngsters might not care, but older Shanghainese agonise over the tongue's slow extinction. The most perfectly preserved forms of Shànghǎihuà survive in rural areas around Shanghai, where Mandarin has less of a foothold. The Shanghainese may remind themselves of the Chinese idiom – jiùde bù qù, xīnde bù lái (旧的不去新的不来; 'If the old doesn't go, the new doesn't arrive') – but it may offer scant consolation.

There are few more stylish places to base yourself in Shanghai than this breathtaking 19-room, four-storey South Bund converted 1930s warehouse right by the Cool Docks. Gazing out onto supreme views of Pudong or into the crisp courtyard, the Waterhouse's rooms are perfection itself. Service can be wanting, though, and it's isolated from the action. There is a lovely rooftop bar.

Hotel Indigo   HOTEL ¥¥¥

(英迪格酒店, Yīngdígé Jiǔdiàn; ☑ 021 3302 9999; www.hotelindigo.com; 585 East Zhongshan No 2 Rd, 中山东二路585号; d¥1500; ❇❡❄; Ⓜ Xiaonanmen) With its quirky lobby – chairs like birdcages; tree branches trapped in cascades of glass jars; sheets of metal riveted to the wall; modish furniture; and funky ceiling lights – towering Hotel Indigo is a stylish South Bund choice. Chic and playful guest rooms feature colourful cushions and whimsical designs, with lovely rugs and spotless bathrooms.

Note that accommodation either looks out onto the Old City (so-so) or the river (stellar). Service is very helpful and the infinity pool is a dream. Regular discounts tame prices by up to 60%.

🏠 French Concession

★ Kevin's Old House   B&B ¥¥

(老时光酒店, Lǎoshíguāng Jiǔdiàn; Map p294; ☑ 021 6248 6800; No 4, Lane 946, Changle Rd, 长乐路946弄4号; ste incl breakfast from ¥800; ❇❡; Ⓜ Changshu Rd) Housed in a secluded 1927 four-storey French Concession villa, this quiet place is run by a friendly, English-speaking owner. Six spacious suites are spread throughout the house, featuring wooden floorboards, traditional Chinese furniture and a few antiques, as well as fridges, flat-screen TVs and washing machines. Suite 328 is the pick of the bunch.

There's an attached Italian restaurant with a long menu of pizza and pasta dishes.

Quintet   B&B ¥¥

(Map p294; ☑ 021 6249 9088; www.quintet-shanghai.com; 808 Changle Rd, 长乐路808号; d incl breakfast ¥900-1100; ❄❇❡; Ⓜ Changshu Rd) This chic B&B has five homey double rooms in a 1930s town house full of character. Some of the rooms are small, but each is decorated with style, incorporating modern luxuries such as large-screen TVs and laptop-sized safes, alongside more classic touches such as wood-stripped floorboards and deep porcelain bathtubs. The loft room comes with a private rooftop terrace.

Staff members sometimes get a barbecue going in the downstairs restaurant terrace in summer. There's no sign – just buzz on the gate marked 808 and wait to be let in. No lift.

Langham Xintiandi   LUXURY HOTEL ¥¥¥

(新天地朗廷酒店, Xīntiāndì Lǎngtíng Jiǔdiàn; Map p294; ☑ 021 2330 2288; www.langhamhotels.com; 99 Madang Rd, 马当路99号; d from ¥1540; ❇❡❄; Ⓜ South Huangpi Rd) Xintiandi has become a magnet for luxury hotels, and they don't come much nicer than this one. Its 357 smart, stylish rooms all feature huge floor-to-ceiling windows, plenty of space to spread out in, and attention to the little details that make all the difference: Japanese-style wooden tubs in some suites, heated bathroom floors, Nespresso machines, VPN wi-fi and fresh flowers.

Amenities include the much-lauded Cantonese restaurant **T'ang Court** (☑ 021 2330 2430; 5th fl, 5楼; meals from ¥250; ⊙ 11.30am-2pm & 5.30-10pm) an indoor pool and the award-winning **Chuan** spa.

🏠 Jing'an

★ Meego Youth Hotel   HOSTEL ¥

(米果青文酒店, Mǐguǒ Qīngwén Jiǔdiàn; ☑ 021 6288 3328; 4th fl, 495 Jiangning Rd, 江宁路495号4楼; dm from ¥100, d ¥260-240; ❡; Ⓜ Changping Rd) The Meego is decorated with stencils of Shanghai's skyline and rooms are modern and clean but compact. Choose between private rooms with city views or budget rooms without windows; dorms sleep four to six people. It's a great location for exploring Jing'an and the prices are hard to beat.

★ Urbn   BOUTIQUE HOTEL ¥¥¥

(雅悦酒店, Yǎ Yuè Jiǔdiàn; Map p301; ☑ 021 5153 4600; 183 Jiaozhou Rd, 胶州路183号; r incl breakfast ¥1260-3000; ❇; Ⓜ Jing'an Temple) 🌿 Within a former post office, China's first carbon-neutral hotel not only incorporates recyclable materials and low-energy products where possible, but also calculates its complete carbon footprint – including staff commutes and delivery journeys – and offsets it by donating money to environmentally friendly projects. The 26 open-plan rooms are beautifully designed using recycled brick and timber from a French Concession *shíkùmén*, with low furniture and sunken living areas that exude space.

Bathtubs are in the bedroom rather than in the bathroom (and sometimes right next to the bed!), while grey slate tiling and textured surfaces lend a distinctly urban vibe. Check out the cool wall behind reception arranged with a mosaic of well-travelled suitcases.

It also has the **URBN Restaurant**, a good alfresco dining spot to hang out in.

🛏 Pudong

Beehome Hostel HOSTEL ¥
(宾家国际青年旅舍, Bīnjiā Guójì Qīngnián Lǚshè; Map p313; ☑ 021 5887 9801; 490 Dongchang Rd, 东昌路490号; dm from ¥100, tw/tr ¥300/370, d ¥330-410; ✽ @ 🛜; Ⓜ Dongchang Rd) If you have to live Pudong-side, this well-tended hostel is a leafy and homey oasis in an otherwise innocuous housing estate. It offers basic but clean rooms, all with private bathrooms (even the dorms), and excellent communal areas – a bar-restaurant, a balcony seating area and a cute, tree-shaded courtyard garden.

There's wi-fi throughout and a laundry room, kitchen and bar. Go through the gate at 490 Dongchang Rd and the hostel is in a lane on the right.

★ Mandarin Oriental Pudong HOTEL ¥¥¥
(浦东文华东方酒店, Pǔdōng Wénhuá Dōngfāng Jiǔdiàn; Map p313; ☑ 021 2082 9888; www.mandarinoriental.com; 111 South Pudong Rd, 浦东南路111号; d ¥1700-2600, ste from ¥2800; ✽ @ 🛜 ⚊; Ⓜ Lujiazui) Slightly tucked away from the Lujiazui five-star hotel melee in a sheltered riverside spot, the 362-room Mandarin Oriental is a visual feast, from the beautiful oval chandeliers and multicoloured glass murals (depicting forests) in the lobby to the excellent dining choices, such as **Fifty 8° Grill**. All five-star expectations are naturally met, but it's the meticulous service that ices this cake.

Sumptuous rooms aside, there's a 24-hour pool and gym, spa and fantastic views. The address may seem a bit stranded, but it's a short walk to the heart of Lujiazui and there's a complimentary shuttle bus within the area.

🍴 Eating

🍴 The Bund & People's Square

★ Jiajia Soup Dumplings DUMPLINGS ¥
(佳家汤包, Jiājiā Tāngbāo; Map p286; 90 Huanghe Rd, 黄河路90号; 12 pork & crab dumplings ¥33, crab only ¥99; ⊙ 7am-8pm; Ⓜ People's Sq) A fixture on Huanghe Road Food Street, this humble tiled restaurant is a real contender for one of Shanghai's best dumpling places, with juicy pork-and-crab *xiǎolóngbāo* served up in bamboo steamers. Point to what you want – include a duck blood soup – dip your dumplings in vinegar, and delight in the flavour. Expect a queue and to share a table.

Yúxìn Chuāncài SICHUAN ¥
(渝信川菜; Map p286; ☑ 021 6361 1777; 5th fl, Huasheng Tower, 399 Jiujiang Rd, 九江路399号 华盛大厦5楼; meals from ¥60; ⊙ 11am-2.30pm & 5-9.30pm; 🛜; Ⓜ East Nanjing Rd) Among Shanghai's best Sichuan restaurants, Yúxìn is a dab hand in the art of blistering chillies and numbing peppercorns. Menu all-stars include the 'mouth-watering chicken' starter (口水鸡, *kǒushuǐ jī*), or opt for the simply smoking spicy chicken (辣子鸡, *làzǐ jī*), the crispy camphor tea duck (half/whole ¥42/73) or catfish in chilli oil.

The occasionally misfiring English menu adds to the experience. ('Impregnable Sibao' anyone?) Take the lift.

★ Yunnan Road Food Street CHINESE ¥
(云南路美食街, Yúnnán Lù Měishí Jiē; Map p286; Ⓜ People's Square, Dashijie) Yunnan Rd has great speciality restaurants and is the spot for an authentic meal after museum-hopping at People's Square. Find Shaanxi dumplings and noodles at No 15, five-fragrance dim sum at **Wǔ Fāng Zhāi** (五芳斋; 28 Yunnan South Rd, 云南南路28号; dumplings from ¥12; ⊙ 7am-10pm), or *yán shuǐ yā* (salted duck, 盐水鸭) and steamed dumplings at **Xiǎo Jīn Líng** (小金陵; 55 South Yunnan Rd, 云南南路55号; dumplings from ¥12; ⊙ 8am-9pm). Don't miss the fly cakes at I'm Waiting For You in Chengdu (p318).

Definitely have a taste of the kebabs at the stand on the corner of Yunnan Rd and Ninghai Rd, where skewered lamb is sold to be eaten with flatbread.

Yang's Fry Dumplings DUMPLINGS ¥
(小杨生煎馆, Xiǎoyáng Shēngjiān Guǎn; Map p286; 97 Huanghe Rd, 黄河路97号; dumplings from ¥12; ⊙ 6.30am-8pm; Ⓜ People's Square) The city's most famous place for sesame-seed-and-spring-onion-coated *shēngjiān* (生煎, fried dumplings) has queues that can stretch to the horizon as eager diners wait for their scalding orders to be dished into mustard-coloured bowls. Watch out for boiling meat juices that unexpectedly jet down your shirt. Per *liǎng* (两, four dumplings) it's ¥12. Order a duck blood soup, fragrant with coriander.

Zero in on the pink frontage to order at the left counter – eight dumplings and a soup (汤, *tāng*) should be sufficient – then join the queue on the right to pick up your order.

I'm Waiting for You in Chengdu STREET FOOD ¥
(我在成都等你, Wǒ Zài Chéngdū Děng Nǐ; Map p286; 27 Yunnan Rd, 云南路27号; fly cakes ¥15; ⊙ 10am-11pm; Ⓜ People's Square, Dashijie) The

best thing about this wackily-named restaurant on Yunnan Rd is its street-front 'fly cake' (印度煎饼, Yìndù jiānbǐng) vendor, where you can buy fantastic pancakes that are stuffed with fresh durian, mango, banana or savoury fillings, seasoned with sesame seeds, wrapped like an envelope and fried to a crispy succulence. Don't miss.

★ **Lost Heaven** YUNNAN ¥¥
(花马天堂, Huāmǎ Tiāntáng; Map p286; ☏ 021 6330 0967; www.lostheaven.com.cn; 17 East Yan'an Rd, 延安东路17号; meals ¥150-180; ⊗11.30am-3pm & 5.30-10.30pm; Ⓜ East Nanjing Rd) Lost Heaven might not have the views that keep its rivals in business, but why go to the same old western restaurants when you can get sophisticated Bai, Dai and Miao folk cuisine from China's mighty southwest? Specialities are flowers (banana and pomegranate), wild mushrooms, chillies, Burmese curries, Bai chicken and superb pǔ'ěr teas, all served up in gorgeous Yunnan-meets-Shanghai surrounds.

The rooftop bar and lounge is a popular spot for a drink.

★ **Ultraviolet** GASTRONOMY ¥¥¥
(紫外线, Zǐwàixiàn; www.uvbypp.cc; Bund, 外滩; dinner from ¥5000; ⊗dinner Tue-Sat; Ⓜ East Nanjing Rd) You've probably paired food and wine before, but what about coupling an illuminated apple-wasabi communion wafer with purple candles and a specially designed cathedral scent and visuals? Welcome to China's most conceptual dining experience – and the only restaurant in Shanghai with three Michelin stars. The evening's diners gather first at Mr & Mrs Bund (p319) for an aperitif before they're whisked away to a secret location.

The meal consists of 22 courses – each accompanied by a different sensory mood (sounds, scents and images). This is Paul Pairet's masterpiece, years in the making. Revolving around his signature mischievous creations, a dinner here is bound to be unlike anything you've ever experienced before.

Reservations must be made online; book months in advance – it's only 10 people a night.

Mr & Mrs Bund FRENCH ¥¥¥
(先生及夫人外滩, Xiānshēng Jí Fūrén Wàitān; Map p286; ☏ 021 6323 9898; www.mmbund.com; 6th fl, Bund 18, 18 East Zhongshan No 1 Rd, 中山东一路18号6楼; mains ¥160-800, 2-/3-course set brunch ¥200/250; ⊗5.30-10.30pm Wed-Sun, to 2am Thu-Sat, brunch 11.30am-2.30pm Sat & Sun; Ⓜ East Nanjing Rd) Chef Paul Pairet's casual bistro

has a mix-and-match menu with a heavy French influence, reimagined and served up with Pairet's ingenious presentation. But it's not just the food you're here for: it's the post-midnight menu deal (two-/three-course meals ¥270/330), the bingo nights and the wonderfully wonky atmosphere. Ring the doorbell for entry.

Brunch (from 11am to 2.30pm on weekends) is another reason to visit, with jugs of Pimm's for ¥180.

M on the Bund EUROPEAN ¥¥¥
(米氏西餐厅, Mǐshì Xīcāntīng; Map p286; ☏ 021 6350 9988; www.m-restaurantgroup.com; 7th fl, 20 Guangdong Rd, 广东路20号7楼; mains ¥200-400; ⊗11.30am-2.30pm & 6-10.30pm; Ⓜ East Nanjing Rd) M exudes a timelessness and level of sophistication that eclipses the razzle-dazzle of many other upmarket Shanghai restaurants. The menu ain't radical, but that's the question it seems to ask you – is breaking new culinary ground really so crucial? Crispy suckling pig and tagine with saffron are, after all, simply delicious just the way they are.

The art deco dining room and 7th-floor terrace overlooking the Bund are equally gorgeous. It's also a heavenly spot for afternoon tea (¥85 to ¥168). Make reservations well in advance.

Atelier de Joël Robuchon FRENCH ¥¥¥
(Map p286; ☏ 021 6071 8888; www.joelrobuchon-china.com; Bund 18, 3rd fl, 18 East Zhongshan No 1 Rd, 中山东一路18号3楼; meals from ¥900; ⊗5.30-11pm daily, 11.30am-2pm Sat & Sun; ❄🔊; Ⓜ East Nanjing Rd) French chef Joël Robuchon has earned two Michelin stars for his Bund 18 restaurant. Much the same as in his other luxury restaurants, this is definitely the place to treat yourself to classic French fare, heavy on butter and foie gras. The decor is dark hues of red and black. Asia's supposedly largest teppanyaki bar sits in the centre.

Downstairs is the **Salon de thé Joël Robuchon** (卢布松茶室, Qiáo Lúbù Sōng Cháshì; sandwiches from ¥25; ⊗10am-9pm) offering an affordable array of sandwiches and cakes.

Hakkasan CANTONESE ¥¥¥
(客家人, Kèjiā Rén; Map p286; ☏ 021 6321 5888; www.hakkasan.com; 5th fl, Bund 18, 18 East Zhongshan No 1 Rd, 中山东一路18号5楼; meals ¥360-700; ⊗5.30-11pm daily, 11am-3pm Fri-Sun; Ⓜ East Nanjing Rd) At this acclaimed Cantonese-cuisine restaurant, it's all about high-end dim sum (such as jasmine-tea-smoked pork ribs) and luxurious mains like crispy Peking duck with imperial caviar. The decor is dark with

EAT LIKE A LOCAL

This is actually than a little trickier than it sounds. If you're wondering how you could not eat like a local, you only need to step into a western restaurant or bar any night of the week – in Shanghai, the temptations to stay in your comfort zone are everywhere. Eating Shanghainese-style may require an initial leap of faith (you want me to eat *what*?), but be brave and challenge your taste buds: with specialities such as freshly pulled noodles, braised pork belly and quick-fried shrimp, you won't regret it.

heavy woods, seductive lighting and intricate Chinese partitions – though it doesn't capitalise on its Bund views.

Wáng Bǎohé Jiǔjiā SHANGHAI ¥¥¥
(王宝和酒家; Map p286; ☑ 021 6322 3673; 603 Fuzhou Rd, 福州路603号; meals ¥80-600, set menu ¥450-800; ⊙ 11am-1.30pm & 5-9pm; Ⓜ People's Square) More than 250 years old, this restaurant's claim to fame rests on its extravagant selection of crab dishes; its popularity reaches an apex during hairy-crab season (October to December). Most diners opt for one of the all-crabs-must-die banquets, but if you're new to hairy crab, you might want to give it a try elsewhere before shelling out for an eight-course meal. Reserve.

Shanghai Old City

Nanxiang Steamed Bun Restaurant DUMPLINGS ¥
(南翔馒头店, Nánxiáng Mántou Diàn; Map p286; 85 Yuyuan Rd, Yuyuan Bazaar, 豫园商城豫园路85号; 12 dumplings on 1st fl ¥22; ⊙ 1st fl 10am-9pm, 2nd fl 7am-8pm, 3rd fl 9.30am-7pm; Ⓜ Yuyuan Garden) Renovated to spanking modernity in 2018, this is Shanghai's most famous dumpling restaurant – some love it, others see an overrated tourist trap. Decide for yourself how the *xiǎolóngbāo* rate, but lines are long and you won't even get near it on weekends. There are three dining halls upstairs, with the prices escalating (and crowds diminishing) in each room.

The takeaway deal (including crab meat) is comparable to what you pay elsewhere for *xiǎolóngbāo,* but the queue snakes halfway around the Yuyuan Bazaar.

★ El Willy SPANISH ¥¥
(Map p286; ☑ 021 5404 5757; www.elwillygroup. com; 5th fl, South Bund 22, 22 East Zhongshan No 2 Rd, 中山东二路22号5楼; 3-course set menus ¥175; ⊙ 11am-2.30pm & 6-10.30pm Mon-Sat; Ⓜ Yuyuan Garden) Ensconced in the stunningly converted South Bund 22, Willy Trullas Moreno's fetching and fun restaurant is a more relaxed

counterpoint to many other overdressed Bund operations. Seasonal scrumptious tapas and paellas are Willy's forte, paired with some serene Bund views beyond the windows. Both the Spanish and the Chinese have a communal approach to eating, so tapas and chopsticks work perfectly.

★ Kebabs on the Grille INDIAN ¥¥
(☑ 021 6152 6567; No 8, Cool Docks, 505 South Zhongshan Rd, 中山南路505号码头8号; meals ¥150, set weekday lunches ¥60; ⊙ 11am-10.30pm; Ⓜ Xiaonanmen) This busy Cool Docks restaurant is a genuine crowd-pleaser, and has alfresco seating by the pond outside. There's a delicious range of tandoori dishes, live table-top grills, vegetarian choices, smooth and spicy daal options, plus an all-you-can-eat Sunday brunch (¥150). Another central branch can be found west of **People's Square** (在格栅烤肉串, Zài Gézhà Kǎoròu Chuàn; Map p286; ☑ 021 3315 0132; 227 North Huangpi Rd, inside Central Plaza, 黄陂北路227号; meals ¥200-350, set lunch ¥55-68; ⊙ 11am-10.30pm; Ⓜ People's Square).

Napa Wine Bar & Kitchen FUSION ¥¥¥
(Map p286; Bund 22, 22 East Zhongshan No 2 Rd, 中山东二路22号; mains ¥168-288, set menus from ¥400; ⊙ noon-2.30pm Tue-Fri, to 4pm Sat & Sun, 6-11pm daily; Ⓜ East Nanjing Rd) One of Shanghai's go-to addresses for fine dining, Napa plates up beautifully presented gastronomic dishes in an elegant Bund setting. The food combines elements of Asian and western cuisines, and, as the name suggests, there's a strong emphasis on wine pairing. A good choice for a serious splurge.

French Concession

★ Jian Guo 328 SHANGHAI ¥
(建国328小馆, Jiànguó Sān'èrbā Xiǎoguǎn; Map p294; ☑ 021 6471 3819; 328 West Jianguo Rd, 建国西路328号; meals from ¥40; ⊙ 11am-2pm & 5-9.30pm; Ⓜ Jiashan Rd) Frequently crammed, this boisterous, narrow, two-floor, MSG-free spot tucked away on Jianguo Rd does

a roaring trade in well-priced Shanghainese cuisine. You can't go wrong with the menu; highlights include deep-fried duck legs, aubergine casserole, spring-onion-oil noodles and yellow croaker (that's a local fish) spring rolls. Plus, the house's famous eight treasure whole duck. Reserve.

★ Wēixiāng Zhāi   NOODLES ¥
(味香斋; Map p294; 14 Yandang Rd, 雁荡路14号; meals from ¥10; ⊙6am-9pm; Ⓜ South Huangpi Rd, Xintiandi) The reason to come to this no-frills local spot is to do as the locals do and scoop up a bowl of *májiàng miàn* (麻酱面, sesame noodles). At just ¥10 to ¥20 for a bowl of hand-pulled noodles, it's no surprise this place is consistently packed. Pay at the counter and clip your ticket to your table.

Green & Safe   INTERNATIONAL ¥
(Map p294; ☑021 5465 1288; 6 Dongping Rd, 东平路6号; meals from ¥58; ⊙8am-midnight; Ⓜ Changshu Rd) 🖋 Expat favourite Green & Safe is the closest thing you'll get to Whole Foods in Shanghai. There's open-plan dining and a restaurant upstairs with an open kitchen. The free-range meat (burgers, racks of lamb) comes from the company's farm. On your way out, stock up on organic wine, fresh produce, pastries, sustainable chocolate and more.

There's all-day brunch, plus happy hour from 8pm to midnight, with ¥28 beers.

Sichuan Citizen   SICHUAN ¥
(龙门阵茶屋, Lóngménzhèn Cháwū; Map p294; ☑021 5424 5886; 2nd fl, 378 Wukang Rd, 武康路378号; meals from ¥70; ⊙11am-3pm & 5-10pm; 🛜🖋; Ⓜ Shanghai Library) The subdued evening lighting and welcoming service concoct a warm and homey atmosphere at this popular outpost of Sichuan cuisine. The extensive photo menu is foreigner-friendly and includes a sizeable vegetarian selection. The *dàndàn* noodles (¥12) are textbook spicy, while the pork wontons in hot oil (¥12) are spot on.

Not all dishes hit the Sichuanese nail on the head though, and the *mápó dòufu* (tofu and pork in a spicy sauce; ¥26) is wide of the mark. Quench it all with a large bottle of Budweiser for ¥30 or one of the great basil-drop cocktails. Service can be slow at busy times.

Uncle Cha's Noodles   CANTONESE ¥
(查爸厅, Chá Cāntīng; Map p294; ☑021 6093 2062; 30 Sinan Rd, 思南路30号; meals from ¥22; ⊙11am-midnight; Ⓜ South Shaanxi Rd) Usually crammed, this Cantonese diner does its best to teleport you to 1950s Hong Kong, with old-style tiled floors, retro stained-glass and whirring ceiling fans. You'll probably have to wait to get a table, so use the time to peruse the menu of classic noodles (wantons, beef brisket, minced pork and more) in advance.

Zhen Yuan Rice Ball   SHANGHAI ¥
(Map p294; 263 Zhaojiabang Rd, 肇嘉浜路263号; pancakes ¥6-12; ⊙9am-4pm; Ⓜ Jinshan Rd) An awesome hole-in-the-wall pancake stall right outside the entrance of Jinshan Rd metro station (opposite Brut Eatery). Delicious, crispy *cōngyóu bǐng* (spring-onion pancakes) made on the spot in a coal-heated oven. Choose from vegetable and pork flavours, spring onion and beef, or spicy dried veg and beef, all of which is baked into the dough. No seating.

Fu's Hong Kong Restaurant   CANTONESE ¥
(福记港式茶粥面; Fújìgǎng Shìchá Zhōumiàn; Map p301; ☑021 3250 1791; 11 South Shaanxi Rd, 陕西南路11号; meals from ¥60; ⊙10.30am-11pm; Ⓜ South Shaanxi Rd) This super low-key Cantonese restaurant has a long menu of traditional southern dishes such as barbecue pork (*char siu*) and fried noodles with beef. A complimentary cup of *hóng chá* (红茶, black tea) while you browse the menu is a bonus. Fu's has an established fan club, so be prepared to wait.

★ Ye Shanghai   SHANGHAI ¥¥
(Yè Shànghǎi, 夜上海; Map p294; ☑021 6311 2323; Xintiandi North Block, 338 South Huangpi Rd, 黄陂南路338号新天地北里; meals from ¥110; ⊙11.30am-2.30pm & 6-10.30pm; Ⓜ South Huangpi Rd, Xintiandi) Ye offers sophisticated, unchallenging Shanghainese cuisine in classy Xintiandi surroundings. The drunken chicken and smoked fish starters are an excellent overture to local flavours, the crispy duck comes with thick pancakes and the sautéed string beans, and the braised beef ribs and bamboo shoots doesn't disappoint either. An affordable wine list gives it a further tick.

Sproutworks   INTERNATIONAL ¥¥
(豆苗工坊, Dòumiáo Gōngfǎng; Map p294; ☑021 6339 0586; www.sproutworks.com.cn; 85 Madang Rd, 马当路185号; meals from ¥30; ⊙10am-10pm Mon-Fri, from 8.30am Sat & Sun; Ⓜ Xintiandi) A smart cafeteria where you're served food at the counter and clear and stack your own plate when you've finished. Unlike school lunches, however, the food is fresh and tasty with awesome flavour combinations spanning Asia to the Mediterranean. Our favourite dish is the pork meatballs in tomato sauce, with a side of brown rice mixed with quinoa and salad.

Choose your own combos from the rotating menu: expect pesto cod, pasta, black-pepper beef stir-fry, honey-soy glazed chicken and teriyaki chicken leg. For lighter eats, there's a full salad bar, soups and gourmet sandwiches.

The Barn by Green & Safe INTERNATIONAL ¥¥

(Map p294; ☑ 021 6386 0140; Xintiandi North Block, 2nd fl, Bldg 22, 太仓路181弄22号新天地北里; meals from ¥48; ⊙11.30am-1.30am; Ⓜ Xintiandi) Part deli, part grocery, plus pizzeria, grill, bakery and brunch...the hugely popular Barn has it all. Its motto is 'eat your way around the world', and the extensive menu offers something for most palates. Ingredients are well sourced, with seasonal veggies and lots of responsibly raised meat options.

Try the seven premium cuts of natural-fed beef steak, plus the choice of dry-aged Angus steaks. The decor is farmhouse chic – head upstairs to find the secret speakeasy The Bunker (p329).

★ Jesse SHANGHAI ¥¥

(吉士酒楼, Jíshì Jiǔlóu; Map p294; ☑ 021 6282 9260; www.xinjishi.com; 41 Tianping Rd, 天平路 41号; meals from ¥160; ⊙11am-4pm & 5.30pm-midnight; Ⓜ Jiaotong University) Jesse is a popular, intimate space. So if you tend to gesture wildly when you talk, watch out with those chopsticks. This is Shanghainese home cooking at its best: dumplings, salted chicken, spicy beef, liquor-soaked crab and Grandma's braised pork, plus plenty of fish (including the jelly variety) and sea cucumbers. Expect to queue.

★ Xibo XINJIANG ¥¥

(锡伯新疆餐厅, Xíbó Xīnjiāng Cāntīng; Map p294; ☑ 021 5403 8330; www.xiboxinjiang.com; 3rd fl, 83 Changshu Rd, 常熟路83号3楼; meals ¥120; ⊙noon-2.30pm & 5.30-11pm; Ⓜ Changshu Rd) Trust Shanghai to serve up a stylish Xinjiang restaurant – you're unlikely to find a place like this in China's wild northwest. It's a little pricey, but super-polished with great service and on-point dishes. Choose mutton, beef skewers, the spicy big-plate chicken, or the dreamy shredded tomato, pepper and onion salad from the region. Xibo gets it right.

It serves cocktails too (also pretty unusual for Xinjiang). There's another branch on Maoming Rd (p324).

Dī Shuǐ Dòng HUNANESE ¥¥

(滴水洞; Map p301; ☑ 021 6253 2689; 2nd fl, 56 South Maoming Rd, 茂名南路56号2楼; meals from ¥120; ⊙11am-midnight; Ⓜ South Shaanxi Rd) Until the beer arrives, the faint breeze from the spreading of the blue-and-white tablecloth by your waiter may be the last cooling sensation you experience at this rustic shrine to Hunan's chilli-laden cuisine. Loved by Shanghainese and expats in equal measure, dishes are ferried in by sprightly peasant-attired staff to tables stuffed with enthusiastic, red-faced diners.

The claim to fame is the Hunan-style cumin-crusted ribs, but there's no excuse not to sample the *làzi jīdīng* (fried chicken with chillies), the excellent Hunan-style fried crab in a clay pot or even the classic boiled frog. Cool down with the crowd-pleasing caramelised bananas for dessert.

★ Lost Heaven YUNNAN ¥¥

(花马天堂, Huāmǎ Tiāntáng; Map p294; ☑ 021 6433 5126; www.lostheaven.com.cn; 38 Gaoyou Rd, 高邮路38号; mains from ¥110; ⊙11.30am-2pm & 5.30pm-midnight; ☑; Ⓜ Shanghai Library) While Lost Heaven has been around for more than a decade, it remains a stylish dinner choice with subdued red lighting and a giant Buddha dominating the main dining area. The Yunnan dishes are delicately flavoured and nicely presented; although the Dali chicken may not be as spicy as it is south of the clouds, the flavours are spot on.

The ancient trail crispy pork is delicious, as is the Yi-style stir-fried spicy beef. There are plenty of veggie options too, including wild vegetable cakes that come with a salsa-like garnish and the Yunnan eggplant with tofu salad.

Bǎoluó Jiǔlóu SHANGHAI ¥¥

(保罗酒楼; Map p294; ☑ 021 6279 2827; 271 Fumin Rd, 富民路271号; meals from ¥68; ⊙11am-late; Ⓜ Changshu Rd, Jing'an Temple) Gather up some friends to join the boisterous crowds at this expanded, highly popular Fumin Rd venue. It's a great place to get a feel for Shanghai's famous buzz. Try the excellent baked eel (保罗烤鳗, *bǎoluó kǎomán*) or pot-stewed crab and pork.

Coffee Tree CAFE ¥¥

(Map p294; Ferguson Lane, 376 Wukang Rd, 武康路376号; meals from ¥110; ⊙9am-10pm; ☎; Ⓜ Shanghai Library) Full of well-heeled diners come weekend mornings, this cafe in Ferguson Lane is a pleasant spot for coffee. Sit on the patio in the courtyard out the front, ringed by brickwork and verdant foliage. The brunches are popular; you can fill up with two courses and a drink for ¥168. Afternoon high tea is ¥288.

Xian Yue Hien
DIM SUM ¥¥

(申粤轩酒楼, Shēnyuèxuān Jiǔlóu; Map p294; ☑ 021 6251 1166; 849 Huashan Rd, 华山路849号; meals from ¥120; ◷ 11am-2.30pm & 5-10pm; Ⓜ Shanghai Library) The Ding Xiang Garden, originally built for the concubine of a Qing dynasty mandarin, is reserved for retired Communist Party cadres, so to peek behind the undulating dragon wall you'll need to dine here. It serves Shanghainese and Cantonese cuisine, but the real draw is the dim sum, served overlooking the pretty lawn on mornings and afternoons.

Afternoon tea is served from 2.30pm to 5pm. Service can be slow. Reserve ahead.

Spice Up
SICHUAN ¥¥

(Map p294; ☑ 021 5266 5186; 2nd fl, 98 Changshu Rd, 常熟路98号2楼; meals ¥120; ◷ 11am-11pm; ⓐ; Ⓜ Changshu Rd) A nice date spot for those who can handle the heat, with plush red chairs and marble tables serving fiery Sichuan-style dishes. Choose from green-pepper chicken to hot-pepper duck tongue, white fish with beancurd and spicy broth, or the classic diced chicken heaped with chilli peppers. Or go wild with some spicy chicken feet.

★ Shintori
JAPANESE ¥¥¥

(新都里无二店, Xīndūlǐ Wú'èr Diàn; Map p294; ☑ 021 5404 5252; 803 Julu Rd, 巨鹿路803号; meals from ¥300; ◷ 11.30am-2pm Fri & Sat, 5.30-10.30pm daily; Ⓜ Jing'an Temple) The industrial-chic interior here resembles a set from a Peter Greenaway film, from the eye-catching open kitchen to the sleek staff running around like an army of ninjas. The dishes (like Peking duck rolls, cold noodles served in an ice bowl, and beefsteak) are excellent, but portions are small. Reserve.

The entrance is hard to find as the place is signless. Look for the doorway in the grey wall and follow the bamboo tree-lined path into the restaurant.

Yongfoo Elite Residence
CHINESE ¥¥¥

(雍福会, Yōngfú Huì; Map p294; ☑ 021 5466 2727; 200 Yongfu Rd, 永福路200号; meals from ¥550; ◷ 11.30am-midnight; Ⓜ Shanghai Library) Although this 1930s residence was once members only, it's since opened to the general public as a restaurant – great news, because the decor is absolutely stunning. Take time out for afternoon dim sum or return later for dinner and drinks to fully appreciate the antique-strewn setting, which includes a gorgeous carved archway from Zhejiang in the garden. Some of the fish dishes are priced by weight. A 15% service charge will be added to the bill.

Bird
INTERNATIONAL ¥¥¥

(Map p294; ☑ 135 0172 6412; 50 Wuyuan Rd, 五原路50号; meals from ¥190; ◷ 6-10.30pm Mon & Tue, noon-3pm & 6-10.30pm Wed-Sun; ⓐⓘ; Ⓜ Changshu Rd) A cute and intimate spot that seats about 20 people on high tables facing a small bar or window. Foodies will enjoy the daring and intriguing veggie-heavy concoctions. Try shaved celery with green garlic puree and parmesan or mushroom ragu with Shanghainese chive oil and raw egg yolk. It's a refreshing change, but the service could be improved.

Good wine list and brunch (Wednesday to Sunday) too.

✖ Jing'an

★ Yang's Fry Dumplings
DUMPLINGS ¥

(小杨生煎馆, Xiǎoyáng Shēngjiān Guǎn; Map p301; 2nd fl, 269 Wujiang Rd, 吴江路269号2楼; 4 fried dumplings from ¥9; ◷ 10am-10pm; Ⓜ West Nanjing Rd) In the mall above a metro exit is this small outlet of the great fried-dumpling chain, specialising in delicious pork and prawn *shēngjiān* (spring-onion-and-sesame-seed-coated dumplings). Pay first then pass your receipt to the kitchen to collect your dumplings. Fishball soup, curry beef soup and rice noodles also available.

★ Sproutworks
INTERNATIONAL ¥

(豆苗工坊, Dòumiáo Gōngfáng; Map p301; www.sproutworks.com.cn; 84 Taixing Rd, 泰兴路84号; meals from ¥30; ◷ 10am-10pm; Ⓜ West Nanjing Rd) A branch of the excellent quick-serve smart cafeteria joint, serving cooked Asian and Mediterranean meals from counter vats. Plus fresh-to-order salads from the salad bar, sandwiches and soups. A clear standout combo is the pork meatballs in tomato sauce with a side of brown rice mixed with quinoa and salad. Clear and stack your own plate when you've finished.

There's another branch in Xintiandi (p321).

★ Brut Eatery
CAFE ¥

(悦璞食堂, Yuèpú Shítáng; Map p294; 698 Yuyuan Rd, 愚园路698号; meals from ¥46; ◷ 8am-10pm; Ⓜ Jiangsu Rd) An extremely popular casual cafe with half a dozen tables, plus steps with cushions and mini side tables out the front. Diners queue and then sit shoulder to shoulder with other patrons for Californian-Chinese chef Jun Wu's creations. The waffles and chicken is a winner – six-spice fried chicken, a large chewy waffle, pickled watermelon radish, jujube honey and candied walnuts.

Other mains range from wild-caught Arctic cod to Korean pork ribs and Asian curries, plus California-style breakfasts plates, pastas and burgers. We haven't had a bad dish yet, and you can't beat the prices. There's another branch on Zhaojiaobang Rd (p323).

Jin Hua
YUNNAN ¥

(金花云南菜馆, Jīnhuā Yúnnán Càiguǎn; Map p301; 408 North Shaanxi Rd, 陕西北路408号; meals from ¥40; ⏰11am-11pm; ✍; Ⓜ West Nanjing Rd) Dressed with tropical plants, vintage lampshades and plastic tablecloths, this casual retro spot serves tasty eats from Yunnan. Order crunchy fried lotus roots with Yunnanese pickles, passion-fruit fish soup or Kunming-style minced meat with tomato and pepper. The rice noodle bowls with soup and heaped veggies are awesome. Most dishes come with tropical touches, like palm leaves or floral garnishes.

Jade Buddha Temple Vegetarian Restaurant
CHINESE ¥

(玉佛寺素斋, Yùfó Sì Sùzhāi; Map p303; 999 Jiangning Rd, 江宁路999号; meals ¥80; ⏰8am-4.30pm; ✍; Ⓜ Changshou Rd) Pull up a seat alongside the monks, nuns and lay worshippers for a vegetarian feast at this Buddhist banquet hall. On the menu are dumplings, noodles, hotpot and mock-meat dishes such as succulent soya Sichuan chicken.

Pho Store
VIETNAMESE ¥

(Map p301; 118 Xikang Rd, 西康路118号; pho bowls from ¥54; ⏰11am-10pm; Ⓜ Jing'an Temple, West Nanjing Rd) This vibrant pop-art decorated hole-in-the-wall has a wonderful selection of hearty bowls of *pho* (noodle soup), vermicelli dishes, fresh *banh mi* (baguette sandwiches) and rice-paper rolls filled with soft-shell crab. Finish with Vietnamese coffee.

Jen Dow Vegetarian Restaurant
CHINESE ¥

(人道素菜小吃, Réndào Sùcài Xiǎochī; Map p301; 153 Yuyuan Rd, 愚园路153号; noodles/set plates from ¥20/35, buffet ¥140; ⏰7am-9pm, buffet 11.30am-2pm & 5.30-9pm; ✍; Ⓜ Jing'an Temple) Your body is a temple, so treat it with respect by dining at this fab ground-floor meat-free restaurant slung out behind the Jing'an Temple. You can slurp up a vast, tasty bowl of noodles densely sprinkled with fresh mushrooms, bamboo shoots, cabbage and carrots for a mere ¥20 – it's a meal in itself. Or the set menus are great value.

Also on hand are vegetarian hotpots (¥55) and a host of other choices, plus Portuguese egg tarts and other baked delicacies at the door. Order fast-food-style from the counter. Upstairs the smarter 2nd floor is a civilised choice with a Chinese and western menu. The blistering and salty *mápó dòufu* (tofu and pork in a spicy sauce) is delicious with mushrooms in place of meat, while the sizzling seafood bake with melted cheese is crisp and filling. Service is efficient; the only fly in the ointment is the Richard Clayderman muzak.

The 3rd floor has a classy buffet, with creative vegetarian fare. Head here Monday evenings for the ¥140 all-you-can-eat feast.

★ Commune Social
TAPAS ¥¥

(食社, Shíshè; ☎021 6047 7638; www.commune social.com; 511 Jiangning Rd, 江宁路511号; tapas ¥38-238, tasting menu ¥629; ⏰11.30am-2.30pm & 5.30-10pm Tue-Sun; Ⓜ Changping Rd) From UK celebrity chef Jason Atherton, this natty Neri & Hu–designed restaurant blends a stylish yet relaxed vibe with sensational tasting dishes, exquisitely presented by chef Scott Melvin. It's divided neatly into an upstairs cocktail bar with terrace, downstairs open-kitchen tapas bar and dessert bar. It's the talk of the town, but has a no-reservations policy, so prepare to queue. The range of tapas menus includes vegetarian options.

★ Xibo
XINJIANG ¥¥

(锡伯新疆餐厅, Xíbó Xīnjiāng Cāntīng; Map p301; ☎021 5299 3983; 2nd fl, Bldg F, No 16, Lane 281, North Maoming Rd, 茂名北路281弄16号F幢2楼; meals ¥100-150; ⏰11.30am-2.30pm & 5.30-10pm; Ⓜ West Nanjing Rd) Named after an ethnic group in China's northwest, this excellent restaurant is a tad pricey compared to other Xinjiang options in Shanghai, but makes up for it in atmosphere and perfectly executed dishes. Tuck into marinated charcoal barbecued eggplant or skewers of lamb dusted in spices, plus traditional bread, fried potatoes, and tangy onion and tomato salads.

★ Din Tai Fung
DUMPLINGS ¥¥

(鼎泰丰, Dǐng Tài Fēng; Map p301; ☎021 6289 9182; 1st fl, Shanghai Centre, 1376 West Nanjing Rd, 南京西路1376号上海商城; 5 dumplings from ¥58, meals from ¥150; ⏰11am-3pm & 5-10pm Mon-Fri, 11am-10pm Sat & Sun; ✍; Ⓜ Jing'an Temple) If you choose one place to try Shanghai's famous pork-and-crab *xiǎolóngbāo* soup dumplings, let it be here. This critically acclaimed restaurant steams them to perfection. With flawless service, Din Tai Fung is as much about the dining experience as it is about the food. Rice, soups and an array of meat dishes are also available. Reserve.

★ Hǎi Dǐ Lāo
HOTPOT ¥¥

(海底捞; ☑ 021 6277 0701; 468 Changshou Rd, 长寿路468号; hotpot per person ¥80-140; ⊗ 24hr; ☎; Ⓜ Changshou Rd) This Sichuanese hotpot restaurant is all about service, and the assault begins the minute you walk in the door. Pre-dining options include shoeshines, manicures and trays of nuts or fresh fruit; once you've actually sat down, the buzz of activity continues with the donning of matching red aprons and a YouTube-worthy noodle-stretching dance performance (order *lāo miàn*, 捞面).

Hǎi Dǐ Lāo sets the standard for sauce bars across the country – make sure your table has enough bowls to fully appreciate the range of flavours available. While it's great for group meals, this is definitely not a place to dine alone or to go on a date.

Méilǒngzhèn Jiǔjiā
CHINESE ¥¥

(梅陇镇酒家; Map p301; ☑ 021 6253 5353; No 22, Lane 1081, West Nanjing Rd, 南京西路1081弄22号; meals from ¥140; ⊗ 11am-1.30pm & 5-9pm; Ⓜ West Nanjing Rd) This esteemed *lǎozìhào* ('old name') lane-house restaurant has been serving delighted diners since the 1930s. The iPad menu mixes Sichuan and Shanghainese tastes, and ranges from the pricey seasoned lamb chops to the more reasonable noodle dishes. The rooms once housed the Shanghai Communist Party headquarters, but are now clad in wood carvings, intricate ceiling panels and photos of foreign dignitaries.

★ Fu 1088
SHANGHAI ¥¥¥

(福1088; Map p294; ☑ 021 5239 7878; 375 Zhenning Rd, 镇宁路375号; meals from ¥400; ⊗ 11am-2pm & 5.30-11pm; Ⓜ Jiangsu Rd) In a 1930s villa, exclusive Fu 1088 has 17 rooms filled with Chinese antiques. Rooms are rented out privately, with white-gloved service and an emphasis on elegant Shanghainese fare with a modern twist.

Together
FUSION ¥¥¥

(Map p294; ☑ 021 5299 8928; 546 Yuyuan Rd, 愚园路546号; meals from ¥250; ⊗ 10am-10pm Mon-Fri, 11.30am-10pm Sat, 11.30am-4.30pm Sun; Ⓜ Jing'an Temple) Foodies will adore this French-Asian minimalist place with an open kitchen and nice red-brick courtyard. It serves uber-creative cold and hot sharing plates, alongside seafood, meaty mains and homemade desserts. Almost too-pretty-to-eat dishes (eg tuna tartare with ponzu) arrive in enamel-style blue-and-white trays and bowls.

While the setting is gorgeous and the flavours are refreshingly bold, the service can be painfully slow.

✕ Pudong

★ Sichuan Folk
SICHUAN ¥

(☑ 021 3111 8055; Room 110, 1368 Shibo Ave, 世博大道1368号110室; meals ¥70; ⊗ 11am-2pm & 5-9pm; Ⓜ China Art Museum) Formerly known as Baguo Buyi, Sichuan Folk is among the most authentic Sichuan food in town, cooked up by the diligent chefs at this famous restaurant at the World Expo site. There's no concessions to the dainty Shanghai palate, so prepare for a spicy firecracker of a meal. It's in a complex opposite the Mercedes-Benz Arena.

Yang's Fry Dumplings
DUMPLINGS ¥

(小杨生煎馆, Xiǎoyáng Shēngjiān Guǎn; Map p313; 1406 Lujiazui Ring Rd, 陆家嘴环路1406号; meals ¥30; ⊗ 8am-9pm; Ⓜ Lujiazui) A short walk from the Oriental Pearl TV Tower brings you to a string of restaurants, including the city's best sesame-seed-and-spring-onion-coated fried dumplings (生煎, *shēngjiān*). It's often hard to get a table, but do as the locals do and order takeaway for snacking on the go.

Food Opera
ASIAN ¥

(食代馆, Shídàiguǎn; Map p313; B2, Superbrand Mall, 168 West Lujiazui Rd, 陆家嘴西路168号正大广场B2楼; meals ¥50; ⊗ 10am-10pm; Ⓜ Lujiazui) Grab a card from the booth (¥10 deposit), load up with credits and then spend, spend, spend on a whole host of open kitchens in this hopping food court. There's Korean, teppanyaki, Japanese noodles, pasta and much more. The spicy *shoyu ramen* at Ramen Play is a good place to start. Just point at what you want and hand over your card.

Sproutworks
HEALTH FOOD ¥¥

(豆苗工坊, Dòumiáo Gōngfáng; Map p313; www.sproutworks.com.cn; B2, Superbrand Mall, 168 West Lujiazui Rd, 陆家嘴西路168号正大广场B2楼; meals ¥90, set lunch from ¥50; ⊗ 10am-10pm; Ⓜ Lujiazui) For a healthy recharge, Sproutworks offers a natural and earthy focus on fresh, wholesome food, in a clean-cut (but rather square) setting. Cleanse your insides with delicious smoothies; load up with brown rice, tasty soups and crisp panini sandwiches; or try freshly tossed salads, fresh juices, home-made desserts and lunch sets. Most dishes are pre-prepared and are ready to go.

There are plenty of branches around town.

Lei Garden   CANTONESE ¥¥

(利苑, Lì Yuàn; Map p313; ☑021 5106 1688; 3rd fl, 8 Century Ave, 世纪大道8号3楼; meals ¥130; ⏰11.30am-3pm & 5.30-9.30pm; Ⓜ Lujiazui) On the 3rd floor of the IFC Mall (p334), Lei Garden is a classy affair serving good-quality Cantonese; it's perfect for a lunch break during a shopping spree. Be sure to reserve ahead.

★ Grand Café   BISTRO ¥¥¥

(Map p313; ☑021 5047 8838; http://shanghai.grand.hyatt.com; Grand Hyatt, Jinmao Tower, 88 Century Ave, 世纪大道88号君悦大酒店; buffet lunch/dinner from ¥300/400; ⏰buffet 11.30am-2.30pm, à la carte 24hr; Ⓜ Lujiazui) On the 54th floor of Jinmao Tower (in the Grand Hyatt lobby), the Grand Café offers stunning panoramas through its glass walls and an excellent-value lunch buffet; pile your plate with endless crab legs, Peking duck, fresh prawns, mini burgers, dumplings, made-to-order noodles...you name it. Book well in advance for a window table.

There's a service charge of 10%.

✖ Hongkou & North Shanghai

★ Yang's Fry Dumplings   DUMPLINGS ¥

(小杨生煎馆, Xiǎoyáng Shēngjiān Guǎn; 2298 North Sichuan Rd, 四川北路2298号; 4 dumplings ¥9; ⏰6.30am-9pm; Ⓜ Hongkou Football Stadium) Hoover up Yang's signature, time-honoured and much-applauded fried *shēngjiān* dumplings in various incarnations from pork to shrimp. Order per *liǎng* (两, four dumplings). If the dining area is full, get yours to go and enjoy them in the nearby **Lu Xun Park** (鲁迅公园, Lǔ Xùn Gōngyuán; 2288 North Sichuan Rd, 四川北路2288号; ⏰6am-7pm, to 9pm summer). Never fear, the soupy goodness inside will remain piping hot by the time you walk there.

★ Xīndàlù   PEKING DUCK ¥¥¥

(新大陆; Map p286; ☑021 6393 1234; www.hyatt.com; 1st fl, Hyatt on the Bund, 199 Huangpu Rd, 黄浦路199号外滩茂悦大酒店1楼; meals from ¥200, roast duck half/whole ¥228/318; ⏰11.30am-2.30pm & 5.30-10pm; Ⓜ Tiantong Rd) Although definitive *Běijīng kǎoyā* (Peking duck) really needs to be flamed up within quacking distance of the Forbidden City, Shanghai's best roast-duck experience imports all the necessary ingredients (including chefs and a special brick oven) direct from the capital. There's also excellent live seafood and crab on the menu. It has a sleek open kitchen and dark wood design.

You'll need to order the duck a few days in advance, and weekend bookings require almost a week's notice. Leave room for the Xīndàlù dessert sensation – a platter of treats, from moon cake to fruit.

✖ West Shanghai

★ Bǎinián Lóngpáo   DUMPLINGS ¥

(百年龙袍; 15 Bei Daijie, Qibao, 七宝古镇北大街15号; 8 dumplings from ¥15; ⏰6.30am-8.30pm; Ⓜ Qibao) This tiny spot at the foot of Qibao's main bridge has by far and away the best *xiǎolóngbāo* ('little steamer buns') on the block. Dumpling fillings include crab, shrimp and pork. For takeaway, the slow-moving queue heads out the door.

★ 1221   SHANGHAI ¥¥

(Yī Èr Èr Yī; ☑021 6213 6585; 1221 West Yan'an Rd, 延安西路1221号; meals from ¥90; ⏰5-11pm; ☑; Ⓜ West Yan'an Rd) No one has a bad thing to say about this dapper expat favourite, and rightly so. Meat dishes start at ¥58 for beef and *yóutiáo* (dough strips), and the plentiful eel, shrimp and squid dishes cost around twice that. Other tempting fare includes roast duck and braised pork.

Things are backed up by a four-page vegetarian menu, including sweet-and-sour vegetarian spare ribs, which are out of this world. The setting (tucked away in an alley) is white tablecloths, cream walls and brown leatherette furniture. Service is fantastic. Reserve.

🍷 Drinking & Nightlife

🍷 The Bund & People's Square

★ Glam   LOUNGE

(魅力, Mèilì; Map p286; 7th fl, 20 Guangdong Rd, 广东路20号7楼; ⏰5pm-late; Ⓜ East Nanjing Rd) The decor here is decidedly bohemian and its cool retro feel makes it one of the Bund's most atmospheric spots for a drink. Cocktail prices are accessible, as is the bar menu, ranging from truffle cheese toasties to soft-serve ice cream.

★ Long Bar   BAR

(廊吧, Láng Bā; Map p286; ☑021 6322 9988; 2 East Zhongshan No 1 Rd, 中山东一路2号; ⏰4pm-1am Mon-Sat, from 2pm Sun; 🛜; Ⓜ East Nanjing Rd) For a taste of colonial-era Shanghai's elitist trappings, you'll do no better than the Long Bar. This was once the members-only Shanghai Club, whose most spectacular accoutrement was a 34m-long wooden bar. Foreign businessmen would sit here according to rank, comparing fortunes, with the taipans (foreign heads of business) closest to the view of the Bund.

It's now part of the **Waldorf Astoria** (华尔道夫酒店, Huá'ěr Dàofū Jiǔdiàn; www.waldorfastoriashanghai.com; r new/old wing from ¥2500/6000; ✴@🛜♨), and the bar's original wood-panelled decor has been painstakingly recreated from old photographs. There's a good selection of old-fashioned cocktails as well as an oyster bar (and jazz, naturally).

★ Barbarossa
BAR

(芭芭露莎会所, Bābālùshā Huìsuǒ; Map p286; People's Park, 231 West Nanjing Rd, 南京西路231号人民公园内; ☉5pm-2am; 🛜; M People's Square) Set back in People's Park alongside a pond, Barbarossa is all about escapism. Forget Shanghai: this is Morocco channelled by Hollywood set designers. The action gets steadily more intense as you ascend to the roof terrace, via the cushion-strewn 2nd floor, where the hordes puff on fruit-flavoured hookahs. At night, use the park entrance just east of the Shanghai History Museum building.

Happy hour (5pm to 8pm) is a good time to visit for two-for-one cocktails.

M1NT
CLUB

(Map p286; ☎021 6391 2811; www.m1ntglobal.com; 24th fl, Cross Tower, 318 Fuzhou Rd, 福州路318号24楼; ☉9.30pm-late Wed-Sat; M East Nanjing Rd) An exclusive penthouse-style club with knockout views and fusion food, but not a lot of dance space. Dress to impress or you'll get thrown into the shark tank. No sports shoes etc.

Nonagon
CAFE

(九边形, Jiǔ Biān Xíng; Map p286; 27 Huqiu Rd, 虎丘路27号; ☉9am-6pm; M East Nanjing Rd) Opposite the Rockbund Art Museum (p284), this elegant local chain has excellent artisanal, locally roasted coffee at reasonable prices. The decor is stylish and minimalist, and the cool interior is the perfect spot for a break.

Pop
BAR

(流行音乐, Liúxíng Yīnyuè; Map p286; ☎021 6321 0909; www.threeonthebund.com; 7th fl, Three on the Bund, 3 East Zhongshan No 1 Rd, 中山东一路3号7楼; ☉11am-late; M East Nanjing Rd) On the top floor of Three on the Bund, Pop's splendid roof terrace is divided into multiple entities, all with choice views of Pudong's hypnotising neon performance. There's always a crowd, whether they're here for the Miami art deco-themed cocktail bar or the Louisiana-style Whisper bar, specialising in American rye whiskies and bourbon.

There's also a stylish restaurant that channels a retro New York brasserie. The menu is mainly western comfort food, with mains from ¥120.

Shook!
BAR

(Map p286; 5th fl, 23 East Zhongshan No 1 Rd, 中山东一路23号5楼; ☉5pm-late; M East Nanjing Rd) Sure, it's not quite as fashionable (or pretentious) as its neighbours, but that's not necessarily a bad thing: the views from Shook!'s rooftop are just as good, and it's a more laid-back spot to enjoy a slice of Shanghai's famed glamour without breaking the bank. Aim for happy hour (5.30pm to 7pm) for ¥55 cocktails.

Sir Elly's Terrace
BAR

(艾利爵士露台, Àilì Juéshì Lùtái; Map p286; www.peninsula.com; 14th fl, Peninsula Shanghai, 32 East No 1 Zhongshan Rd, 中山东一路32号半岛酒店14楼; ☉6pm-midnight Sun-Thu, to 1am Fri & Sat; 🛜; M East Nanjing Rd) Sir Elly's offers some of Shanghai's best cocktails, shaken up with that winning ingredient: 270-degree panoramas taking in Pudong, Suzhou Creek and the Bund. Of course it's not cheap, but the views are priceless. The rooftop terrace opens from April to December.

🍷 Shanghai Old City

Char Bar
BAR

(恰酒吧, Qià Jiǔbā; 30th fl, Hotel Indigo, 585 East Zhongshan No 2 Rd, 中山东二路585号30楼; ☉4.30pm-1am; M Xiaonanmen) This stretch of the Bund is ideal for a rooftop bar and Char ticks all the boxes. The outdoor terrace has some of the finest views over the Huangpu River across to the thrilling neon lights of Pudong. Inside, intimate tables are filled with noisy drinkers dressed to the nines.

Drinks are as pricey as you'd expect (cocktails start at ¥95), but for a taste of textbook Bund glamour, it's worth the splurge.

Mid-Lake Pavilion Teahouse
TEAHOUSE

(湖心亭, Húxīntíng; Map p286; Yuyuan Bazaar, 豫园商城; ☉9am-9pm; M Yuyuan Garden) Next to the entrance to the Yuyuan Gardens is the Mid-Lake Pavilion Teahouse, once part of the gardens and now one of the most famous teahouses in China, visited by Queen Elizabeth II and Bill Clinton, among others. The zigzag causeway is designed to thwart spirits (and trap tourists) who can only travel in straight lines.

The wonderfully lengthy menu recommends suitable brews to drink in each season and the tea (from ¥70) is served elegantly with tiny nibbles.

Old Shanghai Teahouse
TEAHOUSE

(老上海茶馆, Lǎo Shànghǎi Cháguǎn; Map p286; ☑ 021 5382 1202; 385 Middle Fangbang Rd, 方浜中路385号; ☉ 9am-9pm; Ⓜ Yuyuan Garden) A bit like the attic of an eccentric aunt, this wonderfully decrepit 2nd-floor teahouse, overlooking the throng of Old Street (p333), is a temple to the 1930s, with music on scratched records, period typewriters, aged photos, an old fireplace, sewing machines, electric fans, an ancient fridge, oodles of charm and tea (from ¥60), of course.

🍷 French Concession

⭐ Café del Volcán
CAFE

(Map p294; ☑ 156 1866 9291; www.cafevolcan.com; 80 Yongkang Rd, 永康路80号; ☉ 8am-8pm Mon-Fri, from 10am Sat & Sun; 🛜; Ⓜ South Shaanxi Rd) Tiny Café del Volcán offers a refuge from the bustle of Yongkang Rd. The minimalist cafe has just a few wooden box tables sharing the space with the roasting machine. The coffee here is excellent and its signature, aromatic beans come from the owner's coffee plantation in Guatemala – in the family for 120 years.

Choose from pour-over or cafetière brewing methods. Other single-origin beans are from Ethiopia, Kenya, Panama and Yunnan.

⭐ Ars & Delecto
COCKTAIL BAR

(Map p301; ☑ 021 5679 9916; 222 Jinxian Rd, 进贤路222号; ☉ 6pm-2am; Ⓜ South Shaanxi Rd) Parisian-style cafe, with round wooden tables, a long marble bar and simple art deco images on white walls, Ars & Delecto is, without a doubt, one of the best cocktail bars in town. The small but punchy drinks menu has classic tipples, martinis, negronis, whisky sours and highballs, plus signature creations served with serious style.

Depending on what you order, it may come with a dainty sprig of rosemary and citrus, in a teacup or perhaps with a pile of mascarpone on top. Every drink is an experience and taste sensation that should be savoured. Many of the signature cocktails are molecular style; the Crystal Ruby Punch, for example, with mezcal, Calvados, oolong tea, hibiscus and lime, is curdled with dairy to get rid of the acidic punch – the result is a clear and smooth sensation with aromatic layers.

The Odd Couple
COCKTAIL BAR

(Map p294; ☑ 021 6333 2363; www.facebook.com/theoddcoupleshanghai; Xintiandi North Block, Bldg 25, 太仓路181弄25号新天地北里; ☉ 6pm-4am; Ⓜ Xintiandi) Enter this Xintiandi speakeasy via a wall of rainbow LED lights and an enormous Pac-Man screen at the top of the stairs. Inside it's an intimate, thin rectangular space with red lighting, small tables, standing space and a little smoking balcony. The concept comes from two esteemed bartenders, Tokyo's Shingo Gokan and New York's Steve Schneider. Throwback classic cocktails are mixed to perfection.

Choose the '80s-style woo woos, Alabama slammers and Long Island ice teas, or one of the half a dozen signature drinks from each mixologist. The 'Speak Loud' with rum, sherry, bubble tea and matcha from Gokan, and the 'Hello McFly' with mezcal, pink peppercorn and chilly tincture from Schneider are good places to start.

Senator Saloon
COCKTAIL BAR

(Map p294; ☑ 021 5423 1330; www.senatorsaloon.com; 98 Wuyuan Rd, 五原路98号; ☉ 5pm-1am Mon-Fri, to late Sat & Sun; Ⓜ Changshu Rd) From the team behind Sichuan Citizen (p321) comes this classy 1920s Prohibition-style cocktail bar in a quiet spot on Wuyuan Rd. Slink into a dark-wood booth under pressed metal ceilings and dim art deco lights to order a barrel-aged negroni from waitstaff decked out in braces and bow ties. There's a long menu of bourbon and rye-whiskey cocktails; excellent service.

Café des Stagiaires
BAR

(Map p294; ☑ 158 2147 7495; https://shanghai.cafestagiaires.com; 158 Julu Rd, 巨鹿路158号; ☉ noon-2am Mon-Fri, to 4am Sat & Sun; Ⓜ Middle Huaihai Rd) This popular oasis of Francophilia is decked out in hip 'olde worlde' charm with a bar made from stacked suitcases and bistro-like decor, plus windows that fully open out creating a lovely patio atmosphere into the often raucous Found 158 complex. Cocktails include the mint julep, the basil smash and a punchy Sichuan negroni. Happy hour runs weekdays from 5pm to 8pm.

Get a French geography lesson via the wine list: Languedoc, Provence, Côte du Rhône, Loire, Alsace, Bourgogne and Bordeaux are all present. Each table is regularly stocked with addictive chilli peanuts, but it also serves quality charcuterie, cheese and pizza.

⭐ Speak Low
COCKTAIL BAR

(Map p294; ☑ 021 6416 0133; 579 Middle Fuxing Rd, 复兴中路579号; ☉ 7pm-1.30am Sun-Thu, to 2.30am Fri & Sat; Ⓜ South Shaanxi Rd) Speak Low is a speakeasy within a speakeasy within a speakeasy. Once you find your way in through the Ocho bar equipment shop, start with a drink on the 2nd floor; outstanding cocktails run ¥75 to ¥85. Then head upstairs (hint: find China and you'll find the entrance) to the intimate, seating-only bar for expertly crafted Japanese-influenced cocktails from ¥100.

Third-floor signature drinks include the Speak Low – made with Barcardi, matcha tea and sherry, served with chocolates – and the Ladybird, with shiso-infused tequila, served in a wooden sake cup complete with a plum-salt rim. Then head to the even more exclusive 4th floor (if you can find it) where there are lockers in a Japanese-style whisky lounge; purchase a key to get a vintage bottle of liquor and enjoy it with a cigar. Reserve ahead at weekends.

Cotton's   BAR

(棉花酒吧, Miánhuā Jiǔbā; Map p294; ☑ 021 6433 7995; www.cottons-shanghai.com; 132 Anting Rd, 安亭路132号; ⊙ 11am-2am Mon-Thu, to 4am Fri & Sat, to midnight Sun; 🛜; Ⓜ Hengshan Rd, Zhaojiabang Rd) This excellent bar is one of the most pleasant spots in the concession to raise a glass. Ensconced in a converted 1930s villa, the bar's interior has cosy sofas and fireplaces to snuggle around in the winter, and a tiny outdoor terrace on the 2nd floor. The real draw, though, is the garden, which is intimate yet still big enough not to feel cramped.

The drinks and bar snacks, pizzas, burgers, salads and sandwiches are reasonably priced and the crowd is a good mix of locals and expats. You'll have to get here early on weekends to grab a table outside, or book ahead.

1984 Bookstore & Cafe   CAFE

(Map p294; ☑ 021 3428 0911; 11 Hunan Rd, 湖南路11号; ⊙ 10am-8pm; 🛜; Ⓜ Shanghai Library) Big Brother might be watching, but he'd be hard-pressed to find you in this hidden nook of a bookshop-cafe off Hunan Rd. There's no sign, just a metal gate, and you'll need to buzz to get in. Once inside, there's a cosy room with exposed brick walls and a fantastic outdoor courtyard garden; perfect for breakfast or a coffee stop.

It stocks a good range of English and Chinese books (yes, you can pick up a copy of *1984*), canvas tote bags, records and cute notebooks. It also serves smoothies, tea and beer.

Boxing Cat Brewery   BREWERY

(拳击猫啤酒屋, Quánjīmāo Píjiǔwū; Map p294; ☑ 021 6431 2091; www.boxingcatbrewery.com; 82 West Fuxing Rd, 复兴西路82号; ⊙ 5pm-midnight Mon-Wed, 5pm-2am Thu, 3pm-2am Fri, 10am-2am Sat, 10am-midnight Sun; 🛜; Ⓜ Shanghai Library, Changshu Rd) A popular three-floor microbrewery, with a rotating line-up of top-notch beers that range from the Standing 8 Pilsner and Black EyePA to the Right Hook Helles. But that's not all – the kitchen has paired Southern home cooking (gumbo, blackened fish tacos), burgers and beer snacks with the drinks. Come for a pint; stay for dinner.

The Bunker   BAR

(Map p294; ☑ 021 5382 0315; Xintiandi North Block, Bldg 22, 太仓路181弄22号新天地北里; ⊙ 6pm-2am; Ⓜ Xintiandi) This speakeasy is located inside the Green & Safe restaurant (p321) on the 2nd floor, behind a wooden palette–style door. This sophisticated spot is a top choice for a quiet cocktail within Xintiandi. If you're drinking, you can skip the Green & Safe dining queue and order from the menu. Most of the cocktails are excellent, though some are a bit wacky.

The strawberry rice pudding, for example, has Mount Gay rum, sherry, strawberry and cream cheese foam. The Bitter Giuseppe comes with black tea–infused sake, whiskey, Aperol and orange bitters. Cocktails are made using fresh ingredients from Green & Safe's farm.

Dada   CLUB

(115 Xingfu Rd, 幸福路115号; ⊙ 8pm-late; Ⓜ Jiaotong University) This friendly no-frills place stuffed away down an alley near Jiaotong University is one of Shanghai's most popular dives, specialising in cheap drinks and popular weekend dance parties, with local and international DJs. At the time of research, it was temporarily closed, but due to reopen (check before you visit).

Lucca   CLUB

(www.lucca.cc; 390 Panyu Rd, 番禺路390号; ⊙ 6pm-3am; 🛜; Ⓜ Jiaotong University) One of the only LGBTIQ+ clubs in Shanghai, Lucca 390 (formerly 390 Bar) is divided into several sections, with dance floors, bars and mostly techno coming through the speakers. It also hosts a number of events throughout the year, from drag shows and bubble parties to coloured-smoke parties.

🍷 Jing'an

★Sumerian   CAFE

(苏美尔人, Sū Měi Ěr Rén; Map p301; www.sumerian coffee.com; 415 North Shaanxi Rd, 陕西北路415号; ⊙ 7.30am-6pm Mon, to 7.30pm Tue-Sun; 🛜;

Ⓜ West Nanjing Rd) Run by a bright and sunny bunch, good-looking Sumerian packs a lot into a small space. The real drawcard here is the coffee – the cafe roasts its own single-origin beans sourced seasonally from Ethiopia, El Salvador and China. It does good pour-overs and lattes, as well as a nitro and eight-hour cold drip. The homemade bagels are winners too.

★ Tap House
PUB

(扎啤工坊, Zhāpí Gōngfǎng; Map p301; 99 Taixing Rd, 泰兴路99号; ⏰ 11am-1am; ☎; Ⓜ West Nanjing Rd) Part of the trendy **Zhang Garden** (张园, Zhāng Yuán; Map p301; Taixing Rd, 泰兴路; Ⓜ West Nanjing Rd) eating and drinking complex, this brewhouse has a nice outdoor area, rooftop terrace and 20 craft imports on tap. Food is also a highlight with pub and barbecue dishes (mains from ¥65) like pork ribs, sliders and fish and chips. The VPN-enabled wi-fi is handy.

Mokkos Lamu
BAR

(☑ 021 6212 1114; 1245 West Wuding Rd, 武定西路1245号; ⏰ 7pm-2am; Ⓜ Jiangsu Rd) Hidden away on a residential side street, Mokkos is a long-running local fave that specialises in nothing but *shōchū* (a Japanese spirit). Intimate and cheerful, drinkers sit on stools around the curved bar lined with large *shōchū* bottles. There's a choice of wheat, rice or potato varieties. Cash only.

There's a guitar on the wall for regular impromptu jams.

Windows Garage
BAR

(702 West Nanjing Rd, 南京西路702号; ⏰ 11am-late; Ⓜ West Nanjing Rd) One of the cheapest drinking options in town, Windows is a cheery underground dive bar that's been in Shanghai for more than a decade. It serves bargain-basement paint-stripper shots and no-frills beers, plus soak-it-all-up fried foods (from ¥25) and is always a good time. The clientele is a lively mixture of expats, locals and students.

🍺 Pudong

★ Flair
BAR

(Map p313; 58th fl, Ritz-Carlton Shanghai Pudong, 8 Century Ave, 世纪大道8号丽思卡尔顿酒店58楼; ⏰ 5.30pm-late; ☎; Ⓜ Lujiazui) Wow your date with Shanghai's most intoxicating nocturnal visuals from the outdoor terrace on the 58th floor of the Ritz-Carlton, where Flair nudges you that bit closer to the baubles of the Oriental Pearl TV Tower. The chilled-out interior,

designed by the firm Super Potato, is also very cool. Book well in advance for the terrace.

Brew
BAR

(酿, Niàng; ☑ 021 6169 8886; Kerry Hotel, 1388 Huamu Rd, 花木路1388号嘉里大酒店; ⏰ 11am-2am; ☎; Ⓜ Huamu Rd) Ale connoisseurs can earmark this nifty microbrewery bar in the Kerry Hotel, where resident brew-master Leon Mickelson dispenses six on-tap handmade beers (Skinny Green, pils, White Ant, Indian pale ale, Dugite vanilla stout, Mash) and a cider (Razorback). There's a huge range of other bottled beers, and Heineken for those who prefer it.

The bar is sleek and cool without being impersonal, and you can hit the terrace for alfresco park views. Prices are steep, though, so target happy hour (3pm to 8pm).

Patio Lounge
LOUNGE

(Map p313; http://shanghai.grand.hyatt.com; Grand Hyatt, Jinmao Tower, 88 Century Ave, 世纪大道88号君悦大酒店; ⏰ 11.30am-11pm Sun-Thu, to midnight Fri & Sat; Ⓜ Lujiazui) Have a drink or indulge in afternoon tea with the spectacular 33-floor atrium of the Grand Hyatt towering above you in the Jinmao Tower.

100 Century Avenue
BAR

(世纪大道100号, Shìjì Dàdào Yìbǎi Hào; Map p313; ☑ 021 3855 1428; http://shanghai.park.hyatt.com; 91st fl, Park Hyatt, Shanghai World Financial Center, 100 Century Ave, 世纪大道100号柏悦酒店91-92楼; ⏰ 6pm-1am Mon-Thu, to 2am Fri & Sat; ☎; Ⓜ Lujiazui) Pudong keeps its edge honed with two of the highest bars in the world at 100 Century Avenue. It's pretty impressive inside, but the restaurant on the 91st floor has better views than the bars, **Music Room** and **Shanghai Lounge** (on the floor above), as you can get up close to the windows. The bars are closed on Sunday.

Access is through the lobby of the Park Hyatt, on the south side of the building.

🍺 Hongkou & North Shanghai

★ Vue
BAR

(非常时髦, Fēicháng Shímáo; Map p286; www.hyatt.com; 32nd & 33rd fl, Hyatt on the Bund, 199 Huangpu Rd, 黄浦路199号外滩茂悦大酒店32-33楼; entry ¥110; ⏰ 2.30pm-midnight; Ⓜ Tiantong Rd) Take in the extrasensory nocturnal views of the Bund and Pudong from Vue bar at the Hyatt on the Bund, while you raise your glass of bubbly. The cover charge for nonguests includes a drink.

☆ Entertainment

★ JZ Club
JAZZ

(Map p294; Found 158, 158 Julu Rd, 巨鹿路158号; ⊗8pm-2am Sun-Thu, to 4am Fri & Sat; Ⓜ Middle Huaihai Rd) The JZ brand has been in Shanghai for decades, and its newest spot hosts live music every day of the week in an old Shanghai–style jazz club. It's always atmospheric, with velvet red drapes and art deco lighting softly illuminating the space. Look out for the annual **JZ Festival Shanghai** in Expo Park, bringing big-name international jazz artists to Shanghai.

★ Heyday
JAZZ

(Map p294; ☑ 021 6236 6075; 50 Tai'an Rd, 泰安路50号; ⊗6.30pm-2am; Ⓜ Jiaotong University) An intimate jazz bar with an art deco feel and a drinks menu to match Shanghai's decadent era. Cocktails are top notch, with plenty of vintage flavours on the list – orange bitters, cognac and the like. Midweek catch an acoustic set. At the weekends there's a full band, with local acts like Jade Lee and Coco Zhao on the bill.

★ Wooden Box
LIVE MUSIC

(☑ 021 5213 2965; 9 Qinghai Rd, 青海路9号; ⊗10am-midnight; Ⓜ West Nanjing Rd) Down a quiet street, this leafy cabin surrounded by trees is an intimate live venue run by the JZ family with live jazz, and regular acoustic folk and bluegrass sets. The happy hour is excellent and runs from 2pm to 8pm daily.

★ Shanghai Grand Theatre
CLASSICAL MUSIC

(上海大剧院, Shànghǎi Dàjùyuàn; Map p286; ☑ 021 6386 8686; www.shgtheatre.com; 300 Renmin Ave, 人民广场人民大道300号; ⊗box office 9am-8pm; Ⓜ People's Square) Shanghai's state-of-the-art concert venue hosts everything from Broadway musicals to symphonies, ballets, operas and performances by internationally acclaimed classical soloists. There are also traditional Chinese-music performances. Pick up a schedule at the ticket office.

Fairmont Peace Hotel Jazz Bar
JAZZ

(爵士吧, Juéshì Bā; Map p286; ☑ 021 6138 6883; 20 East Nanjing Rd, 南京东路20号费尔蒙和平饭店; ⊗5.30pm-2am; Ⓜ East Nanjing Rd) Shanghai's most famous hotel features Shanghai's most famous jazz band (starts at 7pm), a septuagenarian sextet that's been churning out nostalgic covers such as 'Moon River' and 'Summertime' since the dawn of time. There's no admission fee, but you'll need

to sink a drink from the bar (draught beer starts at ¥70; a White Lady is ¥100).

The original band takes the stage from 7pm to 9.45pm; to get the pulse moving, a 'sultry female vocalist' does her bit from 9.45pm.

House of Blues & Jazz
LIVE MUSIC

(布鲁斯乐爵士之屋, Bùlǔsī Yuè Juéshì Zhīwū; Map p286; ☑ 021 6323 2779; 60 Fuzhou Rd, 福州路60号; ⊗5pm-1am Tue-Sun; Ⓜ East Nanjing Rd) Fittingly dark and divey, this vintage jazz and blues bar exudes plenty of class with its polished heavy wood decor. The house band delivers live jazz or blues from 9.30pm (10pm on Friday and Saturday) to 1am. Sunday night is a free-for-all jam. Entry is free if you're here to eat or drink; happy hour runs to 8pm.

The attached restaurant is set within an atmospheric dining room with an international menu and teppanyaki bar.

★ Shanghai Centre Theatre
ACROBATICS

(上海商城剧院, Shànghǎi Shāngchéng Jùyuàn; Map p301; ☑ 021 6279 8948; www.shanghaicentre.com; Shanghai Centre, 1376 West Nanjing Rd, 南京西路1376号; tickets from ¥180; Ⓜ Jing'an Temple, West Nanjing Rd) The Shanghai Acrobatics Troupe has popular performances here most nights from 7.30pm. It's a short but fun show and is high on the to-do list of most first-time visitors. Buy tickets a couple of days in advance from the ticket office on the right-hand side at the entrance to the Shanghai Centre.

Cathay Theatre
CINEMA

(国泰电影院, Guótài Diànyǐngyuàn; Map p294; 870 Middle Huaihai Rd, 淮海中路870号; tickets ¥35-160; ⊗10am-10.30pm; Ⓜ South Shaanxi Rd) Retro 1932 movie house showing films in 2D and 3D, with some in English. Ticket prices vary depending on the title and movie show times.

Shanghai Conservatory of Music
CLASSICAL MUSIC

(上海音乐学院, Shànghǎi Yīnyuè Xuéyuàn; Map p294; ☑ 021 6431 1792; 20 Fenyang Rd, 汾阳路20号; Ⓜ South Shaanxi Rd) The auditorium here holds classical music performances (Chinese and western) usually on weekends at 7.30pm; the musicians are often the stars of the future. You can buy tickets at the box office at **1155 Huaihai Rd** (☑ 021 6431 8756; 1155 Middle Huaihai Rd, 淮海中路1155号; tickets from ¥80; ⊗9am-5pm; Ⓜ Changshu Rd), which also sells tickets to performances at other venues in the city.

Shanghai Symphony Orchestra Hall
CLASSICAL MUSIC

(上海交响乐团, Shànghǎi Jiāoxiǎngyuè Tuán; Map p294; ☑ bookings 4008210522; www.shsymphony.

com; 1380 Middle Fuxing Rd, 复兴中路1380号; tickets from ¥80; M Changshu Rd) Designed by architects Isozaki Arata and Yasushisa Toyota and opening in 2014, this modern concert venue is now the home of the Shanghai Symphony Orchestra, which has been going strong since 1949. Small chamber music concerts are held most Friday evenings at affordable prices, but they do tend to sell out, so book in advance. Tickets can be bought at the venue's box office or on the website.

MAO Livehouse
LIVE MUSIC

(Map p294; ☑ 021 6445 0086; 3rd fl, 308 South Chongqing Rd, 重庆南路308号3楼; M Dapuqiao) One of the city's best and largest music venues, MAO is a stalwart of the Shanghai music scene, with acts ranging from rock to pop to electronica. Check the Smart Tickets website (www.smartticket.cn) for scheduled events and ticket prices.

Yifu Theatre
CHINESE OPERA

(逸夫舞台, Yìfū Wǔtái; Map p286; ☑ 021 6322 5294; www.tianchan.com; 701 Fuzhou Rd, 人民广场 福州路701号; tickets ¥30-280; M People's Square) One block east of People's Square, this is the main opera theatre in town. The theatre presents a popular program of Beijing, Kun and Yue (Shaoxing) opera. A Beijing opera highlights show is performed several times a week at 1.30pm and 7.15pm; pick up a brochure at the ticket office.

🔒 Shopping

🏛 The Bund & People's Square

★ Shanghai
Museum Art Store
GIFTS & SOUVENIRS

(上海博物馆艺术品商店, Shànghǎi Bówùguǎn Yìshùpǐn Shāngdiàn; Map p286; 201 Renmin Ave, 人民大道201号; ⊙9.30am-5pm; M People's Square) Attached to the Shanghai Museum and entered from East Yan'an Rd, this shop offers a refreshing change from the usual tourist tat. There is an excellent range of books on Chinese art and architecture and a good selection of quality cards, prints and slides, as well as fine imitations of some of the museum's ceramic pieces.

★ Shanghai No 1 Food Store
FOOD

(第一食品商店, Dìyī Shípǐn Shāngdiàn; Map p286; 720 East Nanjing Rd, 南京东路720号; ⊙9.30am-10pm; M People's Square, East Nanjing Rd) Brave the crowds to check out the amazing variety of dried meats, mushrooms, ginseng, chicken

feet and sea cucumber, as well as more tempting snacks including sunflower seeds, nuts, dried fruit, moon cakes and tea. Built in 1925 and redone in 2012, this used to be Sun Sun, one of Shanghai's big department stores.

There are restaurants on the 3rd floor.

Suzhou Cobblers
FASHION & ACCESSORIES

(摩登绣鞋, Módēng Xiùxié; Map p286; www.suzhou-cobblers.com; Unit 101, 17 Fuzhou Rd, 福州路17号101室; ⊙10am-6.30pm; M East Nanjing Rd) Right off the Bund, this cute boutique sells exquisite hand-embroidered silk slippers, bags, hats and clothing. Patterns and colours are based on the fashions of the 1930s, and as far as the owner Denise Huang is concerned, the products are one of a kind. Slippers start at ¥650 and can be made to order.

Blue Shanghai White
CERAMICS

(海晨, Hǎi Chén; Map p286; ☑ 021 6323 0856; www.blueshanghaiwhite.com; Unit 103, 17 Fuzhou Rd, 福州路17号103室; ⊙10.30am-6.30pm; M East Nanjing Rd) Just off the Bund, this little boutique is a great place to browse for a contemporary take on a traditional art form. It sells a tasteful selection of hand-painted Jingdezhen porcelain teacups (from ¥150), teapots and vases, displayed together with the shop's ingeniously designed wooden furniture.

Foreign Languages Bookstore
BOOKS

(外文书店, Wàiwén Shūdiàn; Map p286; 390 Fuzhou Rd, 福州路390号; ⊙10am-6.30pm; M East Nanjing Rd) Open since the 1950s, this monumental red-brick bookshop is Shanghai's best for English-language fiction, nonfiction and travel guides. There's also a stellar selection of Chinese cultural, cooking and language books. Kids' literature is on the 4th floor.

French Concession

★ Lolo Love Vintage
VINTAGE

(Map p294; ☑ 021 6433 9987; 2 Yongfu Rd, 永福路2号; ⊙noon-9pm; M Shanghai Library, Changshu Rd) There are dozens of 1920s brooches and pearl necklaces in glass display cabinets, rock and roll on the stereo and brilliantly kitsch bits and bobs like a stuffed peacock and plastic cactus outside this wacky shrine to 20th-century vintage. The Lolo villa is stuffed with frocks, blouses, tops, shoes and sundry togs spilling from hangers, shelves and battered suitcases.

There's a lovely garden out the front. Find the inconspicuous cream steel doorway on Yongfu Rd, opposite building No 1.

FZH
FASHION & ACCESSORIES

(Map p294; 193 Nanchang Rd, 南昌路193号; ⊙11am-8pm; M South Shaanxi Rd) An independent little indigo shop, selling awesome handmade, hand-dyed blue-tinted garments, using traditional methods. Pick up stylish printed shirts, dresses, T-shirts and more on vintage fabrics. Designer FF Hu will likely be working at the shop and speaks English.

Urban Tribe
CLOTHING

(城市山民, Chéngshì Shānmín; Map p294; www.urbantribe.cn; No 14, Lane 248, Taikang Rd, 泰康路248弄14号; ⊙10am-9.30pm; M Dapuqiao) Urban Tribe is the only contemporary Shanghai label to draw inspiration from the ethnic groups of China and Southeast Asia. The collection of loose-fitting blouses, pants and jackets made of natural fabrics are a refreshing departure from the city's on-the-go attitude and usual taste for flamboyance. It also has a selection of handmade silver jewellery and ceramics.

There's a branch on **Wukang Rd** (城市山民, Chéngshì Shānmín; ☑ 021 6340 0310; 97 Wukang Rd, 武康路97号; ⊙10am-10pm; M Changshu Rd) too.

D.Art
ART

(Map p294; ☑ 021 6385 4401; www.d-art.cn; 63 Nanchang Rd, 南昌路63号; ⊙10am-6pm; M South Huangpi Rd) This charming gallery and shop behind a gate is too easy to miss, but deserves to be found. D.Art packs colourful prints depicting rural Chinese life into all four corners of its pocket-sized space. The eye-catching folk art, initially used as propaganda during the Mao era to glorify farming, is a welcome alternative to more traditional art forms.

Prints, calendars, cards and coasters make perfect gifts. It's on the corner of Nanchang and Sinan Rds through the iron gate.

Huifeng Tea Shop
DRINKS

(汇丰茶庄, Huìfēng Cházhuāng; Map p294; ☑ 021 6472 7196; 124 South Maoming Rd, 茂名南路124号; ⊙9am-9pm; M South Shaanxi Rd) A friendly, reliable tea shop, which has loads of good-quality clay teapots and cups, and a great range of Chinese tea from oolong and green to flower and pǔ'ěr. Sample varieties and make your choice. Good-quality tea ranges from around ¥50 to ¥3000 for 50g. Some English is spoken.

Zhenchalin Tea
DRINKS

(臻茶林, Zhēnchálín; Map p294; ☑ 021 6473 0507; No 13, Lane 210, Taikang Rd, Tianzifang, 泰康路210弄13号; ⊙10am-8.30pm; M Dapuqiao) From the entrance, this looks like just another tea shop, but poke around inside and you'll find specially blended herbal teas from Ayako, a traditional Chinese medicine–certified nutritionist. Peruse the hand-wrapped pǔ'ěr rose, jasmine and peach teas and ceramic and crystal teaware, while staff ply you with tiny cups of ginseng oolong to keep you lingering.

Bags of tea start at around ¥45.

Madame Mao's Dowry
CLOTHING, SOUVENIRS

(毛太设计, Máotài Shèjì; Map p294; ☑ 021 5403 3551; www.madamemaosdowry.com; 207 Fumin Rd, 富民路207号; ⊙10am-7pm; M Jing'an Temple) What better way to brighten up your hall than with a poster of jubilant socialist workers? Madame Mao's Dowry has an emphasis on design during the Mao era. Beyond the Cultural Revolution paintings and prints, there's locally designed clothing, jewellery, ceramics and textiles – including cute bāozi (steamed bun) printed tea towels from Pinyin Press.

Garden Books
BOOKS

(韬奋西文书局, Tāofèn Xīwén Shūjú; Map p301; ☑ 021 5404 8728; 325 Changle Rd, 长乐路325号; ⊙10am-10pm; ☎; M South Shaanxi Rd) The shelves are well stocked at this bookshop-cafe-gelato-bar, with a selection of novels, art books, cookbooks, language references, and books on Shanghai and China. Grab some reading material or a Shanghai postcard, then indulge in a scoop of black sesame ice cream.

There's a postcard mailing service in-store (¥4.50 for international mail).

Shanghai Old City

★ Old Street
GIFTS & SOUVENIRS

(老街, Lǎo Jiē; Map p286; Middle Fangbang Rd, 方浜中路; M Yuyuan Garden) This renovated Qing dynasty stretch of Middle Fangbang Rd is lined with specialist tourist shops, spilling forth with shadow puppets, jade jewellery, embroidered fabrics, kites, horn combs, chopsticks, zǐshā teapots, old advertising posters, banknotes, Tibetan jewellery, the usual knock-off Mao memorabilia, reproduction 1930s posters, old illustrated books and calligraphy manuals, and surreal 3D-dazzle kitten photos.

Following the closure of the long-standing Dongtai Road Antique Market, some interesting items have shown up in these shops, but it's best to assume that nothing is a genuine antique.

South Bund Fabric Market
CLOTHING

(南外滩轻纺面料市场, Nán Wàitān Qīngfáng Miànliào Shìchǎng; 399 Lujiabang Rd, 陆家浜路399号; ⊙8.30am-6pm; M Nanpu Bridge) This old building with more than 100 stalls is one of the best and easiest fabric markets for tourists as many of the stallholders speak a little English. Dresses and suits can be chosen from pattern books or copied from pictures and made up in a dizzying range of fabrics.

Cashmere and wool coats, curtains, suits and leather jackets can all be made to order for a fraction of the price you might spend elsewhere. Take your time when negotiating a price and examining the materials to make a good purchase. If you're not confident tackling the market alone, great **shopping tours** (📋138 1863 2387; www.shoppingtoursshanghai. com; half-day tours from ¥670) are available.

Fuyou Antique Market ANTIQUES, SOUVENIRS
(福佑工艺品市场, Fúyòu Gōngyìpǐn Shìchǎng; Map p286; 459 Middle Fangbang Rd, 方浜中路459号; ⊘9am-5.30pm; Ⓜ Yuyuan Garden) There's a permanent antique market here on the 1st and 2nd floors, but the place really gets humming for the **Ghost Market** on Sunday at dawn, when sellers from the countryside fill up all four floors and then some. Use your best haggling skills.

The range is good, but there's a lot of junk, so you need a shrewd eye if you don't want to pay over the odds.

🄰 Jing'an

★ **Design Republic** HOMEWARES
(设计共和, Shèjì Gònghé; www.thedesignrepublic. com; 511 Jiangning Rd, 江宁路511号; ⊘10am-7pm; Ⓜ Changping Rd) Run by esteemed interior-design duo Neri & Hu – the last word on everything tasteful in Shanghai – Design Republic has set up this multilevel showroom displaying products from acclaimed local and international designers. Within a beautiful red-brick building that was a former police headquarters (c 1909), here you'll encounter anything from Scandinavian furniture to designer glassware, ceramics and accessories.

Jingdezhen Porcelain Artware CERAMICS
(景德镇艺术瓷器, Jǐngdézhèn Yìshù Cíqì; Map p301; 📋021 6253 8865; 212 North Shaanxi Rd, 陕西北路212号; ⊘10am-9pm; Ⓜ West Nanjing Rd) This is one of the best places for high-quality traditional Chinese porcelain. Blue-and-white vases, plates, teapots and cups are some of the many choices available. Credit cards are accepted, and overseas shipping can be arranged.

10 Corso Como FASHION & ACCESSORIES
(Map p301; www.10corsocomo.com; Wheelock Sq, 1717 West Nanjing Rd, 南京西路1717号; ⊘10am-10pm; Ⓜ Jing'an Temple) The first China branch of this glamorous Milan boutique incorporates the same model of 'slow shopping'. Over five floors there's a mix of men's and women's clothing, shoes, homeware, accessories, art books and design pieces. It's mainly international names, with a few Chinese designers. Head upstairs for an art gallery and restaurant.

Pīlíngpālāng CERAMICS
(噼呤啪啷; 📋021 6219 5020; www.pilingpalang. com; Shanghai Centre, Shop 116, 1376 West Nanjing Rd, 南京西路1376号东峰116上海商城; ⊘10am-9.30pm; Ⓜ West Nanjing Rd, Jing'an Temple) You'll find gorgeous vibrant-coloured ceramics, cloisonné and lacquer, in pieces that celebrate traditional Chinese forms while adding a modern and deco-inspired slant. Tea caddies and decorative trays make for great gifts or souvenirs.

🄰 Pudong

IFC Mall MALL
(上海IFC商场, Shànghǎi IFC Shāngchǎng; Map p313; www.shanghaiifcmall.com.cn; 8 Century Ave, 世纪大道8号; ⊘10am-10pm; Ⓜ Lujiazui) This incredibly glam and glitzy six-storey mall beneath the Cesar Pelli–designed twin towers of the Shanghai International Finance Center hosts a swish coterie of top-name brands, from Armani via Prada to Miu Miu and Vuitton and a host of great dining options including Lei Garden and branches of Baker & Spice, Simply Thai and Haiku by Hatsune.

AP Xinyang
Fashion & Gifts Market GIFTS & SOUVENIRS
(亚太新阳服饰礼品市场, Yàtài Xīnyáng Fúshì Lǐpǐn Shìchǎng; ⊘10am-8pm; Ⓜ Science & Technology Museum) This mammoth underground market by the Science & Technology Museum metro station is Shanghai's largest collection of shopping stalls. There are tonnes of merchandise and fakes, from suits to moccasins, glinting copy watches, Darth Vader toys, jackets, Lionel Messi football strips, T-shirts, Indian saris, Angry Birds bags, Bob Marley Bermuda shorts and Great Wall snow globes.

It includes a branch of the **Shiliupu Fabric Market** and a separate market devoted to pearls, the **Yada Pearl Market**. Shop vendors are highly persistent and almost clawing, sending out scouts to wait at the metro exit turnstiles to ensnare shoppers. Haggling is a common language – mixed with much huffing and puffing – so start with a very low offer and take it from there.

Superbrand Mall   MALL

(正大广场, Zhèngdà Guǎngchǎng; Map p313; 168 West Lujiazui Rd, 陆家嘴西路168号; ⊙10am-10pm; Ⓜ Lujiazui) Always busy, this gargantuan shopping mall is also ultrahandy for its dining options, its supermarket in the basement, a kids' arcade on the 6th floor and a cinema on the 8th floor.

West Shanghai

★ Tianshan Tea City   DRINKS

(天山茶城, Tiānshān Cháchéng; 520 West Zhongshan Rd, 中山西路520号; ⊙8.30am-8.30pm; Ⓜ Zhongshan Park, West Yan'an Rd) Running low on loose-leaf oolong and aged *pǔ'ěr* cakes? This three-storey sprawl is hands down the largest collection of tea shops in the city. Taste-test a few to see what you like before you purchase. You probably won't need to leave the ground level, but you'll find a decent selection of teaware and porcelain on the 2nd and 3rd floors.

Information

EMERGENCY

Ambulance	✆ 120
Fire	✆ 119
Police	✆ 110

INTERNET ACCESS

Getting internet access will be a constant source of frustration on your visit to China if you rely heavily on being connected and are used to a lightning-fast service. The Chinese authorities remain mistrustful of the internet, and censorship is heavy-handed. Around 10% of websites are blocked; sites, apps and services such as Google (including Google Maps and Gmail), Dropbox, Facebook, Instagram, Twitter, YouTube and many more are all blocked. Media such as *The New York Times* and *Bloomberg* are also blocked.

In order to get around censored content, you will need to use a VPN (Virtual Private Network) service such as Astrill (www.astrill.com), Express VPN (www.expressvpn.com) or Vypr (www.vyprvpn.com). Note: these must be downloaded *before* you enter China, as they will likely be inaccessible inside the country. They are available for both laptops and mobile devices.

Occasionally email providers can go down, so having a back-up email address set up before you leave home is advisable.

The majority of hostels and hotels have broadband internet access, and many hotels, cafes, restaurants and bars are wi-fi enabled. The wi-fi icon is used in Lonely Planet reviews where it is available. As a general rule, expect internet speeds to be slower than in the West.

MEDIA

Newspapers Imported English-language newspapers can be bought from five-star-hotel bookshops. Local English-language newspapers include the *Shanghai Daily* (www.shanghaidaily.com) and the insipid national *China Daily* (www.chinadaily.com.cn).

Magazines Stacked up in bars, restaurants and cafes, free listings magazines include the monthly *That's Shanghai* (www.thatsmags.com) and the quarterly *Time Out Shanghai* (www.timeoutshanghai.com).

TV Your hotel may have ESPN, Star Sports, CNN or BBC News 24. You can also tune into the censored English-language channel CCTV9 (Chinese Central TV).

MEDICAL SERVICES

Shanghai is credited with the best medical facilities and most advanced medical knowledge in mainland China. The main foreign embassies keep lists of the English-speaking doctors, dentists and hospitals that accept foreigners.

MONEY

Most Chinese people use mobile phones to make payments; non-resident foreigners, however, will generally need to rely on cash. ATMs are plentiful.

POST

The larger tourist hotels and business towers have convenient post offices from where you can mail letters and small packages. **China Post** (中国邮政, Zhōngguó Yóuzhèng) offices and post boxes are green.

Letters and parcels take about a week to reach most overseas destinations; Express Mail Service (EMS) cuts this down to three or four days. Courier companies can take as little as two days. Ubiquitous same-day courier companies (快递, *kuàidi*) can express items within Shanghai from around ¥7 within the same district.

Most major offices open between 8.30am and 6pm daily, sometimes opening until 10pm. Local branches are closed on weekends.

SAFE TRAVEL

Shanghai feels very safe, and crimes against foreigners are rare. Petty theft is unusual, but if you have something stolen, you need to report the crime at the district's **Public Security Bureau** (PSB; 公安局, Gōng'ānjú; ✆ 021 2895 1900; 1500 Minsheng Rd, 民生路1500号; ⊙9am-5pm Mon-Sat) office and obtain a police report.

Traffic & Street Hazards

➥ Crossing the road is probably the greatest danger: develop avian vision and a sixth sense to combat the shocking traffic. Don't end up in an ambulance: Chinese drivers never give way.

* The green man at traffic lights does not mean it's safe to cross. Instead, it means it is *slightly safer* to cross, but you can still be run down by traffic allowed to turn on red lights.

* Bicycles and scooters regularly flout all traffic rules, as do many cars. Bicycles, scooters, mopeds and motorbikes freely take to the pavements, as, occasionally, do cars.

* Older taxis only have seatbelts in the front passenger seat.

* Watch out for scooters whizzing down Shanghai roads without lights at night.

* Don't take an unmarked taxi, as foreigners have been sexually assaulted and robbed. Stick to the larger taxi firms, such as the turquoise Dazhong (p339), gold Qiangsheng (p339), green Bashi (p339) or white **Jinjiang** taxis, and avoid black-market cabs. A registered taxi should always run on a meter and have a licence displayed on the dashboard.

* Other street hazards include discarded neon-light tubes poking from litter bins, open manholes with plunging drops, and welders showering pavements with burning sparks. Side streets off the main drag are sometimes devoid of street lights at night, and pavements can be crumbling and uneven.

TELEPHONE

Long-distance phone calls can be placed from hotel-room phones, though this is expensive without an internet phonecard. You may need a dial-out number for a direct line. Local calls should be free.

Local directory enquiries	☑ 114
Weather	☑ 12121

TOURIST INFORMATION

Shanghai has about a dozen or so rather useless **Tourist Information & Service Centres** (旅游咨询服务中心; Lǚyóu Zīxún Fúwù Zhōngxīn). English is rarely spoken.

TRAVEL AGENCIES

The following agencies can help with travel bookings:

eLong (www.elong.net) Hotel and flight bookings.

Trip (www.trip.com) Excellent online agency, good for hotel, train and flight bookings.

USEFUL WEBSITES

Lonely Planet (www.lonelyplanet.com/shanghai) Destination information, hotel bookings, traveller forum and more.

Shanghaiist (www.shanghaiist.com) Excellent source of news and reviews.

That's Shanghai (www.thatsmags.com) City listings and cultural features for news, events and new openings.

Smart Shanghai (www.smartshanghai.com) Quality listings website, blog entries and sister booking site.

Time Out Shanghai (www.timeoutshanghai.com) Has solid restaurant reviews.

Trip (www.trip.com) For train, plane and hotel bookings.

ⓘ Getting There & Away

Most international passengers reach Shanghai by air. The city has two airports: Pudong International Airport to the east and Hongqiao International Airport on the other side of the city to the west, with most international passengers arriving at the former. Shanghai is China's second-largest international air hub (third-largest including Hong Kong) and if you can't fly direct, you can go via Beijing, Hong Kong or Guangzhou (and a host of lesser international airports in China).

* From the US west coast, figure on a 13- to 14-hour flight to Shanghai or Beijing, and an additional hour or more to Hong Kong.

* From London Heathrow it's about an 11-hour flight to Beijing and 12 to 13 hours to Shanghai and Hong Kong.

* Daily (usually several times a day) domestic flights connect Shanghai to every major city in China.

* Shanghai is linked to the rest of China by an efficient rail network (with numerous high-speed lines) and, to a far lesser extent, long-distance buses.

* Shanghai can be reached by ferry from Osaka, Kobe and Nagasaki in Japan.

Flights, cars and tours can be booked online at lonelyplanet.com/bookings.

AIR

Pudong International Airport (PVG; 浦东国际机场, Pǔdōng Guójì Jīchǎng; ☑ 021 6834 7575, flight information 96990; www.shairport.com) is 30km southeast of Shanghai, near the East China Sea. Most international flights (and some domestic flights) operate from here. If you're making an onward domestic connection from Pudong International Airport, it's crucial that you find out whether the domestic flight leaves from Pudong or Hongqiao, as it will take about 1½ hours to transfer between the two airports.

There are two main passenger terminals, plus a new satellite terminal opened in late 2019, which are easy to navigate. Departures are on the upper level and arrivals on the lower level, where there is a tourist information counter.

Hongqiao International Airport (SHA; 虹桥国际机场, Hóngqiáo Guójì Jīchǎng; ☑ 021 3253 1090, flight information 021 6268 8899; www.shairport.com; 2550 Hongqiao Rd, 虹桥路2550号; Ⓜ Hongqiao Airport Terminal 1, Hongqiao Airport Terminal 2), 18km west of the Bund, has two terminals: the older and less-used **Terminal**

1 (east terminal; halls A and B), and the new and sophisticated **Terminal 2** (west terminal; attached to Shanghai Hongqiao Railway Station, which is served by the Beijing to Shanghai high-speed rail line), where most flights arrive. If flying domestically within China from Shanghai, consider flying from here; it is closer to central Shanghai than Pudong International Airport. If transferring between Hongqiao and Pudong International Airports, note they are a long way apart and it will take at least an hour and a half.

BOAT

Shanghai Port International Cruise Terminal
(上海港国际客运中心, Shànghǎi Gǎng Guójì Kèyùn Zhōngxīn; 500 Dongdaming Rd, 东大明路500号; M International Cruise Terminal) Located north of the Bund and mostly serving cruise ships. A few international passenger routes serve Shanghai, with reservations recommended in July and August. Passengers must be at the harbour three hours before departure to get through immigration.

China-Japan International Ferry Company
(中日国际轮渡有限公司, Zhōngrì Guójì Lúndù Yǒuxiàn Gōngsī; ☑ 021 6595 7988; www.shinganjin.com/index_e.php; 18th fl, Jin'an Bldg, 908 Dongdaming Rd, 东大明路908号金岸大厦18楼; ⊙ 8.30am-11.30am & 1.30-5pm Mon-Fri) Has staggered departures every week to either Osaka or Kobe (46 hours) in Japan on Saturdays at 12.30pm. Fares range from ¥1300 in an eight-bed dorm to ¥6500 in a deluxe twin cabin.

Shanghai International Ferry Company (上海国际轮渡, Shànghǎi Guójì Lúndù; ☑ 021 6537 5111; www.shanghai-ferry.co.jp/english; 15th fl, Jin'an Bldg, 908 Dongdaming Rd, 东大明路908号金岸大厦15楼; ⊙ 8.30am-5pm Mon-Fri) Has departures to Osaka (46 hours) on Tuesdays at 11am. Fares range from ¥1300 in an eight-bed dorm to ¥6500 in a deluxe twin cabin.

Wusongkou International Terminal (吴淞口国际邮轮港, Wúsōngkǒu Guójì Yóulúngǎng, Baoshan Cruise Terminal; No 1 Baoyang Rd, 宝杨路1号; M Baoyang Road) Some cruise ships dock at this north Shanghai terminal (including Royal Caribbean, Princess Cruises and SkySea Cruise), which is 25km from central Shanghai. From the port it's 3km to Baoyang Rd metro station (a 10-minute taxi ride; about ¥16). From Baoyang Rd to People's Square via metro takes around 50 minutes; alternatively, it takes a minimum 40 minutes via taxi (about ¥140).

BUS

As trains are fast, regular and efficient, and traffic on roads unpredictable, travelling by bus is not a very useful way to leave or enter Shanghai, unless you are visiting local water towns. Buses to Beijing take between 14 and 16 hours: it is far faster and more comfortable (but more expensive) to take the 5½-hour high-speed G-class trains to the capital, or even the eight-hour D-class trains.

The huge **Shanghai South Long-Distance Bus Station** (上海长途客运南站, Shànghǎi Chángtú Kèyùn Nánzhàn; 666 Shilong Rd, 石龙路666号; ⊙ 6.30am-8.30pm; M Shanghai South Railway Station) mostly has buses to destinations in south China. Destinations include Suzhou (苏州; ¥38, hourly, 6.39am to 5.25pm), Nanjing (南京; ¥105, one daily), Hangzhou (杭州; ¥80, two daily) and Ningbo (宁波; ¥110, half-hourly, 6.25am to 7.55pm).

Although it appears close to Shanghai Railway Station, the vast **Shanghai Long-Distance Bus Station** (上海长途汽车客运总站, Shànghǎi Chángtú Qìchē Kèyùn Zǒngzhàn; ☑ 021 6605 0000; www.kyzz.com.cn; 1666 Zhongxing Rd, 中兴路1666号; M Shanghai Railway Station) is a pain to get to (taxi is the easiest), but has buses to everywhere, including regular buses to Suzhou (¥38, two hours) and Hangzhou (¥65, 2½ hours), as well as two buses to Nanjing (¥112, 4½ hours, 9.30am and 2.50pm). Buses also journey to Zhouzhuang (¥29, four daily, two hours) and Beijing (¥354, 4pm, one daily, 18 hours).

Regular buses run to Suzhou (苏州; ¥84, three hours, around 15 per day) and Hangzhou (杭州; ¥130, three to 3½ hours, around 14 per day) from the long-distance bus stop at the airport. Buses for Hangzhou, Suzhou and a host of destinations also leave from the **Hongqiao Long-Distance Bus Station** (虹桥长途客运站, Hóngqiáo Chángtú Kèyùn Zhàn; 298 Shenhong Rd, 申虹路298号; M Hongqiao Airport Terminal 2) at Hongqiao Airport Terminal 2.

TRAIN

The only 'international' train to arrive in Shanghai travels from Kowloon (Hung Hom station) in Hong Kong, leaving every other day and taking around 8½ hours. However, the train is an excellent way to arrive in Shanghai from other parts of China. The railway to Lhasa in Tibet began running in 2006, despite scepticism that it could ever be laid, so you can climb aboard a train in Shanghai and alight in Tibet's capital!

The modern **Shanghai Hongqiao Railway Station** (上海虹桥站, Shànghǎi Hóngqiáo Zhàn; 1500 Shengui Rd, 申贵路1500号; M Hongqiao Railway Station) is located at the western end of metro line 10 and on line 2, near Hongqiao International Airport. It's the terminus for the high-speed G-class and other trains, and includes services to Beijing (from ¥552, frequent), Hangzhou (from ¥73, frequent), Hong Kong (around ¥1008, 2.10pm), Nanjing South (from ¥115, frequent) and Suzhou (from ¥32, frequent).

The vast, hectic and sprawling **Shanghai Railway Station** (上海火车站, Shànghǎi Huǒchē Zhàn; 385 Meiyuan Rd, 梅园路385号; M Shanghai Railway Station), located in the north of town, is easily reached by metro lines 1, 4 and 3 and has G-class, D-class and express trains to Beijing (from ¥157, six daily), Hangzhou (from

¥84, three daily), Huangshan (around ¥206, two daily), Nanjing (from ¥92, frequent), Suzhou (¥40, frequent) and Xi'an (¥181, frequent). The main **ticket office** (上海火车站售票处, Shàng-hǎi Huǒchē Zhàn Shòupiàochù; Meiyuan Rd, 梅园路; ⊙5am-12.15am) is outside the station.

Modern **Shanghai South Railway Station** (上海南站, Shànghǎi Nánzhàn; 9001 Humin Rd, 沪闵路9001号; ⊙ticket office 7am-7.30pm; Ⓜ Shanghai South Railway Station) is easily accessed on metro lines 1 and 3. It has trains to southern and southwestern destinations including Guilin (around ¥200, four daily) and Hangzhou (from ¥24, frequent).

A few trains also leave from the renovated **West Station** (上海西站; Shanghai Xīzhàn), including trains to Nanjing (¥190); however, they are infrequent and it's less convenient.

Ticket Offices

There are several options for getting hold of train tickets in Shanghai. You can queue at the ticket offices (售票厅; shòupiàotīng) at train stations, but brace yourself for a long wait. Your hotel will be able to obtain a ticket for you for a commission. Tickets can also be purchased for a small surcharge from travel agencies.

Easiest of all is to book tickets online. Websites and apps like **Trip** (www.trip.com), **China DIY Travel** (www.china-diy-travel.com) and **China Highlights** (www.chinahighlights.com) provide comprehensive schedules, ticket availability and booking services; have them delivered to your hotel (extra fee) or pick them up at the station (go early). The commission should be around ¥30.

ⓘ Getting Around

The rapidly expanding metro and light railway system works like a dream; it's fast, efficient and inexpensive. Rush hour on the metro operates above capacity, however, and you get to savour the full meaning of the big squeeze. Buses can also get stuck in chaotic traffic and be packed during rush hour. And non-Chinese speakers might struggle trying to decipher routes.

TO/FROM THE AIRPORT

Pudong International Airport The warp-speed **Maglev** (磁浮列车, Cífú Lièchē; ☏021 2890 7777; www.smtdc.com; economy one way/return ¥50/80, with same-day air ticket ¥40) train runs to Longyang Rd metro stop on line 2 (¥50, eight minutes); from there you can catch the metro into central Shanghai (from ¥3). Metro line 2 also runs from the airport to central Shanghai (¥7 to People's Sq, 45 minutes). A taxi to the Bund will cost around ¥170 and take approximately one hour, depending on traffic.

Hongqiao International Airport Terminal 2 (where most flights arrive) is connected to downtown Shanghai by metro lines 2 and 10 (¥5, 30 minutes to People's Sq). A taxi to the Bund will cost around ¥110 and take approximately 45 minutes, depending on traffic.

BICYCLES

If you can handle the fumes and menace of Shanghai's intimidating traffic, cycling is a great way to get around town, but you may need to link your journey with public transport if going long distances.

➧ Cars will give you little room; if you're new to Shanghai, allow a few days to adjust.

➧ Make sure that you have your own bicycle cable lock and try to leave your bike at bike parks.

➧ Cyclists never use lights at night and Chinese pedestrians may be in dark clothing, so ride carefully.

Several hostels around town, including **Le Tour Traveler's Rest** (乐途静安国际青年旅舍, Lètú Jìng'ān Guójì Qīngnián Lǘshè; ☏021 6267 1912; www.letourshanghai.com; No 36, Lane 319, Jiaozhou Rd, 胶州路319弄36号; dm from ¥90, r from ¥345; ❋@⊚⧂; Ⓜ Jing'an Temple), can rent you a bike. Or **China Cycle Tours** (☏137 6111 5050; www.chinacycletours.com; House 1, 376 Changle Rd, 长乐路376弄1号; half-day tours from ¥400, rental per day ¥100; Ⓜ Middle Huai-hai Rd) rents bikes on a daily basis and offers cycling tours.

The city also has a huge bike-sharing scheme with two major companies MoBike and Ofo. These are hard for tourists to use but not impossible if you do a little planning in advance (you must have a smartphone, internet, the relevant bike app, and have a topped up WeChat account or have registered on the MoBike app in your home country with your international card before you arrive in Shanghai). Rides cost around ¥1 for 15 minutes and then ¥0.5 for every additional 15 minutes until you dock the bike.

BOAT

There are dozens of ferries ports lining the Huangpu River between Puxi on the west bank and Pudong on the east. Pedestrian tickets are sold for ¥2 at the kiosks at the front of the piers. Among the most useful is the **Shanghai Ferry** (127 East Zhongshan No 2 Rd, 中山东二路127号; one way ¥2; Ⓜ East Nanjing Rd), which operates between the southern end of the Bund and Dong-chang Rd Pier in Pudong, running around every 15 minutes from 7am to 10pm. The **Fuxing Road Ferry** (复兴路轮渡站, Fùxīng Lù Lúndùzhàn; one way ¥2) runs from Fuxing Rd north of the Cool Docks in the South Bund area to Dongchang Rd. Ferries run every 10 to 20 minutes from 6am to 7pm.

BUS

Although sightseeing buses can be extremely handy, the huge Shanghai public bus system is unfortunately very hard to use for foreigners who don't speak or read Chinese. Bus-stop signs and routes are in Chinese only. Drivers and conductors speak little, if any, English, although onboard announcements in English will alert you to when to get off. The conductor will tell you when the bus is arriving at your your stop, if you ask. Bus stops are widely spaced and your bus can race past your destination and on to the next stop up to a kilometre away. Suburban and long-distance buses don't carry numbers – the destination is in characters.

➡ Air-con buses (with a snowflake motif and the characters 空调 alongside the bus number) cost ¥2 to ¥3. The buses without air-con start from ¥1.

➡ The swipeable Transport Card works on many but not all bus routes.

➡ If you can't speak Chinese, have your destination written down in Chinese to show the driver, conductor or even a fellow passenger.

➡ Buses generally operate from 5am to 11pm, except for 300-series buses, which operate all night.

➡ For English-language bus routes in town, go to http://msittig.wubi.org/bus or www.travelchinaguide.com.

CAR & MOTORCYCLE

It is possible to hire a car in Shanghai, but the bureaucratic hurdles are designed to deter would-be foreign drivers – you can't simply pick up a car at Pudong International Airport and hit the road. You will need a temporary or long-term Chinese driving licence.

For most visitors, it is more advisable to hire a car and a driver. A Volkswagen Santana with driver and petrol starts at around ¥700 per day; it might be cheaper to hire a taxi for the day. Ask for more information at your hotel or visit www.chinatour.net.

METRO

The Shanghai metro is fast, cheap, clean and easy, though hard to get a seat on at the best of times (unless you get on at a terminus). The rush hour sees some lines filled beyond capacity, but trains are frequent and the system has rapidly expanded to serve more and more of the city.

➡ At the time of writing, there were 16 lines serving more than 413 stations over 676km, making it the world's largest rapid transit system by length and the second-largest by station numbers.

➡ Current expansion plans include line 18, running between the districts of Baoshan and Pudong. A line connecting Shanghai and Suzhou is under construction and is slated for completion in 2023.

➡ Metro maps are available at most stations. The free tourist maps also have a small metro map printed on them.

➡ The Explore Shanghai app helps you calculate how long your journey will take, how much it will cost and where the nearest metro station is.

➡ Metro station exits can be confusing, so look for a street map (usually easy to find) in the ticket hall before exiting to get your bearings.

➡ To find a metro station, look for the red M.

➡ Wi-fi is available on most metro lines and platforms.

Fares & Tickets

➡ Tickets range from ¥3 to ¥15, depending on the distance.

➡ The rechargeable Transport Card can be used on the metro, some buses, ferries and all taxis.

➡ There can be huge distances between different lines at interchange stations, such as between line 9 and 1 at Xujiahui station, so factor this into your journey time.

TAXI

Shanghai has around 45,000 taxis. They are reasonably cheap, hassle-free and generally easy to flag down, except during rush hour and in summer storms.

Shanghai's main taxi companies include turquoise-coloured **Dazhong** (大众; ☑ 021 96822), gold **Qiangsheng** (强生; ☑ 021 6258 0000) and green **Bashi** (巴士; ☑ 021 96840).

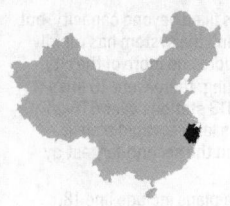

Zhejiang

POP 57 MILLION

Includes →

Best Places to Eat

➡ Green Tea Restaurant (p348)

➡ Xiánhēng Jiǔdiàn (p356)

➡ Zǎozǐshù (p362)

➡ Gāngyāgǒu (p364)

➡ Grandma's Home (p347)

Best Places to Stay

➡ Le Passage Mohkan Shan (p355)

➡ Four Seasons Hotel Hangzhou (p347)

➡ Hofang International Youth Hostel (p347)

➡ Wuzhen Guesthouse (p352)

Why Go?

It's Hangzhou, the handsome capital city, that lands Zhejiang (浙江, Zhèjiāng) on many a traveller's itinerary. Home to picture-perfect landscapes of classical Chinese beauty (and just a short train ride from Shanghai), Hangzhou is the obvious highlight. Yet the province offers so much more. Also within easy striking distance are water towns with spiderweb networks of canals and restored Ming and Qing dynasty merchants' homes (Wuzhen and Nanxun). Among the thousands of islands dotting a ragged and fragmented shoreline is the island of Putuoshan, one of China's four most important Buddhist pilgrimage sites. More intrepid travellers can head west, where ancient villages retain their traditional architecture and bucolic charms. Meanwhile travellers looking for the opposite of intrepid can hole up in one of the stylish resorts nestled among the hillside bamboo groves and tea fields of naturally cool Moganshan.

When to Go
Hangzhou

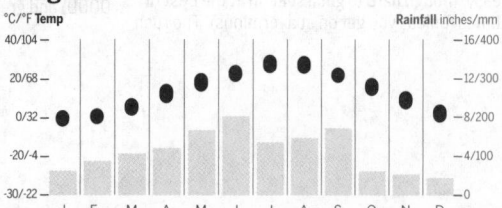

| Late Mar–early May Spring sees low humidity and vegetation turning a brilliant green. | Aug & Sep Flee the simmering lowland heat to the cooler heights of Moganshan. | Late Sep–mid-Nov Steal a march on winter and evade the sapping summer in Hangzhou. |

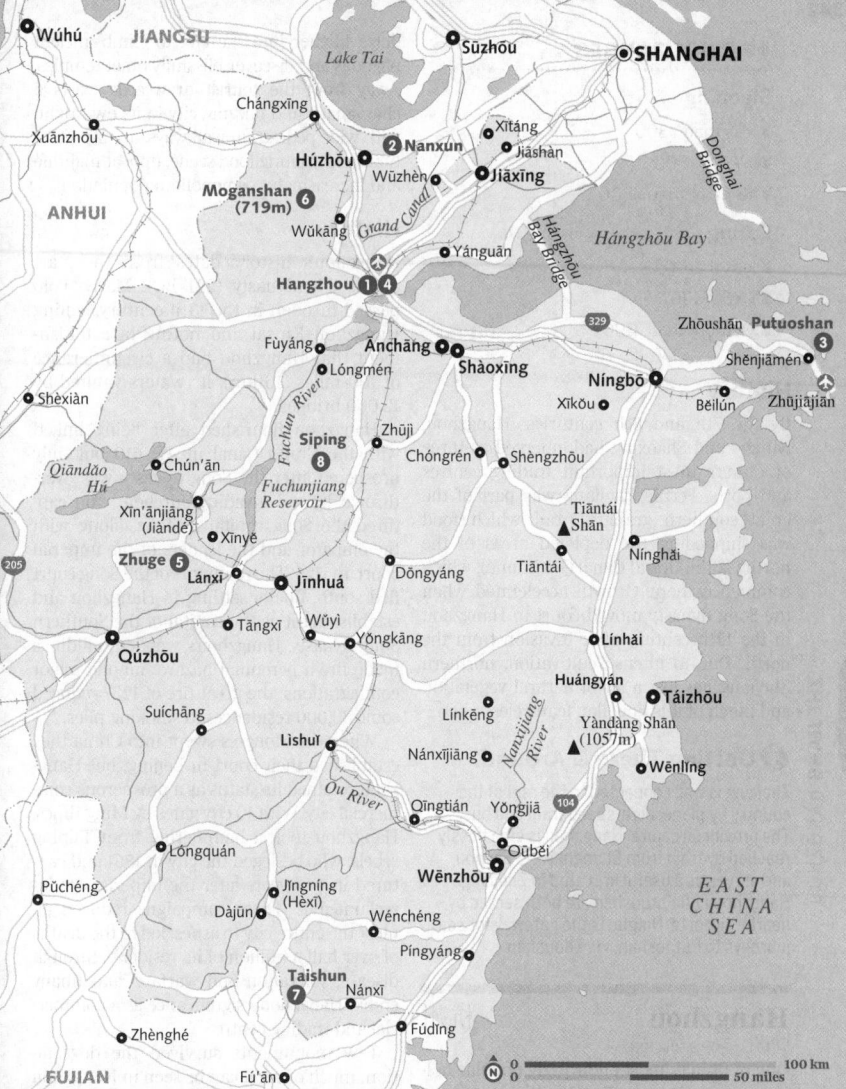

Zhejiang Highlights

1 Hangzhou (p342) Cycling around scenic West Lake, a reflecting pool for willow trees and traditional pavilions.

2 Nanxun (p353) Strolling alongside the waterways of Zhejiang's most charming canal town.

3 Putuoshan (p359) Basking in the glow of the goddess of mercy on a sacred island.

4 Lingyin Temple (p345) Seeking out the 470 Buddhist carvings in the hillsides and grottoes at Lingyin Temple outside central Hangzhou.

5 Zhuge (p357) Exploring the cobblestone alleys of an ancient village designed for maximum feng shui.

6 Moganshan (p354) Trading urban landscapes for the lush forested ones of a 19th-century hill station.

7 Taishun (p363) Riding through the countryside to discover China's best collection of antique covered bridges.

8 Siping (p357) Getting into the rhythms of village life with a homestay.

ℹ PRICE RANGES

Sleeping

¥ less than ¥300

¥¥ ¥300–800

¥¥¥ more than ¥800

Eating

¥ less than ¥60

¥¥ ¥60–120

¥¥¥ more than ¥120

History

By the 7th and 8th centuries, Hangzhou, Ningbo and Shaoxing had emerged as three of China's most important trading centres and ports. Fertile Zhejiang was part of the great southern granary from which food was shipped to the depleted areas of the north via the Grand Canal (Dà Yùnhé), which commences here. Growth accelerated when the Song dynasty moved court to Hangzhou in the 12th century after invasion from the north. Due to intense cultivation, northern Zhejiang has lost a lot of natural vegetation and much of it is now flat, featureless plain.

ℹ Getting There & Around

Zhejiang is well connected to the rest of the country by plane, high-speed train and bus. The provincial capital Hangzhou is effortlessly reached by train from Shanghai and Suzhou, and serves as a useful first stop in Zhejiang. Hangzhou and Putuoshan are both served by nearby airports. Ningbo is the gateway for sea journeys to Putuoshan, via Zhoushan.

Hangzhou   杭州

📞 571 / POP 9 MILLION

One of China's most enduringly popular holiday spots, Hangzhou's (Hángzhōu) dreamy West Lake panoramas and fabulously green hills can easily tempt you into long sojourns. Eulogised by poets and applauded by emperors, the lake has intoxicated the Chinese imagination for aeons. Kept spotlessly clean by armies of street sweepers and litter collectors, its scenic vistas draw you into a classical Chinese watercolour of willow-lined banks, mist-covered hills and the occasional *shíkùmén* (stone-gate house) and old *lǐlòng* (residential lane).

Wonderful as it is, Hangzhou's charms are by no means limited to West Lake scenery – delve further into the city to climb ancient pagodas and discover blissfully quiet temples. Away from the tourist drawcards exists a charismatic and buzzing city in its own right, with wide pedestrian walkways, an unpretentious and exciting food scene, upbeat nightlife and increasingly cosmopolitan population.

History

Hangzhou's history dates from the start of the Qin dynasty (221 BC). Marco Polo passed through in the 13th century, calling Hangzhou Kinsai and noting in astonishment that Hangzhou had a circumference of 100 miles (161km), its waters vaulted by 12,000 bridges.

Hangzhou flourished after being linked with the Grand Canal in AD 610 but fully prospered after the Song dynasty was overthrown by the invading Jurchen, who captured the Song capital Kaifeng, along with the emperor and the leaders of the imperial court, in 1126. The remnants of the Song court fled south, finally settling in Hangzhou and establishing it as the capital of the Southern Song dynasty. Hangzhou's wooden buildings made fire a perennial hazard; among major conflagrations, the great fire of 1237 reduced some 30,000 residences to smoking piles.

When the Mongols swept into China they established their court in Beijing, but Hangzhou retained its status as a prosperous commercial city. With 10 city gates by Ming times, Hangzhou took a hammering from Taiping rebels, who besieged the city in 1861 and captured it; two years later the imperial armies reclaimed it. These campaigns reduced almost the entire city to ashes, led to the deaths of over half a million of its residents through disease, starvation and warfare, and finally ended Hangzhou's significance as a commercial and trading centre.

Few monuments survived the devastation; much of what can be seen in Hangzhou today is of fairly recent construction.

⊙ Sights

★ West Lake   LAKE

(西湖, Xīhú) The very definition of classical beauty in China, West Lake is utterly mesmerising: pagoda-topped hills rise over willow-lined waters as boats drift slowly through a idyll of leisurely charm. Walkways, perfectly positioned benches, parks and gardens around the banks of the lake offer a thousand and one vantage points for visitors to admire the faultless scenery.

Originally a lagoon adjoining the Qiantang River, the lake didn't come into existence until the 8th century, when the governor of Hangzhou had the marshy expanse dredged. As time passed, the lake's splendour was gradually cultivated: gardens were planted, pagodas built, and causeways and islands were constructed from dredged silt.

Celebrated poet Su Dongpo himself had a hand in the lake's development, constructing the **Su Causeway** (苏堤, Sūdī) during his tenure as local governor in the 11th century. It wasn't an original idea – the poet-governor Bai Juyi had already constructed the **Bai Causeway** (白堤, Báidī) some 200 years earlier. Lined by willow, plum and peach trees, today the traffic-free causeways with their half-moon bridges make for restful outings.

Lashed to the northern shores by the Bai Causeway is **Gushan Island** (孤山岛, Gūshān Dǎo), the largest island in the lake and the location of the **Zhejiang Provincial Museum** (浙江省博物馆, Zhèjiāng Shěng Bówùguǎn; 25 Gushan Lu, 孤山路25号; audio guide ¥10; ☉9am-5pm Tue-Sun) **FREE** and **Zhongshan Park** (中山公园, Zhōngshān Gōngyuán). The island's buildings and gardens were once the site of Emperor Qianlong's 18th-century holiday palace and gardens. Also on the island is the intriguing **Seal Engravers Society** (西泠印社, Xīlíng Yìnshè; 31 Gushan Lu, 孤山路31号; ☉9am-4.30pm) **FREE**. Though closed for renovations at the time of research, it's dedicated to the ancient art of carving the name seals (chops) that serve as personal signatures.

The northwest of the lake is fringed with the lovely **Quyuan Garden** (曲院风荷, Qūyuàn Fēnghé) **FREE**, a collection of gardens spread out over numerous islets and renowned for their fragrant spring lotus blossoms. Near Xiling Bridge (Xīlíng Qiáo) is **Su Xiaoxiao's Tomb** (苏小小墓, Sū Xiǎoxiǎo Mù) **FREE**, a 5th-century courtesan who died of grief while waiting for her lover to return. It's been said that her ghost haunts the area and the tinkle of the bells on her gown are audible at night.

The smaller island in the lake is **Xiaoying Island** (小瀛洲, Xiǎoyíng Zhōu), where you can look over at **Three Pools Mirroring the Moon** (三潭印月, Sāntán Yìnyuè), three small towers in the water on the southern side of the island; each has five holes that release shafts of candlelight on the night of the mid-autumn festival. From Lesser Yíngzhōu Island, you can gaze over to **Red Carp Pond** (花港观鱼, Huāgǎng Guānyú) **FREE**, home to a few thousand red carp.

Impromptu opera singing, ballroom dancing and other cultural activities often take place around the lake, and if the weather's fine, don't forget to earmark the eastern shore for sunset over West Lake photos.

It's hardly needed, but musical dancing fountains burst into action at regular intervals throughout the night and day, close to Lakeview Park.

Crowds can be a real issue here, especially on public days off when it can seem as if every holidaymaker in China is strolling around the lake. Escape the jam of people by getting out and about early in the morning – also the best time to spot the odd serene lakeside taichi session. The best way to get around the lake is by bike or on foot.

★**Longjing Tea Village** VILLAGE
(龙井问茶, Lóngjǐng Wènchá, Dragon Well Tea Village; 47 Hupao Lu, 虎跑路47号; ☉8am-5.30pm) **FREE** The lush, green scenery around this tea village up in the hills southwest of West Lake makes for a wonderful break from the bustle of Hangzhou. Visitors can wander through the village and up into the tea plantations themselves. During the spring, which is the best time to visit, straw-hatted workers can be seen picking the tea leaves by hand in the

---

WEST LAKE CRUISE BOATS

Wooden **cruise boats** (游船, Yóuchuán; Hubin Lu, 湖滨路; return trip adult/child ¥50/35; ☉7am-5pm) shuttle from a number of points around West Lake (including Gushan Island, Yue Fei Temple, Red Carp Pond and No 1 Park at the southern end of Hubin Lu) past the **Mid-Lake Pavilion** (湖心亭, Húxīn Tíng) to Xiaoying Island, which has a fine central pavilion and 'nine-turn' causeway. Boats depart either every 20 minutes or when full. Your ticket allows you to take another boat on to Gushan Island or to any of the other cruise-boat docks, but you need to buy another ticket to return.

If you want to contemplate things at a slower pace, hire one of the smaller **six- or 11-person boats** (小船, xiǎo chuán; small/large boat ¥150/180, about one hour) rowed by a boatsperson. Look for them along the causeways. Self-rowing boats are also available, but foreign tourists are not allowed to access these without a Chinese escort.

ZHEJIANG

Hangzhou

1 km
0.5 miles

Hangzhou East
(8km);
Main (18km)

40

Fengqi Lu 凤起路

Xinhua Lu

Hangzhou Old
City Wall Exhibition
Hall (550m);
(30km):

Qingchun Lu 庆春路

Zhejiang University
First Affiliated
Hospital

Jiang Lu

54

48
50
Hangzhou Main
Train Station
Chengzhan

Qingtai Jie 清泰街

Zhonghe Lu

Zhonghe River

Zhongshan Beilu 中山北路

Zhongshan Zhonglu

31
43
Renhe Lu 仁和路

Pinghai Lu 平海路

Longxiangqiao

Youdian Lu

Jiefang Lu

Kaiyuan Lu开元路

Huaguang Lu华光路

Dingan
Rd

45
49

Changsheng Lu 长生路

Xueshi Lu 学士路

42

35 52
53

Xihu Dadao

Laodong Lu

44
8
9

Yan'an Lu 延安路

Fengqi
Rd
39

Wulin Lu 武林路

Hubin Lu 湖滨路

27
38

32
37

Huancheng Xilu 环城西路

CAAC
Office
(200m)

North
(8km)

West Lake

West
Lake
2

6
14

3

4

Baoshi Hill
宝石山

Beishan Lu 北山路

Bai Causeway 白堤

Inner
North
Lake

Gushan
Island

Gushan

24

Gu Hill
25

13

21

5

26

Xiling
Bridge

19

20

12

Su Causeway 苏堤

16

Inner
West
Lake

Qixialing

Yanggongdi

Shuguang Lu 曙光路

West
(5km)

Zheda Lu 浙大路

Yuhuang Lu

Hangzhou
Botanical
Gardens

28

30

Lingyin
Temple
(2km)

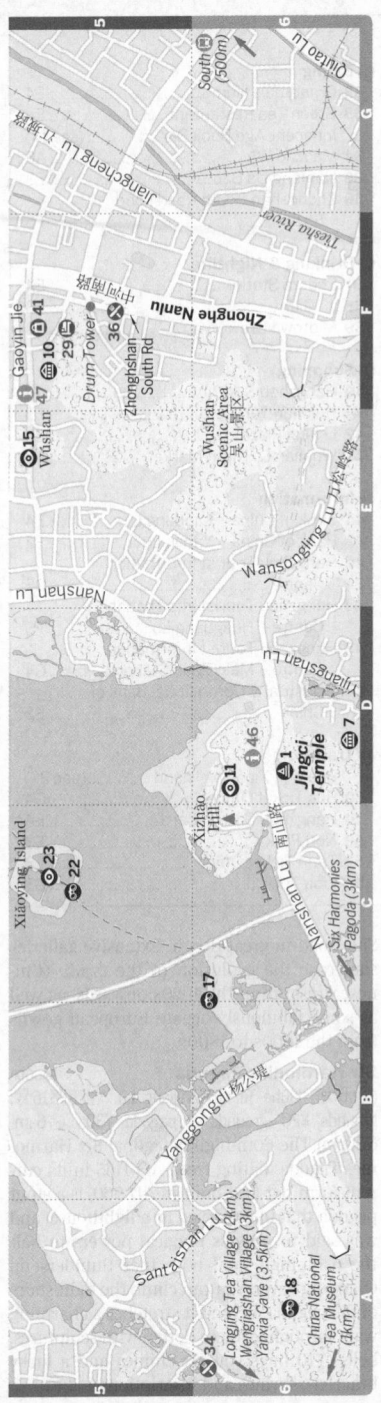

fields, and baskets of the fresh leaves are left out to dry in the sun back in the village.

Stop into any of the casual restaurants and teahouses to taste the *lóngjǐng* (dragon well) tea itself, which is renowned throughout China. It's expensive but has a fine, distinctive flavour.

Well-signposted walking trails lead off from the village into the surrounding hills.

To get to the tourist area, take local bus 27 (¥2, 25 minutes, frequent) from anywhere along the northern shore of West Lake and get off at the Lóngjǐngcháshì (龙井茶室) stop. Last buses at 8pm. A taxi costs about ¥25.

Bus 87 usefully connects most of the sites in the tea plantation area.

★ **Lingyin Temple**   BUDDHIST SITE
(灵隐寺, Língyǐn Sì; ☑0571 8796 8665; http://en.lingyinsi.org; Lingyin Lu, 灵隐路; grounds/temple ¥45/30; ☉7am-5pm; ☒Y2 or K7 to Lingyin stop) Hangzhou's most famous Buddhist temple, Lingyin Temple was originally built in AD 326, but has been destroyed and rebuilt no fewer than 16 times. During the Five Dynasties period (907–960) about 3000 monks lived here. The **Hall of the Four Heavenly Kings** is astonishing, with its four vast guardians and an ornate cabinet housing Milefo (the future Buddha). The **Great Hall** contains a magnificent 20m-high statue of Siddhartha Gautama (Sakyamuni), sculpted from 24 blocks of camphor wood in 1956 and based on a Tang dynasty original.

★ **Jingci Temple**   BUDDHIST SITE
(净慈寺, Jìngcí Sì; 56 Nanshan Lu, 南山路56号; ¥10; ☉6am-5.15pm summer, 6.30am-4.45pm winter) The serene yet monastically active Chan (Zen) Jingci Temple was built in AD 954 and has been fully restored. The splendid first hall contains the massive, foreboding Heavenly Kings and an elaborate red and gold case encapsulating Milefo (the future Buddha) and Weituo (protector of the Buddhist temples and teachings). The main hall – known as the **Great Treasure Hall** – contains a vast seated effigy of Sakyamuni (Buddha).

Qinghefang Old Street   STREET
(清河坊历史文化街, Qīnghéfāng Lìshǐ Wénhuà Jiē; Hefang Jie, 河坊街) At the southern end of Zhongshan Zhonglu is this touristy, crowded and bustling pedestrian street, with makeshift puppet theatres, teahouses, and gift and curio stalls selling everything from stone teapots to boxes of *lóngxūtáng* (龙须糖, dragon whiskers sweets), ginseng and silk. It's also home to

Hangzhou

several traditional medicine shops, including the Huqing Yutang Chinese Medicine Museum, which is an actual dispensary and clinic.

Baoshi Hill HILL
(宝石山, Bǎoshí Shān; ☑0571 8717 9603) FREE Baoshi Hill is one of the loveliest places in Hangzhou to take a hike (p348). Numerous well-kept paths wind through the forest, taking you up steep slopes and past pagodas, West Lake viewpoints and a temple. A perfect escape from the city bustle.

China National Silk Museum MUSEUM
(中国丝绸博物馆, Zhōngguó Sīchóu Bówùguǎn; ☑0571 8706 2129; www.chinasilkmuseum.com; 73-1 Yuhuangshan Lu, 玉皇山路73-1号; ⊙9am-5pm Tue-Sun, noon-5pm Mon) FREE This vast museum is devoted to all things silk, covering fashion, craftsmanship and the historic

Silk Road in great depth. Extensive galleries showcase the evolution of the qípáo (Chinese dress) from the 1920s onwards, as well as some fabulously ornate European gowns from the 1600s to 1800s.

Six Harmonies Pagoda PAGODA
(六和塔, Liùhé Tǎ; 16 Zhijiang Lu, 之江路16号; grounds ¥20, grounds & pagoda ¥30; ⊙6am-6.30pm) The 60m-high octagonal Six Harmonies Pagoda, dating from AD 1165 in its current form but first built in AD 960, is a stout pagoda that once served as a lighthouse, and was said to possess magical powers to halt the 6.5m-high tidal bore that thunders up Qiantang River. You can climb the tight stairs of the pagoda. Behind it stretches a charming walk through terraces dotted with sculptures, bells (¥10 buys you six chimes and a lucky bracelet), shrines and inscriptions.

Huqing Yutang
Chinese Medicine Museum MUSEUM
(中药博物馆, Zhōngyào Bówùguǎn; 95 Dajing Xiang, 大井巷95号; ¥10; ⊙8.30am-5pm) The Huqing Yutang Chinese Medicine Museum has a dispensary and clinic adjoined to the museum. Established by the Qing dynasty merchant Hu Xueyan in 1874, the medicine shop and factory retain the typical style of the period. The museum itself is housed in a lovely, musty old building with a bright courtyard full of medicinal plants.

Leifeng Pagoda PAGODA
(雷峰塔, Léifēng Tǎ; 15 Nanshan Lu, 南山路15号; adult/child ¥40/20; ⊙8am-8.30pm Mar-Nov, to 5.30pm Dec-Feb) Topped with a golden spire, the eye-catching Leifeng Pagoda can be climbed for fine views of the lake. The original pagoda, built in AD 977, collapsed in 1924. During renovations in 2001, Buddhist scriptures written on silk were discovered in the foundations, along with other treasures. There's now a lift and an escalator to help visitors reach the top.

China National Tea Museum MUSEUM
(中国茶叶博物馆, Zhōngguó Cháyè Bówùguǎn; ☑0571 8796 4221; 88 Longjing Lu, 龙井路88号; ⊙8.30am-4.30pm Tue-Sun; ⊑27, 87) **FREE** Not far into the hills of Hangzhou, you'll begin to see fields of tea bushes planted in undulating rows, the setting for the China Tea Museum – 3.7 hectares of land dedicated to the art, cultivation and tasting of tea. Further up are several tea-producing villages, all of which harvest China's most famous variety of green tea, *lóngjǐng* (dragon well), named after the spring where the pattern in the water resembles a dragon.

🛌 Sleeping

Book well ahead in the summer months, at weekends and during the busy holiday periods. Room prices at hostels and some hotels see a significant hike on weekends. Areas near the lake are convenient, atmospheric and upmarket. There are more midrange options closer to Ding'an metro, which still places you within walking and cycling distance of West Lake's eastern shore.

★Hofang International
Youth Hostel HOSTEL ¥
(荷方国际青年旅社, Héfāng Guójì Qīngnián Lǚshè; ☑0571 8706 3299; 67 Dajing Xiang, 大井巷67号; dm ¥56-90, s/d ¥178/208; ❋@🛜) Pleasantly tucked away from the noise down a historic alley off Qinghefang Old Street (p345), this hostel has an excellent location and exudes a pleasant, calm ambience, with attractive rooms, the cheapest of which come with tatami. Note that prices go up by between ¥30 and ¥60 on weekends and holidays. The adjoining hostel cafe is a cosy place to check emails with a coffee.

West Lake 7
Service Apartments APARTMENT ¥¥
(西湖柒号酒店公寓, Xīhú Qīhào Jiǔdiàn Gōngyù; ☑0571 8883 3776; www.westlake7.com; 1 Yuewang Lu, 岳王路1号; d¥320; 🅿🛜) These large and comfortable serviced apartments offer excellent value for money, with facilities including a washing machine, kitchen and speedy wi-fi. The location is not bad, set right next to the Wushan Lu Night Market (p349) and just a few blocks' walk from the West Lake.

★Four Seasons Hotel
Hangzhou HOTEL ¥¥¥
(杭州西子湖四季酒店, Hángzhōu Xīzihú Sìjì Jiǔdiàn; ☑0571 8829 8888; www.fourseasons.com/hangzhou; 5 Lingyin Lu, 灵隐路5号; d¥3020, ste from¥7225; ❋❋@🛜❄) More of a resort than a hotel, the fabulous 78-room, two-pool Four Seasons enjoys a seductive position in lush grounds next to West Lake. Low-rise buildings and three private villas echo traditional China, a sensation amplified by the osmanthus trees, ornamental shrubs, ponds and general tranquillity.

Tea Boutique Hotel HOTEL ¥¥¥
(杭州天伦精品酒店, Hángzhōu Tiānlún Jīngpǐn Jiǔdiàn; ☑0571 8799 9888; www.teaboutiquehotel.com; 69 Qingzhiwu Lu, 青芝坞路69号; d incl breakfast¥630; ❋❋@🛜) A Chinese–Japanese minimalist mood holds sway at this hotel with tea-themed artwork, muted colours, soft lighting and heavy wood in the bedrooms to create a relaxing atmosphere.

🍴 Eating

Hangzhou has endless zones dedicated to the art of feasting – try Gaoyin Jie, a long sprawl of neon-lit restaurants or **Zhongshan South Road Food Street** (中山南路美食街, Zhōngshān Nánlù Měishí Jiē; Zhongshan Nanlu, 中山南路美食街; ⊙5.30pm-late). Many of the smarter restaurants around the West Lake itself also offer good-value and interesting meals.

★Grandma's Home HANGZHOU ¥
(外婆家, Wàipójiā; ☑0571 8502 8700; 147 Nanshan Lu, 南山路147号; mains ¥15-35; ⊙10am-9pm) There's no end to the hype about this restaurant, which now has branches across the

WEST LAKE HILLS WALK

For a manageable and breezy trek into the forested hills above West Lake, walk up a lane called Qixialing, immediately west of the **Mausoleum of General Yue Fei** (岳庙, Yuè Fēi Mù; 80 Beishan Lu, 北山路80号; ¥25; ⊙ 7.30am-5.30pm). The road initially runs past the temple's west wall to enter the shade of towering trees, with stone steps leading you up. At **Ziyun Cave** (紫云洞, Zǐyún dòng, Purple Cloud Cave; 69 Shuguang Lu; ⊙ 6.30am-4.30pm) `FREE` the hill levels out and the road forks; take the right-hand fork towards the Baopu Taoist Temple, 1km further, and the **Baochu Pagoda** (保俶塔, Bǎochù Tǎ; Beishan Jie, 北山街). At the top of the steps, turn left and, passing the **Sunrise Terrace** (初阳台, Chūyáng Tái; ⊙ 24hr) `FREE`, with its West Lake viewing balcony, again bear left. Down the steps, look out for the tiled roofs and yellow walls of the charming **Baopu Taoist Temple** (抱朴道院, Bàopǔ Dàoyuàn; ☑ 0571 8798 1201; ¥5; ⊙ 6am-5pm) to your right; head right along a path to reach it. Come out of the temple's back entrance and turn left towards the Baochu Pagoda and, after hitting a confluence of three paths, take the middle track towards and up **Toad Hill** (蛤蟆峰, Hámá Fēng), which affords supreme views over the lake, before squeezing through a gap between huge boulders to meet the Baochu Pagoda rising ahead. Restored many times, the seven-storey grey brick pagoda was last rebuilt in 1933, although its spire tumbled off in the 1990s. Continue on down and pass through a **páilou** (牌楼) – or decorative arch – erected during the Republic (with some of its characters scratched off) to a series of stone-carved **Ming dynasty effigies**, all of which were vandalised in the tumultuous 1960s, save two effigies on the right. Turn left here and walk a short distance to some steps heading downhill to your right past the remarkable weathered remains of a colossal stone Buddha by the cliff face (with square niches cut in him) – all that remains of the **Big Buddha Temple** (大佛寺, Dàfó Sì). Continue on down to Beishan Lu.

whole country, with eager diners constantly clustering outside. It almost lives up to its reputation, with low prices and generous portions, but dishes do vary enormously in quality. The braised pork and tea-scented chicken are both good bets to get a taste of classic Hangzhou flavours.

★ Green Tea Restaurant HANGZHOU ¥
(绿茶, Lùchá; 3rd fl, Intime Mall, 98 Yan'an Lu, 安路 98号银泰店F3; mains ¥26-68; ⊙ 10.30am-11pm; Ⓜ Ding'an Lu) Often packed, this excellent Hangzhou restaurant, on the 3rd floor of Intime Mall, has superb food. With a bare-brick finish and rows of clay teapots, the low-lit dining room is sleek and trendy. Prices are surprisingly low, with the signature fish-head dish the most expensive thing on the menu at ¥68. Eggplant claypot and a Cantonese bread and ice-cream dessert are also sensational.

Nánfāng Dà Bāo DUMPLINGS ¥
(南方大包; 82 Youdian Lu, 邮电路82号; per bun ¥2-6; ⊙ 6.30am-6.30pm) Who would have thought the humble *bāozi* could taste so good? The fluffy steamed buns served at this small corner stand near the Rénhé Hotel building are simply huge, and come with either pork or a sweet bean filling. The pork ones are sensational, with top-quality meat and a rich gravy.

Innocent Age Book Bar CHINESE ¥
(纯真年代书吧, Chúnzhēn Niándài Shūbā; ☑ 0571 8694 0779; Baochuta, 8 Qianshan Lu, 保俶塔前 山路8号; dishes from ¥22; ⊙ 9.30am-10pm) Enjoy snacks, cakes, tea and coffee on a glorious terrace overlooking the West Lake at this cafe set just down the slope of Baoshi Hill (p346) from Baochu Pagoda. Try the huge and flavoursome bowl of Hangzhou beef noodles for good-value fuel before you continue your walk, or linger indoors with the quiet reading-room atmosphere among shelves full of books.

Máocǎo Wū HANGZHOU ¥
(茅草屋; ☑ 0571 8799 6622; 85 Longjing Lu, 龙井 路85号; mains ¥38-58; ⊙ 9am-2pm & 5-9pm; ☒ 27, 87) Near the China National Tea Museum, this restaurant serves traditional Hangzhou cuisine in a beautiful setting overlooking a pond and surrounded by tea bushes. The melt-in-your-mouth *dōngpō ròu* (东坡肉, braised pork belly) is especially good. Order from the large picture menu display inside.

🍷 Drinking & Nightlife

★ Midtown Brewery PUB
(城中啤酒吧, Chéngzhōng Píjiǔ Bā; ☑ 0571 8159 0433; 1st fl, Shangri-la Hotel, 6 Changshou Lu, 长 寿路6号杭州城中香格里拉大酒店1楼) The craft-beer craze has certainly hit Hangzhou

and the standout place to sample some top-notch craft beers is Midtown Brewery. Housed in the Shangri-la hotel, the beers are brewed on-site and are genuinely outstanding. If you need convincing, order the tasting paddle (¥99) of seven samplers, including pale ale, porter and stout. Service is smooth and the setting smart and contemporary.

★ JZ Club
CLUB

(黄楼爵士俱乐部, Huáng Lóu Juéshì Jùlèbù; ☑ 0571 8702 8298; www.jzclub.cc; 6 Liuying Lu, at 266 Nanshan Lu, 柳营路6号; ⊙7pm-2am) The folk that brought you JZ Club in Shanghai have the live jazz scene sewn up in Hangzhou with this neat three-floor venue in a historic building near West Lake. There are three live jazz sets nightly, with music kicking off at 9.15pm (until 12.30am). There's no admission charge; reserve a seat on Friday and Saturday.

Eudora Station
BAR

(亿多瑞站, Yìduōruìzhàn; ☑ 0571 8791 4760; 101-107 Nanshan Lu, 南山路101-107号; ⊙9.30am-2am) A fab location by West Lake plus a roof terrace, outside seating and great happy-hour deals conspire to make this welcoming watering hole a solid choice. There's sports TV, live music, a good range of imported beers and barbecues that fire up on the roof terrace in the warmer months.

 Shopping

Hangzhou Silk City
SILK

(丝绸城, Sīchóu Shìchǎng; 253 Xinhua Lu, 新华路253号; ⊙8am-5pm) Hangzhou is famous for its silks and there are certainly bargains to be found in this seven-storey market. You'll have to work hard to get them, though. Head straight for the 5th and 6th floors (lower levels just sell regular clothes) to find scarves, slinky nightwear, dresses, qìpáo (traditional Chinese sheath dresses) and other silk items. Vendors will usually let you bargain them down by around 30%.

Wushan Lu Night Market
MARKET

(吴山路夜市, Wúshān Lù Yèshì; Huixing Lu, 惠兴路; ⊙7-10.30pm) This night market doesn't have too much to offer by way of interesting souvenirs, but it's still a pleasant place to stroll for half an hour. Stalls sell knock-off cosmetics and bags, cheap clothes, shoes, plastic jewellery and other knick-knacks to an excited crowd of mostly teenagers. Get the gloves off and haggle if something catches your eye.

Huíchūn Táng
HEALTH & WELLNESS

(回春堂; ☑0571 8780 8117; 117 Hefang Jie, 河坊街117号; ⊙7.15am-8.30pm) One of the country's oldest traditional Chinese medicine (TCM) clinics, Huíchūn Táng is still a fully functioning business with TCM doctors on-site and dried herbs, powders and tonics all available to buy. Help yourself to free herbal tea from the dispenser and sip as you browse the intriguing jars. No English is spoken.

ⓘ Information

MONEY

Bank of China – Laodong Lu (中国银行, Zhōngguó Yínháng; 177 Laodong Lu, 劳动路177

QIANTANG RIVER TIDAL BORE

An often spectacular natural phenomenon occurs every month on Hangzhou's Qiantang River (钱塘江, Qiántáng Jiāng), when the highest tides of the lunar cycle dispatch a wall of water – sometimes almost 9m tall – thundering along the narrow mouth of the river from Hangzhou Bay, at up to 40km/h. Occasionally sweeping astonished sightseers away and luring bands of intrepid surfers, this awesome tidal bore (钱塘江潮, qiántáng jiāngcháo) is the world's largest and can be viewed from the riverbank in Hangzhou, but one of the best places to witness the action is on the northern side of the river at **Yanguan** (盐官, Yánguān), a delightful ancient town about 38km northeast of Hangzhou.

The most popular viewing time is during the **International Qiantang River Tide Observing Festival** (admission to viewing area ¥30; ⊙Sep/Oct), on the 18th day of the eighth month of the lunar calendar (the same day as the mid-autumn festival), which usually falls in September or October. You can, however, see it throughout the year when the highest tide occurs at the beginning and middle of each lunar month; access to the park in Yanguan for viewing the tide is ¥25. The Hangzhou Tourist Information Centre (p350) can give you upcoming tide times. To make it a day trip, a through ticket (¥100) is available in Yanguan to explore the charming historic temples and buildings of the town.

Take a train (¥11, 35 minutes) from Hangzhou Main Train Station (p350) or East Train Station (p350) to Hǎiníng (海宁) and change to bus 109 (¥10, 25 minutes) to Yanguan.

号; ☺9am-5pm) Offers currency exchange plus a 24-hour ATM.

Bank of China – Yanan Lu (中国银行, Zhōngguó Yínháng; 320 Yanan Lu, 延安路320号; ☺9am-5pm) A useful central branch with currency exchange.

Industrial & Commercial Bank of China (ICBC, 工商银行, Gōngshāng Yínháng; 300 Yan'an Lu, 延安路300号) Has a 24-hour ATM.

TOURIST INFORMATION

Asking at, or phoning up, your hostel or hotel for info can be very handy.

Hangzhou Tourist Information Centre (杭州旅游咨询服务中心, Hángzhōu Lǚyóu Zīxún Fúwù Zhōngxīn; ☑0571 8797 8123; Léifēng Pagoda, Nanshan Lu, 雷峰塔 南山路; ☺8am-5pm) provides basic travel info, free maps and tours. Other branches include **Hangzhou main train station** (☑0571 8782 5755; ground fl, Main Train Station, Chengzhan Lu, 城站路; ☺8am-8pm) and **10 Huaguang Lu** (☑0571 8780 9951; 华光路10号; ☺7.30am-8.30pm), just off Qinghefang Old Street.

Travellers Infoline (☑0571 96123; ☺6.30am-9pm) Helpful 24-hour information, with English service.

VISAS

Public Security Bureau (PSB, 公安局, Gōng'ānjú; ☑0571 8728 0600; 35 Huaguang Lu; ☺8.30am-noon & 2-5pm Mon-Fri) You can extend visas here.

ⓘ Getting There & Away

AIR

Hangzhou has flights to all major Chinese cities (bar Shanghai) and international connections to Tokyo, Singapore and other destinations. Several daily flights connect to Beijing and Guangzhou.

Most hotels will also book flights, generally with a ¥20 to ¥30 service charge. The **Civil Aviation Administration of China** (CAAC, 中国民航, Zhōngguó Mínháng; ☑0571 8666 8666; 390 Tiyuchang Lu; ☺7.30am-8pm) office is in the north of town.

BUS

All four bus stations are outside the city centre; tickets can be conveniently bought for all stations from the **bus ticket office** (长途汽车售票处, Chángtú Qìchē Shòupiàochù; Chengzhan Lu, 城站路; ☺6.30am-5pm) right off the exit from Hangzhou Main Train Station. The least convenient station are the North and West bus stations, as neither is connected by metro – only by buses or taxi (about 35 minutes).

Buses leave Shanghai's South Station frequently for Hangzhou's various bus stations (¥80, 2½ hours). Buses to Hangzhou also run every 30 minutes between 10am and 9pm from Shanghai's Hongqiao airport (¥100, two hours). Regular buses also run to Hangzhou from Shanghai's Pudong International Airport (¥120, three hours, 8.40am to 9pm).

Yibu Trip (驿步出行, Yìbù Chūxíng; www.yibutrip.com; Jianguo Nan Lu; ☺7am-6pm) runs buses (¥31, 1½ hours, every 20 to 100 minutes, 7am to 6pm) between its small station northwest of Hangzhou Main Train Station and the car parks of either of the two scenic zones in Wuzhen. Buy tickets before boarding.

Buses from the huge **Hangzhou Main Bus Station** (客运中心站, Kèyùn Zhōngxīn; ☑0571 8765 0678; Jiubao Zhijie, 九堡直街) at Jiubao, in the far northeast of Hangzhou (and linked to the centre of town by metro to Keyun Zhongxin station; a taxi will cost around ¥65) include the following:

Ningbo ¥70, two hours, frequent

Wuzhen ¥35, one hour, 16 daily

Xin'anjiang ¥60, two hours, five daily

Buses from the **North Bus Station** (汽车北站, Qìchē Běizhàn; 766 Moganshan Lu, 莫干山路766号) include the following:

Ningbo ¥70, two hours, frequent

Shanghai ¥80, 2½ hours, frequent

Suzhou ¥73, two hours, frequent

Tongli ¥53-67, two hours, four daily

Buses from the **West Bus Station** (汽车西站, Qìchē Xīzhàn; 357 Tianmushan Lu, 天目山路357号) include Wuyuan (¥140, 4½ hours, 9.20am and 1.40pm) and Xinye (¥61, 2½ hours, 8.20am and 1.50pm) services.

TRAIN

Both of Hangzhou's train stations are conveniently linked to the metro.

The easiest way to travel to Hangzhou from Shanghai Hongqiao Train Station is on the high-speed G- and D- class trains to **Hangzhou East Train Station** (杭州东站, Hángzhōu Dōngzhàn; Dongning Lu, 东宁路). For Beijing, there are just two sleeper options. The overnight Z282 (hard/soft sleeper ¥351/537) departs **Hangzhou Main Train Station** (杭州火车站, Hángzhōu Huǒchēzhàn; ☑0571 8762 2362; Chengzhan Lu, 城站路) at 5.04pm, arriving at 10.22am; and the K102 (hard/soft sleeper ¥344/528) departs at 7.22pm, arriving at 3.43am. The much faster seated G-class trains to Beijing South leave from Hangzhou East Train Station.

A handy **train ticket office** (火车票售票处, Huǒchēpiào Shòupiàochù; 147 Huansha Lu, 浣纱路147号; ☺8am-5pm) is north of Jiefang Lu, just east of West Lake. Other offices are at 72 Baochu Lu (near the turning with Shengfu Lu) and 149 Tiyuchang Lu. Train tickets are also available at certain China Post branches including 10 Desheng Lu and 60 Fengqi Lu.

ⓘ Getting Around

BICYCLE

If you have internet access on your phone, the easiest way rent bikes is to use the English **Mobike** (www.mobike.com) app, which is the only service that accepts international debit/credit cards, and has deals from as little as ¥15 for a month of unlimited rides across China. There are Mobike bikes on virtually every street in Hangzhou.

Without internet, the cheapest way to rent a bike is to use the **Hangzhou Bike Hire Scheme** (☑ 0571 8533 1122; deposit ¥200, incl ¥35 credit). Stations (2700 in total) are dotted in large numbers around the city, in what is one of the world's largest government-run networks. Applying can be a bit time consuming and requires half an hour to apply and the same time again to get a refund on your deposit.

You can now only apply at the **Hangzhou Citizen Card** (杭州市民卡(城南服务厅), Hángzhōu Shìmín Kǎ (Chéngnán Fúwù Tīng); 25 Ding'an Lu, 定安25号; ⊙ 8am-5pm) office next to Intime Mall and Ding'an metro, not from the docks themselves. Take a number and wait about half an hour. Show your passport and pay a deposit of ¥200, which includes ¥35 credit on the swipe card that you will receive on the spot.

To use a bike, swipe the pad at one of the docking stations till you get a steady green light, free a bike and you're away. Return bikes to any other station (ensure the bike is properly docked before leaving it). The first hour on each bike is free, so if you switch bikes within the hour, the rides are free. The second hour on the same bike is ¥1, the third ¥2 and after that it's ¥3 per hour. Note you cannot return bikes outside booth operating hours as the swipe units deactivate (you will be charged a whole night's rental).

Your deposit and unused credit are refunded to you when you return your swipe card (check when it should be returned as this can vary), minus a 1% fee. This requires queueing again at the office.

BUS

Hangzhou has a clean, efficient bus system and getting around is easy (but roads are increasingly gridlocked). 'Y' buses are tourist buses; 'K' is simply an abbreviation of '*kōngtiáo*' (air-con). Tickets cost ¥2 to ¥5. These are popular bus routes:

Bus K7 Connects the Main Train Station to the western side of West Lake and Lingyin Temple.

Tourist bus Y2 Connects the Main Train Station, along Beishan Lu, to Lingyin Temple.

Buses 15 and K15 Connect the North Bus Station to the northwestern area of West Lake.

Buses K4 and 334 Run from downtown to the Six Harmonies Pagoda.

METRO

Hangzhou's metro Line 1 (tickets ¥2 to ¥8; first/last train 6.06am/11.32pm) runs from the southeast of town, through the Main Train Station, along the eastern side of West Lake and on to the East Train Station, the Main Bus Station and the northeast of town. It's useful for getting from the train stations, but not very useful for sightseeing around town. The other three lines are of little use to visitors.

Many other lines are under construction to be ready for the 2022 Asian Games in Hangzhou (and also Shaoxing and Ningbo), including a metro line linking Hangzhou to Shaoxing; and an Airport Express line linking the airport with Hangzhou East Train Station.

TAXI

Metered Hyundai taxis are ubiquitous and start at ¥11; figure on around ¥20 to ¥25 from the main train station (queues can be horrendous) to Hubin Lu.

Wuzhen 乌镇

☑ 0573 / POP 59,000

Like many of the other famous water towns, Wuzhen (Wūzhèn) was part of the Grand Canal and prospered from trade and silk production. It's a major tourist attraction, and with its crowds and rows of souvenir shops it's easy to write off Wuzhen as inauthentic. But then you turn a corner and get a view of an ancient stone bridge curving over a canal or a row of weathered Qing dynasty wooden homes, and realise that this place really is beautiful. It's also easily explored, with good transit links and plenty of English on the ground.

⊙ Sights

The old town is divided into two scenic areas: **Dongzha** (东栅) and **Xizha** (西栅); a combined ticket to visit the two areas costs ¥150. Most of the row homes in both areas have been transformed into museums, galleries and artisan workshops (with giftshops), snack vendors and restaurants. All are free to enter, though you may be required to show your village admission ticket.

The Xizha scenic zone covers more ground than Dongzha, has the visitor centre and is where bus K350 drops passengers off first. For day trippers it makes sense to start here, take the free shuttle to Dongzha and then grab a *sānlúnchē* (pedicab) on Xinhua Lu (新华路), which runs perpendicular to Dongzha's main drag, Dong Dajie, back to the bus station. If you're overnighting in Xizha, you might want to start in Dongzha. Admission tickets are for one day only, but if you spend the night in Xizha you won't need a ticket to enter the next day.

◉ Xizha Scenic Zone

The Xizha scenic zone (p351) is more spread out so feels less packed, even though visitors spend more time here. It is the more photogenic of the two scenic zones as the main street, Xizha Dajie (西栅大街), is criss-crossed with bridges from where you can gaze upon the canals.

Chinese Footbinding Culture Museum
MUSEUM

(三寸金莲馆, Sāncùn Jīnlián Guǎn; 349 Xizha Dajie, Xizha, 西栅大街349号, 西栅; ⊙8am-5pm) With plenty of English, this fascinating museum covers the thousand-year history of female foot-binding in China with examples of the shoes that constituted (as the captions attest to) the Golden Lotus (3in foot) complex that was the freakish mentality of the males at that time. Periodically banned, foot-binding was finally abolished in the 20th century.

Yuelao Temple
BUDDHIST SITE

(月老庙, Yuèlǎo Miào; Xizha, 西栅) Singles and couples alike come here to win the favour of the god of love (who appears here as an old man) by lighting incense and tying red-stringed charms to trees around the temple.

White Lotus Pagoda
BUDDHIST SITE

(白莲塔, Báilián Tǎ; 18 Shifu Nanlu, Xizha, 石佛南路18号, 西栅; ⊙8am-5pm) This seven-storey pagoda is a beacon at the far western end of the Xizha scenic zone. You can climb up to the 3rd floor for excellent views over the Grand Canal.

◉ Dongzha Scenic Zone

The main street of the Dongzha scenic zone (p351), Dongda Jie (东大街) is a narrow path paved with stone slabs and flanked by wooden buildings. There are workshops here turning out indigo-dyed cloth, bamboo weavings and the like. Most sights are open from 8am to 5pm. As the road is narrow it can feel a bit claustrophobic when busy, but Dōngzhà generally sees fewer guests than Xīzhà.

🏃 Activities

Boat Tours
BOATING

(游船, Yóuchuán; Dōngzhà/Xīzhà per person from ¥30/60; ⊙Dōngzhà 8am-5.30pm, Xīzhà 7.30am-9.30pm) At several points along the canals in both scenic zones you can pick up a ride on a traditional wooden boat. Wait for enough passengers to gather or charter one for your group (¥200 for a couple in Xizha; ¥160 for up to four people in Dongzha).

🛏 Sleeping

Wuzhen is a lovely place to stay overnight, although you can easily make it a day trip from either Shanghai or Hangzhou. Only the Xizha scenic zone is set up for overnight guests, with both budget and boutique inns. The visitor centre can make bookings, though you'll need to book ahead on weekends and holiday periods.

★ Wuzhen Guesthouse
GUESTHOUSE ¥¥

(乌镇民宿, Wūzhèn Mínsù; ☑0573 8873 1088; wuzhen1@wuzhen.com.cn; 137 Xizha Dajie, 西栅大街137号; r incl breakfast from ¥590; 🌐) Stretching the length of Xizha Dajie, in the Xizha scenic zone, is this loose collection of canalside, family-run B&Bs in old wooden homes with chic, modern amenities. Prices rise for rooms with river views and verandas, and those in the middle of town (rooms are numbered 1 to 65) are generally considered more desirable as they're away from the main gates.

🍷 Drinking & Entertainment

The Ruyi Bridge Quay (如意桥游船码头, Rúyì Qiáo Yóuchuán Mǎtóu), at the far western end of the Xīzhà scenic zone, is lined with cafes and bars, some of which stay open quite late (but are pricey). There are also a few kiosks on Xizha Dajie where you can fill up your thermos for free with chrysanthemum tea.

Kungfu Boat
LIVE PERFORMANCE

(拳船, Quán Chuán) Ten-minute martial-arts performances are held eight times daily (including 11.10am, 1.30pm, 2.30pm and 3.30pm) on the Kungfu Boat, just inside the main entrance to the Dongzha scenic zone.

ℹ Information

There are ATMs at the main entrances to both scenic zones.

Wuzhen Visitor Centre (乌镇游客服务中心, Wūzhèn Yóukè Fúwù Zhōngxīn; ☑0573 8873 1088; www.wuzhen.com.cn; Hongqiao Lu, 虹桥路; ⊙8am-5.30pm) A large complex at the entrance to the Xīzhà scenic zone, with free left luggage, an accommodation booking counter, admission ticket sales and rest area. Some staff speak a little English. Most tourist buses and the K350 from the bus station terminate or stop at the sprawling car park outside here.

ℹ Getting There & Away

Buses run regularly from Hangzhou Main Bus Station (¥35, 75 minutes, every 30 to 60 minutes, 7am to 6.20pm) to **Wuzhen Bus Station** (乌镇汽车站, Wūzhèn Qìchēzhàn; ☑0573 8871

1014; 521 Qingzhen Lu, 青镇路521号). The last bus returns at 6.25pm. From there take a local bus to get to the scenic zones.

Yibu Trip (p350) runs buses (¥31, 1½ hours, every 20 to 100 minutes, 7am to 6pm) between its small station northwest of Hangzhou Main Train Station and the car parks of either of the two scenic zones in Wuzhen. Buy tickets before boarding.

From Shanghai, buses run roughly every 30 minutes from Shanghai South Bus Station (¥55, two hours); the last return bus is at 5pm. Eight buses (¥37, two hours) also run between Wuzhen and Suzhou train station.

There are two daily buses to Nanxun (¥10, one hour, 8.30am and 1.30pm), but no direct buses in the opposite direction.

ⓘ Getting Around

Bus K350 (¥2, frequent, 6.10am to 7.45pm) runs in a loop from Wuzhen Bus Station – take a sharp right on arrival, within the station – to Xīzhà and Dōngzhà scenic zones and then back to the bus station. A free shuttle bus (every 20 minutes, 7.30am to 5.30pm) runs between the main entrance to both scenic zones. From 7.45pm to 10pm, bus K350 shuttles between the scenic zones only.

Sānlúnchē (pedicabs) can be picked up at Wuzhen Bus Station and on Xinhua Lu (新华路) at the western end of the Dōngzhà scenic zone. Rides between the two zones or the bus station cost ¥10. It is possible to walk between the two zones in 20 minutes.

The 'free ferry' immediately inside the entrance to the Xīzhà scenic zone only takes you across the water to the entrance to the scenic zone proper. There is little to see and not worth the long queues, unless you can't walk the five minutes across the bridges.

Nanxun   南浔

ⓙ 0572 / POP 491,000

Like other towns on the water, **Nanxun** (南浔, Nánxún; ¥100; ⓧ 7.30am-5pm Apr-Oct, 8am-4.30pm Nov-Mar) has arched stone bridges, meandering lanes and old wooden houses. What sets it apart is its fascinating mix of Chinese and European architecture – and comparatively few visitors. Established during the Southern Song dynasty, Nanxun rose to prominence in the Ming and Qing dynasties, when it became a key trading point along the Grand Canal from Beijing to Hangzhou. Merchants made fortunes in silk and translated it into decadent homes. It's now a sprawling city, on the border with Jiangsu province, but the old town within it is well preserved.

⊙ Sights

Nanxun's scenic area stretches a couple of kilometres along a network of canals and is easily walkable in half a day. The waterway along Nanxi Lu (南溪路) is the largest and the most touristy; it runs perpendicular to Dongdajie (东大街), another canal-lined street. From Dongdajie, several bridges cross over to Bǎijiānlóu, the most atmospheric – and least crowded – part. If you arrive by public bus, you'll enter from Bǎijiānlóu.

The main ticket office is at the opposite end of Nanxi Lu, which means you may be able to dodge the admission fee, though you'll need a ticket to enter any of the sights (the ticket covers entry to all of them). The scenic area is well signposted in English.

★ Bǎijiānlóu   HISTORIC SITE
(百间楼, Hundred Room Corridor; Shiyuan Lu, 适园路) Oddly overlooked by most visitors, this 400m stretch of 100 (or so) wooden row houses, flanking a narrow canal, is Nanxun's most charming spot. The buildings here have distinctive blue-black tiles and white walls, creating striking views. Most houses are still lived in by descendants of workers from Nanxun's Ming dynasty (1368–1644) merchant days when goods would arrive from Suzhou along these waters. Today residents run small tea shops on their waterfront patios (try the local water-chestnut cakes).

Zhangshiming's Former Residence   HISTORIC BUILDING
(张石铭旧宅, Zhāng Shí Míng Jiùzhái; ⓙ 0572 303 5035; 51 Renrui Lu, 人瑞路51号; ⓧ 8am-5pm) The grandest of Nanxun's wealthy merchant homes looks like a classic Chinese manor, with ornate carvings in wood, stone and brick – until you reach deep into the interior, which hides a European-style ballroom, complete with crown moulding, crystal chandelier and brocade drapery. Other European touches draw on both Renaissance and baroque styles. The combined effect is both fascinating and bizarre, a well-preserved portrait of the cultural exchange between China and the West at the turn of the last century.

Liu's Former House   HISTORIC BUILDING
(刘氏梯号, Liúshì Tīhào; ⓙ 0572 303 5035; Nanxi Jie, 南西街; ⓧ 8am-5pm) Nicknamed the red house, this intriguing two-faced structure has a traditional Chinese front house and a back one of red brick. It contains baroque-style structures in the northern and southern areas and a courtyard with classical Roman columns, which are a popular selfie spot.

Lesser Lotus Villa
HISTORIC BUILDING

(小莲庄, Xiǎolián Zhuāng; 124 Nanxi Jie, 南西街 124号; ⊙8am-5pm) Nanxun's most famous attraction is this sprawling villa, though its best feature only shines in summer, when the lotus flowers in the courtyard pond blossom into a postcard-worthy sight.

🛏 Sleeping

Nanxun is an easy day trip from Hangzhou, though there are a handful of inns here nestled among the canals if you choose to stay.

Bayside Inn
INN ¥¥

(云水谣客栈, Yúnshuǐyáo Kèzhàn; ☑0572 301 7919; 71 Dongdajie, 东大街71号; d from ¥300; 🕸🛜) The best-value inn on the water in Nanxun has clean, if compact, rooms with modern amenities and friendly staff, who try their best at English. All the rooms are a little different, with many styled with dark wood in an ancient Chinese-house style, so have a look around. Naturally the best ones have windows opening over the canal.

🍴 Eating & Drinking

Tourist restaurants line Nanxi Lu, which runs alongside the town's largest canal. For cheap eats head to Nandongjie (南东街), lined with noodle shops, just over Tongjin Bridge (通津 桥, Tōngjīnqiáo) from Dongdajie.

Nanxun's signature brew is xūndòuchá (熏 豆茶), an eclectic concoction of tea, smoked soy beans, pickled citrus peel, toasted sesame seeds and clove-infused, salt-dried turnip; look for it in the tea shops around Bǎijiānlóu. Dongdajie has cafes with verandas overlooking the canal, many of which morph into bars in the evening.

Zhuàngyuánlóu
NOODLES ¥

(状元楼; Dong Dajie, 东大街; noodles ¥8-13; ⊙5am-10pm) One of Nanxun's local specialties is shuāng jiāo miàn (双浇面), a long thin wheat noodle in a rich, dark soy broth. This is the most popular shop in which to try it, though it looks nearly identical to others (to spot it, look for the coal furnace outside).

ⓘ Getting There & Away

Buses leave every 45 minutes (¥45, 1½ hours) from Hangzhou's North Bus Station (8am to 5.20pm); the last return bus is at 5.20pm. Buses also depart for Shanghai (¥50, two hours, frequent) and Suzhou (¥25, one hour, every 20 to 40 minutes, 7am to 5.50pm).

There is no direct bus from Nanxun to Wuzhen; you'll need to take one of the hourly buses to Jiāxìng (嘉兴; ¥23, one hour) and transfer there for the hourly bus to Wuzhen (¥11, one hour).

Nanxun's bus station is at the back entrance to the scenic area. Cross the overpass and in 50m you'll see a sign pointing you to the main sights.

Moganshan 莫干山

☑0572

Refreshingly cool in summer and sometimes smothered in spectral fog, **Moganshan** (莫干 山, Mògànshān; ☑0572 841 2345; Deqing; admission¥80; ⊙8.30am-4.30pm), 60km northwest of Hangzhou, is famed for its scenic vistas, forested views, towering bamboo and stone villa architecture. It was developed as a hilltop resort (719m) by 19th-century Europeans living in Shanghai. Largely abandoned during the second half of the last century, it is now seeing a new buzz of activity (and construction), reclaiming its reputation as a weekend bolthole for expat tàitai (wives) fleeing the simmering lowland heat. There is visible wealthy privilege to this mountain-cool escape, lending it the nickname 'the Hamptons of China'.

The best way to enjoy Moganshan is just to wander the winding forest paths, taking in some of the architecture en route. There's Shanghai gangster **Du Yuesheng's old villa** (杜月笙别墅, Dù Yuèshēng biéshù) – now serving as a hotel; the villa where Chiang Kaishek spent his honeymoon; a couple of churches (375 Moganshan and 419 Moganshan); and many other villas linked (sometimes tenuously) with the rich and famous, including a **house** (毛主席下榻处, Máo Zhǔxí Xiàtàchù; 126 Moganshan, 莫干山126号) 🆓 where Chairman Mao once napped.

To preserve the mood you will have to work hard to ignore the often slapdash new constructions. Genuine, older villas are identifiable by their irregularly shaped stones.

Besides the attractions on the summit, you can strike out on longer hikes, including a five-hour loop, known colloquially as the 'temple hike', to an old, deserted temple; pick up a map at **Moganshan Lodge** (马克的咖啡 厅, Mǎkè de Kāfēitīng; ☑0572 803 3011; www.mogan shanlodge.com; Songliang Shanzhuang, off Yinshan Jie, 松粮山庄; ⊙9am-9pm, closed Jan & Feb; 🛜🍴♿). Containing Tǎ Mountain (塔山, Tǎ Shān) in the northwest, the **Dakeng Scenic Area** (大坑景区, Dàkēng Jǐngqū) is great for rambling. Many hotels also offer excursions, such as picking tea leaves in the fields nearby.

Moganshan is full of hotels of varying quality, many housed in former villas; room prices nearly double at weekends and some places require a two-night minimum booking. If you come in low season (eg early spring) you can expect good rates. Many hotels either shut up shop or close for renovation over the winter.

Moganshan Fleecity Resort (莫干山离城度假别墅, Mògànshān Líchéng Dùjià Biéshù; ☑0188 5722 9640; www.moganshan395.com; Láolǐngcūn Sānjiǔwù, 劳岭村三九坞; d weekday/weekend from ¥599/799; P⊜❉🅿) 🏊 is halfway up the mountain (meaning you can stay here and dodge the entry fee), surrounded by bamboo (though construction sites inch ever nearer). There are only eight rooms; some have balconies while others have Japanese-style tatami floors. The best part is the food: dinner (¥80 per person) features local produce, like wild mushrooms and bamboo, prepared home-style.

Ensconced within an organic tea plantation, **Le Passage Mohkan Shan** (莫干山里法国山居, Mògànshānlǐ Fǎguóshānjū; ☑0572 805 2958; www.lepassagemoganshan.com; Xiànrénkēng Tea Plantation, Zǐlíng Village, 紫岭村仙人坑茶厂; r weekday/weekend from ¥2680/3180; ⊜🅿❉) 🏊 evokes the glamorous cosmopolitan history of Moganshan perhaps better than the actual villas do. The main house and bungalows were designed by owners Christophe Peres and Pauline Lee to look like a colonial-era hill station, with high ceilings, a wood-burning stove in the salon and a spring-fed swimming pool. The menu at the swanky restaurant includes ham and saucisson cured in-house; the wine cellar is stocked with French bio wines.

The kitchen at **Moganshan Lodge** cooks up roast dinners (by reservation only), full English breakfasts and sandwiches. Grab a book from the shelves (there are many in English) and curl up in one of the vintage armchairs here with a pot of tea. Should you decide to stretch your legs, Moganshan Lodge is your best source for advice and local maps.

🛈 Getting There & Away

The nearest train station is Deqing (德清, Déqīng), a short ride on one of the frequent high-speed trains from Hangzhou East (¥16, 15 minutes). The last return train is at 9.20pm. There are two trains daily from Shanghai Hongqiao (¥94, 1¾ hours, 7.27am and 6.18pm).

You can also go by bus from Hangzhou's main bus station to Deqing (¥18, one hour, six daily).

Now comes the expensive part: getting a taxi from the bus or train station to Moganshan, which will cost ¥120 to ¥150. Most lodgings can arrange transport from Deqing, Hangzhou or even Shanghai – at a mark-up, of course.

Don't take a *sānlúnchē* (three-wheel scooter) as they will drop you at the foot of the mountain.

Shaoxing 绍兴

☑0557 / POP 2.16 MILLION

Sprawling, ancient Shaoxing (Shàoxīng), built on a network of canals, is among the oldest cities in the province. Unlike the more touristy water towns, which have concentrated historic areas, Shaoxing is a contemporary city marbled with the old, where modern housing blocks are shot through with rivulets and whitewashed homes. The city is also the birthplace of many influential and colourful figures, including the writer Lu Xun.

Many of Shaoxing's sights are related to Lu Xun (1881–1936), China's first great modern novelist, who lived here until he went abroad to study. (He later returned to China, but was forced to hide out in Shanghai's French Concession when the Kuomintang decided his books were too dangerous.) These sights are clustered on the busy cobblestone pedestrian area known as **Luxun Native Place** (鲁迅故里, Lǔxùn Gùlǐ; ☑0575 8513 2080; 241 Luxun Zhonglu, 鲁迅中路241号; ⊙8.30am-5pm Mon, to 8.30pm Tue-Sun) **FREE**. The most interesting of the bunch is the **Sānwèi Shūwū** (三味书屋), the one-room schoolhouse where the author studied as a boy. There are also two residences through which you can stroll. Entry is free, but you'll need to show your passport.

From here you can walk north along the quays, some of which are shaded with wooden overhangs, past quiet slices of residential life. The most noteworthy among the numerous stone bridges (some ancient and many still in use) you'll pass is **Bazi Bridge** (八字乔, Bāzì Qiáo; Bazi Qiao Zhijie, 八字桥直街) **FREE**, shrouded in ivy and shaped like the character for lucky number eight (八, bā). It dates from the first years of the 13th century.

Two kilometres west of Bazi Bridge is **Cangqiao Street** (仓桥直街, Cāngqiáo Zhíjiē), a restored stretch of old shophouses, several of which now house cafes and teahouses.

Shaoxing can easily be done as a day trip from Hangzhou, though there are plenty of places to stay here, the nicest of which are around Luxun Native Place, including the **Luxun Native Place Youth Hostel** (老台门鲁迅故里国际青年旅舍, Lǎotáimén Lǔxùn Gùlǐ Guójì Qīngnián Lǚshè; ☑0575 8508 0288; www.yhachina.com; 558 Xinjian Nanlu, 新建南路558号; dm ¥55, d ¥198-398; ❉@🅿). Filling the corridors of a centuries-old courtyard house, this hostel is right in line with the city's other historic sites. The renovations are a bit patchwork, but the rooms are clean and comfortable. There's also a restaurant and lounge where you can unwind with some Shaoxing wine. Staff speak some English and are friendly.

Shaoxing has one of China's oldest wine-making traditions. Amber-coloured, earthy and dry, Shaoxing *jiǔ* (绍兴酒) is available in bars and restaurants around town and is also prevalent in cooking. Cangqiao Street has some atmospheric teahouses and cafes, some serving local rice-wine ice cream. **Xiánhēng Jiǔdiàn** (咸亨酒店; ☑0557 8512 7179; 179 Luxun Zhonglu, 鲁迅中路179号; dishes ¥20-55; ◷10.30am-2.30pm & 4.30-8.30pm) is a fantastic, if touristy, place to sample local food and drink. Dishes include dried broad beans stewed in fennel water (茴香豆, huíxiāng dòu) and 'drunk' river crab (醉蟹, zuì xiè) that has been pickled and cooked with wine vinasse, the residue from the winemaking process. Order Shaoxing wine from the counter out the front. You'll need to first purchase a prepaid card (minimum ¥100), which you'll use to purchase dishes inside. The remaining balance and deposit will be returned to you when you return the card. The restaurant is easily spotted by its outdoor seating, just 150m west of Luxun Native Place.

🛈 Getting There & Away

Frequent high-speed trains run between Hangzhou East (¥15, 20 minutes) and Shaoxing North Station; however, Shaoxing North is far north of the city, either 30 minutes in a taxi (¥50) or an hour on the BRT1 express bus (¥4). Hangzhou Main Train Station has slower K trains (¥13, one to two hours, eight daily) that run from 3.11am to 2pm to **Shaoxing Train Station** (绍兴站, Shàoxīng Zhàn; 200 Chezhan Lu, 车站路200号), which is conveniently downtown.

Ningbo (¥17, every one to two hours) also has K trains to Shaoxing Train Station.

Frequent buses also run from Hangzhou (¥24 to ¥27, one hour) to **Shaoxing Passenger Transport Centre** (绍兴客运中心, Shàoxīng Kèyùn Zhōngxīn; Zhongxing Beilu, 中兴北路), although this bus station is also north of the city centre.

Shaoxing taxis start at ¥7.

Jinhua 金华

☑0579 / POP 4.73 MILLION

As provincial Chinese cities go, Jinhua (Jīnhuá) is an agreeable one, with tree-lined streets and a central river flanked by parkland. It's a useful transport hub and a springboard for visiting the attractive villages of central Zhejiang.

Jinhua's main sight is its **Architecture Park** (金华建筑艺术公园, Jīnhuá Jiànzhù Yìshù Gōngyuán; cnr Qingzhao Lu & Huancheng Lu, 清照路与环城东路交叉口东50米) **FREE**, made up of 16 pavilions, designed by international and domestic architects, strung over 2km along the Yiwu River. It was conceived and curated by the artist Ai Wei Wei, to honour his father, poet and native son Ai Qing. Though the buildings – intended to be coffee shops, libraries, wi-fi-enabled work spaces and the like – are shuttered, it is still a fascinating sight, a modern meditation on memorial architecture. The park is 6km east of central Jinhua. A taxi to the park costs around ¥30, and buses 24, 303 and 528 run here.

Business hotels line Bayi Beilu, the main artery running north to south through the town centre. Frustratingly, only half a dozen hotels in this area accept foreigners, with even many chain brands off limits. If desperate, there are another 20 or so welcoming hotels south, across the river. Hotel booking websites in English only list hotels that accept foreigners.

One of the few hotels to accept foreigners in Jinhua, **Wangjiang Hotel** (望江饭店, Wàngjiāng Fàndiàn; ☑0579 8233 6680; 112 Zhongshan Lu, 中山路112号; d incl breakfast from ¥230; P🐱) is thankfully excellent. The old business hotel has unusual carpeted halls separated by walls so that barely any noise enters the rooms. You might be tempted to stay on to enjoy the lofty city views from your massive room, emerging only for the generous buffet breakfast or the nearby plaza shopping.

Cheap noodle and hotpot joints can be found on Wuyi Lu, which runs diagonally southeast from the train station. Jinhua is famous for its dry-cured ham – so rich and salty it's used more to flavour dishes than to eat on its own – though unfortunately it's largely considered an export and is hard to come by in restaurants in town.

Bank of China (中国银行, Zhōngguó Yínháng; cnr Bayi Beijie & Renmin Donglu, 八一北街人民东路的路口; ◷8.30am-5pm) offers money exchange and has 24-hour ATM. There are several other branches around town.

🛈 Getting There & Away

BUS

The **West Bus Station** (汽车西站, Qìchē Xīzhàn; ☑0579 8321 5888; 2289 Huancheng Xilu, 环城西路2289号), where buses depart for Zhuge, is 500m west of Jinhua Main Train Station; the walk is well signposted. The **South Bus Station** (汽车南站, Qìchē Nánzhàn; Bayi Nanjie, 八一南街), where buses depart for Tangxi (for Siping), is at the southern end of the city.

TRAIN

Jinhua has excellent high-speed train connections, thanks to a modern rail line between Hangzhou and Changsha. Trains stop at **Jinhua Main Train Station** (金华站, Jīnhuá Zhàn; ☑ 0579 8497 2992; 300 Hou Fenglu, 后丰路 300号), but also inconveniently at Jinhua South Train Station (金华南站, Jīnhuá Nánzhàn), 12km east (not south), so check your ticket carefully.

Both stations have services to Hangzhou East (¥74, one hour, frequent), Shanghai Hongqiao (¥147, two hours, frequent) and Wenzhou South (¥77, 1½ hours, 10 daily).

There are services to Huángshān North (¥178, 2¾ hours, one daily) only from Jinhua South Train Station.

ⓘ Getting Around

Bus K11 (¥2) runs from the Jinhua Main Train Station via Jinhua West Bus Station to Jinhua South Bus Station in 45 minutes.

Taxis around town start at ¥8. The 20-minute ride from the west to the south bus station costs around ¥40.

Around Jinhua

Siping   寺平村

☑ 0579 / POP 1600

The tiny village of Siping (寺平村, Sìpíng Cūn; ¥20; ⊙ 8.30am-5pm), 30km west of Jinhua, was founded 700 years ago, and remains a remarkable repository of brick and wood carvings. Its seven original halls, built by generations of the Dai (戴) family, are arranged in the shape of the Big Dipper – to communicate harmony between the human and natural world. The village is blissfully uncommercial, though thanks to a homestay program it's well set up for visitors.

The main entrance to Siping is along the handle of the dipper. On your right will be Liben Hall (立本堂, Lìběn Táng), an early Qing dynasty structure with some wood carvings that remain impressively vivid; keep an eye out for carvings of the bats. In the cosmology of the village, this hall represents the star Phad.

Just a few paces from Chonghou Hall (崇德堂, Chóngdé Táng) is Wǔjiān Huāxuān (五间花轩), marked by flowery brick carvings over the door. This is the birthplace of Dai Yinniang, Siping's most famous historical resident – the village girl who became an imperial concubine. According to legend, when Yinniang was ill as a child, a monk in a vision told her father to construct a well near the house. He did, and after giving his daughter water from it to drink and wash, she became well – and more beautiful. The well still exists, adjacent to the house.

At the base of the dipper, and standing in for the star Alioth, is Chongde Hall. Its brick carving, 'Nine Lions Scrambling for a Ball', is noteworthy as much for its detail as for its seemingly impudent use of five-toed lions (usually an imperial symbol).

The village is well signposted in English. While the halls are the most dramatic structures, many ordinary houses have fantastic carvings as well, depicting popular Chinese symbols of luck, upward mobility and prosperity.

As most people day trip here from Jinhua, the only accommodation in Siping is the 15 homes open to guests through the Jinhua Homestay (www.jinhua-homestay.com; s/d incl 2 meals per person ¥128) program (the small number keeps the village uncrowded). The program began in 2015, with six villages and counting. While Siping has plenty of heritage structures, the homes are modern (with modern amenities); bathrooms are shared. Host families are keen to have guests at their table and to take them around the village. Little English is spoken in the village, but you can make arrangements through the program in English. Contact by email; the website is mainly about the homestay 'scholarships'.

ⓘ Getting There & Away

Bus 502 runs to/from Jinhua's south bus station to Tangxi (汤溪, Tāngxī; ¥5.50, one hour, frequent, 6am to 6.30pm). In Tangxi, pick up a pedicab (¥30) for the last 5km to Siping. If you've booked a homestay, transportation from Tangxi can be arranged.

Zhuge   诸葛

☑ 0579 / POP 4000

Photogenic Zhuge (诸葛八卦村景区, Zhūgé Bāguà Cūn Jǐngqū; ☑ 0579 8860 0026; ¥155; ⊙ 7.30am-5pm summer, 8am-4.30pm winter) (Zhūgě) is a fascinating composition of traditional Chinese village architecture and feng shui planning: the village was designed according to the bāguà (八卦, eight trigrams) of the I Ching. Included in Zhuge's meticulous plans are numerous snaking cobblestone alleyways – some only wide enough for one person to pass – intentionally designed (for purposes of protection) for outsiders to get hopelessly lost. This is naturally one of the pleasures of visiting.

Though Zhuge is one of the most commercialised of the area villages, it remains visibly lived in. Residents are largely descendants of Zhuge Liang, who was a prime minister during the Three Kingdoms period.

Entering from Gaolong Lu (高隆路), proceed downhill and around the corner to reach the lovely, huge **Upper Pond** (上塘, Shàng Táng). At the southern end of the pond, look for a sign leading to **Tianyi Hall** (天一堂, Tiānyī Táng; 7.30am-5pm summer, 8am-4.30pm winter), most noteworthy for its beautiful garden with flowering trees and hundreds of potted plants – all used for Chinese medicine.

Double back and look for **Shouchun Hall** (寿春堂, Shòuchūn Táng; ⊘7.30am-5pm summer, 8am-4.30pm winter) – one of Zhuge's 18 halls – itself a long sequence of chambers and courtyards. Just past it is **Lower Pond** (下塘, Xià Táng) and two additional halls: **Dajing Hall** (大经堂, Dàjīng Táng; ⊘7.30am-5pm summer, 8am-4.30pm winter) – housing a traditional Chinese medicine museum – and, up the steps, the **Yongmu Hall** (雍睦堂, Yōngmù Táng; ⊘7.30am-5pm summer, 8am-4.30pm winter), a fine Ming dynasty hall with an eye-catching central stone door frame.

Eight (the number mirroring the trigrams of the *bāguà*) lanes radiate from **Zhong Pond** (钟池, Zhōng Chí) at the heart of the village. The feng shui symbol of the village, the circular pond resembles the Chinese twin-fish, *yīn-yáng tàijí* diagram, half filled in and the other half occupied with water. You can also spot the black trigrams (八卦, *bāguà*) above some windows of the whitewashed houses.

Overlooking the water is the splendid **Dagong Hall** (大公堂, Dàgōng Táng; ⊘7.30am-5pm summer, 8am-4.30pm winter), a huge, airy space with a pairing of huge black Chinese characters 武 ('Wŭ' or 'Martial') and 忠 ('Zhōng' or 'Loyal') on the walls outside. The memorial hall originally dates from the Yuan dynasty; note its two large and smooth drum stones. The **Prime Minister's Temple** (丞相祠堂, Chéng Xiàng Cítáng; ⊘7.30am-5pm summer, 8am-4.30pm winter), an impressive and massive old hall with some intricately carved cross-beams in the roof, is nearby.

Admission to the village gets you into all the sights described above, so hold on to your ticket.

The vast majority of visitors are day trippers so there is an advantage to overnighting in one of the few guesthouses here. Also the village is beautiful at dusk. **Huāyuán Gōngyù** (花园公寓; ☑0579 8860 0336; 48 Yitai Xiang, 義泰巷48号; r with/without bathroom ¥288/120; ❋) is a quiet choice, set amid the garden at Tianyi Hall, embellished with views over the village rooftops from the 2nd-floor corridor. The cheapest rooms come without shower and have rather flaky ceilings; of the pricier rooms, go for the less damp ones on the 2nd floor. Discounts are common.

Restaurants are dotted around the village, but most are aimed at tourists. Along the eastern edge of the Upper Pond are some more local options, where villagers gather to drink tea and play mahjong and you can get a bowl of noodles for ¥10. **Sunshine House** (昱栈, Yùzhàn; ⊘10am-9.30pm; ☎), overlooking the pond, serves big pots of tea and espresso drinks (¥25 to ¥40). Food carts and fruit sellers gather at the bottom of Gaolong Lu, just outside the village.

ℹ Getting There & Away

Direct buses to **Zhuge Bus Station** (诸葛汽车站, Zhūgě Qìchēzhàn; 330 Guodao, 国道330号) leave roughly hourly from Hangzhou East Train Station (¥60, two hours, 14 daily); there are also two buses from Hangzhou Main Bus Station (¥60, two hours, 8.10am and 12.30pm) and one from the west bus station (¥60, two hours, 2.40pm). Going back to Hangzhou there are 12 buses daily (6.15am to 6.20pm).

From Jinhua West Bus Station, buses depart nine times daily for Zhuge (¥18 to ¥21, one hour, 6.50am to 3.10pm). Return buses (7.15am, 8.50am, 9am, 1.40pm and 5pm) depart from in front of the bus station, on the opposite side of the street.

Buses from Lanxi en route to Xinye swing by Zhuge around 7.45am, 10.20am, 1.30pm and 5.15pm. You'll need to flag one down from the road in front of Zhuge Bus Station. In the return direction, buses from Xinye (¥4, 30 minutes) depart at 6.10am, 8.30am, noon and 3.20pm; the bus drops off at the foot of Gaolong Lu.

ℹ Getting Around

Zhuge Bus Station is on Rte 330, a 15-minute walk from the village. Walk east for 500m until you see the cluster of pedicabs and snack vendors that mark the entrance to Gaolong Lu. At the top of the road (300m) is the entrance to the village. You can also hire a pedicab from the bus station for ¥5. Some drivers will bypass the admission gate and take you straight into the village; note that without a ticket you won't be able to enter any of the ticketed structures (though you are free to walk around).

Xinye 新叶

☎ 0571 / POP 3900

Cut with sparkling streams, decorated with placid ponds and embraced by silent hills, the picturesque village of **Xinye** (新叶, Xīnyè; admission incl all sights ¥78; ☺8am-4pm) is populated by families sharing the surname Ye (叶) and an abundance of free-roaming chickens. A day trip to Xinye is a rare chance to experience traditional Chinese village life surrounded by ancestral halls and residences in Qing and Ming dynasty architecture. The village is laid out in accordance with the traditional five element (五行, *wǔ xíng*) theory, so it's a balanced exercise in feng shui aesthetics. During spring, the village is framed by fields of yellow rapeseed flowers.

◉ Sights

The village is signposted in Chinese; you can get a map at the tourist centre. The admission fee covers all the village sights; hold onto your ticket for entry.

Tuanyun Pagoda PAGODA
(抟云塔, Tuányún Tǎ; ☺8am-4pm) The white and elegant seven-storey Tuányún Pagoda is the definitive image of the village. There is a small pond beside the pagoda.

Wénchāng Hall HISTORIC BUILDING
(文昌阁, Wénchāng Gé; ☺8am-4pm) A signature sight, the Wénchāng Hall contains a portrait of Confucius and an adjacent shrine (土地祠, *Tǔdì Cí*) to the village god (for good harvests). Smudged red Maoist slogans add their own narrative.

Xishan Ancestral Temple TEMPLE
(西山祠堂, Xīshān Cítáng; ☺8am-4pm) Dedicated to the ancestors of the Ye clan, this ancestral hall dates back to the Yuan dynasty.

Hall of Good Order HISTORIC BUILDING
(有序堂, Yǒuxù Táng; ☺8am-4pm) This hall is central to the village; its front door does not open so its accessible side door faces out onto pyramid-shaped Daofeng Mountain (道峰山, *Dàofēng Shān*), across the waters of half-moon shaped South Pond (南塘, *Nántáng*), from where eight alleys radiate out through the village. Originally built in 1290 and rebuilt during the Republic, the hall contains some astonishing wood carvings of a deer, small birds and a monkey in the trees.

Shuangmei Hall HISTORIC BUILDING
(双美堂, Shuāngměi Táng; ☺8am-4pm) This hall is a lovely wood-panelled affair containing intricate and exquisite carvings above its pillars.

🛏 Sleeping & Eating

Most people day-trip to Xinye from Zhuge or Hangzhou. But if you want to immerse yourself in local life, there are several basic guesthouses here; you'll see signs posted around the village. Xinye has just a couple of small eateries, though all guesthouses offer meals.

Dàojīn Rénjiā GUESTHOUSE ¥
(道金人家; **☎** 159 8816 0523; r ¥100) A reliable option inside the village, with well-kept but basic singles and doubles, and meal service. The easiest way to get here from the bus stop is to continue down the main road and then turn right on the market lane; follow it around the bend and look for the white guesthouse down an alley on the right.

ℹ Information

The nearest international ATMs are in Xin'anjiang or Jinhua, or you can try your luck with the local ZJRC (Zhejiang Rural Credit) ATM in the western end of town to see if it now accepts foreign cards.

Xinye Tourist Centre & Ticket Office (新叶 古村售票处, Xīnyè Gǔcūn Shòupiàochù) Sells admission tickets covering the sights.

ℹ Getting There & Away

There is a direct bus service to Xinye from Hangzhou Main Bus Station (¥61, two hours, 7.20am) and also from Hangzhou's west bus station (¥61, two hours, 8.20am and 1.50pm). A return bus leaves at 12.45pm.

Xinye also works as a convenient day trip from Zhuge: buses to Xinye (¥4, 30 minutes) depart at 7.45am, 10.20am, 1.30pm and 5.15pm and return at 6.10am, 8.30am, noon and 3.20pm.

To get to the village from the bus drop-off, turn right and follow the stone path for a few minutes. Note that to get an admission ticket covering the sights, you'll need to go to the Xinye Tourist Centre & Ticket Office at the far southeastern corner of the village.

Putuoshan 普陀山

☎ 0580 / POP 5000

Putuoshan (Pǔtuóshān) – the Zhōushān Archipelago's most celebrated isle and one of China's four sacred Buddhist mountains – is the abode of Guanyin, the eternally compassionate Goddess of Mercy. With pine

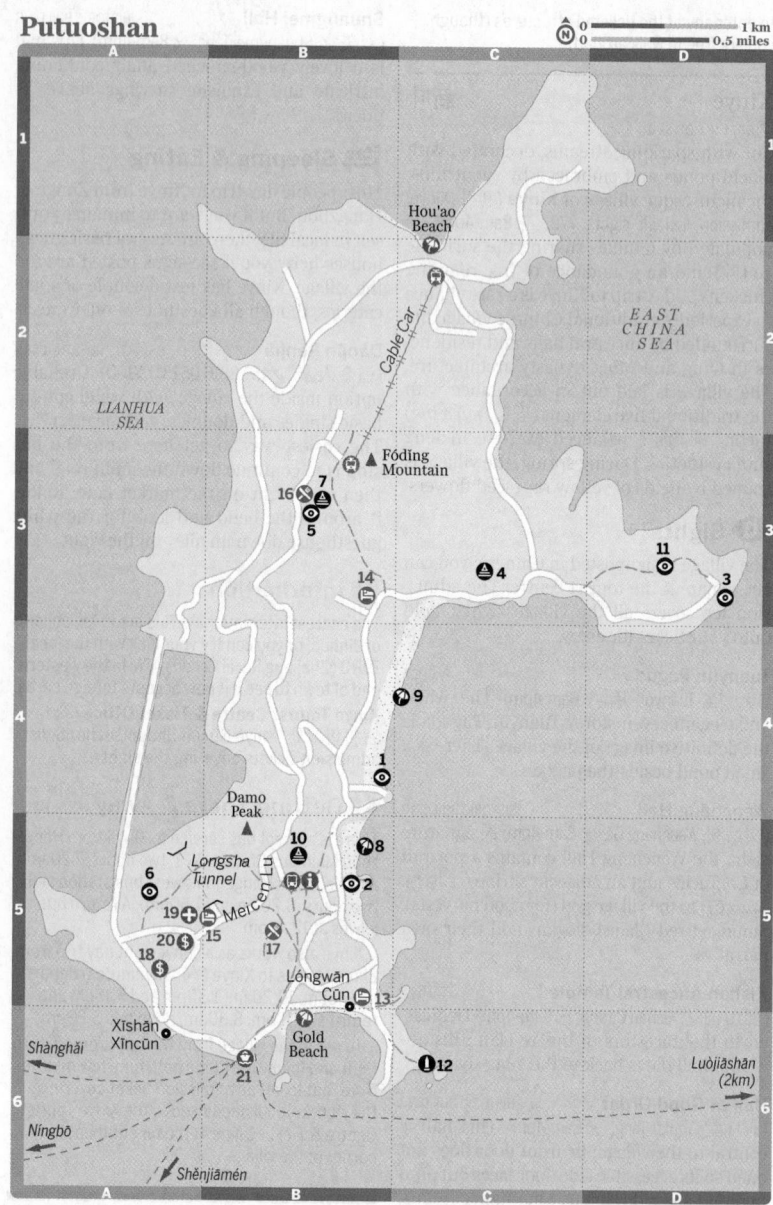

Putuoshan

N 0 — 1 km
0 — 0.5 miles

Hou'ao Beach

Cable Car

EAST CHINA SEA

LIANHUA SEA

Fóding Mountain

16 7
5

14
4
11
3

9

1

Damo Peak

Longsha Tunnel
10
6 8
19 15 2
20 17
18
Lóngwān Cūn 13

Xīshān Xīncūn
Gold Beach
12

Shànghǎi
21

Luòjiāshān (2km)

Níngbō

Shěnjiāmén

ZHEJIANG PUTUOSHAN

groves, sandy beaches, grand temples and hidden grottoes, it is immensely scenic, but also very popular (despite the fact that it is only accessible by boat). Aim for a midweek visit outside of holiday periods.

◉ Sights

Putuoshan's temples are all shrines for the merciful goddess Guanyin. Besides the three main temples, you will stumble upon nunneries and monasteries everywhere you turn, while decorative archways may suddenly

Putuoshan

emerge from the sea mist. Several sights, including Puji Temple, and most amenities are clustered at the southern end of the island, which is easily walkable. If you want to stretch your legs, trails (often empty) line much of the coastline. Pay the entrance fee (summer/winter ¥160/140) before you board the ferry and know that entry to some other sights is extra (usually ¥5).

Sights in Putuoshan don't have addresses, but are well signposted in English.

South Sea Guanyin
STATUE

(南海观音, Nánhǎi Guānyīn; ¥10; ☉8am-5pm) The first thing you see as you approach Putuoshan by boat is this 33m-high glittering statue of Guanyin, overlooking the waves at the southernmost tip of the island. It's the symbol of the island. To get closer to her and 33 other bronze Guanyin images, and for grand seaviews, you'll have to pay an entrance fee and climb hundreds of steps.

Puji Temple
BUDDHIST TEMPLE

(普济禅寺, Pǔjì Sì; ¥5; ☉6am-9pm) Fronted by large ponds and overlooked by towering camphor trees and luohan pines, this restored Chan (Zen) temple stands by the main square and dates from at least the 17th century. Beyond chubby Milefo sitting in a red, gold and green burnished cabinet in the **Hall of Heavenly Kings**, throngs of worshippers stand with incense in front of the colossal main hall. Note the seated 1000-arm effigy of Guanyin in the **Pumen Hall** (普门殿, Pǔmén Diàn).

Fayu Temple
BUDDHIST TEMPLE

(法雨禅寺, Fǎyǔ Chánsì; ☎0580 669 0480; Fayu Lu, 法雨路; ¥5; ☉6am-9pm) Colossal camphor trees and a huge gingko tree tower over this yellow-roof-tiled Chan (Zen) temple, where a vast glittering statue of Guanyin sits resplendently in the main hall, flanked by 18 *luóhàn* effigies. Each *luóhàn* has a name – eg the Crossing the River *luóhàn* or the Long Eyebrows *luóhàn* – and worshippers pray to each in turn. In the hall behind stands a dextrous 1000-arm Guanyin.

Luòjiāshān
ISLAND

(洛伽山) The very small island of Luòjiāshān, southeast of Putuoshan, has its own temples and pagodas and makes for a fun expedition. The ferry (return trip including admission to Luòjiāshān ¥70, 25 minutes) departs at 7am, 8am, 9am and 1pm when conditions are good. You have to take a returning boat two hours later.

Guanyin Cave
CAVE

(观音洞, Guānyīn Dòng; ☉8.30am-4pm; 🛈) **FREE** Crouch with an arched back into this magnificent, smoky and mysterious old grotto with a low, head-scraping ceiling to witness its assembly of Guanyins carved from the rock face along with small effigies of the goddess in porcelain and stone, draped in cloth.

One Hundred Step Beach
BEACH

(百步沙, Bǎibùshā; ☉6am-6pm) The most popular of Putuoshan's beaches has a pretty pagoda perched on terraced rock that always has a crowd. Swimming is allowed between May and August until 6pm.

ZHEJIANG PUTUOSHAN

Foding Mountain
MOUNTAIN

(佛顶山, Fódǐng Shān; ¥5) A steep but beautifully shaded half-hour to 45-minute climb can be made up Foding Mountain – Buddha's Summit Peak – the highest point on the island. This is also where you will find **Huiji Temple** (慧济禅寺, Huìjì Chánsì; ☑ 0580 669 0126; ¥5; ☉ 8am-4pm). Watch devout pilgrims and Buddhist nuns stop every three steps to either bow or kneel in supplication. The less motivated take the **cable car** (索道, suǒdào; one way/return ¥40/70, 6.30am to 5pm).

One Thousand Step Beach
BEACH

(千步金沙, Qiānbù Jīnshā; ☉ 6am-6pm) Putuoshan's largest beach stretches all along the northeast coast of the island – a long unspoilt stretch of blonde sand. Swimming is only permitted between May and August until 6pm, but any time of year it's a lovely place to plonk down on the sand.

🛏 Sleeping & Eating

Most hotels on Putuoshan aim squarely at tour groups and holidaying Chinese, with prices to match. Room rates are generally discounted from Sunday to Thursday. Larger hotels have shuttle buses to/from the pier.

Putuoshan dining is largely seafood and hotel restaurants and therefore expensive. Less expensive are the makeshift restaurants set up by villagers in hillside **Longwan Village** (龙湾村, Lóngwān Cūn); when the weather's good look for plastic tables and chairs. You can also get noodles (from ¥20) on Meicen Lu, just east of the ferry port. The best places to eat are the vegetarian canteens inside the temples; both **Puji** (普济寺素菜馆, Pǔjìsì Sùcàiguǎn; breakfast ¥5, lunch & dinner ¥10; ☉ 5.30-6.30am, 10.30-11am & 4.10-5.10pm; ✐) and **Huiji** (慧济禅寺素菜馆, Huìjì Chánsì Sùcàiguǎn; breakfast ¥5, lunch & dinner ¥10; ☉ 4.30-6.30am, 9am-noon, 3.30-5.30pm; ✐) have them.

Hǎibiān Rénjiā
GUESTHOUSE ¥¥

(海边人家, Seaside Guest House; ☑ 130 5984 6649; 77, Bldg 34, Longwan Village, 龙湾村34幢77号; r from ¥280; ☎) This very clean budget choice up the steps in Longwan Village and not far from Gold Beach in the southeast of the island has 18 rooms with showers (including a sweet attic room with a skylight) and a tip-top, clean ambience.

Putuoshan Hotel
HOTEL ¥¥¥

(普陀山大酒店, Pǔtuóshān Dàjiǔdiàn; ☑ 0580 609 2828; www.putuoshanhotel.com; 93 Meicen Lu, 梅岑路93号; tw/d from ¥1180/1380; ☀ @) Maximising its feng shui by backing onto a green hill, this is a fine choice with a pleasant and uncluttered feel and a convenient location. The rooms have fresh carpet and natural light; service is crisp and professional. Discounts of about 25% are common midweek.

Zǎozishù
VEGETARIAN ¥¥

(枣子树; 84-86 Meicen Lu, 梅岑路84-6号; dishes ¥28-108; ☉ 10.30am-9.30pm; ✐) Far more upmarket (and with prices to match) than a typical temple canteen, Zǎozishù serves up vegetarian delicacies like stir-fried tea mushrooms (干煸茶菇, gānbiān chágū) and stewed papaya with snow lotus seed (瓜田雪莲, guātián xuělián). It's part of the Meicen Restaurants complex; look for the English sign inside that says 'vegetarian life style'.

ℹ Information

Bank of China (中国银行, Zhōngguó Yínháng; 85-7 Meicen Lu, 梅岑路85-7号; ☉ 8am-noon & 1.30-4.30pm) Currency exchange and a 24-hour ATM that accepts international cards. There are several different banks here on what is dubbed 'Financial Street'.

Buddhist Association Puji Hospital (佛教协会普济医院, Fójiào Xiéhuì Pǔjì Yīyuàn; ☑ 0580 609 2388; 95 Meicen Lu, 梅岑路95号; ☉ 8am-5pm) Private hospital with emergency medical services.

Left-luggage Office (行李寄存, Xínglǐ Jìcúnchù; per day ¥5-10; ☉ 6.45am-4.15pm) At the ferry terminal and also at the Zhoushan Putuo Tourist Destination Service Centre as you arrive at the ferry terminal on Zhujiajian.

Tourist Service Centre (旅游咨询中心, Lǚyóu Zīxún Zhōngxīn; ☑ 0580 388 9090; ☉ 6.20am-9.50pm) Friendly, helpful service with some basic English spoken. Free maps in English.

ℹ Getting There & Away

Getting to Putuoshan looks daunting as it requires multiple forms of transportation (most visitors do it on a package tour). Even coming from Ningbo, the nearest major hub, the journey takes a minimum of three hours. However, transfers are seamless and the construction of bridges linking the principal islands of the Zhoushan archipelago to the mainland means the journey is largely made by bus (unless you choose otherwise).

First you need to get to **Puto Central bus station** (普陀长途客运中心站, Pǔtuó chángtú Zhōngxīnzhàn), also called Shenjiamen (沈家门, Shěnjiāmén; though not to be confused with the Shěnjiāmén Central bus station to the southwest), on the island of Zhoushan. Buses depart from Hangzhou south (¥65, four hours, hourly), Ningbo south (¥57, two hours, frequent from 5.55am) and Shanghai south (¥130 to ¥220, 4½ hours, every 40 minutes).

THE BRIDGES OF TAISHUN COUNTY

Scenic, damp Taishun (泰顺, Tàishùn), in southeast Zhejiang, is China's living bridge museum: there are hundreds of covered wooden bridges – many centuries old, in varying stages of preservation and decay – scattered around the countryside. The best of those that are easily accessible are the four clustered around the township of Sixi (泗溪, Sìxī), which sits on the confluence of two streams.

From the main arrival bus stop in Nanxi (南溪, Nánxī), a village within Sixi township, it's a short 400m walk back through the village to **Nanxi Bridge** (南溪桥, Nánxī Qiáo). What this level bridge lacks in grandeur it makes up for in usefulness: built in 1842, it's more local thoroughfare than tourist attraction.

Next head back 200m to the main village junction and turn right. In 1km you can turn right again and take a 3km detour up to **Nanyang Bridge** (南阳桥, Nányáng Qiáo), a level wooden cantilever bridge, built in 1870 and situated in the grassy hills above town. Otherwise veer left for **Xidong Bridge** (溪东桥, Xīdōng Qiáo, Creek East Bridge), in Sixi proper, another 500m away. Easily identified by its dramatic winged roof and deep vermilion staining, this Ming dynasty arched wooden bridge was first built in 1570 and later rebuilt in 1827.

From here, the village is well signposted in English. Follow signs to gracefully arching, covered **Beijian Bridge** (北涧桥, Běijiàn Qiáo, North Stream Bridge), the most picturesque of Sixi's bridges, accessed by stone steps. It was originally built in 1674 and last rebuilt in 1803. Don't miss the 1000-year-old camphor tree just before it.

Just 30m west of Beijian Bridge, at the far end of the village, is the **Covered Bridge Culture Hall** (廊桥文化展厅, Lángqiáo Wénhuà Zhǎntīng; ☉hours vary) FREE, which has models and information (in English) on other noteworthy bridges in the area.

If you find yourself overnighting in Wenzhou, the **Dongou Hotel** (东瓯大酒店, Dōngōu Dàjiǔdiàn; ☎0577 8808 9988; Dongjian Building, Wenzhou Dadao, Wenzhou, 温州大道东建大厦; d/tr from ¥288/388; ❄@), 2.5km from the bus station (and 580m from the main high-speed-train station), is a comfortable choice.

Getting There & Around

To get to Sixi you need to first get to Wenzhou (温州, Wēnzhōu). High-speed trains arrive at **Wenzhou South** (温州南站, Wēnzhōu Nánzhàn), 15km west from downtown, from where you'll need to take a taxi (¥45, 25 minutes) or local bus 131 (¥2, 40 minutes) to **Niushan Transport Centre** (牛山客运中心, Niúshān Kèyùn Zhōngxīn), Wenzhou's central bus station. Sleeper trains arrive at the more convenient main **Wenzhou train station** (温州站, Wēnzhōuzhàn), from where you can catch local buses 21, 23, 27, 60, 91, 94 or 107 (¥2, 12 minutes, frequent) west to Niushan.

At the bus station, buy a ticket to Nanxi (南溪, Nánxī; ¥51, two hours, every 40 minutes, 6.20am to 6.40pm) on the Taishun-bound bus. The last return bus leaves at 5pm; buy your ticket from the stall opposite the Nanxi bus stop, which has the timetable posted. Nanxi is the main arrival village within the Sixi township.

If you're feeling ambitious, you can hire one of the unofficial taxi drivers (¥150 to ¥400, depending on the route) who haunt the Nanxi bus stop to take you around. Make sure the driver understands where to go before setting out, as some might not know the location of all the bridges. A typhoon in 2016 damaged three bridges.

ZHEJIANG PUTUOSHAN

From Putuo Central you'll be immediately funnelled onto a minibus (¥10) that will take you the last 10 minutes east to the dockside **Zhoushan Putuo Tourist Destination Service Center** (舟山旅游目的地服务中心, Zhōushān Lǚyóu Mùdìdì Fúwù Zhōngxīn; 7am to 5pm) on Zhujiajian (朱家尖, Zhūjiājiān), where you get your ferry ticket (¥30) and admission ticket to the island. The crossing from here takes just 10 minutes. Ferries depart between 6.30am and 5.30pm, after which there half-hourly departures until 8.30pm and a last boat at 9.50pm. Ferries are cancelled in very foggy weather, which can strand passengers on the island till morning. Return buses leave the Zhujiajian station adjacent to the ferry station and the KFC.

The other option is the slow **overnight ferry** direct from Shanghai, which takes 12 hours. From Shanghai, the boat leaves at 7.30pm on Monday, Wednesday and Friday, reaching Putuoshan at around 8am. In the other direction, it leaves on Tuesday, Thursday and Saturday at 4pm (winter) or 5pm (summer), reaching Shanghai at around 6am. Tickets cost anywhere from ¥139 (4th class) to ¥499 (special class); it's easy to upgrade (*bǔpiào*) once you're on board. In Putuoshan boats depart from the main **ferry terminal** (普陀山客运码头, Pǔtuóshān Kèyùn Mǎtou; ☑ 0580 609 1121); and in Shanghai from Wusong Passenger Transportation Centre, in the north of the city. On Putuoshan, ferry tickets can be bought at the **ticket office** at the jetty.

The nearest **airport** is at Zhoushan (also known as Putuoshan; Zhōushān) on the neighbouring island of Zhujiajian; get the ferry from the dock.

❶ Getting Around

Minibuses zip from the passenger ferry terminal to various points around the island, including Puji Temple (¥5), One Thousand Step Beach (¥10), Fayu Temple (¥10) and the cable car station (¥10), leaving every 20 minutes or when full between 7am and 4.30pm. There are more bus stations at Puji Temple, Fayu Temple and other spots around the island serving the same and other destinations. If you're heading to Puji Temple and the sights in the south of the island, walking is fine.

Ningbo 宁波

☑ 0574 / POP 5.77 MILLION

An ancient harbour city, Ningbo (Níngbō) has been an important trading port for millennia and was one of those opened during the Treaty of Nanjing in 1842. Today it's one of China's busiest, but for travellers Ningbo is primarily a waypoint on the journey to Putuoshan.

Ningbo has a former foreign concession **Old Bund** (老外滩, Lǎo Wàitān; Jiangxia Jie, 江夏街; Ⓜ Waitan Daqiao), now a vibrant, pedestrian-only entertainment district along the Yong River. The centrepiece is a cobblestone street with strings of fairy lights luring you towards the clubs and live-music bars. If that's too much, walk to the end where the quiet riverside is framed by skyscrapers projected with animations, resembling a miniature of Shanghai's Bund. Get a taxi to drop you off at the corner of Renmin Lu and Yangshan Lu (人民路洋山路的路口); or take the metro and walk 1km, following the water's edge.

Should you find yourself overnighting in Ningbo, the city's main east-west thoroughfare Zhongshan Lu (中山路) is lined with midrange business hotels, including many chains, such as 7 Days Inn. There are more hotels, as well as some more upmarket options (including international chains), in the Old Bund area. With its convenient location just off Zhongshan Lu, 2km either way from the train station or the Old Bund, and just seconds from metro Line 1, **Nanyuan Wenchang**

Business Hotel (南苑文昌商务酒店, Nányuàn Wénchāng Shāngwù Jiǔdiàn; ☑ 0574 5586 3999; 2 Wenchang Lu, 文昌路2号; s/d ¥298/398; ❄ ❇ ❜; Ⓜ Ximen Kou) is an easy choice (less so if just overnighting). Rooms are spacious, clean and modern, and the savvy manager speaks decent English. For overnighters, **Nanyuan Inn** (南苑e家酒店; ☑ 0574 8185 9090; 419 Mayuan Lu, 马园路419号; d from ¥189; ❜), with small but clean and comfortable rooms, is opposite the northern exit of Ningbo Train Station.

Tianyi Plaza (天一广场, Tiānyī Guǎngchǎng; 68 Shuijing Jie, 水晶街68号; ⊙ most stores & restaurants 9am-9pm; Ⓜ Dongmen Kou) is full of everything from budget international fastfood branches to Chinese banquet eating, or a supermarket for self-catering. At the southeast of the plaza, **Gāngyāgǒu** (缸鸭狗; ☑ 0574 8908 1926; Tiānyī Guǎngchǎng, 68 Shuijing Jie, 天一广场, 水晶街68号; dishes ¥12-52; ⊙ 9am-9.30pm; Ⓜ Dongmen Kou) has been making Ningbo's signature dumplings (宁波汤圆, Ningbo tāngyuán; six for ¥16), silky boiled rice cakes stuffed with sugar-spiked ground sesame, since 1926. They also come in more inventive flavours, such as rose (玫瑰, méiguī) and pumpkin (南瓜, nánguā). You can make a meal out of it by ordering some *xiǎolóngbāo* (小笼包, soup dumplings; ¥19 to ¥36). There's a picture menu; look for a bronze sculpture of a dog, duck and dumplings.

❶ Getting There & Around

Buses to Putuo central bus station (普陀中心站, Pǔtuó Zhōngxīnzhàn), also known as Shěnjiāmén (沈家门), from where you can travel onwards to Putuoshan, leave frequently from Ningbo's **South Bus Station** (汽车南站, Qìchē Nánzhàn; 408 Jiaoshuiqiao Lu, 角水桥路408号). Buses also run frequently between the south bus station and Hangzhou (¥70, two hours).

South Bus Station is just next door to Ningbo Train Station from its south exit. Signs show either 'South Coach Terminal' or 'South Bus Station'. Don't confuse it with 'Bus Station S', which is for local buses.

Ningbo has just one **train station** (宁波站, Níngbō Zhàn; ☑ 0574 5616 3111; 19 Nanzhan Donglu, 南站东路19号) for high-speed and ordinary trains, 3km south of downtown. Ningbo is well connected to China's high-speed rail network. Destinations include Hangzhou East (¥71, one hour, frequent), Jinhua (¥145, two hours, five daily) and Shanghai Hongqiao (¥144, two hours, frequent).

Metro Line 1 runs east-west along Zhongshan Lu, stopping at Tianyi Plaza (Dongmen Kou stop) and Old Bund (Lao Waitan stop); rides cost ¥2 to ¥3. Taxis start at ¥11.

Fujian

POP 38.7 MILLION

Best Places to Eat

➡ Lucky Full City Seafood (p370)

➡ Lǎohǎi Wù (p374)

➡ Gǔcuò Cháfáng (p380)

➡ Old Foochow (p383)

➡ Shíjǐnzhāi (p383)

Best Places to Stay

➡ Soul Touch Hotel (p373)

➡ Liangzhu Boutique Lifestyle Hotel (p369)

➡ Xinyuan Hotel (p369)

➡ Tulou Sunshine International Youth Hostel (p377)

➡ Xiamen International Youth Hostel (p369)

Why Go?

Fujian (福建, Fújiàn) is an attractive coastal province with a long seafaring history. As a significant stop on the maritime Silk Road, its cities developed an easy cosmopolitan outlook and visitors are surprised by the traces of the wider world in its architecture, food, language and people.

Xiamen is the star attraction for visitors, with its long seaside promenade and easy access to little Gulang Yu, a hip island enclave just offshore. Many travellers also pass through the area en route to the Taiwanese island of Kinmen.

Away from the coast, the Unesco World Heritage–listed *tǔlóu* (roundhouses) rise out of the countryside and for generations have housed traditional Hakka and Fujianese communities. Further north, the hill station of Wuyi Shan offers year-round hiking opportunities and a memorable river cruise on bamboo rafts.

When to Go
Xiamen

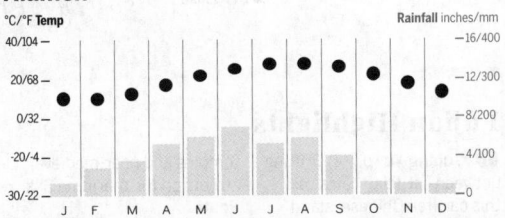

Mar & Apr Sleep in a traditional *tǔlóu* (roundhouse) in spring to experience rural life.

Jun & Sep Relax in one of Gulang Yu's countless cafes and cool off in the sea.

Oct Hike crowd free in lush Wuyi Shan in the north-west.

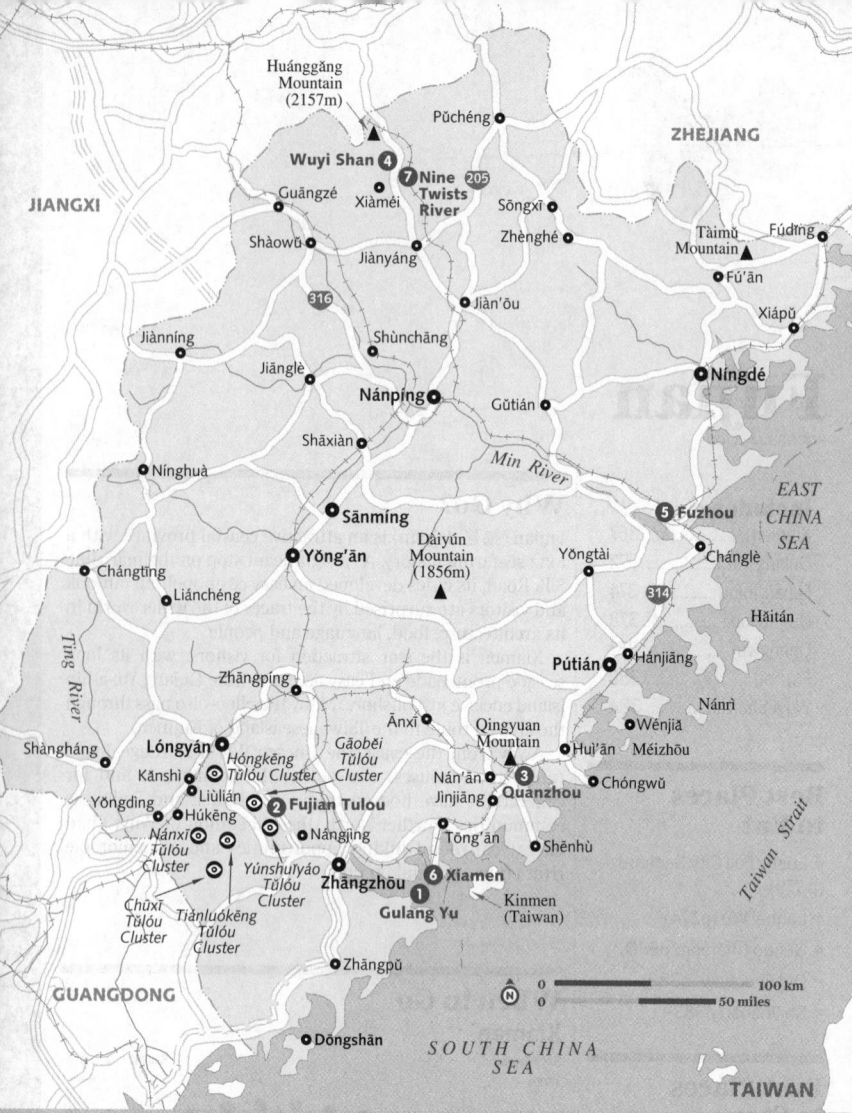

Fujian Highlights

1 **Gulang Yu** (p372) Drifting between cat-filled cafes on this car-free Chinese island with European flair.

2 **Fujian Tǔlóu** (p374) Sleeping in packed earth fortresses like a character from *Game of Thrones*.

3 **Quanzhou** (p378) Exploring the city's multi-faith temples and near-medieval streets on the maritime Silk Route.

4 **Wuyi Shan** (p384) Hiking and cleansing your lungs at a quaint hill station in the province's northwest.

5 **Fuzhou** (p382) Losing yourself in Fuzhou's network of Jin dynasty laneways bathed in the glow of red lanterns.

6 **Xiamen** (p367) Strolling the seaside promenade of one of China's most attractive cities.

7 **Nine Twists River** (p385) Reclining in a rattan chair on a *zhúpái* (bamboo raft) cruise.

History

The coastal region of Fujian, known in English as Fukien or Hokkien, has been part of the Chinese empire since the Qin dynasty (221–207 BC), when it was known as Min. Sea trade transformed the region from a frontier into one of the centres of the Chinese world. During the Song and Yuan dynasties the coastal city of Quanzhou was one of the main ports on the maritime Silk Road, which transported not only silk but also other textiles, precious stones, porcelain and a host of other valuables. The city was home to more than 100,000 Arab merchants, missionaries and travellers.

Despite a decline in the province's fortunes after the Ming dynasty restricted maritime commerce in the 15th century, the resourcefulness of the Fujian people proved itself in the numbers heading for Taiwan, Singapore, the Philippines, Malaysia and Indonesia. Overseas links that were forged continue today, contributing much to the modern character of the province.

Language

Fujian is one of the most linguistically diverse provinces in China. Locals speak variations of the Min dialect, which includes Taiwanese. Min is divided into various subgroups – you can expect to hear Southern Min (Mǐnnán Huà) in Xiamen and Quanzhou, and Eastern Min (Dōng Mǐn) in Fuzhou. Using Mandarin is not a problem.

ⓘ Getting There & Around

Fujian is well connected to the neighbouring provinces of Guangdong and Jiangxi by train and coastal highway. Xiamen and Fuzhou have airline connections to most of the country, including Hong Kong, and Taipei and Kaohsiung in Taiwan. Wuyi Shan has flight connections to China's larger cities, including Beijing, Shanghai and Hong Kong. The coastal freeway also goes all the way to Hong Kong from Xiamen. The D-class train links Xiamen to Shanghai in eight hours.

For exploring the interior, high-speed D trains are more comfortable than travelling by bus, but not always more convenient. Wuyi Shan is linked to Fuzhou, Quanzhou and Xiamen by train. There are also daily flights between Xiamen and Wuyi Shan.

Xiamen 厦门

📞 0592 / POP 3.1 MILLION

Xiamen (Xiàmén), the island city formerly known in western circles as Amoy, is emerging as southern China's most sophisticated city.

ⓘ PRICE RANGES

Sleeping
The following price ranges refer to a double room with bathroom:

¥ less than ¥250

¥¥ ¥250–500

¥¥¥ more than ¥500

Eating
The following price ranges refer to a main meal:

¥ less than ¥40

¥¥ ¥40–100

¥¥¥ more than ¥100

Chinese travellers have long understood the lure of its lengthy seaside promenade and European city architecture, but international 'jetizens' are now joining in the fun.

History

Xiamen was founded around the mid-14th century in the early years of the Ming dynasty, when the city walls were built and the town was established as a major seaport and commercial centre. In the 17th century it became a place of refuge for Ming rulers fleeing the Manchu invaders. Xiamen and nearby Kinmen (金门, Jīnmén) were bases for the Ming armies that, under the command of the general Koxinga, raised their anti-Manchu battle cry, 'Resist the Qing and restore the Ming'.

The Portuguese arrived in the 16th century, followed by the British in the 17th century, and later by the French and the Dutch, all attempting, rather unsuccessfully, to establish Xiamen as a trade port. The port was closed to foreigners in the 1750s and it was not until the Opium Wars that things began to change. In August 1841 a British naval force of 38 ships carrying artillery and soldiers sailed into Xiamen harbour, forcing the port to open. Xiamen then became one of the first treaty ports.

Japanese and western powers followed soon after, establishing consulates and making nearby Gulang Yu a foreign enclave. Xiamen turned Japanese in 1938 and remained that way until 1945.

⊙ Sights

The town of Xiamen is on the island of the same name. It's connected to the mainland by a 5km-long causeway bearing a railway,

Xiamen & Gulang Yu

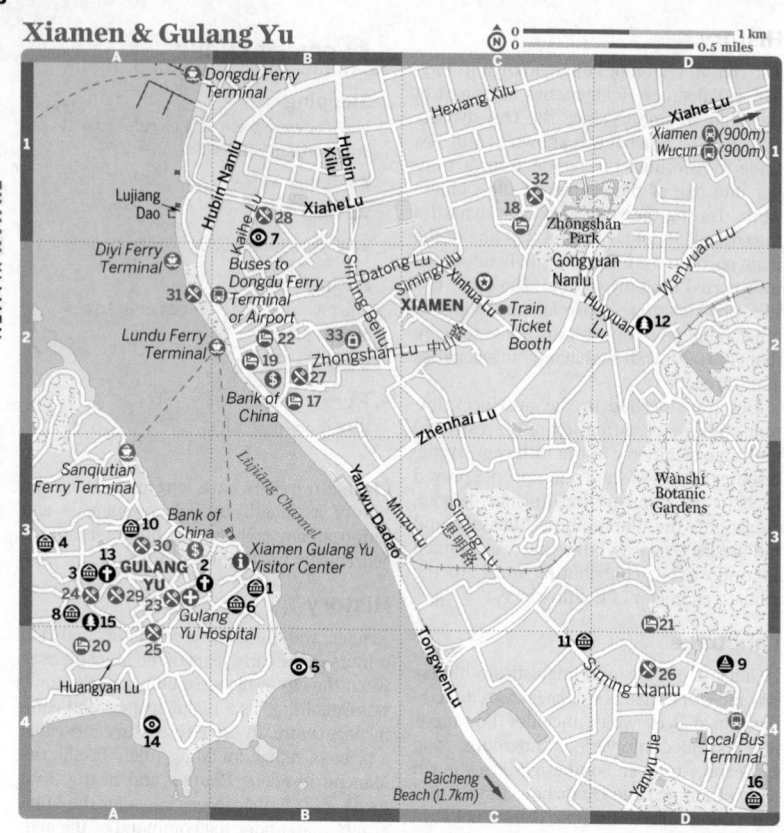

a Bus Rapid Transit (BRT) line, a road and a footpath. The most absorbing part of Xiamen is near the western (waterfront) district, directly opposite the small island of Gulang Yu. This is the old area of town, known for its colonial-era architecture, parks and winding streets. At its heart, though, is the tourist-heavy pedestrianised Zhongshan Lu walking street, which stays hectic until 10pm when it becomes deserted, but makes for a useful point of reference.

Bailuzhou Park
PARK

(白鹭洲公园, Báilùzhōu Gōngyuán; Bailuzhou Lu, 思明区白鹭洲路) Xiamen positions itself as China's most liveable city and this huge green expanse on an islet north of town is a quiet exclamation mark on that claim. Perfect for families or broken souls who need to touch grass for a while.

Kaihe Lu Fish Market
MARKET

(开禾路菜市场, Kāihélù Càishìchǎng; Kaihe Lu, 开禾路; ⊙7am-9pm) In the old district of

Xiamen, this tiny but lively market sells various (weird) sea creatures to a backdrop of *qílóu* (骑楼, shophouses) and a church. Access is from Xiahe Lu, where you can also find some Taiwanese food.

Nanputuo Temple
BUDDHIST SITE

(南普陀寺, Nánpǔtuó Sì; Siming Nanlu; ⊙8am-6pm) **FREE** This Buddhist temple complex on the southern side of Xiamen is one of the most famous temples among the Fujianese, and is also considered a pilgrimage site by dedicated followers from Southeast Asia. The temple has been repeatedly destroyed and rebuilt. Its latest incarnation dates from the early 20th century, and today it's an active and busy temple with chanting monks and worshippers lighting incense.

Baicheng Beach
BEACH

(白城沙滩, Báichéng Shātān; 422 Siming Nanlu, 思明南路422号) You can rarely swim here due to council restrictions, but there are few more convenient places in the city to enjoy

Xiamen & Gulang Yu

FUJIAN XIAMEN

a beautiful natural environment than this beach in the south, especially at sunset. Except on weekends, that is, when every man and his mobile turns up.

Railroad Culture Park   PARK
(铁路文化公园, Tiělù Wénhuà Gōngyuán; Huyuan Lu, 虎园路) The charming 3km walking trail on an abandoned railway track in this park makes a welcome change from the crowds of the city. It is reached by bus 1, 15, 20, 122 or 135; get off at Dashengli (大生里站).

Húlǐ Shān Fortress   NOTABLE BUILDING
(胡里山炮台, Húlǐ Shān Pàotái; ☑0592 208 4184; 2 Cengcuo Anlu, 曾厝垵路2号; ¥25; ◷7.30am-5.30pm) Across Daxue Lu, south of Xiamen University, is this gigantic German artillery post built in 1894. You can rent binoculars to peer over the water to the Taiwanese-occupied island of Kinmen (金门, Jīnmén), formerly known as Quemoy and claimed by both mainland China and Taiwan.

🛏 Sleeping

★ **Xiamen International Youth Hostel**   HOSTEL ¥
(厦门国际青年旅舍, Xiàmén Guójì Qīngnián Lǚshè; ☑0592 208 2345; www.yhachina.com/web-hostel-detail-id-104706; 41 Nanhua Lu, 南华路41号; dm/d/family from ¥80/258/348; ❋@☎) This is the best hostel in Fujian. Spacious mixed dorms share a clean bathroom between up to six

guests; stylish double rooms – some with balcony – would suit a boutique hotel; and the excellent family rooms make it a popular base for the entourage. Reception can be a little regimented, but sunlight pours through the splendid backyard and into the communal lounge room.

★ **Xinyuan Hotel**   BOUTIQUE HOTEL ¥¥
(心远酒店 (轮渡中山路店), Xīnyuǎn Jiǔdiàn; ☑0592 210 0186; 38-40 Shengping Lu, 升平路38-40号; d from ¥305; ❤❋☎) Designer looks for a steal can be snatched up at this small hotel near buzzy Zhongshan Lu walking street. Rooms are compact but feel very comfortable with fresh furnishings, glossy glass showers, soft indirect lighting and techie touches like electric-operated curtains and built-in Bluetooth room speakers. Staff are very friendly, but best of all, the beds are dreamy.

★ **Liangzhu Boutique Lifestyle Hotel**   BOUTIQUE HOTEL ¥¥
(良筑, Liángzhù; ☑0592 207 1322; 22 Huaxin Lu, 华新路22号; r ¥472-658; ❋☎) Old-world hospitality makes a guest appearance at this 1950s chocolate-coloured villa discreetly tucked away in central Xiamen for golden night-time peace. The eight lovely small rooms are designed in themed nostalgia-chic aesthetics – some busier than others – so look at a few before settling, though all are light-filled and decorated with plants. The garden provides a lovely breakfast setting.

DON'T MISS

SANDWORM JELLY

Fancy aspic dishes, or some jelly with a difference? *Tŭsŭndòng* (土笋冻, sandworm jelly) is one of the best loved starters in Fujian. The sandworms are boiled into a jelly mould and the crunchy end product, an aspic dish, is said to be rich in collagen. Locals love eating them with mustard, coriander leaves and turnip slices. You'll find the jelly sold in any streetfood joint, but locals all recommend **Tiānhé Xīmén Tŭsŭndòng** (天河西门土笋冻; ☑0592 865 0170; 33 Douxi Lu, 斗西路33号; snacks from ¥10; ☉8am-10pm), near the west gate of Zhongshan Park.

Hotel Indigo
Xiamen Harbour
BOUTIQUE HOTEL ¥¥¥

(厦门海港英迪格酒店, Xiàmén Hǎigǎng Yíndígé Jiŭdiàn; ☑0592 226 1666; www.hotelindigo.com; 16 Lujiang Dao, 鹭江道16号; d ¥933-1400; ☀☉☎) The small rooms at the sea-facing, luxurious Indigo are accented with chic-coloured sofas and artworks, and have Gulang Yu firmly in their sights. High-tech bathrooms have hidden lighting and many sport bathtubs and windows. Staff work hard to please, especially at check-in where generous discounts are common.

Lujiang Harbourview Hotel
HOTEL ¥¥¥

(鹭江宾馆, Lùjiāng Bīnguǎn; ☑0592 202 2922; www.lujiang-hotel.com; 54 Lujiang Dao, 鹭江道54号; s ¥670-780, d with sea view ¥929-1040; ℗☀@☎) This red-brick darling in the city's prime location has seen a lot in its 60-odd years. A few cracks may have been papered over, but the walls still talk with nostalgia for old Amoy. The large rooms are neatly presented and the beds are heavenly. There's a decent gym and breakfast buffet.

✖ Eating

Kāihé Shāchámiàn
NOODLES ¥

(开禾沙茶面; ☑0592 8666 6291; 126 Xiahe Lu, 厦禾路126号; noodles from ¥12; ☉24hr) *Shāchámiàn* is Fujian's favourite street noodle dish (¥25), sauced with dried fish, onion and chilli. Which animal protein you choose to add on top depends on personal preference – pork and shellfish feature prominently – or you can opt for tofu and egg. This simple shop is identifiable by the yellow characters on the green front panel.

Huángzéhé Peanut Soup Shop
SOUP ¥

(黄则和花生汤店, Huángzéhé Huāshēng Tāngdiàn; ☑0592 202 4670; 22-24 Zhongshan Lu, 中山路20号; snacks ¥4-10; ☉7am-10pm) Since 1945 this humble counter-service diner has filled an unusual craving for sweet local speciality *huāshēng tāng* (花生汤, peanut soup). Other snacks include fried *zăo* (枣, red dates) and *hălìjiān* (海蛎煎, oyster omelette). Get a free reloadable card from the cash register attendants that you swipe to order food; unused credit is refundable.

★ Lucky Full City Seafood
DIM SUM ¥¥

(潮福城, Cháofú Chéng; ☑0592 505 8688; 28 Hubin Beilu, 湖滨北路28号; dim sum ¥16-34, meals from ¥70; ☉10am-1am) If you eat out just once in Xiamen, join the queues for this Cantonese culinary masterclass, and then stack up the exquisite dim sum dishes like egg buns, roasted pigeon and pork dumplings. Catch a taxi here: the driver will know where it is. It also has a **branch** (幸运的全城海鲜点心, Xìngyùn de Quánchéng Hǎixiān Diǎnxīn; 33 Lujiang Dao, 鹭江道33号; ☉8am-2.30am) 200m north of Lundu ferry terminal.

32/HOW Cafe
CAFE ¥¥

(Cherry 32 Cafe; 32 Huaxin Lu, 华新路32号; coffee from ¥45; ☉9am-11pm) If Xiamen starts to wear you down, hide out in this atmospheric Taiwanese coffee shop in an old house near Zhongshan Park. The coffee is brewed with aplomb and the decor is mid-century Europe: velvety reds and browns, towering wine racks, abstract artwork and hard leather lounges. Lean back and percolate.

Dàfāng Sùcàiguǎn
VEGETARIAN ¥¥

(大方素菜馆; ☑0592 209 3236; 3 Nanhua Lu, 南华路3号; dishes ¥35-70; ☉9.30am-9.30pm; ✔) This popular vegetarian restaurant attracts nearly as many devotees as nearby Nanputuo Temple. The tasty soy-based meals are lavishly named and presented. Dishes are large and best shared for variety.

Seaview Restaurant
DIM SUM ¥¥¥

(鹭江宾馆观海厅, Lùjiāng Bīnguǎn Guānhǎitīng; 7th fl, Lujiang Harbourview Hotel, 54 Lujiang Dao, 鹭江道54号7楼; meals from ¥80; ☉8am-11pm) The prime 7th-floor viewing deck in the city also serves decent Fujianese and Hong Kong snacks such as prawn dumplings, sometimes as a buffet. It's ideal for a predinner drink and the sunset may make you linger longer than expected.

ℹ Information

Bank of China (中国银行, Zhōngguó Yínháng; 6 Zhongshan Lu) The 24-hour ATM accepts international cards.

City Medical Consultancy (来福诊所, Láifú Zhěnsuǒ; ☑ 0592 532 3168; 123-1 Xidi Villa Hubin Beilu, 湖滨北路西堤别墅1号之123号; ◷ 8am-5pm Mon-Fri, to noon Sat) English-speaking doctors; expat frequented. Telephone-operated 24 hours. A taxi here from the western entrance of Zhongshan Lu walking street costs about ¥20.

Public Security Bureau (PSB, 公安局, Gōng'ānjú; ☑ 0592 226 2203; 45-47 Xinhua Lu; visa section 8.10-11.45am & 2.40-5.15pm Mon-Sat) Opposite the main post and telephone office. Visa extensions are handled by the visa section (出入证管理处, chūrùjìng guǎnlǐchù) in the northeastern part of the building on Gongyuan Nanlu.

ℹ Getting There & Away

AIR

Air China, China Southern, Xiamen Airlines and several other domestic airlines operate flights between **Xiamen Gaoqi International Airport** (厦门高崎国际机场, Xiàmén Gāoqí Guójì Jīchǎng; www.xiamen-airport.com; 121 Xiangyun Yilu, 翔云一路121号) and all major domestic airports in China. There are innumerable ticket offices around town, many of which are in the larger hotels.

There are direct international flights to/from Bangkok, Jakarta, Kuala Lumpur, Los Angeles, Manila, Osaka, Penang, Singapore and Tokyo.

BOAT

Fast boats (¥14, 20 minutes, every 15 minutes, 6.30am to 9.30pm) leave for the nearby coastal Fujian town of Zhāngzhōu (漳州) from **Diyi Ferry Terminal** (第一码头, Dìyī Mǎtóu, 旅游客运码头, Lǚyóu Kèyùn Mǎtóu; ☑ 0592 298 5551). Boats to Kinmen (金门, Jīnmén), Taiwan (¥150, 30 minutes, hourly) leave from the northeast of the island from **Wutong Ferry Terminal** (五通码头, Wǔtōng Mǎtóu; 2500 Huandao Donglu, 环岛东路2500号) between 8am and 6.30pm.

Ferries to Gulang Yu (¥35 return, 10 minutes, every 20 minutes) now leave the **Dongdu Ferry Terminal** (东渡码头, Dōngdù Mǎtóu, 厦门国际邮轮中心, Xiàmén Guójì Yóulún Zhōngxīn, Xiàmén International Cruise Terminal; 2 Donggang Lu, 东港路2号10) just north of Xiamen. Take **bus 51** (Lujiang Dao, 鹭江道; ¥1; ◷ 6.45am-8.30pm) to the terminal from outside the small light-grey bus station 50m north on Lujiang Dao (鹭江道, Lùjiāng Dào).

BUS

There are three major bus stations in Xiamen. **Hubin Long-Distance Bus Station** (湖滨长途汽车站, Húbīn Chángtú Qìchēzhàn; ☑ 0592 221 5283; 58 Hubin Nanlu, 湖滨南路58号) serves destinations south of Xiamen; tickets can be bought two days in advance at the ticket booth in the **local bus terminal** (Siming Nanlu, 思明南路) adjacent to Xiamen University at the end of Siming Nanlu. Destinations include Guangzhou (¥377, 8½ or 10 hours, two daily), Nanjing County (in Fujian; ¥28, two hours, 11 daily) and Yongding (Tǔlóu; ¥75, four hours, seven daily).

Wucun Bus Station (梧村汽车站, Wúcūn Qìchēzhàn; 925 Xiahe Lu), directly opposite Xiamen's main train station, serves destinations north of the city, including Jinjiang (¥56, 1½ hours, every 20 minutes) and Quanzhou (¥63, two hours, every 20 minutes).

Note that buses to Fuzhou (¥115, four hours, every 20 minutes) and Wuyi Shan (¥191, nine hours, one daily, 9.30am) leave from the far-flung **Fanghu Bus Station** (枋湖客运中心, Fānghú Kèyùn Zhōngxīn; 5 Jinhu Lu, Huli Qu, 湖里区金湖路5号) in the central-north of Xiamen island near Xiamen Gaoqi International Airport. It is much quicker and easier to take a fast train.

TRAIN

All trains departing from **Xiamen Main Train Station** (厦门站; 900 Xiahe Lu, 厦禾路900号) also make a stop at Xiamen North station, 25km north of the city centre; some trains depart only from Xiamen North, requiring a transfer from Xiamen. Tickets can be booked through the **train ticket booth** (☑ 0592 203 8565; cnr Xinhua

---

ℹ BORDER CROSSINGS: GETTING INTO TAIWAN

Ferries ply between Xiamen and Kinmen (金门, Jīnmén) island in Taiwan hourly between 8am and 6.30pm. You can catch the boat from Wutong Ferry Terminal, 8km east of Xiamen's airport; the journey costs ¥160 and takes 30 minutes.

Tickets can only be bought an hour before the departure time. In Kinmen, visas are issued on the spot for most nationalities, but you need a multiple-entry China visa if you want to return to Fujian.

Wutong Ferry Terminal can only be reached by taxi. Expect to pay ¥20 from the airport to the terminal.

Rénmínbì is the only currency accepted in the money-exchange counters at Kinmen's ferry terminal. From Kinmen, there are flights to other major cities in Taiwan.

Lu & Zhongshan Lu; 9am-6pm) behind the Gem Hotel (金后酒店, Jīnhòu Jiǔdiàn). Tickets listed here are from the main train station. Destinations include the following:

Fuzhou ¥94 to ¥151, two to 2½ hours, 25 daily

Hangzhou ¥342 to ¥398, 4¾ to seven hours, five daily

Quanzhou ¥34, one hour, 36 daily

Shanghai ¥471, 5½ hours, one daily

Wuyi Shan ¥163 to ¥197, three to 4½ hours, nine daily

ⓘ Getting Around

BRT Line 1 links the waterfront to both train stations via Xiahe Lu (¥1). Bus 19 runs to the train station from the ferry terminal (¥1). Buses to Xiamen University leave from the train station (bus 1) and from the ferry terminal (bus 2). Taxis start at ¥8, plus a ¥3 fuel surcharge.

Gulang Yu   鼓浪屿

☑ 0592 / POP 15,400

A short hop from the large island city of Xiamen, car-free Gulang Yu (Gǔlàng Yǔ) is a Unesco World Heritage Site that shows off its cross-cultural heritage in its fusion of architectural styles. The island was a turn-of-the-20th-century international enclave where consulates from Europe, America and Japan managed their affairs among banyan trees and vine-strewn villas.

A day or two spent wandering Gulang Yu's museums, tunnels, trails and beaches is a highlight of a visit to Southern China, but for now it's still mostly locals who hang out in the increasingly slick cafe scene. Breathe deeply if the weekend crowds get too heavy; there is sanctuary to be found if you seek it.

History

The foreign community was well established on Gulang Yu by the 1880s, with a daily English newspaper, churches, hospitals, post and telegraph offices, libraries, hotels and consulates. In 1903 the island was officially designated an International Foreign Settlement, and a municipal council with a police force of Sikhs was established to govern it. Today memories of the settlement linger in the many charming colonial-era buildings and the sound of classical piano wafting from speakers (the island is nicknamed 'piano island' by the Chinese). Many of China's most celebrated musicians have come from Gulang Yu, including the pianists Yu Feixing, Lin Junqing and Yin Chengzong.

◉ Sights

Aside from the hawkers on Longtou Lu and Quanzhou Lu, Gulang Yu is an open-air museum perfect for wandering on foot. You can circumnavigate the island's rocky beaches, short cut through human-made tunnels, or make the skip over Sunlight Rock in the middle. The colonial-era architecture is distinctly European, but life spills out into the narrow alleys where hip Chinese snap their way around the incongruously cool cafe scene.

A combo ticket for ¥90 (saving ¥20) includes Sunlight Rock Park, Shuzhuang Garden, Haoyue Garden, the Organ Museum and International Calligraphic Art Gallery and can be bought at any of the included sights.

Sunlight Rock Park   PARK

(日光岩公园, Rìguāng Yán Gōngyuán; 109 Quanzhou Lu, 泉州路109号; ¥50; ⏱5.30am-9pm) Sunlight Rock (Rìguāng Yán), in Sunlight Rock Park, is the island's highest point at 93m and its biggest draw are the views across the island. At the foot of Sunlight Rock is a large colonial-era building known as the **Koxinga Memorial Hall** (郑成功纪念馆, Zhèngchénggōng Jìniànguǎn; Quanzhou Lu, 泉州路; ⏱8-11am & 2-5pm) FREE. Also in the park is **Yīngxióng Hill** (Yīngxióng Shān), near the memorial hall and connected via a cable-car ride. It has an open-air aviary (admission free) with chattering egrets and parrots.

Shuzhuang Garden   GARDENS

(菽庄花园, Shūzhuāng Huāyuán; 7 Ganghou Lu, 港后路7号; ¥30; ⏱7.30am-9pm) The waterfront Shuzhuang Garden on the southern end of the island is a lovely place to linger for a few hours. It has a small *pénzāi* (bonsai) garden, some delicate-looking pavilions and a rock garden with the 12 animal statues of the Chinese zodiac. A piano museum housed within the grounds holds one piano with its original bill of sale from Melbourne at the turn of the 20th century.

Haoyue Garden   GARDENS

(皓月园, Hàoyuè Yuán; 6 Bishan Lu, 璧山路6号; ¥10; ⏱7.30am-6pm) The main feature at this rocky outcrop is an imposing 15.7m statue of Koxinga (aka Zheng Chenggong) in full military dress, visible from a great distance outside the park, even across the water from Xiamen. Koxinga was a Ming loyalist and led the most sustained resistance to the Qing conquest of China, from the Fujian coast and Taiwan.

Organ Museum

MUSEUM

(风琴博物馆, Fēngqín Bówùguǎn; ☑0592 206 3226; 43 Guxin Lu, 鼓新路43号; ¥15; ◷8.15am-6.15pm) Housed in the highly distinctive Bāguà Lóu (八卦楼) building is the Organ Museum, with a fantastic collection including a Norman & Beard organ from 1909. The octagonal-domed building is lit up at night and visible from across the water in Xiamen.

🛏 Sleeping

Gulang Yu has a variety of excellent boutique guesthouses, hotels and hostels. It's a little more expensive than Xiamen, but a very different experience altogether. Note that whatever luggage you bring you will have to carry or wheel from the ferry terminal as there are no cars on the island. Some hotels can prearrange meeting you at the ferry to help cart luggage.

Impression Coast Hotel

BOUTIQUE HOTEL ¥¥

(印象海岸度假别墅旅馆, Lǎo Hǎi Wù Yinxiàng Hǎiàn Dùjià Biéshù Lǚguǎn; ☑592 208 6060; 111 Kangtai Lu, 汇景苑康泰路111号; d ¥398-588, ste from ¥810; ❀🛜) On the very west of the island, conveniently 200m from the Nèicuo'ao Ferry Terminal (where ferries arrive) and near sandy shores, Impression Coast has undergone extensive renovations and oozes boutique beach

vibes. White wicker furniture mixes it with ornate, cushy beds fit for a wedding night. Rooms are bright, clean and reasonable value.

★ Soul Touch Hotel

BOUTIQUE HOTEL ¥¥¥

(聆海酒店, Línghǎi Jiǔdiàn, 老别墅旅馆, Miryam Lǎo Biéshù Lǚguǎn; ☑0592 206 2505; 70 Huangyan Lu, 晃岩路70号; r ¥923-4878; ❀@🛜) The most splendid five-star hotel on the island is located right below Sunlight Rock and affords views across villa roofs and out to sea. Busy staff will meet you at the ferry, help with luggage and show you to the Victorian mansion where rooms have period furniture and decadent beds. The restaurant is superb and there's a courtyard with banyan trees.

🍴 Eating

The cafe scene is a big drawcard. The lanes off Longtou Lu hide terrific little eateries, but anything on the street here will be decent. Let the crowds decide. Local specialities include Amoy pie (a sweet filled pastry) and shark fishballs. We do not recommend eating shark meat, as many shark species are threatened. Shark fin is not used.

Líjì Mùdān Fishball

SEAFOOD ¥

(林记木担鱼丸, Línjì Mùdān Yúwán; 56 Longtou Lu, 龙头路56号; meals from ¥15; ◷10am-9pm) The stakes are high on Longtou Lu, and the

---

HISTORIC BUILDINGS

Old colonial-era residences and consulates are tucked away in the maze of streets leading from the pier, particularly along Longtou Lu and the back lanes of Huayan Lu. Some of Gulang Yu's buildings are deserted and tumbledown, with trees growing out of their sides, as residents cannot afford their upkeep.

Southeast of the pier you will see the two buildings of the **former British Consulate** (永顺卡斯特宾馆, Yǒngshùn Kǎsītè Bīnguǎn; ☑0592 206 8822; 14 Lujiao Lu, 鹿角路14号; r from ¥495), currently running as a hotel, while further along is the cream-coloured former Japanese **Bo'ai Hospital** (1 Lujiao Lu, 鹿角路1号), built in 1936. Up the hill on a different part of Lujiao Lu stands the red-brick **former Japanese Consulate** (日本领事馆, Rìběn Lǐngshìguǎn; 26 Lujiao Lu, 鹿角路26号), just before you reach the magnificent snow-white **Ecclesia Catholica** (鼓浪屿天主教堂, Gǔlàngyǔ Tiānzhǔ Jiàotáng; 34 Lujiao Lu, 鹿角路34号), dating from 1917. The white building next to the church is the **former Spanish Consulate** (西班牙领事馆, Xībānyá Lǐngshìguǎn; 30 Lujiao Lu, 鹿角路30号). Just past the church on the left is the **Huang Rongyuan Mansion** (黄荣远堂, Huángróngyuàn Táng; ☑0592 688 3070; 32 Fujian Lu, 福建路32号; admission & museum ¥88; ◷8.30am-5.30pm), a marvellous pillared building, now the China Records Museum displaying gramophones. Other buildings worth looking at include the Protestant **Sanyi Church** (三一堂, Sānyī Táng; 67 Anhai Lu, 安海路67号), a red-brick building with a classical portico and cruciform-shaped interior on the corner of Anhai Lu (安海路) and Yongchun Lu (永春路). Here is also the handsome **former Law Court** (1-3 Bishan Lu, 璧山路1-3号), now inhabited by local residents.

Doing a circuit of Bishan Lu will take you past a rarely visited part of the island. **Guāncǎi Lóu** (观彩楼; 6 Bishan Lu, 笔山路6号), a residence built in 1931, has a magnificently dilapidated facade. The building stands in stark contrast next to the immaculate **Yizú Shānzhuāng** (亦足山庄; 9 Bishan Lu, 璧山路9号), a structure dating from the 1920s.

staff at Lìjì Mùdàn will shout you into a plastic seat for some of that fishball goodness in soup or on a skewer.

★ Lǎohǎi Wù
CHINESE ¥¥

(捞海坞; ☑ 0592 206 7918; 35 Wudai Lu, 乌垹路35号; meals ¥30-78; ⊙ 9.30am-9pm) It feels like you're cutting through an elegant alley on the way to somewhere else, but stop at the wooden benches for incredible noodle, fish and duck dishes at this friendly indoor-outdoor restaurant loved by Fujianese food fanatics. There's an attached ceramics gallery and cold beer (¥30) available.

Chu Family Coffee
CAFE ¥¥

(褚家园咖啡馆, Chǔjiāyuán Kāfēiguǎn; ☑ 0592 208 3702; 15 Zhonghua Lu, 中华路15号; meals from ¥60; ⊙ 10.30am-9.30pm) A little delight is found in this garden cafe where cats roam and an award-winning barista brews his magic. The western desserts don't skimp on the cream and sweet Earl Grey milk tea is a non-coffee speciality. The pasta and tapas are also fine for a craving.

Babycat Café
CAFE ¥¥

(☑ 0592 206 3651; 773 Houbindong Sanlu, 后滨东三路773号; snacks from ¥15; ⊙ 10am-9pm; 🛜) The sweet Amoy pies are the attraction at Babycat, a dimly lit cafe with wood furniture and feline touches. Go for the red bean or pistachio flavour.

Black Cat Dining Room
MODERN EUROPEAN ¥¥¥

(黑猫餐厅; 14 Yongchun Lu, 鼓浪屿永春路14号; meals ¥80-120; ⊙ 10.30am-9.30pm) A former 1920s dance hall for sailors and diplomats, the Black Cat is now an antiques-filled multi-room restaurant with lots of intimate dining rooms. The menu swings to its own sweet rhythm between Chinese and international. A speciality here is the Taiwanese-style cured sausage.

❶ Information

There are various maps for sale (¥5 to ¥10) in cafes and souvenir shops, some in English.

Bank of China (中国银行, Zhōngguó Yínháng; 2 Longtou Lu, 龙头路2号; ⊙ 9am-7pm) Forex and 24-hour ATM.

Xiamen Gulang Yu Visitor Center (厦门鼓浪屿游客中心, Xiàmén Gǔlàng Yǔ Yóukè Zhōngxīn; Longtou Lu, 龙头路; ⊙ 8.30am-noon & 3pm-5.30pm) Left luggage costs ¥3 to ¥5. Next to the departure ferry terminal on the east of the island, but far from the arrivals terminal on the west.

❶ Getting There & Away

Ferries to Gulang Yu (¥35, 10 minutes, every 20 minutes) now leave from the Dongdu Ferry Terminal (p371) just north of Xiamen, arriving on the western side of the island at **Neicuo'ao Ferry Terminal** (鼓浪屿内厝澳码头, Gǔlàngyǔ Nèicuò'áo Mǎtóu; ☑ 0592 202 3493; 159 Kangtai Lu, 康泰路159号; ⊙ 7am-midnight). Return ferries (two minutes, every 20 minutes) depart from the **Sanqiutian Ferry Terminal** (三丘田码头, Sānqiūtián Mǎtóu) on the northeast of the island, returning visitors to nearby **Lundu Ferry Terminal** (轮渡码头, Lúndù Mǎtóu; 15 Lujiang Dao, 思鹭江道15号) near the Zhongshan Lu walking street on Xiamen, but only between 7pm and 7am (an hour earlier in winter October to May); before 7pm, you can also return to Dongdu from Sanqiutian.

Foreigners cannot depart from, nor arrive at, the Lundu Ferry Terminal between 6.30am and 6.50pm (an hour earlier in winter), only between Dongdu and Neicuo'ao ferry terminals.

Your return trip is included in the original ticket from Dongdu Ferry Terminal, so hold onto it. Some 'luxury' boats (¥50) take fewer passengers and therefore have more space.

To get to Dongdu Ferry Terminal, take the 51 bus (¥1, 30 minutes, frequent) north from outside the small light-grey bus station, across the road from the Lundu Ferry Terminal and 50m north on Lujiang Dao (鹭江道, Lùjiāng Dào).

❶ Getting Around

Circuits of the island can be done by boat (¥20), with half-hourly departures from the passenger ferry terminal off Lujiang Lu between 7.40am and 5pm.

Fujian Tǔlóu

☑ 0597 / POP 43,000

The Hakka and the Mǐnnán (Fujianese) people have lived in the fabled earthen structures known as tǔlóu (土楼) for centuries. Spread across a southwestern section of the province, many are still inhabited and welcome visitors for the day or night. The circular edifices are remarkable for their ingenuity, but the idyllic rural setting lends an ethereal quality hard to find in modern China. Sleeping here and sharing a meal with local families can be life-affirming.

Take note: since Unesco rubber-stamped the region in 2008, tour buses have rumbled in on freshly paved highways. But it's hardly reason to stay away. With more than 30,000 tǔlóu still intact, you can find one to take your fancy.

⊙ Sights

The most notable of the *tŭlóu* are lumped into various clusters in the vicinity of Nanjing County (南靖, Nánjìng; not to be confused with the city Nánjīng, 南京) and Yongding (永定). Only the three most developed clusters – Hongkeng, Tianluokeng and Yunshuiyao – are accessible by public transport. However, bus services are neither frequent nor punctual. Booking a tour or hiring a vehicle is recommended if you want to venture off the beaten path and see more.

⊙ Hongkeng

This cluster is 50km east of Yongding and contains 30 *tŭlóu* of various shapes and sizes including the concentric circles of Zhènchéng Lóu and the tiny round **Rúshēng Lóu**. The cluster is the easiest to access by bus and the most commercialised. From Xiamen's Fanghu Bus Station (p371), four buses (¥70, 3½ hours, 6.40am, 8.30am, 12.40pm and 1pm) go directly to the cluster, which is also known as Tulou Mínsú Wénhuàcūn (土楼民俗文化村). Admission is ¥90 and it's open 8am to 5.30pm.

Zhènchéng Lóu   NOTABLE BUILDING
(振成楼) This most visited *tŭlóu* is a grandiose structure built in 1912, with two concentric circles and 222 rooms. The four storeys of the outer circle are impressive against a mountainous backdrop. The ancestral hall in the centre of the *tŭlóu* is complete with western-style pillars. The locals dub this *tŭlóu wángzĭ* (土楼王子), the prince *tŭlóu*.

Fúyù Lóu   NOTABLE BUILDING
(福裕楼) Along the river, this five-storey square *tŭlóu* boasts some wonderfully carved wooden beams and pillars. Rooms are available here at the Changdi Inn (p377).

⊙ Tianluokeng

A pilgrimage to the earthen castles is not complete if you miss Tianluokeng (田螺坑, Tiánluókēng), which is 37km northeast of Nanjing County and home to arguably the most picturesque cluster of *tŭlóu* in the region. The locals affectionately call the five noble buildings 'four dishes with one soup' because of their shapes: circular, square and the oval **Wénchāng Lóu** (文昌楼).

There's one direct bus (¥50, 3½ hours) to the cluster from Xiamen, leaving at 8.30am.

Make sure your driver, if you've hired one, takes you up the hill for a postcard-perfect view of Tianluokeng.

Cluster admission, which includes entry to Yùchāng Lóu and Tǎxià village, is ¥100 (open 7am to 7pm). A shuttle bus (¥15) from the cluster's ticket office goes to the above two places, but the vehicle won't leave until it gets 10 passengers.

Yùchāng Lóu   NOTABLE BUILDING
(裕昌楼) The tallest roundhouse in Fujian, this vast five-floor structure has 270 rooms and an observation tower to check for marauding bandits. Interestingly this 300-year-old property's pillars bend at an angle on the 3rd floor and at the opposite angle on the 5th floor. Each room and kitchen on the ground floor has its own well.

Tǎxià   VILLAGE
(塔下村) This delightful river settlement boasts several *tŭlóu*-converted guesthouses and it is a great base from which to explore the *tŭlóu* areas. The highlight of the village is the **Zhang Ancestral Hall** (张氏家庙, Zhāngshì Jiāmiào; ⊙ 9am-5pm). It is surrounded by 23 elaborately carved spear-like stones, which celebrate the achievements of prominent villagers.

The bus station in Nanjing runs six buses (¥20, 1½ hours) to the village between 8am and 5.30pm.

⊙ Yunshuiyao

This cluster of 53 buildings, 48km northeast of Nanjing County, is set in idyllic surrounds with rolling hills, verdant farms and babbling streams.

Six buses run from Nanjing County bus station (¥20, one hour) to Yunshuiyao (云水谣) and seven go from Nanjing train station (¥25, one hour) between 8.30am and 5.25pm. Cluster admission is ¥90 (open 8am to 10pm).

Yunshuiyao Village   VILLAGE
(长教村, Yúnshuǐyáo Cūn) Between the Héguì and Huáiyuǎn *tŭlóu* in the Yunshuiyao Tulou Cluster is this beautiful village (formerly known as ancient Chángjiào) where you can sip tea under the big banyan trees and watch water buffalo in the river. The village has a few guesthouses that offer rooms (from ¥100).

Héguì Lóu   NOTABLE BUILDING
(和贵楼) This tallest rectangular *tŭlóu* in Fujian has five storeys and was built on a swamp. It boasts 120 rooms, a school, two wells, and a

WHAT IS A TŬLÓU?

Tŭlóu (literally mud houses) are outlandish, multistorey, fortified mud structures built between the 15th and 20th centuries by the inhabitants of southwest Fujian to protect themselves from bandits and wild animals.

Tŭlóu were built along either a circular or square floor plan. The walls are made of rammed earth and glutinous rice, reinforced with strips of bamboo and wood chips. These structures are large enough to house entire clans, and they did, and still do! They are a grand exercise in communal living. The interior sections are enclosed by enormous peripheral structures that could accommodate hundreds of people. Nestled in the mud walls were bedrooms, wells, cooking areas and storehouses, circling a central courtyard. The later *tŭlóu* had stone firewalls and metal-covered doors to protect against blazes.

The compartmentalised nature of the building meant that these structures were the ancient equivalent of modern apartments. A typical layout would be the kitchens on the ground floor, storage on the next level and accommodation on the floors above this. Some *tŭlóu* have multiple buildings built in concentric rings within the main enclosure. These could be guest rooms and home schools. The centre is often an ancestral hall or a meeting hall used for events such as birthdays and weddings. For defence purposes, there is usually only one entrance for the entire *tŭlóu* and there are no windows on the first three storeys.

It was once believed that these earthen citadels were inhabited solely by the Hakka. They are the people who migrated from northwest China during the Jin dynasty (AD 265–314) to the south to escape persecution and famine, and they eventually settled in Jiangxi, Fujian and Guangdong. While most *tŭlóu* in the vicinity of Yongding County are inhabited by the Hakka, there are far more *tŭlóu* in other counties like Nanjing and Hua'an populated by the indigenous Mǐnnán (Fujianese) people. A key distinguishing feature between the Hakka and Mǐnnán *tŭlóu* is that the former has communal corridors and staircases as well as a central courtyard, while the latter *tŭlóu* puts more emphasis on privacy, eg each unit has its own staircase and patio.

No matter what type or shape of *tŭlóu* you're looking at, many of them are still inhabited by a single clan, and residents depend on a combination of tourism and farming for a living. The *tŭlóu* are surprisingly comfortable to live in, being '*dōng nuǎn, xià liáng*' (冬暖夏凉), or 'warm in winter and cool in summer'. These structures were built to last.

fortified courtyard in front of the entrance. The mammoth structure was built in 1732.

Huáiyuǎn Lóu NOTABLE BUILDING
(怀远楼) This relatively young *tŭlóu* (built in 1909) has 136 equally sized rooms and a concentric ring that houses an ancestral hall and a school.

Gaobei

This cluster is on the road from Xiamen, roughly 45km east of Yongding, from where there are infrequent buses to Gaobei.

Chéngqǐ Lóu NOTABLE BUILDING
(承启楼; ¥50; ⊙7am-7pm) In the village of Gaobei (高北), this 300-year-old *tŭlóu* has 400 rooms and once housed 1000 inhabitants. It's built with elaborate concentric rings, with circular passageways between them and a central shrine. It's one of the most iconic and photographed *tŭlóu,* and it's no surprise that it has been dubbed the king *tŭlóu*.

Chuxi

This lesser-visited yet picturesque five-*tŭlóu* cluster features the 600-year-old **Jíqìng Lóu** (集庆楼), built without using any nails, and is 48km southeast of Yongding. Admission is ¥70 (open 7am to 7pm).

Nanxi

The Nanxi Tulou Cluster, 35km east of Yongding and just south of the Chuxi Tulou cluster, is such a densely packed cluster of large rectangular structures that it is sometimes referred to as the 'Great Wall of Tǔlóu'. Admission is ¥70.

Huánjí Lóu NOTABLE BUILDING
(环极楼) Midway between Yongding and Nanjing County, this four-storey building is a huge roundhouse with inner concentric passages, tiled interior passages and a courtyard. It also sports a *huíyīnbì* (回音壁) – a wall that echoes and resonates to sharp sounds.

Yǎnxiāng Lóu　　　NOTABLE BUILDING

(衍香楼) This lesser-visited and commercialised four-storey *tǔlóu* rises up beautifully next to a river.

Zhongchuan Village　　中川村

This **village** (中川村, Zhōngchuān Cūn) is the ancestral home of the Burmese-Chinese businessman Aw Boon Haw, inventor of the medicinal salve Tiger Balm and owner of (in)famously quirky Haw Par Villa theme park in Singapore. Here you'll find another **villa** (虎豹别墅, Hǔbào Biéshù; ¥30; ⊙8am-5pm), but its scale and decor can't compete with its Singaporean (big) sister. The photos and newspaper clippings of the founder's family displayed are for fans only and will not soothe aching muscles.

More interesting is his family's ancestral hall (胡氏家庙, Húshì Jiāmiào), 100m behind the villa. The shrine, the spear-like pillars that celebrate the achievements of their family members, and the setting itself are spectacular.

☞ Tours

English-speaking visitor numbers are dwarfed by Chinese tourists, so English-speaking guided tours are rare and expensive but can be organised through Xiamen-based **Discover Fujian** (☑0592 398 9901; www.discoverfujian. com; 2 Fanghu Xiyilu, 厦门市湖里区枋湖西一路2号; ⊙9am-6pm Mon-Fri), or Beijing-based **Amazing Fujian Tulou** (www.amazingfuji antulou.com), which plan group tours with an English-speaking guide starting at US$170 per person per day, reservable online. If you don't mind joining a Chinese group tour without an English-speaking guide, Amazing Fujian Tulou also run tours to Chéngqǐ Lóu for US$41 per person.

🛏 Sleeping & Eating

In short, unless you came on a day trip, we strongly recommend spending a night (or two) in a *tǔlóu*, which must rank among the most novel sleeping experiences in the world.

It's not quite roughing it, but it isn't hotel quality either. Some *tǔlóu* have modern facilities, but most are still very basic – a bed, a thermos of hot water and a fan. You might also find that the toilets are outside. Bring a torch and insect repellent.

Most *tǔlóu* owners can also organise a pick-up from Yongding or Nanjing County and transport for touring the area. There are many hotels in Yongding and Nanjing County, but neither town is attractive. Still, it can be convenient to stay if you arrive late, and to find a local taxi driver to scoot you around the following day.

Yunshuiyao (ancient Chángjiào) and Tǎxià villages are other convenient options, with some basic *tǔlóu* guesthouses available.

If you stay in a *tǔlóu*, most families can cook set-menu meals (¥150 to ¥200 for two people; confirm before ordering). Tasty food stalls will do the trick near the Yongding and Nanjing County bus stations if travelling by public transport. Look out for the *níuròu-wán tāng* (牛肉丸汤, beef soup with meatballs) or *niàng dòufǔ* (酿豆腐, braised tofu with pork). Hakka dishes are often braised.

Fuyu Lou Changdi Inn　　　INN ¥

(福裕楼常棣客栈, Fúyù Lóu Chángdì Kèzhàn; ☑0597 553 2800, 1379 9097 962; www.fuyulou. com; Hongkeng Tulou Cluster; d incl breakfast ¥167-222; 🛜) The English-speaking owners are very welcoming at the Changdi Inn. Fans and TVs in the basic rooms don't hurt either. Other bonuses include cold beer, a lending library and bike rental.

★Tulou Sunshine International Youth Hostel　　　HOSTEL ¥

(土楼沐浴阳光国际青年旅舍, Tǔlóu Mùyù Yángguāng Guóji Qīngnián Lǚshě; ☑0596 777 1348; Tǎxià Village; dm/d ¥45/160; @🛜) Part converted *tǔlóu*, part newly built premises, this HI-affiliated hostel is very friendly and far simpler to negotiate than Tǎxià family life. Dorms are clean and very presentable. Carpooling and bike rental can be arranged. Follow the HI signs after you get off the bus at Xueying bridge (雪英桥, Xuěyīng Qiáo) in Tǎxià.

Qìngdé Lóu　　　INN ¥

(庆德楼, ☑1890 6951 868, ext 777; Tǎxià Village; d ¥138-168; ✳🛜) Beautiful lantern-lit nights await in this modern rectangular compound. The 30 modern rooms have air-con and wi-fi. Upstairs rooms are cheaper, but you share a bathroom.

Défēng Lóu　　　INN ¥¥

(德风楼, ☑0597 775 6669; Yunshuiyao Tulou Cluster, Yunshuiyao Village; d ¥140-170; ✳🛜) The *tǔlóu* with the big red star above the entrance is a reliable place to stay. As the villagers move out, the tourists move in, partly for the en suite bathrooms. It's conveniently located just north of the bridge to the Yunshuiyao Tulou Cluster and all buses stop in front of it.

ℹ Getting There & Away

BUS

From Xiamen's Hubin Long-Distance Bus Station (p371), take a bus headed to Nanjing County (¥32, two hours, 12 daily, 7am to 5.30pm). Upon arrival, you can either take the respective buses to some of the clusters or hire a private vehicle to take you there.

Xiamen's Fanghu Bus Station (p371) has buses to Yongding (永定县; ¥75, four hours, seven daily) between 7.10am and 4pm, from where there are infrequent buses to Gaobei Tulou Cluster. Yongding can also be accessed by bus from Guangdong and Longyan (¥25, one hour, regular).

TRAIN

Direct buses are easier than trains to get to the clusters. High-speed D trains link Xiamen and Longyan (¥51, 1½ hours, hourly). Buses, shuttle buses and carpools outside the station will pester you to use them to get to the clusters for between ¥45 to ¥70 per person. A bus to the Hongkeng Tulou Cluster takes about two hours and leaves when full.

ℹ Getting Around

The easiest way to see the *tǔlóu* is to book a tour, or hire a vehicle either from Xiamen, Nanjing County or Yongding. You'll find taxi drivers in Yongding and Nanjing County offering their services for around ¥500 a day (¥800 if you hire for two days), setting off early morning and returning late afternoon. Expect to see two clusters per day.

If you book a place to stay in one of the *tǔlóu*, most owners can help with transport and they usually arrange pick-up from Nanjing County or Yongding.

Quanzhou 泉州

📞 0595 / POP 1.2 MILLION

The role of Quanzhou (Quánzhōu) as an integral part of the maritime Silk Road during Song and Yuan rule is still felt in the city's architecture, cuisine and ethnic diversity. Today it's a handsome if grossly undervisited place – due partly to the lure of nearby Xiamen – but what Marco Polo described in the 13th century as 'one of the two ports in the world with the biggest flow of merchandise' does not easily fade away.

Wandering Quanzhou's ancient stone streets and temples of many faiths creates a rare sense of timelessness in urban China. Hints of a rich Islamic and maritime past are readily visible, and the atmosphere at times feels like a city further west. There are also easy day trips from here to the fascinating historic villages of Chongwu and Xunpu, which have long faced out towards the sea.

⊙ Sights

The centre of town lies between Zhongshan Nanlu, Zhongshan Zhonglu and Wenling Nanlu. This is where you'll find most of the tourist sights. The oldest part of town is to the west, where many narrow alleys and lanes still retain their traditional charm and are waiting to be explored. The southern edge has the modern Wanda Plaza with views across to the Jinjiang River.

★ **Guandi Temple**   TAOIST TEMPLE
(关帝庙, Guāndì Miào; ☑ 0595 2228 6613; 255 Tumen Jie, 涂门街255号; ⊙ 8am-5.40pm) FREE This magnificently carved temple is immediately identifiable by its showy dragon-decorated roofs and a shroud of smoke emanating from furnaces burning prayer books stuffed in by devotees. It's dedicated to Guan Yu, a Three Kingdoms general who was deified as the god of war. Inside the temple are statues of the god and wall panels that detail his life. Busy merchants gather outside. By night the temple is lit up in wonderfully gaudy fairy lights.

Lingshan Islamic Cemetery   CEMETERY
(灵山伊斯兰教圣墓, Língshān Yīsīlán Shèngmù; cnr Donghu Lu & Lingshan Lu, 在东湖路与灵山路的路口; ¥15; ⊙ 8am-5.30pm) Set at the foot of the mountain of Língshān, this leafy cemetery is one of the most intact historic cemeteries in China. Two of Mohammed's disciples are said to be buried here, and you'll also find some granite steles dating from the Ming dynasty. Take bus 7 or 203 and hop off at Shèngmùzhàn (圣墓站).

Kaiyuan Temple   BUDDHIST SITE
(开元寺, Kāiyuán Sì; ☑ 0595 2238 3285; 176 Xi Jie, 西街176号; ⊙ 8am-5.30pm) FREE In the northwest of the city, one of the oldest temples in Quanzhou dates back to AD 686 and is the largest in Fujian. Surrounded by trees, Kaiyuan Temple is famed for its pair of rust-coloured, five-storey stone pagodas, stained with age and carved with figures that date from the 13th century. Behind the eastern pagoda is a **museum** containing the enormous hull of a Song dynasty seagoing junk, which was excavated near Quanzhou in 1974.

Maritime Museum   MUSEUM
(泉州海外交通史博物馆, Quánzhōu Hǎiwài Jiāotōngshǐ Bówùguǎn; 425 Donghu Lu, 东湖

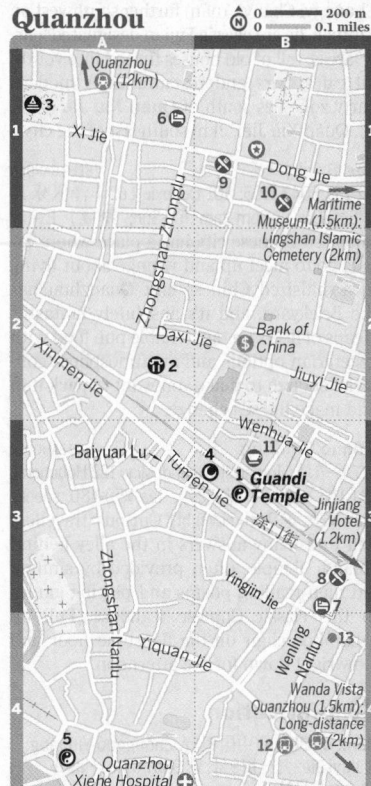

Quanzhou

Quanzhou

路425号; ⊗8.30am-5.30pm Tue-Sun) FREE On the northeastern side of town, this fabulous museum explains Quanzhou's trading history, the development of Chinese shipbuilding and the kaleidoscope of religions in the port's heyday. The Religious Stone Hall and Islamic Culture Hall are highlights, boasting a beautiful collection of gravestones and reliefs of different religions dating from the Yuan dynasty. Take bus 7 or 203 and alight at Qiáoxiāng Tǐyùguǎn (侨乡体育馆).

Qingjing Mosque　　　　　　　MOSQUE
(清净寺, Qīngjìng Sì; 108 Tumen Jie, 涂门街108号; ¥3; ⊗8am-5.30pm) Built by the Arabs in 1009 and restored in 1309, this stone edifice is one of China's only surviving mosques from the Song dynasty. Only a few sections (mainly walls) of the original building survive, largely in ruins. The adjacent mosque is a donation from the government of Saudi Arabia.

🛏 Sleeping

54 Coffee Inn　　　　　　　　GUESTHOUSE ¥
(泉州新街54咖啡客栈, Quánzhōu Xīnjiē Wǔshísì Kāfēi Kèzhàn; ☑0595 2287 5167; 54 Xin Jie, 新街54号; dm ¥85, s & d ¥268; ❄🛜) It's worth the effort to seek out this welcoming red-brick building managed by two friendly women. The four-bed dormitory is excellent value, while the courtyard is a great place to meet other travellers.

**Quanzhou Humei
Holiday Hotel**　　　　　BUSINESS HOTEL ¥¥
(泉州湖美假日酒店, Quánzhōu Húměi Jiàrì Jiǔdiàn; ☑0595 6823 9999; Wenling Nanlu, 温陵南路; tw & d from ¥236; 🅿❄🛜) A great location and small rooms possessing a sense of colour and style in neutral tones lift Humei beyond the business basics, especially in the modern bathrooms. Service is commendably earnest.

C & D Quanzhou Hotel　　　　HOTEL ¥¥¥
(泉州悦华酒店; ☑0595 2801 9999; www.cnd-hotels.com; 129 Citong Xilu, 刺桐西路129号; d ¥679-2200; ❄@🛜) Long-standing C & D is one of the best hotels in the city, with four restaurants, a complete spa and friendly English-speaking staff. Generous rack-rate discounts will please tired travellers. It's about 2km southeast of the centre.

 Eating

You can find the usual noodle and rice dishes served in the back lanes around Kaiyuan Temple (p378) and also along the food street close to Wenling Nanlu. The air-conditioned, clean restaurants and cafes outside Wanda Plaza offer a range of Asian and international choices.

Ānjì Kèjiāwáng   HAKKA ¥¥
(安记客家王; 461 Tumen Jie; meals from ¥50; ⊙11am-9pm) The Ān family are well known across town for their Cantonese-style dim sum, which sneaks a few Hakka delights onto the trolley. The *xiāmǐ chángfěn* (虾米肠粉, shrimp in rice paper) and *xián dànjuǎn* (咸蛋卷, salty egg rolls) will do just nicely thanks.

Sāndé Sùshíguǎn   VEGETARIAN ¥¥
(三德素食馆, Three Virtues Vegetarian Restaurant; ☑595 2227 6705; 124 Nanjun Lu, 南俊路124; meals ¥25-60; ⊙10am-9pm; 🖉) This fine vegetarian restaurant has clear picture menus and more creativity than the typical faux-meat staples. Try any of the simple rice dishes for their delicious chewy textures.

Lánshì Zhōnglóu   HAKKA ¥¥
(蓝氏钟楼肉粽; 9-21 Dong Jie; meals from ¥25; ⊙11am-9.30pm) In an area flush with eateries, this Hakka favourite draws a return crowd for its honest, affordable fare. The signature *hēimǐzòng* (黑米粽, black rice dumplings) and *dànhuángzòng* (蛋黄粽, rice dumpling with yolk) are recommended by staff for a reason.

Drinking & Nightlife

New Overseas Chinese Village west of Zhongshan Park and **Yuanhe 1916 Idea Land** (源和1916创意产业园, Yuánhé 1916 Chuàngyì Chǎnyè Yuán) further southwest on Xinmen Jie are classic Fujian designated 'party' areas, full of old houses turned into youthful cafes, bars and restaurants. A modern party zone lies south of **Quan Xiu Jie** (泉秀街, Quán Xiù Jiē), 2km southeast of the city.

The Brickyard   BEER GARDEN
(☑159 6043 1105; 101 Quanxiu Lu, 丰泽区乐其道6号101; ⊙6pm-2am Tue-Sun; 🛜🅱) Every midsized Chinese city has a place where expats go to meet up and whinge about living in a midsized Chinese city. Quanzhou has the Brickyard, and it's absolutely fantastic. Heaps of beers on tap, reliable pub food with vegetarian options and an atmosphere convivial enough to make you want to pack it in and make the sea change.

Gǔcuò Cháfáng   TEAHOUSE
(古厝茶坊; Tumen Jie Guandi Miao 122 Houcheng, 涂门街关帝庙后城122号; tea ¥50-480, snacks from ¥20; ⊙9am-midnight) Curious travellers will find many answers in the alley behind Guandì Temple, often provided by smiling old men reading poems and playing games in this classic Chinese teahouse. Pull up a bamboo chair on the flagstone floor and slow right down for the afternoon.

ℹ Information

Bank of China (中国银行, Zhōngguó Yínháng; 9 Jiuyi Jie, 九一街9号; ⊙9am-5pm) Has a 24-hour ATM.

Public Security Bureau (PSB, 公安局, Gōng'ānjú; ☑2218 0323; 62 Dong Jie, 东街62号; ⊙visa section 8-11.30am & 2.30-5.30pm) You can extend your visa here.

Quanzhou Xiehe Hospital (泉州协和医院, Quánzhōu Xiéhé Yīyuàn; Tian'an Nanlu, 天安南路) In the southern part of town.

NÁNYĪN: THE SOUL MUSIC OF QUANZHOU

The square in front of **Confucius Temple** (府文庙, Fǔwén Miào; Zhongshan Zhonglu, 鲤城区中山中路; ⊙8am-5.30pm) **FREE** on Tumen Jie is one of the busiest spots in Quanzhou during the day, but once the sun sets, amateur and professional musicians start to gather to practise Nányīn (南音), one of the oldest music genres in China.

The music of Nányīn can be traced as early as Han dynasty, and it was inscribed onto the Unesco Representative List of Intangible Cultural Heritage in 2009. These slow, haunting melodies are performed with Chinese musical instruments like the bamboo flute, the Chinese lute (*pipa*) as well as other percussive instruments like clappers. Sometimes the music is purely instrumental; sometimes it includes ballad singing in the local dialect by a solo singer or by a quartet. The lyrics sung revolve around classical Chinese poems and Buddhist sutras.

The performance in front, and to the right-hand side, of Confucius Temple usually starts at 7pm every night. The shows are free.

ℹ Getting There & Away

BUS

Both **Quanzhou Bus Station** (泉州汽车站, Quánzhōu Qìchēzhàn; cnr Wenling Nanlu & Quanxiu Jie) and the **long-distance bus station** (泉州客运中心汽车站, Quánzhōu Kèyùn Zhōngxīn Qìchēzhàn; cnr Quanxiu Jie & Pingshan Lu) further east along Quanxiu Jie have buses to Guangzhou (¥325 to ¥364, seven hours, four daily) and Shenzhen (¥299, eight hours, two daily). Regular deluxe buses travel to Fuzhou (¥69, 2½ hours, nine daily) and Xiamen (¥55, 1½ hours, frequent).

TRAIN

D trains depart from **Quanzhou Train Station** (泉州站, Quánzhōu Zhàn; 高铁站, Gāotiě Zhàn; Pu Xianlu, 普贤路), 12km northwest from the town centre. Destinations include Fuzhou (¥54 to ¥60, one hour, half-hourly), Shanghai (¥363 to ¥437, six to eight hours, 16 daily) and Xiamen (¥34, one hour, half-hourly).

In town, train tickets can be bought at the **Wenling Nanlu Train Ticket Office** (铁路火车票代售点, Tiělù Huǒchēpiào Dàishòudiǎn; 166 Wenling Nanlu, 温岭南路166号; ⊙9am-6pm) or from the **train ticket office** (火车售票亭, Huǒchē Shòupiàotíng; 675 Quanxiu Jie, 泉秀街675号; ⊙7am-6pm) just east of Quanzhou Bus Station. There's a ¥5 booking fee.

ℹ Getting Around

The local bus network is extensive and most rides cost ¥1. Buses 17 and express K1 run frequently from Quanzhou Train Station to Quanzhou Bus Station (¥1, 70 minutes) and the Long-distance Bus Station (¥1, one hour) respectively, via Zhōnglóu (the Clocktower, 钟楼; ¥1, 40 minutes), at the intersection of Zhongshan Zhonglu and Xijie. Bus 203 links the train station to Maritime Museum and Islamic Cemetery. A taxi from the town centre to the train station costs ¥50. Local bus 15 links both bus stations. Bus 2 goes from the bus station to Kāiyuán Temple. Taxi flagfall is ¥7, then ¥1.80 per kilometre.

Chongwu 崇武

⟁ 0595 / POP 50,000

One of the best-preserved city walls in China can be found in the ancient 'stone city' of Chongwu (Chóngwǔ). The granite walls date back to 1387, stretch over 2.5km and average 7m in height. Scattered around the walls are 1304 battlements and four gates into the city.

The town wall was built by the Ming government as a front-line defence against marauding Japanese pirates, and it has survived the past 600 years remarkably well.

You can also walk along the top of the wall at some points.

If your interest here is solely architectural, enter the old town through a narrow gate roughly 200m before the ticketed entrance. From there you can weave your way past intact 14th-century houses and up towards the wall.

Adjacent to the old town, is the **Chongwu Stone Arts Expo** (崇武石雕工艺博览园, Chóngwǔ Shídiāo Gōngyì Bólǎnyuán; ¥45; ⊙7am-7pm). It is filled with 500 stone carvings made by local craftspeople, a small beach, a lighthouse and some basic seafood restaurants. The open spaces and clean ocean air make it worth the effort, especially if you have kids.

There are a handful of decent hotels within walking distance or a short taxi ride of the old city, but most travellers make day trips from Quanzhou. Holiday Inn moved in and renovated the **West Gulf Holiday Hotel** (湾假日酒店, Wān Jiàrì Jiǔdiàn; ☑0595 2787 7777; www.xswhotel.com; d ¥490-790, ste from ¥1090; ℗❉⊚❄) in 2015, maintaining the beautiful ocean views, large carpeted three-star hotel rooms (some with balcony), friendly service and convenient access to the old town.

The strip of cafes adjacent to the old city serve congee with crab meat (¥20), while many vendors inside the park sell barbecued squid on sticks (¥10). There are comfortable, modern eateries frequented by a younger crowd on the pedestrian-only Xinhua Jie, which is about 2km west of the old town.

Frequent buses depart Quanzhou's long-distance bus station (¥15, 1½ hours), taking you past arrays of stone statues (the area is famed for its stone-carving workshop) before ending up in Chongwu.

From Chongwu, it's best to take the return bus to Quanzhou where numerous connections are available.

A taxi from Quanzhou costs about ¥120 and takes an hour.

Xunpu Village 蟳埔村

The fishing village of Xunpu (Xúnbù Cūn; sometimes Xunbu), some 10km southeast of the city centre of Quanzhou, was on the old trade route of the maritime Silk Road and was perhaps the Arabs' first port of call when they set foot in Quanzhou during the Song dynasty. The village, now under encroaching urbanisation, is still fascinating and you'll find some old houses built with oyster shells behind the main road in the village and older women still wearing flamboyant traditional head ornaments.

The **Mazu Temple** (妈祖庙, Māzǔ Miào) on the knoll in the village is the local centre of worship. It's dedicated to the goddess of seafarers and turns very lively on the 29th day of the first lunar calendar month, the birthday of the protector. All the women in the village turn out in traditional costumes to join in the annual Mazu procession.

A taxi from Quanzhou bus station is about ¥25.

Cao'an Manichaean Temple 草庵摩尼教寺

This quirky **temple** (Cǎo'ān Móníjiào Sì; Huábiǎo Hill, 华表山; ¥20; ⊙8am-6pm) is dedicated to Manichaeism, a religion originating in Persia in the 3rd century, combining elements of Zoroastrian, Christian and Gnostic thought, which reached China in the 7th century.

The well-restored stone complex you see today is a rebuild dating from the Yuan dynasty (14th century). The most remarkable relic in the temple is the 'Buddha of Light', a sitting stone statue in the main hall, which is actually the prophet Mani, founder of Manichaeism, in a Buddhist disguise.

Manichaeism was considered an illegal religion during the Song period and the religion had to operate in the guise of an esoteric Buddhist group. Take a closer look at the statue, and you'll find its hairstyle (straight instead of curly), hand gestures and colour combinations are distinctly different from most representations of the Buddha.

The temple is 19km south of Quanzhou. From the long-distance bus station (p381) in Quanzhou, board a bus to Anhai (安海, Ānhǎi; ¥12) and tell the driver to drop you off at Cǎo'ān Lùkǒu (草庵路口). Then look for the English signage saying Grass Temple and it's a 2km walk uphill. The road is not well marked so taking a taxi is a recommended alternative; a taxi from Quanzhou is around ¥65.

Fuzhou 福州

☑ 0591 / POP 2.8 MILLION

Fuzhou (Fúzhōu) is a handsome provincial capital with charming old town laneways lined with lanterns and traditional architecture pressed up against the backs of shiny shopping plazas. Fuzhou's tea culture is renowned, and you'll find plenty of purveyors along the banks of the Minjiang River. A short trip to the west lies Gu Mountain and its delightful, accessible hiking paths. A new metro makes the centre easy to access, but most visitors pass through en route to other destinations in southern China, so the only tourists you're likely to see will be Chinese.

◉ Sights

★**Sānfāng Qīxiàng** ARCHITECTURE
(三坊七巷; Yangqiao Donglu & Nánhou Jie, 杨桥东路; ⊙24hr) This 'downtown' series of ancient residential buildings is known as 'Three Lanes and Seven Alleys'. Thousands of visitors wander the white-walled streets daily, passing the traditional architecture and the hectic shopping strip on Nanhou Jie, then resting at a cafe on the canal. Constructed in the late Jin dynasty around the 12th century, the residences prospered 400 years later during Ming and then Qing rule. For some peace, duck down quieter side streets, especially by night when red lanterns are illuminated.

Linzexu Memorial Hall MUSEUM
(福州林则徐纪念馆, Fúzhōu Línzéxú Jìniàn Guǎn; ☑0591 8762 2782; 16 Aomen Lu, 澳门路16号; free with ID; ⊙8.30am-5.30pm) FREE The former residence of the anti-opium trade reformer is a surprisingly well-presented museum. It offers an overview of Fuzhou's seafaring history, attractive gardens and courtyards to escape the busy weekend foot traffic. Show your passport for free entry.

Jade Hill Scenic Area PARK
(于山风景区, Yúshān Fēngjǐngqū; ⊙8.30am-5pm) FREE This rocky hill park in the centre of Fuzhou rises above a snow-white **statue of Mao Zedong** (毛主席像, Máo Zhǔxí Xiàng) playing 'traffic cop'. Check out the seven-storey **White Pagoda** (白塔, Bái Tǎ), built in AD 904. At the foot of Jade Hill are the wretched remains of Fuzhou's **Ming dynasty city wall** (明代古城墙遗迹, Míngdài Gǔchéngqiáng Yíjī); originally boasting seven gates, the wall was pulled down for road widening.

🛏 Sleeping

Longdu Hotel BUSINESS HOTEL ¥
(龙都大酒店, Lóngdū Dà Jiǔdiàn; ☑0591 8743 5104; 28 Shangbin Lu, 尚宾路28号; d & tw from ¥240; P☀@☎) The rooms are big enough to swing a suitcase, and the very dated decor and bathtub aren't without their charms, but the real reason to stay here is for a quiet back room in a peaceful area just a short

walk from the action of downtown. It's walkable from Dongjie Kou metro and staff speak some English.

Juchunyuan Inn Fuzhou
HOTEL ¥¥

(福州聚春园驿馆, Fúzhōu Jùchūnyuán Yìguǎn; ☑0591 6303 3888; 22 Gong Xiang, Sānfáng Qīxiàng, 三坊七巷宫巷22号; d ¥415-706; ❀❂@❞) A beautiful inn housed in a historic mansion in the pedestrianised Sānfáng Qīxiàng area. All 56 rooms are modern and tastefully appointed.

Shangri-La Hotel
HOTEL ¥¥¥

(香格里拉大酒店, Xiānggélǐlā Dàjiùdiàn; ☑0591 8798 8888; www.shangri-la.com; 9 Xinquan Nanlu, 新权南路9号; d ¥1450; ❂@❞❀) Overlooking Wuyi Square, this hotel is the finest in Fuzhou, if a little removed from the action of Sānfáng Qīxiàng. The swimming pool, lobby and breakfast spread live up to the brand's reputation. The suites are good value when discounts apply. A taxi from Fuzhou bus station is around ¥25.

🍴 Eating

Sānfáng Qīxiàng is by far the most atmospheric area to eat out in Fuzhou. Its narrow laneways and Ming-style houses have been impeccably maintained, while stylish cafes line small canals. You'll find small eateries on both sides of Nanhou Jie (南后街), which also fills with shoppers on weekends. Food courts are hidden from sight at the basement of plazas. A couple of upmarket vegetarian restaurants are on the entrance road to Jade Hill Scenic Area.

Yonghe Fishballs
SEAFOOD ¥

(永和鱼丸(南后街店), Yǒnghé Yúwán; ☑0591 8767 9539; 89 Nanhou Jie, 南后街89号; snacks ¥12-14; ⊙7am-10pm) Fuzhou is famous for its pork-stuffed fishballs and Yonghe has been fine-tuning its delicious recipe since 1934, with six in a bowl of plain soup. Go for a mixed bowl, which includes mackerel, squid and 'shark' balls (actually just minced white fish), and pull up a window-side seat upstairs in this century-old building for views over bustling Nanhou Jie.

Old Foochow
ZHEJIANG ¥

(老福州, Lǎo Fúzhōu; ☑0591 8361 6985; 5 Hongten Ge, off 55 Bayiqi Zhong Lu, 八一七中路55号洪腾阁5号; ⊙7am-11pm) The antiquated spelling of Fuzhou hints at the old-world chic that's obvious as soon as you plonk down on the green leatherette booths and use a pencil to tick off some Fuzhou favourites from the picture menu, such as *Fúzhōu xiāngyóu xiā* (福州香油虾, sesame oil stir-fried prawns) and the challenging yet moreish *nán jiān gān* (南煎肝, lychee-braised liver).

Shíjīnzhāi
VEGETARIAN ¥

(食锦斋; ☑0591 8751 5500; 332 Tatou Lu, 福清市石竹山道院内332; mains ¥20-30; ⊙9.30am-9pm Mon-Sun; ☑) This reputable, decades-old vegetarian restaurant has a welcoming outdoor area and a variety of mock-meat dishes. It gets busy with workers at lunchtime. It's about 2km east of Sānfáng Qīxiàng.

30ml Coffee Studio
CAFE ¥¥

(☑0591 8789 1230; 78 Húbīn Lù, 湖滨路78号; snacks ¥35-45; ⊙9am-12.30am; ❞) Near the corner of 'Seven Alleys', on the edge of the canal, 30ml is almost too cool for Fuzhou. Here you'll find delicious coffee (¥28 to ¥32), cake, chicken wings, imported fruit beer and the diverse sounds of Cash, Cook, Dylan et al. Reasonable English spoken, with a Chinese sensibility.

ℹ️ Getting There & Away

AIR

Fuzhou airport is 45km southeast of the city centre and has daily flights to Beijing (¥1200, three hours), Guangzhou (¥1100, 1½ hours), Shanghai (¥450, 80 minutes) and Hong Kong (¥800, 1½ hours).

Airport buses leave from at least three locations in town: the Apollo Hotel (阿波罗大酒店, Ābōluó Dàjiǔdiàn; ¥20) on Wuyi Zhonglu, 400m north of the Fuzhou Bus Station, has departures every 20 minutes between 5.30am and 8.30pm; the Fuzhou North Bus Station (¥20) near the Fuzhou Train Station has hourly departures between 6am and 7.30pm; and the South Train Station has departures every hour between noon and 5pm. The trip takes about an hour.

BUS

Fuzhou North Bus Station (福州汽车北站, Fúzhōu Qìchē Běizhàn; 317 Hualin Lu, 华林路317号) is 400m south of Fuzhou Rail Station. Destinations include the following:

Guangzhou ¥280, 18½ hours, five daily

Quanzhou ¥69, 2½ hours, nine daily

Shanghai ¥280, 11½ hours, two daily

Wuyi Shan ¥100, 4 hours, one daily (9.25am)

Xiamen ¥105, 3½ hours, every 20min

Fuzhou Bus Station (福州汽车站, Fúzhōu Qìchēzhàn, South Bus Station; ☑0591 3810 9988; 190 Wuyi Zhonglu, 五一中路190号) services the following destinations:

Guangzhou ¥280, 12 hours, one daily (5pm)

Hong Kong ¥404, 15 hours, four daily

Shenzhen ¥240, 11½ to 13½ hours, two daily

Xiamen ¥115, 3½ hours, every 15min

TRAIN

Fuzhou has a good network of trains to many
major cities. Fast D trains sometimes leave from
the more central **Fuzhou Train Station** (福州站,
Fúzhōu Zhàn; 502 Hualin Lu, 华林路502号), but
more often from the **Fuzhou South Train Station** (福州南站, Fúzhōu Nánzhàn; East of Lulei
Village, Canshan District, 仓山区胪雷路与下洋
路交汇处), 17km southeast of the town centre.

Beijing ¥719 to ¥795, eight to 10½ hours, six
daily

Quanzhou ¥54 to ¥60, one hour, half-hourly

Shanghai ¥309 to ¥378, 4½ to 6½ hours,
half-hourly

Wuyi Shan ¥104 to ¥120, one hour, half-hourly

Xiamen ¥94 to ¥151, two to 2½ hours, every
15 minutes

① Getting Around

Fuzhou has an efficient, comfortable two-line
metro system, new in 2016. Line 1 runs to the
major sights, including Sānfāng Qīxiàng. Most
rides cost ¥2. Fuzhou Rail Station and Fuzhou
South Rail Station are also conveniently connected to the metro. The two stations are both
on Line 1; it takes 42 minutes to get from one
station to the other for ¥5.

Wuyi Shan   武夷山

☑ 0599 / POP 230,000

Despite a long association with domestic travellers, Wuyi Shan (Wǔyí Shān) is a mountain
retreat that retains a sense of untouched natural splendour. Set high up in the northwest
of Fujian, its hiking trails through protected
forests and the famed bamboo rafting trip are
well worth the effort to come here. Try to visit
midweek or in low season (November, March

and April) and you might have the area to
yourself. Avoid visiting during heavy rain (especially during summer months), even if the
hotels and tour organisers advise otherwise.

The Wuyi Shan Scenic Area lies on the west
bank of Chongyang Stream (Chóngyáng Xī).
North of here, the busy resort area (武夷山
旅游度假区, Wǔyíshān lǚyóu dùjià qū) is on
the pleasant east bank and has the most facilities for visitors; from here it's a short bus
ride south to the main, southern entry to the
Wuyi Shan Scenic Area. There are two train
stations, but the east train station is the more
used and is south of the scenic area. In the
north is the north train station and airport.

⊙ Sights & Activities

Wuyi Shan Scenic Area   PARK

(武夷宫; ☑ 0599 525 2884; 3-day access Mar-Nov
¥140, Dec-Feb ¥120, compulsory 1-/2-/3-day shuttle
bus use ¥70/85/95; ⊙ 7am-5pm) Trails within
the scenic area connect all the major sites.
Good walks include the 530m **Great King
Peak** (大王峰, Dàwáng Fēng), accessed
through the main entrance by shuttle bus,
and the 410m **Heavenly Tour Peak** (天游峰,
Tiānyóu Fēng), where an entrance is reached
by road up the Nine Twists River. The main
entrance to the Wuyi Shan Scenic Area is the
south entrance, 3km south of the resort area.
Take bus 6 or 7 (¥1, 22 minutes, frequent) to
the Jǐngqū Nán Rùkǒu (景区南入口) stop.

It's a moderate two-hour walk to Great
King Peak among bamboo groves and steep-
cut rock walls. The trail can be slippery and
wet, so bring suitable shoes.

The walk to Heavenly Tour Peak is more
scenic, with better views of the river and
mountain peaks. But the path is also the
most popular with tour groups. At the northern end of the scenic area, the **Water Curtain
Cave** (水帘洞, Shuǐlián Dòng) is a cleft in the
rock about one-third of the way up a 100m
cliff face. In winter and autumn, water plunges over the top of the cliff, creating a curtain
of spray.

Xiamei   VILLAGE

(下梅古民居群, Xiàméi Gǔmínjū Qún; ¥55; ⊙ 8am-
5pm) This village dates from the Northern
Song dynasty and boasts some spectacular
Qing dynasty architecture from its heyday as
a wealthy tea-trading centre, including about
30 ancient houses. Motorbikes in the Wuyi
Shan resort area can take you 11km (about
20 minutes) northeast to Xiamei (¥50 return
trip). Admission includes a free local guide
(Chinese only) if you wish.

Nine Twists River

RAFTING

(九曲溪, Jiǔqū Xī; boat rides ¥130; ⏰ 7am-5pm) One of the highlights for visitors to Wuyi Shan is floating down the river on *zhúpái* (bamboo rafts) fitted with rattan chairs. Departing from Xingcun (星村, Xīngcūn), 12km west of the resort area, the trip down the river takes over an hour and brings you through some magnificent gorge scenery, with sheer rock cliffs and lush green vegetation. Tickets at park entrances.

🛏 Sleeping & Eating

⭐ **Ancient Street**
Youth Chic Hostel

HOTEL ¥¥

(武夷山旧街五号云起时客栈, Wǔyíshān Jiùjiē Wǔhào Yúnqǐ Shíkèzhàn; ☑ 0599 520 5205; 5 Mantingfeng Lu, 幔亭峰路旧街5号; d/tr from ¥289/359, r with view from ¥429; ⊝ 🕏) The self-claimed 'Youth Chic Hostel' certainly is the first to tap into an ancient-chic vibe for a hotel in the area and is the most relaxing option around. The lobby and attached restaurant resemble stylish tea showrooms and the spacious rooms have an understated cool thanks to soft wood tones. Some rooms sport terrace spas with mountain views.

Wuyi Mountain Villa

LUXURY HOTEL ¥¥¥

(武夷山庄, Wǔyí Shānzhuāng; ☑ 0599 525 1888; www.513villa.com; Wuyi Gong, 武夷宫; d/ste from ¥828/1398; 🕏🕏) This grand residence has been given new life and resembles a palace fit for an emperor. Staff are attentive and match the dressed up marble decor with their own faux-ancient costumes. Tasteful, clean rooms in neutral tones complement the tranquil location at the foot of Great King Peak, which affords excellent relaxing views of greenery and water features.

⭐ **Chui Yan Restaurant**

CHINESE ¥

(炊烟旧街山房菜, Chuīyān Jiùjiē Shānfángcài; ☑ 0599 803 0700; 8 Yunu Fenglu, 玉女峰路8号; mains ¥29-69; ⏰ 11am-3pm & 5.30-9pm) This bamboo-heavy, riverside restaurant buzzes most nights with groups sharing platters of Chinese dishes such as the local speciality of chicken fried with tea leaves and cumin, served in a bamboo basket. Part of a promising trend in Wuyi Shan for chic dining with good-value food that doesn't require a tout.

ℹ Information

Bank of China (中国银行, Zhōngguó Yínháng; Da Wangfeng Lu, 大王峰路; ⏰ 9am-5pm Mon-Fri)

Large branch in the Wuyi Shan resort area with a 24-hour ATM.

ℹ Getting There & Away

AIR

Wuyi Shan's airport, about 15km south of the town and east of the mountain park, has air links to several cities. A taxi should cost about ¥40 to either. Destinations include the following:

Beijing ¥1860, 2½ hours, two daily

Guangzhou ¥1125, two hours, one daily

Shanghai ¥850, 1½ hours, one daily

Xiamen ¥840, one hour, two daily

BUS

Buses run from the long-distance bus station in Wuyi Shan city, about 15km north of the resort area. Destinations include Fuzhou (¥100, four hours, daily) and Xiamen (¥144 to ¥223, nine hours, four daily)

TRAIN

Most trains depart from **Wuyi Shan East Train Station** (武夷山东站, Wǔyíshān Dōng zhàn), 29km southeast of the resort area. Services include the following:

Fuzhou ¥104 to ¥120, one hour, half-hourly

Jinhua ¥135, 1½ hours, hourly

Quanzhou ¥129 to ¥163, two to three hours, hourly

Xiamen ¥163 to ¥197, three to 4½ hours, hourly

Some trains from Fuzhou and elsewhere arrive at **Wuyi Shan North Train Station** (武夷山北站, Wǔyíshān Běi zhàn), 19km northeast of the resort area.

ℹ Getting Around

Bus 6 and 7 run frequently between the resort area (or Wǔyí Mountain Villa) and the long-distance bus station (¥2, 50 minutes) and Wuyi Shan North train station (¥2, 1¼ hours, every 10 minutes); bus 7 goes from the airport (¥1, 30 minutes) to the resort area. The main bus stop in the resort area is Tàiyángchéng Shìchǎng (太阳城市场).

To get from Wuyi Shan East train station to the resort area, take express bus K1 (¥10, 1¼ hours, every 20 minutes), from the right as you exit the station, for six stops to Tàiyáng Chéng Shichǎng; cash only, no change given. A taxi costs about ¥30 to ¥40.

The resort area is small enough for you to walk everywhere. Expect to pay about ¥15 for a motorised trishaw from the resort area to most of the scenic area entrances.

Shanxi

POP 36.5 MILLION

Best Places to Eat

➜ Zǐní Sānliùjiǔ Cūliáng Guǎn (p390)

➜ Haoganggang Lamb Offal (p398)

➜ Jia Jin Yang Hele Noodles (p406)

➜ Fènglín Gé (p391)

➜ Tianyuankui (p402)

➜ Mínjiān Càiguǎn (p405)

Best Places to Stay

➜ Yide Guesthouse (p402)

➜ Jing's Residence (p402)

➜ Atour (p397)

➜ Pipa Hostel (p389)

➜ Luohou Temple Hotel (p396)

Why Go?

Waist-deep in handsome history, Shanxi (山西, Shānxī) is home to an impressive roll call of must-see, ancient sights. Most travellers start with the walled city of Pingyao. Basing yourself here and jumping to the town's surrounding sights is practically all you need: you'll encounter time-worn temples, sprawling Ming- or Qing-dynasty courtyard residences, some of the warmest people in the Middle Kingdom and the opportunity for a day trip to the dizzying mountain cliffs and gorges of Mian Shan.

Travellers shouldn't overlook Datong, a forward-thinking city with a brand-new city wall and a great looking old town, but it's the astonishing cave sculptures at Yungang, outside town, that give expression to the province's other great source of magic: a rich vein of Silk Road Buddhist heritage, which splendidly litters the rolling mountain fastness of Wutai Shan with temples. Add the time-warp walled village, Guoyu, and the still-inhabited cave dwellings of Lijia Shan, and you could find yourself staying longer than planned.

When to Go
Datong

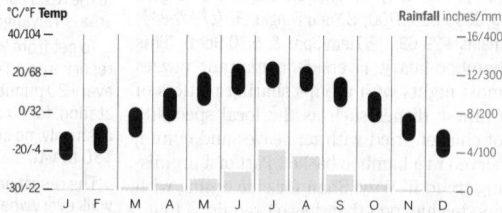

May Cooler than the sapping summer months and not as blustery as early spring.

Late May–early Sep Good time for trips to cooler, mountainous Wutai Shan.

Late Sep Enjoy the comfortable start of the lovely Shanxi autumn.

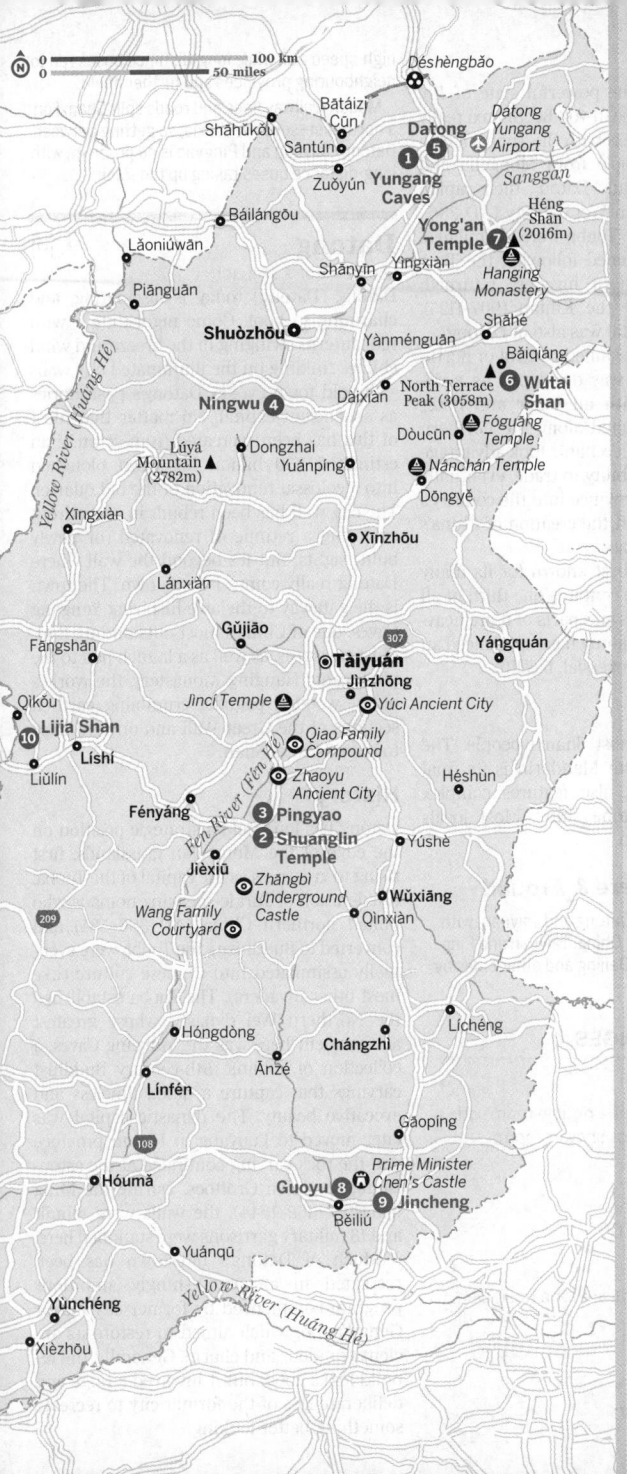

Shanxi Highlights

1 **Yungang Caves** (p392) Discovering the grandeur of the caves' magnificent Buddhist statues.

2 **Shuanglin Temple** (p403) Admiring some of China's most ancient in situ temple statuary.

3 **Pingyao** (p399) Wandering the cobblestone ancient streets of this time-warped, walled town.

4 **Ningwu Ice Cave** (p395) Journeying through a three-million-year-old mountain cave that's frozen year-round.

5 **Datong** (p388) Checking out the lavishly restored city wall and the old town.

6 **Wutai Shan** (p393) Hanging up your traveller's hat in this scenic and mountainous monastic enclave.

7 **Yong'an Temple** (p395) Marvelling at 200m of sublime frescoes at a remote temple.

8 **Guoyu** (p406) Visiting this still-inhabited historical walled village in Shanxi's remote southeast.

9 **Jincheng Museum** (p405) Getting context for an ancient city and its treasures at this highly informative museum.

10 **Lijia Shan** (p404) Walking among tiers of cave dwellings and paddy fields at the Ming dynasty village.

History

Though home to the powerful state of Jin, which split into three in 403 BC, Shanxi really only rose to greatness with the Tuoba, a clan of the Xianbei people from Mongolia and Manchuria who made Datong their capital during the Northern Wei dynasty (AD 386–534). Eventually the Tuoba were assimilated, but as China weakened following the Tang collapse, the northern invaders returned; most notable were the Khitan (907–1125), whose western capital was also in Datong.

After the Ming regained control of northern China, Shanxi was developed as a defensive outpost, with an inner and outer Great Wall constructed along the northern boundaries. Local merchants took advantage of the increased stability to trade, eventually transforming the province into the country's financial centre with the creation of China's first banks in Pingyao.

Today Shanxi is best known for its many mines; the province contains one-third of all China's coal deposits and parts of it are heavily polluted, while Datong has experienced an astonishing, if controversial, facelift.

Language

Jin is spoken by most Shanxi people. The main difference from Mandarin is its final glottal stop, but it also features complex grammar-induced tone shifts. Most locals also speak Mandarin.

ⓘ Getting There & Around

There are airports at Datong and Taiyuan, with flights to cities across China. Taiyuan and Pingyao are connected to Beijing and other cities by high-speed rail, while long-distance buses run to neighbouring provinces and further afield.

Modern railway lines and roads split Shanxi on a northeast–southwest axis, so getting between Datong, Taiyuan and Pingyao is no problem, with long-distance buses taking up the slack.

Datong 大同

📱 0352 / POP 3.5 MILLION

Datong (Dàtóng) today is fascinating, and charming to boot. Come night-time – with red lanterns swinging in the breeze and wind chimes tinkling on the illuminated city walls – the old town evokes Datong's past glories as an ancient capital. No matter that most of this has been recreated from scratch: an estimated ¥50 billion has been ploughed into a colossal renovation of the old quarter. The city wall has been rebuilt in its entirety, enclosing a retinue of renovated (or newly built) sights. But it's beyond the wall where Datong really comes into its own. The town is the gateway to the awe-inspiring Yungang Caves, one of China's most outstanding Buddhist treasures, as well as a launch pad to the photogenic Hanging Monastery, the world's oldest wooden pagoda, crumbling earthen sections of the Great Wall and onward trips to sacred Wutai Shan.

History

Datong has long held a strategic position on the edge of the Mongolian grasslands, first rising to greatness as the capital of the Tuoba. A federation of Turkic-speaking nomads who united northern China (AD 386–534) and converted to Buddhism, the Tuoba were eventually assimilated into Chinese culture (like most other invaders). The Tuoba established the Northern Wei dynasty, whose greatest achievement here was the Yungang Caves, a collection of sublime 5th-century Buddhist carvings that capture a quiet, timeless and evocative beauty. The dynastic capital was later moved to Luoyang in Henan province and the rock carving continued at the astonishing Longmen Grottoes. During the Ming dynasty (1368–1644), the walls were rebuilt and 13 military garrisons were stationed here.

Much of Datong's old town has been recreated in an astonishingly ambitious program commenced by former city mayor Geng Yanbo, which aimed to restore its ancient grandeur and charm. Generally, the rebuild looks good, but it involved a huge and deliberate loss of the former city to recreate something better looking.

⊙ Sights

Nine Dragon Screen
WALLS

(九龙壁, Jiǔlóng Bì; Da Dongjie, 大东街; ¥10; ⊙8am-6.30pm) Emblazoned with nine coiling dragons picked out in coloured glazed tiles, this is one of the finest *yǐngbì* (影壁) spirit walls in China (it has two counterparts in Beijing). It's also the largest, at 45.5m long, 8m high and 2m thick. Built in the Ming dynasty in 1392, the palace it once protected belonged to the 13th son of a Ming emperor and burnt down in 1644. Amazingly, the palace is being rebuilt in its entirety, covering a vast area of town.

★Datong Museum
MUSEUM

(大同市博物馆, Dàtóng Shì Bówùguǎn; ☑0352 242 7185; Taihe Rd, Yudong New District, 御东新区太和路; ⊙9am-5pm Tue-Sun) **FREE** Housed in a contemporary building inspired by a dragon totem, this wonderful museum is chock-full of relics – religious, funereal, military, imperial and quotidian – dating from when Datong was a frontier known as Ping Cheng (平成), between the Chinese and the nomads of the Eurasian steppes, all the way through to the Ming and Qing dynasties. What came before all that? Check out the prehistoric gallery with its animatronic dinosaurs and egg fossils.

Huayan Temple
BUDDHIST SITE

(华严寺, Huáyán Sì; Huayan Jie, 华严街; ¥50; ⊙8am-6.30pm; 🚌38) Built by the Khitan during the Liao dynasty (AD 907–1125), this 66,000-sq-metre temple faces east, not south (it's said the Khitan were sun worshippers) and is divided into two separate complexes. One of these is an active monastery (upper temple), while the other is a museum (lower temple). Dating from 1140, the impressive main hall of the Upper Temple (上华严寺, Shàng Huáyán Sì) is one of the largest Buddhist halls in China, with Ming murals and Qing statues within.

Datong City Wall
FORTRESS

(大同城墙, Dàtóng Chéngqiáng; ⊙8am-10pm) **FREE** This incredible city wall has been rebuilt from the soles up in what must be one of the most ambitious feats of engineering to hit Datong since, well, since the last time it was built. Prior to the rebuild, what was left of the wall had been denuded of bricks and reduced to earthen stumps. At 7.2km in circumference, the wall makes an ambitious jogging circuit, or you can hire a bicycle (¥50) or sit on an electric buggy (¥30). Passport required.

Shanhua Temple
BUDDHIST SITE

(善化寺, Shànhuà Sì; Nansi Jie, 南寺街; ¥50; ⊙8am-6pm) Originally constructed in AD 713 and today standing just inside the city walls, Shanhua Temple was rebuilt during the Jin dynasty. The grand wooden-bracketed Hall of Mahavira at the rear contains five beautiful central Buddhas and expressive statues of celestial generals in the wings. Look out for the impressive and quite colossal turquoise, yellow and ochre five-dragon screen (五龙壁, *wǔlóngbì*). It stands outside the current temple perimeter, so is free to admire.

🛏 Sleeping

Bravo Hostel
HOSTEL ¥

(子鼠丑牛青年旅舍, Zi Shǔ Chǒu Niú Qīngnián Lǚshě; ☑181 3526 3301; www.bravoyouthhostel.com; 8 Qingyuan Jie, 清远街8号; dm ¥40-60, d ¥188; 🅿🐾📶) Set within an attractive period courtyard, this laid-back hostel is strewn with communal couches and offers cluttered dorms (including some unusual dorm 'twins' set in the eaves), and a handful of en suite doubles emblazoned with funky murals. In the heart of the old town (老城区, Lǎochéngqū), it's a short walk to the sights, with several bars nearby.

★Pipa Hostel
HOSTEL ¥¥

(琵琶老店, Pípa Lǎodiàn; ☑0352 378 1666; Block B2 Qingyuan St, 清远街内侧B2座; r from ¥200) A charming hostel with themed rooms overlooking a bright communal area. Good illumination and air-conditioning, abundant USB sockets, and clean toilets more than make up for the smallish rooms. Service is warm (the owner, a great source of information on Datong culture, likes to hang around the breakfast room and talk to guests) and there is complimentary fruit and chocolates daily.

Garden Hotel
HOTEL ¥¥¥

(花园大饭店, Huāyuán Dàfàndiàn; ☑0352 586 5888; www.gardenhoteldatong.com; 59 Da Nanjie, 大南街59号; d & tw incl breakfast ¥1080-1780, tw ¥1380-1580, ste ¥2880-3880; ⊕🅿@📶) The well-appointed rooms at this popular hotel feature down quilts, carved rosewood bed frames and excellent bathrooms. There's an attractive atrium with a cafe lounge, western and Chinese restaurants, plus great staff. Significant discounts (even in high season) knock prices as low as ¥300: excellent value.

The location is fantastic. It's within the city walls right by the old district – you don't have to walk far to visit the sights and soak up the old-town atmosphere.

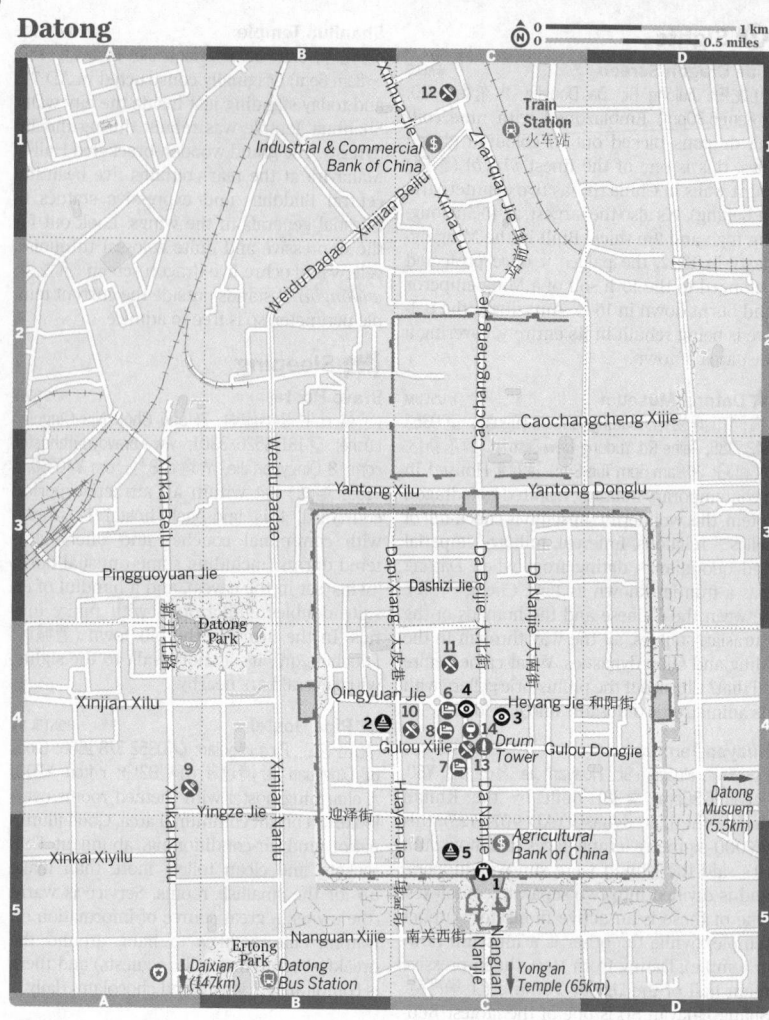

✗ Eating

★ Shuaifujie Islam Lamb Offal

CHINESE ISLAMIC ¥

(清真帅府街羊雜, Qīngzhēn Shuàifújiē Yángzá; ☑ 138 3528 9118; 18 Shuaifu Jie, 帅府街18号; offal noodles ¥8; ⊙ 7-11am) Before hitting the hills, come here for the ultimate protein breakfast: lamb offal! Most locals order the offal with potato-flour noodles (粉羊杂, fěn yángzá). Hardcore fans prefer just offal (纯羊杂, chún yángzá; bowl ¥30, half-bowl ¥15), with steamed bun (馒头, mántou) or fried dough (油饼, yóubǐng) to soak up the soup. Look for the big green sign with white lettering.

Zǐní Sānliùjiǔ Cūliáng Guǎn

CHINESE ¥

(紫泥369粗糧館; 13 Gulou Xijie, 鼓楼西街13号; mains ¥12-60; ⊙ 11.30am-2.30pm & 6-10pm) A large, formal restaurant with attentive service and surprisingly affordable prices. The thick bilingual picture menu covers a huge array of Shanxi and northern Chinese dishes from dumplings and lamb skewers to claypot tofu and rabbit heads.

★ Dōngfāng Xiǎo Miàn

NOODLES ¥

(East Wheat, 东方削面; Yingze Jie, 迎泽街; noodles from ¥6; ⊙ 7am-10pm) Forgive the chainstore decor and endure the long queues (always a good sign) and you'll soon be in noodle heaven at this popular local chain.

Datong

◉ Sights
1	Datong City Wall	C5
2	Huayan Temple	B4
3	Nine Dragon Screen	C4
4	Old Town	C4
5	Shanhua Temple	C5

◉ Sleeping
6	Bravo Hostel	C4
7	Garden Hotel	C4
8	Pipa Hostel	C4

✕ Eating
9	Dōngfāng Xiāo Miàn	A4
10	Fènglín Gé	C4
11	Shuaifujie Islam Lamb Offal	C4
12	Tónghé Dàfàndiàn	C1
13	Zǐní Sānliùjiǔ Cūliáng Guǎn	C4

◎ Drinking & Nightlife
14	Gym Bar	C4

Steaming bowls of the humble Shaanxi speciality *xiāo miàn* (削面) are the stars here; have the noodles with pork (¥8), beef or lamb (each ¥10) and pair them with a variety of side dishes such as spicy cucumbers. A beer will help top it all off.

Tónghé Dàfàndiàn   CHINESE ¥
(同和大饭店; 1 Zhanqian Jie, 站前街1号; dishes ¥16-40; ⊙11am-2pm & 6-9pm) This fantastic, bright and cheery spot alongside the Hóngqí Hotel and a short hop from the train station can look a little intimidating with its big round tables better suited to functions, but solo diners can pull up a chair no problem. There's a huge range of tasty, well-presented dishes on the picture menu, suiting all budgets.

Fènglín Gé   CHINESE ¥¥
(凤临阁; ☑0352 205 9799; near cnr Gulou Xijie & Huayan Jie, 鼓楼西街华严街路口; mains from ¥28; ⊙6.30-9.30am, 11.30am-2pm & 5.30-9pm; ✳🖥) Exquisite and delectable *shāomai* (steamed dim-sum dumplings) are the star of the show at this fancy, period-style restaurant in the heart of the old town. Order by the steamer (笼, *lóng*) or half steamer. The crab *shāomai* are succulent and gorgeous, but not cheap (¥15 each, half steamer ¥45); there's also lamb (¥8 each, half steamer ¥26) and other tempting fillings.

🍷 Drinking & Nightlife

Datong's old town is home to a growing number of touristy bars, with enough for a crawl along Shanhuasi Jie, running parallel to the west wall of Shanhua Temple all the way down to its Nine Dragon Screen. Yet more bars can be found along Gulou Dongjie, many with live music.

★ Gym Bar   CRAFT BEER
(工業革命; Gōngyè Gémìng; Xiǎochīchéng Xiàng, off Gulou Xijie, 鼓楼西街, 小吃城巷内70米; ¥35-65) One of the few quiet, laid-back bars in Datong, you won't find guests singing or playing drinking games here, just an adorable black dog, her friendly owner and Victoria's Secret fashion shows playing on a loop. You can choose from an entire wall of craft beers, including European and American brews, plus Chinese brands. Just help yourself.

ⓘ Information

Agricultural Bank of China (ABC, 中国农业银行, Zhōngguó Nóngyè Yínháng; Da Nanjie, 大南街; ⊙8.30am-5.30pm) ATM and money exchange.

Public Security Bureau (PSB, 公安局城区分局, Gōng'ān Jú Chéngqū Fēnjú; ☑0352 201 4927; Zhengfa Bldg, Xinkai Nanlu, 新开南路政法大楼; ⊙9am-noon & 3-5.30pm Mon-Fri)

ⓘ Getting There & Away

AIR
Located 20km east of the city, Datong's small airport has flights to destinations including Beijing (¥500, one hour), Shanghai (¥1450, 2½ hours), Shenzhen (¥1300, five hours), Taiyuan (¥700, one hour) and Xi'an (¥650, two hours). Buy tickets at www.ctrip.com or www.elong.net.

BUS
Buses from the new **South Bus Station** (新南公路客运站, Xīn nán gōnglù kèyùn zhàn; ☑0352 502 5222; Weidu Dadao, 魏都大道), 9km from the train station, include the following:

Beijing ¥128, four hours, hourly (7.30am to 3pm)

Muta ¥32, 1½ hours, hourly (7.30am to 7pm)

Taiyuan ¥90, 3½ hours, hourly (6.50am to 7pm)

Wutai Shan ¥95, 3½ hours, two daily summer only (8am and 2.30pm)

You can also catch minibuses to some of these destinations from outside the train station.

Buses from the **Main Bus Station** (大同汽车站, Dàtóng Qìchēzhàn; ☑0352 246 4464; Weidu Dadao, 魏都大道) include the following:

Hanging Monastery ¥30, two hours, hourly (7am to 11am)

Hohhot ¥80, 3½ hours, hourly (7.20am to 4.20pm)

Regular buses (¥80) to Hohhot depart hourly from next to the Tónghé Dàfàndiàn by the train station.

Buses (two to three hours; ¥38) depart daily for **Daixian** (代县汽车站, Dàixiàn Qìchē Zhàn) from both Datong bus stations.

TRAIN

A new high-speed line connects Beijing with Datong, cutting the journey time to two hours and bringing a huge influx of new visitors to the city. Departures from Datong also include the following:

Hohhot Hard seat ¥42, three to four hours, 22 daily

Pingyao Hard seat/sleeper ¥63/122, six to eight hours, four daily

Taiyuan Hard seat/sleeper ¥44/98, four to five hours, 10 daily

ⓘ Getting Around

Bus routes are being readjusted due to the massive construction all around town, so expect changes. Buses 4 and 15 run from the train station to the Main Bus Station. Bus 30 takes 30 minutes to run from the train station to the new South Bus Station. Buses 27 and 35 go to the old town from Weidu Dadao. Bus 603 runs to the Yungang Caves.

Taxi flagfall is ¥7. Most drivers will also try to sell you a package deal out to the Yungang Caves and the Hanging Monastery, which, with a bit of bartering, can be had for ¥250 to ¥300.

Yungang Caves 云冈石窟

One of China's most supreme examples of Buddhist cave art, the 5th-century **Yungang Caves** (Yúngāng Shíkū; ☎ 0352 302 6230; Dec-Feb ¥80, Mar-Nov ¥125; ⏰ 8.30am-5.30pm 1 Apr–15 Oct, to 4.50pm 16 Oct–31 Mar) are magnificent. With 51,000 ancient statues and celestial beings, they put everything else in the Shanxi shade. Carved by the Turkic-speaking Tuoba, the Yungang Caves drew their designs from the Indian, Persian and Greek influences that swept along the Silk Road. Work began in AD 460, continuing for 60 years before all 252 caves, the oldest collection of Buddhist carvings in China, had been completed.

Pass through the visitor centre and a recreated temple on a lake before arriving at the caves. You may find some caves shut for restoration and this is done on a rotational basis. Despite weathering, many of the statues at Yungang still retain their gorgeous pigment. The caves that are deeply recessed, in particular, have been well protected from the outside weather, although the penetration of water from above is a constant hazard.

A number of caves were once covered by wooden structures. Many of these are long gone, although the very impressive Caves 5 to 13 are still fronted by recently constructed wooden temples. Past the last set of caves, you can turn off the path down to the slick and informative **museum** (open 9.30am to 4.30pm) detailing the Wei Kingdom and the artwork at the caves. English captions are limited.

Most of the caves, however, come with good dual Chinese/English captions. English-speaking tour guides can be hired for ¥150; their services include a trip to the museum. Note that photography is permitted in some caves but not in others.

To get to the caves, take bus 603 (¥3, 45 minutes) from Datong train station to the terminus. Buses run every 15 minutes. A taxi from Datong is around ¥40 each way. You will pass the rather less appealing but interesting Datong Coal Mine en route.

Daixian

Daixian (or Dai County) is located between Taiyuan and Datong. Tourism has not yet reached its old town, which is quite lively with relics still very much a part of inhabitants' everyday life. The town is small and you can walk from sight to sight.

Smack in the centre of Daixian old town, the 14th-century **Bianjing drum tower** (边靖楼, Biānjìng Lóu; ¥20; ⏰ 8am-6pm) will make up for all the times you felt let down by faux ancient towers or authentic ones you could only admire from afar. The majestic wooden structure, preluded by a dramatic stone staircase, has retained many of its Ming dynasty features. Ascend to the upper floors for a closer look at the simple but beautiful beams and brackets, and a bird's-eye view of the town.

Raised in the Tang dynasty and restored in the Ming, the serene **Confucius Temple** (代县文庙, Dàixiàn Wénmiào; Wenmiao Lu, 文庙路; ¥20; ⏰ 8am-6pm) features gateway arches with striking green glazed tiles, shapely centuries-old trees, and ornate caisson ceilings (藻井, zǎojǐng). In the garden, a Confucius statue stands cloaked in red before yellow school desks on which worshippers have left gifts of candies and apricots. On the altar of the main hall, buns fashioned into the heads of Chinese zodiac animals are offered to the sage.

Buses (¥38, two to three hours) depart daily for Daixian from Datong Bus Station and Datong South Bus Station. The Drum Tower is 610m from Daixian Bus Station, while the Confucius Temple is 60m to the right.

THE GREAT WALL AROUND DATONG

Some 70km northeast of Datong, **Zhenghong** (正宏堡村长城, Zhènghóng Bǎo Cūn Cháng Chéng; Zhènghóngbǎo Village, 正宏堡村) is a sleepy farming village just off the highway, set within the ruins of a *bǎo* (fort) that once served the Great Wall. The fort was one of more than 70 dotting the strategic plains north of Datong. Keep going through the village and you'll reach the Wall proper, which scythes eastwards through untamed canyon country. Opportunities for hiking and canyoning abound, but exercise caution and take water. No public transport, but a return taxi should cost ¥300.

A good place to see some raw sections of the Great Wall is **Deshengbao** (得胜堡), a 16th-century walled fort almost on the border with Inner Mongolia that is now a small farming village. The fort's north and south gates are still standing, as are parts of its walls. Walk through the village (many of its houses are built out of Great Wall bricks) to the north gate and beyond it you'll see wild wall – 10m-high sections of it. To get to Deshengbao, take a minibus to Fengzhen (丰镇; ¥17, one hour) from opposite Tónghé Dàfàndiàn, next to Datong train station. There are about 10 buses a day between 7.15am and 3.45pm. The bus will drop you at the turn-off for Deshengbao, from where it's a 1km walk to the south gate. Heading back, return to the highway and flag down any Datong-bound bus.

Yong'an Temple 永安寺

Yong'an Temple (Yǒng'ān Sì; 200m south of Heshun Beilu, 和顺北路南200米; ¥20; ⊙8am-5pm) at the foothills of Heng Shan (恒山) only unlocks its halls when there are visitors and for a good reason – this poised and serene 13th-century temple is the home of some of the most precious Yuan dynasty coloured frescoes in China. You don't have to be an expert to appreciate the 200m of paintings on the interior walls of the main hall: gorgeous, fragile and surprisingly vivid, quietly telling their religious and secular stories in the half-light.

The temple sells exquisitely printed scrolls of the frescoes with descriptions. Scroll booklets (in English or Chinese) are ¥50 each; and there's a large deluxe box-set with several metres of scrolls that sells for over ¥9000.

Buses depart for Hunyuan (浑源) from Datong's main bus station (p391; ¥31, two hours). A cab ride from downtown Hunyuan to the temple costs ¥50.

Hanging Monastery 悬空寺

Built precariously into the side of a cliff, the Buddhist **Hanging Monastery** (Xuánkōng Sì; ¥115; ⊙8am-7pm summer, 8.30am-5.30pm winter) is made all the more stunning by its long support stilts. The halls hug the contours of the cliff face, connected by rickety catwalks and narrow corridors, which can get very crowded in summer. It's a sight to behold.

Combine your trip to the monastery with a visit to the riveting five-storey **Yingxian Muta** (应县木塔; Yingxian Xijie, 应县西街; ¥50; ⊙7.30am-6.30pm summer, 8am-5.30pm winter),

the world's tallest (67m) and China's oldest wooden pagoda. Constructed with red pine without a single nail, it's often referred to as simply *mùtǎ* (the Wooden Pagoda). The clay Buddhist carvings it houses, including an 11m-high Sakyamuni on the 1st floor, are as old as the pagoda itself. Visitors can only climb to the first two levels, but there are photos of the higher floors to the side of the pagoda.

Many buses departing for Hunyuan (浑源) from Datong's main bus station (¥31, two hours) come to the monastery. If you want to go on to Yingxian Muta, there are frequent buses from Hunyuan (¥14, one hour), or shared taxis make the run from the monastery car park for ¥50 per person (when full). Hourly buses return to Datong until 6pm, or you can travel onto Taiyuan (¥90, 3½ hours, last bus 2.30pm).

Wutai Shan 五台山

📞 0350 / POP 326,600

The mountainous, monastic enclave of Wutai Shan (Wǔtái Shān, Five Terrace Mountains) is Buddhism's sacred northern range and the said to be earthly abode of Manjusri (文殊, Wénshū), the Bodhisattva of Wisdom. Chinese students sitting the ferociously competitive *gāokǎo* (university entrance) exams troop here for a nod from the learned Bodhisattva, proffering incense alongside saffron-robed monks and octogenarian pilgrims.

A powerful sense of the divine holds sway in Wutai Shan, and the port-walled monasteries – the principal sources of spiritual power – find further amplification in the sublime mountain scenery.

The forested slopes overlooking the town eventually give way to alpine meadows where you'll find more temples and great hiking possibilities. Wutai Shan is also famed for its mysterious rainbows, which can appear without rain and are said to contain shimmering mirages of Buddhist beings, creatures and temple halls.

Climate

Wutai Shan is at high altitude and powerful blizzards can sweep in as late as May and as early as September; check ahead to ensure the roads are passable. Winters are freezing with snow; summer months are the most pleasant, but always pack a jacket, as well as suitable shoes or boots for rain, as temperatures fall at night. If you are climbing up the peaks to see the sunrise, warm coats can be hired.

◉ Sights & Activities

Enclosed within a lush valley between the five main peaks is an elongated, touristy town

called Taihuai (台怀), but everyone simply calls it Wutai Shan. It's here that you'll find the largest concentration of temples, as well as all the area's hotels and tourist facilities. The five main peaks are north (北台顶, běitái dǐng), east (东台顶, dōngtái dǐng), south (南台顶, nántái dǐng), west (西台顶, xītái dǐng) and central (中台顶, zhōngtái dǐng).

There's a steep ¥145 entrance fee for the area – including a mandatory ¥50 'sightseeing-bus' ticket (旅游观光车票, lǚyóu guānguāng chēpiào) for transport within the area, valid for three days. Some of the more popular temples charge an additional entrance fee. On the way in, the bus will stop at a large visitor centre where you buy tickets and reboard after your tickets are checked. Note that your bus might drop you behind the main town area, from where you'll need to walk to the main drag. From the main bus station in Wutai Shan, you can jump on a free shuttle bus along the main road to get to different points.

Opportunities for hiking are immense, but there are no good maps and no marked trails.

Wutai Shan

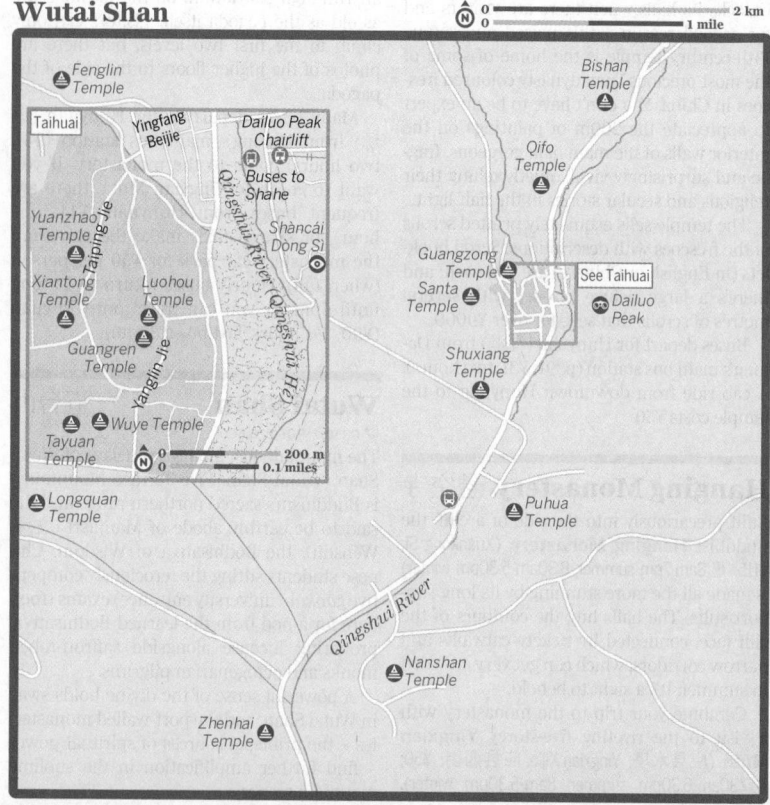

NINGWU ICE CAVE

Also known as Wannian Ice Cave (literally, 'Million-year Ice Cave'), this naturally occurring **ice cave** (万年冰洞, Wànnián Bīngdòng; ¥120; ⊙ 8am-6pm May-Oct) sits 2300m above sea level in the Luyashan Scenic Area (芦芽山景区, Lúyáshān Jǐngqū) near the town of Dongzhai (东寨), 50km west of downtown Ningwu.

The cave was formed three million years ago, during the Quaternary Period of glaciation. Inside, no matter the time of year, you're surrounded by stalactites and ice walls that have been illuminated for visual impact. The cave is not very big – it takes about 30 minutes to see everything unless there's a tour group in front of you, blocking the narrow walkway. Note that on public holidays, particularly the 1st May Labour Day holiday, the line can be long, with waits of up to three hours.

The large Luyashan Scenic Area, which has an assortment of other sights that includes hills, lakes, plains, waterfalls, valleys, each with a separate entrance fee that ranges from ¥20 to ¥120. It is often closed outside the months of May to October.

There are hotels and guesthouses along the two main avenues of Dongzhai: Siyuan Dajie and Fenyuan Dajie. Some do not open in winter when the ice cave and Luyashan Scenic Area are closed.

Buses (¥7, 40 minutes, every 15 minutes, 7.15am to 7pm) depart from in front of **Ningwu Bus Station** (宁武汽车站, Níngwǔ Qìchē Zhàn; Fenghuang Dongjie, 凤凰东街) for Dongzhai, from where a taxi to the cave (23km) is ¥120.

From Ningwu Bus Station, six buses depart daily for Taiyuan (¥50, three hours, 10.35am to 9.34pm).

There are trains to nearby cities from **Ningwu train station** (宁武火车站, Níngwǔ Huǒchē Zhàn; http://hcp.tiexing.com/ningwu/; Railway Station St, 火车站街, Huochezhan Jie) including the following:

Datong ¥11 to ¥25, two to four hours, five daily

Pingyao ¥39 to ¥44, five hours, three daily

Taiyuan ¥26 to ¥29, three to four hours, five daily

Roads lead to the summits of the five main peaks, so you can take a taxi up to one of them before hiking back into town using the road as a bearing. Minibuses run to all five peaks for ¥350 (7.30am departure, 5pm return). They can be found at the big car park by the chairlift to Dailuo Peak.

👁 Taihuai Temple Cluster

More than 50 temples lie scattered in town and across the surrounding countryside, so knowing where to start can be a daunting prospect. Most travellers limit themselves to what is called the **Taihuai Temple Cluster** (台怀寺庙群, Táihuái Sìmiàoqún), about 20 temples around Taihuai itself, among which Tayuan Temple and Xiantong Temple are considered the best. Many temples in Taihuai contain a statue of Manjusri, often depicted riding a lion and holding a sword used to cleave ignorance and illusion.

⭐**Tayuan Temple**   BUDDHIST SITE
(塔院寺, Tǎyuàn Sì; ¥10; ⊙ 8.30am-5pm) At the base of **Spirit Vulture Peak** (灵鹫峰, Língjiù Fēng), Tayuan Temple is the most prominent landmark in Wutai Shan and all pilgrims pass through here to spin the prayer wheels at its base or to prostrate themselves, even in the snow. Even Chairman Mao did his tour of duty, staying in the **Abbot Courtyard** in 1948.

⭐**Xiantong Temple**   BUDDHIST SITE
(显通寺, Xiǎntōng Sì; ¥10; ⊙ 8am-4.30pm) Xiantong Temple – the largest temple in town – was erected in AD 68 and was the first Buddhist temple in the area. It comprises more than 100 halls and rooms. The **Qianbo Wenshu Hall** contains a 1000-armed, multifaced Manjushri, whose every palm supports a miniature Buddha. The squat brick **Beamless Hall** (无梁殿, Wúliáng Diàn) holds a miniature Yuan dynasty pagoda, remarkable statues of contemplative monks meditating in the alcoves and a vast seated effigy of Manjushri.

👁 Further Temples

North beyond Xiantong Temple is a cluster of temples that you can explore. **Yuanzhao Temple** (圆照寺, Yuánzhào Sì; ⊙ 8am-5pm) FREE contains a smaller stupa than the one at Tayuan Temple (p395). A 10-minute walk south down the road, **Shuxiang Temple** (殊像寺, Shūxiàng Sì; ⏰8am-5pm) FREE can be reached up a steep slope beyond its spirit wall by the side of the road; the temple contains Wutai Shan's largest statue of Manjusri riding a lion.

For great views of the town, you can trek, take a **chairlift** (one way/return ¥50/85; ⏰7am to 5pm) or ride a horse (¥50 one way) up to the temple on **Dailuo Peak** (黛螺顶, Dàiluó Dǐng; ¥10), on the eastern side of Qingshui River (清水河, Qīngshuǐ Hé). For even better views of the surrounding hills, walk 2.5km south to the isolated, fortresslike **Nanshan Temple** (南山寺, Nánshān Sì; ⏰8am-6pm) FREE, which sees far fewer tour groups than the other temples and has beautiful stone carvings.

🛏 Sleeping

While Wutai Shan attracts tens of thousands of tourists, accommodation is fairly basic and most hostels are identical in terms of pricing and standard. Luohou Temple has a fabulously clean and tranquil hotel with a 9pm curfew. For cheap lodging, touts are happy to lead you to family-run guesthouses with decent rooms from ¥120. Find one that's close to the main road so you can easily get to the temples.

⭐ **Luohou Temple Hotel** HOTEL ¥¥
(罗睺寺庙宾馆, Luóhóu Sìmiào Bīnguǎn; ☎0350 654 5421; r from ¥200; 🌐) This new guesthouse inside the centrally located Luohou Temple compound has clean rooms with new furniture and a tranquil atmosphere. You can take your meals with the monks here, but you can't stay out later than 9pm.

ℹ Information

ATMs are found in the visitor centre and along the town's main road.

ANCIENT WOODEN TEMPLES

Two of the oldest wooden buildings in China, dating from the Tang dynasty, can be found at **Foguang Temple** (佛光寺, Fóguāng Sì; ¥15; ⏰7.30am-6.30pm) and **Nanchan Temple** (南禅寺, Nánchán Sì; ¥10; ⏰8am-6pm). Not many visitors make it out here, but it's worth the journey for the sheer rarity and the tranquillity. Many of the buses between Wutai Shan and Taiyuan pass through the countryside where they are located, so both can be seen as a day trip.

ℹ Getting There & Away

BUS

Buses from **Wutai Shan bus station** (五台山汽车站, Wǔtái Shān Qìchēzhàn; ☎0350 654 3101) include the following:

Beijing ¥145, five hours, three daily (11am, 1.30pm and 3.30pm)

Datong ¥75, four hours, three daily (7.30am, 9am and 1pm)

Hanging Monastery ¥65, three hours, one daily (7.30am)

Taiyuan ¥75, four to five hours, hourly (6.30am to 4.30pm)

Buses to Shahe (离黛螺顶索道近; ¥25, 1½ hours, hourly, 7am to 3pm) leave from the car park by the chairlift to Dailuo Peak.

TRAIN

The station known as **Wutai Shan** is actually 50km away in the town of Shahe (砂河, Shāhé), from where you can get a minibus taxi (around ¥70) or a bus (¥25) the rest of the way. Destinations include Pingyao (hard seat ¥51, five hours, one daily), Taiyuan (hard seat ¥16 to ¥38, four to five hours, three daily) and Beijing (hard seat ¥50, six to seven hours, two daily).

ℹ Getting Around

The entry fee includes a ¥50 bus ticket, valid for three days, that lets you hop on and off a tour bus running frequently through the town and a little way beyond. The service is available roughly between 7am and 7pm.

Minibuses go to the five plateau (五台顶, Wǔtáidǐng) between 7am to 7pm. Embark at the foot of Dailuo Peak. Tickets are approximately ¥70 for one plateau or ¥350 for a full-day trip to all five.

Taiyuan 太原

☎0351 / POP 4.2 MILLION

Most travellers pass through Shanxi's capital en route to Pingyao or heading north to Datong or Wutai Shan, but Taiyuan (Tàiyuán) is well worth a day or two of your time. It's a huge, modern and cosmopolitan city, but it's not short on history or culture; there's a first-rate museum, a historic park and several notable temples – including a picturesque complex that was a site of water deity worship and former imperial garden – and a cathedral that wouldn't look out of place in Italy.

👁 Sights

⭐ **Twin Pagoda Temple/Yongzuo Temple** BUDDHIST SITE
(双塔寺/永祚寺, Shuāngtǎ Sì/Yǒngzuò Sì; ¥30; ⏰8.30am-5.30pm) These gorgeous twin brick

Taiyuan

Taiyuan

pagodas rise photogenically south of the Nansha River in Taiyuan's southeast. There's not much left of the original Yongzuo Temple, which the pagodas belong to, but the area is well tended with shrubs and greenery. Of the two pagodas, 13-storey **Xuanwen Pagoda** (宣文塔, Xuānwén Tǎ), dating from the reign of Ming emperor Wanli, can be climbed. The adjacent pagoda dates from the same period but is closed.

Cathedral of the Immaculate Conception   CHURCH
(圣母无染原罪主教座堂, Tàiyuán Shèngmǔ Wúrǎn Yuánzuì Zhǔjiào Zuòtáng; 178 Jiefang Lu, 解放路178号) Built in 1870, the neoclassical house of worship was badly damaged during the Boxer Rebellion but today stands magnificently amid modern buildings. The church is often closed, so try to go during Mass when it's definitely open so you can look at the amazing interior – a blaze of white, blue, red and gold. Mass is held from Monday to Friday at 6am, 6.30am, 4.30pm and 6.30pm; and on Sundays, 6.15am, 7.45am, 9am (in English), 10am and 6.30pm.

★ Jinci Temple   HISTORIC SITE
(晋祠, Jìncí; ¥80; ⊙8am-6pm) This sprawling complex sits on the source of the Jin River. The earliest structures and the irrigation canal (which still gushes on rainy days) were built between the 7th and 2nd centuries BC. Over the dynasties, Jinci Temple has been a site for the worship of ancestors, water deities and a plethora of gods; it was also an imperial garden where religious rites and sporting contests were held. The highlights are structures on the central axis, including the magnificent **Hall of the Sacred Mother**.

Take bus 804 or 308 from Taiyuan Train Station (¥5, 45 minutes). Jinci Temple is 25km southwest of downtown Taiyuan.

Shanxi Museum   MUSEUM
(Shānxī Bówùguǎn; ☑0351 878 9015; http://shanximuseum.com; 13 Binhe Xilu Beiduan, 滨河西路北段13号; ⊙9am-5pm Tue-Sun, last entry 4pm) **FREE** This comprehensive museum has three floors that walk you through various aspects of Shanxi culture, from Neolithic jade and Silk Road Buddhist statues to Shanxi merchant culture and opera. The popularity of this latter art form explains why there are so many operatic stages in historic locations and even miniature ones in burial sites. Some exhibits have English captions.

🛏 Sleeping & Eating

★ Atour Hotel   HOTEL ¥¥
(亚朵酒店, Yàduǒ Jiǔdiàn; ☑0351 495 5777; 25 Shuiximen St, 迎泽区，水西门街25号; r ¥448) Good service, a young, easy vibe, and su-

QIAO FAMILY COMPOUND

An 18th-century complex of courtyards, **Qiao Family Compound** (乔家大院, Qiáojiā Dàyuàn; www.qjdywhyq.com; ¥138; ⏰8am-7pm) is a fine example of a traditional private residence in China. Once home to a celebrated merchant, it's an austere yet elegant maze of doorways and courtyards that lead onto a seemingly infinite number of rooms (over 300). The complex is famous as the set of director Zhang Yimou's tragedy *Raise the Red Lantern* (大红灯笼高高挂; 1991) starring Gongli. If you have seen and enjoyed the film, a visit is a must.

Sure enough, the place is festooned with red lanterns, but many fascinating exhibits of Ming- and Qing-era furniture and objects are also displayed, as well as Shanxi opera costumes and props. English signage helps convey northern Chinese traditions and rites to foreign visitors.

The site is massively popular with domestic tour groups so get here as early as you can. While the entrance is glossed up, and souvenir and food stalls besiege the courtyard, the residence is still big enough to flee the crowds: step through one of the many doorways and they magically vanish.

Located 14km southwest of Qiao Family Compound, **Zhaoyu Ancient City** (昭馀古城, Zhāoyú Gǔchéng) is a refreshingly undeveloped ancient town with a **courtyard mansion** (渠家大院, Qújiā Dàyuàn) and Qing dynasty banks. What's more enjoyable, however, is strolling the dusty streets, exploring the teashops – Zhaoyu was founded by tea traders – the fragile and lovely facades, and the quirky western bakery. In summer afternoons, people doze off on barber chairs, on duvets for sale, and in makeshift beds.

To get to both, catch any bus going to Qixian (祁县; ¥25, 1½ hours) from Taiyuan's Jiannan bus station. Tell the driver where you're headed. You can also visit Qiao Family Compound from Pingyao (¥15, 45 minutes, every 30 minutes to 6.40pm).

per-comfortable rooms in Taiyuan's main commercial and business area. The rate includes a solid buffet breakfast with Chinese and western offerings.There are banks, grocery stores, shops and restaurants within walking distance, some open till late.

World Trade Hotel
HOTEL ¥¥¥

(山西国贸大饭店, Shānxī Guómào Dàfàndiàn; ☎0351 868 8888; 69 Fuxi Jie, 府西街69号; d ¥1268-1600, ste ¥2478; ❉@🛜🏊) This dapper, efficient five-star hotel has fine rooms and facilities, including a gym and spa. Its marble lobby is a vast atrium-lit space slung between its two towers. Rooms with a view cost extra. Discounts of 25% to 40% are available.

★Liùwèizhāi
CHINESE ¥

(六味斋; ☎0351 197 9131; junction btwn Liuxiang Nanlu & Qiaotou Jie, 柳巷南路和桥头街交叉路口; set meals ¥36) Behind the grey walls of this period-style low-rise is a famous establishment founded in the Qing dynasty. The ground floor sells cold braised snacks. Ascend to the upper floors and take a seat by the window. The sets give you a bit of everything such as the signature spiced pork (酱肉, *jiàng ròu*) and steamed tubular oat-flour pasta (栲栳栳, *kǎolǎolǎo*).

Haoganggang Lamb Offal
CHINESE ISLAMIC ¥

(郝刚刚羊杂割店, Hǎogānggang Yángzá Gēdiàn; 29 Shuiximen St, 水西门街29号; noodles ¥18-25, dishes ¥42-49; ⏰6am-1pm & 6-9pm) The standard mutton soup (羊肉汤, *yángròu tāng*) or offal soup (羊杂汤, *yángzá tāng*) at this popular chain comprises mutton or offal in broth with noodles. You can add extra meat (加肉, *jiā ròu*) or offal (加羊杂, *jiā yángzá*) for ¥12 or ¥13 a tael (两, *liǎng*). One tael is about 38g. Flaky pastry (油酥饼, *yóusū bǐng*) is ¥1 apiece.

ℹ Information

Agricultural Bank of China (ABC, 中国农业银行, Zhōngguó Nóngyè Yínháng; Yingze Nanjie, 迎泽南街) ATM next to the Jinlin Oriental Hotel.

Bank of China (中国银行, Zhōngguó Yínháng; 47 Wuyi Lu, 五一路47号; ⏰9am-5pm) Foreign exchange and ATM.

Industrial & Commercial Bank of China (ICBC, 工商银行, Gōngshāng Yínháng; Yingze Dajie, 迎泽大街) ATM.

Public Security Bureau (PSB, 公安局, Gōng'ānjú; ☎0351 895 5355; Wuyi Dongjie, 五一东街; ⏰8.30am-5.30pm Mon-Fri) Can extend visas, but they need seven working days to do so.

❶ Getting There & Away

AIR

Destinations from Taiyuan Wusu International Airport include Beijing (¥550), Hangzhou (¥800), Hong Kong (¥1400), Kunming (¥1300), Nanjing (¥600), Shanghai (¥850) and Shenzhen (¥1100).

BUS

Taiyuan's seriously old-school long-distance **bus station** (长途汽车站, Chángtú Qìchēzhàn; Yingze Dajie, 迎泽大街) is 700m west of the train station on Yingze Dajie. Buses travel to the following destinations:

Beijing ¥160, seven hours, eight daily (6.30am to 8.30pm)

Datong ¥117, 3½ hours, every hour (7am to 7pm)

Shanghai ¥409, 17 hours, 2.30pm

Shijiazhuang ¥65, 3½ hours, half-hourly (6am to 8pm)

Xi'an ¥180, eight hours, six daily (6am to 11am)

Zhengzhou ¥152, seven hours, seven daily (6.30am to 8.30pm)

Buses from the **Jiannan Bus Station** (建南站, Jiànnán Zhàn; Jianshe Nanjie, 建设南路), 3km south of the train station:

Jiexiu ¥36, 2½ hours, half-hourly (7.40am to 6.40pm)

Jincheng ¥104, 4½ hours, half-hourly (7am to 7pm)

Pingyao ¥26, two hours, half-hourly (7.30am to 6pm)

Qixian ¥17, two hours, half-hourly (7.30am to 6.30pm)

The **East Bus Station** (东客站, Dōng Kèzhàn; Wulongkou Jie, 五龙口街) has buses to Wutai Shan (¥90, four to five hours, hourly, 6.45am to 6pm).

The **West Bus Station** (客运西站, Kèyùn Xīzhàn; Xijie, South Inner Ring, 南内环西街) has the following services:

Lishi ¥60, three hours, frequent (7am to 7.30pm)

Qikou ¥70, four hours, one daily (10am)

TRAIN

Sample routes from **Taiyuan train station** (火车站, Huǒchē Zhàn) include the following:

Beijing Normal train seat/sleeper ¥78/136, 10 to 11½ hours, four daily

Beijing West G-class train 1st/2nd class ¥197/315, three to five hours, regular

Datong Hard seat/sleeper ¥44/90, four to 5½ hours, 10 daily

Jincheng Hard seat/sleeper ¥54/100, seven hours, four daily

Pingyao ¥17, 1½ hours, frequent

Wutai Shan ¥38, 3½ to 5½ hours, three daily

High-speed trains depart from the new **Taiyuan South train station** (火车南站, Huǒchē Nán-zhàn), 10km south of the old train station in the Beiying (北营) district. The best way to get there is via taxi (¥20, 25 minutes) or bus 861 from the old station. Services include the following:

Beijing West D-/G-class train ¥155/197, three hours, regular

Xi'an North 2nd/1st class ¥179/286, four hours, regular

Zhengzhou East G-class train 2nd/1st class ¥257/412, four hours, five daily

❶ Getting Around

The Taiyuan metro is currently undergoing construction, with the north–south Line 2 due to open in 2020. The west–east–south Line 1 began construction in 2019.

Bus 1 (¥1) runs the length of Yingze Dajie. For the Jiannan Bus Station, the long-distance bus station and the train station, take bus 23 or 611 (¥1) from Yingze Dajie. For the East Bus Station, take any bus (¥1) heading east from Wulongkou Jie. Bus 70 connects the East Bus Station to the South Train Station. Bus 859 (¥1) links the West Bus Station and the train station along Yingze Dajie. A taxi to Jiannan Bus Station costs ¥13. Taxi flagfall is ¥8.

Pingyao 平遥

📞 0354 / POP 502,000

Pingyao (Píngyáo) is China's best-preserved ancient walled town. If you have any China mileage under your belt you'll appreciate the town's age-old charms. While some 'ancient' cities may rustle together an unconvincing display of old city walls, sporadic temples or the occasional ragged alley thrust beneath apartment blocks, Pingyao has managed to keep its beguiling narrative largely intact: red-lantern–hung lanes set against silhouettes of imposing town walls, ancient towers poking into the north China sky, and an entire brood of creaking temples. In recent years, shops on the main commercial streets have developed a penchant for disco lighting, light-box menus and noise-making costumed jesters. But outside these central areas, the ancient city is little changed.

Pingyao is also a living and breathing community where the 30,000-odd locals who reside in the old town hang laundry in courtyards, career down alleyways on bicycles and sun themselves in doorways.

❍ Sights

If you have even the remotest interest in Chinese history, culture or architecture, you could easily spend a couple of days wandering the pinched lanes of Pingyao, stumbling across hidden gems while ticking off all the

SHANXI PINGYAO

well-known sights. You will always find something new, whether it's an ancient temple or alleyway, or an old courtyard house. It's free to walk the streets, but you must pay ¥125 to climb the city walls or enter any of the 18 buildings deemed historically significant. Tickets are valid for three days and can be purchased from near the gate openings and at other ticket offices near the big sights. Opening hours for sights are 8am to 7pm in summer and 8am to 6pm in winter.

★ Pingyao City Walls   HISTORIC SITE

(城墙, Chéng Qiáng) A good place to start your Pingyao experience is the magnificent city walls; they date from 1370 and are among the most complete in the nation. At 10m high and more than 6km in circumference, they are punctuated by 72 watchtowers, each containing a paragraph from Sun Tzu's *The Art of War*. You can wander around the walls gazing down into the old town.

Rishengchang Financial House Museum   MUSEUM

(日升昌, Rìshēngchāng; 38 Xi Dajie, 西大街38号; ⊙8am-7pm) Not to be missed, this museum began life as a humble dye shop in the late 18th century before its tremendous success as a business saw it transform into China's first draft bank (1823), eventually expanding to 57 branches nationwide.

Confucius Temple   CONFUCIAN SITE

(文庙, Wén Miào; Wenmiao Jie, 文庙街; ⊙8am-7pm) Pingyao's oldest surviving building is **Dacheng Hall** (大成殿, Dàchéng Diàn), dating from 1163. It can be found in the Confucius Temple, a huge complex where bureaucrats-to-be came to take the imperial exams. Within the hall, beneath the roosting pigeons, is the seated sage with his fellow disciples.

Pingyao City Tower   TOWER

(市楼, Shì Lóu; Nan Dajie, 南大街) This is the signature structure standing proud above Pingyao, the tallest building in the old town – snap a photo before passing under it en route to other sites. Sadly, you can no longer climb it for city views.

City God Temple   TAOIST SITE

(城隍庙, Chénghuáng Miào; 51 Chenghuangmiao Jie, 城隍庙街51号; ⊙8am-6pm) Within the venerable halls of this astonishing temple, first raised in the Song dynasty, are some intriguing frescoes, including the hall at the very rear of the temple, the **Qǐn Gōng** (寝宫). Also look out for the two-faced fertility goddess in the **Songsheng Dian** (送生殿) – she is the (ferocious-faced) reincarnation mother, responsible for sending out babies to the world. And don't forget to look up at the roofs of the halls, gorgeously decked out in blue-and-green tiles and roof-ridge ornaments.

Pingyao Festival Palace   HISTORIC BUILDING

(平遥电影宫, Píngyáo Diànyǐng Gōng; 153 Xi Dajie, 西大街153号) An abandoned diesel engine factory is now a cinema-restaurant-souvenir shop complex, and the venue of the **Pingyao International Film Festival** (平遥国际电影节, Píngyáo Guójì Diànyǐng Jié; www.pyiffestival.com/index_en/index.aspx; ⊙Oct). There's an open-air theatre and five auditoriums. The cinema, in a cavernous socialist-era building, is open year-round to entertain the cultured with its thoughtfully curated program of art-house and award-winning mainstream films. The film festival and the palace were founded by celebrated Shanxi director Jia Zhangke (贾樟柯). The compound is quiet outside the film festival (October).

Old Town Cinema   NOTABLE BUILDING

(古城电影院, Gǔchéng Diànyǐngyuàn; Nan Dajie, 南大街) This incongruously socialist-era concrete building houses one of the last operating cinemas from the 1960s in China. The building has recently been restored and the facilities upgraded to include a gallery on the history and culture of Pingyao, and a circular-screen viewing hall. Old Town Cinema sits behind a huge dynastic-style doorway on the east side of Nan Dajie.

Xietongqing Draft Bank   MUSEUM

(协同庆票号, Xiétóngqìng Piàohào; Nan Dajie, 南大街; ⊙8am-7pm) First established in 1856, this former bank had underground vaults protected by live-in guards. After checking out the courtyard displays, descend into the cool (literally) vaults and explore the cave-like rooms filled with stacks of faux gold and silver ingots.

Nine Dragon Screen   MONUMENT

(九龙壁, Jiǔlóng Bì; Chenghuangmiao Jie, 城隍庙街) Located close to the Confucius Temple is this magnificent glazed-tile screen wall featuring reliefs of nine different Chinese dragons. It was originally placed at the entrance of a temple in the early Ming dynasty; it was completely damaged after the Cultural Revolution and subsequently rebuilt. This is one of a handful of Nine Dragon screen walls left in China, and one of two in Shanxi; the other one is in Datong (p389).

Pingyao

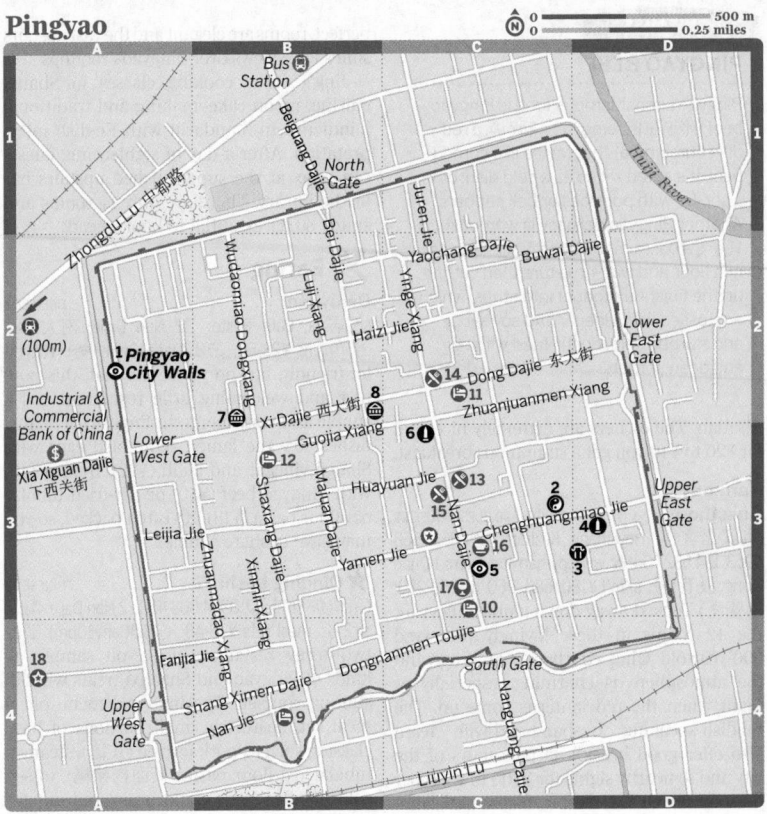

⊨ Sleeping

City Wall Old House
Ji Residence   COURTYARD GUESTHOUSE ¥¥
(平遥城墙老宅冀府, Píngyáo Chéngqiáng Lǎozhái Jìfǔ; ☑ 0354 568 2959; www.citywallcourtyard.com/zh-cn; 16 Luohanmiao Jie, 罗汉庙街16号; r from ¥400) The rooms at this converted courtyard house are quite small, as are the bathrooms, which double up as showers, and the water heaters. On the plus side, it's on a quiet street and the courtyards are relaxing for an evening drink or playing with the cat and Harry the

DON'T MISS

PINGYAO BEEF

Pingyao's most famous food is Pingyao beef (平遥牛肉, píngyáo niúròu), a red-dish cured meat that tastes like corned beef. It's eaten sliced as a cold dish, or in a stir-fry with potatoes or bell peppers. Another Pingyao delicacy is wǎntuōzǐ (碗饦子), a pasta made by steaming plates of a flour and water mixture then cutting up the finished product into strips, which are tossed with vinegar and soy sauce and slurped cold, or stir-fried with egg and bean sprouts.

Alsatian. The owners are extremely nice, and for ¥20 to ¥40 you get a sumptuous breakfast.

Harmony Guesthouse COURTYARD GUESTHOUSE ¥¥

(和义昌客栈, Héyìchāng Kèzhàn; ☑0354 568 4963, 134 5327 0465; www.py-harmony.com; 1 Duan Xiang, 段巷1号; s/tr/f ¥180/580/960, d ¥258-280; ❄@☎) Tucked away down a quiet alleyway, the 42 rooms in these lovingly preserved 300-year-old Qing courtyards are cosy and the atmosphere is charming, especially at night when the red lanterns come on. The English-speaking husband-and-wife team also offer good breakfasts plus tours of the city and to nearby sights for ¥300 to ¥500 per person; as well as ticketing, bike rental, laundry and pick-up.

★ Yide Guesthouse COURTYARD GUESTHOUSE ¥¥¥

(一德客栈, Yídé Kèzhàn; ☑139 0354 7233; 16 Shaxiang Jie, 沙巷街16号; d/tr ¥1050/1280, ste from ¥2980) This impeccable Qing dynasty courtyard house once belonging to a banker and is over 280 years old. Near the entrance, you'll see the original horse tie rings and carriage tracks. There are 26 rooms with kàng (raised platform) beds and two family suites. One suite is the former master bedroom and it is adorned with expensive period furniture.

Jing's Residence COURTYARD HOTEL ¥¥¥

(锦宅, Jǐn Zhái; ☑0354 584 1000; www.jingsresidence.com; 16 Dong Dajie, 东大街16号; r ¥1680, ste ¥2280-2880; ❄@☎) Jing's is a soothing blend of old Pingyao and modern flair that's aimed at sophisticated, upmarket travellers. At 270 years old, the former home of a Qing dynasty silk merchant is sleek and well finished with polished service from the English-speaking staff. The themed courtyards are picture-perfect, rooms are elegant and the vast upstairs suites have views over Pingyao's rooftops.

Jing's offers cooking classes in Shanxi cuisine, moon cake–making and traditional handicraft in Mandarin with English interpretation. After a day of sightseeing, guests can relax at the super-hushed upstairs bar or the library. There are only 14 rooms and suites, so it's essential to book ahead.

✕ Eating

Déjūyuán CHINESE ¥

(德居源, Petit Resto; 82 Nan Dajie, 南大街82号; mains ¥28-50; ☺8.30am-10pm; ☎) Traveller-friendly, but no worse for that, this popular and welcoming little restaurant has a simple and tasty menu (in English) of Shanxi dishes. Try the famed scrambled eggs with Shanxi vinegar and chilli (¥22), fried potato with Pingyao beef (¥50) or stir-fried tubular oat-flour pasta (¥18). It's often packed, so you may have to share a table.

★ Qīnqíng Lúshí Pù CHINESE ¥¥

(亲情炉食铺; ☑0354 568 4111; 2 Nan Dajie, 南大街2号; meal sets ¥38-48; ☺8.30am-10pm) This two-storey restaurant lets you sample all kinds of Pingyao and Shaanxi treats without stuffing yourself. The bilingual menu offers meal sets featuring small portions of local classics, such as pork terrine (皮冻), steamed tubular oat-flour pasta (莜面栲栳栳), tossed cold noodles (碗脱), and grain and nut tea (油茶). It's near the junction between Nan Dajie (南大街) and Xi Dajie (西大街).

Tianyuankui CHINESE ¥¥

(天元奎, Tiānyuánkuí; ☑0354 568 0069; 73 Nan Dajie, 南大街73号; main dishes from ¥28; ☺7.30am-10pm; ☎) With wooden furnishings and helpful staff, this huge restaurant spanning three dining spaces in a courtyard house has a loud and jolly vibe. The iPad English menu has photos of the dishes, making ordering a snap. There's an overwhelming variety of Shaanxi and other favourites, from Cantonese-style blanched greens to Pingyao beef and spicy Sichuan stir-fries.

🍷 Drinking & Nightlife

Cozy Bar BAR

(165 Nan Dajie, 南大街165号; ☺5pm-midnight) This friendly bar owards the south end of Nan Dajie is a good choice, with an English-speaking owner and comfy sofas. The atmosphere is relaxing; this is one of very few bars around without flashing lights and loud music.

Chichi Coffee
CAFE

(池池咖啡馆, Chíchí Kāfēiguǎn; 8 Chenghuang-miao Jie, 城隍庙街8号; coffee from ¥25, cakes ¥28, alcohol from ¥35; ⊙11am-9pm; 🐾) Behind its green doors is a cute-as-piecafe serving some of Pingyao's best espresso, lattes and single-origin brews in a warm setting lined with bookshelves and cosy seats. Come night-time, swap caffeine for simple cocktails and start a conversation with the Fujianese owner Shrew. There are rooms too – they're not at this address, but Shrew can take you there.

☆ Entertainment

Yòujiàn Píngyáo
THEATRE

(又见平遥; 154 Shuncheng Lu, 顺城路154号; tickets from ¥238; ⊙2pm & 7pm Tue-Sun) Ninety minutes of immersive, interactive theatre featuring extravagant sets and mind-blowing visual effects will transport you to ancient Pingyao. The audience walks from set to set to experience the performances before settling down for the finale. The story is about the trials and tribulations of a banking family and the city of Pingyao. The theatre is 100m west of the west city walls.

ⓘ Information

Industrial & Commercial Bank of China
(ICBC, 工商银行, Gōngshāng Yínháng; Xia Xiguan Dajie, 下西关大街) ATM.

Public Security Bureau (PSB, 公安局, Gōng'ānjú; ☑0354 563 5010; off Yamen Jie, 衙门街; ⊙8am-noon & 3-6pm Mon-Fri)

ⓘ Getting There & Away

BUS

Pingyao's **bus station** (汽车新站, Qìchēxīnzhàn; ☑0354 569 0011; Zhongdu Dongjie, 中都东街) has buses to Taiyuan (¥25, two hours, frequent, 6.15am to 8pm), Lishi (¥36, three hours, 7am and 12.30pm), Changzhi (¥58, four hours, 7.50am) and the Qiao Family Courtyard (¥15, 45 minutes, half-hourly).

TRAIN

Pingyao has two train stations: the older **Pingyao Train Station** (平遥站, Píngyáo Zhàn) just north of the city walls, and the new **Pingyao Gucheng Train Station** (平遥古城站, Píngyáo Gǔchéng Zhàn) further away to the south; the latter mainly services high-speed trains. Check to see which station your train is pulling in at.

Tickets for trains (especially to Xi'an) are tough to get in summer, so book ahead. Your hotel/hostel should be able to help. Trains depart for the following destinations:

Beijing D-class train 1st/2nd class ¥294/183, 4½ hours, two daily

Beijing G-class train 1st/2nd class ¥362/226, four hours, one daily

Datong Hard seat/sleeper ¥61/122, six to 7½ hours, four daily

Taiyuan ¥15, 1½ hours, frequent

Taiyuan South D-class train 1st/2nd class ¥46/29, 50 minutes, 22 daily

Xi'an D-class train 1st/2nd class ¥240/150, three hours, seven daily

ⓘ Getting Around

Many hotels and hostels arrange pick-up from the train station, so check up front.

Pingyao can be easily navigated on foot or bicycle (¥10 to ¥15 per day). Bike rental is available all over; most guesthouses offer it and there are many spots along Nan Dajie and Xi Dajie.

From Pingyao Gucheng Train Station, take bus 108 (¥1) to the old town. The old town is only 2.25 sq km; you can get around by walking or hopping on the official tour bus for ¥10 a trip.

A rickshaw will run from Pingyao Train Station and the bus station to the old town for ¥10. A taxi from Pingyao Gucheng Train Station to the old town costs ¥30. Note that taxis are not allowed to enter the old town (for traffic control), so you will be dropped outside the gates of the city wall.

Around Pingyao

★ Shuanglin Temple
BUDDHIST SITE

(双林寺, Shuānglín Sì; ¥40; ⊙8.30am-6.30pm) This fascinating Buddhist temple houses many incredibly rare, sublimely carved Tang, Song and Yuan painted statues. Rebuilt in 1571, it's a mesmerising complex of ancient halls: the interiors of the **Sakyamuni Hall** and flanking buildings are exquisite. The beauty is overwhelming, not just of the painted clay sculptures, which are among the best in China, but also in the backgrounds – the grotto-like niches behind the statues, and the clouds and waves on the relief pieces.

The **Four Heavenly Kings** in the first hall date from the Tang dynasty, and if you go round to the back of that hall, you'll see a stunning relief mural featuring the goddess Guanyin riding a mythical beast, her ladies-in-waiting and guardians on intricately carved clouds of faded green on either side. The **Thousand Buddha Hall** contains a wondrous 1000-arm Guanyin holding different implements in her many hands, while dark-faced Buddha statues hide within the main worship hall. Guanyin is portrayed sitting *lalitasana* (a very lithe and relaxed regal posture) in another hall, while in the **Luohan Hall**, one of the ancient *luóhàn* (arhat) is depicted boozing. In the **Hall of Ksitigarbha**, judges and hell guardians mete out punishment like mutilation and burning.

You can also go up and walk along the wall around the temple. A rickshaw or taxi from town will cost ¥60 return, or you could cycle the 7km here.

Mian Shan
MOUNTAIN

(绵山; incl bus ¥160) With vertiginous and dizzying cliffs alongside a deep gorge, this astonishing mountain area is a splendid day trip from Pingyao. Lined with precariously perched temple architecture, scenic gully walks and breathtaking views, the road snaking around the mountain is an undemanding hike, with buses linking the main sights. From the bus drop-off, it's a short walk to **Dragon Head Temple** (龙头寺, Lóngtóu Sì), from where a long, flat road links to the **Shuǐtāogōu Scenic Area** (水涛沟景区, Shuǐtāogōu Jǐngqū), a few hours' walk away.

Take a train (¥9 to ¥11, 30 minutes, regular) to Jiexiu (介休) from Pingyao train station or take a bus (¥12, one hour) from Pingyao bus station to Jiexiu bus station. Buses (¥11) to Mian Shan leave from in front of the train station, around 300m east along Xinjian Xilu (新建西路) from the long-distance bus station in Jiexiu. Booking a car from Pingyao will cost around ¥350 for the return trip; this can be arranged at hotels.

Qikou
碛口

🎵 0358 / POP 29,000

Separated from neighbouring Shaanxi (Shǎnxī) province by the fast-flowing Yellow River (黄河, Huáng Hé), this tiny Ming River port found prosperity during its Qing heyday when hundreds of merchants lived here, only to lose it when the Japanese army arrived in 1938. Qikou (碛口, Qìkǒu) is well worth visiting for its evocative stone courtyards and cobbled pathways. All wind their way, eventually, up to the Black Dragon Temple, which overlooks the town.

While it's some of its charm due to recent construction, considerable appeal survives. The streets behind the riverfront path are littered with shops selling Shanxi vinegar and old-fashioned bakeries selling delicious buns with date or brown-sugar paste. There's even a Qing dynasty bodyguard agency (镖局, *biāojú*) catering to merchants who were

transferring large amounts of money and other valuables from town to town.

🅞 Sights

Lijia Shan
CAVE

(李家山) This supremely peaceful 550-year-old village, hugging a hillside with terraces of crops running up it, has hundreds of **cave dwellings** (窑洞, *yáodòng*) scaling 11 levels. Once home to more than 600 families, most with the family name Li, today's population is much depleted at around 45. Some stone paths and stairways that twist up the hill date from Ming times; note the rings on some walls that horses were tied to and the ornate stone, brick and wood carvings.

The cave structures look similar at a glance, with red dates and bushels of corn hung out to dry beside the doors, but in fact there are three villages here: **West** (西财主, Xī Cáizhǔ), **East** (东财主, Dōng Cáizhǔ) and the **Chen's** (陈家湾, Chénjiā Wān). The larger West Village has a plain gate but spacious courtyards; East Village has tiny courtyards and a beautiful gate with a metal door knocker (in the past men coming home late at night would knock instead of calling for their wives and giving mischievous mountain spirits ideas). East Village faces terraced fields, and if you follow the path down a little further and look to the left, you see an isolated cluster of homes belonging to the Chen's who were the only inhabitants here before the Li's moved in.

The village is very popular with artists who have come to walk in the footsteps of the late Chinese painter Wu Guanzhong, a pioneer in modern Chinese painting who found inspiration here. The surrounding countryside offers ample opportunities for hikes and there are **homestays** (¥60 including two meals). Accommodation is basic; you'll have to use the public toilets and they are rough.

The village is 3km south of Qikou. To get here, cross the bridge by Qikou's bus stop and follow the river for about 30 minutes until you see a blue sign indicating Lijia Shan. Walk on for about 100m and then take the road up the hill for another 30 minutes and you'll reach the old village. Local cars do a return run for around ¥50 to ¥60.

🛏 Sleeping & Eating

Some locals offer clean beds (with an outhouse) for around ¥60; look for the characters 住宿 (*zhùsù*, accommodation) or 有房 (*yǒufáng*, rooms available). For something more comfortable, with views onto the Yellow River, **Xiángyuánlóng Kèzhàn** (祥元隆客栈; ☑ 0358 458 6666; Yánhuáng Gōnglù, 沿黄公路; r from ¥498) and **Qìkǒu Kèzhàn** (碛口客栈; ☑ 0358 446 6188; Yánhuáng Gōnglù, 沿黄公路; d/tw/tr ¥208/238/388; @) are good choices among the half-dozen guesthouses on Yanhuang Gonglu (沿黄公路).

Restaurants and noodle places line the road leading from the bus station towards **Qìkǒu Kèzhàn**, offering simple dishes from around ¥10 to ¥30. For something tastier and more substantial, head to restaurants by the Yellow River for country cuisine (农家菜, nóngjiā cài). **Mínjiān Càiguǎn** (民间菜馆; ☑ 187 3583 7168; Yánhuáng Gōnglù, 沿黄公路; mains ¥15-158; ⊗ 9am-9.30pm) is a great option.

🛈 Getting There & Around

One bus runs from the West Bus Station in Taiyuan to Qikou (¥70, four hours, 10am). If you miss it, or are coming from Pingyao, you will have to go through nearby Lishi (离石).

Regular buses go from Taiyuan to Lishi (¥60, three hours, frequent, 7am to 7.30pm). There are two daily buses from Pingyao (¥36, three hours, 7am and 12.30pm). From Lishi's long-distance bus station (长途汽车站, chángtú qìchēzhàn), take bus 104 (¥1, 25 minutes) to the Jinian Bei (纪念碑) crossroads where buses to Qikou (¥20, 1½ hours, 7am to 7pm) depart.

There's one daily bus from Qikou to Taiyuan (¥80), but it leaves very early at 5.30am. There are hourly buses to Lishi from Qikou until around 4pm. From Lishi, there are many buses back to Taiyuan (¥70, 7am to 8pm), two to Pingyao (¥45, 8am and 1.40pm) and one to Xi'an (¥183, eight hours, 11.30am).

Transport options are limited in Qikou. Locals will offer to take you to nearby places within two hours' travel time for about ¥50 per one to two people.

Jincheng 晋城

☑ 0356 / POP 500,000

Jincheng (Jìnchéng) has a top-notch museum, a couple of important temples and few other sights, but the surrounding countryside conceals a rich vein of impressive ancient architecture. This small, little-visited city is an ideal launch pad for a historical adventure into Shanxi's southeast.

The area has historically been of strategic military importance and was a site of vibrant commerce and great wealth. It was already known as a town of coal and steel during the Warring States period (475–221 BC). By the Ming and Qing dynasties, Jincheng had become an economic and cultural hub, attracting travelling traders and migrants. Today this glorious past translates into magnificent fort-like settlements, sumptuous official residences, opulent merchant mansions, and ancient temples with some of China's most precious religious art.

All this makes Jincheng an incredibly rewarding stop, particularly if you are continuing south into Henan.

👁 Sights

Jincheng Museum　　　　MUSEUM
(晋城博物馆, Jinchéng Bówùguǎn; ☑ 0356 696 5135; 1263 Fengtai Dongjie, 凤台东街1263号; ⊗ 9am-5pm Tue-Sun; 🚍 4, 5, 13, 19) FREE This remarkable museum gives fascinating context to the fort-like settlements, ancient temples, and vernacular housing around Jincheng. Using fine replicas, 'Ancient Architecture Art of Jincheng' illuminates the raison d'etre of important structures like Old Qinglian Temple. Don't miss the exceptional 28 Lunar Mansions of the Jade Emperor Temple – get your fill of information here as explanations are brief and photos are not allowed.

⭐ **Jade Emperor Temple**　　TAOIST TEMPLE
(府城玉皇庙, Fǔchéng Yùhuáng Miào; ¥10; ⊗ 8am-5.30pm) This picturesque temple littered with Taoist deities is an enjoyable place to visit by any measure. But what makes it exceptional are the painted sculptures of the 28 lunar mansions masterfully personified as scholars and nobility in pensive and playful poses; they're some of China's very best Taoist painted sculptures. You'll find them in the western chamber – on your right as you leave the Jade Emperor Hall. If the door is locked, ask the guard to open it for you.

Qinglian Temples　　　BUDDHIST TEMPLE
(青莲寺, Qīnglián Sì; both temples ¥20; ⊗ 8am-5.30pm) This pair of Green Lotus Temples are among China's oldest in Pure Land Buddhism. They're celebrated for their gorgeous Tang and Song dynasty painted sculptures, some of which, unfortunately, you have to ogle behind glass. The 'young' temple, founded by a monk 1600 years ago, has a beautiful courtyard, 1000-year-old gingko trees and wooden structures all around – nothing grandiose, but poised and elegant. The older temple has a Ming dynasty Tibetan stupa and a main hall with rare painted sculptures.

🛏 Sleeping & Eating

Mehood Theatre Hotel HOTEL ¥¥
(美豪酒店, Měiháo Jiǔdiàn; ☎0356 256 1888; www.mehoodhotels.com; 1888 Zezhou Rd, 泽州路 1888 号; r from ¥220) This new hotel stands out from the rest on this street with its young, design-oriented vibe and attentive service. The rooms are not very big but are pleasant, with spacious beds and a bright palette. There's not much nightlife in Jincheng, so you may also appreciate the massive flat-screen TV.

⭐ **Jia Jin Yang Hele Noodles** NOODLES ¥
(贾晋阳饸饹馆, Jiǎ Jìn Yáng Héle Guǎn; ☎159 0356 6930; 363 Shangnian St, 上辇街363; noodles ¥9-12; ◉11am-2pm & 5-9pm) A tiny shop with rustic decor run by a friendly couple, the noodles here – al dente and delicious – come in clear broth (清汤, qīng tāng) or with pumpkin (金瓜, jīn guā), preserved vegetables (酸菜, suān cài) or braised pork (炖肉, dùn ròu). For ¥5 you get a salad of various types of tofu: strips, hard, scrunched up sheets, you name it.

ℹ Information

On Wenchang Dongjie (文昌东街) you can find a branch of the Bank of China with an ATM (there are many more around town).

ℹ Getting There & Around

Buses depart from the East Bus Station (客运东站, Kèyùn Dōngzhàn). Destinations include the following:

Luoyang ¥50, every 1½ hours, three daily (7.40am to 5.30pm)

Pingyao ¥110, five hours, three daily (7am, 8am and 9.30am)

Taiyuan ¥115, four hours, hourly (6.30am to 6.30pm)

Xi'an ¥180, seven hours, three daily (8.30am, 10.30am and 3.30pm)

Zhengzhou ¥65, 1½ hours, half-hourly (6.15am to 7.30pm)

The few trains that pass Jincheng head to Taiyuan (hard seat/sleeper ¥54/100, seven to eight hours and four daily), Zhengzhou (¥33, 3½ hours, one daily) and there's a handy overnight to Datong (hard sleeper ¥163, 11 hours, 9.59pm).

Buses 2, 3 and 5 (¥1) connect the train station with the East Bus Station. Bus 30 from the train station travels along the main road, Wenchang Dongjie (文昌东街). Taxi flagfall is ¥5.

Guoyu 郭峪古城

The atmospheric walled village of Guoyu (Guōyù Gǔchéng) is the highlight of a trip to this part of Shanxi. Although there's now an entrance fee (¥35), there's little tourist paraphernalia; just the genuine charm of a historic and still inhabited Ming dynasty settlement. The crumbling remains of this one-time fort's south gate and some of its old walls still stand sentry at the entrance to the village close to the road. Walk 200m and it's as if you've stepped back in time. Narrow alleys and stone streets run past courtyard houses, where the locals sit and chatter in their native dialect.

Guoyu's oldest building is **Tāngdì Miào** (汤帝庙), a 600-year-old Taoist temple. It's well preserved with nine rooms and an operatic stage; the latter has Cultural Revolution–era paintings with slogans exhorting the locals to work harder. In the room on the left of the main worship hall (where you'll find a few disconcertingly life-like statues of deities), there are also Communist propaganda slogans on the walls. The temple was a government building during the Cultural Revolution. It's also worth looking inside the former courtyard residence of Minister Chen's grandfather at **1 Jingyang Beilu** (景阳北路1号). Admission is included with the village entrance.

To get here, catch one of the frequent buses headed to Prime Minister Chen's Castle (¥15, 1½ hours, 6.30am to 6pm) from Jincheng's East Station. Guoyu is a 10-minute walk south of the castle. Return transport is scarce, so it's best to take a minibus to the small town of Beiliu (北留; ¥5, 15 minutes), then catch an ordinary bus back to Jincheng (¥12).

⭐ **Prime Minister Chen's Castle** CASTLE
(皇城相府, Huángchéng Xiàngfǔ; ¥120; ◉8am-6pm) This well-preserved, magnificent Ming dynasty castle is the former residence of Chen Tingjing, prime minister under Emperor Kangxi in the late 17th century, and coauthor of China's most famous dictionary. The Chen family rose to prominence as senior officials in the 16th century and the castle walls were originally constructed to keep revolting peasants out. While it may have some tourist trappings today, it remains a riveting maze of battlements, courtyards, gardens and stone archways.

Bus 803 (¥12) runs to the ticket office from Jincheng's East Bus Station every 15 minutes between 6.30am and 6.30pm; the last bus back to Jincheng departs at 5pm or 5.30pm. If there isn't a minibus back to Jincheng, minibuses zip to the small town of Beiliu (北留; ¥5, 15 minutes), where you can catch an ordinary bus back to Jincheng (¥12).

Shaanxi

POP 37.3 MILLION

Best Places to Eat

➜ Sānjiěmèi Jiǎozi (p414)

➜ Hǎiróng Guōtiēdiàn (p414)

➜ Muslim Family Restaurant (p415)

➜ Mǎ Hóng Xiǎochǎo Pàomóguǎn (p414)

Best Places to Stay

➜ Han Tang House (p413)

➜ Han Tang Inn (p413)

➜ Hua Shan Guesthouse (p423)

Why Go?

Shaanxi (陕西; Shǎnxī) is where it all began for China. As the heartland of the Qin dynasty (秦朝), whose warrior emperor united much of China for the first time, Shaanxi was the cradle of Chinese civilisation and the fountainhead of Han culture. Xi'an marked the beginning and end of the Silk Road and was a buzzing capital long before anyone knew of Beijing and its Forbidden City.

Shaanxi's archaeological sites make it an essential destination. Around Xi'an there's an excavated Neolithic village and royal graves, including the tomb of Qin Shi Huang and his Army of Terracotta Warriors, one of the world's foremost heritage sites. The city of Xi'an is also an emergent travellers' hub, with hotels, restaurants, museums, ancient pagodas, and a marvellous city wall and Muslim Quarter.

Rural areas contain fascinating villages barely touched by modernity as well as mountains that once sheltered hermits and sages.

When to Go
Xian

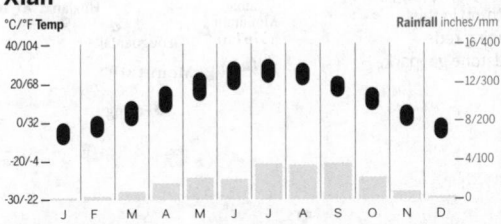

Apr & May Spring breezes and the ideal time to climb Hua Shan.

Sep & Oct The rain's stopped and it's still warm, so hit Xi'an's sights.

Dec Avoid the crowds and maybe get the Terracotta Warriors all to yourself.

Shaanxi Highlights

1 Army of Terracotta Warriors (p418) Gazing down onto the timeless guardians protecting an ancient Qin emperor in the afterlife.

2 Xi'an (p409) Admiring Xi'an's Tang dynasty Big Goose Pagoda, its Muslim Quarter and its glorious old city walls.

3 Hua Shan (p421) Watching the sun rise over the Qinling Mountains from atop Taoism's sacred and dramatic western peak.

4 Hancheng (p423) Exploring this old town with its quaint quarter of buildings dating from the Yuan, Ming and Qing eras.

5 Tomb of Emperor Jingdi (p420) Taking a different look at China's past by perusing these eye-opening excavations.

6 Jingbian Wave Valley (p424) Searching for the most eye-popping photo-op in this stunning red-sandstone geopark.

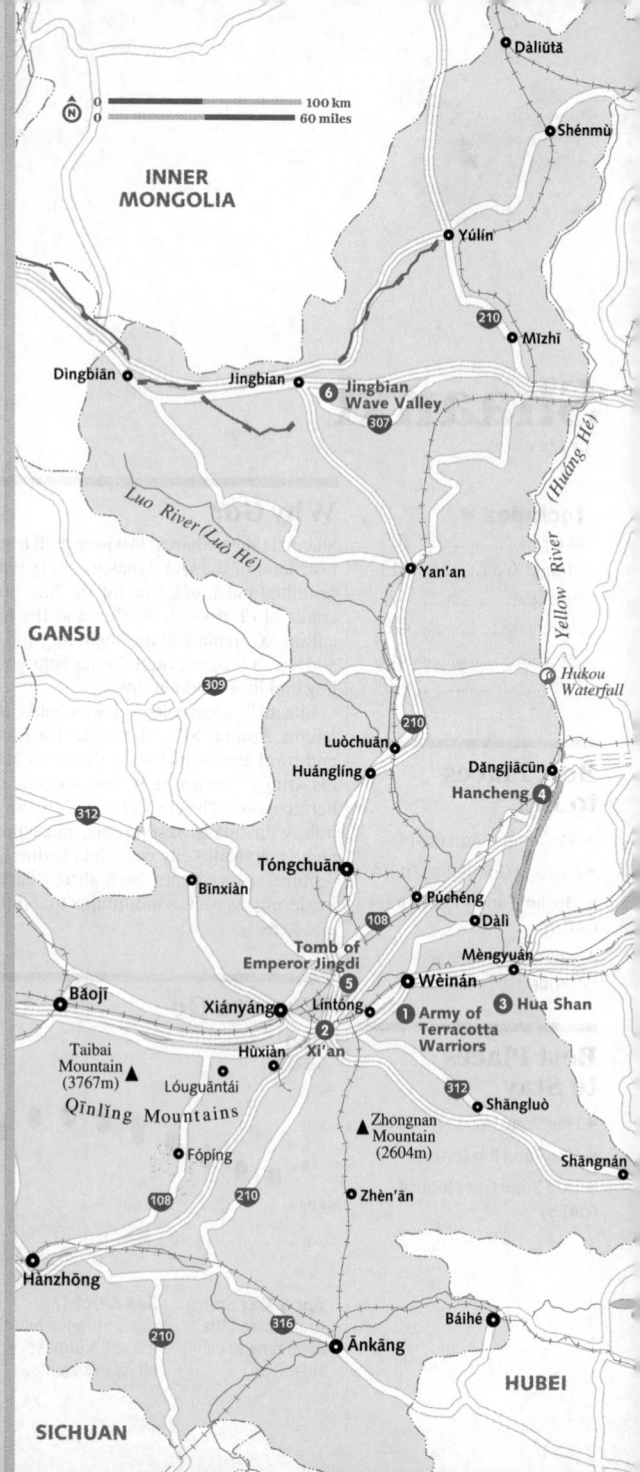

History

Around 3000 years ago, the Zhou people of the Bronze Age moved out of their Shaanxi homeland, conquered the Shang and became dominant in much of northern China. Later the state of Qin, ruling from its capital Xian-yang (near modern-day Xi'an), became the first dynasty to unify much of China. Subsequent dynasties, including the Han, Sui and Tang, were based in Xi'an, then known as Chang'an, which was abandoned for the eastern capital of Luoyang (in Henan) whenever invaders threatened.

Shaanxi remained the political heart of China until the 10th century. However, when the imperial court shifted eastward, the province's fortunes began to decline. Rebellions and famine were followed in 1556 by the deadliest earthquake in history, when an estimated 830,000 people died (the unusually high death toll was attributed to the fact that millions were living in cave homes, which easily collapsed in the quake). The extreme poverty of the region ensured that it was an early stronghold of the CCP (Chinese Communist Party).

Language

Locals like to joke that Xi'an's dialect is the 'real' standard Mandarin – after all, the city was one of the ancient capitals of China. More pedantic linguists, however, prefer to classify the Shaanxi dialect as part of the central Zhongyuan Mandarin group. Generally speaking, the Mandarin spoken in and around Xi'an is pretty clear to students of the language. The Jin Chinese dialect is also spoken in some parts of the province.

Xi'an 西安

029 / POP 5.9 MILLION

Once the terminus of the Silk Road and a melting pot of cultures and religions, as well as home to emperors, courtesans, poets, monks, merchants and warriors, the glory days of Xi'an (Xī'ān; pronounced 'see-an') may have ended in the early 10th century, but a considerable amount of ancient Chang'an, the former city, survives behind the often roaring, modern city. Xi'an's Ming-era city walls remain intact, vendors of all descriptions still crowd the narrow lanes of the warren-like Muslim Quarter, and there are enough places of interest to keep even the most amateur historian riveted.

Most people only spend two or three days in Xi'an; dynastic enthusiasts could easily stay busy for a week. Must-sees include the Army of Terracotta Warriors, the Tomb of Emperor Jingdi, the Xi'an City Walls and the Muslim Quarter, but try to set aside time for its pagodas and museums, plus a side trip to nearby Hua Shan (p421).

Sights

Inside the City Walls

Xi'an City Walls HISTORIC SITE
(西安城墙, Xī'ān Chéngqiáng; ¥54; 8am-8.30pm Apr-Oct, to 7pm Nov-Mar) Xi'an is one of the few cities in China where the imposing old city walls still stand. Built in 1370 during the Ming dynasty, the magnificent 12m-high walls are surrounded by a dry moat and form a rectangle with a perimeter of 14km. Most sections have been restored or rebuilt, and it is possible to walk the walls in their entirety in a leisurely four hours (or around two hours by bike, or at a slow jog).

You can cycle from the South, North, West and East gates, with rental costing ¥45 for 100 minutes (¥200 deposit), while the truly lazy can be whisked around in a golf cart for ¥200. Access ramps are located inside the major gates, with the exception of the South Gate, where the entrance is outside the walls; there's another entrance inside the walls beside the Forest of Stelae Museum (p412). En route, you get to look out over modern-day Xi'an. From this vantage point it's clear that the city is a hotchpotch of the old and new, with the new vastly in the ascendancy. Every

SHAANXI XI'AN

SHAANXI

Xi'an

1 km
0.5 miles

West Station (4.3km)
Daqing Lu
Yuxiangmen

Xiguan Zhengjie
Airport Shuttle (1.2km)

Huancheng Xilu 环城西路

West Gate

1 Xi'an City Walls
6

Huancheng Beilu

Lianhu Lu
Xi Qilu
Lianhu Park
19
7

Qianwei Jie
Sajinqiao
Damashi Jie 大差市街
Qiaozi Kou 桥梓口

Beiguangji Jie
Xiyang Shi
Xi Dajie 西大街
24 Folk House 5
17
Nanyuanmen

Shuncheng Nanlu Xiduan 顺城南路西段
Little Goose Pagoda (1.2km); Tang Dynasty (2km);
Shaanxi History Museum (3km); Xi'an Museum (3km)

North Gate
Anyuanmen 安远门
Bei Da Jie M
Bei Dajie 北大街
Dapi Yuan
Beiyuanmen
13 20
3
18
Defu Xiang 得福巷

Xi'an Central Hospital
Xi Wulu 西五路
Huangcheng Xilu
Houzaimen
Beixin Jie 北新街

Xi Xinjie
Nanchang Xiang 南长巷
11
10
Bank of China
Zhonglou M 钟楼站
Nan Dajie 南大街
9 $ ATM
2 $
22
12 21
Advance Train Ticket Booth
South Gate
Yongningmen 永宁门

Shangde Lu
Shangqin Lu
Dong Xinjie
16
Naxin Jie 南新街
Dongmutou Shi
Shuyuan Xiang 书院巷
4
Duanlümen

Train Station 火车站
Long-Distance Bus Station
Longhai Hotel
Airport Shuttle Bus
Wulukou
Geming Park
Train Ticket Booth
Xi Balu

Jiefang Lu 解放路
Liberation Lu

Dong Balu
Dong Qilu
Dong Liulu
Dong Wulu
Dong Silu
Dong Sanlu
Dong Erlu
23

Huancheng Donglu

Lianbang Dental
Changle Lu
Chaoyangmen
8

East Station (2.7km)
Yongle Lu

Zhongshan Gate

East Gate

Shanglian Lu
Dong Yilu
Dong Dajie 东大街
15
Juhuayuan Lu 菊花园路
Dong Dajie
Dachaishi

Heping Lu 和平路
Heping Men

Shaanxi Grand Opera House (550m)

Xi'an

now and then a slice of old Xi'an, such as Guangren Temple (p412), appears and you are rewarded with a bird's-eye view.

To get an idea of Xi'an's former grandeur, consider this: the Tang city walls originally enclosed 83 sq km, an area seven times larger than today's city centre.

Buses 4, 15 and 201 reach the West Gate; buses 9, 26 and 37 and Line 2 of the metro reach the North Gate; buses 11, 16 and 23 and Line 2 of the underground can get you to the South Gate; and buses 8, 22 and 33 go to the East Gate.

Muslim Quarter   HISTORIC SITE
(回族区; M Zhonglou) The backstreets leading north from the Drum Tower have been home to the city's Hui community (non-Uyghur Chinese Muslims) for centuries, perhaps as far back as the Ming dynasty or further still. The narrow lanes are full of butcher shops, sesame-oil factories, smaller mosques hidden behind enormous wooden doors, men in white skullcaps and women with their heads covered in coloured scarves. It's a great place to wander and is especially atmospheric at night.

Great Mosque   MOSQUE
(清真大寺, Qīngzhēn Dàsì; Huajue Xiang, 化觉巷; Mar-Nov ¥25, Dec-Feb ¥15, Muslims free; ⊙8am-9pm Mar-Nov, to 5.30pm Dec-Feb; M Zhonglou) Bigger than many temples in China, the Great Mosque is a gorgeous blend of Chinese and Islamic architecture and one of the most fas-

cinating sacred sites in the land. The present buildings are mostly Ming and Qing, though the mosque was founded in the 8th century. Arab influences extend from the central minaret (cleverly disguised as a stumpy pagoda) to the enormous turquoise-roofed Prayer Hall (not open to visitors) at the back of the complex, dating from the Ming dynasty.

Bell Tower   HISTORIC SITE
(钟楼, Zhōng Lóu; ¥35, combined Drum Tower ticket ¥50; ⊙8.30am-8.30pm Mar-Oct, to 5.30pm Nov-Feb, last admission 30min before close; M Zhonglou) Occupying a central place at the frantic bullseye intersection of Xi Dajie, Dong Dajie, Bei Dajie and Nan Dajie, the domineering form of the Bell Tower originally housed a huge bell that was rung sonorously at dawn. Initially standing two blocks to the west, it dates from the 14th century and was rebuilt in the 1700s. Musical performances are held inside from 9am to 11.30am and 2.30pm to 5.30pm. It is entered through the underpass on the north side.

Drum Tower   HISTORIC SITE
(鼓楼, Gǔ Lóu; Beiyuanmen; ¥35, combined Bell Tower ticket ¥50; ⊙8.30am-9.30pm Mar-Oct, to 6.30pm Nov-Feb, last admission 30min before close; M Zhonglou) While the Bell Tower originally held a bell that was rung at dawn, the Drum Tower, standing at the foot of the smoky and uproarious street of Beiyuanmen, marked nightfall. It similarly dates from the 14th century and was rebuilt in the 1700s. Musical performances are

held inside from 9am to 11.30am and 2.30pm to 5.30pm. Close by, a **covered market** sells all manner of haggle-worthy goods for souvenirs and gift-giving, leading to the magnificent Great Mosque.

Guangren Temple
BUDDHIST TEMPLE

(广仁寺, Guǎngrén Sì; Guangren Si Lu, 广仁寺路; ◎8am-5.30pm; M Sajinqiao or Yuxiangmen) FREE The sole Tibetan Buddhist temple in the entire province, Guangren Temple dates from the early 18th century, but was largely rebuilt in the 20th century. As a sacred Tibetan Buddhist place of worship, the temple hums with mystery and spiritual energy. Perhaps the most valuable object in the temple resides in the final hall, a golden representation of Sakyamuni that rests upon a Tang dynasty pedestal. There is only one other like it, housed at the Jokhang Temple in Lhasa.

Forest of Stelae Museum
MUSEUM

(碑林博物馆, Bēilín Bówùguǎn; www.beilin-museum.com; 15 Sanxue Jie, 三学街15号; Mar-Nov ¥75, Dec-Feb ¥50; ◎8am-6.45pm Mar-Nov, to 5.45pm Dec-Feb, last admission 45min before close; M Yongningmen) Housed in Xi'an's Confucius Temple, this museum holds more than 1000 stone stelae (inscribed tablets), including the nine Confucian classics and some exemplary calligraphy. The highlight is the fantastic sculpture gallery (across from the gift shop), where animal guardians from the Tang dynasty, pictorial tomb stones and Buddhist statuary muster together. To reach the museum, follow Shuyuan Xiang east from the South Gate.

◉ Outside the City Walls

★Big Goose Pagoda
BUDDHIST PAGODA

(大雁塔, Dàyàn Tǎ; Yanta Nanlu, 雁塔南路; grounds/pagoda ¥40/25; ◎8.30am-5pm; M Dayanta) This seven-storey pagoda, Xi'an's most famous landmark, 4km southeast of the South Gate and formerly within the old (and huge) Tang dynasty city wall, dominates the surrounding modern buildings. One of China's best examples of a Tang-style pagoda (squarish rather than round), it was completed in AD 652 to house Buddhist sutras brought back from India by the monk Xuan Zang. His travels inspired one of the best-known works of Chinese literature, *Journey to the West*.

Xi'an Museum
MUSEUM

(西安博物馆, Xī'ān Bówùguǎn; ☑029 8780 3591; www.xabwy.com; 72 Youyi Xilu, 友谊西路72号; ◎9am-5.30pm Wed-Mon; M Nanshaomen) FREE

Housed in the pleasant grounds of the **Jianfu Temple** is this museum featuring relics unearthed in Xi'an over the years. There are some exquisite ceramics from the Han dynasty, as well as figurines, an exhibition of Ming-dynasty seals and jade artefacts. Don't miss the basement, where a large-scale model of ancient Xi'an gives a good sense of the place in its former pomp and glory.

Jianfu Temple was originally built in AD 684 to bless the afterlife of the late Emperor Gaozong. Also in the grounds is the **Little Goose Pagoda** (小雁塔, Xiǎoyàn Tǎ; grounds free, pagoda ¥30; ◎8.30am-7pm Wed-Mon). The top of the pagoda was shaken off by an earthquake in the middle of the 16th century, but the rest of the 43m-high structure is intact. The pagoda, a rather delicate building of 15 progressively smaller tiers, was built from AD 707 to 709 and housed Buddhist scriptures brought back from India by the pilgrim Yi Jing. Admission to the grounds is free, but climbing up the pagoda requires a ¥30 ticket.

Shaanxi History Museum
MUSEUM

(陕西历史博物馆, Shǎnxī Lìshǐ Bówùguǎn; www.sxhm.com; 91 Xiaozhai Donglu, 小寨东路91号; ◎8.30am-6pm Tue-Sun Apr-Oct, last admission 4.30pm, 9.30am-5pm Tue-Sun Nov-Mar, last admission 4pm; M Xiaozhai) FREE This museum naturally overlaps with Xi'an's surrounding sights but makes for a comprehensive stroll through ancient Chang'an. Most exhibits offer illuminating explanations in English. Don't miss the four original terracotta warrior statues on the ground floor. Go early and expect to queue for at least 30 minutes. In the Sui and Tang section, unique murals depict a polo match, and you'll find a series of painted pottery figurines with elaborate hairstyles and dress, including several bearded foreigners, musicians and braying camels.

Temple of the Eight Immortals
TAOIST SITE

(八仙庵, Bāxiān Ān; Yongle Lu, 永乐路; ¥3; ◎7.30am-5.30pm Mar-Nov, 8am-5pm Dec-Feb; M Chaoyangmen) Xi'an's largest Taoist temple dates from the Song dynasty and is still an active place of worship. Supposedly built on the site of an ancient wine shop, it was constructed to protect against subterranean divine thunder. Scenes from Taoist mythology are painted around the courtyard. Empress Cixi, the mother of the last emperor, stayed here in 1901 after fleeing Beijing during the Boxer Rebellion. The small antique market (p416) opposite is busiest on Sunday and Wednesday.

SHAANXI XI'AN

Tours

One-day tours allow you to see all the sights around Xi'an more quickly and conveniently than if you arranged one yourself. Itineraries differ somewhat, but there are two basic tours: an Eastern Tour and a Western Tour.

Most hostels run their own tours, but make sure you find out what is included (admission fees, lunch, English-speaking guide etc) and try to get an exact itinerary, or you could end up being herded through the Terracotta Warriors before you have a chance to get your camera out. Tours may also include stops you may wish not to include, such as terracotta warrior figurine factories, where you may feel coerced into buying things you don't want.

You can also visit Hukou Waterfall (p425), 150km north on a tour (the usual cost is around ¥380 to ¥400) from a Xi'an city-centre hotel (tours tend to leave at around 6.30am and return by around 9pm as it takes between 4½ and five hours to travel from the waterfall back to town).

Sleeping

All hostels in the city offer similar services, including bike hire, wi-fi, laundry, restaurant and travel services, while others offer a range of cultural activities too. Ask about free pick-up from the train station and book ahead at popular places.

In low season (January to March) you can usually get 20% off at hostels. If you're arriving by air and have not yet booked accommodation, keep in mind that touts may get you discounted rooms at a wide selection of hotels.

★ **Han Tang Inn** HOSTEL ¥
(汉唐驿, Hantang Yi; ☎029 8726 6762, 029 8728 7772; www.itsxian.com; 7 Nanchang Xiang, 南长巷7号, 南长巷7号, ㎞ ¥60-94, s & d ¥136-230; ❄❂❃; ⑭ Zhonglou) This very popular hostel has friendly and helpful staff – some of the best in China – and loads of information and tours of Xi'an. Dorms are compact but clean and have en suite bathrooms. There's a pleasant rooftop terrace with loads of potted plants and trees, ping-pong table and even a sauna!

So Young City Center Hostel HOSTEL ¥
(书院青旅汇亚天寨, Shūyuàn Qīng Lǚ Huì Yà Tiānmí; ☎029 8741 4845; www.soyounghostel.com; 138 Xiyi Lu, 侧西一路138号; ㎞ ¥60-80, d ¥188-280; ⑭ Zhonglou) This hip hostel is the younger sister of Han Tang House and Han Tang Inn and a short walk down the road

from both. It has cleaner, brighter and more modern rooms at similarly reasonable prices. The hostel's Sky Bar (p415) is undeniably the main draw of this place, where you'll be sure to make a friend or two at one of their many themed social nights. The lively Muslim Quarter and city walls are a 20-minute walk away.

Sahara Youth Inn HOSTEL ¥
(撒哈拉青年客栈, Sahala Qīngnián Kèzhàn; ☎029 8728 763; http://site.douban.com/219529; 180 Beiyuanmen, 北院门180号, ㎞ ¥35-60, s & d ¥159; ❂; ⑭ Zhonglou) You'd think staying smack bang in the Muslim Quarter would be noisy, but Sahara is set well back around a quiet Chinese courtyard in a lovely Qing-dynasty building replete with traditional accents. The beds are firm but rooms are clean and peaceful. You can even see the action outside from the rooftop. You'll be tripping over cats too.

Shuyuan Youth Hostel HOSTEL ¥
(书院青年旅舍, Shūyuàn Qīngnián Lǚshè; ☎029 8228 0092; 2 Shuncheng Nanlu Xiduan, 南门里顺城城南路西段2号; ㎞ ¥44-99, s/d ¥338/506; ❄❂❃; ⑭ Yongningmen) The longest-running hostel in Xi'an, this converted residence has three lovely courtyards, and a welcoming and enjoyable atmosphere. The cafe has a pizza oven and serves excellent food, and the lively basement bar (guests get a free beer voucher) is a riot in the evenings. Rooms are simple but clean, the staff are excellent and the location a winner.

★ **Han Tang House** HOSTEL ¥¥
(汉唐居, Hàn Táng Jū; ☎029 8738 9765; www.hantanghouse.com; 32 Nanchang Xiang, 南长巷32号; ㎞ dm/s/d/tr ¥60/168/268/338; ㊀❄❂❃; ⑭ Zhonglou) A hybrid of sorts, this place has dorms and the vibe of a youth hostel but the look and feel of a three-star hotel. The smart rooms are decked out with high-quality dark-wood furnishings, slab floors and comfortable beds, but lighting is a bit gloomy. The downstairs lobby area is fun and staff are friendly and helpful.

Holiday Inn Express HOTEL ¥¥
(西安钟楼智选假日酒店, Xī'ān Zhōnglóu Zhìxuǎn Jiǎrì jiǔdiàn; ☎029 6181 6688; www.ihg.com/holidayinnexpress; 70 Nan Dajie, 南大街70号, d from ¥379; ㊀❄❂; ⑭ Zhonglou) This quite recently renovated, clean, central and modern hotel is comfortable and reliable, with lots of USB sockets in the rooms and modern amenities. The washing machine and tumble dryer can be used for free.

★ Bell Tower Hotel
HOTEL ¥¥¥

(西安钟楼饭店, Xī'ān Zhōnglóu Fàndiàn; ☑029 8760 0000; www.belltowerhtl.com; 110 Nan Dajie, 南大街110号; d incl breakfast ¥900-1200, ste ¥1800-2800; ❀@; MZhonglou) Right by the Bell Tower in the centre of downtown, this decent 300-plus-room, four-star hotel has been in business for more than three decades. The expansive foyer is all marble, gloss and the occasional dash of kitsch; rooms are comfortable but rather dated, while staff are pleasant and welcoming. The pricier ¥1200 doubles look directly onto the Bell Tower.

Sofitel
HOTEL ¥¥¥

(索菲特人民大厦, Suǒfēitè Rénmín Dàshà; ☑029 8792 8888; www.sofitel.com; 319 Dong Xinjie, 东新街319号; d/ste ¥799/1656; ❀❀❀❀; MZhonglou) Grandly housed, the Sofitel is a fine choice, with a soothing, hushed atmosphere and that crucial central location. Rooms are elegant and comfortable, with top-notch bathrooms, while restaurants are excellent and service is professional and courteous. Reception is in the east wing. Room rates change daily, so you can score a deal when business is slow.

✕ Eating

Xi'an has a wide range of restaurants serving cuisine from across China and the world. The Muslim Quarter is an excellent place for snacking, while a good street to wander for a selection of more typically Chinese restaurants is Dongmutou Shi, east of Nan Dajie; the rest of the city is very well supplied with dining places. Hostels all serve western breakfasts and meals with varying degrees of success.

★ Mǎ Hóng

Xiǎochǎo Pàomóguǎn
CHINESE ISLAMIC ¥

(马洪小炒泡馍馆, ☑133 5918 5583; 46 Hongbu Jie, 红埠街46号; dishes ¥17; MBei Da Jie) A superb choice for lamb or beef *pàomó*; you need to grab a seat before 11am, otherwise it's all elbows in ribs. Pay for your dish, take your seat and then break the round bread into a myriad tiny pieces (they *must* be small) to drop into the bowl, and wait for your meat broth to arrive, which will be splashed over the crumbs.

Tóngshèngxiáng
CHINESE ISLAMIC ¥

(同盛祥; 5 Xi Dajie, 西大街5号; ¥16; ⏱7am-10pm; MZhonglou) Famous for its *yángròu pàomó*, which comes two ways: one is called *gānpào* (干泡; dry soak) where the broth is totally soaked up by the bread and the other is *shuǐwéichéng* (水围城) where there is a large amount of broth. Take your pick.

Měishíchéng
CHINESE ¥

(美食城; basement level 2, 2 Nan Dajie, 南大街2号地下二层; mains from ¥20; ⏱10am-9pm; MYongningmen) This smart food court serves a wide choice of food from each corner of China. There's everything from Sìchuān *dàndàn* noodles (*dàndàn miàn*) to roast duck, dumplings, claypot dishes, *ròujiāmó* (shredded pork in a bun) and more. There's no English; just wander past the counters and point at what you want.

Buy a card from the till, loaded with credit, and purchase dishes with it. When you've finished, hand the card back and your deposit and unused credit is returned.

Hǎiróng Guōtiēdiàn
DUMPLINGS ¥

(海荣锅贴店; 67 Zhubashi, 竹笆市67号; mains from ¥12; ⏱10.30am-10pm; MZhonglou) A civilised and restful choice, this place specialises in *guōtiē* (锅贴) 'potsticker' fried dumplings and they are simply delicious. There's six different types to choose from, including a vegetarian choice. There are other dishes on the menu too, including the lovely *tiáozi ròu* (条子肉; ¥32): soft chunks of pork that you squeeze into white buns.

Sānjiěmèi Jiǎozi
DUMPLINGS ¥

(三姐妹饺子, Three Sisters Dumplings; ☑029 8725 2129; 140 Dongmutou Shi, 东木头市140号; dumplings from ¥16; ⏱10.30am-2.30pm & 5-9.30pm; MZhonglou) Weary diners with dumpling fatigue will be inspired by the rustic two-room Three Sisters, with its well-done twist on classics. Try succulent carrot-and-lamb dumplings blanketed in crisp peanuts and fried chives. Or for vegetarians, sample the winning texture of dry and marinated tofu (yes, two types) with the zing of crunchy coriander and a lashing of chilli.

Dǐng Dǐng Xiāng
CHINESE ¥

(顶顶香; 130 Nanyuanmen, 南院门130号; dishes ¥18-60; ⏱10am-10pm; MZhonglou) A clean cafe atmosphere is spread over four floors with aspirational snaps of Europe in scattered picture frames on the walls. A lively well-dressed crowd peers down onto the street, drinking beer and eating Chinese classics such as hotpots with generous servings. The extensive English picture menu includes excellent veg options.

MUSLIM QUARTER EATS

Explore the Muslim Quarter for tasty eating in Xi'an. Common dishes here are *májiàng liángpí* (麻酱凉皮, cold noodles in sesame sauce), *fěnzhēngròu* (粉蒸肉, chopped mutton fried in a wok with ground wheat), the 'Chinese hamburger' *ròujiāmó* (肉夹馍, fried pork or beef in pitta bread, sometimes with green peppers and cumin), *càijiāmó* (菜夹馍, the vegetarian version of *ròujiāmó*) and the ubiquitous *ròuchuàn* (肉串, kebabs).

Best of all is the delicious *yángròu pàomó* (羊肉泡馍), a soup dish that involves crumbling a flat loaf of bread into a bowl and adding noodles, mutton and broth. You can also pick up mouth-watering desserts such as *huāshēnggāo* (花生糕, peanut cakes) and *shìbǐng* (柿饼, dried persimmons), which can be found at the market or in Muslim Quarter shops.

The food market around Xiyangshi Jie (西羊市街) is excellent grazing territory for everything from lamb skewers to walnuts, cakes, pomegranate juice, flatbreads of all sorts, fried potatoes, fragrant tofu and much more.

Muslim Family Restaurant CHINESE ISLAMIC ¥
(回文人家, Huíwén Renjia; ☑ 029 8721 1466; Beiyuanmen, 北院门; dishes ¥10-98; ⊗ 9am-10.30pm; Ⓜ Zhonglou) Right on Beiyuanmen in the heart of the Muslim Quarter, this smart establishment serves classic Muslim dishes such as *ròujiāmó* (¥15), lamb kebabs (¥10 each), beef- or lamb-filled *xiànbǐng* (fried, crispy bread; ¥18 to ¥20), dumplings (¥15 to ¥18) and lovely grilled golden needle mushrooms (¥18).

🍷 **Drinking & Nightlife**

Xi'an's nightlife options range from bars and clubs to cheesy-but-popular tourist shows.

A main bar strip is near the South Gate on leafy Defu Xiang – one of the most pleasant parts of Xi'an to stroll through by day.

Clubs get going early in Xi'an. They are free to get into, but expect to pay at least ¥30 for a beer. Most are located along or off Nan Dajie.

Sky Bar BAR
(书院青旅汇亚天幕, Shūyuàn Qīng Lǚ Huì Yà Tiānmù; ☑ 029 8741 4845; www.soyounghostel.com; 138 Xiyi Nanlu, 西一路138号; drinks ¥15-50; ⊗ 7pm-2am; Ⓜ Zhonglou) The top floor of So Young City Center Hostel (p413) hosts this quirky, loft-style bar full of wooden benches and beams, plants, country flags and a friendly resident cat. There's a vintage Harley Davidson motorbike and sidecar on show too. Weekly specials include Pizza Day and Ladies' Night, and they host calligraphy and cooking lessons, as well as a number of organised city tours. Happy hour is from 8pm to 10pm, with drinks starting at ¥15.

Jamaica Blue BAR
(蓝色牙买加, Lánsè Yámǎijiā; ☑ 029 8738 9765; 32 Nanchang Xiang, 南长巷32号; Ⓜ Zhonglou) Doubling as a good restaurant, enterprising Jamaica Blue gets a daily workout come sundown as a fine and sociable bar, with live crooning at around 9pm some nights. Moreish, finger-lickin' savoury snacks are delivered free to tables. The layout is a squarish mezzanine, looking down into the lobby of a youth hostel below. Staff are polite and efficient.

ParkQin BAR
(秦吧, Qínbā; 2 Shuncheng Nanlu Xiduan, 南门里顺城南路西段2号; Ⓜ Yongningmen) In the basement bowels of the Shuyuan Youth Hostel (p413), this music bar is a tip-top riot and a fun night out. Staff are excellent and very mindful. It has lots of coloured terracotta warrior statues, blues music, balloons and delicious savoury snacks delivered to your table.

Xi'an Brewery BREWERY
(仙麦, Xiān Mài; ☑ 029 8955 7872; www.xianbrewery.com; F1041, Mandy Plaza, 9 Yan'an Rd, Qujiang, 曲江新区雁南一路9号曼蒂广场一层 F1041; beers ¥30-50; ⊗ 4pm-2am Mon-Thu, to 3am Fri & Sat; 🚌 610 from Bell Tower, Ⓜ Big Wild Goose Pagoda, 🚌 609 from South Gate) Xi'an Brewery puts decent craft beer on the city's map. Set over two floors, it offers a fine array of crafted brews. Go for the Citra IPA for tropical flavours or the Milk Stout for something sweeter. If you can't decide, they offer a sample set of six different beers (150ml each). Indoors can be a bit dark, but the outdoor terrace is pleasant and a stone's throw away from the Big Goose Pagoda (p412).

King Garden Bar BAR
(老城根, Lǎo Chénggēn; ☑ 029 8797 3366; ⊗ 7pm-2am; 🔊; Ⓜ Yuxiangmen) Picturesquely located just outside the gate of Yuxiang Men, this slick bar is a cool spot to hang out with Xi'an's high rollers. With illuminated bar top, snappily

attired bar staff, subdued lights and chill-out sounds, the setting is sharp. A lovely outside garden area awaits for the warmer months. A small Tsingtao beer is ¥55, so it's not cheap.

☆ Entertainment

Shaanxi Grand Opera House
LIVE PERFORMANCE

(陕歌大剧院, Shǎngē Dàjùyuàn; ☑ 029 8785 3295; 165 Wenyi Beilu, 文艺北路165号; performance with/without dinner ¥298/198) Also known as the Tang Palace Dance Show, this is cheaper and less flashy than other dinner-dance shows in town. Wenyi Lu starts south of the city walls. You can get a better price by buying your ticket through a reputable hostel or hotel. Performances are from 8pm to 9pm. Take bus 213, 14 or 118.

Tang Dynasty
LIVE PERFORMANCE

(唐乐宫, Tángyuè Gōng; ☑ 029 8782 2222; www.xiantangdynasty.com; 75 Chang'an Beilu, 长安北路75号; performance with/without dinner ¥500/220; Ⓜ Tiyuchang) The most famous dinner theatre in the city stages an over-the-top spectacle with Vegas-style costumes, traditional dance, live music and singing, dubbed into English. Book online for discounts. Performances are from 8pm to 9.10pm.

Buses can take you to the theatre 1.5km directly south of the South Gate.

Fountain & Music Show
LIVE MUSIC

(Dayan Ta Bei Guangchang, 大雁塔北广场; ⊙ 9pm Mar-Nov, 8pm Dec-Feb; Ⓜ Dayanta) Some travellers enjoy spending the evening at the free fountain and music show on Big Goose Pagoda Sq; it's the largest such 'musical fountain' in Asia. Try to get here around 20 minutes early for a good spot.

🔒 Shopping

Stay in Xi'an for a couple of days and you'll be offered enough sets of miniature Terracotta Warriors to form your own army. A good place to search for gifts is the Muslim Quarter, where prices are generally cheaper than elsewhere.

Xiyang Market
MARKET

(西羊市, Xīyáng Shì; Ⓜ Zhonglou) This narrow alley running north of the Great Mosque is a great central stop for souvenirs. With vocal vendors, bargaining is a way of life here. You'll get everything from Terracotta Warriors to shadow puppets, lanterns, tea ware, 'antiques', jade, T-shirts, paintings,

Cultural Revolution memorabilia and whatnot. Quality varies a lot, so look for defects, but bargains can be had.

Temple of the Eight Immortals Antique Market
MARKET

(八仙庵古玩市场, Bāxiānān Gǔwán Shìchǎng; Yongle Lu, 永乐路; Ⓜ Chaoyangmen) A small antique market sells its wares by the Temple of the Eight Immortals (p412) on Sunday and Wednesday mornings.

Northwest Antique Market
MARKET

(西北古玩城, Xīběi Gǔwán Chéng; Dong Xinjie/Shuncheng Donglu, 东新街/顺城东路北段; ⊙ 10am-5.30pm; Ⓜ Chaoyangmen) Serious shoppers can visit the Northwest Antique Market, by Zhongshan Gate. This three-storey warren of shops selling jade, seals, antiques and Mao memorabilia sees far fewer foreign faces than the Muslim Quarter. Dozing street sellers also display their wares south along Shuncheng Donglu (顺城东路北段). As with everywhere, however, examine everything with a critical eye.

ℹ Information

MAPS

Pick up a copy of the widely available *Xi'an Traffic & Tourist Map* (¥12), a bilingual publication with listings and bus routes. It's available at the airport and some bookshops. Chinese-language maps with the bus routes are sold on the street for ¥5 to ¥6. Shuyuan Youth Hostel (p413) has useful free maps with key bus routes. The English-language magazine *Xianese* (www.xianease.com) is available at some hotels and restaurants that cater to tourists.

MEDICAL SERVICES

Xi'an Central Hospital (西安市中心医院, Xī'ān Shì Zhōngxīn Yīyuàn; ☑ 029 6281 2600; www.xaszxyy.com; 161 Xi Wulu, 西五路161号; Ⓜ Beidajie) Centrally located and a short walk from Beidajie metro station.

MONEY

Bank of China (中国银行, Zhōngguó Yínháng; 29 Nan Dajie, 南大街29号; ⊙ 8am-6pm) You can exchange cash and travellers cheques and use the ATM here.

ATM (自动柜员机, Zìdòng Guìyuánjī; ⊙ 24hr) At the southeast corner of the Bell Tower intersection.

TOURIST INFORMATION

Your hotel is your best place for travel advice. Staffed by English speakers, Han Tang House (p413), Han Tang Inn (p413) and the Shuyuan

Youth Hostel (p413) are excellent and resourceful sources of impartial travel information for visitors.

VISAS

Public Security Bureau Exit-Entry Administration Bureau (公安局出入境管理处, Gōng'ānjú Chūrùjìng Guǎnlǐchù; ☑ 029 8727 5934; 2 Keji Lu, 科技路2号; ⊙ 8.30am-noon & 2-6pm Mon-Fri; Ⓜ Kejilu) On the southeast corner of Xixie 7 Lu. Visa extensions take five working days.

ℹ️ Getting There & Away

AIR

Xi'an's **Xianyang Airport** (西安咸阳国际机场, Xī'ān Xiányáng Guójì Jīchǎng; ☑ 029 96788; www.xxia.com/en) is one of China's best connected – you can fly to almost any major Chinese destination from here, as well as several international ones. Most hostels and hotels and all travel agencies sell airline tickets.

Daily flights include Beijing, Chengdu, Guangzhou, Hong Kong, Shanghai and Ürümqi, while international flights fly from Xi'an to London Heathrow, Seoul, Singapore, Bangkok, Tokyo and Nagoya.

BUS

The **Long-distance Bus Station** (长途汽车站, Chángtú Qìchēzhàn; 13 Fengqing Lu, 丰庆路13号) is opposite Xi'an's train station. It's a chaotic place. Note that buses to Hua Shan (6am to 8pm) depart from in front of the train station.

Other bus stations around town include the **East Bus Station** (城东客运站, Chéngdōng Kèyùnzhàn; 103 Changle Zhonglu, 长乐中路103号) and the **West Bus Station** (城西客运站, Chéngxī Kèyùnzhàn; ☑ 029 8463 0000; Zaoyuan Donglu, 枣园东路; Ⓜ Hancheng Lu). Both are outside the Second Ring Rd. Bus K43 travels between the Bell Tower and the East Bus Station, and bus 103 travels between the train station and the West Bus Station. A taxi into the city from either bus station costs between ¥15 and ¥20.

Buses from Xi'an's Long-distance Bus Station include the following:

Luoyang ¥105, five hours, four daily (10am, noon, 1pm, 3pm)

Zhengzhou ¥135, six hours, one daily (10am)

Buses from Xi'an's East Bus Station include the following:

Hancheng ¥75, four hours, half-hourly (8am to 6.30pm)

Hua Shan One way ¥36, two hours, hourly (7.30am to 7pm)

Pingyao ¥160, six hours, five daily (8am, 9.30am, 10.30am, 12.30pm, 4.30pm)

Yan'an ¥93, five hours, every 40 minutes (8.30am to 5.35pm)

TRAIN

Xi'an's **Main Train Station** (Huǒchē Zhàn) is just outside the northern city walls. It's always busy so arrive early for your departure to account for queues and poor signage. Try to buy your onward tickets as soon as you arrive.

Most hotels and hostels can get you tickets (¥40 commission); there's also an **advance train ticket booking booth** (代售火车票, Dàishòu Huǒchēpiào; Nan Dajie, 南大街; ⊙ 8.50am-noon & 1.30-4.30pm) in the ICBC Bank's south entrance and another **train ticket booth** (代售火车票, Dàishòu Huǒchēpiào; Xiwu Lu, 西五路; ⊙ 8am-5pm & 5.30pm-midnight) just west of Wulukou metro station on Xiwu Lu. This is much easier than the hectic crowds in the main ticket hall and commission is only ¥5.

Xi'an is well connected to the rest of the country. For an overnight journey, deluxe Z trains run to/from Beijing West (hard/soft sleeper ¥273/416, 11½ hours), the later departures leaving Xi'an at 7.21pm and 7.27pm and Beijing at 8.12pm and 8.40pm. The Z94 to Shanghai (hard/soft sleeper ¥332/510, 15 hours) departs at 4.46pm and arrives at 8.11am.

From Xi'an's **North Train Station** (Huǒchē Běizhàn) high-speed 'bullet' G trains zip to Beijing West (2nd/1st class ¥825/516, 5½ hours, 10 daily), Luoyang (2nd/1st class ¥280/175, 1½ hours) and Wuhan (2nd/1st class ¥455/728, four hours, nine daily), with other destinations starting in the next several years.

Within Shaanxi, there are regular trains (including several night trains) to Yulin (hard seat/sleeper ¥81/154, six to seven hours, regular) via Yan'an (2nd/1st class ¥96/115, two hours). Buy tickets in advance. There is also an early morning train to Hancheng (¥32.5, three hours) at 7.42am.

ℹ️ Getting Around

TO/FROM THE AIRPORT

Xianyang Airport is about 40km northwest of Xi'an. Shuttle buses run every 20 to 30 minutes from 5.40am to 8pm between the airport and several points in the city, including the **Longhai Hotel** (陇海大酒店, Lónghǎi Dàjiǔdiàn; 306 Jiefang Lu, 解放路306号) (¥26, one hour). Metered taxis into the city charge more than ¥100.

Airport Shuttle Bus (机场大巴, Jīchǎng Dàbā; 306 Jiefang Lu, 解放路306号; ¥25) Runs every 20 minutes from an alley by the Longhai Hotel.

Airport Shuttle Bus (机场大巴, Jīchǎng Dàbā; 207 Laodong Nanlu, 劳动南路207号; ¥25) Another service that leaves regularly for the airport from the Konggang Hotel.

BICYCLE

If you can cope with the congested roads, bikes are a good alternative to taxis and can be hired at the youth hostels.

BUS

If you're itching to try out the public buses, they go to all the major sights in and around the city. Bus 610 is a useful one: it passes the train station, then onto the Bell Tower, Little Goose Pagoda, Shaanxi History Museum and Big Goose Pagoda. Remember that packed buses are a pickpocket's paradise, so watch your wallet.

METRO

The Xi'an metro system (西安地铁, Xī'ān dìtiě) currently runs to four lines: Lines 1, 2, 3 and 4, with more under construction. Rides cost ¥2 to ¥5 depending on distance. Line 1 has a stop at the Banpo Neolithic Village. Trains run between around 6.10am and 11.15pm.

TAXI

Taxi flagfall is ¥9. It can be very difficult to get a taxi in the late afternoon, when the drivers change shifts. Bicycles are a good alternative.

Around Xi'an

The ranging plains and flat ochre farmland around Xi'an are strewn with early imperial tombs, many of which still await excavation. Unless you have a particular fascination for archaeology and imperial burial sites, you can probably come away satisfied after visiting a couple of them. The Army of Terracotta Warriors is obviously the most famous site, but it's really worth the effort to get to the Tomb of Emperor Jingdi (p420) as well.

Tourist buses run to almost all the sites from in front of Xi'an's main train station, with the notable exception of the Tomb of Emperor Jingdi.

East of Xi'an

★ **Army of Terracotta Warriors** HISTORIC SITE
(兵马俑, Bīngmǎyǒng; www.bmy.com.cn; adult/
student Mar-Nov ¥150/75, Dec-Feb ¥120/60;
☺ 8.30am-6pm Mar-Nov, to 5.30pm Dec-Feb, last
admission 1hr before close) The Terracotta Army isn't just Xi'an's premier sight: it's one of the most famous archaeological finds in the world. This subterranean life-size army of thousands has silently stood guard over the soul of China's first unifier for more than two millennia. Either Qin Shi Huang was terrified of the vanquished spirits awaiting him in the afterlife or, as most archaeologists believe, he expected his rule to continue in death as it had in life.

Whatever the case, the guardians of his tomb – who date from the 3rd century BC – today offer some of the greatest insights we have into the world of ancient China.

The discovery of the army of warriors was entirely fortuitous. In 1974 peasants drilling a well uncovered an underground vault that eventually yielded thousands of terracotta soldiers and horses in battle formation. Throughout the years the site became so famous that many of its unusual attributes are now well known; in particular the fact that no two soldier's faces are alike.

The on-site **wrap-around theatre** gives a useful primer on how the figures were sculpted. You can also employ a guide (low/ high season ¥150/200) or try the audio guide (¥40, plus ¥200 deposit), although the latter is somewhat useless, being difficult to understand and not very compelling.

After this, visit the site in reverse, which enables you to build up to the most impressive pit for a fitting finale.

Start with the smallest pit, **Pit 3**, containing 72 warriors and horses; it's believed to be the army headquarters due to the number of high-ranking officers unearthed here. It's interesting to note that the northern room would have been used to make sacrificial offerings before battle. In the next pit, **Pit 2**, containing around 1300 warriors and horses, you can examine five of the soldiers up close: a kneeling archer, a standing archer, a cavalryman and his horse, a mid-ranking officer and a general. The level of detail is extraordinary: the expressions, hairstyles, armour and even the tread on the footwear are all unique.

The largest pit, **Pit 1**, is the most imposing. Housed in a building the size of an aircraft hangar, it is believed to contain 6000 warriors (only 2000 are on display) and horses, all facing east and ready for battle. The vanguard of three rows of archers (both crossbow and longbow) is followed by the main force of soldiers, who originally held spears, swords, dagger-axes and other long-shaft weapons. The infantry were accompanied by 35 chariots, though these, made of wood, have long since disintegrated.

Almost as extraordinary as the soldiers is a pair of bronze chariots and horses unearthed just 20m west of the Tomb of Qin Shi Huang. These are now on display, together with some of the original weaponry and a mid-ranking officer you can see up close, in a huge modern museum called the **Qin Shi Huang Emperor Tomb Artefact Exhibition Hall** (秦始皇帝陵文物陈列厅, Qínshǐhuángdìlíng Chénliètīng).

Around Xi'an

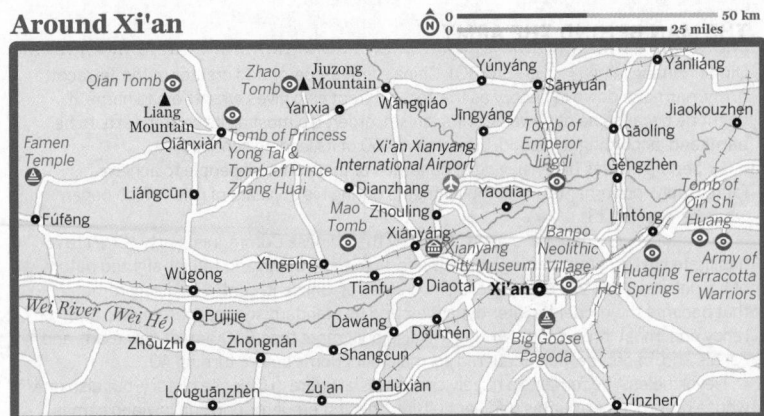

You can take photographs, although signs forbid using flash photography (widely ignored) or tripods.

Among rather tacky souvenir offerings, you can get your own warrior statue personalised with your own face (¥100) or have a photo taken next to a fake warrior (¥10). You can also pick up all manner of terracotta ornamentation – from warrior paperweights to life-size statues – from the souvenir shop in the theatre building. There's also a **Friendship Store** for jade, jewellery and so forth.

The Army of the Terracotta Warriors is easily reached by public bus. From Xi'an train station take one of the air-conditioned buses, either 914 or 915 (¥8, one hour), which depart every four minutes from 6am to 7pm. Take the bus to the last stop; the buses also travel via the **Huaqing Hot Springs** (华清池, Huáqīng Chí; adult Mar-Nov ¥110, Dec-Feb ¥80, child under 1.2m free, cable car one way/return ¥45/70; ⊙7am-7pm Mar-Nov, 7.30am-6.30pm Dec-Feb) and the Tomb of Qin Shi Huang (which is included in the Terracotta Army). The car park for the vehicles is a 15-minute walk from the site, but you can take an electric buggy (¥5) instead if you want. If you want to eat here, there's a good cafe in the theatre building; and after you exit to walk back to the car and bus park, you will take another route past a whole assortment of restaurants and fast food, including a McDonald's. Buses head back to town from the parking lot.

Tomb of Qin Shi Huang
HISTORIC SITE
(秦始皇陵, Qín Shǐhuáng Líng; incl Terracotta Warriors adult/student Mar-Nov ¥150/75, Dec-Feb ¥120/60; ⊙8am-6pm Mar-Nov, to 5pm Dec-Feb) In its time this tomb must have been one of the grandest mausoleums the world had ever seen. Historical accounts describe it as containing palaces filled with precious stones, underground rivers of mercury and ingenious defences against intruders. The tomb reputedly took 38 years to complete, and required a workforce of 700,000 people. It is said that the artisans who built it were buried alive within, taking its secrets with them.

Archaeologists have yet to enter the tomb but probes and sensors have been sent inside. Levels of mercury inside exceed 100 times normal concentrations, adding credence to some of the legends. Since little has been excavated there isn't much to see but you can climb the steps to the top of the 76m-high mound for a fine view of the surrounding countryside.

The Terracotta Warriors bus from Xi'an train station stops at the tomb, which is 2km west of the warriors.

North & West of Xi'an

Many imperial tombs (皇陵, huáng líng) dot the Guanzhong plain around Xi'an. They are sometimes included on tours from Xi'an, but most aren't so as to be destinations in themselves. By far the most impressive is the **Qian Tomb** (乾陵, Qián Líng; Mar-Nov ¥122, Dec-Feb ¥98, incl Tomb of Princess Yong Tai & Tomb of Prince Zhang Huai; ⊙8am-6pm), where China's only female emperor, Wu Zetian (AD 625–705) – from when Tang dynasty Chang'an was at its cultural zenith – is buried with her husband Emperor Gaozong, whom she succeeded. The long **Spirit Way** (神道, Shéndào) – an outdoor, paved path leading to the imperial tomb – is lined with

THE MAN BEHIND THE ARMY

Qin Shi Huang (秦始皇; 259–210 BC), China's first emperor and creator of the Terracotta Army, has gone down in history as the sort of tyrant who gives tyrants a bad name. It might be because he outlawed Confucianism, ordered almost all its written texts to be burnt and, according to legend, buried alive 460 of its leading scholars.

Or perhaps it was his enslaving of hundreds of thousands of people to achieve his (admittedly monumental) accomplishments during his 36 years of rule (which began when he was just 13).

In recent years, there have been efforts by the Chinese Communist Party (CCP) to rehabilitate him, by emphasising both his efforts to unify China and the far-sighted nature of his policies. A classic overachiever, he created an efficient, centralised government that became the model for later dynasties; and he standardised measurements, currency and, most importantly, writing. He also built more than 6400km of new roads and canals and, of course, he conquered six major kingdoms before turning 40.

Nevertheless, he remains a hugely controversial figure in Chinese history, but also one whose presence permeates popular culture. The first emperor pops up in video games, in literature and on TV shows. He's also been the subject of films by both Chen Kaige and Zhang Yimou (*The Emperor and the Assassin* and *Hero*), while Jet Li played a thinly disguised version of him in the 2008 Hollywood blockbuster *The Mummy: Tomb of the Dragon Emperor*.

enormous, lichen-encrusted sculptures of animals and officers of the imperial guard, culminating with 61 (now headless) statues of Chinese ethnic group leaders who attended the emperor's funeral. The mausoleum is 85km northwest of Xi'an. Tour bus 2 (¥25, 8am) runs close to here from Xi'an train station and returns in the late afternoon.

Nearby are the **tombs** (永泰公主墓、章怀太子墓, Yǒngtài Gōngzhǔ Mù, Zhāng Huái Tàizǐ Mù; Mar-Nov ¥122, Dec-Feb ¥82 incl admission to Qian Tomb) of Princess Yong Tai and Prince Zhang Huai, both of whom fell foul of Empress Wu, before being posthumously rehabilitated. Other notable tombs are the **Zhao Tomb** (昭陵, Zhāo Líng; ¥40), where the second Tang emperor Taizong is buried, and the **Mao Tomb** (茂陵, Mào Líng; Dec-Feb ¥60, Mar-Nov ¥80), the resting place of Wudi (156–87 BC), the most powerful of the Han emperors.

★ **Tomb of Emperor Jingdi** TOMB
(汉阳陵, Hàn Yánglíng; Mar-Nov ¥90, Dec-Feb ¥65; ◎8.30am-7pm Mar-Nov, to 6pm Dec-Feb) This tomb, also referred to as the Han Jing Mausoleum, Liu Qi Mausoleum and Yangling Mausoleum, is the burial place of the Han-dynasty emperor Jingdi (188–141 BC) and is quite possibly Xi'an's most underrated highlight. If you only have time for two sights outside Xi'an, make it the Army of Terracotta Warriors and this impressive museum and tomb. Unlike the warriors, though, it's not inundated with visitors so you'll have elbow room to fully appreciate what you're seeing.

Much influenced by Taoist precepts, Emperor Jingdi based his rule upon the concept of *wúwéi* (无为, nonaction or noninterference) and did much to improve the life of his subjects: he lowered taxes greatly, used diplomacy to cut back on unnecessary military expeditions and even ameliorated punishments meted out to criminals. The contents of his tomb are particularly interesting, as they reveal more about daily life than martial preoccupations – a total contrast with the Terracotta Army.

The site has been divided into two sections: the museum and the tomb's excavation area. The **museum** holds a large display of expressive terracotta figurines (more than 50,000 were buried here), including eunuchs, servants, domesticated animals and even female cavalry on horseback. The figurines originally had movable wooden arms (now gone) and were dressed in colourful silk robes.

Inside the **tomb** are 21 narrow pits, some of which have been covered by a glass floor, allowing you to walk over the top of ongoing excavations and get a great view of the relics. In all 81 burial pits are believed to be here.

To get here, take Xi'an metro Line 2 to Shitushuguan station. Outside exit D take bus 4 (¥1) to the tomb, which leaves at 8.30am, 9.30am, 10.30am, noon, 1.30pm, 3pm, 4pm and 5pm, returning to the Xi'an metro station at 9am, noon, 4pm and 5pm.

Alternatively, tours (around ¥160 per person) are usually arranged by guesthouses.

The tomb is 20 minutes from the airport, so makes an easy stop-off by taxi.

Famen Temple BUDDHIST SITE
(法门寺, Fǎmén Sì; Mar-Nov ¥120, Dec-Feb ¥90; ⏰8am-6pm) Dating way back to the 2nd century AD, this temple was built to house parts of a sacred finger bone of the Buddha, presented to China by India's King Asoka who undertook the distribution of Sakyamuni's relics. The older section is worth a visit and you can join the queue of pilgrims who shuffle past the finger bone. The real reason to make the trip out here is the superb **museum** and its collection of Tang-dynasty treasures.

Reaching Famen Temple is quite an expedition, but direct buses head to the sacred site 115km northwest of town. Tour bus 2 (¥25, 8am) from Xi'an train station runs to the temple and returns to Xi'an at 5pm.

Hua Shan 华山

♩ 0913

One of Taoism's five sacred mountains, the granite domes of Hua Shan (Huá Shān) used to be home to hermits, sages and Taoist mystics (some of whom could fly, they say). These days, though, the trails that wind their way up to the five peaks are populated by droves of day-trippers drawn by the dreamy scenery. And it is spectacular. There are knife-blade ridges and twisted pine trees poking from crevices and clinging to ledges, while the summits offer transcendent panoramas of green mountains and countryside stretching away to the horizon. Taoists hoping to find a quiet spot to contemplate the *dào* (道) may be disappointed, but everyone else seems to revel in the tough climb and those who overnight can bask in the first warming glow of sunrise.

⊙ Sights & Activities

There are three ways up the mountain (adult/student ¥180/90) to the **North Peak** (北峰; Běi Fēng), the first of five summit peaks. Two of these options start from the eastern base of the mountain, at the North Peak cable-car terminus. The first option is handy if you don't fancy the climb: an Austrian-built **cable car** (北峰索道, Běifēng Suǒdào; one way/return ¥80/160; ⏰7am-7pm) will lift you silently (bar the on-board announcements) to the North Peak in eight scenic minutes, though you may have to queue for over an hour at busy times.

The second option is to work your way to the North Peak under the cable-car route. This takes two sweaty hours, and two sections of 50m or so are literally vertical, with nothing but a steel chain to grab onto and tiny chinks cut into the rock for footing. It's why this route is called the 'Soldiers Path'.

The third option is the most popular, but it's still hard work, taking between three and five hours. A 6km path leads to the North Peak from the village of Hua Shan, at the base of the mountain (the other side of the mountain from the cable car). It's pretty easy for the first 4km, but after that it's all steep stairs.

The village at the trailhead is a good place to stock up on water and snacks; these are also available at shops on the trail but prices double and triple the further you head up the mountain. There's no need to fork out for the white cotton gloves purveyed by loud old ladies; they insist the rust on the chains at the steepest sections will come off on your hands, but in our experience this was not the case.

If you want to carry on to the other peaks, then count on a minimum of eight hours in total from the base of Hua Shan. To spare your knees you can take the cable car to the North Peak and then climb to the other peaks, before ending up back where you started. It takes about four to five hours to complete the circuit in this fashion, and it's still fairly strenuous and some sections are exhausting. In places, it can be a little nerve-racking too. Hua Shan has a reputation for being dangerous, especially when the trails are crowded or if it's wet or icy, so exercise caution.

The scenery is sublime. Along **Blue Dragon Ridge** (苍龙岭, Cānglóng Lǐng), which connects the North Peak with the **East Peak** (东峰; Dōng Fēng), **South Peak** (南峰; Nán Fēng) and **West Peak** (西峰; Xī Fēng), the way has been cut along a narrow rock ridge with impressive sheer cliffs on either side.

The **West Peak cable car** (西峰索道, Xīfēng Suǒdào; one way/return ¥140/280; ⏰7am-7pm) is less crowded than the North Peak cable car and the 20-minute ride offers clear views of all the other peaks at the top, but it is also more expensive.

The South Peak is the highest at 2160m and the most crowded. The East Peak isn't as busy, but all three rear peaks afford great views when the weather cooperates. If possible, avoid weekends when foot traffic is heaviest.

At the South Peak thrill-seekers can try the **Plank Walk** (长空栈道, Chángkōng Zhàndào; ¥30); a metal ladder leads down to

Hua Shan

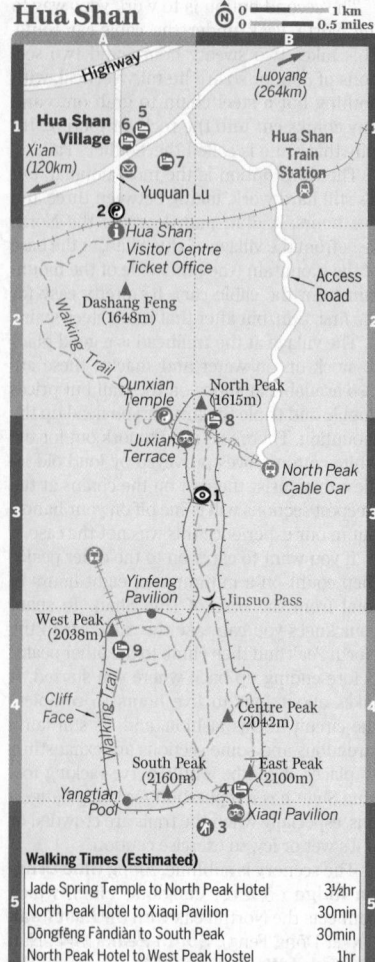

N 0 ——— 1 km
0 ——— 0.5 miles

Walking Times (Estimated)

Jade Spring Temple to North Peak Hotel	3½hr
North Peak Hotel to Xiaqi Pavilion	30min
Dōngfēng Fàndiàn to South Peak	30min
North Peak Hotel to West Peak Hostel	1hr

minated. The idea is to start around 11pm and be at the East Peak for sunrise; you get to see the scenery on the way down.

Jade Spring Temple   TAOIST SITE
(玉泉院, Yùquán Yuàn) This large Taoist temple awaits climbers taking the 6km walk from Hua Shan village to the North Peak and lies just before the ticket office.

🛏 Sleeping & Eating

You can either stay in Hua Shan village or on one of the peaks. Prices for a bed triple during public holidays. It's best to phone ahead to check on room availability and prices on the mountain, but you'll probably need a Chinese speaker. Mountain hotels are basic, with no showers and shared bathrooms.

In the village, there are a couple of hostels and other cheapies, plus some decent hotels.

Take your own food or eat well before ascending, unless you like to feast on instant noodles and processed meat – proper meals are very pricey on the mountain. Along Yuquan Lu in town, every other outlet sells *ròujiāmó* (shredded pork or beef in a bun) for around ¥8 – perfect for stocking up on calories if you're climbing up the mountain.

Huá Shān Bǎoliánjū
Guójì Qīngnián Lǚshě   HOSTEL ¥
(华山宝莲居国际青年旅舍; ☑ 0913 436 8010; Huashan Lu, 华山路; dm ¥60, s & d ¥198; ❉ 🕾) This particularly clean, smart but rather soulless hostel has a lot of exposed brickwork, especially in the lobby and the shower rooms. Rooms are comfortable, if characterless. It's on the main road, so there's a lot of traffic outside.

a path made from wooden boards that hover above a 2000m vertical drop. Thankfully, the admission fee includes a harness and karabiners that you lock onto cables, but even with these safety features it's scary as hell. At peak times, and even in the slow season, queues can get seriously long here.

There is accommodation on the mountain, most of it basic and overpriced, but it does allow you to start climbing in the afternoon, watch the sunset and then spend the night, before catching the sunrise from either the East Peak or South Peak. Some locals make the climb at night, using torches (flashlights) and some of the paths are illu-

Hua Shan Huayi Youth Hostel HOSTEL ¥
(华山华驿青年旅舍, Huá Shān Huáyì Qīngnián Lǚshě; ☏ 0913 436 0385; Dongmian Xiang, Lianhua Shanzhuang, 莲花山庄东面巷; dm ¥30-55, r ¥128; ❄ ⑤) This white tiled hostel in the east of Hua Shan village is a reasonable and friendly choice, with a very quiet setting, way back from the main road. There's a pleasant courtyard, with sunloungers upstairs and excellent views of the mountain, but English is poor. Doubles are good value, although the beds are a bit hard.

West Peak Hostel HOSTEL ¥
(西峰旅社, Xīfēng Lǚshè; dm ¥100) Rustic and basic, but also the friendliest place on the mountain. It shares its premises with an old Taoist temple.

North Peak Hotel HOTEL ¥¥
(北峰饭店, Běifēng Fàndiàn; 云台山庄, Yúntái Shānzhuāng, Yuntai Hotel; ☏ 157 1913 6466; dm ¥130-230, d/tr/q ¥820/1100/1140) The busiest of the peak hotels, this is a friendly enough place with clean enough rooms with views; the 'eight-human' dorm is the cheapest. It's also home to Hua Shan Coffee, with its fantastic views.

Dōngfēng Fàndiàn HOTEL ¥¥¥
(东峰饭店, ☏ 0913 430 1312; dm/q ¥80/1480, d & tr ¥1240) The top location on the East Peak for watching the sunrise also has the best restaurant. Triples and quads have views from upstairs.

Hua Shan Guesthouse HOTEL ¥¥¥
(华山客栈, Huàshān Kèzhàn; ☏ 0913 465 8111; www.517huashan.com; 2 Yuquan Lu, 玉泉路2号; d ¥241-763, ste ¥890-1939; @ ⑤) This excellent and very friendly place in the village is huge and is the best place in the area. You can usually nab one of the rooms for under ¥300.

🍷 Drinking & Nightlife

Hua Shan Coffee CAFE
(华山咖啡, Huàshān Kāfēi; North Peak Hotel; coffee from ¥38; ⊙ 8.30am-5pm, 24hr summer) At the end of your slog, sit down for some restorative caffeine and watch the sun going down through the panoramic windows at this comfy cafe by the North Peak Hotel.

ℹ Information

Buy your tickets for admission to Hua Shan either at **Hua Shan Visitor Centre Ticket Office** (华山游客中心售票处, Huá Shān Yóukè Zhōngxīn Shòupiàochù), if taking the bus, or at the start of the climb in the village of Hua Shan.

ℹ Getting There & Away

From Xi'an to Hua Shan, catch one of the private buses (¥36, two hours, 6am to 8pm) that depart when full from in front of Xi'an train station. You'll be dropped off on Yuquan Lu, which is also where buses back to Xi'an leave from 7.30am to 7pm; they depart from the lot opposite the **post office** (Yuquan Lu). Coming from the east, try to talk your driver into dropping you at the Hua Shan highway exit if you can't find a direct bus. Don't pay more than ¥10 for a taxi into Hua Shan village. There are few buses (if any) going east from Hua Shan; pretty much everyone catches a taxi to the highway and then flags down buses headed for Yuncheng, Taiyuan or Luoyang.

Eight high-speed G-class trains (2nd/1st class ¥55/90, 32 minutes) run daily from Xi'an North train station to **Hua Shan North train station** (华山北站, Huáshān Běizhàn; Huayue Dadao, 华岳大道) between 9.19am and 9.06pm. In the other direction, the first/last train back to Xi'an leaves at 6.26am/9.17pm. Slower trains (¥20, 90 minutes) also link Xi'an with **Hua Shan train station** (华山站, Huáshān Zhàn), a different station that services slower trains.

ℹ Getting Around

Regular buses (free) connect Hua Shan North train station with the Hua Shan Visitor Centre Ticket Office. A taxi will cost you around ¥20. Regular buses (¥3.50) also connect Hua Shan train station with Hua Shan Visitor Centre Ticket Office.

Shuttle buses (one way/return ¥20/40) to the North Peak cable car (p421) run from the Hua Shan Visitor Centre Ticket Office; shuttle buses (one way/return ¥40/80) also run to the West Peak cable car (p421) from here. A free bus runs to the Hua Shan Visitor Centre Ticket Office from the bus station near the foot of the main steps that lead to the Jade Spring Temple on Yuquan Lu. It can be a long wait, though, so you can take a taxi from the village for ¥10, or walk (20 minutes).

Hancheng 韩城

☏ 0913 / POP 59,000

Hancheng (Hánchéng) is best known for being the home town of Sima Qian (145–90 BC), China's legendary historian and author of the *Shiji* (史记, Records of the Grand Historian). Sima Qian chronicled different aspects of life in the Han dynasty and set about arranging the country's already distant past in its proper (Confucian) order. He was eventually castrated and imprisoned by Emperor Wudi, after defending an unsuccessful general.

For its historical textures and ambience, Hancheng is a great side trip from Xi'an.

JINGBIAN WAVE VALLEY

If you haven't seen red sandstone Danxia rock formations in China before, Jingbian Wave Valley (波浪谷火焰丹霞区, Bōlànggǔ Huǒyàn Dānxiáqū) outside Yan'an is an absolute stunner. What's more, not too many people know of it yet, so a powerful sense of space and freedom reigns in the contours of striated rock sculpted by aeons of wind into fanciful and highly photogenic forms. It's a photographer's paradise.

The largest Danxia landscape in Shaanxi, extending 750km north to south and between 10km and 70km from east to west, it has several viewing points you can visit: viewing points Nos 2 (火焰丹霞, huǒyàn dānxiá) and 3 (水上丹霞, shuǐshàng dānxiá) are both hypnotically attractive, but at the time of writing No 1 (地心丹霞, dìxīn dānxiá) viewing point was not open. You might find some locals keen to take you to viewpoint No 5 (apparently not open to the public yet) and they ask around ¥150 per person. The red sandstone takes on different complexions depending on weather conditions – eg after rain – while the best times to visit are early in the morning or late afternoon.

Buses (¥50.50, 2½ hours) run from Yan'an South Bus Station to the town of Jingbian, from where you can hire a car there and back for around ¥350.

You can also get to Jingbian from Xi'an long-distance bus station, with six buses (¥145) a day running to Jingbian. One direct train also departs Xi'an train station at 10.38am (hard seat/sleeper ¥86/181, 7½ hours) to Jingbian. If heading from Xi'an, it's fastest to go by train (2nd/1st class ¥96/115, two hours, regular) from Xi'an North train station to Yan'an first and then take a bus. Tours also head here from Xi'an, so it's worth asking at your hotel.

In Jingbian town, you will find not many hotels take foreigners, though one that does is the central **Jingbian Diamond International Hotel** (靖边钻石国际大酒店, Jìngbiān Zuànshí Guójì Dàjiǔdiàn; ☑0912 491 2777; 63 Xixin Jie, 西新街63号; r from ¥299).

Built upon a hill, the new town (新城, xīnchéng) at the top is dusty and unremarkable, and is where you'll find hotels, banks and transport. But the more atmospheric old town (古城, gǔchéng) at the bottom of the hill boasts a handful of historic sights. The unique Ming dynasty village of Dangjiacun is 9km further east.

⊙ Sights

Dangjiacun
HISTORIC SITE

(党家村; ¥60; ⊙7.30am-6.30pm) This lovely and perfectly preserved 14th-century village nestles in a sheltered location in a loess valley. Once the home of the Dang clan (党家), successful merchants who ferried timber and other goods across the Yellow River, it has since subsided into a quintessential farming community. The village is home to 125 greybrick courtyard houses, which are notable for their carvings and mix of different architectural styles. The elegant six-storey tower is a **Confucian Hall** (文星阁; Wénxīng Gé).

As with so many small villages, many of the families have moved out and their homes are now exhibition showrooms, so the village feels rather lifeless. However, it's well worth a wander to explore the old alleys and admire the historic architecture.

Dangjiacun is 9km northeast of Hancheng. To get here, take a minibus (¥4, 20 minutes) from the bus station to the entrance road, from where it's a pleasant 2km walk through fields to the village. A taxi from Hancheng is another option (¥35 to ¥40).

Confucius Temple
CONFUCIAN SITE

(文庙, Wénmiào; 学巷, Xue Xiang; ¥15; ⊙8am-5.30pm) In the heart of the old town, the tranquil and hoary Confucius Temple is the pick of the sights in Hancheng. The weathered Yuan, Ming and Qing buildings possess an understated sense of how long they have stood the test of time, along with the dramatic towering cypress trees (often associated with Confucian sites), halfmoon pool and glazed dragon screens. The city museum holds peripheral exhibits in the wings.

Buying a ticket for the Confucius Temple gets you admission to the City God Temple too. Bus 102 (¥1) runs here from the southwest corner of Huanghe Dajie, close to the bus station. A taxi is ¥10.

Yuanjue Pagoda
MONUMENT

(园觉寺塔, Yuánjué Sìtǎ; ⊙6am-6pm) Looming over the old town and dating to the Tang dynasty, but rebuilt in 1958, this pagoda also acts as a memorial to Red Army soldiers killed fighting the Kuomintang. It's sadly impossible to climb the pagoda itself, but the steep ascent to it offers panoramic views over the old town nonetheless. To get here, make a sharp right turn when leaving the City God Temple and take the first major right you come to.

City God Temple CONFUCIAN SITE
(城隍庙, Chénghuáng Miào; Huangmiao Xiang, 隍庙巷; ¥15; ☉8am-5pm) At the back of the Confucius Temple is the City God Temple (Chenghuang Temple), in a lane lined with Ming dynasty courtyard houses. An antediluvian temple has apparently been here since the Zhou dynasty, but this whole site has undergone renovation through the dynasties and in recent years. The main attraction is the **Sacrificing Hall**, with its intricate roof detail, where gifts were offered to the divine protector of the city. Admission gets you entrance to the Confucius Temple too.

🛏 Sleeping & Eating

There is a fair number of business-style hotels and lower midrange places in town, albeit nowhere special. For something completely different, spend the night in Dangjiacun, where basic dorm beds in some of the courtyard houses are available for around ¥30 to ¥35. If a local doesn't approach you, just ask and you'll be pointed in the right direction. Places are pretty relaxed about taking foreigners.

Restaurants and noodle outfits litter the new town and there's a fair choice in the old town (don't expect many English menus though). If you spend the night in Dangjiacun, the guesthouses there offer simple and cheap home cooking.

Tiānyuán Bīnguǎn HOTEL ¥
(天园宾馆; ☏0913 529 9388; Longmen Dajie Beiduan, 龙门大街北段; s & d ¥120-140; ❄@) A few doors down from the main bus station, this place has simple but serviceable rooms.

Yínhé Dàjiǔdiàn HOTEL ¥¥
(银河大酒店; ☏0913 529 2555; Longmen Dajie Nanduan, 龙门大街南段; r from ¥398; ❄@🛜) This upmarket option offers comfortable accommodation and healthy discounts of around 50%. From the bus station turn left and walk on the main road for about 10 minutes. The name means the 'Milky Way Hotel'.

ℹ Information

A branch of the **Bank of China** (中国银行, Zhōngguó Yínháng; cnr Huanghe Dajie & Jinta Zhonglu; ☉8am-6pm) is close to the bus station. It has a 24-hour ATM and can change cash.

ℹ Getting There & Away

Buses (¥75, three hours, seven daily) leave from Xi'an's East Bus Station for **Hancheng bus station** (韩城汽车站; Longmen Dajie, 龙门大街) from 6.20am to 7.05pm. Buses back to Xi'an run until 6.30pm. There are two buses per day from to Hancheng to Hua Shan (¥45, two hours) at 7am and noon. There are also two daily buses to Yan'an (¥80, eight hours) at 6.50am and 8am.

Three trains (¥33, just over three hours) run between Xi'an and Hancheng from 8am to 6.10pm. There's also a less useful slow train at 2.20am. From Hancheng, the daily K610 train rumbles towards Beijing (hard sleeper ¥256, 15 hours) via Pingyao (¥105, six hours) and Tàiyuán (¥123, eight hours), departing at 2.13pm.

Yan'an 延安

☏0911 / POP 107,000
When the diminished communist armies arrived at Yan'an (Yán'ān) at the end of the Long March, it signalled the beginning of Yan'an's brief period in the sun. For 12 years, from 1935 to 1947, this backwater town was the CCP (Chinese Communist Party) headquarters, and it was in the surrounding caves that the Party established much of the ideology that was put into practice during the Chinese revolution.

Beyond the SUVs and shopping malls, Yan'an's livelihood is still tied to the CCP; endless tour groups of mostly middle-aged 'red tourists' pass through each year on the trail of Mao and his cohorts. Few foreigners make it here, so expect some attention.

◎ Sights

Hukou Waterfall WATERFALL
(壶口瀑布, Húkǒu Pùbù; peak/off-peak ¥100/85) The largest waterfall on the Yellow River (黄河; Huánghé) and the second largest waterfall in China (only the Huangguoshu Waterfall in Guizhou province is bigger), Hukou Waterfall is sometimes associated with neighbouring Shanxi province, though it can be seen from the Shaanxi side at this point where the Yellow River cleaves the two provinces. The waters of the Yellow River are constricted at this point, being pinched between the mountains, so they gush at speed. Buses run from Yan'an (return ¥81).

The volume of water varies according to the time of year, with greater and more dramatic flows during the heavier rains and water flows from April to around October. Winter can also be a photogenic time to travel, when the you get to see a sparkling and frozen ice fall instead.

A shuttle bus (¥30) takes you from the tourist centre drop-off to the falls themselves. Try to avoid public holidays when it can be very busy indeed.

Bao Pagoda
PAGODA

(宝塔; Bǎo Tǎ; Baota Shan, 宝塔山; ¥65; ⊙7am-7pm Mar-Nov, to 8pm Dec-Feb) Yan'an's most prominent landmark on a hill overlooking town, Bao (Treasure) Pagoda dates from the Song dynasty. For an extra ¥10, you can climb the very narrow steps and ladders of the pagoda for unrestricted views of the city. The pagoda is most beautifully illuminated at night.

Yangjialing Revolution Headquarters Site
HISTORIC SITE

(杨家岭革命旧址, Yángjiālíng Gémìng Jiùzhǐ; Yangjialing Lu, 杨家岭路; ⊙8am-6pm Mar-Nov, 8.30am-5pm Dec-Feb) FREE Perhaps the most interesting of the revolutionary sites and located 3km northwest of the town centre, you can see the assembly hall here where the first central committee meetings were held, including the seventh national plenum, which formally confirmed Mao as the leader of the party and the revolution. It's always fun watching tourists pose in old CCP uniforms in front of the podium.

Zaoyuan Revolution Headquarters Site
HISTORIC SITE

(枣园革命旧址, Zǎoyuán Gémìng Jiùzhǐ; Zaoyuan Lu; 枣园路; ⊙8am-6pm Mar-Nov, to 5pm Dec-Feb) FREE The communist leadership took refuge here between 1943 and 1947, on land allocated by a wealthy merchant. The leafy grounds are perhaps the most attractive of the revolutionary sites. It is 4km past the Yangjialing site.

Yan'an Revolution Museum
MUSEUM

(延安革命简史陈列馆, Yán'ān Gémìng Jiǎnshǐ Chénlièguǎn; Shengdi Lu; 圣地路; ⊙8am-6pm) FREE By far the flashest building in town is the Yan'an Revolutionary Memorial Hall (延安革命纪念馆, Yán'ān Gémìng Jìniàn-guǎn), fronted by a statue of Mao and housing this museum. It offers an excellent, if obviously one-sided, account of the CCP's time in Yan'an and the Sino-Japanese War. More English captions would be nice, but there are plenty of photos of the good old days and other exhibits that are self-explanatory. Bus 1 (¥1) runs here.

Qingliang Mountain
PARK

(清凉山, Qīngliáng Shān; ¥31; ⊙7am-7pm Mar-Nov, to 5.30pm Dec-Feb) This was the birthplace of the CCP propaganda machine: Xinhua News Agency and the *Liberation Daily* started life here when the place was known as 'Information Mountain'. Now, it's a pleasant hillside park with good city views, some nice trails and a few sights, including **Ten Thousand Buddha Cave** (万佛洞, Wànfó Dòng) dug into the sandstone cliff beside the river. The cave has relatively intact Buddhist statues.

Fenghuangshan Revolution Headquarters Site
HISTORIC SITE

(凤凰山革命旧址, Fènghuángshān Gémìng Jiùzhǐ; Fenghuangshan Lu, 凤凰山路; ⊙8am-5pm Mar-Nov) FREE This was the first site occupied by the communists after their move to Yan'an (Mao Zedong lived here from 1937 to 1938), before being abandoned because it was too exposed to enemy aircraft fire. There's a photo to exhibit about Norman Bethune, the Canadian doctor who became a hero in China for treating CCP casualties in the late 1930s.

🛏 Sleeping & Eating

There are few budget options in Yan'an, but you can usually net a plush room for less than ¥200. Avoid the hotels near the train station – they're only slightly cheaper than those in town and are usually very grim.

The bustling **night market** (大东门便民夜市) just off Erdao Jie (二道街) fires up at around 6pm, sizzling through to around 4am. Expect lamb and squid kebabs, noodles, *dòufu* (tofu) and all manner of other street food. Lamb kebabs are around ¥10 for three.

★ Yàshèng Dàjiǔdiàn
HOTEL ¥¥¥

(亚圣大酒店; ☑0911 266 6000; Erdaojie Zhongduan; 二道街中段; tw ¥336-400, ste ¥897; ❋ 🐾) Located in the centre of town with some rooms facing Bao Pagoda, this excellent hotel has stylish, modern, comfortable and well-equipped rooms. A decent restaurant is on the top floor. You can usually get a room from around ¥200. Access the hotel from the back of the street, via the car entrance gate.

Hǎishèng Jiǔdiàn
HOTEL ¥¥¥

(海盛酒店, Daqiaojie; ☑0911 821 3333; Daqiao Jie; 大桥街; s & tw incl breakfast ¥398, ste ¥498; ❋ 🐾) There may be a brash preponderance of gold and marble kitsch in the foyer, but there are smart rooms at hand. Staff seem eager to please, even as English skills falter. In a town

MIZHI

Mizhi (米脂, Mǐzhǐ) is famed as the home town of Li Zicheng, proto-communist and would-be emperor, as well as for the alleged beauty of its women.

Way off the tourist circuit about 70km south of Yulin, it's a sleepy place with a small presence of the Hui ethnic minority; you will be the sole foreigner in town and possibly the only visitor of any description. There are attractive terraced fields in the surrounding hills and some of the local population still live in caves (窑洞, yáodòng) and homes carved out of the hillsides, while the small old quarter, with its narrow alleys and dilapidated courtyard homes, is a fascinating place to wander.

The principal sight in Mizhi is the **Li Zicheng Palace** (李自成行宫, Lǐ Zìchéng Xínggōng; Xinggong Lu, 行宫路; ¥20; ⊙8am-5pm), a well-preserved and compact palace built in 1643 at the height of Li's power. Set against a hillside, there's a statue of the man himself, pavilions housing exhibits about Li and notable Mizhi women, and a pagoda. There's also a fine theatre where music performances and plays were held, sometimes for three days at a time, to celebrate Li's victories. To reach the palace, walk east on Xinggong Lu. It's a 10- to 15-minute walk from the bus station.

Turning left immediately after leaving Li Zicheng Palace puts you in the appealing heart of the **old quarter** of Mizhi, where many of the original, late Ming–dynasty courtyard homes survive, albeit in particularly run-down condition.

Getting There & Away

Mizhi is an easy day trip from Yulin or you could stop here to/from Yan'an. Frequent buses (¥22, two hours) run from Yulin's main (south) bus station; ask to get off at Jiulong Bridge (九龙桥, jiǔlóng qiáo), which is a little closer to the palace. Buses to Mizhi from Yan'an (¥60, 3½ hours, three daily) depart at 1.20pm, 2.20pm and 3.10pm. From Xi'an there's one direct bus daily at 7am to Mizhi (¥122) from the north bus station (9 Bei'erhuan Xiduan).

of overpriced hotels this isn't a bad option, with rates often falling to around ¥198.

ℹ Information

Bank of China (中国银行, Zhōngguó Yínháng; Daqiao Jie; 大桥街; ⊙8am-5pm) On the corner of Daqiao Jie and Erdao Jie, this branch has a 24-hour ATM. There are many other ATMs around town too.

ℹ Getting There & Away

From Xi'an's East Bus Station (汽车东站, qìchē dōngzhàn), there are buses to Yan'an (¥93, four hours) every 40 minutes from 8.30am to 5.35pm. The schedule back to Xi'an is very similar. Buses arrive and depart from the South Bus Station (汽车南站, qìchē nánzhàn), obliquely across the way from the train station on Qilupu Jie, although some buses run to the better located East Bus Station in Yan'an, so check first.

At Yan'an's East Bus Station (汽车东站, qìchē dōngzhàn), a short walk from the far side of Da Bridge (大桥, Dà Qiáo), there are buses to Yulin (¥49, four hours) every hour from 5.30am to 5pm. Local buses to Mizhi (¥59.50, four hours) depart at 9.15am, 1.20pm and 2.10pm. Buses also run hourly from here to Xi'an (¥93, four hours) between 7.30am and 5pm.

Heading west, there are departures to Yinchuan in Ningxia (¥72, 10 hours); buses leave at 5.30am, 9.30am and 10.30am, while sleepers leave at 4.30pm and 5.30pm. You can also get into Shanxi and Henan from here.

Frequent high-speed trains run to Xi'an North (2nd/1st class ¥96/115, two hours), and there are slow trains from Xi'an train station (hard seat/sleeper ¥51/105, four hours). Regular trains also run to Yulin (hard seat/sleeper ¥42/96; four hours).

ℹ Getting Around

The Revolution Headquarters sites can be reached by taking bus 1, which runs along the road east of the river and then heads up Shengdi Lu. This bus starts at the train station. Bus 8 also passes these places and can be caught from Da Bridge.

Bus K22 runs from the train station to a stop near the Yàshèng Dàjiǔdiàn, the Hǎishèng Jiǔdiàn and the centre of town. A taxi from the train station into town costs ¥10 to ¥15. Taxi flagfall is ¥5.

Yulin   榆林

☑ 0912 / POP 92,000

Thanks to extensive coal mining and the discovery of natural gas fields nearby (though you'll see wind farms as well as oil wells on the way up from Yan'an), Yulin (Yúlín), a one-time garrison town on the fringes of Inner Mongolia's Mu Us Desert, is booming. Despite all the construction, there's enough interesting stuff to make this a good place to break a trip if you're following the Great Wall, heading north on the trail of Genghis Khan or wandering west to the Hui culture of Yinchuan. If you're on the road from Yan'an, look out for *yáodòng* (cave dwellings) perforating the hillsides until the land becomes desert.

Parts of Yulin's earthen **city walls** are still intact, especially running along Changcheng Nanlu, while the main north–south pedestrian street in the elongated old town (divided into Beidajie and Nandajie) has several restored buildings. The lovely **Lingxiao Pagoda** looks down on the town from near the centre of Yulin and is gorgeously illuminated at night. The **Drum Tower** (鼓楼, Gǔlóu; Bei Dajie, 北大街) is in the same area, overlooking a pleasant and *rènào* (bustling) neighbourhood come evening. The tower was first erected in 1380 and destroyed several times (the current tower dates from the early 20th century). With several restaurants and antique shops, the whole street is a nice place to wander.

Seven kilometres north of the Yulin bus station, on the outskirts of town, are some badly eroded sections of the Great Wall and an imposing Ming-era four-storey **beacon tower** (镇北台, Zhènběitái; ¥30; ☉7.30am-7.30pm, later in summer) that dates from 1607 (and has been much restored recently). You can climb to the top for long views and also walk past old eroded and wind-blasted sections of wall and the stump of a disintegrated watchtower. There are also two old surviving Siberian elm trees that Yulin (literally Siberian Elm Forest) is named after; the tree species, now virtually wiped out here, once grew in abundance along the river. Bus 5 (¥1) runs here from Changcheng Nanlu (长城南路), about 200m west of the main bus station. Take the bus to Zhenbeitai, which is the last stop, walk in the same direction a further 30m and then turn right; you will see the beacon tower on the hilltop.

There is no shortage of places to stay in Yulin, but not everywhere will take foreigners so you may need to hunt around and face rejection. The **Jingdu Holiday Hotel** (晶都假日酒店, Jīngdū Jiàrì Jiǔdiàn; ☎0912 354 9966; 3 Yuyang Zhonglu, 榆阳中路3号; r ¥138-158, ste & tr

¥188), with its comfortable and very presentable rooms, and the spacious and smart **Jinyu Hotel** (金域大酒店, Jīnyù Dàjiǔdiàn; ☎0912 233 3333; 6 Xinjian Nanlu, 新建南路6号; s incl breakfast ¥218, tw ¥178-260, ste ¥598; ✳@☎) are exceptions. Both are right at the heart of the action, near all the central sights of note, and not far from the bus station.

A selection of street stalls can be found cooking up snacks in the evenings around the Drum Tower area.

ℹ Getting There & Away

AIR

There are several daily flights from Yulin to Xi'an (from ¥300) as well as two flights daily to Shanghai (¥1920) and three flights per day to Beijing (¥945).

BUS

Yulin has two bus stations. If you get off the bus inside the town walls (near the South Gate), you are at the main (south) bus station (汽车站, qìchē zhàn); the regional (north) bus station (客运站, kèyùn zhàn) is 3.5km northwest on Yingbin Dadao, near the intersection with Changcheng Beilu.

The main bus station has regular buses to Xi'an (¥166 to ¥181, eight hours) from 7.25am to 7.30pm. You can also get buses to Yan'an (¥87, five hours, half-hourly) from 7.25am to 5pm, to Yinchuan (¥127, five to six hours, eight daily), and to Taiyuan (¥122, eight hours, 6.50am and 12.20pm).

The regional bus station has buses to Baotou (¥84, four hours, hourly, 7am to 5.30pm) in Inner Mongolia and to Dongsheng (¥66, regular, 7.10am to 6.40pm). The buses to Dongsheng pass by Genghis Khan's Mausoleum. Five buses a day also leave from here to Xi'an (¥170, eight hours). There are also three buses per day to Jingbian at 7.30am, 1.20pm and 3pm.

TRAIN

The train station is 4km west of the main bus station. There are trains to Xi'an (hard seat/hard sleeper ¥47/101, six to seven hours, regular) via Yan'an. There are also regular trains north to Baotou (hard seat ¥47, four to five hours). There is also a handy sleeper trundling to Beijing (hard seat/hard sleeper ¥116/214, 12½ hours, 11.10pm).

ℹ Getting Around

Taxis around town and to the train station will cost you ¥6. Bus 1 (¥1) runs between the two bus stations. Bus 7 (¥1) runs between the main bus station and the train station.

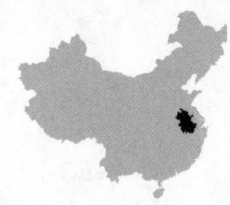

Anhui

POP 62 MILLION

Best Places to Eat

➡ Lǎo Jiē Yīlóu Shíyè (p433)

➡ Pig's Heaven Inn (p438)

➡ Qiyuan Vegetarian (p446)

➡ Gāotāng Húndūn (p432)

Best Places to Stay

➡ Pig's Inn Bishan (p438)

➡ Long Lane Inn (p437)

➡ Ancient Town Youth Hostel (p432)

➡ Imperial Guard Boutique Hotel (p439)

Why Go?

Fantastical mountainscapes and well preserved villages make Anhui (安徽, Ānhuī) the perfect antidote to the brashness of China's larger cities. The main attraction is unquestionably Huangshan, a jumble of sheer granite cliffs wrapped in cottony clouds that inspired an entire school of ink painting during the 17th and 18th centuries. But the often-overlooked peaks of nearby Jiuhua Shan, where Buddhists bless the souls of the recently departed, have a hallowed aura that offers a strong contrast to Huangshan's stunning natural scenery.

At the foot of these ranges are strewn the ancient villages of the province formerly known as Huizhou. With distinctive whitewashed walls and black-tiled roofs augmented by lush surroundings of buckling earth, bamboo and pine forest, they are among the most picturesque in the country.

Anhui's top sights are clustered in its southeast corner. Easy to navigate and within striking distance of Shanghai, this is rural China at its accessible best.

When to Go

Tunxi

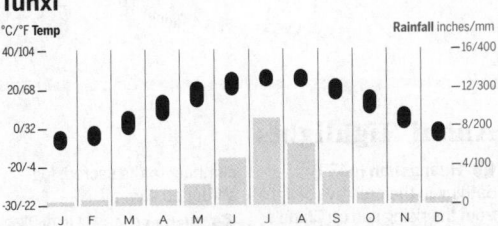

Mar & Apr Pack a camera to catch the flowering yellow rapeseed in the villages around Shexian.

Oct Autumn days are best for climbing Huangshan.

Dec The snow-capped rooftops of Xidi's Huizhou houses look a picture.

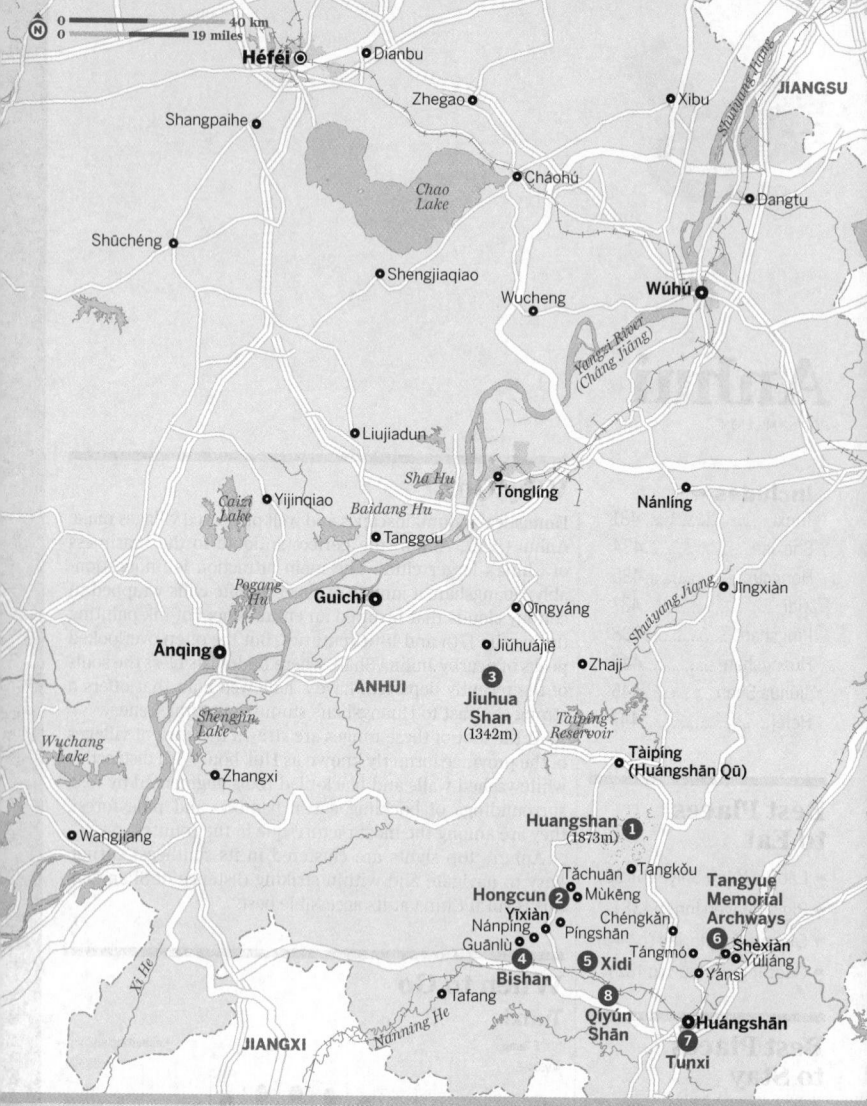

Anhui Highlights

1 Huangshan (p439) Bathing in the first rays of light from the rising sun on China's most iconic mountain.

2 Hongcun (p435) Delving into the back alleys and marvelling at the waterways of this ancient Anhui village.

3 Jiuhua Shan (p445) Joining Buddhist pilgrims in climbing to the sacred, fog-shrouded summit.

4 Bishan (p438) Living like a Qing dynasty merchant at the Pig's Inn Bishan.

5 Xidi (p437) Wandering the lanes of a white-walled village, a living museum of traditional architecture.

6 Tangyue Memorial Archways (p434) Standing in awe of this grand procession of stone archways.

7 Tunxi Old Street (p431) Sampling local snacks and Huangshan's famous tea.

8 Qiyun Shan (p435) Exploring the grottoes and temples of this Taoist haven.

History

The provincial borders of Anhui were defined by the Qing government, bringing together two highly disparate geographic regions and cultures: the arid, densely populated North China Plain and the mountainous terrain south of the Yangzi River (Cháng Jiāng). The region has a long, long history, with excavation sites in the Yangzi River basin turning up some of the oldest evidence of human settlement in Eurasia. During the Three Kingdoms Period many battles were fought here (and warlord Cao Cao was a native son).

Impoverished for much of history and today a primary source of China's hardworking army of *āyí* (nannies), rural Anhui's fortunes have begun to reverse. Some say the massive infrastructure improvements in the hitherto remote areas are partly due to former president Hu Jintao, whose ancestral clan hails from Jixi County. Hu comes from a long line of Huizhou merchants, who for centuries left home to do business or fill official posts elsewhere, but would never fail to complete their filial duty and send their profits back home (much of it by way of large homes and ceremonial structures).

Getting There & Around

The historic and tourist sights of Anhui gather in the south around the town of Tunxi (also known as Huangshan Shì), which has an airport and high-speed train station. High-speed trains connect Tunxi with Shanghai, Beijing, Xi'an, Nanjing, Hangzhou, Fuzhou, Changsha and other cities, departing from and arriving at Huangshan North Train Station, 18km north of town.

Within mountainous Anhui, buses are plentiful and the best way to get around. However, as the main sights are clustered in one region, hired taxis are also an option for groups.

Tunxi 屯溪

📞 0559 / POP 156,000

Ringed by low-lying hills, the old trading town of Tunxi (Túnxī; also called Huangshan Shì; 黄山市, literally 'Huangshan City') is the main springboard for trips to Huangshan and the surrounding Huizhou villages. Compared with the region's capital, Hefei, Tunxi makes for a far, far better base.

⊙ Sights

Tunxi's historic heart is the restored Old St (老街, Lao Jie). Unless you're travelling to nearby villages or the atmospheric Taoist hilltop

centre **Qiyun Shan** (p435), there's little else to see.

Tunxi Old Street   STREET

(屯溪老街, Túnxī Lǎojiē) Running a block in from the river, Old St is lined with restored Ming-style Huizhou buildings. It's definitely touristy – every block is a loop of tea shops and snack vendors – but it's pretty nonetheless, and pleasant for an evening stroll.

Wancuilou Museum   MUSEUM

(万粹楼博物馆, Wàncuìlóu Bówùguǎn; 143 Lao Jie, 老街143号; ¥50; ⊙ 8.30am-8.30pm) This fascinating private collection of ceramics, painted scrolls and religious carvings is displayed as they were meant to be – in the halls of a wealthy merchant's house. The house itself, three storeys high, with an open-air atrium over a fishpond, is also something to behold.

☞ Tours

Youth hostels offer day trips to the villages of Xidi and Hongcun (expect to pay around ¥250 including transport, admission fees and lunch) and to Huangshan (around ¥350). They can also arrange tickets for a shuttle bus from Old St to Huangshan (¥22, one hour, 6.15am) and pack you a lunch.

The Huangshan Tourist Distribution Center (p444), inside the long-distance bus station, runs day trips (p433) and tourist shuttles to surrounding villages, and sells discounted tickets.

🛏 Sleeping

Tunxi's Old St is an established traveller base, with excellent hostels and boutique hotels in restored wooden homes.

Tunxi

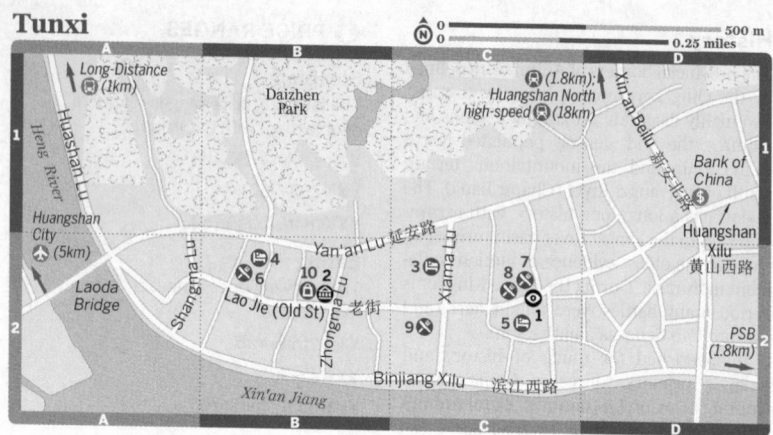

★**Ancient Town Youth Hostel** HOSTEL ¥
(小镇国际青年旅社, Xiǎozhèn Guójì Qīngnián Lǚshè; ☑0559 252 2088; www.yhahs.com; 11 Sanma Lu, 三马路11号; dm ¥42-47, d & tw ¥150-242; ❈@☎) Started by some former tour guides, this hostel ticks all the right boxes, with a well-stocked bar, movie room, friendly and informative English-speaking staff, bike rental and organised tours. Dorms are spacious and comfy, but the cheapest of the (clean) twin rooms lack natural light and the quality varies, so check them out first and compare.

Old Street Hostel HOSTEL ¥
(老街国际青年旅舍, Lǎojiē Guójì Qīngnián Lǚshè; ☑0559 254 0386; www.hiourhostel.com; 266 Lao Jie, 老街266号; dm without/with shower ¥55/65, d ¥168; ❈@☎) With a convenient location and good rooms, this place clearly has an appeal that extends beyond the backpacking crowd. The four-person dorms come with proper mattresses and some have private bathrooms; private rooms are spartan but spacious and comfortable. There's a cafe-bar on the 2nd floor, overlooking Lao Jie. Helpful staff speak English and are happy to help make travel arrangements.

Hui Boutique Hotel BOUTIQUE HOTEL ¥¥
(黄山徽舍品酒店, Huángshān Huīshèpǐn Jiǔdiàn; ☑0559 235 2003; 3 Lihong Xiang, 老街李洪巷3号; d ¥580-880; ❈☎) In a Qing dynasty building with a landscaped courtyard, down a quiet lane off Old St, this is a cloistered and atmospheric place to stay. The 1st-floor rooms (the cheaper ones) have been shoddily modernised, but the 2nd-floor ones have antique rosewood beds and more natural light. Look for online discounts to soften the tariff.

✕ Eating

Old St is full of restaurants and stalls selling classic local snacks like *xièké huáng* (蟹壳黄, 'yellow crab shells') – actually baked buns stuffed with meat or vegetables that just look like crab shells. You will also find a lot of pickled vegetables as well as local delights such as vacuum-packed fermented Mandarin fish.

Cheaper street eats and fast-food restaurants congregate just east of the eastern entrance and also along the river on Binjiang Xinlu.

★**Gāotāng Húndūn** DUMPLINGS ¥
(高汤馄饨; 1 Haidi Xiang, 海底巷1号; wontons ¥10; ⊙7am-10pm; ☑) Duck down a little alley opposite 120 Lao Jie for what is essen-

tially an ancient food cart inside an even more ancient Qing dynasty home – run by a 12th-generation *húndùn* (wonton) seller and his family. The speciality is obviously the wontons, made to order and with superthin skin, though there are other dishes, like fried *jiǎozi* (stuffed dumplings), on the menu too.

Měishí Rénjiā HUIZHOU ¥
(美食人家; 245 Lao Jie, 老街245号; dishes ¥5-118; ☉10.30am-2pm & 5-10.30pm) Crowd-pleasing Měishí Rénjiā has something for everyone: if you want to dig in deep on local specialities, you can find *chòu guìyú* (臭鳜鱼, fermented mandarin fish; ¥118). If you just want something light and cheap, you can snack on various *bāozi* (steamed buns stuffed with meat or vegetables; from ¥5). Belly-warming claypots cost ¥25 to ¥40.

Tóngjùlóu Huīcài HUIZHOU ¥¥
(同聚楼徽菜; ☑0559 257 2777; 216 Lao Jie, 老街216号; mains ¥22-70; ☉11am-9pm) With a corner positioning at the heart of Lao Jie, this 90-year-old restaurant is a fun place to sample Huizhou cuisine. Various stews and dishes of braised meat are arranged in claypots, so take a look and see what you fancy, order up, grab some beers and claim an outside table.

★ **Lǎo Jiē Yīlóu Shíyè** HUIZHOU ¥¥¥
(老街一楼食业; ☑0559 235 9999; 247 Lao Jie, 老街247号; mains ¥28-138; ☉11am-1.30pm & 5-8.30pm) Considered the best restaurant on Old St, this is the place to splash out on Huizhou delicacies, like *tiánluó* (田螺, pond snails), here braised in a plate-licking concoction of soy sauce and spices. Also excellent is the Huizhou *wēisānbǎo* (徽州煨三宝), a stew of 'three treasures' – salt-cured pork, thin skins of tofu tied in decorative knots, and puffs of fried tofu stuffed with meat.

 Drinking & Nightlife

Zhongma Lu off Old St has a string of cute coffee shops and bars, all with free wi-fi; coffee and beer starts at about ¥20. Most open around 10am and close up around 10pm.

 Shopping

★ **Xie Yu Da Tea** FOOD & DRINKS
(谢裕大茶行, Xiè Yù Dàcháháng; 149 Lao Jie, 老街149号) Old St is lined with tea shops but Xie Yu Da Tea is the real deal, founded by Xie Zhengan (1838–1910), the man who first marketed Huangshan's now famous *máofēng* (毛峰) tea. Literally 'fur peak', the subtle, slightly floral green tea gets its name from an almost-indiscernible peach fuzz.

ℹ Information

Bank of China (中国银行, Zhōngguó Yínháng; cnr Xin'an Beilu & Huangshan Xilu, 新安北路黄山西路的路口; ☉8am-5.30pm) Changes travellers cheques and major currencies; 24-hour ATM.

Public Security Bureau (PSB, 公安局, Gōng'ānjú; ☑0559 251 2929; 108 Changgan Donglu, 长干东路108号; ☉8am-noon & 2.30-5pm) For visa extensions and police assistance.

ℹ Getting There & Away

AIR

Daily direct flights from **Huangshan City Airport** (黄山市飞机场, Huángshānshì Fēijīchǎng) include the following:

Guangzhou ¥960, two hours, one daily

Qingdao ¥957, 1¾ hours, one daily

Shenzhen ¥1108, two hours, one daily
Flights usually depart late in the evening.

BUS

The **long-distance bus station** (客运总站, Kèyùn Zǒngzhàn; ☑0559 256 6666; 31 Qiyun Dadao, 齐云大道31号; ☉5.45am-5.50pm) is roughly 2km west of the train station on the outskirts of town. Destinations include the following:

Hangzhou ¥98, three hours, hourly (6.50am to 6.20pm)

Jingdezhen ¥61, 3½ hours, three daily (9.15am, noon and 2.10pm)

Nanjing ¥114, 5½ hours, eight daily (7.40am to 5.50pm)

Shanghai ¥132, five hours, 10 daily (last bus 4.20pm)

Suzhou ¥128, six hours, three daily (5.40am, 6.50am and 7.20pm)

Wuyuan ¥45, two hours, one daily (8.30am)
Within Anhui, buses go to these destinations:

Hefei ¥88, four hours, hourly (6.45am to 5pm)

Jiuhua Shan ¥63, 3½ hours, one daily (1.30pm)

Shexian ¥7, 45 minutes, frequent services (6am to 5pm)

Yixian ¥13, one hour, frequent services (6am to 5pm)

Buses to Huangshan go to the main base at Tangkou (¥20, one hour, every 20 minutes, 6am to 5pm) and on to the north entrance, Taiping (¥36, two hours). There are also minibuses to Tangkou (¥20) from in front of the train station (6.30am to 5pm) that leave when full.

Inside the bus station (to the right as you enter) is the separate Huangshan Tourist Distribution Center (p444) with tourist buses following three routes to popular destinations.

Bus 1 Qiyun Shan (¥12, 45 minutes), Xidi (¥14, one hour) and Hongcun (¥20, 1½ hours); hourly 8am to 4pm, last return bus 5pm

Bus 2 Tangmo (¥5.50, 45 minutes), Tangyue (¥6, one hour), Huizhou Old Town (¥8, 75 minutes)

and Yuliang (¥9, 90 minutes); 8am, 10am, 2pm and 4pm, last return bus 4pm

Bus 3 Chengkan (¥10, 40 minutes); hourly 8am to 11am and 1pm to 4pm, last return bus 4pm

TRAIN

Numerous high-speed trains depart **Huangshan North station** (黄山北站; Huángshān Běizhàn) for Hangzhou (¥190, 90 minutes), Shanghai (¥290, three hours), Beijing (¥548, 6½ hours) and to a lesser extent Nanjing (¥232, four hours).

Regular-service trains also depart from the older Huangshan station in central Tunxi.

❶ Getting Around

Bus 2 (¥2) runs between the bus station and Old St; bus 12 (¥2) runs between Huangshan train station and Old St.

Taxi flagfall is ¥7, but most drivers who hang out around Old St refuse to use the meter. Grab one from Binjiang Xilu instead, or pay the accepted fares from Old St: long-distance bus station or main train station ¥10; high-speed train station (Huángshān Běizhàn) ¥50.

Shexian 歙县

☑ 0559 / POP 490,000

Shexian (Shèxiàn) is 25km northeast of Tunxi and can be visited as a day trip. The town was formerly the grand centre of the Huizhou culture, serving as its capital. Today the city's classic Old Town is the main sight. The nearby port of Yuliang harbours an architectural heritage entirely different from the other Huizhou villages. Shexian is also the jumping-off point for visiting the memorial archways of Tangyue, the best collection of their kind in the region.

❍ Sights

A combined ticket (¥220) for Huizhou Old Town, Tangmo and Tangyue Memorial Archways is a good deal if you plan to visit everything; it also includes entry to the village of Chengkan.

Huizhou Old Town VILLAGE
(徽州古城, Huīzhōu Gǔchéng; adult/child & senior ¥80/50; ☉8am-5pm) The entrance to the old town is marked by **Yanghe Gate** (阳和门, Yánghé Mén), a double-eaved, wooden gate tower that dates from the Song dynasty. To the left are two stone *xièzhì* (獬豸, a legendary beast) and straight ahead, the main attraction: the magnificent **Xuguo Archway** (许国石坊, Xǔguó Shífáng). This is China's sole surviving four-sided decorative archway, with 12 lions (18 in total if you count

the cubs) seated on pedestals around it and a profusion of bas-relief carvings of other mythical creatures.

Tangyue Memorial Archways MONUMENT
(棠樾牌坊群, Tángyuè Páifāng Qún; www.paifang qun.com; adult/student ¥100/50, child & senior free; ☉7.30am-5.30pm) Over generations, the Bao (鲍) family constructed these seven carved stone *páifāng* (牌坊, memorial arches), stretching east to west in the fields outside their village, to consecrate their ancestors for feats of service and piety. Three are from the Ming dynasty, four from the Qing. Placards (in English) describe the acts – some touching, some gruesome – that earned such high esteem. Tourist bus 2 runs from Tunxi's Tourist Distribution Center, calling at Tangyue (¥6, one hour) before continuing to Tangmo.

Tangmo VILLAGE
(唐模; adult/student ¥80/50, child & senior free; ☉8am-5pm) A narrow village stretching along a central canal, Tangmo is usually uncrowded, though it's by no means uninteresting. According to village lore, the original Tang dynasty settlers planted two ginkgo trees: only one grew, and that became the site of the village. The **tree** (银杏, *yínxìng*), in the centre of the village, is thick and full of leaves, still bearing fruit 1300-plus years later.

★ Chengkan VILLAGE
(呈坎, Chéngkǎn; ¥107; ☉8am-5pm) Designed around the *bāguà*, the eight trigrams of the *I Ching*, which match up with eight surrounding hills, Chengkan is a highly photogenic village that hasn't yet been completely restored, with arched bridges over waterways cloaked with lilies. Buildings are in various states of repair and visitors are far fewer than at villages more firmly on the tourist map. An S-shaped stream snakes through the middle, carving the symbol for yin and yang deep into the heart of the village.

Yuliang VILLAGE
(渔梁, Yúliáng; ¥30, child & senior free; ☉9am-5pm) Little-visited Yulang is a historic riverine port village on the Lian River (练江, Liàn Jiāng). The cobbled and picturesque alley of **Yuliang Jie** (渔梁街) houses former transfer stations for the wood, salt and tea that plied the river; the tea shop at No 87 is an example. Note the firewalls separating the houses along the road. The attraction with most historical significance is the 138m-long granite **Yuliang Dam** (渔梁坝, Yúliáng Bà) across the river; it's believed to be 1400 years old.

🛏 Sleeping

Tunxi has more accommodation options and makes for a better base; however, you could go for a quiet night in atmospheric Yuliang, though sleeping options are basic.

Yuliang Farm Hotel   HOMESTAY ¥
(渔梁农家饭店, Yúliáng Nóngjiā Fàndiàn; ☑ 0559 653 9731; 147 Yuliang Jie, 渔梁街147号; d ¥60-80) Midway down Yuliang's narrow, cobblestone lane you can find small, clean, modern rooms above a restaurant. There's an English sign out the front.

Jiangnan Deyuelou Hotel   HOTEL ¥¥
(江南得月楼, Jiāngnán Déyuèlóu; ☑ 0559 653-1378; 110 Huiyuan, 徽园110; d ¥439; @ 🛜) This choice on the east side of the entrance for Huizhou Old Town is set in a traditional-style building with clean rooms and decent views from the 2nd floor.

ℹ Information

Bank of China (中国银行, Zhōngguó Yínháng; Huizhou Lu, 徽州路; ⊙8am-5.30pm) ATM and currency exchange; across from the entrance to Old Town.

ℹ Getting There & Away

Regular high-speed trains run from Huangshan station in Tunxi to Shexian (Huangshan) North Train Station (¥9 to ¥15, eight minutes), departing from around 7.30am to roughly 5.30pm. Buses from Tunxi's long-distance bus station also run regularly to Shexian (¥7, 45 minutes, frequent 6am to 5pm).

Tourist bus 2 runs from Tunxi's Tourist Distribution Center (p444) at 8am, 10am, 2pm and 4pm, to Tangmo (¥5.50, 45 minutes), stopping at Tangyue (¥6, one hour) and Huizhou Old Town (¥8, 75 minutes) before terminating in Yuliang (¥9, 90 minutes). The last bus returns to Tunxi at 4pm.

ℹ Getting Around

You can try to use tourist bus 2 to get around, but hiring a pedicab to take you to the sights (¥40/80 for a half/full day) is more convenient. Getting return cabs in Yuliang and Tangmo can be tricky.

Bus 702 (¥1) runs from Shexian North Train Station to Yuliang via Huizhou Old Town.

To reach Tangyue, take bus 701 (¥1) to the Yinyue Guangchang stop and change to bus 2.

Qiyan Shan   齐云山

Qiyun Shan (Qíyún Shān; Mar-Nov ¥75, Dec-Feb ¥55; ⊙8am-5pm Mon-Fri, 7.30am-5.30pm Sat & Sun; P) means 'mountain as high as the clouds' and it's an apt description: though not actually

that high (just 585m) its peaks do pierce the low-lying, ghostly puffs of mist that regularly envelop the region. Long venerated by Taoists, the reddish sandstone rock provides a mountain home to temples, many built into the mountain itself, and the monks who tend to them. It's a 45-minute bus trip west of Tunxi.

Most tour groups get dropped off at a back entrance, so if you arrive by public bus you'll likely be on your own for the 75-minute climb up stone steps to the ticket office. Just beyond, **Zhenxian Cave** (真仙洞府, Zhēnxiān Dòngfǔ) houses a complex of Taoist shrines in grottoes and niches gouged from the sandstone cliffs. Further on, seated within the smoky interior of the vast and dilapidated **Xuán Tiān Tàisù Gōng** (玄天太素宫) is an effigy of Zhengwu Dadi, a Taoist deity. A further temple hall, the **Yùxū Gōng** (玉虚宫), is erected beneath the huge brow of a 200m-long sandstone cliff, enclosed around effigies of Zhengwu Dadi and Laotzu.

A village – seemingly plonked in the middle of the mountain range – stretches along **Moonlight Street** (月华天街, Yuehua Tian Jie). Most residents operate restaurants and snack stands from their homes.

The bus from Tunxi will likely drop you off on the side of the road, from where you'll walk through a village to **Dengfeng Bridge** (登封桥, Dēngfēng Qiáo). Return buses sometimes hang around the bridge; otherwise wait at the side of the road for buses coming from Yixian. The last bus from Yixian to Tunxi departs at 5pm; the last tourist bus departs at 4pm. Buses (¥12) also run to Qiyun Shan from the transport hub next to Huangshan North station.

Hongcun   宏村
☑0559 / POP 4000

The Unesco World Heritage Site of Hongcun (Hóngcūn; ¥104; open 7am to 5.30pm), is the most-visited and best-known of the Huizhou villages. It is a standout example of ancient feng shui planning, a perfect marriage of symbolism and function, predicated on a sophisticated network of waterways. Founded in the Song dynasty, the village was remodelled in the Ming dynasty by village elders, under the direction of a geomancer, to suggest an ox; its still-functioning waterway system represents the animal's entrails.

⊙ Sights

Hongcun has crescent-shaped **Moon Pond** (月沼, Yuè Zhǎo) at its heart, or rather at its

ZHAJI

Stuffed with old stone bridges and creaking, whitewashed ancient buildings, the charming, very pretty and large village of **Zhaji** (查济古镇, Zhājǐ Gǔzhèn; Nov-Feb ¥60, Mar-Oct ¥80) dates originally back to the Sui and Tang dynasties, though most of the structures you will see are from the Ming (80 in all) and Qing dynasty (109).

The settlement differs from other villages in the region as it is much further to the north of Tunxi and is not actually a Huizhou village. Look out for the elegant and fine **Rusong Pagoda** (如松塔, Rúsōngtǎ) whose name means 'Like a Pine Tree Pagoda'. The view down onto **Xuxi Street** (许溪街, Xuxi Jie) is a lovely perspective, while the exquisite **Honglou Bridge** (红楼桥, Hónglóu Qiáo) is a picture. However, the best way to infuse yourself with the charms of the village is to wander through its alleys and lanes.

Frequent high-speed trains (¥51.50, 43 minutes) run from Huangshan North Train Station to Jingxian (泾县, Jīngxiàn), from where buses (¥11, one hour) run from the bus station alongside the train station to Zhaji.

stomach – as that's what the pond represents in the village's ox-shaped layout. Larger **South Lake** (南湖, Nán Hú), built later, is another stomach; **Leigang Mountain** (雷岗山, Léigǎng Shān), to the north, is the head. The busy square by **Hongji Bridge** (宏际桥, Hóngjì Qiáo) on the West Stream is shaded by two ancient trees (the 'horns' of the ox), a red poplar and a ginkgo.

The village has long been the stronghold of the Wang (汪) clan, although the person who designed the village's water system was not of the same clan but was a woman named Hu Zhong. Her portrait was worshipped in the **Wangshi Ancestral Hall** (汪氏宗堂). If the **bridge** at the entrance to the village looks familiar, it's because it featured in the opening scene of Ang Lee's *Crouching Tiger, Hidden Dragon*. The picturesque Moon Lake also features in the film. Built by a salt merchant, the Chengzhi Hall (p436) dates from 1855.

Other notable buildings include the **Utopian Residency** (桃源居, Táoyuán Jū), with its elaborate carved wood panels, and the **South Lake Academy** (南湖书院, Nánhú Shūyuàn), which enjoys an enviable setting beside tranquil South Lake. Overlooking Moon Pond is a gathering of further halls, chief among which is the dignified **Lexu Hall** (乐叙堂, Lèxù Táng), a hoary Ming antique from the first years of the 15th century.

Chengzhi Hall HISTORIC SITE

(承志堂, Chéngzhì Táng; Shangshuizhen Lu, 上水圳路) Flung up by a salt merchant, the Chengzhi Hall dates from 1855 and has 28 rooms, adorned with fabulous woodcarvings, 2nd-floor balconies and light wells. Peepholes on top-floor railings are for girls to peek at boy visitors and the little alcove in the mahjong room was used to hide the concubine. The now-faded gold-brushed carvings are said to have required 100 taels of the expensive stuff and took over four years to reach completion and full fruition.

Mukeng Zhuhai FOREST

(木坑竹海; ¥40; ⏱7.30am-5pm) A rich and dense forest of feathery bamboo, Mukeng is most famous as the setting for the breathtaking zero-gravity bamboo-top fight scenes in *Crouching Tiger, Hidden Dragon*. You can't quite get to the exact spot where the magical swordplay was enacted, but you can hike 1km up the ridge for views over the grove of golden plumes. You can also walk across a dramatically perched and rather nerve-racking **glass bridge** (¥60).

Tachuan VILLAGE

(塔川; ¥20; ⏱7.30am-5pm) Tachuan is a favourite with photographers, especially in the early spring, when the rapeseed blooms, and in the autumn, when the leaves of the old-growth trees turn vivid colours. Year-round you can stroll the flagstone walking path through the village, past residents tending their rice and tea fields. From afar, the village looks like a pagoda (hence the name; the 'tǎ' in Tachuan means 'pagoda'; the full name means 'Pagoda River') as it's built across the steps of foothills.

🛏 Sleeping

Qíng Hé Yuè HOSTEL ¥

(清和月; ☎139 5596 8814, 0559 217 1713; 28-29 Hou Jie, 后街28-29号; dm/d ¥60/380; ❉🖥) This great choice has tidy, though small, six-bed dorm rooms with showers. Across the alleyway a 200-year-old villa houses the double rooms. All guests are free to use the common areas in the old house, the highlight of which is the 3rd-floor veranda, from where you can look out over the village rooftops. Friendly staff speak good English.

⭐ **Long Lane Inn** BOUTIQUE HOTEL ¥¥
(宏村一品更楼, Hóngcūn Yīpǐn Gēng Lóu; ☑ 0559 554 2001; 1 Shangshui Zhen, 上水甽1号; r incl breakfast ¥380-1280; ❄ ➚) Housed in a gorgeous Ming dynasty villa, Long Lane Inn is a tourist attraction in its own right. There are nine different rooms, some with traditional rosewood Chinese four-poster beds, arranged around a courtyard. It's in a quiet corner of the village, away from the tourist scrum. Mornings start with birdsong and a good Chinese breakfast.

✖ Eating & Drinking

Vendors sell local specialities like *chòu dòufu* (臭豆腐, 'stinky' fermented tofu) and *gāncài shāobing* (干菜烧饼, dried vegetable cakes). The one on the edge of Moon Pond is particularly good. Plenty of restaurants in town cater to tourists. There's a row of cheaper joints just outside the village, on the other side of Hongji Bridge.

Hongcun has a smattering of cafes that serve good coffee and morph into bars in the evening, though pretty much everything shuts down around 9pm.

❶ Getting There & Away

Tourist bus 1 runs to Hongcun (¥20, 1½ hours) via Xidi from Tunxi's Huangshan Tourist Distribution Centre, leaving hourly from 8am to 4pm. Return buses run hourly from 8am to 5pm. The fare from Hongcun to Xidi (30 minutes) and Pingshan (15 minutes) is ¥6. Buses (¥30) also run to Hongcun and Xidi from the train station in Tunxi.

From Hongcun you can travel onwards to Tangkou, for Huangshan (¥15, one hour, hourly 6.50am to 2.50pm).

❶ Getting Around

There are several bicycle rental shops (出租自行车, *chūzū zìxíngchē*; ¥40 per day) outside the village, on the modern street opposite Hongji Bridge.

Taxis and pedicabs can be picked up in front of the village. A pedicab ride to Tachuan and Mukeng Zhuhai costs ¥30. You'll need to negotiate for the driver to wait for you as returning pedicabs are rare.

Xidi 西递

☑ 0559 / POP 1000

Typical of the elegant Huizhou style, Xidi's 124 surviving buildings reflect the wealth and prestige of the prosperous merchants who settled here. Its Unesco World Heritage Site status means **Xidi** (西递, Xīdì; ¥104; ☉ 7am-5pm) enjoys a lucrative tourist economy, yet it remains a picturesque tableau of slender lanes, cream-coloured walls topped with horse-head gables, roofs capped with dark tiles, and doorways ornately decorated with carved lintels. From here you can head out further into the countryside, to explore less-visited villages such as Nanping, Guanlu and Bishan.

◉ Sights

Dating from AD 1047, the village has for centuries been a stronghold of the Hu (胡) clan, descended from the eldest son of the last Tang emperor who fled here in the twilight years of the Tang dynasty. The magnificent three-tiered Ming dynasty decorative arch, the **Húwénguāng Páifāng** (胡文光牌坊), at the entrance to the village, is an ostentatious symbol of Xidi's former standing.

Numerous other notable structures are open for inspection, including **Diji Hall** (迪吉堂, Díjí Táng) and **Zhuimu Hall** (追慕堂, Zhuīmù Táng), both on Dalu Jie (大路街). **Jing'ai Hall** (敬爱堂, Jìng'ài Táng) is the town's largest building, a multipurpose hall where wedding ceremonies and clan meetings were held and punishments meted out. Back in the day, women weren't allowed inside. **Xiyuan** (西园) is a small house known for its exquisite stone carvings on the windows. Unlike regular carvings, these are carved on both sides.

Paths lead out from the village to nearby hills where there are suitable spots for picture-postcard panoramas of the village (though a mobile-phone tower blights the landscape). If you want to avoid the crowds, you'll have to start early or hang out late: tour groups start roaming around at 7am and only trickle out at 5pm or so.

Nanping VILLAGE
(南屏, Nánpíng; ¥43; ☉ 8am-5pm) Labyrinthine Nanping has a history of more than 1100 years. However, it's relatively recent history that draws most visitors, particularly film fans: much of Zhang Yimou's 1989 tragedy *Judou* was filmed inside the village's **Xuzhi Hall** (叙秩堂, Xùzhì Táng). Props from the film and behind-the-scenes photographs from the filming are on display inside the dramatic 530-year-old hall. Parts of Ang Lee's 1999 *Crouching Tiger, Hidden Dragon* were filmed next door in the Ming dynasty **Kuiguang Hall** (奎光堂, Kuíguāng Táng).

ANHUI PINGSHAN

Guanlu VILLAGE

(关麓, Guānlù; ¥35; ⊙8am-5pm) This small village's drawcard sights are the extravagant **households** (八大家, bādàjiā) of eight rich brothers. Each Qing-dynasty residence shares similar elegant Huizhou features, with interior courtyards, carved wood panels and small gardens. A distinctive aspect of the residences is their elegantly painted ceilings, the patterns and details of which survive. Each an independent entity, the households are interconnected by doors and linked together into a systemic whole.

🛏 Sleeping & Eating

Xidi and nearby Bishan have two of the most attractive boutique hotels in the region so spending the night is recommended.

There are plenty of indistinguishable restaurants, cafes and snack vendors here. The best meals in town are served at the Pig's Heaven Inn at the back of the village – it's well worth the trouble of finding it.

★ Pig's Heaven Inn BOUTIQUE HOTEL ¥¥

(猪栏酒吧, Zhūlán Jiǔbā; ☑138 5590 6765; http://blog.sina.com.cn/zhulanjiuba; Renrang Li, Xidi, 西递镇仁让里; s/d incl breakfast ¥390/610; ❊@☎) 🍃 When Shanghai artist Li Guoyu discovered this Ming dynasty home it was being used as a pigsty (hence the name). She painstakingly restored it, adding an eclectic blend of vintage furniture and mid-20th-century memorabilia. Cheaper rooms may be pokey but all guests can make use of the common areas, including a 3rd-floor veranda overlooking the village rooftops.

Xidi Travel Lodge HOTEL ¥¥

(西递行馆, Xīdì Xíngguǎn; ☑0559 515 6999; 西递; d incl breakfast from ¥358; ℗❊@☎) This can't-miss-it property, just behind the main gate to Xidi village, is a sprawling multi-building affair with comfortable rooms, its own restaurant and alfresco cafe. All rooms have modern showers, flat-screen TVs and faux antique furnishing, while some have balconies. Get a room facing the small tea garden.

★ Pig's Inn Bishan BOUTIQUE HOTEL ¥¥¥

(猪栏酒吧璧山, Zhūlán Jiǔbā Bìshān; ☑0559 517 5555; http://blog.sina.com.cn/zhulanjiuba; Bishan, 璧山村; tw/d incl breakfast ¥790/910; ❊☎) 🍃 There is no better way to experience the extravagant villas of the Huizhou merchants than to spend a few days living in one, waking for breakfast overlooking the courtyard, and spending a rainy afternoon in the wood-panelled study. At this nine-room boutique hotel, inside a Qing dynasty home masterfully restored by Shanghai artist Li Guoyu, you can do exactly that.

🔒 Shopping

Librairie Avant-Garde BOOKS

(先锋书店, Xiānfēng Shūdiàn; Bishan, 璧山; ⊙10am-noon & 1-6pm) An unlikely bookshop in an unlikely place, this is the Bishan branch of the stupendous Nanjing bookshop, Librairie Avant-Garde, coaxed into existence by a pair of Beijing artists who relocated to the village. While the open-air courtyard of a restored ancestral hall may not be the best environment for books (it's awfully damp), it certainly is stunning.

ℹ Getting There & Away

Tourist bus 1 runs to Xidi (¥14, one hour) from Tunxi's Huangshan Tourist Distribution Center (p444), leaving hourly from 8am to 4pm. From Xidi buses leave hourly for Hongcun (¥6, 30 minutes), stopping at Pingshan (¥6, 15 minutes). From the bus hub next to Huangshan North Station, buses run to Xidi (¥23, one per hour, 8.30am to 6pm).

For Tangkou you'll need to first get a bus to Hongcun.

For all other onward travel, you'll need to first get to Yixian (¥3, 20 minutes, every 30 minutes, 7.30am to 3.30pm), the nearest transit hub. From Yixian, it's possible to travel on to Jiuhua Shan (¥50, 3½ hours, two daily, 6.50am and 1.15pm), Hangzhou (¥91, two daily, 8.15am and 1.35pm) and Shanghai (¥151, two daily, 7.20am and 2.20pm). There are also frequent buses between Yixian and Tunxi's long-distance bus station (¥14, one hour).

ℹ Getting Around

To get to Guanlu and Nanping, you'll need to first travel to Yixian, where minibuses (¥3, every 30 minutes, 7am to 4pm) depart and stop at both villages. Minibuses also travel to Bishan (¥2, 15 minutes, hourly, 7.30am to 3.30pm).

It's easier to pick up a taxi in Xidi than a pedicab. A taxi ride to Nanping or Guanlu costs around ¥40; to Bishan, ¥20.

Pingshan 屏山

☑0559 / POP 3050

Pingshan (Píngshān), first settled in the Tang dynasty, was once the largest village in the county, with 38 ancestral halls and 13 archways. Its stature made it a target during the Cultural Revolution; only a handful of these structures remain. The lack of grand halls means that Pingshan sees few visitors; most who do come are art students sitting with easels in shady corners. With its canal lined with rose bushes, meandering cobblestone lanes and whitewashed homes, the village does make a pretty picture. Just a few kilometres away is Xiuli, a repository of restored old buildings.

⊙ Sights

Pingshan (¥50; ⊘7.30am-5pm) village was designed as a boat riding through the waves of hills (and historical forces), its residential houses likened to cabins. Some noteworthy structures include **Píngshān Gŏngzhì** (屏山拱峙), the only gate still standing, and **Shuguangyu Hall** (舒光裕堂, Shūguāngyù Táng), the only painted *ménlóu* (门楼, gate house) in Huizhou. The nearly 300-year-old **Imperial Guard Temple** (御前侍卫寺, Yùqián Shìwèi Sì), with its glorious entranceway of elaborately carved stone, has been artfully refashioned into a gorgeous boutique hotel.

At the northern tip of the village is the rouge-coloured, 900-year-old **Sāngū Miào** (三姑庙, Three Goddess Temple). In the temple's main hall are the Sānshèng Lóngnǚ (Three Sacred Dragon Girls) with 18 *luóhàn* (arhat, 罗汉) in attendance.

Yixian Xiuli Cinema Village HISTORIC BUILDING
(黟县秀里影视村, Yìxiàn Xiùlǐ Yǐngshìcūn; Xiuli, 秀里; ¥50) Xiuli, which opened in 2007, is a collection of 100-plus historic structures from around Yixian County that were left in ruins because their owners couldn't afford to maintain them. Here they've been restored and given new life, with art deco touches adding extra cachet. What could be a tourist trap is actually an arrestingly beautiful, if artificial, village, curated with a film-maker's eye (it's the pet project of film producer and frequent Zhang Yimou collaborator Zhang Zhenyan).

🛏 Sleeping

Pingshan and Xiuli both have beautiful boutique hotels, though unless you're also planning to splash out on a driver, neither makes for a convenient base. Budget accommodation in Pingshan caters exclusively to classes of art students who book en masse. Xiuli has just one hotel and is very quiet.

Xiuli Huizhou Culture Hotel BOUTIQUE HOTEL ¥¥
(秀里徽州庄园精品文化酒店, Xiùlǐ Huīzhōu Zhuāngyuán Jīngpǐn Wénhuà Jiǔdiàn; ☑0559 518 2979; Xiuli, 秀里; r ¥600-6000; ❉ 🛜 🌊) Filling several restored buildings inside the Yixian Xiuli Cinema Village, this boutique hotel has 31 rooms of various configurations, from humble doubles to sprawling family suites, decorated with a careful selection of antiques. Guests can take advantage of the pool, inside another refitted historic hall, with colourful, Mondrian-esque window panes.

★**Imperial Guard Boutique Hotel** BOUTIQUE HOTEL ¥¥¥
(御前侍卫艺术精品酒店, Yùqián Shìwèi Yishù Jīngpǐn Jiǔdiàn; ☑133 5909 1777, 0599 555 2777; imperial_guard@163.com; Pingshan, 屏山村; d & tr incl breakfast ¥921-2000, 3-bed detached house ¥3995; ❉ 🛜) All that was left of the nearly 300-year-old Imperial Guard Temple was the facade. Film producer Zhang Zhenyan reinvented the rest using beams salvaged from other structures and concession-era antiques. The result is this swoon-worthy, 10-room boutique hotel, favoured by movers and shakers of the Chinese film world. Zhang's son, who speaks fluent English, and his wife manage the place.

❶ Getting There & Away

Pingshan and Xiuli are in between Hongcun and Xidi. Hourly buses running to and from the two villages can drop you off in Pingshan or Xiuli (¥6, 15 minutes); tell the driver when you get on the bus where you want to get off. You can try to hail the same bus from the side of the road going back, though this isn't always possible and it's nearly impossible to pick up a cab at either village. As such, it's best to visit these two areas with a hired taxi or pedicab from Xidi.

Huangshan   黄山

☑ 0559

When its granite peaks and twisted pines are wreathed in spectral folds of mist, the idyllic views of Huangshan (Huángshān; literally 'Yellow Mountain') easily nudge it into the select company of China's top 10 – nay, top five – sights. Legions of poets and painters have drawn inspiration from Huangshan's iconic beauty. Yesterday's artists seeking an escape from the hustle and bustle of the temporal world have been replaced by crowds of tourists, who bring the hustle and bustle with them: the mountain is inundated with tourist traffic at choke points, so the magic can rapidly evaporate, especially during holiday periods and weekends. But Huangshan still rewards visitors with moments of tranquillity, and the unearthly views are simply breathtaking.

Climate

Locals claim that it rains more than 200 days a year up on the mountain. Allow yourself

Huangshan

N 0 — 1 km
0 — 0.5 miles

NORTH SEA

Taiping (5km)

Purple Cloud Peak (1700m)

6

Beginning to Believe Peak (1683m)

Bank of China

Beihai Clinic

5 12 3

14

9 Tianhai Lake

White Goose Ridge (1770m)

White Goose Ridge Station

EAST SEA

West Sea Canyon Cable Car

4

Tianhai Station

Bright Summit Peak (1841m)

West Sea Canyon Trail

11

WEST SEA

Aoyu Peak (1780m)

Huangshan 1

Lotus Flower Peak (1873m)

Cloud Valley Cable Car

7

Lianrui Peak (1776m)

Jade Screen Peak (1770m)

15

Jade Screen Tower Station

Heavenly Capital Peak (1810m)

Cloud Valley Station

2

Jade Screen Cable Car

10

Taohua River

Mercy Light Pavilion Station

Purple Stone Peak (1682m)

8

Huangshan Front Gate

Taohua River

East Bus Station

TANGKOU

16

Huangshan Scenic Area Emergency Medical Center

Tunxi (30km) 13 Bank of China

Huangshan

several days and climb when the forecast is best. Spring (April to June) generally tends to be misty, which means you may be treated to some sublime scenery, but you're just as likely to encounter a dense fog that obscures everything except for a line of yellow ponchos extending up the trail. Summer (July to August) is the rainy season, though storms can blow through fairly quickly. Autumn (September to October) is generally considered to be the best travel period. Even at the height of summer, average temperatures rarely rise above 20°C (68°F) at the summit, so come prepared. Summit hotels usually offer warm jackets for sunrise watchers.

⊙ Sights & Activities

Buses from Tunxi drop you off at the **Tourist Distribution Center** (新国线客车站, Xīnguóxiàn Kèchēzhàn; Tangchuan Lu, 汤川路) in the tourist village 2km south of Tangkou, the town at the southern foot of Huangshan. The area around the bus station is a base for climbers; you can stock up on supplies (maps, rain gear and food), store luggage (¥10 per bag per day) and arrange onward transport here. Tangchuan Lu runs north to the town itself, where you can find amenities such as China Post and banks with international ATMs.

Tangkou Town is small: basically two streets, Yanxi Zonglu and Yanxi Xilu, on either side of a river; look for the stairs leading down from the bridge on Tangchuan Lu.

Huangshan Summit   VIEWPOINT
The summit's huge network of connecting trails and walks meander up, down and across several different peaks. More than a few visitors spend several nights on the peak, and the **North Sea** (北海, Běihǎi) sunrise is a highlight for those staying overnight. **Refreshing Terrace** (清凉台; Qīngliáng Tái) is five minutes' walk from Beihai Hotel (p443) and attracts sunrise crowds. Lucky visitors

are rewarded with the luminous spectacle of *yúnhǎi* (literally 'sea of clouds'): idyllic pools of mist that settle over the mountain, filling its chasms and valleys with fog.

The staggering and other-worldly views from the summit reach out over huge valleys of granite and enormous formations of rock, topped by gravity-defying slivers of stone and the gnarled forms of ubiquitous Huangshan pine trees (*Pinus taiwanensis*). Many rocks have been christened with fanciful names by the Chinese, alluding to figures from religion and myth. **Beginning to Believe Peak** (始信峰, Shǐxìn Fēng; 1683m), with its jaw-dropping views, is a major bottleneck for photographers. En route to the North Sea, pause at the **Flower Blooming on a Brush Tip** (梦笔生花; Mèngbǐ Shēnghuā), a 1640m-high granite formation topped by a pine tree. Clamber up to **Purple Cloud Peak** (丹霞峰, Dānxiá Fēng; 1700m) for a long survey over the landscape and try to catch the sun as it descends in the west. Aficionados of rock formations should keep an eye out for the poetically named **Mobile Phone Rock** (手机石, Shǒujī Shí), near the top of the Western Steps.

If you're coming via cable car, the hike between **White Goose Ridge station** (白鹅岭站, Bái'élíng Zhàn) and **Jade Screen Tower station** (玉屏楼站, Yùpínglóu Zhàn) takes 3½ hours – though you'd be missing out if you didn't explore the summit further.

Eastern Steps   HIKING
A medium-fast climb of the 7.5km Eastern Steps from **Cloud Valley Station** (云谷站, Yúngǔ Zhàn), at 890m, to **White Goose Ridge** (白鹅峰, Bái'é Fēng; 1770m) can be done in 2½ hours. The route is pleasant, but lacks the awesome geological scenery of the Western Steps. In spring, wild azalea and weigela add gorgeous splashes of colour to the wooded slopes.

ANHUI HUANGSHAN

ASCENDING & DESCENDING THE MOUNTAIN

Regardless of how you ascend **Huangshan** (黄山, Yellow Mountain; www.chinahuangshan. gov.cn; Mar-Nov ¥230, Dec-Feb ¥150, child 1.2-1.4m ¥115, under 1.2m free), you will be stung by a dizzying entrance fee. You can pay at the Eastern Steps near the Cloud Valley Station or at the Mercy Light Pavilion Station (p442), where the Western Steps begin. Shuttle buses (¥19) run to both places from Tangkou.

Three basic routes will get you up to the summit: the short, hard way (Eastern Steps; the longer, harder way (Western Steps); and the very short, easy way (cable car). It's possible to do a 10-hour circuit going up the Eastern Steps and then down the Western Steps in one day, but you'll have to be slightly insane, in good shape and you'll definitely miss out on some of the more spectacular, hard-to-get-to areas.

A basic itinerary would be to take an early morning bus from Tunxi, climb the Eastern Steps, hike around the summit area, spend the night at the top, catch the sunrise and then hike back down the Western Steps the next day, giving you time to catch an after-noon bus back to Tunxi. Most travellers do opt to spend more than one night on the sum-mit to explore all the various trails. Don't underestimate the hardship involved; the steep gradients and granite steps can wreak havoc on your knees, both going up and down.

Most sightseers are packed (and we mean *packed*) into the summit (p441) area above the upper cable car stations, consisting of a network of trails running between various peaks, so don't go expecting peace and quiet. The volume of visitors is mounting every year and paths are being constantly widened at bottleneck points where scrums develop. The highlight of the climb for many independent travellers is the lesser-known West Sea Canyon (p443) hike, a more rugged, exposed section where most tour groups do not venture.

Make sure you bring enough water, food, warm clothing and rain gear before climbing. Bottled water and food prices increase the higher you go as porters carry everything up. As mountain paths are easy to follow and English signs plentiful, guides are unnecessary.

Much of the climb is comfortably shaded and although it can be tiring, it's a doddle compared with the Western Steps.

Slow-moving porters use the Eastern Steps for ferrying up their massive, swaying loads of food, drink and building materials, so considerable traffic plies the route. While clambering up, note the more ancient flight of steps that makes an occasional appearance alongside the newer set.

Purists can extend the Eastern Steps climb by several hours by starting at the Front Gate – also called the **South Gate** (南 大门, Nán Dàmén) – where a stepped path crosses the road at several points before linking with the main Eastern Steps trail.

Western Steps
HIKING

The 15km Western Steps route has some stel-lar scenery, but it's twice as long and stren-uous as the Eastern Steps (p441), and much easier to enjoy if you're clambering down rather than gasping your way up. If you take the cable car up the mountain, just do this in reverse. The Western Steps descent begins at the **Flying Rock** (飞来石; Fēilái Shí), a boul-der perched on an outcrop.

The steps go over **Bright Summit Peak** (光 明顶, Guāngmíng Dǐng; 1841m), from where

you can see **Aoyu Peak** (鳌鱼峰, Áoyú Fēng; 1780m), which resembles two turtles! South of Aoyu Peak en route to Lotus Flower Peak, the descent funnels you down through **Gleam of Sky** (一线天, Yīxiàn Tiān), a remarkably nar-row chasm – a vertical split in the granite – pinching a huge rock suspended above the heads of climbers. Further on, **Lotus Flower Peak** (莲花峰, Liánhuā Fēng; 1873m) marks the highest point, but is occasionally sealed off, preventing ascents. **Lianrui Peak** (莲蕊峰, Liánruǐ Fēng; 1776m) is decorated with rocks whimsically named after animals, but save some energy for the much-coveted and stag-gering climb – 1321 steps in all – up **Heavenly Capital Peak** (天都峰, Tiāndū Fēng; 1810m) and the stunning views that unfold below. As elsewhere on the mountain, young lovers have padlocks engraved with their names up here and lash them for eternity to the chain railings. Access to Heavenly Capital Peak (and other peaks) is sometimes restricted for maintenance and repair (especially if the steps have become dangerous), so keep those fingers crossed when you go!

At the halfway point is **Banshan Temple** (半山寺; Bànshān Sì), which literally means halfway temple. At the bottom of the steps is **Mercy Light Pavilion** (慈光阁站, Cíguānggé

Zhàn), which has been repurposed as the cable car station. From here, you can pick up a minibus back to Tangkou (¥20) or continue walking 1.5km to the hot-springs area.

West Sea Canyon
HIKING

(西海大峡谷, Xīhǎi Dàxiágǔ) A strenuous and awe-inspiring 8.5km hike, the West Sea Canyon route descends into a gorge (Xīhǎi Dàxiágǔ) with some impressively exposed stretches (not for those with vertigo), taking a minimum four hours to complete. You can access the canyon at either the northern entrance, near the Paiyunlou Hotel, or the southern entrance, near the **Baiyun Hotel** (白云宾馆, Báiyún Bīnguǎn; ☑ 0559 558 2708; dm/d ¥388/1880; ❋ 🛜) aka White Clouds Hotel.

Avoid this region in bad weather as things can get hairy. A good option to start would be at the northern entrance. From there, you'll pass through some rock tunnels and exit onto the best bits of the gorge. Here, stone steps have been attached to the sheer side of the mountain – peer over the side for some serious butt-clenching views down. Don't worry, there are handrails. If you're pressed for time or don't have the energy to stomach a long hike, do a figure-eight loop of **Ring Road 1** (一环上路口, Yīhuán Shàng Lùkǒu) and **Ring Road 2** (二环上路口, Èrhuán Shàng Lùkǒu), and head back to the northern entrance. Sure, you'll miss some stunning views across lonely, mist-encased peaks, but you'll also miss the knee-killing dip into the valley and the subsequent climb out to the southern entrance.

The **West Sea Canyon Cable Car** (西海大峡索道, Xīhǎi Dàxiá Suǒdào; one way ¥80; ⊙6am-4.30pm Mar-Nov) runs between **Tianhai Station** (天海站, Tiānhǎi Zhàn), at the southern entrance, and the bottom of the valley in a startling three minutes.

Huangshan Hot Springs
HOT SPRINGS

(黄山温泉, Huángshān Wēnquán; ¥298; ⊙10.30am-11pm) Costing more than admission to the mountain itself, a stop here is definitely an indulgence. Still, after a long day (or several) of hiking, the tubs, filled with natural spring water, are heavenly and may just seem worth it. There are many to choose from, including ones steeped in Chinese medicinal herbs.

Shuttle buses (¥11) run from Tangkou to the hot springs or from the lower stations of both cable cars (¥8). But if you're coming from the Western Steps, the 1.5km walk down here from the cable car station passes several waterfalls. Don't walk on the road: look for the sign to the pedestrian path at the bottom of the car park.

🛏 Sleeping

Huangshan visits should ideally include nights on the summit, though this is not essential. Room prices rise on Saturday and Sunday, and are astronomical during major holiday periods (when you need to book ahead). It's possible to camp at select, though not scenic, points on the mountain, such as the plaza in front of the Beihai Hotel You'll need to ask for permission and pay a fee of ¥180.

🛏 On the Mountain

Paiyunlou Hotel
HOTEL ¥¥

(排云楼宾馆, Páiyúnlóu Bīnguǎn; ☑ 0559 231 7070; dm/d/tr ¥280/1280/1480; ❋ 🛜) With an excellent location near Tianhai Lake (Tiānhǎi Hú) and the entrance to the West Sea Canyon, plus three-star comfort, this place is recommended for those who prefer a slightly more tranquil setting. None of the regular rooms have views, but the newer dorms have unobstructed vistas and come with TVs and attached showers. Discounted dorms fall to ¥210 and doubles are usually ¥680.

Beihai Hotel
HOTEL ¥¥¥

(北海宾馆, Běihǎi Bīnguǎn; ☑ 0559 558 2555; www.beihaihotelhuangshan.com; dm ¥300, d ¥1081-5062; ❋ @ 🛜) This is the best located hotel, but the four-star Beihai is also the busiest and lacks charm. Situated a 1.2km walk from the top of the Cloud Valley cable car, there's professional service, money exchange, a cafe and 30% discounts during the week. Larger doubles have older fittings than the smaller, better-fitted-out doubles (same price). The cheaper doubles are in the three-star compound across the square.

Yupinglou Hotel
HOTEL ¥¥¥

(玉屏楼宾馆, Yùpínglóu Bīnguǎn; ☑ 0559 558 2288; www.hsyplhotel.com; dm/d ¥400/1380; ❋ 🛜) A 10-minute walk to the right from the top of the **Jade Screen cable car** (p445) this four-star hotel is perched on a spectacular 1660m-high lookout just above the Welcoming Guest Pine Tree (迎客松, Yíngkèsōng). Aim for the doubles at the back, as some rooms have small windows with no views. Discounts generally bring doubles down to around ¥780 and dorm beds to about ¥150.

🛏 Tangkou

In the tourist village around the bus station chain hotels, like 7 Days Inn and Green Tree Inn, offer rooms for around ¥200. Mediocre midrange hotels geared to tour groups line Tangchuan Lu all the way to Tangkou Town, where rooms are a little cheaper; remember to look at rooms first and ask for discounts before committing. Many hotels in town offer transport to and from the Tourist Distribution Center (p441).

Grapevine Hotel HOTEL ¥
(黄山葡萄藤酒店, Huángshān Pútáoténg Jiǔdiàn; ☑ 0559 556 7377; 92 Tangchuan Lu, 汤川路92号; r from ¥80; ❋ ⚛) With sketches on the wall, this hotel has a youthful feel lacking at most hotels around the mountain. Rooms are basic but clean. It's just past the post office, before the bridge on the way to Tangkou Town (a 30-minute walk from the bus station).

Zhongruihuayi Hotel HOTEL ¥¥
(中瑞华艺大酒店, Zhōngruìhuáyì Dàjiǔdiàn; ☑ 0559 556 6888; www.huayihotel.cn; 119 Tangchuan Lu, 汤川路119号; r from ¥480; ❋ ⚛) Though this white four-star hotel doesn't look like much from the outside, it has the nicest rooms in Tangkou. Staff can help with bus and flight bookings and there's a free shuttle bus to the bus station.

✕ Eating

The tourist village next to the Tourist Distribution Center (p441) has numerous, nearly identical restaurants (dishes ¥10 to ¥100). There are supermarkets here, too, for loading up with snacks for the mountain assault.

For street food head into Tangkou where there are a few vendors on Yanxi Jie near the bridge. Most hotel restaurants offer buffets (breakfast ¥60; lunch and dinner ¥100 to ¥140) plus a selection of standard dishes (fried rice ¥50), though getting service outside meal times can be tricky. It's usually a better deal to sign up for a meal plan at your hotel.

❶ Information

Huangshan Tourist Distribution Center (黄山市旅游集散中心, Huángshān Lǚyóu Jísàn Zhōngxīn; ☑ 0559 255 8358; 31 Qiyun Dadao, 齐云大道31号; ⊙ 8.30am-5.30pm) Inside the bus station (to the right as you enter), the separate Huangshan Tourist Distribution Center has special tourist buses to popular destinations. Return buses operate hourly from 8am to 4pm, with a break from noon to 1pm.

MEDICAL SERVICES & POLICE

Huangshan Scenic Area Emergency Medical Center (黄山风景区卫生防疫中心, Huángshān Fēngjǐngqū Wèishēng Fángyì Zhōngxīn;

☑ 0559 562 436) On the east side of the river in Tangkou Town.
Beihai Clinic (北海医疗急救中心, Běihǎi Yīliáo Jíjiù Zhōngxīn; ☑ 0559 556 2555; ⊙ 8am-10pm) Opposite Beihai Hotel.
Police Station (派出所, pàichūsuǒ; ☑ 0559 558 1388) Opposite Beihai Hotel.

MONEY

Bank of China (中国银行, Zhōngguó Yínháng; Yanxi Jie, Tangkou, 沿溪街; ⊙ 8am-5pm) Southern end of Yanxi Jie with a 24-hour ATM.
Bank of China (中国银行, Zhōngguó Yínháng; ⊙ 8-11am & 2.30-5pm) Changes money and has an ATM that accepts international cards. Opposite Beihai Hotel.

❶ Getting There & Away

BUS

Buses from Tunxi (aka Huangshan Shi) take around one hour to reach Tangkou from either the long-distance bus station (¥20, frequent, 6am to 5pm) or the train station (¥20, departs when full, 6.30am to 5.30pm; may leave as late as 8pm in summer).

Buses back to Tunxi (¥20) from Tangkou depart on roughly the same schedule, and can be flagged down on the road to Tunxi. The last bus back leaves at 5.30pm.

The main bus depot for both long-distance buses to and from Tangkou and tourist buses around Huangshan is the Tourist Distribution Center (p441). Destinations include the following:
Hangzhou ¥110, 3½ hours, regular (6.50am to 6.20pm)
Hefei ¥98, four hours, regular (6.50am to 5.20pm)
Jiuhua Shan ¥54, 2½ hours, twice daily (6.30am and 2.20pm)
Nanjing ¥110, five hours, eight daily
Shanghai ¥135, 6½ hours, regular (6.10am to 6.10pm)
Wuhan ¥235, nine hours, two daily (8.40am and 5.30pm)
Yixian ¥17, one hour, four daily (8am, 9.30am, 1.40pm and 3.30pm; stops at Hongcun and Xidi)

TAXI

A taxi between Tunxi and the Huangshan Scenic Area should cost around ¥200; to the villages of Yixian ¥110 to ¥140.

❶ Getting Around

CABLE CAR

Cloud Valley Cable Car (云谷索道, Yúngǔ Suǒdào; one way Mar-Nov ¥80, Dec-Feb ¥65; ⊙ 7.30am-4.30pm) Runs from Cloud Valley Temple to White Goose Ridge, bypassing the Eastern Steps. Beware the long queues, especially during the holiday periods: it's best to arrive very early or late (if you're staying on the summit).

Jade Screen Cable Car (玉屏索道, Yùpíng Suǒdào; one way Mar-Nov ¥90, Dec-Feb ¥75; ⏱7am-4.30pm) Runs from Mercy Light Pavilion to Jade Screen Tower (p441) , just below the Yupinglou Hotel (p443), bypassing the Western Steps.

The West Sea Canyon Cable Car (p443) runs between Tianhai Station (p443), at the southern entrance, and the bottom of the West Sea Canyon valley.

SHUTTLE BUS

Official tourist shuttles run from the Tourist Distribution Center (p441) to Hot Springs (p443) (¥11), Cloud Valley Station (p441) (¥19) and Mercy Light Pavilion Station (p442) (¥19), departing every 20 minutes from 6am to 6.30pm, though they usually wait until enough people are on board. If you're staying in Tangkou Town, you can get the buses at the **east bus station** (东岭换乘分中心; Dōnglíng Huànchéng Fēnzhōngxīn; Tangchuan Lu, 汤川路) on Tangchuan Lu.

Jiuhua Shan 九华山

☑ 0566

The Tang dynasty Buddhists who determined Jiuhua Shan to be the earthly abode of the Bodhisattva Dizang (Ksitigarbha), Lord of the Underworld, chose well. Often shrouded in an other-worldly fog that pours in through the windows of its cliff-side temples, **Jiuhua Shan** (Jiǔhuá Mountain; Nine Flower Mountain; Feb-Nov ¥160, Dec-Jan ¥140) has a powerful gravitas, heightened by the devotion of those who come here to pray for the souls of the departed. It is one of China's four most sacred Buddhist peaks and there are dozens of active temples here, housing a population of some 500-plus monks and nuns.

The mountain is not untouched by commercialism, however; the hawkers of overpriced joss sticks and jade carvings come together with the ochre-coloured monasteries, flickering candles and the low, steady drone of Buddhist chanting emanating from pilgrims' smartphones to concoct an atmosphere both of this world and of another one entirely.

History

Jiuhua Shan was made famous by the 8th-century Korean monk Kim Kiao Kak (Jin Qiaojue), who meditated here for 75 years and was posthumously proclaimed to be the reincarnation of Dizang. In temples, Dizang is generally depicted carrying a staff and a luminous jewel, used to guide souls through the darkness of hell.

◉ Sights & Activities

Buses will let you off at Jiuhuashan bus station (九华山汽车站, Jiǔhuàshān qìchēzhàn), the local bus terminus and main ticket office where you purchase your ticket for the mountain. You'll also then need to buy a return shuttle-bus ticket (¥50, 20 minutes, half-hourly) from the counters on the left of the admission-ticket windows. The shuttle bus goes to Jiuhua village (九华镇), halfway up the mountain (or, as locals say, at roughly navel height in a giant Buddha's pot belly). The shuttle terminates at the bus station just before the gate (大门, dàmén) leading to the village, from where the main street (芙蓉路, Furong Lu; also called Jiuhua Jie, 九华街) heads south past hotels and restaurants.

Zhiyuan Temple · BUDDHIST TEMPLE
(祇园寺, Zhǐyuán Sì; ⏱6.30am-8.30pm) **FREE** Just past the village's main entrance on your left, worshippers hold sticks of incense to their foreheads and face the four directions at this enticingly esoteric yellow temple. Pilgrims can join chanting sessions in the evening, starting around 5pm.

Huacheng Si · BUDDHIST TEMPLE
(化成寺, Huàchéng Sì; ⏱6.30am-8.30pm) **FREE** Set back off the road, behind a pond, Huacheng Si was originally founded in the Tang dynasty (though the current structure is not that old). It has ornately carved lions guarding the main steps (one male and one female as Chinese lions traditionally are), colourful eaves and beams, and three huge golden representations depicting the past, present and future Buddhas.

Baisui Gong · BUDDHIST TEMPLE
(百岁宫, Bǎisuì Gōng; ⏱6am-5.30pm) **FREE** A 30-minute hike up the ridge behind Zhiyuan Temple leads you to Baisui Gong, an active temple built into the cliff in 1630 to consecrate the Buddhist monk Wu Xia, whose shrunken, embalmed body is coated in gold and sits shrivelled within an ornate glass cabinet in front of a row of pink lotus candles. A **cable car** (百岁宫缆车, Bǎisuì Gōng Lǎnchē; one way/return ¥55/100; ⏱7am-5.30pm) also makes the journey, departing from just off Furong Lu.

Jiuhua Shan Summit · HIKING
(九华山巅, Jiǔhuá Shān Diān) Hiking the summit of Jiuhua Mountain alongside pilgrims following a **stone trail** (天台正顶, Tiāntái Zhèng Dǐng) shaded by pines and bamboo is the highlight of a journey to the mountain.

To begin the full-day hike from the village, walk up Furong Lu for 450m and look for a sign on your left pointing up to **Huixiang Pavilion** (回香阁, Huíxiāng Gé).

From here to the summit takes four to five hours; count on about two to three hours to get back down to the village. Follow the path along the front of **Tonghui Nunnery** (通慧庵, Tōnghuì Ān) as the gentle incline transitions to steep stone steps. The 750m trek up to Huíxiāng Pavilion takes around 20 minutes. Above you reach the towering seven-storey **10,000 Buddha Pagoda** (万佛塔, Wàn Fó Tǎ), fashioned entirely from bronze and prettily lit at night. Continuing along, the path dips into a pleasant valley, passing **Roushen Temple** (肉身寺, Ròushén Sì) and **Welcoming Guest Pine** (迎客松, Yíngkè Sōng) en route to **Phoenix Pine** (凤凰松, Fènghuáng Sōng). From here, the two-hour, 4km walk to the summit, **Tiantai Peak** (天台正顶, Tiāntái Zhèng Dǐng; 1304m) is tough going, passing small temples and nunneries.

The summit is slightly damp, with mist shrouding the area. Within the faded **Tiantai Temple** (天台寺, Tiāntái Sì) on Tiantai Peak, a statue of the Dizang Buddha is seated within the **Dizang Hall** (地藏殿, Dìzàng Diàn), while from the magnificent **10,000 Buddha Hall** (万佛楼, Wànfó Lóu) above, a huge enthroned statue of the Dizang Buddha gazes at the breathless pilgrims mustering at his feet. The beams above your head glitter with rows of thousands of Buddhas.

There's another trail to your right before the main stairs to the Tiantai Temple. This one leads you to one of the highest and quietest points of the mountain, **Shiwang Peak** (十王峰, Shíwáng Fēng; 1344m), where you can stop and let the rolling fog sweep past you. This trail will also take you to Tiantai Temple, with far fewer crowds.

An easier route is to take a bus (return trip included with the ¥50 shuttle bus ticket) from Jiuhua village up to Phoenix Pine, from where a **cable car** (天台索道, Tiāntái Suǒdào; one way/return ¥85/160; ⏱ 6.50am-5pm) runs to the summit in five minutes. Note that from the terminus of the cable car, it's still a 1km climb up steps to Tiantai Temple.

🛏 Sleeping & Eating

Numerous in Jiuhua village, restaurants historically served only vegetarian food, though now some do offer meat. Look for dishes (¥10 to ¥100) featuring bamboo and mushrooms of all colours and shapes harvested from the mountain.

Zhayuan Temple (p445) serves vegetarian meals (5.30am, 10.40am and 4.40pm; ¥10) to the public after the monks have eaten, though often runs out of food due to its popularity.

Baisuigong Xiayuan Hotel HOTEL ¥¥
(百岁宫下院, Bǎisuìgōng Xiàyuàn; 🕿 0566 283 3122, 139 0566 7465; 1 Huacheng Lu, 化成路1号; r ¥360-1380; 🕸🖨) Pleasantly arranged around an old temple, this hotel combines the right atmosphere with a good location. Standard rooms are just that: simple but comfortable enough. It's right beside Julong Hotel, opposite Zhiyuan Temple (p445).

Julong Hotel HOTEL ¥¥¥
(聚龙大酒店, Jùlóng Dàjiǔdiàn; 🕿 0566 283 1368; Furong Lu, 芙蓉路; d & tw ¥1280-1480; 🕸🖨) Just 50m from the main gate, the long-standing Julong has friendly staff and quality rooms decked out with TVs and good bathrooms. Discounts knock rooms down to around ¥690 on weekdays and ¥890 on weekends. It's opposite Zhiyuan Temple (p445), off Furong Lu. Buffet breakfast is ¥68.

★ **Qiyuan Vegetarian** VEGETARIAN ¥¥
(祇园素斋, Qíyuán Sùzhāi; Shàngkètáng Bīnguǎn, 上客堂宾馆; dishes ¥28-188, buffet ¥88; ⏱ 11am-2pm & 5-8pm; 🖨) Come here to sample (and study) the exotic edible fungi, shoots and roots of the mountain. Dishes range from humble Chinese chestnuts flavoured with osmanthus (a flowering shrub; 桂花板栗, guìhuā bǎnlì; ¥30) to prized 'stone ear' mushrooms (石耳, shí'ěr; ¥188), a kind of lichen that grows on rock and is believed to possess medicinal properties.

🛈 Information

Bank of China (中国银行, Zhōngguó Yínháng; 65 Huacheng Lu, 化城路65号; ⏱ 9am-4.30pm) Foreign exchange and 24-hour international ATM. West of the main square, halfway up Huacheng Lu.

🛈 Getting There & Away

Buses from Jiuhuashan bus station (九华山汽车站, Jiǔhuàshān qìchēzhàn; the bus terminus and main Jiuhua Mountain ticket office) run to the following destinations:

Hangzhou ¥127, five hours, two daily (9.25am and 12.45pm)

Hefei ¥88, 3½ hours, hourly (last bus at 4.50pm)

Huangshan ¥54, three hours, two daily (7.20am and 2.30pm)

Nanjing ¥80, three hours, 10 daily

Shanghai (Hutailu Bus Station) ¥145, six hours, three daily (5.55am, 1.45pm and 3.55pm)

Tunxi ¥70, 3½ hours, two daily (7.20am and 1.30pm)

Wuhan ¥155, six hours, one daily (7am)

Yixian ¥60, 2½ hours, two daily (7.30am and 12.30pm)

The nearest high-speed train station is Chizhou (池州, Chízhōu). Buses depart hourly (¥12, one hour, 7am to 4.50pm) for Jiuhuashan bus station from the bus station next to the train station. Chizhou can be reached from Shanghai (¥221, four hours, four daily) and Hefei (¥69 to ¥91, 90 minutes, nine daily).

ⓘ Getting Around

The ¥50 shuttle ticket includes four bus rides: from the main ticket office to Jiuhua village (the base for the mountain ascent), from the village to **Phoenix Pine cable car station** (凤凰松站, Fènghuáng Sōng Zhàn) and back to the village, and from the village back to the main ticket office (first bus 7am, last bus 5pm). The Tiantai Cable Car (p446) runs up from the Phoenix Pine cable car station to the summit at Tiantai and the Baisui Gong Cable Car (p445) runs up to the eponymous temple from Furong Lu in the village below.

To get to Phoenix Pine, catch the bus (every 30 minutes or when full) from the bus station north of the main gate (cross the bridge on the right after the Julong Hotel, p446). On busy days you may need to queue for more than two hours for the cable car to/from the peak.

Hefei 合肥

📞 0551 / POP 7.8 MILLION

Hefei (Héféi) is the capital of Anhui. Besides the excellent museum, the city is quite a workaday and typical provincial city, with a limited amount to divert tourists from heading to the south of the province and Anhui's highlight sights.

⊙ Sights

Anhui New Provincial Museum　MUSEUM
(安徽省博物馆新馆, Ānhuīshěng Bówùguǎn Xīnguǎn; www.ahm.cn; 268 Huaining Lu, 怀宁路268号; ⊙9am-5pm Tue-Sun) FREE To get to grips with Anhui, it's well worth taking a half-day to explore this four-floor museum. Exhibits begin with Palaeolithic artefacts (some are replicas) mined from the earliest known settlements in Eurasia, which happen to be in Anhui. Other exhibitions cover the region's Three Kingdoms Period history (including a replica of Cao Cao's fabulous jade burial suit) and the symbolism evoked by Huizhou architecture and artworks. The building itself is quite a sight to behold.

The museum is 10km southwest of downtown, about a ¥30 taxi ride. Passport required.

Former Residence of Li Hongzhang　HOUSE
(李鸿章故居, Lǐ Hóngzhāng Gùjū; www.lihongzhang.org.cn; Huaihe Lu, 淮河路; ¥20; ⊙8.30am-6pm Apr-Oct, to 5.30pm Nov-Mar) Li Hongzhang, born to farmers in Hefei, rose to become a key official in the late Qing dynasty, playing a part in China's modernisation (and also in the signing of the much maligned unequal treaties foisted upon China). Set among the hubbub of the Huaihe Lu pedestrian street, this building is his restored former home and now serves as a museum with some English explanations on the man's life and politics.

Lord Bao Park　PARK
(包公园, Bāo Gōngyuán; 72 Wuhu Lu, 芜湖路72号; ⊙8am-6pm) FREE This pretty park with a central pond is named for native son Lord Bao, aka Bao Zheng, an official in the Northern Song dynasty (960–1279). There are several sights (joint admission ¥50) here relating to Bao, the highlight of which is **Lord Bao's Tomb** (包公墓园, Bāogōng Mùyuán). There's also **Bao Gong Temple** (包公祠, Bāogōng Cí), with a 3m-tall statue of Lord Bao, and **Qingfeng Tower**, a 42m pavilion built in 1999 to mark the 1000th anniversary of his birth.

🛏 Sleeping & Eating

Budget chain hotels can be found around the train station and on Huaihe Lu Buxing Jie. Midrange ones are located on the main commercial street of Changjiang Zhonglu.

For food, head to the pedestrianised Huaihe Lu Buxing Jie. The side streets have cheap eats and there's everything from fast-food chains to noodle shops. A night market sets up in the area too. An abundance of all kinds of snack food from all over China can be found on Lei Jie (罍街) off Ningguo Nanlu (宁国南路), which is generally hopping at breakfast time and late at night.

Green Tree Inn　HOTEL ¥
(格林豪泰, Gélín Háotài; 📞0551 6265 0988; www.998.com; 24 Hongxing Lu, 红星路24号; d ¥209; ※@🛜) This reliable, modern, midrange chain hotel offers compact, cheap and clean accommodation in a 24-room branch along a quiet residential street. There's food and shopping within walking distance.

Holiday Inn Express Downtown　HOTEL ¥¥¥
(Héféi Zhōngxīn Zhìxuǎn Jiàrì Jiǔdiàn, 合肥中心智选假日酒店; 📞0551 6570 6888; 279 Changjiang Zhonglu, 长江中路279号; d from ¥479; P※@🛜)

Hefei's best midrange deal is this well-located branch of the Holiday Inn (not to be confused with all the other branches in town). It's centrally located in a building shared by a bookshop and cafe (enter the hotel around the back). Rooms are modern, clean and comfortable. Look for 50% discounts online.

Drinking & Nightlife

The little alley Dongxi Xiang (东西巷), off Shuguang Lu (曙光路), is a colourful and fun strip of tiny bars and cafes with a DIY vibe – a refreshing change from the usual KTV (karaoke). The whole area is known as 中隐于市 (*zhōng yǐn yú shì*) and is a 15-minute taxi ride from downtown, just south of Tunxi Lu (屯溪路).

Shipyard BAR
(造船厂咖啡店, Zàochuánchǎng Kāfēidiàn; 50 Shuguang Lu, 曙光路50号; ⊙2pm-2am) Founded by a Frenchman, popular expat hang-out Shipyard has decent burgers (¥55), Guinness on tap (¥60), mojitos (¥55), bottles of Heineken (¥25) and live music on weekends. If it gets too loud or the cigar smoke gets too pungent, retreat to the small courtyard out the back. In the afternoon, coffee is brewed up.

ⓘ Information

Bank of China (中国银行, Zhōngguó Yínháng; Wuwei Lu, 无为路; ⊙8.15am-5pm) Branches on Wuwei Lu and Shouchun Lu, with currency exchange and international ATMs.
Civil Aviation Ticket Center (民航合肥售票中心, Mínháng Héféi Shòupiào Zhōngxīn; ☏0551 637 7777; 212 Shouchun Lu, 寿春路212号; ⊙8am-6pm) Air and train tickets.

ⓘ Getting There & Away

AIR

Hefei Xinqiao International Airport (合肥新桥国际机场, Héféi Xīnqiáo Guójì Jīchǎng; ☏0551 6377 7888; http://hfairport.com) is 32km northwest of Hefei. If you go for the earliest flights of the day, they are often cheap.

Daily flights include the following:
Beijing ¥1760, two hours, four daily
Guangzhou ¥1080, two hours, seven daily
Shanghai ¥1130, one hour, two daily
Xiamen ¥910, 1½ hours, four daily

BUS

Centrally located **Hefei long-distance bus station** (合肥长途汽车站, Héféi Chángtú Qìchēzhàn; 168 Mingguang Lu, 明光路168号; ⊙5.30am-9pm), near Xiaoyaojin Park, has buses to destinations in the surrounding provinces, including the following:
Hangzhou ¥138, six hours, 10 daily
Nanjing ¥63, 2½ hours, hourly (6.55am to 5.30pm)
Shanghai ¥145, six hours, every 40 minutes (6.40am to 7pm)
Wuhan ¥148, six hours, one daily (9am)

Buses to Jiuhua Shan (¥88, 3½ hours, every 40 minutes, 6.40am to 6pm) leave from the **tourist bus station** (旅游汽车站, Lǚyóu Qìchēzhàn; Zhanqian Jie, 站前街), 500m west of the train station.

Buses to Tunxi (¥98, four hours, 7.50am, 10.10am, 1pm and 3.20pm) via Huangshan (¥98, 3½ hours) depart from the **east bus station** (合肥汽车东站, Héféi Qìchē Dōngzhàn; 281 Dangtu Lu, 当涂路281号), 5km east of the city centre.

The so-called **main bus station** (客运总站, Kèyùn Zǒngzhàn; Zhanqian Jie, 站前街), just outside the train station, is actually for local buses only.

TRAIN

Most (but double-check your ticket) high-speed trains depart from the new **Hefei South station** (合肥火车南站, Héféi Huǒchē Nánzhàn), 6km southeast of the city centre. Express D and G trains head to the following destinations:
Beijing ¥427, 4½ hours, hourly
Huangshan North ¥141, one hour 40 minutes, frequent
Nanjing South ¥61, one hour, frequent
Shanghai Hongqiao ¥182–202.5, 2½ to 3½ hours, frequent
Wuhan and Wuhan Hànkǒu ¥133, two hours, frequent

Regular-service trains depart from **Hefei train station** (合肥火车站, Héféi Huǒchēzhàn), 4km northeast of the city centre:
Beijing Hard/soft sleeper ¥141/262 to ¥262/398, 11 to 14 hours, six daily
Shanghai Hard/soft sleeper from ¥173/268, 6½ to 8½ hours, seven daily

ⓘ Getting Around

Hefei has a new metro system that currently runs to two lines: north–south running Line 1 (running south from Hefei Train Station) and east–west running Line 2. Both lines intersect at Dadongmen station (大东门, Dàdōngmén). Most journeys within the city centre will cost ¥2. In an ambitious expansion, the system is expected to eventually have 15 lines.

The city also has an extensive local bus system (all rides ¥1) though it isn't particularly helpful for visitors, like most city bus systems in China. Metered taxis start at ¥8. The 25-minute ride from Hefei South station to the city centre should cost ¥25; from Hefei train station expect to pay ¥20.

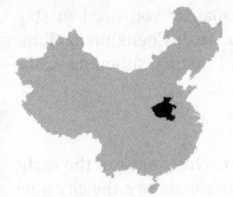

Henan

POP 109 MILLION

Best Places to Eat

➡ Xisi Square Night Market (p468)

➡ Niūniú Dàpánjī (p460)

➡ Hé Jì (p452)

➡ Old Town Night Market (p461)

Best Places to Stay

➡ Lanyue Inn (p457)

➡ Kungfu Hostel (p457)

➡ Sofitel (p452)

➡ Luoyang Anximen Youth Hostel (p460)

Why Go?

The stereotype of Henan (河南, Hénán) as a slow-moving and impoverished province may cause affluent Chinese to roll their eyes at its mention, but Henan's heritage takes us back to the earliest days of Chinese antiquity. Ancient capitals rose and fell in Henan's north, where the capricious Yellow River (Huáng Hé) nourished the flowering of a great civilisation.

Henan is home to China's oldest surviving Buddhist temple and one of the country's most astonishing collections of Buddhist carvings, the Longmen Grottoes. There is also the Shaolin Temple, that legendary institution where the martial way and Buddhism found an unlikely but powerful alliance. Henan's inability to catch up with the rest of the land perhaps helps to explain why the unusual village of Nanjiecun still sees a future in Maoist collectivism. Henan is also home to the excellent walled town of Kaifeng and the 1000-year-old craft of woodblock printing in Zhuxian Zhen.

When to Go
Zhengzhou

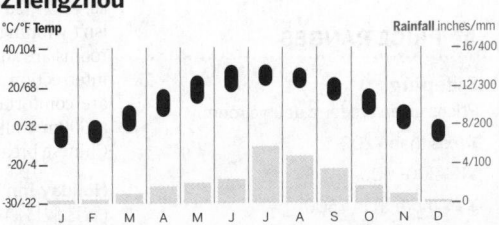

Apr Luoyang is a blaze of floral colour during the peony festival in spring.

Jun Take a pause from the heat with a trip to cool Guoliang up in the mountains.

Sep & Oct Catch the lovely and fleeting north China autumn.

History

It is believed that the first Shang capital, perhaps dating back 3800 years, was at Yanshi, west of modern-day Zhengzhou. Around the mid-14th century BC, the capital is thought to have moved to Zhengzhou, where its ancient city walls remain visible.

Henan again occupied centre stage during the Song dynasty (AD 960–1279), but political power deserted it when the government fled south from its capital at Kaifeng following the 12th-century Jurchen invasion.

Modern Henan has been poor and strife-prone. In 1975 Henan's Banqiao Dam collapsed after massive rainfall, leading to a string of other dam failures that caused the deaths of 230,000 people. In the 1990s a scandal involving the sale of HIV-tainted blood led to a high incidence of AIDS in several Henan villages.

ℹ Getting There & Around

Zhengzhou is the main regional rail hub; high-speed G-class and D-class trains zip between Zhengzhou, Luoyang and, to a lesser extent, Kaifeng.

Luoyang has a small airport, but Zhengzhou is the main hub for flying to/from Henan.

Zhengzhou 郑州

📞 0371 / POP 10.14 MILLION

The provincial Henan capital of Zhengzhou (Zhèngzhōu) is a rapidly modernising, smog-filled metropolis with few relics from its ancient past (due to Japanese bombing in WWII). The city is a major transport hub and access point for the Shaolin Temple and the left-field Maoist collective of Nanjiecun. Although Zhengzhou can largely be zipped

---

ℹ PRICE RANGES

Sleeping

Prices given are for a double room.

¥ less than ¥200

¥¥ ¥200–500

¥¥¥ more than ¥500

Eating

Prices given are for a meal for one.

¥ less than ¥35

¥¥ ¥35–100

¥¥¥ more than ¥100

---

through, don't despair if you need to stay here for a night or two: Chenghuang Temple, good food and quality shopping malls help to pass the time.

⊙ Sights

Despite a history reaching back to the earliest chapters of Chinese history, the city now only has a few sights of interest to travellers.

Most worthwhile is the bustling 600-year-old **City God temple** (城隍庙, Chénghuáng Miào; 4 Shangcheng Lu, 商城路4号; ⊙9am-5pm; 🚌2) FREE. Worshippers leave its trees festooned with red ribbons and its entrances swirling with incense smoke. There is an opera stage in the temple and a small exhibition of opera costumes on the right side of the complex.

Henan Museum (河南博物院, Hénán Bówùyuàn; http://english.chnmus.net; 8 Nongye Lu, 农业路8号; ⊙9am-4.30pm Tue-Sun Mar-Sep, to 4pm Oct-Feb; 🚌93, Y27) FREE has an impressive collection that at the time of writing was on limited display due to renovation. Take your passport as ID for admission. The museum is around 2km north of Jinshui Lu; a taxi there will cost about ¥20.

Zhengzhou's eastern outskirts are marked by long, high mounds of earth, the remains of the **old city walls** (商代城墙遗址, Shāngdài Chéngqiáng Yízhǐ) FREE. There are a few small parks around the entrances and you can climb up to explore the mounds.

🛏 Sleeping

At the time of research, only international chains and a select few domestic hotels were accepting foreigners.

AnXinBoKe Hotel HOTEL ¥¥
(安信铂客酒店, Ān Xìn Bó Kè Jiǔdiàn; 33 Jiefang Lu, 解放路33号; d ¥200-340; ❇🖥) This hotel isn't winning any awards for cleanliness but rooms are surprisingly quiet (there is a large intersection outside the front door), beds are comfortable and February 7 Sq is only a 600m walk away. Rates include a simple Chinese breakfast.

Holiday Inn Express HOTEL ¥¥
(智选假日酒店, Zhìxuǎn Jiàrì Jiǔdiàn; 📞6595 6600; www.hiexpress.com.cn; 115 Jinshui Lu, 金水路115号; d/ste ¥350/480; 🖥, Ⓜ) A good-value option with regular discounts, the Holiday Inn has neat rooms spread across two buildings next to the Sofitel. The breakfast buffet has something for everyone, staff are very

Henan Highlights

1 **Shaolin Temple** (p455) Fathoming the martial mysteries of Shaolin boxing and hiking the surrounding peaks.

2 **Longmen Grottoes** (p462) Admiring the artistry of 1500-year-old Bodhisattvas carved into a cliff wall.

3 **Luoyang** (p458) Taking a trip back in time to ancient burial sites, tombs and temples in the 'cradle of Chinese civilisation'.

4 **Guoliang** (p463) Discovering unreal scenery from the clifftop village and hiking in the Mountains of the Ten Thousand Immortals.

5 **Kaifeng** (p465) Climbing a Northern Song dynasty pagoda and feasting at night markets in this ancient city.

6 **Zhuxian Zhen** (p470) Getting acquainted with the ancient craft of Chinese woodblock printing.

7 **Nanjiecun** (p454) Rediscovering communism at China's last surviving Maoist commune.

Zhengzhou

HENAN ZHENGZHOU

Zhengzhou

helpful and there's a handy bus stop out the front on Jinshui Lu.

Sofitel

HOTEL ¥¥¥

(索菲特国际饭店, Suǒfēitè Guójì Fàndiàn; ☑ 0371 6595 0088; www.sofitel.com; 115 Jinshui Lu, 金水路115号; d from ¥678; ➋✳@🛎🏊; Ⓜ Yanzhuang) Rooms at the five-star Sofitel are excellent. Muted gold and brown tones provide a soothing counterpoint to Zhengzhou's chaotic street life, and plusher rooms are filled with plenty of modern conveniences, including Nespresso machines and swivel TVs.

✖ Eating & Drinking

A short walk north of the train station is the busy February 7 Sq (二七广场, Erqī Guángchǎng), also called Erqi Sq, with nearby shops, restaurants and a market area.

There is a good selection of food stands and barbecue joints on Gong'er Jie (工二街) just behind Hé Jì restaurant. For guaranteed smoke-free dining, all of the malls around February 7 Sq have food courts, many with English menus, and relatively swish restaurants.

Jingwu Lu off Jinshui Rd is home to a handful of welcoming bars serving international beers and with occasional live music.

If you're willing to venture slightly further afield, there are one or two good expat options north of the museum, near Lazy Taps.

Hé Jì

HENAN ¥

(合记; 3 Renmin Lu, 人民路3号; noodle soup ¥17-29; ⏱10.30am-10pm; Ⓜ Renmin Rd) For years, this Zhengzhou stalwart has been drawing raucous crowds for its nourishing noodles served in deliciously oily mutton broth (烩面, huìmiàn).

Place your order with a green-shirted staff member: basic (优质, yōuzhì) or deluxe (特优, tèyōu), with a bit more meat. Servings can be small (小, xiǎo) or large (大, dà). Help yourself to tea at the tea station. Add coriander and chilli to taste and slurp your soup straight from the bowl. The pickled garlic is for eating on the side.

Huāyù Chuān Jiǔjiā · SICHUAN ¥¥

(花豫川酒家; ☑ 6622 2356; 11th fl David Mall, 大卫城店11层; dishes ¥68-198; ⊙ 11am-2pm & 5.30-9.30pm; ❄ 🈂; 🅜 Erqi Sq) This extremely popular chain restaurant has accommodating staff and an easy-to-read menu of delicious Sichuan dishes as well as flavoursome steamed dumplings (¥16). Beer is hardly icy cold, although the complimentary jelly desserts more than make up for it.

You may have to take a number and wait for a table.

Lazy Taps · CRAFT BEER

(啤休, Pí Xiū; ☑ 5550 1775; www.lazytaps.com; 6-209 Lan Bao Wan Gui Ren Jie, 蓝堡湾贵人街 6-209号; ⊙ 5pm-1am; 🈂; 🅜 Line 2, Dongfenglu) Giving Zhengzhou's iffy beer scene a good kick in the pants, this upstairs bar has 20 beers on tap, including some brewed by the Lazy Taps microbrewery in Anhui, and a good selection of fresh, bottled goodies. The food menu is dominated by terrifically spicy Sichuan snacks (¥28). Prices for a small tap beer start at ¥45.

Lazy Taps is a 1km walk west of Dongfenglu metro station, and a ¥20 taxi from the centre.

🛈 Information

Agricultural Bank of China (中国农业银行, Zhōngguó Nóngyè Yínháng, ABC; Renmin Lu, 人民路) Twenty-four-hour ATM.

Bank of China (中国银行, Zhōngguó Yínháng; 8 Jinshui Lu, 金水路8号; ⊙ 9am-5pm Mon-Fri) North of the Sofitel, on Jinshui Lu. Has 24-hour ATMs.

Henan Pharmacy (河南大药房, Hénán Dàyàofáng; ☑ 6623 4256; 19 Renmin Lu, 人民路19号; ⊙ 24hr) Large, helpful pharmacy right next to a metro exit.

Public Security Bureau (公安局出入境管理处, Gōng'ānjú Chūrùjìng Guǎnlǐchù, PSB; ☑ 0371 6962 5990; 66 Huanghe Nanlu, 黄河南路66号; ⊙ 9am-noon & 2-5pm Mon-Fri; 🅜 Huanghenanlu) For visa extensions; in the north of town.

Train Ticket Booking Office (火车预售票处, Huǒchē Yùshòupiàochù; ☑ 0371 6835 6666; 35 Zhengxing Jie, 正兴街35号; ⊙ 8am-8pm) For a ¥5 commission, skip waiting in line and buy train tickets here.

🛈 Getting There & Away

AIR

Zhengzhou Airport is 37km southeast of town. Flights include the following:

Beijing ¥900, frequent

Chengdu ¥580, frequent

Hong Kong ¥1500, two daily

Shanghai ¥480, frequent

BUS

The **long-distance bus station** (郑州长途汽车站, Zhèngzhōu chángtú qìchēzhàn) is opposite the train station. Destinations include the following:

Dengfeng ¥27, two hours, half-hourly

Kaifeng ¥10, two hours, every 15 minutes

Linying ¥40, 2¼ hours, hourly

Luoyang ¥35, three hours, half-hourly

Shaolin Temple ¥28, two hours, four daily (7.30am to 11am)

TRAIN

Zhengzhou is a major rail hub located at the intersection of several major lines. There are two principal stations, both of which have similar connections: the **main train station** (火车站, huǒchē zhàn) and the high-speed **east train station** (郑州东站, Zhèngzhōu dōngzhàn). Both stations are on metro line 1.

For a small commission, skip waiting in line and get tickets at the advance booking office.

High-speed trains departing from Zhengzhou East Station include the following:

Beijing West ¥315, 2½ to 3½ hours, frequent

Kaifeng ¥24, 30 minutes, frequent

Luoyang Longmen ¥66, 40 minutes, frequent

Nanjing South ¥318, four hours, frequent

Shanghai ¥448, five hours, frequent

Xi'an North ¥229, 2½ hours, frequent

Trains departing from Zhengzhou station include the following:

Kaifeng ¥13, 50 minutes, frequent

Luoyang ¥20, 1½ hours, frequent

Nanjing Seat/sleeper ¥93/163 six to nine hours, frequent

Shanghai Hard/soft sleeper ¥223/349, nine to 13 hours, frequent

Xi'an Seat/sleeper ¥72/129, six to 8½ hours, frequent

🛈 Getting Around

The **airport bus** (飞机巴士, fēijī bāshì; ¥20, 80 minutes, half-hourly from 6.30am to 8.30pm) leaves from the long-distance bus station. A taxi costs around ¥85 and takes 50 minutes.

Bus 26 travels from the train station past February 7 Sq, along Renmin Lu and Jinshui Lu. Local buses cost ¥1 to ¥2.

The east–west Line 1 of the metro (tickets from ¥2) runs through the train station, up Renmin Lu and Jinshui Lu to the Central Business District, eventually passing the east train station. Note that the main train station metro stop only exits on the west side and is not conveniently accessed from the front of the train station.

Line 2 runs north–south following Zijingshan Lu, while Line 5 loops around the edges of the city. Line 3 will only open in 2020 at the very earliest.

Taxi fares start at ¥8 (¥10 at night).

Nanjiecun 南街村

☑ 0395 / POP 3400

Nanjiecun (Nánjiēcūn) is China's very last Maoist collective (gōngshè), and a visit here is a surreal trip back in time – a journey to the puritanical and revolutionary China of the 1950s, when Chairman Mao was becoming a supreme being, money was yesterday's scene and the menace of karaoke had yet to be prophesied by even the most paranoid party faithful.

The first inkling you have arrived in an entirely different world comes from the roads: relatively clean, tree-lined streets run in straight lines with a kind of austere socialist beauty (or, perhaps, the quiet menace of an autocratic sci-fi dystopia), past factories, schools, and rows of identikit blocks of workers' flats emblazoned with vermilion communist slogans. There are no advertising billboards, but beatific portraits of Chairman Mao gaze down on all.

To find your way into the collective, head down the main drag, Yingsong Dadao (颍松大道), to the rainbow-arch-adorned East Is Red Square. A short stroll to the left brings you to **Chaoyang Gate Square** (朝阳门广场, Cháoyángmén Guǎngchǎng).

East Is Red Square SQUARE

(东方红广场, Dōngfānghóng Guǎngchǎng) In this square, guards maintain a 24-hour vigil at the foot of a statue of Chairman Mao, and portraits of Marx, Engels, Stalin and Lenin (the original 'Gang of Four') rise up on all four sides. Behind the ensemble, a tri-coloured rainbow proclaims 'Mao Zedong thought will shine forever'. The square is deluged in shrill propaganda broadcast from speakers in true 1950s style, kicking off at 6.15am daily.

Nanjiecun Instant Food Company FACTORY

(8 Guangming Lu; ⊙ 7.30am-6pm) FREE You don't have to join a tour to visit this noodle factory, which employs more than 500 people in the collective. Enter at the east end and go upstairs to reach the windows onto the factory floor, where you'll see the noodles being shaped, cooked and packaged, ready for export to Germany, Australia, Canada and the UK.

The factory outlet by the exit has its wider product range on display (made in a second factory in Nanjiecun), including the 'Pocky' sticks that it supplies to Tesco.

Nan Jie Cun Hotel HOTEL ¥

(南街村宾馆, Nánjiēcūn Bīnguǎn; ☑ 885 1270; north side of East Is Red Sq, 东方红广场北侧; d ¥200) For the full Nanjiecun experience, this hotel offers the same stark cleanliness and communist charm that you'll find about town. Long, red-carpeted halls give way to simple rooms with private bathrooms. No need to book ahead – the hotel is usually deserted.

❶ Information

Tourist Service Centre (游客服务中心, Yóukè Fúwù Zhōngxīn; Qianjin Beilu, 前进北路; ⊙ 7.30am-5.30pm) You can safely avoid the Tourist Service Centre (off the west end of Yingsong Dadao), as they'll ask you to buy an admission ticket (¥90) that you don't actually need to visit Nanjiecun. If you do take up their offer, it comes with a whiz around town on an electric cart, combined with a Chinese-language tour of the noodle factory and the underwhelming cultural park.

❶ Getting There & Away

From Zhengzhou bus station, buses (¥40, 2¼ hours) run south every hour between 8.10am and 7.40pm to the bus station at Linying (临颍), from where it's a ¥8 sānlúnchē (pedicab) journey south to Nanjiecun.

Song Shan & Dengfeng 嵩山、登封

☑ 0371 / POP 727,000

In Taoism, Song Shan (嵩山, Sōng Shān) is considered the central mountain (中岳, zhōngyuè) of the five sacred peaks, symbolising earth (土, tǔ) among the five elements and occupying the axis directly beneath heaven. Despite this Taoist persuasion, the mountains are also home to one of China's most famous and legendary Zen (禅, Chán) Buddhist temples: the inimitable Shaolin Temple. Two main mountains crumple the area, the 1494m-high Mt Taishi and the 1512m-high Shaoshi Shan (少室山, Shàoshì Shān) whose peaks compose Song Shan about 80km west of Zhengzhou.

At the foot of Mt Taishi, 12km southeast of the Shaolin Temple and 74km from Zhengzhou, sits the squat little town of Dengfeng (登封, Dēngfēng). While tatty in parts, it's prettily fringed by mountains, and travellers use it as a base for trips to surrounding sights or exploratory treks into the hills.

◉ Sights & Activities

In Dengfeng, Zhongyue Dajie (中岳大街) is the main east–west street; Shaolin Dadao (少林大道) runs parallel to the south.

A bunch of buildings in Dengfeng have recently been renumbered. When you're looking for a specific address, don't be fooled if the street number is completely different from what you were expecting.

Dengfeng is hemmed by the mountains of Song Shan, with the Shaolin Scenic Area to the west and Mt Taishi to the north.

A few kilometres east of Dengfeng, the ancient and hoary **Zhongyue Temple** (中岳庙, Zhōngyuè Miào; Shaolin Dadao, 少林大道; ¥30; ⊙8am-5pm) is an underrated but important Taoist monastery complex that dates back to the 2nd century BC. Embedded in a mountainous background, with monks garbed in traditional dress and sporting topknots, the temple is less visited and exudes a more palpable air of reverence than its Buddhist sibling, the Shaolin Temple.

◉ Shaolin Scenic Area

The largely rebuilt **Shaolin Temple** (少林寺, Shàolín Sì; incl with Scenic Area ticket; ⊙8am-5.30pm Mar-Sep, to 5pm Oct-Feb) is a commercialised victim of its own incredible success. A frequent target of war, the ancestral home of *wǔshù* was last torched in 1928, and the surviving halls – many of recent construction – are today assailed by relentless waves of selfie-shooting tour groups. The temple's claim to fame, its dazzling *gōngfu* (kung fu) based on the movements of animals, insects and sometimes mythological figures, guarantees that martial arts clubs around the world make incessant pilgrimages.

A satisfying visit to the Shaolin Temple requires, rather than bestows, a Zen mentality (to handle the visiting hordes and looped recordings broadcast from competing loudspeakers). But if you explore away from the main areas, you could spend an entire day or two visiting smaller temples, climbing the surrounding peaks and eking out crumbs of solitude.

Coming through the main entrance, you'll pass several *wǔshù* schools; the students practising in the red uniforms belong to Shaolin Tagou – the world's biggest *gōngfu* school. On the right, about 500m in, is the **Wushu Training Centre** (武术馆, Wǔshù Guǎn; incl with Scenic Area ticket; ⊙9.30am, 10.30am, 11.30am, 2pm, 3pm, 4pm, 5pm), with shows featuring novices tumbling around and breaking sticks and metal bars over their heads – an integral part of the Shaolin experience, though some may find parts of the performance uncomfortable to watch.

The main temple itself is another 600m along. Many buildings, such as the main **Daxiong Hall** (大雄宝殿, Dàxióng Bǎodiàn; reconstructed in 1985), burned to the ground in 1928. Although the temple seems to have been founded in approximately the year AD 500 (accounts vary), some halls only date back as far as 2004. Among the oldest structures at the temple are the decorative arches and stone lions, both outside the main gate.

At the very rear, the **West Facing Hall** (西方圣人殿, Xīfāng Shēngrén Diàn) has depressions in the floor, famously (and apocryphally) the result of generations of monks practising their stance work, and huge colour frescoes. Always be on the lookout for the ubiquitous Damo (Bodhidharma), whose bearded Indian visage gazes sagaciously from stelae or peeks out from temple halls.

Past the main temple on the right, the **Pagoda Forest** (少林塔林, Shàolín Tǎlín), a cemetery of 248 brick pagodas, which includes the ashes of eminent monks, is well worth visiting. Not all of the pagodas are ancient; see if you can spot the one with a car, camera and laptop computer on the frieze!

Between the main temple and the Pagoda Forest, paths lead up **Wuru Peak** (五乳峰, Wǔrǔ Fēng). Flee the tourist din by heading towards the peak to see the **cave** (达摩洞, Dámó Dòng) where Damo (Bodhidharma) meditated for nine years; it's 4km uphill with lots of steps towards the end. From the base, you may spot the peak and the cave, marked by a large, white Bodhisattva figure. En route to the cave, detour to the **Chuzu Temple** (初祖庵, Chūzǔ Ān), a quiet and battered counterpoint to the other temple. Its main hall, with Northern Song frescoes, is the oldest timber structure in the province (c 1125).

At 1512m above sea level and reachable on the Songyang Cableway (嵩阳索道, Sōngyáng Suǒdào; return ticket ¥50), **Shaoshi Shan** (少室山, Shàoshì Shān) is the

BODHIDHARMA AND HIS SOLE SHOE

Called Damo (达摩) by the Chinese, Bodhidharma was a 5th-century Indian monk who travelled to the Shaolin Temple, bringing Chán (禅, Zen) Buddhism to China in the process. The monk is also traditionally revered for establishing the breathing and meditation exercises that lay the foundations of Shaolin Boxing. Bodhidharma's bearded, heavy-browed and serious expression can be seen in temples across China, especially Chán temples. Accomplishments and legends swarm around his name: he is said to have sat in a cave silently staring at a wall for nine years.

Damo is also often depicted carrying a shoe on a stick. Folklore attests that he was spotted wandering in the Pamir Mountains holding a single shoe. When the news reached the Shaolin Temple, it caused consternation as Bodhidharma had previously passed away and was buried nearby. His grave was opened and discovered to contain nothing but a solitary shoe.

area's tallest summit. The area beyond the cable car is home to the peak, and to **Erzu Nunnery** (二祖庵, Èrzǔ Ān) with four wells where you can sample its various tasting waters (¥10): sour, sweet, peppery and bitter.

Perhaps the most famous hike, however, is to neighbouring **Sanhuangzhai** (三皇寨, Sānhuángzhài), which takes about six hours return and covers 9km one way (and 7398 steps!). The path goes past precipitous cliffs along a roller coaster of a route that often hugs the striated rock face to the 782-step **Rope Bridge** (连天吊桥, Lián Tiān Diào Qiáo). The scenery is superb.

Consider bypassing the initial 3km with the **Shaolin Cableway** (少林索道, Shàolín Suǒdào; one way/return ¥70/120), which conveys you effortlessly to the start of the most dramatic section. No matter how you do this hike, start early and be prepared for some noise – it's very popular and the echoes are a big draw. Once you get to the first suspension bridge (one hour), most people turn around and the crowds thin out considerably. If you go further, you'll reach **Songshan Monastery**, the majestic structure hugging the high-up cliffs. The grounds aren't open to the

public, which means the monastery actually looks its best from a distance, where you can appreciate the tenacity of its location. (When the monastery was restored in 2005, all the cement and tiles were brought in on foot.)

To do this hike one way – probably the most satisfying option – you can start from the end (catch a cab to Sanhuangzhai from Dengfeng; aim for ¥50) and walk towards Shaolin. You can do it the other way too, but you're at the mercy of the drivers (assuming there are any) when you finish. Note that the bridge may be closed at times for repair or during inclement weather.

To reach the Shaolin Temple, take a bus (¥5, 15 minutes) from Dengfeng's west bus station or main station (¥5). A taxi to the temple from Dengfeng will cost ¥30 to ¥40. Alternatively, take a minibus from either Luoyang (¥19, two hours) or Zhengzhou (¥29, two hours).

From the ticket office, it's then a 20-minute walk to the actual temple (passing the Wushu Training Centre on the way); electric carts (one way/return ¥15/25, 7.30am to 6pm) run from the ticket office to the main temple entrance and beyond.

Note that tickets to the scenic area (including all hikes) are valid for 10 days, except for the temple itself, which can only be visited once on the date of purchase. If you stay in the park overnight without a ticket, you'll need to purchase one at the temple (¥30) and negotiate for entry into the Wushu show (¥20).

◉ Taishi Shan

Songyang Academy   HISTORIC BUILDING

(嵩阳书院, Sōngyáng Shūyuàn; ¥30; ⊙ 6.30am-5.30pm Mar-Nov, 7am-5pm Dec-Feb) At the foot of Mt Taishi sits one of China's oldest academies, the lush and well-tended Songyang Academy, a building complex that dates from AD 484 and rises up the hill on a series of terraces. In the courtyard are two cypress trees believed to be around 4500 years old – and they're still alive.

Both bus 2 and bus 6 (¥1) run to the Songyang Academy.

Taishi Shan   MOUNTAIN

(太室山, Tàishì Shān; ¥50; ⊙ 6.30am-5.30pm Mar-Nov, 7am-5pm Dec-Feb) Arguably the best hike in the area, Taishi Shan serves as a much quieter counterpoint to Shaolin Temple. It's not for slackers, however; like all Chinese mountains, the steps go straight up, and these ascend a leg-busting 1000m in altitude before reaching **Junji Peak** (1492m). Along the way you'll pass some fantastical landscapes and a host of ravaged temples, the most interesting being **Laomu Cave** (老母洞, *lǎomǔ dòng*), where according to one legend Laotzu lived for six years while writing the *Tao Te Ching*.

If you want to make a day of it, it's possible to do a loop, descending past **Fawang Temple** (法王寺, Fǎwáng Sì) on the return trip. Ask for directions at Tianye Temple.

Be sure to bring plenty of water: even though there are snack vendors with loudspeakers at every peak on the way up, there aren't so many on the loop back.

At Fawang Temple, you can either bargain for a minivan ride back to the entrance or walk the 10-minute track to the oldest brick pagoda in China, **Songyue Pagoda** (嵩岳塔, Sōngyuè Tǎ), which was built in the year 509.

The entrance to Taishi Shan is behind Songyang Academy; take bus 6 or 2 to get here. Don't forget to pick up a map (地图, *dìtú*) with your ticket and figure on spending six hours hiking (return).

🛏 Sleeping

Luxury sleeping options are non-existent – if you'd prefer an international hotel with English-speaking staff and nonsmoking rooms, stay in Zhengzhou and visit Shaolin as a day trip. Dengfeng has a handful of budget options in town.

Kungfu Hostel
HOSTEL ¥

(功夫客栈, Gōngfù Kèzhàn; ☑ 6274 8889; www. kungfuhostel-shaolintemple.com; 20 Wangzhigou, Shaolin Temple Grounds, 少林景区内王指沟20号院; dm/d ¥80/198; ❄ 🛜) If waking up to the sounds of crowing roosters and beating all the crowds to the Shaolin Temple sounds like your cup of *chá*, don't miss the opportunity to stay in this peaceful village inside the scenic area. Simple rooms are spread across two buildings: if you can't find any staff, check the other building.

Make sure you reserve in advance – it's hard to find (about a 30-minute walk from the ticket office), and you need to purchase a ticket before you check in (unless it's after 6pm). Staff can help arrange private martial arts classes too.

Dengfeng Climb Hostel
HOSTEL ¥

(登封攀登国际青年旅舍, Dēngfēng Pāndēng Guójì Qīngnián Lǚshě; ☑ 138 3853 6111; Songyang Lu, 嵩阳路; dm/d ¥40/160; ❄ 🛜) The simple and friendly Climb Hostel has a comfortable bar and a pool table and is enviably close to the entrance to Taishi Shan. The dorms are a bit

cramped and have thin mattresses, but are still good for the price. Located in the north of town, it can be a bit tricky to reach on foot, though. Bus 6 runs almost here from the bus station (last stop, then ask directions).

★ Lanyue Inn
BOUTIQUE HOTEL ¥

(揽岳客栈, Lǎnyuè Kèzhàn; ☑ 6295 2555; 9 Dongsanshi Xiang, 东三十巷9号; s/d ¥189/199) Down an alley off Chongfu Lu, this little hotel has helpful staff and large rooms with comfortable beds and private bathrooms. Thoughtful room decorations include a tea set, calligraphy station and unobtrusive sex-toy vending machine (requires QR payment). The mountain views over Dengfeng are spectacular from the higher floors, and a simple egg-and-bread breakfast is delivered to your door each morning.

Shaolin Hotel
HOTEL ¥¥

(少林宾馆, Shàolín Bīnguǎn; ☑ 6016 1616; 66 Zhongyue Dajie, 中岳大街66号; d from ¥238; ❄ 🛜) Enthusiastic staff, a good location and easy discounts make this midrange hotel a half-decent choice. Rooms are tidy enough but don't expect them to be spotless.

Look for the white building on the corner of Guan Shi Jie (opposite the night market) with the yellow-and-red sign. It's a ¥7 taxi ride from the bus station. Discounts of ¥100 available.

🍴 Eating

Shaolin Temple has stands selling instant noodles, bread, snacks and water. There is a

---

WǓSHÙ OR GŌNGFU?

When planning to study Chinese martial arts, the first question you should ask is: shall I learn *wǔshù* (武术) or *gōngfù* (功夫)? There may be considerable overlap, but there are crucial differences.

Wǔshù is a more recently coined term that's strongly associated with athletic martial arts displays and competition-based martial arts patterns or forms. *Gōngfù* (kung fu), however, is more about the development of internal and more esoteric skills, rather than physical prowess or mainstream athleticism.

If you're lucky enough to see a martial arts master break a piece of ceramic from a bowl and grind it to dust with his bare fingers, this is *gōngfù*, not *wǔshù*.

restaurant on the right, at the beginning of the track towards Damo Cave.

In Dengfeng, the local speciality is thickly cut handmade soup noodles (烩面, *huì miàn*). Head to the intersection of Aimin Lu (爱民路) and Songshan Lu (嵩山路) for a good choice of restaurants.

There are a heap of hole-in-the-wall restaurants and snack stalls on Dongguan Jie (东关街).

The **night market** (Guangming Lu; meals from ¥6-20) opposite Shaolin Hotel (p457) has plenty of goodies on offer for the adventurous diner. If entrails on sticks aren't your thing, opt for vegetable kebabs or a hearty *jīdànbǐng* (鸡蛋饼, egg-filled roll).

☆ Entertainment

Shaolin Zen Music Ritual LIVE PERFORMANCE (禅宗少林音乐大典, Chánzōng Shàolín Yīnyuè Dàdiǎn; www.czslyydd.com; tickets ¥199-999; ⊙8.15pm) This elaborate zen-themed light-and-music show, directed by Tan Dun, is set against the magnificent backdrop of Shaoshi Shan. Music is prerecorded but the choreography and dancing is all real.

ℹ Information

Bank of China (中国银行, Zhōngguó Yínháng; 52 Zhongyue Dajie, 中岳大街52号; ⊙9am-5pm Mon-Fri) Has a 24-hour ATM and foreign exchange.

ℹ Getting There & Away

Most intercity buses run from the main bus station (总站, zǒng zhàn), including the following:
Kaifeng ¥40, three hours, two daily (7.20am and 12.10pm)
Luoyang ¥25, two hours, seven daily
Zhengzhou ¥10 to ¥32, two hours, half-hourly

ℹ Getting Around

The **main bus station** is in the east of town; jump on bus 1 (¥1) to reach Zhongyue Dajie and the town centre. There's also a **west bus station** (西站, xī zhàn), which runs a bus service to the Shaolin Temple.

Taxi flagfall is ¥5, though many drivers insist on a ¥10 flat fee.

Luoyang 洛阳

☑ 0379 / POP 2 MILLION

Access point for the incredible Longmen Grottoes outside town, Luoyang (Luòyáng) was one of China's true dynastic citadels. The city was the prosperous capital of 13 dynasties, until the Northern Song dynasty shifted its capital east along the Yellow River to Kaifeng in the 10th century. The mighty Sui and Tang dynasty walls formed an imposing rectangle north and south of the Luo River, while worshippers flocked to 1300 Buddhist temples through the city.

Luoyang was once the very centre of the Chinese universe and the eastern capital of the resplendent Tang dynasty. Attempts have been made to recreate the enormous Ming and Tang palace complex near the frenzied intersection of Zhongzhou Zhonglu and Dingding Lu, although very little remains of the city's glorious past.

◉ Sights

Luoyang Museum MUSEUM (洛阳市博物馆, Luòyáng Shì Bówùguǎn; Wenbo Lu, 文博路; ⊙9am-4.30pm Tue-Sun) FREE This huge museum, situated out of the action south of the river, has fascinating displays across two huge floors and is one of the few places where you can get any kind of perspective on ancient Luoyang. There's an absorbing collection of three-colour Tang dynasty *sāncǎi* porcelain; the city's rise is traced through dynastic pottery, bronzeware and other magnificent objects. An audio guide (¥40) is also available. Bring your passport.

Lijing Gate HISTORIC BUILDING (丽景门, Lìjǐng Mén; Xi Dajie, 西大街; ¥35; ⊙8am-9pm summer, shorter hours rest of year) Originally built in the Sui dynasty, this gate separated the palace area from the city's residential quarters. It was reconstructed in 2002 and renovated in 2014. Up top you'll find the Town God's Temple, the Hall of Nine Dragons (nine well-known emperors), a gallery commemorating the 104 emperors who made Luoyang their capital, and views over the Old Town.

Luoyang Old Town AREA (老城区, lǎochéngqū) Any Chinese city worth its rice has an Old Town. Within Luoyang's is this scenic area comprising a plethora of water-banquet restaurants, costume shops and the occasional creaking monument, namely the lovely brick **Wenfeng Pagoda** (文峰塔, Wénfēng Tǎ), originally built in the Song dynasty.

Bring your passport for access or skip the theme-park area entirely and make your way to the more atmospheric **Drum Tower** (鼓楼, Gǔ Lóu) rising up on Dong Dajie (东大街).

Luoyang

Luoyang

⊙ Sights

🛏 Sleeping

✖ Eating

ℹ Information

ℹ Transport

Mingtang Tiantang Scenic Area   PAGODA
(明堂天堂景区, Míngtáng Tiāntáng Jǐngqū; ¥120; ⊙8.30am-9pm) It's difficult to miss this enormous pagoda and hall, recreated on the original site of the Ming and Tang palace complex. The most impressive element of each is the sheer scale of the structures, which you can easily appreciate from outside without forking out for a ticket.

Inside the **Hall of Enlightenment** (明堂, Míngtáng) is a decadent gilt throne room, and stage for daily belly-dancing performances. On the basement floor of the **Heavenly Hall** (天堂, Tiāntáng), you can view the actual remains (read: stumps) of the original structure. The top floor has an exceptional panorama of the area.

Eastern Zhou Royal Horse & Chariot Pits   MUSEUM
(周王城天子驾六博物馆, Zhōuwángchéng Tiānzi Jiàliù Bówùguǎn; 226 Zhongzhou Zhonglu, 中洲中路226号; ¥30; ⊙8.30am-6pm; 🚍4, 5, 41, 56) A huge statue of six rearing horses marks this two-hall underground museum, where the principal draw is the in-situ remains of a Zhou emperor's royal horses – that were buried alive when the emperor passed on.

The ¥10 audio guide helps with a much-needed explanation of the unearthed remains.

Wangcheng Square   SQUARE
(王城广场, Wángchéng Guángchǎng; Zhongzhou Zhonglu, 中州中路) This square is the cacophonous meeting place for locals who come to play chess and cards, practise calligraphy, stroll with grandchildren, play instruments and work on their dance moves. Catch the square at its busiest and you could say it

HENAN LUOYANG

WORTH A TRIP

ANCIENT TOMBS MUSEUM

Towards the airport, about 7km north of town, the superb but little-visited **Ancient Tombs Museum** (古墓博物馆, Gǔmù Bówùguǎn; Airport Rd, 机场路; ☺9am-4.30pm Tue-Sun) FREE has three main exhibits: 20 reconstructed tombs (spanning five main dynasties, or over 1000 years), recreated using original building materials; original tomb murals; and a Northern Wei royal burial mound. Grab an audio guide (¥20) on the way in and let loose your inner Indiana Jones: stand inside 2000-year-old tombs to admire delicately carved panels and faded frescoes.

If you haven't seen a *lóngxǐ* (singing fountain bowl) before, it's worth springing ¥5 for a demonstration and the chance to try your hand at making the unique sound and 'boiling water' effect.

Many of the relics from these tombs are kept at Luoyang Museum (p458). Visiting the tombs first makes it easier to visualise the museum exhibits in context.

To get here, take bus 83 north from the train station (¥1, 20 minutes). A taxi will run about ¥30.

represents a good chunk of Chinese society in a nutshell; it's also busy at night.

Wangcheng Park　　PARK
(王城公园, Wángchéng Gōngyuán; Zhongzhou Zhonglu, 中洲中路; ☺6am-9pm winter, to 9.30pm summer) One of Luoyang's indispensable green lungs, this park is the site of the annual Peony Festival. There's also a small **amusement park** (rides ¥20), complete with miniature train.

✨✨ Festivals & Events

Peony Festival　　CULTURAL
(洛阳牡丹文化节, Luòyáng Mǔdān Wénhuà Jié; Wangcheng Park, 王城公园; ☺Apr) The annual peony festival floods Wangcheng Park with colour and crowds of floral aficionados, photographers and flower vendors.

🛌 Sleeping

Luoyang has a decent range of hotels in every budget bracket dotted around the city.

Luoyang Anximen Youth Hostel　　HOSTEL ¥
(洛阳安喜门青年旅舍, Luòyáng Ānxǐmén Qīngnián Lǚshè; ☎150 3670 3503; 306 Zhongzhou Donglu, 中州东路306号; 4-bed dm ¥80, d ¥160) Super close to the night market and right in front of a bus station, Anximen Hostel has a great location. It has lovely new facilities, including a roof garden and a (loud) bar on the same floor as the dorms. Rooms look smart and are cleaned daily. Private rooms are particularly great value; dorms are basic but secure.

Staff don't speak much English but communicate via apps and can arrange group trips to the grottoes and Shaolin Temple.

If you fancy street food for breakfast, a handful of places pop up each morning on Jifu Jie (集市街), 50m west of the hostel.

★ Christian's Hotel　　BOUTIQUE HOTEL ¥¥¥
(克丽司汀酒店, Kèlìsītīng Jiǔdiàn; ☎6326 6666; 56 Jiefang Lu, entrance on Tanggong Xilu, 解放路56号; d from ¥1999; ❄@⊚) This boutique hotel scores points for its variety of themed rooms, each with large plush beds and a kitchen-dining area. Do you go for Tang dynasty style or white walls and a circular bed? Regardless, you'll be thanking the eponymous Christian each time you step into the room. Outside of April, discounts usually slash rates in half.

Next door, the **Today Mall** (新都汇, Xīndùhuì) has a few restaurants.

🍴 Eating

Luoyang's famous 'water banquet' (水席, *shuǐxí*) is much discussed on China's culinary grapevine. The main dishes of this 24-course meal are soups served up with the speed of flowing water – hence the name.

Sweet-tooths will find their groove on the west side of Lijing Gate (p458), where small shops specialise in traditional biscuits and rice cakes, many of which are beautifully presented with peony powder and delicate petals.

Niūniū Dàpánjī　　XINJIANG ¥
(妞妞大盘鸡; ☎166 3942 9610; Yiyong Dongjie, 义永洞街; small/medium/large ¥45/68/88; ☺9am-2pm & 5-10pm) A Xinjiang speciality, *dàpánjī* (大盘鸡, big-plate chicken) is a spicy chicken, potato and pepper stew; halfway through the meal, handmade noodles and greens are added to the mix – the ensemble is absolutely delicious. This is the only dish it serves, so you can be assured it does it well!

A small portion feeds two people, and the large is recommended for four to six people. If you're coming here solo, the lovely owners will be happy to rustle up a (generous) single serving for ¥35.

Yiyong Dongjie is packed with cheery outdoor restaurants serving beer and barbecue. It's a lot less hectic here than at similar places around the night market.

Old Town Night Market STREET FOOD ¥
(十字街夜市, Shízìjiē Yèshì; Xinghua Jie, 兴华街; meals ¥10-50; ⊙6pm-1am) Festooned with brightly lit red lanterns, this lively night market has a cornucopia of snacks. The market is now cash-free, meaning that if you aren't able to pay with WeChat or Alipay, you'll need to purchase a payment card (¥10). Look for the red tent and table halfway along the market.

Zhēn Bù Tóng Fàndiàn Chinese HENAN ¥¥
(真不同饭店; ☑ 6399 5080; 369 Zhongzhou Donglu, 中州中路369号; dishes ¥30-68; ⊙11am-2pm & 4.30-8.30pm) A huge place behind a colourful green, red, blue and gold traditional facade. If you can rustle up a large group, this is the place to come for a water banquet experience. But if 24 courses and ¥688 seems a little excessive, you can simply pick out your own selection of dishes from the water banquet menu.

ⓘ Information

Industrial & Commercial Bank (工商银行, Gōngshāng Yínháng, ICBC; 228 Zhongzhou Zhonglu, 中州中路228号; ⊙9am-5pm Mon-Sat) Huge branch; foreign exchange and 24-hour ATM.
Luoyang Central Hospital (洛阳市中心医院, Luòyáng Shì Zhōngxīn Yīyuàn; ☑ 6389 2222; 288 Zhongzhou Zhonglu, 中州中路288号) Accepts foreigners. There is a 24-hour pharmacy across the street.

ⓘ Getting There & Away

AIR
Luoyang has its own airport but most people fly into or out of Zhengzhou (p453), which has more regular connections and much cheaper flights.

BUS
Regular departures from the **long-distance bus station** (洛阳一运汽车站, Luòyáng Yīyùn Qìchēzhàn; 51 Jinguyuan Lu, 金谷园路), located diagonally across from the train station, include the following:
Dengfeng ¥24, three hours, every 40 minutes (5.30am to 5.40pm)
Kaifeng ¥60, four hours, hourly (8.25am to 4pm)
Shaolin Temple ¥19, two2 hours, every 40 minutes (5.30am to 12.30pm)
Zhengzhou ¥35, three hours, half-hourly

Buses to Dengfeng and Zhengzhou also depart from the less frantic **Jinyuan bus station** (锦远汽车站, Jǐnyuǎn Qìchēzhàn), just west of the train station.

TRAIN
Luoyang's **Longmen Station** (洛阳龙门站, Lùoyáng Lóngmén Zhàn), over the river in the south of town, is the high-speed station. The **main train station** (洛阳火车站, Lùoyáng Huǒchē Zhàn) has slower trains.

Tickets can be bought online, at the station and through a **train ticket agency** (火车售票处, Huǒchē Shòupiàochù; 9 Renmin Xilu, 人民西路9号; ⊙8am-noon & 1-5pm). Try to book ahead of time, as tickets can sometimes be in short supply.

Destinations departing the main train station:
Beijing West Seat/sleeper ¥105/196, 7½ to 11 hours, seven daily
Kaifeng Hard seat ¥30, three hours, frequent departures (1pm to 9.40pm)
Nanjing Seat/sleeper ¥112/224, eight to 13 hours, 12 daily
Shanghai Seat/sleeper ¥142/262, 11 to 17 hours, 11 daily
Xi'an Seat/sleeper ¥63/118 five hours, frequent in mornings and afternoons but no trains between 10.30am and 3pm
Zhengzhou Seat ¥20, two hours, frequent departures

Destinations from Luoyang Longmen Station include the following:
Beijing West G train 1st/2nd class ¥589/368, four hours, 12 daily
Kaifeng North G train 1st/2nd class ¥144/90, one hour, 11 daily
Nanjing G train 1st/2nd class ¥626/383, four hours, frequent departures
Shanghai D train sleeper ¥650, 8½ hours, two daily (9.48pm and 10.02pm)
Shanghai Hongqiao G train 1st/2nd class ¥844/513, five to six hours, frequent departures
Wuhan 1st/2nd class ¥483/302, three hours, regular departures
Xi'an North D train 2nd class ¥120, two hours, one daily (8.07am)
Xi'an North G train 1st/2nd class ¥280/175, 1¾ hours, frequent departures
Zhengzhou G train 1st/2nd class ¥90/60, 40 minutes, frequent departures

ⓘ Getting Around

Luoyang Beijiao Airport is 12km north of the city. On the west side of the long-distance bus station, bus 83 (¥1.5, 45 minutes) runs to/from Jinguyuan Lu (金谷园街). A taxi to/from the train station costs about ¥35.

Buses 5 and 41 go to the Old Town from the same stop on Jinguyuan Lu, running via Wang-cheng Sq. Bus 49 (among others) runs from Longmen station to the centre of town.

Taxis are ¥5 at flagfall, making them good value. Expect to pay about ¥30 from the Old Town to Longmen station and ¥22 to the main train and bus station area.

At the time of writing, a two-line metro system was under construction, and blocking off whole swaths of the city. If you plan to do a lot of walking, expect detours.

Around Luoyang

★ **Longmen Grottoes**   BUDDHIST SITE
(龙门石窟, Lóngmén Shíkū; ¥90, English-speaking guide for west grottoes ¥100; ⊙ 8am-6.30pm Apr-Oct, to 5.30pm Nov-Jan, to 6pm Feb & Mar) The ravaged grottoes at Longmen constitute one of China's handful of surviving masterpieces of Buddhist rock carving. A sutra in stone, the epic achievement of the Longmen Grottoes was commenced by chisellers from the Northern Wei dynasty after the capital relocated here from Datong in the year AD 494. Over the next two centuries, more than 100,000 images and statues of Buddha and his disciples emerged from over a kilometre of limestone cliff wall along the Yi River (伊河, Yī Hé).

The grottoes are scattered in a line on the west and east sides of the river. Most of the significant Buddhist carvings are on the west side, but a small crop can also be admired after traversing the bridge to the east side. Admission also includes entry to a temple and garden on the east side. English captions are rudimentary, although some carvings have English audio descriptions available via WeChat.

After you've seen the west side, you can take a boat (¥25) back to the main entrance to get a riverside view of the grottoes (note that you can't re-enter the west side once you leave). On the east side, electric carts (¥10) can take you to a variety of locations. All in all, it's a 3km walk; expect to spend at least three hours here.

The grottoes are 13km south of Luoyang and can be reached by taxi (¥30); bus 81 (¥1.5, 50 minutes) from the west side of the long-distance bus station on Jinguyuan Lu (金谷园街); or bus 53 from Zhongzhou Donglu. A taxi from Longmen station will cost ¥15. On the way back, be prepared to haggle or take the bus.

A disheartening amount of decapitation disfigures the statuary at this Unesco World Heritage Site. In the early 20th century, many effigies were beheaded by unscrupulous collectors or simply extracted whole, many ending up abroad in such institutions as the Metropolitan Museum of Art in New York, the Atkinson Museum in Kansas City and the Tokyo National Museum. Many statues have clearly just had their faces crudely bludgeoned off, vandalism that probably dates from the Cultural Revolution and earlier episodes of anti-Buddhist fervour. The elements have also intervened, wearing smooth the faces of many other statues.

➡ **West Side**

Work began on the **Three Binyang Grottoes** (宾阳三洞, Bīnyáng Sān Dòng) during the Northern Wei dynasty. Despite the completion of two of the grottos during the Sui and Tang dynasties, statues here all display the benevolent expressions that characterised Northern Wei style. Traces of pigment remain within the three large grottoes and other small niches honeycomb the cliff walls. Nearby is the **Moya Three Buddha Niche** (摩崖三佛龛, Móyá Sānfó Kān), with seven figures that date from the Tang dynasty.

The Tang dynasty **Ten Thousand Buddha Grotto** (万佛洞, Wànfó Dòng) dates from 680. In addition to its namesake galaxy of tiny bas-relief Buddhas, there is a fine effigy of the Amitabha Buddha. Note the red pigment on the ceiling.

The most physically imposing and magnificent of all the Longmen carvings, the vast **Losana Buddha Statue Grotto** (奉先寺, Fèngxiān Sì) was created during the Tang dynasty between 672 and 675; it contains the best examples of sculpture, despite evident weathering and vandalism. Nine principal figures dominate: the Buddha, two disciples, two Bodhisattvas, two heavenly kings and two guardians. The 17m-high seated central Buddha is said to be modelled on Losana, whose face is allegedly modelled on Tang empress and Buddhist patron Wu Zetian, who funded its carving.

The Tang figures tend to be more three-dimensional than the Northern Wei figures, while their expressions and poses also seem more natural. In contrast to the otherworldly effigies of the Northern Wei, many Tang figures possess a more fearsome ferocity and muscularity, most noticeably in the huge guardian figure in the north wall.

➡ **East Side**

Although the **east side grottoes** (东山石窟, Dōngshān Shíkū) lack comparable grandeur

– many are even gated shut – there are still some gems to seek out here. The first stop you'll come across after crossing the bridge is the **Leigutai Architectural Site** (擂鼓台建筑遗址, Léigǔtái Jiànzhù Yízhǐ), which takes visitors through an earlier excavation, with various Tang and Song relics on display. It's through a pair of doors at the top of the steps.

Although badly faded, the delicate **Thousand Arm and Thousand Eye Guanyin** (千手千眼观音龛, Qiānshǒu Qiānyǎn Guānyīn Kān) in Grotto 2132 is a splendid bas-relief dating from the Tang dynasty, revealing the Goddess of Mercy framed in a huge fan of carved hands, each sporting an eye.

Further is the eastern side's largest site, the **Reading Sutra Grotto** (看经寺洞, Kàn Jīng Sìdòng), with a carved lotus on its ceiling and 29 expressive *luóhàn* (arhats) around the base of the walls.

At the top of a steep flight of steps, the **Xiangshan Temple** (香山寺, Xiāngshān Sì) nestles against a hill. It was first built in 516 and has been repeatedly restored. Look for the villa which once belonged to Chiang Kaishek, built in 1936 to celebrate his 50th birthday.

The final stop is a lovely garden built around the **tomb of Bai Juyi** (白居易墓地, Bái Jūyì Mùdì), a poet from the Tang dynasty. It's a peaceful, leafy place with windy and secluded paths. Rest your tired feet at the shady alfresco **cafe**, where you can get tea (from ¥98), snacks and instant noodles.

White Horse Temple BUDDHIST MONASTERY
(白马寺, Báimǎ Sì; ¥35, audio guide ¥20; ⏱7.40am-6pm) Although its original structures have all been replaced and older Buddhist shrines may have vanished, this vast, active monastery outside Luoyang is regarded as China's first surviving Buddhist temple, originally dating from AD 68. When two Han dynasty court emissaries went in search of Buddhist scriptures, they met two Indian monks in Afghanistan; the monks returned to Luoyang on white horses carrying Buddhist sutras and statues. The impressed emperor built the temple for the monks; it's also their resting place.

More than 500 years later, the monk Xuanzang began his 'journey to the west' pilgrimage from here, and served as the abbot of White Horse Temple upon his return.

In Mahavira hall, it is astonishing to note that the main sculpture is hollow and weighs only 5kg. Outside, keep an eye out for the bronze 'longevity peach' – give it a good rub, then brush your hands over your head or whichever body part you think might need a little extra luck.

Tucked amid the smoky incense burners and usual Buddhist halls are some unusual sights; plan on spending at least two hours here. In the back of the complex, beneath a raised hall, is the **Shiyuan Art Gallery** (释源美术馆, Shìyuán Měishùguǎn), displaying temporary exhibitions. Also in the back of the complex is a surprisingly chic **teahouse** (止语茶舍, zhǐyǔ cháshě), an excellent place to take refuge and relax with a bowl of weak tea (free; help yourself from the warmer).

West of the historic grounds is the remarkable **International Zone**, featuring Thai, Burmese and Indian Buddhist temples. It's certainly worth strolling around.

At the opposite end of the grounds are **gardens** and the ancient 12-tiered **Qiyun Pagoda** (齐云塔, Qíyún Tǎ), encircled by worshippers. People say that if you stand 20m back from the pagoda and clap your hands, the echo sounds like a croaking frog.

The temple is 13km east of Luoyang, around 40 minutes away on bus 56 from the Xīguān (西关) stop. Bus 58 from Zhongzhou Donglu in the Old Town also runs here.

Guoliang 郭亮

🔊 0373 / POP 400
On its clifftop perch high up in the Mountains of the Ten Thousand Immortals (万仙山, Wànxiān Shān) in north Henan, this high-altitude stone hamlet was for centuries sheltered from the outside world by a combination of inaccessibility and anonymity. Guoliang (Guōliàng) shot to fame as the bucolic backdrop to a clutch of Chinese films, which firmly embedded the village in contemporary Chinese mythology.

Today the village attracts legions of artists, who journey here to capture the unreal mountain scenery on paper and canvas. Joining them are Chinese tourists who get disgorged by the busload. For a more isolated mountaintop experience, come on an out-of-season weekday when it's more tranquil. New buildings have sprung up but the original dwellings – climbing the mountain slope – retain their simple, rustic charms. Long treks beneath the marvellous limestone peaks more than compensate for the hard slog of journeying here.

WHAT TO WEAR

At 1700m above sea level and approximately 6°C (42.8°F) colder than Zhengzhou, Guoliang is cool enough to be devoid of mosquitoes year-round (some locals say), but pack warm clothes for winter visits, which can be bone-numbing. Visiting in low season may seem odd advice, but come evening the village can be utterly tranquil, and moonlit nights are intoxicating.

◉ Sights & Activities

Several kilometres before the village, you'll need to purchase an admission ticket to the **Wanxian Shan Scenic Area** (¥115); the required ticket includes free transport on the park's green shuttle buses. Bring your passport.

All of the **village dwellings**, many hung with butter-yellow *bàngzi* (sweetcorn cobs), are hewn from the same local stone that paves the slender alleyways, sculpts the bridges and fashions the picturesque gates of Guoliang village. Swallowed up by new construction, the original village can be easy to miss – it's on the right and up the hill from the rest of town.

Most buses from the ticket office terminate at the **Long Corridor in the Cliffs** (绝壁长廊, Juébì Chángláng), leaving visitors to walk through for a closer perspective on the plunging cliffs, with dramatic views from the tunnel carved through the rock. Before this tunnel was built by hand (between 1972 and 1978) by a local man called Shen Mingxin and several others, the only way into the village was via the **Sky Ladder** (天梯, Tiān Tī) – steep Ming dynasty steps hewn from the local stone.

The stairs have no guard rails and have fallen into disrepair, making them off limits to visitors, but the 2km walk from the village is among the area's most scenic. To get here, take the left fork of the road heading back from the village towards the tunnel and walk for 2km.

On the other side of the precipice from the village, across the bridge, a small row of cottages, set almost on the edge of the cliff, is **Yáshàng Rénjiā** (崖上人家), four family compounds that date back to the Ming dynasty. Nearby, there's a viewing platform that sits atop a pillar of rock; step across the walkway for astonishing views into the canyon.

Alternatively, head up the valley through the strip of street stalls and hotels to get to the start of a 5km circuit. From the end of the street, it's an additional 1.3km to the starting point of the loop. (Sadly, the mood of the area has been spoilt in parts by the addition of several constructed oddities, including a mini zip line and a drain-like slide ride from the top of the mountain.) If you start on the left-hand set of steps, you'll first go past the awe-inspiring curtain of rock above the **Shouting Spring** (喊泉, Hǎn Quán). According to local lore, its flow responds to the loudness of your whoops (it doesn't, but the site is predictably a riot of noise). You'll also pass the peaceful **Old Pool** (老潭, Lǎo Tán), which is thankfully out of earshot of the spring. Further along is the **Red Dragon Cave** (红龙洞, Hónglóng Dòng), now closed, and after a few steep flights of stairs, the slide ride (¥30) and then the small **White Dragon Cave** (白龙洞, Báilóng Dòng; ¥20), which you can skip with no regrets. The last sight is a set of steps that lead up to **Pearl Spring** (珍珠泉, Zhēnzhū Quán), a fissure in the mountain from which pours out cool, clear, spring water. You can, of course, do the loop in the opposite direction.

Take the time to visit the western half of the scenic area. Most shuttles leaving from the lower end of the Long Corridor will take you to the village under Sun Moon Star Rock (400m up the road from Nanping). From here, it's a 1500m walk to **Black Dragon Pool**, which is at least 28m deep (the shape of the pool has thus far made it impossible to measure any deeper). Above the pool is a stunning 40m-tall waterfall. For a longer walk, wooden steps lead from the pool high up into the mountain. Take your own water with you.

🛏 Sleeping & Eating

There are hotels galore in Guoliang village, most heading up the valley, though there are also rooms along the road by Yáshàng Rénjiā. All offer identical two-star quality, with hot showers, private squat toilets, wi-fi and TVs (no toiletries or towels though). Rooms cost ¥50 to ¥100 depending on size and orientation. Prices are a bit higher during the summer but negotiable in the low season and on weekdays.

Small restaurants are everywhere you turn, with most attached to one of the innumerable village guesthouses. Expect a sampling of classic Chinese dishes and noodles, costing in the range of ¥25 to ¥60.

ℹ Information

There are no ATMs and there is nowhere to change money in Guoliang.

ℹ Getting There & Away

You can reach Guoliang from Xinxiang (新乡, Xīnxiāng), between Anyang and Zhengzhou. Fast trains run from Zhengzhou east train station to Xinxiang east train station (¥31, 20 minutes). From here, you'll need to take a cab to Xinxiang's **main bus station** (客运总站, kèyùn zǒngzhàn; about ¥20, 25 minutes) to catch the bus to Huixian (辉县; ¥7, 45 minutes), which runs regularly. Bus 66 (¥1) also runs to the main bus station.

From Huixian, seven buses (¥15, 1¾ hours, first/last bus 7.20am/5.25pm) leave the **bus station** (辉县站, Huīxiàn zhàn) for Wanxian Shan ticket office. Here, you will need to buy a ticket and hop on the green shuttle, which will take you the rest of the way to the Long Corridor in the Cliffs.

To return, take the green shuttle from the bottom of the Long Corridor to the western half of the park. If you get dropped at Nanping (南坪, Nánpíng; 25 minutes), walk the 400m up the road to the restaurant area near Rì Yuè Xīng Shí (日月星石). From here, minibuses depart for Xinxiang (¥25) at 6.20am, 9am, noon, 1pm, 1.30pm, 3pm and 5pm. If there are only a few people on the bus, it may only go as far as Huixian.

ℹ Getting Around

Electric carts (¥20 return) run to the trail for the Shouting Spring loop (1.3km). Follow the signs and you'll find the carts waiting at the edge of the village.

To get to the western section of the park, hop on a shuttle in the direction of Nanping (ask the driver) at the bottom of the Long Corridor. The shuttle will either drop you in Nanping or, even better, at the restaurant area 400m up the road.

Kaifeng 开封

📞 0378 / POP 2.23 MILLION

More than any other of Henan's ancient capitals, Kaifeng (Kāifēng) makes an effort to recall its former grandeur. The walled town has character: you may have to squint a bit and sift the reproductions from its genuine historical narrative, but the city still offers up an intriguing display of age-old charm, magnificent market food, relics from its long-vanished apogee, and colourful chrysanthemums, the city flower (Kaifeng is also known as Júchéng, or 'Chrysanthemum Town').

You won't see soaring skyscrapers, though – one reason being that buildings requiring deep foundations are prohibited, for fear of destroying the ancient northern Song dynasty city below.

History

Once the prosperous capital of the Northern Song dynasty (AD 960–1126), Kaifeng was established south of the Yellow River, but not far enough to escape the river's capricious wrath. After centuries of flooding, the city of the Northern Song largely lies buried 8m to 9m deep in hardened silt. Between 1194 and 1938 the city flooded 368 times, an average of once every two years.

By the early 13th century Kaifeng had a whopping one million inhabitants and likely was the most populous city in the world. An important stop along the Silk Road, Kaifeng was also the first city in China where Jewish merchants settled when they arrived. Sadly, little remains of Kaifeng's once thriving Jewish community – all that remains of Kaifeng Synagogue is a well with an iron lid in the boiler room of the Kaifeng Traditional Chinese Medicine Hospital and the name of the brick alley south of the hospital – Jiaojing Hutong (教经胡同, Teaching the Torah Alley). A small Christian and Catholic community also lives in Kaifeng alongside a much larger local Muslim Hui community.

◉ Sights

★ Temple of the Chief Minister BUDDHIST TEMPLE
(大相国寺, Dà Xiàngguó Sì; www.daxiangguosi.com; 36 Ziyou Lu, 自有路36号; ¥40; ⊙8am-5pm Dec-Feb, to 6.30pm Jun-Aug, to 6pm rest of year) First founded in AD 555, this frequently rebuilt temple vanished along with Kaifeng in the early 1640s, when rebels breached the Yellow River's dykes. During the Northern Song, the temple covered a massive 34 hectares and housed over 10,000 monks. The show-stopper today is the mesmerising **Four-Faced Thousand Hand Thousand Eye Guanyin** (四面千手千眼观世音, Sìmiàn Qiānshǒu Qiānyǎn Guānshìyīn), towering within the octagonal **Arhat Hall** (罗汉殿, Luóhàn Diàn), beyond the **Hall of Tathagata** (大雄宝殿, Dàxióng Bǎodiàn).

Kāifēng Fǔ HISTORIC SITE
(开封府; north side, Baogong East Lake, 包公湖北岸; ¥65; ⊙7.30am-7pm Mar-Nov, to 5.30pm Dec-Feb) This reconstructed site of the government offices of the Northern Song has daily theatricals commencing outside the gates – the doors are thrown open and

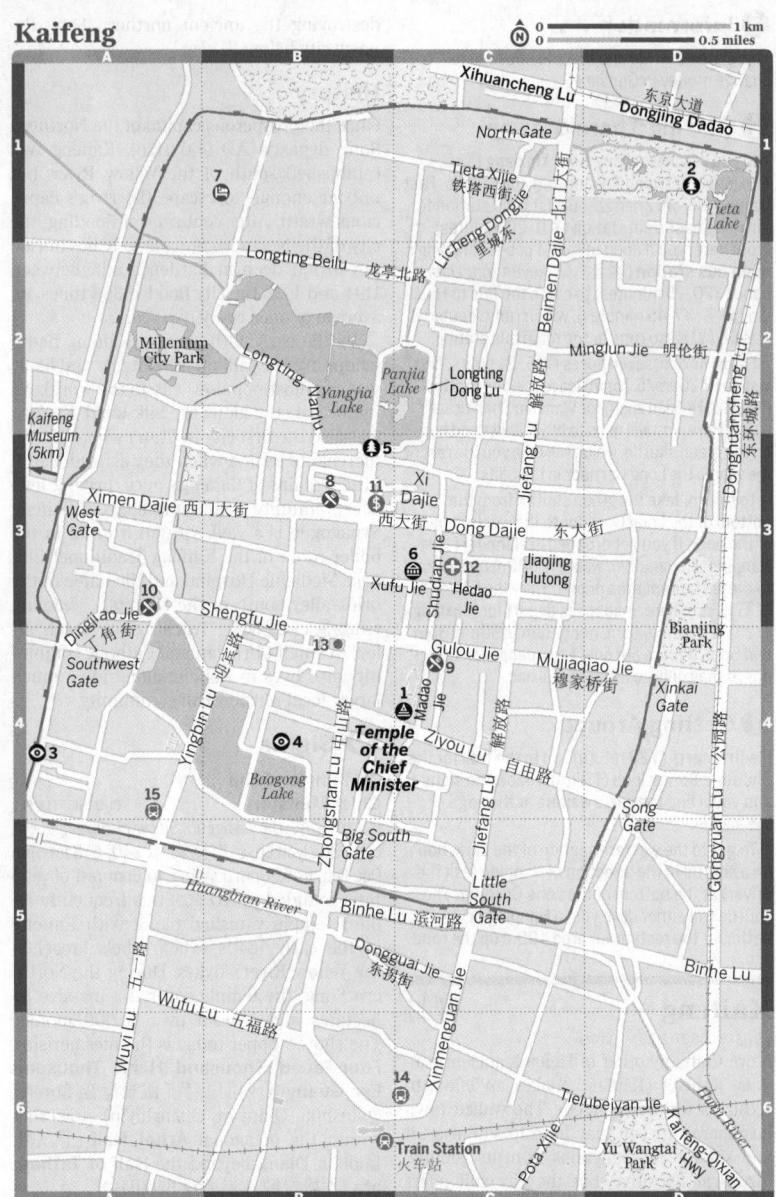

0   1 km
0   0.5 miles

Xihuancheng Lu

东京大道
Dongjing Dadao

North Gate

Tieta Xijie
铁塔西街

Tieta
Lake

7

Licheng Dongjie 里城东街

Beimen Dajie 北门大街

Longting Beilu 龙亭北路

Minglun Jie 明伦街

Donghuancheng Lu 东环城路

Millenium
City Park

Longting Nanlu

Yangjia
Lake

Panjia
Lake

Longting
Dong Lu

Jiefang Lu 解放路

Kaifeng
Museum
(5km)

5

Ximen Dajie 西门大街

West
Gate

8

11

Xi
Dajie
西大街

Dong Dajie 东大街

Jiaojing
Hutong

6

12

Xufu Jie

Shudan Jie

Hedao
Jie

Bianjing
Park

10

Dingjiao Jie
丁角街

Shengfu Jie

13

Gulou Jie

Mujiaqiao Jie 穆家桥街

Xinkai
Gate

Southwest
Gate

Yingbin Lu 迎宾路

Zhongshan Lu 中山路

9

1

Madao
Jie

**Temple
of the
Chief
Minister**

Ziyou Lu 自由路

Jiefang Lu

Song
Gate

3

4

Baogong
Lake

Big South
Gate

Little
South
Gate

Huangbian River

Binhe Lu 滨河路

Binhe Lu

15

Dongguai Jie 东拐街

Wufu Lu 五福路

Wuyi Lu 五一路

Ximenguan Jie 西门关街

14

Tielubeiyan Jie 铁路北沿街

Kaifeng-Qixian Hwy

Huiji River

Train Station
火车站

Pota Xijie

Yu Wangtai
Park

Gongyuan Lu 公园路

costumed actors play period scenes, complete with cracking whips and the sound of gongs. Drumming, kung-fu displays and Chinese-language plays are staged inside throughout the day. Drama aside, the site is one of Kaifeng's better recreations of Song imperial life, with English explanations,

martial parade grounds, a prison and several appearances by the famed Judge Bao.

Kaifeng City Walls   WALLS
(城墙, Chéng Qiáng) FREE Kaifeng is ringed by a relatively intact, much-restored Qing dynasty wall, which you can climb up at various

Kaifeng

points. There's precious little to see from up top and it can be punishingly hot on a sunny day (bring plenty of water and a hat). In fact, the best way to appreciate the bastion is to walk alongside it at ground level, through various small parks and with plenty of local life to observe.

Today's bastion was built on the foundations of the Song dynasty Inner Wall (内城, Nèichéng). Rising up outside was the mighty, now buried Outer Wall (外城, Wàichéng), a colossal construction containing 18 gates, which looped south of Po Pagoda.

Po Pagoda   BUDDHIST PAGODA
(繁塔, Pó Tǎ; Pota Xijie, 繁塔西街; ¥15; ⏰9am-5.30pm) This stumpy pagoda from 974 is the oldest Buddhist structure in Kaifeng and was originally a nine-storey hexagonal building, typical of the Northern Song style. The pagoda is clad in tiles decorated with 108 different Buddha images – note that most of the Buddhas on the lower levels have had their faces smashed off. The pagoda is all that survives of Tianqing Temple (天清寺, Tiānqīng Sì), but worshippers still flock here to burn incense and pray.

Across from the entrance, **Yuwangtai Park** (禹王台公园, Yǔwángtái Gōngyuán) is popular with local families, with its five flower gardens, small temple, revolutionary memorial and children's playground.

You'll find the pagoda hidden down alleyways east of the train station. Cross southward under the railway tracks from the corner of Huayuan Jie and Houzhuang Jie. From here follow the path, along with any red arrows spray-painted on the walls. Buses 8, 12 and 15 get relatively close; ask the driver to let you off at the right stop, or grab a taxi.

Shanshangan Guild Hall   HISTORIC BUILDING
(山陕甘会馆, Shānshǎn'gān Huìguǎn; 85 Xufu Jie, 徐府街85号; ¥25; ⏰8am-6pm Mar-Nov, 8.30am-6.30pm Dec-Feb) This tiny, elaborately styled guild hall was built as a lodging and meeting place during the Qing dynasty by an association of merchants from Shanxi (山西), Shaanxi (陕西) and Gansu (甘肃) provinces. You can delve into the exhibition on historic Kaifeng and see a fascinating diorama of the old Song city – with its palace in the centre of town – and compare it with a model of modern Kaifeng. Note the ornate carvings on the roof beams.

Kaifeng Museum   MUSEUM
(开封博物馆, Kāifēng Bówùguǎn; ☎2393 3624; Zhengkai Dadao, near Wu Dajie, 郑开大道与五大街交叉口; ⏰9am-5pm Tue-Sun) FREE Housed in a colossal fortress 10km west of town, the Kaifeng Museum contains a modest collection of archaeological finds, woodblock prints and historical objects, along with a sizeable exhibition on Zhang Zeduan's Qingming painting (p468). The audio guide (¥20 with ¥200 deposit) is helpful for lending context to the displays.

Get here on bus 56 from Zhongshan Zhongduan (¥1, 45 minutes, every 25 minutes), or by taxi (¥25). Bring your passport.

Iron Pagoda Park   PARK
(铁塔公园, Tiě Tǎ Gōngyuán; 210 Beimen Dajie, 北门大街210号; ¥30; ⏰8am-6pm Mar-Nov, 7.30am-6.30pm Dec-Feb) Kaifeng's most iconic landmark is a magnificent 11th-century Iron Pagoda (55m tall) at the centre of a pleasant park. The gorgeous, glazed-brick edifice,

named for its rust-coloured tiles, is the oldest and tallest of its kind in China. You can climb its narrow stairs for an additional ¥35. Take bus 1 from Zhongshan Lu; alternatively, a taxi will cost ¥10.

🎆 Festivals & Events

Chrysanthemum Festival   CULTURAL
(🕐 Oct) Millions of chrysanthemums are on full display at **Longting Park** (龙亭公园, Lóngtíng Gōngyuán; 📞 0371 566 0316; Zhongshan Lu, 中山路; ¥35; 🕐 8am-6pm Mar-Nov, to 5.30pm Dec-Feb) and elsewhere around the city during this autumn festival. In 2015 botanists grafted 641 flowers together, earning a spot in the Guinness World Records for the largest number of chrysanthemum species on one plant.

🛏 Sleeping

At the time of research, Kaifeng had closed the majority of hotels to foreigners, with the exception of a few midrange and top-end options. Staying overnight is the best way to catch a night market, but the rest of the city can easily be seen on a day trip from Zhengzhou.

Jinjiang Inn (Longting Park)   HOTEL ¥¥
(锦江之星　龙亭店, Jǐnjiāng zhī xīng lóng tíng diàn; 📞 2599 6666; 99 Xi Dajie, 西大街99号; d ¥228-289) Smack bang in the restaurant area just south of Longting Park, this budget branch has reasonable rates, large rooms, daily cleaning and a 24-hour reception.

Pullman Hotel   HOTEL ¥¥¥
(铂尔曼酒店, Bó'ěrmàn Jiǔdiàn; 📞 0371 2358 9999; www.pullman.accorhotels.com; 16 Longting Beilu, 龙亭北路16号; d from ¥1800; 🅿❄🌐📶🏊) Set in expansive, park-like grounds, Kaifeng's

top hotel choice is enormous and peaceful. Rooms are stylish, with tasteful depictions of the city's famous sights on the walls and opulent marble bathrooms with deep below-floor tubs. Discounts of 65% make this an excellent, affordable luxury choice, especially if you plan to get around town in a taxi or rent a bicycle (¥20).

🍴 Eating & Drinking

Kaifeng is particularly famous for its snacks and night markets, and you'll find several food streets popping up in the evenings around town. Xisi Square is the best of the night markets; the Drum Tower night market is more central but gets the most crowded.

Specialities to keep an eye out for include *chǎo liángfěn* (开封炒凉粉, stir-fried mungbean jelly with soy and shallots), *yángròu kàngmó* (羊肉炕馍, lamb in a parcel of bread) and *chǎo suānnǎi* (炒酸奶, yoghurt frozen on an icy grill then mixed with dried fruit and sunflower seeds).

Baiqiyuan Gourmet Park   FOOD HALL ¥
(百奇源美食广场, Bǎiqíyán Měishí Guǎngchǎng; 4th fl, New Mart Mall, 388 Ximen Dajie, 西门大街388号新玛特4楼; meals from ¥15; 🕐 10am-8pm) This hawker-style food court offers plenty of easy-to-order meals, with noodles, dumplings, fried rice, tempting soups and delicious choose-your-own-ingredient stir-fries on offer.

Xisi Square Night Market   STREET FOOD ¥
(西司广场夜市, Xīsī Guǎngchǎng Yèshì; Dingjiao Jie, 丁角街; meals from ¥15; 🕐 6.30pm-late) Join the scrum weaving between stalls busy with hustling and hollering vendors cooking up *chuan'r* (串儿, things on sticks), *náng* bread, cured beef, hearty *jiānbǐng guǒzi*

ALONG THE RIVER DURING THE QINGMING FESTIVAL

Now held in the Forbidden City and widely acknowledged as China's first *shén* (godly) painting, *Along the River During the Qingming Festival* was completed by Zhang Zeduan (张择端) in the early 12th century. These days, you'll see versions of it everywhere in Kaifeng. Museums, parks and bridges have it in carved wood and stone bas-relief; it's found in scale dioramas, souvenir posters and advertising; and there's even a theme park modelled after it.

The long (about 25cm x 529cm) painting depicts life in Kaifeng during the Song dynasty. The painting is packed to the gills with details of the period: boats unloading goods at a harbour, an inn crowded with customers and children playing on the streets. When the original is displayed in Beijing, queues to see it last hours. Art enthusiasts will no doubt recognise later copies of the work, some of which are equally famous – the 1737 version, presented to Emperor Qianlong, is now held in Taipei's national Palace Museum.

Versions in Kaifeng include the scale diorama in the Shanshangan Guild Hall (p467) and the replica in the Kaifeng Museum (p467).

(煎饼裹子, pancakes with chopped onions), sweet potatoes, roast rabbit, Kaifeng-style *xiǎolóngbāo* (steamed dumplings) and peanut cake (花生糕, *huāshēng gāo*). Take your snacks for a stroll or pull up a plastic chair and order an accompanying beer or two.

Take bus 24 to get here.

Gulou Night Market STREET FOOD ¥
(鼓楼夜市, Gǔlóu Yèshì; Sihou Jie, 寺后街; meals from ¥20; ⊙6.30pm-late) Kaifeng's bustling night market wraps around the Drum Tower, sprawling in various directions, and serves the usual run of point-and-grill kebabs and steamers of soup dumplings. It's always crowded with locals out enjoying themselves.

There is veritable hotchpotch of stalls, with non-food offerings ranging from jeans and children's toys to on-the-spot tattoos and nail art.

Dào Xiāng Jū HENAN ¥
(稻香居, ☑2288 4603; 73 Song Duyu Jie, 宋都御街73号; dishes ¥20-68; ⊙10am-2pm & 5-9pm) This no-fuss restaurant, specialising in *guōtiē* (锅贴, potsticker dumplings), serves as a welcome break from the night markets. Service is fast and the menu has a few pictures that help with pointing. If you don't feel like dumplings, the menu also has a long list of home-style Henan dishes on offer.

Guangying Cafe CAFE
(光影咖啡, Guāngyǐng Kāfēi; ☑2261 1622; 69 Song Duyu Jie, 宋都御街69号; ⊙9am-10pm; 🛜) Guangying Cafe is a breath of fresh air in Kaifeng. Come here for cold drip coffee, generous lattes and icy-cold craft beer. The food service is slow but worth the wait: the hand-cut potato wedges, ¥28, particularly hit the spot.

As you make yourself comfortable in the cushioned chairs, be mindful not to sit on a lounging cat (there are at least two).

ℹ️ Information

Bai Shi Kang Pharmaceutical (百氏康医药, Bǎi Shìkāng Yīyào; ☑139 3863 0323; Dong Dajie, 东大街; ⊙7.30am-9.30pm) Small, well-stocked pharmacy with helpful staff. Bring a translation app.

Bank of China (中国银行, Zhōngguó Yínháng; cnr Xi Dajie & Zhongshan Lu, 西大街与中山路交叉口; ⊙9am-5pm Mon-Sat) Has a 24-hour ATM.

Kaifeng Central Hospital (开封市中心医院, Kāifēng Shì Zhōngxīn Yīyuàn; ☑0371 2567 1288; 85 Hedao Jie, 河道街85号) Located right in the heart of town.

ℹ️ Getting There & Away

AIR

The nearest airport is at Zhengzhou. The **airport shuttle** (机场巴士, Jīchǎng Bāshì; ¥40; ⊙1½hr, hourly 4.40am-6.40pm) runs from the corner of Gulou Jie and Jiefang Lu. Tickets can be bought at either of the IATA Air Ticket Offices.

Alternatively, the train from Songcheng Lu can make the trip to Zhengzhou's Xinzheng Airport in one hour (¥30, every 1½ hours, 6.20am to 8.30pm).

BUS

Buses leave from the main **long-distance bus station** (开封长途汽车中心站, Kāifēng Chángtú Qìchē Zhōngxīnzhàn; Zhongshan Lu, 中山路), opposite the train station, including the following:

Anyang ¥63, four hours, half-hourly

Luoyang ¥60, three hours, hourly

Xinxiang ¥31, three hours, hourly

Zhengzhou ¥10, 1¾ hours, every 15 minutes

Buses also run from the **west long-distance bus station** (开封长途汽车西站, Kāifēng chángtú qìchē xīzhàn; Yingbin Lu, 迎宾路), including the following:

Anyang ¥63, four hours, half-hourly

Dengfeng ¥40, three hours, two daily (9.30am and 1.25pm)

Xinxiang ¥31, three hours, six daily

Zhuxian Zhen ¥5, one hour, every 15 minutes

Note that almost all buses to Zhengzhou terminate at its east train station; to get into town from there, either take the metro or the transfer bus running between the two train stations.

TRAIN

Kaifeng's train station is in the south of town, an ¥8 taxi-ride from Zhongshan Lu. Rail options – and tickets – from Kaifeng are limited; your options are much better with a connection in Zhengzhou.

Most trains from Zhengzhou come from Zhengzhou east train station, terminating at Kaifeng North or Songcheng Lu, each a ¥20 cab ride from Kaifeng.

Trains departing from Kaifeng North Train Station include the following:

Anyang K train hard seat ¥30, three hours, frequent; G train 1st/2nd class ¥144/90, one hour, six daily

Beijing West Hard sleeper ¥195, 12 hours, two daily

Luoyang Hard seat ¥30, 2½ hours, eight daily (few tickets available)

Shanghai G train 1st/2nd class ¥701/423, 4½ hours, 10 daily; K train hard/soft sleeper ¥221/337, 11½ hours, five daily (few tickets available)

Xi'an Seat/sleeper ¥81/168, nine hours, frequent (few tickets available)

Xinxiang East 1st/2nd class ¥88/55 one hour, two daily (8am and 3.15pm)

Zhengzhou East Hard seat ¥18 to ¥24, 30 minutes, frequent departures

❶ Getting Around

Zhongshan Lu is a good place to catch buses (¥1) to most sights. Taxis (flagfall ¥5, pollution tax ¥1) are the best way to get about.

Avoid pedicabs as they frequently rip off tourists.

Zhuxian Zhen   朱仙镇

☏ 0371 / POP 38,630

Zhuxian Zhen (Zhūxiān Zhèn), where the 1000-year-old craft of woodblock printing (木板年画, mùbǎn niánhuà) is still practised, is known as one of China's four 'ancient' towns: the other three are Hankou (trade), Jingdezhen (porcelain) and Foshan (silk). An easy day trip from Kaifeng, the woodblock prints here are a sure highlight for anyone interested in traditional Chinese arts and crafts.

The expertly baked naan (flat bread; ¥2), sold by Muslim vendors in the street, may just be some of the freshest bread you'll eat in your life.

At the time of writing, Zhuxian's charming main drag had been engulfed by enormously dusty roadworks. All the buildings were intact, but you may have to clamber over some rough sections to reach the two temples and the Yin family workshop.

Heading 700m or so south off the main road along a wide stone path will take you to the **mosque** (朱仙清真寺, Zhūxiān Qīngzhēn Sì) FREE, originally founded in the Northern Song and featuring elaborately carved beams and lintels.

Guanyu Temple   TEMPLE

(关庙, Guān Miào; ¥10; ⊙8am-5pm) Dedicated to Guandi, the god of war and protection (among other things), this temple was originally built during the Ming dynasty (then dedicated to the god of wealth); the present structure dates back to 1708. Consisting of a single hall, there is not much to see here besides the building and a twisted pine tree – touch the top branch for fortune, the rear for longevity, or the middle for a promotion.

Yue Fei Temple   TEMPLE

(岳飞庙, Yuè Fēi Miào; ☏ 2675 8556; ¥30; ⊙8am-6pm summer, 8.30am-5pm winter) Dedicated to the Southern Song military hero Yue Fei, this temple was first founded in 1478. The weatherbeaten temple hasn't seen much restoration, and has a refreshing sense of time and place that is difficult to find in most popular temples.

Don't be surprised to come across the 'five kneeling traitors' statues of the corrupt officials who persecuted Yue Fei and were instrumental in the hero's execution. The officials were not punished in their lifetimes but statues like these were erected posthumously at Yue Fei's mausoleum in Hangzhou. Visitors are encouraged to give the traitors a little whip (whips provided) as they pass by.

★ Yínshì Lǎo Tiānchéng   ARTS & CRAFTS

(尹氏老天成; ☏ 0371 2671 2924; ⊙9am-4pm) The artist/owner of this woodblock printing workshop, Mr Yin (尹), is a fifth-generation artisan whose family has been in business for more than 200 years. A beautifully bound box of prints, with English explanations, housed in a wooden presentation box costs ¥300 (but if you're nice, he may knock a little off the price). Located 100m east of the Yue Fei Temple.

❶ Getting There & Away

As it's an easy day trip from Kaifeng, there is no need to spend the night in Zhuxian.

Head to Kaifeng's west bus station (p469), from where bus 306 (¥5, one hour, every 15 minutes) runs all the way to Zhuxian. The driver can let you off at the mosque, or you can get off at a busy thoroughfare closer to the centre of town. The last bus from Zhuxian leaves at 6pm.

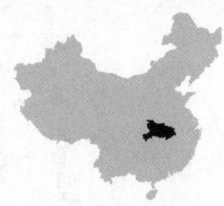

Hubei

POP 59 MILLION

Best Places to Eat

➡ Xiǎo Bèiké (p476)

➡ Shěnjì Shāokǎo Hǎixiān (p475)

➡ Fangweng Restaurant (p481)

Best Places to Stay

➡ Ivorll International Youth Hostel (p475)

➡ Tomolo (p475)

➡ Shangri-La Hotel (p475)

➡ Wudang International Youth Hostel (p479)

Why Go?

Many travellers find themselves drifting into Hubei (湖北, Húběi) through the Three Gorges, the precipitous marvel that's a continuation of Chongqing's uniquely lush and hilly landscape. This classic trip down the Yangzi is the perfect introduction to Hubei's natural beauty.

Sliced by rivers and dappled with lakes, Hubei's western regions are dominated by stunning mountain scenery, from the national parks of Shennongjia and Enshi to the historic Taoist retreat of Wudang Shan. In 1944 the only variety of redwood growing outside of the USA, the dawn redwood, was discovered in these mountains.

While eastern Hubei is better known for its industrial belt rather than scenic beauty, the region's central location has ensured it played a key role in China's history. Vestiges spanning thousands of years, from the ancient state of Chu to the modern Wuchang Uprising – which led to the downfall of dynastic China – are woven into the province's very fabric.

When to Go
Wuhan

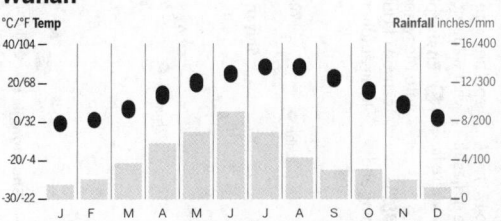

Mar & Apr Rhododendrons are in bloom and the Three Gorges cruises are warm and breezy.

Sep–Nov The stupefying summer heat has finally lifted.

Nov–Mar Dustings of snow mean Wudang Shan at its prettiest. Hold that taichi pose.

Hubei Highlights

1 Wudang Shan (p478)
Learning taichi on the majestic cloud-covered slopes where it all began.

2 Shennongjia (p482)
Misty mountain-hopping and spotting rare monkeys in this vast wilderness area.

3 Enshi (p483) Descending into the waterfall-strewn canyon of Hubei's Tujia and Miao autonomous region.

4 Wuhan (p473) Breaking for coffee, beer and barbecue in central China's biggest city.

5 Yichang (p480) Tackling the Three Gorges from this humble river town, rather than the better-known Chongqing.

6 Jingzhou (p477)
Exploring the historic gates, city walls and ancient artefacts of Jingzhou.

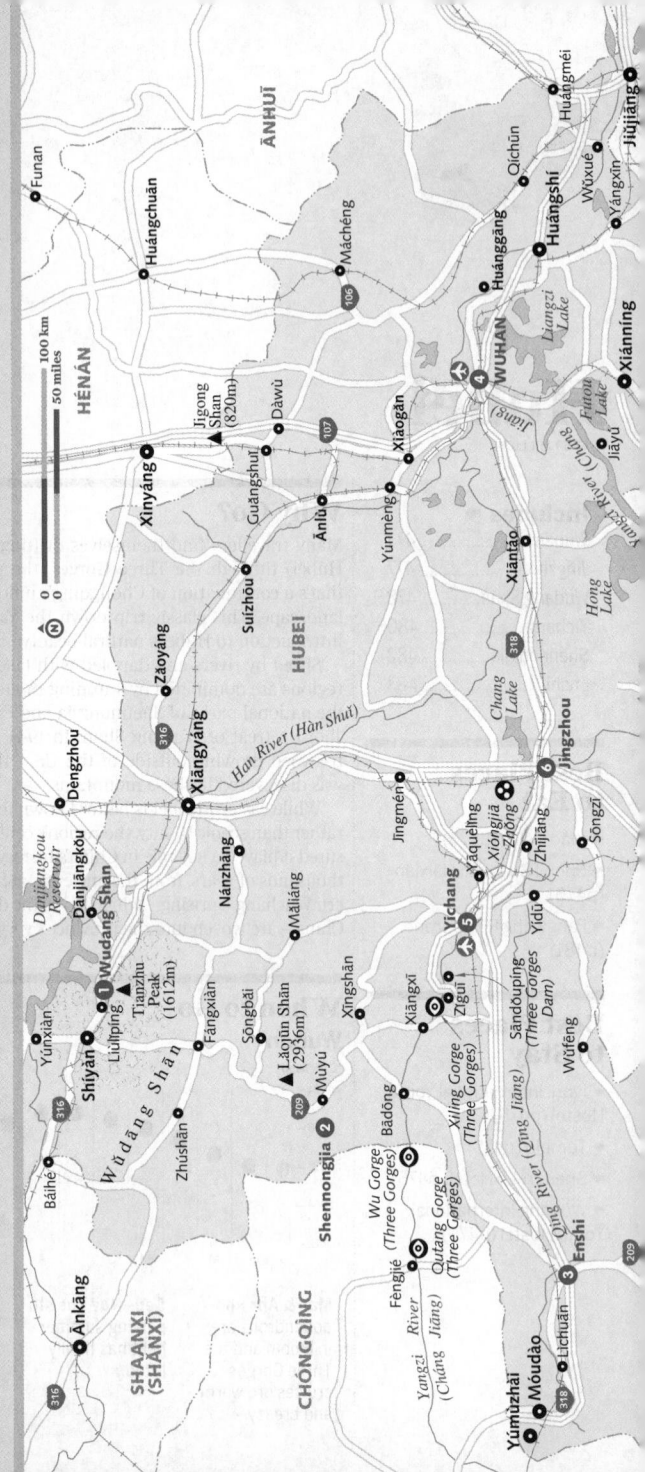

History

The Hubei area first came to prominence during the Eastern Zhou (700–221 BC), when the powerful Chu kingdom, based in present-day Jingzhou, was at its height. Hubei again became pivotal during the Three Kingdoms (AD 220–280). The Chinese classic *The Romance of the Three Kingdoms* (*Sān Guó Yǎnyì*) makes much reference to Jingzhou. The mighty Yangzi River (Cháng Jiāng) ensured prosperous trade in the centuries that followed, especially for Wuhan, China's largest inland port and stage of the 1911 uprising, which led to the fall of the Qing and the creation of the Republic of China.

Language

Hubei has two dialects of northern Mandarin – southwest Mandarin and lower-mid Yangzi Mandarin – while in the southeast many people speak Gan, a dialect from Jiangxi.

ℹ Getting There & Around

Wuhan is a major transport hub and Hubei is consequently well connected to the rest of China by high-speed rail, air and the occasional bus.

Rail travel between most of the destinations within the province is the easiest, fastest and the cheapest way to get around.

Wuhan 武汉

♪ 027 / POP 7.98 MILLION

Wuhan (Wǔhàn) has matured from the sprawling convergence of three independent cities to central China's main industrial and commercial centre. While there's not much in the way of cultural sites, Wuhan is a major transport hub so you may find yourself here for a night or two.

The Yangzi and Han rivers open up the densely packed streets, flowing by parks, lakes and a concession-era entertainment district in Hankou, the pick of the three former cities. This is not a place of penny postcards, but for those travelling through the middle of the Middle Kingdom, it's a good place to get your urban fix.

◎ Sights

Hubei Provincial Museum   MUSEUM
(湖北省博物馆, Húběi Shěng Bówùguǎn; www.hbww.org; 156 Donghu Lu, 东湖路156号; ⊙9am-5pm Tue-Sun; Ⓜ Dongting) FREE The highlights of Hubei's Provincial Museum are

excavations from the Tomb of Marquis Yi of Zeng (c 433 BC): there are bronze wares, weaponry and musical instruments – including one of the world's largest, a remarkable five-tonne set of 65 double-tone bronze bells. Half-hour chime bell performances (¥30) are given thrice daily (10.30am, 2pm and 3pm) during the week, with an extra performance at 11.30am on the weekend. Other exhibits here include Palaeolithic fossils and Neolithic bronzes and pottery. Passport required.

The museum is by the enormous East Lake (东湖, Dōng Hú). Bus 411 runs here from the Yellow Crane Tower. Line 8 on the metro will eventually stop here too.

Hubei Museum of Art   MUSEUM
(湖北美术馆, Húběi Měishùguǎn; www.hbmoa.com; 1 Sanguandian, Donghu Lu, 东湖路三官殿1号; ⊙9am-5pm Tue-Sun; Ⓜ Dongting) FREE Focusing on modern Chinese art, the first two floors here are dedicated to temporary exhibits, while the 3rd floor features a permanent collection tracing the development of art in Hubei in the 20th century. Don't expect anything too provocative, but as it's right next door to the Provincial Museum it's certainly worth a visit.

Bus 411 runs here from the Yellow Crane Tower.

Yellow Crane Tower   HISTORIC SITE
(黄鹤楼, Huánghè Lóu; Wuluo Lu, 武珞路; ¥70; ⊙8am-6pm, to 5pm winter) Wuhan's mythical crane, immortalised in the 8th-century poetry of Cui Hao, has long flown, but the city landmark remains perched atop Snake Hill. The tower has been rebuilt often since the original was constructed in AD 223, and

---

ℹ PRICE RANGES

Sleeping
Prices given are for a double room with private bathroom.

¥ less than ¥150

¥¥ ¥150–500

¥¥¥ more than ¥500

Eating
Prices given are for a meal for one.

¥ less than ¥40

¥¥ ¥40–100

¥¥¥ more than ¥100

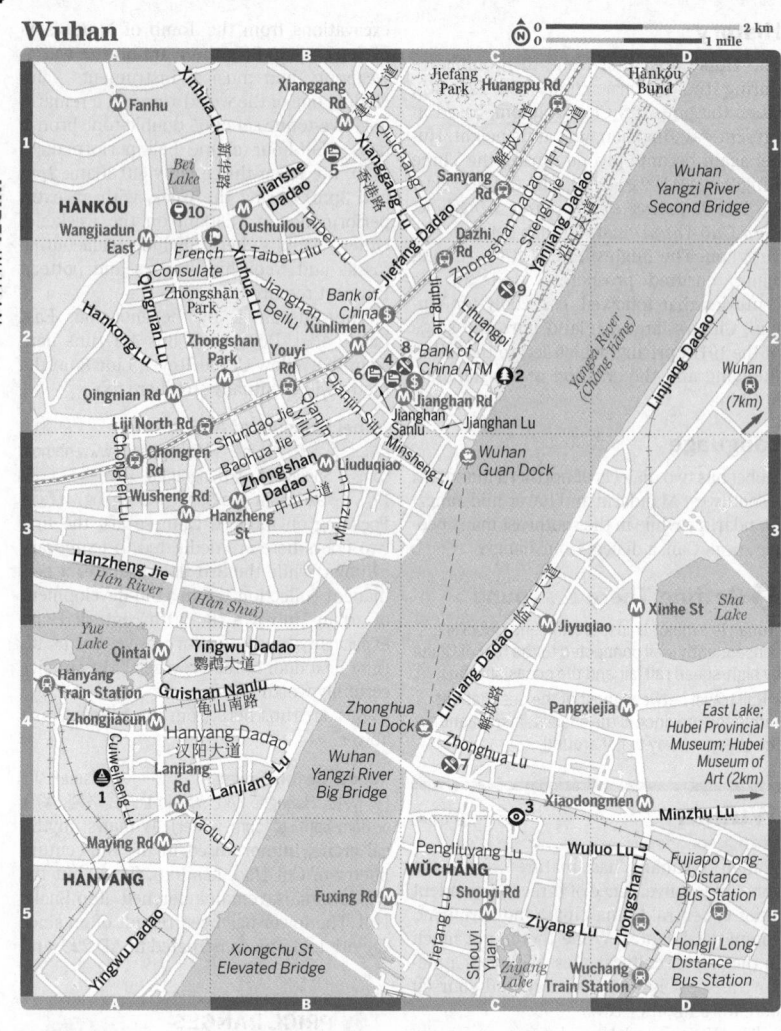

Wuhan

◉ Sights
1 Guiyuan Temple A4
2 Hankou Bund C2
3 Yellow Crane Tower C4

⬛ Sleeping
4 Dorsett Wuhan B2
5 Shangri-La Hotel B1
6 Tomolo B2

❌ Eating
7 Hubu Alley C4
8 Shěnjì Shāokǎo Hǎixiān C2
9 Xiǎo Bèiké C2

◉ Drinking & Nightlife
10 Brussels Beer Garden A1

today's five-storey, yellow-tiled version is a 1980s remake of the Qing tower that burned down in 1884.

Bus 411 runs between the tower and the provincial museum. The Dongtinmen stop on metro Line 7 will get you close, while Line 5 will eventually run directly here.

Hankou Bund PARK

(汉口江滩, Hànkǒu Jiāngtān; Ⓜ Jianghan Rd)
FREE The Hankou Bund is a roughly 4km
stretch of curated park running parallel to
the Yangzi where locals gather to amble
or gossip. There are some tea houses and
bars, a few historic buildings, mahjong and
chess boards, and some green areas. Mostly,
though, it's locals escaping the concrete and
posing for photos, especially around sunrise
and sunset.

Guiyuan Temple BUDDHIST TEMPLE

(归元寺, Guīyuán Sì; 20 Cuiweiheng Lu, 翠微横
路20号; ¥10; ⏱ 7.30am-5pm; Ⓜ Zhongjiacun)
An afternoon at this revered 350-year-old
Buddhist temple can fluctuate between serenity and chaos, depending on the tour buses.
Pass a large rectangular pond where turtles
cling like shipwrecked sailors to two metal
lotus flowers and examine the magnificently
burnished cabinet housing Milefo in the first
hall. Also seek out the more than 500 statues
of enlightened disciples in the **Hall of Arhats**
(罗汉堂, Luóhàn Táng). Completed in 1890,
after nine years in the making, they remain
in pristine condition.

🛏 Sleeping

Hankou is the most pleasant place to stay
in Wuhan, but as the metro system is quite
extensive, it's not too hard to get around if
you're based elsewhere.

★ Ivorll International Youth Hostel
HOSTEL ¥

(象牙国际青年旅舍, Xiàngyá Guójì Qīngnián
Lǚshè; ☑ 181 8610 0399; 3rd fl, Weiduoli Bldg,
218 Luoyu Lu, 珞瑜路218号维多利大厦3层;
dm/d from ¥60/180; ✸ 🛜; Ⓜ Guangbutun) The
only real hostel in Wuhan, Ivorll is a stylish
choice, with a pleasing blue-and-white colour scheme and thoughtful design touches
throughout. There are eight-bunk and four-
bunk dorms, both with privacy curtains, and
a stylish cafe and cocktail bar offer an easy
escape from Wuhan's crowds. Although it's
in Wuchang, it has a great location steps
from the metro.

Tomolo BOUTIQUE HOTEL ¥¥

(天美乐饭店, Tiānměilè Fàndiàn; ☑ 027 8275
7288; 56 Jianghan Sanlu, 江汉三路56号; r ¥348;
✸ 🛜; Ⓜ Xunlimen, Jianghan Rd) Tomolo is a
Wuhan brand known for style and panache.
You'll enjoy the giant rooms with a sofa, coffee table and large bed, and the bathrooms
feature stylish tiling and power showers.
While rooms could use a refresh, you can't
beat the online rates (from ¥200). Great location in the heart of Hankou, with plenty of
street food at your doorstep.

Dorsett Wuhan HOTEL ¥¥

(武汉帝盛酒店, Wǔhàn Dìshèng Jiǔdiàn; ☑ 027
6882 2899; www.dorsetthotels.com/wuhan; 118
Jianghan Erlu, Hankou, Hong Kong & Macau Centre,
江汉二路118号新世界百货时尚广; r ¥428-600;
✸ 🛜; Ⓜ Xunlimen, Jianghan Rd) With a handy
location in the heart of Hankou, the Dorsett
is an attentive and efficient four-star hotel.
Rooms are large, some with leather furniture
and rainforest showers, though not all have
windows. There's a Hong Kong–style cafe,
small gym and staff that speak some English.

Shangri-La Hotel LUXURY HOTEL ¥¥¥

(香格里拉大酒店, Xiānggé Lǐlā Dàjiǔdiàn; ☑ 027
8580 6868; www.shangri-la.com; 700 Jianshe Dadao,
建设大道700号; r from ¥615; ⊙ ✸ @ 🛜; Ⓜ Xianggang Rd) One of Wuhan's top international
hotels, the Shangri-La gets good marks for
service and its convenient Hankou location.
Room design is a bit dated (some renovations
were taking place during our last visit), but
the comfort level meets expectations.

🍴 Eating

Wuhan's speciality is *règānmiàn* (热干面;
from ¥5), delicious sesame paste noodles
sold in small shops everywhere.

In Hankou, Jiqing Jie (吉庆街) and its extension, Jianghan Sanlu (江汉三路), are great
places to look for small restaurants and street
food, especially *shāokǎo* (烧烤, barbecue) on
the former and noodles on the latter.

Hubu Alley STREET FOOD ¥

(户部巷小吃, Hùbù Xiàng Xiǎochī; noodles from
¥6) Hubu Alley is famous among locals for
street food, from noodles and steamed buns
to duck intestines and pigs' feet. Crowds here
can be intense on weekends and holidays. It's
off Minzhu Lu, just west of the Yellow Crane
Tower in Wuchang.

Shěnjì Shāokǎo Hǎixiān HUBEI ¥¥

(沈记烧烤海鲜; 100-4 Jianghan Erlu, 江汉二路
100附4号; skewers ¥7-42, noodles ¥36-65; ⏱ 11am-
1am; Ⓜ Jianghan Rd, Xunlimen) Not your typical
noodle stand, this popular spot specialises
in two things: seafood *règānmiàn* (sesame
noodles) served in a huge bowl that will easily
feed two, and barbecued skewers. The noodles
come with crab legs (蟹脚面, *xièjiǎomiàn*;
¥68) and clams (圣子面, *shèngzǐmiàn*; ¥38)

– the literal translation of the latter is 'Jesus noodles'!

On the barbecue menu, the potatoes (土豆, *tǔdòu*) are particularly good. Look for the Santa decal on the front window.

Xiǎo Bèiké
CHINESE ¥¥¥

(小贝壳; 129 Dongting Jie, 洞庭街129号; dishes ¥32-168; ⊙11am-9.30pm; Ⓜ Dazhi Rd) This stylish restaurant, with lovely tree-shaded terrace seating, offers an excellent range of pan-Chinese cuisine, with dishes from Hubei, Sichuan and Chongqing featuring highly. In addition to seafood, it prepares delicious variations of roasted duck, chicken and goose. It's on the corner of Dongting Jie and Cai'e Lu (蔡锷路); the sign on the terrace fencing reads 'Petits Coquille Restaurant'.

Drinking & Nightlife

In Hankou, pedestrian Lihuangpi Lu (黎黄陂路), formerly in the Russian concession, has pleasant Western-style cafes and is good place for a relaxing drink. South of East Lake, on the other side of the Yangzi, are a few indie-style bars where you can catch live music.

Brussels Beer Garden
BAR

(☑ 027 8556 6465; www.brusselsbg.com; 8-8 Xibeihu Lu, 西北湖路8附8号; ⊙5pm-2am; Ⓜ Wangjiadun East) Stop by Bei Lake for a great selection of Belgian brews and yummy mini pizzas and burgers.

Wuhan Prison
BAR

(Guoguang Bldg, Lumo Lu, 鲁磨路国光大厦A座半地下室; ⊙9pm-2am; Ⓜ Optics Valley Sq) This long-standing, grungy Wuchang dive was opened by longtime punk musician Wu Wei (of seminal band SMZB), and is a popular expat hangout. It's up an alley around the corner from Vox.

★ Vox Livehouse
LIVE MUSIC

(☑ 027 8759 6030; https://site.douban.com/voxwuhan; 118 Lumo Lu, 鲁磨路118号; ⊙hours vary; Ⓜ Optics Valley Sq) Vox Livehouse is Wuhan's indie music venue of choice. Cover charge ranges from free to ¥220; call or check online for opening dates. It's on the south side of East Lake.

ⓘ Information

Many ATMs here state they accept foreign cards, but in reality they don't. Bank of China is the most reliable.

Bank of China (中国银行, Zhōngguó Yínháng; 819 Jinghan Dadao, 京汉大道819号;

⊙8.30am-5.30pm; Ⓜ Xunlimen) Centrally located in Hankou, with exchange services and a 24-hour ATM.

Bank of China (中国银行, Zhōngguó Yínháng; 593 Zhongshan Dadao, 中山大道593号; ⊙24hr; Ⓜ Hanjiang Rd) Handy ATM near the Jianghan Rd metro station.

Public Security Bureau Exit & Entry Division (PSB, 公安局出入境管理处, Gōng'ānjú Chūrù Jìngguǎn Lǐchù; ☑ 027 8539 5370; 7 Jinqiao Dadao, 金桥大道117号; ⊙8.30am-noon & 2.30-5.30pm; Ⓜ Citizen's Home) Can extend visas. Right next to the Citizen's Home (市民之家, Shìmín Zhijiā) metro station.

ⓘ Getting There & Away

AIR

Tiānhé International Airport (天河国际机场; Tiānhé Guójì Jīchǎng, WUH; ☑ 027 96577; Ⓜ Tianhe International Airport) is central China's main hub, and roughly 30km north of Wuhan. There are daily flights to all major Chinese cities, as well as direct international flights to Kuala Lumpur, London, New York, Paris, San Francisco, Seoul, Singapore, Sydney and Tokyo.

Use www.elong.net or www.trip.com to book flights.

BUS

None of the long-distance bus stations are particularly useful for travellers, as most destinations of interest are now served primarily by train. In Wuchang, the main two stations are **Fujiapo long-distance bus station** (傅家坡汽车客运站; Fùjiāpō Qìchē Kèyùnzhàn; 358 Wulou Lu, 五楼路358号; Ⓜ Zhongnan Rd) and **Hongji long-distance bus station** (宏基长途汽车站, Hóngjī Chángtú Qichēzhàn; 519 Zhongshan Lu, 中山路519号; Ⓜ Wuchang Railway Station).

TRAIN

Wuhan is an important rail hub with connections to most major cities. There are three stations: **Hankou Train Station** (汉口火车站; Hànkǒu Huǒchēzhàn; 2nd Ring Rd, 二环线; Ⓜ Hankou Railway Station), **Wuchang Train Station** (武昌火车站; Wǔchāng Huǒchēzhàn; 642 Zhongshan Lu, 中山路642号; Ⓜ Wuchang Railway Station), and **Wuhan Train Station** (武汉火车站; Wǔhàn Huǒchēzhàn; Baiyun Lu, 白云路; Ⓜ Wuhan Railway Station). Wuhan is high-speed trains only, Hankou is high-speed and regular trains, and Wuchang is primarily regular trains.

Services from all stations include the following:

Enshi D-train 2nd class ¥155 to ¥184, four hours, frequent

Jingzhou D-train 2nd class ¥57 to ¥89, 1½ hours, frequent

Shiyan (Wudang Shan) D-train 2nd/1st class from ¥141/225, 3¾ to 4½ hours, four daily

Yichang D-train 2nd class ¥70 to ¥121, two hours, frequent

Services from Hankou station include the following:

Beijing West G-train 2nd/1st class ¥522/835, 4½ to six hours, frequent

Shanghai Hongqiao D-train 2nd/1st class ¥315/503, 4½ to 6½ hours, frequent

Wudang Shan K-train hard seat/sleeper ¥69/130, 5½ to 6½ hours, four daily

Services from Wuchang station include the following:

Beijing West Hard seat/sleeper ¥153/280, 11 to 15½ hours, frequent

Shanghai South K-train hard sleeper from ¥248, 14 to 17 hours, three daily

Xi'an Z-train hard sleeper from ¥221, 11 hours, four daily

Services from Wuhan station include the following:

Beijing West G-train 2nd/1st class ¥521/833, 4½ to six hours, frequent

Changsha G-train 2nd/1st class ¥165/265, 1½ hours, frequent

Guangzhou G-train train 2nd/1st class ¥464/739, four hours, frequent

Hong Kong G-train 2nd/1st class ¥679/1083, 4¾ hours, one daily (2.20pm)

Shanghai Hongqiao G-train 2nd/1st class from ¥289/473, four to 6½ hours, nine daily

Xi'an North G-train 2nd/1st class ¥455/728, five hours, 15 daily

ⓘ Getting Around

TO/FROM THE AIRPORT

Metro Line 2 serves the airport, conveniently running through central Hankou (¥7) and on to Wuchang (¥8), from 6am to 10.30pm. There are also seven airport bus lines, serving destinations such as the Fujiapo long-distance bus station in Wuchang (Line 1, ¥32, one hour, 7am to 8pm) and the Wuhan train station (Line 5, ¥37, 9am to 8pm). A taxi into Hankou is about ¥100.

FERRY

Ferries (¥5, 8.45am to 5.25pm) make swift daily crossings of the Yangzi between **Zhonghua Lu Dock** (中华路码头; Zhōnghuá Lù Mǎtóu) and **Wuhan Guan Dock** (武汉关码头; Wǔhàn Guān Mǎtóu).

METRO

Wuhan's metro system (地铁, dìtiě) included nine lines on our last trip, with rapid expansion slated to continue for the foreseeable future. Fares are ¥2 to ¥10 and trains run (roughly) from 6am to 10.30pm. Signs are bilingual and the electronic ticket machines have an English option. All important transport hubs are linked via metro.

Jingzhou 荆州

☏ 0716 / POP 1.22 MILLION

The former capital of the Chu kingdom from 689 to 278 BC, Jingzhou (Jīngzhōu) is an old city even by Chinese standards, and an easy stopover for those travelling by bullet train between Wuhan and Yichang. While traces of the more recent past can be discerned through a few rebuilt temples within the city walls, the main reason to come here is to visit the interesting museum, which holds a number of ancient artefacts. Also worth a visit is Xióngjiā Zhǒng (p478), the best known of several Chu burial sites scattered across the surrounding countryside.

◉ Sights

The walled section of Jingzhou is approximately 3.5km from east to west and 2.5km from north to south, with impressive city gates at each cardinal point, as well as several lesser gates. Jingzhou has tried to reinvent itself as a tourist destination of late, but truthfully, many of the sights included on the town's through ticket (not obligatory) are lacking interest.

Passing through the wall at **New East Gate** (新东门, Xīn Dōngmén), which you will do if you're on a bus from the train station, you'll have Jingzhou Nanlu (荆州南路) stretching out in front of you, and you'll see the older **East Gate** (老东门, Lǎo Dōngmén) off to your right.

Jingzhou City Wall　　　　　HISTORIC SITE

(城墙, Chéngqiáng; through ticket ¥115; ◷ 7am-5.30pm) Jingzhou's original city wall was a tamped mud wall dating from the Eastern Han dynasty, and was later clad in stone during the Five Dynasties and Ten Kingdoms. The oldest surviving sections today, around South Gate, are Song, but most date from the Ming and Qing. Small sections of the wall are open and charge admission: the **East Gate** or Binyang Tower (东门, Dōngmén; ¥35), **South Gate** (南门, Nánmén; ¥6), **North Gate** (¥18; 北门; Běimén) and **West Gate** (西门, Xīmén; ¥6).

Jingzhou Museum　　　　　MUSEUM

(荆州博物馆, Jīngzhōu Bówùguǎn; 166 Jingzhou Zhonglu, 荆州中路166号; ◷ 9am-4pm Tue-Sun) 𝗙𝗥𝗘𝗘 At this small but surprisingly good museum you'll find wonderful artefacts unearthed from Chu tombs around the area. The jade and porcelain halls are marvellous, and there is a collection of old silks that appear to float in their cabinets. The highlight is the incredibly well-preserved 2000-year-old body of a man found in his tomb with ancient tools, clothing and even food; the airtight mud seal around his crypt helped preserve him.

Buses 15, 21, 25 and 32 from the train station all pass nearby; tell the driver where you are going.

Xióngjiā Zhǒng
ARCHAEOLOGICAL SITE

(熊家冢; ¥85; ⊙8.30am-5.20pm) Forty kilometres north of Jingzhou, the 2300-year-old tombs of Xióngjiā Zhǒng are the source of a large collection of jade – on display at the Jingzhou Museum (p477) – while there is a fascinating and huge collection of skeletal horses and chariots in a section of the tomb in a hangar-like museum that is open to visitors.

To get here, catch the bus (¥12, 70 minutes) at the station (客运枢纽站, kèyùn shūniǔ zhàn) next to the train station. It runs from 7.30am to 4.50pm, departing roughly every three hours. As there is only one bus shuttling back and forth, you're best off trying to get one of the two morning departures. A taxi will be at least ¥100 return.

🛏 Sleeping & Eating

There are a few Chinese chain hotels near the East Gate, but not all of them accept foreigners. Jingzhou can be visited as a day trip from Wuhan or Yichang, though you'll want to get an early start if you plan on visiting the tombs.

There are scores of small nondescript noodle places and home-style restaurants within the city walls.

Oyo Hotel
HOTEL ¥

(坤宁源馆, Kūnníngyuán Bīnguǎn; ☑0716 416 1616; 1 Huangjintang Lu, 黄金堂路1号; r ¥138; ❀🔊) A reliable Chinese chain hotel, Oyo has decent, inexpensive rooms and a good location not far from the East Gate.

ℹ Information

Bank of China (中国银行, Zhōngguó Yínháng; 42-1 Huangjintang Lu, 黄金堂路42-1号; ⊙8.30am-5pm Mon-Fri, 9am-4pm Sat & Sun) Foreign exchange and 24-hour ATM.

ℹ Getting There & Away

BUS

There's no reason to take the bus here, but if you do, you'll find yourself 5km southeast of town at the Shashi Long-Distance Bus Station (沙市长途汽车站, Shāshì Chángtú Qìchēzhàn). Destinations include the following:

Shiyan (for Wudang Shan) ¥145, five hours, two daily (7am and noon)

Wuhan (Fujiapo) ¥70, four hours, hourly, two daily (9am to 4pm)

TRAIN

D- and G-class trains link Jingzhou's train station (火车站, huǒchē zhàn) with the following:

Enshi 2nd/1st class ¥96/153, 2½ hours, regular

Wuhan 2nd/1st class ¥70/85, two hours, regular

Yichang East 2nd/1st class ¥33/52, 40 minutes, regular

ℹ Getting Around

From the train station, buses 15 and 21 run to the East Gate and then proceed west through the walled city, turning south just before the museum. Buses 25 and 32 run from the station to the North Gate, and then also trundle along the walled city's main street.

From the bus station, take bus 101 to the East Gate. All buses are ¥1. Taxis are only ¥5, making them an inexpensive alternative.

Wudang Shan 武当山

☑ 0719

There are not many places in the world quite like Wudang Shan (Wǔdāng Shān), the wellspring of the gentle art of taichi. Misty clouds cover Taoist courtyards where masters and disciples make slow, flowing moves in unison, while travellers make the long, sweat-soaked ascent up thousands of stone steps. The 'No 1 Taoist Mountain in the Middle Kingdom' is more than a place of pilgrimage, however; its flora contains elixirs for natural health remedies sold on every second precipice and its mountain views rival any in China. Press away from the crowds and you'll find unmarked paths to moss-strewn temples and ethereal splendour.

◉ Sights

The town's main road, Taihe Lu (太和路), runs east–west, passing the main entrance to the mountain at its eastern end. Everything of interest in town is either on or near this road.

Wudang Shan
MOUNTAIN

(武当山; Wǔdāng Shān; ¥235; ⊙7am-6.45pm) Wudang Shan attracts a diverse array of climbers, from Taoist pilgrims with knapsacks and porters shouldering paving slabs and sacks of rice, to tired parents piggybacking young kids and bright-eyed octogenarians hopping along. It's a gruelling climb but the scenery is worth every step; several Taoist temples line the route (where you can take contemplative breathers) and you'll see the occasional Taoist inscription or trees garlanded with scarlet ribbons.

Ascents start from the huge **Tourist Centre complex** (游客中心, Yóukè Zhōngxīn) near the east end of town. From the ticket office you need to board a shuttle to either the cable car (24km, 45 minutes) or to Nanyan (26km, one hour), from where you can hike up a very steep 4km trail to the top – figure on at least two hours. The **cable car** (索道, Suǒdào; up/down ¥90/80) gets you close to the summit, but you'll still need at least half an hour of steep climbing from here.

If you're hiking, consider getting off the shuttle before Nanyan at the beautiful, turquoise-tiled **Zixiao Palace** (紫霄宫, Zǐxiāo Gōng; Purple Cloud Temple; ¥15). From here, a small stone path leads up to Nanyan (45 minutes). At Nanyan, you have the choice of two paths, the more direct route, or the slightly longer path that passes by the cliffside **Nanyan Palace** (南岩宫, Nányán Gōng).

About halfway up is the red-walled **Cháotiān Temple** (朝天宫, Cháotiān Gōng), housing a statue of the Jade Emperor and standing on an old, moss-hewn stone base. From here you have a choice of two ascent routes, via the 1.4km **Ming dynasty route** (the older, Back Way) or the 1.8km **Qing dynasty path** (the 'Hundred Stairs'). The shorter but more exhausting Ming route ascends via the Three Heaven's Gates, including the stupefying climb to the **Second Gate of Heaven** (二天门, Èrtiān Mén). You can climb by one route and descend by the other. Temple ruins, fallen trees, shocking inclines and steep steps misshapen by centuries of footslogging await you.

Near the top, the Nanyan trail passes by the cable car exit; from here, you'll need to ascend to and pass through the magnificent Taihe Palace and **Forbidden City** (紫金城, Zǐjīn Chéng; ¥27), with its 2.5m-thick stone walls hugging the mountainside and balustrades adorned with lovers' locks. You can then stagger to the summit and magnificent views outside the Golden Hall, constructed entirely from bronze, dating from 1416 and in dire need of some buffing up. A small statue of Zhenwu – Ming emperor and Wudang Shan's presiding Taoist deity – peeks out from within.

THE BIRTH OF TAICHI

Zhang Sanfeng (张三丰), a semi-legendary Wudang Shan monk from the 10th or 13th century (depending on what source you read), is reputed to be the founder of the martial art *tàijíquán* (literally 'Supreme Ultimate Boxing') or taichi. Zhang had grown dissatisfied with the 'hard' techniques of Shaolin Boxing and searched for something softer and more elusive. Sitting on his porch one day, he became inspired by a battle between a huge bird and a snake. The sinuous snake used flowing movements to evade the bird's attacks. The bird, exhausted, eventually gave up and flew away. Taichi is closely linked to Taoism, and many priests on Wudang Shan practise some form of the art.

Courses

★ **Wudang Daoist Traditional Kungfu Academy**   SPORTS
(武当道教功夫学院, Wǔdāng Dàojiào Gōngfu Xuéyuàn; ☎ 135 9788 6695; www.wudangwushu.com; Shanshui Jie, Taiji Lake, 太极湖山水街) Dozens of taichi schools pepper these parts – all with similar sounding names – but this one is the largest and most well established. All courses include martial arts, qigong and meditation training, and cover all accommodation and meal expenses. The main campus is by Taiji Lake, though the original school is located by Zixiao Temple on the mountain.

Sleeping & Eating

Travellers can either sleep in town or on the mountain – long-term martial-arts students, on the other hand, will probably want to make arrangements through their school. The hostel in town is a reliable and convenient choice, though the hotels around Nanyan and the chairlift often come with superb views. Expect to pay from ¥250 and up on the mountain.

There are plenty of basic meals sold at all major points on the mountain. In town, restaurants line the main road, Taihe Lu.

Wudang International Youth Hostel   HOSTEL ¥
(武当山国际青年旅舍, Wǔdāngshān Guójì Qīngnián Lǚshè; ☎ 0719 566 2333; 2 Gongyuan Lu, 公园路2号; dm/tw ¥58/120; ❋ ⓐ) English-speaking staff, good info on visiting the mountain and

a nice cafe and bar on the ground floor – this hostel has more going for it than anywhere else in town. Rooms show some wear and beds are a bit hard, but overall they're comfortable and clean. It's a 10-minute walk west (down the hill) from the park entrance.

Nányán Bīnguǎn
HOTEL ¥¥

(南岩宾馆; ☑ 0719 568 9182; Nanyan, 南岩停车场; r ¥300-400; ❈ ☎) This is our top pick for on-mountain accommodation. Rooms are in great shape and even have a hint of style, and there's a pleasant outdoor terrace overlooking the valley below. Even on busy weekends it doesn't seem to fill up. It's on the main plaza where the Nanyan bus drops you off.

☆ Entertainment

A Dream of Wudang
LIVE PERFORMANCE

(梦幻武当, Mènghuàn Wǔdāng; Taiji Lake, 太极湖; tickets from ¥130; ⊙ 8pm Fri & Sat) This taichi-themed dance show is held on Friday and Saturday nights at Taiji Lake, east of town.

❶ Information

Bank of China (中国银行, Zhōngguó Yínháng; 1 Taihe Zhonglu, 太和中路1号; ⊙ 8.30am-noon & 2-5pm Mon-Fri) 24-hour ATM.

❶ Getting There & Away

AIR

Shiyan Wudangshan Airport (十堰武当山机场, Shíyàn Wǔdāngshān Jīchǎng, WDS) is in Shiyan, 20km northwest of Wudang Shan, and serves many major cities in China. Airport Bus 1 (快线1号线; kuàixiàn yīhào xiàn) runs between the airport and Wudang Shan from 7.40am to 5.40pm daily (¥15, 40 minutes).

BUS

There is no bus station in Wudang Shan. There are a few buses that will drop you nearby from elsewhere in Hubei, but to leave you'll definitely want to take the train.

Bus 202 (¥4, 6am to 6pm) runs between Wudang Shan and the two nearest train stations: **Wudangshan** (武当山站; 30 minutes) and **Shiyan** (十堰站; one hour). The bus drops you off near the entrance to the mountain.

TRAIN

Wudangshan station is closer to town but has fewer services; roughly half of Shiyan trains stop there. For high-speed trains, you can transfer at the nearby city of Xiangyang (襄阳).

Wudang Shan trains include the following:

Wuhan K-train hard seat/hard sleeper ¥69/138, six to eight hours, three daily

Xiangyang Hard seat/hard sleeper ¥24/78, two hours, regular

Yichang East Hard seat/hard sleeper ¥55/113, five hours, one daily (4.19pm)

Shiyan trains include the following:

Beijing West Hard seat/hard sleeper ¥164/316, 15¾ to 21½ hours, four daily

Changsha Hard seat/hard sleeper ¥112/219, 11½ hours, three daily

Chengdu Hard seat/hard sleeper ¥124/242, 11½ to 16 hours, six daily

Shanghai Hard sleeper ¥370, 22 to 26 hours, four daily

Wuhan D-train 2nd/1st class ¥155/246, 4¼ hours, four daily

Wuhan T-/K-train hard seat/sleeper ¥72/145, 5½ to 8¼ hours, five daily

Xi'an Hard sleeper ¥113, six hours, one daily (1am)

Yichang 宜昌

☑ 0717 / POP 1.46 MILLION

Yichang (Yíchāng) is a small, compact city known as the culmination point for many a Three Gorges cruise. There is not a lot to do for the waylaid traveller here – other than get psyched for, or decompress from, the boat trip – but the Yangzi offers an attractive backdrop to the urban hum.

◉ Sights

Three Gorges Dam
DAM

(三峡大坝, Sānxiá Dàbà) **FREE** The huge, hulking Three Gorges Dam is the world's largest dam due to its length (2.3km) rather than its height (101m), and while it isn't the most spectacular dam, it is worth a peek. You can't walk on it, but there's a tourist viewing area to the north. The easiest way to visit from Yichang is to join a half-day tour (in Chinese) leaving from the Three Gorges Tourist Centre (¥100, departures 8am and 2pm).

Three Gorges Village
VILLAGE

(三峡人家, Sānxiá Rénjiā; ¥180; ⊙ 8am-5.30pm) This recreated village is definitely tacky and overrun on weekends, but nonetheless a convenient way to take in the stunning views near **Xiling Gorge** (西陵峡, Xīlíng Xiá). The Three Gorges Tourist Centre runs trips here for ¥210, which include bus fare, admission and a boat ride – this is a much better deal than trying to get there yourself. Departures are at 8am and 9.50am.

👉 Tours

River Cruise
BOATING

(游船, Yóuchuán; half-/full day ¥168/358) If you're interested in a getting a glimpse of the Yangzi but don't have time for the full trip to Chongqing, the Three Gorges Tourist Centre runs half- and full-day tours upstream. The half-day trip takes a boat towards the Xiling Gorge and back, and then returns via bus; the full-day tour sails to the dam and back.

Both tours depart at 8.30am; you'll need to board at 7.30am.

🛏 Sleeping & Eating

Sanmao Youth Hostel
HOSTEL ¥

(三毛青年旅舍, Sānmáo Qīngnián Lǚshè; ☑0717 627 8543; Room 1101, 11th fl, Nanbei Tiancheng, 2 Tian Jie, 夷陵大道万达南北天城天街2号1101; dm/s ¥50/168; ❉ 🛜) The selling point of this simple hostel is a great little outdoor terrace to chill on. Located on the 11th and 12th floors of an apartment building near the Three Gorges Tourist Centre, dorms here sleep four or six, and there's also a single room. Read the directions closely when you book as it's quite tricky to find.

Bus 1 from the East Train Station runs here. Some English spoken.

Ramada Yichang Hotel
HOTEL ¥¥

(华美达宜昌大酒店, Huáměidá Yíchāng Dàjiǔdiàn; ☑0717 652 8888; www.ramadayichang.com.cn; 27 Yunji Lu, 云集路27号; r from ¥300; ❉ 🛜) Rooms here won't win any awards for style, but they're more than comfortable and generally a great deal. Staff can help book cruises and onward travel, though their English is limited.

Wanda Plaza
FOOD HALL ¥

(万达广场, Wàndá Guǎngchǎng; 166 Yanjiang Dadao, 沿江大道166号; meals ¥8-70; ⊙9am-9pm) Across the street from the Three Gorges Tourist Centre, this popular mall has a good selection of restaurants on the 3rd and 4th floors, as well as a number of outdoor stalls around the back on the ground level.

Fangweng Restaurant
HUBEI ¥¥¥

(放翁酒家, Fàngwēng Jiǔjiā; ☑0717 886 2179; Nanjin Guan Sanyoudong Bridge, 南津关三游洞桥头; dishes ¥60-160; ⊙11am-8.30pm) At Xiling Gorge, 13km north of Yichang, is a peculiar restaurant perched precariously against a cliff. Claimed to be the ninth 'cave restaurant' in the world, the cuisine is distinctly Hubei, the service brisk and the view quite amazing. Taxis know it well (about ¥80 one way).

ℹ Information

Three Gorges Tourist Centre (三峡游客中心, Sānxiá Yóukè Zhōngxīn; ☑0717 690 0802; 142 Yanjiang Dadao, 沿江大道142号; ⊙7am-8pm) This ticket office and information centre is the place to go for all things Three Gorges, from day trips to cruises upstream. Minimal English is spoken, but staff members are helpful. They sell three- and four-day cruises on tourist boats and five-day cruises on luxury boats.

Prices and basic descriptions for day trips are posted on the wall in English near the information desk, at the far right of the building. There are no boats here, but buses for all trips depart directly from the centre.

Yichang is a large city and ATMs are not too hard to find. China Bank has an **ATM** (中国银行, Zhōngguó Yínháng; 193 Yiling Dadao, 夷陵大道193号; ⊙24hr) behind the Wanda Plaza, near the Three Gorges Tourist Centre.

ℹ Getting There & Away

AIR

Daily flights from **Three Gorges Airport** (三峡机场, Sānxiá Jīchǎng) include Beijing (¥1100), Guangzhou (¥860), Shanghai (¥1080) and Xi'an (¥640).

BUS

Yichang's main **long-distance bus station** (客运中心站; Kèyùn Zhōngxīn Zhàn) is next to the East Train Station, about 8km southeast of downtown. Don't confuse it with the former long-distance bus station (长途汽车站, chángtú qìchēzhàn) in the city centre, which only has buses to local destinations.

Yichang is connected to most destinations by rail, but there are some services from the main long-distance bus station. They include the following:

Jingzhou ¥55, 1½ hours, three daily (8.50am, 11.50am and 3pm)

Muyu (for Shennongjia) ¥76, 3½ hours, three daily (9.30am, noon and 2.30pm)

Wudang Shan ¥133, 4½ hours, two daily (8.40am and 1pm)

Wuhan (Hongji) ¥100, 4½ hours, one daily (11.50am)

TRAIN

Yichang's **East Train Station** (火车东站; Huǒchē Dōngzhàn) is the station that almost all trains use. Destinations include the following:

Beijing West G-train 2nd/1st class ¥630/1008, eight hours, two daily (8.18am and 2pm)

Chengdu East D-train 2nd/1st class ¥259/415, seven hours, 15 per day

Chongqing North D-train 2nd/1st class ¥162/259, four hours, frequent

Enshi D-train 2nd/1st class ¥63/101, two hours, frequent

Jingzhou D-train 2nd/1st class ¥33/52, 40 minutes, frequent

Shanghai Hongqiao D-train 2nd/1st class ¥423/676, 6½ to 8¼ hours, 10 daily

Shiyan (Wudang Shan) K-train hard seat/hard sleeper ¥63 to ¥118, 5¼ hours, one daily (7.40pm)

Wuhan D-train 2nd/1st class from ¥108/173, two to three hours, regular

ℹ Getting Around

Airport shuttle buses (¥20) run to and from the former long-distance bus station (1½ hours), also stopping at the main long-distance bus station (40 minutes). Buses leave two hours before outgoing flights and meet all incoming flights.

Local buses cost ¥2. Useful routes for frequently running buses include the following:

Bus b1 24-hour route that connects the East Train Station with the Three Gorges Tourist Centre (45 minutes)

Bus b9 East Train Station to the former long-distance bus station in the city centre (50 minutes)

Shennongjia 神农架

☑ 0719 / POP 9100

Hubei's natural beauty is on show in the northeast of the province, especially around the vast, misty wilderness area known as Shennongjia (Shénnóngjià). Golden snub-nosed monkeys, giant salamanders, 3000m peaks that hold snow through spring, and lower-elevation wetlands come together to form an enchanting and uniquely Chinese nature reserve. Oh, and lest we forget, this is also the supposed stamping ground of none other than yěrén (野人), China's very own Bigfoot.

While it's not easy to get to, even the sputtering bus ride here is a show-stopper, making it an interesting detour for the intrepid. Remember that transportation is infrequent, so you'll need to spend at least two nights here in order to have one full day in the park. The town of Muyu (木鱼, Mùyú; elevation 1216m) is the main jumping-off point, where you can find a number of hotels, restaurants and basic provisions.

◉ Sights

Shennongjia International Ecotourism Area NATIONAL PARK

(神农架国际生态旅游区, Shénnóngjià Guójì Shēngtài Lǚyóu Qū; 5-day pass ¥269; ⊗6.30am-5.30pm) Shennongjia is a vast wilderness area, and what you visit is largely determined by your driver, fellow passengers and available time; however, there are definitely some areas that are worth trying to get to. Seeing the rare **golden snub-nosed monkey** (川金丝猴, chuān jīnsīhóu) is a highlight for most, and Xiǎolóngtán (小龙潭), about 10km from the entrance, is one place to spot them.

Shénnóngdǐng (神农顶), 20km from the entrance, is the highest peak in the park (3105m) and can be climbed in summer – figure on two to three hours. The wetlands surrounding **Dajiu Lake** (大九湖, Dàjiǔ Hú; additional ¥60 shuttle bus fee may be in effect) also get high marks from travellers, though this is considerably further away and requires a minimum half-day commitment. Other places of interest include several waterfalls and a **stone forest** (板壁岩, Bǎnbìyán).

All in all, when the weather is good, the scenery here is spectacular. However, you should always be prepared for mist and rain. In winter snow is common (there's even a mini bunny slope for first-time skiers), and may remain on the ground through April.

🛏 Sleeping & Eating

There is a good selection of basic and midrange hotels spread throughout Muyu.

Yuèhǎi Kèzhàn HOTEL ¥

(月海客栈; ☑ 156 2950 2789; 21 Muyu Lu, 木鱼路21号; d ¥140; ❋ 🛜) The midrange rooms here rival some of the more expensive options in town. Good central location.

Shuanglin Hotel HOTEL ¥

(双林酒店, Shuānglín Jiǔdiàn; ☑ 0719 345 2803; 25 Muyu Lu, 木鱼路25号; r from ¥80; ❋ 🛜) The modest Shuanglin Hotel has tidy rooms and welcoming management.

Shíyúnfù CHINESE ¥¥

(食云府; ☑ 0719 345 4111; 40 Muyu Lu, 木鱼路40号; dishes ¥15-88; ⊗11am-9pm) Comfy booths, lattice screens and some traditional-style murals make this an attractive place to dine. Local tea is included with meals.

ℹ Information

The ATM at the **ICBC Bank** (工商银行, Gōngshāng Yínháng) at the top of Muyu village theoretically accepts foreign cards, but to be safe you should bring cash.

ⓘ Getting There & Away

AIR

The small **Shennongjia Hongping Airport** (神农架红坪机场, Shénnóngjià Hóngpíng Jīchǎng) has three daily flights to and from Wuhan (from ¥410, 1¼ hours). The airport is about 70km north of Muyu; at the time of writing, there was only one shuttle running daily (¥50, 1½ hours) once all flights had arrived, so don't miss it.

BUS

Buses leave from the **station** (汽车站, qìchēzhàn), which is at the end (top) of the town. If you've booked lodging in advance, ask the driver to drop you off on the way. Theoretically, foreigners aren't allowed to continue north to Wudang Shan from Muyu because the route passes through a military zone. However, on our last visit the driver claimed this route was now open – if you go this way, bear in mind that there is a risk you will be forced to disembark midway and turn around. Destinations include the following:

Badong (Wu Gorge) ¥56, three hours, one daily (9.50am)

Shiyan (Wudang Shan) ¥86, 4½ hours, one daily (8.30am)

Yichang ¥65, 3½ hours, three daily (7.30am, 10am and 2.30pm)

ⓘ Getting Around

There are no official taxis here and no local buses. The only way to get to and around the park is to hire a private driver: you can hire an entire minivan (¥400 to ¥500 for the day) or you can join up with a group and split the cost (¥100), which in Chinese is called pīnchē (拼车). This is a common option; get to the bus station around 7am to find a driver as they usually leave from out the front by 7.30am. Alternatively, ask your hotel to help you arrange this.

Drivers have set itineraries they usually follow, and if you join a group of local tourists you should expect more of an emphasis on taking pictures and less on walking around. Of course, it does depend on the group. If you'd rather have more of a wilderness experience, put together a like-minded group ahead of time (ideally with at least one person who can speak some Chinese) to ensure you can get off the beaten path.

Shuttles do run around the park (¥60), but these are really designed for tour groups and not set up for individual travellers.

Enshi 恩施

☎ 0718 / POP 780,000

Wedged into Hubei's southwestern border region is a picturesque tableau of crumpled green mountains and terraced tea fields, as well as the occasional giant cliff face that's high enough to catch a rock climber's eye. Seat of the Tujia and Miao Autonomous Prefecture, Enshi (Ēnshī) is a low-key town whose main claim to fame is the Grand Canyon. OK, not *that* Grand Canyon, but instead a swath of impressive cliffs that tower over some lovely countryside below.

While the area can't compare to the grander landscapes of Zhangjiajie or Shennongjia, it's still beautiful, and the location along a main rail line makes for a convenient summer getaway for those in the sweltering cities of Chongqing and Wuhan.

ⓞ Sights

If you have time to kill, **Tǔsī Chéng** (土司城; 138 Tusi Lu, 土司路138号; ¥45; ⓣ 7.30am-7pm), a recreated fortified Tujia town, is a pleasant park to stroll through but hardly a must-see. It's a ¥17 taxi ride from the train station.

Enshi Grand Canyon NATURE RESERVE
(恩施大峡谷, Ēnshī Dàxiágǔ; all-inclusive ticket ¥285; ⓣ ticket sales 8.30am-4pm) Encompassing sheer limestone cliffs and a series of waterfalls cascading down the side of a narrow river gorge, Enshi has some marvellous scenery. It's divided in two sections: the **lower gorge** (云龙地缝, Yúnlóng Dìfèng; translated on signs as 'Yunlong Crack'; elevation 1034m) and the upper clifftop area, **Seven Star Village** (七星寨, Qīxīng Zhài; elevation 1704m). The river gorge is relatively short with several lovely waterfalls, while the clifftop is more of a hike, eventually opening up to far-reaching views over the valley floor.

Ticket prices are quite confusing for the uninitiated – you can choose to visit both areas or just one, with optional extras like the cable car adding to the final price.There are additional add-ons inside the park too, such as a long series of escalators descending from the upper section to the final bus stop – this costs an extra ¥30, though you can choose to walk instead. We recommend visiting both areas if you have a full day, and while the cable car is nice, you can save about ¥100 by taking the bus instead and walking from the last bus stop – note that you will need to change buses to do this.

Now for the caveat: this is a popular destination that was not designed with big crowds in mind. The lower gorge in particular is very narrow and subject to excruciatingly long bottlenecks for the better part of an hour – get there as early (or late) as possible to avoid this.

The upper gorge will take about 2½ hours to walk and can also get quite crowded. The first hour or so is just OK, and it's not until you reach Ancient Elephant Mountain that the views really start to impress. The iconic formation here is **A Stick of Incense** (一炷香, Yī Zhù Xiāng), a slender and supremely photogenic limestone spire.

All told, you should expect to spend about five to seven hours here. There are plenty of vendors serving simple meals (fried potatoes are a speciality) and drinks.

Enshi Grand Canyon is 50km northwest of town; buses (¥25, 1½ hours) leave regularly from the bus station (across from the train station) from 6.30am to 5.30pm – it's a very scenic ride. The last bus back is at 6pm.

Nŭ'ér Chéng   CULTURAL CENTRE
(女儿城; off Jinlong Dadao, 金龙大道; ⊙9am–11pm) FREE This Tujia-focused outdoor mall-like area is Enshi's favourite option for nightlife. Local song-and-dance performances (featuring the usual communist-approved 'minority circle dance') are held throughout the day, but the most popular show takes place around 7.30pm nightly. Show up early to grab dinner at one of the innumerable street stalls, sample some local tea and browse the handicrafts displays and shops.

It's quite a hike from the train station area – bus 31 from the local bus lot across from the station terminates nearby (¥2, one hour, last bus around 7.30pm), after which you'll need to walk for 10 minutes (ask for directions), or you can take a much quicker taxi for ¥30. There are also a few hotels based here.

🛏 Sleeping & Eating

Enshi has plenty of middling hotels where you can get a room for around ¥100, particularly in the apartment blocks opposite the train station (across the street and to the right as you exit). Nü'er Cheng has some more upmarket choices, though it is further

away from the stations and less convenient for getting to the canyon.

Both the apartment blocks and Nü'er Cheng also have a good selection of local Tujia restaurants come evening. The main strip in town is Xueyuan Lu (学院路), across from Minority University.

Enshi More Mountain YHA   HOSTEL ¥
(恩施多山国际青年旅舍, Ēnshī Duōshān Guójì Qīngnián Lûshè; ☑0718 8966 628; Bldg 26, Nü'er Cheng, Cultural Creativity Garden, Ma'anshan Lu, 马鞍山路女儿城文化创意园26栋; dm ¥60, d from ¥180; 🕸 ⚛) This stylish hostel has an atmospheric location in Nü'er Cheng as well as a nice cafe/bar. Beds are in four- or six-bed dorms, and there are also comfortable private rooms. It is far from the train and bus stations, though. Take bus 31 (¥2, one hour) from the train station to the last stop and then walk for 10 minutes.

Alternatively, take a much faster taxi (¥30). Limited English.

ⓘ Getting There & Away

BUS

The **bus station** (汽车客运中心, qìchē kèyùn zhōngxīn) is across from the train station, on your left as you exit. Catch a bus to the Grand Canyon or direct to Zhangjiajie (¥111, 4½ hours, departs 9am).

TRAIN

Enshi is on the railway line connecting Chongqing and Wuhan.

Trains leaving from the train station (火车站, huǒchē zhàn) include the following:

Chongqing 2nd/1st class ¥100/159, 2½ hours, frequent

Jingzhou 2nd/1st class ¥96/153, 2½ hours, frequent

Wuhan 2nd/1st class ¥171/274, four hours, frequent

Yichang 2nd/1st class ¥63/101, 1¾ hours, frequent

Jiangxi

POP 45.2 MILLION

Best Places to Eat

➡ Lao San Yang (p488)

➡ Taste of Caimi (p488)

➡ Youshi Kafei (p496)

➡ Guangming Teahouse (p497)

➡ Niu Gu Fen (p494)

Best Places to Stay

➡ Jingdezhen International Youth Hostel (p494)

➡ Brook Hotel (p497)

➡ Shenming Kezhan (p497)

➡ Go Home Hotel (p498)

Why Go?

Rarely explored by foreign travellers, the luscious province of Jiangxi (江西, Jiāngxī) offers a bucolic entrée into semi-rural Chinese life. It's a succulent, green place, connected by waterways of natural and human design, rice paddies teeming with bird life and fields draped in wildflowers. Tea seemingly grows out of every patch of land until dramatic mountain ranges, swirling with mist, rise up at its edges.

Jiangxi has joined the high-speed rail circuit and now there's a new breed of local, prosperous traveller. They come here for the story-book villages around Wuyuan, the remote mountain parks of great spiritual significance and the 'white gold' of Jingdezhen, the porcelain capital of China.

The cities here are small, manageable and surprisingly pleasant, but it's the irresistible countryside villages, with their traditional architecture and their altogether slower pace of life, which are the real highlight of a visit to this charming pocket of southeast China.

When to Go
Nanchang

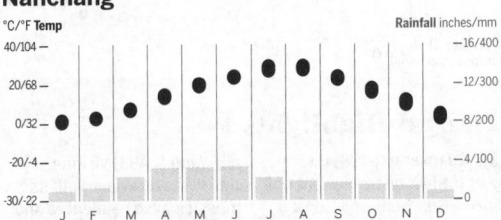

Mar Rapeseed fields burst into yellow around Wuyuan's intact Song and Qing villages.	**Late May–early Jun** Pink rhododendrons bloom across the Sanqing Shan and Lushan canopies.	**Sep–Nov** The ideal climate for visiting Jiangxi: dry and relatively mild.

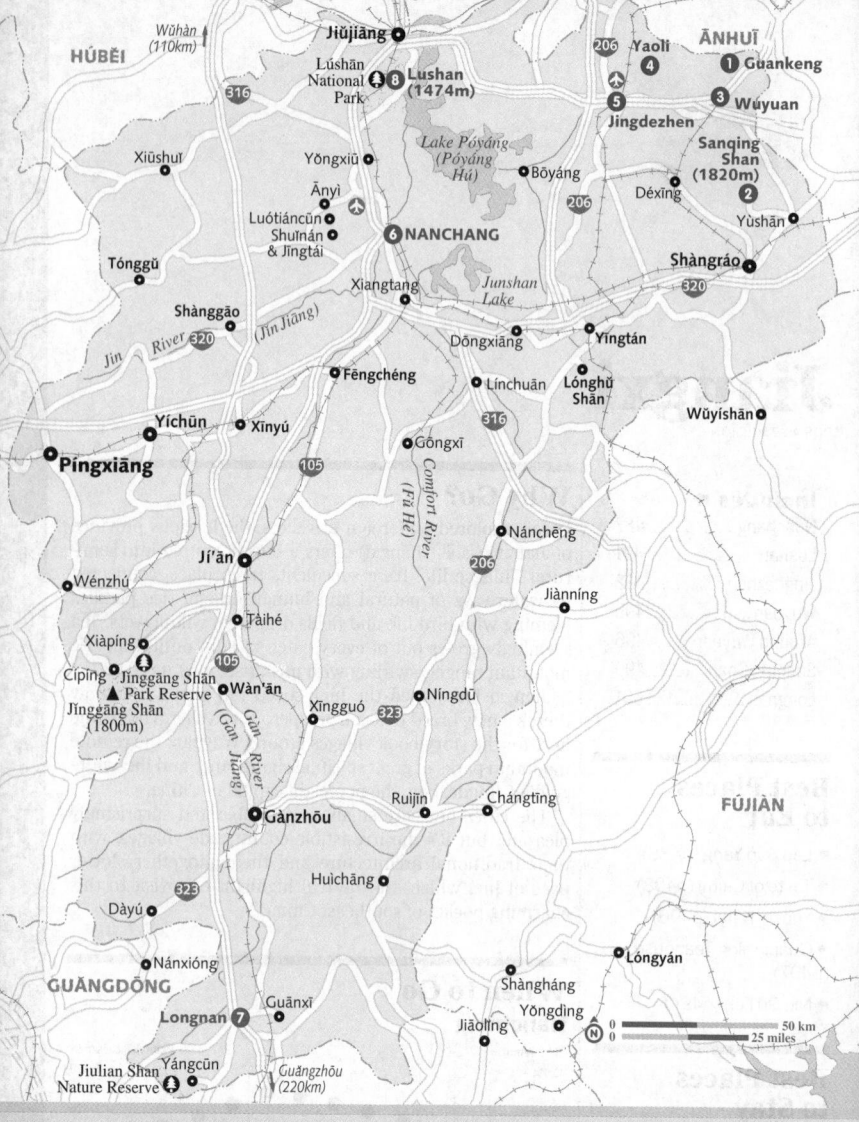

Jiangxi Highlights

1 **Guankeng** (p498) Hiking over the hills on the ancient trail linking Guankeng and Lingjiao.

2 **Sanqing Shan** (p499) Looking over a forest of granite spires in one of eastern China's spectacular national parks.

3 **Wuyuan** (p495) Cycling around the Wuyuan countryside, stopping off at ancient Huizhou villages.

4 **Yaoli** (p493) Visiting this riverside village with its moss-cloaked residences and traditional pottery kilns.

5 **Jingdezhen** (p492) Shopping for exquisite teaware in the revitalised arts districts of the porcelain capital of China.

6 **Nanchang** (p487) Tucking into Jiangxi's fresh and fiery

cuisine in this energetic riverside capital's restaurants.

7 **Longnan** (p501) Exploring southern Jiangxi's Hakka country and its fortified villages.

8 **Lushan** (p491) Seeking respite from the heat in this former Communist Party summer playground atop a misty national park.

History

Jiangxi's Gan River Valley was the principal trade route that linked Guangdong with the rest of the country in imperial times. Its strategic location, natural resources and long growing season have ensured that the province has always been relatively well off. Jiangxi is most famous for its imperial porcelain (from Jingdezhen), although its contributions to philosophy and literature are perhaps more significant, particularly during the Tang and Song dynasties.

Peasant unrest arose in the 19th century when the Taiping rebels swept through the Yangzi River Valley. Rebellion continued into the 20th century, and Jiangxi became one of the earliest bases for the Chinese communists.

Language

Most Jiangxi natives speak one of innumerable local variants of Gàn (赣), a dialect whose name is also used as a shorthand for the province. Gàn is similar (some say related) to the Hakka language, spoken in southern Jiangxi.

ℹ Getting There & Away

Nanchang is connected by air to most major cities in China. There's also a small airport at Jingdezhen. Bullet trains link most of the main destinations with other parts of the country, and will soon reach down to Longnan too.

ℹ Getting Around

As with the rest of China, long-distance buses are on the decline, slowly being usurped by high-speed trains, which are quicker, more frequent and often cheaper than buses. Unlike overnight sleeper trains, tickets for high-speed trains are generally easy to come by – just turn up at the train station and buy a ticket for the next available train; you'll rarely have to wait more than an hour or so. Within towns and cities, local buses cost ¥1 to ¥2 (carry exact change). Around the villages, you may sometimes have to resort to motorbike taxis if you're in a hurry, though there's always a bus for those who are willing to wait.

Nanchang 南昌

✈ 0791 / POP 2.5 MILLION

Known reverently in textbooks for fomenting Chinese Communist Party (CCP) rule, Nanchang (Nánchāng) now galvanises support for its attractive, tree-lined streets and easy urban charm. It's a handy base for Jiangxi's immediate country to the north and is now on a number of bullet-train lines.

◎ Sights & Activities

Bayi Park PARK

(八一公园, Bāyī Gōngyuán; Zhongshan Lu, 中山路)
A focal point for locals, and one of the most pleasant spots in town, this lakeside park attracts groups of Chinese, young and old, walking, dancing, singing and laughing the night away. Best enjoyed just after dusk or at dawn.

Tengwang Pavilion MONUMENT

(腾王阁, Téngwáng Gé; Rongmen Lu, 榕门路; ¥50; ⊗7.30am-6.30pm summer, 8am-5pm winter; Ⓜ Wanshou Palace) This nine-storey pagoda, now part of landscaped riverside grounds, is the city's drawcard monument. It was first erected during Tang times, but destroyed and rebuilt no fewer than 29 times, most recently in 1989. Each floor (including two basement floors) contains museum exhibitions of varying interest, and some of the floors have viewing balconies overlooking the river.

Shengjin Pagoda HISTORIC BUILDING

(绳金塔, Shéng Jīn Tǎ; Shengjinta Jie, 绳金塔街)
FREE This rebuilt, 58m-tall Tang-dynasty pagoda can't be climbed, but is attractive, and surrounded by other recently reconstructed features (an outdoor stage, a small garden, a huge bronze bell) to create a pleasant area for families to hang out in. The pagoda, which is lit up at night, has been rebuilt several times throughout history, most recently in 1985.

Youmin Temple BUDDHIST SITE

(佑民寺; Yòumín Sì; 181 Minde Lu, 民德路181号; ¥2; ⊗9am-5pm) Once hidden down a knot of alleyways, this large still-active, yellow-walled temple is now the centrepiece of a newly landscaped area immediately north of

---

ℹ PRICE RANGES

Sleeping

The following price ranges are for a standard double room:

¥ less than ¥100

¥¥ ¥100–300

¥¥¥ more than ¥300

Eating

The following price ranges are for a meal for one:

¥ less than ¥30

¥¥ ¥30–60

¥¥¥ more than ¥60

Bayi Park. The temple was heavily damaged during the Cultural Revolution, but still contains some notable statuary.

Former Headquarters of the Nanchang Uprising
MUSEUM

(八一南昌起义纪念馆, Bāyī Nánchāng Qǐyì Jìniànguǎn; 380 Zhongshan Lu, 中山路380号; ⊘9am-5pm Tue-Sun) FREE Wartime paraphernalia for rainy days and enthusiasts of the CCP. Admission free with passport.

Tengwang Pavilion River Cruise
CRUISE

(滕王阁游轮, Téngwánggé Yóulún; off Rongmen Lu; ¥110; ⊘8pm) Every evening a one-hour cruise takes passengers along the Gan River, past the beautifully illuminated Tengwang Pavilion and back. Snacks and drinks can be bought on board.

🛏 Sleeping

Letu International Youth Hostel
HOSTEL ¥

(乐途国际青年旅舍, Lètú Guójì Qīngnián Lǚshě; ☑0791 8523 9191; 253 Shengjinta Jie (Mei Shi Jie), 绳金塔街253号 (美食街); dm ¥35-45, d & tw ¥108-128; 🅿🛜) Pretty much the only low-budget lodgings in Nanchang that will accept foreigners, this OK hostel is on the city's ye-olde 'snack' street (美食街, Měi Shí Jiē), so you won't go hungry. Dorms are well kept but small, while the private rooms are also compact but bright and airy. The lobby doubles up as a bar come evening. Not much English spoken.

Ibis Nanchang Bayi Memorial Hall
HOTEL ¥¥

(宜必思南昌八一馆地铁站酒店, Yíbìsī Nánchāng Bāyīguǎn Dìtiě Zhàn Jiǔdiàn; ☑187 0553 3211; https://ibis.accorhotels.com; 217 Zhongshan Lu, 中山路217号; r from ¥209; 🅿🛜) This new, friendly budget branch of the international hotel chain Ibis offers great value and a central location. Rooms are on the small side, and most are lacking in natural light, but they are all clean, comfortable and modern, and come with powerful, hot showers. No English spoken, but expect a warm welcome. Breakfast is available, and is free with some rooms.

Swiss Grand Nanchang
LUXURY HOTEL ¥¥¥

(南昌瑞颐大酒店, Nánchāng Ruìyí Dàjiǔdiàn; ☑0791 8777 7777; www.swissnanchang.cn; 69 Yanjiang Bei Lu, 沿江北路69号; r incl breakfast from ¥900; 🅿🛜) On the mighty Gan River is Nanchang's finest high-end hotel, doing the Swiss efficiency model proud. Rooms are understated and spacious with big-window views of barges and bridges. Staff provide real expertise on the area and can arrange trips around the province. There's a spa, a swimming pool and multiple restaurants, including the 61st-floor **Sky Lounge**.

Galactic Classic International Hotel
HOTEL ¥¥¥

(嘉莱特精典国际酒店, Jiāláitè Jīngdiǎn Guójì Jiǔdiàn; ☑0791 8828 1888; www.glthp.com; 2 Bayi Dadao, 八一大道2号; r incl breakfast from ¥600; 🅿🛜) It's not quite out of this world, but this classy luxury hotel near the train station has quite the futuristic exterior. Rooms are spacious and modern, with espresso machines, city views from the bathtubs and even TV screens in the bathroom mirrors.

🍴 Eating

Nanchang is food crazy. Many city-centre streets are jam-packed with restaurants, though few have English menus. Streets that are particularly good hunting grounds are **Shengjinta Jie Snack Street** (绳金塔街美食街, Shéngjīntǎ Jiē Měi Shí Jiē; Sheng Jin Ta Jie, 绳金塔街; ⊘11am-1pm), Jimazhuang Jie (系马桩街, south off Bayi Park), Dashun Xiang (大顺巷, a little alley west of Bayi Park, off Zhongshan Lu), and Chuanshan Lu (船山路), which is lined on both sides with buzzing restaurants specialising in *xiǎo lóng xiā* (小龙虾, spicy crayfish).

Lao San Yang
JIANGXI ¥¥

(老三样, Lǎo Sān Yàng; 437 Chuanshan Lu, 船山路437号; most dishes ¥16-45; ⊘11am-1.30pm & 4.45-8.30pm) Promising to 'keep the real taste of Old Nanchang', this wildly popular no-frills restaurant has a youthful vibe, a Communist Revolutionary theme and a menu full of spicy Jiangxi deliciousness. The house speciality, a large tin tray of *xiǎo lóngxiā* (小龙虾, spicy crayfish; ¥108), needs to be shared by at least two people, but the rest of the menu has normal-sized dishes.

Bǎi Cǎo Xiāng
CHINESE ¥

(百草香; Minde Lu, 民德路; dishes ¥17-23; ⊘9am-10pm) If having to choose from long, impenetrable menus is starting to make your head spin, consider seeking out this tiny, modern place that offers just three versions of one simple, filling dish: a meat pot with rice. All you have to decide is whether you want chicken (鸡肉, *jī ròu*), beef (牛肉, *niú ròu*) or pork ribs (排骨, *pái gǔ*).

Taste of Caimi
JIANGXI ¥¥

(小柴米, Xiǎo Chái Mǐ; 428 Ruzi Lu, 孺子路428号; dishes ¥20-80; ⊘10am-2pm & 4.30-9pm) This clean, comfortable, air-con-cooled restaurant

Nanchang

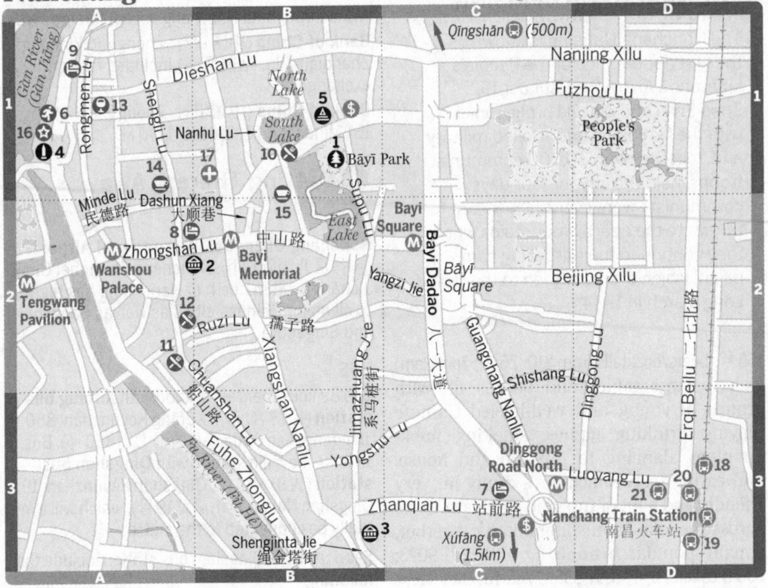

Map content:

Qīngshān (500m)

Nanjing Xilu

Fuzhou Lu

Dieshan Lu

North Lake

People's Park

Rongmen Lu

Shengli Lu

Nanhu Lu

South Lake

Minde Lu 民德路

Dashun Xiang 大顺巷

Bāyī Park

Zhongshan Lu 中山路

Bayi Memorial

Wanshou Palace

Tengwang Pavilion

Ruzi Lu

Chuanshan Lu 船山路

Xiangshan Nanlu

Fuhe Zhonglu

Fu River 抚河路

East Lake

Sunu Lu

Bayi Square

Bayi Dadao

Bāyī Square

Yangzi Jie

Beijing Xilu

Guangchang Nanlu

Shishang Lu

Jimazhuang Jie 紫马桩街

Yongshu Lu

Dinggong Road North

Zhanqian Lu 站前路

Shengjinta Jie 绳金塔街

Xúfāng (1.5km)

Luoyang Lu

Diinggong Lu

Erqi Beilu 二七北路

Nanchang Train Station 南昌火车站

has large windows overlooking the street and a menu that includes Jiangxi specialities such as _jiàng huáng niú ròu_ (酱黄牛肉, spicy stir-fried beef), _lǎo huǒ mèn yā_ (老火焖鸭, duck stew) and _chì tāng guì yú_ (翅汤桂鱼, mandarin fish soup). Little English is spoken, but staff are friendly and courteous, and there's a clear photo menu.

🍷 Drinking & Entertainment

Nanchang has a friendly, youthful vibe, best experienced in the many bars and clubs around the northwest corner of Bayi Park.

Helen's (Bayi Park)   BAR
(海伦司小酒吧（八一公园店）, Hǎilúnsī Xiǎo Jiǔbā (Bāyī Gōngyuán Diàn); 156 Minde Lu, 民德路

THE NANCHANG UPRISING

The Nanchang Uprising is known as the first appearance of the People's Liberation Army. On 1 August 1927, Zhou Enlai and Zhu De broke ranks with the Nationalist-controlled military and, together with 30,000 communist troops, held the city for four days. The communists were eventually forced to retreat to the nearby mountains where they continued their gruelling campaign, which eventually led to the fabled Long March in 1934.

156号; beers/cocktails from ¥10/26; ⊘7pm-2am) Helen's large tables and booths fill with groups of young and well-heeled Chinese playing drinking games, smoking hookah pipes, dancing to hip-hop and house, and eating tasty snacks. It's dimly lit, very friendly and a lot of fun, and there are views across the lake from some booths. Another, equally popular **branch** (☑0791 8671 9023; 536 Dieshan Lu, 叠山路536号) is further west on Dieshan Lu.

Sober   CAFE
(30 Baihuazhou Lu, 百花洲路30号; coffee ¥20-55, craft beer from ¥20; ⊘noon-midnight; 🛜) A trendy but chilled-out cafe serving drip coffee as well as espresso-machine brews. Also has a small selection of bottled craft beers. It's one of a handful of cutesy cafes along this quiet lakeside lane.

Rive Gauche Arts Cafe   CAFE
(左岸艺文咖啡馆, Zuǒ'àn Yìwén Kāfēi Guǎn; Minde Lu, 民德路; drinks ¥30-60; ⊘10.30am-midnight) This Parisian-themed bar-cafe on busy Minde Lu is remarkably cool for a second-tier Chinese city. The owner has sourced antiques and bric-a-brac from across Europe to create an intimate, kooky venture where you can sip martinis or hot espressos in period splendour.

Tengwang Theatre   DANCE
(滕王戏园, Téngwáng Xìyuán; Tengwang Pavilion; ¥30; ⊘10am, 11.30am, 1.30pm, 3pm & 4.30pm) This small theatre within the grounds of Tengwang Pavilion puts on short but high-quality performances of traditional dance and music five times a day. An outdoor evening show (7.30pm, also ¥30) is put on in the main square in front of the pavilion.

❶ Information

ATMs throughout Nanchang accept foreign cards.
Bank of China (中国银行, Zhōngguó Yínháng; Zhanqian Xilu, 站前西路) Includes foreign exchange.

Bank of China (中国银行, Zhōngguó Yínháng; 161 Minde Lu, 民的路161号) ATM.

❶ Getting There & Away

AIR

Nanchang Changbei International Airport (南昌昌北国际机场, Nánchāng Chāngběi Guójì Jīchǎng), 28km north of Nanchang, has flights to all major Chinese cities as well as Bangkok and Singapore.

BUS

Bus 89 links the train station with **Xufang bus station** (徐坊客运站, Xúfáng Kèyùnzhàn; 850 Jinggangshan Dadao, 井冈山大道850号). Bus 18 links the train station with **Qingshan bus station** (青山客运站, Qīngshān Kèyùnzhàn; 19 Qingshan Nanlu, 青山南路19号), which will eventually be connected to the metro.

Services from Qingshan bus station include the following:
Lushan ¥60, 2½ hours, one daily (9.30am)
Wuyuan ¥101, 3½ hours, one daily (1.20pm)
  Services from Xufang bus station include the following:
Ganzhou ¥120, 5½ hours, one daily (2.50pm)
Jingdezhen ¥85, three hours, roughly hourly (7am to 7.30pm)
Jiujiang ¥45, two hours, two daily (9.50am and 1pm)
Yingtan ¥50, three hours, three daily (9.45am, 1pm & 3.20pm)
Yushan ¥85, four hours, one daily (11.20pm)

TRAIN

Most (but not all) bullet trains leave from Nanchang's colossal **west train station** (南昌西站, Nánchāng Xīzhàn; Xizhan Jie, 西站街), which is connected to the metro. The **main station** (南昌火车站, Nánchāng Huǒchēzhàn; Erqi Nanlu, 二七南路) is more central. Shuttle bus 1 (高铁巴士1号线, gāotiě bāshì yīhàoxiàn; ¥5, 45 minutes, half-hourly, 6am to 11pm) also links the two train stations.

❶ Getting Around

TO/FROM THE AIRPORT

Airport buses (机场大巴, jīchǎng dàbā; ¥15, 50 minutes) leave every 20 minutes from 5.30am to 9pm from the north side of the train-station square. A taxi to the airport (机场, jīchǎng) costs around ¥120.

METRO

Lines 1 and 2 of Nanchang's metro (地铁, dì tiě) are up and running, though both will be further extended. They link the two train stations and many of the central sights. Tickets are ¥2 to ¥5 for single trips, and trains run from around 6.30am to 10.30pm.

Numerous local buses run from different points outside the main train station; **Bus 52** (高铁巴士1号线, Gāotiě Bāshì Yīhàoxiàn; Nánchāng Train Station, Nánchāng Huǒchēzhàn, 南昌火车站) goes to Tengwang Pavilion, via Bayi Sq and Zhongshan Lu (but returns a different route). Bus 5 goes to Shengjin Pagoda and its namesake snack street.

Lushan 庐山

☑ 0792

The drive up to Lushan (Lúshān) weaves through thick forest and low-hanging clouds until you reach a town indelibly inked in the Chinese consciousness. Long revered as a Buddhist centre and as a spiritual retreat for European missionaries, Lushan infiltrated the public imagination as the official summer residence of the Chinese Community Party.

The Taiping Rebellion in the mid-19th century destroyed most of the spiritual sites, though some 20th-century European-style villas still dot the hillsides. These days, however, most people come simply to escape the scorching summer heat of Nanchang (it's particularly popular at weekends).

When it's not covered in mist, walking around here is pleasant: there are plenty of viewpoints, some waterfalls and a few notable villas to head for. Buy a bilingual map (地图, dìtú; ¥6) in **Xinhua Bookstore** (新华书店, Xīnhuá Shūdiàn; 11 Guling Zhengjie, 牯岭政街11号), opposite the main square – called Central Park (街心公园, Jiēxīn Gōngyuán) – and head off in whatever direction takes your fancy.

Venturing in any direction from the town of Lushan will take you into the wilds of one of the most ethereal environments in this province. The 300-sq-km **Lushan National Park** (庐山国家公园, Lúshān Guójiā Gōngyuán; ¥160) is best known for its strange rock formations that seem almost perennially covered in cloud. Loads of hiking trails are clearly marked and often paved. You pay to enter upon arrival at the foot of the mountain; all accommodation, restaurants and hiking trails are at the top.

Sandiequan Waterfall (三叠泉瀑布, Sāndiéquán Pùbù), the three-tiered waterfall inside Lushan National Park, is a highlight and just reward for hikers. The ascent of 1600m will test your knees, but press on to the top (or take the cable car) for tremendous, misty vistas.

There are dozens of hotels lining the main road. As always, prices are negotiable, especially during the week and in low season. Formerly Daziran Youth Hostel, **Pine Gate Hotel** (松门山舍, Sōng Mén Shān Shě; ☑ 153 5013 6003, 0792 829 6327; 1 Hubei Lu, 湖北路1号; dm/d from ¥50/110; ⊞ @ 🛜), perched on a hillside just below road level, has had a lick of paint but is still the same friendly, youthful place it was before. Dorms are very spacious and private rooms are bright and clean. Young staff have limited English but are helpful and welcoming. It's about a 1km walk from the bus station; turn left off the main drag after Mancat Coffee, onto Henan Lu, and it's about 500m along on your right. Alternatively, **Lushan Hotel** (庐山饭店, Lúshān Fàndiàn; ☑ 0792 828 5430; 4 Guling Jie, 古岭街4号; s/d from ¥78/128) is pretty ordinary but cheap and close to the bus stand. It's on the left as you walk towards the main drag. English sign.

There are plenty of restaurants on the main drag in Lushan, and a branch of the modern Shanghai cafe chain, Mancat Coffee, was just about to open when we were last here. There's not much English in the restaurants, but some picture menus are available.

🛈 Getting There & Around

There's one direct bus to Lushan from Nanchang's Qingshan bus station at 9.30am (sometimes two or three in July); the return leaves Lushan at 3pm. Otherwise, you'll have to first go to the small city of **Jiujiang** (九江, Jiǔjiāng) at the foot of the mountain, then catch a bus up to Lushan (¥16.5, one hour, hourly or when full, 6.50am to 5pm) from there. The last bus back down to Jiujiang from Lushan is at 5.30pm.

Lushan bus stand (庐山车站, Lúshān chēzhàn) is through a small tunnel. To get to the main drag, walk back through the tunnel and turn left. Sometimes you'll be dropped just before the tunnel.

It's much easier to catch a train to **Jiujiang train station** (九江火车站, Jiǔjiāng huǒchē zhàn) than a bus (which are slower and fewer). The train station and **Jiujiang bus station** (九江车总站, Jiujiang chē zǒng zhàn) are linked by local bus 15 (¥1) and are just three stops apart.

Note: don't make the mistake of catching a train to Lushan train station, which is on the wrong side of the mountain with no public transport links up the mountain. If you do end up there, take local bus 901 (¥4, 45 minutes) to Jiujiang train station.

Hop-on hop-off **sightseeing buses** (观光车, guānguāng chē; ¥70 for a seven-day ticket) start from the bus stand in Lushan and go to all the main sights.

Jingdezhen   景德镇

☑ 0798 / POP 1.6 MILLION

The undisputed porcelain capital of China (and therefore the world), Jingdezhen (Jīngdézhèn) has been producing the finest-quality ceramics for more than 1700 years. The imperial kilns have long been extinguished, but Jingdezhen still boasts a booming porcelain industry, including a thriving contemporary scene in three captivating arts districts.

Even those unaccustomed to the ways of the wheel will be stoked by the range of glazed wares on offer at the many small galleries around town, and although little of the city's architectural heritage remains, it is well worth a day or two getting to know more about the precious 'white gold'.

◉ Sights & Activities

★ Sculpture Factory   ARTS CENTRE

(雕塑瓷厂, Diāosù Cíchǎng; 139 Xinchang Donglu, 新厂东路139号; ⊙9.30am-6pm) FREE

This tree-lined street, and the pathways that branch off it, form a kind of porcelain-production arts district, which is a centre for contemporary ceramics in China. Some of the world's leading porcelain artists work and teach here and visitors can wander freely around the kilns, workshops and small factories as the latest masterpieces are being sculpted. Along with Ceramics Art Avenue, this is also the most pleasant place in town to shop for ceramics, including tea sets.

While here, ceramics enthusiasts should pay a visit to the **Pottery Workshop** (乐天陶社, Lètiān Táoshè; ☑ 0798 844 0582; www.pottery workshop.com.cn; residencies incl accommodation & meals per week ¥2800). Casual visitors can ask to look around. Staff speak English, and there's a nice little cafe on-site.

Jingdezhen

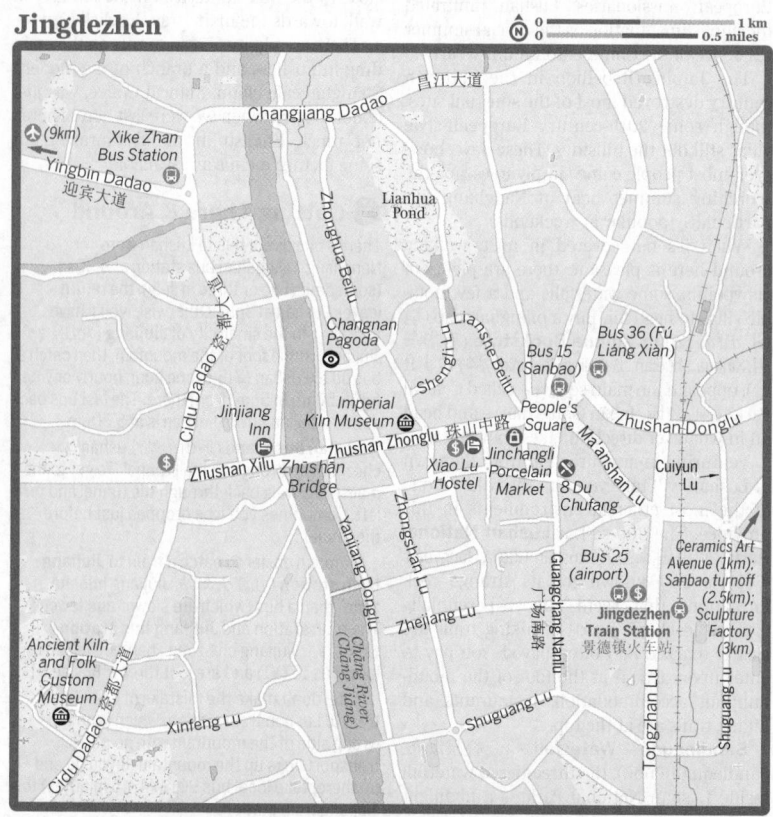

YAOLI

Situated on the banks of the Yao River (瑶河, Yáo Hé), and surrounded by forested hills and tea plantations, **Yaoli Ancient Village** (瑶里古镇, Yáolǐ Gǔzhèn), 90 minutes from Jingdezhen, is a gorgeous rural getaway.

Like Jingdezhen, Yaoli was one of China's original centres for porcelain production, and there's an ancient kiln site you can visit here. The village itself is made up of elegant, moss-covered, stone-walled courtyard homes, many of which are still lived in, and wandering its tight, riverside pathways is a treat.

It's free to walk around the village, but you need to buy a ¥30 ticket to enter the three most notable buildings: **Shigang Scenery** (狮冈胜览, Shīgāng Shènglǎn), **Chen Yi's Former Residence** (陈毅旧居, Chényì Jiùjū) and the **Cheng Ancestral Hall** (程氏宗祠, Chéngmín Zōngcí). You can buy the ticket at the main ticket office by the car park, or at the entrance to any of the three buildings.

Also well worth visiting is the **Ancient Kiln** (古窑, Gǔyáo; ¥20), about 3km beyond the village (away from Jingdezhen); walk along the country road and you'll see the entrance on your right. It contains a collection of sights, all strung out along a riverside walk (give yourself at least an hour here). Don't miss the Song dynasty 'dragon kiln' (龙窑, lóngyáo), which was built up a slope to increase the heat of the kiln's fire.

Another ticket (¥110) allows you entry to the three notable village buildings, the Ancient Kiln and three other sights within the surrounding scenic area, though you'll need transport to visit them as they are some distance away.

Simple restaurants, teahouses and family-run guesthouses (农家乐, nóngjiālè) are dotted around the village, including cute, riverside **Pingchang Renjia** (平常人家; ☎150 7980 8902; Yáolǐ Gǔzhèn, 瑶里古镇; r¥100; ❋🛜), to your left as you enter the old village proper.

Buses to Yaoli (瑶里, ¥6, one hour, 10 daily, 7.30am to 5pm) leave roughly hourly from **Fu Liang Xian Bus Station** (浮梁县汽车站, Fú Liáng Xiàn Qìchē Zhàn), 7km north of town. To get to the bus station, take **bus 36** (Guangchang Beilu, 广场北路; ¥2, 25 minutes, 7am to 7.30pm) from Er Yuan (二院) bus stop near People's Square, or from outside Sculpture Factory, and get off at Fuliang Xian Yancao Gongsi (浮梁县烟草公司, Fúliáng Xiàn Yāncǎo Gōngsī) bus stop, a 200m walk from the bus station; turn left at the large roundabout in front of you, and the station is soon on your right. The last bus back from Yao Li leaves at 5pm.

Bus 1, which runs along Zhushan Zhonglu in the centre of town, stops outside the south gate of the complex, as does bus 908 from North Train Station, and bus 28 from Xīkè Zhàn Bus Station and Jingdezhen Train Station. Get off at Caojialing (曹家岭) bus stop, then walk through the archway opposite.

Ceramics Art Avenue
ARTS CENTRE

(陶溪川, Táoxīchuān; ☎079 8844 0866; 150 Xinchang West Rd, 新厂西路150号; ⊙10am-10pm) This large, modern ceramics hub opened in 2016 with the aim of regenerating the city. Built on the site of an old 1950s ceramics factory it features multiple renovated red-brick industrial buildings, the largest of which houses a **museum** (¥20, 9am to 9pm) containing original stone-firing kilns. The smaller surrounding buildings accommodate galleries and shops that display the ceramic creations of local and international students and artists. A good sprinkling of restaurants and cafes, and a craft-beer bar, fill the rest of the space.

You pass the place on the way to Sculpture Factory. Get off bus 1 at Zhāngshù Xià (樟树下) bus stop and walk back 50m.

Sanbao International Ceramic Valley
ARTS CENTRE

(三宝国际瓷谷, Sānbǎo Guójì Cígǔ; Sanbao Lu, 三宝路; ⊙10am-6pm) **FREE** About 2km or 3km south of the Sculpture Factory and Ceramics Art Avenue is a third ceramic arts district, known simply as San Bao (三宝), which is strung out for a couple of kilometres along a forested valley. Here you'll find pottery workshops, galleries and cafes all along Sanbao Lu, a road that follows the valley to Sanbao Village.

To get here take bus 15 from People's Sq (人民广场, Rénmín Guǎngchǎng) to its terminus, then walk left out of the small bus station and then right onto Sanbao Lu. You can also catch bus 15 from opposite Ceramics Art Avenue.

🛌 Sleeping

⭐ Jingdezhen International Youth Hostel
HOSTEL ¥

(景德镇国际青年旅舍, Jǐngdézhèn Guójì Qīng-niánlǚshè; ☑0798 844 8886, 189 7980 6717; jdzhostel@hotmail.com; south end of Sculpture Factory, 139 Xinchangdong Lu, 新厂东路139号 (雕塑瓷厂前门口内; dm ¥45-55, r ¥138-178) Located just inside the Sculpture Factory arts district, about 3km east of the town centre, this is the best hostel in Jingdezhen, with a lovely ground-floor cafe-bar area and clean but slightly poky rooms. Some staff speak English. No website, but you can book through www.yhachina.com.

Xiao Lu Hostel
HOSTEL ¥

(晓庐青年酒店, Xiǎo Lú Qīngnián Jiǔdiàn; ☑0798 829 8999; Zhushan Zhonglu, 珠山中路; r from ¥108; ❄🤖) The private rooms here (no dorms) are excellent value: cheap yet large and bright, and with tables, chairs and strong wi-fi.

Jinjiang Inn
HOTEL ¥¥

(锦江之星, Jǐnjiāng Zhīxīng; ☑0798 857 1111; www.jinjianginns.com; 1 Zhushan Xilu, 珠山西路1号; r from ¥189; ❄🤖) A comfortable, well-run chain hotel overlooking the river and Zhushan Bridge. Rooms are bright and clean. Breakfast costs ¥22 extra. Buses 5 and 1 go here.

🍴 Eating & Drinking

Jingdezhen's restaurants are the typical second-tier city range of delicious street fare, working-class restaurants and pan-Chinese banquet halls. Dig in.

Ceramics Art Avenue has a couple of low-key bars and is decent for evening drinks.

Niu Gu Fen
JIANGXI ¥

(牛骨粉, Niú Gǔ Fěn; Xinchang Xilu, 新厂西路; dishes ¥8-20; ⏱8.30am-10.30pm) Nevermind the fancy-pants places inside Ceramics Art Avenue: try some of the great-value no-frills restaurants opposite. Order the speciality *niú gǔ fěn* (牛骨粉, beef-rib noodles) at this place, for example, and you'll get a filling bowl of noodles plus a side bowl of succulent, spicy, beef ribs to chomp on too, all for just ¥16. English menu.

8 Du Chufang
JIANGXI ¥¥

(八渡厨房, Bādù Chúfáng; 57 Guangchang Nanlu, 广场南路57号; mains ¥20-50; ⏱11am-9.30pm) The most popular of numerous places to eat on this stretch, this modern restaurant serves Jiangxi specialities such as *niúqì chōngtiān* (牛气冲天, spicy beef claypot), *xiāngcūn lǎodòufu* (乡村老豆腐, village-style tofu) and *hóngshāo huángyātou* (红烧黄丫头, braised river fish).

ℹ️ Information

ICBC Bank (Zhongshan Zhonglu, 中山中路) ATM.
Bank of Communications (24 Zhongshan Xilu, 中山西路24号) ATM; there's another ATM on **Tongzhan Lu** (Tongzhan Lu, 同栈路).

ℹ️ Getting There & Away

AIR
There are direct flights from **Jingdezhen Luojia Airport** (景德镇罗家机场, Jǐngdézhèn Luójiā Jīchǎng) to many Chinese cities, including Beijing.
Local bus 25 (Zhejiang Lu, 浙江路) (¥2, 45 minutes, 6am to 6.30pm) goes from Jingdezhen Train Station to the airport, via People's Sq, Zhushan Zhonglu and Xike Zhan Bus Station.

BUS
Jingdezhen's main bus station is called **Xike Zhan** (西客站, Xīkè Zhàn; Yingbin Dadao, 迎宾大道). Services include the following:
Jiujiang ¥50, 90 minutes, four daily (8am, 11am, 2.30pm and 5pm)
Nanchang ¥50, three hours, hourly (6.50am to 7.30pm)
Wuyuan ¥28, one hour, three daily (7am, 10.30am and 3.30pm)
Yingtan ¥60, 2½ hours, four daily (7.40am, 9.15am, 1.40pm and 4.30pm)
Yushan ¥91, four hours, one daily (8.20am)

TRAIN
Bullet-train services stop at the new **Jingdezhen North Train Station** (景德镇北站, Jǐngdézhèn Běi Zhàn).
Services from **Jingdezhen Train Station** (景德镇火车站, Jǐngdézhèn Huǒchē Zhàn; Tong-zhan Lu, 通站路) (景德镇火车站; Jǐngdézhèn Huǒchē Zhàn) include the following:
Beijing K-train hard sleeper ¥337, 24 hours, one daily (5.22am)
Nanchang K-train hard seat ¥47, 4½ to five hours, two daily (7.36am and 2pm)

ℹ️ Getting Around
Local buses cost ¥2 per trip; exact change is needed. Handy ones include the following:
Bus 901 Jingdezhen North Train Station to People's Sq (人民广场, Rénmín Guǎngchǎng)
Bus 902 Jingdezhen North Train Station to Xike Zhan Bus Station
Bus 25 Jingdezhen Train Station to the airport via People's Sq and Zhushan Zhonglu

Wuyuan 婺源

☑ 0793 / POP 135,000

Wuyuan (Wùyuán) is home to some of south-eastern China's most immaculate views. Parcelled away in this hilly pocket is a scattered cluster of picturesque Huīzhōu villages, where old China remains preserved in enticing panoramas of ancient bridges, trickling streams and stone-flagged alleyways.

Despite lending its name to the entire area, the main town of Wuyuan itself is a fairly bog-standard town, but it's the transport hub, has some comfortable hotels, and you can arrange bicycle hire here for cycling trips into the far more arresting countryside.

The area is enjoying a renaissance among domestic tourists, so expect the crowds at the more popular villages on weekends.

Of the myriad villages, 12 have been officially opened up to tourism and are ticketed, including Likeng (p497), Xiaoqi (p496), Wangkou (p496) and the twin villages of Sixi and Yancun (p498). Smaller, more remote villages such as Guankeng (p498) and Lingjiao (p496) are still free to enter. There are three types of tickets:

➡ Single village entrance ticket (门票, *mén piào*; ¥60)

➡ Twelve village one-day pass (联票, *lián piào*; ¥150)

➡ Twelve village five-day pass (通票, *tōng piào*; ¥210)

🏃 Activities

Cycling

Though you can reach most of Wuyuan's villages by bus, cycling gives you more freedom to village-hop around the surrounding countryside. Roads are in good nick (some have cycle lanes) and are well signposted in pinyin as well as Chinese characters. You can pick up a Chinese map of the area from Xinhua Bookstore (p496).

One possible two- to three-day trip is the 130km circuit from Wuyuan, passing Likeng, Xiaoqi and the Duanxin Reservoir (段莘水库, Duànxīn Shuǐkù), before looping back to Wuyuan via Qinghua (p498) and Sikou. Follow Wengong Beilu north out of Wuyuan to pick up road signs to the villages.

How long the circuit takes you depends on how much time you spend in each village, but the total cycling time (not including side trips to villages such as Guankeng

and Lingjiao, both 30 minutes from the main road) is about seven or eight hours. You could do it in two days, but taking three days makes more sense.

Some roads are hilly, but the only really tough climb is the one-hour slog from Jiangling up to the Duanxin Reservoir.

Individual cycling times from Wuyuan to various villages:

Likeng one hour

Wangkou 90 minutes

Xiaoqi 2½ hours

Guankeng 4½ hours

Sikou one hour

Qinghua 90 minutes

In Wuyuan, numerous places rent bikes, including **Merida Bike Shop** (美利达自行车, Měilìdá Zìxíngchē; ☑ 0793 734 1818, 135 1703 3662; Liangli Shanlu, 凉笠山路二环路南段; bike rental per day from ¥30; ◎ 8am-9pm), which has good-quality second-hand mountain bikes for ¥50 per day (including helmet and lock; deposit ¥1000), plus some older bikes for ¥30. It's a short walk from Old North Bus Station; turn left out of the station, first left, right at the end, and it's on your left.

Walking

Many of Wuyuan's villages are linked by time-worn postal roads (驿道, *yìdào*) that today provide hikers with the perfect excuse to explore the area's gorgeous backcountry: imagine wild azalea, wisteria and iris blooms dotting steep hills cut by cascading streams and you're off to the right start.

Most trails are difficult to navigate without help from a local, but one fabulous 8km-long, three-hour trail linking the rarely visited villages of Guankeng (官坑, Guānkēng) and Lingjiao (岭脚, Lǐngjiǎo) has bilingual signposts along its route, so can be done independently.

The path takes you up and over a pass, and has numerous steps, so it's not feasible if you've cycled out here.

Follow the hiking sign beside the guesthouse Guankeng Fandian, in Guankeng village, and head straight upstream. After the second pavilion (near the top of the pass) turn left, then right immediately afterwards, to continue on the path to Lingjiao, from where you can catch a bus back to Wuyuan (¥20, 90 minutes, 7am, 11.30am and 1pm).

🛏 Sleeping & Eating

In Wuyuan, Wengong Beilu (文公北路) is lined with hotels and restaurants. Out in the countryside, pretty much every village has accommodation (住宿, zhùsù) of some sort, most of which will serve great home-cooked meals. Expect to pay around ¥60 to ¥80 for a room, and about ¥30 to ¥40 for a meal.

Yíngdū Bīnguǎn   HOTEL ¥
(迎都宾馆; ☎ 0793 734 8620; 13 Wengong Nan-lu, 文公南路13号; r ¥100; ❀@🛜) A central budget hotel with large, bright rooms, and a friendly welcome despite no English being spoken. Get bus 1 to People's Hospital (人民 医院, Rénmín Yīyuàn); it's to your left as you face the hospital.

Youshi Kafei   CAFE ¥¥
(有时咖啡, Yǒushí Kāfēi; Shū Xiāng Lù, 书乡路; coffee from ¥20, dishes ¥30-70; ⊙10.30am-11pm; ❀🛜) This modern, comfortable, 1st-floor cafe is the only place for miles that does freshly ground coffee, but it also does western food (avocado sandwiches, salads, mini burgers, pizza) as well as beer and wine, and it has an English menu. Walk along the road opposite the Yingdu Binguan hotel on Wengong Nanlu, then turn right at the end and it's on your right.

ℹ Information

ATMs are plentiful in Wuyuan, but not in the villages (apart from Qinghua), so load up with cash in Wuyuan.

Xinhua Bookstore (新华书店, Xīnhuá Shūdiàn; Tianyou Xilu, 天佑西路; ⊙8am-8pm) Pick up a Wuyuan map (婺源地图; Wùyuán dìtú; ¥6 to ¥8) here to help with cycling around the country-side. If they've sold out, try QY bookshop 100m further on, on the right.

ℹ Getting There & Away

Wuyuan Bus Station (婺源汽车站, Wùyuán qìchēzhàn; Caishi Dadao, 才士大道) is about 2km west of town. Bus services include the following:

Nanchang ¥100, 3½ hours, one daily (8am)
Sanqing Shan (east section) ¥26, 1½ hours, two daily (8.10am and 1.20pm)
Yushan ¥43, 2½ hours, two daily (8.10am and 1.20pm)

Services from the smaller, more hectic **Old North Bus Station** (老北站, Lǎo Běizhàn; Wen-gong Beilu, 文公北路) include the following:
Guankeng ¥23, 2½ hours, 6.30am, two daily (8.30am and 3.20pm)

Likeng ¥8, 20 minutes, every 20 minutes (6.30am to 6.30pm)
Lingjiao ¥16, 90 minutes, roughly hourly (7.50am to 3.50pm)
Qinghua (via Sikou) ¥10, 30 minutes, half-hourly (7am to 5pm)
Xiaoqi ¥15, one hour, hourly (6.30am to 3.30pm)

Wuyuan's fairly new **train station** (婺源火车站, Wùyuán Huǒchēzhàn) is an impressive structure, 4km southeast of the centre. Motorcycle taxis line the exit to take you to the various villages.

ℹ Getting Around

Local bus 1 (¥2, 6am to 6pm) goes from Wuyuan Bus Station forecourt to Old North Bus Station and People's Hospital before terminating at the train station. Bus 3 also links the train and bus stations.

It's relatively easy to bus hop your way from village to village if you stick to the more popular villages. Buses, for example, shuttle between Wuyuan and Jiangwan – via Likeng and Wangkou – every 20 minutes until 5pm. Likewise, there are frequent services along the Wuyuan–Qinghua road, via Sikou.

If you're trying to get to a more remote village, consider taking a motorcycle taxi. Expect to pay at least ¥40 for a 10km ride.

Around Wuyuan

Lingjiao   岭脚

Lingjiao is best known as one end of the old Qing postal route that now serves as one of Wuyuan's most spectacular and manageable hikes. The village itself is magical and pristine. There is not much to do, but it has a couple of basic restaurants for pre- or post-hike sustenance, and a few simple guest-houses should you get stuck here.

Wangkou   汪口

Less popular than some of the other ticketed villages, Wangkou, 9km northeast of Likeng, enjoys a fine location beside a rushing weir at the confluence of two large rivers.

Xiaoqi   晓起

About 35km from Wuyuan, Xiaoqi dates from AD 787. There are actually two villages here: the larger, more touristy lower Xiaoqi (下晓起, Xià Xiǎoqī) and the much quieter upper Xiaoqi (上晓起, Shàng Xiǎoqī), where you'll find a fascinating old **tea factory** (传统生态茶作坊, chuántǒng shēngtài chá

Around Wuyuan

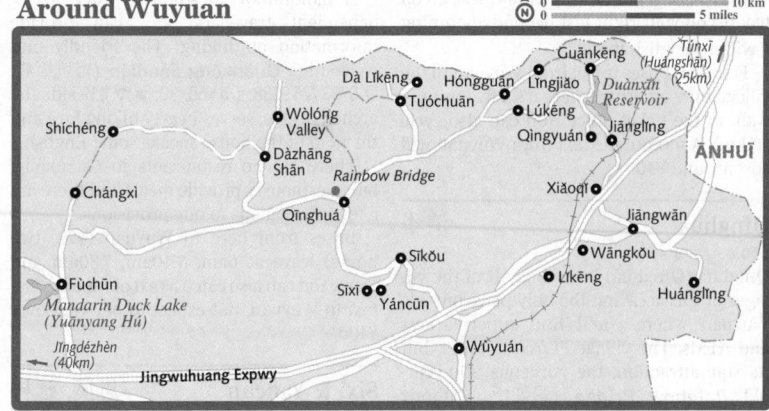

zuòfang). The two are linked by a time-worn, 500m-long stone pathway. Both parts of the village have accommodation.

Likeng 李坑

☎ 0793 / POP 3000

Likeng (Lǐkēng) is the most popular village in the area due to its Song dynasty houses and buzzing laneways. The walk in from the car park, past rice paddies and the main local temple, is beautiful, despite the high-speed train line now running overhead. Once at the village proper, winding, lantern-strewn pathways follow a trickling brook with punters offering lifts on bamboo barges. Narrow footbridges cross the water, and after sunset visitors fill the riverside lanes for chrysanthemum tea, rice wine and trinkets, snapping photos of rooftops glowing under red lanterns and old-fashioned street lamps.

Note, there is another Likeng in the north of the county, though it's usually referred to as Da Likeng (大李坑, Dà Lǐkēng, Big Likeng).

Likeng's highly photogenic focal point hinges on the confluence of its two streams, traversed by the hump of the 300-year-old **Tongji Bridge** (通济桥, Tōngjì Qiáo) and signposted by the **Shenming Pavilion** (申明亭, Shēnmíng Tíng). The pavilion, with its wooden benches polished smooth with age, is a favourite local meeting point.

Among the *báicài* (Chinese cabbage) draped from bamboo poles and chunks of cured meat hanging out in the air from crumbling, mildewed buildings, notable structures include the **Patina House** (铜录

坊, Tónglù Fáng), erected during Qing times by a copper merchant, the rebuilt **old stage** (古戏台, gǔxìtái), where Chinese opera and performances are still held during festivals, and spirit walls erected on the riverbank to shield residents from the sound of cascading water.

Entrance to the village is ¥60, and it is included in the 12 village pass.

Accommodation is easy to find with plenty of choices on either side of both streams. The friendly, family-run **Brook Hotel** (傍溪居, Bàng Xī Jū; ☎ 0793 737 0086, 151 8036 7092; limin608058@126.com; r from ¥100; ❀ ᯤ), on your right as you walk into the village, is the most accustomed to foreign guests on account of the welcoming owner 'Linda' being able to speak some English. Rooms are clean and spacious, and the food (dishes ¥12 to ¥48) cooked up by Linda's in-laws is delicious.

With a choice location overlooking Shenming Pavilion and the two rushing weirs, and river-view rooms decked out in gorgeous traditional Chinese furniture, **Shēnmíng Kèzhàn** (申明客栈, Shēnmíng Kèzhàn; ☎ 134 7932 8482; r from ¥300; ❀ ᯤ), a small guesthouse above a teashop, is worth a bit of a splurge. No English spoken.

Cheap snack sellers line the paths, while slightly overpriced restaurants fill up after dark for atmospheric lantern-lit suppers. Serving some of the best food in Likeng, the charming **Guangming Teahouse** (光明茶楼, Guāngmíng Chálóu; ☎ 0793 737 0999; mains ¥15-58; ❀ ᯤ) acts as an informal thoroughfare to the best photo spot in the village, perched above the village stream. It's a lovely spot to try the local hóng lǐyú (红鲤鱼,

red carp), or a pot of Wuyuan's finest green tea. It's on your right just beyond Shenming Pavilion. English menu.

Frequent buses travel from Wuyuan to the village turn-off, from where it's a five-minute walk to the ticket office. You can also cycle (12km). A motorcycle taxi from Wuyuan will cost around ¥40.

Qinghua 清华

☑ 0793 / POP 40,000

Qinghua (Qīnghuá) is the biggest of the villages in this area and the only place outside Wuyuan where you'll find supermarkets and ATMs. The village is free to enter, but its star attraction, the gorgeous 800-year-old **Rainbow Bridge** (彩虹桥, Cǎihóng Qiáo; entrance ¥60, or with the 12 village ticket), is one of the area's ticketed sights. The charming, narrow, traffic-free street called **Lao Jie** (老街, Old Street), which runs parallel to the river close to the bridge, contains Qinghua's most interesting architecture. An alleyway off Lao Jie, called Dai Fu Xiang (大夫巷), leads to the ticket office for Rainbow Bridge.

There are a few simple guesthouses (客栈, kèzhàn) on Lao Jie including **Měiqín Kèzhàn** (美琴客栈; ☑ 134 3793 1684; 309 Lao Jie, Qinghua, 清华老街309号; r ¥60; ❄ ⓢ), a welcoming family-run place with large rooms and clean bathrooms with squat toilets. The large, well-run **Qīnghuá Bīnguǎn** (清华宾馆; ☑ 0793 724 2789; Zhengfu Lu, 镇政府路; r ¥138; ❄ ⓢ) is one of a few business hotels up on Zhengfu Lu.

Buses to Wuyuan (via Sikou; ¥9, 30 minutes, half-hourly, 6.50am to 5pm) and Lingjiao (30 minutes, roughly hourly, 8.30am to 4.30pm) leave from the turn-off into the town, by the river. There's also one daily bus to Jingdezhen (¥25, two hours, 7.20am).

Guankeng 官坑

☑ 0793 / POP 600

Rarely visited Guankeng (Guānkēng) is set between two valleys in the north of the county. It may lack the architectural heritage of its neighbours, but the absence of tour buses more than compensates.

The village is best known in travel circles as the start or end point of a wonderful three-hour hike to the equally quiet village of Lingjiao.

A handful of guesthouses cater to independent travellers, and can provide information on hiking. The friendly and welcoming **Guānkēng Fàndiàn** (官坑饭店; ☑ 0793 725 9588; s/d ¥60/80; ❄ ⓢ), beside the arched bridge, serves hearty hiking fare and the man of the house speaks some English.

There are no restaurants in Guankeng, but guesthouses provide meals and there are a few small shops to buy provisions.

Buses from here to Wuyuan (¥22, two hours) leave at 6am, 6.40am, 7.30am and 11am. You can also catch a taxi or motorcycle-taxi to Wuyuan, but expect to pay well over ¥100.

Sixi & Yancun 思溪, 延村

☑ 0793 / POP 30,000

Less hectic than other parts of Wuyuan, but with a small independent travel scene and stunning natural surrounds, these charming twin villages are a convenient alternative to staying in Likeng.

Sixi (Sīxī) and Yancun (Yáncūn) are quintessential Qing chic, with the prow-shaped, covered wooden **Tongji Bridge** (通济桥, Tōngjì Qiáo) at Sixi's entrance dating from the 15th century. Follow the signs to the numerous Qing dynasty residences, making sure not to miss the large **Jingxu Hall** (敬序堂, Jìngxù Táng). A 15-minute walk back along the road, towards Sikou, brings you to Yancun, Sixi's more homey sibling, where you'll find yet more Qing architecture.

Admission to the pair of villages costs ¥60; or you can use the 12 village ticket.

The most appealing place to stay in any of the villages around Wuyuan is **Go Home Hotel** (归去来兮, Guīqù Láixī; ☑ 0793 733 5118; Yancun Village, 延村; r incl breakfast from ¥398; ❄ ⓢ), an immaculately renovated boutique hotel housed in a 270-year-old former residence. Each room is different (ask to see them all) but decorated beautifully with period wooden furniture. There's no website, but you can book a room through www.ctrip.com (search for Guiqulaixi Hotel).

You can also stay outside the paid area in Sikou town at **Wángjiā Huīyuàn** (王家徽院; ☑ 150 0703 7380, 0793 733 5679; Sikou Town (Sixi Village side), 思口镇 (思溪侧); d/tw from ¥300/350; ❄ ⓢ), where two brothers and their father have recreated a period mansion using their own incredibly deft touch and indefatigable work ethic. The result is splendid and makes a handy alternative to staying within Sixi village proper, a 2km walk away. It's on the right as you walk along the road from Sikou to Sixi.

It's an easy one-hour cycle from Wuyuan, along a road with a painted cycle path. Alternatively, take any Wuyuan to Qinghua bus (¥5, 20 minutes, frequent) and get off at Sikou (思口). Motorbike taxis will take you the rest of the way (¥5), or just you can walk it (3km).

Sanqing Shan 三清山

📞 0793

The best scenery in Jiangxi province is here at Sanqing Shan (Sānqīng Shān). The drive in, along dripping-wet, thickly forested river gorges, is spectacular enough, but the views from the hiking trails on top of the mountain will take your breath away.

Sānqīng means 'The Three Pure Ones', and you won't find a mountain park in China more serendipitous than this triumvirate of natural majesty, believed to resemble Taoism's three most important deities. Concrete may encroach underfoot, and a cable car whir overhead, but consider the architectural feat as you hike around sheer rock face, looking out onto a forest of fantastical granite spires and a gorgeous canopy sprinkled with white rhododendron blooms. Entrance to the park is ¥120.

Unlike Huang Shan, its more famous neighbour to the north, Sanqing Shan has a spiritual legacy and has been a place of retreat for Taoist adepts for centuries. Views are spectacular in any season, reaching a climax amid the flowering buds of late May.

The main town near the mountain park is Yushan; this is where you'll find the train and bus station.

⊙ Sights & Activities

Hiking is the activity you come for, or at least some kind of gazing into the great abyss. There are enough trails that you could easily spend two days up here, though a long day hike is doable. There are two main access points: the southern section (南部, *nán bù*) and the eastern section (东部, *dōng bù*). You can buy maps (¥5), or photograph the ones on the signboards.

Estimated hiking times from the southern-section trailhead are as follows:

➡ top of southern-section cable car: 1½ hours

HOW TO 'DO' SANQING SHAN

Nothing beats staying on top of a mountain so, if you're able to carry all your luggage, take the bus from Yushan to either the southern or eastern sections, hike to the summit, stay overnight, then hike down to the other section the following day to catch a bus back to Yushan. Alternatively, stay the night in Yushan and leave your luggage there, then catch an early bus to the mountain – it's quite possible to hike from one section to the other in one day and then catch the bus back to Yushan. If you arrive at the mountain late, or miss the last buses back to Yushan, there are plenty of hotels and guesthouses at both the southern and eastern trailheads. The southern is smaller and quieter, but you'll always find a room somewhere.

➡ top of eastern-section cable car: three hours

➡ bottom of eastern-section cable car: five hours

➡ Nanqing Garden loop and back: four hours

West Coast Trail HIKING
(西海岸, Xī Hǎi'àn) The spectacularly exposed West Coast Trail was built into the cliff face at an average altitude of 1600m. This trail eventually leads to the secluded Taoist Sanqing Temple, established during the Ming dynasty.

Sunshine Coast Trail HIKING
(阳光岸, Yángguāng Àn) The Sunshine Coast Trail winds through a forest of ancient rhododendrons, sweet chestnut, bamboo, magnolia and pine, and even features a glass-floored observation platform. There are lots of steps here; take it on the way back from the Taoist Sanqing Temple.

Nanqing Garden MOUNTAIN
(南清苑, Nánqīng Yuàn) Sanqing Shan's main summit area is known as Nanqing Garden, and includes a looping trail that wends beneath strange pinnacles and connects the southern and eastern sections.

Taoist Sanqing Temple TAOIST SITE
(三清宫, Sānqīng Gōng) Established during the Ming dynasty, this is one of the few Taoist

temples in Jiangxi to have survived the Cultural Revolution.

🛌 Sleeping

You can sleep in three areas: on the summit, at either of the trailheads, or in the town of Yushan. Prices rise at weekends.

🛌 Yushan Town

Fāngfāng Bīnguǎn GUESTHOUSE ¥
(芳芳宾馆; ☑187 7931 6629, 0793 220 5890; off Renmin Dadao, Yushan, 玉山县人民大道日景现代城; s/d/tw ¥60/80/100; 🕸🛜) The best value of numerous hotels near Yushan bus station (left then second left), Fangfang has large, clean rooms, and bathrooms with squat toilets.

International Trade Hotel HOTEL ¥¥
(国贸大酒店, Guómào Dàjiǔdiàn; ☑0793 235 3922; Renmin Beilu, Yushan, 玉山县人民北路汽车站对面; r incl breakfast from ¥168; 🅿🕸🛜) Opposite Yushan bus station, this midrange business hotel is smart and spacious.

🛌 Trailheads

Nánqīng Kèzhàn GUESTHOUSE ¥
(南清客栈; ☑138 7930 6267, 0793 218 0019; southern entrance, 三青山南部（索道站附近）; r from ¥100) This simple guesthouse beside the start of the southern trail and the cable car is ideal to rest up in before you start your hike. The owners speak some English.

Hilton Sanqingshan Resort HOTEL ¥¥¥
(三清山希尔顿度假酒店, Sānqīngshān Xīěrdùn Dùjià Jiǔdiàn; ☑0793 223 3333; Sanqing Shan southern section, Sānqīngshān fēngjǐng míngshèngqū nánbù, 三清山风景名胜区南部; r without/with breakfast from ¥550/750; 🅿🕸@🛜🛝) Sanqing Shan's best hotel has genuine luxury throughout. It's by the bus drop-off point at the southern section.

🛌 Mountain Summit

Rìshàng Bīnguǎn HOTEL ¥¥
(日上宾馆; ☑0793 218 9377; Sanqing Shan southern section, 三清山南部，Sānqīngshān nánbù; r from ¥260; 🕸🛜) About a 10-minute climb from the southern chairlift is the welcoming, pale-blue Rìshàng, with a stupendous viewing deck and neat, renovated rooms. If it's full, you won't go wrong with the options either side.

Nǔshén Bīnguǎn HOTEL ¥¥¥
(女神宾馆; ☑218 9300; Mountain summit, east side; r from ¥480; 🕸🛜) A comfortable choice, situated 20 minutes' walk past the top of the eastern chairlift.

🍴 Eating

Lánzhōu Lāmiàn NOODLES ¥
(兰州拉面; Renmin Dadao, 人民大道; noodles ¥9-19, other dishes ¥12-35; ⏱9.30am-midnight) The noodles at this tiny restaurant, located 100m left out of Yushan bus station, are pulled fresh while you wait, and there are more than 30 different types. There's a bunch of rice dishes on offer too, plus good English descriptions and clear photos of most dishes on the wall.

ℹ️ Getting There & Away

Sanqing Shan is accessed via the town of Yushan (玉山), which has bus links to Wuyuan and train links to many other places. The daily buses between Wuyuan and Yushan also swing by the eastern section of Sanqing Shan.

Buses from **Yushan bus station** (玉山汽车站, Yùshān qìchēzhàn) include the following:

Sanqing Shan ¥17, 80 minutes, hourly (6.30am to 5pm)

Wuyuan ¥45, 2½ hours, two daily (7.55am and 1.20pm)

Yushan has two stations: the main **train station** (玉山火车站, Yùshān huǒchēzhàn) and **Yushan South Train Station** (玉山火车南站, Yùshān Huǒchē Nánzhàn), which has bullet-train services.

ℹ️ Getting Around

Local bus 6 (¥2, 6.30am to 6.30pm) links Yushan bus station with Yushan South Train Station, 6km from town.

Yushan bus station is a 3km walk from Yushan Train Station (walk north out of the train station, take any right then, after 1km, turn left at the main road and the bus station is eventually on your right). A motor-rickshaw or taxi costs around ¥10.

Sanqing Shan buses run from Yushan bus station to the start of both the eastern section and southern section – make sure you specify your destination, as no buses link the two sections and they are at least 20km apart. The last buses back to Yushan leave just after 5pm.

A **cable car** (三清山索道, Sānqīng Shān Suǒdào; up/down ¥70/50; ⏱8am-5.30pm) rides part way up both sections of the mountain. The eastern ride is more spectacular, but leaves you further from the West Coast Trail.

Longnan 龙南

☎ 0797 / POP 152,000

You may have heard of Fujian's famous circular *tǔlóu* (土楼, roundhouses). Well, Jiangxi has its very own, equally marvellous rectangular versions, called *wéi lóng wū* (围龙屋). In the verdant Hakka countryside in the south of the province, there are estimates of some 370 such dwellings surrounding the town of Longnan (Lóngnán) alone. These unusual structures have housed neighbouring families for generations in earthen, fortified compounds; the villages of Guanxi (关西, Guānxī) and Yangcun (杨村, Yángcūn) are the most accessible.

☉ Sights

The most convenient and fun place to base yourself in Longnan is Bingjiang Sq (滨江广场, Bīnjiāng Guǎngchǎng), a small, tree-shaded, riverside square dotted with shops, restaurants and night-time barbecue stands, and a favourite local hangout come evening. It's also well served by local buses.

★ Yànyì Wéi   HISTORIC BUILDING

(燕翼围; ¥10) The jewel in the crown of Jiangxi's *wéi lóng wū*, this fascinating, 350-year-old, four-storey structure is the tallest of a number of crumbling old fortified residences in the vicinity of the village of Yancun. Mercifully, it has yet to be targeted by the local tourism industry, and is still lived in by villagers. You can wander around freely (be respectful of the residents, of course), and you can even climb all four storeys. The ¥10 entrance fee is rarely enforced.

To get here, take a bus to the village of Yangcun (杨村, Yángcūn; ¥12.5, 80 minutes, frequent) from Longnan's small bus station at 99 Longding Dadao, 200m from Binjiang Sq. The fortress is 200m from the main drag; cross the river and turn right through the arch.

Wǔdāng Shān   MOUNTAIN

(武当山; ¥80; ◉8am-5.30pm) Not to be confused with Hubei province's more famous and much larger Wudang Shan, and also known as Xiǎo Wǔdāng (小武当, Little Wudang), this group of spectacular, weathered sandstone peaks rewards an easy one-hour climb with stunning views of the surrounding subtropical forest. The bus to Yangcun village from Longnan's small bus station at 99 Longding Dadao stops here en route (¥10, 50 minutes, frequent).

🛏 Sleeping & Eating

There's a cluster of budget hotels overlooking Binjiang Sq, the best value and friendliest of which is **Xinxing Binguan** (新兴宾馆, Xīnxìng Bīnguǎn; ☎0797 353 6288; Binjiang Sq, 滨江广场; d from ¥88; ❄@🅢). For something more upmarket, head 3km east of Binjiang Sq to **Fuye Hotel** (富野酒店, Fùyě Jiǔdiàn; 500 Jinshui Dajie, 金水大道500号; r incl breakfast from ¥298; 🅿❄🅢), a smart midranger that's served by bus 1; get off at the post office stop (邮政, yóu zhèng).

Binjiang Sq has several small restaurants and, come evening, roadside barbecues spring up along the river beside it.

ⓘ Getting There & Around

Four direct trains to Longnan run from Nanchang (hard seat ¥75, six to seven hours, 8.19am, 12.33pm, 3.50pm and 4.16pm), but there are plenty more trains from Nanchang to Ganzhou (赣州, Gànzhōu; ¥62, four to five hours) from where you can either hop on another train to Longnan (¥19, 1½ hours) or take one of the hourly buses (¥55, two hours, until 6.25pm) from the **bus station** (客运站, kèyùn zhàn), which is opposite the train station and to the left a bit. There is also one bus a day to Ganzhou (¥120, 5½ hours, 2.50pm) from Nanchang's Xufang bus station, but you'll miss the connecting bus to Longnan if you take this.

If you get stranded in Ganzhou, there's a YHA youth hostel opposite the train station (and next to the bus station), which has spacious, capsule dorm beds for ¥50 and private rooms for ¥98.

Buses from Ganzhou to Longnan will stop at Longnan's **long-distance bus station** (长途汽车站, chángtú qìchēzhàn), 3.5km east of the town centre, from where you can take local bus 1 to Binjiang Sq. Some of them will continue on to the small bus station at 99 Longding Dadao (龙鼎大道99号), which is a 200m walk from Binjiang Sq; turn left as you exit the station.

Trains from Longnan back to Nanchang leave at 8.30am, 1.56pm, 8.09pm and 11.09pm.

The extremely handy local bus 1 (¥2) goes from Longnan train station, 10km east of town, past the long-distance bus station and on to Binjiang Sq.

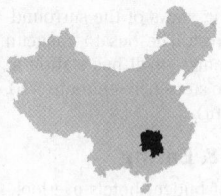

Hunan

POP 68.6 MILLION

Best Places to Eat

➡ Huǒgōngdiàn (p506)

➡ Zuì Xiāngxī (p519)

➡ Miss Yang Restaurant (p519)

➡ Máo Jiā Fàndiàn (p508)

Best Places to Stay

➡ 1982 International Youth Hostel (p513)

➡ Rose Courtyard Hotel (p518)

➡ Lu Shu Homestay (p505)

➡ Yinji Inn (p518)

➡ Hostel Geographer (p514)

Why Go?

As the birthplace of Mao Zedong, Communist Party cadres might wax lyrical about the sacred standing of Hunan (湖南; Húnán) in the annals of Chinese history, but it's the province's dramatic scenery that is the real draw. A magnificent landscape of isolated mountain ranges and jagged peaks envelops more than 80% of the province. The most astonishing example is found at the phantasmagorical Zhangjiajie, one of China's most surreal national parks. Here, as in other parts of the province, geological marvels thrust up majestically from green vales fed by tributaries in the fertile Yangzi River basin.

People have long made a home amid Hunan's natural wonders, taming the rocky slopes into terraces of lush fields, and their distinctive cultures live on in charming villages and towns, the most alluring being the historic riverside settlement of Fenghuang.

When to Go
Changsha

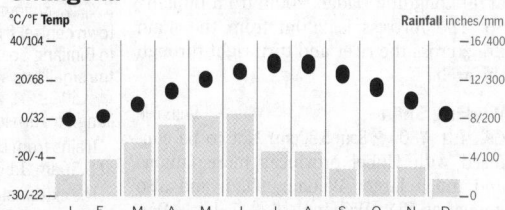

| Apr & May After a chilly winter, spring brings welcome warmth and mountain blooms. | Sep & Oct Temperatures cool after a scorching summer. Autumnal leaves emblazon Zhangjiajie. | Dec–Feb Tour groups diappear from Fenghuang. Zhangjiajie is sometimes brushed with snow. |

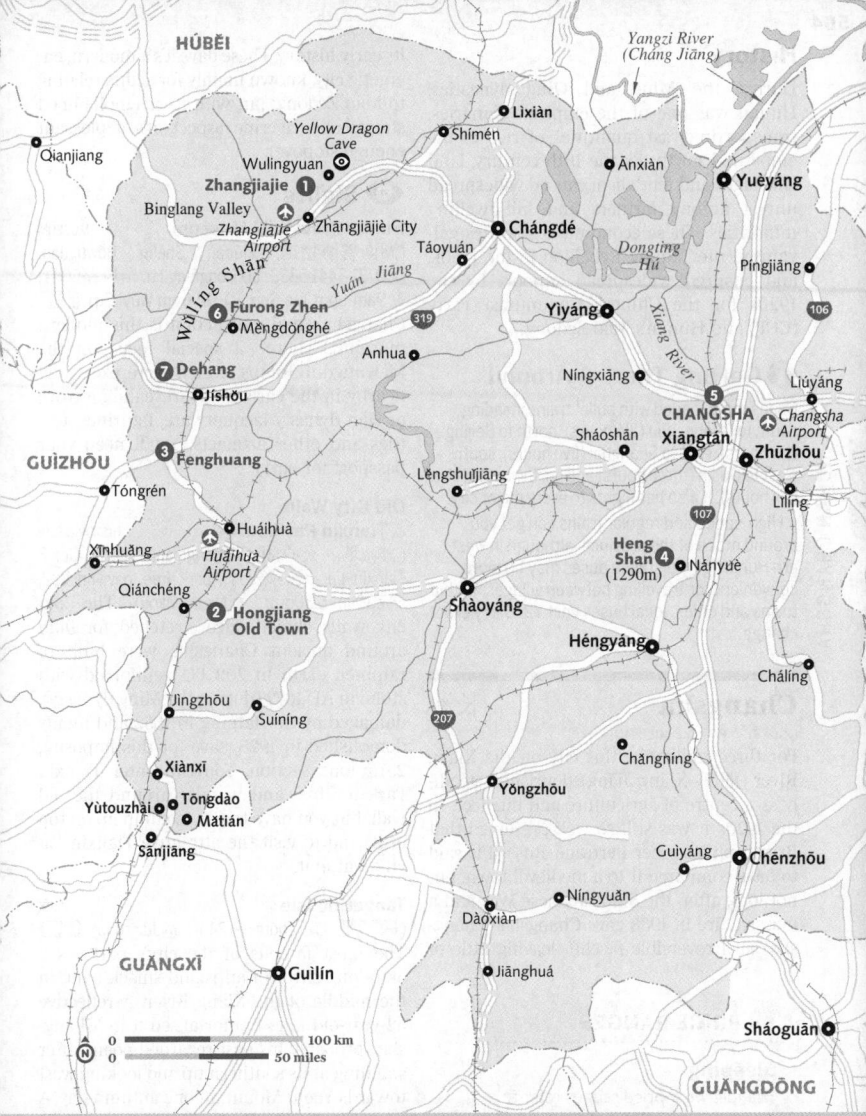

Hunan Highlights

1 **Zhangjiajie** (p510) Hiking among the otherworldly peaks of one of China's most spectacular national parks.

2 **Hongjiang Old Town** (p519) Meandering around Hongjiang's and Qianyang's river towns, and checking out their good-looking crop of ancient buildings.

3 **Fenghuang** (p516) Finding your way through the alleys of this one-time border town in the evening, marvelling at its lights.

4 **Heng Shan** (p509) Ascending the slopes of the sacred Taoist mountain.

5 **Changsha** (p504) Sampling authentic, chilli-laden

xiāng cài (Hunan cuisine) in the food-loving provincial capital.

6 **Furong Zhen** (p520) Sizing up the magnificent waterfall alongside this quaint old town.

7 **Dehang** (p515) Hiking off in search of waterfalls amid the gorgeous greenery of west Hunan.

History

During the Ming and Qing dynasties, Hunan was one of the empire's granaries, transporting vast quantities of rice to the embattled north. By the 19th century, land shortages and feudalism caused widespread unrest among farmers and hill-dwelling minorities. These economic disparities galvanised the Taiping Rebellion in the 1850s, and ensured widespread support by the 1920s for the Chinese Communist Party (CCP) and Hunan's Mao Zedong.

🛈 Getting There & Around

Changsha is loaded with bullet trains, heading south to Guangzhou (2½ hours), north to Beijing (six hours), east to Shanghai (five hours), southwest to Guilin (three hours) and northwest to Xi'an (six hours). It also has flights to every major city.

High-speed and regular trains can get you around much of the province, although in western Hunan long-distance buses may be more convenient for travelling between villages. Within towns and cities, local buses cost ¥2. Carry exact change.

Changsha 长沙

♪ 0731 / POP 4.3 MILLION

For three millennia, this city on the Xiang River (湘江, Xiāng Jiāng) flourished steadily as a centre of agriculture and intellect. In the 1920s it was still so well preserved that British philosopher Bertrand Russell is said to have compared it to a medieval town, but not long after, the Sino-Japanese War and a massive fire in 1938 gave Changsha (Chángshā) an irreversible facelift, leaving little of

its early history. These days it's a modern, energetic city, known mainly for sights relating to Mao Zedong, but with its magnolia-lined streets and riverine aspect, it's a pleasant enough stopover.

⊙ Sights

Hunan Provincial Museum   MUSEUM
(湖南省博物馆, Húnán Shěng Bówùguǎn; ☑ 0731 8441 5833; 50 Dongfeng Lu, 东风路50号; ⊙ 9am-5pm Tue-Sun; 🚌 112 from Wuyi Sq) FREE
Changsha's main attraction is this modern museum. There's a special focus on the Mawangdui Tombs, which were excavated nearby in the early 1970s, revealing a trove of Han dynasty lacquerware, figurines, textiles and other artefacts. You'll need your passport for entry.

**Old City Walls
& Tianxin Pavilion**   HISTORIC SITE
(古城墙、天心阁, Gǔchéngqiáng, Tiānxīn Gé; 3 Tianxin Lu, 天心路3号; park free, pavilion ¥32; ⊙ 7.30am-5.30pm; Ⓜ Nanmenkou) The old city walls, which once stretched for 9km around ancient Changsha, were built of rammed earth in 202 BC, reinforced with stone in AD 1372 (during the Ming dynasty), damaged by the Taiping in 1852 and finally demolished in 1928, save for this imposing 251m-long section. You can enter Tianxin Park for free and wander around the old wall, but you have to pay to climb up on top of it, and to visit the attractive Tianxin Pavilion atop it.

Tangerine Isle   PARK
(橘子洲, Júzi Zhōu; ⊙ 24hr; Ⓜ Juzizhou) FREE
The most famous of the city's parks is a 5km-long sliver of an island smack bang in the middle of the Xiang River. A reflective 32-year-old Mao immortalised it in 'Changsha', probably his best-regarded poem, after standing at its southern tip and looking west towards Yuelu Mountain one autumn day. A towering granite bust of a youthful Chairman with flowing locks now stands at the spot – but faces in a new direction.

🛏 Sleeping

Changsha does not have a great selection of accommodation. There are a few hostels, not always near metro stops, and there's little in the way of midrange hotels apart from the usual Chinese chains, which don't always accept foreigners.

🛈 PRICE RANGES

Sleeping

The following price ranges refer to a double room with bathroom.

¥ less than ¥150

¥¥ ¥150–400

¥¥¥ more than ¥400

Eating

The following price ranges refer to a meal for one.

¥ less than ¥40

¥¥ ¥40–80

¥¥¥ more than ¥80

Changsha

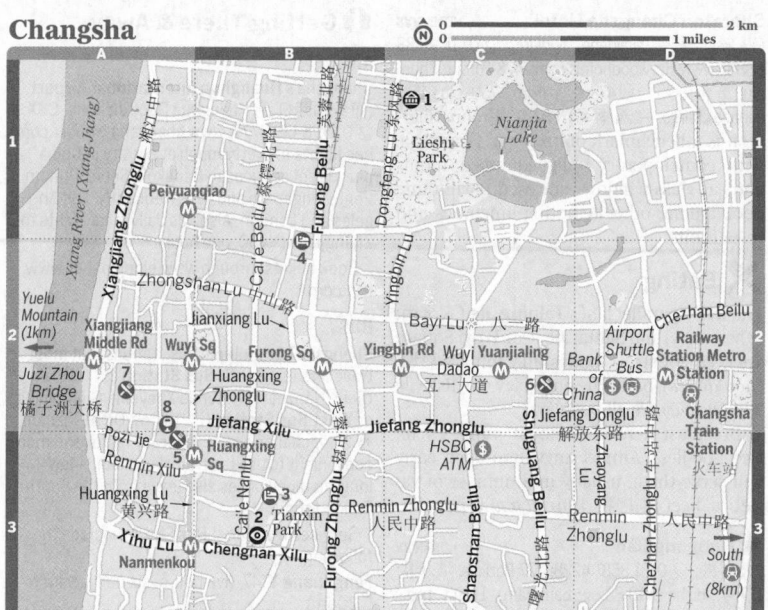

Changsha

◎ Sights
1 Hunan Provincial Museum......................C1
2 Old City Walls & Tianxin Pavilion..........B3

⊟ Sleeping
3 Old Street International Youth
   Hostel..B3
4 Sheraton Changsha Hotel.....................B2

⊗ Eating
5 Huǒgōngdiàn...A3
6 Huǒgōngdiàn – Wuyi Dadao.................C2
7 Taiping Jie...A2

◎ Drinking & Nightlife
8 Jiefang Xilu...A2

Zhongtian Hibiscus
Land International Hostel   HOSTEL ¥
(中天芙蓉国际青年旅舍, Zhōngtiān Fúróng
Guó Guójì Qīngnián Lǚshè; ☑0731 8521 5518; 277
Fenglin Rd, 枫林路277号; dm/d ¥45/128; ❈☏;
Ⓜ Yingwanzhen) Up a peaceful alleyway, this
dependable hostel has reasonably spacious
four- and eight-bed dorms with lockers and
shared bathrooms, plus a few private rooms
(double to quad). There's laundry and a 2nd-
floor terrace, though not a lot in the way of
atmosphere. It's a short walk from the metro
station, on the west side of the river. Some
English spoken.

Old Street International
Youth Hostel   HOSTEL ¥
(古巷国际青年旅舍, Gǔxiàng Guójì Qīngnián
Lǚshè; ☑0731 8225 3500; 56 Duzheng Jie, 都正
街56号; dm/d ¥42/130; ❈☏; Ⓜ Huangxing Sq)

This small Hostelling International place,
parcelled away along the restored old street
of Duzheng Jie, has a fabulous location in
a charming area not far from Changsha's
nightlife. The staff are friendly and speak
English. Bus 124 runs here from the South
Train Station (one hour).

★ Lu Shu Homestay   BOUTIQUE HOTEL ¥¥
(麓墅旅馆, Lùshù Lǚguǎn; ☑0731 8857 3049; 289
Fenglin Yilu, 枫林一路289号; r ¥155-355; ❈☏;
Ⓜ Yingwanzhen) Set in an old brick house and
owned by an architect, this is Changsha's
cosiest hotel by a long shot. Decor mixes
contemporary sensibilities with the odd antique to superb effect – there's a lovely sitting
room, patio, adjacent cafe and even a 2nd-
floor tatami terrace. Book in advance (try
www.trip.com).

Sheraton Changsha Hotel HOTEL ¥¥¥
(喜来登酒店, Xǐláidēng Jiǔdiàn; ☎0731 8488
8888; www.starwoodhotels.com; 478 Furong Zhonglu, 芙蓉中路一段478号; r from ¥750, plus 15%
service charge; ▣❄🛜🏊) The 380-room Sheraton is a benchmark of luxury in Changsha,
with contemporary, fully equipped rooms
and a glass-window enclosed swimming
pool, among other tempting amenities and
restaurants.

✕ Eating

The lively parallel lanes **Taiping Jie** (太平街;
☉ hours vary) and Santai Jie near Wuyi Square
are great for street food: stinky tofu (臭豆腐,
chòu dòufu), barbecue and spicy crayfish (龙
虾, *lóngxiā*) are all popular.

Breakfast here is all about *mǐfěn* (米粉),
rice noodles). Almost anywhere open early
will serve them, usually in a number of varieties; beef (牛肉粉, *niúròu fěn*) is popular.

★ Huǒgōngdiàn HUNAN ¥¥
(火宫殿; ☎0731 8581 4228; 127 Pozi Jie, 坡子街
127号; dishes ¥18-88; ☉6am-2am) Don't miss
the experience of eating this culinary landmark, established in 1747 and set around a
small temple courtyard. Downstairs has a
Hunan menu and dim sum trolley; upstairs
is the self-service area (perhaps easier to
navigate), presenting an array of small dishes, steamed buns, skewers, soups and much
more. Portions are inexpensive but small, so
come prepared to spend.

The **Wuyi Dadao branch** (火宫殿五一
大道店; 93 Wuyi Dadao, 五一大道93号; dishes
¥5-88; ☉11am-2pm & 5pm-2am; Ⓜ Yuanjialing),
near the train station, is less atmospheric,
but slightly cheaper and has a photo menu.

🍷 Drinking & Nightlife

Jiefang Xilu (解放西路; Ⓜ Wuyi Sq) is Changsha's club central with KTV (karaoke) joints
and clubs; **Hualongchi Xiang** (化龙池巷;
Ⓜ Huangxing Sq) is another popular strip for
nightlife, off the shopping strip Huangxing
Zhonglu.

❶ Information

ATMs all over town take foreign cards.
Bank of China (中国银行, Zhōngguó Yínháng;
43 Wuyi Dadao, 五一大道43号; Ⓜ Railway
Station) By the Shanshui Trends Hotel. Has a
currency exchange.
HSBC ATM (汇丰银行, Huìfēng Yínháng; 159
Shaoshan Lu, 韶山路159号) 24-hour ATM in
Dolton Hotel lobby.

❶ Getting There & Away

AIR

Changsha's **Huanghua International Airport**
(黄花国际机场, Huánghuā Guójì Jīchǎng, CSX;
☎0731 8479 8777; www.changsha-airport.com)
has flights to pretty much every city in China
plus direct services to Bangkok, Seoul, Phnom
Penh, Singapore and, less frequently, Los Angeles and London. Also has daily local flights to
Zhangjiajie (¥450, one hour).

Book tickets through www.elong.net or www.
trip.com.

BUS

Changsha has multiple bus stations, but most
travellers use **South Bus Station** (汽车南站,
Qìchē Nánzhàn; Ⓜ Tiedao Xueyuan, Guihuaping)
or **West Bus Station** (汽车西站, Qìchē Xīzhàn;
Ⓜ Wangchengpo). It's generally faster and more
convenient to use the train if you can. A few
long-distance buses also leave from the South
Train Station.

Services from West Bus Station include the
following:
Fenghuang ¥147, five hours, six daily (9am to
5.20pm)
Jishou ¥136, 4½ hours, nine daily (8.30am to
6.30pm)
Zhangjiajie ¥119, four hours, hourly (8.20am
to 7pm)

The South Bus Station is 17km from the city – to
get here, take metro Line 1 to Tiedao Xueyuan
and then change to bus 388. Alternatively, get
off at the Guihuaping metro stop and then take
a taxi. Services from South Bus Station include
the following:
Fenghuang ¥158, five hours, one daily (3.40pm)
Heng Shan ¥45, three hours, eight daily
Shaoshan ¥32, 1½ hours, seven daily

TRAIN

Changsha has services to many other major
cities by high-speed rail. Bullet trains leave from
the West Square of **Changsha South Train
Station** (长沙南站, Chángshā Nánzhàn). Regular
trains leave from **Changsha Train Station** (长沙
火车站, Chángshā Huǒchēzhàn).

Bullet trains from Changsha South Train
Station include the following:
Beijing West 2nd class ¥649, 5¾ to seven
hours, 15 daily (7.10am to 5.05pm)
Guangzhou South 2nd class ¥294, 2½ hours,
regular (7am to 9pm)
Guilin 2nd class ¥182, three hours, regular
(6.53am to 5pm)
Heng Shan West 2nd class ¥65, 30 minutes,
regular (7am to 8.47pm)
Huaihua South 2nd class ¥153, 1¾ hours,
regular (6.52am to 8pm)

MAO: THE GREAT HELMSMAN

Mao Zedong was born in the village of Shaoshan in 1893, the son of 'wealthy' peasants. Mao worked beside his father on the 8-hectare family farm from age six and was married by 14.

At 16, he convinced his father to let him attend middle school in Changsha. In the city, Mao discovered Sun Yatsen's revolutionary secret society. When the Qing dynasty collapsed that year, Mao joined the republican army but soon quit, thinking the revolution was over.

At the Hunan County No 1 Teachers' Training School, Mao began following the Soviet socialism movement. He put an ad in a Changsha newspaper 'inviting young men interested in patriotic work to contact me', and among those who responded were Liu Shaoqi, who would become president of the People's Republic of China (PRC), and Xiao Chen, who would be a founding member of the Chinese Communist Party (CCP).

Mao graduated in 1918 and went to work as an assistant librarian at Peking University, where he befriended more future major CCP figures. By the time he returned to teach in Changsha, Mao was active in communist politics. Unlike orthodox Marxists, Mao saw peasants as the lifeblood of the revolution. The CCP was formed in today's Xīntiāndì area in Shanghai in 1921, and soon included unions of peasants, workers and students.

In April 1927, following Kuomintang leader Chiang Kaishek's attack on communists, Mao was tasked with organising what became the 'Autumn Harvest Uprising'. Mao's army scaled Jinggang Shan, on the border with Jiangxi province, to embark on a guerrilla war. The campaign continued until the Long March (p974) in October 1934, a 9600km retreat that ended up in Yan'an in Shanxi province. Mao emerged from the Long March as the CCP leader.

Mao forged a fragile alliance with the Kuomintang to expel the Japanese, and from 1936 to 1948 the two sides engaged in betrayals, conducting a civil war simultaneously with WWII. Mao's troops eventually won, and the PRC was established on 1 October 1949.

As chairman of the PRC, Mao embarked on radical campaigns to repair his war-ravaged country. In the mid-1950s he began to implement peasant-based and decentralised socialist developments. The outcome was the ill-fated Great Leap Forward (p977) in the late 1950s and the chaos of the Cultural Revolution (1966–76; p977).

China saw significant gains in education, women's rights and average life expectancy under Mao's rule; however, by most estimates, between 40 million and 70 million people died during that era of change, mainly from famine. Five years after Mao's death, Deng Xiaoping famously announced Mao had been 70% right and 30% wrong in an effort, some say, to tear down Mao's cult of personality. Yet today Mao remains revered as the man who united the country, and he is still commonly referred to as the 'Great Leader', 'Great Teacher' and 'supremely beloved Chairman'. His image hangs everywhere – in public places, schools, taxis, restaurants and living rooms – but exactly what he symbolises now is the question that China grapples with today.

HUNAN CHANGSHA

Shanghai Hongqiao 2nd class ¥478, five to 7½ hours, regular (7.06am to 6.12pm)

Shaoshan South 2nd class ¥31, 25 minutes, regular (7.18am to 6.05pm)

Wuhan 2nd class ¥165, 1½ hours, regular (7.30am to 9.30pm)

Services from Changsha Train Station include the following:

Beijing Z-train hard sleeper ¥364, 14 hours, seven daily

Guangzhou T/K-train hard sleeper ¥193, seven to eight hours, 13 daily

Jishou K-train hard seat/sleeper ¥75/150, 7½ hours, three daily

Wuhan K-train hard seat ¥54, four hours, eight daily

Zhangjiajie K-train hard seat/sleeper ¥55/113, 5½ hours, six daily

ⓘ Getting Around

Taxi flagfall is ¥8; ¥10 after 10pm.

TO/FROM THE AIRPORT

The airport is 26km east of the city centre. The **Maglev** (磁浮, Cífú; ¥20, 7am to 10.30pm) zips passengers from the airport to South Train Station in 20 minutes – but then you have to take the metro into the city.

Airport shuttle buses (机场巴士, Jīchǎng Bāshì; Wuyi Dadao, 五一大道; ¥19; Ⓜ Railway Station) depart from the Shanshui Trends Hotel (山水时尚酒店, Shānshuǐ Shíshàng Jiǔdiàn) on Wuyi Dadao near the train station, every 20 minutes between 5am and 10.30pm, and take 40 minutes.

A taxi from the city centre is about ¥100.

METRO

Handy Line 2 of Changsha's metro (地铁, dìtiě; tickets ¥2 to ¥6) goes from Changsha South Train Station to Changsha Train Station then along Wuyi Dadao to Tangerine Isle and on to the West Bus Station. Line 1 runs north to south, intersecting Line 2 at Wuyi Sq. Metro trains run from 6.30am to 10.30pm. Lines 3, 4 and 5 are now open, and Line 6 is expected to open in 2021.

Shaoshan 韶山

📞 0731 / POP 118,000

More than 20 million people make the pilgrimage each year to Mao Zedong's rural home town, where the Great Helmsman's childhood home is frozen in time. The swarms of young and old drop something to the tune of ¥6 billion annually in Shaoshan (Sháoshān). Mao statues alone are such big business that each must pass inspection by no fewer than five experts checking for features, expression, hairstyle, costume and posture. The 6m-high bronze statue of Mao erected in 1993 in Mao Zedong Sq is considered a model example.

Only 130km southwest of Changsha, Shaoshan is easily done as a day trip, so there's little reason to spend the night here.

⊙ Sights

Shaoshan was once a village, but these days it's been entirely paved over and rebuilt for tourism, with little to remind you that there was once a community living here. Only a handful of the popular sights have a genuine connection to Mao. It's extremely confusing to find your way around, so your best strategy is to board the bus at the visitor centre and follow the crowds.

Former Residence of
Mao Zedong   HISTORIC SITE

(毛泽东故居, Máo Zédōng Gùjū; ⊘8.30am-5pm) FREE Surrounded by lotus ponds and rice paddies, this modest mud-brick house is like millions of other country homes except that Mao was born here in 1893. By most accounts, his childhood was relatively normal, and he returned briefly in 1921 as a young revolutionary and firebrand. On view are some original furnishings, photos of Mao's parents and a small barn. No photography or backpacks are allowed inside (lockers are provided). A passport is required to get the free ticket.

Nan'an School   HISTORIC SITE

(南岸私塾, Nán'àn Sīshú; ⊘8.30am-5pm) FREE Mao began his education in this simple country school, next door to his childhood home.

Relic Hall of Mao Zedong   MUSEUM

(毛泽东遗物馆, Máo Zédōng Yíwùguǎn; ⊘9am-4.30pm) FREE This museum includes everyday artefacts used by the Great Helmsman, clothing he wore and photos from his life; it benefits from good English captions.

Shao Peak   MOUNTAIN

(韶峰, Sháo Fēng; incl cable car ¥60; ⊘8am-5pm) This cone-shaped mountain is visible from the village. On the lower slopes is the **forest of stelae**: stone tablets engraved with Mao's poems. You can hike to the summit, where there's a **lookout pavilion**; this takes about an hour.

Dripping Water Cave   PARK

(滴水洞, Dī Shuǐ Dòng; ¥60; ⊘8am-5.30pm) Mao secluded himself here for 11 days in June 1966, 3km outside of Shaoshan village, to contemplate the start of the Cultural Revolution. His retreat was actually a low-slung, concrete and steel bunker (not the cave, which was a few kilometres away). Members of the Mao clan are entombed nearby.

✗ Eating

There are a handful of restaurants here, like **Máo Jiā Fàndiàn** (毛家饭店; Shaoshan Village, 韶山; mains ¥25-65; ⊘11am-8pm), serving Mao's favourite dish, *Máo jiā hóngshāoròu* (毛家红烧肉, Mao family red-braised pork). We're curious, however, what Mao's favourite menu item at the visitor centre's KFC would have been.

ⓘ Getting There & Away

The fast-train service (2nd/1st class ¥31/51) zips regularly to **Shaoshan South Train Station** (韶山南站, Sháoshān Nánzhàn) from Changsha South Train Station between 7.18am and 6.05pm, making it the fastest way to reach Shaoshan. The journey takes a mere 25 minutes. The last train back to Changsha departs at 5.34pm. Reserve tickets ahead.

If you can't get a seat on the train, you can always take the bus (¥32, 1½ hours). They run from Changsha's South and West bus stations to the **Shaoshan Bus Station** (韶山汽车站, Sháoshān Qìchēzhàn).

ⓘ Getting Around

Tourist buses run regularly from Shaoshan's train and bus stations (¥3) to the visitor centre

(游客中心, *yóukè zhōngxīn*), which serves as Shaoshan's main entrance. At the visitor centre, you'll need to buy a bus ticket (¥20) to take you around to Shaoshan's various sights, which are quite spread out.

Heng Shan 衡山

♪ 0734

About 130km south of Changsha rises the southernmost of China's five sacred Taoist mountains – Heng Shan (Héng Shān) – to which emperors came to make sacrifices to heaven and earth. The ancients called it Nányuè (南岳, Southern Mountain), a name it now shares with the town at its base. The imperial visits left a legacy of Taoist temples and ancient inscriptions in the region scattered amid gushing waterfalls, dense pine forests and terraced fields cut from lush canyons. Bring extra layers, as the weather can turn quickly and the summit is often cold and wet.

◉ Sights & Activities

Heng Shan   MOUNTAIN

(衡山; Héng Shān; ¥84) Seventy-two peaks spanning 400km comprise the Heng Shan range, but most visitors focus on Zhurong Peak, rising 1290m above sea level.

The lung- and knee-busting 13km ascent up winding paths, steep staircases and, in places, a road busy with tourist shuttle buses, takes around four hours one way, although it can fill the best part of a day if you take in the many temples en route. Alternatively, a combination of bus and cable-car up and walking down can take as little as three hours.

If you want to take the bus, buy the transportation ticket (¥44/78 one way/return, including cable car), along with your entrance ticket, on the 2nd floor of the modern tourist centre (p510), where you can pick up a map (地图; *dìtú*) and visit a small museum. Buses depart directly from here to the mountain's **halfway point** (半山亭, Bànshān Tíng; 15 minutes). From there, you can either take the cable car to **Nántiānmén** (南天门; five minutes), or change to another bus. From Nántiānmén, it's a 30-minute hike to Zhurong Peak.

Note, the mountain is open 24 hours, but the buses and cable car only run until around 5.30pm. It's worth packing a raincoat, although you can buy plastic ponchos from hawkers.

If you decide to hike up the mountain (a wise choice, as you'll miss most of the temples

if you take the bus), it's nicer to start up the tree-lined road 300m east of the tourist centre marked by the stone **Shengli Archway** (胜利坊, Shènglì Fāng). This road leads to another entrance and then to a tranquil path that winds 5km past lakes, waterfalls and streams in **Fanyin Valley** (梵音谷, Fànyīn Gǔ), almost to the cable car departure point at Bànshān Tíng. Along the way, you can stop to see the colourful figures of Taoist and Buddhist scripture on display in **Shenzhou Temple** (神州祖庙, Shénzhōu Zǔmiào), along with the grand and dignified **Nanyue Martyrs Memorial Hall** (南岳忠烈祠, Nányuè Zhōngliècí), dedicated to the anti-Japanese resistance, and a **stele** inscribed with a dedication from Kuomintang leader Chiang Kaishek celebrating the pine forest. Before you jump on the cable car, take a break at **Xuándōu Guàn** (玄都观), an active Taoist temple. The couplet carved at the entry reminds weary climbers that the path of righteousness is long, so don't give up halfway through!

The next 4.5km up to Nántiānmén frequently takes the busy road and scattered staircases, but there are plenty more inspiring temples along the way. Once you reach Nántiānmén, it's a chilly (outside of July and August) 30-minute ascent to the peak.

At the top is **Zhu Rong Palace** (祝融殿, Zhù Róng Diàn), an iron-tiled, stone structure built for Zhu Rong, an ancient official who devised a method of striking stones to create sparks. After his death, he became revered as the god of fire.

Nanyue Temple   TAOIST, BUDDHIST

(南岳大庙, Nányuè Dàmiào; ¥63 May-Oct, ¥43 Nov-Apr; ⊙ 7am-5.30pm) This huge Taoist and Buddhist temple dates from the Tang dynasty and was moved from Heng Shan summit to its foot in the Sui dynasty and then rebuilt many times, most recently in the Qing dynasty. Each carved panel in the main pavilion's balustrade tells a legend of one of Heng Shan's peaks. The main entrance is the south gate, but the back entrance is just opposite the Heng Shan tourist centre.

🛏 Sleeping & Eating

Heng Shan can easily be visited as a day trip, but if you're planning to hike the entire way, you may want to spend the night to give you more time. Hotels near the middle of the mountain charge around ¥200; those at the top charge about ¥500. You can also stay in town.

There are plenty of nondescript restaurants in town and occasional snack stalls on the hike. Accommodation places cook up meals on the mountain, although they can be pricey.

Wàngrì Tái Jiēdàizhàn
HOTEL ¥¥

(望日台接待站, Wàngrì Tái Jiēdàizhàn; ☑ 0734 566 3188; Wàngrì Tái; r ¥500; 🕸 🛜) The mountain's highest accommodation, this place is just a 10-minute walk below Zhùróng Peak (up to your right as you are climbing), and has small but modern twin rooms with air-con–heaters, TV, bathroom and wi-fi. Cooked meals also available (mains ¥30 to ¥60).

Zushi Temple
GUESTHOUSE ¥¥

(祖师殿, Zǔshī Diàn; near Nántiānmén, 南天门附近; d ¥348; @) The rooms in this Taoist temple are spartan for sure, but the views are magic and vegetarian rice meals are served up throughout the day. It's a five-minute walk from the cable-car station by Nántiānmén – turn left as you exit the cable car.

ⓘ Information

Tourist Centre (游客服务中心, Yóukè Fùwù Zhōngxīn; Jinsha Lu, 金沙路; ◷7am-5.30pm) Has leaflets, maps, a small museum and left-luggage service.

ⓘ Getting There & Away

Fifteen bullet trains run from Changsha South Station (2nd/1st class ¥65/100, 30 minutes, 7am to 8.47pm) to **Heng Shan West Station** (衡山西站; Héng Shān Xīzhàn), 7km from Nanyue.

Returning to Changsha, 12 bullet trains leave Heng Shan West Station between 9.14am and 9.40pm.

A few buses (¥46, 2½ hours) run between Changsha and Nanyue Bus Station, but they only depart when they fill up.

ⓘ Getting Around

Local buses wait at the West Train Station to take passengers to Nányuè (¥6, 15 minutes), where they drop you off at the **Nanyue Bus Station** (南岳汽车站; Nányuè Qìchēzhàn; 287 Hengshan Lu, 衡山路287号). From the bus station, city buses 1 and 2 (free) run to the tourist centre and Nanyue Temple. Bus 1 is more direct.

Zhangjiajie
张家界

☑ 0744 / POP 1.7 MILLION

Rising from the subtropical and temperate forests of northwest Hunan, Zhangjiajie (Zhāngjiājiè) has a concentration of quartzite-sandstone formations found nowhere else in the world. Some 243 peaks and more than 3000 pinnacles and spires dominate the scenery in this Unesco-protected park. If caught in the right light or when the early-morning mountain mist rolls in around them, the effect is otherworldly.

For thousands of years, this was a remote land known mainly to three minority peoples: Tujia, Miao and Bai. It is also home to more than 3000 distinct plant species as well as diverse fauna. You'll see lots of macaques on the main trails (remember, they are wild so don't feed them), while endangered species such as the Chinese giant salamander, Chinese water deer and the elusive clouded leopard (only their tracks have been seen) lurk deep in the park's wilderness.

Most travellers base themselves in the gateway town of Wulingyuan, at the main park entrance. All trains and most buses, however, arrive in the much larger Zhangjiajie city, which also has accommodation options and is 28km south of the park.

ⓞ Sights

★ Zhangjiajie National Forest Park
NATIONAL PARK

(张家界国家森林公园, Zhāngjiājiè Guójiā Sēnlín Gōngyuán; 4-day pass adult/student ¥228/116; ◷7am-8pm) Among China's crop of surreal landscapes, Zhangjiajie has got to be a contender for one of the most impressive. A forest of spectacularly weathered spires rises up out of a verdant valley that's filled with dripping moss, fragrant blossoms and acrobatic monkeys. Come dusk, the ensemble is serenaded by a chorus of chirping insects.

The national park encompasses 690 sq km, and deciding where to go can be a daunting task. Your hotel should provide you with a map and also help you plan out a route best suited for your needs.

The first thing to know is that there are two primary entrances: the main gateway town of Wulingyuan (武陵源, Wǔlíngyuán) and the less-developed Forest Park (森林公园, Sēnlín Gōngyuán). There are other entrances as well, but you won't use them unless you've booked lodging there.

Regardless of the entrance you take, all itineraries start on the valley floor and climb up to the top of the spires, where the main scenic areas are found. You can make use of cable cars, a glass elevator, a mini monorail and a network of free shuttle buses to get

Zhangjiajie

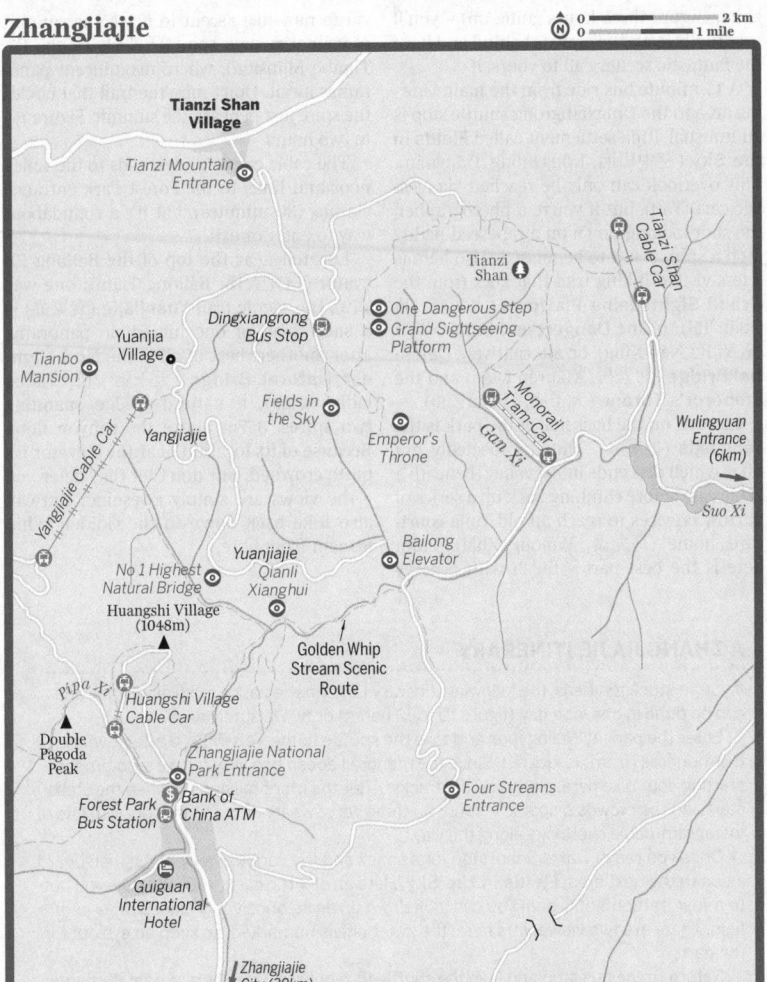

around, but however you do it, you'll still need to walk a fair amount.

If you're starting in Wulingyuan, you'll need to queue for a bus to either the chairlift or the monorail (hikers go to the monorail) at the entrance – don't get in the wrong line, and don't get intimidated by the sheer chaos and theme park–like crowds here. The park is big enough to absorb vast numbers of people, and if you're hiking most of the way, you'll have no trouble finding solitude.

If you start at the Forest Park, you'll need to hike roughly two hours along the flat valley floor to the elevator, or begin climbing up to the upper section after an hour.

In total, there are five main scenic areas: Tianzi Shan, Yangjiajie, Yuanjiajie, Golden Whip Stream and Huangshi Village. You can't see all the areas in one day, so plan accordingly.

Weather wise, it's extremely hot and humid from April through September. Rain is common, so come prepared.

Tiānzǐ Shān (天子山) is at the top of the plateau near the Wulingyuan entrance, and enjoys many of the park's more spectacular viewpoints. It can be reached directly by cable car (¥72), which makes the main lookouts quite crowded, but if you use the stairs instead – follow the monorail and keep going (figure three hours going up) – you'll eventually leave the crowds behind and have the fantastic scenery all to yourself.

A 15-minute bus ride from the main viewing area to the Dingxiangrong shuttle stop is an unusual Tujia settlement called **Fields in the Sky** (空中田园, Kōngzhōng Tiānyuán). This overlook can only be reached via electric cart (¥50), but if you're a photographer, the shot looking down on a rapeseed paddy atop a spire is not to be missed. Also here is a less-visited hiking trail that goes from the **Grand Sightseeing Platform** (大观台, Dà Guān Tái) to **One Dangerous Step** (一步难行, Yī Bù Nán Xíng), or, alternatively, **Celestial Bridge** (仙人桥, Xiānrén Qiáo) and the **Emperor's Throne** (天子座, Tiānzǐ Zuò).

Located on the backside of the park is the **Yángjiājiè** (杨家界). This unexpectedly fun hike, which descends into a valley (beneath a cable car) before climbing back up a series of narrow crevices to reach an old Tujia courtyard home (乌龙寨, Wūlóng Zhài). From here is the best part – finish with a nervy

via ferrata–like ascent to reach the summit of your very own spire (天波府, Tiānbō Fǔ, Tianbo Mansion), where magnificent panoramas await. Don't miss the trail that circles the spire just beneath the summit. Figure 1½ to two hours.

The cable car (¥76) descends to the valley floor and links to the Forest Park entrance via bus (30 minutes), but it's a roundabout way to enter or exit.

Located near the top of the Bailong Elevator (白龙天梯; Báilóng Tiāntī; one way ¥72), the scenic trail **Yuánjiājiè** (袁家界) is a succession of one incredible panorama after another: best of all is the **No 1 Highest Natural Bridge** (天下第一桥, Tiānxiàdìyī Qiáo), a natural bridge spanning two spires, 357m above the canyon floor. Because of its location near the elevator it's quite crowded, but don't let that deter you – the views are simply awesome. You can also hike back down to the Golden Whip Stream from here.

A ZHANGJIAJIE ITINERARY

If you're stuck for ideas, the following itinerary takes in the park's main highlights, and can be done in one long day (figure 10 to 12 hours) or two leisurely days.

Enter the park at Wulingyuan and take the shuttle to the **Ten-Mile Gallery**, where the monorail (tram) is located. Since the monorail doesn't go very far, we recommend starting your hike here, alongside the tracks. After the monorail ends is when the steps start and the crowds disperse – count on three very sweaty hours to the top, with lots of Instagrammable overlooks along the way.

Once you reach Tianzi Shan, stop for a snack and the various viewpoints, then board a bus to the next area, **Fields in the Sky**. Here an electric cart (¥50) will take you out to a Tujia settlement, where you can look down on an inconceivably placed rapeseed field. There are two viewpoints here; the lower one is unmarked, so keep an eye out for the path.

Return to the bus stop and take the shuttle to Yangjiajie. From here, a path descends into a valley, then climbs back up the other through a series of narrow fissures in the rock and past another Tujia settlement, eventually reaching the top of a pinnacle, which must be ascended via a steel ladder. Don't skip this area, unless you are afraid of heights. Figure on two hours for the return trip.

The next stop is Yuanjiajie, from where you can follow a 90-minute path to some of the park's most famous vistas, including the **No 1 Highest Natural Bridge** and the **Heavenly Pillar**.

From here, you can take the shuttle to the **Bailong Elevator** (the world's highest outdoor lift; ¥72), descend to the valley floor, and then board another shuttle to take you all the way back to the park entrance at Wulingyuan. Be forewarned that the queues to board the final shuttle can be very long (up to an hour) at the end of the day, but you don't have much of a choice, unless you are returning to Zhangjiajie city instead of Wulingyuan.

If you'd rather enter the park at the slightly quieter Forest Park entrance instead, you can follow Golden Whip Stream to either the elevator or the steps climbing up the cliff at Qiānlǐ Xiānghuì (千里相会), which leads to Yuanjiajie. From here, you can do the trip in reverse, though remember you'll have to exit the park at Wulingyuan.

On the canyon floor, the **Golden Whip Stream** (金鞭溪, Jīnbiān Xī) area is a peaceful, flat trail meandering 5.7km east from the Forest Park entrance to the Bailong Elevator, a cliffside lift rising 335m in under two minutes to the Yuanjiajie area. If you'd rather walk the whole way, about halfway to the elevator are steps climbing up the cliff to Yuanjiajie (one hour). This is Zhangjiajie's main access route if coming from Forest Park.

From the Forest Park entrance, there is an early opportunity for a bird's-eye view of the towers from **Huangshi Village** (黄石寨, Huángshí Zhài), a 3km loop on a plateau 1048m up. It's a two-hour slog up 3878 stone steps, or a half-hour by bus, then cable car (one way ¥70).

Tianmen Mountain   MOUNTAIN
(天门山, Tiānmén Shān; off Yingbin Lu, 迎宾路; ¥258; ⏰ 6.30am-4pm) Visible from anywhere in Zhangjiajie City, this distinctive mountain range features **Tiānmén Dòng** (天门洞), a prominent keyhole cut through the mountainside. The seriously lengthy 7km-long **Tianmen Mountain Cable Car** (天门山索道, Tiānmén Shān Suǒdào) is Asia's longest, and takes half an hour to hoist you up. The cable car is included in your entrance ticket. There are several glass-bottomed walkways at the top.

It's a 10-minute walk to the cable-car station from Zhangjiajie's bus and train stations. Follow the main street leading north from the train station until you see the entrance on your left. Keep the cable car on your left as you go.

Zhangjiajie Grand Canyon   GORGE
(张家界大峡谷, Zhāngjiājiè Dàxiágǔ; ¥219) The Grand Canyon's primary attraction is the world's highest (300m) and longest (430m) glass bridge, which famously closed a mere two weeks after opening in 2016 when officials realised that visitation was going to exceed their projections by a factor of 10. If that didn't clue you in, we'll say it again: this is a very crowded place. Unless you're excited about seeing the bridge, you can skip it. No cameras allowed.

🏃 Activities

With more than 40 caves hidden along the banks of the Suoxi River and the southeast side of Tiānzǐ Shān, the region offers ample opportunities to **raft** (漂流, piāoliú) and tour caves. Your lodging should be able to organise day trips – expect to pay between ¥200 and ¥250. Trips usually run from June through September.

🛏 Sleeping

Most hotels are in either Wulingyuan or Zhangjiajie city (known as 'Yongding' on booking websites). The other park entrances also have a few options. There are easily over 100 hotels in the area, but the vast majority have no English-speaking staff. The most competent places will send instructions in English detailing the hotel's location and transportation options immediately after booking.

🛏 Wulingyuan

★ 1982 International Youth Hostel   HOSTEL ¥
(1982初见客栈, Yījiǔbā'èr Chūjiàn Kèzhàn; ☎ 0744 555 5866; 1 Tuofeng Lu, 武陵源区驼峰路1号; dm ¥33, d from ¥170; ❄@🛜) The top pick in Wulingyuan, this hostel features spacious double rooms with faux lattice decor, six-person dorms and a huge 2nd-floor cafe and restaurant with a pool table and evening movies. Its sister hostel, Wulingyuantuniu, is also a good choice, though rooms aren't as nice. The staff speak English at both places and will help plan park itineraries.

Laundry is ¥10.

Wulingyuantuniu Youth Hostel   HOSTEL ¥
(武陵源途牛青年旅舍, Wǔlíngyuán Túniú Qīngnián Lǚshè; ☎ 0744 555 5444; off Jundi Lu, 武陵源区军邸路; dm ¥30-35, d ¥130-180; ❄🛜) Amenities are minimal (no food or laundry), but the staff speak English and are full of good advice for planning your day. It's just around the corner from the Wulingyuan park entrance and a seven-minute walk from the bus station. Good wi-fi.

Floral Hotel   HOTEL ¥¥
(花筑酒店, Huāzhù Jiǔdiàn; ☎ 0744 595 8998; 327 Jundi Lu, 武陵源区军邸路327号; d ¥200; ❄🛜) Bright modern rooms with a touch of style make this a good midrange choice in Wuyuan. To get here, turn left out of the bus station, make another left onto Jundi Lu, and the hotel will be on your left after five minutes or so. Basic English spoken.

🛏 Zhangjiajie City

Mini Inn   HOTEL ¥
(觅你客栈, Mìnǐ Kèzhàn; ☎ 166 0744 8606; Pengjiapu District, off Guanli Lu, 张家界市官黎坪彭家

HUNAN ZHANGJIAJIE

BINGLANG VALLEY

If you speak some Chinese and want to get well off the beaten track, the staggeringly beautiful **Binglang Valley** (槟榔谷, Bīngláng Gǔ) and its caves, natural arches and vertiginous cliffs, 90 minutes by bus from town, makes for a sublime overnight expedition. You begin by descending through a beautiful flat valley called **Moon Valley** (月之谷, Yuè Zhi Gǔ), surrounded by cliffs, before climbing to a vast cave called **Cathedral Gate** (教堂们, Jiàotáng Mén), after which you thread through a bamboo forest to make your way towards a 1km-long **subterranean cave**.

On the way you will pass the **Two Layer Cave** (双层洞, Shuāngcéng Dòng) before reaching the astonishing **Angel Castle** (天使城, Tiānshǐ Chéng) – a formation of vast cliffs that encircles you – with the **Angel Gate** (天使门, Tiānshǐ Mén) at the far end, a further cave that drills through the entire cliff to the far side.

A low-hanging cave entrance on the far side of the valley leads to the **Mí Cave** (迷洞, Mí Dòng), but whatever you do, don't enter without a guide and a headlamp. It's 1km long, pitch black, devoid of mobile signal and if you take a wrong turn, you could easily get lost. But it's an astonishing experience. One section is full of litter, not dropped by visitors, but swept in by river waters that flow in here during the rainy season (though usually only to a shallow depth). Eventually – after about half an hour of walking in the dark – you will see the faint glow of the exit, a cavernous opening leading to a breathtaking valley called **Star Valley** (星之谷, Xīng Zhī Gǔ) surrounded by colossal limestone cliffs. Give a good shout: the echo acoustics are phenomenal.

Not far away is **Binglang Hole** (槟榔孔, Bīnláng Kǒng), another natural cave leading through to the other side, from where you can make your way back to the bus drop-off point. Locals still use the naturally formed cave to reach villages on the far side, thus avoiding a circuitous detour.

To reach Binglang Valley, take a taxi (¥20) to the pick-up point (大庸桥西站, dàyōng-qiáo xīzhàn) in Zhangjiajie City and then take a bus (¥17, 90 minutes, 8.30am) towards Qīng'ān Píng (青安坪) and disembark at Bīnglángǔ Nóngjiā Lè (槟榔谷农家乐), simply the name of a family homestead by the valley access point. The return buses are at 8.30am and 1.30pm, which means you'll likely need to stay the night. The **Fùguì Shānzhuāng** (富贵山庄; ☑153 8744 3719; r ¥100; P) can arrange lodging and a guide (¥200, no English), but make sure you ask your Zhangjiajie hotel for help in arranging everything as the bus schedules and pick-up point are subject to change.

铺小区; r ¥100-180; ❄☎) A stylish midrange option, the Mini Inn is consistently booked up, so make reservations well in advance. It's part of the Penjiapu guesthouse district, a 10-minute walk down Guanli Lu left out of the train and bus stations.

Hostel Geographer
HOSTEL ¥

(地理学家客栈, Dìlǐ Xuéjiā Kèzhàn; ☑173 4269 3636; Pengjiapu District, off Guanli Lu, 张家界市官黎坪彭家铺小区; dm ¥36, d ¥92-115; ❄☎) Great-value rooms at the Geographer come with hot showers and industrially cool decor – there are even floor-to-ceiling windows in some double rooms. The downstairs lounge serves coffee and meals, and can provide other extras like ticket booking and laundry service (though at ¥40 it's comparatively expensive). English spoken.

It's also part of the Penjiapu guesthouse district.

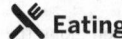 Forest Park

Guiguan International Hotel
HOTEL ¥¥¥

(桂冠国际酒店, Guìguān Guójì Jiǔdiàn; ☑0744 571 2999; Forest Park entrance, 森林公园; d ¥680-1280; ❄☎) If you want to get away from the crowds, this peaceful four-star hotel is a short walk before you reach the Forest Park entrance and is interspersed with pleasant courtyard gardens sprouting magnolias and water features. The most affordable standard rooms are discounted to ¥460, which is quite reasonable; rooms with mountain view will set you back more.

✗ Eating

Snack stalls line all the main hiking trails around the park. Expect fried potatoes, noodles, fried cakes and bowls of kudzu-root jelly (the clear gelatinous stuff – try it!). Local restaurants are plentiful in both Wulingyuan and Zhangjiajie city.

ℹ Information

There are ATMs in Zhangjiajie city and at the Wulingyuan and Forest Park entrances.

ℹ Getting There & Away

AIR

Zhangjiajie Hehua Airport (张家界荷花机场, Zhāngjiājiè Héhuā Jīchǎng; ☏ 0744 823 8417) is 6km southwest of Zhangjiajie City and about 36km south of Wulingyuan.

There are flights to Beijing, Changsha, Chengdu, Chongqing, Guangzhou, Shanghai, Xi'an and other domestic destinations. Use www.trip.com to book.

BUS

Buses leave from **Central Bus Station** (中心汽车站, Zhōngxīn Qìchēzhàn; ☏ 0744 822 2417), right beside Zhangjiajie train station, to destinations including the following:

Changsha ¥120, 4½ hours, hourly (7am to 7pm)
Fenghuang ¥80, four hours, six daily (8.30am, 9.30am, 12.30pm, 2.30pm, 3.30pm and 5.20pm)
Furong ¥30, 1½ hours, hourly (7.30am to 5pm)

A few buses also run direct from **Wulingyuan Bus Station** (武陵源汽车站, Wǔlíngyuán Qìchēzhàn), allowing you to bypass Zhangjiajie city. These include the following:

Changsha ¥103, 4½ hours, three daily (8.20am, 1.20pm and 3pm)
Fenghuang ¥105, 4½ hours, two daily (8.30am and 2.30pm)

TRAIN

Zhangjiajie has rail connections with a number of cities around China; however, seats are limited and sell out quickly. Book as far in advance as possible. The **train station** (火车站, Huǒchēzhàn; ☏ 0744 214 5182) is right beside Central Bus Station. Destination include the following:

Beijing Hard/soft sleeper ¥370/581, 24 to 28 hours, three daily (12.37pm, 1.22pm and 2.35pm)
Changsha Hard seat ¥55 to ¥84, 4½ to 5½ hours, seven daily
Huaihua Hard seat ¥38, 3½ to 4½ hours, 12 daily
Jishou Hard seat ¥20, two hours, 12 daily
Yichang Hard seat/sleeper ¥44/101, five hours, two daily (5.53am and 9.03am)

ℹ Getting Around

TO/FROM THE AIRPORT

A taxi from the airport costs about ¥30 to Zhangjiajie city and ¥160 to Wulingyuan. To reach the airport from the city, take local bus 4 (¥2, 5.30am to 8.30pm) from outside the Tianmen Mountain Cable Car; the journey takes around 30 minutes.

TO/FROM THE PARK

Shuttle buses travel every 10 minutes from Zhangjiajie Central Bus Station to the three park entrances, from roughly 6.30am to 7pm: Wulingyuan (武陵源; ¥13, one hour), Forest Park (森林公园, Sēnlín Gōngyuán; ¥12, 50 minutes), and Tianzi Shan (天子山; ¥12, one hour, less frequent). Buses also run between the entrance points (¥10, 30 minutes), allowing you to bypass Zhangjiajie city if need be. Buy tickets on board the bus.

Once inside the park, all buses are free with your park ticket, and run from 7am to roughly 8pm or whenever the last visitors leave.

A taxi from the city to Wulingyuan costs around ¥160, and to the Forest Park entrance costs around ¥120.

Dehang 德夯

☏ 0743 / POP 500

Set against a backdrop of forested peaks, the Miao village of Dehang (Déhāng; ¥80) is a fabulous place to spend the night and explore the surrounding scenery with short and easy-to-follow hikes.

While the town has been largely rebuilt, there's no denying its magnificent setting. Just past the main square are two separate trails: the **Nine Dragon Stream Scenic Area** (九龙溪景区, Jiǔlóngxī Jǐngqū), which leads to the 216m-tall **Liusha Waterfall** (流沙瀑布, Liúshā Pùbù), one of China's tallest (although very skinny), and the lovely **Yuquanxi Scenic Area** (玉泉溪景区, Yùquánxī Jǐngqū).

Liusha Waterfall concludes a lovely walk beyond the village. You can climb up behind the curtain of water, which is fun, though slippery. It takes about two hours to get to the waterfall and back, walking alongside a stream and through a verdant canyon. Don't miss the smaller waterfall on your right, about halfway along.

In the **Yuguanxi Scenic Area**, a 2.6km-long hike follows a path along the Yuquan Stream, past terraced fields and delightful views. Cross the **Jade Spring Gate** (玉泉门, Yùquán Mén) to make your way to a waterfall and, if you've the energy, climb the steps up to the Tianwen Platform (天问台, Tiānwèn Tái) for glorious views.

Simple guesthouses (客栈, kèzhàn) are found throughout town and adjacent to the gurgling stream (past the circular performance venue). Rooms are all ¥100 and come with wi-fi. There's a loud nightly performance (in Chinese) at 7pm, but otherwise it's a very peaceful place to stay.

Restaurants are clustered throughout town. Hawkers also proffer small bites, including skewers of grilled fish, tiny crabs and grubs.

ⓘ Getting There & Away

Dehang is accessed from the town of Jishou (吉首). Bus 11 runs from the Jishou train station to Aizhai (挨寨; ¥3, 40 minutes, 6.30am to 6pm). From Aizhai, it's a 3.5km walk to town (you may be able to convince the driver to take you all the way, but don't count on it). When returning to Jishou, ask the ticket office to call a driver to take you to Aizhai.

Next to the train station, you can catch frequent buses to Fenghuang (¥25, one hour, 7am to 5.30pm), Huaihua (¥42, two hours, 7.20am to 5.40pm) and Changsha (¥120, five hours, 7.20am to 6.30pm) from Jishou's north bus station.

Frequent trains serve Zhangjiajie (¥19.50, about two hours, 6.30am to 5pm) and, less frequently, Huaihua (¥16.50, about two hours, 8am to 9pm).

Fenghuang 凤凰

☑ 0743 / POP 57,000

Once a frontier town, Fenghuang (Fènghuáng) marked the boundary between the Han civilisations of the central plains and the Miao (苗), Tujia (土家) and Dong (侗) minorities of the southwest mountains. Protective walls went up in the Ming dynasty, but despite the implications Fenghuang prospered as a centre of trade and cultural exchange. Its diverse residents built a breathtaking riverside settlement of winding alleys, temples and rickety stilt houses, which these days attract tourists by the bucketload. Do try to stay overnight – the town is bursting with accommodation options, and the sight of an illuminated Fenghuang at night is quite awesome.

◉ Sights

Wandering aimlessly is the best way to experience the charms of the **old town** (古城, gǔchéng). The back alleys, especially outside the city walls to the north and east, is a trove of shops, ancestral halls and courtyard homes. You'll see the exteriors of a few temples too; however, on our last visit they were all closed or repurposed for other uses.

Strolling through the old town is free, though in order to enter the featured buildings you'll need a **through ticket** (通票,

tōngpiào; ¥128), which grants you two-day access to nine sights plus a half-hour boat trip on the river. The ticket office is at the **North Gate** (北门城楼, Běimén Chénglóu; ⓢ 8am-11pm). Alternatively, you can pick and choose what you want to see – as many sights are of minimal interest and have no English explanations, this might be a better plan. Individual tickets cost ¥30 to ¥40 per sight.

Sights are generally open 8am to 6pm. Come nightfall, much of the old town is dazzlingly illuminated, making it one of the most photogenic sights in China.

◉ Inside the City Wall

Fenghuang City Wall   HISTORIC SITE
(城墙, Chéngqiáng) Restored fragments of the city wall lie along the south bank of the Tuo River. Carvings of fish and mythical beasts adorn the eaves of the North Gate Tower, one of four original main gates. Another, the **East Gate Tower** (东门城楼, Dōngmén Chénglóu; ¥30 or through ticket), is a twin-eaved tower of sandstone and fired brick.

Hong Bridge   BRIDGE
(虹桥, Hóng Qiáo; ¥30 or through ticket for upstairs galleries) In the style of the Dong minority's Wind and Rain bridges, this attractive structure vaults the waters of the Tuo River and is illuminated at night. Like some other sights in Fenghuang, it's best viewed from a distance.

Chaoyang Temple   TAOIST TEMPLE
(朝阳宫, Cháoyáng Gōng; 41 Wenxing Jie, 文兴街41号) **FREE** This small, one-time Taoist temple is now home to a silversmithing training centre.

Wanshou Temple   HISTORIC SITE
(万寿宫, Wànshòu Gōng; ¥40 or through ticket) Built in 1755, this assembly hall north of Wanming Pagoda served as the Jiangxi guildhall for almost 200 years. It now has dance performances every half-hour from 8.30am to noon, and houses an art gallery with temporary exhibits (no English).

Yang Family Ancestral Hall   HISTORIC SITE
(杨家祠堂, Yángjiā Cítáng; Laocai Jie, 老菜街; ¥40 or through ticket) Built in 1836, this building's exterior (by the door) still has some faded slogans from the Cultural Revolution. There are two lovely black-and-white frescoes of mythical animals on the rear walls of the main hall. From 8.30am to noon there are half-hourly performances of Miao rituals.

Fenghuang

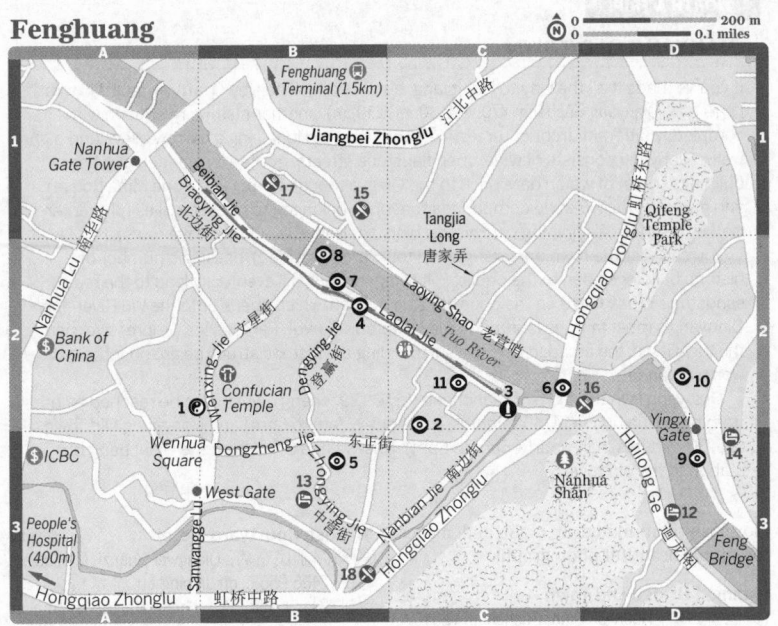

Fenghuang

🅞 Sights
1 Chaoyang Temple A2
2 Chongde Hall C2
3 East Gate Tower C2
4 Fenghuang City Wall B2
5 Former Home of Shen Congwen B3
6 Hong Bridge C2
7 North Gate Tower B2
8 Stepping Stones B2
9 Wanming Pagoda D3
10 Wanshou Temple D2
11 Yang Family Ancestral Hall C2

🛏 Sleeping
12 A Good Year D3
13 Shi'er Hao Shiguang Hostel B3
14 Yinji Inn D3

🍴 Eating
15 Miss Yang Restaurant B1
16 Soul Cafe D2
17 Soul Too B1
18 Zuì Xiāngxī B3

Chongde Hall
HISTORIC SITE

(崇德堂, Chóngdé Táng; Shijia Long, 史家弄; ¥40 or through ticket) The town's wealthiest resident, Pei Shoulu, has his personal collection of antiques on display in his former residence on Shijia Long. The collection of carved wood lintels, decorative woodwork and inscribed wooden wall plaques is simply gorgeous.

Former Home of Shen Congwen
HISTORIC SITE

(沈从文故居, Shěn Cóngwén Gùjū; 21 Zhongying Jie, 中营街21号; ¥40 or through ticket) The famous modern novelist was born here in 1902. (His tomb is east of town.) His most

famous novel – *Border Town* (边城) – is definitely worth a read.

🅞 Outside the City Wall

The north bank of the river offers lovely views of Fenghuang's diàojiǎolóu (吊脚楼, stilt houses). Cross by **stepping stones** – best navigated when sober – or the wooden footbridge (木头桥, mùtóu qiáo). Huilong Ge, along the south bank east of the city walls, is also a delightful place to stroll.

Wanming Pagoda
PAGODA

(万名塔, Wànmíng Tǎ) This elegant and slim pagoda was built during the reign of Emperor Jiaqing. It cannot be climbed, but is

HUNAN FENGHUANG

QIANYANG OLD TOWN

If you've made it all the way to Hongjiang, don't overlook nearby **Qianyang Old Town** (黔阳古城, Qiányáng Gǔchéng; ¥70; ⏱8.30am-5.30pm), another historic river town with a completely different architectural style. In contrast to Hongjiang's narrow alleys and high walls, Qianyang consists of wide-open flagstone streets, fronted by wooden clapboard buildings (most of which date back to the Qing, although there is also one Ming house) and grander *yinziwu*-style compounds that once belonged to noble families (characterised by a series of adjoining courtyards, high exterior walls and concave roofs).

You can visit the town on a self-guided tour (map provided), passing a number of historic buildings open to the public. Following the tour will eventually lead to the red sandstone **West Gate** on the opposite side of town, which opens onto the Wu River and Qianyang's most famous landmark, the **Hibiscus Tower**. Perhaps less impressive than the town itself, the arcaded gardens surrounding the historic structure are nonetheless worth a wander.

Qianyang is in the town of Qiancheng (黔城, Qiánchéng), which can be reached by bus from both Huaihua (¥14, 45 minutes, half-hourly, 7am to 6pm) and Hongjiang Old Town (¥6, 30 minutes, half-hourly, 6am to 6pm). Buses 1 and 2 run from the Qiancheng bus station to the old town.

gloriously illuminated at night and makes for simply beautiful photographs.

Huangsi Bridge Old Town
VILLAGE

(黄丝桥古城, Huángsī Qiáo Gǔchéng; ¥20) A Tang dynasty military outpost, this village is well preserved and of interest to architecture buffs. Located 25km west of town, you'll need to take a taxi here; it's ¥160 return trip.

Southern Great Wall
ARCHITECTURE

(南方长城, Nánfāng Chángchéng; ¥45) The Ming dynasty defensive wall, 13km west of town, once stretched to Guizhou province. It's been largely rebuilt, though it does provide nice views of the countryside.You'll need to take a taxi here; it's ¥120 return trip.

🛏 Sleeping

Fenghuang is stuffed with guesthouses (客栈, kèzhàn). River-view rooms come at a premium, but may also be a bit damp. All places have wi-fi, but reception can be bad in many rooms, so check first. Look for the sign 今日有房, which means 'rooms available'; book ahead for weekends and holidays. Aircon may cost an extra ¥20 at some places.

Shi'er Hao Shiguang Hostel
HOSTEL ¥

(十二号时光国际青年旅舍, Shí'èr Hào Shíguāng Guójì Qīngnián Lǚshě; ☑0743 350 0302, 137 6210 6759; 12 Zhongying Jie, 中营街12号; dm ¥35, d from ¥108; ❅⏵) A friendly, laid-back hostel with a quiet, back-alley location on historic Zhongying Jie. The eight-person bunks are a bit cramped, but the doubles are bright and comfortable. Basic English.

★ Rose Courtyard Hotel
HOTEL ¥¥

(蔷薇院子民宿店, Qiángwēi Yuànzi Mínsùdiàn; ☑177 7436 9553; off Jinping Lu, 金水桥头江北新村22号; r ¥98-286) There's a lot to like at this stylish hotel: it's got soft beds, excellent English-speaking staff who go out of their way to help, useful information, and a great location next to a market. It's just down the street from the bus station, near the old town. Rooms are spread out over two buildings.

A Good Year
GUESTHOUSE ¥¥

(一年好时光, Yī Nián Hǎo Shíguāng; ☑0743 322 2026; 91 Huilong Ge, 迴龙阁91号; r ¥168-228; ❅⏵) There are just 10 rooms in this sweet, wood-framed inn on the river; all have balconies, but six have fantastic river views (¥228) and swinging chairs. The owners are welcoming (but no English) and the location is quiet and secluded, tucked away a fair distance along Huilong Ge. Take a taxi to Feng Bridge (凤桥, Féng Qiáo) and cross from there.

Yinji Inn
BOUTIQUE HOTEL ¥¥¥

(印记客栈, Yìnjì Kèzhàn; ☑0743 322 6994, 186 0743 3537; 24-25 Baoziwan Lu, 豹子湾路24-25号; d¥265-557; ❅⏵) With a terrace perched above the Wanming Pagoda and fine views of the river and Hong Bridge come nightfall, this boutique property done up in grey brick and wood accents is the best choice for upmarket lodging in Fenghuang. You'll need to climb some stairs to access the hotel. English is spoken.

Eating

★ Zuì Xiāngxī
HUNAN ¥¥

(醉湘西; ☏ 134 0743 6565; 97 Hongqiao Zhong-lu, 虹桥中路97号; dishes ¥18-68; ⏲ 11am-9pm)
One of Fenghuang's most popular restau-rants, the speciality here is a type of fish stew (石锅鱼, *shíguō yú*), cooked at your ta-ble in a delectable broth. It's a Chinese menu only, but the owner speaks some English and the red stars indicate house specialities. Also good is the cauliflower drypot (干锅有机花菜, *gānguō yǒujī huācài*), loaded with chillies and garlic.

Miss Yang Restaurant
HUNAN ¥¥

(杨小姐的餐厅, Yángxiǎojiě de Cāntīng; 48 Laoying Shao, 老营哨48号; dishes ¥25-88; ⏲ 10am-10pm)
Specialising in local cuisine, particularly that of the Miao and Tujia people, such as Tuo River fish (沱江小鱼, *Tuó Jiāng xiǎoyú*), this intimate restaurant serves tasty de-lights in an atmospheric upstairs setting of varnished-wood furniture and colourful cushions. It also does a classic Jiangxi chick-en stew called *sān bēi jī* (三杯鸡), and its cured pork (腊肉, *là ròu*) dishes are superb.

Soul Cafe
ITALIAN ¥¥

(亦素咖啡, Yìsù Kāfēi; 17 Huilong Ge, 回龙阁17号; mains ¥38-65; ⏲ 8.30am-11.30pm; 🛜) This upmarket cafe serves proper coffee (from ¥28) and the setting is lovely, with sofas, comfy chairs, lampshades everywhere and river views. If you want to push the boat out, there are imported wines, Cuban cigars and hookah pipes (¥90).

A **second location** (16 Laoying Shao, 老营哨16号) is across the river.

ⓘ Information

You can change money at the **Bank of China** (中国银行, Zhōngguó Yínháng; Nanhua Lu, 南华路; ⏲ 9am-5pm Mon-Fri). A branch of **ICBC** (工商银行, Gōngshāng Yínháng; Nanhua Lu, 南华路; ⏲ 9am-5pm Mon-Sat) is a bit further down.

People's Hospital (人民医院, Rénmín Yīyuàn; ☏ 0743 322 1199; Hongqiao Xilu, 虹桥西路)
Southwest of town near the Fenghuang Nanlu intersection.

ⓘ Getting There & Away

Buses from Fenghuang bus terminal (汽车客运总站, qìchē kèyùn zǒngzhàn) include the following:

Changsha West ¥162, 5½ hours, nine daily (7.30am to 5.30pm)

Guilin ¥180, 6½ hours, one daily (11am)

Huaihua South Station ¥40, 80 minutes, hourly(8am to 6pm)

Jishou ¥22, one hour, frequent (6.30am to 7.30pm)

Wulingyuan ¥100, 4½ hours, two daily (9am and 2.30pm)

Zhangjiajie ¥82, 3½ hours, eight daily (9am to 5pm)

There are also frequent buses to Tongren (铜仁; ¥25, 1½ hours, 7am to 4.30pm), from where you can change for Zhenyuan in Guizhou province.

ⓘ Getting Around

Taxis charge a flat ¥10 to ¥15 from the bus sta-tion to hotels around town. No meters.

Hongjiang Old Town 洪江古商城

☏ 0745 / POP 61,000

This little-known town boasts an extraordi-nary history as a Qing dynasty financial and trading centre, due to its fortuitous location at the confluence of the Yuan (沅江, Yuán Jiāng) and Wu (巫水, Wū Shuǐ) rivers. At one time it was the main opium-distribution hub in southwest China. Dating as far back as the Northern Song dynasty, the surround-ing city is mostly modern now, but the past lives on in the remarkable old town.

While not as visually dramatic as Feng-huang, Hongjiang is culturally more inter-esting, with a better selection of buildings that can be visited and fewer tour groups wandering the streets. On the road between Huaihai and Hongjiang is another rarely visited old town, Qianyang.

The **old town** (洪江古商城, Hóngjiāng Gǔ Shāngchéng; Xingfu Lu, 幸福路; ¥90; ⏲ 8am-5pm) can be visited in half a day, and undu-lates in a delightful, higgledy-piggledy, often steep, maze of narrow stone-flagged alleys and lanes. English and Chinese signposts point the way to the more worthy buildings, most of which have been fully restored.

Notable buildings include the tax office, an opium shop, a brothel, a pharmacy, a newspaper office, ancestral halls, courtyard homes of prominent merchants and sever-al guildhalls (会馆, *huìguǎn*), including the superb facade of the **Taiping Palace** (太平宫, Tàipíng Gōng). The main entrance is off Xingfu Lu, across the smaller Wu River from the bus station.

On our last visit, foreigners were prohibit-ed from spending the night in either Hong-jiang or Qianyang. However, it's worth calling

Qianyang's **Hibiscus Guesthouse** (芙蓉客栈, Fúróng Kèzhàn; ☑ 181 7451 8515; Yanhe Xilu, 沿河西路; r ¥148-188; ❉ ☎), set in a charming old wooden building by the river, to see if the situation has changed, as the setting is lovely. If both towns remain closed, the only place to spend the night is in Huaihua.

❶ Getting There & Away

BUS

Don't confuse Hongjiang Old Town with Hongjiang City (洪江市, Hóngjiāng Shì), the town 30km west. The old town is most easily reached via the town of Huaihua (怀化).

Buses to and from Hongjiang Old Town (¥25, 80 minutes, half-hourly, 6.30am to 6.40pm) and Qiancheng depart from Huaihua's south station.

Buses to and from Fenghuang (¥40, one hour, hourly, 7am to 6pm) use the Huaihua west train and bus station (西站, xīzhàn), but there are also direct buses (80 minutes, hourly, 10am to 6pm) to and from the south train and bus station (南站, nánzhàn), which is more convenient if you can catch one.

Local bus 12 (¥2) links Huaihua's west and south stations.

Buses back to Huaihua from Hongjiang Old Town (6.30am to 6pm) leave from the **bus station** (洪江汽车站, Hóngjiāng Qìchēzhàn; 416 Nanyue Lu, 南岳路416号). It's a 15-minute walk to the old town across the bridge from the bus station, or a ¥5 taxi ride.

TRAIN

High-speed trains run regularly from Huaihua to Changsha (¥150, 1½ to 2½ hours) from the south station. Regular trains to Jishou (¥17, 1½ hours) and Zhangjiajie (¥38, 3½ hours) run frequently from the west station.

Furong Zhen   芙蓉镇

☑ 0743 / POP 17,000

The road between Jishou and Zhangjiajie runs through hills, terraced fields and minority villages, and past rivers and lush, verdant scenery via the Tujia settlement of Furong (Fúróng Zhèn), an old town elevated to fame in the 1986 film *Hibiscus Town*. Until around 10 years ago, the town was simply called Wang Village (王村, Wáng Cūn), before being renamed in honour of the movie. Wandering down the steps of the old riverside town is charming, but the main draw is the gushing waterfall alongside the hamlet, splendidly illuminated come nightfall.

Wandering down the village (¥80) main street, which descends in steps to the wharf and the You River at its foot, is a charming excursion. Historic buildings on the way down include the **Guanyin Hall** (观音阁, Guānyīn Gé; No 105) and the **Tóngzhù Guǎn** (铜柱馆; No 15). The highlight, however, is the **Furong Zhen Waterfall** (芙蓉镇瀑布, Fúróng Zhèn Pùbù), which divides the village and can be crossed via stepping stones to the far side, affording the most amazing views of the town, especially at sundown as the lights begin twinkling. Have a camera ready.

There are numerous hotels and guesthouses in and around the old town where you can find a double room with shower for the night for around ¥150 to ¥250. Hotels in the new town go for about ¥100.

There are a few restaurants as you walk down the main steps to the river, with tables overlooking the waterfall, which serve up a variety of local and regional dishes. Expect to pay around ¥20 to ¥40 per dish.

Regular buses (¥30, one hour) run between Jishou north bus station and Furong Zhen from 7.30am to 5pm. Buses (¥30, 90 minutes) run hourly from the bus station in Furong Zhen to Zhangjiajie between 7.30am and 5pm. It's a dusty 2km walk from the bus station (汽车站, qìchēzhàn) to the old town (古镇, gǔzhèn). Unfortunately, the green carts whisking visitors around near the old town go to the tour bus parking lot, not the bus station.

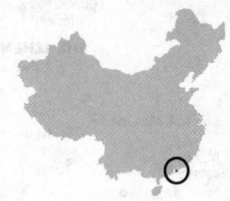

Hong Kong

♪ 852 / POP 7.45 MILLION

Best Places to Eat

➡ Kau Kee Restaurant (p543)

➡ Old Bailey (p543)

➡ Aberdeen Fish Market Yee Hope Seafood Restaurant (p545)

➡ Yè Shanghai (p545)

➡ Seventh Son (p545)

Best Places to Stay

➡ Peninsula Hong Kong (p542)

➡ Hotel Indigo (p541)

➡ Upper House (p541)

➡ Helena May (p540)

Why Go?

Like a shot of adrenaline, Hong Kong quickens the pulse. Skyscrapers march up jungle-clad slopes by day and blaze neon by night across a harbour criss-crossed by freighters and motor junks. Above streets teeming with traffic, five-star hotels stand next to ageing tenement blocks.

The very acme of luxury can be yours, though enjoying the city need not cost the earth. The HK$2.50 ride across the harbour must be one of the world's best-value cruises. A meander through a market offers similarly cheap thrills. You can also escape the crowds – just head for one of the city's many country parks.

It's also a city that lives to eat, offering diners the very best of China and beyond. Hong Kong, above all, rewards those who grab experiences by the scruff of the neck, who'll try that stinky tofu, explore half-deserted villages or stroll beaches far from neon and steel.

When to Go
Hong Kong

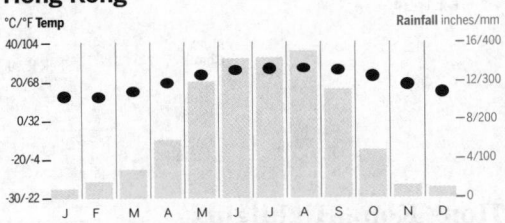

Mar–May Asia's top film festival and deities' birthdays beckon beyond a sea of umbrellas.	**Jun–Sep** Get hot (beach, new wardrobe), get wet (rain, beer): antidotes to sultry summers.	**Nov–Feb** Hills by day; arts festival by night; celebrate Chinese New Year under Christmas lights.

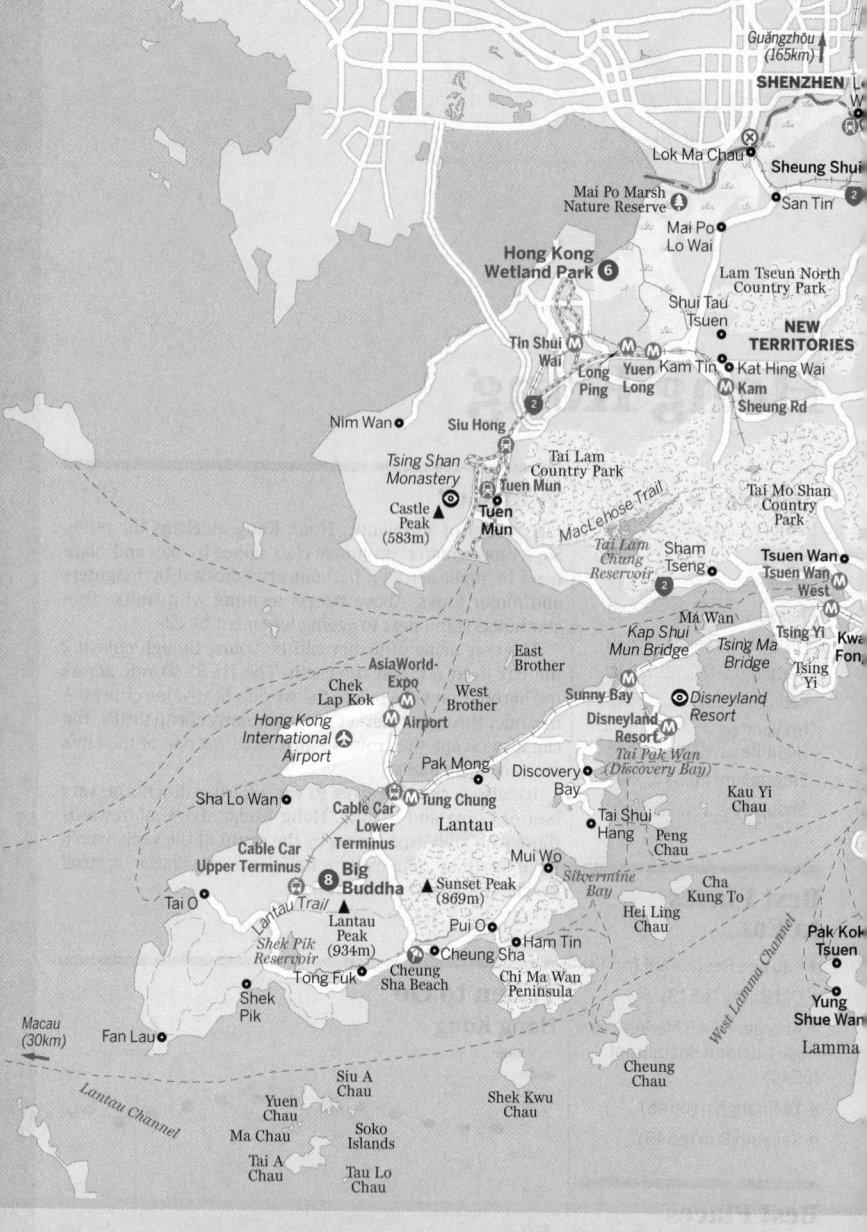

Hong Kong Highlights

1 Ferries (p534) Crossing Victoria Harbour on the legendary Star Ferry.

2 Victoria Peak (p526) Taking the steep ascent on the Peak Tram.

3 Hong Kong teahouses Sitting with locals and sipping 'pantyhose' milk tea at a *cha chaan tang* (teahouse) such as Lan Fong Yuen (p543).

4 Man Mo Temple (p527) Soaking up the incensed air at this famous temple.

5 Temple Street Night Market (p533) Taking in the sights, sounds and smells.

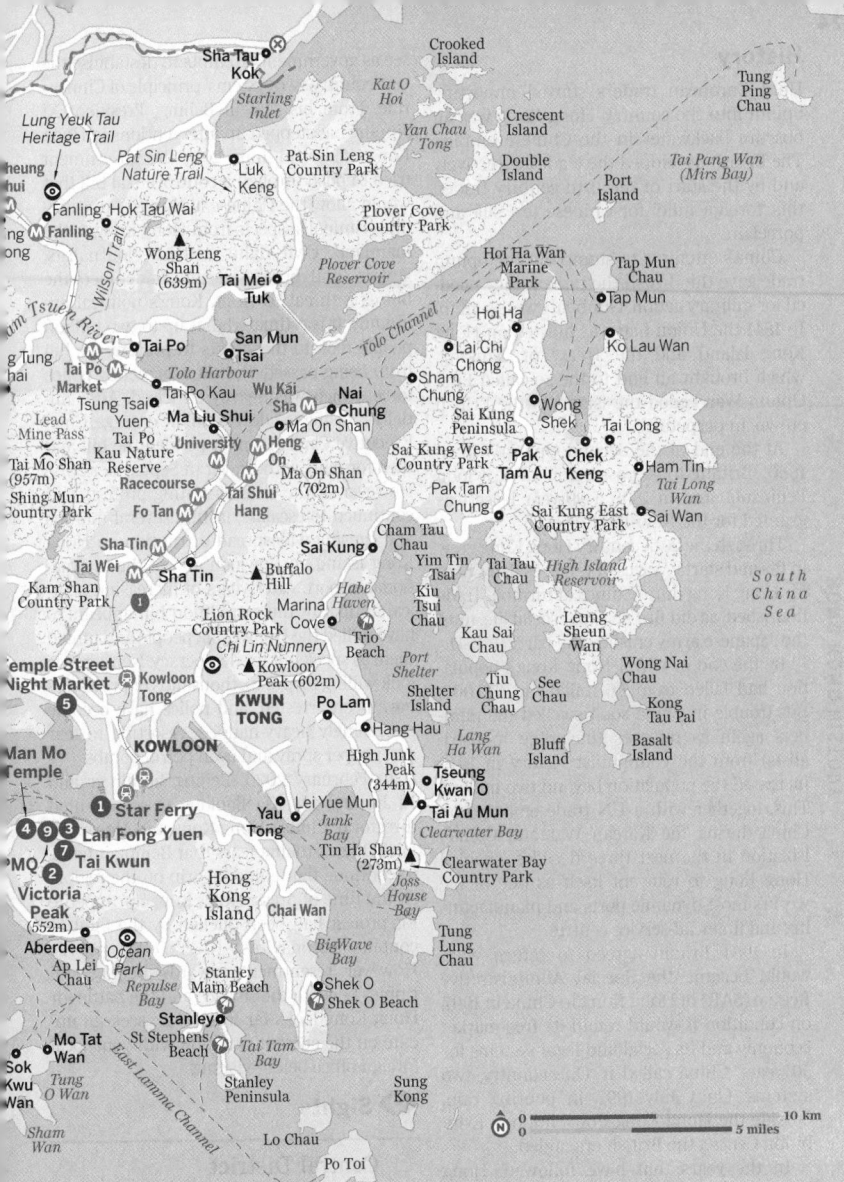

History

Until European traders started importing opium into the country, Hong Kong was an obscure backwater in the Chinese empire. The British developed the trade aggressively and by the start of the 19th century traded this 'foreign mud' for Chinese tea, silk and porcelain.

China's attempts to stamp out the opium trade gave the British the pretext they needed for military action. Gunboats were sent in. In 1841 the Union flag was hoisted on Hong Kong Island and the Treaty of Nanking, which brought an end to the so-called First Opium War, ceded the island to the British crown 'in perpetuity'.

At the end of the Second Opium War in 1860, Britain took possession of Kowloon Peninsula, and in 1898 a 99-year lease was granted for the New Territories.

Through the 20th century Hong Kong grew in fits and starts. Waves of refugees fled China for Hong Kong during times of turmoil. Trade flourished, as did British expat social life, until the Japanese army crashed the party in 1941.

By the end of WWII Hong Kong's population had fallen from 1.6 million to 610,000. But trouble in China soon swelled the numbers again as refugees (including industrialists) from the communist victory in 1949 increased the population beyond two million. This, together with a UN trade embargo on China during the Korean War and China's isolation in the next three decades, enabled Hong Kong to reinvent itself as one of the world's most dynamic ports and manufacturing and financial-service centres.

In 1984 Britain agreed to return what would become the Special Administrative Region (SAR) of Hong Kong to China in 1997, on condition it would retain its free-market economy and its social and legal systems for 50 years. China called it 'One country, two systems'. On 1 July 1997, in pouring rain, outside the Hong Kong Convention & Exhibition Centre, the British era ended.

In the years that have followed, Hong Kong has weathered major storms – an economic downturn, the outbreak of the SARS virus and increasing political activism among Hong Kong's youth. A deluge of tourists from mainland China, which now make up nearly 70% of the territory's visitor numbers, and soaring rents are changing the urban fabric of Hong Kong. A nagging mistrust of the government hangs in the air.

Two decades on from the handover, many Hong Kongers are worried about what they see as government attempts to destabilise the 'one country, two systems' principle of Chinese rule. From his seat in Beijing, President Xi Jinping has stepped up interventions in Hong Kong affairs. In June 2019 the government tried to push through a controversial bill that would allow the Chinese authorities to extradite criminal suspects from Hong Kong to the mainland. Civil rights activists, journalists, lawyers and businesses all condemned the bill as a threat to Hong Kong's political autonomy. It is estimated that up to two million people took to the streets to prevent the bill from being passed. Protest was met by police force, which was heavily criticised. After initially refusing to address public outrage, Chief Executive Carrie Lam suspended the bill and then formally withdrew it in September 2019. However, at the time of writing protests had continued to escalate, lasting several months and causing widespread disruption on Hong Kong Island, in Kowloon and at the international airport. After years of increasing political antipathy, the extradition bill appears to have rallied the Hong Kong people and united them to speak out for democracy. Neither side look willing to give in, thousands of protestors have been arrested, and police have become increasingly heavy-handed, resorting to tear gas, pepper spray and even petrol bombs.

In February 2020, Beijing hardliner and Xi Jinping ally Xia Baolong was appointed director of China's Hong Kong and Macau Affairs Office, stoking fears that Beijing intends to continue tightening its grip on the region. At the time of press, Hong Kongers' appetite for protest had been quelled by the fight to contain coronavirus (COVID-19; p1047). However resentment towards Beijing still ripples beneath the surface and the battle for Hong Kong looks far from over: seek an update on the current situation with your local foreign office before visiting.

◉ Sights

◉ Central District

The minted heart of Asia's financial hub is crammed with corporate citadels, colonial relics and massive monuments to consumerism. It's where you'll find the stock exchange, the Mandarin Oriental, Prada and world-class restaurants and bars, all housed in a compelling mix of modern architecture and heritage digs. Dynamic day and night, Central and its raucous bedfellows, Lan Kwai Fong and Soho, are where well-heeled Hong Kongers come to work and play.

Central Hong Kong & Kowloon

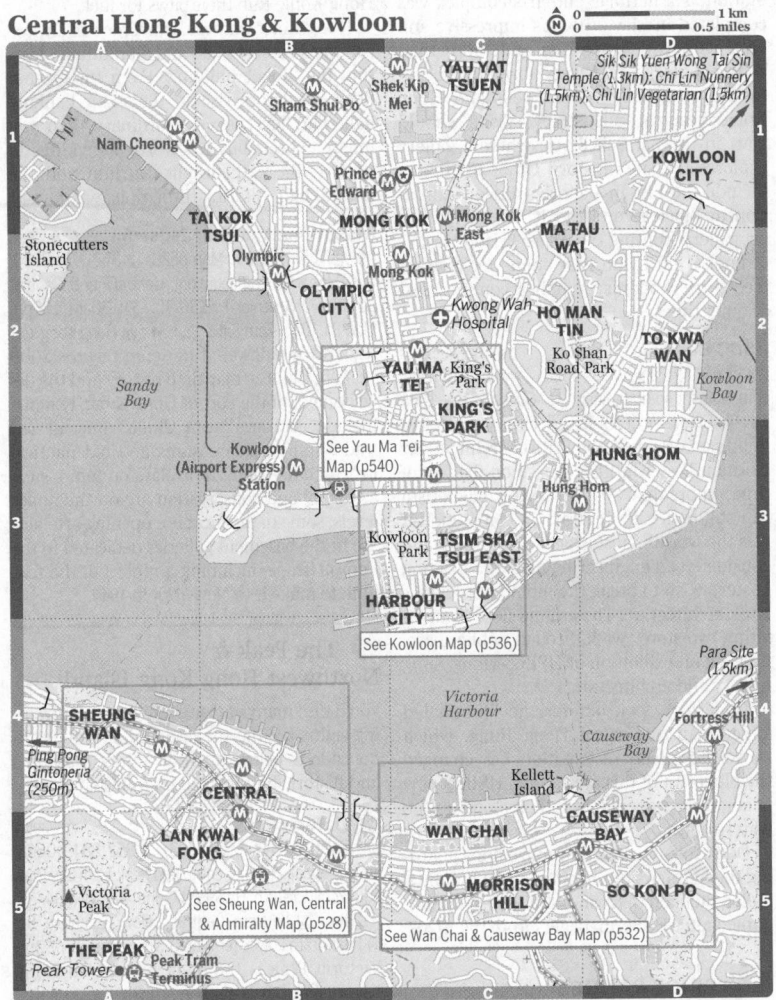

★ **Peak Tram**   FUNICULAR

(Map p528; ☎ 852 2522 0922; www.thepeak.com.
hk; Lower Terminus, 33 Garden Rd, Central; adult/
child & senior return HK$52/23, one way HK$37/14;
⊙ 7am-midnight; ⓜ Central, exit J2) This ca-
ble-hauled funicular railway has been scaling
the 396m ascent to the highest point on Hong
Kong Island since 1888. A ride on this clank-
ing tram is a classic Hong Kong experience,
with vertiginous views over the city as you
ascend the steep mountainside. It's become
so popular that the whole experience is being
upgraded with larger trams and a bigger lower terminus. A five-month service suspension

in 2020 should allow work to be completed
in 2021.

The Peak Tram runs every 10 to 15 minutes from 7am to midnight; using an Octopus card to pay for the ticket will help reduce
your queuing time. Note that the ticket office
will push the fare that includes entry to the
Sky Terrace 428 viewing deck (HK$84/99 per
one way/return).

★ **Tai Kwun**   MUSEUM, ARTS CENTRE

(Map p528; ☎ 852 3559 2600; www.taikwun.hk;
10 Hollywood Rd, Lan Kwai Fong; ⊙ 10am-11pm,
visitor centre to 8pm) **FREE** The long-awaited

reinvention of Hong Kong's Central Police Station as a heritage and arts complex was completed in May 2018. It's impressive and vast, with two courtyards and more than a dozen blocks that were formally dormitories, an armoury, prison cells and Hong Kong's central magistracy. Visits should start in the Barrack Block, where a gallery explores the site's history. Other highlights include the Life in Victorian Prison exhibition in Block 12 and the JC Contemporary art gallery fronting the upper Prison Yard.

Book a Tai Kwun Pass online for guaranteed entry; walk-ins are only accommodated at quiet times.

HSBC Building   NOTABLE BUILDING
(滙豐銀總大廈; Map p528; www.about.hsbc.com.hk/hsbc-in-hong-kong; 1 Queen's Rd, Central; MCentral, exit K) FREE This remarkable building, designed by British architect Sir Norman Foster in 1985, has stood the test of time – more than 30 years on, its magnetism can still be felt in Central. On completion it was the world's most expensive building and considered an engineering marvel, reflecting Foster's wish to break the mould of previous bank architecture. The ground floor is an inviting two-storey walk-through public space, housing an exhibition of HSBC's Hong Kong history and architecture.

Underfoot, look out for the illuminated street map of Central Hong Kong, which shows how land reclamation has changed the blueprint of this area; when HSBC's new headquarters opened in 1986 it stood on the waterfront.

Don't miss the pair of bronze lions guarding the harbourside entrance of the building. Called Stephen (left) and Stitt (right), they're named after HSBC managers from the 1920s.

Both bear shrapnel scars from the Battle of Hong Kong. Rub their paws for luck.

Hong Kong Chinese, irreverent as always, call the 52-storey glass and aluminium structure the 'Robot Building'. From the ground floor, escalators rise to the main banking hall. This level is more ordinary than you might expect, but it's worth ascending to gaze at the cathedral-like atrium and the natural light filtering through its windows.

Hong Kong Maritime Museum   MUSEUM
(香港海事博物館; Map p528; ☑852 3713 2500; www.hkmaritimemuseum.org; Central Pier 8, Central; adult/child & senior HK$30/15; ⊗9.30am-5.30pm Mon-Fri, 10am-7pm Sat & Sun; 🚾; MHong Kong, exit A2) This multilayered museum records 2000 years of Chinese maritime history and the development of the Port of Hong Kong. Exhibits include ceramics from China's ancient sea trade, shipwreck treasures and old nautical instruments. Modern displays on topics such as diving and conservation are on the upper levels; some of the most eye-opening artefacts are in the basement galleries dedicated to the Canton Trade, including a replica of the first junk to make it to New York in 1847.

◉ The Peak &
Northwest Hong Kong Island

You'll find many of Hong Kong's most intriguing sights around the Peak and in the neighbourhoods below it, from quirky museums and historic buildings to fragrant temples.

★Victoria Peak   VIEWPOINT
(維多利亞山頂; Map p528; ☑852 2849 0668; www.thepeak.com.hk; combined Peak Tram Sky Pass adult/child return HK$99/47, one way HK$84/38; ⊗24hr; 🚌15 from Central, below Exchange Sq, ⓇPeak Tram Lower Terminus) Standing at 552m, Victoria Peak is the highest point on Hong Kong Island. It is also one of the most visited spots by tourists, and it's not hard to see why. Sweeping views of the metropolis, verdant woods and easy but spectacular walks are all reachable in just eight minutes from Central via Hong Kong's 125-year-old, gravity-defying Peak Tram (p524). Predictably, it's become a money-making circus with restaurants and two shopping malls, but there's still magic up here if you can get past that.

The Peak Tram's upper terminus spits you out at the Peak Tower. Ascend to Level 5 and you'll reach the **Sky Terrace 428**, so named because it stands at 428 metres above sea level. In Hong Kong terms, this is the top of

One Day

Catch a tram up to Victoria Peak (p526) for great views of the city, stopping for lunch in Central on the way down. Head to historic Man Mo Temple (p527) and the Tai Kwun (p525) centre before boarding the Star Ferry (p534) to Kowloon. Enjoy the views along Tsim Sha Tsui East Promenade as you stroll over to the Hong Kong Museum of History (p534). Dine on budget Michelin-starred roast goose at Yat Lok (p543) in Central. After dinner, stroll to Quinary (p547) for cocktail wizardry in Soho.

Two Days

In addition to the above, you could go to Aberdeen (p533) for a boat ride, then seafood and shopping. After dark, head to the Temple Street Night Market (p533) in Kowloon for more shopping and street food.

the world and you'll be greeted with panoramic 360-degree views of Hong Kong's forest of skyscrapers, the harbour and Kowloon beyond (if you can dodge the Instagrammers and official photographer touting for business in front of the best framed view).

If you're not bothered about the highest point, and even if you are, it's worth seeking out the **Lions View Point Pavilion** – a far more charming lookout with a cute Chinese pagoda and gate, bristling with lion statues. This is where elderly locals come to sit and enjoy the view. It's a signposted two-minute walk from the tram's upper terminus.

Some 500m to the northwest of the upper terminus, up steep Mt Austin Rd, is the site of the old governor's summer lodge, which was burned to the ground by Japanese soldiers during WWII. The beautiful gardens still remain, however, and have been refurbished with faux-Victorian gazebos, sundials, benches and stone pillars. They are open to the public; it takes about 30 minutes to get up here and your reward is that it's blissfully peaceful. Head past the gardens and you'll find a second lookout point with island and sea views.

For longer walks, including the 3.5km **Morning Trail**, pick up maps from the Hong Kong Visitor Centre (p554) in the disused tram beside the Peak Tower, or download the Enjoy Hiking Hong Kong app.

★ Man Mo Temple   TAOIST TEMPLE

(文武廟; Map p528; ☑852 2540 0350; 124-126 Hollywood Rd, Sheung Wan; ⊙8am-6pm; ☒26) One of Hong Kong's oldest temples and a declared monument, atmospheric Man Mo Temple is dedicated to the gods of literature ('Man'), holding a writing brush, and of war ('Mo'), wielding a sword. Built in 1847 during the Qing dynasty by wealthy Chinese mer-

chants, it was, besides a place of worship, a court of arbitration for local disputes when trust was thin between the Chinese and the colonialists.

Pak Sing Ancestral Hall   TEMPLE

(廣福祠; Kwong Fuk Ancestral Hall; Map p528; 42 Tai Ping Shan St, Sheung Wan; ⊙8am-5pm; ☒26) In the 19th century many Chinese who left home in search of better horizons died overseas. As it was the wish of traditional Chinese to be buried in their home towns, this temple was built in 1856 to store corpses awaiting burial in China, and to serve as a public ancestral hall for those who could not afford the expense of bone repatriation. Families of the latter have erected 3000 memorial tablets for their ancestors in a room behind the altar.

★ PMQ   ARTS CENTRE

(元創方; Map p528; ☑852 2870 2335; www.pmq. org.hk; S614, Block A, PMQ, 35 Aberdeen St, Soho; ⊙building 7am-11pm, shops noon-8pm; ☒26, Ⓜ Central, exit D2) This arts and lifestyle hub occupies the multistorey modernist building complex of the old married police quarters (c 1951). Dozens of small galleries and shops, including a branch of G.O.D (p551). peddle local design in the form of hip handmade jewellery, clothing, housewares and more, making the PMQ a terrific place to hunt for nontacky souvenirs. There are also several restaurants and cafes, a breezy central courtyard hosting pop-ups and street art, and a large space on the top floor with rotating free exhibitions.

The site's earliest incarnation was a temple built in 1843, which was subsequently replaced by Central School, where Nationalist leader Dr Sun Yatsen once studied. Remnants of the school remain. PMQ is bounded by Hollywood Rd (north), Staunton St (south), Aberdeen St (east) and Shing Wong St (west).

Sheung Wan, Central & Admiralty

Hotel Jen (1.4km);
BlackSalt Tavern (1.4km);
Little Creatures (2.3km);
Sun Hing Restaurant (2.3km)

Western Harbour
Crossing

Hong Kong–Macau
Ferry Terminal

59

Connaught Rd W

Chung
Kong Rd

Des Voeux Rd W

58

P

57

53

54

Pier Rd

P

Tramway

Ko Shing St

Queen St

Wilmer St

Bonham Strand W

Wing Lok St

New Market St

14

Morrison St

Mar Wa La

Tramway

CTS Express
Coach

Ping Pong
Gintoneria
(500m)

Queen's Rd W

52

Possession St

44

18

Bonham Strand E

M

Wing Lok St

Wing Wo St

Gilman's

Hollywood
Road
Park

27

Burd St

Cleverly St

Hiller St

Queen's Rd Central

Gilman's
Bazaar

King George V
Memorial Park

Pak Sing
Ancestral Hall

13

SHEUNG
WAN

Lok Ku Rd

Jubilee
St

High St

Hospital Rd

Bonham Rd

Po Yan St

New St

5

Sai St

Tung St

10

22

29

24

Gough St

Staunton St

43

11

Stanley St

Park Rd

Queen Mary
Hospital
(2km)

Pound La

Blake
Garden

40

Tai Ping Shan St

Po Hing Fong

Ladder St

Man Mo
Temple

4

Hollywood Rd

PMQ

7

Aberdeen St

Peel St

Gage St

16

Lyndhurst Tce

Conduit Rd

Seymour Rd

Castle Rd

Bridges St

Caine Rd

Shing Wong St

35

23

38

25

41

SOHO

34

36

Robinson Rd

MID-LEVELS

Elgin St

Shelley St

Central Mid-Levels
Escalator

46

37

Old Bailey St

28

Tai
Kwun

8

Wyndham St

Chancery La

Arbuthnot Rd

Mosque St

Pok Fu Lam
Country
Park

Robinson Rd

Old Peak Rd

9 Victoria
Peak
(552m)

THE PEAK

Mt Austin Rd

Peak Tower (300m);
Hong Kong Island
HKTB Centre (350m)

May Rd

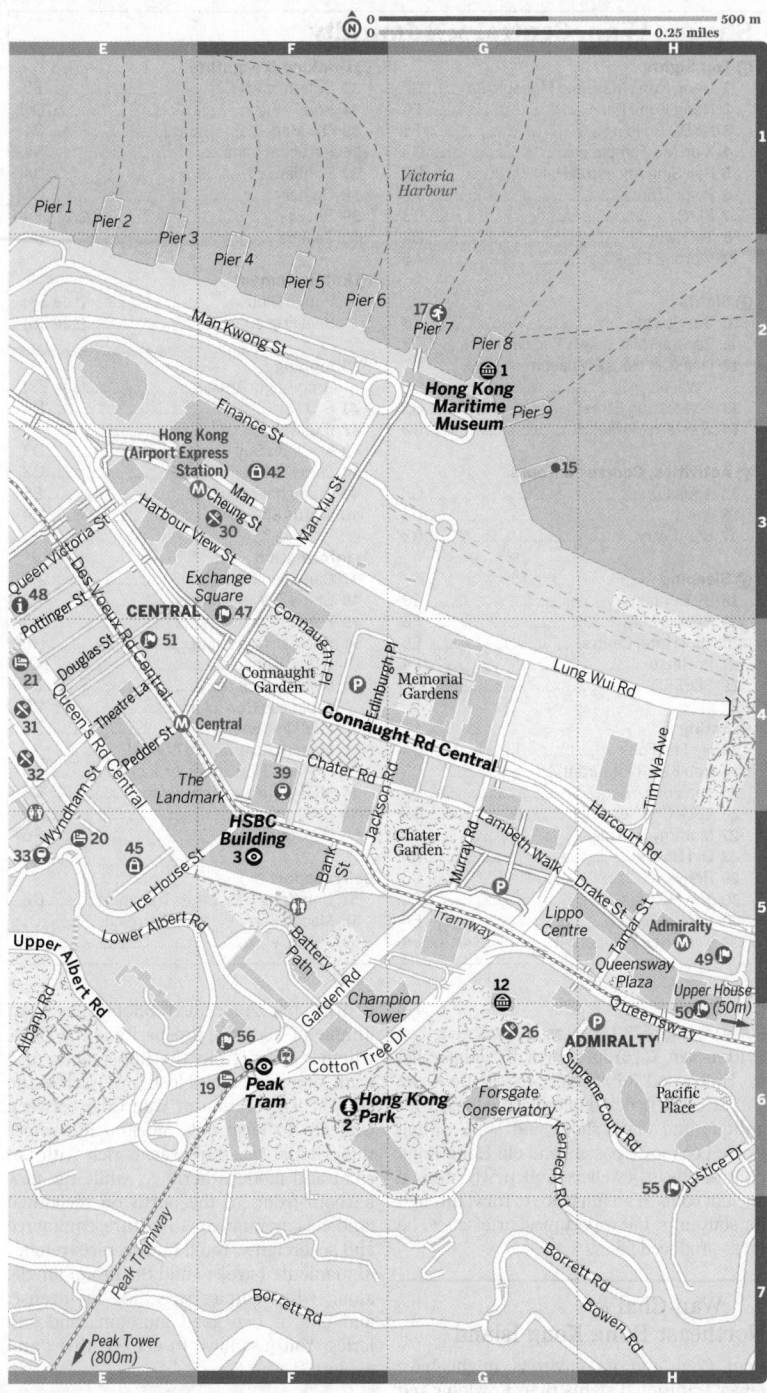

0
0

500 m
0.25 miles

Victoria
Harbour

Pier 1
Pier 2
Pier 3
Pier 4
Pier 5
Pier 6
Pier 7
Pier 8
Pier 9

Man Kwong St

17

**Hong Kong
Maritime
Museum**

1

15

Finance St

Hong Kong
(Airport Express
Station)

42

Man
Cheung St

30

Harbour View St

Man Yiu St

Exchange
Square

Queen Victoria St

48

Pottinger St

Das Voeux Rd Central

CENTRAL

47

51

Connaught Pl

Connaught
Garden

Edinburgh Pl

Memorial
Gardens

Lung Wui Rd

Douglas St

Theatre La

21

31

32

Queen's Rd Central

Pedder St

M Central

Connaught Rd Central

Chater Rd

Jackson Rd

Murray Rd

Lambeth Walk

Harcourt Rd

Tim Wa Ave

Wyndham St

20

33

45

**The
Landmark**

39

**HSBC
Building**
3

Bank St

Chater
Garden

Drake St

Tamar St

Admiralty

49

Ice House St

Lower Albert Rd

Upper Albert Rd

Battery
Path

Tramway

Lippo
Centre

**Queensway
Plaza**

M

Upper House
(50m)

50

Albany Rd

Garden Rd

Champion
Tower

12

26

ADMIRALTY

Queensway

Supreme Court Rd

**Pacific
Place**

56

6

**Peak
Tram**

19

Cotton Tree Dr

**Hong Kong
Park**
2

**Forsgate
Conservatory**

Kennedy Rd

55

Justice Dr

Peak Tramway

Borrett Rd

Bowen Rd

Borrett Rd

Peak Tower
(800m)

Sheung Wan, Central & Admiralty

Cat Street AREA
(摩囉街; Map p528; Upper Lascar Row, Sheung Wan; ⊙10am-6pm; 🚊26) Just north of (and parallel to) Hollywood Rd is Upper Lascar Row, aka 'Cat Street', a pedestrian-only lane lined with antique and curio shops and stalls selling Bruce Lee movie posters and old Hong Kong photos, cheap jewellery and newly minted ancient coins. It's a fun place to trawl through for souvenirs, but expect most artefacts to be mass-produced fakes.

◎ Wan Chai & Northeast Hong Kong Island

Wan Chai and its environs might have fewer traditional sights than Kowloon and Central, but this claustrophobic, east-west jumble of high-rise prosperity *is* the sight, whether ogled from the upper deck of a tram, or at street level losing yourself in the crowds. The section of Wan Chai between Queen's Rd East and Johnston Rd, where the original coastline was, is rich with ancient and modern heritage, while the new harbour-front, to the north on reclaimed land, has monuments to culture, commerce and sovereignty. You'll find scenic stretches of manicured green amid the urban jungle, along with temples wreathed in incense, and one or two good museums and galleries. You just have to get out there and explore.

★**Hong Kong Park** PARK
(香港公園; Map p528; ☑ 852 2521 5041; www.lcsd.
gov.hk/en/parks/hkp; 19 Cotton Tree Dr, Admiralty;
⏰ 6am-11pm; 🚻; Ⓜ Admiralty, exit C1) A hillside
oasis squeezed between Central and Admiralty, Hong Kong Park was built in 1991 over
part of the former Victoria Barracks. Terraced
landscaping connects tree-lined pathways
with various family-friendly attractions such
as its fountain plaza, waterfall, playground,
aviary and museum. Lotus-filled pools with
gliding koi carp and turtles basking on rocks
are a draw for local photographers, who jostle
for position to give their images that dramatic
skyscraper backdrop.

Tin Hau Temple TEMPLE
(天后廟; Map p532; 10 Tin Hau Temple Rd, Causeway Bay; ⏰ 7am-5pm; Ⓜ Tin Hau, exit B) Hong
Kong Island's most famous Tin Hau (Goddess
of the Sea) temple has lent its name to an entire neighbourhood, a metro station and a
street. It has been a place of worship for 370
years and, despite renovations, imparts an air
of antiquity, particularly in the intricate stone
carvings near the entrance and the ceramic
figurines from Shíwān decorating the roof.
The main altar contains an effigy of the goddess with a blackened face.

**Flagstaff House
Museum of Tea Ware** MUSEUM
(旗桿屋茶具文物館; Map p528; ☑ 852 2869
0690; 10 Cotton Tree Dr, Admiralty; ⏰ 10am-6pm
Wed-Mon; Ⓜ Admiralty, exit C1) FREE Built in
1846 as the home of the commander of the
British forces, Flagstaff House is the oldest
colonial building in Hong Kong still standing
in its original spot. Its colonnaded verandas
exude a Greek Revival elegance, complemented by the grace of the teaware from the
11th to the 20th centuries: bowls, brewing
trays, sniffing cups (used particularly for
enjoying the fragrance of the finest oolong
from Taiwan) and teapots made of porcelain
or purple clay from Yíxīng.

👁 **Aberdeen &
South Hong Kong Island**

The southern part of Hong Kong Island lays
claim to Hong Kong's richest fishing culture.
You'll see the homes, markets and temples, both traditional and modern, of Hong
Kong's 'people of the water'. The island's
south is also home to a Victorian dairy, an
ancient waterfall, art galleries in lofty warehouses, and popular sunbathing spots. And

of course, there's **Ocean Park** (海洋公園;
☑ 852 3923 2323; www.oceanpark.com.hk; Ocean
Park Rd; adult/child 3-11yr HK$498/249; ⏰ 10am-
6pm Mon-Fri, to 7pm Sat & Sun; 🚻; Ⓜ Ocean Park),
a theme park undergoing a mega expansion.

Aberdeen Promenade WATERFRONT
(香港仔海濱公園; Ⓜ Wong Chuk Hang, exit B)
Tree-lined Aberdeen Promenade runs from
west to east on Aberdeen Praya Rd across the
water from Ap Lei Chau. On its western end
is sprawling **Aberdeen Wholesale Fish Market** with its industrial-strength water tanks
teeming with marine life. It's pungent and
grimy, but 100% Hong Kong. Before reaching
the market, you'll pass berthed house boats
and seafood-processing vessels. (We detected
a karaoke parlour or two as well.)

Young Master Brewery BREWERY
(少爺麥啤; www.youngmasterales.com; Ground
fl, Sungib Industrial Centre, 53 Wong Chuk Hang Rd,
Wong Chuk Hang; tour HK$100; ⏰ 4.30-6.30pm
Mon-Fri, noon-6pm Sat; Ⓜ Wong Chuk Hang, exit
A2) Young Master Ales has moved to a new
street-level location in Wong Chuk Hang.
Merchandise is sold in the front, while at
the back, the brewing system, with its ageing
barrels, whirs, hisses and grinds away. The
small-batch, nonfiltered, chemical-free beers
range from crisp to robust, and have funky
names inspired by Hong Kong pop culture
like Fake Blood, a tribute to kung fu movies.
Book online for the Saturday hour-long guided tours (English 1pm, Cantonese 4pm). You
cannot imbibe on the premises, but you can
buy beer to take away.

Stanley VILLAGE
(赤柱) This crowd-pleaser is best visited on
weekdays. **Stanley Market** (赤柱市集; Stanley Village Rd, Stanley; ⏰ 10am-6pm; 🚌 6, 6A, 6X,
260) is a maze of alleyways that has bargain
clothing (haggling is a must!), while **Stanley Main Beach** (赤柱正灘; 🚌 6A, 14) is for
beach-bumming and windsurfing. With
graves dating back to 1841, **Stanley Military
Cemetery** (赤柱軍人墳場; ☑ 852 2557 3498;
Wong Ma Kok Rd, Stanley; ⏰ 8am-5pm; 🚌 14, 6A),
500m south of the market, is worth a visit.

👁 **Kowloon**

Kowloon has most of Hong Kong's major
museums, its busiest and most beguiling
Taoist temple complex (p534), and some of
the liveliest street markets. Pockets of fading colonial heritage, including old churches and police stations, reward the casual

Wan Chai & Causeway Bay

Tung Po Seafood
Restaurant (1.2km)

Victoria Harbour

Causeway Bay

Kellett Island

Cargo Handling Basin

Hong Kong Convention & Exhibition Centre

Expo Dr

Expo Dr E

2

Victoria Park Rd

Gordon Rd

Tsing Fung St

Victoria Park

Electric Rd

Hing Fat St

King's Rd

Tin Hau   M   1
Tin Hau Temple

Hung Hing Rd

Tonnochy Rd

Wan Shing St

CAUSEWAY BAY

Cannon St

14   6
Kingston St   Gloucester Rd
11

WAN CHAI

17
Harbour Rd

Jaffe Rd

Paterson St

Island Beverley

Causeway Rd

21
19   20

Gloucester Rd

18

Fleming St

Stewart Rd

Marsh Rd

Canal Rd

Causeway Bay   M
13

Kai Chiu Rd
Pak Sha Rd
Jardine's Bazaar
Yun Ping Rd
Lee Garden Rd
Hysan Ave

Yee Wo St   St Shelter
Irving St

10

Tung Lo Wan Rd

Wun Sha St

Pennington St

WAN CHAI

Jaffe Rd

Lockhart Rd

Wan Chai
M

8

Fenwick St

Liard Rd

Hennessy Rd

5

3

23

Tak Yan St

Yat Sin St

Morrison Hill Rd

Bowrington Rd

Russell St

Percival St

Russell St

22

SO KON PO

Kai Ling Path
Eastern Hospital Rd
Tai Hang Rd

Admiralty (1km)

Thomson Rd
16
Johnston Rd

Wan Chai Rd

Heard St

MORRISON HILL

Yiu Wa St
Leighton Rd

Leighton Rd

CAROLINE HILL

Tai Hang Rd

15

9

Cross St

Kennedy Rd

Chun Yuen St

Stone Nullah La

Queen's Rd E
4

Ruttonjee Hospital
Wan Chai Park

Stubbs Rd

Hau Tak La

Sports Rd

Wong Nai Chung Rd

LEIGHTON HILL

Caroline Hill Rd

Link Rd

TAI HANG

Lovers' Rock (800m)

HAPPY VALLEY

Happy Valley Racecourse

12

Wan Chai & Causeway Bay

wanderer, while Yau Ma Tei is the place to go to soak up what vibes linger of yesteryear Hong Kong, especially along Shanghai St. Many of Kowloon's attractions revolve around views of the Hong Kong Island skyline, which can be best appreciated from the Kowloon waterfront and various well-positioned bars and restaurants.

⭐**Tsim Sha Tsui East Promenade** HARBOUR
(尖沙嘴東部海濱花園; Map p536; Salisbury Rd, Tsim Sha Tsui; Ⓜ East Tsim Sha Tsui, exit J) One of the finest city skylines in the world has to be that of Hong Kong Island, and the promenade here is one of the best ways to get an uninterrupted view. It's a lovely place to stroll around during the day, but it really comes into its own in the evening, during the nightly **Symphony of Lights** (Kowloon waterfront; ⊙ 8-8.20pm), a spectacular sound-and-light show involving dozens of buildings on the Hong Kong Island skyline.

The **Avenue of Stars** (星光大道), revamped with a new design in 2019, pays homage to the Hong Kong film industry and its stars, with more than 100 handprints and sculptures.

The promenade starts just west of **Victoria Dockside** parallel to Salisbury Rd, an ambitious 279,00-sq-metre development of offices, retail, art galleries and the ultraluxe Rosewood Hotel. It then carries on eastwards almost all the way to the Hong Kong Coliseum and Hung Hom train station.

It gets especially crowded during the Chinese New Year fireworks displays in late January/early February and in June during the **Dragon Boat Festival**.

Shanghai Street   STREET
(上海街; Map p540; Yau Ma Tei; Ⓜ Yau Ma Tei, exit C) Strolling down Shanghai St will return you to a time long past. Once Kowloon's main drag, it's flanked by shops selling Chinese wedding gowns, sandalwood incense and Buddha statues, plus mahjong parlours and an old pawn shop (at the junction with Saigon St). This is a terrific place for souvenirs – fun picks include wooden moon-cake moulds stamped with images of fish, pigs or lucky sayings, bamboo steamer baskets, long chopsticks meant for stirring pots, and pretty ceramic bowls.

⭐**Temple Street Night Market**   MARKET
(廟街夜市; Map p540; Temple St, Yau Ma Tei; ⊙ 6-11pm; Ⓜ Yau Ma Tei, exit C) When night falls and neon buzzes, Hong Kong's liveliest market rattles into life. Covering multiple city blocks from Man Ming Lane in the north to Nanking St in the south, Temple St is cleaved in two by the **Tin Hau Temple** (天后廟; ☑ 852 2385 0759; www.ctc.org.hk; ⊙ 9am-5pm) complex. In the 1920s, vendors gathered there to serve temple-goers; a century on, the crowds descend nightly for cheap clothes and watches, street food, trinkets and teaware. Marked prices are mere suggestions – this is a place to bargain.

Sik Sik Yuen Wong Tai Sin Temple
TAOIST TEMPLE

(嗇色園黃大仙祠; ☑852 2351 5640, 852 2327 8141; www.siksikyuen.org.hk; 2 Chuk Yuen Village, Wong Tai Sin; donation HK$2; ⊙7am-5pm; Ⓜ Wong Tai Sin, exit B2) A devout ensemble of halls, shrines, pavilions and altars, this busy temple is a destination for all walks of Hong Kong society, from pensioners and business people to parents and young professionals. Some come to pray, others to divine the future with *chim* – numbered bamboo 'fortune sticks' that are shaken out of a box on to the ground (they're available free from the right of the main temple). Take the noted numbers to an attendant fortune-teller to be read.

★Chi Lin Nunnery
BUDDHIST MONASTERY

(志蓮淨苑; ☑852 2354 1888; 5 Chi Lin Dr, Diamond Hill; ⊙nunnery 9am-4pm, garden 7am-7pm; Ⓜ Diamond Hill, exit C2) FREE One of Hong Kong's most arresting and tranquil escapes, this Buddhist complex, originally dating from the 1930s, was rebuilt completely of wood (and not a single nail) in the style of the Tang dynasty in 1998. Amid lotus ponds, immaculate bonsai tea plants and bougainvillea, silent nuns deliver offerings of fruit and rice to Buddha and arhats (Buddhist disciples freed from the cycle of birth and death), or chant behind intricately carved screens.

★Hong Kong Museum of History
MUSEUM

(香港　史博物館; Map p536; ☑852 2724 9042; http://hk.history.museum; 100 Chatham Rd S, Tsim Sha Tsui; ⊙10am-6pm Mon & Wed-Fri, to 7pm Sat & Sun; ☻; Ⓜ Tsim Sha Tsui, exit B2) FREE Prepare to be whisked through millennia of Hong Kong history at this extraordinary museum, starting with prehistory (don't linger, the best is yet to come) and ending with the territory's return to China in 1997. Highlights of the 'Hong Kong Story' include a recreation of an entire arcaded street in Central from 1881, a full-sized fishing junk, lots of informative video theatre exhibits (including an even-handed stab at the Opium Wars) – and so much more.

Kowloon Park
PARK

(九龍公園; Map p536; www.lcsd.gov.hk; cnr Nathan & Austin Rds, Tsim Sha Tsui; ⊙5am-midnight; ☻; Ⓜ Tsim Sha Tsui, exit C2) Built on the site of a barracks for an Indian regiment of the British Army, Kowloon Park is an oasis of greenery and a refreshing escape from the Nathan Rd hustle. Pathways wind between banyan trees, gardens, fountains and a flamingo pond; go early to see elderly locals performing taichi.

On Sundays from 2.30pm, martial-arts and dragon dances are performed at 'Kung Fu Corner' at the park's **Sculpture Walk**. The **Hong Kong Heritage Discovery Centre** (free) has exhibitions relating to old Hong Kong, but kids will prefer the **Aviary** and the extensive **swimming facilities** (九龍公園游泳池; ☑852 2724 3577; adult/concession Mon-Fri HK$17/8, Sat & Sun HK$19/9; ⊙6.30am-noon, 1-5pm & 6-10pm; ☻).

◉ New Territories

The New Territories offer much cultural and natural interest. Ancient walled villages (Sha Tau Kok, Sheung Shui, Fanling, Yuen Long), wetlands teeming with birds and aquatic life (Yuen Long), temples (Tsuen Wan, Sha Tin, Fanling), a solid museum in Sha Tin, and generous expanses of unspoiled country are just some of its attractions. Notably, Sai

---

STAR FERRY

You can't say you've 'done' Hong Kong until you've taken a ride on a **Star Ferry** (天星小轮; Map p528; ☑852 2367 7065; www.starferry.com.hk; Central Pier 7, Central; adult HK$2.20-3.70, child HK$1.50-2.20; ⊙every 6-12min, 6.30am-11.30pm; Ⓜ Hong Kong, exit A2), that wonderful fleet of electric-diesel vessels with names like *Morning Star, Celestial Star* and *Twinkling Star*. Try to take your first trip on a clear night from Kowloon to Central. It's not half as dramatic in the opposite direction.

At any time of the day, the journey, with its riveting views of skyscrapers and jungle-clad hills, must be one of the world's best-value cruises. At the end of the 10-minute journey, a hemp rope is cast from the back of the boat and caught with a billhook, the way it was in 1888 when the first boat docked.

The cheapest fares are only available on the lower deck, but the views are a little better and there are less fumes on the top deck; it's more expensive to ride on weekends and public holidays.

Want more? Star Ferry also runs a 60-minute **Harbour Tour** (HK$110 to HK$230) with pick-ups at Tsim Sha Tsui, Central and Wan Chai. Get tickets at the piers.

LANTAU'S PO LIN MONASTERY & BIG BUDDHA

Po Lin (寶蓮禪寺; ☑852 2985 5248; Lantau Island; ☉8am-6pm) is a huge Buddhist monastery and temple complex that was built in 1924. Today it seems more of a tourist honeypot than a religious retreat, attracting hundreds of thousands of visitors a year and still being expanded. Most of the buildings you'll see on arrival are new, with the older, simpler ones tucked away behind them. The big draw is the enormous seated bronze Buddha, a must-see on any Hong Kong trip.

Commonly known as the 'Big Buddha', the Tian Tan Buddha is a representation of Lord Gautama some 23m high (or 26.4m with the lotus), or just under 34m if you include the podium. It was unveiled in 1993, and today it still holds the honour of being the tallest seated bronze Buddha statue in the world.

The most spectacular way to get to the plateau is by the 5.7km **Ngong Ping 360** (昂平360纜車; www.np360.com.hk; adult/child/senior one way from HK$160/75/105, return from HK$235/110/155; ☉10am-6pm Mon-Fri, 9am-6.30pm Sat, Sun & public holidays; 🅿), a cable car linking Ngong Ping with the centre of Tung Chung, where there's an MTR station.

Kung Peninsula has fabulous hiking trails, delicious seafood and attractive beaches. And, of course, there's the awe-inspiring Hong Kong Unesco Global Geopark.

★Hong Kong Global Geopark   PARK
(香港地質公園; www.geopark.gov.hk) Part of the Unesco Geopark network, this spectacular geopark consists of two regions of formations: volcanic rock from 140 million years ago that often appears as stacks of visually stunning hexagonal columns; and sedimentary rock from 400 million years ago comprising uniquely shaped sandstone and siltstone. The best way to experience all or part of the eight site groups dispersed over 50 sq km is by joining a guided tour. Contact the **Volcano Discovery Centre** (火山探知館; ☑852 2394 1538; www.volcanodiscoverycentre.hk; Sai Kung Waterfront Park; ☉9am-5pm, exhibition 9.30am-4.30pm; 🅿; 🚌92, 299X). **Sea Kayak Hong Kong** (☑852 9313 9165; www.seakayakhongkong.com; 54 Lo So Shing Village, Sok Kwu Wan) 🚣 runs kayaking tours of the Geopark.

★High Island Reservoir East Dam   DAM
(萬宜水庫東壩) Handsome architecture, the South China Sea, and 140-million-year-old volcanic rocks make this one of Hong Kong's most breathtaking places. High Island Reservoir East Dam is the most easily accessible part of Hong Kong Global Geopark and the only place where you can touch the hexagonal rock columns. The scenery is surreal and made even more so by the presence of thousands of dolosse (huge reinforced concrete blocks shaped like jacks) placed along the coast to break sea waves.

A dedicated green minibus (route 9A) runs between Sai Kung's Pak Tam Chung and East Dam (HK$11.30), but it only operates on Sundays and public holidays between 3pm and 7pm. You could also take bus 94 from Sai Kung Bus Terminus to Pak Tam Chung, then walk 9km along Tai Mong Tsai Rd and Sai Kung Man Yee Rd, following **MacLehose Trail** Stage 1, to East Dam.

A taxi to East Dam from Sai Kung Town takes about 30 minutes and costs HK$160, but you may need to call a taxi service for the return trip. Be prepared to offer an extra HK$50 or more when placing your request in order to land a ride. Alternatively, Live Nature (www.ecotoursaikung.com) runs tours to the dam.

Lai Chi Wo   VILLAGE
(荔枝窩; hakkahomelcw@gmail.com; Plover Cove Country Park) Part of Hong Kong Global Geopark, 400-year-old Lai Chi Wo is Hong Kong's best-preserved Hakka walled village and has an intact woodland. With 200 houses, ancestral halls, temples, and a breezy square fringed by old banyans, it is a sight to behold. There are 90-minute guided tours every Sunday and public holiday (usually at 11am and 1.30pm), as well as bespoke tours available on weekdays; all must be booked two weeks in advance by email.

Green minibus 56K leaves Fanling MTR station for Luk Keng at 30-minute intervals on weekdays, and 10- to 30-minute intervals on Saturdays, Sundays and public holidays. From Luk Keng, it's a two-hour walk to Lai Chi Wo.

Hong Kong Heritage Museum   MUSEUM
(香港文化博物館; ☑852 2180 8188; www.heritagemuseum.gov.hk; 1 Man Lam Rd, Sha Tin;

Kowloon

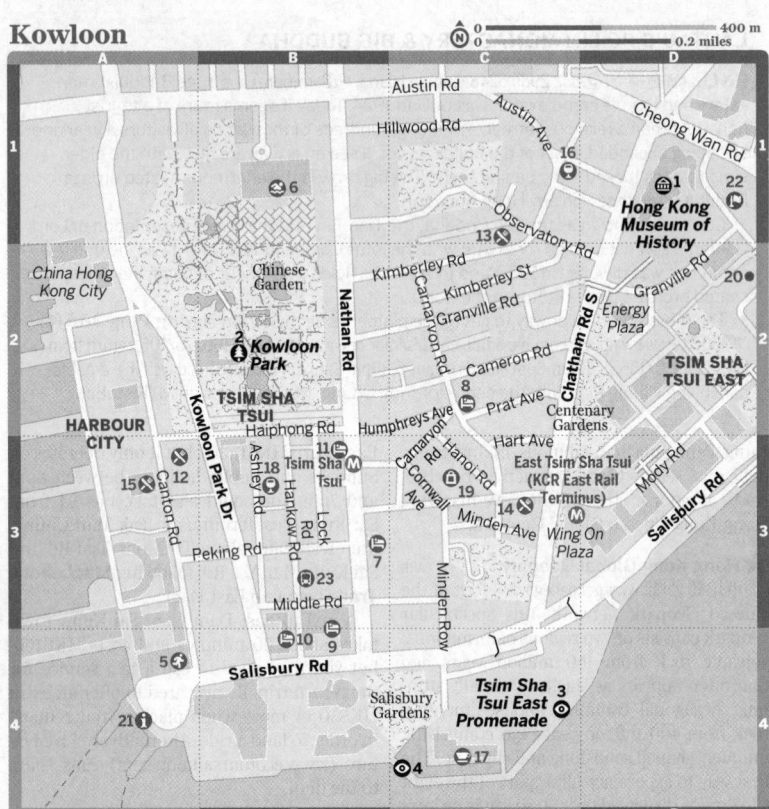

Kowloon

⊗ 10am-6pm Mon & Wed-Fri, to 7pm Sat & Sun; 🖈; M Che Kung Temple, exit A) Southwest of Sha Tin town centre, this spacious, high-quality museum inside an ugly building gives a peek into local history and culture. Highlights include a children's area with interactive play zones, the Cantonese Opera Heritage Hall, where you can watch old operas with English subtitles, and an elegant gallery of Chinese art. There's also a Jin Yong exhibit, with some 300 items illustrating the life and works of martial arts novelist Dr Louis Cha, aka Jin Yong.

Ping Shan Heritage Trail   HISTORIC BUILDING
(屏山文物徑; ☏ 852 2617 1959; Hang Tau Tsuen, Ping Shan, Yuen Long; ⊗ ancestral halls & Tsui Sing Lau Pagoda 9am-1pm & 2-5pm Wed-Mon; M Tin Shui Wai, exit E) Hong Kong's first-ever heritage trail features historic buildings belonging to the Tangs, the first and the most powerful of the 'Five Clans'. Highlights of the 1km trail include Hong Kong's oldest pagoda, **Tsui Sing Lau Pagoda** (聚星樓; Ping Ha Rd) **FREE**, the magnificent **Tang Clan Ancestral Hall** (鄧氏宗祠) **FREE**, a temple, a study hall, a well and **Ping Shan Tang Clan Gallery** (屏山鄧族文物館; ⊗ 10am-5pm Tue-Sun Oct-Feb, to 6pm Mar-Sep; ⊞ Ping Shan) **FREE** inside an old police station built by the British as much to monitor the coastline as to keep an eye on the clan.

Cross Tsui Sing Rd from the ground floor of the MTR station and you'll see the pagoda. Set aside two hours for the trail.

Hong Kong Wetland Park   PARK
(香港濕地公園; ☏ 852 3152 2666; www.wetland park.gov.hk; Wetland Park Rd, Tin Shui Wai; adult/concession HK$30/15; ⊗ 10am-5pm Wed-Mon; 🖈; ⊞ 967, ⊞ 705) This 60-hectare ecological park is a window on the wetland ecosystems of the northwest New Territories. The natural trails, bird hides and viewing platforms make it a handy and excellent spot for birdwatching. The futuristic grass-covered headquarters houses interesting galleries, a film theatre, a cafe and a viewing gallery. If you have binoculars, bring them; otherwise be prepared to wait to use the fixed points in the viewing galleries and hides.

To reach Hong Kong Wetland Park, take the MTR West Rail to Tin Shui Wai and board light-rail line 705, alighting at the Wetland Park stop. It can also be reached directly from Hong Kong Island: jump on a 967 bus at Admiralty MTR bus station.

⊙ Outlying Islands

From the winding streets and isolated beaches of Cheung Chau and Peng Chau to the monasteries and hiking trails of Lantau and the seafood restaurants of Lamma, Hong Kong's Outlying Islands offer a host of sights and activities.

The sheer size of **Lantau**, Hong Kong's largest island, makes for days of exploration. The north tip of the island, home to the airport, Disneyland and the high-rise Tung Chung residential and shopping complex, is highly developed. But much of the rest of Lantau is still entirely rural. Here you'll find traditional fishing villages, empty beaches and a mountainous interior criss-crossed with quad-burning hiking trails.

Most visitors come to Lantau to visit Mickey or see the justly famous 'Big Buddha' statue, but be sure you get beyond the north side for a taste of a laid-back island where cows wander down the middle of the road, school kids gather seaweed with their grandparents in the shallow bays, and the odd pangolin is said to still roam the forested hillsides.

Lamma, Hong Kong's laid-back 'hippy island', is easily recognisable at a distance by the three coal chimneys crowning its hilly skyline. The chimneys stand out so much because Lamma, home to 6000 or so people, is otherwise devoid of high-rise development. Here it's all about lush forests, hidden beaches and chilled-out villages connected by pedestrian paths. You won't see any cars here, but be prepared for spotting the odd snake.

Most visitors arrive in Yung Shue Wan, a counterculture haven popular with expats.

Small, dumb-bell-shaped **Cheung Chau** is a popular getaway thanks to its beaches and its cute downtown, near the main pier, lined with snack shops and stores. Many of these operate out of village homes. Come here for an afternoon of temple and village touring, noshing on fish balls and exploring the rocky coastline. Or stay for a weekend at one of the many holiday rentals and treat yourself to a day of windsurfing lessons followed by an alfresco seafood dinner at a harbourside restaurant.

Hong Kong Disneyland   AMUSEMENT PARK
(香港迪士尼樂園; ☏ 852 183 0830; www.hong kongdisneyland.com; adult/child HK$639/475; ⊗ 10.30am-8pm; 🖈; M Disney Resort Station) Disneyland serves as a rite of passage for the flocks of Asian tourists who come daily to steal a glimpse of one of America's most

HONG KONG SIGHTS

famous cultural exports. It's divided into seven areas – Main Street USA, Tomorrowland, Fantasyland, Adventureland, Toy Story Land, Mystic Point and Grizzly Gulch – but it's still quite tiny compared to the US version, and most of the attractions are geared towards families with small children.

A *Frozen*-themed zone will unveil in 2020 and an entire Marvel-themed area is launching in phases till 2023.

Disneyland is linked by rail with the MTR at Sunny Bay station on the Tung Chung line; passengers just cross the platform to board the dedicated train for Disneyland Resort station and the theme park. Journey times from Central/Kowloon/Tsing Yi stations are 37/28/16 minutes respectively.

🏃 Activities

Despite the metropolis of glass and steel at its heart, Hong Kong is an outdoorsy city offering countless ways to enjoy the water and the outlandish natural environment that pushes against the city's urban spaces. Hiking trails abound, there's a thriving keep-fit culture, and dozens of spas and massage centres cater for relaxation-seekers.

★ Lantau Peak   HIKING

(Fung Wong Shan; Lantau Island; 🚌 3M) Known as Fung Wong Shan (Phoenix Mountain) in Cantonese, this 934m-high peak is the second-highest in Hong Kong after Tai Mo Shan (957m) in the New Territories. The view from the summit is absolutely stunning, and on a clear day it's possible to see Macau 65km to the west. Watching the sun rise from the peak is a popular choice among hardy hikers. Some choose to stay at the **Ngong Ping SG Davis Hostel** (昂坪戴維斯青年旅舍; 📞852 2788 1638; www.yha.org.hk; Ngong Ping; dm/tent/r from HK$150/300/380; 🚌2 from Mui Wo, or 21, 23 from Tung Chung) and leave around 4am for the two-hour summit push.

If you're hiking Lantau Peak as a day trip, take the MTR to Tung Chung, then take bus 3M to Pak Kung Au (tell the driver where you're getting off beforehand). From here, you'll follow the markers for section 3 of the **Lantau Trail** (鳳凰徑), ascending the peak and then descending the steps into Ngong Ping. This 4.5km route takes about three hours.

Tai Tam Waterworks Heritage Trail   HIKING

(大潭水務文物徑; South Hong Kong Island ; 🚌6) This scenic 5km trail runs past reservoirs and a handsome collection of 20 historic waterworks structures – feats of Victorian utilitarian engineering that include bridges, aqueducts, valve houses, pumping stations and dams, many still working.

The trail, which ends at Tai Tam Tuk Raw Water Pumping Station, takes about two hours. Enter at Wong Nai Chung Gap near the luxury flats of Hong Kong Parkview, or at the junction of Tai Tam Rd and Tai Tam Reservoir Rd. On weekends you'll see residents taking a walk with their dogs, kids, maids, chauffeurs and nannies.

From Central Exchange Sq station, bus 6 takes you to Wong Nai Chung Reservoir. Walk east along Tai Tam Reservoir Rd.

★ Tai Long Wan Hiking Trail   HIKING

(大浪灣遠足郊遊徑; Sai Kung Peninsula ; 🚌 village bus 29R) The northern end of Sai Kung Peninsula has several wonderful hikes that will take you through some of Hong Kong's most pristine scenery. The breathtaking 12km Tai Long Wan Hiking Trail, which starts from the end of Sai Wan Rd and passes through beautiful coves including Sai Wan, Tai Long Wan and Chek Keng, is a perennially popular option. On weekdays you're likely to have the trail to yourself. The walk takes five to six hours.

Take the village bus 29R at Chan Man Rd (the stop is in front of McDonald's), get off at the last stop – Sai Wan Ting (西灣亭), literally West Bay Pagoda – and start the hike there. Departures are more frequent on Sundays and public holidays. A taxi ride will be less than HK$160. The trail ends at Pak Tam Au, from where you can catch a minibus back to Sai Kung town.

Hong Kong Dolphinwatch   WILDLIFE WATCHING

(香港海豚觀察; Map p536; 📞852 2984 1414; www.hkdolphinwatch.com; 15th fl, Middle Block, 1528A Star House, 3 Salisbury Rd, Tsim Sha Tsui, Kowloon; adult/child HK$460/230; ⏱cruises Wed, Fri & Sun) 🌿 Hong Kong Dolphinwatch was founded in 1995 to raise awareness of Hong Kong's endangered pink dolphins. The organisation conducts dolphin-spotting cruises (three to four hours) three times weekly as long as enough people sign up. Advance booking is required. It claims that 97% of cruises sight at least one dolphin; if none are spotted, passengers are offered a free trip.

Iyara   SPA

(Map p528; 📞852 2545 8638; www.iyaradayspa. com; 1st fl, 26 Cochrane St, Lan Kwai Fong; manicure/pedicure/massage from HK$250/350/780;

⊙ 10am-8pm) Many of Hong Kong's city spas are positively cave-like, in low-lit high-rises with no windows. Iyara, however, is more like a secret garden. It's run by friendly Thais who use organic, natural products. Floor-to-ceiling windows at eye level with the Central–Mid-Level Escalator provide entertainment while getting a manicure or foot massage with a (free) glass of wine.

☞ Tours

Kayak and Hike   HIKING, WATERSPORTS
(☑ 852 9300 5197; www.kayak-and-hike.com; HK$800) The seven-hour Sai Kung Geopark kayak tour provides an exciting option for exploring the beauty of Sai Kung. It takes you to a kayak base at nearby Bluff Island in a speed boat or junk, from where you paddle to a beach to enjoy swimming and snorkelling. Departs 8.30am from Sai Kung old pier.

Hong Kong Foodie Tour   FOOD & DRINK
(☑ 852 2850 5006; www.hongkongfoodietours.com; adult/child from HK$750/540; ⊙ Mon-Sat) Regular group tours crawl Hong Kong's local food joints with native guides; it's also one of the only operators covering further-flung food haunts in the New Territories. There are four options: Central and Sheung Wan, Sham Shui Po, the Tai Po Market, and Temple Street Night Market. Walks run every day of the week except Sunday.

Big Foot Tours   CULTURAL
(☑ 852 8192 9928; www.bigfoottour.com; group tour per person HK$750, 1- or 2-person private tour HK$2200) Professional small group and private tours that really get behind the scenes of daily Hong Kong life. Group tours focus on New Territories neighbourhoods, their monasteries and so on. Private itineraries can focus on food (want to try snake soup?), architecture, nature or whatever strikes your fancy, and guides are full of interesting facts.

Aqua Luna   BOATING
(Map p528; ☑ 852 2116 8821; www.aqualuna.com.hk; Central Pier 9, Central; from HK$160) Professional harbour tours on traditional Chinese wooden junk boats, with a covered upper level and comfy deck seating. Lots of options run on different days, including a hop-on, hop-off harbour tour, a trip to Stanley, a Symphony of Lights (p533) evening cruise, and a recommended dim sum lunch cruise (HK$450) on Mondays and Fridays. Tours depart from Central and then pick up from Tsim Sha Tsui Pier 1.

✸✸ Festivals & Events

Hong Kong Arts Festival   PERFORMING ARTS
(香港藝術節; www.hk.artsfestival.org; tickets from HK$150; ⊙ Feb-Mar) A feast of music and performance arts, ranging from classical to contemporary, by hundreds of local and international talents.

Art Basel Hong Kong   ART
(香港巴塞爾藝術展; www.artbasel.com/hong-kong; ⊙ Mar) The Hong Kong edition of the world's premier art fair is a mega event where hundreds of galleries, thousands of artists, and art collectors from around the world flock to Hong Kong for five days of buying, selling, mingling and viewing. Satellite happenings are hosted by galleries across town, but big shows are at the **Hong Kong Convention & Exhibition Centre** (香港會議展覽中心; Map p532; www.hkcec.com; 1 Expo Dr, Wan Chai; ☐ 18).

Hong Kong International Film Festival FILM
(香港國際電影節; www.hkiff.org.hk; tickets from HK$55; ⊙ Mar-Apr) One of Asia's top film festivals, the HKIFF has been running for more than 40 years. It screens the latest art-house and award-winning movies from around the world for two to three weeks straddling the Easter holidays. Those who miss the festival can catch screenings all year round at regular cinemas through the festival's Cine Fan program (http://cinefan.com.hk). The same organisation also runs the **Summer International Film Festival** in August.

Cheung Chau Bun Festival   FOOD & DRINK
(長洲太平清醮; www.cheungchau.org; Apr/May) Taking place over four days in late April or early to mid-May, Cheung Chau's annual Bun Festival is one of Hong Kong's unique cultural experiences. Honouring the Taoist god Pak Tai, the festival involves days of parades, music and sweet buns galore. The main event is the scramble up the 'bun tower' – whoever grabs the top bun first wins.

Hong Kong International Dragon Boat Races   SPORTS
(香港國際龍舟邀請賽; www.hkidbr.sportsoho.com; ⊙ May or Jun) For several days around the fifth day of the fifth lunar month, as has been the custom for hundreds of years, dragonboaters race in waterways all over Hong Kong. It's also around this time that the government-hosted Hong Kong International Dragon Boat Carnival takes place at Victoria Harbour. The event features thousands

Yau Ma Tei

Yau Ma Tei

◎ Top Sights
1 Shanghai Street.....................................B1
2 Temple Street Night Market..............B1

◎ Sights
3 Tin Hau Temple C2

✕ Eating
4 Mido Café B2

⊕ Entertainment
Canton Singing House.................(see 4)

⊙ Shopping
5 Yue Hwa Chinese Products
Emporium C3

of the world's top dragon-boaters over three exciting days of racing and partying.

Clockenflap
MUSIC

(香港音樂及藝術節; www.clockenflap.com; Central harbourfront; tickets 1-day HK$930-1000, 3-day HK$1720; ⊙ Nov or Dec) Hong Kong's largest outdoor music festival incorporates international, regional and local live music of a mostly indie variety, as well as art installations and pop-ups. Acts that have played the festival include New Order, the Libertines, A$AP and Massive Attack.

🛏 Sleeping

Notorious for its boxy rooms, you won't get much bang for your buck in Hong Kong hotels. That said, service is usually very good and there's plenty of diversity, from dorm beds to chic apartments and palatial suites. Most hotels on Hong Kong Island are between Sheung Wan and Causeway Bay; in Kowloon, they fall around Nathan Rd, where you'll also find budget places. All rooms have air-conditioning, and all but the cheapest rooms have in-room wi-fi and cable TV in English.

🛏 Central District

★ Mini Hotel Central
BOUTIQUE HOTEL $

(Map p528; ☑ 852 2103 0999; www.minihotel.hk/central; 38 Ice House St, Central; s/d from HK$400/460; @ 🛜) We've seen glasses of wine in ritzy Central more expensive than this budget hotel. Of course for this price there has to be a trade-off, and in Mini Hotel Central it's thin walls and 10-sq-metre rooms. Look beyond that, though, and it's an excellent deal: clean, stylish and modern, with glass-walled marbled bathrooms. The location could not be better.

★ Helena May
HOTEL $

(梅夫人婦女會主樓; Map p528; ☑ 852 2522 6766; www.helenamay.com; 35 Garden Rd, Central;

s/d HK$630/820, studios HK$900-1040; ☎; 🖵23, Ⓜ Central, exit J2) If you like the Peninsula's colonial setting but not its price tag, this grand dame could be your cup of tea. Founded in 1916 as a social club for single European women, it is now a private club for both sexes of all nationalities, and a hotel with women-only rooms in the main building and popular en suite studios in an annexe that allows men.

Pottinger BOUTIQUE HOTEL $$$
(Map p528; ☎852 2308 3188; www.thepottinger. com; 74 Queen's Rd Central, enter from Stanley St, Central; r HK$2320-4000, ste from HK$5000; ☎; Ⓜ Central, exit D2) In the heart of Central, this unobtrusive boutique hotel has 68 airy, white-and-cream rooms with marble bathrooms and subtle Asian touches: carved wooden screens, calligraphy work, black-and-white photos of old Hong Kong. Free Fuji water is a nice touch. The Envoy, its excellent hotel bar, is a tribute to Sir Henry Pottinger, Hong Kong's first governor and the hotel's eponym.

The Peak & Northwest Hong Kong Island

SLEEEP CAPSULE HOTEL $
(Map p528; ☎852 9604 6049; www.sleeep. io; 242 Queen's Rd Central, Sheung Wan; capsule per hour/12hr/night from HK$149/399/499; ☎; Ⓜ Sheung Wan, exit A2) 🌿 Frazzled city workers sometimes bunk into this award-winning futuristic hotel by the hour to recalibrate, and it's easy to see why: an aura of calm akin to a meditation studio surrounds SLEEEP – Hong Kong's first capsule hotel. There are only eight capsules, with shared shower facilities. The hotel is on the steps between Queen's Rd Central and Gough St.

★ Hotel Jen HOTEL $$
(☎852 2974 1234; www.hoteljen.com/hongkong; 508 Queen's Rd W, Shek Tong Tsui; r from HK$800; ☎🏊; Ⓜ HKU, exit B2) Now part of the Shangri-La group, Hotel Jen feels more luxurious than its price tag suggests. The high-ceilinged, modern rooms are supercomfy with plump beds, and harbour views cost just a fraction more. In Hong Kong's stifling summers, the rooftop pool (with dreamy harbour views!) is a coveted amenity, and a rare one to find on Hong Kong Island at this price.

99 Bonham BOUTIQUE HOTEL $$
(Map p528; ☎852 3940 1111; www.99bonham.com; 99 Bonham Strand, Sheung Wan; r from HK$1500; @☎; Ⓜ Sheung Wan, exit A2) This hotel has 84 unusually large rooms (for Hong Kong).

They are stylishly minimalist, with luxury bathrooms and washed in a neutral palette. The hotel also has a small gym with free refreshments, free laundry on each floor, and a rooftop terrace with loungers and resplendent views. Extra handy is the mobile phone with free data and local calls for use during your stay.

Wan Chai & Northeast Hong Kong Island

Check Inn HOSTEL $
(卓軒旅舍; Map p532; ☎852 2955 0175; Flat A, 2nd fl, Kwong Wah Mansion, 269-273 Hennessy Rd, Wan Chai; dm/s/d from HK$160/500/600; @☎; Ⓜ Wan Chai, exit A2) Clean, spacious and brightly lit dorms are furnished with huge bunk beds and lockers at this well-located Wan Chai hostel. The reception and hang-out area (2nd floor) has sofas, free coffee and iMacs facing a wall of windows. Friendly staff host the occasional activity for guests, such as hiking up Victoria Peak.

★ Hotel Indigo DESIGN HOTEL $$
(Map p532; ☎852 3926 3888; www.hotelindigo. com; 246 Queen's Rd E, Wan Chai; r from HK$1600; @☎🏊; Ⓜ Wan Chai, exit A3) With an enticing location on hip Queen's Rd East, and colourful, tech-forward rooms that are exceedingly spacious for the price, Indigo is an excellent mid- to upper-range proposition. A petite pool and quiet bar high up on the rooftop seal the deal.

Upper House BOUTIQUE HOTEL $$$
(☎852 2918 1838; www.upperhouse.com; 88 Queensway, Pacific Pl, Admiralty; r/ste from HK$5200/18,000; @☎; Ⓜ Admiralty, exit F) For ultraluxe living in designer style, there is no finer Hong Kong hotel – provided you're willing to forgo a pool. Piggybacking on to the top floors of the JW Marriott (hence the 'Upper'), even the smallest rooms, the Studio 70s, are twice as large as other top-end digs and have walk-in closet, complimentary minibar and deep-soaking tub with a view.

Kowloon

★ Hop Inn on Carnarvon HOSTEL $
(Map p536; ☎852 2881 7331; www.hopinn.hk; 9th fl, James S Lee Mansion, 33-35 Carnarvon Rd, Tsim Sha Tsui; dm HK$150-340, s HK$430-580, d HK$540-850; @☎; Ⓜ Tsim Sha Tsui, exit A2) A sofa-strewn lounge, adjoining roof terrace and obligatory cheap beer fridge make this laid-back hostel a

CHUNGKING MANSIONS

Say 'budget accommodation' and 'Hong Kong' in one breath and everyone thinks of Chungking Mansions (36-44 Nathan Rd, Tsim Sha Tsui; M Tsim Sha Tsui, exit D1). Built in 1961, CKM is a labyrinth of homes, guesthouses, Indian restaurants, souvenir stalls and foreign-exchange shops spread over five 17-storey blocks in the heart of Tsim Sha Tsui. According to anthropologist Gordon Mathews, it has a resident population of about 4000 and an estimated 10,000 daily visitors. More than 120 different nationalities – predominantly South Asian and African – pass through its doors in a single year.

Though standards vary significantly, most of the guesthouses at CKM are clean and quite comfortable. It's worth bearing in mind, however, that rooms are usually the size of cupboards and you have to shower right next to the toilet. The rooms typically come with air-con and TV and, sometimes, a window. Virtually all have wi-fi and some even offer daily housekeeping and luxuries like toothbrushes!

Bargaining for a bed or room is always possible, though you won't get very far in high season. You can often negotiate a cheaper price if you stay more than, say, a week, but never try that on the first night – stay one night and find out how you like it before handing over more rent. Once you pay, there are usually no refunds.

Though there are dozens of ever-changing hostels in Chungking Mansions, some reliable ones include **Dragon Inn** (龍滙賓館; Map p536; ☑ 852 2367 7071; www.dragoninn. info; Flat B, 3rd fl, B Block; s HK$180-400, d HK$360-660, tr/q HK$480/520; ☎) and **Holiday Guesthouse** (Map p536; ☑ 852 2316 7152, 852 9121 8072; Flat E1, 6th fl, E Block; s HK$300-600, d HK$350-700; ☎).

great place to wind down after a day pounding the mean streets of Kowloon. Polished concrete floors lead to neatly swept singles, doubles, triples and four- to eight-person dorms, several with murals by local artists.

Urban Pack
HOSTEL $
(休閒小窩; Map p536; ☑ 852 2732 2271; www.urban-pack.com; Unit 1410, 14th fl, Haiphong Mansion, 99-101 Nathan Rd, Tsim Sha Tsui; dm HK$150-300, r from HK$500; ☎; M Tsim Sha Tsui, exit A1) A laid-back, sociable hostel with a great location between Kowloon Park and Harbour City, Urban Pack is run by two friendly Canadian-Chinese, Albert and Jensen. Compact dorms with privacy blinds, doubles and twin bunk rooms occupy various units of a commercial building, with separate areas for hanging out. A tour program includes bar crawls and Happy Valley races.

Salisbury YMCA
HOTEL $$
(香港基督教青年會; Map p536; ☑ 852 2268 7888; www.ymcahk.org.hk/thesalisbury; 41 Salisbury Rd, Tsim Sha Tsui; s/d/ste from HK$920/1280/2280; @☎☒; M East Tsim Sha Tsui, exit L6) If you can manage to book a room at this fabulously located YMCA hotel, you'll be rewarded with professional service. The 372 rooms and suites are comfortable but basic, but the views of the harbour would cost five times as much at the Peninsula next door.

★ Peninsula Hong Kong
HOTEL $$$
(香港半島酒店; Map p536; ☑ 852 2920 2888; www.peninsula.com; Salisbury Rd, Tsim Sha Tsui; r/ste from HK$4120/6440; @☎☒; M Tsim Sha Tsui, exit E) Lording it over the southern tip of Kowloon, the throne-like Peninsula (c 1928) is one of the world's great hotels. It was once called 'the finest hotel east of Suez', and your dilemma will be how to get here: landing on the rooftop helipad or arriving in one of the hotel's 16-strong fleet of Rolls Royce Phantoms.

Another dilemma is choosing which of the 300 classic, modern Chinese-influenced rooms is for you; staying in the 20-storey annexe offers spectacular harbour views, but the original building has glorious heritage interiors. Taking afternoon tea here is a wonderful experience – dress neatly and be prepared to queue for a table.

🛏 New Territories

Mojo Nomad
HOSTEL $
(☑ 852 3728 1000; www.mojonomad.com; 100 Shek Pai Wan Rd, Aberdeen; dm HK$250-350, d/f from HK$780/1390; ☒@☎; ☐ 31, 42, 48, 71, 72) One of Hong Kong's best budget options, Mojo Nomad has 196 beds and 64 rooms spread over 20 floors a street shy of Aberdeen Typhoon Shelter and its moored boats. The divine view is displayed to full effect by wall-to-wall windows in the harbour-facing rooms (which includes all family rooms). Units overlooking

a hillside cemetery are HK$20 to HK$40 cheaper. Dormitory beds drop to HK$160 to HK$190 in the off season.

T Hotel
HOTEL $$

(T酒店; ☑852 3717 7388; www.thotel.edu.hk; VTC Pokfulam Complex, 145 Pok Fu Lam Rd, Pok Fu Lam; r/ste from HK$990/2940; ⊕❄@🛜; 🚌7, 91 from Central, 973 from Tsim Sha Tsui) Ah, we almost don't want to tell you about this gem! The 30-room T in the serene neighbourhood of Pok Fu Lam is entirely run by students of the hospitality training institute. The young trainees are attentive, cheerful and eager to hone their skills. Rooms, all on the 6th floor, are sparkling and spacious, with ocean or mountain views.

🍴 Eating

One of the world's top culinary capitals, the city that worships the God of Cookery has many a demon in the kitchen, whether it's Cantonese, Sichuanese, Japanese or French. So deep is the city's love of food and so broad its culinary repertoire that whatever your gastronomic desires, Hong Kong will find a way to sate them. The answer could be a bowl of wonton noodles, freshly steamed dim sum, a warm pineapple bun wedged with butter, a pair of the sweetest prawns, your first-ever stinky tofu, or the creations of the latest celebrity chef.

🍴 Central District

★ Yat Lok
CHINESE $

(一樂燒鵝; Map p528; ☑852 2524 3882; 34-38 Stanley St, Central; meals HK$56-180; ⊗10am-8.30pm; Ⓜ Central, exit D2) Be prepared to bump elbows with locals at this tiny, basic joint known for its roast goose. Anthony Bourdain gushed over the bird. The leg is the most prized cut and the general rule is the more you pay, the better your meat will be; meals include rice or slippery noodles.

Little English is spoken, but there's a menu. Takeaway is also available.

★ Lan Fong Yuen
CAFE $

(蘭芳園; Map p528; ☑852 2544 3895; 2 & 4A Gage St, Central; meals from HK$60, minimum spend HK$28; ⊗7.30am-6pm Mon-Sat; 🚌5B) This rickety facade hides an entire cha chaan tang (tea cafe). Lan Fong Yuen (1952) is believed to be the inventor of the 'pantyhose' milk tea, and droves of Instagrammers come to worship here, drink in hand. Over a thousand cups of the strong and silky brew are sold daily along-side pork-chop buns, instant noodles and other delicious hasty tasties.

Tim Ho Wan
DIM SUM $

(添好運點心專門店; Map p528; ☑852 2332 3078; www.timhowan.hk; Shop 12A, Level 1, Hong Kong Station, Central; meals HK$100-150; ⊗9am-9pm; Ⓜ Hong Kong, exit E1) Opened by a former Four Seasons chef, Tim Ho Wan was the first-ever budget dim sum place to receive a Michelin star. Many relocations and branches later, this iteration beneath **IFC Mall** (Map p528; ☑852 2295 3308; www.ifc.com.hk; 8 Finance St, Central; Ⓜ Hong Kong, exit F) may be bland-looking but the star is still tucked snugly inside its tasty titbits (the shrimp dumplings are excellent). Expect to wait 15 to 40 minutes for a seat.

★ Old Bailey
CHINESE $$

(Map p528; ☑852 2877 8711; www.oldbailey.hk; 2nd fl, JC Contemporary, Tai Kwun, Old Bailey St, Soho; meals from HK$300; ⊗noon-3pm & 6-11pm, lounge bar noon-11pm; 🛜🍽; 🚌26) The joy of Old Bailey begins with its snazzy Herzog & de Meuron–designed interior that mixes mid-century-modern Scandi with Chinese design principles, and the sweeping outdoor terrace that overlooks Tai Kwun and Soho's skyscrapers. The food lives up to its surroundings, with dishes like Longjing-tea-smoked pigeon, pork belly with spindly shimeji mushrooms and juicy *xiao long bao* (soup dumplings) with Sichuan peppercorns.

Ho Lee Fook
HONG KONG $$

(Map p528; ☑852 2810 0860; www.holeefook.com.hk; Ground fl, 3-5 Elgin St, Soho; meals from HK$400; ⊗6-10.45pm Sun-Thu, to 11.45pm Fri & Sat; 🛜; Ⓜ Central, exit D2) As irreverent as its name suggests, this buzzy underground spot does a winkingly modern take on retro Chinatown cuisine. Fat prawn toasts are served with Kewpie mayo, the char siu (barbecued pork) uses upmarket Kurobuta pork, and prawn *lo mein* is spangled with crunchy fried garlic and slicked with shellfish oil. It's justifiably popular and the atmosphere is see-and-be-seen, despite nightclub-level darkness.

🍴 The Peak & Northwest Hong Kong Island

★ Kau Kee Restaurant
NOODLES $

(九記牛腩; Map p528; ☑852 2850 5967; 21 Gough St, Central; meals from HK$50; ⊗12.30-10.30pm Mon-Sat; Ⓜ Sheung Wan, exit E2) You can argue till the noodles go soggy about

HONG KONG EATING

CHA CHAAN TANG

Teahouses (茶餐廳, *cha chaan tang*) are cheap and cheery neighbourhood eateries that appeared in the 1940s serving western-style snacks and drinks to those who couldn't afford Earl Grey and cucumber sandwiches. Their menus have since grown to include more substantial Chinese and soy sauce western dishes.

Some teahouses have bakeries creating European pastries with Chinese characteristics, such as pineapple buns (菠蘿包, *bo law bao*), which don't contain a trace of the said fruit, and cocktail buns, which have coconut stuffing (雞尾包, *gai may bao*).

whether Kau Kee has the best beef brisket in town. Whatever the verdict, the meat – served with toothsome noodles in a fragrant beefy broth – is hard to beat. During the 90 years of the shop's existence, film stars and politicians have joined the queue for a table.

Sun Hing Restaurant · DIM SUM $

(新興食家; ☑ 852 2816 0616; Ground fl, 8C Smithfield Rd, Kennedy Town, Western District; meals HK$50; ◷ 3am-4pm; ☐ 101) Many a drunken Soho reveller has trudged westward after a long night seeking cheap dim sum, but to no avail. Then just before they pass out, there appears, vision-like, Sun Hing in all its scrumptious glory! They weep. True story, though some say tears are shed over the runny 'Golden Sauce' custard bun (流沙包) – don't leave without ordering some.

Little English is spoken, but there's an English menu and staff will also wave you over to point at what you want in baskets on a table at the side of the cafe.

★ Little Bao · FUSION $$

(Map p532; ☑ 852 2194 0202; www.little-bao.com; 9 Kingston Street, Causeway Bay; meals HK$250-400; ◷ 6-11pm Mon-Fri, noon-4pm & 6-11pm Sat, noon-4pm & 6-10pm Sun; ☎◢; Ⓜ Central, exit D2) A trendy diner that wows with its *bao* (Chinese buns) – snow-white orbs crammed with juicy meat and slathered with Asian condiments – and fusion sharing dishes. Its signature pork-belly *bao* with hoisin ketchup, and truffle fries with shiitake tempeh might just be the greatest meal you have in Hong Kong. Go early to put your name on the waiting list – no reservations.

BlackSalt Tavern · ASIAN $$

(☑ 852 3702 1237, reservations by Whatsapp 852 5173 3058; www.tavern.blacksalt.com.hk; Ground fl, 1 South Lane, Shek Tong Tsui; meals from HK$300; ◷ 6-11pm Tue-Thu, noon-3pm & 6pm-midnight Fri & Sat, noon-3pm & 6-11pm Sun; ☎◢; Ⓜ HKU, exit B2) Black Salt is the friendly neighbourhood restaurant we'd all like to have around the corner. In 2018 it moved into a bigger space in Shek Tong Tsui and added a craft beer menu. Dishes are a delicious, accomplished mashup of South Asian cuisines, including fancy Kathmandu *momo* dumplings, Sri Lankan *kothu roti* and Indian *mattar paneer* with melt-in-the-mouth homemade curds.

Rōnin · JAPANESE $$$

(Map p528; ☑ 852 2547 5263; www.roninhk.com; Ground fl, 8 On Wo Lane, Sheung Wan; meals from HK$500; ◷ 6pm-midnight Mon-Sat; ☎; Ⓜ Sheung Wan, exit E2) With just 24 counter seats locked down behind an unmarked door, Rōnin has all the hallmarks of a coveted Soho dining spot before you've even seen the daily changing menu. Plates – all delicious and inventive – are organised by raw, smaller and bigger, and include revelations like succulent blackpilsner-battered smoked tilefish and crunchy palm-sized crabs with *yuzu* and sesame.

✖ Wan Chai & Northeast Hong Kong Island

On Lee Noodle · NOODLES $

(☑ 852 2513 8398; 22 Main St E, Shau Kei Wan; noodles from HK$40; ◷ 9am-7pm; Ⓜ Shau Kei Wan, exit B2) Quiveringly tender beef brisket is the big draw here, eaten with noodles either in a soup or 'stirred' with soy sauce (you still get a little bowl of beefy soup to drink). Add extras such as fish balls, wontons, or more brisket if hungry. It's the perfect pit stop when visiting the nearby Hong Kong Museum of Coastal Defence.

★ Lock Cha Tea Shop · VEGETARIAN, CHINESE $

(樂茶軒; Map p528; ☑ 852 2801 7177; www.lockcha.com; Ground fl, KS Lo Gallery, 10 Cotton Tree Dr, Hong Kong Park, Admiralty; dim sum HK$28-35, tea from HK$38; ◷ 10am-8pm, closed 2nd Tue of month; ◢; Ⓜ Admiralty, exit C1) Set in the lush environs of Hong Kong Park, Lock Cha serves fragrant Chinese teas and vegetarian dim sum in an antique-styled environment designed to resemble a scholar's quarters. There are traditional music performances on Saturday (7pm to 8.30pm; free) and Sunday (4.30pm to 6.30pm; HK$150). Do call to reserve a seat.

Kam's Roast Goose
CANTONESE **$**

(甘牌燒鵝; Map p532; ☑ 852 2520 1110; www.krg. com.hk; 226 Hennessy Rd, Wan Chai; meals HK$80-200; ⊙ 11.30am-9.30pm; Ⓜ Wan Chai, exit A2) Expect to queue for half an hour or more to worship at the oily altar of perfectly roasted goose. A spin-off from Central's famed **Yung Kee Restaurant** (鏞記; Map p528; ☑ 852 2522 1624; www.yungkee.com.hk; 32-40 Wellington St, Lan Kwai Fong; lunch from HK$150, dinner HK$250-500; ⊙ 11am-11pm; 🅰; Ⓜ Central, exit D2), Michelin-starred Kam's still upholds the same strict standards in sourcing and roasting. The best cut is the upper thigh (succulent but less fatty), which can be had with steamed rice or seasoned noodles.

Besides the crisp-skinned fowl, other barbecued meats such as roast suckling pig are well worth sinking your teeth into. If you don't mind ordering your goose to take away, you can get it almost straight away.

Samsen
THAI **$$**

(泰麵; Map p532; ☑ 852 2234 0001; 68 Stone Nullah Lane, Wan Chai; dishes from HK$118; ⊙ noon-2.30pm & 6.30-11pm; Ⓜ Wan Chai, exit D) One bite of Samsen's delectable pad thai and Queen's Rd E becomes Khao San Rd; but at this hip little gem presided over by an Aussie chef, the good ol' backpacker staple is pimped up with plump tiger prawns, paired with zingy Thai salads and washed down with Moonzen craft beer. Expect to queue.

Tung Po Seafood Restaurant
MARKET, CANTONESE **$$**

(東寶小館; ☑ 852 2880 5224, 852 2880 9399; 2nd fl, Java Rd Wet Market, Municipal Services Bldg, 99 Java Rd, North Point; meals HK$200-600; ⊙ 5.30pm-midnight; Ⓜ North Point, exit A1) You're guaranteed a hearty repast at any *dai pai dong* (大牌檔, food stall) atop Java Rd Wet Market, but at Tung Po (and its sister spot, 店小二), you'll discover fusion Cantonese with a higher price tag and a dash of eccentricity. Thursday to Saturday, it's Hong Kong's most riotous dinner, as bowls of beer are downed to blaring '90s R&B. Cash only.

★ Seventh Son
CANTONESE **$$**

(家全七福; Map p532; ☑ 852 2892 2888; www. seventhson.hk; 3rd fl, Wharney Guangdong Hotel, 57-73 Lockhart Rd, Wan Chai; meals from HK$350; ⊙ 11.30am-2.30pm & 6-10.30pm; Ⓜ Wan Chai, exit C) Worthy spin-off from the illustrious and famously wallet-unfriendly **Fook Lam Moon** (福臨門; Map p536; ☑ 852 2366 0286; www. fooklammoon-grp.com; Shop 8, 1st fl, 53-59 Kimberley Rd, Tsim Sha Tsui; meals HK$400-2000; ⊙ 11.30am-2.30pm & 6-10.30pm; Ⓜ Tsim Sha Tsui, exit B1) – aka Tycoon's Canteen, for its clientele of movie stars and politicians – Seventh Son reproduces FLM's home-style dishes to a T, and a few extravagant seafood numbers as well. The food here is excellent, prices are fair, plus you get the treatment FLM reserves for regulars.

⊁ Aberdeen & South Hong Kong Island

★ Aberdeen Fish Market Yee Hope Seafood Restaurant
CANTONESE, SEAFOOD **$$**

(香港仔魚市場二合海鮮餐廳; ☑ 852 2177 7872; 102 Shek Pai Wan Rd, Aberdeen; meals from $350; ⊙ 4am-3pm; 🚌 107, Ⓜ Wong Chuk Hang, exit B) Hidden in Hong Kong's only wholesale fish market, this understated eatery run by fishers is truly an in-the-know place for ultra-fresh seafood. There's no menu, but tell them your budget and they'll source the best sea creatures available, including ones not often seen in restaurants. There's no English sign; look for the nondescript one-storey yellow building with a green roof at the end of the fish market.

⊁ Kowloon

Mido Café
CAFE **$**

(美都餐室; Map p540; ☑ 852 2384 6402; 63 Temple St, Yau Ma Tei; meals HK$45-150; ⊙ 8.30am-8pm Thu-Tue; Ⓜ Yau Ma Tei, exit B2) Kowloon's most famous tea cafe, this highly instagrammable *cha chaan tang* (teahouse; c 1950) with mosaic tiles and metal latticework stands astride a street corner that comes to life at sundown. Go upstairs and take a seat next to a wall of iron-framed windows overlooking Tin Hau Temple (p533).

★ Ye Shanghai
DIM SUM **$$**

(夜上海; Map p536; ☑ 852 2376 3322; www. elite-concepts.com; 6th fl, Marco Polo Hotel, Harbour City, Canton Rd, Tsim Sha Tsui; meals HK$300-800; ⊙ 11.30am-3pm & 6-10.30pm; Ⓜ Tsim Sha Tsui, exit C2) Dark woods and subdued lighting inspired by 1920s Shanghai impart an air of romance to this otherwise bustling restaurant serving exquisite Shanghainese and Zhejiang classics – tea-smoked duck, sweet and sour 'squirrel' fish and unctuous steamed pork belly. The only exception to this Jiangnan harmony is the Cantonese dim sum being served at lunch, though that too is excellent.

★ **Chi Lin Vegetarian** VEGETARIAN, CHINESE $$

(志蓮素齋, 龍門樓; Long Men Lou; Map p525; ☑ 852 3658 9388; 60 Fung Tak Rd, Nan Lian Garden; meals from HK$200; ⊙ noon-3pm & 6-9pm Mon-Fri, noon-9pm Sat & Sun; ✔; Ⓜ Diamond Hill, exit C2) Savour organic wild mushrooms with rice or noodles, and impeccable veggie dim sum such as steamed asparagus with lily bulbs and truffle, as an artificial waterfall cascades over enormous windows at this refined Chinese restaurant in the ornamental **Nan Lian Garden**. If you're coming to the Chi Lin Nunnery (p534) next door, it's a must visit.

Do reserve ahead, especially on weekends, and note the minimum charge of HK$120 per person at lunch (and a little more for dinner).

Din Tai Fung SHANGHAI $$

(鼎泰豐; Map p536; ☑ 852 2730 6928; www.dintaifung.com.hk; Shop 130, 3rd fl, Silvercord, 30 Canton Rd, Tsim Sha Tsui; meals HK$150-300; ⊙ 11.30am-10pm; ✔; Ⓜ Tsim Sha Tsui, exit C1) DTF's steamers of perfectly pleated *xiao long bao* (Shànghǎi-style dumplings) have made this Taiwanese chain an Asia-wide institution. Order them wrapped with pork, crab, veggies or even truffle. Queues are the norm and there are no reservations, but service is excellent. Must-eats also include the fluffy steamed pork buns and the greasy-but-oh-so-good fried pork chop.

Spring Deer PEKING DUCK $$

(鹿鳴春飯店; Map p536; ☑ 852 2366 4012; 1st fl, 42 Mody Rd, Tsim Sha Tsui; meals HK$150-500; ⊙ noon-2pm & 6-10pm; Ⓜ East Tsim Sha Tsui, exit P3) Hong Kong's most authentic Northern Chinese–style roast lamb is served at this long-standing locals' favourite. Better known is the perfectly bronzed Peking duck, carved thick and served with traditional *shāobǐng* bread as well as the more usual steamed pancakes. Service can sometimes be as welcoming as a Beijing winter, c 1967. Booking is essential.

✗ New Territories

The New Territories whips up Hong Kong's best Hakka and walled village cuisines (Yuen Long and Fanling) and makes a solid bowl of noodles (Tai Po, Yuen Long and Fanling). Waterfront areas in Sai Kung, Tuen Mun (Sam Shing Hui) and Po Toi O fishing village feature exciting seafood places. Laudable village kitchens can be found in Tai Mo Shan and Sha Tau Kok, and world-famous roast goose in Tsuen Wan and Tai Po.

Sun Kwai Heung CHINESE $

(新桂香燒臘; ☑ 852 2556 1183; 17, Kam Tam Yun House, 345 Chai Wan Rd, Chai Wan; meals from HK$47; ⊙ 8.30am-9pm; Ⓜ Chai Wan, exit C) This off-the-beaten-track shop has unbeatable Cantonese barbecue and none of the lines of better-known places. Char siu (barbecued pork) emerges from the roaster, edges beautifully bronzed and caramelised, several times a day.

★ **Yue Kee Roasted Goose Restaurant** CANTONESE $$

(裕記大飯店; ☑ 852 2491 0105; www.yuekee.com.hk; 9 Sham Hong Rd, Sham Tseng; meals HK$180-500; ⊙ 11am-11pm; 🚌 minibus 302 from Tai Wo Hau MTR) In an alley lined with roast-goose restaurants, 60-year-old Yue Kee is the king. Order gorgeous plates of coppery-skinned charcoal-roasted goose (half is plenty for four people) and sample house specialities including soy-braised goose web (feet), wine-infused goose liver and stir-fried goose intestines. If that's not your speed, there are plenty of standard Cantonese dishes on offer. Book ahead. Yue Kee is a Michelin-starred restaurant.

Loaf On CANTONESE, SEAFOOD $$

(六福館; ☑ 852 2792 9966; 49 See Cheung St, Sai Kung; dishes from HK$150; ⊙ 11am-11pm; 🚌 1) The motto here is: eat what they hunt. This three-storey Michelin-starred restaurant is where fish freshly caught from Sai Kung waters in the morning lands on customers' plates by midday. The signature fish soup and steamed fish sell out fast. There is no English signage, but it's identifiable by a lone dining table set outside and the shiny brass sign. Reservations recommended.

Sha Tin 18 CANTONESE, CHINESE $$

(沙田18; ☑ 852 3723 7932; Hyatt Regency Hong Kong, 18 Chak Cheung St, Sha Tin; meals HK$350-800; ⊙ 11.30am-3pm & 5.30-10.30pm Mon-Fri, from 10.30am Sat & Sun; Ⓜ University) Sha Tin 18's Peking duck (half/whole HK$538/848) has put this hotel restaurant, adjacent to the Chinese University, in the gastronomic spotlight. Book your prized fowl 24 hours in advance, and tantalise your taste buds in three ways – pancakes with the crispy skin, meat and leeks; duck soup; and wok-fried minced duck. The Asian fusion desserts here are also famous.

🍷 Drinking & Nightlife

Energetic Hong Kong knows how to party and does so visibly and noisily. That said, don't be surprised that many of the city's bars are hidden inside skyscrapers; would it be Hong Kong if it were otherwise? You can find any type of bar or pub you want, but boozing will cost you dearly as alcohol is one of the few things that is taxed in this city: follow the happy hours.

Central District

★ Quinary
COCKTAIL BAR

(Map p528; ☑️852 2851 3223; www.quinary.hk; 56-58 Hollywood Rd, Soho; ⊙5pm-1am Mon-Sat; 🔊; Ⓜ Central, exit D2) Consistently voted one of the world's top 50 bars, Quinary is a sleek, moodily lit cocktail bar that attracts a well-dressed crowd. Its gifted mixologists create homemade infusions of spirits and the Asian-inspired cocktails are delicious, theatrical marvels. Signature creations include the Quinary Sour (whisky, homemade liquorice syrup and bonito flakes) and the Instagram-killing Earl Grey Caviar Martini with whipped air.

★ Pontiac
BAR

(Map p528; ☑️852 2521 3855; 13 Old Bailey St, Lan Kwai Fong; ⊙3pm-1am Mon-Sat, happy hour 5-8pm; 🔊; 📖26) There's something indescribably comfortable about the Pontiac, which rocks to a different tune from most of the cheesy bars in LKF. It's a skinny, open-fronted, graffiti-covered dive that's wholly run by women, with a string of bras hanging behind the bar to let you know who's in charge. Alternative music, friendly vibe and HK$30 happy-hour beers: what's not to love?

Iron Fairies
COCKTAIL BAR

(Map p528; ☑️852 2603 6992; www.facebook.com/theironfairieshongkong; lower ground fl, 1-13 Hollywood Rd, Lan Kwai Fong; ⊙6pm-2am Mon-Thu, 5pm-3am Fri & Sat, 5pm-2am Sun; 🔊; 📖26) Australian Ashley Sutton is a master of theatre and his bar is unlike anything else in Hong Kong. Ten thousand butterflies flutter from copper threads attached to the ceiling in an underground cave designed to mimic a blacksmith's foundry where tables are piled with fairies forged from iron. It's beautifully surreal, and the mixology ain't bad either.

Sevva
COCKTAIL BAR

(Map p528; ☑️852 2537 1388; www.sevva.hk; 25th fl, Prince's Bldg, 10 Chater Rd, Central; ⊙noon-midnight Mon-Thu, to 2am Fri & Sat; 🔊; Ⓜ Central, exit H) If there was a million-dollar view in Hong Kong, it'd be the one from the balcony of flashy Sevva – skyscrapers so close you can see their arteries of steel, with the harbour and Kowloon in the distance. At night it takes

your breath away, but the prices will too – expect to pay a minimum HK$160 for a glass of wine.

Book ahead if you want a couch on the balcony in the evening, though you can also perch at a standing table or simply go out for photos.

Colette's Art Bar
BAR

(Map p528; ☑️852 2521 7251; www.hkfringe colettes.com; 2nd fl, 2 Lower Albert Rd, Lan Kwai Fong; ⊙noon-3pm Mon, noon-3pm & 4.30-10pm Tue-Thu, to 12.30am Fri, 4.30pm-12.30am Sat; Ⓜ Central, exit D1) Bargain-hunters and thirsty shoestringers rejoice: happy hour runs from 4.30pm to 10pm at arty Colette's, which makes it one of the cheapest bars in Central. It's in a lovely corner heritage building (the Fringe Club) that was once a dairy farm, and has a hidden balcony with alfresco seating. It packs out for its weekday vegetarian lunch buffet (HK$118 with drink).

Petticoat Lane
GAY & LESBIAN

(Map p528; ☑️852 2808 2738; www.petticoatlane. club; Basement, 57-59 Wyndham St, Lan Kwai Fong; ⊙6pm-2am Mon & Sun, to 3am Tue, to 4am Wed & Thu, to 5am Fri, 8pm-5am Sat; Ⓜ Central, exit D2) Central's best LGBTIQ+ night out is Petticoat Lane, a basement club with sparkling foliage hanging above the bar, a dance floor, a small outdoor terrace and gender-neutral toilets. The vibe is inclusive and its weekly 'Wednesgay' evenings with topless bartenders include free-flow Absolut vodka (10pm to 11pm) for all and sundry. There's a drag show every night at midnight.

The Peak & Northwest Hong Kong Island

★ Old Man
COCKTAIL BAR

(Map p528; ☑️852 2703 1899; www.theoldman hk.com; Lower ground fl, 37-39 Aberdeen St, Soho; ⊙5pm-2am Mon-Sat, to midnight Sun; Ⓜ Central, exit D2) If Ernest Hemingway was still alive today, the chances are he'd love this tiny no-sign speakeasy named after his novel *The Old Man and the Sea* with a neo-cubist portrait of Papa himself looking down approvingly from behind the bar. The atmosphere is friendly rather than pretentious and the mixology is exceptionally creative, with elements like gruyere, sous-vide pandan leaves and nori dust (cocktails HK$100).

Ping Pong Gintoneria
BAR

(☑️852 9835 5061; www.pingpong129.com; 135 Second St, Sai Ying Pun; ⊙6-11pm; 🔊; Ⓜ Sai Ying

Pun, exit B2) Behind a closed red door, stairs lead down into a cavernous former ping-pong hall, now one of Hong Kong's coolest bars. The drink here is gin – the neon-illuminated bar stocks more than 50 types from across the globe, served in a variety of cocktails both classic and creative (G&Ts from HK$110). The crowd is arty, and the decor is even artier.

Little Creatures
MICROBREWERY

(☑852 2833 5611; www.littlecreatures.hk; Ground fl, 5A New Praya, Kennedy Town; ⊙9am-11pm Mon-Thu, to midnight Fri, 8am-midnight Sat, 8am-11pm Sun; ☜) This Australian import has the most visitor-friendly microbrewery set-up in Hong Kong. It occupies a vast space (for Hong Kong) just back from the waterfront; a cathedral of reclaimed wood and hoppy aromas. You'll find all the classic brews here, plus an increasing selection of local experiments like mangosteen ale. The western-style pub grub and brunch is top-notch.

Teakha
TEAHOUSE

(茶家; Map p528; ☑852 2858 9185; www.teakha. com; Shop B, 18 Tai Ping Shan St, Sheung Wan; ⊙9am-6pm Mon & Wed-Fri, 8.30am-7pm Sat & Sun; ☜; ☒26) Fancy organic tea concoctions are best enjoyed with the homemade drop scones in this modern interpretation of a Chinese teahouse, just off the main street in the impossibly hip Tai Ping Shan St area. The cute teaware makes a good souvenir.

Wan Chai & Northeast Hong Kong Island

★Second Draft
CRAFT BEER

(Map p532; ☑852 2656 0232; 98 Tung Lo Wan Rd, Tin Hau; ⊙4pm-1am Mon-Thu, to 2am Fri, noon-2am Sat, to 1am Sun; ☒Tin Hau, exit B) Tall windows wrap around a magisterial sweep of wooden bar at this Tai Hang neighbourhood gastropub, the sort of civilised joint where everybody knows everybody. A curated line-up of local beers favours the faultless Young Master brewery (450ml pours around HK$80), or go for an organic wine, paired with creative nibbles such as edamame with crispy chicken skin.

On weekends, it's also a breezy spot to stop by for lunch or single-origin coffee.

Botanicals
BAR

(Botanical Bar; Map p532; ☑852 2866 3444; www. thepawn.com.hk; 1st fl, 62 Johnston Rd, Wan Chai; ⊙noon-1am Sun-Thu, to 2am Fri & Sat; ☒Wan Chai, exit A3) On the 1st floor of gorgeous heritage pile the Pawn, Botanicals draws after-work imbibers to its stylish twin bars and colonial-chic veranda for wines by the glass, craft beers and playful cocktails (after 5pm) including 10-cask negronis (HK$100 to HK$140) concocted from a variety of gin infusions, boutique vermouths and herbal additions.

Skye Bar
BAR

(Map p532; ☑852 2839 3327; 22nd fl, Park Lane Hotel, 10 Gloucester Rd, Causeway Bay; ⊙noon-1am; ☒Causeway Bay, exit E) The views are to die for at this open-air rooftop gem jutting out from the corner of the Park Lane Hotel. Treat yourself to a glass of Perrier-Jouët champers (HK$170) at the curvaceously sociable bar as you drink in one of the most magnificent harbour panoramas in the city. Ah, Hong Kong.

🍷 Kowloon

Bound
BAR

(☑852 2396 6488; https://bound.business.site; 32 Boundary St, Prince Edward; ⊙2pm-2.30am; ☜; ☒Prince Edward, exit D) You could squish a dozen Hong Kong bars together and they still wouldn't have as much personality as this boho hang-out with its art-adorned walls, flashes of pink neon, indie playlist and craft-beer fridge. Bound could almost be the HQ of a hip marketing agency, but don't be put off – staff are really nice, and the coffee is fabulous.

★InterContinental Lobby Lounge
CAFE, BAR

(Map p536; ☑852 2721 1211; www.hongkong-ic. intercontinental.com; Hotel InterContinental Hong Kong, 18 Salisbury Rd, Tsim Sha Tsui; ⊙7am-1am; ☜; ☒East Tsim Sha Tsui, exit J) What's that sound? No, it's not the chink of cup and saucer, it's your jaw hitting the marble floor as you gaze, enraptured, at Hong Kong's most fabulous harbour views through a wall of glass. It's enough to make anybody feel like a somebody, and all you have to do is order a (very expensive) drink.

Lobby Lounge is also an ideal venue from which to watch the evening light show (p533) at 8pm.

Kowloon Taproom
CRAFT BEER

(Map p536; ☑852 2861 0355; www.kowloon-tap room.com; Ground fl, 26 Ashley Rd, Tsim Sha Tsui; ⊙2pm-2am Mon-Fri, 1pm-2am Sat & Sun; ☜; ☒Tsim Sha Tsui, exit H) Plugging a crafty gap in the market between TST's hotel bars and same-same sports dives, Kowloon Taproom pours a dozen, local-only craft beers from Lion Rock, Heroes and the like, astride a fry-heavy snack list including battered 'IPA' fish and chips. The grungy, open-fronted space, its bare walls pasted with posters, is a fine people-watching perch. Beers from HK$60.

Chicken HOF & Soju
BEER HALL

(李家; Lee Family Chicken; Map p536; ☑ 852 2375 8080; 84 Kam Kok Mansion, Kimberley Rd, Tsim Sha Tsui; ⊙ 2pm-6am; Ⓜ Jordan, exit D) In the middle of a Korean neighbourhood, this dark little venue hides an authentically tatty *chimeak* (chicken and beer) bar. Korean lager starts at a wallet-friendly HK$32, and you'll need plenty of it (*soju* chasers optional) to wash down a hearty order of crisp fried chicken.

☆ Entertainment

Hong Kong's arts and entertainment scene is healthier than ever. The increasingly busy cultural calendar includes music, drama and dance hailing from a plethora of traditions. The schedule of imported performances is nothing short of stellar. And every week, local arts companies and artists perform anything from Bach or stand-up to Cantonese opera and English versions of Chekhov plays.

★ Happy Valley Racecourse
HORSE RACING

(跑馬地馬場; Map p532; ☑ 852 2895 1523; www.hkjc.com; 2 Sports Rd, Happy Valley; HK$10; ⊙ races 7.15-10.50pm Wed Sep-Jun; ☒ Happy Valley) An outing at the races is one of the quintessential Hong Kong things to do, especially if you're around during the weekly Wednesday-evening races. Punters pack into the stands and trackside, with branded beer stalls, silly wigs and live music setting up an electric party atmosphere.

To bet, you must first exchange cash for betting vouchers inside the stands, then use the machine terminals (which have English settings and instructions). Stewards will help.

The first horse races were held here way back in 1846. Now meetings are held both here and at the newer and larger (but less atmospheric) **Sha Tin Racecourse** (沙田賽馬場; Penfold Park, Sha Tin; race-day public stands HK$10, tourist balcony zone HK$80-150; Ⓜ Racecourse) in the New Territories. Check the website for details on betting and tourist packages. Take the eastbound Happy Valley tram to the final stop and cross the road to the racecourse. You can use an Octopus card to enter the turnstiles.

Peel Fresco
JAZZ

(Map p528; ☑ 852 2540 2046; www.peelfresco.com; ground fl, 49 Peel St, Soho; ⊙ 5.30pm-late; ☒ 13, 26, 40M) Charming Peel Fresco has live jazz every day of the week, with local and overseas acts on an intimate stage close enough for listeners to chink glasses with musicians. It's small, relaxed and friendly, and there's no better place in Soho than here curled up with a drink when the action starts (around 7pm weekdays and 9pm weekends); come a little early to secure a seat.

A cover charge of up to HK$150 can apply if the act is an international recording artist, but often the gigs are free.

★ Canton Singing House
LIVE MUSIC

(艷陽天; Map p540; 49-51 Temple St, Yau Ma Tei; HK$20; ⊙ 3-7pm & 8pm-5am; Ⓜ Yau Ma Tei, exit C) The oldest and most atmospheric of Temple St's singalong parlours, Canton resembles a film set with mirror balls and glowing shrines. Singers take to the stage one after another to belt out the oldies; some customers applaud between glugs of beer, while others are too busy with card games. Every character in here looks like they have a story to tell.

Each session features 20 singers, all with a fan following. Patrons tip a minimum of HK$20 if they like a song. Even if you don't, it's nice to tip every now and then for the experience – just slip your money into the box on stage. For HK$100, you can sing a number yourself. They have a few western classics, and you can bet the keyboard player will know them.

This Town Needs
LIVE MUSIC

(☑ 852 9869 7865; www.facebook.com/thistown needs; 1st fl, 6 Shung Shun St, Yau Tong; bands local HK$180-350, international HK$280-500; Ⓜ Yau Tong, exit A2) This Town Needs...more underground music venues like this, staging 10 to

---

ⓘ TICKET BOOKING SERVICES

Urbtix (☑ 852 2111 5999; www.urbtix.hk; ⊙ booking hotline 10am-8pm) is the booking portal for tickets to shows at venues operated by the government's Leisure and Cultural Services Department. Book online and pick up your tickets at one of its many counters around Hong Kong; see the website for locations. There's also a My Urbtix booking app.

Another outlet that sells tickets to plays, concerts and other cultural events is **Hong Kong Ticketing** (☑ 852 3128 8288; www.hkticketing.com; ⊙ booking hotline 10am-8pm).

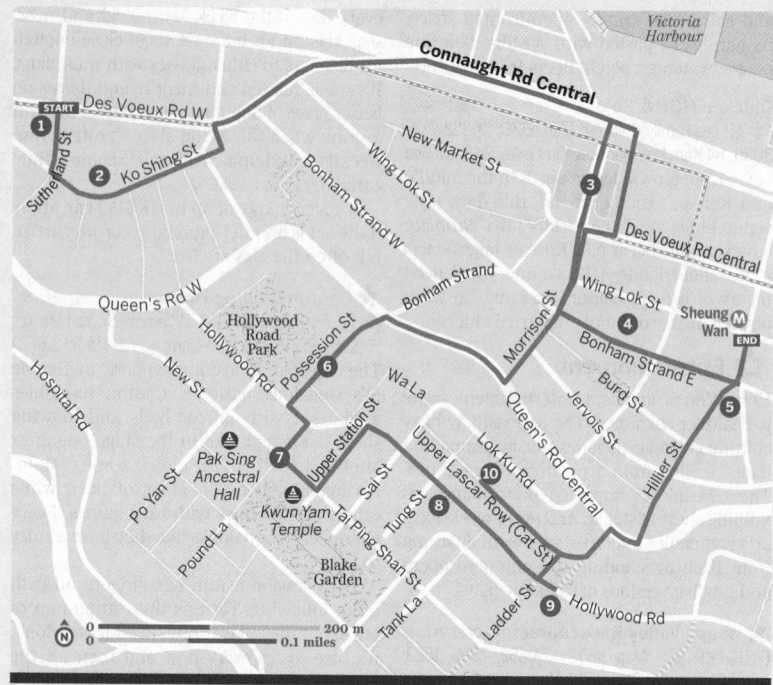

🏃 Walking Tour
Hong Kong's Wholesale District

START SUTHERLAND ST STOP, KENNEDY TOWN TRAM
END SHEUNG WAN MTR STATION, EXIT B
LENGTH 1.5KM; ONE HOUR

Set off from the Sutherland St stop. Have a look at Des Voeux Rd W's many ❶ **dried seafood shops** piled with all manner of desiccated sea life. Walk south to Ko Shing St to browse the medieval-looking goods on offer from the ❷ **herbal-medicine traders**.

At the end of Ko Shing St, re-enter Des Voeux Rd W and head northeast. Continue along Connaught Rd W, where you'll find the attractive colonial building that houses the ❸ **Western Market** (西港城; ☎852 6029 2675; 323 Des Voeux Rd Central & New Market St; ⊙10am-7pm).

At the corner of Morrison St, walk south onto Bonham Strand where you'll find ❹ **Lam Kie Yuen Tea Co** (p551). This friendly tea shop might let you sample some of its astounding selection of Chinese brews.

Take a quick detour continuing east down Bonham Strand to ❺ **Mammy Pancake**

(媽咪雞蛋仔; 32 Bonham Strand E; waffles from HK$24; ⊙12.30-9pm) for a takeaway egg waffle and iced tea. Backtrack to climb up ❻ **Possession St**, where British marines planted the Union Jack flag in 1841, then take a left into Hollywood Rd, before turning right to ascend Pound Lane to where it meets Tai Ping Shan St. Here you'll see three charming ❼ **temples** (p527).

Head southeast down Tai Ping Shan St, keeping an eye out for street art, then turn left to descend Upper Station St to the start of Hollywood Rd's ❽ **antique shops**. There's a vast choice of curios and rare treasures.

Continue on Hollywood Rd to ❾ **Man Mo Temple** (p527), one of the oldest and most significant temples in the territory.

Take a short hop to the left down Ladder St to Upper Lascar Row, home of the ❿ **Cat Street Market** (p527), which is well stocked with inexpensive Chinese memorabilia. Ladder St brings you back to Queen's Rd Central; head north until you hit Wing Lok St and you'll find yourself at exit A1 of Sheung Wan MTR station.

15 gigs monthly in a hip warehouse space in the coastal Kowloon burb of Yau Tong. Formerly known as Hidden Agenda, TTN is a much expanded rebranding, now offering an exhibition space and movie screenings (1pm to 8pm; days vary) as well as a bar during live shows.

Fringe Club
LIVE MUSIC

(藝穗會; Map p528; ☎ 852 2521 7251, theatre bookings 852 2521 9126; www.hkfringeclub.com; 2 Lower Albert Rd, Lan Kwai Fong; ☎; Ⓜ Central, exits D1, D2, G) The Fringe offers original music most Friday and Saturday nights, with jazz, rock and world music getting the most airplay. The intimate theatre hosts eclectic local and international performances other nights. It's in a Victorian listed building (c 1892) that was part of a dairy farm, and the distinctive red-and-white brickwork on its facade is known as 'blood and bandages'.

🔒 Shopping

Hong Kong is renowned as a place of neon-lit retail pilgrimage. This city is positively stuffed with swanky shopping malls and brand-name boutiques. All international brands worth their logos have shops here. These are supplemented by the city's own retail trailblazers and an increasing number of creative local designers. Together they are Hong Kong's shrines and temples to style and consumption.

🔒 Central District

★ Wattis Fine Art
ANTIQUES

(Map p528; www.wattis.com.hk; 2nd fl, 20 Hollywood Rd, Lan Kwai Fong; ☎ 11am-6pm Mon-Sat; 🚌 26) This upstairs gallery has an outstanding collection of antique maps, lithographs, photos and posters for sale. Rarely will you find such an extensive homage to Asian history, covering not just Hong Kong and Macau but also Chinese cities like Shanghai and Southeast Asian destinations such as Borneo, Myanmar (Burma), Malaka and Mumbai. Enter from Old Bailey St.

★ G.O.D.
GIFTS, HOUSEWARES

(Goods of Desire; Map p528; ☎ 852 2805 1876; www.god.com.hk; 48 Hollywood Rd, Soho; ☎ 11am-9pm) Goods of Desire – or G.O.D. – is a cheeky local lifestyle brand, selling homewares, clothes, books and gifts with retro Hong Kong themes. Fun buys include aprons printed with images of Hong Kong's famous neon signs, bed linen with themes like koi fish, and reasonably priced cheongsam tops in modern fabrics and colours; great for souvenirs. There's several other branches, including in PMQ (p527).

Kowloon Soy Company
FOOD & DRINKS

(九龍醬園; Map p528; ☎ 852 2544 3695; www.kowloonsoy.com; 9 Graham St, Central; ☎ 8.30am-6pm Mon-Sat; Ⓜ Central, exit D1) *The* shop (c 1917) for artisanal, naturally fermented soy sauce, premier cru yellow-bean sauce (Chinese miso) and other high-quality condiments; it also sells preserved eggs (皮蛋, *pei darn*) and pickled ginger (酸姜, *suen geung*), which are often served together at restaurants. Did you know that preserved eggs, being alkaline, can make young red wines taste fuller-bodied? Just try it.

The owner speaks excellent English and can help guide you through the range.

Shanghai Tang
CLOTHING, HOMEWARES

(上海灘; Map p528; ☎ 852 2525 7333; www.shanghaitang.com; Shanghai Tang Mansion, 1 Duddell St, Central; ☎ 10.30am-8pm; Ⓜ Central, exit D1) This elegant four-level shop is a local institution, and one of the few places in Central that specialises in luxury Chinese style. It's the place to go if you fancy a body-hugging *qípáo* (cheongsam) with a modern twist, a Chinese-style clutch or a lime-green mandarin jacket. Shanghai Tang also stocks beautiful chinoiserie-style homewares; don't expect to find much below HK$1000.

Arch Angel Antiques
ANTIQUES

(Map p528; ☎ 852 2851 6848; 70 Hollywood Rd, Soho; ☎ 9.30am-6.30pm; 🚌 26) Though the specialities are ancient porcelain and tombware, Arch Angel packs a lot more into its two floors: it has everything from old ink drawings and terracotta horses to palatial furniture, with friendly staff to help you navigate the well-displayed stock. Prices range from about HK$3000 to HK$1 million.

🔒 The Peak & Northwest Hong Kong Island

Sheung Wan is a hub for small independent traders and an excellent place to pick up locally designed souvenirs, particularly around Tai Ping Shan St and in the PMQ (p527) centre.

Lam Kie Yuen Tea Co
FOOD & DRINKS

(林奇苑茶行; Map p528; ☎ 852 2543 7154; www.lkytea.com; Ground fl, 105-107 Bonham Strand E, Sheung Wan; ☎ 9am-6pm Mon-Sat; Ⓜ Sheung Wan, exit A2) This shop, which has been around since

1955, is testament to just how much tea there is in China. From unfermented to fully fermented, and everything in between, there's simply too much to choose from. But don't panic – the owner will offer you a tasting. Lovely (pricey!) teaware is also sold here.

Wan Chai & Northeast Hong Kong Island

★ Kapok
FASHION & ACCESSORIES

(Map p532; ☑ 852 2520 0114; www.ka-pok.com; 8 Sun St, Wan Chai; ⊙ 11am-8pm, to 6pm Sun; Ⓜ Admiralty, exit F, Wan Chai, exit B1) In the hip Star St area, this Hong Kong–born boutique has combined two old shops to create a new 1500-sq-ft flagship. It stocks a fastidiously curated selection of luxe-cool mens- and womenswear labels (plus its own brand, a Paris design collaboration), along with bags and quirky design gifts. A cafe counter means you can sip single-origin espresso as you browse.

Fashion Walk
CLOTHING

(Map p532; www.fashionwalk.com.hk; Causeway Bay; ⊙ office 10am-11pm; Ⓜ Causeway Bay, exit D4) A mostly street-level fashion-shopping mecca spanning four streets in Causeway Bay – Paterson, Cleveland, Great George and Kingston. It's where you'll find big names such as Comme des Garçons, Sandro and Kiehl's, but also high-street favourites, up-and-coming local brands and shops with off-the-rack high-street labels.

Eslite
BOOKS

(誠品; Map p532; ☑ 852 3419 6789; 8th-10th fl, Hysan Pl, 500 Hennessy Rd, Causeway Bay; ⊙ 10am-10pm Sun-Thu, to midnight Fri & Sat; ♿; Ⓜ Causeway Bay, exit F2) You could waste hours inside this swanky three-floor Taiwanese bookshop, which features a massive collection of English and Chinese books and magazines, a shop selling gorgeous stationery and leather-bound journals, a cafe, a bubble-tea counter and a huge kids' toy and book section.

Wan Chai Computer Centre
ELECTRONICS

(灣仔電腦城; Map p532; 1st fl, Southorn Centre, 130-138 Hennessy Rd, Wan Chai; ⊙ 10am-10pm; Ⓜ Wan Chai, exit B1) Buy a drone, build a custom gaming PC, or repair the iPhone screen you cracked on that Lan Kwai Fong bar crawl. You can do it all and more at this gleaming, beeping warren of tiny electrical shops.

Kowloon

★ Yue Hwa Chinese Products Emporium
DEPARTMENT STORE

(裕華國貨; Map p540; ☑ 852 3511 2222; www.yuehwa.com; 301-309 Nathan Rd, Jordan; ⊙ 10am-10pm; Ⓜ Jordan, exit A) This five-storey behemoth is one of only a few old-school Chinese department stores left in the city. Products include silk scarves, traditional Chinese baby clothes and embroidered slippers, cheap and expensive jewellery, pretty patterned chopsticks and ceramics, plastic acupuncture models and calligraphy equipment. The top floor is all about tea, with vendors offering free sips. Food is in the basement.

Ladies' Market
MARKET

(通菜街, 女人街; Tung Choi Street Market; www.ladies-market.hk; Tung Choi St, Mong Kok; ⊙ noon-11.30pm; Ⓜ Mong Kok, exit D3) The Tung Choi Street Market is a cheek-by-jowl affair offering cheap clothes and trinkets. Vendors start setting up their stalls as early as noon, but it's best to get here between 1pm and 6pm when there's much more on offer. Beware, the sizes stocked here tend to suit the lissom Asian frame. A terrific place to soak up local atmosphere.

K11 Select
ACCESSORIES, CLOTHING

(Map p536; Shop 101, K11 Mall, 18 Hanoi Rd, Tsim Sha Tsui; ⊙ 10am-10pm; Ⓜ Tsim Sha Tsui, exit D2) In the K11 mall, this shop – like a mini department store – is a funky destination for clothing and accessories, much of it by Hong Kong designers. Matter Matters employs bold colours and iconic geometric graphics on its bags and gifts. Hip multibrand shop Kapok has menswear and unisex accessories.

ℹ Information

ACCESSIBLE TRAVEL

People with mobility issues face substantial obstacles in Hong Kong, particularly on Hong Kong Island, because of its extremely hilly topography, pedestrian overpasses and crowded – often obstructed – streets. Those with hearing or visual impairments will find several aids to help them, including Braille panels in lift lobbies and audio units at traffic signals.

EMERGENCY & IMPORTANT NUMBERS

To make a phone call to Hong Kong, dial your international access code, Hong Kong's country code, then the eight-digit number.

Hong Kong country code	☑ 852
International access code	☑ 001
Local directory enquiries	☑ 1081
Police emergency	☑ 999
Police	☑ 852 2527 7177
Antiscam public helpline	☑ 18222
Weather/tropical cyclone warning enquiries	☑ 187 8200

INTERNET ACCESS

Free wi-fi is available in virtually all hotels, at the airport, in MTR stations, on some buses and in various public areas including shopping malls, key cultural and recreational centres, and almost all urban cafes and bars. In short, Hong Kong is well hooked up.

Computer access If you don't have a smartphone, tablet or laptop, desktop computers are available for guests at some hotels and in some public locations, including Hong Kong's Central Library.

Portable wi-fi devices Some hotels now offer portable wi-fi devices as a free add-on for guests, or have them available to hire for a nominal fee.

Wi-fi hotspots There are more than 15,000 public hotspots in Hong Kong. They will pop up as 'CSL' or 'Wi.Fi.HK' on your device; you can search where the latter hotspots are by downloading the Wi.Fi.HK mobile app.

LGBTIQ+ TRAVELLERS

Hong Kong has a small but growing LGBTIQ+ scene and the annual Pride Parade in November now attracts rainbow flag-wavers by the thousands. That said, Hong Kong Chinese society remains fairly conservative, and it can still be risky for gay and lesbian individuals to come out to family members or their employers. It is not common to see LGBTIQ+ couples making displays of affection in public.

In 1991 the Crimes (Amendment) Ordinance removed criminal penalties for homosexual acts between consenting adults over the age of 18. Since then LGBTIQ+ groups have been lobbying for legislation to address the issue of discrimination on the grounds of sexual orientation, but the government has been criticised for failing to recognise and embrace the community.

In July 2018 there was a landmark ruling by Hong Kong's Court of Final Appeal, stating that the same-sex partner of a British expat should be granted a spousal visa – a move that has given the local LGBTIQ+ community hope that change (and, importantly, greater equality) is on the horizon.

Dim Sum Magazine (www.dimsum-hk.com) Hong Kong's first free gay lifestyle magazine covers local lifestyle, news and entertainment.

Pink Alliance (www.pinkalliance.hk) For information about LGBTIQ+ culture and events in Hong Kong.

MEDICAL SERVICES

Hong Kong Baptist Hospital (瑪嘉烈醫院; ☑ 852 2339 8888; www.hkbh.org.hk; 222 Waterloo Rd, Kowloon Tong) Private.

Princess Margaret Hospital (瑪嘉烈醫院; ☑ 852 2990 1111; www.ha.org.hk; 2-10 Princess Margaret Hospital Rd, Lai Chi Kok) Public, with a 24-hour accident and emergency service.

Queen Elizabeth Hospital (伊利沙伯醫院; Map p540; ☑ 852 3506 8888; 30 Gascoigne Rd, Yau Ma Tei; ☐ 112, Ⓜ Jordan, exit B2) Public.

Queen Mary Hospital (瑪麗醫院; ☑ 852 2255 3838; www3.ha.org.hk/qmh; 102 Pok Fu Lam Rd, Pok Fu Lam; ☐ 30X, 40M, 90B, 91, minibus 8, 10) Public, with a 24-hour accident and emergency service.

Ruttonjee Hospital (律敦治醫院; Map p532; ☑ 852 2291 2511; www.ha.org.hk; 266 Queen's Rd E, Wan Chai; Ⓜ Wan Chai, exit A3) Public hospital in Wan Chai with 24-hour A&E.

MONEY

The local currency is the Hong Kong dollar (HK$). ATMs are widely available; international debit/credit cards are accepted in most places except budget Cantonese restaurants.

➡ Most ATMs are linked up to international money systems such as Cirrus, Maestro, Plus and Visa Electron.

➡ Withdrawal fees will typically be between HK$20 and HK$50 per transaction, and the local ATM provider may levy an extra surcharge.

➡ American Express (Amex) cardholders can withdraw cash from AEON ATMs in Hong Kong if they have signed up to Amex Express Cash service before arrival.

NEWSPAPERS & MAGAZINES

There are several English-language newspapers and radio stations in Hong Kong.

China Daily (www.chinadaily.com.cn) The Beijing mouthpiece prints an English-language edition and covers news from across Asia.

South China Morning Post (www.scmp.com) The city's biggest daily broadsheet toes the government line, has an excellent website and is a good source of both current affairs and lifestyle news, particularly new restaurant reviews.

Time Out Hong Kong (www.timeout.com/hong-kong) The international what's-on guide has a dedicated Hong Kong edition with its finger on the pulse of local life, especially events, eating and drinking.

OPENING HOURS

Some shops and restaurants are closed on the first and second days of the Lunar New Year;

some for a longer period of time. The following list summarises standard opening hours.

Banks 9am to 4.30pm or 5.30pm Monday to Friday, 9am to 12.30pm Saturday

Museums 10am to between 5pm and 9pm; many close on Mondays as well as sometimes on Sundays

Offices 9am to 5.30pm or 6pm Monday to Friday (lunch hour 1pm to 2pm)

Restaurants 11am to 3pm and 6pm to 11pm

Shops Usually 10am to 8pm

POST

Hong Kong Post (www.hongkongpost.hk) is generally excellent; local letter delivery takes one to two working days and there is Saturday delivery. The staff at most post offices speak English. Mailboxes on the streets are green and clearly marked in English.

SAFE TRAVEL

Hong Kong is generally a safe city to travel around, even alone at night, but always use common sense. Some things to keep in mind:

➡ Stick to well-lit streets if walking after dark; note the MTR is perfectly safe to use at night.

➡ Regarding shopping scams, retailers of genuine antiques should be able to provide certification proving authenticity; as a general rule, assume trinkets in markets are reproductions.

➡ Hong Kong has its share of pickpockets. Carry as little cash and as few valuables as possible, and if you put a bag down, keep an eye on it. If robbed, obtain a loss report for insurance purposes at the nearest police station. See 'e-Report Centre' at www.police.gov.hk.

TELEPHONE

As in the rest of the world, public telephones are increasingly rare. More and more hotels are including free mobile handsets with 4G data and free local calls as part of the room deal.

International Direct Dial (IDD) service If the phone you're using has registered for the IDD 0060 service (or if you have the IDD Global Calling Card), dial 0060 first, then 852, and then the number; rates will be cheaper at any time.

Rates All local calls in Hong Kong are free. However, hotels charge from HK$3 to HK$5 for local calls from your room landline.

Mobile Phones

The Hong Kong Tourist Board sells a prepaid Tourist SIM, which includes 4G mobile data, unlimited CSL wi-fi hotspot usage and unlimited calls. A five-day pass costs HK$88 and includes 3GB of data; the eight-day pass is HK$118 for 8GB. It can be purchased at 1O1O Centers, including the one on level five of the Arrivals Hall at Hong Kong International Airport, at 7-Elevens and at the HKTB Visitor Centre on Kowloon's

Star Ferry Concourse. Other SIM-card options are available at CSL shops and 7-Elevens.

Coverage Mobile phones work everywhere, including in the harbour tunnels and on the MTR.

Handsets There are CSL (www.hkcsl.com) shops all over the city that sell cheap handsets and mobile accessories, should you need to replace your phone while in Hong Kong.

Rates Local calls cost between 6¢ and 12¢ a minute (calls to the mainland are about HK$1.80–3.50 per minute with IDD 0060 – significantly more without it).

TOURIST INFORMATION

Hong Kong Tourism Board (www.discover hongkong.com) visitor centres have helpful and welcoming staff, and reams of information – most of it free. There are two branches in town, plus visitor centres in the airport, at the West Kowloon Train Station, and in the passenger clearance building at Hong Kong Port (connecting with the new bridge to Macau).

Hong Kong International Airport (Chek Lap Kok; ☺8am-9pm) In Halls A and B on the arrivals level in Terminal 1.

Kowloon (香港旅遊發展局; Map p536; ☺8am-8pm; 🚢Star Ferry) On the Star Ferry Visitor Concourse, right by the ferry terminal.

Lo Wu (羅湖旅客諮詢及服務中心; Map p611; 2nd fl, Arrival Hall, Lo Wu Terminal Bldg, New Territories; ☺6.30am-midnight) Self-service kiosk at the border crossing to Shēnzhèn, mainland China.

The Peak (港島旅客諮詢及服務中心; www. discoverhongkong.com; Peak Piazza, The Peak; ☺11am-8pm; Peak Tram) In a vintage tram, between the Peak Tower and the Peak Galleria.

TRAVEL AGENCIES

China Travel Service (CTS; 中國旅行社; Zhōngguó Lǚxíngshè; ☑customer service 852 2998 7888, tour hotline 852 2998 7333; www. ctshk.com) For tours to the mainland; also has a China visa service.

Forever Bright Trading Limited (Map p536; ☑852 2369 3188; www.fbt-chinavisa.com.hk; Room 916-917, Tower B, New Mandarin Plaza, 14 Science Museum Rd, Tsim Sha Tsui East, Kowloon; ☺8.30am-6.30pm Mon-Fri, to 1.30pm Sat; Ⓜ East Tsim Sha Tsui, exit P2) For China visas.

Jebsen Holidays (☑852 3180 6799; www. concorde-travel.com) The old Aussie-run Concorde Travel is now part of Jebsen.

Splendid Tours & Travel (☑852 2316 2151; www.splendid.hk) Ticketing, visa and tours services.

WEBSITES

Lonely Planet (lonelyplanet.com/china/hong-kong) Destination information, hotel bookings, traveller forum and more.

Discover Hong Kong (www.discoverhongkong. com) The Hong Kong government's user-friendly website for travel information.

Hong Kong Observatory (www.hko.gov.hk) Weather information including forecasts.

ℹ️ Getting There & Away

Most international travellers arrive and depart via Hong Kong International Airport. Travellers to and from mainland China can use ferry, road or rail links to Guangdong and points beyond. Hong Kong is also accessible from Macau via ferry or the Hong Kong–Zhuhai–Macau Bridge.

More than 100 airlines operate between Hong Kong International Airport and some 190 destinations around the world. Flights include New York (16 hours), Los Angeles (14 hours), Sydney (9½ hours), London (13 hours) and Beijing (3½ hours).

There are regular buses connecting Hong Kong with major destinations in neighbouring Guangdong province. Regular trains run to Guangzhou (two hours), Beijing (24 hours) and Shanghai (19 hours). The opening of Kowloon West Railway Station in September 2018 has dramatically reduced train journey times, with regular high-speed services to destinations including Shenzhen, Guangzhou and Beijing. Visas are required to cross the border to the mainland.

Frequent scheduled ferries link the China Ferry Terminal in Kowloon and/or the Hong Kong–Macau Ferry Terminal on Hong Kong Island with a string of towns and cities on the Pearl River Delta, including Macau. The journey time to Macau on the high-speed ferries is one hour, compared with 30 minutes using the bridge.

Flights, cars and tours can be booked online at lonelyplanet.com.

AIR

There are flights between Hong Kong and around 50 cities in mainland China, including Beijing, Chengdu, Kunming and Shanghai. One-way fares are a bit more than half the return price. Hong Kong is the hub city for Cathay Pacific (www. cathaypacific.com), a five-star airline.

Other carriers include the following:

Air China (www.airchina.hk) The national carrier, based in Beijing.

Cathay Dragon (www.cathaypacific.com) Owned by Cathay Pacific, Cathay Dragon was previously known as 'Dragonair'; its flight schedules have been amalgamated into the main website. It specialises in regional flights to mainland China.

Hong Kong Airlines (www.hongkongairlines. com) Cheaper airline covering nearly 40 destinations in Asia Pacific and North America.

Hong Kong International Airport

Designed by British architect Norman Foster, the **Hong Kong International Airport** (HKG; ☑ 852

2181 8888; www.hkairport.com) is on Chek Lap Kok, a largely reclaimed area off Lantau's northern coast. Highways, bridges (including the 2.2km-long Tsing Ma Bridge, one of the world's longest suspension bridges) and a fast train link the airport with Kowloon and Hong Kong Island.

The two terminals have a wide range of shops, restaurants, cafes, ATMs and money changers.

China Travel Service (p554) has a counter at Arrivals Hall A in Terminal 1 and can organise China visas (which normally takes two to five working days).

BOAT

Regular scheduled ferries link the China Ferry Terminal in Kowloon and/or the **Hong Kong–Macau Ferry Terminal** (Shun Tak Centre; Map p528; Shun Tak Centre, 200 Connaught Rd Central, Sheung Wan) in Sheung Wan on Hong Kong Island with a string of towns and cities on the Pearl River Delta – but not central Guangzhou or Shenzhen.

Mainland destinations from Hong Kong include the following:

Shékǒu 30 minutes

Zhōngshān 70 minutes

Zhūhǎi 70 minutes

SkyPier is a fast ferry service that links Hong Kong airport with nine Pearl River Delta ports including Shenzhen, Guangzhou and Macau. The service enables travellers to board ferries directly without clearing Hong Kong customs and immigration. Book a ticket prior to boarding from the ticketing counter at Transfer Area E2 at least 60 minutes before ferry departure time. For more information, see the 'Mainland Connections' tab under Transport on the airport website (www.hongkongairport.com).

BUS

The Hong Kong–Zhuhai–Macau Bridge opened in 2018. From the Hong Kong port area, a 24-hour licensed shuttle-bus service operates daily to both Macau and Zhuhai, with departures every five to 15 minutes. A one-way daytime/night-time trip costs HK$65/70. Bus services A11, A21, A22, A29, A31, A33X, A35, A36 and A41 have been extended from the airport to reach the port area and shuttle pick-up.

CTS Express Coach (Map p528; ☑ 852 3604 0118; www.hkctsbus.com) Buses to mainland China.

Eternal East Cross Border Coach (Map p536; ☑ 852 3412 6677; www.eebus.com; 1st fl, Kai Seng Commercial Centre, 4-6 Hankow Rd, Tsim Sha Tsui; ⊙ 9am-7.30pm) Mainland destinations from Hong Kong that include Shenzhen, Guangzhou and other Guangdong cities.

TRAIN

The Kowloon West high-speed rail terminus opened in September 2018. Costing HK$9 billion, the terminus comprises joint immigration and customs for travel to mainland China and is partly governed by mainland laws. Built to hook up to mainland China's high-speed rail infrastructure, it has roughly halved the minimum time it takes to reach Guangzhou, to 48 minutes, and makes Shenzhen accessible in just 14 minutes. You can also catch direct high-speed trains from here to Beijing (nine hours) and Shanghai (seven hours). Tickets can be booked on the MTR website (www. highspeed.mtr.com.hk).

Nonbullet intercity trains to Guangzhou and the rest of Guangdong province and further afield leave from Hung Hom station in Kowloon.

Intercity train tickets can be purchased at the Intercity Through Train Customer Service Centre in Hung Hom Station, and ticket offices at Mong Kok East, Kowloon Tong and Shatin MTR stations, plus the Tourist Services counter at Admiralty MTR station and through approved agents such as China Travel Service. Sales open 30 days in advance.

Shenzhen

→ Dozens of the new high-speed trains per day leave from West Kowloon rail terminus calling at Shenzhen's Futian and North stations; you pass through mainland border and customs control before departure.

→ The first high-speed train to Shenzhen departs West Kowloon at 7am, with the last at 10.50pm.

→ The journey takes 14 minutes to Futian (2nd class/1st class/business HK$77/124/232) and around 20 minutes to Shenzhenbei (about HK$10 extra). Prices are pegged against the RMB so expect minor price fluctuations.

→ There are also two foot-border crossings for Shenzhen, at Lo Wu and Lok Ma Chau, both of which have their own station on the MTR East Rail line, 200m from the mainland border.

→ The MTR's Tourist Cross-Boundary Travel Pass (one/two consecutive days HK$100/140) allows unlimited travel on the MTR and two single journeys to/from Lo Wu or Lok Ma Chau stations.

→ The first MTR trains to Lo Wu/Lok Ma Chau leave Hung Hom station at 6.30am and the last at midnight/10.30pm; the trip takes about 45/49 minutes.

→ The border crossing at Lo Wu opens at 6.30am and closes at midnight. The crossing at Lok Ma Chau is open around the clock.

→ Lo Wu is the main checkpoint for foot passengers and tourists. Queues can be bad at both checkpoints during peak times.

Guangzhou

→ Dozens of the new high-speed trains per day leave from West Kowloon rail terminus for Guangzhou South station (2nd class/1st class/ business HK$245/368/514); you pass through mainland border and customs control before departure.

→ The journey takes around an hour.

→ Slower MTR intercity trains leave Hung Hom station for Guangzhou East train station; the trip takes approximately two hours.

Beijing & Shanghai

→ High-speed trains to Beijing West Railway Station (2nd class/1st class/business HK$1225/1962/3833) depart at 8.05am, arriving at 5.01pm the same day.

→ High-speed trains to Shanghai Hongqiao Railway Station (2nd class/1st class/business HK$1147/1873/3570) depart at 11.10am, arriving at 7.27pm the same day.

→ MTR intercity trains run between Hung Hom and both Shanghai and Beijing, departing on alternate days.

ⓘ Getting Around

MTR The ultramodern Mass Transit Railway is the quickest way to get to most urban destinations. Most lines run from 6am to just after midnight.

Bus Extensive and as efficient as the traffic allows, but can be bewildering for short-term travellers.

Ferry Fast and economical, and you get spectacular harbour views at no extra cost.

Tram Runs east to west along Hong Kong Island; convenient and great fun if you're not in a hurry.

Taxi Cheap compared with Europe and North America. Most taxis are red; green ones operate in certain parts of the New Territories; blue ones on Lantau Island. All run on meters.

Minibus Vans with a green or red roof that cover areas not reachable by bus; green are the easiest for travellers to use.

TO/FROM THE AIRPORT

The **Airport Express line** (⌨ 852 2881 8888; www.mtr.com.hk; one way Central/Kowloon/ Tsing Yi HK$115/105/70; ⊗10min, 5.50am-1.15am) is the fastest (and most expensive, other than a taxi) way to get to and from the airport. The trains have plug sockets and free wi-fi.

Departures From 5.54am to 12.48am heading to Central, calling at Tsing Yi island and then Kowloon en route to the city; the full trip takes 24 minutes. Tickets are available from vending machines at the airport and train stations.

Fares There is a marginal saving if you book a return rather than single; one-way is also HK$5 cheaper if you use an Octopus card or buy online. Return fares for Central/Kowloon/Tsing Yi, valid for a month, cost HK$205/185/120. Children three to 11 years pay half-price. An Airport Express Travel Pass allows three days of mostly unlimited travel on the MTR and Light Rail and one-way/return trips on the Airport Express (HK$250/350).

TAXI FARES FROM THE AIRPORT

DESTINATION	FARE (HK$)
Central, Admiralty, Wan Chai, Causeway Bay (Hong Kong Island)	315-370
Tsim Sha Tsui, Jordan, Yau Ma Tei, Mong Kok, Hung Hom (Kowloon)	265-270
Sha Tin (New Territories)	290
Tsuen Wan (New Territories)	225
Tung Chung (Lantau)	60
Disneyland (Lantau)	140

In addition to the fares listed, passengers officially have to pay HK$6 for every piece of baggage that is carried inside the baggage compartment.

Shuttle buses Airport Express also operates shuttle buses on Hong Kong Island (H1 to H4) and in Kowloon (K1 to K5), with free transfers for passengers between Central and Kowloon stations and major hotels. The buses run every 15 to 20 minutes between 6.12am and 11.12pm. Schedules and routes are available at www.mtr.com.hk/en/customer/services/complom_free_bus.html.

AsiaWorld-Expo The Airport Express is the same train that deposits visitors at the AsiaWorld-Expo venue; a two-minute journey in the opposite direction to the city centre.

Bus

There are good bus links to/from the airport. These buses have plenty of room for luggage, and announcements are usually made in English, Cantonese and Mandarin notifying passengers of hotels at each stop. For more details on the routes, check the Transport section at www.hkairport.com.

Departures Buses run every 10 to 30 minutes from about 6am to around midnight. Airport buses use the designation 'A' ahead of their route number. There are also quite a few night buses (designated 'N').

Fares Major hotel and guesthouse areas on Hong Kong Island are served by the A11 (HK$40) and A12 (HK$45) buses; the A21 (HK$33) covers similar areas in Kowloon. Bus drivers in Hong Kong do not give change, but it is available at the ground transportation centre at the airport, as are Octopus cards. Normal returns are double the one-way fare. Unless otherwise stated, children aged between three and 11 years and seniors over 65 pay half-fare.

Tickets Buy your ticket at the booth near the airport bus stand.

BICYCLE

Cycling in urbanised Kowloon or Hong Kong Island would be suicide, but in the quiet areas of the islands (including southern Hong Kong Island) and the New Territories, a bike can be a lovely way to get around. It's more recreational than a form of

transport, though – the hilly terrain will slow you down (unless you're mountain biking). Be advised that shops and kiosks renting out bicycles tend to run out early on weekends if the weather is good.

BOAT

Ferries to the Outlying Islands depart from the Central Piers. The nearest MTR station is Hong Kong; follow the elevated walkway east out of the IFC Mall (MTR exit A1 or A2) and then due north to reach the piers (follow signs for the Star Ferry). Tickets can be bought on the day from kiosks at the entrance to each pier.

Cheung Chau Ferries run every half-hour from Pier 5. One-way fares start from HK$13.60; tickets for the fast ferry cost about 50% more.

Discovery Bay Ferries depart from Pier 3 every 15 to 30 minutes around the clock (less frequent after midnight). One-way fares start from HK$46; the trip takes 25 minutes. On Saturdays and Sundays, four ferries a day usually go from here to Disneyland Resort, but at the time of writing this service was suspended due to typhoon damage; check ahead.

Lamma Ferries depart from Pier 4 to Lamma Island's main town of Yung Shue Wan every half-hour to an hour until around 11.30pm. Some departures head to the smaller town of Sok Kwu Wan. One-way fares start from HK$17.80.

Lantau and Peng Chau Ferries depart from Pier 6, heading to the Lantau village of Mui Wo (every 30 to 50 minutes). One-way fares start at HK$15.90.

Star Ferry

➡ There are two Star Ferry (p534) routes, but by far the more popular is the one running between Central (Pier 7) and Tsim Sha Tsui. The other links Wan Chai with Tsim Sha Tsui.

➡ There are two ticket types: upper deck (slightly more expensive) and lower deck. Fares are nominally higher on weekends and public holidays.

➡ Buy a ticket at one of the payment kiosks or use an Octopus card (most convenient).

BUS

Hong Kong's extensive bus system will take you just about anywhere in the territory, but it's not always easy to follow. Since Kowloon and the northern side of Hong Kong Island are so well served by the MTR, most visitors use the buses primarily to explore the southern side of Hong Kong Island, the New Territories and Lantau Island.

Departures Most buses run from 5.30am or 6am until midnight or 12.30am. There are a small number of night buses that run from 12.45am to 5am or later, designated with the letter 'N'.

Fares Bus fares cost HK$4.50 to HK$47, depending on the destination. Fares for night buses cost from HK$7.50 to HK$33. You will need exact change or an Octopus card.

Bus stations On Hong Kong Island the most important bus stations are the terminus in Central underneath Exchange Sq and the one on Queensway at Admiralty. From these stations you can catch buses to Aberdeen, Repulse Bay, Stanley and other destinations on the southern side of Hong Kong Island. In Kowloon the Star Ferry bus terminal has buses heading up Nathan Rd and to the Hung Hom train station.

Route information Figuring out which bus you want can be difficult. Citybus (www.nwstbus.com.hk) and New World First Bus, owned by the same company, plus Kowloon Motor Bus (www.kmb.hk) provide user-friendly route searches on their websites. KMB also has a route app for smartphones.

Lantau Most parts of Lantau Island are served by New Lantao Bus (www.newlantaobus.com). Major bus stations are located in Mui Wo ferry terminal and Tung Chung MTR station.

Minibus

Minibuses are vans with no more than 19 seats. They come in two varieties: red and green.

Green minibuses (HK$4 to HK$24) Cream-coloured with a green roof or stripe, they make designated stops and operate fixed fares, much like regular buses. You must put the exact fare in the cash box when you get in or you can use your Octopus card. Two useful routes are the 6 (HK$7.40) from Hankow Rd in Tsim Sha Tsui to Tsim Sha Tsui East and Hung Hom station in Kowloon, and the 1 (HK$10.20) to Victoria Peak from next to Hong Kong station. There's a good directory of routes, costs and frequencies at www.16seats.net.

Red minibuses Cream-coloured with a red roof or stripe, they pick up and discharge passengers wherever they are hailed or asked to stop along fixed routes. Information such as the destination and price are only displayed in Chinese.

CAR & MOTORCYCLE

Hong Kong's maze of one-way streets and dizzying expressways isn't for the faint-hearted. Traffic is heavy and finding a parking space is difficult and very expensive. If you are determined to see Hong Kong under your own steam, do yourself a favour and rent a car with a driver.

Road rules Vehicles drive on the left-hand side of the road in Hong Kong, as in the UK, Australia and Macau, but not in mainland China. Seat belts must be worn by the driver and all passengers, in both the front and back seats. Police are strict and give out traffic tickets at the drop of a hat.

Driving licence Hong Kong allows most foreigners over the age of 18 to drive for up to 12 months with a valid licence from home. It's still a good idea to carry an International Driving Permit (IDP) as well. Car-rental firms accept IDPs or driving licences from your home country; drivers must usually be at least 25 years of age.

TRAIN

The Mass Transit Railway is the name for Hong Kong's rail system comprising underground, overland and Light Rail (slower tram-style) services. Universally known as the 'MTR', it is clean,

TICKETS & PASSES

Octopus card (www.octopuscards.com) A rechargeable smartcard valid on the MTR and most forms of public transport. The card costs HK$150 (HK$70 for children and seniors), which includes a HK$50 refundable deposit (minus a HK$9 handling fee if returned within 90 days) and HK$100 worth of travel. Octopus fares are about 5% cheaper than ordinary fares on the MTR. You can buy one and recharge at any MTR station; the minimum rechargeable amount is HK$50. Exact change is required to travel on buses and trams so Octopus is the most convenient way to pay. A Tourist Octopus card is also available for HK$39 with no stored value and no deposit required; the normal card is better value.

Airport Express Travel Pass (one way/return HK$250/350) As well as travel to/from the airport, it allows three consecutive days of mostly unlimited travel on the MTR, Light Rail and MTR Bus.

MTR Tourist Day Pass (adult/child HK$65/30) Valid on the MTR for 24 hours after the first use.

fast and safe, and transports around four million people daily.

It costs only slightly more than bus travel (fares HK$5 to HK$55), and is the quickest way to get to most destinations in Hong Kong. Routes, timetables and fares can be found at www.mtr.com.hk.

There are around 90 stations on nine underground and overland lines, and a Light Rail network that covers the northwest New Territories. Smoking, eating and drinking are not permitted in MTR stations or on the trains, and violators are subject to a fine of HK$2000 to HK$5000.

Departures Trains run every two to 14 minutes from around 6am to sometime between midnight and 1am.

Exits MTR exit signs use an alphanumerical system and there can be as many as a dozen to choose from. There are easy-to-navigate maps of the local area in each ticket hall; use them to decipher which exit will serve you best.

Fares Tickets are extremely cheap compared with those in many other world cities: between HK$5 and HK$30, though fares to stations bordering mainland China (Lo Wu and Lok Ma Chau) cost up to HK$55. Children aged between three and 11 years and seniors over 65 pay half-fare. Ticket machines accept notes and coins, and dispense change.

Tickets Once you've passed through the turnstile to begin a journey you have 90 minutes to complete it before the ticket becomes invalid. If you have underpaid (by mistake or otherwise), you can make up the difference at an MTR service counter next to the turnstiles.

Peak hours If possible, it's best to avoid the rush hours: 7.30am to 9.30am and 5pm to 7pm weekdays.

TAXI

Hong Kong taxis are a bargain compared with those in other world-class cities. With more than 18,000 cruising the streets of the territory, they're easy to flag down, except during rush hour, when it rains or during the driver shift-change period (around 4pm daily). Taxi drivers in Hong Kong always use their meter.

Taxis are colour-coded:

Red with silver roofs Urban taxis – those in Kowloon and on Hong Kong Island. Can go anywhere except Lantau.

Green with white tops New Territories taxis.

Blue Lantau taxis.

You need to take a red taxi in New Territories if your destination is in Hong Kong, Kowloon or the city centres of the new towns in New Territories.

TRAM

Hong Kong's venerable old trams are tall, narrow double-deckers. They are slow, but they're cheap and a great way to explore the city above ground level. Try to get a seat at the front window on the upper deck for a first-class view while rattling through the crowded streets.

➧ The flat fare is HK$2.60 for adults and HK$1.30 for kids. Drop your coins (exact change only) into the box beside the driver, or use the Octopus touch pad.

➧ Use the turnstiles at the back of the trams to get on; pay at the front when you disembark.

➧ The route is very simple, moving along one set of tracks that runs along the northern coast of Hong Kong Island (with a couple of minor offshoots), from Kennedy Town in the west to Shau Kei Wan in the east.

➧ Hong Kong Tramways also offers an hour-long **TramOramic Tour** (☏ 852 2548 7102; www.hktramways.com; adult/child HK$95/65), which lets you experience the city on an open-top, 1920s-style tram with an audio guide.

HONG KONG GETTING AROUND

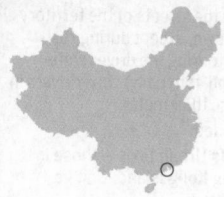

Macau

☎ 853 / POP 648,550

Best Places to Eat

➡ Tapas de Portugal (p573)

➡ Clube Militar de Macau (p573)

➡ Sum Yuen (p574)

➡ Espaço Lisboa (p574)

Best Places to Stay

➡ MGM Cotai (p572)

➡ Morpheus (p572)

➡ 5Footway Inn (p572)

Why Go?

Known as the 'Vegas of China', Macau is indeed an epicentre of gambling and glitz. While luxury entertainment here is world-class, the city has much more to offer than that. Macau was a Portuguese colony for 300 years, a heritage marked by a wonderful cultural hybridity that manifests itself in all aspects of life: Chinese temples stand on maritime-themed Portuguese tiles; the sound of Cantonese permeates streets with Portuguese names; and when you're hungry, it could be Chinese dim sum, *pastéis de nata* (Portuguese egg tarts) or Macanese *minchi* (ground meat stir-fried with potatoes) that come to the rescue.

Macau Peninsula holds the Unesco World Heritage–crowned old city centre. Further south are the former islands of Taipa and Coloane, joined together by a strip of reclaimed land named Cotai. Taipa has lovely Macanese houses and quaint boutiques; Cotai hosts the new megacasinos; while Coloane is a laid-back village with shipyards and beaches.

When to Go
Macau

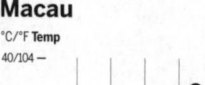

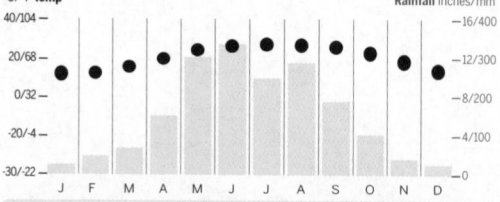

Mar–May The city celebrates the arts and deities' birthdays as mist hangs over the harbour.

Jun–Sep Days are spent in shady temples and outdoors at dragon boat races; nights are aglow with fireworks.

Oct–Feb Music and motor sports feature in a high-octane run-up to Christmas and New Year.

History

Portuguese galleons first visited southern China to trade in the early 16th century, and in 1557, as a reward for clearing out pirates, they obtained a leasehold for Macau. The first Portuguese governor of Macau was appointed in 1680, and as trade with China grew, so did Macau. However, after the Opium Wars between the Chinese and the British, and the subsequent establishment of Hong Kong, Macau went into a long decline.

In 1999, under the Sino–Portuguese Joint Declaration, Macau was returned to China and designated as a Special Administrative Region (SAR). Like Hong Kong, the pact ensures Macau a 'high degree of autonomy' in all matters (except defence and foreign affairs) for 50 years. The handover, however, did not change Macau socially and economically as much as the termination of the gambling monopoly in 2001. Casinos mushroomed, redefining the city's skyline, and tourists from mainland China surged, fattening up the city's coffers.

Yet the revenue boost, coupled with government policies (or the lack thereof), also led to income inequality and a labour shortage. Macau residents are also increasingly critical of their chief executive's pro-Beijing stance.

The government tightened its anti-money-laundering laws in 2017, which will subject casinos to stricter controls and regulations from 2020.

Language

Cantonese and Portuguese are the official languages of Macau, though not many people actually speak Portuguese. English and Mandarin are reasonably well understood, though the former is harder to find here than in Hong Kong.

☉ Sights

You'll find the lion's share of Macau's museums, churches, gardens and interesting architecture on the peninsula. In 2005 Unesco recognised this wealth by adding the Historic Centre of Macau, comprising eight squares and 22 historic buildings, to its World Heritage list. At many of the heritage sites, seniors over 60 and children under 11 are admitted free – just ask. The Macau Museum Pass (MOP$50) allows entry to a half-dozen museums for six months.

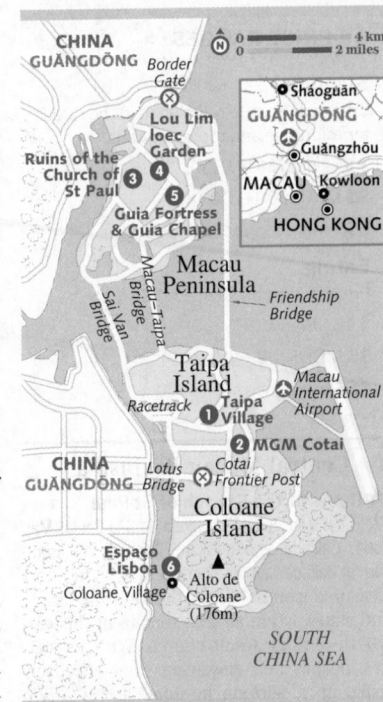

Macau Highlights

❶ **Taipa Village** (p569) Munching on Macanese snacks while visiting shrines, cafes and art spaces in this charming old village.

❷ **MGM Cotai** (p569) Wandering in a massive indoor garden with exotic plants, and sampling pastries and sweets by a celebrity chef.

❸ **Ruins of the Church of St Paul** (p562) Admiring the sculptures and engravings on the towering facade of a 17th-century cathedral that stands dramatically on a knoll.

❹ **Lou Lim Ieoc Garden** (p566) Exploring maze-like spaces in this public park, its bamboo groves and lotus ponds built by a 19th-century tycoon.

❺ **Guia Fortress & Chapel** (p567) Taking the cable car to handsome Guia Fortress and its gorgeous chapel, part of a 17th-century colonial complex atop a hill.

❻ **Espaço Lisboa** (p574) Indulging in a long lunch of garlicky clams and fried *bacalhau* (dried salted cod) at this Michelin-crowned Portuguese institution in Coloane.

ℹ PRICE RANGES

. . . .

Sleeping

Breakfast is usually included in the rates for midrange and top-end hotels.

$ less than MOP$800

$$ MOP$800–2000

$$$ more than MOP$2000

Eating

Prices based on a two-course meal:

$ less than MOP$200

$$ MOP$200–400

$$$ more than MOP$400

◉ Central Macau Peninsula

★ **Ruins of the Church of St Paul**   RUINS
(大三巴牌坊, Ruinas de Igreja de São Paulo; Map p564; Calçada de São Paulo; 🚌 8A, 17, 26, disembark at Luís de Camões Garden) FREE The most treasured icon in Macau, the towering facade and stairway are all that remain of this early-17th-century Jesuit church. With its statues, portals and engravings that effectively make up a 'sermon in stone' and a *Biblia pauperum* (Bible of the poor), the church was one of the greatest monuments to Christianity in Asia, intended to help the illiterate understand the Passion of Christ and the lives of the saints.

The church was designed by an Italian Jesuit and built by early Japanese Christian exiles and Chinese craftsmen between 1602 and 1640. It was abandoned after the expulsion of the Jesuits in 1762 and a military battalion was stationed here. In 1835 a fire erupted in the kitchen of the barracks, destroying everything, except what you see today. At the top is a dove, representing the Holy Spirit, surrounded by stone carvings of the sun, moon and stars. Beneath the Holy Spirit is a statue of the infant Jesus, and around it, stone carvings of the implements of the Crucifixion (the whip, crown of thorns, nails, ladder and spear). In the centre of the third tier stands the Virgin Mary being assumed bodily into heaven along with angels and two flowers: the peony, representing China, and the chrysanthemum, representing Japan. To the right of the Virgin is a carving of the tree of life and the apocalyptic woman (Mary) slaying a seven-headed hydra; the Japanese kanji next to her read: 'The holy mother tramples the heads of the dragon'. To the left of the central statue of Mary, a 'star' guides a ship (the Church) through a storm (sin); a carving of the devil is to the left. The fourth tier has statues of four Jesuit doctors of the church: (from left) Blessed Francisco de Borja; St Ignatius Loyola, the founder of the order; St Francis Xavier, the apostle of the Far East; and Blessed Luís Gonzaga.

★ **St Lazarus Church District**   AREA
(瘋堂斜巷, Calcada da Igreja de São Lázaro; Map p568; 🚌 7, 8) A lovely neighbourhood with colonial-style houses and cobbled streets makes for some of Macau's best photo ops. Designers and other creative types like to gather here, organising arty events.

★ **Mandarin's House**   HISTORIC BUILDING
(鄭家大屋, Caso do Mandarim; Map p564; ☑ 853 2896 8820; www.wh.mo/mandarinhouse; 10 Travessa de António da Silva; ⊙ 10am-5.30pm Thu-Tue; 🚌 18, 28B) FREE Built around 1869, the Mandarin's House, with over 60 rooms, was the ancestral home of Zheng Guanying, an influential author-merchant whose readers included emperors, Dr Sun Yatsen and Chairman Mao. The compound features a moon gate, tranquil courtyards, exquisite rooms and a main hall with French windows, all arranged in that labyrinthine-style typical of certain Chinese period buildings. There are guided tours in Cantonese on weekends.

★ **Church of St Joseph**   CHURCH
(聖若瑟聖堂, Capela do Seminario São José; Map p568; Rua do Seminário; ⊙ 9am-6pm; 🚌 9, 16, 18, 28B) St Joseph's, which falls outside the tourist circuit, is Macau's most beautiful model of tropicalised baroque architecture. Consecrated in 1758 as part of the Jesuit seminary, it features a scalloped canopy and a staircase leading to the courtyard from which you see the arresting white-and-yellow facade of the church and its dome. The latter is the oldest dome ever built in China. The interior, with its three altars, is lavishly ornamented with overlapping pilasters and attractive Solomonic 'spiral' columns.

★ **Sir Robert Ho Tung Library**   LIBRARY
(何東圖書館; Map p568; ☑ 853 2837 7117; 3 Largo de St Agostinho; ⊙ 2-8pm Mon, 8am-8pm Tue-Sun; 🚌 9, 16, 18) This charming building, founded in the 19th century, was the country retreat of the late tycoon Robert Ho Tung, who purchased it in 1918. The colonial edifice, featuring a dome, an arcaded facade, Ionic columns and Chinese-style gardens, was given a mod-

ern extension by architect Joy Choi Tin Tin in 2006. The new four-storey structure in glass and steel has Piranesi-inspired bridges connecting to the old house and a glass roof straddling the transitional space.

★ Chapel of Our Lady of Penha   HISTORIC BUILDING
(西望洋聖母堂, Capela de Nossa Senhora da Penha; Map p564; Penha Hill; ⊙10am-5pm; 🚌3, 9, 16) This graceful chapel atop Penha Hill was raised as a place of pilgrimage for Portuguese sailors in the 17th century, purportedly by survivors of a ship that had narrowly escaped capture by the Dutch. Most of what you see though came about in 1935. In the courtyard is a marble statue of Our Lady of Lourdes facing the sea; symmetrical staircases lead down to a grotto of the saint, complete with pews and altar. The chapel is visible across the lake.

Leal Senado   HISTORIC BUILDING
(民政總署大樓; Map p568; 🖉853 2857 2233; 163 Avenida de Almeida Ribeiro; ⊙9am-9pm Tue-Sun; 🚌3, 6A, 18A, 26A, 33, disembark at Almeida Ribeiro) Facing Largo do Senado is Macau's most important historical building, the 18th-century 'Loyal Senate', which houses the Instituto para os Assuntos Cívicos e Municipais (IACM; Civic and Municipal Affairs Bureau). It is so-named because the body sitting here refused to recognise Spain's sovereignty during the 60 years that it occupied Portugal. In 1654, a dozen years after Portuguese sovereignty was re-established, King João IV ordered a heraldic inscription that is displayed inside the Leal Senado's entrance hall.

Inside the entrance hall is the **IACM Temporary Exhibition Gallery** (民政總署臨時展覽廳; 🖉853 2836 6866; www.icm.gov.mo/en/ events) FREE with rotating art exhibitions. On the 1st floor is the **Senate Library** (民政總署圖書館; 🖉853 2857 2233; ⊙1-8pm Mon-Sat) FREE, which has a collection of some 19,000 books, and wonderful carved wooden furnishings and panelled walls.

Monte Fort   FORT
(大炮台, Fortaleza do Monte; Map p568; Praceta do Museu de Macau; ⊙7am-7pm; 🚌7, 8, disembark at Social Welfare Bureau) FREE Just east of the Ruins of the Church of St Paul, from which it is separated by a pebbled path and picturesque foliage, Monte Fort was built by the Jesuits between 1617 and 1626 to defend the College of the Mother of God against pirates. It was later handed over to the colonial government. Barracks and storehouses were designed to allow the fort to survive a two-year siege, but the cannons were fired only once, during the aborted attempt by the Dutch to invade Macau in 1622.

Lou Kau Mansion   HISTORIC BUILDING
(盧家大屋, Casa de Lou Kau; Map p568; 🖉853 8399 6699; www.wh.mo/loukau; 7 Travessa da Sé; ⊙10am-5.30pm Tue-Sun; 🚌3, 4, 6A, 8A, 19, 33) FREE Built around 1889, this Cantonese-style mansion with southern European elements belonged to merchant Lou Wa Sio (aka Lou Kau), who also commissioned the Lou Lim Ieoc Garden (p566). Behind the grey facade, an maze of open and semi-enclosed spaces blurs the line between inside and outside.

Church of St Dominic   CHURCH
(玫瑰堂, Igreja de São Domingos; Map p568; Largo de São Domingos; ⊙10am-6pm; 🚌3, 6A, 26A) Smack in the heart of Macau's historic centre, this sunny yellow baroque church with a beautiful altar and a timber roof was

MACAU SIGHTS

MACAU IN ONE DAY

Start in the Largo do Senado area, where you can have a look inside the gorgeous Senate Library, before wandering up to the Ruins of the Church of St Paul. Check out the handsome building housing Cinematheque Passion (p576), Macau's arthouse cinema, at Travessa da Paixão just under the ruins. Spend an hour in the Macau Museum (p566) to give it all some context, and take in the views from Monte Fort just outside. Have lunch at Clube Militar de Macau (p573), before wandering back through the tiny streets towards the Inner Harbour port and A-Ma Temple (p567). Jump on a bus to laid-back Coloane Village (p570). Have an egg custard tart from Lord Stow's Bakery (p574) before exploring the religious spaces, dried-seafood stalls and old shipyards. Bus it to the magnificent Morpheus (p572) in Cotai to gawp at its splendour and perhaps take a luxurious afternoon tea, then head to Taipa for some easy sightseeing. The old Taipa Village (p569) and the lakeside Taipa-Houses Museum (p569) are highlights, as is dinner at cosy Tapas de Portugal (p573). Return to Macau Peninsula for wine and jazz at Macau Soul (p575) or live indie bands at Live Music Association (p576).

Macau Peninsula

N 0 ——————————— 500 m
0 ——————————— 0.25 miles

The Garden (1.2km)

Ilha Verde

Av do Conselheiro Borja

Rotunda da Amizade

Av Norte do Hipódromo

Av Leste do Hipódromo

Rua de Maio

Rua de Canal Novo

Av do Nordeste

E do Arco
11

Av do General Castelo Branco

Inner Harbour

Av do Almirante Lacerda

24

Av do Coronel Mesquita

Tv de Praia

Estrada de Ferreira

Montanha Russa Garden

Rua dos Pescadores

Rua de Brás da Rosa

Rua Horta e Costa

22

Rua de Francisco Xavier Pereira

Cemetery

Rua do Visconde Paço de Arcos

Reservoir

Tv da Corda

Rua de Entre Campos

Estrada de Adolfo de Loureiro

Av do Conselheiro Ferreira de Almeida

23

Estrada de Coelho do Amaral

12 ⊚ 13

Rua de Silva Mendes

Tv do Túnel

⊚ 10

Praça de Luís de Camões

9

25

28

14

Guia Hill

Maçau Maritime Ferry Terminal

Rua de Tomás Vieira

Rua do Almirante Costa Cabral

16

Flora Garden

Rua de Terminal Marítimo

TurboJet

19

29

5 Ruins of the Church of St Paul

Tap Seac Square

17

Guia Fortress & Chapel
2

Rua de São Paulo

Qiantshan Waterway

Rua do Campo

Calçada do Gaio

Rua de Mallaca

565

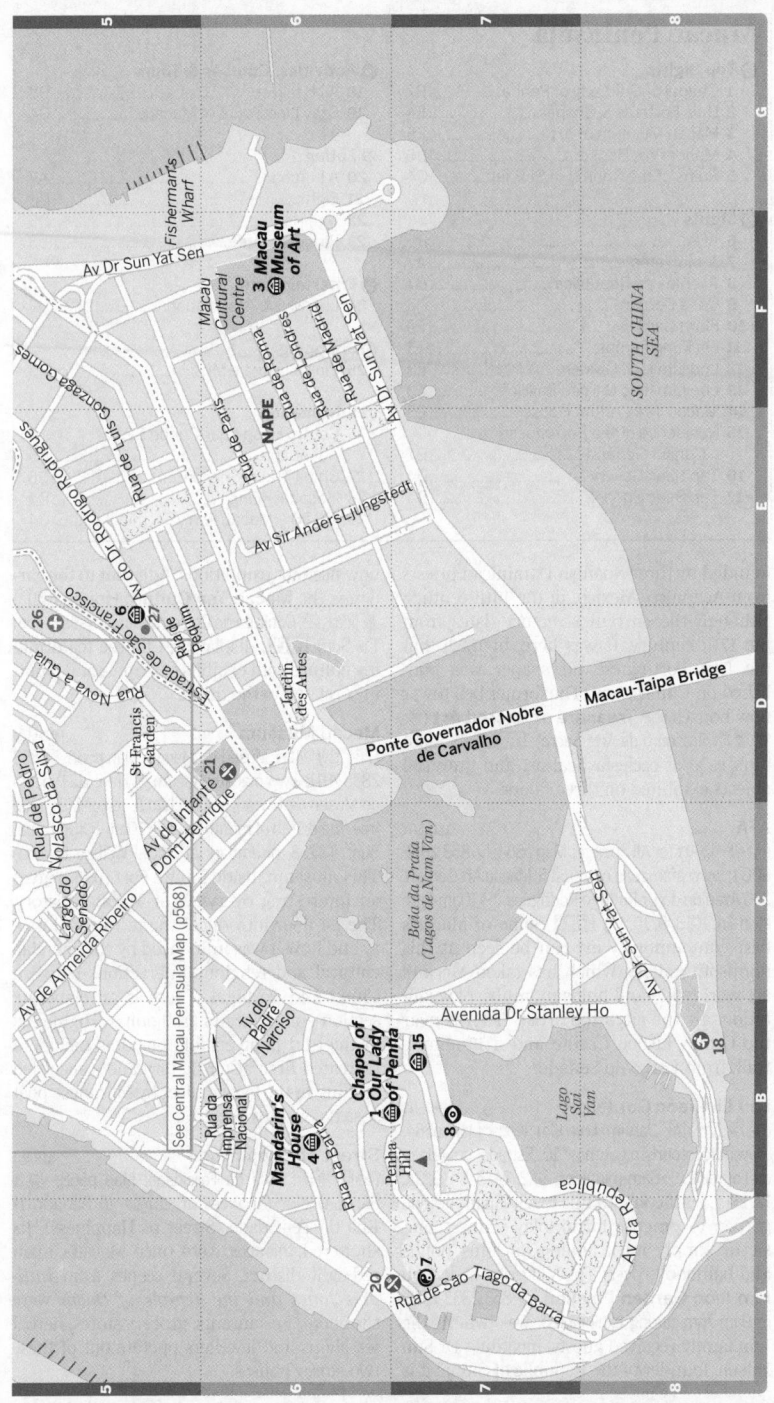

Fisherman's Wharf

Av Dr Sun Yat Sen

3 Macau Museum of Art

Macau Cultural Centre

NAPE

Rua de Roma
Rua de Londres
Rua de Madrid
Av Dr Sun Yat Sen

Rua de Paris

SOUTH CHINA SEA

Rua de Luís Gonzaga Gomes

Av do Dr Rodrigo Rodrigues

Av Sir Anders Ljungstedt

26
9
27

Rua Nova à Guia

Estrada de São Francisco

Rua de Pádua

Jardim des Artes

Macau-Taipa Bridge

Ponte Governador Nobre de Carvalho

St Francis Garden

Av do Infante 21 Dom Henrique

See Central Macau Peninsula Map (p568)

Rua de Pedro Nolasco da Silva

Largo do Rua de Imprensa Nacional

Av de Almeida Ribeiro

Baía da Praia (Lagos de Nam Van)

Av Dr Sun Yat Sen

Avenida Dr Stanley Ho

18

Tv da Padre Narciso

Chapel of 1 Our Lady of Penha

15

Mandarin's House 4

Rua da Barra

8

Penha Hill

Lago Sai Van

Av da República

20
7

Rua de São Tiago da Barra

Macau Peninsula

founded by three Spanish Dominican priests from Acapulco, Mexico, in the 16th century, although the current structure dates from the 17th century. It was here, in 1822, that the first Portuguese newspaper was published on Chinese soil. The former bell tower now houses the **Treasure of Sacred Art** (聖物寶庫, Tresouro de Arte Sacra) FREE, an Aladdin's cave of ecclesiastical art and liturgical objects exhibited on three floors.

AFA GALLERY
(全藝社, Art for All Society; Map p564; ☎ 853 2836 6064; www.afamacau.com; 1st fl, Macau Art Garden, 265 Avenida do Dr Rodrigo Rodrigues; ◎10am-7pm Mon-Fri; 🚌3, 9, 10, 17) FREE Some of Macau's best contemporary art can be seen at this nonprofit gallery, which has taken Macau's art worldwide and holds monthly solo exhibitions by the city's top artists. AFA is near the Grand Lisboa Casino and a 15-minute walk from Largo do Senado.

Lou Lim Ieoc Garden GARDENS
(盧廉若公園, Jardim Lou Lim Ieoc; Map p564; www.macaotourism.gov.mo; 10 Estrada de Adolfo de Loureiro; ◎6am-midnight; 🚌2, 2A, 5, 8A, 9, 9A, 12, 16) Locals come to this lovely Suzhou-style garden to practise taichi, play Chinese music or simply relax among its lotus ponds and bamboo groves. The Victorian-style **Lou Lim Ieoc Garden Pavilion** (☎853 2833 7676; ◎9am-7pm during exhibitions) was where the Lou family received guests, including Dr Sun Yatsen, founder of the Republic of China; it is

now used for exhibitions. Adjacent to the garden is the **Macao Tea Culture House** (澳門茶文化館, Caultura do Chá em Macau; ◎9am-7pm Tue-Sun) FREE, displaying Chinese tea-drinking culture with exhibits of teapots and paintings related to the drink.

Macau Museum MUSEUM
(澳門博物館, Museu de Macau; Map p568; ☎853 2835 7911; www.macaumuseum.gov.mo; 112 Praceta do Museu de Macau; adult/child & senior MOP$15/free, Tue & 15th of month free; ◎10am-5.30pm Tue-Sun; 🚌7, 8, disembark at Social Welfare Bureau) This museum inside Monte Fort (p563) gives an interesting overview of Macau's history. The 1st floor introduces the territory's history and how it was influenced by commercial, cultural and religious interactions between China and Portugal. There is an elaborate section on Macau's religions. Highlights of the 2nd floor on folk customs include a recreated firecracker factory and a recorded reading in the local dialect by Macanese poet José dos Santos Ferreira.

Street of Happiness STREET
(福隆新街; Rua da Felicidade; Map p568; 🚌3, 6A, 26A) Not far west of Largo do Senado is Rua da Felicidade (Street of Happiness). Its shuttered terraces were once Macau's main red-light district. Several scenes from *Indiana Jones and the Temple of Doom* were shot here. Restaurants, grocery stores, herbal tea shops and jewellers operate out of these two-storey houses.

◉ Southern Macau Peninsula

★ Macau Museum of Art   MUSEUM

(澳門藝術博物館, Museu de Arte de Macau; Map p564; ☎ 853 8791 9814; www.mam.gov.mo; Macau Cultural Centre, Avenida Xian Xing Hai; ⊙ 10am-6.30pm Tue-Sun; ☐ 1A, 8, 12, 23) **FREE** This excellent five-storey museum has well-curated displays of art created in Macau and China, including paintings by western artists such as George Chinnery, who lived in the enclave. Other highlights are ceramics and stoneware excavated in Macau, Ming and Qing dynasty calligraphy from Guangdong, ceramic statues from Shiwan (Guangdong) and seal carvings. The museum also features 19th-century western historical paintings from all over Asia, and contemporary Macanese art.

Avenida da República   AREA

(民國大馬路; Map p564; ☐ 6, 9, 16) Banyan-lined Avenida da República, along the northwest shore of Sai Van Lake, is Macau's oldest Portuguese quarter. There are several grand colonial villas not open to the public here. The former Bela Vista Hotel, one of the most storied hotels in Asia, is now the **Residence of the Portuguese Consul-General** (葡國駐澳門領事官邸, Consulado-Geral de Portugal em Macau; 8-10 Rua do Comendador Kou Ho Neng). Nearby is the ornate **Santa Sancha Palace**, once the residence of Macau's Portuguese governors, and now used to accommodate dignitaries. Not too far away are beautiful, abandoned art deco–inspired buildings.

A-Ma Temple   TAOIST TEMPLE

(媽閣廟, Templo de A-Ma; Map p564; Rua de São Tiago da Barra; ⊙ 7am-6pm; ☐ 1, 2, 5, 6B, 7) A-Ma Temple was probably already standing when the Portuguese arrived, although the present structure may date from the 16th century. It was here that fisherfolk once came to replenish supplies and pray for fair weather. A-Ma (aka Tin Hau and Mazu) is a sea goddess from whom the name Macau is derived. It's believed that when the Portuguese asked the locals the name of the place, they were told 'A-Ma Gau' (A-Ma Bay).

◉ Northern Macau Peninsula

★ Guia Fortress & Chapel   FORT, CHAPEL

(東望洋炮台及聖母雪地殿聖堂, Fortaleza da Guia e Capela de Guia; Map p564; Flora Gardens; ⊙ fortress 9am-6pm, chapel 10am-5.30pm; ☐ 2, 2A, 6A, 12, 17, 18, Flora Gardens stop) **FREE** As the highest point on the peninsula, Guia For-

tress affords panoramic views of the city. At the top is the small but stunning **Chapel of Our Lady of Guia**, built in 1622 and retaining almost 100% of its original features, including frescoes with both Portuguese and Chinese details that are among Asia's most important. Next to the chapel stands the oldest modern **lighthouse** (c 1865) on the China coast – a commanding 15m-tall structure, often open every Saturday and Sunday in July.

The entrance to the fortress has an attractive display of old typhoon signals that were hoisted during storms – large metallic physical symbols of the strong-wind numbering system adopted by Macau (and Hong Kong). Inside the fortress is an information gallery on the chapel and the complex. On the other side of the fortress is a tunnel showing old photos and replicas of how things used to look when it was an air-raid shelter.

You could walk up to the fortress and chapel, but it's easier to take the Guia cable car that runs from the entrance of **Flora Gardens** (二龍喉公園, Jardim da Flora; Travessa do Túnel; cable car one way/return MOP$2/3; ⊙ garden 6am-midnight daily, cable car 8am-6pm Tue-Sun; 🚶; ☐ 2, 17, 18), Macau's largest public park.

Casa Garden   HISTORIC BUILDING

(東方基金會會址; Map p564; 13 Praça de Luís de Camões; ⊙ garden 9.30am-6pm daily, gallery open only during exhibitions 9.30am-6pm Mon-Fri; ☐ 8A, 17, 26) **FREE** This beautiful colonial villa and park were built in 1770 as a merchant's residence. It later became the headquarters of the British East India Company when it was based in Macau in the early 19th century. The property has a small gallery that puts on excellent exhibitions with a cross-cultural (Portuguese and Macanese/Chinese) aspect. Visitors can wander the gardens.

Lin Fung Temple   BUDDHIST TEMPLE

(蓮峰廟, Lin Fung Miu; Map p564; Avenida do Almirante Lacerda; ⊙ 7am-5pm; ☐ 1A, 8, 8A, 10, 28B) Dedicated to Kun Iam, the Goddess of Mercy, this graceful Temple of the Lotus was built in 1592, and underwent several reconstructions. It used to host mandarins from Guangdong province when they visited Macau, the most famous being Commissioner Lin Zexu, who was credited with stamping out the opium trade. His statue stands in the entrance courtyard. The temple has beautiful religious art.

Tap Seac Square   SQUARE

(塔石廣場, Praca do Tap Seac; Map p564; ☐ 7, 8) This beautiful square is surrounded by important historic buildings from the 1920s,

Central Macau Peninsula

Central Macau Peninsula

such as the Cultural Affairs Bureau, Central Library, Library for Macau's Historical Archives and **Tap Seac Gallery** (塔石藝文舘, Galeria Tap Seac; ☑853 2836 6866; www.icm.gov.mo/ts; 95 Avenida Conselheiro Ferreira de Almeida; ⊙10am-9pm) FREE. It was designed by Macanese architect Carlos Marreiros. Marreiros also created the Tap Seac Health Centre, a contemporary interpretation of Macau's neoclassical buildings.

⊙ The Islands

The islands of Taipa and Coloane are one big island these days. Land reclamation has created a connecting strip known as Cotai (conflation of 'Coloane' and 'Taipa'). Head to Taipa for dining and shopping in the narrow streets of old Taipa Village. Visit Cotai to gamble and gawk at the biggest casinos on earth. Go south to Coloane for beachy getaways and long Portuguese lunches.

★ Taipa Village   VILLAGE
(氹仔舊城區; Map p572; ☑22, 26, 33) The historical part of Taipa is best preserved in this village in the south of the district. An intricate warren of alleys holds traditional Chinese shops and some excellent restaurants, while the broader main roads are punctuated by colonial villas, churches and temples. Rua da Cunha, the main pedestrian drag, is lined with vendors hawking free samples of Macanese almond cookies and beef jerky, and tiny cafes selling egg tarts and *serradura* pudding.

Avenida da Praia, a tree-lined esplanade with wrought-iron benches, is perfect for a leisurely stroll.

Taipa Houses-Museum   MUSEUM
(龍環葡韻住宅式博物館, Casa Museum da Taipa; Map p572; ☑853 8988 4000; www.icm.gov.mo/en/housesmuseum; Avenida da Praia, Carmo Zone, Taipa; ⊙10am-6.30pm Tue-Sun; ☑11, 15, 22, 28A, 30, 33, 34) FREE Before being converted into a museum, the pastel-coloured villas (c 1921) here were the summer residences of wealthy Macanese. The **Macanese Living Museum** is a permanent display of local history and culture, while two of the other houses are reserved for rotating exhibitions spanning art, religion, architecture and food culture. There's a large and attractively landscaped lotus pond out the front, with the towering casinos of Cotai in the distance, that art students like to sketch.

MGM Cotai   CASINO
(美獅美高; Map p561; ☑853 8806 8888; www.mgm.mo/en/cotai; Avenida da Nave Desportiva; ⊙24hr) In the MGM Cotai's atrium, the walls are hung with LED screens showing razor-sharp images of landscapes from all over the world. These are interspersed with vertical gardens where purportedly 2000 plant species grow, including extinct 19th-century botanicals revived from seed banks. Topping it off is a glass canopy larger than a football field. It's quite an experience to traverse this space – lofty and futuristic, but with the grandeur and transience of an old train station.

★ Ká Hó Church of Our Lady of Sorrows   CHURCH
(九澳七苦聖母小堂, Missão de Nossa Senhora das Dores; Estrada de Nossa Senhora de Ká Hó, Nossa Senhora Village, Coloane; ☑15, 21A) Tent-like with a long, slanting roof, like hands in prayer, this church was raised in the Ká Hó

leper colony in 1966. It was built for use by the female leprosy patients staying at the **leprosarium** (前九澳痲瘋病院; off Estrada de Nossa Senhora de Ká Hó), along with their families and caretakers. Italian architect Oseo Acconci designed the simple and graceful structure. The sturdy wooden door has planks echoing the angularity of the roof and the bell tower. The bronze crucifix was by another Italian, Francisco Messima.

Coloane Village   VILLAGE

(路環村; Map p574) Coloane's 'urban centre' is an old fishing village on its southwestern coast. It is marked by **Tam Kung Temple** (譚公廟; Avenida de Cinco de Outubro; ⊙8.30am-5.30pm; 🚌15, 21A, 26A) to the south and Lai Chi Vun Village (p571) to the north, with winding alleys, tiny squares, temples and modern villas in between. Coloane Village retains an idyllic air, especially in the late afternoon when the tour groups have left. Attractions here include delicious Portuguese and Macanese restaurants, the **Chapel of St Francis Xavier** (聖方濟各教堂, Capela de São Francisco Xavier; Rua do Caetano, Largo Eduardo Marques; ⊙9.30am-5.30pm) and a couple of small temples.

Macau Giant Panda Pavilion   ZOO

(大熊貓館; Pavihao do Panda Gigante de Macau; 🗐853 2888 0087; www.macaupanda.org.mo; Estrada de Seac Pai Van Park, Coloane; adult/child under 12yr MOP$10/free; ⊙9.30am-5pm Tue-Sun; ♿; 🚌15, 21A, 25, 26, 26A, 50) Coloane offers a convenient and inexpensive opportunity to see pandas. The pair of cuddly ones are kept inside a purpose-built pavilion inside **Seac Pai Van Park** (石排灣郊野公園; ⊙8am-6pm) **FREE**. There are six hour-long viewing sessions daily, from 10am to 4pm. While waiting for your turn, you can check out the peacocks, monkeys and toucan.

To get here, take any bus with a stop at Seac Pai Van Park; there are plenty of them originating in different places in Macau.

🏃 Activities & Tours

While Macau is no adventure paradise, it offers a taste of everything from spectator sport to extreme sport. For more ways to get those endorphins flowing, visit www.iam.gov.mo (click 'Municipal Facilities').

Hac Sa Reservoir Park   HIKING

(黑沙水庫郊野公園; 🗐853 2833 7676; Estrada de Hác Sá, Coloane; pedal boat per 30min for 2 people MOP$20; ♿) This park roughly circling Hác Sá Reservoir is the best place in Macau for

outdoor family fun. There are barbecue and picnic areas, a campsite and several signposted hiking trails that include a 45-minute family route and a 90-minute path that runs all the way up to **A-Ma Cultural Village** (媽祖文化村, Aldeia Cultural de A-Má; Estrada do Alto de Coloane; ⊙temple 9am-6pm). On weekends and public holidays (10am to 5pm), you can hire pedal boats and canoes in the water park, or send your child sliding down a grassy slope.

AJ Hackett   ADVENTURE SPORTS

(Map p564; 🗐853 988 8656; http://macau.ajhackett.com; Macau Tower, Largo da Torre de Macau; bungee/skywalk per person MOP$3788/888; ⊙11am-7.30pm Mon-Thu, 10am-9pm Fri, to 10pm Sat & Sun Sep-Jun, extended hours Jul & Aug) New Zealand-based AJ Hackett organises all kinds of adventure climbs, bungee jumps and more on the Macau Tower. Rates include a T-shirt, certificate, AJ Hackett membership card and other perks; bungee jumps include a free skywalk. Book online.

Gray Line Tours of Macau   TOURS

(澳門錦倫旅行社; Map p564; 🗐853 2833 6611; www.grayline.com.hk; Room 1015, Ground fl, Macau Ferry Terminal; tours per person from MOP$880) This Hong Kong–based travel agency offers day tours in Macau, with return-trip ferry tickets from Hong Kong included in the price. Tours are based around heritage and the Cotai casino strip, and the ferry tickets and tour can be booked for different days if you're staying overnight in Macau. Limousine tours with a private guide and customised itinerary are also available (from MOP$4950).

🎭 Festivals & Events

The blend of Cantonese and Portuguese culture and religious occasions creates an intriguing succession of holidays and festivals in Macau. Chinese festival dates are usually calculated according to the lunar calendar.

Procession of Our Lady of Fatima RELIGIOUS

(⊙May) A celebration of Macau's Portuguese heritage, this event draws thousands of Catholics into the streets, where they parade from St Domingo's to Penha Chapel in honour of a purported 1917 sighting of the Virgin Mary in Portugal.

★ Tam Kong Festival   PARADE

(譚公誕; ⊙May/June) Tam Kong Festival is huge in Coloane. The birthday of the sea deity falls on the eighth day of the fourth lunar month (May or June), with festivities lasting three to five days. Highlights include a dazzling parade by residents dressed in traditional Chinese, Portuguese or fusion costumes; free Cantonese opera in a massive bamboo theatre that springs up by the harbour each year around this time; Portuguese folk dance and juggling; and lots of traditional food.

Feast of the Drunken Dragon   CULTURAL
(醉龍節; ⊙May/Jun) One of Macau's unique festivals: on the evening of the eighth day of the fourth month of the lunar calendar (in May or June), local fishmongers and fishermen perform drunken dances with a wooden dragon and parade through the streets distributing free 'longevity rice'.

Macau Formula 3 Grand Prix   SPORTS
(www.macau.grandprix.gov.mo/en; ⊙Nov) Macau's biggest sporting event of the year is held in the third week of November.

🛏 Sleeping

The Macau Peninsula has a range of accommodation, from dated-but-serviceable business hotels at low price points to international luxury brands. Cotai has casino hotels, many offering excellent weekday deals. Coloane is home to a handful of beachy inns and two HI-affiliated hostels (the only ones in the city).

Love Lane Seven Inn   INN $
(戀愛七號旅館; Map p568; ☑853 2836 6490; www.lovelane7.com; 7 Travessa da Paixão;

COLOANE'S STILT HOUSES & SHIPYARDS

Coloane is the only place in Macau with very visible vestiges of its past as a fishing and shipbuilding village.

Chopsticks in the Sea

Stilt houses and shipyards (or skeletons of them) dot coastal Rua dos Navegantes. These huts of colourful corrugated metal, extending like chunky chopsticks into the harbour, were once landing spots for houseboats. Dried seafood shops occupy some of them, such as Tong Kei Dried Fish at Largo do Cais, the square near the lovely old Coloane pier (Ponte Cais de Coloane).

Lai Chi Vun Village

A slope on the right of the Servicos de Alfangega building at the square connects to Lai Chi Vun Village (荔枝碗村, 'Lychee Bowl Village'), an area synonymous with Macau's old shipbuilding industry. The village has sparked much recent debate among conservation advocates who believe the shipyards should be kept and restored, developers who think otherwise, and the government who agreed to stop tearing down the structures. You can see the cavernous cadavers of a dozen shipyards lined up on the left side of the road. Their gates are often open during the day and if you like atmospheric abandoned spaces, you can enter for a peek and to take pictures, but beware of dogs.

Shipbuilding in Macau

Shipbuilding, the crafting of wooden fishing junks and dragon boats, as well as their demolition, was one of Macau's oldest and most important industries. The city was a port for four centuries, one built by seafarers and fisherfolk. At its heyday in the 1940s and '50s, Macau's shipbuilders' skills were much sought after and there were close to 10,000 fishermen and over 30 shipyards in the city, mostly in the coastal villages. But the industry began declining from the 1970s, through the '80s and '90s, to the early 2000s when the last vessels were made. This was due to various factors – the market shifting to mainland China where production costs were cheaper, the popularity of metal boats, which were less time-consuming to make, and water pollution in the Pearl River Delta.

Conservation & Repurposing

The Macau government bulldozed two shipyards in the 2010s, then halted due to a public outcry. There's been much talk of revitalising the shipyards into a museum, inns and boutiques, and everything in between. At the time of writing, the site is awaiting heritage classification. It is expected that at least some of the shipyards will be restored and revitalised. In the meantime, the docks remain forlorn witnesses to an important slice of Macau's modern history.

The Islands – Taipa

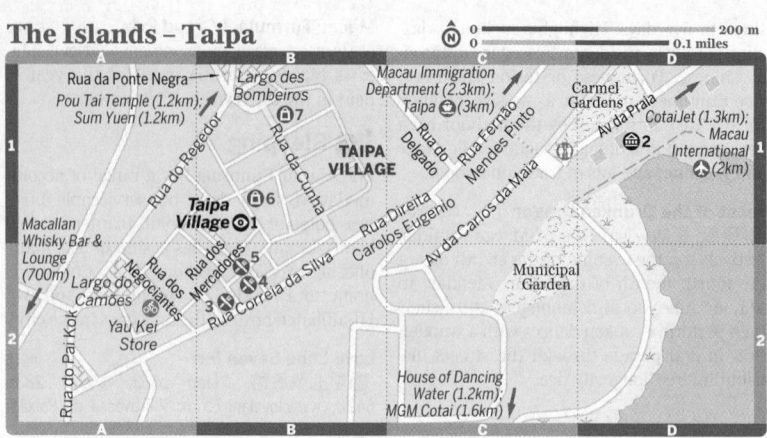

MACAU SLEEPING

d MOP$450-850, f MOP$750-950; ⊖✳🛜; 🚌8A, 17, 26) Occupying several floors behind a pink-and-green facade are seven rooms with stained-glass windows: a large family one with two double beds; four standard rooms with private showers; and two small rooms with communal showers. Historical relics are dispersed throughout the building, including a century-old herbal cabinet and auspicious stone engravings.

★ 5Footway Inn
INN $$

(五步廊旅舍; Map p568; ☑ 853 2892 3118; 8 Rua de Constantino Brito; d/tr from MOP$620/930; ⊖✳🛜; 🚌1, 2, 5, 7, 10) Converted from a love motel, 5Footway Inn has 24 small clean rooms, vibrant paintings in communal areas and excellent English-speaking staff. Breakfast isn't offered, but there's free tea and coffee on tap. It's opposite the Sofitel Macau at Ponte 16, which means you can take its free shuttle

buses to and from the ferry terminal. The rate drops to MOP$500 on off-season weekdays.

★ MGM Cotai
CASINO HOTEL $$$

(美獅美高梅; Map p561; ☑ 853 8806 8888; www.mgm.mo/en/cotai; Avenida da Nave Desportiva, Cotai; r incl breakfast from MOP$2000; ⊖✳@🛜🏊) MGM Cotai has 1400 impeccable rooms, including duplex sky-lofts and studios, all in a light and refreshing palette. There's also a gym with panoramic views, and a chic and soothing spa. But the star here is the four-storey atrium (p569) just past the reception lobby. Booking seven or more days in advance will get you a 15% discount.

★ Morpheus
CASINO HOTEL $$$

(摩珀斯酒店; ☑ 852 8868 8888; www.cityof-dreamsmacau.com; City of Dreams, Estrada do Istmo, Cotai; r incl breakfast from MOP$2700; ⊖✳@🛜🏊) Designed by the late Zaha Hadid, Morpheus, with 770 spacious rooms, is the flagship luxury hotel of the City of Dreams (p576). The exoskeleton of the building has strong lines that are visible from the interior, where generous stretches of white let them speak for themselves, as in a museum.

✴ Eating

Besides Macanese food, Macau was once the place to go for authentic Portuguese in Asia, and that proverbial bowl of cheap but ethereal Chinese noodles. It still is, but the proliferation of luxury casino-hotels has broadened the city's culinary repertoire. Now foodies make epicurean pilgrimages to the former Portuguese colony where top-notch Chinese, Japanese and European restaurants, including Michelin-star winners, can be found.

🍴 Macau Peninsula

★ Riquexó Cafe
MACANESE $

(利多咖啡屋; Map p564; ☎ 853 2856 5655; 69 Avenida de Sidónio Pais; meals from MOP$60; ☺noon-9.30pm) Modest Riquexó is *the* place for tasty, no-frills Macanese. Take your pick of the daily options, which may include *minchi,* a homey dish of minced meat sautéed with diced potatoes and seasoned with soy and Worcester sauce, then sit down in the cafe and look at the old photos of Macau.

Nga Heong
BURMESE $

(雅馨緬甸餐廳; Map p564; ☎ 853 2855 2711; 27 Rua de Fernao Mendes Pinto; noodles from MOP$30; ☺7.30am-5pm; ❄; ☐23, 32) In Macau's Three Lamps district, an area known for its Burmese immigrants, this popular greasy spoon with two adjacent shops dishes out homestyle Burmese like coconut chicken noodles, fish soup noodles with banana blossom, and shrimp-paste-fragrant greens. There's an English menu with pictures.

★ Clube Militar de Macau
PORTUGUESE $$

(陸軍俱樂部; Map p568; ☎ 853 2871 4000; 975 Avenida da Praia Grande; meals MOP$200-500; ☺1.30-3.15pm & 7-11pm Mon-Fri, noon-3.15pm & 7-11pm Sat & Sun; ❄; ☐6, 28C) In a distinguished colonial building, with fans spinning lazily above, the Military Club takes you back in time to a quieter Macau. Simple and delicious Portuguese fare is complemented by reasonably priced wines and cheeses. The MOP$200 lunch buffet is great value, though à la carte offers more culinary refinement and a chance to taste the famous *leitão* (suckling pig).

Reservations advised for dinner and weekends.

A Lorcha
MACANESE, PORTUGUESE $$

(船屋葡國餐廳; Map p564; ☎ 853 2831 3193; www.alorcha.com; 289 Rua do Almirante Sérgio; meals MOP$200-400; ☺12.30-3pm & 6.30-10pm Wed-Mon; ❄⚲; ☐1, 5, 10) 'The Sailboat' is listed in every guidebook. One reason for its popularity is that it's within walking distance of the A-Ma Temple. If you go not expecting outstanding creativity, you'll enjoy its solid Portuguese and Macanese fare. Portions are generous. Bookings recommended.

★ Eight
CANTONESE $$$

(8餐廳; Map p564; ☎ 853 8803 7788; www.grandlisboahotel.com; 2nd fl, Grand Lisboa Hotel, Avenida de Lisboa; mains MOP$480-3000; ☺11.30am-2.30pm Mon-Sat, 10am-3pm Sun, also 6.30-10.30pm daily; ℗❄☎; ☐3, 10, 28B) The Eight is a stellar three-Michelin-starred restaurant and model of Cantonese culinary refinement inside the Grand Lisboa. You can dine on a 'simple' meal of roast meat and Cantonese soup cooked to perfection, or splurge on marine delicacies such as abalone, to the accompaniment of water cascading down a wall and crystal-dripping chandeliers. Reservations a must.

The eight-course tasting menu (MOP$2800 per person) lets you sample a bit of everything.

🍴 The Islands

★ Tapas de Portugal
TAPAS $

(葡意園; Map p572; ☎ 853 2857 6626; http://tapasdeportugal.com.mo; 9 Rua dos Clérigos, Taipa; tapas from MOP$75; ☺noon-11pm; ☐22, 26) Tantalising Portuguese-style tapas are on offer at this cosy, warm-toned restaurant by the owner of Michelin-lauded **António** (安東尼奧; ☎ 853 2888 8668; map p572; www.antoniomacau.com; 7 Rua dos Clérigos; meals MOP$550-1200; ☺11.30am-4pm & 6pm-midnight; ❄). There are over 40 to choose from and savour with Portuguese wine. After your lamb tenderloin bruschetta, suckling pig pie and scrambled eggs with asparagus and Iberico sausage on toast, you can order a main course of duck rice or the Macanese classic, African chicken.

Tai Lei Loi Kei
CHINESE $

(大利來記; Map p572; ☎ 853 2882 7150; www.taileiloi.com.mo; 35 Rua dos Clérigos, Taipa; buns MOP$40; ☺8am-6pm; ⚲; ☐22, 26) South China's most famous pork-chop bun is made here – a shop founded in 1968 as a street stall by the mother of the current owner. Succulent slices of pork (or slivers of fish) are coupled with warm, chewy buns that emerge from the

MACAU EATING

MACAU CHOW

A typical Macanese menu features an enticing stew of influences from Chinese, Asian and Portuguese cuisines, and the cooking of former Portuguese colonies in Africa, India and Latin America. Coconut, tamarind, chilli, jaggery (palm sugar) and shrimp paste can all feature. A famous Macanese speciality is *galinha à africana* (African chicken), made with coconut, garlic and chillies. Other popular dishes include *casquinha* (stuffed crab), *minchi* (minced pork or beef cooked with potatoes and onions) and *serradura* (a milk pudding).

The Islands – Coloane

Hon Kei Hand-Whipped Coffee (250m);
Macau Giant Panda Pavilion (1.2km); Seac Pai Van Park (1.2km);
A-Ma Cultural Village (2.7km).

Fishing Boats

Lai Chi Wan

Largo do Matadouro

COLOANE VILLAGE

Rua Da Tassara

⊗5 ⊗4

Estrada do Campo

Seac Pai Van Park

Alto de Coloane (170m)

Lai Chi Wan

Av de Cinco de Outubro

Rua do Caetano

🅟1

Largo da Fonte

Rua da Cordoaria

Estrada de Cheoc Van

Cheoc Van Bay (Bamboo Bay)

Restaurante Fernando (1.3km); Hac Sa Reservoir Park (2km)

Rua do Estaleiro

Av da Republica

3🅟

Largo Tam Kong Miu

SOUTH CHINA SEA

The Islands – Coloane

◎ Sights

⊗ Eating

oven daily at 2pm sharp. Earlier in the day you can try soft rolls or sweet pineapple buns.

Lord Stow's Bakery
BAKERY $

(澳門安德魯餅店; Map p574; ☑853 2888 2534; www.lordstow.com; 1 Rua do Tassara, Coloane; egg tarts MOP$10; ☺7am-10pm) Though the celebrated English baker Andrew Stow has passed away, his **cafe** (☑853 2888 2174; 9 Largo do Matadouro, Coloane; egg tarts MOP$10; ☺9am-6pm; ❄) and the original Lord Stow's Bakery here keep his memory alive by serving his renowned *pastéis de nata* (warm egg-custard tart with a flaky crust) and cheesecake (MOP$24 to MOP$28) in different flavours, including mango and green tea.

★ Sum Yuen
VEGETARIAN, CHINESE $$

(心橡素食; ☑853 2881 2698; www.facebook. com/sumyuenmacau; 5 Estrada Lou Lim Ieok,

Taipa; meals MOP$200-400; ☺10.30am-3pm & 5.30-10.30pm; ❄🅿♿; ☐21A, 22, 25, 26A, 28A) You can pick from over 150 creative dishes at this modern restaurant at **Pou Tai Temple** (菩提禪院, Pou Tai Un). Avocado, yam and eggplant figure on the menu, in the form of sushi, teppanyaki or pudding, as do mushrooms and bamboo piths as soup or stir-fry. The cooking style is Chinese, with nods to Japan, Europe and Southeast Asia.

Restaurante Fernando
PORTUGUESE $$

(法蘭度餐廳; ☑853 2888 2264; www.fernando-restaurant.com; 9 Estrada de Hác Sá, Coloane; meals MOP$200-450; ☺noon-9.30pm; ♿; ☐21A, 25, 26A) Possibly Coloane's most famous restaurant, sprawling Fernando's contains two separate dining rooms and a large courtyard bar. Devoted customers and travellers pack the chequered-tablecloth-covered tables to chow on plates of garlicky clams, golden roast suckling pig and piles of codfish rice. Expect lines during peak lunch and dinner times, especially on weekends. There's a fee for paying by card, so bring cash.

★ Espaço Lisboa
PORTUGUESE, MACANESE $$$

(里斯本地帶; Map p574; ☑853 2888 2226; 8 Rua das Gaivotas, Coloane; meals MOP$250-800; ☺noon-3pm & 6.30-10pm; ♿; ☐21A, 25, 26A) 'Lisbon Space' is unique for its Portugal-inspired decor inside a Chinese village house. This two-storey restaurant in Coloane Village is known for its classic Portuguese dishes, including several tasty versions of *açorda* – bread cooked to a paste with eggs, olive oil and parsley; our favourite is the one with seafood that originated in the Alentejo region. On weekdays the restaurant offers a two-course set menu for MOP$88.

★ Jade Dragon   CANTONESE $$$
(譽瓏軒; ☑853 8868 2822; www.cityofdreams-macau.com; Level 2, Shops at the Boulevard, City of Dreams, Cotai; dim sum MOP$28-88, meals from MOP$800; ◷noon-3pm & 6-11pm) At three-Michelin-starred Jade Dragon, the genius of a Cantonese master is applied to top-notch ingredients and the results are mesmerising. We've all had barbecued pork and dumplings, but the real highlights here are its lychee-wood roasted goose or Kegani crab-meat pockets. The restaurant claims to consult experts on the health benefits of its creations (though we suspect the glistening barbecued goose was exempted).

🍸 Drinking & Nightlife

🍷 Macau Peninsula

★ Macau Soul   BAR
(澳感廊; Map p568; ☑853 2836 5182; www.macausoul.com; 31A Rua de São Paulo; ◷3-10pm Wed & Thu, to midnight Fri-Sun; ☐8A, 17, 26) An elegant haven in wood and stained glass. On most nights, Thelonious Monk jazz music fills the air as customers chat with the owners and dither over their 400 Portuguese wine options, including some rare varietals. Opening hours vary; phone ahead. Cash only.

★ Single Origin   COFFEE
(單品; Map p568; ☑853 6698 7475; 19 Rua de Abreu Nunes; ◷noon-8pm; ☎; ☐2, 4, 7, 7A, 8) This airy corner cafe opened by coffee professional Keith Fong makes a mean shot of espresso (coffees from MOP$30). You can choose your poison (single origin, of course) from a daily selection of 10 beans. If you can't decide, the well-trained baristas are more than happy to help.

★ Beer Temple   PUB
(Map p568; ☑853 2835 2803; www.facebook.com/beertemple.patiolazaro; 4 Pátio Sao Lázaro; ◷noon-2am; ☎; ☐3,4,6A,19) As the name suggests, the craft beer selection here is huge. If you can't decide, tell the staff your preference – fruit-forward, dry and bitter, or smelling like a pine forest – and they'll pick something out for you. Consume in the bar area with the high ceiling, loud music and shiny black surfaces.

🍷 The Islands

★ Macallan Whisky Bar & Lounge   BAR
(☑853 8883 2221; www.galaxymacau.com; 2nd fl, Galaxy Macau, Estrada da Baía de Nossa Senhora da Esperança, Cotai; ◷5pm-1am Mon-Thu, to 2am Fri & Sat; ☐25, 25X) Macau's best whisky bar is a traditional affair featuring oak panels, Jacobean rugs and a real fireplace. The 400-plus whisky labels include single malts from Ireland, France, Sweden and India, and a 1963 Glenmorangie. The 5pm to 8pm happy hour means you get your age in years discounted as a percentage from your drink (30 years old = 30% off, 100 years old = free).

★ Goa Nights   BAR
(果阿之夜; Map p572; ☑853 2856 7819; www.goanights.com; 118 Rua Correia da Silva, Taipa; ◷5pm-1am Tue-Sun; ☐22, 26) With lotus-shaped light stencils on the walls, intimate Goa is a cocktail bar that plays on the Portuguese-India theme. The menu, resembling an ancient map, introduces nine aromatic concoctions that allude to Portuguese explorer Vasco da Gama through ingredients such as raw turmeric and chorizo fat. The most interesting, we felt, was the smooth, fruity and spice-fragrant 'Lisbon'.

Hon Kei Hand-Whipped Coffee   CAFE
(漢記手打咖啡; ☑853 2888 2310; S-26, Lai Chi Vun Village, Coloane; ◷8am-6pm Thu-Tue; ☎; ☐15, 26, 26A, 50) At this thriving cafe next to shipyards, instant coffee is hand-whipped with sugar to create a peanut-buttery texture. The owner Mr Leong was a shipyard worker who built this shanty with old wood after an arm injury left him unfit for his job. Besides coffee (MOP$20), patrons enjoy egg sandwiches and noodles with Spam at shared tables in the semi-open space. The cafe is a 15-minute walk north of Lord Stow's Bakery (p574) near the entrance to Coloane Village, past the Ponte Cais de Coloane pier and the shipyards of Lai Chi Vun Village. It's on the left side of the road.

☆ Entertainment

Macau's nightlife may be dominated by the ever-expanding casino scene, but a number of interesting live-music venues have also sprung up about town. For entertainment/ cultural events listings, check out the bi-monthly *CCM+* and monthly *Destination Macau* available free at MGTO outlets and larger hotels.

★ **House of Dancing Water** THEATRE
(水舞間; ☑ ticket hotline 853 8868 6767; www.the-houseofdancingwater.com; City of Dreams, Estrada do Istmo, Cotai; tickets adult MOP$600-1500, child MOP$480-800; ☐ 35, 50) *The House of Dancing Water*, Macau's most expensively made show, is a breathtaking melange of stunts, acrobatics and theatre designed by Franco Dragone, the former director of Cirque du Soleil. The magic revolves around a cobalt pool the size of several Olympic-sized swimming pools. Over, around, into and under this pool a cast of 80, dressed in glorious costumes, performs hair-raising stunts.

★ **Live Music Association** LIVE MUSIC
(LMA; 現場音樂協會; Map p564; ☑ 853 2875 7511; www.facebook.com/lma.macau; 11th fl, Flat B, San Mei Industrial Bldg, 50 Avenida do Coronel Mesquita; ☐ 7, 17, 18A) *The* go-to place for indie music in Macau, this excellent dive inside an industrial building hosts live acts from Macau and overseas. There are two or three bands a week, with past performers including Cold Cave, Buddhistson, Mio Myo and Pet Conspiracy. See the Facebook page for what's on.

City of Dreams CASINO
(新濠天地, COD; ☑ 853 8868 6688; www.city-ofdreamsmacau.com; Estrada do Istmo, Cotai; ☉ 24hr; ☎ 🔓; ☐ 25, 26A, 35, 50) In addition to a sprawling gaming floor, this colossal hotel-casino-mall complex is home to four sleek hotels, several restaurants (including award-winners), kilometres of malls, and theatres large enough to host regional video-game competitions. The 1600-sq-metre **Kids' City** is a sophisticated indoor climbing facility that evokes an enlarged futuristic Lego set.

A free shuttle bus to City of Dreams operates from Macau Ferry Terminal and other locations (see website for details).

Cinematheque Passion CINEMA
(戀愛電影館; Map p568; ☑ 853 2852 2585; www.cinematheque-passion.mo; 11-13 Travessa da Paixão; tickets adult/student & senior MOP$60/30; ☉ ticket office 10am-11.30pm, archive 10am-8pm Tue-Sun; ☐ 2, 3, 4, 6, 7) An attractive yellow house shelters Macau's art-house cinema and film archive. There are regular screenings of Macanese movies and films about the city;

most films come with English subtitles. Even if you're not here for the flicks, it's worth going through the lobby to the back to see the garden with the shapely trees and a view of the Ruins of the Church of St Paul.

🛍 Shopping

There are old shops on Rua dos Ervanários and Rua de Nossa Senhora do Amparo near the Ruins of the Church of St Paul where you can look at antiques (and imitations). Shops selling pork jerky, egg rolls and almond biscuits are everywhere. Portuguese canned seafood, wine and ham seems to be all the rage now, with vendors appearing all over town.

Macau Peninsula

★ **Loja das Conservas** FOOD
(澳門葡式辣魚店, LCM Shop of Canned Macau; Map p568; ☑ 853 6571 8214; www.facebook.com/lojas conservasmacau; 9 Travessa do Aterro Novo; ☉ 11am-9pm; ☐ 4, 8A, 18A, 19) This beautiful shop carries dozens of canned seafood brands (representing hundreds of varieties) from Portugal, all labelled with details on the history of the the product. You'll find not only excellent sardines, tuna and mackerel but also sea bream, *bacalhau* (salted cod), octopus and *sangacho de atum* (tuna blood).

★ **Pin-to Livros e Musica** BOOKS
(邊度有書有音樂; Map p564; ☑ 853 2833 0909; www.facebook.com/pg/pintolivros; 47 Rua de Coelho do Amaral; ☉ 1-9pm Tue-Sun; ☐ 3, 18, 26A) One of Macau's best independent bookshops, Pin-to (which means 'where' in Cantonese) has a strong curation of titles in art and culture, including some in Portuguese and in English. The collections reflect the taste of owner Anson who can sometimes be seen reading by the staircase. You'll also find a dozen or so jazz and esoteric CDs, and two resident cats.

Taipa

★ **Cunha Bazaar** GIFTS & SOUVENIRS
(官也墟; Map p572; www.cunhabazaar.com; 33-35 Rua da Cunha; ☉ 9.30am-10pm; ☐ 22, 26, 33) This four-storey shop on the corner of Taipa Village's Rua do Cunha pedestrian street has the mother lode of made-in-Macau gifts, T-shirts, candies and more. You'll find traditional foods such as almond biscuits and jerky on the ground floor, while the 1st floor is dedicated to goods bearing the image of Macau's own Soda Panda.

BRIGHT LIGHTS, SIN CITY

Macau's gambling industry goes back to the 16th century when migrant labourers from China would gather to play a game called 'fan tan' in makeshift stalls on the streets and alleys near the harbour. But it wasn't until the 19th century when neighbour Hong Kong surpassed the port of Macau in importance that the government legalised gambling to boost revenue, and the city gained a reputation for being a gambling centre.

Rise of the Megacasinos

Since the early 2000s, megacasinos boasting celebrity-chef restaurants, top-tier fashion boutiques and rooms with excessive luxuries have been sprouting in the city, especially in the Cotai area. The change began when casino mogul Stanley Ho's monopoly ended in 2002 and Las Vegas operators set up shop in competition. The trend peaked in 2014 when Macau's gaming revenue surpassed all of the world's major gambling jurisdictions combined.

However, at around the same time, the industry suffered a blow from Beijing's anti-corruption crackdown. The move targeted the ultra-wealthy, many of whom happened to be VIPs at Macau's casinos. Gaming revenue plummeted for two years, but in August 2016 things started looking up again and in 2018 Macau's gaming revenue more than tripled that of Las Vegas.

There are currently more than 40 casinos in Macau, with more in the pipeline. Macau Peninsula has most of the older, smaller casinos, while the Cotai area is home to the new breed of casino-hotel-shopping-entertainment behemoths.

Indoor Smoking Ban

A welcome change for many, and a very visible one too, is that Macau's casinos are no longer the smoke-filled halls they once were where players had to squint to see their cards. Smoking is now prohibited in all indoor areas in Macau, and while casinos (and the airport) are allowed to have smoking lounges, the law now requires new lounges of a higher standard to better protect casino employees from secondhand smoke.

Casino Culture

Table games are the staple at casinos here – mostly baccarat, then roulette and a dice game called *dai sai* (big small). You'll hardly hear any whooping and clunking – slot machines make up only 5% of total casino winnings (versus Vegas' 60%). Drunks are also hard to come by, as Chinese players believe that booze dulls their skill. Over 80% of gamblers and 95% of high rollers come from mainland China. The latter play inside members-only rooms where the total amount wagered on any given day can exceed a small country's GDP.

For recreational players, the only thing to watch out for is harassment by tip hustlers – scam artists who hang around tables acting like your new best friend. They may steal your chips, nag you for a cut or try to take you to a casino that will tip them for bringing clients.

Casinos are open 24 hours. To enter, you must be 21 years or older and neatly dressed.

★**Cool ThingzZ & Portuguese Spot** FOOD & DRINKS
(葡國小天地; Map p572; ☑853 2857 6873; 2 Rua das Gaivotas; ☺11am-10pm; ☒22, 26) Portuguese products in Macau are booming these days, and this bright and welcoming shop stocks wines, olive oil, sweets and canned seafood, as well as cockerel-themed cushions.

ⓘ Information

ACCESSIBLE TRAVEL

Macau is not exactly friendly to travellers with disabilities. The historical part of Macau sits on a hilly landscape and pavement is often uneven, though some major sights do have provisions for disability access. The newer parts, such as around the Cotai Strip, are flat and have wider streets.

Macau law requires accessible facilities in public buildings (usually in the form of a ramp) and disabled parking bays in public car parks. Traffic lights generally have audible signals to help the sight-impaired cross the street.

Public transport, including taxis, is not equipped to accommodate people with physical disabilities. The airport is quite accessible, but accessing the ferries from Hong Kong to Macau will require assistance from the staff.

EMERGENCY & IMPORTANT NUMBERS

Police, fire & ambulance	☑ 999
24hr tourist emergency hotline	☑ 110, 112
International directory assistance	☑ 101
Local directory assistance	☑ 181
Country dialling code	☑ 853

INTERNET ACCESS

➤ You can access free public wi-fi in select government premises, tourist hotspots and public areas under a unified brand name 'FreeWiFi. MO' (www.freewifi.mo/en).

➤ Most cafes and hotels in Macau have free wi-fi.

➤ You can also buy prepaid phonecards from CTM, ranging from MOP$50 to MOP$100, to enjoy mobile broadband; or buy a mobile broadband pass for unlimited internet access for three days (MOP$100) or seven days (MOP$200).

➤ CTM, Three, SmarTone and China Telecom offer prepaid SIM cards (from MOP$50) with comparable coverage and services; all except China Telecom requires a SIM-unlocked, GSM-compatible phone.

LGBTIQ+ TRAVELLERS

Gay culture is not particularly visible in Macau, though a handful of activists and lawmakers are seeking to change that. Gay and lesbian travellers are unlikely to be bothered by locals, though displays of affection may bring stares. Rainbow of Macau (www.rainbow.mo), the territory's only gay-rights association, has information about the state of same-sex civil rights.

MEDICAL SERVICES

Two of Macau's hospitals have 24-hour emergency services.

Centro Hospitalar Conde São Januário (山頂醫院; Map p564; ☑ 853 2831 3731; Estrada do Visconde de São Januário; ⊙ 24hr emergency) Southwest of Guia Fort.

Hospital Kiang Wu (鏡湖醫院; Map p564; ☑ 853 2837 1333; Estrada de Coelho do Amaral; ⊙ 24hr emergency) Northeast of the ruins of the Church of St Paul.

MONEY

Macau's currency is the pataca (MOP$). Most ATMs allow you to choose between patacas and Hong Kong dollars. Credit cards are readily accepted at Macau's hotels, larger restaurants and casinos. You can also change cash and travellers cheques at the banks lining Avenida da Praia Grande and Avenida de Almeida Ribeiro, as well as at major hotels.

POST

Correios de Macau, Macau's postal system, is efficient and inexpensive.

Macau's **general post office** (郵政總局; ☑ 853 2857 4491; cnr Largo do Senado & Avenida de Almeida Ribeiro; ⊙ 9am-6pm Mon-Fri, to 1pm Sat) is in Largo do Senado. EMS Speedpost is available here.

Other companies can also arrange express forwarding, including DHL, FedEx and UPS.

SAFE TRAVEL

➤ Violent crime against visitors in Macau is rare, but pickpocketing and other street crime can occur in busy areas.

➤ Take extra caution with passports and valuables in crowded areas and when visiting casinos late at night.

TELEPHONE

Local calls are free from private telephones; at a public payphone they cost MOP$1 for five minutes. Most hotels will charge you MOP$3.

All payphones permit International Direct Dialling (IDD) using an Easy Call phonecard available for purchase from CTM for MOP$100. Rates are cheaper from 6pm to 9am on weekdays.

TOURIST INFORMATION

The **Macau Government Tourist Office** (旅遊局; ☑ 853 8397 1120, tourism hotline 853 2833 3000; www.macautourism.gov.mo; Edifício Ritz, Largo do Senado; ⊙ 9am-6pm) is a well-organised and helpful source of information. It dispenses a large selection of free literature, including pamphlets on everything from Chinese temples and Catholic churches to fortresses, gardens and walks. The MGTO also runs a 24-hour tourist hotline.

There are half a dozen MGTO outlets scattered all over Macau, including at the **MGTO – Macau Ferry Terminal** (旅遊局外港碼頭分局; Map p564; ☑ 853 2872 6416; Macau Ferry Terminal, Outer Harbour; ⊙ 9am-10pm) and the mezzanine level of the **airport** (澳門旅遊局, Macau Government Tourism Office; ☑ 853 2886 1436; www.macau tourism.gov.mo; Macau International Airport; ⊙ 9am-10pm; 🚌 21, 26, AP1). There are also Hong Kong branches at Hong Kong International Airport (p1033) and **Shun Tak Centre** (澳門政府旅遊局旅客詢問處 – 香港分行; Map p532; ☑ 853 2857 2287; www.macautourism.gov.mo; 336-337 Shun Tak Centre, 200 Connaught Rd Central, Hong Kong; ⊙ 9am-8pm).

The **Macau Cultural Affairs Bureau** (www. icm.gov.mo) lists Macau's cultural offerings month by month.

VISAS

UK travellers can enter Macau with just their passports for six months. Most other travellers can do the same between 30 and 90 days, including citizens of Australia, Canada, the EU, New Zealand, South Africa and the US. Travellers who do require visas can get them, valid for 30 days, on arrival in Macau. They cost MOP$100/50/200 per adult/child/family. You can apply for a visa extension from the Taipa branch of the **Immigration Department Office Building** (出入境事務廳; Serviço de Migração; ☑ 853 2872 5488; Immigration Department Office Bldg, Estrada de Pac On, Taipa; ⊙ 9am-5pm Mon-Fri).

Nationals of Australia, Canada, the EU, the UK, New Zealand and most other countries (but not US citizens) can purchase their China visas at Zhuhai on the border, but it will ultimately save you time if you get one in advance as lines can be long. Express visas (MOP$1250 plus photos) are available in Macau or Hong Kong from **China Travel Service** (CTS; 中国旅行社, Map p564; Zhōngguó Lǚxíngshè; ☑ 853 2870 0888; www.cts.com.mo; Nam Kwong Bldg, 207 Avenida do Dr Rodrigo Rodrigues; ⊙ 9am-5pm Mon-Sat), usually in two to five working days.

ⓘ Getting There & Away

Most travellers arrive in Macau by ferry from Hong Kong. If you are coming from mainland China, you can take the ferry or a bus from Guangdong, or fly from select cities in mainland China. In October 2018, the world's longest sea bridge opened in the Pearl River Delta, connecting Macau with Hong Kong by road, cutting the cost and time of the journey.

Macau International Airport is connected to a number of destinations in Asia. If you are coming from outside Asia and destined for Macau, your best option is to fly to Hong Kong International Airport (p1033) and take a ferry to Macau without going through Hong Kong customs.

AIR

Located on Taipa Island, **Macau International Airport** (澳門國際機場; Map p561; www.macau-airport.com) is only 20 minutes from the city centre. It has frequent services to destinations including Bangkok, Chiang Mai, Kaohsiung, Kuala Lumpur, Manila, Osaka, Seoul, Singapore, Taipei, Tokyo and Beijing.

Many passengers arrive to Macau via Hong Kong International Airport, which has more international connections and is linked to Macau via ferry and bridge.

BOAT

Ferry and catamaran tickets can be booked in advance at the ferry terminals, through travel agencies or online. You can also buy tickets on the spot, though advance booking is recommended if you plan to travel on weekends or public holidays, as tickets are often in high demand. There is a standby queue at the pier for passengers wanting to travel before their ticketed sailing. You need to arrive at the pier at least 15 minutes before departure, but you should allow 30 minutes

because of occasional long queues at immigration. You are limited to 20kg of carry-on luggage in economy class, but oversized or overweight bags can be checked in.

To/From Hong Kong

The vast majority of travellers make their way from Hong Kong to Macau by ferry. The journey takes just an hour and there are frequent departures throughout the day, with reduced service between midnight and 7am.

Most ferries depart from the Hong Kong–Macau Ferry Terminal (p559) on Hong Kong Island or the China Ferry Terminal in Kowloon, and arrive at the **Macau Maritime Ferry Terminal** (澳門外港客運碼頭,Terminal Marítimo de Passageiros do Porto Exterior; Map p564) – also known as the Outer Harbour Ferry Terminal – or the Taipa Ferry Terminal.

TurboJet (噴射飛航; ☑ Hong Kong enquiries 852 2859 3333, Macau 853 2855 5025, toll-free mainland China & Taiwan 00800 3628 3628; www.turbojet.com.hk; economy/superclass Mon-Fri MOP$160/355, Sat & Sun MOP$175/360, night crossing MOP$200/380) has regular departures from the Hong Kong–Macau Ferry Terminal (every 15 minutes) and the China Ferry Terminal (every 30 minutes to 3½ hours) to Macau from 7am to midnight, and less frequent service after midnight.

CotaiJet (金光飛航; ☑ 853 2885 0595; www.cotaiwaterjet.com; regular/1st class Mon-Fri MOP$171/293, Sat & Sun MOP$186/310, after 5pm MOP$211/338; 🚌 26, N2, 36) has high-speed catamarans connecting the Hong Kong–Macau Ferry Terminal and the **Taipa Ferry Terminal** (氹仔客運碼頭, Terminal Marítimo de Passageiros da Taipa; 🚌 26, N2, 36) every 30 minutes between 7am and midnight. Free shuttles at the ferry terminal in Taipa will take you to destinations along the Cotai Strip.

To/From Mainland China

TurboJet has 12 departures from the Macau Maritime Ferry Terminal daily to the port of Shekou (economy/super class MOP$257/412, one hour) in Shenzhen. Twelve ferries return from Shekou between 8am and 7.45pm. TurboJet also has four departures to Shenzhen airport (MOP$252/437, one hour) from 10.30am to 6pm.

Yuet Tung Shipping Co (粵通船務有限公司; ☑ 853 2885 0272; Point 11A Inner Harbour, Inner Harbour Ferry Terminal) has ferries connecting Macau (Taipa Ferry Terminal) with Shekou (MOP$210, 70 minutes, 10 daily), departing between 8.30am and 10.30pm. Book at the ferry terminal.

BUS

Macau is an easy gateway by land into mainland China. Simply take bus 3A, 27 or AP1 (MOP$6) to the Border Gate (關閘, Portas do Cerco; 6am to

1am) and walk across. A second – and much less busy crossing – is the Cotai Frontier Post (路氹邊檢大樓; 24 hours) on the causeway linking Taipa and Coloane, which allows visitors to cross the Lotus Flower Bridge by shuttle bus (MOP$5) to Hengqin in Zhuhai. Buses 15 (MOP$6, every 30 to 35 minutes, 6am to 8pm) and 50 (MOP$6, every 12 to 26 minutes, 7.30am to 10.15pm) will drop you off at the crossing.

If you want to travel further afield in China, buses run by **Kee Kwan Motor Road Co** (歧關車路有限公司; ☑ 853 2893 3888; ⊙ 9am-9.30pm) leave the bus station at the Border Gate. Buses for different locations in Guangzhou (about MOP$90, three hours) depart every 30 minutes or so. There are also a number of buses to Zhongshan (MOP$50, one hour).

In 2018 the long-anticipated Hong Kong–Zhuhai–Macau Bridge opened to traffic, reducing transit times and costs for getting around the Pearl River Delta. A 24-hour licensed shuttle-bus service (HK$65 to HK$70, every five to 15 minutes, 6am to midnight and every 15 to 30 minutes overnight) operates daily from Macau Port to Hong Kong Port, where you can pick up local buses to the airport and city. Bus 101X runs between Macau Port and central Macau Peninsula.

ⓘ Getting Around

TO/FROM THE AIRPORT

Take bus 26 (MOP$6) from the airport to Coloane and Taipa; it goes between airport, Taipa Ferry Terminal and A-Ma Temple.

The airport bus AP1 (MOP$6) leaves the airport and zips around Taipa before heading to the Macau Maritime Ferry Terminal and the Border Gate. The bus stops at a number of major hotels en route and departs every five to 12 minutes from 6am to 1.20am. Buses AP1X and 26 also run from the airport to the Border Gate (Portas do Cerco) for onward journeys to China.

Other services include buses to Praça de Ferreira do Amaral on Macau Peninsula (MT1 and N2).

The Macau Maritime Ferry Terminal (p579) is linked directly to Hong Kong International Airport by TurboJet (HK$270/205/150 per adult/child/infant, 70 minutes), which has four ferries operating between 7.15am and 9.45pm from Hong Kong, and two in the opposite direction, at 11am and 6pm.

You can also travel to Taipa Ferry Terminal (p579) from Hong Kong International Airport via CotaiJet (HK$270/205 per adult/child, 65 minutes), which has two ferries from Hong Kong at 2.15pm and 4.15pm, and five ferries between 7.55am and 3.55pm in the other direction. There are also some night sailings. However, this ferry service is for transit passengers only. It is not applicable to passengers originating in Hong Kong.

A taxi from the airport to the town centre should cost about MOP$70, plus a surcharge of MOP$5. Large bags cost an extra MOP$3.

BICYCLE

Bikes can be rented in Taipa Village from **Yau Kei Store** (友記士多; ☑ 853 2882 7975; 11 Rua dos Negociantes, Taipa; per hour MOP$25; ⊙ 10am-7pm; ☐ 11, 15, 22, 28A). You are not allowed to cross the Macau–Taipa bridges on a bicycle.

PUBLIC TRANSPORT

Public buses and minibuses run by **TCM** (www. tcm.com.mo) and **Transmac** (☑ 853 2827 1122; www.transmac.com.mo) operate from 6am until shortly after midnight. All routes charge a standardised fare (MOP$6), which is dropped into a box upon entry (exact change only), or you can pay with a Macau Pass smart card that allows you to enjoy a discount of MOP$3 or MOP$4 per trip. The Macau Pass can be purchased from various supermarkets and convenience stores and costs MOP$130 at first purchase, which includes a non-refundable fee of MOP$30. A minimum of MOP$50 is required to add money to the card each time. Expect buses to be very crowded.

The *Macau Tourist Map* has a full list of bus-company routes and it's worth picking one up from one of the Macau Government Tourist Office (MGTO) outlets. You can also check the routes on the TCM website. The two most useful buses on the peninsula are buses 3 and 3A, which run between the Maritime Ferry Terminal and the city centre, near the post office. Both continue up to the border crossing with the mainland, as does bus 3X, and can be boarded along Avenida de Almeida Ribeiro. Bus 12 runs from the ferry terminal, past the Lisboa Hotel and then up to Lou Lim Ieoc Garden and Kun Iam Temple. The best services to Taipa and Coloane are buses 21A, 25 and 26A. Buses to the airport are AP1, 26, MT1 and MT4.

Free shuttle buses run from the ferry terminals and the border gates to the casinos of Cotai; anyone can ride, not just hotel guests.

TAXI

Taxis are a convenient and inexpensive option in Macau. The flagfall charge is MOP$19 for the first 1.6km, and MOP$2 for every 240m thereafter. A MOP$5 surcharge applies to taxi trips boarded at Macau International Airport, Taipa Ferry Terminal, the University of Macau and journeys from Macau Peninsula to Coloane. From Taipa to Coloane, the surcharge is MOP$2. There are plenty of taxi queues around the casinos in Cotai, but expect long lines and refusals to take you to far-flung locations (ie Coloane).

For a taxi, call either 853 8500 0000 or 853 2828 3283, or have your hotel call a taxi for you. You can also try using the Macau Taxi Fare app. There's no Uber in Macau.

Guangdong

POP 104 MILLION

Best Places to Eat

➜ Guangzhou Restaurant (p591)

➜ Zheng's Private Kitchen (p615)

➜ Panxi Restaurant (p591)

➜ Supin (p590)

➜ Bingsheng Taste (p591)

➜ Fán Lóu (p608)

Best Places to Stay

➜ LN Garden Hotel (p605)

➜ Guangdong Victory Hotel (p589)

➜ Shenzhen Loft Youth Hostel (p607)

➜ Zaiyang Inn (p615)

Why Go?

Guangdong's unique culture and natural beauty fly under the radar and have yet to be discovered by many travellers, so you may have a plethora of sublime sights (not to mention great dim sum) all to yourself.

Northern Guangdong (广东, Guǎngdōng) is home to some wild and wondrous landscapes. In the blue pine forests of Nanling, the music of waterfalls and windswept trees boomerangs in your direction. If it's Unesco-crowned heritage you're after, Kaiping's flamboyant watchtowers and the stylised poses of Cantonese opera will leave you riveted. What's all the fuss about Hakka culture? Find out in Meizhou and Chaozhou.

Historically Guangdong was the starting point of the Maritime Silk Road and the birthplace of revolution. On the scenic byways of the Pearl River delta, you'll uncover the glory of China's revolutionary past, while on the surfbeaten beaches of Hailing Island, an ancient shipwreck and its treasures await.

When to Go
Guangzhou

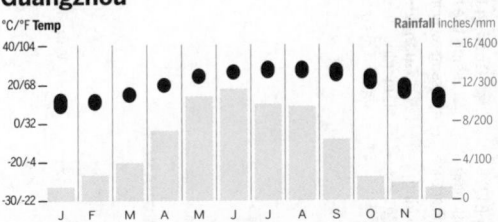

Apr–Jun Verdant paddy fields contrast with the built wonders of Kaiping and Meizhou.

Jul–Sep Blue pines and stained-glass windows offer respite from summer.

Oct–Dec The typhoons and heat are gone; this is the best time to visit.

Guangdong Highlights

1 Nankou Village (p617) Being awed by the crouching dragons of Hakka architecture.

2 Foshan (p594) Visiting the home town of two kung fu legends.

3 Guangji Bridge (p614) Crossing the majestic passageway in Chaozhou.

4 Guangzhou (p583) Lunching on dumplings in a garden restaurant.

5 Shenzhen (p603) Witnessing China's tech capital buzz with commerce at its technology malls.

6 Nanling National Forest Park (p601) Falling asleep to the whispered symphony of an ancient forest after a day's hike.

7 Yangjiang (p597) Visiting silken beaches of Shili Yintan Beach and an 800-year-old shipwreck.

8 Kaiping (p596) Climbing dramatic Unesco-crowned watchtowers.

9 Chayang (p618) Being mesmerised by the labyrinthine streets of the old town.

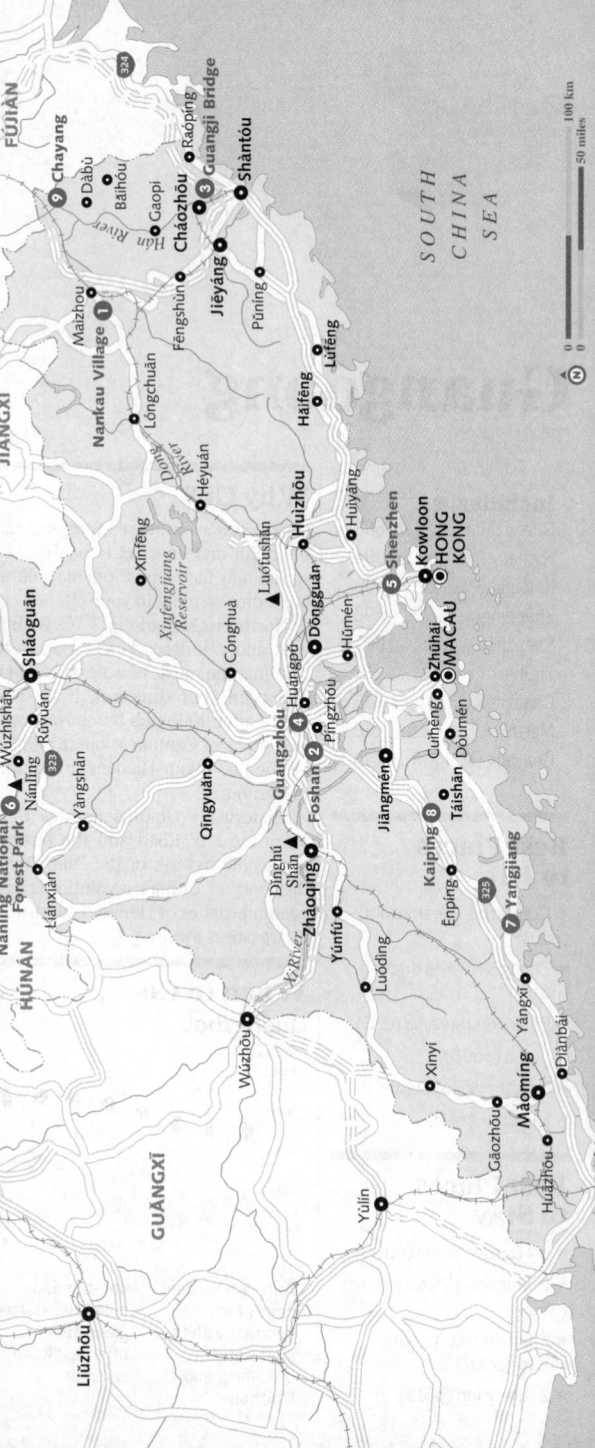

History

Guangdong has had contact with the outside world for nearly two millennia. Among the first outsiders to arrive were the Romans, who appeared in the 2nd century AD. By the Tang dynasty (618–907), a sizeable trade with the Middle East and Southeast Asia had developed.

The first Europeans to settle here were the Portuguese in 1557, followed by the Jesuits who established themselves in Zhaoqing. The British came along in the 17th century and by 1685 merchant ships from the East India Company were calling at Guangzhou. In 1757 an imperial edict gave the *cohong*, a local merchants' guild, a monopoly on China's trade with foreigners, who were restricted to Shamian Island. Trade remained in China's favour until 1773, when the British shifted the balance by unloading 1000 chests of Bengal opium in Guangzhou. Addiction spread in China like wildfire, eventually leading to the Opium Wars.

In the 19th century Guangdong was a hotbed of reform and revolt. Among the political elites who sowed revolutionary ideas here was Sun Yatsen, who later became the first president of the Republic of China.

The 20th century saw Guangdong serve as the headquarters of both the Nationalist and Communist Parties, and endure great suffering during the Cultural Revolution. After the implementation of the 'open door' policy in 1978, it became the first province to embrace capitalism. The province's continued economic success has made it a leading export centre for consumer goods.

Language

The vast majority of the people of Guangdong speak Cantonese, a dialect distinct from Mandarin and also spoken in Hong Kong. Though it enjoys a less exalted status than the national dialect, Cantonese is older and better suited than Mandarin for the reading of classical poetry, according to many scholars. In 1911 Cantonese lost out to Mandarin by a mere one vote to become the national language of China.

ⓘ Getting There & Around

Airports at Guangzhou and Shenzhen run domestic and international flights, while those in Zhuhai, Meizhou and Chaozhou bring every major city within a three-hour flight of the sights.

Long-distance buses are the transportation with the most frequent departures between major areas in Guangdong.

High-speed rail connects Guangdong to its provincial neighbours Guangxi, Hunan, Jiangxi and Fujian.

The fastest trains on the northeast–southwest axis head for Nanchang (four hours), Wuhan (four hours), Xi'an (nine hours) and Beijing (eight to 10 hours). A well-developed network of convenient, older rail lines and expressways spans the entire province. Metro and light rail in Guangzhou, Shenzhen, Zhuhai and Foshan are connected to major and high-speed train stations.

Guangzhou 广州

🗓 020 / POP 13 MILLION

Guangzhou (Guǎngzhōu), once better known internationally as Canton, has been China's busiest trading centre for centuries. Despite breakneck redevelopment up to and after the 2010 Asian Games, much of the metropolis still hums along at a pleasantly sedate pace, where narrow, leafy streets conceal temples and mosques, pockets of colonial-era heritage, traditional dim sum eateries, distinctive *qílóu* shophouses and Lingnan architecture. Equally, you can embrace modernity via the 21st-century architectural landmarks of the showpiece Zhujiang New Town, such as Zaha Hadid's Opera House and the slim-waisted Canton Tower, rising up over the Pearl River, which cuts a lazy course through the city.

History

Guangzhou's history is one dominated by trade and revolution. Since the Tang dynasty, it had been China's most important southern port and the starting point for the Maritime Silk Road, a trade route to the West. It became a trading post for the Portuguese in the 16th century, and later for the British.

After the fall of the Qing dynasty in 1911, the city was a stronghold of the republican forces led by Sun Yatsen and, subsequently, a centre of activity for the Chinese Communist Party (CCP) led by Mao Zedong.

During the post-1949 years of China's self-imposed isolation, the Canton Trade Fair was the only platform on which China did business with the West.

In 2010 Guangzhou held the Asian Games, which meant a wide-ranging facelift for the city, from improved transport networks to new landmark buildings and cultural institutions.

◉ Sights

★ **Shamian Island**　　　HISTORIC SITE
(沙面岛, Shāmiàn Dǎo; Ⓜ Lines 1 & 6 to Huangsha, exit F) Don't depart Guangzhou without an amble through the concession-era gem that is Shamian Island. The central east–west drag is a time-warp boulevard of faded European-style buildings shaded by columns of banyan trees. It's a charming setting and the backdrop to many a wedding photo shoot. Choose a quiet time of day, and duck into side streets where you can peek into lived-in residences with wooden staircases and cracked Victorian floor tiles.

Canton Customs Mansion　　NOTABLE BUILDING
(粤海关旧址, Yuè Hǎiguān Jiùzhǐ; Ⓙ 020 8101 3617; 29 Yanjiang Xilu, 沿江西路29号; ⊘ 9am-4pm Wed; Ⓜ Line 6 to Culture Park, exit A) **FREE**
The Guangdong customs building (c 1916) is one of the most impressive concession-era structures remaining along the waterfront. Designed by a British architect in neoclassical style, it is crowned with a bell tower that chimes at 8am and 8pm.

★ **Qingping Chinese Medicine Market**　　　MARKET
(清平市场, Qīngpíng Shìchǎng; 23-25 Zhuji Lu, 珠玑路23-25号; ⊘ 9am-7pm; Ⓜ Line 1 & 6 to Huangsha, exit E) Just north of the channel that divides Shamian Island from the city, this tumbledown market is a sensory delight, with open-fronted vendors arranged beneath an arcade and in the tiny alleys behind. You'll find ginseng, goji berries, Sichuan peppercorns, giant mushrooms and countless other restorative tonic essentials.

Just over the bridge, **Shamian Traditional Chinese Medical Centre** (沙面国医馆, Shāmiàn Guóyīguǎn; Ⓙ 020 8121 8383; 85-87 Shamian Beijie, Shamian Island, 沙面北街 85-87号; full-body massage per hour from ¥238; ⊘ 11am-1.30am; Ⓜ Line 1 & 6 to Huangsha, exit F) is a professional clinic specialising in Chinese medical treatments, where qualified therapists will pummel you back into order.

★ **Chen Clan Ancestral Hall**　　HISTORIC SITE
(陈家祠, Chénjiā Cí; Ⓙ 020 8181 4559; 903 Kangwang Beilu, 康王北路903号; ¥10; ⊘ 8.30am-5pm; Ⓜ Line 1 to Chenjiaci, exit D) An all-in-one ancestral shrine, Confucian school and 'chamber of commerce' for the Chen clan, this compound was built in 1894 by the residents of 72 villages in Guangdong, where the Chen lineage is predominant. There are 19 buildings in the traditional Lingnan style, all featuring exquisite carvings, statues and paintings, and decorated with ornate scrollwork throughout.

Temple of the Six Banyan Trees　　BUDDHIST SITE
(六榕寺, Liùróng Sì; Ⓙ 020 8339 2843; 87 Liurong Lu, 六榕路87号; ¥5, pagoda ¥10; ⊘ 8am-5pm; Ⓜ Line 2 to Sun Yatsen Memorial Hall, exit D1) This Buddhist temple complex was first built in AD 537 to enshrine Buddhist relics brought over from India and placed in the octagonal **Decorated Pagoda** (Huā Tǎ). The temple was given its current name by the exiled poet Su Dongbo in 1099, who waxed lyrical over the banyans in the courtyard. Though not the original trees, the current banyans are over 170 years old. You can see the character's 'six banyans' (liùróng) that Su wrote above the gates.

Huaisheng Mosque　　MOSQUE
(怀圣寺, Huáishèng Sì; Ⓙ 020 8333 3593; 56 Guangta Lu, 光塔路56号; ⊘ dawn-dusk; Ⓜ Line 1 to Ximenkou, exit B) You can't miss the 36m-high minaret thrusting up over Guangta Lu like a lighthouse. Enter just east of it and you can stroll all the way through the complex to the main prayer hall with its tapering Chinese roof shading rows of west-facing prayer mats.

Guangxiao Temple　　BUDDHIST SITE
(光孝寺, Guāngxiào Sì; Ⓙ 020 8108 8867; 109 Guangxiao Lu, 光孝路109号; ¥5; ⊘ 6am-5pm; Ⓜ Line 1 to Ximenkou, exit C) The 'Bright Filial Piety Temple' is the oldest temple site in Guangzhou, dating from the 4th century. By the time of the Tang it was well established as a centre of Buddhist learning in southern China. Bodhidharma, the founder of Zen

AN OPERATIC STROLL ON ENNING LU

Enning Lu is not just a showcase of old Guangzhou's Qílóu (騎樓) architecture – the early-20th-century arcaded buildings that line the street – it's also a window into the performance past of this historic neighbourhood.

The first stop is **Bahe Academy** (八和会馆, Bāhé Huìguǎn; 117 Enning Lu, 恩宁路117好; Ⓜ Line 1 to Changshou Lu, exit D2), a guild hall for Cantonese opera practitioners. The original academy opened in 1889 to provide lodging, schooling, and medical and funeral services to Cantonese opera troupes. It's now a gathering place for retired artists. It is not open to the public, but you can see the original 3m-tall wooden door from 1889, the only item that survived a bombing by the Japanese in 1937. The door was also used during the Great Leap Forward as a parking plank for 4-tonne vehicles, and clearly survived that as well.

Just past the academy is a huge faux-historic complex set around the old waterway that houses the **Cantonese Opera Art Museum** (open 9am to 4pm).

A block further on, you'll reach Yongqing Fang (永庆坊), an alleyway running north under a stone from Enning Lu. Turn left into the second smaller lane here; at No 7-1 you'll find **Luányú Táng** (銮舆堂; 7-1, 2nd Alley, Yongqing Fang, Enning Lu, 恩宁路永庆坊二巷; ⏱10am-3pm), a 200-year-old union for actors playing martial-arts and acrobatic roles in Cantonese opera. The union still gives martial-arts training for the stage to children, and its members come for operatic 'jamming' sessions on the 2nd floor. Visitors may be let in at their discretion.

Doubling back into the first lane here, the last unit was the **ancestral home of Bruce Lee** (1st Alley, Yongqing Fang, Enning Lu, 恩宁路永庆坊一巷; ⏱9am-5pm) **FREE**, the kung fu (gōngfū) icon, whose father Lǐ Hǎiquán (李海泉) was – you guessed it – a Cantonese opera actor and a member of that union. You can enter the old house, which has been stripped back to the bare bricks and is now an exhibition space displaying historic photographs of the surrounding neighbourhood.

If you're inspired keep walking north as Enning Lu becomes equally pleasant Longjin Xilu, then reward yourself with dim sum at Panxi Restaurant (p591) when you reach Lìwān Lake Park.

Enning Lu is easily reached from Changshou Lu metro station or from Shamian Island.

Buddhism, taught here. Most of the current buildings date from the 19th century or later, including a double-eaved main hall containing a 10m-tall Buddha statue.

Dōngshān   HISTORIC SITE

(东山区, Dōngshān Qū; Xinhepu Lu, 新河浦路; Ⓜ Line 1 to Dongshankou, exit E) Tree-lined streets Xinhepu Lu (新河浦路), Xuguyuan Lu (恤孤院路) and Peizheng Lu (培正路) in the historic Dōngshān area offer a welcome respite from the city. Here you'll find schools and churches raised by American missionaries in the 1900s, and exquisite villas commissioned by overseas Chinese and military bigwigs of the Kuomintang.

Guangdong Museum of Art   MUSEUM

(广东美术馆, Guǎngdōng Měishùguǎn; ☏020 8735 1468; www.gdmoa.org; 38 Yanyu Lu, 烟雨路 38号; ⏱9am-5pm Tue-Sun; 🚌89, 131A, 194) **FREE** On the southern shoreline of Ersha Island (Èrshā Dǎo), this colossus of an art museum showcases the works of important Cantonese artists and has been the site of the Guangzhou

Triennale. It's a little tricky to get to; taxi is your best bet (¥25 from Shamian Island).

Mausoleum of the Nanyue King   MAUSOLEUM

(南越王墓, Nányuèwáng Mù; ☏020 3618 2920; www.gznywmuseum.org; 867 Jiefang Beilu, 解放北路867号; adult/child ¥12/free; ⏱9am-4.45pm; Ⓜ Line 2 to Yuexiu Park, exit E) You'll feel like Indiana Jones/Lara Croft (select as preferred) as you descend the two-millennia-old steps into an actual Han dynasty tomb. This was the final resting place of Zhao Mo, second king of the Nanyue Kingdom, entombed here in 122 BC with over a dozen sacrificial servants. The remains of a concubine lies under glass – a shroud of bone dust.

Yuexiu Park   PARK

(越秀公园, Yuèxiù Gōngyuán; ☏020 8666 1950; 988 Jiefang Beilu, 解放北路988号; ⏱6am-10pm; Ⓜ Line 2 to Yuexiu Park, exit B1) **FREE** A crenellated roadway between attractions in this hilly park is actually a (heavily restored) slab of Guangzhou's long-departed city wall, built during the Ming dynasty. Entering via the park's west

Guangzhou

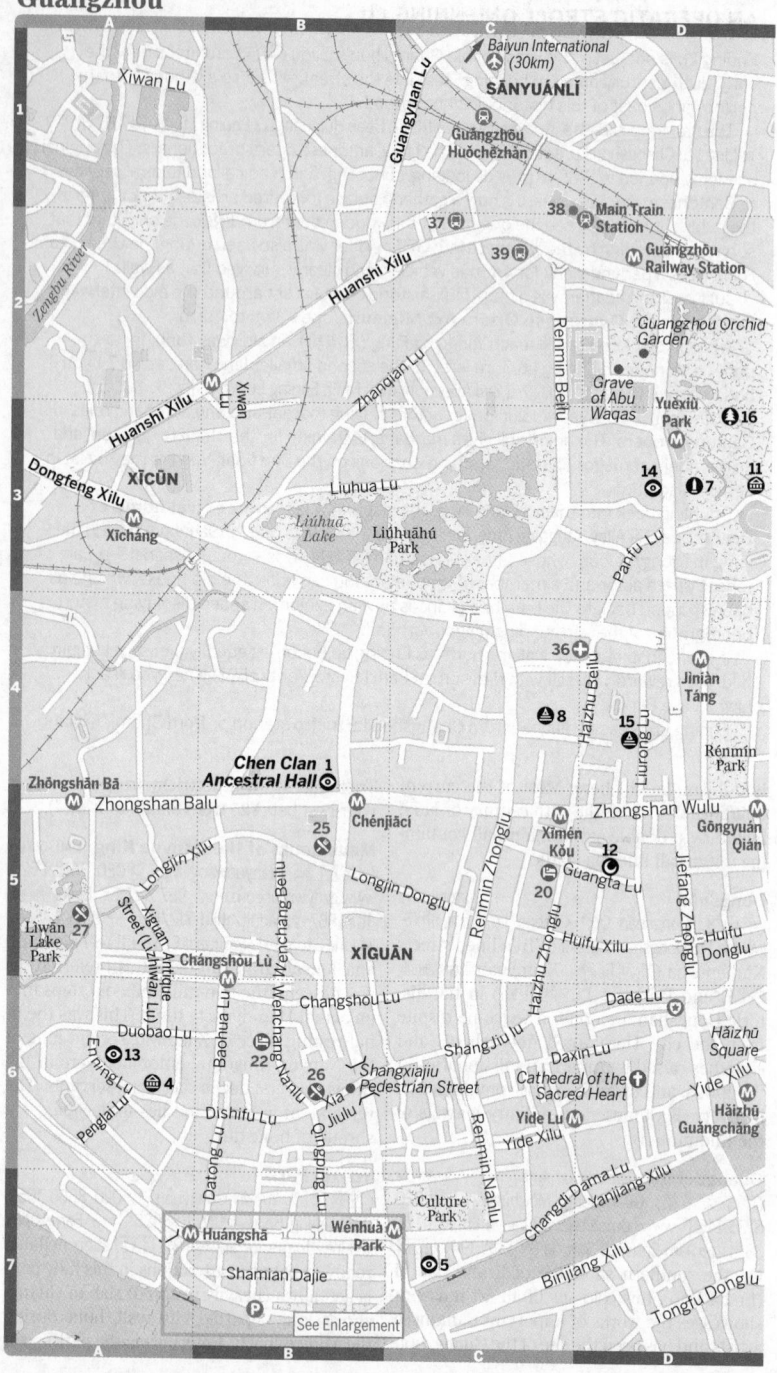

GUANGDONG

Baiyun International
(30km)

SĀNYUÁNLǏ

Guangyuan Lu

Xiwan Lu

Guǎngzhōu
Huǒchēzhàn

37

38 ● Main Train
Station

M Guǎngzhōu
Railway Station

39

Huanshi Xilu

Zhanqian Lu

Renmin Beilu

Guangzhou Orchid
Garden

Grave
of Abu
Waqas

Yuèxiù
Park

16

Huanshi Xilu

Xiwan
Lu

XĪCŪN

Dongfeng Xilu

M
Xīcháng

Liuhua Lu

Liúhuā
Lake

Liúhuāhú
Park

14

7

11

Pantu Lu

36

M Jiniàn
Táng

Rénmín
Park

Haizhu Beilu

8

15

Liurong Lu

Zhōngshān Bā

**Chen Clan 1
Ancestral Hall**

M
Zhongshan Balu

25

Chénjiācí

Ximén
Kǒu

12

Guangta Lu

Zhongshan Wulu

M
Gōngyuán
Qián

Longjin Xilu

Xiguan
Antique
Street (Lizhwan Lu)

Wenchang Beilu

Longjin Donglu

XĪGUĀN

20

Renmin Zhonglu

Haizhu Zhonglu

Huifu Xilu

Jiefang Zhonglu

Huifu
Donglu

Liwān
Lake
Park

27

Chángshòu Lù

Baohua Lu

Changshou Lu

Shangjiu Lu

Dade Lu

Hǎizhū
Square

Duobao Lu

13

Enning Lu

4

Datong Lu

Dishifu Lu

Wenchang Nanlu

22

26

Qingping Lu

Jiulu

Xia

Shangxiajiu
Pedestrian Street

Daxin Lu

Cathedral of the
Sacred Heart

Yide Lu

Yide Xilu

Changdi Dama Lu

Yide Xilu

Hǎizhū
Guǎngchǎng

Penglai Lu

Renmin Nanlu

Yanjiang Xilu

M Huángshā

Wénhuà
Park

Culture
Park

5

P

Shamian Dajie

See Enlargement

Binjiang Xilu

Tongfu Donglu

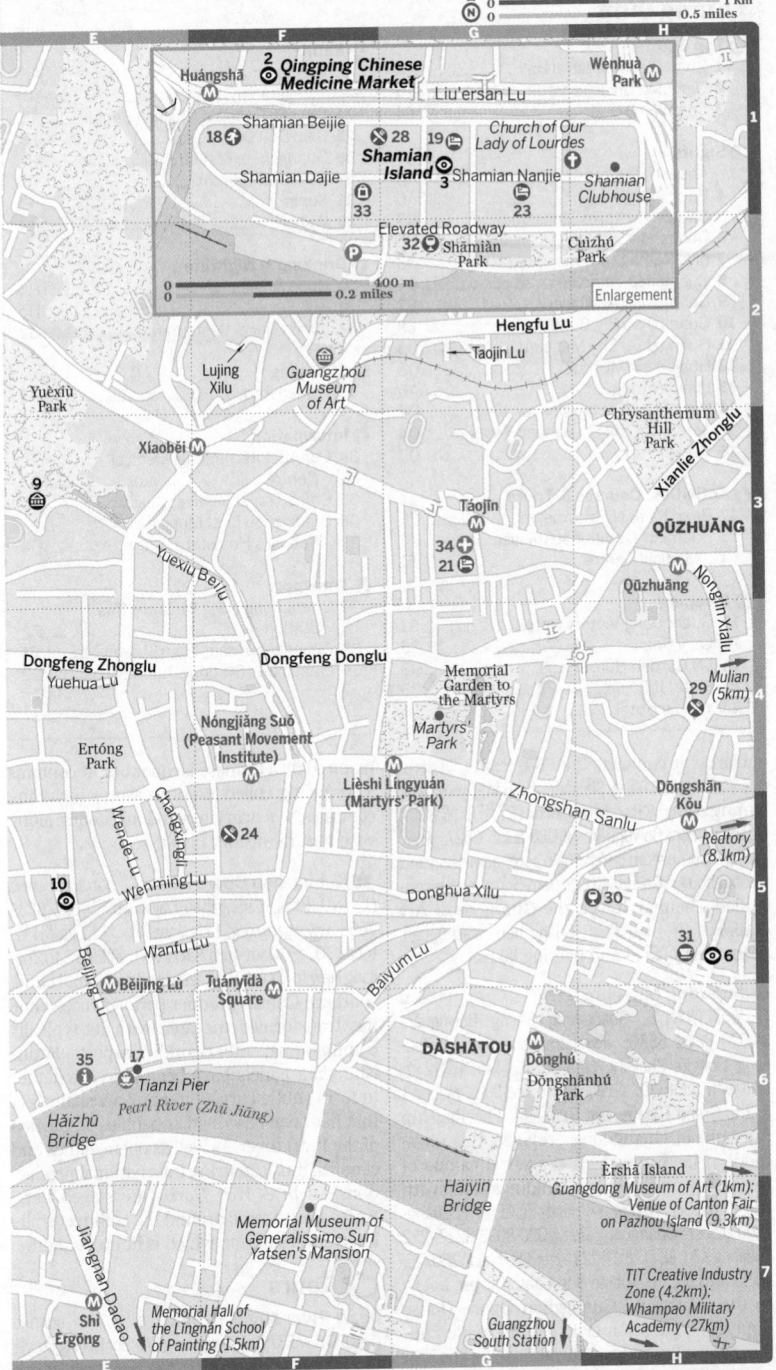

Guangzhou

entrance, it connects the **Five Rams Statue** (五羊石像; Wǔ Yáng Shíxiàng; ◎6am-9pm), the **Guangzhou City Museum** (广州市博物馆, Guǎngzhōushì Bówùguǎn; ☑020 8355 0627; www. guangzhoumuseum.cn/en/main.asp; admission incl Guangzhou Art Gallery ¥10; ◎9am-5pm) in the red-walled Zhenhai Tower, the **Guangzhou Art Gallery** (广州美术馆, Guǎngzhōu Měishùguǎn; ◎9am-5pm) FREE and boating lakes.

Guangdong Museum　　　MUSEUM
(广东省博物馆, Guǎngdōng Shěng Bówùguǎn; ☑020 3804 6886; www.gdmuseum.com; 2 Zhujiang Donglu, Zhujiang New Town, 珠江东路2号; free with photo ID; ◎9am-4pm Tue-Sun; Ⓜ Line 1 & 2 to Grand Theatre, exit B) FREE The flagship museum of Guangdong province, this ultra-modern institution was conceived as one of the city's new showpiece buildings along with the **Canton Tower** (广州电视观光塔, Guǎngzhōu Diànshì Guānguāng Tǎ; ☑020 8933 8222; 222 Yuejiang Xilu, 阅江西路222号; adult/child ¥150/75; ◎9am-10.30pm; Ⓜ Line 3 to Canton Tower, exit D) to the south and Guangzhou Opera House opposite – part of a civic plan to make Zhujiang New Town the cultural heart of the city.

Inspired by a Chinese lacquer box, it contains a sprawling collection of treasures including ceramics, woodcarvings and ink stones, along with natural-history displays.

★**Guangzhou Opera House**　NOTABLE BUILDING
(广州大剧院, Guǎngzhōu Dàjùyuàn; ☑020 3839 2666; www.gzdjy.org; 1 Zhujiang Xilu, 珠江西路1号; tour ¥30; ◎10am-4pm Sat & Sun; Ⓜ Line 3 to Zhujiang New Town, exit B1) Designed by Zaha Hadid, southern China's premier performance venue has transformed the area with its typically commanding, otherworldly aspect. Futuristic glass panels have been woven together to form subtle curves, creating a visual effect that has been described as pebbles on the bed of the Pearl River. As well as opera, dance and classical music, touring international productions, such as *War Horse,* are staged here. You're free to stroll around the architecturally interesting exterior, which is lit up at night.

☞ Tours

Pearl River Night Cruise　BOATING
(☑020 8375 3751; 150 Yanjiang Xilu, cnr Beijing Lu, 沿江西路150号; cruises ¥150-200; ◎6-10pm; Ⓜ Line

6 to Haizhu Sq, exit D) An evening cruise on the Pearl River is a fun way to see the shoreline in all its neon pomp. Boats leave from **Tianzi Pier** (p594; five-minute walk west of the metro, or a 1.5km stroll along the river from Shamian Dao) and do an hour loop as far as Ersha Island. Passport required.

✨ Festivals & Events

Birthday of the Fire God   CULTURAL
(⏱ 28th day of the 9th lunar month) On the birthday of the Fire God (华光师傅, Huáguāng Shīfu), usually around November, Bahe Academy (p585) guild hall throws a banquet for the opera industry (closed to the public). From early morning, gongs and drums sound as ceremonies are performed at nearby Luányú Táng (p585), open to all. Hundreds show up for the day-long feasting that takes place both indoors and on the pavement.

Canton Trade Fair   FAIR
(China Import & Export Fair; ☎ 020 2608 8888; www.cantonfair.org.cn; ⏱ Apr-May & Oct-Nov) Dating from 1957, the Canton Trade Fair is held twice yearly on Pazhou Island south of the Pearl River. It's a massive event that sees thousands of business people descend on the city, with a resultant spike in hotel prices.

🛏 Sleeping

For atmosphere and walkability, try historic Xiguan in Lìwān District, stretching from Shamian Island (p584) in the south to Chen Clan Ancestral Hall (p584). For international luxury, there are high-spec and (relatively) affordable options in Tianhe District, near East Railway Station, and Zhujiang New Town.

Prices rocket during the Canton Trade Fair.

Shamian Island, the heritage heart of Guangzhou's Xiguan area, is an atmospheric place to stay with several hotels occupying restored concession-era buildings.

★ Lazy Gaga   HOSTEL ¥
(春田家家, Chūntián Jiājiā; ☎ 020 8192 3232; 215 Haizhu Zhonglu, 海珠中路215号; dm/d/tw/tr from ¥63/200/200/250; ❈ @ 🛜; Ⓜ Line 1 to Ximenkou, exit B) In a buzzy local 'hood a quick stagger from the metro and within walking distance of many Xiguan sights, Lazy Gaga offers cheerful rooms and communal areas with pool table, cheap beer and movie screenings.

★ Guangdong Victory Hotel   HOTEL ¥¥
(胜利宾馆, Shènglì Bīnguǎn; ☎ 020 8121 6688; www.vhotel.com; 53-54 Shamian Beijie, 沙面北街 53-54号; r from ¥500; ❈ @ 🛜; Ⓜ Line 1 & 6 to Huangsha, exit F) One of a handful of heritage buildings you can bed down in on Shamian Island, the Victory is divided in two: the west wing is the oldest and more atmospheric, carved out of the former HSBC bank building; there you can bag a room with a grand balcony.

Motel 168   HOTEL ¥¥
(莫泰酒店(广州华林国际玉器城店), Mòtài Jiǔdiàn; ☎ 020 8167 0029; 4 fl, 107 Wenchang Nanlu, 文昌南路107号4楼; d & tw from ¥267; ❄ ❈ 🛜) This chain hotel is plusher than the norm and the best value near Shangxiajiu Pedestrian Street. Diffused lighting, wall-mounted TV panels, and bathrooms with dark faux-tiles and deep washbasins hint at designer digs. Large blackout curtains and a self-service laundry room are practical plusses. English-speaking front desk staff are the friendliest around.

Yuehai Hotel   HOTEL ¥¥
(Customs Hotel, 悦海宾馆, Yuèhǎi Bīnguǎn; ☎ 020 8110 2388; 35 Shamian Dajie, 沙面大街 35号; r from ¥450; ❈ @ 🛜; Ⓜ Line 6 to Culture Park, exit E) If you're soaking up the colonial vibes on Shamian Island (p584), you might as well go the whole hog and bed down in a heritage building. Yuehai Hotel, formerly a customs house, is a good choice. Spacious, modernised rooms encircle a handsome four-floor inner atrium, service is warm, and it serves dim sum for breakfast. Good discounts online.

Aloft Guangzhou Tianhe   HOTEL ¥¥¥
(广州天河雅乐轩酒店, Tiānhé Yǎ Yuè Xuān Jiǔdiàn; ☎ 020 3802 8888; www.marriott.com; 365 Tianhe Beilu, 天河北路365号; d from ¥915; ❈ @ 🛜 ❄; Ⓜ Line 3 to Linhexi, exit C) Decent deals can be had at this midrange tower hotel that opened in 2016. Spotless rooms are zesty and modern with a few designer touches, and for your *rénmínbì* you get city views and a large indoor swimming pool.

Westin Guangzhou   HOTEL ¥¥¥
(广州海航威斯汀酒店, Guǎngzhōu Hǎiháng Wēisītīng Jiǔdiàn; ☎ 020 2886 6868; www.starwood hotels.com; 6 Linhe Zhonglu, 林和中路6号; d/ste from ¥1279/2155; ❈ @ 🛜 ❄; Ⓜ Line 3 to Linhexi, exit D) A safe bet if you're craving a dose of western-style comfort, the Westin has courteous staff, well-appointed rooms and a handy location close to restaurants and Guangzhou's east train station.

GUANGDONG GUANGZHOU

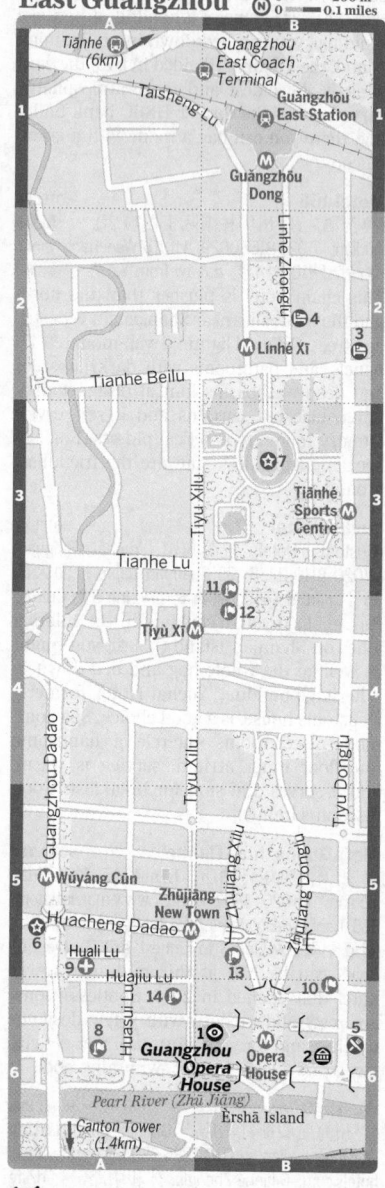

East Guangzhou

lunch; at dinner restaurants often switch to banquet fare like roast meats, seafood and stir-fries. You'll also find many small eateries selling wonton noodles, congee and milk-based desserts.

★ Supin
CAFE ¥

(速品家, Sùpǐn Jiā; ☎ 199 2843 8323; 67 Shami-an Beijie, 沙面岛沙面北街67号; mains ¥38-78; ⊙10am-10pm; 🌐🚺; Ⓜ Line 6 to Huangsha, exit F) The gleaming interior of this Shamian mansion conversion is all glass, marble and chandeliers, baiting you to photograph it. Equally social-media shareable are organic dishes such as salmon with pine nuts and strawberries, and chicken, mango and kale salad. Seafood servings are a little stingy but egg tarts and fruit smoothies keep most young visitors happy.

★ Diǎn Dōu Dé
DIM SUM ¥

(点都德; ☎ 020 8170 0813; 587 Longjin Zhonglu, 龙津中路587号; dim sum ¥13-30; ⊙10.30am-2pm & 4.30-10pm; Ⓜ Line 1 to Chen Clan Academy, exit A) With around 25 branches in Guangzhou, Diǎn Dōu Dé is one of the best-loved names in dim sum, turning out delicious shrimp dumplings, *shāomài* (烧卖, shrimp and pork dumplings), rice rolls, durian puffs and all the other favourites on an epic scale, while still keeping the vibe traditional.

✖ **Eating**

Guangzhou is rich in Cantonese dining options, with several esteemed dim sum (点心, *diǎnxīn*) chains boasting a dozen or more branches. Dim sum (also known as 'yum cha' here) is mainly eaten for breakfast or

Guangzhou Restaurant DIM SUM ¥

(广州酒家, Guǎngzhōu Jiǔjiā; 2 Wenchang Nanlu, 文昌南路2号; dim sum per dish ¥9-31; ⏱7-10am, 11am-3pm & 5.30-10pm; Ⓜ Line 1 to Changshou Lu, exit D2) The grand master of dim sum, this is reckoned to be Guangzhou's oldest restaurant, still churning out bamboo steamers of deliciousness the traditional way, but without the trolleys. There's no English dim sum menu, but the classics are pictured. Note that dim sum is only served at breakfast and lunch; evenings are reserved for banquet-style Cantonese fare, which can be underwhelming.

Dayang Coconut Chicken Soup SOUP ¥

(达扬原味炖品, Dáyáng Yuánwèi Dùnpǐn; ☑020 8352 0983; 304 Dezheng Zhonglu 304, 德政中路 304号; soup ¥20; ⏱noon-midnight; Ⓜ Line 1 to Nongjiangsuo, exit A) Cooking chicken soup in a coconut with its own sweet coconut water is as delicious as it sounds. Then add superfood goji berries, bamboo and stewed chicken (they're black silky hens). This hole-in-the-wall eatery split across three metal tables is nonstop busy.

Big Buddha Temple Vegetarian VEGETARIAN ¥

(大佛寺素食阁, Dàfósì Sùshí Gé; 23 Beijing Lu, 北京路23号; dishes from ¥40; ⏱11am-2pm & 5.30-9pm; ☎✉; Ⓜ Line 1 & 2 to Gongyuanqian, exit D) On the 2nd floor of the main building of the **Big Buddha Temple** (大佛古寺, Dàfógǔsì; ☑020 8333 5678⏱24hr, statues 9am-4pm), you'll find this sprawling veggie banquet hall of rough-hewn timber tables, costumed servers and an iPad picture menu presenting mockmeat Canto fare.

★**Panxi Restaurant** DIM SUM ¥

(泮溪酒家, Pànxī Jiǔjiā; ☑020 8172 1328; 151 Longjin Xilu, 龙津西路151号; dishes from ¥40; ⏱7am-9pm; Ⓜ Line 1 to Changshou Lu, exit E) Set in Liwan Lake Park amid ornamental gardens interlinked with pools, courtyards and corridors, Panxi is typical of Guangzhou's garden restaurants, designed to give the effect of 'every step, a vista' (一步一景). Choose from several separate dining rooms – some huge and brightly lit, others more intimate – serving classic dim sum alongside refined Canto fare.

★**Bingsheng Mansion** CANTONESE ¥¥

(公馆炳胜, Gōngguǎn Bǐng Shèng; ☑020 3803 5888; 5th fl, 2 Xiancun Lu, Zhujiang New Town, 珠江新城冼村路2号首府大厦1-4楼; dishes from ¥68; ⏱10am-3pm & 5-10pm Mon-Fri, from 9am Sat & Sun; Ⓜ Line 1 & 2 to Grand Theatre, exit B) One of only eight restaurants awarded a star in the inaugural 2018 Guangzhou Michelin

guide, this is the upmarket flagship of the esteemed Bingsheng chain, serving creative riffs on Canto classics in an elegant dining space with multiple private rooms. A must-try for carnivores is the signaturechar siu pork, marinated for 24 hours, then roasted to charred, sticky loveliness.

★**Bingsheng Taste** CANTONESE ¥¥

(炳胜品味, Bǐngshèng Pǐnwèi; ☑020 8751 8682; 168 Tianhe Donglu, 天河东路168号; dishes from ¥48; ⏱11am-midnight; Ⓜ Line 3 to Shipaiqiao, exit C) This marvellous restaurant, one of several branches of Guangzhou's highly regarded chain that also boasts upmarket editions like Bingsheng Mansion and 'Little Bingsheng' (小炳胜, Xiǎo Bǐngshèng), serves hit after hit. Along with delectable Cantonese roast goose, pork and rice-noodle stir-fries, you can savour the freshwater-fish dishes of Shùndé (a town south of Guangzhou) and Cantonese-style sashimi (刺身, cìshēn).

Wilber's EUROPEAN ¥¥

(☑020 3761 1101; 62 Zhusigang Ermalu, 竹丝岗 二马路62号; mains ¥68-280; ⏱5pm-midnight; ☎; Ⓜ Line 1 to Dongshankou, exit C) Tucked away on the fringes of Yuexiu District, gay-friendly Wilber's gets top marks for cocktails and atmosphere, and the food isn't far behind. You can dine on snacks at the bar, or opt for well-presented, multicourse menus (¥350) in the swish restaurant. Look for the restored concession-era villa with whitewashed walls and patio.

🍷 Drinking & Nightlife

★**Hope & Sesame** COCKTAIL BAR

(庙前冰室, Miàoqián Bīngshì; ☑189 9841 8723; www.hopeandsesamegz.com; 58 Miaoqian Xijie, 庙 前西街58号; ⏱7pm-2am; Ⓜ Line 1 to Dongshankou, exit D) The booze boffins at this speakeasy have an on-site lab with bubbling stills for bespoke spirit infusions, resulting in some of the most creative top-shelf cocktails in China. Though they are masters of their craft, the vibe is louche and playful, with chatty bartenders and live jazz from 8.45pm till midnight. Book two days ahead if coming on Friday or Saturday.

Lucy's Bar & Restaurant BEER GARDEN

(露丝酒吧餐厅, Lùsī Jiǔbā Cāntīng; ☑020 8136 6203; 3 Shamian Nanjie, 沙面南街3号; ⏱11am-midnight; Ⓜ Line 6 to Culture Park, exit E) A welcoming spot for a beer and a bite on Shamian Island, Lucy's rocks some retro neon signage out the front and a big patio

YUYIN MOUNTAIN VILLA

One of Guangdong's four famous classical gardens, **Yuyin Mountain Villa** (余荫山房, Yúyīn Shānfáng; ☏ 020 3482 2187; Bei Dajie, Nancun Village, 南村镇北大街; adult/child ¥18/9; ☉ 8am-5.30pm; M Line 7 to Banqiao, exit A) is graceful property on the outskirts of the city was built in 1871 by an official of the Qing court. It incorporates the landscaping styles of Suzhou and Hangzhou, and the features of Lingnan architecture. The result is a photogenic collection of courtyards, pavilions, terraces, halls and water features.

Highlights include the **Waterside Pavilion**, which commands a different vista on each of its eight sides, and the **Deep Willow Room** with its 'Manchu' windows (满洲窗, mǎnzhōu chuāng) of coloured glass, designed to create the illusion of the passing seasons by altering the hue of the garden scenery.

A dessert shop on the premises is famous for ginger milk curd (姜汁撞奶, jiāngzhī zhuàngnǎi; ¥10), a pudding-type treat made by adding the squeezed juice of fresh ginger to heated buffalo's milk.

It's a 20-minute walk from the metro station to Yuyin Mountain Villa. A taxi from central Guangzhou should cost about ¥80 to ¥100.

from which to sup beers, wine and cheap tropical cocktails. If you need to refuel, there's a menu of backpacker-style grub such as sandwiches, fried rice and Thai curries.

Kuí Yuán CAFE
(逵园, ☏ 020 8765 9746; 2nd fl, 9 Xuguyuan Lu, 恤孤院路9号; ☉ 11am-9pm; 🛜; M Line 1 to Dongshankou, exit D) A heritage gem in the historic Dongshan area, Kuí Yuán has a sunny cafe with balcony terrace on its top floor serving coffee, cakes and cocktails. The ground floor has a gallery and the 2nd floor a stylish boutique. Built in 1922, the house is notable for its western architectural features that include colonnaded verandas and a portico.

☆ Entertainment

★ 191 Space LIVE MUSIC
(191Space 音乐主题酒吧, 191 Space Yīnlè Zhǔtí Jiǔba; ☏ 020 8737 9375; 191 Guangzhou Dadao Zhonglu, 广州大道中路191号; ☉ 8pm-2am; M Line 5 to Wuyangcun, exit A) Two steps from the metro exit, 191 Space is a throbbing dive that features live indie gigs from China and overseas every weekend.

Tianhe Stadium FOOTBALL
(天河体育场, Tiānhé Tiyùchǎng; http://gzfc.evergrande.com; 299 Tianhe Lu, 天河路299号; M Line 1 to Tianhe Sports Center, exit C) This 58,000-capacity stadium is the home of Guangzhou Evergrande Taobao FC, the more decorated of the city's two Chinese Super League soccer teams. One of the richest clubs in Asia, at the time of research they boasted at least three Brazilian players and Italian legend Fabio Cannavaro as manager.

🛍 Shopping

Xīguān Rénjiā ANTIQUES
(西关人家; ☏ 135 7000 8431; 8-2 Shamian 4 Jie, 沙面四街8号; ☉ 10am-10pm; M Line 6 to Culture Park, exit E) The magpie owners here have accumulated all manner of treasures (OK, and plenty of tat), displayed in the grand surrounds of a former concession-era mansion on Shamian Island. Want an old Chinese radio for your mantelpiece? No problem. They also have postcards, Mao trinkets and other gift-y goods. Look for the 'Antique and gift shop' sign above the door.

TIT Creative Industry Zone CLOTHING
(TIT创意园, TIT Chuàngyì Yuán; ☏ 020 8422 1810; 397 Xingang Zhonglu, 新港中路397号; ☉ 10am-7pm; M Line 3 & 8 to Kecun, exit A) Inside the leafy compound of a communist-era textile factory are boutiques selling a variety of locally designed clothing, from office wear to lacy dresses, along with art installations and a couple of funky cafes.

Fangcun Tea Market MARKET
(芳村茶叶市场, Fāngcūn Cháyè Shìchǎng; 500 Fangcun Dadao Zhong, 芳村大道中500号; ☉ 9am-6pm; M Line 1 to Fangcun, exit C) More for oolong aficionados than casual browsers, this is a wholesale area spanning block after block of tea shops, along with entire malls selling leaves and teaware.

Tianhe Computer Markets ELECTRONICS
(天河电脑城, Tiānhé Diànnǎochéng; 502 Tianhe Lu, 天河路502号; ☉ 10am-9pm; M Line 3 to Shipaiqiao, exit B) You'll find hundreds of bargain-basement microelectronics retailers in shops and malls straddling this part of Tianhe Lu.

ⓘ Information

China Travel Service office (CTS, 中国旅行社, Zhōngguó Lǚxíngshè; 20th fl, 195-197 Yanjiang Zhonglu, 沿江中路195-197号; ⊘ 8.30am-6pm Mon-Fri, 9am-5pm Sat & Sun; Ⓜ Line 2 & 6 to Haizhu Sq, exit F) Just east of Haizhu Sq; a useful source of travel information.

Life of Guangzhou (www.lifeofguangzhou. com) Regularly updated tourist info for visitors.

That's Guangzhou (www.thatsmags.com/ guangzhou) Restaurant and nightlife listings with an expat focus.

MEDICAL SERVICES

EurAm Medical Center (康辰国际医疗中心, Kāngchén Guójì Yīliáo Zhōngxīn; ☑ 020 3758 5328, 020 3759 1168; www.eurammedicalcenter. com; 1st fl, Ocean Pearl Building, 15 Huali Lu, 华利路15号远洋明珠大厦1层; ⊘ 8am-8pm & 24hr emergency; Ⓜ Line 5 to Zhujiang New Town, exit B1) Receives excellent feedback for its English-speaking European, American and Chinese doctors and Singaporean and Japanese dentists.

Guangzhou First Municipal People's Hospital (广州第一人民医院, Guǎngzhōu Dìyī Rénmín Yīyuàn; ☑ 020 8104 8888; www.gzhosp.cn; 1 Panfu Lu, 盘福路1号; Ⓜ Line 2 to Sun Yat-sen Memorial Hall, exit D2) Medical clinic for foreigners on the 1st floor.

VISAS

Visitors from over 50 countries entering Baiyun International Airport or **Shenzhen Bao'an International Airport** (深圳宝安国际机场, Shēnzhèn Bǎo'ān Guójì Jīchǎng; ☑ 0755 2345 6789; http:// eng.szairport.com; Jichang Nanlu, Bao'an Qu, 宝安区机场南路; Ⓜ Line 11 to Airport) with an onward ticket to a third country are allowed the 144-hour Transit Visa Exemption.

PSB Exit & Entry Office (公安局出入境管理处, Gōng'ān Jú Chū Rùjìng Guǎnlǐ Chù; ☑ 020 8311 5800, 020 8311 5808; 155 Jiefang Nanlu, 解放南路155号; ⊘ 8-11.30am & 2.30-5pm; Ⓜ Line 2 & 6 to Haizhu Sq, exit B3)

ⓘ Getting There & Away

AIR

About 40km north of the city, **Baiyun International Airport** (白云国际机场, CAN, Báiyún Guójì Jīchǎng; ☑ 020 3606 6999; www.gbiac. net; Ⓜ Line 3 to Airport South or Airport North) has flights to all major airports in China as well as direct flights to Australia and countries in Southeast Asia.

BUS

Guangzhou has many long-distance bus stations with services to destinations in Guangdong, southern Fujian, eastern Guangxi and further afield. There are frequent buses to Foshan (¥17 to ¥30, 45 minutes), Kaiping (¥65, two hours),

Shenzhen (¥55 to ¥70, two hours) and Zhuhai (¥60, two hours) from Tianhe Bus Station, Fangcun Bus Station (from metro Kēngkǒu), Guangzhou East Coach Terminal and Guangdong Long-Distance Bus Station.

Deluxe buses ply the Guangzhou–Shenzhen freeway to Hong Kong, which is the easiest route to travel. Buses to Hong Kong and its airport (from ¥110, 3½ hours) leave from Hotel Landmark Canton near Haizhu Sq station or China Hotel near Yuexiu Park station every 30 minutes.

Buses via Zhuhai to Macau (¥80, 2½ hours) leave frequently from Tianhe Bus Station (7.40am to 8pm).

Tianhe Bus Station (天河客运站, Tiānhé Kèyùnzhàn; ☑ 020 3709 0062; www.tianhebus.com; Yanling Lu, 燕玲路; Ⓜ Line 3 & 6 to Tianhe Coach Terminal, exit B) Most frequent departures to destinations in Guangdong; accessible by metro.

Fangcun Bus Station (芳村客运站, Fāngcūn Kèyùnzhàn; ☑ 020 8140 5555; 51 Huadi Dadao, 花地大道中51号; Ⓜ Line 1 to Kengkou, exit B) Accessible by metro. Destinations include within Guangdong, Fujian and Jiangxi.

Guangzhou East Coach Terminal (广州东站汽车客运站, Guǎngzhōu Dōngzhàn Kèyùnzhàn, Guangzhou City Bus Station; ☑ 020-8770-5008; 43 Yudong Xilu, 禺东西路43号; Ⓜ Lines 1 & 3 to Guangzhou East Railway Station, exit H) Behind Guangzhou East Railway Station. Good for destinations within Guangdong; departures aren't as frequent as from other stations.

Guangdong Long-Distance Bus Station (广东省汽车客运站, Guǎngdōng Shěng Qìchē Kèyùnzhàn; ☑ 020-8666-1297; 147-149 Huanshi Xilu, 环市西路145-149号; Ⓜ Line 2 & 5 to Guangzhou Railway Station, exit F) West of the Guangzhou train station. There's a smaller long-distance bus station (广州市气车客运站, Guǎngzhōu Shì Qìchēzhàn) under the footbridge.

Liuhua Bus Station (流花车站, Liúhuā Chēzhàn; 188 Huanshi Xilu, 环市西路188号; Ⓜ Line 2 & 5 to Guangzhou Railway Station, exit D4) Opposite Guangzhou main train station. Destinations include Chaozhou and Shantou.

TRAIN

Guangzhou's three major train stations serve destinations all over China. You can book train tickets in advance at www.trip.com, and collect them at the station by presenting your passport and booking number at a ticket office window. The first or last ticket window is usually marked for soldiers and foreigners, with shorter queues.

Light rail to Zhuhai (¥70, one hour, frequent) also leaves from Guangzhou South Railway Station.

From **Guangzhou Main Train Station** (广州站, Guǎngzhōu Zhàn; 159 Huanshi Xilu, 环市西路159号; Ⓜ Line 2 & 5 to Guangzhou Railway Station) services run to Lhasa (¥447, 53 hours, one daily, 11.45am) and Zhaoqing (¥16 to ¥65, 1¼ to two hours, frequent).

From **Guangzhou East Railway Station** (广州火车东站, Guǎngzhōu Huǒchē Dōngzhàn; 1 Dongzhan Lu, 东站路1号; Ⓜ Lines 1 & 3 to Guangzhou East Railway Station) services run to Shanghai (¥206 to ¥377, 16½ hours, one daily, 6.12pm) and Shenzhen (¥80, 1½ hours, frequent).

The station has bullet trains to Shenzhen and slower trains as far as Harbin in northern China, and is also the terminal station for the Guangzhou–Hong Kong through train to Hung Hom station (¥179, two hours, 8.19am to 9.32pm).

ⓘ Getting Around

TO/FROM THE AIRPORT

Airport shuttle buses (¥17 to ¥32, 35 to 70 minutes, every 20 to 30 minutes, 5am to 11pm) leave from half a dozen locations, including the LN Garden Hotel (p605) and Tianhe Bus Station (p593). A taxi to/from the airport should cost between ¥150 and ¥200.

Metro Line 2 links the airport's two terminals (with Airport South serving Terminal 1 and Airport North serving Terminal 2) with Guangzhou East Railway Station. The ride takes 40 minutes (¥8, 6.10am to 11pm), or 70 minutes to Beijing Lu station.

BOAT

The Pearl River is a useful and overlooked means of getting across the city, sometimes helping to avoid multiple metro line changes. A DIY river tour costs from ¥2. Ferry piers near sights include the following.

Dashatou Wharf (大沙头游船码头, Dàshātóu Yóuchuán Mǎtóu) Used by main river-tour boats. It's next to Haizhu Sq station.

Tianzi Pier (天字码头, Tiānzì Mǎtóu; ferry one-way ¥2; Ⓜ Line 6 to Beijing Lu) At the southern end of Beijing Lu shopping street, with frequent ferries to Canton Tower. The Pearl River Night Cruise (p588) departs from here.

Xidi Pier (西堤码头, Xīdī Mǎtóu) Just east of Shamian Island.

BUS

Guangzhou has a large network of public buses (¥1) and bus rapid transport (BRT; ¥2), with live locations on Chinese map apps (Chinese only).

METRO

Guangzhou has 13 metro lines in operation from around 6am to 11.30pm, with distance-based fares from ¥2 to ¥14. There is also the Guangzhou–Foshan line linking the two cities on regular metro tickets and passes.

Transit passes (羊城通, yáng chéng tōng) are available at metro stations from ¥70 (¥20 deposit included). The deposit is refundable at designated stations, including Tiyu Xilu and Gongyuanqian. The passes can be used on all public transport, including public taxis. There are also one-day (¥20) and three-day (¥50) metro passes available. Both allow unlimited metro use within the specified period and do not require a deposit.

TAXI

Taxis are abundant in the city, with flagfall at ¥10 for the first 2.5km and ¥2.6 for every additional kilometre, plus a ¥1 fuel surcharge.

Chinese taxi-hailing app DiDi has an English-language version, which can be useful at busy periods. Note that you will only be able to hail regular metered taxis payable with cash and not private cars unless you have an electronic payment method such as WeChat Pay, Alipay or an international debit/credit card.

Foshan   佛山

🗐 0757 / POP 6 MILLION

Foshan (Fóshān; literally 'Buddha Hill') was famous for its ceramics in the Ming dynasty. Today it's better known as the birthplace of two kung fu icons, Wong Fei Hung and Ip Man (Bruce Lee's master); the Wing Chun style of kung fu developed here. An easy half-hour metro ride lets day-trippers from Guangzhou have a taste of where Buddhist beliefs meet martial-arts practices.

◉ Sights

★Nanfeng Ancient Kiln
Artists' Village   ARTS CENTRE

(南风古灶, Nánfēng Gǔzào; 🗐 0757 8278 0606; 6 Gaomiao Lu, Shiwan, 高庙路6号; ¥25; ◎8am-5pm; 🚌137) This lovely ceramics town of stone-paved paths in Shiwan (石湾, Shíwān) is worth snooping around for its artisans' ceramics workshops and the two ancient 'dragon kilns' of more than 30m in length. The modern Bruce Lee statues celebrating the local Wing Chun school of kung fu are also photogenic. Shiwan, 2km from downtown Foshan, was once China's most important ceramics production centre. Much of the Ming dynasty pottery you see at museums comes from here (those in most shops here, however, are mass-produced copies).

★Zumiao   TAOIST SITE

(祖庙, Zǔmiào; 🗐 0757 8228 6913; www.fszumiao.com; 21 Zumiao Lu, 祖庙路21号; ¥20, incl Nanfeng Ancient Kiln ¥35; ◎8.30am-6pm; Ⓜ Zumiao, exit A) The 11th-century Zumiao temple is believed to be the site where Cantonese opera flourished. The art is still performed today during festivals to entertain the gods...and the tourists. Sharing the complex are a Confucius temple (c 1911) and memorial halls dedicated to two martial artists born in Foshan – Wong Fei Hung (aka Huang Fei Hong) and Ip Man – and kung fu cinema in general.

There are daily performances (10am, 2.15pm and 3.30pm) of kung fu and lion dance. Cantonese opera performances are held at 1.30pm on the 1st and 15th of every month. The temple runs martial-arts classes for children every summer. Call 0757 8222 1680 for details.

Lingnan World HISTORIC BUILDING
(佛山岭南天地, Fúshān Lǐngnán Tiāndì; Tiandi Lu, Chancheng Qu, 天地路禅城区; ⊙10am-10pm; 🚍101, 105) A photogenic collection of restored medicinal shops, Chinese liquor stores and old villas from the Qing dynasty and Republic era are now occupied by swanky boutiques, upmarket eateries and trendy bars. A relaxing place to pass a few lazy hours sipping coffee or filling up your social media with snaps.

Liang Garden GARDENS
(梁园, Liáng Yuán; ☑ 0757 8224 1279; Songfeng Lu, 松风路; ¥10; ⊙9am-5pm; 🚍205, 212) This tranquil residence of a family that produced painters and calligraphers was built during the Qing dynasty. Designed in a Lingnan style, it delights with ponds, willow-lined pathways and, in summer, trees heavy with wax apples and jackfruit. Like Yuyin Mountain Villa near Guangzhou, it's one of the four great classical gardens. Liáng Garden is north of Rénshòu Temple and 300m north of the Bank of China (中国银行, Zhōngguó Yínháng).

🛏 Sleeping & Eating

In this temple town, vegetarian restaurants are dotted on-site or nearby. A local speciality is the shrimp wonton noodle soup.

Foshan Marco Polo HOTEL ¥¥¥
(马哥孛罗酒店, Mǎgē Bóluó Jiǔdiàn; ☑ 0757 8250 1888; www.marcopolohotels.com; 97 Renmin Lu, 人民路97号; r/ste from ¥839/1522; @ 🛜 🅿; Ⓜ Zumiao, exit C) Arguably the most opulent place to stay in town is the five-star Marco Polo perched over the lake in Foshan. Things have been well maintained in recent years with neat black-and-white bathrooms and soft-coloured armchairs in the light-filled rooms, but heritage touches like old lifts and sweeping stairwells remain to remind you of its fine pedigree.

Renshengyuan Vegetarian VEGETARIAN ¥
(仁生缘素食, Rénshēngyuán Sùshí; ☑ 0757 8225 2171; 22 Zumiao Lu, 祖庙路22号; mains ¥23-38; ⊙11am-2.30pm & 5-8.30pm; 🍴; Ⓜ Zumiao, exit A) Very good vegetarian dishes include plenty of fresh greens and mock meats, made to be shared. Enter the large, neat restaurant from the laneway opposite Renshou Temple.

Yingji Noodle Shop NOODLES ¥
(应记面家, Yìngjì Miànjiā; ☑ 0757 8228 1679; 112 Lianhua Lu, 莲花路112号; noodles ¥7-12; ⊙6am-11pm; 🚍106, 118) This excellent noodle shop opposite Lianhua Supermarket (莲花超市, Liánhuā Cháoshì) is the go-to place in Foshan for noodles with shrimp wonton (鲜虾云吞面, xiānxiā yúntūnmiàn).

❶ Getting There & Away

Buses depart from **Foshan bus station** (佛山汽车站, Fóshān Shěng Qìchēzhàn; ☑ 0757 8223 2940; 6 Fenjiang Zhonglu), 400m south of the train station. Destinations include Shenzhen (¥105, 2½ hours, every 30 minutes) and Zhuhai (¥84, three hours, every 30 to 60 minutes).

Buses (¥18) run hourly between Guangzhou's Guangdong long-distance bus station and **Zumiao bus station** (祖庙车站, Zǔmiào

---

THE MAKING OF A NATIONAL LEGEND

Foshan-born Wong Fei Hung (1847–1924) is one of China's best-known folk heroes. Although a consummate gōngfū (kung fu) master in his lifetime, he didn't become widely known until his story was merged with fiction in countless movies made after 1949, most by Hong Kong directors, such as Hark Tsui's Once Upon a Time in China, starring Jet Li. Sadly, Wong spent his later years in desolation, after his son was murdered and his martial-arts school was destroyed by fire. Regardless, an astonishing 106 movies (and counting!) have celebrated this son of Foshan, resulting in the world's longest movie series and the creation of a national legend.

Another Foshan hero, Ip Man (1893–1972) rose to fame as a Wing Chun master at the outset of WWII. He fled to Hong Kong in 1949 where he founded the first Wing Chun school. His most famous student was Bruce Lee. Ip Man was immortalised in Wong Kar-wai's award-winning The Grandmaster and a series of semibiographical movies starring Donnie Yen.

Chēzhàn; 104 Jianxin Lu, 建新路104号), a block east of Zumiao metro station.

Trains go to Guangzhou (¥10 to ¥24, 30 minutes, 21 daily).

The metro is the easiest way to get between Guangzhou and Foshan, via the Guǎngfó line (¥6, 30 to 60 minutes), with regular Guangzhou tickets. Get out at Zumiao in Foshan for the most sights.

From Hong Kong, there is no direct train but a transfer in Shenzhen or Guangzhou makes things almost seamless. A typical trip including transfer via Guangzhou totals 1½ to two hours and costs about ¥230; via Shenzhen North, it's two hours and ¥160.

⊕ Getting Around

Buses 101 and 134 (¥2) link the train station to Zumiao and Shiwan.

Taxis start at ¥8 for the first 2km, costing ¥2.60 for every additional 1km.

Kaiping 开平

📞 0750 / POP 680,000

Kaiping (Kāipíng), 140km southwest of Guangzhou, is home to one of the most arresting human-constructed attractions in Guangdong – the Unesco-crowned *diāolóu* (碉楼), eccentric watchtowers featuring a fusion of Eastern and Western architectural styles. Out of the approximately 3000 original *diāolóu*, only 1833 remain.

Downtown Kaiping is pleasant, especially the section near the Tanjiang River (潭江), where you'll see people fishing next to mango and wampee trees.

Kaiping is also the home of many overseas Chinese. Currently, 720,000 people from the county are living overseas – 40,000 more than its local population. Chinese tourists abound and it's worth dedicating at least one whole day to *diāolóu* hunting, as most require renting a bike or taxi.

⊙ Sights

A combo ticket for seven sights, including Li Garden and the villages of Zili, Jinjiangi and Maijianglong, costs ¥180. It's only available at Li Garden and Zili village. The price for just Li Garden and one village is ¥150. A village alone costs from ¥50 to ¥80. Some towers charge an extra ¥5 to ¥10 to let you in.

★ **Zili**   VILLAGE
(自力村, Zìlì Cūn; 📞 0750 267 9078; ⊙ 8.30am-5.30pm) FREE Zili, 11km west of Kaiping, has the largest collection of *diāolóu* historic watchtowers in the area, though only a few of the 15 are open to the public. The most stunning is **Míngshí Lóu** (铭石楼), which has a veranda with Ionic columns and a hexagonal pavilion on its roof. It appeared in the film *Let the Bullets Fly*. **Yúnhuàn Lóu** (云幻楼) has four towers known as 'swallow nests',

---

KAIPING'S BIZARRE TOWERS

Scattered across Kaiping's 20km periphery are *diāolóu* – multistorey watchtowers and fortified residences displaying a flamboyant mix of European, Chinese and Moorish architectural styles. The majority were built in the early 20th century by some of the villagers who made a fortune working as labourers overseas. They brought home fanciful architectural ideas they'd seen in real life and on postcards, and built the towers as fortresses to protect their families from bandits, flooding and Japanese troops.

The oldest *diāolóu* were communal watchtowers built by several families in a village. Each family was allocated a room within the citadel, where all its male members would go to spend the night to avoid being kidnapped by bandits. These narrow towers had sturdy walls, iron gates and ports for defence and observation. The earliest *diāolóu* were also watchtowers, but ones equipped with searchlight and alarm. They are located at the entrances to villages.

More than 60% of *diāolóu*, however, combined residential functions with defence. Constructed by a single family, they were spacious and featured a mix of decorative motifs. As the builders had no exposure to European architectural traditions, they took liberties with proportions, resulting in outlandish buildings that seem to have leapt out of an American folk-art painting or a Miyazaki animation.

These structures sustain a tower-like form for the first few floors, then, like stoic folk who have not forgotten to dream, let loose a riot of arches and balustrades, Egyptian columns, domes, cupolas, corner turrets, Chinese gables and Grecian urns.

each with embrasures, cobblestones and a water cannon.

Li Garden
HISTORIC SITE

(立园, Lì Yuán; ☑0750 267 8888; ¥100; ⏱8.30am-5.30pm) About 15 minutes by taxi west from Kaiping in Tangkou town (塘口镇, Tǎngkǒu zhèn), Li Garden has a fortified mansion built in 1936 by a wealthy Chinese American. The delightful interiors feature Italianate motifs and gardens have artificial canals, footbridges and dappled pathways.

Diāolóu here include the oldest of the historic towers, **Yínglóng Lóu** (迎龙楼), found in Sanmenli village (三门里, Sānménlǐ), and the fortified villas of **Majianglong** (马降龙, Mǎjiànglóng) village.

Jinjiangi Historic Village
VILLAGE

(锦江里, Jǐnjiānglǐ; ⏱9am-5pm) The highlights in this village, 20km southwest of Kaiping, are the privately run **Ruìshí Lóu** (瑞石楼; ¥20; ⏱hours vary) and **Shēngfēng Lóu** (升峰楼). The former (c 1923) is Kaiping's tallest *diāolóu* and comprises nine storeys, topped off with a Byzantine-style roof and a Roman dome. The latter is one of very few *diāolóu* that had a European architect.

Nánxìng Xié Lóu
HISTORIC BUILDING

(南兴斜楼, 边筹筑楼, Biānchóu Zhùlóu, Leaning Tower) FREE In Nanxing village, Nánxìng Xié Lóu was built in 1903 and tilts severely to one side, with its central axis over 2m off-centre.

🛏 Sleeping

Tribe of Diaomin
HOSTEL ¥

(碉民部落, Diāomín Bùluò; ☑0750 261 6222; 55 Tangkou, Tangkou Village, 塘口镇塘口街55号2-3层; dm/d/tr ¥52/148/188; ▣❄🛜) A bicycle club has brought to life an ancient building, revived as a boutique hostel. Tiled private rooms have soft-lighting, flat-screen TVs, air purifiers and some views of the lush surrounding village; dorms feel like classrooms with wooden beds and high ceilings. Spacious common areas, a bar and restaurant all feature exposed beams and retro-China antiques.

Pan Tower Hotel
BUSINESS HOTEL ¥¥

(潭江半岛酒店, Tánjiāng Bàndǎo Jiǔdiàn; ☑0750 233 3333; www.pantower.com; 2 Zhongyin Lu, 中银路2号; r ¥700-1700; ▣❄🛜) *The* place to stay in Kaiping. Spacious rooms have curved window nooks for peering wistfully across the water. Pan Tower is on an islet on the Tanjiang River and only accessible by taxi (¥15 from Kaiping bus station, five minutes away).There's an on-site restaurant serving western food if you want to stay put.

🍴 Eating & Drinking

Many villagers in Zili village serve rustic dishes cooked with home-grown ingredients inside their homes. Popular items include free-range chicken (走地鸡, *zǒudìjī*) for ¥28 a catty (斤, *jīn*; 500g), and rice cooked with baby eel (黄鳝饭, *huángshàn fàn*; ¥70).

A drink in a small bar or cafe along the warmly lit river is a popular way to enjoy the early evening.

Cháojiāngchūn
CHINESE ¥¥

(潮江春酒楼, Cháojiāngchūn Jiǔlóu; ☑0750 221 9963; 42 Zhangsha Mushalu, 长沙幕沙路42号; mains ¥28-98; ⏱11.30am-2.30pm & 5.30-10pm) This excellent restaurant serves the local speciality – braised wild-grown goose (狗仔鹅, *gǒuzǎi é*). The steamed tofu with shredded taro and ground pork (肉碎芋丝蒸豆腐, *ròusuì yùsī zhēng dòufu*) and salt-baked chicken (手撕鸡, *shǒusījī*) are also delicious.

ℹ Getting There & Around

Kaiping has two bus stations that are linked by local buses 7 and 13: **Yici Bus Station** (义祠汽车总站, Yìcí Zǒngzhàn; ☑0750 221 3126; 30 Liangyuan, cnr Mucun Lu, 良园路30号) at the northern end of town and **Kaiping Bus Station** (开平汽车总站, Kāipíng Qìchē Zǒngzhàn; ☑0750 233 3442; 28 Xijiao Lu, 西郊路28号) in the centre.

From both Yici and Kaiping bus stations, local buses (from ¥4) go to Chikan and some of the *diāolóu*. But as the *diāolóu* are scattered over several counties, your best bet is to hire a taxi for the day. A full day costs around ¥600, but you can negotiate. Otherwise hiring a bike is possible to see a handful of *diāolóu*.

Yangjiang
阳江

☑0662 / POP 2.7 MILLION

Yangjiang (Yángjiāng) is a city on the southwestern coast of Guangdong and a useful gateway to seaside attractions. While downtown Yangjiang is unexciting, picturesque Hailing Island (海陵岛, Hǎilíng Dǎo), 50km or an hour's drive away, is home to some of the finest beaches in the province, including **Shi-li Yintan Beach** (十里银滩, Shílǐ Yíntān; Hǎilíng Island, Jiāngchéng District, 江城区海陵岛南面; ⏱6.30am-6pm summer, 8am-7pm rest of year). Literally '10 miles of silver beach', this is the most beautiful and the longest stretch of coastline in the area. On the southern shore of Hailing

Island, it's also where you'll find the **Maritime Silk Road Museum** (广东海上丝绸之路博物馆, Guǎngdōng Hǎishàng Sīchóu Zhīlù Bówùguǎn; ☑ 0662 368 1111; www.msrmuseum.com; Shili Yintan beach; ¥80, English audio guide free; ⊙ 9am-5.30pm) of Guangdong, purpose-built to house an 800-year-old Song dynasty shipwreck that was wholly salvaged near the island.

Ten minutes by pedicab from Shili Yintan beach, **Dajiaowan Beach** (大角湾, Dàjiǎowān; 38 Haibin Lu, Zhapo Zhen, 闸坡镇海滨路38号; ¥51; ⊙ 6.30am-6pm May-Oct, 8am-6pm Nov-Apr) is a central, relatively clean beach in the lively Zhapo (闸坡, Zhápō) resort area. A ¥51 ticket gives you two days' unlimited entry. Lockers and showering facilities are available for ¥10 and ¥5 respectively.

If money is not an issue, stay on Hailing Island – either in the up-and-coming resort area near the museum or in Zhapo. **Hailing Crowne Plaza** (海陵岛皇冠假日酒店, Hǎilíngdǎo Huángguān Jiàrì Jiǔdiàn; ☑ 0662 386 8888; www.ihg.com/crowneplaza; Shili Silver Beach, 十里银滩; r ¥1749-3800; P ✱ @ ☎ ✉) is the most luxurious place to stay on the island, offering 313 top-notch rooms, its own stretch of beach, a spa, swimming pools, barbecues and child-minding services. Downtown Yangjiang has the cheapest sleeping options. **7 Days Inn** (7天连锁酒店, Qītiān Liánsuǒ Jiǔdiàn; ☑ 0662 321 7888; www.7daysinn.cn; 37 Dongfeng Erlu, 东风二路37号; r ¥127-187; ✱ ☎) has cheerful rooms.

Zhapo has plenty of similar seafood restaurants. Pick what you want from the tanks, agree on prices, and it'll be cooked for you. Seafood items cost ¥30 to ¥230 per 500g/1 catty (斤, jīn; 500g); non-seafood dishes are between ¥20 and ¥90. Most eateries pay drivers commission for bringing customers – it's better to choose a restaurant yourself.

The beachfront of Hailing Island gets a buzz happening at night, with good places to drink, mostly for the partial water views. Prices come down considerably a street or two back.

ℹ Getting There & Away

Yangjiang Main Bus Station (阳江汽车客运总站, Yángjiāng Qìchē Kèyùn Zǒngzhàn; ☑ 0662 316 9999; Xiping Beilu) has direct services to the following:

Foshan ¥80 to ¥95, three hours, six daily (8.30am to 2.50pm)

Guangzhou ¥72 to ¥95, 3½ hours, frequent (6.05am to 7.20pm)

Hong Kong ¥170 to ¥260, six hours, four daily (8am to 5pm)

Kaiping ¥50, four hours, four daily (8.45am to 5pm)

Shenzhen ¥120, four to five hours, 14 daily (8am to 8.30pm)

Zhuhai ¥100, 3½ to four hours, frequent (8am to 7.30pm)

One block east, Yangjiang's **No 2 bus station** (阳江二运汽车站, Yángjiāng Èryùn Qìchēzhàn; ☑ 0662 342 9168; 666 Shiwan Beilu) has direct services to the following:

Guangzhou ¥85, three hours, frequent (6.10am to 7pm)

Kaiping Yici ¥45 to ¥60, two hours, two daily (2.05pm and 4.50pm)

Shenzhen ¥135, five hours, 11 daily (7.40am to 8.30pm)

Zhuhai ¥100, 3½ to four hours, frequent (7am to 7.30pm)

ℹ Getting Around

Local buses run every 20 minutes to Zhapo from No 2 bus station (¥13, one hour, 6.30am to 9pm) and the main station (¥13 to ¥20, one hour, 6am to 9.30pm).

Zhapo and the museum area on Hailing Island are connected by pedicabs (¥10 to ¥15, 10 minutes). A taxi from downtown Yangjiang to the Maritime Silk Road Museum of Guangdong costs ¥100 (one hour).

Zhaoqing 肇庆

☑ 0758 / POP 3.9 MILLION

Bordered by lakes and limestone formations, the leisurely town of Zhaoqing (Zhàoqìng) in western Guangdong province was where Jesuit Mateo Ricci first set foot in China in 1583. It makes a comfortable base to explore the octagon-shaped bāguà villages.

◉ Sights

Seven Star Crags Park PARK
(七星岩公园, Qīxīng Yán Gōngyuán; ☑ 0758 230 2838; ¥78; ⊙ 8am-5.30pm) The landscape of limestone hills, grottoes and willow-graced lakes in this massive, busy park is beautiful, so it's a pity the authorities try so hard – the caves are illuminated like nightclubs and boat rides cost extra (¥15 to ¥60). The easiest way to navigate between sights is to use the battery-operated carts (¥15 to ¥30 per person). If you just want a quick jaunt, it's possible to walk around the lake without entering (or paying).

Zhaoqing Ancient City Walls HISTORIC SITE
(肇庆古城, Zhàoqìng Gǔchéng) FREE Zhaoqing's city walls were built during several

Zhaoqing

periods – the lowest part with large mud bricks are Song dynasty; above that is Ming; then a Qing extension featuring smaller bricks. Anything above that was built yesterday. Interestingly, there are alleyways and dwellings at the top. The **River View Tower** and **Cloud-Draped Tower** here are only open to dignitaries.

🛏 Sleeping & Eating

Shanshui Trends Hotel　BUSINESS HOTEL **¥¥**
(山水时尚酒店, Shānshuǐ Shíshàng Jiǔdiàn; ☑0758 285 9999; 36 Xijiang Beilu, 西江北路36号; d & tw ¥207-326, tr/ste from ¥360/537, all incl breakfast; ⊕❄@🛜) A decent option for the price and location, if you don't mind slightly thin walls (pray for a quiet neighbour) and small TV screens. There are more than 200 rooms in this hotel that's adjacent to a shopping centre.

Kuaihuolin Restaurant　CANTONESE **¥**
(快活林食家, Kuàihuolín Shíjiā; ☑0758 285 1332; Xijiang Beilu, 西江北路, 水果市场侧; mains ¥26-45; ⊙11am-2.30pm & 5pm-2am) If you're in the mood for seafood, this restaurant near a fruit market will overwhelm with its options. It's wildly popular and, at peak times, can get slightly chaotic. But the food is great. Try the grilled sand shrimp (白灼沙虾, báizhuó shāxiā; ¥26) and the fish soup

with tofu and parsley (芫茜豆腐黄骨鱼汤, *yánqiàn dòufu huánggǔyú tāng;* ¥37). Chinese picture menu.

Bōhǎilóu CHINESE ¥
(波海楼; ☐ 0758 230 2708; Yuanxi Yilu, 苑西一路; dim sum ¥10-32; ◷ 11.30am-1.30pm & 5.30-7.30pm) This restaurant with lake views serves Zhaoqing delicacies such as sticky rice dumplings (裹蒸粽, *guǒzhēngzòng*), containing beans, pork, chestnuts and egg yolk, and fox-nuts buns (茨实包, *císhí bāo*). It's a 10-minute walk from the western entrance of Seven Star Crags Park. Bus 19 (¥2) from the entrance passes here.

ⓘ Information

Bank of China (中国银行, Zhōngguó Yínháng; Duanzhou Wulu; ◷ 9am-5pm Mon-Sat)

ⓘ Getting There & Around

Zhaoqing Main Bus Station (肇庆汽车客运总站, Zhàoqìng Qìchē Kèyùn Zǒngzhàn; ☐ 0758 223 5173; 17 Duanzhou Silu, 端州四路17号) has frequent services to Guangzhou (¥40 to ¥55, 1½ hours, frequent, 6.15am to 9.30pm), Shenzhen (¥100, three hours, frequent, 7.30am to 7.30pm) and Zhuhai (¥100, 3½ hours, 13 daily, 7.40am to 6.30pm).

The **East Bus Station** (肇庆城东客运站, Zhàoqìng Chèngdōng Kèyùnzhàn; ☐ 0758 271 8474; 13 Duanzhou Sanlu, 端州三路13号), around 1.5km east of the main bus station, has services to Kaiping (¥55, two hours).

Boats (¥35, 30 minutes, frequent to 5pm) ferry passengers slowly across to a tiny island in Dinghu Shan Reserve.

Fast trains link Zhaoqing with Guangzhou (¥24 to ¥65, 45 to 80 minutes, frequent).

Bus 12 links the train station (¥2, every 10 minutes) and main bus station with the ferry pier. A taxi to the train station from the centre costs about ¥15.

Bāguà Villages 八卦村

Two villages, exceptional for their shape and feng shui, make great excursions from Zhaoqing. These '*bāguà* villages' (*bāguà cūn*) are designed according to *bāguà*, an octagon-shaped Taoist symbol with eight trigrams representing different phases in life.

Around 15km southeast of downtown Zhaoqing, **Xiangang village** (蚬岗镇, Xiǎngǎng Zhèn), founded in the Ming dynasty, is large and lively and has a market at its entrance. Its 16 ancestral halls, some opulent, are open only on the first and 15th days of the

lunar month. Board bus 308 (¥12, one hour) at **Qiaoxi Bus Station** (桥西汽车站, Qiáoxī Qìchē Zhàn) in Zhaoqing to get here.

At 700-year-old **Licha village** (黎槎村, Líchá Cūn; ¥25; ◷ 8.15am-5.30pm), 21km southeast of Zhaoqing, houses, many with wok-handle roofs and bas-relief sculptures, radiate from a taichi (a symbol of yin and yang) on a central terrace, turning the village into a maze. Most residents have emigrated to Australia; only the elders remain. Bus 315 leaves for Licha (¥12, 40 minutes, every 15 minutes) from behind Zhaoqing's Qiaoxi Bus Station.

Dinghu Shan Reserve 鼎湖山

The 11.3-sq-km **Dinghu Shan Reserve** (鼎湖山自然保护区, Dǐnghúshān Zìrán Bǎohù Qū; ☐ 0758 262 2510; Shangshan Lu, 上山路; ¥78; ◷ 5.30am-5.30pm) lies 18km northeast of Zhaoqing and offers great walks among lush vegetation, rare trees and roaring waterfalls, making for a relaxing day trip. A wooden boat will ferry you to a butterfly reserve on a tiny wooded island on Ding Lake (Dǐnghú). From there, a guide will take you on an hour-long hike through a scenic forest with ponds and waterfalls, to emerge near **Baoding Garden** (宝鼎园, Bǎodǐng Yuán), which has the world's largest *dǐng*, a three-legged ceremonial cauldron. Battery-operated carts (¥20) are useful for navigating the reserve.

Qingyun Temple (庆云寺, Qìngyún Sì) may look a little gaudy, but the site was built in 1636, making it one of Guangdong's 'four oldest temples' (广东四大名刹, *guǎngdōng sì dà míngshā*). What's more, it's surrounded by towering ancient banyans, and it's where you'll find the great Qingyun Vegetarian Restaurant. Here you can sample the famous **Dinghu Vegetarian Dish** (鼎湖上素, Dǐnghú Shàngsù; ¥68), supposedly an invention by monks around here. If ordering tea, make sure it's regular tea (普通茶, *pǔtōngchá*; ¥3 per person) and not an exotic variety that will inflate your bill by ¥30 to ¥100.

Bus 21 (¥2) goes to Dinghu Shan from the **local bus station** (Duanzhou Silu) in Zhaoqing. Dinghu Shan's local bus station is on Duanzhou Silu.

Qingyuan 清远

☐ 0763 / POP 3.7 MILLION

The industrial town of Qingyuan (Qīngyuǎn) is where to set off for a scenic jaunt down the

Beijiang River (北江, Běijiāng) on popular boat trips. Four-hour cruises (¥380 to ¥600 for the whole boat, depending on size) leave from Qingyuan's Wuyi dock (五一码头, Wǔyī Mǎtóu), heading past ancient pagodas to the Buddhist temple complex of **Feilai** (飞来寺, Fēilái Sì; boat ¥20; ⏱7.30am-5pm; 🅿). Though it has been around for more than 1400 years, the complex was destroyed by a landslide in 1997 and subsequently rebuilt. The mountaintop pavilion offers terrific views of the river gorge below.

The admission fee to the monastery at **Feixia** (飞霞, Fēixiá; 📞0763 378 0128; ¥40; ⏱10am-9pm), 4km upstream from Feilai, includes an eight-minute ride (every 15 minutes) to the Taoist relics uphill. **Cangxia Ancient Cave** (藏霞古洞, Cángxiá Gǔdòng; c 1863) is a maze of whispering shadows, abandoned courtyards and crumbling alleys connected by arboured paths. Further up, there is a pagoda; further down, a nunnery.

Most people do Qingyuan boat tours as a day trip from Guangzhou. If you do get stuck, there are budget hotels (from ¥120) a block or two back from the docks.

You can buy seafood from the floating market at Feixia and your boatman will cook it for you at no extra charge. Make sure you do so after sightseeing. Boat operators are known to return produce to vendors in exchange for cheaper versions when you're not looking.

To visit Feilai Temple and Feixia on a day trip from Guangzhou, catch one of the five high-speed trains from Guangzhou South train station in the daytime to Qingyuan (¥40 to ¥60, 24 minutes). There are another seven nearly identical trains later in the day for ¥120. Don't confuse Qingyuan (清远, Qīngyuǎn) here in Guangdong with Qingyuan (清原, Qīngyuán) in northeastern Liaoning (辽宁, Liáoníng).

Buses run every 25 minutes from Guangzhou's long-distance bus stations (¥42 to ¥47, 70 to 80 minutes, 6.30am to 9pm).

It's a 15-minute walk from Qingyuan station to Qingyuan's Wuyi dock. Turn right as you leave the station.

Nanling National Forest Park 南岭

📞0751 / POP 2000

Lying 285km north of Guangzhou, the Nanling (Nánlǐng, Southern Mountains) ranges stretch from Guangxi to Jiangxi provinces, separating the Pearl River from the Yangzi.

The range in Guangdong, home to the only ancient forests in the province, is a reserve for old-growth blue pines, a species unique to this part of Guangdong. Hiking in **Nanling National Forest Park Reserve** (南岭国家森林公园, Nánlǐng Guójiā Sēnlín Gōngyuán; 📞0751 523 2038; 327 Xian Dao, Rǔyuán Yao Autonomous Region, 乳源瑶族自治区县道327号; ¥80; ⏱7am-6pm) is the best way to take in the area's mountain vistas and natural wonders, passing pummelling waterfalls and clear tranquil pools.

The Nanling National Forest Park entrance is at the southern end of the village of **Wuzhishan** (五指山, Wúzhǐshān), which is small enough to cover on foot. Farmers nearby do their weekly shopping and stock clearance at Wuzhishan's lively Sunday market. Staying in **Orange House** (橙屋, Chéngwū; 📞0751 523 2929; d ¥398-498, Ranger House tr ¥198; ❄@) here will give you access to the park the next day. Just get your ticket and receipt stamped at the hotel.

The best way of getting around is to hire a car from Wuzhishan. For between ¥350 and ¥500 you can hire one for the whole day. The driver can drop you at one end of the trail and wait for you at the other. A one-way trip to the lower entrance of the trail to Little Yellow Mountain costs ¥120.

There are four trails, most of which can be completed in under three hours.

From Wuzhishan it's 6km to the start of the trails to Pùbù Chángláng waterfalls and Water Valley, and another 6km to **Little Yellow Mountain** (小黄山, Xiǎo Huángshān). The 12km-long trail is a challenging hike through a forest of blue pines. The view of rolling mountain ranges from the crest (1608m) is spectacular.

The easiest of the four walks through Nanling National Forest Park, is a 6km trail that follows a stream and leads you through the steep-sided gorges and crystalline pools of **Water Valley** (亲水谷, Qīnshuǐgǔ). The 3.5km **Waterfall Trail** (瀑布长廊, Pùbù Chángláng) is a short but interesting trail that takes you past roaring waterfalls.

The longest (28km) and most difficult of the four trails through Nanling National Park is the **No 4 Trail** (四号林道, Sìhào Líndào) to **Shíkēngkōng** (石坑空). At 1902m, Shíkēngkōng is the highest peak in Guangdong and straddles the boundary between Guangdong and Hunan.

As camping inside Nanling National Forest Park is prohibited, the only option is to stay in Wuzhishan. There are a couple of

Overseas Chinese Town (OCT)

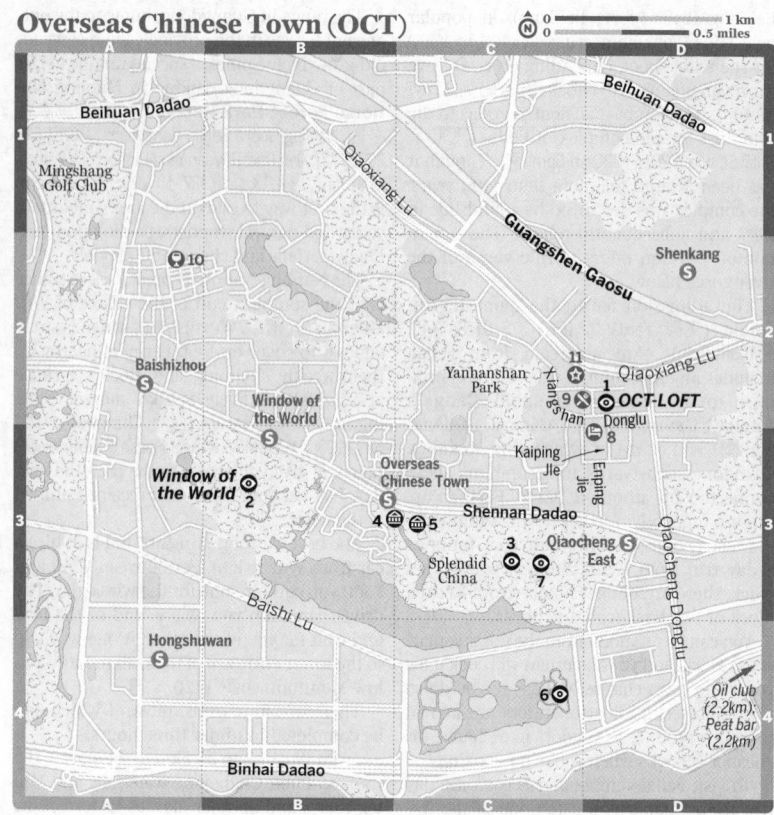

zhāodàisuǒ (招待所, basic lodgings), where you can get a room from ¥90.

Bring snacks and water as the only reliable places to get food are in Wuzhishan. **Feng's Kitchen** (冯家菜, Féngjiācài; ☑138 2799 2107; mains ¥13-45; ⊙10am-10pm) is a farmer restaurant that cures its own meat and grows its own vegetables (¥13 per plate). Reservations necessary. Mr Feng can arrange for car hire of any duration. It's 1km northeast of the park entrance.

ⓘ Getting There & Away

BUS

Shaoguan (韶关) is your gateway to Nanling. Buses leave Guangzhou long-distance bus station (¥75 to ¥95, 3½ hours) for Shaoguan's **Xihe Bus Station** (西河汽车站, Xīhé Qìchēzhàn; ☑0751 875 4176; Huimin Nanlu, Shaoguan, 韶关市惠民南路) every hour (6.50am to 8.30pm).

If you miss the bus to Shaoguan, catch a bus to Ruyuan (乳源, Rǔyuán; ¥10, one hour, every 15 minutes). From Ruyuan, three buses to Wuzhishan (Wúzhǐshān; ¥10) leave at 9am, 12.45pm and 4.30pm, or you can hire a taxi (¥90).

In Wuzhishan, buses to Shaoguan leave at 7.30am, 12.30pm and 3.30pm.

TRAIN

High-speed trains leave from Guangzhou South Railway Station (¥105, 51 minutes, frequent) for **Shaoguan Train Station** (韶关站, Sháoguān Zhàn; Shaoguan Dadao, Shaoguan, 韶关市武江区赤水村韶关大道附近). From there, board bus 22 and get off at Xihe Bus Station. Buses to Wuzhishan (¥22, two hours) depart at 8am, 11.45am and 3.30pm.

Guangzhou Main Train Station has trains (¥38, 2½ hours, frequent) that stop over at **Shaoguan East Train Station** (韶关东站, Sháoguān Dōng-zhàn; ☑0751 617 2222; 56 Nanshaolu, Jiang Qu, Shaoguan, 韶关市浈江区南韶路56号). Buses to Wuzhishan leave at 7.45am, 11.15am and 3.15pm.

Overseas Chinese Town (OCT)

Shenzhen 深圳

📞 0755 / POP 12.53 MILLION

The gleaming manifestation of China's economic miracle, Shenzhen (Shēnzhèn) has risen from the marshy Pearl River Delta into one of the world's most mega megacities in less time than it took London's St Paul's Cathedral to be built. Millions of migrants have been drawn to its golden gates from the Chinese countryside since the 1980s; now Shenzhen attracts high-flying tech graduates and global corporations.

But it's not all work, work, work. This free-spirited, forward-looking metropolis has thriving arts, nightlife and music scenes, multicultural dining and oodles of shopping. And when you step away from the skyscrapers and malls you'll discover fascinating 'urban villages': poor but vibrant migrant worker communities that were once clan villages before the city swallowed them up.

◉ Sights

★ OCT-LOFT
ARTS CENTRE

(华侨城创意文化园, Huáqiáochéng Chuàngyì Wénhuàyuán; www.octloft.cn; 2 Jinxiu Beilu, Nánshān District, 南山区锦绣北街2号; ⊙10am-5.30pm; M Line 1 to Qiaocheng East, exit A, Line 2 to Qiaocheng North, exit B) By far the best place for strolling or simply hanging out in the city is the breezy OCT-LOFT complex, a warren of repurposed communist-era factories crisscrossed by cobbled laneways. It's also a great place to browse a multitude of contemporary art spaces in between pit stops at the area's excellent cafes, design shops, music venues, bars, restaurants and Shenzhen's best bookshop (p610).

★ Lianhua Shan Park
PARK

(莲花山公园, Liánhuā Shān Gōngyuán; 6030 Hongli Lu, Futian District, 福田区红荔路6030号; ⊙6am-10.30pm; ♿; M Line 4 to Lianhua North, exit A2, Line 3, 4 to Children's Palace, exit F2) FREE It's an easy half-hour amble up to the top of this tropical hill in the heart of Futian District for Shenzhen's best skyline photographs. Appropriately, you'll be sharing the mind-blowing vistas with Deng Xiaoping (in statue form), whose economic reforms in the 1980s made this whole crazy mess of prosperity possible.

★ Dafen Oil Painting Village
ARTS CENTRE

(大芬村, Dàfēncūn; Buji, Lónggǎng District; ⊙9am-6pm; M Line 3 to Dafen, exit A1) FREE This folksy urban village of narrow lanes and alleys is a pleasure to visit in itself, but what makes Dafen simply unmissable is the hundreds of art studios and shops churning out reproduction oil paintings by hand, from Van Gogh's sunflowers (yours for less than ¥100) to enormous, gilt-framed scenes of mounted cavalry or galleons at sea rendered in lavish detail, costing upwards of ¥2000. Or why not go pop art with a Mona Lisa–meets-Minions mash-up?

★ Sunrise Art Center
GALLERY

(太阳山艺术中心, Tàiyáng Shān Yìshù Zhōngxīn; 📞0755 2871 6049; www.sunrise-art.com.cn; 23 Laowei, Dafen Oil Painting Village, 大芬村老围23号; ¥20; ⊙9.30am-6.30pm; M Line 3 to Dafen, exit A1) Built from the vestiges of a century-old Hakka home, this idyllic courtyard gallery was created by Chen Qiuzhi, a contemporary ink artist from Anhui province. Several galleries display his work, and the wonderful cafe is just the spot to kick back with a tea or coffee after browsing the surrounding Dafen Oil Painting Village.

★ Design Society
GALLERY

(设计互联, Shèjì Hùlián, Sea World Culture & Arts Center; 📞0755 2667 1187; www.designsociety.cn; 1187 Wanghai Lu, Shekou, 蛇口望海路1187号; ⊙10am-10pm; M Line 2 to Sea World, exit A) FREE China's first dedicated museum of design, this architectural landmark opened with media fanfare in 2017 on the Shekou shore with its

LINGNAN CULTURE

Lingnan (岭南, Lǐngnán) culture is an important part of broader Cantonese culture and it manifests itself most notably in food, art, architecture and Cantonese opera. Culturally Lingnan was a hybrid and a late bloomer that often went on to reverse-influence the rest of the country. Its development was also fuelled by the ideas of the revolution to end feudalism. Boundaries between refined and pedestrian are relaxed and there's an open-mindedness towards modernity.

Place

Lingnan, literally South of the Ranges, refers to the region to the south of the five mountain ranges that separate the Yangzi River (central China) from the Pearl River (southern China). Traditionally, Lingnan encompassed several provinces, but today it's become almost synonymous with Guangdong.

People

The term 'Lingnan' was traditionally used by men of letters on the Yangzi side as a polite reference to the boonies, where 'mountains were tall and emperors out of sight', as a Chinese saying goes. These northerners regarded their southern cousins as less robust (physically and morally), more romantic and less civilised. But being far-flung had its benefits. Lingnan offered refuge to people not tolerated by the Middle Kingdom; and played host in various diasporas in Chinese history to migrants from the north, such as the Hakkas in Meizhou. This also explains why some Cantonese words are closer in pronunciation to the ancient speech of the Chinese.

Lingnan School of Painting (1900–50)

The Lingnan painters were an influential lot who ushered in a national movement in art in the first half of the 20th century.

Traditionally Chinese painters were literati well versed in calligraphy, poetry and Confucian classics. These scholar-artists would later become imperial bureaucrats, and as they were often stationed somewhere far away from home, they expressed their nostalgia by recreating the landscapes of their childhood villages from memory.

The founding masters of the Lingnan School of Painting, however, studied abroad, where they were exposed to Japanese and European art. China, during the Qing dynasty, was being carved up by Western powers. Sharing the ideals of the revolutionaries, these artists devoted themselves to a revolution in art by combining traditional techniques with elements of Western and Japanese realist painting.

The New National Painting, as it came to be called, featured a bolder use of colours, more realism and a stronger sense of perspective – a style that was more accessible to the citizenry of China's new republic than the literati painting of the past.

You can see Lingnan paintings at the Guangdong Museum of Art (p585) and the **Memorial Hall of the Lingnan School of Painting** (岭南画派纪念馆, Lǐngnán Huàpài Jìniànguǎn; ☑ 020 8401 7167; www.lingnans.org; Guǎngzhōu Měishù Xuéyuàn, 257 Changgang Donglu, 广州美术学院昌岗东路257号; ⊙ 9am-5pm Tue-Sun; Ⓜ Line 8 to Xiaogang, exit A) **FREE**.

Lingnan Architecture

The Lingnan school of architecture is one of three major schools of modern Chinese architecture, alongside the Beijing and Shanghai schools. It was founded in the 1950s, though earlier structures exhibiting a distinctive local style had existed since the late Ming dynasty (1600s). The features of the Lingnan school are lucidity, openness and an organic incorporation of nature into built environments.

ANCIENT

Examples of this style of architecture include schools, ancestral halls and temples of the Ming and Qing dynasties. The Chen Clan Ancestral Hall (p584) in Guangzhou and Zumiao (p594) in Foshan are prime illustrations of this style.

Vernacular Lingnan-style houses are more decorative than their austere northern cousins. The 'wok-handle' houses (锅耳屋, *guō'ěr wū*) in Licha village (p600) near Zhaoqing have distinctive wok-handle-shaped roofs that also serve to prevent the spread of fire. You'll also see in Licha village bas-relief sculpting and paintings (浮雕彩画, *fúdiāo cǎihuà*), intricate and colourful, above windows or doors, portraying classical tales, birds, flowers and landscapes.

MODERN

Excellent examples of this style of architecture, appearing in the late Qing dynasty, are the Xiguan houses on Enning Road (p585) in Guangzhou, with their grey bricks and stained-glass windows. These windows were products of the marriage between Manchurian windows (满洲窗, *mǎnzhōu chuāng*), simple contraptions consisting of paper overlaid with wood, and coloured glass introduced to Guangzhou by Westerners. It's said that when a foreign merchant presented the empress dowager with a bead of coloured glass, she was so dazzled by its beauty that she reciprocated with a pearl. Panxi Restaurant (p591) in Guangzhou and Yuyin Mountain Villa (p592) have Manchurian windows embedded with coloured glass.

CONTEMPORARY

The garden-restaurants and garden-hotels that proliferated between the 1950s and 1990s are examples of contemporary architecture. Guangzhou's **LN Garden Hotel** (花园酒店, Huāyuán Jiǔdiàn; ☑ 020 8333 8989; www.gardenhotel.com; 368 Huanshi Donglu, 环市东路368号; r/ste from ¥1000/2000; ✴ @ 🛜 ⛱; Ⓜ Line 5 to Taojin, exit A), Guangzhou Restaurant (p591) and Panxi Restaurant (p591) all contain elaborate indoor gardens complete with trees and waterfalls, and make use of glass to blur the boundary between built and natural environments.

These indoor Edens were fashioned after the private Lingnan-style gardens of wealthy families, such as Liang Garden (p595) in Foshan, which together with the imperial gardens of Peking and the scholars' gardens of Jiangnan, constituted the three main types of Chinese gardens.

Cantonese Opera

Cantonese opera is a regional form of Chinese opera that evolved from theatrical forms of the north and neighbouring regions. Like Peking opera, it involves music, singing, martial arts, acrobatics and acting. There's elaborate face painting, glamorous period costumes and, for some of the roles, high-pitched falsetto singing. But compared to its northern cousin, it tends to feature more scholars than warriors in its tales of courtship and romance.

You don't have to understand or even like Cantonese opera to appreciate it as an important aspect of Cantonese culture – there's no shortage of related attractions, such as Bahe Academy (p585) and Luányú Táng (p585) in Guangzhou, a festival, and a props speciality shop in Chaozhou.

Cantonese Cuisine

There's a saying 'Good food is in Guangzhou' (食在广州, *shí zài Guǎngzhōu*). Regional bias aside, Cantonese food is very good. The most influential of the eight major regional cuisines of China, it's known for complex cooking methods, an obsession with freshness and the use of a wide range of ingredients.

Many Cantonese dishes depend on quick cooking over high heat – these require skills (versus patience over a stew) that are less common in other regional cuisines. Dishes such as sweet-and-sour pork, crab shell au gratin and tempura-style prawns show an open-mindedness to foreign ideas.

When it comes to haute cuisine, even northern cooks would acknowledge the superiority of their Cantonese colleagues in making the best of expensive items such as abalone. Also, much of the costliest marine life to grace the Cantonese table, such as deep-sea fish and large prawns, simply doesn't grow in inland rivers.

famous founding partner, London's V&A Museum. A focus on contemporary concerns is present in shows that have included the story of China through comics and cutting-edge local designers. The fabulous building, designed by Japanese architect Fumihiko Maki, has plenty of room for humongous exhibitions, an excellent cafe (plus a small rooftop coffee kiosk with ocean views) and a dim sum restaurant.

★ **Window of the World** AMUSEMENT PARK
(世界之窗, Shìjiè Zhīchuāng; http://en.szwwco.com; 9037 Shennan Dadao, 深南大道9037号; adult/child ¥200/100; ⊘ 9am-10pm; 🚇; M Line 1, 2 to Window of the World, exit H1) It's 'Around the World in 80 Minutes' (OK, more like half a day) at this endearingly kitsch theme park set in well-tended gardens. From the Houses of Parliament to the Pyramids, the world's great monuments are realised, tackily, in miniature. Some aren't so small – the Eiffel Tower clocks in at an impressive 108m, and Niagara Falls is quite the sight.

Ping An Finance Centre NOTABLE BUILDING
(平安国际金融中心, Píng'ān Guójì Jīnróng Zhōngxīn; 5033 Yitian Lu, Futian District, 益田路5033号; M Line 1 to Shopping Park, exit D) The fourth-tallest building in the world when it topped out in 2015, the Ping An Finance Centre (599m) rises like a glass pencil above Shenzhen's ever-blooming Futian District. The Free Sky Observation Deck offers suitably jaw-dropping views on a clear day.

Museum of Contemporary Art & Planning Exhibition NOTABLE BUILDING
(MOCAPE; 当代艺术与城市规划展览馆, Dāngdài Yìshùyǔ Chéngshì Guīhuà Zhǎnlǎn Guǎn; 184 Fuzhong Lu, Futian District, 福田区福中路184号; 10am-5pm Tue-Sun; M Line 3, 4 to Children's Palace, exit A2) FREE One of those thrillingly space-age, 'only in China' architectural projects, this gargantuan exhibition space designed by Coop Himmelb(l)au anchors Shenzhen's Fútián Cultural District. Opened in 2016, the exterior is a vast curve of chrome planted among the city's high-rises, while the entrance hall is a soaring atrium with a cloud-like mirrored art installation (perfect to take selfies in). Gallery spaces within house temporary exhibitions with an emphasis on contemporary art and design.

Shenzhen Museum MUSEUM
(深圳博物馆新馆, Shēnzhèn Bówùguǎn Xīnguǎn; 📞 0755 8812 5550; www.shenzhenmuseum.com; East Gate, Block A, Citizens' Centre, Fuzhong Sanlu, 福中路市民中心A区; ⊘ 10am-6pm Tue-Sun; M Line 4 to Shimin Zhongxin, exit B) FREE The hulking Shenzhen Museum provides a decent enough introduction to Shenzhen's brief but breakneck march into modernity, both before and after the implementation of Deng Xiaoping's policies of reform. Highlights include propaganda art popular in the 1940s and the colourful scale models in the folk-culture hall.

Litchi Park PARK
(荔枝公园, Lìzhī Gōngyuán; 1001 Hongling Zhonglu, cnr Shennan Zhonglu, 红岭中路1001号南门; 🚇; M Line 1, 2 to Grand Theatre, exit A) FREE When big-city fatigue sets in, you can seek refuge in this spacious inner-city park. It may still get busy but here the mood is created by musicians, elderly taichi practitioners, couples crossing faux-ancient bridges and a small lake. There are a few kids' amusement rides and paddleboats for rent.

★ Festivals & Events

Bi-City Biennale of Urbanism\Architecture CULTURAL
(UABB; 深港城市\建筑双城双年展; http://szhkbiennale.org; ⊘ Dec-Mar) This excellent arts festival installs itself into various parts of the city for a few months every two years, presenting thought-provoking exhibitions and events on issues faced by rapidly urbanising cities like Shenzhen. Previous event venues include Futian Railway Station, and Nantou Old Town, one of Shenzhen's 'urban villages' – congested communities of transient workers from rural communities.

Midi Music Festival MUSIC
(谜笛音乐节, Mídí Yīnyuè Jié; www.midifestival.com; Shenzhen Universiade Sports Center, 3001 Longxiang Dadao, 龙翔大道3001号; 1-/2-day tickets at the door ¥240/440; ⊘ 31 Dec-1 Jan; S Line 3 to Universiade station, exit 3) Founded by Beijing's Midi School of Music in the late '90s, Midi Music Festival has evolved into one of China's largest rock and indie music events, head-banging its way into other major Chinese cities. Shenzhen got its first taste of Midi in 2013, and the fest now returns annually on New Year's Eve and New Year's Day.

🛏 Sleeping

With multiple disparate centres, the conundrum in Shenzhen is choosing *where* to stay. High-rise Futian District has the most luxury hotels, while scruffier Luohu District is stuffed with budget and midrange business hotels – the best orbit Laojie metro. Shekou, in the

Luohu

Fán Lóu (500m); Summer Tea House (800m) Shēnzhèn North (23km); Shēnzhèn ✈ (43km)

Dàfēn Oil Painting Village (4km)

Laojie

Shennan Donglu

Muslim Hotel Restaurant (900m)

Bank of China

Guomao

Jiabin Lu

Youyi Lu

Huaqiang Bei Commercial St (2.2km); Huaqiang Electronics World (2.2km); Crown Technology Park (11km); Shekou Port (20km)

Hongling South

Grand Theatre

Ludancun

Chunfeng Lu

Binhe Dadao

Binhe Dadao

HSBC

Shenzhen Tourist Office

Shēnzhèn Train Station

Luohu Bus Station

HONG KONG

Luohu

Luohu Border

Lo Wu Information Centre

GUANGDONG SHENZHEN

Luohu

◎ Sights
1 Litchi Park A1

🛏 Sleeping
2 Renaissance Shenzhen Luohu D2
3 Shangri-La D3
4 ZTL Hotel C1

🍴 Eating
5 Yunlaiju Vegetarian D1

---

city's west, has decent midrange and upmarket options, but is further from the sights. Consider anywhere in range of OCT-LOFT (p602), one of the most pleasant, central areas, though with pricier digs.

★ **Shenzhen Loft Youth Hostel**   HOSTEL ¥
(深圳侨城旅友国际青年旅舍, Shēnzhèn Qiáochéng Lǚyǒu Guójì Qīngnián Lǚshè; ☑ 0755 8609 5773; OCT-LOFT, 7 Xiangshan Dongjie, Nán-shān District, 华侨城香山东街7号; dm/d/f from ¥95/300/600; ☺ 🕸 @ 🛜; Ⓜ Line 1 to Qiaocheng East, exit A) Located in a tranquil part of OCT-LOFT, near the junction of Enping Jie and Xiangshan Dongjie, this immaculate YHA hostel has over 50 private rooms with showers and dormitory-type triples with shared bathrooms. The industrial building previously served as factory workers' lodgings. An adjoining cafe offers breakfast and drinks.

ZTL Hotel   HOTEL ¥
(中泰来大酒店, Zhōng Tài Lái Dà Jiǔdiàn; ☑ 0755 6688 6388; 57 Yongxin Jie, Jiefang Lu, 解放路永新街57号; d from ¥388; 🕸 @ 🛜; Ⓜ Line 1, 3 to Laojie, exit D) You get a lot for your money at this older hotel on a pedestrianised shopping and eating street in the very centre of Dongmen. It has spacious (though dimly lit) rooms, marble bathrooms and huge comfy beds – but also the lingering whiff of stale smoke, even on the no-smoking floors.

Renaissance
Shenzhen Luohu   LUXURY HOTEL ¥¥

(彭年酒店, Péng Nián Jiǔdiàn; ☑ 0755 2518 5888; www.marriott.com; 2002 Jiabin Rd, 嘉宾路2002号; d/ste from ¥688/1488; ✳@중; Ⓜ Line 1 to Guomao, exit B) This luxury hotel has been recently renovated and reborn from the Panglin Hotel. The grand marble lobby, splendid fountains on the forecourt, outdoor pool and 50th-floor revolving restaurant with views of Shenzhen and Hong Kong remain, but have been elevated to Marriott standards. Fresh, bright rooms have neutral tones, and bathrooms feature angular design touches, but rates stay affordable.

Shangri-La   HOTEL ¥¥¥

(香格里拉大酒店, Xiānggélǐlā Dàjiǔdiàn; ☑ 0755 8233 0888; www.shangri-la.com/shenzhen; 1002 Jianshe Lu, 建设路1002号; d ¥950-1400, ste ¥1800; Ⓟ@중❄; Ⓜ Line 1 to Luohu, exit E2) One of the first luxury hotels in Shenzhen, the Shangri-La has seen millions of suited traders and Hong Kong shoppers pass through its marble lobby over the years, unsurprising considering its location overlooking the Luohu border crossing. Service remains exemplary, and rooms are considerably cheaper (though smaller) than the newer Futian Shangri-La. The outdoor pool is a big plus.

✗ Eating

Locals say that for the best food, go north to Guangzhou or south to Hong Kong. That's doing Shenzhen a disservice, which, given its migrant population, is home to a huge diversity of food from all over China. Dim sum and Cantonese fare is ubiquitous too, with most of the famous Guangdong chains represented.

★ Hoi Fan   CANTONESE ¥

(开饭, Kāifàn; ☑ 0755 8322 6165; Central Walk Shopping Mall, 3 Fuhua Yilu, Futian District, 福田区福华一路3号怡景中心城; dishes from ¥35; ◷ 11am-10pm; Ⓜ Line 1, 4 to Convention & Exhibition Center, exit B) Get an iced lemon coke with your 'kung fu' crispy duck at this fun contemporary Canto chain, originally from Guangzhou. The bilingual picture menu presents all manner of treats from roast-meat platters to Cantonese 'sweet and sour' fried eggs, steamed beef with preserved pickles and tender claypot chicken.

★ Fán Lóu   DIM SUM ¥

(繁楼; ☑ 0755 8211 5186; 2nd fl, 2078 Baoan Nanlu, 宝安南路2078号2楼; dim sum ¥8-27; ◷ 8am-10pm; Ⓜ Line 3, 9 to Hongling, exit C2) Excellent dim sum is served in square steamer baskets at this friendly and highly affordable restaurant. The tick-box picture menu is Chinese only; a simple payment key using Chinese characters denotes how much each dish costs. Note the mandatory ¥6 per person zuò fèi (sitting fee), which includes your choice of tea – pǔ'ěr (fermented tea from Yúnnán) is traditional.

Muslim Hotel Restaurant   CHINESE ISLAMIC ¥

(穆斯林宾馆大餐馆, Músīlín Bīnguǎn Dàcānguǎn; ☑ 0755 8225 9664; 2nd fl, Muslim Hotel, 2013 Wenjing Nanlu, 罗湖区文锦南路2013号; dishes ¥38-128; ◷ 10am-11pm; Ⓜ Line 9 to Wenjin, exit D) Enjoy juicy roast mutton from the great plains of northern China at this halal restaurant run by Hui (Chinese Muslims). The roast lamb legs, tender boiled ribs or dàpán jī ('big plate' stewed chicken) are best for groups, but solo diners can gorge on Lanzhou noodle soup or bǎn miàn – chewy noodles stir-fried with tomatoes, peppers, carrots and mutton.

Summer Tea House   VEGETARIAN ¥

(静颐茶馆, Jìngyí Cháguǎn; ☑ 0755 2557 4555; www.jingyi2000.com; 7th & 8th fl, Jintang Daxia, 3038 Bao'an Nanlu, 综合大厦宝安南路3083号; dishes ¥50-80; ◷ 9am-11pm; ✐; Ⓜ Line 9 to Yuanling, exit C) An unexpected oasis of tranquillity in a dull office block, this wood-panelled teahouse has deep armchairs just begging for your bottom and a creative, all-veggie menu of mock-meat dishes. You could easily while away a couple of hours here sipping tea (¥6) and grazing on sweet dim sum snacks (¥45).

Yunlaiju Vegetarian   VEGETARIAN ¥

(云来居素食馆, Yúnláijū Sùshíguǎn; ☑ 0755 8238 3253; 4th fl, Dongmending Meishijie, Renmin Beilu, 人民北路东门町美食街4层; dishes around ¥40; ◷ 10am-10pm; ✐; Ⓜ Line 1, 3 to Laojie, exit C) A soothing respite from the street-food bedlam below, this spacious restaurant serves a range of tasty vegetarian dim sum, hand-pulled noodle dishes, mock meat and more. You might even see a local monk or two popping in for a bite.

★ Phoenix House   CANTONESE ¥¥

(凤凰楼, Fènghuánglóu; ☑ 0755 8207 6338, 0755 8207 6688; 4002 Huaqiang Beilu, East Wing, Pavilion Hotel, 华强北路4002号; lunch ¥60-100, dinner ¥100-350; ◷ 8am-10pm; Ⓜ Line 3, 7 to Huaxin, exit C) This is one of the most popular Cantonese chains in town, so expect noisy waits for a table after 11.30am. Must-try dim sum here are the sweet durian puffs (榴莲酥, liúlián sū) and chén cūn fěn (陈村粉), a speciality from the Guangdong foodie heartland of

Shunde County, consisting of rice roll sheets steamed with pork and gravy.

Magpie FUSION ¥¥

(喜鹊派餐厅, Xǐquè Pài Cāntīng; ☑ 0755 8652 8782; 125, Block A5, OCT-LOFT, 华侨城东部工业区北区A5-125号; dishes ¥60-188; ☺ 5pm-2am Tue-Sun, kitchen to 10.30pm; Ⓜ Line 2 to Qiaocheng North, exit B) Dine on small-plate fusion fare at this hip and stylish restaurant in OCT-LOFT (p602). The Chinese chef owners draw inspiration from their Manchurian roots with ambitious creations such as horsemeat tartare with sweet-potato crisps and venison Bolognese. There's definitely some molecular trickery at play, not least in the impressive cocktails.

Drinking & Nightlife

You have to dig a little for great nightlife in Shenzhen, but when you do you're sure to strike gold. Boutique cocktail speakeasies are opening faster than you can muddle a mojito. That's Shenzhen (www.thatsmags. com/shenzhen) is a handy source on what's hot and happening.

One of the liveliest concentrations of bars and clubs in Shenzhen can be found in Coco Park, an upmarket shopping complex in high-rise Futian District, which has its own, fairly commercial bar street and plenty of restaurants.

★ Oil CLUB

(油, Yóu; ☑ 0139 8989 3959; www.facebook.com/Oil-clubShenzhen; 11a Tairan Dasha, Tairan Balu, 车公庙泰然八路深然大厦11A号; around ¥80; ☺ 10pm-late Fri & Sat; Ⓜ Line 9 to Xiasha, exit D) Quite possibly the best underground club in China, Oil is a compact, sweaty chapel to electronic beats, the darker and more esoteric the better. An adjoining cocktail bar (open nightly) provides the perfect prelude to Oil's weekend parties, which have been known to keep raging until 7am. Check its socials for upcoming events.

Peat COCKTAIL BAR

(☑ 1812 627 3323; 2nd fl, Block A, Tairan Dasha, Tairan Ba Lu, 泰然八路泰然大厦A座2楼; ☺ 6.30pm-2am) Bartenders clamber up stepladders to access their impressive cache of whiskies (some 500 to 600 bottles) in this smart bar sharing the same office-block location as nightclub Oil, though the vibe is completely different. Whisky-based cocktails (from ¥90) are the sort of smoky, booze-heavy drinks you twirl nonchalantly in your palm as you brood over life's great questions, cigar optional.

Bionic Brew CRAFT BEER

(百优精酿啤酒, Bǎi Yōu Jīng Niàng Píjiǔ; ☑ 136 2466 8864; http://bionicbrew.com; Shop A1-1F02, 24 Shahe Jie Pedestrian St, Baishizhou, 白石洲沙河街道商业步行街24栋A1-1F02铺; ☺ 5.30pm-1am Sun-Thu, to 2am Fri & Sat; Ⓜ Line 1 to Baishizhou, exit A) Shenzhen's very own craft-beer brand, American-run Bionic Brew, pours four core beers as well as guest brews from elsewhere in China. But the best thing about this tiny, open-fronted bar is its thrillingly local setting, hemmed in by raucous *shāokǎo* (barbecue) joints in one of Shenzhen's few remaining 'urban villages'.

HEYTEA TEAHOUSE

(喜茶, Xǐ Chá; ☑ 0755 8663 6383; www.heytea. com; B2 fl, Central Walk Mall, 3 Fuhua Yilu, 怡景中心城福华一路3号; ☺ 10am-10.30pm; Ⓜ Line 1, 4 to Convention & Exhibition Center, exit B) You haven't been to Guangdong unless you've tasted cheese tea. (This is not something we ever expected to print!) There are umpteen branches of HEYTEA across Shenzhen, where folks queue with a sup big cups of milk tea topped with its trademark layer of cheesy foam (¥17), and take a selfie, of course. Say cheese!

☆ Entertainment

For indie bands and underground DJs, Shenzhen is becoming a mandatory China tour stop after Beijing and Shanghai. See SZ Party (www.shenzhenparty.com) for current events.

★ B10 Live House LIVE MUSIC

(B10现场, B10Xiànchǎng; ☑ 0755 8633 7602; http://b10live.cn; OCT-LOFT, Xiangshan Dongjie, 香山东街华侨城创意文化园; prices vary; Ⓜ Line 2 to Qiaocheng North, exit B) From hair metal to experimental jazz, all genres are equal at this warehouse live-music venue that welcomes eclectic performers from around the world. The musical heartbeat of OCT-LOFT (p602), B10 is also the principal host venue for the **OCT-LOFT Jazz Festival** (www.octloft jazz.com; ☺ Oct) and **Tomorrow Music Festival** (http://b10live.cn/tomorrowfestival; ☺ May).

Brown Sugar Jar LIVE MUSIC

(红糖罐, Hóngtáng Guàn; ☑ 186 6588 8524; 9 Gongye Liulu, Shekou, 圈创101空间蛇口 工业六路9号; tickets around ¥80; ☺ 2pm-midnight Sun-Thu, to 2am Fri & Sat; Ⓜ Line 2 to Shuiwan, exit D) The long-established Brown Sugar Jar has several locations in Shenzhen, but this is its main live house, a cavernous, warehouse-style space buried deep in Shekou district that hosts local and overseas folk, indie and alternative acts most weekends from 9pm.

🔒 Shopping

The best gets in Shenzhen are homegrown tech gadgets, many of which can be found along **Huaqiang Bei Commercial St** (华强北商业街, Huáqiángběi Shāngyèjiē; Huaqiang Beilu, 华强北路; ⊘ around 9am-7pm; Ⓜ Line 2, 7 to Huaqiangbei) – though avoid Chinese mobile phones, many of which won't officially work with the Google Play Store, unless you are tech savvy. You can also pimp out your crib with reproduction Da Vinci canvases from Dafen Oil Painting Village (p602).

★ **Old Heaven Books**   BOOKS
(旧天堂书店, Jiùtiāntáng Shūdiàn; ☑ 0755 8614 8090; oldheavenbooks@gmail.com; Shop 120, Bldg A5, OCT-Loft, Xiangshan Dongjie, 香山东街华侨城创意园北区A5栋120铺; ⊘ 11am-10pm; Ⓜ Qiaochengdong, exit A) A delicious bookshop specialising in cultural and academic titles, Old Heaven also doubles as a vinyl-music shop, cafe, live venue and community creative hub. It's a great place to plug in and catch up on that travel blog over a hazelnut latte. Performances take place here during the OCT-LOFT Jazz Festival (p609).

★ **Huaqiang Electronics World**   ELECTRONICS
(华强电子世界(深圳二店), Huáqiáng Diànzǐ Shìjiè; 1007-1015 Huaqiang Beilu, 华强北路1007-1015号; ⊘ 9.30am-6.30pm; 🅿; Ⓜ Line 7 to Huaqiangbei, exit D2) Miniscule spy cameras, jiving robots, e-skateboards and air-conditioned jackets (yep!) – for a sea of innovative, cut-price kidult toys, head to this multifloor electronics mall on Huaqiang Bei Commercial St. Haggling is the norm, with terrific bargains to be had.

ℹ Information

Buy the Shenzhen-only visa (¥168 for most nationalities, ¥304 for Brits; Chinese currency only) at the **Luohu border** (⊘ 7am-11.30pm), Huangang (9am to 1pm and 2.30pm to 5pm) or **Shekou** (⊘ 9am-1pm & 2.30-5pm).

At the time of research, US citizens were eligible to get the five-day visa, but the cost (over ¥900) is steep, so it makes more sense to organise a tourist visa in advance through the normal channels.

Bank of China (中国银行, Zhōngguó Yínháng; Int Finance Bldg, 2022 Jianshe Lu, 建设路2022号; ⊘ 9am-5.30pm Mon-Fri, to 4pm Sat & Sun; Ⓜ Line 1 to Guomao, exit E)

HSBC (汇丰银行, Huìfēng Yínháng; Shangri-La Hotel, 1002 Jianshe Lu, 香格里拉大酒店; ⊘ 9am-5pm Mon-Fri, 10am-6pm Sat; Ⓜ Line 1 to Luohu, exit E2)

Public Security Bureau (PSB; 公安局, Gōng'ānjú; ☑ 0755 8249 8710; 4018 Jiefang Lu, 解放路4018号; ⊘ 24hr) Can handle visa extensions.

Shenzhen Tourist Office (深圳旅游咨询中心, Shenzhen Tourist Consultation Centre; ☑ 0755 8232 3045; ground fl, Shenzhen Train Station, east exit; ⊘ 9am-6pm) Free and reasonably detailed maps available on request at this office at Shenzhen train station.

ℹ Getting There & Away

AIR

Shenzhen Bao'an International Airport (p593) has daily flights to all major destinations in China and direct flights further afield to Southeast Asia, Australia and Europe.

BOAT

Shekou Port (轮渡码头, Lúndù Mǎtóu; ☑ 0755 2669 1213; Shekou Gang, 蛇口港; Ⓜ Line 1 to Luohu, exit A) has regular boat services to Hong Kong and Macau (take subway Line 2 to Shekou Port then catch the free shuttle bus).

Hong Kong International Airport ¥270, 30 minutes, 14 daily (7.45am to 9pm)

Hong Kong–Macau Ferry Terminal, Central ¥120, one hour, nine daily (7.45am to 7.15pm, from 9am weekends)

Macau Maritime Ferry Terminal ¥210, one hour, 13 daily (8am to 7.45pm)

Taipa Temporary Ferry Terminal (Macau) ¥210, one hour, nine daily (9.15am to 9pm)

Jiuzhou Port (Zhuhai) ¥120, one hour, 30 to 60 minutes (7.30am to 9.30pm)

You can also catch a ferry at Shenzhen Airport's **Fuyong Ferry Terminal** (福永码头, Fúyǒng Mǎtóu; ☑ 0755 2345 5300; 1001 Xin Gangwu Matou Dadao, 新港务码头大道1001号) to Hong Kong and Macau.

Macau Maritime Ferry Terminal ¥196, 80 minutes, six daily (8.45am to 5.30pm)

Sky Pier, Hong Kong International Airport ¥295, 40 minutes, four daily (8.35am, 10.15am, 1.15pm and 5pm)

BUS

Buses depart to Guangzhou (¥50 to ¥70, two hours, 7am to 10pm) every 20 minutes from **Luohu Bus Station** (罗湖汽车站, Luóhú Qìchēzhàn; ☑ 0755 8232 1670; beneath Luohu Commercial City; Ⓜ Line 1 to Luohu, exit B). You can also reach other Guangdong cities from here, including Dongguan, Zhongshan, Chaozhou and Shantou.

For buses to more distant destinations across China, head to Shenzhen's **Yinhu Bus Station** (银湖汽车站, Yínhú Qìchē Zhàn; Shangbubei Lu, 上步北路; Ⓜ Line 9 to Yinhu, exit D).

TRAIN

Dozens of high-speed trains per day shuttle between Shenzhen's Futian and North stations, and Hong Kong's West Kowloon rail terminus; you pass through mainland border and customs control before departure on both ends and don't have to get off the train when crossing the border. The first high-speed train to West Kowloon departs Shenzhen North at 6.44am, the last at 10.36pm. One-way 2nd-class tickets cost ¥75.

You can also catch the newer high-speed line in the other direction to Guangzhou South departing from Shenzhen North.

Shenzhen Train Station (深圳站, Shēnzhèn Zhàn; 1 Jianshe Lu, 建设路1号; Ⓜ Line 1 to Luohu, exit E1) is the most convenient station for the adjacent Luohu area, Luohu Bus Station and Luohu Border. **Shenzhen North Train Station** (深圳北站, Shēnzhèn Běi Zhàn; 28 Zhiyuan Zhonglu, 致远中路28号) is the main station for high-speed trains and is 16km north of Luohu, but is conveniently connected to the metro on Lines 4 and 5.

Shenzhen's metro also meets Hong Kong's Mass Transit Railway (MTR) at Luohu (Line 1) and Futian Checkpoint (Line 4). Passengers have to disembark and cross border control on foot.

Normal intercity services to Guangzhou depart from Shenzhen Train Station (¥80, 1½ hours), Futian train station (¥80, 50 minutes) and Shenzhen North station (¥75, 30 minutes).

ⓘ Getting Around

Around 30km northwest of the city centre, Shenzhen's airport is connected by two metro lines, 1 and 11. It takes 70 minutes to get to Luohu for Shenzhen railway station or the crossing into Hong Kong (¥9).

There are around 10 airport buses connecting various parts of Shenzhen. Airport bus Line 2 goes to Shenzhen railway station/Luohu border crossing (¥20, one hour, every 15 minutes, 7.45am to midnight).

A taxi to the airport from Luohu district should cost ¥200.

You can also take a boat from Shenzhen airport's Fuyong Ferry Terminal to Hong Kong and Macau.

Shenzhen has an excellent public transport network, with eight metro lines in operation at the time of research and more in the works. Distance-based fares start from ¥2, with tokens purchased from bilingual machines (you'll need ¥1 coins or ¥5 notes).

One-day travel passes can be bought at metro-station service booths for ¥20, good for both metro and buses. Most bus trips in town cost around ¥1 to ¥2.

Flagfall for taxis is ¥12.50 (¥16 from 11pm to 6am), with a ¥4 fuel surcharge and ¥2.40 for every additional kilometre. For trips out of the city, you can usually negotiate a fee in advance.

Dapeng Fortress 大鹏所城

This Ming dynasty **walled town** (Dàpéng Suǒchéng; Dapeng Town, Longgang District, 龙岗区 大鹏市; adult/student & senior ¥20/10; ⏱10am-6pm; 🚌E26 to Dapeng bus station) was erected 600 years ago to shore up the coastline against marauding Japanese pirates, and later became embroiled in the Opium Wars with the British in the 19th century. Old houses in narrow alleyways (some operating as restaurants and shops), fortress gates, temples, wells and other relics are the main attractions, many spruced up for visitors.

It's a bit of a mission to get here by public transport. From Futian bus station, take bus E26 to Dapeng bus station (¥10, 60km). Change to local bus B753 for the final 4km to the fortress (or take a taxi). The total journey time is around 2½ to three hours from Shenzhen. A taxi (one hour) should cost about ¥400 to ¥500 for the return trip (negotiated in advance).

Zhuhai 珠海

🗹 0756 / POP 1.6 MILLION

Zhuhai is close enough to Macau for a day trip without any maniacal driving. Never too hot or too frosty, Zhuhai (Zhūhǎi) is the just-right popular Chinese getaway – especially in summer – with plenty of seaside glitz. Yet it remains laid-back, and what helps it really shine is the natural beauty of its gardens and an attractive, relatively clean port.

⊙ Sights

Lover's Road STREET
(情侣路, Qínglǚ Lù) This balmy promenade starts at Gongbei (拱北, Gǒngběi), at the border with Macau, and sweeps north for 28km along the coast, passing some of Zhuhai's most coveted real estate. The section near Tangjia Public Garden is the most beautiful. There are kite and bicycle rentals along the way, and snack booths at night.

Zhuhai

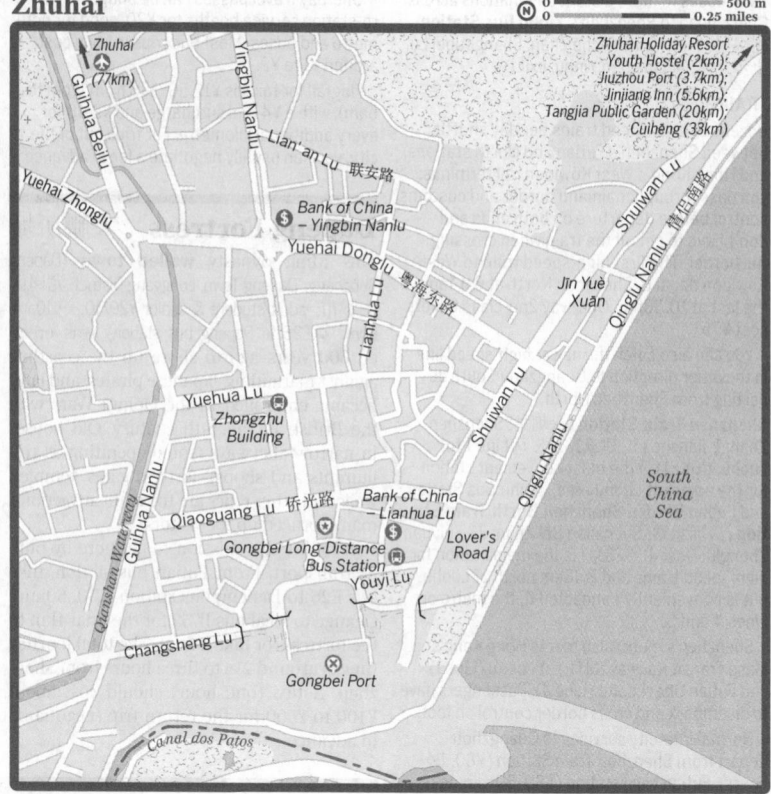

🛏 Sleeping

Zhuhai Holiday Resort Youth Hostel
HOSTEL ¥

(国际青年学生旅馆, Guójì Qīngnián Xuéshēng Lǚguǎn; ☑0756 333 3838; www.zhuhai-holitel. com; 9 Shihua Donglu, 石花东路9号; dm ¥68) Hidden away inside the Zhuhai Holiday Resort (珠海度假村, Zhūhǎi Dùjiàcūn) in Jídà, this hostel has two eight-bed dorms. Take bus 99 to get there.

Jinjiang Inn
INN ¥¥

(锦江之星, Jǐnjiāng Zhīxīng; ☑0756 221 9899; 1058 Fenghuang Nanlu, 凤凰南路1058号; r ¥225-410; ❋❓) The best of several branches in Zhuhai, this one is 50m from Lover's Road, and 300m from Wanzaisha Sq (湾仔沙广场, Wānzǐshā Guǎngchǎng). Rooms are bright and clean, though those facing the street can be a tad noisy. Not all staff members speak English, but they're helpful and courteous. A reliable and affordable option.

🍴 Eating & Drinking

Gongbei (拱北, Gǒngběi) near the Macau border has restaurants, bars and street hawkers.

The Garden
INTERNATIONAL ¥

(健康园餐饮, Jiànkāngyuán Cānyǐn; ☑0756 830 5190; www.thegarden.com.cn; Unit 3115, New Century Plaza, 376 Changsheng Lu, 昌盛路376号新世纪广场3115号; mains ¥40-68; ⊘10.30am-10.30pm; ❋❓) If you're craving a break from Chinese food, the Garden might please you with some international bistro favourites, such as Greek feta salad, lasagne, good steaks and salmon, couscous and a nice selection of wines.

Jīn Yuè Xuān
DIM SUM ¥¥

(金悦轩; ☑0756 813 3133; 1st-3rd fl, Block B, Rihua Commercial Sq, 265 Qinglu Nanlu, 情侣南路265号日华商业广场; meals ¥100-130; ⊘9am-10pm) For some of the best dim sum and Cantonese cuisine in Zhuhai, head to this elegant restaurant before 11am to secure a table.

☆ Entertainment

Zhuhai Live Bar LIVE MUSIC
(珠海現場酒吧, Zhūhǎi Xiànchǎng Jiǔbā; ☑0756
3352 580; 45 Jidayuan Linlu, 吉大园林路45号;
☉7pm-late) A dive bar that hosts local and
international gigs nightly from 9pm within
its graffitied walls. The music can be pop,
rock and everything in between. It's across
the road from Xinhai Building (信海大厦,
Xìnhǎi Dàxià), between Pingan Insurance
Building (平安保险, Píngān Bǎoxiǎn) and
Chunxing Restaurant (春兴酒家, Chūnxīng
Jiǔjiā). Get here by bus 23 or 43.

ℹ Information

Visas (¥168 for most nationalities, ¥304 for
Brits) valid for three days are available at the
border (open 8.30am to 12.15pm, 1pm to 6.15pm
and 7pm to 10.30pm). US citizens must buy a
visa in advance in Macau or Hong Kong.

Visa extensions can be arranged at the **Public
Security Bureau** (PSB; 公安局, Gōng'ānjú;
☑0756 888 5277; 1038 Yingbin Nanlu, 迎宾南
路1038号).

Bank of China (中国银行, Zhōngguó Yínháng;
cnr Yingbin Nanlu & Yuehai Donglu; ☉9am-
5.30pm Mon-Fri, to 4pm Sat & Sun) has another
branch on **Lianhua Lu** (中国银行, Zhōngguó
Yínháng; Lianhua Lu; ☉9am-5.30pm Mon-Fri, to
4pm Sat & Sun).

ℹ Getting There & Away

AIR

Zhuhai Jinwan Airport (珠海金湾机场;
☑0756 777 8888; www.zhairport.com), 45km
southwest of the centre, serves various destinations in China, including Beijing, Shanghai and
Chengdu. An expansion in 2019 has equipped
the airport for new flights to Hong Kong.

BOAT

Hong Kong–bound jetcats leave from **Jiuzhou
Port** (九州港, Jiǔzhōu Gǎng; ☑0756 333 3359)
for China Ferry Terminal, Kowloon (¥175, 70
minutes, six daily, 8am to 5pm), Hong Kong
International Airport (¥290, one hour, 9.30am,
12.40pm, 3.30pm and 6.30pm) and Hong
Kong–Macau Ferry Terminal, Central (¥150, 70
minutes, hourly, 8am to 9.30pm).

Ferries leave Jiuzhou Port for Shenzhen's Shekou Port (p610) (¥150, one hour, every 30 minutes, 8am to 9.30pm); ferries leave Shekou for
Jiuzhou every 30 minutes (7.30am to 9.30pm).

Local buses 3, 4, 12, 23, 25 and 26 go to Jiuzhou Port.

BUS

Gongbei Long-Distance Bus Station (拱北汽
车客运站, Gǒngběi Qìchē Kèyùn Zhàn; ☑0756
888 5218; Lianhua Lu) at **Gongbei Port** (拱北码
头, Gǒngběi Mǎtóu) runs regular buses between
6am and 9.30pm, including the following:

Foshan ¥84, three hours, every 30 to 60 minutes
Guangzhou ¥60, two hours, frequent
Kaiping ¥60, 2½ to three hours, every 40
minutes
Shantou ¥180, 5½ hours, six daily
Shenzhen ¥80, three hours, every 30 minutes
Zhaoqing ¥100, 3½ hours, 13 daily

LIGHT RAIL

Guangzhou–Zhuhai Light Rail (广珠城轨,
Guǎng Zhū Chéngguǐ; ☑0756 9510 5105)
connects Zhuhai North station (珠海北站; from
the north exit) and Guangzhou South station
(¥70, one hour, frequent). Zhuhai North station
can be reached by buses K1, 3A and 998.

ℹ Getting Around

An airport shuttle bus runs between Zhuhai Jinwan Airport and the city centre (¥25 to ¥30, 50
to 70 minutes, every 30 to 60 minutes, 7.30am
to 6pm) along five different routes in both directions. The most popular end destinations are
Jiuzhou Port and the **Zhongzhu Building** (中珠
大厦, Zhōngzhū Dàshà; cnr Yuehua Lu & Yingbin
Nanlu). A taxi to the centre costs about ¥150.

Flagfall for taxis is ¥10 for the first 3km, then
¥0.60 for each additional 250m.

Chaozhou 潮州

☑0768 / POP 2.7 MILLION
Charming Chaozhou (Cháozhōu) was once a
thriving trading and cultural hub in southern China, rivalling Guangzhou. Today it
still preserves its distinct dialect, cuisine
and opera. Chaozhou is best appreciated at
a leisurely pace, so do consider spending a
night here.

Paifang Jie (牌坊街, Street of Memorial
Arches), running 1948m from north to south
in the old quarter, has signage to the main
sights and is a good place to orient yourself.
It's made up of Taiping Lu (太平路; 1742m)
and Dongmen Jie (东门街; 206m).

◉ Sights

Sights abound in Chaozhou but admission
charges can add up. Before you go sightseeing, buy a combo ticket (¥80) from **Jinlong
Travel Service** (金龙旅行社, Jīnlóng Lǚxíngshè; ☑0768 222 1437; 39 Huangcheng Nanlu;
☉9am-5.30pm), located across Huangcheng
Nanlu from the southern entrance of Street
of Memorial Arches. Tickets are good for
two days and cover six or seven sights.

Chaozhou

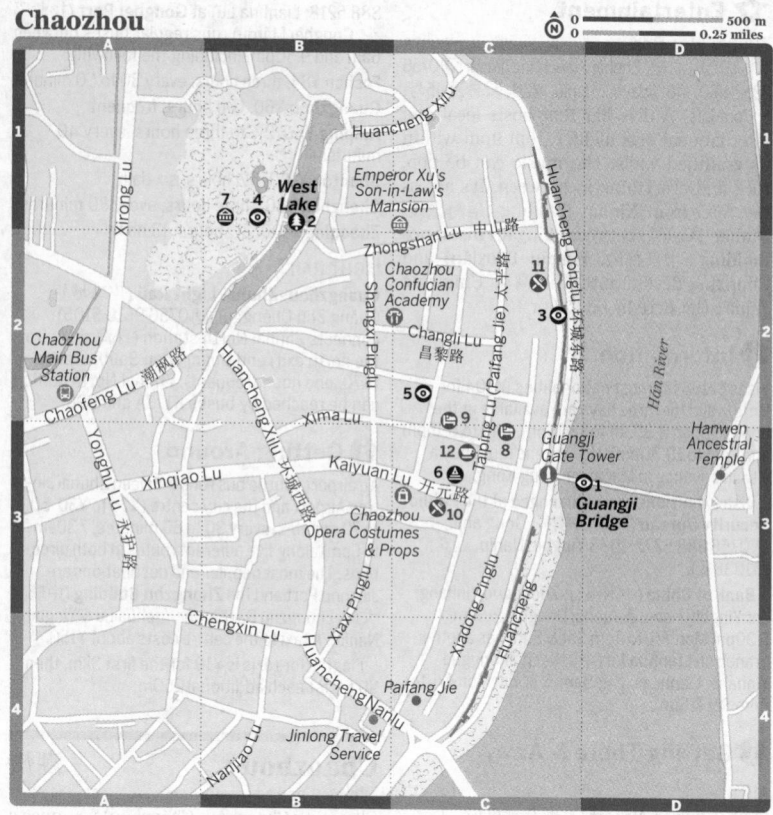

Chaozhou

◎ Top Sights
1 Guangji Bridge	D3
2 West Lake	B1

◎ Sights
3 Chaozhou City Wall	C2
4 Hanbi Building	B1
5 Jilue Huang Temple	C2
6 Kaiyuan Temple	C3
7 Phoenix Building	B1

☰ Sleeping
8 Fucheng Inn	C3
9 Zaiyang Inn	C2

⊗ Eating
10 Lianhua Vegetarian	C3
11 Zheng's Private Kitchen	C2

⊕ Drinking & Nightlife
12 Pinyu Teahouse	C3

★ **West Lake**　　　　　　　　　　PARK
(西湖, Xīhú; ☎ 0768 222 0731; Huancheng Xilu, 环
城西路; ⊙8am-11pm) **FREE** The moat of ancient Chaozhou is a lake inside a park well
loved by locals. Around the lake are a few
notable buildings. **Hanbi Building** (涵碧楼,
Hánbì Lóu; ⊙9am-5pm Tue-Sun) served as a military office during anti-warlord expeditions in
1925. Sitting on a knoll is **Phoenix Building**
(凤楼, Fènglóu; ⊙6am-6pm) **FREE**, with its

bird-like shape, iron moongate, gourd-shaped
ceiling openings, and quirky interior spaces
formed by the fowl's anatomy.

★ **Guangji Bridge**　　　　　　　BRIDGE
(广济桥, Guǎngjǐ Qiáo; ☎ 0768 222 2683; ¥20;
⊙10am-5.30pm Mon-Fri, from 9am Sat & Sun)
Originally a 12th-century pontoon bridge
with 86 boats straddling the Hán River,
Guangji Bridge suffered repeated destruction
over the centuries. The current version is a

brilliant, faux-ancient passageway with 18 wooden boats hooked up afresh every morning and 24 stone piers topped with pagodas.

A ticket allows you one crossing. If you want to come back, remember to tell the staff 'I want to come back' (我要回来, 'wǒyào huílai') before leaving the bridge.

Jilue Huang Temple   TEMPLE
(己略黄公祠, Jǐluè Huánggōngcí; ☑ 0768 225 1318; 2 Tie Xiang, Yian Lu; ¥10; ◐ 8.30am-5pm) The highlights here are the ancient Chaozhou woodcarvings decorating the walls and thresholds – most single pieces took a decade to complete. The art form is famous for its rich and subtle details, intricate designs and exquisite craftsmanship. Emerging 1000 years ago, it flourished during the Qing dynasty, which was also when this small temple (1887) was built. It's a short walk from Paifang Jie. No English explanations.

Kaiyuan Temple   BUDDHIST SITE
(开元寺, Kāiyuán Sì; ☑ 0768 222 5571; 32 Kaiyuan Lu, 开元路32号; ◐ 6am-5.30pm) FREE Built in AD 738, Chaozhou's most famous temple has old bodhi trees and an embarrassment of statues, including one of a 1000-arm Guanyin. Roof tiles can be daubed by a calligraphist (by donation) with your wishes, to be later installed in the complex ceiling.

Chaozhou City Wall   HISTORIC SITE
(潮州古府城墙, Cháozhōu Gǔfǔ Chéngqiáng; ◐ 24hr) FREE The remains of the ancient city wall run alongside and back from the river. You can walk on the top of most sections.

🛏 Sleeping & Eating

The most convenient area to stay to see the sights is near Guangji Bridge and Paifang Jie. The glut of lower-midrange options and chain hotels tend to be further out, near the main bus station or city centre.

Food is generally good in Chaozhou. On Paifang Jie you'll find street food such as some of China's best beef balls with noodles (牛丸粉, niúwán fěn) and oyster omelette (蚝烙, háolào), though prices can be a little more local just a block away. There are also a number of trendy cafes, all offering free wi-fi.

★ Zaiyang Inn   HOTEL ¥
(载阳客栈, Zàiyáng Kèzhàn; ☑ 0768 223 1272; 15 Zaiyang Xiang, Taiping Lu, 太平路, 载阳巷15号; r ¥315-410; 🕾) This classy Qing-style inn with graceful courtyards and antique woodcarvings is *the* place to stay in Chaozhou. Rooms

are small but clean and far from street noise, though wooden-gate-style doors might feel too exposed for some. Prices more than double during holidays. Located in an alley off Paifang Jie; ¥10 by pedicab from the main bus station.

Fucheng Inn   HOTEL ¥
(府城客栈, Fǔchéng Kèzhàn; ☑ 0768 222 8585; 9 Fensi Houxiang, Taiping Lu, 太平路, 分司后巷9号; s/d ¥158/208; 🕾🕾) In an old building inside an alley off Paifang Jie, Fucheng Inn offers decent accommodation and opportunities to meet fellow travellers. Rooms on the ground floor can be noisy. It's ¥10 by pedicab from the main bus station (汽车总站).

★ Lianhua Vegetarian   CHINESE ¥
(莲华素食府, Liánhuá Sùshífǔ; ☑ 0768 223 8033; 9 Kaiyuan Guangchang, 2nd fl, 开元广场9号2楼; mains ¥18-48; ◐ 11am-2pm & 5-8.30pm; ☑) An excellent vegetarian restaurant opposite Kaiyuan Temple with delicacies such as lotus-flowers on skewers. The menu also features Chaozhou specialities, including delightful desserts on the last page.

★ Zheng's Private Kitchen   CHINESE ¥¥
(郑厨私房菜, Zhèngchú Sīfángcài; ☑ 0768 399 1310; 1 Shangdong Pinglu, 上东平路1号; per person ¥50-100; ◐ 11.30am-2.30pm & 5.30-8.30pm) A private kitchen that whips up impressive Chaozhou-style seafood dishes. Ask a Mandarin- or Cantonese-speaking friend to call and book at least a day in advance. Also tell them your budget per person. Shark fin is a speciality here; be sure to mention if you don't want it. Eating shark fin is not recommended, as preparing the dish involves cutting the fin off the shark and then throwing the shark back into the water for it to die a painful and lingering death.

🍷 Drinking & Nightlife

★ Pinyu Teahouse   TEAHOUSE
(品羽茶居, Pǐnyǔ Chájū; ☑ 134 3559 3009; 15 Xima Lu, 西马路15号; per hour ¥30; ◐ 10am-10pm) A lovely place for a tea experience with an English speaker in a minimalist, modern-meets-ancient Chinese teahouse. You pay for a taste test of bottomless different Chaozhou teas and learn the difference between exquisite brews, such as oolong winter versus spring tea, and how to pour tea. If you're lucky, the owner might play one of the Chinese musical instruments on display.

ⓘ Getting There & Away

Services from **Chaozhou Main Bus Station** (潮州汽车总站, Cháozhōu Qìchē Zǒngzhàn; ☏ 0768 220 2552; 2 Chaofeng Lu) include the following:

Guangzhou ¥150, six to seven hours, eight daily (8am to 11.55pm)

Meizhou ¥80, two hours, six daily (8.30am to 3pm)

Raoping ¥19, one hour, 13 daily (6.30am to 6.30pm)

Shanghai ¥389, 20 hours, daily (2.45pm)

Shantou ¥17, one hour, 13 daily (7am to 6.40pm)

Shenzhen ¥120 to ¥140, five hours, five daily (8am to 11pm)

Xiamen ¥100, 3½ hours, four daily (7am to 2.20pm)

Zhuhai ¥140, 9½, two daily (8.30am and 9.10pm)

A taxi to **Chaozhou's train station**, 8km west of the centre, costs about ¥35. Services include Guangzhou (¥91 to ¥167, seven to 8½ hours, 8.27am, 2pm and 11.13pm) and Shantou (¥9.50, 35 minutes, 6.50am, 11.48pm and 8.57pm).

Dàoyùnlóu

China's largest octagonal *tǔlóu* (土楼, Hakka earthen house), **Dàoyùnlóu** (道韵楼; ☏ 0768 835 4633; ¥20; ☉ 8am-6pm) is located in Raoping (饶平, Ráopíng), 53km northeast of Chaozhou. Some 600 villagers once resided in this stunning complex built in 1587; today only 160 remain. Ascend to the upper floors from unit 18 to admire the views and frescoes.

Buses to Raoping (¥22, one hour) leave from Chaozhou Main Bus Station. Change to a bus to the village of Sānráo (三饶镇; ¥13) in Raoping, another 50km away. From there, motor-rickshaws will take you to Dàoyùnlóu (¥5, 10 minutes).

At the time of research the building was being partially renovated without word of when things would be completely open. Call ahead to see if they are receiving visitors.

Shantou   汕头

☏ 0754 / POP 4.9 MILLION

If you like history, the port town of Shantou (Shàntóu) has a couple of interesting sites on its outskirts that can be covered on a day trip from Chaozhou. The subtropical climate and beaches add a marine vibe to the otherwise industrial city.

Sitting atop **Tashan Park** (塔山风景区, Tǎshānfēngjǐngqū), 25km north of Shantou's city centre, the **Cultural Revolution Museum** (文革博物馆, Wēngé Bówùguǎn; ¥10; ☉ 9.30am-5.30pm) is the only museum in China that honours the victims of the Cultural Revolution. Names and inscriptions are engraved on the walls. Take eastbound bus 102 from the long-distance bus station to Tǎshān Lùkǒu (塔山路口). After the 45-minute ride, cross the road and walk 800m to the park entrance, then another 3.5km uphill (take the path on the left).

Chen Cihong Memorial Home (陈慈黉故居, Chén Cíhóng Gùjū; ☏ 0754 8578 6955; Qian Mei Cun, Longdou, 隆都镇前美村; ¥40; ☉ 8.30am-5.30pm) is an attractive complex was built by a businessman who made his fortune in Thailand in the 19th century. He had the region's best raw materials shipped here and assembled in imaginative ways that incorporated Asian, Western and Moorish motifs. Board the northbound bus 103 from People's Square (eastern edge) in Shantou. The hour-long ride north will cost you ¥7.

It is more pleasant to stay in the old town of Chaozhou, but if you do want more than a day trip in Shantou, there are perfectly fine accommodation options, with chain hotels near the bus stations, starting from ¥100.

Buses run from Chaozhou (¥18, one hour, 13 daily, 7am to 6.40pm). Shantou's main bus station and CTS bus station run buses every 30 minutes to an hour to Chaozhou (¥17, one hour, 8.20am to 4.10pm), Guangzhou (¥110 to ¥120, 4½ to 5½ hours, 6.40am to 11pm) and Meizhou (¥75 to ¥90, 2½ hours, 6.20am and 5pm).

Meizhou   梅州

☏ 0753 / POP 5 MILLION

Meizhou (Méizhōu), populated by the Hakka (客家; Kèjiā in Mandarin) people, is home to China's largest cluster of 'coiled dragon houses' or *wéilóngwū* (围龙屋). Specific to the Hakka, these are dwellings arranged in a horseshoe shape evocative of a dragon napping at the foot of a mountain. You'll also see *tǔlóu* (roundhouses) dotting the fields like mysterious flying saucers, and a jumble of other architectural treasures.

Meizhou's sleepy **Old Street** (梅州老街, Méizhōu Lǎojiē; Lingfeng Lu, 凌风路) covers four blocks on Lingfeng Lu. There's not much to see by way of building design, but there are traditional industries that cannot be found elsewhere producing fishing implements, funereal and wedding accessories, and more. Walk through the vehicular passage in the brown building opposite Huáqiáo Dàxià (華僑大廈) at 12 Jiangbian Lu (江边路) and you'll see it.

◉ Sights

Hakka Park PARK
(客家公园, Kèjiā Gōngyuán; 2 Dongshan Dadao, 东山大道2号; ⊙Xianqin Bldg 8.30am-5.10pm, Dafu Bldg 8.30-11.30am & 2-5.30pm; 🚌1, 6) Pebbled paths and a willow-fringed pond make this small park on the north bank of the Meijiang River a delight to stroll around in. The **Hakka Museum** (客家博物馆, Kèjiā Bówùguǎn; ☑0753 225 8830; ⊙9am-5.30pm Tue-Sun) FREE here offers a quick warm-up to the culture of Hakkaland, and there are a couple of interesting 1930s buildings – Xianqin Building (先勤樓, Xiānqínlóu), a courtyard-style Hakka house; and the East–West hybrid Dafu Building (達夫樓, Dáfūlóu), which evokes a pseudo-Western train terminal drawn by Japanese animator Miyazaki.

The **Huang Zunxian Memorial** (黄遵宪纪念馆, Huáng Zūnxiàn Jiniànguǎn; ⊙9am-5pm) FREE is a famous Qing dynasty writer's home.

Meizhou Thousand Buddha Pagoda TEMPLE
(梅州千佛塔寺, Méizhōu Qiān Fó Tǎsì; ☑0753 229 0362; www.qianfotasi.com; Xuezi Dadao Dong, Meijiang Qu, 梅江区学子大道东; ⊙7am-6pm; 🚌20 to terminus, or 6 to Gangbei) FREE Cast in AD 965, there are indeed 1000 buddha statues (250 on each side) of varying sizes on the iron pagoda that sits on a 36m-high tower. The complex itself surprises with each turn as it takes you through an ascending journey of white, columned temples, statues built into a faux cliff, long, open corridors, bridges and finally the towering pagoda and (hazy) views across Meizhou. The complex emphasises gold and colour, reminiscent of Thai temples. A taxi here costs about ¥35.

Nankou Village VILLAGE
(南口镇, Nánkǒu Zhèn) This quiet village about 17km west of Meizhou is where you'll see fine examples of *wéilóngwū*, dwellings nestled between paddy fields and the hills, like dragons in repose. If you make your way to the back of Dōnghuá Lú (东华卢) and Déxīn Táng (德馨堂), you'll see rooms arranged in a semi-circle on an undulating slope, like the coiled body of a dragon. Another of the old houses, Nánhuá Yòulú (南华又庐) charges an admission of ¥12.

Bus 9 from Meizhou's local bus terminal and buses to Xìngníng (兴宁; ¥15, every 20 minutes) from Meizhou's main bus station go to Nankou. Once you get off, walk 1km to the village entrance. The last bus back departs at 4.30pm. A one-way taxi ride costs around ¥35.

🛏 Sleeping & Eating

The local speciality is wok-tossed Hakka noodles (腌面, *yānmiàn*) smothered in minced pork, resembling spaghetti Bolognese. You'll find stalls all over town dishing up the noodles from 9pm long into the night.

Jinjiang Inn HOTEL$
(锦江之星旅馆, Jǐnjiāng Zhīxīng Lǚguǎn; ☑0753 218 9999; www.jinjianginns.com; 88 Binfang Dadao, 彬芳大道88号; d¥156-263; ❄️📶) Near the city centre and a short walk from the Jiangnan bus station south of the river. Modern rooms are warm in mood and tone and come with movies on demand, strong wi-fi, large comfy beds and small but spotless bathrooms. A taxi from the train station costs ¥20.

Royal Classic Hotel HOTEL$$
(皇家名典酒店, Huángjiā Míngdiǎn Jiǔdiàn; ☑0753 867 7777; 35 Dongmen Lu, 东门路35号; r¥263-1278, ste¥1888-2888; 🅿️📶) This glitzy Hong Kong–owned hotel is the tallest building around and has clean, quiet rooms, with wide, comfortable beds. Lifts can only be activated with guest room card-keys, which makes it feel safe. The extravagant breakfast buffet (¥50 per person) in the revolving restaurant offers a good selection of local delicacies.

Weilong Coiled Dragon House Restaurant HAKKA$
(围龙屋星园酒家, Wéilóng Wūxīngyuán Jiǔjiā; ☑0753 233 1315; 41 Fuqi Lu, 富奇路190号; mains ¥33-120; ⊙9.30am-2.30pm & 5-9.30pm) From inside a maze-like 19th-century Hakka house, this atmospheric eatery serves local dishes such as salt-baked chicken (盐焗鸡, *yánjú jī*; ¥58) and pork braised with preserved vegetables (梅菜扣肉, *méicài kòuròu*; ¥48). The manager speaks English. A taxi here from Meizhou centre costs ¥15.

Dabu Handmade Noodles NOODLES$
(大埔手工面馆, Dàbù Shǒugōng Miànguǎn; ☑1598 648 3326; 99-9 Bingfang Dadao Nan, 彬芳大道99-9号; soup ¥5, noodles ¥8-15; ⊙6.30am-2pm & 5pm-2am) This neighbourhood shop whips up al dente Hakka tossed noodles (腌面, *yānmiàn*) and pig-innards soup (三及第汤, *sānjídì tāng*). The strands also come stir-fried (炒面, *chǎomiàn*). Bus 4, which runs from Meizhou train station, a 15-minute walk away, stops here; disembark at Méiyuán Xīncūn (梅园新村).

ⓘ Getting There & Away

Meizhou's airport (梅县机场, Méixiàn Jīchǎng), 4km south of town, has direct flights to Guangzhou (¥700, one hour, daily) and Taichung (¥1500, 1½ hours, daily) in Taiwan.

Meizhou has two bus stations and a **local bus terminal** (市公共汽车总站, Shì Gōnggòng Qìchēzhàn; cnr Meijiang Dadao & Xinzhong Lu, 梅江大道新中路路口): the **Main Bus Station** (梅州粤运汽车总站, Méizhōu Yuèyùn Qìchē Zǒngzhàn; ☐ 0753 222 2427; 2 Meishi Lu, 梅石路2号), north of the river, and **Jiangnan Bus Station** (梅州粤运江南汽车站, Meizhou Yueyun Jiangnan Qiche Zhan; ☐ 0753 226 9568; 38 Binfang Dadao, 彬芳大道38号) to the south. Most buses to Meizhou drop you off at the former. Destinations include the following:

Chaozhou ¥80, two hours, six daily (10.20am to 3.45pm)

Chaoyang ¥28, 1½ hours, three daily (8.15am, 11.35am and 2.30pm)

Guangzhou, ¥165 to ¥193, five hours, 15 daily (7am to 10.30pm)

Hong Kong ¥280, eight hours, two daily (7.40am and 2.40pm)

Shantou ¥69, 2½ hours, 13 daily (8am to 5.20pm)

Shenzhen ¥178 to ¥187, six hours, 10 daily (6.45am to 5pm)

Yongding ¥49, three hours, two daily (6am and 12.45pm)

The train station, south of town, has four daily trains to Guangzhou (¥65 to ¥117, 5¾ to 6¼ hours, 12.12am, 10.30am, 4.48pm and 10.53pm) and two early trains to Yǒngdìng (¥19 to ¥32, two hours, 2.30am and 3.14am).

ⓘ Getting Around

A taxi ride into Meizhou town centre from the airport costs about ¥20. Buses 3 and 11 also go into town.

Bus 6 links the airport and train station to both bus stations. Anywhere within the city by taxi should cost no more than ¥25.

Most sights are scattered in different villages, and almost inaccessible by public transport, so it makes more sense to hire a taxi for a day. Expect to pay about ¥450.

Dabu 大埔

☑ 0753 / POP 540,000

Dabu (Dàbù) sits on the border with Fujian, in the easternmost part of Guangdong, about 89km from downtown Meizhou. It's encircled by mountains and rivers, which means beautiful natural scenery and nicely preserved old towns.

Downtown Dabu is a typical small city of monotone, low-level buildings, where the wildest entertainment is locals playing Russian poker on the street, but there is no shortage of food and facilities, making it a useful base or crossroad for day trips to surrounding areas.

Many people make day trips from Meizhou, but if you find yourself stuck, **Ruijin Hotel** (瑞锦酒店, Ruìjǐn Jiǔdiàn; ☐ 0753 518 5688; www.ruijin-hotel.com; 2nd St, Long Shan, Neihuan Xilu, 内环西路龙山二街; r ¥888-988, ste ¥1688-1988; ❋◎✿☎) is a great place to stay. The hotel is a 20-minute walk from Dabu bus station (大埔汽车客运站, Dàbù Qìchē Kèyùn Zhàn). Take the station's southern exit and turn left to Neihuan Xilu (内环西路), then walk three blocks south. The hotel will be on your right.

Your best bet for food are the tiny eateries on **Dabu Gourmet Street** (大埔美食街, Dàbù Měishì Jiē; Huliao Tongyen Lu; snacks ¥2-12; ⊙ 8am-5pm). Comb its 330m for Dabu and Hakka snacks such as pancakes (薄饼, *báobǐng*) and bamboo-shoot dumplings (笋板, *sǔnbǎn*).

ⓘ Getting There & Away

Dabu is sometimes written as 'Dapu' on bus or train timetables.

Meizhou has buses to Dabu from Jiangnan bus station every 30 minutes (¥24, one hour).

Buses head daily from **Dabu Long-Distance Bus Station** (大埔汽车客运站, Dàbù Qìchē Kèyùn Zhàn) to the following:

Chaozhou ¥67, three hours, one daily (8.10am)

Chayang ¥5, 30 minutes, two daily (5pm and 5.30pm)

Guangzhou ¥238, 6½ hours, eight daily (7.30am to 7.30pm)

Meizhou ¥24, one hour, frequent

Shantou ¥78, three hours, two daily (6.50am & 12.30pm)

Shenzhen ¥226, six hours, five daily (8.20am to 3.30pm)

Xiamen ¥105, 4½ hours, one daily (6.40am)

Meizhou (¥25, one hour, 2.30am and 1.24pm) has two trains, one very early, daily to Dabu. Return trains to Meizhou leave at 3.47pm and 11.10pm.

Chayang Old Town 茶阳古镇

☑ 0753 / POP 55,000

People still take long siestas in lazy Chayang (Cháyáng Gǔzhèn), 27km from downtown Dabu County. Its old streets (老街, *lǎojiē*) with pillared arcades are nice to lose yourself in for a couple of hours.

Beautiful **Xuan Villa** (旋庐, Xuánlú; 115 Dahua Lu, 大华路115号) was built in 1936 by a wealthy Malaysian-Chinese member of a secret society tied to Sun Yatsen. Parts of the building doubled up as an air-raid shelter. If the owners let you in, you'll see crumbling but elegant staircases and sweeping balconies with views of tea fields.

This weather-beaten, three-storey **Soviet Department Store Building** (百货大楼, Bǎihuò Dàlóu; Shengli Lu, 胜利路), just opposite Chayang Guesthouse (茶陽賓館, Cháyáng Bīnguǎn), was a department store built in the 1950s with Soviet funds. Patches of yellow paint still cling onto its facade, and you can make out Mao-era slogans on its red pillars.

The handsome granite **Memorial Arch of the Father & Son Graduates** (父子进士牌坊, Fùzǐ Jìnshì Páifāng; Dabu High School, Jinshan Lu, 大埔中学, 金山路, 茶阳镇) from 1610 stands before a school. The arch was set up by the Ming government to commemorate a father and son who were both successful candidates in the imperial exams.

Most people just pass through Chayang and stay in Meizhou, but if you get stuck there are a few simple budget options in the south of town, and a clean business hotel at the roundabout (there's only one) on the northern side with rooms for around ¥100.

There are noodle joints, snacks and even a more upmarket seafood option, but for more variety head to Meizhou or Chaozhou.

Buses run to Chayang from Dabu (¥5, 30 minutes, 5pm and 5.30pm) and Jiangnan bus station in Meizhou (¥28, 1½ hours, half-hourly, 7.10am to 6pm).

Baihou Old Town 百侯镇

☑ 0753 / POP 30,300

Scenic Baihou (Bǎihóu Zhèn) is known for its Qing dynasty buildings. These were the stately residences and public spaces of the Yang (楊) family, a family known for the number of scholars and government officials it nurtured. Baihou literally means 'a hundred noblemen'.

Buildings with a flamboyant hybrid style tend to cluster around the southern end of town, while ancestral halls and village houses are in the north. Between them are winding paths, peanut vines, longan and wampi trees, and a huge lily pond.

GUANGDONG'S LARGEST CIRCULAR EARTHEN CASTLE

The majestic 400-year-old 'house of calyx', 120km east of Meizhou, is the largest circular **earthen castle** (花萼楼; 151 Xiang Dao, 乡道151; admission ¥10; ⊗ 9am-4pm) in Guangdong. It comes complete with three rings and stone walls more than 1m thick. There's no public transport to Huā'è Lóu. A taxi from Dabu costs ¥100 and takes about an hour to travel 36km on neglected hilly roads.

Lack of upkeep and old age (it dates from the early 18th century) mean **Qinan Villa** (企南軒, Qǐnán Xuān) looks a bit like a princeling-turned-pauper. The stone carvings around its elegant arches and the terraces fringed with urn-shaped balusters are now overgrown with black moss and weeds. The villa was built as a study with 27 rooms in the early decades of the Qing dynasty.

Inhabited by the third and fourth generations of the founder, a pharmaceutical merchant, **Zhaoqing Hall** (肇庆堂, Zhàoqìng Táng; ¥30; ⊗ 8.30am-noon & 2-5pm) is a balmy courtyard residence (c 1914) featuring stone, wood and ceramic carvings, and stained-glass windows from Italy. The stately two-storey structure in front of it was the study quarters of the younger members of the family.

An eye-catching, early-20th-century mansion, the **Haiyuan Inn** (海源客栈, Hǎiyuán Kèzhàn) combines Southeast Asian features, Western details and the attributes of a hakka (走马楼; zǒumǎ lóu), a two-storey residence with a wide wooden corridor that keeps the rooms safe and dry.

Although there is loads of potential for a tourist town, options for sleeping here are virtually nil as most people still move on and stay in nearby Meizhou.

There are a handful of simple places to eat in the Baihou Tourist Area (百侯旅游区, Bǎihóu Lǚyóu Qū) and around the bus station (百侯客运站, Bǎihóu Kèyùn Zhàn), 1km north.

All southbound buses from Dabu pass through Baihou (¥7). Tell the driver you want to get off at Baihou Tourist Area (百侯旅游区, Bǎihóu Lǚyóu Qū). From Dabu, it's 20 minutes (11km).

Hainan

POP 9 MILLION

Best Places to Eat

➡ A Bo Po Salt Roasted Chicken (p625)

➡ Haikou Qilou Snack Street (p625)

➡ Wàngjiǎo Měishí Diàn (p634)

➡ Sea Story (p631)

➡ Banqiao Seafood Market (p625)

Best Places to Stay

➡ Haikou Banana Youth Hostel (p624)

➡ Qionghai Boao Xishe Guesthouse (p630)

➡ Le Méridien Resort & Spa (p631)

➡ Narada Resort & Spa (p629)

Why Go?

China's largest tropical island boasts all the balmy weather, coconut palms and gold-sand beaches you could ask for. Down at Sanya it's see-and-be-seen on the boardwalks or you can escape altogether at some of Asia's top luxury resorts. Thatched huts and banana pancakes haven't popped up anywhere yet, but there's a hint of hipness coming from the east-coast beachside towns, and the budding surf scene is helping to spread the gospel of chill out.

Money is pouring into Hainan (海南, Hǎinán) these days to ramp up the luxury quotient. You can cruise on the high-speed rail, but cycling is still the better way to get around. When you've had enough of a lathering on the coast, the cool central highlands are an ideal place to be on two wheels. The good roads, knockout mountain views, and concentration of Li and Miao, the island's first settlers, give the region an appealing distinction from the lowlands.

When to Go
Sanya (Dadonghai)

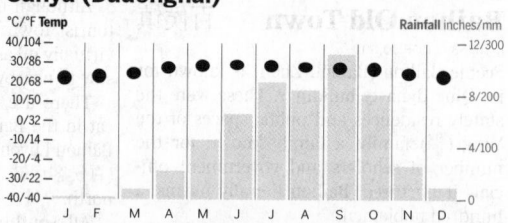

Apr–Sep Low season is hot, hot, hot, but ideal for hotel bargains.

Oct–Mar Cool dry months are perfect for cycling under the blue South China sky, but it's high season for accommodation.

Nov–Jan Winter winds blow in the island's best surfing season.

History

Until the economic boom of the last 30 years, Hainan had been a backwater of the Chinese empire. The first Han settlements appeared on the coast almost 2000 years ago, but the island was largely ignored by a series of dynasties, and was known as the 'tail of the dragon', 'the gate of hell' and a place best used as a repository for occasional high-profile exiles such as the poet Su Dongpo and the official Hai Rui.

More recently, China's first communist cell was formed here in the 1920s and the island was heavily bombarded and then occupied by

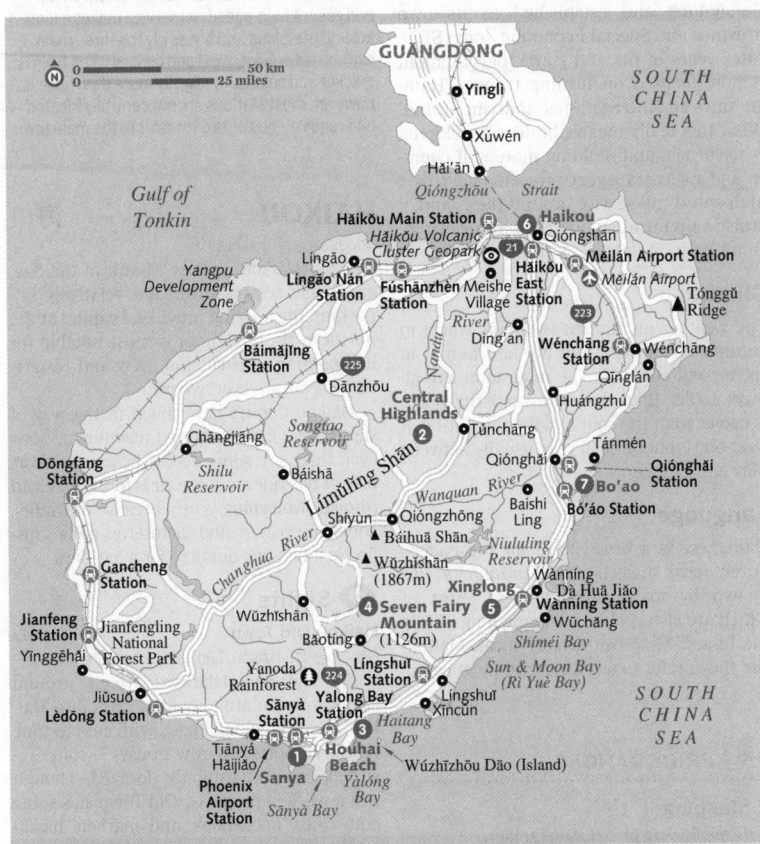

Hainan Highlights

1 Sanya (p632) Soaking up the sun, sand and cocktails at China's top seaside resort; the beaches here are probably the best in China.

2 Central Highlands (p628) Cycling through the island's mountainous spine, home of the Li and Miao ethnic groups.

3 Houhai Beach (p633) Taking surfing lessons and

chilling out at laid-back guesthouses right on the beach.

4 Seven Fairy Mountain (p628) Hiking and soaking in hot springs surrounded by rainforest.

5 Xinglong (p632) Getting a whiff of Hainan's unexpected coffee scene in Xinglong and enjoying a strong brew with locals.

6 Banqiao Seafood Market (p625) Bargaining for fresh local seafood at one of the most popular seafood markets in Haikou.

7 Bo'ao (p629) Taking in traditional villages and empty beaches – just be sure to avoid it during its major annual economic conference.

the Japanese during WWII. Li and Han Chinese guerrillas waged an effective campaign to harass the Japanese forces but the retaliation was brutal – the Japanese executed a third of the island's male population. Even today resentment over Japanese atrocities lingers among the younger generation.

In 1988 Hainan was taken away from Guangdong and established as its own province and Special Economic Zone (SEZ). After years of fits and starts, development is now focused on turning tropical Hainan into an 'international tourism island'. What this really means, besides developing every beach, and building more golf courses and mega-transport projects (such as a high-speed rail service around the island, a cruise-ship terminal and even a spaceport), is not entirely clear.

Climate

The weather on Hainan is largely warm in autumn and winter, and hot and humid in spring and summer. The mountains are always cooler than the coast, and the north is cooler than the south. Hainan is hit by at least one typhoon each year, usually between May and October.

Language

Hainanese is a broad term for the baker's dozen local dialects of *Hǎinán Mǐn* (it's known by many other names), most of which are also spoken in Guangdong. While the Li and Miao can usually speak Mandarin, they prefer to use their own languages.

ℹ️ PRICE RANGES

Sleeping
The following price ranges refer to a double room with bathroom.

¥ less than ¥200

¥¥ ¥200–600

¥¥¥ more than ¥600

Eating
The following price ranges refer to a main course or meal.

¥ less than ¥30

¥¥ ¥30–100

¥¥¥ more than ¥100

ℹ️ Getting There & Around

Both Haikou and Sanya have international airports. Haikou, the capital city on the island's north coast, is the point of entry for long-distance buses and trains coming from the mainland. And yes, there's no bridge: even trains cross the Qiongzhou Strait on the ferry.

Getting around most of Hainan is both cheap and easy. A high-speed rail service makes a loop around the island and buses ply the three main expressways (east, west and central). The train is quicker and costs only slightly more than buses; however, most stations are not centrally located and require a bus or taxi transfer to the main town.

HAIKOU 海口

📍 0898 / POP 2.2 MILLION

Haikou (Hǎikǒu) means 'Mouth of the Sea', and while sea trade remains relatively important, the buzzing provincial capital at the northern tip of Hainan is most notable for its booming construction. New and restarted projects are everywhere.

Haikou doesn't have much in the way of sights, save for its restored downtown; however, there are some decent beaches a short bike or bus ride away, the air is fresh and clean (though worsening yearly because of traffic), and some visitors find themselves quite satisfied just hanging out here for a few days.

⊙ Sights

Haikou Old Town   AREA
(海口老街, Hǎikǒu Lǎo Jiē; Zhongshan Lu, 中山路) The pedestrianised streets around Zhongshan Lu are a looking glass into Haikou's French colonial past, with cobblestone blocks of porticoed row houses – some restored, some charmingly decayed. Though still a work in progress, 'Old Town' has some cute cafes, bookshops, and markets hawking handicrafts and spices, while down the smaller side streets you can still see active scenes of local life.

Hainan Museum   MUSEUM
(海南省博物馆, Hǎinán Shěng Bówùguǎn; 68 Guoxing Dadao, 国兴大道68号; ⊙9am-5pm Tue-Sun, last admission 4.30pm; 🚌43) **FREE** This modern colossus of a building should be your first stop when you arrive in Hainan. The displays on ethnic minorities, as well as Hainan's 20th-century history, which included fierce resistance against the Japanese and later Nationalists, are particularly informative (and in English too!). The museum is

Haikou

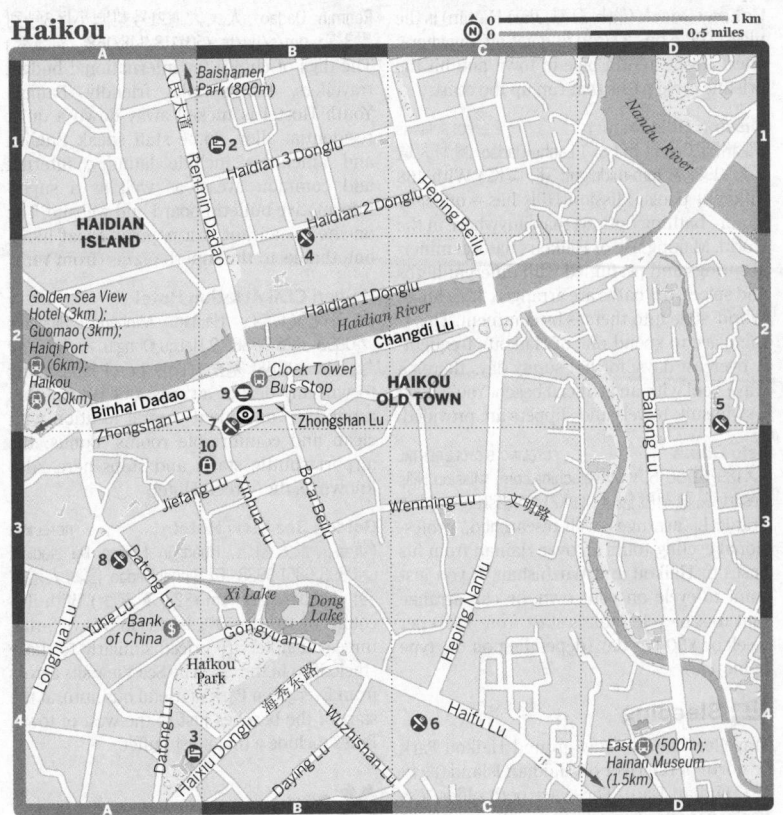

Haikou

◎ Sights
1 Haikou Old Town B2

🛏 Sleeping
2 Haikou Banana Youth Hostel B1
3 Hainan Civil Aviation Hotel A4

✕ Eating
4 A Bo Po Salt Roasted Chicken B2
5 Banqiao Seafood Market D2

6 Carrefour C4
7 Guangfulong Wontons B2
8 Haikou Qilou Snack Street A3

🍷 Drinking & Nightlife
9 Square Out Space Cafe B2

🛍 Shopping
10 Xinhua Bookstore B3

about 2km southeast of Haikou Park, along the river. Passport required.

Five Officials Memorial Temple TEMPLE
(五公祠, Wǔgōng Cí; 169 Haifu Dadao, 海府大道 169号; Oct-Apr ¥20, May-Sep ¥17; ⊗8am-6pm, last entry 5.30pm; 🚌37) Hainan wasn't always a desirable holiday destination. In earlier times it was considered a remote part of the Chinese empire and used as a place of banishment for disgraced court officials. This Ming temple is dedicated to five such officials. Famous Song dynasty poet Su Dongpo, banished to Hainan for his 'radical' writing and beliefs, is commemorated here as well. The temple is about 2km southeast of Haikou Park, a short walk from the east bus station.

🏃 Activities & Tours

A few kilometres west of the city centre is a long stretch of sandy beaches, of which

Holiday Beach (假日海滩, Jiàrì Hǎitān) is the nicest. Take bus 37 (¥2) and get off anywhere; alternatively, rent a bike in town and hit the pristine cycle paths that run up the coast.

Mission Hills Resort
HOT SPRINGS

(观澜湖, Guàn Lán Hú; 1 Lanhu Dadao, 澜湖大道1号; ¥198; ☺1pm-midnight; 🚻; 🚌K2) With 168 different pools, Mission Hills has – officially – more bathing options than anywhere in the world. Making use of Haikou's natural mineral springs and perfumed with different herbs and spices, the baths are arranged 'It's a Small World' style into themes by continent. This is the place to spend one of Haikou's frequently overcast days; for hot sunny days there's a wave pool with an artificial beach. You'll need a swimsuit; towels and slippers are provided.

Velo China
CYCLING, BICYCLE RENTAL

(☎18976175016; www.velochina.com; Mission Hills Resort, 观澜湖度假区; 🚌K2) English-speaking Frank Li arranges well-researched, professional cycling tours all over Hainan from his bases in Haikou and Wuzhishan. If you just want to cycle on your own, he can arrange that too; bicycle rentals start from ¥500 per week or ¥80 per day (depending on the type of bicycle).

🛏 Sleeping

Travellers tend to stay around Haikou Park or north of the river on Haidian Island (海甸岛, Hǎidiàn Dǎo). These are both older, less flashy neighbourhoods (especially compared with the western sections of the city), but all your life-support systems, including banks, food and travel agents, can be found here.

★ Haikou Banana Youth Hostel
HOSTEL ¥

(海口巴纳纳国际青年旅舍, Hǎikǒu Bānànà Qīngnián Lǔshè; ☎0898 6628 6780; www.haikou hostel.com; 3 Dong, 6 Bieshu Liyuan Xiaoqu, 21 Renmin Dadao, 人民大道21号梨园小区6号别墅3栋; dm/s/tw/tr ¥50/118/148/168; 🚻@🛜) The digs of choice for international budget travellers, the simple, friendly Banana Youth Hostel is tucked away down a quiet residential alley. Some staff speak English and amenities include laundry, internet and common areas, as well as a super-informative bulletin board and website. The on-site restaurant is a popular expat hang-out, thanks to the superb pizzas (from ¥45).

Hainan Civil Aviation Hotel
HOTEL ¥

(海南民航宾馆, Hǎinán Mínháng Bīnguǎn; ☎0898 3128 9888; 9 Haixiu Donglu, 海秀东路9号; r from ¥168; 🚻🛜) This hotel isn't going to win any design awards, but it's solid all around: a convenient central location with clean and comfortable rooms. Bonus: the airport shuttle starts and stops here. Also known as the 'Green Hotel'.

Golden Sea View Hotel
HOTEL ¥¥¥

(黄金海景大酒店, Huángjīn Hǎijǐng Dà Jiǔdiàn; ☎0898 6851 9988; 67 Binhai Dadao, 滨海大道67号; r incl breakfast from ¥825; 🅿🚻🛜) With discounts of 40% to 50%, rooms in this well-run, three-star hotel are priced similarly to those stuck deep in the city. The Sea View sits across from Evergreen Park (a useful bus hub), at the start of the beaches just to the west of town. Rates include a breakfast buffet.

🍴 Eating

Haikou is a great place to sample Hainanese cooking. Though much of the city's street-food scene has been, unfortunately, moved into hawker markets following a city-wide 'clean-up' campaign, you can still find barbecue stalls lining up from around 9pm on Haidian 2 Donglu, between Renmin Dadao and Heping Beilu.

ℹ VISA-FREE ENTRY TO HAINAN

Citizens of 59 qualifying countries can gain 30 days of visa-free entry to Hainan if for a visa-waiver is applied for through a registered travel agency or tour operator. You must arrive at either Haikou or Sanya on an international direct flight (so if you transfer in-country you are not eligible). You are not entitled to travel to mainland China on this visa.

Another, less reliable, visa-free method of entering Hainan is the 15-day visa-on-arrival scheme open to travellers from countries with diplomatic relations with China – except for the US and France. Again, it is only valid for entry into Haikou or Sanya on direct international flights. The cost varies between ¥168 and ¥1000, and you'll need this in cash. However, keep in mind that arbitrary approval processes apply here and there are lots of reports of travellers being rejected. You may also encounter difficulty even boarding your flight as ground crew may not be aware of the visa regulations.

HAINAN LOCAL FOOD

Hainan residents are proud of the natural flavours of the meat and produce raised here under blue skies and in red soil mostly free from industrial contamination and, as a result, they tend to cook with a light hand. Rather than vinegar, you'll be given calamansi (a type of citrus) to mix with soy sauce.

The best places to sample local specialities are Haikou Qilou Snack Street and the area around Sanya's No.1 Farmers Market. Dishes to look out for include the following:

Bàoluófěn (抱罗粉) Rice noodles in beef or pork stock and often topped with peanuts; usually found at street stalls.

Dongshan goat (东山羊, *dōng shānyáng*) A black-wool mountain goat fed camellias and orchids, and stewed, roasted or cooked in coconut milk, or used in soups.

Fried ice (炒冰, *chǎobīng*) Blended tropical fruit that is then 'fried' on a cold plate until it turns thick like sorbet.

Hele crab (和乐蟹, *Hélè xiè*) Steamed crab, from Hele near Wanning, served with ginger and vinegar; it's best eaten in autumn.

Jiaji duck (加积鸭, *Jiājī yā*) Steamed duck from Jiaji (the alternative name for Qionghai).

Lingao suckling pig (临高乳猪, *Língāo rǔzhū*) Whole-roasted pig served with its crisp skin intact.

Qīngbǔliáng (清补凉) A sweet coconut soup loaded with any number of fillings, such as fruit, quail eggs, red beans and macaroni; a market staple.

Wenchang chicken (文昌鸡, *Wénchāng jī*) Poached chicken raised on a diet of rice and peanuts.

Haikou Qilou Snack Street   HAINAN ¥

(海口骑楼小吃街, Hǎikǒu Qílóu Xiǎochī Jiē; 2-1 Datong Lu, 大同路2-1号; dishes ¥6-30; ⏰7am-2am) This marvellous colonial arcade is the repository of many of the street vendors swept off the street in the clean-up campaign and is easily the best place to sample local Hainanese dishes. On weekends and busy nights, expect opera and other traditional performances on the stage in the open atrium. There's plenty of seating.

Guangfulong Wontons   DUMPLINGS ¥

(廣福隆馄饨, Guǎngfúlóng Húntun; 107 Daxing Xilu, 大兴西路107号; meals from ¥8; ⏰24hr; ❄) This Haikou institution in Old Town does a brisk business in scalding bowls of wonton soup. A 'small' is plenty filling. There's a picture menu.

★ A Bo Po Salt Roasted Chicken HAINAN ¥¥

(海口美兰阿卜婆女盐焗鸡店, Hǎikǒu Měilán Ā Bo Pó Nǚ Yánjú Jī Diàn; Shop c1-10, Shuicheng Community B, Erdong Lu, 二东路水岸星城b小区c1-10号铺面; chicken from ¥88; ⏰11am-11pm; ❄ 🌐; 🚌18) *Ā bo pó* (阿卜婆) means 'grandma' in Hainanese, though we'd also translate it as 'best chicken ever'. Indeed made by a 70-something grandma, the chicken here is buried in sea salt and baked for four hours, then sealed in plastic to pull in all the juices. Just tear into it with your hands (plastic gloves are provided).

Banqiao Seafood Market   SEAFOOD, MARKET ¥¥

(板桥海鲜广场, Bǎnqiáo Hǎixiān Guǎngchǎng; 8 Banqiao Lu, 板桥路8号; meals per person from ¥30; ⏰4pm-late; 🚌37) For a fresh seafood dinner with lots of noise, smoke and toasting, head to the hectare of tables at the Banqiao Seafood Market, known island-wide. First bargain for the raw ingredients from the market – local oysters for ¥5 or enormous tiger prawns for ¥20 per 100g – and then have one of the restaurants cook it up for you.

Drinking & Nightlife

Guomao (国贸, Guómào) is the newest downtown area, with the flashiest nightlife. Along Hadian 5 Xilu, in front of the south gate of Hainan University, you'll find bars popular with students.

Small stands selling lemon drinks and teas are plentiful. *Liángchá* (凉茶, cool tea) is a little medicinal in taste but locals swear it helps cool the body's fires on a hot day.

Drunk Bear BAR

(白熊酒馆, Báixióng Jiǔguǎn; 111 Daykun Chaye Yuan, Guomao Beilu, 国贸北路大坤茶叶园111号; draught beer ¥40; ⏰5pm-late; 🐾) With half a dozen local craft brews on tap, this Guomao watering hole is a favourite among expats and beer-loving locals alike.

Square Out Space Cafe CAFE

(房外空间, Fángwài Kōngjiān; 3-4F, 68 Zhongshan Lu, 中山路68号3-4楼; coffee/mains from ¥32/36; 🐾) With calming blue and white interiors, and ample windows that let in what breeze there is in Haikou, this charming cafe and art space is a cooling and quiet place to hang out. As well as staging its own musical performances in the evenings, the cafe is also a good place to find out what cultural events, such as concerts and theatre performances, are happening in the city.

🛍 Shopping

Xinhua Bookstore BOOKS

(新华书店, Xīnhuá Shūdiàn; 10 Jiefang Xilu, 解放西路10号; ⏰9am-10pm) Xīnhuá Bookstore has good maps if you are cycling.

ℹ Information

ATMs are plentiful around town.

Bank of China (中国银行, Zhōngguó Yínháng; 10 Datong Lu, 大同路10号; ⏰8.30am-5pm, ATM 24hr) Changes money and travellers cheques.

ℹ Getting There & Away

AIR

Haikou's **Meilan Airport** (美兰国际机场, Měilán Guójì Jīchǎng; www.mlairport.com; 🚌K4), 25km to the east of town, is well connected to most of China's major cities, including Hong Kong and Macau, with international flights to Bangkok, Singapore, Kuala Lumpur and Taipei. Low-season one-way domestic fares are cheap. Destinations include Beijing, Guangzhou and Shanghai.

BUS

Long-distance buses to the mainland depart from **Haiqi Port Bus Station** (海汽港口汽车客运站, Hǎiqì Gǎngkǒu Qìchē Kèyùn Zhàn; 96 Binhai Dadao, 滨海大道96号; 🚌37), far to the west of town. Destinations include the following:

Guangzhou ¥252, 10 hours, hourly from 2pm

Guilin ¥322, 12 hours, one daily (3.30pm)

Nanning ¥280, nine hours, four daily (10.10am, 2.30pm, 4.30pm and 7pm)

Buses from the **east bus station** (汽车东站, Qìchē Dōng Zhàn; 148 Haifu Lu, 海府路148号),

1.5km south of downtown, go to the following destinations:

Qionghai ¥32, 1½ hours, every 20 minutes

Sanya ¥50, 3½ hours, every 30 to 60 minutes

Wenchang ¥21, 1½ hours, every 15 minutes

TRAIN

Haikou Railway Station (海口站, Hǎikǒu Zhàn; Yuehai Dadao, 粤海大道, 🚌37), the main train station, is in the northwest corner of the city. Bus 37 (¥2) connects the train station and the **Clock Tower bus stop** (钟楼, Zhōng Lóu; 20 Changdi Lu, 长堤路20号); for destinations in the southern part of the city, take bus 40 (¥2).

There are four trains daily to/from Guangzhou (hard/soft sleeper ¥261/412, 11 to 14 hours). Buy tickets (¥5 service fee) at the train station.

High-Speed Train

High-speed trains running down the east coast to Sanya mostly start from **Haikou East Railway Station** (海口东站, Hǎikǒu Dōngzhàn; Fengxiang Xilu, 凤翔西路; 🚌K4), in the southeast corner of the city. Trains down the west coast depart from Haikou Railway Station, on the western side.

Trains departing from the east railway station include the following:

Qionghai ¥40, 50 minutes, half-hourly

Sanya ¥100, two hours, half-hourly

Wanning ¥59, 1½ hours, half-hourly

ℹ Getting Around

TO/FROM THE AIRPORT

An airport shuttle bus (¥20, half-hourly, 5.30am to 9.30pm) runs to/from Hainan Civil Aviation Hotel in downtown. Public bus K4 (¥6, regular, 6.30am to 9.30pm) runs down Renmin Dadao, past Banana Youth Hostel, and along Binhai Dadao, stopping at **Evergreen Park** (万绿园, Wànlùyuán; Binhai Dadao, 滨海大道; 🚌37, K4, 3), slightly east of Golden Sea View Hotel.

A taxi costs around ¥80 to downtown; negotiate the price. The high-speed rail also has a stop at the airport; this train will take you to the Haikou East Railway Station.

BUS

Both Haikou's city centre and Haidian Island are easy to get around on foot. The bus system (¥1 to ¥2) is decent, though it often takes transfers to get around. Key bus hubs include Clock Tower and Evergreen Park, both serviced by the handy bus 37.

Most tourist buses depart from Evergreen Park, while some also leave from a stop near **Baishamen Park** (白沙门公园, Báishāmén Gōngyuán; Renmin Dadao, 人民大道; 🚌K4) on Haidian Island. For the Haikou Volcanic Cluster

CYCLING HAINAN

Hainan is a great destination for recreational touring. You're rarely more than an hour from a village with food and water, and never more than a few hours from a town with a decent hotel. At the same time, you'll find most of your riding is out in nature or through pretty farming valleys, not urban sprawl. Roads, even to minor villages, are generally in excellent condition (and new ones are being created regularly). Preparation time for a tour can be minimal.

Around Haikou

A network of narrow, paved lanes connects the picturesque villages around the Haikou Volcanic Cluster Geopark, which are perfect for a day or afternoon trip. Velo China (p624) runs short, one- to three-hour cycling tours (free with the cost of bicycle rental, which starts at ¥80) that leave daily at 9am and 3pm from in front of the Mission Hills Resort (p624); for reservations call Frank on 189 7617 5016.

East Coast

The most popular of the multiday routes, because it is largely flat, runs from Haikou to Sanya along the eastern highway, covering about 300km. The main road runs somewhat inland, though, so if you want to strike out along the coast, you'll need a good map to follow the small roads that run to the seaside villages.

Central Highlands

This is the most spectacular ride, if you have the stamina for it. The central highway, which runs 300km from Haikou to Sanya via Wuzhishan, has a good shoulder most of the way, and allows for endless side trips up small country roads and stops in tiny villages. The major towns in this area are **Tunchang** (屯昌, Túnchāng) and **Qiongzhong** (琼中, Qióngzhōng), the latter a major settlement for the Miao.

After a day riding through the lush Tunchang county valley, the route climbs into some fine hill country around Shiyun (什运, Shíyùn). The village, 32km southwest of Qiongzhong, sits on a grassy shelf above a river and is worth a look around. Local cyclists recommend the 42km side trip from here up a wooded canyon to Baisha (白沙, Báishā).

After Shiyun you can look forward to a long climb (at least 10km), followed by a long fast descent into Wuzhishan. If you are continuing on to Sanya, the road is one long, steep downhill after the turn-off to Baoting.

Bicycle Rental

If you're not bringing your own wheels, you can rent decent-quality mountain bikes at Haikou Banana Youth Hostel (p624) from ¥30 a day. The hostel's website has detailed information on cycling Hainan. Velo China (p624) also rents mountain and touring bicycles (from ¥80/500 per day/week) and can arrange custom tours with English-speaking guides. Six-day tours, which include hotel accommodation, bicycle rental and maintenance, picnic lunch and insurance, start at ¥2860 per person.

Maps

Road maps are available at Xinhua Bookstore in Haikou. It's worth noting that people in Hainan call bikes *dānchē* (单车). Buses will accept bicycles in the hold, but trains require you to box them up.

Geopark take tourist bus 游1 (¥15, 45 to 50 minutes, 8.30am to 3.30pm). Bus K2 goes to the Mission Hills Resort (p624; ¥2, 45 minutes, 6.30am to 9pm).

TAXI

Taxis charge ¥10 for the first 3km. They're easy to spot, but difficult to catch on large roads because of roadside barriers.

AROUND HAIKOU

Haikou Volcanic Cluster Geopark VOLCANO
(雷琼世界地质公园, Léiqióng Shìjiè Dìzhì Gōngyuán; Shishan Town, 石山镇; Oct-Apr ¥60, May-Sep ¥50; ⊙ 8.30am-6pm; 🚌 1) While this geopark encompasses about 108 sq km of rural countryside, the main attraction here is a corny tourist park surrounding a (genuinely cool) extinct volcano cone. Make haste past

THE LI & MIAO

The Li, who today number over one million and can only be found on Hainan, were the island's first-known settlers, likely immigrating from southern China several thousand years ago. The Li were followed by the Miao (H'mong), who can also be found across stretches of northern Vietnam, Laos and Thailand; their arrival pushed the Li into the central highlands. When Han settlers arrived in big numbers during the Qing dynasty (1644–1911), they pushed the Miao, who in turn pushed the Li even further into the mountains.

Today both populations occupy some of the most rugged terrain on the island, in the forested areas covering the Limuling mountain range that stretches down the centre of the island. Since 1987 several counties in the central highlands have been designated as Li and Miao autonomous regions, which afford the minority groups a degree of independent governance.

Visitors to the central highlands will see visual markers of Li culture, including architecture adorned with traditional geometric symbols and children in school uniforms hemmed with colourful embroidery.

the snack stands and gift kiosks to descend the stairs winding down into the lushly vegetated crater, which feels more like a cave. Then climb back up for luscious views of the countryside all the way to the sea.

The geopark entrance is about 18km southwest of Haikou. A taxi to the park costs ¥60. From here, it's an easy walk to nearby Mei She Village.

Mei She Village　　　　HISTORIC SITE
(美社村, Měi Shè Cūn) Photogenic Mei She was built out of the rough grey volcanic stone so prevalent in this part of Hainan. Wander the quiet back alleys and gawp at the castle-like, five-storey gun tower in the town centre. It was built in the early 20th century to protect the village from bandits. The village is a 20-minute walk from the Haikou Volcanic Cluster Geopark entrance.

CENTRAL HIGHLANDS

📞 0898

Hainan's reputation rests on its tropical beaches, but for many travellers it's in this region of dark-green mountains and terraced rice-growing valleys that they make genuine contact with the island's culture. Baoting, with its rainforest and hot springs, is the most accessible destination. With more time, and especially if you're on two wheels, you can head to Wuzhishan and Qiongzhong and their surrounding villages.

Until recently, Han Chinese had left almost no footprint here, and even today visible signs of Chinese culture, such as temples or shrines, are very rarely seen. Instead, the region is predominantly Li and Miao – minority

ethnic groups who have lived a relatively simple subsistence existence for most of their time on the island. Indeed, groups of Li living as hunter-gatherers were found in the mountainous interior of Hainan as recently as the 1930s. Today they are by far the poorest people on Hainan.

The central highlands have a good range of accommodation, from luxurious rainforest resorts to village guesthouses. Transport hubs like Wuzhishan City have business hotels around the bus station if you find yourself stuck.

One of the joys of visiting the highlands is getting to feast on wild mountain vegetables (野菜, yěcài) and free-range duck and pork. On the pavements, Li women sell *zhú tǒng fàn* (竹筒饭, rice baked in fragrant bamboo stalks; ¥10).

Travelling in the region is easy, as a decent bus system links major and minor towns. Key transit hubs include Wuzhishan and Qiongzhong.

Baoting　　　保亭

📞 0898 / POP 170,000

Baoting (Bǎotíng) is a well-developed town with a large population of Li and Miao people. It is the gateway to the **Mt Qixian Hot Springs National Forest Park** (七仙岭温泉国家森林公园, Qīxiānlǐng Wēnquán Guójiā Sēnlín Gōngyuán), where the main attraction is the ridge of jagged, spear-like crags that make up **Seven Fairy Mountain** (七仙岭, Qīxiānlǐng; ¥50; ⊙ticket office 7.30am-4pm), named for its dramatic seven pinnacles. It's a three-hour return trip to the top of the first pinnacle along a stepped path through a dense, healthy rainforest buzzing with bird and insect life. The final 100m climb to the peaks runs up a pitted slope with chains and railings in place to aid your near-vertical climb. The views from the top are worth the effort. With no shuttle bus and no gimmicks (such as glass bridges), this is a much more authentic way to experience Hainan's rainforest than visiting the forest parks closer to Sanya. The mountain entrance and hot-springs area are 8km out of town.

Budget accommodation is hard to find in town, although there's an ever-growing number of hot-spring resorts in the area. The **Narada Resort & Spa** (七仙岭君澜度假酒店, Qīxiān Lǐng Jūnlán Dùjià Jiǔdiàn; ☑0898 8388 8888; www.naradahotels.com; Mt Qixian Hot Springs National Forest Park, 七仙岭国家森林温泉公园内; r from ¥2488; P✳︎☎︎✶︎❄︎) is an elegant surprise in the middle of the peaceful (though increasingly developed) rainforest. The 222 bright, airy rooms are done up in wood with ethnic minority art; the manicured grounds are spotted with fruit trees; and the bathtubs, behind screens on the veranda, are filled with natural hot-spring water. If you don't want to stay, Baoting is easily visited as a day trip from Sanya.

Baoting's old town, around the county hall bus stop (县政府, Xiàn Zhèng Fǔ), has a better selection of restaurants than the area around the main bus station. The area around the bus station has some amenities, including restaurants and an ATM.

There's little nightlife to speak of in Baoting, unless the locals entice you into a round (or several) of *jiǔ niàng* (酒酿, sweet, and potent, homemade rice wine). Most visitors, however, are safely ensconced in resorts.

❶ Getting There & Away

There are frequent buses to Baoting's **bus station** (保亭车站, Bǎotíng Chēzhàn) from Sanya (¥22, two hours). The last bus back to Sanya from Baoting station leaves at 7pm.

There are also three buses per day (¥22, two hours, 8am, 10.50am and 1pm) directly to Mt Qixian Hot Springs National Forest Park. You'll need to get a bus back to Sanya from the main station.

❶ Getting Around

To get to Mt Qixian Hot Springs National Forest Park from Baoting's bus station, you can take bus 1 (¥1, 10 minutes) to Xiàn Zhèng Fǔ (县政府) and then transfer to bus 2 (¥3, 15 minutes) to the entrance of the park, though it's easier to catch one of the motorcycle taxis that will be waiting outside the station (¥30). Don't catch a motorcycle with a sidecar as they lack the power to make it the last 4km from the hot springs area up to the park entrance.

From the Narada Resort & Spa, a shuttle bus can take you to the entrance of Mt Qixian Hot Springs National Forest Park (¥30, return). Free shuttle buses for guests run between the hotel and Baoting town (15 minutes), Lingshui high-speed train station (one hour) and Sanya Phoenix Airport (two hours); reserve when you book.

EAST COAST

☑0898

Hainan's east coast is a series of spectacular palm-lined beaches, long bays and headlands, most of which are, unfortunately, not usually visible from the main roads, not even at bicycle level. With the best beaches developed or being developed, there is little reason to make a special trip out here (Bo'ao being the exception) unless you are surfing and wish to stay at a resort. Biking or motorcycling is another story, however, as there are endless small villages and rural roads to explore and even a few near-deserted bays.

In the past, the east coast was the centre of Han settlement. If you are coming from the highlands you will start to notice temples, grave sites, shrines and other signs of Chinese culture dotting the landscape.

We've heard reports of travellers camping on the undeveloped beaches with no trouble, although bear in mind that this is technically illegal for international visitors to China. There are camping facilities at Da Hua Jiao (大花角, Dà Huā Jiǎo), a pretty beach with bobbing fishing boats at the end of the outstretched finger of land due east of Wanning.

Frequent high-speed trains and buses run down the eastern side of the island, stopping at Qionghai (for Bo'ao), Wanning (for Shimei and Ri Yue Bays) and Lingshui.

Note that the eastern highway runs quite a bit inland; if you're keen to cycle along the coast, you'll need a good map to navigate the tiny roads that flit in and out of the waterfront towns.

Bo'ao　博鳌

☑0898 / POP 29,000

Bo'ao (Bó'áo) is an unpretentious (though rapidly developing) beach town surrounded by pretty countryside. It makes a convenient stop for cyclists. Just to the west are small villages of stone and brick buildings where locals dry rice in the middle of the lanes, and burn incense for their local folk deities in small shrines.

Officially Bo'ao is starting to cover a large area, but the 'downtown' blocks, where most travellers both stay and eat, are tiny. The beach is a five-minute walk away.

Avoid visiting during, or the week before, the Bo'ao Forum for Asia (BFA), an annual April meet-up of top-level officials, academics and economists exclusively from the Asia region. The town is pretty much closed off under the scrutiny of high-level security (there are even warships in the harbour).

⊙ Sights

Bo'ao Bay
BEACH

(博鳌湾, Bó'áo Wān) Bo'ao's beach is a long, narrow strip of golden sand, just a few hundred metres east of the town's main road. If you plan to swim, head at least 500m north to avoid dangerous currents. The best stretches are even further north, particularly around the Asia Bay resort hotel. The beach is popular with local kitesurfers.

Bo'ao Temple
BUDDHIST MONASTERY

(东方文化苑, Dōngfāng Wénhuàyuàn, Courtyard of Eastern Culture; ¥22; ⊙8am-5pm; P) The highlight of this modern Buddhist temple complex, 3km west of the town centre, is the enormous statue of the many-armed and many-headed Guanyin, the towering pagoda, and the views over the delta. After getting the bus out, you can easily walk back to town along the quieter paths that run north of the main road, taking in some of the villages along the way.

Cai Family Former Residence
HISTORIC SITE

(蔡家宅, Càijiā Zhái; Liú Kè Cùn, 留客村; ⊙9am-5pm) FREE This sprawling, and pleasantly decaying, mansion was built in 1934 by several brothers who made their fortune in the Indonesian rubber industry. The building was abandoned in 1937 after the Japanese invaded Hainan, and later became a guerrilla outpost for resistance fighters. In 2006 it was declared a heritage site and these days you can wander around inside for a look if the caretaker is about.

It's about 8.5km from downtown. Bus 13 (¥2, regular departures) will drop you off on the main road (ask for the stop for 莫村 Mò Cūn). From there walk west along the road, staying left at the junction, and continuing for around 3km through green fields

and collections of handsome old and new houses. Alternatively, make an afternoon bike ride out of it: head west out of Bo'ao and when the road ends at a junction turn left (south) and cross two long bridges. After crossing the second bridge, head right at the English sign, near where the bus drops off. A *sānlúnchē* (三轮车, pedicab) will cost around ¥60 for the return trip.

⊟ Sleeping

Bo'ao has resorts that looked like they beamed in from Dubai and a growing number of guesthouses and hostels. Note that hostels often book out completely with cycling tours; you'll want to book in advance.

★ Qionghai Boao Xishe Guesthouse
GUESTHOUSE ¥

(琼海博鳌喜舍客栈, Qiónghǎi Bó'áo Xǐshè Kèzhàn; ☑0898 6260 9018; 49 Yudai Lu, 玉带路 49号; r from ¥126; P ⊙ ✲ @ ☎) The owners of this simple yet stylish guesthouse are extremely friendly, and will almost certainly invite you to take tea with them. As a bonus, they have a cute dog (who loves head rubs), and the guesthouse is five minutes' walk from the beach. Perfect.

Bo'ao Golden Coast Hot Spring Hotel
RESORT ¥¥¥

(博鳌金海岸温泉大酒店, Bó'áo Jīnhǎi'àn Wēnquán Dàjiǔdiàn; ☑0898 6277 8888; 8 Jinhai'an Dadao, 金海岸大道8号; r from ¥1380; P ✲ ✲ ☎) One of the more classically resort-like options in town, this sprawling complex has more than 300 rooms, an enormous pool, manicured lawns, and several restaurants and bars. In the off-season (most of the year), when discounts upwards of 50% are available, it's great value.

✗ Eating & Drinking

Bo'ao has a good spread of eating options. Around 4pm each day, look for the stalls at the intersection of Haibin Lu and Ao Sheng Jie selling succulent Jiaji duck (加积鸭, *Jiājī yā;* sold by weight), a Hainan speciality. It sells out quickly. On the main streets there are abundant grocery stores and fruit stands. Seafood lovers should head to the beach to check out the catch of the day.

The beach road leading running parallel to the coast has been redeveloped into a 'Seaside Bar Street' lined with open-air bars and cafes, which are lit up in the evenings.

★ Sea Story
SEAFOOD, CAFE ¥¥

(海的故事, Hǎide Gùshì; dishes ¥28-138; ⊙11.30am-late; ✸✿) Bo'ao's most famous restaurant is surprisingly un-flashy, cobbled together from driftwood and with a courtyard full of weathered old fishing junks. The kitchen turns out excellent local and Southeast Asian dishes (think barbecued spare ribs and curried prawns). Outside, the breezy, seaside deck is an ideal spot for evening drinks.

ⓘ Information

Bank of China (中国银行, Zhōngguó Yínháng; 122 Haibin Lu, 海滨路122号) Has a 24-hour ATM. At the intersection of Haibin Lu and Ao Wang Jie.

Leisure Travel (海南逍遥国际旅游, Hǎinán Xiāoyáo Guójì Lǚyóu; ☑ 0898 32129339; 60-3 Haibin Lu, 海滨路60-3号; ⊙7.30am-10pm) Sells high-speed train tickets for a booking fee of ¥5. It's across from an ABC Bank, near the intersection with Bo Ai Jie.

ⓘ Getting There & Away

BUS

From Haikou's east bus station, catch a bus to the main station in Qionghai (琼海车站; ¥27, 1½ hours, every 20 to 30 minutes) then cross the street and look for the bus stop just down the road to the left. Catch bus 2 to Bo'ao (¥6, 30 minutes, frequent). Passengers are dropped off on Haibin Lu, the town's main street. All transport from Bo'ao passes through Qionghai.

TRAIN

Bo'ao has its own high-speed train station, 17km west of the main town. You can either get a taxi to town (¥40) or take the bus 13 (¥6), which drops you off on Haibin Lu, Bo'ao's main street. Destinations include the following:

Haikou ¥45 to ¥53, 40 to 60 minutes, four daily (8.15am, 12.16pm, 12.45pm and 7pm)

Sanya ¥55, one hour, four daily (7.53am, 9.59am, 4.07pm and 5.29pm)

Qionghai also has a high-speed station with more frequent trains to and from Haikou and Sanya. To get to Bo'ao from Qionghai Station, catch bus 7 (¥2) from in front of the station, then transfer to bus 2 (¥6). Ask the driver where to change. Alternatively, take one of the many taxis (¥50) that wait at the station.

ⓘ Getting Around

There is a handful of shops around town renting bicycles (¥50 per day), though it's common for tour groups to have reserved all the stock in advance. Otherwise it's easy to walk around.

Bus 2 runs along Haibin Lu to Bo'ao Temple and back.

Shimei Bay & Ri Yue Bay

This is a wild, rocky stretch of coastline. Shimei Bay is now lined with resorts, but Ri Yue Bay, further southwest, is still largely undeveloped and is popular with local surfers. Both bays have strong currents and aren't considered safe for casual swimmers.

With its blue water, golden sand and shady coconut trees, it's no surprise that several large resorts have staked their claim to **Shimei Bay** (石梅湾, Shíméi Wān). Still, if you're after a little relaxation among affordable luxury you'd do worse than stay here for a couple of days – the **Le Méridien Resort & Spa** (石梅湾艾美度假酒店, Shíméi Wān Àiměi Dùjià Jiǔdiàn; ☑ 0898 6252 8888; https://le-meridien.marriott.com; Shimei Bay Tourist Holiday Zone, 石梅湾旅游度假区; d from ¥598; ℙ✿✸✿✿) is a solid choice. Some of the villas have direct access onto Shimei Bay beach, as well as their own private pools. Elsewhere, standard rooms are enormous, with quality fixtures and spacious balconies. Some staff speak English. The hotel operates a shuttle bus to and from Wanning high-speed

SURFING ON HAINAN

Surfing is slowly gaining a following in China, and Hainan is without question the centre of that budding scene. Conditions are never going to make this the next Indonesia, but every level, from beginner to advanced, can find suitable waves.

If you want to try your hand at the sport, Dadonghai and Houhai get decent waves from May to September and are suitable for absolute novices (especially quiet Houhai). Ri Yue Bay is prime from November to January, but it's possible to surf all year. With up to five breaks, the area is suitable for all levels; advanced surfers can try their luck on the Ghost Hotel waves. Unlike further south, Ri Yue Bay gets a bit chilly and overcast in the winter months, so light wetsuits are recommended.

Rentals and lessons are available year-round through Jalenboo Surf Club (p632) in Ri Yue Bay and Jile Hotel (p634) on Houhai Beach. During summer you can find rentals and basic lessons in Sanya at Sanya Backpackers (p634).

train station (¥5 one way, 40 minutes). Check ahead for times and to reserve.

If you like your ocean slate-blue and unpredictable (and largely resort free), **Ri Yue Bay** (日月湾, Rì Yuè Wān, Sun & Moon Bay) is for you. Colour is provided by local surfers rather than the usual flotilla of inflatable children's toys. The beachside restaurant (open 10am to midnight) run by the friendly people at **Jalenboo Surf Club** (戒浪不冲浪俱乐部; Jièlàngbù Chōnglàng Jùlèbù; ☑188 8914 4033, 0898 6225 4626; www.surfinghainan.net; board/wetsuit rental per day ¥100/30; ◷8am-9pm) is a good place to hang out. Hainan's original surf community offers two-hour lessons for ¥400, as well as gear rental. Ri Yue Bay has just one combined hotel and hostel. Travellers report camping with no trouble (although it's technically illegal for foreigners in China) but you'll need to bring your own gear.

The most direct way to get here is on the bus that runs down the eastern expressway between Haikou and Sanya: ask the driver to drop you off at the exit for Ri Yue, from where it's a 500m walk down the ramp to the shore. Only the lower-class green buses will stop, so check when you buy a ticket. From Sanya you'll have to buy a ticket to Wanning (万宁, Wànníng; ¥34, two hours, six daily); from Haikou, buy one to Lingshui (陵水, Língshuǐ; ¥54, three to four hours, seven daily). You can also take a taxi from Xinglong for around ¥50.

If you're cycling down the eastern highway, note that the expressway (which runs closer to the coast here) blocks your access to the beach. A smaller coastal road runs from Shimei Bay to Ri Yue Bay.

Xinglong   兴隆

☑ 0898 / POP 25,800

Xinglong (Xīnglóng) is a hot-spring town that is home to communities of overseas Chinese who returned from Southeast Asia in the 1950s. While the town itself is quiet and not especially attractive, it is set among some lush tropical countryside and makes a good stopping place for those cycling or travelling along the east coast.

During the early 20th century, many Hainanese left for Southeast Asia in search of a higher standard of living. In the 1950s, when the new government offered them free farmland, some returned, settling in communities around Xinglong – and bringing coffee back with them. Downtown Xinglong

is full of cafes selling locally produced coffee (¥6) and Indonesian-style sweets. Every year local coffee houses compete in tasting competitions to decide the best brews. **Rasa Enak** (桥咖, Qiáo Kā; 3 Xing Sheng Zhonglu, 兴生中路3号; ◷6am-4pm) is a laid-back place in which to sample a local brew, served in beautiful gold-plated cups. You won't find cafe latte here: locals take their coffee black or with a drop of condensed milk to add sweetness. Head west from the bus station (万宁兴隆车站, Wànníng Xīnglóng Chēzhàn) to the centre of town to find coffee houses.

There are several high-end resorts in nearby Shimei Bay (p631) but otherwise Xinglong is best visited as a day trip from Sanya. Buses run from Sanya to Xinglong (¥31, two hours, six daily).

The nearest train station is in Wanning (万宁), where regular trains arrive from Haikou (¥59, 75 minutes), Qionghai (¥19, 20 minutes) and Sanya (¥40, 45 minutes). Direct buses (¥5, 40 minutes) to Xinglong town meet the trains at the station.

SANYA   三亚

☑ 0898 / POP 580,500

China's premier beach community claims to be the 'Hawaii of China', but 'Moscow on the South China Sea' is more like it. The modern, hyper-developed resort city has such a steady influx of Russian holidaymakers these days that almost all signs are in Cyrillic as well as Chinese. Middle-class Chinese families are increasingly drawn to the golden shores of Sanya (Sānyà) as well.

While the full 40km or so of coastline dedicated to tourism is usually referred to as Sanya, the region is actually made up of three distinct zones. Sanya Bay is home to the bustling city centre and a long stretch of beach and hotels aimed at locals and mainland holidaymakers. Busy, cheerfully tacky Dadonghai Bay, about 3km southeast, beyond the Luhuitou Peninsula (鹿回头岭, Lùhuítóu Lǐng), is where most western travellers stay. A further 15km east, at exclusive Yalong Bay, the beach is first-rate, as is the line of plush international resorts.

◉ Sights

Sanya Bay   BEACH

(三亚湾, Sānyà Wān; ☐27) The long sandy strip off the city centre at Sanya Bay is where you'll find crowds of mostly mainland Chinese tourists kicking back. In little covered

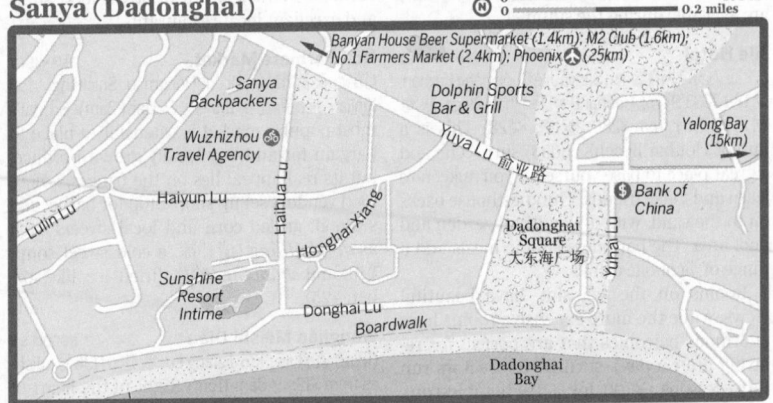

Sanya (Dadonghai)

areas locals play music, sing, write characters in the sand and so on. There's a long pathway for strolling in the cool evenings, and if the tide is out a little, you can walk on the sand for many kilometres. In the evenings it's fun to watch the lights on Phoenix Island (the awesome cruise-ship terminal).

Dadonghai Bay   BEACH
(大东海湾, Dàdōnghǎi Wān; 🚌2,8) Dadonghai Bay sports a wider beach than Sanya and has a shaded boardwalk running along most of its length. The setting, in a deep blue bay with rocky headlands, is simply gorgeous, but it does get busy here. At night, half the crowd is knocking back beers and eating crabs at the boardwalk restaurants, while the other half is still bobbing in the sea under the light of the moon.

Yalong Bay   BEACH
(亚龙湾, Yàlóng Wān; 🚌15) Yalong Bay is the most picture-perfect of Sanya's beaches, though jet skis and banana boats do buzz through (there are roped-off swimming areas in the shallows). This is resort central, with all the attendant luxuries. Budget travellers will want to head to the main plaza for fast-food and coconut stands.

China's beaches are theoretically open to everyone, but at Yalong Bay there can be a quasi-official entry fee if you're not staying at one of the beachfront resorts. To avoid any sporadically enforced fees, walk through one of the hotels rather than entering the beach from the main square. No one will bother you.

Houhai Beach   BEACH
(后海湾, Hòuhǎi Wān; 🚌28) A crescent-shaped sandy beach about 30km northeast of Dadonghai, Houhai Bay, which is in **Tenghai** village (滕海村, Ténghǎi Cūn), is the place for those looking to get away from the crowds. Be prepared though: the entrance to Tenghai is also the gateway to Wuzhizhen Island, one of Sanya's major tourist spots, and is extremely busy with cars and coaches parking up for the ferry. Once you're through the crowds, however, Houhai is the most low-key of the Sanya area beaches and a popular place for beginner surfers.

The village is fast developing and the pick of the hotels, including Jile Hotel (p634), line the beach. There are also plenty of small restaurants and fruit stands around.

🛏 Sleeping

A glut of hotel rooms makes even luxury resorts affordable in Sanya. Dadonghai Bay is the place to head for midrange and budget lodgings catering to the international set. Houhai Beach has a row of beachside guesthouses and a backpacker vibe. The top-end resorts are at Yalong Bay, in a private area of palm-lined roads and landscaped grounds. Outside peak periods 30% to 60% discounts are common everywhere.

Sanya Backpackers   HOSTEL ¥
(三亚阳光国际青年旅舍, Sānyà Yángguāng Guójì Qīngnián Lûshě; ☑0898 8895 5890; Villa 1, Luming Community, 2 Haihua Lu, 海花路2号鹿鸣小区1号别墅; dm ¥45, s & d ¥95; ⊖❀🛜) Although getting a little tired, this hostel is a more intimate and friendly place than others in town. Set in a whitewashed building in a residential compound, it's also an oasis. Simple backpacker dishes are available, and there's a bar (which can get noisy) for hanging out in the evenings.

Surf lessons and board rentals (¥150 per day) are available during the summer.

Jile Hotel
GUESTHOUSE ¥¥

(三亚人尔冲浪客栈, Sānyà Jílè Chōnglàng Kèzhàn; ☑ 189 7633 9475; Houhai Bay, Tenghai village, 滕海村后海湾; r from ¥280; ❈ 🛜; 🖥 28) This is a hub of Houhai Beach's (p633) surf scene and a great place to base yourself if you're keen to learn and make friends. The guesthouse backs on to the sand, with a wonderful garden and pool area. The bar offers simple meals and a range of alcoholic drinks.

Rooms on the sea side have beautiful views, while the more expensive rooms have enormous balconies that are perfect for relaxing after a day's surfing. Instructors run intro lessons (¥800 for a 1½-hour lesson), and boards are available to rent.

Sunshine Resort Intime
RESORT ¥¥¥

(三亚银泰阳光度假酒店, Sānyà Yíntài Yángguāng Dùjià Jiǔdiàn; ☑ 0898 8821 0888; www.resortintime. com; 88 Haihua Lu, 海花路88号; r from ¥1989; ❂❈❈🛝) This great little resort right by the beach has surprisingly large and leafy grounds with a barbecue area near the pool. The rooms aren't the most spacious, but those with sea views are set at a perfect angle to take in the bay. Nonsmoking floors are available. Discounts of over 50% are common.

Ritz-Carlton
RESORT ¥¥¥

(金茂三亚亚龙湾丽思卡尔顿酒店, Jīnmào Sānyà Yàlóngwān Lìsī Kǎěrdùn Jiǔdiàn; ☑ 0898 8898 8888; www.ritzcarlton.com; 2 Qingmei Lu, Yalong Bay, 青梅路2号; r from ¥4000; 🅿❈❈🛜🛝; 🖥 27) While some of Yàlóng Bay's palatial resorts can feel a bit like ghost towns due to Sanya's overbuilding, the Ritz is always abuzz. Well-heeled matrons sip tea on the grand patio, princelings splash down waterslides in the kids' pool, and young couples lie on the wide, sugar-white beach. Rooms are large and airy, all white linen and elegant mahogany, and can be had for a fraction of the advertised price out of season.

✕ Eating

The entire beachfront at Dadonghai is one long strip of restaurants, bars and cafes, most of which are overpriced and not terribly good, even if the overall atmosphere is cool, shady and scenic. When ordering seafood, be sure to settle on a price beforehand – Sanya has had some fairly infamous restaurant scams. The area around the No.1 Farmers Market is full of street-food stalls and excellent local restaurants.

No.1 Farmers Market
MARKET ¥

(第一农贸市场, Dì Yī Nóngmào Shìchǎng; 155 Xinjian Jie, 新建街155号; ☺ 11am-2am) Sanya's most popular market is ostensibly a place to bargain for and buy locally grown produce, but its real appeal lies on the fringes, where food vendors set up shop. Stop for barbecued seafood, grilled corn and local sweets such as *qīngbǔliáng* (清补凉, a cold sweet soup; ¥10) and *chǎobīng* (炒冰, 'fried' ice, like sorbet; ¥25).

Wàngjiǎo Měishí Diàn
NOODLES ¥

(旺角美食店; 136 Jiefang Lu, 新建街136号; dishes from ¥12; ☺ 8am-11pm) Right in the heart of the action around the No.1 Farmers Market, this colourful place has all the Hainanese classics: *bàoluófěn* noodles (抱罗粉; ¥12, choose from meat or seafood) and Wenchang chicken (文昌鸡, *Wénchāng jī*; ¥55) as well as fried ice (炒冰, *chǎobīng*; ¥20 to ¥25) and coconut jelly (椰子冻, *yēzi dòng*; ¥25) for dessert.

Casa Mia Italian Restaurant
ITALIAN ¥¥

(卡萨米亚意大利餐厅, Kǎsà Mǐyà Yìdàlì Cāntīng; ☑ 0898 8888 9828; 88 Sanya Wan Lu, 三亚湾路88号; mains ¥58-98; ☺ 11.30am-10pm; ❈🛜; 🖥 8) A jaded traveller might pooh-pooh the thought of finding top-notch Italian in a Chinese resort town. But they'd be wrong. Casa Mia has truly divine pizzas, pastas (try the special seafood linguine) and classics such as veal scallopini. The wine list is nothing to sneeze at either. The terrace gets a nice breeze from Sanya Bay across the street.

🍷 Drinking & Nightlife

Most of the after-hours fun is in Sanya and Dadonghai Bay. Times Coast Bar Street, on Yuya Lu, where it crosses the river, is the nexus of Sanya's club scene.

Banyan House Beer Supermarket
BAR

(榕树屋啤酒超市, Róngshù Wū Píjiǔ Chāoshì; 22 Yuya Lu, 榆亚路22号; beer from ¥25; ☺ 4pm-1am; 🛜) Tucked on the riverside beside Chaojian Bridge (the more easterly of the two bridges that connect Dadonghai to downtown Sanya), this bar has a pleasant outdoor seating area and a huge range of international bottled beers. Choose your drink from the well-stocked fridges and enjoy with some simple bar snacks or barbecued meat.

Sunset Bar
COCKTAIL BAR

(日落吧, Rì Luò Bā; Mandarin Oriental Hotel, 12 Yuhai Lu, 文华东方酒店榆海路12号; ⏱11am-1am; 🐾) A two-for-one happy hour (5pm to 7pm) makes this terrace bar at the cool and collected Mandarin Oriental almost a good deal. Watch the sun drop behind the headland while sipping a signature ginger lycheetini (¥90). Smoothies from ¥60.

Dolphin Sports Bar & Grill
PUB

(海豚美式餐厅酒吧, Hǎitún Měishì Cāntīng Jiǔbā; 📱0898 8821 5700; 95 Yuya Lu, 榆亚路95号; beer from ¥25; ⏱11am-2am; 🐾) International tourists and expats mingle with locals at this always-packed western-style pub. Wash down a (very good) cheeseburger with a pint while watching football on the multiple TVs, or wait until after 10pm, when the live music starts up and the crowd really gets rolling. Friendly servers speak impeccable English.

M2 Club
CLUB

(12 Yuya Lu, 榆亚路12号; ⏱9pm-3am; 🐾) You've got to dress the part to get into M2, one of the swankier clubs on Sanya's Times Coast Bar Street – think lots of hair gel, high heels, skinny suits, minidresses etc. Chinese big shots wheel and deal by the bar, while the younger crowd dances to earsplitting EDM.

ℹ Information

Bank of China (中国银行, Zhōngguó Yínháng; cnr Yuya Lu & Yuhai Lu, 榆亚路和榆海路口; ⏱8.30am-5pm) Has money exchange and a 24-hour ATM.

ℹ Getting There & Away

Sanya's Phoenix Airport has international flights to Singapore, Hong Kong, Malaysia, Thailand, Taiwan and Japan, as well as to Beijing, Guangzhou and Shanghai.

Sanya high-speed train station (三亚站, Sānyà Zhàn; 10 Yuxiu Lu, 育秀路10号) is closest to Sanya Bay. A taxi will cost ¥50 for the 20-minute ride to Dadonghai. Destinations include the following:

Haikou ¥99, two hours, regular

Qionghai ¥49, one hour, regular

Yalong Bay also has a **high-speed station** (亚龙湾站, Yàlóngwān Zhàn), which is 10km from the resort area.

Frequent buses and minibuses to most parts of Hainan depart from the **long-distance bus station** (三亚汽车站, Sānyà Qìchēzhàn; 425 Jiefang Lu, 解放路425号), in busy central Sanya.

ℹ Getting Around

BUS

Sanya has a good local bus system. Useful services include the following:

Buses 2 and **8** (¥2, 40 minutes, frequent) Sanya bus station to Dadonghai Bay.

Bus 4 (¥2, 1¼ hours, frequent) Connects Sanya high-speed train station with Dadonghai.

Bus 15 (¥5, 45 minutes, frequent) Dadonghai Bay to Yalong Bay.

Bus 27 (¥2 to ¥10, frequent) Runs between the airport, Sanya Bay, Yalong Station and Yalong Bay.

Bus 28 (¥12, 1¼ hours, frequent) Travels to Tenghai village (for Houhai Beach) from Dadonghai.

ELECTRIC SCOOTER

Lots of shops around Dadonghai offer electric scooters (电动车, diàndòng chē; known as e-bikes) for hire – **Wuzhizhou Travel Agency** (蜈支洲岛, Wúzhīzhōu Dǎo; 2-9 Haihua Lu, 海花路2-9号; e-bikes per day ¥50; ⏱8.30am-9pm) is central and reasonably priced. You don't need a driving licence so e-bikes are a cheap and convenient way to zip around Sanya – you can get as far as 60km on one charge, which is more than enough for a day's exploring. You'll need either ¥500 or a passport as a deposit.

TAXI

Taxis charge ¥10 for the first 2km. A taxi from Sanya to Dadonghai Bay costs ¥15 to ¥20, and from Dadonghai Bay to Yalong Bay it's ¥70.

Guangxi

POP 51 MILLION

Best Places to Eat

➡ Luna (p651)

➡ First Oyster (p662)

➡ Zhongshan Lu Market (p654)

Best Places to Stay

➡ Secret Garden (p651)

➡ Alila Yangshuo (p647)

➡ This Old Place Youth Hostel (p652)

➡ Dong Village Hotel (p645)

➡ Longji Vita Hotel (p643)

Why Go?

Guangxi (广西, Guǎngxī) conjures up visions of cycling and bamboo-rafting upon shimmering river waters beneath the sublime karst peaks of Yangshuo and hiking between ethnic villages in the lofty Longji Rice Terraces. That's not all though: you can take selfies in front of the dramatic Danxia landscape (a type of landform) at Tianmen Mountain and Bajiaozhai National Geopark, and get sprayed by the mighty waterfall of Detian or splashed by live seafood in Beihai's Vietnamese quarter.

What's more, you'll be contemplating the 2000-year-old Huashan cliff murals from a boat and comparing the poetry of the Dong villages at Chengyang to the beauty of Japan's Kyoto.

After you've had your fill of wonders above ground, you'll be plunging into the subterranean forests of Leye and soaking your feet in the underground streams of Tongling Grand Canyon. Doing it all in reverse also makes sense, for Yangshuo is the perfect conclusion to any expedition.

When to Go
Guilin

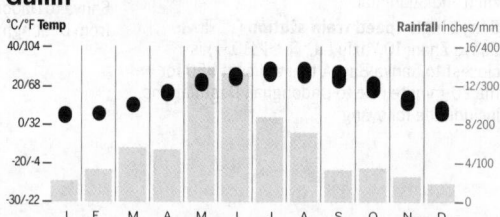

Mar The flowering rapeseed adds splashes of yellow to the fields around Yangshuo's karst peaks.

Jun–Sep Rain turns rice terraces into mirrors and fattens waterfalls.

Sep & Oct The gulf breeze keeps things cool as you stroll around Weizhou Island.

Guangxi Highlights

1 **Yangshuo** (p645) Cycling past scenery straight out of a painting alongside the Yulong River.

2 **Longji Rice Terraces** (p642) Trekking among stilt houses and fields that cascade down the slopes.

3 **Sanjiang** (p644) Stopping by the bridge, drum towers and cedar-wood homes of the artistic Dong people.

4 **Bajiaozhai National Geopark** (p641) Watching the drama of Danxia geology unfold before you.

5 **Leye Geopark** (p661) Being awestruck by the surreal nature of the geopark's massive sinkholes and their caverns.

6 **Huashan Cliff Murals** (p661) Taking in the beauty of 2000-year-old tribal rock murals that decorate the cliffs along the picturesque Zuǒ River.

7 **Beihai** (p657) Exploring the old seaside quarter and taking a trip to the volcanic island of Weizhou.

History

In 214 BC a Qin dynasty army attempted to assimilate the Zhuang people, living in what is now called Guangxi, into their newly formed Chinese empire. But while the eastern and southern parts submitted, the western extremes remained largely controlled by hill-tribe chieftains.

Major tribal uprisings occurred in the 19th century, the most significant being the Taiping Rebellion (1850–64), which became one of the bloodiest civil wars in human history, resulting in 20 million deaths.

Communist bases were set up in Guangxi following the 1929 Baise Uprising led by Deng Xiaoping, although they were eventually destroyed by Kuomintang forces. Much of Guangxi fell briefly under Japanese rule following highly destructive WWII invasions.

Today the Zhuang, China's largest minority group, makes up 32% of Guangxi's population, which led to the province being reconstituted in 1955 as the Guangxi Zhuang Autonomous Region. As well as Zhuang, Miao and Yao, Guangxi is home to significant numbers of Dong people.

Language

Travellers with a grasp of Mandarin (Pǔtōnghuà) will have few problems navigating Guangxi's vast sea of languages. Cantonese (Guǎngdōnghuà), known as Báihuà in these parts, is the language of choice in Nanning, Pingxiang and Daxin, but most people also understand Mandarin. Visitors will also hear a number of minority languages being spoken, such as Zhuang, Dong and Yao.

ℹ PRICE RANGES

Sleeping

The following price ranges refer to a double room with bathroom.

¥ less than ¥150

¥¥ ¥150–¥400

¥¥¥ more than ¥400

Eating

The following price ranges refer to a main course.

¥ less than ¥40

¥¥ ¥40–¥100

¥¥¥ more than ¥100

Guilin 桂林

📋 0773 / POP 5.19 MILLION

Guangxi's second-largest city, Guilin (Guìlín) has the hallmarks of most Chinese megapolises, but it feels much more relaxed given its spectacular setting among the jagged-peak limestone karsts that surround it. It was China's first city to develop tourism after 1949, and for decades, children's textbooks proclaimed 'Guilin's landscape is the best under heaven' (桂林山水甲天下). It was the darling of Chinese politicians, the star city proudly presented to visiting dignitaries. Today Guilin's natural endowments still amaze, yet, thanks to imperfect urban planning, there is a pervasive feeling that the city is past its prime.

Guilin serves as a convenient base to plan trips to the rest of the province. It's clean, modern and offers plenty of greenery among its city lakes and the majestic Li River. Star Wars fans may recognise the surrounding karst peaks from *Revenge of Sith*, which was used as the set location for the Wookiee planet, Kashyyyk.

👁 Sights & Activities

★ Rong Lake   LAKE

(榕湖, Róng Hú) Rong Lake (literally, Banyan Lake), named for an ancient Chinese banyan on its shore, and its adjoining **Shan Lake** (杉湖, Shān Hú) are an oasis of calm in the urban hub of Guilin. It has no shortage of local charm, with a walking track leading through lush gardens with ornate bridges and Chinese pavilions that dot the shimmering water.

Sun & Moon Twin Pagodas   PAGODA

(日月双塔, Rìyuè Shuāng Tǎ; Shan Lake, 杉湖; ¥35; ⏰ 8am-10pm) Elegantly embellishing the scenery of Shan Lake, the Sun and Moon Twin Pagodas, beautifully illuminated at night, are the highlight of a stroll around Guilin's two central lakes. The octagonal, seven-storey Moon Pagoda (月塔, Yuè Tǎ) is connected by an underwater tunnel to the 41m-high Sun Pagoda (日塔, Rì Tǎ), one of the few pagodas with a lift.

Two Rivers Four Lakes   BOATING

(二江四湖, Èr Jiāng Sì Hú) This boat ride around Guilin does a loop of the Li River and the city's lakes. Prices vary from ¥170 to ¥340 for 90 minutes, depending on the time of day (it costs more at night). Pretty much every Guilin hotel and tourist information service centre can arrange the tour.

Guilin

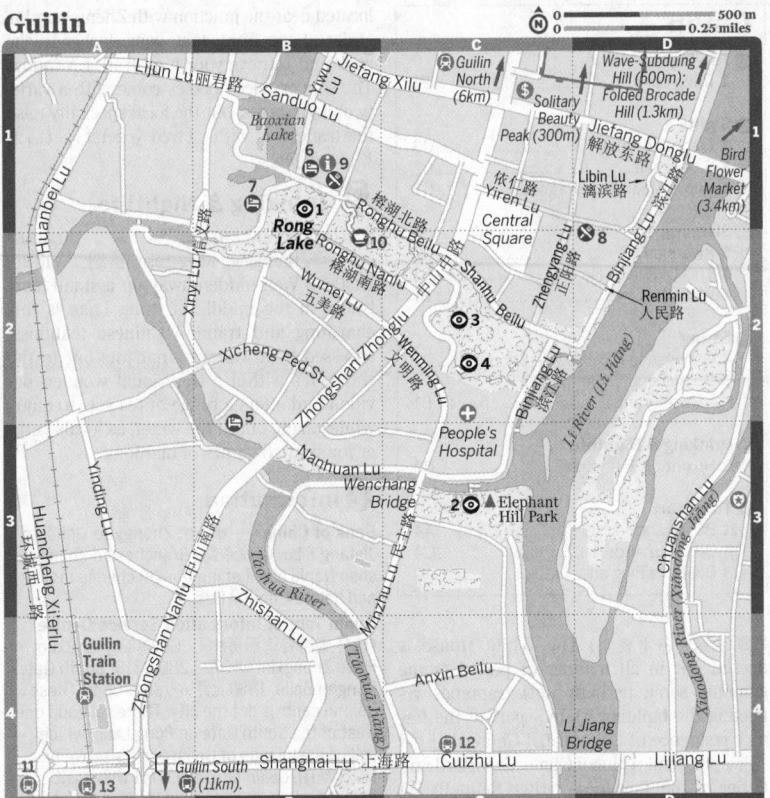

👉 Tours

Guilin Cycling Tours CYCLING
(📱 152 9680 7701, 0773 381 0665; www.guilincycling
tours.com; tours from ¥800) Pedal out among
Guangxi's famed countryside with this recommended operator which organises an assortment of cycling excursions from Guilin. Trips
last anywhere from one day to several weeks
exploring the local region and beyond. It also
rents quality mountain bikes that you can
pick up from This Old Place Hostel.

🛏 Sleeping

This Old Place Hostel HOSTEL ¥
(老地方国际青年旅舍, Lǎodìfāng Guójì Qīngnián
Lǚshè; 📱 0773 281 3598; www.guilinhostel.net; 2 Yiwu
Lu, 翊武路2号; dm ¥30-50, d without view ¥120-140,
with view ¥140-160, f from ¥225; 🌐 ❄ @ 🛜) One of
Guilin's most popular hostels, This Old Place
has a wonderful location down a leafy street
across from Baoxian Lake, and is a 10-minute
walk to the main eating and shopping areas.

Private rooms are spacious and comfortable,
while four-bed dorms come equipped with
powerpoints and curtains. It's a good spot to
chill out, particularly its rooftop terrace with
amazing karst-peak views.

★ Riverside Inn INN ¥¥
(桂林九龙水岸别院酒店, Guìlín Jiǔlóng Shuǐ àn
Bié Yuàn Jiǔdiàn; 📱 0773 258 0215; riversideinn2015@
outlook.com; 5 Zhumu Xiang, 南门桥竹木巷5号; d
¥180-400; ❄ @ 🛜) A former hostel, this attractive inn by the peaceful Taohua River (桃花
江) has ditched the dorms to focus squarely
on its boutique-style rooms. They feature a
classy decor of traditional adornments, modern bathrooms and a handsome blonde-wood
finish. If you want to treat yourself, go the
honeymoon suite with a private outdoor tub
on the balcony overlooking the river.

White House BOUTIQUE HOTEL ¥¥¥
(白公馆, Bái Gōngguǎn; 📱 0773 899 9888; Bldg
4, 16 Ronghu Beilu, 榕湖北路16号4栋; d/ste from

Guilin

¥980/1760; ⊖❄@🛜) The White House is decked out in all manner of period (some genuine, some perhaps not) trappings reflecting the building it's in – part of the former residence of General Bai Chongxi (白崇禧), a powerful regional Guangxi warlord and father of the Taiwanese writer Kenneth Pai Hsien-yung (白先勇). Spacious guestrooms are lavishly appointed, featuring a mini-spa and high-thread-count bedding.

🍴 Eating

Gongcheng Yaofei Oil Tea Restaurant
GUANGXI ¥

(恭城瑶妃御品油茶餐馆, Gōngchéng Yáofēi Yùpǐn Yóuchá Cānguǎn; 📞0773 280 1688; 2-4 Rongyin Rd, 榕荫路2-4; mains ¥8-62; ⊗9am-9pm) One for those seeking out regional specialities is this atmospheric restaurant just north from the Song dynasty South Gate. It's a fitting place to sample Guilin oil tea (油茶; ¥3), a hot brew prepared from fried tea leaves and pork fat to which peanuts, rice puffs and scallions are added – it's an acquired taste favoured by Guangxi's ethnic minority people.

Chongshan Rice Noodle Shop
NOODLES ¥

(崇善米粉店, Chóngshàn Mǐfěn Diàn; 📞0773 282 6036; 5 Yiren Lu, 依仁路5号; noodles ¥4-12; ⊗6.30am-11.30pm) A good place to sample Guilin noodles is this canteen-style restaurant

located near the junction with Zhengyang Lu. Order at the front, take your docket to the cook and retrieve your food from a window. The slippery rice noodles come with a variety of ingredients, but the local speciality (also the tastiest) is with stewed vegetables (卤菜粉, *lǔcài fěn*).

🍷 Drinking & Nightlife

Huxinting Teahouse   TEAHOUSE
(湖心亭, Húxīntíng; Rong Lake, 榕湖; ⊗10am-10.30pm) Well hidden away on a small leafy island in the middle of Rong Lake is this charming and tranquil Chinese teahouse, accessed by a walkway that juts out to the water. It's within a traditional wooden pavilion and offers a range of tea sets to enjoy while gazing out to the water, as locals gather for spirited games of mahjong.

ℹ Information

Bank of China (中国银行, Zhōngguó Yínháng; Jiefang E Lu, 解放东路) Branches on Zhongshan Nanlu and Jiefang Donglu change money and have 24-hour ATMs.

Guilin Tourist Information Service Centre (桂林旅游咨询服务中心, Guìlín Lǚyóu Zīxún Fúwù Zhōngxīn; 📞0773 280 0318; South Gate, Ronghu Beilu, 榕湖北路; ⊗8am-6pm) These helpful centres dot the city. There's a good one west of the South Gate on Rong Lake, which sells a useful map of Guilin and its surrounds (桂林地图, Guìlín dìtú; ¥6). Visit www.visit guilin.org for an overview of things to do, tours and accommodation listings.

People's Hospital (人民医院, Rénmín Yīyuàn; 📞0773 282 0816; www.glrmyy.com; 70 Wenming Lu, 文明路70号) This large, well-equipped hospital is a designated International SOS service provider, and the teaching hospital of several universities in Guilin.

Public Security Bureau (公安局, Gōng'ānjú, PSB; 📞0773 582 9930; 16 Shijiayuan Lu, 七星区施家园路16号; ⊗8.30am-noon & 3-6pm Mon-Fri) Visa extensions. Located by Xiaodong River and 500m south of the Seven Stars Park. A taxi from downtown will cost around ¥20.

ℹ Getting There & Away

AIR

Direct flights from Guilin Liangjiang International Airport (两江国际机场, Liǎngjiāng Guójì Jīchǎng) include Beijing, Chengdu, Chongqing, Haikou, Guangzhou, Hong Kong (Xianggang), Kunming, Shanghai and Xi'an. International destinations include Seoul, Korea (Hancheng), and Osaka, Japan (Daban).

GUANGXI GUILIN

BUS

Guilin's main terminal for long-distance buses is the **South Bus Station** (桂林汽车客运南站, Guìlín Qìchē Kèyùn Nán Zhàn; off Kaifeng Lu, 桂林市象山区凯风路西侧, 茶店西路南侧; 🚌 K99), rather inconveniently located 15km south of town.

The **North Bus Station** (桂林汽车客北站, Guìlín Qìchē Běizhàn; 76 Beichen Lu, 北辰路76号; 🚌 18, 32, 99, 100) has buses to Ziyuan (¥35 to ¥45, every 20 minutes, 6.40am to 7.40pm) for Bajiaozhai National Geopark.

Direct shuttles for the Longji Rice Terraces are booked through lodges in Dazhai and Ping'an. Both departures are from hotels across from Guilin train station: Dazhai is from **HongKong Hotel** (香江饭店, Xiāngjiāng Fàndiàn, HongKong Hotel; 141 Xihuan First Lu, Guilin Train Station, 象山区西环一路141号), while Ping'an is at **Oriental Pearl Hotel** (桂林东方明珠大酒店, Dōngfāngmíngzhū Dà Jiǔdiàn, Oriental Pearl Hotel; 25 Shanghai Lu, Guilin Train Station, 象山区 上海路25号); both cost around ¥50, and take three to four hours. Otherwise, by public transport you can take a bus to Longsheng and the Longji Rice Terraces either from the **North Bus Station** (桂林汽车客北站, Guìlín Qìchē Běizhàn; 76 Beichen Lu, 北辰路76号; 🚌 18, 32, 99, 100) (¥40, two hours, eight daily) departing every 1½ hours from 8.30am to 5.20pm, or **Qintan Bus Station** (琴潭汽车站, Qíntán Qìchē Zhàn; 31 Cuizhu Lu, 翠竹路31号; 🚌 2, 12, 26, 32, 85, 91) (¥40, two hours, every 40 minutes, 6.10am to 7pm).

TRAIN

High-speed trains are by far the best means of travel, both significantly faster and cheaper than buses. Most trains leave from Guilin Station (桂林站, Guìlín Zhàn), but some may leave from Guilin North Train Station (桂林北站, Guìlín Běizhàn), 9km north of the city centre. It's best to book a few days in advance.

ℹ Getting Around

TO/FROM THE AIRPORT

The airport is 30km west of the city. Half-hourly shuttle buses (from ¥20) run from the **Civil Aviation Hotel** (民航大厦, Mínháng Dàshà, Guilin Civil Aviation Hotel; 18 Shanghai Lu, 市象山区上海路18号) between 6am and 9pm. From the airport, shuttle buses meet every arrival. A taxi costs about ¥100 to ¥120 (40 minutes). There are also eight daily buses to Yangshuo (¥50, 9.30am to 8pm) that depart from the airport.

BICYCLE

Guilin's sights are all within cycling distance. Many hostels can arrange bicycles for rent (¥20 to ¥50 per day). For quality bikes and recommended tours, get in touch with Guilin Cycling Tours (p639), which offers bike rental at This Old Place Hostel (p639).

TAXIS

Taxis are the most convenient means of getting around town, with short jaunts costing around ¥10 to ¥15.

Jiangtouzhou Ancient Town 江头洲古城

The 1000-year-old village of **Jiangtouzhou** (Jiāngtóuzhōu Gǔchéng; ¥20) is tucked away among farmland 32km north of Guilin. The mostly abandoned village has layers of old-world charm, with its labyrinth of cobblestone alleyways lined with stone houses dating from the Ming and Qing dynasties, and where blocks of tofu are laid out to set in the courtyards. Its residents are descendants of the philosopher Zhou Dunyi (周敦颐), who is famed for his essay on virtue, 'Love of the Water-Lily'.

The flower is a decorative motif throughout the village and inside the ancestral hall. A short walk across from the village is a picturesque lotus flower garden, which offers a wonderful photo op with karst peaks looming in the background; entry is ¥10, but views from outside are equally lovely.

Jiangtouzhou is a two- to three-hour bike ride from Guilin. Alternatively, take an orange minibus on the stretch of Zhongshan Beilu near Guilin North Train Station to Lingchuan (灵川; ¥3, 40 minutes). Get off at Tanxia Lukou (潭下路口), zip across the road and change to bus 309 for Jiuwu (九屋; ¥3, 45 minutes). Arriving in Jiuwu, it's a 15-minute walk to Jiangtouzhou. Buses stop running around 5.30pm. Otherwise a return taxi from Guilin will set you back ¥200.

Ziyuan 资源

📞 0773 / POP 167,000

Ziyuan county (Zīyuán), built around the pristine Zi River, is a gateway to geological gems of Danxia (丹霞, *dānxiá*) topography, such as Bajiaozhai National Geopark and Guilin Tianmen Mountain Scenic Area.

It's located about 107km north of Guilin. While it's possible to visit as a day trip, most folk base themselves in the sprawling, gritty town of Ziyuan to explore the main sights.

Bajiaozhai National Geopark (八角寨, Bājiǎozhài; Meixi Xiang Fúzhú Village, 梅溪乡, 福竹村; ¥30; ⊙8am-5pm) is named after eight Danxia stone peaks that lie near the border with Hunan. Round, isolated, featuring ring-like troughs and leaning 45 degrees, these spectacular formations resemble snails sunning themselves after the rain. It's a 1½-hour loop walking trail, so you don't need to retrace your steps from the carpark. The trail winds along steep cliffs, collapsed boulders, plunging gorges, a Buddhist monastery, glass walkways and bamboo forests.

Tianmen Mountain Scenic Area (桂林天门山风景区, Guìlín Tiānménshān Fēngjǐng Qū; adult/child ¥30/15, cable car 1 way/return ¥58/110; ⏲8.30am-5pm, cable car 9.20am-4.40pm), not to be confused with Tianmen Mountain in Zhangjiajie, Hunan, is home to proud cliffs, sharp ravines and dramatic waterfalls of Danxia topography, but also lush subtropical foliage, clusters of ash-brown dwellings and crumbling roadside shrines. Tourist development here, however, has taken some of its natural wonder away. There are multiple viewing spots along hiking trails in the park, including a U-shaped deck with a transparent floor – a 1½- hour return walk or you can take the cable car.

For a good night's sleep, **Haoting Grand Hotel** (资源豪廷大酒店, Zīyuán Háotíng Dà Jiǔdiàn; ☑0773 436 8678, 133 2173 5898; 118 Chéngběi Kāifāqū, 城北开发区118号; d/ste from ¥190/480; ❄❈🛜) in the northern area of town is a very good choice.

There are plenty of places to eat in Ziyuan itself, with the best quality restaurants located to the north of town. **Xiao Shi Hou Xiang** (小食侯湘; Binjiang Lu, 滨江路; mains ¥20-59; ⏲9.30am-9pm; ❈🛜) sits on a scenic stretch of the Zijiang River and serves up spicy Hunan cuisine. On the way up to the Bajiaozhai car park, you'll pass a few farm restaurants. The chicken hotpot (土鸡火锅, tǔjī huǒguō), made with free-range fowl and just-picked vegetables, is divine.

Buses leave Guilin's North Bus Station for Ziyuan (¥35 to ¥45, 2½ hours) every 20 minutes from 6.40am to 7.40pm. There are also two buses to Longsheng (¥38, three hours) for the Longji Rice Terraces, departing at 8.40am and 12.50pm.

A car directly from Guilin to Tianmen Mountain or Bajiaozhai National Geopark (two hours one way) will cost around ¥750.

From downtown Ziyuan, you can hire a car to Tianmen Mountain, 30 minutes away, for around ¥200, or to Bajiaozhai National Geopark, 45 minutes away, for slightly more. The driver will wait for you to hike, but take their mobile number in case you need extra time. If you do both places on the same day it'll cost you around ¥300 to ¥350, but you'll

need to start no later than mid-morning and spend only a few hours at each destination.

Longji Rice Terraces 龙脊梯田

☑0773

This part of Guangxi is famous for its breathtaking vistas of terraced paddy fields cascading in swirls down into a valley. For hundreds of years, the paddy fields of Longji Rice Terraces (Lóngjǐ Tītián) remained unknown to travellers, then everything changed in the 1990s when a photographer named Li Yashi (李亚石) moved here. His images of the scenery amazed the world and put Longji (literally 'Dragon's Back') firmly on the tourist trail.

You'll find the most spectacular views around the villages of Ping'an (平安, Píng'ān), a Zhuang settlement; **Dazhai** (大寨, Dàzhài), a mesmerising Yao village; and **Tiantouzhai** (田头寨, Tiántóuzhài), which sits slightly further above Dazhai.

On arrival at Dazhai or Ping'an you'll be charged an ¥80 entrance fee to access the area, which is valid for the entirety of your stay, so be sure to hold on to your ticket.

◉ Sights & Activities

As hiking is a way of life here, bring a day pack and leave your luggage in Guilin or at the main ticket office in Dazhai or Ping'an (storage per day ¥15). Otherwise, villagers will carry your bags for ¥50 apiece.

While the Dazhai to Ping'an trek is the most popular, you can take a number of **short walks** from each village to the fabulous viewing points, which are all signposted. Given there are some 13 villages in the Longji region, there are plenty of rewarding hikes beyond Dazhai, Ping'an and Tiantouzhai.

★ **Rice Terraces** VIEWPOINT
(龙脊梯田, Lóngjǐ Tītián) Longji's famed rice terraces have been luring travellers to the region for decades to witness some of China's most spectacular scenery. Rising to 1000m, they are an amazing feat of farm engineering on hills dotted with minority villages. There are two main areas to see: the **Ping'an terraces**, the most established of the region's rice fields; and the **Jinkeng terraces**, with life-affirming viewpoints around Dazhai and Tiantouzhai.

On the Ping'an side, one of the most sublime and beautiful images rewards the climb up to the **Nine Dragons & Five Tigers Viewing Point** (九龙五虎观景点, Jiǔlóng Wǔhǔ

Guānjǐngdiǎn) with its astonishing, curvaceous layers of terraces. It's around a 30-minute walk above Ping'an. The oldest field is over 700 years old; you pass it just before making your ascent to Dazhai.

Smaller, but equally impressive, is the view at **Seven Stars Chase the Moon** (七星伴月), 700m east of Ping'an, where the striped, swirled patterns of the terraces resemble the contours of a giant thumbprint. From here you can make your way down the stairs to the atmospheric **old village** (古壮; one hour return) with century-old buildings set among rice fields immersed in a sea of cloud.

From the Jinkeng side, the signature outlook is from **Golden Buddha Peak** (金佛顶, Jīnfó Dǐng), offering astounding views of sculpted terraces that are reached via the **cable car** (大寨 缆车, Dàzhài Lǎnchē; single/return adult ¥55/100, child ¥30/50; ⏰ 9am-5pm) from Dazhai or a one-hour hike (one way) from Tiantouzhai. Also don't miss the sublime vistas from **Music From Paradise** (西山韶乐, Xishan Shaoyue), a 40-minute hike from Tiantouzhai, or at **Thousand Layers to Heaven** (大界天层天梯, Dajie Qianceng Titian), famous for its ethereal sunrise, a 30-minute walk from Tiantouzhai.

Dazhai to Ping'an Trek
WALKING

For many, the four-hour trek between the villages of Dazhai and Ping'an (via Tiantouzhai) offers the quintessential Longji experience – taking you right among the photogenic rice terraces with its famed viewpoints. Be aware that there are almost no signposts for this hike, and you will meet numerous sign-less forks in the path. Maps. Me offers a reliable route.

🛏 Sleeping & Eating

Ping'an, Dazhai and Tiantouzhai all offer excellent backpacker choices, along with midrange hotels offering more comfort. Most involve anything from a 20- to 50-minute hike from the parking lot, but villagers can carry your bags for ¥50 apiece. There's also the option to stay in traditional wooden homes for around ¥40 per night per bed. Nearly all guesthouses offer food, and most restaurants have English menus (¥15 and ¥100).

🛏 Ping'an

★Longji International Youth Hostel
HOSTEL ¥

(龙脊国际青年旅舍, Lóngjǐ Guójì Qīngnián Lǚshè; ☎0773 758 3265; yha-longji@qq.com; Ping'an Village, 平安村; dm/d/tr from ¥40/128/168; ❄@🛜) One of the first accommodation options you find walking into Ping'an, this thoroughly pleasant, friendly and amenable hostel has decent rooms in a kind of *Twin Peaks* wooden surrounds setting. Aim for one of the rooms in the newly renovated attached building, featuring well-decorated, comfortable rooms with modern bathrooms. Dorms, on the other hand, are no-frills. Excellent for local info.

★Longji Vita Hotel
INN ¥¥¥

(龙脊草木生活, Lóngjǐ Cǎomù Shēnghuó; ☎182 9010 2861; 2869131462@qq.com; Ping'an Village, 平安村; r incl breakfast ¥380-800; ❄🛜) Offering some of the finest views you'll get in Longji is this memorable inn overlooking the spectacular **Seven Stars Chase the Moon** rice terrace. All rooms feature stunning panoramic outlooks, but it's worth upgrading for a balcony. Rooms are comfortable with all the mod cons, but the cutesy Chinese decor may be too quirky for some tastes.

🛏 Dazhai

Minority Inn & Cafe
GUESTHOUSE ¥

(龙脊咖啡客栈, Lóngjǐ Kāfēi Kèzhàn; ☎183 7637 4170, 0773 758 5605; Dazhai, 大寨; r ¥100; ❄🛜) Perched above Dazhai village on the trail leading up to Tiantouzhai, this small guesthouse has a terrace and an owner who speaks excellent English. It's about a 20-minute walk (1km) uphill from the village's main gate.

🛏 Tiantouzhai

★Dragon's Den Hostel
HOSTEL ¥

(大寨青年旅舍, Dàzhài Qīngnián Lǚshè; ☎132 5731 5769, 182 7838 7610; www.facebook.com/dragonsdenhostel; Tiantouzhai, 田头寨; dm ¥35-55, r with shared/private bathroom ¥100/140; ➡❄🛜) One of Longji's most social hangouts is this friendly backpacker in the hilltop village of Tiantouzhai. It's a scenic spot, with each of the rooms in the sprawling, creaky wooden inn featuring fabulous rice-terrace views. Dorms are four- and five-bed rooms, while spartan private rooms have either sit-down or squat toilets. It's a 40-minute climb from Dazhai.

Salad Days Inn
GUESTHOUSE ¥

(龙胜吾悠山舍, Lóngshèng Wú Yōu Shān Shě; ☎181 7830 0588; Tiantouzhai, 田头寨; dm/d/q ¥60/260/400; ❄🛜) With its contemporary furniture, hanging lamps and exposed brick, Salad Days offers a boutique alternative to Tiantouzhai's rickety inns. Its lounge is the undisputed highlight, with comfy couches and gallery windows looking out to superb rice terrace views. Rooms are modern and comfortable, but show signs of wear, while there's a dorm option for budget travellers.

ℹ Getting There & Away

From April to October, the lodges in Longji Rice Terraces can arrange a shuttle service from Guilin to Dazhai (three hours) or Ping'an (2½ hours). The price is usually ¥50 per person and reservations at least one day in advance are a must; however, they also take other passengers if seats are available. For Dazhai and Tiantouzhai, shuttles depart from HongKong Hotel (p641) at 8am, 9.30am, 10.30am, 12.30pm, 2.30pm and 3.30pm. For Ping'an, two daily buses depart from the Oriental Pearl Hotel (p641) at 9am and 2pm. Both are within close proximity to Guilin train station.

There's also a direct shuttle service to Dazhai from Yangshuo (¥90, 4½ hours) departing at 8am, 9am and 1pm.

For public transport from Guilin, head to the city's North Bus Station (p641) or Qintan Bus Station (p641). Here you can take a bus to Longsheng (龙胜; ¥40, 1½ hours, every 30 minutes 6am to 7pm) and ask to get off at Heping (和平). From the road junction (or the ticket office three minutes' walk away), minibuses trundle between Longsheng and the rice terraces, stopping to pick up passengers to Dazhai or Ping'an. Regular buses depart for Dazhai (one way/return ¥30/40, 1½ hours, every 40 minutes 7.10am to 5.30pm), but are less frequent for Ping'an, with six buses daily buses departing Longsheng (¥20/30, one hour, 7.30am, 9am, 11am, 1pm, 3pm and 5pm).

To continue to Sanjiang, catch a bus (¥22, two hours, every 30 minutes) from Longsheng bus station; the last bus is at 6pm. The bus runs scenically along the river to Sanjiang.

If you're renting a car from Guilin, count on paying around ¥400 one way for the 110km journey.

ℹ Getting Around

You can walk between Ping'an and Dazhai (four hours), but to catch a bus from Dazhai to Ping'an you first need to take a bus to Erlong Bridge (二龙桥, Èrlóng Qiáo; ¥15), then another (though much less frequent) bus to Ping'an (¥10). The same applies in the other direction. Alternatively, you could arrange a taxi for the 6km leg between Ping'an and Erlong Bridge for ¥50. A taxi between Ping'an and Dazhai costs ¥150.

For Tiantouzhai, it's a 40-minute walk from the bus stand in Dazhai. Otherwise, if you have a booking with a guesthouse, you can arrange a complimentary bus shuttle (five to six per day); though at the time of research there remained doubts whether this would remain a permanent service.

Most rice terraces involve anywhere from a 20-minute walk to 1½-hour walk. If you're short on time or energy, you can take the cable car (p643) up to Golden Buddha Peak from Dazhai.

Sanjiang   三江

📞 0772 / POP 367,707

While riverside Sanjiang (Sānjiāng) is a rather hectic, nondescript city, for tourists it serves as a convenient springboard to the ethereal Dong villages and their architectural wonders in Chengyang (程阳), 18km north of the city.

Set among picturesque countryside of verdant rice fields, scenic rivers and mountains, Chengyang comprises eight adjoining villages that are inhabited by the ethnic minority Dong people. Each features an ornate, traditional drum tower, charming wooden architecture, nail-less bridges and fertile vegetable gardens. The homes are simple one- or two-storey cabins made of chocolate-toned cedar bark that exude an ancient grace evocative of Kyoto. The Dong are known for their exquisite carpentry and each home is a celebration of that skill.

◉ Sights

★ **Chengyang Bridge**   BRIDGE
(程阳桥, Chéngyángqiáo, Wind & Rain Bridge; Linxi, 林溪) In the district of Chengyang, around 18km north of Sanjiang, Chéngyángqiáo is the grandest of over 100 nail-less Wind and Rain Bridges in the area. This photogenic black-and-white structure (78m) was built from cedar and stone over 12 years in the early 1900s, and features towers with upturned eaves, pavilions where people gather to socialise or take shelter from the elements, and a sweeping corridor with handrails and benches.

For superb views over the bridge, eight villages and beyond, take the 20-minute trek up to the **Lai Nu Pavilion**, which is appropriately named 'beauty' in the Dong language. To get here, cross Chengyang Bridge and take a right, and after 200m you'll reach the signed trailhead. The path loops over to the other side of town, so you don't need to backtrack.

🛏 Sleeping

Chengyang has a number of atmospheric guesthouses near the bridge. Sanjiang itself has many hotels, especially along Furong Lu (芙蓉路), not far from the east bus station, but the town is not a particularly appealing place.

DON'T MISS

DRUM TOWERS

A drum tower resembles a flamboyant, multi-eaved pagoda plonked on a rectangular pavilion; many are found in Dong villages in the region. The taller ones are built entirely of cedar. Donate a few coins as you enter, and look up at the receding beams and the scale-like tiles. Some towers have a fire pit. Once the social and religious heart of the village, they're now colonised by old men watching TV and playing ping pong.

Most villages still have their old drum tower too – by comparison a much smaller and squat structure – that's the domain for elderly ladies to sit and gossip. Each of the drum towers is built in the village main square, and is faced by an opposing stage on which tables are often set up for mahjong games.

Among the drum towers in the Chengyang area, you can't miss **Ma'an's** ornate 60-year-old wooden tower, along with the newer, but more impressive-sized towers, in the villages of **Yan** and **Ping**, which stand more than 25m high. The granddaddy of towers, however, is in Sanjiang, with its monumental 42.6m-high structure that dominates the main square along the river.

⭐ **Dong Village Hotel** INN ¥¥
(程阳桥侗家宾馆, Chéngyángqiáo Dòngjiā Bīnguǎn; ☑ 0772 858 2421; Chengyangqiao, 程阳桥; d/tr ¥180/240; ❄ ❋ ☎) This popular inn, run by friendly, English-speaking owner Michael Yang, is superbly located right by the bridge. Rooms, connected by a creaking staircase, are spacious and attractively decorated and come with balconies, air-con and modern bathrooms. It's a 20-minute walk from the main road where the bus drops you off, about 100m to the right of the bridge.

Yeste Hotel HOTEL ¥¥
(耶斯特酒店, Yésītè Jiǔdiàn; ☑ 0772 862 6888, 400 009 1199; www.yestehotel.com; Furong Lu, Sanjiang, 芙蓉路; d ¥115-398; ❋ ☎) In case you needed to stay in Sanjiang itself, this reasonably glossy three-star hotel has clean, spacious and comfortable rooms. Staff are not that used to dealing with foreigners, but are very friendly. It's conveniently located in between the east and west bus stations.

⭐ **Entertainment**

Pingzha Performing Arts Centre TRADITIONAL MUSIC
(表演中心, Biǎoyǎn Zhōngxīn; Ping Village, 平潭; adult ¥30; ⊙ 10.30am & 3.30pm) In the village of Ping, 800m northwest of Chenyang Bridge, is this open-air stage that hosts daily traditional Dong music and dance performances. If there are enough people there's also an evening performance held at 7.30pm.

ℹ **Information**

In Sanjiang, **ICBC** (工商银行, Gōngshāng Yínháng; 22 Dongxiang Dadao, 侗乡大道22号) cannot change money, but has a 24-hour ATM.

The **tourist office** (旅游服务中心, Lǚyóu Fúwù Zhōngxīn; ☑ 0772 858 1288; 19 Dongxiang Dadao, 侗乡大道19号; ⊙ 8am-6pm) on Dongxiang Dadao will do its best to help, however English-language proficiency is limited to conversing via translation apps.

ℹ **Getting There & Away**

For Chengyang Bridge, take the half-hourly bus (¥4, 30 minutes, 7.30am to 5.30pm) bound for Linxi (林溪). It departs from the main road outside the west bus station, located 200m on your first right after you cross the bridge. If you miss the last bus, you'll likely find private minivans to Linxi (the fare is the same but they won't leave until they're full). Otherwise a taxi costs ¥70.

High-speed trains arrive and depart from the **Sanjiang South Train Station** (三江南站, Sānjiāng Nánzhàn), located 9km south of town, reached by bus 4 (¥3) that passes through the city centre.

Heading north towards Hunan and Fenghuang, you'll need to go to Sanjiang Train Station (三江县站, Sānjiāng Xiàn Zhàn), around 10km north of town. There's one train per day from here to Huaihua ((¥33, 4¼ hours) at 7.14pm.

For a ¥5 commission, you can get train tickets from a **ticket office** (Huǒchē Shōupiàochù; opposite Bird's Nest, Dongxiang Dadao, 侗乡大道, 鸟巢对面; ⊙ 9am-noon & 1-6pm) opposite the Bird's Nest (三江侗乡鸟巢, Sānjiàng Dòngxiāng Niǎocháo) on Dongxiang Dadao, which is just beyond the tourist office.

Yangshuo 阳朔

☑ 0773 / POP 308,296

Yangshuo (Yángshuò) is one of China's gold-ticket draws. The once-peaceful settlement is now a collage of Chinese tour groups, bewildered westerners, pole-dancing bars, construction and the glue that binds any tourist hotspot together – touts. Come evening, Xijie is all thumping music and bristling with selfie-sticks, but go up a few flights to a hotel rooftop bar and behold the ethereal beauty of the surrounding karsts, their peaks lit up by searchlights.

◉ Sights & Activities

Yangshou is very much an outdoors destination, and there are many ways to enjoy the superb natural scenery, from cycling, hiking and bamboo rafting, to rock climbing, river trekking and caving.

The most accessible of Yangshuo's limestone peaks is **Green Lotus Peak** (Bilian Peak, 碧莲峰, Bìlián Fēng; ¥22; ⏱8am-6pm), which overlooks Xijie and the Li River, and can be climbed in half an hour. **Ma Shan** (马山) better known as the Yangshuo TV Tower, is one for more adventurous types. It's to the south of town and doesn't come with an admission fee; this one-hour climb offers stupendous views. It's tricky to find, so to get here take the route marked on Maps.Me. **Yangshuo Park** (阳朔公园, Yángshuò Gōngyuán) is a short walk west of Xijie and that's where you'll find **Man Hill** (西郎山, Xīláng Shān) 'bowing' to **Lady Hill** (小姑山, Xiǎogū Shān).

Don't overlook going for a walk along the **Li River** (Lijiang Jiāngbīn Dào, 漓江江滨道; Binjiang Lu, 滨江路), to get away from the crowds and take in beautiful panoramas of karst peaks, glittering river water and green bamboo. It's a stunning sight, and you can walk for a fair distance along the bank of the river, past folk practising taichi, and see what coming to Yangshuo is all about.

Wandering Dao
WELLNESS
(☎189 7868 6637; www.wanderingdao.com; Furong Lu 8, 芙蓉街8号) Quebec-born owner Daniel, and his wife Chen, run this wellness centre upstairs from their vegetarian restaurant. They offer a long list of Daoist treatments, meditation, yoga, massage and natural medicines, as well as cleansing and detox programs. There's also an onsite tourmaline sauna and a small gym. Check the website for its full range of options.

⛟ Tours

★ Bike Asia
CYCLING
(自行车亚州, Zìxíngchē Yàzhōu; ☎0773 882 6521; www.bikeasia.com; 5 Furong St, 芙蓉街5号; guide per day incl lunch from ¥340; ⏱8am-6.30pm Mar-Dec; 🚲) Bike Asia offers English-speaking

guides and a range of themed tours that take in anything from mountain-biking and cooking to family-oriented trips. It's also good for DIY travellers, and offers the best equipment and advice on trips; bike rental is ¥70 to ¥100 per day (deposit ¥300) and includes a helmet, repair kit and a self-guided tour map.

🛏 Sleeping

Yangshuo teems with hotels run by English-speaking staff, and virtually all provide wi-fi access and air-con. While the Xijie neighbourhood is stuffed with choices, quieter and more attractive lodgings lie on the outskirts.

Bella's Inn
GUESTHOUSE ¥
(阳朔贝拉的小院, Yángshuò Bèi Lā De Xiǎo Yuàn; ☎136 7786 1677; 10 Fuhou Lane, 府后巷10号贝; d from ¥80; 🅿🖥) One for budget travellers who aren't into the whole backpacker scene is this stylish guesthouse run by the friendly, English-speaking Bella. Rooms are sparsely furnished with polished concrete floors and have comfy beds, fast wi-fi, reliable air-con and functional bathrooms. Head up to its rooftop terrace to enjoy pleasing karst views.

Green Forest Hostel
HOSTEL ¥
(Travelling with Hostel, 瓦舍, Wǎshě; ☎0773 888 2686; greenforest_yangshuo@yahoo.com; 3rd fl, Zone A, Business St, Chengzhongcheng, Diecui Lu, 叠翠路, 城中城, 城南商业街A区3楼; dm ¥30-50, r ¥120-200; 🅿@🖥) This hostel's attractiveness is highlighted by the rundown building it's in. Rooms are painted white with colourful accents and have earth-toned furnishings; communal areas are flooded in natural light. Dorms come with curtains and power points, while private rooms are modern and comfortable. There's a lounge at reception with a bar, tour info and an attached cafe.

C Source West Street Residence
HOTEL ¥¥
(禧朔源西街公馆, Xǐshuòyuán Xijiē Gōngguǎn; ☎0773 882 9489; www.csourceweststreetresidence. com; 79 Xijie, 西街79号; r/ste from ¥320/500; 🅿@🖥) Set a bit back from heaving Xijie is this hotel in a 270-year-old-plus building that was once part of a Jiangxi Guildhall (江西会馆). Elegant, swish rooms are stylishly and traditionally Chinese and modern, although the effect is spoiled by the cheap green lettering out front.

River View Hotel
HOTEL ¥¥
(望江楼酒店, Wàngjiānglóu Jiǔdiàn; ☎0773 882 2688; www.riverview.com.cn; 25 Binjiang Lu, 滨江路 25号; r ¥328-658; 🅿@🖥) If you prefer staying downtown but want to avoid the crowds, this

Yangshuo

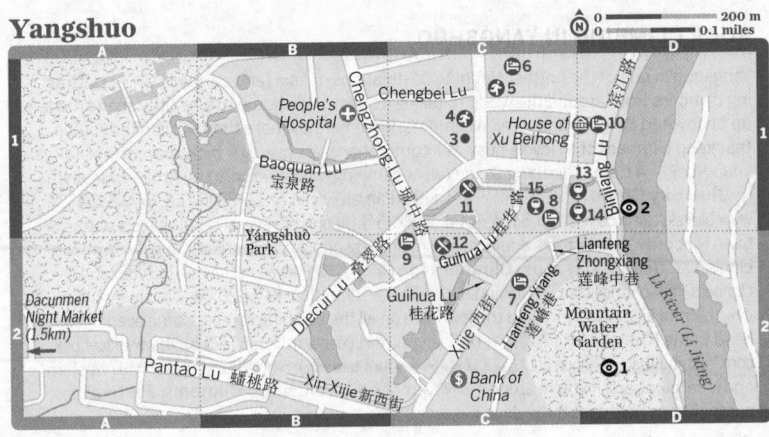

good-value hotel is a decent bet. The balcony rooms overlook the Li River and feature a good balance between traditional Chinese style and western comforts. The restaurant (p648) on the ground floor is a wonderful choice, too.

★**Alila Yangshuo**　　　BOUTIQUE HOTEL ¥¥¥
(阿丽拉阳朔糖舍, Ālìlā Yángshuò Táng Shě; ☑0773 888 3999; www.alilahotels.com/yangshuo; 102 Dongling Lu, 东岭路102号; r incl breakfast from ¥2250; ✵❋❋) One of Yangshuo's most memorable stays is this old, Chinese sugarbeet factory – complete with Cultural Revolution slogans – that's been converted into a hub of luxury and design. Set among limestone karst peaks, its location is stunning, and one you can bask in from its opulent infinity pool. Room design is sleek, minimalist and modernist-inspired with ambient lighting and stylish industrial touches.

✗ Eating

In Yangshuo you can find anything from wood-fired pizza and chicken korma to full English breakfasts, vegan cuisine and outposts of US fast-food empires.

Local specialities include *tiánluóniàng* (田螺酿; stuffed snails) and *píjiǔ yú* (啤酒鱼; beer fish). The fish with the least bones are *jiàngǔyú* (剑骨鱼) and the bigger and cheaper ones *máogǔyú* (毛骨鱼). Almost all restaurants have English menus.

Mood Food Cafe　　　VEGETARIAN ¥
(☑189 7868 6637; www.wanderingdao.com; Furong Lu 8, 芙蓉街8号; mains ¥28-55; ☉8am-10pm; ☎✐) Cooking up some of the best international cuisine in Yangshuo, Mood offers a long menu of wholefood, vegetarian and vegan dishes. Most items are made from scratch, ranging from nourishing bowls loaded with superfoods, along with veggie plates,

ROCK CLIMBING IN YANGSHUO

Yangshuo is one of the hottest climbing destinations in Asia (and certainly China), attracting climbers from around the world to tackle its peaks. It's home to a healthy scene made up of devoted Chinese and foreign climbers, lured here by more than 900 bolted routes that keep climbers of all levels busy. For comprehensive coverage, pick up a copy of *Yangshuo Rock – A China Climbing Guide* (www.climbingyangshuo.com) by Andrew Hedesh.

Blue Sky Climb (蓝天攀岩俱乐部, Lántiān Pānyán Jùlèbù; ☑ 137 8843 7131, 0773 882 4337; www.blueskyclimb.com; 2nd fl, 5 Furong Rd, 芙蓉街5号) is one of several reputable operators in town that offer guided trips, equipment hire and lessons. And if you want to get *in* with the climbing fraternity, stay at the **Climbers Inn** (攀岩客栈, Pānyán Kèzhàn; ☑ 138 7837 9347; climbers-inn@hotmail.com; 21 Guihua Lu, 桂花路21号; dm/r from ¥40/120; 🌐🛜), run by the ever-helpful Lily, who'll give you the lowdown on all the climbing routes. Come evenings, head to the **Rusty Bolt** (生锈的螺栓, Shēng Xiù de Luóshuān; ☑ 135 1773 1064; www.facebook.com/rustyboltbar; 7 Guihua Lu, 桂花路7号; ⊙ 6.30pm-late; 🛜), a dive bar popular with western and local climbers. If you're around in November, the **Yangshuo Climbing Festival** has competitions held over three days.

soups and salads, to comfort food such as veggie burgers and nachos.

River View Hotel Restaurant
GUANGXI, WESTERN ¥

(望江楼餐厅, Wàngjiānglóu Cāntīng; ☑ 0773 882 2688; www.riverview.com.cn; 25 Binjiang Lu, 滨江路25号; mains ¥12-98; ⊙ 7.30am-11.30pm; 🌐🍴) Just a street removed from traffic-choked Diecui Lu, this place offers good food, quiet surrounds and attractive prices, with river views to boot. There's an English menu with pizzas and burgers, and a Chinese one with all the usual suspects and the likes of Yangshuo beer duck and excellent vegetarian options. Good breakfasts too.

Lèngwá Shǎnxī Fēngwèiguǎn
CHINESE ¥

(愣娃陕西风味馆; 21 Diecui Lu, 叠翠路21号; mains from ¥10; ⊙ 8.30am-11pm) This small and simple Shanxi eatery specialises in the addictive *ròujiāmó* (肉夹馍; flat-bread buns filled with beef or pork and peppers) and *biángbiángmiàn* (flat Shanxi noodles; the character for *biáng* is the most complicated in Mandarin, and impossible to reproduce here). One *ròujiāmó* is ¥10 and two are almost a meal; a bowl of *biángbiángmiàn* is ¥30.

Dacunmen Night Market
MARKET ¥

(大村门夜市, Dàcūnmén Yèshì; Pantao Lu, 蟠桃路; ⊙ 5pm-late) This night market is a culture-filled slice of Yangshuo life. Watch locals sniffing out the best spices, haggling over snails or tucking into a hotpot. It's a 30-minute walk from Xijie. After you pass the petrol station on Pantao Lu, look for the fire station on the left, behind which is the night market.

Lucy's
INTERNATIONAL ¥¥

(露茜, Lùxī; 30 Guihua Lu, 桂花路30号; mains ¥30-148; ⊙ 7am-midnight; 🌐🛜) With graffiti-splattered walls, Lucy's is quite an institution. Western and Chinese food are done with equal aplomb: aim for one of the terrace seats upstairs overlooking the tourist traffic below. There's shepherd's pie (¥58), beer fish (¥128), crispy duck (¥48), sizzling beef platter (¥55), tuna spaghetti (¥40) and more, plus full English brekkies (¥38).

🍷 Drinking & Nightlife

Yangshuo's West St area is stuffed with bars, but there are few of character and taste, and many are cheesy. Just off Xijie is where German beer gardens sit alongside generic western-style cafes. Among all this there are a handful of quality drinking spots attracting cool locals and travellers.

★ Demo Bar
CRAFT BEER

(☑ 191 7831 5450; www.facebook.com/demobar; 31-34 Binjiang Lu, 滨江路31-34号; beer from ¥30; ⊙ noon-late Tue-Sun; 🛜) With a prime riverfront location overlooking karst peaks, Demo's outdoor terrace is the perfect spot to come for a sundowner of quality craft beers. Its four beers on tap are all from Trip Smith microbrewery in Guiyang, with a pale ale, IPAs and a seasonal to go with a menu of pizzas. It attracts a cool crowd of local musos.

Kaya
BAR

(☑ 186 7735 0084; 31 Xianqian Jie, beside Shuangyue Bridge, 县前街31号双月桥旁边; drinks ¥20-50; ⊙ 7.30pm-3am; 🛜) Bars that do not play C-pop or hire pole dancers have a hard time surviving in Yangshuo, which makes this 'Jamaica pub' an anomaly. Run by dreadlocked owner-DJ Topper, Kaya has reggae performances, to go with bass and dubstep, along with quality Chinese craft beers in the fridge. Entry is via the clothes store downstairs, giving it a speakeasy feel.

Zermo Coffee COFFEE
(cnr Furong Lu & Fuxian Alley; coffee from ¥20; ⏰10am-9pm; 🛜) Down a leafy street is this chic microroaster doing pour-over coffees brewed using single-origin beans from Yunnan, Central America and Ethiopia. Its plant-filled, contemporary decor will suit freelance travellers looking for a workspace.

Mojo Bar BAR
(露天酒吧, Lùtiān Jiǔbā; 6th fl, Alshan Hotel, 18 Xijie, 西街18号阿里山大酒店六楼; ⏰7pm-3am; 🛜) Way above the throngs choking Xijie, Mojo Bar – on the 6th floor and roof of the Alshan Hotel – has the most amazing outdoor terrace with wraparound views of the *Avatar*-like karst landscape. It's regarded as the place to kick on into the night, with pool and cheap beer (Tsingtao ¥20): it's where things get loose late in the evening.

⭐ Entertainment

Impressions Liu Sanjie PERFORMING ARTS
(印象刘三姐, Yìnxiàng Liú Sānjiě; 📞0773 881 7783; tickets ¥200-680, children free-¥90; ⏰7.30-8.30pm & 9.30-10.30pm) The busiest show in town is directed by filmmaker Zhang Yimou, who also directed acclaimed films such as *Raise the Red Lantern* and *House of Flying Daggers*. Six hundred performers take to the Li River each night with 12 illuminated karst peaks serving as a backdrop. Book at your hotel for discounts and transport to/from the venue (1.5km from town).

ℹ️ Information

Travel agencies are all over town. Backpacker-oriented cafes and most hotels can also often dispense good advice. Shop around for the best deals.
Bank of China (中国银行, Zhōngguó Yínháng; Xijie, 西街; ⏰9am-5pm) Foreign exchange and 24-hour ATM for international cards.
People's Hospital (人民医院, Rénmín Yīyuàn; 📞0773 882 2472; 26 Chengzhong Lu, 城中路 26号) English-speaking doctors available.

ℹ️ Getting There & Away

AIR
The closest airport is in Guilin. There are eight daily buses to the airport (¥50) departing from Yangshuo South Bus Station. A taxi ride is about ¥300 (one hour), or ¥240 with DiDi.

BUS
Yangshuo's buses leave from the **South Bus Station** (汽车南站, Qìchē Nánzhàn; courtyard of the Agriculture Mechanisation Management Bureau, 321 Guodao, 国道321号, 农业机械化管理局); however, at the time of writing there was some talk of this relocating to a new location outside town.

Direct bus links are as follows:
Guilin ¥27, one hour, every 15 to 20 minutes 6.45am to 8.30pm
Guilin Airport ¥50, 1½ hours, eight daily 7am to 7pm
Huangyao ¥61, 2½ hours, two daily (9.40am and 2.10pm)
Nanning ¥140, six hours, 10am
Xingping ¥10, one hour, every 15 minutes 6.30am to 6pm
Yangdi ¥10, one hour, every 20 minutes 6am to 6pm

Buses for Yangshuo train station depart from the **terminal** (Yangshuo Transportation Centre, 凤鸣停车场; Kangzhan Lu, 康战路), 500m south from the South Bus Station.

There's also a direct bus to Longji Rice Terraces, which is booked through the hotels in Dazhai, departing at 8am, 9am and 1pm from varying locations.

TRAIN
While there's no train station in the town itself, Yangshuo Train Station, 14km away near Xingping, has regular high-speed trains. To get here you'll need to take the bus (¥20, 50 minutes).

ℹ️ Getting Around

Most places in town can be reached by taxi for under ¥20. Bicycles can be rented at almost all hostels and from streetside outlets for ¥20 per day. A deposit of ¥200 to ¥500 is standard, but don't hand over your passport. For quality mountain bikes, head to Bike Asia (p646).

Bike-rental operators will rent you an electric scooter (from ¥150 per day) or petrol scooter (from ¥200) without asking to see a driver's licence. Scooters can make the going easier, but be aware that if you don't have a Chinese driver's licence, you will probably not be insured (international driving licences are not accepted in China) and things could get complicated and costly in the event of an accident.

Around Yangshuo

The countryside of Yangshuo and the region through which the Li River (漓江, Lí Jiāng) and its tributary waterways flow offer weeks of exploration by bike, boat, foot or any

Around Yangshuo

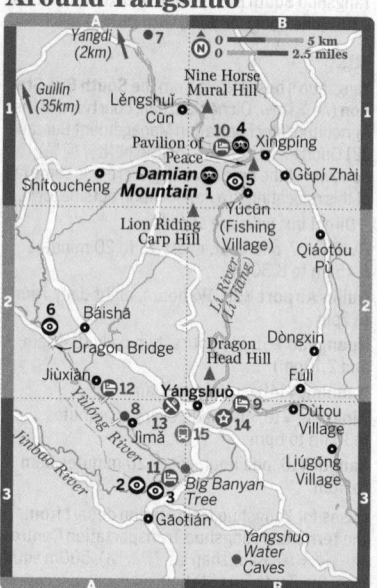

combination thereof. Scenes that inspired generations of Chinese painters are the standard here: wallowing water buffalo and farmers tending their crops against a backdrop of limestone peaks. Some of the villages come alive on market days, which operate on a three-, six- and nine-day monthly cycle. The Yulong River, the very pretty tributary of the Li River, courses through this region, making for fantastic day trips, with riverside villages to explore, ancient settlements to stop by and verdant hills to climb.

◎ Sights

Moon Hill
HILL

(月亮山, Yuèliàng Shān; ¥15) A 30-minute – extremely sweaty – climb up steps to the magnificent natural arch that adorns Moon Hill (380m) is rewarded with both lost calories and some exhilarating views of surrounding peaks and the tapestry of flat fields in the lowlands. Load up with liquids in hot weather, and be prepared to be pounced on by hawkers flogging water.

Longtan Village
VILLAGE

(龙潭村, Lóngtán Cūn; ¥16; ⊙8am-6pm) This fascinating village about 1.5km beyond Moon Hill is a treasure trove of traditional Qing dynasty architecture. Beyond the initial, slightly cheesy scenic area at the beginning,

you reach the village proper, where you can get lost in a maze of tight lanes. Look out for the old **Opium Den** (烟馆, Yānguǎn) at No 89 Longtan Cun, which didn't close till 1940, and note the village's carved upturned lintels, astonishingly regular brickwork and ample distribution of Cultural Revolution slogans.

Yulong River
RIVER

(遇龙河, Yùlóng Hé; from ¥180) The scenery along this small river about 6km southwest of Yangshuo is breathtaking, and best enjoyed by bamboo raft. Though the set-up for the rafting has become very touristy and over-regulated (it's now all ticketed and you have to wear a lifejacket), once you're out on the water it's a relaxing way to take in the views. The rafts are constructed using bamboo planks and poled by a boatman, but fitted with chairs and a tacky umbrella.

⚓ Courses

Yangshuo Cooking School
COOKING

(阳朔烹饪学校, Yángshuò Pēngrèn Xuéxiào; ☎137 8843 7286; Chaolong Village; Zhāoyáng Cūn, 朝阳

村; per person¥190) A bucolic setting overlooking rice fields and karst peaks is the location for this classy cooking school. Here you can learn to make a variety of Chinese cuisine, including local dishes such as beer fish.

🛌 Sleeping

Some of Yangshuo's best sleeping options lie scattered among the peaks and hills around the town, in the lush Li River and Yulong River region, making it the area of choice to base yourself for either short or extended stays.

Wada Hostel Yulong River HOSTEL ¥

(和田旅馆玉龙河, Hétián Lüguǎn Yùlóng Hé; ☑147 9601 6001; www.wadahostel.com/en/yangshuo; 146 Chaoyang Village, 朝阳村146号; dm ¥25-50, d ¥100-180, tr ¥128-236; ❄@ 🛜) One of few genuine budget places out this way is this long-established hostel that's now opened a branch here in Chaoyang Village, 5km from Yangshuo. Modern dorms are equipped with personal lamps, powerpoints and the privacy of curtains, while private rooms are basic but spacious and some have karst views. It has a small cafe and bicycle hire (per day ¥20).

Phoenix Pagoda
Fonglou Retreat BOUTIQUE HOTEL ¥¥

(凤楼岁月, Fènglóu Suìyuè; ☑0773 877 8458, 180 7730 5230; 98 Fenglou Village, Gaotian Town, 高田镇, 凤楼村98号; d ¥320-380, f ¥560; ⊖❄@🛜) The 12 rooms here have wide balconies overlooking the hills, furniture made from local materials, wi-fi and no TV. The Taiwanese owner Jerry has tips on hiking and biking. It's around a ¥40 taxi ride from downtown Yangshuo.

★ Tea Cozy Hotel BOUTIQUE HOTEL ¥¥¥

(水云阁, Shuǐyún Gé; ☑135 0783 9490, 0773 881 6158; www.yangshuoteacozy.com; 212 Báishā Zhèn, Xiatang Village, 白沙镇夏棠村212号; r ¥580, ste ¥680-980; ❄@🛜🏊) What makes Tea Cozy a true winner is not the 18 traditional-style balcony rooms (though these are wonderful in themselves), but the exceptional service by the English-speaking staff. Also laudable are the culinary skills of the restaurant staff (mains ¥20 to ¥128), while its pool offers superb views of the bucolic countryside and karst peaks.

★ Secret Garden BOUTIQUE HOTEL ¥¥¥

(秘密花园酒店, Mìmì Huāyuán Jiǔdiàn; ☑0773 877 1932; www.yangshuosecretgarden.com; Jiuxian Village, 旧县村; r ¥498-888; ❄@🛜) Middlesbrough-born South African designer Ian Hamlinton (nicknamed 'Crazy One' by the

locals) has energetically and lovingly converted a cluster of Ming dynasty houses in the village of Jiuxian into a gorgeous western-style boutique hotel with a choice selection of classy rooms. Its restaurant does burgers and pizzas, along with local Guangxi cuisine and homemade wine made using seasonal fruits.

🍴 Eating

★ Luna ITALIAN ¥¥

(☑0773 877 8169; www.yangshuoguesthouse. com; 26 Moon Hill Village (Li Village), Gaotian Town, 月亮村 (历村) 26号, 高田镇; mains ¥30-70; ⏱7.30am-11pm; 🛜) This fine rooftop restaurant experience is one of Yangshuo's best. The view of Moon Hill isn't quite as amazing as it used to be – thanks to a neighbour building a stack opposite – but it's still sublime. And the food remains top-notch: the rigatoni *alla amatriciana* (smoked bacon, onion and tomato) is lovely, but the whole menu's a winner. Romantic, delightful, highly appetising.

❶ Getting There & Away

The region is best reached from Yangshuo by a combination of bus, bike and taxi. Bikes can be hired from rental operators along Xi Jie, especially towards the southern end, where you can also rent electric and petrol scooters. Buses to this region depart from Yangshuo; you can jump aboard them along Pantao Lu. If you plan to come by taxi, the area around Moon Hill can be tricky due to a restriction on non-local cars entering the traffic-control zone from 8am to 5.30pm; however, cars arranged by local guesthouses are able to pass.

❶ Getting Around

The best way to explore this region is by bike, leisurely cycling through the flatlands of this karst region. Hiking is also an option and boating trips are available too.

Xingping 兴坪

☑0773 / POP 43,000

Some say Xingping (Xìngpíng) is just like Yangshuo before the latter became a honeypot, for better or worse. This 1750-year-old town has loads of history and is certainly attractive; the landscape you'll see here is printed on the back of China's ¥20 banknote.

Travellers still come here for its yesteryear flavours, and though things have become a lot busier, once the rush hour of tourist boats has passed, by mid-afternoon, you'll see the town return back to its languid self. It's also worth adding time here to cross the river and explore the villages and country-side by bicycle or scooter.

◉ Sights & Activities

★ Damian Mountain VIEWPOINT
(达米安山, Dámǐān Shān) FREE For truly spectacular outlooks over the region's famed karst topography, take the sweaty 45-minute trek up to the top of this jungle-clad mountain. Combined with views of the Li River, the sight of these jagged limestone peaks stretching endlessly into the horizon is astounding. While the path up is clearly visible, finding the trailhead can be tricky; take the route labelled on Maps.Me. Otherwise the team at Nirvana Organic Farm can assist with directions.

Laozhai Hill VIEWPOINT
(老寨山, Lǎozhài Shān) Just on the edge of town, Laozhai Hill is the most accessible of Xingping's limestone peaks, a tough 300m climb that'll reward you with life-affirming outlooks of the Li River and its superb karst surrounds. It's around 35 minutes to walk up the stairs, with a few small ladders to keep things interesting.

Twenty Yuan View VIEWPOINT
(二十元景色, Èrshí Yuán Chákàn) To get the same perspective as the image emblazoned on the ¥20 note (with that obligatory snap of money in hand), cross the bridge at the harbour and walk for 20 minutes until you reach the multiple viewpoints set along the riverfront.

Xingping Fishing Village VILLAGE
(鱼村, Yúcūn) Miraculously untouched during the Sino-Japanese War and the Cultural Revolution, this 400-year-old village has friendly residents and vernacular houses similar to those at Xingping. The 1½-hour hike (one way) takes you through the scenic countryside among farmland, fruit orchards and stunning views; otherwise you can opt for one of the tourist ferries from Xingping (¥60) that stop off here.

Xingping Ancient Stage HISTORIC SITE
(兴平古戏台, Xìngpíng Gǔ Xìtái; ⏰9am-5pm)
FREE The highlight of Xingping's old street is this well-preserved and attractive Qing dynasty opera stage and museum (Chinese captions only). You can see intricate carvings depicting operatic scenes and slash marks made by prop weaponry on the pillars. If you want to take pictures, an old man may collect a ¥1 donation from you. The trendy-looking **Master Cafe** is in the same compound.

Bamboo Rafting BOATING
(per person ¥80) For those looking to get out on to the water, the 'bamboo' rafts (actually constructed from PVC tubes, and powered by an outboard motor) are a popular choice. They putt along a dramatic stretch of the Li River from Yangdi to Nine Horse Mountain, offering fantastic, all-encompassing views.

🛏 Sleeping & Eating

Xingping's rural setting makes it a great place to stay overnight.

Some excellent dining options can be found in Xingping, complementing the town's attractiveness as an overnight option.

★ This Old Place Youth Hostel HOSTEL ¥
(老地方, Lǎo Dìfang; ☑0773 870 2887; www.top xingping.com; 5 Rongtan Lu, 榕潭街5号; dm ¥30-50, s/d/q from ¥80/135/200; ❄@�) At the far end of town near the river is this popular hostel with a lovely backpacker vibe. Split over two buildings, rooms are really pleasant; the south-facing ones in the new wing are the best. Its rooftop terrace has magnificent views, and is best enjoyed digging into a wood-fired pizza with a cold beer.

Nirvana Organic Farm Inn GUESTHOUSE ¥¥
(涅槃生态庄园酒店, Nièpán Shēngtài Zhuāngyuán Jiǔdiàn; ☑189 7739 8982; www.nirvanaorganicfarm. com; Dahebei Village, Dahebei Cūn, 大河背村; d ¥220-389; ❄�) � Offering a chilled-out and less touristy alternative to Xingping is this relaxed guesthouse set in the countryside on a small, organic permaculture farm. It's the site of a former primary school, of which the rooms on the ground floor offer tatami seating and garden views, while upstairs has rooms with balcony and karst views.

To get here you'll need to take the small pontoon across the river at Xingping, from where it's a five-minute bike ride, or a 20-minute walk. Otherwise, call ahead to arrange someone to pick you up.

ℹ Getting There & Away

High-speed trains connect Xingping with Guilin, Nanning, Guangzhou and other destinations via Yangshuo train station, 8km northeast of town; buses (¥5, 10 minutes) depart Xingping every 15 minutes for the station, from 6.30am to 6pm.

Regular buses depart from Xingping to Yangshuo (¥10, one hour), with the last departure at 6pm. There's also a bus to Guilin (¥35, two hours), but the train is a much faster and more economical option.

ⓘ Getting Around

While the immediate area is lovely to explore by foot, to venture further into the countryside, it's best to hire a bicycle (¥25) from This Old Place for the day. A small pontoon ferry (¥5) will punt you across the Li River from 7.30am to 6.30pm.

If you want to get out on the water your only options are the bamboo raft or motorised boat cruises (¥60); both are very touristy, but you can't fault the views.

Huangyao 黄姚

☑ 0774 / POP 62,000

Huangyao (Huángyáo) is one of Guangxi's most picturesque villages, with many movies filmed here; *The Painted Veil*, starring Edward Norton, is possibly the most well known. This is fitting given it feels more like a film set than a living, working town, with the town existing these days solely for tourism.

Bucolic charm permeates the lovingly preserved 900-year-old village, though Huangyao struggles to cope with the influx of roving tour groups and housing them all. There's plenty on its eight streets to ensure the ¥100 entry fee is well spent, including two massive 500-year-old Chinese banyans that have wound their way up from the river's edge.

Guōjiā Dàyuàn (郭家大院; 44 An Dongjie, 安东街44号) is one of the village's most standout historical buildings, named after the Guo family that lived here. The compound includes ornate architectural features, including circular doorways, a picturesque lake and temple.

🛏 Sleeping & Eating

Given the infrequency of public transport here, most visitors have no choice but to spend the night in Huangyao. There's no shortage of accommodation options, some very comfortable, generally inexpensive and with plenty of Qing-dynasty charm.

Huangyao is famous for its condiments and chilli salsa, which you'll see and smell everywhere. Many of the guesthouses and accommodation choices can cook up good food, but there are some excellent places to eat around the villages.

Heterotopias Club BOUTIQUE HOTEL ¥¥
(异托邦会馆, Yìtuōbāng Huìguǎn; ☑ 181 7679 6519; heterotopias@126.com; 49 Anle Jie, 安乐街49号; r ¥152-250; 🌬 ❈ @ 🐾) With its cultured, civilised air and eight elegant rooms, Heterotopias sits inside an old courtyard complex. The owners are intellectual types and the

hotel's white walls and minimalist aesthetic showcase their literary collection and paintings by their artist friends to great effect.

Yanimu GUESTHOUSE ¥¥
(一念一梦客栈, Yīniànyīmèng Kèzhàn; ☑ 0774 672 2477; 66 Anle Jie, 安乐街66号; r ¥158-188; ❈ 🐾) This sweet little traditional place is buried away down an alley, and features an attractive courtyard with a leafy canopy. Some of the rooms are squashy and lacking in natural light, so try to take a look at a few. The English-speaking owners have numerous other places in the village if this one is full.

★ **Dailong Farmer Restaurant** GUANGXI ¥
(带龙桥龙家饭庄, Dàilóngqiáo Lóngjiā Fànzhuāng; Zhongxing Jie, 中兴街; mains ¥20-138; ⏱ 7am-8pm) Rarely does a famous eatery (it's been featured countless times by the media) uphold its culinary excellence, but that's precisely why patrons keep returning to feast on steamed spare ribs (豆豉蒸排骨, dòuchǐ zhēng páigǔ), stuffed tofu (豆腐酿, dòufu niàng) and other deliciousness on the riverbank. It's at the start of Dailong Bridge.

ⓘ Getting There & Away

Two direct buses run daily from Guilin (¥61, 3½ hours, 9am and 1.30pm) via Yangshuo (2½ hours, 9.40am and 2.10pm); for the latter, you'll be transferred via minivan to meet the bus. The return buses usually leave at 8.20am and 2pm, though the service is erratic, so check before you leave. If returning to Yangshuo, you'll be dropped off at the junction from where you'll have to wait for bus 1 to take you the remainder of the short journey into town.

It's a 20-minute walk into the old town from the bus station, or you can take a passing pedicab (¥2).

If you miss the last bus from Huangyou, you may have to take a bus to Hezhou (贺州; ¥18, two hours) and change to a Guilin service (¥55 to ¥80, 2½ to 3½ hours). The last bus from Hezhou is at around 5.10pm, but you're much better off catching a fast D-class train (1st/2nd class ¥108/68, one to 1½ hours) from Hezhou to Guilin that departs frequently until 9.50pm.

Nanning 南宁

☑ 0771 / POP 7.1 MILLION

In many ways, Nanning (Nánníng) is a typical provincial capital with few sights of note, but many of its streets are lined with trees and shaded with a bountiful canopy of leaves, affording welcome shade. It's also a relaxing and friendly place to recharge your batteries before leaving for, or coming from, Vietnam. It makes for a refreshingly non-touristy destination and one where you'll eat well and get local cultural insights. The brilliant metro system helps to tame the town's distances.

⊙ Sights

South Lake Park
PARK

(南湖名树博览园, Nánhú Míngshù Bólǎnyuán; MNanhu) FREE This 193-hectare park, around 2.5km east of downtown, has dozens of species of trees including some rare ones, but you don't have to be a botanist to enjoy it. The setting by the river is lovely and some of the foliage is simply interesting to look at, or read a book beneath. There are also lawns to nap on and a lake to stroll around while you watch the locals fish.

Guangxi Museum
MUSEUM

(广西博物馆, Guǎngxī Bówùguǎn; cnr Minzu Dadao & Gucheng Lu, 民族大道古城路的路口; ◎9am-4.30pm Tue-Sun; MMinzu Sq) FREE This fairly interesting museum showcases Qing ceramics, art and calligraphy with Guangxi characteristics, and the customs of ethnic minorities. The collection of ancient copper drums is one of China's best. It's been closed for several years as it undergoes renovation, and is estimated to reopen in 2020.

Yangmei
VILLAGE

(扬美, Yángměi; ¥10) A former market town on the Yong River (邕江, Yōng Jiāng), Yangmei was founded a millennium ago and flourished in the 17th century, earning the nickname 'Little Nanning'. Spend a couple of hours wandering the cobbled streets, munching on fried fish (from ¥4), steamed rice rolls (¥4) and local starfruit (¥5 per catty) as you walk. The pace is slow and you're free to peep into the designated Ming and Qing dynasty homes.

Buses for Yangmei leave from **West Bus Station** (南宁市货运西站, Nánníngshì Huòyùn Xīzhàn, Nanning City Freight West Station; cnr Daxue Lu & Luban Lu, 大学路鲁班路的路口; MLuban Lu) near the corner of Daxue Lu (大学路) and Luban Lu (鲁班路) in the northeast of town; take metro Line 1. Departures and returns are from 8.30am to 6pm (¥17, two hours, every 50 minutes). The last bus back from Yangmei leaves at 4pm, but can get packed so arrive early for a seat.

🛏 Sleeping

Hechang Business Hotel
HOTEL ¥

(和昌商务宾馆, Héchāng Shāngwù Bīnguǎn; ☑151 7791 1198; 3065796765@qq.com; 14 Zhutang Lu, 竹塘路14号; d from ¥80; ❄🛜; MMacun) Basic and a bit grimy, so business hotel it ain't; instead, Hechang's appeal lies in its budget price, functional amenities (fast wi-fi, reliable air-con and hot water) and its English-speaking owner, Miranda. Another plus is the local neighbourhood, with its alleys lined with tasty dumpling restaurants and nearby produce market. It's a 20-minute walk from the Macun metro station.

South Face Hostel
HOSTEL ¥

(South Face青年旅舍; ☑151 7791 9708; 12th fl, 6 Yuanhu South Lu, 青秀区园湖南路6号南湖6号大厦二单元1201室; dm ¥80; ❄🛜; MMacun) This unconventional, and pricier than usual, 'hostel' is essentially a residential apartment fitted with bunk beds. While it caters primarily to Chinese backpackers, it remains one of Nanning's few genuine budget options. There's a kitchen and laundry, and it's handily located for the metro. It's on the 12th floor, so the city views up here are good.

Wanxing Hotel
HOTEL ¥¥¥

(万兴酒店, Wànxīng Jiǔdiàn; ☑0771 238 1000; Unit 1, 42 Beining Jie, 北宁街42-1号; d¥438-788, tr/ste ¥888/1688; ❄@🛜; MChaoyang Sq) One of those seemingly characterless urban hotels that actually turn out to be very good. There's an uncluttered, marble-clad foyer overseen by very helpful staff, and rooms are comfortable, if unsurprising. Efficient and value for money; on the corner with Gonghe Lu.

🍴 Eating

Nanning is a culinary destination, and you'll find an eclectic mix of local and regional Chinese cuisine on offer.

★ Zhongshan Lu Market
STREET FOOD ¥

(中山路; Zhongshan Lu, 中山路; snacks ¥5-10; ◎6pm-4am) Don't come to Nanning without visiting the pulsating night market along Zhongshan Lu each evening. It gets absolutely jam-packed, so it's not one for claustrophobes, and features endless rows of stalls cooking up skewers of all descriptions, from grilled meats and seafood to spiders and scorpions.

Amou Delicious Eats
GUANGXI ¥

(阿谋美食, Āmóu Měishí; Gucheng Lu, 古城路; mains from ¥32; ◎9am-10.30pm; ❄🛜; MMinzu

Nanning

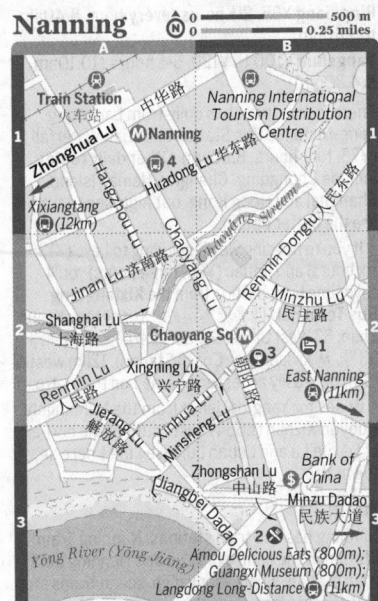

Nanning

Sq) Unique and flavourful ethnic dishes served on a photogenic Wind and Rain Bridge or in a dining room. There's a huge range of ethnic food, from fried pork belly dipped in rice wine (么佬族乳香肉饼甜酒, *melǎozú rǔxiāng ròubǐng tiánjiǔ*) to fragrant *máonán* beef (毛南香牛扣, *máonán xiāngníukòu*). There's a photo menu.

Ganjiajie Lemon Duck GUANGXI ¥¥
(甘家界牌柠檬鸭, *Gānjiājiè Pái Níngméngyā*; ☑ 0771 585 5585; 12-2 Yuanhu Lu, 园湖路12-2号; mains ¥30-110; ⊙ 11am-10pm; Ⓜ Macun) One of several branches in town, the star here is the tasty lemon duck (柠檬鸭, *níngméngyā*), a Nanning dish that cooks the fowl with pickled lemon peel, ginger, garlic and chilli. You'd be quackers not to try it. Choose from two types of duck: we recommend the more tender cherry duck (樱桃谷鸭, *yīngtáo gǔyā*).

Drinking & Nightlife

Nanning's nightlife is an ever-evolving scene; you'll find a decent choice of pubs, bars and clubs spread across the city.

Kong BAR
(Kong酒吧, Kong Jiǔbā; Lane 3, 33 Gecun Lu, 市青秀区葛村路三巷33号; ⊙ 8.30pm-2.30am) A tiny but classy inner-city bar where you'll get a friendly welcome as you prop yourself up at the bar to order from a selection of its well-made cocktails. It's down a small walkway off Gecun Lu.

WOW Hangout BAR
(Wow南宁, Wow Nánníng; ☑ 152 7297 9337; Zuanshi Sq, 3rd fl, 66 Xhaoyang Lu, 朝阳路66号, 钻石广场3楼; beers from ¥12, cocktails from ¥25; ⊙ 5pm-5am; Ⓜ Chaoyang Sq) One of downtown's best drinking choices is this pub-style venue that's popular with young Chinese professionals, students and expats here to unwind with scarily cheap mixer drinks served by the bucket. The music is loud, so it's not great for conversation, but it has a fun boozy atmosphere, and things often get loose later in the night.

☆ Entertainment

Hope Live LIVE MUSIC
(侯朋现场, Hóupéng Xiànchǎng; 1st Floor, ASEAN Shengtiandi, 8 Zhongyue Lu, 青秀区中越路8号东盟盛天地负一楼; tickets ¥50-120; ⊙ from 8pm; Ⓜ ASEAN Business District) The spot to tap into Nanning's underground music scene is this live house with an unlikely location inside a shopping mall. Most evenings it hosts local punk and indie bands. It's a bit tricky to find, but it's down the stairs opposite from KFC.

ⓘ Information

The useful *Street Map of Nanning* (南宁街道图; Nánníng Jiēdào Tú; ¥6), in English and Chinese, can be found at bookshops and kiosks around town.

Bank of China (中国银行, Zhōngguó Yínháng; Chaoyang Lu, 朝阳路; ⊙ 9am-5pm Mon-Fri; Ⓜ Chaoyang Sq) Has branches around town with 24-hour ATMs that accept international cards.

China International Travel Service (中国国际旅行社, Zhōngguó Guójì Lǚxíngshè, CITS; ☑ 0771 568 3808; 8 Zhongyue Lu, 中越路8号盛天地步行街; ⊙ 8am-11pm; Ⓜ ASEAN Busi-

ℹ️ BORDER CROSSINGS: VIETNAM FROM NANNING

Six daily buses run to Hanoi (河内, Henei; ¥177, 7½ to eight hours) via Friendship Pass (友谊关, Yǒuyì Guān). Four departures (8.20am, 9.10am, 10.20am and 12.50pm) leave from **Nanning International Tourism Distribution Centre** (南宁国际旅游集散中心, Nánníng Guójì Lǚyóu Jísàn Zhōngxīn; ☎ 0771 210 2362; 10 You'ai Nanlu, 友爱南路10号; ⊗ 7.30am-8.30pm; Ⓜ Nanning Station), and two (9am and 1.40pm) leave from Langdong Long-Distance Bus Station. Note that you'll have to get off and walk across the border at Friendship Pass before boarding another bus to Hanoi.

Alternatively, there's a daily train from Nanning train station to Hanoi (soft sleeper ¥300, 11½ hours, 6.05pm). There are also four trains and regular buses daily to Pingxiang.

Pingxiang ¥65, 2½ hours (every hour, 8.40am to 7.40pm)

Yangshuo ¥100 to ¥120, 5½ hours (10.10am & 4.30pm)

There is one direct bus daily from Langdong Long-Distance Bus Station to Detian Waterfall (¥75, four hours, 8.30am). Other daily routes include Chongqing, Chengdu, Hainan Island, Shanghai and Hong Kong, but high-speed trains are the better option.

If you're heading west, including to Leye (¥135, six hours) and Detian (¥65, three hours) you'll save time by departing from the **Xixiangtang Bus Terminal** (西乡塘客运站, Xīxiāngtáng Kèyùn Zhàn; 63 West University Lu, 西乡塘区大学西路63号; Ⓜ Xixiangtang Coach Station), 12km west of town but easily accessed by Line 1 on the metro.

Buses for Yangmei leave from the Nánníngshì Huóyùn Xīzhàn (p654), just south of the corner of Daxue Lu and Luban Lu; take Line 1 here on the metro.

TRAIN

Nanning has two train stations: Nanning Train Station at the centre of town and Nanning East train station, where many high-speed trains stop and depart from.

Three trains go to Pingxiang (¥30, four to five hours, 7.53am, 3.26pm and 6.05pm) near the Vietnam border. Each one stops at Chongzuo (¥18, 2½ hours) and Ningming (¥26, 3½ to four hours).

Booth 16 in the train station sells international tickets to Hanoi.

---

ness District) Has some English-speaking staff and can issue 30-day Vietnam visas (¥280).

Public Security Bureau (公安局, Gōng'ānjú, PSB; ☎ 0771 577 2570; 18 Jiangbei Ave, Qingxiu District, 市青秀区江北大道凌18号; ⊗ 9am-4.30pm Mon-Fri) Has several offices offering 30-day visa extensions, including this one located 3km south from Chaoyang Sq.

ℹ️ Getting There & Away

AIR

Direct daily flights from Nanning Wuxu International Airport include Beijing, Shanghai, Xi'an, Kunming, Guangzhou and Hong Kong. You can also fly to a number of other destinations in Asia, including Bangkok, Kuala Lumpur, Singapore and Hanoi.

BUS

The main **Langdong Long-Distance Bus Station** (琅东客运站, Lángdōng Kèyùnzhàn; east end of Minzu Dadao, 民族大道东端; Ⓜ Nanning Langdong Bus Terminal), 5km east of the city centre (linked on Line 1 of the Nanning metro), has direct buses to pretty much everywhere, although you may be dropped at one of the other bus stations, also on the outskirts, when arriving. There's a downtown ticketing office on Chaoyang Lu near **CAAC** (中国民航, Zhōngguó Mínháng, CAAC; ☎ 0771 243 1459; 82 Chaoyang Lu, 朝阳路82号; ⊗ 24hr). Destinations from Langdong Long-Distance Bus Station include the following:

Guilin ¥110 to ¥128, five hours (four buses daily, 10.05am, 11.30am, 4.40pm, 9.10pm)

ℹ️ Getting Around

The airport shuttle bus (¥20, 50 minutes) leaves every 30 minutes from the **Nanning Civil Aviation Hotel** (民航饭店, Mínhang Fàndiàn; 82 Chaoyang Lu, 区朝阳路82号; ⊗ 5.30am-10.30pm; Ⓜ Nanning Station) from 5.30am to 10.30pm, or the **Wharton Hotel** (广西沃顿国际大酒店, Guǎngxī Wòdùn Guójì Dà Jiǔdiàn; 88 Minzu Ave, 青秀区民族大道88号; ¥20; ⊗ 5.30am to 9pm) until 9pm.

Bus 301 (¥3, 1½ hours) also runs to the airport from Chaoyang Guangchang (朝阳广场) every 20 minutes, a cheaper but slower option. Otherwise a taxi is ¥120, or ¥85 for a DiDi ride-share car.

Though Nanning has an extensive bus network, its impressive metro system is the best means of getting around. It comprises three lines and links it with all the major bus and train stations, and points of interest. Tokens cost ¥2 to ¥4, depending on how far you're travelling. It's very user-friendly with English signage and announcements.

A taxi ride from Langdong Long-Distrance Bus Station or East Nanning train station to downtown is around ¥40. Flagfall is ¥9. The DiDi rideshare platform offers a cheaper alternative to taxis.

Beihai 北海

☑ 0779 / POP 1.5 MILLION

Beihai (Běihǎi; literally 'North Sea') – called *baakhoi* in the local *baíhuà* dialect – is famed among Chinese tourists for its **Silver Beach** (银滩; Yíntān) **FREE**, dubbed 'number one beach on earth' in tourism brochures (it ain't). A far more charming and unique selling point, however, is the lovely and crumbling Old Quarter, a delightful vignette of colonnaded streets and colonial-era architecture. It's lovely in the right light, and with a fine cafe and hotel, the old town is the place to settle down for a day or two to ease into Beihai's lazy seaside rhythms.

◉ Sights

Beihai's **old streets** (老街, lǎojiē) usually refer to Zhongshan Lu (中山路) and Zhuhai Lu (珠海路), once part of old Beihai's trading hub, which are now home to sleepy residences of the city's older population. Built a century ago, the streets spread from west to east and are flanked by recently restored 19th-century *qílóu* buildings (arcade houses) housing an alarming number of pearl shops.

Start your stroll at the western end of Zhuhai Lu. Look for the small white arch inscribed with the Chinese characters 升平街 (Shengping Jie), the road's former name. This street has been paved over and offers visitors an atmospheric walk.

Former British Consulate Building
HISTORIC BUILDING

(英国领事馆旧址; Yīngguó Lǐngshìguǎn Jiùzhǐ; Beihai No 1 Middle School, 1 Beijing Lu, 北京路1号) Beihai's first consulate of a western country is a whitewashed edifice built in 1885 that now sits inside the grounds of the Beihai No 1 Middle School. The building faces you as you stand in front of the school; the guard will let you in for a peek if you're nice.

Former German Consulate Building
HISTORIC BUILDING

(德国领事馆旧址; Déguó Lǐngshìguǎn Jiùzhǐ; 2 Beijing Lu, 北京路2号) Across the street from the Former British Consulate Building is this charming two-storey yellow structure built in 1905.

Maruichi Drugstore
HISTORIC BUILDING

(丸一药房; Wányī Yàofáng; 104 Zhuhai Zhonglu, 珠海中路104号) **FREE** This historic building was disguised as a pharmacy that allowed the Japanese to pursue espionage activities in the 1930s.

GUANGXI BEIHAI

LOCAL KNOWLEDGE

CHOW DOWN IN OVERSEAS TOWN

Beihai is the place to feast on fresh seafood – it's excellent and abundant. Yet at the most visible seafood restaurants, especially those near Silver Beach, customers pay through the nose for a plate of squid.

This is because cab and pedicab drivers get a cut for bringing customers to these places – up to 50% of the bill! With that kind of incentive, some drivers will work hard to lure you to the spots that pay them. Insist on going elsewhere and they may feign ignorance of the location, or take you to their pet eatery and pretend it's the one you're after.

But there are exceptions to the rule. Seafood restaurants that don't overcharge can be found in Overseas Town (侨港镇, Qiáogǎng Zhèn), 4km away from Silver Beach. OT was established in 1979 to settle Vietnamese Chinese refugees who had arrived near the shores of Beihai. Most of the arrivals were fishermen who brought their unique mix of Chinese and Vietnamese culture to the area. There are no sights as such, but the pervasive Sino-Vietnamese atmosphere is quite unique. Note how written Vietnamese is abundantly used alongside Chinese on shopfronts.

Ask a driver to take you to Overseas Town (without mentioning a restaurant), then walk to your destination; alternatively, simply take bus 5 from Beibuwan Sq (北部湾广场, Běibùwān Guǎngchǎng), which runs direct to Qiaogang Market (侨港市场, Qiáogǎng Shìchǎng). The whole town is only 1.1 sq km. The string of outdoor restaurants here has a classic Southeast Asian feel, where you can dine outdoors on Vietnamese street food, accompanied by cold beer. The piping hot, fresh and delicious steamed rice rolls (粉卷, fěnjuǎn) at **Kieu Viet Vietnam Banh Cuon** (侨越越南卷粉汤粉; Qiáoyuè Yuènán Juǎnfěn Tāngfěn; 14 Fengsheng Jie, Qiaonan Lu, Overseas Town, 侨港镇, 丰盛街侨南路14号; rice rolls ¥2-5; ☉ 7am-1am) are a winner.

Beihai

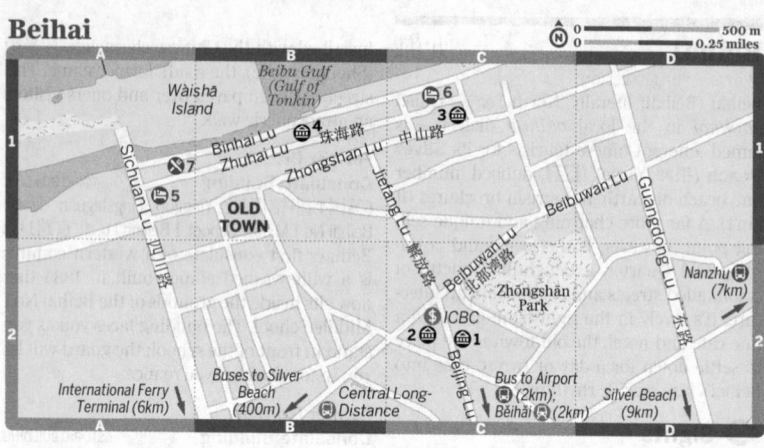

Beihai

Former Post Office   HISTORIC BUILDING
(大清邮政北海分局旧址; Dàqīng Yóuzhèng Běi-hǎi Fēnjú Jiùzhǐ; cnr Zhongshan Donglu & Haiguan Lu, 中山东路和海关路的路口; ⊙9am-noon & 2.30-5.30pm Wed-Sun) FREE Dating from 1896, this attractive edifice now serves as a tiny museum devoted to relics of the Qing dynasty postal system. No English captions, nor photos allowed indoors.

🛏 Sleeping

Beihai has a reasonable spread of accommodation, including a handful of budget guesthouses in close proximity to either the old town or Silver Beach. There are a few decent midrange and international chain hotels too.

Across from the central bus station, you'll find many *zhāodàisuǒ* (招待所; basic lodgings) along Huoshaochuang Wuxiang (火烧床五巷) for around ¥40; some may not take foreigners.

Mango Guesthouse   GUESTHOUSE ¥
(芒果宿客栈; Mángguǒ Sù Kèzhàn; ☏177 7791 6741; 296259547@qq.com; 64 Zhuhai Lu, 珠海东路64号 芒果; d¥78-148; ❄⊛ 🛜) By far the best budget choice in Beihai is this relaxed guesthouse at the eastern end of historic Zhuhai Lu. With its eponymous mango tree standing out front, it's an attractive spot, and the basic rooms are brightened with classy touches and decorative bedspreads. English-speaking manager Frank goes well beyond the scope of the job to help out.

WBS Hostel   GUESTHOUSE ¥
(WBS青年旅舍; WBS Qīngnián Lǚshě; ☏130 1484 8095; 16 Guangdong Lu, 广东路16; dm/d¥55/105; ❄⊛🛜) Tucked away off the main road just up from Silver Beach, and conveniently located for the ferry terminal and Overseas Town (p657), WBS Hostel makes for a solid, if unremarkable, budget choice. It has both dorms and private rooms, but it lacks atmosphere and there are no sea views as claimed. No English spoken.

Backpacker Inn   INN ¥¥
(老道精舍; Lǎodào Jīngshě; ☏0779 203 0605; 155 Zhuhai Lu, 珠海路155号; d¥198-288; ❄⊛🛜) Sharing space with a cafe is this attractive inn perched at the western end of the atmospheric old-town street Zhuhai Lu. Non-backpackers should not be put off by the name: this is far more comfy hotel than hostel. Its 14 spacious rooms are Mediterranean in style, with upholstered bay windows to enjoy complimentary filter coffee and a good novel.

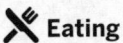 **Eating**

The old town is full of stalls selling steamed rice rolls (粉卷, *fěnjuǎn*) and shrimp pancakes (虾饼, *xiābǐng*). Overseas Town (p657) is where you'll find Vietnamese cuisine and reasonably priced seafood feasts.

Aunty Li's Shrimp Pancakes GUANGXI ¥
(李姨虾饼店; Lǐyí Xiābǐng Diàn; 110 Zhuhai Lu, 珠海路110号; pancakes ¥5; ⊙8am-4pm) Dried shrimp pancakes (虾饼; *xiābǐng*) are a delicacy here and nobody does them better than this hawker stall opposite the historic Beihai Christ Church.

 Drinking & Nightlife

The best and most atmospheric part of town for a drink is along Zhuhai Lu.

Old Town Coffee, Bar & Restaurant CAFE
(老道咖啡; Lǎodào Kāfēi; ☎0779 203 1828; 155 Zhuhai Lu, 珠海路155号; drinks ¥10-45; ⊙8am-midnight; 🛜) Come by this atmospheric old-town cafe with distressed exposed brickwork for top-notch house-roasted coffees, with a choice of beans from Indonesia to Ethiopia. In the evenings the upper floors morph into a bar with regular live music. It also does an all-day western menu of burgers, sandwiches etc (dishes ¥18 to ¥38).

ℹ️ **Information**

ICBC (中国工商银行; Zhōngguó Gōngshāng Yínháng; Beijing Lu, 北京路号) Has a 24-hour ATM for international cards.

ℹ️ **Getting There & Away**

AIR

Beihai Fucheng Airport is 21km northeast of the town centre, from where there are daily flights to Beijing and Shanghai.

BOAT

The **International Ferry Terminal** (国际客运港; Guójì Kèyùn Gǎng; ☎0779 306 9988, 0779 307 1866; www.laiu8.cn; off Yintan Middle Lu, 银海区银滩旅游区18号; ⊙7am-7pm) on the road to Silver Beach (bus 3, ¥2) has boats to Weizhou Island. Boats also sail to Haikou (¥140 to ¥500, 12 hours) on Hainan Island at 6pm.

BUS

There are two main bus stations: the **Central Long-Distance Bus Station** (北海和信客运中心; Běihǎi Héxìn Kèyùn Zhōngxīn; Beibuwan Zhonglu, 北部湾中路) and the newer, inconveniently located **Nanzhu Bus Station** (南珠汽车站; Nánzhū Qìchē Zhàn; cnr Beihai Dadao & Nanzhu Dadao,

北海大道南珠大道路口). From the central bus station, bus 2 (¥2) goes to the train station.

Direct buses from the Central Long-Distance Bus Station run to Guangzhou (¥200, nine hours, 8.30pm) and Haikou (¥180, four hours, 7.20am). From Nanzhu bus station there are regular buses to Guangzhou (¥200, six daily) and one daily bus to Zhuhai (¥250, 7½ hours, 10.30am).

To reach Nanning or Guilin, take the high-speed train.

TRAIN

Eighteen high-speed trains run daily to Beihai train station (北海站) from Nanning East station (1st/2nd class ¥92/58, 1½ hours, 7.48am to 9.07pm), along with regular trains from Guilin (1st/2nd class ¥291/183, 4¼ hours, 7.50am to 5.04pm) and Sanjiang (¥350/219, 5¼ hours, four daily).

In the other direction, regular high-speed trains run to Nanning train station and Nanning East train station (6.52am to 8.36pm) from Beihai. Tickets to onward destinations can be bought from the **train station ticket office** (北海火车站位; Běihǎi Huǒchē Zhàn Wèi; Beijing Lu, 北京路; ⊙8.10am-noon & 2-5pm) for a ¥5 fee.

ℹ️ **Getting Around**

Airport shuttle buses (¥20, 50 minutes) leave from outside the train station at the **Hampton at Hilton Hotel** (Beihai City Terminal; 北海机场巴士总站; 138 Beijing Lu, Hampton at Hilton Hotel, 北京路138号), with nine daily departures from 6.30am to 9pm.

Pingxiang 凭祥

📞0771 / POP 110,000

Guangxi's gateway to Vietnam (越南, Yuenan), Pingxiang (Píngxiáng) is a market town with a dusty, end-of-the-world feel. Everyone passing through is on their way to Vietnam, rather than visiting Pingxiang specifically. There are no real sights of note and no reason to linger, unless you're heading to nearby Ningming (宁明县), a springboard for exploring the stunning Huashan Cliff Murals (p661).

At the Chinese side of the Sino-Vietnamese border, the **Friendship Pass Scenic Area** (友谊关景区, Yǒuyìguān Jǐngqū; ¥42; ⊙8.30am-6pm) is a quite attractive park sprinkled with old buildings, including a yellow French colonial number erected by the Qing government, and the virile-looking **Friendship Pass Tower**, rebuilt in 1957 on the original 2000-year-old site with battlements and ramparts.

You can find simple places to sleep on Beida Lu (北大路) behind the bus station, with air-con and wi-fi, ranging from ¥50 to ¥150.

ℹ️ GETTING TO/FROM VIETNAM FROM PINGXIANG

The Friendship Pass (友谊关, Yǒuyì Guān) border is located about 18km south of Pingxiang on the Chinese side, and several kilometres from the obscure town of Dong Dang on the Vietnamese side; the nearest Vietnamese city (Liangshan; Lang Son in Vietnamese) is 18km away. The border is open from 8am to 9pm Chinese time (China is one hour ahead of Vietnam), but some travellers have reported that passports aren't always stamped after around 4.30pm.

To get to the border crossing, take a pedicab or taxi (about ¥35 to ¥40) from Pingxiang. From there it's a 600m walk to the Vietnamese border post. Onward transport to Hanoi, located 164km southwest of the border, is by bus or train via Lang Son.

If you're heading into China from Friendship Pass, catch a minibus to Pingxiang's bus or train station, from where there's regular onward transport to Nanning and beyond.

There are still reports of Lonely Planet's *China* being confiscated by border officials at Friendship Pass. We advise copying vital information and putting a cover over your guidebook just in case. Note that all bags are searched as you walk into the train station. Once you leave Pingxiang, you won't have a problem.

Look for the Chinese characters 宾馆 (*bīnguǎn*; hotel).

Xiangcheng International Hotel (祥城国际大酒店, Xiángchéng Guójì Dàjiǔdiàn; ☏ 0771 802 2666; 2 Beida Lu, 北大路; r incl breakfast from ¥298; ✳ 🛜) is definitely one of the more comfortable places to stay in Pingxiang.

Given its proximity to the Vietnam border, unsurprisingly Pingxiang has a number of good spots for Vietnamese food, including the popular **Yazhuang Vietnamese Restaurant** (雅庄越式风味馆, Yǎzhuāng Yuèshì Fēngwèi Guǎn; ☏ 0771 858 8123, 0771 852 2886; 78 Pingshan Lu, 屏上路78号; dishes ¥45-65; ⏲ 7.30am-2.30pm & 4.30-9pm). Turning left from the bus station will take you to rice and noodle stalls.

Turn right from the bus station's front entrance onto Yingxing Lu (银兴路) to find the **Bank of China** (中国银行, Zhōngguó Yínháng; off Beida Lu).

Regular buses depart from **Pingxiang bus station** (凭祥 巴士总站, Píngxiáng Bāshì Zǒngzhàn; ☏ 0771 852 0958; 222 Beida Lu, 北大路222号) for Ningming (¥10, 40 minutes) every 20 minutes from 6.20am to 6pm, and for Nanning (¥82, three hours) until 8pm.

Trains leave Pingxiang Station (凭祥站, Píngxiáng Zhàn) for Ningming (¥9, 45 minutes) at 6.05am, 10.10am and 2pm, en route to Nanning (¥30, four to five hours). The train station is 3km south of the bus station and pedicabs (about ¥5) link the two.

Detian Waterfall 德天瀑布

Detian Waterfall (Détiān Pùbù, Ban Gioc Waterfall; ¥80; ⏲ 8am-5pm) belongs to the Chungui River (春归河, Chūnguīhé), which flows between China and Vietnam. The river is only 30m across in this upstream section, which means that people on both sides can see each other going about their business. It's not grand like Niagara Falls, but it's the largest falls spanning two countries in Asia, with the added buzz of being surrounded by karst peaks. The best months to see the waters in their glory are between July and November.

The falls drop in three stages to create cascades and small pools. Swimming is not allowed, but bamboo rafts (from ¥30) will take you up to the spray. You can also legally cross the Vietnamese border at the 53rd merestone – tourists love taking selfies stepping into what's officially Vietnamese territory.

There is only one direct bus from Nanning's International Tourism Distribution Centre (¥75, four hours, 7.30am), which stops en route at Langdong bus station (8.30am). The direct bus from the falls back to Nanning leaves at 3pm.

Otherwise you will have to take a bus first to Daxin (大新; from ¥45, 2½ hours, regular departures) from Nanning's Xixiangtang Bus Station, and then switch to a bus headed to Detian (德天; ¥15, two hours, hourly), a further 60km. A cab costs around ¥150.

Tongling Grand Canyon 通灵大峡谷

Located in Baise prefecture (百色市), Jingxi County (靖西县), **Tongling Grand Canyon** (Tōnglíng Dàxiá Gǔ; ¥115; ⏲ 8am-5pm) means 'Connected to the Spirit World'. You will certainly feel spiritual as you descend narrow flights of stairs down to a large cavern, with flickering bulbs and the roar of an underground river. Emerging past the cave, you venture through a thick tropical forest into a series of wild gorges, and past vaulted cliffs with hanging stalactites and dramatic waterfalls that end in crystal pools framed by boulders.

You can walk around some of the waterfalls into the cool, otherworldly caves beyond. But you can't go near the tallest one, which has a drop of 170m and a splash of hundreds of metres in the summer.

From the canyon's exit, walk 30 minutes uphill to the entrance car park, where you can ask your driver to meet you. Alternatively, vans can take you there for ¥5.

There are buses from Jingxi south bus station that make the hour-long trip (¥14) to the canyon every 20 to 30 minutes until 7pm. Look for those headed for Hurun town (湖润镇, Húrùnzhèn).

The best way to get to Jingxi from Nanning is to take the train (¥44, 3½ hours, 8.24am and 1.17pm). Otherwise there are regular buses from Nanning's Xixiangtang bus station for Jingxi (¥90 to ¥130, four hours).

Leye 乐业

📞 0776 / POP 157,000

Guangxi's highest county, Leye (Lèyè) is perched on the western edge of the province, a fine springboard to the surrounding underground caves, primeval forests and natural sinkholes, and an opportunity to get off the beaten path to a less-visited part of the province.

There are 28 naturally formed and highly impressive sinkholes (天坑, tiānkēng) here, including six major ones. The town itself has a scenic setting enclosed by green-forested mountains, and, given its far-flung location, travellers here will likely receive more attention from friendly, curious locals than elsewhere in Guangxi.

⊙ Sights

★ **Dashiwei Scenic Area** CAVE
(大石围风景区, Dashiwei fengjing qu; www.lfgeopark.com; Leye Geopark, 乐业世界地质公园; ¥98, combined ticket ¥158; ⊙ 8.30am-4.30pm) Located 15km northwest from Leye is this geopark famous for its sinkholes set amid an environment of karst landforms, caves and underground rivers. From the ticket office, you're transferred to an electric cart for a 20-minute ride to visit two sinkholes. The first resembles a giant meteor crater, after which it's named, while the more spectacular Dashiwei Tiankeng (大石围天坑) is the largest of Leye's sinkholes.

Dashiwei is accessed from two viewpoints, of which the most dramatic is via an illuminated cave that leads to a memorable natural arch that opens to astonishing views of the sinkhole. You can also follow the stairs

---

WORTH A TRIP

HUASHAN CLIFF MURALS

Close to the Vietnam border, the enigmatic **Huashan Cliff Murals** (花山岩画, Huàshān Shíhuà; ¥82), 2000-year-old rock paintings of people and animals on sheer cliff faces, are one of the undisputed highlights of Guangxi. The red-painted murals are believed to be the work of ancestors of the Zhuang, but remain shrouded in mystery.

The primitive ochre-coloured figures are depicted hands raised and knees bent, accompanied by pictures of drums and animals – features that suggest celebration of harvest or victory. As the cliff paintings are in the process of being restored, some sections will likely be covered in scaffolding; however, you'll still be able to get a full appreciation of the murals.

The admission fee includes a 2½-hour boat ride on a spectacular section of the Zuo River (左江, Zuǒ Jiāng). The boat generally leaves at 10.30am, 11.30am, 1.30pm and 2.30pm; outside these times, you can hire a private boat for ¥400.

The only way to see this ancient wonder is by boat from the village of Panlong (攀龙), commonly known as Huashan Shanzhai (花山山寨). Trains and buses that run between Nanning and Pingxiang stop at Ningming, from where it's a 40-minute taxi ride (¥50) to the boat dock; grab the driver's mobile number to arrange a pickup.

Should you find yourself overnighting in Ningming, the **Lido Business Hotel** (骊都商务大酒店, Lídōu Shāngwù dà Jiǔdiàn; 📞 0771 861 0298; Xingning Ave West, Ningming, 兴宁大道西, 新汽车站对面, 宁明县; r incl breakfast from ¥130; ❀ ☎) is tasteful, well managed and conveniently located across from the bus station. Its classy Vietnamese restaurant (open 7am to 10.30pm, mains ¥38 to ¥98) is another reason to drop by.

SKY PITS

Sinkholes (天坑. *tiānkēng*), literally 'sky pits' in Chinese, are depressions in the land caused by the collapse of the surface layer. This happens when bedrock made of a soluble substance such as limestone is eroded by underground water, forming caves that perforate the interior rock, which may eventually collapse inwards. Some sinkholes have openings into the caves below or to the underground rivers that have eroded its interior. Some are also carpeted by primeval forests that have sought purchase upon them.

down beyond the cave to one of three viewing platforms for cloud-level views of the surrounding karst ranges. At the time of research, a glass-viewing platform was being constructed. In total, count on spending two hours here. Every 20 to 30 minutes, between 8am and 4.30pm, a bus leaves Leye for Dashiwei Sinkhole (¥7, 30 minutes). Catch it from the car park diagonally opposite the People's Hospital (人民医院, Rénmín Yīyuàn).

★ Chuandong Sinkhole
CAVE

(穿洞天坑, Chuāndòng Tiānkēng; www.lfgeopark. com; Leye Geopark, 乐业世界地质公园; ¥75, combined ticket ¥158; ⊗8.30am-5.30pm) A one-hour walking circuit loops you past limestone caves, primeval vegetation and an underground river in this sinkhole that reaches 312m in height. Trek to the sinkhole's bottom via an ethereal-looking cavern with a hole in its roof: around noon, a shaft of light shines through the hole to illuminate the cavern floor, reminiscent of *Raiders of the Lost Ark*.

Luomei Lotus Cave
CAVE

(罗妹莲花洞, Luōmèi Liánhuā Dòng; Tongle Lu, 同乐路; ¥80, combined ticket ¥158; ⊗8am-5pm) This 970m-long underground river cave shelters the world's largest collection of lotus-shaped limestone formations. While the artificial illumination spoils the natural beauty, giving the cave an unmistakable Disneyland atmosphere, it's also hard not to be dazzled by the psychedelic lighting effect in each of its many chambers. The cave is handily located 200m north of the bus station.

🛏 Sleeping & Eating

There are several hotels where foreigners can stay, so you won't be stuck without a roof or bed for the night. Rooms start at around ¥75 and come with air-con and ensuite bathrooms. Xingle Lu is a good place to start looking.

Noodle shops can be found along Xingle Lu (兴乐路), an ¥8 pedicab ride from the train station. From Xingle Lu, it's a ¥5 ride or a 10-minute walk west towards Tongle Zhonglu (同乐中路), where you'll find vendors selling snacks and fruit.

City Comfort Inn
HOTEL ¥¥

(城市便捷酒店, Chéngshì Biànjié Jiǔdiàn; ☑0776 255 9888; 1/14 Lotte Lu, Lètiān Lu, 乐天路14栋 1单元; r incl breakfast from ¥180; ☺❋🐾) The best choice in town is this centrally located, modern hotel with spacious, bright and comfortable rooms. Management is friendly and helpful. Rooms are supposed to be nonsmoking, though some reek of stale cigarettes.

★ First Oyster
BARBECUE ¥

(第一生蚝, Dìyī Shēngháo; Lotte Lu, Lètiān Lu, 乐天路; skewers ¥3-10; ⊗8pm-2am) Come evening, head to this no-frills barbecue joint for a delicious array of seasoned skewers cooked on its streetside charcoal grill. Choose from juicy mushroom and tofu skewers, grilled Beihai oysters, charcoal-grilled eggplant with garlic and shallots, and a mix of tasty lamb, beef and succulent crispy-skinned chicken wings. There's a fridge full of cold beers to wash it down.

ℹ Getting There & Away

There are two daily buses from Nanning Langdong bus station (¥135, six hours, 8.20am and 10.10am), but it's quicker to take it from Xixiangtang Bus Terminal (¥135, five hours, 9am, 10.10am and 12.40pm), 12km west of Nanning's city centre.

Otherwise take the high-speed train from Nanning to Baise (1st/2nd class ¥132/83, 1½ hours), from where there are regular local buses to Leye (¥60, three to four hours).

From Baise, you can also take a bus to Jingxi (¥48 to ¥63, two hours) and transfer to Deitan's Hurun Town Bus Station (湖润镇客运汽车站, Húrùnzhèn Kèyùn Qìchēzhàn; ¥10).

The main station in Leye is on the southern end of Tongle Lu (同乐路) and the town is 1km north. The best way to get around is via pedicab – short rides cost about ¥10.

ℹ Getting Around

The easiest way to see the sights in Leye is to hire a taxi for half a day (from ¥250).

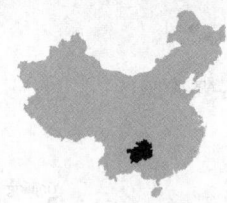

Guizhou

POP 35.1 MILLION

Best Places to Eat

➜ Old Kaili Sour Fish Restaurant (p667)

➜ Shanzai Vegetarian Meal (p667)

➜ Nóngjiā Fàn Xiāng (p676)

➜ Màizi Shānzhuāng (p681)

Best Places to Stay

➜ Yǒngfúróng Jìngxīn Jū (p675)

➜ He House (p667)

➜ Indigo Lodge (p673)

➜ Double Tree Hilton (p678)

➜ Kuanju Lingjiang Riverview Private Hotel (p684)

Why Go?

Despite being a popular destination with domestic travellers, Guizhou (贵州, Guìzhōu) remains largely unknown to travellers outside China – and what a travesty of justice. The province has two of the country's largest and most spectacular natural features – a waterfall and a cave – while outside the capital, Guiyang, it's pretty much green hills and valleys, flowing rivers and limestone formations to the horizon.

Guizhou's people are as diverse as its environment. Around 37% of the province's population consists of more than 18 ethnic minorities. Flitting around the Dong and Miao villages in the east of the province is like an anthropological dream sequence. Nearby is the ancient riverside settlement of Zhenyuan, as striking as Guilin to the south, where Chinese tourists chuckle into their hot-and-spicy sour fish soup that they still have it all to themselves.

When to Go
Guiyang

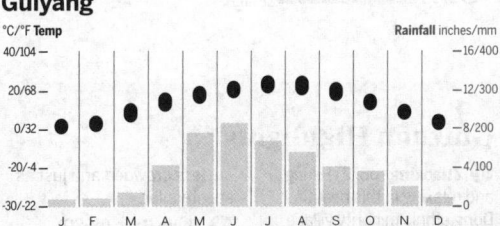

Jan Follow the birdsong to Caohai Lake, where birdwatchers flock each winter.

Jul & Aug See the region's waterfalls at their fullest and most awesome.

Oct & Nov Toast the Miao New Year in the traditional villages around Kaili.

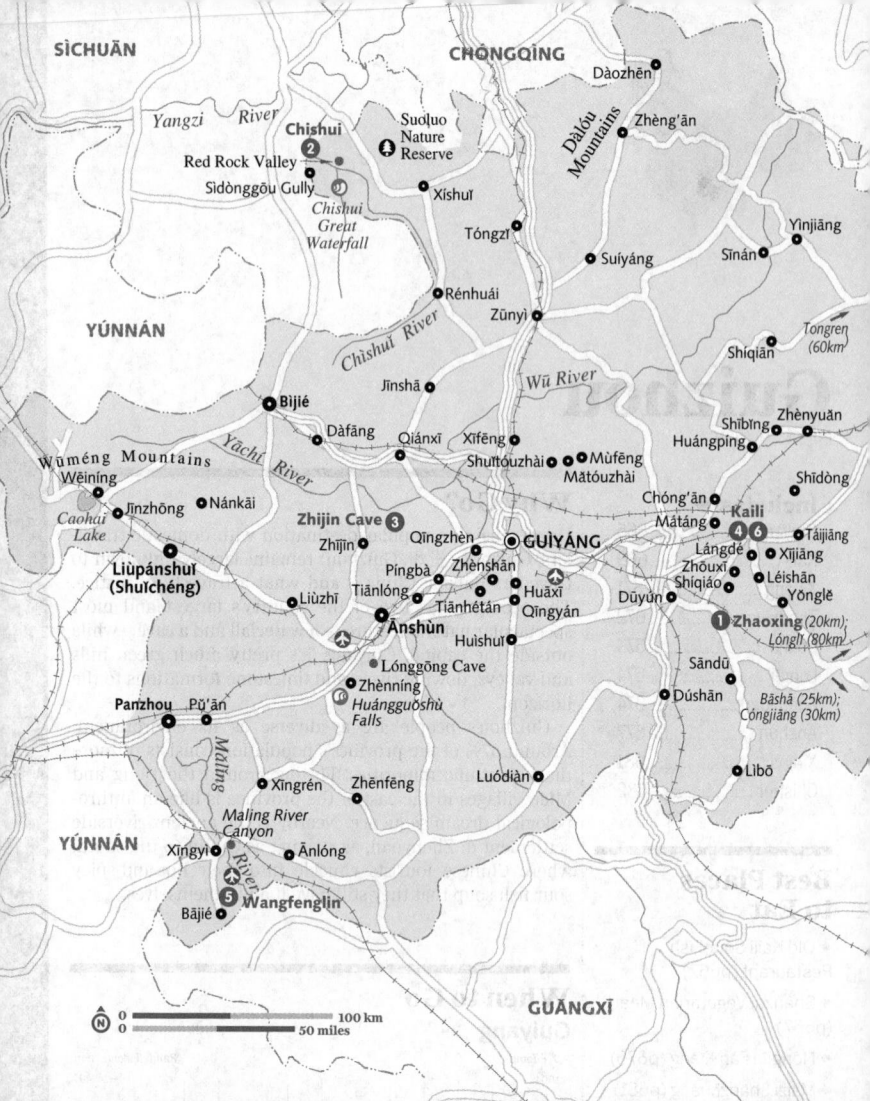

Guizhou Highlights

1 Zhaoxing (p672) Hiking and relaxing in this beautiful Dong ethnic minority village, which, at night, resembles something from a fantasy epic.

2 Chishui Great Waterfall (p683) Admriing this natural marvel: Huangguoshu Falls might be the province's poster child, but the falls at Chishui are less crowded and just as spectacular.

3 Zhijin Cave (p680) Descending into the largest cavern in China, where millennia-old formations create an underground karst palace.

4 Kaili (p669) Hopping between the tiny Miao villages nestled in the hills around this important market town.

5 Wanfenglin (p681) Marvelling at the beautiful karst mountains of this under-visited region: hire an electric bike for total travel freedom.

6 Festivals (p668) Partying with the locals at one of the thousand-odd celebrations held in Guizhou each year, such as Miao New Year.

History

Chinese rulers set up an administration in this area as far back as the Han dynasty (206 BC–AD 220), but it was merely an attempt to maintain some measure of control over Guizhou's non-Han tribes.

It wasn't until the Sino-Japanese war, when the Kuomintang made Chongqing their wartime capital, that the development of Guizhou began. Most of this activity ceased at the end of WWII; industrialisation of the area wasn't revived until the Chinese Communist Party (CCP) began construction of the railways.

Despite an expanding mining industry, Guizhou's GDP per capita remains the lowest in all China.

Language

Mandarin Chinese is spoken by the Han majority, although with a distinctive local accent. Thai and Lao are spoken by some, and Miao-Yao (Hmong-mien) dialects by the Miao and Yao.

ⓘ Getting There & Away

You can fly to more than 40 destinations within China from the squeaky clean and spacious **Guiyang Longdongbao International Airport** (贵阳龙洞堡国际机场, Guìyáng Lóngdòng Bǎo Guójì Jīchǎng), including all major Chinese cities plus direct flights to Taipei (Taiwan), Hong Kong, Bangkok, Seoul and Singapore.

High-speed trains radiate out from Guiyang, connecting the city with other major destinations around China, including Guangzhou, Xi'an and Shanghai. It's easy to combine southeastern Guizhou with a trip to Guangxi province – you can even start your journey in Hong Kong.

Sleeper trains to Chengdu, Kunming and Guilin are popular. You can enter Guizhou by train from Hunan through the back door from Huaihua to Zhenyuan.

ⓘ Getting Around

The high-speed train is very handy for the southern half of the province, cutting journey times significantly between most of the major areas of interest. Regular trains serve smaller towns and cities, while buses are useful for northern Guizhou. New expressways access the more remote western areas of the province. Roads in the main tourist areas are generally good but between smaller cities and villages they remain a work in progress.

Guiyang   贵阳

⬛ 0851 / POP 3.1 MILLION

Guiyang (Guìyáng) is an unpretentious, relatively youthful provincial capital under seemingly continual construction. While it may not leap out at the traveller, there are some interesting sights and affordable fine hotels, and the city's location makes it a perfect base for exploring the surrounding southern countryside, especially Huangguoshu Falls, the ethnic villages around Kaili, and historic Zhenyuan.

The city passed through the hands of various warring states until it became established during the Yuan dynasty in 1283. While Guiyang has not featured prominently in the annals of Chinese history, it has since emerged from the smoke of the country's industrial boom.

⊙ Sights

Jiaxiu Pavilion   NOTABLE BUILDING
(甲秀楼, Jiǎxiù Lóu; 8 Cuiwei Xiang, 翠微巷8号; ◷ 9am-5pm, last entry 4.30pm) **FREE** Constructed during the Ming dynasty in 1598, this triple-roofed pavilion perched atop a boulder is Guiyang's most iconic landmark. Built to celebrate the local people as 'the finest and most talented under heaven', the structure contains slabs of marble and an impressive art and calligraphy collection.

Cuiwei Garden   BUDDHIST TEMPLE
(翠微公园, Cuìwēi Gōngyuán; 8 Cuiwei Xiang, 翠微巷8号; ◷ 9am-5pm, last entry 4.30pm) **FREE** This city park features a restored Ming dynasty temple with some picturesque pavilions. It's a pleasant place to find some respite from the city noise.

ⓘ PRICE RANGES

Sleeping
Price per room (either twin or double):

¥ less than ¥200

¥¥ ¥200–400

¥¥¥ more than ¥400

Eating
Prices per meal:

¥ less than ¥50

¥¥ ¥50–100

¥¥¥ more than ¥100

Guiyang

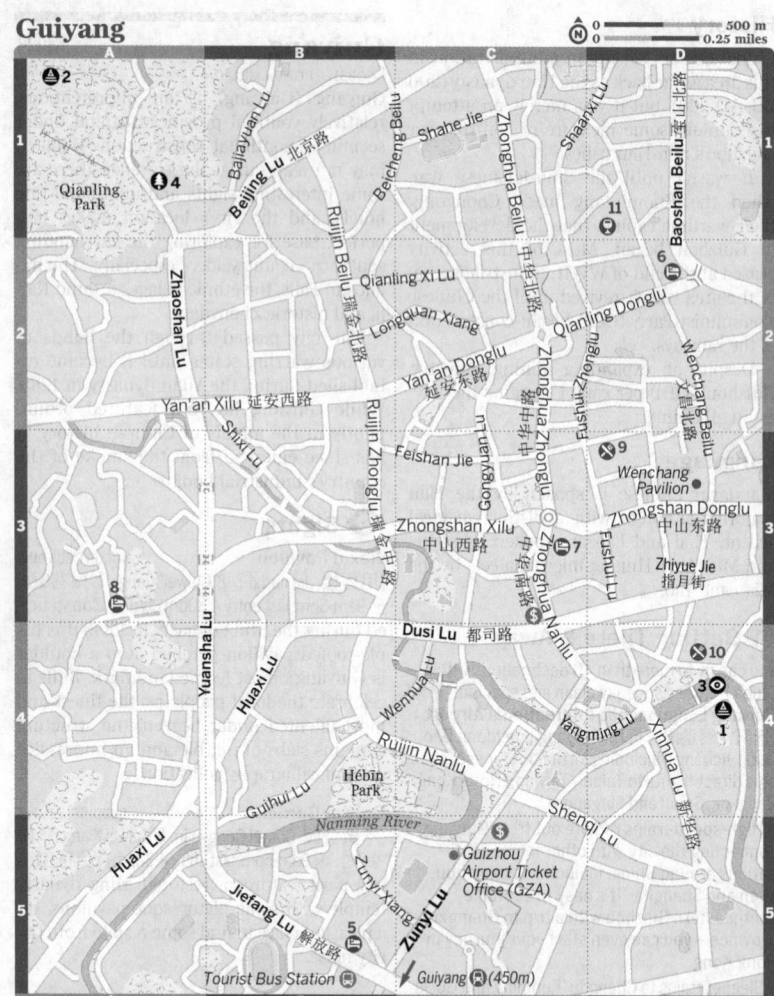

Qianling Mountain Park

PARK

(黔灵山公园, Qiánlíng Shān Gōngyuán; ¥5; ⏰24hr; 🚌1, 2) Qianling Mountain Park, in the northwest of the city, is more forest than park. It's a great escape from the crowds and city noise and has some lovely paths up to the Hongfu Temple.

Hongfu Temple

BUDDHIST TEMPLE

(弘福寺, Hóngfú Sì; 187 Zao Shanlu, 枣山路187号; ¥2, cable car one way/return ¥20/30; ⏰7am-6pm, cable car 9am-5pm; 🚌) Guiyang's best attraction is a temple complex hidden inside Qianling Mountain Park to the north of the city. Near the top of 1300m Qianling

Mountain (黔灵山, Qiánlíng Shān), Hongfu Temple dates back to the 17th century and is reached via an easy 40-minute walk (or a cable car if you don't feel up to it). The on-site monastery has a decent vegetarian restaurant in the rear courtyard.

🛏 Sleeping

Shu Hostel

HOSTEL ¥

(贵阳墅国际青年驿栈, Guìyáng Shù Guójì Qīngnián Yìzhàn; 📞181 9828 7383; 86 Zhongshan Nan-lu, 中山南路86号; dm/tw ¥60/120; ❄🤝; 🚌261) This quiet and friendly hostel has clean, if a little rundown, dorm rooms, and spacious shared bathrooms. The walls are covered in

Guiyang

useful information on travelling around the province, while the central space is good for meeting other travellers.

Hanting Express HOTEL ¥¥
(汉庭连锁酒店, Hàntíng Liánsuǒ Jiǔdiàn; ☑0851 8855 1888; www.htinns.com; 188 Fangyuan Sq, Jiefang Lu, 解放路方源广场188号; tw/d ¥219/239; ⊛@☢; 🚇Line 1) Very convenient for the train station, this efficient chain hotel is a good-value overnighter. Rooms are spotless (if a little tight) and free coffee awaits guests in the lounge. Walk north up Zunyi Lu and turn left along Jiefang Lu; it's on the far side of the road.

★He House BOUTIQUE HOTEL ¥¥¥
(和舍酒店, Héshè Jiǔdiàn; ☑0851 8682 5888; 219 Baoshan Beilu, 宝山北路219号; tw/d ¥498/508; Ⓟ⊛☢) Housed in a large white gallery space in a converted building, He House is Guiyang's best independent hotel. Open-plan rooms are oversized and crisply prepared with original artworks and high-quality bathroom amenities. Service is earnest but staff are knowledgeable about the city. The on-site restaurant has a limited selection; the breakfast buffet has a colourful continental variety.

Novotel HOTEL ¥¥¥
(贵阳诺富特酒店, Guìyáng Nuòfùtè Jiǔdiàn; ☑0851 8588 1888; www.accorhotels.com; 8 Zhonghua Nanlu, 中华南路8号; d¥448; ⊜⊛☢; 🖥1,2) Centrally located with clean, spacious rooms. Staff are courteous and speak a little English. The hotel has a basic but well-equipped fitness centre and a top-floor revolving bar that serves cocktails and craft beers.

✖ Eating

Guiyang is a haven for fans of street food, and stalls serving up barbecue, steaming bowls of rice noodles or sour fish soup can be found all over the city. In warm weather, head to Qianling Donglu (黔灵东路) for late-night alfresco dining. On the city's frequent rainy days, explore the bustling food courts housed in the underpasses below many major road junctions.

★Shanzai Vegetarian Meal VEGETARIAN ¥
(善哉膳斋, Shànzāi Shànzhāi; ☑0851 8561 4480; 8 Xihu Lu, 西湖路8号; dishes from ¥11am-9pm; ⊛☢) The beautiful rooftop terrace of this vegetarian restaurant has some of the best views and food in Guiyang. All dishes are stylishly presented and combine interesting and unique flavours. The signature dish is the enthusiastically named *shànzāi shànzāi* (善哉善哉; ¥48), which literally means 'excellent excellent', and combines stir-fried vegetables with crunchy bits of fried dough stick, walnuts and tofu skin.

★Old Kaili Sour Fish Restaurant GUIZHOU ¥
(老凯俚酸汤鱼, Lǎo Kǎilǐ Suāntāngyú; ☑0851 8584 3665; 12 Shengfu Lu, 省府路12号; dishes from ¥40; ⊙11am-9.30pm; ⊛☢) This local institution has two branches, but the one on Shengfu Lu has superior service and atmosphere (both have Miao waitstaff in traditional garb). Everyone comes for *suāntāngyú* (酸汤鱼; sour fish soup), a Miao delicacy and Guizhou's most famous dish. Choose a fish from the tank and point to the vegetables you'd like; your soup is made to order. Delicious.

Shù Chú GUIZHOU ¥
(树厨; ☑0851 8582 6853; 8 Zhonghua Nanlu, 中华南路8号; dishes from ¥26; ⊙11am-9pm; ⊛☢; 🖥1, 2) Next door to the Novotel is this homely restaurant set inside a courtyard of a former private residence. The menu here errs on the spicy side, although the fish-flavoured pork (鱼香肉丝, *yúxiāng ròusī*; ¥46) doesn't pack too much heat, while the 'oil residue' vermicelli (油渣炒粉丝, *yóuzhā chǎo fěnsī*; ¥36) is tastier than it sounds – a colourful mix of crunchy vegetables and crispy pork with noodles.

🍷 Drinking & Nightlife

Guiyang is a modest party capital by contemporary Chinese standards, but that doesn't mean you can't dance the night away with friendly strangers. Aim for the cool bars in the alleys around Qianling Donglu.

CELEBRATING WITH THE LOCALS, GUIZHOU-STYLE

Minority celebrations are lively events that can last for days at a time, and often include singing, dancing, horse racing and buffalo fighting.

One of the biggest is the **lusheng festival**, held in either spring or autumn, depending on the village: a *lúshēng* is a reed instrument used by the Miao people. Other important festivals include the **Dragon Boat Festival** (端午节, Duānwǔ Jié; ⊙ Jun), the **hill-leaping festival** and the **'sharing the sister's meal' festival** (equivalent to Valentine's Day in the west). Bull or bird fights are held at many of the celebrations, which, while not usually to the death, might be distressing to animal-loving visitors. The **Miao New Year** is celebrated on the first four days of the 10th lunar month in Kaili, Guading, Zhouxi and other Miao areas.

All minority festivals follow the lunar calendar, so dates vary from year to year. They will also vary from village to village and shaman to shaman.

★ **Trip Smith**   CRAFT BEER

(☑ 18984872915; 27 Yujia Xiang, 余家巷27号; beer from ¥30; ⊙ 4-11pm; ☎) Tucked down one of the many alleys off Qianling Dong Lu, Trip Smith is a small, happening bar that brews its own beer and serves better-than-average western fare, including pretty decent burgers (¥68). In warm months the outdoor seating area is packed with local beer lovers keen to sample the 10 brews on offer, including IPAs, stout, porter, bitter, pilsener and wheat beer.

ⓘ Information

Guiyang has plentiful banks and ATMs. **Bank of China** (中国银行; Zhōngguó Yínháng; 30 Dusi Lu, 都司30号; ⊙ 9am-5pm) has an ATM and offers all the services you need. Another **branch** (中国银行; Zhōngguó Yínháng; 56 Zunyi Lu, 遵义路56号; ⊙ 9am-5pm) can be found on Zunyi Lu.

ⓘ Getting There & Away

AIR

Guiyang Longdongbao International Airport (p665) is around 10km east of the city and has departures to destinations across mainland China, as well as to Hong Kong and Macau.

The **airport ticket office** (贵州省机场集团售票处, Guìzhōu Shěng Jīchǎng Jítuán Shòupiào Chù; ☎ 0851 859 77777; 264 Zunyi Lu, 遵义路264号; ⊙ 8am-7pm) is around 1km north of the **train station** (贵阳火车站, Guìyáng Huǒchēzhàn; 1 Sitong Jie, 四通街1号; Ⓜ Line 1). Airport buses depart every 30 minutes from here (¥10, 20 minutes, 8am until last flight departures).

A taxi from the airport will cost around ¥65.

BUS

The **Jinyang long-distance bus station** (贵阳金阳客车站, Guìyáng Jīnyáng Kèchēzhàn; Hangzhou Lu, 杭州路; ☐ 219) is in the western suburbs, 15km northwest of central Guiyang. Take bus 219 (¥2, 6.30am to 10pm) from the train station; a taxi will cost ¥50. Destinations include the following:

Anshun ¥35, 1½ hours, every 15 minutes (7am to 9pm)

Chishui ¥150, six hours, three daily (9am, 11am and 4pm)

Weining ¥130, six hours, two daily (12pm and 4pm)

For Kaili (¥60, 2½ hours, every 20 minutes, 8am to 8pm) and Congjiang (¥150, seven hours, 9am and 11am), head to the **east bus station** (客运东站; Kèyùn dōngzhàn; ☐ 229) on the eastern outskirts of town. Bus 229 (¥2) runs here from Jinyang bus station; a taxi is about ¥30.

TRAIN

Guiyang North Train Station (贵阳火车北站, Guìyáng Huǒchē Běizhàn; Beizhan Jie, 北站街; Ⓜ Line 1) is useful for reaching the increasing number of cities in Guizhou (and beyond) that are serviced by high-speed rail lines.

To reach destinations that don't yet have high-speed train stations, head to Guiyang's central train station. Destinations include the following (prices are for hard seats):

Caohai (for Weining) ¥50.50, five to eight hours, three daily (7.05am, 11.40am and 11.56pm)

Zhenyuan ¥41.40, three to four hours, seven daily (6.05am to 3.20pm)

ⓘ Getting Around

At the time of research, Guiyang had just one metro line, but expect this to change as new lines are opened. Line 1 connects the central Guiyang Train Station and Guiyang North Train Station (p668), passing through the downtown area. Trains run from 6.30 to 1am, with tickets costing ¥2 to ¥8.

Guiyang has an extensive and cheap bus network. Tickets to most destinations cost ¥1 to ¥2. Many of the local buses start and terminate their routes in the square in front of the train station.

Taxi flag fall is ¥10; late at night it increases to ¥11.

Qingyan 青岩

☑ 0851

With its winding, stone-flagged streets and restored city walls, Qingyan (Qīngyán) makes a pleasant diversion from modern Guiyang. A former Ming-era military outpost dating back to 1378, Qingyan was once a traffic hub between the southwest provinces, leaving the village with Taoist temples and Buddhist monasteries rubbing up against Christian churches and menacing watchtowers.

To access most of the town's major sights, including the city walls, you need to buy the ¥60 ticket. To enter only the old town, tickets cost ¥10.

Some of Qingyan's places of worship are still active; make sure to visit the tranquil **Yingxiang Temple** (迎祥寺, Yíngxiáng Sì; 6 Yingxiang Lu, 迎祥寺路6号), on a side street populated by fortune tellers; also compare the current, minimalist **Catholic Church** (天主教堂, Tiānzhǔ Jiàotáng; 56 Xi Mingqing Lu, 西明清街56号) with the now disused – but much more impressive – 19th-century original next door.

With steep climbs, a walk of the 1300m-long restored **city walls** (古镇城墙, Gǔzhèn Chéngqiáng) offers quite a workout as well as great views of the town. Tickets are, in theory, required but this didn't seem strictly enforced when we visited.

There are loads of cheap food stalls inside the city gates selling everything from pig-feet stew to deep-fried potato cakes and tofu balls.

There is no real nightlife in Qingyan but there are some nice cafes and teahouses dotted around the town centre, including **Bǎi Wú Yī Yòng Shūdiàn** (百无一用书店; 134 Qingyan Dong Jie, 青岩东街134号; tea from ¥48, coffee from ¥18; ☺9am-9pm; ☎). This bookshop hides a wonderful teahouse and coffee shop out back, housed in a beautiful old wooden building that opens out onto a tranquil garden. The friendly staff speak a little English.

Qingyan is about 30km south of Guiyang and makes for an easy day trip. Bus 203 runs here from the bus terminus at Guiyang Train Station (¥10, one to two hours, regular departures 6.30am to 9pm). Stay on until the end of the line. The same bus runs back to the station (¥10). A taxi will cost around ¥100 one way.

Kaili 凯里

☑ 0855 / POP 522,601

The largest city in eastern Guizhou, Kaili (Kǎilǐ) is a bustling industrial centre for the region. It might not be beautiful, but it's a lively, friendly place and a decent base – or at the very least a transit point – for planning your forays into nearby ethnic minority villages in the gorgeous surrounding countryside.

☞ Tours

Wu Min TREKKING, CULTURAL
(Louisa) (☑15885835852; wuminlouisa@hotmail.com) Wu Min, also known as Louisa, a local Miao woman, runs treks to remote Miao and Dong villages that come highly recommended. She can also organise **homestays**, as well as arrange for visitors to study the Miao and Dong languages and learn local dances; she speaks English well.

🛏 Sleeping

New Mill Inns HOSTEL ¥
(新磨坊连锁酒店, Xīn Mòfāng Liánsuǒ Jiǔdiàn; ☑13728035935, 18185533972; 26 Yingpan Donglu, 营盘东路26号; tw & d from ¥120; ❀☎) This hostel, tucked down an alleyway off Yingpan Donglu, has clean, basic rooms that are a bit rundown in places. Beds are softer than you might expect and the private bathrooms have western-style toilets. Friendly staff.

Hexie Dunpu Hotel HOTEL ¥¥
(和谐敦普酒店, Héxié Dūnpǔ Jiǔdiàn; ☑0855 229 9999; 70 Shaoshan South Rd, 山南路70号; d incl breakfast ¥360; ❀☎; ☐2) Centrally located, impeccably clean and with excellent wi-fi, the Hexie Dunpu Hotel makes a comfortable base in Kaili. It offers a decent Chinese buffet breakfast and has a restaurant that serves up classic local dishes at reasonable prices.

Zong Heng Hotel HOTEL ¥¥¥
(纵横大酒店, Zònghéng Dàjiǔdiàn; ☑0855 869 8888; 5 Ningbo Lu, 宁波路5号; tw/d incl breakfast ¥368/418; P❀☎; ☐2) A well-established four-star hotel with spacious, modern rooms that make a good base for a family or small group. Carpets and communal areas are tired, but the restaurant cooks up delicious Chinese food.

✖ Eating

Savoury crêpes, potato patties, barbecues, tofu grills, noodles, hotpot, *shuǐjiǎo* (boiled

Kaili

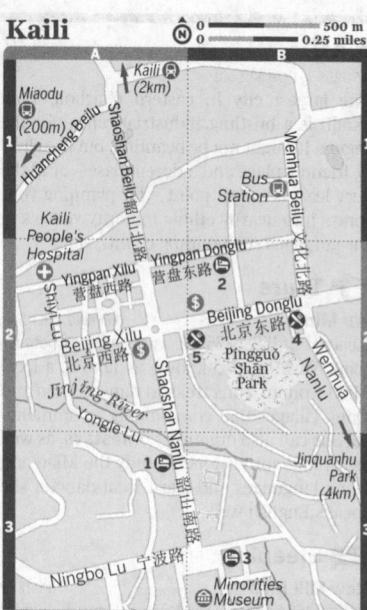

dumplings) and wonton soup overflow at reasonable prices at Kaili's street stalls. Look for *guōtiēdiàn* (锅贴店, dumpling snack restaurants) selling *guōtiē* (锅贴, fried dumplings) and Shanghai-style *xiǎolóngbāo;* there are several on Wenhua Beilu. Also head to the **night market** (夜市, Yèshì; Niuchangba Lu, 牛场坝路; ⊙5pm-2am), packed with locals and open till the wee hours.

Lǐxiǎng Miànshídiàn   NOODLES ¥
(理想面食店; 2 Wenhua Nanlu, 文化南路2号; dishes from ¥7; ⊙7am-7.30pm) This friendly cafe with blue plastic furniture serves simple dishes such as beef soup noodles (牛肉汤粉面, *niúròu tāng fěnmiàn*; ¥10) and handmade soup dumplings (汤饺, *tāngjiǎo*; ¥10). It's handy for a morning meal prior to village-hopping: try the pumpkin porridge (南瓜粥, *nánguā zhōu*; ¥4) or the egg pancake (鸡蛋饼, *jīdàn bǐng*; ¥6) for breakfast.

Kuàihuó Línliànghuān Zhài   CHINESE ¥
(快活林亮欢寨; 98 Huancheng Xilu, 环城西路98号; soup ¥38-48; ⊙11am-10pm; ☎; ☐20) The pick of the local sour soup venues gets the nod due to the high turnover of customers, the bubbly service and the sharp, tangy flavour. Take control of the chilli before someone else does! It's 2km west of the city centre.

ℹ Information

Bank of China (中国银行, Zhōngguó Yínháng; 6 Shaoshan Nanlu, 韶山南路6号; ⊙9am-5pm) This main branch has all services and an ATM. A second branch on **Beijing Donglu** (中国银行; Zhōngguó Yínháng; 11 Beijing Donglu, 北京东路11号; ⊙9am-5pm) will also change cash. Many other ATMs around town accept foreign cards.

ℹ Getting There & Away

For departures from Guiyang Longdongbao International Airport, buses (¥70, three to five hours, nine daily, 7am to 5pm) leave hourly or so from the **bus station** (凯里客车站, Kǎilǐ Kèchē Zhàn; ☑ 0855 825 1025; 25 Wenhua Beilu, 文化北路25号).

Kaili's bus station has departures to the following destinations:

Congjiang ¥78, five hours, six daily (9am to 5pm)

Guiyang ¥70, three hours, nine daily (8am to 5pm)

Leishan ¥22, 50 minutes, every 40 minutes (7am to 4.20pm)

Rongjiang ¥50, 4½ hours, every 40 to 50 minutes (7.30am to 6.20pm)

Xijiang ¥6, 80 minutes, every 50 minutes (7.50am to 5.40pm)

Zhenyuan ¥35, two hours, seven daily (8.40am to 7.30pm)

Minibuses to most local Miao villages depart from the **Miaodu Bus Terminal** (苗都客运站, Miáodōu Kèyùnzhàn; 358 Huancheng Beilu, 环城北路358).

High-speed trains depart from **Kaili South** (凯里南站, Kǎilǐ Nánzhàn; Jinhui Dadao, 金汇大道; ☐ 20, 21) with regular arrivals from and departures to Guiyang (¥58.50, 38 minutes), Shanghai (¥694, eight to nine hours) and Kunming (¥267, three to four hours), among others.

Kaili's **train station** (凯里站, Kǎilǐ Zhàn; 237 Qingjiang Lu, 清江路237号; ☐20) is a couple of kilometres north of town. Regular trains run to Guiyang (¥28.50, two to three hours), Zhenyuan (¥14.50, 1½ hours) and Huaihua (¥41.50, four hours).

ℹ Getting Around

Most bus fares cost ¥1 in Kaili. Taxi flag fall is ¥6. When arriving at the main station, you'll have

VILLAGE HOPPING AROUND KAILI

Kaili is surrounded by numerous charming Miao villages, most of which are accessible by minibus from the Miaodu Bus Terminal. Alternatively, you could hire a local driver – Mr Yang (mobile 15186785081) is a reliable option.

Matang (麻塘, Mátáng), 18km northwest of Kaili, is the home of the Gejia, renowned wax batik artisans. A worthwhile 30-minute walk through rice fields from here brings you to the village of **Shilongzhai** (石龙寨, Shílóngzhài), populated by another sub-branch of the Miao called the Xijia.

Nanhua (南华, Nánhuá), roughly 15km southeast of Kaili, is famous for its stilted buildings that seem to cling onto the valley wall above the Bala River. All of these traditional wooden dwellings are built with interlocking joints and sophisticated joinery methods – not a single nail, screw or bolt was used in their construction.

Zhouxi (舟溪, Zhōuxī), 15km southwest of Kaili, has a massive water buffalo fighting ring that is edged by ornate wooden walkways. When the ring is not in use during festivals, villagers use it to dry off long lengths of the indigo-dyed material that Zhouxi is famous for.

Shiqiao (石桥, Shíqiáo), 35km southwest of Kaili, is renowned for its traditional paper-making that local families still make a living from. Visitors can have a go at making their own paper.

to negotiate with drivers to bring you into town – they won't put the meter on. A good starting price is ¥20 (the equivalent journey the opposite way should cost around ¥12).

Langde 郎德

📞 0855 / POP 500

With its superb extant Miao architecture, cobbled pathways and spectacular valley setting, tiny Langde (Lángdé; ¥50) naturally draws visitors eager to experience traditional village life. While most visit on a day trip, if you choose to spend a night or two here, by nightfall you'll find yourself almost alone with the locals, who are members of the 'Long Skirt Miao' ethnic group. At night, enjoy the village's bucolic tranquillity. During the day, explore the hiking trails that radiate up and along the valley, taking you through beautiful fir forests to several nearby villages.

Langde's *diàojiǎolóu* (吊脚楼, literally 'hanging feet buildings') take advantage of the village's position up the sides of a valley. The fronts of these typical Miao buildings are supported by pillars while the backs are suspended on stilts that keep the building level with the hillside. An architectural wonder, many are held together without the use of nails or rivets, simply locked together with a system of wooden joints.

Local families offer rooms for around ¥70 (prices negotiable), while there are also homestay options in the village, including **Měi Hā Lè Miáo Jiā** (美哈乐苗家; 📞 15286313929,

15121457288; tw with/without bathroom ¥188/120; 🛜). Bathrooms have squat toilets and firm beds but are clean and well taken care of. It's near the tourist information centre at the front of the village, up some stairs to the right of the souvenir stall square.

Homestay hosts will rustle up some simple home cooking to visitors staying overnight in the village.

Langde can be reached by public bus from Kaili, 27km away. Buses will stop on the main road above the village, near the ticket office. From here, it's a 2km walk down the valley to Langde, or you can take a shuttle bus (¥5).

Xijiang 西江

📞 0855 / POP 6000

Xijiang (Xījiāng; ¥90), tucked away in the undulating greenery of Leigong Mountain (雷公山, Léigōng Shān), is the largest Miao settlement in China at roughly 1200 wooden homes. Like many neighbouring Miao villages, the town is famous for its embroidery and silver ornaments (the Miao believe that silver can dispel evil spirits).

With its stunning setting and easy access from Kaili, the town has been given over entirely to tourism. This manifests itself in a high entrance fee, crowds of day trippers, scheduled performances of traditional folk dancing and streets of standard Chinese souvenir shops. On the flip side, it also means plenty of places to eat, a wide variety of accommodation and little through traffic as

DON'T MISS

LANGDE WELCOMING CEREMONY

Although nowadays put on for tourists, the traditional welcome ceremony in Langde (p671) is still very atmospheric. Villagers clad in traditional dress line the terraces at the front of the village playing *lúshēng* reed pipes, singing greetings and offering visitors oxen horns of rice wine. Feel free to have a try of the potent spirit as the horn is offered to you, although if you don't want to drink it's OK to politely decline.

visitors are forced to park their cars at the entrance. The town's setting is stunning and there are some hiking opportunities through still-used farmland and quiet forests.

To escape the crowds, head away from the town on paths that weave through rice paddies, sidestepping farmers and water buffalo, and recharge your soul in the surrounding hills. A lovely trek is the 50-minute hike past terraced fields and rice paddies over the hills to Kaijue Miao Village (开觉苗寨, Kǎijué Miáozhài) and Kaijue Waterfall (开觉瀑布, Kǎijué Pùbù) a bit further beyond.

Xijiang is full of quality (and therefore pricier) guesthouses and hotels, although many families will also offer basic homestay rooms. The bohemian **998 Hostel** (☑15808555223; tw ¥300-320, d ¥320; ✸ ☎) is pretty and quiet and has stunning views out across Xijiang. **Miao Family Guesthouse** (苗寨人家, Miáo Zhài Rénjiā; ☑0855 334 8688, 18212337355; No 5, Group 2, Neinan Guicun, 内南贵村二组5号; tw & d ¥200-220; ✸ ☎) has clean comfortable rooms, some decorated with local artwork.

ⓘ Getting There & Around

From Kaili, buses run every 50 minutes between 7.50am and 5.40pm (¥16, one hour); there are regular buses back to Kaili from 8.20am to 4.10pm. There are also five buses per day from Xijiang to Kaili south high-speed train station (¥25, one hour, 9am to 3.30pm) for connections to Guiyang, and one bus a day directly to Guiyang's east bus station (¥95, four hours, 3pm).

Alternatively, heading south and east, there are buses to Leishan (¥12, 1½ hours, 6.30am to 5.40pm), from where you can head south towards Rongjiang (榕江, Róngjiāng), and high-speed train connections onto Congjiang and destinations in Guangxi.

From the ticket office, buses (¥5) run down the valley to the town. A site-seeing shuttle bus (¥5 per section) can ferry you between various points of interest, up some of the town's steep hills.

Zhaoxing 肇兴

☑ 0855 / POP 4000

Dreamy Zhaoxing (Zhàoxīng) has emerged from its stunning natural seclusion as a drawcard for visitors looking to experience life in a Dong village. The beautiful wooden housing is overshadowed only by the Wind and Rain bridges, reminiscent of a fantasy epic. Then there are the five drum towers that call forth generations of ritual and celebration.

Away from the main street, which is undeniably touristy, Zhaoxing remains a working farming village, where most people still speak only their native Dong language and little has changed for generations. For the time being at least, Zhaoxing seems to be striking the right balance between tourism and preserving the local way of life.

Entry to the village is ¥80 and tickets are valid for three days. For day trips out of Zhaoxing, make sure you carry your ticket for re-entry.

The colossal **Dazhai Gate** (大寨门, Dàzhài Mén) is Zhaoxing's most spectacular example of a wind and rain bridge, an architectural feature unique to Dong villages. These entirely wooden structures, built with long covered corridors, usually served as a village's main entrance, as well as a fine shelter from bad weather. Dazhai Gate is particularly beautiful at night when golden lighting gives it an almost fantastical quality.

🏃 Activities

From Zhaoxing, there is some wonderful hiking and the chance to explore several nearby Dong villages. Be sure not to miss the following.

Tang'an (堂安, Tǎng'ān) Head east out of Zhaoxing on a well-marked path through stunning rice terraces, and two hours later you reach Tang'an, a village so essentially Dong it's been named a living museum. There are also hourly buses (¥10, 20 minutes) from a **small bus station** in Zhaoxing if you don't fancy the walk.

Jitang (己塘, Jǐtáng) Follow the road that leads southwest out of Zhaoxing village. When you get to a small car park, head left up a steep hill and continue along the road for a couple of hours to reach pretty Jitang, which has its own drum tower. Be careful as you'll be sharing the road with cars and motorcycles.

🛏 Sleeping

There are lots of good-quality hotels and guesthouses in Zhaoxing. Locals might also put you up in a homestay – ask around for rooms from ¥50.

Wangjiang Lou Hostel HOSTEL ¥
(望江楼客栈, Wàngjiānglóu Kèzhàn; ☑ 15086213158, 0855 613 0269; tw & d ¥158; ✴@🛜) Family-run place by the river, with fresh and clean wooden rooms featuring hot showers and sit-down toilets.

★ Creekside Inn GUESTHOUSE ¥¥
(溪舍.田园, Xīshě. Tiányuán; ☑ 0855 613 0097, 13595115991; 53597675@qq.com; beside the Rentuan Drum Tower, 仁团鼓楼旁; d ¥252, breakfast ¥25; ➖✴🛜) This family-run guesthouse has one of the nicest locations in Zhaoxing – at the quieter, eastern edge of the village – with fabulous views overlooking the rice terraces. Split across two locations, the original riverside location has slightly larger rooms while the nearby newer building has a wonderful rooftop seating area. Both have clean, comfortable ensuite rooms.

Indigo Lodge LODGE ¥¥
(青定阁, Qīngdìnggé; ☑ 0855 609 8933, 18375274959; 202 Sheng Dao, 202省道; d from ¥298; ✴🛜) Indigo is indicative of the increasing professionalism of the Dong villages in catering to the travel community: hip, understated luxury; impeccable customer service; and a real understanding of how to maximise your visit to the region. Lit up at night, it's a beauty. Walk-ins can usually negotiate a discount.

🍴 Eating & Drinking

You won't go hungry or thirsty in Zhaoxing – head to the main street for an abundance of restaurants and small bars, many with picture menus for easier ordering.

Nóngfū Rénjiā CHINESE ¥
(农夫人家, next to Dragon Bridge, 龙桥旁边; dishes from ¥10; ☉ 7am-9pm) Next to the Dragon Bridge (龙桥, Lóngqiáo) this simple homestyle restaurant has pictures for easier ordering and a lovely riverside terrace. The braised aubergine (红烧茄子, hóngshāo qiézi) served with a bowl of white rice is delicious and vegetarian.

⭐ Entertainment

Cultural performance LIVE PERFORMANCE
(Performance Sq, 表演场; included in entrance ticket; ☉ 10am, 8pm) Twice daily performances of traditional Dong singing and dancing with the accompanying narration translated into English on LED signs by the stage.

ℹ Getting There & Away

Getting to Zhaoxing is easy thanks to the Guangdong-to-Guiyang high-speed train line. Zhaoxing's nearest station is **Congjiang** (从江站, Cóngjiāng Zhàn), 6km west of the village ticket office. From the station, minibuses (¥10) will ferry you to the village itself, via the ticket office.

Congjiang has departures to the following destinations:

Guangdong ¥216, three to four hours, 12 daily (9.39am to 7.59pm)

Guilin ¥59.50, 50 to 75 minutes, 17 daily (8.47am to 7.59pm)

Guiyang ¥107, 1½ hours, 15 daily (10.57am to 9.09pm)

A **bus station** (车站, Chēzhàn) at the western end of the village, just north of the beautiful Dazhai Gate, has departures for day trips to Basha and Liping (for Longli).

Basha 岜沙

☑ 0855 / POP 2500

Visiting historic Basha (Bāshā) is like stepping back in time to the Tang or Song eras. The local men wear period clothes with daggers secured to their belts and tote antique rifles that, despite strict gun control laws in the rest of China, the government allows them to keep. Meanwhile, the women parade in full Miao rig with their hair twisted in a curl on top of their heads.

LOCAL KNOWLEDGE

INDIGO IN ZHAOXING

The Dong are indigo growers and Zhaoxing is a major producer of the dark blue cotton cloth that many local people still wear. All around the village you'll see lengths of dyed cotton hanging up to dry as well as women coating the material in egg white before beating it with heavy mallets to achieve a lustrous sheen. The rhythmic pounding of these mallets on the cloth will be the soundtrack to your stay in Zhaoxing.

Basha is made up of six hamlets sprawled across a beautiful valley – the surrounding countryside is superb.

Basha has not escaped mass tourism. A ticket to enter the village (8am to 6pm) is ¥40 (plus ¥20 for the bus from the ticket office to the village entrance). There are three cultural performances each day (¥40, 9.30am, 11.30am and 3.30pm) and at 9am, 11am and 3pm the men will welcome you to the village with a traditional gun salute.

You can find very rudimentary rooms for ¥30 and a couple of decent guesthouses, including **Gǔfēngzhài Qīngnián Lǚguǎn** (古风寨青年旅馆; ☑ 13885549720; dm/tw/d ¥50/168/238; @ 🛜), the pick of the village, although you might have to ask around to find the owner. The views of the surrounding valley alone are worth the stay, but there's also real pride in the presentation of the modest private rooms and spotless dorms. Walk down the path to the left of the village square to find it.

Basha has a few barbecued meat stalls and rice noodle (米粉, *mǐfěn*) places, as well as a couple of larger restaurants.

It's easiest to visit Basha on a day trip from Zhaoxing – three buses per day leave Zhaoxing for the ticket office at Basha village (¥60 return, one hour, 7.30am, 9.30am and 1.30pm). Buses then return to Zhaoxing at 11am, 1.30pm and 5pm.

Longli 隆里

☑ 0855 / POP 180,000 (COUNTY LEVEL)

Stranded in splendid isolation amid fields and rice paddies near the Hunan border, Longli (Lónglǐ) is a former garrison town populated by the descendants of Han soldiers sent to 'protect' the Ming empire from the 'pesky' Miao. One of the province's 'eco-museums' – that is, a real-life village – Longli is fascinating for its stone buildings that have more in common with the architecture of east China's Anhui and Jiangxi provinces than the wooden buildings of nearby Miao and Dong villages.

Enter Longli via the ivy-covered Qingyang Gate (青阳门, Qīngyáng Mén) and take an hour's stroll to savour its warren of narrow cobblestone streets, passing brightly painted frontages of the stone buildings, lovely courtyards, pavilions, temples and town walls. Be sure to walk along the remaining city wall, starting to the right of Qingyang Gate as you enter.

After serving under the Ming emperors, who paid their army wages, the residents of Longli were largely abandoned by Qing dynasty rulers who had other military priorities. As a consequence, activity in the town shifted to education and **Longbiao Academy** (龙标书院, Lóngbiāo Shūyuàn) **FREE** was just one seat of learning set up to serve local scholars. Inside, there's an interesting map depicting Longli at the height of its military power.

If you want to stay overnight, **Gǔchéng Jiǔdiàn** (古城酒店; ☑ 13638554888, 0855 718 0018; next to the east gate entrance, 隆里古城东大门旁; tw ¥100; ❄ 🛜) has basic rooms with western-style toilets and is located in the square in front of the Qingyang Gate (eastern) entrance.

A few basic restaurants set up when the tourist buses pass through; otherwise, cuisine on offer caters to local tastes. You might see villagers selling live bamboo rats (野竹鼠, *yězhú shǔ*) to take home for the pot.

🛈 Getting There & Away

Longli is easiest visited as a day trip from Zhaoxing, an hour's drive away. Expect to pay around ¥600 for a car and driver, depending on your bargaining skills. Mr Huang is a reliable local driver (mobile 18785546476), or you can ask your hotel to help you organise a car.

There is no direct bus to Longli from Zhaoxing – you must first take a bus to Liping (黎平, Lípíng). Buses to Liping leave Zhaoxing village itself four times a day from Congjiang high-speed station (¥30, 1½ hours, 7.10am, 9am, 11am and 12.50pm). In Liping, transfer to a bus bound for Longli (¥20, one hour, regular departures from around 8am to 4pm).

Zhenyuan 镇远

☑ 0855 / POP 40,000

Zhenyuan (Zhènyuǎn) is the highlight for many visitors to southern China thanks to its unruffled charm, high density of historical sights, gorgeous locale by the Wuyang River (Wǔyáng Hé), and relative obscurity in the eyes of international travellers. In some neighbouring provinces, places half as delightful draw twice the number of visitors.

A former outpost on the trade route from Yunnan to Hunan, Zhenyuan by day is pleasantly quiet, and small enough to explore comfortably on foot. When evening comes, its riverfront buildings are illuminated in dreamy golden lighting and its surprisingly lively nightlife scene kicks into gear.

⊙ Sights

Qīnglóng Dòng
TEMPLE

(青龙洞, Green Dragon Cave; 14 Dongxia Jie, 东峡街14号; ¥60; ⊙8am-5pm) Across the river from the old town, the epic vertical warren of temples, grottoes, corridors and caves of Qīnglóng Dòng rises up against Zhonghe Mountain (中和山, Zhōnghé Shān). Flooded with lights at night, it forms a sublime backdrop to the town. Put aside a good hour for exploration: it's a labyrinth and there's a lot to see, including some choice panoramas.

★ Zhusheng Bridge
BRIDGE

(祝圣桥; Zhùshèng Qiáo) The most photographed sight in town, Zhenyuan's old bridge is a gorgeous and robust span of arches topped with a three-storey pavilion, leading visitors across the water to Qīnglóng Dòng. It's an impressive sight. Views along the river from the bridge at night are serene, with Qīnglóng Dòng splendidly lit up.

Sifangjing Xiang
AREA

(四方井巷) Four old and well-preserved alleys lead north away from the river: Sifangjing Xiang, Fuxing Xiang, Renshou Xiang and Chongzikou Xiang. Wander along Sifangjing Xiang and peek at its namesake Sìfāngjǐng (Four Directions Well), with its three deities overlooking the water, capped with red cloths. Note the magnificently made stone steps of this alley and the gorgeous old residences – a picture at night, when they're dressed with red lanterns.

★ Shiping Mountain Scenic Area
MOUNTAIN

(石屏山景区, Shípíng Shān Jǐngqū; Shuncheng Jie, 顺城街; ¥30) A strenuous 30-minute climb up this mountain above town takes you through quiet forest to the remains of the Miaojiang Great Wall and the **Four Officials Temple** (四官殿, Sìguān Diàn) FREE. En route, a pretty pavilion perched on the cliff-edge offers a welcome rest point, as well as gorgeous panoramic views of the town and surrounding valleys.

Miaojiang Great Wall
WALLS

(苗疆长城, Miáojiāng Chángchéng) Accessed with your ticket to the Shiping Mountain Scenic Area, the remains of this 16th-century wall, built to protect Zhenyuan, are quite remarkable. You can walk on top of the wall for a fair distance as it undulates across the peaks – the views of the surrounding mountains are glorious. Be careful in wet weather when the stone is slippery.

Tiexi Gorge
GORGE

(铁溪景区, Tiěxī Jǐngqū; ¥50; ☒7) A trip to the pleasant Tiexi Gorge offers the chance to plunge along rocky trails shaded by overhanging trees. Don't miss the Dragon Pool (龙潭, Lóngtán) and Jiguan Mountain (鸡冠岭, Jīguān Lǐng). Food vendors are scattered along the 2½-hour walk to the mountain, ensuring you won't go hungry.

☞ Tours

River cruises (30 minutes, 9am to 10.30pm, ¥60 before 6pm, ¥80 after) are available in Zhenyuan; buy tickets at the office next to **Yumen Wharf** (禹门码头, Yǔmén Mǎtóu; Xinglong Jie, 兴隆街), which is identifiable by the decorative arch.

Travel agents line Xinglong Jie; you should also be able to book tours around the area through your hotel.

🛏 Sleeping

There are rooms everywhere in the old town, with new guesthouses opening up steadily, often above restaurants. Don't expect any spoken English. Rooms south of the river get the amplified sound of trains rumbling by, while all riverside hotels have a front-row seat to loud nightly karaoke performances in bars along the river. Ask for discounts.

Ren Zai Zhenyuan Youth Hostel
HOSTEL ¥

(人在镇远青年客栈, Rén Zài Zhènyuǎn Qīngnián Kèzhàn; ☏13885544870; Chongzikou Xiang, 冲子口巷; dm/tw/d ¥50/148/128; ❋⑦) Cheerful hostel with nicely decorated rooms and dorms, some with views of the charming surrounding lanes. Comfortable high-quality bedding. Squat toilets only in bathrooms.

Yǒngfúróng Jìngxīn Jū
BOUTIQUE HOTEL ¥¥

(永福荣静心居; ☏13378550003; Xinglong Jie, 兴隆街; d from ¥279; ❋⑦) Stylishly decorated rooms, comfortable beds and friendly reception staff. Rooms overlooking the river enjoy beautiful views but are noisy thanks to nightly karaoke sessions in bars along the opposite riverbank. Wi-fi is a little patchy.

★ Daheguan Hotel
HOTEL ¥¥¥

(大河关宾馆, Dàhéguān Bīnguǎn; ☏18685551211, 0855 571 0188; Shuncheng Jie, 顺城街; tw & d ¥388-688; ❋⑦) The faux-period wooden courtyard at the Daheguan passes the authenticity test well enough, but it's the corner location, classy finishing and luxurious beds that help make this the best hotel in town.

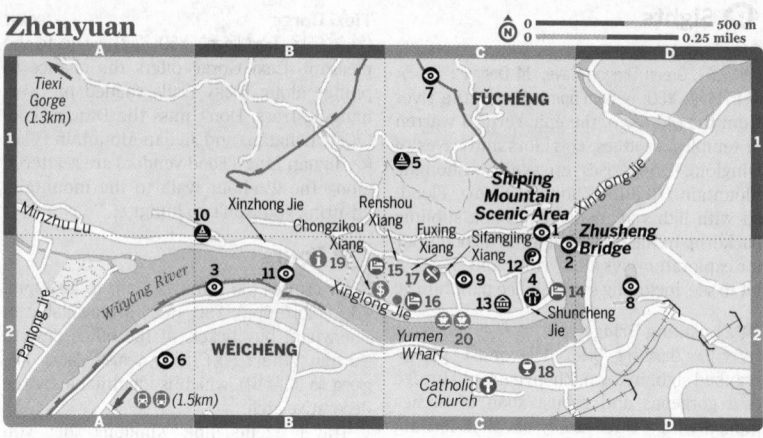

Zhenyuan

🍴 Eating

Xinglong Jie is full of restaurants, many aimed at tourists. Look out for urns of locally brewed alcohol, such as *báijiǔ* (白酒) grain wine and corn wine (包谷酒, *bāogǔjiǔ*).

In warmer months, locals flock to the outdoor seating areas of the riverside hotpot restaurants. Best enjoyed in a group; to order, just point to what the next table is having.

★ **Nóngjiā Fàn Xiāng** CHINESE ¥
(农家饭香; ☑ 18608558672; Sifangjing Xiang, 四方井巷; dishes from ¥15; ⊙ from 10am) At the top of Sifangjing Xiang (p675), and with a lovely terrace, this quiet family-run restaurant serves up Guizhou-style dishes including smokey cured bacon with ferncakes (蕨粑腊肉, *juébā làròu*). It also has classics such as shredded potato with green pepper (青椒土豆丝,

qīngjiāo tǔdòusī) and egg-fried rice (鸡蛋炒饭, *jīdànchǎofàn*).

🍷 Drinking & Nightlife

After daytime tranquillity, come nightfall Zhenyuan somewhat surprisingly becomes a party town. Revellers gather at raucous hotpot joints or blast out Chinese pop songs at various karaoke bars along the southern riverbank, their voices echoing around the hills until around 11pm. Pretty much all bars in town feature live bands of varying quality.

Yǐ Mèng Wéi Mǎ BAR
(以梦为马; Riverside Boardwalk, 河滨栈道; beer from ¥40; ⊙ 2-11pm; 🛜) Artsy bar on the southern bank of the river, with bottled international beers and so-so cocktails. Also has tea and coffee, and a small selection of bar snacks. It's in an area of similar bars;

look for the comfy outdoor seating area with pastel-coloured cushions.

ⓘ Information

Industrial & Commercial Bank of China (中国工商银行, Zhōngguó Gōngshāng Yínháng; Xinglong Jie, 兴隆街; ⊙9am-5pm) Has an ATM; takes foreign cards.

Zhenyuan Tourist Information Centre (镇远旅游咨询服务中心, Zhènyuǎn Lǚyóu Zīxún Fúwù Zhōngxīn; Xinglong Jie, 兴隆街; ⊙8am-8pm) Has basic maps of Zhenyuan.

ⓘ Getting There & Away

The best way to reach Zhenyuan from Guiyang is by train. The **train station** (火车站, Huǒchēzhàn) is southwest of the town, not far from Wuyanghe Bridge (舞阳河大桥, Wǔyánghé Dàqiáo). It's a good 20-minute walk to the old town from the train station, so either buy your ticket out of Zhenyuan when you arrive at the station or book tickets in advance at the downtown **Train Ticket Booking Office** (火车票代售点, Huǒchēpiào Dàishòu Diǎn; ☑0855 5723261; 21 Xinglong Jie, 兴隆街21号; ⊙8.30am-5.30pm) for a commission (¥5).

The **bus station** (镇远汽车站 Zhènyuǎn Qìchēzhàn) is opposite the train station. Bus services include the following destinations:

Baojing ¥15, one to 1½ hours, three daily (10.20am, 12.30pm and 3.20pm)

Kaili ¥50, 1½ to two hours, hourly (7am to 7.30pm)

Tongren ¥60, two hours, two daily (11am and 5pm)

ⓘ Getting Around

Zhenyuan is small enough to walk around but a couple of bus routes are useful and have stops outside the tourist information centre. **Bus 1** starts at the train station and heads to the main strip at Xinglong Jie (¥2, 20 minutes). **Bus 7** runs to Tiexi Gorge (¥2, 30 minutes) along Xinglong Jie.

Taxis are cheap and plentiful, although you'll only likely need them to get to and from the train and bus stations (¥8, 15 minutes). Alternatively, you can walk it in about 20 minutes.

A **ferry** (¥1; ⊙6am-7.30pm) can punt you across the river.

Around Zhenyuan

Baojing 报京

Baojing (Bàojīng) is a Dong minority village with fine examples of stilted *diàojiǎolóu* (吊脚楼) architecture. The village is also known for its **seed-sowing festival** (播种节, *bōzhǒngjié*) – held on the third day of the third lunar month, it's a lively celebration of dancing and courtship rituals.

Baojing is located 40km from Zhenyuan. Three buses (¥15, 10.20am, 12.30pm and 3.20pm) run there daily from Zhenyuan's bus station, the journey takes one to two hours. There is one bus back to Zhenyuan at 4pm.

Fanjing Mountain 梵净山

Guizhou's northeastern flanks are home to some of southern China's most densely populated wildlife. The 2572m **Fanjing Mountain** (Fànjīng Shān; ¥110) is a sacred Buddhist site and nature reserve known for rare plant species and the elusive golden monkey (金丝猴, jīnsīhóu). Precariously balanced and oddly shaped rock structures reward climbers (or those who brave the cable car).

Spring and autumn are the best seasons to visit Fanjing Mountain, but check the weather before you go as it is often fogged out; clear days offer spectacular views. (Bear in mind too that the animals here are very retiring.)

You can make a long day trip from Zhenyuan. Negotiate with a local driver to take you on the four-hour round trip and wait for you while you climb the mountain – Mr Yang is reliable (mobile 15186785081). Expect to pay around ¥700 for the day.

Anshun 安顺

☑0851 / POP 765,310

Anshun (Ānshùn) is an unassuming provincial city that makes a convenient base for travel around western Guizhou. The prime attraction is Hongshan Lake, especially when lit up at night; it's fringed by a gorgeous walking track leading up to two temples. Once a marvellous historical city ringed by a town wall, the city's heritage has largely vanished and now it's the surrounding sights that are the real draws. Shoppers can look out for batik, kitchen knives and the lethal Anjiu brand of alcohol.

🛏 Sleeping

Anshun doesn't receive many foreign visitors so there is a limited number of hotels that can accommodate international travellers. If your Chinese is up to it, try your luck at one of the guesthouses (旅馆, *lǚguǎn*) near the train station for a cheap room. Otherwise, stay further into town or closer to the lake.

Anshun

N 0 —— 500 m
0 —— 0.25 miles

Anshun

◎ Sights
1 Anshun City Walls	B2
2 Donglin Temple	B2
3 Lóngwáng Miào	A2
4 Wénmiào	A2

⊟ Sleeping
5 Double Tree Hilton Anshun	A1
6 Xīxiùshān Bīnguǎn	B3

⊗ Eating
Bǎinián Lǎozìhao	(see 6)

ⓘ Transport
7 Anshun Train Station	B4

first class. The international breakfast buffet will fill you for the day.

✗ Eating

Anshun is chock-full of street-food options, with locals crowding out the many food tents and stalls that set up on streets such as Nanshui Lu and around the train station. The arterial roads off happening Gufu Jie also hide food stalls and tiny restaurants, while the northern side of Hongshan Lake has some charming small cafes that serve basic food.

Bǎinián Lǎozìhao   DUMPLINGS ¥
(百年老字号; 25 Zhonghua Nanlu, 中华南路25号1; dumplings from ¥8) The Shanghai-style steamed buns, dumplings and pot stickers served here are good for a quick and cheap bite. To order, simply point to a picture or one of the bamboo steamers out front. Also serves congee (粥, zhōu; from ¥3) for breakfast.

ⓘ Information

Bank of China (中国银行, Zhōngguó Yínháng; 19 Zhonghua Nan Lu, 中华南路19号; ◷9am-5pm) Offers all services and has an ATM. There are many other ATMs around town.

ⓘ Getting There & Away

AIR

Anshun Huangguoshu Airport (安顺黄果树机场, Ānshùn Huángguǒshù Jīchǎng; Jichang Lu, 安顺市西秀区机场路) is around 8km from downtown Anshun and has departures to destinations across China.

Bus 9 (¥2) runs from the airport to the **east bus station** (东客运站, Dōng Kèyùnzhàn; Liangliu Lu, 两六路; ☐2, 16, 19), stopping on Zhonghua Xilu. A taxi will cost around ¥20.

Xīxiùshān Bīnguǎn   HOTEL ¥¥
(西秀山宾馆; ☐0851 3333 7888; 63 Zhonghua Nanlu, 中华南路63号; r incl buffet breakfast from ¥268; ❋❀) A point of difference here is the variety of rooms across three buildings. Go for one near the garden courtyard (where stray cats soak up the sun), or nab a suite if you feel the need to stretch out. Bathrooms could do with an overhaul but linens are clean and hot water abundant. Check the wi-fi in your room before committing.

Double Tree Hilton Anshun   HOTEL ¥¥¥
(安顺百灵希尔顿逸林酒店, Ānshùn Bǎilíng Xīěrdùn Yìlín Jiǔdiàn; ☐0851 3366 9666; www.doubletree3.hilton.com; 42 Hongshanhu Lu, 虹山湖路42号; d from ¥700; ❋@☎❀) This gigantic hotel towering over Hongshan Lake like a grounded spaceship is the only high-end option in Anshun, so it's a good thing that it's quietly fabulous. Views from the plush lake rooms are stunning, especially at night, and the pool, gym and yoga studio are all

BUS

The **north bus station** (客车北站, Kèchē Běizhàn; 🚍 6, 16) has buses to Zhijin town (for Zhijin Cave, p680). Almost every other bus leaves from the east bus station, 9km east of the city centre. Bus 16 (¥2) connects the two bus stations, running along Zhonghua Nanlu (there's a stop opposite the Xīxiùshān Bīnguǎn hotel. A taxi from downtown Anshun to the east station is ¥25 to ¥30.

Local bus timetables for destinations around Anshun can be confusing and subject to change, so it's always best to check exact timings on the day you want to travel. General departures from the east bus station include the following:

Huangguoshu Falls ¥25, one hour, every 30 minutes (7.20am to 5pm)

Jiuzhou (for Yunshan) ¥8, 40 minutes, every eight minutes (7am to 7pm)

Longgong Caves ¥15, 40 minutes, every 30 minutes (7.30am to 4pm)

Pingba (for Tianlong) ¥15, 40 minutes, every 30 minutes (7.30am to 6.30pm)

Xingyi ¥109, four hours, six daily (9am to 5pm)

TRAIN

Anshun has two train stations – the **main station** (火车站, Huǒchē zhàn; 1 Zhonghua Nanlu, 中华南路1号; 🚍 1, 2, 6, 19) in downtown and the newer **Anshun West high-speed station** (安顺西站, Ānshùn Xī Zhàn; Fumin Lu, 富民路; 🚍 19), 9km southwest of town. Most trains heading east from both stations stop in Guiyang.

The more conveniently located Anshun Station has a ticket office where you can buy tickets for both stations.

Around Anshun

Yunshan   云山屯

One of eight Ming-era fortified villages in the area, **Yunshan** (Yúnshān Tún; ¥50; ⊙9am-6pm) is a gem. Protected by a wall and a main gate, and overlooked by the Yunjiu Mountain (云鹫山, Yúnjiù Shān), the settlement is a charming portrait of rural Guizhou. At the heart of the almost deserted village stands a rickety **Money God Temple** (财神庙, Cáishén Miào) opposite an ancient pavilion. Don't miss the chance to walk up to **Yunjiu Temple** (云鹫寺, Yúnjiù Sì) at the top of Yunjiu Mountain for some wonderful views. To reach Yunshan, take a bus bound for Jiuzhou (旧州, Jiùzhōu; ¥8, 40 minutes, regular, around 7am to 7pm) from Anshun's east bus station. The bus will drop you off on the main road northeast of the

village. It's a 15-minute walk through a modern area of houses to reach the entrance gates to Yunshan. To get back, flag down any Anshun-bound bus back on the main road or a bus bound for nearby Qiyanqiao (七眼桥, Qīyǎnqiáo) and then take a bus back to Anshun. From Qiyanqiao you can also transfer to buses for Tianlong.

Tianlong   天龙

POP 5000

You only need around a couple of hours to explore this interesting village not far outside Anshun. Tianlong (Tiānlóng) is a well-preserved Tunpu village (屯堡, túnpǔ), its settlements erected by Ming dynasty garrison troops posted here during the reign of Hongwu to help quell local uprisings and consolidate control. Coming from the middle and lower reaches of the Yangzi River, the soldiers brought their customs and language with them. Han descendants of these 14th-century soldiers live in Tianlong today. The local women are notable for their turquoise tops with embroidered hems; other local idiosyncrasies include distinct colloquialisms: the local expression for a thief is a *yèmāozi* (夜猫子, 'night cat'). Admission to the village is ¥35; it's an additional ¥25 to climb Tiantai Mountain.

Complementing the village's drystone walls and narrow alleyways, the architectural highlight here is the **Tianlong Primary School** (天龙学堂, Tiānlóng Xuétáng), an impressive and distinctive school building. The **Three-Religion Temple** (三教寺, Sānjiào Sì) is a creakingly dilapidated shrine dedicated to Taoism, Confucianism and Buddhism.

A well-signed 30-minute walk will bring you to the forested **Tiantai Mountain** (天台山, Tiāntáishān; ¥25; 1138m), which has the astonishing **Wulong Temple** (伍龙寺, Wǔlóng Sì) **FREE** at its summit. This combined hilltop fortress and temple emerges surreally from the summit like something out of a fairy tale. If it's closed, ask the guard kindly and the doors will likely be opened for you. In a hall at the rear sits a lithe figure of Guanyin, illuminated by a guttering candle; a further hall displays exhibits relating to local *dìxì* theatre. Afterwards, climb to the Dayuetai terrace to gaze out over the glorious countryside. You can also reach the summit on a shuttle bus from the ticket office.

To reach Tianlong, hop on a bus for Pingba (平坝, Píngbà; ¥15, 40 minutes, every 30 minutes, 7.30am to 6.30pm) from Anshun's east bus station. Buses will drop you off on the

WORTH A TRIP

ZHIJIN CAVE

The monstrously long (10km) **Zhijin Cave** (织金洞, Zhījīn Dòng; Mar-Nov ¥100, Dec-Feb ¥110, plus shuttle bus ¥10; ☉9am-5pm Mar-Nov, to 4.30pm Dec-Feb) is the biggest in the country – a visit will satisfy everyone from hardcore spelunkers to wide-eyed tourists with a penchant for subterranean beauty. Pockets open up to 150m high to reveal Zhijin's organic splendour twisting upward like a stone forest.

Tickets to the cave, which is 15km outside Zhijin and 125km north of Anshun, include a compulsory two-hour Chinese-only tour (minimum 10 people). The tour covers some 6km of the cave, up steep, slippery steps at times, and there are English captions at the main points along the way. Solo travellers visiting outside peak summer months or Chinese holidays should be prepared for what can be a tedious wait while enough people roll up to form a group.

Zhijin is doable as a day trip from Anshun. Buses leave Anshun's north bus station (p679) regularly (¥35, one hour, from around 7am). From the bus station in Zhijin, you'll need to get a shuttle bus to the cave (¥10, 40 minutes). Buses run from Zhijin back to Anshun until around 6.30pm, although check last departure times. Alternatively, you can take a train to Zhijin from Anshun station (p679; ¥15.50, 1½ hours, four daily) and then transfer to a shuttle bus (¥10) to the caves. The last train departs from Zhijin at 6.17pm.

From Guiyang, a bus leaves the tourist bus station on Jiefang Lu at 8am (return ¥70, two hours) and returns between 4pm and 5pm – check with the driver for exact return time.

main road – walk down the smaller road with an archway across its entrance to get to Tianlong. To return, flag down any Anshun-bound bus or minibus on the main road.

Longgong Cave 龙宫洞

Even though the feeling is overwhelmingly tacky – coloured lights, awkward commentary and boats full of tourists – there is something sublime about the water-borne cave expedition winding through 20 hills. **Longgong** (Lónggōng Dòng, Dragon Palace; ¥150; ☉8.30am-6pm Mar-Oct, 9am-5.30pm Nov-Feb) is 23km south of Anshun and a fairly easy day trip from there.

Huangguoshu Falls 黄果树大瀑布

Hugely popular among domestic travellers for good reason, the 77.8m-tall, 81m-wide *dàpùbù* (大瀑布, great waterfall) is China's largest waterfall and understandably Guizhou's number-one natural attraction. From June to October in particular, these falls really rock the local landscape with their cacophony, while rainbows from the mist dance about Rhinoceros Pool below. Don't miss groping your way through the dripping natural corridor in the rock face of the 134m-long Water Curtain Cave (水帘洞, Shuǐlián Dòng), behind Huangguoshu itself.

The cascades are actually part of a 450-sq-km cave and karst complex discovered when engineers explored the area in the 1980s to gauge the region's hydroelectric potential. Nowadays, the area is a designated national park that features other natural attractions apart from the falls. Going underground into the colossal caves within the geological Tianxing Qiao Scenic Area (天星桥景区, Tiānxīng Qiáo Jǐngqū) is a quite awe-inspiring sideshow, especially if you do not have time for the Longgong or Zhijin Caves. Doupotang Waterfall (陡坡塘景区, Dǒupōtáng Jǐngqū) is one of Guizhou's widest waterfalls. Visiting can get extremely crowded, especially on weekends and holidays.

Transport around the park is handled by a system of one-way shuttle buses that stop firstly at Tianxing Qiao Scenic Area, then go to the main Huangguoshu Falls and then onto Doupotang Scenic Area. Buses then return back to the main entrance.

You can do Huangguoshu Falls as a long day trip from Guiyang, while it's an easier one from Anshun. There are accommodation options in Huangguoshu village, but there is little need to overnight here. From Anshun, bus timings can vary but generally leave the east bus station (p678) every 30 minutes or so from around 7.20am until 5pm (¥25, one hour); buses back to Anshun run until around 7pm, although do check these timings when you visit. For a quicker and easier trip, arrange a car and driver through your hotel. A coach from Guiyang to the falls leaves at 8am (¥60, two hours) from the tourist bus station on Jiefang Lu and returns to Guiyang at 5pm.

Xingyi　兴义

♪ 0859 / POP 335,250

In the southwestern corner of Guizhou, on the borders with Yunnan and Guanxi, lies the beautiful region of Xingyi (Xīngyì). The city itself is unremarkable – most people come to spend time in the magical karst mountain landscape of the Wanfenglin Scenic Area.

Nearby, the Maling River Canyon is an incredible natural site: a 74km-long gouge in the earth, underpinned by the Maling River and its groundwater. Visitors can walk along a section of the canyon, passing underneath 100m-high waterfalls. Higher above still, the stunning Maling Gorge Arch Bridge seems to cling onto the edges of the canyon itself.

⊙ Sights

Wanfenglin Scenic Area　AREA

(万峰林景区, Wànfēnglín Jǐngqū, Forest of Ten Thousand Peaks; ¥80; 🚍19) The karst hills of the Wanfenglin Scenic Area raise up like the knobbly back of a sleeping dragon, surrounded by charming villages, carefully tended rice paddies and winding rivers lined with banana trees. In February and March, golden rape flowers carpet the floor between the peaks, while in summer purple azalea flowers punctuate the endless green. Highlights include the riverside Upper and Lower Nahui villages, inhabited by people of the Buyi ethnic minority, and the spectacular Wanfo Temple built into a karst hillside.

Even though there is, in theory, an entrance fee (¥80), this wasn't enforced during our visit. There is also a shuttle bus (¥50) that whisks visitors around key areas of interest, including a spectacular viewpoint across the area. The absolute best way to experience Wanfenglin, however, is under your own steam – it's easy to hire an electric scooter (¥50 per day) or bike (¥15 per day) for a couple of days of glorious independent exploration, a rarity in Chinese scenic areas.

Wanfo Temple　BUDDHIST TEMPLE

(万佛寺, Wànfó Sì; ⊙8am-5.30pm) FREE Built in a natural cave on the face of a karst hill at the very southern tip of the Wanfenglin Scenic Area, the Wanfo Temple is spectacular. Originally built during the Ming dynasty, the current temple opened in 2007. The cave that houses the Buddha Sakyamuni and his two disciples is said to be able to hold 10,000 people. There are wonderful views of the karst landscape from the cave.

Maling River Canyon　CANYON

(马岭河峡谷, Mǎlíng Hé Xiágǔ; Near National Road 324, 324国道附近; ¥60; ⊙7.30am-6pm; 🚍) The Maling River Canyon is a geological wonder, a 74km rift in the earth's surface caused by the surging Maling River and its groundwater. Paths down each side of the canyon and two suspension bridges allow you to do a loop of the valley, taking you past just some of the 100 waterfalls that crash down into the river below.

Maling Gorge Arch Bridge　BRIDGE

(马岭河拱桥, Mǎlíng Hé Gǒngqiáo) The first bridge built to cross the Maling River Canyon, this elegant concrete arch bridge is impressive when viewed while walking through the gorge 143m below.

🛏 Sleeping & Eating

While there are hotels in downtown Xingyi, it's much nicer to base yourself in one of the many lovely guesthouses within the Wanfenglin Scenic Area. Upper Nahui Village (上纳灰村, Shàng Nàhuī Cūn) is a good bet as it has a local bus service as well as a beautiful setting by the river.

There are small restaurants and supermarkets in all of the villages dotted around Wanfenglin.

Sound Of Nature Inn　GUESTHOUSE ¥¥

(兴义天籁八音客栈, Xīngyì Tiānlài Bāyīn Kèzhàn; ☑15117332242, 0859 311 6246; Wanfenglin Scenic Area, 万峰林景区; r incl breakfast ¥200; ◉❄🛜) Sound of Nature Inn has friendly owners, beautiful rooms decorated with local artwork and plenty of outdoor space from which to admire the rolling hills of Wanfenglin. Plus points too for the communal water fountains to top up your own water container rather than use plastic bottles.

Màizi Shānzhuāng　CHINESE ¥

(麦子山庄; Upper Nahui Village, 上纳灰村; dishes from ¥18; ⊙9am-9pm) On the western edge of Upper Nahui village and with a lovely outdoor seating area, this restaurant serves up delicious dishes such as green pepper pork (青椒炒肉丝, qīngjiāo chǎo ròusī; ¥30), soy sauce braised fish (红烧鱼, hóngshāo yú; ¥68) and egg-fried rice (鸡蛋饭, jīdàn fàn; ¥35).

❶ Getting There & Away

AIR

Xingyi's **Wanfenglin Airport** (兴义机场, Xīngyì Jīchǎng) has flights to destinations in western China, including Chengdu, Kunming and Guiyang.

WEINING

On the historically significant trade route between north Yunnan and Sichuan, the small town of Weining (威宁, Wēiníng) is now better known as the site of **Caohai Lake** (草海湖, Cǎohǎi Hú; Grass Sea Lake), which sits on its western edge. As a wintering spot for a host of different birds, between November and March the lake attracts birdwatchers from across the globe – the rare black-necked crane is the signature find. Lovely trails explore much of the lake, but the best way to get a close-up view of the birds is to cruise around the lake on a punt. Buy tickets at the **ticket office** (江家湾, Jiāngjiā Wān; boat hire per 1/2/3hr ¥120/240/360; ☺8.30am-5.30pm) at the end of the path leading to the lake, rather than from the touts lurking nearby. Avoid the height of summer when the lake turns to mush, and out of season when access to the lake is restricted (and the town is extremely quiet).

For budget rooms, try the bus station area and nearby Jianshe Donglu, where you should be able to net a room for around ¥100. **Yinghe Hotel** (迎鹤大酒店, Yínghè Dà Jiǔdiàn; ☑0857 633 0078; Bin Hai Dadao, 滨海大道; tw ¥179; ❉☏) has clean and spacious rooms, friendly staff and a decent Chinese buffet breakfast. There are few good choices near the lake itself.

With a large population of Hui, you'll find Muslim *yángròu fěn* (羊肉粉, lamb rice noodles) and *niúròu fěn* (牛肉粉, beef rice noodles) places all over town, especially around the bus station area. A local delicacy is dragonfly larvae, consumed fried.

Getting There & Away

Weining's **train station** (草海站, Cǎohǎi Zhàn; Middle Section of Heye Lu, 荷叶路中段) is 6km west of the town centre, connecting the town to points east in Guizhou, west into nearby Yunnan and north to Sichuan. Note that the station's official name is Caohai (草海, Cǎohǎi).

Leaving Weining from the **bus station** (凤山客运站, Fèngshān Kèyùn Zhàn; Huancheng Lu, 环城路), you can backtrack to Guiyang (¥130, five to six hours, three daily, 9am, 12pm and 3pm), or take a bus south to Xuanwei in Yunnan (¥65, five to six hours, six daily, 7.30am to 2.20pm), where you can transfer to a bus for Kunming. From Weining, there is also a daily direct bus to Kunming (¥130, 10 hours, 10.30pm).

BUS

The bus from Anshun to Xingyi crosses the spectacular Malinghe Bridge Shankun, which, at 241m, is one of the highest bridges in the world. The views from the bridge, down the Maling River Canyon, are breathtaking.

Hourly buses (¥109, four hours, 8am to 5pm) leave from **Xingyi's west bus station** (兴义客运西站, Xìngyì Kèyùn Xī Zhàn; Pingdong Dadao, 坪东大道) to Anshun. Other departures include the following:

Kunming ¥128, four hours, four daily (8.30am, 11am, 2pm and 4.30pm)

Liupanshui ¥120, four hours, three daily (8.30am, 10.30am and 2pm)

Nanning ¥150, eight hours, one daily (9.30am)

TRAIN

Xingyi lies on the Nanning to Kunming rail line. The **train station** (兴义站, Xìngyì Zhàn; 2 Baiyun Lu, 白云路2号) is northeast of the city centre and has departures to the following destinations (prices are for a hard-seat ticket):

Kunming ¥51.50 to ¥53.50, six hours, five daily (1.54am, 3.50am, 4.11am, 5.08am and 2.53pm)

Nanning ¥69, six to eight hours, five daily (2.29am, 1.01pm, 2.20pm, 4.39pm, 10.46pm)

❶ Getting Around

Bus 19 (¥2) runs from the Wanfenglin Scenic Area to the centre of downtown Xingyi – you can connect to Bus 4 (¥2) for the west bus station.

A special tourist line (景区专线公交, jǐngqū zhuānxiàn gōngjiāo; ¥5, one hour, regular departures 7am to 7.30pm) connects General Bridge (将军桥, Jiāngjūn Qiáo), in the centre of Wanfenglin, with Maling River Canyon.

You'll find yourself having to negotiate fares with taxi drivers here. Expect to pay around ¥60 to get to Wanfenglin from the west bus station.

Chishui 赤水

☑0851 / POP 80,800

The northwestern tip of the province is centred on the handsome town of Chishui (Chìshuǐ), which hugs the eponymous red-running river famed for its role in the salt trade. While the town proper is easily walked in an afternoon, just outside town are deep gorges and valleys flanked by towering cliffs hewn out of red sandstone – a World Heritage–listed feature known as *dānxiá* – and a profusion of waterfalls, as well as luxuriant bamboo and fern forests that date to the Jurassic era. Exploring this region will keep nature lovers busy for days.

The town sits on the east bank of the Chishui River (Chìshuǐ Hé). Cross the town's main bridge (Chìshuǐ Dàqiáo) to the other side and you're in Jiuzhi (九支, Jiǔzhī) in Sichuan. The river was the site of many fabled crossings by the Red Army.

◉ Sights

It's hard to imagine a more dramatic landscape. The locals claim the region has 4000 waterfalls, and some are spectacular – everywhere you look they're gushing into the rivers that run red from the colour of the earth (Chishui means 'red water') and which cut through valleys and gorges covered in lush foliage. If that wasn't enough, there are huge forests of bamboo and Alsophila plants – giant ferns that date back 200 million years and were once the food of dinosaurs.

To see the waterfalls at their fullest and loudest, come during the rainy season (July to September).

Chishui Great Waterfall   WATERFALL
(赤水大瀑布, Chìshuǐ Dà Pùbù; ¥80; ⊙8am-4.30pm Mar-Nov, to 4pm Dec-Feb; 🚍Tourist Express Line 4) The under-visited understudy to the famous Huangguoshu Falls in the south is a 76m-high beauty pummelling into the pools below. Even standing 100m away, you will get drenched if the wind is right.

To get to the falls, you'll first need to take a minibus from Chishui (¥12, 1½ hours, from 6.50am to around 4.30pm) to the falls ticket office. From there, you can ride to the falls on a shuttle bus (one way/return ¥10/20) – it's a 10-minute walk from the drop-off point down steep steps to the falls. Alternatively, you can walk along the opposite side of the river along a shaded path. You'll need three to four hours to do the whole thing on foot.

Sidonggou Gully   AREA
(四洞沟谷, Sìdònggōu Gǔ; ¥75, shuttle bus 1 way/return ¥20/30; ⊙8am-5pm Apr-Nov, to 4.30pm Dec-Mar) This 4.5km-long valley is forested with ancient ferns and dotted with gushing cataracts. Paths follow both sides of a river; gushing minifalls lead to four 'proper' waterfalls. The biggest and most impressive is the last, the 60m-high White Dragon Pond Waterfall (白龙潭瀑布, Báilóngtán Pùbù). You can get really close to the falls here. The circuit takes about three hours.

Swallow Rock
National Forest Park   NATIONAL PARK
(燕子岩国家森林公园, Yànziyán Guójiā Sēnlín Gōngyuán; ¥45; ⊙8am-5pm Mar-Nov, to 4.30pm Dec-Feb; 🚍Tourist Express Line 4) Swallow Rock is lesser known than Suolou Nature Reserve, mostly because it doesn't have the bamboo, but it's just as stunning if you're after *dānxiá* (red sandstone) formations and impressive cascades. It's around 9km from Chishui Great Waterfall; the bus to the waterfall from Chishui also passes by the park.

Suoluo Nature Reserve   NATURE RESERVE
(桫椤国家级自然保护区, Suōluó Guójiā Jí Zìrán Bǎohù Qū; ¥50; ⊙8am-5pm Apr-Nov, to 4.30pm Dec-Mar) This reserve was established to protect the Alsophila ferns that grow in abundance here. Today, the prehistoric plants still dwarf visitors. It's also the site of a bamboo forest, known as the **Bamboo Sea** (竹海, Zhúhǎi).

From the bus drop-off point, you'll need to negotiate with locals to take you the remaining 4km to the park entrance. Make sure they wait to take you back. This section of the journey may be difficult out of peak season: considering hiring a car and driver in Chishui.

Hongshi Yegu Scenic Spot   NATIONAL PARK
(红石野谷, Hóngshí Yěgǔ, Red Rock Valley; ¥30; ⊙7.30am-6pm) The highlight of this park is the distinct, ochre sandstone rock face that resembles honeycomb. The formation is part of the extensive *dānxiá* landscapes that make up this area.

🛏 Sleeping & Eating

Chishui has a range of modern, three-star hotels dotted around the centre of the town. Hotels closer to the river are nearer to the after-dark action, when outdoor hotpot restaurants fill up and locals enjoy a waterside stroll or dance.

Popular restaurants are scattered in the area around Hebin Dadao Zhonglu, near the Chishui River, where there are also simple outdoor bars for an evening beer. The main drag of Renmin Xilu has hole-in-the-wall eateries serving noodle and rice dishes, dumplings and the ever-present pigs trotters. There are also street-food stalls, supermarkets and a few hotpot places scattered along Renmin Beilu.

Chishui Hotel   HOTEL ¥
(赤水大酒店, Chìshuǐ Dàjiǔdiàn; ☎0851 2288 1566; 281 Renmin Xilu, 人民西路281号; tw & d ¥168; ❀@🛜) A little tired in the paint and plaster-

GUIZHOU CHISHUI

ing, but nonetheless a welcoming hotel with spacious rooms featuring English-language movies and strong internet connections. The beds are spine-aligningly firm.

Kuanju Lingjiang
Riverview Private Hotel HOTEL ¥¥
(赤水宽居·聆江180°河景别院, Chìshuǐ Kuānjū·Língjiāng 180° Héjǐng Biéyuàn; ☑ 0851 2287 0888; Bldg 7, Hebin Zhong Lu, 河滨中路7号楼; d ¥220; P ✳ 🛜) The floorboards, stylish interior design and quality fittings surpass anything you'll find elsewhere in town.

Zhongyue Hotel HOTEL ¥¥
(中悦大酒店, Zhōngyuè Dàjiǔdiàn; ☑ 0851 2282 3888; 69 Nanzheng Jie, 南正街69号; tw & d ¥268-388; ✳ @ 🛜) When you crave the anonymity of a large hotel, this option will deliver discretion, soft carpets and powerful showers. Buffet breakfast included.

❶ Information

There's a branch of the **Agricultural Bank of China** (中国农业银行, Zhōngguó Nóngyè Yínháng, ABC; 4 Hebin Xilu, 河滨西路4号; ⊙ 9am-5pm) with a 24-hour ATM on Hebin Xilu, near the river. There are many other ATMs around town.

Note that you cannot change money in either Chishui or Jiuzhi, so bring extra cash with you or plan to use ATMs.

❶ Getting There & Away

Chishui's **tourist coach station** (旅游长途汽车客运站, lǚyóu chángtú qìchē kèyùn zhàn; 84 Hebin Dadao Zhonglu, 河滨大道中路84号) is on the riverfront opposite Sichuan, a ¥5 cab ride from Renmin Xilu. Destinations include the following:

Chengdu ¥105, five hours, three daily (7.50am, 9.10am and 3pm)

Chongqing ¥90, 2½ hours, six daily (6.10am to 5pm)

Guiyang ¥150, 6¼ hours, three daily (7.30am, 9.30am and 3pm)

Zunyi ¥120, four hours, seven daily (7.10am to 4.50pm)

❶ Getting Around

Buses for very local destinations leave from the minibus station next door to the tourist coach station. Minibus timetables can be erratic so it's always best to confirm timings on the day you want to travel. Destinations include the following:

Chishui Great Waterfall ¥12, 1½ hours, nine daily (6.50am to 4.30pm)

Hongshi Yegu ¥6, 40 minutes, seven daily (7.20am to 4.10pm)

Jinsha ¥12, 1½ hours, hourly (6am to 5pm)

Sidonggou Gully ¥8, 30 minutes, hourly (7am to 5pm)

Alternatively, tourist express line buses (旅游直通车, lǚyóu zhítōng chē) take visitors to various attractions from the **tourist service centre** (赤水游客中心, Chìshuǐ yóukè zhōngxīn; 🚍 Tourist Express Line 1). Tourist bus 3 (¥25, 8am to 11.30pm) travels to Jinsha (for Suoluo Nature Reserve). Tourist bus 4 (¥15, 8am to 11pm) stops at Swallow Rock and Chishui Great Waterfall. Tourist bus 5 (¥15, 8am to 11.30pm) serves Datong old town and Sidonggou Gully.

As sights are scattered, consider hiring a car and driver to help you scoop them all up. Ask your hotel reception to help you find a driver. Expect to pay ¥500 to ¥700 per day, depending on your bargaining skills. Negotiating with a local taxi driver might be cheaper.

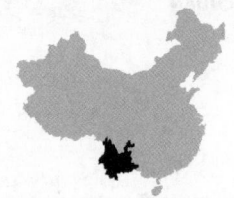

Yunnan

POP 47.705 MILLION

Why Go?

Yunnan (云南, Yúnnán) is the most diverse province in all China, both in its extraordinary mix of peoples and in the splendour of its landscapes. That combination of superlative sights and many different ethnic groups has made Yunnan *the* trendiest destination for China's exploding domestic tourist industry.

More than half of the country's minority groups reside here, providing a glimpse into China's hugely varied mix of humanity. Then there's the eye-catching contrasts of the land itself: dense jungle sliced by the Mekong River in the far south; soul-recharging glimpses of the sunset over rice terraces in the southeastern regions; snowcapped mountains as you edge towards Tibet.

Infrastructure development makes travel here easier than ever, but you'll need time to see it all – whatever time you've set aside for Yunnan, double it.

Best Places to Eat

➜ 1 Restaurant (p722)
➜ Yánquán Nóngjiā (p711)
➜ Shípíng Huìguǎn (p693)
➜ Les Petites Écuries (p719)

Best Places to Stay

➜ Linden Centre (p710)
➜ Interval Time Guesthouse (p733)
➜ Tea Horse Guesthouse (p724)
➜ Old Theatre Inn (p713)

When to Go
Kunming

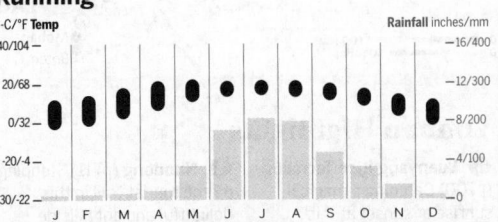

Apr & May Look for wildflower blooms offset by the brilliant white of snow-covered peaks.

Jul & Aug Head for mountains and glaciers around Deqin for prime hiking.

Dec & Jan Escape China's winter in Kunming, the city of eternal spring, or further south in Xishuangbanna.

Yunnan Highlights

1 Yuanyang Rice Terraces (p700) Catching a magical sunrise or sunset at this incredible synthesis of natural beauty and constructed innovation.

2 Yubeng (p733) Hiking to mountain lakes and waterfalls from a quaint Tibetan village in the shadow of Kawa Karpo.

3 Nuodeng (p711) Stepping off the tourist trail in this delightful ancient hillside village.

4 Shaxi (p711) Exploring the ancient Tea Horse Road from the heart of an attractive historic village.

5 Bingzhongluo (p735) Heading towards the edges of

the map in this village in the remote Nujiang Valley.

6 Jianshui (p698) Enjoying classic architecture in a mixture of styles (and great barbecue).

7 Lugu Lake (p725) Lazing around the shores of this stunning lake – or punting about in a dugout canoe.

History

With its remote location, harsh terrain and diverse ethnic make-up, Yunnan was once considered a backward place populated by barbarians.

The early Han emperors held tentative imperial power over the southwest and forged southern Silk Road trade routes to Myanmar (Burma). From the 7th to mid-13th centuries, though, two independent kingdoms, the Nanzhao and Dali, ruled and dominated the trade routes from China to India and Myanmar. It wasn't until the Mongols swept through that the southwest was integrated into the Chinese empire as Yunnan. Even so, it remained an isolated frontier region, more closely aligned with Southeast Asia than China.

Today, Yunnan is still a strategic jumping-off point to China's neighbours. Despite its geographical isolation, much of the province has modernised rapidly in recent years.

Language

Many different dialects are spoken in Yunnan. Most belong either to the Tibeto-Burman family (eg the Naxi language) or the Sino-Tibetan family (eg the Lisu language).

ℹ️ Getting There & Around

AIR

Kunming's airport is the sixth-busiest in China, handling over 47 million passengers per year. There are daily flights to most major cities, as well as to an increasing number of international destinations. Lijiang is well connected to a number of cities in China and internationally, while Dali, Shangri-la and Jinghong have surprisingly good connections within China.

BOAT

One adventurous route out of Yunnan in the past was to travel down the Mekong by cargo boat from Jinghong to northern Thailand. Recent security threats have put off most passengers, but it is still possible to hitch a ride.

ROAD

Expressways link Kunming with Dali, east to Guizhou and Guangxi, southwest past Baoshan to Ruili and past Jinghong to the Laos border. An expressway is also being built from Kunming to Hekou on the Vietnam border and beyond to Hanoi. To remote destinations within Yunnan, bus is still often the only way in or out.

TRAIN

Railways link Yunnan to Guizhou, Guangxi, Sichuan and beyond. In Yunnan itself development of the railways has been slower than elsewhere in China due to difficult topography, but the region is finally catching up to the rest of the country and more rail lines are currently under development. The main route for travellers is the line from Kunming to Dali and Lijiang, which will soon continue on to Shangri-la. Also in the works are rail links with Ruili, Xishuangbanna, and international extensions into Laos and on to Thailand.

CENTRAL YUNNAN

Central Yunnan covers a big swathe of land, including key destinations such as the capital Kunming, old-school travellers favourite Dali, and the surrounding Erhai Lake and mountains of Cang Shan, as well as the legendary rice terraces of Yuanyang, perhaps Yunnan's finest photo opportunity.

But central Yunnan is also where you'll find some of the region's least visited highlights: the former Tea Horse Road caravan oasis of Shaxi, the ancient Bai village of Nuodeng and the historic old towns of Jianshui and Weishan, whose streets are lined with wooden houses, courtyard homes, temples and drum and bell towers.

Kunming 昆明

📋 0871 / POP 6.6 MILLION

Kunming (Kūnmíng) has long been known as one of China's most liveable cities. Known as the 'Spring City' for its equable climate, it remains a very pleasant place to kick back for a few days. For visitors who haven't succumbed to the laid-back attitude of the place, there are plenty of temples and national parks nearby to keep you busy during the day and a fair few craft breweries and cool bars to hold your attention at night.

ℹ️ PRICE RANGES

Sleeping

¥ less than ¥200

¥¥ ¥200–350

¥¥¥ more than ¥350

Eating

¥ less than ¥40

¥¥ ¥40–60

¥¥¥ more than ¥60

Of course, like other Chinese cities, the face of Kunming is constantly changing and most old neighbourhoods have been torn down to make way for shopping malls and towering new residential complexes. Traffic jams, unknown even a few years ago, are now a common occurrence. Yet the essentially easy-going nature of Kunming is, thankfully, still the same.

History

The region of Kunming has been inhabited for 2000 years, but it wasn't until WWII that the city really began to expand, when factories were established and refugees, fleeing from the Japanese, started to pour in from eastern China. As the end point of the famous Burma Road, a 1000km-long haul from Lashio in Myanmar, the city played a key role in the Sino-Japanese War. Renmin Xilu marks the tail end of the road.

After the war, the city returned to being overlooked and isolated. When China opened to the West, however, tourists noticed the province, and Kunming used its gateway status to the rest of Yunnan to become one of the loveliest cities in southwest China.

Now, as Beijing looks to boost China's already significant economic presence in Southeast Asia, new transport routes south from Kunming are being constructed. In particular, work has finally started on the long-touted high-speed railway designed to link Kunming with Vientiane in Laos and Bangkok in Thailand. In the not-too-distant future, maybe as early as 2021, travellers will be able to jump on a train in Kunming and arrive in Vientiane the same day.

⊙ Sights

★ **Golden Temple**   BUDDHIST TEMPLE
(金殿风景名胜区, Jīndiàn Fēngjǐng Míngshèngqū; ☑ 871 6501 4511; Chuanjin Lu, 穿金路; ¥25; ⊙ 7.30am-6pm) The Golden Temple Scenic Area is equal parts religious space, forest park, botanical garden and open-air sculpture museum; it covers 118 hectares on the northwestern outskirts of the city. The obvious highlight is the namesake Qing dynasty shrine, the largest bronze temple in China, which shines magnificently under the bright Yunnan sun.

Numerous buses from the centre stop out front, or take the metro to the North Bus Station and transfer to Bus 57.

Dounan Flower Market   MARKET
(斗南花市, Dòunán Huāshì; Chenggongqu Xianhua Dadao, 呈贡区鲜花大道; ⊙ 8am-6pm; Ⓜ Dounan) China's largest flower market is a riot of colours and smells, and a charming place to wander for an hour and see the diversity of species on offer. Try to get here early, when the morning auctions are happening, for the most action.

From Metro Line 1's Dounan station, walk southwest a little over 1km. Most days you'll be able to follow the crowd.

Yunnan Provincial Museum   MUSEUM
(云南省博物馆, Yúnnán Shěng Bówùguǎn; ☑ 871 6728 6223; www.ynmuseum.org; 6393 Guangfu Lu, 广福路6393号; ⊙ 9am-5pm Tue-Sun) FREE Originally built in 1951, this museum's relocation in 2015 gave it a thoroughly modern 60,000 square metres of exhibition space. Displays span the prehistoric to the present day; expect a broad overview of Yunnan's past through well-curated exhibitions, though English captions are at times frustratingly limited. Enter on the southeast side of the building, and visit the quality on-site cafe for a coffee or tea if you find your feet dragging. Free baggage storage is also available.

From Metro Line 1's Erji Road station, catch Bus 169 and ride for six stops. You can also get here directly from the Yunnan Nationalities Museum, though Bus 165 covers the 20 intervening stations in an agonisingly slow hour of traffic.

Green Lake Park   PARK
(翠湖公园, Cuìhú Gōngyuán; ☑ 871 6531 8808; 67 Cuihu Nanlu, 翠湖南路67号; ⊙ 6am-10pm) FREE Come here to people-watch, practise taichi or just hang with the locals and stroll through winding lines that meander through the 22 hectares of ponds and pavilions. The roads surrounding the park are lined with wannabe trendy cafes, teahouses and shops. In November, everyone in the city awaits the return of the local favourites: red-beaked seagulls. It's a treat watching people, er, 'flock' to the park when the first one shows up.

Yuantong Temple   BUDDHIST TEMPLE
(圆通禅寺, Yuántōng Chán Sì; ☑ 871 6519 3762; 42 Yuantong Jie, 圆通街42号; ¥6; ⊙ 8am-5.20pm) This Zen Buddhist temple is the largest Buddhist complex in Kunming and a popular draw for both pilgrims and locals. It's more than 1200 years old, but has been refurbished many times. To the rear, a hall has been added with a statue of Sakyamuni, a gift from Thailand's king.

THE STONE FOREST

Inscribed on UNESCO's World Heritage list in 2007 as part of the South China Karst, Kunming's **Stone Forest Scenic Area** (石林风景区, Shílín Fēngjǐngqū; ☑ 871 6771 1439; Shilin Yizu Autonomous County, 石林彝族自治县; adult/child ¥130/65; ⊙ sunrise-sunset) is undeniably beautiful – but extremely popular with tour groups and independent travellers alike. It's worth the cost and trip from Kunming, but plan to spend most of the day exploring the outlying pathways of the park. Or else skip the scenic area entirely and wander the surrounding country (which is, after all, the same landscape without the ticket cost).

During the July/August torch festival, activities like wrestling, bullfighting, singing and dancing are held at a natural outdoor amphitheatre by Hidden Lake, south of Shilin.

At the bus station are a handful of fast-food joints if you haven't brought snacks. Check all prices before you order, as overcharging is not uncommon.

Four daily buses leave from Kunming's East Station (¥34, 1½ hours, 9am, 10.30am, 12pm, 5.30pm) for the Stone Forest Scenic Area. Buses and minibuses return roughly hourly from the Scenic Area until 6pm. From the Stone Forest Bus Station to the scenic area entrance, a 3km trip, electric carts charge ¥25 each way.

Confucian Temple CONFUCIAN TEMPLE
(文庙, Wén Miào; 96 Renmin Zhonglu, 人民中路 96号; ⊙ 7.30am-6pm) FREE Originally built in 1276 and completely rebuilt to current form in 1690, after decades of neglect Kunming's Confucian Temple has undergone extensive renovations in the last 50 years. It serves as a sort of community centre for locals practising taichi, taking classes or just playing cards and gossiping. It's one of the best spots in the city for people-watching.

Kunming Museum MUSEUM
(昆明市博物馆, Kūnmíngshì Bówùguǎn; ☑ 871 6315 3359; www.kmmuseum.com; 93 Tuodong Lu, 拓东路93号; ⊙ 9.30am-5pm) FREE While the centrepiece of the museum is the Dharani Pillar, a 6.7m carved stone pillar from the Kingdom of Dali, exhibitions range through a strong focus on WWII history and an interesting collection of porcelain, as well as numerous rotating temporary exhibitions. English captions aren't always widely available, but it's still a diverting series of displays.

Zhenqing Temple TAOIST TEMPLE
(真庆观, Zhēnqìng guān; ☑ 871 6312 5250; 82 Tuodong Lu, 拓东路82号; ⊙ 8am-5.30pm) FREE Dwarfed by the surrounding tower blocks, this quaint Taoist temple is an island of calm in the midst of the city. The compound has expanded significantly since first built, but the original construction dates to the Ming Dynasty in 1419.

Yunnan Nationalities Museum MUSEUM
(云南民族博物馆, Yúnnán Mínzú Bówùguǎn; ☑ 871 6431 1385; 1503 Dianchi Lu, 滇池路1503 号; ⊙ 9am-4.30pm Tue-Sun) FREE On the northeast corner of Diān Chí (p696), the Yunnan Nationalities Museum is reputedly the largest minorities museum in China. The ground-floor exhibition of local cultures, customs and costumes is comprehensive and comes with proper English captions.

To get here catch Bus A1 from the city centre, or from Kunming Railway Station catch Bus 24 or 44.

Don't confuse this with the Yunnan Nationalities Village across the street, a large park with reconstructions of 'traditional' villages of 26 of Yunnan's minority groups, which some visitors will find objectionable on account of elephant performances and the general theme-park atmosphere.

East Pagoda PAGODA
(东寺塔, Dōngsì Tǎ; ☑ 871 6810 6361; 63 Shulin Jie, 书林街63号; ⊙ 9am-5pm) FREE The East Pagoda is a Tang structure that was, according to Chinese sources, destroyed by an earthquake (western ones say it was destroyed by the Muslim revolt in the mid-19th century) and renovated as recently as 1983. The small surrounding park is a hang-out for senior citizens.

🛏 Sleeping

Some of the best hostels and guesthouses in all Yunnan can be found in Kunming, as well as the full range of budget, midrange and luxury hotels. Many are dotted around Green Lake Park and the surrounding area, which is a convenient central location for sightseeing (if poorly connected to transit options), while the cheapest places are in the streets north of the train station.

Kunming

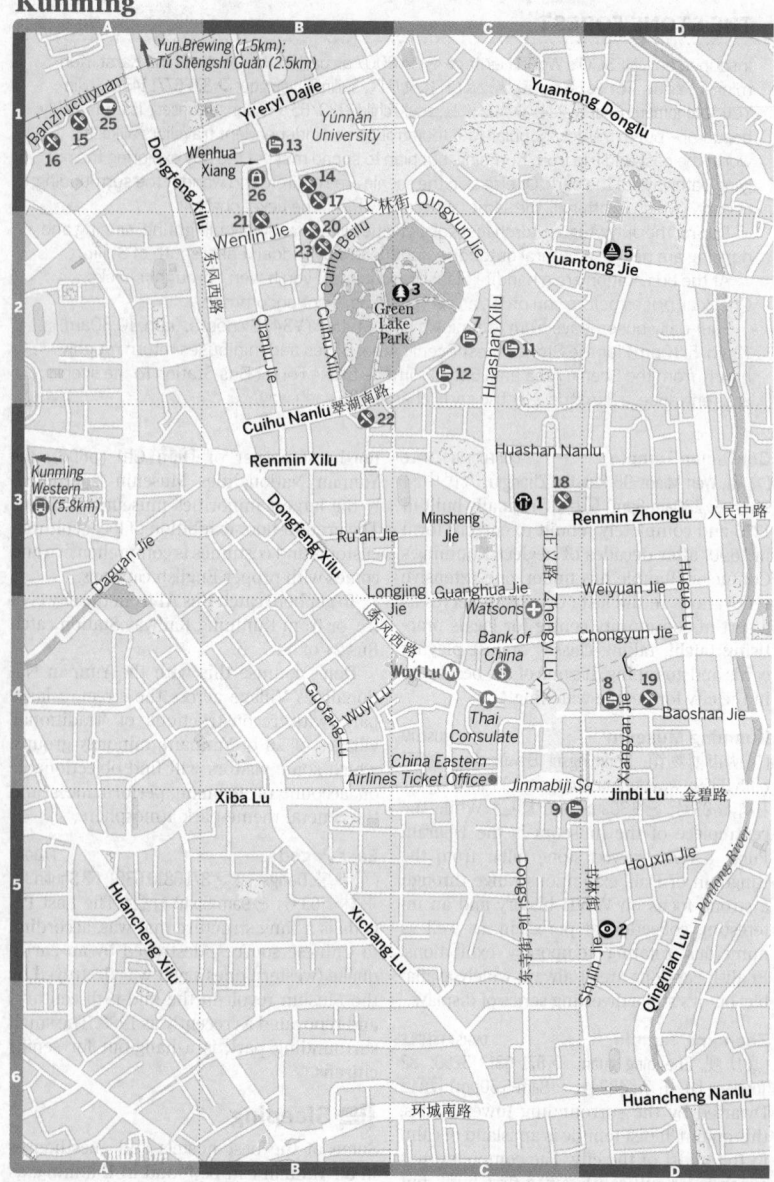

★**Lost Garden Guesthouse** GUESTHOUSE ¥¥
(一丘田七号客栈, Yīqiū Tiánqīhào Kèzhàn; ☑871
6511 1127; www.lostgardenguesthouse.com; 7 Yíqiū
Tian, 一丘田7号; dm/r ¥60/200; ⊛❉@◆)
Tucked in the side streets off Green Lake,
this oasis amid white-brick apartment
blocks has nouveau Dali decor with wood
furniture, antiques and a pleasant lounge.
Rooms are spread across two adjoining
buildings. It's tricky to locate: start by following the alley to the right of Green Lake
Hotel, then take the first left and look for the
sign pointing left.

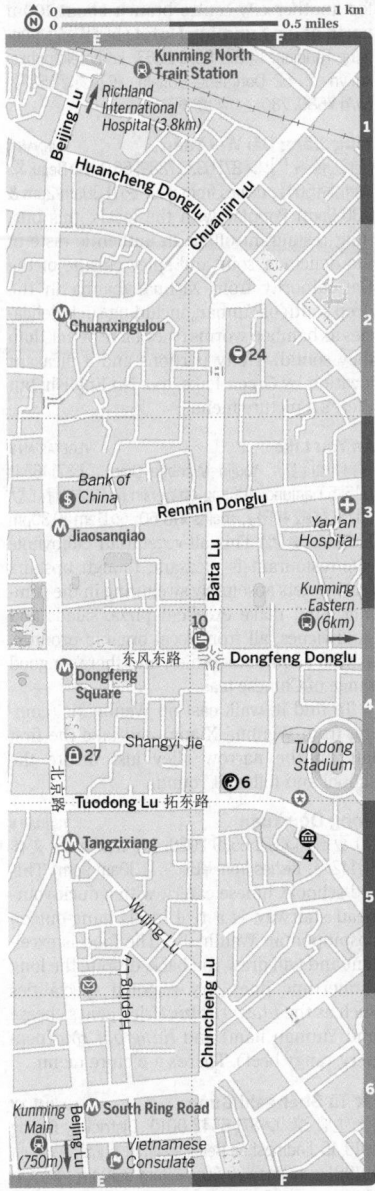

Kunming

Sights

Sleeping

Eating

Drinking & Nightlife

Shopping

★ **Kunming Upland Youth Hostel** HOSTEL ¥¥
(昆明倾城国际青年旅社, Kūnmíng Qīng-
chéng Guójì Qīngnián Lûshè; ☑ 871 6337 8910;
1330971349@qq.com; 92 Huashan Xilu, 华山西路92
号; 8-/16-bed dm ¥55/45, s ¥178, d ¥228-258; @ 🛜)
This large, friendly place aims to impress
with its sharp red-and-black decor, welcoming kitchen and bar plus inside and outdoor
communal areas with all the amenities backpackers are looking for. Dorms come with
big lockers and power outlets. It has English-
speaking staff and a handy location near
Green Lake. Bikes can be rented for ¥30 a day.

It's just off Huashan Xilu, near the back
entrance of the landmark Green Lake Hotel.

Yúndà Bīnguǎn HOTEL ¥¥
(云大宾馆, Yunnan University Hotel; ☑ 871 6503
4179; www.ynuhotel.com; Yieryi Dajie, 一二一
大街; r ¥280-300; ✳🛜) Conveniently close

Ask for a room towards the back as there's
a noisy school across the road.

They also serve a decent coffee and breakfast from 8am, one of the earliest options for
western breakfast in the centre.

to the restaurant and bar hub of Wenhua Xiang and Wenlin Jie, the Yúndà's rooms are not exactly exciting but do the job. The hotel is divided into two, with the cheaper rooms with hard beds in the wing across the road from the main entrance. It's popular and books up completely, so reserve in advance.

Hump Hostel
HOSTEL ¥¥

(驼峰客栈, Tuófēng Kèzhàn; ☑871 6464 7888; info@thehumphostel.com; Jinmabiji Guangchang, Jinbi Lu, 金碧路金马碧鸡广场; dm ¥68-88, d/tw ¥298/328; @ 🛜) Kunming's liveliest hostel, in part because of its rooftop bar and close proximity to many drinking spots and restaurants, this one's mostly for the party crowd. The hostel itself has clean and big dorms (six to twelve beds); the private rooms are large, too, although the beds can be a bit hard.

★ Hotel Arts
BOUTIQUE HOTEL ¥¥¥

(海院艺术酒店; ☑871 6311 1558; 173 Baoshan Jie, 宝善街173号; tw/d ¥558/668; ❄🛜) Built around a tranquil garden space, large rooms here offer sitting areas overlooking the street below. It's one of the most pleasant options in the city, and the neighbourhood is flush with bars and restaurants.

Green Lake Hotel
HOTEL ¥¥¥

(翠湖宾馆, Cuihú Bīnguǎn; ☑871 6515 8888; www.greenlakehotelkunming.cn; 6 Cuihu Nanlu, 翠湖南路6号; r incl breakfast from ¥998; ❄❄@🛜❄) Proud but subdued, this icon of Kunming *hôtellerie* history has a fabulous location opposite Green Park, and has kept up with modernity with a tasteful 2015 renovation and top-notch service. The panorama from the top floors is worth the price alone. Discounts are often available on their website, and there are Chinese, Japanese and western restaurants on-site.

✖ Eating

Kunming is a fine place to sample Yunnan's most famous dish: 'across-the-bridge noodles' (过桥米线, *guòqiáo mǐxiàn*), but you'll find restaurants serving food from every corner of the province. For all manner of foreign restaurants head to Wenhua Xiang and the streets surrounding nearby Yunnan University.

Jiàn Xīn Yuán
YUNNAN ¥

(建新园; 195 Baoshan Jie, 宝善街195号; mains ¥7-40; ⊙24hr; 🛜) Authentic Yunnan cuisine, including well-regarded 'across-the-bridge noodles', that won't break the bank and is available around the clock. There's a lot to like about this simple local chain. Look

for another city-centre branch about 100m north of the **Kunming Hotel** (昆明饭店, Kūnmíng Fàndiàn; ☑871 6316 2063; kmhotel@public.km.yn.cn; 52 Dongfeng Donglu, 东风东路52号; tw/d ¥680/780; ❄❄🛜).

Yíng Jiāng Dǎi Wèi Yuán
YUNNAN ¥

(盈江傣味园; ☑871 6533 7889; 66 Cuihu Beilu, 翠湖北路66号; dishes from ¥20; ⊙11.30am-2pm & 5.30-9pm) Popular with the locals, this bustling restaurant offers an authentic taste of the delicious, sour and spicy cuisine of the Dai minority from Xishuangbanna in the deep south of Yunnan, including such delicacies as bamboo worms (they taste better than they sound). Hefty portions and a pleasant location by Green Lake, too. No English, but there's a picture menu.

As You Like
VEGETARIAN ¥

(有佳面包店, Yǒujiā Miànbāo Diàn; ☑871 6541 1715; 5 Tianjundian Xiang, off Wenlin Jie, 文林街红豆园,天君殿巷5号; mains ¥18-60; ⊙11am-10.30pm Tue-Sun; 🛜🍴) This all-vegetarian cubbyhole cafe/restaurant is pleasant, though upstairs seating gets absolutely sweltering in the summer. Staff make excellent pizza, salads and sandwiches, all from local organic produce, as well as fine smoothies, and there's a good range of Chinese teas.

To find it, walk east on Wenlin Jie (coming from Wenhua Xiang) and take the first left up the narrow alley just before the school and follow it round.

Hóng Dòu Yuán
YUNNAN ¥

(红豆圆; ☑871 6539 2020; 142 Wenlin Jie, 文林街142号; dishes from ¥15; ⊙11.30am-9pm) This old-school Chinese eatery, with a duck-your-head stairway, is a real locals hang-out on cosmopolitan Wenlin Jie. The food is excellent and will draw you back, despite the long dinnertime lines. Try regional specialities such as the *táozá rǔbǐng* (fried goat's cheese and Yunnan ham) and *liáng bái ròu* (peppery, tangy beef). There's a picture menu.

★ Tǔ Shēngshí Guǎn
YUNNAN ¥¥

(土生食馆; ☑871 6542 0010; District B, Jinding 1919, 15 Jindingshan Beilu, 金鼎山北路15号金鼎1919B区; mains ¥26-60; ⊙9am-9.30pm; 🛜) On the ground floor of a converted warehouse a couple of kilometres northwest of the city centre, this family-run place strictly uses locally sourced organic ingredients for its selection of flavourful Yunnan dishes and Chinese favourites. The veggies and homemade tofu are outstanding and the atmosphere relaxed; there's a small outside area.

No English spoken, but there's an English menu.

Prague Cafe
CAFE ¥¥

(布拉格咖啡馆, Bùlāgékāfēi Guǎn; ☑871 6533 2764; 40 Wenlin Jie #5, 文林街40号附5; mains from ¥40; ◎9am-9pm; ☏) Breakfast, sandwiches, salads and more are available at this long-standing favourite for coffee lovers.

Cantina
ITALIAN ¥¥

(意老夫子意大利餐厅, Yìlǎofūzi Yìdàlì Cāntīng; ☑180 8827 1192; 9 Hongshan Donglu, Backstreet Block, Bldg 11-1, 虹山东路9号版筑翠园商铺11幢一层1号（麦当劳隔壁）; mains from ¥42; ◎10.30am-11pm Tue-Sun; ☏) This large, light-filled Italian-run venue is set around an attractive central bar. There's a wide selection of pizza, pasta and panini (from ¥28), steaks and more. Good wine list, aperitifs, and cocktails, plus there are daily lunch specials (from ¥49).

It's inside the Banzhucuiyuan complex northwest of the centre. To find it, walk a little east of the McDonald's.

Humdinger
GASTROPUB ¥¥

(玩啤, Wánpí; ☑871 6360 1611; www.humdingerpub.com; 111 Zhengyi Lu, 正义路111号; mains ¥22-98; ◎5.30pm-2.30am; ☏) Despite the giant vats on show, this place is much more of a restaurant than a bar. Expect a mixed menu of western and Chinese food – burgers and brats alongside spicy beef noodles and BBQ chicken feet – to complement a range of beers brewed in-house. Locals love it, packing it out every evening.

Brooklyn Pizzeria
PIZZA ¥¥

(布鲁克林批萨店, Bùlǔkèlín Pīsàdiàn; ☑871 6539 1208; www.brooklynpizza.com; 6-8, Bldg 12 Banzhucuiyuan, 4 Hongshan Donglu, 虹山东路4号版筑翠园12栋6-8商铺; mains ¥45-73, pizzas from ¥65; ◎11am-10pm; ☏) Pizza, pasta, salads, sandwiches: the list continues. If you're looking for western comfort food, this is the place. It's unsurprisingly popular with the expat crowd. Find it northwest of the centre of town, in a busy pocket of restaurants and bars.

Salvador's
INTERNATIONAL ¥¥

(萨尔瓦多咖啡馆, Sà'ěrwǎduō kāfēiguǎn; ☑871 6531 5811; www.salvadors.cn; 76 Wenhua Xiang, 文化巷76号; mains from ¥30; ◎9am-11.30pm; ☏) Always busy with travellers and students, Salvador's is now a Kunming staple. With a Mexican/Mediterranean food theme, as well as solid breakfasts, good coffee and a decent range of teas, it caters for all hours of the day. In the evening, you can hang around the bar and watch as Kunming's hipsters and youth parade along Wenhua Xiang.

★ Shípíng Huìguǎn
YUNNAN ¥¥¥

(石屏会馆; ☑871 6362 7222; 24 Zhonghe Xiang, 中和巷24号; mains ¥28-138; ◎10am-noon & 1.30-8.30pm) Try authentic Yunnan cuisine in a beautifully restored heritage courtyard building with outdoor seating – this is one of our favourite restaurants in the city. No English menus (or spoken), but digital tablet menus do have photos. There are a handful of inexpensive dishes, including well-executed stinky tofu, but overall expect this to be a splurge.

🍷 Drinking & Nightlife

Foreigners congregate in the bars on and around Wenhua Xiang and Banzhucuiyuan. Head to the Kūndū Night Market area and Jinmabiji Sq for Chinese-style clubs and bars.

★ Uncle John's Craft Beer
CRAFT BEER

(约翰叔叔的啤酒墙, Yuēhàn Shūshu de Píjiǔ Qiáng; ☑138 8850 0050; 2nd fl, Bldg 12 Banzhucuiyuan, 11 Hongshan Donglu, 虹山东路11号版筑翠园电影院2楼; ◎5.30pm-2am; ☏) The new second branch of a long-standing Kunming favourite is far more accessible, and the long wooden bar is fairly inviting as well. You'd have to try quite hard to sample the whole range of Uncle John's brews (some of which are made on-site), but luckily there's a sampler paddle to help things along.

★ M For Maker
COFFEE

(梵米客, Fàn Mǐkè; ☑138 8882 3050; #6, Bldg 14 Banzhucuiyuan, 9 Hongshan Donglu, 虹山东路9号版筑翠园14栋一层6号; ◎10.30am-9pm; ☏) Yunnanese and Ethiopian beans are roasted on-site and served as delightfully balanced brews at this tiny, unprepossessing coffee shop beyond Brooklyn Pizzeria.

O'Reilly's Beer Garden
BEER GARDEN

(爱尔兰酒吧啤酒花园, Ài'ěrlán Jiǔbā Píjiǔ Huāyuán; ☑136 6875 7476; 52 Dongfeng Donglu, 东风东路52号; ◎10am-2am; ☏) This Yunnan-based chain of Irish pubs actually hits pretty close to the mark with a massive beer list (though disappointingly no Chinese options) and spirits and cocktails, as well as a short but appetising selection of western and Chinese dishes. On breezy Kunming nights, the patio area is a delight, particularly if you make it over during happy hour.

It's inside the commercial annexe of the Kunming Hotel, accessible directly from Dongfeng Donglu.

Yun Brewing   CRAFT BEER

(云酿, Yún Niàng; ☑871 6531 1927; 5 Kunjian Lu, 昆建路5; ⊘11am-2am; 🛜) Sixteen homebrews, a fridge full of imports and a fun-loving vibe all recommend this as one of the better craft-beer places in Kunming.

The brewpub sits just behind the **108 Loft Complex** (108智库空间, 108 Zhìkù Kōngjiān), a creative space with sometimes-open art galleries and a handful of other bars and restaurants.

EGO   CRAFT BEER

(☑181 0105 4707; #3, Bldg 11, Qicai Junyuan, Baita Lu, 白塔路七彩俊园11栋3号商铺; ⊘9.30am-2am) Along with a handful of their own drinkable home brews here, there's a long list (and cooler full) of domestic and import craft offerings to complement a menu of pub grub.

Shopping

Yunnan specialities are marbled batik from Dali, jade from Ruili, minority peoples embroidery, musical instruments and spotted-brass utensils.

Yunnanese tea is an excellent buy and comes in several varieties, from bowl-shaped bricks of smoked green tea called *tuóchá*, which have been around since at least Marco Polo's time, to leafy black tea that rivals some of India's best.

Tianfu Famous Teas   TEA

(天福茗茶, Tiānfú Míngchá; ☑871 6718 0701; 41 Shangyi Jie (cnr Beijing Lu), 尚义街41号; ⊘9am-10pm; Ⓜ Dongfeng Square) This place offers most types of teas grown in Yunnan, including the famed *pǔ'ěr* tea, and there are sometimes English-speaking staff available to help foreign shoppers make a selection.

Mandarin Books   BOOKS

(漫林书苑, Mànlín Shūyuàn; ☑871 6551 6579; www.mandarinbooks.cn; 52 Wenhua Xiang, 文化巷52号; ⊘9am-10pm) Good spot for novels and a selection of travel writing in English and other languages, as well as books on Yunnan itself and a small selection of maps of the province.

ⓘ Information

MEDICAL SERVICES

Richland International Hospital (瑞奇德国际医院, Ruìqídé Guójì Yīyuàn; ☑871 6574 1988; 1st fl, Shangdu International Tower, 1208 Beijing Lu, 北京路1208号尚都国际大厦一楼; ⊘8.30am-5pm; Ⓜ Beichen) Most of the doctors are Chinese, but English is spoken here. Standards are generally

good and prices are reasonable. It's on the bottom three floors of the Shangdu International Tower. A taxi ride from the city centre costs around ¥30 or it's a short walk north of the Beichen station on the Metro Line 2.

Watsons (屈臣氏, Qūchénshì; ☑871 6836 9201; 68 Zhengyi Jie, 正义路68号; ⊘10am-10.30pm) Western cosmetics and basic medicines. Other branches around town.

Yan'an Hospital (延安医院, Yán'ān Yīyuàn; ☑871 6321 1073; 245 Renmin Donglu, 人民东路245号) Has a foreigners' clinic, but not a lot of English is spoken.

MONEY

Many ATMs around town accept international cards.

Bank of China (中国银行, Zhōngguó Yínháng; ☑871 6319 2915; 515 Beijing Lu, 北京路515号; ⊘9am-5.30pm; Ⓜ Jiaosanqiao) All necessary services and has an ATM.

Bank of China (中国银行, Zhōngguó Yínháng; ☑871 6361 2090; 16 Dongfeng Xilu, 东风西路16号; ⊘9am-5.30pm Mon-Fri; Ⓜ Wuyi Road) Will change foreign currency and travellers cheques.

PUBLIC SECURITY BUREAU

Public Security Bureau (PSB, 公安局, Gōng'ānjú; ☑871 6335 7157; 118 Tuodong Lu, 拓东路118号; ⊘9-11.30am & 1-5pm Mon-Fri) Stop by for information on visa extensions.

SAFE TRAVEL

As always, take special precautions against pickpockets at and around the train and long-distance bus stations. There have been a number of travellers who've reportedly been drugged and robbed on overnight sleeper buses.

TOURIST INFORMATION

Most of the backpacker hotels and some of the cafes can assist with travel queries and they are usually the best places to get travel advice.

ⓘ Getting There & Away

AIR

Kunming's airport is located 25km northeast of the city.

It has direct services to/from North America, Europe and Australia. International flights to Asian cities include Bangkok (from ¥433), Hong Kong (from ¥804), Vientiane (from ¥704), Yangon (from ¥975) and Kuala Lumpur (from ¥606).

China Eastern Airlines (东方航空售票中心, Dōngfāng Hángkōng Shòupiào Zhōngxīn; ☑871 6515 4119, 95530; 21st fl, China Merchant's Bank Tower, Huguo Jie, 护国街道招银大厦21楼; ⊘8.30am-5pm) issues tickets for any Chinese airline but the office only offers discounts on certain flights.

ⓘ BORDER CROSSINGS: LAOS & VIETNAM

Getting to Laos

A daily bus from Kunming to Vientiane (¥587, 25 hours) leaves from the south bus station at 6pm. Alternatively, take a bus to Mohan (¥260 to ¥301, 10 hours), on the border with Laos; these depart at 12.20pm and 8pm. While the Lao Consulate in Kunming does issue visas, for most nationalities it will be more convenient to get a visa on arrival at the border.

Getting to Vietnam

The only way to get overland to Vietnam from Kunming for now is by bus or train to the border town of Hekou, and then a local bus to the Lao Cai border checkpoint.

Official proceedings at this border crossing can be frustrating – Chinese officials have been known to confiscate Lonely Planet guides because they show Taiwan as a different country to China, while Vietnamese customs officers have been known to ask for bribes. Just keep your cool.

From the Vietnamese side of the border, it's a 15-minute walk to the Lao Cai train station and onward connections into Vietnam.

On the Chinese side, the **border checkpoint** is technically open from 8am to 11pm but don't bank on anything after 6pm. Set your watch when you cross the border – the time in China is one hour later than in Vietnam. Visas are unobtainable at the border crossing.

Daily flights from Kunming go to most major cities across China, including Beijing (from ¥782), Guangzhou (from ¥450) and Shanghai (from ¥800). There are regional services to Lhasa in Tibet (¥1960) and within Yunnan, including Baoshan (from ¥395), Lijiang (from ¥320), Tengchong (from ¥490) and Xiaguan/Dali (from ¥320).

BUS

Kunming's bus stations are located on the outskirts of the city.

Buses departing the **southern bus station** (南部客运站, Nánbù Kèyùnzhàn) include the following:

Jianshui ¥81, 3½ hours, 13 daily (7.30am to 8.30pm)

Jinghong ¥223 to ¥247, eight hours, 19 daily (8.40am to 10pm)

Yuanyang ¥147, seven hours, three daily (10.20am, 12.30pm and 6pm)

Buses departing the **western bus station** (西部客运站, Xībù Kèyùnzhàn) include the following:

Baoshan ¥167 to ¥233, nine hours, 15 daily (8.30am to 10pm)

Chuxiong ¥55 to ¥58, two to three hours, every 15 minutes (7.15am to 7.20pm)

Dali ¥110 to ¥160, four to five hours, every 30 minutes (8am to 7.20pm)

Lijiang ¥184 to ¥238, seven hours, nine daily (9.30am to 8.30pm)

Ruili ¥200 to ¥300, 12 hours, thirteen daily (8.30am to 9pm)

Shangri-la ¥208 to ¥249, 12 hours, six daily (8.30am to 8.30pm)

Tengchong ¥230 to ¥289, 11 hours, 12 daily (9am to 9.10pm)

Buses departing the **eastern bus station** (东部客运站, Dōngbù Kèyùnzhàn) include the following:

Hekou ¥149, eight hours, six daily (8am to 7.30pm)

Shilin ¥34, two hours, four daily (9am, 10.30am, noon and 5.30pm)

Allow plenty of time to get to the bus stations (60 to 90 minutes). Lines 1 and 2 of the metro run between the north and south bus stations via the north and central railway stations. Line 3 connects the west and east stations.

TRAIN

The following information is for travel on high-speed trains:

Beijing 1st/2nd class ¥1878/1148, 11 to 12 hours, two daily

Chengdu 1st/2nd class ¥798/488, 5½ to 6½ hours, seven daily

Guangzhou 1st/2nd class ¥876/535, seven to eight hours, 16 daily

Guiyang 1st/2nd class ¥358/213, two to three hours, 42 daily

Shanghai 1st/2nd class ¥1475/879, 11 to 12 hours, four daily

Xi'an 1st/2nd class ¥1904/623, 11 hours, one daily

Limited services exist within Yunnan, with work underway for further extension of the local network to Shangri-la and Ruili and for international connections to Laos and Vietnam. They include the following:

Dali 1st/2nd class ¥231/145, two hours, 23 daily

Heijing hard seat/sleeper ¥86/23, two to three hours, two daily

Hekou hard/soft seat ¥55/87, six to seven hours, two daily

Jianshui hard/soft seat ¥33/50, three hours, three daily

Lijiang 1st/2nd class ¥351/216, three to four hours, 10 high-speed daily

Trains depart for most destinations from the **main train station** (昆明站, Kūnmíng Zhàn) as well as the **north** (昆明北站, Kūnmíng Běizhàn) and **south** (昆明南站, Kūnmíng Nánzhàn) stations, all of which are connected by the Line 1 and Line 2 metros. The distance between the north and south stations is significant – allow up to two hours to get between the two on the metro, with another 30 minutes or more to get through security and walk to your platform.

❶ Getting Around

TO/FROM THE AIRPORT

Ignore the many unofficial taxi touts who will approach you after you exit customs. Always take an official cab. Metered taxis charge ¥80 to ¥90 into town, depending on traffic and where you are going, including a ¥10 toll en route.

Line 6 of the Kunming Metro connects the airport to the east bus station (¥3, 15 minutes), where it's possible to change to Line 3 and continue on to Dongfeng Square (¥5) in about one hour, including transfer time.

Airport buses (24 hours, regular/express ¥13/25) run to/from the airport every 30 minutes on three different routes, the most convenient being the one that runs to the main train station, the north train station and western bus station.

From the airport's long-distance bus station, regular departures leave for the following destinations:

Baoshan ¥219, nine hours, four daily, 11am to 5.30pm

Dali ¥220, five hours, three daily, 12pm to 4.30pm

Jinghong ¥288, eight hours, 9am & 2.30pm

Shilin ¥45, two hours, 10 daily, 9.20am to 7pm

BUS

Bus fares within the city are ¥1, though trips to outlying suburbs may run as high as ¥4; most require exact change. City buses all run from 6.30am to 8pm, many with slightly longer hours.

Bus 2 runs from the train station to Government Sq (Dongfeng Guangchang) and then near Green Lake past the Confucian Temple to Huangtupu (where you can transfer for a minibus to the Bamboo Temple).

TRAIN

Three metro lines are now operational in Kunming, though they're marked as four (Line 1 turns into Line 2 without passengers needing to switch trains), and two more lines are in the works.

Fares range from ¥2 to ¥7 based on travel distance, and all trains run at least from 6.40am to 10.20pm. For now, the most useful stops include the train and bus stations, as well as Government Sq (Dongfeng Guangchang) in the centre of town.

Around Kunming

There are some grand sights within a 15km radius of Kunming, but getting to most of them is time-consuming and you'll find the majority of them extremely crowded (weekdays are best to avoid the crowds).

If you don't have much time, the Bamboo Temple and Xi Shan are the most interesting. Both have decent transport connections. Dian Lake has terrific circular-tour possibilities of its own, particularly for ardent cyclists.

Bamboo Temple BUDDHIST TEMPLE
(筇竹寺, Qióngzhú Sì; ☑ 871 6818 1881; Heiqiong Lu, 黑筇路; ⊙ 8am-5pm) FREE Tucked away atop a winding mountain road up the forested hills northwest of the city centre, this serene temple is definitely one to be visited by sculptors as much as by those interested in temple collecting. Raised during the Tang dynasty in 639 AD, it was refitted in the Qing Dynasty by master Sichuan sculptor Li Guangxiu and his apprentices, featuring 500 *luóhàn* (罗汉, arhats or noble ones) in a fascinating mishmash of superb realism and head-scratching exaggerated surrealism.

Li and his mates pretty much went gonzo in their excruciating, seven-year attempt to perfectly represent human existence in statuary. Check out the 70-odd surfing Buddhas, riding the waves on a variety of mounts – blue dogs, giant crabs, shrimp and turtles. So lifelike are the sculptures that they were considered in bad taste by Li Guangxiu's contemporaries (some of whom no doubt appeared in caricature), and upon the project's completion he disappeared into thin air.

The temple is about 12km northwest of Kunming. Take a bus to Huangtupo (黄土坡, Huángtǔpō; Bus 2 runs here from the Confucian Temple bus stop), from where minibus C61 (¥8 per person) runs to the Bamboo Temple. If you visit around midday the temple kitchen prepares a simple vegetarian lunch for ¥10 per person, and the all-day teahouse on-site makes a pleasant stop as well.

Diān Chí LAKE
(滇池, Dian Lake) The shoreline of Dian Chi, located to the south of Kunming, is dotted

with settlements, farms and fishing enterprises, and tourist resorts. The lake is elongated – about 40km from north to south – and covers an area of 300 sq km. Plying the waters are *fānchuán* (pirate-sized junks with bamboo-battened canvas sails). The area around the lake is mainly for scenic touring and hiking, and there are some fabulous aerial views from the ridges at Dragon Gate in Xi Shan.

Xi Shan 西山

The craggy forested range of Xi Shan (Xī Shān) on the western side of Dian Chi lake makes for a great day trip from Kunming. The area is full of walking trails (some have very steep sections), quiet temples, gates and lovely forests – including an area known as the 'mini stone forest' for its rocky outcrops. Try to avoid the weekends, when Kunmingers come here in droves.

⊙ Sights

The temples and trails of the lower sections of Xi Shan are free to visit, while entrance to the large Dragon Gate area atop the mountain requires an entry ticket.

Taihua Temple　　　BUDDHIST TEMPLE
(太华寺, Tàihuá Sì; ☉8am-5pm) **FREE** The courtyard of the Ming dynasty Taihua Temple houses a fine collection of flowering trees, including magnolias and camellias, and is a popular to place to relax on the way up or down the mountain.

The road from Huating Temple winds 2km up to the turn-off for Taihua, but if you're travelling on foot look for the pleasant Taihua Ancient Road (太华古道, Tàihuá Gǔdào) that climbs above the bus road, on a 1.3km track of stone staircases and pathways.

Huating Temple　　　BUDDHIST TEMPLE
(华亭寺, Huáting Sì; ☉8am-5pm) **FREE** Towards the bottom of the mountain is Huating Temple, a country temple of the Nanzhao kingdom believed to have been constructed in the 11th century. It's one of the largest in the province and its numerous halls are decorated with arhats.

From the metro station, walk about 3km up the main Xishan road (or catch the tourist bus, which picks up and drops off just outside the temple).

Dragon Gate　　　HISTORIC SITE
(龙门, Lóng Mén; ☏ 871 6842 6668; ¥30; ☉8.30am-5.30pm) On the upper reaches of Xi Shan, the

Around Kunming ⊕

See Kunming Map (p690)

Around Kunming

⊙ Top Sights
1 Golden Temple	B1

⊙ Sights
2 Bamboo Temple	A1
3 Huating Temple	A2
4 Taihua Temple	A2
5 Yunnan Nationalities Museum	B2
6 Yunnan Provincial Museum	B2

'Dragon Gate Scenic Area' is a collection of pavilions, temples and grottoes scattered along the mountaintop. The highlight is the eponymous **Longmen Grottoes**, a series of passages carved deep into the cliffside between 1781 and 1835, punctuated with small shrines and incredible views across to Dian Chi lake.

Lingxu Pavilion　　　VIEWPOINT
(凌虚阁, Língxū Gé) One of the topmost publicly accessible points of Xi Shan, this large pavilion inside the Dragon Gate scenic area offers breathtaking views of Dian Chi lake as a reward for the equally breathtaking climb.

Sānqīng Gé　　　TAOIST TEMPLE
(三清阁; ☉8.30am-5.30pm) Towards the bottom of the Longmen area, this was a country villa of a Yuan dynasty prince that was later turned into a temple dedicated to the three main Taoist deities (*sānqīng* refers to the

highest level of Taoist enlightenment). It now features a delightful series of panels depicting legends surrounding the Longmen Grottoes.

ℹ️ Getting There & Around

Xishan Park is the western terminus of Metro Line 3. Just south of the metro station, tourist buses (¥12) shuttle visitors 6km up the mountain road to the Dragon Gate ticket office and **chairlift** (龙门索道, Lóngmén Suǒdào; one-way ¥25; ⏱9am-5pm), passing by Huating and Taihua Temples en route.

From the ticket office and chairlift, electric carts (¥10) cover the 1.5km section of road up to the bottom of the actual grottoes. It's a pleasant, shaded walk, with no other traffic apart from the carts.

From the top of the Dragon Gate grottoes section, it's possible climb a little further to the chairlift and return to the base, or continue further upwards to the Lingxu Pavilion and incredible panoramic views of Kunming and Dian Chi, then descend on a short side trail to the Dragon Gate South Entrance (龙门景区南门, Lóngmén Jǐngqū Nánmén).

While no public transport serves the south entrance, private vans often wait to shuttle travellers between there and the metro for ¥40 per vehicle, making a one-way through-hike of the mountain utterly practical.

Heijing   黑井

☑️ 0878

Time-warped Heijing (Hēijǐng) has been known for salt production for centuries and is still an important producer of the 'white gold', as well as home to a sizeable Hui Muslim community. Heijing has retained much of its period architecture and is a great place to wander for a day or two, marvelling at the old gates, temples and shady narrow alleys. The village makes a fine stopping-off point if you want to take the route less travelled between Dali and Kunming.

The ¥30 entry fee at the main gate (a couple of kilometres before the village) includes admission to **Dalong Ci** (大龙祠, Dàlóng Cí), the clan meeting hall, and **Guyan Fang** (古盐坊, Gǔyán Fáng), an old salt production facility. The latter offers brief descriptions of the history of salt production, although none in English. You can find it by walking east from the village for about 15 minutes. A few old salt wells around the village can also be inspected: look out for the **Black Cow Well** (黑牛井, Hēiniú Jǐng), just south of Dalong Ci.

A small tourist office near the first bridge can point the way to the various sites.

Wu Family Courtyard   HISTORIC BUILDING
(武家大院, Wǔjiā Dàyuàn; ☎878 489 0358) The best-known courtyard home in town was once owned by local salt magnate Wu Weiyang, who was summarily executed by communist forces in 1949. You can walk around the courtyard, or take tea here.

Wang Family Courtyard   INN ¥
(王家大院, Wángjiā Dàyuàn; ☎878 489 0506; r ¥100; 🛎) A family-run guesthouse, the rooms here are set around a pleasant courtyard. They're not huge and the bathrooms are simple (squat toilets), but it's a peaceful place and the courtyard is perfect for stargazing come nightfall.

ℹ️ Getting There & Away

The best option to reach Heijing is local train 6162 (¥22.50, three hours), departing Kunming at 6.54am and arriving at 10.04am. The train stops a couple of kilometres from the village but horse-drawn buggies and minivans (¥5 to ¥10 per person) meet the train to make the journey here. Going the other way, train 6161 departs at 8.39pm and reaches Kunming at 11.22pm.

The alternative is to take the frequent buses from Kunming (¥55) or Dali (¥75) to county capital **Chuxiong** (楚雄, Chǔxióng). From Chuxiong's main bus station, take a taxi (¥15) to the east bus station (东客运站, dōng kèyùnzhàn), where there are buses to Heijing (¥19, 2½ hours) every hour between 9am and 3.55pm. From Heijing, buses to Chuxiong leave from outside the market at the end of the village from 6.40am to 2.30pm.

Jianshui   建水

☑️ 0873 / POP 531,460

Jianshui (Jiànshuǐ) is a charming town of old buildings surrounded by a much larger modern city. The architecture is constantly being 'facelifted', but still retains much of its distinct character. The locals, who are a mix of Han, Hui and Yi, are friendly.

⊙ Sights

Classic architecture surrounds you here, and not just in the old-style back alleys. Virtually every main street has a historically significant traditional structure. The architecture is especially intriguing because of the obvious mixture of central plains and local styles. Many old buildings, despite official decrees positing them as state treasures, have been co-opted for other purposes, so the trick – and the fun – is trying to spot them.

Twin Dragon Bridge
BRIDGE

(双龙桥, Shuānglóng Qiáo; ☑ 873 766 4447) This beautiful 30m bridge across the confluence of the Lu and Tachong Rivers features 17 arches, so many that it took two periods of the Qing dynasty to complete the project in 1839. It's 3km from the western side of town. Minivans (¥3, 7am to 6pm) run here from Jianshui's Hong Yun bus station, and will let travellers out at an intersection 300m from the bridge.

Swallow's Cavern
CAVE

(燕子洞, Yànzi Dòng; Highway 323, 323国道; ¥55; ⊘9am-5pm) Set inside a small nature reserve, this large cave complex is split into two – one high and dry, the other low and wet. The natural quiet of the popular wet cave is diluted a bit by bright neon lighting and a small shopping complex, as well as the drone of free motorboats that ferry tourists back to the cave mouth, but the hundreds of thousands of swallows flying around in spring and summer are a delightful touch of wildlife.

Zhu Family Garden
HISTORIC SITE

(朱家花园, Zhūjiā Huāyuán; ☑ 873 766 7115; 16 Hanlin Jie, 翰林街16号; ¥35; ⊘8am-8pm) This spacious 20,000-sq-metre complex, which includes 42 separate courtyards, is a fascinating example of Qing-era architecture. Comprising ancestral buildings, family homes, ponds and lovely gardens, it took 30 years to build. The Zhu family made its fortune through its mill and tavern, and went on to dabble in everything from tin in Gejiu to opium in Hong Kong, eventually falling victim to the political chaos following the 1911 revolution.

Confucian Temple
CONFUCIAN TEMPLE

(文庙, Wénmiào; ☑ 873 765 3333; Lin'an Lu, 临安路; ¥40; ⊘8am-6.30pm) Jianshui's most famous temple was modelled after the temple in Confucius' hometown of Qufu (Shandong province) and finished in 1285; it covers 7.5 hectares and is the third-largest Confucian temple in China. The temple operated as a school for nearly 750 years – its academic credentials were such that more than half of all Yunnan's successful candidates in imperial examinations during this period came from Jianshui.

🛏 Sleeping

Typha Youth Hostel
HOSTEL ¥

(草芽青年旅舍, Cǎoyá Qīngnián Lǚshě; ☑ 873 765 2451; yhajianshui@yahoo.com; 89 Ruyi Xiang,

如意巷89号; dm/s/d ¥30/70/90; ✳@🛜) This is a legit hostel with a cosy communal area, bike hire (¥30 per day) and sound travel advice; it's also a good place to book a tour of the surrounding area. Dorms are clean and come with lockers; the private rooms are compact but OK.

To find it, walk 30m west of the Confucian Temple and turn down an alley on the left-hand side of the road.

Lin'an Inn
INN ¥¥

(临安客栈, Lín'ān Kèzhàn; ☑ 873 765 5866; lin-aninn@hotmail.com; 32 Hanlin Jie, 翰林街32号; r ¥238-328; ✳🛜) In a prime location in the heart of the old town and with well-kept rooms. The biggest draw here is the great communal courtyard, which is very pleasant for a beer in the evening, but the rooms are comfortable too. It rents bikes for ¥30 per day.

Huáqīng Jiǔdiàn
HOTEL ¥¥

(华清酒店; ☑ 873 766 6166; 146 Hanlin Jie, 翰林街146号; r ¥188-328; ✳🛜) Decorated in a neo-Qing dynasty style, the rooms here are a nice size and some come with small terraces. The staff are friendly and offer a great English map of the old town.

🍴 Eating

Jianshui is legendary for its *qìguō* (汽锅), a stew often infused with medicinal herbs and served in earthenware pots. Expect to pay ¥40 to ¥50 per pot. Jianshui is also well-known for barbecue (烧烤, *shāokǎo*) and you'll find many cubbyhole restaurants grilling away, particularly along Hanlin Jie.

Āmáo Qīngzhēn Shāokǎo
BARBECUE ¥

(阿毛清真烧烤; ☑ 134 0892 7657; 6 Shuyuan Jie, 书院街6号; barbecue skewers from ¥2; ⊘5pm-1am) This is the place to eat delicious barbecue on tiny stools. Everything – fish, meat, veggies, tofu – is on display, so just pick and choose. It's tucked down an alley off Hanlin Jie south of the Zhu Family Garden. If you can't find it, ask around: everyone knows it.

Fújí Cài
CHINESE ¥¥

(福籍菜; ☑ 873 765 5889; 363 Lin'An Lu, 临安路363号; mains ¥28-88; ⊘9.30am-8.30pm) Local delicacies, including the herbal stew *qìguō* (汽锅; ¥38) and a wide range of Chinese dishes served in a renovated courtyard home make this one of the nicer full-service restaurants in Jianshui. Find it around 350m west of the Confucian Temple.

ℹ Getting There & Away

BUS

The main Jianshui bus station is 2km north of Chaoyang Gate. Buses to Swallow's Cavern depart hourly from 7am (¥11, one hour), with the last returning from the caves at 7pm. Other destinations include the following:

Hekou ¥65 to ¥77, five hours, four daily (7.26am to 10.57am)

Jinghong ¥225, eight to ten hours, two daily (1pm & 4pm)

Kunming ¥81, three to four hours, 24 daily (7am to 7.35pm)

Nansha ¥31, two to three hours, 12 daily (7.15am to 6.40pm)

Xinjie ¥43, three hours (11.34am)

For local destinations, including the Twin Dragon Bridge, head to Hongyun Bus Station (红运客运站, Hóngyùn Kèyùnzhàn), just north of the old town's north gate at the corner of Chaoyang Beilu and Beizheng Jie.

TRAIN

Six daily departures connect Jianshui's train station to Kunming (1st/2nd class ¥95/59, two to three hours, 8.50am to 8.01pm); in the opposite direction three daily trains link the city to Hekou (hard/soft seat ¥30/47, two to three hours, 2.24pm to 6.26pm).

ℹ Getting Around

Bus 919 (¥2) links the train station with the bus station and old town, while buses 13 and 15 link the bus station and old town. A taxi from the main bus station to the old town is ¥7.

Yuanyang Rice Terraces 元阳

📱 0873

Yuanyang (Yuányáng) is a wonderful region of hilltop villages and intricate rice terraces cascading down surrounding hillsides. It's a palette of colours at sunrise and sunset, and a place for spirit-recharging treks through centuries-old rice-covered hills with a few water buffalo eyeing you contentedly nearby.

Yes, it's hard not to become indulgent when describing these *tītián* (梯田, rice terraces), hewn from the rolling topography by the Hani people throughout the centuries. They cover roughly 125 sq km and are one of Yunnan's most stunning sights.

◉ Sights

The terraces around dozens of outlying villages have their own special characteristics, often changing with the daylight. Bilingual maps are available at many hotels in town. Bear in mind that the terraces are at their most extraordinary in winter when they are flooded with water, which the light bounces off in spectacular fashion. Avoid visiting at Chinese public holidays, when prices for minibuses go sky-high (¥600 and more per day).

A combined ¥70 ticket gets you access to the Duoyishu, Bada, and Laohuzui terraces.

★ Bada Rice Terrace   VIEWPOINT
(坝达梯田, Bàdá Tītián; combined ticket ¥70; ⏰ 6am-8pm) Bada is one of the finest rice terraces at Yuanyang to catch the sunset at. If you only have time for one terrace, this is it.

Duoyishu Rice Terrace   VIEWPOINT
(多依树梯田, Duōyīshù Tītián; combined ticket ¥70; ⏰ 6am-8pm) Located about 25km from Xinjie, this rice terrace has the most awesome sunrises. As it's walking distance from Pugaolao it's an easy choice for the morning.

Quanfuzhuang Rice Terrace   VIEWPOINT
(全福庄梯田; Quánfúzhuāng Tītián) **FREE** Quanfuzhuang is a less-crowded – and free – alternative to Duoyishu, and has easy access via trails that reach the terraces from near a roadside viewing platform.

Laohuzui Rice Terrace   VIEWPOINT
(老虎嘴梯田, Lǎohǔzuǐ Tītián; combined ticket ¥70; ⏰ 6am-8pm) Among the rice terraces at Yuanyang this was once one of the most mesmerising places to watch the sunset, but a recent landslide has sadly destroyed some of the surrounding terraces. It's also known as Mengpin (勐品梯田, Měngpǐn Tītián), after the name of the closest village.

🛏 Sleeping

Xinjie and Pugaolao have the greatest concentration of hotels and guesthouses. Of the two, Pugaolao is by far the nicer place to stay.

ℹ Getting There & Away

Xinjie is the main transport hub for the Yuanyang terraces, with daily buses from the bus station to and from Kunming, Jianshui and Hekou, as well as minivans to the surrounding villages. There are also many buses to the same destinations from Nansha, an hour away from Xinjie by minivan, where some buses to Yuanyang will deposit unsuspecting travellers.

While buses run to all the villages from the bus station, you are much better off arranging your own transport, or hooking up with other travellers to split the cost of a sunrise or sunset drive. Minivans and motor-rickshaws congregate just below the hotel Yúntī Shùnjié Dàjiǔdiàn and on the street west of the bus station. Expect to pay ¥200 to ¥400 in peak season for a minivan for driving and a two-hour wait, depending on distance. Less comfortable motor-rickshaws can be had for ¥150 and up.

Xinjie 新街

📶 0873 / POP 74,575

Xinjie (Xīnjiē) makes a useful base for exploring the Yuanyang Rice Terraces, even if it is a bit grubby. The bus station is a minute's walk uphill from Titian Sq, the town's hub and a nice viewpoint for the surrounding hills.

Basic restaurants surround Titian Sq and the commercial pedestrian street down the stairs from here.

Yúntī Shùnjié Dàjiǔdiàn HOTEL ¥

(云梯顺捷大酒店; 📞 873 562 1588; Titian Square, 梯田广场; d ¥136; 🛜) Just off Titian Sq and a few minutes from the bus station, this place is the best of the centrally located hotels. Rooms are clean and compact, but wi-fi is available only in the lobby. Prices go up during festival periods.

Yǐngyǒuliàn Jiǔdiàn HOTEL ¥

(影友恋酒店; 📞 873 562 4591, 159 8737 4367; caihuimei2006@163.com; r ¥60-80; 🛜) It's basic (the price is a clue) and even a bit grimy, but some rooms have western toilets and the wi-fi connection is strong. Owner Belinda speaks English well and will help arrange transport to the outlying villages – she's the real reason to stay. To get here, walk uphill from the bus station for 500m and it's on your left.

ⓘ Getting There & Away

There are two buses daily from Xinjie to Kunming (¥173, seven hours, 9.30am & 12.30pm), two to Hekou (¥60, six hours, 7.30am and 10.10am) and one to Jianshui (¥44, three hours, 4.30pm).

Minivans leave when full from just outside the station to Duoyishu's Pugaolao village (¥15) and down the hill to Nansha (¥15) from around 7.30am to 6pm. From Nansha, many more buses run to points around Yunnan and beyond, but for Xishuangbanna you'll have to transfer in Jianshui.

Pugaolao 普高老

📶 0873 / POP 980

In-the-know travellers base themselves in picturesque Pugaolao (Pǔgāolǎo) in Duoyishu (多依树, Duōyīshù), a Hani village

Yuanyang Rice Terraces

Map Distances	
Xinjie to Nansha	30km
Xinjie to Longshuba	4km
Xinjie to Qingkou	6km
Xinjie to Quanfuzhuang	10km
Xinjie to Mengpin/Laohuzui	18km
Xinjie to Bada	16km
Xinjie to Duoyishu	25km

an hour by minivan from Xinjie. The rice terraces are all around you here and when not gazing out on them, you can experience something of traditional village life as you dodge the water buffalo, chickens and pigs that wander the stone paths of the village and the mud walls of the surrounding terraces. It's a perfect place for catching the sunrise from the roof of your guesthouse.

🛏 Sleeping & Eating

There are two restaurants on the main road above the village, but none in Pugaolao itself. All guesthouses offer meals, although they are often pricier than they would be elsewhere.

Sunny Guesthouse GUESTHOUSE ¥

(多依树阳光客栈, Duōyīshù Yángguāng Kèzhàn; 📞 159 8737 1311; sunny_guesthouse@163.com; dm ¥40, d ¥120-200; 🌬 🛜) This guesthouse now offers quite a range of comfortable rooms, from those that have huge windows overlooking the rice terraces to ones with tiny windows facing the next building. There's a roof terrace, a couple of communal areas and one large dorm that may or may not be in service when you visit. Friendly owner Lucian speaks excellent English.

Belinda's Backpackers Guesthouse GUESTHOUSE ¥

(影友漫步客栈, Yǐngyǒumànbù Kèzhàn; 📞 159 8737 4367; caihuimei2006@163.com; dm/r ¥35/120; 🛜) Like her operation in Xinjie, Belinda's guesthouse in Pugaolao is a little rough-and-ready, but the private rooms have western toilets and Belinda's tours of the area – especially some little-visited villages – get good

VILLAGE MARKETS

Villages across Yuanyang play host to weekly morning markets, but the schedule changes based on the traditional Chinese zodiac, with different villages connected to different signs of the calendar. Ask at your guesthouse where to head on a given day.

feedback. It's at the top of the village, just down from the highway.

Timeless Hostel Yuanyang HOSTEL ¥ (久居元阳客栈, Jiǔ Jū Yuányáng Kèzhàn; ☑153 6837 6718; yuangyang.timeless@gmail.com; dm/d ¥45/120; ❂☎) In the heart of the village, with fresh dorms and rooms, a roof terrace with decent views, an amiable communal area and English-speaking staff. Bikes can be hired for ¥30 per day and staff can offer advice on potential hiking routes, as well as organise transport to other villages.

❶ Getting There & Away

Minivans (¥15 per person, one hour) leave from outside Xinjie's bus station from 6.30am to 6pm. They return to Xinjie on the the same schedule and can be hailed on the main road.

Erhai Lake 洱海湖

☑0872

The seventh-largest freshwater lake in China, Erhai Lake (Ěrhǎi Hú; 'Ear-Shaped' Lake) covers 250 sq km. Beyond the well-known Dali Old Town it's dotted with villages to visit and surrounded by a ring road great for bike rides, all with the verdant Cangshan Mountains towering in the background.

Caicun (才村, Cáicūn), a pleasant little village east of Dali (¥1.50 on bus 2), is a nexus of water transport. All boat travel is on 'official' vessels. Expect to pay ¥180 for a three-hour trip across the lake to the **Luoquan Peninsula** (罗荃半岛, Luōquán Bàndǎo). Catch bus 2 from Dali to get here; boats run roughly from 8.30am to 4.30pm.

On the east side of the lake, the beautiful waterside town of **Shuanglang** (双廊, Shuāngláng) is extremely popular with domestic tourists. The old town (¥10) is a labyrinth of winding old alleys and traditional homes sitting on a little peninsula that juts into the lake. A 2km pedestrian street leads to the ferry port and ticket office for **Nanzhao Customs Island** (南诏风情岛, Nánzhào Fēngqíng Dǎo; Shuanglang, 双廊). This pleasant island has gardens, parks, a 17.5m-tall marble statue of Avalokiteshvara (Chenresig; aka Guanyin) and a hotel. Boats to the island cost ¥50 per round-trip, which includes admission.

The other east-side highlight, close to Wase, is **Putuo Island** (普陀岛, Pǔtuó Dǎo) and the 15th Century **Lesser Putuo Temple** (小普陀寺, Xiǎopǔtuó Sì; Putuo Island, 普陀岛), set on an extremely photogenic rocky outcrop. A taxi from Shuanglang is ¥50 each way, or else hire a bicycle and stop off along the way.

Roads encircle the lake, so it's possible to do a loop (or partial loop) of the lake by **mountain bike**. A bike path goes from Caicun to Tao Yuan Port, which makes a great day trip (though most travellers turn around at Xizhou). Some hardcore cyclists continue right around the lake; the full loop is around 98km. The lack of boats means you're looking at an overnight stay or an extremely long ride in one day.

❶ Getting There & Away

Xiaguan is the transport hub of the region, home to the train station and airport as well as a number of bus stations serving points near and far. Smaller towns, particularly Dali, also have limited services to locations in Yunnan.

Xiaguan 下关

☑0872 / POP 235,300

Xiaguan (Xiàguān), on the southern shore of Erhai Lake, is a transport hub for travellers headed to Dali Old Town a few kilometres further up the highway. Confusingly, Xiaguan is also often referred to as Dali (大理, Dàlǐ) on tickets, maps and buses.

There's little reason to stay in Xiaguan – you only need to come here to catch a bus or train (or to extend a visa). If you're waiting for a bus and need to eat, the roads close to the bus and train stations are jammed with restaurants offering similar menus.

❶ Getting There & Away

AIR

Xiaguan airport (DLU) is 15km from the town centre. Buy air tickets online or at an agency in Dali Old Town. A handful of flights leave daily for Kunming (from ¥420); four fly to Guangzhou (from ¥952); six to Chengdu (from ¥742); three to Beijing (from ¥1272); and two to Xishuangbanna (from ¥560). In the high season service extends to other major Chinese airports – check online.

Airport buses (¥15, 30 minutes) run to the train station from 6.30am to 4pm. Taxis cost ¥40 from Xiaguan or ¥100 from Dali.

BUS

Remember that when departing, the easiest way to Kunming or Lijiang is to get a bus from Dali Old Town. Bus tickets for nearly all destinations can be booked in Dali – this is often the easiest way as it will save you a trip to Xiaguan (although you will pay a service fee of ¥10 to ¥15). Xiaguan has four bus stations.

The following departures are from the Express Bus Station (快速汽车客运站, Kuàisù Qìchē kèyùnzhàn):

Chuxiong ¥75, 2½ hours, four daily (10am, 1pm, 3.40pm and 5.30pm)

Fugong ¥137, eight hours, one daily (10am)

Kunming ¥110, four to five hours, every 10 minutes (8.30am to 10.30pm)

Liuku ¥71, four hours, hourly (7.20am to 8pm)

Ruili ¥171, eight hours, three daily (8.30am, 1.40pm and 3pm)

Yunlong (for Nuodeng) ¥43, three hours, 14 daily (7.30am to 4.30pm)

The following departures are from the Xingsheng Bus Station (兴盛客运站, Xīngshèng Kèyùnzhàn), which is also referred to as South Bus Station (客运南站, Kèyùn Nánzhàn):

Baoshan ¥77 to ¥82, 2½ hours, 11 buses daily (8am to 8.30pm)

Kunming ¥145, five hours, 15 buses daily (7.20am to 7.30pm)

Tengchong ¥140, five hours, five daily (8.50am, 10.30am, 12.30pm, 2pm and 4.40pm)

Weishan ¥17, 1½ hours, every 20 to 30 minutes (7am to 6.45pm)

Departures from the North Bus Station (汽车客运北站, Qìchē Kèyùn Běizhàn) include the following:

Deqin ¥197, 12 hours, one daily (6.30pm)

Jianchuan (for Shaxi) ¥41, 2½ hours, every 20 to 30 minutes (6.25am to 6.50pm)

Lijiang ¥56 to ¥80, three hours, 16 daily (8am to 6.10pm)

Shangri-la ¥106, seven hours, 15 daily (7am to 6.30pm)

Shuanglang ¥13, 1½ hours, every 30 minutes (8am to 3.04pm)

If you want to head to **Jinghong** (¥220, 12 hours, 8.20am, 9.40am and 11am), you need the Dali Bus Terminal (大理汽车客运站, Dàlǐ Qìchē kèyùnzhàn) just northeast of the train station.

Bus 8 to Dali Old Town (¥3, 35 minutes) leaves from a handful of locations. Bus 8 runs from the train station to the north bus station and on to a car park at the north of the Dali Old Town. There is also an unnumbered 'special line' (专线, zhuānxiàn) bus that leaves from the train station

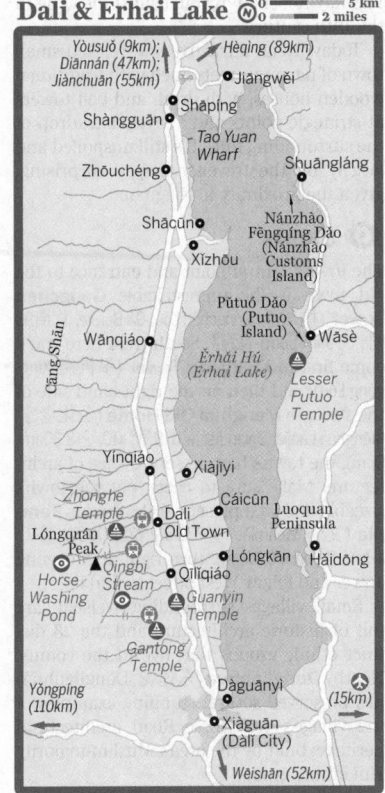

Dali & Erhai Lake

and passes Dali's west gate en route to the Three Pagodas. If you want to be sure of where to disembark, ask for *Dali gǔchéng* (Dali Old Town).

Within Xiaguan, Bus 21 (¥2) connects the train station, express bus station and south bus station.

TRAIN

Xiaguan's train station is called 'Dali', and all trains stop here; there is no station in the Old Town.

There are 24 trains daily to Kunming's main train station (1st/2nd class ¥231/145, two hours, 7.40am to 9.14pm); three daily to Guangzhou (1st/2nd class ¥943/590, twelve hours, 10.05am to 11.53am); and five trains daily to Lijiang (hard/soft seat ¥34/49, two to three hours, 10.18am to 6.06pm).

Weishan 巍山

☎ 0872 / POP 46,470

Weishan (Wēishān) is the heart of a region populated by Hui and Yi, once the centre of the powerful Nanzhao kingdom; from here the Hui rebel Du Wenxiu led an army in the

Panthay Rebellion revolt against the Qing in the 19th century.

Today it's an attractive and relaxed small town of narrow streets lined with traditional wooden houses, with drum and bell towers at strategic points and a lovely backdrop of the surrounding hills. It's still unspoiled and largely off the traveller map – surprising, given the proximity to Xiaguan.

◎ Sights

The town's central point and entrance to the old town is the unmistakable **Gongchen Tower** (拱辰楼, Gǒngchén Lóu; 93 Bei Jie, 北街93 号; ⊙9am-5pm) FREE. South from here you'll come first to **Xinggong Tower** (星拱楼, Xīnggǒng Lóu), and then on the right-hand side of the street to **Menghua Old Home** (蒙化老家, Měnghuà Lǎojiā; 8 Nan Jie, 南街8号; ¥10; ⊙8.30am-9pm), the town's best-preserved slice of architecture. Make sure to check out the town's sizeable and well-preserved **Confucius Temple** (文庙, Wénmiào; ☑872 612 7287; Xi Jie, 西街; ¥3; ⊙8.30am-5.30pm): turn right at Xinggong Tower and follow West Street to find it.

Small villages surrounding Weishan are full of historic architecture and the 23 distinct ethnic groups that live in the county. Nearby **Donglianhua** (东莲花, Dōngliánhuā) has preserved several stunning examples of the village's Tea Horse Road architectural heritage, built by the area's Muslim-majority Hui ethnic group.

Nanzhao Museum   MUSEUM

(南诏博物馆, Nánzhào Bówùguǎn; ☑872 612 2523; 1 Baguo Jie, 报国街1号; ⊙9am-4pm) FREE Architecture and artefacts describe the rise and importance of the Nanzhao kingdom, as well as offer brief introductions to the many ethnic groups that inhabit the region, using surprisingly good multilingual signage. Look for a sign just south of the Gongchen Tower that points the way.

Wēibǎo Shān   MOUNTAIN

(巍宝山; ☑872 218 1798; ¥60) Weibao Mountain, about 10km south of Weishan, has a relatively easy hike to its peak at around 2500m. During the Ming and Qing dynasties it was the zenith of China's Taoism, and you'll find some superb Taoist murals; the most significant are at **Wenchang Palace** (文昌宫, Wénchāng Gōng) and **Changchun Cave** (长春洞, Chángchún Dòng). Birders in particular love the mountain; the entire county is a node on an international birding flyway.

There are no buses here. Head to the street running east of Gongchang Tower in Weishan to pick up a taxi to the mountain, or ask your hotel to arrange one. Expect to pay ¥100 to ¥150 for the round trip; you'll need the driver to wait for you.

🛏 Sleeping & Eating

Línyè Bīnguǎn   HOTEL ¥

(林业宾馆; ☑872 612 0761; 24 Xixin Jie, 西新 街24号; d ¥150-200; ❈ 🛜) A few minutes' walk west of the Gongchang Tower, with big rooms and a strong wi-fi connection. Staff are friendly, if not exactly helpful.

Báilùyuán   GUESTHOUSE ¥¥

(白露原; ☑152 1950 0258; 19 Bei Jie, 北街19 号; r ¥300; 🛜) Out front this is a lovely teahouse which opens in the afternoon and also serves coffee and juices, but out back you can stay in what's effectively your own little courtyard home, with a small garden and a very comfortable and tastefully decorated loft bedroom. It's not always open if there are no guests, so call ahead.

Lǎowáng Guòjiāng Ěrsī   YUNNAN ¥

(老王过江饵丝; 160 Bei Jie, 北街160号; mains ¥11-22; ⊙7am-3pm) Your options here are small, medium, or large: there's only one dish on the menu at Weishan's most highly recommended restaurant for ěrsī (饵丝) rice noodles. Dip the cut noodles in the broth and slurp it all up together at this busy shop 100m north of the Xinggong Tower.

❶ Getting There & Away

Xiaguan's Xingsheng bus station has buses to Weishan (¥17, 1½ hours, every 20 to 30 minutes, 7am to 6.45pm). The last return to Xiaguan is 5.30pm.

No public transport runs to Weibao Mountain, but a private taxi return with around three hours of waiting time should cost ¥100 to ¥150.

Dali Old Town   大理古城

☑0872 / POP 82,570

Dali Old Town (Dàlǐ Gǔchéng), the original backpacker hang-out in Yunnan, was once *the* place to chill, with its stunning location sandwiched between mountains and Erhai Lake. Loafing here for a couple of weeks was once an essential part of the Yunnan experience.

In recent years, domestic tourists have discovered Dali in a big way and the scene has changed accordingly. Instead of dreadlocked westerners, it's young Chinese who

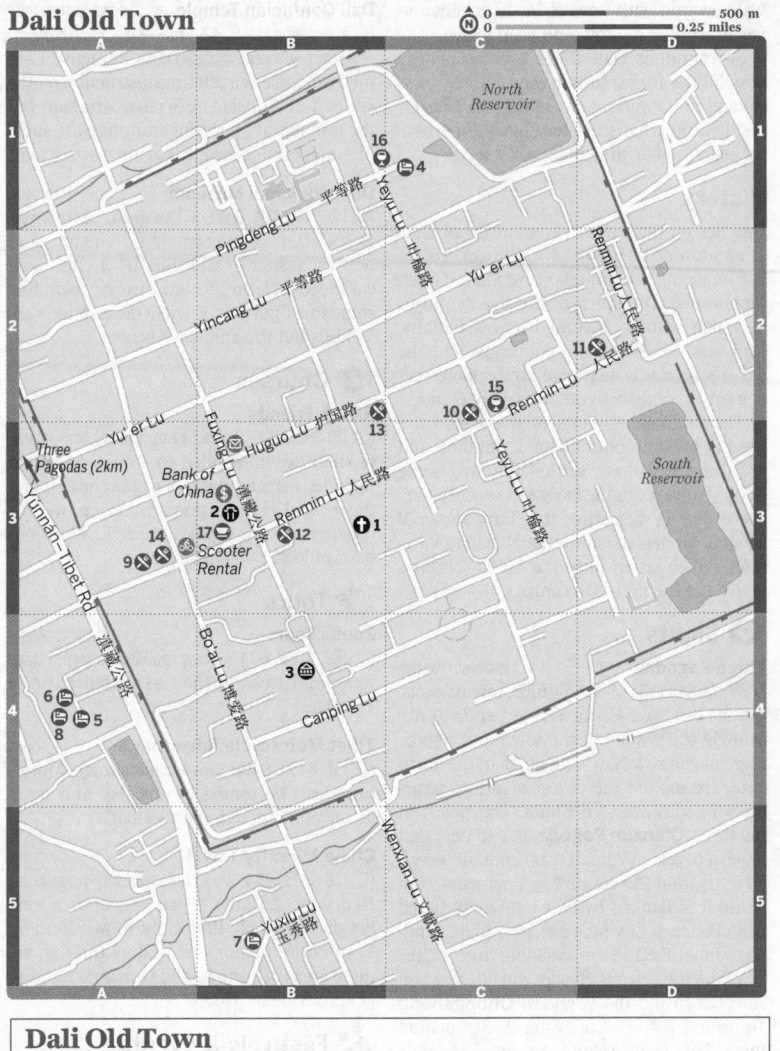

Dali Old Town

⊚ Sights
1 Dali Catholic Church	B3
2 Dali Confucian Temple	B3
3 Dali Municipal Museum	B4

⊕ Activities, Courses & Tours
China Minority Travel	(see 7)

⊜ Sleeping
4 Dragonfly Guesthouse	C1
5 Five Elements	A4
6 Jade Emu	A4
7 Jim's Tibetan Hotel	B5
8 Lily Pad Inn & International Guest House	A4

⊗ Eating
9 Bakery No 88	A3
10 Cháimǐduǒ	C2
11 Duan's Kitchen	D2
12 Méizi Jǐng	B3
13 Serendipity	B2
14 Sweet Tooth	A3

⊝ Drinking & Nightlife
15 Chateau Pirates	C2
16 Craft Beer House	B1
17 Tang Cafe	B3

walk around with flowers in their hair, and facelifts of the old town proceed apace.

Surrounding Dali there are fascinating possibilities for exploring, especially by bicycle and in the mountains above the lake. Or you can do what travellers have done here for years – eat, drink and make merry.

History

Dali lies on the western edge of Erhai Lake at an altitude of 1900m, with a backdrop of the imposing 4000m-tall Cang Shan (Green Mountains). For much of the five centuries in which Yunnan governed its own affairs, Dali was the centre of operations, and the old city retains a historical atmosphere that is hard to come by in other parts of China.

The main inhabitants of the region are the Bai, who number about 1.5 million and are thought to have settled the area some 3000 years ago. In the early 8th century they succeeded in defeating the Tang imperial army before establishing the Nanzhao kingdom, which lasted until the Mongol hordes arrived in the mid-13th century.

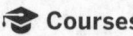 Sights

Three Pagodas
BUDDHIST PAGODA

(三塔寺, Sān Tǎ Sì; ☑ 872 266 6158; www.dalisanta. net; 214 Guodao, 214国道; ¥75; ☺ 7am-7pm) Absolutely *the* symbol of the town and region, these pagodas, a 2km walk north of the north gate, are among the oldest standing structures in southwestern China. The tallest of the three, **Qianxun Pagoda**, has 16 tiers that reach a height of 70m. It was originally erected in the mid-9th century by engineers from Xi'an. It is flanked by two smaller 10-tiered pagodas, each of which are 42m high. Guided tours in English are available from ¥120.

While the price is cheeky considering you can't go inside the pagodas, **Chongsheng Temple** (崇圣寺, Chóngshèng Sì) behind them has been rebuilt to an incredible degree along the design of the destroyed Nanzhao-era original, and is well worth exploring. Just inside the main entrance, the **Chong Sheng Vegetarian Buffet** serves lunch (¥20, 11.30am to 1pm).

Dali Catholic Church
CHURCH

(大理天主教堂, Dali Tiānzhǔ Jiàotáng; 6 Xinmin Lu, 新民路6号) FREE It's worth checking out Dali's Catholic Church. Dating back to 1927, it's a beautiful blend of Bai-style architecture and classic Christian theology and church design. Mass is held here every Sunday at 9.30am.

Dali Confucian Temple
CONFUCIAN TEMPLE

(文庙, Wénmiào; 42 Yita Lu, 一塔路42号; ☺ 7.30am-9.30pm) FREE Dali's attractive Confucian Temple is a 2014 reconstruction on the site of the original Qing dynasty structure, but the grounds are peaceful and there are small museum exhibits inside that are worth a look.

Dali Municipal Museum
MUSEUM

(大理市博物馆, Dàlǐ Shì Bówùguǎn; 111 Fuxing Lu, 复兴路111号; ☺ 9am-5pm) FREE The museum houses a small collection of archaeological pieces relating to Bai history, including some fine figurines. English descriptions are lacking, but the ambience is nice.

 Courses

Rice & Friends
COOKING

(☑ 151 2526 4065; www.riceandfriends.com; classes ¥180) Recommended cooking school that includes trips to markets to purchase ingredients and tips on preparation, as well as cooking classes. Classes are held daily, but need at least two participants.

☞ Tours

Zouba Tours
CYCLING, HIKING

(☑ 188 4082 6047; www.zoubatours.com) Bike tours and treks to the less-visited parts of Yunnan.

Tibet Motorcycle Adventures
TOURS

(☑ 151 8499 9452; www.tibetmoto.de) Motorbikes can be rented by the day and tours arranged (although not to Tibet).

China Minority Travel
CULTURAL

(☑ 138 8723 5264; www.china-minority-travel.com) Henriette, a Dutch expat, can offer a long list of trips, including tours to Muslim and Yi minority markets as well as through remote areas of Yunnan and Guizhou. Enquire at Jim's Tibetan Hotel.

✵ Festivals & Events

Third Moon Fair
CULTURAL

(三月节, Sānyuè Jié) Merrymaking – along with endless buying, selling and general horse-trading (but mostly partying) – takes place during the Third Moon Fair, which begins on the 15th day of the third lunar month (usually April) and ends on the 21st day.

Three Temples Festival
CULTURAL

(绕三灵, Ràosān Líng) The Three Temples Festival is held between the 23rd and 25th days of the fourth lunar month (usually May).

The first day starts at Dali's south gate and ends at Sacred Fountainhead Temple (Shèngyuán Sì) in Xizhou, where there is all-night dancing and singing. From there, revellers move on to Jīnguì Temple (Jīnguì Sì), before returning by way of Majiuyi Temple (Mǎjiǔyì Sì).

Torch Festival
CULTURAL

(火把节, Huǒbǎ Jié) The Torch Festival is held on the 24th and 25th days of the sixth lunar month (normally July) and is likely to be the best photo op in the province. Flaming torches are paraded at night through homes and fields. Locals throw pine resin at the torches, causing minor explosions everywhere. According to one local guesthouse owner, 'it's total madness'.

🛏 Sleeping

Jade Emu
HOSTEL ¥

(金玉缘中澳国际青年旅舍, Jīnyùyuán Zhōng'ào Guójì Qīngnián Lǚshè; ☑872 267 7311; www.jade-emu.com; Ximen Cun, 西门村; 8-/6-/4-bed dm ¥30/35/40, r ¥168; ❀ @ 🛜) Smack in the shadow of Cang Shan and now spread over a complex of buildings, the Jade Emu is massive and has everything a traveller could need. The dorms are more comfortable than most and the private rooms are spacious, clean and bright, while the new boutique annexe is perfect for flashpackers. Staff are efficient and friendly.

There's a big, outdoor communal area with bar and pool table, and a separate movie room. They also arrange tours and bus tickets. Next door is their own cafe-cum-bookshop and restaurant La Dolce Vita.

Five Elements
HOSTEL ¥

(五行国际客栈, Wǔ Xíng Guójì Kèzhàn; ☑130 9985 0360; fiveelementsdali@gmail.com; Ximen Cun, 西门村; 6-/4-bed dm ¥30/45, r ¥128; ❀ 🛜) This place has a popular following with backpackers, thanks to the low prices and friendly vibe. Dorms need more storage space but are reasonably sized, while the private rooms are a decent deal for the price. The best are very comfortable and set around a pleasant garden where the manager grows organic veggies. Bike hire is available.

Lily Pad Inn & International Guest House
HOSTEL ¥

(百合青年旅舍, Bǎihé Qīngnián Lǚshě; ☑872 267 7807; Ximen Cun, 西门村; 4-/6-bed dm ¥40/50, d ¥128; 🛜) One of a growing number of hostels located just outside the old town and near the west gate, this relaxed, peaceful guesthouse is set around two plant-filled courtyards. Dorms are a little cramped and it's all a little run-down, but the English-speaking staff are helpful.

Dragonfly Guesthouse
GUESTHOUSE ¥¥

(清亭客栈, Qīngtíng Kèzhàn; ☑872 266 2182; 200 Pingdeng Rd, 平等路200号; 6-/4-bed dm ¥50/80, s/d ¥185/256; ❀ @ 🛜) This newish place gets great reviews, and the dorm beds are certainly among the most comfortable in Dali. All the rooms are sizeable and have decent bathrooms, while there's a roof terrace with views towards the lake and mountains, and a basic restaurant. It's 15 minutes' walk from the centre of town at the northern end of Yeyu Lu.

Jim's Tibetan Hotel
HOTEL ¥¥

(吉姆和平酒店, Jímǔ Hépíng Jiǔdiàn; ☑872 267 7824; jimstibetanhotel@gmail.com; 4 Yuyuan Xiang, 玉苑巷4号; s/d ¥280 incl breakfast; ❀ 🛜) The rooms here are some of the most distinctive in Dali, styled with Tibetan motifs and packed with antique Chinese-style furniture (even if the bathrooms are looking their age now). There's also a garden, rooftop terrace, restaurant and bar. Travel services and tours can be booked, and bikes and scooters can be hired.

🍴 Eating

Bai food makes excellent use of local flora and fauna. Specialities include *rǔbǐng* (goat's cheese) and *ěr kuài* (饵块; toasted rice 'cakes'). Given the proximity of Erhai Lake, try *shāguō yú* (沙锅鱼), a claypot fish casserole/stew made from salted Erhai Lake carp – and, as a Bai touch, magnolia petals.

Bakery No 88
CAFE ¥

(88号西点店, Bāshíbā Hào Xīdiàndiàn; ☑872 267 9129; 17 Renmin Lu, 人民路17号; meals from ¥25; ⏱8.30am-9.45pm; 🛜) Spread across two floors and with a small garden, this popular, smoke-free haven of tranquillity has excellent sandwiches, pastas and soups, all prepared with local produce, as well as fine breads and cakes. It also sells German sausages and beer.

Sweet Tooth
CAFE ¥

(甜点屋, Tiándiǎn Wū; ☑872 266 3830; 79 Bo'ai Lu, 博爱路79号; cakes from ¥25, sandwiches from ¥28; ⏱8.30am-10.30pm; 🛜) Owned and run by a culinary arts graduate, the homemade ice cream and desserts here are simply inspiring. There's also fine coffee, proper English tea and healthy fruit and yoghurt shakes. Breakfast is served from 8.30am to noon.

YUNNAN ERHAI LAKE

MARKETS AROUND DALI

Travellers have a market to go to nearly every day of the week. Every Monday at **Shaping** (沙坪), about 30km north of Dali, there is a colourful Bai market (Shāpíng Gǎnjí). From 10am to 2.30pm you can buy everything from food products and clothing to jewellery and local batik.

Regular buses to Shaping (¥11, one hour) leave from just outside the west gate. By bike, it will take about two hours at a good clip.

Markets also take place in **Shuanglang** (双廊, Shuāng Láng; Tuesday), **Shaba** (沙坝, Shābà; Wednesday), **Yousuo** (右所, Yòusuǒ; Friday morning) and **Jiangwei** (江尾, Jiāngwěi; Saturday). **Xizhou** (喜洲, Xǐzhōu) and **Zhoucheng** (州城, Zhōuchéng) have daily morning and afternoon markets, respectively. **Wase** (挖色, Wāsè) also has a popular market every five days with trading from 9am to 4.30pm. Thanks to the lack of boats, travellers now have to slog to Xiaguan's east bus station for buses to Wase (¥20).

Many guesthouses and hostels in Dali offer tours or can arrange transport to these markets for around ¥150 per half-day.

Duan's Kitchen   YUNNAN ¥¥
(小段厨房, Xiǎoduàn Chúfáng; ☎153 0872 7919; 12 Renmin Lu, 人民路12号; dishes from ¥30-58; ☺11.30am-9pm; 🛜) Now so popular that you can expect to queue for a table, this place is set around a cosy and cute courtyard. The dishes are an interpretation of Bai cuisine rather than 100% the real deal, but the ingredients are absolutely local. There's also a nice plum-infused liquor that's worth sampling.

Méizi Jǐng   YUNNAN ¥¥
(梅子井; ☎872 267 1578; 130 Renmin Lu, 人民路130号; dishes ¥25-98; ☺10am-9pm) This charmingly authentic Bai restaurant is composed of three grey-brick courtyards each containing small seating nooks where you can feast on traditional local cuisine. The English menu features some erratic translations ('garlic loofah tip', anyone?), but the 'braised chicken' or 'wild mushroom' dishes are both fine starting points, as are the small bottles of aged house-made plum liquor.

It's tucked off Renmin Lu opposite the vegetable market.

Serendipity   AMERICAN ¥¥
(大理美国小馆, Dàlǐ Měiguó Xiǎoguǎn; ☎872 251 0086; 53 Guangwu Lu, 广武路53号; mains from ¥38; ☺8am-11pm; 🛜) Busy, American-run diner with a traditional counter to sit around and a solid menu of properly cooked burgers, steaks, pasta and salad, as well as hefty, top-notch breakfasts. There's some outdoor seating in the alley that is rather quieter than Dali's main drag.

Cháimǐduō   INTERNATIONAL ¥¥¥
(柴米多; ☎872 256 9967; 204 Nan Yeyu Lu, 叶榆路南204号; mains ¥38-98; ☺10am-9.30pm; 🛜) Look for occasionally innovative combinations of all-organic Yunnan ingredients sourced from the proprietors' own farm outside Dali. It features an open kitchen, faux-rustic design and a large outside area to eat in. The starters don't really deliver but the mains are a hit.

🍷 Drinking & Nightlife

Tang Cafe   CAFE
(唐咖, Táng Kā; ☎872 256 0560; 350 Renmin Lu Zhongduan, 人民路中段350号; ☺9am-10pm; 🛜) One sip of the flat white here and you'll swear you're in Melbourne, or at least Sydney. A rooftop terrace sweetens the deal, as does a small but tempting brunch menu.

Craft Beer House   CRAFT BEER
(182 Pingdeng Lu, 平等路182号; ☺1pm-4am; 🛜) In a quiet corner of the old town, this fun place carries European and American craft brews plus some locally produced 'foreign' options (¥39 to ¥69). There are no Chinese craft beers, unfortunately, but there's live music sometimes. It's the kind of bar you'd open for your friends to hang out at, which appears to be exactly the story here.

Chateau Pirates   CRAFT BEER
(海盗酒堡, Hǎidào Jiǔbǎo; ☎189 8723 1290; 55-2 Nan Yeyu Lu, 叶榆路南55-2号; ☺4pm-12.30am; 🛜) Chinese craft beer (including one Dali offering) from a hole-in-the-wall taproom with just a few barstools and one tiny table. If you're peckish, the place next door will bring over fish 'n' chips and bacon sandwiches.

🔒 Shopping

Dali is famous for its marble blue-and-white batik printed on cotton and silk. There are many clothes shops around Dali. Most can also make clothing to your specifications – which will come as a relief when you see how small some of the ready-made items are.

ℹ Information

All hostels and guesthouses and many hotels offer travel advice, arrange tours and book tickets for onward travel. There are also numerous travel agencies and cafes that will book bus tickets and offer all manner of tours. They can be expensive unless you can get a group together.

Bank of China (中国银行, Zhōngguó Yínháng; ☑ 872 266 0191; 333 Fuxing Lu, 复兴路333号; ⊗ 9am-5pm Mon-Fri) Changes cash and travellers cheques, and has an ATM that accepts all major credit cards.

ℹ Getting There & Away

The golden rule: almost all buses advertised to Dali actually go to Xiaguan. Coming from Lijiang and Shangri-la, most Xiaguan-bound buses stop at the eastern end of Dali Old Town to let passengers off before continuing on to Xiaguan's north bus station.

From Kunming's west bus station there are numerous buses to Dali (¥110 to ¥160, four to five hours, every 30 minutes from 7.15am to 7.20pm). Heading north, it's easiest to pick up a bus on the roads outside the west or east gates; buy your ticket in advance from your guesthouse or a travel agent and they'll make sure you get on the right one. (You could hail one yourself to save a surcharge but you're not guaranteed a seat.)

From Dali Old Town (near the west gate) you can catch a bus to Kunming for ¥150; it runs seven times a day. There are also frequent buses from the old town to Lijiang (¥80) and Shangri-la (¥110).

Buses run regularly to Xizhou (¥7, 30 minutes) and other local destinations from outside the west gate.

ℹ Getting Around

From Dali, a taxi to Xiaguan airport takes 45 minutes and costs around ¥100; to Xiaguan's train station it costs ¥50.

Bikes and scooters are the best way to get around and can be hired at numerous places from ¥40 to ¥180 per day; higher-priced scooter rentals have a larger battery capacity and can make longer trips. Try the **scooter rental** (出租大功率电动车, Chūzū Dàgōnglǜ Diàndòngchē; ☑ 138 8725 8079; Bo'ai Lu; rental per day ¥50-120; ⊗ 8am-8pm) stand on Bo'ai Lu.

Buses (¥2, 30 minutes) marked 大理 (Dàlǐ) run between the old town and Xiaguan from as early as 6.30am to around 7pm; wait along the highway and flag one down.

Bus 4 (¥2, 30 minutes) travels between Dali's west gate and Xiaguan's North Bus Station.

Bus 8 runs between Dali's east gate and central Xiaguan (¥3, 45 minutes), passing close to the North, Express and Xingsheng bus stations, then terminating at the Xiaguan Train Station. There is also a bus marked Dali Special Service (大理专线, Dàlǐ Zhuānxiàn) that runs past the west gate to and from the train station every 15 to 20 minutes from 6.30am (¥5, 30 minutes).

Bus C2 (¥2, 30 minutes) travels from Caiyun Port to the northern edge of Dali Old Town and then down the western side to the west gate.

Cang Shan   苍山

The verdant 4000m-plus peaks of the Cang Shan range (Cāng Shān) rise imposingly above Dali and offer the best managed hikes in the area. Most travellers head first for Zhonghe Temple, on the side of 4088m Zhonghe Mountain (中和山, Zhōnghé Shān), and then follow the Jade Belt Road along the contours of the mountainside to Gantong Temple.

⊙ Sights & Activities

Admission to Cang Shan (¥35) entitles visitors to see all the cultural and natural sites on the mountain but doesn't include the chairlifts or cable car. It is possible to hike up the mountain, a sweaty two to three hours for those in moderately good shape. Keep your eyes peeled for elusive red pandas, which have been spotted here in the past.

Branching out from either side of Zhonghe Temple (p710) is the **Jade Belt Road** (玉带路, Yùdài Lù) a paved and easily walkable flat trail that winds along the face of the mountains, taking you in and out of lush valleys and past streams and waterfalls. From the temple it's a nice 6km walk to the Qilongnu Pools (p710) and the middle station of the Horse Washing Pond Cable Car, followed by a further 5km south to the **Gantong Temple Cable Car** (感通索道, Gǎntōng Suǒdào; one-way/return ¥50/80; ⊗ 8.30am-4.30pm) top station and a viewpoint overlooking the **Qingbi Xi Gorge**. Carry on a final 4km to the topmost section of Gantong Temple (p710), from where you can continue down the road via **Guanyin Temple** (观音堂, Guānyīn Táng) and pick up a Dali-bound bus.

Alternatively take the **cable car** (洗马潭索道, Xǐmǎ Tán Suǒdào; ☑ 872 228 9977; return

¥300; ⊙9am-4pm) up to the Horse Washing Pond, high in the mountain range, where Kublai Khan set up his base in the late 13th century.

Gantong Temple
BUDDHIST TEMPLE

(感通寺, Gǎntōng Sì) Originally constructed in the Tang dynasty, this was once the most important temple in the Dali area. Only one of the original 36 halls remains, but reconstruction continues apace and in its forested mountainside setting the atmosphere is magnificent.

Most notable is the uppermost temple (just uphill for visitors arriving on the stone path descending from the Jade Belt Road) for the delicate, manicured gardens and wonderful teahouse (10.30am to 6pm) inside. Pay whatever you like for the tea, leave a ¥100 deposit for the glassware, and pick a spot to relax for a while.

Qilongnu Pools
NATURAL POOL

(七龙女池, Qīlóngnǚ Chí) This series of attractive pools and cascades is said to have been the favourite bathing spot of an Erhai dragon king's seven daughters. The path up is quite steep, but worthwhile.

Qingbi Stream
RIVER

(清碧溪, Qīngbì Xī) Mountain spring that gushes into three basins, with an impressive waterfall during the rainy season. The combination of the clear water and the stones in the basins give the water an attractive green-blue colour that delights local visitors.

Zhonghe Temple
BUDDHIST TEMPLE

(中和寺, Zhōnghé Sì) This temple on the side of Zhonghe Mountain is small and pretty but of little note otherwise. There is a small restaurant on-site with basic dishes, plus tea, coffee and beer.

Horse Washing Pond
LAKE

(洗马潭, Xǐ Mǎ Tán) Kublai Khan used this place as a base back in the late 13th century. On a clear day, views from the cable car and pond are stunning.

🛏 Sleeping & Eating

It is not permitted for travellers to stay overnight on the mountainside; the few guesthouses that once existed here have all been shuttered.

Each of Cang Shan's temples has at least one simple restaurant, and snacks are available for purchase about halfway along the Jade Belt Road at the Horse Washing Pond Cable Car's middle station.

ℹ Getting There & Around

The starting point for numerous footpaths up Cang Shan is walking distance from Dali's Old Town. For the most popular, walk about 200m north of the Zhonghe Chairlift base station to the riverbed and a rarely staffed checkpoint. Follow the left bank for about 50m and walk through the cemetery, then follow the path zigzagging under the chairlift. When you reach some stone steps, you're near the top. This is but one of several paths up to Zhonghe Temple, and one of many that climbs up the mountainside.

From Dali Old Town's South Gate, tourist shuttles (¥8) run to and from the Gangtong Cable Car's lower station throughout the day. Taxis run from the old town to Zhonghe Temple Chairlift (¥15), Horse Washing Pond Cable Car (¥20), and Gantong Temple Cable Car (¥30).

Most independent travellers hike or take a cable car up to either of the two main temples and follow the Jade Belt Road across the mountain towards the other temple, perhaps stopping at the Horse Washing Pond Cable Car to ride up to the pool and back.

Zhonghe Chairlift (中和索道, Zhōnghé Suǒdào; one-way ¥30; ⊙9am-5pm) is the obvious choice for an early start, as it's the closest to Dali. Gantong Temple Cable Car (p709) is less convenient to the old town, but is served by public transport. Horse Washing Pond Cable Car (p709) can be taken from the lower station (return ¥300) near the old town or from the middle station (¥140) on the Jade Belt Road near the Qilongnu Pools. The entire ride from bottom to top takes around 40 minutes.

Xizhou
喜洲

📱 0872 / POP 54,940

A trip to the old town of Xizhou (Xīzhōu) for a look at its well-preserved Bai architecture is a lovely stop, and some travellers make it their base for exploring the area around Dali.

Yan Family Compound
HISTORIC BUILDING

(严家大院, Yánjiā Dàyuàn; 📞 872 245 4198; Sifang Jie, 四方街; ¥25; ⊙8.30am-6pm) This traditional Bai-style wooden courtyard home was constructed by businessman Yan Zizheng in the early 1900s, using the fortune he made from trading along the Tea Horse Road (p712). Don't miss the small entrance off the 4th courtyard to the 'No 5 Garden', and an underground air-raid shelter. There's surprisingly good English signage throughout the complex.

★ Linden Centre
HOTEL ¥¥¥

(喜林苑, Xǐ Lín Yuàn; 📞 872 245 2988; www.lindencentre.com; 5 Chengbei Cun, 城北村5号; d/ste incl breakfast ¥880/1480; @🛈) This tradition-

Sidebar: YUNNAN ERHAI LAKE

al Bai stone-and-wood courtyard home has been turned into a very smart boutique hotel with 16 rooms, all of which are set around a courtyard, have balconies and come with antique furniture (but modern bathrooms). The first courtyard is open to curious visitors, as is the terrific upstairs terrace bar (noon to 10pm) overlooking the agrarian landscape surrounding Xizhou.

Xīzhōu Pòsū Bābā
YUNNAN ¥

(喜洲破酥粑粑; ☑ 139 8856 5525; ¥10; ⊙ 9am-5pm) Local 'baba' cakes are for sale from street stalls around Xizhou, but the best we've tasted in town are from this friendly chef, who sets up shop just southwest of the entrance to the Yan Family Compound.

ⓘ Getting There & Away

You can catch a local bus (¥7, 30 minutes, 7am to 6pm) from the west or east gates in Dali. Return buses leave from the main highway on the west side of Xizhou, just south of the moon bridge.

Nuodeng
诺邓

☑ 0872 / POP 1200

In existence for over 1150 years, the anachronistic hamlet of Nuodeng (Nuòdèng) has one of the highest concentrations of Bai in Yunnan and some of the best preserved buildings in the entire province. The area has managed to maintain traditional village life, with ponies and donkeys clomping up the steep flagstone streets past traditional mudbrick buildings with ornate gates, many of which date back to the Ming and Qing dynasties.

It's finally starting to hit the radar of both domestic and foreign tourists, but for now Nuodeng is still very peaceful and a delightful place to kick back for a while.

◉ Sights

After crossing the bridge at the bottom of the village you'll see one of the original **salt wells,** located inside a wooden shed. The town is built upon a steep hill and winding up along the alleys you'll pass through an impressive **Wooden Archway** (木牌坊, Mù Páifāng) just before the final steps to the restored **Confucian Temple** (孔庙, Kǒngmiào), notable as one of few in China that show the sage dressed as a commoner (also check out the detailed frescoes still visible on the ceiling). Just beyond is the picturesque 16th-century **Yuhuang Pavillion** (玉皇阁, Yùhuáng Gé).

Village daily life is centred on the small **market square,** a good place to catch some sun and gab with the local elders.

🛏 Sleeping & Eating

Good Life Hostel
HOSTEL ¥

(古道坊客栈, Gǔdàofāng Kèzhàn; ☑ 186 0125 2967; 292970620@qq.com; dm ¥50, d without/with bathroom ¥120/160; ☎) This beautiful terraced courtyard home is near the bottom of the village. Rooms are generally small and dark, but common spaces are inviting. To find it, head for the stone steps leading uphill from the bridge where rickshaws arrive and depart, and follow the signs. They can cook simple Chinese dishes, too.

Fùjiǎ Liúfāngyuàn Kèzhàn
INN ¥

(復甲留芳苑客栈; ☑ 872 572 3466; 502609@qq.com; d ¥100-120, ste ¥200; ☎) Expect big rooms and sit-down toilets at this friendly, family-run guesthouse set around a lush garden of bougainvillea. The new annexe offers very comfortable rooms and a terrace overlooks the village – perfect for sunrises and stargazing. It's in the northern section of the village but a bit hard to find; call ahead and they'll come and meet you.

★ Yánquán Nóngjiā
YUNNAN ¥¥

(盐泉农家; ☑ 872 552 5111; dishes ¥15-100; ⊙ 11am-8pm) The one genuine restaurant in the village is also one of the most famous in Yunnan, after being featured on the hit Chinese TV show *A Bite of China.* People come from far and wide to sample *shúhuǒtuǐ* (熟火腿; ¥40), a slightly salty cured ham that's the local speciality. It tastes fantastic, as do the all-natural veggies and tofu.

ⓘ Getting There & Away

Buses (¥43, three hours, 14 daily, 7.10am to 4.30pm) leave from Xiaguan's express bus station to the sleepy county seat **Yunlong** (云龙, Yúnlóng), from where you can take a three-wheel rickshaw or minivan (¥15 to ¥20) the final 7km to Nuodeng. Buses back to Xiaguan leave on the same schedule. There is also one daily bus to Kunming (¥175, seven to eight hours, 9.30am) and to Jianchuan (¥51, four to five hours, 8.30am), where travellers can transfer for Shaxi.

Shaxi
沙溪

☑ 0872 / POP 6,000

The tiny hamlet of Shaxi (Shāxī) is an evocative throwback to the days of the Tea Horse Road – you can almost hear the clippety-clop of horses' hooves and shouts of traders. It is by far the best preserved of the caravan oasis towns from the era – and the only one with a functioning market, held on Friday, when Bai and Yi villagers converge on the town to trade in goods and livestock.

The village's courtyards, wooden houses and narrow, winding streets make it a popular location for period Chinese movies and TV shows, and there are plenty of domestic day trippers visiting from Dali. However, this is still a wonderfully relaxed place where you can spend the night sitting by the river under a canopy of stars and listening to the frogs croaking in the rice paddies.

◉ Sights & Activities

Sideng Jie (寺登街, Sìdēng Jiē) is the ancient town street leading off the main road, running 300m downhill past an alley that leads to the Ouyang House and on to the old square – dominated by the prominent theatrical stage (古戏台, gǔxìtái) of **Three Terraced Pavilion** (魁星阁, Kuíxīnggé; Shiji Guangchang, 市集广场), something of a rarity in rural Yunnan. Opposite is **Xingjiào Sì** (兴教寺, Xìngjiào Temple; Shiji Guangchang, 市集广场; ¥20; ◎ 9am-5pm), the only Ming dynasty Bai Buddhist temple.

Exit the old town's east gate and head south along the Hui River (惠江, Huì Jiāng), cross the ancient Yujin Bridge (玉津桥, Yùjīn Qiáo),

and you're walking the same trail as the horse caravans once rode. If you look hard enough, you'll still be able to see hoofprints etched into the rock, or so the locals claim. Ponies can be rented for ¥120 an hour by the river, if you want to ride part of the trail yourself.

Beyond the small old town, the main activity here is walking. The guesthouses in town have maps that can get you started and keep you busy for days, with Horsepen 46 among the best sources of information for walks to White Dragon Pool, hidden mountain lakes and quiet mountain temples.

Shíbǎoshān NATURE RESERVE, HISTORIC SITE
(石宝山; ☑ 872 868 6280; ¥40; ◎ 9am-5pm) Wandering anywhere along the forested trails and stone pathways throughout Shibao Mountain makes for a pleasant day trip out of Shaxi, but the real highlights of the area are the Tangera temples and carvings. The **Shizhongshan Grottoes** (石钟山石窟, Shízhōngshān Shíkū) have the most impressive concentration, most dating to the Nanzhao Kingdom and depicting the state's political and religious life. Also worth a visit is **Baoxiang Temple** (宝相寺, Bǎoxiāng Sì) for fantastic views of the rolling mountains beyond Shaxi.

No public transport runs here. Walk up any of the numerous trails from Shaxi in around two hours, or take a minivan to the access road turn-off 12km north of the village. You'll have to walk the last 2km to the entrance.

THE TEA HORSE ROAD

Less known than the Silk Road, but equally important in terms of trade and the movement of ideas, people and religions, the Tea Horse Road (茶马古道, Chámǎgǔdào) linked southwest China with India via Tibet. A series of caravan routes, rather than a single road, which also went through parts of Sichuan, Myanmar (Burma), Laos and Nepal, the trails started deep in the jungle of Xishuangbanna. They then headed north through Dali and Lijiang and into the thin air of the Himalayan mountains on the way to the Tibetan capital Lhasa, before turning south to India and Myanmar.

Although archaeological finds indicate that stretches of the different routes were in use thousands of years ago, the road really began life in the Tang dynasty (AD 618–907). An increased appetite for tea in Tibet led to an arrangement with the Chinese imperial court to barter Yunnan tea for the prized horses ridden by Tibetan warriors. By the Song dynasty (AD 960–1279), 20,000 horses a year were coming down the road to China, while in 1661 alone some 1.5 million kilograms of tea headed to Tibet.

Sugar and salt were also carried by the caravans of horses, mules and yaks. Buddhist monks, Christian missionaries and foreign armies utilised the trails as well, to move between Myanmar, India and China. In the 18th century the Chinese stopped trading for Tibetan horses and the road went into a slow decline. Its final glory days came during WWII, when it was a vital conduit for supplies from India for the Allied troops fighting the Japanese in China. The advent of peace and the communist takeover of 1949 put an end to the road's long history.

Ouyang House
HOUSE

(欧阳大院, Ōuyáng Dàyuàn; off Sideng Jie, 寺登街; ¥10) Constructed in the late Qing dynasty, this courtyard home is a superb example of three-in-one Bai folk architecture, in which one wall protected three yards/residences. Sadly, most of it is currently closed to the public – people still live here – although for a small fee you can poke your head inside for a quick look.

🛏 Sleeping

Horsepen 46
HOSTEL ¥

(马圈46客栈, Mǎjuàn Sìshíliù Kèzhàn; ☑872 472 2299; www.horsepen46.com; 46 Sideng Jie, 寺登街46号; dm ¥35, r ¥90-120; @🛜) Popular guesthouse with compact rooms surrounding a sunny little courtyard. There's a laid-back traveller vibe here, with daily communal dinners (¥25). There's also laundry and bike hire (¥20 per day). The helpful English-speaking staff can provide info on hikes and activities in the area. It's tucked away to the right of the stage in the village square.

Tea and Horse Caravan Trail Inn
INN ¥¥

(古道客栈, Gǔdào Kèzhàn; ☑872 472 1051; www.shaxitrip.com; 83 Sideng Jie, 寺登街83号; d ¥80-280; 🛜) There are a couple of cheap rooms without bathrooms at this friendly place. The more expensive ones are a significant step up and come with good beds and decent bathrooms, as well as being set around a large and pleasant garden. Turn left into the last alley off Sideng Jie just before reaching the main square.

★ Old Theatre Inn
GUESTHOUSE ¥¥¥

(戏台会馆, Xìtái Huìguǎn; ☑872 472 2296; www.shaxichina.com; Duànjiādēng Village, 段家登; r incl breakfast ¥460; @🛜) This boutique guesthouse has been lovingly restored out of a 260-year-old Chinese theatre and inn. There are only five very comfortable rooms here, all with photogenic views towards the nearby mountains, so book ahead. It's located 3km north of Shaxi; you can rent a bike (¥20) to get around.

Non-guests may want to visit on Thursdays at 6pm, when a local orchestra puts on a performance that includes dinner (¥60).

🍴 Eating & Drinking

Pear Blossom
Vegetarian Restaurant
VEGETARIAN ¥

(梨花素菜馆, Líhuā Sùcàiguǎn; Diantou Village, 甸头村; mains ¥25-40; ⏰9.30am-6pm; 🛜🚲) Operating in the forecourt of the restored

Pear Orchard Temple (慈荫庵, Cíyīnān) the delightfully clever menu here presents Shaxi dishes made primarily with ingredients locally sourced from farms in the surrounding Diantou Village.

Hungry Buddha
ITALIAN, VEGETARIAN ¥¥

(大嘴佛, Dàzuǐ Fó; www.soundinner.com/yunnan; 36 Sideng Jie, 寺登街36号; mains ¥32-92; ⏰11.30am-9pm Tue-Sun; 🛜🚲) The most sophisticated eatery in town and one of the most notable in all Yunnan, with a mouth-watering all-vegetarian Italian menu utilising locally produced ingredients across the authentic menu. The range of options is limited but delicious, and there's a proper wine list, too.

There are only 10 spots at the wooden counter where you eat and watch your meal being prepared, so grab one early.

Gong Ho
AMERICAN ¥¥

(工合, Gōng Hé; Sideng Jie, 寺登街; mains ¥40-88; ⏰11am-9pm) Pasta, steak, burgers and beer. The menu may be simple but the service is friendly and it's excellent food. Find it off a side alley just before Sideng Jie meets market square.

Corvus Corax
CAFE

(渡鸦, Dùyā; ☑150 5328 9386; ⏰10am-7.30pm) Perhaps the best coffee to be had in Shaxi is available at this tiny cafe and roastery just south of the old town square.

ℹ Getting There & Away

From Jianchuan (剑川, Jiànchuān), minivans (¥15, one hour) run to and from Shaxi from 6.30am until 5pm.

Moving on, you'll have to backtrack to Jianchuan. There are buses every 20 to 30 minutes to Xiaguan (¥41, 2½ hours) between 6.40am and 5.30pm. To Lijiang (¥28, two hours) there are six daily buses between 8.20am and 5.30pm. A daily bus to Kunming (¥168, seven hours) leaves at 9.30am, and two daily buses depart for Shangri-la (¥50, four hours) at 9am and 10am.

NORTHWEST YUNNAN

Northwest Yunnan is a gorgeous blend of soaring mountains, pristine lakes and dizzyingly deep gorges and valleys. This is the part of Yunnan to head to for epic hikes, whether in the shadow of the 6000m peaks around Deqin or through the impressive Tiger Leaping Gorge. But the region is also home to Lugu Hú, a vast lake that straddles the Yunnan–Sichuan border and is home to the Mosuo people, the last matriarchal society in the world. If that wasn't enough, there are also the towns of Shangri-la, with its intriguing blend of Tibetan and Han Chinese culture, and Lijiang, a Unesco World Heritage Site that draws in both domestic and foreign visitors en masse.

❶ Getting There & Away

Lijiang and Shangri-la are the only places in Northwest Yunnan with airports and train stations (the railway is scheduled to reach Shangri-la in 2020), and from them you can connect to destinations across Yunnan and beyond. Lugu Lake's new airport makes getting there far easier to get to than before, but services are limited. Buses remain the main way to get around this region; with roads winding through mountain passes, journey times can be long.

Lijiang 丽江
☑ 0888 / POP 70,000

How popular is this time-locked place? Lijiang's (Lìjiāng) maze of cobbled streets, rickety (or rickety-looking, given gentrification) wooden buildings and gushing canals suck in over *eight million* people a year. So thick are the crowds in the narrow alleys that it can feel like they've all arrived at the same time.

But remember the 80/20 rule: 80% of the tourists will be in 20% of the places. Get up early enough and you can often beat the crowds. And when they do appear, that's the cue to hop on a bike and cycle out to one of the nearby villages.

◉ Sights

Lijiang Old Town   HISTORIC SITE
(丽江古城, Lìjiāng Gǔchéng; ¥80) The old town is centred on busy and touristy **Old Market Square** (四方街, Sìfāng Jiē), with the **Waterwheel** (大水车, Dàshuǐchē) defining the northern edge and the lively **Zhongyi Market** (忠义市场, Zhōngyì Shìchǎng; 148 Guyou Xiang, 古佑巷148号; ⊙9am-9pm) marking the southern

limit (which is a good stop for a slice of old Lijiang's trading traditions or just some afternoon street food). The surrounding lanes are dissected by a web of artery-like canals that once brought the city's drinking water from Yuquan Spring, on the far outskirts of what is now Black Dragon Pool Park.

Several wells and pools are still in use around town (but hard to find), including **White Horse Dragon Pool** (白马龙潭, Báimǎlóng Tán; 1 Dong Dajie, 东大街1号). Where there are three pools, these were designated into pools for drinking, washing clothes and washing vegetables.

Much of the joy of the old town is to be had in wandering small twisting lanes that open into small courtyards, hidden teahouses or tiny temples like **Puxian Temple** (普贤寺, Pǔxián Sì; 73 Chongren Xiang, 崇仁巷73号; ⊙8.30am-5pm) FREE. Don't stress too much about seeing it all – but do make sure to climb the flanks of **Lion Hill** (狮子山, Shīzi Shān; ☑888 510 6290; ¥35; ⊙8am-6.30pm) at some point for sweeping views of the old town and mountains.

Black Dragon Pool Park   PARK
(黑龙潭公园, Hēilóngtán Gōngyuán; ☑888 518 8041; 1 Minzhu Lu, 民主路1号; ¥50; ⊙7am-8pm) On the northern edge of town is Black Dragon Pool Park; the view from here of Jade Dragon Snow Mountain is an obligatory photo stop in southwestern China. The **Dongba Cultural Institute** (东巴文化研究所, Dōngbā Wénhuà Yánjiūsuǒ; Black Dragon Pool Park, 黑龙潭公园; ⊙9am-5pm Mon-Fri) is part of a renovated complex on the hillside inside, an interesting stop for Naxi cultural artefacts and scrolls featuring the unique Naxi pictograph script.

Trails lead up Elephant Hill (象山, Xiàng Shān) to a dilapidated gazebo and then across a spiny ridge past a communications centre and back down the other side, making a nice morning hike (but bring your passport to register before you start the hike).

The park is included in the all-encompassing Lijiang Old Town entrance ticket, but in practice this is the only place it seems to be checked.

Museum of Dongba Culture   MUSEUM
(东巴文化博物馆, Dōngbā Wénhuà Bówùguǎn; ☑888 545 7517; Jiaoyu Lu, back entrance of Black Dragon Pool Park, 教育路黑龙潭公园后门口; ⊙8.30am-5.30pm) FREE The Museum of Dongba Culture houses displays on Naxi dress and culture, Dongba pictographic script, Lijiang's old town and the dubious

JADE DRAGON SNOW MOUNTAIN

Jade Dragon Snow Mountain (玉龙雪山, Yùlóng Xuěshān; ¥100; ⊙cable cars 7am-6pm) soars to some 5596m, and the massif's thirteen peaks dominate the skyline of the surrounding regions. Undeniably beautiful, the national park is also undeniably overcrowded – a classic case of over-tourism, compounded by a lack of any nature trails or hiking areas whatsoever. If you're looking for pristine nature, consider Tiger Leaping Gorge or a day hike out of Baisha. If you just want to get up close and personal with peaks, though, visit Jade Dragon Snow Mountain.

Buses (¥15, one hour) from Lijiang arrive at a parking area where you can purchase tickets for the various cable cars and chairlifts that ascend the mountain, but before you even arrive at the service centre you'll need to pony up ¥100 for the entrance fee. This grants you entrance to the service centre and surrounding **Dry Sea Meadow** (干海子, Gānhǎizi), but not much more.

This is also where the **Impression Lijiang** (印象丽江, Yìnxiàng Lìjiāng; Yulong Snow Mountain National Scenic Area, 玉龙雪山国家级风景区; ¥280; ⊙1pm) show is held, a mega song-and-dance performance. Note that if you are going to the performance you will also have to pay the park admission fees. Most independent travellers skip this, but those booking an organised tour may find it included in the package price.

From the bus drop-off, a counter on the right sells tickets for separate cable cars to **Yak Meadow** (牦牛坪, Máoniú Píng) and **Spruce Meadow** (云杉坪, Yúnshān Píng). Cable-car trips for both Yak Meadow (¥45) and Spruce Meadow (¥40) also require a bus transfer (¥20 round-trip); you could conceivably walk it, but the road to the Yak Meadow cable car is 20km from the visitor centre. Just below the Spruce Meadow cable car station (and served by bus) are the **Blue Moon Valley** (蓝月谷, Lányuè Gǔ) and the **White Water River** (白水河, Báishuǐ Hé) that runs through it. In summer, when crowds for the cable cars are long (up to four hours' wait), many travellers just do the trip to the lake and Yak Meadow or Spruce Meadow.

If you have the time to wait for it, the main draw of Jade Dragon Snow Mountain is **Glacier Park** (冰川公园, Bīngchuān Gōngyuán). Ride up nearly 3km of cable car to an elevation of 4506m, where a 200m wooden pathway gets visitors right up next to the mountain's largest glacier. Buy cable car (¥120) and bus transfer (¥20 round-trip) tickets from a separate ticket office east of where buses from Lijiang drop passengers, across from the Impression Lijiang theatre. In the high season, expect to wait an hour or more for a bus transfer to the cable-car station and then a further three to four hours for the cable car itself. It can get cold and windy at the top in midsummer; you'll see plenty of domestic tourists wearing rented down jackets, and you'd be well advised to pack your own warm clothes for the trip.

Buses (¥15, one hour) returning to Lijiang leave every 20 minutes until 5pm from a parking lot just between the Glacier Park ticket office and the Impression Lijiang theatre. The line is not numbered, so look for Yulong Xueshan (玉龙雪山, Yùlóng Xuěshān) in Chinese.

claim that the region is the 'real' Shangri-la; it's worth a visit if you're passing by. Find it just outside Black Dragon Pool Park's northern entrance.

Mu Family Mansion　　　HISTORIC SITE
(木氏土司府, Mùshì Tǔsīfǔ; ☑888 512 2572; ¥40; ⊙8.30am-5.30pm) The home of a Naxi chieftain, the Mu Family Mansion was heavily renovated (more like built from scratch) after the devastating earthquake that struck Lijiang in 1996. Limited captions do very little to introduce the Mu family's history, but for many the beautiful grounds are reason enough to visit. Entrance is not included in the Old Town ticket.

 **Tours**

Lijiang Guides　　　TOUR
(☑137 6900 1439; www.lijiangtravel.info; per day from ¥200) Lijiang-based guide Keith Lyons runs tours and treks, specialising in the area outside Lijiang but extending throughout Yunnan and across the borders of neighbouring provinces.

✷✷ **Festivals & Events**

Torch Festival　　　CULTURAL
(火把节, Huǒbǎ Jié; ⊙Jul) The torch festival is also celebrated by the Bai in the Dali region and the Yi all over the southwest. The origin of this festival can be traced back to

Lijiang

N 0   500 m
   0   0.25 miles

Bus 6 to
Shuhe and
Baisha

Xin Dajie

6

Xiàng Shān
(Elephant Hill)

Black
Dragon
Pool

1

2

Yu River

Mao
Square

Shangri-la Dadao

Yuyuan Lu

Bank of
China

YUNNAN

Fuhui Lu   福慧路

Lijiang Express
(400m)

Shangri-la Dadao

Minzhu Lu   民主路

Main Entrance
to the
Old Town

8

Garden Inn (250m);
October Inn (650m)

Jinhong Lu

Xinyi Jie

Jishan
Xiang

3

Bus to Jade
Dragon Snow
Mountain (Old
Town Entrance)

Xinhua Jie

Dong Dajie

22

16

Mishi Xiang

OLD TOWN

14

18

Wuyi Jie

Wenzhi Xiang

20

10

Shīzi Shān
(Lion Hill)

Old Market
Square

17

Bar St

19

21

4

11

Qiyi Jie

7

13

Chongren Xiang

5

15

Guangbi Xiang

NEW TOWN

Minzhu Lu   民主路

9

Bus to Jade Dragon
Snow Mountain
(Zhongyi Market)

23

12

Changshui Lu

Lijiang ⓡ Station
(500m)

Lijiang

the Nanzhao kingdom, when the wife of a man burned to death by the king eluded the romantic entreaties of the monarch by leaping into a fire.

These days, flaming torches are paraded through the streets to much merriment, for three days from the 24th day of the sixth lunar month.

Sanduo Festival CULTURAL
(三朵节, Sānduǒ Jié; ⊘ Apr) Held on the 13th day of the third lunar month, this festival sees Naxi people offering a sacrifice – normally a goat – to their patron saint Sanduo. The biggest celebration takes place at the Sanduo Temple (三朵寺, Sānduǒ Sì) on Jade Dragon Snow Mountain, where there's a big market and much revelry.

🛏 Sleeping

Rising rents mean that most backpacker guesthouses have relocated to just outside the old town, either north or south. Nevertheless, there are still well over a thousand places to stay in the old town, with more appearing all the time. Many have fewer than 10 rooms. In peak season (especially public holidays), prices double (or more) and you'd do well to book early.

New Youth Inn HOSTEL ¥
(新青年旅舍, Xīn Qīngnián Lǚshě; ☑ 888 535 3000; 185 Xianghe Lu, 祥和路185号; dm/r ¥38/100; 🖭) Bright, modern rooms and common spaces are to be found at this popular Chinese-market hostel, complemented by excellent views over the old town from the 3rd-floor terrace. Not much English is spoken here, but the location just outside the

old town south gate is convenient without being in the crush of crowds.

Water Ripples Inn INN ¥
(水涟漪精品客栈, Shuǐ Liányī Jīngpǐn Kèzhàn; ☑ 182 7527 4061; 75 Chongren Xiang, Qiyi Jie, 七一街崇仁巷75号; r ¥110) The seven modern rooms around a small courtyard here are excellent value, especially considering their location in the centre of the old town just beside Puxian Temple. There's a house dog as well.

October Inn GUESTHOUSE ¥
(汤姆家客栈, Tāngmǔ Jiā Kèzhàn; ☑ 139 8704 6967; www.october-inn.com; 69-1 Xuantian Xiang, Beimen Jie, 北门街玄天巷69-1号; 8-/4-bed dm ¥30/35, d & tw ¥160; 🖭) A secluded, increasingly popular guesthouse with excellent spacious dorms, a handful of private rooms – book ahead – and a cool roof terrace with great views. There are daily communal dinners (¥25) and bike hire is ¥30. It's a steep, 15-minute climb from the old town; call ahead and they'll pick you up when you arrive in Lijiang.

Friendly owner Tom helps coordinate group trips to popular nearby destinations, including van transfers to Tiger Leaping Gorge.

YUNNAN LIJIANG

KEEPING THE GOOD FORTUNE

An interesting local historical story has it that the original Naxi chieftain, whose former home is the Mu Family Mansion (p715), would not allow the old town to be girded by a city wall because drawing a box around the Chinese character of his family name would change the character from *mù* (木, 'wood') to *kùn* (困, 'surrounded' or 'hard-pressed').

Garden Inn
GUESTHOUSE ¥

(丽江文庙国际客栈, Lìjiāng Wénmiào Guójì Kèzhàn; ☑ 151 0887 3494; www.mayhostel.wix.com/gardeninn; 7 Wenmiao Xiang, Beimen Jie, 文庙巷7号, 北门街; dm ¥40, d ¥180-200; @ 🤶) Just outside the old town – the views are good but you'll have to carry your luggage up some stairs – this popular but peaceful hostel has dark, compact dorms (but the beds have proper mattresses). Private rooms are big, with shared balconies, and there's a roof terrace. There's a small communal area and the helpful staff can arrange tours.

Cǎiyúnjiān Kèzhàn
INN ¥¥

(彩云间客栈; ☑ 137 7816 3214; 42 Xianwen Xiang, Guangyi Jie, 光义街现文巷42号; r ¥200) Set behind an entrance that seems more like a temple than a guesthouse, this makes a great base for exploring the old town thanks to its modern stylings and an unbeatable location due south of the Old Market Square.

★ Blossom Hill Neverland
BOUTIQUE HOTEL ¥¥¥

(花间堂, Huājiān Táng; ☑ 133 6888 6376; 97 Wenzhi Xiang, Wuyi Jie, 五一街文治巷97号; d ¥488-1288; ❄ 🤶) There are only a handful of massive rooms, all built around a central courtyard filled with the sounds of classical music and burbling (artificial) brooks, at this very popular boutique inn in the heart of the old town. Bathrooms are modern and large, while each room comes with its own collection of antiques and wood furnishings.

Staff are helpful and there's a small common area with a library. It's essential to book ahead.

Intercontinental Lijiang
HOTEL ¥¥¥

(丽江和府洲际度假酒店, Lìjiāng Héfǔ Zhōujì Jiàrì Jiǔdiàn; ☑ 888 558 8888; www.intercontinental.com; 276 Xianghe Lu, 祥和路276号; r ¥1200-2700; ❄ @ 🤶 ☁) The most popular luxury hotel in the old town – a magical space with lofty ceilings, little gardens and epic views of the Jade Dragon Snow Mountain. The bathrooms are the finest in town, the beds huge and comfy. Other amenities include two restaurants, a swimming pool, day spa and children's play room. Discounts of 25% are sometimes available.

 Eating

Baba (粑粑, *bābā*) is the Lijiang local speciality – thick Naxi flatbreads of wheat, served plain or stuffed with meat, vegetables or sweets. There are always several Naxi items on menus, including the famous 'Naxi omelette' (*baba* with a layer of eggs and tomato cooked on top) and 'Naxi sandwich' (goat's cheese, tomato and fried egg between two pieces of *baba*). Try locally produced *qīng méi jiǔ* (a plum-based wine with a 500-year history) – it tastes like a semisweet sherry.

Tiāntiān Xiān
YUNNAN ¥

(天天鲜; ☑ 139 8704 1292, 888 518 4933; 47 Wangjiazhuang Xiang, Wuyi Jie, 五一街王家庄巷47号; mains ¥12-42; ⏰ 11.30am-9pm) Locals flock here for the superb grilled fish and chicken and soy-bean-paste dishes (get here before 7pm or they will have run out). But all the Naxi specialities on offer are fantastic and great value. No English spoken, but there is an English menu. To find it, look for

---

THE NAXI

Lijiang has been the homeland of the 300,000-odd Naxi (纳西, Nàxī; *na*-see; also spelled Nakhi and Nahi) minority for about the last 1400 years. The Naxi descend from ethnically Tibetan Qiang tribes and lived until recently in matrilineal families. Since local rulers were always male it wasn't truly matriarchal, but women still seemed to run the show.

The Naxi matriarchs maintained their hold over the men with flexible arrangements for love affairs. The *azhu* (friend) system allowed a couple to become lovers without setting up joint residence. Both partners would continue to live in their respective homes; the boyfriend would spend the nights at his girlfriend's house but return to live and work at his mother's house during the day. Any children born to the couple belonged to the woman, who was responsible for bringing them up. The man provided support, but once the relationship was over, so was the support. Children lived with their mothers and no special effort was made to recognise paternity. Women inherited all property and disputes were adjudicated by female elders.

There are strong matriarchal influences in the Naxi language. Nouns enlarge their meaning when the word for 'female' is added; conversely, the addition of the word for 'male' will decrease the meaning. For example, 'stone' plus 'female' conveys the idea of a boulder; 'stone' plus 'male' conveys the idea of a pebble.

RELIGIOUS SITES AROUND LIJIANG

There are a number of historic monasteries around Lijiang, all Tibetan in origin and belonging to the Karmapa (Red Hat) sect. Most were extensively damaged during the Cultural Revolution and there's not much monastic activity nowadays.

Jade Peak Monastery (玉峰寺, Yùfēng Sì; ☑ 888 519 0164; Yufeng Si Lu, 玉峰寺路; ¥17; ◷ 8am-5.30pm), one of the region's last functional Tibetan monasteries, is on a hillside about 6km past Baisha. The monastery sits at the foot of Yùlóng Xuěshān (5500m) and was established in 1756. The monastery's main attraction nowadays is the **Camellia Tree of 10,000 Blossoms** (Wànduǒ Shānchá). Ten thousand might be something of an exaggeration, but locals claim that the tree produces at least 4000 blossoms between February and April. A monk on the grounds risked his life to keep the tree secretly watered during the Cultural Revolution.

Lijiang is also famed for its **temple frescoes**, most of which were painted during the 15th and 16th centuries by Tibetan, Naxi, Bai and Han artists; many were restored during the later Qing dynasty. They depict various Taoist, Chinese and Tibetan Buddhist themes and can be found on the interior walls of temples in the area. Remember, though, that the Cultural Revolution caused havoc around here so many are desecrated in various ways.

Frescoes can be found in Baisha and on the interior walls of **Dajue Palace** (Dàjué Gōng) inside Shuhe's **Longquan Temple** (Lóngquán Sì).

---

the three characters with 'Daily Fresh' written in English underneath them.

Sifang Food Court
YUNNAN ¥

(四方美餐坊, Sìfāng Měicānfāng; 17 Sifang Jie, 四方街17号; snacks from ¥20; ◷ 9am-late; ▣) Snackers should not miss this open-air food market where vendors sell appetising bite-size treats, some of which are native to Lijiang. Try the *Nàxī kǎo qiézi* (纳西烤茄子, Naxi grilled eggplant), served in a boat-shaped crust; *tǔ dòu bǐng* (土豆饼, Naxi potato pancake), and *Nàxī kǎolà cháng* (纳西烤腊肠, Naxi grilled, salty sausage) made with pork, fat and pepper.

For dessert, try the delightful *Nàxī nuomi tuán* (纳西糯米团), a sticky rice ball stuffed with either *hóngdòushā* (红豆沙, red bean), *shūcài* (蔬菜, vegetable) or *ròu* (肉, meat). There are other similar open-air food markets scattered around the old town.

Tiān Hé Cāntīng
YUNNAN ¥

(天和餐厅; ☑ 139 8887 6492; 139 Wenzhi Xiang, Wuyi Jie, 五一街文治巷139号; mains ¥16-68; ◷ 24hr) It's hard to find a neighbourhood-style restaurant in the old town, or one that doesn't also serve western food, but this very solid, family-run place hits the spot with a mix of authentic Naxi dishes and Chinese staples like dumplings, noodles and hotpots.

Amayi Naxi Snacks
YUNNAN ¥¥

(阿妈意纳西饮食院, Āmǎyì Nàxī Yǐnshí Yuàn; ☑ 888 530 9588; Wuyi Jie, 五一街; mains ¥18-88; ◷ 11am-10pm) The name doesn't do justice to the very authentic selection of Naxi cuisine on offer at this calm courtyard restaurant. There are fantastic mushroom dishes (when in season), as well as *zhútǒng fàn* (rice packed in bamboo). It's down an alley off Wuyi Jie, east of the Stone Bridge.

N's Kitchen
INTERNATIONAL ¥¥

(二楼小厨, Èrlóu Xiǎochú; ☑ 888 512 0060; 2nd fl, 17 Jishan Xiang, Xinyi Jie, 新义街积善巷17号2楼; breakfast from ¥20, mains from ¥28; ◷ 9am-10pm; ☎) Clamber up the steep stairs for one of the best breakfasts in town, a monster burger or a fine Yunnan coffee from a window seat overlooking the small square below. The owner is a reliable source of travel info, too, and can arrange bus tickets.

★ Les Petites Écuries
YUNNAN ¥¥¥

(小马厩, Xiǎo Mǎjiù; ☑ 888 518 9333; 9 Yigu Xiang, Nanmen Jie, 南门街依古巷9号; mains ¥42-108; ◷ 10am-9.30pm; ☎🖉) High-end Yunnanese cuisine fills most of the menu at this Yunnanese–French collaboration, in an upmarket setting on the south side of the old town. Bring a group of three or four and try the Yunnan Nations Platter, a selection of 10 to 15 small dishes representative of the region's breadth of flavours.

🍷 Drinking & Nightlife

Two Cats
CAFE

(两只猫咖啡, Liǎngzhī Māo Kāfēi; ☑ 150 1222 1480; 2nd fl, 50 Xinhua Jie, 新华街50号2楼; ◷ 8.30am-late; ☎) Coffee, cakes and a small selection of booze make up the menu at this little cafe on the eastern flank of Lion Hill, but really what keeps us coming back is the incredible views of the old town from the terrace.

Stone the Crows BAR
(乌鸦飞了, Wūyā Fēile; ☑ 888 510 6771; 134 Wenzhi Xiang, 文治巷134号; ⊙ 6pm-late; 🛜) Worth checking out is this foreign-owned, endearingly ramshackle bar with a good range of foreign beers and a mixed crowd of locals (many musicians who play in the nearby bars come here) and westerners. There's a pool table and decent pub food: pizza, pies and burgers. It gets going later rather than earlier.

☆ Entertainment

Naxi Music Academy LIVE MUSIC
(纳西古乐会, Nàxī Gǔyuè Huì; ☑ 888 512 7971; 86 Xinyi Jie Mishi Xiang, 新义街密士巷86号; tickets ¥120-160; ⊙ 8pm) Attending a performance of this orchestra inside a beautiful building in the old town is a good way to spend an evening in Lijiang. Not only are all two dozen or so members Naxi, but they play a type of Taoist temple music (known as *dòngjīng*) that has been lost elsewhere in China.

The pieces they perform are said to be faithful renditions of music from the Han, Song and Tang dynasties, and are played on original instruments.

ⓘ Information

Crowded, narrow streets are a pickpocket's heaven, and solo women travellers have reported being mugged when walking alone at night in isolated areas or in remote sections of Elephant Hill in Black Dragon Pool Park.

Bank of China (中国银行, Zhōngguó Yínháng; ☑ 888 512 2491; 42 Yuyuan Lu, 玉缘路42号; ⊙ 9am-5pm) This branch has an ATM and is convenient for the old town. There are ATMs in the old town, too.

Public Security Bureau (PSB, 公安局; Gōng'ānjú; ☑ 888 513 2310, 888 518 8437; 110 Taihe Xilu, 太和西路110号; ⊙ 8.30-11.30am & 2.30-5.30pm Mon-Fri) Come here for visa extensions. Located on the west side of the Government Building. A taxi will cost ¥15 from the city centre.

ⓘ Getting There & Away

AIR

Lijiang's airport (LJG) is 28km south of town. From Lijiang there are frequent departures to Kunming (from ¥362), as well as multiple daily flights to Beijing (¥1160), Chengdu (¥742), Chongqing (¥514), Guangzhou (¥962), Shanghai (¥1422) and Xishuangbanna (¥430).

International options directly into Lijiang include flights from Taipei (¥1746) and Kuala Lumpur (¥868).

BUS

The main **Lijiang bus station** (丽江客运站; Lìjiāng Kèyùn Zhàn) south of the old town handles long-distance departures; to get here, take bus 8 or 11 (¥1; the latter is faster) from Minzhu Lu. Destinations include the following:

Baishuitai ¥60, five hours, (irregular service at 9am)

Chengdu ¥308, 20 hours, one daily (1pm)

Jianchuan (for Shaxi) ¥28, two hours, six daily (8.20am to 5.30pm)

Kunming ¥238, seven hours, four daily (9am to 8pm)

Lugu Lake ¥61 to ¥85, 4½ hours, two daily (9am and 10am)

Ninglang (for Lugu) ¥49 to ¥69, three hours, 14 daily (8am to 4.30pm)

Shangri-la ¥62, 3½ hours, 19 daily (7.30am to 5.10pm)

Tiger Leaping Gorge ¥35, two hours, one daily (8.30am; Lijiang to Shangri-la buses also stop at Qiaotou, the hike's starting point)

Xiaguan ¥79 to ¥93, three hours, 27 daily (7.10am to 7pm)

Xishuangbanna ¥242, 16 hours, one daily (7.30am)

West of the old town, the **express bus station** (丽江高快客运站, Lìjiāng Gāokuài Kèyùnzhàn; ☑ 888 516 9758; 925 Xianggelila Dadao, 香格里大道925号) serves a smaller selection of the same places. Destinations include the following:

Kunming ¥238, seven hours, 10 daily (9am to 6.30pm)

Lugu Lake ¥71, 4½ hours, two daily (8.30am and 9.30am)

Shangri-la ¥68, 3½ hours, six daily (8.20am to 3.30pm)

Xiaguan ¥79, three hours, six daily (7.30am to 7.30pm)

TRAIN

There are five trains daily from Lijiang Railway Station (丽江火车站, Lìjiāng Huǒchē Zhàn) to Dali (¥34 to ¥49, two to three hours, 7.35am to 3pm) and six fast trains to Kunming (1st/2nd class ¥220/351, three hours, 8.25am to 7.10pm). The line is scheduled to reach Shangri-la by 2020.

Note that the former train station, now known as Lijiang East station, no longer serves any passenger traffic.

ⓘ Getting Around

Bus 6 (Xiangshan Shichang, 象山市场; ⊙ 6.45am-6.30pm; ¥1) runs from Xiangshan Shichang (象山市场, Xiàngshān Shìchǎng) to Shuhe Old Town and Baisha, terminating several kilometres before Yuhu village.

Buses to Jade Dragon Snow Mountain (¥15) run from several points around the old town, including the **main entrance** (888 516 5873; Old Town Bus Stop, 古城口站; ¥15; 7am-4pm) and **Zhongyi Market** (Zhongyi Market Bus Stop, 忠义市场; ¥15; 7am-4pm).

Buses 8A and 8B (¥1) make loops in opposite directions between Xiangshan Shichang, the express bus station, the long-distance bus station, and Minzhu Lu (for the old town and Black Dragon Pool Park).

Bus 16 (¥1) travels between the railway station, express bus station, Xiangshan Shichang and Black Dragon Pool Park.

Bus 17 (¥1) starts at Xiangshan Shichang and ends at Yuhu village.

Bike hire is available at many hostels (¥30 per day). Taxi flagfall is ¥8, but taxis are not allowed into the old town.

Baisha 白沙

 0888 / POP 8,160

By far the most serene spot around Lijiang, Baisha (Báishā) is a small village near several old temples, behind which Jade Dragon Snow Mountain serves as an imposing backdrop. It makes a great bike trip from Lijiang or an ideal spot for lazing and cycling the surrounding area for a day or two.

Located on the plain north of Lijiang, Baisha was the capital of the Naxi kingdom until Kublai Khan made it part of his Yuan empire (1271–1368). Today it's known as a centre of Naxi embroidery; you'll see examples of local handiwork throughout the village.

Dabaoji Palace PALACE
(大宝积宫, Dàbǎojī Gōng; ¥50; 8.30am-5.30pm) The main historical draw of Baisha is the impressive collection of frescoes located inside the small complex, the earliest of which date to 1385. In addition to those that line the walls of the palace, look for those in the **Liuli Temple** (琉璃殿, Liúlí Diàn) and **Dading Pavilion** (大定阁, Dàdìng Gé), which are inside the same complex.

Baisha There
International Youth Hostel HOSTEL ¥
(白沙那里青年旅舍, Báishā Nàlǐ Qīngnián Lǔshè; 888 534 0550; baishathere@hotmail.com; 6 Sanyuan Village, 三元村6号; dm/rm ¥35/118; @) A fine place for chilling out away from the crowds of Lijiang, this laid-back hostel built around a small courtyard garden makes a nice base for exploring the surrounding villages. Dorms are bright, while the private rooms are spacious and comfortable;

Around Lijiang

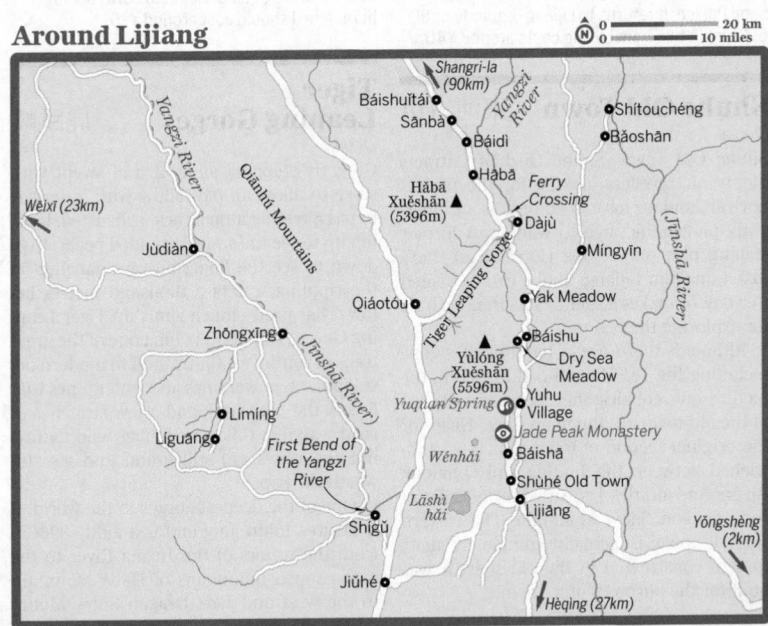

upstairs rooms have great mountain views. Bike hire is ¥30 per day.

★ Me Let

CAFE

(米良, Mǐliáng; ☑130 9744 0079; 14 Sānyuán Village; 三元村14号; ⏰9am-6pm Mon-Sat; 🐾) Of the many fantastic cafes in Baisha, and there are surprisingly many, Me Let stands apart for its selection of and passion for coffee, as well as for the fantastic garden in which to sit. The cafe is locally famous for its home-made plum juice, which also comes in an alcoholic version.

Baisha Naxi Embroidery Institute

ARTS & CRAFTS

(白沙锦绣艺术院, Báishā Jǐnxiù Yìshùyuàn; ☑137 6900 3543; www.lijiangethnicembroidery. com; 17 Sanyuan Village, 三元村17号; ⏰9am-5.30pm) Even if you're not in the market for handmade embroidery it's worth stopping by the institute, which is an active centre for teaching traditional Naxi embroidery to local women. Even the shop is full of museum-quality pieces. Don't miss the small side gallery of painting and embroidery featuring traditional Naxi pictographs.

ℹ Getting There & Away

Baisha is a one-hour bike ride from Lijiang. Otherwise, take bus 6 (¥1, 30 minutes) from Lijiang, which drops you right beside the Dabaoji Palace. It returns to Lijiang regularly until 6.30pm. A taxi from Lijiang costs around ¥40.

Shuhe Old Town 束河古镇

☑0888 / POP 34,950

Shuhe Old Town (Shùhé Gǔzhèn) attracts plenty of travellers looking for the perfect portrait, and we have to admit it is an inherently photogenic area to wander. A former staging post on the Tea Horse Road that's just 4km from Lijiang, Shuhe can be visited in a day, or makes a slightly less frenetic base for exploring the region.

Although there are a handful of sights, including the Tea Horse Road Museum, the picturesque cobblestone alleys and streets of the old town are the main draw. Head for the original section of town, which is sandwiched between the Jiuding and Qinglong Rivers and nestles beneath the foothills of Jade Dragon Snow Mountain. The eastern side of town is actually completely new; though constructed in the old style, it was built for the purposes of tourism.

Tea Horse Road Museum

MUSEUM

(茶马古道博物馆, Chá Mǎ Gǔdào Bówùguǎn; ☑888 517 4636; ¥30; ⏰8.30am-5.30pm) Exhibits here are heavy on artefacts and historic photos of the Tea Horse Road era, but light on English signage. The main reason to visit is the building itself, tastefully restored to retain much of the original material.

Lazy Tiger Inn

B&B ¥¥¥

(懒老虎客栈, Lǎn Lǎohǔ Kèzhàn; ☑151 2609 9450; www.lazytigerinn.com; 54 Zhonghe Lu, 中和路54号; r ¥466, ste ¥566-668 incl breakfast) This intimate courtyard-home guesthouse run by a Chinese-Canadian couple is one of the most pleasant spaces in Shuhe Old Town, but with only six rooms it can book up fast. Discounts are available in low season.

★ 1 Restaurant

YUNNAN ¥¥¥

(壹餐厅, Yī Cāntīng; ☑888 513 6681; 14 Renli Lu, 仁里路14号; dishes ¥28-128; ⏰11am-9pm; 🐾) Built into a historic courtyard house once owned by a trader of the Tea Horse Road era, the restaurant's very modern menu features Yunnanese and Naxi specialties and even a few truffle dishes. Ask if a table is available out on the patio overlooking the old town.

ℹ Getting There & Away

Getting to Shuhe from Lijiang is easy, with local buses 5 and 6 (¥1, 20 minutes) both running here. A taxi should cost around ¥20.

Tiger Leaping Gorge 虎跳峡

☑0887

Gingerly stepping along a trail swept with scree to allow an old fellow with a donkey to pass; resting atop a rock, exhausted, looking up to see the snow-shrouded peaks, then down to see the lingering rays dancing on the rippling waters a thousand metres below. That pretty much sums up Tiger Leaping Gorge (Hǔtiào Xiá), long one of the great treks of southwest China. Add in modern development, power lines and water pipes that follow the high trail, and a few stretches of road walking: this is no longer wild nature, but the views are still grand and it's still worth the trip.

One of the deepest gorges in the world, it measures 16km long and is a giddy 3900m from the waters of the Jinsha River to the snowcapped mountains of Haba Mountain to the west and Jade Dragon Snow Mountain to the east.

Tiger Leaping Gorge

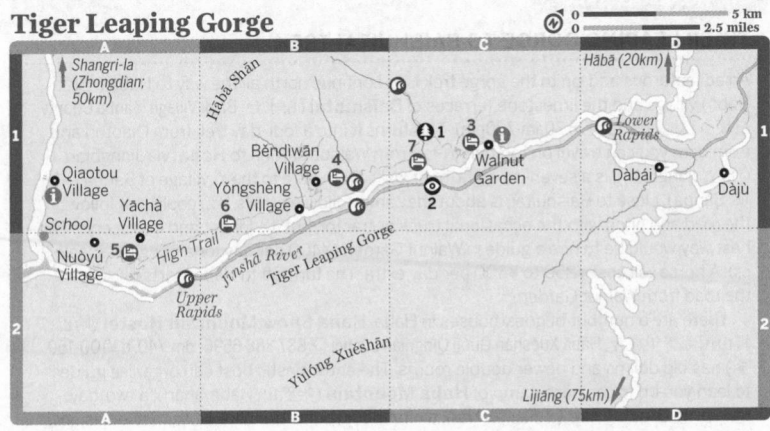

0 — 5 km
0 — 2.5 miles

Tiger Leaping Gorge

🏃 Activities

There are two trails: the higher and the lower; the latter follows the road and is best avoided. While the scenery is stunning wherever you are in the gorge, it's absolutely sublime from the high trail. Make sure you don't get too distracted by all that beauty, though, and so miss the blue signs and red arrows that help you avoid getting lost on the trail.

At the time of research, a new highway was being tunnelled through part of the gorge, resulting in a diversion at the start of the high trail which makes the route an hour or so longer. From the **Qiaotou ticket office** (regular/student ¥45/25), it's seven hours to Bendiwan, nine hours to Middle Gorge (Tina's Guesthouse), or 10 hours to Walnut Garden. It's much more fun, and a lot less exhausting, to do the trek over two days. By stopping overnight at one of the many guesthouses along the way, you'll have the time to appreciate the magnificent vistas on offer at almost every turn of the trail.

Ponies can be hired (¥200) to take you to the gorge's highest point.

🏃 The High Route

The main hiking route along the higher road starts 1km past the main ticket office, where you'll need to buy a ticket (regular/student admission ¥45/25). Walk through **Qiaotou** (桥头, Qiáotóu), past the school for five minutes or so, then head up the paved road that forks to the left. After about 2.5km on the road, look for the blue sign pointing to the High Trail just beyond a tiny settlement. The serious climbing starts straight away with a steep ascent, but levels out a bit around 3.3km in, and then descends into **Nuoyu** (诺余, Nuòyú) village and past the Naxi Family Guesthouse (p724).

The toughest section of the trek comes after Nuoyu, when the trail is a paved path until it winds up the 28 Bends, or turns, that lead to the highest point of the gorge. Count on six hours at a standard pace to get through here and to reach **Yacha** (牙叉, Yāchà) village and the Tea Horse Guesthouse (p724).

It's a relatively straightforward walk on to **Bendiwan** (本地湾, Běndìwān), following the road out of Yacha until the trail drops into a foot path at a sign for Halfway Guesthouse (p725). The stretch that follows is among the most beautiful scenery of the entire hike, detouring up small side canyons and with incredible views of the massif throughout. About 1½ hours on from Bendiwan, you begin the descent to the road on slippery, sometimes precarious paths. Watch your step here; if you twist an ankle, it's a long hop down.

After the path meets the road at Tina's Guesthouse (p725), there's a good detour that leads down to the Middle Rapids and **Tiger Leaping Stone** (虎跳石, Hǔ Tiào Shí; ¥15),

TIGER LEAPING GORGE TO BAISHUITAI TREK

An adventurous add-on to the gorge trek is to continue north all the way to Haba (哈巴, Hābā) village and the limestone terraces of **Baishuitai** (白水台; Baidi Village, Sanba County, 三坝乡白水村; ¥30; ☉6.30am-7.30pm). This turns it into a four-day trek from Qiaotou and from here you can travel on to Shangri-la. From Walnut Garden to **Haba**, via Jiangbian (江边, Jiāngbiān), is a seven- to-eight-hour walk. From here to the Yi village of Sanba (三坝, Sānbà), close to Baishuitai, is about the same, following trails. You could just follow the road and hitch with the occasional truck or tractor, but it's longer and less scenic. The best way would be to hire a guide in Walnut Garden (¥400 per day for an English speaker). A horse will cost ¥250 to ¥300 per day extra. The turn-off to Haba starts 6km down the road from Walnut Garden.

There are a number of guesthouses in Haba. **Haba Snow Mountain Hostel** (哈巴 雪山国际青年旅舍, Hābā Xuěshān Guójì Qīngnián Lǚshě; ☎887 886 6596; dm ¥40, d ¥100-150; ☎) has old dorms and newer double rooms. The enthusiastic host can organise guides to lead you up to the base camp of **Haba Mountain** (哈巴山, Hābā Shān), a two-day trek, or to **Black Lake** (黑海, Hēi Hǎi), a nine-hour round-trip hike. Note that locals now charge a ¥200 'protection fee' per person for access to the mountain, supposedly going towards conservation efforts.

The irregular bus to Sanba passes Tina's Guesthouse around 1pm (¥40, two hours) and Walnut Garden shortly thereafter, but only if the road is open. One bus from Baishuitai to Shangri-la goes through Sanba around noon (¥24, two hours). Minivans frequently ply these routes so flagging down a ride isn't too tough.

If you plan to hike the route alone, assume you'll need all provisions and equipment for extremes of weather. Ask for local advice before setting out.

where a tiger is once said to have leapt across the river, thus giving the gorge its name. Locals charge ¥15 to go down the path and it's a two-hour round trip. At the bottom of this insanely steep trail locals charge another ¥15 for one viewpoint but another spot is free. From the bottom of the gorge the beautiful 'Ray of Sunshine' trail (another ¥15) heads downstream for a one-hour walk to **Walnut Garden** (核桃园, Hétáo Yuán), where you'll find Sean's Spring Guesthouse and **Chateau de Woody** (山白脸旅馆, Shānbáiliǎn Lǚguǎn; ☎139 8875 6901; sgrlwoody@163.com; dm/d ¥30/120; ☎). If you get to the eastern **ticket office** (regular/student admission ¥45/25), you've passed the guesthouses.

Many hikers stay at Tina's, stay overnight, and head on to Lijiang or Shangri-la the next day. Those continuing to Walnut Garden can take the trail along the river or use an alternative trail that keeps high (where the path descends to Tina's), crosses a stream and a '**bamboo forest**' (竹林, Zhúlín) before descending into Walnut Garden. If you are debating where to spend the night, Walnut Garden is far more attractive than Tina's.

🛏 Sleeping & Eating

There are numerous accommodation options along the trek through the gorge; you'll find them generally every hour or two as you go. In the unlikely event that everywhere is full, basic rooms will be available with a local. We've never heard of anyone who had to sleep rough in the gorge.

All the guesthouses double as restaurants and shops, where you can have meals, or pick up water and snacks. A few hardy vendors can be found along the high trail as far as Běndiwān, selling water, fruit and chocolate bars.

★ **Tea Horse Guesthouse**   GUESTHOUSE ¥
(茶马客栈, Chámǎ Kèzhàn; ☎139 8870 7922; dm/d ¥35/150; ☎) Just above Yāchà village, this ever-expanding place has a reasonable restaurant – it makes a sensible lunch stop – as well as a small spa and massage parlour, but the main draw is the indescribably beautiful view from the upstairs terrace. The cheapest rooms share bathrooms; the most expensive are very big and have good beds, modern bathrooms and shared balconies.

Naxi Family Guesthouse   GUESTHOUSE ¥
(纳西雅阁, Nàxī Yǎgé; ☎139 9875 8424, 0887 880 6928; www.yunnantrekking.com; dm/d ¥30/120; ☎) This is an incredibly friendly, well-run place (with organic veggies and wines), set around a pleasant courtyard; as an overnight

stop, however, it will be of use mostly to travellers hiking eastwards towards Qiaotou.

Tina's Guesthouse　　　　　GUESTHOUSE ¥
(中峡旅店, Zhōngxiá Lǚdiàn; ☑ 887 820 2258; tina999@live.com; Middle Tiger Leaping Gorge, 中虎跳峡; 8-/3-bed dm ¥30/50, d ¥120-280; @ 🖘) Almost a package-holiday operation, with travellers funnelled to and from the gorge. Tina's lacks the charm of its competitors, but it's efficiently run, has plenty of beds and the location is perfect for those too knackered to make it to Walnut Garden. Pricier upstairs rooms have excellent views.

Halfway Guesthouse　　　　GUESTHOUSE ¥¥
(中途客栈, Zhōngtú Kèzhàn; ☑ 131 7079 5128; Bèndiwān; dm ¥40, d ¥120-300; 🖘) Once the simple family home of a local guy collecting medicinal herbs, this is now a busy and constantly expanding operation set around a courtyard and with a great roof terrace. The vistas here are awe-inspiring and among the best of any lodging in the gorge; the view from the communal toilets alone is worth the price of a bed.

Sean's Spring Guesthouse　　GUESTHOUSE ¥¥
(山泉客栈, Shānquán Kèzhàn; ☑ 0887 820 2223, 158 9436 7846; www.tigerleapinggorge.com; Walnut Garden; dm ¥60, r ¥180-300; 🖘) One of the original guesthouses on the trail. The eponymous Sean is a true character, a good source of travel info and one of the few locals seriously concerned with the gorge's environmental well-being. There are 28 rooms here, including a couple of cheapies; the best have great views of Jade Dragon Snow Mountain. The meals are all-organic and tasty.

❶ Getting There & Away

From Lijiang's long-distance bus station there is one direct bus a day to Tiger Leaping Gorge at 8.30am (¥35, two hours). Otherwise, catch any bus to Shangri-la (¥62, 3½ hours, 19 daily, from 7.30am to 5.10pm) and get off at Qiaotou – you'll walk about an extra hour to join the hiking route.

Some travellers get a minivan (¥35 per person) to the start of the walking track, organised through their guesthouse in Lijiang. The minivan can usually deliver extra luggage to the guesthouse of your choice (generally Tina's, allowing you to hike the gorge and then head directly to Shangri-la without backtracking to Lijiang).

Returning to Lijiang from Qiaotou, buses start passing through from Shangri-la at around 9.30am; the last one rolls through at around 8pm. The last bus to Shangri-la passes through at around 6.30pm. Guesthouses also coordinate with one bus a day to both Lijiang (¥40) and Shangri-la (¥45) at 3.30pm, and it's possible to get on either from Walnut Garden as well.

There is one daily bus to Baishuitai from Lijiang at 9am (¥38, five hours), though it doesn't reliably run every day. It passes Tina's around 1pm and Walnut Garden shortly thereafter.

Lugu Lake　　　　泸沽湖

☑ 0888 / ELEV 2690M

Straddling a remote stretch of the Yunnan-Sichuan border, Lugu Lake (Lúgū Hú) is an absolutely idyllic place, even with growing numbers of domestic tourists. Your first sight of the 50-sq-km body of water, surrounded by lushly forested slopes, will take your breath away – as will the 2690m elevation. Upon entering the area you'll be expected to purchase a ¥70 ticket.

The area is home to several Tibetan, Yi and Mosuo (a Naxi subgroup) villages. The

---

❶ DANGERS OF THE TREK

The gorge hike is not to be taken lightly. Even for those in good physical shape, it can be a workout and tough on the knees. The path is alarmingly narrow in places, making it sometimes dangerous. When it's raining (especially in July and August), landslides and swollen waterfalls can block the paths, in particular on the low road. (The best time to come is May and the start of June, when the hills are afire with plant and flower life.)

A few people – including a handful of foreign travellers – have died in the gorge. During the past decade, there have also been cases of travellers being assaulted on the trail. It's safer in all ways not to do the hike alone – though it is rare that anybody reports serious problems.

Check with cafes and lodgings in Lijiang or Qiaotou for trail and weather updates. Most have fairly detailed gorge maps; just remember they're not to scale and are occasionally out of date.

You can buy water along the way at the guesthouses on the route, but make sure to bring plenty of sunscreen and lip balm.

VILLAGES AROUND LUGU LAKE

Villages are scattered around the outskirts of the lake. **Luoshui** (洛水, Luòshuǐ) is the biggest and most developed, and where the bus will drop you. As well as guesthouses, restaurants and a few cafes with English menus and western food, there are the inevitable souvenir shops and a handful of bars with music. Away from them, though, the dominant night-time sound is the lapping of the lake.

Most travellers move quickly to **Lige** (里格, Lǐgé), 9km further up the road, tucked into a bay on the northwestern shore of the lake. Although guesthouses make up most of the place, along with restaurants serving succulent barbecue, the nights here are lovely. If you want a less touristy experience, then you need to keep village-hopping around the lake to the Sichuan side. Top votes for alternative locations are Luowa (洛瓦, Luòwǎ), Wuzhiluo (五支罗, Wǔzhīluó) and Zhaojiawan (赵家湾, Zhàojiāwān).

Mosuo are the last practising matriarchal society in the world and many other Naxi customs lost in Lijiang are still in evidence here.

⊙ Sights

From lakeside villages Luoshui and Lige you can punt about with local Mosuo by dugout canoe – known by the Mosuo as 'pig troughs' (*zhūcáo chuān*). Expect to head for **Liwubi Island** (里务比岛, Lǐwùbǐ Dǎo), the lake's largest (where you can throw a stone into Sichuan), or second-largest **Heiwae** (黑瓦俄岛, Hēiwǎé Dǎo), both of which feature small temples. Boat-trip prices are posted at the wharves in Luoshui and Lige, though in low season it's certainly worth trying to haggle. Boats run roughly from 8.30am to 5pm.

Mosuo Folk Custom Museum   MUSEUM
(摩梭民俗博物馆, Mósuō Mínzú Bówùguǎn; ☑888 581 2345; Luoshui; ¥30; ⊙9am-5pm) This museum in Luoshui is set within the traditional home of a wealthy Mosuo family, and the obligatory guide will explain (in Chinese only) how the matriarchal society functions. There is also an interesting collection of photos taken by Joseph Rock in the 1920s.

🛏 Sleeping & Eating

Gēwǎ Yínhú Yuèpàn   HOTEL ¥
(戈瓦银湖月畔; ☑135 4134 4144; 26 Binhe Lu, Luoshui, 滨河路26号; rm ¥150-200) Tucked away on the quieter northern stretch of Luoshui's lakefront road, the 2nd-floor rooms with balconies overlooking the lakeside here are among the best value on Lugu.

Husi Teahouse   HOSTEL ¥
(湖思茶屋, Húsī Cháwū; ☑888 588 6960; www.husihostel.com; Luoshui; dm ¥45-50, rm ¥128-280; @🕾) The old man of the Lugu Lake hostels, this multistorey complex of dorms and private rooms is still a mainstay. The more expensive rooms come with excellent lake views. There's a big communal area with computers and a restaurant serving Chinese food and average western meals, while the coffee is the best of the few places in town that serve it.

Lǚxíngzhě Zhǐjiā   HOTEL ¥¥¥
(旅行者之家; ☑888 588 1196; Lige; rm ¥380-420; 🕾) On the edge of the Lige peninsula, all the rooms here come with decent views, but the 2nd-floor views are tremendous and worth the small price increase. They're a little overpriced but the bathrooms are a cut above the rest in the village. In the attached restaurant, try Lugu Lake fish (泸沽湖鱼, Lúgū Hú yú) or sausage (香肠, xiāngcháng).

Zhāxī Cāntīng   BARBECUE ¥¥
(扎西餐厅; ☑888 588 1055; Lige; dishes ¥25-100; ⊙11am-11pm; 🕾) Lively restaurant and barbecue joint that's great for the local speciality, Mosuo pork (from ¥50), which you cook yourself on tabletop wood-fired grills. It's popular anytime, but the atmosphere becomes particularly festive in the evenings when cold beer washes down the superb barbecue.

ℹ Getting There & Away

On arrival at the Lugu Lake Scenic Area, you'll be expected to briefly step off to buy a ticket. Make a note of your bus number so you can find it in the parking lot on the far side.

AIR

Ninglong Luguhu Airport (NLH), 42km southwest of Luoshui, has daily flights to Kunming (from ¥462), Chongqing (from ¥576), and Chengdu (from ¥519) in the high season.

A local Airport Express Bus (机场快线, Jīchǎng Kuàixiàn) connects the airport to Luoshui's bus station (¥30). Return trips are timed to depart Luoshui based on flight departures.

BUS

From the tiny Luoshui bus station (洛水客运站, Luòshuǐ Kèyùnzhàn) there are two daily buses to Lijiang (¥71, 4½ hours) at 9am and 10am, though in high season there may be up to nine. Tickets should be bought at least a day in advance. You can also catch one of the regular minivans to Ninglang (宁蒗, Nínglàng; ¥30, one hour), from where there are three buses daily to Lijiang. Daily buses to Xichang (西昌, Xīchāng) in Sichuan depart at 11am (¥110, seven hours).

For Lige you'll need to change for a minibus in Luoshui (¥20 per person, 30 minutes) or hire a bike.

Shangri-la   香格里拉

☑ 0887 / POP 173,000 / ELEV 3200M

Shangri-la (Xiānggélǐlā), formerly known as Zhongdian (中甸, Zhōngdiàn) and sometimes 'Gyalthang' in Tibetan, is where you really start to breathe in the Tibetan world – if you can breathe at all, given the altitude.

Home to one of Yunnan's most important monasteries and surrounded by mountains, lakes and grassland, it's also the last stop in Yunnan before a rough five- to six-day journey to Chengdu via the Tibetan townships and rugged terrain of western Sichuan.

The town is divided into two distinct sections: the larger modern side and the old quarter. A devastating fire in January 2014 sent much of the old town up in smoke, but it's now been almost completely rebuilt. Most of the places you'll visit in the new town are within walking distance of the old town, making getting around easy.

Plan your visit for between March or April and October. During winter, Shangri-la is still busy but it gets very cold indeed, although spectacular mountain views can be the reward for braving the frigid temperatures.

In mid- to late June, the town hosts a **horse-racing festival** that sees several days of dancing, singing, eating and, of course, horse racing. Accommodation is tight at this time.

⊙ Sights

The mountains surrounding Shangri-la are a wonderful place for getting off the beaten track, with plenty of trekking and horse-riding opportunities, as well as little-visited monasteries and villages. However, the remote sights are difficult to reach independently given the lack of public transport.

YUNNAN SHANGRI-LA

SHANGRI-LA: FACT & FICTION

At first it seemed like a typically overstated tourist campaign: 'Shangri-la Found'. Only they weren't kidding. In November 1997 'experts' had established with 'certainty' that the fabled 'Shangri-la' of James Hilton's 1933 bestseller *Lost Horizon* was, indeed, in Deqin County.

Hilton's novel (later filmed by Frank Capra and starring Ronald Coleman and Jane Wyatt) tells the story of four travellers who are hijacked and crash-land in a mountain utopia ruled by a 163-year-old holy man. This 'Shangri-la' is in the Valley of the Blue Moon, a beautiful fertile valley backed by a perfect pyramid peak, Mt Karakul.

The claim is based primarily on the fact that Deqin's Kawa Karpo peak resembles the 'pyramid-shaped' landmark of Mt Karakul. Also, the county's blood-red valleys with three parallel rivers fit a valley from *Lost Horizon*.

One plausible theory is that Hilton, writing the novel in northwest London, based his descriptions of Shangri-la on articles by Joseph Rock that he had read in *National Geographic* magazine, detailing Rock's expeditions to remote parts of Lijiang and Deqin. Hilton's invented place name 'Shangri-la' may have been a corruption of the word *Shambhala*, a mystical Buddhist paradise.

After Deqin staked its claim to the name Shangri-la, rival bids popped up around Yunnan. Cízhōng in Wěixī County pointed out that its Catholic churches and Tibetan monasteries live side by side in the valley. Meanwhile, Dàochéng, just over the border in Sichuan, had a strong bid based around the pyramid peak of its mountain Channa Dorje and the fact that Rock wrote about the region in several articles.

Cynics have had a field day with this and the resulting hijacking of the concept, part of which was to establish tourism as an industry to replace logging, which had been banned.

Shangri-la is at its heart surely a metaphor. As a skinny-dipping Jane Wyatt says in the film version of the book: 'I'm sure there's a wish for Shangri-la in everyone's heart...'

Shangri-la

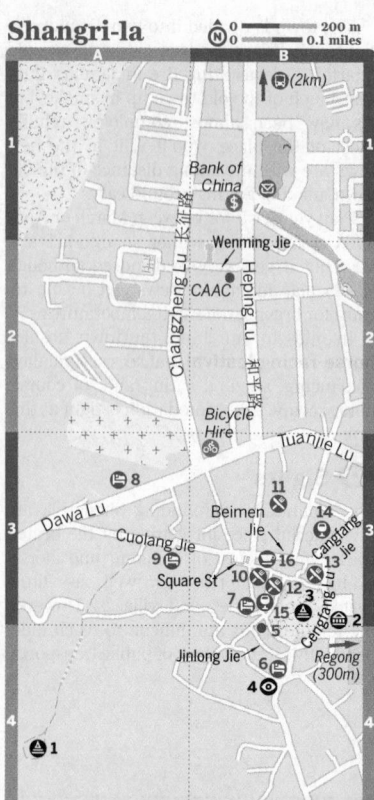

Deqin Tibetan Autonomous Prefecture Museum   MUSEUM

(迪庆藏族自治州博物馆, Díqìng Zàngzú Zìzhìzhōu Bówùguǎn; ☑887 822 6610; Yueguang Square, 月光广场; ⊗9am-5pm) FREE Attractive modern permanent exhibitions on local history, folk traditions and religious culture make this a worthwhile stop before or after the Guishan Buddhist Temple (even if English captions are somewhat limited). Rotating exhibitions are hit or miss, but have a look at whatever is on. It also makes a strange counterpoint to the heavily propagandistic **Long March Museum** across the square.

Guishan Buddhist Temple   BUDDHIST TEMPLE

(龟山大佛寺, Guīshān Dàfó Sì; 9 Lunholang, 伦火廊9号) FREE Atop 'Great Turtle Hill' in the heart of the old town, this modern temple stands on the site of an original 1667 construction consecrated to a replica of the Sakyamuni statue in Lhasa's Jokhang Temple.

Shangri-la Thangka Academy   CULTURAL CENTRE

(唐卡学会, Tángkǎ Xuéhuì; ☑887 888 1612; 31 Jinlong Jie, 金龙街31号; ⊗9am-9pm) Thangka master Lobsang Khudup trains young students in painting and Buddhist philosophy here. Even if you're not in the market to buy, it's worth stopping in to see the process of creation.

Ganden Sumtseling Gompa   MONASTERY

(松赞林寺, Sōngzànlín Sì; 尼旺路, Níwàng Lù; ¥55; ⊗7am-7pm) This 300-year-old Tibetan monastery complex about 4km north of the old town is home to around 600 monks. Extensive rebuilding has robbed the monastery of some of its charm, but it remains the most important in southwest China and is definitely worth the visit. Bus 3 runs here from anywhere along Changzheng Lu (¥1). From the main gate where the tickets are sold you can catch a tourist bus (¥10 one-way) or walk the final 2km to the monastery.

Gyalthang Ringha Monastery   BUDDHIST TEMPLE

(大宝寺, Dàbǎo Sì; ¥20) One of the oldest Buddhist temples in Yunnan, local monks claim this small hilltop temple in a walled forest reserve is at least 500 years old and perhaps much older. Don't miss the delightful time-worn murals on the walls of the main hall.

The temple is around 19km east of Shangri-la just beyond Siya (司牙, Sīyá) village. No public transport goes all the way to the temple, but it's a good end point for a bike ride or a stop en route if you're hiring a taxi to Pudacuo.

Pudacuo National Park   LAKE

(普达措国家公园, Pǔdácuò Guójiā Gōngyuán; ☑ 887 823 2529; ¥100; ⊙ ticket office 7.30am-4pm) China's first national park, this collection of small mountain lakes is about 25km east of Shangri-la. From the visitor centre, a 20-minute bus ride drops travellers on the shore of **Shudu Lake** (属都湖, Shǔdū Hú). Follow the 3.3km wooden boardwalk around the shore of the lake, where buses wait to whisk you back to the visitor centre.

Bǎijī Sì   BUDDHIST TEMPLE

(百鸡寺, 100 Chickens Temple) **FREE** For the best views over Shangri-la, head to this delightfully named and little-visited temple. The temple has a couple of monks inside and a handful of chickens wandering around outside. To get here, walk along the narrow paths behind Kersang's Relay Station, past the deserted temple, continue uphill and you'll see it on the left. It's busiest in the mornings, when locals come to make offerings.

Nàpà Hǎi   LAKE

(纳帕海) **FREE** Some 7km northwest of Shangri-la you'll find the seasonal Napa Sea, surrounded by a large grassy meadow that pushes right up to the mountains. Between September and March it attracts many rare species, including the black-necked crane. Outside of these months, the lake dries up and you can see high numbers of yaks and cattle grazing. During the wet season, the small road that circles the lake makes an excellent bike or motorbike day trip from Shangri-la.

👉 Tours

Caravane Liotard   TOURS

(☑ 188 0693 2184; www.caravane-liotard.com; 91 Jinlong Jie, 金龙街91号) Named after a legendary French explorer, this French-run outfit specialises in adventure tours along the former routes of the Tea Horse Road. Enquire at Flying Tigers Cafe (p730).

Khampa Caravan   TOURS

(康巴商道探险旅行社, Kāngbā Shāngdào Tànxiǎn Lǚxíngshè; ☑ 887 828 8648; www.khampacaravan.

com; Jinlong Jie, 金龙街; ⊙ 9am-noon & 2-5.30pm Mon-Fri) This well-established, Tibetan-run outfit organises some excellent treks and overland journeys – inside Tibet, too – that get good feedback, as well as homestays with Tibetan families. The company also runs a lot of sustainable development programs within Tibetan communities. See www.shangrila association.org for more details.

🛏 Sleeping

There is a wide choice of guesthouses and hotels here, with the cheapest digs (¥60 and up per room) to be found around the bus station, but much nicer accommodation in and around the old town. Despite Shangri-la's often glacial night-time temperatures, some cheaper guesthouse and hotel rooms are not heated.

Tavern   GUESTHOUSE ¥

(仁和客栈, Rénhé Kèzhàn; ☑ 887 888 1147; christinhe@hotmail.com; 47 Cuolang Jie, 措廊街 47号; dm ¥40, d without/with bathroom ¥90/120; 🐾@🛜) The private rooms here are distinctive, with Tibetan motifs and big comfortable beds. Dorms are more basic, but there's a nice communal area with a big stove to keep warm by and a small garden and efficient staff. Western, Korean and Naxi meals are available. The 11pm curfew may be a problem for some.

Kersang's Relay Station   INN ¥

(格桑藏驿, Gésāng Zàng Yì; ☑ 887 822 3118; kersangs@yahoo.com; 1 Yamenlang, Jinlong Jie, 衙 门廊1号, 金龙街; dm ¥40, r ¥150-200; @🛜) Rooms at this friendly Tibetan-run place are cosy, with modern bathrooms, and come with much-needed electric blankets. There's a communal lounge, pleasant staff and a cool rooftop terrace with great views of Guishan Buddhist Temple. Upper-floor rooms are more expensive, but if you appreciate a view it's worth the price.

Desti Hostel   HOSTEL ¥¥

(背包十年青年公园, Bēibāo Shínián Qīngnián Gōngyuán; ☑ 130 3860 8855; Chenni Village, 称 尼村; dm ¥45-60, d ¥280-380; @🛜) Unusual upmarket hostel located in a huge converted Tibetan house in a village just outside town, close to the grasslands and mountains. Tibetan-run, it has numerous communal areas, while dorms are heated and come with individual reading lights, USB sockets and comfy beds. Private rooms retain the original wood features of the former house.

WEIXI

Around Shangri-la are any number of sights: villages, mountains, meadows, ponds and *chörten* (Tibetan stupas) waiting to be explored.

Local travellers rave about **Weixi** (维西, Wéixī), an area 80km southwest of Shangri-la sometimes known as 'the Rocky Mountains of Yunnan' for their visual similarity to the mountain range in Colorado. There are four buses a day to Weixi (¥74, five hours; 8.50am, 10.30am, noon and 2pm) from Shangri-la's bus station; bear in mind that it's a bad road.

The real draw here is the chance to interact with the local villagers. You can herd yaks, help a Tibetan family farm before eating with them, study Tibetan and *thangka* painting, ride horses or trek into the mountains. It's a 20-minute bike ride from town.

Kevin's Trekker Inn GUESTHOUSE ¥¥
(龙门客栈, Lóngmén Kèzhàn; 887 822 8178; 138 Dawa Lu, 达娃路138号; d ¥138-298; @) Staff at this guesthouse are friendly, helpful and full of tips for exploring the area. It has a cosy lounge and rooms that range from the cheap and boxy to the very comfortable, with good bathrooms and views over the newly rebuilt old town. It's located just off Dawa Lu behind the Long Xiang Inn.

Red Hill B&B B&B ¥¥¥
(红坡客栈, Hóngpō Kèzhàn; 187 0887 1463; www.redhillbnb.com; Hongpo Village, 红坡村; r ¥650-750;) With large, bright rooms and beautiful common areas overlooking Hongpo village and the snowy mountains in the distance, you may never want to leave this little American-run B&B about 12km east of Shangri-la. It's small and books up quickly, though, so reserve well in advance. They can arrange transfers from town.

Arro Khampa Hotel BOUTIQUE HOTEL ¥¥¥
(阿若康巴南索达庄园, Āruòkāngbā Nánsuǒdá Zhuāngyuán; 887 888 1007; arrokhampa@vip. sina.com; 15 Jinlong Jie Donglang, 金龙街东廊15 号; d ¥980;) Hushed boutique hotel with 18 swish rooms set around a flagstone courtyard. Excellent beds and bathrooms, and the underfloor heating keeps everything toasty warm. There's a restaurant offering Chinese and Tibetan dishes on-site, and a nice bar terrace with a fire pit and excellent views of Guishan Buddhist Temple.

✗ Eating

Silent Holy Stones TIBETAN ¥
(静静的嘛呢石, Jìngjìngde Manishí; 887 828 6627; 1 Zuobarui, 作巴瑞号; dishes ¥18-58; 8am-10.30pm;) Long a favourite spot for

local Tibetans, this relaxed and welcoming place specialises in yak-meat hotpots (from ¥148). Great *mómo* (馍馍, Tibetan dumplings) too, which come with a spicy dipping sauce, as well as a small selection of vegetable and mushroom dishes.

★**Flying Tigers Cafe** INTERNATIONAL ¥¥
(飞虎, Fēihǔ; 887 828 6661; 91 Jinlong Jie, 金龙 街91号; mains ¥40-98; 11am-10.30pm Mon-Sat;) French-run bistro in a hundred-year-old courtyard house, with the finest wine list in town (from ¥30 a glass) and a diverse local and international menu that utilises local ingredients. Try the house-made mushroom ravioli or the yak burger. There's also an extensive bar menu of cocktails and, of course, Shangri-La Beer. You may even find yourself coming back.

Xiao Cai Cafe INTERNATIONAL ¥¥
(小菜咖啡, Xiǎocài Kāfēi; 139 8878 8737; 19 Dugushuo, 独古硕19号; dishes ¥20-98; 9am-10pm;) Built into a hundred-year-old wooden building rebuilt in original form after the 2014 fire, this small cafe just off the main square is one of the prettiest places in town. There's a nice range of Chinese and western dishes on the menu, plus coffee and sweets.

Kailash TIBETAN, CHINESE ¥¥
(格拉夏餐吧, Gélāxià Cānba; 887 822 5505; 20 Beimen Ji, Laojie Xiang, 北门街20号老街巷; dishes ¥15-68; 10am-10pm;) This reliable long-standing restaurant serves up a mix of Tibetan, Indian and Chinese dishes in a Tibetan-teahouse atmosphere. It's down Old Street (老街, Lǎo Jiē) alley just off Beimen Jie: look for the gateway marking the entrance.

Compass INTERNATIONAL ¥¥
(舒灯库乐, Shūdēng kùlè; 887 822 3638; 3 Chilang Gang, 池廊冈3号; mains from ¥40; 9am-10pm Tue-Sun;) Bustling spot for a fine breakfast, and a popular hang-out for international travellers. Salads, steaks, pasta and pizzas are all available, as well as a few generic Asian dishes. Great cakes and coffee;

it's nonsmoking, too. It's an ideal place to take a break from sightseeing, plus there's a small selection of handicrafts if you need to pick up souvenirs.

Drinking & Nightlife

★ Raven
BAR

(乌鸦酒吧, Wūyā Jiǔbā; ☑ 887 881 1663; 11 Chigu Lang, 池古廊11号; beers from ¥20; ⏰ 7pm-late; 🛜) Raven is the best bar in town and one of the best in northwest Yunnan, with a huge range of beers and spirits and a small selection of pub food. There's a big bar counter to sit around, sofas to sink into, New York–style pizzas (from ¥45), a pool table and decent sounds.

Shangri-La Beer Bar
CRAFT BEER

(香格里拉啤酒吧, Xiānggélǐlā Píjiǔ Bā; 17 Dong Lang, 东廊17号; ⏰ 7pm-late) Drink Shangri-la's favourite local craft beer straight from the source – they've got all the varieties on tap, plus a handful of international wines, beers and spirits.

Yunnan Arabica Coffee
COFFEE

(云南小粒咖啡, Yúnnán Xiǎolì Kāfēi; ☑ 186 8797 5198; 43 Beimen Jie, 北门街43号; ⏰ 9.30am-10pm) Local beans and a handful of sweets at this local coffee chain will see you through a day of sightseeing around Shangri-la.

ℹ Information

Altitude sickness can be a problem here and most travellers need a couple of days to acclimatise.

Bank of China (中国银行, Zhōngguó Yínháng; Chicika Jie, 池慈卡街; ⏰ 9am-5pm Mon-Fri) Has a 24-hour ATM and changes US dollars. Many other ATMs around town take foreign cards too.

Public Security Bureau (PSB, 公安局; Gōng'ānjú; ☑ 887 822 6834; Kangzhu Dadao, 康珠大道; ⏰ 9am-noon & 2.30-5.30pm Mon-Fri) Shangri-la is an excellent place to extend your visa, the local police being both accommodating and friendly, although new regulations mean the process can take between three and seven days. The PSB office is on the outskirts of town. Bus 2 (¥1) runs here from Changzheng Lu.

ℹ Getting There & Away

AIR

Shangri-la Airport (DIG) is 5km from town and is sometimes referred to as Diqing or Deqen – note that there is currently no airport at Deqin.

There are eight flights daily to Kunming (¥520) and daily flights to Chengdu (¥610), Shanghai (¥1322) and Xishuangbanna (¥580). In peak season one daily flight also leaves for Lhasa (¥2480). Flights for other domestic destinations also leave from the airport but these can change from week to week. If booking online, you need to type in 'Diqing' for the airport name.

BUS

Note that bus tickets may refer to either Shangri-la or Zhongdian, but usually the former. Destinations from Shangri-la include the following:

Baishuitai ¥35, two hours, one daily (9.10am)

Daocheng ¥133, 11 hours, one daily (8am)

Deqin ¥62, four hours, five daily (8.20am, 9.20am, 10.30am, 12.30pm and 2.30pm)

Jianchuan ¥50, five hours, two daily (9.15am and 2.50pm)

Kunming ¥223 to ¥264, 10 hours, four daily (8.30am, 2pm, 6pm and 7pm)

Lijiang ¥62 to ¥68, four hours, every 30 minutes (7.20am to 4pm)

Xiaguan ¥101 to ¥123, seven hours, seven daily (8am to 6.30pm)

If you're up for the bus-hopping trek to Chengdu in Sichuan, you're looking at a minimum of three to four days' travel (often five to six) at some very high altitudes – you'll need warm clothes. Note that for political reasons this road may be closed at any time of the year (if the ticket seller at the bus says 'come back tomorrow', it's closed indefinitely for sure).

If you can get a ticket, the first stage of the trip is to Daocheng in Sichuan. From there you'll hop through Litang and Kangding and finally to Chengdu.

ℹ OVERLAND TO TIBET

At the time of writing it is once again possible to enter Tibet overland from Shangri-la with the proper contacts and permits, as long as you are part of an organised group with a tour agent. If you're tempted to try and sneak in, then think again. There are many checkpoints operating on the road between Shangri-la and Lhasa; you will be caught, fined, detained, escorted to Chengdu by the police and deported at your own expense. Any local person believed to have assisted you (for example by giving you a ride) will get into worse trouble.

It is possible to fly to Lhasa from Shangri-la, but flights are cheaper from elsewhere (Kunming and Chengdu), and you'll still need to be part of an organised group with all the necessary permits (p942).

Roads out of Shangri-la can be temporarily blocked by snow at any time from November to March. Bring a flexible itinerary.

TRAIN

A railway from Lijiang to Shangri-la has been under construction and is expected to be operational in 2020.

❶ Getting Around

The bus station is 2.5km north of the old town, straight up Xiangbala Dadao. Aside from walking, the easiest way to the old town (古城, gǔchéng) is to take local bus 1 (¥1) west along Kangding Lu until it turns south into Changzheng Lu and terminates at a stop just northwest of the old town.

From the same old town stop, bus 3 (¥1) heads up to Ganden Sumtseling Gompa.

Bikes can be hired from ¥30 a day and electric motorbikes from ¥120, including at the small **bicycle hire** (出租, Chūzū; ☑ 139 8879 9184; Changzheng Lu, 长征路; ⊙ 9am-7pm) shop on Changzheng Lu just outside the old town.

Deqin & Kawa Karpo   德钦

☑ 0887

Deqin (Déqīn) lies in some of the most ruggedly gorgeous scenery in China. Snugly cloud-high at an average altitude of 3550m, it rests in the shadow of one of China's most magical mountains, Kawa Karpo (梅里雪山, Méilǐ Xuěshān); at 6740m, it is Yunnan's highest peak and straddles the Yunnan–Tibet border.

More than 80% of locals are Tibetan, though two dozen other minorities also live here, including one of the few settlements of non-Hui Muslims in China. The town of Deqin itself is unattractive and mostly a staging post to the nearby mountains of Meili Snow Mountain National Park (梅里雪山国家公园, Méilǐ Xuěshān Guó Jiā Gōng Yuǎn) in surrounding Deqin county; all of which are incorporated by the Díqìng Tibetan Autonomous Prefecture (迪庆藏族自治州, Díqìng zàngzú zìzhìzhōu).

Beyond the town, the villages of Feilaisi, Mingyong and Yubeng serve the needs of travellers with guesthouses and restaurants.

◎ Sights

Travellers stop in the tiny strip of civilisation known as **Feilaisi** (飞来寺, Fēilái Sì) primarily for the sublime sunrise views over the Meili Snow Mountain Range peaks of Kawa Karpo and 6054m Miacimu (神女, Shénnǚ), whose spirit is the female counterpart of Kawa Karpo. Sadly, the weather doesn't always cooperate, often shrouding the peaks in mist. October and November are the likeliest months for your sunrise photo op.

Approximately 10km southwest of Deqin, a cluster of guesthouses and restaurants surround the main road leading to a viewing platform (¥40 entrance fee, valid for three consecutive days) at the end of town, the ticket for which also includes access to the small **Feilai Temple** (飞来寺, Fēilái Sì; ¥40; ⊙ 24hr). If you'd rather skip the fee, walk downhill about 200m past the end of the small wall that blocks mountain views along the main road.

Accommodation options in Feilaisi are largely overpriced, but if you're going to overnight here you may as well splurge a little on rooms with a view just opposite the viewing platform. **Méilǐ Yìjū** (梅里逸居; ☑ 151 2609 9176; rm ¥380-580) is the best bet, though expensive, while **Zàng Jí Wáng Shāngwù Jiǔdiàn** (藏吉王商务酒店; ☑ 887 302 2558; d ¥218-280; ☎) represents a less comfortable but more budget-friendly option.

Shared taxis from Deqin run regularly to Feilaisi from ¥10 per person or ¥40 per vehicle.

A separate entry ticket is required at each of the major tourist areas of the Feilaisi viewing deck, Yubeng and the Mingyong Glacier; all tickets can be purchased at the entrance to any area.

Mingyong Glacier   GLACIER
(明永冰川, Míngyǒng Bīngchuān; Mingyong; ¥55; ⊙ 8am-6pm) Tumbling off the side of Kawa Karpo peak is the 12km-long Mingyong Glacier. At over 13 sq km, it is not only the lowest glacier in China (around 2200m) but also an oddity – a monsoon marine glacier, which basically translates as having an ecosystem that couldn't possibly be more diverse: tundra, taiga, broadleaf forest and meadow. Sadly, this natural wonder is also retreating at an alarming – and increasing – rate.

The mountain, representing the embodiment of the warrior god Kawa Karpo, has been a pilgrimage site for centuries and you'll still meet a few Tibetan pilgrims, some of whom circumambulate the mountain over seven days in autumn. Surrounding villages are known as 'heaven villages' because of the dense fog that hangs about in spring and summer.

The way to the glacier leads up from Mingyong's central square. The visitor centre sells tickets (¥75 round-trip) for electric

YUBENG & KAWA KARPO HIKES

The principal reason to visit Deqin is the chance to hike to the foot of Kawa Karpo. The main destination is **Yubeng** (雨崩, Yǔbèng) village, from where you can make day hikes to mountain meadows, the Ice Lake and the fabulous Sacred Waterfall.

The five- to six-hour (10km) trek to Yubeng starts at the **Xidang Hot Spring** (西当温泉, Xīdāng Wēnquán), about 6km uphill past Xidang village. You'll pay the ¥55 entry fee for Yubeng here if you haven't already. Jeeps (¥200 per person, one hour) make the trip from the hot spring to Yubeng – they use the same road as hikers and don't slow down to pass, so remain vigilant if you're on foot.

While it is possible to overnight at simple guesthouses in Xidang (from ¥30), it's actually more efficient to overnight in **Feilaisi**, from which shared vans will deposit you directly at the hot spring. The drive from Feilaisi to Xidang takes 1½ hours.

Yubeng consists of two sections. You first arrive in 'Upper Yubeng', which contains more guesthouses, then the trail continues another 1km to 'Lower Yubeng'. Booking ahead at peak periods is a good idea, but in other seasons the abundance of rooms here rarely get full. Dorm beds in Upper Yubeng are available from ¥40 and private rooms start at ¥120. Of special note is the **Interval Time Guesthouse** (间隔时光, Jiàngé Shíguāng; ☑ 180 0887 8300; Upper Yubeng; dm/d ¥50/220; 🛜), which has knowledgable staff and decent food. Lower Yubeng is slightly cheaper (from ¥35 for dorm beds, or ¥120 for private rooms) with the **Mystic Waterfall Lodge** (神瀑客栈, Shénpù Kèzhàn; ☑ 887 841 1082; Lower Yubeng; dm/d ¥35/120; 🛜) of similar quality to other options, but in the nicest location right at the bottom of the village. Guides in the village cost around ¥200 per day. Supplies (food and water) are pricey in Yubeng, so stock up in Feilaisi.

From Yubeng village there are loads of trekking possibilities, though only the two main hikes are signposted. It's a five- to six-hour round-trip (11.6km) on foot or horseback (¥250) to the **Ice Lake** (冰湖, Bīng Hú) from Upper Yubeng, passing through rhododendron and pine forests and through the nearly pristine Xiaonong mountain pasture – site of the base camp for ill-fated Japanese climbing expeditions in 1991 and 1996.

From Lower Yubeng a 10.8km trail leads up to the **Sacred Waterfall** (神瀑, Shénpù), roughly a four- to five-hour round-trip, along a gentler slope through another beautiful forested valley. Another small lake sits high in the mountains here (around 4350m), but it's inaccessible while snow remains and even in ideal conditions you'll need a guide and a very early start.

Leaving the village, many travellers hike 14km to **Nínóng** (尼农) village by the Mekong River, a two- to four-hour downhill trek that includes a lovely one-hour section along a rocky path with steep drops down to the river below – if you are prone to vertigo, head back to Xidang instead. Vans run to Deqin and Feilaisi from Ninong for ¥30 per person or ¥200 for the whole van. If you are stuck, walk 6km to Xidang, where there's more transport.

Other options for hiking in the region include the legendary Kawa Karpo kora, a 12-day pilgrim circumambulation of Meili Snow Mountain. However, half of it is in the Tibetan Autonomous Region, so you'll need a permit to do it, and you'll definitely need a guide.

carts to shuttle you 3.6km up to the start of the walk; you can also follow the same road on foot. From the end of the cart road it's a steady uphill of 2.5km via a new staircase that rises nearly 500 vertical metres – the old horse path is visible below, but there are only a few spots where it's accessible. At the top is **Lotus Temple** (莲花庙, Liánhuā Miào), which offers incredible views of the glacier framed by prayer flags and *chörten* (Tibetan stupas). It's home to a single monk who lives here for a month at a stretch without leaving the mountain.

Mingyong village consists of only a couple of hotels, restaurants and shops. You can overnight in the very basic **Renqin Hotel** (仁钦酒店, Rénqīn Jiǔdiàn; ☑ 139 8871 4330; Mingyong; d ¥80; 🛜). From Deqin, irregular private minibuses to Mingyong leave from the bridge near the market at the top end of town (¥20 per person), or you can hire your own for around ¥150. If you're coming from Yubeng, you could also hike a high trail to Mingyong from Xidang in around three hours if you hoof it.

The road from Deqin descends into the dramatic Mekong Gorge. Six kilometres before Mingyong the road crosses the Mekong River and branches off to Xidang. There is a checkpoint here where you will need to show your national park ticket or buy one if you haven't already.

Sleeping & Eating

The best places to stay are located in Yubeng village, though some travellers will need to overnight in Feilaisi en route – conveniently also a spectacular place to catch sunrise over the peaks of Kawa Karpo.

Guesthouses double as restaurants across the region. Feilaisi and Deqin also have plenty of stand-alone restaurants.

Getting There & Away

For Shangri-la, four daily buses leave from Deqin's small bus station on the main street (¥62, four hours, 9.30am, 10.30am, 12.30pm and 4pm). There are also daily buses to Lijiang (¥122, eight hours, 7.30am), Kunming (¥277, 16 hours, 2pm) and Xiaguan (¥197, 12 hours, 3pm).

Buses depart for both Xidang and Mingyong daily at 3pm (¥30, one hour), but for both destinations a more efficient option is the private shared vans that cover the same routes. Shared taxis also make the short trip to Feilaisi for ¥10 per person or ¥40 per car.

A shared van from Feilaisi to Xidang Hot Spring will cost ¥30 per person or ¥180 for the whole van. You could also hike all the way down from Feilaisi using local roads and paths, but the way is steep and the path often crumbling, so this is only for the sure-footed.

NUJIANG VALLEY 怒江大峡谷

The 320km-long Nujiang Valley (Nùjiāng Dàxiágǔ) is one of Yunnan's best-kept secrets. The Nujiang (known as the 'Salween' in Myanmar; its name in Chinese means 'Raging River') is the second-longest river in Southeast Asia and a Unesco World Heritage Site.

Sandwiched between the Gaoligong mountains and Myanmar to the west, Tibet to the north and the imposing Biluo Mountain to the east, the gorge holds nearly a quarter of China's flora and fauna species, and half of China's endangered species. The valley also has a mix of Han, Nu, Lisu, Drung and Tibetan nationalities, and even the odd Burmese trader. And it's simply stunning – all of it.

Like other parts of rural Yunnan, change is coming to the Nujiang Valley. The local government is touting investment opportunities in everything from truffle farms to stone quarries, and the main towns – Liuku and Fugong especially – are booming, with new apartment blocks and shops appearing and Han migrants arriving in numbers. Though the region has long been kept remote by poor road access, a new highway all the way to Gongshan was nearing completion at the time of research.

Nevertheless, the Nujiang remains one of only two rivers that have not been dammed in all China and the signs are that it will, thankfully, stay that way. And getting here remains a pain, which is a good thing in terms of keeping the valley as pristine as is possible in China. Plans have been announced to blast a road from Gongshan in the northern part of the valley to Deqin, and another from the village of Bingzhongluo even further north into Tibet. Given the immense topographical challenges, these schemes are a long way off. But you should make sure to get here before they happen.

Getting There & Away

All traffic enters via Liuku. From there, you trundle for hours up the valley, marvelling at the scenery, and then head back the way you came. Travellers, though, should be prepared for roads that can be impassable due to heavy rain and/or landslides en route to Bingzhongluo and beyond.

Liuku 六库

☎ 0886 / POP 184,835

Liuku (Liùkù) is the lively, pleasant capital of the prefecture. Divided by the Nujiang River, it's the main transport hub of the region and growing fast. Although it's of little intrinsic interest, it's pleasant enough to stroll through while overnighting before an early bus. The larger surrounding area is known as Lushui (泸水, Lúshuǐ), which you may sometimes see on bus timetables.

Sleeping & Eating

To eat, head to the riverbank north of the bus station, where lots of restaurants serve Chinese dishes and hotpot in a newly constructed development.

Riverside Handpick Hotel HOTEL ¥¥
(江之畔精选酒店, Jiāngzhī Pànjīngxuǎn Jiǔdiàn; ☎ 886 666 9888; 16 Xueshan Lu, 雪山路16号; r

¥258-358; ❀ 🛜) Bright rooms with big balconies close to the bus station make this a nice splurge for travellers who need to overnight in Liuku before catching an early bus. More expensive rooms have river views. From the bus station, turn left towards the river and walk about 100m.

Qīngjiāng Jiǔdiàn
HOTEL ¥¥

(清江酒店; ☎ 886 305 2888; 150 Xueshan Lu, 雪山路150号; r ¥228) In the newest section of town about 450m south of the bus station. Rooms are large and squeaky clean.

ℹ Information

You will likely have to register your passport at a police checkpoint about 30 minutes before entering Liuku.

Bank of China (中国银行; Zhōngguó Yínháng; ☎ 886 362 8143; Nujiang Dadao, 怒江大道; ⊙ 9am-5pm) Located uphill from the bus station. Other ATMs around town take foreign cards.

ℹ Getting There & Away

Nujiang airport was reportedly slated to open in late 2019, but at time of research the only access was still by bus. The bus station is located south of the old town and across the river; if you can't find a ride up the valley try the informal minibus stand to the west of the main bridge to the old town, where it's occasionally also possible to take a minibus directly to Bingzhongluo (from ¥300, but be prepared to bargain).

Services from the bus station include the following:

Baoshan ¥53, four hours, five daily (8.30am, 12.30pm, 2.30pm, 3.30pm and 5pm)

Fugong ¥35, four to five hours, five daily (8am to 12.40pm)

Gongshan ¥107, eight to nine hours, one daily (9am)

Kunming ¥202, eight hours, three daily (8.30am, 10am and 6.30pm)

Ruili ¥117, five hours, one daily (7.40am)

Tengchong ¥63, six hours, three daily (7am, 9am and 11am)

Xiaguan ¥93, four to five hours, nine daily (7am to 7pm)

Fugong   福贡

☐ 0886 / POP 98,620

Hemmed in by steep cliffs on all sides, the landscape around Fugong (Fúgòng) offers some of the best scenery in the Nujiang Valley and has a large Lisu population. The town itself is unremarkable, although it is expanding rapidly (it has working ATMs

now). Fugong is roughly halfway up the valley and the best place to break your journey if you get a late start from Liuku.

A number of similarly priced restaurants serving the same dishes and display cases to pick and choose from can be found along Wenhua Lu, the main road through Fugong.

Róngdū Shāngwù Jiǔdiàn
HOTEL ¥¥

(荣都商务酒店; ☎ 886 889 4666; 2 Shiyue Jie, 石月街2号; tw ¥260; ❀ 🛜) On the corner of the bus station street and the main drag, this hotel offers clean, large and modern rooms (with sit-down toilets) and has a good wi-fi connection. Discounts of more than 50% are standard.

ℹ Getting There & Away

There are five daily buses to Liuku (¥49, four to five hours) between 7am and 10.45am. For Bingzhongluo you'll have to wait for the bus from Liuku to pass by, which happens around noon, but there's a good chance there won't be any free seats.

Your best bet to Gongshan is to take a shared minivan (¥150 per person). They start running from 7.30am and you'll find them just east of the bus station. From Gongshan, shared minivans run to Bingzhongluo (¥30 per person). Minivans also run to Liuku (¥80 per person) far more frequently than buses.

There are also two daily buses to Kunming (¥265, 12 hours, noon and 1.30pm) and one to Xiaguan (¥137, nine hours, 8am).

Bingzhongluo   丙中洛

☐ 0886 / POP 6,465

The main reason to come to the Nujiang Valley is to visit isolated, friendly Bingzhongluo (Bǐngzhōngluò), a farming village set in a beautiful, wide and fertile bowl and populated primarily by Tibetan and Nu communities. Just 35km south of Tibet and close to Myanmar, it's a great base for hikes into the surrounding mountains and valleys.

The area is at its most beautiful in spring and early autumn. Don't think about coming in the winter, as even in the drier seasons the road is regularly closed by landslides.

Potential short hops include heading south along the main road for 2km to the impressive 'first bend' of the Nujiang River, or north along a gravel road more than 20km long that passes a 19th-century church and several villages, with a side path to a Nu village at **Qiunatong**.

Longer three- or four-day treks include heading to the Tibetan village of **Dimaluo** (迪麻洛, Dímáluò) and then onto the village of **Yongzhi** (永芝, Yǒngzhī). From Yongzhi it's another two hours' walk to the main road from where you can hitch a ride to Deqin. It is a demanding trek that can really only be done from late May until September as the 3800m pass is too difficult to cross in heavy snow.

There's a small selection of restaurants, and all the guesthouses and hostels prepare meals.

❶ Getting There & Away

Take a bus from Liuku to Gongshan (¥107, eight to nine hours, one daily, 9am), where you can connect for regular buses to Bingzhongluo (¥30, one hour). To return, transport for Liuku leaves regularly from both Gongshan and Fugong.

TENGCHONG COUNTY

Scrunched up against Myanmar in a rarely touristed corner of Yunnan, Tengchong County (腾冲县, Téngchōng Xiàn) is home to varied landscapes that include thick forests, dormant volcanoes, minority villages, and steaming hot springs.

Tengchong city has been revamped thoroughly but is still a pleasant enough base with interesting World War II history, while nearby Heshun's traditional village architecture speaks to the region's legacy as a base for many migrants who found their fortunes overseas.

Tengchong   腾冲

☑ 0875 / POP 644,765

With volcanoes in the immediate vicinity, lots of hot springs and great hiking potential, there's plenty to explore in this neck of the woods. Tengchong (Téngchōng) itself is a bit of an oddity – it's one of the few places in China that, though much of the old architecture has been demolished, remains a pleasant place to hang out, with oodles of green space and a friendly, low-key populace.

◉ Sights

Much of the old-time architecture is now gone, but a few OK places for a random wander are still to be found. Tengchong's proximity to Myanmar (Burma) means there are many jade and teak shops around town.

National Memorial Cemetery   CEMETERY
(国殇墓园, Guóshāng Mùyuán; Tiansheng Shequ, 天成社区; ⊗ 9am-4.40pm) This touching

cemetery and museum is dedicated to the soldiers who fought and died to defend Yunnan during World War II, including those fighting on behalf of the United States and other Allied nations. Particularly poignant sections are dedicated to the fighter pilot squadron known as the Flying Tigers and to the objectionable conduct of invading armies in Yunnan. Passport required.

Laifeng Temple   BUDDHIST TEMPLE
(来凤寺, Láifēng Sì; 34 Shangxi Jie, 上西街34号) FREE Surrounded by lush pine forest, this Buddhist temple on the edge of Laifeng Shan National Forest Park feels like a secluded sanctuary yet remains a hub of local life.

Dieshuihe Waterfall   WATERFALL
(叠水河瀑布, Diéshuǐhé Pùbù; ☑ 875 514 1499; Baofeng Lu, 宝峰路; ¥10; ⊗ 7am-7pm) On the western edge of town, this large park is a pleasant place for a stroll or a picnic. Just inside the entrance is the small Xianle Temple (仙乐观, Xiānlè Guān), the path past which leads down to a viewing platform of the 46m waterfall. At the top of a hilltop path, opposite the staircase down to the waterfall, is the small Longguang Hall (龙光台, Lóngguāng Tái), which is pleasantly quiet but architecturally uninteresting.

Laifeng Shan National Forest Park   PARK
(来凤山国家森林公园, Láifēng Shān Guójiā Sēnlín Gōngyuán; ☑ 875 515 5283; ⊗ 8am-7pm) On the southwestern edge of town, walk through the lush pine forests of this park to Laifeng Temple or make the sweaty hike on any number of dirt and concrete paths up to the summit, where the **Wenbi Pagoda** (文笔塔, Wénbǐ Tǎ) stands as a landmark visible from anywhere in Tengchong.

🛏 Sleeping & Eating

Tengchong Royal Orchid Boutique Hotel   HOTEL ¥
(腾冲御庭兰花精品酒店, Téngchōng Yùtíng Lánhuā Jīngpǐn Jiǔdiàn; ☑ 875 515 5855; Huangxue Xiaoqu, 簧学小区; d ¥179; ☻) Large rooms and friendly staff make this place a joy, even if it has more of a business-hotel vibe than something truly boutique.

Yudu Hotel   HOTEL ¥¥¥
(玉都大酒店, Yùdū Dàjiǔdiàn; ☑ 875 513 8666; 15 Tengyue Lu, 腾越路15号; d ¥978; ❈ ☻) There are 130 rooms at this comfortable, professionally run place and they are routinely discounted by a whopping 70% to 80%, making them a great deal. Some come with computers; all

Tengchong

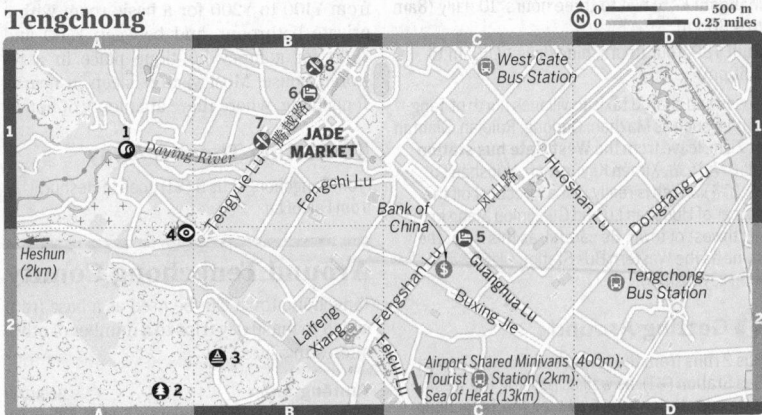

Tengchong

⦿ Sights

1 Dieshuihe Waterfall...............................A1
2 Laifeng Shan National Forest Park A2
3 Laifeng Temple.......................................B2
4 National Memorial Cemetery A2

🛏 Sleeping

5 Tengchong Royal Orchid Boutique
    Hotel...C2
6 Yudu Hotel...B1

✕ Eating

7 Héfēngyuán Cāntīng...............................B1
8 Yíngxiāngyuán Cāntīng..........................B1

have decent bathrooms. Don't expect to hear any English, though. It's on the corner of Tengyue Lu and Guanghua Lu.

Yíngxiāngyuán Cāntīng   YUNNAN ¥

(盈香园餐厅; ☑182 8853 3320; 7 Hongxing Xiaoqu, 红星小区7号; dishes ¥18-45; ⏰11am-9.30pm; 🛜) This popular local place has a wide menu of Yunnan and broader Chinese dishes to choose from, as well as a cooler display to pick and mix for those who want to customise their own meal.

Héfēngyuán Cāntīng   YUNNAN ¥¥

(河风园餐厅; ☑875 513 2758; 182 Hepan Xiaoqu, 河畔小区182号; dishes ¥20-58; ⏰7.30am-9pm) Eat outside in a large, pleasant courtyard. Try the local cured ham, huǒtuǐ (火腿), or point and choose from the wide range of fish, meat and veggies on display. No English spoken, but the staff are welcoming. It's right by the bridge over the river: look for the five red characters painted on the wall.

ℹ Information

Bank of China (中国银行, Zhōngguó Yínháng; ☑875 518 3307; cnr Fengshan Lu & Buxing Jie; ⏰8.30am-5pm) Has a 24-hour ATM and will change cash and travellers cheques. There are other ATMs around town that take foreign cards too.

ℹ Getting There & Away

AIR

Tengchong 'Hump' Airport (腾冲驼峰机场, Téngchōng Tuófēng Jīchǎng), 12km south of town, has six flights daily to Kunming (from ¥580). The name evokes the route over the Himalayas flown by WWII pilots to support the war effort in Yunnan.

BUS

Tengchong's **Tourist Bus Station** (腾冲旅游客运站, Téngchōng Lǚyóu Kèyùnzhàn; ☑875 516 1526; Rehai Lu, opposite Xiake Hotel, 热海路霞客酒店对面) is in the south of town. A taxi to the centre costs ¥15. Buses to most points east of Tengchong arrive and depart from here. Destinations include the following:

Baoshan ¥63, 2½ hours, every 40 minutes (8am to 7pm)

Kunming ¥218 to ¥289, 11 hours, nine daily (9am to 8pm)

Lijiang ¥195, 10 hours, one daily, 10.50am)

Liuku ¥58, six hours, three daily (10am, 11am and noon)

Xiaguan ¥130, 5½ hours, four daily (10.30am, noon, 2pm and 7pm)

Tengchong Bus Station (腾冲客运站, Téngchōng Kèyùnzhàn; 223 Yuanji Xiaoqu, 元吉小区223号), on Dongfang Lu, is used primarily for buses headed towards the Myanmar (Burma) border. Destinations include the following:

Mangshi ¥45, two to three hours, 10 daily (8am to 4.30pm)

Ruili ¥80, four hours, nine daily (7.50am to 3.50pm)

Buses and shared taxis to villages north of Tengchong, such as Mazhan, Gudong, Ruidian, Diantan or Zizhi, leave from the **West Gate bus station** (西门客运站, Xīmén Kèyùnzhàn; Huoshan Lu, 火山路), which is really just a forecourt off the corner of Huoshan Lu and Guaijinlou Xiang in the northwest of town. Be careful, as this is not the same as the Western Bus Station (西部客运站, Xībù kèyùnzhàn).

ⓘ Getting Around

Bus 2 runs from the town centre to the Tourist Bus Station (¥1), as well as passing the West Gate bus station. Bus 6 passes the Tengchong bus station on Dongfang Lu (¥1) en route to Heshun. Taxis charge ¥6 to hop around town.

Minivans (机场面包车, Jīchǎng Miànbāochē; cnr Rehai Lu & Fecui Lu; ¥10) run to the airport from just south of the junction of Feicui Lu and Rehai Lu. Taxis to the airport charge approximately ¥40.

Heshun 和顺

☏ 0875 / POP 6,000

Located 2km southwest of Tengchong, Heshun (Héshùn) somewhat retains the feel of a traditional Chinese village with cobbled streets, even if there are an ever-increasing number of jade and jewellery shops here. But it's still far from overwhelmed by day trippers and there are some great old buildings in the village, providing lots of opportunities for photography or a relaxing stroll.

The village has a small **World War II Museum** (滇缅抗战博物馆, Diānmiǎn Kàngzhàn Bówùguǎn), a famous old **library** (和顺图书馆, Héshùn Túshūguǎn; ☏ 875 515 0182; ⊙ 8am-7.30pm) and a few interesting courtyard residences and temples. There's an admission fee (¥55) to enter the village itself, payable at the main entrance from 7am to 8.30pm. Most of the sites will check your ticket so hang on to it; they're open generally from 8am to 8pm.

Leading south from the village entrance is a waterfront walking path along the shore of Mallard Lake (野鸭湖, Yěyā Hú) to three restored Qing dynasty temples that are all included in the village entry fee: Liu Family Temple (刘氏宗祠, Liúshì Zōngcí), Li Family Temple (李氏宗祠, Lǐshì Zōngcí), and Yuanlong Pavilion (元龙阁, Yuánlóng Gé).

There are many inns and guesthouses scattered through the village. Expect to pay from ¥100 to ¥200 for a basic room with a private bathroom, and between ¥500 and ¥800 for a fancy boutique place in a restored house. Most visitors sleep in nearby Tengchong, where there are plenty of hotels.

ⓘ Getting There & Away

From Tengchong, bus 6 (¥1) goes to Heshun from Feicui Lu.

Around Tengchong County

Téngchōng town can be used as a base from which to make day trips to a number of other interesting sites.

Yúnfēng Shān   MOUNTAIN

(云峰山, Cloudy Peak Mountain; ☏ 875 585 6901; ¥40; ⊙ 8am-6pm) Dotted with 17th-century temples and monastic retreats, Taoist holy mountain Yunfeng Shan is 47km north of Tengchong. It's possible to take a **cable car** (云峰山索道, Yúnfēngshān Suǒdào; one way/return ¥90/160; ⊙ 8am-6pm) close to the top, from where it's a 20-minute walk to **Sanqing Temple** (三清殿, Sānqīng Diàn) on the summit at 2449m. Luzu Temple (吕祖殿, Lǔzǔ Dià), just below the top, serves up a solid vegetarian buffet from 10am to 6pm.

You can walk up the mountain in about 2½ hours or down in around 45 minutes, but repetitive large stairs can be hard on the knees.

To get to the mountain, go to the West Gate bus station in Tengchong and catch a bus (¥10) or shared taxi (¥15 per person) to Gudong (固东, Gùdōng), and then switch to a shared taxi (¥10) or taxi (¥30) to the base of the mountain – you'll probably want to arrange a pick-up time or take the driver's phone number. From the parking lot a golf cart (¥5) takes you to the entrance, or else it's a 1½ km walk. Hiring a vehicle from Tengchong for the return trip will cost about ¥300 to ¥350. On the way back to Tengchong the road passes through Mazhan, where it's possible to detour to the Volcano Park on the same trip.

Volcano Park   VOLCANO

(火山公园, Huǒshān Gōngyuán; ☏ 875 513 3333; Mazhan Village, 马站县; ¥35; ⊙ 8am-6pm) Hike to the top of Tengchong's dormant volcanoes and peer down into the former inferno; it's all very verdant now, but the view's still nice. Though on a clear day visitors can see a handful of the 97 volcanoes in the vicinity of Tengchong, only 2050m Big Empty Hill (大空山, Dàkōng Shān) and 1937m Small Empty Hill (小空山, Xiǎokōng Shān) are currently possible to climb.

Sea of Heat
HOT SPRINGS

(热海, Rèhǎi; ☑ 875 513 3333; www.rehaispa.com; ¥50; ⊙ 8am-8pm) A steamy collection of hot springs, geysers and streams (but no actual sea), located about 12km southwest of Tengchong. The cost of admission allows you to wander the tree- and plant-lined stone paths to admire the geothermal activity – some of the springs reach temperatures of 102°C.

A few of the outdoor springs in the scenic area offer swimming, with a nice warm-water swimming pool, plus indoor baths, from ¥150 to ¥300. Much better value is the **Baths Valley** (浴谷温泉, Yùgǔ Wēnquán; ☑ 875 513 3333; ¥288; ⊙ 8am-1am) complex.

A special bus service (热海专线, Rèhǎi Zhuānxiàn; ¥3) leaves Tengchong's Tourist Bus Station for the Sea of Heat regularly from 7am to 8pm. Alternatively, taxis from the city charge around ¥40.

DEHONG PREFECTURE

Dehong Dǎi and Jingpo Autonomous Prefecture (德宏傣族景颇族自治州, Déhóng Dǎizú Jǐngpǒzú Zìzhìzhōu) juts into Myanmar in the far west of Yunnan. Once a backwater of backwaters, from the late 1980s the region saw tourists flock in to experience its raucous border atmosphere.

That's dimmed quite a bit and most Chinese tourists in Dehong are here for the trade from Myanmar that comes through Ruili and Wanding. Burmese jade is the most desired commodity and countless other items are spirited over the border.

Ruili
瑞丽

☑ 0692 / POP 180,630

Ruili (Ruìlì) was notorious as recently as the 1990s as a haven for drug and gem smugglers, prostitution and various other iniquities that plague border towns worldwide. The government cleaned it up in the late 1990s (on the surface anyway) and today you're more likely to stumble into a shopping mall than a den of thieves. Still, it has an edge to it, thanks to its proximity to a notoriously anarchic region of Myanmar and a thriving gem market operated largely by Burmese traders. And with its palm-tree-lined streets, bicycle rickshaws and steamy climate, it has a distinctly laid-back, Southeast Asian feel.

The minority villages nearby are also good reason to come and it's worth getting a bicycle and heading out to explore.

⊙ Sights

Ruili Market
MARKET

(瑞丽市场, Ruìlì Shìchǎng; ⊙ 6am-7pm) This is one of the most colourful and fun markets in all Yunnan, with a real swirl of ethnicities, including Dai, Jingpo, Han and Burmese, as well as the odd Bangladeshi and Pakistani trader. Get here in the morning, when the stalls are lined with Burmese smokes, tofu wrapped in banana leaves, freshly made noodles, cosmetics and pharmaceuticals from Thailand, clothes – you name it.

Jade Market
MARKET

(珠宝街, Zhūbǎo Jiē; Zhubao Jie, 珠宝街; ⊙ 9am-9pm) Ruili's jade market is the centre of town in all senses. Burmese jade sellers run some of the shops here and for a moment you may even forget you are still in China.

Golden Duck Pagoda
PAGODA

(金鸭塔, Jīnyā Tǎ; Renmin Lu, 人民路; ⊙ 7am-8pm) FREE This pagoda is on the southwestern outskirts of Ruili on the main road. An attractive stupa set in a temple courtyard, it was established to mark the arrival of a pair of golden ducks that brought good fortune to what was previously an uninhabited marshy area.

🛏 Sleeping

Irrawaddy International Youth Hostel
HOSTEL ¥

(伊洛瓦底国际青年旅舍, Yīluòwǎdǐ Guójì Qīngnián Lǔshě; ☑ 189 8824 3100; 7 Youyi Lu, 友谊路 7号; dm ¥30, d ¥80-120; ❈ 🛜) This hostel on a quiet, residential street in the north of town likes to fly under the radar: it's hard to find any English-language information about it. But the dorms and rooms are bright and reasonably well kept, the bathrooms have sit-down toilets, the staff are cheerful and speak a little English and there's a pleasant communal area and garden. It's a 15-minute walk from Nanmao Jie, or a ¥8 taxi ride.

MINORITY GROUPS

The most obvious minority groups in Dehong are Burmese (normally dressed in their traditional sarong-like *longyi*), Dai and the Jingpo – known in Myanmar (Burma) as the Kachin, a minority group long engaged in armed struggle against the Myanmar government.

Ruili

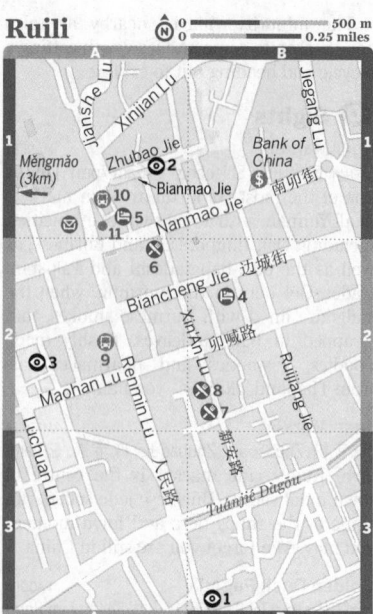

N 0 ——— 500 m
0 ——— 0.25 miles

lish menu, but if you're in doubt try the signature Myanmar beef curry (咖喱牛肉, *gālí niúròu*).

Lántiān Xiǎochī   YUNNAN ¥
(蓝天小吃; ☑ 159 6920 3446; 66 Xin'an Lu, 新安路66号; dishes from ¥8; ⊙ 7am-9pm) Fantastic, popular place for noodles at any time of day, but especially breakfast. It's also good for Burmese-style salads, Thai fried rice dishes and fruit juices. No English menu, but there are pictures on the wall to choose from.

Bo Bo's Cold Drinks Shop   CAFE ¥
(步步冷饮店, Bùbù Lěngyǐndiàn; ☑ 692 412 3643; 43 Nánmǎo Jie, 南卯街43号; drinks ¥5-15, dishes ¥10-20; ⊙ 10am-11.30pm; 🛜) This Ruili institution is busy from early to late, with Burmese waiters clad in their native, sarong-like *longyi* hustling as they serve up fantastic fruit juices, Burmese-style milky tea, ice cream and cakes. They also do simple but tasty rice and noodle dishes. Look for the English sign on Xin'An Lu and go upstairs to the large, 2nd-floor covered terrace.

ⓘ Information

Bank of China (中国银行, Zhōngguó Yínháng; ☑ 692 414 2219; 8 Nanmao Jie, 南卯街8号; ⊙ 8.30am-5.30pm) Provides all the usual services. There are many other ATMs around town that take foreign cards. You can also change/find US dollars at the jade market.

ⓘ Getting There & Away

An expressway from Baoshan to Ruili is scheduled for completion in 2022 and perhaps one day in the not-too-distant future there will be a high-speed rail link from Kunming that will extend into

Mingrui Hotel   HOTEL ¥
(明瑞宾馆, Míngruì Bīnguǎn; ☑ 692 410 8666; 98 Nanmao Jie, 南卯街98号; d ¥80; ✳🛜) Big, bright and clean rooms are basic but in a handy central location, although that means it can be noisy. Strong wi-fi connection. It's down an alley off the northern side of Nanmao Jie, close to the intersection with Xinan Lu. More Burmese is spoken here than Mandarin.

Biānchéng Jiǔdiàn   HOTEL ¥¥
(边城酒店; ☑ 692 415 6669; 85 Biancheng Jie, 边城街85号; d ¥200-328; ✳🛜) This place in the centre of town has comfortable beds in clean, large rooms, power showers, good wi-fi and efficient staff (but little English spoken). The most expensive rooms are themed – think Superman decor – and have round beds. No English sign; look for the large, sand-coloured building close to the corner with Ruijiang Lu.

✗ Eating

Jue Jue Delicious Foods   BURMESE ¥
(觉觉味道, Jué Jué Wèidào; ☑ 692 414 1281; 74 Xin'An Lu, 新安路74号; dishes ¥18-48; ⊙ 11.30am-11.30pm; 🛜) Travellers dreaming of the culinary possibilities just across the border can drop by here for delicious Burmese cuisine from *lyongi*-clad waiters. There's no Eng-

Myanmar (Burma) via Ruili, if talked-about plans ever come to fruition.

AIR

There are 20 or more daily flights from Mangshi to Kunming (from ¥580), as well as limited services to Beijing and Shanghai. You can buy tickets at **China Eastern Airlines** (东方航空公司, Dōngfāng Hángkōng Gōngsī; ☑ 692 411 1111; 15 Renmin Lu, 人民路15号; ⊗ 9am-9pm) or online.

Mangshi Airport is a 1½-hour drive from Ruili. Taxis in Ruili charge ¥300 for the trip, though it's possible to share with other passengers on the way to or from the airport. Alternatively, take the regular bus to Mangshi city and transfer to local bus 6 (¥1) or a local taxi (¥20) for the airport.

BUS

The new **Ruili Passenger Terminal** (瑞丽综合客运枢纽站, Ruìlì Zōnghé Kèyùn Shūniǔ Zhàn; 234 Sheng Dao, 234省道) is on the northeastern outskirts of Ruili. Taxis charge a flat ¥15 to the centre of town; buses 6 and 9 (¥2, 6.30am to 9pm) also travel here from the centre of Ruili. Destinations include the following:

Baoshan ¥93, six hours, nine daily (8.10am to 5pm)

Jinghong ¥405, 22 hours, one daily (9.30am)

Kunming ¥295 to ¥331, 12 hours, five daily (8.30am, noon, 3pm, 5pm and 7.30pm)

Mangshi ¥41, 1½ hours, every 30 minutes (7am to 7pm)

Tengchong ¥80 to ¥90, four hours, six daily (8.30am to 3.50pm)

Xiaguan ¥171 to ¥192, nine hours, three daily (9am, 10am and 3pm)

Minivans and buses for local destinations cruise around town: flag them down on Nanmao Jie and Renmin Lu. Destinations include Wanding (¥15), Zhangfeng (¥15) and Nongdao (¥8).

🛈 Getting Around

Bus 1 (¥5; ⊗ 8am-7pm) to Nongdao (弄岛, Nòngdǎo) runs every 20 minutes down Renmin Lu, including a stop at Tuanjie Jiancai (团结建材, Tuánjié Jiàncái) near the Golden Duck Pagoda, en route to many of the villages along the old highway west of town.

Bus 5 (¥2; ⊗ 6.30am-9pm) goes to the Golden Pagoda to the east of Ruili, and is most conveniently boarded at a stop just west of the Jade Market.

A flat rate for a taxi ride inside the city should be ¥6, and is up for negotiation from there. There are also motorcycle taxis and cycle rickshaws, but with no set prices you'll need to negotiate.

Around Ruili

Just past the Golden Duck Pagoda (p739), on the southwestern outskirts of Ruili, is a crossroads and a small wooden temple. The road to the right (west) leads to the villages of **Jiexiang** (姐相, Jiěxiàng) and **Nongdao** (弄岛, Nóngdǎo), and on the way are a number of small temples, villages and stupas. None are spectacular but the village life is interesting and there are often small markets near the temples.

The first major Dai temple is **Hansha Zhuang Temple** (喊沙奘寺, Hǎnshā Zhuāng Sì; Jiedong Cun, 姐东村) FREE, a fine wooden structure with a few resident monks. It's set a little off the road and a green tourism sign marks the turn-off. The surrounding Dai village is interesting.

Another 20 minutes or so west down the road, look out for a turn on the right side of the road marked as Huyu (户育, Hùyù), 200m before a Sai Jing Petrol Station (赛静加油站, Sàijìng Jiāyóuzhàn). Turn right and follow the narrow paved road through the fields to **Léizhuāngxiāng** (雷奘相, Jiexiang Xiang, 姐相乡) FREE, Ruili's oldest stupa, which dates back to the middle of the Tang dynasty.

In between the two major temples, on the south side of the road, is what appears to be a collection of temples but is actually 'One Village Two Countries'. It's a theme park staffed by workers from Myanmar (Burma) to serve as 'authentic' tourist attractions, and best avoided.

🛈 BORDER CROSSINGS

At the time of writing it was not possible for independent third-country nationals to travel across the border at Jiegao, though there were rumours that it may be possible as part of a tour group. The only way to go is by air from Kunming. Visas are available at the embassy in Beijing or in Kunming at the **Myanmar Consulate** (缅甸领事馆, Miǎndiàn Lǐngshìguǎn; ☑ 871 816 2804; www.mcgkunming.org; Kunming Diplomat Compound, 99 Yingbin Lu, 迎宾路99号; ⊗ visa section 9am-noon & 1-2pm Mon-Fri; Ⓜ Erji Road).

XISHUANGBANNA REGION

North of Myanmar and Laos, Xishuangbanna (西双版纳, Xīshuāngbǎnnà) is the Chinese approximation of the original Thai name of Sip Sawng Panna (12 Rice-Growing Districts). Better known as Bǎnnà, the area has become China's mini-Thailand, attracting tourists looking for sunshine, water-splashing festivals and jungle treks. Xishuangbanna Dai Autonomous Prefecture, as it is known officially, is subdivided into the three counties of Jinghong, Menghai and Mengla.

Banna is home to some of the best food in all China. Sour and spicy Dai food in particular is excellent, drawing on both Chinese and Southeast Asian influences. Dai dishes include barbecued fish, eel or beef cooked with lemongrass or served with peanut and tomato sauce. The region's fertile earth guarantees superb fruit and vegetables too.

Environment

Xishuangbanna has myriad plant and animal species, although scientific studies have shown the tropical rainforest areas of Banna are now acutely endangered. The jungle areas that remain contain a handful of tigers, leopards and golden-haired monkeys. The number of elephants has doubled to 250, up 100%

from the early 1980s; the government now offers compensation to villagers whose crops have been destroyed by elephants, or who assist in wildlife conservation. In 1998 the government banned the hunting or processing of animals, but poaching is hard to control.

People

About one-third of the million-strong population of this region are Dai; another third or so are Han Chinese and the rest are a conglomerate of minorities that include the Hani, Lisu and Yao, as well as lesser-known hill tribes such as the Aini (a subgroup of the Hani), Jinuo, Bulang, Lahu and Wa.

Climate

The region has two seasons: wet and dry. The wet season is between May and October, when it rains ferociously, although not every day and only in short bursts. From September to April there is less rainfall, but thick fog often descends during the late evening and doesn't lift until 10am or even later.

November to March sees temperatures between 12° and 26°C. The hottest months of the year are from April to September, when you can expect up to 35°C or more.

Xishuangbanna

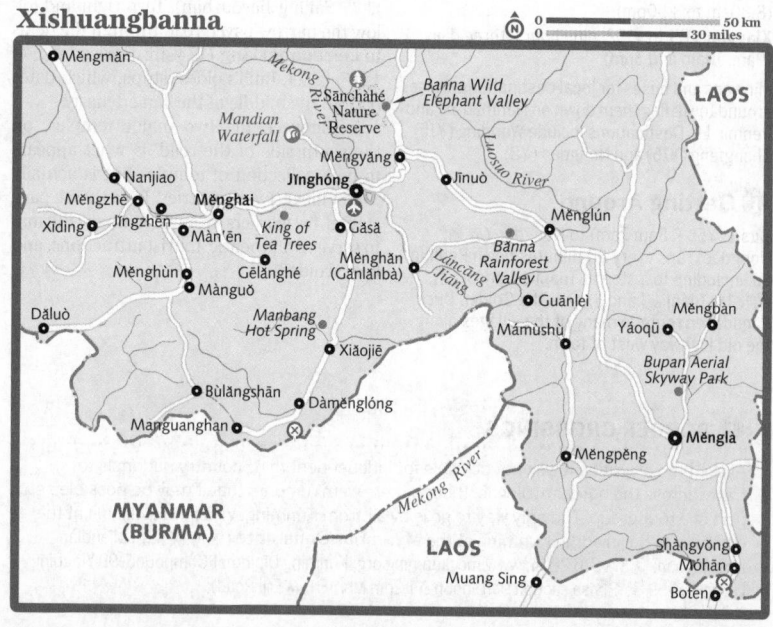

XISHUANGBANNA VILLAGES

Visiting the numerous minority villages is the major draw here. You could spend weeks doing so, but even with limited time most destinations in Xishuangbanna are only two or three hours away by bus. Note that to get to the most isolated villages, you'll often first have to take the bus to a primary (and uninteresting) town and stay overnight there, since only one bus per day – if that – travels to the tinier villages.

Market lovers rejoice – it's an artist's palette of colours in outlying villages. The most popular markets are the Thursday market in Xiding and Menghun's Saturday market. Daily markets in Menghai and Menghan are worth a stop if you're passing through, but are less photogenic than village markets and not necessarily destinations on their own.

Take note: it can feel like every second village begins with the prefix 'Meng' and it isn't unheard of for travellers to end up at the wrong village entirely because of communication problems. Have your destination written down in script before you head off.

ℹ️ Getting There & Away

Jinghong is the main transport hub for Xishuangbanna, with air and bus connections to the rest of Yunnan. Menghai, about an hour west of Jinghong by bus, is another key transport node for reaching many of Xishuangbanna's outlying villages, including Xiding and Menghun. Frequent buses from Jinghong's Banna Bus Station travel to Menghai's bus station, where you can pick up buses and minivans to the villages.

You can also get direct buses from Jinghong to destinations in Laos, including Luang Nam Tha and Luang Prabang, while there's also the possibility of hitching a ride on a cargo boat down the Mekong to northern Thailand. There is still no overland access to Myanmar from here.

Jinghong　　景洪

📞 0691 / POP 600,000

Jinghong (Jǐnghóng) – meaning 'City of Dawn' in the local Dai language – has expanded enormously, both in terms of infrastructure and interest to domestic tourists, especially those looking for a taste of Southeast Asia without even leaving the Middle Kingdom. The once-sleepy capital of Xishuangbanna Prefecture is now very much a tourist town, though it sees relatively few international visitors and remains laid-back despite the increasingly snarled traffic.

◉ Sights

Tropical Flower & Plants Garden GARDENS
(热带花卉园, Rèdài Huāhuìyuán; 📞 691 212 0493; www.xsbnrdhhy.com; 99 Xuanwei Dadao, 宣慰大道 99号; ¥40; ◷ 7.30am-6pm) This terrific botanic garden, found west of the town centre, is one of Jinghong's better attractions. Admission gets you into a series of gardens where you can view over a thousand different types of plant life grouped by species and connected by meandering stone paths. It's all very calm and colourful.

🛏️ Sleeping

There are hotels and hostels aplenty in Jinghong. Basic guesthouses are sometimes available in the villages, or locals will offer a bed. Make sure to pay for it: the going rate is around ¥60 for a bed and meal.

Zouyi Youth Hostel HOSTEL ¥
(走一国际青年旅舍, Zǒuyī Guójì Qīngnián Lǚshě; 📞 136 2871 3988; 6 Zhuanghong Lu, 庄洪路6号; dm ¥30, r ¥80-120) Although rooms feel a bit institutional, the top-floor patio and convenient location (close to the Banna and long-distance bus stations) make this an appealing choice.

Home Inn HOTEL ¥
(如家酒店, Rújiā Jiǔdiàn; 📞 691 219 0688; www.homeinns.com; 2 Manting Lu, 曼听路2号; d ¥129-179; ❋ 🕸 🛜) Nothing to write home about, but this chain hotel offers big rooms with modern bathrooms in a convenient central location. Some rooms smell like old cigarettes, so check before you move in. Efficient and friendly staff.

Jing Land Hotel HOTEL ¥¥¥
(鲸兰大酒店, Jīnglán Dàjiǔdiàn; 📞 691 212 9999; 6 Jingde Lu, 景德路6号; d ¥320-1180; ❋ 🛜 🏊) Sporting two enormous elephants at its entrance, this is one of Jinghong's unmissable landmarks. The rooms are a little plain and compact for the price, but this is the only four-star place with such a central location – and a swimming pool. Rooms are routinely discounted by 20% out of season and it takes western credit cards.

Jinghong

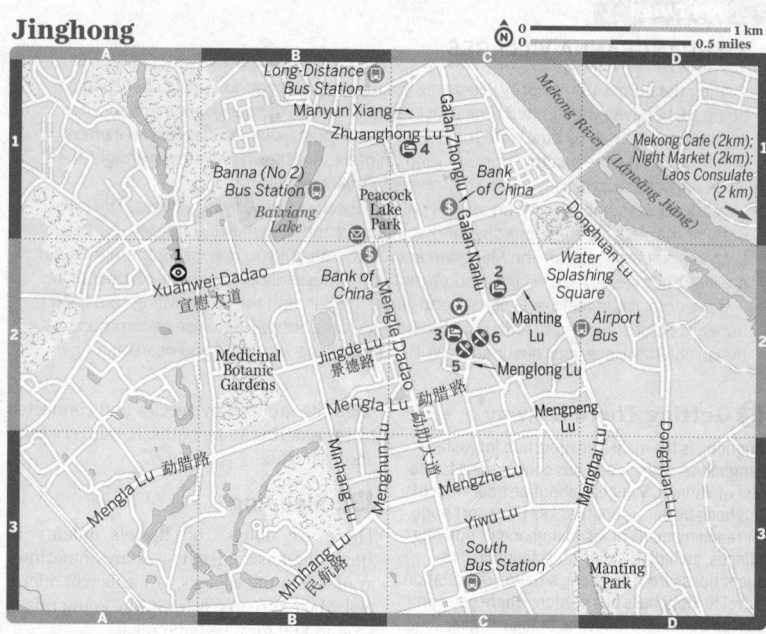

✕ Eating

Dai dishes include grilled fish or beef cooked with lemongrass, or served with peanut or tomato sauces. The most authentic Dai restaurants are located on the outskirts of town and serve up big set-meal feasts, so get a group together; ask at the Meimei Café for directions. In the centre, Menghai Lu, Mengpeng Lu and Menghun Lu all have a handful of Dai restaurants.

Thai Restaurant
THAI ¥

(财春青, Cáichūnqīng; ☑ 691 216 1758; 193 Manting Lu, 曼听路193号; mains ¥16-40; ⊙ 9.30am-9.30pm; 🐕) If you're not making the trek overland to Southeast Asia, get your Thai fix at this ever-reliable open-air restaurant. It's not the most upmarket Thai place in town,

but it's certainly the busiest and there's a huge range of dishes to choose from.

Jinghong Night Market
MARKET ¥

(景洪夜市, Jǐnghóng Yèshì; Ganbai Jie, Shuishang Renjia, Gaozhuang Xishuangjing, 告庄西双景水上人家赶摆街; dishes from ¥2; ⊙ 8pm-late) All manner of Dai and Yunnan eats are on display in the centre of this redeveloped east bank complex, and the market is close to the riverbank where Chinese-style bars congregate. For a taxi from the centre of town it's ¥15 to ¥20, or else bus 2 will drop you off relatively close.

★ Meimei Cafe
INTERNATIONAL ¥¥

(美美咖啡, Měiměi Kāfēi; ☑ 691 216 1221; www.meimei-cafe.com; 107-108 Menglong Lu, 勐龙路107-108号; dishes ¥28-55; ⊙ 9am-1am; 🐕) This is the first of all the western-style cafes in town and still the best. Choose from Dai and Chinese, burgers and breakfast, Belgian beer and espresso drinks; the menu has it all and everything we've tried has been good. The website is also a great source of local info (if a bit dated) and much of the same info can be found on-site in a binder kept behind the bar.

Mekong Cafe
INTERNATIONAL ¥¥

(湄公咖啡, Méigōng Kāfēi; ☑ 691 222 6588; mekong cafe@163.com; 1-1201, Ganbai Jie, Shuishang Renjia, Gaozhuang Xishuangjing, 告庄西双景水上人家

DON'T MISS

FESTIVALS & EVENTS

During festivals, booking same-day airline tickets to Jinghong can be extremely difficult. Hotels in Jinghong town are booked solid and prices usually triple. Most people end up commuting from a nearby Dai village. Festivities take place all over Xishuangbanna, so you might be lucky further away from Jinghong.

Water-Splashing Festival (泼水节, Pōshuǐjié; ⊙ mid-Apr) Celebrated at the same time as in Thailand and Laos, the three-day water-splashing festival washes away the dirt, sorrow and demons of the old year and brings in the happiness of the new. Jinghong celebrates it from 13 to 15 April; dates in the surrounding villages may vary. The actual splashing only occurs on the last day. Foreigners earn special attention, so prepare to be drenched all day.

Closed-Door Festival (傣族关门节, Dǎizú Guānmén Jié; ⊙ Jul) This Dai festival marks the start of the farming season, running from July to October, a time when marriages or festivals are banned. Traditionally, this is also the time of year that men aged 20 or older are ordained as monks for a period of time.

Open-Door Festival (傣族开门节, Dǎizú Kāiménjié; ⊙ Oct) The farming season ends with the Dai minority's Open-Door Festival, when everyone lets their hair down again to celebrate the harvest.

赶摆街1-1201号; dishes from ¥26; ⊙ 9am-1am; 🛜) This long-standing presence has a prime location overlooking the riverbank close to the night market in the newly developed bar strip. It still serves up a wide-ranging mix of western and Chinese food, as well as many foreign ales and decent wine. The attached travel agency specialises in eco-treks and is a reliable source of information and guides.

ℹ Information

Very occasionally, we get reports from travellers who have been drugged and then robbed on the Kunming–Jinghong bus trip. Be friendly but aware, accept nothing from strangers, and never leave your stuff unattended when you hop off for a break.

Bank of China (中国银行, Zhōngguó Yínháng; ☑ 691 212 3131; 39 Mengle Dadao, 勐泐大道39号; ⊙ 8.30am-5pm Mon-Fri) Changes travellers cheques and foreign currency, and has an ATM machine. There are others on Minhang Lu and Galan Zhonglu, including this **branch** (中国银行, Zhōngguó Yínháng; ☑ 691 212 3187; 96 Galan Zhonglu, 嘎兰中路96号; ⊙ 8.30am-5pm Mon-Fri, 8.30am-noon & 3-5pm Sun).

ℹ Getting There & Away

AIR

Xishuangbanna Gasa International Airport (JHG) is 4km southwest of the city.

There are around 40 daily flights to Kunming (from ¥452) but in April (when the water-splashing festival is held) you'll still need to book tickets in advance to get in or out. There

are also daily flights to Dali (from ¥362) and Lijiang (¥352), as well as increasing numbers of flights that connect with cities across China via Kunming.

Lao Airlines has one direct flight each Sunday from Jinghong to Luang Prabang in Laos (¥900).

BUS

The **long-distance bus station** (长途客运站, Chángtú Kèyùnzhàn; 16 Mengle Dadao, 勐泐大道16号) has daily buses to Luang Nam Tha (¥108, six hours, 10.40am) and Vientiane (¥348, 18 hours, 6.30am) in Laos. Every other day there's also a bus to Luang Prabang in Laos (¥198, 10 hours, 7.30am). Destinations also include the following:

Jianshui ¥260, eight to nine hours, two daily (9.30am and 10.30am)

Kunming ¥260, eight hours, 11 daily (8.30am to 9.50pm)

Lijiang ¥298, 14 to 16 hours, one daily (8am)

Ruili ¥503, 14 to 16 hours, one daily (9am)

Xiaguan ¥267, 10 to 12 hours, two daily (8.30am and 5.30pm)

To explore Xishuangbanna go to the No 2 bus station, also known as the **Banna bus station** (版纳客运站, Bǎnnà Kèyùnzhàn; 第二客运站, Dì'èr Kèyùnzhàn; 3 Minhang Lu, 民航路3号). Destinations include the following:

Menghai ¥19 to ¥21, 1½ hours, every 20 minutes (7am to 7.40pm)

Menghan (Ganlanba) ¥10, one hour, every 20 minutes (7.40am to 7pm)

Menglun ¥23, 1½ hours, every 20 minutes (7.40am to 9.30pm)

Mohan ¥80, four hours, three daily (9.20am, 1.10pm and 3.30pm)

For buses to **Damenglong** (¥19, two hours, every 15 minutes, 11.15am to 6pm), head to the **south bus station** (客运南站, Kèyùn Nánzhàn; 77 Menghai Lu, 勐海路77号), which also has departures to Kunming.

TRAIN

At the time of research a train line was under construction between Kunming and Jinghong and onwards to the Laotian border at Mohan. Predicted for completion sometime in 2020, when operational it will reduce travel times between Kunming and Jinghong to just 2½ hours.

❶ Getting Around

Jinghong is small enough that you can walk to most destinations, but a bike makes exploring nearby villages easier and can be rented from some guesthouses for ¥30 a day.

Bus 1 (¥1) connects all three bus stations along Mengle Dadao.

Bus 2 (¥1) connects the Tropical Flower & Plants Garden to the two northern bus stations and onwards across the river to the night market area.

Taxi flagfall is ¥8, but you may struggle to get drivers to use their meters.

Menglun   勐伦

📞 0691 / POP 26,610

Rare and exotic plant species and the song of wild tropical birds are the tourist draw in Menglun (Měnglún), home to the largest botanic gardens in all of China. Otherwise, the town is an unremarkable strip of hotels and restaurants just beyond the gardens.

Menglun is an easy day trip from Jinghong and there is little reason to stay here. But if you need to, there are a couple of basic hotels close to the bus station that charge from ¥50 to ¥120; **Jīnjiāngyuán Jiàrì Jiǔdiàn** (金江源假日酒店; 📞 691 871 7555; Menglun Jie, 勐伦街; r ¥120; @ 🛜) is the best of the bunch. The Royal Lily Hotel, inside the park, is not great quality and fairly poor value at ¥320.

There are simple restaurants on the same road as the bus station and on the road leading to the Tropical Botanical Garden. For friendly vibes and delicious Laotian fare, look for the **Lǎowō Rénjiā** (老挝人家; 📞 182 8808 9086; mains ¥10-30; ⏱ 10am-11pm).

Tropical Botanical Garden   GARDENS
(热带植物园, Rèdài Zhíwùyuán; 📞 691 871 5914; http://english.xtbg.cas.cn; Highway 213, 213国道; ¥80; ⏱ 8am-6pm) Lovely tropical gardens – the largest botanic gardens in all China – with many rare plant species and decent English and Latin signage. Don't miss the Distinctive Plant Collection. In addition to the main manicured sections of the gardens, the much larger East Area is home to acres of mostly undisturbed tropical rainforest, great for quiet wandering away from the crowds.

WORTH A TRIP

HIKING IN XISHUANGBANNA

Hikes around Xishuangbanna used to be among the best in China – you'd be invited into a local's home to eat, sleep and drink *mǐjiǔ* (rice wine). Growing numbers of visitors have changed this in many places, while rubber and banana plantations are having an increasingly deleterious effect on the environment.

It's still possible to find villages that see very few foreigners and remain pristine, but they are remote. Don't expect to roll up in Jinghong and the next day to be in a village that hasn't seen a foreigner before. And don't automatically expect a welcome mat and a free lunch because you're a foreigner, either.

If you do get invited into someone's home, try to establish whether payment is expected. If it's not, leave an offering or modest gift (ask at the backpacker cafes to find out what's considered appropriate), even though the family may insist on nothing.

Also, take care before heading off. It's a jungle out there – literally – so go prepared, and make sure somebody knows where you are and when you should return. In the rainy season, you'll need to be equipped with proper hiking shoes and waterproof gear. You'll need water purification tablets, bottled water or a water bottle able to hold boiled water, as well as snacks and sunscreen. Seriously consider taking a guide. You won't hear much Mandarin on the trail, let alone any English. Expect to pay around ¥300 per day.

The Mekong Cafe (p744) in Jinghong can arrange treks and guides. The Meimei Cafe (p744) doesn't organise treks but does have lots of details in binders so you can find your own way, including info on self-guided hikes to the villages of Zhanglang, Bulangshan and Manmai as well as a handful of day-hike options nearer to Jinghong.

On-the-spot visas for Laos can be obtained at the Mohan border, which is 600m south of the bus station. The price will depend on your nationality (generally US$30 to US$42), and is payable in USD or either local currency. You can also pick one up at the **Laos Consulate** (老挝驻昆明总领事馆驻景洪领事办公室, Lǎowōzhù Kūnmíngzǒng Lǐngshìguǎn Zhùjǐnghóng Lǐngshì Bàngōngshì; ☑ 691 221 9355; 2nd fl, Bldg 2, Gaozhuang Xishuangjing, Xuanwei Dadao, 宣慰大道, 告庄西双景综合楼2楼; ⊘ 8.30-11.30am & 2.30-4.30pm Mon-Fri) in Jinghong. The **Chinese checkpoint** (国际口岸, Guójì Kǒu'àn; ☑ 691 812 2684; Dongmeng Dadao, 东盟大道; ⊘ 9am-10pm) is generally not much of an ordeal. Don't forget that Laos is an hour behind China.

Apart from the one bus from Mohan to Luang Prabang in Laos, a daily bus also runs to Luang Prabang from Jinghong. The daily bus to Vientiane from Kunming stops at Mohan, but you're not guaranteed a seat if you try to board here and it has filled up previously.

No matter what anyone says, there should be no charge to cross. Once your passport is stamped (double-check all stamps), you can jump on a motor-rickshaw to take you 3km into Laos for around ¥10. There are guesthouses on both the Chinese and Laos sides; people generally change money on the Laos side at better rates.

ℹ️ Getting There & Away

Menglun is located east of Menghan. To and from Jinghong's Banna station there are buses to Menglun (¥23, 75 minutes, every 20 minutes, 7.40am to 9.30pm). From Menglun there are buses to and from Mengla (¥37, two hours, every 20 minutes, 8am to 6pm), and two buses to Kunming (¥265, nine hours, 11.20am and 8pm). Most Jinghong and Mengla buses stop at the west entrance of the Tropical Botanical Garden to drop off and pick up tourists.

Damenglong 大勐龙

☑ 0691 / POP 30,000

Damenglong (Dàměnglóng) has seen rapid development, like much of Xishuangbanna. It's still a drowsy place though and, a couple of pagodas aside, is traditionally just a staging point for hikes to the surrounding minority villages. Bear in mind that rubber plantations have made the countryside here less pristine than it once was.

◉ Sights

White Bamboo Shoot Pagoda PAGODA

(曼飞龙塔, Mànfēilóng Tǎ; ¥80) Surrounded by bamboo stands and rubber plantations, this pagoda dates back to 1204 and is Damenglong's premier attraction. According to legend, the pagoda's temple was built on the location of a hallowed footprint left behind by the Sakyamuni Buddha, who is said to have visited Xishuangbanna. If you have an interest in ancient footprints you can look for it in a niche below one of the nine stupas. The temple has been renovated in recent years.

The pagoda is easy to get to: just walk back along the main road towards Jinghong for 2km until you reach a small village with a temple on your left. From here there's a path up the hill: it's about a 20-minute walk up 400 or so steps through the jungle. A motor-rickshaw from Damenglong is ¥10, or ask to be let off on the way from Jinghong.

Black Pagoda PAGODA

(黑塔, Hēi Tǎ; 布朗塔, Bùlǎng Tǎ) FREE Just above the centre of town is a Dai monastery with a steep path beside it leading up to the Black Pagoda – you'll notice it when entering Damenglong. The pagoda itself is actually gold, not black. Take a 15-minute stroll up and have a chat with the few monks in residence, but the views of the surrounding countryside are more interesting than the temple itself.

🛏️ Sleeping & Eating

There's no reason to stay in Damenglong: it's either an easy day trip from Jinghong, or just a place to catch a bus to the jumping-off point for hikes into the countryside. If you need a room here, they're available along the main drag for ¥80 and up. There are simple restaurants and Dai barbecue places scattered throughout the village.

ℹ️ Getting There & Away

Buses to Damenglong (¥19, 1½ hours, every 20 minutes, 6.10am to 6pm) leave from Jinghong's south bus station. Often just the last two characters, 'Měnglóng', are written on buses; the 'Da' character (大, Dà) is generally not displayed. Buses for the return trip run on the same schedule.

YUNNAN DAMENGLONG

Sichuan

POP 80.1 MILLION

Best Places to Eat

➡ Zhao Family Crispy Duck (p770)

➡ Are Tibetan Restaurant #1 (p758)

➡ Dōng Zǐ Kou Zhāng Lǎo Èr Liáng Fěn (p758)

➡ Mǎ Wàng Zi (p759)

Best Places to Stay

➡ Zhilam Hostel (p777)

➡ Flipflop Lounge Hostel (p757)

➡ The Temple House (p757)

➡ Khampa Nomad Ecolodge & Arts Center (p782)

Why Go?

It's fitting that an ancient form of opera and magic called *biànliǎn* (face-changing) originated here, for Sichuan (四川, Sìchuān) is a land of many guises. Capital Chengdu shows a modern face, but just beyond its ring roads you'll find a more traditional landscape of mist-shrouded, sacred mountains, and a countryside scattered with ancient villages and cliffs of carved Buddhas.

Central Sichuan is also home to the giant panda, the most famous face in China. In the south, expect a veil of history and a muted beauty that sees far fewer travellers than the rest of the region. To the north the visage changes again into a fairyland of alpine valleys and blue-green lakes. Sichuan's Tibetan side appears as you venture west. This is Kham, one of the former Tibetan prefectures: a vast landscape of plateau grasslands and glacial mountains where Tibetan culture still thrives and you're certain to have your most challenging, yet most magical, experiences.

When to Go
Chengdu

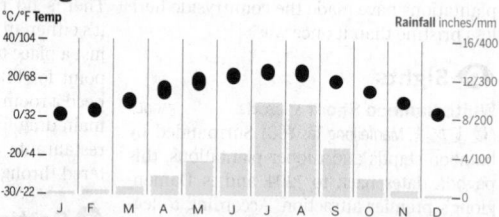

March–May
Prime time for Chengdu; not too humid, peach blossoms and little rain.

July & August In the west the warm grasslands bloom in technicolour and festivals abound; time for hiking in the mountains.

September & October Turquoise glacial lakes in the west amid autumn leaves; summer heat of Chengdu begins to subside.

History

Sichuan's early history was turbulent. The region was the site of various breakaway kingdoms, ever skirmishing with central authority, but it was finally wrested under control and established as the capital of the Qin empire in the 3rd century BC. It was here that the kingdom of Shu (a name by which the province is still known) ruled as an independent state during the Three Kingdoms period (AD 220–80).

During the Warring States period (475–221 BC), local governor and famed engineer Li Bing managed to harness the flood-prone Min River (岷江, Mín Jiāng) on the Chuanxi plain with his revolutionary weir system; the Dujiangyan Irrigation Project still controls flooding, and supplies Chengdu and 49 other provincial cities with water 2200 years after it was constructed. It's one of the reasons the Sichuan basin is synonymous with fertile soil.

Another more recent factor was the efforts of Zhao Ziyang, the Party Secretary of Sichuan in 1975. After the Great Leap Forward, when an estimated 10% of Sichuan's population died of starvation, Ziyang became the driving force behind agricultural and economic reforms that restored farming output. He reinstated the 'Responsibility System', whereby plots of land were granted to farming families on the proviso that they sold a quota of crops to the state. Any additional profits or losses would be borne by the families. This household-focused approach was so successful that it became the national model. Sichuan continues to be a major producer of the nation's grain, soybeans and pork.

Catastrophe struck the region on 12 May 2008, when the Wenchuan earthquake measuring 7.9 on the Richter scale hit the province's central region. Some sources reported it killed more than 88,000 people, as many as 10,000 of them school children, and left millions more injured or homeless. The rebuilding effort cost over a trillion yuan and the destruction was so complete in some areas that it has taken many years for the work to be completed. The main road linking Chengdu with Jiuzhaigou took four years to reopen, and travellers on that route will now see that brand-new villages have risen from the rubble.

Earthquakes continue to rock the region on a regular basis. In mid 2019 a series of quakes hit the area around Yibin, causing a number of fatalities and structural damage.

Language

Sichuanese is a Mandarin dialect, but with its fast clip, distinctive syntax and five tones instead of four, it can challenge standard Mandarin speakers. Two phrases easily understood are *yàodé* (pronounced 'yow-day', meaning 'yes' or 'OK') and *méidé* (pronounced 'may-day', meaning 'no').

Sichuan's other major languages belong to the Tibeto-Burman family and are spoken by Tibetans and Yi minorities. Don't expect much help from standard phrasebooks. In western Sichuan, Tibetan dialects vary from region to region. Hiring a guide for this area makes sense, but ensure that they are a native Tibetan speaker rather than Chinese (many Chinese guides to the region don't speak Tibetan).

ⓘ Getting There & Away

Chengdu serves as the province's transit hub. Smooth expressways to many towns and cities near Chengdu as well as to parts of eastern and western Sichuan make for short trips to many destinations. There are no expressways in the north or west of Sichuan (though some are under construction) but all but the most minor roads – or those over the highest passes – are still in pretty good condition. Tunnels that bore straight through the heart of mountains have cut journey times considerably on main roads in the west. Weather conditions are unpredictable at high elevations, and hazards ranging from landslides to snow-blocked roads are common,

---

ⓘ PRICE RANGES

Sleeping

The following price ranges refer to a double room. Unless otherwise stated, private bathroom is included in the price.

¥ less than ¥200

¥¥ ¥200–400

¥¥¥ more than ¥400

Eating

The following price ranges refer to a main course.

¥ less than ¥30

¥¥ ¥30–50

¥¥¥ more than ¥50

Sichuan Highlights

1 Yading Nature Reserve (p794) Making multiday pilgrimage treks around the stunning holy mountains.

2 Tagong (p780) Striding across windswept grasslands and sleeping in Tibetan nomad tents.

3 Emei Shan (p765) Rising with the sun above the forested slopes at this cool, misty retreat.

4 Giant Panda Breeding Research Base (p752) Meeting China's cuddly national icon.

5 Dzongsar Valley (p790) Exploring this beautiful valley dotted with ancient temples and home to thousands of monks.

6 Grand Buddha (p769) Peering over the toenails of the world's largest Buddha statue in Le Shan.

7 Dzogchen (p787) Being dazzled by the scale of this monastery complex and then dazzled again by the epic mountain scenery.

8 Four Sisters Mountain (p796) Hiking at the foot of Sichuan's second-highest mountain and taking in the panorama from the top of the Haizi Valley.

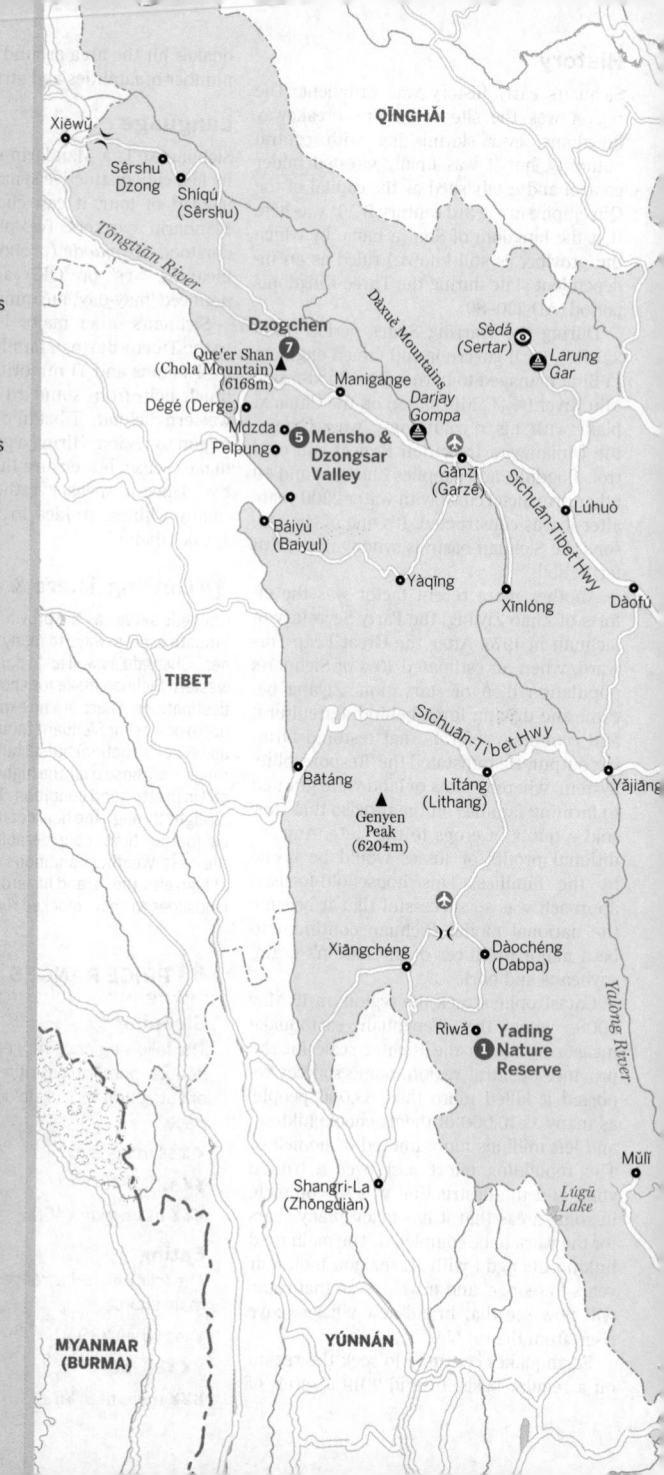

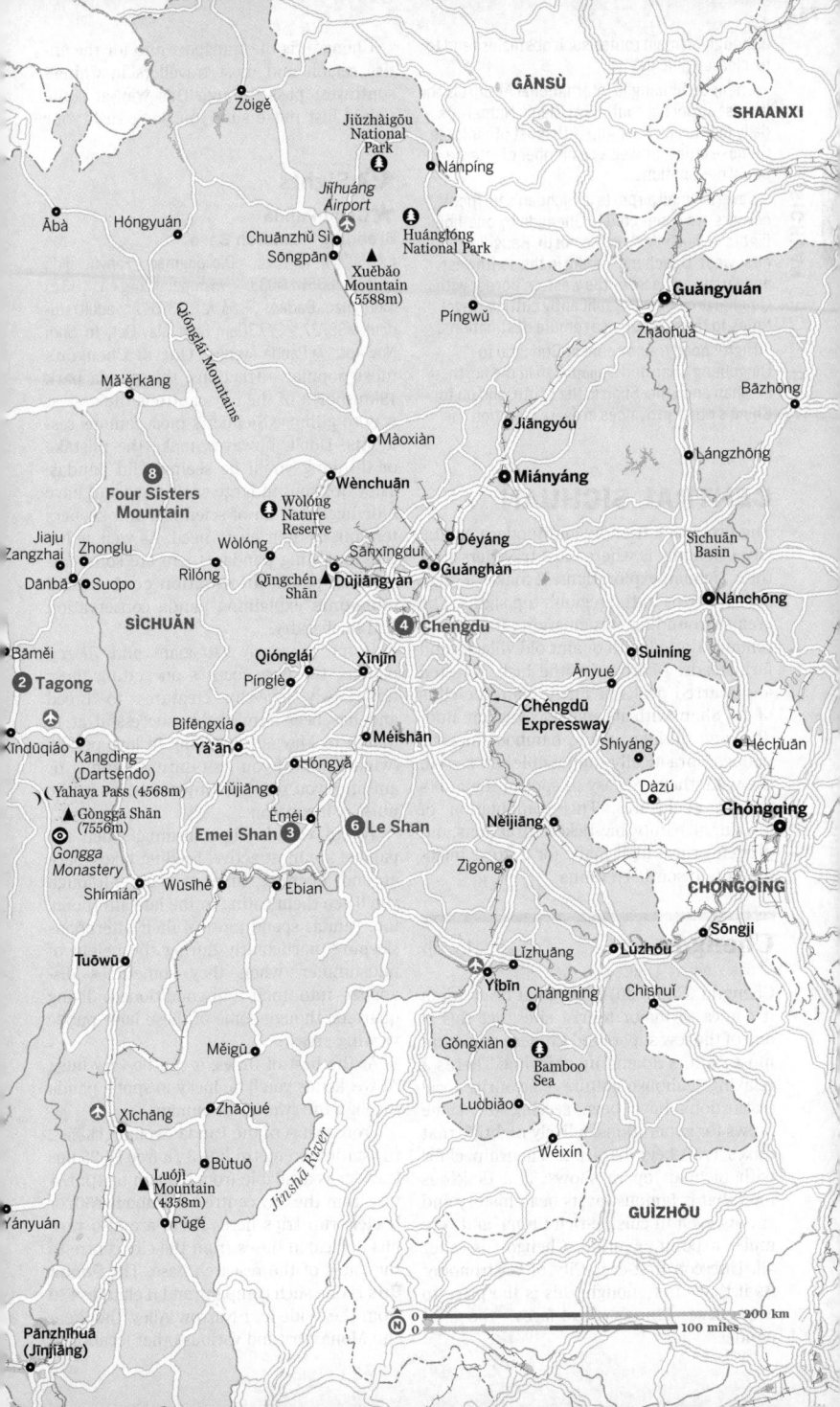

although on main routes such obstacles tend to be cleared quickly.

Chengdu Shuangliu International Airport is the largest airport in southwest China. Numerous daily flights link Chengdu with most other large Chinese cities, as well as a number of international destinations.

Several small airports in Sichuan's furthest corners are connected to Chengdu by one-hour flights — Jiuzhaigou in the north, Kangding in the near west, Daocheng-Yading in the southwest, and Yushu just across the western border with Qinghai province – significantly cutting travel times to these otherwise remote destinations.

High-speed trains connect Chengdu to Qingcheng Shan and Dujiangyan in the north, Le Shan and Emei Shan in the south, and on to China's other provinces in every direction.

CENTRAL SICHUAN

The province's friendly and modern capital city, Chengdu, is where most travellers start their Sichuan explorations. It makes a great base for trips to the region's top sights. The area surrounding this emerging metropolis remains dotted with quaint old villages and farmsteads. Nearby rise the lush, forested and scarred peaks of Emei Shan, the cliffs of Le Shan with its massive ancient Buddha, and, hidden in the bamboo thickets, pandas; practically impossible to see in the wild, they are easy to spot in the area's reserve enclosures. This combination of buzzing urbanity, big-ticket attractions and peaceful rural idyll make for a great introduction to southern China.

Chengdu 成都

☑ 028 / POP 14.42 MILLION

Chengdu (Chéngdū) is no great draw when it comes to major tourist sites, yet this is one of the few supersized Chinese cities that most visitors do end up enjoying. There's a relaxing teahouse culture – favourite local institutions have been serving the same brews for generations; a lively nightlife that mixes craft-beer bars and superhip clubs with Sichuan opera shows; and delicious food that is famous for its heat, history and variety even in cuisine-rich China, and very much a point of pride: Chengdu is, after all, Unesco's first-ever City of Gastronomy. As if that's not enough, this is the place to come to see China's cutest faces – the giant pandas.

Chengdu is the transport hub for the entire region and most travellers in China's southwest pass through this way at some point. Just make sure you don't rush your visit.

◉ Sights

★ Giant Panda Breeding Research Base   ZOO

(大熊猫繁育基地, Dàxióngmāo Fányù Jīdì; ☑028 8351 0033; www.panda.org.cn; 1375 Xiongmao Dadao, 熊猫大道1375号; adult/student ¥55/27; ⊙7.30am-6pm May-Oct, to 5pm Nov-Apr; Ⓜ Panda Avenue) One of Chengdu's most popular attractions, this panda park 18km north of the city centre is the easiest way to glimpse Sichuan's most famous residents. Don't, however, make the mistake of thinking you'll be seeing wild pandas. They are kept in large enclosures and have a dedicated team of scientists and keepers tending to their every need. As well as living, breathing pandas, there are some fascinating panda information centres and museums explaining panda conservation and husbandry.

Home to nearly 120 giant and 76 red pandas, the base focuses on getting these notoriously love-shy creatures to breed and has been remarkably successful at it. March to May is the 'falling in love period' (wink wink). If you visit during summer or autumn, you may see tiny newborns in the nursery incubators.

Try to visit in the morning, when the pandas are most active. Feeding takes place around opening time at 8am, although you'll see them eating in the late afternoon, too. Pandas spend most of their afternoons sleeping, particularly during the height of midsummer, when they sometimes disappear into their (air-conditioned) living quarters, though some of these have public viewing areas.

At the best of times, it can be very busy. At weekends you'll be lucky to spot a panda through the swarms of humans.

From exit A of the Panda Avenue (熊猫大道) station on metro line 3 , a free D025 bus transfer is available from 8.30am to 4pm. A taxi from the city centre costs about ¥50, or hostels run trips here. There are also various dedicated buses from the city centre to the gates of the research base. The Panda Bus is one such company and it charges ¥10 from the Wide and Narrow Alley, the Wenshu Monastery and various other locations.

★**Chengdu Museum**   MUSEUM
(成都博物馆, Chéngdū Bówùguǎn; ☎028 6291 5593; www.cdmuseum.com; west side of Tianfu Sq, 天府广场西侧; ◉9am-8.30pm Tue-Sun May-Oct, to 8pm Nov-Apr; Ⓜ Tianfu Square) FREE Spanning ancient Shu and pre-Qin dynasties to the Revolutionary era and modern Chengdu, this spectacular five-storey museum (completed in 2016) is packed with historical and cultural relics of the city's past. Don't miss the two 'Puppetry and Shadow Plays of China' galleries on the top floor, with excellent examples of the art from across the country. There are also some interesting temporary exhibitions in the basement. Signage is in English. Bring a passport for entry.

★**Wenshu Monastery**   BUDDHIST TEMPLE
(文殊院, Wénshū Yuàn; 66 Wenshuyuan Lu, 文殊院路66号; ◉7am-9pm; Ⓜ Wenshu Monastery) FREE This Tang dynasty monastery is dedicated to Wenshu (Manjushri), the Bodhisattva of Wisdom, and is Chengdu's largest and best-preserved Buddhist temple. The air is heavy with incense and the low murmur of chanting; despite frequent crowds of worshippers, there's still a sense of serenity and solitude. At weekends free Chinese- and English-language tours of the complex run frequently. Look for the stand advertising them inside the main courtyard.

Chengdu Art Gallery   GALLERY
(成都市美术馆, Chéngdū Shì Měishùguǎn; ☎028 8663 3667, 028 8627 5483; www.cdcaa.net; 80 Xiatongren Lu, 下同仁路80号; ◉9am-5pm Tue-Sun; Ⓜ Wide and Narrow Alley) FREE Rotating exhibitions of classical-style Chinese art in a traditionally styled courtyard building that's almost as artistic as the paintings within. It's a real haven of calm from the frenetic crowds on the Wide and Narrow Alley pedestrian streets you take to access it.

Sichuan Museum   MUSEUM
(四川博物院, Sìchuān Bówùyuàn; ☎028 6552 1888, 028 6552 1569; www.scmuseum.cn; 5 Huanqing Hualu, 浣青华路5号; ◉9am-9pm Tue-Sun May-Oct, to 8pm Nov-Apr; ◻19, 82, 165) FREE Aficionados of Chinese history will enjoy a stop here for a look at Sichuan's past through Shu-era calligraphy and painting, bronze works and ceramics, and a nice gallery of Buddha statues unearthed during archaeological works at the Ming dynasty Wanfo Temple (万佛寺). The hall focusing on the region's ethnic minorities is also fascinating (even more so if you're heading west to Tibet). Most signage is in English. Bring your passport for entry.

Jinsha Site Museum   MUSEUM
(金沙遗址博物馆, Jīnshā Yízhǐ Bówùguǎn; ☎028 8730 3522; www.jinshasitemuseum.com; 227 Qingyang Dadao, 青羊大道227号; ¥70; ◉8.30am-8pm Tue-Sun May-Oct, to 6.30pm Nov-Apr; also Mon Jan-Feb & Jul-Aug; Ⓜ Jinsha Site Museum) In 2001 archaeologists made a historic discovery in Chengdu's western suburbs: they unearthed a major site containing ruins of the 3000-year-old Shu kingdom. This excellent, expansive museum includes the excavation site and beautiful displays of many of the uncovered objects, which were created between 1200 and 600 BC.

The 6000 or so relics here include both functional and decorative items, from pottery and tools to jade artefacts, stone carvings and ornate gold masks. A large number of elephant tusks were also unearthed here.

Use exit C of the Jinsha Site Museum station on metro line 7; the ticket office is about 400m north.

An audio guide (in English) is ¥10 with a ¥200 deposit.

Wuhiu Temple   BUDDHIST TEMPLE
(武侯祠, Wǔhóu Cí; ☎028 8555 2397; www.wuhouci.net.cn; 231 Wuhouci Dajie, 武侯祠大街231号; adult/student ¥50/25; ◉8am-8pm May-Oct, to 6.30pm Nov-Apr; ◻1, 21, 26) Located adjacent to Nanjiao Park and surrounded by mossy cypresses, this temple (rebuilt in 1672) honours several figures from the Three Kingdoms period, namely legendary military strategist Zhuge Liang and Emperor Liu Bei (his tomb is here). Both were immortalised in the Chinese literature classic, *Romance of the Three Kingdoms* (Sān Guó Yǎnyì).

Qingyang Temple   TAOIST TEMPLE
(青羊宫, Qīngyáng Gōng; 9 Huanlu Xi Er Duan, 一环路西二段9号; ¥10; ◉8am-6pm; ◻11, 27, 45) Alongside **Culture Park** (文化公园, Wénhuà Gōngyuán; ◉6am-10pm; ⊡) FREE, this is Chengdu's oldest and most extensive Taoist temple. Qingyang (Green Ram) Temple dates from the Zhou dynasty, although most of what you see is Qing. A highlight is the unusually squat, eight-sided pagoda, built without bolts or pegs. There's also a popular teahouse (tea from ¥10) inside towards the back.

People's Park   PARK
(人民公园, Rénmín Gōngyuán; 9 Citang Jie, 祠堂街9号; ◉6.30am-10pm; Ⓜ People's Park) FREE On weekends, locals fill this park with dancing,

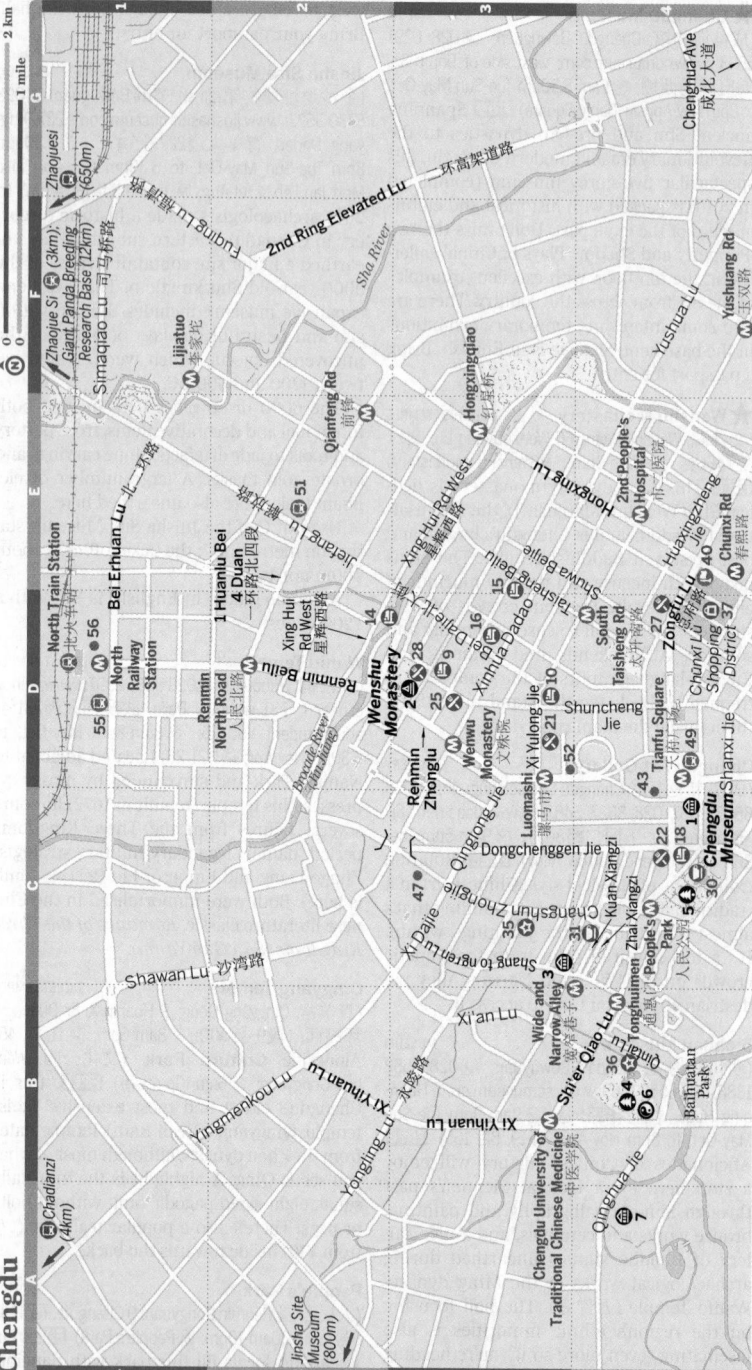

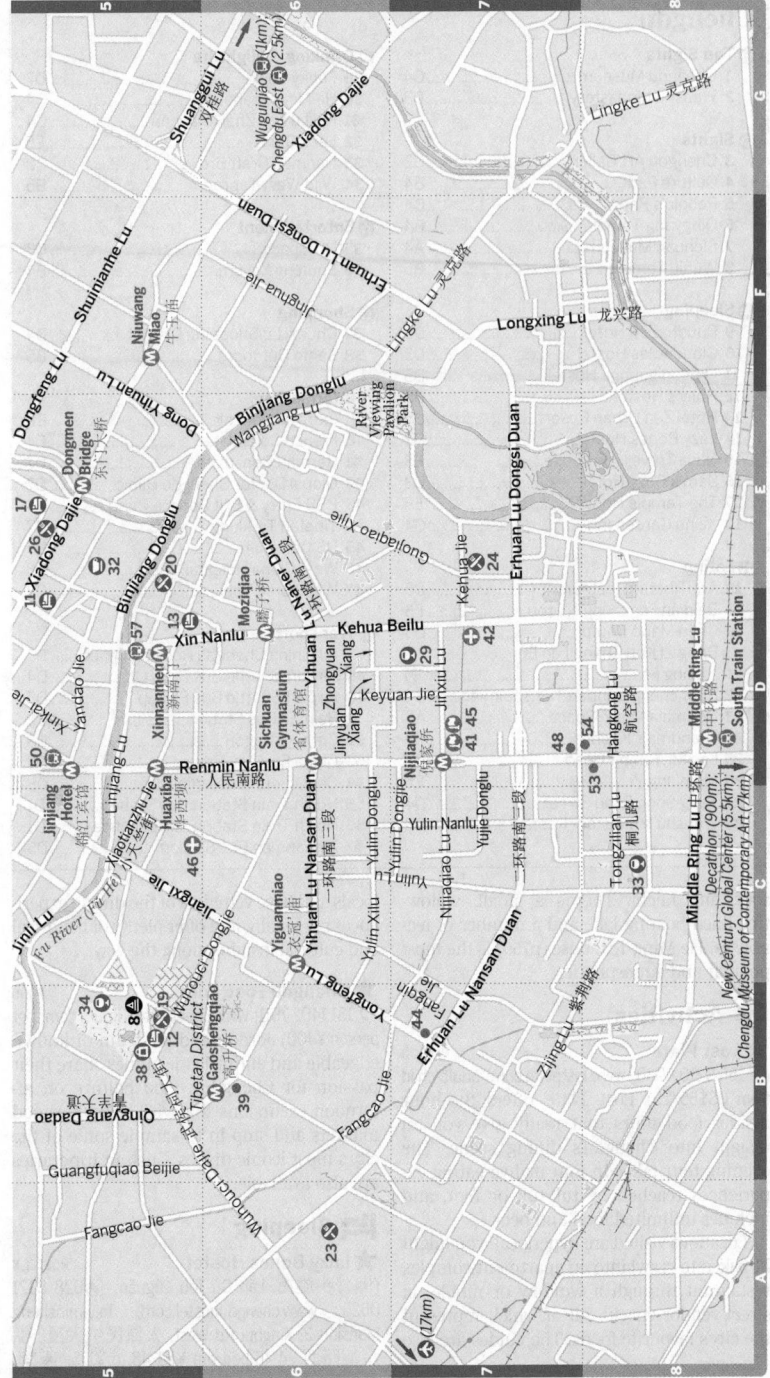

Chengdu

song and taichi. There's a small, willow-tree-lined boating lake and a number of teahouses: He Ming Teahouse (p759) is the most popular and atmospheric.

🏃 Activities

★ Lost Plate
FOOD

(☑156 9210 9030; www.lostplate.com; adult/child from US$55/25) Lost Plate offers 3½-hour insider food tours that really give you an insight into Chengdu's dining scene. The evening tour takes in four or five eating experiences reached by tuk-tuk or foot, and includes unlimited food and beer.

Locations visited are hyperlocal: you might be asked to crawl into an apartment-complex restaurant through a window or nibble on street-vendor snacks, all of which represent the city's favourite foods. The guides are also locals and have vetted all of the dining experiences personally, and offer plenty of historical and cultural insights along the way.

★ Chengdu Food Tours
FOOD

(☑151 1402 7611; www.chengdufoodtours.com; per person ¥400) Jordan and his team of knowledgeable and enthusiastic guides share their passion for Chengdu's food culture on afternoon excursions that visit neighborhood markets and stop in to sample some of the city's most iconic dishes. Custom itineraries are also available.

🛏 Sleeping

★ Lazy Bones Hostel
HOSTEL ¥

(懒骨头旅馆, Lǎn Gú Tóu Lǚguǎn; ☑028 8321 0525; www.chengduhostel.com; Taiyiminsheng Mansion 2, Xinghui Rd West, 太原民生大厦2号, 星汇路西; 4-/6-bed dm ¥58/48, d ¥175; ❈🅡;

Ⓜ Wenshu Monastery) Excellent hostel aimed at poshpackers rather than backpackers. Pristine dorms have private bathrooms and a maximum of just six beds while the private rooms, with fancy tile work, are as good as many a hotel room. There's a cool street-side wooden terrace, loads of travel facilities, advice and tours, good western breakfasts and clued-up, English-speaking staff.

Cloud Atlas Hostel HOSTEL ¥
(云图国际青年旅舍, Yúntú Guójì Qīngnián Lǚshě; ☑ 028 8334 6767; cloudatlashostel@163.com; 288 Shuncheng Jie, 顺城街288号; dm ¥39-59, s/d ¥109/119; ❄ ❋ �ⓦ; Ⓜ Luomashi) Excellent facilities, great coffee, lots of common space – this artsy hostel with bright, 'building-block' furnishings and spotless bathrooms has it all. It's large enough to feel a bit institutional on the dorm floors, but that just means there are tonnes of new friends to be made. Look for it inside the entrance to the Zhufeng Jiudian (珠峰酒店).

Nova Traveller's Lodge HOSTEL ¥
(成都乐浮国际青年旅舍, Chéngdū Lèfú Guójì Qīngnián Lǚshě; ☑ 028 8695 0016; www.dragontown.com.cn; 10 Taisheng Beilu, 太升北路10号; dm from ¥55, r ¥148-218; ❋ ⓦ; Ⓜ South Taisheng Rd) Clean, bright and quiet; the staff here make the collection of good facilities into a truly warm hostel. Standard private rooms are on the small side, so upgrade to one of the spacier deluxe rooms. There are frequent movie nights, a range of day trips and an inviting alfresco cafe, plus the staff speak superb English.

Holly's Hostel HOSTEL ¥
(九龙鼎青年客栈, Jiǔlóngdǐng Qīngnián Kèzhàn; ☑ 028 8554 8131; hollyhostelcn@yahoo.com; 246 Wuhouci Dajie, 武侯祠大街246号; 4-/6-bed dm ¥50/40, s/d ¥165/218; ❋ @ ⓦ; ▯ 27, 45) Prepare for trips out west by plugging yourself in to Chengdu's small Tibetan district, which surrounds this welcoming hostel. Holly's has bright, comfortable and four- to six-bed dorms, plus English-speaking staff, bike rentals (¥20) and a nice rooftop cafe (western and Chinese mains ¥10 to ¥50). Staff can also help with permits to Lhasa.

★ Xishu Garden Inn HOSTEL ¥¥
(探索西部青年旅舍, Tànsuǒ Xībù Qīngnián Lǚshě; ☑ 028 6210 5818; www.hiwestchina.com; Suite 5, 19 Dongcheng Gennanjie, 东城根南街19号附5号; dm ¥40-45, d ¥220; ❋ ⓦ; Ⓜ People's Park) Superfriendly English-speaking staff,

bold jungle-green rooms with panda motifs and an unbeatable location beside People's Park make this one of our favourite hostels in the city; not to mention the great rooftop terrace that caps it all off. The only drawback is that the dorms contain a LOT of beds (10 or 22!).

★ Flipflop Lounge Hostel HOSTEL ¥¥
(拖板鞋青年旅舍, Tuō Bǎnxié Qīngnián Lǚshě; ☑ 028 6250 0185; www.chengduhostel.com; 98 Dongsheng Jie, 东升街98号; 10-/6-/4-bed dm ¥69/89/109, d ¥189-299; ❋ @ ⓦ; Ⓜ Chunxi Rd) Currently the ciy's best hostel, this lively place offers travellers all the usual services plus a few rare gifts – a pool table, a rooftop terrace, and experienced help when it comes to onward travel. The dorm beds are made of rough timber and have a fair amount of privacy, while the private rooms are more hotel than hostel.

It has fun daily events such as dumpling parties, singing competitions (okay maybe that's not so fun...), barbecues and communal hotpot dinners. Slightly more expensive than other hostels, here you're paying for the hip(ster) vibe and 10-minute walk to Chunxi Rd and Tai Koo Li.

Sam's Cozy Hotel HOTEL ¥¥
(成都九龙鼎客栈, Chéngdū Jiǔlóngdǐng Kèzhàn; ☑ 028 6016 7761; samtour1991@163.com; 37 Zaojunmiao Jie, 灶君庙街37号; r from ¥200; ❋ ⓦ; Ⓜ Wenshu Monastery) Sam's is a long-standing, solid budget hotel with nicely aged rooms with huge mirrored walls. Check a few rooms first as some are a step up the quality ladder from others. Quiet location near Wenshu Monastery. Some English spoken.

★ The Temple House LUXURY HOTEL ¥¥¥
(博舍酒店, Bóshè Jiǔdiàn; ☑ 028 6636 9999; www.thetemplehousehotel.com; 81 Bitieshi Jie, 笔帖式街81号; r from ¥1615; ❋ ⓦ ❄; Ⓜ Chunxi Rd) Cool to its core, every room is hip and understated with elegant stylings and modern amenities that come together perfectly around a traditional-style courtyard. Superb location bang in the middle of an upmarket, city-centre neighbourhood. Discounts of 25% are available outside of high season when booking directly.

Hotel Zen Urban Resort BOUTIQUE HOTEL ¥¥¥
(朴院禅文化精品酒店, Pǔyuànchán Wénhuà Jīngpǐn Jiǔdiàn; ☑ 028 8505 1088; www.zenurbanresort.com; 14 Longjiang Lu, 龙江路14号; r from ¥310; ❋ ⓦ; Ⓜ Xinnanmen) Very good value, boutique

hotel with dark wood tones and a peaceful inner courtyard that all give a sense of an older, more traditional China. Cheaper rooms don't have windows and are a little cramped. Good breakfast is included and there's decent street food available all around the hotel.

BuddhaZen Hotel　　　BOUTIQUE HOTEL ¥¥¥
(圆和圆佛禅客栈, Yuánhéyuán Fúchán Kèzhàn, ☐ 和☐; ☑ 028 86929898; www.buddhazen-hotel.com; B6-6 Wenshufang, 青羊区文殊坊B6-6号; s/d/ste incl breakfast from ¥468/568/788; ✿@☎; Ⓜ Wenshu Monastery) Set in a tranquil courtyard building, this boutique hotel near Wenshu Monastery blends traditional decor with modern comforts and a taste of Buddhist philosophy. You can ponder life while sipping tea on your private balcony, circling the sand garden or soaking in a wooden tub at the spa. It's lovely here.

✖ Eating

Given that Chengdu has reportedly the highest density of restaurants and teahouses of any city in the world, and is the first city in Asia to be named a Unesco City of Gastronomy, your most memorable moments here are likely to involve food.

Several temples, including Wenshu Monastery, have popular vegetarian restaurants that are generally open only for lunch.

★ Dòng Zǐ Kou Zhāng Lǎo Èr Liáng Fěn　　NOODLES ¥
(洞子口张老二凉粉; 39 Wenshuyuan Lu, 文殊院路39号; mains ¥12; ⊘ 8.30am-7.30pm Apr-Oct, to 6.30pm Nov-Mar; Ⓜ Wenshu) A city classic that's always packed at lunchtime, but just squeeze onto the end of one of the benches and tuck into the house special: *tián shuǐ miàn*, which is a tongue-tingling, mind-blowing bowl of thick, sugary noodles in a spicy sauce. Try it once and you'll come back day after day.

Bǎinián Fěnzhēng Niúròu　　SICHUAN ¥
(百年粉蒸牛肉; 33 Zhimin Lu, 致民路33号; mains ¥12-88; ⊘ 11.30am-8pm; Ⓜ Xinnanmen) Drop in at this little hole in the wall for friendly vibes and fiery flavours – the namesake 'Century Steamed Beef' (¥22) is particularly nice, but you'll want to order a cold one to cool off the spice.

Dōngchéng Dàndàn Tiánshuǐmiàn SICHUAN ¥
(东城担担甜水面; ☑ 028 8625 8168; 13 Dongchenggen Shangjie, 东城根上街13号; mains ¥10-16; ⊘ 7.30am-10pm; Ⓜ People's Park) There are lots of reasons to recommend this neighborhood place just up from People's Park. We could talk about watching the food being prepared through the glass kitchen-front, or how it's like an upmarket street-food joint, but the real reason locals pour in here is for the simple, flavourful bowls of local classic *dàndàn* noodles (担担面; ¥10).

Tang Song Food Street　　STREET FOOD ¥
(春熙坊唐宋美食街, Chūnxīfāng Tángsòng Měishí Jiē; 29 Zongfu Lu, 总府路29号; mains from ¥12; ⊘ 10am-10.30pm; Ⓜ Chunxi Rd) This reconstructed ancient alleyway is jam-packed with tourists and Chengdu favourites like *chāoshǒu* (抄手, wontons; ¥12) and *chuàn-chuàn xiāng* (串串香, the skewer version of the Chongqing hotpot; ¥2 to ¥5). Musical performances reverberate in the indoor space in the evening. Look for the wooden sign and doors near Lotte KTV.

★ Drolmala Music Space　　TIBETAN ¥¥
(倬玛啦音乐空间; ☑ 028 8746 4169; Jinke Shuangnanzhan 80, Xiyiduan 2nd Ring Rd, 金科双南站西一段二环路80号; mains ¥20-80; ⊘ noon-2am; Ⓜ Hongpailou) Drolmala is something of a social centre for the young of Chengdu's big Tibetan community. This superb space mixes fabulous modern Tibetan cuisine with regular, live world music (when we dropped by a contemporary Kazak folk band was playing) and a happening bar that attracts a good crowd of Tibetans and in-the-know Chinese and expats. Food is served until 10pm.

★ Are Tibetan Restaurant #1　　TIBETAN ¥¥
(阿热藏餐老店, Arè Zángcān Lǎodiàn; ☑ 028 8551 0112; 3 Wuhouci Dongjie, 武侯祠东街3号; mains ¥18-118; ⊘ 9am-10pm; ☎; Ⓜ Gaoshengqiao) Not only will you not find no better Tibetan food in Chengdu, you'd be hard-pressed to find better Tibetan food anywhere in Tibet. Choose from a delicious range of Tibetan staples, from *tsampa* (roasted barley flour; ¥20) to *thugpa* (noodles in soup; ¥18). Or go for the house special: *Are Covered*, a thin, crispy pancake spread over fried yak meat.

Chén Mápó Dòufu　　SICHUAN ¥¥
(陈麻婆豆腐; ☑ 028 8674 3889; 197 Xi Yulong Jie, 西玉龙街197号; mains ¥22-58; ⊘ 11.30am-2.30pm & 5.30-9pm; Ⓜ Luomashi) The plush flagship of this famous chain is a great place to experience *mápó dòufu* (麻婆豆腐; small/large ¥12/20) – soft, house bean curd with a fiery sauce of garlic, minced beef, fermented soybean, chilli oil and Sichuan pepper. It's one of Sichuan's most famous dishes and

SICHUAN FOOD

Sichuan food is one of the four great regional Chinese cuisines, with famously spicy dishes that keep diners warm in the cold, damp winters and sweating in the hot, humid summers. From a ¥10 bowl of *dāndàn* noodles (noodles served with preserved vegetables in a spicy sauce) to a multicourse family feast or a bubbling vat of hotpot, the variety in Sichuan is nearly endless and the heat is unrelenting.

➡ **Huǒguō** (火锅) Hotpot; more a food style than a dish – a boiling vat of spicy (or not) oil cooks all manner of meat, veggies, intestines and more.

➡ **Gōngbào jīdīng** (宫爆鸡丁) Spicy chicken with peanuts.

➡ **Gānbiān sìjìdòu** (干煸四季豆) Dry-fried green beans.

➡ **Mápó dòufu** (麻婆豆腐) Spicy beancurd 'invented' by a pock-marked woman.

➡ **Shuǐzhǔ yú** (水煮鱼) Boiled fish in a fiery sauce.

➡ **Huíguō ròu** (回锅肉) Pork, simmered with spices and then stir-fried.

➡ **Yúxiāng qiézi** (鱼香茄子) Sliced eggplant, simmered in a sweet/sour/spicy sauce.

➡ **Dàndàn miàn** (担担面) Pickled veggies, minced pork, chilli and green onions over a bowl of noodles.

➡ **Máyóujī** (麻油鸡) Sesame-oil chicken.

➡ **Chuānběi liángfěn** (川北凉粉) The local take on a national favourite: mung-bean noodles served cold and drowning in spices.

---

this restaurant's speciality. Nonspicy choices are available, too.

Lao Ma Rabbit Head　　　　　SICHUAN ¥¥
(老妈兔头; Lǎomā Tùtóu; ☎ 132 1902 5349; 22 Jinsi Jie, 金丝22号; rabbit head ¥12, mains ¥12-68; ⊗ 8.30am-10pm; Ⓜ Wenshu Monastery) It's said that people will fly across China to eat rabbit head (兔头, *tùtóu*) in Chengdu and this restaurant cooks it better than most. Order by the piece, kinda spicy (五香, *wǔxiāng*) or pretty spicy (麻辣, *málà*). When it comes break open the jaw, split open the skull, and don't miss the best bits down in the cranial cavity.

**Wenshu Monastery
Restaurant**　　　　　　　　VEGETARIAN ¥¥
(文殊院素宴厅, Wénshūyuàn Sùyàn Tīng; southeast cnr of Wenshu Temple, Wenshuyuan Lu, 文殊院路; dishes ¥12-48, tea from ¥68; ⊗ 9.30am-11pm; ☑; Ⓜ Wenshu Monastery) This excellent volunteer-staffed vegetarian restaurant and the atmospheric teahouse that surrounds it are on Wenshu Monastery's grounds. There's also a coffee shop in a separate pavilion in the first courtyard.

★ **Mǎ Wàng Zi**　　　　　　　SICHUAN ¥¥¥
(马旺子; ☎ 028 6423 1923; 1 Dongkang Shijie, 东糠市街1号; mains ¥25-89; ⊗ 11.30am-2pm & 5.30-8.30pm Mon-Fri, 11.30am-2.15pm & 5.30-8.45pm Sat & Sun; ☑; Ⓜ Chunxi Rd) This high-end Sichuan

joint does everything right, from service and cuisine to ambience, but it's decidedly popular so you'd do well to make reservations beforehand.

Grandma's Kitchen　　　　INTERNATIONAL ¥¥¥
(奶奶的厨房, Nǎinai de chúfáng; ☎ 028 8555 3856; 22 Renmin South Lu, 人民南路22号; mains ¥68-88; ⊗ 9am-10pm; Ⓜ Nijiaqiao) Carefully presented, tasty western dishes such as chili con carne or Hungarian goulash as well as crisp, refreshing salads are served to a largely local lunchtime crowd who squeeze onto the faded wooden picnic benches. If you just need a liquid pause, they serve delicious juices and have a wide range of coffees. The exotic cheesecake is a triumph.

🍷 Drinking & Nightlife

Sichuan does teahouses better than anywhere else in China, and an afternoon in a leafy park's teahouse is a quintessential experience. Chengdu has plenty of options for the harder stuff too, including raucous bar strips but also craft-beer joints, refined cocktail bars and upmarket clubs.

For the latest on Chengdu's nightlife, check out More Chengdu (www.morechengdu.com).

★ **He Ming Teahouse**　　　　　TEAHOUSE
(鹤鸣茶馆, Hèmíng Cháguǎn; People's Park, 人民公园; ⊗ 9am-8pm; Ⓜ People's Park) Always

lively, this century-old spot is the most famous teahouse in Chengdu and the ideal place to fritter away an afternoon with a bottomless cup of tea (¥13 to ¥30) and a view over the endlessly absorbing park life. Neat tea-pouring performances can be organised for ¥280. Ear cleanings (¥20) available daily.

★ **Kǎi Lú Lǎo Zhái Cháyuán** TEAHOUSE
(庐恺老宅茶园; ☑ 180 3041 6632; 11 Kuan Xiangzi, 宽巷子11号; ⊙ 10am-10pm; ☎; Ⓜ Wide & Narrow Alley) For 200 years, one of the city's most venerable teahouses has been tucked away in a peaceful courtyard behind a stone archway off frenetic Kuan Alley, the distant hum of which is more than countered by the sound of zither music that plays in the background. These days there's wi-fi, but that seems to be about all that has changed. Tea from ¥48; snacks ¥12.

Let's Grind COFFEE
(☑ 181 1163 4646; 39 Jiangtingtang Bajie, 江亭镗钯街39号; ⊙ 8am-7pm; ☎; Ⓜ Chunxi Rd) In-the-know locals call this some of the best coffee in Chengdu, and we're inclined to agree. It certainly has the best selection of brews we've seen in town, and the beans are roasted locally and ground fresh for each cup.

Funky Town BAR
(时髦的小镇, Shímáo De Xiǎo Zhèn; ☑ 0182 8005 9632; www.facebook.com/FunkyTownChengdu; 58-3 North Kehua Lu, 北科华路58-3号; ⊙ 7pm-2am; Ⓜ Nijiaqiao) Tiny, hole-in-the-wall bar where three people constitute a full house. There's a single sofa inside and a table and couple of chairs on the pavement outside, and the whole thing is held together by skateboard and street art stickers and attitude. The best part of it is that people can bring along any vinyl they like and they'll play it.

Wild West Taproom CRAFT BEER
(美西啤酒, Měixī Píjiǔ; ☑ 028 8557 8927; 30 Zhangwu Jie, off Jinli Guije, 章武街30号; ⊙ 9am-midnight; ☐ 1, 21, 26) Sample some (or perhaps all) of this Chengdu-based brewer's eleven different ales at its taproom off Jinli Gujie. The four- to 10-glass samplers are particularly good value and the potato wedges go with it all very nicely.

Nanmen Craft Brewery CRAFT BEER
(南门精酿, Nánmén Jīngniàng; ☑ 028 8508 2366; 7 Tongzilin Lu, 桐梓林路7号; ⊙ 5pm-2am; Ⓜ Tongzilin) Craft beer, a convivial atmosphere and an eye-catching bar built around the brewing vats and equipment combine for a great thirst-quenching stop in Tongzilin. Sidle up to the bar and ask a bartender to help you find your personal preference of the numerous house brews, or choose from the wide menu of Chinese speciality beers.

☆ **Entertainment**

Chengdu is the birthplace of Sichuan opera, which dates back more than 250 years. Besides glass-shattering songs, performances feature slapstick, martial arts, men singing as women, acrobatics and even fire breathing. An undoubted highlight is *biànliǎn* (变脸; face changing), where performers change character in a blink by swapping masks, manipulating face paint and other conjuring tricks performed as entertainment.

★ **NU Space** LIVE MUSIC
(纽空间, Niǔ Kōngjiān; ☑ 028 8746 1983; www.facebook.com/nuspacechengdu; 9 Kuixinglou Jie, 奎星楼街9号; concerts ¥120-200; ⊙ 9am-10pm Sun-Thu, to 11pm Fri & Sat; Ⓜ Wide & Narrow Alley) This combination cafe, bookshop, gallery and performance space at the head of delightfully hip Kuixinglou Jie makes a nice stop to unwind after the overenthusiastic crowds of Wide and Narrow Alley, or to get pumped up by touring domestic and foreign artists from a wide range of genres. Check its Facebook page for show dates and timing.

★ **Shǔfēng Yǎyùn** CHINESE OPERA
(蜀风雅韵; ☑ 028 8776 4530; www.cdsfyy.com; Culture Park, 文化公园内面; tickets ¥140-320; ⊙ ticket office 3-9.30pm, nightly shows 8-9.30pm; ♿; Ⓜ Tonghuimen) This famous century-old theatre and teahouse puts on excellent 1½-hour shows that include music, puppetry and Sichuan opera's famed fire breathing and face changing. Come at around 7.15pm to watch performers putting on their elaborate make-up and costumes. For ¥50 to ¥100, kids (and adults) can try on garb and have a costume artist paint their face.

At weekends it sometimes stages an additional 3pm performance.

🔒 **Shopping**

Fancy-pants shopping centres dot the city, with the highest concentration around the **Chunxi Lu Shopping District** (春熙路步行街, Chūnxīlù Bùxíngjiē; Ⓜ Chunxi Rd) east of Tianfu Sq. For traditional Tibetan shopping options, try the shops in the Tibetan neighbourhood southeast of Wuhou Temple.

Outdoor enthusiasts gearing up for mountain trips should head to **Sanfo Outdoors** (三夫户外, Sānfū Hùwài; ☑ 028 8507 9586; www.sanfo.com; 243 Wuhouci Dajie, 武侯祠大街243号; ◷10am-8pm; M Gaoshengqiao) or **Decathlon** (迪卡侬运动超市, Díkǎnóng Yùndòng Chāoshì; ☑ 028 8531 0388; www.decathlon.com.cn; 199 Duhui Lu, 都会路199号; ◷10am-10pm; M South Train Station).

ℹ Information

HEALTH

Global Doctor Chengdu Clinic (环球医生, Huánqiú Yīshēng; ☑ 028 8522 6058, 24hr emergency 139 8225 6966; 2nd fl, 9-11 Lippo Tower, 62 Kehua Beilu, 科华北路62号力宝大厦2层9-11号; ◷9am-6pm Mon-Sat; M Nijiaqiao) English- and Chinese-speaking doctors and a 24-hour emergency line; staff can even make house visits.

West China Hospital SCU (四川大学华西医院, Sìchuān Dàxué Huáxī Yīyuàn; ☑24hr emergency assistance in Chinese & English 028 8542 3712, appts 028 8558 6698; www.eng.cd120.com; 37 Guoxue Xiang, 国学巷37号; M Huaxiba) This hospital complex is China's largest and is among the most well regarded. Foreigners should head for the International Hospital here, where doctors and some staff speak English. Note that some treatments without qualifying insurance may require a deposit.

TOUR COMPANIES

Skip the gazillion Chinese travel agencies around town and head to the travel desks at one of Chengdu's many excellent hostels, or try the following:

Extravagant Yak (☑028-8510 8093; www.extravagantyak.com; 11th fl, Rome Plaza Gaosheng Center 1117, 2 Gaoshengqiao Donglu, 高升桥东路2号罗马假日广场 高盛中心1117室; ◷9am-6pm Mon-Fri; M Gaoshengqiao)

Haiwei Trails (☑Mobile 013988756540; www.haiweitrails.com)

Kham Voyage (☑183 8218 6668; www.kham-voyage.com)

Mystic Tibet Tours (☑971 556 2272, 182 0971 5464; www.mystictibettours.com)

Tibetan Trekking (☑028 8597 6083; www.tibetantrekking.com; Room 35, 10th fl, Yulin Fengshang, 47 Yongfeng Lu; 47永丰路丰尚玉林商务港5楼; ◷9am-noon & 2.30-5pm Mon-Fri; M Yiguanmiao)

Windhorse Tour (风马旅游, Fēngmǎ Lǚyóu; ☑028 8559 3923; www.windhorsetour.com; Suite 2103, 21st fl, Bldg C, 1 Babao Lu, 八宝街1号万和苑C座2103室; ◷9am-6pm; M Luomashi)

VISAS

PSB Entry & Exit Service Centre (成都市出入境接待中心, Chéngdūshì Chūrùjìng Jiēdài Zhōngxīn; ☑028 8640 7067; www.chengdu.gov.cn; 2 Renmin Xilu, 人民西路2号; ◷9am-noon & 1-5pm Mon-Fri; M Tianfu Square) Visa extensions (in seven working days), residence permits and paperwork for lost passports are on the 3rd floor. It's in the building behind the Mao statue's right hand, to the left of the Sichuan Science & Technology Museum.

ℹ Getting There & Away

AIR

You can fly directly to **Chengdu Shuangliu International Airport** (成都双流国际机场, Chéngdū Shuāngliú Guójì Jīchǎng; ☑028 8570 2649; www.chengdu-airport.net; Shuangliuqu Jichang Donglu, 双流区机场东路; M Shuangliu International Airport), 18km west of the city, from nearly any other major Chinese city in less than three hours. There are also direct international flights from Amsterdam, Bangkok, Doha, Frankfurt, Kathmandu, Kuala Lumpur, London, Melbourne, San Francisco, Seoul, Singapore, Tokyo and many more destinations.

Many travellers fly from here to Lhasa (¥892 to ¥2200; prepare for palpable oxygen deprivation upon arrival). Flights to destinations within Sichuan include Kangding (¥500 to ¥930), Jiuzhaigou (¥830 to ¥1239) and Daocheng-Yading (¥570 to ¥1228), with Ganzi airport still under construction at the time of research.

Many hostels can book tickets, and the major Chinese airlines are also bookable online.

Air China Chengdu Booking Office (国航世界中心, Guóháng Shìjiè Zhōngxīn; ☑028 85958021, 95583; www.airchina.com.cn; 1 Hangkong Lu, 人民南路四段航空路1号; ◷8.30am-5pm; M Tongzilin) By Tongzilin metro station, on the north side of Hangkong Lu.

Cathay Dragon (国泰港龙航空, Guótài Gǎnglóng Hángkōng; ☑400 888 6628; www.cathaypacific.com; 5th fl, Sheraton Chengdu Lido Hotel, 15 Renmin Zhonglu 1st Section, 人民中路1段15号天府丽都喜来登饭店5楼; ◷9am-5pm Mon-Fri; M Luomashi) Rather than visiting in person, it's possible to book tickets (in English) by phone; 24 hours.

China Eastern Airlines (中国东方航空公司, Zhōngguó Dōngfāng Hángkōng Gōngsī; ☑028 67993985, 95530; www.ceair.com; Suite 1504, Shangshan International Bldg, 46 Renmin Nanlu 4th Section, 人民南路四段46号附1号1504室; ◷9am-4.30pm; M Tongzilin) Directly outside Tongzilin metro Exit B.

China Southern Airlines (中国南方航空, Zhōngguó Nánfāng Hángkōng; ☑9553921; www.csair.com; 15th fl, New Hope Tower, 45 Renmin Nanlu 4th Section, 人民南路四段45号

新希望大厦15室; ⊘ 8.30am-5.30pm; Ⓜ Tongzilin) Near Tongzilin metro station, just south of Hangkong Lu.

BUS

The main bus station for tourists is **Xinnanmen** (新南门汽车站, Xīnnánmén Qìchēzhàn; 2 Xinnanlu, 新南路2号; ⊘ 6.30am-6.30pm; Ⓜ Xinnanmen), officially the central tourist station; 旅游客运中心. Two other useful stations are **Beimen** (北门客运站, Běimén Kèyùnzhàn; ☑ 028 8333 4126; 197 Yihuanlu Beisiduan, 一环路北四段197号; ⊘ 6am-7.30pm; Ⓜ Qianfeng Rd), also called North Gate, and **Chadianzi** (茶店子). Be prepared to be dropped at any one of these (and other) bus stations when arriving in Chengdu. For Sanxingdui Museum, transfer via the town of Guanghan from **Zhaojuesi bus station** (昭觉寺汽车站, Zhāojuésì Qìchēzhàn; 88 Zhaoqing Henglu, 昭青横路88号; Ⓜ South Zhaojuesi Rd). If you end up at Shiyangchang bus station (石羊场公交站), local bus 28 (¥2) connects it to Xinnanmen and Beimen bus stations, as well as **North train station bus station** (火车北站汽车站, Huǒchē Běizhàn Qìchēzhàn; Ⓜ North Railway Station). Limited buses also depart directly from the **airport bus station** (双流客运站).

Destinations from Xinnanmen Station include the following:

Emei Shan ¥42, 2½ hours, hourly (7.40am to 7.40pm)

Jiuzhaigou ¥141, nine hours, one daily (8am). Extra morning buses run in July and August. Note: these buses pass Songpan (eight hours), but you may have to pay the full fare even if you get off at Songpan.

Kangding ¥114-135, seven hours, two daily (7.10am and 2pm)

Le Shan ¥46-53, two hours, every 20 minutes (7.20am to 7.35pm)

Pingle ¥33, three hours, six daily (7.30am to 5.15pm)

Ya'an (for Bifengxia) ¥48, 2½ hours, hourly (7.30am to 7.30pm)

Zigong ¥60, 3½ hours, two daily (9am and 2pm)

TRAIN

Chengdu's two main train stations are **Chengdu North train station** (火车北站, huǒchē běizhàn) and the newer **Chengdu East train station** (火车东站, huǒchē dōngzhàn), both of which connect directly to the metro.

Hotels and hostels can book tickets, usually for a ¥5 fee.

Destinations from Chengdu North Train Station include the following:

The **North train station ticket office** (火车北站售票处, Huǒchē Běizhàn Shòupiàochù; Huochezhan Guangchang, 火车站广场; ⊘ 24hr; Ⓜ North Railway Station) is in the separate building on your right as you approach the station.

Emei Shan hard seat/sleeper ¥23/77, 2½ hours, four daily (6.26am to 2.20pm)

Kunming K seat/hard sleeper ¥141/261, 18 to 20 hours, two daily (1pm and 2.20pm)

Lhasa hard/soft sleeper ¥668/1062, 36 hours, alternate days (9.37pm)

Qīngcheng Shan C seat ¥10, 45 minutes, frequently (6.40am to 7.20pm)

Xi'an seat/hard sleeper ¥112/208, 10 to 17 hours, five daily (7.36am to 10.16pm)

Zigong seat/hard sleeper ¥40/131, five to six hours, three daily (8.58am, 10.10am, 10.50am)

Daily D/G-class trains depart from Chengdu East train station for the following:

Chongqing 1st/2nd class ¥233/146, 1¾ hours, frequently (6.40am to 10.15pm)

Emei Shan 1st/2nd class ¥104/65, 1½ hours, seven daily (7.07am to 7.09pm)

Wuhan 1st/2nd class ¥587/366, eight to 10 hours, frequently (6.43am to 11.51pm)

Yibin seat/hard sleeper ¥110/176, 1½ to two hours, frequently (8.54am to 11.33pm)

Sichuan's high-speed train line stops at the airport (p761) on the way to two of the province's major tourist destinations:

Emei Shan 2nd/1st class ¥56/68, one hour, nine daily (7.54am to 9.10pm)

Le Shan 2nd/1st class ¥46/55, one hour, 10 daily (7.54am to 9.10pm)

ⓘ Getting Around

TO/FROM THE AIRPORT

From Chengdu Shuangliu International Airport, airport shuttle buses cover five routes, reaching all corners of the city. **Bus route 1** goes to the Minshan Hotel in the city centre. **Buses for route 2** (机场班车, Jīchǎng Bānchē; Tianfu Square, 天府广场; ¥12; ⊘ 6am-10pm; Ⓜ Tianfu Square) – for most purposes this is the most useful bus route – reach the South train station (which also has a metro connection) and then stops frequently along Renmin Lu to the North train station. **Route 3** heads to the East train station via the South train station. **Route 5** connects with Chadianzi bus station for western Sichuan departures. **Route 4** is of the least use to most tourists. It goes to the convention and exhibit centre.

To return by bus to the airport, the easiest bus **pick-up** (机场班车, Jīchǎng Bānchē; ¥12; ⊘ 6am-10pm; Ⓜ Jinjiang Binguan) is north of Minshan Hotel outside Jinjiang Hotel metro station.

From the airport, metro line 10 connects to line 3 (for the city centre) and 7 (south train station) at Taipingyuan, but it involves a bit of schlepping if you're travelling with luggage. Airport metro stations can be found in terminals 1 and 2. Depending on where in the city you're aiming for, the cost is around ¥4 to ¥5. Allow around 25 minutes (with transfers) to travel from the city centre to the airport.

A taxi costs ¥80 to ¥150. Most guesthouses offer airport pick-up services for slightly more.

BUS

You can get almost anywhere in Chengdu by bus, as long as you can decipher the labyrinthine routes. Stops are marked in Chinese and English and some post route maps. Fares within the city are usually ¥2.

Bus 1 Wuhou Temple–City centre–Beimen bus station–Zhaojuesì bus station

Bus 16 Chengdu North train station–Renmin Lu–Chengdu South train station

Bus 28 Shiyangchang bus station–Sichuan University–Xīnnanmen bus station–Chunxi Rd–Beimen bus station–Chengdu North train station

Bus 82 Chadianzi bus station–Jinsha Site Museum (stop is 金沙遗址东门)–Sichuan Museum–Culture Park–Wuhou Temple–Xinnanmen bus station

Bus 83 Chengdu North train station bus station–Zhaojue Si bus station

METRO

If you'll be using the metro extensively, it's worth buying a Tiānfǔ Tōng Kǎ (天府通卡) rechargeable payment card (¥25), which also works for local buses. Look for kiosks at the airport and Tianfu Square metro station, exit A, among other stations. Signage and information is in English as well as Chinese.

Line 1 links Chengdu North and South Railway Stations, running the length of Renmin Lu and beyond.

Line 2 links Chengdu East Railway Station with the city centre on an east–west route via Chunxi Rd, meeting line 1 at Tianfu Square before continuing west to Chadianzi bus station.

Line 3 runs to nearby the Giant Panda Breeding Research Base and Xinnanmen bus station, ending at Taipingyuan for the connection to the airport.

Line 4 is of use to tourists mainly for Chengdu West Railway Station.

Line 7 rings the city, stopping in at Chengdu's North, South and East Railway Stations as well as the Jinsha Site Museum.

Line 10 runs from both airport terminals to Taipingyuan, where it's possible to transfer to line 3.

Rides cost ¥2 to ¥10 depending on the distance covered. Stations have bilingual signs, maps and ticket machines.

AROUND CHENGDU

Dujiangyan   都江堰

☑ 028 / POP 630,000

Two Unesco World Heritage sites in Dujiangyan (Dūjiāngyàn), 60km northwest of Chengdu, make for very different glimpses into the history of Sichuan. Qingcheng Shan, most notably famous as the birthplace of Taoism, offers the chance to hike through misty forests past cascading waterfalls and ancient temples with views back down to the Chengdu plains. The Dujiangyan Irrigation System, the first in the world to control river flooding without the use of dams, is right in the thick of the modern city of Dujiangyan: a look into how ancient engineering marvels still play a role in the life of modern China.

◉ Sights

Qingcheng Shan   TAOIST SITE
(青城山, Azure City Mountain; Front Mountain adult ¥90, student/child/elderly ¥45, Back Mountain ¥20/10; ☺8am-5.30pm) Covered in lush, dripping forests, the sacred mountain of Qingcheng Shan has been a Taoist spiritual centre for more than 2000 years. Its beautiful trails are lined with ginkgo, plum and palm, and there are caves, pavilions and centuries-old wooden temples to explore.

Visitors can experience two sides of the mountain. The main entrance is on the mountain's front side (前山, Qián Shān) and leads to paths that wind past 11 important Taoist sites. Those interested in hiking will prefer the quieter and more scenic back mountain (后山, Hòu Shān), accessed 40km northwest. In either case, to actually enjoy the views, avoid major holidays when masses of tourists arrive to pay tribute to their ancestors.

The trails at **Qian Shan** lead to a summit of only 1260m, a relatively easy climb – four hours up and down, even easier via the **cable car** (one way/return ¥35/60). Snack stands are scattered along the mountain trails, and several of the major temples have small restaurants.

If you want to spend the night, a few temples on Qian Shan welcome guests. Most atmospheric is the fantastic Shangqing Temple (p764), a Qing-dynasty rebuild of the original Jin-dynasty temple in the middle of a forest near the top of the mountain,

SICHUAN DUJIANGYAN

WORTH A TRIP

SANXINGDUI MUSEUM

The **Sanxingdui Museum** (三星堆博物馆; Sānxīngduī Bówùguǎn; ☑ 0838 5500349; www. sxd.cn; 133 Xi'An Lu, Guǎnghàn, 广汉市西安路133号; ¥80, audio guide ¥10; ⊙ 8.30am-6.30pm, last entry 5pm), 40km north of Chengdu in Guanghan (广汉), exhibits relics of the Shu kingdom, a cradle of Chinese civilisation dating from 1200 BC to 1100 BC. Some archaeologists regard these artefacts, which include stunningly crafted, angular and stylised bronze masks, as even more important than Xi'an's Terracotta Warriors. Art and anthropology buffs will need at least a half day here, though budding archaeologists may be disappointed by the lack of access to the dig site itself.

Throughout the 20th century, farmers around Guanghan continually unearthed intriguing pottery shards and dirt-encrusted jade carvings when digging wells and tilling their fields. However, war and lack of funds prevented anyone from investigating these finds. Finally, in September 1986, archaeologists launched a full-scale excavation and made a startling discovery when they unearthed the site of a major city dating back to the Neolithic age in the upper reaches of the Yangzi River (Cháng Jiāng). It was previously believed that the oldest civilisations were concentrated around the Yellow River (Huáng Hé).

Buses to the site depart Chengdu's Xinnanmen bus station (¥50 return, one hour, 9.30am) and return from the museum around 3pm. Alternatively, buses from Chengdu's Zhaojue Si station (¥12, 1½ hours, 7am to 8pm) head to Guanghan's tourist bus station (广汉客运中心) – transfer to local bus 10 (¥2, 6.30am to 8pm) for the remaining 10km to the site. A bus from the site back to Zhaojue Si station leaves at 4.10pm, otherwise buses depart the tourist bus station for Xinnanmen every 10 minutes (¥16, 6.40am to 6.50pm).

with guest rooms and a restaurant/teahouse attached. Alternatively, the **Tianshi Cave Temple** (天师洞, Tiānshī Dòng; r from ¥120) has slightly less-welcoming rooms, but is on a quieter stretch of the mountain.

Hou Shan, the back of the mountain, has 20km of rugged pathways – expect a six-hour round-trip hike to the 2128m summit, where you'll find **Baiyun Temple** (白云寺, Báiyún Sì); the **cable cars** at Jinli (one way/return ¥30/55) and Baiyun (one way/return ¥45/80) can shave a couple of hours off the hike. You can find some guesthouses (山庄, shānzhuāng) at **Youyi Village** (又一村, Yòuyī Cūn), around halfway up the mountain's west side, of which **Jiachun Villa** (佳派山庄, Jiāchún Shānzhuāng; ☑ 155 2838 2949; Youyi Village, 又一村; Yòuyī Cūn; r from ¥100; ❄ 🛜) is among the best.

Dujiangyan Irrigation System   HISTORIC SITE
(都江堰灌溉系统, Dūjiāngyàn Guàngài Xìtǒng; adult ¥80, student/child/elderly ¥45, shuttle to Yùlěi Pavilion one-way/rtn ¥10/15; ⊙ 8am-6pm Mar-Nov, to 5.30 Dec-Feb) This Qin dynasty waterworks project (completed in 256 BC) is the oldest and only surviving non-dam irrigation system in the world. Still used to control the water levels of the Mín Jiāng, this scenic area is studded with historic temples,

forested hills and hilltop pagodas, as well as coursing waters.

🛏 Sleeping

Joy 100 Hotel   HOTEL ¥
(幸福驿站, Xìngfú Yìzhàn; ☑ 028 8711 2999; 194 Xinfu Lu, 幸福路194号; r ¥85; ❄ 🛜) Of several Chinese hotel chains with a presence in Dujiangyan Ancient Town, this is the best combination of value and location. Clean rooms, friendly staff and, most importantly, an easy walk from both Lidui Gongyuan Station and the entrance to the Dujiangyan Irrigation System. Little English is spoken.

Shangqing Temple   GUESTHOUSE ¥
(上清宫, Shàngqīng Gōng; d from ¥80; ❄) This Qing dynasty rebuild of the original Jin-dynasty temple is set in the forest near the top of the mountain; guest rooms are basic but comfortable, though avoid the shared bathrooms. It has a restaurant (dishes ¥18 to ¥30) and a teahouse (tea from ¥10). No English menus, but there are a handful of photos to point at.

ⓘ Getting There & Away

There are two high-speed rail routes from Chengdu's North Train Station to the Dujiangyan sites.

For the Dujiangyan Irrigation System, take a train to Lidui Gongyuan (离堆公园; ¥15, 33 minutes, 6.02am and 9.21pm). From there, walk out of the station to Dujiangyan Dadao (都江堰大道), turn left through the reconstructed city wall, and walk until the road ends at the site's entrance.

For Qingcheng Shan, take the train to Qingcheng Shan station (青城山; ¥15, 37-49 minutes, 6.02am to 10.17pm). Pick up bus 101, 104, 106 or 109 (¥2, 15-40 minutes, every 10 minutes from 6.56am to 6.30pm) to the main gate (Qián Shān), or a tourist bus (中巴车; ¥25 return, 40 minutes) to Hou Shsn. Tourist buses leave when full and sweep past the main gate en route, but only stop for passengers if there are empty seats. A taxi will cost around ¥10.

Emei Shan 峨眉山

📞 0833 / POP 423,070

A cool, misty retreat from Sichuan basin's heat, Emei Shan (3099m) is one of China's four sacred Buddhist Mountains (the others being Putuo Shan, Wutai Shan and Jiuhua Shan. This excludes sacred Buddhist mountains in the Tibetan regions). A farmer built the first Buddhist temple near Jinding summit in the 1st century. That temple stood until it was gutted by fire in 1972, and many of the more than 150 temples on the mountain suffered fires or looting over the centuries but around 30 have been maintained and restored in various degrees. Reconstructed in the 9th century, Wannian Temple is the oldest surviving temple on the mountain.

Beyond its rich cultural heritage, the mountain also stands on the edge of the eastern Himalayan highlands and hosts a diverse range of plants and animals, all of which helped place it on Unesco's World Heritage list.

When to Go

The best time to visit is June to October, when the mist burns off by early afternoon. Epic crowds arrive in July and August; weekends from spring to autumn are always busy. Avoid national holidays at all costs. Snowfall generally begins around November on the upper slopes. In winter you can rent crampons to deal with ice and snow, and jackets (rental ¥30, ¥170 deposit) to stave off the cold. Expect rain and mist throughout the year.

Average temperatures are as follows:

	Jan	Apr	Jul	Oct
Emei town	7°C	21°C	26°C	17°C
Summit	-6°C	4°C	12°C	4°C

⦿ Sights & Activities

The entry ticket (adult ¥160/student and seniors ¥90, winter ¥110/55) gets you access to most sites on the mountain but does not include rides on the three buses to the main routes up or into a few of the temples. You will also need to pay a compulsory 'insurance' fee (¥5). You will need your passport to buy a ticket.

Most rewarding is walking the whole way starting from Baoguo Temple, but most opt to ride to Wannian depot (for easy access to the cable car) or to Wuxiangang depot (an easy walk to poetic Qingyin Pavilion and other important sights). The Leidongping bus drops off closest to the summit, just an hour or two short of Jinding Peak (or half an hour up to the upper cable car).

Regardless of your starting point, getting a feel for the place takes at least a full day, ideally two or three. Wander the wooden temples, hurry past the macaques demanding tribute for safe passage, then find shelter in a monastery guesthouse and wake up in time to welcome the sunrise. The early morning light refracting in the cool mist has been heralded since ancient times as Buddha's Halo, and the sea of clouds stretching out to the horizon is enough to make even the most jaded traveller feel a little bit closer to the heavens.

Jinding Temple BUDDHIST TEMPLE

(金顶寺, Jīndǐng Sì, Golden Summit) This temple is at the Golden Summit (Jīndǐng; 3079m), commonly referred to as the mountain's highest peak. This temple is a striking modern renovation, covered with glazed tiles and surrounded by white marble balustrades. In front, the prominent 48m-tall golden statue of multidimensional Samantabhadra (十方普贤, Shífāng Pǔxián) honours mountain protector Pǔxián, and was added in 2006 though it's already showing signs of decay.

Fading statues aside, the views at sunset and sunrise, as golden light illuminates the clouds below, are a highlight of any visit to Emei. The mountain's highest point (3099m) is actually nearby Wanfo Ding (Ten Thousand Buddha Summit), but it has been closed to visitors for some years now.

Emei Shan

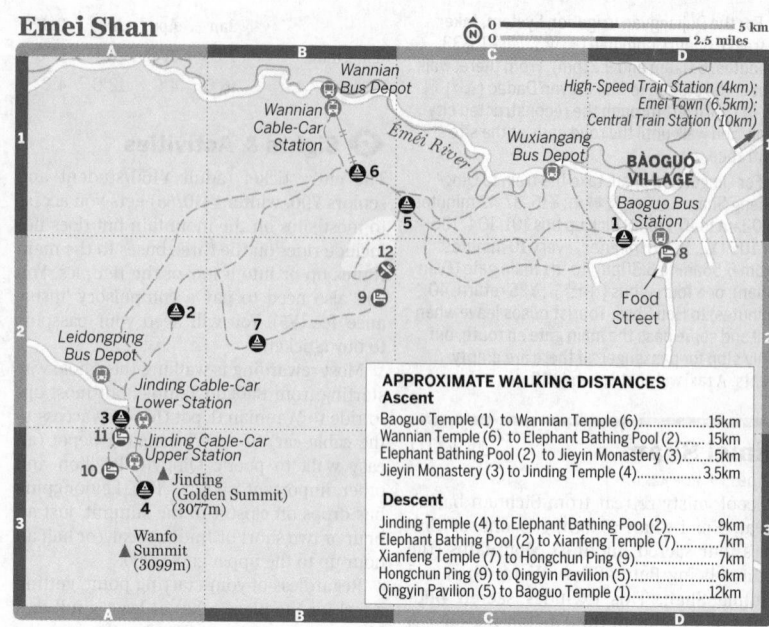

APPROXIMATE WALKING DISTANCES

Ascent

Baoguo Temple (1) to Wannian Temple (6)....................15km
Wannian Temple (6) to Elephant Bathing Pool (2).......15km
Elephant Bathing Pool (2) to Jieyin Monastery (3)........5km
Jieyin Monastery (3) to Jinding Temple (4).................3.5km

Descent

Jinding Temple (4) to Elephant Bathing Pool (2)..............9km
Elephant Bathing Pool (2) to Xianfeng Temple (7)............7km
Xianfeng Temple (7) to Hongchun Ping (9)....................7km
Hongchun Ping (9) to Qingyin Pavilion (5)....................6km
Qingyin Pavilion (5) to Baoguo Temple (1)...................12km

Emei Shan

◎ Sights

1	Baoguo Temple	D1
2	Elephant Bathing Pool	A2
3	Jieyin Monastery	A2
4	Jinding Temple	A3
5	Qingyin Pavilion	C1
6	Wannian Temple	B1
7	Xianfeng Temple	B2

⌂ Sleeping

8	Happy Hotel	D2
9	Hóngchún Píng	B2
10	Jīndǐng Dàjiǔdiàn	A3
	Me & Hostel	(see 8)
11	Tàizǐ Píng	A3
	Teddy Bear Hotel	(see 8)

⊗ Eating

12	Hard Wok Cafe	B2

Baoguo Temple
BUDDHIST MONASTERY

(报国寺, Bàoguó Sì; Emei Shan Lu, 峨眉山路; ¥8; ⊙7am-7.30pm) Constructed in the 16th century, this temple (550m) features beautiful gardens of rare plants, as well as a 3.5m-high porcelain Buddha dating back to 1415, which is housed near the **Sutra Library**. This is not included in the Emei Shan entrance ticket, but as it lies outside the scenic area you won't need the ticket to visit.

Jieyin Monastery
BUDDHIST MONASTERY

(接引寺, Jiēyǐn Sì) A large main hall and several smaller shrines mark the starting point of the final push to Jinding Peak. To take the cable car to Jinding, you'll have to walk up 1.5km from Leidongping to here.

Wannian Temple
BUDDHIST MONASTERY

(万年寺, Wànnián Sì; ¥10) Reconstructed in the 9th century, Wannian Temple (1020m) is the oldest surviving Emei temple. It's dedicated to the man on the white elephant, the Bodhisattva Pǔxián (also known as Samantabhadra), the Buddhist Lord of Truth and patron of the mountain. This 8.5m-high statue cast in copper and bronze dates from AD 980 and weighs an estimated 62,000kg. If you can manage to rub the elephant's hind leg, good luck will be cast upon you.

Qingyin Pavilion
BUDDHIST TEMPLE

(清音阁, Qīngyīn Gé) Named 'Pure Sound Pavilion' after the soothing sounds of the waters coursing around rock formations, this temple (710m) is built on an outcrop in the middle of a fast-flowing stream. Rest in one of the small pavilions here while you appreciate the natural 'music' of the water.

Xianfeng Temple BUDDHIST MONASTERY
(仙峰寺, Xiānfēng Sì) Somewhat off the beaten track on the long way round to the peak, this carefully tended monastery (1752m) is backed by rugged cliffs and surrounded by fantastic scenery. Entrance to the nearby Jiulao Cave is ¥10.

Elephant Bathing Pool BUDDHIST MONASTERY
(洗象池, Xǐxiàng Chí) According to legend, Elephant Bathing Pool (2070m) is where Pǔxián flew his elephant in for a nice scrub, but today there's not much of a pool to speak of. Or flying elephants for that matter. There are some elephant statues, though. Being almost at the crossroads of both major trails, the temple here is sometimes packed with pilgrims and often crowded with curious monkeys.

🛏 Sleeping

The tourist district in Emei town surrounds Baoguo Temple and the travellers bus station, where most people will spend a night on their way to and from the mountain. The real draw, though, is sleeping on the mountain itself, in one of the many basic temple-run guesthouses.

🛏 On the Mountain

Hóngchún Píng MONASTERY ¥
(洪椿坪; ☑0833 509 9043; dm ¥50, tw ¥60-130; 🛜) The smartest temple accommodation

on the mountain is at a comfortable 1120m, tucked away in a quiet stretch of forest. Rooms are simple, with wi-fi and shared bathrooms. Approximate walking times from base/summit are three/six hours. Friendly monks-in-residence and a contemplative location make this a great place to sleep if you're not aiming to summit for sunrise.

Tàizǐ Píng MONASTERY ¥
(太子坪; dm ¥50) Blankets are musty and dorms could use a good cleaning, but this closest monastery to Jinding Peak is predictably popular with backpackers. It's about 40 minutes from here up to the peak, so set your alarm early. You'll need to leave your passport with staff for the duration of your stay.

Jīndǐng Dàjiǔdiàn HOTEL ¥¥¥
(金顶大酒店; ☑0833 509 8088; Jinding, 金顶; r incl breakfast from ¥1280; ❈🛜) This conveniently placed mountain hotel makes an efficient base for catching both sunset and sunrise (it's just moment's walk to the summit temples). However, it's outrageously overpriced for most of the year (in the dead of winter some decent discounts might be available).

🛏 In Town

Me & Hostel HOSTEL ¥
(我和旅馆, Wǒ hé lǚguǎn; ☑0833 5098 699; Baoguo Lu, 报国路; dm ¥40, r ¥100; ❈🛜) Smart new hostel with six-bed dorms and bright, spotless and well-thought-out private rooms. There's friendly English-speaking staff and – the highlight of the place – a delightful cafe

---

EMEI SHAN HIKING ROUTES

There are many combinations of paths, buses, cable cars and monastery rest stops on Emei Shan; below are some possibilities. Estimated times exclude breaks, which you will certainly need after all those stairs.

➡ **One day** Take the bus from Baoguo station to Wannian bus depot (45 minutes, ¥20), then hike to the Golden Summit (five hours) with the help of both **cable cars** (万年索道站; Wànnián Suǒdàozhàn; ascent ¥65, descent ¥45; ⊘ 6.40am-6pm). Catch a ride from Leidongping bus depot (1½ hours, ¥50) back to Baoguo Village.

➡ **Two days** Take the bus from Baoguo station to Wannian bus depot, then hike to the summit (6½ hours). Sleep in a hotel at the peak or descend for a monastery, but either way make it back up to the top for sunrise. On the way down, turn right a short distance past Elephant Bathing Pool and take the more scenic path, via Xianfeng Temple, to Wuxiangang depot (eight hours) for a ride back to the village (30 minutes, round trip ¥40).

➡ **Three days** Hoof it up and down the mountain (20 hours or more in total). To see all the sights the mountain has to offer, ascend via Wannian Temple and descend via Xianfeng Temple. (Perhaps make offerings to sore muscles at each – you'll be taking a break anyway.)

serving a range of teas and coffees. Disappointingly, no other food is available so you'll need to go elsewhere for a meal.

Happy Hotel HOTEL ¥¥
(幸福树酒店, Xìngfú Shù Jiǔdiàn; ☎ 400 823 0917; 31 Baoguo Village, 4th group, 报国村4组31号; r incl breakfast from ¥158; P ❀ 🛜) This straightforward, very tidy hotel has super-value rooms and a surprisingly good, reasonably priced Chinese restaurant (a rarity in Baoguo Village). The friendly staff speak English and there's bike rental, too.

⭐ **Teddy Bear Hotel** HOSTEL ¥¥
(玩具熊酒店, Wánjùxióng Jiǔdiàn; ☎ 0833 559 0135; www.teddybear.com.cn; 43 Baoguo Lu, 报国路 43号; r incl breakfast from ¥100; ❀ 🛜) If you can get past the theme (bears, bears, everywhere), this very clean, long-standing backpacker hotel offers nice rooms and English-speaking staff that provide solid, hostel-style travel services plus decent coffee and western food. There's always a good crew of international and Chinese travellers staying.

🍴 Eating

On the mountain most temples have dining halls serving filling vegetarian stir-fry for ¥20 to ¥30, and you're never far from a trailside food stall selling simple dishes, instant noodles (方便面, *fāngbiàn miàn*), tea and snacks. The unexpected but welcome Hard Wok Cafe is one of few that have an English menu.

In Baoguo Village, restaurants and supermarkets abound. **Haochi Jie** (好吃街, Food St) is crammed with places serving Sichuan dishes (¥15 to ¥40).

Hard Wok Cafe CAFE ¥
(晓鱼小餐店, Xiǎoyú Xiǎocāndiàn; ⏱ hours vary) As surprising as it is delightful, this tiny cliffside cafe reaches beyond the standard Sichuan noodle menu to include *jiānbing* (煎饼; ¥25), something between a crêpe and a pancake. Apple and honey? Chocolate and banana? Mix and match to your stomach's content. It's about 15 minutes downhill from Hongchun Ping.

ⓘ Getting There & Away

The town of Emei (峨眉山市, Éméi Shān Shì) is the transport hub and lies 6.5km east of the park entrance. Most buses terminate at Emei Shan central station (峨眉山客运中心, Éméi Shān kèyùn zhōngxīn), directly opposite Emei Railway Station (峨眉火车站, Éméi Huǒchēzhàn). If you

ask, some drivers will go all the way to the more convenient Baoguo Village bus station (报国汽车站) – which confusingly is also known as the Emei Shan tourist bus station (峨眉山旅游客运中心, Éméi Shān lǚyóu kèyùn zhōngxīn) – for ¥10 more. The High-Speed Train Station (高速列车站, Gāosù Lièchē Zhàn) is the closest to Baoguo Village, around 4km away.

A taxi from Emei town to Baoguo Village is about ¥25 or from the High-Speed Train Station to Baoguo Village is around ¥6 to ¥8. Most guesthouses will pick you up if you arrange it with them in advance. Local bus 8 (¥1.5) connects the Emei town train station with the park entrance.

BUS

While it's not possible to travel directly to Baoguo from most long-distance destinations, the following long-distance buses do leave from Baoguo:

Chengdu South ¥46, 2½ hours, every two hours (9am to 5pm)

Chongqing ¥130, six hours (8.30am)

Le Shan ¥11, 45 minutes, every 30 minutes (8am to 5.30pm)

Yibin ¥76, four hours, four daily (7.10am, 10.30am, 12.50pm and 4.30pm)

Destinations from Emei Shan central station include the following:

Hongya (for Liujiang) ¥19, 1½ hours, frequently (8am to 5pm)

Kangding ¥121, seven hours, one daily (9.50am)

Ya'an ¥46, three hours, four daily (8.10am, 9.30am, 12.30pm and 2.20pm)

Zigong ¥65, three hours, frequently (7.40am to 5.10pm)

TRAIN

Chengdu C/K&T ¥65/27, 1½ to 2¾ hours, 13 daily (7.13am to 9.20pm)

Kunming K seat/hard sleeper ¥124/215, 15½ hours, one daily (4.02pm)

Le Shan C ¥11, 15 minutes, seven daily (7.13am to 9.06pm)

ⓘ Getting Around

Buses from **Baoguo bus station** (报国车站, Bàoguó Chēzhàn) travel to three depots on the mountain: **Wuxiangang** (五显冈车站, Wǔxiǎngǎng Chēzhàn) (30 minutes, round trip ¥40), about a 20-minute walk below Qingyin Pavilion; **Wannian** (万年车站, Wànnián Chēzhàn) (45 minutes; round trip ¥40), beside the Wannian cable car (p767) and a half-hour walk below Wannian Temple; and **Leidongping** (雷洞坪车站; Léidòngpíng Chēzhàn) (1½ hours, round trip ¥90), a half-hour walk from the **Jinding cable car** (下金顶索道站; Xià Jīndǐng Suǒdàozhàn; ascent ¥65, descent ¥55, return ¥120; ⏱ 5.30am-6.30pm). If you return via a different depot, you may have to pay a small surcharge.

Buses run frequently from around 6am to 5pm (7am to 4pm in winter). The last buses head down the mountain at 6pm (5pm in winter). Don't be late for the last bus as it won't wait. The roads up the mountain are very winding and not all your fellow bus passengers will be good travellers. Expect the lovely aroma of car sickness to fill the bus.

Local city buses (¥1.50) run every 30 minutes or so between Emei town's main transit hubs and Baoguo bus station. The standard fare is ¥1.50.

Le Shan 乐山

📞 0833 / POP 1.62 MILLION

With fingernails larger than the average human, the world's largest ancient Buddha draws plenty of tourists to the relaxed riverside town of Le Shan (Lè Shān). This Unesco World Heritage Site is an easy day trip from Chengdu or stopover en route to or from Emei Shan, but the laid-back vibe and higher-quality accommodation options may convince you to linger.

⊙ Sights

★ **Le Shan Grand Buddha** BUDDHIST STATUE
(乐山大佛, Lè Shān Dàfó; adult ¥80, children, students & seniors ¥40; ⊙ 7.30am-6.30pm Apr–early Oct, 8am-5.30pm early Oct–Mar) Le Shan's serene, 1200-year-old Grand Buddha sits in repose, carved from a cliff face overlooking the confluence of three busy rivers: the Dadu, Min and Qingyi. The Buddhist monk Haitong conceived the project in AD 713, hoping that Buddha would protect the boats and calm the lethal currents.

It was 90 years after Haitong's death that the project was completed, but afterwards the river waters obeyed. Believers credited Buddha's grace; others pointed to the construction process, in which piles of surplus rocks reshaped the rivers and changed the currents.

At 71m tall, he is indeed grand. His shoulders span 28m, and each of his big toes is 8.5m long. His ears are 7m. Their length symbolises wisdom and the conscious abandonment of materialism. It is said that heavy gold baubles left Siddartha's earlobes elongated even after he was no longer weighed down by material things. Inside the body, hidden from view, is a water-drainage system to prevent weathering,

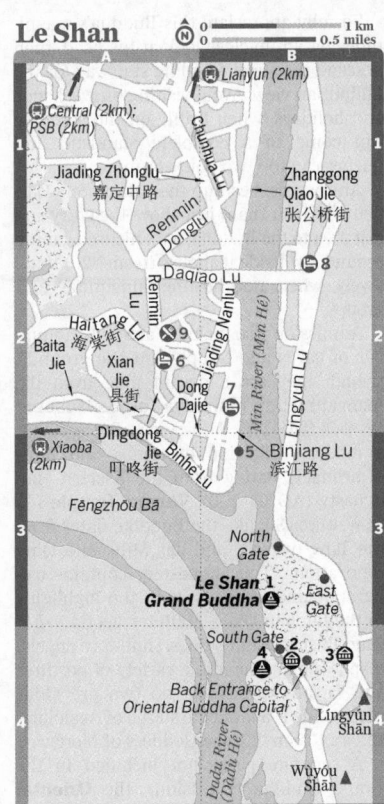

Le Shan

although he is showing his age and soil erosion is an ongoing problem.

To fully appreciate this Buddha's magnitude, get an up-close look at his head, then descend the steep, winding stairway for the Lilliputian view. Avoid visiting on weekends and holidays, when traffic on the staircase can come to a complete standstill and queues can top two hours or more.

Afterwards, head up the path to Su's Garden (苏园, Sū Yuán) just above the entry and exit area to the Buddha, a manicured garden around a cliffside teahouse (from ¥20) that's lovely when not hosting lunchtime tour groups.

Admission also includes access to a number of caves and temples on the grounds, though they are a decent hike from the main attraction. **Mahaoya Tombs Museum** (麻浩崖墓博物馆, Máhàoyámù Bówùguǎnhas a modest collection of tombs and burial artefacts dating from the Eastern Han dynasty (AD 25–220). **Wuyou Temple** (乌尤寺, Wūyóu Sì), like the Buddha, dates from the Tang dynasty, and has Ming and Qing renovations. This monastery contains calligraphy and artefacts, with the highlights in the Luohan Hall – 1000 terracotta *arhat* (Buddhist celestial beings, similar to angels) displaying an incredible variety of postures and facial expressions: no two are alike. Also inside is a fantastic statue of Avalokiteshvara (Guanyin), the Goddess of Mercy.

A separate park (not included in the Grand Buddha admission), the **Oriental Buddha Capital** (东方佛都, Dōngfāng Fódū; ☑0833 230 1177; ¥80; ⊙8am-6pm), houses a collection of 3000 Buddha statues and figurines from across Asia, including a 170m-long reclining Buddha, one of the world's longest. There is an entrance near the Grand Buddha's south gate; otherwise exit and take bus 3 or 13 (¥1) to the Oriental Buddha Capital (东方佛都, Dōngfāng Fódū) stop. The entrance is further than it looks on the park maps.

Tours

Sightseeing Cruises
BOATING
(游船, Yóuchuán; Le Shan Dock, 乐山港; 20min round trip ¥70, children under 12yr free; ⊙7.30am to 6.30pm Apr-Oct, from 8am winter) Tour boats leave regularly from Le Shan dock, passing by the cliffs for views of Dafo, which reveal two guardians in the cliff-side not visible from land. The ride is short and, when busy, there's no guarantee you'll get much of a view of the Giant Buddha because the cruise boats tend to battle one another for the prime view; you might find your view obstructed by another boat.

Sleeping

Haiyun International Youth Hostel
HOSTEL ¥
(海韵国际青年旅社, Hǎiyùn Guójì Qīngnián Lǔshě; ☑0833 209 0999; 59 Renmin Nanlu, 人民南路59号; dm ¥58-68, r from ¥148) The only hostel in Le Shan and it's a good one. Rooms and dorms are painted in striking primary colours and throughout the building there are pictures of old China, Marilyn Monroe and cartoon figurines (quite the contrast!). The English-speaking staff can advise how to get around and where to eat in the area. Dorms have four or eight beds.

Peace Inn Hotel
GUESTHOUSE ¥¥
(和平饭店, Hépíng Fàndiàn; ☑0833 210 3366; 3 Long Hong Lu, 3龙洪路; r from ¥148; ❀ ☎) Small, family-run guesthouse where each of the six arty rooms are different, but all have modern, tiled bathrooms. The owners don't speak much English, but they do have big, welcoming smiles. It's a short walk to the Grand Buddha.

Jiayun Mingtai Hotel
HOTEL ¥¥¥
(嘉运明泰大酒店, Jiā Yùn Míng Tài Dà Jiǔdiàn; ☑0833 209 0999; 26 Binjiang Lu, 26滨江路; d incl breakfast ¥220-260; ❀ ☎) This is an impressive new addition to the Le Shan hotel scene. River-facing rooms have big, free-standing bathtubs overlooking the chocolate brown river while the (noisy) road-facing rooms have giant, wall-projected TV's that made us feel like we were in a lecture theatre. Needless to say, the road-facing rooms are to be avoided.

Staff are sweet and there's a delightful teahouse (open to all; ¥20) that is an ideal place from which to watch the river rapids.

Eating

★Zhao Family Crispy Duck
BARBECUE ¥
(赵记油烫甜皮鸭, Zhàojì Yóutàng Tiánpíyā; ☑0833 211 4196; 169 Xincun Jie, 新村街169号; meals ¥25; ⊙9am-9pm) Foodies flock to this simple but superb restaurant for its speciality – sweet, crispy roast duck (*jīn*; ¥22). The draw is the skin, which is best described as duck candy, a miraculously ungreasy bite of heaven. Eat it while it's hot – in the middle of the sidewalk with your bare hands, if necessary. Look for the sign 'Zhaoyazi, 赵鸭子'.

ⓘ Getting There & Away

BUS

Le Shan has three main bus stations, all within 5km of each other. Buses from Chengdu's Xinnanmen station usually arrive at **Xiaoba Bus Station** (肖坝旅游车站, Xiàobà Lǚyóu Chēzhàn), the main tourist station. The **Central Bus Station** (乐山客运中心车站, Lè Shān Kèyùn Zhōngxīn Chēzhàn) and **Lianyun Bus Station** (联运车站, Liányùn Chēzhàn) are also useful.

Note: if you're heading to Emei Shan, it's better to use Xiaoba Bus Station, as buses from there go all the way to Baoguo (¥11, 45 minutes, every 30 minutes from 7am to 5pm). There is also another bus (¥5) which stops multiple times on the way between Le Shan and Baoguo, taking up to 1½ hours.

Other services from Xiaoba Bus Station include the following:

Chengdu ¥46 to 53, two hours, every 20 minutes (7am to 7pm)

Chongqing ¥147, 4½ hours, frequent (7am to 6pm)

Emei Town ¥8, 30 minutes, every 30 minutes (7.30am to 6pm)

Ya'an ¥46, 2½ hours, hourly (8.40am to 5.30pm)

Zigong ¥50, three hours, hourly (8.10am to 5.30pm)

TRAIN

High-speed trains depart Leshan for Chengdu's South and East Train Stations (first/second class ¥81/51, 50 minutes to 1¼ hours, 22 daily, 7.26am to 9.35pm) and Emei Shan (¥11, 15 minutes, nine daily, 7.06am to 8.21pm).

ⓘ Getting Around

Local buses cost ¥1. Destinations include the following:

Bus 1 Xiaoba Bus Sstation–Jiazhou Hotel–town centre–Lianyun bus station

Bus 6 Xiaoba Bus Station–Renmin Nanlu–Public Security Bureau

Bus 8 Xiaoba Bus Station–town centre–Le Shan dock

Bus 9 Central Bus Station–town centre–Le Shan dock

Bus 13 Xiaoba Bus Station–town centre–Oriental Buddha Capital–Grand Buddha–Wuyou Temple

---

Ya'an 雅安

📱 0835 / POP 1.53 MILLION

Chinese travellers head to the sprawling city of Ya'an (Yǎ'ān) as a hub for activities like picking tea leaves on the hills of Mengshan (蒙山, Méngshān) or watching sunrise from above the clouds at Bull's Back Mountain (牛背山, Niúbèishān), but for foreigners the primary draw is the Bifengxia Panda Base, a short way out of the city. It's a treat to glimpse any one of the estimated 2380 surviving pandas in the world (1864 wild pandas and 520 captive), but with bustling Chengdu 150km east, you can get a sense of their natural habitat here. Cubs in the 'panda kindergarten' climb high into the trees in their reasonably pleasant enclosures, while humans can hike along a forested river gorge with waterfalls and stunning scenery surrounding the main attraction.

⊙ Sights

★ **Ya'an Bifengxia Panda Base** ZOO

(雅安碧峰峡大熊猫基地; Bìfēngxiá Dàxióngmāo Jīdì; ☎ 0835 231 8020; ¥118; ⊙ 9am–noon & 1-4pm, kindergarten feeding 9.30am & 3pm) Ya'an Bifengxia Panda Base was established in prime forest in Ya'an in 2003 for research purposes rather than tourism, and its mission expanded in 2008 following the earthquake that severely damaged its sister reserve at Wolong. Bifengxia is now home to 80 pandas, some of which may eventually be returned to the wild.

The panda centre is 3km away from the ticket office in the main car park where the minibus drops passengers. Pick up a map and store bags for free at the tourist information office. Turn left out of the ticket office then take the free lift (乘电梯, chéngyúntī; 8am to 7.30pm) down 50 storeys to the foot of the gorge for a 7.5km nature walk to the panda centre entrance. It takes about two hours to reach the centre via the concrete paths passing tall waterfalls, imaginatively named mountains, and a small collection of hanging coffins (悬棺, xuánguān) en route.

Although this panda base does get chaotically busy at weekends and in holidays in general, it's much quieter and therefore a more enjoyable visit than the Giant Panda Breeding Research Base in Chengdu. The walk along the valley to the pandas adds to the pleasure of a visit.

🛌 Sleeping

Those staying overnight can sleep in the park at **Qiáotóu Nóngjiālè** (桥头农家乐; ☎ 138 8243 7340; 200m uphill from Panda Base bus drop-off, 碧峰峡小西天前行200米; r ¥120), a basic guesthouse just beyond the end of the gorge hike, uphill from the panda centre. A handful of guesthouses and restaurants are also by the park entrance, including the park-owned **Bìfēngxiá Dàjiǔdiàn** (碧峰峡大酒店; ☑ 0835 231 8017; Bifengxia tourist centre, 碧峰峡游客中心; r ¥100; ✳ 🛜), but leaving the area to spend the night there won't allow re-entrance to the park on the same ticket.

Ya'an city itself has masses of accommodation options; most are aimed at business travellers.

❶ Getting There & Away

There's a near-endless succession of buses from Chengdu's Xinnanmen station (¥47) to Ya'an's Ximen bus station (西门车站, Xīmén chēzhàn), but for Bifengxia get off before this at the tourist bus station (旅游车站, lǚyóu chēzhàn) where minibuses (¥5, 45 minutes) wait to take you to the Panda Base. The last bus back to Chengdu from the tourist bus station leaves at 7pm, or it's also possible to continue on to Qionglai (邛崃; ¥26, one hour) for transfers to the historic town of **Pingle** (平乐古镇, Pínglè Gǔzhèn).

From Ya'an's Ximen bus station, you can head on to various other destinations:

Emei town ¥44, two hours, six daily (8.50am to 5.20pm)

Kangding ¥93, 2½ hours, five daily (8am to 1pm)

Le Shan ¥46, 2½ hours, nine daily (8.50am to 4.50pm

A pedicab between Ya'an's two bus stations costs ¥6. At the tourist bus station, the left-luggage office (9.30am to 6.30pm) holds bags for ¥1 per hour.

SOUTHERN SICHUAN

Not often on the radar of foreign tourists, steamy southern Sichuan is for those who enjoy digging into history and exploring the quiet side of nature. With dinosaur fossils and lush bamboo forests, as well as some stellar teahouses, there's plenty to enjoy here.

Zigong 自贡

☑ 0813 / POP 2.67 MILLION

This intriguing riverside city has been an important centre of Chinese salt production for almost 2000 years. Remnants of that industry make up part of an unconventional list of sights that includes the world's deepest traditional salt mine and China's first dinosaur museum. Zigong (Zìgòng) is also a clear contender for the most atmospheric teahouses anywhere in Sichuan – and thus

by definition, China – so there's plenty of opportunity to just put your feet up for a day.

◉ Sights

★ Dinosaur Museum MUSEUM

(恐龙馆, Kǒnglóng Guǎn; ☑ 0813 580 1235; www.zdm.cn; 238 Dashan Pu, Da'an District, 大安区大山铺238号; adult ¥4, with 3D movie ¥80, student/elderly ¥40, with 3D movie ¥60, child free; ⏰8.30am-6pm; 🚌35) Relive your childhood palaeontology fantasies at this spectacular dinosaur museum. It was the first museum of its kind in China and is arguably one of the best dinosaur museums in the world. Built on top of the Dashanpu excavation site, which has one of the world's largest concentrations of dinosaur fossils, the museum has a fine collection of reassembled skeletons as well as partially excavated fossil pits.

The first publicised finds here were made in 1972. The huge numbers of fossils, mostly dating from the rarely seen early and middle Jurassic periods, baffled archaeologists at first. It is now believed that floods swept them here en masse. Budding palaeontologists will appreciate the *Huayangosaurus taibaii,* the most primitive and complete stegosaur ever discovered, as well as the incredibly rare skin fossil specimens on display. A child-friendly movie screens at 10am, 11am, 2.30pm and 3.30pm daily.

Take bus 35 (¥1, 25 minutes) uphill from the city centre (it's about a 45-minute journey).

Shenhai Salt Well HISTORIC SITE

(燊海井, Shēnhǎi Jǐng; ☑ 0813 510 6214; 289 Da'an Jie, 大安街289号; adult ¥22, student/child/elderly ¥11; ⏰8.30am-5.30pm) This fascinating museum is also a working salt mine. Its 1001m-deep artesian salt well was the world's deepest well when it was built in 1835 and it remains the deepest salt well ever made using percussion drilling, a technique invented here and later applied throughout the world.

Many pieces of original equipment, including a 20m-high wooden derrick that towers above the tiny, 20cm-wide mouth of the well, are still intact. On the 2nd floor of the salt house, rows of cauldrons bubble away day and night over fires powered by natural gas, the mine's other product, until only fluffy white piles of glistening salt remain.

There are excellent English captions explaining the process, from how bamboo was once used to siphon brine from beneath the earth to how soy milk is added to clarify it. Bags of the salt (from ¥3.50) are sold from the window to the right when you exit.

Take bus 5 or 35 (¥1, six stops) uphill from the city centre.

Salt Industry History Museum MUSEUM
(盐业历史博物馆; Yányè Lìshǐ Bówùguǎn; ☏0813 220 2083, 0813 220 8581; 89 Dongxing Si, 东兴寺89号; adult ¥20, student/child/elderly ¥10, guide ¥60; ◷8.30am-5.30pm) Housed in an ornate 270-year-old guild hall, this unique museum documents the course of the region's salt industry, which dates to the first century CE. Salt was at one time valued more than gold, and by the late 19th century industrious salt merchants had turned Zigong into a leading industrial centre.

Sleeping & Eating

There are plenty of Sichuan restaurants in the tourist district by the river, serving spicy favourites from across the province. For a quicker fix, head down the **walking street** (自贡商业步行街, Zìgòng Shāngyè Bùxíngjiē; snacks & meals from ¥9; ◷7am-9pm) for cheap noodles and steamed dumpling (包子) stands. Of course, ask for a bit of local salt.

Xiongfri Holiday Hotel HOTEL ¥¥
(雄飞假日酒店, Xióngfēi Jiàrì Jiǔdiàn; ☏0813 211 8888; www.jiarihotel.com; 193 Jiefang Lu, 解放路193号; r incl breakfast from ¥200; ❇☎) This large and somewhat faded business hotel is within close reach of Zigong's riverside sights and the Shizi Kou (十字口) bus stop. Competition among hotels mean that rates are unusually low, which puts it within range of budget travellers.

Drinking & Nightlife

★**Wangye Temple** TEAHOUSE
(王爷庙, Wángyé Miào; 3 Binjiang Lu, 滨江路3号; ◷8.30am-11pm) Housed within the ochre walls of a 100-year-old guild hall of boatmen and merchants, this lively teahouse (officially known as 临江茶楼, Línjiāng Chálóu) is one of the most atmospheric in Sichuan. Tea costs ¥12 to ¥20.

Huanhou Palace TEAHOUSE
(桓侯宫, Huánhóu Gōng; Zhonghua Lu, 中华路; ◷7am-9pm) This teahouse (tea ¥5 to ¥8) is located inside an 1868 butchers guild hall. Its dramatic stone facade opens up onto a tree-shaded courtyard with an old stone stage framed on all sides by beautiful wooden carvings. The antique dealers who share the

space generally don't cut into the tranquility – unless you make eye contact.

Getting There & Away

The main **bus station** (客运总站, Kèyùn Zǒngzhàn; ☏0813 820 9777; 817 Dangui Dajie, 丹桂大街817号) is a short way south of the river. Destinations include the following:

Chengdu ¥73 to ¥84, 2½ hours, about every 20 minutes (6.30am to 7pm)

Chongqing ¥76, three hours, every half hour (8.20am to 6.30pm)

Emei Shan ¥60, 3½ hours, four daily (9.10am, 11.50am, 1.30pm and 4pm)

Le Shan ¥50, three hours, 13 daily (7am to 5.30pm)

Yibin ¥28, one hour, every 30 minutes (7.10am to 7pm)

Train services from Zigong are limited. Go to Yibin (¥11, 2 hours, one daily, 9.15am) and take a train from the much busier station there.

Yibin 宜宾

☏0831 / POP 595,000

Where the Min and Jinsha River converge to become the mighty Yangzi River, Yibin (Yíbīn) has stood as a town of great strategic military importance throughout history, although there's few visible reminders of the city's long past. Today it's a relatively modern mid-sized city, making it a convenient travel hub for trips to old town Lizhuang, the Bamboo Sea and Luobiao's hanging coffins.

There's a lively **night market** (东街, Dong Jie) with stalls serving diǎndiǎn xiāng màocài (点点香冒菜, skewers boiled in a spicy sauce). In the daytime, look for Yíbīn ránmiàn (宜宾燃面), a spicy, fried noodle dish with a crushed peanut and minced-meat sauce that is a local favourite.

Jingmao Hotel HOTEL ¥¥
(经贸宾馆, Jīngmào Bīnguǎn; ☏0831 701 0888, 0831 513 7222; 108 Minzhu Lu, 民主路108号; tw ¥220; ❇☎) In the middle of the action, this no-frills hotel is clean and serves its purpose. Discounts of up to 20% make it a bargain in this town.

Getting There & Away

BUS

Most travellers arrive at **Gaoke bus station** (高客站, Gāokè zhàn). Departures from here include the following:

Chengdu ¥104 to 106, four hours, frequent (7.30am to 7pm)

Le Shan ¥56, four hours, hourly (8.20am to 5.30pm)

Zigong ¥28, one hour, frequent (7am to 7.20pm)

Head across town to **Nanke bus station** (南客站, *Nánkè zhàn*) for buses to Lizhuang (¥4, 35 minutes, every 15 minutes from 6.15am to 7.30pm), the Bamboo Sea (¥22, 1½ hours, 9.30am) and Luobiao (¥33, three hours, 2.05pm).

Travellers may find the nearby cities of Changning and Gongxian have more direct buses to the Bamboo Sea and Luobiao.

TRAIN

Trains leaving from **Yibin train station** (火车站, *huǒchē zhàn*) include the following:

Chengdu high-speed train from ¥107, 1½ hours, 15 daily (6.42am to 8.51pm)

Zigong ¥11 to ¥19, 2½ hours, one daily (4.08pm)

Bamboo Sea 蜀南竹海

☎0831 / POP 3000

Looking like it's straight out of a Chinese film set, south Sichuan's Bamboo Sea (Shǔnán Zhúhǎi), which is protected as the **Shunan Zhuhai National Park** (蜀南竹海国家公园, Shǔnán Zhúhǎi Guójiā Gōngyuán; ¥110 Jan-Nov, ¥60 Dec), is a world removed from the bustling cities in the centre of the province. Wander through forests of this fast-growing grass (some species of bamboo can grow up to 91cm in a single day!), in an atmosphere so quiet that you can actually seem to hear it growing, or float through the foggy sky on either of the two cable cars. While the park is generally more optimised for travellers with vehicles than those on foot, the interconnected trails in the centre of the park, looping around still forest lakes and along temple-crowded cliff sides, make it worth the trip.

Sights & Activities

The villages of Wanling (万岭), at the west gate, and Wanli (万里), near the east gate, are the main settlements inside the park. It's about 11km from one to the other if you follow the road the whole way.

Two cable cars (索道, *suǒdào*) ease the journey considerably, and are a great way to see the forest from another angle. The **Guanguang cable car** (观光索道, Guānguāng Suǒdào; one way/return ¥30/40; ⏲8am-5pm) near Wanling takes you on a 25-minute ride over a stunning forest and past steep cliffs. There's a pleasant one-hour walk along the Mo Brook (墨溪, Mò Xī) that loops through the forest just past the cable-car entrance.

From the end of the Guanguang cable car, either follow the signs for a free lift to the **Daxiagu cable car** (大峡谷索道, Dàxiágǔ Suǒdào; one way/return ¥20/30; ⏲8.30am-5.30pm), a 10-minute ride traversing a dramatic gorge, or walk to the junction at Sanhe Jie (三合界) where you can find a small selection of accommodation and food.

From both Daxiagu or Sanhe Jie your destination is the same: the trails that trace through the scenic area, which includes a number of small lakes and caves with picturesque names like 'Sea within the Sea' (海中海) and 'Cave of the Immortals' (仙禹洞). Either way, at the end of the paths you'll need to retrace your steps or head back via the opposite route.

If you end up with extra time in Wanling at the end of the day, the nearby **Forgotten Worries Valley** (忘忧谷, Wàngchén Gǔ) makes for a nice two-hour walk from the village and back past a number of progressively larger waterfalls.

Sleeping

Settle in a hotel in Wanling, with the friendly Yang family's tidy, basic **Joan's Guesthouse** (晶鑫园衣家乐, Jīngxīn Yuán Yījiālè; ☎135 4771 7196; www.snzhjourney.com; West gate, 200m past the small bridge on Wanling's main square, 小桥广场往观云亭方向前行200米左手边; r ¥120-160; ❄📶) on the road above the village or at the **Chéngbīnlóu Jiǔdiàn** (承宾楼酒店; ☎0831 498 0104; Wanling village square, 蜀南竹海小桥（西大门前1公里）; s/tw ¥220/280; ❄📶) on the main square.

Getting There & Around

Buses into the park stop at the west gate to allow you to get off and buy your entrance ticket, before passing through Wanling village and then terminating at Wanli.

There are two direct buses from Wanli to Yibin (¥22, two hours, 7am and 2pm). Both pass Wanling (40 minutes) and, if you ask, will drop you at the junction for Changníng (one hour; 15km from the main western park entrance), where you can change for Gongxian to get to Luobiao. Smaller local buses shuttle every 15 minutes between Wanling and Changning (¥6, 7am to 6pm).

Motorbike taxis can take you between the two main villages (around ¥60, 45 minutes) if you decide not to walk.

WESTERN SICHUAN

West of Chengdu, green tea becomes butter tea, gentle rolling hills morph into jagged snowy peaks and the Mandarin *nǐ hǎo!* gives way to Tibetan *tashe deleg!*

This is the Garze Tibetan Autonomous Prefecture, a territory that corresponds roughly with the Kham (in Chinese 康巴, Kāngbā), one of old Tibet's three traditional provinces. It is home to more than a dozen distinct Tibetan tribes, the largest being the Khampas, historically fierce warriors and horsemen.

Each season brings its own rugged beauty. In spring and summer many remote towns and monasteries can feel abandoned as villagers head out to harvest *byar rtswa dgun bu* (虫草, *chóngcǎo*) – cordyceps in English – a medicinal caterpillar fungus that grows on the alpine slopes and retails for outrageous amounts in lowland China and increasingly throughout the world.

ℹ️ Information

At these elevations, altitude sickness and acute mountain sickness (AMS) are very real concerns, especially for those looking to get out into nature for long periods. Acclimatise slowly and carefully, and if you start to suffer from AMS symptoms descend immediately to lower elevations.

Western Sichuan endures up to 200 freezing days per year, but sunny summer days can be blistering. This, combined with the high altitude, can leave new arrivals vulnerable to bad sunburn in addition to altitude sickness. Pack layers and take a couple of days to acclimatise when you arrive and as you continue to gain elevation.

Kangding 康定

📞 0836 / POP 134,000 / ELEV 2560M

Coming from the Chengdu area, there are two main gateways into Tibetan Sichuan. One is Danba, but far more popular is Kangding (Kāngdìng; known in Tibetan as Dartsendo or Dardo), the capital of the Garze Tibetan Autonomous Prefecture.

Set in a steep river valley at the confluence of the raging Zheduo and Yala Rivers (the Dar and Tse in Tibetan), Kangding offers an easy introduction to Tibetan culture and a couple of days here allows you to acclimatise while still being in range of mountains like enormous Gongga Shan to the south, one of nearly two dozen peaks over 6000m within a few hours' drive.

This town has long stood as a trading centre between the Tibetan and Han, with sizeable Hui and Qiang minority populations also part of the mix; you'll find elements of all these cultures represented here. Golden-roofed monasteries, a city-centre mosque and several large churches attest to the town's diversity.

🔵 Sights

Nánwú Sì   BUDDHIST TEMPLE
(南无寺, Lhamo Tse; Lucheng Nanlu, 炉城南路; ⊘ 7am-9pm) FREE This temple belongs to the Gelugpa (Yellow Hat) sect of Tibetan Buddhism and is the most active monastery in the area. Walk south along the main road, cross the river and keep going for about 200m until you see a small sign ('南無村') for the monastery on your right. Follow the road straight uphill on a steep road to the gold-capped roofs.

Jingang Si   BUDDHIST TEMPLE
(金刚寺; Dordrak Lhakang; Lucheng Nanlu, 炉城南路; ⊘ 7am-9pm) FREE A short way south of town, along the main road, is this 400-year-old Nyingma (Red Hat sect) monastery. To get there, turn right from the main road into an archway labelled '金刚村'.

Guānyīn Sì   BUDDHIST TEMPLE
(观音寺; 9 Paomashan Donglu, 跑马山东路9号; ⊘ 7am-6pm) FREE Looming over Kangding on the lower slopes of Paoma Shan, above the three main halls of the temple, is a path that leads on to several pagodas and another remote prayer hall. Continue following the same path to reach the scenic area around the **Pǎomǎ Sì** (跑马寺, Dentok Lhakang; ¥50; ⊘ 8am-6pm).

Ānjué Sì   BUDDHIST TEMPLE
(安觉寺, Ngachu Gompa; 52 Yanhe Xilu, 沿河西路52号; ⊘ 7am-6.30pm) This central temple's two small halls built around a colourful central courtyard have roots dating back to 1652, but it's been much rebuilt in the centuries since. It was said to have been established by the fifth Dalai Lama. Despite its illustrious beginnings, it's today suffering from an ever-decreasing number of monks (currently just 28).

🏃 Activities

The mountains looming over Kangding are ideal for day walks and a great way of safely acclimatising and preparing yourself for the high altitude adventures that lie just to

Kangding (Dartsendo)

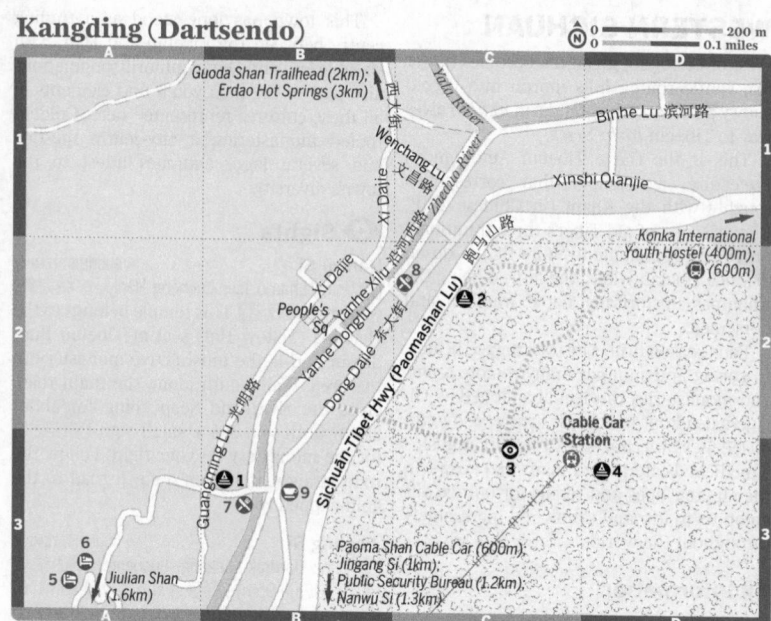

Kangding (Dartsendo)

the west. For most walks you'll need a guide, which can be arranged easily through any of the main guesthouses and hostels.

Jiǔlián Shān   MOUNTAIN

(九连山) **FREE** The best way of acclimatising and getting fit for adventures further west is to climb the beautiful Mt Jiulian. The trail rises steeply through forest but the top is a rolling grassland plateau of between 3500 and 4000m, beyond which horses and yaks graze and there might even be the odd

nomad tent. Access it behind Zhilam Hostel, which can provide maps and guides (advisable) for guests.

If you've just arrived in town from lower elevations, be sure to spend at least one day resting before climbing up.

Paoma Shan   MOUNTAIN

(跑马山, Dentok Rawo; ¥50; ⊙8am-6pm) Paoma Shān is the famed mountain of the *Kāngdìng Qíng Gē* ('Kangding Love Song'), one of China's most enduring folk songs, and will appeal the most to those who are familiar with the ditty. It's an easy ascent on foot, or take the **cable car** (索道, Suǒdào; 36 Xiangyang Jie, 向阳街36号; one way/return adult ¥35/55, child (rtn only) ¥25; ⊙9am-6pm) halfway up for excellent views of the town and surrounding peaks and valleys. You have to pay to go all the way up the stepped path, past ribbons of prayer flags and the Pǎomǎ Sì (p775).

⭐ Festivals & Events

Circling the Mountain Festival   RELIGIOUS

(转山节, Zhuǎnshānjié) Kangding's biggest annual festival takes place on Paoma Shan on the eighth day of the fourth lunar month (normally in May) to commemorate the birthday of the Historical Buddha, Sakyamuni. White and blue Tibetan tents cover the hillside and there's wrestling, horse racing and visitors from all over western Sichuan.

🛌 Sleeping

Konka International Youth Hostel HOSTEL ¥
(贡嘎国际青年旅舍, Gònggā Guójì Qīngnián Lûshě; ☑ 0836 281 7788, 189 9048 1279; 3rd fl, 59 Dongguan Yinle Guangchangjie, 东关音乐广场街 59号3楼; dm ¥35-40, d ¥150; ☎) The most convenient option for transiting bus travellers, this sprawling hostel has slightly scrappy dorms (six or eight beds) and rooms. Some English is spoken and staff can help arrange self-guided excursions into the mountains, even loaning outdoor gear. Lively communal dinners include vegetarian options (¥18 to ¥24 per person). Just 50m to the left (west) of the bus station.

★ **Zhilam Hostel** HOSTEL ¥¥
(汇道客栈, Huìdào Kèzhàn; ☑ 0836 283 1100; www.zhilamhostel.com; 72 Baitukan Xiang, 白土坎巷72号; dm ¥50, r with/without bathroom from ¥160/240, family ¥460; @☎) Run by an American family, this fabulous hillside hostel is a comfortable base in Kangding. It provides all manner of top-end hostel services, from camping-gear rental to good western food (served in a nomad tent built into the dining room!) and travel advice. It's a winding 10-minute walk uphill from the city centre.

Zhilam is also a reliable resource for wilderness adventures, and can arrange guides and transport to trek the Gongga Shan circuit, visit nearby Muge Cuo lake or other adventures.

Kangding Guozhuang Boutique Home Stay GUESTHOUSE ¥¥
(康定国庄精品民宿, Kāngdìng Guó Zhuāng Jīngpǐn Mínsù; ☑ 0836 2830 083; 75 Bai Tu Kan, 75白土侃; tent ¥100, d from ¥280; ☎) Attractive guesthouse with a covered dining terrace surrounded by a virtual rainforest of tropical flowers. The green motif continues inside where each of the homely rooms has floral touches and quality furnishings. The apple pancakes are a special treat after a few weeks of yak meat out in the high grasslands.

CLOSED AREAS

As in most Tibetan areas of China, restrictions on foreign tourists visiting certain areas are common. In general, most of western Sichuan is normally open to tourists, but at the time of research there were some travel restrictions in place. Seda, which is home to the massive Larung Gar Five Sciences Buddhist Academy, has been closed to foreigners for some years though rumours were swirling at the time of research that it might be about to reopen (according to the regional government it is now possible to visit, but the local government is still refusing tourists entry). Also closed was Yaqing in Baiyu county, which is home to the extraordinary Yarchen Gar Buddhist Institute; even Chinese visitors are currently banned from visiting here. Although it's officially only these two towns that are closed, in reality the whole of Baiyu county, including the main town of Baiyu, is closed to foreigners.

The official reason for the closures is that the monastery towns have grown too fast and with little in the way of planning, sewage systems or fire-safety systems, and that the government was therefore demolishing certain buildings in order to improve safety and hygiene. However, many local people and Tibetan groups report that mass demolitions of the monks' and nuns' housing is taking place simply because the monasteries are seen to be becoming too large and powerful and attracting too many people from other parts of Tibet and China. There are widespread reports in the international media of forced relocations and 're-education' of monks and nuns.

Due to these closures we have been unable to conduct on-the-ground research in Seda, Yaqing and Baiyu.

Foreigners are forbidden from travelling individually overland from Sichuan into the Tibetan Autonomous Region (西藏, Xīzàng) as Tibet's far eastern prefecture of Chamdo (昌都地区, Chāngdū Dìqū), which borders Sichuan, is usually off limits. During March (a time of holy celebrations and politically sensitive anniversaries), Tibet is often completely closed to foreigners. This closure has extended to Sichuan's Aba and Ganzi Prefectures before as well, though not in recent years.

Hostels keep up with the latest information, or check the China and Tibet branches of Lonely Planet's online forum, Thorn Tree (www.lonelyplanet.com/thorntree).

EATING TIBETAN

While there's plenty of decent Sichuan cuisine available throughout most of the region, you should really use this opportunity to delve into the radically different world of Tibetan cuisine. From a breakfast of sticky porridge-like *tsampa* to a lunch of raw yak meat in a remote nomad tent, eating in western Sichuan is always an adventure.

English	Local (Kham) Tibetan pronunciation	Tibetan script	Chinese pronunciation	Chinese script
Butter tea	bo-ja	བོད་ཇ།	sūyóu chá	酥油茶
Noodles	took-ba	ཐུག་པ།	zàngmiàn	藏面
Rice, potato and yak-meat stew	sham-dre	ཤ་འབྲས།	gālí niúròu fàn	咖喱牛肉饭
Roasted barley flour	tsom-ba	རྩམ་པ།	zānbā	糌粑
Salted black tea	ja nak-bo	ཇ་ནག་པོ།	yán hóngchá	盐红茶
Tibetan yoghurt	sho	ཞོ།	suānnǎi	酸奶
Vegetable dumplings	tse-momo	ཚལ་མོག་མོག	sùcài bāozi	素菜包子
Yak-meat dumplings	sha-momo	ཤ་མོག་མོག	niúròu bāozi	牛肉包子
'A little more'	dee-tse mong-wa go	དེ་ཚེ་མང་བ་དགོས།	háiyào yīdiǎnr	还要一点
'It's enough!'	te-drig-song!	དའ་འགྲིགས་སོང་།	chī bǎole!	吃饱了!

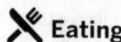 Eating

Mágē Miàn
NOODLES ¥

(麻哥面; 59 Yanhe Xilu, 沿河西路59号; noodles ¥11-13; ⊙24hr) A local classic, this hole-in-the-wall place right in the town centre draws crowds of locals for its house special: *ma'gē miàn* (麻哥面) – noodles topped with a spicy mince-meat sauce in small (一两, *yīliǎng;* ¥11) or large (二两, *èr liǎng;* ¥13) servings.

Malaya Tibetan Restaurant
TIBETAN ¥¥

(玛拉亚藏餐, Mǎlāyà Zàngcān; ☏ 0836 287 7111; 6th fl, 14 Yanhe Donglu, 沿河东路14号6楼; dishes from ¥25-40; ⊙11am-9pm; ☜) A friendly restaurant-cum-teahouse serving upmarket Tibetan dishes in a dining room decorated with *mani* stones (stones inscribed with mantras) and with views out over the city. If you need inspiration from the menu, try the yak-meat burger (meat stew topped with flatbread; ¥68) or the Tibetan-style beef dumplings (藏式牛肉包子; ¥28). Despite the fairly high prices, the food is only so-so.

Located above the fast-food joint Dico's (德克士); walk up then take the elevator to the 6th floor.

Drinking & Nightlife

Himalayan Coffee & Trading Co.
CAFE

(喜马拉雅咖啡, Xǐmǎlāyǎ Kāfēi; ☏ 0836 7524 329; 54 Dong Dajie, 东大街54号; ⊙7.30am-11pm; ☜) The best coffee in town is served at this bright, cool and busy place near the big yak sculpture. Wraps, pizzas, house-baked pastries, waffles and wi-fi satisfy other common traveller cravings – though at homeland prices. Even for nonsmokers the 'VIP' balcony out back makes for great people-watching over the street below.

ⓘ Information

Public Security Bureau (PSB, 公安局, Gōng'ānjú; ☏ 0836 281 1415; 213 Luchengnan Lu, 213鹿城南路; ⊙8.30am-5pm) Visa-extension service that takes three working days. First-time extensions only.

ⓘ Getting There & Away

AIR
Kangding Airport is 43km west of town and has between one and two daily flights to Chengdu (from ¥1000) and two weekly flights to Chongqing (¥1280, 12.40pm Tuesday and Thursday).

Pick up the airport shuttle (¥35, 1½ hours, 8am, 10am & 1.30pm) in front of the Airport

Hotel (also signed as the Xiang Yun Hotel – 翔云酒店 – from the street front). Tickets can be bought on the bus.

BUS

Kangding is a major transport hub in Sichuan, and travellers can transfer from here to most of the province. The **bus station** (Sichuan-Tibet Hwy, 川藏公路) is a 10-minute walk north from the centre of town (a taxi there is ¥7). Shared taxis also leave from outside the bus station (the vehicles aren't actually parked here; instead, look for the group of men loitering on the street outside the station). They head to most western Sichuan destinations listed here, including to Chengdu (¥150 to 200), Tagong (¥50 to ¥80) and Ganzi (around ¥150). Ask for either private hire (包车, bāochē) or a shared vehicle (拼车, pīnchē).

Destinations from the bus station include the following:

Baiyu ¥233, 18 hours (6am; stops overnight in Ganzi; book the day before)

Chengdu ¥114 to ¥135, six hours, hourly (6am to 4.30pm)

Chongqing ¥235, 12 hours (7am)

Danba ¥52, three hours, two daily (7.30am and 2.30pm)

Daocheng ¥155, 10 hours (6am)

Ganzi ¥124, eight hours (6am)

Le Shan ¥114, seven hours (6am)

Litang ¥102, eight hours (7am)

Tagong ¥63, three hours (3pm)

Xiangcheng ¥174, 15 hours (6am)

Ya'an ¥66 to ¥73, four hours, seven daily (6am to 4pm)

Northern Garze Prefecture

This is the Tibet you always dreamt of. A vast region where cold and barren grasslands collide with soaring mountain peaks. Where nomads with wind-reddened faces march with their yaks to the far horizon and snaking queues of pilgrims spin prayer wheels and walk a *kora* (pilgrim circuit) or two around thousand-year-old temples.

Once the realm of great kingdoms and marauding nomads, today the prefecture is only just being rediscovered by outsiders. Most are coming for one of two things: spiritual satisfaction in the countless temples and monasteries, or satisfaction of the soul by walking some of high Asia's best – and least-known – trekking routes.

Bring warm clothing; it can be frigid at these elevations even in midsummer. Bus services can be unreliable, and at times the government closes all or part of the region to foreign travellers with no notice. This is no place to be in a hurry.

Danba 丹巴

♪ 0836 / POP 70,000 / ELEV 1893M

Danba (Dānbā; known as Rongtrak in Tibetan; 1893m) straddles a dramatic gorge near the confluence of three rivers, and makes an interesting alternative to Kangding as a gateway into or out of western Sichuan.

The town is far from picturesque and isn't very exciting, but in the surrounding hills are clusters of gorgeous and traditional stone Jiarong Tibetan and Qiang villages with ancient watchtowers and welcoming homestays. These are the real reason for coming all the way out here.

☉ Sights

The 30m- to 60m-high ancient stone towers scattered throughout the villages overlooking the Dadu River were built by the Qiang between 700 and 1200 years ago. Some enterprising families have opened theirs up to travellers (¥10 to ¥20) who are willing to climb log ladders 6m up to the entrance.

Household towers were signs of status, and were used to store precious goods (and family members during wartime). Village towers were taller, built for conducting religious rituals, demarcating borders and passing smoke signals. In wartime, they were used to launch assaults against Tibetan marauders and the Qing army.

You can string together some nice day walks strolling between the towers and villages. There are lots of big shady trees and deep green fields of crops set against a backdrop of mountain spires.

★ Zhonglu VILLAGE

(中路) Comparatively remote Zhonglu, 13km from Danba, is less a village and more a collection of grand, traditional stone houses spread across a lush, green mountain slope. It's blissfully cool and quiet, and though there's not much to actually do (the energetic could hike up to the mountain ridge behind the village) it's a peaceful place to rest up and to acclimatise if you'll be heading further west afterwards. Many of the houses have watchtowers that you can visit.

Jiaju Zangzhai VILLAGE

(甲居藏寨; adult/student ¥50/25) Of all the pretty villages in the hills around here, Danba tourism's pride and joy is Jiaju, 12km northwest of town and perched at the top of a multiswitchback road that winds up a steep river gorge. With fruit trees, charming Tibetan stone houses and homestays, Jiaju's quaint architecture will pull in travellers for a half-day (or longer) visit.

Suopo
VILLAGE

(梭坡) Danba's nearest village with watchtowers is a 1½- to two-hour walk along the river. A resourceful family has rebuilt the wooden base levels of a tower next to their home; visitors can climb up the inside from their rooftop (¥15). Don't worry about finding them: they, or a 'friend' of theirs, will find you.

To get to Suopo, turn east out of Danba's cluster of hostels and follow the river. Turn down the track beside the small police station after about 5km, then cross the small suspension bridge and keep walking up to the village. Look for stone steps under some large trees up to your left, just after you reach the village's first couple of buildings. These steps lead to the nearest towers.

🛏 Sleeping

While there are plenty of midrange hotels in town, as well as a couple of hostels with dorm beds, the real reason for venturing out here is to stay in one of the increasingly luxurious 'homestays' (although they're often touted as homestays, nowadays they're more like guesthouses or boutique hotels) in the villages surrounding the town.

Zhaxi Zhuokang ~
Backpackers Hostel
HOTEL ¥

(扎西卓康国际青年旅舍, Zháxī Zhuōkāng Guójì Qīngnián Lǚshè; ☑189 9049 0656; 35 Sanchahe Nanlu, 三岔河南路35号; dm ¥30, tw ¥110; ☎) This is traveller central in Danba proper; the friendly English-speaking management can arrange minibus rides and extended treks to natural springs and remote villages off the tourist map. Rooms are decidedly average but tidy, while the common area is an inviting place to hang out. It's a 25-minute walk from the bus station (keep the river on your left) or a ¥5 taxi ride.

★ Joy Mystery Hotel
BOUTIQUE HOTEL ¥¥¥

(欢乐秘境酒店, Huānlè Mìjìng Jiǔdiàn; ☑083 6898 1111; Zhonglu Xiang, Kegeyi Cun, 中路乡克格依村; s/d incl meals ¥898/1099; ❄☎❄) So, you thought travel in Kham was going to be tough? Think again! At this sublime 15-room boutique hotel, set in a renovated 700-year-old building complete with its own temple, life is all about luxurious textiles, walk-in Italian rain showers, delicious meals (included in room rates) and pre-breakfast laps in the infinity pool.

Hán é Zhuāngyuán
BOUTIQUE HOTEL ¥¥¥

(罕é庄园, Hán é zhuāngyuán; ☑135 1844 0006; Zhonglu; d incl breakfast from ¥480; ☎❄) High up above Zhonglu village, this traditional whitewashed stone building set in a large flower garden has been converted into a fantastic boutique hotel adorned with antique furnishings. Spacious rooms do away with beds and just have the comfy mattresses placed on low wooden platforms. From the roof terrace, there are astounding views in all directions. Excellent meals are served.

❶ Getting There & Away

For Tagong, take a minibus (¥65, three hours) from the west end of town, via Bamei (¥43, two hours). Minibuses also head to Four Sisters Mountain (¥50-60, three hours) via Xiaojin (¥30, two hours). Bus destinations include the following:

Chengdu ¥135, nine hours, two daily (7.30am, 8am)

Ganzi ¥103, nine hours, one daily (7am)

Kangding ¥51, 3½ hours, two daily (7am, 3pm)

Tagong
塔公

☑0836 / POP 8990 / ELEV 3718M

With giant temple and monastery complexes that bustle with monks, nuns and pilgrims, spectacular rolling grasslands dotted with yaks and full of hiking possibilities, plus some great places to stay (including homestays with genuine nomads), the small Tibetan town of Tagong (Tǎgōng; Lhagang) and its surrounding grasslands offer plenty of excuses to linger.

On the road from Kangding is a sea of *mani* stones carved (and spray-painted) with ཨོཾ་མ་ཎི་པདྨེ་ཧཱུྃ (*om mani padme hum*), the mantra of Buddha's path. Explore this terrain on horseback or foot, sip real yak-butter tea, then fall asleep in tents under the stars like a Tibetan nomad. You're certain to end up staying longer than originally planned.

◎ Sights

★ Ser Gyergo Nunnery
BUDDHIST MONASTERY

(和平法会, Hépíng Fǎhuì) FREE Known locally as *ani gompa* (Tibetan for 'nunnery'), Hépíng Fǎhuì is home to around 500 nuns and more than 100 monks. Lama Tsemper was a revered hermit who spent much of his life meditating in a cave about two hours' walk across the grasslands from Tagong. Nuns would bring him food and look after him, so when he requested a temple be built here just before his death in the 1980s it was decided that a nunnery be built too.

Lama Tsemper's remains are in a *chörten* (Tibetan stupa) inside the original cave; you may have to ask a nun to unlock the door to look inside. Below the cave is the temple and a huge *mani* wall as big as the temple itself, which has its own *kora* that attracts many pilgrims. On the far hill, and overlooking the site, is a huge new building containing the nuns residences and kitchens; a little further uphill from that is a large walled complex containing a new monastery and monks residences called the Mùyǎ Dàsì (木雅大寺). On the opposite hill is a sky burial site. Here you will find the area where the bodies are cut up and left and a tree in which braids of hair, necklaces, glasses and other personal objects of the deceased are hung. You should not visit the sky burial site if a burial is taking place, but when nothing is happening nobody seems to mind you having a respectful look around. In between all the temples are tiny, fragile wooden houses of more nuns. All are painted a blood-red colour. The whole complex is growing fast as more and more nuns and monks arrive. You could easily spend a full day exploring this extraordinary complex, chatting to the people who live here and walking the *kora* with the pilgrims.

Getting to the nunnery is half the fun and a super little 4km walk from town over the hills and with views over the distant snow peaks. Ask for directions from any of the popular traveller hotels and hostels.

Lhagang Monastery BUDDHIST MONASTERY
(塔公寺, Tǎgōng Sì; Tagong Guangchang, 塔公广场; ¥20; ⊙5am-6pm) The story goes that when Princess Wencheng, the Chinese bride-to-be of Tibetan king Songtsen Gampo, was on her way to Lhasa in 640, a precious statue of Jowo Sakyamuni Buddha toppled off one of the carts in her entourage. A replica of the statue was carved on the spot where it landed and a temple built around it.

The busy complex contains a number of temples. The one where the statue fell is on the far right as you enter. The original, which is the most revered Buddha

image in all of Tibet, is housed in Lhasa's Jokhang Temple. As a result, it is said that praying in Tagong is the spiritual equivalent of praying in Lhasa itself. Also make note of the beautiful 1000-armed Chenresig (Avalokiteshvara) in the hall to the left, and the impressive garden of *chörtens* behind the monastery. In the early morning and evening lots of local people make a *kora* around the complex.

You can also visit the Sakya Monastic School across the river; exit the monastery and walk straight down the main road, turn right at the police station, cross the bridge and walk another 800m. Monks-in-training sit face-to-face on cushions, debating Buddhist texts. After seven years they will be able to join the others in Lhagang.

Golden Temple BUDDHIST TEMPLE
(木雅金塔, Mùyǎ Jīntǎ; ¥10; ⊙6am-6pm) The glimmering roof and stupa-lined walls of this temple are set against the fantastic backdrop of the snowy mountains across the grasslands. Inside it's a more sedate affair, but the prayer-wheel-lined walls and central

temple hall are worth a wander for those with spare time in town.

🏃 Activities

Horse riding (per person per day for one/two/three people ¥720/570/540 with meals and homestay) and guided grassland hikes (per person per day ¥200) can be arranged through Khampa Nomad Ecolodge (bespoke itineraries available). The ecolodge also organises treks through the grasslands and nearby mountain ranges.

You can hike into the grasslands on your own. One popular option is the two-hour hike from the town south to Ser Gyergo (p780); ask Khampa Cafe for directions.

🛌 Sleeping

Khampa Cafe GUESTHOUSE ¥
(康巴咖啡, Kāngbā Kāfēi; ☎ 183 0287 9858; www.khampacafe.com; Tagong Guangchang, 塔公广场; r ¥100-200; 🛜) A Czech/local couple run this popular guesthouse and cafe overlooking Tagong's main square. There is just one shared bath, but the double and triple bedrooms are comfortable and clean. The top-floor cafe is also the most popular hang-out in town, with a selection of western and Tibetan dishes, plus real coffee.

**★ Khampa Nomad
Ecolodge & Arts Center** LODGE ¥¥¥
(康巴牧民环保艺术客栈, Kāngbā Mùmín Huánbǎo Yìshù Kèzhàn; ☎ 136 8449 3301; www.definitelynomadic.com; dm/d incl breakfast ¥160/620; 🛜) 🍃 Tibetan/American couple Djarga and Angela run this superb ecolodge way out in the grasslands. There are only four cosy rooms (one of them can just about fit in a family of four) with wooden furnishings and picture-frame window views over a snowy mountainscape. There's a small dorm plus a sauna and hot tub that's bliss after a long walk.

Angela can advise on hiking routes and nomad homestays in the area, and rents tents and sleeping bags for ¥60. The breakfast spread is the best in Kham and they also do delicious meals (¥60 to 120).

From Tagong the lodge is a 15-minute taxi ride (¥60; mention Angela and most local drivers know where to go) or a three-hour hike. Contact the lodge for details on either.

🍴 Eating & Drinking

Khampa Cafe BAR
(康巴咖啡, Kāngbā Kāfēi; ☎ 183 0287 9858; www.khampacafe.com; Tagong Guangchang, 塔公广场;

⏱ 8am-10pm) By far the most popular place in town with travellers is the top-floor patio of the Khampa Cafe. They serve a tasty selection of Tibetan staples as well as steaks, burgers and pasta. A selection of local and international beers plus a healthy dose of travel camaraderie make this nightlife central.

ℹ️ Getting There & Away

Buses pass through town en route to Ganzi (¥120, six hours, 9am) and Kangding (¥40, two hours, 9am). If these are full, minibuses leave from the main square (which is also where the buses stop) to Litang (¥150, seven hours), Ganzi (¥100 to ¥150) and Kangding (¥50 to ¥70).

For destinations north it's also possible to take a shared minivan to Bamei (八美; ¥20, one hour), where you'll have your pick of minivans to places such as Danba (¥30, two hours) and Ganzi (¥50 to ¥70, seven hours).

Yulongsi Valley & Mt Gongga Shan

Gongga Shan (贡嘎山, Gòng gā shān; 7556m), also known locally as Minya Konka, is the highest mountain in Sichuan and the third-highest mountain in the world outside of the Himalaya. It sits at the centre of a dense cluster of snowy peaks and is considered one of the holiest mountains in Tibet. It's also one of the most dangerous. So far only 24 people have stood on the mountain summit, while 37 have died trying. While we don't suggest you try climbing it, we do suggest you trek around the base and explore its side valleys. It's one of the most scenically impressive areas in the entire Tibetan plateau. There are a number of different approaches to the mountain but perhaps the most rewarding area to base yourself, both before and after treks, is the remote but sublime Yulongsi Valley where tourism is just starting to take off.

◎ Sights

The Gongga massif covers a huge area. We cover just the trekking around the mountain itself, the Gongga Monastery and walks around it, plus the Yulongsi Valley and Yaha Valley.

The Yaha and Yulongsi valleys and the Gongga monastery are all to the west of the mountain and can be accessed by road from the town of Xinduqiao to the west of Kangding. From Xinduqiao a road runs south and gives access to the Yaha Valley. This is the lowest valley and the one furthest from the

OFF THE BEATEN TRACK

HIKING GONGKAR TSO

There's a memorable day hike from the Yulongsi Valley to a beautiful mountain lake and some lofty vantage points high above that's worth considering if you don't have time to do a full circuit of Gongga Shan. On still, clear days the mountains are beautifully reflected in the lake water.

The trail starts from the first collection of solid stone houses that you reach in the valley (when coming in from the north over the Yahaya Pass). Cross over the bridge, turn right and walk to the last farmhouse at the end of this side valley. A clear and obvious trail heads uphill to the start of the valley to the right of the farmhouse. Keep to the right-hand side of the stream. After 45 minutes you'll clamber up onto a grassy ridge and be greeted with a breathtaking view over the snowy peaks to the east.

The trail turns sharp left (west) and heads laboriously upwards. Soon all the trees and shrubs fade away to be replaced with heathers and scree slopes. The trail now ambles in a more gentle fashion to a bowl between two mountain peaks and a small lake (4600m). It's a two-hour walk from the farmhouse to this lake. If you still have energy left (and some oxygen in your lungs!) then you can follow a trail up beyond the lake to a low crest marked with prayer flags. From here you can head up to the summit of a ridge on your right (north). It's a short, steep and breathless climb to the top but from this lofty 4810m viewpoint you're rewarded with a magnificent vista of rolling grassland peaks and the ice walls of the enormous Gongga massif. Retrace your steps back down to the village. Allow four to five hours for the entire walk.

mountain but, with fields of wheat, gushing rivers and beech-tree woodlands, it's a very beautiful area (in autumn especially, when the leaves change colour). From the head of this valley a rough dirt road zigzags sharply upwards to the Yaha Pass (4641m) and a view over the entire western side of the Gongga massif that can make you want to drop to your knees in praise. The road then takes a rollercoaster downward ride to the bleaker and much colder Yulongsi Valley. At first you won't see much sign of human life bar the occasional nomad tent. Further along the valley a few small villages of large stone houses appear. Few crops grow this high up though, so even the people living in these houses are yak herders. An excellent walk heads to a hidden mountain lake from the first of these villages. Further down the valley still, a turn-off leads up to another pass and, eventually, the Gongga Monastery right at the foot of the massif. However, at the time of research this road was closed for repairs and it wasn't possible to reach the monastery.

★ **Gongga Monastery**   BUDDHIST MONASTERY
(贡嘎寺, Gòng Gǎ Sì) Set at an altitude of 3941m and cut off from the outside world by winter snows for months on end, the Gongga Monastery (also known as the Minya Konka Monastery) has an unforgettable location with views directly over to the glaciers of

Gongga Shan. The small monastery dates from 1285 and is of the Kagyu, or Black Hat, sect of Tibetan Buddhism. There are some impressive wall murals within the main prayer hall.

 Activities

The routes around Mt Gongga Shan (7556m), the highest mountain in Sichuan, form arguably the most spectacular trekking area in western Sichuan. There are a number of different trekking routes; most are five- to six-day circuits and each trekking agency will have its preferred routes. In all cases though, expect a hard, cold trek in a region with highly changeable weather. Most treks start at Kangding with a full day's drive to the chosen trailhead.

Sleeping

In the gentle charms of the rural Yaha Valley there are a number of attractive homestays and one superb guesthouse. On the other side of the spectacular Yaha Pass in the wild and bleak Yulongsi Valley and also around the Gongga Monastery are further homestays (around ¥100 with meals). These are very basic, with hard wooden beds, limited electricity, outdoor pit toilets and no washing facilities. But it's a great experience.

DON'T MISS

DARJAY GOMPA

Darjay Gompa (大金寺, Dàjīn Sì) is one of the most venerated monasteries in the prefecture; the reasoning behind the name 'Big Golden Temple' becomes apparent as soon as it appears on the horizon. There are two large halls surrounded by a small village that consists primarily of monks' brightly painted wooden houses. You may have to track down a monk to unlock (开门, kāimén) the temple halls. Keep an eye out for the fantastic sand mandalas the monks make from time to time.

Darjay Gompa is 30km west of Ganzi on the road to Manigange. It costs around ¥20 to get here from Ganzi in a shared minivan, at least ¥40 in a private taxi. A short walk from the Darjay Gompa is the basic but atmospheric **Talam Khang guesthouse and temple** (大金寺旅馆, Dàjīn Sì Lǚguǎn; ☑ 135 5851 9090, 187 8366 2272; camping/dm/s/d ¥30/40/100/200), with snowcapped mountains to one side, and rolling grasslands and a river to the other. To get here from Darjay Gompa, exit from the monastery's back gate and walk about 15 minutes along the dirt road. Walk towards the white stupa furthest on the left, keeping the grassland villages on your right. You'll see the temple as you come over the hill.

All homestays are clearly signed and you can normally just turn up and ask for a room.

Players Inn   GUESTHOUSE ¥¥
(球员旅馆, Qiúyuán lǚguǎn; ☑ 133 5084 4881; Yaha Valley, 雅哈谷; r with/without bathroom ¥240/180; ☎) This well-organised guesthouse with an attractively decorated dining area has sparkling rooms with a bright and summery decoration scheme and windows overlooking fields of wheat. There's 24-hour hot water, decent wi-fi, and coffee for breakfast. It's right up towards the head of the valley, close to where the sealed road turns into a dirt road heading to the Yaha Pass.

❶ Getting There & Away

There's no reliable public transport to the Yulongsi Valley or to the Gongga Monastery, so you'll need to hire a car and driver (ask at hostels in Kangding or Chengdu). If you're on an organised trek arranged through agencies in Kangding or Chengdu, the tour company will arrange all transport.

Ganzi   甘孜

☑ 0836 / POP 68,525 / ELEV 3475M

It's easy to spend a couple of days in the lively market town of Ganzi (Gānzī; Garzê) exploring the beautiful nearby countryside, which is scattered with Tibetan villages and large monasteries surrounded by snowcapped mountains. The fast-growing town itself is home to some large and busy monasteries and interesting markets full of cordyceps (a half-caterpillar, half-fungus that's gathered in nearby grasslands and used in the rest of China as a general energy booster and retails for outrageous sums of money) dealers and small shops stacked with prayer wheels and monks clothing.

⦿ Sights

★**Degongbu Temple**   BUDDHIST TEMPLE
(德贡布; Dégòngbù; Deba Cun, 德巴村) FREE
Surrounded by the mud-brick buildings belonging to the smaller of Ganzi's two Tibetan quarters, this 13th-century temple's two dimly lit halls (one historic, the other finished in 2007) are filled with the smell of yak-butter candles and the sound of spinning prayer wheels as locals make a small kora (circumambulation of a sacred site done as a pilgrimage) around both the exterior and interior of the compound. It's one of the most atmospheric temples in Kham.

Garze Gompa   BUDDHIST TEMPLE
(甘孜寺; Gānzī Sì; ¥10; ⊙approx 9am-6pm) North of the town's old Tibetan quarter is Ganzi's largest monastery, dating back more than 500 years and glimmering with gold (some of it even real!). Encased on the walls of the main hall are hundreds of small golden Shakyamunis (Buddhas). In a smaller hall down the hill to the west is an awe-inspiring statue of Jampa (Maitreya or Future Buddha) dressed in a giant silk robe, with a tooth of the historical Buddha embedded in the right big toe.

🛏 Sleeping

⭐ DzachuSama Hostel   HOSTEL ¥¥
(📞083 6752 3882; www.dzachusama.com; 133 QingKe PuDi, 邮政编码 133; dm ¥45, d ¥270; 🛜) This traditionally styled, large and bright American-owned hostel has some of the most luxurious private rooms you could hope to find in a hostel, all with Tibetan accents. The bathrooms even have big wooden bathtubs. The four- and eight-bed dorms are equally impressive. Staff can organise treks and excursions in the area.

There's a big garden with a vegetable patch, trampoline and children's toys (it's very child-friendly here) and the sunny terrace cafe (open to non-guests) serves burgers, pizzas, steaks, loads of types of coffee and a super breakfast. There's even a book swap.

It's a short way north of the city centre in a quiet, traditional neighbourhood.

Yong Kang Hotel   HOTEL ¥¥
(甘孜雍康大酒店, Yǒngkāng Fàndiàn; 📞083 6752 666; 99 Jichang Ave, 甘孜县新区路99号; r incl breakfast ¥238; 🛜) Good-value modern hotel with a little too much in the way of gold paint. It's bang in the city centre (get a rear-facing room to ensure a quiet night) and beds are comfy and amply cushioned. The rooftop restaurant offers epic mountain views. Popular with small group tours.

🍴 Eating

Ai Xin Dangao   BAKERY
(爱心蛋糕, Ài Xīn Dàn Gāo; Dong Dajie, 东大街; cakes ¥5-8; ⏱7.30am-10pm) Your breakfast dreams are answered at this delightful, and unexpected, European-style bakery selling custard tarts, croissants, small pizzas and other savoury snacks as well as juices and pots of jam. Sadly there's no coffee available.

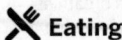

SICHUAN NORTHERN GARZE PREFECTURE

OFF THE BEATEN TRACK

HIKING THE CHOLA MOUNTAINS

Travel west from Manigange and very quickly a daunting range of rock and ice rises up off the plateau in front of you. This is the Chola Mountains (雀儿山, Què'ér Shān). At its highest point, the range reaches 6168m. Although such a dominant feature of the landscape, the mountains are little explored by trekkers and few Chinese or Tibetan tour companies can tell you much about them. If you have a private vehicle though, there is a superb five-hour round trip (roughly 12km) hike you can make into the range that will take you past a turquoise lake and into a jagged cirque of peaks.

Drive from Manigange towards Dzogchen. Just as the main road starts to climb up towards the pass separating the two towns you will see a small concrete track turning off on your left. Follow this track for four kilometres until the road comes to an abrupt end above the silky turquoise waters of Ngor Lake. Beyond the lake, a great shaft of jagged snow-covered mountains blocks the end of the valley. This is Mt Ngodong (elevation unknown) and local people consider it a holy mountain.

From the lake, a fairly obvious trail follows its western edge before heading over wet meadows that in spring and summer become a carpet of butter-yellow flowers. After 45 minutes you will see a group of prayer flags just off to your right. The trail veers downhill slightly to the milky-coloured river. Remove your boots and wade across. It's shallow but even in summer it's bone-numbingly cold. Continue along the east bank of the river following the obvious trail (there's also a trail on the west side of the river but it's indistinct, overgrown and passes directly below some terrifyingly sheer cliff faces that suffer from frequent rockfalls – avoid this route). After around an hour and a half you will come to some dilapidated herders huts and the trail drops down to the river and – hopefully – a precarious stick bridge (this might get washed away after heavy rains, in which case you will need to find somewhere to wade carefully across). Back on the west bank of the river, the trail bends around the back of the vertical cliff face (look up towards the top of these cliffs and you might spot some caves; locals say that one of these caves contains the magic treasure of an important lama) and after half an hour you'll top a final rise and find yourself face to face with a cirque of mountains that look like torn dinosaur fangs. At this point the valley has widened a little and there's a small boggy meadow with little pools of water and big boulders to sit and picnic on. To head back, just retrace your steps.

SICHUAN NORTHERN GARZE PREFECTURE

SEDA & THE LARUNG GAR FIVE SCIENCES BUDDHIST ACADEMY

Seda (色达; Sertar), home to **Larung Gar Five Sciences Buddhist Academy** (喇荣五明佛学院, Lǎróng Wǔmíng Fó Xuéyuàn), the largest Buddhist academy in the world, used to offer those foreigners lucky enough to visit an incredible glimpse into the life of monks and nuns.

However, this is a politically sensitive town and since July 2016 the town and academy have been firmly closed to foreign tourists, with the possibility of fines and compulsory trips to Chengdu for those caught in the area.

Larung Gar, which sits at a breathless 4000m, was founded in 1980 by 30 disciples gathering at the modest home of their charismatic leader Khenpo Jikphun. Many more soon arrived. Today the two main halls that anchor the valley floor – the nunnery (女金室, nǔjīn shì), distinguished with three *darchen* (flag poles) in front, and the massive main monastery (大金室, dàjīn shì) – are thoroughly surrounded by a hive of subsidiary chapels and low-slung living quarters that blanket the valley in crimson. Devoted pilgrims climb to the ridge to prostrate before a huge chorten (Tibetan stupa) and walk the *kora*, spinning prayer wheels.

At the time of research rumours were swirling that Larung Gar might be about to reopen to foreign tourists. Ask with Tibetan specialist tour companies for the latest.

Lake Mamosarovor Tibetan Restaurant
TIBETAN ¥

(玛旁雍措藏餐馆, Mǎpángyōngcuò Zàngcānguǎn; Dong Dajie, 东大街; mains ¥25-50; ⊙ 8.30am-midnight; 🛜) The friendly Tibetan family that runs this restaurant serves a few local Sichuan favourites and a much wider variety of Tibetan dishes, including raw yak meat. Afterwards, enjoy one of their selection of teas from across the Tibetan regions.

ℹ️ Getting There & Away

The new Ganzi Gesar Airport (50km north) opened in late 2019.

Scheduled bus services run from the new **bus station**, to the east of the city centre, to the following destinations:

Chengdu ¥231, 18 hours (6.10am)

Danba ¥104, eight hours (6.30am)

Kangding ¥124, 11 hours, two daily (both at 6.30am)

Litang ¥81, six hours (9am)

Minivans leave from a **station** in the centre of the city and head to the following:

Dege ¥100, six to seven hours

Litang ¥120, six to seven hours

Manigange ¥40, two to three hours

Manigange 马尼干戈

📞 0836 / POP 3850 / ELEV 2988M

There's not much going on in Manigange (Mǎnígāngē; Manigango) itself, a small transit town halfway between Ganzi and Dege. The surrounding hills do offer wonderful hiking opportunities, though, and the main draw near the town (the magnificent Yilhun Lha-Tso lake) makes it well worth spending a full day in the area.

On hilltops to either side of Manigange are the relatively new Yazisi and Lajiasi temples, the views from both of which also take in the mountains that ring the grasslands surrounding the city.

Yilhun Lha-tso
LAKE

(玉隆拉措, Yùlónglācuò; ¥30; ⊙ 6am-9pm) It is said King Gesar's beloved concubine Zhumu was so taken by these stunning turquoise-blue waters that her heart fell in. This now-holy glacial lake, 8km southwest of Manigange, is still awe inspiring. Follow a small dirt track around the north edge of the lake to a marshy plain at the far end, from which you can take in the spectacular views of peaks and glaciers from right up close. Locally, this area is also known as 新路海 (Xīnlù Hǎi).

Manigange Pani Hotel
HOTEL ¥

(马尼干戈怕尼酒店, Mǎnígāngē Pàní Jiǔdiàn; 📞 0836 822 2788, 183 8366 2210; r ¥180-300; 🛜) Not just the town's best hotel, this is also the town's only proper hotel. The rooms are well kept and have everything you might need for a comfortable night, but they're certainly not the height of luxury. The restaurant (mains ¥25 to ¥40, open 7am to 10pm) is the best place to eat in town, too.

Burgers & Pizza INTERNATIONAL ¥

(汉堡和比萨饼, Hànbǎo Hé Bǐsàbǐng; ☑136 9834 1637; mains ¥10-40; ⊙9am-9pm; 🛜) This popular, clean, canteen-like place is a surprise in remote little Manigange. Peruse the easy-to-understand picture menu and take your pick from reasonable (for Kham) burgers and pizzas, yak steaks, ice cream and decent coffee.

❶ Getting There & Away

Buses depart daily from the car park of the Manigange Pani Hotel for Dege (¥40, three hours, 4.30pm) and Ganzi (¥40, three hours, 7pm). Heading northwest to Dzogchen, there are only minibus taxis and demand is so little that normally you'll have to do a private hire for ¥300.

Dzogchen   竹庆寺

ELEV 3850M

Wedged between high, glacial mountain peaks on the northern side of the Chola Mountains is the vast monastery and *shedra* (Buddhist college) complex of Dzogchen (Zhú Qìng Sì), one of the most important seats of the Nyingma (Red Hat) sect. Exploring this massive and ever-expanding complex of temples, prayer halls, stupas and meditation retreats alone could keep you busy for a day or three, but there's more to Dzogchen than spirituality. With snow-capped mountain peaks on one side and rolling grasslands with wandering yaks and nomads on the other there's plenty of scope here for several days of exciting walking.

⊙ Sights

★**Dzogchen Gompa** BUDDHIST MONASTERY

(竹庆寺, Zhú Qìng Sì; www.dzogchenmonastery. cn) FREE Backed by mountains, the massive Dzogchen monastery complex sits halfway up a steep ridge overlooking a valley dotted with stupas, *shedras*, dormitory blocks, and further chapels and prayer halls. One of the most important seats of the Nyingma (Red Hat) sect, the monastery was originally established in 1685 but almost everything you see today was rebuilt with flamboyance from the 1980s onward. Visiting the monastery and other Buddhist sites in the valley takes at least a day.

In Tibetan, 'Dzogchen' means 'Great Perfection'; the monastery is so named because it's supposed to be the perfect place to study the Vajrayana Buddhist tradition and the site is regarded as one of the holiest places in the Tibetan world. As such, over the years thousands of Buddhist practitioners have come to the valley to study at the renowned *shedra*. Today the monastery's popularity means it's continuing to grow and many of the students studying here are actually Han Chinese. Currently, there are around 300 registered monks and nuns, but many hundreds more are present at any one time.

The main part of the complex contains three different prayer halls. After you've finished exploring these, clamber uphill for ten minutes to the prayer-flag-lined ridge just above from where there are stunning views. Afterwards, descend down to the valley floor and walk up towards the head of the valley. Along the way you'll pass the main *shedra* on your left, accommodation blocks for students, further smaller temples and a large stupa that's a near-exact copy of the famous Boudhanath Stupa in Nepal (though without the atmosphere of that one), before finally arriving right at the end of the valley and a nunnery. On the mountain slopes above are remote meditation caves.

From around 8am to noon daily, monks gather in the main prayer hall to pray and chant. Interested visitors are welcome to sit in and watch.

🏃 Activities

To the southwest of the monastery complex a thick wall of mountains and glaciers seals off the end of the valley. By contrast, to the north of the village the mountains fade away to fertile, rolling grasslands that are ideal for yaks. It all makes for a wonderfully diverse – and as yet totally undeveloped and little known – hiking scene.

The best day walk is a full day (eight hours return) hard hike to three high toothpaste-blue lakes set among scree slopes, right at the foot of one of the mountain's glaciers. The trail starts from the ridge above the main monastery, crosses over to the other side of the valley and then turns south and rises sharply up into the mountains. It's an obvious trail but a guide is still a very wise idea (ask at the monastery guesthouse).

A shorter walk (three to four hours return) goes from the nunnery at the far end of the valley straight up through old-growth pine forest to various meditation caves (if there are people using the caves then don't disturb them by approaching too close). The route will also take you past a number of gorgeous waterfalls.

There's also a longer, two-day trek that traverses around the back of the mountains and over a high pass right next to a glacier. We haven't walked it, but locals tell us it's a very tough, cold and high hike, for which you must be properly prepared.

For a different kind of hiking, the grasslands leading away from the northern end of the village have all manner of walking possibilities. Just take your pick of hills to climb or valleys to pace, and go and explore. Be warned that there are quite a few nomads out here and you should always give their dogs a very wide berth.

For all these walks it's sensible to take a local guide (ask in the guesthouses), warm and waterproof clothing, and some food.

🛏 Sleeping & Eating

The village centre has a few basic restaurants selling Tibetan staples, and there's a decent restaurant at the monastery accommodation.

Along Hotel   HOTEL¥
(沿着酒店, Yánzhe Jiǔdiàn; ☎135 4746 0000; r with/without bathroom ¥260/130; 🛜) Close to being completed at the time of research, it was obvious that this place in the centre of the village was going to be the best of a couple of basic options here. Rooms have thick mattresses and some have attached bathrooms. There's also a restaurant serving Chinese and Tibetan dishes.

Dzogchen International
Buddhist Exchange Centre   HOTEL¥¥
(大圆满国际佛教交流中心, Dà yuánmǎn Guójì Fójiào Jiāoliú Zhōngxīn; ☎199 0478 3193; r from ¥260; 🛜) The huge monastery guesthouse is the best place to stay in Dzogchen, offering plain but clean and quiet rooms in a blissful valley setting with amazing mountain views from some rooms. The showers have ample hot water and there's wi-fi in the lobby. There's also a large, institutional-feeling restaurant serving Sichuan dishes (¥15 to ¥20).

ℹ Getting There & Away

All transport to and from Dzogchen is by minibus, and even that's limited. A seat to Ganzi is ¥70 and there are normally one or two vans a day leaving from the centre of the village. To get to Yushu in Qinghai is ¥150, but very few people travel this route so you might have to do a private hire (¥120 to ¥1300).

Dege   德格

📱 0836 / POP 81.500 / ELEV 3334M

Surrounded by an old Tibetan quarter of red-painted stone houses, the heart of Dege (Dégé; Derge) is the large Buddhist Scripture Printing Press. More than a mere printing house, this is both a hugely important repository of Tibetan Buddhist texts and a major pilgrimage site, around which hordes of local townsfolk and nomadic herders make endless circumambulations.

The printing press is a fascinating spectacle that makes the long journey to Dege well worthwhile, even if the new part of the town is one of the least attractive urban areas in western Sichuan.

◎ Sights

★**Bakong Scripture**
Printing Press   BUDDHIST MONASTERY
(德格印经院, Dégé Yinjīngyuàn; www.degepark hang.org; Bagong Jie, 巴宫街; ¥50; ⊙8.30-11.30am & 2-5pm) This fascinating 1729 printing press houses an ongoing printing operation that still uses traditional woodblock printing methods and maintains more than 290,000 scripture plates, an astonishing 70% of Tibet's literary heritage. It's the biggest and most important of three such printing presses (the others are in Lhasa and Gansu). It's more than just a mere printing house though; this is a religious and pilgrimage site, and throughout the day and early evening scores of pilgrims circumambulate the outside of the building.

Have a look in the main hall, protected from fire and earthquakes by the guardian goddess Drölma (Tara). There are some nice murals in the two ground-floor chapels (bring a torch). Afterwards, head up the stairs on the left-hand side of the courtyard to examine the wood-block storage chambers before climbing a steep ladder up to the main attraction: pairs of printers working together to ink and press more than 2500 prints each day at lightning speed. In a side room on the same floor, you'll find the senior printers making larger and more complex prints of Tibetan gods on paper and coloured cloth. Aside from a brief interlude during China's Cultural Revolution, these printers have been in operation continuously since the founding of the monastery in much the same atmosphere as they work in today.

The wood blocks are engraved with scriptures from all of the Tibetan Buddhist orders, as well as Bön (苯教), a religion that predates

WORTH A TRIP

BAIYU & THE PELYUL GOMPA

Those looking to get a small taste of the spectacle of Buddhist village life can do so at **Pelyul Gompa** (白玉祖寺, Báiyù Zǔsì) FREE, a monastery encircled by a swathe of small white houses clinging to the mountainside above the modern town of Baiyu (白玉, Báiyù) on the narrow floor of the gorge below.

The original monastery, built in 1665, grew to be one of the six most influential monasteries of the Nyingma (Red Hat) sect. It has been restored and rebuilt several times, and at its height had more than 1000 monks before it was destroyed during the Cultural Revolution. The monastery was rebuilt in 1982 with a combination of private and government funds.

The monastery has a small printing operation in a building just uphill from the main halls. On the 2nd floor, you can watch carvers create delicate script in reverse as they cut away intricate designs out of small wooden blocks.

The monastery village infrastructure remains rudimentary; raw sewage flows onto the paths after rains. There are no restaurants or guesthouses, so head back down into the modern town below where there are a couple of decent places to stay and eat.

At the time of research Baiyu was closed to foreign tourists and we were unable to conduct on-ground research. The general consensus among locals though was that the town and monastery would reopen to tourists within a short time. Check with tour companies in Kangding or Chengdu.

the arrival of Buddhism in Tibet. These ancient writings cover astronomy, geography, music, medicine and Buddhist classics, including two of the most important Tibetan sutras. A set of 555 woodblock plates, written in Hindi, Sanskrit and Tibetan, describes the history of Indian Buddhism and is the only surviving copy in the world.

On the way out, don't miss the steep ladder that gives access to the paper-cutting rooms upstairs and a small rooftop shrine beyond.

You aren't generally allowed to take photos inside.

To get here, turn right out of the bus station, then left over the bridge and keep walking straight up the hill.

Gonchen Monastery　　BUDDHIST MONASTERY
(德格寺, Dégé Sì; Bagong Jie, 巴宫街; ⊙6am-8pm) FREE Fronted with a large collection of stupas and prayer wheels, this imposing building stands on what has been the site of a monastery since the 15th century and a place of worship for far longer. From the Bakong Printing Press, walk through the courtyard out front and uphill to the left for about 200m. At the time of research, some of the chapels were undergoing renovations but others were still open.

🛏 Sleeping & Eating

Dege Hotel　　HOTEL ¥¥
(德格宾馆, Dégé Bīnguǎn; ☑ 0836 822 6666; 11 Gesa'er Dajie, 格萨尔大街11号; r old/new block from ¥380/480; ❉ ⧉) This government-run

place is the town's original hotel. It has rooms split between two riverside blocks. All are large and classically styled with private baths and some even have lovely mountain views. Turn left out of the bus station, cross the bridge, and follow the signs to turn right down the lane into the hotel courtyard.

Ying Jin Yuan Hotel　　HOTEL ¥¥
(英金园宾馆, Yīng Jīn Yuán Bīnguǎn; ☑ 187 8366 9126; Chamashang Jie, 茶马上街; r from ¥285; ⧉) There seems to be a near-countless number of modern, high-rise tower-block hotels lining the main street. This one is one of the better-value options. The large rooms have polished wooden floors and wine-red bedspreads, plus TVs and desks. Get a river-facing room in order to avoid street noise. The receptionist speaks a little English.

Delicious Vegetarian Dege Shop　　TIBETAN ¥
(美味素食德格店, Měiwèi Sùshí Dé Gé Diàn; Chamashang Jie, 茶马上街; buffet ¥30; ⊙9am-10pm) Classy and relaxed vegetarian restaurant serving a bargain-priced lunch buffet full of your 'five-a-day' greens. Follow up with green tea and enjoy the peace. It shares a building with a slightly simpler restaurant selling more traditional Tibetan dishes. Turn left out of the bus station and it's across the intersection.

🛈 Getting There & Away

With roads improved and mountain tunnels easing what was, until just a couple of years ago, a fraught journey over lofty, snow-bound mountain passes, once-remote Dege is no longer quite so cut off from the rest of western Sichuan as it once was.

The frontier to the Chamdo Prefecture of the Tibet Autonomous Region (西藏, Xīzàng) is just to the west of the town, but it's been many years since foreign tourists were allowed to cross over it.

A bus leaves from Dege at 6am, heading for Kangding (¥217, 12 hours) via Ganzi (¥84, four hours). There is also a bus at 9am for Manigange (¥40, two hours) and minivans to Ganzi (¥80) and Manigange (¥60).

Minibuses to Baiyu (¥80, two hours), though less reliably available, enable a loop back towards Ganzi via several small monastery towns; for the first hour or so of the trip the highway traces the Yangzi River border with Tibet and pays off in views towards the small hamlets and towering mountains just beyond.

Vehicles to the Dzongsar Valley cost ¥50. They may take a while to fill.

Buses and minibuses leave from a small **bus station** right in the town centre. For the vehicles to the Dzongsar Valley, ask among the drivers loitering about on the opoosite side of the road from the bus station. They don't have their vehicles with them so can be a little hard to pick out.

Dzongsar Valley

From Dege a small, narrow road winds up a tight gorge that cooks in the summer sun and freezes under the cold fingers of winter. Travelling along it, mighty stone walls leer menacingly out over the puny road and the river crashes over the rocks below. Then, just as you start to wonder if you'll ever reach your destination, the walls of the gorge peel back and reveal a paradisal valley where small stone villages are surrounded by terraced fields of barley, old-growth pine forests clamber up hillsides ribboned in waterfalls and hundreds of red-robed monks pray in ancient monasteries. If there is such a thing as the archetypical lost Shangri-la, then the beautiful and peaceful Dzongsar Valley has to be it.

The main village in the valley is called Mensho (门绍, Mén Shào), but everyone just knows the place as Dzongsar after the main monastery here.

⊙ Sights

★**Dzongsar Monastery**   BUDDHIST MONASTERY
(宗萨寺, Zōng Sà Sì; www.khyentsefoundation.org) FREE One of the oldest, most important and certainly most visibly impressive

monastery complexes in Kham, the remote Dzongsar Monastery sits on a sharp ridge above the main village of the Dzongsar Valley. The monastery was originally founded in 746 by a Bönpo lama, but has been much reconstructed since and, considering its importance, is quite a small structure, though it's none the less magical for it.

In the late 13th century a new Sakya monastery was established on the site of the Bön monastery (Bön was the religion that predated Buddhism on the Tibetan plateau) and the monastery has remained a part of that school of Tibetan Buddhism ever since. However, it has also played an important role in the Rimé movement and is known for its openness to most Tibetan Buddhism schools. The complex contains a number of chapels, one of which houses the ashes of the first and second Rinpoche Dzongsar, who were leading figures in the 19th-century Rimé movement.

Colourful traditional wooden housing for the monks is clustered around the monastery and along the valley floor below. It's down on the valley floor that the large and highly regarded *shedra* (Buddhist college) is located. Around 1900 monks study here. Many of them have studied previously in India and some will likely want to practise their English with you. The colourful buildings and constant ebb and flow of monks moving around the complex make for a wholly exotic and mystical place to explore. Come to the *shedra* in the early evening and you might catch the courtyard full of hundreds of debating monks. What makes the place so utterly charming is the absolute dearth of other tourists.

🏃 Activities

As soon as you arrive in the valley you're going to want to lace up your hiking boots. The scenery is a simply exquisite mix of forests, flower meadows, gushing rivers, small stone villages and red-walled monasteries, all overlooked by a thick hulk of high mountains.

There are endless different routes but the most popular (though still walked by very few foreigners) is the long day walk (better still as an overnight camping trip). It goes from the end of the road currently being cut towards the head of the valley to a small glacial lake right at the foot of the mountains. The road was still being constructed when we walked this route, but we have been assured it will not go beyond the first meadow and will be for tourism access only. The trail is very obvious and ascends only gently throughout its course but it's a long walk if you go all the way to the glacial lake and back in a day (allow 10 to 12 hours). The route follows the length of the milky-blue Menchu River, passing by a couple of smaller lakes and taking you through strands of pine forest and over open meadows where yaks graze. Eventually the land buckles up a bit and becomes steadily rockier before the trail arrives at the glacier lake. This makes a good place to camp for the night before walking back the next day. Along the way you will pass by a few stone herders' cottages, and if anyone is around it's highly likely that they will invite you in for some butter tea. In the higher, remoter and more forested reaches of the valley, keep your eyes peeled for wildlife, including some of the valley's large bear population.

Other possible routes include a steep day-long trek from the valley floor to a high and often frozen lake set among scree slopes in a mountain bowl. Another possibility is a half-day hike from the main Dzongsar monastery up onto the hill behind it and from where there are great views over the valley. There is also a nunnery up towards the end of the valley and from here a number of different ridge and hill walks are possible.

🛏 Sleeping

There's a basic place to stay in Mensho village but by far the best base is five kilometres further up the valley in the village of Mdzda.

★ **Khyenle**   GUESTHOUSE ¥¥
(📞135 5019 4096; www.khyenle.com; Mdzda village, 夏勒; r incl breakfast from ¥200; 🛜) 🌿
This peaceful guesthouse is part of a renowned art centre and is run by a fluent English-speaking Tibetan woman and her family. At the time of research, simple but spotless and comfortable rooms with shared bathrooms were available, but they were also in the process of constructing some more luxurious options with bathrooms.

Tasty Tibetan and western meals (¥40) are served in the traditional Tibetan guestroom downstairs. The owners can organise English- and French-speaking guides for hikes and monastery visits. While you're here check out the workshops behind the guesthouse where beautiful statues are created using the Lost Wax technique. Works from here are regularly displayed in top-end galleries and showrooms around the world.

OFF THE BEATEN TRACK

YAQING

Centred on the **Yarchen Gar Buddhist Institute** (亚青邬金禅林, Yàqīng Wūjīn Chánlín; Yaqing Si, 亚青寺) FREE and the massive community of monks and nuns that live here as students of the Dharma, until 2019 Yaqing (亚青, Yàqīng) offered an in-depth look into monastic life and was one of the most eye-opening sights in western Sichuan. However, in May 2019 the authorities closed the town to all outsiders (including Chinese and Tibetans) and began to demolish housing. The authorities say that this demolition has been for health and safety reasons; Tibetan-rights groups say that there have been mass forced relocations and that many nuns have been sent to 're-education camps'.

All access to the area was closed at the time of research and we were unable to visit. Check with Tibet specialist tour companies in Kangding or Chengdu to see if the town has reopened.

ℹ Getting There & Around

There's no official public transport to the valley, but private cars make the journey most days from Dege and will take passengers for around ¥50. It can take a long time for enough passengers to roll up. Organise through the minibus drivers who gather outside Dege bus station.

Once you get to the valley, however, you really do need your own transport as everything is quite spread out. Therefore it makes more sense to come here with a car and driver hired elsewhere; note that it's best to have a local Tibetan driver.

Southern Garze Prefecture

Travelling through the southern reaches of western Sichuan takes you through vast grasslands dotted with alpine lakes, shiny gold-roofed monasteries and temples, and grazing yaks against a background of snowy peaks that seem to reach to the sky.

Journeying along this 2140km route is slightly easier than taking the northern route, but it's still not for the faint-hearted; settlements are far and few and high altitude is a factor as much as ever. Warm clothing and sunscreen are a must. However, as the Kangding–Litang–Xiangcheng–Shangri-la journey has become a popular route into

Yunnan province, road conditions have vastly improved and so have the services available to travellers in the region.

Litang 理塘

📞 0836 / POP 51,300 / ELEV 3886M

Rich grasslands flecked with nomad encampments stretch away from the dizzyingly high (3886m) town of Litang (Lǐtáng; Lithang) and, off in the hazy distance, hills heap and buckle up into soaring mountain peaks. Both the scenery and the altitude will leave you breathless, and getting out to see it – whether on horse, motorcycle or foot – calls for spending at least a couple of days here.

For Tibetans, Litang occupies another exalted space as the birthplace of holy men, including the seventh and 10th Dalai Lamas and many revered lamas. Their birthplace and the town's large monastery, Chöde Gompa, draw devoted pilgrims from afar.

⊙ Sights

★ Former Residence of the 7th Dalai Lama
BUDDHIST TEMPLE

(仁康古屋, Rénkāng Gǔwū; Renkang Gujie, off Genie Xilu, 仁康古街, 格聂西路; ⊙ 9.30am-5pm) FREE Kelzang Gyatso (1708–57), the seventh Dalai Lama, was born in a cold, dark, cave-like room in the basement of this house during a period of intense political struggle. He eventually grew into a visionary leader, and under his rule Tibet established a national archive, instituted civil-service training programmes and formalised the Tibetan government structure. While the building is officially open from 9.30am to 5pm, in practice the hours are erratic. Chinese tourists are normally forbidden from entering inside the building.

Not all Tibetans shared the belief Gyatso was the reincarnate; to escape the ongoing civil war, the Dalai Lama was raised and educated largely in exile. Qing Emperor Kangxi issued a proclamation affirming his identity, and in 1720 sent his son and troops to install the Dalai Lama to power in Lhasa. Mongol uprisings, rebellions and several coups later, the Dalai Lama gained the support of the clergy and the people.

The main house is a series of rooms crowded with devotees lost in prayer, and displays of sacred relics of the Dalai Lama and the 13 other lamas born here. If you ask, the guardian will show you the exact spot where Gyatso was born. There is a small footprint visible in the rock, plus a number of other auspicious signs and markings. Tibetan Buddhist or not, a visit here can be a deeply powerful experience, especially if there are many other pilgrims present.

Gyatso's descendants still live in the house next door and it's likely that it will be one of them who shows you around.

The area around the house has recently been completely renovated in a sympathetic style and is now one of the more attractive urban neighbourhoods in all of the Tibetan regions.

Khampa Museum
MUSEUM

(康巴博物馆, Kāng Bā Bówùguǎn; Renkang Gujie, off Genie Xilu, 仁康古街, 格聂西路; ⊙ 9am-noon, 2-6pm & 7-10pm) FREE This traditional 200-year-old family house has been totally renovated and turned into an interesting ethnographic museum that recreates life in a typical Kham house and also looks at nomadic life and culture. There's good English signage and – thankfully – no political propaganda. In the future, there's likely to be a small entry charge.

OFF THE BEATEN TRACK

HIKING AROUND MT GE'NYEN

The brooding mountain massif southwest of Litang tops out with Mt Ge'nyen (格聂峰, Géniè Fēng; 6204m). Considered one of Tibet's 24 holy mountains, until recently the area had been little explored by international trekkers. However, as road access to the area improves this is starting to change. There are a number of different walking routes possible, ranging from one or two days to a week or more. Some of the guesthouses in Litang can help you organise exciting treks in the area, as can the better Tibetan specialist tour companies.

The best base for the mountains is the spectacular Kampo Nenang monastery and surrounding village, which sit at an elevation of 4150m, deep within the massif just east of Mt Ge'nyen. Founded in 1164, it's one of the oldest Karmapa monasteries in Tibet. The atmospheric monastery has a simple guesthouse and a number of day (or longer) walks can be undertaken from here.

White Temple Park
PARK

(白塔公园; Báitǎ Gōngyuán; Baita Lu, 白塔路) **FREE** Circle the White Temple (白塔, Báitǎ) with worshippers as they recite mantras and spin the massive, house-sized prayer wheel, or join the locals just hanging out in the surrounding park. From the main intersection, it's five minutes' or so walk down Xingfu Xilu (幸福西路).

Chöde Gompa
BUDDHIST MONASTERY

(长青春科尔寺, Chángqīngchūn Ke'ěr Sì; ⊙6am-11pm) **FREE** At the northern end of town, the large Chöde Gompa is a Tibetan monastery that was built for the third Dalai Lama (1543–1588). Inside is a statue of Sakyamuni, believed to have been carried from Lhasa by foot. Don't miss climbing onto the roof of the main hall on the far right for great views of the Tibetan homes leading up to the monastery, as well as the grasslands and mountains beyond.

⭐ Festivals & Events

Litang Horse Festival
CULTURAL

(⊙Early Aug) Banned for some years after a nomad grabbed the microphone and made political statements, the Litang Horse Festival has finally been brought back to life. Held over the first week of August, it attracts masses of nomads, all of whom are keen to prove that they are the bravest and fastest rider.

Don't think of this festival as a gentle afternoon down at the local race track, however. These are wild races where a drop or two of spilled blood is neither here nor there. To prove their bravery and horsemanship, riders will lean right out over the side of the horse so that their heads are almost touching the ground as the horse gallops along the uneven grasslands.

Smaller races are held frequently throughout the region in the summer months and, with no official government involvement, these are often far more authentic – and even more wild – affairs. Finding one of these events is, however, just a case of right place, right time. Ask around at the Tibetan-owned hotels and if you do chance upon one it's best to go with a Tibetan rather than a Chinese guide.

🛏 Sleeping

Litang Summer International Youth Hostel
HOSTEL ¥

(理塘的夏天国际青年旅舍, Lǐtáng de Xiàtiān Guójì Qīngnián Lǚshě; ☑180 1579 1574; litang summer@gmail.com; 47 Ping'an Lu, 平安路47号; dm ¥40, r from ¥140; 🕸) This lively youth hostel has cheerful rooms with colourful, warm bedding and a sociable bar downstairs. Staff speak English and are clued in to travellers' needs. Hike this mountain? Find this unmapped route? Make me breakfast (¥20)? They'll make it happen.

Potala Inn
HOTEL ¥

(布达拉大酒店, Bùdálá Dàjiǔdiàn; ☑0836 8326 366; Chenghe Xilu, 城河西路; dm ¥25-30, s/d/tr ¥100/120/150; 🕸) While the Tibetan-style twins with private bathrooms can be nice, the dorms with shared bathrooms could use a bit of a revamp. Some rooms are much nicer than others, so look first. Considering the low price it's not bad at all. Some English is spoken.

Night of Grassland
GUESTHOUSE ¥¥

(草原之夜, Cǎoyuán Zhīyè; ☑0836 532 2655, 135 0829 3569; 28 Ping'an Lu, 平安路28号; r ¥130-240; 🕸) Smart twin rooms with private bathrooms are set around a garden courtyard on a quiet side road. Squat toilets only in the cheap rooms while the more expensive rooms even have nifty oxygen machines for the O_2 deprived. It's popular with groups road-tripping in the summer, so call ahead (although little English is spoken). In high season it offers a good western breakfast.

🍴 Eating

⭐ Yúnduān Yī Yè
INTERNATIONAL ¥¥

(云端一叶; ☑173 4032 0689; Renkang Gujie, off Genie Xilu, 仁康古街, 格聂西路; mains ¥20-50; ⊙9am-11pm; 🕸) Laid-back, relaxed new restaurant full of sofas and with a first-floor dining room overlooking the birthplace of the 7th Dalai Lama. The menu is a meeting of east and west with classic Sichuan dishes sharing the table with steaks, pastas, fruit salads and more. If you're not hungry just pop in for one of the herbal teas.

It closes for two random days each month.

Hope
CAFE ¥¥

(希望; ☑139 8904 8204; ⊙9am-9pm Mar-Dec) Wonderful little cafe-restaurant in the middle of the old Tibetan neighbourhood and just down from the Chöde Gompa. Smiley staff will whip you up a tasty light meal such as yak ribs or soup. They also brew a range of teas and coffees and bake some delicious cakes, including one you won't get at home: yak yoghurt cake.

DON'T MISS

YADING NATURE RESERVE

The magnificent **Yading Nature Reserve** (亚丁风景区, Yàdīng Fēngjǐngqū; ☎0836 572 2666; entry incl shuttle bus ¥270; ☉7.30am-5.40pm), 140km south of Daocheng, centres around three sacred snowcapped mountains, a holy trinity encircled by forested valleys, crystal-clear rivers and glacier-fed lakes. These are, quite simply, some of the most stunning landscapes you'll ever see. There are opportunities to hike, ride and camp here.

Locals have worshipped these mountains for more than 800 years. The three peaks – Chenresig (compassion), Chana Dorje (power) and Jampelyang (wisdom) – represent bodhisattvas in Tibetan Buddhism. Even for nonbelievers, walking the 35km *kora* (转山, holy hike) around the highest peak, Chenresig (仙乃日, Xiānnǎirì), which tops out at 6032m, can be a hugely meaningful experience.

The clockwise circuit around Chenresig begins at **Longtong Ba** (龙同坝, Lóngtóng Bà) and takes at least 12 hours of serious hiking. To avoid one very long day, many use the campsites located about halfway, just below the first pass beyond Five-Colour Lake. You have to bring all your own gear and supplies. (Though you'll pass locals living in simple stone huts, under park rules they are not supposed to take you in.) Remember to keep the mountain on your right, and to always take the right-hand turn when there's a choice of paths. There is a longer, four-day, 110km hike that adds a circuit around 5958m **Chana Dorje** (夏郎多吉, Xiàláng Duōjí), which begins and ends at the same place as the *kora*.

These hiking trails are all around 4000m above sea level, so acclimatise properly and pack for a serious expedition before you set off. Guides are available for hire at Longtong Ba.

If you don't have the time (or energy) for a full circuit, there are day-hike options that see far more visitors. Take the shuttle bus from the ticket office into the park to just beyond the small settlement of Longtong Ba. From here hike 2km to the 800-year-old **Chonggu Monastery** (冲古寺, Chōnggǔ Sì), where you can pick up electric carts (one way/return ¥50/80, 6km, 20 minutes) into the **Luorong Grassland** (洛绒牛场, Luòróng Niúchǎng), which offers incredible views of the trinity and is as far as most tourists go. The other direction, uphill from Chonggu Monastery, is a 40-minute (1km) uphill hike to **Zhuoma La** (卓玛拉, Zhuómǎ Lā) and a small lake. This lake, just in the shadow of Chenresig's north face, is particularly impressive in spring when surrounded by blooming azalea flowers.

It's worth continuing another 5km (three hours) from the Luorong Grasslands to **Milk Lake** (牛奶海, Níunǎi Hǎi) and stunning **Five-Colour Lake** (五色海, Wǔsè Hǎi). You can also ride guided mules (return ¥300) for this segment, but keep in mind that even on four legs the round-trip journey takes 5½ hours on a steep, rocky trail. Riders must dismount multiple times to scramble alongside their ride for about a kilometre.

Take a shared minibus (per person ¥50, 2½ hours) from Daocheng to the small town of **Riwa** (日瓦), where you buy tickets for the reserve. The ticket includes a mandatory ¥120 shuttle-bus fee, so take the park shuttle bus the last 32km into the park (50 minutes); it stops first in Yading village and then 3km later at Longtong Ba.

There are guesthouses and places to eat in **Yading village** (亚丁村). To get an early start on the *kora*, sleep in a guesthouse in Yading then catch the 7.30am shuttle the last few kilometres down to Longtong Ba. Buses within the park run from the visitors centre between 7.20am and 5.40pm, and back from Longtong Ba between 9am and 7.30pm.

The best times to visit the reserve are May to June and September to early October.

ℹ Getting There & Away

The big new **bus station** is out on the far eastern edge of town. Destinations include the following:

Batang ¥64 to ¥69, 3½ hours (noon and 5pm)

Chengdu ¥230, 14 hours (6am)

Daocheng ¥57 to ¥62, four hours (noon and 5pm)

Ganzi ¥84, four hours (9.30am)

Kangding ¥106, six hours (7am)

Xiangcheng ¥76, five hours, two daily (both around noon)

Tickets to points west are only sold the day of departure, once it has been verified that space is available. Minivans (around ¥40 more expensive than buses) loiter outside the bus station to fill the void.

Daocheng 稻城

☑ 0836 / POP 32,300 / ELEV 3760M

Daocheng (Dàochéng; Dabpa) packs bags of rural charm, despite the fact that its small town centre has been modernised. It makes a lovely base for exploring the magnificent Yading Nature Reserve a couple of hours to the south, but don't discount the appeal of the town itself. After Yading, you can easily fill another couple of days here walking or cycling around boulder-strewn wetlands, hills and barley fields, all of it dotted with villages and Tibetan monasteries. Spring brings some of the clearest skies, while autumn is particularly beautiful as a blaze of red leaves and grass electrifies the landscape.

⊙ Sights

Namgyal Tallinn　BUDDHIST STUPA
(尊胜塔林, Zūnshèng Tǎlín) FREE Join locals in the *kora* walk circling this stupa that is dedicated to the Shakyamuni Buddha, or climb up to the covered pavilions on the hilltop just above for views of Daocheng city and the surrounding foothills. The stupa is around 500m outside of town, just across the main bridge.

🛏 Sleeping

Yading Backpackers Hostel　HOSTEL ¥
(亚丁人社区国际青年旅舍, Yàdīng Rén Shèqū Guójì Qīngnián Lûshě; ☑ 0836 572 8994; 58 Dexi Lu, 德西路58号; dm ¥30-50, tw ¥120; ☎) The dorms and rooms at this helpful hostel are a bit cramped but the whole place has a lot of Tibetan atmosphere and there's a quiet courtyard overhung with prayer flags. English-speaking staff can help arrange excursions, rides and luggage storage.

Péng Sōng Cuò　HOTEL ¥¥
(彭松措精品客栈, ☑ 0836 571 8581; 128 Dexi Lu, 德西路128号; r ¥110; ☎) The lodgings in this Tibetan-style courtyard house by the river are standard hotel rooms with private, modern baths. All have wi-fi. Turn left out of the bus station, walk past the beginning of Dexi Lu and then turn left just before the bridge. The hotel is a short distance down on the right.

ℹ Getting There & Away

A bus leaves Daocheng daily at 7.40am, for the mammoth journey to Chengdu (¥269, 18 hours). There's a daily morning bus to Litang (¥65, three

hours, 6.10am), which continues onto Kangding (¥155, six hours). Going the other way there's a bus to Shangri-la (Zhongdian; ¥108, 10 hours, 6.10am) in Yunnan province, via Xiangcheng (¥45, three hours).

Minibuses, which gather across the street from the **bus station**, are also popular for Litang and Xiangcheng. Prices are negotiable, but expect to pay ¥20 or ¥30 more per seat than bus prices. Frequency depends on demand but count on at least one a day. For Yading Nature Reserve (¥50, two hours) minibuses are the only option.

Daocheng-Yading Airport, 43km north, has several flights daily to Chengdu (from ¥1300, one hour) and five flights weekly to Chongqing (¥1700). Minibuses (机场拼车, *jīchǎng pīnchē*) leave from near the town square (¥50, 50 minutes, around three hours before departures). Turn right out of the bus station, left before the square; the airport minibuses leave from a car park just before the first intersection on the left.

Xiangcheng 乡城

☑ 0836 / POP 55,000 / ELEV 2977M

The valley town of Xiangcheng (Xiāngchéng; Chaktreng) is a good spot to break your journey into or out of Yunnan province if you can't bear it all in one go. It benefits from a microclimate that keeps temperatures here slightly warmer than everywhere else around it, making it a particularly comfortable stop, with a number of small villages nearby that make for pleasant wandering.

Bsampeling Monastery　BUDDHIST MONASTERY
(桑披岭寺, Sāngpīlíng Sì; 27 Tongsha Xiang, 同沙巷27号; ¥15; ⊙ 5am-10.30pm) Originally established in 1669, but much rebuilt, this collection of monastery buildings at the top end of town commands fine views of the surrounding hills. Take the stairs up to the 2nd and 3rd floors of the main structure for great close-up views of the large Buddha statues within and an excellent rooftop vantage over the town, respectively.

The main road is dotted with restaurants offering similar menus of Sichuan favourites.

Zha Xi Grand Hotel　HOTEL ¥¥
(扎西大酒店; Xiangbala North, 香巴拉北; r incl breakfast from ¥261; ☎) Large hotel aimed squarely at Chinese tour groups but the reasonable prices and big, warm rooms with work desks and rather over-the-top bedheads mean that anyone will be happy kipping here.

ⓘ Getting There & Away

Two buses leave daily at 6am. One goes south into Yunnan to Shangri-la (Zhongdian; ¥85, seven hours); the other goes to Kangding (¥145, 10 hours). Note that tickets to Litang are not sold on the Kangding-bound bus, even though it's en route; take a shared minivan instead (¥76 to ¥80, 4½ hours).

A passing bus to Daocheng (¥45, three hours, 2.30pm) sometimes has seats, otherwise a shared minivan to Daocheng is around ¥70.

NORTHERN SICHUAN

In the north of Sichuan the land buckles up into mountains that reach for the heavens; in the valleys in-between the glacial peaks are dense forests and exquisite lakes, around which some of China's most alluring hiking trails twist and turn. It's in this area that the famed (but partially closed) **Jiuzhaigou National Park** can be found, as well as the lesser-known (but almost equally attractive) Huanglong National Park. Elsewhere in the north, you can swing into some stirrups in the one-horse town of Songpan, which is used by travellers as a base for multiday horseback expeditions into the wilderness. Finally, if you're looping around towards western Sichuan and Danba, take time as well for the stunning valleys and panoramic peak-filled landscapes of Four Sisters Mountains en route.

Four Sisters Mountain 四姑娘山

☑ 0837 / POP 2900 / ELEV 3151M

Established as a national park in 1994 and declared a Unesco World Heritage Site in 2006, Four Sisters Mountain (Sìgūniang Shān) is famous among Chinese tourists as one of the most impressive natural areas of the entire country. At a magnificent 6250m the fourth of the Four Sisters, pyramid-shaped Yaomei Feng, comes in as the second-highest peak in all of Sichuan.

Composed of three distinct valleys with a combined area of 450 sq km, the park has plenty of hiking and rock climbing for adventurous travellers looking to test their mettle. Anything beyond a day hike will require a permit and a local guide, but these peaks are well known among climbers and you may well see a group headed back down after a successful attempt.

◉ Sights

★ Haizi Valley
NATIONAL PARK

(海子沟, Hǎizi Gōu; ☑ 0837 279 1999; adult/student ¥60/30 Apr-Oct, ¥40/20 Nov-Mar; ⊙ ticket office 7am-5.30pm Apr-Oct, from 8am Nov-Mar) Considered by many the most beautiful of the three valleys in the Four Sisters Mountain area, Haizi Valley's eponymous lakes and majestic views of the Four Sisters peaks make it hard to disagree. It's a steep walk for much of the way, so acclimatise in the other valleys first if possible. The entrance to the 19km-long valley is about 500m from the tourist centre, up an obvious staircase to the right of the building.

The most popular day hike is to the pastures at Dajianbao (3750m) which makes for a decent 15km round-trip hike and rewards with majestic mountain views. An excellent overnight hike (ask in your guesthouse for help finding camping gear and a guide) is to the **Eldest Sister Peak Protection Station** at 4400m. It's right at the foot of the mountains and the imposing glaciers.

At the time of research, a wooden walkway was being constructed along the valley. Once this is complete, visitor numbers are likely to shoot up as the tour bus crowds arrive.

Shuangqiao Valley
NATIONAL PARK

(双桥沟, Shuāngqiáo Gōu; ¥80, student/off-season ¥50; ⊙ ticket office 7.30am-5.30pm) The longest of the three main valleys in the Four Sisters Mountain area is also the most accessible to tourists, with a wooden boardwalk that runs for about 30km of the valley's 40km length, and regular shuttle buses running throughout the day. Shuttle tickets are ¥70, not including the 7km transfer from Rilong, but if you want to get to the most impressive scenery at the far end of the valley it's the only way to do it in a day.

Changping Valley
NATIONAL PARK

(长坪沟, Chángpíng Gōu; ¥70, student/off-season ¥50; ⊙ ticket office 8am-4pm) While the first hour or so of the valley walk is on a wooden boardwalk, after that it's muddy trails through yak-filled pastures and dense forests all the way to the end. There's a shuttle (included in park entry) from the tourist centre to within the park just past Zhangmu Village, but from there you'll need to be prepared to walk the rest of the way up the 29km valley trail.

🛏 Sleeping & Eating

⭐ A Lee Ben Hostel
HOSTEL ¥

(阿里本青年旅舍, Ālǐběn Qīngnián Lǚshě; ☑ 180
9043 8688; 49 Changping Village, 长坪村49号;
dm ¥40-50, d ¥160-210; ☎) Take a look at all
this place offers: a pool table, underfloor
heating, info on local sites and an English
menu in the cafe, and you'll probably – and
rightly – come to the conclusion that this
is a model hostel. Private rooms are plush,
while dorms are very comfortable and have
private curtains and a large, clean shower.

Lotus Inn
INN ¥¥

(莲花客栈, Liánhuā Kèzhàn; ☑ 136 0808 6250;
Changping Village, 长坪古街; r incl breakfast ¥200;
☎) The elegant private rooms here, with
thick, colourful blankets for the frequent
cold nights, will make it worth the splurge
for some, while the ground-floor cafe/bar
(open 4pm to 11pm) is a local gathering
point for cold beer (¥15) to round off the day.
Some English is spoken.

Alan Kezhan
CHINESE ¥

(艾伦科赞, Ài Lún Kē Zàn; Changping Village, 长
坪古街; mains ¥18-25; ☎ 8am-10pm) The most
attractive restaurant in the village has tables
made from old doors and genuinely impressive photo art on the walls. But this is more
than just eye-candy: the food is also great.
Don't miss the wild mushrooms with chick-
en. It's also the only place that does a western breakfast, and it has real coffee (¥35).

ℹ Information

Whether you're looking to buy tickets, pick
up free maps (地图, dìtú) of the park, or have
questions about exploring the three main valleys (only Chinese spoken), the **Four Sisters
Mountain Tourist Centre** (四姑娘山游客中
心, Sìgūniángshān Yóukè Zhōngxīn; Changping
Village; ☎ 7.30am-5.30pm) is the place to do it.
The building is at the eastern end of Rilong, at
the entrance to the Changping Valley.

If you're hoping to camp or climb (climbing
permit ¥150, plus ¥30 per day) inside any of the
valleys of the national park, the **Hùwài Zhōngxīn**
(户外中心; G350; ☎ 9am-4.30pm) is where you
will have to come in order to find your mandatory
guide (from ¥300 per day). The office is on the
road into Rilong, 500m past the Changping
Valley turn-off, on the right.

ℹ Getting There & Away

Two buses (¥105, seven to nine hours) per day
pass through Rilong on the way to Chengdu.

Otherwise, arrange a seat in a shared vehicle
(¥150) through your hostel.

In the other direction frequent minibuses and
share taxis head to Xiaojin (minibus/share taxi
¥10/25, two hours), from which a transfer to
Danba is ¥30 (1½ hours).

Huanglong National Park
黄龙景区

ELEV 3600M

The still fairly unknown **Huanglong National Park** (Huánglóng Jǐngqū; ☑ 0837 724
9958, 0837 724 9188; www.huanglong.com;
Apr–mid-Nov/mid-Nov–Mar ¥170/60, cable car
¥80; ☎ 8am-5pm) is a stunning valley with
terraces of coloured limestone ponds in
blues, greens, oranges, yellows and white.
The best time to come from is June to October, ideally during mild July and August.
Outside of this period, lack of water in the
pools significantly reduces the visual impact of the park.

Visiting the park essentially means a
three- to four-hour moderate hike up and
down a small valley on wooden boardwalks.
The walk starts by taking a cable car (9am to
5pm; ¥80), which drops you in a deep forest.
A path then leads you up a few kilometres to
the start of the main sights, and then down
again to the entrance – some 8km of long
ascents and descents in all.

At this elevation (3600m), it always pays to
bring a jacket, waterproofs and other warm
clothing, as well as plenty of sun cream.

There are a few expensive tour-group hotels nearby, but most people visit as a day
trip from Songpan or Jiuzhaigou.

To get here, two daily buses depart Jiuzhaigou (¥46, three hours, 7am and 7.30am);
travellers arriving on early-morning flights
can take an airport shuttle (¥120, 1½ hours)
directly to Huanglong. There's also one return bus to Jiuzhaigou (¥46, 3pm) and a
minibus (¥120, departs when full) by the
visitor centre. To get to Songpan, take the
Jiuzhaigou bus and ask the driver to drop
you at Chuanzhu Si (川主寺; one hour),
from where you can catch a shared taxi to
Songpan (¥60).

Langzhong
阆中

☑ 0817 / POP 242,535

An endless sea of black-tile roofs with waves
of swooping eaves, flagstone streets lined

WORTH A TRIP

JIUZHAIGOU NATIONAL PARK

Jiuzhaigou National Park (九寨沟风景名胜区, Jiǔzhàigōu Fēngjǐng Míngshèngqū; ☑ 0837 773 9753; www.jiuzhai.com), an enchanting Unesco World Heritage Site, is one of Sichuan's and even China's star attractions. More than two million people visit annually – or rather, used to visit annually – to gawk at its famous bluer-than-blue lakes, rushing waterfalls and deep woodlands backlit by snowy mountain ranges.

In 2017 the park closed after suffering damage from a 7.0-magnitude earthquake, in addition to erosion in some areas caused by over-tourism. The park reopened to tourism in late September 2019. Initially, however, it is only open to those on organised tours and there is a limit of 5000 entries per day. It's unknown if and when the park will reopen to independent travellers. If you want to visit, book as far in advance as you can through a Chengdu tour company.

The park has an informative multilanguage website (www.jiuzhai.com) although it hasn't been updated to reflect the current situation in the park. There is a **visitors centre** (沟口游客中心; Gōukǒu Yóukè Zhōngxīn; park entrance; 沟口; adult ¥110; ☺ 7am-2pm) by the **park entrance**, but it might not be open during the park closure.

There's a seemingly endless supply of hotels around Pengfeng Village (彭丰村, Péng-fēng Cūn), the area near the park entrance. With the current dearth of visitors there will be stiff competition between hotels for your custom.

Even if independent travellers can't visit the park itself, it's still possible to visit areas around the park. One of the best ways of doing so is through the **Ecotourism Program** (九寨扎如沟生态旅游, Jiǔzhài Zhārú Gōu Zhēngtài Lǚyóu; ☑ 0837 773 7070; www.zharu.jiuzhai. com; 2nd fl, Heye Guesthouse, 荷叶迎宾馆二楼; Tours 1/2/3 days ¥560/1320/1960) operating inside the neighbouring Zharu Valley. Visitors can hike and camp in a region believed to contain at least 40% of the plant species that exist across China.

In the past there were more than a dozen daily flights linking Chengdu and other cities with Jiuzhaigou Airport. With the closure of the park, the number of flights has dramatically decreased and there are now only occasional flights to and from Chengdu.

Jiuzhaigou Central Bus Station is just 2km east of the park entrance. Services include buses to Chengdu (¥155, 6 hours, one daily at 8am), Huanglong National Park (¥46, three hours, two daily at 7am and 7.30am) and Songpan (¥49, two hours, two daily at 6am and 1pm).

---

with tiny shops, and temples atop hills of mist overlooking the river. It's all here in the town of Langzhong (Lángzhōng), Sichuan's capital city for 20 years during the Qing dynasty and now home to the province's largest grouping of extant traditional architecture.

Other foreign visitors are rare, which means you may get to enjoy this constructed work of art all to yourself.

◉ Sights

Langzhong's architecture is a blend of northern *táiliáng* (抬梁; pillars and beams) and southern *chuāndòu* (穿斗; through-joint) styles that allow for a variety of dramatic roof shapes under which shelter North China *sìhéyuàn* (四合院; courtyard) and South China garden styles.

Most of the main sights are covered by a combination ticket (adult/student ¥110/60).

Jinping Park
MOUNTAIN

(锦屏山, Jǐnpíng Shān; ¥25; ☺ 8am-6pm) Considered an essential element of the feng shui balance of ancient Langzhong and holy to Taoists, Jinping is dotted with pavilions, temples and caves. To get here, catch a ferry (¥3, from 8am to 6pm) across the river from the wharf just below the Huaguang Tower.

Jinping Gate
TOWER

(锦屏门, Jǐnpíng Mén; ☺ 8am-6.30pm) Originally constructed in 1371 and renovated in 1767, the current version of Jinping Gate is a 2010 rebuild. Join art students sketching from the top and at the same time take in the great view out over the old town's slate rooftops. Access it via the staircase just off Nan Jie, a street running parallel to Dadong Jie.

Zhang Fei Temple
TEMPLE

(张飞庙, Zhāngfēi Miào; Xi Jie, 西街; ¥58; ☺ 8am-6.30pm) This temple is the tomb of local boy

Zhang Fei, a respected general during the kingdom of Shu and hero of the *Three King-doms* epics, who administered the kingdom from here until his murder in the year 221. The interesting complex consists of four courtyards and a number of Ming-era halls and other structures. In the centre of the complex is Zhang Fei's tomb, topped with a statue of the man himself and two demons.

Imperial Examination Hall HISTORIC BUILDING
(贡院, Gòng Yuàn; Xuedao Jie, 学道街; ¥50; ⊙8am-6.30pm) The best-preserved Qing-era imperial examination hall in China, with a number of in-character actors on hand to pose for photographs. The museum shows the development of the Chinese language but English-language information panels are disappointingly limited. Located on Xuedao Jie (学道街), which is parallel to Wumiao Jie, one block north.

🛏 Sleeping & Eating

Popular local fare includes *zhāngfēi niúròu* (张飞牛肉; preserved water-buffalo beef, from ¥25 per packet), which makes a great road-trip snack. Places to eat abound throughout the old town and in the modern city streets just to the east.

⭐ Ancient Hotel HISTORIC HOTEL ¥¥
(杜家客栈, Dùjiā Kèzhàn; ☑0817 622 4436; 63 Xiaxin Jie, 下新街63号; r from ¥380; ❋🏠) Hotels don't come with much more history than this appropriately named place. It was founded as a hotel during the Tang dynasty and is still the place to stay in Langzhong. There are multiple attractive courtyards, lots of weathered and termite-chewed timber, deliciously comfortable beds, and even an open-air stage (performances Friday and Saturday from 8pm to 10pm).

Lee's Courtyard HOTEL ¥¥¥
(李家大院, Lǐjiā Dàyuàn; ☑0817 623 6500; 47 Wumiao Jie, 武庙街47号; r from ¥450; ❋🏠) This is the most upmarket option in the old town, with luxe bedding, fully equipped bathrooms and private balconies. After renovations a couple of years ago, this ancient courtyard hotel, built in 1506, sparkles like a five-star hotel and is priced to match. The in-house restaurant is about the best place in town to eat.

ℹ Getting There & Away

Buses to Chengdu's Beimen bus station leave Langzhong's **bus station** (七里客运中心汽车站, Qīlǐ kèyùn zhōngxīn qìchēzhàn) frequently between 6.30am and 5.50pm (¥97; four hours). There are also buses to Chongqing (¥105, five daily, four hours, 7.50am to 3pm).

Songpan 松潘
📞0837 / POP 67,975 / ELEV 3014M

Tilt your (Tibetan) cowboy hat low over your eyes, buckle on your spurs and gallop out into the giant mountain peaks. Horse trekking into the woods and mountains is the main draw of the laid-back, historic town of Songpan (Sōngpān), a holdover from its role as a major trading centre on the Tea Horse Road (茶马路, Chá Mǎ Lù). The hiking is also good, so there's a healthy backpacker population to swap travel tales with.

Much of the old town has been rebuilt in recent years, but architecturally it still holds much of its visual appeal and finding the touches of true history hidden throughout makes it feel even more special. In midwinter (December to March) Songpan slows down and some businesses close; however, even in the cold, horse trekking is still possible.

👁 Sights

Songpan's partially rebuilt **city wall** may be less than 10 years old, but its **ancient gates** are original Ming dynasty structures dating back some 600 years. Note the horse carvings at the foot of the two south gates, half swallowed up by the ever-rising level of the road. The only original part of the **old wall** is by the rebuilt **West Gate** (西大门, Xī Dàmén; ⊙9am-6pm), which overlooks the town from its hillside perch far above.

Two wooden **covered bridges** (古松桥, Gǔsōng Qiáo; and 映月桥, Yìng Yuè Qiáo), the bases of which are genuinely old, span the Min River. On the western side of the Yingyue Bridge is **Guanyin Temple** (观音阁, Guānyīn Gé) FREE, a small temple near the start of a hillside trail that offers good views over Songpan en route to the West Gate.

Shangniba Monastery BUDDHIST MONASTERY
(上泥巴寺, Shàngníbā Sì) FREE A two-hour hike or horse ride east over the hills from Songpan, this small Tibetan Buddhist monastery sits in a picturesque valley among small minority villages. One-day horse trips often head out here for a roughly five-hour round trip, including a stop for lunch.

Songpan

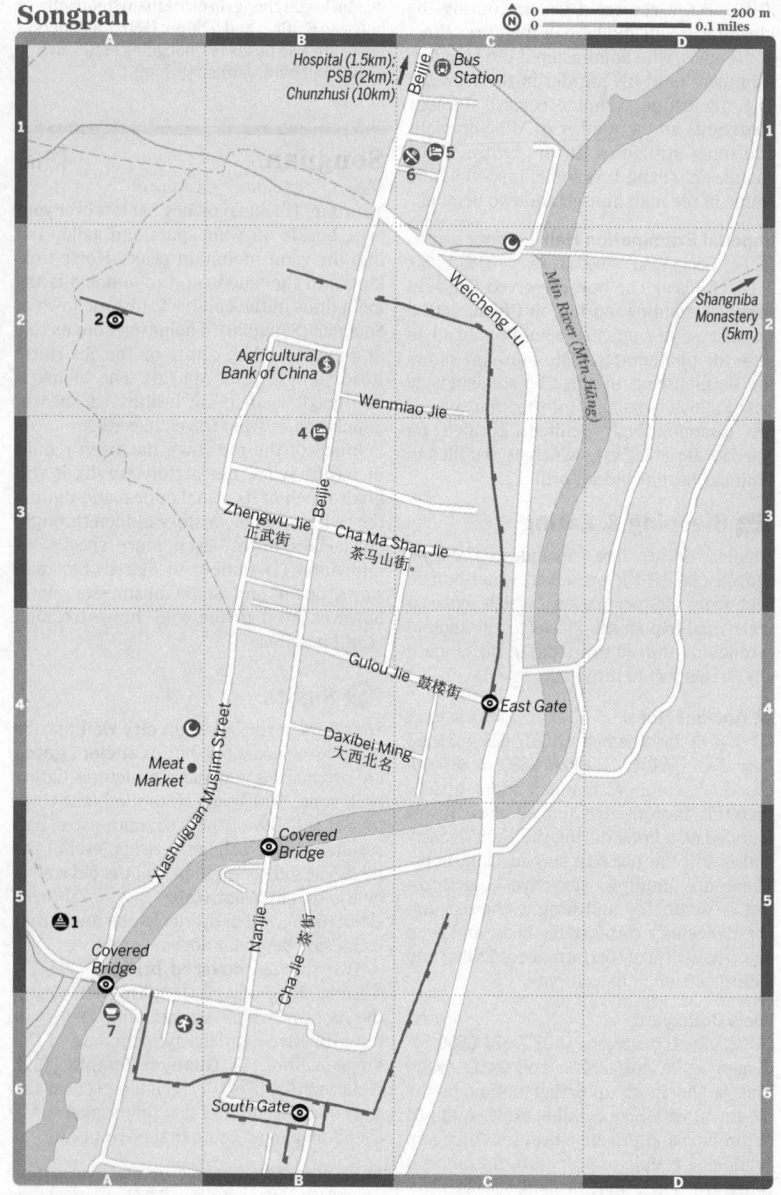

Activities

One of the most popular ways to experience the alpine forests and lakes surrounding Songpan is by signing up for a horse trek. Many people rate this experience as a highlight of their travels in this region. Guides lead you through otherwise unseen territory to remote campsites aboard not-so-big, very tame horses. Food and gear are all provided.

One of the most popular routes is a three- or four-day trek through unspoilt scenery to **Ice Mountain** (雪宝顶, Xuěbǎodǐng), a spectacular peak. A three-day trek to **Qicang Valley** (七藏沟, Qīcáng Gōu) passes several technicolour lakes.

Rates are all-inclusive of gear, horses and meals. Your guides take care of setting up tents and cooking, unless you want to. The only additional charges are park entry fees for some of the trips (you are told of these before you set out), and tips, should you be inclined.

The majority of travellers seem happy with their services, but we do sometimes receive reports of guides careless about environmental impact. Also, some travellers have had trouble getting refunds, particularly when the weather turned, which it often does. If you don't speak Chinese or Tibetan, we recommend booking through local and Chengdu hostels, which will help you negotiate details such as the terms for a refund.

Qíqílè Mǎduì   HORSE RIDING
(骑奇乐马队; ☏ 189 0904 3667, 0837 723 4138; Nanjie, Yingyue Xiang, 南街映月巷; per day per person from ¥200; ☉8.30am-7pm) This well-run outfitter covers the usual local favourites and further afield to northerly Zoige (若尔盖, Ruò'ěrgài; eight days) and southward to Hong Yuan (红原; 10 days). Daily prices include food, tent rental and all other costs, aside from admission to any national parks included in the route (which are outlined up front). Little English is spoken.

🛏 Sleeping

★ Emma's Guesthouse   GUESTHOUSE ¥
(小欧洲青年旅舍, Xiǎo Ōuzhōu Qīngnián Lǚshě; ☏131 0837 2888, 0837 723 1088; emmachina@hotmail.com; Shunjiang Cun, 顺江村; dm ¥48-60, r ¥160-180, ste ¥200-300; ❇☎) Friendly and helpful owner Emma speaks excellent English and it's her influence that really turns this guesthouse into something special. She can arrange horse treks, book onward transport and organise tours to nearby national parks and sights. The rooms and small dorms are simple, but bright and clean with private bathrooms, and heaters and electric blankets for the cold months.

Amdo Coffee House Inn   HOTEL ¥¥
(安多房子咖啡客栈, Ānduō Fángzi Kāfēi Kèzhàn; ☏0837 723 2178, English 135 1596 0964; Beijie, North Gate, 北街农行旁; s/d without bathroom from ¥200; ☎☎) In a stylish wooden structure just inside the old town's North Gate, this hip guesthouse with English-speaking staff, unusually comfy beds and a historical touch packs in all the modern conveniences plus airport pick-up (¥120). Some rooms are small, so head downstairs to the cafe for real coffee (¥20) and a big window perfect for people-watching.

🍴 Eating & Drinking

Emma's Kitchen   CAFE ¥¥
(小欧洲西咖啡餐厅, Xiǎo Ōuzhōu Xī Kāfēi Cāntīng; ☏131 0837 2888, 0837 723 1088; emmachina@hotmail.com; Shunjiang Beilu, 顺江北路; mains ¥18-58; ☉8am-midnight; ☎) Songpan's main traveller hang-out is this laid-back cafe with wi-fi and fresh coffee, pizza and other western fare, along with a range of Chinese and Tibetan dishes. It's a good place to meet other travellers. Emma is exceedingly knowledgable and can sort out almost anything from laundry to tickets and picnic lunches for your horse trek.

Yùyuàn Nóngjiālè   TEA GARDEN
(御苑农家乐; across the bridge from Guanyin Temple, 古镇南桥; ☉8am-7pm) Set in an open-air garden with an eclectic array of furnishing, this family-run teahouse (tea from ¥3, dishes from ¥8) has a number of shady nooks that make for a great place to unwind after a long day hiking or horse riding. It's on the old-town side of the covered bridge.

ⓘ Information

The ATMs at the **Agricultural Bank of China** (中国农业银行, Nóngyè Yínháng; Shunjiang Beilu, 顺江北路) accept Visa and MasterCard, though many travellers report problems accessing their

802

POOMPOB ANANTARAK/SHUTTERSTOCK ©

RICHARD GOULD/EYEEM/GETTY IMAGES ©

1. Yading Nature Reserve (p794)
The stunning landscape around these three peaks allows for hiking, riding and camping.

2. The Golden Summit, Emei Shan (p765)
The Jinding Temple and golden statue of Samantabhadra are to be found at 3079m. Samantabhadra honours the mountain protector Pǔxián.

3. Ancient bridge in Le Shan (p769)
The world's largest ancient Buddha is not the only draw in this relaxed riverside town.

4. Pandas in Chengdu (p752)
One of the region's most popular attractions, the Giant Panda Breeding Research Base is focused on getting these creatures to breed. Beware massive crowds.

PHILIPPE LEJEANVRE/GETTY IMAGES ©

foreign accounts. It's best to bring a decent amount of cash with you.

❶ Getting There & Away

Buses leaving Songpan's **bus station** (汽车站, Qìchēzhàn; Shunjiang Beilu, 顺江北路) include the following:

Chengdu ¥113, 8½ hours, four daily (6am, 7am, 9.30am and 12.30pm)

Huanglong National Park ¥29, 1½ hours, three daily (6am, 7am and 2pm)

Jiuzhaigou ¥50, two hours, two daily (9am and 1pm)

Zoige ¥55, three hours, two daily (10am and 2.30pm)

Wolong Giant Panda Garden 臥龍自然保護區

📋 028 / POP 5345

China's leading panda conservation centre and, almost certainly, the best place to see pandas in China, the **Wolong Giant Panda Garden** (臥龍自然保護區, Wòlóng Zìránbǎohùqū; 📋 028 8733 1272; Wolong; adult/senior/child ¥90/60/45; ⊙ 9am-5pm) and surrounding nature reserve suffered devastating damage in the 2008 Sichuan earthquake and many of its captive pandas were moved to other centres for their own safety. Reconstruction is now complete, however, and the pandas are back living in large cages surrounded by thick bamboo forests (which are themselves home to genuine wild – but impossible to see – pandas). They're obviously quite happy being back here because they've already started to breed, and some captive-bred pandas have been released into the wild.

The reserve's distance from Chengdu (140km) means visitor numbers are far lower here than at any other panda site and during the week it's possible to have the entire place almost entirely to yourself. In a private vehicle it's easy to stop here en route to the Four Sisters Mountains.

There are a couple of basic roadside hotels in the village of Wolong, a short (but steep) walk downhill from the panda garden entrance.

There are no direct buses from Chengdu to Wolong. Take a share taxi to Dujiangyan (¥25) and change there for buses to Wolong. If you're heading to the Four Sisters Mountains in a private vehicle, it's easy to stop here for a couple of hours on the way.

Chongqing

POP 30.48 MILLION

Best Places to Eat

➡ Zēng Lǎo Yāo Yú Zhuāng (p823)

➡ Mang Hot Pot (p825)

➡ Xiǎomiàn (p826)

Best Places to Stay

➡ Travelling With Hostel (p810)

➡ Westin Chongqing (p823)

➡ Only Cafe & Backpacker (p810)

➡ Somerset (p810)

➡ Ming & Qing Dynasty Inn (p810)

Why Go?

Chongqing municipality (重庆市, Chóngqìng Shì) may be a relatively recent creation, having been carved out of Sìchuan in 1997, but with its eponymous city driving the economy of western China, it's now one of the most important regions in the whole country. Understandably, many confuse the larger administrative 'municipality' with the city itself – keep in mind that the former is really a province, consisting of dozens of large towns and lots of verdant, hilly countryside.

Thanks to the mighty Yangzi River (Cháng Jiāng), which powers its way through here, this region has long been one of strategic military importance. The river was responsible for creating one of China's greatest natural wonders, the magnificent Three Gorges.

Humans have left their indelible mark as well, with a panoply of ancient Buddhist sculptures, rural riverside villages and, of course, the megalopolis that is Chongqing: one of the five largest cities in all China.

When to Go
Chongqing

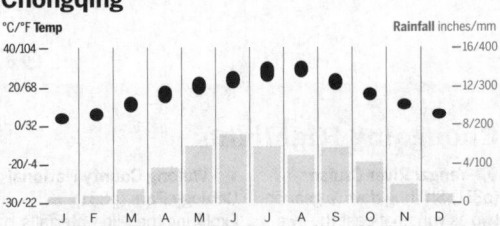

Apr & May Misty rain has replaced winter chill; it's already hot, but still manageable.

Jul & Aug Temperatures top 40°C, humidity is maxed out and the city resembles a steam bath.

Sep & Oct Pleasant temperatures; a good time to explore the countryside.

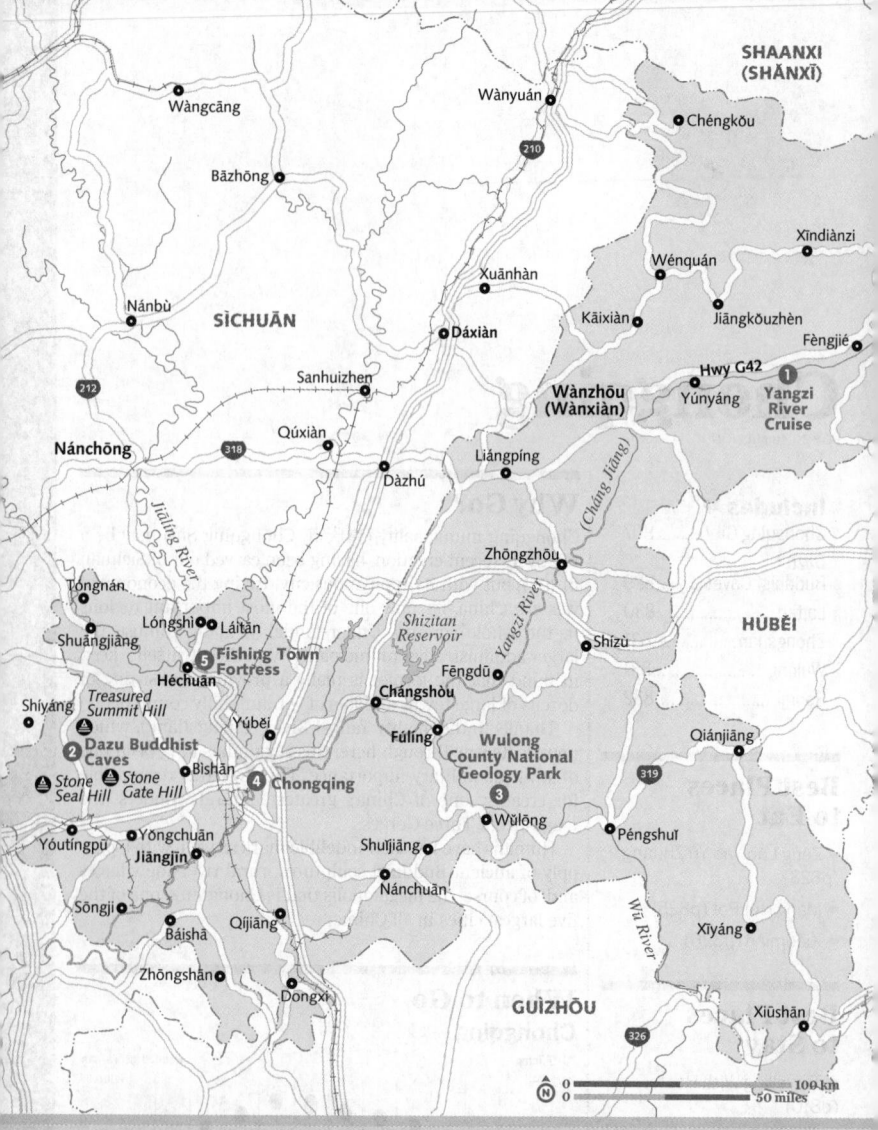

Chongqing Highlights

1 **Yangzi River Cruise** (p811) Shifting down a gear or two as you float past the awe-inspiring Three Gorges.

2 **Dazu Buddhist Caves** (p829) Admiring the exquisite artwork of these ancient cliff carvings.

3 **Wulong County National Geology Park** (p831) Exploring the wild waterfalls and karst formations of this mountain wilderness area.

4 **Hotpot** (p823) Embracing the heat and banishing damp with the world's most mouth-numbing (and eye-watering)

hotpot in one of Chongqing's numerous restaurants.

5 **Fishing Town Fortress** (p830) Hiking the overgrown ruins of a Song dynasty stronghold.

History

Stone tools unearthed along the Yangzi River valleys show that humans lived in this region two million years ago. The ancient Ba kingdom ruled from here more than 2000 years before subsequent Qin, Sui and Southern Song dynasty rulers took over. From 1938 to 1945, Chongqing City (then romanised as 'Chungking') became the Kuomintang's wartime capital. It was here that representatives of the Chinese Communist Party (CCP), including Zhou Enlai, acted as 'liaisons' between the Kuomintang and the communists headquartered in Yan'an, Shaanxi province.

Refugees from all over China flooded into the city during WWII. More followed when the construction of the Three Gorges Dam displaced over one million people.

In 1997 Chongqing separated from Sichuan province and became an autonomous municipality, eventually joining Beijing, Shanghai and Tianjin as one of the only municipal areas under direct control of the central government.

The city was the backdrop for one of modern China's biggest political scandals in 2012 when Gu Kailai, the wife of Chongqing's Communist Party boss Bo Xilai, was convicted of murdering a British business associate, Neil Heywood. Allegations of corruption, extortion and espionage surrounded the case, as well as rumours that political rivals in Beijing felt threatened by Bo's populist policies and wanted him out of the way. Both Bo and his wife were sentenced to life in prison.

Language

In addition to standard Mandarin Chinese, Chongqing residents also speak Sichuanese. It's a Mandarin dialect, but pronunciation is different enough that it's often difficult for those who speak standard Chinese to understand. Two words visitors will often hear are *yàodé* (pronounced 'yow-day', meaning 'yes' or 'OK') and *méidé* (pronounced 'may-day', meaning 'no').

ⓘ Getting There & Around

Chongqing is well connected with the rest of the country and the world via bus, rail and air. The road network has improved, but getting around rural areas is still relatively slow, often involving lengthy bus rides.

Chongqing City   重庆

🎧 023 / POP 15.35 MILLION

The most important city in western China and the economic engine of the upper Yangzi, Chongqing City (Chóngqìng) is a massive and enthralling urban sprawl. Chongqing makes up for a lack of top-notch sights with fantastic food and charismatic geography: its steep hills at the confluence of the Yangzi and Jialing Rivers are a prelude to the even more dramatic scenery of the Three Gorges.

Be aware that navigating some parts of the city on foot, particularly near the riverbanks, can be like a real-life game of chutes and ladders. Something that looks close on a map might be separated by hundreds of vertical feet – expect to climb lots of stairs while absolutely drenched in sweat, or save your energy and hail taxis with abandon.

When we last visited, a new port area for Three Gorges cruises at Chaotianmen was in the midst of reopening.

⊙ Sights

The city centre is the peninsula at the confluence of the Yangzi and Jialing rivers. This area is called Yuzhong (渝中区), and the busy urban core at its eastern tip is known as Jiefangbei (解放碑). To the north of Yuzhong across the Jialing River is Jiangbei (江北区). To the south across the Yangzi is Nan'an (南岸区). West of Yuzhong is Shapingba (沙坪坝区), home to several universities.

Huguang Guild Hall   MUSEUM
(湖广会馆, Húguǎng Huìguǎn; 🎧 023 6393 0287; Dongshuimen Zhengjie, 东水门正街; ¥30; ⊙9am-6pm; Ⓜ Xiaoshizi) You could spend several hours poking around the beautifully restored buildings in this gorgeous museum complex, which once served as a community headquarters for

---

ⓘ PRICE RANGES

Sleeping

¥ less than ¥200

¥¥ ¥200–500

¥¥¥ more than ¥500

Eating

¥ less than ¥50

¥¥ ¥50–80

¥¥¥ more than ¥80

Chongqing City

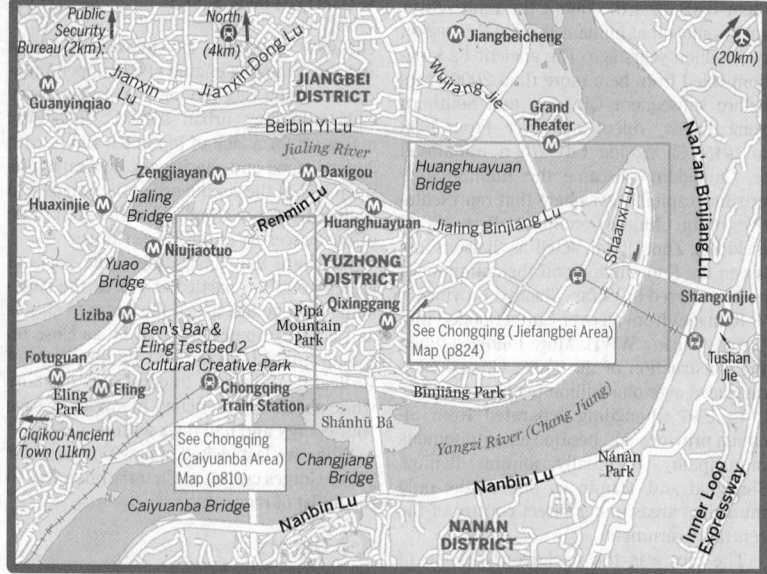

immigrants from the Hu (Hunan and Hubei) and Guang (Guangdong and Guangxi) provinces, who arrived in Chongqing several hundred years ago. There are rooms filled with artwork and furniture, a **temple**, a **teahouse** and several stages for Chinese **opera performances** (held daily at 3.30pm).

At the time of research, neighbourhood construction meant that access to the Hall from central (upper) Chongqing was very hard to locate (the hall is under the bridge). If construction is ongoing, keep asking the way – or take a taxi.

Hongya Cave
AREA

(洪崖洞, Hóngyá Dòng; 56 Cangbai Lu, 沧白路 56号; M Xiaoshizi) Not a cave, but a Disney-esque recreation of the old stilt houses that once lined Chongqing's riverfronts, this 11-storey shopping, dining and entertainment complex anchors the city's tourism scene. Here, you can get a foot massage, buy a jade bracelet, eat a dinner of spicy skewers and down a beer or cup of tea or coffee, all in one place. It's cheesy good fun and at night, the lit-up complex is fairly spectacular.

Luohan Temple
BUDDHIST TEMPLE

(罗汉寺, Luóhàn Sì; Luohan Si Jie, 罗汉寺街; ¥10; ⊗8am-5pm; M Xiaoshizi) Built around 1000 years ago, this still-active temple is now sandwiched between skyscrapers. A notable feature is the corridor flanked by intricate rock carvings found just after you enter the complex, but the main attraction here is **Arhat Hall** (罗汉堂, Luóhàn Táng), off to your right just after the corridor. It contains 500 terracotta arhats (a Buddhist term for those who have achieved enlightenment and who pass to nirvana at death).

Chongqing Ancient City Gates
RUINS

(古城门, Gǔchéngmén) Sadly, only fragments remain of Chongqing's once-magnificent Ming dynasty city wall, which stretched 8km around the Jiefangbei peninsula and was more than 30m tall in places. Of the 17 gates that punctuated the wall before demolition began in 1927, two are still standing. The renovated **Dōngshuǐ Mén** (东水门) is plumb beneath the Donshuimen Bridge along the pleasant Dongshuimen Old Street. Larger and partly restored is **Tōngyuán Mén** (通远门; M Qixinggang, exit 1), a short walk from Qixinggang metro station.

Ciqikou Ancient Town
OLD TOWN

(磁器口古镇, Cíqíkǒu Gǔzhèn; Shapingba; M Ciqikou, exit 1) The opportunity to snatch a glimpse of old Chongqing makes it worth riding some 45 minutes out to Shapingba district, on the Jialing River west of the centre. Through the archway that is the entrance to the town, most of the late-Ming buildings in this sprawling complex have been restored. The main drag can feel like a carnival, especially on weekends, but away from the central street, a living village remains.

You can easily lose yourself in the narrow lanes. And there's plenty to eat here, both in the alleys and overlooking the river. It's also worth poking your head inside **Bǎolún Sì** (宝轮寺; ¥5; ⊙7am-6pm), one of Ciqikou's only remaining temples. Its main building is more than 1000 years old. The alley the temple is on, Heng Jie (横街), is one of the most pleasant places to explore.

When we passed through, a new sightseeing ferry running between Chaotianmen and Ciqikou was slated to open following the renovation of the port.

Three Gorges Museum   MUSEUM
(三峡博物馆; Sānxiá Bówùguǎn; 236 Renmin Lu, 人民路236号; ⊙9am-5pm Tue-Sun; Ⓜ Zengjiayan, exit A) FREE This sleek museum showcases the history of settlement in the Chongqing region. There's the inevitable exhibition on the Three Gorges, including a model of the dam, as well as clothing and artwork relating to southwest China's minority groups. Some exhibits have better English captions than others.

Pipa Mountain Park   PARK
(枇杷山公园; Pípá Shān Gōngyuán; 74 Pipa Shanzheng Jie, 枇杷山正街74号; ⊙6am-10pm; Ⓜ Qixinggang) FREE For views of the city skyline, climb 345m Pipa Mountain Park, the highest point on the Chongqing peninsula. During the day, residents bring their songbirds to the park for air and group warbling.

Liberation Monument   MONUMENT
(解放碑, Jiěfàngbēi; Ⓜ Linjiangmen) This clock tower monument at the heart of Chongqing commemorates China's victory over Japan in WWII. The surrounding pedestrian streets are now home to the city's most luxurious shopping, with international clothing and watch brands aplenty, and outposts of global chains filling the surrounding malls.

🏃 Activities

Chongqing looks best from the water, especially at night when the city flashes with neon. The so-called **two-river cruises** (两江游船, Liàng Jiāng Yóuchuán; Chaotianmen Docks; 朝天门码头; day/night cruise ¥80/138) last for 40 minutes to an hour, leaving during the day (10.45am to 6pm) and evening (7pm to 10pm) from Chaotianmen Docks, and can be a fun way to get an alternative view of this sprawling metropolis.

Evening cruises are much more popular and worthwhile. Buy your tickets directly down at the docks, by the river at Hongya Cave, or at your hotel if they have a travel agency.

★ **Ronghui Hot Springs**   HOT SPRINGS
(融汇温泉城, Rónghuì Wēnquán Chéng; ☎023 6530 0378; 6 Huiquan Lu, Shapingba, 沙坪坝区汇泉路6号; entry ¥169; ⊙10am-midnight Sun-Thu, 24hr Fri & Sat; 👶; Ⓜ Yanggongqiao) The Chongqing area is famed for its hot springs, and Ronghui is the most popular and easily accessible resort inside the city limits. Visitors relax in the lushly landscaped grounds, soaking in dozens of spring-fed indoor and outdoor pools, some steeped with medicinal Chinese herbs, others with essential oils, and still others featuring an array of jets.

Complete the experience with a full-body exfoliation (¥39), massage (from ¥139), pedicure or have your feet nibbled in the fish pool (free). Three towels are included with admission, but you'll need to bring a swimsuit. There's a kids' water playground,

---

THE LARGEST CITY IN THE WORLD?

Chongqing is sometimes mistakenly referred to as the most populous city in the world. It isn't. Much of the confusion stems from the fact that the administrative designation for the larger entity ('municipality' or 市) suggests that it consists solely of a massive metropolitan area surrounded by suburban sprawl.

While Chongqing City is, in fact, enormous, the actual 'municipality' is much larger, encompassing 82,400 sq km – for comparison, that's bigger than Scotland and only slightly smaller than South Carolina. And like both of those places, the municipality includes everything from a capital city to large towns, rural villages, plenty of farmland and even wilderness. But no matter how you slice it, it hardly qualifies as a principally urban area. Figures for the municipal population are just over 30 million but, for now anyway, the city of Chongqing itself only has 15 million inhabitants, meaning it's still smaller than Shanghai, Beijing and Guangzhou.

Chongqing (Caiyuanba Area)

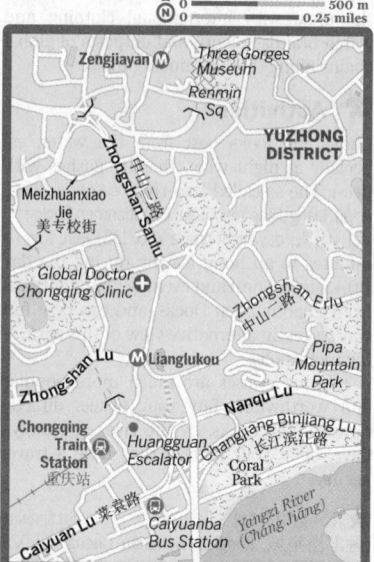

but many families just take their children right into the hot springs with them.

The resort is a short taxi ride from Yanggongqiao metro station, which is about 30 minutes from downtown on line 1. The Radisson next door is the best place to pick up a taxi after you're finished.

★ **Yangzi River Cable Car**　CABLE CAR
(长江索道, Chángjiāng Suǒdào; Jiefang Donglu, 解放东路; one way/round trip ¥20/30; ☺ 7.30am-10.30pm; Ⓜ Xiǎoshízi, exit 5) A ride on the creaky old Yangzi River cable car is slightly disconcerting, but gives you a wonderful bird's-eye view of the murky waters and the cityscape beyond. It drops you off near the riverside bar and restaurant strip on Nan'an Binjiang Lu.

🛏 Sleeping

Only Cafe & Backpacker　HOSTEL ¥
(弱水咖啡国际青旅; Ruòshuǐ Kāfēi Guójì Qīnglǚ; ☑ 130 0230 2740; 31st fl, Yangguang Xingzuo Bldg, 9 Minsheng Lu, 民生路9号阳光星座31楼11号; dm ¥70; 🌐🛜; Ⓜ Jiaochangkou) Run by a lovely globe-trotting, coffee-loving couple, the Only Cafe moved to these stylish new penthouse digs in 2019. Expect updated amenities in the eight-bed dorms (reading lights, bed-side mobile chargers, lockers), as well as a fridge, microwave, laundry and loads of great local tips. At the top-floor retro-chic cafe, they

even roast their own beans. Twenty-four-hour check-in available.

Travelling With Hostel　HOSTEL ¥
(瓦舍旅行酒店, Wǎshè Lǚxíng Jiǔdiàn; ☑ 023 6303 3925; www.chongqingtravellingwith.com; 4th fl, Yuya Bldg, 7 Zhongxing Lu, 中兴路7号渝亚大厦4楼; dm ¥32-50, d ¥124-200; 🌐🛜; Ⓜ Jiaochangkou, exit 4) Travelling With is much nicer than its location (on the 4th floor of a commercial building, no elevator) might suggest. It's the only hostel in Chongqing with a reliably social bar and common area, populated largely by a mix of international and Chinese travellers. Friendly employees speak English and are happy to help you book train tickets or tours. Rooms run the gamut from eight-person mixed dorms to comfy doubles with private baths.

Bindun Langyi Hotel　HOTEL ¥¥
(宾顿朗逸酒店, Bīndùn Lǎngyì Jiǔdiàn; ☑ 023 6366 0777; 6F, 118 Zourong Lu, 邹容路118号都市广场B座6楼; r ¥308-468; 🌐🛜) This central option has taken inspiration from the minimalist Apple look, with lots of light wood and modern touches. It's not international standard, but it's better than other hotels in this price range. Breakfast included; some English spoken.

Somerset　HOTEL ¥¥
(盛捷解放碑服务公寓, Shèngjié Jiěfàngbēi Fúwù Gōngyù; ☑ 023 8677 6888; www.somerset.com; 108 Minzu Road, 9F, Block B, Hejing Bldg, 民族路108号合景大厦B栋9楼; ste from ¥400; 🌐🖥🛜📶; Ⓜ Xiaoshizi) If you're looking for short-term apartment-style accommodation, consider this welcoming suite hotel, perched high above the noise of central Jiefangbei. Spacious modern suites, from studios to one- and two-bedroom apartments, come with kitchenettes and laundry machines. The large number of long-term international guests means there are communal activities, like Friday movie nights, not found in traditional hotels.

Ming & Qing Dynasty Inn　HOTEL ¥¥
(明清客栈, Míngqīng Kèzhàn; ☑ 023 6371 7295; 23 Xiahong Xuexiang, near the Huguang Guild Hall, 长江滨江路湖广会馆下洪学巷23号; r ¥400-1200; 🌐🛜) This Qing dynasty courtyard hotel with a lovely downstairs teahouse (open to nonguests) could be the nicest boutique setting in Chongqing, but it comes with several caveats: it's somewhat hard to find, the riverside location is not convenient for getting around (lots of steps), rooms are on the small side and English is limited. It is peaceful though.

Cruising the Yangzi

Taking a boat down the Yangzi River (长江, Cháng Jiāng) – China's longest and most scenic waterway – is all about the journey rather than the destination. It isn't just an escape from marathon train journeys and agonising bus rides, but a chance to kick back as an astonishing panorama slides by at a sedate pace which allows time for contemplation and relaxation. Cruising the Yangzi is a truly unique experience, one that gets you up close with mostly domestic travellers allowing time for real interaction. Jump aboard.

Contents

Xiling Gorge (p480)

The Route

The journey puts you adrift on China's mightiest – and the world's third-longest – waterway, the gushing 6300km Yangzi River. Starting life as trickles of snowmelt in the Tanggula Mountains of southwestern Qinghai, the river then spills from Tibet, swells through seven Chinese provinces, sucks in water from hundreds of tributaries and rolls powerfully into the Pacific Ocean north of Shanghai.

Apocryphally the handiwork of Yu the Great, a legendary architect of the river, the gorges – Qutang, Wu and Xiling – commence just east of Fengjie in Chongqing province and level out west of Yichang in Hubei province, a distance of around 200km. The principal route for those cruising the Yangzi River is therefore between the cities of **Chongqing** and **Yichang**.

The route can be travelled in either direction, but most passengers journey downstream from Chongqing. Travelling upstream from Yichang is slower and hence ensures a less crowded boat. Going downstream, cruises are typically four days, three nights; going upstream, cruises are five days, four nights. However, you can shorten the trip to as little as two or three days by starting (or ending) in Fengjie or Wanzhou – cruise operators will arrange your bus transport to/from Chongqing.

If you buy your ticket from an agency, ensure you're not charged upfront for the sights along the way, as you may not want to visit them all. Some of the sights are underwhelming and entrance fees are as steep as the surrounding inclines. The only ticket truly worth buying in advance

Yangzi River (Chang Jiang)

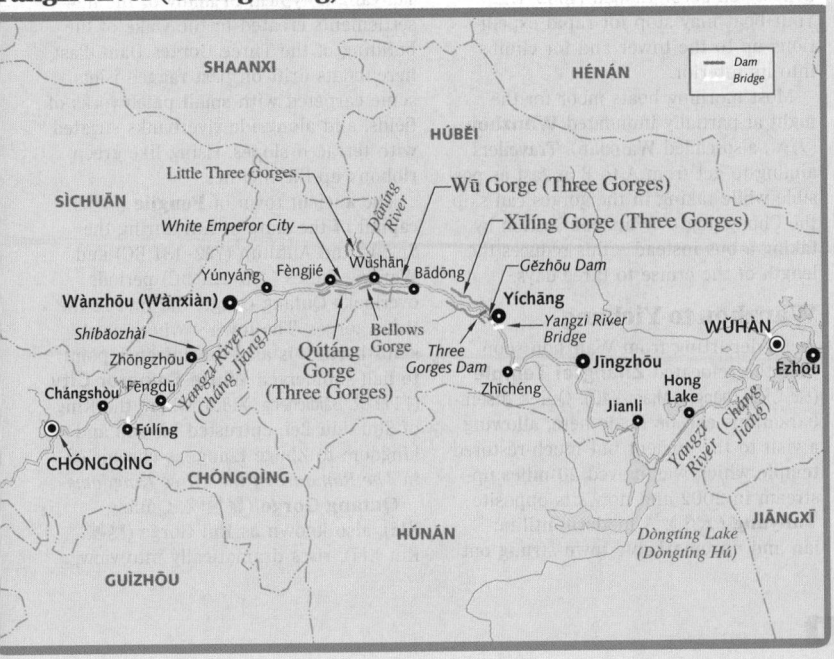

is for the popular and worthwhile Little Three Gorges tour, which is often full.

Chongqing to Wanzhou

The initial stretch is slow-going and unremarkable, although the dismal view of factories gradually gives way to attractive terraced countryside and the occasional small town.

Passing the drowned town of Fuling (涪陵), the first port of call is at **Fengdu** (丰都), 170km from Chongqing city. Long nicknamed the City of Ghosts (鬼城, Guǐchéng), the town is just that: inundated in 2009, its residents were moved across the river. This is the stepping-off point for crowds to clamber up **Ming Mountain** (名山; Míng Shān; adult ¥95, cable car ¥20), with its theme-park crop of ghost-focused temples.

Drifting through the county of Zhongzhou, the boat takes around three hours to arrive at **Shíbǎozhài** (石宝寨; Stone Treasure Stockade; ¥150; ⊙8am-4pm) on the northern bank of the river. A 12-storey, 56m-high wooden pagoda built on a huge, river-water-encircled rock bluff,

WHEN TO GO

Dec–Mar The low season; rates are cheaper and the journey is more serene.

Apr & May The best weather, with fewer crowds than in summer.

Jun–Aug Chinese summer holidays means crowded, kid-filled boats.

Oct & Nov Cooler climes but still crowded.

the structure dates to the reign of Qing dynasty emperor Kangxi (1662–1722). Your boat may stop for rapid expeditions up to the tower and for climbs into its interior.

Most morning boats moor for the night at partially inundated **Wanzhou** (万州, also called Wanxian). Travellers aiming to get from A to B as fast as possible while taking in the gorges can skip the Chongqing to Wanzhou section by taking a bus instead – this reduces the length of the cruise to three days.

Wanzhou to Yichang

Boats departing from Wanzhou soon pass the relocated **Zhangfei Temple** (张飞庙; Zhāngfēi Miào; ¥40). Quick disembarkations can be made here, allowing a visit to the ancient but much-restored temple which was moved 20 miles upstream in 2002 and now sits opposite **Yunyang** (云阳). A modern, utilitarian and unremarkable town strung out

along the northern bank of the river, Yunyang is typical of many of the new settlements created in the wake of the building of the Three Gorges Dam. Past here, boats drift on past ragged islets, some carpeted with small patchworks of fields, and alongside riverbanks striated with terraced slopes, rising like green ribbons up the inclines.

The ancient town of **Fengjie** (奉节), capital of the state of Kui during the Spring and Autumn (722–481 BC) and Warring States (475–221 BC) periods, overlooks Qutang Gorge, the first of the three gorges. The town – where most ships berth – is also the entrance point to half-submerged **White Emperor City** (白帝城; Báidìchéng; ¥180), where the King of Shu, Liu Bei, entrusted his son and kingdom to Zhuge Liang, as chronicled in *The Romance of the Three Kingdoms*.

Qutang Gorge (瞿塘峡, Qútáng Xiá), also known as Kui Gorge (夔峡, Kuí Xiá), rises dramatically into view,

towering into huge vertiginous slabs of rock, its cliffs jutting out in jagged and triangular chunks. The shortest and narrowest of the three gorges, 8km-long Qutang is over almost as abruptly as it starts, but is considered by many to be the most awe-inspiring. The gorge offers a dizzying perspective onto huge strata despite having some of its power robbed by the rising waters. On the northern bank is **Bellows Gorge** (风箱峡, Fēngxiāng Xiá), where nine coffins were discovered, possibly placed here by an ancient tribe.

After Qutang Gorge the terrain folds into a 20km stretch of low-lying land before boats pull in at the riverside town of **Wushan** (巫山), situated high above the river. Most boats stop at Wushan for five to six hours so passengers can transfer to smaller boats for trips along the **Little Three Gorges** (小三峡; Xiǎo Sānxiá; ticket ¥240-280) on the Daning River (大宁河, Dàníng Hé).

The landscape is gorgeous and you're right up close to it, and many travellers insist that the narrow gorges are more impressive than their larger namesakes. Some tours include a 40-minute ride on local fishing boats here, or further excursions to the Little Little Three Gorges (小小三峡, Xiǎo Xiǎo Sānxiá).

Back on the Yangzi River, boats pull away from Wushan to enter the middle Wu Gorge, under a bright-red bridge. Some of the cultivated fields on the slopes overhanging the river reach almost illogical angles.

Wu Gorge (巫峡; Wū Xiá) – the Gorge of Witches – is stunning, cloaked in green and carpeted in shrubs, its sides frequently disappearing into ethereal layers of mist. About 40km in length, its towering cliffs are topped by sharp, jagged peaks on the northern bank. A total of 12 peaks cluster on either side, including **Goddess Peak** (神女峰, Shénnǚ Fēng) and **Peak of**

1. Misty sunset near the Three Gorges Dam (p480) 2. View along the Yangzi near the Three Gorges

BAMBOOME/GETTY IMAGES ©

1. Shíbǎozhài Pagoda (p813) 2. Three Gorges Dam (p480)
3. Yangzi River near Lijiang (p714) 4. Gate to White Emperor City
(p814)

the Immortals (集仙峰, Jíxiān Fēng). If you're fortunate, you'll catch the sunrise over Goddess Peak.

Boats continue floating eastward out of Wu Gorge and into Hubei province, along a 45km section before reaching the last of the three gorges. At this time, many boats offer the option of a two-hour trip on motorised dragon boats along **Jiuwan Stream** (九畹溪, Jiǔwǎn Xī) and nearby tributaries of the Yangzi. Some travellers enjoy the experience, although the scenery isn't as inspiring as that of the Little Three Gorges.

At 80km, **Xiling Gorge** (西陵峡, Xīlíng Xiá) is the longest and perhaps least spectacular gorge; sections of the gorge in the west have been submerged. Note the slow-moving cargo vessels, including long freight ships loaded with mounds of coal, ploughing downriver to Shanghai. The gorge was traditionally the most hazardous, where hidden shoals and reefs routinely holed vessels, but it has long been tamed, even though river traffic slows when the fog reduces visibility.

Apart from the top-end luxury cruises, tour boats no longer pass through the monumental **Three Gorges Dam**, although some tours offer the option of a visit to the dam by bus. Once you disembark, it's about an hour by bus to Yichang – check to see if this is included or if you'll need to take public transport.

Boats

There are two types of boat: luxury cruises and tourist boats. Cabins on the top-end cruises are like comfy hotel rooms, complete with TV, private balconies and daily maid service. Tourist boats are more basic, with simple private rooms.

Luxury Cruises

The most luxurious passage is on international-standard cruise ships (豪华游轮, *háohuá yóulún*), where maximum comfort and visibility accompany a leisurely agenda. Trips normally depart Chongqing and include shore visits to all the major sights (Three Gorges Dam, Little Three Gorges etc), allowing time to tour the attractions (often secondary to the scenery). Cabins have air-con, TV (perhaps satellite), fridge/minibar and sometimes wi-fi (generally unusable). These vessels are aimed at both Chinese and western tourists and are ideal for travellers with time, money and negligible Chinese skills. Top-end cruises feature daily buffet meals, generally including both western and Chinese food. Seating is assigned, and meals are included in your ticket price. The average duration for such a cruise going downstream is three nights and four days.

Fares range from about ¥2000 (from Chongqing) to ¥2800 (from Yichang), but will vary according to the season. You can also book online ahead of time; some of these trips will incorporate the cruise as part of an all-inclusive package and take in other must-see sights in China as well.

1. Exploring the Wu Gorge (p815)
2. Setting out from Little Three Gorges (p815)
3. Aerial view of a ferry on its way to Wuhan

Tourist Cruise Ships

Typically departing from Chongqing around 9pm, ordinary tourist cruise ships (普通游轮, *pǔtōng yóulún*) usually take just under 40 hours to reach Yichang (including three nights on board). Some boats stop at all the sights; others stop at just a few. They are less professional than the luxury tour cruises and are squarely aimed at domestic travellers (Chinese food, little English spoken).

Expect early starts: the public-address system starts going off after 6am. Cabins in all classes are fairly basic, but come with AC and a TV and usually have a small attached bathroom with a shower (although that doesn't mean hot water).

Many travellers now book packages that take you first by bus from Chongqing to either Wanzhou or Fengjie,

BEST TOP-END CRUISES

Viking River Cruises (☑US 800-706-1483; www.vikingrivercruises.com; from US$4299) Very luxurious cruise, offering five-day cruises from Chongqing to Wuhan, as part of a two-week tour of China.

Century Cruises (☑023 6294 9888; www.centuryrivercruises.com) Claims to be the most luxurious cruise service on the Yangzi. Ships, service and facilities are among the best on the river.

Victoria Cruises (☑US 800-348-8084; www.victoriacruises.com) Comfortable four-day trips between Chongqing and Yichang. Older boats than some other operators, but has excellent English-speaking guides.

where you board a vessel for the rest of the trip. This reduces the journey by one or two nights – prices may be the same for either option when travelling downstream.

In theory, you can buy tickets on the day of travel, but booking one or two days in advance is recommended. Fares vary, although not by much, depending whether you buy your ticket from a hostel, agency or direct from the ticket hall. Always ensure you know exactly what the price includes.

Approximate fares are as follows:

Chongqing to Yichang (4 days) 1st class only ¥1280

Wanzhou to Yichang (3 days) 1st/2nd/3rd class ¥1080/880/780, two-/four-/six-bed cabin

Fengjie to Yichang (2 days) 1st/2nd/3rd class ¥1080/880/780, two-/four-/six-bed cabin

From Yichang to Chongqing, tourist boats only run to Fengjie or Wanzhou. To make the entire journey, you will need to book a luxury cruise. The bus to the dam is included in the price, as is the bus to Chongqing after you disembark.

Yichang to Wanzhou (4 days) 1st/2nd class ¥980/850

Yichang to Fengjie (3 days) 1st/2nd class ¥900/820

1. The Wu Gorge (p815) 2. Deck of a luxury cruise ship sailing along the Yangzi 3. View of boats cruising along the Three Gorges

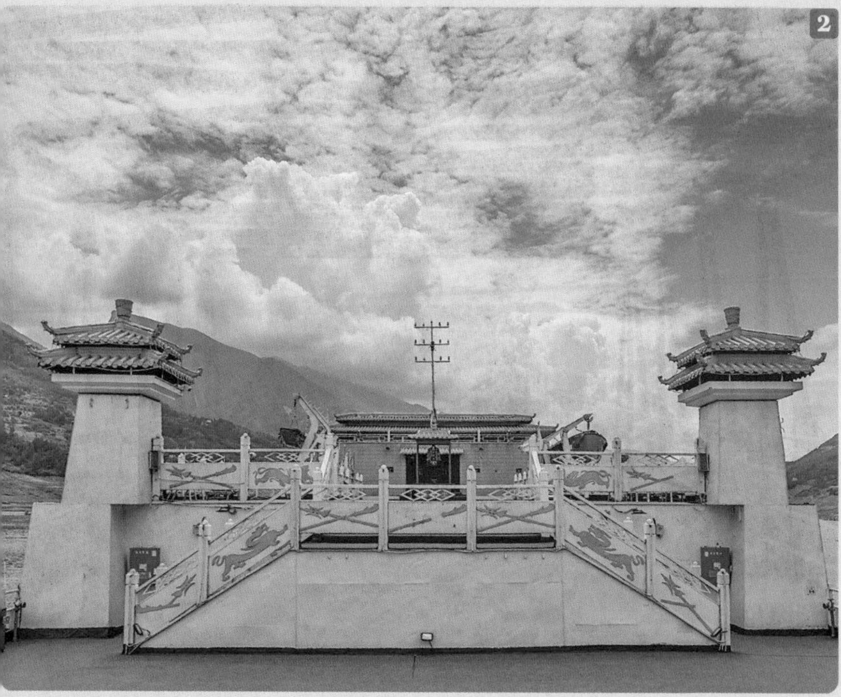

2

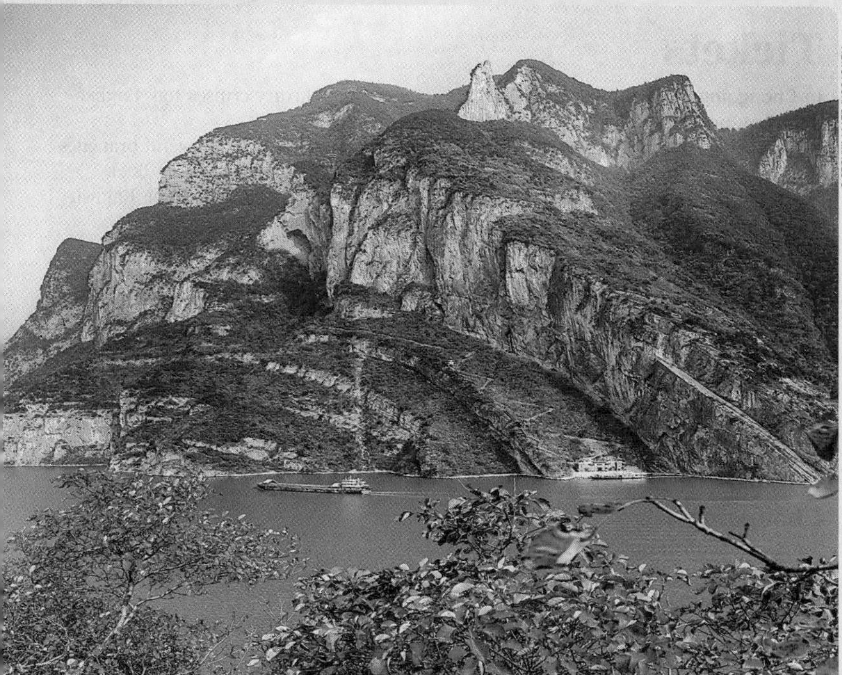

VIEWSTOCK/GETTY IMAGES ©

Boarding at the Three Gorges Dam (p480)

Tickets

In Chongqing most hotels, travel agents and ferry-port ticket halls can sell you a trip on either the luxury cruise ships or the ordinary tourist boats. The process may become more centralised after the completion of the new dock area, however.

In Yichang, it's very simple – head to the Three Gorges Tourist Centre (p481). It sells everything from day trips to luxury cruises upstream at a fair price.

The price of your ticket should include the one-hour shuttle bus ride between Yichang and the cruise port about 45km upstream.

Chongqing

Travelling With Hostel (p810) mostly sells tickets for the ordinary tourist boats, but can arrange luxury cruises too. English-speaking staff.

CITS (p827) is one of several branches in town, with an emphasis on booking Three Gorges cruises. Some English spoken.

Online Booking

If you want to travel on a specific day, you can book luxury cruises in advance. It will be more expensive, though the selection process should be easier to navigate. Ensure that the website you are booking through can accept payments from foreign credit cards. Try www.yangtze-river-cruises.com or www.yangtze.com.

Westin Chongqing HOTEL ¥¥¥
(解放碑威斯汀酒店, Jiěfàngbēi Wēisītīng Jiǔdiàn;
☎023 6380 6666; https://westin.marriott.com;
222 Xinhua Lu, 新华路222号; r from ¥1200;
😊❄🅿🛜; Ⓜ Xiaoshizi) With a lobby on the
51st floor, views over the Yangzi and to the
hills beyond it won't get much better. A light
colour palette, hardwood accents and a deft
modern touch make the rooms here a touch
more stylish than those of its competitors,
though service can be uneven. There's also a
spa and several classy dining options.

Harbour Plaza HOTEL ¥¥¥
(重庆海逸酒店, Chóngqìng Hǎiyì Jiǔdiàn; ☎023
6370 0888; www.harbour-plaza.com; 68 Zourong
Lu, 邹容路68号; r from ¥800; ❄🛜🅿; Ⓜ Jiaochangkou) Renovated in 2018, the modern,
white-themed rooms at this centrally located
hotel include LED mirrors and Chinese tea
sets in each room. All come with wide-screen
TV, fridge and safe, and English is spoken.
That said, it's not quite at the level of other
luxury brands in the city. You can often get
discounts of up to 25%.

✖ Eating

Chongqing is all about hotpot (火锅, huǒguō):
a fiery cauldron of eye-watering làjiāo (辣椒,
chillies) and mouth-numbing huājiāo (花椒,
Sichuan peppercorn) into which deliciously
fresh ingredients are dipped, from vegetables
and tofu to all types of fish and meat. It's a
meal best sampled with a group, and hotpot
restaurants tend to be among the liveliest
you'll find.

★ Zēng Lǎo Yǎo Yú Zhuāng SICHUAN ¥¥
(曾老幺鱼庄; ☎023 6392 4315; 220 Changjiang
Binjiang Lu, 长江滨江路220号; mains ¥28-78;
⊙24hr) Outside, it's a seething mass of people crowded around tables. Inside, it's even
more packed as you enter a former bomb
shelter – white-tiled walls and a rock roof.
This Chongqing institution is a unique, utilitarian dining experience, with all strata of
society in search of the signature fish dish

HOTPOT MENU

The best hotpot restaurants are entirely local affairs so you have about as much chance of finding an English menu as you have of being able to eat the thing without your nose running.

As with many dishes in Chongqing, the first thing to establish when ordering hotpot is what sort of broth you want (this typically costs from ¥25 to ¥50) and how hot you want it – bù là (不辣, not spicy, but in Chongqing this will still be spicy), wēi là (微辣, mildly spicy), zhōng là (中辣, medium spicy), zuì là (最辣, very spicy) and jiā má jiā là (加麻加辣, extra, extra spicy). Do not underestimate a hotpot's bite. This part of China is renowned for fiery food, and it doesn't come spicier than hotpot.

Then you'll be given a Chinese menu checklist of raw ingredients that you will later cook in your pot. Some places serve ingredients on skewers (串串, chuàn chuàn) instead of the menu – these are self-service and makes choosing your meal somewhat easier. When you're done, the discarded skewers are weighed, and your total price is tallied according to the weight.

Here are some of our favourites for you to look out for on the menu:

➜ yángròu juǎn (羊肉卷, wafer-thin lamb slices)

➜ féi niúròu (肥牛肉, beef slices)

➜ xiān máodǔ (鲜毛肚, fresh tripe, usually lamb)

➜ xiān yācháng (鲜鸭肠, strips of duck intestine)

➜ lǎo dòufu (老豆腐, tofu slabs)

➜ ǒu piàn (藕片, slices of lotus root)

➜ xiān huánghuā (鲜黄花, chrysanthemum stalks)

➜ tǔ dòu (土豆, potato slices)

➜ bái cài (白菜, cabbage)

➜ mógu (蘑菇, mushrooms)

➜ mù'ěr (木耳, wood ear mushrooms)

➜ kōngxīn cài (空心菜, water spinach)

Chongqing (Jiefangbei Area)

CHONGQING

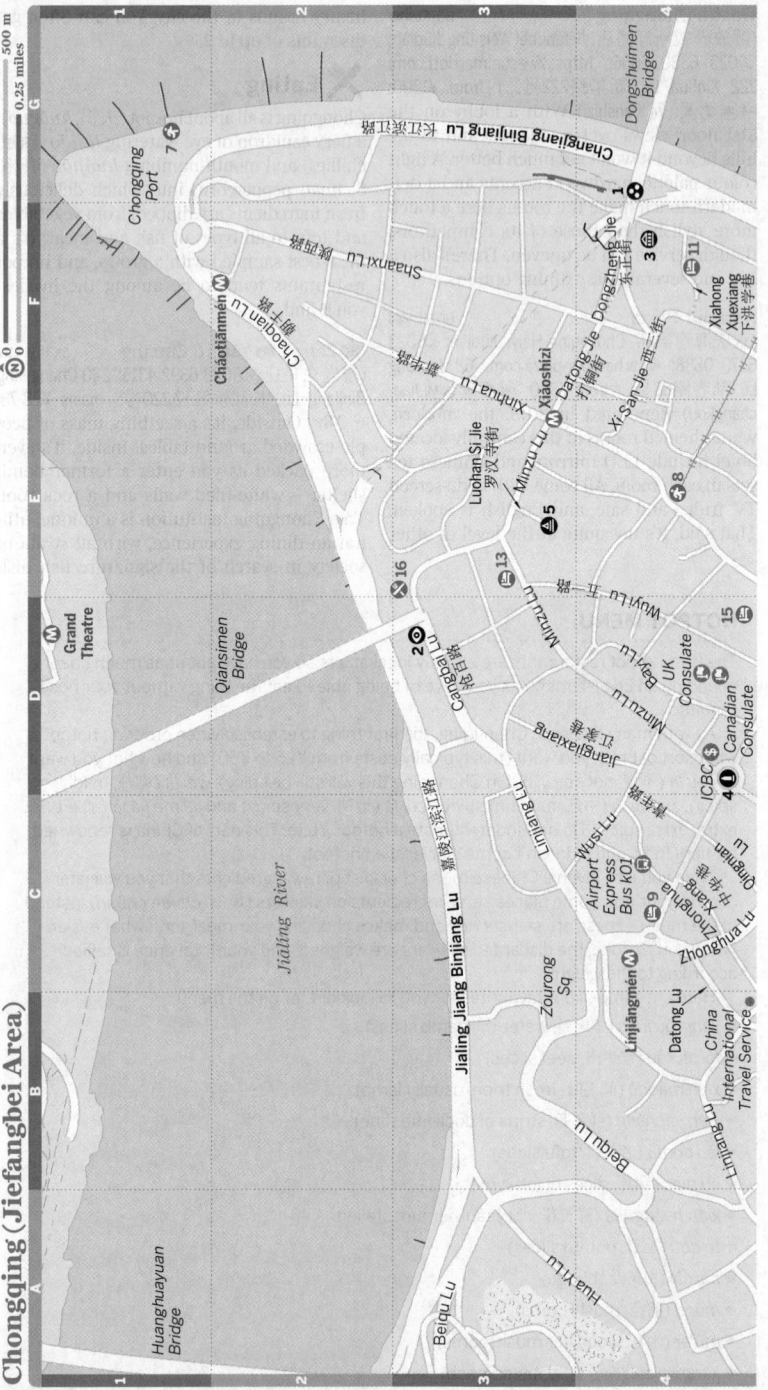

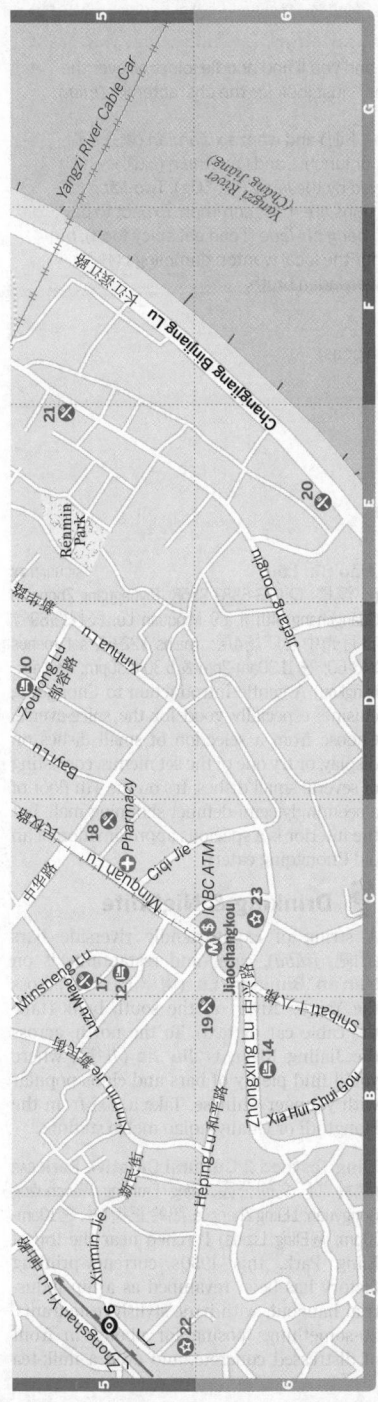

Chongqing (Jiefangbei Area)

(鲫鱼, *jìyú,* carp) and the simply sublime spare ribs (排骨, *páigǔ*).

As always, it's best to eat in a group and be prepared to wait for a table. But it never closes, so you can roll up anytime. No English menu, so point at the picture menu or at what other diners are eating.

Mang Hot Pot   HOTPOT ¥¥
(莽子老火锅, Mǎngzi Lǎo Huǒguō; ☏ 02363718492; 7 Luzu Miao, 鲁祖庙10号; broth ¥28-35, dipping ingredients ¥6-30; ⊗ 11am-2am; Ⓜ Jiaochangkou) A real locals fave with some of the tastiest (and spiciest) hotpot in town. You sit on wooden benches around your table and bubbling broth. Expect to see male diners with their shirts off, beer bottles close to hand. It's up the alley at the end of Qingnian Lu in the midst of the flower market on the left-hand side.

There's a wooden sign with English and a picture of a man. No English menu.

Shùnfēng 123 Coco   SICHUAN ¥¥
(顺风 123 Coco; ☏ 023 6383 3123; 5th fl, Bayi Plaza, 238 Bayi Lu, 八一路238号八一广场5楼; dishes ¥12-68; ⊗ 11am-9pm; Ⓜ Jiaochangkou) A trendy

CHONGQING NOODLES

Chongqingers are particularly fond of noodles and you'll find noodle joints all over the region. They rarely have English menus or signs – just look for the character 面 (*miàn*, noodles) and you're good to go.

Specialities here include the spicy *xiǎomiàn* (小面) and *wānzá xiǎomiàn* (豌杂小面, with crunchy peas) – often eaten for breakfast or lunch – and *liángmiàn* (凉面), which are served cold. Noodles in Chongqing are served by the *liǎng* (两; 50g). Two-*liǎng* (二两, *èr liǎng*) or three-*liǎng* (三两, *sān liǎng*) portions are most common. Expect to pay between ¥6 and ¥12 for a bowl. Remember: *wǒ néng chī làde* (I can eat spicy food); *bù yào tài là* (not too spicy, please). Also look out for the local wonton dumplings (抄手, *chāoshǒu*), which are served in a chilli-and-ginger-laden broth.

Menu Decoder

➡ *wānzá xiǎomiàn* (豌杂小面, spicy noodles with peas)

➡ *liángmiàn* (凉面, cold noodles)

➡ *niúròu miàn* (牛肉面, beef noodles)

➡ *jīdàn miàn* (鸡蛋面, egg noodles)

➡ *suānlà fěn* (酸辣粉, tangy glass noodles)

➡ *féicháng miàn* (肥肠面, pig intestine noodles)

Sichuan, 123 Coco goes beyond the same old, same old with a bit of modern culinary flair (and questionable interior design). There's no English, but there is a heat index and starred specials, like charred chillies and pork (特色炒肉, *tèsè chǎoròu*), which pairs nicely with an ice-cold mango juice.

Zhào'èr Huǒguō　　　　HOTPOT ¥¥
(赵二火锅; ☑ 023 6671 1569; 128 Jiefang Donglu, 3rd fl, 解放东路128号世纪龙门大厦三楼; dipping ingredients ¥5-38; ⏰ 11am-2pm & 5.30pm-midnight) Highly popular, Zhào'èr's hotpot is rightly lauded. There are various options: the nine-sectioned pot (九宫锅, *jiǔgōng guō*) allows you to separate the flavours of your raw ingredients, although the broth is shared; while the two-sectioned *yuānyang guō* (鸳鸯锅) has a clear broth that is separated completely from the spicy one. It's a bit out of the way. No English sign or menu. Look for the archway with yellow characters against a red backdrop and walk up the stairs to the left.

Liúyīshǒu Huǒguō　　　　HOTPOT ¥¥
(刘一手火锅; ☑ 023 6161 8555; 46 Cangbai Lu, 3rd fl, 沧白路46号南国丽景大厦3楼; broth ¥48, dipping ingredients ¥7-46; ⏰ 11am-1am; Ⓜ Xiaoshizi) The hotpot here is excellent, and the atmosphere is congenial, but the real attraction is the view: you dine as you gaze out across the Jialing River. You'll be pushed to find a riverview table at peak meal times. Take the lift three doors to the right of Home Inn.

Xiǎo Bīn Lōu　　　　SICHUAN ¥¥
(小滨楼; ☑ 023-6383 8858; Riyueguang Zhongxin Guangchang, 4th fl, 89 Minquan Lu, 民权路89号日月光中心广场4层; mains ¥22-68, set menus ¥43-60; ⏰ 11.30am-2pm & 5.30-8.30pm; Ⓜ Jiaochangkou) A gentle introduction to Chongqing cuisine, especially good for the spice-averse. Choose from a selection of small dishes on display, or try one of the set menus, consisting of several small dishes. It's on the 4th floor of a seemingly semi-defunct shopping mall, but the interior is a spacious approximation of an old Chongqing eatery.

🍷 Drinking & Nightlife

A string of expat-friendly riverside bars (酒吧, *jiǔbā*), cafes and restaurants is on **Nan'an Binjiang Lu** (南岸滨江路) across the Yangzi River on the south bank (take the cable car or taxi). To the north, across the Jialing River, is **Jiu Jie** (九街), where you'll find plenty of bars and clubs popular with younger Chinese. Take a taxi from the Hongtudì or Guanyinqiao metro stations.

Eling Testbed 2 Cultural Creative Park BAR
(鹅岭二厂文创公园, Élíng Èrchǎng Wénchuàng Gōngyuán; 1 Eling Zhengjie, 鹅岭正街1号; ⏰ 10am-10pm; Ⓜ Eling, Liziba) Perched near the top of Eling Park, this 1950s currency-printing factory has been revamped as a hip industrial hangout, with bars, stylish restaurants, 20-somethings posing for photos in front of distressed concrete, and even a milk-tea

truck. Come at night for cool views looking out over the neon-lit cityscape.

It's a 15-minute walk uphill from either metro station or a short cab ride.

Ben's Bar CRAFT BEER
(笨精酿啤酒, Bèn Jīngniàng Píjiǔ; ☑023 6326 4179; Bldg 7, Eling Testbed 2 Cultural Creative Park, 1 Eling Zhengjie, 鹅岭正街1号二广文创公园7号; ⊙2pm-midnight, Mon-Thu, from noon Fri-Sun; Ⓜ Eling, Liziba) Part of the Eling Park scene, American-run Ben's is a low-key place to get your craft-beer fix – of the 15 brews on tap, our favourite was the house-brewed Sichuan peppercorn ale. It also serves burgers and pizzas.

Harp Irish Pub BAR
(竖琴爱尔兰酒吧, Shùqín Ài'ěrlán Jiǔbā; ☑023 6880 0136; Chongqing Tiandi, 化龙桥重庆天地; ⊙4pm-midnight; 🛜) By far the best spot in town to catch live sport, especially the English Premier League, NBA and NFL. Strong selection of foreign brews and decent pub grub: fish and chips, pizzas, burgers and salads, as well as Mexican dishes. Also has a pool table and is nonsmoking. It's in a complex of bars and restaurants a ¥25 taxi ride from the centre.

☆ Entertainment

Nuts Live House LIVE MUSIC
(坚果, Jiān Guǒ; ☑133 5037 9029; https://site. douban.com/nutslivehouse; B1-21, Deyi Fashion Mall, Xinhua Lu, 新华路得意世界负一楼; ⊙7pm-2am Tue-Sat; Ⓜ Jiaochangkou) Fabulous, belowground club that's *the* place to catch live music. Local bands take to the stage every weekend, but it also hosts any act of note passing through. Live music runs from ¥30 to ¥150.

Chongqing Sichuan Opera House THEATRE
(重庆市川剧院, Chóngqìngshì Chuānjùyuàn; ☑023 6371 0153; 76 Jintang Jie, 金汤街76号; tickets ¥40) Holds a 2½-hour performance of Sichuan opera every Saturday afternoon.

🛍 Shopping

For top-name brands, head to the glitzy shopping malls around the Liberation Monument (p809). For souvenirs, try the unashamedly touristy Hongya Cave (p808), or head to Ciqikou Ancient Town (p808).

ℹ Information

MEDICAL SERVICES

Pharmacy (桐君阁大药房, Tóngjūngé Dàyàofáng; 55 Minquan Lu, 民权路55号; ⊙8am-9.30pm; Ⓜ Jiàochǎngkǒu) Western medicine, ground floor; Chinese medicine, 1st floor.

Global Doctor Chongqing Clinic (环球医生重庆诊所, Huánqiú Yīshēng Chóngqìng Zhěnsuǒ; ☑023-8903 8837; Suite 701, 7th fl, Office Tower, Hilton Hotel, 139 Zhongshan Sanlu, 中山三路139号希尔顿酒店商务楼7层701室; ⊙9am-5pm Mon-Fri) A 24-hour emergency service is available by dialling the general clinic number.

MONEY

ATMs are everywhere; many accept foreign cards.

ICBC (Industrial & Commercial Bank of China; Gōngshāng Yínháng; 工商银行; Minzu Lu, 民族路; ⊙9am-4pm; Ⓜ Jiaochangkou) On Minzu Lu beside Liberation Monument. Has a dedicated money-exchange facility.

ICBC (工商银行; Gōngshāng Yínháng; Minquan Lu, 民权路; ⊙24hr; Ⓜ Jiaochangkou) 24-hour ATM.

TRAVEL AGENCIES

At the time of writing a total renovation of the port area in Chaotianmen, the tip of the peninsula, was underway (expected completion date late 2019). This area will contain new ticket halls and docks and may be a better place to buy Three Gorges cruise tickets in the future. Always compare prices and boat options with at least two operators before purchasing.

Travelling With Hostel (p810) can arrange tours of all types (including Three Gorges cruises), with better English-language speakers than the travel agencies and ticket offices around town. It charges minimal commission.

CITS (中国国际旅行社; Zhōngguó Guójì Lǚxíngshè; ☑023 6799 1233; www.cits.net; 132 Minsheng Lu, 民生路132号; ⊙9am-midnight) One of several branches in town, with an

---

CHONGQING'S STILT HOUSING

Once a striking feature of the Chongqing skyline, stilt houses (吊脚楼, *diàojiǎo lóu*) were in many ways the predecessor to the modern skyscraper, expanding vertically rather than horizontally to save space. Their design also served to keep family units in close quarters despite the uneven terrain of hilly Chongqing. They were built on a bamboo or fir frame that was fitted into bore holes drilled into the mountain side, and their thin walls were stuffed with straw and coated with mud to allow for cooling ventilation in a city that swelters in summer.

You'll no longer see any stilt housing in the city, but some survives in the villages around Chongqing municipality, particularly in Zhongshan.

emphasis on booking Three Gorges cruises. Some English spoken.

VISAS

Public Security Bureau (PSB; 公安局出入境管理处, Gōng'ānjú Chūrù Jìngguǎn Lǐchù; ☑ 023 6396 1944; 555 Huanglong Lu, 黄龙路555号; ☉ 9am-noon & 2-5pm; Ⓜ Tangjia Yuanzi, exit 2) Extends visas. Accessed from Ziwei Zhilu (紫薇支路). Take metro line 3 to Tangjia Yuanzi. Leave from exit 2, go up the escalator, turn left then first right, then keep going until you see the large building with flags on your right (10 minutes). Call for a recorded list of requirements in English.

ⓘ Getting There & Away

Chongqing is well connected to the rest of China via rail, bus and air. There are also numerous direct flights to other parts of Asia and beyond.

AIR

Chongqing Jiangbei International Airport (重庆江北国际机场, Chóngqìng Jiāngběi Guójì Jīchǎng; CKG; www.airport-chongqing. com; Ⓜ Jiangbei Airport) is 25km north of the city centre. In addition to extensive domestic connections (including Hong Kong and Lhasa), it also has direct international flights, including, among others: London, Los Angeles, Melbourne, New York, Paris, Singapore and Sydney. As always, it's easiest to book online. Try www.trip. com or www.elong.net.

BOAT

Chongqing is the starting point for hugely popular cruises down the Yangzi River through the magnificent Three Gorges. All boats dock at the port area in Chaotianmen.

BUS

Chongqing has several long-distance bus stations, but most buses use **Caiyuanba Bus Station** (菜园坝汽车站, Càiyuánbà Qìchēzhàn; Caiyuan Lu, 菜园路; Ⓜ Lianglukou) beside the old train station. There is no English spoken.

One of the world's longest **escalators** (皇冠大扶梯, Huángguān Dàfútī; ¥2; ☉ 6.45am-10pm) connects the bus station with the Lianglukou metro station (located much higher up the hill). The bottom entrance is hidden on the far side of the train station square — you'll definitely appreciate it more on the way up!

Destinations include the following:

Chengdu (成都; Sichuan) ¥77, four hours, every hour (9am, 12.10pm and 4.40pm)

Chishui (赤水; Guizhou) ¥70, 3½ hours, six daily (7.40am to 6.30pm)

Dazu (大足) ¥43, two hours, hourly (7.40am to 6.20pm)

Hechuan (合川) ¥29, 1½ to two hours, half-hourly (8.10am to 6.10pm)

Yibin (宜宾; Sichuan) ¥97, four hours, half-hourly (7.10am to 7.40pm)

Yongchuan (永川) ¥34, 1½ to two hours, hourly (7am to 9pm)

Buses for **Jiangjin** (江津; ¥24, 1½ hours, half-hourly, 6.50 am to 7.50pm) leave from the smaller Hall 3 (3号) across the street; take the underpass.

TRAIN

All high-speed trains use Chongqing's North Station, West Station or (less frequently) Shapingba Station; some local trains still use the older station at Caiyuanba, known simply as Chongqing Station. Try to get a ticket to/from the North Station, as the West Station is far away and hard to reach – pay particularly close attention to trains for/from Chengdu. The West Station will eventually be connected to the metro via line 5 and the Loop line.

North Station (重庆北站, Chóngqìng Běizhàn) is divided into two *unconnected* parts – the North Square side (北广场, Běi Guǎngchǎng) and the South Square side (南广场, Nán Guǎngchǎng). All high-speed trains leave from the North Square and all regular trains leave from the South Square, but try to double-check with someone when purchasing tickets to avoid any unpleasant surprises. You cannot get from the South Square to the North Square except by metro (line 10). It's a big place, so give yourself extra time to navigate. All ticket sales are on the ground floor level (outside) in Ticket Hall 1. If you're picking up prebooked tickets, you can also do that one floor down (up from the metro) at Ticket Hall 3.

Destinations from the North Station include the following:

Beijing West G-class 1st class/2nd ¥1267/792, 12 hours, one daily (9.30am)

Beijing West Z-, T-, K-class hard sleeper from ¥418, 19 to 31 hours, six daily

Chengdu East D-/G-class seats ¥97/154, 1¼ to 2¼ hours, frequent

Shanghai Hongqiao D-class seat from ¥585, 10½ to 12 hours, seven daily

Wuhan D- & G-class seat from ¥270, 6½ to 7½ hours, frequent

Xi'an North D-class seat from ¥280, five hours, three daily (2.16pm, 6.04pm and 6.32pm)

Destinations only departing from the West Station include the following:

Guilin D-class 1st class/2nd from ¥400/250, 4½ to five hours, frequent

Kunming G-class 1st class/2nd from ¥564/342, four to five hours, frequent

ⓘ Getting Around

TO/FROM THE AIRPORT

Metro Line 3 goes from the airport into town (¥7, 45 minutes, 6.30am to 10.30pm). Note: the metro may be signposted as 'Light Rail' in some places at the airport.

A taxi should cost anywhere from ¥50 to ¥75 depending on your destination.

The **Airport Express Bus k01** (机场快线 k01 路, Jīchǎng Kuàixiàn Yīlù; ¥15, 45 min) operates half-hourly from the first flight to the last, running from the airport to central Chongqing (near Jiefangbei); it's most useful for late-night arrivals. The city stop is located across from the Guotai Plaza Mall, in between Wusi Lu and Zourong Lu.

BUS

Tourist buses T480A and T480B run between Hongya Cave, the Yangzi River Cable Car, and Huguang Guild Hall (among other places) from 9am to 6pm, and cost ¥10 per ride or ¥30 for a 24-hour pass. They come every 20 minutes. Local bus fares are ¥2, though the metro is more convenient and easier to navigate.

METRO

Chongqing's metro system had eight lines at the time of writing, with more on the way. Fares are ¥2 to ¥10 and trains run (roughly) from 6.30am to 10.30pm. Signs are bilingual and the electronic ticket machines have an English option. The airport and all major train and bus stations (except, at the time of research, for the West Train Station) are connected to the metro system.

TAXI

Taxi flag fall is ¥10. A taxi from Jiefangbei to Shapingba should cost around ¥45.

Dazu Buddhist Caves 大足石刻

The superb rock carvings of Dazu (Dàzú Shíkū) are a Unesco World Heritage Site and one of China's four great Buddhist cave-sculpture sites, along with those at Dunhuang, Luoyang and Datong. The Dazu sculptures are the most recent of the four, and the artwork here is distinctly more Chinese in style – with ghosts, monsters and Confucian influences – when compared with its Silk Road counterparts.

Scattered over roughly 40 sites are thousands of cliff carvings and statues, dating from the Tang dynasty (9th century) to the Song dynasty (13th century). The main groupings are at Treasured Summit Hill and North Hill.

◉ Sights

Treasured Summit Hill ARCHAEOLOGICAL SITE
(宝顶山, Bǎodǐng Shān; ¥115, joint ticket with North Hill ¥140; ⊙ 8.30am-6pm) If you only have time

for one Dazu stop, make it this, the largest and most impressive of the sites. Of all the stunning sculptures here, which are believed to have been carved between 1174 and 1252, the centrepiece is a 31m-long, 5m-high reclining Buddha depicted entering nirvana, with the torso sunk into the cliff face. Next to the Buddha, protected by a temple, is a mesmerising gold Avalokiteshvara (Guanyin, the Goddess of Mercy).

Treasured Summit Hill differs from other cave sites in that it incorporates some of the area's natural features – a sculpture next to the reclining Buddha, for example, makes use of an underground spring.

The site is about 15km northeast of Dazu town and is accessed by buses from town. Dazu has two bus stations: old and new. Buses from Chongqing drop you at Dazu's old bus station (老站, lǎozhàn). Buses from Chengdu drop you at Dazu's new bus station (新站, xīnzhàn). Bus 205 (¥3, 30 minutes) runs direct from both stations. Once at the site, it's a shadeless 25-minute walk from where the bus drops you off to the entrance to the sculptures (electric carts do less than half of the walk for ¥10). Buses returning from Treasured Summit Hill run until 6.30pm.

North Hill ARCHAEOLOGICAL SITE
(北山, Běi Shān; ¥70, combination ticket with Treasured Hill Summit ¥140; ⊙ 8.30am-6pm) This site, originally a military camp, contains some of the region's earliest carvings. The dark niches hold several hundred statues. Some are in poor condition, but it is still well worth a visit.

The pleasant, forested North Hill is about a 30-minute hike from Dazu town; turn left out of the old bus station and keep asking the way. It's about ¥10 in a taxi.

Buddha Vairocana Cave CAVE
(毗卢洞, Pílú Dòng) The truly adventurous might like to catch a bus to the tiny town of Shiyang (石羊, Shíyáng), which has a little-seen collection of Song dynasty Buddhist rock carvings.

Buses to Shiyang, just over the border in Sichuan province, leave from Dazu's old bus station. When you get there, keep asking for Pílú Dòng (毗卢洞); it's walking distance. From Shiyang, you can continue by bus to Chengdu.

Stone Gate Hill & Stone Seal Hill ARCHAEOLOGICAL SITE
If you're really into Buddhist rock carvings, try to get out to the rarely visited sculptures at **Stone Gate Hill** (石门山, Shímén Shān),

FISHING TOWN FORTRESS

Famed throughout China for being one of the great ancient battlegrounds, the 700-year-old **Fishing Town Fortress** (钓鱼城, Diàoyú Chéng; ¥60; ⊙8.30am-5pm) is perched on top of a 300m-tall hill at a bend in the Jialing River. The Yangzi Basin was the last stand of the Southern Song dynasty and famously, in the 13th century, the fortress withstood the mighty Mongol armies for an incredible 36 years, during which time an estimated 200 battles were fought here.

The fortress was protected by an 8km-long, 30m-tall double wall, punctuated with eight gate towers. Much of the outer wall and all the main gates remain today; some partly restored, others crumbling away. There is little here in terms of facilities apart from a noodle vendor or two, but it's a fascinating and peaceful place to walk around. Narrow stone pathways lead you through the forest, past Buddhist rock carvings, temples, engraved poems, bamboo groves, the wall and its gateways and some fabulous lookout points. Sights not to miss include the serene, 11m-long, 1000-year-old **Sleeping Buddha** (卧佛, Wòfó), cut into the overhang of a cliff; **Huguo Temple** (护国寺, Hùguó Sì), dating from the Tang dynasty, although largely rebuilt; and the **Imperial Cave** (黄洞, Huángdòng), an ancient drainage passage with steps leading down to it, clinging to the outside of the fort wall.

Three high-speed trains running to Hechuan from Chongqing North train station (from ¥20, 25 minutes, 7.17am, 7.58am, 8.54am) are the best way to get here, but they often sell out – book ahead. Alternatively, you can take the much longer bus ride from Caiyuanba station (¥29, 1½ to two hours, half-hourly, 8.10am to 6.10pm).

Once in Hechuan, you'll need to take a taxi to the fortress. It's about ¥25 from the train station and ¥10 from the bus station. The last train back to Chongqing is at 9.43pm; the last bus is at 7pm.

19km southeast of Dazu, or those at **Stone Seal Hill** (石篆山, Shízhuàn Shān), 20km southwest of town. You'll have to take a taxi (about ¥90 to Shizhuan Shan).

South Hill
ARCHAEOLOGICAL SITE

(南山, Nán Shān; ¥5; ⊙8.30am-6pm) This modest site really only has one set of carvings, but makes a nice appetiser before you delve into the main courses at North Hill and Treasured Summit Hill. It's behind the old bus station and takes around 15 minutes to walk to. It's ¥10 in a taxi.

🛏 Sleeping & Eating

Dazu is usually visited as a day trip from Chongqing. If you plan to stay overnight, there are several hotels in Dazu city, though many don't accept foreigners.

There are plenty of eating options near the Dazu bus stations. Treasured Summit Hill has stalls serving simple meals at both the entrance and exit. Group tours of the area include a lunch stop.

❶ Getting There & Away

Astute travellers may notice that bullet trains serve Dazu South Station. However, this station is one hour by bus (30km) from Dazu city, and thus doesn't really save you any time if you're coming from Chongqing.

Buses from Dazu old station (老站, lǎozhàn) include the following:

Chongqing ¥43, two hours, every 20 minutes (6.20am to 6pm)

Hechuan (for Fishing Town Fortress) ¥30, 1½ hours, frequent (8am to 5pm)

Jiangjin (for Zhongshan) ¥50, two hours, two daily (7.50am and 2pm)

Shiyang ¥12, one hour, every 40 minutes (7.20am to 5.20pm)

Yongchuan (for Songji) ¥22, 1½ hours, every 30 minutes (7am to 5.30pm)

Buses from Dazu new station (新站, xīnzhàn) include the following:

Chengdu ¥85, 2½ hours, four daily (7.50am to 2.30pm)

Leshan ¥90, four hours, one daily (8am)

Zigong ¥60, two hours, one daily (8am)

Laitan 涞滩古镇

📋 023 / POP 24,430

The main attraction in Laitan (Láitān Gǔzhèn), a walled village overlooking the Qu River, is Erfo Temple's towering Buddha, carved into a hillside and surrounded by more than 1000 mini statues. The Erfo Temple is divided in two, with a less interesting upper temple (¥10) and the main **lower temple** (二佛寺, Èrfó Sì; ¥20; ⊙8am-5.30pm), where you'll find the vast Buddha sculpture, which dates back to the Tang and Song dynasties. It's one of the largest in the Sichuan area (the temple name, Second Buddha, refers to the fact that it is smaller than the Leshan Buddha, which is number one). At the time of writing, the statue was closed for restoration.

Allow time to wander around the picturesque village, checking out the small shops and Qing architecture. As Laitan is accessed from the town of Hechuan, it's easy to combine it with a trip to nearby Fishing Town Fortress. Three high-speed trains run to Hechuan from Chongqing North train station (from ¥20, 25 minutes, 7.17am, 7.58am, 8.54am), but they often sell out – book ahead. Alternatively, you can take the much-longer bus to Hechuan.

From Hechuan's main bus station (客运中心站; *kèyùn zhōngxīn zhàn*), there are direct buses to Laitan (¥11, one hour, six daily, 7.10am to 4.10pm) as well as regular buses to Longshi (¥11, one hour). From Longshi, minibuses (¥2, five minutes) leave for Laitan from outside the bus station.

The last train back to Chongqing is at 9.43pm; the last bus is at 7pm.

Zhongshan 中山

☑ 023 / POP 20,500

Chongqing's once-ubiquitous stilt houses have all but disappeared from the city itself, but visit the gorgeous riverside village of Zhongshan (Zhōngshān) and you'll find plenty of them to gawp at. The **old town** (古镇, *gǔzhèn*) is essentially one long street lined with wooden homes on stilts above the riverbank. Walk down to the river and look up to see their support structures. You can also hike along the other side of the river.

Most residents have turned their front rooms into storefronts. While some hawk souvenir trinkets, others sell locally made products such as chilli sauce or jugs of rice wine. Popular snacks include squares of smoked tofu (烟熏豆腐, *yānxūn dòufu*) and sweet doughy rice cakes filled with ground nuts.

There are a few simple local guesthouses in town (rooms ¥30 to ¥100). Look for signs saying 住宿 (*zhùsù*, lodgings). Most are small but clean and the more expensive rooms have their own bathrooms and great river views.

Several local restaurants and guesthouses will cook up a meal for you. Look for *gǔzhèn lǎolàròu* (古镇老腊肉, cured pork fried with green chillies), *héshuǐ dòufu* (河水豆腐, river water tofu) and *yě cài* (野菜, a type of spinach).

To get here from Chongqing, change buses at Jiangjin (江津), from where buses leave for Zhongshan (¥19.50, one hour 45 minutes, hourly, 5.30am to 5.30pm). The last bus back to Jiangjin is around 4.20pm. The last bus from Jiangjin back to Chongqing is at 6pm – try to get a bus to Caiyuanba Station (¥27, 1½ hours), which is more central; other buses run to Longtousi Station (¥27, two hours). You can also head south into Guizhou province from Jiangjin, via Zunyi (遵义; ¥107, 3½ hours, 9.10am and 2.10pm), or north to the caves at Dazu (大足; ¥51, two hours, 7.50am and 2pm).

Wulong 武隆喀斯特

☑ 023 / POP 351,000 (WULONG COUNTY)

Head three or so hours southeast of Chongqing City and you enter Wulong (Wǔlóng Kāsītè), a dramatic landscape where deep ravines cut through the thickly forested hills, while waterfalls plunge into mighty rivers, and jagged limestone karst formations rise up towards the sky. Mostly off the map for foreign travellers, the Wulong County National Geology Park is a fantastic place to experience this wild scenery.

◎ Sights

Wulong County
National Geology Park PARK

(武隆国家地质公园, Wǔlóng Guójiā Dìzhí Gōngyuán) About 20km from the town of Wulong, this fairy-tale landscape of gorges, sinkholes, natural bridges and mossy caves lies deep within the mountains about three hours from Chongqing. The park has three main areas: Three Natural Bridges, **Qingkou Tiankeng Scenic Area** and Furong Cave (p832). Most visitors come to Wulong via organised tours from Chongqing, which usually stop at the Three Natural Bridges area, home to three magnificent natural bridges you can gaze at from beneath.

Three Natural Bridges NATURAL FEATURE

(天生三桥, Tiānshēng Sān Qiáo; ¥125; ⏱9am-4.30pm) Towering above huge, hollowed-out limestone sinkholes, these natural bridges (you don't walk across them) are the highest in the world. A wander through the mossy, green gorge beneath the bridges takes about two hours. A vertiginous glass elevator takes you into the gorge; once down, sedan-chair carriers will try to offer you a lift and electric trams whisk the hiking-averse up the hill back to the bus terminal.

Longshui Gorge
CANYON

(龙水峡, Lóngshuǐ Xiá; ¥115; ⏰8.30am-4.30pm) A tall glass elevator lowers you to the floor of this deep gorge, created by the flow of an ancient river. It takes an hour or two to wander the length of the canyon, exploring dripping caves and traversing elevated pathways over milky green waters. Numerous waterfalls along the rocky gorge walls mean you can expect to get a little damp.

Furong Cave
CAVE

(芙蓉洞, ¥150; ⏰8.30am-4.30pm) This vast karst cavern is hung with dripping stalactites and lined with surreal rock formations, all lit up with multicoloured stage lights. Follow a guide along the raised pathway for some 2km, passing stone 'waterfalls' and rocks shaped like dragons or Buddhas.

From the Wulong bus station, shuttle buses run to Furong Cave, or you can take a taxi. Admission prices are lower in winter.

🛏 Sleeping

Yuzhu Garden Hotel
HOTEL ¥¥

(武隆瑜珠花园酒店, Yúzhū Huāyuán Jiǔdiàn; ☎023 7779 9888; www.yuzhugardenhotel.com; 16 Furong Xilu, 芙蓉西路16號; r from ¥300) If you're planning on staying overnight in Wulong town, this international-style riverfront hotel is your best bet. Despite its luxury trappings, some guests have reported hard beds, though that's par for the course in this part of the world. It has a Chinese restaurant, and is an easy walk from other restaurants and a market.

ℹ Getting There & Away

Visiting the park as an independent traveller can be done, but it is time-consuming and expensive. While there are a few trains (¥25, two hours, 7am, 2.50pm, 7.50pm) to the unremarkable town of Wulong from Chongqing, the main sights are 22km northeast of there. Some buses do run from Wulong to the different gateway towns for each sight, but given the time constraints, hiring a taxi for the day is best. Each site also has a separate (and pricey) admission ticket, while the restaurants and hotels scattered around the park are expensive.

The best way to visit is as part of a group on a day tour. Expect to pay ¥350 to ¥400 (bring your passport), which will include all transport, lunch and admission to the Three Natural Bridges and at least one other site, usually Longshui Gorge. Travelling With Hostel (p810) in Chongqing can arrange tours, which depart at 7am and return around 7pm.

Songji
松溉

♪023 / POP 50,000

Winding cobblestone alleyways housing temples, teahouses, old gateways and some wonderful courtyard homes dominate this still-lived-in Ming dynasty village on the banks of the Yangzi River. Deep in southwest Chongqing, Songji (Sōngjì) is a genuine community, rather than just a tourist destination, and sees very few foreigners, making it a pleasant place to wander.

To guide yourself around the lanes, take a photo of the large wooden bilingual map at the entrance to the old town (古镇, gǔzhèn), just down towards the river from where the bus drops you off.

If you're looking for a focus, seek out the **Chen Family Compound** (陈家大院, Chén Jiā Dàyuàn; ¥2), the historic home of the village's most prominent family. This sprawling structure once contained more than 100 rooms. What remains of the compound is much smaller, but its walls are extensively decorated with family photos and memorabilia. Actress/director Joan Chen (Chen Chong), who starred in Bernardo Bertolucci's *The Last Emperor* and Ang Lee's *Lust, Caution*, is the most famous family member. It's tricky to find; ask for directions.

On a bluff above the river, about a 20-minute walk from the old town, is the **Dongyu Temple** (东狱庙, Dōngyù Miào), home to a 9.5m-tall Buddha and some gruesome dioramas depicting various hells (impaling, scalding, having your tongue ripped out).

Most of Songji's few visitors come on a day trip. There is one **hotel** (Songshan Binguan, 松山宾馆; ☎023 4954 6078; 9 Binjiang Jie, Old Town, 滨江街9号; r from ¥100; ⚒🛜) in the old town as well as a few options in the new town. **Gǔzhèn Jiǔdàwǎn** (古镇九大碗; Songzi Shan, 松子山; dishes ¥20-50; ⏰11am-6.30pm), a nicely renovated old ancestral temple, has been turned into a restaurant and teahouse, and has reasonably priced dishes.

ℹ Getting There & Away

There's one direct bus from Chongqing (¥41, 1½ to two hours, 1.20pm). Otherwise, catch a bus to Yongchuan (¥34, 1½ to two hours), from where buses to Songji (¥12, 70 minutes) leave every 20 to 30 minutes from the *kèyùn zhōngxīn* (客运中心) station (you may be dropped off at a different nearby station, a ¥5 taxi ride away). The last bus back to Yongchuan leaves Songji at about 5.50pm. The last bus from Yongchuan to Chongqing leaves around 6.10pm.

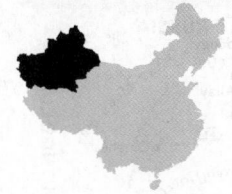

Xinjiang

POP 22.1 MILLION

Best Natural Scenery

➡ Shipton's Arch (p845)

➡ Flaming Mountains (p842)

➡ Tian Chi Lake (p840)

➡ Kanas Lake Nature Reserve (p854)

➡ Bulunkou Lake (p849)

Best Ancient Sights

➡ Bezeklik Cave Complex (p841)

➡ Jiaohe Ruins (p841)

➡ Gaochang (p842)

➡ Melikawat Ruins (p851)

➡ Zaghunluq Ancient Mummy Tomb (p852)

Why Go?

China's largest province, Xinjiang (新疆, Xīnjiāng) is the homeland of the Muslim Uyghurs and a fast-changing region where ancient and modern push up against each other in surprising ways. High-speed railways cross the Martian-like landscapes, linking cities in hours rather than days, and the regional capital Ürümqi is a forest of high-rise apartments and glass skyscrapers; yet, in the Silk Road oases of Kashgar, Hotan and Turpan, life goes as it has for centuries, based around the mosque, the teahouse and the bazaar.

Despite the military and police presence here due to years of unrest, Xinjiang offers extraordinary natural beauty and fascinating Central Asian history and culture. This province of 'Chinese Turkestan' offers insights into China's past and its unsettled multicultural present, and glimpses of some of the most sublime landscapes on earth.

When to Go

Ürümqi

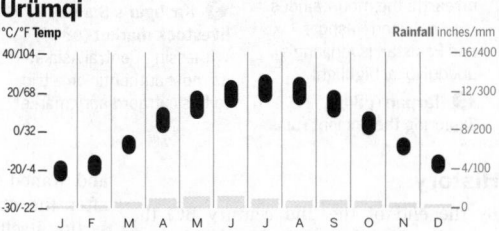

Mar Nowruz (New Year) festivals are held in Kazakh and Kyrgyz villages.	May Sunny days and cool breezes make this one of the best times to visit Xinjiang.	Sep Sublime autumnal colours at Kanas Lake and Hemu.

Xinjiang Highlights

❶ Karakoram Highway (p849) Travelling quite possibly one of the most extraordinary road journeys on earth; the mountainous road between Kashgar and Pakistan is Xinjiang's unequivocal highlight.

❷ Turpan (p841) Exploring the ancient ruins, magnificent mountain landscapes and Buddhist caves surrounding this laid-back oasis town.

❸ Kashgar's Sunday livestock market (p846) Witnessing Central Asia at its most authentic on a trip to this extraordinary market.

❹ Hotan Sunday market (p850) Choosing between silk, spices, jade and carpets at this centuries-old bazaar.

❺ Kanas Lake Nature Reserve (p854) Heading into Xinjiang's remote north to see the magnificent scenery of this mountainous nature reserve.

History

By the end of the 2nd century BC, the expanding Han dynasty had pushed its borders west into what is now Xinjiang. Military garrisons protected the fledgling trade routes, as silk flowed out of the empire in return for the strong Ferghana horses needed to fight nomadic incursions from the north. Chinese imperial rule waxed and waned over the centuries, shrinking after the collapse of the Han and reasserting itself during the 7th-century Tang, though central control was tenuous at best. A Uyghur kingdom based at Khocho (now known as the ruined city of Gaochang in Turpan) thrived from the 8th century and oversaw the Central Asian people's transformation from nomads to farmers and from Manichaeans to Buddhists.

It was during Kharakhanid rule in the 10th to 12th centuries that Islam took hold in Xinjiang. In 1219, Ili (modern Yining), Hotan and Kashgar fell to the Mongols and their various successors controlled the whole of Central Asia until the mid-18th century, when the Manchu army marched into Kashgar.

In 1865, a Kokandi officer named Yaqub Beg seized Kashgaria, proclaimed a short-lived independent Turkestan, and made diplomatic contacts with Britain and Russia. The Manchu army eventually returned and two decades later Kashgaria was formally incorporated into China's newly created Xinjiang (New Frontier) province. With the fall of the Qing dynasty in 1911, Xinjiang came under the chaotic and violent rule of a succession of Muslim and Chinese warlords, over whom the Kuomintang (the Nationalist Party) had very little control. In the 1930s and 1940s there was an attempt in both Kashgar and Ili to establish an independent republic of East Turkestan, but both were short-lived.

Since 1949 the Chinese government's main social goal in Xinjiang has been to keep a lid on ethnic separatism, dilute local culture, and flood the region with Han Chinese. Economically, the 'Develop the West' campaign has used the region's oil resources to ramp up the local economy. But this has led to an increase in Han settlers, which has exacerbated ethnic tensions. In a telling statistic, Uyghurs once composed 90% of Xinjiang's population; today they make up less than 50%. But despite the unease and resentment of the native population, Xinjiang remained peaceful throughout the 1990s and early 2000s as China began to open up to the outside world.

However, in 2008 street protests and bomb attacks rocked the province, and in 2009 communal violence between Han and Uyghur civilians in central Ürümqi led to around 200 deaths and 1700 injuries, according to Chinese police reports. Protests, riots and terrorist acts have continued to simmer ever since. In 2014 a knife attack at a train station in Kunming (Yunnan province) that killed 29 and injured 143 was blamed on Uyghur separatists. The next month, two attackers stabbed people at the Ürümqi train station before setting off vest explosives. A few weeks later, a suicide car and bomb attack on a market in Ürümqi ended with 31 killed and 90 injured. As a direct result, the Chinese authorities launched a huge security crackdown, the 'Strike Hard Campaign against Violent Terrorism', the results of which can still be seen on any street corner in the province. Hundreds of Uyghurs were sentenced to long jail terms and dozens were executed. In 2016 Chen Quanguo, known for his hardline policies, became party secretary in Xinjiang. Since then, reports have circulated of unverified numbers of Uyghurs, Kazakhs, Hui, Kyrgyz and other ethnic and religious minorities being sent to government-run 'Vocational Education and Training Centers' for re-education.

The current situation remains tense. As long as Uyghur resentment continues to be fuelled by what they view as economic marginalisation, cultural restrictions, ethnic discrimination and outright oppression, violence looks likely to remain a threat in the province. However, apart from the heavy police and security measures present, including checkpoints, metal detectors and other security scans, Xinjiang remains open to travellers.

❶ Information

Old Roads Tours (www.oldroadtours.com) Kashgar-based travel agency run by a local Uyghur family. Can organise full tours of Xinjiang, including permits for the Karakoram Highway.

❶ Getting There & Away

You can fly between Xinjiang and most large Chinese cities, as well as to several Central Asian capitals and a couple of cities further afield, including Moscow, Tehran, Dubai, Seoul and Vienna.

There are overland border crossings with Pakistan (Khunjerab Pass), Kyrgyzstan (Irkeshtam and Torugart Passes) and Kazakhstan (Nur Zholy, Alashankou, Tacheng and Jimunai). The remote Qolma (Kulma) Pass to Tajikistan appears officially closed to foreigners, though since 2017 a number of travellers, including cyclists, have reported transiting through this crossing. There

---

❶ PRICE RANGES

Sleeping

¥ less than ¥150

¥¥ ¥150–300

¥¥¥ more than ¥300

Eating

¥ less than ¥30 (for a main course)

¥¥ ¥30–50

¥¥¥ more than ¥50

XINJIANG HISTORY

SAFE TRAVEL

Due to the unrest and terrorism that has been a rare – but recurring – feature of life in Xinjiang since 2008, and which most recently peaked again in 2014, the province today has a very visible military and police presence, which can unnerve some. The main function of these patrols is to deter public protests in the cities, and to check the passports of anyone travelling by train or bus. It's essential that you carry your passport with you at all times; you're simply asking for trouble otherwise. The main annoyance for travellers is the sheer amount of time that just getting into a train station can take, or the number of stops a long-distance bus is obliged to make, during which Chinese citizens will be required to disembark to have their IDs scanned. As foreign passports cannot be scanned in this way, you may or may not be required to disembark yourself; await instructions at each checkpoint. Note that you may not bring cigarette lighters, a pocket knife, scissors or anything that could potentially be used as a weapon, however seemingly innocuous, onto any bus or train.

are no buses to this pass. The rest of these are served by chartered car or bus; Alashankou is China's only rail link to Central Asia.

Heading back into mainland China, the obvious route is the high-speed train line following the Silk Road through Gansu.

ⓘ Getting Around

Xinjiang is enormous (slightly bigger than Iran), and getting around usually takes time, money or both. The bus is the standard way to get around, and while bus journeys are cheap, new laws forbidding drivers to drive overnight and constant document checks along the way have increased travel times over the past few years. Buses are often sleepers, which means you're on either the top (cheaper) or bottom (pricier) bunk, arranged in three lines down the middle of the bus. On-board entertainment usually includes kung fu-film marathons cranked to the hilt. Shared taxis run along many of the bus routes, taking up to half as long, and costing twice as much as buses. Shared taxis only depart when full.

In 2015 the Ürümqi–Lanzhou high-speed railway line opened, massively cutting travel times across Eastern Xinjiang. In the west of the province, train journeys are not nearly as fast, but they're a lot of fun on overnight sleepers – a great way to meet locals.

Flying around the province can save a lot of time and tickets are often discounted by up to 60%. Be aware that flights can sometimes be cancelled for lack of passengers or due to bad weather, but if you have more money than time, this is a good way to claw some back.

CENTRAL XINJIANG

Bound by deserts and mountain ranges, much of present-day Central Xinjiang would have been completely familiar to Silk Road traders on the Northern Route to Kashgar. Today the largest and most important city in the region is Xinjiang's capital, Ürümqi, though for travellers the ancient cities around Turpan, the Tian Shan mountains, and the Buddha caves of Kuqa are the bigger draws.

ⓘ Getting There & Away

Most people fly into Ürümqi, though the high-speed railway link now connects the regional capital to the rest of China, including stops at both Hami and Turpan.

Ürümqi　乌鲁木齐

📞 0991 / POP 3.1 MILLION

In Xinjiang's capital, Ürümqi (Wūlǔmùqí), high-rise apartments form a modern skyline that will soon dash any thoughts of spotting wandering camels and ancient caravanserais. The vast majority of its inhabitants are Han Chinese, and the city is one of the least typical of Xinjiang, though glimpses of the distant Tian Shan mountains provide a taste of the extraordinary landscapes awaiting you elsewhere.

As a fast-growing Central Asian hub, the city does business with traders from Beijing to Baku and plays host to an exotic mix of people. Indeed, it's hard to imagine where else in the world you'll see Chinese, Arabic, Latin and Cyrillic script so commonly side-by-side. This truly is Central Asia.

Ürümqi is not a historic city, but its museum is excellent and there are some atmospheric Uyghur districts. Most travellers pass through the provincial capital at some point, and many find their stay to be surprisingly enjoyable.

⊙ Sights

★ Xinjiang Autonomous Region Museum
MUSEUM

(新疆自治区博物馆, Xīnjiāng Zìzhìqū Bówùguǎn; ☑ 0991 455 2826; 581 Xibei Lu; ⊙ 10.30am-4.30pm Tue-Sun) FREE Xinjiang's massive provincial museum is a must for Silk Road aficionados. The highlight is the locally famous 'Loulan Beauty', the first of half a dozen 3800-year-old desert-mummified bodies of Xinjiang's erstwhile Indo-European inhabitants. Other exhibits include some amazing silks, decorative arts, pottery and sculpture, a collection of white jade and an introduction to the traditions of each of the province's minorities. From the Hóngshān Intersection, take bus 7 for four stops and ask to get off at the museum (bówùguǎn).

An English-language audio guide is available; you'll need to leave a ¥200 deposit at the tourist centre by the entrance.

Hongshan Park
PARK

(红山公园, Hóngshān Gōngyuán; 40 Hongshan Beilu, Yi Xiang; 红山路北一巷40号; park free, pagoda ¥20; ⊙ dawn-dusk) More of an amusement park than a natural wonder, Hongshan Park is nevertheless a great place to stroll and enjoy the good city views, particularly from the 18th-century hilltop pagoda, which has become something of a city icon. The main southern entrance is to the north of the Xidaqiao Intersection – it can be hard to find

---

ⓘ BORDER CROSSINGS

To Kyrgyzstan

There are two passes into Kyrgyzstan: the Torugart Pass, which leads to Naryn and then Bishkek in the north; and the Irkeshtam Pass, which goes to Osh in the south.

Going through the Irkeshtam Pass and on to Osh is straightforward, and there may be sleeper buses available from Kashgar's **international bus station** (国际汽车站; Guójì Qìchēzhàn; ☑ 138 9916 8559, 138 9914 0624). You can also charter a car through a Kashgar agency, though no special permits or guides are needed for this route.

Crossing the Torugart Pass involves more red tape, for which you will need a travel agency's help. You will also need to have arranged transport on the Kyrgyz side, which travel agents can organise in Naryn or Bishkek. The pass is open year-round to foreigners (weather permitting), though taxis cannot go here; only cars with permits allowing them to make the journey may pass. Cyclists can go from Kyrgyzstan into China this way, but need to have proof of travel-agency arranged transport on the Chinese side through customs.

Most travellers do not need a visa to enter Kyrgyzstan, so the red tape is at least simplified in that respect.

To Pakistan

Trips from Kashgar to Sost in Pakistan are done in two stages – there is no direct bus. Take a bus to Tashkurgan from Kashgar's local bus station (p849), and then stay overnight at Tashkurgan, before continuing the following morning on a minibus to Sost (which runs only Monday to Friday).

Officially, the border opens daily between 1 April and 1 November. However, the border can open late or close early depending on conditions at the Khunjerab Pass, and is always closed on weekends. The Chinese customs and immigration formalities are dealt with beforehand at Tashkurgan (3km down the road towards Pakistan). Then it's 126km to the last checkpost at Khunjerab Pass, the actual border, where your documents are checked again before you head into Pakistan. Pakistan immigration formalities are performed at Sost. Pakistani visas are not available to tourists on arrival (and visas are difficult to get in Beijing), so arrive in China with a visa obtained in your home country. Check the current situation as this could change.

To Tajikistan

The 4362m Qolma (Kulma) Pass linking Kashgar with Murghab (via Tashkurgan) opened in 2004 to local traders, and some travellers have reported success passing through here, though officially it is closed to international travellers. You'll require a Tajik visa (some nationalities are eligible for an e-visa) beforehand. A more reliable option is to travel via Irkeshtam Pass in Kyrgyzstan.

Ürümqi

N

0 — 500 m
0 — 0.25 miles

Yema International Business Clubhouse (4km);
Kazakhstan Consulate (5km)

High-speed
(8km)

Kelamayi Xilu

Nanhu Nanlu

(13km)

Xibei Lu

Xinjiang
1 Autonomous
Region
Museum

XINJIANG

Hetan Gonglu

Youhao Nanlu

Kyrgyzstan
Consulate

South Lake
Square (Nánhú
Guǎngchǎng)

Xihong Lu

Xinmin Lu

Binhe Nanlu

Nanliangpo Lu

China Southern
Ticket Office

Hóng
Shān

3

Hongshan Lu

Hóngshān
Intersection

Youhao Nanlu

Xidàqiáo
Intersection

Guangming Lu

光明路 North
Gate
(Běi Mén)

SHAYIBAK

Buses to
Tiān Chí

Xinhua Beilu

Jianshe Lu

Jiefang Beilu

Yangzijiang Lu

Wenhuagong
Lu

Gongyuan Beijie 公园北街

4

Minzhu Lu

民主路

Heping Canal

Main Bus
Station

Ürümqi
International
Bus Station

Renmin Lu 人民路

Zhongshan Lu

Hongqi Lu

Wenhua Lu

South
Gate
(Nán Mén)

Wuyi Lu 五一路

Qitai Lu 奇台路

Xinhua Nanlu

Mashi Xiang

Changjiang Lu 长江路

Huanghe Lu 黄河路

Hetan Jie
和田街

Hetan Dongyijie

Longquan Jie 龙泉街

Jiefang Nanlu

Heping Nanlu 和平南路

Train Ticket
Booking
Office

Ürümqi
Train Station

5

Qiantangjiang Lu

Hetan Gonglu

South
(2.5km)

Rendezvous
(2.5km)

2

Ürümqi

◎ Top Sights
1 Xinjiang Autonomous Region
   Museum A2

◎ Sights
2 Erdaoqiao Market D7
3 Hongshan Park....................................C3
4 People's Park.......................................C5

ⓘ Transport
5 Ürümqi South Station A7

your way in elsewhere, as the park is fenced off with totalitarian relish.

People's Park   PARK
(人民公园, Rénmín Gōngyuán; 3 Youhao Nanlu; 友好南路3号; ⊙dawn-dusk) FREE A green oasis with manicured grounds and a ceremonial pagoda in its centre, around which visitors may paddle little boats in the summer months. Like most parks here, its perimeters are sealed with high fences and razor wire: enter either via the park's north or south entrance.

Erdaoqiao Market   BAZAAR
(二道桥市场, Èrdàoqiáo Shìchǎng; 589 Jiefang Lu; 🚌1, 7, 912) FREE The Erdaoqiao Market and nearby **International Bazaar** (Guójì Dàbāzhá) have undergone extensive 'redevelopment' in recent years and are now aimed more at Chinese tour groups than Uyghur traders. Planted in the bazaar is a replica of the Kalon Minaret from Bukhara in Uzbekistan (though the 12th-century original doesn't have a lift inside it). The surrounding streets are worth a stroll for their Uyghur markets and snack stalls.

🍴 Eating & Drinking

Ürümqi has the greatest variety of cuisine available in Xinjiang, whether it be the ad hoc Uyghur street food that takes over entire neighbourhoods in the evenings, or the more formal restaurants offering cuisine from all regions of China and beyond.

Ürümqi has small patches of nightlife, though partying and drinking are somewhat muted here compared to other cities of a similar size. The largest variety of bars and clubs is situated along the western side of People's Park.

ⓘ Information

Public Security Bureau (PSB; 公安局; Gōng'ānjú; 🕿 0991 281 0452, ext 3456; 30

Nanhu Donglu; 南湖东路30号; ⊙10am-1.30pm & 4-6pm Mon-Fri) It's far preferable to avoid having to renew your visa in Ürümqi; it is normally possible here, though it might take three weeks.

ⓘ Getting There & Away

AIR
Ürümqi Diwopu International Airport is a big hub; international destinations include Almaty (Kazakhstan), Bishkek (Kyrgyzstan), Baku (Azerbaijan), Tbilisi (Georgia), Islamabad (Pakistan), Seoul (South Korea), Dubai (UAE), Moscow (Russia), Dushanbe (Tajikistan), Tashkent (Uzbekistan) and Tehran (Iran). Some of these flights are seasonal, however, and schedules change with great regularity.

You can get to Ürümqi by direct flights from almost anywhere in China and a number of destinations within Xinjiang. China Southern runs by far the most flights to and around Xinjiang, and has a central booking office in the **Southern Airlines Pearl International Hotel** (南方航空收票处; Nánfāng Hángkōng Shòupiàochù; 🕿 0991 450 4998; www.csair.com; 576 Youhao Nanlu).

BUS
There are four long-distance bus stations in Ürümqi, which serve destinations in various directions. The most useful station is the **Southern Suburb Passenger Transport Station** (南郊客运站; Nánjiāo Kèyùnzhàn; 1 Yan'erwo Lu; 燕尔窝路1号), which has buses to the south including Kashgar, Turpan and Korla. You can reach this station by the metro and buses 51 or 7.

Tourist **buses to Tian Chi** (return ¥50) leave from the northern end of People's Park.

TRAIN
High-speed trains depart and arrive from Ürümqi's giant, super-modern **main railway station** (乌鲁木齐站; Wūlǔmùqí Zhàn; 1 Gaotie Beilu; 高铁北六路1号). The high-speed line stretches to Lanzhou and, from there, the rest of the Chinese high-speed rail network. Destinations include multiple daily services to Turpan (1st/2nd class ¥82/51.50, one hour), Hami (1st/2nd class ¥266/166.50, three hours) and Lanzhou (1st/2nd class ¥882/551, 12 hours).

Ürümqi South (乌鲁木齐南站; Wūlǔmùqí Nánzhàn; 135 Nanzhan Lu; 南站路135号), the city's old train station, handles all non-high-speed services to and from the regional capital, including services to the south of Xinjiang, as well as international connections to Almaty in Kazakhstan. Tickets can be purchased at the international ticket window; bring cash.

Both stations are surrounded by an incredible number of security points, passport checks, ticket controls and X-ray points – even by local standards. Do give yourself plenty of time to get to either station before catching your train.

❶ Getting Around

Ürümqi's metro system opened in 2018 with one line connecting the airport to the city centre (Nanmen Station).

The fastest and most useful buses are the BRT (Bus Rapid Transit) expresses, which dodge traffic by having their own bus lanes. BRT 1 runs from the main railway station to Hongshan Intersection and then north up Beijing Nanlu. BRT 3 runs from the south bus station to People's Sq and the South Lake Sq. Fares are a flat ¥1 – drop a note or coin into the box at the ticket gates.

Other useful buses (¥1, pay the driver as you board, no change given) include bus 7, which runs up Xinhua Lu from the south bus station through the Xidaqiao and Hongshan Intersections, and bus 52 from the train station to Hongshan Intersection.

Taxis are everywhere and cost a standard ¥10 per journey for the first few kilometres, rising quickly after that.

Tian Chi Lake 天池

The rugged Tian Shan range was well known to travellers along the northern Silk Road, who had to traverse its southern edge if they had any hope of making progress. Modern travellers have it far easier and plan trips into the mountains for fun, especially to stunning Tian Chi Lake (Tiān Chí; literally 'heavenly lake'). This high-altitude lake is extremely popular with domestic tourists, but you can still escape the worst of the crowds, who either stick to the paved paths on the northern end or ride overpriced boats across the lake.

◉ Sights

Tian Chi Lake LAKE

(天池, Tiān Chí; Heavenly Lake; ¥215) Two thousand metres up in the Tian Shan range is Tian Chi, a small, long steely-blue lake nestled below the view-grabbing 5445m **Peak of God** (博格达峰, Bógédá Fēng). Scattered across the alpine pine and spruce-covered slopes are Kazakh yurts and lots of sheep. It was a paradise described in Vikram Seth's wonderful travelogue *From Heaven Lake*; and still is for some.

There are dirt roads, boardwalks and trails to various peaks at Tian Chi, or it's a seven-hour hike around the lake (if the whole path is open, which it may not be – check before you set out). For an easy walk, try the path up to **Little Heavenly East Lake** (东小天池, Dōng Xiǎo Tiānchí). There are also commercialised temples to explore on both the east and west shores.

⏢ Sleeping & Eating

At the time of writing it was not possible for international visitors to stay overnight at Tian Chi, though in the past local Kazakh nomads offered yurt stays near the lake

---

❶ BORDER CROSSING: GETTING TO KAZAKHSTAN

A regular bus departs every evening for Almaty from **Ürümqi International Bus Station** (乌鲁木齐国际运输汽车站; Wūlǔmùqí Guójì Yùnshū Qìchēzhàn; ☎ 0991 587 8637; Shayibake District, 236 Gaotie Beiwu Lu, 沙依巴克区高铁北五路236号), next to the main bus station. You can expect hold-ups lasting several hours at the Korgas customs post. A longer but more pleasant trip is to break the journey with a stay in Yining.

Trains currently depart Ürümqi twice weekly for Almaty, Kazakhstan (via Alashankou), on Monday and Saturday at 11pm. The journey takes a slow 24 hours, a number of which are spent at Chinese and Kazakh customs.

The Monday service carries on to the Kazakh capital of Nur-Sultan (Astana), taking 38 hours, total.

Tickets can be purchased in the lobby of the Yà'ōu Jiǔdiàn (next to the train station) or at the railway station ticket window 12 (no English spoken). The booking office regulations are worth noting: on Monday you can buy same-day train tickets; Wednesday and Thursday you can buy tickets for the next Saturday and Monday; Saturday you buy same-day tickets and tickets for next Monday.

If you are one of the minority who need a visa for Kazakhstan (most westerners can travel there visa-free these days), you can as a last resort apply for a 30-day tourist visa at the **Kazakhstan Consulate** (哈萨克斯坦共和国驻; Hāsàkè Sītǎn Gònghéguó Zhù; ☎ 0991 369 7585; pvs-urumqi@yandex.ru; 216 Kunming Lu) in Ürümqi.

In the summertime you may encounter some food and snack-sellers set up around the lake, but it's best to pack a lunch as there are no bricks-and-mortar restaurants to fall back on.

ⓘ Getting There & Around

Tourist buses (return ¥50, 2½ hours) to the Tian Chi main gate leave Ürümqi at 9am from the north gate of People's Park, and return around 7pm. Buy your ticket from the office inside the small pagoda next to the entrance to the park.

From the main gate (where you purchase an entry ticket), you must take the park's own bus (included in park entry ticket) for the 30-minute ride to another car park, which itself is still 1km before the lake. You can walk from the final lot or take a shuttle (¥10).

Turpan   吐鲁番

☏ 0995 / POP 637,000

Turpan (Tǔlǔfān) is China's Death Valley. At 154m below sea level, it's the second-lowest depression in the world and the hottest spot in China. In July and August, temperatures soar above 40°C and even 50°C, forcing the local population to sleep on their roofs and visiting tourists into a state of semi-torpor.

Despite the heat, the ground water and fertile soil of the Turpan depression has made this a veritable oasis in the desert, evidenced by the nearby centuries-old remains of ancient cities, imperial garrisons and Buddhist caves. The city itself has a mellow vibe to it, and recovering from a day's sightseeing over a cold Xinjiang beer under the grape vines on a warm summer evening is one of the joys of travelling through the province.

◉ Sights

★Jiaohe Ruins   RUINS
(交河故城, Jiāohé Gù Chéng; ¥70) Also called Yarkhoto, Jiaohe was established by the ancient Jushi kingdom as a garrison town in the 2nd century BC. It's one of the world's largest (6500 residents once lived here), oldest (1600 years old) and best-preserved ancient cities, inspiring with its scale, setting and palpable historical atmosphere. Get an overview of the site at the central governor's complex, then continue along the main road past a large monastery to a 'stupa grove' with a 10m-tall pagoda surrounded by 100 smaller pagoda bases.

While far busier than the similar ruins at Gaochang (p842), these are definitely the most impressive of the two, mainly due to the sheer number of surviving structures and the dramatic location, on a hillside with wide views in all directions. The ruins are 10km west of Turpan. There's no public transport; a taxi (¥30) takes 20 minutes, or you can cycle.

★Bezeklik Cave Complex   CAVE
(柏孜克里克千佛洞, Bózīkèlǐkè Qiānfó Dòng; ¥40) This cave complex, which dates from the 6th to 14th centuries, is located in a mesmerising desert landscape. Bezeklik means 'Place of Paintings' in Uyghur and the murals painted in the 11th century represented a high point in Uyghur Buddhist art. Sadly, German, Japanese and British teams removed most of the site's distinctive cave art in the early 20th century, and only a few caves can be entered today. However, the location is gorgeous and well worth the trip.

A return taxi should cost around ¥80.

Tuyoq   VILLAGE
(吐峪沟, Tǔyùgōu; ¥30) Set in a green valley fringed by the Flaming Mountains, this mudbrick village offers a fascinating glimpse of traditional Uyghur life and architecture. It has been a pilgrimage site for Muslims for centuries, as on the hillside above is the Hojamu Tomb, a *mazar* (a tomb of a saint or holy person), said to hold the first Uyghur to convert to Islam. The *mazar* is not open to non-Muslims. The rest of the village is great for strolling.

Visiting Tuyoq is a little like time travel, save for the odd awkwardly parked Landcruiser on its narrow, crooked streets. Don't leave without trying some of the locally produced mulberry juice or dried berries, available near the tomb entrance.

Emin Minaret   ISLAMIC SITE
(苏公塔, Sūgōng Tǎ; ¥50; ◷10am-6.30pm; 🚌6) Built to honour Turpan general Emin Hoja, this splendid 44m-high mud-brick structure

is the tallest minaret in China. Named *Sūgōng Tǎ* after Emin's son Suleiman, who oversaw its construction (1777–78), its bowling-pin shape is decorated with an interesting mix of geometrical and floral patterns: the former reflect traditional Islamic design, the latter Chinese. You can't climb the interior steps of the minaret itself, but the rest of the grounds, including the adjacent mosque, are open.

The minaret is 3km southeast of the centre of Turpan. Biking or strolling is a fun way to get here when the weather isn't too hot. The dusty, tree-lined Uyghur streets in this traditional neighbourhood give a fascinating glimpse into old Turpan.

Flaming Mountains
MOUNTAIN

(火焰山, Huǒyàn Shān; ¥40) Near the Bezeklik Caves in Turpan are the Flaming Mountains, which appear at midday like multicoloured tongues of fire. The Flaming Mountains were immortalised in the classic Chinese novel *Journey to the West*, in which Sun Wukong (the Monkey King) used his magic fan to extinguish the blaze.

From the official viewpoint you can explore the site on foot, although the mountains are visible for free anywhere on the dramatic drives to the Bezeklik Cave Complex (p841), Gaochang and Tuyoq (p841).

Turpan Museum
MUSEUM

(吐鲁番博物馆, Tǔlǔfān Bówùguǎn; 1268 Muna'er Lu; 木纳尔路1268号; ⊙10am-6.30pm Tue-Sun) FREE Xinjiang's second-largest museum houses a rich collection of relics recovered from archaeological sites across the Turpan Basin, including a superb collection of dinosaur fossils, dinosaur eggs

and various species of ancient rhino. Upstairs there's a ghoulish gallery of local mummies. Pop in here before signing up for a regional tour; the photos of nearby sites at the entrance might help you decide which ones to visit.

Entry is free, but you need to present ID and collect a ticket downstairs, as well as pass a security check. No thongs (flip-flops) allowed.

Gaochang
RUINS

(高昌故城, Gāochāng Gù Chéng; Khocho; Karakhoja; admission incl electric buggy ¥100; ⊙8.30am-5pm) Dating from the 1st century, Gaochang rose to power during the Tang dynasty in the 7th century and became the Uyghur capital in AD 850. It was a major staging post on the Silk Road until it burnt in the 14th century. Though the earthen city walls, once 12m thick, are clearly visible, not much else is left standing other than a large Buddhist monastery in the southwest. It's 30km from Turpan.

To the north, adjacent to an adobe pagoda, is a two-storey structure (half underground) that is purportedly the ancient palace. There is good signage in English in front of each structure, and the sheer scale of the place is incredible. Walking is possible but, due to its size, Gaochang is best covered by bike or electric buggy.

Astana Tombs
TOMB

(阿斯塔那古墓区, Āsītǎnà Gǔmùqū; Astana; ¥40; ⊙8am-9pm summer, 10.30am-6.30pm winter) The small Uyghur village of Astana contains this ancient imperial cemetery, chiefly of interest for the mummies you normally see in museums in the exact positions in which they were discovered. However, as just one of the three subterranean graves you can visit on the walking tour contains mummies, it may well seem an expensive visit. The most interesting finds are now in museums in Ürümqi and Turpan. There's a colourful Friday bazaar in the village.

🛏 Sleeping

Turpan has plenty of decent sleeping options, including several charming and innovative midrange hotels set amid the vineyards on the outskirts of town. Travellers recommend the **Silk Road Lodges** (www.silkroadlodges. com) set in a traditional village 2km east of the city centre.

XINJIANG'S CLIMATE

Xinjiang's climate is one of extremes. Turpan is the hottest spot in the country – temperatures of 54°C have been recorded in the summer months – while the Tarim and Jungar Basins aren't much cooler. Spring (April and May) is a much better time to travel temperature-wise, though frequent sandstorms can sometimes obscure the landscape. Winters (November to March) see the mercury plummet below 0°C throughout the province, although March is a good time to catch some festivals. Late May, June, September and (especially) October are the best times to visit.

Eating & Drinking

The string of restaurants that set up tables under the vine trellises on pedestrianised **Qingnian Lu** are a fine place to savour a cold drink and bowl of *laghman* (pulled noodles; ¥15). Nearby **Bezeklik Lu** is known as 'the eating street' locally, and has lots of choice between more formal Uyghur and Chinese restaurants.

Turpan's nightlife is centred on its night markets, where locals gather to eat and drink. Gaochang Lu has a number of options, as well as a bazaar set up in Tourism Culture Square (Lǚyóu Wénhuà Guǎngchǎng, 旅游文化广场). Despite being a largely Uyghur city, alcohol is widely available. One pleasant place for an evening drink is the string of bars along pedestrianised Qingnian Zhonglu.

Getting There & Away

Turpan is connected by high-speed rail via **Turpan North Station** (吐鲁番北站; Tǔlǔfān Běi Zhàn), 12km northwest of the city centre. A taxi from the city centre costs ¥30, or you can take bus 202 (¥1). From here, several trains a day go to Ürümqi (1st/2nd class ¥82/51, one hour) and Hami (1st/2nd class ¥184/115, two hours).

The old train station, simply known as Turpan, is actually at Daheyan (大河沿), a whopping 45km north of Turpan. From here, you can get non-high-speed services to Kuqa (hard/soft sleeper ¥161/244, 6½ to 7½ hours) and Kashgar (hard/soft sleeper ¥299/456, 15 to 22 hours). A taxi here costs around ¥150, or take a shared taxi (¥40 per person) from Turpan's **passenger transport centre** (客运中心, Kèyùn Zhōngxīn; 545 Chun Shu Lu; 椿树路545号).

Buses run regularly to Ürümqi (3½ hours), and a daily bus goes to Hami (six hours).

Getting Around

Taxi flag fall is ¥5. Bicycles (about ¥5 per hour) can be hired from many hostels and hotels.

The best way to see Turpan's scattered sights is to hire a driver for a day or two (around ¥500 per car per day). Don't underestimate the desert heat: bring plenty of water, sunscreen, sunglasses and a hat.

Hami 哈密

☑ 0902 / POP 580,000

Hami (哈密, Hāmì; Kumul in the Uyghur language), with its famously sweet melons, was a much-anticipated stop on the Silk Road for ancient travellers. It's still worth a break today, with its green and well-kept city centre and a few interesting sights that can keep you busy for a day if you're travelling between Turpan and Dunhuang.

At the time of writing, Hami could be visited independently as long as you're on a standard tourist visa. Those that require an invitation letter (eg a business visa) must travel on a guided tour.

Sights

Hami Kings Mausoleum TOMB

(哈密王陵, Hāmì Wánglíng; Huancheng Lu, 环城路; adult/student ¥40/20; ⏰9am-8pm Apr-Sep, 10am-7pm Oct-Mar) The chief reason to visit Hami is for this wonderfully serene complex of tombs containing the nine generations of Hami kings who ruled the region from 1697 to 1930. The blue- and green-tiled main tomb is the resting place of the seventh king, Muhammed Bixir, with family members and government ministers housed in Mongolian-style buildings to the side. Facing it is the rather garish facade of the Etigar mosque, which has a wonderful colonnaded interior.

Barkol Lake LAKE

(巴里坤湖, Bālǐkūn Hú) If the summer heat of Hami is unbearable, take a day trip out to the cooler climes of Barkol Lake (Bālǐkūn Hú), on the north side of the Tian Shan. Kazakh herders set up their yurts here in summer and offer horse riding for ¥10 per hour. Sadly it's not possible to swim, but the bucolic setting and views are well worth the trip.

To reach the yurts, first take a bus from Hami's central bus station to Bālǐkūn town (¥30, three hours, hourly between 8.30am and 5.30pm). From Bālǐkūn it's 16km to the yurts. A return taxi starts at ¥50. Along the route from Hami, keep an eye out for the remains of ancient beacon towers slowly disintegrating by the roadside.

Hami Museum MUSEUM

(哈密博物馆, Hāmì Bówùguǎn; Huancheng Lu, 环城路; ⏰10am-1pm & 3.30-6.30pm Tue-Sun) FREE This mildly interesting three-floor museum spotlights mummies and dinosaurs found in the region, including several impressively preserved fossilised nests of dinosaur eggs, and, for a reason we were unable to glean, an enormous display of plastic food. Sadly there's almost no English signage.

Kumul Muqam Heritage Centre MUSEUM

(哈密木卡姆传承中心, Hāmì Mùkǎmǔ Chuánchéng Zhōngxīn) The extraordinary exterior of this eye-catching building is perhaps its most impressive feature, and is well worth checking out as it's next to the main museum in Hami. Inside, the large display focuses specifically on *muqam,* the classical form of Uyghur music.

✗ Eating & Drinking

There are plenty of eating options in Hami, particularly around the Guangdong Lu and Tianshan Beilu intersection, and near the train station.

Hami is a sleepy town with little nightlife. Alcohol is widely available, however, and most locals head to Chinese restaurants if they want a night out.

❶ Getting There & Around

Hami is connected by high-speed rail with Ürümqi (1st/2nd class ¥266/166, three hours) and Turpan (1st/2nd class ¥184/115, two hours). For some ticket sites you'll need to use Hami's other name, Kumul.

Long-distance buses depart for Dunhuang, Turpan and Ürümqi from the **south bus station** (南郊客运站, *nánjiāo kèyùnzhàn*) on Tuanjie Lu. For services to Dunhuang, try to buy a ticket one day in advance.

Local buses 10 and 14 (¥1) run from outside the train station through the centre of the city to the south bus station.

Kuqa   库车

☑ 0997 / POP 76,000

The ancient town of Kuqa (Kùchē), once a major centre of Buddhism and now a largely Han Chinese–dominated modern city, is worth a stopover between Ürümqi and Kashgar for its bazaar, old town and some interesting excursions to the surrounding desert ruins.

As a once-thriving city-state, known as Qiuci, Kuqa was famed in Tang-era China for its music and dancers. Kumarajiva (AD 344–413), the first great translator of Buddhist sutras from Sanskrit into Chinese, was born here to an Indian father and Kuqean princess, before later being abducted to central China to manage translations of the Buddhist canon. When the 7th-century monk Xuan Zang passed through nearby Subashi, he recorded that two enormous 30m-high Buddha statues flanked Kuqa's western gate, and that the nearby monasteries housed more than 5000 monks.

At the time of writing, a number of travellers had reported heavy security in Kuqa,

including police escorts in some instances and a number of accommodations being shut down at short notice. While it is technically possible to visit, travellers should be aware of the realities on the ground and that they may face delays or extra searches/security during their stay.

⊙ Sights

Kizil Thousand Buddha Caves   CAVE
(克孜尔千佛洞, Kèzǐ'ěr Qiānfó Dòng; ¥70; ⊘10.30am-7pm) This is the largest cave-art site in Xinjiang and the earliest major Buddhist cave complex in all of China. In its day, the site would have been comparable to the Mogao Grottoes (p884), although sadly only a handful of the 236 caves are open and the once-dazzling wall art has been largely destroyed by early archaeologists and religious zealots. The drive here is still beautiful, though, crossing bleak and empty landscapes and jagged mountains.

The interior murals date from the 3rd to the 8th centuries and, as ancient Kuqa was an ethnically diverse place, artisans were inspired by Afghan, Persian and Indian motifs and styles brought via the Silk Road. The heavy use of blue pigment in middle-period murals is a Persian influence, for example. Each cave is generally built the same way, with two chambers and a central vaulted roof. The roof contains murals of the Buddha's past lives (so-called Jātaka tales) and, unique to Kizil, the pictures are framed in diamond-shaped patterns. Several caves were stripped bare by German archaeologist Albert Von le Coq in the early 20th century, only for the treasures to be destroyed during WWII. Note the richly decorated roof of Cave 8, where the Buddha's golden robes have been systematically removed over the centuries.

The site is 75km northwest of Kuqa. Private transfer is the only way to get here, and a return taxi will cost around ¥250 and takes 90 minutes each way. Most people combine the trip with one to Sūbāshí, even though you have to return to Kuqa between the two sights. Reckon on paying ¥350 for both.

Subashi   RUINS
(苏巴什故城, Sūbāshí Gùchéng; ¥25; ⊘10am-7pm) Subashi was a Buddhist complex that thrived from the 3rd to 13th centuries. It's less visited than other ancient cities in Xinjiang, but with its starkly beautiful desert setting it's worth the 23km trip northeast

of Kuqa. There are a number of ruined buildings that you visit, though the best preserved one is the pagoda on the far side of the site (the main path takes you there), where brickwork and some decoration can still be seen.

Most people just go to the western complex, with its large central *vihara* (monastery) and two pagodas, but the dramatic eastern complex across the Kuqa River is worth the hike, though it was being renovated at the time of research. A return taxi to Subashi costs about ¥150; you'll need to pay for extra waiting time if you want to visit the eastern ruins.

Kuche Royal Palace   MUSEUM
(库车原世袭回部亲王府, Kùchē Yuán Shìxí Huí Bù Qīnwáng Fǔ; Qiuci Palace; Linjiu Jie; 林基路街; ¥55; ⊙10am-7.30pm; 🚌) Located in the old town, 3.5km west of the centre, is the rebuilt Kuche Palace, the residence of the kings of Kuche until the early 20th century. The exhibits tend towards the mundane and are slightly bizarre, but a visit can be entertaining. The last Kuche king, Dawud Mahsut, died in 2014 and is buried in the ancestral hall at the back of the compound.

The museum has a good collection of Buddhist frescoes, some from the nearby Kumtura and Simsim caves, and there are human remains from the surrounding desert ruins. Nearby is a rebuilt section of Qing dynasty city wall.

✖ Eating & Drinking

There's plenty of choice for eating in Kuqa, though in a largely Han Chinese city most options are for Chinese food.

❶ Getting There & Away

The **bus station** (汽车站, qìchēzhàn) is in the town centre on Tianshan Zhonglu, and the train station is a further 5km southeast.

The train station is southeast of the centre. A taxi costs ¥10. There are daily non-high-speed trains to Kashgar (hard/soft sleeper ¥182/275, 8½ to 11 hours) and Ürümqi (hard/soft sleeper ¥190/285, eight to 10 hours).

The small airport, 35km west of the city, has daily flights to Ürümqi (from ¥360, one hour) on China Southern and Tianjin Airlines. A taxi there costs around ¥50.

❶ Getting Around

Taxi rides are a standard ¥5 per trip within the town centre, with pedicabs, tractors and donkey carts around half this.

SOUTHWEST XINJIANG

The Uyghurs' heartland is the southwest of Xinjiang, known as Kashgaria, the rough but mellifluous-sounding historical name for the western Tarim Basin. Consisting of a ring of oases lined with poplar trees, it was a major Silk Road hub and has bristled with activity for more than 2000 years, with the weekly bazaars remaining the centre of life here to this day.

The centre of the region is undoubtedly the ancient city of Kashgar, one of the absolute highlights of any visit to Xinjiang. Another highlight is the breathtaking scenery along the Karakoram Hwy between Kashgar and remote Tashkurgan.

Kashgar   喀什

📶 0998 / POP 507,000

Locked away in the westernmost corner of China, closer to Tehran and Damascus than to Beijing, Kashgar (Kāshí) has been the epicentre of regional trade and cultural exchange for more than two millennia.

In recent years, modernity has swept through Kashgar, bringing waves of Han migrant workers; huge swathes of the old city have been bulldozed in the name of 'progress'. Only a tiny section of the 'real' Old Town remains today.

Yet, in the face of these changes, the spirit of Kashgar lives on. Uyghur craftsmen and artisans still hammer and chisel away as they have done for centuries, traders haggle over deals in the boisterous bazaars and donkey carts still trundle their way through the narrow alleyways. Do not miss the city's Sunday livestock market, which remains a fascinating sight, no matter how many tour buses roll up.

◎ Sights

★ Shipton's Arch   NATURAL FEATURE
(阿图什天门, Ātúshí Tiānmén; Tushuk Tagh; ¥45; ⊙10am-7.30pm) This extraordinary natural rock arch (the rather prosaic Uyghur name means simply 'mountain with a hole in it') is one of the tallest on earth. The first westerner to describe it was Eric Shipton, the last British consul-general in Kashgar, during his visit to the region in 1947. Successive expeditions attempted to find it without success until a team from *National Geographic* rediscovered the arch in 2000. Located 80km northwest of Kashgar, it's a half-day excursion.

Kashgar

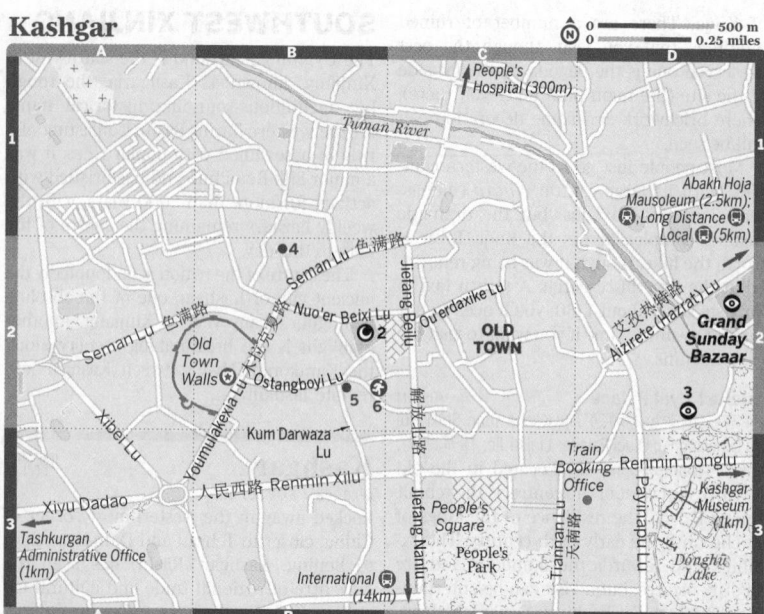

Kashgar map

Kashgar

The first part of the trip involves an hour's drive towards the Irkeshtam Pass, followed by another 20km ride and then a 45-minute hike through a sublimely lunar landscape, hemmed in on all sides by sheer cliffs. At times you'll be scrambling through the narrowest part of the gorge over small ladders and staircases, until your final ascent to the arch itself, which takes you up a long wooden staircase. Kashgar-based tour operators can arrange a day trip with guide for ¥600 to ¥800, or you can simply take a taxi and walk from the car park yourself, as the route is well signposted. Bring sturdy shoes, a sun hat and water.

★ **Sunday Livestock Market**   MARKET
(动物市场, Dòngwù Shìchǎng, Mal Bazaar; ⊙8am–6pm Sun) No visit to Kashgar is complete without a trip to the Livestock Market, which takes place once a week on Sunday. The day begins with Uyghur farmers and herders trekking into the city from nearby villages. By lunchtime, just about every saleable sheep, camel, horse, cow and donkey within 50km has been squeezed through the bazaar gates. It's dusty, smelly and crowded, and most people find it wonderful, though some visitors may find the treatment of the animals upsetting.

Trading at the market is swift and boisterous between the old traders; animals are carefully inspected and haggling is done with finger motions. Keep an ear out for the phrase '*Bosh-bosh!*' ('Coming through!') or you risk being ploughed over by a cartload of fat-tailed sheep.

★ **Grand Sunday Bazaar**   MARKET
(大巴扎, Dàbāzhā; Yengi Bazaar; Aizirete Lu; 艾孜热特路; ⊙daily) Kashgar's main bazaar is open every day but really kicks it up a gear on Sunday. Step through the jam-packed entrance and allow your five senses to guide you through the market; spices and teas are an obvious highlight, as are silk, *doppa* (traditional Uyghur hats) and carpets, all of which

can be seen in abundance. There's so much variety that locals joke that only chicken milk cannot be found amid this mercantile chaos.

A section on the northern side of the market contains everything of interest to foreign visitors, including the spice market, musical instruments, fur caps, kitschy souvenirs and carpets.

Kashgar Old Town
OLD TOWN

(喀什老城区, Kāshí Lǎo Chéngqū) The Old Town is the soul of Kashgar, and as such the government has spent much of the past two decades knocking it down block by block and building a modern replacement. Yet it's still possible to see some of the remaining alleyways: check out the neighbourhood near Donghai Lake in the eastern part of the city. Around Jiefang Lu there are also alleys lined with Uyghur workshops and adobe houses that have withstood the passage of time.

Where they exist, houses range in age from 50 to 500 years old and the lanes twist haphazardly through neighbourhoods where Kashgaris have lived and worked for centuries. It's a great place for strolling, peeking through gates, chatting to the locals and admiring the craftspeople as they bang on tin and chase copper.

Traditional houses in Kashgar, rarely more than two storeys high, are built with poplar timber and mud bricks. Walls are very thick but usually unadorned on the outside. The inner courtyards and balconies, however, are decorated with woodcarvings and hangings.

At the eastern end of Seman Lu stands a 10m-high section of the Old Town walls, which are at least 500 years old. Much of the rest of the Old Town has now been enclosed by modern walls.

Id Kah Mosque
MOSQUE

(艾提尕尔清真寺, Ài Tígǎ'ěr Qīngzhēn Sì; Id Kah Sq; ¥45; ☺ dawn-dusk outside of prayer times) The yellow-tiled Id Kah Mosque, which dates from 1442, is the spiritual and physical heart of the city. Enormous (it's the largest mosque in Xinjiang), its courtyard and gardens can hold 20,000 people during the annual Qurban Baiyram (Eid). Non-Muslims may enter, but not during prayer time. Dress modestly, including a headscarf for women. Take off your shoes if entering carpeted areas and be discreet when taking photos.

Mor Pagoda
RUINS

(莫尔佛塔, Mò'ěr Fótǎ; ¥30; ☺ dawn-dusk) At the end of a 45km drive northeast of Kashgar are the ruins of Ha Noi, a Tang-dynasty town built in the 7th century and abandoned in the 12th century. Little remains apart from an enigmatic pyramid-like structure and the impressive four-tiered Mor Pagoda. A round-trip taxi, including waiting time, should cost around ¥200.

Abakh Hoja Mausoleum
TOMB

(香妃墓, Xiāngfēimù, Abakh Hoja Maziri; Afaq Khoja Mausoleum; Haohan Village; 浩罕村; ☺ dawn-dusk) This 3-hectare mausoleum complex was built by the Khoja family, who ruled the region in the 17th and 18th centuries. Widely considered the holiest Muslim site in Xinjiang, it's a major pilgrimage destination and a beautiful piece of Islamic architecture, located on the northeastern outskirts of town.

Founded as a religious school by Yusuf Khoja, the mausoleum was built in 1640 with further halls and mosques being added over the next three centuries. Not only does it house the remains of Yusuf, but dozens of Khoja family members are also interred here. These include Yusuf's son Abakh Hoja, a famed 17th-century Sufi and political leader (and after whom the mausoleum is named), and according to legend, Iparhan, Abakh Hoja's granddaughter.

Known to the Chinese as Xiang Fei, the 'Fragrant Concubine' of the Emperor Qianlong, Iparhan remains a potent symbol of the Chinese–Uyghur divide. To the Han, she was the beloved but homesick concubine of the Emperor and thus a symbol of national unity. To the Uyghur she was a resistance leader (or the wife of one) who was captured and taken to Beijing where she died (and was likely buried) broken-hearted, or was killed by the Emperor's mother.

The mausoleum complex has an irregular design so all the mosques face Mecca at a slightly different angle. South are the main stone gate, with its striking blue tiles, and the High and Low Mosques. These mosques form a typical pairing in Uyghur religious architecture and are known as summer and winter mosques: their open-sided and closed structures, respectively, allow for prayer during the different seasons. Note the wooden and painted columns here, carved in 1926, with their *muqarnas* capitals (a traditional Persian design likened to hanging stalactites).

The Great Mosque is in the west of the complex, while the small Green Mosque (which also has summer and winter halls) is in the north. The domed mausoleum, the tallest structure in the complex, is east, and is surrounded by a graveyard wall with four colourful towers in the corners. The most striking feature, however, is the exterior of mismatched tiles, the result of piecemeal repairs over the years.

Kashgar Museum MUSEUM
(喀什博物馆; Kāshí Bówùguǎn; 19 Tawu Guzi Lu;塔吾古孜路19号; ⊘10am-7pm) FREE This regional museum is not as good as some of the other excellent local museums in Xinjiang, but it's free and includes an incredible 6th-century Buddhist urn and a mummy amid the otherwise rather forgettable collection.

☞ Tours

Kashgar Offbeat Tours TOURS
(☑138 9913 6195; https://kashgar.culture-travel.net) Local English-speaking Uyghur-carpet dealer Ablimit 'Elvis' Ghopor organises citywide cultural trips, with a special emphasis on Uyghur classical music and the Kashgar carpet market. He also offers tours and treks to Karakul and the Taklamakan Desert.

China Silk Road Tours TOURS
(Uigher Tours; ☑180 9377 1979, 0937 883 5452; www.silkroadtours.com.cn; 144 Seman Lu, Chini Bagh Royal Hotel) English-speaking Ali Tash runs this highly recommended agency offering tours and travel between Kashgar and Xi'an along the Northern Silk Road (via Turpan),

---

WHICH TIME IS IT?

All of China officially runs on Beijing time (*Beijing shíjiān*). Xinjiang, several time zones removed from Beijing, however, unofficially runs duelling clocks: while the Chinese tend to stick to the official Beijing time, the locals set their clocks to unofficial Xinjiang time (*Xīnjiāng shíjiān*), two hours behind Beijing time. Thus 9am Beijing time is 7am Xinjiang time. Most government-run services, such as banks, post offices, bus stations and airlines, run on Beijing time, generally operating from 10am to 1.30pm and from 4pm to 8pm to cater to the time difference. Uyghurs will often automatically use Xinjiang time – a political statement as much as anything else – so always double-check which clock they're using when making plans!

---

as well as trips to Muztagh Ata (7509m). Bike hire in Kashgar can also be arranged.

You may also be invited into Ali's home and have the opportunity to take Uyghur cooking lessons if you book a tour.

🛏 Sleeping

Despite being Xinjiang's biggest tourist draw, Kashgar's accommodation options remain fairly mediocre, especially in the midrange category. There are now a number of well-run hostels, however, so budget travellers are well catered for, at least.

✗ Eating & Drinking

Kashgar is one of the best places in Xinjiang to try the full gamut of Uyghur food. There are two excellent night markets and an incredible bazaar, and street food is available on almost every corner of the expansive Old Town.

Drinking options are fairly limited in Kashgar – Chinese restaurants and hotel bars are your best bets for alcohol. Nightlife takes place more in the city's night markets than in bars or clubs, and you'll often find families even with little children out very late during the hot summer months.

🔒 Shopping

For serious shopping go to the Old Town, ready to bargain. Kum Darwaza Lu is a good starting point. The Grand Bazaar has a decent selection but prices tend to be higher. Hats, teapot sets, copper- and brassware, kebab skewers and Uyghur knives are among the best souvenirs.

ⓘ Information

Public Security Bureau (PSB; 公安局; Gōng'ānjú; 346 Youmulake Xiehai'er Lu; 尤木拉克协海尔路346号; ⊘8.30am-5.30pm) May be able to issue one-month visa extensions.

First People's Hospital (地区第一人民医院; Dìqū Dìyī Rénmín Yīyuàn; 66 Yingbin Dadao; 迎宾大道66号) North of the river.

ⓘ Getting There & Away

AIR
Also known as Kashi Airport, Kashgar's busy airport has more than a dozen daily flights to and from Ürümqi (from ¥550, two hours).

The airport is 13km northeast of the town centre. A taxi costs ¥15 to ¥20 but drivers often ask for double this. Insist on a meter being used, and avoid the touts in the arrivals hall. Sightseeing Buses (游览观光) 1 and 2 (¥2) go from the airport from People's Sq and Id Kah Mosque, from where it's an easy walk to most hotels.

BUS

Kashgar's bus stations are prone to changing locations. The long-distance and local bus stations are next to each other near the train station, around 7km northwest of the Old Town, while the international bus station is 14km south of the Old Town.

The **long-distance bus station** (汽车客运站; Qìchē Kèyùnzhàn; National Hwy 315; 315国道) handles buses to the north of the region, including to Kuqa (12 hours), Turpan (22 hours), and Ürümqi (24 hours).

All Ürümqi and Turpan buses go through Kuqa, but a ticket to Kuqa on these services is far pricier (¥255) as you have to buy a ticket to Turpan, so you're much better off using the cheaper 7pm service that terminates in Kuqa.

Buses heading south use the **local bus station** (公共汽车站; Gōnggòng Qìchē Zhàn; National Hwy 315; 315国道), which is located next door to the long-distance bus station. Destinations from here include Hotan (10 hours), Karghilik (four hours), Tashkurgan (six hours), Yarkand (three hours) and Yengisar (1½ hours).

Bus 20 connects the Old Town to all three bus stations.

An alternative to taking a bus to Tashkurgan is to take a faster shared taxi, which leaves when full from the **Tashkurgan Administration Office** (塔什库尔干办事处; Tǎshíkù'ěrgān Bànshìchù; 166 Xiyu Dadao Lu; 西域大道166号).

TRAIN

Kashgar's **train station** (喀什火车站; Kāshí Huǒchē Zhàn; National Hwy 315; 315国道) is 7km northeast of the Old Town, and there are regular connections to the rest of the region, including the following destinations:

Hotan hard/soft sleeper ¥130/194, four to seven hours, six daily

Karghilik 叶城 hard/soft sleeper/hard seat ¥94/135/40, 2½ to 3½ hours

Ürümqi hard/soft sleeper ¥325/497, 17¾ to 24½ hours, six daily

Yengisar 英吉沙 hard/soft sleeper/hard seat ¥68/101/12, 45 minutes

Yarkand 莎车 hard/soft sleeper/hard seat ¥86/131/28, 1½ to 2½ hours

ⓘ Getting Around

Taxi flagfall is ¥5, and nowhere in town should cost more than ¥15.

Useful bus routes are numbers 2 (Jiefang Lu north to the international bus station and the airport), 9 (international bus station to the Chini Bagh Hotel and Sèmǎn Bīnguǎn), 20 (China Post

to Abakh Hoja Tomb) and 28 (Id Kah Mosque to the train station).

Karakoram Highway   中巴公路

The Karakoram Hwy (KKH; Zhōngbā Gōnglù) over the Khunjerab Pass (4693m) is one of the world's most spectacular roads and China's gateway to Pakistan. For centuries this route was used by caravans plodding down the Silk Road. Khunjerab means 'valley of blood' as local bandits used to take advantage of the terrain to slaughter merchants and plunder their wares. Upgraded roads make the going much easier than it once was, though a proposed railway linking China to Pakistan has yet to be developed.

The main (and practically the only) town between Kashgar and Pakistan is Tashkurgan, a surprisingly modern and sprawling town with a devastatingly beautiful mountain setting. This is where the bus journey to Pakistan begins, and it's also as far as most travellers not entering Pakistan itself are able to go.

⊙ Sights

Bulunkou Lake   LAKE
(布伦库勒湖;, Bùlúnkùlēi Hú) This absolute wonder of nature is the first of the big plateglass lakes you meet as you head up to Tashkurgan on the Karakoram Hwy. Backed by sublime sand mountains and often without a single ripple in its waters, it's an astonishing sight on a calm day, when the landscape is perfectly mirrored in the lake. It's currently totally deserted, though it looked like some form of construction was beginning when we were there, suggesting that mass tourism can't be far away.

Karakul Lake   LAKE
(喀拉库勒湖, Kālākùlēi Hú) Extraordinarily beautiful Karakul Lake sits below the soaring snowcapped peak of Muztagh Ata (7509m)

and has a couple of small Kyrgyz settlements along its western shore. Famed for its perfect reflections of the surrounding mountains, it's a popular stop between Kashgar and Tashkurgan, though the overnight yurt and homestays of years past are no longer available to international travellers.

Tashkurgan Fort FORT

(古石头城, Gŭ Shítóu Chéng; ¥30; ⊙10am-7pm) The 1400-year-old stone (*tash*) fortifications (*kurgan*) of this fort give the town of Tash-kurgan on the Karakorum Hwy its name. The ruins were one of the filming locations for the movie *The Kite Runner*. The boggy valley below is dotted with Tajik yurts in summer (as well as a network of walkways for tourists) and offers some spectacular views.

Tomb of Mahmud Kashgari TOMB

(穆罕默德喀什噶里墓, Mahèmùdé Kāshén Gálǐmù; adult ¥30) Mahmud Kashgari was a beloved local 11th-century scholar, travel-ler and writer. His renovated tomb, about 2.5km from the market on the edge of Upal Hill in Upal (Wùpà'ěr in Chinese) is a po-tential side excursion on the way up the Karakoram Hwy.

🛏 Sleeping & Eating

Unless you plan to do an expedition, your hotel choices are limited to the decent se-lection in Tashkurgan. The yurts and stone huts on the shore of Karakul Lake are no longer allowed to accept international trav-ellers and camping is not allowed.

Tashkurgan has plenty of simple eating options and some decent shopping at the town bazaar. Elsewhere on the Karakoram Hwy you will need to take supplies.

ℹ Getting There & Away

In 2019 regulations reportedly changed, requiring international travellers to be on a guided tour through a licensed travel agency to travel the Karakoram Hwy. Travellers report that this trip can be booked through the **Kashgar Tourist Service Centre** (📞158 0904 2877, 0998 283 1196; kashgar7@hotmail.com; Ostangboyi Lu; ⊙10am-8pm).

There are almost no settlements on the road between Kashgar and Tashkurgan, so be sure to take everything you need, including warm cloth-ing, food and drink. If you plan to continue into Pakistan, it's essential to have a Pakistani visa already in your passport.

SOUTHERN SILK ROAD

The Silk Road east of Kashgar splits into two threads in the face of the Taklamakan Desert, the second-largest sandy desert in the world. The northern thread follows the modern road and railway to Kuqa and Turpan. The southern road charts a more remote course between desert sands and the towering Pamir and Kunlun mountain ranges.

This off-the-grid journey takes you far into the Uyghur heartland, as well as deep into the ancient multiethnic heritage of the region. You're as likely to come across a cen-turies-old tiled mosque as you are the ruins of a Buddhist pagoda from the 4th century.

Hotan 和田

📞0903 / POP 322,000

An ancient Silk Road city with a long and illustrious history, Hotan (Hétián) is never-theless moving quickly and relentlessly into the modern age. Indeed, today it can be hard at first to imagine that this was once the fo-cal point of the ancient kingdom of Khotan (224 BC to AD 1006), or that later it became an important junction of the southern Silk Road from where trade routes led into India.

But get off the busy main avenues and enter the fabulous bazaar or wonderfully varied night market and you'll quickly get a sense of this important Uyghur city's his-tory and culture. The main reason to come here today is to explore several ancient sites around the city, or simply to shop for jade, silk, carpets and all manner of other things at Hotan's various markets.

◎ Sights

★ **Hotan Sunday Market** MARKET

(星期天市场, Xīngqítiān Shìchǎng; Taibei Donglu, 台北东路; ⊙dawn-dusk) Hotan's most popular attraction is its weekly Sunday market. The covered market bustles every day of the week, but on Sundays it swamps the northeast part of town, reaching fever pitch between noon and 2pm Xinjiang time. The most interesting parts are the *doppi* (skullcap) bazaar, the col-ourful *atlas* (tie-dyed, handwoven silk cloth) to the right of the main entrance and the *gil-im* (carpet) bazaar, across the road. Nearby Juma Lu (加买路) is filled with traditional medicine and spice shops.

The small but authentic Sunday livestock bazaar is about 2km further east, near the Yurungkash River on Donghuan Beilu.

Rawaq Stupa ARCHAEOLOGICAL SITE
(热瓦克佛寺, Rèwǎkè Fósì; Rawak Stupa; National Hwy 217; 217国道; ¥20) This 9m-tall ruin is the largest of the southern Silk Road Buddhist stupas yet discovered. Built between the 3rd and 5th centuries for a wealthy Khotanese monastery, it might have been visited by the Chinese monk Faxian in AD 401 on his way to India. It was certainly explored by archaeologist Aurel Stein, who excavated the site in 1901, and declared it a magnificent ruin. Stein's original work also uncovered 91 large Buddhist statues (now all sadly gone).

Rawaq is about 50km north of Hotan and it's best to go with a guide who knows the site, as taxi drivers have been known to get lost.

Melikawat Ruins RUINS
(玛利克瓦特古城, Mǎlìkèwǎtè Gǔchéng; ⏰dawn-dusk) The deserts around Hotan are peppered with the faint remains of abandoned cities. The most interesting are those of Melikawat, 25km south of town, a Tang dynasty settlement with wind-eroded walls, Buddhist stupas and the remains of pottery kilns. Some scholars believe Melikawat was a capital city of the Yutian state (206 BC to AD 907), an Indo-European civilisation that thrived during the height of the Silk Road. A taxi to Melikawat should cost about ¥100.

Hotan Cultural Museum MUSEUM
(和田博物馆, Hétián Bówùguǎn; Beijing Xilu; ⏰10am-1.30pm & 4-7.30pm, closed Wed) FREE Hotan's museum is relatively small but well curated and has items labelled in English. The main attractions are a fine painted wooden coffin and two 1500-year-old Indo-European mummies unearthed from the nearby Imam Musa Kazim Cemetery who are so well preserved that you can still see the patterns on their shoes. There are also some fascinating finds from ancient Niya, including a large wooden pillar, a 2000-year-old bow and arrow and wooden tablets engraved with Indian-influenced Kharoshthi script.

Mazar of Imam Asim TOMB
FREE A few kilometres beyond the village of Jiya lies the tomb complex of Imam Asim (Tomb of Four Imams). It's a popular pilgrimage site, particularly during May, and you may see groups of Uyghurs praying and

SOUTHERN SILK ROAD TRAVEL RESTRICTIONS

At the time of research, most of the towns along the traditional Southern Silk Road route, including Yarkand (莎车, Shāchē), Karghilik (叶城, Yèchéng) and Cherchen (且末, Qiěmò) were difficult for visitors to access. A number of travellers reported that they were turned away from towns by police, told there were no hotels accepting foreign travellers, or told that sights were closed and escorted out of town or sent back to Kashgar. Hotan remained open, though security was reported to be very tight. If you want to travel east of Hotan, you may need to apply for a permit, and your best bet is to book your trip through an authorised Xinjiang travel agency or tour operator.

chanting at the desert shrine, which is slowly being engulfed by the Taklamakan Desert. It's best to arrange a visit here through a travel agency or guide, as travellers have reported being turned away by police if arriving on their own.

Hotan Foreign Trade Carpet Factory FACTORY
(和田地区外贸地毯厂, Hétián Dìqū Wàimào Dìtǎn Chǎng; ⏰10am-7pm) FREE On the eastern bank of the Yurungkash River is this large factory (*gilim karakhana* in Uyghur). It's primarily set up for group visits but it's perfectly possible for individual travellers to look around the various halls when open. Even with up to 10 weavers, 1 sq m of wool carpet takes 20 days to complete, and the finished items are very impressive. The factory is 5km east of the city centre.

❶ Getting There & Away

Hotan airport – 10km southwest of town – has regular flights to Ürümqi on various national airlines.

There are two bus stations in Hotan. The **main bus station** (客运站, Kèyùnzhàn; Taibei Xilu) serves Kashgar (seven to 10 hours), Kuqa (eight hours) and Ürümqi (25 hours).

The **east bus station** (东郊客运站, Dōngjiāo Kèyùnzhàn), 2km east of the centre, has buses to Cherchen (10 hours). Shared taxis may be harder to come by nowadays due to Xinjiang's security restrictions, but you can try your luck near the stations.

THE SILK ROAD

Nomadic trading routes across Asia and Europe had existed for thousands of years but what we now call the Silk Road, an intercontinental network connecting the East and West, began to take shape in the 2nd century BC. At the time, the Mediterranean had already been linked to Central Asia by Alexander the Great (and his Roman successors), and China, in its need to defend itself from marauding Xiongnu, was about to do its part.

In 138 BC the Emperor Wudi sent envoy Zhang Qian to negotiate an alliance with the Yuezhi, a Central Asian people being driven west by the Xiongnu. On his return (after much hardship which included being kidnapped twice), Zhang piqued the emperor's interest with tales of wealthy neighbouring kingdoms, powerful horses, and trade of Chinese goods, including silk, that had already reached these regions. Over the next two centuries, the Han experienced endless setbacks as they sought to defeat the Xiongnu and secure safe passage from Gansu through Xinjiang, but eventually formal trade with Central Asia was established.

Owing as much to continuous political instability as geographical challenges, there was never any one route that goods travelled along, much less a single road; the name Silk Road was coined in 1877 by German geographer Ferdinand von Richtofen. The loose, fragile and often dangerous network of ancient times had its Chinese start in Chang'an (modern Xi'an) and from there proceeded up the Hexi Corridor to Dunhuang. At this great oasis town it split north and south to circumvent the unforgiving Taklamakan Desert. The routes then met again at Kashgar, where they once more split to cross the high, snowy Pamir, Karakorum and Tian Shan Mountains to connect with Samarkand (and eventually Iran and Constantinople), India and the Russian Volga.

Despite the distances that goods could reach, almost all trade was small scale and local: large caravan teams were rare unless travelling as official envoys, and goods were seldom

Hotan is connected to the main Xinjiang railway line, though not by high-speed rail. The vast **train station** (和田火车站; Hétián Huǒchē Zhàn) is 5.5km north of the city centre.

Kashgar soft seat/hard sleeper ¥130/107, four to six hours, several daily

Ürümqi hard/soft sleeper ¥397/611, 25 hours, three daily

❶ Getting Around

Metered taxis start at ¥5; figure on ¥15 to the train station and ¥30 to the airport. Buses crisscross the city and cost a flat fare of ¥1.

Cherchen 且末

📞 0996 / POP 60,000

Emerging from any direction into the dusty oasis town of Cherchen (Qiěmò) is an unforgettable experience, as you'll have had to pass through hundreds of kilometres of desert just to get here. Indeed, the town itself is struggling against being swallowed up by the massive Taklamakan Desert to its north, and dust storms and hazy days are common here.

The predominantly Uyghur town is fairly unremarkable, but pleasant enough, with a couple of interesting sights nearby that

are worth stopping off for if you're passing through. At the time of research, international travellers were advised to book any travel to Cherchen through a travel agency to make necessary arrangements for visiting sights and to avoid delays due to security.

◉ Sights

Toghraklek Manor HISTORIC BUILDING
(托乎拉克庄园, Tuōhūlākè Zhuāngyuán) The main sight in Cherchen itself is this fine example of early-20th-century Kasghgarian architecture, built in 1911 for a local warlord. The compound has half a dozen rooms, with carved walls, bamboo ceilings and bright carpets, though sadly none of the original furniture remains and the whole site requires quite a bit of imagination to evoke Cherchen a century ago. It's 2.5km west of town.

Travellers have reported some difficulties accessing the site – best advice is to take a taxi or, better yet, hire a guide or go ask for access at the museum, otherwise local police may become suspicious.

Zaghunluq Ancient Mummy Tomb TOMB
(扎滚鲁克古墓群, Zāgǔnlǔkè Gǔmùqún; ¥30) This 2600-year-old tomb contains 13 naturally mummified Mongol bodies, still

carried more than a few hundred kilometres by any one group. An average day's journey was 15km to 20km and traders often made lengthy stops at oasis towns to plan their next stage.

In addition to silk, which was often used as currency, goods included spices, nuts, fruit, metals, leather products, chemicals, glass, paper, precious gems, gold, ivory, porcelain and exotic animals, including the powerful Ferghana horse much prized by the Chinese. It was the exchange of ideas, technology and culture, however, that is the true legacy of the Silk Road.

Buddhism entered China via the Silk Road, and later allowed Chinese monks to travel to Gandhara and India for direct study and the gathering of primary texts. In copying Buddhist cave art, the Chinese created some of the finest examples in locations such as Mogao and Kizil. Going in the other direction, fine Chinese tricoloured pottery had influence across Central Asia, the Middle East and Europe.

The heyday of Silk Road trade began in the 6th century under the stable but militarily strong Tang dynasty. Chang'an became one of the most cosmopolitan capitals in the world, with an estimated 5000 foreigners, including Indians, Turks, Iranians, Japanese and Koreans permanently settled there. Trade declined and then stabilised under Mongolian rule of China, but by the 14th century, sea routes were supplanting the slow and still dangerous overland routes. By the 16th century, the Silk Road network had reverted to obscure local trading and never recovered its former importance.

In June 2014, at the behest of China, Kazakhstan and Kyrgyzstan, Unesco listed the 5000km Tian Shan Corridor of the Silk Roads as a World Heritage Site. The designation highlights not just the obvious pagodas, palaces, cave art and remains of the Great Wall (including beacon towers and forts), but also the caravanserai and way stations that provided relief and lodging for traders. Hopefully in the coming years the listing will encourage more conservation and research and not be seen as a licence for unfettered tourist development.

sporting shreds of colourful clothing. What's particularly interesting here is that unlike the mummies on display in the various regional museums, you get a real sense of how the bodies were buried, including the depth, which makes it amazing they were ever found. The site is a further 4km west of the Toghraklek Manor, on the edge of the desert.

Cherchen Museum MUSEUM
(且末县博物馆, Qiěmò Xiàn Bówùguǎn) Relics from Cherchen's main sights are on display at this regional museum, alongside displays ranging from yetis in the Altun Tagh mountains to the travels of explorer Sven Hedin. Sadly there's almost no labelling in English. It's in the northwest of town: the second of three buildings along the south side of the huge government square.

NORTHERN XINJIANG

The north of Xinjiang is both geographically and culturally very different from the rest of the province; here thick evergreen forests, rushing rivers and isolated mountain ranges are home to Tuvan and Kazakh nomads, and while the Han Chinese population is

growing, as it is throughout Xinjiang, you'll still find markedly different landscapes and people here. The entire north of Xinjiang was closed to foreigners until the 1990s, due to the proximity of the Russian, Mongolian and Kazakh borders, but today the region is developing fast as both a tourist and trade centre.

❶ Getting There & Away

There are airports in both Yining and Altay (阿勒泰, Ālètài), both with multiple daily connections to Ürümqi, as well as the summer-only Burqin Kanas Airport near the popular Kanas Lake Nature Reserve. Bus and train travel to the region is far cheaper, but also far more time consuming. From Yining, you can continue overland by bus into neighbouring Kazakhstan.

Bu'erjin 布尔津

📞 0906 / POP 70,000

Bu'erjin (Bù'ěrjīn), also known as Burqin, is 620km north of Ürümqi, and marks the end of the desert-like Jungar Basin and the beginning of the lusher sub-Siberian birch forests and mountains to the north. The town's population is mainly Kazakh, but there are also Russians, Han, Uyghur and Tuvans.

The town has clear architectural influences from nearby Russia. Though there's little to see and do, it's a pleasant place to start or end a journey to the magnificent Kanas Lake Nature Reserve.

🛏 Sleeping

Bu'erjin has many hotels, though only a handful accept foreigners. Rates peak between July and September and are heavily discounted at other times.

✗ Eating & Drinking

There is a range of street food and small noodle bars on pedestrian Baihuayuan Lu, between Kanase Lu and Baihu Lu, where you can get simple meals until late at night. The **Bu'erjin Night Market** (河提夜市; Hétí Yèshì; Hebin Lu; mains from ¥10; ⊘ 7pm-midnight May-Sep) is along the river embankment and is a great place to eat, even if it lacks the raucous atmosphere of similar markets in Hotan or Kashgar.

ℹ Getting There & Around

There are several buses a day from Bu'erjin's **bus station** (32 Kanase Lu) to Ürümqi (10 hours) as well as Altay (1½ hours).

Buses also run from here to Jimunai (吉木乃镇; two hours) on the border with Kazakhstan.

There is no train station in Bu'erjin. The closest station is Beitun (北屯), from where you have to catch a shared taxi or bus the final 90km. Make sure to buy your return train tickets in advance.

Taxi flagfall in town is ¥5.

Kanas Lake Nature Reserve 喀纳斯湖自然保护区

Stunning Kanas Lake (哈纳斯湖, Hānàsī Hú) is a long finger of water surrounded by soaring mountain peaks nestled in the southernmost reaches of the Siberian taiga ecosystem, pinched in between Mongolia, Russia and Kazakhstan. Most of the local inhabitants are Kazakh or Tuvan, though Chinese tourists (and the occasional foreigner) descend on the place in droves during the summer months.

Many visitors come hoping for a cameo by the Kanas Lake Monster, China's Nessie, who has long figured in stories around yurt campfires to scare the kids. She appears every year or two, bringing loads of journalists and conspiracy hounds.

The whole area is only easily accessible from April to October, with ice and snow making transport difficult at other times. The gorgeous autumn colours peak around mid-September.

🛏 Sleeping & Eating

Chartering a car makes this a day trip, but if you want to spend more time, there are hotels at the main Jiǎdēngyù gate to the park, and in the park at the tourist base and in Kanas Village.

There are plenty of eating options available at the tourist facilities at the Jiǎdēngyù gate and small noodle restaurants in Kanas Village.

ℹ Getting There & Away

Travellers use either Bu'erjin or Beitun (北屯) as a jumping-off point to reach Kanas Lake. Some travellers report it's possible to visit in a long day trip from Bu'erjin or Altay by hiring a private driver, which cuts travel time to four to five hours each way.

Public buses from Bu'erjin are sporadic. From Beitun's bus station (next door to the train station), you may be able to catch a shuttle bus (¥100, seven hours) to the Jiǎdēngyù gate.

From Ürümqi, there are two overnight trains – the K9749 and K9791 – calling at Beitun (hard/soft sleeper ¥174/263, eight to 10 hours) and then Altay (hard/soft sleeper ¥197/298, nine to 11 hours). These depart at 8.13pm and 11.10pm.

WORTH A TRIP

HEMU

This gorgeous little Tuvan village of **Hémù** (禾木; ¥50) is an alternative place to base yourself when you visit Kanas Lake. It's 70km southeast of the lake, but far less crowded come the summer months. May and June are great times to visit, when the blossom is thick on the trees, while September is a riot of autumnal colours.

Yining 伊宁

☑ 0999 / POP 542,000

Located on the historic border between the Chinese and Russian empires, Yining (Yīníng; Yili or Gulja) has long been subject to a tug-of-war between the two sides. The city was occupied by Russian troops between 1872 and 1881, and in 1962 there were major Sino–Soviet clashes along the Ili River (Yīlí Hé). There are no unmissable sights here but it's a pleasant, little-visited stop en route to Sayram Lake, or a good place to break an overland journey to Kazakhstan.

In 2014 the stadium in Yining was the site of a mass trial in which 55 Uyghurs were charged with terrorist activities. At least one death sentence was handed down. A similar mass trial was held in 1997 and is the subject of Nick Holdstock's book *The Tree That Bleeds* (2011).

◉ Sights

People's Square   SQUARE
(人民广场, Rénmín Guǎngchǎng) The heart of the city is People's Sq, a popular place to fly kites. It's rather a well-tended plaza with ornamental trees and is surrounded by local government buildings. The south side is lined with ice cream, fruit and kebab stands.

🛏 Sleeping

As a busy overland stopover between China and Kazakhstan, Yining has a fair range of accommodation in varied price ranges. According to travellers, at the time of writing the **Metropolo Jinjiang Hotel** (20 Shenzhen Lu) was accepting foreigners.

WORTH A TRIP

SAYRAM LAKE

Vast **Sayram Lake** (赛里木湖, Sàilǐmù Hú; ¥70), 120km north of Yining and 90km west of Bole, is an excellent spot to get a taste of the Tian Shan range (Tengri Tagh in Kazakh). The lake is especially colourful in June and July, when the alpine flowers are in full bloom. In the height of summer, there are Kazakh yurts scattered around the lake, willing to take boarders.

From Yining bus station, take the special Sayram Lake tourist bus (return ¥80, three hours). Departures are at 9am and 10am, returning at 5pm. Chartering a car or taxi will cost around ¥400.

🍴 Eating & Drinking

Just to the south of town is a line of open-air restaurants where you can sit and watch the mighty Ili River (Ili Daria in Uyghur, Yìlí Hé in Chinese) slide by over a bottle of honey-flavoured *kvass* (a fermented drink made from rye bread).

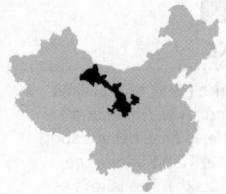

Gansu

POP 25.6 MILLION

Best Places to Eat

➜ Mazilu Beef Noodles (p860)

➜ Zhāixīng Gé (p879)

➜ Yunnan Mama's Kitchen (p870)

➜ Tara Cafe & Restaurant (p865)

Best Places to Stay

➜ Nirvana Hotel (p865)

➜ Silk Road Dunhuang Hotel (p878)

➜ Ganzhou Hotel (p874)

➜ Huálián Bīnguǎn (p860)

➜ Overseas Tibetan Hotel (p865)

Why Go?

Synonymous with the Silk Road, the slender province of Gansu (甘肃, Gānsù) flows east to west along the Hexi Corridor, the gap through which goods and ideas once streamed between China and Central Asia. The constant flow of commerce left Buddhist statues, beacon towers, forts, chunks of the Great Wall and ancient trading towns in its wake. Gansu offers an entrancingly rich cultural and geographic diversity. Historians immerse themselves in Silk Road lore, art aficionados swoon before the wealth of Buddhist paintings and sculptures, while adventurers hike through desert rockland, ascend sand dunes and tread along high-mountain paths well worn by Tibetan nomads. The ethnic diversity is equally astonishing: throughout the province, the local Hui Muslims act as though the Silk Road lives on; in Xiahe and Langmusi a pronounced Tibetan disposition holds sway, while other minority groups such as the Bao'an and Dongxiang join in the colourful minority patchwork.

When to Go
Lanzhou

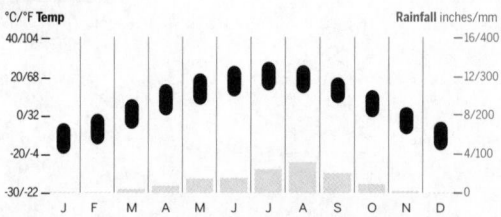

Feb & Mar Join the Tibetan pilgrims for the magnificent Monlam Festival in Xiahe.

Apr & May Before the full heat of summer switches on.

Sep & Oct For crisp northern Gansu autumnal colours, blue skies and cooler climes.

History & People

Although the Qin dynasty had a toehold on eastern Gansu, the first significant push west along the Hexi Corridor came with the Han dynasty. An imperial envoy, Zhang Qian (Chang Ch'ien), was dispatched to seek trading partners and returned with detailed reports of Central Asia and the route that

Gansu Highlights

1 Mogao Grottoes (p880) Making your pilgrimage to one of the most important Buddhist sites on the Silk Road.

2 Bǐnglíng Sì (p864) Gazing up at the giant Buddha carved into a desert cliff at this remote temple by the Yellow River.

3 Big Buddha Temple (p873) Feeling Lilliputian next to the colossal head of the reclining Buddha in his ancient temple hall.

4 Maijishan Grottoes (p884) Clambering up nerve-rattling catwalks to discover these ancient Buddhist caves.

5 Singing Sands Dune (p882) Trudging up these colossal sand dunes to seek out breathtaking views.

6 Labrang Monastery (p862) Going with the Tibetan flow around the *kora* at Gansu's most important monastery.

7 Langmusi (p869) Hiking to your heart's content around this chilled-out Tibetan town.

8 Jiayuguan Fort (p875) Feeling the Gobi wind in your hair, standing on the ramparts of this ancient fortress.

9 Yadan National Park (p882) Seeing the sun setting over eerie desert rock formations.

would become known as the Silk Road. The Han extended the Great Wall through the Hexi Corridor, expanding their empire in the process.

Travellers and merchants from as far as the Roman Empire entered the Middle Kingdom along the Silk Road, and as trade grew, so did the small way-stations set up along its route; these grew into towns and cities that form the major population centres of modern Gansu. The streams of traders from lands east and west also left their mark in the incredible diversity of modern Gansu, and Buddhism found itself conveyed into China along these mercantile routes. The Buddhist grottoes at Mogao, Maijishan and elsewhere are testament to the great flourishing of religious and artistic schools along the Silk Road.

The mixing of cultures in Gansu eventually led to serious tensions, which culminated in the Muslim rebellions of 1862 to 1877. The conflict left millions dead and virtually wiped out Gansu's Muslim population. Ethnic tensions have never fully left the province, as the pro-Tibetan demonstrations in Xiahe in 2008 and 2012 illustrate.

Though remote from the investment banks and manufacturing hubs along the east coast of China, Gansu is not a poor province and a palpable air of prosperity can be felt in towns such as Dunhuang. Gross Domestic Product has been growing at a higher rate than the already blistering national average and massive investments in wind energy are fuelling the transformation of both the natural and urban landscapes.

Gansu is home to a large collection of minority peoples, including the Hui, Mongols,

ⓘ PRICE RANGES

Sleeping
The following price ranges are for a double room in Gansu.

¥ less than ¥150

¥¥ ¥150–500

¥¥¥ more than ¥500

Eating
The following price ranges are for a meal in Gansu.

¥ less than ¥30

¥¥ ¥30–80

¥¥¥ more than ¥80

Tibetans and Kazaks, though the dominant group is the Han.

ⓘ Getting There & Away

Lanzhou Zhongchuan International Airport has flights around the country; other airports such as Dunhuang, Jiayuguan and outside Xiahe only have a handful of flights to major cities, with fewer flights in the winter.

LANZHOU 兰州

📞 0931 / POP 2.9 MILLION

At China's cartographic bullseye, Lanzhou (Lánzhōu) marks the halfway point for overlanders trekking across the country. Growing up on a strategic stretch of the Yellow River (黄河, Huáng Hé), and sitting between competing Chinese and Central Asian empires, Gansu's elongated capital city frequently changed hands, reflected today in its mix of ethnic groups and cultures. These days, Lanzhou is perhaps most well known for its favourite food – Lanzhou beef noodles (牛肉拉面, niúròu lāmiàn) – and with several excellent night markets, this is an excellent place to sample the delights of Chinese Silk Road fare.

⊙ Sights

White Pagoda Temple BUDDHIST SITE
(白塔寺, Báitǎ Sì; White Pagoda Park, Binhe Zhonglu, 白塔山公园宾河中路; ⊙7am-8pm) FREE
This temple, built during the Yuan dynasty (1206–1368) for a fallen Tibetan monk, stands on a hilltop in lovely **White Pagoda Park** (白塔山公园, Báitǎ Shān Gōngyuán) on the northern bank of the Yellow River and provides excellent city and river views on a clear day. The brick-and-stone pagoda is at the top of the hill, engraved around its base with the names of marauding visitors from more recent decades, before it became a protected monument.

White Cloud Temple TAOIST TEMPLE
(白云观, Báiyún Guàn; Binhe Zhonglu, 宾河中路; ⊙7am-6.30pm) FREE Originally founded in the 8th century, this expansive, much rebuilt and active Taoist temple features five halls and was among the most important Quanzhen-order temples during the Qing dynasty. The Jade Emperor sits within his namesake hall, while the final hall is devoted to the 'Three Clear Ones'. The temple is frequented by a large number of Taoist monks and nuns, with their distinctive dark clothes.

Lanzhou

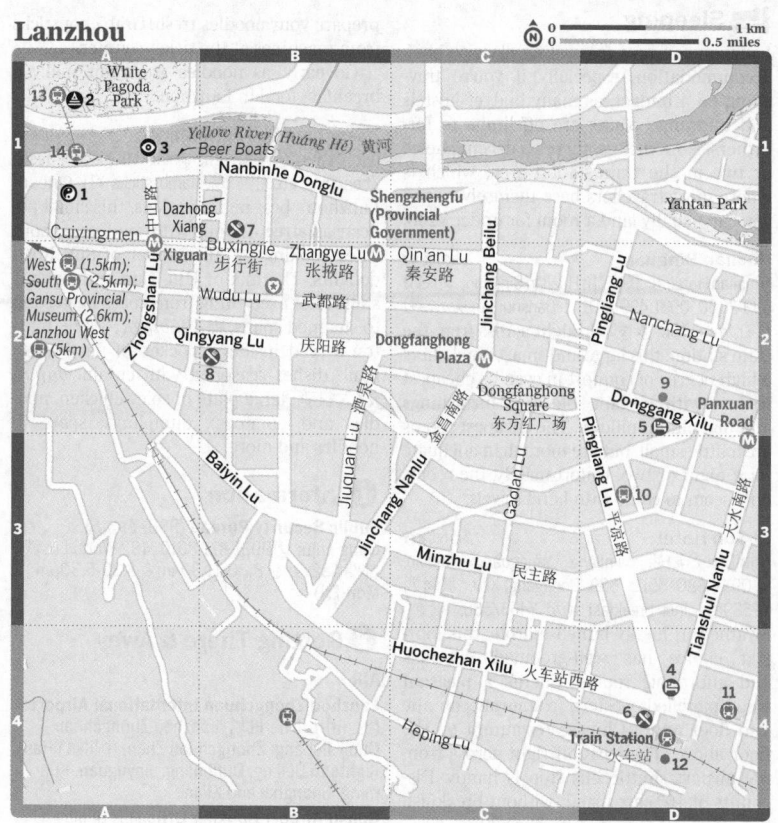

Lanzhou

◎ Sights
1 White Cloud Temple A1
2 White Pagoda Temple A1
3 Zhongshan Bridge A1

🛏 Sleeping
4 Huálián Bīnguǎn D4
5 JJ Sun Hotel D2

🍴 Eating
6 Mazilu Beef Noodles D4
7 Mazilu Beef Noodles B1
8 Zhengning Lu Night Market B2

ℹ Transport
9 Gansu Airport Booking Office D2
10 Lanzhou East Bus Station D3
11 Lanzhou Main Bus Station D4
12 Lanzhou Train Station D4
13 Upper Cable Car Station A1
14 Yellow River Cable Car A1

Gansu Provincial Museum   MUSEUM
(甘肃省博物馆, Gānsù Shěng Bówùguǎn; ☏ 0931 233 9131; 3 Xijin Xilu, 西津西路3号; ⊙ 9am-5pm Tue-Sun) FREE This museum has an intriguing collection of Silk Road artefacts with English descriptions, including inscribed Han-dynasty wooden tablets used to relay messages along the Silk Road, and dinosaur skeletons. The graceful Eastern Han (25 BC–AD 220) bronze horse galloping upon the back of a swallow is known as the 'Flying Horse of Wuwei'. Unearthed at Leitai near Wuwei, it has been proudly reproduced across northwestern China. Take your passport. Bus 1 (¥1, 40 minutes) runs here from Lanzhou train station.

🛏 Sleeping

Lanzhou can be a frustrating place to book accommodation, especially if you're travelling on a budget, as many budget hostels and midrange places are off limits to foreigners. Nonetheless, there's a decent choice or two in the train-station area, which is where most travellers base themselves, and you can usually land a room for under ¥200.

Huálián Bīnguǎn   HOTEL ¥¥
(Hualian Hotel, 华联宾馆; Huálián Bīnguǎn; ☑ 0931 499 2000, 0931 499 2101; 1 Tianshui Lu, 天水路1号; r from ¥198; ﹡ 🔊) Straight across from the train station, this large and smart hotel offers a high degree of comfort in even its cheapest rooms, with elegant, old-style furnishings and big, plump pillows. The cheapest rooms are a little small, but are more than adequate for a night or two. Unfortunately, the rooms only seem to come with hand towels.

JJ Sun Hotel   HOTEL ¥¥¥
(锦江阳光酒店, Jǐnjiāng Yángguāng Jiǔdiàn; ☑ 0931 880 5511; 589 Donggang Xilu, 东岗西路589号; incl breakfast tw/d ¥466/566; ﹡ @) Swathed in highly buffed marble, this four-star choice has well-groomed, spacious and affordable rooms. There's a pleasant wood-panelled western restaurant on the 2nd floor and a Chinese restaurant on the floor above. The location right across from the airport shuttle bus stop is handy. Discounts of 40% are usual; without breakfast, the price comes down another ¥30.

🍴 Eating

Lanzhou is famous for its *niúròu lāmiàn* (牛肉拉面), beef soup with hand-pulled noodles and a spicy topping. There are plenty of places to try the dish, including on Huochezhan Xilu (left as you exit the train station), and Dazhong Xiang near the **Zhongshan Bridge** (Zhōngshān Qiáo, 中山桥; Zhongshan Lu, 中山路). These streets are also lined with restaurants serving dumplings and noodle dishes. Most have picture menus.

⭐ Mazilu Beef Noodles   NOODLES ¥
(马子禄牛肉面, Mǎzìlù Niúròu Miàn; ☑ 0931 845 0505; 86 Dazhong Xiang, 大众巷86号; noodles ¥8; ⏲ 6.30am-2.30pm) In business since 1954, this place has locals flocking here for steaming bowls of the city's most well-known export: spicy hand-pulled noodles. Join the queue inside the door and ask for *niúròu miàn* (牛肉面). You'll be given a ticket, which you take to the kitchen counter where chefs will prepare your noodles fresh. Grab chopsticks from machines at the ticket counter.

Go early, as noodles are traditionally a breakfast food in Lanzhou.

Zhengning Lu Night Market   MARKET ¥
(正宁路小吃夜市, Zhèngníng Lù Xiǎochī Yèshì; Zhengning Lu, 正宁路; lamb sticks ¥1) One of Lanzhou's best night markets, this small pedestrian street is lined with vendors on both sides cooking up all manner of Silk Road delights. The mix of Hui, Han and Uyghur stalls offer everything from goat's head soup to steamed snails, *ròujiābǐng* (肉夹饼, mutton served inside a 'pocket' of flat bread), lamb dishes seasoned with cumin, *dàpán jī* (大盘鸡, large plate of spicy chicken, noodles and potatoes), dumplings, spare-rib noodles and more.

ℹ Information

Public Security Bureau (PSB, 公安局, Gōng'ānjú; ☑ 0931 871 8610; 482 Wudu Lu, 武都路482号; ⏲ 8.30-11.30am & 2.30-5.30pm Mon-Fri)

ℹ Getting There & Away

AIR

Lanzhou Zhongchuan International Airport (兰州中川国际机场, Lánzhōu Zhōngchuān Guójì Jīchǎng; Zhongchuan Zhen, 中川镇) Has flights to Beijing, Dunhuang, Jiayuguan, Kunming, Shanghai and Xi'an.

Gansu Airport Booking Office (甘肃机场集团售票中心, Gānsù Jīchǎng Jítuán Shòupiào Zhōngxīn; ☑ 0931 888 9666; 616 Donggang Xilu, 东岗西路616号; ⏲ 9am-6pm) Can book all air tickets at discounted prices.

BUS

Lanzhou has five bus stations, though the most useful are the main bus station, the south bus station and the west bus station. Buses also head to top ticket destinations from Lanzhou Zhongchuan International Airport. The **Lanzhou Main Bus Station** (兰州客运中心, Lánzhōu Kèyùn Zhōngxīn; 338 Huochenzhan Donglu, 火车站东路338号) is just east of Lanzhou Train Station. Many bus journeys back into Lanzhou end up at the east bus station or the south bus station. For most journeys along the Hexi Corridor, it is faster to take the train.

Journeys to and from the south of Gansu, including to Xiahe, go through the **south bus station** (汽车南站, Qìchē Nánzhàn). A taxi to the train station costs ¥45 and takes 45 minutes, or take bus 111 (¥1).

Services from the main bus station are as follows:

Hezuo ¥75, four hours (8.30am)

Pingliang ¥118, six hours, hourly (7.30am to 7.30pm)

Yinchuan ¥140, six hours, eight per day (7.30am to 5.30pm)

The following services depart from the south bus station. Frustratingly, tickets can only be purchased there, though can be bought just before departure:

Hezuo ¥75, four to five hours, every 20 minutes (7am to 5.50am)

Linxia ¥44, three hours, every 30 minutes (7am to 7.30pm)

Xiahe ¥75, four hours, nine daily (7.30am to 4pm)

Note: there is no direct bus from Lanzhou to Langmusi. Go to Hezuo and change.

The **west bus station** (兰州汽车西站, Lánzhōu Qìchē Xīzhàn; 456 Xijin Donglu, 西津东路 456号) has six departures to Liujiaxia (¥23, 2½ hours, 8am to midday), useful if you are heading to Bǐnglíng Sì. It's perhaps handy to know that the **east bus station** (兰州汽车东站, Qìchē Dōngzhàn; ☏ 0931 841 8411; 276 Pingliang Lu, 平凉路276号) also has two departures per day to Liujiaxia (¥25, 2½ hours, 1.30pm and 2.30pm).

If flying into Lanzhou, three buses for Xiahe (¥110, four hours) and Hezuo (¥125, four hours) also leave from the Terminal 1 Bus Station at Lanzhou Zhongchuan International Airport; five buses per day also depart from the same terminal bus station for Linxia (¥80, three hours).

TRAIN

Lanzhou is the major rail link for trains heading to and from western China. The city has two train stations: the centrally located **Lanzhou Train station** (兰州火车站, Lánzhōu Huǒchēzhàn; Huochezhan Donglu, 火车站东路) and **Lanzhou West Train Station** (兰州西火车站, Lánzhōu Xīhuǒchēzhàn; 187 Jinxi Lu, 津西路187号). Both stations serve the Lanzhou–Xinjiang high-speed rail line and airport trains, though the most frequent departures go from Lanzhou Station.

In high season buy your onward tickets at least a couple of days in advance to guarantee a sleeper berth. For Dunhuang, double-check whether you are getting a train to the town itself or Liuyuan, which is 180km away. Four slow overnight sleepers roll daily to Dunhuang, which can be useful; two fast trains leave every morning for the 8½-hour journey.

From Lanzhou Station, there are trains to the following destinations:

Dunhuang 1st/2nd-class seat ¥523/327, 8½ hours, two fast trains daily (6.33am and 11.58am); hard/soft sleeper ¥289/426, 13 to 14 hours, four trains daily; the remaining trains go to Liuyuan

Jiayuguan 1st/2nd-class seat ¥349/218, 5½ hours; hard/soft sleeper ¥190/319, nine hours

Ürümqi 1st/2nd-class seat ¥882/551, 12 hours; hard/soft sleeper ¥397/611, 18 to 22 hours

Wuwei Hard/soft seat ¥47/72, 3½ hours, regular departures

Xi'an Hard/soft sleeper ¥174/296, eight to nine hours, regular departures

Zhangye West 1st/2nd-class seat ¥244/153, four hours, three daily

Zhongwei Hard seat/soft sleeper ¥47/186, five to six hours, regular departures

From Lanzhou West Train Station, there are trains to the following destinations:

Jiayuguan South 1st/2nd-class seat ¥344/215, six hours, 12 daily

Tianshui South 1st/2nd class ¥99/83, 1½ hours, regular departures

Ürümqi 1st/2nd-class seat ¥882/551, 12 hours, four daily

Xi'an North 1st/2nd class seat ¥232/175, three hours, regular departures

Xining 1st/2nd-class seat ¥93/58, two hours, regular departures

Zhangye West 1st/2nd-class seat ¥239/150, four hours, 12 daily

ⓘ Getting Around

Lanzhou is a huge, sprawling place so give yourself plenty of time to get around, especially if you have a morning bus or train to catch, as both taxis and city buses tend to get caught in traffic.

Lanzhou's new metro system (tickets ¥2 to ¥6) currently runs one line, with a second under construction. Not terribly useful for travellers, Line 1 runs from Chenguanying in the west to Donggang in the east. Line 2 is under construction and is scheduled to commence operation in 2021.

Public buses cost ¥1; taxis are ¥7 for the first 3km. A taxi to Lanzhou South Bus Station costs around ¥35 (45 minutes).

A cable car runs from the **Yellow River Cable Car Station** (黄河索道, Huánghé Suǒdào; down/up/return adult ¥30/45/55, child ¥15/20/25; ☐ 34) to the **Upper Cable Car Station** (黄河索道上站, Huánghé Suǒdào Shàngzhàn) for easy access to White Pagoda Temple.

SOUTHERN GANSU

Mountainous and largely verdant, the southern part of Gansu is a sight to behold. The Tibetan-inhabited areas around Xiahe and Langmusi are the principal enticements here – perfect stopovers for overlanders heading to or from Sichuan or as destinations in their own right. Southwest of Lanzhou, the inspiring vistas of the Yellow River and the Buddhist grottoes of Bǐnglíng Sì, carved out of dusty desert cliffs, remain some of the best-kept secrets in the country.

Xiahe 夏河

☎ 0941 / POP 80,000

The alluring monastic town of Xiahe (Xiàhé) attracts an astonishing band of visitors: backpack-laden students, insatiable wanderers, shaven-headed Buddhist nuns, Tibetan pilgrims in their most colourful finery, camera-toting tour groups and dusty, itinerant beggars. Most visitors are rural Tibetans, whose purpose is to pray, prostrate themselves and seek spiritual fulfilment at holy Labrang Monastery, around which Xiahe has grown up.

In an arid mountain valley at 2920m above sea level, Xiahe has a certain rhythm about it and visitors quickly tap into its fluid motions. The rising sun sends pilgrims out to circle the 3km *kora* (pilgrim path) that rings the monastery. Crimson-clad monks shuffle into the temples to chant morning prayers. It's easy to get swept up in the action, but some of the best moments come as you set your own pace, wandering about town or in the splendid encircling mountains.

◉ Sights

Labrang Monastery covers much of Xiahe and a ticket to the monastery includes the main buildings on a guided tour. Several other buildings have their own admission fees, and tickets for those can be purchased at small ticket offices or from attendants at the entrances. In general, opening hours for the monastery's buildings are 8am to 5pm, although you can wander the grounds from very early in the morning, and many pilgrims begin walking the *kora* before dawn, a good time to join in.

★ **Labrang Monastery** BUDDHIST TEMPLE
(拉卜楞寺, Lābǔléng Sì; Renmin Xilu, 人民西路; tour ¥40; ⊙8am-6pm) With its succession of squeaking prayer wheels (3km in total), hawks circling overhead and the throb of Tibetan longhorns resonating from the surrounding hills, Labrang is a monastery town unto itself. Many of the chapel halls are illuminated in a yellow glow by flickering yak-butter lamps, their strong-smelling fuel scooped from voluminous tubs. Even if Tibet is not on your itinerary, the monastery sufficiently conveys the mystique of its devout persuasions, leaving indelible impressions of a deeply sacred domain.

In addition to the chapels, residences, golden-roofed temple halls and living quarters for the monks, Labrang is also home to six *tratsang* (monastic colleges or institutes), exploring esoteric Buddhism, theology, medicine, astrology and law. No photography is allowed within the temple halls, with a ¥500 fine in some places.

Labrang Monastery was founded in 1709 by Ngagong Tsunde (E'angzongzhe in Chinese), the first-generation Jamyang (a line of reincarnated Rinpoches or living Buddhas

---

DON'T MISS

WALK LIKE A TIBETAN

Following the 3km **inner kora** (pilgrim path) encircling Labrang Monastery is perhaps the best approach to grasping the giant temple's layout, scale and significance. The *kora* is lined with long rows of squeaking prayer wheels, whitewashed *chörtens* (Tibetan stupas) and chapels. Tibetan pilgrims in trainers, with beads in their hands and sunhats on their heads, old folk, mothers with babies and children, shabby nomads and curious visitors walk in meditative fashion clockwise along the path (called *zhuǎnjìngdào*, 'scripture-turning way' in Chinese), rotating prayer wheels as they go. Look also for the tiny meditation cells on the northern hillside.

For a short hike, the more strenuous **outer kora** takes about an hour and climbs high above the monastery. To reach the start, head past the monastery's western edge. About one block into the Tibetan village look for a large signpost (in Tibetan but it's the only one around) on the right. Follow the alley up to the right, and make your way to the ridge, where you wind steeply uphill to a collection of prayer flags and the ruins of a **hermitage**. The views of the monastery open up as you go along. At the end of the ridge there's a steep descent into town.

Xiahe

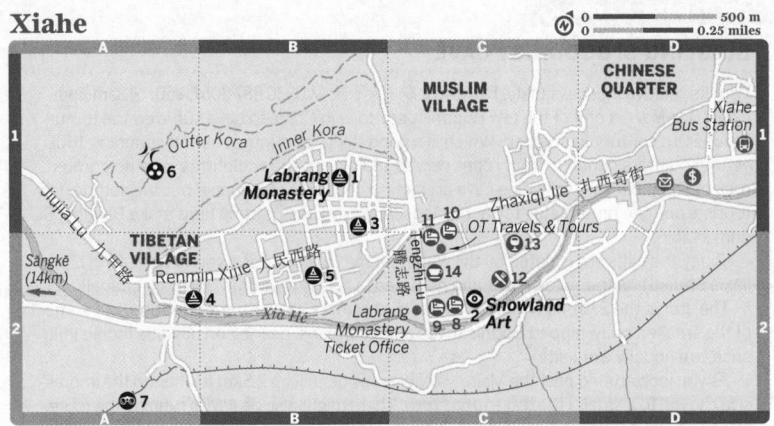

ranking third in importance after the Dalai and Panchen lamas, from nearby Ganjia. The monastery is one of the six major Tibetan monasteries of the Gelugpa order (Yellow Hat sect of Tibetan Buddhism). The others are Ganden (p946), Sera (p946) and Drepung (p945) monasteries near Lhasa; Tashilhunpo Monastery (p949) in Shigatse; and Kumbum Monastery (p921) outside Xining in Qinghai.

At its peak, Labrang housed nearly 4000 monks, but their ranks greatly declined during the Cultural Revolution. Modern Labrang is again such a popular destination for young disciples that numbers are currently capped at 1800 monks, with about 1600 currently in residence, drawn from Qinghai, Gansu, Sichuan and Inner Mongolia.

Main Buildings

The only way to visit the interior of the most important buildings is on a tour (no photos allowed inside buildings), which generally includes the **Institute of Medicine**, the **Manjushri Temple**, the **Serkung** (Golden Temple) and the main **Prayer Hall** (Grand Sutra Hall) – an amazing sight, steeped in mystery and where you may be treated to the spectacle of lamas chanting in the courtyard outside – plus a **museum** of relics and yak-butter sculptures. English-language **tours** (per person ¥40) leave the monastery's **ticket office** (拉卜楞寺售票处, Lābǔléng Sì Shòupiàochù; ⊙ 8am-5pm mid-Apr–mid-Oct, 9am-4pm mid-Oct–mid-Apr) around 10.15am and 3.15pm most days, and although there is plenty to see, they can feel a bit rushed. Outside those times you can latch on to a Chinese tour, with little lost even if you don't understand the language, but be aware you must purchase the ¥40 ticket to gain entrance to any of the buildings' interiors. Even better is to show up at around 6am or 7am, when the monks come out to pray and chant. At dusk the hillside resonates with the throaty sound of sutras being chanted behind the wooden doors.

Other Buildings

The rest of the Labrang can be explored by walking the **inner kora**, a 3.5km-long pilgrim path and the world's longest stretch of prayer wheels. Although many of the temple

GANSU XIAHE

BǏNGLÍNG SÌ BUDDHIST CAVE

With its relative inaccessibility, **Bǐnglíng Sì** (炳灵寺; ☏0930 887 9057; ¥50; ☉8am-6pm, closed Dec-Mar) is one of the few Buddhist grottoes in China to have survived the tumultuous 20th century unscathed. Which is a good thing, as during a period spanning 1600 years, sculptors dangling from ropes carved 183 niches and sculptures into the porous rock of steep canyon walls. The cave art can't compare to Dunhuang, but the setting, few tourists and the remarkable terraced landscapes you pass getting here make Bǐnglíng Sì unmissable.

Today the cliffs are isolated by the waters of the Liujiaxia Reservoir (刘家峡水库, Liújiāxiá Shuǐkù) on the Yellow River and hemmed in by a ring of dramatic rock citadels.

The star is the 27m-high **seated statue of Maitreya**, the future Buddha, but some of the smaller, sway-hipped Bodhisattvas and guardians, bearing an obvious Indian influence, are equally exquisite.

As you loop around past the Maitreya cave, consider hiking 2.5km further up the impressive canyon to a small **Tibetan monastery**. There might also be 4WDs running the route.

You can visit Bǐnglíng Sì as a day trip from Lanzhou or en route to Xiahe via Linxia. Take a boat or taxi from the town of Liujiaxia. Six buses depart from Lanzhou's west bus station (¥23, 2½ hours, 8am to midday) to Liujiaxia bus station. Two later buses (¥25, 2½ hours, 1.30pm and 2.30pm) also run daily to Liujiaxia from the east bus station in Lanzhou, but these will arrive too late for a trip to the grottoes. From Liujiaxia, you will need to take a 10-minute taxi (¥6) to the boat ticket office at the dam (大坝, dàbà). Try to catch the earliest buses possible from Lanzhou (starting at 8am) to avoid getting stuck on the way back. The last return bus to Lanzhou leaves at 6.30pm.

Covered speedboats (seating nine people) cost ¥700 for the one-hour journey. The boat ticket office will refuse to make the trip unless the boat is full, so independent travellers may have to wait for a small group to form; expect to pay around ¥150 per person in this case. In summer, you should have no trouble finding a seat, but in shoulder season, you may find yourself stranded. Note that no boats run from December to March.

Surprisingly, the much more scenic (and flexible) route to the caves is by hiring a private car (¥250 to ¥300 return). Out of Liujiaxia, the road runs high into the rugged hills above the reservoir, and for 90 minutes you will twist and turn, dip and rise through a wonderland of corn-growing terraces laddering and layering every slope, mound, outcrop and ravine. The final descent to the green-blue reservoir, with its craggy backdrop, is sublime. Driver touts ply the bus station in Liujiaxia; bargain hard for a good deal.

If heading to Linxia after the grottoes, there are frequent buses (¥21, three hours) from the station at Liujiaxia.

You can also opt to stay overnight in Liujiaxia for a less rushed experience. The **Dorsett Hotel** (临夏刘家峡帝豪大酒店, Línxià Liújiāxiá Dìháo Dà Jiǔdiàn; ☏0930 888 8888; 169 Huanghe Lu, Liujiaxia, 黄河路169号, 刘家峡; tw/d ¥230/250; ❄⊞) at the north end of town is a good option with huge rooms overlooking the Yellow River.

halls are padlocked shut, there are a couple of separate smaller chapels you can visit, though they can often be closed for unexplained reasons. Some charge admission. Among the most popular are the three-storey **Barkhang** (Printing Temple; ¥10), the monastery's traditional printing temple, as well as the **Hall of Hayagriva** (马头明王殿, Mǎtóu Míngwáng Diàn, Hall of Horsehead Buddha; ¥10) with its enchanting murals, and the golden **Gongtang Pagoda** (贡唐宝塔, Gòngtáng Bǎotǎ, Gòngtáng Chörten; ¥20), which offers incredible views over the whole monastery from its roof. The **Lower Tantric College** (下续部学院, *xiàxùbù xuéyuàn*) contains some riveting tantric figures and a shrine at the rear with ancient murals. Women are not allowed to enter the **Hùfǎ Shéndiàn** (护法神殿, Hall of Protecting the Law). The large wall of a walled garden can also be seen, part of the monk's living quarters (no admission).

Access to the rest of the monastery area is free, and you can easily spend several hours just walking around and soaking up the atmosphere in the endless maze of mudpacked walls. The Tibetan greeting in the local Amdo dialect is *Cho day mo?* ('How do you do?') – a great icebreaker.

The best morning views of the monastery come from the **Thangka Display Terrace** (FREE), a popular picnic spot, or the forested hills south of the main town.

You'll need a ticket to enter the main monastery complex between mid-June and mid-October, when most visitors are in Xiahe, but at other times you will find you can just wander in and around the monastery (though you may not be able to access individual halls).

Tours

Guided tours of the surrounding area can be arranged by **OT Travels & Tours** (☑1390 941 9888, 0941 712 2642; www.overseastibetan hotel.com/TravelAgency.htm; 77 Renmin Xijie, 人民西街77号; ☉8am-9pm), the couple who runs Nirvana Hotel and the staff at Snowy Mountain Cafe (p866). Most guesthouses in town can also help with day-trip arrangements.

Festivals & Events

Monlam Festival RELIGIOUS
(Great Prayer Festival) This festival starts three days after the Tibetan New Year, which is usually in February or early March, with significant days accompanied by spectacular processions and prayer assemblies. Monlam Festival finishes with a creative display of monk-sculpted butter lanterns lighting up the 15th evening (and full moon) of the New Year.

Sleeping

Xiahe has long been a travellers destination, and is loaded with small guesthouses, inns and hotels catering to a variety of budgets. Most are located at the west end of Renmin Xilu/Zhaxiqi Jie near the entrance to Labrang Monastery.

Many hotels here utilise solar to power their hot-water supplies: showering in the evening offers the best chance for hot water in many places.

★ **Overseas Tibetan Hotel** HOTEL ¥
(华侨饭店, Huáqiáo Fàndiàn; ☑0941 712 2642; www.overseastibetanhotel.com; 77 Renmin Xijie, 人民西街77号; dm/d ¥50/300; ☎) This well-run, large and popular 40-room place is a Xiahe mainstay, offering comfortable rooms, wi-fi that reaches every corner, solar-powered hot water, laundry service and affable staff. The modern and refurbished doubles have clean enclosed showers, flat-screen TVs and cushy, thick mattresses. Dorm beds are four to a

room, with shared shower. Expect discounts of 20% in quiet periods.

It's owned by Losang, an energetic, likeable Tibetan with faultless English who's in touch with the wants of travellers. Useful services include the OT Travels & Tours travel agency, transport arrangements and the **Everest Cafe** with western set breakfasts with yak yoghurt (¥30).

Labrang Red Rock International Hostel HOSTEL ¥
(拉卜楞红石国际青年旅馆, Lābǔléng Hōngshí Guójì Qīngnián Lǚguǎn; ☑0941 712 3698; 253 Yagetang, 雅鸽塘253号; dm/d ¥50/150; @☎) Quietly tucked away south of much of the action, this Tibetan-themed hostel has pinewood rooms, solar-powered hot showers and an attractive floorboard restaurant-bar area as you walk in. Doubles are clean with futon-style beds, and YHA cardholders get a discount. Washing is ¥15 per load.

★ **Nirvana Hotel** HOTEL ¥¥
(德吉园, Déjíyuán; ☑0941 718 1702; www.nirvana-hotel.net; 247 Yagetang, 雅鸽塘247号; d ¥300; ❀@☎) ✎ Run by a friendly, English-speaking Tibetan-Dutch couple, Nirvana's cosy rooms are decorated tastefully in traditional Tibetan style, with giant, comfy beds. Small details make its slightly higher prices worthwhile: international plug boards, free coffee/tea/bottled water and toiletries. The bonus of having Nirvana's popular bar-restaurant (p866) downstairs and the friendliness of the proprietors make this a haven in this part of China.

Eating

For those who can't make it to Tibet, Xiahe provides an opportunity to develop an appetite for the flavours of the Land of Snows, whether it's momo (dumplings), *tsampa* (a porridge of roasted barley flour), yak-milk yoghurt or throat-warming glasses of the local barley-based firewater (*chang* in Tibetan; *qīngkèjiǔ*, 青稞酒 in Chinese).

Tara Cafe & Restaurant TIBETAN ¥
(268 Yagetang, 雅鸽塘268号; dishes ¥16-46; ☉8.30am-10pm) This traditionally styled and highly colourful restaurant on the ground floor of **Tara Guesthouse** (卓玛旅社, Zhuōmǎ Lǚshè; ☑0941 712 1274; dm ¥40, d ¥320, s/tw per bed without bathroom ¥85/100; ☎) is very good-looking indeed and serves excellent baked Tibetan dumplings (烤藏包, *kǎozàngbāo*; ¥36) and other Tibetan and Chinese

GANSU XIAHE

dishes, and is popular with monks for its many vegetarian options and salads. Tara also serves coffee (from ¥15) and beer.

Nirvana Restaurant & Bar   TIBETAN ¥

(德吉园, Déjíyuán; ☎ 0941 718 1702; www.nirvana-hotel.net; 247 Yagetang, 雅鸽塘247号; dishes ¥15-35; ⊗ 9am-9pm; ❋ 🐾) 🍴 This inviting, bright restaurant serves Tibetan dishes, such as the popular yak hotpot (¥25) and *tsampa* (¥20), as well as western favourites and breakfasts (¥28). The welcoming, casual vibe makes leaving Nirvana difficult, as does the long booze menu, which includes imported beers (from ¥20), coffee, shakes, smoothies, cocktails (from ¥30) and hot toddy (¥40) for those cold nights.

Snowy Mountain Cafe   CAFE ¥

(雪山餐厅, Xuěshān Cāntīng; Fengqing Pedestrian St, 风情步行街; mains from ¥15) This chilled-out choice was moving at the time of writing, but its former incarnation served a menu of Tibetan, Chinese and western staples, as well as a full-service bar. The Tibetan-style noodles and yak steak were crowd-pleasers at its late spot, and there was also a nice western breakfast menu, including a set menu of eggs, toast, yoghurt and tea/coffee.

🍷 Drinking & Nightlife

There isn't a huge nightlife scene in Xiahe, owing largely to the town's monastic

sensibilities, but several guesthouses have attached bar-cafes. Nirvana Restaurant & Bar has the best booze selection in town, including locally brewed Gansu craft beer and homemade barley spirits. Snowy Mountain Cafe also has a decent selection and sells the usual Chinese beers as well as Budweiser.

Norden Cafe   CAFE

(诺尔丹咖啡, Nuò'ěrdān Kāfēi; Tengzhi Lu, 腾志路; tea ¥15; 🐾) Traveller-friendly cafe with warm pine-wood interior serving homemade cakes, soups and burgers, plus excellent tea and coffee. Lovely big window seats overlook Labrang Monastery's ticket office (p863). Service is first rate.

🛍 Shopping

Xiahe is an excellent place to look for Tibetan handicrafts, from cowboy hats and Tibetan trilbies to *chuba* (Tibetan cloaks), monks boots, strings of prayer flags and *thangka* (Tibetan sacred art) paintings. Stacks of handicraft shops line Zhaxiqi Jie east of the monastery, and there's a good cluster of *thangka* shops, with artists busy at work, south of Norden Cafe towards the Labrang Red Rock International Hostel.

ℹ Information

Xiahe is located at nearly 3000m in altitude, and some travellers experience mild altitude

GANSU XIAHE

SNOWLAND ART

A visit to **Snowland Art** (www.snowlandart.org) – an art studio where visitors can meet and talk to Tibetan students, and buy artworks, *thangka*, handicrafts and souvenirs – is a must for anyone interested in art, Tibetan culture and the potential of youth. Training gifted Tibetan youngsters in art – employing western art techniques and introducing them to the history of western art at the same time – the studio is run by Tenzin Dolma (Kristel Ouwehand), who originally hails from Canada.

Tenzin's explorations brought her to a Tibetan monastery in South India, living in the monastic community as the sole woman and foreigner. After 10 years teaching English and art within the monastery, Tenzin emerged from her monastic life proficient in the Tibetan language. She then lived in Sichuan, Qinghai and Xiahe, developing Snowland Art along the way; the school now has its own building, housing 15 young Tibetan artists, Tenzin's husband, three cats and a dog.

Tenzin's purpose is to provide an ethics-based learning environment for young artists, exposing them to art and international people and cultures. She takes in talented kids from disadvantaged families, who graduate from their five-year live-in program with skills and confidence.

Tenzin also oversees rock-painting workshops for children over the age of five and has plans for workshops in butter sculptures and sand painting (you will need to book two days in advance). All proceeds from art and handicraft sales go back into supporting the school and its mission.

sickness when they arrive. The most common complaints are headache, fatigue and dizziness. Take care not to overexert yourself, especially for the first 24 hours while you acclimatise.

ICBC (工商银行, Gōngshāng Yínháng; 13 Renmin Dongjie, 人民东街13号; ⏰ 8.30am-4pm) Has an ATM that accepts international cards and exchanges major currencies.

China Post (中国邮政, Zhōngguó Yóuzhèng; 8 Renmin Xijie, 人民西街8号; ⏰ 8am-6pm)

ⓘ Getting There & Away

AIR

Gannan Xiahe Airport (甘南夏河机场, Gānnán Xiàhé Jīchǎng), 65km south of Xiahe, has flights to several cities, including Xi'an, Lhasa, Chengdu and Yinchuan. Book flights online in English at www.ctrip.com.

BUS

The following bus services depart from **Xiahe** (汽车站, Qìchēzhàn; ⏰ 6am-6pm):

Hezuo ¥22, 1½ hours, every 30 minutes (8.10am to 5.20pm)

Langmusi ¥72, 3½ hours, one daily (7.40am)

Lanzhou ¥76, 3½ hours, six daily (6.30am, 7.30am, 8.30am, 12.10pm, 2.30pm and 2.55pm)

Linxia ¥32, two hours, every 30 minutes (6am to 5.25pm)

Tongren ¥32, three hours, two daily (8am and 2pm)

Xining ¥79, six hours, one daily (7am)

If you can't get a direct ticket to/from Lanzhou, take a bus to Linxia or Hezuo and change there. If heading to Xining, note that buses run there every 40 minutes from Tongren.

Around Xiahe

Sangke Grasslands   AREA

(桑科草原, Sāngkē Cǎoyuán) Expanses of open grassland dotted with Tibetans and their grazing yak herds highlight a trip to the village of Sangke, 14km from Xiahe. Development has turned the area into a bit of a small circus, complete with touristy horse rides and fake yurts, but there is good hiking in the nearby hills and you can keep going to more distant and pristine grasslands in the direction of Amchog.

You can cycle to Sangke from Xiahe in about one hour. A taxi costs ¥50 return, or ¥250 for an English-speaking guide and driver; enquire at Snowy Mountain Cafe. The grasslands are lushest in summer. If you want to spend more time up here, the Nirvana Resort (p868) and the Norden Camp (p868) are both here.

Ganjia Grasslands   AREA

(甘加草原, Gānjiā Cǎoyuán) The Ganjia Grasslands, 34km from Xiahe, aren't as pretty as those at nearby Sangke, but there is more to explore. From Xiahe a bumpy road crosses the Naren-Ka pass (impassable after long rains) before quickly descending into wide grasslands dotted with herds of sheep and backed by ever-more-dramatic mountain scenery.

Past Ganjia Xian village, a side road climbs 12km to **Nekhang**, a cave complex where pilgrims lower themselves down ropes and ladders into two sacred underground chambers. A Dutch traveller fell to his death here in 2006 so it is inadvisable to penetrate too far into the cavern, though the front section – where a lama left a sacred hand print on the rock – is safe. A kind of makeshift barrier is in place to stop explorers from investigating the cave to any great depth. The **gorge** alongside the cave can be explored on a long and thrilling hike: indeed, it's possible to keep exploring for days.

Just up the road from the caves is **Trakkar Gompa** (白石崖寺, Báishíyá Sì; ¥30), a monastery of 90 monks set against a stunning backdrop of vertical rock formations and with sweeping views of the grasslands. From Trakkar it's a short drive to the 2000-year-old Han dynasty village of **Bajiao** (八角城, Karnang), whose remarkable 12-sided walls still shelter a small living community. From the village it's a short 5km diversion to the renovated **Tseway Gompa** (作海寺, Zuòhǎi Sì; ¥20), one of the few Bön monasteries in Gansu. Make sure you circumnavigate any holy site counterclockwise in the Bön fashion (the opposite direction from the usual way). There are great views of Bajiao from the ridge behind the monastery.

A four- to five-hour return trip to the Ganjia Grasslands costs around ¥180 for a taxi from Xiahe. An English-speaking driver and guide costs ¥450 for the full return trip and can be arranged at Snowy Mountain Cafe.

🛏 Sleeping

Norden Camp   CABIN ¥¥¥

(诺尔丹营地, Nuòěrdān Yíngdì; www.nordentravel. com; cabin incl 3 meals for 2 ¥3925, tent inc 3 meals for 2 ¥2400; ⏰ May-Oct; 🛜) This selection of

LINXIA & ITS MINORITY COMMUNITIES

Linxia (临夏; population 250,000) is a centre of Chinese Islam settled by ancient Silk Road Muslims and now populated by their descendants. At one time known as Hezhou (河州, Hézhōu), the city, which holds a strategic location at the junction of the Silk Road and several north–south trade routes meant it was, for centuries, an important commercial centre. These crossing roads brought Muslim teachers from Central Asia and further afield, some of whom stayed and went on to turn Linxia into an important centre for Chinese Islamic scholarship, particularly Sufism. The city itself is occasionally used by travellers (and monks) to break up the trip between Xiahe and Lanzhou or Qinghai. Linxia is home to more than 80 mosques and *gōngbĕi* (拱北, Sufi master's shrine complexes) dotted all over town.

Spilling over a ridge high above Linxia and home to both Hui and Dongxiang minorities, the little market town of **Suonanba** (锁南坝, Suǒnánbà; population 12,000) has a single street that's a hive of activity, with locals trading livestock and occasional shepherds shooing flocks about.

The town is sometimes also called Dongxiang (东乡, Dōngxiāng) after the surrounding county. The Dongxiang people speak an Altaic language and are believed to be descendants of 13th-century immigrants from Central Asia, moved forcibly to China after Kublai Khan's Middle East conquest.

Dahejia (大河家, Dàhéjiā; population 4500), with sweeping views over the Yellow River, towering red cliffs and (in summer) verdant green terraces, is a kaleidoscope of colour. The surrounding area is home to a significant population of Bao'an (保安族), Muslims who speak a Mongolic language. The Bao'an are famed for producing knives and share cultural traits with the Hui and Dongxiang. Their Mongol roots are evident during summer festivals, when it is possible to see displays of wrestling and horse riding.

To Suonanba, frequent minibuses (¥7, one hour) head up on the pleasant journey past terraced fields from Linxia's east bus station.

You can visit Dahejia when travelling on the road between Linxia and Xining. Most buses between the two will stop here. From Linxia you can also catch a frequent minibus (¥25, three hours) from the station (城郊汽车站, chéngjiāo qìchē zhàn) on the outskirts of town.

pinewood log cabins, with decks and composting toilets, as well as khullu yak fibre and wood-floor tents, is very scenically located by a river in the Sangke Grasslands. It's certainly an attractive, pastoral and quite luxurious proposition, though prices are almost as high as the altitude. The camp is full board, with a menu that draws on local and seasonal ingredients.

Nirvana Resort
CHALET ¥¥¥

(德吉林卡, Déjílínkǎ; www.nirvanaresort-xiahe.com; Sangke Grasslands, 桑科草原; chalet ¥2000, family chalet ¥2600; ☺May–mid-Oct; ☎) On the cusp of opening at the time of writing, these lovely all-rustic, all-wood 60-sq-metre chalets (a dozen in all), operated by the folk at the Nirvana Restaurant (p866) in Xiahe, are positioned with large windows looking out onto the expansive grasslands and overlooking a river. Each chalet features running water and a bar-restaurant is at hand. Transport can be arranged.

Hezuo 合作

☑ 0941 / POP 90,000

The regional capital of Gannan (甘南, Gānnán) prefecture, Hezuo (Hézuò) mainly serves as a transit point for travellers plying the overland route between Gansu and Sichuan provinces. The city is also the site of the staggering Milarepa Palace, a bewitching Tibetan temple ranging spectacularly over nine floors.

Hezuo is a fairly compact town, with a large public square roughly halfway between the two bus stations. You will frequently see the name spelt 安多合作 (Āndūo Hézuò) – Anduo (安多) being the Chinese for Amdo, one of the three regions of Tibet.

◉ Sights

★ Milarepa Palace
Buddhist Temple
BUDDHIST TEMPLE

(九层佛阁, Sekhar Gutok, Jiǔcéng Fógé; ¥20; ☺7am-6pm) A towering nine-storey layer cake of a temple, the Milarepa Palace is both deeply steeped in mystery and unusual in the

Tibetan world as different spiritual leaders from varying sects are worshipped on each floor. The exterior is quite modern, but the interior conveys a seasoned, creaky and musty sense of age coupled with a powerful sense of devotion from the worshippers who flock here and prostrate themselves at the main gate. A taxi here costs ¥2 to ¥3 from the main bus station.

The Milarepa's ground floor is a powerful spectacle: a galaxy of Bodhisattvas, Buddhist statues and yak-butter lamps illuminating celestial figures. Climb upstairs to a further rich display of lamas and living Buddhas. More deities muster on the 4th floor and an unsettling array of fearsome, turquoise tantric effigies awaits on the 6th floor. The 8th floor houses effigies of Sakyamuni and Guanyin, with views over the hills and town.

If the weather obliges with blue skies, the temple makes for a superb photo-op, especially with Tibetan pilgrims circling the outside wall. The town's main monastery, **Tso Gompa** (合作寺, Hézuò Sì, Hezuo Monastery; Nawulu, 那吾路; ⊙8am-6pm) FREE, is next door, with its various stupas and halls, some of which you may find open.

You can find the temple about 2km from the bus station along the main road towards Xiahe.

⌣ Sleeping & Eating

There is an ample supply of Sichuan restaurants along the main roads and a good choice of dining options around the main square.

Táoyuán Dàjiǔdiàn HOTEL¥
(桃园大酒店; ☑0941 822 3366; 206 Dangzhou Jie, 当周南街206号; s & tw inc breakfast from ¥288, ste ¥688; ☀⊡) Staff are welcoming at this centrally located hotel (one of a small handful permitted to accept foreigners in Hezuo), though their English is rather limited; rooms are comfortable and pleasant.

ⓘ Getting There & Away

Hezuo is where buses from Zoigê (Ruò'ěrgài), in Sichuan, and Langmusi and Xiahe meet. There is no train station here, but you can book tickets between other stations and destinations at the **train booking office** (火车票售票点, Huǒchēpiào Shòupiàodiǎn; ⊙8.30am-noon & 1.30-5pm) within the north bus station on Zhihema Lu.

Services from the **north bus station** (合作汽车北站, Hézuò Qìchē Běizhàn; Zhihema Lu, 知合玛路) include the following:

Lanzhou ¥74, four hours, every 30 minutes

Linxia ¥31, 1½ hours, every 25 to 30 minutes

Xiahe ¥22, one hour, every 30 minutes (7am to 4pm)

Xining ¥92, 6½ hours, one daily (7.30am)

From the **south bus station** (合作南站, Hézuò Nánzhàn; Tongqin Jie, 通钦街) destinations include the following:

Langmusi ¥50, three hours, three daily (6.30am, 10.20am and noon), the bus to Zöigê also goes via Langmusi

Zoigê (Ruò'ěrgài) ¥80, 3½ hours, one daily (7.30am)

Langmusi 郎木寺

☑0941 / POP 4500 / ELEV 3325M

Straddling the border between Sichuan and Gansu, Langmusi (Lángmùsì; Taktsang Lhamo in Tibetan) is an expanding alpine Amdo Tibetan village nestled among steep grassy meadows, evergreen forests of slender pine trees, crumbling stupas, piles of *mani* stones, and snow-clad peaks. The village is a delightful place surrounded by countless red and white monastery buildings, flapping prayer flags, and the mesmerising sound of monks chanting at twilight.

The White Dragon River (白龙江, Báilóng Jiāng) divides the town in two, and the Sichuan side has quickly become the far more comfortable part to stay in. From where the bus drops you off, most of the budget accommodation and restaurant options lie along this main street or just beside, with the Kerti Gompa up a small street on the left and Serti Gompa on a hillside to the right beyond the river.

◉ Sights

Kerti Gompa BUDDHIST MONASTERY
(格尔底寺, Gé'ěrdǐ Sì; ¥30; ⊙6.30am-8pm) Rising up on the Sichuan side of White Dragon River is this monastery – otherwise dubbed the Sichuan Monastery – built in 1413, home to around 700 monks and composed of six temples and colleges. Try catching a glimpse of student monks in class by visiting the monastery in the morning and late afternoon. The admission is valid for two days.

🏃 Activities

Hiking

Bountiful hiking opportunities radiate in almost every direction from Langmusi. For all-day or overnight treks, including to **Huagaishen Shan** (华盖神山, Huágàishén Shān; 4200m), all the horse-trekking companies and most of the hostels in town can arrange a local guide.

Southwest of Kerti Gompa is **Namo Gorge** (纳摩峡谷, Nàmó Xiágǔ), which makes for an excellent two- to three-hour (return) hike. The gorge contains several sacred grottoes, one dedicated to the Tibetan goddess Palden Lhamo, the other a stone-tablet-labelled **Fairy Cave** (仙女洞, Xiānnǚ Dòng), where monks sometimes chant inside, which gives the town its Tibetan name (lángmù means 'fairy'). Cross rickety bridges flung over the gushing stream, trek past piles of *mani* stones and prayer flags, and hike on into a splendid ravine. After about 30 minutes of clambering over rocks you reach a grassy plain surrounded by towering peaks.

A popular trek is the hike along the White Dragon River to the **river's source** (白龙江源头, Báilóng Jiāng Yuántóu), where domestic hikers go in search of *chóngcǎo* (虫草), a coveted herb used in Chinese medicine.

Another lovely walk heads out over the hills along a narrow paved road from the stupa at Serti Gompa (you must pay admission to pass through) to the small village of **Jikehe Cun** (吉科合村, Jíkēhé Cūn). This hike can be combined with the hike to the White Dragon River source. When you reach the village, simply follow the loop and then head down a dirt path towards the valley below. Watch out for local dogs.

For glorious views over Langmusi, trek up the coxcomb-like **Red Stone Mountain** (红石崖, Hóngshí Yá). To start, turn right one street back (heading out of Langmusi) from the intersection where the bus drops off.

Horse Trekking

The mountain trails around Langmusi offer spectacular riding opportunities. There are two outfits in town offering similar one- to four-day treks overnighting at nomads' tents and with the option of climbing nearby peaks along the way. Both **Langmusi Tibetan Horse Trekking** (☎0941 667 1504; www.langmusi.net; ⊗8am-10pm) and **Wind Horse Trekking** (郎木寺白龙马队, Lángmùsì Báilóng Mǎduì; ☎151 0944 1588; www.windhorse-trekking.com; ⊗8am-8pm) have English-speaking staff and are good sources of travel information.

🛏 Sleeping

★ Trachung Tsang   HOTEL ¥
(扎琼仓青年客栈, Zhāqióngcāng Qīngnián Kèzhàn; ☎151 0941 3440; Langmusi Zhen, 郎木寺镇; dm ¥50, d with/without shower ¥220/150; 🛜 🧖) This endearing choice up the hill on the Sichuan side has a comfortable range of doubles and dorm accommodation. The operation is run by Huasang, an environmentalist who has put the sustainable management of the grasslands at the core of his work, reflected in the on-site museum. The stove-heated library–common room is lovely (and the only wi-fi area).

Boke Youth Hostel   HOSTEL ¥
(泊客青年旅舍, Bókè Qīngnián Lǚshè; ☎188 0666 1900; dm ¥30, s & d ¥60, f ¥180; ❀🛜) This Kung-fu Panda mural-decorated hostel offers large and clean doubles and pretty good dorms too, along with an open and uncluttered main lounging zone. Head back from the bus drop-off towards the highway; it's not far down the road on the left inside a courtyard.

Yong Zhong Hotel   HOTEL ¥
(永忠宾馆, Yǒngzhōng Bīnguǎn; ☎0941 667 1032; downhill from Kerti Gompa, 农村信用杜隔壁; tw ¥180-220; ❀🛜) On the Sichuan side of town is this decent enough family-run hotel with small and bright rooms with air-con and 24-hour hot water. On street level keep an eye out for the shoe shop through which you access the hotel. Expect discounts of 45%.

🍴 Eating

Hangzhou Dumplings   DUMPLINGS ¥
(杭州小笼包, Hángzhōu Xiǎolóngbāo; ☎152 5754 5988; dishes ¥10-68; ⊗7am-10pm, later in Jul & Aug; 🛜) This friendly family-run restaurant offers a wide range of Chinese dishes and breakfasts such as *yóutiáo* (fried dough sticks), *dòujiāng* (warm soya milk), *tsampa* and *xiǎolóngbāo* (steamed dumplings). There is an English menu, but note that many of the prices are out of date so you'll need to compare to the regular menu to confirm.

Yunnan Mama's Kitchen   YUNNAN ¥
(缘滋缘味, Yuánzī Yuánwèi; ☎139 8879 3187; dishes ¥12-68; ⊗9am-10pm Apr-Oct; 🛜) Mr Wang and the folk from Dali in Yunnan

at this family-run restaurant are a bundle of fun. Sample the five or six flavours of strong homemade *qīngkē báijiǔ* (Chinese barley spirit) and you might be too. Popular with travellers for the *guòqiáo mǐxiàn* (Yunnanese hotpot) and colossal servings of classics such as *shuǐzhǔ niúròu* (boiled yak meat in spicy broth; ¥45).

Black Tent Cafe
TIBETAN ¥¥

(黑帐蓬咖啡, Hēi Zhàngpeng Kāfēi; dishes ¥20-55; ⊙8am-10pm; 🛜) This upstairs place has a comfortable Tibetan-style interior with expensive coffee, plus breakfasts, sandwiches and other western dishes and desserts. It's run by the folk at Langmusi Tibetan Horse Trekking. The cafe is just along from the bus drop-off.

❶ Information

There's nowhere to change money and no ATMs that accept foreign cards, so get plenty of cash before you arrive in Langmusi.

❶ Getting There & Away

There's one daily bus to Zoigê (Ruò'ērgài; ¥30, 2½ hours) at 7.20am, which arrives with time to connect with the bus to Songpan. There are two to three daily buses to Hezuo (¥50, three hours), departing at 6.30am (summer only), 7.20am and noon. Take the only direct bus to Xiahe (¥72, 4½ hours) at 2pm, for frequent buses to Xiahe. There are no direct buses to Lanzhou, you will first need to go to Hezuo.

Guesthouses may be able to coordinate a seat to Chuanzhusi or Jiuzhaigou (¥150, six hours) on the bus that passes by on the main highway at around 3pm, otherwise you'll have to change in Hezuo.

For the latest scheduling info see www.lang musi.net.

HEXI CORRIDOR

Bound by the Qilian Shan (祁连山, Qílián Shān) range to the south and the Mazong Shan (马鬃山, Mǎzōng Shān, Horse's Mane Mountains) and Longshou (龙首山, Lóngshǒu Shān, Dragon's Head Mountains) mountains to the north, the pinched, narrow and dramatic Hexi Corridor (河西走廊, Héxī Zǒuláng) is the crux around which the province is formed. This valley was once the sole western passage in and out of the Middle Kingdom.

Wuwei
武威

⏲ 0935 / POP 1.81 MILLION

Wuwei (Wǔwēi) stands at the strategic eastern end of the Hexi Corridor. It was from here, two millennia ago, that the emperors of China launched their expeditionary forces into the unknown west, eventually leading them to Jiayuguan and beyond. Temples, tombs and traditional gates hint at Wuwei's Silk Road past, while the rapidly modernising city has some pleasant squares and pedestrian streets. Though the town is famous for the Flying Horse of Wuwei that was discovered here and is dotted with an intriguing collection of temples and a very attractive pagoda, some of the most absorbing sights lie outside the city: the Buddhist carvings at the Tiantishan Grottoes and the earthen remains of the Great Wall in Changchengxiang.

◉ Sights

Haizang Temple
BUDDHIST TEMPLE

(海藏寺, Hǎizàng Sì; Liangzhou District, Jinsha Township, 凉州区金沙乡; ⊙9am-5pm) FREE A fascinating active monastery with a minute pavilion to the right of the entrance containing a well whose 'magic waters' (神水, *shénshuǐ*) are said to connect by subterranean streams to a Holy Lake (圣湖, *Shènghú*) in the Potala Palace in Lhasa. Drinking the water is said to cure myriad ailments. Bus 5 (¥2) towards Haizang Gongyuan (海藏公园) or a taxi (¥10) will take you the short trip outside town to Haizang Park entrance (¥2); the temple is out back.

Wuwei Confucius Temple
CONFUCIAN TEMPLE

(武威文庙, Wénmiào; 43 Chongwen Jie, 崇文街43号; ¥30; ⊙8am-6pm) This large Ming-era temple complex divides into two sections: the Confucian Temple and the Wenchang Hall, both fine examples of traditional architecture. An important stele featuring the extinct Xixia language carved onto one side and a Chinese translation on the other served as a sort of Rosetta stone that allowed researchers to understand the once unintelligible Xixia texts. The stele is today housed in the **museum** (西夏博物馆, Xīxià Bówùguǎn; 179 Chongwen Jie, 崇文街179号; incl in ticket to Confucius Temple; ⊙8.30am-5.30pm Tue-Sun) (free with temple ticket) on the left flank of the square as you exit the temple.

Kumarajiva Pagoda
BUDDHIST PAGODA

(罗什寺, Luóshí Sì; 66 Bei Dajie, 北大街66号; ⊙8am-6pm) FREE This elegant 12-storey

GANSU WUWEI

brick pagoda dates from AD 488 and is surrounded by a tranquil complex of both unpainted and colourful wooden temple halls with old folk gossiping under trees. Dedicated to Kumarajiva, the great translator of Buddhist sutras (who lived here for 17 years and whose tongue was buried beneath the pagoda), the original 17th-century structures were toppled during a great earthquake in 1927 and rebuilt.

Sleeping & Eating

Xiliang Hotel   HOTEL ¥¥
(西凉大酒店, Xīliáng Dàjiǔdiàn; ☏ 0935 596 5599; 58 Yingbin Lu, 迎宾路58号; d inc breakfast from ¥228; ❋❔) Right opposite the main train station, this hotel is certainly handy. Spacious, bright and very smart rooms have large TVs, work desk, modern furnishings and swish shower rooms. The breakfast is Chinese, though there is toast too.

Liangzhou Food Street   MARKET ¥
(凉州美食街, Liángzhōu Měishíjiē; Pedestrian St, 步行街; dishes ¥7-20) This warren of covered pedestrian alleys within bustling Liangzhou Market (凉州市场, Liángzhōu Shìchǎng) packs in dozens of snack stands, hawker stalls and small, hole-in-the-wall restaurants in a blaze of garish red neon signs. Lots of easy foods on a budget, from simple fried noodles (炒面, chǎomiàn) to barbecue, fried dumplings, hotpot and Sichuan dishes. Expect to be pretty well fed for little more than ¥10.

❶ Getting There & Away

BUS

Express buses to Lanzhou (¥65) and cities such as Zhangye (¥58, regular) and Jiayuguan (¥96, 11.30am) in the Hexi Corridor run from the **main bus station** (Yingbin Lu, 迎宾路) on the corner of Yingbin Lu and Zhengyang Lu, though trains are faster and cheaper and generally more plentiful. The bus station has a daily bus (9.10am) to Bayanhot in Inner Mongolia and also south to Linxia (8.30am), if you are headed towards Xiahe; there are also two buses daily (¥130; 7am and 10am) to Yinchuan in Ningxia.

TRAIN

There are two train stations in Wuwei: the old **main station** (Yingbin Lu, 迎宾路), located at the south end of Yingbin Lu and the newer **Wuwei south station** (武威南站, Wǔwēi Nánzhàn; Wunan Jie, 武南街), much further away to the southeast of town. Both have similarly frequent departures to the main cities in Gansu, though direct trains to Dunhuang only run from Wuwei station. The overnight trains to Dunhuang are

a good choice, bringing you into Dunhuang between around 7am and 9am. The following trains leave from Wuwei station in the main:

Jiayuguan Hard seat/sleeper ¥69/130, 4½ to six hours, regular departures

Lanzhou Hard/soft seat ¥47/72, 3½ hours, every 20 to 30 minutes

Zhangye Hard/soft seat ¥41/61, two to three hours, every 20 to 30 minutes

Zhongwei (Ningxia) Seat/hard sleeper ¥41/95, three to four hours, nine daily

From Wuwei station only:

Dunhuang Hard/soft sleeper ¥239/346, 10 hours (four overnight trains per day direct to Dunhuang at 9.26pm, 10.09pm, 10.40pm and 10.52pm; other trains drop you off at Liuyuan).

Around Wuwei

The two real highlights of Wuwei are both to be found a short way outside of the city (but in opposite directions from one another).

Changchengxiang

Great Wall   ARCHAEOLOGICAL SITE
(长城乡长城; Changchengxiang, 长城乡) Running between fields near the village of Changchengxiang (itself named after the Great Wall), this section of Great Wall makes for an interesting excursion from Wuwei. The wall runs for around 600m, a brick-less, tamped-earth fortification that dates to the Ming dynasty. Jump on one of the buses (¥6, one hour) to Changcheng (长城) from the main bus station and ask to be dropped off at the Ming Great Wall (明长城, Míng Chángchéng).

Tiantishan Grottoes   CAVE
(天梯山石窟, Tiāntīshān Shíkū; Dengshan Village, 灯山村; ¥30; ⏰8.30am-6.30pm) By the Huangyanghe Reservoir (黄羊河水库, Huángyánghé Shuǐkù), it's hard to appreciate how massive the 15m-high Shakyamuni Buddha statue at Tiantishan Grottoes is until you reach his truck-sized feet to peer up at his outstretched hand emerging from the cliff face. These 1600-year-old carvings stand majestically in the open air, but the real star is the Buddha, his enormous feet protected from the reservoir's flood by a giant, half-moon dam around which you can walk to see him from varying vantages.

There are 17 caves here containing ancient murals (tigers, black dragons), along with some scroll paintings. Only one is open to the public, however, as many suffered devastation after a large earthquake in 1927. In 1959 many of the relics from lower caves were moved to Gansu Provincial Museum (p859) to make way for the construction of the reservoir. Two sets of stairs also lead to the dam floor, allowing worshippers to descend and light incense.

To reach the grottoes, take a bus (¥10; first/last bus 7am/5.30pm) to Haxi (哈溪, Hāxī) and tell the driver you are heading to the grottoes; he will tell you where to get off, then you will need to walk around 2km to the grottoes. To return to Wuwei, walk back to the drop-off and wait for a bus back (the last bus returns at 5.30pm). Alternatively, hire a driver or take a taxi from Wuwei (¥200 per half-day).

Zhangye   张掖

📞 0936 / POP 260,000

Smack-dab in the middle of the Hexi Corridor, the chilled-out city of Zhangye (Zhāngyè) has a relaxed atmosphere that belies its historical status as an outpost connecting Central Asia to the Chinese empire via the Silk Road. Marco Polo is said to have spent a year here around 1274 – he provided a detailed description of Zhangye (by its historical name, Campichu) in *The Travels of Marco Polo*. Even the name Zhangye alludes to its Silk Road importance: 张掖 is a shortening of '张国臂掖，以通西域', which translates as 'Extending the arm of the nation to its Western Realm'.

Today, Zhangye is a useful base from which to explore the otherwordly landscapes of the Danxia Geopark and the ancient cliff temples at Mǎtí Sì. In town, one of Asia's largest reclining Buddhas is ensconced in a beautifully preserved ancient wooden temple, which, according to legend, was the birthplace of Mongol warrior Kublai Khan.

👁 Sights

⭐ Big Buddha Temple   BUDDHIST SITE

(大佛寺, Dàfó Sì; www.zydfs.com; Dafosi Xiang, 大佛寺巷; ¥40; ⏰8am-6pm) Originally dating to 1098 (Western Xia dynasty), this stunning temple contains an astonishing 35m-long sleeping Buddha – China's largest of this variety and among the biggest clay and wood reclining Buddhas in Asia – surrounded by mouldering arhats (Buddhists who have achieved enlightenment) and Qing dynasty murals. The hall in which Buddha lies is one of the few wooden structures from this era still standing in the land; note the panels of the main doors to the hall and their ancient paintwork.

There is a gallery above the reclining Buddha, which you sadly cannot climb. No photography is allowed in the main hall. The former Wansheng Hall further on now contains an exhibition showcasing Buddhist artefacts as well as an explanation of the history of the temple and the town (in Chinese only) and some fascinating models of how the Big Buddha statue was constructed over a wooden frame. A further hall is devoted to a display of golden Buddhist sutras associated with the temple. At the very rear rises up an impressive white clay stupa (土塔, tǔtǎ) dating from the Ming dynasty, similar in style to Miaoying Temple White Dagoba in Beijing.

The Shanxi Guild Hall at the northeast corner of the temple is also worth investigating. Dating to 1724, this Qing-era complex was used as a meeting place and includes rare intact wooden stage and platform viewing areas.

To reach the temple from the drum tower, head south on Nan Dajie for about 1km and turn right along Minzhu Xijie before heading left down Dafosi Xiang to the ticket office which is on the right (the temple entrance is a bit further down on the left).

Xilai Wooden Pagoda   PAGODA

(西来寺, Xīlái Sì; cnr Minzhu Xijie & Xianfu Jie, 民主西街县府街的路口; ¥25; ⏰8am-6pm Apr-Oct, to 5pm Nov-Mar) Zhangye's main square is dominated by this good-looking and elegant nine-tiered brick and wooden pagoda. Though first built during the Northern Zhou dynasty (AD 557–588), the current 27.4m structure is a thorough reconstruction from 1926 and looks quite recent upon inspection, although is traditionally styled. Admission buys you a ticket to the top, which offers views over the city.

🛏 Sleeping & Eating

Mingqing Jie (明清街, Míngqīng Jiē; mains from ¥10; ⏰9am-9.30pm) is an alley of faux-Qing architecture lined with dozens of clean, friendly restaurants with picture menus. To find it, head 300m west of the drum tower along Xi Dajie. Local specialities include lǎoshǔfěn (老鼠粉, rice-flour noodles; literally 'mouse vermicelli') and cuōyúmiàn (搓鱼面, twisted fish noodles), so named because they are hand-twisted into oblong pointed shapes resembling small fish.

★ Ganzhou Hotel
HOTEL ¥

(甘州宾馆, Gānzhōu Bīnguǎn; ☎0936 888 8822; 11 Nan Dajie, 南大街11号; incl breakfast small/big r from ¥128/188, ste from ¥248) Running since 1971, this excellent hotel combines hardworking and very friendly staff with a very central location just south of the Bell and Drum Tower. The cheapest rooms are not so big, but are fine, otherwise you can upgrade to a huge twin for ¥188 or nab a suite for just ¥248. Rooms are comfortable and wi-fi is good.

Xīnyǒnghéng Niúròu Lāmiàn
NOODLES ¥

(鑫永恒牛肉拉面; Nan Dajie, 南大街; noodles ¥7-13; ⏰24hr) Round-the-clock hours make this a decent pit-stop at any time of the day or night. For ¥7 you can devour a deep, clear, fresh, zesty and filling bowl of beef noodles (牛肉面, niúròumiàn) with sesame seeds and spring onions and top it off with an egg (¥1; 鸡蛋, jīdàn) if you so wish. Other types of noodle are also on offer, including cold noodles and stir-fried noodles.

❶ Getting There & Away

BUS

Zhangye has three bus stations, in the south, east and west. The main **bus station** (张掖汽车站, Zhāngyè Qìchēzhàn; Xihuan Lu, 西环路) is the most useful, with the most frequent departures. Destinations include Xining, Golmud, Jiayuguan, Lanzhou, Dunhuang and Wuwei, though it's much faster, cheaper and far easier to take a train.

TRAIN

Zhangye is an important stop along the high-speed rail line connecting Lanzhou and Ürümqi in Xinjiang. High-speed trains depart from the huge **Zhangye West Railway Station** (张掖西站, Zhāngyè Xīzhàn) for Lanzhou via Xining in Qinghai province. Two high-speed trains depart daily from Zhangye West Railway Station for Dunhuang. Services include the following:

Dunhuang 1st/2nd class ¥278/174.50, four hours, two daily (11.18am and 4.28pm)

Jiayuguan South 1st/2nd class ¥105/66, 1½ hours, regular departures

Lanzhou West 1st/2nd class ¥239/149.50, four hours, regular departures

Tianshui 1st/2nd class ¥338/232.50, five to six hours, four daily

Ürümqi 1st/2nd class ¥642/401.50, seven hours, four daily

Xining 1st/2nd class ¥147/91.50, two hours, regular departures

Slower departures for Wuwei and destinations further east go from **Zhangye Railway Station** (张掖火车站, Zhāngyè Huǒchēzhàn), locally known as lǎozhàn (老站, old station), including the following:

Dunhuang Hard/soft sleeper ¥189/267, 7½ hours, seven daily; many day trains go to Liuyuan on the high-speed line. The Y667 overnighter is handy as it departs at 11.34pm and pulls into Dunhuang at 5.53am.

Wuwei Seat/hard sleeper ¥41/131.50, 2½ to three hours, every 20 to 30 minutes

There is a **train booking office** (火车票代售点, Huǒchēpiào Dàishòu Diǎn; 12 Oushi Jie, 欧式街12号; ⏰8am-noon & 1-6pm) on Oushi Jie. To get there walk west of the drum tower and turn right (north) when you reach Oushi Jie.

❶ Getting Around

A taxi from any of the bus stations to the hotels costs ¥4 to ¥5. Bus 4 runs past the west bus station from Dong or Xi Dajie.

The old train station is 7km northeast of the city centre, and a taxi will cost ¥10, or take bus 1 (¥1) which runs between the train station and the south bus station, traversing the central part of town. The west railway station is 3.5km from the centre of town, reachable on bus 22 or Xīn 1 (新1路). Shared taxis depart from in front of the station for ¥10 per person.

Zhangye Danxia National Geopark

The swirling orange, yellow, white and brown lunar landscape of **Zhangye Danxia National Geopark** (张掖丹霞国家地质公园, Zhāngyè Dānxiá Guójiā Dìzhí Gōngyuán; incl tourist bus ¥75; ⏰6am-8pm) is the result of sandstone and mineral deposits that have eroded into odd shapes over the course of millennia. Infrastructure was installed inside the park after it was named a national geopark in 2011, making it – for better or worse – very accessible to tourists. Wooden stairs and platforms allow visitors to reach the tops of the hills without damaging the delicate landscape and offer views over the coloured strata.

There are five observation stops, reached by hop-on, hop-off tourist bus from either the west or north entrance; you can spend as long as you wish at each stop. Stop No 4 is the best-looking, with iridescent hills rolling off in a long panorama. Some advice: choose a clear day for your visit, otherwise it could be a bit of a let-down. The park opens early and shuts late for a reason: the best time to visit (and photograph) the landscape is at sunrise or sunset.

The wooden walkways channel visitors into confined areas, so there is little opportunity to explore the park and its full possibilities and it is also hard to get close-ups of the landscape and its colours, unless you have a telephoto lens. Take water with you and don a sunhat on a hot day (there is no shade).

From Zhangye, a taxi to both Mǎtí Sì and Danxia will cost around ¥350 to ¥400, or a taxi to just the geopark will cost about ¥150 to ¥200 (depending on your bargaining skills). If you speak Chinese, you can try local travel agents who run tours to the geopark for around ¥120.

Mati Village 马蹄乡

📞 0936

Carved into the cliff sides in the foothills of the grand Qilian Mountains (Qílián Shān), the venerable Buddhist grottoes of Mǎtí Sì make for a fine short getaway from the hectic small towns along the Hexi Corridor. The tiny tourist village of Mati Village (Mǎtí Xiāng) serves as a gateway to the temples. There's excellent hiking in the nearby hills, and a small range of very simple accommodation and food from May to September. Come in July to see the mountain valleys carpeted in blue wildflowers.

There are several good day hikes around Mǎtí Sì, including the five-hour loop through pine forest and talus fields to the Línsōng Waterfall (临松瀑布, Línsōng Pùbù) and back down past Sword Split Stone (剑劈石, Jiànpīshí). For unrivalled panoramas, take the steep ascent of the ridge starting across from the white chörten (Tibetan stupa) just above the village at Sānshísāntiān Shíkū (三十三天石窟).

Mǎtí Sì CAVE

(马蹄寺; 📞 0936 889 1610; http://mt.ichuangsi.com; ¥74; ⊙ 8.30am-6pm) Mǎtí Sì translates as 'Horse Hoof Monastery', a reference to when a heavenly horse left a hoof imprint in a grotto. Between the 5th and 14th centuries a series of caves were almost as miraculously built in sheer sandstone cliffs and filled with carvings, temples and meditation rooms. The caves are reached via twisting staircases, balconies, narrow passages and platforms that will leave your head spinning.

The grottoes are not in one area but spread over several sections. The most accessible are the **Thousand Buddhas Caves** (千佛洞石窟, Qiān Fó Dòng Shíkū) just past the entrance gate to the scenic area. Within

this complex is the **Puguang Temple**, where you'll find the relic of the aforementioned horse hoof imprint. The **Mati Si North Caves** (马蹄寺北石窟, Mǎtí Sì Běi Shíkū) are above the village (2km up the road from the Thousand Buddhas Caves) and feature the more dizzying platforms as well as a large grotto with a tall golden Buddha.

Mǎtí Sì is 65km south of Zhangye, and one or both of the main caves may be closed outside of April to September. The best way to get here is to hire a taxi in Zhangye (¥160 round trip, including the temple drive).

Jiayuguan 嘉峪关

📞 0937 / POP 231,000

You approach Jiayuguan (Jiāyùguān) through the forbidding and desiccated lunar landscape of north Gansu. It's a fitting setting, as Jiayuguan marks the symbolic end of the Great Wall, the western gateway of China proper and, for imperial Chinese, the beginning of the back of beyond. One of the defining points of the Silk Road, a Ming dynasty fort was erected here in 1372 and Jiayuguan came to be colloquially known as the 'mouth' of China, while the narrow Hexi Corridor, leading back towards the nèidì (内地, inner lands), was dubbed the 'throat'.

In the town itself, you'll need some imagination to conjure up visions of the Silk Road, as the modern city of Jiayuguan is a place of straight roads, identikit blocks and manufacturing. But Jiayuguan Fort and the Great Wall sites outside town are an essential part of Silk Road lore and most certainly worth a visit.

⊙ Sights

With the exception of the Weijin Tombs (p876), all the sites are covered by purchasing a through ticket (通票, tōngpiào) to Jiayuguan Fort; admission fees quoted for individual sites are for entry without admission to the fort. Through tickets can be purchased at any of the three sites.

★ Jiayuguan Fort FORT

(嘉峪关城楼, Jiāyùguān Chénglóu; Guancheng Nanlu, 关城南路; ¥120; ⊙ 8.30am-8pm, to 6pm in winter) One of the classic images of western China, this huge fort once guarded the narrow pass between the snowcapped Qilian Shan peaks and the Hei Shan (Black Mountains) of the Mazong Shan range.

Built in 1372, it was named the 'Impregnable Defile Under Heaven'. Although the Han

Jiayuguan

Chinese often controlled territory far beyond here, this was the last major stronghold of imperial China – the end of their 'civilised world', beyond which lay only desert demons and the barbarian armies of Central Asia.

Towards the eastern end of the fort is the **Gate of Enlightenment** (光化楼, Guānghuá Lóu) and on the west side is the **Gate of Conciliation** (柔远楼, Róuyuǎn Lóu), from where exiled poets, ministers, criminals and soldiers would have ridden off into oblivion. Each gate dates from 1506 and has 17m-high towers with upturned flying eaves and double gates that would have been used to trap invading armies. On the inside are horse lanes with steps leading up to the top of the inner ramparts where you can wander around. Back on ground level, you can also see a former **stage** for performances, opposite a sizeable **Guandi Temple** (Guāndì Miào). Note the wall of the **Wenchang Pavilion** next to the Guandi Temple, which is still covered in a large, yellow and flaking **Maoist slogan** from the Cultural Revolution.

Near the fort entrance gate is the excellent **Jiayuguan Museum of the Great Wall** (嘉峪关长城博物馆, Jiāyùguān Chángchéng Bówùguǎn; incl in through ticket to Jiayuguan Fort; ☉8.30am-6pm) **FREE**, which has some interesting exhibits about the Wall and its history in this part of China.

Overhanging Great Wall HISTORIC SITE
(悬壁长城, Xuánbì Chángchéng; adult ¥21, incl in through ticket to Jiayuguan Fort; ☉8.30am-8pm, to 6pm winter) Running north from Jiayuguan Fort (p875), this section of the Great Wall is believed to have been first constructed in 1539, though it was reconstructed in 1987.

It's a reasonably energetic hike up the equivalent of 55 flights of stairs to excellent views of the desert, power stations and the distant, glittering snowcapped peaks from the watchtower at the top (which you can climb up). The Wall is about 9km north of the fort.

First Beacon Platform of the Great Wall HISTORIC SITE
(长城第一墩, Chángchéng Dìyī Dūn; ¥22, incl in through ticket to Jiayuguan Fort; ☉8.30am-8pm, to 6pm winter) Atop a 56m-high cliff overlooking the Taolai River south of Jiayuguan, a large, crumbling and wind-eroded chunk of packed earth is all that remains of this beacon platform, believed to be the first signalling tower along the western front of the Great Wall. Views over the river and bare gorge below are impressive and you can walk alongside lengthy attached vestiges of adobe Ming-era Great Wall. An excellent museum affords an exhaustive look at the Great Wall and its history here.

Weijin Tombs TOMB
(新城魏晋壁画墓, Xīnchéng Wèijìn Bìhuàmù; ¥35; ☉8.30am-8pm) These tombs date from approximately AD 220–420 (the Wei and Western Jin periods) and contain extraordinarily fresh brick-wall paintings (some sadly ineptly retouched) depicting scenes of everyday life, from making tea to picking mulberries for silk production. There are thousands of tombs in the desert 20km east of Jiayuguan, but only one is currently open to visitors, that of a husband and wife. There is a small **museum** that's also worth a look; it's the only area where photos are permitted.

🛏 Sleeping & Eating

Wanhui Holiday Hotel HOTEL ¥¥
(万辉假日酒店, Wànhuī Jiàrì Jiǔdiàn; ☎0937 637 8666; 78 Xinhua Beilu, 新华北路78號; d/ste from ¥188/328; ✳@🛜) This snazzy and pretty snappy midrange option has a handy location on Xinhua Beilu in the centre of town with bright, clean rooms with modern facilities. Good discounts if you book online.

Jingtie Market MARKET ¥
(镜铁小吃城, Jìngtiě Xiǎochīchéng; Xinhua Zhonglu, 新华中路; ☉10am-10pm) At this busy market load up on lamb kebabs, *ròujiāmó* (肉夹馍, pork sandwiches), *shāguō* (claypot) dishes, barbecue, Sichuan cuisine, beef noodles, roast duck, dumplings and more. There's a whole batch of small restaurants on the north side of the market that offer sit-down meals.

ⓘ Getting There & Away

AIR

Jiayuguan Airport (嘉峪关机场, Jiāyùguān Jīchǎng) has flights to Beijing, Shanghai, Xi'an, Lanzhou, Hangzhou, Chengdu and other destinations, but most people arrive by bus or train.

BUS

Jiayuguan's **bus station** (嘉峪关汽车站, Jiāyùguān Qìchēzhàn; 312 Lanxin Xilu, 兰新西路 312号) is by a busy four-way junction on Lanxin Xilu, next to the main budget hotels. It is cheaper and quicker to take a train, but bus destinations include Dunhuang, Lanzhou, Wuwei and Zhangye.

TRAIN

Jiayuguan has two train stations. The **main train station** (嘉峪关站, Jiāyùguān Zhàn; Zhanqian Lu, 站前路) is southwest of the town centre. Bus 1 runs here from Xinhua Zhonglu (¥1). A taxi costs ¥10.

Jiayuguan South Station (嘉峪关南站, Jiāyùguān Nánzhàn) serves the high-speed rail line that connects Lanzhou to Xinjiang. It is located 8km southeast of the town centre. Bus 10 (¥1) runs from the south station to the Jiayuguan Hotel and the centre of town – get off at the Jiugang Binguan (酒钢宾馆) stop. A taxi costs ¥30.

Trains from the south station include the following:

Dunhuang 1st/2nd class ¥174/109, 2½ hours, three daily

Lanzhou West High-speed 1st/2nd class ¥344/215, 5½ hours, 10 daily

Ürümqi High-speed 1st/2nd-class seat ¥538/336, six hours, four daily

Zhangye West 1st/2nd class ¥105/66, one hour 20 minutes, 11 daily

Trains from the main train station include:

Wuwei Seat/hard sleeper ¥69/168, four to six hours, regular departures

Direct trains to Dunhuang are labelled as such. Beware of the more frequently scheduled trains to Liuyuan – a lengthy 180km away from Dunhuang. Train tickets can be booked in town at the **post office** (铁路客票代售点, Tiělù Kèpiào Dàishòudiàn; Xinhua Zhonglu, 新华中路; ⊙9am-6pm Mon-Fri, to 5pm Sat & Sun).

Dunhuang 敦煌

☑0937 / POP 186,000

The fertile Dunhuang (Dūnhuáng) oasis has for millennia been a refuge for weary Silk Road travellers. Most visitors stayed long enough only to swap a camel; but some stayed, building the forts, towers and cave temples that are scattered over the sur-

rounding area. These sites, along with some dwarfing sand dunes and desertscapes, make Dunhuang a magnificent place to visit.

Despite its remoteness, Dunhuang's per-capita income is among the highest in China, thanks to a push into wind and solar energy production. The town is thoroughly modern, but has maintained its distinctive desert-sanctuary ambience – with clean, tree-lined streets, slow-moving traffic, bustling markets, budget hotels, cafes and souvenir shops.

Though relatively small, it's a clean and terrific walking town with wide footpaths and narrow alleys opening up into squares, markets and the lives of ordinary citizens.

◎ Sights

★ Dunhuang Museum   MUSEUM
(敦煌博物馆, Dūnhuáng Bówùguǎn; ☑0937 882 2981; Mingshan Lu, 鸣山路; ⊙8am-6pm) FREE
On the road to Singing Sands Dune (p882) is this sparkling museum that takes you on an artefact-rich journey through the Dunhuang area (from prehistoric to Qing dynasty times) via hallways designed to make you feel as if you were exploring the caves. Don't miss the splendid to-scale recreation, decorated with soft pigment, of Cave 45. Another highlight is the excellent **Fan Yanyan Centre of Silk Arts** display, with its eye-catching styling and gorgeous silk pieces. Take your passport.

ⓒ Tours

Ask at any hostel or **Charley Johng's Cafe** (风味餐馆, Fēngwèi Cānguǎn; ☑0937 388 2411; Mingshan Lu, 鸣山路; dishes ¥6-36; ⊙8am-10pm; 🛜) for tourist info; they can also help with tours, from camel treks to overnight camping excursions and day trips. Bus tours (¥100) that include visits to Yadan National Park (p882) and Jade Gate Pass (p883) and Sun Pass (p883) depart daily from Dunhuang and can also be arranged at Charley Johng's. Be aware you'll have to pay for admission to each site separately during the tour.

⛏ Sleeping

Dunhuang Hotel   HOTEL ¥
(敦煌饭店, Dūnhuáng Fàndiàn; ☑0937 884 0088; 18 Mingshan Lu, 鸣山路18号; r ¥119-189) On the corner of Mingshan Lu and Xiyu Lu and so highly central, this hotel is overseen by helpful staff, with an attractive staircase leading up to rooms that even at the cheap end are entirely adequate and comfortable, furnished in dark wood. The ¥149 doubles

Dunhuang

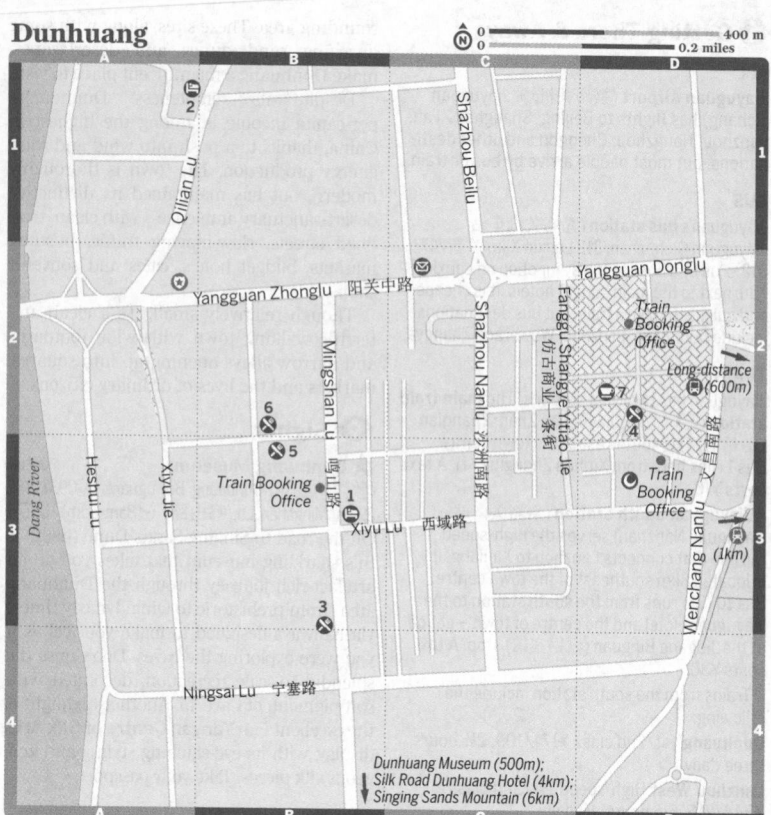

GANSU DUNHUANG

Dunhuang

🛏 Sleeping
1 Dunhuang Hotel B3
2 Shazhouyi International Youth
   Hostel...A1

✖ Eating
3 Charley Johng's Cafe..........................B3
4 Shazhou Night Market.......................D2
5 Speciality Snack Street......................B3
6 Suǒfěiyà Qīngzhèn Fànguǎn..............B2

🍷 Drinking & Nightlife
7 Memory Box Cafe D2

are very spacious and appear more pleasant than the pricier ¥189 rooms. Breakfast is an extra ¥20.

**Shazhouyi International
Youth Hostel**   HOSTEL ¥
(敦煌沙州驿国际青年旅舍,   Dūnhuáng
Shāzhōuyì Guójì Qīngnián Lǚshè; ☎ 0937 880 8800;

8 Qilian Lu, 祁连路8号; dm/d ¥40/120; P ⊛ ❄ 🖤)
This hostel is plant- and light-filled, inviting you to lounge and plan one of the offered tours. Dorm beds are comfy with modern shared bathrooms. Doubles are bright and spacious. The street is traffic heavy and rather out on a limb, but the Shazhou Night Market is a 10-minute walk away through a leafy park. English spoken.

Silk Road Dunhuang Hotel   HOTEL ¥¥¥
(敦煌山庄, Dūnhuáng Shānzhuāng; ☎ 0937 888 2088; www.dunhuangresort.com; Dunyue Lu, 敦月路; d & tw ¥1200-1500, ste ¥2500-15,000; ❄ @ 🖤)
This stand-alone four-star resort is tastefully designed with Central Asian rugs, a cool stone floor and Chinese antiques. The hotel's rooftop restaurant has without doubt the best outdoor perch in Dunhuang with amazing views of Singing Sands Dune (p882). It's located south of town on the road to the dunes; a taxi costs ¥10, or take minibus 3 (¥2). Discounts of 20% to 40% often available.

✕ Eating

For *niúròu miàn* (牛肉面, beef noodles) head to any of a number of restaurants along Xiyu Lu. The **night market** (沙洲夜市, Shāzhōu Yèshì; btwn Yangguan Donglu & Xiyu Lu; ⊙4pm-late) is the most popular spot for food in the city. The great length of **Speciality Snack Street** (特色小吃街; Tèsè Xiǎochījiē) is an excellent choice for a selection of Chinese snacks and homestyle favourites.

Suǒfēiyà Qīngzhèn Fànguǎn XINJIANG ¥
(索菲亚清真饭馆; Wenmiao Xiang, 文庙巷; mains ¥12-70) Come to this small and friendly Muslim restaurant down Confucian Temple Alley (Wenmiao Xiang) for lamb kebabs (羊肉串, *yángròuchuàn;* ¥2 each), roast lamb with cumin (孜然羊肉, *zīrǎn yángròu;* ¥70), spicy chicken chunks (辣子鸡块, *làzi jīkuài;* ¥20) or a piquant tiger salad (老虎菜, *lǎohǔ cài;* ¥12). Look for the green restaurant front. The name in Chinese means 'Sophia Muslim Restaurant'.

It's located just north of Speciality Snack Street.

★Zhāixīng Gé INTERNATIONAL ¥¥
(摘星阁, Silk Road Dunhuang Hotel; Dunyue Lu, 敦月路; dishes ¥32-138; ⊙7am-1pm & 4.30pm-midnight) Part of the Silk Road Dunhuang Hotel, this rooftop restaurant is ideal for a meal (the western buffet breakfast is excellent) or a sundowner gazing out over the golden sand dunes. There's everything from pumpkin-and-potato soup to Russian borscht, chicken curry, rib-eye steak and thick-crust pizza. A good wine list and cocktails are at hand as well as relaxing traditional Chinese music.

🍷 Drinking & Nightlife

★Memory Box Cafe CAFE, BAR
(时光盒子咖啡馆, Shíguāng Hézi Kāfēi Guǎn; ☑0937 881 9911; room 106a, 7th Bldg, Fengqing City; juice ¥25, beer ¥15; ⊙10am-midnight; 🛜) This comfy and eclectically designed cafe with ample greenery, high ceiling, voluminous glass windows, a vast aquarium with huge, colourful fish and lots of neat little compartmentalised tables to sit down at serves a range of drinks and Chinese and western snacks, including Illy coffee and some imported beers. It also has a few nice seats out front in warmer weather.

ℹ Information

Public Security Bureau (PSB, 公安局, Gōng'ānjú; ☑0937 886 2071; Yangguan Zhonglu, 阳关中路; ⊙8am-noon & 3-6.30pm Mon-Fri) Two days needed for visa extension.

ℹ Getting There & Away

AIR
Apart from November to March, when there are only flights to/from Lanzhou and Xi'an, there are regular flights to/from Beijing, Lanzhou, Shanghai, Ürümqi, Hangzhou, Kunming, Nanjing and Xi'an.

BUS
From Dunhuang's **bus station** (长途汽车站, Chángtú Qìchēzhàn; ☑0937 885 3746; Sanwei Lu, 三危路; ⊙7am-8pm daily) you can catch buses to Jiayuguan and Lanzhou (though trains are cheaper and faster), as well as to the following destinations:

Golmud ¥150, eight hours, one daily (9am)

Jiayuguan ¥95, 4½ hours, 11 daily (8am to 7.30pm)

Liuyuan (柳园) ¥46, three hours, 10 daily (9.30am to 7.30pm)

TRAIN
Dunhuang's **station** (敦煌站, Dūnhuángzhàn; Yangguan Dadao, 阳关大道) is 10km east of town, but for some destinations, such as Beijing West and Ürümqi, you'll have to leave from Liuyuan Station, a crazy 180km away.

Jiayuguan South 1st/2nd class ¥174/109, 2½ hours, three high-speed trains daily (there are more slower trains too)

Lanzhou West 1st/2nd class ¥518/324, eight hours, two high-speed trains daily; three other slower trains leave from Dunhuang station and more trains leave from Liuyuan Station

Turpan (from Liuyuan Station) Hard seat/hard sleeper ¥93/208, six to eight hours; high-speed trains go from Liyuan South to **Turpan North**, 1st/2nd class ¥312/196, three hours, four daily

Ürümqi (from Liuyuan Station) Hard sleeper/soft sleeper/high-speed 2nd-class seat ¥239/346/247, five to nine hours; high-speed trains leave from Liuyuan South

Tickets can be booked at the **train booking office** (车票代售点, Chēpiào Dàishòu Diǎn; Tianma Jie, 天马街; ⊙9am-5.30pm, 8am-7pm summer) to the rear of the mosque, at the **office** (火车票发售点, Huǒchē Piào Fāshòu Diǎn; Mingshan Lu, 鸣山路; ⊙9am-5pm) within the post office on Mingshan Lu or at the upstairs **office** (火车票发售点, Huǒchē Piào Fāshòu Diǎn; Xinglong Jie, 兴隆街; ⊙8am-noon & 1.30-5pm) in the Shazhou Night Market area.

❶ Getting Around

The train station is 12km from the centre of town, on the same road as the airport. A taxi will cost around ¥35.

If you are heading to Liuyuan train station (for trains to Ürümqi and high-speed rail), catch a bus or shared taxi (per person ¥45) from the front of the bus station. Give yourself at least three hours to get to Liuyuan station (including waiting for the taxi to fill up with other passengers).

Taxis around town start at ¥5.

You can rent bikes from travellers cafes for ¥5 per hour.

Around Dunhuang

Most people visit the Mogao Grottoes in the morning, followed by the Singing Sands Dune in the late afternoon to catch the sunset. Note that it can be 40°C in the desert during the summer so go prepared with water, a sunhat and snacks.

★ **Mogao Grottoes** CAVE
(莫高窟, Mògāo Kū; A ticket ¥258, B ticket ¥100, C ticket ¥50; ☺8am-6pm Apr-Nov, 9am-5.30pm Dec-Mar) The Mogao Grottoes are considered one of the most important collections of Buddhist art in the world. At its peak during the Tang dynasty (618–907), the site housed 18 monasteries, more than 1400 monks and nuns, and countless artists, translators and calligraphers.

English-language tours, running at 9am, noon and 2.30pm, are included in the ¥258 'A' ticket admission price, which gives you access to eight caves; the alternative ¥100 'B' ticket is for Chinese-language tours, with access to four caves.

Due to a massive increase in visitor numbers (including school tours), the access procedure has undergone a revamp and all visitors to the Mogao Grottoes now have to go via the visitor centre a few kilometres outside of central Dunhuang. The ¥258 'A' ticket includes transport to the grottoes, access to four museums and admission to two 30-minute films, one on the history of the area and the Silk Road, and one that allows close-up computer-generated views of cave interiors not normally open to visitors, in an IMAX-style theatre at the visitor centre. From the visitor centre, purchasers of both 'A' and 'B' tickets are shuttled to the caves 15km down the road in dedicated coaches. The ¥100 'B' ticket is only for those who

have a good understanding of the Chinese commentary (and includes transport to the Mogao Grottoes and access to three museums). After the tour, you are free to wander around the site and catch whatever coach you like back to the visitor centre at your own leisure, but you won't be allowed back into any of the caves. The ¥50 'C' ticket only covers access to the films in the cinema at the visitor centre.

'A' tickets are limited to 6000 tickets per day; 'B' tickets are limited to 12,000 tickets per day. Purchasing tickets is not straightforward. 'A' tickets must be purchased in advance either online at the caves' official website (Chinese-language website only; Chinese phone number and Chinese ID card most inconveniently required for purchase at the time of writing) or in Dunhuang from the (also) inconveniently located **Mogao Grottoes Reservation and Ticket Center** (莫高窟参观预约售票中心, Mògāo Kū Cānguān Yùyuē Shòupiào Zhōngxīn; Yangguan Dadao, 阳关大道迎宾花园北区15号楼102号), a separate booking office in the east of town where staff speak English. During the high season, you should buy your ticket a day or more in advance from the Mogao Grottoes Reservation and Ticket Center.

Of the 492 caves, 20 'open' caves are rotated fairly regularly. Entrance is strictly controlled – it's impossible to visit them independently. On the 'A' ticket, you will be given a roughly two-hour tour of eight caves, which should include the famous **Hidden Library Cave** (cave 17), the two **big Buddhas** including the vast 35.5m tall Buddha in **Cave 96** (behind the iconic seven-storey pagoda) and another 26m-tall Buddha statue, the vast reclining Buddha, in **Cave 148**, as well as a chance to see rare fragments of manuscripts in classical Uyghur and Manichean. The cheaper 'B' ticket gives you access to half the number of caves and may be useful if time is tight (but remember the tour on the 'B' ticket is in Chinese only).

Photography is prohibited inside the caves. If it's raining or snowing or there's a sand storm, the site will be closed.

➡ **History**

Wealthy traders and important officials were the primary donors responsible for creating new caves, as caravans made the long detour past Mogao to pray or give thanks for a safe journey through the treacherous wastelands to the west. The traditional date ascribed to the founding of the first cave is AD 366.

ℹ TICKETS TO MOGAO GROTTOES

Though you used to be able to buy tickets to the Mogao Grottoes directly at the entrance, the sight's popularity has meant that advance purchase is now necessary. If you're an independent traveller, this isn't as easy as it sounds. You can buy your ticket online in advance at www.mgk.org.cn, but the website is amazingly still Chinese-language only (as it has been for many years), plus you will need a Chinese mobile phone number and a Chinese ID and domestic payment method.

Bearing all this in mind, you will almost certainly need to go to the Mogao Grottoes Reservation and Ticket Center a fair distance away from the centre of town to reserve your ticket; if it is the high summer season, you will need to go a day in advance (and take your passport). During slower periods, you should be able to get your ticket on the day from the visitor centre. Most hotels and hostels in Dunhuang can also book tickets for you, but may levy a surcharge. The ¥258 'A' tickets include an English-language guide and are limited to 6000 tickets per day; ¥100 'B' tickets include a Chinese-language guide and are limited to 12,000 tickets per day.

The caves fell into disuse for about 500 years after the collapse of the Yuan dynasty and were largely forgotten until the early 20th century, when they were 'rediscovered' by a string of foreign explorers.

➡ Northern Wei, Western Wei & Northern Zhou Caves

These, the earliest of the Mogao Caves, are distinctly Indian in style and iconography. All contain a central pillar, representing a stupa (symbolically containing the ashes of the Buddha), which the devout would circle in prayer. Paint was derived from malachite (green), cinnabar (red) and lapis lazuli (blue), expensive minerals imported from Central Asia.

The art of this period is characterised by its attempt to depict the spirituality of those who had transcended the material world through their asceticism. The Wei statues are slim, ethereal figures with finely chiselled features and comparatively large heads. The northern Zhou figures have ghostly white eyes.

➡ Sui Caves

The Sui dynasty (AD 581–618) was short-lived and very much a transition between the Wei and Tang periods. This can be seen in the Sui caves at Mogao: the graceful Indian curves in the Buddha and Bodhisattva figures start to give way to the more rigid style of Chinese sculpture.

The Sui dynasty began when a general of Chinese or mixed Chinese–Tuoba origin usurped the throne of the northern Zhou dynasty and reunited northern and southern China for the first time in 360 years.

➡ Tang Caves

The Tang dynasty (AD 618–907) was Mogao's high point. Painting and sculpture techniques became much more refined, and some important aesthetic developments, notably the sex change (from male to female) of Guanyin and the flying apsaras, took place. The beautiful murals depicting the Buddhist Western Paradise offer rare insights into court life, music, dress and architecture of Tang China.

Some 230 caves were carved during the religiously diverse Tang dynasty, including two impressive grottoes containing enormous, seated Buddha figures. Originally open to the elements, the statue of Maitreya in cave 96 (believed to represent Empress Wu Zetian, who used Buddhism to consolidate her power) is a towering 35.5m tall, making it the world's third-largest Buddha. The Buddhas were carved from the top down using scaffolding, the anchor holes of which are still visible.

➡ Post-Tang Caves

Following the Tang dynasty, the economy around Dunhuang went into decline, and the luxury and vigour typical of Tang painting began to be replaced by simpler drawing techniques and flatter figures. The mysterious Western Xia kingdom, which controlled most of Gansu from 983 to 1227, made a number of additions to the caves at Mogao and began to introduce Tibetan influences.

➡ Getting There & Away

The Mogao Grottoes are 25km (30 minutes) southeast of Dunhuang, but tours start and end at the visitor centre, about 5km from Mingshan Lu near the train station. A green

SILK ROAD RAIDERS

In 1900 the Taoist priest and self-appointed guardian of the Mogao Grottoes (p880), Wang Yuanlu, discovered a hidden library (in cave 17, alongside the Taoist Sanqing Gong Taoist temple), filled with tens of thousands of immaculately preserved manuscripts and paintings, dating as far back as AD 406.

It's hard to describe the exact magnitude of the discovery, but stuffed into the tiny cave were texts in rare Central Asian languages, military reports, music scores, medical prescriptions, Confucian and Taoist classics, and Buddhist sutras copied by some of the greatest names in Chinese calligraphy – not to mention the oldest printed book in existence, the *Diamond Sutra* (AD 868). In short, it was an incalculable amount of original source material regarding Chinese, Central Asian and Buddhist history.

Word of the discovery quickly spread and Wang Yuanlu, suddenly the most popular bloke in town, was courted by rival archaeologists Aurel Stein and Paul Pelliot, among others. Following much pressure to sell the cache, Wang Yuanlu finally relented and parted with an enormous hoard of treasure. On his watch close to 20,000 of the cave's priceless manuscripts were whisked off to Europe for the paltry sum of £220.

Today, Chinese intellectuals – bitter at the sacking of the caves – deride Stein, Pelliot and others for making off with what they consider to be national treasures. Defenders of the explorers point out that had the items been left alone, there is a chance they could have been lost during the ensuing civil war or the Cultural Revolution.

minibus (one way ¥3) leaves for the visitor centre every 30 minutes from 8am to 5pm from outside the Silk Road Yiyuan Hotel (丝路怡苑宾馆, Sīlù Yíyuàn Bīnguǎn). A taxi costs ¥20 one way, and taxis generally wait outside the visitor centre right by where the green minibuses wait, so it's easy to find one on the way back.

★ **Singing Sands Dune**   OASIS
(鸣沙山, Míngshā Shān; ¥120; ⊙6am-7.30pm) Six kilometres south of Dunhuang at Singing Sands Dune, the desert meets the oasis in most spectacular fashion. From the sheer scale of the dunes, it's easy to see how Dunhuang gained its moniker 'Shāzhōu' (Continent of Sand). The view across the undulating desert and green poplar trees below is awesome.

You can bike to the dunes in 20 minutes from the centre of Dunhuang. Bus 3 (¥2) shuttles between Shazhou Lu and Mingshan Lu and the dunes from 7.30am to 9pm. A taxi costs ¥20 one way.

The climb to the top of the dunes – the highest peak swells to 1715m – is sweaty work, but worth it. Rent a pair of bright-orange shoe protectors (防沙靴, fángshāxuē; ¥15) or just shake your shoes out later as most people do. A wooden ladder/walkway is half buried in the sand so you can get a decent footing on the deep sand.

At the base of the colossal dunes is a famous pond, **Crescent Moon Lake** (月牙泉, Yuèyáquán). The dunes are a no-holds-barred tourist playpen, with dune buggies, 'dune surfing' (sand sledding), paragliding, microlighting and helicopter flights. But it's not hard to hike away to enjoy the sandy spectacle in peace. The dunes look their most photogenic either first thing in the morning or towards dusk.

Tickets are good for three days' entry. To avail of this, you must ask the security staff at the gate as you exit – facial recognition software is employed.

Camel rides are available at the dunes.

The drive down Mingshan Lu to the dunes is also astonishing as this vast mountain of sand suddenly appears from the shimmering heat at the end of the road.

Yadan National Park   DESERT
(雅丹国家地质公园, Yǎdān Guójiā Dìzhì Gōngyuán; ¥120; ⊙8am-5.30pm) The weird, eroded desert landscape of Yadan National Park is 180km northwest of Dunhuang, in the middle of the Gobi Desert's awesome nothingness. A former lake bed that eroded in spectacular fashion some 12,000 years ago, the strange rock formations provided the backdrop to the last scenes of Zhang Yimou's film *Hero*. Tours (included in the price) are confined to group minibuses (with regular photo stops) to preserve the natural

surrounds, but the desert landscape here is so dramatic you will still feel like you're at the ends of the earth.

To get to Yadan you have to pass through (and buy a ticket to) the Jade Gate Pass and Sun Pass. The best way to get here is to take one of two daily **minibus tours**: the first departs at 7am (¥120 per person; returning by 7pm) and can be booked through Charley Johng's Cafe (p877). There is also a sunset tour (¥88 per person) which sets off 8.30am and returns at 11pm. Tours include the Jade Gate Pass, Sun Pass and the **Western Thousand Buddha Caves** (西千佛洞, Xī Qiānfó Dòng; ¥40; ⊗8.30am-5pm) as well as a section of Han dynasty Great Wall. Tour prices don't include entrance fees to the individual sights.

Jade Gate Pass   HISTORIC SITE
(玉门关, Yùmén Guān; Jade Gate ¥60, South Pass ¥40) The Jade Gate Pass, 78km west of Dunhuang, was originally a military station. Together with Sun Pass, it formed part of the Han dynasty series of beacon towers that extended to the garrison town of Loulan in Xinjiang. Admission includes entry to a section of Han dynasty **Great Wall** (101 BC), impressive for its antiquity and lack of restoration; and the ruined city walls of **Hecang Cheng** (河仓城, Hécāng Chéng), 15km down a side road.

Sun Pass   HISTORIC SITE
(阳关, Yángguān; ¥50; ⊗8am-8pm) This Han dynasty military post was one of the two most important gates marking the end of the Chinese empire along the ancient Silk Road. Today, a dusty museum chronicles some of the site's artefacts, but the real draw is the crumbling beacon tower atop **Dundun Hill** (墩墩山, Dūndūnshān), where a modern viewing platform offers generous vistas of the surrounding Taklamakan Desert.

Sometimes also referred to as the South Pass due to its geographical location as the sunny and southern side of the hill, this site marked the start of the southern route westward through Miran in Xinjiang, while the Jade Gate Pass was its northern twin. The pass is noted in several early Chinese poems, which speak with sadness about the finality of a traveller's departure through the gate and into the western world beyond, presumably never to return.

EASTERN GANSU

Tianshui   天水
☑0938 / POP 3.27 MILLION
Tianshui's (Tiānshuǐ) splendid Buddhist caves at nearby Maijishan entice a consistent flow of visitors. Though the city is not a draw in and of itself, it is a pleasant place to spend the night on the way to or from Maijishan and there's enough dining and sleeping options to keep you occupied on your way through. The city has developed a waterside promenade and park along the Wei River that is both a relaxing and romantic place for a stroll or evening beer.

Modern Tianshui is actually two very separate districts 15km apart: there is the railhead sprawl, known as Maiji Qu (麦积区, Màijī Qū), and the central commercial area to the west, known as Qinzhou Qu (秦州区, Qínzhōu Qū), where you'll arrive if coming in by bus. The two sections are lashed together by a long freeway that runs along the river.

⊙ Sights

Confucian Temple   CONFUCIAN TEMPLE
(文庙, Wénmiào; Zhonghua Xilu, Qinzhou, 秦州区中华西路) The lovely Confucian Temple is testament to the grandeur of old Qinzhou. Today the temple is open to all, a gorgeous haven of peace and tranquillity, exuding a sense of introspective calm. A statue of Confucius greets you as you enter, while behind rise up ancient cypresses, newly planted maples and a lovely, verdant space extends before the main hall, where Confucius is revered. Note the red ribbons everywhere, entreating Confucius to bestow exam success upon local hard-working pupils and scholars.

Fuxi Temple   BUDDHIST TEMPLE
(伏羲庙, Fúxī Miào; off Jiefang Lu, Qínzhōu, 秦州区解放路; ¥20; ⊗8am-5.40pm) This hoary Ming dynasty temple was founded in 1483 in honour of Fuxi, the father and emperor of all Chinese people. A statue of Fuxi is in the main hall, surrounded by traditional symbols such as bats, dragons and peonies, motifs also observable in the elegantly carved woodwork. The hall ceiling's original paintings of the 64 hexagrams (varying combinations of the eight trigrams used in the *I Ching*) is an astonishing sight. A 1000-year-old cypress tree is also in the grounds.

🛏 Sleeping & Eating

Tasty *ròujiāmó* (肉夹馍, shredded pork or beef in a bun) and other fine snack foods can be found along Shangbu Lu Pedestrian St, a pedestrian street a block directly south of the train station in Maiji Qu. A large choice of restaurants can be found in Qinzhou Qu.

Dōngān Fàndiàn
HOTEL ¥

(Dongan Hotel, 东安饭店; Longchang Lu, 陇昌路; r from ¥138; 🌐 🎧) This rather old-school hotel only opened in 2003 but already possesses a seasoned, throwback air, which is actually good news. Service is friendly, though English skills are very limited, while rooms are spacious and comfortable, decorated with traditional brown furniture and priced low. Find the hotel a short walk east of the train station. The downside is you have to pay for towels (¥15).

Tianshui Garden Hotel
HOTEL ¥¥

(天水花园酒店, Tiānshuǐ Huāyuán Jiǔdiàn; 📞 152 4937 3206; 1 Longchang Xilu, Màijī Qū, 麦积区隆昌西路1号; d ¥238; 🌐 @ 🎧) With a classical, bombastic portico crowned with angels and friendly staff snapping to attention at the front desk, this hotel is handily located directly across from the train station on the corner. It's modern and clean, though could do with a bit of a revamp.

★ Qīngxiāngyuán Lǎozìhào
Niúròu Lāmiàn
NOODLES ¥

(清香园老字号牛肉面馆; Shangbu Lu Pedestrian St, 商埠路步行街; dishes ¥8-35; ⏰24hr) Grab a ticket from the kiosk out front of this Muslim restaurant and collect your beef noodles (*niúròu miàn;* ¥8) from the kitchen window inside. The noodles are excellent, infused with dollops of scarlet-red chilli oil. For extra meat, ask for *jiāròu niúròumiàn* (加肉牛肉面; ¥15). There's no English sign, but it's the green-and-white place roughly opposite a small branch of ICBC bank.

ℹ Getting There & Away

BUS

Buses leave from the long-distance bus station in Qinzhou or the Tianshui West Bus Station (also in Qinzhou), but it is more convenient to take the fast train for Lanzhou and for destinations in southern Gansu; the high-speed line has dried up many of the buses. It is also faster to take the train to Pingliang.

TRAIN

Fast 'G' and 'D' bullet trains run to **Tianshui South Railway Station** (天水南站, Tiānshuǐ Nánzhàn; Xihuang Dadao Zhonglu, 義皇大道中路), located to the south of Maiji Qu. Trains from Tianshui South Railway Station include the following:

Jiayuguan South 1st/2nd class ¥443/298, seven hours, three daily

Lanzhou 1st/2nd class ¥83/68, 80 minutes, every 30 minutes

Xi'an North 1st/2nd class ¥132/93, one hour 40 minutes, regular departures

Xining 1st/2nd class ¥192/141, four hours, six daily

Zhangye West 1st/2nd class ¥338/233, six hours, three daily

Slower 'K' and 'T' trains rumble into **Tianshui Railway Station** (天水站, Tiānshuǐzhàn; Longchang Llongchangluu, 陇昌路) in Maiji Qu, which is close to hotels and restaurants. Tianshui Railway Station is on the Xi'an–Lanzhou rail line, with many daily trains in each direction, but it's only really useful for heading to Pingliang, or for the slow overnight train to Dunhuang, which sets off mid-afternoon and arrives the next morning. Trains from Tianshui Railway Station include the following:

Chengdu Hard seat/hard sleeper ¥149/273, 16 hours, one daily (9.56pm)

Dunhuang Hard seat/hard sleeper ¥178/350, 18 hours, one daily (2.57pm)

Pingliang Hard seat/soft seat ¥29/44, three hours, two per day (8.23am and 2.46pm)

ℹ Getting Around

Taxis shuttle passengers between Qinzhou Qu and the train station in Maiji Qu. It costs ¥10 per person (¥40 for the whole taxi); taxi flag-fall is ¥10. Alternatively, take the much slower bus 1 or 6 (¥3, 40 minutes) which departs from a stop at the southwest corner of Tianshui Railway Station, on Longchang Lu (陇昌路).

To get from Tianshui South Railway Station to Tianshui Railway Station, jump on bus 58 (¥1).

Around Tianshui

★ Maijishan Grottoes
CAVE

(麦积山石窟, Màijīshān Shíkū; Maijishan, 麦积山; grottoes ¥90, scenic area alone ¥25; ⏰8.30am-4.30pm) Set among wild, green mountains southeast of Tianshui, the grottoes of Maijishan hold some of the most famous Buddhist rock carvings along the Silk Road. The cliff sides of Maijishan are covered with 221 caves holding more than 7800 sculptures carved principally during the Northern Wei and Zhou dynasties (AD 386–581). The rock face rises in a steep ascent, with the hundreds of grottoes connected by a series of constructed walkways clinging to the sheer cliff.

Within the hard-to-miss Sui dynasty trinity of Buddha and two Bodhisattvas is the largest statue on the mountain: the cave's central effigy of Buddha tops out at 15.7m. During restoration works on the statue in the late 1980s, a handwritten copy of the Sutra of Golden Light was discovered within the Buddha's fan.

Vertigo-inducing catwalks and steep stairways cling to the cliff face, affording close-ups of the art. It's not certain just how the artists managed to clamber so high; one theory is that they created piles from blocks of wood reaching to the top of the mountain before moving down, gradually removing them as they descended.

A considerable amount of pigment still clings to many of the statues – a lot of which are actually made of clay rather than being hewn from rock – although you frequently have to climb up steps to peer at them through tight mesh grills with little natural illumination; sometimes it can be hard to see much, but other statues are as clear as day. Most of the more impressive sculptures decorate the upper walkways, especially at cave 4.

A new visitor centre, complete with post office and rather spooky face recognition technology, has gone up 3km from the grottoes, meaning that you still have to walk this distance uphill to get to the statuary, or you can take one of the sightseeing buses (观光车, *guānguāng chē*; ¥15) that regularly depart from the road just beyond the ticket office.

An English-speaking guide charges ¥50 for a group of up to five. It may be possible to view normally closed caves (such as cave 133) for an extra fee of ¥500 per group.

The admission ticket includes entry to **Ruiying Monastery** (瑞应寺, Ruìyìng Sì), at the base of the mountain, which acts as a small museum of selected statues. Across from the monastery is the start of a trail to a **botanic garden** (植物园, *zhíwùyuán*), which allows for a short cut back to the entrance gate through the forest.

The grottoes are the highlight of the much larger **Maijishan Scenic Area** (麦积山景区, Màijīshān Jǐngqū), which has considerable hiking potential if you want to make a day of it, passing waterfalls, observation terraces, mountains, valleys and temples. One activity is climbing **Xiāngjí Shān** (香积山); for the trailhead, head back towards the visitor centre where the sightseeing bus drops you off and look for a sign to the hill down a side road to the left. You can purchase a cheaper ticket (¥25) for just the scenic area if you wish, but it will not permit you to visit the grottoes.

If you're hungry, there's a huge collection of stalls serving noodles and other local dishes near the ticket office. Most dishes are priced at ¥10.

To reach Maijishan, take bus 34 (¥5 one way, one hour, every 15 minutes) from the bus shelter in the southeast corner of Tianshui Railway Station. The bus terminates at the Maijishan ticketing office. At the time of writing, the road to the grottoes was being much widened to accommodate a greater volume of vehicle traffic to the sight.

GANSU AROUND TIANSHUI

Ningxia

POP 6.3 MILLION

Best Places to Eat

➜ Tóng Xīn Chūn (p890)

➜ Guó Qiáng Shǒu Zhuā (p890)

➜ Sulai Special Beef Bone (p895)

➜ Laobaishi Flatbread and Stewed Meat (p897)

Best Places to Stay

➜ Atour (p897)

➜ Flow Youth Hostel (p890)

➜ Holiday Inn (p890)

Why Go?

With its raw terrain of dusty plains and stark mountains, sliced in two by the Yellow River, there's a distinct *Grapes of Wrath* feel to Ningxia (宁夏). Outside the cities is a timeless landscape where farmers till the hard yellow earth just like their ancestors did.

Yet Ningxia was once the front line between the Mongol and Han Chinese empires. Wondrous art and architecture from the Xixia empire and the Jin and Liao dynasties fills museums and historic sites. Then there's the royal tombs of Xixia, as well as rock carvings that predate the emperors, plus the chance to camp out under the desert sky or float down the Yellow River on a traditional raft. Being the homeland of the Muslim Hui ethnic minority adds another unique layer to Ningxia's culture.

Best of all, Ningxia sees few foreign visitors, so it seems like you have the place all to yourself.

When to Go
Yinchuan

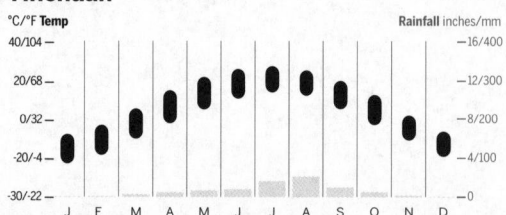

Jun–Aug Just after sandstorm season, nature glows by day, with warm, dry nights.

Sep & Oct It's cooling down and time to hike, camp or sand-surf on the dunes of the Tengger Desert.

Nov The Yellow River festival in Yinchuan features concerts and folk dancing.

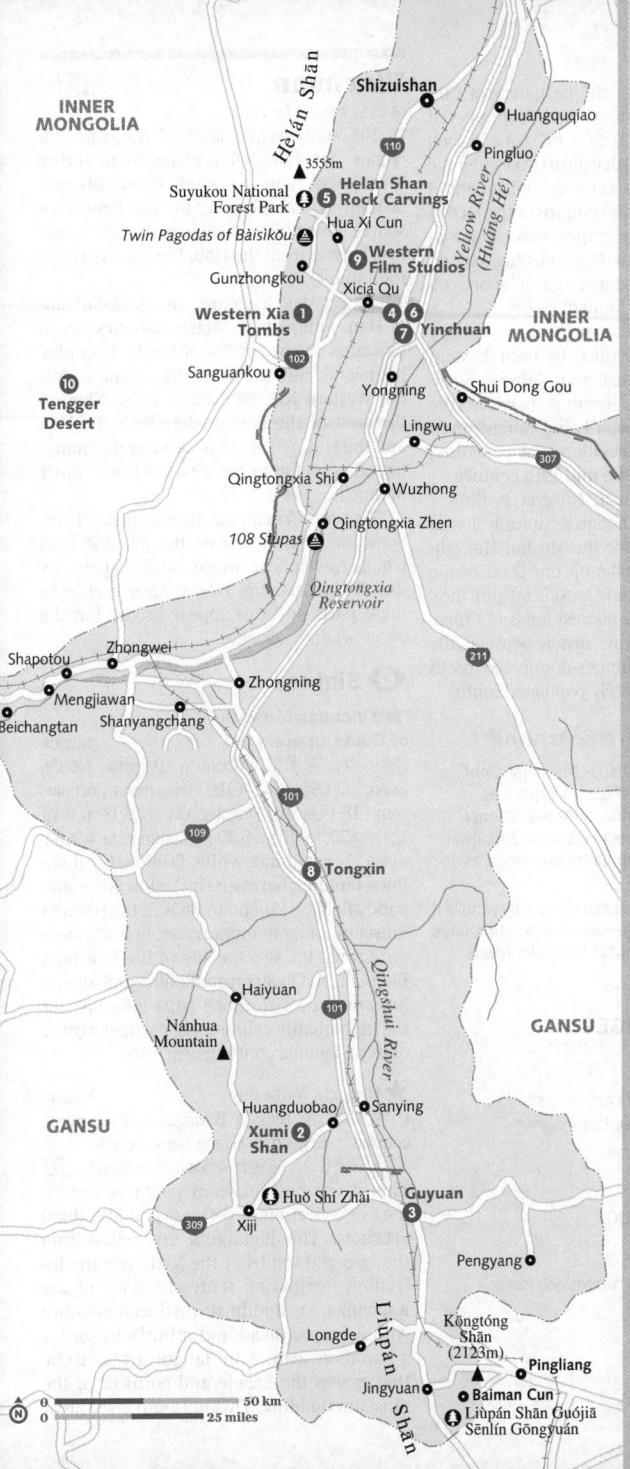

Ningxia Highlights

① **Western Xia Tombs** (p893) Visiting these imperial tombs outside Yinchuan, a rare reminder of a long-vanished culture.

② **Xūmí Shān** (p896) Exploring these little-visited Buddhist grottoes with their hundreds of statues.

③ **Guyuan Museum** (p896) Learning about the Silk Road through the treasures at this wonderful museum.

④ **Mutton** (p890) Feasting on Ningxia's famously succulent and tender mutton.

⑤ **Helan Shan Rock Carvings** (p892) Admiring unique rock carvings that date back thousands of years.

⑥ **Xinyi Market** (p889) Shopping, feasting and people-watching at this busy market.

⑦ **Yinchuan Museum of Contemporary Art** (p888) Enjoying Chinese and Islamic contemporary art at this modern museum.

⑧ **Great Mosque** (p898) Getting way off the beaten track at Tongxin's Ming-era mosque.

⑨ **Western Film Studios** (p892) Navigating fake deserts and fortresses in this film studio.

⑩ **Tengger Desert** (p895) Hopping on a camel to trek into the dunes for an overnight stay.

History

Ningxia had been on the periphery of Chinese empires ever since China's first imperial dynasty, the Qin (221–206 BC), but it took centre stage in the 10th century AD when the Tangut people declared the establishment of the Xixia (Western Xia) empire in the face of Song opposition. The empire was composed of modern-day Gansu, Ningxia, Shaanxi and western Inner Mongolia, but it soon collapsed in the face of Mongol might.

The Mongol retreat in the 14th century left a void that was filled by both Muslim traders from the west and Chinese farmers from the east. Tensions between the two resulted in Ningxia being caught up in the great Muslim Rebellion that convulsed northwest China in the mid-19th century.

Once part of Gansu, Ningxia is China's smallest province, although technically it is an autonomous region for the Muslim Hui ethnic minority, who make up one-third of the population, rather than an official province. It remains one of the poorest areas of China, with a sharp economic divide between the more fertile, Han Chinese–dominated north and the parched, sparsely populated south.

ⓘ Getting There & Around

Ningxia's capital Yinchuan is the major flight hub, although Zhongwei has an airport, as does Bayanhot (for connections within Inner Mongolia). Trains connect Yinchuan, Zhongwei and Guyuan with neighbouring provinces, as do long-distance buses.

Ningxia is so small you can cross it by vehicle in a few hours. Buses go everywhere, sometimes slowly, while trains connect the major towns.

ⓘ PRICE RANGES

Sleeping

The following prices are for a double room with shower or bathroom.

¥ less than ¥250

¥¥ ¥250–400

¥¥¥ more than ¥400

Eating

The following price ranges are for a main course.

¥ less than ¥30

¥¥ ¥30–50

¥¥¥ more than ¥50

Yinchuan 银川

☑ 0951 / POP 2 MILLION

In the sun-parched land of Ningxia, Yinchuan (Yínchuān) has managed to thrive. The Tangut founders wisely chose this spot as their capital, planting the city between a source of water (the Yellow River) and a natural barrier from the Gobi Desert (the Helan mountains).

Modern-day Yinchuan is predominantly Han, although its many mosques reveal its status as the capital of the Hui peoples' homeland. But the most interesting sights, the Western Xia Tombs and Helan Shan to the west of the city, predate both the Han and the Hui. Yinchuan is also a handy jumping-off point for longer trips to western Inner Mongolia.

The name Yinchuan means 'Silver River'. Some say it comes from the alkaline land which can appear white, while others say that it's because the Yellow River is clear in these parts and can appear bright, but the exact origin is obscure.

◎ Sights

★ Yinchuan Museum of Contemporary Art MUSEUM

(银川当代美术馆, Yínchuān Dāngdài Měishù Guǎn; ☑ 0951 842 6111; www.moca-yinchuan.com; 12 Hele Rd, Xingqing Qu, 兴庆区禾乐路 12号; ¥20; ⊙ 10am-5.30pm summer, to 4.30pm winter) Located in a white, fashionably fluid-lined building between the Yellow River and paddy fields is Yinchuan MOCA, the premier museum for contemporary art in northwestern China. It's also the site of the Yinchuan Biennale. Art lovers from Beijing and Shanghai are known to make trips here just for the high-quality exhibitions, particularly the ones on Islamic contemporary art.

★ Ningxia Museum MUSEUM

(宁夏博物馆, Níngxià Bówùguǎn; www.nxbwg.com/en/; 6 Renmin Guangchang Donglu, 人民广场东路6号; ⊙ 9am-4.50pm Tue-Sun) FREE This cavernous museum contains an extensive collection of rock art and Silk Road artefacts. The highlights are relics from the imperial tombs of the Xixia empire, including fascinating representations of the Kalaviṅka, a Buddhist mythical creature with a human head and a bird's torso; it's a common feature in Tangut art and one that graces the facade and cornices of the museum building. This museum gives great

Yinchuan

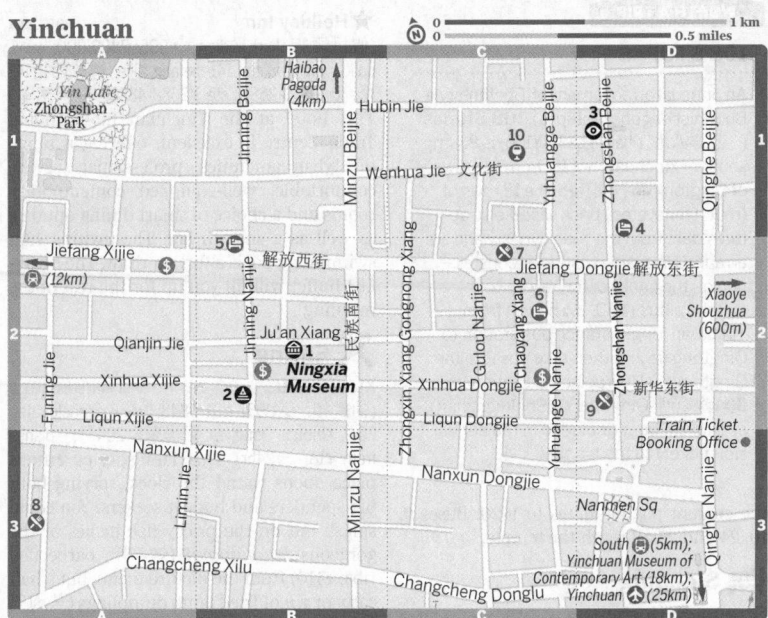

Yinchuan

context to the history of Ningxia, especially pertaining to Xixia and Silk Road culture.

Xinyi Market
MARKET

(信义市场, Xìnyì Shìchǎng; 48 Zhongshan Beijie, Xingqing Qu, 兴庆区, 中山北街48号) At this busy market with lanes flanked by mounds of local produce, the assortment of chilli peppers is astounding – all shapes, sizes and hotness levels: dried, ground, fried and fresh. Here vendors make manakish and

Chinese buns from scratch, extract chilli oil with old-fashioned presses, and weigh spices. Fruit is good and cheap here.

Haibao Pagoda
BUDDHIST PAGODA

(海宝塔, Hǎibǎo Tǎ; Hǎibǎo Park, Minzu Beijie, 民族北街的海宝公园; ¥10; ⊙9am-5pm) This fantastically well-preserved pagoda in the north of town is a beauty. Its cross-shaped (from above), straight-edged and tapering form was exquisitely built. The pagoda was damaged during the 2008 Sìchuan earthquake, so sadly can no longer be climbed. Also known as North Pagoda (北塔, Běitǎ), the structure was possibly originally built in the 5th century, before being toppled by an earthquake in 1739. It was then rebuilt in its current form in 1771.

Chengtiansi Pagoda
BUDDHIST PAGODA

(承天寺塔, Chéngtiānsì Tǎ; junction btwn Jinning Nanjie & Xinhua Xijie, 进宁南街和新华西街路口; admission ¥10, climb pagoda ¥20; ⊙9am-5pm Tue-Sun, to 5.30pm summer) Climb the 11 storeys of steep, narrow stairs of this brick pagoda topped with a green spire for 360-degree views of Yinchuan. The octagonal pagoda is also known as Xītǎ (西塔, West Pagoda) and dates back almost 1000 years to the Western Xia dynasty, though it has been rebuilt several times since, especially after it toppled during the great Ningxia earthquake of 1738;

WORTH A TRIP

108 STUPAS

An unusual arrangement of Tibetan-style Buddhist *dagobas* (stupas), **108 Stupas** (一百零八塔, Yìbǎilíngbā Tǎ; ¥100) is 83km south of Yinchuan, not far from the town of Qingtongxia (青铜峡). The 12 rows of (much renovated) brick vaselike structures date from the Yuan dynasty and are arranged in a large triangular constellation on the banks of the Yellow River.

Take a bus (¥30, 2½ hours) from Yinchuan long-distance bus station to Qingtongxia and then take bus 2 to the Qingtongxia Hydroelectric Station (青铜峡水电站, Qīngtóngxiá Shuǐdiànzhàn) and take a boat (included in the admission ticket) to the far bank.

the current pagoda dates to 1820. Buses 9, 10, 24 and 25 all reach the temple.

🛏 Sleeping

Flow Youth Hostel   HOSTEL ¥
(浮游国际青年旅社, Fúyóu Guójì Qīngnián Lǚshè; ☑ 177 0950 4177; 52 Yizhi Alley, Gulou Nanjie, 鼓楼南街，意志巷52号; 4-/6-person dm ¥55/60, d ¥160-180) A hostel with compact and comfortable four- and six-person dorms and double en-suite rooms. Girls dorms are on the 2nd floor. Decor is upbeat and modern, with a warm and welcoming palette. There are a number of bookshelves stacked with magazines and travel-related literature, and a pleasant balcony area overlooking a quiet street.

The hostel runs tours to the beach and/or desert daily during the peak season from May to September, and weekly outside of that. Day trips are ¥300 per person, desert trips involving overnight camping are ¥900 per person, and three-day excursions are ¥2600.

Yinchuan Hotel   HOTEL ¥
(银川宾馆, Yínchuān Bīnguǎn; ☑ 0951 603 7666; 28 Yuhuangge Nanjie, 玉皇阁南街28号; d ¥148-258; ☎) Yes, it's an old-school clunker. Yes, a pompous grand classical portico greets you. Yes, a vast dusty chandelier hangs from its capacious lobby ceiling. But the location is excellent, and the rooms are huge and a bargain. For ¥148 you acquire a colossal room with swirly carpet, flat-screen TV, and more-than-acceptable beds. Note that lower-floor rooms facing the street can be noisy.

★**Holiday Inn**   HOTEL ¥¥¥
(假日酒店, Jiàrì Jiǔdiàn; ☑ 0951 7800 000; www.holidayinn.com.cn; 141 Jiefang Xijie, 解放西街141号; d ¥600-2688, ste ¥2688-4888; ❋❅❂✿) This hotel at the Yinchuan International Trade Centre is excellent, offering a range of stylish amenities, professional service, comfortable, well-equipped contemporary rooms and a choice of smart dining options, as well as a smooth bar. The inviting 18m swimming pool is a further draw. The breakfast buffet will fill you up for the rest of the morning.

🍴 Eating

Xiānhè Lóu   CHINESE ISLAMIC ¥
(仙鹤楼, ☑ 0951 401 3848; www.xianhelou.net; 204 Xinhua Dongjie, 新华东街204号; dishes from ¥18; ☻24hr) This fantastic, cavernous place opens round the clock, serving both big spenders and budget seekers. You could splash out on the pricey fish dishes or the gorgeous *kǎoyángpái* (烤羊排, barbecued ribs; ¥110) from the picture menu, but a half catty or *jīn* of fried lamb dumplings (羊肉煎饺, *yángròu jiānjiǎo*; ¥30) makes a filling meal for one, arriving with a crimson soy sauce and chilli dip.

★**Tóng Xīn Chūn**   CHINESE ISLAMIC ¥¥
(同心春; ☑ 0951 412 2991; 269 Funing Nanjie, 富宁南街269号; main dishes ¥18-48; ☻10am-10pm) Locals regard this unassuming decades-old establishment as one of the best places to try Ningxia cuisine, in particular, mutton. The bonus is that it's one of the few Hui shops in the city that strictly enforces the no-smoking rule. The *shǒu zhuā* lamb (手抓羊肉; catty/half-catty ¥85/45) is sublime, succulent and melt-in-your-mouth, with the right lean-fat ratio.

Guó Qiáng Shǒu Zhuā   CHINESE ISLAMIC ¥¥
(国强手抓; ☑ 0951 601 5266; 3 Yinjiaqu Beijie, Jinfeng Qu, 金凤区，尹家渠北街3号; main dishes ¥36-108) An elegant branch of a well-known restaurant, Guo Qiang Shǒu Zhuā is best known for *shǒu zhuā* (hand-grabbed) boiled mutton, which comes in different cuts. Quite a few things on its massive picture menu are also worth trying, such as mutton and sticky rice sausage (焖肚子), misleadingly labelled 'braised belly', and sauteed knife-shaved noodles (炒刀削面, *chǎo dāoxiāo miàn*).

Quánjùdé   PEKING DUCK ¥¥
(全聚德; 51 Jiefang Dongjie, 解放东街51号; half-duck ¥80; ☻11am-10pm) If you pine for Peking

duck, Quánjùdé steps up to the plate. For ¥80 you get half a duck – a meal for one – served with cucumber, scallions and hoisin sauce. Purists maintain that the best Peking duck is served within earshot of the Forbidden City, but as a Beijing institution, Quánjùdé is a close second.

 Drinking & Nightlife

For live rock and a laid-back feel, the **Liang-yuan Bar** (凉缘酒吧; 127 Wenhua Dongjie, 文化东街127号; beer from ¥30; ⊙10.30am-1am; 🛜) is a great choice near the action at the centre of town.

After Nine Bar BAR
(☑177 9519 4784; 上海西路万达中心B座3-102; per person ¥140; ⊙7pm-2am) A quiet, dimly lit cocktail and whisky bar with sleek decor that wouldn't look out of place in Shanghai or Guangzhou, with smartly dressed servers. The handcrafted cocktails, concocted with their stock of 200 types of liqueur, are decent, but the main draw is the secluded atmosphere.

ℹ Information

Bank of China (中国银行, Zhōngguó Yínháng; 170 Jiefang Xijie, 解放西街170号; ⊙8am-noon & 2.30-6pm) You can change travellers cheques and use the 24-hour ATM at this main branch. Other branches change cash only.

Bank of China (中国银行, Zhōngguó Yínháng; Xinhua Dongjie, 新华东街; ⊙9am-5pm Mon-Sat)

Bank of China (中国银行, Zhōngguó Yínháng) ATM only.

Public Security Bureau (PSB; 公安局, Gōng'ānjú; 217 Yuhuangge Beijie, 217 玉皇阁北街; ⊙8.30am-noon & 2.30-6.30pm Mon-Fri) For visa extensions. It's on a busy intersection near a hospital, large park and schools. Take bus 3 from the Drum Tower.

ℹ Getting There & Away

AIR

Yinchuan Hedong International Airport (银川河东国际机场, Yínchuān Hédōng Guójì Jīchǎng) is located by the Yellow River, 24km southeast of the Drum Tower and Xīngqìng Qū. Flights connect Yinchuan with Beijing (¥1100), Chengdu (¥1100), Guangzhou (¥1300), Shanghai (¥1100), Ürümqi (¥1200) and Xi'an (¥500). Buy tickets at www.ctrip.com or www.elong.net.

The airport is 25km from the Xìngqìng Qū (Old City) centre; buses (¥20, 30 minutes, every 30 minutes, 6am to 10pm) arrive and leave from in front of the Civil Aviation Administration of China office on Changcheng Donglu, just south

---

THE EAST IS RED (WINE)

Wine is hot in China. A bottle of red is a status symbol for a wining and dining Chinese upper middle class: in 2013 China became the world's largest red-wine consumer, overtaking France and Italy by glugging (or at least purchasing) 155 million cases of the stuff. Consumption per capita in China remains lower than in Europe, but sales of the tipple tripled from 1997 to 2013, and continue to grow.

In China 80% of the wine consumed is red. The colour red (*hóng*) is a positive and vibrant colour: strongly associated with wealth, power and good fortune, so red wine is the way to go (especially for men; Chinese women incline more to white).

In 2018 China was the world's ninth-biggest wine producer, just ahead of Portugal, with Ningxia, Shandong and Xinjiang the most prominent wine-producing regions. The first commercial vines were planted in 1982 by large Chinese wineries like Great Wall and the following years saw a flurry of investment by international names such as LVMH (of Moët fame) and Pernod Ricard.

By 2019 Ningxia had about 170 wineries and some 90,000 acres of vines. There are plans to develop another 3200 acres between the base of the Helan mountains and the Yellow River into 50 small boutique wineries. By 2022 it is expected that Ningxia's vineyard area will double and wine production will increase by four times.

Taste-wise, Ningxia wine, like most other Chinese wines, has moved beyond striving for the technical precision of a 'proper' cabernet sauvignon to developing its own character. Though the wines may not yet have the same full flavours of their European cousins, domestically the region is esteemed for its merlot, cabernet sauvignon and 'Chinese Cabernet' Gernischt grape varieties. Try Ningxia's distinctively light, herbaceous wine *putaojiu* with live jazz or Tibetan music in Yinchuan at Liangyuan Bar, a five-minute walk north of the Drum Tower.

of Nanmen Sq. A taxi to/from the airport costs around ¥60.

BUS

Yinchuan has two bus stations: North and South. The North Bus Station, commonly known as the Tourism Bus Station, has services to scenic spots in Helan Shan. The main **South Bus Station** (银川汽车站; Yínchuān qìchēzhàn) is 5km south of Nanmen Sq on the road to Zhongwei. Departures run to the following destinations:

Bayanhot ¥30, two to three hours, every 40 minutes (7.45am to 5.20pm)

Guyuan ¥68 to ¥90, four hours, every 20 minutes (7.15am to 6.54pm)

Lanzhou ¥140, six hours, every 45 minutes (8.05am to 5.05pm)

Xi'an ¥181, 10 hours, five daily (8.30am to 7pm), last three are sleepers

Yan'an ¥136, six to seven hours, three daily (8.50am to 11.10pm)

Zhongwei ¥35 to ¥53, two to three hours, every 30 minutes (7.20am to 6.15pm)

Some buses north to Inner Mongolia also go from the northern (tourism) bus station (北门车站; běimén chēzhàn). Bus 316 (¥1) trundles between it and the main bus station. From the southern terminal the express buses (kuàikè) to Zhongwei and Guyuan are far quicker than the local buses that stop at every village along the way.

TRAIN

Yinchuan is on the Lanzhou–Beijing railway line, which runs via Hohhot (nine to 10 hours) and Datong (12 to 13½ hours) before reaching Beijing (18 to 20 hours). If you're heading for Lanzhou, the handy overnight K815 train (hard/soft sleeper ¥123/186, seven to nine hours) leaves at 10.40pm, arriving at around 7am. For Xi'an, the K1615 (hard/soft sleeper ¥178/274, 15½ hours) leaves Yinchuan at 4.56pm, arriving in Xi'an at 8.17am. The **train station** (银川火车站, Yínchuān Huǒchē Zhàn; 1 Huibei Xiang, Shanghai Xilu, 上海西路, 惠北巷1号) is in Jīnfèng Qū.

A **train ticket booking office** (Yinchuan South Bus Station, 1 Shengli St, 银川客运站南站, 胜利街一号; ⊙8am-noon & 1-7pm) can be found at the South Bus Station.

ℹ Getting Around

Between 6am and 11.30pm green BRT bus 1 (¥1) runs from the southern bus terminal (from the bus shelter in the middle of the road) to Nanmen Sq (10 minutes) in Xìngqìng Qū, via Nanmen Sq and along Jiefang Jie and on to the train station in Xīxià Qū (40 to 50 minutes). Buses 45 (¥1, 6.20am to 8pm) and 521 (¥1, 7am to 10.30pm) also run from the train station to Nanmen Sq.

Helan Shan 贺兰山

📞 0951

The rugged Helan Shan (Helan mountains) have long proved an effective barrier against both nomadic invaders and the harsh Gobi winds. They were the preferred burial site for Xixia monarchs, and the foothills are today peppered with graves and honorific temples.

It's best to stock up with snacks and bring your own food as the area around Suyukou National Forest Park and the Helan Shan rock carvings is not well supplied with restaurants. If you're going to the Western Film Studios, the nearby **Silk Road Food Street** (丝绸之路美食街; Sīchóu Zhīlù Měishí Jiē; Zhenbeibu Zhen, Xixia Qu, 银川市西夏区镇北堡镇) has more than adequate options for a simple meal.

Most visitors come to Helan Shan on a day-trip excursion from Yinchuan.

⊙ Sights

★**Helan Shan Rock Carvings** ARCHAEOLOGICAL SITE
(贺兰山岩画, Hèlánshān Shíhuà; 📞0951 601 0049; ¥70; ⊙8am-6pm) The most significant sight in Helan Shan is these ancient rock carvings dating from 1000 to 10,000 years ago. Over 2000 pictographs depict animals, faces, hunting and copulation scenes, as well as inscriptions of Xixia characters praising the Buddha. They are remnants of the early nomadic tribes who lived in the steppes north of China. Admission includes entry to a museum on ancient rock art and a ride to the valley containing the rock carvings.

The pièce de résistance here is supposedly the image of the Rastafarian-like sun god (climb the steps up the hill on the far side of the valley), but the steps leading to it were closed off at the time of research. Bus Y2 (游二路; ¥15, 1½ hours) goes to the Rock Carvings from Xinyue Sq (新月广场, Xīnyuè Guǎngchǎng) in Yinchuan; get off at the last stop. The last bus back to town is at 3.30pm.

★**Western Film Studios** FILM LOCATION
(镇北堡西部影城, Zhènběibǎo Xībù Yīngchéng; www.chinawfs.com; ¥80; ⊙8am-6pm; 🅿) This wacky film studio is where famed Chinese movies like *Red Sorghum* and many Hong Kong classics by Stephen Chow, Jackie Chan, Sammo Hung and Tsui Hark were shot. If you're a Chinese-language film buff, you may recognise some of the sets. But even if you're not, it's fun to explore the fake

WESTERN XIA TOMBS

Like giant beehives scattered on the arid eastern slope of the Helan mountains, the **Western Xia Tombs** (西夏王陵, Xīxià Wánglíng; ¥68, van ¥20; ⏱ 8am-5.30pm, to 6pm summer) are Ningxia's most celebrated sight. The earliest tombs were built a millennium ago by Li Yuanhao, founder of the kingdom. There are nine tombs, plus 250 lesser tombs, in an area of 50 sq km. The one you'll see (Tomb No.3) belongs to Li – constructed as a 23m-tall wooden pagoda, now weathered to its earthen core. The tomb site is fashioned like a miniature city with towers, city walls and temple.

Permits, usually organised through local tour operators, are required to see the other tombs, but you will pass them if you opt to get to Li Yuanhao's burial place by van.

The examples of Buddhist art in the good site museum (8am to 5.30pm) offer a rare glimpse into the ephemeral Western Xia (or Xixia) culture, and point to clear artistic influences from neighbouring Tibet and Central Asia. There are also many fascinating artefacts excavated from Li Yuanhao's tomb.

The Xixia Tombs have applied for inclusion in the Unesco World Heritage List for 2020.

The tombs are 33km west of Yinchuan. A return taxi costs from around ¥200 (including waiting time). Regular buses (¥15, every 30 minutes, 7am to 7pm) run past the tombs from the bus station next to the Nánguān Mosque, not far from South Gate Square (南门广场, Nánmén Guǎngchǎng); you will need to tell the driver you want to get off at the tombs. From the South Gate, you could also take bus 2 or 4 to its terminus in Xixia Qu and then take a van (around ¥50 each way) from there. As the site is on the road towards Bayanhot, you can get off any bus heading that way.

villages, fortresses and other recreations of China's windswept, deserty 'Wild West', but be prepared to jostle with domestic tourists for good pictures.

To get here, take bus 303 (¥5) or any buses with the words Western Film Studios (西部影城) from Yinchuan Train Station.

Suyukou National Forest Park PARK (苏峪口国家森林公园, Sūyùkǒu Guójiā Sēnlín Gōngyuán; ☎ 0951 207 9103; ¥60; ⏱ 7am-5pm) This park is a good place to start exploring Helan Shan. The 5km northbound trail is quite challenging in parts and takes you to the highest point in the park (just under 3000m above sea level). There are shorter and easier routes or you can combine hiking with a ride on the cable car (up/down ¥50/30) straight up to cool pine-covered hills.

The forest park can be glorious in winter. It's also home to the **Suyukou Ski Resort** (苏峪口滑雪场, Sūyùkǒu Huáxuěchǎng; ☎ 0951 503 5959, 0951 2079 103; ¥150-320; ⏱ 8am-5.30pm from Dec; 🚌), northwest China's largest ski resort. The downhill action gets going in mid-December. Bus Y2 (游二路; ¥15, 1½ hours) goes to the Suyukou National Forest Park from Xinyue Sq (新月广场, Xīnyuè Guǎngchǎng) in Yinchuan; get off at the second-last stop. The last bus back to town is at 3.30pm.

ℹ Getting There & Around

Bus Y2 (游二路; ¥15, two hours) goes to the Helan Shan rock carvings from Xinyue Sq (新月广场, Xīnyuè Guǎchǎng) in Yinchuan; the bus also stops at the Suyukou National Forest Park, the stop prior to the rock carvings.

Alternatively, you can hire a taxi to take you to and around the Helan Shan area for about ¥500 to ¥700 per day (including a lunch break), depending how many sights you want to pack in. You can hire a minibus (¥200 return) from Yinchuan Train Station to do a loop of the sights, or combine them with a visit to the Western Xia Tombs (around ¥300).

Zhongwei 中卫

☏ 0955 / POP 1.2 MILLION

With its wide streets and relaxed feel, Zhongwei (Zhōngwèi) – 167km to the southwest of Yinchuan – easily wins the prize for Ningxia's best-looking, most laid-back, friendliest city. The streets radiating from the Drum Tower and Gao Temple Park were given an expensive makeover not long ago: many trees were planted and buildings were given a period look. This whole area is colourfully illuminated at night, making it ideal for an after-dinner stroll and some people-watching. Zhongwei makes a good base for a trip up the Yellow River or further afield into the Tengger Desert.

Zhongwei

⊙ Sights

Gao Temple
TEMPLE

(高庙, Gāo Miào, High Temple; Gulou Beijie, 鼓楼北街; ⊙7.30am-7pm) This is one of China's most extraordinary temples. The three faiths of Buddhism, Confucianism and Taoism are revered here; it has an unusual roofline because its halls and shrines are stacked cluster by cluster on a slope. Check out the unnerving **Arhat Hall** (罗汉堂, Luóhàn Táng), which contains 500 arhats, many in grotesque guises and postures. The drawcard oddity is **Dì Gōng** (地宫), a maze-like shelter converted into a Buddhist hell.

The eerie, dimly lit tunnels contain numerous scenes of the damned having their tongues cut out, eyes poked out, being sawed in half or stoked in the fires of hell, while their screams echo all around. The ceiling

is very low, so prepare to crouch your way through. Look for the signs to 'The Infernal'.

The name of the temple becomes clear after you exit the **Hall of Heavenly Kings** (天王殿, Tiānwáng Diàn) to climb some seriously steep steps to the halls high above. After your climb, you are greeted by woodwork in a blaze of gold, blue, green and vermilion paint. To the rear, a reclining Buddha lies supine in most relaxed fashion within the **Sleeping Buddha Hall** (卧佛殿, Wòfó Diàn), while side halls are dedicated to Guanyin and other Bodhisattvas as a host of obscure Taoist deities peek out from smoky shrine niches in the walls.

Shapotou
DESERT

(沙坡头, Shāpōtóu; winter/summer ¥65/80; ⊙7am-6pm; ⊡) The desert playground of Shapotou, 17km west of Zhongwei, lies on the fringes of the Tengger Desert at the dramatic convergence of sand dunes, the Yellow River and lush farmlands. It's based around the Shapotou Desert Research Centre, which was founded in 1956 to battle the ever-worsening problem of desertification in China's northwest.

These days, though, Shapotou is more of an amusement park. The main office is a massive service centre, with a post office and a large number of shops. You can zipline (¥100) on a wire across the Yellow River, go sand-sledding (¥50), camel riding (¥80 to ¥120) and bungee jumping (¥180).

It's also a good place to raft the churning Yellow River. The traditional mode of transport on the river for centuries was the *yángpí fázi* (leather raft), made from sheep or cattle skins soaked in oil and brine and then inflated. From Shapotou you can roar upstream on a speedboat and return on a traditional raft. Prices range from ¥100 to ¥260, depending on how far you go.

The ticket office sells an assortment of tickets covering various combinations of activities. Once you enter, staff will approach you to explain and sell you packages.

If you want to flee the crowds for the sands, off-road buggies (¥300 to ¥1500) taking up to three passengers are available for hire. Tourist buses wheel visitors around (¥10 to ¥20) from point to point.

Shāpō Shānzhuāng is a basic but comfortable hotel near the dunes. Meals are available.

Bus 2 (¥5, 45 minutes) from the bus station (客运总站, *kèyùn zǒngzhàn*) runs between Zhongwei and Shapotou from 7.30am to 6.30pm. You can also pick it up on Changcheng Xijie about 200m past the Gao Temple on the opposite side of the road. Taxis cost ¥30 each way.

🛏 Sleeping

Flourish International Hotel   HOSTEL ¥¥
(金土木国际酒店, Jīntǔmù Guójì Jiǔdiàn; ☑ 0955 650 2222; 51 Gulou Dongjie, 鼓楼东街51号; r from ¥328) A ridiculously grand hotel with a lofty lobby and an eclectic assortment of Europe-inspired architectural and decorative features. Despite the hotel's aesthetic eccentricities, the service of its staff, from front desk to the servers at breakfast, is laudable, and the rooms on all of its 18 floors are very comfortable.

Zhōngwèi Dàjiǔdiàn   HOTEL ¥¥
(中卫大酒店; ☑ 0955 702 5555; 66 Gulou Beijie, 鼓楼北街66号; incl breakfast d & tw ¥320-498, f ¥498, ste ¥698; ❋ ☎) This smart hotel has large, comfortable rooms with decent-sized beds and attractive rosewood furniture. Discounts are available outside peak season, bringing room prices down to the ¥228 mark, making it a bargain.

🍴 Eating

**Zhongwei Shangcheng
Night Market**   MARKET ¥
(中卫商城夜市, Zhōngwèi Shāngchéng Yèshì; off Xinglong Nanjie, 兴隆南街旁边; dishes ¥10-28; ☺ 4pm-4am) A Dante's Inferno of flaming woks and grills, the night market is made up of countless stalls in alleys running left off Xinglong Nanjie (which is lined with Chinese-style bars). Among the tonnes of cheap food, two favourites to check out are *ròujiāmó* (肉夹馍, pork or beef stuffed in bread) and *shāguō* (砂锅, mini hotpot), as well as the ever-present pulled noodles (拉面, *lāmiàn*).

⭐ **Sulai Special Beef Bone** CHINESE ISLAMIC ¥¥
(苏莱特色啃牛骨头, Sūlái Tèsè Kěn Niúgǔtou; 58 Changcheng Dongjie, 长城东街58号; pork bone per catty ¥48) This cosy Hui restaurant specialises in stewed pork bone (牛骨头, *niúgǔtou;* catty ¥48). The bones are laden with meat and best eaten Genghis Khan–style – with your hands (you get gloves for that). There are a plethora of other Ningxia dishes on the picture menu, including shredded local chicken (手撕土鸡, *shǒusī tǔjī;* ¥48) and stewed oxtail (炖牛尾, *dùn niúwěi;* ¥68), all delectable.

Xiang Shan Lamb   CHINESE ISLAMIC ¥¥
(香山羊羔肉, Xiāngshān Yánggāo Ròu; 262 Gulou Nanjie, 鼓楼南街262; lamb dishes from ¥78;

☺ 11am-10pm) The tender, succulent cuts at this lamb specialist are boiled, braised, grilled or flash-fried with chives, chilli and potatoes – all done masterfully and captured on the picture menu. Portions tend to be big, even for side dishes (our pickled cabbage arrived looking like the whole cabbage). The decor is surprisingly attractive in a retro sort of way.

ℹ Getting There & Away

BUS

The long-distance bus station (汽车客运总站, qìchē kèyùn zǒngzhàn) is 2.5km east of the Drum Tower, along Gulou Dongjie. Take bus 2, which runs to the train station, or a taxi (¥7, 10 minutes). Destinations include the following:

Guyuan ¥70, two hours, two daily (10.10am and 2.30pm); express bus (快车, *kuàichē*)

Tongxin ¥26, two hours, five daily (from 9am)

Yinchuan ¥53, 2½ hours, every 45 minutes (7.20am to 6pm); express bus

Buses to Xi'an (¥180, eight hours, 6pm) run every other day from in front of the train station.

TRAIN

You can reach Yinchuan in 2½ hours (¥25, regular), though you'll be dropped off closer

---

WORTH A TRIP

TENGGER DESERT

If you fancy playing Lawrence of Arabia or Mad Max, make a trip out to the Tengger Desert (腾格里沙漠, Tenge Shamo), a mystical landscape of shifting sand dunes and the occasional herd of two-humped camels. Shapotou lies on the southern fringe, but it's definitely worth heading deeper into the desert to avoid the crowds. The sun is fierce out here, so you'll need a hat, sunglasses and plenty of water. Nights are cool, so bring a warm layer.

Ningxia Desert Travel Service (宁夏沙漠旅行社, Níngxià Shāmò Lǚxíng-shè; ☑ 186 0955 9777, 0955 702 7776) in Zhongwei offers overnight camel treks through the desert, with a visit to the Great Wall by car, for ¥500 per person per day for a group of four. The price includes transport, food and a guide. Ask your guide to bring along a sand sled for a sunset surfing session. Drinking beers around the campfire under a starry sky tops off the experience. The desert trek can be combined with a rafting trip down the Yellow River.

to the city centre in Yinchuan if you take the bus. It's 5½ hours to Lanzhou (hard seat/hard sleeper ¥47/92, 10 daily) and 12½ hours to Xi'an (hard/soft sleeper ¥158/243, five daily). For Guyuan (¥33, 3½ hours, seven daily) take the Xi'an train. A **train ticket office** (火车票代售点, Huǒchēpiào Dàishòudiàn; cnr Yingli Nanjie & Gulou Xijie, 应理南街鼓楼西街路口) can be found in the west of town.

ℹ️ Getting Around

Bus 2 (¥5) runs to **Shapotou** from the main bus station, running along Changcheng Lu, taking 45 minutes. The first bus departs at 6.30am and the last bus returns at 9.30pm.

Guyuan 固原

📞 0954 / POP 1.6 MILLION

An expanding but still small and historic city that dates to the 6th century, Guyuan (Gùyuán) makes a convenient base for exploring little-visited southern Ningxia. Largely populated by easygoing Hui Muslims and a large Han community, the city sees few foreigners, so expect some attention from the locals. An important but abandoned and neglected vestige of the town's history is its **City Wall** (固原城墙, Gùyuán Chéngqiáng; Kaicheng Lu, 开城路).

◉ Sights

★ **Xūmí Shān** CAVE

(须弥山; ¥60; ⊙ 8am-5pm) Cut honeycomb-like into five sandstone hills, 55km northwest of Guyuan, are 132 magnificent grottoes housing 300 Buddhist statues. They date back 1400 years, from the Northern Wei to the Sui and Tang dynasties, when this region was an important gateway in the eastward spread of Buddhism and the westward movement of goods on the Silk Road. Cave 5 contains the largest statue, a colossal Maitreya, standing 20.6m high.

A little further uphill, the finest statues are protected by the 6th-century **Yuánguāng Temple** (圆光寺, Yuánguāng Sì; caves 45 and 46) and the 7th-century **Xiànggúo Temple** (相国寺, Xiànggúo Sì; cave 51), where you can walk around the interior and examine the artwork up close – amazingly, the pigment on several of the statues is still visible in places, despite the obvious weathering.

To reach the caves, buses run from Wenhua Xilu, by the two big hospitals opposite the Xiaochi night market, to Sanying (三营; ¥8, one hour), from where you'll need to take a taxi for the 40km return trip (¥120 including waiting time) to Xūmí Shān. Between May and October, buses run direct to Xūmí Shān (¥20, 90 minutes, 7.30am, 1.30pm, 5.30pm) from near the hospitals.

Liùpán Shān Guójiā Sēnlín Gōngyuán PARK

(六盘山国家森林公园, Liupan Mountain National Forest Park; 📞 0954 564 8319; ¥65; ⊙ 7.30am-5pm) Those on the trail of Genghis Khan will want to visit southern Ningxia's Liùpán Shān, where some maintain the great man died in 1227. Legend attests that the Mongol emperor fell ill and came here to ingest medicinal plants native to the area, but perished on its slopes (though it's much more likely he died elsewhere). The mountain is now a protected area.

A walking trail leads 3km up a side valley to a waterfall. About 5km further up the main valley is a clearing with some stone troughs and tables that locals say were used by the Mongols when they came 800 years ago in search of respite from the heat.

To get here, take a bus from Guyuan's main bus station to Jingyuan (泾源; ¥20, 90 minutes) and then hire a taxi for the final 18km to the reserve (¥100 return). A return taxi from Guyuan will cost around ¥230.

Huǒ Shí Zhài NATIONAL PARK

(火石寨, Fire Rock Fort; 📞 0954 390 6999; ¥65; ⊙ 8am-6pm) The centrepiece of this geopark is its Danxia landform, with its dramatic red rocks and steep cliffs. This is not the most impressive Danxia in China but it's attractive enough. Studded into cliff-faces are shrines and temples, reachable via vertiginous steps, while pagodas perch on peaks and hiking paths snake between the various rocky formations. The light is best in the late afternoon.

For an extra ¥45, you can walk over a gorge on a glass suspension bridge. Huǒ Shí Zhài is best explored in combination with Xūmí Shān, 30km away. Hiring a car from Guyuan to visit both places will cost between ¥350 and ¥400. Alternatively, a cab can take you on the half-hour journey from Xūmí Shān to Huǒ Shí Zhài for about ¥80.

Guyuan Museum MUSEUM

(固原博物馆, Gùyuán Bówùguǎn; 133 Xicheng Rd, 西城路133号; ⊙ 9am-5pm Tue-Sun) FREE The collection of relics at this excellent museum features Neolithic pottery, lacquer coffin paintings from the Northern Wei dynasty, Tangut ceramics and Silk Road artefacts from Roman coins and Persian ewers to Buddhist statues, most of which were excavated in villages or found in tombs in and around the region. As an early stop on the northern bypass of the eastern Silk Roads, Guyuan was a site of vigorous cultural exchange between civilisations, nomadic and otherwise.

🛏 Sleeping

Liùpánshān Bīnguǎn
HOTEL ¥

(六盘山宾馆; ☑ 0954 202 1666; 35 Zhongshan Nanjie, 中山南街35号; s ¥168, d ¥148-178, ste ¥600; ✳ 🤶) The rooms at this long-standing hotel are not the freshest, but they are decent and quiet, and staff, although not used to dealing with foreigners, are helpful. Wi-fi reception in some rooms is rather weak, but regular discounts make it cheap.

Atour
HOTEL ¥¥

(亚朵酒店, Yà Duǒ Jiǔdiàn; ☑ 0954 292 9888; Bldg 19, Taihe Jiayuan, Wenhua Xijie, Yuanzhou District, 原州区，文化西街，泰合嘉园19号; r ¥309-429) An excellent find in this far-flung city, modern Atour has well-trained staff, cheerful contemporary decor, and bright, comfortable rooms. The breakfast offers well-made western and Chinese selections and lots of fruit, and instead of the usual complimentary Chinese tea, there is Twinings Earl Grey. It's 900m from Guyuan Museum, a 10-minute jaunt along Xicheng Rd.

🍴 Eating

The **Xiaochi Night Market** (小吃城, Xiǎochī Chéng; 44 Wenhua Donglu, 文化东路44号; dishes from ¥11; ⏰ noon-dawn) is an excellent place to sample the local Hui food. There are plenty of decent restaurants and noodle shops, as well as grocery stores and fruit shops, on both sides of Wenhua Xijie, heading east from Atour Hotel.

⭐ Laobaishi Flatbread and Stewed Meat
XINJIANG ¥

(老白师泡馍烩肉, Lǎobáishī Pàomó Huìròu; Wenhua Xijie, opposite Atour Hotel, 文化西街东段, 亚朵酒店对面; pàomó per bowl ¥19-50; ⏰ 7am-10pm) This three-storey establishment is famous for its *pàomó* – a Xi'an and Xinjiang delicacy of mutton (羊肉泡馍, *yángròu pàomó*) or beef (牛肉泡馍, *niúròu pàomó*) in an aromatic broth, served with unleavened flatbread. You eat by breaking the bread into small pieces and letting them soak in the broth until they're soft and full of flavour, but not soggy.

You get to choose the amount of meat you'd like: half a catty (半, *bàn jīn*) or two (二, *èr*), three (三, *sān*) or four (四, *sì*) taels

(两, *liǎng*). One tael is 50g and one catty equals 16 taels. If you're quite hungry, half a catty is a good option.

ℹ Information

Bring cash; precious few ATMs in this part of the world accept foreign cards.

ℹ Getting There & Away

AIR

Guyuan Liupanshan Airport (固原六盘山机场, Gùyuán Liùpánshān Jīchǎng) is just under 9km from town, with flights to Yinchuan, Xi'an, Chongqing and Shanghai.

BUS

The **long-distance bus station** (固原汽车站, Gùyuán Qìchēzhàn; ☑ 0954 266 2905) is about 4km west of central Guyuan's hotels and museum. No buses connect with town; a taxi costs ¥5 to ¥7. There are frequent buses to Tongxin (¥26 to ¥33, 1½ hours), Xi'an (¥120, six hours) and Yinchuan (¥70 to ¥90, four hours), as well as the following destinations:

Lanzhou ¥100, six hours, three daily (8am, 2.40pm and 3.30pm)

Tianshui ¥85, six hours, one daily (10.40am)

Zhongwei ¥70, two hours, two daily (10.10am and 3pm)

TRAIN

Guyuan is on the Zhongwei–Baoji railway line. Sleeper tickets are near impossible to get and the majority of trains depart in the middle of the night. To get to the train station, on Guxi Lu in the northwest of town around 4km away from the Liùpánshān Bīnguǎn, take bus 1 or a taxi (¥5). Destinations include the following:

Lanzhou Seat ¥75, hard sleeper ¥152, eight to 9½ hours, two daily (5.32pm and 11.30pm)

Xi'an Hard/soft sleeper ¥110/166, seven to 8½ hours, four daily (12.51am, 3.08am, 3.56am and 11.56pm)

Yinchuan Seat/hard sleeper ¥51/96, six hours, six daily (1.25am to 1.53pm)

The **Train Ticket Booking Office** (火车售票处, Huǒchē Shòupiàochù; 6 Zhongshan Nanjie, 中山南街6号; ⏰ 8am-noon & 2-4pm) is at the post office on Zhongshan Nanjie.

Tongxin
同心

☑ 0953 / POP 400,000

South of Zhongwei, the Han Chinese-dominated cities of northern Ningxia give way to the Hui heartland. Journeying here takes you deep into rural Ningxia, through villages of mud-brick houses where the minarets of the numerous mosques tower over the endless cornfields.

Tongxin (同心, Tóngxīn) has a very strong Muslim feel. There are always students in residence at the mosque training to be imams and they will greet you with a *salaam alaikum* and show you around. Tongxin is also one of the few places in China outside of southern Xinjiang where you'll see women in veils and covered from head to toe in black.

Great Mosque
MOSQUE

(清真大寺, Qīngzhēn Dà Sì; ¥15) Of all the mosques in Ningxia, the most hallowed is the Great Mosque. Dating back to the 14th century (although the present mosque was built in 1573 and then renovated in 1791), it was the only one of Ningxia's 1000-odd mosques to avoid the ravages of the Cultural Revolution. As such, it's a near-perfect example of Ming- and Qing-era temple architecture. Not until you get up close and notice

the crescents that top the pagoda roofs does it become apparent that it's a mosque.

Most travellers visit Tongxin as a day trip from Zhongwei. If you get stuck here, try **Huí Chūn Bīnguǎn** (回春宾馆; ☑ 0953 803 1888; Yinping Xijie, 银平西街; r from ¥148; ❀), opposite the bus station. For slightly longer stays, options abound on Yù Hǎi St (豫海街) close to the intersection with Cháng Zhēng St (长征街).

There are plenty of noodle, lamb, dumpling and Hui restaurants in the roads and alleys near the mosque and scattered around town.

🛈 Getting There & Away

There are frequent express buses between Tongxin and Yinchuan (¥60, three hours), making a long day trip possible. The last bus back to Yinchuan leaves at 5.30pm. You could also visit from Zhongwei (¥26, 2½ hours), or stop for a couple of hours if you are heading further south to Guyuan (¥26, two hours).

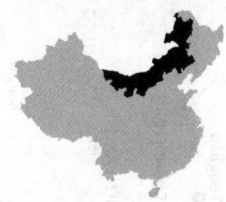

Inner Mongolia

POP 24.7 MILLION

Best Places to Eat

➡ Grandma (p904)

➡ Zhōngguān Miàn (p912)

➡ Dàndàn Tóngguōshuàn (p904)

Best Places to Stay

➡ Inner Mongolia Hotel (p904)

➡ Alashan Hotel (p912)

➡ Shèngbǐdé Zhuāngyuán (p910)

➡ Shangri-La Hotel (p903)

Why Go?

Mongolia. The name alone stirs up visions of nomadic herders, thundering horses and, of course, the warrior-emperor Genghis Khan.

Travellers heading north of the Great Wall might half expect to see Mongol hordes galloping through the vast grasslands. The reality is rather different: the 21st-century Chinese province of Inner Mongolia (内蒙古, Nèi Měnggǔ) is a wholly separate place from the neighbouring country of Mongolia itself. The more-visited south of the province is industrialised, prosperous and very much within the realm of China's modern economic miracle.

Having said that, Inner Mongolia is more than nine times the size of England and the Mongolia of your dreams can be found off the tourist route, amid the shimmering sand dunes of the Badain Jaran Desert or the vast grasslands in the north. Some effort is required to reach these areas, but the spectacular scenery can make it an unforgettable journey.

When to Go
Hohhot

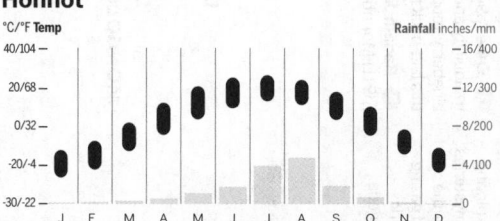

May Good weather and shoulder season equals good value.

Jul Hohhot and other regions host the annual Naadam festival.

Aug & Sep The best time to see the grasslands and ride Mongolia's famed horses.

Inner Mongolia Highlights

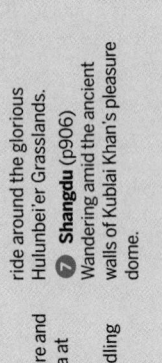

1 **Hohhot** (p902) Exploring the colourful esoteric mysteries of Tibetan Buddhism at the temple of Dà Zhào, and gazing at the astonishing tantric statues at the Wuta Pagoda.

2 **Enhe** (p909) Finding tranquillity and sampling blueberry-topped yoghurt at this laid-back farming town.

3 **Badain Jaran Desert** (p911) Mounting a camel and setting off in search of massive dunes.

4 **Shi Wei** (p910) Wandering alongside the river at sunset and gazing into Russia from this delightful village.

5 **Bayanhot** (p910) Discovering Alashan culture and about west Inner Mongolia at the Alashan Museum.

6 **Haila'er** (p908) Saddling up and going for a horse ride around the glorious Hulunbei'er Grasslands.

7 **Shangdu** (p906) Wandering amid the ancient walls of Kublai Khan's pleasure dome.

---

250 km
125 miles

RUSSIA

MONGOLIA

ULAANBAATAR

Choibalsan

Erenhot

Zabaikalsk
Mǎnzhōulǐ

Xiqi
Dōngqi
Dálái Hú
Hūlún Nur
Jinzhānghàn Grassland Camp
Haila'er
Bugt
Zālántún
À'érshān
Bèi'ěr Hú

Qiqha'er

JILIN
Jiāgédáqí
Enhe (80km);
Shi Wei (180km)

Ulanhot

Tōngliáo

CHÁNGCHŪN

SHÉNYÁNG

LIAONING
Dāndōng
Liaodong Bay
Bo Sea
Korea Bay

Sonid Youqi
Xilinhot
Bairin Zuoqi
Chìfēng
Chéngdé

Zhengxiangbai Qi
Sānggēn Dálái
Shangdu
Shangdu
Duōlún
Zhenglánqi

HEBEI
Zhāngjiākǒu
Dàtóng

Xīlāmùrén
Jíníng
Hohhot

BEIJING

SHANXI

Bayan Obo
Wùyuán Wudang Lamasery
Bāotóu
Dàqí
Dōngshèng
Ordos
Ejin Horo
Genghis Khan Mausoleum

Línhé
Dèngkǒu
Yellow River (Huáng Hé)
Resonant Sand Gorge
Wǔshénqí

Wùhǎi
Bayanhot
Guāngzōng Sì
Tengger Desert

Ējìnà Qí
Khara Khoto
Badain Jaran Desert

Álāshān Youqi
Mínqín
Shāndān Xiàn
Zhāngyè
Héxībǎo

GANSU
Jiāyùguān
Jiǔquán

QINGHAI

YÍNCHUĀN

History

The nomadic tribes of the northern steppes have always been at odds with the agrarian Han Chinese, so much so that the Great Wall was built to keep them out. But it acted more like a speed bump than an actual barrier to the Mongol hordes.

Genghis Khan and grandson Kublai rumbled through in the 13th century, and after conquering southern China in 1279 Kublai Khan became the first emperor of the Yuan dynasty. But by the end of the 14th century the Mongol empire had collapsed, and the Mongols again became a collection of disorganised roaming tribes. It was not until the 18th century that the Qing emperors finally gained full control of the region.

A divide-and-conquer policy by the Qing led to the creation of an 'Inner' and 'Outer' Mongolia. The Qing opened up Inner Mongolia to Han farmers, and waves of migrants came to cultivate the land. Outer Mongolia was spared this policy and, with backing from the USSR, it gained full independence in 1921.

Now Mongolians make up only 15% of Inner Mongolia's population. Most of the other 85% are Han Chinese, with a smattering of Hui, Manchu, Daur and Ewenki.

Inner Mongolia's economy boomed in recent years thanks to extensive mining of both coal and rare earth minerals. That growth came at great environmental cost. The mines swallowed up pastureland at alarming rates and desertification has been the root cause of the dust storms that envelop Beijing each spring. Only the far north of the region, where the economy is largely based on cattle ranching and tourism, has escaped heavy industrialisation.

For a look at how Inner Mongolia fared during the Cultural Revolution and how traditional ways of life were impacted by politics and ideology, find a copy of the semi-autobiographical novel *Wolf Totem* (2009) by Jiang Rong.

Climate

Siberian blizzards and cold air currents rake the Mongolian plains from November to March. June to August brings pleasant temperatures, but the west is scorching hot during the day.

The best time to visit is between July and September, particularly to see the grasslands, which are green only in summer. Make sure you bring warm, windproof clothing, as even in midsummer it's often windy, and evening temperatures can dip to 10°C or below.

Language

The Mongolian language is part of the Altaic linguistic family, which includes the Central Asian Turkic languages and the now defunct Manchurian. Although the vertical Mongolian script (written left to right) adorns street signs, almost everyone speaks standard Mandarin.

❶ Getting There & Around

Inner Mongolia borders Mongolia and Russia. There are border crossings at Erenhot (Mongolia) and Manzhouli (Russia), which are stopovers on the Trans-Mongolian and Trans-Manchurian Railways, respectively. To Mongolia, you can also catch a local train to Erenhot, cross the border and take another local train to Ulaanbaatar (with the appropriate visa). Possible international air connections include Hohhot to Ulaanbaatar or Haila'er to Ulaanbaatar.

Trains and long-distance buses reach Hohhot, Baotou and other large towns from neighbouring provinces.

Inner Mongolia is vast and stupendously long from east to west, so you may find yourself flying at least once, especially when accessing the northeast of the province and the far west. Otherwise you'll be relying on a mixture of trains and long-distance buses. The far west of Inner Mongolia has airports at Ejina Qi, Alashan Youqi and Bayanhot, collapsing distances within the region; buses are another option for the far west (but there are no train lines).

---

❶ PRICE RANGES

Sleeping

The following prices are for a double room with shower or bathroom.

¥ less than ¥200

¥¥ ¥200–400

¥¥¥ more than ¥400

Eating

The following price ranges indicate the cost of a main course.

¥ less than ¥30

¥¥ ¥30–50

¥¥¥ more than ¥50

Hohhot 呼和浩特

📞0471 / POP 2.86 MILLION

Founded by Altan Khan in the 16th century, the good-looking capital of Inner Mongolia is an increasingly prosperous city. Hohhot (known in Mandarin as 呼和浩特, Hūhéhàotè) means 'Blue City' in Mongolian, a reference to the arching blue skies over the grasslands. Streets are attractively tree-lined (although the roads are traffic-snarled) and there are some truly astonishing Tibetan Buddhist temples in town – more than enough to keep you busy for a day or two before heading to the hinterlands. Helpfully, most of the sights congregate in the same part of town, making sightseeing a doddle. Note that the cumbersome name of the city is often colloquially shortened to 呼市 (Hūshì).

👁 Sights

★ Dà Zhào   MONASTERY
(大召; Danan Jie, 大南街; admission ¥35, guide ¥90, joint ticket with Xílìtú Zhào ¥50; ⊙8am-7pm)
This spectacular Tibetan Buddhist temple is the oldest and largest temple in the city. Also called 'Immeasurable Temple' (无量寺, Wúliàng Sì) in Chinese, the complex was originally built in the 16th century and much enhanced in the following century. A very sacred place and a fascinating introduction to the mysterious ways of Tibetan Buddhism, Dà Zhào attracts pilgrims from across the land, who prostrate themselves fully in prayer on boards in front of the magnificent altars through the temple.

Look for the amazing-looking and blue-faced **Medicine Buddha** (药师佛, Yàoshī Fó) seated in his namesake hall and garbed in the most astonishing fashion. Also seek out the many-armed golden deity in the esoteric **Mizong Hufa Hall** (密宗护法殿, Mìzōng Hùfǎ Diàn), the central tantric deity within the **Shengle Jingang Hall** (胜乐金刚殿, Shènglè Jīngāng Diàn) and the huge jade Buddha residing in the **Jade Buddha Hall** (玉佛殿, Yùfó Diàn). The temple is also home to a 2.55m silver effigy of Sakyamuni, contained within the **Buddha Hall** (佛堂, Fótáng). Note the **Changshuo Stupa** (长寿佛塔, Chángshòu Fótǎ), draped in prayer flags. In other halls, pilgrims walk in clockwise fashion around altars, twirling prayer wheels, lost in prayer.

The plaza south of the temple is popular with kite flyers and is great for people-watching. There's an attractive decorative archway and a vast statue of Altan Khan (1507–82), the Mongol founder of the city and ruler who began building the temple.

★ Wuta Pagoda   PAGODA
(五塔寺, Wǔtǎ Sì; Wutasi Houjie, 五塔寺后街; ¥35; ⊙8am-6pm) Rising up at the rear of the Five Pagoda Temple, this striking, Indian-influenced, five-tiered pagoda was completed in 1732. Its main claim to fame is the Mongolian **star chart** around the back (protected behind glass), though the engraving of the Diamond Sutra (in Sanskrit, Tibetan and Mongolian), extending around the entire base of the structure, is in much better condition. Another fascinating aspect of the temple is the 'Temple Culture Exhibition of Hohhot' Hall, containing a mesmerising array of **tantric statues**.

Guanyin Temple   BUDDHIST SITE
(观音寺, Guānyīn Sì; E'erduosi Dajie, 鄂尔多斯大街) **FREE** Its colossal halls capped in saffron tiles visible from a huge distance away, this massive temple is dedicated to the Goddess of Mercy, Guanyin. The vast **statue** of the 1000-arm Guanyin within the **Yuantong Treasure Hall** (圆通宝殿, Yuántōng Bǎodiàn) is simply staggering. The head of the three-faced statue wears a tower of several heads on top. Within the **Great Treasure Hall** are vast seated effigies of the past, present and future Buddhas as well as the 18 luóhàn (arhats).

Xílìtú Zhào   MONASTERY
(席力图召; Da'nan Jie, 大南街; ¥25; ⊙7.30am-6.30pm) East across the road from the Dà Zhào temple is this simple, peaceful monastery, which is also known as Xiǎo Zhào or Yanshou Temple (延寿寺, Yánshòu Sì). The temple is the official residence of Hohhot's 11th Living Buddha (he actually works elsewhere). Monks chant here at 9am and 3pm.

Inner Mongolia Museum   MUSEUM
(内蒙古博物院, Nèi Měnggǔ Bówùyuàn; 27 Xinhua Dongdajie, 新华东大街27号; ⊙9am-5.30pm Tue-Sun) **FREE** This massive museum in the northeastern section of town has a distinctive sloping roof supposed to resemble the vast steppes of Mongolia. It's one of the better provincial museums, with a focus on Mongolian culture, from an excellent dinosaur exhibition to Genghis Khan and the space age.

🎎 Festivals & Events

Naadam   SPORTS
(⊙Jul) The week-long summer festival known as Naadam (literally meaning 'Games' in Mongolian) is the most famous knees-up in Inner Mongolia, featuring traditional Mongolian

Hohhot

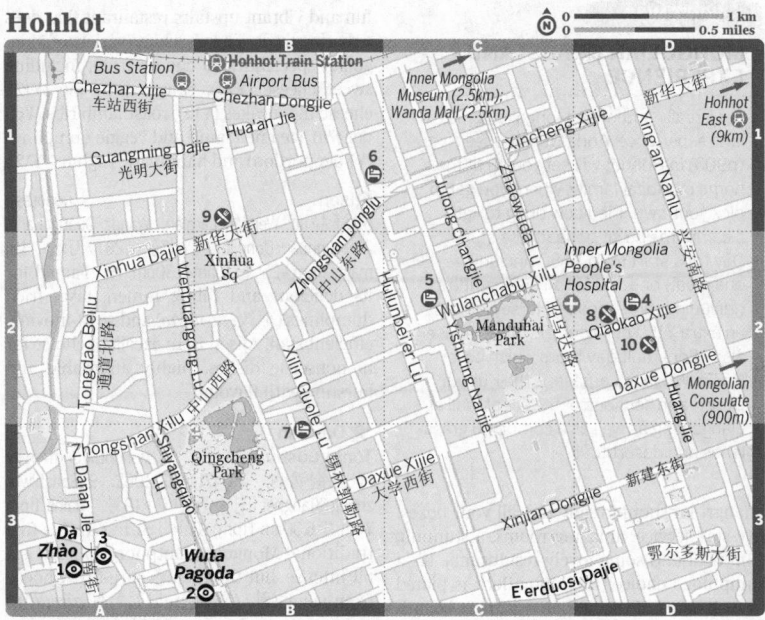

Hohhot

sports such as archery, wrestling and horse racing. The competitions and festivities take place at Gegentala and at various grassland areas in early July when the grass is green. Book local tours at your accommodation.

🛏 Sleeping

Anda Guesthouse HOSTEL ¥

(安达旅馆, Āndá Lûguǎn; ☑ 0471 691 8039, 159 475 19807; www.andaguesthouse.com; middle section of Qiaokao Xijie, 桥靠西街中段; dm/d with shared bathroom ¥50/170; 🛜) Thrust down a rather charmless alley, this friendly place has compact five-bed dorms and unadorned but pleasant enough doubles. There's an inviting, small lounge, kitchen facilities and a cute, sunny courtyard where a yurt is stuffed. Staff are eager to show

off Mongolian culture and organise loads of trips to the grasslands as well as to the Kubuqi Desert and Naadam.

Jinjiang Inn HOTEL ¥¥

(锦江之星, Jínjiāng Zhīxīng; ☑ 0471 666 8111; www. jinjianginns.com; 6 Xinhua Dajie, 新华大街6号; s ¥199, d ¥239-309; ❄🛜) This large, pleasant and snappy branch of the ultra-efficient chain hotel is located in a tower, with very clean if somewhat characterless rooms in a decent location. The hotel has a very good restaurant attached; breakfast is an extra ¥18. The hotel also arranges tours to the grasslands.

Shangri-La Hotel HOTEL ¥¥¥

(☑ 0471 336 6888; www.shangri-la.com; 5 Xilin Guole Nanlu, 锡林郭勒南路5号; d/ste ¥1388/4588; ⊖❄🛜🏊) The exemplary, 365-room

MONGOLIAN GRASSLAND EXPERIENCE

For a really authentic Mongolian grassland experience, Anda Guesthouse (p903) in Hohhot will set you up at the home of a local family, where you get to pick your own dried cow dung to light a campfire and sit beneath the stars. Day trips start from ¥480 (including one meal) or ¥580 for an overnight trip (including three meals). Horse riding is an extra ¥150 per hour. The guesthouse also offers multiday tours which cover Bái Tǎ, Wudang Lamasery, the Kubuqi Desert and sections of the Great Wall at Liangcheng as well as a combined grasslands and desert tour.

Shangri-La should really tick all your boxes: five-star service, amazing rooms, a stunning 25m pool and some lovely restaurants. It's a sumptuous choice: the lobby floor is plated in lush acres of the smoothest, most beautifully coloured marble and staff are always on hand to help. It's often possible to get large discounts.

Inner Mongolia Hotel   HOTEL ¥¥¥
(内蒙古饭店, Nèi Měnggǔ Fàndiàn; ☏0471 693 8888; 31 Wulanchabu Xilu, 乌兰察布西路31号; r from ¥1480; ❀@☎☒) Despite competition from upmarket western and Asian chains, this 14-storey high-rise remains one of Hohhot's best, featuring fine renovated rooms with big comfy beds, a pool and a health centre. The **cafe-bar** (☺8am-1am; ☎) on the ground floor is both elegant and restful for afternoon tea or an evening cocktail, and a smart restaurant serves Inner Mongolian cuisine. Discounts of 60% outside the peak summer season.

✗ Eating

A decent selection of Mongolian and Chinese restaurants can be found down **Huang Jie** (黄街), which is lined with about 40 small eateries. A standout Mongolian choice north of Xinhua Sq in the centre of town is Grandma.

★Grandma   MONGOLIAN ¥
(格日勒阿妈, Gérìlè Āmā; ☏0471 333 0055; Xilin Guole Beilu, 锡林郭勒北路; mains from ¥12; ☺7am-2pm & 5-9pm; ☎) Overlooked by a portrait of Genghis Khan, diners love this colourful, fun and vibrant upstairs restaurant that does a roaring trade. There's a huge variety of Mongolian specialities to choose from, including sweet cheese (¥10), camel meat pie (¥12), cheese mooncakes (¥12), roast lamb ribs (¥68 per jīn), steamed lamb and veggie dumplings (¥7 per portion) and handmade yoghurt (¥12).

Ajisen   NOODLES ¥
(味千拉面, Wèiqiān Lāmiàn; Wanda Guangchang, 26 Xinhua Dongjie, 新华东街26号万达广场; mains from ¥25; ☺10am-9.30pm; ☎) Famed for its delicious and filling ramen, tasty fried dumplings (煎饺, jiānjiǎo) and swift-moving, efficient staff, Ajisen is an excellent choice for no-nonsense dishes, highly affordable and bursting with flavour.

★Dàndàn Tóngguōshuàn   MONGOLIAN, HOTPOT ¥¥
(旦旦铜锅涮; ☏0471 662 1062; 9 Sanshiwuzhong Xiangnei, 三十五中巷内9号; mains from ¥40; ☺6.30am-11pm) The lighting in this fine traditional Mongolian hotpot restaurant is a bit intense, but the menu's sure-fire. Choose from spicy (辣, là) or mild (清淡, qīngdàn) broth, or a yuānyāng (鸳鸯, hot one side, mild the other) pot into which you scald your beef and lamb strips and piles of mushrooms, potatoes and other veggies.

ℹ Information

Exit-Entry Administration Bureau (出入境管理处, Chūrùjìng Guǎnlǐchù; ☏0471 669 9318; 501 Hailaer Donglu, 海拉尔东路501号; ☺8.30am-noon & 2.30-5pm Mon-Fri) For visa extensions and other enquiries.

Inner Mongolia People's Hospital (内蒙古自治区人民医院; ☏0471 662 0000; www.nmgyy.cn; 20 Zhaowuda Lu, 昭乌达路20号)

ℹ Getting There & Away

AIR

Hohhot Baita International Airport (呼和浩特白塔国际机场, Hūhéhàotè Báitǎ Guójì Jīchǎng) is 15km east of the city. Daily flight destinations (routes are reduced in winter) include Beijing, Xi'an, Haila'er, Manzhouli and Shanghai. International destinations include Ulaanbaata, Bangkok and seasonal flights to Moscow.

Book flights on www.trip.com.

The **airport bus** (机场巴士, Jīchǎng Bāshì; ¥15; 40 minutes) runs from 5.30am to the last flight. Between 10am and 10pm, the bus runs every half an hour, less regularly outside those hours. There are three lines, but the most useful route for travellers is line 1, which runs in a loop along Xinhua Dongjie, then north to the train station before heading east along Beiyuan Dongjie (北垣东街) back to the airport. You can pick it up at the train station. Lines 2 and 3 run into town via Hohhot East Train Station. A taxi to the airport will cost ¥50 (flagfall ¥8).

BUS

Hohhot's **main bus station** (长途汽车站c chángtú qìchēzhàn; Chezhan Xijie, 车站西街) is next door to Hohhot Train Station. Destinations include the following:

Baotou ¥50, two hours, every 30 minutes (7am to 7pm)

Beijing ¥150, six to eight hours (9.30am, 1.30pm and 6.20pm)

Datong ¥88, four hours, hourly (7.20am to 4.30pm)

Dongsheng ¥72, three hours, every 30 minutes (6.30am to 7.25pm)

TRAIN

Hohhot has two train stations: **Hohhot Train Station** (呼和浩特火车站, Hūhéhàotè Huǒchēzhàn; Chezhan Xijie, 车站西街), and **Hohhot East Train Station** (呼和浩特东站, Hūhéhàotè Dōngzhàn; Wantong Lu, 万通路), around 9km to the east. Most useful trains leave from Hohhot Train Station. Sleeper tickets are hard to come by in July and August; hotel travel desks can book them for a ¥30 commission. From Hohhot, trains go to the following destinations:

Baotou 1st/2nd class ¥77/49, one hour, regular departures

Beijing Hard seat/hard sleeper ¥80/169, nine to 14 hours, regular departures

Datong Hard seat/hard sleeper ¥38/98, three to four hours, regular departures

Erlian (Erenhot) Hard seat ¥54, hard/soft sleeper ¥136/242, 8½ hours (9.42am and 11.13pm)

Lanzhou Hard seat/hard sleeper ¥142/262, 17 hours, five daily

Xilinhot Hard seat/hard sleeper ¥91/169, 9½ hours, four daily

Yinchuan Hard seat/hard sleeper ¥93/208, eight hours, regular departures

ⓘ Getting Around

A metro system is under construction, with two lines due to open by 2020 and eventually running to five lines. Useful bus routes include bus 1, which runs from the Hohhot Train Station to the old part of the city past Zhongshan Xilu, and

---

ⓘ BORDER CROSSINGS: GETTING TO MONGOLIA

The Chinese-owned direct K3 train runs between Beijing and Ulaanbaatar, the Mongolian capital, on Wednesday, departing Beijing at 7.27am (hard/deluxe soft sleeper ¥1310/2041, 30 hours). The Mongolian-owned K23 (hard/soft/deluxe sleeper ¥1310/1881/2041) also departs Beijing at 7.27am on Tuesday (sometimes on Monday, it can vary). The same train stops in Erlian (二连浩特, Èrliánhàotè, Erenhot, hard sleeper ¥186, 13 hours), at the Mongolian border. Erenhot is listed on Chinese train timetables as Erlian (二连).

There are also six daily buses from Hohhot to Erlian (¥95, six hours), leaving between 8am and 1.30pm; as they depart more regularly, buses are more practical than the train, although the overnight train at 11.13pm is very useful. From Erlian you can catch a jeep across the border (about ¥80) and continue to Ulaanbaatar on the daily 5.50pm local train.

A train also runs from Hohhot to Ulaanbaatar on Monday and Friday, leaving at 9.59pm and taking 30 hours. Two trains run from Hohhot to Erlian: the 6856 (hard seat ¥54) departs at 9.42am and arrives in Erlian at 6.28pm; the overnight T4202 (hard/soft sleeper ¥136/242) from Baotou leaves Hohhot at 11.13pm, pulling into Erlian at 6.50am.

To fly from Hohhot to Ulaanbaatar, you usually need to go via Beijing, though there are direct flights during the peak season on some days. Book online at www.trip.com. Flights can be reduced in winter.

For a Mongolian visa, go to the **Mongolian Consulate** (蒙古领事馆, Měnggǔ Lǐngshìguǎn; ☏ 0471 490 2262, 0471 490 2531; Unit 1, Bldg 5, Wulan Residential Area, Dongying Nanlu, Sai Han District, 赛罕区东影南路乌兰小区五号楼一单元; ☺9am-noon Mon, Tue & Thu) in Hohhot. The 30-day visa costs ¥260 and takes four days to process. A rush visa (¥495) can be obtained the following day. US citizens do not need a visa to visit Mongolia for visits of up to 90 days; for citizens of Israel, it's 30 days visa-free. To find the consulate, travel east on Daxue Dongjie, turn left on Dongying Nanlu and look for the consulate 200m on the left. Go early.

There are also consulates in Erlian (p906) and **Haila'er** (☏ 0470 811 2896, 0470 811 2897; 6 Baihua Xilu, 白桦西路6号). A 30-day rush tourist visa (¥495) can be obtained the next day.

bus 33, which runs east on Xinhua Dajie from the Hohhot Train Station. Buses 19 (¥1) and 83 (¥1) run to the East Train Station. Taxi flag fall is ¥8.

Erlian 二连

📞 0479 / POP 75,000

Most travellers who reach Erlian (Èrlián; in Mongolian Ereen or Erenhot; also known as 二连浩特, Èrliánhàotè in Chinese) are travelling overland between China and Mongolia on the Trans-Mongolian Railway. A small city (by Chinese standards) just over the border from Zamyn-Üüd, Erlian has a dusty outpost feel. Apart from being the main China–Mongolia land crossing for rail travellers, Erlian is also known as a 'dinosaur town' thanks to the discovery of several dinosaurs in the surrounding areas.

Mongolian Consulate (Menggu Lingshiguan, 蒙古领事馆; 📞 0479 752 4240; http://ereen. consul.mn; 1206 Youyi Beilu, 友谊北路1206号; ⏰ 8.30am-5.30pm Mon-Fri) Walk north Youyi Beilu for 15 minutes until you see the Mongolian flags on your left. A 30-day rush tourist visa can be issued on the same day you apply; bring one passport-sized photo. To find the consulate from the train station, walk west up Xinhua Dajie and turn right onto Youyi Lu or take a taxi (¥6).

There aren't a lot of sleeping options open to international travellers in Erlian. If you need to stay overnight, travellers report that the **Erenhot Rurouni Youth Hostel** (Chahar'er Jie) is a passable budget option, while the **Naxiduo Hotel Heart Posthouse** (Konglong Jie) offers very large rooms and a central location.

ⓘ Getting There & Away

AIR

Erenhot Saiwusu International Airport (二连 浩特赛乌素机场, Èrliánhàotè Sàiwùsù Jīchǎng; G208) is 27km south of the city. There are regular flights to/from Beijing, Hohhot and Tongliao as well as daily international flights in summer to Ulaanbaatar with Hunnu Air.

BUS

Getting same-day train tickets out of Erlian is darn near impossible for Beijing, so most people opt for the bus. The **international bus station** (二连浩特市国际汽车站, Èrliánhàotèshì Guójì Qìchēzhàn; Chaha'er Jie, 察哈尔街) is halfway between the consulate and the train station, from where buses run to Beijing (¥220, six buses from 2pm to 4.30pm), Hohhot (¥95, six per day) and Datong (¥136, one daily).

In Beijing, buses depart/arrive at the Xinfadi bus station (新发地客运站, Xīnfādì Kèyùnzhàn), beyond the fourth ring road in the southeast of the capital. Five buses (¥180) run between 5.40pm and 6.20pm. There is also a very slightly earlier departure (¥180) at 5.30pm from the Yongdingmen bus station (永定门客运站, Yǒngdìngmén Kèyùnzhàn). Try to get there early to get a ticket.

Shangdu 上都

📞 0479 / POP 83,000 (ZHENGLANQI)

The 'very fine marble palace' described by explorer Marco Polo and eulogised and immortalised by poet Samuel Taylor Coleridge as a 'stately pleasure-dome' is today little more than a vast prairie with vague remnants of its once mighty walls, but it continues to have an allure that is far greater than the sum of its remaining parts.

Today Xanadu, or Shangdu (Shàngdū) as it was actually called, is accessed via the small gateway town of Zhenglanqi (正蓝旗).

History

Conceived by Kublai Khan, grandson of Genghis and the first Yuan emperor, Shangdu's lifespan as the summer capital was relatively brief. Construction of the city started in 1252 and lasted four years, serving as Kublai Khan's summer palace away from his palace in Zhongdu (Khanbaliq), the Yuan dynasty capital in today's Beijing. Shangdu was overrun and destroyed by Ming forces in 1369.

Shangdu actually consisted of three distinct cities: the outer city, the imperial city and the palace city. All that is visible now are the outer and inner walls, which are ticketed (admission ¥50), though there is a museum of the ruins here too. The site was listed as a Unesco World Heritage site in June 2012.

◎ Sights

Xanadu Ruins   RUINS
(元上都遗址, Yuán Shàngdū Yízhǐ; ¥50) Surrounded by the Jinlianchuan Grasslands, there is not a huge amount to see of the palace remains. From the yurt where you buy your ticket, it's another 1.5km to the outer walls (a golf buggy will take you for ¥10). From there, you can walk another 500m to the inner ramparts. Paths through the wildflower-covered grassland that has swallowed up the city offer the chance for pleasant strolls and reflective musings on the vagaries of history.

GENGHIS KHAN MAUSOLEUM

Located 130km south of the large and uninspiring city of Baotou in the middle of nowhere is the **Genghis Khan Mausoleum** (成吉思汗陵园, Chéngjí Sīhàn Língyuán; mid-Apr–mid-Oct ¥170, mid-Oct–mid-Apr ¥150; ⏱8am-6pm), China's tribute to the great Mongol warlord. Unfortunately, old Genghis Khan (成吉思汗, Chéngjí Sīhàn) is not buried here (his resting place has never been found). Instead, the mausoleum's existence is justified by an old Mongol tradition of worshipping Genghis Khan's personal effects, including his saddle, bow and other items. Kublai Khan established the cult and handed over care for the objects to the Darhats, a Mongol clan.

Darhat elders kept the relics inside eight white tents, which could be moved in times of warfare. In the early 1950s the government decided to build a permanent site for the relics and constructed this impressive triple-domed building, in the traditional Mongolian style. By then, most of the relics had been lost or stolen (everything you'll see here is a replica). But even today, some of the guards at the site still claim descent from the Darhat clan. The ticket includes entry to a museum with information on Genghis and Monglian culture.

The nearest city to the site is the ho-hum city of Baotou, but even from here there is currently only one bus (¥47, two hours, 9.10am) to Chengling (成陵, Chénglíng) from the forecourt of the Donghe Bus Station in Donghe. As you'll be dropped off by the side of the road, you'll then have to catch a taxi (¥15) the final 7km to the mausoleum, or beg for a lift from a returning restaurateur (dining at his restaurant is a good way of paying him back). All buses from Baotou to Yulin pass by Chengling, so that is also an option (same in the other direction, if you are coming from north Shanxi).

There are 11 trains (hard seat ¥18, 80 minutes) per day from Baotou to Dongsheng West train station, 60km from the tomb. There are also regular buses (¥34, two hours, every 20 to 30 minutes, 8am to 7pm) from Baotou to Dongsheng, from where buses run to the mausoleum.

To move on, take a cab back to a small tourist village (with shops, hotels and restaurants) to flag down any Dongsheng-bound bus at the roundabout. Buses should pass by regularly till about 4pm. From Dongsheng (东胜) you can connect to Baotou (¥34), Hohhot (¥65, four hours, hourly) and other regional destinations as well as Yulin in north Shanxi province.

At the roundabout, there are also share taxis to Ejin Horo Qi (伊金霍洛旗, Yijīn Huòluò Qí; ¥15 to ¥20 per person), known as 'Yī Qí', from where you can get a bus to Hohhot (¥70, 4½ hours, last bus 3pm).

Xanadu Ruins Museum MUSEUM

(元上都遗址博物馆, Yuán Shàngdū Yízhǐ Bówùguǎn; ⏱9am-4.30pm) **FREE** This museum is very important to visit for the scale models that give a realistic impression of the sheer ambition of Shangdu, as well as for relics from the site, including ceramics, statues and decorative and structural pieces of the original palace, which crucially put the ancient complex into context.

🛏 Sleeping & Eating

You can find a good selection of restaurants on and around Shangdu Dajie, including barbecue places, hotpot restaurants and noodle bars, as well as teahouses. Worite Beilu (沃日特北路), off Shangdu Dajie, also has a strong choice of noodle places, dumplings and barbecue restaurants.

Jiādì Shāngwù Bīnguǎn HOTEL ¥

(佳帝商务宾馆; ☎0479 422 0555; Shangdu Dajie, 上都大街; tw from ¥128; 🖥) This modern business-style hotel towards the west end of Shangdu Dajie has clean and affordable rooms.

188 Liánsuǒ Bīnguǎn HOTEL ¥¥

(188 连锁宾馆; ☎0479 423 9188; Jinlianchuan Dajie, 金莲川大街; r/ste ¥288/388; ❄🖥) A fresh place with very clean and spacious rooms, this hotel is in a building right by the bus station.

ℹ Information

At the time of writing, no bank ATMs accepted foreign cards, so bring enough cash with you.

ℹ Getting There & Away

Although Shangdu signifies distant wonders in the western imagination, in truth it's not that isolated (275km northwest of Beijing). But it does feel rather remote, partly because of the huge empty prairie it sits in, and also because getting here requires some effort. Hohhot's bus station by the train station has buses to Zhenglanqi (¥132, six to seven hours, 7am, 7.35am, 9am and 2pm), also just known as Lanqi (蓝旗). From Zhenglanqi it's about a 20km taxi ride (¥200 return) to Shangdu. Buses return to Hohhot at 7.20am.

Haila'er 海拉尔

📞 0470 / POP 350,000

Northern Inner Mongolia's largest city, Haila'er (Hǎilā'ěr) is a busy, rather ordinary place. Don't fret, the city isn't the draw: surrounding the town range the expansive Hulunbei'er Grasslands, a vast prairie that begins just outside the city and rolls northwards towards the Russian and Mongolian borders, seemingly forever. Superbly lush and deeply verdant come July and August, the grasslands are a fantastic sight and *the* place in Inner Mongolia to saddle up a horse.

The immediate area around Haila'er sees several inevitably touristy yurt camps where you can eat, listen to traditional music and sometimes stay the night. Although they're not places where Mongolians actually live, you can still learn a bit about Mongolian culture, and the wide-open grasslands are a gorgeous setting.

For a more authentic experience, travel further away, although staying with local families in the grasslands is not easy to organise unless you speak some Mandarin (or Mongolian).

◎ Sights

Ewenki Museum MUSEUM

(鄂温克族博物馆, Èwēnkè Bówùguǎn; Yimin Lu, 伊敏路; ⊙8.30-11.30am & 2.30-5.30pm) FREE Roughly 20,000 Ewenki people live in northern Inner Mongolia, most of them in the Hulunbei'er Grasslands surrounding Haila'er. Glimpse some of their history and culture at this modern museum. Traditionally herders, hunters and farmers, the Ewenki are one of the few peoples in China to raise reindeer. You can see a *chum*, a wigwam-style portable dwelling that the Ewenki traditionally used. The museum is on the southeastern edge of town. Regular minibuses (¥4, 15 minutes) run here from Buxing Jie beside the Busen shopping centre.

☞ Tours

North of Haila'er are few permanent settlements, just the yurts of herders with their flocks of sheep and cows and strings of Mongolian ponies set in some of the greenest grasslands you will ever see. Closer to the Russian border, the rolling prairie becomes more wooded, as spindly white pine trees appear. Bring along binoculars if you want to have a closer look at the Russian villages across the border.

The bus journey to Labudalin itself gives you magnificent views of the grasslands as they roll past.

If you speak Chinese, you can hire a private car from around ¥500 per day to take in the sights around Haila'er: contact Mr Liu (刘师父, Liú Shīfù; 159 4775 3673). During busier seasons, he can find Chinese travellers to carpool (拼车, *pīnchē*) with. He has set itineraries that cover Enhe, Shi Wei and Manzhouli.

⭐ Festivals & Events

Naadam SPORTS

(⊙Jul) The Haila'er Naadam (sports festival) is held annually in July on the grasslands just north of town. You'll see plenty of exciting wrestling, horse racing and archery. The city is, however, flooded with tour groups from across China at this time, making it difficult to find a room, and hotel prices double.

🛏 Sleeping & Eating

On summer nights Buxing Jie and the surrounding alleys become a hub of outdoor *shāokǎo* (barbecue) places that are good for a beer and meeting the locals.

Jinzhanghan Grassland Camp TOURIST GER CAMP ¥

(金帐汗草原, Jīnzhànghàn Cǎoyuán; 📞133 2700 0919; yurt per person ¥100; ⊙Jun–early Oct) Set along a winding river about 40km north of Haila'er, this grasslands camp has a spectacular setting, even if it is aimed at tourists. You can pass an hour or so looking around and sipping milk tea, spend the day horse riding (per hour ¥200) or hiking, or come for an evening of dinner, singing and dancing.

If you want to stay the night, the yurts are ¥100 per person. There's no indoor plumbing, but there is a communal toilet hut. To get here, you'll have to hire a taxi from Haila'er (about ¥300 return) or join one of the

Chinese group tours (sign up at your hotel or at the booth at the Haila'er train station).

About 2km before the main camp there are a couple of unsigned family-run camps. Prices for food, accommodation and horse rental are about half what you pay at Jin-zhanghan, but they are rather less organised. To skip the tourist-run camps, push further north through the grasslands towards Enhe and Shi Wei.

Bèi'ěr Dàjiǔdiàn   HOTEL ¥¥

(贝尔大酒店, Bei'er Hotel; ☑ 0470 835 8455; 36 Zhongyang Dajie, 中央大街36号; d incl breakfast ¥880-980; ❀ 🛜) With a large bright lobby, welcoming staff and well-maintained rooms, this is a very good midrange choice. It's advisable to book ahead here, especially in July and August, when the crowds descend. Discounts frequently knock rooms down to a very affordable ¥230, so don't be frightened by the official rates.

🚹 Getting There & Away

AIR

Hulunbei'er Haila'er Airport (呼伦贝尔海拉尔机场, Hūlúnbèi'ěr Hǎilā'ěr Jīchǎng) Direct daily flights to Beijing (two hours), Hohhot (2¼ hours) and Shanghai (3½ hours). Go to www.trip.com to book flights.

Hunnu Air (☑ +976 7000 1111; www.hunnuair.com) Flies to Ulaanbaatar in Mongolia every Monday and Friday. Book tickets online.

Airport buses (¥5) connect to all flights and depart from the train station roughly 1½ hours before departure. A taxi to the airport from town costs ¥30.

BUS

The **Long-Distance Bus Station** (长途车站, Chángtú Chēzhàn) in the Hedong district east of the river has buses to the following destinations:

Labudalin ¥38, two hours, half-hourly (7am to 5.30pm)

Manzhouli ¥37, three hours, hourly (8am to 5.30pm)

On the Hexi side, there are also regular buses to Labudalin (¥38, two hours) from the **Gōnglù Kèyùn Shòupiàochù** (公路客运售票处), a bus ticket office on the corner of Chezhan Lu facing the train station.

TRAIN

Trains from **Haila'er Train Station** (海拉尔站) include the following:

Manzhouli Hard seat ¥23 to ¥29, two hours, 12 daily

Harbin (Hā'ěrbīn) Hard/soft sleeper ¥102/223, 10 to 11 hours, nine daily

Qiqiha'er Hard seat/hard sleeper ¥72/136, seven to eight hours, eight daily

Beijing Hard/soft sleeper ¥240/453, 29 hours, two daily

The train station is in the northwestern part of town. A taxi to the city centre is ¥7.

🚹 Getting Around

Buses 1, 3, 7 and 9 run from the train station past Bèi'ěr Dàjiǔdiàn (Bei'er Hotel). Bus 18 runs from the Long-Distance Bus Station in Hedong to the train station, while taxis charge ¥12. Taxi fares start at ¥6.

Enhe   恩和

☑ 0470 / POP 2570

The small township of Enhe (Ēnhé), located 70km north of Labudalin en route to Shi Wei, is a charming village brimming with an unhurried and authentic atmosphere. Surrounded by hills and acres of lush grass, a low-key and very unhurried vibe survives. A large number of residents are of Chinese-Russian origin; many look purely Russian. Here, herders milk their cows outside their properties when they aren't taking them out to pasture. The local yogurt – mixed with wild blueberry sauce – is on sale everywhere.

Horse rides start run from around ¥50 to ¥100. You can hire bikes (from ¥10 per hour) – an excellent way to get about – or go for hikes.

There's quite a choice of Russian minority family-run places offering accommodation in the village, where you can usually get a room with bright sheets for around ¥100; in terms of accessibility, travel info and affordability, the **Enhe Grasslands International Hostel** (呼伦贝尔恩和牧场国际青年旅舍, Hūlúnbèi'ěr Ēnhé Mùchǎng Guójì Qīngnián Lǔshě; ☑ 0470 694 2277; www.yhachina.com; Enhe, 恩和; dm from ¥45, d & tw ¥200-360, tr/q ¥280/360; ☺ May-Oct; 🛜) is a good choice. Most hotels shut up shop during the glacial winter months, opening again in spring.

🔘 Sights

Russian Minority Folk Museum   MUSEUM

(俄罗斯族民俗博物馆, Éluòsīzú Mínsú Bówùguǎn) **FREE** In a traditional wooden building with a Russian Orthodox chapel topped with a bronze roof and a cross, this sweet museum has a charming collection of objects relating to the Russian minority that lives here, from farming equipment to old record players and stuffed animals that roam the borderlands, including a wild-eyed lynx.

ℹ Getting There & Away

To get here from Haila'er, you need to travel first to Labudalin (拉布达林; ¥36, two hours, half-hourly, 6.30am to 5.30pm). Labudalin (sometimes called E'erguna; 额尔古纳) has two daily direct buses (¥15, two hours) to Enhe, at 12.10am and 2.30pm. Buses return to Labudalin in the morning at 8.30am and 9.30am. Shi Wei–bound buses (¥15) run from the crossroads by the provincial government (县政府, xiànzhèngfǔ) building at around 11.15am and 5.15pm.

Shi Wei   室韦

📞 0470 / POP 1800

A small Russian-style town of log cabins located right on the E'erguna River, which marks the border with Russia, Shi Wei (Shì Wěi) is deep within the glorious grasslands. Shi Wei itself is no longer the backwater it once was and the commercial summer tourist season gets busy with domestic visitors, although very few foreigners make it up here, especially out of season. But it's fun to ride a horse along the riverbank (¥50 to ¥100) while gazing at the Russian village on the opposite bank, or sitting down to some Russian food. Look for wooden stages on both sides of the river: each country used to host performances for their neighbours! Taking the backcountry roads here, through the elm forests, is another attraction.

For a closer look at Russia, you can walk to the **Friendship Bridge** (友谊桥, Yǒuyì Qiáo; ¥20; ⊗ 8am-5pm), though many visitors are happy to just walk along the **wooden walkway** that overlooks the river and Russian border immediately north of the village. Chinese tourists pose for photos at the foot of the bridge connecting the two countries before wandering down to a hut to buy Russian chocolate and souvenirs. Taxis can take you to **Linjiang** (临江) – a less touristy border village with a lovely natural setting – for around ¥100 return. You can also find accommodation in Linjiang but will need to head back to Shi Wei if you want to get the bus back to Labudalin.

There is nowhere to take out or change money in Shiwei, so come prepared.

🛏 Sleeping & Eating

In Shi Wei, families have turned their homes into guesthouses and/or restaurants, often named after Russian-minority families, with names such as Dounia's Delicacy Manor or Sonya's Family. You can get a room for around ¥100 to ¥300. There are also larger all-wood hotels and a large tourist hotel capped with onion domes that glow with neon at night on the main drag.

Shèngbǐdé Zhuāngyuán   HOTEL ¥¥¥
(圣彼得庄园; 📞 0470 697 6678; Zhongyang Jie, 中央街; d ¥980-1080, ste ¥1180; ⊗ May-Oct; 🅿 🛜) You can usually get a room for around ¥220 unless you turn up during the peak season at this comfortable and cosy, large all-wood affair, which looks like something right out of *Twin Peaks*. You'll get a large timber room fashioned from logs (with wooden ceiling). Like virtually every hotel, it shuts for the winter. The name means the 'St Peter Manor'.

ℹ Getting There & Away

From Haila'er, first travel to Labudalin (拉布达林; ¥38, two hours, half-hourly, 6.30am to 5.30pm), and from two daily direct buses go to Shi Wei (¥45, four hours), at 9.30am and 3.30pm. Buses return to Labudalin at 8am and 1pm but make sure you buy your ticket in advance to secure a seat. Alternatively, take a bus (¥15) first to Enhe and then wait for the bus coming through to Shi Wei (¥15).

Bayanhot   阿拉善左旗

📞 0483 / POP 140,000

If coming from Ningxia, Bayanhot (Ālāshàn Zuǒqí; also called 巴彦浩特, Bāyànhàotè) can serve as a handy one-stop introduction to Mongol culture, its language, food and the vast deserts and high blue skies of far western Inner Mongolia. The town is also the gateway to the fantastic temple Guǎngzōng Sì and has a crop of interesting sights of its own, including the excellent, modern museum and the traditional architecture of the Qīnwáng Fǔ. Despite the dearth of railways, the airport links Bayanhot with Alashan Youqi (for the Badain Jaran Desert) and Ejina Qi (for Khara Khoto) in Inner Mongolia, so access from further afield has been greatly simplified.

◉ Sights

★ **Qīnwáng Fǔ**   HISTORIC BUILDING
(亲王府; ⊗ 9am-6pm) **FREE** This fabulous courtyard palace is the former home of the local prince, the Alashan Qin Wang. A well-restored, Qing-era complex of buildings

and courtyards, the palace has photos of the last prince (1903–68) and his family, plus some of their personal effects, but it's the splendid traditional layout and architecture that steals the show.

★ **Alashan Museum**   MUSEUM
(阿拉善博物馆, Ālāshàn Bówùguǎn; Ande Jie, 安德街; ⊙9am-6pm) **FREE** This superb museum affords a fascinating insight into Alashan and Mongolian culture. English captions are sporadic, which is a shame, but there's a wealth of objects to explore. The Dinosaur Gallery on the 1st floor is very professional, but the upstairs galleries are exemplary, with displays of Mongolian clothing, saddles and Buddhist instruments, as well as a range of sacred masks and a *thangka*. There's also a gallery on ancient stone carvings and a model of Khara Khoto in its heyday.

Guǎngzōng Sì   MONASTERY
(广宗寺; May-Oct ¥80, Nov-Apr ¥40; ⊙8am-5pm) Once one of the most magnificent monasteries in Inner Mongolia, Guǎngzōng Sì has a stunning setting in the Helanshan mountain foothills 38km south of Bayanhot. At its height, some 2000 monks lived here and so important was the monastery that the main prayer hall, Gandan Danjaling Sum, contains the remains of the sixth Dalai Lama inside the golden stupa that dominates it. Locals call the temple Nán Sì (南寺, South Temple) and taxi drivers frequently refer to it that way.

Tragically, and as was the fate for many, the monastery was demolished during the Cultural Revolution; a 1957 photo in the main prayer hall gives you an idea of how big it once was. The temples have since been rebuilt, but a hotel, yurt restaurants and a tacky shopping street have been added to the complex to entice domestic tour groups.

There are good walking trails in the mountains behind the complex; take the path to the right of the main temple and follow it for one hour to a grassy plateau with fantastic views.

From Bayanhot, a taxi to the monastery and back is around ¥200, but the driver may not want to wait for long (in this case

---

OFF THE BEATEN TRACK

FAR WEST INNER MONGOLIA

The golden deserts, shimmering lakes and ruined cities of western Inner Mongolia are fantastic places for adventures far from the beaten track. With airports in the three major towns across the region – Bayanhot, Alashan Youqi (阿拉善右旗) and Ejina Qi (额济纳旗) – providing links to Hohhot and Xi'an, the Badain Jaran Desert and ancient town of Khara Khoto is more accessible than before. Yet this remains a vast and infrequently explored area offering some of the most photographic landscapes you can hope to locate in China.

The remote but stunning **Badain Jaran Desert** (巴丹吉林沙漠, Bādānjílín Shāmò) (the world's fourth-largest desert) is a mysterious 49,000-sq-km landscape of desert lakes, Buddhist temples and towering dunes. The dunes here are among the tallest in the world, some topping 460m (taller than the Empire State Building). The tallest are static with a solid core, and do not move. The closest town in the region, Alashan Youqi (阿拉善右旗), is a 30-minute drive from the dunes.

The ruined Tangut city of **Khara Khoto** (黑城, Hēichéng, Black City; ¥10; ⊙8am-7pm) was built in 1032 and captured by Genghis Khan in 1226 (his last great battle). Khara Khoto continued to thrive under Mongol occupation, but in 1372 an upstart Ming battalion starved the city of its water source, killing everyone inside. Six hundred years of dust storms nearly buried Khara Khoto, until the Russian explorer PK Kozlov excavated and mapped the site, recovering hundreds of Tangut-era texts (now kept at the Institute of Oriental Manuscripts in St Petersburg). Located about 25km southeast of Ejina Qi, the allure of Khara Khoto is the remoteness of the site and surrounding natural beauty. A great time to visit is late September to early October when the poplar trees are changing colours; but be warned that every hotel room in Ejina Qí will be booked out at this time.

There are hotels that accept foreigners in Bayanhot and Alashan Youqi, but not all hotels accept foreigners in Ejina Qi (额济纳旗) and sometimes permits are required to visit (though not at the time of writing); it's perhaps best to visit the town as a day trip or arranged through a tour company such as **China Hiking** (☑1565 2200 950; www.chinahiking.cn).

he will naturally charge more). If going on to Yinchuan (your taxi driver can drop you at the highway where you can stop any Yinchuan-bound bus), look out for the crumbling, yet still mighty, remains of the Great Wall at Sanguankou (三关口, Sānguānkǒu). Some sections are up to 10m high and 3m wide.

Yánfú Sì
BUDDHIST TEMPLE

(延福寺; ⊙8am-noon & 3-6pm) FREE The original Mongol town of Bayanhot was centred on this 18th-century temple. Completed in 1742, it once housed 200 lamas; around 30 are resident here now. The **Hall of the Three Buddhas** is an authentic and dusty shrine housing its namesake trinity of Buddha in various incarnations, while the **Money God Temple**, in one of the side halls, sees the shining Money God himself, flanked by ferocious Tibetan Buddhist deities, gazing out over flickering, burning wicks suspended in oil.

🛏 Sleeping & Eating

Alashan Hotel
HOTEL ¥¥

(阿拉善宾馆, Ālāshàn Bīnguǎn; ☑ 0483 221 1889; www.alsbg.com; 42 Hoxud Lu, 和硕特路42号; ⊙d ¥300-433, ste ¥580-980; ❀❈☏) This smart and sparkling four-star hotel is the best in town, with very swish and comfortable rooms in the main block. Cheaper rooms are located in the other buildings on the other side of the courtyard, with discounts of around 40% in effect most of the time. The airport bus leaves from the main gate.

Āndá Jiàrì Jiǔdiàn
HOTEL ¥¥

(安达假日酒店, Āndá Holiday Hotel; ☑ 0483 877 0999; Tuerhute Beilu, next to long-distance bus station, 土尔扈特北路汽车站旁边; r incl breakfast ¥170-400; ❀❈☏) This decent hotel is excellently located for that early-morning bus to Baotou or Alashan Youqi. Rooms are bright, spacious and quiet, though getting a bit scuffed, with excellent

discounts regularly bringing the cheapest twins down to around ¥130. Staff have very limited English and there have been occasional reports of indifference.

Zhōngguān Miàn
NOODLES ¥

(中关面; Yabulai Lu, 雅布赖路; noodles ¥8-30; ⊙10.30am-10pm) This noodle bar to the west of New Century Sq serves up some fine and filling noodles: aim for the oil-splashed noodles (油泼面, yóupōmiàn; small/big ¥12/14) for flavoursome noodles with diced spring onions, or the tomato and egg noodles (番茄鸡蛋面, fānqié jīdànmiàn; small/big ¥13/15), but there are many more. Most noodles come either dry (干拌, gānbàn) or in soup (汤面, tāngmiàn).

❶ Getting There & Away

AIR

Bayanhot is served by **Alxa Left Banner Bayanhot Airport** (阿拉善左旗巴彦浩特机场, Ālāshàn Zuǒqí Bāyànhàotè Jīchǎng), to the southwest of town. Joy Air flights connect Bayanhot with Alxa Right Banner Badanjilin Airport, Ejin Banner Taolai Airport, Xi'an, Baotou and Tianjin; China Express Airlines flies to Hohhot and Chongqing. Snow can scupper flights, so be prepared for delays.

BUS

Buses depart every 40 minutes from Yinchuan's south bus station for Bayanhot (¥30, two to three hours) between 7.20am and 6pm (you could stop off at the Western Xia Tombs). In the other direction, the first bus leaves Bayanhot at 7am, the last departs at 6.05pm; some buses run to Yinchuan train station. If you want to travel further west into Inner Mongolia from Bayanhot there are three buses in the morning to Ejina Qi (¥140, eight hours), at 8am, 9am and 9.20am. One daily bus goes to Alashan Youqi (阿拉善右旗; ¥121, seven hours) at 7.50am. There is a bus to Baotou (¥120, eight to nine hours) at 7.10am, there are two buses to Hohhot (¥176, nine hours) and one bus per day to Dongsheng (¥131) at 9.30am.

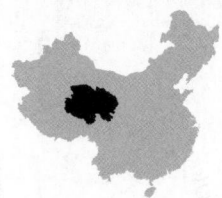

Qinghai

POP 5.6 MILLION

Best Places to Eat

➡ Snow Mountain Creamery (p917)

➡ Ah Ma La (p917)

➡ Mǎzilù Niúròumiàn (p917)

➡ Dreamland (p925)

Best Places to Stay

➡ Rebgong Norbang Travel Inn (p925)

➡ Gesar Palace Hotel (p929)

➡ Sofitel Xining (p917)

➡ Starway Hotel (p917)

Why Go?

Big, bold and beautifully barren, Qinghai (青海, Qīnghǎi), larger than any country in the EU, occupies a vast swathe of the northeastern chunk of the Tibetan Plateau. As far as Tibetans are concerned, this is Amdo, one of old Tibet's three traditional provinces. Much of what you'll experience here will feel more Tibetan than Chinese; there are monasteries galore, yaks scattered across the hills by the thousands and nomads camped out across high-altitude grasslands.

Rough-and-ready Qinghai, which means 'Blue Sea' in Chinese, is classic off-the-beaten-track territory, often with a last frontier feel to it. Travelling here can be a little inconvenient, but that is part of what makes the province so very special: seclusion is everywhere. Indeed, Qinghai delivers all the adventure you may need, with heavy doses of solitude among middle-of-nowhere high-plateau vistas, Martian-like red mountains, mouthwatering cuisine and encounters with remote communities of China's ethnic minorities.

When to Go
Xining

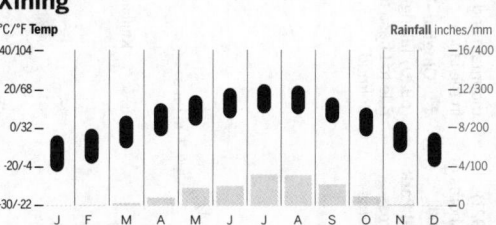

Jan & Feb Tibetan New Year (Losar), with lots of pilgrims and celebrations at monasteries.

Jul & Aug Grasslands at their greenest; landscape dotted with nomad tents.

Sep Safest and most comfortable time for hiking around Mt Amnye Machen.

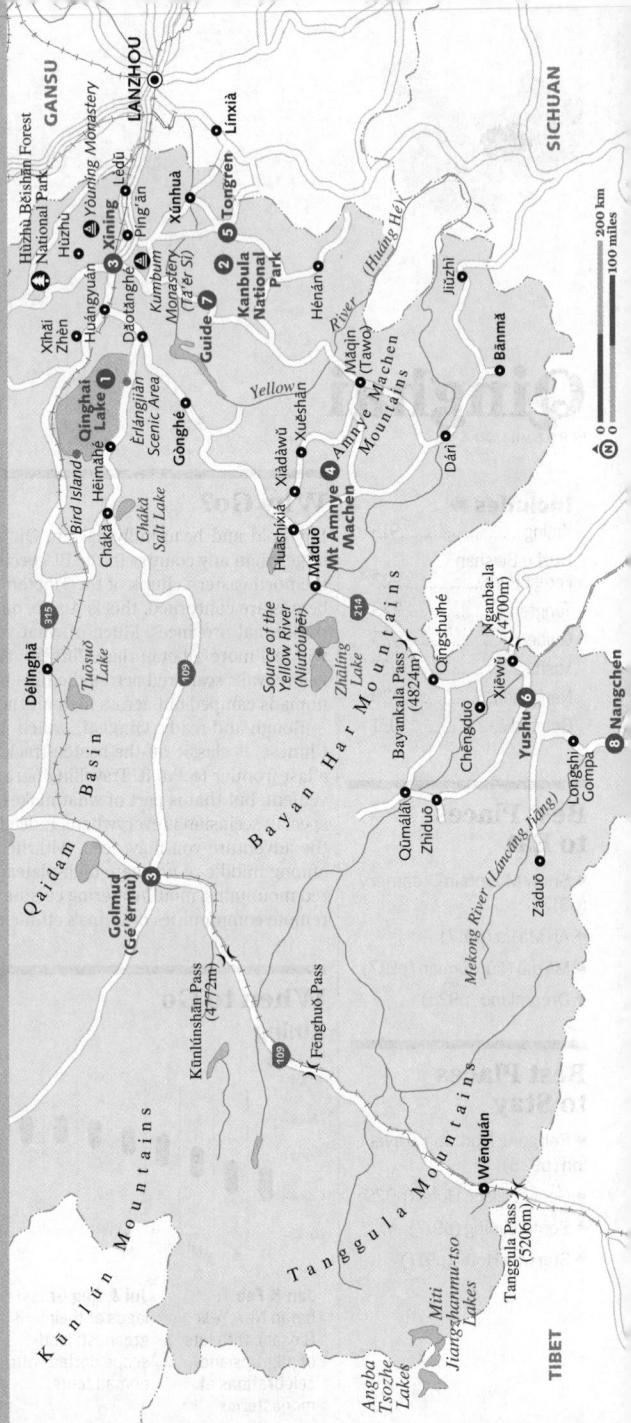

Qinghai Highlights

1 Qinghai Lake (p921)
Cycling along on the shores of
the largest lake in China.

2 Kanbula National Park
(p924) Gazing out across
some of the most sublime
mountain and river panoramas
in the land.

3 Qinghai–Tibet Railway
(p920) Taking the iconic train
ride to Lhasa from Xining or
Golmud.

4 Mt Amnye Machen
(p926) Joining pilgrims on a
trek on eastern Tibet's most
sacred mountain.

5 Tongren (p923) Buying a
thangka straight from the easel.

6 Yushu (p927) Immersing
yourself in all the textures and
hues of Tibet in this welcoming
high-altitude town.

7 Guide (p925) Gazing
at the world's largest prayer
wheel, turned by the crystal-
clear waters of the Yellow River.

8 Nangchen (p929)
Exploring the scenery and
monasteries around this small
town near the border with Tibet.

History

The northern Silk Road passed through what is now Qinghai province, and in 121 BC the Han dynasty established a military base near modern Xining to counter Tibetan raids on trading caravans.

During the Yarlung dynasty, a time of great expansion of Tibetan power and influence, Qinghai was brought directly under Lhasa's control. After the collapse of the dynasty in AD 842, local rulers filled the ensuing power vacuum, some nominally acting as vassals of Song dynasty emperors.

In the 13th century all of Qinghai was incorporated into the Yuan empire under Genghis Khan. During this time the Tu began to move into the area around Huzhu, followed a century or so later by the Salar Muslims into Xunhua.

After the fall of the Yuan dynasty, local Mongol rulers and the Dalai Lamas in Lhasa wrestled for power. The Qing emperors restored the region to full Chinese control, setting it up as a prefecture with more or less the same boundaries as today. As in the past, however, they left administrative control in the hands of local elites.

Qinghai became a province of China in 1928 during the republican era, though at the time it was under the de facto control of the Muslim Ma clan. When the People's Republic of China was established in 1949, Qinghai retained its provincial borders and capital city, Xining.

In the late 1950s an area near Qinghai Lake (青海湖, Qīnghǎi Hú) became the centre of China's nuclear weapons research program. During the next 40 years, at least 30 tests were held at a secret base, the Qinghai Mine.

In April 2010 Yushu, a Tibetan town in remote southwest Qinghai, was devastated by a 7.1-magnitude earthquake. Thousands died – some say tens of thousands – but the rebuilding effort was swift and Yushu's main centre reopened as a tourist destination in early 2014.

Today, the province is experiencing rapid growth. It's not uncommon to see large apartment blocks under construction in provincial towns (though in some places many of the finished apartments remain empty). Highways have been constructed to facilitate faster movement around the province, while huge investment in wind energy has seen wind farms sprout up, taking advantage of the big gusts that sweep across Qinghai.

ⓘ Getting There & Around

Off-the-beaten-track overland routes include south into Sichuan, at Aba or Shiqu, and north into Gansu or Xinjiang from Golmud (check before going as foreigners travelling this way may need a special permit). Zhangye, Lanzhou and Xi'an are quickly reachable by high-speed train. Urumqi in Xinjiang can also be reached on high-speed train. Xining Caojiabao International Airport has flights across the land.

Routes southwest into Tibet are remote and are almost always closed to foreigners altogether.

Most people arrive by train, usually into Xining, but after that train lines are limited, so long-distance buses are the best way to get around. In more remote areas you'll often have no option but to hire a private car and driver. Some areas north of Qinghai Lake have been closed to foreigners for years; usually this means you cannot spend the night, but it can be hard to get bus tickets without a travel permit from the PSB.

Xining 西宁

☑ 0971 / POP 2.2 MILLION

Situated on the eastern edge of the Tibetan Plateau, this lively and hugely diverse provincial capital makes a good base from which to dive into the surrounding sights and on to the more remote regions of Qinghai and beyond. Though many travellers use Xining (Xīníng) as a jumping-off or landing point from the Qinghai–Tibet Railway, it's also a wonderful place to encounter the province's varied cultures – Muslim (Hui, Salar and Uyghur), Tibetan and Han Chinese – it's a rich culinary mix that these groups bring together. There's superb food and a scattering of tempting cafes as well as

ⓘ PRICE RANGES

Sleeping
The following price ranges refer to a private double room.

¥ less than ¥200

¥¥ ¥200–320

¥¥¥ more than ¥320

Eating
The following price ranges refer to a meal for one.

¥ less than ¥30

¥¥ ¥30–50

¥¥¥ more than ¥50

an outstanding museum of Tibetan culture, some beautiful temples and mosques, plus the remains of the old city wall, so try not to race through without putting aside some time to explore.

⊙ Sights

★ Tibetan Culture & Medicine Museum
MUSEUM

(藏文化博物馆, Zàng Wénhuà Bówùguǎn; ☑ 0971 531 7881; www.tibetanculturemuseum.org; 36 Jing'er Rd, 经二路36号; north hall free, south hall ¥60; ◔ 9am-6pm May-Sep, to 5pm Oct-Apr; ☑ 1, 34, 65, 66, 84) **FREE** Exhibitions in the north hall focus on Tibetan medicine, astronomy and science. Many visitors come for the 618m-long *thangka* scroll in the south hall – the world's longest – which charts most of Tibetan history. Completed in 1997, it's not very old but it is unbelievably long and took 400 artists four years to complete. There's a decent amount of signage in English. A guided tour in English of the north hall is ¥200 and for the south hall it's ¥360.

The museum is located on the far northwest side of Xining. Bus 1 (¥1, 50 minutes) goes here from the public bus terminal by the train station (get off at 新乐花园). A taxi costs about ¥20 from the city.

★ Nanguan Mosque
MOSQUE

(南关清真寺, Nánguān Qīngzhènsì; 23 Nanxiao Jie, 南小街23号; ◔ 4-11pm) This beautiful and recently constructed mosque is really quite an astonishing sight. Built from marble and a variety of other stones and carved tilework, the entire complex is a photogenic opportunity. The **main prayer hall** is usually out of bounds to non-Muslims (although you may also be allowed in), but you are certainly welcome to wander the grounds.

Dongguan Grand Mosque
MOSQUE

(东关清真大寺, Dōngguān Qīngzhēn Dàsì; 25 Dongguan Dajie, 东关大街25号; ◔ 7am-8pm) **FREE** As becomes quickly evident to even the most casual observer, about one-third of Xining's population is Muslim, and although the city's biggest mosque may not be the prettiest, it's one of the largest mosques in China and is certainly an imposing sight. Friday lunchtime prayers regularly attract 50,000 worshippers, who spill out onto the streets before and afterwards. And, during Ramadan (斋月), as many as 300,000 come here to pray, with police closing off the streets to traffic.

Nánshān Gōngyuán
PARK

(南山公园; Nanshan Lu, 南山路; ◔ temples 9am-5pm; ☑ 16, 103) **FREE** This park, which is also known as Fènghuáng Shān (凤凰山), rises above Xining south of town. The grounds are home to two Buddhist temples: **Nánchán Sì** (Nánchán Sì, 南禅寺; 93 Nanshan Lu, 南山路93号) **FREE** and **Fǎchuáng Sì** (法幢寺). In between them is a path that leads up to the hill where you'll find more walking paths and panoramic views of the city. Fortune tellers assemble on the steps on they way up, charging ¥30.

Xining City Wall
RUINS

(青唐城遗址, Qīngtáng Chéng Yízhǐ; Kunlun Zhonglu, 昆仑中路) **FREE** One or two isolated sections of Xining's Tang dynasty city wall still remain, the most accessible being this short stretch within a park on Kunlun Zhonglu. It is part of the south wall of ancient Qingtang city and was built in 1034, though different portions were erected, repaired or left to crumble over subsequent centuries. The wall's remains – an overgrown dirt embankment – aren't all that impressive; however, the tiered pathways that wind through the park make for a pleasant stroll.

🛏 Sleeping

Hehuang Memory Youth Hostel
HOSTEL ¥

(河湟记忆青年旅舍, Héhuáng Jìyì Qīngnián Lǚshè; ☑ 189 9722 3551; Longhua Jiayuan, 295 Kunlun Donglu, 昆仑东路295号龙华佳园; dm ¥58; ❄ ❀; ☑ 83) This cheerful hostel has clean six- and eight-bed dorms and friendly, English-speaking staff, but the real draw is the cosy communal lounge lined with bookshelves and offering a decent beer selection. In high season, western and Chinese food is available. Pros: great atmosphere and cheap prices. Cons: it's a bit far away from everything and there are squat loos. BYO toilet paper.

Lete Youth Hostel
HOSTEL ¥

(理体青年旅舍, Lǐtǐ Qīngnián Lǚshè; ☑ 0971 820 2080; xnletehostel@gmail.com; 15th fl, Bldg 5, International Village Apts, 2-32 Jiancai Xiang, 建材巷国际村公寓5号楼15层; dm ¥40-55, d with/without bathroom ¥140/70; ☜) A warren of rooms high up in a tall building, this backpacker haunt has been running for years, and everything is slightly faded. Someone here usually speaks some English and most guests are Chinese, but you can usually find fellow travellers for joint tours (arranged by the hostel). There's a pleasant common area with long views. Bike rental is ¥40 per day.

Starway Hotel HOTEL ¥¥

(星程酒店，Xīngchéng Jiǔdiàn；☏0971 811 9333; 7 Dong Dajie, 东大街7号; d ¥199-249, tw/ste/f ¥229/299/309; ☏) This smart midrange option has a very central location right on Dong Dajie: you won't find much English spoken here but rooms are spacious, tidy and modern with work desks, coffee and water provided, and clean en-suite bathrooms. Wi-fi works well, even with a VPN. Ask if breakfast is included as they may just throw it in, otherwise it's an extra ¥25.

Sofitel Xining LUXURY HOTEL ¥¥¥

(索菲特大酒店, Suǒfēitè Dàjiǔdiàn；☏0971 766 6666; www.sofitel.accorhotels.com; d/ste ¥800/1120; ❋❊@☏; ❑9,31,106) Xining's first foreign five-star hotel, the Sofitel guarantees a plush stay: rooms have soft beds, and large bathrooms have bathtubs and giant showers. Expect reasonable discounts.

✗ Eating

Xining is an excellent place to sample Tibetan and Hui (Chinese Islamic) cuisines. For Chinese Islamic food, head to Dongguan Dajie, near Dongguan Grand Mosque, or the northern stretch of Nanxiaojie. **Mojia Jie** is a traditional snack street with lots of point-and-go options and local dives; the **Mazhong Snack Centre** (马忠食府, Mǎzhōng Shífǔ; 11-16 Mojia Jie, 莫家街11-16号; dishes from ¥15; ☺6.30am-11.30pm) is a reliable, bustling choice for its variety of dishes and flavours. **Limeng Business Pedestrian Street** has western fast food, chain restaurants and bars.

★ **Mǎzilù Niúròumiàn** NOODLES ¥

(马子禄牛肉面; 6 Jiaotong Xiang, 交通巷6号; noodles from ¥8; ☺6.30am-8.30pm) Classic beef noodle fare at this Muslim restaurant with a long pedigree as a brand. The standard bowl of lip-smacking beef noodles (牛肉面, niúròumiàn) is ¥8 and with extra beef it's ¥18; an egg (鸡蛋, jīdàn) on the side will cost you a mere ¥1.50. Round it all off with a delightful bowl of sweet milk and egg pudding (牛奶鸡蛋醪糕, niúròu jīdàn láogāo; ¥10), sprinkled with red wolfberries and black sesame seeds: seriously delicious.

★ **Snow Mountain Creamery** ICE CREAM ¥¥

(雪山冰淇淋, Xuěshān Bīngqílín; ☏0971 827 8334; www.snowmountaincreamery.com; Bandao Buxingjie, 半岛步行街; mains from ¥30; ☺9.30am-10pm; ☏❖) This two-tier American-run spot is a winner and a must-do for fans of superb,

---

ℹ HOTEL BLUES

Scoring a hotel room in Xining and popular tourist spots around Qinghai during the summer months can be surprisingly difficult, especially for international travellers, as not all places have a licence to accept non-Chinese guests. Book your room or dorm bed as early as possible, at the very least one week in advance, especially in July and August; when you book, double-check that the hotel or hostel is permitted to take foreign guests. There is nothing worse than paying for your room online and then arriving to find you are not allowed to stay. Foreigners are not officially allowed to spend the night in Xihai Zhen and other parts of the area north of Qinghai Lake, which makes it even more of a squeeze on choices of places to stay.

---

handmade ice cream (¥15 a scoop), coffee, comfort and the whole Mountain Creamery shebang. Your fingers could be reaching for the yak pizza or yak cheese burger too, or if you're nodding off on one of the sofas, Snow Mountain roasts, grinds and brews its own coffee for that on-the-spot, wide-eyed pick-me-up.

The menu is superb, with an adorable range of pizzas, expertly made – from cheese pizza to yak pepperoni – along with fill-me-up burgers and sizzling chicken dishes, plus fries on the side. Baked goodies are at hand for sticky-finger moments: brownies, dark-chocolate pastries, bagels with cream cheese. The upstairs mezzanine is a recommended bolt-hole, surveying the vast coffee roaster and views out back while snuggling into a sofa that is hard to leave. The charming, young American family in charge has seven kids, so this is a seriously family-friendly spot.

★ **Ah Ma La** TIBETAN ¥¥

(阿妈啦; 120 Nanshan Donglu, 南山东路120号; dishes ¥15-150; ☺10am-10.30pm) Delish Tibetan food, tacky decor, English-speaking Tibetan boss, picture menu. That pretty much sums up the Ah Ma La experience. Slide into a booth seat and order up authentic Tibetan dishes such as yak tongue and mómo (馍馍, dumplings) and wash it down with Lhasa beer. The restaurant is along Nanshan Donglu, opposite the Tibetan Hospital.

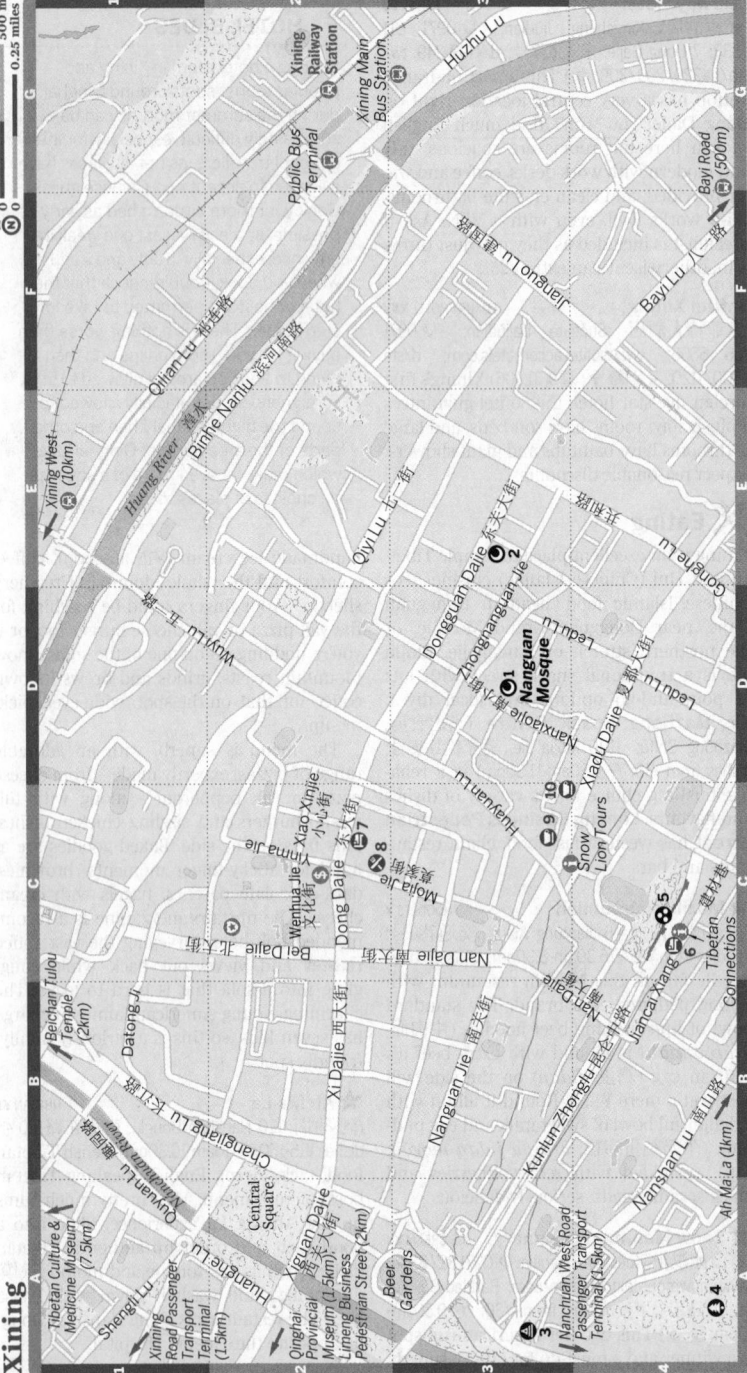

Xining

Xining

At the time of writing, Ah Ma La was opening another restaurant just round the corner on Jianxin Lu.

🍷 Drinking & Nightlife

Coffee Top   CAFE
(☑187 0978 5067; Xiadu Dadao, 夏都大道; ⊙9am-10pm) This Tibetan place is a top choice for a coffee, or a Tibetan breakfast (*tsampa* porridge with honey; ¥22) at the start of your Xining day. There's Bob Marley, a charcoal ceiling, books scattered around, comfy sofas and even a picture of pre-fire Notre Dame. There's a pleasant spot on a raised platform at the back where you can stake your claim.

Greenhouse   CAFE
(古林坊咖啡, Gǔlínfáng Kāfēi; ☑0971 820 2710; 222-22 Xiadu Dajie, 夏都大街222-22号; ⊙9.30am-10.30pm; 🛜) Greenhouse has a charming, rustic split-level wood interior, super-comfy leather sofas and some of the best coffee in town (from ¥25). You can also munch on pizzas, burgers, sandwiches (from ¥33), cake, scones or tiramisu to a mellow music selection. Plenty of plugs and free wi-fi, mercifully nonsmoking, and there's a shelf or two of books aloft.

🔒 Shopping

★ **Amdo Craft Shop**   ARTS & CRAFTS
(安多手工铺面, Ānduō Shǒugōng Pùmiàn; ☑0971 816 9740; www.amdocraft.com; Hutai Sanxiang, Jiesen Huayuan Xinanmen, 虎台三巷, 杰森花园西南门; ⊙9am-8pm) Dedicated to training and helping Tibetan nomads to produce handicrafts, Amdo Craft returns profits from all sales to Tibetan communities. Browse an excellent selection of yak milk soap, tops, coats, mittens, baby blankets, jewellery, children's socks and shoes and much more, all made from natural resources: yak and sheep wool (and yak milk).

ℹ️ Information

Bank of China (中国银行, Zhōngguó Yínháng; 22 Dong Dajie, 东大街22号; ⊙9am-5pm Mon-Fri, 10am-4pm Sat & Sun) Has a number of large branches around town that exchange cash and have foreign-friendly ATMs.

Public Security Bureau (公安局, Gōng'ānjú, PSB; 35 Bei Dajie, 北大街35号; ⊙8.30-11.30am & 2.30-5.30pm Mon-Fri) Can extend visas.

ℹ️ Getting There & Away

AIR

Xining Caojiabao International Airport (西宁曹家堡国际机场, Xīníng Cáojiābǎo Guójì Jīchǎng; www.qhaport.com) is 27km east of the city. There are daily flights to Beijing, Chengdu, Dunhuang, Shanghai, Yushu, Golmud, Tianjin, Xi'an and other cities across China.

Shuttle buses run to the airport from the main bus station (¥21) between 8am and 6.30pm; tickets are sold at window 11. Buses (¥21) also run from the Bayi Road bus station.

A taxi from the airport to central Xining costs ¥110, or ¥150 to the Sofitel.

BUS

Xining has way too many bus stations for a city of its size. Most buses leave from the **Xining Main Bus Station** (西宁客运车站, Xīníng Kèyùn Chēzhàn) beside the main railway station, but some buses leave from one of the four other stations. For arrivals to Xining by bus or train, local buses depart from the Public Bus Terminal by the train station. Visitors to Xihai Zhen will need a travel permit from the PSB in Xining before buying a bus ticket.

From Xining Main Bus Station, there are buses to the following destinations:

Bird Island ¥66, 4½ hours, 7.45am

Chaka (direct to the lake) Single/return ¥100/240, five hours, one daily (10am)

Chaka ¥65.50, five hours, seven daily (7.45am to 3.30pm)

Golmud ¥164.50, 15 hours, four daily (2pm, 5pm, 5.30pm and 6pm)

ℹ TRAVEL AGENCIES & TOUR COMPANIES

There are some excellent Tibetan-run tour companies based in Qinghai. The following are all highly recommended.

Mystic Tibet Tours (☏ 182 0971 5464; www.mystictibettours.com; Rm 902, Bldg 7/2 Bandao Xinjiayuan, Bayi Lu, 八一路半岛新家园7/2号楼 902室) One of the better agencies in town, run by an English-speaking Tibetan guide, Gonkho. Arranges tours and treks around Tibet, particularly Amdo and Amnye Machen.

Snow Lion Tours (☏ 0971 816 3350; www.snowliontours.com; Office 408, Xiadu Dasha Bldg, Xiadu Dajie, 夏都大街夏都大厦408室; ⊙ 9am-6pm) Run by a knowledgeable English-speaking Tibetan, Wangden; arranges treks, camping with nomads and Tibet permits.

Tibetan Connections (☏ 186 9725 9259; www.tibetanconnections.com; Apt 1209, 12th fl, Bldg 5, International Village, Jiancai Xiang, 建材巷国际村公寓5号楼18层1209室) This tour company focuses on more remote parts of Amdo and Kham but can arrange trips into Tibet.

Elevated Trips (☏ 199 1732 4924, 133 0978 7215; www.elevatedtrips.com) Capable outfit offering off-the-beaten track experiences across the Tibetan Plateau with a focus on small groups.

Heimahe ¥44, four hours, two daily (8.30am and 9.30am)

Hezuo (Gansu) ¥85, five to six hours, one daily (7.45am)

Huzhu Beishan National Forest Park ¥30, four hours, two daily (noon and 2pm)

Kanbula National Park ¥22.5, 2½ hours, every 30 minutes (10.30am to 5pm)

Kumbum Monastery Single/return ¥25/50, 45 minutes (10am)

Lanzhou ¥65, three hours, hourly (8am to 6.30pm)

Linxia ¥61, five hours, six daily

Maduo ¥111, eight hours, 8.30am (other buses go to the intersection)

Qinghai Lake Single/return ¥50/100, three hours (9.30am)

Tongren ¥40, four hours, every 40 minutes (7.30am to 5.30pm)

Wuwei ¥95, 7.40am, 9am (noon and 8.15pm)

Xiahe (Gansu) ¥79.50, 4½ hours, one daily (8.20am)

Xihai Zhen ¥25, 2½ hours, every 25 minutes (7.30am to 5.30pm)

Yinchuan ¥150, seven to eight hours (9am)

Yushu ¥229, 15 hours, eight daily (11am to 6.30pm)

Bayi Road Bus Station (八一路汽车站, Bāyī Lù Qìchē Zhàn; cnr Bayi Lu & Huangzhong Lu, 八一路和湟中路路口) runs buses to Tongren (¥35, four hours, every 30 minutes, 7.40am to 5pm) and Youning Monastery (¥12, 70 minutes, 10.30am). A daily bus (one way/return ¥50/100, three hours each way) also runs to Qinghai Lake at 9.30am, returning at 3.30pm.

Nanchuan West Road Passenger Transport Terminal (南川西路客运站, Nánchuān Xilù Kèyùn Zhàn; 48 Nanchuan Xilu, 南川西路48号; ☐ 23, 33, 37) has buses to Guide (¥26, two hours, every 20 minutes, 7.45am to 5.40pm) and Maduo (¥100, eight hours, 8am).

Public Bus Terminal (公交车站, Gōngjiāo Chēzhàn) has a bus to Pingan (¥5, two hours, every five minutes) and also serves as the terminal station for local buses.

The **Xinning Road Passenger Transport Terminal** (新宁路客运站, Xīnníng Lù Kèyùn Zhàn; Xinning Lu, 新宁路), 2.5km northwest of the city, has buses to Ledu (¥21, one hour, every 15 minutes, 7am to 6.45pm) and regular buses to Huzhu (¥14, 45 minutes).

TRAIN

Xining Railway Station (火车站, Huǒchē Zhàn) is on the high-speed rail line between Lanzhou in Gansu province and Ürümqi in Xinjiang. Regional trains also start/stop at Xining West Railway Station (火车西站, Huǒchē Xīzhàn), about 10km west of the city centre.

Lhasa-bound trains pass through or start/terminate at Xining (hard/soft sleeper ¥540/826, 22 hours) on their way along the now world-famous Qinghai–Tibet Railway. Make sure to have all your Tibet papers in order and get tickets well in advance.

Destinations include the following:

Beijing Hard/soft sleeper ¥398/601, 18 to 24 hours

Chengdu Hard/soft sleeper ¥247/377, 14½ to 17 hours

Dunhuang 1st/2nd class ¥425/266, six hours

Jiayuguan South 1st/2nd class ¥251/157, 3½ hours

Golmud Seat/hard sleeper ¥112/208, seven to 10 hours

Lanzhou West 1st/2nd class ¥93/58, two hours

Ürümqi 1st/2nd class ¥789/493, 10 hours

Xi'an North 1st/2nd class ¥325/233, five to six hours

Zhangye West 1st/2nd class ¥147/92, two hours

ⓘ Getting Around

City buses cost ¥1 to ¥2 per ride. A handy route is bus 1, which runs from the public bus terminal at the train station to the Tibetan Culture Museum, a 45-minute ride.

Taxis are easy to flag and cost ¥8 for the first 3km and ¥1.40 per kilometre thereafter. Ignore the touts at stations.

While it's best to catch official buses from the stations, some travellers prefer to take a shared taxi/minibus to Guide or Kumbum Monastery; for both destinations you can find drivers near or in the parking space under the bridge at the corner of Kunlun Zhonglu and Changjiang Lu.

Around Xining

Kumbum Monastery 塔尔寺

One of the great monasteries of the Gelugpa (Yellow Hat) sect of Tibetan Buddhism, **Kumbum Monastery** (Tǎ'ěr Sì; ¥80; ⊗8.30am-6pm) was built in 1577 on hallowed ground – the birthplace of Tsongkhapa, founder of the sect. It's of enormous historical significance, and hundreds of monks still live here, but the atmosphere can feel a bit overrun, perhaps because it's such a big tourist draw. The artwork and architecture, however, remain impressive.

Nine temples are open, each with its own characteristics. The most important is the **Grand Hall of Golden Tiles** (大金瓦殿, Dàjīnwǎ Diàn), where an 11m-high *chörten* (Tibetan stupa) marks the spot of Tsongkhapa's birth. You'll see pilgrims walking circuits of the building and prostrating outside the entrance. Also worth seeking out is the **Yak Butter Scripture Temple** (酥油花馆, Sūyóuhuā Guǎn), which houses sculptures of human figures, animals and landscapes carved out of yak butter. The hall is incredibly ornate, with an interior emblazoned with colour.

Kumbum is located 27km from Xining in the town of Huangzhong. Bus 909 (¥4, one hour) runs from the public bus terminal at the train station in Xining to the monastery every six minutes between 6.30am and 6.40pm. Get off at the last stop and walk up the hill to the monastery. The last bus back from the monastery is at 7pm. A faster, direct and nonstop bus (one way/return ¥25/50) also leaves Xining main bus station at 10am each day.

Qinghai Lake 青海湖

China's largest lake, Qinghai Lake (Qīnghǎi Hú, Lake Kokonor; elevation 3600m) is nearly six times the size of Singapore and is a huge draw for tour groups. It may be busy during the high season, but views of the lake backdropped by mountains still make the trek out worthwhile. The bright yellow

---

WORTH A TRIP

YOUNING MONASTERY

Well known throughout the Tibetan world, the 17th-century hillside **Youning Monastery** (佑宁寺, Yòuníng Sì; ⊗8am-6pm) in the Huzhu Tuzu (互助土族, Hùzhù Tǔzú) Autonomous County is considered one of the greats of the Gelugpa order. The monastery lies at the edge of a forested valley, and many chapels perch wondrously on the sides of a cliff face. Give yourself a couple of hours to explore the entire picturesque area.

Famous for its academies of medicine and astrology, its scholars and its living Buddhas (*tulku*), Youning Monastery (Rgolung in Tibetan) was instrumental in solidifying Gelugpa dominance over the Amdo region. The monastery was founded by the Mongolian 4th Dalai Lama, and over time became a religious centre for the local Tu (themselves a distant Mongolian people). At its height, more than 7000 monks resided here; these days there are probably fewer than 200, all of whom are Tu. Expansion works continue in the main complex. Three kilometres up the road from the main complex is a small *kora* that takes you to a smaller temple and up the surrounding hills.

A daily bus (¥12, 90 minutes, 10.30am) departs from Bayi Road Bus Station. Otherwise, take a bus to Ping'an (¥8, 40 minutes) from Xining's Public Bus Terminal. From there, you'll need to hire a taxi (one way/return ¥70/100, 30 minutes), Alternately, if you have a group, you could hire a private car or taxi (return ¥400) from Xining. The monastery is about 25km north of Ping'an.

rapeseed flower season, which runs through the summer, is another draw for floral fans and photographers, as are the views of the huge dunes of Sand Island facing the Er-langjian Scenic Area.

Plenty of Chinese tourists zip in for whistle-stop one- or two-day guided tours, but the lake is also popular with more adventurous types who rent bikes for a more leisurely circuit around the lake. Avoid the lake on the weekends and public holidays when traffic slows to a crawl.

◉ Sights

Chaka Salt Lake LAKE
(茶卡盐湖, Chákǎ Yánhú; ¥50) Located 25km west of Qinghai Lake past Heimahe, this salt lake is a popular side trip for a stunning optical illusion that occurs between noon and 4pm daily where, on a clear day, you can capture amazing photographs of skies and people mirrored onto the lake's surface. In order to get the best portraits on the lake, wear something bright (yellow, blue and red are great). Black and grey are hipster cool but they don't show up very well in images.

The K6961, a daily train (hard seat/hard sleeper ¥62.50/155.50, four hours, 8.25am) from Xining to Chaka (茶卡站, Chákǎ Zhàn) drops you just at the tourist entrance of the lake, a short distance from the lake itself. The train returns at 4.30pm so you could do the salt lake as a long day trip if you aren't coming from the main lake. A daily bus departs the main bus station in Xining at 10am (one way/return ¥100/240, five hours) and drops you at Chaka town, 2km from the lake, where waiting taxis will take you the rest of the way for ¥30; the bus returns later in the afternoon.

From Heimahe, you can flag down a bus to Chaka (roughly noon and 1.25pm) or hire a private car (¥320 return).

Bird Island ISLAND
(鸟岛, Niǎo Dǎo; high/low season ¥150/130) This island (a peninsula, in fact) on China's largest lake is the breeding ground for thousands of wild geese, gulls, cormorants, sandpipers, extremely rare black-necked cranes and other bird species. Perhaps the most interesting are the bar-headed geese that migrate over the Himalaya to spend winter on the Indian plains, and have been spotted flying at altitudes of 10,000m. In 2019 Bird Island was closed indefinitely to allow ecological regeneration, so check with your hotel to see if it has reopened.

🛏 Sleeping

Qīnghǎi Hú Qíshí Guójì Qīngnián Lǚshè HOSTEL ¥
(青海湖奇石国际青年旅舍; ☑ 0974 851 9313; G109, Heimahe, 黑马河国道109; dm ¥50-70, d ¥180-220; 🕿) Handy hostel with OK rooms, located at the eastern end of the main street in Heimahe. It's nothing special but you can find other travellers for shared trips to Bird Island (¥80 per person or ¥340 per car) and Chaka Salt Lake (¥80 per person or ¥320 per car). Staff can also organise a driver to take you to the shore for sunrise (¥25 per person).

ℹ Getting There & Around

One way to see the sights around Qinghai Lake is by hiring a private car and driver (¥500 to ¥600 per day from Xining). Alternatively, all-inclusive overnight stays and multiday trips can be organised through travel agencies in Xining. Touts abound at every bus station in Xining; bargain hard and you could score a great deal on a shared taxi.

You can also take a taxi from Xining to Xihai Zhen (西海镇), from where you can rent bikes to tour the lake, though you will need a travel permit from the PSB if you wish to take the bus. Note that foreigners are not permitted to spend the night in Xihai Zhen.

On public transport, buses for Qinghai Lake depart Xining's main station at 9.30am (one way/return ¥50/100, three hours each way); the bus returns at 3.30pm. Buses also leave at the same time for the Erlangjian Scenic Area from Xining's Bayi Lu bus station. You can flag down regular returning buses on the main road as well as buses going on to Heimahe.

A daily train runs from Xining to Chaka (¥62.50, 8.25am, four hours). If you take this route, you can work your way back towards Xining across two days by taking a bus back and stopping along Heimahe (黑马河), zipping up to Bird Island and then looping back down to Erlangjian Scenic Area and then back to Xining. A daily bus also departs the main bus station in Xining at 10am (one way/return ¥100/240, five hours) and drops you at Chaka town, 2km from the lake, where waiting taxis will take you the rest of the way for ¥30; the bus returns later in the afternoon.

Cycling sections of the lake or the full 360km tour around the lake are popular activities. Xihai Zhen has quality bicycle-hire shops, though foreigners are not allowed to spend the night here and you will need to obtain a travel permit from the PSB if you wish to travel to Xihai Zhen by bus. Bike rental outfits can also be found near the Erlangjian Scenic Area on the south side of the lake, but these are generally for short-period rentals and not for more ambitious journeys around the lake. Tour companies such as Elevated Trips (p920) can arrange transport and collection for bikes and cyclists to any point around the lake.

Xihai Zhen 西海镇

📞 0970 / POP 12,000

A tidy little town (until the 1990s called 'Atomic Town', as the People's Republic of China designed and developed its nuclear arsenal here), Xihai Zhen (Xīhǎi Zhèn) is 43km east of Qinghai Lake; travellers come to rent bicycles for a tour round the lake. There's not much to see in town, so plan on getting here early, picking up your bikes, grabbing supplies and then hitting the road.

Xihai Zhen is small and easy to get around on foot. With more than 20 bicycle-rental stores, you're spoilt for choice. Foreigners are not permitted to spend the night here and if you want to arrive by bus, you will need to have a travel permit from the PSB.

Bike rental ranges from ¥100 to ¥400 per day, depending on the model. All are solid brand-name bikes and rental includes panniers, helmet, tool kit and spares. The sun gets harsh so be sure to bring sunscreen, long-sleeved riding gear, sunglasses and a bandana.

The full circuit round the lake is 360km and takes four days but you can drop your bikes off at various stops along the lake if you don't fancy riding all the way. Ask the store where you can drop them off. Stores can also suggest itineraries and offer discounted accommodation with hotel partners around the lake.

The main bus station is on the east end of Yuanzi Lu (原子路). Regular buses run to Xining (¥25, two hours) from 7.30am to 5pm; from Xining, however, you will need to obtain a travel permit to Xihai Zhen before buying your bus ticket (and these can be hard to obtain), so you will probably need to hire a car and driver or take a taxi (expect to pay ¥300 each way).

Huzhu Beishan Forest Park 互助北山国际森林公园

📞 0972 / POP 11,150

Here is proof, should you need it, that Qinghai has incredibly diverse landscapes: an alpine forest located 100km northeast of Xining with an elevation that spans 2200m to 4000m. Within are farming communities, ranging mountain goats, family restaurants, birch forests, waterfalls, lakes and plenty of hiking opportunities. The **Huzhu Beishan Forest National Park** (Hùzhù Běishān Guójiā Sēnlín Gōngyuán; incl mandatory transport ticket ¥82) is popular with Xining folk seeking a weekend retreat, so go during the week for the optimum experience.

This is superb hiking territory, with forest panoramas, chilly waterfalls, shimmering lakes, sublime valleys, mountain views and all the fecundity of nature. If you're game, you can hike 7km up to the tiny Heavenly Lake (天池, Tiānchí) at 3000m elevation. Your ticket includes a tourist car that you can hop on and off.

Local homestays (农家乐, nóngjiālè) are available (expect to pay around ¥100), or stay at the **Cáilúnduō Sēnlín Nóngzhuāng** (才伦多森林农庄; 📞 155 9722 9788; cailunduo@ sina.com; dm/d ¥60/260, f per bed ¥100; 🅿 🛜 🌐), a sprawling lodge with 19 comfortable rooms, a BBQ patio, riverside pagodas and a restaurant wing. While short on English, the owners are high on service. Sample the in-house brewed highland barley *báijiǔ* (clear liquor) and pick local dishes (from ¥15) such as yak and wild mushrooms from an English menu. Get the tourist car to drop you off at Cáilúnduō (才伦多), 4km from the main gate. There are some good trails behind the lodge that lead up the back mountain for good views.

The forest park is 100km northeast of Xining. From Xining, there's a daily 9am bus (¥36, four hours) from the main bus station by the train station. Be aware that it may stop in the town of Huzhu (互助) for 45 minutes. Coming back, there's a 4pm bus that returns to Xining.

Tongren 同仁

📞 0973 / POP 93,000

Tongren (Tóngrén; Rebkong in Tibetan) is set on the slopes of the wide and fertile Gu-chu river valley. For several centuries now, the villages outside the monastery town of Tongren have been famous for producing some of the Tibetan world's best *thangkas* (scroll paintings) and painted statues, so much so that an entire school of Tibetan art is named after the town. Visiting Wútún Sì monastery not only gives you a chance to meet the artists, but also to purchase a painting or two, fresh off the easel.

The local populace is a mix of Tibetans and Tu. Aside from the monasteries, the valley and surrounding hills are easily explored on foot.

WORTH A TRIP

KANBULA NATIONAL FOREST PARK

The desert scenery outside of Tongren comes to a pinnacle in the **Kanbula National Forest Park** (坎布拉国家森林公园, Kǎnbùlā Guójiā Sēnlín Gōngyuán; incl bus & boat tour ¥250; ⊘8am-6pm) where flaming-red mountains meet the turquoise waters of a reservoir created by the damming of the Yellow River. A nervous-sweat-inducing road snakes up through the park's peaks, past sleepy Tibetan villages and colourful prayer flags waving high on the wind.

For a fantastic perspective on the park and its simply beautiful greens, purples, sapphires and blues of the mountains, waters and sky over Kanbula, climb the long wooden steps up to the vast **Big Buddha** (大佛, Dàfó) – a huge and unfinished (at the time of writing) peak-top statue at the end of the stairs. The views from here are simply knock-out.

Alas, the park no longer allows private cars unless you're a) coming from Guide or b) in a local car. This means being shunted on the pricey but decent fixed bus-and-boat tour (roughly three hours), but this way won't allow you to explore the huge territory of the park. You can skip the entrance fee and fully experience the park, including plenty of photo stops, by going with a local taxi driver (¥100 if you find at least one other person to share with).

The alternative route is to find a private driver to bring you here from Guide (¥400 per day), or join a tour with one of the recommended outfits in Xining, which will allow you to see much more of the park, as they should provide four-wheel-drive transport. To get here from Xining, buses (¥22.50) run every 30 minutes from the main bus station between 10.30am and 5pm. You'll be dropped 7km from the park entrance. Taxis will take you there for ¥10. The last bus returns at 4.30pm or so, so make sure you get out early otherwise you'll have to stay the night where the bus drops you or hitch back.

◉ Sights

Wútún Sì   MONASTERY
(吾屯寺; per monastery ¥30) This two-monastery complex is the place to head if you're interested in Tibetan art. The **Upper (Yango) Monastery** (吾屯上寺, Wútún Shàngsì) is closest to Tongren, while the **Lower (Mango) Monastery** (吾屯下寺, Wútún Xiàsì) is larger and may offer the chance to see monks painting. The monks will show you around and you can usually ask to see a showroom or workshop. The resident artists are no amateurs – commissions for their *thangka* come in all the way from Lhasa.

Artwork is usually of an exceptionally high quality, but expect to pay hundreds of rénmínbì for the smallest painting, thousands for a poster-sized one and tens or even hundreds of thousands for the largest pieces. There are a handful of showrooms outside the Lower Monastery where you can browse and buy.

The Lower Monastery is easily recognisable by eight large *chörten* (Tibetan stupas) out front and a new triple Buddha statue. While there, check out the 100-year-old **Jampa Lhakhang** (Jampa Temple) and the newer chapels dedicated to Chenresig and Tsongkhapa.

The Upper Monastery includes a massive modern *chörten* as well as the old *dukhang* (assembly hall) and a chapel dedicated to Maitreya (Shampa in Amdo dialect). The interior murals painted by local artists are superb.

Bus 1 runs here; a taxi will cost around ¥15.

Gomar Gompa   BUDDHIST MONASTERY
(郭麻日寺, Guōmárì Sì; ¥10; ⊘8am-6pm) Across the Gu-chu river valley from Wútún Sì is the mysterious 400-year-old Gomar Gompa, a charming monastery that resembles a medieval walled village. There are around 30 monks living in whitewashed mud-walled courtyards with a few temples you can visit. The huge *chörten* (Tibetan stupa) outside the monastery entrance was built in the 1980s and is the biggest in Amdo. You can climb it, but remember to always walk clockwise.

To get here, turn left down a side road as you pass the westernmost of the eight *chörten* outside Wútún Sì's Lower Monastery. Follow the road 1km across the river and turn right at the end on a main road. Then head up the track towards the giant *chörten*. Further up the valley is **Gasar Gompa**, marked by its own distinctive eight *chörten*. Note that women may not be allowed into the Gomar Gompa or Gasar Gompa.

Lóngwù Dàsì
MONASTERY

(隆务大寺, Rongwo Gonchen Gompa; ☑ 0973 872 2762; Dehelong Nanlu, 德合隆南路; ¥60; ☺ 8am-6pm) Tongren's main monastery is a huge and fascinating maze of renovated chapels and monks' residences, dating from 1301. It's a superb place to wander and explore, and you'll need one or two hours. Your ticket includes entry into eight main halls, although you may be able to peek inside others, too. There are more than 500 resident monks, and every day dozens of them go into the courtyard outside the **Hall of Bodhisattva Manjusri** (文殊殿, Wénshū Diàn) to take part in animated, hand-clapping debates on Buddhist philosophy.

🛏 Sleeping & Eating

Règòng Sìhéjí Bīnguǎn
HOTEL ¥

(热贡四合吉宾馆; ☑ 0973 879 7988; 14 Dehelong Nanlu, 德合隆南路14号; d/tr from ¥120/130; ☎) Ignore the dusty facade: this hotel has a colourful lobby that leads up through gold hallways to bright and clean rooms with flat-screen TVs and well-maintained bathrooms. It's well placed on Tongren's main road, about 200m before Lóngwù Sì. The hotel proudly declares it accepts foreigners with its sign 'Foreign-related hotel'.

★ Rebgong Norbang Travel Inn
HOTEL ¥¥

(热贡诺尔邦旅游客栈, Règòng Nuò'ěrbāng Lǚyóu Kèzhàn; ☑ 0973 872 6999, 138 9753 5393; www.nuoerbang.com; Xuelian Donglu, 雪莲东路; d ¥188-300; ste ¥400-500; ☒@☎) The Norbang is an excellent choice in Tongren and offers fantastic value with stylings that are almost boutique-hotel. Forgo the generic western-style rooms, and pay a little extra to bunk in a traditional Tibetan-style room with wooden platform beds, ornate ceiling, polished wood flooring and large and very clean sparkling shower rooms. Breakfast is ¥10 extra (upstairs on the top floor).

Dreamland
TIBETAN ¥¥

(梦土庄园; 78 Dong Ge'er Lu, 东格尔路78号; mains from ¥25; ☺ 10am-2am; ☎) This lovely up-stairs 3rd-floor restaurant is a very enjoyable experience. Nab a seat in a curtained cubicle for privacy; English skills of the staff are not so good, but the selection is all photographically depicted on the iPad menu. Select between baked mushrooms, seasoned roast-lamb ribs, substantial meat-filled bread, tasty vegetable rolls and a host of other dishes.

Find it down a small curving alleyway opposite the Regong Hotel (热贡宾馆, Règòng Bīnguǎn); enter the courtyard garden and take the stairs up to the 3rd floor.

ℹ Information

China Construction Bank ATM (建设银行, Jiànshè Yínháng; 47 Zhongshan Lu, 中山路47号) is foreign-card friendly but it would pay to take enough cash to Tongren with you.

ℹ Getting There & Away

The scenery on the road from Xining is awesome, as it follows a tributary of the Yellow River through steep-sided gorges. There are regular daily buses to Xining (¥40, four hours, 7.20am to 6.30pm). A freeway is being constructed and when complete should cut travel time by an hour. For Xiahe (¥28, three hours, 8am) and Linxia (¥45, four hours, 8am) try to buy your ticket one day in advance.

Guide
黄河

☑ 0974 / POP 101,771

As the Yellow River (Huáng Hé) flows down from the Tibetan Plateau it makes a series of sharp bends, powering its way past ancient Guide (贵德, Guìdé – pronounced 'gway-duh'), where the water turns turquoise. The river, popular with Chinese tourists, was to provide a tourism lifeline to the town and the government's plans began with the old town (古城, gǔchéng), still largely enclosed within its crumbling 10m-high mud walls.

Buildings may have been knocked down, and faux new-old ones were built, but contained within the old town are crumbling ruins and residents clinging on to life in packed earthen houses. It's the space between the old and new which makes Guide so intriguing. Wandering along the remains of the Qing dynasty walls through the back lanes behind the old town towards the Yellow River offers a glimpse of China that may no longer be here in the next few years.

◉ Sights & Activities

You can rent bikes in the old town or at the start of Nanbinhe Lu (from ¥15 per hour) to cycle along the Yellow River. Boat rides float down the river from **Shuǐ Chē Guǎng Chǎng** (水车广场; Nanbinhe Lu, 南滨河路).

★ Guide National Geological Park
PARK

(贵德国家地质公园, Guìdé Guójiā Dìzhì Gōngyuán; 101 Provincial Rd, 省道101; ¥60; ☐ 11) In the stunning multicoloured clay scenery of Danxia Canyon (丹霞峡谷, Dānxiá Xiágǔ), this geopark offers walking trails in among

HIKING MT AMNYE MACHEN

The 6282m peak of Machen Kangri, or **Mt Amnye Machen** (阿尼玛卿, Ānímǎqīng), is Amdo's most sacred mountain – it's eastern Tibet's equivalent to Mt Kailash in western Tibet. Tibetan pilgrims travel for weeks to circumambulate the peak, believing it to be home to the protector deity Machen Pomra. The circuit's sacred geography and wild mountain scenery make it a fantastic, adventurous trekking destination.

The full circuit takes around 11 days (including transport to/from Xining), though tourists often limit themselves to a half circuit. Several monasteries lie alongside the route. With almost all of the route above 4000m, and the highest pass hitting 4600m, it's essential to acclimatise before setting off, preferably by spending a night or two at the nearby Maduo (玛多; 4290m). The best months to trek are May to October, though be prepared for snow early and late in the season.

Since local public transport is almost nonexistent, most trekkers go on an organised tour. Expect to pay around US$180 per person per day, all-inclusive in a group, and double or triple that if you are going solo. Tour agencies in Xining also take trekkers on an alternative (nonpilgrimage) route through parts of Mt Amnye Machen that are less disturbed by the highway.

If you do want to try venturing out on your own, you can take the bus (¥91.50) to Huashixia (花石峡) or Maduo and then hitch or hire a shared minivan (¥300 to ¥400 per person) to Xiadawu (下大武).

In Xiadawu the starting point for the *kora* (holy hike; pilgrim circuit) path is at Guru Gompa (格日寺, Gérì Sì), and from here follow the road east. After three days the road peters out near Xueshan (雪山, Xuěshān), from where you can hitch a ride to Maqin (玛沁, Mǎqìn). If you intend to continue past Xueshan you'll need to ask a local to show you the *kora* path. In Xiadawu, a guide costs ¥150 to ¥200 per day, and it's about the same price for a packhorse or yak. You'll need to be fully sufficient and bring a tent, sleeping bag etc.

Unfortunately, a recently completed road project has now cut through the region, disturbing the equilibrium, and the full *kora* from Xiadawu is now broken up by the highway and bridges; it's still doable, but guides recommend travellers do the half *kora* from Tsam Nak Kham Do and continue clockwise to Xiadawu, from south to north. This route is less disjointed, more continuous and more pleasant. If doing the half *kora* from Tsam Nak Kham Do, first take a bus (¥95, 7½ hours) from Xining Nanchuan Xilu bus station (南川西路客运站, Nánchuān Xīlù Kèyùnzhàn) to Maqin and then get a ride to Tsam Nak Kham Do.

red and orange hills that have eroded into otherworldly shapes. Set against the contrasting blue Qinghai skies and teal waters of the Yellow River, this is a lovely spot to spend an afternoon wandering and taking photos, or exploring the peculiar geology of this part of the Tibetan Plateau.

There's a museum with decent signs and maps in English, and well-kept paths allow for easy access to the geological formations, making this a leisurely walk rather than a back-country hike. Admission includes a Chinese-speaking guide (which you can politely decline) and you can also save ¥20 by declining the tourist electric car (观光车, Guānguāng Chē). Once inside, there are opportunities to go off-piste and clamber up the dirt mounds between canyons, but do take care as you're on your own and the wind can really whip up. Water can be purchased

at the entrance. You can also hike up the Tongtianxia (通天峡) trail to the top of one of the peaks for views of the Yellow River.

The park is located about 20km north of Guide. Local bus 11 (¥3) stops here, though the last bus is at around 12.30pm, so you will need to wait on the far side of the road for a bus heading to Guide from Xining; the driver will charge you ¥5 for the journey. If you're coming from Xining by bus, you can ask the driver to drop you here. Keep an eye on the landscape on the drive from Guide: there are stupefying rock forms on the way to the park, with dry mountains on one side and lush valley on the other. A taxi will cost around ¥40 or you can wait at the exit gate of the bus station and get on a bus heading towards Xining and tell the driver you're stopping here.

★ China Fortune Wheel BUDDHIST SITE

(中华福运轮, Zhōnghuá Fúyùnlún; Nanbinhe Lu, 南滨河路; ¥70; ⏰8.30am-6pm) This enormous, gold-plated Tibetan prayer wheel is turned with the aid of rushing water from the Yellow River. The prayer wheel is 27m tall, 10m in diameter and weighs 200 tonnes, earning it a spot in the *Guinness World Records* as the world's largest prayer wheel. On a clear day it is quite a beautiful sight, positioned above a recently built rectangular pool of shimmering, sapphire water, with the line of sublime mountains behind and the Yellow River sandwiched between.

Inside the wheel are 200 copies of the Kangyur text, and the base contains a large prayer hall where you can see one of the prayer-wheel-shaped gear wheels turning. There is also an exhibition devoted to prayer wheels, while on the 2nd floor of the wheel is a stupendous collection of modern *thangka*.

The glittering exterior of the wheel is decorated with resplendent bodhisattvas and jewelled Buddhist motifs. From the far side of the pool, the entire apparatus makes for an extraordinary photographic image.

The wheel is located in a dedicated park along the Yellow River, which can be reached on foot by following Huanghe Nanlu behind Yuhuang Pavilion and turning left at the large suspension bridge (itself a great spot for catching sunset over the river). You can rent bikes in the old town or at the start of Nanbinhe Lu (from ¥15 per hour) to cycle alongside the Yellow River.

🛏 Sleeping

Guide has a generally lousy choice of accommodation options for foreigners. Most of the small and cheaper hotels do not take non-Chinese; others may take you and then throw you out later once they check with the PSB. All this means you are unfairly steered towards the much pricier end of the market, which although comfortable, does not give you much flexibility as to where to stay.

Qinghai Guide Hot Spring Hotel HOTEL ¥¥

(温泉宾馆, Wēnquán Bīnguǎn; ☑0974 855 3534; 355 Yingbin Lu, 迎宾路355号; d/ste ¥200/550; ❄@🛜🏊) The hotel is starting to show its age, but this is a decent choice for foreigners, with clean rooms, a heated pool (¥50 per use), a spa and pleasant garden grounds. There are no hot springs per se on-site; instead, the hotel claims to have piped water from the springs into its pool and taps. Located 1km west of the bus station.

Jinheyuan International Hotel HOTEL ¥¥¥

(金河源国际饭店, Jīnhéyuán Guójì Fàndiàn; Yingbin Donglu, 迎宾东路; d/ste ¥420/700; ℗❄@🛜) This glossy hotel offers bright, spacious and fully equipped rooms decorated to a high standard, with automatic lights in shower rooms and large, comfortable beds. Staff speak limited English and the breakfast buffet is Chinese-food only (with no coffee). It's obliquely opposite the bus station, so not in the old town and a bit stranded, but a taxi is only ¥6 to most sights.

ℹ Getting There & Away

There are very regular buses to Xining (¥26, two hours, 7.40am to 5.45pm) and several other destinations around Qinghai. If you are heading to Tongren, you will need to either return to Xining or take a bus (¥33) first to Adai (阿代) and from there continue to Tongren (but it's probably faster and more reliable to return to Xining).

Yushu 玉树

🌐 0976 / POP 380,000 / ELEV 3681M

A beautifully located, welcoming and endlessly rewarding Tibetan town, Yushu is one of the most idyllic places in the entire land. Tragically levelled in an earthquake in 2010, Yushu (Yùshù; Jyekundo is the name of the town, while Yushu is the prefecture) has been entirely rebuilt and has bounced back to regain its popularity as one of Qinghai's best adventure-travel destinations. Getting here is not such a struggle as it once was: though you can still take the 12-hour bus journey from Xining, you can fly in and out too. Aim to spend as long as you can here to walk the *kora* above Jyekundo Dondrubling Monastery and circumambulate the colossal Seng-ze Gyanak Mani Wall before delving into the surrounding region – the town is a superb high-altitude launching pad for the grasslands, mountain passes, monasteries, rivers and diversity of flora and fauna nearby.

◉ Sights

Reportedly there are a staggering 246 monasteries located around Yushu county. On a clear day, just the sight of the prayer-flag-carpeted peaks about town is enough to draw you to do the *kora* around Jyekundo Dondrubling Monastery (p928) or further into the hills. Minivans ply the 35km route from Yushu to Xiewu, where you will find **Drogon Gompa** (歇武寺, Xiēwǔ Sì; ⏰8am-6pm) and a landscape dotted with monasteries as well as a simply beautiful terrain that is perfect for hiking.

★ Yushu Museum
MUSEUM

(玉树州博物馆, Yùshùzhōu Bówùguǎn; Qionglong Lu, 琼龙路) This huge and excellent museum is a must-see to put some of the region's history and culture into perspective, including informative and well-presented sections on the geography, rivers, fauna and flora as well as religious culture and folk history. Don't miss the fascinating photographic exhibition on the ground floor that catalogues the history of the local people by way of photographs reaching all the way back to the early 20th century and through the dark days of the Cultural Revolution.

★ Jyekundo
Dondrubling Monastery
MONASTERY

(结古寺, Jié Gǔsì; Jiegusi Lu, 结古寺路; ◷8am-6pm) FREE First built in 1398, the Jyekundo Dondrubling Monastery suffered heavy damage from the 2010 earthquake (the main prayer hall was completely destroyed and a number of resident monks were killed). The monastery has since been rebuilt and it's dramatically located on a ridge perched above town. It's a very active place: you may see young monks playing football. Hike up north into the hills above the temple to follow the clockwise *kora* through a huge encampment of prayer flags.

Seng-ze Gyanak Mani Wall
BUDDHIST SITE

(新寨嘉那嘛呢石堆, Xīnzhài Jiānà Máni Shíduī; Xinzhai Village, 新寨) FREE Completely rebuilt after suffering extensive damage in the 2010 earthquake, this site is thought to be the world's largest *mani* wall (piles of stones with Buddhist mantras carved or painted on them). Founded in 1715, the *mani* comprises an estimated 2.5 billion mantras, piled one on top of the other over hundreds of square metres. It's an astonishing sight that (literally) grows as you circumambulate the wall with the pilgrims.

🎭 Festivals & Events

Horse Festival
CULTURAL

(Yùshù Sàimǎ Jié, 玉树赛马节; ◷mid-late Jul) Yushu's spectacular three-day horse festival features traditional horse and yak races, Tibetan wrestling, archery, shooting and dance. The festival is held at different parts of the county each year, with a mega, multi-county affair occurring every four to five years. Check for the latest before you make this part of your itinerary.

DON'T MISS

PRINCESS WENCHENG TEMPLE

Dedicated to the Tang dynasty Chinese Princess Wencheng, who was instrumental in converting her husband and Tibetan king, Songtsen Gampo, to Buddhism in the 7th century, the small, sacred and age-seasoned **Princess Wencheng Temple** (文成公主庙, Wénchéng Gōngzhǔ Miào; ◷8am-6pm) marks the spot where the princess (and possibly the king) paused for a month en route from Xi'an to Lhasa. It's said to be Qinghai's oldest Buddhist temple; the inner chapel contains a rock carving (supposedly self-arising) of Vairocana (Nampa Namse in Tibetan), the Buddha of primordial wisdom, which allegedly dates from the 8th century.

To the left is a statue of King Songtsen Gampo.

Fifteen kilometres south of Yushu, the small temple is set against the cliff and suffered minor damage from the 2010 Yushu earthquake. Look around the surrounding rock faces for ancient rock and scripture carvings. Do allow time to explore the nearby hills and marvel at the sprawling spider's web of blue, red, yellow, white and pink prayer flags that runs up the slopes, down the slopes and over the ravine and road, covering every inch of land.

A steep trail (a popular *kora* route for pilgrims) ascends from the end of the row of eight *chörtens* to the left of the temple. At the end of the trail head up the grassy side valley for some great hiking and stunning open views.

Private minibuses (¥200 return) depart from outside the long-distance bus terminal in Yushu, or a taxi costs about ¥100 to ¥120 return. Consider stopping by on the way to the airport if you are flying out of Yushu as the temple is en route and the taxi driver should only ask for a bit extra to visit.

🛏 Sleeping

Jiégǔ Sì Dàjiǔdiàn
HOTEL ¥¥
(结古寺大酒店; ☏0976 680 2222; Qionglong Lu, 琼龙路; d ¥180-240; 🛜) A stuffed antelope with a wooden tongue greets visitors to this large and decent hotel with faded yet spacious Chinese-style rooms. Rooms all come with independent wi-fi, TV, kettle, desk and shower. The hot water is rather lukewarm and you need to let it run for quite a while beforehand. Discounts lower rates to around ¥150. Located 250m east of the main square.

★ Gesar Palace Hotel
HOTEL ¥¥¥
(Yùshù Gésàěr Wángfǔ Fàndiàn, 玉树格萨尔王府饭店; ☏0976 882 1999; 9 Minzhu Lu, 民主路9号; d inc breakfast ¥500-1000; 🛜🏊) Located 100m west of the town square, and towering over the local buildings, is the town's best hotel, flooded with traditional Tibetan decor in the cavernous lobby. Rooms feature comfortable beds, tasteful dark-wood panels and modern toilets. Service is friendly and comfort levels make this a good choice. Discounts regularly bring rooms down to ¥290.

🍴 Eating & Drinking

Rose of Sharon Bistro
CAFE ¥¥
(玫瑰西点咖啡, Méiguì Xīdiǎn Kāfēi; Minzhu Lu, 民主路; dishes from ¥30; ⏰9.30am-10.30pm; 🛜) This large and modern upstairs restaurant-cafe has a tasty menu, efficient staff, comfy rows of sofas and decent views of the hills (though it's a bit heavy on the classical music). On the iPad menu are dishes such as highland rib of lamb (¥99), spicy dry pot chicken (¥76), *gongbao* chicken (¥52), nine-flavour eggplant stew (¥36) and *mapo dòufu* (¥38).

★ Josai Pub
PUB
(乔赛洋餐吧, Qiáosài Yángcānba) With guitars lying around on the sofas, a pool table and superb views of Yushu, the river and hills from the veranda, this excellent choice also has a good menu of grilled meats and pizza. There's a fridge just inside the door where the Blue Barley beer chills alongside the Hoegaarden; cocktails and coffee are also served. The friendly owner Sai speaks English.

ℹ️ Information

Gesartour (☏139 0976 9192; www.gesartour.com; 🌐) The best way to see the region is via a private vehicle, and English-speaking Tibetan manager Tsebtrim can organise a bunch of different options based on your interests. You'll get a great wealth of regional and Tibetan knowledge from Tsebtrim and his guides as well as myriad suggestions and tips. Tsebtrim also has a lovely traditional-style guesthouse in the Xinzhai part of town; contact him for details.

ℹ️ Getting There & Away

AIR

One of the highest airports in the world, **Yushu Batang Airport** (玉树巴塘机场, Yùshù Bātáng Jīchǎng) is 25km south of town. There are daily flights to Xining, with some services to Xi'an. There is considerable variance in the price of tickets to Xining, so choose your flying date with some caution and allow some flexibility if possible. As Yushu is at a high altitude, it can be a good idea to take the bus up and fly out.

A taxi to the airport will cost around ¥80. Consider tying in a trip to and from the airport by taxi with a visit to the Princess Wencheng Temple, which is not far away.

BUS

Yushu's **long-distance bus terminal** (玉树长途客运站, Yùshù Chángtú Kèyùn Zhàn; Xihang Lu, 西航路) has buses to Xining (seat ¥191, 8.30am, 9am, noon, 1pm, 4pm, 5pm, 5.30pm, 6pm); the journey takes 12 hours. The later-afternoon buses may stop off during the night for several hours for a rest.

Other destinations include Chengdu (¥500, daily, 9am), Lhasa (¥502, 9am, every third day), Chongqing (¥550, 10am, every other day), Nangchen (¥50, 9.30am, three to four hours) and Maduo (¥83).

Long-distance minibuses also depart from outside the long-distance bus terminal, bound for Nangchen (¥50, three to four hours) but leaving only when full. Vehicles also depart when full for Ganzi (¥170, five to seven hours) in Sichuan. Ask around for other destinations. Minibuses for other parts of Qinghai, including Nangchen, also leave from another minivan square located on Shuangyong Jie (双拥街), 550m north of the long-distance bus terminal. Buses to Ganzi (¥150) and Chengdu also leave from a point on Qionglong Lu down the road towards Gesar Sq from the Jiégǔ Sì Dàjiǔdiàn.

Nangchen
囊谦

☏0976 / POP 130,000 (COUNTY) / ELEV 3630M

The scenic county of Nangchen (Nángqiān), a former Tibetan kingdom, is the end of the line for most travellers. The drive from Yushu to the dusty little county capital of Sharda (香达镇, Xiāngdá Zhèn; 3630m), colloquially referred to as Nangchen, takes you past some incredibly diverse landscapes filled with mountains, valleys, monasteries, rushing rivers and a plethora of animals and flora. You'll be tempted to stop the driver to take photos along every bend in the road.

Further south is the Qinghai–Tibet border, with roads to Riwoche and Chamdo, but foreigners aren't allowed access; however, a wonderland of jaw-dropping scenic sights lies scattered in the hills, valleys and rivers around Nangchen, so aim to spend several days exploring.

⊙ Sights

Gading Gompa
BUDDHIST MONASTERY

(嘎丁寺, Gādīng Sì; ⊘8am-6pm) Nestled on a piece of land within a horseshoe bend in the Dzichu River, Gading makes for one of the most stunning photos you could take in the region. The monastery itself is nothing special, but hike up the hill opposite for views across both sides of the valley. When you're done, pitch a tent and have a picnic along the river. The monastery is 15km from Nangchen (a car will cost ¥350 return).

Dana Gompa
BUDDHIST MONASTERY

(达那寺, Dánǎ Sì; ⊘8am-6pm) The stunning Dana Gompa is remote and the road out from Nangchen takes you across a valley towards 4000m elevation. Once there, you'll find the province's largest nunnery. Getting out here is expensive and drivers will ask ¥1200 for the 320km return journey. It can be included on a tour itinerary.

Naygyama Gompa
BUDDHIST TEMPLE

(⊘8am-6pm) Some 10km south of Nangchen is an atmospheric *kora* path sitting beside a wide section of the Za Qu River (扎曲), which swells to become the Mekong River. The nunnery here isn't much to look at but the *kora* wends you round a small hill past stupas, fluttering prayer flags and carved stones.

Gar Gompa
BUDDHIST MONASTERY

(尕尔寺, Gǎ'ěr Sì; ⊘8am-6pm) Nestled on the ridge of a forested mountain about 70km south of Nangchen is this picturesque monastery. Wildlife is prevalent in the area, including blue sheep and monkeys. It's a popular spot for birdwatchers. A taxi from Nangchen costs about ¥550 return.

Sajiya Gompa
BUDDHIST MONASTERY

(萨迦寺, Sàjiā Sì; ⊘8am-6pm) The most recognisable of the Buddhist monasteries scattered around Nangchen, this one is perched on a hill above town like an old manor and its *kora* is popular with locals. You can hike even further up the hill behind the *gompa*

for excellent views of the valley and the Za Qu River (扎曲). Located 4.5km west of town.

🛏 Sleeping

Dōngfāng Bīnguǎn
HOTEL ¥

(东方宾馆, Dōngfāng Bīnguǎn; ☑152 9702 5483; Xiangda Nanjie, 香达南街; d ¥150; 🕲) This Salar-run hotel is simple with reasonably clean bathrooms and hot showers, bright rooms with fresh linen and heating in the winter. Located in an unfinished and unlikely looking brick block as you head 100m south down Xiangda Nanjie on the corner with Zhaxi Alley (扎西巷).

Travellers report that sometimes this hotel has issues registering foreigners. Your best bet is to ask when you arrive.

Lóngzhū Dàjiǔdàn
HOTEL ¥¥

(龙珠大酒店; ☑0976 887 3999; 43 Xiangda Dongjie, 香达东街43号; s ¥248, d ¥268-288, ste ¥488; 🕲) This business-style hotel with the colourful portico is a good choice for a decent level of comfort and service in town. Exit the bus station and turn right to follow Xiangda Dongjie along and down the hill and round the corner; the hotel is on the left.

ⓘ Information

Agricultural Bank of China ATM (农业银行, Nóngyè Yínháng; 109 Xiangda Dongjie, 香达东街109号) Accepts foreign cards in theory, but bring some cash from Yushu or Xining to be safe.

ⓘ Getting There & Around

From **Nangchen bus station** (襄谦汽车站, Nángqiàn Qìchēzhàn; 25 Xiangda Dongjie, 香达东街25号) on the main road, one daily bus goes to Xining (¥264, 15 to 18 hours) departing at 10am. Book at least one day in advance.

To reach Yushu (¥50, three hours), most locals travel by shared minibuses, which assemble on the main road outside Nangchen's bus station. Note that everyone entering Nangchen from Yushu will be asked for their ID on the way, so you will need to disembark the bus and go through a checkpoint. Foreigners may be invited in for a chat, or you may just be waved through after your passport has been inspected.

Nangchen itself is a dusty town where you're likely to see stray dogs and mountain goats trotting beside cows on the main street. You'll need to hire a taxi to see many of the sights around town, or contact Gesartour (p929) in Yushu for a trip out here via the back roads. The route takes twice as long to travel but offers plenty of picturesque stops.

Golmud 格尔木

📱 0979 / POP 186,000 / ELEV 2800M

For three decades Golmud (Gé'ěrmù) faith-fully served overlanders as the last jump-ing-off point before Lhasa. Bedraggled backpackers hung around the city's truck depot trying to negotiate a lift to the 'Roof of the World'. But since the completion of the Qinghai–Tibet Railway, this lonesome back-water has become a very marginal town, as most Tibet-bound travellers board the train elsewhere and blow right through. Today, there is little reason to visit and it's only of use to travellers trying to get between Lhasa and Dunhuang (in Gansu) or Huatugou (en route to Xinjiang).

🛏 Sleeping & Eating

Qīnggǎng Bīnguǎn HOTEL ¥¥

(青港宾馆; ☎ 0979 723 9888; 17 Jiangyuan Nanlu, 江源南路17号; d incl breakfast ¥218) The closest option to the train station, this corner hotel has clean, modern rooms and a not-bad Chi-nese breakfast spread. It's 300m north of the train station along Jiangyuan Nanlu.

★ Qíjì Shǒugōng Miànpiàn Fāng CHINESE ISLAMIC ¥

(祁记手工面片坊; Bayi Zhonglu, 八一中路; noodles ¥13-15, dishes ¥5-50; ☺ 9am-10.30pm) An unexpected gem, this noodle joint has both style that wouldn't look out of place in Beijing and substance by way of delicious handmade miànpiàn (面片, noodle slices). With its almost-Scandi decor and friendly service, it's not hard to return here for noo-dles, suānnǎi (酸奶, yoghurt), cold dishes and other chunkier meat options displayed in a glass case.

🛈 Information

China International Travel Service (中国旅行社, Zhōngguó Lǔxíngshè, CTS; ☎ 0979 725 8858; Rm 303, 3rd fl, 46 Kunlun Zhonglu Wumao Dajiudian, 昆仑中路46号物贸大酒店 3楼303室; ☺ 8.30am-6pm Mon-Fri) The only place in town that can arrange Tibet permits, though it takes seven to 10 days. Best used as a last resort.

The **Public Security Bureau** (公安局, Gōng'ānjú, PSB; 6 Chaidamu Dong Lu; ☺ 8am-noon & 2.30-5pm Mon-Fri) can extend visas.

🛈 Getting There & Away

AIR

Golmud's airport is 15km west of town. Daily flights go to Xining, Lhasa and Zhengzhou.

BUS

There are buses to a number of destinations in Qinghai and neighbouring provinces from Golmud's **main bus station** (格尔木长途车站, Gé'ěrmù Chángtú Chēzhàn; ☎ 0979 845 3688; 23 Jiangyuan Nanlu, 江源南路23号) including Dunhuang (¥115, 10 hours, 9am), Huatugou (¥106 to ¥129, six hours, 9.30am and 10am) and Xining (¥140, 11 to 14 hours, 2pm). A bus also leaves for Xining (¥156) at 4pm from the **Taishan Lu bus station** (格尔木泰山路汽车站, Gé'ěrmù Tàishānlù Qìchēzhàn; Taishan Zhonglu, 泰山中路). There is also a bus to Charklik (若羌, Ruòqiāng; ¥228, 12 hours, 10am) in Xinjiang from the main bus station.

TRAIN

Trains to Lhasa (hard/soft sleeper ¥404/610, 14 hours) depart from **Golmud Railway Station** (格尔木火车站, Gé'ěrmù Huǒchē Zhàn; ☎ 0979 722 2222; Yingbin Lu, 迎宾路) late in the evening or past midnight; you'll need your Tibet permit to be in order to board. Trains also go to Xining (hard/soft sleeper ¥208/346, seven hours).

Tibet

AREA 1.23 MILLION SQ KM / POP 3.2 MILLION

Best Places to Eat

➡ Third Eye (p951)

➡ Wordo Tibetan Courtyard (p951)

➡ Snowland Restaurant (p942)

➡ Tibetan Family Kitchen (p942)

Best Places to Sleep

➡ Kyichu Hotel (p940)

➡ Yeti Hotel (p949)

➡ Songtsam Choskyi Linka Lhasa (p940)

➡ Yak Hotel (p940)

➡ House of Shambhala (p940)

Why Go?

For many visitors, the highlights of Tibet will be of a spiritual nature: magnificent monasteries, prayer halls of chanting monks, and remote cliffside meditation retreats. Tibet's pilgrims – from local grandmothers murmuring mantras in temples heavy with the aromas of juniper incense to hardcore professionals walking or prostrating themselves around Mt Kailash – are an essential part of this experience. Tibetans have a level of devotion and faith that seems to belong to an earlier age. It is fascinating, inspiring and endlessly photogenic.

Tibet's other big draw is the beauty of the highest plateau on earth. Geography here is on a humbling scale and every view is illuminated with spectacular mountain light. Your trip will take you past turquoise lakes, across huge plains dotted with yaks and nomads' tents, and over high passes draped with colourful prayer flags. Hike past the ruins of remote hermitages, stare at the north face of Everest or make an epic trip along some of the world's wildest roads. The scope for adventure is limited only by your ability to get permits.

When to Go
Lhasa

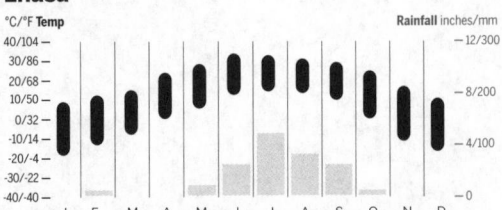

May–Sep The warmest weather makes travel, trekking and transport easiest.	**Apr & Oct–Nov** The slightly colder weather means fewer travellers and a better range of vehicles.	**Dec–Feb** Very few people visit Tibet in winter, so you'll have key attractions largely to yourself.

History

Recorded Tibetan history began in the 7th century AD, when the Tibetan armies began to assemble a great empire. Under King Songtsen Gampo, the Tibetans occupied Nepal and collected tribute from parts of Yunnan. Shortly afterwards, the Tibetan armies moved north and took control of the Silk Road and the great trade centre of Kashgar, even sacking the imperial Chinese city of Chang'an (present-day Xi'an). Tibetan expansion came to an abrupt halt in 842 with the assassination of anti-Buddhist King Langdarma; the region subsequently broke into independent feuding principalities. The increasing influence of Buddhism ensured that the Tibetan armies would never again leave their high plateau.

By the 7th century, Buddhism had spread through Tibet, though it had taken on a unique form, as it adopted many of the rituals of Bön (the indigenous animist pre-Buddhist belief system of Tibet) including the prayer flags, pilgrimage circuits and sacred landscapes you'll see across modern Tibet.

From the 13th century, power politics began to play an increasing role in religion. In 1641 the Gelugpa ('Yellow Hat' order) used the support of Mongol troops to crush the Sakyapa, their rivals. It was also during this time of partisan struggle that the Gelugpa leader adopted the title of Dalai Lama (Ocean of Wisdom), given to him by the Mongols. From here on out, religion and politics in Tibet became inextricably entwined and both were presided over by the Dalai Lama.

With the fall of the Qing dynasty in 1911, Tibet entered a period of de facto independence that was to last until 1950. In this year a resurgent communist China invaded Tibet, claiming it was 'liberating' more than one million Tibetans from feudal serfdom and bringing it back into the fold of the motherland.

Increasing popular unrest in response to Chinese land reform resulted in a full-blown revolt in 1959, which was crushed by the People's Liberation Army (PLA). Amid popular rumours of a Chinese plot to kidnap him, the Dalai Lama fled to India. He was followed by an exodus of 80,000 of Tibet's best and brightest, who now represent the Tibetan government-in-exile from Dharamsala, India.

The Dalai Lama, who has referred to China's policies on migration as 'cultural genocide', is resigned to pushing for autonomy rather than independence, though even that concession has borne little fruit. The Chinese, for their part, seem to be waiting for him to die, positioning themselves to control the future politics of reincarnation. The Dalai Lama's tireless insistence on a non-violent solution to the Tibet problem led to him winning the Nobel Peace Prize in 1989, but despite global sympathy for the Tibetan cause, few nations are willing to raise the issue and place new business deals with China's rising economic superpower at risk.

The Chinese are truly baffled by what they perceive as the continuing ingratitude of the Tibetans. They claim that Tibet pre-1950 was a place of abject poverty and feudal exploitation. China, they say, has brought roads, schools, hospitals, airports, factories and rising incomes.

Many Tibetans, however, cannot forgive the destruction in the 1950s and 1960s of hundreds of monasteries and shrines, the restrictions on religious expression, the continued heavy military presence, economic exploitation and their obvious second-class status within their own land. Riots and protests in the spring of 2008 brought this simmering dissatisfaction out into the open, as Lhasa erupted into full-scale riots and protests spread to other Tibetan areas in Gansu, Sichuan and Qinghai provinces. The Chinese response was predictable: arrest, imprisonment and an increased police presence in

TIBET HISTORY

ℹ **PRICE RANGES**

Eating

The following price ranges refer to a standard dish in Chinese restaurants or a main course in western restaurants. There are no additional taxes, though some higher-end places may add a service charge.

¥ less than ¥30

¥¥ ¥30–80

¥¥¥ more than ¥80

Sleeping

The following price ranges refer to a standard double room before discounts. Unless otherwise stated, breakfast is not included.

¥ less than ¥200

¥¥ ¥200–400

¥¥¥ more than ¥400

Tibet Highlights

1 Lhasa (p935) Rubbing shoulders with Tibetan pilgrims in this holy city.

2 Samye Monastery (p947) Exploring the mandala-shaped chapels and stupas at Tibet's first monastery.

3 Mt Kailash (p955) Erasing the sins of a lifetime on the three-day pilgrim circuit.

4 Gyantse Kumbum (p948) Marvelling at the murals of angels and demons in the 108 chapels of this architectural wonder.

5 Friendship Highway (p952) Seeing all the highlights of Tibet at your own pace on one of Asia's great road trips.

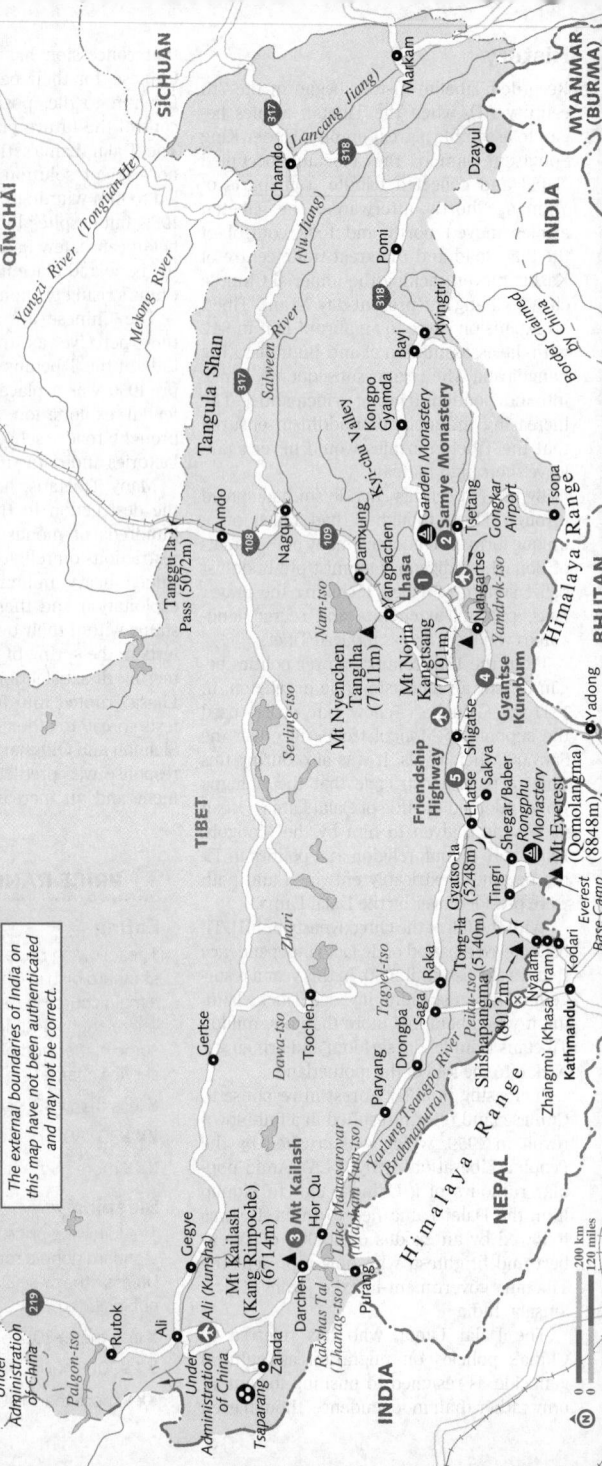

The external boundaries of India on this map have not been authenticated and may not be correct.

many monasteries. The increasing desperation felt by many Tibetans has led to a spate of self-immolations by Tibetans across the region, including two in Lhasa's Barkhor Circuit in 2012.

As immigration and breakneck modernisation continue, the government is gambling that economic advances will diffuse the Tibetans' religious and political aspirations. It's a policy that has so far been successful in the rest of China. Whether it will work in Tibet remains to be seen.

Climate

Most of Tibet is a high-altitude desert plateau at more than 4000m. Days in summer (June to September) are warm, sunny and generally dry, but temperatures drop quickly after dark. It's always cool above 4000m and often freezing at night, though thanks to the Himalayan rain shadow there is surprisingly little snow in the Land of Snows. Sunlight is very strong at these altitudes, so bring plenty of high-factor sunscreen and lip balm.

Language

Most urban Tibetans speak Mandarin in addition to Tibetan. Even in the countryside you can get by with basic Mandarin in most restaurants and hotels, since they are normally run by Mandarin-speaking Han or Hui Chinese. That said, Tibetans are extremely pleased when foreign visitors at least greet them in Tibetan, so it's well worth learning a few phrases. Very few Tibetans outside of the tourism industry speak English.

🛈 Getting There & Away

For most international travellers, getting to Tibet will involve at least two legs: first to a gateway city such as Kathmandu (Nepal) or Chengdu (China), and then into Tibet.

The most popular options from the gateway towns into Tibet are as follows:

➡ International flight from Kathmandu to Lhasa

➡ Domestic Chinese flight to Lhasa from Chengdu, Kunming, Xining, Beijing or many others

➡ Train via Qinghai to Lhasa, starting in Xining, Lanzhou, Beijing or other Chinese cities

➡ The overland drive from Kathmandu to Lhasa via the new crossing at Kyirong, along the Friendship Hwy

At the time of writing, bureaucratic obstacles to entering Tibet from China were many and involved signing up for a preplanned and prepaid tour. The situation from Nepal is even trickier because of group-visa requirements. Political events, both domestic and international, can mean that regulations for entry into Tibet change overnight. Nerves of steel are definitely useful when arranging flights and permits. Always check on the latest developments before booking flights.

Note that it can be very hard to get hold of air and train tickets to Lhasa around the Chinese New Year and the week-long holidays around 1 May and 1 October.

Flights, hotels and tours can be booked online at www.lonelyplanet.com/bookings.

🛈 Getting Around

Tibet's transport infrastructure has developed rapidly in recent years. Most of the main highways are now paved. Airports are springing up across the plateau and the railway line is slowly extending beyond Lhasa. In 2011 Tibet's Metok county was the very last of China's 2100 counties to be connected by road.

Car The only way to travel around Tibet at the moment, since foreign travellers have to hire private transport as part of their obligatory tour.

Train Great for getting to and from Tibet but of limited use inside Tibet, unless you are just taking a short trip from Lhasa to Shigatse and back.

Bus Lots of services, but foreigners are currently not allowed to take buses or shared taxis in Tibet.

LHASA ལྷ་ས 拉萨

📞 0891 / ELEV 3650M / POP 530,000

The centre of the Tibetan Buddhist world for over a millennium, Lhasa (Lāsà, literally the 'Place of the Gods') remains largely a city of wonders. Your first view of the red-and-white Potala Palace soaring above the Holy City raises goosebumps and the charming whitewashed old Tibetan quarter continues to preserve the essence of traditional Tibetan life. It is here in the Jokhang, an other-worldly mix of flickering butter lamps, wafting incense and prostrating pilgrims, and the encircling Barkhor pilgrim circuit, that most visitors first fall in love with Tibet.

These days the booming boulevards of the modern city threaten to overwhelm the winding alleyways and backstreet temples of the Tibetan old town, but it is in the latter that you should focus your time. If possible, budget a week to acclimatise, see the sights and roam the fascinating backstreets before heading off on a grand overland adventure.

Lhasa

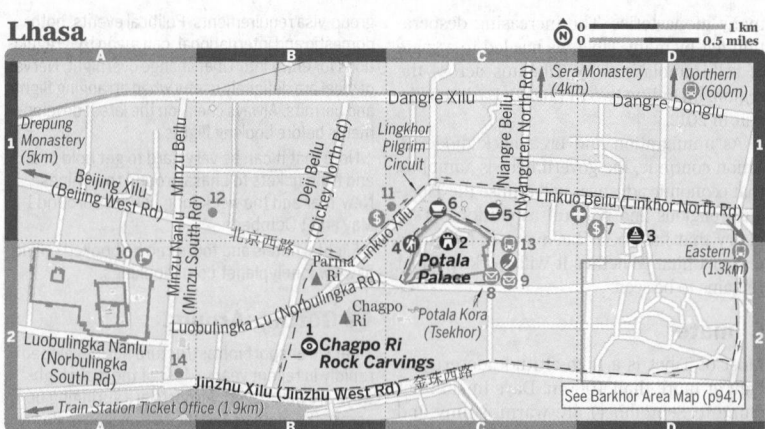

◉ Sights

★ Potala Palace
PALACE

(ནོ་ཏ་ལ, 布达拉宫, Bùdálā Gōng; 35 Beijing Dong-lu, 北京中路35号; May-Oct ¥200, Nov-Apr ¥100; ⏱9.30am-3pm Nov-Apr, 9am-3.30pm May-Oct, interior chapels close 4.30pm) The magnificent Potala Palace, once the seat of the Tibetan government and the winter residence of the Dalai Lamas, is Lhasa's cardinal landmark. Your first sight of its towering, fortress-like walls is a moment you'll remember for years. An architectural wonder even by modern standards, the palace rises 13 storeys from 130m-high Marpo Ri (Red Hill) and contains more than 1000 rooms. Pilgrims and tourists alike shuffle open-mouthed through the three storeys, past the dozens of magnificent chapels, golden stupas and prayer halls.

The first recorded use of the site was in the 7th century AD, when King Songtsen Gampo built a palace here. Construction of the present structure began during the reign of the fifth Dalai Lama in 1645 and took divisions of labourers and artisans more than 50 years to complete. It is impressive enough to have caused Chinese premier Zhou Enlai to send his own troops to protect it from the Red Guards during the Cultural Revolution.

The layout of the Potala Palace includes the rooftop **White Palace** (Kharpo Podrang) (the eastern part of the building), used for the living quarters of the Dalai Lama, and the central **Red Palace** (Marpo Podrang), used for religious functions. The most stunning chapels of the Red Palace house the jewel-bedecked golden *chörten* (Tibetan stupa) tombs of several previous Dalai Lamas. The apartments of the 13th and 14th Dalai Lamas, in the White Palace, offer a more personal insight into palace life.

Tickets for the Potala are limited and your guide will need to book a time slot several days in advance. Arrive at the palace an hour or so before your allotted time. After a security check (no water or lighters allowed), follow the other visitors to the stairs up into the palace. Halfway up you'll pass the ticket booth, where you'll buy your ticket. Note that if you arrive later than the time on your voucher (or if you forget your voucher) you can be refused a ticket. Photography isn't allowed inside the chapels.

★ **Jokhang Temple**　　　BUDDHIST TEMPLE
(ᠵᠣᡍᠠᠩ, 大昭寺, Dàzhāo Sì; Bakuo Xijie, 八廓西街; adult ¥85; ⊙ 8.15-noon & 3-5.30pm, most chapels closed after noon) The 1300-year-old Jokhang Temple is the spiritual heart of Tibet: the continuous waves of awestruck pilgrims prostrating themselves outside are a testament to its timeless allure. The central golden Buddha image here is the most revered in all of Tibet.

The Jokhang was originally built to house an image of Buddha brought to Tibet by King Songtsen Gampo's Nepalese wife. However, another image, the Jowo Sakyamuni, was later moved here by the king's other wife (the Chinese Princess Wencheng), and it is this image that gives the Jokhang both its name and its spiritual potency: Jokhang means 'chapel of the Jowo'.

The two-storeyed Jokhang is best visited in the morning, though the crowds of yak-butter-spooning pilgrims can be thick. Access is possible in the afternoon through a side entrance, but only the ground-floor chapels can be viewed (and then only through a grille) and there are no pilgrims.

★ **Chagpo Ri Rock Carvings**　　HISTORIC SITE
(药王山, Yàowáng Shān; 41 Beijing Zhonglu, 北京中路41号; ¥10; ⊙ dawn-dusk) This hidden corner of Lhasa features more than 5000 painted rock carvings that were created on the back side of Chagpo Ri over the course of a millennium. Throughout the day, pilgrims perform full-body prostrations in front of the images, while stone carvers at the far end of the courtyard contribute to a large chörten built entirely of the carvers' *mani* stones. The best way to visit the area is as part of the Lingkhor pilgrim route.

Barkhor Square　　　　　SQUARE
(八角广场, Bājiǎo Guǎngchǎng) For your first visit to the Barkhor, enter from Barkhor Sq,

a large plaza that was cleared in 1985. The square has been a focus for violent political protest on several occasions, notably in 1998 (when a Dutch tourist was shot in the shoulder) and most recently in 2008. The square is now bordered by metal detectors, riot-squad vehicles, fire-extinguisher teams (to prevent self-immolations) and rooftop surveillance. Despite the stream of selfie-taking tourists, the atmosphere is one of occupation or siege.

★ Festivals & Events

Saga Dawa　　　　　　RELIGIOUS
(⊙ May/Jun) The 15th day (full moon) of the fourth lunar month sees huge numbers of pilgrims walking and prostrating along the Lingkhor and Barkhor pilgrim circuits. Follow the locals' cue and change ¥10 into a fat wad of one-*máo* notes to hand out as alms during the walk.

Drepung Festival　　　　RELIGIOUS
(⊙ Jul) The 30th day of the sixth lunar month is celebrated with the hanging at dawn of a huge *thangka* at Drepung Monastery. Lamas and monks perform opera in the main courtyard.

Tsongkhapa Festival　　　RELIGIOUS
(⊙ Dec) Much respect is shown to Tsongkhapa, the founder of the Gelugpa order, on the anniversary of his death on the 25th day of the 10th lunar month. Check for processions and monk dances at the monasteries at Ganden, Sera and Drepung.

⌇ Sleeping

The Tibetan eastern end of town is easily the most interesting place to be based, with accommodation options in all budgets. There are dozens of shiny, characterless hotels scattered around other parts of town. You might find yourself in one of these if you arrive on a tour or book a hotel online.

Flora Hotel　　　　　　HOTEL ¥
(哈达花神旅馆, Hǎdáhuāshén Lǚguǎn; ☑ 891 632 4491; florahtl@hotmail.com; Hebalin Lu, 河坝林路; d incl breakfast ¥185; ☎) The Flora is a well-run and reliable hotel in the interesting Muslim quarter (it's run by a Nepali Muslim). Nice touches include a laundry service and English-speaking staff. The tiled rooms are clean and spacious, though the bathrooms are a bit crummy. Rooms face inwards so are quiet. Budget tour groups from Kathmandu often stay here.

TIBET TRAVEL RESTRICTIONS

Travel to the Tibet Autonomous Region (TAR) is radically different from travel to the rest of China; a valid Chinese visa is not enough to visit Tibet. You'll also need several permits, foremost of which is a Tibet Tourism Bureau (TTB) permit, and to get these you have to book a tour. At a minimum you will need to hire a guide for your entire stay and transport for any travel outside Lhasa.

Travel regulations to Tibet are constantly in flux, dependent largely on political events in Lhasa and Beijing. Don't be surprised if the permit system is radically different from how we describe it. In fact, expect it. One of the best places for updated information is the dedicated Tibet page of Lonely Planet's Thorn Tree, at www.lonelyplanet.com/thorntree.

Start your tour planning at least two months in advance. Agencies need two to four weeks to arrange permits.

Tibet Tourism Bureau (TTB) Permit

Without a Tibet Tourism Bureau (TTB) permit you will not be able to board a flight or train to Tibet or cross overland from Nepal and you will not be able to secure the other permits you need to continue travelling throughout Tibet.

How these rules are interpreted depends on the political climate in Tibet. These days you can only get a TTB permit through a tour agency in Tibet (agencies outside Tibet can arrange trips, but ultimately they book through a Tibetan-based agency). Everything must be arranged beforehand, including any trekking.

To get a permit you need to undertake the following steps:

➡ Work out an itinerary detailing exactly where you want to go in Tibet

➡ Pay for a guide for every day of your tour, including arrival and departure days, at a rate of around ¥250 to ¥300 per day

➡ Hire a vehicle for all transport outside Lhasa

➡ Agree on a price and send a deposit, normally through PayPal or a bank transfer (check the transfer charges)

➡ Send a scan of your passport information pages and Chinese visa

➡ Arrange an address in China (usually that of a hotel, guesthouse or local agency) to receive your posted TTB permit, if flying to Lhasa

What your tour actually involves depends on the agency. Some offer all-inclusive tours, while others will arrange transport, a guide and permits but leave accommodation, food and entry fees up to you. You can book your own train or air ticket to Lhasa or have the agency arrange this. Some airline offices and online booking agencies will sell flights to Lhasa to foreigners, but others won't unless you can show you have a TTB permit.

You need to have the original permit in your hands in order to board a flight to Lhasa, so most agencies arrange to post the permit through an agency or hostel. This can cost anything from ¥25 for normal post (four working days) to ¥180/280/380 for 36-/24-/18-hour express post. A photocopy or scan of an original TTB permit is currently all that is required to board a train to Tibet, which saves on postage fees. The permit is actually free, though most agencies charge a few hundred *yuán* per person for the bureaucratic runaround.

Agencies can only apply for some permits 15 days before departure, so there is invariably a last-minute rush to get permits posted to you in time. Travel restrictions and closures occur without warning, especially during religiously significant dates, if there is a major political meeting in Beijing or if there are any political disturbances in Tibet.

TTB permits are not issued in March due to the anniversary of several politically sensitive dates. Assuming the political situation is calm, permits normally start to be reissued in the last week of March and agencies only know the new season's permit regulations for sure by the end of March. The last-minute nature and uncertainty that comes with this obviously complicates booking train and flight tickets; we recommend booking a fully refundable ticket if possible and taking out trip-cancellation insurance in case your permits fail to materialise.

Tour Agencies in Tibet

In general, Tibetan tour agencies are not as professional as agencies in neighbouring Nepal or Bhutan. You'll need to stay on top of the permit process, double check all communications and make sure the places on your itinerary match your permits, especially in eastern or western Tibet.

The following companies in Lhasa are experienced in arranging customised trips.

For good information on responsible tour companies and ecotourism initiatives in Tibet, visit www.tibetecotravel.com.

Shigatse Travels (☑891 633 0489; www.shigatsetravels.com; Yak Hotel, 100 Beijing Donglu, 北京东路100号) Top-end tours from a large agency that uses European trip managers.

Spinn Café (风转咖啡馆, Fēngzhuǎn Kāfēiguǎn; ☑139 9908 8152; www.cafespinn.com; 3rd floor, 7-9 Beijing Xilu, 北京西路7-9号3楼; ⊙1-7pm) Contact Kong/Pazu.

Tibet Highland Tours (☑139 0898 5060; www.tibethighlandtours.com; Danjielin Lu) Contact Tenzin or Dechen.

Tibet Native Tours & Travel (☑139 8909 4160; www.tibetnative.com; 38 Yutuo Lu, 宇拓路38号; ⊙9am-5pm Mon-Fri) This Tibetan-run agency gets great reviews. Contact Sonam Gyatso.

Tibet Roof of World International Travel (☑136 5952 6699, 891 633 0982; www.tibet traveladventure.com; 25 Sela Nanlu) Offers budget tours, treks and private cultural trips across Tibet. Contact Migmar.

Tibet Travellers (☑189 0899 0100; www.tibettravelers.com; Yutok Lu) Owner Tenzin Dondup is experienced at organising custom tours.

Tibet Wind Horse Adventure (☑891 683 3009; www.windhorsetibet.com; B32 Shenzheng Huayuan, Sera Beilu) Top-end trips, strong on trekking and rafting.

Visit Tibet Travel and Tours (☑028 8325 7742; www.visittibet.com; Jiaji Lu) Can arrange Nepal add-ons.

Tour Agencies Elsewhere in China

There are several companies outside the TAR that can arrange tours in Tibet; many are based in the Tibetan areas of China and operate through local contacts in Lhasa. If catching the train from Xining, it's handy to use an agency there to help arrange hard-to-find train tickets and permit pick-up.

One recommended agency that is particularly knowledgeable when arranging Tibet tours is US-based **Himalaya Journey** (www.himalayajourney.com), which has an office in Lhasa and utilises only local Tibetan guides.

Alien's Travel Permits & Military Permits

Once you have a visa and have managed to wangle a TTB permit, you might think you're home and dry. Think again. Your agency will need to arrange an alien's travel permit for most of your travels outside Lhasa.

Travel permits are *not* needed for Lhasa or places just outside the city such as Ganden Monastery, but most other areas do technically require permits. Permits are most easily arranged in the regional capital. Agencies can only arrange a travel permit for those on a tour with them.

Sensitive border areas – such as Mt Kailash, the road to Kashgar and the Nyingtri region of eastern Tibet – also require a military permit and a foreign-affairs permit. For remote places such as the Yarlung Tsangpo gorges in southeastern Tibet, the roads through Lhoka south of Gyantse or for any border area, you will likely be unable to get permits even if you book a tour. Regions can close at short notice. The majority of Chamdo prefecture has been closed since 2010, effectively blocking overland trips from Sichuan and Yunnan, but as of 2018 limited areas surrounding the G318 highway are now open to tourists. You'll have to check the current situation with your travel agent, but overland entry from Yunnan and southern Sichuan now appears to be possible.

Tibet Bike Hostel HOSTEL ¥

(风马飞扬旅舍, Fēngmǎ Fēiyáng Lǚshě; ☑891 679 0250; www.tibetbike.com; 5-1 Beijing Zhonglu Erxiang, 北京中路二巷5-1号; dm ¥60, d ¥208-298; ☏) This modern courtyard hostel (north of Beijing Donglu behind the Yak Hotel) is a decent option, especially if you speak some Chinese and want to connect with the many overland Chinese cyclists here. The en-suite rooms are bright, modern and good value, varying in size according to price, and the three-bed dorms come with shared hot showers and free washing-machine access.

Dongcuo International Youth Hostel HOSTEL ¥

(东措国际青年旅馆, Dōngcuò Guójì Qīngnián Lǚshè; ☑891 627 3388; yhalhasa@hotmail.com; 10 Beijing Donglu, 北京东路10号; dm ¥30-55, s/d/tr ¥140/180/200, r without bathroom ¥80-120; @☏) This hostel attracts mainly Chinese backpackers, though a few foreign travellers find their way here. Rooms are smallish but well maintained, with wooden floors and crisp white sheets, but the graffiti-covered walls beloved by Chinese backpackers add to the slightly grim, institutional feel. The hot water is best at night. Prices drop in April and rise in July and August.

★ Yak Hotel HOTEL ¥¥

(亚宾馆, Yà Bīnguǎn; ☑891 630 0009; www.yak-hotel.com; 100 Beijing Donglu, 北京东路100号; d ¥200-250, r VIP ¥880; ❊@☏) The ever-popular Yak has matured in recent years from backpacker hang-out to tour-group favourite, upgrading to a range of comfortable en-suite rooms. The best rates are through an online booking website such as Trip.com. The location is perfect and the 5th-floor breakfast bar offers great views of the Potala.

Tashi Choeta Tibetan Folk Hotel HOTEL ¥¥

(扎西曲塔风情大酒店, Zhāxī Qūtǎ Fēngqíng Dàiǔdiàn; ☑139 8998 5865; www.tashichoeta.com; 21 Beijing Donglu, 3rd Alley, 北京东路三巷21号; d/tr ¥388/528; ❊@☏) This new hotel has a great location on the edge of the old town, with 58 comfortable and fresh Tibetan-style rooms ranged around a sunny internal atrium of Tibetan-style seating. It's down an alley off Beijing Donglu so is quiet. There's another branch in Shigatse.

★ Kyichu Hotel HOTEL ¥¥¥

(吉曲饭店, Jíqǔ Fàndiàn; ☑891 633 1541; www.lhasakyichuhotel.com; 149 Beijing Donglu; r incl breakfast ¥480; ❊@☏) The renovated Kyichu is a friendly and well-run choice that's very popular with repeat travellers to Tibet. Rooms are comfortable and pleasant, with wooden floors, underfloor heating, Tibetan carpets and private bathrooms, but the real selling points are the location, the excellent service and – that rarest of Lhasa commodities – a peaceful garden courtyard (with espresso coffee). Reservations recommended.

★ Songtsam Choskyi Linka Lhasa BOUTIQUE HOTEL ¥¥¥

(松赞曲吉林卡, Sōngzàn Qūjí Línkǎ; ☑891 674 7666; www.songtsam.com; Sicholing; d incl breakfast ¥1180-1680; ❊☏) Lhasa's most stylish accommodation comes thanks to the Songtsam chain, which runs seven boutique lodges in the Tibetan area of Yunnan. The 50 rooms here are scattered in nine stone-and-wood villas and are spacious, stylish and very comfortable, with separate living rooms and bedrooms, and private balconies. Upper-floor rooms have distant views of the Potala (¥200 extra).

★ House of Shambhala BOUTIQUE HOTEL ¥¥¥

(桌玛拉宫, Zhuōmǎlā Gōng; ☑891 632 6533; 7 Jiri Erxiang, 吉日二巷7号; d incl breakfast ¥590-1015; ☉closed mid-Jan–end Mar; @) Hidden in the old town in a historic Tibetan building, the romantic, boutique-style Shambhala mixes the neighbourhood's earthy charm with buckets of style and a great rooftop lounge, making it perfect for couples who prefer atmosphere over mod cons. The 13 rooms, decorated in natural wood and slate with antique Tibetan furniture, vary only in size.

🛈 PERMITS

Lhasa is currently the only part of Tibet that doesn't require you to hire pricey transport. The only time you will be asked for your Tibet Tourism Bureau (TTB) permit is when you check into a hotel, which your guide will help you with. No other permits are required for the city or surroundings.

At the time of research you had to visit the main monasteries of Drepung, Sera and Ganden and Jokhang Temple and Potala Palace in the company of your guide, but other parts of the city were fine to explore by yourself.

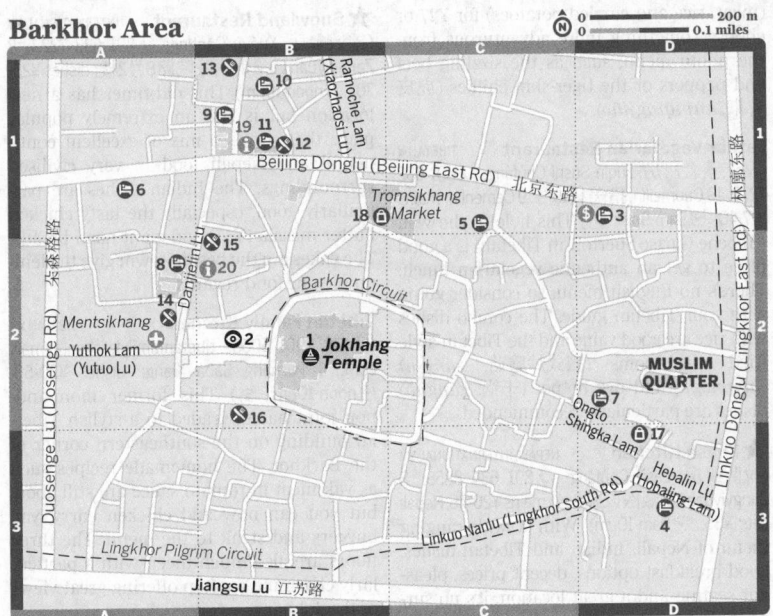

Barkhor Area

◎ Top Sights
1 Jokhang Temple B2

◎ Sights
2 Barkhor Square B2

◎ Sleeping
3 Dongcuo International Youth
   Hostel D1
4 Flora Hotel D3
5 House of Shambhala C1
6 Kyichu Hotel A1
7 Shambhala Palace D2
8 Shangbala Hotel A2
9 Tashi Choeta Tibetan Folk Hotel B1
10 Tibet Bike Hostel B1
11 Yak Hotel B1

◎ Eating
12 Dunya B1
13 Father Vegetarian Restaurant B1
14 Lhasa Kitchen A2
15 Snowland Restaurant B2
16 Tibetan Family Kitchen B2

◎ Drinking & Nightlife
Summit Cafe .... (see 8)

◎ Shopping
17 Dropenling D3
18 Tromsikhang Market B1

◎ Information
19 Shigatse Travels B1
20 Tibet Highland Tours B2

✕ Eating

The best Tibetan, Nepali and western restaurants are in the Tibetan quarter around Barkhor Sq. Almost all places offer decent breakfasts. Most serve lunch and dinner, but you will struggle to find a meal after about 10pm. For the flashiest Chinese restaurants you'll have to head to the western districts.

**Seyzhong Nongze
Bösey Restaurant**   TIBETAN ¥
(金藏特宝藏餐, Jīnzàng Tèbǎo Zàngcān; ☑891 633 3347; Ramoche Lam; dishes ¥15-35) Superconvenient if you're visiting the next-door **Ramoche Temple** (ར་མོ་ཆེ, 小昭寺; Xiǎozhāo Sì; ¥30; ☺7.30am-8pm), this pleasant upstairs Amdo Tibetan restaurant offers great views over the street below from the low Tibetan-style tables. Try the set meal of *shemdre*

(meat, rice and curried potatoes) for ¥27 or choose something more adventurous from the photo menu, such as the sizzling beef and peppers or the tiger-skin chillies (虎皮青椒, hǔpíqīngjiāo).

Father Vegetarian Restaurant TIBETAN ¥
(父亲素食厨房, Fùqīn Sùshí Chúfáng; ☑ 891 632 7279; 19 Cuomeilin, 措美林19号, 9 Cemenlin; mains ¥17-40; ⊙ 9am-9pm; ☑) This hole in the wall ('Yebche Gartse Suertob' in Tibetan) is a good place to get an authentic vegetarian lunch. There's no English menu, so consider going with your Tibetan guide. The combo dishes with rice are good value and the Tibetan-style fried mushrooms (藏式炒蘑菇, zāngshì chǎomógu) and dry hotpot (干锅, gānguō) dishes are particularly recommended.

★ **Lhasa Kitchen** NEPALI, INTERNATIONAL ¥¥
(拉萨厨房, Lāsà Chúfáng; ☑ 891 634 8855; 8 Zangyiyuan Lu, 藏医院路8号; mains ¥20-45, Nepali sets ¥35; ⊙ 9am-10pm) With a wide-ranging menu of Nepali, Indian and Tibetan dishes, good breakfast options, decent prices, pleasant seating and a great location, it's no surprise that this is an extremely popular place with tour groups and locals alike. The menu covers everything from vegetable *dopiaza* (onion-based curry) to chicken sizzlers. Service can be brusque.

★ **Snowland Restaurant** INTERNATIONAL ¥¥
(雪域餐厅, Xuěyù Cāntīng; ☑ 891 633 7323; 8 Zangyiyuan Lu, 2 fl, 藏医院路8号2楼; dishes ¥25-70; ⊙ noon-10pm) This old-timer has a new location but is still an extremely popular place that serves a mix of excellent continental and Nepali food in very civilised surroundings. The Indian dishes are particularly good, especially the tasty chicken butter masala (¥55) and giant naan breads. The cakes are the best in town; give the lemon pie our fond regards.

Tibetan Family Kitchen TIBETAN ¥¥
(☑ 138 8901 5053; tibetanfamilykitchen@gmail. com; 1 Pozhang Saba Xiang; dishes ¥30-50; ⊙ noon-10pm; ☎) This former mom-and-pop joint has upgraded to a stylish Tibetan building on the southeastern corner of the Barkhor. The homemade recipes such as yak meat in tomato sauce are still good, but you can now add chicken curry, yak burgers and steak to the menu. The three floors are also much nicer, with a particularly charming rooftop offering great views of the Jokhang.

🍷 Drinking & Nightlife

★ **Summit Cafe** CAFE
(顶峰咖啡店, Dǐngfēng Kāfēidiàn; ☑ 891 691 3884; www.thetibetsummitcafe.com; 1 Danjielin

---

LHASA IN...

Two Days

On arrival in Lhasa you need at least two days to adjust to the altitude; you can expect to be tired and headachey most of the time. We recommend adding an extra day and taking the first day very easy.

Start at Barkhor Square (p937), finding your legs on a relaxed stroll around the Barkhor Circuit before visiting the Jokhang (p937). Grab lunch at nearby Snowland Restaurant (p942) or Lhasa Kitchen (p938). In the afternoon head to Sera Monastery (p946) to catch the monks debating. If your headache's gone, round off the day with a cold Lhasa Beer at **Dunya** (☑ 891 633 3374; 100 Beijing Donglu, 北京东路100号; dishes ¥40-80; ⊙ 11am-10pm, earlier opening Jul-Sep; ☎) or on the roof of **Shambhala Palace** (香巴拉宫, Xiāng-bālā Gōng; ☑ 891 630 7779; 16 Tiebeng Gang, 铁蹦岗6号; r incl breakfast ¥389-489; ⊙ closed mid-Jan–end Mar; ᠗ ☎).

On day two visit the Potala Palace (p936) at your allotted time and then spend the afternoon losing yourself in the fascinating old town.

Four Days

With four days you could leave the Potala until day three, and add on a stroll around the **Potala Kora**, grabbing some sweet tea en route. On day four leave the city on a day trip out to Ganden Monastery (p946), visiting the hermitage caves of **Drak Yerpa** (ཕུག་ཡར་པ, 扎叶巴寺, Zhā Yèbā Sì; ¥30; ⊙ 9am-5pm) on the way back. Try to budget some time for handicraft shopping at Dropenling (p943) and to explore an off-the-beaten-path chapel such as the Lho Rigsum Lhakhang.

Lu, 丹杰林路1号; coffee ¥22-27, mains ¥50-80; ⊙9am-8.30pm; 🛜) With authentic espresso coffee and smoothies, free wi-fi and melt-in-your-mouth cheesecakes, plus salads, paninis, pizza and American-style breakfast waffles and pancakes, this coffeehouse is mocha-flavoured nirvana. It's in the courtyard of the **Shangbala Hotel** (香巴拉酒店, Xiāngbālā Jiǔdiàn; 🖉891 632 3888; d ¥470-560, ste ¥800; ❊🛜), a stone's throw from the Jokhang. There are other, less appealing branches around town.

Dzongyab Lukhang
Park Teahouse East   TEAHOUSE
(龙王潭风经情茶园, Lóngwángtán Fēngqíng Cháyuán; tea ¥5-12) One of two good Tibetan-style teahouse restaurants in pleasant Dzongyab Lukhang Park, perfect for a break after a visit to the Potala or for snapping photos in the charming local park. Don't miss the traditional Tibetan-style line dancing on the stages outside the teahouse every morning until lunchtime.

Grab a thermos of sweet tea or try a cheap lunch of *shemdre* (meat and curried potatoes; mains ¥15 to ¥20). There's a second identical **teahouse** (tea ¥5-12) in the northwest corner of the park.

🔒 Shopping

★ Dropenling   ARTS & CRAFTS
(桌番林, Zhuōfānlín; 🖉891 636 0558; 11 Qiacaigang Lu, 恰彩岗路11号, 11 Chaktsalgang Lam; ⊙9am-8pm) ⬮ This impressive nonprofit enterprise aims to bolster traditional Tibetan handicrafts in the face of rising Chinese and Nepali imports. Products are unique and of high quality, and they are made using traditional techniques (natural dyes, wool not acrylic etc) updated with contemporary designs. Ask about the two-hour artisan walking tour of Lhasa's old town (¥50 per person, minimum five people).

Tromsikhang Market   MARKET
(冲赛康市场, Chōngsàikāng Shìchǎng; 31 Beijing Zhonglu, 北京中路31号; ⊙8am-6pm) This bazaar-like area in the old town has the widest selection of dried fruit and nuts (imported from Xinjiang) and is the place to buy such Tibetan specialities as *tsampa* (roasted-barley flour), *churpi* (dried yak cheese) and yak butter. Khampa-style cowboy hats are for sale in the streets outside.

ⓘ Information

EMERGENCY NUMBERS

Ambulance	☎120
Fire	☎119
Police	☎11

INTERNET ACCESS
Almost all hotels and some cafes, including the Summit Cafe, offer free wi-fi to patrons.

MEDICAL SERVICES
120 Emergency Centre (急救中心, Jíjiù Zhōngxīn; 🖉891 633 2462, emergency 120; 16 Linkuo Beilu, 林廓北路16号) Part of People's Hospital. Consultations cost around ¥150.

Tibet Military Hospital (西藏军区总医院, Xīzàng Jūnqū Zǒngyīyuàn; 🖉891 685 8120; 66 Niangre Beilu, 娘热北路66号) Travellers who have received medical attention confirm that this place is the best option (if you have an option).

MONEY
Changing cash and using ATMs is generally easy in Lhasa. Stock up on cash here for the rest of your trip through Tibet.

Bank of China Main Office (中国银行, Zhōngguó Yínháng; 7 Linkuo Xilu, 林廓西路7号; ⊙9am-1pm & 3.30-6pm Mon-Fri, 10.30am-4.30pm Sat & Sun) West of the Potala, this is the only place to arrange a credit-card advance (3% commission) or a bank transfer. The ATMs outside the building are open 24 hours.

Bank of China – Beijing Donglu (中国银行, Zhōngguó Yínháng; 95-103 Beijing Donglu, 北京东路95-103号; ⊙24hr) The most conveniently located branch is fully automated, with a currency-exchange machine that converts cash currencies much more quickly than the main bank branch. Bring your cleanest notes, as the machine can be fussy. ATMs dispense cash 24 hours a day. It's just west of the Banak Shol Hotel.

Bank of China – Duosenge Lu (🖉891 633 8778; 37 Duosenge Beilu, 朵森格北路37号; ⊙9.30am-5.30pm Mon-Fri, 10.30am-4pm Sat & Sun) If you actually need to talk to a human to change money, this bank branch is the closest to the Tibetan old town.

POST
China Post (中国邮政, Zhōngguó Yóuzhèng; 🖉891 624 1443; 33 Beijing Zhonglu, 北京中路33号; ⊙9am-6.30pm) Counter three sells packaging for parcels. Express Mail Service (EMS) is also here. Leave parcels unsealed until you get here, as staff will want to check the contents for customs clearance.

Heaven Tibet Post Office (天上西藏邮局, Tiānshàng Xīzàng Yóujú; ☑ 891 624 1443; 33 Beijing Zhonglu, 北京中路33号; ⊙ 9.30am-6.30pm) This branch of China Post, just east of the main office, is the easiest place to buy stamps for international postcards (¥5) and letters (¥6.50). It sells a wide range of post-cards. Look for the fun range of Tibet-themed ink stamps you can put on your envelope or postcard for free.

SAFE TRAVEL

If you fly straight into Lhasa, remember to take things easy for your first day or two.

➡ It's not uncommon to feel breathless, suffer from headaches and sleep poorly because of the altitude.

➡ Don't attempt the steps up to the Potala for the first few days and drink lots of fluids.

➡ Armed-police posts and riot-squad teams currently occupy every street corner in the old town. Most Tibetans ignore them, but you should take care not to photograph any military posts or armed patrols.

TELEPHONE

China Mobile (中国移动通信, Zhōngguó Yídòng Tōngxìn; Beijing Donglu, 北京东路; ⊙ 9am-7pm Mon-Sat) This is the easiest place to get a local SIM card for your mobile phone. Choose from data, calls or a mixture of both. It's a fairly complicated procedure and you'll likely need a local ID card, so go with your guide. Expect to pay around ¥120 for a month of data.

ⓘ Getting There & Away

While there are a number of ways to get to Lhasa, the most popular routes are by air from Chengdu (in Sichuan), by train from Xining, and overland or by air from Kathmandu.

AIR

Modern Gongkar airport is 66km from Lhasa, via a new expressway and Gala Shan tunnel.

Flying out of Lhasa is considerably easier than flying in. No permits are necessary (except your visa for mainland China) – just turn up at the **Civil Aviation Authority of China office** (CAAC, 中国民航, Zhōngguó Mínháng; ☑ 0891-682 5430; 42 Niangre Beilu; ⊙ 9am-6pm) and buy a ticket. In August and around national holidays, you'd be wise to book your ticket at least a week in advance. At other times you'll generally get a 30% discount off the full fare.

To book a ticket you'll need to complete a form, get a reservation and then pay the cashier (cash only). Sample full fares include ¥1680 to Chengdu, ¥3310 to Beijing (check as only some flights are direct), ¥1950 to Xiahe, ¥1060 to Yushu and ¥1900 to Xining. Booking online is also an option.

Air China (中国国际民航, Zhōngguó Guójì Mínháng; ☑ 891 681 9777; www.airchina.com. cn; 67 Beijing Zhonglu, 北京中路67号; ⊙ 9am-7.30pm)

China Southern (中国南方航空, Zhōngguó Nánfāng Hángkōng; ☑ 891 681 8366; www.

THE WORLD'S HIGHEST TRAIN RIDE

There's no doubt the Qinghai–Tibet train line is an engineering marvel. Topping out at 5072m, it is the world's highest railway, snatching the title from a Peruvian line. The sta-tistics speak for themselves: 86% of the line is above 4000m, and half the track lies on permafrost, requiring a cooling system of pipes driven into the ground to keep it frozen year-round to avoid a rail-buckling summer thaw. Construction of the line involved build-ing 160km of bridges and elevated track, seven tunnels (including the world's highest) and 24 hyperbaric chambers, the latter to treat altitude-sick workers.

Aside from environmental concerns, many local Tibetans are deeply worried about the cultural and political impact of the train. The trains unload thousands of tourists and immigrants into Lhasa every day.

The authorities stress the economic benefits of the line: highly subsidised, it has decreased transport costs for imports by up to 75%. But Tibetans remain economically marginalised. More than 90% of the 100,000 workers employed to build the line came from other provinces and few, if any, Tibetan staff members work on the trains. The US$4.1 billion cost of building the line is greater than the amount Beijing has spent on hospitals and schools in Tibet over the past 50 years.

As ambitious as the current line is, connecting Lhasa with the rest of China was only the beginning. An extension to Shigatse opened in 2014, and a new railway line under construction will expand the line east to Tsetang, Nyingtri and Sichuan province, start-ing/ending at Chengdu. While this undoubtedly eases travel and provides a comfortable and romantic method of transport into Tibet, travellers should remain mindful of the impact on the culture and delicate ecology of this special region.

csair.com; 33 Beijing Zhonglu, 北京中路33号;
⊙9.30am-6pm)

Tibet Airlines (西藏航空, Xīzàng Hángkōng;
☑891 683 0088; www.tibetairlines.com.cn; 1
Minzu Nanlu, 民族南路1号; ⊙10am-5pm)

TRAIN

It's possible to ride the rails up onto the Tibetan
plateau to Lhasa, and even beyond to Shigatse.
There are daily trains to/from Beijing, Xi'an,
Shanghai and Guangzhou and four daily to/from
Xining or Lanzhou, and every other day to/from
Chengdu and Chongqing. The train station is
4km southwest of town.

Train services were extended from Lhasa to
Shigatse in 2014. Fares for the three-hour trip
cost around ¥41 for a hard seat or ¥120/176
for a hard/soft sleeper. Trains depart Lhasa at
8.30am (Z8801) and 3.20pm (Z8803), returning
from Shigatse at 12.05pm and 6.40pm. If your
tour agency can secure tickets you can add
Shigatse onto a Lhasa trip without having to fork
out for pricey vehicle hire.

It's only a question of time before rail services
extend from Lhasa to Tsetang in the Yarlung
Valley.

You can buy train tickets up to two months in
advance at the Lhasa **train station ticket office**
(⊙7am-10pm) or the more centrally located
city ticket office (火车票代售处, Huǒchēpiào
Dàishòuchù; Beijing Donglu; commission ¥5;
⊙8am-5.40pm). You'll need your passport.
Note that it's generally much easier to get tickets from Lhasa than to Lhasa.

A taxi to/from the train station costs around
¥30.

ℹ Getting Around

For those travellers based in the Tibetan quarter
of Lhasa, most of the major inner-city sights are
within fairly easy walking distance. For sights
such as the Norbulingka over in the west of town,
it's better to jump in a taxi (¥10).

TO & FROM THE AIRPORT

Most agencies send a guide and vehicle to pick
up their clients from the airport. Most charge
around ¥300, either directly or as part of your
tour fee.

Airport buses (☑891 682 7727; Niangre
Beilu; ¥30) leave up to 10 times a day (¥30, 1¼
hours) between 5am and 8pm from beside the
CAAC building and are timed to meet flights.
From the airport, buses wait for flights outside
the terminal building. Some agencies will let
their tourists travel by airport bus as long as
they buy a return ticket for the guide. Buy tickets
on the bus.

A taxi to the airport costs around ¥200.

BUS

Buses (¥1) are frequent on Beijing Donglu, and if
you need to get up to western Lhasa, this is the
cheapest way to do it. That said, route maps are
in Chinese only, so if you aren't with your guide
it's easiest to just take an inexpensive taxi.

PEDICAB

There is no shortage of pedicabs plying the
streets of Lhasa, but they require endless haggling and are only really useful for short trips
(around ¥7). At least most are Tibetan-owned.
Always fix the price before getting in.

PUBLIC TRANSPORT

At the time of research, foreigners were not
allowed to travel on public transport out of
Lhasa, with the possible exception of buses to
the airport.

TAXI

Taxis charge a standard fare of ¥10 for the first
3km (then ¥2 per subsequent kilometre), resulting in a ¥10 ride within the city centre.

AROUND LHASA

Drepung Monastery འབྲས་སྤུངས་ 哲蚌寺

ELEV 3800M

Drepung was once one of the world's largest monasteries and its ancient prayer halls
and self-contained college temples are still
a highlight of Tibet. It is bigger and more
sprawling than Sera Monastery, so budget
half a day here, longer if you want to walk
the lovely *kora*.

Drepung Monastery   BUDDHIST MONASTERY
(Zhébàng Sì; ¥60; ⊙9.30am-4pm, smaller chapels
close at 3pm) Along with Sera and Ganden
Monasteries, Drepung functioned as one of
the three 'pillars of the Tibetan state', and it
was purportedly the largest monastery in
the world, with around 7000 resident monks
at its peak. Drepung means 'rice heap', a
reference to the white buildings dotting
the hillside. The 1½-hour *kora* around the
15th-century monastery, 8km west of Lhasa,
is among the highlights of a trip to the city.

The kings of Tsang and the Mongols
savaged the place regularly; oddly, the Red
Guards pretty much left it alone during
the Cultural Revolution. With concerted
rebuilding, Drepung once again resembles
a monastic village and around 600 monks
reside here. At lunchtime you can see the

novices bringing in buckets of *tsampa* (roasted-barley flour) and yak-butter tea. In the afternoon you can often witness Tibetan-style religious debating (lots of hand slapping and gesticulating). The best way to visit the monastery is to follow the pilgrim groups or the yellow signs.

Nearby **Nechung Monastery**, a 10-minute walk downhill, was once the home of the Tibetan state oracle and is worth a visit for its blood-curdling murals.

Bus 25 (¥1) runs from Beijing Donglu to the foot of the Drepung hill, from where minivans (¥2) run up to the monastery. Most tourists take a taxi from the Barkhor area for around ¥60.

★ Drepung Kora   WALKING

This lovely *kora* climbs up to around 3900m and so probably should not be attempted until you've had a couple of days to acclimatise in Lhasa. The path passes several rock paintings, climbs past a high wall used to hang a giant *thangka* during the Shötun festival, peaks at a valley of prayer flags, and then descends to the east via an encased Drölma (Tara) statue and several more rock carvings. There are excellent views along the way.

The **Monastery Restaurant** (mains ¥7-12; ⊙10am-3pm) near the bus stop serves reviving sweet tea by the glass or thermos (¥7), as well as bowls of *shemdre* (meat and curried potatoes) and vegetable momos (dumplings).

❶ Getting There & Away

Located about 8km west of central Lhasa, the easiest way to get out to Drepung is by taxi from the Barkhor for ¥40. To save some pennies, take bus 18, 25 or 16 (¥1), all of which run from Beijing Donglu to a stop at the foot of the Drepung hill. From here minivans (¥2) run up to the monastery bus stop.

Ganden Monastery   དགའ་ལྡན་ 甘丹寺

ELEV 4300M

Ganden Monastery (Gāndān Sì; ¥50; ⊙9am-4pm) was the first Gelugpa monastery and has been the main seat of this major Buddhist order ever since. If you only have time for one monastery excursion outside Lhasa, Ganden – 60 km from the city – is the best choice. With its stupendous views of the surrounding Kyi-chu Valley and its fascinating *kora*, Ganden makes for an experience unlike those at the other major Gelugpa monasteries in the Lhasa area.

Ganden is also the start of the popular wilderness trek to Samye Monastery. Make sure you visit the monastery in the morning, as many chapels are closed in the afternoon.

★ Ganden Kora   WALKING

The Ganden *kora* is simply stunning and should not be missed. There are superb views over the braided Kyi-chu Valley along the way and there are usually large numbers of pilgrims and monks offering prayers, rubbing holy rocks and prostrating themselves along the path. There are two parts to the walk: the high *kora* and the low *kora*. The high *kora* climbs Angkor Ri south of Ganden and then drops down the ridge to join up with the low *kora*.

Tourists are generally not allowed to stay overnight at Ganden, but there is a guesthouse here, so check with your tour agency.

Basic food is available at the **monastery restaurant** (dishes ¥13-20), and the **shop** sells basic supplies.

❶ Getting There & Away

The road from Lhasa follows a new highway east, from which a paved road switchbacks the steep final 12km to the monastery. Vehicle hire for a day trip costs around ¥500.

On the way back to Lhasa, pilgrims traditionally stop for a visit at Sanga Monastery, set at the foot of the ruined Dagtse Dzong (or Dechen Dzong; *dzong* means fort).

Sera Monastery   སེ་ར་དགོན་པ་ 色拉寺

Sera Monastery (Sèlā Sì; 1 Sela Lu, 色拉路1 号, 1 Sera Lam; ¥50; ⊙9am-4pm; 🚌22, 23) was one of Lhasa's two great Gelugpa monasteries, second only to Drepung. Its once-huge population of around 5000 monks has now been reduced by 90% and building repairs are still continuing. Nevertheless, the monastery is worth a visit, particularly in the morning, when the chapels are at their most active, but also between 3pm and 5pm (not Sunday), when debating is usually held in the monastery's debating courtyard. Chapels start to close at 3pm, so it makes sense to see the monastery chapels before heading to the debating.

The pleasant **monastery restaurant** (dishes ¥3-8; ⊙10am-3pm) is worth a stop for tea and momos.

From Sera Monastery it's possible to take a taxi northwest for a couple of kilometres to little-visited **Pabonka Monastery** (པ་བོང་ཁ་དགོན་པ་, 帕邦喀寺, Pàbāngkā Sì; ⊙dawn-dusk) **FREE**. Built in the 7th century by King Songtsen Gampo, this is one of the most ancient Buddhist sites in the Lhasa region.

Just 5km north of Lhasa, Sera is a short bus ride on bus 16, 20, 22 or 25 to a stop at the monastery. A taxi (¥20) is the easiest option.

Ü   དབུས་

Ü (དབུས་) is Tibet's heartland and contains almost all the landscapes you'll find across the plateau, from sand dunes and meandering rivers to soaring peaks and juniper forests. Due to its proximity to Lhasa, Ü is the first taste of rural Tibet that most visitors experience, and you can get off the beaten track surprisingly easily here. Fine walking opportunities abound, from day hikes and monastery *koras* to overnight treks.

Ü is the traditional power centre of Tibet, and home to its oldest buildings and most historic monasteries. The big sights, such as Samye, are unmissable, but consider also heading to lesser-visited places such as the Drigung and Yarlung Valleys, or to smaller monasteries like Dratang and Gongkar Chöde. Make it to these hidden gems and you'll feel as though you have Tibet all to yourself.

Samye   བསམ་ཡས་ 桑耶镇

The monastic town of Samye (Sāngyé Zhèn) is home to the the beautiful Samye Monastery, deservedly the most popular destination for travellers in the Ü region. As Tibet's first monastery and the place where Tibetan Buddhism was established, the monastery is also of major historical and religious importance. Surrounded by barren mountains and rolling sand dunes, the monastery has a quiet magic about it that causes many travellers to rate it as the highlight of Ü.

If you are heading to Everest Base Camp or the Nepali border, a trip here will only add one day to your itinerary. You may have to detour briefly to the nearby town of Tsetang (རྩེད་ཐང་ ; 泽当; Zédāng) for your guide to pick up the required travel permit.

◉ Sights

★ **Samye Monastery**   BUDDHIST MONASTERY
(བསམ་ཡས་དགོན་པ་, 桑耶寺, Sāngyē Sì; ⊙dawn-dusk) About 170km southeast of Lhasa, on the north bank of the Yarlung Tsangpo (Brahmaputra River) is Samye, the first monastery in Tibet. Founded in 775 by King Trisong Detsen, Samye is famed not just for its pivotal history but for its unique mandala design: the Main Hall, known as **Ütse** (¥35; ⊙dawn-dusk), represents Mt Meru, the centre of the universe, while the outer temples represent the oceans, continents, subcontinents and other features of the Buddhist cosmology.

As renovation work continues at Samye, the original *ling* (royal) chapels – lesser, outlying chapels that surround the Ütse – are slowly being restored. Wander around and see which are open. Aside from the Ütse, none require any entry fees.

★ **Chim-puk Hermitage**   BUDDHIST SITE
(མཆིམས་ཕུ་སྒྲུབ་གནས, 青朴修行地, Qīngpò Xiūxíngdì) **FREE** Chim-puk Hermitage is a collection of cave shrines northeast of Samye that grew up over the centuries around the meditation retreat of Guru Rinpoche. Chim-puk's Tantric practitioners were once famed for their ability to protect fields from hailstorms. It is a popular excursion for travellers overnighting at Samye. Make sure your agency knows in advance that you want to visit or you'll have to haggle over the return 20km trip.

⛺ Sleeping & Eating

Tashi Guesthouse & Restaurant   GUESTHOUSE ¥
(扎西旅馆, Zhāxī Lǚguǎn; ☏189 8993 7883; dm/r without bathroom ¥60/120; ☎) Pleasant two-, four- and five-bed dorms with clean foam beds above a restaurant by the East Gate. If things are busy, you may have to pay for all beds in a room to keep it private. The nice teahouse restaurant downstairs (8.30am to 10.30pm) has an English menu of Tibetan and Chinese staples from ¥15 to ¥30 per dish.

Samye Monastery Guesthouse   HOTEL ¥¥
(桑耶寺宾馆, Sāngyésì Bīnguǎn; ☏0893-783 6666; d with/without bathroom ¥240/200, tr ¥300; ☎) This huge modern hotel is the default option for most visitors. Although devoid of monastic charm, the carpeted double rooms are comfortable (check for barking dogs

when choosing your room), have a hot-water shower and the only western toilets in town. The cheaper doubles share a bathroom down the hall (no showers).

Friendship Snowland Restaurant CHINESE ✗
(Gangjong Pönda Sarkhang, 雪域同胞藏餐旅馆, Xuěyù Tóngbāo Zángcān Lǚguǎn; ☑ 136 1893 2819, 136 5958 4773; dishes ¥16-50; ☺ 8.30am-11pm; ☎) The backpacker-inspired menu at this pleasant Tibetan-style restaurant includes banana pancakes, hash browns and omelettes, making this your best breakfast bet. Good Chinese and Tibetan dishes are also available, as well as yak sizzlers.

Monastery Restaurant TIBETAN ✗
(dishes ¥15-28; ☺ 8am-8pm; ✍) Expect loads of atmosphere, sunny outdoor seating, a vegetarian menu and pilgrims galore at this welcoming place within the monastery compound. Fried Chinese dishes are the best options for food, but you can also just sit around and drink sweet tea like the locals.

ℹ Getting There & Away

A highway connects Samye to Lhasa in 1½ hours or less, but this will get even shorter when the direct highway between Lhasa and Samye opens within the next few years.

Leaving Samye it's possible to take a new bridge across the Yarlung Tsangpo, 17km west of Samye, to head directly to Mindroling, Dratang or Gongkar without backtracking.

TSANG གཙང

The historical province of Tsang is either the first or last place that most travellers experience in Tibet, and the setting for two of Asia's great mountain drives: out to far western Tibet and across the Himalaya to Nepal. The great overland trip across Tibet – from Lhasa along the Friendship Hwy to the Nepali border via Gyantse, Shigatse and Mt Everest Base Camp – goes straight through Tsang, linking most of Tibet's highlights on one irresistible route. Along the way is a scattering of atmospheric Tibetan monasteries and historic towns, an adventurous detour to the base of Mt Everest and multitudes of snowy peaks and moonlike landscapes to behold. Dozens of smaller monasteries just off the highway offer plenty of scope to get off the beaten track and experience an older Tibet.

Gyantse རྒྱལ་རྩེ 江孜

☑ 0892 / ELEV 4000M / POP 15,000

Lying on a historic trade route between India and Tibet, Gyantse (Jiāngzī) has long been a crucial link for traders and pilgrims journeying across the Himalaya. It was once considered Tibet's third city, behind Lhasa and Shigatse, but in recent decades has been eclipsed by fast-growing towns such as Bayi and Tsetang. Perhaps that's a good thing, as Gyantse has managed to hang on to its small-town charm and laidback atmosphere.

Gyantse's greatest sight is Gyantse Kumbum, the largest *chörten* remaining in Tibet and one of its architectural wonders, but there's plenty more to see. With good hotels and restaurants, Gyantse is the town in Tibet that most warrants an extra day to explore little-visited nearby monasteries or wander the town's charming back streets.

The drive from Gyantse to Shigatse takes around two hours, but allow half a day with stops en route.

◎ Sights

★**Gyantse Kumbum** BUDDHIST STUPA
(རྒྱལ་རྩེ་སྐུ་འབུམ་, 江孜千佛塔, Jiāngzī Qiānfótǎ; incl with Palcho Monastery; ☺ 7am-7pm) Commissioned by a local prince in 1427 and sitting beside Palcho Monastery, Gyantse Kumbum is the town's foremost attraction. This 32m-high *chörten*, with its white layers trimmed with decorative stripes and crownlike golden dome, is awe-inspiring. But the inside is no less impressive, and in what seems an endless series of tiny chapels you'll find painting after exquisite painting (*kumbum* means '100,000 images').

It costs a worthwhile ¥10 for photos (not included in the ticket, bring cash).

Palcho Monastery BUDDHIST MONASTERY
(白居寺, Báijū Sì, Pelkor Chöde Monastery; high/low season ¥60/30; ☺ 9.30am-6pm, some chapels closed 1-3pm) The high red-walled compound in the far north of Gyantse houses Palcho Monastery, founded in 1418. The main assembly hall is of greatest interest, but there are several other chapels to see. There's a small but visible population of 80 monks and a steady stream of prostrating, praying, donation-offering pilgrims doing the rounds almost any time of the day.

Gyantse Dzong
FORT

(江孜宗, Jiāngzī Zōng) The main reason to make the 20-minute climb to the top of this 14th-century fort is for the fabulous views of Palcho Monastery and Gyantse's white-washed old town below. Most visitors drive up halfway to the top but you can walk via the road leading west out of the old town. Unfortunately, the fort is closed to visitors, but it dominates the view from almost everywhere in Gyantse.

🛏 Sleeping & Eating

⭐ Yeti Hotel
HOTEL ¥¥

(雅迪花园酒店, Yǎdí Huāyuán Jiǔdiàn; ☑892 817 5555; 11 Weiguo Lu; d incl breakfast ¥328; ☻❀@🛜) The three-star Yeti is easily the best option in Gyantse, offering 24-hour piping hot water, clean, spacious rooms, quality mattresses and reliable wi-fi, so make sure you reserve in advance. The western-style cafe and excellent lobby Chinese restaurant serve everything from Sichuan favourites and yak steak to pizza, alongside a decent buffet breakfast.

Tashi
NEPALI, INTERNATIONAL ¥¥

(扎西餐厅, Zhāxī Cāntīng; Yingxiong Nanlu; mains ¥20-50; ⊙8.30am-9pm; 🛜🍴) This Nepali-run place (a branch of Tashi in Shigatse) whips up tasty and filling curries, pizza, pastas and yak sizzlers. It also has the best range of western breakfasts. The decor is Tibetan but the Indian films and Nepali music give it a head-waggling subcontinental vibe.

Shigatse
གཞིས་ཀ་རྩེ 日喀则

☑0892 / ELEV 3840M / POP 120,000

Tibet's second-largest city and the traditional capital of Tsang province, Shigatse (Rìkāzé) is a modern, sprawling city, with wide boulevards humming with traffic. As you drive in across the plains, the sight of the Potala-lookalike Shigatse Dzong, high on a hilltop overlooking the town, will probably fire your imagination, but the fort is empty and most of what you see dates from a 2007 reconstruction. The real draw here is Tashilhunpo Monastery. Since the Mongol sponsorship of the Gelugpa order in the 17th century, Tashilhunpo has been the seat of the Panchen Lama, the second-most important spiritual figure in Tibetan Buddhism after the Dalai Lama.

History

The town of Shigatse, formerly known as Samdruptse, has long been an important trading and administrative centre. The Tsang kings exercised their power from the *dzong* (fort) and the fort later became the residence of the governor of Tsang.

Tashilhunpo Monastery is one of the six great Gelugpa (Yellow Hat sect) institutions, along with Drepung, Sera and Ganden Monasteries in Lhasa, and Kumbum (Tǎ'ěr Sì) and Labrang in Amdo (modern Gansu and Qinghai provinces). It was founded in 1447 by Genden Drup, a disciple of Tsongkhapa, the Yellow Hat sect founder himself. Genden Drup was retroactively named the first Dalai Lama and he is enshrined in a stupa inside Tashilhunpo. Despite this important association, Tashilhunpo Monastery was initially isolated from mainstream Gelugpa affairs, which were centred in the Lhasa region.

The monastery's standing rocketed when the fifth Dalai Lama declared his teacher – then the abbot of Tashilhunpo – to be a manifestation of Öpagme (Amitabha). Thus Tashilhunpo became the seat of an important lineage: the Panchen ('great scholar') Lamas. Unfortunately, with the establishment of this lineage of spiritual and temporal leaders – second only to the Dalai Lamas – rivalry was introduced to the Gelugpa order.

⊙ Sights

⭐ Tashilhunpo
Monastery
BUDDHIST MONASTERY

(བཀྲ་ཤིས་ལྷུན་པོ་, 扎什伦布寺, Zhāshílúnbù Sì; ¥100; ⊙9am-6.30pm) One of the few monasteries in Tibet to weather the stormy seas of the Cultural Revolution, Tashilhunpo remains relatively unscathed. It is a pleasure to explore the cobbled lanes twisting around its aged buildings. Covering 70,000 sq metres, the monastery is now the largest functioning religious institution in Tibet – home to around 950 monks – and one of its great monastic sights. The huge golden statue of the Future Buddha is the largest gilded statue in the world.

Summer Palace
of the Panchen Lamas
PALACE

(བདེ་ཆེན་སྐལ་བཟང་ཕོ་བྲང་, 德庆格桑颇彰, Déqìng Gésāng Pōzhāng; ¥60; ⊙9.30am-noon & 3.30-6pm) Though it ranks far below Tashilhunpo, if you have extra time in Shigatse, pay a visit to this walled palace complex at the southwestern end of town. The original

Shigatse

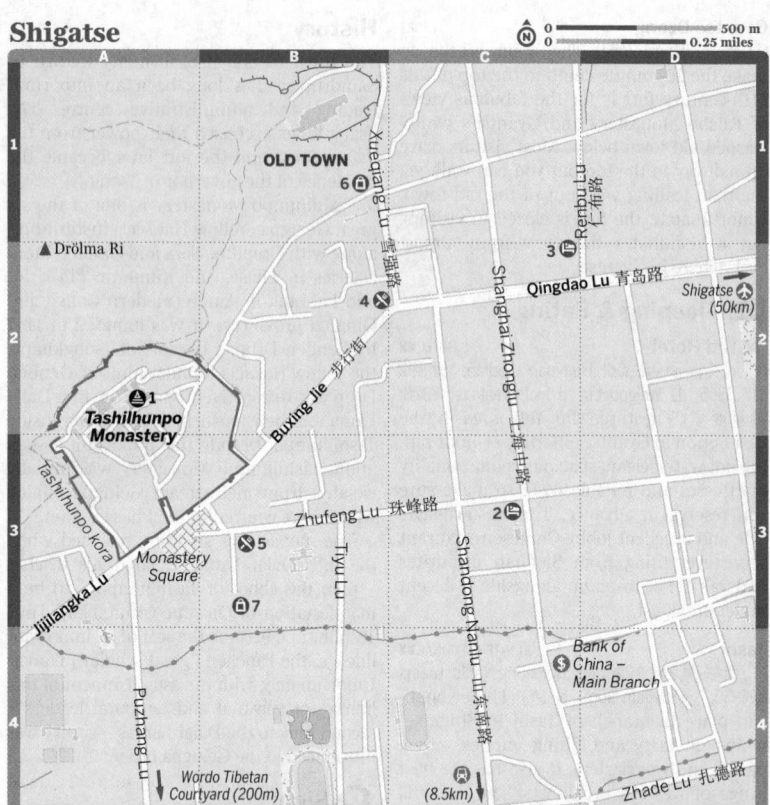

OLD TOWN

▲ Drölma Ri

Tashilhunpo Monastery

Monastery Square

Bank of China – Main Branch

↓ Wordo Tibetan Courtyard (200m)

↓ (8.5km)

Shigatse (50km) →

Zhade Lu 扎德路

Xueqiang Lu 雪强路
Buxing Jie 步行街
Tashilhunpo kora
Jijilangka Lu
Puzhang Lu
Tiyu Lu
Zhufeng Lu 珠峰路
Shanghai Zhonglu 上海中路
Shandong Nanlu 山东南路
Renbu Lu 仁布路
Qingdao Lu 青岛路

Shigatse

⦿ Top Sights
1 Tashilhunpo Monastery A2

🛏 Sleeping
2 Qomolangzong Hotel............................C3
3 Tibet Zangba Hotel C2

🍴 Eating
4 Tashi Choeta...B2
5 Third Eye B3

🛍 Shopping
6 Shigatse Tibetan Market.....................B1
7 Tibet Gang Gyen Carpet Factory B3

---

palace was built in 1844 by the seventh Panchen Lama, Tenpei Nyima, and later destroyed; the current complex was built in 1955 by the 10th Panchen Lama. It's known in Tibetan as the Dechen Kalzang Podrang.

Nartang Monastery BUDDHIST MONASTERY
(纳唐寺, Nàtáng Sì) FREE Just a few kilometres outside of Shigatse, this 12th-century Kadampa monastery is famed for woodblock printing the Nartang canon in the 18th century. Treasures in the assembly hall include small statues of Denba Tortumba said to have the power to control lightning; a mantra written in stone by the first Dalai Lama; and the self-arising stone horns and footprints of the wild yak that helped install the monastery's foundation stones.

🎊 Festivals & Events

Tashilhunpo Monastery Festival CULTURAL
During the second week of the fifth lunar month (around June/July), Tashilhunpo Monastery becomes the scene of a three-day festival, featuring masked dances, the creation of a sand mandala and the unveiling of three huge *thangkas*, one for each day of the festival.

🛏 Sleeping

Shigatse has a good range of decent hotels, most with wi-fi and 24-hour hot water.

Tibet Zangba Hotel HOTEL ¥¥
(藏巴大酒店; Zàngbā Dàjiǔdiàn; ☑ 892 866 9888; 9 Renbu Lu; d/tr ¥280/340; ❊ ☎) This three-star hotel is a good choice with fresh rooms that are modern and carpeted, with fairly modern bathrooms and lots of Tibetan touches. There's a connected Tibetan restaurant. Rooms at the back have stellar views of Tashilhunpo Monastery. No nonsmoking rooms.

Gesar Hotel HOTEL ¥¥¥
(格萨尔酒店; Gésà'ěr Jiǔdiàn; ☑ 892 880 0088; Longjiang Zhonglu, 龙江中路; r standard/deluxe incl breakfast ¥380/480; ❊ @ ☎) This four-star giant has clean and modern Tibetan-style rooms, each decorated with its own *thangka* of Gesar Ling, and a pleasant rooftop teahouse, though the location in the southern suburbs is a bit of a drag. The deluxe rooms are huge and there's 24-hour hot water, but the glass-walled bathrooms won't work unless you and your roommate are close friends.

Qomolangzong Hotel HOTEL ¥¥¥
(乔穆朗宗酒店; Qiáomùlǎngzōng Jiǔdiàn; ☑ 892 866 6333; cnr Shanghai Zhonglu & Zhufeng Lu, 上海中路和珠峰路交叉路口; d incl breakfast ¥978; ❄ ❊ ☎) This plush four-star hotel opened in 2014, offering an impressive lobby of stone and wood, and extremely spacious western-style rooms. Some of the upper-floor rooms have views of Tashilhunpo Monastery. There is a top-floor teahouse-restaurant with beautiful views over the city. Surprisingly little English is spoken.

🍴 Eating

Tashi Choeta DUMPLINGS, TIBETAN ¥
(Xueqiang Lu; 8 dumplings ¥20) This bright restaurant offers Amdo-style food, namely steamed yak-meat momos. And there's Lhasa Beer to wash them down with. Watch the chefs at work inside a glassed-in kitchen at the entrance. The picture menu (no English) is on the wall above. Point out what you want, pay at the counter and choose any table.

★ Third Eye NEPALI ¥¥
(雪莲餐厅, Xuělián Cāntīng; ☑ 892 883 8898; Zhufeng Lu; dishes ¥25-50; ⊙ 9am-10pm) A Nepali-run place that is popular with both locals and tourists. Watch as locals sip *thugpa* (Tibetan noodle soup) while travellers treat their tastebuds to the city's best Indian curries and sizzlers. The chicken tikka masala and the yak steak are both excellent. It's upstairs, next to the Gang Gyan Orchard Hotel.

★ Wordo Tibetan Courtyard TIBETAN ¥¥¥
(吾尔朵大宅院, Wú'ěrduǒ Dà Zháiyuàn; ☑ 892 882 3994; 10 Zhade Xilu; dishes ¥50-70; ⊙ 9.30am-11pm) For something a bit special, head out to this stylish Tibetan restaurant near the Summer Palace of the Panchen Lamas (p949). Sit in one of Tibet's loveliest courtyards, bedecked in swirling prayer flags, and enjoy super-fresh Tibetan specialities such as curried potatoes and potato momos, as well as more ambitious (and pricey) offerings such as roast leg of lamb (¥320).

🛍 Shopping

Shigatse Tibetan Market ARTS & CRAFTS
(Bangjiakong Lu; ⊙ 10am-6pm) In this grimy, open-air market in Shigatse's old town you can pick up low-grade Tibetan crafts and souvenirs, such as prayer wheels, rosaries and jewellery. Bargain hard. The street market just to the east is the best place to get a Tibetan *chuba* (cloak).

If you walk further up the street past the market, you may encounter small shops where prayer flags are being made.

Tibet Gang Gyen Carpet Factory HOMEWARES
(西藏刚坚地毯厂, Xīzàng Gāngjiān Dìtǎn Chǎng; ☑ 139 0892 1399; 9 Zhufeng Lu; ⊙ 9am-1pm & 3-7pm Mon-Sat) This workshop employs local women to weave high-quality wool carpets. Upon arrival you'll be directed to the workshop, where you can watch the craftswomen work, some singing as they weave, dye, trim and spin; you're free to take photos.

ℹ Information

Bank of China – Main Branch (中国银行, Zhōngguó Yínháng; ☑ 892 882 2932; 10 Shanghai Zhonglu, 上海中路,10号; ⊙ 9.30am-6pm Mon-Fri, 11am-4pm Sat & Sun)

Public Security Bureau (PSB, 公安局, Gōng'ānjú; ☑ 892 882 2244; 9 Jilin Lu, 吉林路9号; ⊙ 9.30am-12.30pm & 3.30-6pm Mon-Fri, 10am-1.30pm Sat & Sun) Your guide will likely have to stop here for half an hour to register and/or pick up an alien's travel permit for the Friendship Hwy, Everest Base Camp or western Tibet. It's in the southern suburbs, near the Gesar Hotel.

ℹ Getting There & Around

Tibet Airlines operates daily flights from Shigatse's Peace Airport, 45km east of town, to

FRIENDSHIP HIGHWAY (NEPAL TO TIBET)

The 1000km-or-so stretch of road between Kathmandu and Lhasa is without a doubt one of the most spectacular in the world.

The old route via the border crossing at Kodari (1873m) and Zhangmu (2250m) was badly affected by Nepal's 2015 earthquake and remains closed to international traffic.

The main Nepal–Tibet border crossing has shifted to Rasuwagadhi at the meeting of Nepal's Langtang region and Tibet's Kyirong Valley. Chinese travellers have been using the border crossing for a few years now, but it was only opened to foreigners in 2017. It's a spectacular and little-explored route that allows you to combine a trek in Nepal's Langtang region with a visit to lovely Peiku-tso on the Tibetan side.

The section of road on the Tibetan side is paved, but the Nepali road is slow going, especially during the monsoon months from June to September. Figure on an entire day from Rasuwagadhi to Kathmandu and consider hiring a 4WD for the trip (Rs 16,000).

The new Kyirong route joins the former Kodari route just north of the Lalung-la (4845m) on the Friendship Hwy and continues to Tingri.

It is essential to watch out for the effects of altitude sickness during the early stages of this trip. If you intend to head up to Everest Base Camp (5150m), you really need to slip in a rest day at Tingri or Kyirong. In terms of acclimatisation it is better to fly to Lhasa and then travel back to Kathmandu, rather than the other way around.

China is 2¼ hours ahead of Nepali time.

Chengdu (¥1850). China Eastern also runs two flights a week to Shanghai Hongqiao, stopping in Xi'an (¥3920).

The 250km train spur line from Lhasa to Shigatse opened in late 2014 and international travellers can now theoretically take these trains as part of their guided tour. Though this option may be a lot faster, travelling by train means you miss many opportunities to visit some of the lesser-known monasteries en route from Lhasa, and also the chance to stand breathless at some of the region's high mountain passes.

Central Shigatse can be comfortably explored on foot but many of the hotels are a short drive away. For short trips around town you can use a taxi – anywhere in town costs ¥10.

Lhatse　　拉孜

☑ 0892 / ELEV 3950M

The modern town of Lhatse (Lāzī) is a convenient overnight stop for travellers headed to western Tibet. Lhatse is more or less a one-street town with a small square near the centre. The 3km-long main street runs east–west and used to be part of the Friendship Hwy, but this has now been diverted to the north. Passing traffic will mostly be heading to Everest Base Camp, the Tibet–Nepal border or the turn-off for western Tibet, about 6km out of town past a major checkpoint.

If you have time to kill, you could visit the renovated Changmoche Monastery at the western end of town.

Lhatse is located approximately 150km southwest of Shigatse and some 30km west of the Sakya turn-off.

Lhatse Tibetan Farmer's Hotel　　HOTEL ¥¥
(拉孜农民旅馆, Lāzī Nóngmín Lǚguǎn; ☑ 892 832 2333; 27 Laozhongni Lu, 老中尼路27号; d ¥280; ☎) This courtyard guesthouse has long been popular with foreign travellers. There is an older block of basic rooms with shared squat bathrooms, but the back block offers modern en-suite rooms with Tibetan decor and 24-hour hot water (check the water before handing over your cash).

The hotel also has one of the better **restaurants** (mains ¥15-30) in Lhatse.

Sakya　　萨迦

☑ 0892 / ELEV 4320M

A detour to visit the small town of Sakya (Sàjiā) is a treat on any trip down the Friendship Hwy. The draw is Sakya Monastery, which ranks as one of the most atmospheric, impressive and unique monasteries in Tibet. Moreover, Sakya occupies a pivotal place in Tibetan history.

In recent years Sakya has transformed from a village into a town and the area around the monastery has been developed by a private company to include a huge car park and a hefty entry fee, but Sakya still feels off the grid.

The town is southwest of Shigatse, about 25km off the Southern Friendship Hwy, accessed via a half-paved road through a pretty farming valley.

Sakya is a 25km detour off the Friendship Hwy. En route you'll pass the impressive ridgetop Tonggar Choede Monastery. Just 5km before Sakya at Chonkhor Lhunpo village is the Ogyen Lhakhang, where local farmers go to get blessings from relics said to be able to prevent hailstorms.

★ **Sakya Monastery**   BUDDHIST MONASTERY
(萨迦寺, Sàjiā Sì; ¥45; ⊙9am-6pm) The immense, grey, thick-walled southern monastery is one of Tibet's most impressive constructed sights, and one of the largest monasteries – home to about 200 monks. Established in 1268, it was designed defensively, with watchtowers on each corner of its high walls. Inside, the dimly lit hall exudes a sanctity and is on a scale that few others can rival. Morning is the best time to visit as most chapels are closed over the lunch period.

🛏 Sleeping & Eating

Most people do not stay overnight in Sakya, as the monastery can be visited en route from Shigatse to Lhatse or Shegar, but there are a couple of hotels if you wish to spend more time.

Sakya Farmer's Taste Restaurant TIBETAN ¥
(萨迦农民美食厅, Sàjiā Nóngmín Měishítīng; ☑892 824 2221; Benzhida Donglu, 班智达东路; dishes ¥20-35) Overlooking Sakya's main street, this Tibetan place is located upstairs and has a cosy atmosphere amid Tibetan decor. The waiters are friendly and will help explain the various Tibetan and Chinese dishes available. The food is tasty but portions are small.

Everest Region

For most travellers, Everest Base Camp has become the most popular destination in Tibet, offering the chance to gaze on the magnificent north face of the world's tallest peak, Mt Everest (珠穆朗玛峰, Zhūmùlǎngmǎ Fēng; 8848m). The Tibetan approach provides far better vistas than those on the Nepali side, and access is a lot easier as a road runs all the way to base camp.

Everest's Tibetan name is generally rendered as Qomolangma, and some 27,000 sq km of territory around Everest's Tibetan face have been designated as the Qomolangma Nature Reserve.

Most visitors are content with early-morning views of the mountain from Rongphu Monastery and Everest Base Camp, though adventurous travellers can add in some explorations on foot to their itinerary, and exiting the region via the little-used dirt road to Tingri offers a lot of wow-factor in the form of Himalaya eye-candy.

★ **Everest Base Camp**   BASE
(ཇོ་མོ་གླང་མའི་ལམ་ཁ་ཟིག, 珠峰基地营, Zhūfēng Jīdìyíng) Everest Base Camp (5150m) was first used by the 1924 British Everest expedition. Tourists are no longer allowed to visit the climbing expedition base camp, so most people have their photo taken at the 'Mt Qomolangma Base Camp' marker instead.

In February 2019 Tibet's Everest Base Camp was closed to all visitors to allow for continued clean-up and environmental restoration efforts, begun in 2018 with the removal of 8 tonnes of garbage. The climbers' base camp reopened in mid-2019 for those with climbing permits, and a new camp for non-climbing tourists has been put into operation beside Ronghpu Monastery, where the mountain views are essentially the same as those from the previous tourist camp.

Tour vehicles are now allowed only as far as the new Everest Base Camp tourist centre in the Tibetan village of Chödzom, where travellers must change for government-managed eco-friendly buses (¥120 round-trip) for the remaining 20km to Ronghpu Monastery.

There is no public transport to Everest Base Camp. It's either trek in or come with your own vehicle. From Chay it's 91km to Base Camp; from Tingri it's around 70km on an unpaved road.

Rongphu Monastery   BUDDHIST MONASTERY
(绒布寺, Róngbù Sì; ¥25) Although religious centres have existed in the region since around the 8th century, Rongphu Monastery (4980m) is now the main Buddhist centre in the valley. While not of great antiquity, Rongphu can at least lay claim to being the highest monastery in Tibet and, thus, the world. It's worth walking the short *kora* path around the monastery's exterior walls. The monastery and its large *chörten* make for a superb photograph with Everest casting its head skyward in the background.

ℹ SLEEPING AT EVEREST BASE CAMP

Since the opening of the new Everest Base Camp tourist camp, sleeping options at Everest now boil down to the simple rooms at the **Rongphu Monastery Guesthouse** (绒布寺招待所, Róngbù Sì Zhāodàisuǒ; ☑ 136 2892 1359; dm ¥60, tw without bathroom ¥200) or at tent camps a few hundred metres away. Conditions are quite basic, especially in the shared pit latrines.

ℹ Information

Apart from a normal Tibet Travel Permit, there is a required entry ticket for the Qomolangma Nature Reserve to visit the Everest region, either at the main turn-off from the Friendship Hwy or in Tingri. The ticket costs ¥400 per vehicle plus ¥180 per passenger. Your guide (but not driver) will also need a ticket. Make sure you are clear with your travel agency about whether this cost is included in your trip (it usually isn't).

Your passport and Tibet Travel Permit will be checked at a major checkpoint 6km west of Shegar, where you'll have to walk through a security check in person. Queues can be long here, especially after lunch, as even Chinese and local Tibetans need to register to enter the border region.

Tickets are checked again just before Rongphu Monastery. If you are driving in from Tingri, you'll go to the checkpoint at Lungchang. A final checkpost at Rongphu, just before base camp, will also check your permits.

Tingri   དིང་རི་ 定日

☑ 0892 / ELEV 4330M

The village of Tingri (Dìngrì or Tingri Gankar) comprises a gritty kilometre-long strip of restaurants, guesthouses, loose cattle and truck-repair workshops lining the Friendship Hwy. Generally called Old Tingri, it overlooks a sweeping plain bordered by towering Himalayan peaks (including Everest) and is a common overnight stop for tours heading to or from western Tibet or Nepal, as well as climbing groups coming and going from the nearby peaks. On clear days there are stunning views of Cho Oyu from Tingri. It's pretty much a one-street town: Hwy 318 juts through the centre, where you'll find all of the hotels and restaurants.

Tingri is on the last stretch of the G318 between Lhatse and the Nepal border. Though the previous crossing at Zhangmu is now closed, a smaller road connects across to the new border crossing further east at Kyirong. The turn-off from the Friendship Hwy is located at Km5265 near Xiamude (夏木德), just before the Lalung-la. This then passes north of Shishapangma base camp and south of Peiku-tso (both stunning) to join the road from Saga before climbing to the high Kongtang-la pass into the Kyirong Valley.

An atmospheric unpaved road leads the 70km way between Tingri and Everest Base Camp. Adventurous travellers making a loop back to Lhasa should consider taking this route to really get off the beaten track in truly unspoilt, lunar-like mountainscapes.

Qomolangma Nature Reserve Ticket Office   TOURIST INFORMATION
(☑ 156 9262 6148) Entry tickets to Qomolangma Nature Reserve are available at this office within the compound of the **Snow Leopard Guesthouse** (雪豹客栈, Xuěbào Kèzhàn; ☑ 0892-826 2711; d/tr ¥280/320; 🖭).

Kangar Hotel   HOTEL ¥¥
(岗嘎宾馆, Gǎnggā Bīnguǎn; ☑ 892 826 5777; d/tr ¥260/360; 🖭) This option on the east end of Tingri is wellrun, with western-style rooms and modernish bathrooms, a sunroof sitting area, a restaurant and great views of the mountains. Water pressure can be iffy upstairs, while rooms on the ends of the corridors can get cold due to the lack of sunlight. Still, your best bet in town.

NGARI   མངའ་རིས་

Tibet's far wild west has few permanent settlers but is nevertheless a lodestone to a billion pilgrims from three major religions (Buddhism, Hinduism and Jainism). They are drawn to the twin spiritual power places of Mt Kailash and Lake Manasarovar, two of the world's most fabled and far-flung destinations. Also hidden here are the enigmatic ruins of past kingdoms, entire cities consisting of cave dwellings and some of Tibet's most beautiful remaining murals.

This part of Ngari is a huge, expansive realm of salt lakes, Martian-style deserts, grassy steppes and snow-capped mountains. It's a mesmerising landscape, but it's also intensely remote: a few tents and herds of yaks may be all the signs of human existence you'll come across in half a day's drive.

The tarmacking of the 500km section of road from Saga to Hor Qu means you can now drive from Lhasa to Mt Kailash in as little as three (long) driving days, something unheard of just a decade ago. Resist the temptation to rush, however, and take time to appreciate the scenery and acclimatise.

Saga is the last major town along the southern route and a usual overnight stop, conveniently placed at the junction of roads from Lhasa and Nepal. From here it's a full day's drive to Darchen. If you have a bit of time, consider visits en route to Dargyeling and Tradun monasteries.

If you wish to visit Everest Base Camp en route to Kailash, you can go via the stunning lake views of Peiku-tso before swinging up to Saga.

Darchen & Mt Kailash དར་ཆེན། གངས་རིན་པོ་ཆེ། 塔钦、冈仁波齐峰

☏ 0897 / ELEV 4670M

Going to Ngari and not attempting a *kora* around holy Mt Kailash (Kang Rinpoche, Precious Jewel of Snow in Tibetan) is inconceivable. Kailash dominates the region physically and spiritually, with the sheer awesomeness of its surreal four-sided summit and through the combined faith of over one billion people.

The mountain has been a lodestone to pilgrims and travellers for centuries but until recently few had had set their eyes on it. Improved road conditions are changing this. Large numbers of Indian pilgrims visit the mountain between July and August and hardy Chinese tourists are starting to discover the region.

Mt Kailash is accessed via the grubby town of Darchen (དར་ཆེན།, 塔钦, Tǎqīn), a rapidly expanding settlement of hotel compounds and pilgrim shops. Almost everyone spends a night here before setting off on the *kora*, and many spend a second night after the trek to grab a hot shower and check emails.

Darchen is 3km north of the main Ali–Saga road, about 22km from Barkha, 107km north of Purang, 330km southeast of Ali and a lonely 1200km from Lhasa.

🏃 Activities

The age-old path around Mt Kailash is one of the world's great pilgrimage routes and completely encircles Asia's holiest mountain. With a 5650m pass to conquer, this *kora* is a test of both the mind and the spirit.

There's some gorgeous mountain scenery along this trek, including close-ups of the majestic pyramidal Mt Kailash, but just as rewarding is the chance to see and meet your fellow pilgrims, many of whom have travelled hundreds of kilometres on foot to get here. Apart from local Tibetans, there are normally dozens of Hindus on the *kora* during the main pilgrim season (June to September). Most ride horses, with yak teams carrying their supplies. There are also plenty of Chinese tourists.

The route around Mt Kailash is a simple one: you start by crossing a plain, then head up a wide river valley, climb up and over the 5650m Drölma-la, head down another river valley, and finally cross the original plain to the starting point. It's so straightforward and so perfect a natural circuit that it's easy to see how it has been a pilgrim favourite for thousands of years.

The Mt Kailash trekking season runs from mid-May until mid-October, but trekkers should always be prepared for changeable weather. Snow may be encountered on the Drölma-la at any time of year and the temperature will often drop well below freezing at night. The pass tends to be snowed in from early November to early April.

The *kora* is becoming more and more popular. A tent and your own food are always a nice luxury, but there is now accommodation and simple food at Drira-puk and Zutul-puk. Guides can even book you a room here in advance. Bottled water, beer, instant noodles and tea are available every few hours at teahouse tents. Natural water sources abound, but you should bring some means of water purification. A dirt road now encircles two-thirds of the *kora*, but traffic is light and it's fairly easy to avoid.

Horses, yaks and porters are all available for hire in Darchen, the gateway town to the *kora*. Big groups often hire yaks to carry their supplies, but yaks will only travel in pairs or herds, so you have to hire at least two. Horses are an easier option but are surprisingly expensive because they are in great demand by Indian pilgrims. Most hikers carry their own gear or get by with the services of a local porter (¥210 per day for a minimum of three days). All guides and pack animals have to be arranged through a central **office** (冈仁波齐牛马运输服务中心, Gǎngrén Bōqí Niúmǎ Yùnshū Fúwù Zhōngxīn; ☏ 133 2257 5733) in Darchen.

Your guide will register your group with the **PSB** (公安局, Gōng'ānjú; ☑ 0897-260 7018; ⊙ 24hr) in Darchen. The entrance fee to Mt Kailash is ¥150 per person and is paid at a large entry gate before you arrive in Darchen.

🛏 Sleeping & Eating

Most travellers spend a night in Darchen before the *kora*. Bigger places can be fully booked with large groups of Indian pilgrims during the summer months of June, July and August.

Almost all hotels and even restaurants offer free wi-fi. On the *kora* you can use your mobile phone's 3G connection to go online.

Supplies on the Mt Kailash *kora* are limited to instant noodles, beer and the occasional plate of fried vegetables, so stock up on snacks in Darchen's supermarkets before heading off.

★ Drira-puk Monastery Guesthouse
GUESTHOUSE ¥

(☑ 181 8907 5323; old/new room dm ¥20/80) The quietest and most comfortable accommodation option at Drira-puk is a bed in the monastery guesthouse, which has comfortable new rooms but limited food.

Himalaya Kailash Hotel
HOTEL ¥¥¥

(喜马拉雅冈仁波齐酒店, Xǐmǎlāyǎ Gāngrénbōqíí Jiǔdiàn; ☑ 897 859 500, 139 8997 4987; r ¥580-880; ⊙ May-Oct) Just what you didn't expect in Darchen: a four-star giant, with 102 rooms spread over half a dozen blocks. The grand lobby is impressive and surprisingly stylish, and the comfortable carpeted rooms come with electric blanket and heater. No competition, if it's in your budget.

Qinghai Salar Noodle Shop
CHINESE ISLAMIC ¥

(青海撒拉尔面馆, Qinghai Sālāěr Miànguǎn; mains ¥22-28; 🛜) There's a good range of excellent-value and tasty noodle or rice sets at this tiny but superclean place run by Salar Muslims, an ethnic group from Qinghai. The picture menu on the wall makes ordering a breeze.

Lake Manasarovar
མ་ཕམ་མཚོ་

玛旁雄错

ELEV 4580M

Sacred Lake Manasarovar (Mapham Yumtso, or Victorious Lake, in Tibetan; Mǎpáng Xióngcuò, in Chinese) is the most venerated of Tibet's many lakes and perhaps its most beautiful. With its sapphire-blue waters, sandy shoreline and snow-capped-mountain backdrop, Manasarovar is immediately appealing, and a contrast to the often forbidding terrain of Mt Kailash.

Most visitors base themselves at picturesque Chiu village, site of Chiu Monastery, on the northwestern shore of the lake. Indian pilgrims often drive around the lake, immersing themselves in the sacred waters at some point. You'll also see Tibetan pilgrims walking the four-day kora path around the lake, or inching round on a 40-day prostration.

If you have the time, it's worthwhile travelling around the eastern side of the lake, visiting Seralung and Trugo monasteries en route, and preferably overnighting. It's an easy day slotted in between Hor Qu and Darchen.

The lake area has a one-time admission fee of ¥150 per person (the Mt Kailash fee does not cover this).

There are over a dozen simple guesthouses at Chiu, between the monastery and the lake, with four- or five-bed rooms all costing around ¥65 per bed per night, and sharing a single set of outdoor pit toilets. There's not much to choose between them except perhaps the availability of food and where the big groups are staying. Most are only open May to October.

Chiu, at the northwestern corner of the lake, is 15km south of Barkha junction, from where it is 22km west to Darchen or 22km east to Hor Qu.

The eastern shore of the lake is accessible from Hor Qu, from where a dirt road continues all the way around the lake to Chiu. From Hor Qu it's 8km to Seralung Monastery and a further 24km to Trugo. From Trugo a second dirt road cuts west to join the main paved road south to Purang.

Understand China

History

The epic sweep of China's history can suggest prolonged epochs of peace occasionally convulsed by sudden breakup, internecine division or external attack, yet for much of its history China has been in conflict either internally or with outsiders. The Middle Kingdom's size and shape may have continuously changed – from tiny beginnings by the Yellow River (Huáng Hé) to the subcontinent of today – but an uninterrupted thread of history runs from its earliest roots to the full flowering of Chinese civilisation.

From Oracle Bones to Confucius

The earliest 'Chinese' dynasty, the Shang, was long considered apocryphal. However, archaeological evidence – cattle bones and turtle shells in Henan covered in mysterious scratches, recognised by a scholar as an early form of Chinese writing – proved that a society known as the Shang developed in central China from around 1766 BC. The area it controlled was tiny – perhaps 200km across – but Chinese historians have argued that the Shang was the first Chinese dynasty. By using Chinese writing on 'oracle bones', the dynasty marked its connection with the Chinese civilisation of the present day.

Sometime between 1050 and 1045 BC, a neighbouring group known as the Zhou conquered Shang territory. The Zhou was one of many states competing for power in the next few hundred years, but developments during this period created some of the key sources of Chinese culture that would last till the present day. A constant theme of the first millennium BC was conflict, particularly the periods known as the 'Spring and Autumn' (722–481 BC) and 'Warring States' (475–221 BC).

The Chinese world in the 5th century BC was both warlike and intellectually fertile, in a way similar to ancient Greece during the same period. From this disorder emerged the thinking of Confucius (551–479 BC), whose system of thought and ethics underpinned Chinese culture for 2500 years. A wandering teacher, Confucius dispensed lessons in personal behaviour and statecraft, advocating an ordered and ethical society obedient towards hierarchies and inclined towards ritual. Confucius' desire for an ordered and ethical world was a far cry from the warfare of his times.

So far some 7000 soldiers in the famous Terracotta Army have been found near Xi'an. The great tomb of the first emperor still remains unexcavated, though it is thought to have been looted soon after it was built.

TIMELINE	c 4000 BC	c 1700 BC	c 600 BC
	The first known settlements appear along the Yellow River. The river remains a central cultural reference point for the Chinese throughout history.	Craftsmen of the Shang dynasty master the production of bronzeware (in the form of ritual vessels) in one of the first examples of multiple production in history.	Laotzu (Laozi), founder of Taoism, is supposedly born. The folk religion of Taoism goes on to coexist with later arrivals such as Buddhism in a reflection of Chinese religion's syncretic, rather than exclusive, nature.

Early Empires

The Warring States period ended decisively in 221 BC. The Qin kingdom conquered other states in the central Chinese region and Qin Shi Huang proclaimed himself emperor. The first in a line of dynastic rulers that would last until 1912, Qin Shi Huang would be portrayed in later histories as particularly cruel and tyrannical, but the distinction is dubious: the ensuing Han dynasty (206 BC–AD 220) adopted many of the short-lived Qin's practices of government.

Qin Shi Huang oversaw vast public works projects, including walls built by some 300,000 men, connecting defences into what would become the Great Wall. He unified the currency, measurements and written language, providing the basis for a cohesive state.

Establishing a trend that would echo through Chinese history, a peasant, Liu Bang (256–195 BC), rose up and conquered China, founding the Han dynasty. The dynasty is so important that the name Hàn (汉, 漢) still refers to ethnic Chinese and their language (汉语, Hanyu, 'language of the Han'). Critical to the centralisation of power, Emperor Wu (140–87 BC) institutionalised Confucian norms in government. Promoting merit as well as order, he was the first leader to experiment with examinations for entry into the bureaucracy, but his dynasty was plagued by economic troubles, as estate owners controlled more and more land. Indeed, the issue of land ownership would be a constant problem throughout Chinese history to today. Endemic economic problems and the inability to exercise control over a growing empire, coupled with social unrest that included an uprising by Taoists (known as the Yellow Turbans), led to the collapse and downfall of the Han.

Han trade along the Silk Road demonstrated clearly that China was fundamentally a Eurasian power in its relations with neighbouring peoples. To the north, the Xiongnu (a name given to various nomadic tribes of Central Asia) posed the greatest threat to China. Diplomatic links were also formed with Central Asian tribes, and the great Chinese explorer Zhang Qian provided the authorities with information on the possibilities of trade and alliances in northern India. During the same period, Chinese influence percolated into areas that would later become known as Vietnam and Korea.

Evidence from Han dynasty (206 BC–AD 220) tombs suggests that a popular item of cuisine was a thick vegetable and meat stew, and that flavour enhancers such as soy sauce and honey were also used.

Disunity Restored

Between the early 3rd and late 6th centuries AD, north China witnessed a succession of rival kingdoms vying for power while a potent division formed between north and south. Riven by warfare, the north succumbed to non-Chinese rule, most successfully during the northern Wei dynasty (386–534), founded by the Tuoba, a northern people who

551 BC	214 BC	c 100 BC	c 100 BC
The birth of Confucius. Collected in *The Analects*, his ideas of an ethical, ordered society that operated through hierarchy and self-development would dominate Chinese culture until the early 20th century.	Emperor Qin indentures thousands of labourers to link existing city walls into one Great Wall, made of tamped earth. The brick cladding of the bastion dates from the much later Ming dynasty.	The Silk Road between China and the Middle East takes Chinese goods to places as far flung as Rome.	Buddhism first arrives in China from India. This religious system ends up thoroughly assimilated into Chinese culture and is now more powerful in China than in its country of origin.

embraced Buddhism and left behind some of China's finest Buddhist art, including the famous caves outside Dunhuang. A succession of rival regimes followed until nobleman Yang Jian (d 604) reunified China under the fleeting Sui dynasty (581–618). His son Sui Yangdi contributed greatly to the unification of south and north through construction of the Grand Canal, which was later extended and remained China's most important communication route between south and north until the late 19th century. After instigating three unsuccessful incursions onto Korean soil, resulting in disastrous military setbacks, Sui Yangdi faced revolt and was assassinated in 618 by one of his high officials.

Ban Zhao was the most famous female scholar in early China. Dating from the late 1st century AD, her work *Lessons for Women* advocated chastity and modesty as favoured female qualities.

The Tang: China Looks West

Tang rule (618–907) was an outward-looking time, when China embraced the culture of its neighbours – marriage to Central Asian people or wearing Indian-influenced clothes was part of the era's cosmopolitan élan – and was influenced by the cultures of distant nations that reached the country along the Silk Road. The Chinese nostalgically regard the Tang as their cultural zenith, with Chinatowns around the world still called Tangrenjie (Tang People Streets) to this day. The output of the Tang poets is still regarded as China's finest, as is Tang sculpture, while the dynasty's legal code became a standard for the whole East Asian region.

The Tang was founded by the Sui general Li Yuan, with his achievements consolidated by his son Taizong (r 626–49). Chang'an (modern Xi'an) became the world's most dazzling capital, with its own cosmopolitan foreign quarter, a population of one million people, a market where merchants from as far away as Persia mingled with locals, and an astonishing city wall that eventually enveloped 83 sq km. The city exemplified the Tang devotion to Buddhism, with 91 temples recorded in the city in 722, but a tolerance of, and even absorption with, foreign cultures allowed other faiths a foothold, including Nestorian Christianity, Manichaeism, Islam, Judaism and Zoroastrianism.

Two Nestorian monks smuggled silkworms out of China in AD 550, divulging the jealously guarded method of silk production to the outside world.

Taizong was succeeded by a unique figure – Chinese history's sole reigning woman emperor, Wu Zetian (r 690–705). Under her leadership the empire reached its greatest extent, spreading well north of the Great Wall and far west into inner Asia. Her strong promotion of Buddhism, however, alienated her from the Confucian officials and in 705 she was forced to abdicate in favour of Xuanzong, who would preside over the greatest disaster in the Tang's history: the rebellion of An Lushan.

Xuanzong appointed minorities from the frontiers as generals in the belief that they were so far removed from the political system and society that they would not harbour ideas of rebellion. Nevertheless, it was An Lushan, a general of Sogdian-Turkic parentage, who took advantage of his command in north China to make a bid for imperial power. The

874	c 1000	1215	1286
The Huang Chao rebellion breaks out, which helps reduce the Tang empire to chaos and leads to the fall of the capital in 907.	The major premodern inventions – paper, printing, gunpowder and the compass – are commonly used in China. The economy begins to commercialise and create a countrywide market system.	Genghis Khan conquers Beijing as part of his creation of a massive Eurasian empire under Mongol rule. The Mongols overstretch themselves, however, and neglect good governance.	The Grand Canal is extended to Beijing. Over time the canal becomes a major artery for the transport of grain, salt and other important commodities between north and south China.

fighting lasted from 755 to 763, and although An Lushan was defeated, the Tang's control over China was destroyed forever. It had ceded huge amounts of military and tax-collecting power to provincial leaders to enable them to defeat the rebels, and in doing so dissipated its own potency. A permanent change in the relationship between the government and the provinces formed. Prior to 755 the government had an idea of who owned what land throughout the empire, but after that date the central government's control was permanently weakened. Even today the dilemma has not been fully resolved.

In its last century the Tang withdrew from its former openness, turning more strongly to Confucianism, while Buddhism was outlawed by Emperor Wuzong from 842 to 845. The ban was later modified, but Buddhism never regained its previous power and prestige. The decline of the Tang dynasty was marked by imperial frailty, growing insurgencies, upheaval and chaos.

The Song: Conflict & Prosperity

Further disunity – the fragmentary-sounding Five Dynasties or Ten Kingdoms period – followed the fall of the Tang until the northern Song dynasty (960–1127) was established. The Song dynasty existed in a state of constant conflict with its northern neighbours. The northern Song was a rather small empire coexisting with the non-Chinese Liao dynasty (which controlled a belt of Chinese territory south of the Great Wall that then marked China's northern border) and less happily with the western Xia, another non-Chinese power that pressed hard on the northwestern provinces. In 1126 the Song lost its capital, Kaifeng, to a third non-Chinese people, the Jurchen (previously an ally against the Liao). The Song was driven to its southern capital of Hangzhou for the period of the southern Song (1127–1279), yet the period was culturally rich and economically prosperous.

The full institution of a system of examinations for entry into the Chinese bureaucracy reached fruition during the Song. At a time when brute force decided who was in control in much of medieval Europe, young Chinese men sat tests on the Confucian classics, obtaining office if successful (most were not). The system was heavily biased towards the rich, but was remarkable in its rationalisation of authority, and lasted for centuries. The classical texts set for the examinations became central to the transmission of a sense of elite Chinese culture, even though in later centuries the system's rigidity meant it failed to adapt to social and intellectual change.

China's economy prospered during Song rule, as cash crops and handicraft products became far more central to the economy, and a genuinely China-wide market emerged, which would become even stronger

HISTORY THE SONG: CONFLICT & PROSPERITY

The oldest surviving brick pagoda in China is the Songyue Pagoda, on Song Shan in Henan province, dating from the early 6th century.

The Tang saw the first major rise to power of eunuchs (*huàn-guān*). Often from ethnic minority groups, they were brought to the capital and given positions within the imperial palace. In many dynasties they exercised real influence.

1298–99	1406	1557	c 1600
Marco Polo pens his famous account of his travels to China. Inconsistencies in his story have led some scholars to doubt whether he ever went to China at all.	Ming Emperor Yongle begins construction of the 800 buildings of the Forbidden City. This complex, along with much of the Great Wall, shows the style and size of late-imperial architecture.	The Portuguese establish a permanent trade base in Macau, the first of the European outposts that will eventually lead to imperialist dominance of China until the mid-19th century.	The period of China's dominance as the world's greatest economy begins to end. By 1800 European economies are industrialising and clearly dominant.

during the Ming and Qing dynasties. The sciences and arts also flourished under the Song, with intellectual and technical advances across many disciplines. Kaifeng emerged as an eminent centre of politics, commerce and culture.

The cultural quirk of foot binding appears to have emerged during the Song dynasty. For much of the next few centuries it became a Chinese social norm.

Mongols to Ming

The fall of the Song reinforced notions of China's Eurasian location and growing external threats. Genghis Khan (1167–1227) was beginning his rise to power, turning his gaze on China. He took Beijing in 1215, destroying and rebuilding it. His successors seized Hangzhou, the southern Song capital, in 1276. The court fled and, in 1279, southern Song resistance finally crumbled. Kublai Khan, grandson of Genghis, now reigned over all of China as emperor of the Yuan dynasty. Under Kublai the entire population was divided into categories of Han, Mongol and foreigner, with the top administrative posts reserved for Mongols, even though the examination system was revived in 1315. The latter decision unexpectedly strengthened the role of local landed elites: since elite Chinese could not advance in the bureaucracy, they decided to spend more time tending their large estates instead. Another innovation was the introduction of paper money, though overprinting created a problem with inflation.

The Mongols ultimately proved less adept at governance than warfare, with their empire succumbing to rebellion and eventual vanquishment within a century. Ruling as Ming emperor Hongwu, Zhu Yuanzhang established his capital in Nanjing, but by the early 15th century the court had begun to move back to Beijing, where a hugely ambitious reconstruction project was inaugurated by Emperor Yongle (r 1403–24), building the Forbidden City and devising the layout of the city we see today.

Though the Ming tried to impose a traditional social structure in which people stuck to hereditary occupations, the era was in fact one of great commercial growth and social change. Women became subject to stricter social norms (for instance, widow remarriage was frowned upon), but female literacy also grew. Publishing, via woodblock technology, burgeoned and the novel appeared.

Emperor Yongle, having usurped power from his nephew, was keen to establish his own legitimacy. In 1405 he launched the first of seven great maritime expeditions. Led by the eunuch general Zheng He (1371–1433), the fleet consisted of more than 60 large vessels and 255 smaller ones, carrying nearly 28,000 men. The fourth and fifth expeditions departed in 1413 and 1417, and travelled as far as the present Middle East. The great achievement of these voyages was to bring tribute missions to the capi-

Toilet paper was first used in China as early as the 6th century AD, when it was employed by the wealthy and privileged for sanitary purposes.

1644	1689	1793	1823
Beijing falls to peasant rebel Li Zicheng and the last Ming emperor Chongzhen hangs himself in Jingshan Park; the Qing dynasty is established.	The Treaty of Nerchinsk is signed, delineating the border between China and Russia. This is the first modern border agreement in Chinese history, as well as the longest lasting.	British diplomat Lord Macartney visits Beijing with British industrial products, but is told by the Qianlong emperor that China has no need of his merchandise.	The British are importing roughly 7000 chests of opium annually – with about 63.5kg of opium per chest, enough to supply one million addicts – compared with 1000 chests in 1773.

tal, including two embassies from Egypt. The emperors who succeeded Yongle had little interest in continuing the voyages, however, and China dropped anchor on its global maritime explorations.

The Great Wall was re-engineered and clad in brick, while ships also arrived from Europe, presaging an overseas threat that would develop from entirely different directions. Traders were quickly followed by missionaries, and the Jesuits, led by the formidable Matteo Ricci, made their way inland and established a presence at court. Ricci learned fluent Chinese and spent years agonising over how Christian tenets could be made attractive in a Confucian society with distinctive norms. The Portuguese presence linked China directly to trade with the New World, which had opened up in the 16th century. New crops, such as potatoes, maize, cotton and tobacco, were introduced, further stimulating the commercial economy. Merchants often lived opulent lives, building fine private gardens (as in Suzhou) and buying delicate flowers and fruits.

The Ming was eventually undermined by internal power struggles. Natural disasters, including drought and famine, combined with a menace from the north: the Manchu, a nomadic warlike people, who saw the turmoil within China and invaded.

The Qing: the Path to Dynastic Dissolution

After conquering just a small part of China and assuming control in the disarray, the Manchu named their new dynasty the Qing (1644–1911). Once ensconced in the (now torched) Forbidden City, the Manchu realised they needed to adapt their nomadic way of life to suit the agricultural civilisation of China. Threats from inner Asia were neutralised by incorporating the Qing homeland of Manchuria into the empire, as well as that of the Mongols, whom they had subordinated. Like the Mongols before them, the conquering Manchu found themselves in charge of a civilisation whose government they had defeated, but whose cultural power far exceeded their own. The result was quite contradictory: on the one hand, Qing rulers took great pains to win the allegiance of high officials and cultural figures by displaying a familiarity and respect for traditional Chinese culture; but on the other hand, the Manchu rulers enforced strict rules of social separation between the Han and Manchu. The Qing flourished most greatly under three emperors who ruled for a total of 135 years: Kangxi, Yongzheng and Qianlong.

Much of the map of China that we know today derives from the Qing period. Territorial expansion and expeditions to regions of Central Asia spread Chinese power and culture further than ever. The expansion of the 18th century was fuelled by economic and social changes. The

A Chinese woodblock-printed copy of the *Diamond Sutra*, kept in the British Library, is the earliest dated printed book, created in AD 868. Visit the library website (www.bl.uk/onlinegallery/sacredtexts/diamondsutra.html) to turn the pages of the sutra online.

1839	1842	1856	1898
The Qing official Lin Zexu demands that British traders at Guangzhou hand over 20,000 chests of opium, leading the British to provoke the First Opium War in retaliation.	The Treaty of Nanjing concludes the First Opium War. China is forced to hand over Hong Kong Island to the British and open up five Chinese ports to foreign trade.	Hong Xiuquan claims to be Jesus' younger brother and starts the Taiping uprising. With the Nian and Muslim uprisings, the Taiping greatly undermines the authority of the Qing dynasty.	Emperor Guangxu permits major reforms, including new rights for women, but is thwarted by the Dowager Empress Cixi, who has many reformers arrested and executed.

discovery of the New World by Europeans in the 15th century led to a new global market in American food crops, such as chillies and sweet potatoes, allowing food crops to be grown in more barren regions, where wheat and rice had not flourished. In the 18th century the Chinese population doubled from around 150 million to 300 million people.

Historians now take very seriously the idea that in the 18th century China was among the most advanced economies in the world. The impact of imperialism would help commence China's slide down the table, but the seeds of decay had been sown long before the Opium Wars of the 1840s. Put simply, as China's size expanded, its state remained too small. China's dynasty failed to expand the size of government to cope with the new realities of a larger China.

War & Reform

For the Manchu, the single most devastating incident was not either of the Opium Wars, but the far more destructive anti-Qing Taiping Rebellion of 1850–64, an insurgency motivated partly by a foreign credo (Christianity). Established by Hakka leader Hong Xiuquan, the Heavenly Kingdom of Great Peace (Taiping Tianguo) banned opium and intermingling between the sexes, made moves to redistribute property and was fiercely anti-Manchu. The Qing eventually reconquered the Taiping capital at Nanjing, but upwards of 20 million Chinese died in the uprising.

The events that finally toppled the dynasty, however, came in rapid succession. Foreign imperialist incursions continued and Western powers nibbled away at China's coastline. Shanghai, Qingdao, Tianjin, Gulang Yu, Shantou, Yantai, Weihai, Ningbo and Beihai would all either fall under semi-colonial rule or enclose foreign concessions. Hong Kong was a British colony and Macau was administered by the Portuguese. Attempts at self-strengthening were dealt a brutal blow by the Sino-Japanese War of 1894–95. Fought over control of Korea, it ended with the humiliating destruction of the new Qing navy. Not only was Chinese influence in Korea lost, but Taiwan was also ceded to Japan.

Japan itself was a powerful Asian example of reform. In 1868 Japan's rulers, unnerved by ever-greater foreign encroachment, had overthrown the centuries-old system of the Shōgun, who acted as regent for the emperor. An all-out program of modernisation, including a new army, constitution, educational system and railway network, was launched, all of which gave Chinese reformers a lot to ponder.

One of the boldest proposals for change, which drew heavily on the Japanese model, was the program put forward in 1898 by reformers including the political thinker Kang Youwei (1858–1927). However, in September 1898 the reforms were abruptly halted, as the Dowager Empress Cixi, fearful of a coup, placed the emperor under house arrest and

In the 18th century the Chinese used an early form of vaccination against smallpox that required not an injection but rather the blowing of serum up the patient's nose.

1898	1900	1904–05	1905
The New Territories adjoining Kowloon in Hong Kong are leased to the British for 99 years, eventually returning, along with the rest of Hong Kong, in 1997.	The Hanlin Academy in Beijing – a centre of Chinese learning and literature – is accidentally torched by Chinese troops during the Boxer Rebellion, destroying its priceless collection of books.	The Russo-Japanese War is fought entirely on Chinese territory. The victory of Japan is the first triumph by an Asian power over a European one.	Major reforms in the late Qing dynasty include the abolition of the 1000-year-long tradition of examinations in the Confucian classics to enter the Chinese bureaucracy.

executed several of the leading advocates of change. Two years later Cixi made a decision that helped to seal the Qing's fate. In 1900 north China was convulsed by attacks from a group of peasant rebels whose martial arts techniques led them to be labelled the Boxers, and who sought to expel foreigners and kill Chinese Christian converts. In a major miscalculation the dynasty declared its support for the Boxers in June. Eventually a multinational foreign army forced its way into China and defeated the uprising, which had besieged the foreign Legation Quarter in Beijing. The imperial powers then demanded huge financial reparations from the Qing. In 1902 the dynasty reacted by implementing the Xinzheng (New Governance) reforms. This set of reforms, now half-forgotten in contemporary China, looks remarkably progressive, even set against the standards of the present day.

The Cantonese revolutionary Sun Yatsen (1866–1925) remains one of the few modern historical figures respected in both China and Taiwan. Sun and his Revolutionary League made multiple attempts to undermine Qing rule in the late 19th century, raising sponsorship and support from a wide-ranging combination of the Chinese diaspora, the newly emergent middle class and traditional secret societies.

The end of the Qing dynasty arrived swiftly. Throughout China's southwest, popular resentment against the dynasty had been fuelled by reports that railway rights in the region were being sold to foreigners. A local uprising in the city of Wuhan in October 1911 was discovered early, leading the rebels to take over command in the city and hastily declare independence from the Qing dynasty. Within a space of days, then weeks, most of China's provinces did likewise. Provincial assemblies across China declared themselves in favour of a republic, with Sun Yatsen (who was not even in China at the time) as their candidate for president.

> Qing emperor Kangxi sponsored a vast encyclopedia of Chinese culture, which is still read by scholars today.

The Republic: Instability & Ideas

The Republic of China lasted less than 40 years on the mainland (1912–1949) and continues to be regarded as an unstable period in modern Chinese history, when the country was under threat from what many described as 'imperialism from without and warlordism from within'. Yet there was also breathing room for new ideas and culture.

Sun Yatsen returned to China and only briefly served as president, before having to make way for militarist leader Yuan Shikai. In 1912 China held its first general election, and it was Sun's newly established Kuomintang (Nationalist; Guómíndǎng, literally 'Party of the National People') party that emerged as the largest grouping. Parliamentary democracy did not last long, as the Kuomintang itself was outlawed by Yuan, and Sun had to flee into exile in Japan. However, after Yuan's death in 1916, the country split into rival regions ruled by militarist

1908	1911	1912	1915
Two-year-old Puyi ascends the throne as China's last emperor. Local elites and new classes such as businessmen no longer support the dynasty, leading to its ultimate downfall.	Revolution spreads across China as local governments withdraw support for the dynasty, and instead back a republic under the presidency of Sun Yatsen (fundraising in the US at the time).	Yuan Shikai, leader of China's most powerful regional army, goes to the Qing court to announce that the game is up. On 12 February the last emperor, six-year-old Puyi, abdicates.	Japan makes the '21 demands', which would give it massive political, economic and trading rights in parts of China. Europe's attention is distracted by WWI.

warlord-leaders. Supposedly 'national' governments in Beijing often controlled only parts of northern or eastern China and had no real claim to control over the rest of the country. Also, in reality, the foreign powers still had control over much of China's domestic and international situation. Britain, France, the US and the other Western powers showed little desire to lose those rights, such as extraterritoriality and tariff control.

Shanghai became the focal point for the contradictions of Chinese modernity. By the early 20th century, Shanghai was a wonder not just of China but of the world, with skyscrapers, art deco apartment blocks, neon lights, women (and men) in outrageous new fashions, and a vibrant, commercially minded, take-no-prisoners mindset. The racism that accompanied imperialism was visible every day, as Europeans kept themselves separate from the Chinese. Yet the glamour of modernity was undeniable too, as workers flocked from rural areas to make a living in the city, and Chinese intellectuals sought out French fashion, British architecture and American movies. In the prewar period Shanghai had more millionaires than anywhere else in China, yet its inequalities and squalor would also inspire the first congress of the Chinese Communist Party (CCP) in 1921.

DIRTY FOREIGN MUD

Although trade in opium had been banned in China by imperial decree at the end of the 18th century, the cohong (local merchants' guild) in Guangzhou helped ensure that it continued, and fortunes were amassed on both sides. When the British East India Company lost its monopoly on China trade in 1834, imports of the drug increased to 40,000 chests a year.

In 1839 the Qing government sent Imperial Commissioner Lin Zexu to stamp out the opium trade once and for all. Lin successfully blockaded the British in Guangzhou and publicly burned the 'foreign mud' in Humen. Furious, the British sent an expeditionary force of 4000 men from the Royal Navy to exact reparations and secure favourable trade arrangements.

What would become known as the First Opium War began in June 1840 when British forces besieged Guangzhou and forced the Chinese to cede five ports to the British. With the strategic Yangzi River city of Nanking (Nanjing) under immediate threat, the Chinese were forced to accept Britain's terms in the Treaty of Nanking.

The treaty abolished the monopoly system of trade, opened the 'treaty ports' to British residents and foreign trade, exempted British nationals from all Chinese laws and ceded the island of Hong Kong to the British 'in perpetuity'. The treaty, signed in August 1842, set the scope and character of the unequal relationship between China and the West for the next half-century.

1916	1926	1927	1930s
Yuan Shikai tries to declare himself emperor. He is forced to withdraw and remain president, but dies of uraemia later that year. China splits into areas ruled by rival militarists.	Kuomintang and communists unite under Soviet advice to bring China together by force, then establish a Kuomintang government.	Kuomintang leader Chiang Kaishek turns on the communists in Shanghai and Guangzhou, having thousands killed and forcing the communists to turn to a rural-based strategy.	Cosmopolitan Shanghai is the world's fifth-largest city (the largest in the Far East), supporting a polyglot population of four million people.

The militarist government that held power in Beijing in 1917 provided 96,000 Chinese to serve on the Western Front in Europe in support of the Allies, not as soldiers but as trench-diggers and labourers. This involvement in WWI led to one of the most important events in China's modern history: the student demonstrations of 4 May 1919.

Double-dealing by the Western Allies and Chinese politicians who had made secret deals with Japan led to an unwelcome discovery for the Chinese diplomats at the Paris Peace Conference in 1919. Germany had been defeated, but its Chinese territories – such as Qingdao – were not to be returned to China but would instead go to Japan. Five days later, on 4 May 1919, some 3000 students gathered in front of the Gate of Heavenly Peace in central Beijing, and then marched to the house of a Chinese government minister closely associated with Japan. Once there, they broke in and destroyed the house. Over in a few hours, the event immediately found a place in modern Chinese folklore.

The student demonstration came to symbolise a much wider shift in Chinese society and politics. The May 4th Movement, as it became known, was associated closely with the New Culture, underpinned by the electrifying ideas of 'Mr Science' and 'Mr Democracy'. In literature, a May Fourth generation of authors wrote works attacking the Confucianism that they felt had brought China to its current crisis, and explored new issues of sexuality and self-development. The CCP, later the mastermind of the world's largest peasant revolution, was created in the intellectual turmoil of the movement, with many of its founding figures associated with Peking University, including Chen Duxiu (dean of humanities), Li Dazhao (head librarian) and the young Mao Zedong, a mere library assistant.

Ping-pong (*pīngpāngqiú*) may be China's national sport (*guóqiú*), but it was invented as an after-dinner game by British Victorians who named it wiff-waff and first used a ball made from champagne corks.

The Northern Expedition

After years of vainly seeking international support for his cause, Sun Yat-sen found allies in the newly formed Soviet Russia. The Soviets ordered the fledgling CCP to ally itself with the much larger 'bourgeois' party, the Kuomintang. Their alliance was attractive to Sun: the Soviets would provide political training, military assistance and finance. From their base in Guangzhou, the Kuomintang and CCP trained together from 1923 in preparation for their mission to reunite China.

Sun died of cancer in 1925. The succession battle in the party coincided with a surge in antiforeign feeling that accompanied the May Thirtieth Incident when 13 labour demonstrators were killed by British police in Shanghai on 30 May 1925. Under Soviet advice the Kuomintang and CCP prepared for their 'Northern Expedition', the big 1926 push north that was supposed to finally unite China. In 1926–27 the Soviet-trained National Revolutionary Army made its way slowly north, fighting,

1931	1935	1937	1939
Japan invades Manchuria (northeast China), provoking an international crisis and forcing Chiang to consider anti-Japanese, as well as anticommunist, strategies.	Mao Zedong begins his rise to paramount power at the conference at Zunyi, held in the middle of the Long March to the northwest, while on the run from the Kuomintang.	The Japanese and Chinese clash at Wanping, near Beijing, on 7 July, sparking the conflict that the Chinese call the 'War of Resistance', which only ends in 1945.	On 3–4 May Japanese carpet bombing devastates the temporary Chinese capital of Chongqing. From 1938 to 1943 Chongqing is one of the world's most heavily bombed cities.

bribing or persuading its opponents into accepting Kuomintang control. The most powerful military figure turned out to be an officer from Zhejiang named Chiang Kaishek (1887–1975). Trained in Moscow, Chiang moved steadily forward and finally captured the great prize, Shanghai, in March 1927. However, a horrific surprise was in store for his communist allies. The Soviet advisers had not impressed Chiang and he was increasingly convinced that the communists aimed to use their cooperation with the Kuomintang to seize control themselves. Instead, Chiang struck first. Using local thugs and soldiers, Chiang organised a lightning strike by rounding up CCP activists and union leaders in Shanghai and killing thousands of them.

The first railroad in China was the Woosung Railway, which opened in 1876, running between Shanghai and Wusong. It operated for less than a year before being dismantled and shipped to Taiwan.

Kuomintang Rule

Chiang Kaishek's Kuomintang government officially came to power in 1928 through a combination of military force and popular support. Marked by corruption, it suppressed political dissent with great ruthlessness. Yet Chiang's government also kick-started a major industrialisation effort, greatly augmented China's transport infrastructure and successfully renegotiated what many Chinese called 'unequal treaties' with Western powers. In its first two years, the Kuomintang doubled the length of highways in China and increased the number of students studying engineering. The government never really controlled more than a few (very important) provinces in the east, however, and China remained significantly disunited. Regional militarists continued to control much of western China, the Japanese invaded and occupied Manchuria in 1931, and the communists re-established themselves in the northwest.

In 1934 Chiang Kaishek launched his own ideological counterargument to communism: the New Life Movement. This was supposed to be a complete spiritual renewal of the nation through a modernised version of traditional Confucian values, such as propriety, righteousness and loyalty. The New Life Movement demanded that the renewed citizens of the nation must wear frugal but clean clothes, consume products made in China rather than seek luxurious foreign goods, and behave in a hygienic manner. Yet Chiang's ideology never had much success. Against a background of massive agricultural and fiscal crisis, prescriptions about what to wear and how to behave lacked popular appeal.

The Long March

The communists had not stood still, and after Chiang's treachery most of what remained of the CCP fled to the countryside. A major centre of activity was the communist stronghold in impoverished Jiangxi province, where the party began to try out systems of government that would eventually bring them to power. However, by 1934 Chiang's previously in-

1941	1941	1943	1946
In the base area at Yan'an (Shaanxi), the 'Rectification' program begins, remoulding the Communist Party into an ideology shaped principally by Mao Zedong.	The Japanese attack the US at Pearl Harbor. China becomes a formal ally of the US, USSR and Britain in WWII, but is treated as a secondary partner at best.	Chiang Kaishek negotiates an agreement with the Allies that, when Japan is defeated, Western imperial privileges in China will end forever, marking the twilight of Western imperial power in China.	Communists and the Kuomintang fail to form a coalition government, plunging China back into civil war. Communist organisation, morale and ideology all prove key to the communist victory.

effective 'extermination campaigns' were making the CCP's position in Jiangxi untenable and the Red Army found itself increasingly encircled by Nationalist troops, prompting the CCP to commence its legendary Long March. Travelling over 6400km, just 4000 of the original 80,000 communists who set out eventually arrived, exhausted, in distant Shaanxi province in the northwest, far out of the reach of the Kuomintang. It seemed possible that within a matter of months, however, Chiang would attack again and wipe them out.

The approach of war saved the CCP. There was growing public discontent at Chiang Kaishek's seeming unwillingness to fight the Japanese, a perception that was perhaps unfair. The Kuomintang had undertaken retraining of key regiments in the army under German advice, and also started to plan for a wartime economy from 1931, spurred on by the Japanese invasion of Manchuria. Events came to a head in December 1936, however, when the Chinese militarist leader of Manchuria (General Zhang Xueliang) and the CCP kidnapped Chiang. As a condition of his release, Chiang agreed to an openly declared United Front – the Kuomintang and communists would put aside their differences and join forces against Japan.

War & the Kuomintang

China's status as a major participant in WWII is often overlooked or forgotten in the West. The Japanese invasion of China, which began in 1937, was merciless, with the notorious Nanjing Massacre (also known as the Rape of Nanjing) just one of a string of war crimes committed by the Japanese Army during its conquest of eastern China. The government had to operate in exile from the far southwestern hinterland of China, as its area of greatest strength and prosperity, China's eastern seaboard, was lost to Japanese occupation.

It is now acknowledged that both the Kuomintang and the communists played important roles in defeating Japan. Chiang, not Mao, was the internationally acknowledged leader of China during this period, and despite his government's multitude of flaws, he maintained resistance to the end. However, his government was also increasingly trapped, having retreated to Sichuan province and a temporary capital at Chongqing. Safe from land attack by Japan, the city still found itself under siege, subjected to some of the heaviest bombing in the war. From 1940 supply routes were cut off as the road to Burma was closed by Britain, under pressure from Japan, and Vichy France closed connections to Vietnam. Though the US and Britain brought China on board as an ally against Japan after the bombing of Pearl Harbor on 7 December 1941, the Allied 'Europe First' strategy meant that China was always treated as a secondary theatre of war. Chiang Kaishek's corruption and leadership qualities

Paul French's *Midnight in Peking* (2012) is a gripping true-crime murder-mystery book examining the brutal murder of Pamela Werner, daughter of a retired British diplomat, in 1937 Peking.

1949	1957	1958	1961
Mao Zedong stands on top of the Gate of Heavenly Peace in Beijing on 1 October, and announces the formation of the People's Republic of China (PRC), saying, 'The Chinese people have stood up'.	A brief period of liberalisation occurs under the 'Hundred Flowers Movement', but criticisms of the regime lead Mao to crack down and imprison or exile thousands of dissidents.	During the Taiwan Straits Crisis, Mao's government fires missiles near islands under the control of Taiwan in an attempt to prevent a rapprochement between the US and USSR in the Cold War.	Mass starvation is a consequence of the Great Leap Forward. Politburo members Liu Shaoqi and Deng Xiaoping reintroduce limited market reforms, which lead to their condemnation during the Cultural Revolution.

were heavily criticised, and while these accusations were not groundless, without Chinese Kuomintang armies (which kept one million Japanese troops bogged down in China for eight years), the Allies' war in the Pacific would have been far harder. The communists had an important role as guerrilla fighters, but did far less fighting in battle than the Kuomintang.

The real winners from WWII, however, were the communists. They undertook important guerrilla campaigns against the Japanese across northern and eastern China, but the really key changes were taking place in the bleak, dusty hill country centred on the small town of Yan'an, capital of the CCP's largest stronghold. The 'Yan'an way' that developed in those years solidified many CCP policies: land reform involving redistribution of land to the peasants, lower taxes, a self-sufficient economy, ideological education and, underpinning it all, the CCP's military force, the Red Army. By the end of the war with Japan, the communist areas had expanded massively, with 900,000 troops in the Red Army, and party membership at a new high of 1.2 million.

Chiang Kaishek's New Life Movement and the Chinese Communist Party ideology were attempts to mobilise society through renewal of the individual, but only the communists advocated class war.

Above all, the war with Japan had helped the communists come back from the brink of the disaster they had faced at the end of the Long March. With their common enemy defeated following the Japanese surrender in 1945, the Kuomintang and communists then resumed fighting in 1946 and after three long years of heavy combat, the CCP finally seized victory in 1949. On 1 October 1949, Mao declared the establishment of the People's Republic of China in Beijing's Tian'anmen Square.

Chiang Kaishek fled to the island of Formosa (Taiwan), which China had regained from Japan after WWII. He took with him China's gold reserves and the remains of his air force and navy, and set up the Republic of China (ROC), naming his new capital Taipei (台北, Táiběi).

Mao's China

Mao's China desired, above all, to exercise ideological control over its population. It called itself 'New China', with the idea that the whole citizenry, down to the remotest peasants, should find a role in the new politics and society. The success of Mao's military and political tactics also meant that the country was, for the first time since the 19th century, united under a strong central government.

Most Westerners – and bourgeois Western influences – were swiftly removed from the country. The US refused to recognise the new state at all. However, the 1950s marked the high point of Soviet influence on Chinese politics and culture. Mao's experiences had convinced him that only violent change could shake up the relationship between landlords and their tenants, or capitalists and their employees, in a China that was still highly traditional. The first year of the regime saw 40% of the land redistributed to poor peasants. At the same time, one million or so

1966	1972	1973	1976
The Cultural Revolution breaks out, and Red Guards demonstrate in cities across China. The movement is marked by violence as a catalyst for transforming society.	US President Richard Nixon visits China, marking a major rapprochement during the Cold War and the start of full diplomatic relations between the two countries.	Deng Xiaoping returns to power as deputy premier. The modernising faction in the party fights with the Gang of Four, who support the continuing Cultural Revolution.	Mao Zedong dies, aged 83. The Gang of Four are arrested by his successor and put on trial, where they are blamed for all the disasters of the Cultural Revolution.

Workers' statue, Tian'anmen Square (p75), Beijing

people condemned as 'landlords' were persecuted and killed. The joy of liberation was real for many Chinese, but campaigns of terror were also real and the early 1950s was no golden age.

As relations with the Soviets broke down in the mid-1950s, the CCP leaders' thoughts turned to economic self-sufficiency. Mao, supported by Politburo colleagues, proposed the policy known as the Great Leap Forward (Dàyuèjìn), a highly ambitious plan to harness the power of socialist economics to boost production of steel, coal and electricity. Agriculture was to reach an ever-higher level of collectivisation. Family structures were broken up as communal dining halls were established: people were urged to eat their fill, as the new agricultural methods would ensure plenty for all, year after year.

1980	1987	1988	1989
The one-child policy is enforced. The state adopts it as a means of reducing the population, but at the same time it imposes unprecedented control over the personal liberty of women.	*The Last Emperor*, filmed in the Forbidden City, collects an Oscar for Best Picture, and marks a new openness in China towards the outside world.	The daring series *River Elegy* (Héshāng) is broadcast on national TV. It is a devastating indictment of dictatorship and Mao's rule in particular, and is banned in China after 1989.	Hundreds of civilians are killed by Chinese troops in the streets around Tian'anmen Sq. No official reassessment has been made, but rumours persist of deep internal conflict within the party.

However, the Great Leap Forward was a horrific failure. Its lack of economic realism caused a massive famine that killed tens of millions – historian Frank Dikötter posits a minimum figure of 45 million deaths in his *Mao's Great Famine* (2010), a figure greater than the total number of casualties in WWI. Yang Jisheng's *Tombstone: The Great Chinese Famine, 1958–1962* (2012) conservatively estimates there were 36 million deaths. Yet the return to a semi-market economy in 1962, after the Leap had comprehensively ended, did not dampen Mao's enthusiasm for revolutionary renewal. This led to the last and most fanatical of the campaigns that marked Mao's China: the Cultural Revolution of 1966–76.

Cultural Revolution

Mao had become increasingly concerned that post-Leap China was slipping into 'economism' – a complacent satisfaction with rising standards of living that would blunt people's revolutionary fervour. Mao was particularly concerned that the young generation might grow up with a dimmed spirit of revolution. For these reasons Mao decided upon a massive campaign of ideological renewal, in which he would attack his own party.

Still the dominant figure in the CCP, Mao used his prestige to undermine his own colleagues. In the summer of 1966 posters in large, handwritten characters appeared at prominent sites, including Peking University, demanding that figures such as Liu Shaoqi (president of the PRC) and Deng Xiaoping (senior Politburo member) must be condemned as 'takers of the capitalist road'. Top leaders suddenly disappeared from sight, only to be replaced by unknowns, such as Mao's wife Jiang Qing and her associates, later dubbed the 'Gang of Four'. Meanwhile, an all-pervasive cult of Mao's personality took over. One million youths at a time, known as Red Guards, would flock to hear Mao in Tian'anmen Sq. Posters and pictures of Mao were everywhere. The Red Guards were not ashamed to admit their tactics were violent. Immense violence permeated throughout society: teachers, intellectuals and landlords were killed in their thousands. Encouraged to smash remnants of the past, homes were raided and antiquities looted or destroyed by Red Guards, while imperial and religious sites across China were defaced, damaged or demolished.

While Mao initiated and supported the Cultural Revolution, it was also genuinely popular among many young people (who had less to lose and more to gain). However, police authority effectively disappeared, creative activity came to a virtual standstill and academic research was grounded.

The Cultural Revolution could not last. Worried by the increasing violence, the army forced the Red Guards off the streets in 1969. The early

The ghostly shadows of Cultural Revolution slogans can be hard to find in large and modern cities, but are quite a common sight in rural destinations such as the towns of Pingyao and Fenghuang and small historic villages across China.

1997	2001	2004	2006
Hong Kong is returned to the People's Republic of China. Widespread fears that China will immediately interfere directly in its government prove wrong, but its politics become more sensitive to Beijing.	China joins the World Trade Organization, giving it a seat at the top table that decides global norms on economics and finance.	The world's first commercially operating Maglev train begins scorching a trail across Shanghai's Pudong district, reaching a top speed of 431km/h.	The Three Gorges Dam is completed. Significant parts of the landscape of western China are lost beneath the waters, but energy is also provided for the expanding Chinese economy.

1970s saw a remarkable rapprochement between the US and China: the former was desperate to extricate itself from the quagmire of the Vietnam War; the latter, terrified of an attack from the now-hostile USSR. Secretive diplomatic manoeuvres led, eventually, to the official visit of US President Richard Nixon to China in 1972, which began the reopening of China to the West. Slowly the Cultural Revolution began to cool down, but its brutal legacy survives today. Many of those guilty of murder and violence re-entered society with little or no judgement or punishment, while today's CCP discourages open analysis and debate of the 'decade of chaos'.

Reform & Protest

Mao died in 1976, to be succeeded by the little-known Hua Guofeng (1921–2008). Within two years Hua had been outmanoeuvred by the greatest survivor of 20th-century Chinese politics, Deng Xiaoping. Deng had been purged twice during the Cultural Revolution, but after Mao's death he was able to reach supreme leadership in the CCP with a radical program. In particular, Deng recognised that the Cultural Revolution had been highly damaging economically to China. He enlisted a policy slogan originally invented by Mao's pragmatic prime minister, Zhou Enlai – the 'Four Modernisations'. The party's task would be to set China on the right path in four areas: agriculture, industry, national defence, and science and technology.

To make this policy work, many of the assumptions of the Mao era were abandoned. The first highly symbolic move of the 'reform era' (as the post-1978 period is known) was the breaking down of the collective farms. Farmers were able to sell a proportion of their crops on the free market, and urban and rural areas were also encouraged to establish small local enterprises. 'To get rich is glorious,' Deng declared, adding, 'It doesn't matter if some areas get rich first'. As part of this encouragement of entrepreneurship, Deng designated four areas on China's coast as Special Economic Zones (SEZs), which would be particularly attractive to foreign investors.

The new freedoms that the urban middle classes enjoyed created the appetite for more. After student protests demanding further opening up of the party in 1985–86, the prime minister (and relative liberal) Hu Yaobang was forced to resign in 1987 and take responsibility for allowing social forces to get out of control. He was replaced as general secretary by Zhao Ziyang, who was more conservative politically, though an economic reformer. In April 1989 Hu Yaobang died, and students around China used the occasion of his death to organise protests against the continuing role of the CCP in public life. At Peking University, the breeding ground of the May Fourth demonstrations of 1919, students declared

Read *The Cultural Revolution: A People's History, 1962–1976* (2016) by Frank Dikötter for the history; see Zhang Yimou's film *To Live* (1994) to understand the emotions.

2008	2008	2008	2009
Beijing hosts the Summer Olympic Games and Paralympics. The Games go smoothly and are widely considered to be a great success in burnishing China's image overseas.	Violent riots in Lhasa, Tibet, again put the uneasy region on centre stage. Protests spread to other Tibetan areas in Gansu, Sichuan and Qinghai provinces.	A huge 8.0-magnitude earthquake convulses Sichuan province, leaving 87,000 dead or missing and rendering millions homeless.	July riots in Ürümqi leave hundreds dead as interethnic violence flares between Uyghurs and Han Chinese. Beijing floods the region with soldiers and implements a 10-month internet blackout.

the need for 'science and democracy', the modernising watchwords of 80 years earlier, to be revived.

In spring 1989 Tian'anmen Sq was the scene of an unprecedented demonstration. At its height, nearly a million Chinese workers and students, in a rare cross-class alliance, filled the space in front of the Gate of Heavenly Peace, with the CCP profoundly embarrassed to have the world's media record such events. By June 1989 the numbers in the square had dwindled to only thousands, but those who remained showed no signs of moving. Martial law was imposed and on the night of 3 June and early hours of 4 June, tanks and armoured personnel carriers were sent in. The death toll in Beijing has never been officially confirmed, but it seems likely to have been in the high hundreds or even more. Hundreds of people associated with the movement were arrested, imprisoned or forced to flee to the West.

For some three years, China's politics were almost frozen, but in 1992 Deng, the man who had sent in the tanks, made his last grand public gesture. That year he undertook what Chinese political insiders called his 'southern tour', or *nánxún*. By visiting Shenzhen, Deng indicated that the economic policies of reform were not going to be abandoned. The massive growth rates that the Chinese economy has posted ever since have justified his decision. Deng also made another significant choice: grooming Jiang Zemin – the mayor of Shanghai, who had peacefully dissolved demonstrations in Shanghai in a way that the authorities in Beijing had not – as his successor by appointing him as general secretary of the party in 1989.

Deng died in 1997, the same year that Hong Kong returned to China under a 'one country, two systems' agreement with the UK, which would maintain the ex-British colony's independence in all aspects except defence and foreign affairs for the next 50 years. Macau followed suit two years later. Faced with a multitude of social problems brought on by inequalities spawned by the Deng years, President Jiang Zemin, with Zhu Rongji as premier, sought to bring economic stability to China while strengthening the centralised power of the state and putting off much-needed political reforms. Faced with a protest of up to 10,000 Falun Gong adherents outside Beijing's Zhongnanhai in April 1999, Jiang branded the movement a cult and sought its eradication in China through imprisonment and detention, backed up by a draconian propaganda campaign.

One product of the new freedom of the 1980s was a revived Chinese film industry. *Red Sorghum* (1988), the first film directed by Zhang Yimou, was a searingly erotic film of a type that had not been seen since 1949.

Twenty-first-century China

Jiang Zemin was succeeded in 2002 by President Hu Jintao, who made further efforts to tame growing regional inequality and the poverty scarring rural areas. China's lopsided development continued, however, de-

2010	2011	2012	2013
A huge 7.1-magnitude earthquake in the Qinghai region of the far west flattens the remote town of Yushu in April, killing thousands..	Two high-speed trains collide in July near Wenzhou in Zhejiang province, killing 40 people, the first and only fatal high-speed rail crash in China to date.	After the heaviest rainfall in 60 years, Beijing is inundated with epic summer floods; 77 people are killed by the floodwaters and 65,000 evacuated.	In December the total length of China's national high-speed rail network reaches a staggering 10,000km, making it the world's longest.

spite an ambitious program to develop the western regions. By 2009 an inflow of US$325 billion had dramatically boosted GDP per capita in the western regions, but a colossal prosperity gap survived and significant environmental challenges – from desertification to water shortages and soil erosion – persisted.

The question of political reform found itself shelved, partly because economic growth was bringing prosperity to so many, albeit unevenly. Property prices, especially in the richer eastern coastal provinces, were rocketing and the export and investment-driven economy was thriving. For some the first decade of the 21st century was marked by spectacular riches – the number of dollar billionaires doubled in just two years – and property prices began moving dramatically beyond the reach of the less fortunate, while bringing wealth to the more fortunate. This period coincided with the greatest migration of workers to the cities the world has ever seen.

China responded to the credit crunch of 2007 and the downturn in Western economies with a stimulus package of US$586 billion between 2008 and 2009. Property and infrastructure construction enjoyed spectacular growth, buffering China from the worst effects of the global recession, but the export sector contracted as demand dried up overseas. A barrage of restrictions on buying second properties attempted to flush speculators from the market and tame price rises. These policies partially worked, but millions of flats across China lay empty – bought by investors happy to see prices rise.

Vice president from 2008, Xi Jinping replaced Hu Jintao as president in 2013. Pledging to root out corruption, Xi also sought to instigate reforms, including the abolition of both the one-child policy and the *láojiào* (re-education through labour) system. These reforms, however, were matched by a growing zeal for internet and social-media controls and a domestic security budget that sucked in more capital than national defence.

Xi inherited a China that was a tremendous success story, but one that remained beset with problems. Despite resilient and ambitious planning (including a massive expansion of the high-speed rail network, a space program, some of the world's tallest buildings), the Chinese economy remained fundamentally imbalanced. During his tenure Xi has sought to shift China's economy from this over-reliance on exports by stimulating domestic consumption and at the same time launching a powerful anti-corruption drive. Xi has also worked hard on the presentation of his public persona, in a drive that some observers have likened to a personality cult. The abolition of the two-term presidential limit in 2018 only amplified concerns, ratcheted up further by revelations China was detaining up to a million Uyghurs against their will in detention centres

2014	2015	2017	2018
Malaysia Airlines Flight 370 disappears while flying from Kuala Lumpur to Beijing, with 152 Chinese passengers (of a total of 239 people) on board.	Satellite imagery reveals that China has been rapidly constructing an airfield at Fiery Cross Reef in the Spratly (Nánshā) Islands, part of territory also claimed by Vietnam, the Philippines and Taiwan.	China launches its first domestically constructed aircraft carrier, the Type 001A aircraft carrier, the second carrier in China's People's Liberation Army Navy..	The China National Space Administration launches the Chang'e-4 lunar probe to land on the far side of the moon.

in the Xinjiang autonomous region. Political reform found itself on the back-burner as China sought to consolidate its economic achievements, all the while confronting US President Donald Trump over an increasingly drawn-out and fractious trade war, as storm clouds gathered above the competing claims over the reefs, shoals and islands of the South China Sea.

First identified in December 2019 in Wuhan, Hubei province, but not declared a pandemic by the World Health Organization (WHO) till two and a half months later, Covid-19 went on to become one of the most lethal pandemics in human history, with almost 3.5 million deaths at the time of writing. Though the precise origin of the outbreak remains unknown, the first cases were associated with the Huanan Seafood Market in Wuhan. Several doctors at Wuhan Central Hospital, including Li Wenliang (who later died from Covid-19), were reprimanded by police for 'spreading false rumours' regarding the new virus at the end of December. On 21 January 2020, the WHO tweeted that it was evident there was 'at least some human-to-human transmission' of the virus and just two days later, Wuhan and other cities in Hubei province were quickly put into lockdown. On 30 January, the WHO finally designated Covid-19 a Public Health Emergency of International Concern (PHEIC), though by then the virus had spread abroad. Despite periodic small-scale outbreaks within its borders, China ran a largely successful campaign of not re-importing the virus by closing its borders to foreign nationals in March 2020 and began a huge programme to vaccinate its citizens from early 2021.

2019

China is rebuked by 22 nations that call upon it to stop its program of the detention of a million or more Uyghurs in Xinjiang province.

2019

Covid-19 is first detected in Wuhan, Hubei province, in December 2019; the city and other cities of the province are put into lockdown the following month.

People of China

The stamping ground of roughly one-fifth of humanity, it would be wrong to assume China is largely homogeneous. Even though Han Chinese – the majority ethnic type in this energetic and bustling nation – constitute over nine-tenths of the population, you only have to travel a bit further and turn a few more corners to come face-to-face with a diverse group of indigenous people that make an invaluable contribution to the language and culture of modern China.

Ethnicity

Han Chinese

Han Chinese (汉族, Hànzú), the predominant clan among China's 56 recognised ethnic groups, make up the lion's share of China's people – 92% of the total figure. When we think of China – from its writing system to its visual arts, calligraphy, history, literature, language and politics – we tend to associate it with Han culture.

Distributed throughout China, the Han Chinese are, however, predominantly concentrated along the Yellow River, Yangzi River and Pearl River basins. Taking their name from the Han dynasty, the Han Chinese themselves are not markedly homogenous. China was ruled by non-Han Altaic (Turk, Tungusic or Mongolian) invaders for long periods, most demonstrably under the Yuan dynasty (Mongols) and the long Qing dynasty (Manchu), but also under the Jin, the Liao and other eras.

The Han Chinese display further stark differences in their rich panoply of dialects, which fragments China into a frequently baffling linguistic mosaic, though the promotion of Mandarin has blurred this considerably. The common written form of Chinese using characters (汉字, Hànzi – or 'characters of the Han'), however, binds all dialects together.

The Non-Han Chinese

A glance at the map of China reveals that the core heartland regions of Han China are central fragments of modern-day China's huge expanse. The colossal regions of Tibet, Qinghai, Xinjiang, Inner Mongolia and the three provinces of the northeast (Manchuria – Heilongjiang, Jilin and Liaoning) are all historically non-Han regions, some areas of which remain essentially non-Han today.

Many of these regions are peopled by some of the remaining 8% of the population – China's 55 other ethnic minorities, known collectively as *shǎoshù mínzú* (少数民族, minority nationals). The largest minority groups in China include the Zhuang (壮族, Zhuàng zú), Manchu (满族, Mǎn zú), Miao (苗族, Miáo zú), Uyghur (维吾尔族, Wéiwú'ěr zú), Yi (彝族, Yí zú), Tujia (土家族, Tǔjiā zú), Tibetan (藏族, Zàng zú), Hui (回族, Huízú), Mongolian (蒙古族, Ménggǔ zú), Buyi (布依族, Bùyī zú), Dong (侗族, Dòng zú), Yao (瑶族, Yáo zú), Korean (朝鲜族, Cháoxiǎn zú), Bai (白族, Bái zú), Hani (哈尼族, Hāní zú), Li (黎族, Lí zú), Kazakh (哈萨克族, Hāsàkè zú) and Dai (傣族, Dǎi zú). Population sizes differ dramatically, from the sizeable Zhuang in Guangxi to small numbers of Menba (门巴族, Ménbā zú) in Tibet. Ethnic labelling can be quite fluid: the round-

The Naxi created a written language more than 1000 years ago using an extraordinary system of pictographs – the only hieroglyphic language still in use today.

house-building Hakka (客家; Kèjiā) were once regarded as a separate minority, but are today considered Han Chinese. Ethnic groups also tell us a lot about the historic movement of peoples around China – the Bonan minority, found in small numbers in a few counties of Qinghai and Gansu, are largely Muslim but show marked Tibetan influence and are said to be descended from Mongol troops once stationed in Qinghai during the Yuan dynasty.

China's minorities tend to cluster along border regions, in the northwest, the west, the southwest, the north and northeast of China, but are also distributed throughout the country. Some groups are found in just one area (such as the Hani in Yunnan). Others, such as the Muslim Hui, live all over China.

Wedged into the southwest corner of China between Tibet, Myanmar (Burma), Vietnam and Laos, fecund Yunnan province alone is home to more than 20 ethnic groups, making it one of the most ethnically diverse provinces in the country.

Despite Manchu culture once ruling over China during the Qing dynasty (1644–1911), possibly fewer than 50 native speakers of the Manchu language survive today, though the closely related Xibo language is spoken by around 20,000 descendants of Xibo tribes resettled in Xinjiang in China's northwest in the 18th century.

The Chinese Character

David Eimer's *The Emperor Far Away: Travels at the Edge of China* (2014) is a riveting journey through China's periphery, from the deserts of Xinjiang and the mountains of Tibet to the tropical jungles of Xishuangbanna and the frozen wastes of far-northern Heilongjiang.

Shaped and sculpted by Confucian principles, the Chinese are thoughtful and discreet, subtle but also pragmatic. Conservative and sometimes introverted, they tend to favour dark clothing over bright or loud colours, while their body language is typically reserved and undemonstrative, yet their minds are alert and attentive.

The Chinese can be both delightful and mystifyingly contradictory. One moment they will give their seat to an elderly person on the bus or help someone who is lost, and the next moment they will entirely ignore an old lady who has been knocked over by a motorbike.

Particularly diligent, the Chinese are inured to the kind of hours that would prompt a workers' insurrection elsewhere. This is partly due to a traditional culture of hard work, but is also a response to insufficient social-security safety nets and an anxiety regarding economic and political uncertainties. The Chinese impressively save much of what they earn, emphasising the virtues of prudence and caution. Despite this restraint, however, wastefulness can be breathtaking when 'face' is required: mountains of food are often left on restaurant dining tables, particularly if important guests are present.

Chinese people can be deeply generous. Don't be surprised if a person you have just met on a train invites you for a meal in the dining carriage. They will almost certainly insist on paying, grabbing the bill from the waiter either with impressive subterfuge or with blinding alacrity. If you do spot what is going on, they will tenaciously resist your attempts to help out.

The Chinese are also an exceptionally dignified people. They are proud of their civilisation and history, their written language and their inventions and achievements. This pride rarely comes across as arrogance, however, and can be streaked with a lack of self-assurance. The Chinese may, for example, be very gratified by China's new-found world status, but may squirm at the mention of food safety or pollution.

The modern Chinese character has been shaped by recent political realities, and while Chinese people have always been reserved and circumspect, in today's China they can appear even more prudent. Impressive mental gymnastics are performed to detour contentious domestic polit-

CHINA'S DEMOGRAPHICS

➡ Population: 1.43 billion

➡ Birth rate: 12.1 births per 1000 people

➡ People over 65: 11.3%

➡ Annual urbanisation rate: 2.42%

➡ Male to female ratio: 1.17:1 (under 15s)

➡ Life expectancy: 75.8 years

ical issues, which can make the mainland Chinese appear complicated, despite their reputation for being straightforward.

China's 'One-Child Policy'

Disbanded in 2016, the 'one-child policy' (actually a misnomer) was railroaded into effect in 1979 in a bid to keep China's population to one billion by the year 2000 (a target it failed to meet); the population of China is actually expected to peak at around 1.5 billion in the next decade. In January 2016 the regulation was officially amended to a two-child policy.

The policy was harshly implemented at first, but rural revolt led to a softer stance. Nonetheless it generated considerable bad feeling between local officials and the rural population. All non-Han minorities were exempt from the one-child policy; Han Chinese parents who were both single children could have a second child and this was later expanded to all couples if at least one of them was a single child. Rural families were allowed to have two children if the first child was a girl, but some had upwards of three or four kids. Additional children often resulted in fines, with families having to shoulder the cost of education themselves, without government assistance. Official stated policy opposed forced abortion or sterilisation, but allegations of coercion continued as local officials strove to meet population targets. In 2014 the film director Zhang Yimou was fined US$1.2 million for breaking the one-child policy.

Families who abided by the one-child policy often went to horrifying lengths to ensure their child was male, with female infanticide, sex-selective abortion and abandonment becoming commonplace. In parts of China this resulted in a serious imbalance of the sexes – in 2010, 118 boys were born for every 100 girls. In some provinces the imbalance has been even higher. It was estimated that by 2020 Chinese men could potentially outnumber women by 35 million.

Another consequence of the one-child policy has been a rapidly ageing population, with more than a quarter of the populace predicted to be over the age of 65 by 2050. The 2016 abolition of the one-child policy has sought to adjust these profound imbalances.

China has a high literacy rate of 96.4% for the whole population, a huge improvement on a literacy rate of just 78% in 1990.

Women in China

Equality & Emancipation

Growing up in a Confucian culture, women in China traditionally encountered great prejudice and acquired a far lowlier social status to men. The most notorious expression of female subservience was foot binding, which became a widespread practice in the Song dynasty. Female resistance to male-dominated society could sometimes produce inventive solutions, however – discouraged from reading and writing, women in Jiangyong county (Hunan) once used their own invented syllabic script (partly based on Chinese) called nûshū (女书) to write letters to each other (which men found incomprehensible).

Local ladies in Lou Lim Ieoc Garden (p566), Macau

Women in today's China officially share complete equality with men, though, as with other nations that profess sexual equality, the reality is often far different. Chinese women do not enjoy strong political representation and the Chinese Communist Party (CCP) remains a largely patriarchal organisation. Iconic political leaders from the early days of the CCP were men and the influential echelons of the party persist as a largely male domain. There has never been a female member of the Standing Committee of the Communist Party's Politburo.

Chairman Mao famously said that women 'hold up half the sky' and the Communist Party after 1949 tried to outlaw old customs and put women on equal footing with men. It abolished arranged marriages and encouraged women to get an education and join the workforce. By the 1970s China had the world's largest female workforce. Women were allowed to keep their maiden name upon marriage and leave their property to their children. In its quest for equality during this period, however, the Communist Party seemed to 'desexualise' women, fashioning instead a kind of idealised worker/mother/peasant paradigm.

China has almost 90 cities with populations of five to 10 million people, and more than 170 cities with between one and five million people.

Chinese Women Today

According to the 2017 Hurun Report, 49 of the world's 78 self-made female billionaires are in China. High-profile, successful Chinese women are very much in the public eye, but the relative lack of career opportunities for females in other fields also suggests a continuing bias against women in employment.

Women's improved social status today has meant that more women are putting off marriage until their late 20s or early 30s, choosing instead to focus on education and career opportunities. This has been enhanced by the rapid rise in house prices, further encouraging women to post-pone marriage (and having children) till a later age. Premarital sex and cohabitation before marriage are increasingly common in larger cities and lack the stigma they had 20 years ago. A survey by Chinese sexologist Li Yinhe revealed that 15.5% of Chinese people had sex before marriage in 1989, but by 2014 that figure had leapt to 71%.

In a sign of growing confidence among the female workforce, a young Beijing woman won the first-ever gender discrimination lawsuit in China in 2014. However, feminist activism remains an uphill struggle. After thousands of students and individuals signed #MeToo petitions in 2018 demanding action against sexual harassment, many of the petitions were deleted by censors on social media. Intense political pressure is applied to women's right activists, partly out of fear that these rights may cross over to more general human rights concerns and partly because the Chinese state seeks to suppress and weaken all forms of organised advocacy.

For an absorbing and eye-opening account of migrant workers in to-day's hard-nosed economy, get hold of a copy of *Factory Girls: from Village to City in a Changing China* (2008) by Leslie T Chang.

China's popula-tion is expected to peak in the next decade and will be overtaken as the world's most populous nation in around 2027 by India.

Religion & Philosophy

Ideas have always possessed an extraordinary potency and vitality in China. The 19th-century Taiping Rebellion fused Christianity with revolutionary principles of social organisation, almost sweeping away the Qing dynasty in the process and leaving 20 million dead. The momentary incandescence of the Boxer Rebellion drew upon a volatile cocktail of martial-arts practices and superstition, blended with xenophobia, while the chaos of the Cultural Revolution further illustrates what can happen in China when ideas assume the full supremacy they seek.

Religion Today

China has always had a pluralistic religious culture, and though statistics in China are a slippery fish, an estimated 400 million Chinese today adhere to a particular faith, in varying degrees of devotion. The Chinese Communist Party (CCP) made strident efforts after 1949 to supplant religious worship with the secular philosophy of communism, but since the abandonment of principles of Marxist-Leninist collectivism, this policy has significantly waned.

Religion in China is enjoying an upswing as people return to faith for spiritual solace at a time of great change, dislocation and uncertainty. The hopeless, poor and destitute may turn to worship as they feel abandoned by communism and the safety nets it once provided. Yet the educated and prosperous are similarly turning to religious belief for a sense of guidance and direction in a land many Chinese suspect has become morally bereft.

Religious belief in China was traditionally marked by tolerance. Though the faiths are quite distinct, some convergence exists between Buddhism, Taoism and Confucianism, and you may discover shrines where all three faiths are worshipped. Guanyin, the Buddhist Goddess of Mercy, finds her equivalent in Tianhou (Mazu), the Taoist goddess and protector of fisherfolk, and the two goddesses can seem almost interchangeable. Other symbioses exist: elements of Taoism and Buddhism can be discerned in the thinking of some Chinese Christians, while the Virgin Mary finds a familiar toehold in the Chinese psyche owing to her resemblance, in bearing and sympathetic message, to Guanyin.

The CCP today remains deeply fearful of ideas and beliefs that challenge its authority. Proselytising is not permitted and religious organisation is regulated and monitored, while organisations such as Falun Gong (a quasi-Buddhist health system) can be deemed cults and banned outright. The mass internment of up to several million Uyghurs and other Muslim minorities in northwest China for re-education in what Beijing terms 'correct thought' is evidence of a hardening attitude to devotion among Muslims. Alongside this mass internment, a number of mosques have been razed and signs of religious conservatism (eg long beards and the wearing of veils in public) have been banned, while the region of Xinjiang has effectively been turned into a police state, with endless security checks and high-tech surveillance creating an Orwellian society.

FALUN GONG

Falun Gong – a practice that merges elements of qigong-style regulated breathing and standing exercises with Buddhist teachings, fashioning a quasi-religious creed in the process – literally means 'Practice of the Dharma Wheel'. Riding a wave of interest in qigong systems in the 1990s, Falun Gong claimed as many as 100 million adherents in China by 1999. The technique was banned in the same year after more than 10,000 practitioners stood in silent demonstration outside Zhongnanhai in Beijing, following protests in Tianjin when a local magazine published an article critical of Falun Gong. The authorities had been unnerved by the movement's audacity and organisational depth, construing Falun Gong as a threat to the primacy of the Chinese Communist Party. The movement was branded a cult (邪教, xiéjiào) and a robust, media-wide propaganda campaign was launched against practitioners, forcing many to undergo 're-education' in prison and labour camps. After the ban the authorities treated Falun Gong believers harshly and reports surfaced of adherents dying in custody. Accusations of torture also persist, while several reports have pointed to industrial-scale harvesting of organs of Falun Gong prisoners, including David Matas and David Kilgour's 2009 book *Bloody Harvest: Organ Harvesting of Falun Gong Practitioners in China*. The Chinese government denies the charges. Falun Gong remains an outlawed movement in China to this day.

Buddhism

Although not an indigenous faith, Buddhism (佛教, Fójiào) is the religion most deeply associated with China and Tibet. The religion has seen periods of growth, decline, persecution and grand resurgence through China's history, and while Buddhism's authority may have long ebbed, the faith still exercises a powerful sway over China's spiritual inclinations. Many Chinese may not be regular temple-goers but they may harbour an interest in and an affiliation with Buddhism – they could be described as being 'cultural Buddhists', with a strong affection for Buddhist civilisation.

Chinese towns with any history to their name usually have several Buddhist temples, but the number is well down on pre-1949 figures. The small Hebei town of Zhengding, for example, has four Buddhist temples, but at one time had eight. Beijing once had hundreds, compared to the 20 or so you can find today.

A large number of Buddhist temples are also active monasteries; others may also provide accommodation. Some temples are free to enter, while for others there is an admission fee, especially if the temple is famed for a particular statue, pagoda or temple hall. You may discover pagodas standing alone in the middle of nowhere; these are almost always the remains of vanished temples, as pagodas were traditionally built within temple grounds.

Some of China's greatest surviving artistic achievements are Buddhist in inspiration. The largest and most ancient repository of Chinese, Central Asian and Tibetan Buddhist artwork can be found at the Mogao Grottoes in Gansu, while the carved Buddhist caves at both Longmen and Yungang are spectacular pieces of religious and creative heritage. To witness Buddhism at its most devout, consider a trip to Tibet, where the faith permeates local life to a profound degree.

Anyone interested in Tibetan Buddhism will find Inner Mongolia easier to reach than Tibet. The province is home to many important and historic lamaseries, including Dà Zhào in Hohhot, Wudang Lamasery and Guǎngzōng Sì.

Origins

Founded in ancient India around the 5th century BC, Buddhism teaches that all of life is suffering, and that the cause of this anguish is desire, itself rooted in sensation and attachment. Suffering can only be overcome by following the eightfold path, a set of guidelines for moral behaviour, meditation and wisdom. Those who have freed themselves from suffering and the wheel of rebirth are said to have attained nirvana or enlightenment.

The term Buddha generally refers to the historical founder of Buddhism, Siddhartha Gautama, but is also sometimes used to denote those who have achieved enlightenment.

Siddhartha Gautama left no writings; the sutras that make up the Buddhist canon were compiled many years after his death.

Buddhism in China

Like other faiths such as Christianity, Nestorianism, Islam and Judaism, Buddhism originally reached China via the Silk Road. The earliest recorded Buddhist temple in China proper dates back to the 1st century AD, but it was not until the 4th century that Buddhism gained mass appeal. Buddhism's sudden growth during this period is often attributed to its sophisticated ideas concerning the afterlife (such as karma and reincarnation), a dimension unaddressed by either Confucianism or Taoism. At a time when existence was especially precarious, spiritual transcendence was understandably popular.

As Buddhism converged with Taoist philosophy (through terminology used in translation) and popular religion (through practice), it went on to develop into something distinct from the original Indian tradition. The most famous example is the esoteric Chan school (Zen in Japanese), which originated sometime in the 5th or 6th century and focused on attaining enlightenment through meditation. Chan was novel not only in its unorthodox teaching methods, but also because it made enlightenment possible for laypeople outside the monastic system. It rose to prominence during the Tang and Song dynasties, after which the centre of practice moved to Japan.

Beyond Tibet, China has four sacred Buddhist mountains, each one the home of a specific Bodhisattva. The two most famous mountains are Wutai Shan and Emei Shan, respectively ruled over by Wenshu and Puxiang.

Buddhist Schools

Regardless of its various forms, most Buddhism in China belongs to the Mahayana school, which holds that since all existence is one, the fate of the individual is linked to the fate of others. Thus Bodhisattvas – those who have already achieved enlightenment but have chosen to remain on earth – continue to work for the liberation of all other sentient beings. The most popular Bodhisattva in China is Guanyin, the Goddess of Mercy.

Ethnic Tibetans and Mongols within China practise a unique form of Mahayana Buddhism known as Tibetan or Tantric Buddhism (Lǎma Jiào). Tibetan Buddhism, sometimes called Vajrayana or 'Thunderbolt Vehicle',

GUANYIN

The boundlessly compassionate countenance of Guanyin (观音), the Buddhist Goddess of Mercy, can be encountered in temples across China. The goddess (more strictly a Bodhisattva or a Buddha-to-be) goes under a variety of aliases: Guanshiyin (观世音, literally 'Observing the Cries of the World') is her formal name, but she is also called Guanzizai, Guanyin Dashi and Guanyin Pusa, or, in Sanskrit, Avalokiteshvara. Known as Kannon in Japan, Guanyam in Cantonese and Quan Am in Vietnam, Guanyin shoulders the grief of the world and dispenses mercy and compassion. Christians will note a semblance to the Virgin Mary in the aura surrounding the goddess, which at least partially explains why Catholicism (and Christianity in general) found a slot in the Chinese consciousness.

In Tibetan Buddhism her earthly presence manifests itself in the Dalai Lama, and her home is the Potala Palace in Lhasa. In China her abode is the island of Putuoshan in Zhejiang province, the first two syllables of which derive from the name of her palace in Lhasa.

In temples throughout China, Guanyin is often found at the very rear of the main hall, facing north (most of the other divinities, apart from Weituo, face south). She typically has her own little shrine and stands on the head of a big fish, holding a lotus in her hand. On other occasions she has her own hall, often towards the rear of the temple.

has been practised since the early 7th century AD and is influenced by Tibet's pre-Buddhist Bon religion, which relied on priests or shamans to placate spirits, gods and demons. Generally speaking, the faith is much more mystical than other forms of Buddhism, relying heavily on mudras (ritual postures), mantras (sacred speech), yantras (sacred art) and esoteric initiation rites. Priests called lamas are believed to be reincarnations of highly evolved beings – the Dalai Lama is the supreme patriarch of Tibetan Buddhism.

Taoism

A home-grown philosophy-cum-religion, Taoism (道教, Dàojiào) is also perhaps the hardest of all China's faiths to penetrate and grasp. Controversial, paradoxical and – like the Tao itself – impossible to pin down, it is a natural counterpart to rigid Confucianist order and responsibility.

Taoism predates Buddhism in China and much of its religious culture connects to a distant animism and shamanism, despite the purity of its philosophical school. In its earliest and simplest form, Taoism draws from *The Classic of the Way and Its Power* (Taote Jing; Dàodé Jīng), penned by the sagacious Laotzu (Laozi, c 580–500 BC), who left his writings with the gatekeeper of a pass as he headed west on the back of an ox. Some Chinese believe his wanderings took him to a distant land in the west where he became Buddha.

The Classic of the Way and Its Power is a work of astonishing insight and sublime beauty. Devoid of a godlike being or deity, Laotzu's writings instead endeavour to address the unknowable and indescribable principle of the universe, which he calls Dao (道, dào, 'the Way'). Dao is the way or method by which the universe operates, so it can be understood to be a universal or cosmic principle.

The 5000-character book, completed in terse classical Chinese, somehow communicates the nebulous power and authority of 'the Way'. The book remains the seminal text of Taoism, and Taoist purists see little need to look beyond its revelations.

One of Taoism's most beguiling precepts, wúwéi (inaction) champions the allowing of things to naturally occur without interference. The principle is enthusiastically pursued by students of Taiji Quan, Wuji Quan and other soft martial arts who seek to equal nothingness in their bid to lead an opponent to defeat himself.

Confucianism

The very core of Chinese society for the past two millennia, Confucianism (儒家思想, Rújiā Sīxiǎng) is a humanist philosophy that strives for social harmony and the common good. In China its influence can be seen in everything from the emphasis on education and respect for elders to the patriarchal role of the government.

Confucianism is based upon the teachings of Confucius (Kongzi; p237), a 6th-century BC philosopher who lived during a period of constant warfare and social upheaval. While Confucianism changed considerably throughout the centuries, some of the principal ideas remained the same – namely an emphasis on five basic hierarchical relationships: father-son, ruler-subject, husband-wife, elder-younger and friend-friend. Confucius believed that if each individual carried out his or her proper role in society (a son served his father respectfully while a father provided for his son, a subject served his ruler respectfully while a ruler provided for his subject, and so on) social order would be achieved. Confucius' disciples later gathered his ideas in the form of short aphorisms and conversations, forming the work known as *The Analects* (论语, Lúnyǔ).

Early Confucian philosophy was further developed by Mencius (Mengzi) and Xunzi, both of whom provided a theoretical and practical foundation

China's oldest surviving Buddhist temple is the White Horse Temple in Luoyang. Other more ancient Buddhist temples may well have existed but have since vanished.

Confucius Institutes around the world aim to promote Chinese language and culture internationally, while simultaneously developing its economic and cultural influences abroad.

RELIGION & PHILOSOPHY TAOISM

for many of Confucius' moral concepts. In the 2nd century BC, Confucianism became the official ideology of the Han dynasty, thereby gaining mainstream acceptance for the first time. This was of major importance and resulted in the formation of an educated elite that served both the government as bureaucrats and the common people as exemplars of moral action. During the rule of the Tang dynasty an official examination system was created, which, in theory, made the imperial government a true meritocracy. However, this also contributed to an ossification of Confucianism, as the ideology grew increasingly mired in the weight of its own tradition, focusing exclusively on a core set of texts.

Nonetheless, influential figures sporadically reinterpreted the philosophy – in particular Zhu Xi (1130–1200), who brought in elements of Buddhism and Taoism to create Neo Confucianism (Lǐxué or Dàoxué), which remained a dominant social force up until the 1911 revolution toppled the imperial bureaucracy. In the 20th century modernist writers and intellectuals decried Confucian thought as an obstacle to modernisation and Mao further levelled the sage in his denunciation of 'the Four Olds'. But feudal faults notwithstanding, Confucius' social ethics have resurfaced in government propaganda, where they lend authority to the leadership's emphasis on 'harmony' (héxié).

Christianity

The explosion of interest in Christianity (基督教, Jīdūjiào) in China over the last decade or two is unprecedented except for the wholesale conversions that accompanied the tumultuous rebellion of the pseudo-Christian Taiping in the 19th century.

Christianity first arrived in China with the Nestorians, a sect from ancient Persia that split with the Byzantine Church in AD 431 and arrived in China via the Silk Road in the 7th century. A celebrated tablet – the Nestorian Tablet – in Xi'an records their arrival. Much later, in the 16th century, the Jesuits arrived and were popular figures at the imperial court, though they made few converts. Large numbers of Catholic and Protestant missionaries established themselves in China in the 19th century, but the community left after the formation of the People's Republic of China in 1949.

Some estimates point to as many as 100 million Christians in China today. However, the exact population is hard to calculate as many groups – outside the four official Christian organisations – lead a strict underground existence (in what are called 'house churches') out of fear of a political clampdown.

Churches (教堂, jiàotáng) are not hard to find and most towns will have at least one. Cities such as Shanghai, Beijing, Datong, Taiyuan and Qingdao (and many other large towns) have cathedrals, most of them dating from the 19th and early 20th centuries.

There is growing evidence of official unease at the spread of Christianity and its association with universal human rights and values, and perennial fears of the infiltration of Western ideas that will compete with the primacy of state dogma. Christmas celebrations are periodically banned in various towns and cities to promote traditional Chinese culture instead. Online Bible sales were banned in 2018 to help limit the circulation of Christian concepts.

The removal of crosses and spires from churches has also been reported in several provinces in recent years, while others have been demolished, or had surveillance cameras installed inside.

Islam

Islam (伊斯兰教, Yīsīlán Jiào) in China dates from the 7th century, when it was first brought to China by Arab and Persian traders along the Silk

Kaifeng in Henan province is home to the largest community of Jews in China. The religious beliefs and customs of Judaism (犹太教, Yóutài Jiào) have died out, yet the descendants of the original Jews still consider themselves Jewish.

During the Cultural Revolution, many Christian churches around China served as warehouses or factories, a utilitarian function that actually helped preserve many of them. They were gradually rehabilitated in the 1980s.

THE CHURCH OF ALMIGHTY GOD

One byproduct of the recent explosion of interest in Christianity in China and the widespread number of unofficial 'house churches' has been the emergence of Christian heresies, with large numbers of devoted followers. Chief among these is the Church of Almighty God (www.holyspiritspeaks.org), which teaches that a Chinese woman named Yang Xiangbin is the second Christ.

After being blacklisted in 2000, Yang Xiangbin and the founder of the cult, Zhao Weishan, fled to the US. It was only when some followers killed a 37-year-old woman in a branch of McDonald's in Shandong, after she refused to give them her mobile-phone number, that the organisation came to greater public attention.

Directly opposed to the Chinese Communist Party (CCP), which it terms the Great Red Dragon, the organisation continues to aggressively recruit adherents in China, though its members live a largely underground and secretive existence.

Road. Later, during the Mongol Yuan dynasty, maritime trade increased, bringing new waves of merchants to China's coastal regions, particularly the port cities of Guangzhou and Quanzhou. The descendants of these groups, now scattered across the country, gradually integrated into Han culture, and are today distinguished primarily by their religion. In Chinese they are referred to as the Hui.

Other Muslim groups include the Uyghurs, Kazakhs, Kyrgyz, Tajiks and Uzbeks, who live principally in the border areas of the northwest. It is estimated that 1.5% to 3% of Chinese today are Muslim.

The mass internment of Muslim Uyghurs, Kazakhs, Kyrgyz, Hui and various other ethnic Turkic Muslims in re-education camps since 2014 is further evidence of a hard-line policy against what the state terms 'Islamist extremism', though this seems to include any depth of devotion to Islam. The internment camps are reportedly detaining hundreds of thousands of Muslims, though figures of up to three million detainees have been posited. In Xinjiang long beards and the wearing of veils in public places have been banned. Mosques have also been razed as the state seeks to limit their number.

Animism

A small percentage of China's population is animist, a primordial religious belief akin to shamanism. Animists see the world as a living being, with rocks, trees, mountains and people all containing spirits that need to live in harmony. If this harmony is disrupted, restoration of this balance is attempted by a shaman who is empowered to mediate between the human and spirit world. Animism is most widely believed by minority groups and exists in a multitude of forms, some of which have been influenced by Buddhism and other religions.

Communism & Maoism

Ironically (or perhaps intentionally) Mao Zedong, while struggling to uproot feudal superstition and religious belief, sprang to godlike status in China via a personality cult. By weakening the power of deities, Mao found himself replacing those very gods his political power had diminished. In the China of today, Mao retains a semi-deified aura.

Communism remains the official guiding principle of the CCP. However, young communist aspirants today are far less likely to be ideologues than pragmatists seeking to advance within the party structure.

Chinese communism owes something to Confucianism. Confucius' philosophy embraces the affairs of man and human society and the relationship between rulers and the ruled, rather than the supernatural

Believing he was the son of God and brother of Jesus Christ, Hakka rebel Hong Xiuquan led the bloody and tumultuous pseudo-Christian Taiping Rebellion against the Qing dynasty from 1856 to 1864.

world. Establishing a rigid framework for human conduct, the culture of Confucianism was easily requisitioned by communists seeking to establish authority over society.

With the collapse of the Soviet Union in 1989, Beijing became aware of the dangers of popular power and sought to maintain the coherence and strength of the state. This has meant that the CCP still seeks to impose itself firmly on the consciousness of Chinese people through patriotic education, propaganda, censorship, nationalism and the building of a strong nation.

Communism also holds considerable nostalgic value for elderly Chinese who bemoan the erosion of values in modern-day China and pine for the days when they felt more secure and society was more egalitarian. Chairman Mao's portrait still hangs in abundance across China, from drum towers in Guangxi province to restaurants in Beijing, testament to a generation of Chinese who still revere the communist leader.

President Xi Jinping has faced accusations of attempting to build a personality cult, allowing himself to be nicknamed Xi Dada (Big Daddy Xi), a kind of perennially good, sympathetic and paternal figurehead for the nation, with his citizens' best interests always at heart. The removal of the two-term limit for the Chinese president in 2018 – which Deng Xiaoping warned against decades before – has effectively permitted Xi Jinping to stay on as president indefinitely.

An inspiring read, *God is Red: The Secret Story of How Christianity Survived and Flourished in Communist China* (2011) by Liao Yiwu, himself not a Christian, relates his encounters with Christians in contemporary China, set against a background of persecution and surging growth for the faith.

Nationalism

In today's China '-isms' (主义, *zhǔyì* or 'doctrines') are often frowned upon. Any *zhǔyì* may suggest a personal focus that the CCP would prefer people channel into hard work instead. 'Intellectualism' is considered suspect as it may ask difficult questions, and 'idealism' is deemed non-pragmatic and potentially destructive, as Maoism showed.

China's one-party state has reduced thinking across the spectrum through propaganda and censorship, dumbing down an educational system that emphasises patriotic learning. This in turn, however, helps spawn another '-ism': nationalism.

Nationalism is not restricted to Chinese youth, but it is this generation – with no experience of the Cultural Revolution's terrifying excesses – that most closely identifies with its message. The *fēnqīng* (angry youth) have been swept along with China's rise – while they are no lovers of the CCP, they yearn for a stronger China that can stand up to 'foreign interference' and dictate its own terms.

The CCP actively encourages strong patriotism, but is nervous about its transformation into aggressive nationalism and the potential for disturbance. Much nationalism in the PRC has little to do with the CCP but everything to do with China – while the CCP has struggled at length to identify itself with China's civilisation and core values, it has been only partially successful. With China's tendency to get quickly swept along by passions, nationalism is an often unseen but quite potent force, most visibly flaring up into the periodic anti-Japanese demonstrations that can convulse large towns and cities.

Arts & Architecture

China is custodian of one of the world's richest cultural and artistic legacies. Until the 20th century, China's arts were deeply conservative and resistant to change, but revolutions in technique and content over the last century fashioned a dramatic transformation. Despite this evolution, China's arts – whatever the period – embrace a common aesthetic that embodies the very soul and lifeblood of the nation.

Aesthetics

In reflection of the Chinese character, Chinese aesthetics have traditionally been marked by restraint and understatement, a preference for oblique references over explicit explanation, vagueness in place of specificity and an avoidance of the obvious while inclining towards the veiled and subtle. Traditional Chinese aesthetics sought to cultivate a more reserved artistic impulse, principles that compellingly find their way into virtually every Chinese art form, from painting, sculpture and ceramics to calligraphy, film, poetry, literature and beyond.

As one of the central strands of one of the world's oldest continuous civilisations, China's aesthetic traditions are tightly woven into Chinese cultural identity. It was not until the fall of the Qing dynasty in 1911 and the appearance of the New Culture Movement that China's great artistic traditions began to rapidly transform. In literature the stranglehold of classical Chinese loosened to allow breathing space for *báihuà* (colloquial Chinese) and a progressive new aesthetic started to flower, ultimately leading to revolutions in all of the arts, from poetry to painting, theatre and music.

It is hard to reconcile China's great aesthetic traditions with the devastation inflicted upon them since 1949. Confucius advocated the edifying role of music and poetry in shaping human lives, but 5th-century philosopher Mozi was less enamoured with them, seeing music and other arts as extravagant and wasteful. The communists took this a stage further, enlisting the arts as props in their propaganda campaigns, and permitting the vandalism and destruction of much traditional architecture and heritage. Many of the arts have yet to recover fully from this deterioration, even though opening up and reform prompted a vast influx of foreign artistic concepts and, to a degree, a revival of China's traditional art forms.

The most abstract calligraphic form is grass or cursive script *(cǎoshū)*, a highly fluid style of penmanship that even Chinese people have difficulty reading.

Calligraphy

Although calligraphy (书法, *shūfǎ*) has a place among most languages that employ alphabets, the art of calligraphy in China is taken to unusual heights of intricacy and beauty in a language that is alphabet-free and essentially composed of images.

To fully appreciate how perfectly suited written Chinese is for calligraphy, it is vital to grasp how written Chinese works. A word in English represents a sound alone, but a written character in Chinese combines both sound and a picture. Indeed, the sound element of a Chinese character – when present – is often auxiliary to the illustration of a visual image, even if that image is abstract.

Furthermore, although some Chinese characters were simplified in the 1950s as part of a literacy drive, most characters have remained unchanged for thousands of years. This helps explain why Chinese calligraphy is the trickiest of China's arts to comprehend for Western visitors, unless they have a sound understanding of written Chinese. The beauty of a Chinese character may be partially appreciated by a Western audience, but for a full understanding it is also essential to understand the meaning of the character (or characters).

Painting

Traditional Painting

Unlike Chinese calligraphy, Chinese painting is highly accessible. For this reason traditional Chinese paintings – especially landscapes – have long been treasured in the West for their beauty.

The five fundamental brushstrokes necessary to master calligraphy can be found in the character 永, which means eternal or forever.

As described in Xie He's 6th-century-AD treatise, the *Six Principles of Painting*, the chief aim of Chinese painting is to capture the innate essence or spirit *(qì)* of a subject and endow it with vitality. The brush line, varying in thickness and tone, was the second principle (referred to as the 'bone method') and is the defining technique of Chinese painting. Traditionally it was imagined that brushwork quality could reveal the artist's moral character. As a general rule, painters were less concerned with achieving outward resemblance (that was the third principle) than with conveying intrinsic qualities.

Early painters dwelled on the human figure and moral teachings, while also conjuring up scenes from everyday life. By the time of the Tang dynasty, a new genre, known as landscape painting, had begun to flower. Reaching full bloom during the Song and Yuan dynasties, landscape painting meditated on the environment surrounding man. Towering mountains, ethereal mists, open spaces, trees and rivers, and the effects of light and dark were all exquisitely presented in ink washes on silk. Landscape paintings attempted to capture the metaphysical and the absolute, drawing the viewer into a particular realm where the philosophies of Taoism and Buddhism found expression. Humanity is typically a small and almost insignificant subtext to the performance. The purpose of the dreamlike painting sought to draw the viewer in rather than impose itself on the observer.

Modern Art

Socialist Realism

After 1949 classical Chinese techniques were abandoned and foreign artistic techniques imported wholesale. Washes on silk were replaced with oil on canvas and China's traditional obsession with the mysterious and ineffable made way for concrete attention to detail and realism.

In 2011 an ink-and-brush painting by artist Qi Baishi (1864–1957) sold for ¥425 million (US$65 million) at auction.

By 1970 Chinese artists had aspired to master the skills of socialist realism, a vibrant communist-endorsed style that drew from European neoclassical art, the lifelike canvases of Jacques-Louis David and the output of Soviet Union painters. The blunt style had virtually nothing to do with traditional Chinese painting techniques, instead being saturated with political symbolism and propaganda.

The entire trajectory of Chinese painting had been redirected virtually overnight. Vaporous landscapes were substituted with hard-edged panoramas; traditional Taoist and Buddhist philosophy was overturned and humans became the masters of nature and often the most dominant theme. Dreamy vistas were out; smoke stacks, red tractors and muscular peasants were in.

Propaganda Art

Another art form that found a fertile environment during the Mao era was the propaganda poster. Mass-produced from the 1950s onwards and replicated in their thousands through tourist markets across China today, the colourful Chinese propaganda poster was a further instrument of social control in a nation where aesthetics had become subservient to communist orthodoxy.

With a prolific range of themes from chubby, well-fed Chinese babies to the Korean War, the virtues of physical education, the suppression of counter-revolutionary activity and paeans to the achievements of the Great Leap Forward or China as an earthly paradise, propaganda posters were ubiquitous. The golden age of poster production ran through to the 1980s, only declining during Deng Xiaoping's tenure and the opening up of China to the West.

The success of visual propaganda lay in its appeal to a large body of illiterate or semiliterate peasants. The idealism, revolutionary romanticism and vivid colouring of Chinese propaganda art brought hope and vibrancy to a time that was actually often colourless and drab, while adding certainty to an era of great hardship and struggle.

Post-Mao

It was only with the death of Mao Zedong in 1976 that the shadow of the Cultural Revolution – when Chinese aesthetics were conditioned by the threat of violence – began its retreat and the individual artistic temperament was allowed to thrive afresh.

Painters such as Luo Zhongli employed the realist techniques gleaned from China's art academies to depict the harsh realities etched in the faces of contemporary peasants. Others escaped the suffocating confines of socialist realism to navigate new horizons. A voracious appetite for western art brought with it fresh concepts and ideas, while the ambiguity of precise meaning in the fine arts offered a degree of protection from state censors.

One group of artists, the Stars, found retrospective inspiration in Picasso and German Expressionism. The ephemeral group had a lasting impact on the development of Chinese art in the 1980s and 1990s, paving the way for the New Wave movement that emerged in 1985. New Wave artists were greatly influenced by western art, especially the iconoclastic Marcel Duchamp. In true nihilist style, the New Wave artist Huang Yongping destroyed his works at exhibitions in an effort to escape from the notion of 'art'. Political realities became instant subject matter as performance artists wrapped themselves in plastic or tape to symbolise the repressive realities of modern-day China.

Beyond Tian'anmen

The Tian'anmen Square protests in 1989 fostered a deep-seated cynicism that permeated artworks with loss, loneliness and social isolation. An exodus of artists to the West commenced. This period also coincided with an upsurge in the art market as investors increasingly turned to artworks and money began to slosh about.

Much post-1989 Chinese art dwelled obsessively on contemporary socioeconomic realities, with consumer culture, materialism, urbanisation and social change a repetitive focus. More universal themes became apparent, however, as the art scene matured, and artists who left China in the 1990s returned, setting up private studios and galleries.

Cynical realists Fang Lijun and Yue Minjun fashioned grotesque portraits that conveyed hollowness and mock joviality, tinged with despair. Born in the late 1950s, Wang Guangyi took pop art as a template for his

Chinese individuals and companies are also purchasing non-Chinese art masterpieces. In 2015 Claude Monet's *Bassin aux nymphéas, les rosiers* sold for US$20.4 million at auction to the Dalian Wanda Group.

ironic pieces, fused with propaganda art techniques from the Cultural Revolution.

Born just before the Cultural Revolution in 1964 and heavily influenced by German expressionism, Zeng Fanzhi explored the notions of alienation and isolation – themes commonly addressed by Chinese artists during this period – in his *Mask* series from the 1990s. Introspection is a hallmark of Zeng's oeuvre. In 2008 Christie's in Hong Kong sold Zeng Fanzhi's painting *Mask Series 1996 No. 6* (featuring masked members of China's communist youth organisation, the Young Pioneers) for US$9.7 million, which is the highest price yet paid for a modern Chinese artwork.

Also born in the early 1960s, Zhang Dali is another artist who gave expression to social change and the gulf between rich and poor, especially the circumstances of the immigrant worker underclass in Beijing.

Major art festivals include Beijing's 798 International Art Festival, China International Gallery Exposition and Beijing Biennale, the Shanghai Biennale, Guangzhou Triennial and Hong Kong's one-day Clockenflap festival.

Contemporary Directions

Most artists of note and aspiration gravitate to Beijing (or Shanghai) to work. Today's China provides a huge wellspring of subject matter for artists, tempered by the reality of political censorship and the constraints of taboo. Themes that can seem tame in the West may assume a special power in China, so works can rely upon their context for potency and effect.

Ai Weiwei, who enjoys great international fame partly due to his anti-authoritarian stances, exemplifies the dangerous overlap between artistic self-expression, dissent and conflict with the authorities. He was arrested in 2011 on charges of tax evasion and held for 81 days.

Working collaboratively as Birdhead, Shanghai analogue photographers Ji Weiyu and Song Tao record the social dynamics and architectural habitat of their home city in thoughtful compositions. Beijing-born Ma Qiusha works in video, photography, painting and installations on themes of a deeply personal nature. In her video work *From No.4 Pingyuanli to No.4 Tianqiaobeili,* the artist removes a bloody razor blade from her mouth after narrating her experiences as a young artist in China. Born in 1982, Ran Huang works largely in film but across a spectrum of media, conveying themes of absurdity, the irrational and conceptual. Shanghai artist Shi Zhiying explores ideas of a more traditional hue in her sublime oil-paint depictions on large canvases of landscapes and religious and cultural objects. Also from Shanghai, Xu Zhen works with provocative images to unsettle and challenge the viewer.

A dark and Gothic image in the West, the bat is commonly used in Chinese porcelain, wood designs, textiles and artwork as it is considered a good-luck omen.

Ceramics

China's very first vessels, dating back more than 8000 years, were simple handcrafted earthenware pottery, primarily used for religious purposes. The invention of the pottery wheel during the late Neolithic period, however, led to a dramatic technological and artistic leap.

Over the centuries Chinese potters perfected their craft, introducing many new and exciting styles and techniques. The spellbinding artwork of the Terracotta Warriors in Xi'an reveals a highly developed level of technical skill achieved by Qin-dynasty craftsmen. Periods of artistic evolution, during the cosmopolitan Tang dynasty, for example, prompted further stylistic advances. The Tang dynasty 'three-colour ware' is a much-admired type of ceramic from this period, noted for its vivid yellow, green and white glaze. Demand for lovely blue-green celadons grew in countries as distant as Egypt and Persia.

The Yuan dynasty saw the first development of China's standout 'blue and white' *(qīnghuā)* porcelain. Cobalt-blue paint from Persia was applied as an underglaze directly to white porcelain with a brush, with the vessel then covered with another transparent glaze and fired. This technique was perfected during the Ming dynasty and such ceramics became hugely popular all over the world, eventually acquiring the name 'China-ware', whether produced in China or not.

Although many kilns were established in China, the most famous was at Jingdezhen in Jiangxi province, where royal porcelain was fired. Jingdezhen remains an excellent place to visit ceramic workshops and purchase various types of ceramic wares, from Mao statues to traditional glazed urns. The Shanghai Museum has a premier collection of porcelain, while several independent retailers in Beijing, Shanghai and Hong Kong also sell more modish and creative pieces.

Sculpture

The earliest sculpture in China dates from the Zhou and Shang dynasties, when small clay and wooden figures were commonly placed in tombs to protect the dead and guide them on their way to heaven.

With the arrival of Buddhism, sculpture turned towards spiritual figures and themes, with sculptors frequently enrolled in huge carving projects for the worship of Sakyamuni. Influences also arrived along the Silk Road from abroad, bringing styles from as far afield as Greece and Persia, via India. The magnificent Buddhist caves at Yungang in Shanxi province, for example, date back to the 5th century and betray a noticeable Indian influence.

The most superlative examples are at the Mogao Grottoes at Dunhuang in Gansu province, where well-preserved Indian and Central Asian–style sculptures, particularly of the Tang dynasty, carry overtly Chinese characteristics – many statues feature long, fluid bodies and have warmer, more refined facial features.

Beyond its grottoes, other mesmerising Chinese sculpture hides away in temples across China. The colossal statue of Guanyin in Puning Temple in Chengde is a staggering sight, carved from five different types of wood and towering over 22m in height. Shuanglin Temple outside Pingyao in Shanxi province is famed for its astonishing collection of painted statues from the Song and Yuan dynasties. The Shanghai Museum also has a splendid collection of Buddhist sculpture.

Jade

Jade (玉, yù) has been revered in China since Neolithic times. Because of its hardness and strength, the stone was first used for making tools, but later appeared on ornaments and vessels for its decorative value. During the Qin and Han dynasties, it was believed that jade was empowered with magical and life-giving properties, and the dead were buried with jadeware. Opulent jade suits, meant to prevent decomposition, have been excavated from Han tombs, while Taoist alchemists consumed elixirs of powdered jade in their quest for immortality.

Bronze Vessels

Apocryphal tradition ascribes the first casting of bronze – an alloy of copper, tin and lead – to the legendary Xia dynasty some 5000 years ago.

Shang dynasty ritual bronzes are marvellous specimens, often fabulously patterned with tāotiè, a kind of fierce, mythical animal design. Many Zhou dynasty vessels bear inscriptions describing wars, ceremonial events and the appointment of officials. Though now they wear a deep, dark-green patina, originally they would have been burnished a bright gold colour, so their appearance and aesthetic effect would have been markedly different from what we see today.

In 2010 a Qing dynasty Chinese vase sold for £53.1 million after being discovered in the attic of a house in northwest London and put up for auction.

The *I Ching* (*Yijīng*; Book of Changes) is the oldest Chinese text and is used for divination. It comprises 64 hexagrams, composed of broken and continuous lines, that represent a balance of opposites (yin and yang), the inevitability of change and the evolution of events.

Literature
Classic Novels

Until the early 20th century, classical literature (古文, *gǔwén*) had been the principal form of writing in China for thousands of years. A breed of purely literary writing different from spoken Chinese, classical Chinese maintained divisions between educated and uneducated Chinese, putting literature beyond the reach of the common person and fashioning a cliquey lingua franca for Confucian officials, scholars and the erudite elite.

Classical novels evolved from the popular folk tales and dramas that entertained the lower classes. During the Ming dynasty they were penned in a semi-vernacular (or 'vulgar') language, and are often irreverently funny and full of action-packed fights.

Probably the best-known novel outside China is *Journey to the West* (Xīyóu Jì). Written in the 16th century, it follows the misadventures of a cowardly Buddhist monk (Tripitaka; a stand-in for the real-life pilgrim Xuan Zang) and his companions – a rebellious monkey, lecherous pigman and exiled monster-immortal – on a pilgrimage to India.

Written by Cao Xueqin and one of the most famous tales in Chinese literature, the *Dream of the Red Mansions* (Hónglóu Mèng) is an elaborate 18th-century novel penned in a vernacular, semiclassical form of Chinese. Also known as *The Story of the Stone,* the lavish tale relates the decline of an aristocratic family, affording a captivating overview of the mores and manners of upper-class Qing society.

The Book and the Sword by Jin Yong/Louis Cha (2004) is China's most celebrated martial-arts novelist's first book. The martial-arts genre (*wǔxiá xiǎoshuō*) is a direct descendant of the classical novel.

Classical Poetry

The earliest collection of Chinese poetry is the *Book of Songs* (Shījīng), which includes more than 300 poems dating back to the 6th century BC, gathered together by royal musicians who lived in the many feudal states clustered along the banks of the Yellow River during the Zhou dynasty. Centred on themes of love, marriage, war, agriculture, hunting and sacrifice, the poems were originally meant to be sung.

China's greatest early poet is Qu Yuan, who lived during the Warring States period (475–221 BC) and is known for his romantic, lyrical poetry.

The Tang dynasty is considered to be the golden age of Chinese poetry, when two of China's greatest poets – Li Bai and Du Fu – lived and created some of the most beautiful and moving poems in classical Chinese. During the Song dynasty, a lyric form of poetry called *cí* emerged, expressing feelings of passion and desire. Su Shi (Su Dongpo) is the most famous poet from this period.

Following is an example of a piece of classical Chinese poetry from the Tang dynasty by the poet-painter Wang Wei (王维; AD 699–759), entitled 'Deer Park'. Notice how the number of characters are the same on each line (five on each line) creating a perfect balance in syllables, while the final characters of the first (人, 'ren') and third lines (林, 'lin') rhyme. The last characters of the second (響, 'xiang') and fourth lines (上, 'shang') also rhyme and resonate together (that they still rhyme after more than 1200 years is also astonishing). The meaning of each individual character is added sequentially in the line below each original Chinese line, with a translation into modern English at the end:

鹿柴

空山不見人

(empty mountain not see people)

但聞人語響

(but hear people speak sound)

返景入深林

(again reflection enters deep forest)
復照青苔上。
(again shine green moss upon)

Deer Park
People are unseen in the empty mountains
But the sound of voices carries
The reflected scene enters the deep forest
To shine once more on the green moss.

Modern Literature

Early 20th-Century Writing

Classical Chinese maintained its authority over literary minds until the early 20th century, when it came under the influence of the West.

Torch-bearing author Lu Xun wrote his short story, *Diary of a Madman*, in 1918. It was revolutionary stuff. Apart from the opening paragraph, which is composed in classical Chinese, Lu's seminal and shocking fable is cast entirely in colloquial Chinese.

For Lu Xun to write his short story in colloquial Chinese was explosive: readers were finally able to read language as it was spoken. *Diary of a Madman* is a haunting and unsettling work, and from this moment onwards mainstream Chinese literature would be written as it was thought and spoken: Chinese writing had been instantly revolutionised.

Other notable contemporaries of Lu Xun include Ba Jin (*Family;* 1931), Mao Dun (*Midnight;* 1933), Beijing author Lao She (*Rickshaw Boy/ Camel Xiangzi;* 1936) and the modernist playwright Cao Yu (*Thunderstorm;* 1934). Lu Xun and Ba Jin also translated a great deal of foreign literature into Chinese.

Published by the Chinese University of Hong Kong Research Centre for Translation, *Renditions* (www. cuhk.edu.hk/ rct/renditions/ index.html) is an excellent journal of Chinese literature in English translation, covering works from classical Chinese to modern writing.

Contemporary Writing

A growing number of contemporary voices have been translated into English, but far more exist in Chinese only. The provocative Nobel Prize–winning Mo Yan (*Life and Death are Wearing Me Out;* 2008), Yu Hua (*To Live;* 1992) and Su Tong (*Rice;* 1995) have written momentous, harrowing historical novels set in the 20th century.

Zhu Wen mocks the get-rich movement in his brilliantly funny short stories, published in English as *I Love Dollars and Other Stories of China* (2007). It's a vivid and comic portrayal of the absurdities of everyday China.

'Hooligan author' Wang Shuo (*Please Don't Call Me Human;* 2000) is one of China's bestselling authors with his political satires and convincing depictions of urban slackers. Alai (*Red Poppies;* 2002), an ethnic Tibetan, made waves by writing in Chinese about early-20th-century Tibetan Sichuan – whatever your politics, it's both insightful and a page-turner.

Exiled author Ma Jian writes more politically critical work. His 2001 novel *Red Dust* was a Kerouacian tale of wandering China as a spiritual pollutant in the 1980s. Banned in China, his 2008 novel *Beijing Coma* is set against the Tian'anmen demonstrations of 1989 and their aftermath. Ma Jian's latest book is *China Dream* (2018), a dystopian parody of the 'China Dream' national-rejuvenation maxim dreamed up by President Xi Jinping.

China's most renowned dissident writer, Gao Xingjian, won the Nobel Prize for Literature in 2000 for his novel *Soul Mountain,* an account of his travels along the Yangzi after being misdiagnosed with lung cancer.

The Three-Body Problem, the first novel of a science-fiction trilogy by Liu Cixin, was received with great international acclaim and was the first Asian book to garner the Hugo Award for Best Novel in 2015.

For a taste of contemporary Chinese short-story writing with both English and Chinese, buy a copy of *Short Stories in Chinese: New Penguin Parallel Text* (2012). *The Picador Book of Contemporary Chinese Fiction* (2006) brings together a range of different contemporary voices and themes into one accessible book.

Film

Early Cinema

Wolf Totem (2009) by Jiang Rong is an astonishing look at life on the grasslands of Inner Mongolia during the Cultural Revolution and the impact of modern culture on an ancient way of life.

The moving image first came to the Middle Kingdom in 1896, when Spaniard Galen Bocca unveiled a film projector and blew the socks off wide-eyed crowds in a Shanghai teahouse. Shanghai's cosmopolitan verve and exotic looks would make it the capital of China's film industry, but China's very first movie – *Conquering Jun Mountain* (an excerpt from a piece of Beijing opera) – was actually filmed in Beijing in 1905.

Shanghai opened its first cinema in 1908. In those days cinema owners would cannily run the film for a few minutes, stop it and collect money from the audience before allowing the film to continue. The golden age of Shanghai filmmaking came in the 1930s when the city had more than 140 film companies. Its apogee arrived in 1937 with the release of *Street Angel*, a powerful drama about two sisters who flee the Japanese in northeast China and end up as prostitutes in Shanghai; and *Crossroads,* a clever comedy about four unemployed graduates. Japanese control of China eventually brought the industry to a standstill and sent many film-makers packing.

Communist Decline

China's film industry was stymied after the Communist Revolution, which sent film-makers scurrying to Hong Kong and Taiwan, where they played key roles in building up the local film industries that flourished there. Cinematic production in China was co-opted to glorify communism and generate patriotic propaganda. The days of the Cultural Revolution (1966–76) were particularly dark. Between 1966 and 1972, just eight movies were made on the mainland, as the film industry was effectively shut down.

Resurgence

It wasn't until September 1978, two years after the death of Mao Zedong, that China's premier film school – the Beijing Film Academy – reopened. Its first intake of students included Zhang Yimou, Chen Kaige and Tian Zhuangzhuang, who are considered masterminds of the celebrated 'Fifth Generation'.

The cinematic output of the Fifth Generation signalled an escape from the dour, colourless and proletarian Mao era, and a second glittering golden age of Chinese filmmaking arrived in the 1980s and 1990s with their lush and lavish tragedies. A bleak but beautifully shot tale of a Chinese Communist Party cadre who travels to a remote village in Shaanxi province to collect folk songs, Chen Kaige's *Yellow Earth* aroused little interest in China but proved a sensation when released in the West in 1985.

It was followed by Zhang's *Red Sorghum* (1989), which introduced Gong Li and Jiang Wen to the world. Gong became the poster girl of Chinese cinema in the 1990s and the first international movie star to emerge from the mainland. Jiang, the Marlon Brando of Chinese film, has proved both a durable leading man and an innovative, controversial director of award-winning films such as *In the Heat of the Sun* (1994) and *Devils on the Doorstep* (2001).

Rich, seminal works such as *Farewell My Concubine* (1993; Chen Kaige) and *Raise the Red Lantern* (1991; Zhang Yimou) were garlanded with praise, receiving standing ovations and winning major film awards. Their directors were the darlings of Cannes; Western cinemagoers were entranced. Many Chinese cinema-goers also admired their artistry, but some saw Fifth Generation output as pandering to the Western market.

In 1993 Tian Zhuangzhuang made the brilliant *The Blue Kite*. A heartbreaking account of the life of one Beijing family during the Cultural Revolution, it so enraged the censors that Tian was banned from making films for a decade.

Contemporary Film

The ensuing Sixth Generation film directors eschewed the luxurious beauty of their forebears, and sought to capture the angst and grit of modern urban Chinese life. Their independent, low-budget works put an entirely different and more cynical spin on mainland Chinese filmmaking, but their darker subject matter and harsh film style (frequently in black and white) left many Western viewers cold.

A graduate of the Beijing Film Academy and associated with the Sixth Generation, Jia Zhangke emerged as a highly acclaimed film-maker, adhering to a realist, and some say minimalist, style. His meditative and compassionate look at the social impact of the construction of the Three Gorges Dam on local people, *Still Life* (2006), scooped the Golden Lion at the 2006 Venice Film Festival. Jia established the Pingyao International Film Festival in 2017.

Similarly educated at the Beijing Film Academy, controversial Sixth Generation director Lou Ye has a prolific and notable portfolio of sensual and atmospheric films. The tragic, noirish experience of *Suzhou River* (2000) is perhaps his best-known work, but *Summer Palace* (2006), *Spring Fever* (2009) and the violent *Mystery* (2012) maintained his reputation as an enfant terrible of China's censorship-laden film industry.

Historical *wuxia* (martial arts) cinema is enduringly popular in China and typified much filmmaking in the noughties, with larger-than-life films such as *Hero* (2002; Zhang Yimou), *House of Flying Daggers* (2004; Zhang Yimou) and *The Banquet* (2006; Feng Xiaogang) leading the way. Epic historical war dramas such as *Red Cliff* (2008–09; John Woo) and *The Warlords* (2007; Peter Chan) belong to a similar genre.

Traditional Music

Musical instruments have been unearthed from tombs dating from the Shang dynasty, while Chinese folk songs can be traced back at least that far.

Unlike in the West, traditional Chinese music has long valued tone over melody and uses a pentatonic scale. Music in China is also considered to have cosmological significance with musical harmony finding a parallel in dynastic harmony.

Traditional Chinese musical instruments include the two-stringed fiddle (*èrhú*), four-stringed lute (*pípa*), four-stringed banjo (*yuèqín*), two-stringed viola (*húqín*), horizontal flute (*dízi*), piccolo flute (*bāngdí*), vertical flute (*dòngxiāo*) and zither (*gǔzhēng*). A lot of emphasis is placed on percussion.

China's ethnic minorities have preserved their own folk-song traditions. A trip to Lijiang gives you the opportunity to appreciate the local Naxi Music Academy (p720) orchestra.

For a taste of Kazakh folk music from northwest Xinjiang province, listen to *Eagle* (2009) by Mamer, an intriguing collection of songs described as 'Chinagrass' by their composer.

Chinese Opera

Contemporary Chinese opera, of which the most famous is Beijing opera (京剧, *Jīngjù*), has a continuous history of some 900 years. Evolving from a convergence of comic and ballad traditions in the Northern Song period, Chinese opera brought together a disparate range of forms: acrobatics, martial arts, poetic arias and stylised dance.

Operas were usually performed by travelling troupes who had a low social status in traditional Chinese society. Chinese law forbade mixed-sex performances, forcing actors to perform roles of the opposite sex. Opera troupes were frequently associated with homosexuality in the public imagination, contributing further to their lowly social status.

Formerly, opera was performed mostly on open-air stages in markets, streets, teahouses or temple courtyards. The shrill singing and loud percussion were designed to be heard over the public throng, hence their piercing qualities.

Opera performances usually take place on a bare stage, with the actors taking on stylised stock characters who are instantly recognisable to the audience. Most stories are derived from classical literature and Chinese mythology, and tell of disasters, natural calamities, intrigues or rebellions.

As well as Beijing opera, other famous Chinese operatic traditions include Cantonese opera, Kunqu (from the Jiangnan region), Min opera (from Fujian) and Shanghai opera.

Architecture

Traditional Architecture

Four principal styles governed traditional Chinese architecture: imperial, religious, residential and recreational. Whatever the style, Chinese buildings traditionally followed a similar basic ground plan, consisting of a symmetrical layout oriented around a central axis – ideally running north–south to conform with basic feng shui (风水, *fēngshuǐ*) dictates and to maximise sunshine – with an enclosed courtyard (院, *yuàn*) flanked by buildings on all sides.

In many aspects imperial palaces are glorified courtyard homes (south-facing, with a sequence of courtyards, side halls and perhaps a garden at the rear) completed on a different scale and with more defensive features and decorative embellishments.

Religious Architecture

Chinese Buddhist, Taoist and Confucian temples tend to follow a quite strict, schematic pattern. All temples are laid out on a north–south axis in a series of halls, with the main door of each hall facing south.

The sequence of halls and buildings is interspersed with open-air courtyards, allowing the weather to permeate the temple and permit *qì* (气, spirit) to circulate, stale air to disperse and incense to be burned.

Buddhist Temples

Once you have cracked the logic of Buddhist temples, you will see how most temples conform to a basic pattern, which rarely varies. The first hall and portal to the temple is generally the **Hall of Heavenly Kings** (天王殿, Tiānwáng Diàn) – which is sometimes also called the Mountain Gate (山门; Shānmén) – where a sedentary, central statue of the rotund Bodhisattva Maitreya is flanked by the stern and often fearsome Four Heavenly Kings. Behind is the first courtyard, where the **Drum Tower** (鼓楼, Gǔlóu) and **Bell Tower** (钟楼, Zhōnglóu) may rise to the east and west.

The main hall of Buddhist temples is usually the **Great Treasure Hall** (大雄宝殿, Dàxióngbǎo Diàn), sheltering glittering statues of the past, present and future Buddhas, seated in a row. This is the main focal point for worshippers at the temple. On the east and west interior wall of the hall are often 18 *luóhàn* (arhats – Buddhists who have achieved enlightenment) in two lines, either as statues or paintings. In some temples, they gather in a throng of 500, housed in a separate hall, usually called the **Luohan Hall** (罗汉殿, Luóhàn Diàn). A statue of Guanyin (观世音菩萨, Guānshìyīn Púsà, the Goddess of Mercy; p988) frequently stands at the rear of the main hall, facing north, atop a fish's head or a rocky outcrop.

The rear hall may be where the sutras (Buddhist scriptures) were once stored, in which case it will be called the **Sutra Storing Building** (藏经楼, Cángjīnglóu). Conceived to house the remains of Buddha and later other Buddhist relics, sutras, religious artefacts and documents, a **pagoda** (塔, Tǎ) may rise above the main halls or may be the only surviving fragment of an otherwise destroyed temple.

Taoist Temples

Taoist shrines are not as plentiful and are generally more nether-worldly than Buddhist shrines, though the basic layout echoes Buddhist temples. They are decorated with a distinct set of motifs, including the *bāguà* (八卦, eight trigrams) formations, reflected in eight-sided pavilions and halls, and the Taiji yin/yang *(yīn/yáng)* diagram. Effigies of Laotzu, the Jade Emperor and other characters popularly associated with Taoist myth, such as the Eight Immortals, Guandi and the God of Wealth, are customary.

Taoist door gods, similar to those in Buddhist temples, often guard temple entrances. The main hall is usually called the **Hall of the Three Clear Ones** (三清殿, Sānqīng Diàn), devoted to a triumvirate of Taoist deities. Pagodas are generally absent at Taoist temples as they are Buddhist in function.

Taoist monks (and nuns) are easily distinguished from their shaven-headed Buddhist confrères by their long hair, twisted into topknots, straight trousers and squarish jackets.

Confucian Temples

Unless they have vanished or been destroyed, Confucian temples can be found in the old town district of ancient settlements throughout China and are typically very quiet havens of peace and far less visited than Buddhist or Taoist temples. The largest Confucian temple in China is at Qufu in Shandong, Confucius' birthplace.

Confucian temples are called either Kǒng Miào (孔庙) or Wén Miào (文庙) in Chinese and bristle with stelae celebrating local scholars, some supported on the backs of *bìxì* (mythical tortoiselike dragons). A statue of Kongzi (Confucius) usually resides in the main hall (大成殿; Dàchéng Diàn), overseeing rows of dusty musical instruments and flanked by disciples and philosophers.

Contemporary Architecture

Architecturally speaking, anything goes in today's China. You only have to look at the Pudong skyline to discover a melange of competing designs, some dramatic, inspiring and novel, others rash. The display represents a nation brimming with confidence, zeal and money.

Most of the top names in international architecture have designed at least one building in China in the past decade. Impressive examples of modern architecture include the National Stadium (aka the 'Bird's Nest') and the CCTV Headquarters in Beijing; and the art deco-esque Jinmao Tower, the towering Shanghai World Financial Center, Tomorrow Square and the Shanghai Tower in Shanghai. In Guangzhou the Zaha Hadid–designed Guangzhou Opera House is an astonishing contemporary creation, both inside and out.

For something rather different, Jinhua Architecture Park, a project of artist Ai Weiwei, is an abandoned, overgrown, mouldering yet thought-provoking collection of modern memorial pavilions (designed by such names as Herzog & de Meuron), slowly returning to nature. They can be found in Jinhua, Zhejiang province.

China's Landscapes

The world's third-largest country, China swallows up an immense 9.5 million sq km, only surpassed in area by Russia and Canada. So whatever floats your boat – verdant bamboo forests, sapphire Himalayan lakes, towering sand dunes, sublime mountain gorges, huge glaciers or sandy beaches – China's landscapes offer a simply jaw-dropping diversity.

The Land

Straddling natural environments as diverse as subarctic tundra in the north and tropical rainforests in the south, this massive land embraces the world's highest mountain range and one of its hottest and most forbidding deserts, to the steamy, typhoon-lashed coastline of the South China Sea. Fragmenting this epic landscape is a colossal web of waterways, including one of the world's mightiest rivers – the Yangzi (长江; Cháng Jiāng).

Mountains

China has a largely mountainous and hilly topography, commencing in precipitous fashion in the vast and sparsely populated Qinghai–Tibetan plateau in the west and levelling out gradually towards the fertile, well-watered, populous and wealthy provinces of eastern China.

This mountainous disposition sculpts so many of China's scenic highlights, from the glittering Dragon's Backbone Rice Terraces of Guangxi to the incomparable stature of Mt Everest, the stunning beauty of Jiuzhaigou National Park in Sichuan, the ethereal peaks of misty Huangshan in Anhui, the vertiginous inclines of Hua Shan in Shaanxi, the sublime karst geology of Yangshuo in Guangxi and the volcanic drama of Heaven Lake in Jilin.

Averaging 4500m above sea level, the Qinghai–Tibetan region's highest peaks thrust up into the Himalayan mountain range along its southern rim. The Himalayas, on average about 6000m above sea level, include 40 peaks rising dizzyingly to 7000m or more. Also known as the planet's 'third pole', this is where the world's highest peak, Mt Everest – 'Zhūmùlǎngmǎ fēng' being the Chinese form of its Tibetan name – thrusts up jaggedly from the Tibet–Nepal border.

This vast high-altitude region (Tibet alone constitutes one-eighth of China's landmass) is home to an astonishing 37,000 glaciers – 14.5% of the world's total glacier mass – and the third-largest body of ice on the planet after the Arctic and Antarctic. This enormous body of frozen water ensures that the Qinghai–Tibetan region is the source of many of China's largest rivers, including the Yellow (Huáng Hé), Mekong (Láncāng Jiāng) and Salween (Nù Jiāng) Rivers and, of course, the mighty Yangzi. Global warming, however, is inevitably eating into this glacial volume and though experts argue over how quickly it is melting, Xinhua reported that some 7600 sq km (18% of the total glacier mass in Tibet) of ice has vanished since the 1950s.

This mountain geology further corrugates the rest of China, continuously rippling the land into spectacular mountain ranges. There's the

China has earmarked a staggering US$140 billion for an ambitious programme of wind farms; ranging from Xinjiang province to Jiangsu province in the east, the huge wind farms were due for completion in 2020.

breathtaking 2500km-long Kunlun range, the mighty Karakoram mountains on the border with Pakistan, the Tian Shan range in Xinjiang, the Tanggula range on the Qinghai–Tibetan plateau, the Qinling mountains and the Greater Khingan range (Daxingan Ling) in the northeast.

Deserts

China contains head-spinningly huge – and growing – desert regions that occupy almost one-fifth of the country's landmass, largely in its mighty northwest. These are inhospitably sandy and rocky expanses where summers are staggeringly hot and winters bone-numbingly cold, but as destinations they offer sublime visuals.

The Silk Road into China steered its epic caravan-laden course through this entire region, ferrying slow-moving fleets of camels heavily burdened with merchandise and bringing languages, philosophies, customs and peoples from the far-flung lands of the Middle East.

North towards Kazakhstan and Kyrgyzstan from the plateaus of Tibet and Qinghai is Xinjiang's Tarim Basin, the world's largest inland basin. This is the location of the mercilessly thirsty Taklamakan Desert – China's largest desert and the world's second-largest mass of sand after the Sahara Desert.

The harsh environment shares many topographical features with the neighbouring nations of Afghanistan, Kyrgyzstan and Kazakhstan, and is almost the exact opposite of China's lush and well-watered seaboard southern provinces. Indeed, the Continental Pole of Inaccessibility (the spot on land furthest from the ocean) is located in Xinjiang, at a point near the border with Kazakhstan.

The Tarim Basin is bordered to the north by the lofty Tian Shan range – home to the glittering Tian Chi Lake – and to the west by the mighty Pamirs, which border Pakistan. Also in Xinjiang is China's hotspot, the Turpan Basin. Known as the 'Oasis of Fire' and 'China's Death Valley', it gets into the record books as China's lowest-lying region and the world's second-deepest depression after the Dead Sea in Israel.

China's most famous desert is, of course, the ever-expanding Gobi, though most of it lies outside the country's borders. In little-visited Western Inner Mongolia, the awesome Badain Jaran Desert offers travellers spectacular journeys among remote desert lakes and colossal, fixed sand dunes over 460m in height. Further west lie the famous grasslands and steppes of Inner Mongolia.

Rivers & Plains

The Yangzi (the 'Long River') is one of the longest rivers in the world (and China's longest). Its watershed of almost 2 million sq km – 20% of China's landmass – supports 400 million people. Dropping from its source high on the Tibetan plateau, it runs for 6300km to the sea, with the last few hundred kilometres across virtually flat alluvial plains. In the course of its sweeping journey, the river (and its tributaries) fashions many of China's scenic spectacles, including Tiger Leaping Gorge and the Three Gorges, and cuts through a string of huge and historic cities, including Chongqing, Wuhan and Nanjing, before surging into the East China Sea north of Shanghai. As a transport route, the river is limited (especially with the advent of high-speed rail), but the Three Gorges cruise is China's most celebrated and impressive river journey.

At about 5460km in length and the second-longest river in China, the Yellow River (黄河; Huáng Hé) is touted as the birthplace of Chinese civilisation and has been fundamental in the development of Chinese society. The mythical architect of China's rivers, the Great Yu, apocryphally noted 'Whoever controls the Yellow River controls China'. From its source

China's Bayan Obo Mining District in Inner Mongolia produces around 45% of the world's rare earth metals, elements essential for the production of mobile phones, high-definition TVs, computers, wind turbines and other products.

In 2010 six of China's *dānxiá* (eroded reddish sandstone rock), karst-like geological formations, were included in Unesco's World Heritage List. The list includes Chishui in Guizhou province. The rocks can also be seen outside Zhangye in Gansu.

in Qinghai, the river runs through North China, meandering past or near many famous towns, including Lanzhou, Yinchuan, Baotou, Hancheng, Jincheng, Luoyang, Zhengzhou, Kaifeng and Ji'nan in Shandong, before exiting China north of Dongying (though the watercourse often runs dry nowadays before it reaches the sea).

Fields & Agriculture

China's hills and mountains may surround travellers with a dramatic backdrop, but they are a massive agricultural headache for farmers. Small plots of land are eked out in patchworks of earth squashed between hillsides, or rescued from mountain cliffs and ravines, in the demanding effort to feed 20% of the world's population with just 10% of its arable land.

As only 15% of China's land can be cultivated, hillside gradients and inclines are valiantly levelled off, wherever possible, into bands of productive terraced fields. Stunning examples of rice terraces – beautiful in the right light – can be admired at the Yuanyang Rice Terraces in Yunnan and the Dragon's Backbone Rice Terraces in Guangxi.

Wildlife

China's vast size, diverse topography and climatic disparities support an astonishing range of habitats for animal life. The Tibetan plateau alone is the habitat of more than 500 species of birds, while half of the animal species in the northern hemisphere exist in China.

It is unlikely you will see many of these creatures in their natural habitat unless you are a specialist, or have a lot of time, patience, persistence, determination and luck. But there are plenty of pristine reserves within relatively easy reach of travellers' destinations such as Chengdu and Xi'an, and even if you don't get the chance to see animals, the scenery is terrific. Try Yading Nature Reserve in Sichuan, Mengda Nature Reserve in Qinghai, Sanchahe Nature Reserve in Yunnan, Fanjingshan in Guizhou, Shennongjia in Hubei, Wuzhishan in Hainan, Kanas Lake Nature Reserve in Xinjiang and Changbai Shan, China's largest nature reserve, in Jilin.

Mammals

China's towering mountain ranges form natural refuges for wildlife, many of which are now protected in parks and reserves that have escaped the depredations of loggers and dam builders. The barren high plains of the Tibetan plateau are home to many large animals, such as the chiru (Tibetan antelope), snow leopard, Tibetan wild ass, wild sheep and goats, and wolves. In theory many of these animals are protected, but in practice poaching and hunting still threaten their survival.

One of the aims of the Three Gorges Dam is to help prevent flooding on the Yangzi River. The river has caused hundreds of catastrophic floods, including the disastrous inundation of 1931, in which an estimated 145,000 people died.

TOP BOOKS ON CHINA'S ENVIRONMENT

➡ *When a Billion Chinese Jump* (2010) Jonathan Watts

➡ *China as a Polar Great Power* (2018) Anne Marie Brady

➡ *China's Environmental Challenges* (2012) Judith Shapiro

➡ *The River Runs Black: The Environmental Challenge to China's Future* (2010; 2nd edition) Elizabeth Economy

➡ *The China Price: The True Cost of Chinese Competitive Advantage* (2008) Alexandra Harney

The beautiful and retiring snow leopard, which normally inhabits the highest parts of the most remote mountain ranges, sports a luxuriant coat of fur against the cold. It preys on mammals as large as mountain goats, but is unfortunately persecuted for allegedly killing livestock.

The Himalayan foothills of western Sichuan support the greatest diversity of mammals in China. Aside from giant pandas, other mammals found in this region include the panda's small cousin – the raccoon-like red panda – as well as Asiatic black bears and leopards. Among the grazers are golden takin, a large goat-like antelope with a yellowish coat, argali sheep and various deer species, including the diminutive mouse deer.

The sparsely populated northeastern provinces abutting Siberia are inhabited by reindeer, moose, bears, sables and Manchurian tigers.

The tropical rainforests of Yunnan province, particularly the area around Xishuangbanna, support Indo-Chinese tigers and herds of Asiatic elephants.

The wild mammals you are most likely to see are several species of monkeys. The large and precocious Père David's macaque is common at Emei Shan in Sichuan. Macaques can also be seen on Hainan's Monkey Island. Several other monkey species are rare and endangered, including the beautiful golden monkey of Fanjingshan and the snub-nosed monkey of the Yunnan rainforests. But by far the most endangered is the Hainan gibbon, numbering just a few dozen individuals on Hainan Island thanks to massive forest clearance.

The giant panda (*xióngmāo* – literally 'bear cat') is western Sichuan's most famous denizen, but the animal's solitary nature makes it elusive for observation in the wild, and even today, after decades of intensive research and total protection in dedicated reserves, sightings are rare. It's a notoriously fickle breeder (the female is only on heat for a handful of days each spring); there are approximately 1864 pandas in the Chinese wilds, according to World Wildlife Fund. The easiest way to see pandas outside of zoos is at the Giant Panda Breeding Research Base just outside Chengdu, or at the Ya'an Bifengxia Panda Base, also in Sichuan.

The dawn redwood (*Metasequoia*), a towering (growing up to 60m) and elegant fine-needled deciduous Chinese tree, dates to the Jurassic era. Once considered long extinct, a single example was discovered in 1941 in a Sichuan village, followed three years later by the discovery of further trees.

Birds

Most of the wildlife you'll see in China will be birds, and with more than 1300 species recorded, including about 100 endemic or near-endemic species, China offers some fantastic birdwatching opportunities, with spring usually the best time.

Among China's more famous large birds are cranes, with nine of the world's 14 species having been recorded here. In Jiangxi province, on the lower Yangzi, a vast series of shallow lakes and lagoons was formed by stranded overflow from Yangzi flooding. High numbers of waterfowl and other birds, including ducks, geese, herons and egrets, inhabit these swamps year-round. Although it is difficult to reach, and infrastructure for birdwatchers is practically nonexistent, birders are increasingly drawn to the area in winter, when many of the lakes dry up and attract flocks of up to five crane species, including the endangered, pure-white Siberian crane.

Recommended destinations include Zhalong Nature Reserve, one of several vast wetlands in Heilongjiang province. Visit in summer to see breeding storks, cranes and flocks of wildfowl before they fly south for the winter. Beidaihe, on the coast of the Bohai Sea, is well known for migratory birds. Other breeding grounds and wetlands include Qinghai Lake in Qinghai, Caohai Lake in Guizhou, Jiuzhaigou in Sichuan and Mai Po Marsh in Hong Kong.

Most birdwatchers and bird tours head straight for Sichuan, which offers superb birding at sites such as Wolong. Bird Tour Asia (www.bird tourasia.com) has popular tours to Sichuan, Tibet, Qinghai, eastern China and southeast China, and also provides custom tours.

Plants

China is home to more than 32,000 species of seed plant and 2500 species of forest tree, plus an extraordinary plant diversity that includes some famous 'living fossils' – a diversity so great that Jilin province in the semifrigid north and Hainan province in the tropical south share few plant species.

Apart from rice, the plant probably most often associated with China and Chinese culture is bamboo, of which the country boasts some 300 species. Bamboos grow in many parts of China, but bamboo forests were once so extensive that they enabled the evolution of the giant panda, which eats virtually nothing else, and a suite of small mammals, birds and insects that live in bamboo thickets. Most of these useful species are found in the subtropical areas south of the Yangzi, and the best surviving thickets are in southwestern provinces such as Sichuan.

Many plants commonly cultivated in Western gardens today originated in China, among them the ginkgo tree, a famous 'living fossil' whose unmistakable imprint has been found in 270-million-year-old rocks.

Deciduous forests cover mid-altitudes in the mountains, and are characterised by oaks, hemlocks and aspens, with a leafy understorey that springs to life after the winter snows have melted. Among the more famous blooms of the understorey are rhododendrons and azaleas, and many species of each grow naturally in China's mountain ranges. Although they are best viewed in spring, some species flower right through summer. One of the best places to see them is at Sichuan's Wolong Nature Reserve.

A growing number of international wildlife-travel outfits arrange botanical expeditions to China, including UK-based Naturetrek (www. naturetrek.co.uk), which arranges tours to Yunnan, Sichuan and the Tibetan plateau.

Endangered Species

Almost every large mammal you can think of in China has crept onto the endangered species list, as well as many of the so-called 'lower' animals and plants. The snow leopard, Indo-Chinese tiger, chiru antelope, crested ibis, Asiatic elephant, red-crowned crane and black-crowned crane are all endangered.

Deforestation, pollution and hunting and trapping for fur, body parts, medicine, food delicacies and sport are all culprits. The Convention on International Trade in Endangered Species of Wild Fauna and Flora (CITES) records legal trade in live reptiles and parrots, and high numbers of reptile and wildcat skins. The number of such products collected or sold unofficially is anyone's guess.

Despite the threats, a number of rare animal species cling to survival in the wild. Notable among them are the Chinese alligator in Anhui, the giant salamander in the fast-running waters of the Yangzi and Yellow Rivers, the Yangzi River dolphin in the lower and middle reaches of the river (though there have been no sightings since 2002), and the pink dolphin of the Hong Kong islands of Sha Chau and Lung Kwu Chau. The giant panda is confined to the fauna-rich valleys and ranges of Sichuan.

CHINA'S LANDSCAPES WILDLIFE

By 2019 China had invested in a nationwide fleet of 421,000 electric buses, a staggering 99% of the world total.

The World Health Organization estimates that air pollution causes more than 1.4 million fatalities per year in China, while around 300 million rural Chinese do not have access to safe drinking water.

The Environment

China may be vast, but with two-thirds of the land covered in mountains, desert or uncultivable area, the remaining third is overwhelmed by the people of the world's most populous nation. For the first time in its history, China's city dwellers outnumbered rural residents in 2011, with an urbanisation rate set to increase to 65% by 2050. The speed of development – and the sheer volume of poured concrete – is staggering. During the next 15 years, China is expected to build urban areas equal in size to 10 New York Cities; a staggering one billion Chinese could be urban residents by 2030.

Beyond urban areas, deforestation and overgrazing have accelerated the desertification of vast areas of China, particularly in the western provinces. Deserts now cover almost one-fifth of the country and China's dustbowl is the world's largest, swallowing up 200 sq km of arable land every month. The Gobi Desert is the world's fastest-growing desert, consuming 3600 sq km of grassland annually.

China has been undertaking a huge tree-planting programme, increasing its forest coverage from 8.6% in 1949 to 21.7% in 2017.

A Greener China?

China is painfully aware of its accelerated desertification, growing water shortages, shrinking glaciers, acidic rain, contaminated rivers, caustic urban air and polluted soil. The government is keenly committed, on a policy level, to the development of greener and cleaner energy sources. China's leaders are also seeking to devise a more sustainable and less wasteful economic model for the nation's future development.

China is, however, the world's largest carbon emitter. There is evidence of bold thinking though: in 2010 China announced it would pour billions into developing electric and hybrid vehicles; Beijing committed itself to overtaking Europe in renewable-energy investment by 2020; wind-farm construction (in Gansu, for example) continues apace; and China leads the world in the production of solar cells. Coal use began declining from 2013, though 59% of China's energy was provided by coal in 2018, reflecting a second annual increase in a row. There are worries that China may recently have put emissions reduction on the back-burner due to its slowing economy and growing costs.

SOUTH–NORTH WATER DIVERSION PROJECT

With only around 7% of the world's water resources but almost 20% of its population, China faces a worsening water crisis. Farmers in the arid north are draining aquifers that have taken thousands of years to accumulate, while industry in China uses three to 10 times more water per unit of production than developed nations. Meanwhile water usage in large cities such as Beijing and Tianjin continues to climb as migrants flood in from rural areas.

To combat the crisis the Chinese Communist Party (CCP) embarked on the construction of the US$81-billion South–North Water Diversion Project, a vast network of pumping stations, canals and aqueducts (as well as a tunnel under the Yellow River) designed to divert 3.8 million Olympic swimming pools' worth of water yearly from the Yangzi River to the parched regions of China's north. The first stage began operating in 2013. Calculations, however, suggested that by 2020 only 5% of Beijing's water requirements would be met by the diverted water.

There are also concerns about pollution in the Yangzi River becoming progressively concentrated as water is extracted, while Yangzi cities such as Nanjing and Wuhan are increasingly uneasy that they will be left with a water shortfall. In 2016 it was revealed that lakes along the Yangzi River had reported up to a 40% drop in water inflow.

Public protests – sometimes violent – against polluting industries have proliferated in recent years across China and have scored a number of notable victories, including the 2012 demonstrations in Shifang (Sichuan), which led to the cancellation of a planned US$1.6 billion copper-smelting facility. A 2013 survey in China revealed that 78% of people would demonstrate if polluting industries were constructed near their homes. Much of the agitation is the result of health concerns, as cancer is now the leading cause of death in China, with 7500 deaths per day as a result of the disease (lung cancer being the most prevalent form).

China Dialogue (www.china dialogue.net) is a resourceful dual-language website that seeks to promote debate on China's immense environmental challenges.

Martial Arts of China

Unlike Western fighting arts – savate, kick-boxing etc – Chinese martial arts are deeply impregnated with religious and philosophical values. And, some might add, a morsel or two of magic. Many eminent exponents of *gōngfū* (功夫) – better known in the west as kung fu – were devout monks or religious recluses who drew inspiration from Buddhism and Taoism and sought a mystical communion with the natural world. These were not leisurely pursuits, but were closely entangled with the meaning and purpose of life.

Styles & Schools

China lays claim to a bewildering range of martial-arts styles, from the flamboyant and showy, inspired by the movements of animals (some legendary) or insects (such as Praying Mantis Boxing), to schools more empirically built upon the science of human movement (eg wing chun). On the outer fringes lie the esoteric arts, abounding with metaphysical feats, arcane practices and closely guarded techniques.

Several Chinese styles of *gōngfū* (kung fu) include drunken sets, where the student mimics the supple movements of an inebriate.

Many fighting styles were once secretively handed down for generations within families and it is only relatively recently that outsiders have been accepted as students. Some schools, especially the more obscure styles, have been driven to extinction partly due to their exclusivity and clandestine traditions.

Some styles also found themselves divided into competing factions, each laying claim to the original teachings and techniques. Such styles may exist in a state of schism, while other styles have become part of the mainstream – the southern Chinese martial art of wing chun in particular has become globally recognised, largely due to its associations with Bruce Lee.

Unlike Korean and Japanese arts such as taekwondo or karate-do, there is frequently no international regulatory body that oversees the syllabus, tournaments or grading requirements for China's individual martial arts. Consequently students of China's myriad martial arts may be rather unsure of what level they have attained and it is often down to the individual teacher to decide what to teach students, and how quickly.

Fujian white crane is a southern Chinese fighting style invented by a woman called Fang Qiniang, who based the art's forms and strategy of attack and defence on careful observation of the bird's movements.

Hard School

Although there is considerable blurring between the two camps, Chinese martial arts are often distinguished between hard and soft schools. Typically aligned with Buddhism, the hard or 'external' (外家, *wàijiā*) school tends to be more vigorous, athletic and concerned with the development of power. Many of these styles are related to Shaolin boxing and the Shaolin Temple in Henan province.

Shaolin boxing is forever associated with Bodhidharma, an ascetic Indian Buddhist monk who visited the Shaolin Temple and added a series of breathing and physical exercises to the Shaolin monks' sedentary meditations. The Shaolin monks' legendary endeavours and fearsome physical skills became known throughout China and beyond.

Soft School

Usually inspired by Taoism, the soft or 'internal' Chinese school (内家, *nèijiā*) develops pliancy and softness as a weapon against hard force. Taichi (*tàijí quán*) is the best-known soft school, famed for its slow and lithe movements and an emphasis on cultivating *qì* (energy). Attacks are met with yielding movements that smother the attacking force and lead the aggressor off balance. Other soft schools include the circular moves of *bagua zhang* and the linear boxing patterns of *xíngyì quán*, based on five basic punches – each linked to one of the five elements of Chinese philosophy – and the movements of 12 animals.

Zhang Sanfeng, the founder of taichi, was supposedly able to walk more than 1000 *li* (around 560km) a day; others say he lived for more than 200 years!

Forms

Most students of Chinese martial arts – hard or soft – learn forms (套路; *tàolu*), a series of movements linked together into a pattern, which embody the principal punches and kicks of the style. In essence, forms are unwritten compendiums of the style, to ensure passage from one generation to the next. The number and complexity of forms varies from style to style: taichi may only have one form, though it may be very lengthy (the long form of the Yang style takes around 20 minutes to perform). Five ancestors boxing has dozens of forms, while wing chun only has three empty-hand forms.

Qigong

Closely linked to both the hard and especially the soft martial-arts schools is the practice of qigong (气功, *qìgōng*), a technique for cultivating and circulating *qì* (energy) around the body. *Qì* can be developed for use in fighting to protect the body, as a source of power or for curative and health-giving purposes.

Qì can be developed in a number of ways – by standing still in fixed postures, or with gentle exercises, meditation and measured breathing techniques. Taichi itself is a moving form of qigong cultivation, while at the harder end of the spectrum a host of qigong exercises aim to make specific parts of the body impervious to attack.

The linear movements and five punches of the internal Chinese martial art, body-mind boxing (*xíngyì quán*), possibly evolved from spear-fighting techniques.

Bagua Zhang

One of the more esoteric and obscure of the soft Taoist martial arts, *bagua zhang* (八卦掌, *bāguà zhǎng*; eight trigram boxing, also known as *pa-kua)* is also one of the most intriguing. The *bagua zhang* student wheels around in a circle, rapidly changing direction and speed, occasionally thrusting out a palm strike.

Bagua zhang draws its inspiration from the trigrams (an arrangement of three broken and unbroken lines) of the classic *Book of Changes* (*Yì-jīng* or *I Ching*), the ancient oracle used for divination. The trigrams are typically arranged in circular form and it is this pattern that is traced

BOOKS ON CHINESE MARTIAL ARTS

If you can track down a copy, John F Gilbey's *The Way of a Warrior* is a tongue-in-cheek, expertly written and riveting account of the Oriental fighting arts and their mysteries.

For metaphysical pointers, soft-school adherents can dip into Laotzu's terse but inspiring *The Classic of the Way and Its Power*.

A couple of very useful books (both in print at the time of writing) on *bagua zhang* include *Pa-Kua: Chinese Boxing for Fitness & Self-Defense* (Robert Smith; Blue Snake Books) and *A Short Guide to Baguazhang Circle Walking* (Edward Hines). If you can get hold of the magnificent short story 'Pop Songs and Pa-kua' (in *The Way of a Warrior* by John F Gilbey aka Robert Smith; North Atlantic Books), do so.

out by the *bagua zhang* exponent. Training commences by just walking the circle so the student gradually becomes infused with its patterns and rhythms.

A hallmark of the style is the exclusive use of the palm, not the fist, as the principal weapon. The palm can transmit a lot of power and is also better protected than the fist as it is cushioned by muscle.

The student must become proficient in the subterfuge, evasion, speed and unpredictability that are hallmarks of *bagua zhang*. Force is generally not met with force, but deflected by the circular movements cultivated in students through their meditations upon the circle. Circular forms – arcing, twisting, twining and spinning – are the mainstay of all movements, radiating from the waist.

Despite being dated by historians to the 19th century, *bagua zhang* is quite probably a very ancient art. Beneath the Taoist overlay, the movements and patterns of the art suggest a possibly animistic or shamanistic origin, which gives the art its timeless rhythms.

Praying mantis master Fan Yook Tung once killed two stampeding bulls with an iron-palm technique.

Wing Chun

Conceived by a Buddhist nun from the Shaolin Temple called Ng Mui, who taught her skills to a young girl called Wing Chun (詠春), this is a fast and dynamic system of fighting that promises quick results for novices. Wing chun (*yǒng chūn*) was the style that taught Bruce Lee how to move and, though he ultimately moved away from it to develop his own school, wing chun had an enormous influence on the Hong Kong fighter and actor.

Wing chun emphasises speed over strength and evasion – rapid strikes and low kicks are its hallmark techniques. Forms are simple and direct, dispensing with the pretty flourishes that clutter other styles.

Iron shirt (*tiěshān*) is an external kung fu (*gōngfū*) qigong training exercise that circulates and concentrates the *qi* (energy) in certain areas to protect the body from impacts during a fight.

The art can perhaps best be described as scientific. There are none of the animal forms that make other styles so exciting and mysterious. Instead wing chun is built around its centre-line theory, which draws an imaginary line down the human body and centres all attacks and blocks along that line. The line runs through the sensitive regions: eyes, nose, mouth, throat, heart, solar plexus and groin and any blow on these points is debilitating and dangerous.

The three empty hand forms – which look bizarre to non-initiates – train arm and leg movements that both attack and defend this line. None of the blocks stray beyond the width of the shoulders, as this is the limit of possible attacks, and punches follow the same theory. Punches are delivered with great speed in a straight line, along the shortest distance between puncher and punched. All of this gives wing chun its distinctive simplicity and economy of movement.

Survival Guide

Directory A–Z

(with lots of preparation and prebooking). High-speed trains are generally far more accessible than older rolling stock. Many urban metro systems are quite accessible as they are relatively modern systems, so a fair number of stations have lifts. Accessible toilets can be found in shopping malls in large cities and also at airports, but squat loos elsewhere can make travelling very difficult.

Download Lonely Planet's free *Accessible Travel* guides from http://lptravel.to/AccessibleTravel.

Accommodation

Booking Services

Booking online can help you secure a room and obtain a good price, but remember that you should be able to bargain down the price of your room at hotel reception (except at youth hostels and the cheapest hotels) or over the phone. To secure accommodation, always plan ahead and book your room in advance during the high season. Airports at major cities often have hotel-booking counters that offer discounted rates.

Trip.com (www.trip.com) Excellent hotel booking, air and train ticketing website, with English helpline. Useful app available.

Agoda (www.agoda.com) Generally efficient for hotel bookings.

Accessible Travel

China is not easy to navigate for travellers with limited mobility, but travel in a wheelchair is possible in the large cities by staying at top-end accommodation

eLong (www.elong.net) Hotel and air ticket booking, with English helpline.

Camping

There are few places where you can legally camp, and as most of China's flat land is put to agricultural use, you will largely be limited to remote, hilly regions. Camping is more feasible in wilder and less-populated parts of west China, but be aware it is not strictly legal as you should register your whereabouts with the PSB.

In certain destinations with camping possibilities, travel agencies and hotels will arrange overnight camping trips or multiday treks, in which case camping equipment will be supplied. Camping on the Great Wall is technically illegal, but the watchtowers are often used for pitching tents or rolling out a sleeping bag (if you do, make sure to clean up after yourself and take care of the Wall).

Courtyard Hotels

Largely confined to Beijing, courtyard hotels are a good choice for a more traditional experience. Arranged around traditional sìhéyuàn (courtyards), rooms are on ground level. Courtyard hotels are charming and romantic, but are often expensive and rooms are small, in keeping with the dimensions of courtyard residences. Facilities will be limited, so don't expect a swimming pool, gym or subterranean garage.

Budget Business Chain Hotels

Dotted around much of China, budget business chain hotels can sometimes be a decent alternative to old-school two- and three-star hotels, with rooms around the ¥180 to ¥300 mark. Their sheer universality means you can usually find accommodation (but look at the rooms first). They often have membership/ loyalty schemes, or online deals, which make rooms

cheaper. Breakfast is sometimes included.

Although most of these branches accept foreigners, the odd one does not. Chains include:

Jinjiang Inn (www.jinjianginns. com)

7 Days Inn (www.7daysinn.com)

Home Inn (www.bthhotels.com)

Ibis (www.accorhotels.com)

For higher standards of comfort (with breakfast included) try **Holiday Inn Express** (www.ihg.com/holidayinn express).

Guesthouses

The cheapest of the cheap are China's ubiquitous and rather grimy guesthouses (招待所, zhāodàisuǒ), often found clustered near train or bus stations, but also dotted around cities and towns. The majority are upstairs, accessed through a small door leading up narrow stairs from the street. Not all guesthouses accept foreigners, and Chinese-language skills may be crucial in securing a room. Rooms (doubles, twins, triples, quads) are primitive and grey, with tiled floors and possibly a shower room or shabby bathroom. Showers may be communal.

Other terms for guesthouses, or signs signifying guesthouse accommodation, are as follows:

➜ 旅店 (lǚdiàn)

➜ 旅馆 (lǚguǎn)

➜ 有房 (yǒufáng) means 'rooms available'

➜ 今日有房 (jīnrì yǒufáng) means 'rooms available today'

➜ 住宿 (zhùsù) means 'accommodation'

Homesteads

In more rural destinations, small towns and villages, you should be able to find a homestead (农家, nóngjiā) with a small number of rooms in the region of ¥50. Bargaining is possible; you will not need to register. The owner will be more than happy to cook up meals for you as well. Showers and toilets are generally communal.

Hostels

If you're looking for efficiently run budget accommodation, turn to China's youth-hostel sector. **Hostelling International** (www.yhachina. com; English functionality) hostels are generally well run. Other private youth hostels scattered around China are unaffiliated and standards at these may be variable. Book ahead in popular towns as rooms can go fast.

Superb for meeting like-minded travellers, hostels are typically staffed by youthful English speakers who are also well informed on local sightseeing and transport. The foreigner-friendly vibe in hostels stands in marked contrast to many stiffer Chinese hotels. Double rooms in youth hostels are frequently better than midrange equivalents and often just as comfortable and better located. These places may be cheaper (but

---

TRAVELLER RESTRICTIONS

The majority of hotels in China still do not have the authorisation to accept foreigners as guests. This can be a source of frustration when you find yourself steered towards pricier midrange and top-end lodgings. As a useful general rule, if a hotel can be booked on major websites such as booking.com and Agoda, it will usually be able to accept foreign guests.

To see if a hotel accepts foreign guests, ask '*zhège bīnguǎn shōu wàiguórén ma?*' (这个宾馆收外国人吗?).

BOOK YOUR STAY ONLINE

For more accommodation reviews by Lonely Planet authors, check out http://lonelyplanet.com/hotels/. You'll find independent reviews, as well as recommendations on the best places to stay..

not always: some hostels have prices similar to or higher than midrange hotels, so do compare), or can arrange better-value tours. Laundry, book lending, kitchen facilities, bike rental, lockers and a noticeboard, bar and cafe should all be available, as well as possibly a pool, ping pong, movies, game consoles and other forms of entertainment. Soap, shower gel and toothpaste are generally not provided, though you can purchase them at reception; the same is often (but not always) the case with towels. Be aware that some so-called 'International Youth Hostels' do not actually accept foreigners, so check.

Dorms usually cost between ¥40 and ¥55 (with discounts of around ¥5 for members). They typically come with bunk beds, but may have standard beds. Most dorms won't have en-suite showers, though some do; they should have air-con (except in cooler regions). Many hostels also have doubles, singles, twins and sometimes even family rooms. Prices vary but are often around ¥100 to ¥250 for a single or double (again, with discounts for members). Hostels can arrange ticketing or help you book a room in another affiliated youth hostel.

Book ahead – online if possible – as rooms are frequently booked out, especially at weekends or in busy holiday periods. In popular destinations (such as Hangzhou), hostels may charge elevated rates on Friday and Saturday.

Hotels

Hotels vary wildly in quality within the same budget bracket. The star rating system employed in China can sometimes be misleading: hotels may be awarded four or five stars when they are patently a star lower in ranking. Deficiencies may not be immediately apparent, so explore and inspect the overall quality of the hotel – viewing the room up front pays dividends.

Breakfast at many older-style midrange hotels is often Chinese: porridge (粥, zhōu), fried vegetables and noodles, buns (馒头, mántou) and boiled eggs. Coffee is usually provided and perhaps bread, a toaster, jam, marmalade and butter. At more international hotels, western-style breakfast will be provided.

China has few independent hotels of real distinction, so it's generally advisable to select chain hotels that offer a proven standard of international excellence. Shangri-La, Marriott, Hilton, St Regis, Ritz-Carlton, Marco Polo and Hyatt all have a presence in China and can generally be relied upon for high standards of service and comfort.

Note the following:

➡ Most rooms are twins rather than doubles, so be clear if you specifically want a double.

➡ Virtually all hotel rooms, whatever the price bracket, will have air-conditioning and a TV.

➡ English proficiency may be poor, even in some five-star hotels.

➡ Late-night telephone calls or calling cards from 'masseurs' and prostitutes can be expected in some budget and lower midrange hotels.

➡ All hotel rooms are subject to a 10% or 15% service charge, though the price quoted usually includes this.

➡ Most midrange and top-end hotels accept credit cards and also WeChat Pay and Alipay.

➡ In China there are several words for 'hotel':
bīnguǎn (宾馆)
dàfàndiàn (大饭店)
dàjiǔdiàn (大酒店)
fàndiàn (饭店)
jiǔdiàn (酒店)

Temples & Monasteries

Some temples and monasteries (especially on China's sacred mountains) provide accommodation. They are cheap but austere, may not have running water or electricity, and have very early check-out times.

Checking In & Out

At check-in you will need your passport; a registration form will ask what type of visa you have. For most travellers the visa will be L (travel visa). A deposit (押金, yājīn) is required at most hotels, which will be paid either with cash or by providing your credit-card details. International credit cards are generally only accepted at midrange hotels or chain express hotels and top-end accommodation, so always have cash just in case. If you pay your deposit in cash, you will be given a receipt and the deposit will be returned to you when you check out.

You usually have to check out by noon. Hotel policy regarding late check-out varies, so ask.

Rooms & Prices

On the whole, China's accommodation choices offer superb value for money. In most top-ticket towns it's not hard to find a comfortable and spacious room for between ¥100 and ¥200.

Accommodation is divided by price category, identified by the symbols ¥ (budget), ¥¥ (midrange) or ¥¥¥ (top end) – accommodation prices vary across China, so one region's budget breakdown may differ from another. It is common for hotel receptions to have a wall-mounted board with hyperinflated prices that aren't actually in use. We list the 'true' rack rate, which generally reflects the most you are ever expected to pay. However, at most times of the year discounts are in effect, which can range from 10% to 60% off.

Rooms come with private bathroom or shower room, unless otherwise stated. Rooms are generally easy to procure, but reserve ahead in popular tourist towns (such as Hangzhou), especially for weekend visits or during the hectic holiday periods when rooms fill up quickly.

Most rooms in China fall into the following categories:

Double rooms (双人房、标准间, *shuāng rén fáng* or *biāozhǔn jiān*) In most cases, these are twins, ie with two beds.

One-bed rooms/singles (单间, *dānjiān*) This is usually a room with one double-sized bed (only rarely a single bed).

Large-bed rooms (大床房, *dàchuáng fáng*) Larger than a one-bed room, with a big double bed.

Suites (套房, *tàofáng*) Available at most midrange and top-end hotels.

Dorms (多人房, *duōrénfáng*) Usually, but not always, available at youth hostels (and at a few hotels).

HOTEL DISCOUNTS

Always ignore the rack rate and ask for the discounted price or bargain for a room, as discounts usually apply everywhere except youth hostels (except for hostel members) and the cheapest accommodation. Discounts of 10% to 60% off the tariff rate (30% is typical) are the norm, available by simply asking at reception on arrival, by phoning in advance to reserve a room, or by booking online at Trip.com or Booking.com.

Apart from during the busy holiday periods (the end of April and first few days of May, the first week of October and Chinese New Year), rooms should be priced well below the rack rate and are rarely booked out. In some towns (such as Hangzhou or Guangzhou) there may be a pricier weekend rate (Friday and Saturday).

HOTEL TIPS

➡ The standard of English spoken is often better at youth hostels than at midrange or some high-end hotels.

➡ Your hotel can help with bus and train ticketing, for a commission.

➡ Almost every hotel has a left-luggage room, which should be free if you are a guest.

➡ Bargaining for a room is often possible.

➡ Ask your hotel concierge for a local map.

➡ When you go out, take a hotel business card with the address in Chinese on it to show to a taxi driver.

➡ If using a VPN, some public wi-fi networks may have firewalls in place that block and may slow down connections or break the connection altogether. Turning off the VPN may help restore the connection.

Booking Ahead

Reserving a room, even if only for the first night of your stay, is the best way to ensure a smooth start to your trip. These phrases should see you through a call if English isn't spoken.

Hello	你好	Nǐhǎo
I would like to book a room	我想订房间	Wǒ xiǎng dìng fángjiān
a single room	单人间	dānrén jiān
a double room	双人间	shuāngrén jiān
My name is...	我叫...	Wǒ jiào...
from... to... (date)	从...到...	cóng... dào...
How much is it per night/ person?	每天/个人多少钱?	Měi tiān/gè rén duōshǎo qián?
Thank you	谢谢你	Xièxie nǐ

Electricity

There are three types of plugs used in China – three-pronged angled pins, two flat pins (the most common), or two narrow round pins. Electricity is 220 volts, 50 cycles AC.

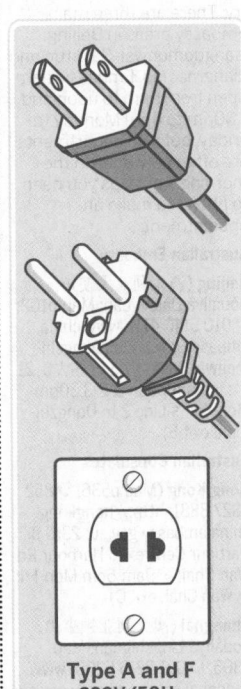

Type A and F
220V/50Hz

Type I
230V/50Hz

Embassies & Consulates

Embassies are located in Beijing, with consulates scattered around the country. There are three main embassy areas in Beijing: Jianguomenwai, Sanlitun and Liangmaqiao. Embassies are open from 9am to noon and 1.30pm to 4pm Monday to Friday, but visa departments are often only open in the morning. For visas you need to phone to make an appointment.

Australian Embassy

Beijing (澳大利亚大使馆, Àodàlìyà Dàshǐguǎn; Map p102; ☑010 5140 4111; www.china. embassy.gov.au; 21 Dongzhimenwai Dajie, 东直门外大街21号; ⊗9am-noon & 2-3.30pm Mon-Fri; ⑤Line 2 to Dongzhimen, exit E)

Australian Consulates

Hong Kong (Map p536; ☑852 2827 8881; http://hongkong. china.embassy.gov.au; 23rd fl, Harbour Centre, 25 Harbour Rd, Wan Chai; ⊗9am-5pm Mon-Fri; ⓜWan Chai, exit C)

Shanghai (澳大利亚领事馆, Àodàlìyà Lǐngshìguǎn; Map p305; ☑021 2215 5200; www. shanghai.china.embassy.gov.au; room 2101, 22nd fl, CITIC Sq,

1168 West Nanjing Rd, 南京西路1168号中信泰富广场22楼; ⊗9am-4pm Mon-Fri; ⓜWest Nanjing Rd)

Guangzhou (澳大利亚驻广州总领事馆, Àodàlìyà Zhù Guǎngzhōu Zǒng Lǐngshìguǎn; Map p594; ☑020 3814 0111; 12th fl, Development Centre, 3 Linjiang Dadao, 临江大道3号; ⓜLine 5 to Zhujiang New Town, exit B1)

Canadian Embassy

Beijing (加拿大大使馆, Jiānádà Dàshǐguǎn; Map p102; ☑010 5139 4000; www.china.gc.ca; 19 Dongzhimenwai Dajie, 东直门外大街19号; ⊗8.30-11am Mon-Fri & 1.30-3pm Tue & Thu; ⑤Line 2 to Dongzhimen, exit E)

Canadian Consulates

Hong Kong (Map p532; ☑852 3719 4700; 5th fl, Tower 3, Exchange Sq, 8 Connaught Pl, Central; ⓜCentral, exit A)

Shanghai (加拿大领事馆, Jiānádà Lǐngshìguǎn; Map p305; ☑021 3279 2800; www. canadainternational.gc.ca; 8th fl, 1788 West Nanjing Rd, 南京西路1788号8楼; ⊗8.30am-5pm; ⓜJing'an Temple)

Chongqing (Map p828; ☑023 6373 8007; www.canadainternational.gc.ca; Suite 1705, 17th fl, Metropolitan Tower, 68 Zourong Lu, 邹容路68号大都会商厦17层)

Guangzhou (加拿大驻广州总领事馆, Jiānádà Zhù Guǎngzhōu Zǒng Lǐngshìguǎn; ☑020 8611 6100; 26th fl, Tai Koo Hui Tower 1, 385 Tianhe Lu, 天河路385号太古汇一座26楼; ⓜLine 3 to Shipaiqiao, exit C)

French Embassy

Beijing (法国大使馆, Fàguó Dàshǐguǎn; Map p102; ☑010 8531 2000; www.ambafrance-cn. org; 60 Tianze Lu, 天泽路60号; ⊗8.30am-noon Mon-Fri, 9am-noon last Sat of month; ⑤Line 10 to Liangmaqiao, exit B)

French Consulates

Hong Kong (Map p532; ☑852 3196 6100; www.consulfrance-hongkong.org; 26th fl, Tower II, Admiralty Centre, 18 Harcourt Rd, Admiralty; ⊗8.30am-12.30pm Mon-Fri; ⓜAdmiralty, exit C2)

Shanghai (法国领事馆, Fǎguó Lǐngshìguǎn; ☑021 6010 6050; www.consulfrance-shanghai. org; 18th fl, Bldg A, Soho Zhongshan Plaza, 1055 West Zhongshan Rd, 中山西路1055号中山广场A座18楼; ⊗8.15am-12.15pm Mon, from 8.45am Tue-Fri)

Chengdu (法国驻成都总领事馆, Fǎguózhù Chéngdūzǒng Lǐngshìguǎn; Map p758; ☑028 6666 6060, emergency 177 2982 1930; www.cn.ambafrance.org/-Chengdu-Consulat-; 30th fl, Times Plaza, 2 Zongfu Lu, 总府路2号时代广场30楼; ⊗9am-12.30pm & 2.15-6pm Mon-Thu, to 4.30pm Fri; ⓜChunxi Rd)

Shenyang (Map p187; ☑024 2319 0000; 34 Nanshisan Weilu, 南十三纬路34号)

Guangzhou (法国驻广州总领事馆, Fǎguó Zhù Guǎngzhōu Zǒng Lǐngshìguǎn; Map p594; ☑020 2829 2000; 19th fl, Kaihua International Center, 5 Xiancun Lu, 冼村路5号凯华国际中心18层1901-1907室; ⓜLine 1 & 2 to Grand Theatre, exit B)

Wuhan (法国领事馆, Fǎguó Lǐngshìguǎn; Map p478; ☑027 6579 7900; https://cn.ambafrance.org; 17th Fl, New World International Trade Center, 568 Jianshe Dadao, 建设大道568号新世界国贸大厦17层; ⓜQushuilou)

German Embassy

Beijing (德国大使馆, Déguó Dàshǐguǎn; Map p102; ☑010 8532 9000; www.china.diplo.de; 17 Dongzhimenwai Dajie, 东直门外大街17号; ⊗8am-noon & 1-5pm Mon, to 5.30pm Tue-Thu, 8am-noon & 12.30-3pm Fri; ⑤Line 2 to Dongzhimen, exit E)

German Consulates

Hong Kong (Map p532; ☑852 2105 8788; www.hongkong. diplo.de; 21st fl, United Centre, 95 Queensway, Admiralty; ⊗8.30-11.30am Mon-Fri; ⓜAdmiralty, exit C2)

Shanghai (德国领事馆, Déguó Lǐngshìguǎn; Map p298; ☑021 3401 0106; www.shanghai. diplo.de; 181 Yongfu Rd, 永福路181号; ⊗8.30-11.30am; ⓜShanghai Library)

Chengdu (德国领事馆, Déguó Lǐngshìguǎn; Map p758; ☎028 8528 0800, emergency only 137 3060 0952; www.chengdu.diplo.de; 25th fl, Western Tower, 19 Renmin Nanlu 4th Section, 人民南路4段19号威斯顿联邦大厦25层; ⏲9am-noon Mon-Fri, telephone consultation 8am-5pm Mon-Thu, to 2pm Fri; Ⓜ Nijiaqiao)

Guangzhou (德国驻广州总领事馆, Déguó Zhù Guǎngzhōu Zǒng Lǐngshìguǎn; Map p594; ☎020 8313 0000; 14th fl, Main Tower, Yuèhǎi Tiānhé Bldg, 208 Tianhe Lu, 天河路208号粤海天河城大厦14楼; Ⓜ Line 1 & 3 to Tiyu Xilu, exit C)

Indian Embassy

Beijing (印度大使馆, Yìndù Dàshǐguǎn; ☎010 8531 2500; www.eoibeijing.gov.in; 5 Liangmaqiao Beijie, 亮马桥北街5号; ⏲8.30am-5.30pm Mon-Fri; Ⓢ Line 10 to Liangmaqiao, exit B)

Indian Consulate

Hong Kong (Map p532; ☎852 3970 9900; www.cgihk.gov.in; Unit A, 16th fl, United Centre, 95 Queensway, Admiralty; ⏲9am-5.30pm Mon-Fri)

Irish Embassy

Beijing (爱尔兰大使馆, Ài'ěrlán Dàshǐguǎn; Map p102; ☎010 8531 6200; www.irishembassy.cn; 3 Ritan Donglu, 日坛东路3号; ⏲9am-12.30pm & 2-5pm Mon-Fri; Ⓢ Line 1 to Yonganli, exit A1)

Irish Consulates

Hong Kong (Map p532; ☎852 2535 0700; www.dfa.ie/irish-consulate/hong-kong; 20th fl, 33 Des Voeux Rd Central, Central; ⏲10am-noon & 2.30-4.30pm Mon-Fri; Ⓜ Central, exit C)

Shanghai (爱尔兰领事馆, Ài'ěrlán Lǐngshìguǎn; Map p305; ☎021 6010 1360; www.embassyofireland.cn; 700a Shanghai Centre, 1376 West Nanjing Rd, 南京西路1376号上海商城700a室; ⏲9.30am-4.30pm Mon-Fri; Ⓜ Jing'an Temple, West Nanjing Rd)

Japanese Embassy

Beijing (日本大使馆, Rìběn Dàshǐguǎn; ☎010 8531 9800; www.cn.emb-japan.go.jp; 1 Liangmaqiao Dongjie, 亮马桥东街1号; ⏲9-11.30am & 1-4.30pm; Ⓢ Line 10 to Liangmaqiao, exit B)

Japanese Consulates

Hong Kong (Map p532; ☎852 2522 1184; www.hk.emb-japan.go.jp; 46-47th fl, 1 Exchange Sq, 8 Connaught Pl, Central; ⏲9.15am-noon & 1.30-4.45pm Mon-Fri; Ⓜ Central, exit D1)

Shanghai (日本领事馆, Rìběn Lǐngshìguǎn; ☎021 5257 4766; www.shanghai.cn.emb-japan.go.jp; 8 Wanshan Rd, 万山路8号; ⏲9am-12.30pm & 1.30-5.30pm Mon-Fri)

Qingdao (☎0532 8090 0001; 45th fl, 59 Xianggang Donglu; ⏲9-11am & 1.30-4pm)

Kazakh Embassy

Beijing (哈萨克斯坦大使馆, Hāsàkè Sītǎn Dàshǐguǎn; Map p102; ☎010 6532 4189, 010 6532 6182; www.mfa.gov.kz/en/beijing; 9 Sanlitun Dongliu Jie, 三里屯东六街9号; ⏲10am-1pm Mon-Fri; Ⓢ Line 10 to Liangmaqiao, exit D)

Kazakh Consulate

Ürümqi (哈萨克斯坦共和国驻, Hāsàkè Sītǎn Gònghéguó Zhù; ☎0991 369 7585; pvs-urumqi@yandex.ru; 216 Kunming Lu)

Kyrgyz Embassy

Beijing (吉尔吉斯斯坦大使馆, Jí'ěrjísīsītǎn Dàshǐguǎn; ☎010 6468 1348; www.kyrgyzstanembassy.net; 18 Xiaoyun Lu, 霄云路18号; ⏲applications 9-11am Mon, Wed & Fri; Ⓢ Line 10 to Sanyuanqiao, exit C2)

Kyrgyz Consulate

Ürümqi (吉尔吉斯斯坦共和国驻; Jí'ěrjísī Sītǎn Gònghéguó Zhù; Map p842; 38 Hetan Beilu; ⏲noon-2pm Mon-Fri)

Laotian Embassy

Beijing (老挝大使馆, Lǎowō Dàshǐguǎn; Map p102; ☎010 6532 1224; laoemcn@public.east.cn.net; 11 Sanlitun Dongsijie, 三里屯东三街11号; Ⓢ Line 10 to Agricultural Exhibition Center, exit D2)

Laotian Consulates

Hong Kong (Map p532; ☎852 2544 1186; 14th fl, Arion Commercial Centre, 2-12 Queen's Rd West, Sheung Wan; ⏲9am-noon & 1.30-5pm)

Kunming (老挝领事馆, Lǎowō Lǐngshìguǎn; ☎871 6316 8916; LaoKun02@public.km.yn.cn; Kunming Diplomat Compound, 6800 Caiyun Beilu, 彩云北路6800号; ⏲9am-1.30pm Mon-Fri; Ⓜ Erji Road)

Jinghong (老挝驻昆明总领事馆驻景洪领事办公室, Lǎowōzhù Kūnmíngzǒng Lǐngshìguǎn Zhùjǐnghóng Lǐngshì Bàngōngshì; ☎691 221 9355; 2nd fl, Bldg 2, Gaozhuang Xishuangjing, Xuanwei Dadao, 宣慰大道, 告庄西双景综合楼2楼; ⏲8.30-11.30am & 2.30-4.30pm Mon-Fri)

Mongolian Embassy

Beijing (蒙古大使馆, Ménggǔ Dàshǐguǎn; Map p102; ☎010 6532 1203; www.beijing.mfa.gov.mn; 2 Xiushui Beijie, 秀水北街2号; Ⓢ Line 1 to Yonganli, exit A1; has a separate **visa section** (Map p102; ☎010 6532 1203, 010 6532 6512; www.beijing.mfa.gov.mn; 2 Xiushui Nanjie, 秀水南街2号; ⏲visa application 9am-noon Mon-Fri, passport collection 4-5pm Mon-Fri; Ⓢ Line 1 to Yonganli, exit A1).

Mongolian Consulates

Hohhot (蒙古领事馆, Měnggǔ Lǐngshìguǎn; ☎0471 490 2262, 0471 490 2531; Unit 1, Bldg 5, Wulan Residential Area, Dongying Nanlu, Sai Han District, 赛罕区东影南路乌兰小区五号楼一单元; ⏲9am-noon Mon, Tue & Thu)

Erlian (Menggu Lingshiguan, 蒙古领事馆; ☎0479 752 4240; http://ereen.consul.mn; 1206 Youyi Beilu, 友谊北路1206号; ⏲8.30am-5.30pm Mon-Fri)

Haila'er (蒙古领事馆, Mènggǔ Lǐngshìguǎn; ☎0470 811 2896, 0470 811 2897; 6 Baihua Xilu, 白桦西路6号)

Myanmar Embassy

Beijing (缅甸大使馆, Miǎndiàn Dàshǐguǎn; Map p102; ☎010 6532 0359; www.myanmarembassy.com; 6 Dongzhimenwai Dajie, 东直门外大街6号; ⏲9am-5pm Mon-Fri, visa 9.30-11.30am; Ⓢ Line 10 to

Agricultural Exhibition Center, exit D2)

Myanmar Consulate

Kunming (缅甸领事馆, Miǎndiàn Lǐngshìguǎn; ☏871 816 2804; www.mcgkunming. org; Kunming Diplomat Compound, 99 Yingbin Lu, 迎宾路99号; ◷visa section 9am-noon & 1-2pm Mon-Fri; Ⓜ Erji Road)

Nepali Embassy

Beijing (尼泊尔大使馆, Níbó'ěr Dàshǐguǎn; Map p102; ☏010 6532 1795; www.nepalembassy. org.cn; 1 Sanlitun Xiliujie, 三里屯西六街1号; ◷10am-noon & 3-4pm Mon-Fri; Ⓢ Line 10 to Agricultural Exhibition Center, exit A, or Liangmaqiao, exit D)

Nepali Consulates

Hong Kong (Map p540; ☏852 2369 7813; 715 China Aerospace Tower, Concordia Plaza, 1 Science Museum Rd, Tsim Sha Tsui; Ⓜ Hung Hom, exit D1)

Lhasa (尼泊尔领事馆, Níbó'ěr Lǐngshìguǎn; Map p940; ☏139 0890 8377; https://lxa.nepal consulate.gov.np/; 12 Beijing Xilu, 北京西路12号; ◷10am-6pm Mon-Fri)

Netherlands Embassy

Beijing (荷兰大使馆, Hélán Dàshǐguǎn; Map p102; ☏010 8532 0200; www.netherlands worldwide.nl/countries/china; 4 Liangmahe Nanlu, 亮马河南路4号; ◷9am-12.30pm & 2-5.30pm Mon-Fri; Ⓢ Line 10 to Liangmaqiao, exit B)

Netherlands Consulates

Hong Kong (Map p536; ☏852 2599 9200; www.netherlands andyou.nl; Suite 3001, 30th fl, Central Plaza, 18 Harbour Rd, Wan Chai; ◷9am-noon & 2-4.30pm Mon-Fri)

Shanghai (荷兰领事馆, Hélán Lǐngshìguǎn; ☏021 2208 7288; www.netherlandsworldwide. nl; 10th fl, Tower B, Dawning Center, 500 Hongbaoshi Rd, 红宝石路500号东银中心东塔10楼; ◷9am-noon & 1-5.30pm Mon-Fri)

Guangzhou (荷兰驻广州总领事馆, Hélán Zhù Guǎngzhōu Zǒng Lǐngshìguǎn; Map p594; ☏020 3813 2200; www.nether landsworldwide.nl/countries/ china; 14th fl, Teem Tower, 208 Tianhe Lu, 天河路208号粤海天河大厦14楼; Ⓜ Line 1 & 3 to Tiyu Xilu, exit C)

New Zealand Embassy

Beijing (新西兰大使馆, Xīnxīlán Dàshǐguǎn; Map p102; ☏010 8532 7000; www.mfat.govt.nz; 1 Ritan Dong'erjie, 日坛东二街1号; ◷8.30am-noon & 1-5pm Mon-Fri; Ⓢ Line 1 to Yonganli, exit A1)

New Zealand Consulates

Hong Kong (Map p536; ☏852 2525 5044; www.eit.ac.nz; Room 6501, 65th fl, Central Plaza, 18 Harbour Rd, Wan Chai; ◷8.30am-1pm & 2-5pm Mon-Fri; Ⓜ Wan Chai, exit C)

Shanghai (新西兰领事馆, Xīnxīlán Lǐngshìguǎn; ☏021 5407 5858; www.nzembassy.com; 2801-2802a & 2806b-2810, 5 Corporate Ave, 150 Hubin Rd, 湖滨150号; ◷8.30am-noon & 1-5pm Mon-Fri; Ⓜ South Huangpi Rd)

Guangzhou (新西兰驻广州总领事馆, Xīnxīlán Zhù Guǎngzhōu Zǒng Lǐngshìguǎn; ☏020 8667 0253; 30th fl, Tai Koo Hui, 385 Tianhe Lu, 天河路385号太古汇一座26楼; Ⓜ Line 3 to Shipaiqiao, exit C)

North Korean Embassy

Beijing (北朝鲜驻华使馆, Běi Cháoxiǎn Zhùhuá Shǐguǎn; Map p102; ☏010 6532 1186; 11 Ritan Beilu, 日坛北路11号; Ⓢ Line 6 to Dongdaqiao, exit D)

North Korean Consulate

Shenyang (☏024 8685 2742; 37 Beiling Dajie, 北陵大街37号)

Pakistani Embassy

Beijing (巴基斯坦大使馆, Bājīsītǎn Dàshǐguǎn; Map p102; ☏010 6532 2504; www.pakbj. org.pk; 1 Dongzhimenwai Dajie, 东直门外大街1号; ◷9-11.30am Mon-Fri; Ⓢ Line 10 to Agricultural Exhibition Center, exit A)

Russian Embassy

Beijing (俄罗斯大使馆, Èluósī Dàshǐguǎn; Map p102; ☏010 6532 1381, visa section 2-6pm Mon-Fri 010 6532 1267; www. russia.org.cn; 4 Dongzhimen Beizhongjie, 东直门北中街4号; ◷9am-noon Mon-Fri; Ⓢ Lines 2, 13 to Dongzhimen, exit A)

South Korean Embassy

Beijing (南韩大使馆, Nánhán Dàshǐguǎn; ☏010 8531 0700; http://overseas.mofa.go.kr/cn-zh; 20 Dongfang Donglu, 东方东路20号; ◷9am-5pm; Ⓢ Line 10 to Liangmaqiao, exit B)

South Korean Consulates

Shenyang (Map p187; ☏024 2385 3388; 37 Nanshisan Weilu, 南十三纬路31号)

Qingdao (☏0532 8897 6001; 88 Chunyang Lu, 春阳路88号; ◷9am-6pm Mon-Fri summer, to 5pm Mon-Fri winter)

Thai Embassy

Beijing (泰国大使馆, Tàiguó Dàshǐguǎn; Map p102; ☏010 8531 8700; www.thaiembbeij. org; 21 Guanghua Lu, 光华路21号; ◷8.30am-noon & 2-5.30pm; Ⓢ Lines 1, 2 to Jianguomen, exit B)

Thai Consulates

Shanghai (泰王国领事馆, Tàiwángguó Lǐngshìguǎn; ☏021 5260 9899; www.thaishanghai. com; 18 Wanshan Rd, 万山路18号; ◷visa office 9.30-11.30am Mon-Fri; Ⓜ Yili Rd)

Kunming (泰国领事馆, Tàiguó Lǐngshìguǎn; Map p694; ☏871 6316 8916; 18th fl, Shuncheng Twin Tower, East Bldg, 18 Dongfeng Xilu, 东风西路18号顺城东塔18楼; ◷visa section 9am-11.30am Mon-Fri; Ⓜ Wuyi Road)

UK Embassy

Beijing (英国大使馆, Yīngguó Dàshǐguǎn; Map p102; ☏010 5192 4000; www.gov.uk; 11 Guanghua Lu, 光华路11号; ◷9am-noon Mon, Tue, Thu & Fri; Ⓢ Line 1 to Yonganli, exit A1)

UK Consulates

Hong Kong (Map p532; ☏852 2901 3000; www.gov.uk/ government/world/hong-kong; 1 Supreme Court Rd, Admiralty; ◷8.30am-5.15pm Mon-Fri; Ⓜ Admiralty, exit F)

Shanghai (英国领事馆, Yīngguó Lǐngshìguǎn; Map p305; ☏021 3279 2000; http://ukinchina. fco.gov.uk; 17th fl, Garden Sq, 968 West Beijing Rd, 京西路968号花园广场17楼; ◷9am-5pm Mon-Fri; Ⓜ Jing'an Temple, West Nanjing Rd)

Chongqing (Map p828; ☑️023 6369 1500; www.gov.uk/world; Suite 2801, 28th fl, Metropolitan Tower, 68 Zourong Lu, 邹容路68号大都会商厦28层)

Guangzhou (英国驻广州总领事馆, Yīngguó Zhù Guǎngzhōu Zǒng Lǐngshìguǎn; Map p594; ☑️020 8314 3000; 22nd fl, Guangzhou Int Finance Centre, 5 Zhujiang Xilu, 珠江西路5号广州国际金融中心22层; Ⓜ️Line 3 to Zhujiang New Town, exit C)

US Embassy

Beijing (美国大使馆, Měiguó Dàshǐguǎn; ☑️010 8531 3300; https://china.usembassy-china.org.cn; 55 Anjialou Lu, off Liangmaqiao Lu, 亮马桥安家楼路55号; ⏰by appointment; Ⓢ️Line 10 to Liangmaqiao, exit B)

US Consulates

Hong Kong (Map p532; ☑️852 2523 9011; https://hk.usconsulate.gov; 26 Garden Rd, Central; ⏰8.30am–noon & 1.30-4pm Mon-Fri; Ⓜ️Central, exit J2)

Shanghai (美国领事馆, Měiguó Lǐngshìguǎn; Map p305; ☑️emergency for US citizens 021 8011 2400; https://china.usembassy-china.org.cn; 8th fl, Westgate Tower, 1038 West Nanjing Rd, 南京西路1038号梅龙镇广场8楼; ⏰8-11.30am Mon-Fri; Ⓜ️West Nanjing Rd)

Chengdu (美国领事; Měiguó Lǐngshìguǎn; Map p758; ☑️028 8558 3992; https://china.usembassy-china.org.cn; 4 Lingshiguan Lu, 领事馆路4号; ⏰1-4pm Tue, Thu & Fri; Ⓜ️Nijiaqiao)

Guangzhou (美国驻广州总领事馆, Měiguó Zhù Guǎngzhōu Zǒng Lǐngshìguǎn; Map p594; ☑️020 3814 5000; 43 Huajia Lu, 华就路43号; Ⓜ️Line 5 to Zhujiang New Town, exit B1)

Shenyang (Map p187; ☑️024 2322 1198; 52 Shisi Weilu, 十四纬路52号)

Vietnamese Embassy

Beijing (越南大使馆, Yuènán Dàshǐguǎn; Map p102; ☑️010 6532 1155; https://vnembassy-beijing.mofa.gov.vn; 32 Guanghua Lu, 光华路32号; ⏰9am-5pm Mon-Fri; Ⓢ️Line 1 to Yonganli, exit A1)

Vietnamese Consulates

Hong Kong (Map p536; ☑️852 2591 4517, 852 2835 9318; www.mofa.gov.vn; 15th fl, Great Smart Tower, 230 Wan Chai Rd, Wan Chai; ⏰9am-5.30pm Mon-Fri; Ⓜ️Wan Chai, exit A3)

Kunming (越南领事馆, Yuènán Lǐngshìguǎn; Map p694; ☑️871 6352 2669; 5th fl, Kewah Plaza, 155 Beijing Lu, 北京路155号红塔大厦5室; ⏰9am-noon & 1.30-5pm Mon-Fri; Ⓜ️South Ring Road)

Food

Cooking plays a central role in both Chinese society and the national psyche. When Chinese people meet, a common greeting is '*Nǐ chīfàn le ma?*' ('Have you eaten yet?'). Work, play, romance, business and family all revolve around food. The catalysts for all manner of enjoyment, meals are occasions for pleasure and entertainment, to clinch deals, strike up new friendships and rekindle old ones. To fully access this tasty domain on home soil, all you need is a visa, a pair of chopsticks, an adventurous palate and a passion for the unusual and unexpected.

Insurance

Carefully consider a travel-insurance policy to cover theft, loss, trip cancellation and medical eventualities. Travel agents can sort this out for you, though it is often cheaper to find good deals with an insurer online or with a broker.

Some policies specifically exclude 'dangerous activities' such as scuba diving, skiing and even trekking/hiking. Check that the policy covers ambulances and an emergency flight home.

Paying for your airline ticket with a credit card often provides limited travel accident insurance – ask your credit-card company what it's prepared to cover.

You may prefer a policy that pays doctors or hospitals directly rather than reimbursing you for expenditures after the fact. If you have to claim later, ensure you keep all documentation.

Worldwide travel insurance is available at www.lonelyplanet.com/travel-insurance. You can buy, extend and claim online anytime – even if you're already on the road.

Internet Access

Wi-fi accessibility in hotels, cafes, restaurants and bars is generally good. The best option is to bring a smartphone, tablet or laptop, or purchase a local SIM card on arrival. Chain restaurants and cafes with free wi-fi sometimes still require a Chinese phone number to receive a login code and the prompt for that may just be in Chinese.

The Chinese authorities maintain strong controls on internet access. Around 10% of websites are blocked. The list is constantly changing, but includes sites and apps such as Facebook, Twitter, Instagram, Google-owned sites (YouTube, Google Maps, Gmail, Google Drive), WhatsApp, Snapchat, Dropbox and many international media outlets, so plan ahead.

Without a VPN (virtual private network) on your phone, tablet or laptop, expect to go cold turkey on social media (and even emails) for the duration of your trip, unless you use you own carrier's roaming service, which may be prohibitively expensive. Bear in mind that many popular VPN services themselves become blocked, so ask around or check online before committing to a service. The government (which uses VPNs itself) had vowed to block all such services eventually, but at time of research was yet to do so.

The VPN you use may sometimes interfere with your wi-fi connection and make it harder to get online when using public wi-fi, in which case you will need to turn off the VPN in order to access wi-fi. A VPN must be installed on devices before departing for China. VPNs can function less well or stop working entirely during politically sensitive times on the annual calendar. It's a good idea to use two VPNs so you have a back-up in case one is twitchy or not working.

Language Courses

Learning Chinese in China is big business. Weigh up the course fees and syllabus carefully and check online reviews – some schools are pricey and may use teaching methods unsuited to westerners. Consider where you would like to study: the Beijing accent and setting has obvious cachet, but a course in a setting such as Yangshuo can be delightful. For Cantonese courses, head to Hong Kong, Macau or Guangzhou.

Legal Matters

China does not officially recognise dual nationality or the foreign citizenship of children born in China if one of the parents is a PRC national. If you have Chinese and another nationality you may, in theory, not be allowed to visit China on your foreign passport. In practice Chinese authorities are unlikely to know if you own two passports, and should accept you on a foreign passport. Dual-nationality citizens who enter China on a Chinese passport are subject to Chinese laws and are legally not allowed consular help. If over 16 years of age, carry your passport with you at all times as a form of ID (in recent years, passport checking in China has become far more common).

Gambling is officially illegal in mainland China, as is distributing religious material.

China takes a particularly dim view of opium and all its derivatives; trafficking in more than 50g of heroin can lead to the death penalty. Foreign passport holders have been executed in China for drug offences. Random drug testing can be conducted on foreign nationals entering China. If you test positive you can be prosecuted irrespective of where the drugs were consumed. There can also be an uptick in arrests of foreigners for drug offences during times of tension between China and other nations.

The Public Security Bureau (PSB) likes to know where everyone is staying. Hotels will supply the PSB with the necessary documentation, including a photocopy of your passport information page and visa details as well as, sometimes, your onward travel plans. If, however, you are staying with a friend in China, you will need to register your place of residence with the PSB within 24 hours. This procedure is time-consuming as you will need to identify the PSB office responsible for registering foreign residents and you will need to take along proof of address, a copy of your friend's ID and your passport.

Be aware that there can be an increase in arrests of foreigners during times of international friction. After a senior Huawei senior executive was arrested in Canada for extradition to the US in December 2018, two Canadian citizens were arrested on spying charges and Chinese courts also sentenced two Canadians to death on drug smuggling charges.

The Chinese criminal justice system does not ensure a fair trial and defendants are not presumed innocent until proven guilty. If arrested, most foreign citizens have the right to contact their embassy.

Passports

You are required to carry your passport (护照, *hùzhào*) with you at all times – police may carry out random checks, all hotels require it for check-in, and many sightseeing spots and museums require passports for entry. It is also mandatory to present your passport when buying train tickets.

Take an ID card with your photo in case you lose your passport, and make digital copies or photocopies of your passport: your embassy may need these before issuing a new one. You must report the loss to the local Public Security Bureau (PSB), which will issue you with a 'Statement of Loss of Passport'.

LGBTI+ Travellers

Greater tolerance exists in big cities such as Beijing and Shanghai than in the more conservative countryside, but even in urban areas, gay and lesbian public displays of affection can raise an eyebrow. You will often see Chinese friends of the same sex holding hands or putting their arms around each other, but this usually has no sexual connotation. There are gay bars and clubs in the major cities, but it is far more common for people to socialise on apps. A same-sex couple staying in a hotel room with only one bed will rarely attract any resistance or comments (at least not to their faces).

There is certainly an increasingly confident scene in Shanghai, as indicated by the numerous gay bars and the annual, event-stuffed **Shanghai Pride** (www.shpride.com; ☉Jun).

In 2016 China banned the depiction of gay people on television. In 2018 videos were circulated online showing two women being assaulted by security staff at 798 Art District for wearing rainbow badges in support of LGBTQ rights.

Surprisingly gay networking app Grindr isn't blocked in China, and neither are local apps Blued and Aloha. While Blued (mostly for hookups) and Aloha are aimed at men, there's Lespark (拉拉公园) and Rela (热拉) for women.

The following resources are useful for gay travellers:

Danlan (淡蓝; www.danlan.org) Chinese-only news and lifestyle.

Spartacus International Gay Guide (www.spartacusworld.com/en) Best-selling guide for gay travellers; also available as an Apple App.

Utopia (www.utopia-asia.com/tipschin.htm) Tips on travelling in China and a complete listing of gay bars nationwide.

Money

ATMs are plentiful in big cities and towns. Credit cards less widely used; always carry cash.

ATMs

Bank of China 24-hour ATMs are plentiful, and you can use Visa, MasterCard, Cirrus, Maestro Plus and American Express to withdraw cash. All ATMs accepting international cards have dual-language ability. The network is largely found in sizeable towns and cities. ATMs at the Industrial & Commercial Bank of China (ICBC) may work with international cards, but not everywhere. We list ATMs that take international cards for each destination, unless they do not exist, in which case you will be advised to take enough cash.

The exchange rate on ATM withdrawals is similar to that for credit cards, but there is a maximum daily withdrawal amount. Note that banks can charge a withdrawal fee for using the ATM network of another bank, so check with your bank before travelling.

Keep your ATM receipts so you can exchange your yuán when you leave China.

To have money wired from abroad, visit Western Union or Moneygram.

Cash

The Chinese currency is the rénmínbì (RMB), or 'people's money'. The basic unit of RMB is the yuán (元, ¥), which is divided into 10 jiǎo (角), which is again divided into 10 fēn (分). Colloquially the yuán is referred to as kuài, and jiǎo as máo (毛). The fēn has so little value these days that it is rarely used.

The Bank of China issues RMB bills in denominations of ¥1, ¥2, ¥5, ¥10, ¥20, ¥50 and ¥100. Coins come in denominations of ¥1, 5 jiǎo, 1 jiǎo and 5 fēn. Paper versions of the coins remain in circulation.

Hong Kong's currency is the Hong Kong dollar (HK$), which is divided into 100 cents. Bills are issued in denominations of HK$10, HK$20, HK$50, HK$100, HK$500 and HK$1000. Copper coins are worth 50c, 20c and 10c, while the $5, $2 and $1 coins are silver and the $10 coin is nickel and bronze. The Hong Kong dollar is pegged to the US dollar at a rate of US$1 to HK$7.80, though it is allowed to fluctuate a little.

Macau's currency is the pataca (MOP$), which is divided into 100 avos. Bills are issued in denominations of MOP$10, MOP$20, MOP$50, MOP$100, MOP$500 and MOP$1000. There are copper coins worth 10, 20 and 50 avos and silver-coloured MOP$1, MOP$2, MOP$5 and MOP$10 coins. The pataca is pegged to the Hong Kong dollar at a rate of MOP$103.20 to HK$100. In effect the two currencies are interchangeable and Hong Kong dollars, including coins, are accepted in Macau. Chinese rénmínbì is also accepted in many places in Macau at one-to-one. You can't spend patacas anywhere else, however, so use them before you leave Macau. Prices quoted are in yuán unless otherwise stated.

Credit Cards

In large tourist towns, credit cards are relatively straightforward to use, but don't expect to be able to use them everywhere and it's always a good idea to carry enough cash. The exception is in Hong Kong, where international credit cards are accepted almost everywhere (though some shops may try to add a surcharge to offset the commission charged by credit-card companies, which can range from 2.5% to 7%). Check to see if your credit-card company charges a foreign transaction fee (usually between 1% and 3%) for purchases in China.

Where they are accepted, credit cards often deliver a slightly better exchange rate than banks. Money can also be withdrawn at certain ATMs in large cities on credit cards such as Visa, MasterCard and Amex.

Mobile Payment Apps

Their use is complicated for foreign visitors, but local Chinese use WeChat (微信, wēixìn, WeChat Pay) and

Alipay (支付宝, *zhīfùbǎo*) apps to pay for virtually everything from taxi rides and market vendors, to hotels and even donating to beggars in the street. Cash is, for the moment, still widely accepted, but China is increasingly a cashless society. Neither WeChat nor Alipay was useful for visitors at the time of writing as it was necessary to link a Chinese bank account to your digital wallet before funds could be received from any source. Check the latest before you head to China as things could change. It is still fine to use cash (or credit cards, where they are accepted) in most instances.

For a visitor the only accessible system that allows foreign cards is Apple Pay, which is accepted where you see the Apple Pay or QuickPass logos. Payments are made by holding your compatible device against the payment machine and verifying with your fingerprint.

Moneychangers

It's best to wait till you reach China to exchange money as the exchange rate will be better. Foreign currency and travellers cheques can be changed at border crossings, international airports, branches of the Bank of China, tourist hotels and some large department stores. Hours of operation for foreign-exchange counters are 8am to 7pm (later at hotels). Top-end hotels will generally change money for hotel guests only. The official rate is given almost everywhere and the exchange charge is standardised, so there is little need to shop around for the best deal.

Australian, Canadian, US, UK, Hong Kong and Japanese currencies and the euro can be changed in China. In some backwaters it may be hard to change lesser-known currencies; US dollars are still the easiest to change.

Keep at least a few of your exchange receipts. You will need them if you want to exchange any remaining yuán you have at the end of your trip.

Taxes & Refunds

When shopping, tax is already included in the displayed prices. Nearly all of the major cities offer a tax refund for foreign tourists on purchases made in the previous 90 days; the list of provinces offering the service keeps expanding. The 11% tax is refunded at the airport and all items must leave China with you. Goods have a minimum purchase of ¥500 from the one store.

Travellers Cheques

With the prevalence of ATMs across China, travellers cheques are not as useful as they once were and cannot be used everywhere, so always ensure you carry enough ready cash. You should have no problem cashing travellers cheques at tourist hotels, but they are of little use in budget hotels and restaurants. Most hotels will only cash the cheques of guests. If cashing them at banks, aim for larger ones such as the Bank of China or ICBC.

Stick to the major companies such as Amex and Visa. In big cities travellers cheques are accepted in almost any currency, but in smaller destinations it's best to stick to currencies such as US dollars or UK pounds. Keep your exchange receipts so you can change your money back to its original currency when you leave.

Opening Hours

China officially has a five-day working week; Saturday and Sunday are holidays.

Banks, offices and government departments 9am to 5pm (or 6pm) Monday to Friday; may close for two hours in the afternoon. Many open Saturday, some Sunday.

Post offices Generally open daily (9am to 5pm).

Restaurants Around 10.30am to 11pm; some shut at 2pm and reopen at 5pm or 6pm.

Bars Open late afternoon, shut midnight or later.

Shops, department stores and shopping malls Daily 10am to 10pm.

Post

The international postal service is generally efficient, and airmail letters and postcards will probably take between five and 10 days to reach their destinations. Domestic post is swift – perhaps one or two days from Guangzhou to Beijing. Intracity post may be delivered the same day it's sent.

China Post (www.china post.com.cn) operates an express mail service (EMS) that is fast, reliable and ensures that the package is sent by registered post. Not all branches of China Post have EMS.

Major tourist hotels have branch post offices where you can send letters, packets and parcels. Even at cheap hotels you can usually post letters from the front desk. Larger parcels may need to be sent from the town's main post office. Some post offices may also have a train ticket office or desk where you can purchase train tickets without having to go to the train station; a ¥5 commission is usually levied.

In major cities, private carriers such as **United Parcel Service** (☏800 820 8388; www.ups.com), **DHL** (☏95380; www.logistics.dhl/cn-en/home. html), **Federal Express** (Liánbāng Kuàidì; ☏800 988 1888; www.fedex.com/en-cn/ home.html) and **TNT Skypak** (☏800 820 9868; www.tnt. com) have a pick-up service as well as drop-off centres; call their offices for details.

If you are sending items abroad, take them unpacked with you to the post office to be inspected; an appropriate box or envelope will be found for you. Most post offices offer materials for packaging (including padded envelopes, boxes and heavy brown paper), for which you'll be charged. Don't take your own packaging as it will probably be refused. You will also need to show your passport or other ID.

Public Holidays

The People's Republic of China has a number of national holidays. Not all of the following holidays result in leave. It's not a great idea to arrive in China or go travelling during the big holiday periods as hotel prices reach their maximum and transport can become very tricky.

New Year's Day 1 January

Chinese New Year 12 February 2021, 1 February 2022, 22 January 2023; a week-long holiday for most.

International Women's Day 8 March

Tomb Sweeping Festival First weekend in April; a popular three-day holiday period.

International Labour Day 1 May; for many, a three-day holiday.

Youth Day 4 May

International Children's Day 1 June

Dragon Boat Festival 25 June 2020, 14 June 2021, 3 June 2022

Birthday of the Chinese Communist Party 1 July (not a public holiday)

Anniversary of the Founding of the People's Liberation Army 1 August

Mid-Autumn Festival 1 October 2020, 21 September 2021, 10 September 2022

National Day 1 October; the big one – a week-long holiday.

Safe Travel

Crime

Travellers are more often the victims of petty economic crime, such as theft, than serious crime. Foreigners are natural targets for pickpockets and thieves – keep your wits about you and make it difficult for thieves to get at your belongings.

High-risk areas in China are train and bus stations, city and long-distance buses (especially sleeper buses), hard-seat train carriages and public toilets.

Women should be aware of the dangers when travelling solo. Even in Beijing, single women taking taxis have been taken to remote areas and robbed by taxi drivers.

If something of yours is stolen, report it immediately to the nearest Foreign Affairs Branch of the Public Security Bureau (PSB; 公安局, Gōng'ānjú). Staff will ask you to fill in a loss report before investigating the crime.

A loss report is crucial so you can claim compensation if you have travel insurance. Be prepared to spend many hours, perhaps even several days, organising it. Make a copy of your passport in case of loss or theft.

Emergency Numbers

Ambulance	120
Fire	119
Police	110

Scams

Watch out for any solicitations to go to teahouses or expensive cafes in cities such as Shanghai, as you could be left with a huge bill.

Taxi scams at Beijing's Capital Airport are legendary – always join the queue at the taxi rank and insist that the taxi driver uses his or her meter. Try to avoid pedicabs and motorised three-wheelers wherever possible – there are widespread complaints against pedicab drivers who originally agree on a price and then insist on an alternative figure once you arrive at the destination (language complications will work against you).

Watch out for itinerant monks asking for donations to their temple as a fair number are bogus. If you wish to donate to a temple, visit the temple and do so there.

Be alert at all times if you decide to change money or buy tickets (such as train tickets) on the black market, which we can't recommend.

Always be alert when buying unpriced goods (which is a lot of the time): foreigners are frequently ripped off. Always examine your restaurant bill carefully for hidden extras and if paying by credit card, ensure there are no extra charges.

Transport

Traffic accidents are the major cause of death in China for people aged between 15 and 45, and the World Health Organization (WHO) estimates there are 700 traffic deaths per day in China (with 60% being vulnerable road users, such as pedestrians, cyclists and motorbike riders). The proliferation of fast e-bikes (electric bikes) added to the mortality rate (so much so that several cities, including Shenzhen, have either restricted their use or banned them).

Seat-belt use on long-distance buses has improved greatly over recent years, and on-board announcements and checks ensure passengers have their seat belts fastened. Taxi drivers continue, however, to insist you don't need to use seat belts – it can often be impossible to find seat belts in the rear seats of taxis. Sit in the front if there is space.

Your greatest danger in China will almost certainly be crossing the road, so develop 360-degree vision and a sixth sense. Electric cars and 'hoverboards' can approach quite silently. Crossing only when it is safe to do so could keep you perched at the side of the road in perpetuity, but don't imitate the local tendency to cross without looking. Note that cars frequently turn on red lights in China, so the green 'walk now' figure does not always mean it is safe to cross.

Government Travel Advice

The following government websites offer travel advisories and information on current hotspots.

Australian Department of Foreign Affairs (www.smart traveller.gov.au)

British Foreign Office (www. gov.uk/foreign-travel-advice)

Canadian Department of Foreign Affairs (https://travel. gc.ca/travelling/advisories)

US State Department (http:// travel.state.gov)

Telephone

Nearly everybody in China has a mobile phone. Landlines and calling cards are rare. Some hotels will give you unlimited local or national calls. Regions and towns through China have their own area codes.

Country code (China/ Hong Kong/ Macau)	☑86/ 852/ 853
International access code	☑00
Directory assistance	☑114

Mobile Phones

A mobile phone should be the first choice for calls, but ensure your mobile is unlocked for use in China if taking your own. SIM cards can be bought at the arrivals area at major airports.

Many international messaging apps, including WhatsApp and Viber, are inaccessible in China, though some people are able to access Skype (www.skype. com). Communication through Chinese app WeChat (微信, Wēixìn; www.wechat. com), which virtually all Chinese use, is standard practice between both friends and small businesses and is

not considered unprofessional. (Note that although Chinese also use the word 'app', they spell it out as 'a-p-p'.)

Data SIM-card plans start at under ¥70 for 500MB of data and 200 minutes of China calls per month. You will be warned about cancelling this service before leaving the country to avoid a hefty bill should you return. For this reason, and the language barrier, it can be more convenient (if more expensive) to pick up a SIM card on arrival at an airport in the major cities. Though more expensive, 3G Solutions (www.3gsolutions. com.cn) offers a range of mobile data and voice packages with pre-booking online, and will have the SIM card delivered to your accommodation on the day you arrive in China.

If you want to get a SIM card independently, China Unicom offers the most reliable service with the greatest coverage. China Mobile or China Unicom outlets can sell you a standard prepaid SIM card, which cost from ¥60 to ¥100 and include ¥50 of credit. (You'll be given a choice of phone numbers. Choose one without the unlucky number 4, if you don't want to irk Chinese colleagues.)

When your prepaid credit runs out, top up by buying a credit-charging card (充值卡, chōngzhí kǎ) from outlets. Cards are also available from newspaper kiosks and shops displaying the China Mobile sign.

Buying a mobile phone in China is also an option as they are generally inexpensive. Make sure the phone uses W-CDMA, which works on China Unicom and most carriers around the world, and not TD-SCDMA, which works only on China Mobile and not international carriers. Android phones bought in China won't support Google apps at all (be it in China or your home country).

Landlines

If making a domestic call, look out for very cheap public phones at newspaper stands (报刊亭, bàokāntíng) and hole-in-the-wall shops (小卖部, xiǎomàibù); you make your call and then pay the owner. Domestic and international long-distance phone calls can also be made from main telecommunications offices and 'phone bars' (话吧, huàbā). Cardless international calls are expensive and it's far cheaper to use an internet phone (IP) card, though these can be hard to find.

Public telephone booths are rarely used now in China, but may serve as wi-fi hotspots (as in Shanghai).

Phone Cards

Beyond Skype, using an internet phone (IP) card on your mobile or a landline phone is much cheaper than calling direct, but these days they can be very hard to find. To use one you simply dial a local number, punch in your account number followed by a PIN number, and finally the number you wish to call. English-language service is usually available.

Some IP cards can only be used locally, while others can be used nationwide, and some can't be used for international calls – make sure you buy the right card (and don't forget to check the expiry date).

Time

The 24-hour clock is commonly used in China. Despite China's breadth, there is just one time zone: UTC+8. (You can find UTC+6 used in Tibet and Xinjiang, though it is not official.)

Tourist Information

Poor and entirely inadequate tourist information has always been one of the banes of travelling around China. An enduring and highly perplexing resistance to staffing tourist information centres with enthusiastic and polite English-speaking staff means that such information points are often little better than useless. While you may be able to find literature and maps, you may also discover yourself being steered (for commercial reasons) onto a tour. In this regard China compares most unfavourably with countries such as South Korea or Japan.

Far better information generally exists online or at youth hostels; the latter are frequently staffed by proficient English speakers who show a genuine interest in promoting travel within their region. It may be worth contacting the China National Tourist Office (www.cnto.org) prior to travelling to China, but don't expect to see CNTO offices dotted helpfully around the country. It serves more as an overseas tourist portal. Once you are in China, you are at the mercy of a mishmash of often ad hoc tourist offices.

Visas

Check your local Chinese embassy website for the latest information on obtaining a visa to visit China during the Covid-19 pandemic. At the time of writing, only a limited range of people (for example those with residence permits for China) could obtain a visa to visit China; they would need to provide a health declaration form from the Chinese embassy (issued if evidence is supplied of negative nucleic acid and IgM antibody tests for Covid-19, taken no more than 48 hours before travel to China) or prove that they had been inoculated with a vaccine produced in China (unavailable in some countries). Entry to China is then followed by a 14-day quarantine.

Otherwise, no particular difficulties exist for travellers entering China. Chinese immigration officers are scrupulous and highly bureaucratic, but not overly officious. The main requirements are a passport that's valid for travel for six months after the expiry date of your visa, and a visa. Travellers arriving in China will receive a health declaration form and an arrivals form to complete.

For Mainland China

Apart from visa-free visits to Hong Kong and Macau, 24-hour visa-free exemptions and useful 144-hour and 72-hour visa-free transit stays (for visitors from 53 nations) to a number of cities and regions, including Beijing, Tianjin, Hebei, Shanghai, Jiangsu, Zhejiang, Qingdao, Shandong, Guangdong province, Chengdu, Xi'an, Liaoning province, Guilin, Chongqing and Kunming, you will need a visa to visit China. Citizens from Japan, Singapore, Brunei, San Marino, Mauritius, the Seychelles, the Bahamas and a handful of other nations do not require a visa to visit China. There remain a few restricted areas in China that require an additional permit from the PSB. Permits are also required for travel to Tibet, a region that authorities can suddenly bar foreigners from entering.

Visa requirements and restrictions continuously change, so always check with your Chinese embassy or Visa Application Service Centre about the latest regulations.

Your passport must be valid for at least six months after the expiry date of your visa (nine months for a double-entry visa) and you'll need at least one entire blank page in your passport for the visa. For children under the age of 18, a parent must sign the application form on their behalf.

Citizens from the US, UK, Canada and Israel can apply for long-term, multiple-entry Chinese visas with a validity of between two and 10 years.

These usually entitle the bearer to stay in China for 60 days per entry, and to come and go without having to reapply for a new visa each time.

At the time of writing the visa application process had become more rigorous. In many countries the visa application service has been outsourced from the Chinese embassy to the Chinese Visa Application Service Centre (www.visaforchina.org), which levies an extra administration fee. You'll need to book an appointment and prepare your application online beforehand. Applicants will need to have their fingerprints scanned as part of the application process. Visa Application Service Centres are open Monday to Friday.

At the time of writing, applicants were required to provide the following:

➡ A copy of flight confirmation showing onward/return travel.

➡ For double-entry visas, flight confirmation showing all dates of entry and exit.

➡ If staying at hotels in China, confirmation from each hotel (these can be booked on reservation platforms such as booking.com for the purposes of proof and later cancelled or amended).

➡ If staying with friends or relatives, a copy of the information page of their passport, a copy of their China visa and a letter of invitation from them.

➡ You may be required to show you have sufficient funds in your bank account for each day you plan to spend in China. Check with your Chinese embassy or at www.visaforchina.org for the latest application requirements.

At the time of writing, prices for a standard single-entry 30-day visa were as follows:

➡ £151 for UK citizens

➡ US$140 for US citizens

➡ C$142 for Canadian citizens

CUSTOMS REGULATIONS

Chinese customs officers generally pay tourists little attention. 'Green channels' and 'red channels' at the airport are clearly marked. You are not allowed to import or export illegal drugs, or animals and plants (including seeds). Pirated DVDs and CDs are illegal exports from China – if found they will be confiscated. You can take Chinese medicine up to a value of ¥300 when you depart China.

Duty free you're allowed to import:

➡ 400 cigarettes (or the equivalent in tobacco products)

➡ 1.5L of alcohol

➡ 50g of gold or silver

Also note:

➡ Importation of fresh fruit and cold cuts is prohibited.

➡ There are no restrictions on foreign currency, but you should declare any cash exceeding US$5000 or its equivalent in another currency.

Objects considered antiques require a certificate and a red seal to clear customs when leaving China. Anything made before 1949 is considered an antique, and if it was made before 1795 it cannot legally be taken out of the country. To get the proper certificate and red seal, your antiques must be inspected by the **State Administration of Cultural Heritage** (国家文物局, Guójiā Wénwù Jú; Map p82; ☑010 5679 2211; www.sach.gov.cn; 83 Beiheyan Dajie, 北河沿大街 83号; ☑8.30am-5pm; ⑤Lines 6, 8 to Nanluoguxiang, exit B, or Line 5 to Zhangzizhonglu, exit D) in Beijing.

➡ A$109 for Australian citizens

➡ €126 for French, German, Italian, Dutch and Spanish citizens

➡ US$40 for citizens of other nations

Prices are higher for double-entry or multiple-entry visas, and significantly higher for visas valid for two, five or 10 years.

A standard, 30-day single-entry visa can be issued in four to five working days; express visas will be more expensive.

A standard 30-day visa is activated on the date you enter China, and must be used within three months of the date of issue. To stay longer you can extend your visa in China.

Hong Kong is a good place to pick up a China visa. Visas can be arranged by **China Travel Service** (CTS; 中國旅行社; Zhōngguó Lǚxíngshè; ☑customer service 852 2998 7888, tour hotline 852 2998 7333; www.ctshk.com), the mainland-affiliated agency, as well as a good many hostels and guesthouses and most Hong Kong travel agents.

At the time of writing, holders of Canadian, Australian, New Zealand, US and most EU passports can get a single visa on the spot for around HK$150 at the Lo Wu border crossing, the last stop on the MTR's East Rail. This visa is for a maximum stay of five days within the confines of the Shenzhen Special Economic Zone (SEZ). However, the rules about who can get what change frequently, the queues for these visas can be interminable, and there have been reports of tourists being rejected on shaky grounds (such as certain passport stamps).

Taking that into consideration, it is highly recommended that you shell out the extra money and get a proper China visa before setting off, even if you're headed just for Shenzhen. If you have at least a week to arrange your visa yourself, you can go to the **China Visa Application Service Centre** (Map p536; ☑852 2992 1999; www.visaforchina.org; 20th fl, Capital Centre, 151 Gloucester Rd, Wan Chai; ☑9am-5pm Mon-Fri; ⓂWan Chai, exit A3) in Hong Kong. For further details see www.fmprc.gov.cn.

Be aware that political events can suddenly make visas more difficult to procure or renew.

When asked about your itinerary on the application form, list standard tourist destinations; if you are considering going to Tibet or western Xinjiang, just leave it off the form. The list you give is not binding. Those working in media or journalism may want to profess a different occupation; otherwise a visa may be refused or a shorter length of stay than requested may be given.

For Hong Kong

At the time of writing, most visitors to Hong Kong, including citizens of the EU, Australia, New Zealand, the USA and Canada, could enter and stay for 90 days without a visa. British passport holders get 180 days, and South Africans 30 days. Anyone requiring a visa or wishing to stay longer than the visa-free period must apply before travelling to Hong Kong. See www.fmprc.gov.cn for your nearest Chinese consulate or embassy where the application must be made.

If you visit Hong Kong from China, you will need a double-entry, multiple-entry or new visa to re-enter China. Visas can be arranged by **China Travel Service** (CTS; 中國旅行社; Zhōngguó Lǚxíngshè; ☑customer service 852 2998 7888, tour hotline 852 2998 7333; www.ctshk.com).

For Macau

Most travellers, including citizens of the EU, Australia, New Zealand, the USA, Canada and South Africa, can enter Macau without a visa for between 30 and 90 days. British passport holders get 180 days. Most other nationalities can get a 30-day visa on arrival, which will cost MOP$100/50/200 per adult/child under 12/family.

If you're visiting Macau from China and plan to re-enter China, you will need to be on a multiple- or double-entry visa, or reapply for a visa. Nationals of Australia, Canada, the EU, the UK, New Zealand and most other countries (but not US citizens) can purchase their China visas at Zhuhai on the border, but it will ultimately save you time if you get one in advance as lines can be long. Express visas (MOP$1250 plus photos) are available in Macau or Hong Kong from China Travel Service, usually in two to five working days.

Visa Types

There are 12 categories of visas:

Type	English Name	Chinese Name
C	Flight attendant	乘务; chéngwù
D	Resident	定居; dìngjū
F	Business or student	访问; fǎngwèn
G	Transit	过境; guòjìng
J1	Journalist (more than six months)	记者1; jìzhě 1
J2	Journalist (less than six months)	记者2; jìzhě 2
L	Travel	旅行; lǚxíng
M	Commercial and trade	贸易; màoyì
Q1	Family visits (more than six months)	亲属1; qīnshǔ 1
Q2	Family visits (less than six months)	亲属2; qīnshǔ 2
R	Talents/needed skills	人才; réncái
S1	Visits to foreign relatives/private (more than six months)	私人1; sīrén 1
S2	Visits to foreign relatives/private (less than six months)	私人2; sīrén 2
X1	Student (more than six months)	学习1; xuéxí 1
X2	Student (less than six months)	学习2; xuéxí 2
Z	Working	工作; gōngzuò

Visa Extensions

FOR MAINLAND CHINA

The Foreign Affairs Branch of the local Public Security Bureau (PSB) deals with visa extensions. We list PSB offices that can grant visa extensions, where an office authorised to administer such extensions exists.

First-time extensions of 30 days are usually easy to obtain on single-entry tourist visas, but must be done at least seven days before your visa expires – a further extension of a month may be possible, but you may only get another week. Travellers report generous extensions in provincial towns, but don't bank on this. Popping across to Hong Kong to apply for a new tourist visa is another option. Note that if you enter Hong Kong (or Macau) on a single-entry visa and do not extend or obtain a new visa, you will not be able to re-enter the PRC.

Extensions to single-entry visas vary in price, depending on your nationality; most nationalities pay ¥160. At the time of writing, US travellers needed to pay ¥760 and UK citizens around ¥500. Expect to wait up to seven days for your visa extension to be processed.

The penalty for overstaying your visa in China is up to ¥500 per day, and you may even be banned from returning to China for up to 10 years if you overstay by more than 11 days. Some travellers have reported having trouble with officials who read the 'valid until' date on their visa incorrectly. For a one-month travel (L) visa, the 'valid until' date is the date by which you must enter the country (within three months of the date the visa was issued), not the date on which your visa expires.

FOR HONG KONG

For tourist-visa extensions, enquire at the **Hong Kong Immigration Department** (Map p536; ☑852 2824 6111; www.immd.gov.hk; 2nd fl, Immigration Tower, 7 Gloucester Rd, Wan Chai; ⊗8.45am-4.30pm Mon-Fri, 9-11.30am Sat; ⓜWan Chai, exit C). Extensions (HK$160) are not readily granted unless there are extenuating circumstances, such as illness.

FOR MACAU

If your visa expires, you can obtain a single one-month extension from the **Macau Immigration Department** (出入境事務廳; Serviço de Migração; ☑853 2872 5488; Immigration Department Office Bldg, Estrada de Pac On, Taipa; ⊗9am-5pm Mon-Fri).

Residence Permits

Residence permits can be issued to English teachers, business people, students and other foreigners who are authorised to live in the PRC. Permits range from one to five years – depending on certain criteria the applicant must be able to meet – and allow unlimited exits and re-entries. International students who graduate from a Chinese university are now eligible to apply for a residence permit valid for two years. Since 2018 highly skilled foreigners (those working in high-tech and new technology, plus research and development, among other professions) can also apply for permanent residency.

To get a residence permit you first need to arrange a work permit (normally obtained by your employer), health certificate and temporary visa ('Z' type visa for most foreign employees).

You then must go to the Public Security Bureau with your passport, health certificate, work contract or permit, your employer's business registration licence or representative office permit, your employment certificate (from the Shanghai Labour Bureau), the temporary residence permit of the local PSB where you are registered, passport photos, a letter of application from your employer and around ¥400 for a one-year permit. In all, the process usually takes two to three weeks. Expect to make several visits and always carry multiple copies of every document. In most cases your employer will take care of much of the process for you.

Visa-Free Transits

Citizens from 53 nations (including the US, Australia, Canada, France, Brazil and the UK) can stay in Beijing, Tianjin and parts of Hebei for 144 hours (six days) without a visa as long as they are in transit to other destinations outside China and have a third-country visa and an air ticket out of China. Similarly, those citizens can transit through these individual regions and/or cities: Shanghai, Jiangsu and Zhejiang; Liaoning province; Guangdong province; Chengdu, Xiamen, Kunming, Wuhan and Qingdao (and Shandong province). You are permitted to travel within each region but not between them, so you can travel within Beijing, Tianjin and Hebei but not from that region to Shanghai.

Chongqing, Harbin, Xi'an, Guilin and Changsha also exercise a 72-hour (three-day) visa-free policy, with the same conditions. Three-day visitors are not allowed to leave the transit city. Chongqing and Xi'an are expected to move to the 144-hour policy in the near future.

China also exercises a 24-hour visa-free transit policy for most nationalities: you don't need a visa for transits of less than one day. It's applicable at most airports, except those in Shenzhen, Fuzhou, Yanji and Mudanjiang. You'll need a ticket to a third country with a confirmed seat.

For visa-free transit you must abide by these requirements:

➡ You must inform your airline at check-in.

➡ Upon arrival, find the dedicated immigration counter.

➡ Your transit time is calculated from just after midnight, so you may have a little more than 72 or 144 hours.

➡ If you're not staying at a hotel, you must register with a local police station within 24 hours of arriving.

➡ Hong Kong, Macau and Taiwan are eligible third countries.

➡ Visitors on the 72-hour visa-free transit must leave China from the same airport of entry. The exception is certain cities adopting the 144-hour visa-free transit scheme, where visitors may enter or leave from land or sea ports. Check your eligibility as the rules change quickly and new cities are being added.

Hainan Island has a scheme that gives you 30 days visa-free travel if you book your trip through a registered travel agency on the island.

Volunteering

Large numbers of westerners work in China with international development charities such as Voluntary Service Overseas (VSO). A placement in China offers an excellent opportunity to get first-hand experience of local life, while contributing to the community and learning Chinese at the same time.

Adventure China (www.adventurechina.com) Various volunteering programmes in summer camps and beyond.

International Volunteer HQ (www.volunteerhq.org) Volunteer projects based in and around Xi'an, focussing mainly on English teaching, special-needs care and summer outreach teaching projects.

World Teach (www.worldteach.org) Volunteer teachers (mostly for English, but also other subjects and skills).

VSO (www.vsointernational.org) Improving education and livelihood and fighting poverty.

Work

It is essential to have the appropriate visa and paperwork to engage in work, and penalties for illegal employment can include detention and deportation.

The English language is a resource that remains in high demand. With recognised ELT qualifications, such as TEFL, and/or experience, teaching in larger cities can be both financially rewarding and provide an opportunity to learn Chinese and travel within China. Salaries at schools in cities such as Beijing start from around ¥14,000 to ¥18,000 per month for qualified teachers; an accommodation stipend is also sometimes provided. You could also try approaching organisations such as the British Council (www.britishcouncil.org), which runs teacher placement programmes in China.

Transport

GETTING THERE & AWAY

Air

Airports & Airlines

Hong Kong, Beijing and Shanghai are China's principal international air gateways; Baiyun International Airport in Guangzhou is also a major gateway.

Baiyun International Airport (白云国际机场, CAN, Báiyún Guóji Jīchǎng; ☑020 3606 6999; www.gbiac.net; ⓂLine 3 to Airport South or Airport North) In Guangzhou; receiving an increasing number of international flights.

Capital Airport (北京首都国际机场, Běijīng Shǒudū Guóji Jīchǎng; PEK; ☑010 6454 1100; www.beijing-airport.com) Beijing's international airport; three terminals.

Chengdu Shuangliu International Airport (成都双流国际机场, Chéngdū Shuāngliú Guóji Jīchǎng; ☑028 8570 2649; www.chengdu-airport.net; Shuangliuqu Jichang Donglu, 双流区机场东路; ⓂShuangliu International Airport) Serving Chengdu in Sichuan province, west China and linked to more than 50 international destinations.

Daxing International Airport (北京大兴国际机场, Běijīng Dàxīng Guóji Jīchǎng) Opened in late 2019, Beijing's vast new airport is the capital's second

international airport and the world's biggest.

Hong Kong International Airport (HKG; ☑852 2181 8888; www.hkairport.com) On an island off the northern coast of Lantau and connected to the mainland by several spans.

Kunming Changshui International Airport The sixth-busiest airport in China, handling more than 47 million passengers per year and serving an increasing number of international destinations.

Pudong International Airport (PVG; 浦东国际机场, Pǔdōng Guóji Jīchǎng; ☑021 6834 7575, flight information 96990; www.shairport.com) In Shanghai's east; international flights.

China doesn't have one single national airline, but has large airlines that operate both domestic and international flights. The biggest are **Air China** (www.airchina.com), Shanghai-based **China Eastern Airlines** (www.ceair.com), and **China Southern Airlines** (www.cs-air.com), based in Guangzhou. They fly to China from the US, Europe, Australia/New Zealand and other parts of Asia. Benefits can include a generous checked-luggage allowance, and sometimes a night's accommodation when stopping over on the way to other destinations – great for visa-free travel. Multiple international carriers also fly to China along similar routes.

Some smaller airlines that offer international flights to China:

AirAsia (www.airasia.com)

Asiana Airlines (www.flyasiana.com)

Cathay Dragon (www.cathaypacific.com)

Tickets

The cheapest tickets to Hong Kong and China exist on price-comparison websites or in discount agencies in Chinatowns around the world. Budget and student-travel agents offer cheap tickets, but the real bargains are with agents that deal with the Chinese, who regularly return home. Airfares to China peak between June and September.

The cheapest flights to China are with airlines requiring a stopover at the home airport, such as Air France to Beijing via Paris, or Malaysia Airlines to Beijing via Kuala Lumpur.

The best direct ticket deals are available from China's international carriers, such as China Eastern Airlines, Air China and China Southern Airlines.

Departure Tax

Departure tax is included in the price of a ticket.

Land

China shares borders with Afghanistan, Bhutan, India,

Kazakhstan, Kyrgyzstan, Laos, Mongolia, Myanmar (Burma), Nepal, North Korea, Pakistan, Russia, Tajikistan and Vietnam – the borders with Afghanistan, Bhutan and India are closed. There are also official border crossings between China and its special administrative regions, Hong Kong and Macau.

Lonely Planet *China* guidebooks may be confiscated by officials, primarily at the Vietnam–China border.

Note that borders can suddenly close; this is an issue that can particularly affect border crossings in Xinjiang.

Kazakhstan

Border crossings from Ürümqi to Kazakhstan are via border posts at Korgas, Alashankou, Tacheng and Jimunai. Ensure you have a valid Kazakhstan visa (obtainable, at the time of writing, in Ürümqi, or from Beijing) or China visa.

Apart from Alashankou, which links China and Kazakhstan by train, all other border crossings are by bus; you can generally also get a bike over, however. Two trains weekly (32 hours) run between Ürümqi and Almaty, and one train per week runs to Astana.

Remember that borders open and close frequently due to changes in government policy; additionally, many are only open when the weather permits. It's always best to check with the **Public Security Bureau** (PSB; 公

安局; Gōng'ānjú; Map p842; ☑0991 281 0452, ext 3456; 30 Nanhu Donglu; 南湖东路30号; ☺10am-1.30pm & 4-6pm Mon-Fri) in Ürümqi for the official line.

Kyrgyzstan

There are two routes between China and Kyrgyzstan: one between Kashgar and Osh, via the Irkeshtam Pass; and one between Kashgar and Bishkek, via the dramatic 3752m Torugart Pass.

Laos

From the Mengla district in China's southern Yunnan province, you can enter Laos via Boten in Luang Nam Tha province (from Mohan on the China side), while a daily bus runs between Vientiane and Kunming south bus station, and also from Jinghong to Luang Nam Tha and also to Luang Prabang.

On-the-spot visas for Laos are available at the border, the price of which depends on your nationality (you cannot get a China visa here). Alternatively, you can obtain a visa for Laos from the Lao consulate in Kunming.

Mongolia

From Beijing the Trans-Mongolian Railway trains and the K23 train run to Ulaanbaatar. There are also trains and regular buses between Hohhot and the border town of Erlian (Erenhot). Mongolian visas can be acquired in Beijing, Hohhot, Haila'er or Erlian.

Myanmar (Burma)

The famous Burma Road runs from Kunming in Yunnan province to the Burmese city of Lashio. The road is open to travellers carrying permits for the region north of Lashio, though you can legally cross the border in only one direction – from the Chinese side (Jiegao) into Myanmar. However, at the time of writing it was not possible for independent third-country nationals to travel across the border at Jiegao, though there were rumours that it may be possible as part of a tour group. The only way to go is by air from Kunming. Visas are available at the embassy in Beijing or the Myanmar consulate in Kunming.

Nepal

The 865km road connecting Lhasa with Kathmandu is known as the Friendship Hwy, currently only traversable for foreign travellers in rented vehicle. It's a spectacular trip across the Tibetan plateau, with the highest point being Gyatso-la Pass (5248m).

Visas for Nepal can be obtained in Lhasa, at the border at Kodari, or in Beijing.

When travelling from Nepal to Tibet, foreigners still have to arrange transport through tour agencies in Kathmandu. Access to Tibet can, however, be restricted for months at a time without warning.

CLIMATE CHANGE & TRAVEL

Every form of transport that relies on carbon-based fuel generates CO_2, the main cause of human-induced climate change. Modern travel is dependent on aeroplanes, which might use less fuel per kilometre per person than most cars but travel much greater distances. The altitude at which aircraft emit gases (including CO_2) and particles also contributes to their climate change impact. Many websites offer 'carbon calculators' that allow people to estimate the carbon emissions generated by their journey and, for those who wish to do so, to offset the impact of the greenhouse gases emitted with contributions to portfolios of climate-friendly initiatives throughout the world. Lonely Planet offsets the carbon footprint of all staff and author travel.

North Korea

Visas for North Korea are not especially hard to arrange, though it is not possible to travel independently so you will need to be on a pre-planned tour. Those interested in travelling to North Korea on tours from Beijing should contact **Koryo Tours** (Map p102; ☑010 6416 7544; www.koryogroup.com; 27 Beisanlitun Nan, 北三里屯南27号; Ⓢ Line 2 to Dongsi Shitiao, exit C, or Line 10 to Tuanjiehu, exit A).

Four international express trains (K27 and K28) run between Beijing train station and Pyongyang.

Pakistan

The exciting trip on the Karakoram Hwy, said to be the world's highest public international highway, is an excellent way to get to or from Chinese Central Asia. There are buses from Kashgar for the two-day trip to the Pakistani town of Sost via Tashkurgan when the pass is open. Chinese customs and immigration procedures take place in Tashkurgan, not actually at the border.

Pakistani visas are no longer available to tourists on arrival (and visas are difficult to get in Beijing), so the safest option is to arrive in China with a visa obtained in your home country. Check the current situation as this could change. Proof of a recent polio vaccination is required by the Chinese side, especially if you have spent some time in Pakistan.

Russia

The train from Harbin East to Vladivostok is no longer running, but you can take the train to Suifenhe and take an onward connection there.

The Trans-Mongolian (via Erlian) and Trans-Manchurian (via Harbin) branches of the Trans-Siberian Railway run from Beijing to Moscow. Obtain your Russian visa at the Russian embassy in Beijing.

There are also border crossings 9km from Manzhouli and at Heihe.

Tajikistan

In recent years it has been hard for foreigners to enter China here, but at the time of writing the Qolma (Kulma) Pass, linking Tashkurgan with Murghab, was open to foreign travellers (and has been since around 2017). The pass is not open on Saturday or Sunday. Obtain your visa at the Tajikistan Embassy in Beijing.

Vietnam

Visas are unobtainable at border crossings. Vietnam visas can be acquired in Beijing, Kunming, Hong Kong and Nanning. China visas can be obtained in Hanoi.

FRIENDSHIP PASS

China's busiest border with Vietnam is at the obscure Vietnamese town of Dong Dang, 164km northeast of Hanoi. The closest Chinese town to the border is Pingxiang in Guangxi province, about 10km north of the actual border gate.

Seven Hanoi-bound buses run from Nanning via the Friendship Pass. Twice-weekly trains (T5 and T6) connect Beijing and Hanoi (via Nanning), while a daily train (T8701 and T8702) links Hanoi with Nanning.

HEKOU

The Hekou–Lao Cai border crossing is 468km from Kunming and 294km from Hanoi. At the time of writing, the only way to reach Vietnam via Hekou was by bus from Kunming.

MONG CAI

A little-known border crossing is at Mong Cai in the northeast corner of Vietnam, just opposite the Chinese city of Dongxing and around 200km south of Nanning.

River

The fast river ferries from Jinghong in Yunnan to Chiang Saen in Thailand have been suspended for many years now, though it is still possible to hitch a ride on a cargo boat.

Rail

In addition to the Trans-Siberian and Trans-Mongolian rail services (p1039), the following routes can be travelled by train:

➡ Almaty (Kazakhstan) to Ürümqi

➡ Astana (Kazakhstan) to Ürümqi

➡ Beijing to Hanoi (Vietnam)

➡ Beijing to Ulaanbaatar (Mongolia)

➡ Hohhot to Ulaanbaatar (Mongolia)

➡ Hung Hom station in Kowloon (Jiǔlóng; Hong Kong) or Hong Kong (West Kowloon) station to Guangzhou, Shanghai, Beijing, Xiamen, Fuzhou, Guilin, Guiyang, Kunming, Tianjin and other cities

➡ Pyongyang (North Korea) to Beijing

A good resource is the website The Man in Seat Sixty-One (www.seat61.com).

Sea

Japan

There are weekly ferries between Osaka and Kōbe and Shanghai. The weekly ferry from the Tianjin International Cruise Home Port to Kōbe (神户; Shénhù) had been suspended indefinitely at the time of writing.

Check in two hours before departure for international sailings.

South Korea

International ferries connect the South Korean port of

Sea Routes

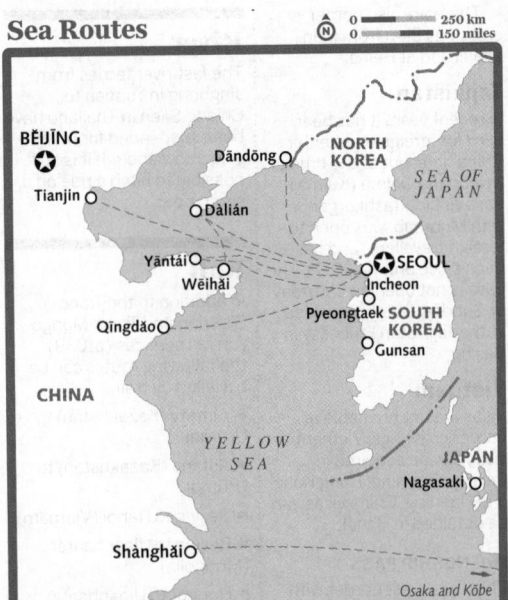

0 — 250 km
0 — 150 miles

BEIJING

Dāndōng

NORTH KOREA

SEA OF JAPAN

Tianjin

Dàlián

Yāntái
Wēihǎi

SEOUL
Incheon
Pyeongtaek SOUTH KOREA
Gunsan

Qīngdǎo

CHINA

YELLOW SEA

JAPAN
Nagasaki

Shànghǎi

Osaka and Kōbe

Incheon with Qingdao, Yantai, Tianjin, Dalian and Dandong. Ferries also sail from Yantai to Pyeongtaek. Tickets are generally available from offices at relevant ports in China.

Taiwan

Daily ferries ply the route between Xiamen and Kinmen Island in Taiwan, from where you can fly to major Taiwanese cities. You can also catch a ferry from Fuzhou's Langqi ferry terminal to Taiwan's archipelago of Matsu, from where there are boats to Keelung and flights to other cities in Taiwan.

GETTING AROUND

Air

China's air network is extensive and growing fast. Air safety and quality have improved considerably, but the speed of change and crowded skies can impact on

reliability, and flight delays are very common. When deciding between flying and using high-speed rail, remember that trains almost always leave on time.

Planes vary in style and comfort, but service has vastly improved over recent years. You may get a hot meal, or just a small piece of cake and an airline souvenir. On-board announcements are delivered in Mandarin and English.

Shuttle buses to airports usually run from Civil Aviation Administration of China (CAAC; Zhōngguó Mínháng) offices, train stations, some hotels or bus stations in towns and cities throughout China, often running via other stops. For domestic flights, arrive at the airport two hours before departure.

Remember to keep your baggage receipt label on your ticket as you might need to show it when you collect your luggage.

Departure tax is included in the price of a ticket.

Airlines

The CAAC is the civil aviation authority for numerous airlines. Some of the listed airlines also have subsidiary airlines. Not all Chinese airline websites have English-language capability.

Air China (www.airchina.com)

Chengdu Airlines (☑in Chengdu 028 6666 8888; www.chengduair.cc)

China Eastern Airlines (www.ce-air.com)

China Southern Airlines (☑in Guangzhou 4006 695 539; www.csair.com/en) Serves a web of air routes, including Beijing, Shanghai, Xi'an and Tianjin.

Hainan Airlines (☑in Hainan 0898 95339; www.hainanairlines.com)

Shandong Airlines (☑95369; www.shandongair.com.cn)

Shanghai Airlines (☑in Shanghai 95530; www.ceair.com) Owned by China Eastern Airlines.

Shenzhen Airlines (☑in Shenzhen 95361; www.shenzhenair.com)

Sichuan Airlines (☑in Chengdu 95378; www.scal.com.cn)

Spring Airlines (☑021 6252 0000; www.ch.com) Has connections between Shanghai and tourist destinations such as Qingdao, Guilin, Xiamen and Sanya.

Tianjin Airlines (☑in Tianjin 95350; www.tianjin-air.com)

Tibet Airlines (☑4008 0891 88; www.tibetairlines.com.cn; ⊙7am-9pm) Domestic connections all over China from Lhasa.

Tickets

Except during major festivals and holidays, tickets are easy to purchase, with an oversupply of airline seats. For the best deals, purchase tickets online. Discounts are common, except when flying into large cities such as Shanghai and Beijing on the weekend, when the full fare can be the norm. Fares are calculated according to one-way travel, with return tickets simply costing twice the single fare. If flying from Hong Kong or Macau to mainland China, note that these are classified as international flights – it is much cheaper to travel overland into Shenzhen, Zhuhai or Guangzhou and fly from there.

Bicycle

Bikes (自行车, zìxíngchē) are an excellent method for getting around China's cities and tourist sights. They can also be invaluable for exploring the countryside and surrounding towns.

Hire

Station-less bike-sharing systems in cities such as Beijing, Shanghai, Chengdu, Lanzhou, Xi'an and Xiamen have the potential to be useful, but at the time of writing were very hard to use for travellers. At basic minimum you'll need a smartphone with internet and SMS access (for verification, so data-only SIM cards are insufficient). You'll also need to download the app and complete the registration process, which involves submitting photos of your passport. The final hurdle is the killer: you'll need to use WeChat or Alipay apps, with credit loaded on them, and at the time of writing you needed a Chinese bank account to do this.

Other local public bike-hire schemes are, by and large, not foreigner-friendly either, so generally the best places to try are youth hostels, which rent out bicycles – as do many hotels, though the latter are more expensive.

Touring

Cycling through China allows you to go when you want, to see what you want and at your own pace. It can also be an extremely cheap, as well as a highly authentic, way to see the land.

You will have virtually unlimited freedom of movement but, considering the size of China, you will need to combine your cycling days with trips by train, bus, boat, taxi or even planes, especially if you want to travel particularly steep regions, or areas where the roads are poor or the climate is cold.

A basic packing list for cyclists includes a good bicycle-repair kit, sunscreen and other sun protection, waterproofs, fluorescent strips and camping equipment. Ensure you have adequate clothing, as many routes will be taking you to considerable altitude. Road maps in Chinese are essential for asking locals for directions.

Bike China Adventures (www.bikechina.com) arranges tours and is a good source of information for cyclists coming to China.

Boat

Boat services within China are very limited, especially with the massive growth of high-speed rail and expressways. They're most common in coastal areas, where you are likely to use a boat to reach offshore islands such as Putuoshan or Hainan, or the islands off Hong Kong. The Yantai–Dalian ferry will probably survive because it saves hundreds of kilometres of overland travel, though a superlong undersea tunnel remains on the drawing board. Construction – if commenced – would take almost 20 years.

The best-known river trip is the three-day boat ride along the Yangzi (Cháng Jiāng) from Chongqing to Yichang. The Li River (Lí Jiāng) boat trip from Guilin to Yangshuo is a popular tourist ride.

Hong Kong employs an out-and-out navy of vessels that connect with the territory's myriad islands, and a number of boats run between the territory and other parts of China, including Macau, Zhuhai, Shekou (for Shenzhen) and Zhongshan.

Bus

Long-distance bus (长途公共汽车, chángtú gōnggòng qìchē) services are extensive and reach places you cannot access by train. With the increasing number of intercity highways, journeys are getting quicker. Some services have reduced frequencies or have vanished altogether due to the appearance of high-speed train routes, but in provinces with limited rail services (eg Qinghai), the bus is still king.

The standard of buses and service has vastly improved in China over the last few years, partly due to competition from high-speed train routes but also as a general raising of the bar to meet more international levels. Routes between big cities sport large, clean and comfortable fleets of private buses, some equipped with toilets and hostesses handing out snacks, mineral water and checking you have fastened your seat belt. Shorter and more far-flung or distant routes can still rely on rattling minibuses into which as many fares as possible are crammed and which may only depart when full and then may trawl the streets looking for fares.

Sleeper buses (卧铺客车, wòpù kèchē) ply popular long-haul routes, costing around double the price of a normal bus service. Many buses have been upgraded over the last few years, so you can now expect reasonable comfort, though they generally will not have onboard toilets and will stop for toilet breaks, when smokers will huddle in packs by the roadside. If an overnight train follows the same route, opt for that, for comfort and the conviviality of the experience. You may find older-style sleeper buses on other routes, in which case prepare for more cramped conditions and less cleanliness.

Bus journey times should be used as a rough guide only. You can estimate times for bus journeys on non-highway routes by calculating the distance against a speed of 25km/h.

All cities and most towns have one or more long-distance **bus station** (长途汽车站, chángtú qìchēzhàn), generally located in relation to the direction in which the bus heads. Where there are multiple stations, each station is generally named after a compass point (north bus station, east bus station etc). Most bus stations have a left-luggage counter. Your bags will be scanned either before you are allowed into the ticketing hall or before you board the bus, but checks are less stringent than on the rail network.

In many cities the train station forecourt doubles as a bus station.

Tickets

Tickets are generally cheaper and easier to get than train tickets; turn up at the bus station and buy your ticket on the spot. The earlier you buy, the closer to the front of the bus you will sit, though you may not be able to buy tickets prior to your day of travel. You will need your passport to purchase a bus ticket.

Tickets can be harder to procure during national holiday periods.

To check the times of buses and ticket prices, consult either Ctrip (www.ctrip.com) or Bus365 (www.bus365.com), though both are Chinese-language only.

Dangers & Annoyances

Breakdowns can be a hassle, and some rural roads and provincial routes (especially in the southwest, Tibet and the northwest) remain in not-so-good condition. Precipitous drops, potholes, dangerous road surfaces and reckless drivers mean

accidents remain common. Long-distance journeys can also be cramped and noisy. Lack of seat belts is not the issue it once was, though you may still find buses without seat belts in more far-flung areas.

Note the following when travelling by bus:

➡ Take plenty of warm clothes on buses to high-altitude destinations in winter. A breakdown in frozen conditions can prove lethal for those unprepared.

➡ Take a lot of extra water on routes across areas such as the Taklamakan Desert.

Car & Motorcycle

To hire a car or motorcycle in China you must hold a valid People's Republic of China driving licence. Foreign driving licences or even those supported by an International Driving Permit (IDP) are simply not accepted. E-bikes and e-scooters generally do not have the same restrictions. If you wish to travel around by car, you will need to hire one with a driver or book a taxi for the day or half-day (or however long you wish). To drive in Hong Kong and Macau, you will need an IDP.

Cars in China drive on the right-hand side of the road. Even skilled drivers will be unprepared for China's roads – in the cities, cars lunge from all angles and chaos abounds.

Local Transport

Long-distance transport in China is good, but local transport is less efficient, except in cities with metro systems. The choice of local transport is diverse but vehicles can be slow and over-burdened, and the network confusing for visitors. Hiring a car is often impractical, while hiring a bike can be inadequate. Unless the town

is small, walking is often too tiring.

On the plus side, local transport is cheap, taxis are usually ubiquitous and affordable, and clean and efficient metro systems continue to rapidly expand in large tourist towns.

Bus

With extensive networks, buses are an excellent way to get around towns, but foreign travellers rarely use them and you will often be the only non-Chinese person on the bus. When boarding a bus, point to your destination on a map and the conductor (seated near the door) will sell you the right ticket. The conductor will usually tell you where to disembark, provided they remember (which they usually do). In conductor-less buses you put money for your fare into a slot near the driver as you embark. A variety of bus apps such as 车来了 (chēláile; 'the bus is coming') can inform you of the arrival time of the next bus, but they are only available in Chinese.

➡ Fares are very cheap (usually ¥1 to ¥2), but buses may be packed.

➡ In cities such as Beijing, Shanghai and Hong Kong, a locally purchased transport card can be used on the buses.

➡ Alipay and WeChat Pay can be used on many buses.

➡ Navigation is tricky for non-Chinese speakers as bus routes at bus stops are generally listed in Chinese, without pinyin.

➡ In Beijing, Shanghai and other large tourist cities and towns, stops will also be announced in English.

➡ Always have change ready if there is no conductor on the bus.

➡ Buses with snowflake motifs are air-conditioned.

➡ Traffic can make things slow.

➡ Disembark through the back door.

Subway, Metro & Light Rail

Going underground or using light rail is fast, efficient and cheap. Most networks are either very new or relatively recent and can be found in a rapidly growing number of cities, including Beijing, Chengdu, Chongqing, Dalian, Guangzhou, Hangzhou, Harbin, Hong Kong, Kunming, Qingdao, Shanghai, Shenyang, Shenzhen, Suzhou, Tianjin, Wuhan, Xiamen and Xi'an. Transport cards for use on metro systems can be purchased in large cities such as Hong Kong, Beijing and Shanghai, and many metro systems also take WeChat Pay and Alipay.

Taxi

Taxis (出租汽车, chūzū qìchē) are cheap and easy to find. Taxi rates per kilometre are clearly marked on a sticker on the rear side window of the taxi; flagfall varies from city to city, and depends on the size and quality of the vehicle. Most taxis have meters but they may only be switched on in larger towns and cities. If the meter is not used (on an excursion out of town, for example, or when hiring a taxi for the day or half-day), negotiate a price before you set off and write the fare down. If you want the meter used, ask for dǎbiǎo (打表). Also ask for a receipt (发票, fāpiào) – if you leave something in the taxi, you can have the car located by its vehicle number printed on the receipt. If paying in cash, you may find that

drivers no longer carry much change; carry small notes when hailing a cab. You can generally pay the taxi driver using WeChat Pay or Alipay, if you wish. WeChat has a useful ride-hailing function through DiDi Chuxing (滴滴出行; www.didiglobal.com), the most popular mobile-phone taxi-hailing app on the China market (Uber sold its market share to DiDi Chuxing in 2016).

Other Local Transport

A variety of ramshackle transport options exist across China; always agree on a price in advance.

➡ Motor pedicabs are enclosed three-wheeled vehicles (often the same price as taxis).

➡ Pedicabs are pedal-powered versions of motor pedicabs.

➡ Motorbike riders also offer lifts in some towns for what should be half the price of a regular taxi. You must wear a helmet – the driver will provide one.

Train

For information on train travel, see the China by Train chapter (p1036).

China by Train

Trains are the best way to travel long distances around China in reasonable speed and comfort. They are also adventurous, exciting, fun, practical and efficient, and ticket prices are reasonable to boot. Colossal investment over recent years has put high-speed rail at the heart of China's rapid modernisation drive. You really don't have to be a trainspotter to find China's railways a riveting subculture – as a plus you'll get to meet the Chinese people at their most relaxed and sociable.

At the Station

As you arrive at the train station to board your train (and sometimes before you can access the main ticket hall), you will have your ticket checked against your passport. Then you will need to put your bag on a conveyor belt through a scanner that checks for prohibited items, including knives (your pocket knife may be confiscated, so leave your best Swiss Army knife at home) and aerosols (anything over 120mL). It is a better idea to buy necessities (eg shoe freshener) in China that are manufactured in low-enough-volume cans to be allowed onto trains. If an item is prohibited and you are prevented from taking it aboard the train, you can arrange for it to be sent to wherever you are going, by

express delivery. That is the only option, other than throwing it away. You will also need to walk through a metal detector and security personnel will quickly check you with a wand.

In old-style stations (such as Beijing West Train Station) you will have to find the correct waiting-room number, displayed on an illuminated screen as you walk in. Some more modern stations (such as Shanghai Hongqiao Train Station) are more straightforward and intelligently designed, without waiting rooms. Instead your platform number will appear on the screen.

Aboard the Train

Trolleys of food and drink are wheeled along carriages during the trip, but prices are high and the selection is limited. You can also load up on mineral water and snacks at stations, where hawkers sell items from platform stalls. Long-distance, older-type trains should have a canteen carriage (餐厅车厢, cāntīng chēxiāng); they are sometimes open through the night.

If taking a sleeper train you will generally be required to exchange your paper ticket for a plastic or metal card with your bunk number on it. The conductor then knows when you are due to disembark, and will wake you

in time to return your ticket to you.

CHINA'S TRAIN NETWORK

One of the world's most extensive rail networks penetrates every province in China and high-speed connections are suddenly everywhere. In line with China's frantic economic development and the pressures of transporting 1.4 billion people across the world's third-largest nation, expansion of China's high-speed rail network over the past decade has been simply mind-boggling.

The network currently totals more than 127,000km in length, 29,000km of which is high-speed rail track. Thousands of kilometres of track are laid every year, with high-speed trains zipping across the land since 2007, shrinking China's once-daunting distances. State-of-the-art train stations have continuously appeared as if from nowhere, primarily to serve high-speed links. Most of these new stations are located in city outskirts and are given a name corresponding to their position in relation to the city in question eg Xi'an North, Zhangye West or Guangzhou South. The highly anticipated Xi'an–Chengdu line has cut travel times from 13 hours to around four hours, and

TRAIN ROUTES

Route	Duration	Fare
Beijing–Datong	6½hr	Hard seat/sleeper ¥54/145
Beijing–Hong Kong (West Kowloon)	9hr	2nd/1st class ¥1077/1724
Beijing South–Hangzhou East	5hr	2nd/1st class ¥539/907
Beijing South–Qingdao	4½hr	2nd/1st class ¥314/524
Beijing South–Shanghai Hongqiao	4-6hr	2nd/1st class ¥553/933
Beijing South–Tianjin	30min	2nd/1st class ¥55/88
Beijing West–Guilin North	8½-10½hr	2nd/1st class ¥804/1287
Beijing West–Kunming South	11-12½hr	2nd/1st class ¥1148/1878
Beijing West–Lhasa	41hr	Hard/soft sleeper ¥763/1189
Beijing West-Pingyao	4hr	2nd/1st class ¥183/294
Beijing West–Xi'an North	4½-6hr	2nd/1st class ¥516/825
Guangzhou–Hong Kong (West Kowloon)	1hr	2nd/1st class ¥215/323
Shanghai Hongqiao–Nanjing South	1½hr	2nd/1st class ¥135/230
Kunming–Guilin West	4hr	Hard seat/sleeper ¥374/616
Kunming–Lijiang	3½hr	Hard/soft sleeper ¥220/351
Kunming South–Chengdu East	6hr	Hard seat/sleeper ¥488/798
Pingyao–Xi'an North	3hr	2nd/1st class ¥150/240
Shanghai–Lhasa	47hr	Hard seat/sleeper ¥403/839
Shanghai Hongqiao–Hangzhou East	1hr	2nd/1st class ¥73/117
Shanghai Hongqiao–Hong Kong (West Kowloon)	8hr	2nd/1st class ¥1008/1647
Shanghai Hongqiao–Shenzhen North	8-11½hr	2nd/1st class ¥568/909
Shanghai Hongqiao–Wuhan	4-6hr	2nd/1st class ¥315/503
Shanghai Hongqiao–Xiamen North	5-8hr	2nd/1st class ¥388/621
Shanghai Hongqiao–Xi'an North	6-11hr	2nd/1st class ¥670/1095
Shenzhen North–Guilin North	3hr	2nd/1st class ¥240/364
Ürümqi–Kashgar	17hr	Hard/soft sleeper ¥326/498
Wuhan–Guangzhou South	4hr	2nd/1st class ¥464/739
Xi'an North–Luoyang Longmen	1½hr	2nd/1st class ¥175/280

similar stories have been repeated across China. The only cities and regions to date not penetrated by high-speed rail are Tibet, Ningxia and Macau.

High-speed D, G and C class trains have also put the squeeze on numerous domestic air routes and the punctuality of trains sees far fewer delays than air travel. Some bus routes have also disappeared, or cut the frequency of services, due to the competition from high-speed rail. There is even talk of extending links through Kyrgyzstan, Tajikistan, Uzbekistan, Turkmenistan, Iran and Turkey to Bulgaria. Down south, China is also planning a high-speed link from Kunming in Yunnan to Singapore, via Laos, Thailand and Malaysia.

TRAIN TRAVEL

Trains are generally highly punctual in China and are usually a safe (and convivial) way to travel. Train stations are often conveniently close to the centre of town, though high-speed train stations may be a considerable distance from the town or city centre.

Travelling on sleeper berths at night means you can frequently arrive at your destination first thing in the morning, saving a night's hotel accommodation. Think ahead, get your tickets early and you can sleep your way around a lot of China.

Some tips regarding train travel:

➡ Don't wait to board your train until the last minute, as queues outside the main train station entrance can be shocking.

➡ Keep passports handy when entering a station as the name on your ticket will be checked against the name on your passport.

➡ On a nonsleeper, ask a member of staff or a fellow passenger to tell you when your station arrives.

➡ Keep your ticket after disembarking the train as there can be checks when exiting the platform and ticket-fed turnstiles in some newer stations.

TRAIN TYPES

Chinese train numbers are usually (but not always) prefixed by a letter, designating the category of train.

High-Speed Trains

The fastest, most luxurious and expensive (and now most common) intercity trains are the streamlined, high-speed G, D and C trains, which rapidly shuttle between major cities. D class trains were the first high-speed trains to appear and glide around China, offering substantial comfort and regular services. Their temperature-regulated 1st-class carriages have mobile and laptop chargers, and seats are two abreast with ample legroom and TV sets. Second-class carriages have five seats in two rows. G class trains are even faster, and have now largely superseded the D class trains on major routes. Smoking is not permitted on high-speed trains. C class trains are mostly used for rapid commuter-type hops between neighbouring cities.

Regular Trains

The old-style express classes, dwindling in number, include the overnight Z class trains, while further down the pecking order are older and more basic T and K class trains. Toilets will generally be the squat variety on these. While high-speed trains are truly nonsmoking, the older trains allow smoking between carriages.

TICKETS

It is possible to upgrade (补票, *bǔpiào*) your ticket once aboard your train. If you have a standing ticket, for example, find the conductor and upgrade to a hard seat, soft seat or hard sleeper (if there are any available).

Soft Sleeper

Soft sleepers are a very comfortable way to travel, and work perfectly as mobile hotels. Tickets cost much more than hard-sleeper tickets but often sell out, so book early. Soft sleepers vary between trains and the best are on the D and Z class trains. All Z class trains are soft-sleeper trains, with very comfortable, up-to-date berths. A few T class trains also offer two-berth compartments, with their own toilet.

Tickets for upper berths are slightly cheaper than for lower berths. Expect to share with total strangers. If you are asleep, an attendant will wake you to prepare you to disembark, so you will have plenty of time to ready your train. Available on some lines, two-bed deluxe soft sleepers usually have a toilet and sink. VIP sleepers – essentially three-bed compartments that one person can book in their entirety – are available on the Kunming–Lijiang route.

Soft-sleeper carriages contain the following:

➡ four air-conditioned bunks (upper and lower) in a closed compartment

➡ bedding on each berth and a lockable door to the carriage corridor

➡ meals, flat-screen TVs on some routes

➡ power/USB sockets

➡ a small table and stowing space for your bags

➡ a hot-water flask for drinking (plain or for tea) or making instant noodles, filled by an attendant (one per compartment)

TRAVELLING THE TRANS-SIBERIAN RAILWAY

Rolling out of Europe and into Asia, through eight time zones and over 9289km of taiga, steppe and desert, the Trans-Siberian Railway and its connecting routes constitute one of the most famous and most romantic of the world's great train journeys.

There are, in fact, three railways. The 'true' Trans-Siberian line runs from Moscow to Vladivostok, but the routes traditionally referred to as the Trans-Siberian Railway are the two branches that veer off the main line in eastern Siberia for Beijing.

Since the first option excludes China, most readers here will be choosing between the Trans-Mongolian and the Trans-Manchurian railway lines. The Trans-Mongolian route (Beijing to Moscow; 7865km) is faster, but requires an additional visa and another border crossing – on the plus side, you also get to see some of the Mongolian countryside. The Trans-Manchurian route (Beijing to Moscow; 9025km) is longer.

Trans-Mongolian Railway

Trains offer deluxe two-berth compartments (with shared shower), 1st-class four-berth compartments and 2nd-class four-berth compartments. Tickets for hard/deluxe soft sleeper to Moscow cost ¥3793/6080, ¥1310/2041 to Ulaanbaatar and ¥2799/4470 to Novosibirsk. Ticket prices are cheaper if you travel in a group. The K23 service departs on either Monday or Tuesday (hard/soft sleeper ¥1310/1881, 7.27am, 30 hours) and terminates at Ulaanbaatar the following day.

From Beijing Train K3 leaves Beijing Train Station on its five-day journey to Moscow at 7.27am every Wednesday, passing Ulaanbaatar and Novosibirsk before arriving in Moscow the following Monday at 1.58pm.

From Moscow Train K4 leaves at 11.55pm on Tuesday, arriving in Beijing Train Station the following Monday at 2.35pm. Departure and arrival times may fluctuate slightly.

Trans-Manchurian Railway

Trains have 1st-class two-berth compartments and 2nd-class four-berth compartments; prices are similar to those on the Trans-Mongolian Railway (p1043).

From Beijing Train K19 departs Beijing Train Station at 11pm on Saturday, arriving in Moscow (via Manzhouli) the following Friday at 2.13pm.

From Moscow Train K20 leaves Moscow at 11.45pm on Saturday, arriving at Beijing Train Station the following Saturday at 5.49am. Departure and arrival times may fluctuate slightly.

Buying Tickets

Book well in advance (especially in summer); in Beijing tickets can be purchased at Beijing train station or booked in central Beijing from **CITS** (China International Travel Service, 中国国际旅行社, Zhōngguó Guójì Lǚxíngshè; Map p82; ☑010 6512 0507; Beijing International Hotel, 9 Jianguomennei Dajie, 北京国际饭店建国门内大街9号; ⊙9am-noon & 1.30-5pm Mon-Fri, to noon Sat; ⑤Lines 1, 2 to Jianguomen, exit A), for a ¥50 mark-up. Tickets can also be booked with a mark-up through **China DIY Travel** (www.china-diy-travel.com; 6 Chaoyang Park Nanlu, 朝阳公园南路6号).

Visas

Travellers will need Russian and Mongolian visas for the Trans-Mongolian Railway and a Russian visa for the Trans-Manchurian Railway, as well as a Chinese visa. These can often be arranged along with your ticket by travel agents such as **China International Travel Service** (CITS; www.cits.net).

Hard Sleeper

Hard sleepers are available on slower and less modern T, K and N class trains, as well as trains without a letter prefix. As with soft sleepers, they serve very nicely as an overnight hotel.

There is a small price difference between the numbered berths, with the lowest bunk (下铺, xiàpù) the most expensive and the highest

REGULAR TRAINS

TYPE	PINYIN	CHINESE	TOP SPEED
Z class (express)	zhídá	直达	160km/h
T class	tèkuài	特快	140km/h
K class	kuàisù	快速	120km/h

bunk (上铺, shàngpù) the cheapest. The top bunk has little headroom and puts you near the speakers. As with soft sleepers, an attendant will wake you well in advance of your station.

Hard-sleeper tickets are the most difficult of all to buy; you almost always need to buy them a few days in advance, so plan ahead. Expect the following:

➡ doorless compartments with half a dozen bunks in three tiers

➡ sheets, pillows and blankets on each berth

➡ a no-smoking policy (though you can smoke in between the carriages)

➡ lights and speakers out at around 10pm

➡ a hot-water flask, filled by an attendant (one per compartment)

➡ trolleys passing by selling food and drink

➡ power/USB sockets in the aisle

➡ a rack above the windows for stowing your baggage, though anything heavy or larger than a carry-on suitcase will need to be stored in the aisle

➡ squat toilets at each end of the carriage

Seats

High-Speed Trains

First-class (一等, yīděng) and 2nd-class (二等, èrděng) soft seats are available on D, C and G class high-speed trains. G class trains also offer business class and/or VIP seats, which include a hot meal and added comfort, and in some cases a seat that folds down into a bed.

First-class comes with TVs, mobile phone and laptop charging points, a snack pack and seats arranged two abreast.

Second-class soft seats are also very comfortable, and staff are very courteous throughout. Overcrowding is not permitted and power points are available.

Regular Trains

Soft-seat class is more comfortable but not as common as hard-seat class. Hard-seat class is found on T and K class trains and trains without a number prefix; a handful of Z class trains have hard seats. Hard-seat class generally has padded seats, but it can be hard on your sanity, especially long haul.

You should get a ticket with an assigned seat number. If seats have sold out, ask for a standing ticket, which gets you on the train, where you may find a seat or can upgrade. Otherwise you will have to stand in the carriage or between carriages (with the smokers). If you find someone sitting in your seat (which is common), just show them your ticket and they will move.

Buying Tickets

The Achilles heel of China's overburdened rail system, buying tickets can be a pain.

Most tickets are one-way only, with prices calculated per kilometre and adjustments made depending on class of train, availability of air-con, type of sleeper and bunk positioning.

Some tips on buying train tickets:

➡ Never aim to get a sleeper ticket on the day of travel – plan and purchase ahead.

➡ Most tickets can be booked 28 days in advance of your departure date when booking in person at ticket offices, or 30 days in advance of the travel date when booking online.

➡ Buying tickets for hard-seat carriages at short notice is usually no hassle, but it may be a standing ticket rather than a numbered seat.

HIGH-SPEED TRAINS

TYPE	PINYIN	CHINESE	TOP SPEED
G class	gāotiě	高铁	350km/h
D class	dòngchē	动车	250km/h
C class	chéngjì	城际	200km/h

TRAIN TICKETS

TICKET TYPE	PINYIN	CHINESE
soft sleeper	*ruǎnwò*	软卧
hard sleeper	*yìngwò*	硬卧
soft seat	*ruǎnzuò*	软座
hard seat	*yìngzuò*	硬座
standing ticket	*wúzuò* or *zhànpiào*	无座\站票

➡ When bought at the train station, tickets can be purchased with cash, WeChat Pay, Alipay or bank cards that are part of the Chinese UnionPay network.

➡ You will need your passport when buying a ticket (the number and your name is printed on your ticket) at all train ticket offices. Your name will also appear on tickets bought online.

➡ All automated ticket machines require Chinese ID – your passport will not work, so you will need to queue at the ticket window.

➡ As with air travel, buying tickets around the Chinese New Year and the 1 May and 1 October holiday periods can be very difficult.

➡ Tickets on many routes (such as to Lhasa) can be very hard to get in July and August; consider flying to distant destinations.

➡ Expect to queue for up to 30 minutes or more for a train ticket at the station; ticket offices outside of the station are often less busy.

➡ Avoid black-market tickets: your passport number must be on the ticket for it to be valid.

➡ Obtaining refunds for lost train tickets is arduous and involves purchasing a new ticket and getting a refund at the other end once it has been proved no one occupied your seat.

➡ If you miss your D or G class train, you will be allowed to take the next available train on the same day only at no charge. For all other trains, your ticket is forfeited (unless your connecting train was late).

➡ Booking tickets on apps lets you avoid missing out. A fee of ¥20 to ¥40 applies, and tickets still need to be picked up from a ticket collection window (often with a queue) at any train station, or the ticket can be delivered for a fee.

➡ Note that the lighter tickets are to be hand-checked when you board the train, while the stiffer variety are designed to be passed through the machine.

Your ticket will display the following:

➡ the train number

➡ the name of your departure and destination stations in Chinese and pinyin

➡ the time and date of travel

➡ your carriage and seat (or berth) number

➡ the ticket price

➡ your passport number and your name

Ticket Offices & Buying Online

Ticket offices (售票厅, *shòupiàotīng*) at train stations are usually to one side of the main station entrance. Automated ticket machines operate on some routes, but never accept foreign passports as ID. At large stations there should be a window staffed by someone with basic English skills. Queues are generally quite long, but are much shorter these days as so many Chinese travellers either buy their tickets online or use the automated ticket machines.

Alternatively, independent train ticket offices usually exist elsewhere in town, where tickets can be purchased for a ¥5 commission without the same kind of queues; we list these where possible. The number of these ticket offices is dwindling, however, as more and more Chinese buy tickets online. Larger post offices may also sell train tickets. Your hotel will also be able to rustle up a ticket for you for a commission, and so can a travel agent.

The China Train Booking (www.chinatrainbooking.com) app can be a useful way to reserve a ticket; you will need to collect your ticket from the train station or have it delivered for a charge. Booking tickets online at the official China Rail website (www.12306.cn; Chinese language only) is only possible with a Chinese bank card and Chinese ID. You can book a ticket over the phone on (area code +) 95105105, but the service is in Chinese only. You pay upon collection of your reserved ticket at the train station.

It's cheaper to buy your ticket at the station, but tickets can be bought online at the following (China DIY Travel is the cheapest) and collected from any train station before travel:

VIEW STOCK/ALAMY STOCK PHOTO ©

Qinghai–Tibet Railway (p948)

China DIY Travel (www.china-diy-travel.com; 6 Chaoyang Park Nanlu, 朝阳公园南路6号)

Trip.com (www.trip.com)

You can also find English-language train timetables on these websites.

To get a refund (退票, *tuìpiào*) on an unused ticket, look for the specifically marked windows at large train stations, where you can get from 80% to 95% of your ticket value back, depending on how many days prior to the departure date you cancel.

Resources

China DIY Travel (www.china-diy-travel.com; 6 Chaoyang Park Nanlu, 朝阳公园南路6号)

China Highlights (www.chinahighlights.com/china-trains)

The Man in Seat 61 (www.seat61.com/China.htm)

Travel China Guide (www.travelchinaguide.com)

Health

China is a reasonably healthy country in which to travel. Some health issues should be noted, though pre-existing medical conditions and accidental injury (especially traffic accidents) account for most life-threatening problems while travelling in China.

Outside of the major cities, medical care is often inadequate, and food and water-borne diseases are common. Malaria is still present in some parts of the country, and altitude sickness can be a problem, particularly in Tibet.

In case of accident or illness, it's best just to get a taxi and go to hospital directly.

Advice here is a general guide only and does not replace the advice of a doctor trained in travel medicine.

Before You Go
Health Insurance

➡ Even if you are fit and healthy, don't travel without health insurance – accidents happen.

➡ Declare any existing medical conditions you have (the insurance company *will* check if your problem is pre-existing and will not cover you if it is undeclared).

➡ You may require extra cover for adventure activities such as rock climbing or skiing.

➡ If you're uninsured, emergency evacuation is expensive; bills of more than US$100,000 are not uncommon.

➡ Ensure you keep all documentation related to any medical expenses you incur.

Vaccinations

Specialised travel-medicine clinics stock all available vaccines and can give specific recommendations for your trip. The doctors will consider your vaccination history, the length of your trip, activities you may undertake and any underlying medical conditions, such as pregnancy.

➡ Visit a doctor six to eight weeks before departure, as most vaccines don't produce immunity until at least two weeks after they're given.

➡ Ask your doctor for an International Certificate of Vaccination (otherwise known as the 'yellow booklet'), listing all vaccinations received.

➡ The only vaccine required by international regulations is for yellow fever.

Proof of vaccination against yellow fever is only required if you have visited a country in the yellow-fever zone within the six days prior to

CORONAVIRUS

In December 2019, a new virus surfaced in a food market in Wuhan, the capital of Hubei province. Officially named Covid-19, the virus spread worldwide, despite Wuhan and other cities in Hubei province going into lockdown in late January 2020. The virus causes a range of range of respiratory illnesses which can lead to death, especially in the elderly and vulnerable. At the time of writing, almost 3.5 million people had died from contracting Covid-19. China closed its borders to foreign visitors in March 2020; at the time of writing, only a restricted number of foreigners could enter China with stringent conditions attached to the visa application system, including the provision of a document of health (issued if evidence is supplied of negative nucleic acid and IgM antibody tests for Covid-19, taken no more than 48 hours before travel to China) or proof of vaccination with a Chinese-made vaccine, followed by two weeks quarantine upon arrival in China. For the latest information on the virus, including safety precautions and travel advice, visit www.who.int/emergencies/diseases/novel-coronavirus-2019..

HEALTH ADVISORIES

It's usually a good idea to check your government's travel advisory website for health warnings before departure.

Australia (www.dfat.gov.au/travel)

Canada (www.travelhealth.gc.ca)

New Zealand (www.safetravel.govt.nz)

UK (www.gov.uk/foreign-travel-advice)

USA (www.cdc.gov/travel)

entering China. If you are travelling to China directly from South America or Africa, check with a travel clinic as to whether you need a yellow-fever vaccination.

RECOMMENDED VACCINATIONS

The World Health Organization (WHO) recommends the following vaccinations for travellers to China:

Adult diphtheria and tetanus (ADT) Single booster recommended if you've not received one in the previous 10 years. Side effects include a sore arm and fever. An ADT vaccine that immunises against pertussis (whooping cough) is also available and may be recommended by your doctor.

Hepatitis A Provides almost 100% protection for up to a year; a booster after 12 months provides at least another 20 years' protection. Mild side effects such as a headache and sore arm occur in 5% to 10% of people.

Hepatitis B Now considered routine for most travellers. Given as three shots over six months, though a rapid schedule is also available. There is also a combined vaccination with hepatitis A. Side effects are mild and uncommon, usually a headache and sore arm. Lifetime protection results for 95% of people.

Measles, mumps and rubella (MMR) Two doses of MMR is recommended unless you have had the diseases. Occasionally a rash and a flu-like illness can develop a week after receiving the vaccine. Many adults under 40 require a booster.

Typhoid Recommended unless your trip is less than a week.

The vaccine offers around 70% protection, lasts for two to three years and comes as a single shot. Tablets are also available, though the injection is usually recommended as it has fewer side effects. A sore arm and fever may occur. A vaccine combining hepatitis A and typhoid in a single shot is now available.

Varicella If you haven't had chickenpox, discuss this vaccination with your doctor.

The following immunisations are recommended for travellers spending more than one month in the country, or those at special risk:

Influenza A single shot lasts one year and is recommended for those over 65 years of age or with underlying medical conditions such as heart or lung disease.

Japanese B encephalitis A series of three injections with a booster after two years. Recommended if spending more than one month in rural areas in summer, or more than three months in the country.

Pneumonia A single injection with a booster after five years is recommended for all travellers over 65 years of age or with underlying medical conditions that compromise immunity, such as heart or lung disease, cancer or HIV.

Rabies Three injections in all. A booster after one year will then provide 10 years' protection. Side effects are rare – occasionally a headache and sore arm.

Tuberculosis A complex issue. High-risk adult long-term travellers are usually recommended to have a TB skin test before and after travel, rather than vaccination. Only one vaccine is given

in a lifetime. Children under five spending more than three months in China should be vaccinated.

Pregnant women and children should receive advice from a doctor who specialises in travel medicine.

Medical Checklist

Recommended medical items for a personal medical kit:

➡ Antibacterial cream, eg mucipirocin

➡ Antibiotics for diarrhoea, including norfloxacin, ciprofloxacin or azithromycin for bacterial diarrhoea, or tinidazole for giardia or amoebic dysentery

➡ Antibiotics for skin infections, eg amoxicillin/clavulanate or cephalexin

➡ Antifungal cream, eg clotrimazole

➡ Antihistamine, eg cetirizine for daytime and promethazine for night-time

➡ Anti-inflammatory, eg ibuprofen

➡ Antiseptic, eg Betadine

➡ Antispasmodic for stomach cramps, eg Buscopan

➡ Decongestant, eg pseudoephedrine

➡ Diamox if going to high altitudes

➡ Elastoplasts, bandages, gauze, thermometer (but not mercury), sterile needles and syringes, safety pins and tweezers

➡ Indigestion tablets such as Quick-Eze or Mylanta

➡ Insect repellent containing DEET

➡ Iodine tablets to purify water (unless you're pregnant or have a thyroid problem)

➡ Laxative, eg coloxyl

➡ Oral-rehydration solution (eg Gastrolyte) for diarrhoea, diarrhoea 'stopper' (eg loperamide) and antinausea medication (eg prochlorperazine)

➡ Paracetamol

➡ Permethrin to impregnate clothing and mosquito nets

→ Steroid cream for rashes, eg 1% to 2% hydrocortisone

→ Sunscreen

→ Thrush treatment, eg clotrimazole pessaries or Diflucan tablet

→ Urinary infection treatment, eg Ural

Websites
Centers for Disease Control & Prevention (www.cdc.gov)

Lonely Planet (www.lonely planet.com)

World Health Organization (www.who.int/ith) Publishes the excellent *International Travel & Health*, revised annually and available online.

Further Reading
→ *Healthy Travel – Asia & India* (Lonely Planet) Handy pocket size, packed with useful information.

→ *Travellers' Health* by Dr Richard Dawood.

→ *Travelling Well* (www.travellingwell.com.au) by Dr Deborah Mills.

Tips for Taking Medications to China
In China you can buy some medications over the counter without a doctor's prescription, but not all, and in general it is not advisable to buy medications locally without a doctor's advice. Fake medications and poorly stored or out-of-date drugs are also common, so try to bring your own.

→ Pack medications in their original, labelled containers.

→ If you take any regular medication, bring double your needs in case of loss or theft.

→ Take a signed and dated letter from your physician describing your medical conditions and medications (using generic names).

→ If carrying syringes or needles, ensure you have a physician's letter documenting their medical necessity. If you have a heart condition, bring a copy of an ECG taken just prior to travelling.

In China

Availability & Cost of Health Care
Good clinics catering to travellers can be found in major cities. They are more expensive than local facilities, but you may feel more comfortable dealing with a western-trained doctor who speaks your language. These clinics usually have a good understanding of the best local hospital facilities and close contacts with insurance companies should you need evacuation. As a rough idea of cost, the private section of a large hospital in Beijing dedicated to foreigners will charge about ¥500 upfront for a consultation, plus another ¥500 for an X-ray. Waiting times are roughly an hour for each step.

Infectious Diseases
DENGUE
This mosquito-borne disease occurs in some parts of southern China. There is no vaccine so avoid mosquito bites – the dengue-carrying mosquito bites day and night, so use insect-avoidance measures at all times. Symptoms include high fever, severe headache and body ache. Some people develop a rash and diarrhoea. There is no specific treatment – just rest and paracetamol. Do not take aspirin.

HEPATITIS A
A problem throughout China, this food- and waterborne virus infects the liver, causing jaundice (yellow skin and eyes), nausea and lethargy. There is no specific treatment for hepatitis A; you just need to allow time for the liver to heal. All travellers to China should be vaccinated.

HEPATITIS B
The only sexually transmitted disease that can be prevented by vaccination, hepatitis B is spread by contact with infected body fluids. The long-term consequences can include liver cancer and cirrhosis. All

travellers to China should be vaccinated.

JAPANESE ENCEPHALITIS
Formerly known as 'Japanese B encephalitis', this is a rare disease in travellers, though vaccination is recommended if you're in rural areas for more than a month during summer, or if spending more than three months in the country. No treatment is available; one-third of infected people die, while another third suffer permanent brain damage.

MALARIA
Malaria has been nearly eradicated in China; it is not generally a risk for visitors to the cities and most tourist areas. It is found mainly in rural areas in the southwestern region bordering Myanmar, Laos and Vietnam, principally Hainan, Yunnan and Guangxi. More limited risk exists in the remote rural areas of Fujian, Guangdong, Guizhou and Sichuan. Generally medication is only advised if you are visiting rural Hainan, Yunnan or Guangxi.

To prevent malaria:

→ Avoid mosquitoes and take antimalarial medications (most people who catch malaria are taking inadequate or no antimalarial medication).

→ Use an insect repellent containing DEET on exposed skin (natural repellents such as citronella can be effective, but require more frequent application).

→ Sleep under a mosquito net impregnated with permethrin.

→ Choose accommodation with screens and fans (if it's not air-conditioned).

→ Impregnate clothing with permethrin in high-risk areas.

→ Wear long sleeves and trousers in light colours.

→ Use mosquito coils.

→ Spray your room with insect repellent before going out for your evening meal.

WATER

In general, you should never drink the tap water in China, even in five-star hotels. Boiling water makes it safe to drink, but you might prefer to buy bottled mineral water.

Follow these tips to avoid becoming ill:

➤ Never drink unboiled tap water.

➤ Water fountains at the major airports are clearly marked if they are safe to drink from.

➤ Bottled water is generally safe – check that the seal is intact at purchase.

➤ Avoid ice.

➤ Avoid fresh juices – they may have been watered down.

➤ At very high altitudes, boil water for an extra minute as water bubbles at a lower temperature.

➤ The best chemical purifier is iodine. It should not be used by pregnant women or those with thyroid problems.

➤ Water filters should also filter out viruses. Ensure your filter has a chemical barrier such as iodine and a pore size of less than 4 microns.

RABIES

An increasingly common problem in China, this fatal disease is spread by the bite or lick of an infected animal, most often a dog. Seek medical advice immediately after any animal bite and commence post-exposure treatment. The pre-travel vaccination means the post-bite treatment is greatly simplified.

Follow these instructions if an animal bites you:

➤ Gently wash the wound with soap and water, and apply an iodine-based antiseptic.

➤ If you are not vaccinated, you will need to receive rabies immunoglobulin as soon as possible, followed by a series of five vaccines over the next month. Those who have been vaccinated require only two shots of vaccine after a bite.

➤ Contact your insurance company to locate the nearest clinic stocking rabies immunoglobulin and vaccine. Immunoglobulin is often unavailable outside of major centres, but if you have had a bite that has broken the skin, it's crucial that you get to a clinic that

has immunoglobulin as soon as possible.

SCHISTOSOMIASIS (BILHARZIA)

This disease occurs in the central Yangzi River (Cháng Jiāng) basin, carried in water by minute worms that infect certain varieties of freshwater snail found in rivers, streams, lakes and, particularly, behind dams. The infection often causes no symptoms until the disease is well established (several months to years after exposure); any resulting damage to internal organs is irreversible. Effective treatment is available.

➤ Avoid swimming or bathing in fresh water where bilharzia is present.

➤ A blood test is the most reliable way to diagnose the disease, but the test will not show positive until weeks after exposure.

TYPHOID

Typhoid is a serious bacterial infection spread via food and water. Symptoms include headaches and a high and slowly progressive fever, perhaps accompanied by a dry cough and stomach pain. Vac-

cination is not 100% effective, so still be careful what you eat and drink. All travellers spending more than a week in China should be vaccinated against typhoid.

Traveller's Diarrhoea

Between 30% and 50% of visitors will suffer from traveller's diarrhoea within two weeks of starting their trip. In most cases the ailment is caused by bacteria and responds promptly to treatment with antibiotics.

Treatment consists of staying hydrated – rehydration solutions such as Gastrolyte are best. Antibiotics such as norfloxacin, ciprofloxacin or azithromycin will kill the bacteria quickly. Loperamide is just a 'stopper' and doesn't cure the problem; it can be helpful, however, for long bus rides. Don't take loperamide if you have a fever, or blood in your stools. Seek medical attention if you do not respond to an appropriate antibiotic.

➤ Eat only at busy restaurants with a high turnover.

➤ Eat only freshly cooked food.

➤ Avoid food that has been sitting around in buffets.

➤ Peel all fruit, cook vegetables and soak salads in iodine water for at least 20 minutes.

➤ Drink bottled water.

Traditional Chinese Medicine

Traditional Chinese Medicine (TCM) views the human body as an energy system in which the basic substances of *qì* (气, vital energy), *jīng* (精, essence), *xuè* (血, blood) and *tǐyè* (体液, body fluids, blood and other organic fluids) function. The concept of *yīn* (阴) and *yáng* (阳) is fundamental to the system. Disharmony between yin and yang, or within the basic substances, may be a result of internal causes (emotions), external causes (climatic conditions) or miscellaneous causes (work, exercise, stress etc). Treatment includes acupuncture, massage, herbs, diet and qì gōng (气功), which seeks to bring these elements back into balance. Treatments can be particularly useful for chronic diseases and ailments such as fatigue, arthritis, irritable bowel syndrome and some chronic skin conditions.

Be aware that 'natural' does not always mean 'safe' – there can be drug interactions between herbal medicines and western medicines. If using both systems, ensure you inform each practitioner what the other has prescribed.

Environmental Hazards

AIR POLLUTION

Air pollution is a significant problem in many Chinese cities, and many locals wear face masks. People with underlying respiratory conditions should seek advice from their doctor prior to travel to ensure they have adequate medications in case their condition worsens. Take treatments such as throat lozenges and cough-and-cold tablets.

ALTITUDE SICKNESS

There are bus journeys in Tibet, Qinghai and Xinjiang where the road goes above 5000m. Acclimatising to such extreme elevations takes several weeks at least, but most travellers come up from sea level very fast – a bad move! Acute mountain sickness (AMS) results from a rapid ascent to altitudes above 2700m. It usually commences within 24 to 48 hours of arriving at altitude, and symptoms include headache, nausea, fatigue and loss of appetite (feeling much like a hangover).

If you have altitude sickness, the cardinal rule is that you must not go higher as you are sure to get sicker and could develop one of the more severe and potentially deadly forms of the disease: high-altitude pulmonary oedema (HAPE) and high-altitude cerebral oedema (HACE).

Both are medical emergencies and, as there are no rescue facilities similar to those in the Nepal Himalaya, prevention is the best policy.

AMS can be prevented by 'graded ascent'. It is recommended that once you are above 3000m you ascend a maximum of 300m daily, with a rest day every 1000m. You can also use a medication called Diamox as a prevention or treatment for AMS, but you should discuss this first with a doctor experienced in altitude medicine. Diamox should not be taken by people with a sulphur-drug allergy.

If you have altitude sickness, rest where you are for a day or two until your symptoms resolve. There is no way of predicting who will suffer from AMS, but certain factors predispose you to it: rapid ascent, carrying a heavy load, and having a seemingly minor illness such as a chest infection or diarrhoea. Make sure you drink at least 3L of non-caffeinated drinks daily to stay well hydrated.

HEAT EXHAUSTION

Dehydration or salt deficiency can cause heat exhaustion. Take time to acclimatise to high temperatures, drink sufficient liquids and avoid physically demanding activity.

Salt deficiency is characterised by fatigue, lethargy, headaches, giddiness and muscle cramps. Salt tablets may help, but adding extra salt to your food is better.

HYPOTHERMIA

Be particularly aware of the dangers of trekking at high altitudes or simply taking a long bus trip over mountains. In Tibet it can go from being mildly warm to blisteringly cold in minutes – blizzards can appear from nowhere.

Progress from very cold to dangerously cold can be rapid due to a combination of wind, wet clothing, fatigue and hunger, even if the air temperature is above freezing. Dress in layers – silk, wool and some artificial fibres are good insulating materials. A hat is important, as a lot of heat is lost through the head. A strong, waterproof outer layer (and a space blanket for emergencies) is essential. Carry basic supplies, including food containing simple sugars, and fluid to drink.

Symptoms of hypothermia are exhaustion, numb skin (particularly the toes and fingers), shivering, slurred speech, irrational or violent behaviour, lethargy, stumbling, dizzy spells, muscle cramps and violent bursts of energy.

To treat mild hypothermia, first get the person out of the wind and/or rain, remove their clothing if it's wet, and replace it with dry, warm clothing. Give them hot liquids – not alcohol – and high-calorie, easily digestible food. Early recognition and treatment of mild hypothermia is the only way to prevent severe hypothermia, a critical condition that requires medical attention.

INSECT BITES & STINGS

Bedbugs don't carry disease, but their bites are very itchy. Treat the itch with an antihistamine.

Lice inhabit various parts of the human body, most commonly the head and pubic areas. Transmission is via close contact with an affected person. Lice can be difficult to treat, but electric lice combs/detectors can be effective (pick one up before travelling). Otherwise you may need numerous applications of an antilice shampoo such as permethrin. Pubic lice (crab lice) are usually contracted from sexual contact.

Ticks are contracted by walking in rural areas, and are commonly found behind the ears, on the belly and in armpits. If you have had a tick bite and experience symptoms such as a rash, fever or muscle aches, see a doctor. Doxycycline prevents some tick-borne diseases.

Language

Discounting its many ethnic minority languages, China has eight major dialect groups: Pǔtōnghuà (Mandarin), Yue (Cantonese), Wu (Shanghainese), Minbei (Fuzhou), Minnan (Hokkien-Taiwanese), Xiang, Gan and Hakka. These dialects also divide into subdialects.

It's the language spoken in Běijīng that is considered the official language of China. It's usually referred to as Mandarin, but the Chinese themselves call it Pǔtōnghuà (meaning 'common speech'). Pǔtōnghuà is variously referred to as Hànyǔ (the Han language), Guóyǔ (the national language) or Zhōngwén or Zhōngguóhuà (Chinese). With the exception of the western and southernmost provinces, most of the population speaks Mandarin (although it may be spoken there with a regional accent). In this chapter, we have included Mandarin, Cantonese, Tibetan, Uyghur and Mongolian.

MANDARIN

Writing

Chinese is often referred to as a language of pictographs. Many of the basic Chinese characters are in fact highly stylised pictures of what they represent, but around 90% are compounds of a 'meaning' element and a 'sound' element.

A well educated, contemporary Chinese person might use between 6000 and 8000 characters. To read a Chinese newspaper you need to know 2000 to 3000 characters, but 1200 to 1500 would be enough to get the gist.

Theoretically, all Chinese dialects share the same written system. In practice, Cantonese adds about 3000 specialised characters of its own and many of the dialects don't have a written form at all.

WANT MORE?

For in-depth language information and handy phrases, check out Lonely Planet's *China Phrasebook*. You'll find it at **shop.lonelyplanet.com**

Pinyin & Pronunciation

In 1958 the Chinese adopted pinyin, a system of writing their language using the Roman alphabet. The original idea was to eventually do away with Chinese characters. However, tradition dies hard, and the idea was abandoned.

Pinyin is often used on shop fronts, street signs and advertising billboards. Don't expect all Chinese people to be able to use pinyin, however. In the countryside and the smaller towns you may not see a single pinyin sign anywhere, so unless you speak and read Chinese you'll need a phrasebook with Chinese characters.

Below we've provided pinyin alongside the Mandarin script.

Vowels

a	as in 'father'
ai	as in 'aisle'
ao	as the 'ow' in 'cow'
e	as in 'her' (without 'r' sound)
ei	as in 'weigh'
i	as the 'ee' in 'meet' (or like a light 'r' as in 'Grrr!' after c, ch, r, s, sh, z or zh)
ian	as the word 'yen'
ie	as the English word 'yeah'
o	as in 'or' (without 'r' sound)
ou	as the 'oa' in 'boat'
u	as in 'flute'
ui	as the word 'way'
uo	like a 'w' followed by 'o'
yu/ü	like 'ee' with lips pursed

Consonants

c	as the 'ts' in 'bits'
ch	as in 'chop', but with the tongue curled up and back
h	as in 'hay', but articulated from further back in the throat
q	as the 'ch' in 'cheese'
sh	as in 'ship', but with the tongue curled up and back
x	as the 'sh' in 'ship'
z	as the 'ds' in 'suds'
zh	as the 'j' in 'judge' but with the tongue curled up and back

The only consonants that occur at the end of a syllable are n, ng and r.

In pinyin, apostrophes are occasionally used to separate syllables in order to prevent ambiguity, eg the word píng'ān can be written with an apostrophe after the 'g' to prevent it being pronounced as pín'gǎn.

Tones

Mandarin is a language with a large number of words with the same pronunciation but a different meaning. What distinguishes these homophones (as these words are called) is their 'tonal' quality – the raising and the lowering of pitch on certain syllables. Mandarin has four tones – high, rising, falling-rising and falling, plus a fifth 'neutral' tone that you can all but ignore. Tones are important for distinguishing meaning of words – eg the word ma has four different meanings according to tone, as shown below. Tones are indicated in pinyin by the following accent marks on vowels:

high tone	mā (mother)
rising tone	má (hemp, numb)
falling-rising tone	mǎ (horse)
falling tone	mà (scold, swear)

Basics

When asking a question it is polite to start with qǐng wèn – literally, 'May I ask?'.

Hello.	你好。	Nǐhǎo.
Goodbye.	再见。	Zàijiàn.
How are you?	你好吗?	Nǐhǎo ma?
Fine. And you?	好。你呢?	Hǎo. Nǐ ne?
Excuse me.		
(to get attention)	劳驾。	Láojià.
(to get past)	借光。	Jièguāng.
Sorry.	对不起。	Duìbùqǐ.
Yes./No.	是。/不是。	Shì./Bùshì.
Please ...	请……	Qǐng ...
Thank you.	谢谢你。	Xièxie nǐ.
You're welcome.	不客气。	Bù kèqi.

What's your name?
你叫什么名字?   Nǐ jiào shénme míngzi?

My name is ...
我叫……   Wǒ jiào ...

Do you speak English?
你会说英文吗?   Nǐ huìshuō Yīngwén ma?

I don't understand.
我不明白。   Wǒ bù míngbái.

KEY PATTERNS – MANDARIN

To get by in Mandarin, mix and match these simple patterns with words of your choice:

How much is (the deposit)?
(押金)多少?   (Yājīn) duōshǎo?

Do you have (a room)?
有没有(房)?   Yǒuméiyǒu (fáng)?

Is there (heating)?
有(暖气)吗?   Yóu (nuǎnqì) ma?

I'd like (that one).
我要(那个)。   Wǒ yào (nàge).

Please give me (the menu).
请给我(菜单)。   Qǐng gěiwǒ (càidān).

Can I (sit here)?
我能(坐这儿)吗?   Wǒ néng (zuòzhèr) ma?

I need (a can opener).
我想要(一个开罐器)。   Wǒ xiǎngyào (yīge kāiguàn qì).

Do we need (a guide)?
需要(向导)吗?   Xūyào (xiàngdǎo) ma?

I have (a reservation).
我有(预订)。   Wǒ yǒu (yùdìng).

I'm (a doctor).
我(是医生)。   Wǒ (shì yīshēng).

Accommodation

Do you have a single/double room?
有没有(单人/套)房?   Yǒuméiyǒu (dānrén/tào) fáng?

How much is it per night/person?
每天/人多少钱?   Měi tiān/rén duōshǎo qián?

campsite	露营地	lùyíngdì
guesthouse	宾馆	bīnguǎn
hostel	招待所	zhāodàisuǒ
hotel	酒店	jiǔdiàn
reception	总台	zǒng tái
air-con	空调	kōngtiáo
bathroom	浴室	yùshì
blanket	被子	bèizi
bed	床	chuáng
cot	张婴儿床	zhāng yīng'ér chuáng
hair dryer	吹风机	chuīfēngjī
safe	保险箱	bǎoxiǎnxiāng
sheet	床单	chuángdān
towel	毛巾	máojīn
window	窗	chuāng

SIGNS – MANDARIN

入口	Rùkǒu	**Entrance**
出口	Chūkǒu	**Exit**
问讯处	Wènxùnchù	**Information**
开	Kāi	**Open**
关	Guān	**Closed**
禁止	Jìnzhǐ	**Prohibited**
厕所	Cèsuǒ	**Toilets**
男	Nán	**Men**
女	Nǚ	**Women**

Directions

Where's (a bank)?
(银行) 在哪儿?   (Yínháng) zài nǎr?

What's the address?
地址在哪儿?   Dìzhǐ zài nǎr?

Could you write the address, please?
能不能请你   Néngbunéng qǐng nǐ
把地址写下来?   bǎ dìzhǐ xiě xiàlái?

Can you show me where it is on the map?
请帮我找它在   Qǐng bāngwǒ zhǎo tā zài
地图上的位置?   dìtú shàng de wèizhi?

Go straight ahead.
一直走。   Yīzhí zǒu.

Turn left.
左转。   Zuǒ zhuǎn.

Turn right.
右转。   Yòu zhuǎn.

at the traffic lights	在红绿灯	zài hónglǜdēng
behind	背面	bèimiàn
far	远	yuǎn
in front of ...	……的前面	... de qiánmian
near	近	jìn
next to	旁边	pángbiān
on the corner	拐角	guǎijiǎo
opposite	对面	duìmiàn

Eating & Drinking

What would you recommend?
有什么菜可以   Yǒu shénme cài kěyǐ
推荐的?   tuījiàn de?

What's in that dish?
这道菜用什么   Zhèdào cài yòng shénme
东西做的?   dōngxi zuòde?

That was delicious.
真好吃。   Zhēn hǎochī.

The bill, please!
买单!   Mǎidān!

Cheers! 干杯!   Gānbēi!

I'd like to reserve a table for ...
我想预订   Wǒ xiǎng yùdìng
一张……   yìzhāng ...
的桌子。   de zhuōzi.

  (eight) o'clock （八）点钟 (bā) diǎn zhōng

  (two) people （两个）人 (liǎngge) rén

I don't eat ... 我不吃……   Wǒ bùchī ...

fish	鱼	yú
nuts	果仁	guǒrén
poultry	家禽	jiāqín
red meat	牛羊肉	niúyángròu

Key Words

appetisers	凉菜	liángcài
bar	酒吧	jiǔbā
bottle	瓶子	píngzi
bowl	碗	wǎn
breakfast	早饭	zǎofàn
cafe	咖啡屋	kāfēiwū
chidren's menu	儿童菜单	értóng càidān
(too) cold	（太）凉	(tài) liáng
dinner	晚饭	wǎnfàn
dish (food)	盘	pán
food	食品	shípǐn
fork	叉子	chāzi
glass	杯子	bēizi
halal	清真	qīngzhēn
highchair	高凳	gāodèng
hot (warm)	热	rè
knife	刀	dāo
kosher	犹太	yóutài
local specialties	地方小吃	dìfang xiǎochī
lunch	午饭	wǔfàn
main courses	主菜	zhǔ cài
market	菜市	càishì
menu (in English)	（英文）菜单	(Yīngwén) càidān
plate	碟子	diézi
restaurant	餐馆	cānguǎn
(too) spicy	（太）辣	(tài) là
spoon	勺	sháo
vegetarian food	素食食品	sùshí shípín

Meat & Fish

beef	牛肉	niúròu
chicken	鸡肉	jīròu
duck	鸭	yā

fish	鱼	yú
lamb	羊肉	yángròu
pork	猪肉	zhūròu
seafood	海鲜	hǎixiān

Fruit & Vegetables

apple	苹果	píngguǒ
banana	香蕉	xiāngjiāo
bok choy	小白菜	xiǎo báicài
carrot	胡萝卜	húluóbo
celery	芹菜	qíncài
cucumber	黄瓜	huángguā
fruit	水果	shuǐguǒ
grape	葡萄	pútáo
green beans	扁豆	biǎndòu
guava	石榴	shíliu
longan	龙眼	lóngyǎn
lychee	荔枝	lìzhī
mango	芒果	mángguǒ
mushroom	蘑菇	mógū
onion	洋葱	yáng cōng
orange	橙子	chéngzi
pear	梨	lí
pineapple	凤梨	fènglí
plum	梅子	méizi
potato	土豆	tǔdòu
radish	萝卜	luóbo
spring onion	小葱	xiǎo cōng
sweet potato	地瓜	dìguā
vegetable	蔬菜	shūcài
watermelon	西瓜	xīguā

Other

bread	面包	miànbāo
butter	黄油	huángyóu
egg	蛋	dàn
herbs/spices	香料	xiāngliào
pepper	胡椒粉	hújiāo fěn
salt	盐	yán
soy sauce	酱油	jiàngyóu
sugar	砂糖	shātáng
tofu	豆腐	dòufu
vinegar	醋	cù
vegetable oil	菜油	càiyóu

Drinks

beer	啤酒	píjiǔ
Chinese spirits	白酒	báijiǔ
coffee	咖啡	kāfēi
(orange) juice	(橙)汁	(chéng) zhī
milk	牛奶	niúnǎi
mineral water	矿泉水	kuàngquán shuǐ
red wine	红葡萄酒	hóng pútáo jiǔ
rice wine	米酒	mǐjiǔ
soft drink	汽水	qìshuǐ
tea	茶	chá
(boiled) water	(开)水	(kāi) shuǐ
white wine	白葡萄酒	bái pútáo jiǔ
yoghurt	酸奶	suānnǎi

Emergencies

Help!	救命!	Jiùmìng!
I'm lost.	我迷路了。	Wǒ mílù le.
Go away!	走开!	Zǒukāi!
There's been an accident. 出事了。		Chūshì le.
Call a doctor! 请叫医生来!		Qǐng jiào yīshēng lái!
Call the police! 请叫警察!		Qǐng jiào jǐngchá!
I'm ill. 我生病了。		Wǒ shēngbìng le.
It hurts here. 这里痛。		Zhèlǐ tòng.
Where are the toilets? 厕所在哪儿?		Cèsuǒ zài nǎr?

Shopping & Services

I'd like to buy ... 我想买……	Wǒ xiǎng mǎi ...
I'm just looking. 我先看看。	Wǒ xiān kànkan.
Can I look at it? 我能看看吗?	Wǒ néng kànkan ma?
I don't like it. 我不喜欢。	Wǒ bù xǐhuan.

QUESTION WORDS – MANDARIN

How	怎么	Zěnme
What	什么	Shénme
When	什么时候	Shénme shíhòu
Where	哪儿	Nǎr
Which	哪个	Nǎge
Who	谁	Shuí
Why	为什么	Wèishénme

NUMBERS – MANDARIN

1	一	yī
2	二/两	èr/liǎng
3	三	sān
4	四	sì
5	五	wǔ
6	六	liù
7	七	qī
8	八	bā
9	九	jiǔ
10	十	shí
20	二十	èrshí
30	三十	sānshí
40	四十	sìshí
50	五十	wǔshí
60	六十	liùshí
70	七十	qīshí
80	八十	bāshí
90	九十	jiǔshí
100	一百	yībǎi
1000	一千	yīqiān

How much is it?
多少钱？ Duōshǎo qián?

That's too expensive.
太贵了。 Tàiguì le.

Can you lower the price?
能便宜一点吗？ Néng piányi yīdiǎn ma?

There's a mistake in the bill.
帐单上 Zhàngdān shàng
有问题。 yǒu wèntí.

ATM	自动取款机	zìdòng qǔkuǎn jī
credit card	信用卡	xìnyòng kǎ
internet cafe	网吧	wǎngbā
post office	邮局	yóujú
tourist office	旅行店	lǚxíng diàn

Time & Dates

What time is it?
现在几点钟？ Xiànzài jǐdiǎn zhōng?

It's (10) o'clock.
(十)点钟。 (Shí) diǎn zhōng.

Half past (10).
(十)点三十分。 (Shí) diǎn sānshífēn.

morning	早上	zǎoshang
afternoon	下午	xiàwǔ
evening	晚上	wǎnshàng

yesterday	昨天	zuótiān
today	今天	jīntiān
tomorrow	明天	míngtiān
Monday	星期一	xīngqī yī
Tuesday	星期二	xīngqī èr
Wednesday	星期三	xīngqī sān
Thursday	星期四	xīngqī sì
Friday	星期五	xīngqī wǔ
Saturday	星期六	xīngqī liù
Sunday	星期天	xīngqī tiān
January	一月	yīyuè
February	二月	èryuè
March	三月	sānyuè
April	四月	sìyuè
May	五月	wǔyuè
June	六月	liùyuè
July	七月	qīyuè
August	八月	bāyuè
September	九月	jiǔyuè
October	十月	shíyuè
November	十一月	shíyīyuè
December	十二月	shí'èryuè

Transport

boat	船	chuán
bus (city)	大巴	dàbā
bus (intercity)	长途车	chángtú chē
plane	飞机	fēijī
taxi	出租车	chūzū chē
train	火车	huǒchē
tram	电车	diànchē

Buses & Trains

I want to go to ...
我要去…… Wǒ yào qù ...

Does it stop at (Harbin)?
在(哈尔滨)能下 Zài (Hā'ěrbīn) néng xià
车吗？ chē ma?

At what time does it leave?
几点钟出发？ Jǐdiǎnzhōng chūfā?

At what time does it get to (Hángzhōu)?
几点钟到 Jǐdiǎnzhōng dào
(杭州)？ (Hángzhōu)?

Can you tell me when we get to (Hángzhōu)?
到了(杭州) Dàole (Hángzhōu)
请叫我, 好吗？ qǐng jiào wǒ, hǎoma?

I want to get off here.
我想这儿下车。 Wǒ xiǎng zhèr xiàchē.

When's the ... (bus)?	……(车) 几点走？	... (chē) jídiǎn zǒu?
first	首趟	shǒutàng
last	末趟	mòtàng
next	下一趟	xià yītàng

A ... ticket to (Dàlián).	一张到 (大连)的 ……票。	Yīzhāng dào (Dàlián) de ... piào.
1st-class	头等	tóuděng
2nd-class	二等	èrděng
one-way	单程	dānchéng
return	双程	shuāngchéng

aisle seat	走廊的 座位	zǒuláng de zuòwèi
cancelled	取消	qǔxiāo
delayed	晚点	wǎndiǎn
platform	站台	zhàntái
ticket office	售票处	shòupiàochù
timetable	时刻表	shíkè biǎo
train station	火车站	huǒchēzhàn
window seat	窗户的 座位	chuānghu de zuòwèi

Taxis

I'd like a taxi to depart at (9am).
我要订一辆出租车，
(早上9点钟)出发。
Wǒ yào dìng yīliàng chūzū chē, (zǎoshàng jiǔ diǎn zhōng) chūfā.

I'd like a taxi now.
我要订一辆出租车，
现在。
Wǒ yào dìng yīliàng chūzū chē, xiànzài.

I'd like a taxi tomorrow
我要订一辆出租车，
明天。
Wǒ yào dìng yīliàng chūzū chē, míngtiān.

Where's the taxi rank?
在哪里打出租车？
Zài nǎli dǎ chūzū chē?

Is this taxi free?
这出租车有人吗？
Zhè chūzū chē yǒurén ma?

Please put the meter on.
请打表。
Qǐng dǎbiǎo.

How much is it (to this address)?
(到这个地址)
多少钱？
(Dào zhège dizhǐ) duōshǎo qián?

Please take me to (this address).
请带我到
(这个地址).
Qǐng dàiwǒ dào (zhège dizhǐ).

Cycling

bicycle pump	打气筒	dǎqìtǒng
child seat	婴儿座	yīng'érzuò
helmet	头盔	tóukuī

CANTONESE

Cantonese is the most widely used Chinese language in Hong Kong, Macau, Guǎngdōng, parts of Guǎngxī and the surrounding region. Cantonese speakers use Chinese characters, but pronounce many of them differently from a Mandarin speaker. Also, Cantonese adds about 3000 characters of its own to the character set. Several systems of Romanisation for Cantonese script exist, and no single one has emerged as an official standard. In this chapter we use Lonely Planet's pronunciation guide, designed for maximum accuracy with minimum complexity.

Pronunciation

In Cantonese, the ng sound can appear at the start of a word. Words ending with the consonant sounds p, t, and k are clipped. Many speakers, particularly young people, replace the n with an l at the start of a word – eg náy (you) often sounds like láy. Where relevant, our pronunciation guide reflects this change.

The vowels are pronounced as follows: a as the 'u' in 'but', ai as in 'aisle' (short), au as the 'ou' in 'out', ay as in 'pay', eu as the 'er' in 'fern', eui as eu followed by i, ew as in 'blew' (short, with lips tightened), i as the 'ee' in 'deep', iu as the 'yu' in 'yuletide', o as in 'go', oy as in 'boy', u as in 'put', ui as in French oui.

Tones in Cantonese fall on vowels (a, e, i, o, u) and on n. The same word pronounced with different tones can have a different meaning, eg gwàt (dig up) vs gwàt (bones). There are six tones, divided into high- and low-pitch groups. High-pitch tones involve tightening the vocal muscles to get a higher note, while lower-pitch tones are made by relaxing the vocal chords to get a lower note. Tones are indicated with the following accent marks: à (high), á (high rising), à (low falling), á (low rising), a (low), a (level – no accent mark).

Basics

Hello.	哈佬。	hàa·ló
Goodbye.	再見。	joy·gin
How are you?	你幾好 啊嗎？	láy gáy hó à maa
Fine.	幾好。	gáy hó
Excuse me.	對唔住。	deui·ǹg·jew
Sorry.	對唔住。	deui·ǹg·jew
Yes./No.	係。/不係。	hai/ǹg·hai
Please ...	唔該……	ǹg·gòy ...
Thank you.	多謝。	dàw·je

What's your name?
你叫乜嘢名？
láy giu màt·yé méng aa

NUMBERS – CANTONESE

1	一	yàt
2	二	yi
3	三	sàam
4	四	say
5	五	ńg
6	六	luk
7	七	chàt
8	八	baat
9	九	gáu
10	十	sap
20	二十	yi·sap
30	三十	sàam·sap
40	四十	say·sap
50	五十	ńg·sap
60	六十	luk·sap
70	七十	chàt·sap
80	八十	baat·sap
90	九十	gáu·sap
100	一百	yàt·baak
1000	一千	yàt·chìn

My name is ...
我叫…… ngáw giu ...

Do you speak English?
你識唔識講 láy sìk·ńg·sìk gáwng
英文啊？ yìng·mán aa

I don't understand.
我唔明 。 ngáw ńg mìng

Accommodation

campsite	營地	yìng·day
guesthouse	賓館	bàn·gún
hostel	招待所	jiù·doy·sáw
hotel	酒店	jáu·dim

Do you have a ... room? 有冇……房？ yáu·mó ... fáwng

double 雙人 sèung·yàn
single 單人 dàan·yàn

How much is it per ...? 一……幾多錢？ yàt ... gáy·dàw chín
night 晚 máan
person 個人 gaw yàn

Directions

Where's ...? ……喺邊度？ ... hái bìn·do

What's the address? 地址係？ day·jí hai

left	左邊	jáw·bìn
on the corner	十字路口	sap·ji·lo·háu
right	右邊	yau·bìn
straight ahead	前面	chìn·min
traffic lights	紅綠燈	hùng·luk·dàng

Eating & Drinking

What would you recommend?
有乜嘢好介紹？ yáu màt·yé hó gaai·siu

That was delicious.
真好味 。 jàn hó·may

I'd like the bill, please.
唔該我要埋單 。 ńg·gòy ngáw yiu màai·dàan

Cheers!
乾杯！ gàwn·buì

I'd like to book a table for ... 我想訂張檯……嘅 。 ngáw séung deng jèung tóy ... ge
(eight) o'clock (八)點鐘 (bàat) dím·jùng
(two) people (兩)位 (léung) ái

bar	酒吧	jáu·bàa
bottle	樽	jèun
breakfast	早餐	jó·chàan
cafe	咖啡屋	gaa·fè·ngùk
dinner	晚飯	máan·faan
fork	叉	chàa
glass	杯	buì
knife	刀	dò
lunch	午餐	ńg·chàan
market	街市 (HK)	gàai·sí
	市場 (China)	sí·chèung
plate	碟	díp
restaurant	酒樓	jáu·làu
spoon	羹	gàng

Emergencies

Help! 救命！ gau·meng
I'm lost. 我蕩失路 。 ngáw dawng·sàk·lo
Go away! 走開！ jáu·hòy

Call a doctor!
快啲叫醫生！ faai·dì giu yì·sàng

Call the police!
快啲叫警察！ faai·dì giu gíng·chaat

I'm sick.
我病咗 。 ngáw beng·jáw

Shopping & Services

I'd like to buy ...
我想買······ ngáw séung máai ...

How much is it?
幾多錢? gáy·dàw chín

That's too expensive.
太貴啦 。 taai gwai laa

There's a mistake in the bill.
帳單錯咗 。 jeung·dàan chaw jáw

internet cafe	網吧	máwng·bàa
post office	郵局	yàu·gúk
tourist office	旅行社	léui·hàng·sé

Time & Dates

What time is it?
而家幾點鐘? yi·gàa gáy·dím·jùng

It's (10) o'clock. (十)點鐘 。 (sap)·dím·jùng

Half past (10). (十)點半 。 (sap)·dím bun

morning	朝早	jiù·jó
afternoon	下晝	haa·jau
evening	夜晚	ye·máan
yesterday	寢日	kàm·yat
today	今日	gàm·yat
tomorrow	听日	tìng·yat

Transport

boat	船	sèwn
bus	巴士 (HK)	bàa·sí
	公共	gùng·gung
	汽車 (China)	hay·chè
train	火車	fáw·chè

A ... ticket to (Panyu).
一張去 (番禺)嘅······飛 。 yàt jèung heui (pùn·yèw) ge ... fày

1st-class	頭等	tàu·dáng
2nd-class	二等	yi·dáng
one-way	單程	dàan·chìng
return	雙程	sèung·chìng

At what time does it leave?
幾點鐘出發? gáy·dím jùng chèut·faa

Does it stop at ...?
會唔會喺······停呀? wuí·ng·wuí hái ... tìng aa

At what time does it get to ...?
幾點鐘到······? gáy·dím jùng do ...

TIBETAN

Tibetan is spoken by around six million people, mainly in Tibet. In urban areas almost all Tibetans also speak Mandarin.

Most sounds in Tibetan are similar to those found in English, so if you read our coloured pronunciation guides as if they were English, you'll be understood. Note that â is pronounced as the 'a' in 'ago', ö as the 'er' in 'her', and ü as the 'u' in 'flute' but with a raised tongue. A vowel followed by n, m or ng indicates a nasalised sound (pronounced 'through the nose'). A consonant followed by h is aspirated (accompanied by a puff of air).

There are no direct equivalents of English 'yes' and 'no' in Tibetan. Although it may not be completely correct, you'll be understood if you use la ong for 'yes' and la men for 'no'.

Hello.
བཀྲ་ཤིས་བདེ་ལེགས། ta·shi de·lek

Goodbye.
(if staying)
ག་ལེར་ཕེབས། ka·lee pay

(if leaving)
ག་ལེར་བཞུགས། ka·lee shu

Excuse me.
དགོངས་དག gong·da

Sorry.
དགོངས་དག gong·da

Please.
ཐུགས་རྗེ་གཟིགས། tu·jay·sig

Thank you.
ཐུགས་རྗེ་ཆེ། tu·jay·chay

How are you?
ཁྱེད་རང་སྐུ་གཟུགས་ kay·râng ku·su
བདེ་པོ་ཡིན་པས། de·po yin·bay

Fine. And you?
བདེ་པོ་ཡིན། ཁྱེད་རང་ཡང་ de·bo·yin kay·râng·yâng
སྐུ་གཟུགས་བདེ་པོ་ཡིན་པས། ku·su de·po yin·bay

What's your name?
ཁྱེད་རང་གི་མཚན་ལ་ kay·râng·gi tsen·lâ
ག་རེ་རེད། kâ·ray·ray

My name is ...
ངའི་མིང་ལ་ ... རེད། ngay·ming·la ... ray

Do you speak English?
ཁྱེད་རང་དབྱིན་ཇི་སྐད་ kay·râng in·ji·kay
ཤེས་ཀྱི་ཡོད་པས། shing·gi yö·bay

I don't understand.
ཧ་གོ་མ་སོང་། ha ko ma·song

How much is it?
གོང་ག་ཚོད་རེད། gong kâ·tsay ray

Where is ...?
... ག་བར་ཡོད་རེད། ... ka·bah yö·ray

UYGHUR

Uyghur is spoken all over Xīnjiāng. In China, Uyghur is written in Arabic script. The phrases in this chapter reflect the Kashgar dialect.

In our pronunciation guides, stressed syllables are indicated with italics. Most consonant sounds in Uyghur are the same as in English, though note that h is pronounced with a puff of air. The vowels are pronounced as follows: a as in 'hat', aa as the 'a' in 'father', ee as in 'sleep' (produced back in the throat), o as in 'go', ö as the 'e' in 'her' (pronounced with rounded lips), u as in 'put', and ü as the 'i' in 'bit' (with the lips rounded and pushed forward). Stressed syllables are in italics.

Basics

Hello.	ئەسسالامۇ	as·saa·laa·mu
	ئەلەيكوم.	a·lay·kom
Goodbye.	خەير·خوش.	hayr·hosh
Excuse me.	كۆرۈوچەكگە	ka·chü·rüng ga
	قانداق	kaan·daak
	باردۇ؟	baar·i·du
Sorry.	كۆرۈوچەك.	ka·chü·rüng
Yes.	ھەئە.	ee·a·a
No.	ياق.	yaak
Please.	مەھرەھەممەھت.	ma·ree·am·mat
Thank you.	رەخمەت سىزگە.	rah·mat siz·ga

How are you?

قانداق	kaan·daak
ئەھۋالىڭىز؟	a·ee·vaa·li·ngiz

Fine. And you?

ياخشى، سىزچۇ؟	yaah·shi siz·chu

What's your name?

سىزنىڭ	siz·ning
ئىسمىڭىز نىمە؟	is·mi·ngiz ni·ma

My name is ...

مىنىڭ ئىسمىم ...	mi·ning is·mim ...

Do you speak English?

سىز ئىنگگىلىزچە	siz ing·gi·lis·ka
بىلەمسىز؟	bi·lam·siz

I don't understand.

چۈشەنمىدىم.	man chu·shan·mi·dim

How much is it?

قانچە پۇل؟	kaan·cha pool

Where is ...?

... نەدە؟	... na·da

MONGOLIAN

Mongolian has an estimated 10 million speakers. The standard Mongolian in the Inner Mongolia Autonomous Region of China is based on the Chahar dialect and written using a cursive script in vertical lines (ie from top to bottom), read from left to right. So if you want to ask a local to read the script in this section, just turn the book 90 degrees clockwise. Our coloured pronunciation guides, however, should simply be read the same way you read English.

Most consonant sounds in Mongolian are the same as in English, though note that r in Mongolian is a hard, trilled sound, kh is a throaty sound like the 'ch' in the Scottish *loch*, and z is pronounced as the 'ds' in 'lads'. As for the vowels, ē is pronounced as in 'there', ô as in 'alone', ö as 'e' with rounded lips, öö as a slightly longer ö, u as in 'cut' and ü as in 'good'.

Stressed syllables are in italics.

Basics

Hello.		sēn bēn nô
Goodbye.		ba·yur·tē
Excuse me./Sorry.		ôch·lē·rē
Yes.		teem
No.		oo·gway
Thank you.		ba·yur·laa

How are you?

sēn bēn nô

Fine. And you?

sēn sēn
sēn nô

What's your name?

tan·nē al·dur

My name is ...

min·nee nur ...

Do you speak English?

ta ang·gul hul
mu·tun nô

I don't understand.

bee oil·og·sun·gway

How much is it?

hut·tee jôs vē

Where's ...?

... haa bēkh vē

GLOSSARY

apsara – Buddhist celestial being

arhat – Buddhist, especially a monk, who has achieved enlightenment and passes to nirvana at death

běi – north; the other points of the compass are *dōng* (east), *nán* (south) and *xī* (west)

biānjiè – border

biéshù – villa

bīnguǎn – hotel

bìxì – mythical tortoiselike dragon

Bodhisattva – one who is worthy of nirvana and remains on earth to help others attain enlightenment

Bon – pre-Buddhist indigenous faith of Tibet

bówùguǎn – museum

CAAC – Civil Aviation Administration of China

cadre – Chinese government bureaucrat

cāntīng – restaurant

cǎoyuán – grasslands

CCP – Chinese Communist Party

chau – land mass

chéngshì – city

chí – lake, pool

chop – carved name seal that acts as a signature

chörten – Tibetan *stupa*

CITS – China International Travel Service

cūn – village

dàdào – boulevard

dàfàndiàn – large hotel

dàjiē – avenue

dàjiǔdiàn – large hotel

dǎo – island

dàpùbù – large waterfall

dàqiáo – large bridge

dàshà – hotel, building

dàxué – university

déhuà – white-glazed porcelain

dìtiě – subway

dōng – east; the other points of the compass are *běi* (north), *nán* (south) and *xī* (west)

dòng – cave

dòngwùyuán – zoo

fàndiàn – hotel, restaurant

fēng – peak

fēngjǐngqū – scenic area

gé – pavilion, temple

gompa – monastery

gōng – palace

gōngyuán – park

gōu – gorge, valley

guān – pass

gùjū – house, home, residence

hǎi – sea

hǎitān – beach

Hakka – Chinese ethnic group

Han – China's main ethnic group

hé – river

hú – lake

huáqiáo – overseas Chinese

Hui – ethnic Chinese Muslims

huǒchēzhàn – train station

huǒshān – volcano

hútòng – a narrow alleyway

jiāng – river

jiǎo – unit of *renminbi*; 10 jiǎo equals 1 *yuán*

jiàotáng – church

jīchǎng – airport

jiē – street

jié – festival

jīn – unit of weight; 1 *jīn* equals 600g

jīngjù – Beijing opera

jìniànbēi – memorial

jìniànguǎn – memorial hall

jiǔdiàn – hotel

jū – residence, home

junk – originally referred to Chinese fishing and war vessels with square sails; now applies to various types of boating craft

kang – raised sleeping platform

KCR – Kowloon–Canton Railway

kora – pilgrim circuit

Kuomintang – Chiang Kaishek's Nationalist Party; now one of Taiwan's major political parties

lama – a Buddhist priest of the Tantric or Lamaist school; a title bestowed on monks of particularly high spiritual attainment

lǐlòng – Shànghǎi alleyway

lín – forest

líng – tomb

lìshǐ – history

lóu – tower

LRT – Light Rail Transit

lù – road

lǚguǎn – guesthouse

luóhàn – Buddhist, especially a monk, who has achieved enlightenment and passes to nirvana at death; see also *arhat*

mahjong – popular Chinese game for four people; played with engraved tiles

mǎtou – dock

mén – gate

ménpiào – entrance ticket

Miao – ethnic group living in Guìzhōu

miào – temple

MTR – Mass Transit Railway

mù – tomb

nán – south; the other points of the compass are *běi* (north), *dōng* (east) and *xī* (west)

páilou – decorative archway

pinyin – the official system for transliterating Chinese script into roman characters

PLA – People's Liberation Army

Politburo – the 25-member supreme policy-making authority of the Chinese Communist Party

PRC – People's Republic of China

PSB – Public Security Bureau; the arm of the police force set up to deal with foreigners

pùbù – waterfall

qì – life force

qiáo – bridge

qìchēzhàn – bus station

rénmín – people, people's

renminbi – literally 'people's money'; the formal name for the currency of China, the basic unit of which is the *yuán*; shortened to RMB

sampan – small motorised launch

sānlún mótuōchē – motor tricycle

sānlúnchē – pedal-powered tricycle

SAR – Special Administrative Region

sēnlín – forest

shān – mountain

shāngdiàn – shop, store

shěng – province, provincial

shì – city

shí – rock

shìchǎng – market

shíkū – grotto

shíkùmén – literally 'stone-gate house'; type of 19th-century Shànghǎi residence

shòupiàochù – ticket office

shuǐkù – reservoir

sì – temple, monastery

sìhéyuàn – traditional courtyard house

stupa – usually used as reliquaries for the cremated remains of important *lamas*

tǎ – pagoda

thangka – Tibetan sacred art

tíng – pavilion

wān – bay

wǎngbā – internet café

wēnquán – hot springs

xī – west; the other points of the compass are *dōng* (east), *běi* (north) and *nán* (south)

xī – small stream, brook

xiá – gorge

xiàn – county

xuěshān – snow mountain

yá – cliff

yán – rock or crag

yóujú – post office

yuán – basic unit of *renminbi*

yuán – garden

zhào – lamasery

zhāodàisuǒ – guesthouse

zhíwùyuán – botanic gardens

zhōng – middle

Zhōngguó – China

zìrán bǎohùqù – nature reserve

Behind the Scenes

SEND US YOUR FEEDBACK

We love to hear from travellers – your comments keep us on our toes and help make our books better. Our well-travelled team reads every word on what you loved or loathed about this book. Although we cannot reply individually to your submissions, we always guarantee that your feedback goes straight to the appropriate authors, in time for the next edition. Each person who sends us information is thanked in the next edition – the most useful submissions are rewarded with a selection of digital PDF chapters.

Visit **lonelyplanet.com/contact** to submit your updates and suggestions or to ask for help. Our award-winning website also features inspirational travel stories, news and discussions.

Note: We may edit, reproduce and incorporate your comments in Lonely Planet products such as guidebooks, websites and digital products, so let us know if you don't want your comments reproduced or your name acknowledged. For a copy of our privacy policy visit lonelyplanet.com/privacy.

OUR READERS

Many thanks to the travellers who used the last edition and wrote to us with helpful hints, useful advice and interesting anecdotes:
Adrian Fawcett, Aitor Saenz, Amy Hendricks, Ana Castillo García, Ana Paula Zarpellon Derboven, Andrew Bain, Antonia Viazis, Bernhard Bouzek, Callum Berryman, Dan Stevens, Danny Verheij, Dieter Suter, Elena Bernardis, Federico Ferrari, Francisco Sevillano, Gabriel Budel, Gary Chow, Giulia Trabacchin, Inge Haby, Inge Koolstra, Jedidiah Carosaari, Jennifer Freeman, Jirina and Zdenek Slanina, Johannes Kneitz, Jonathan Schwab, Julie Woods, Kai-Kai Toh, Katharin Tai, Liao Fangxu, Lim Zi Xiang, Lise and Brecht, Luc Lebon, Maarten Senepart, Mandy Yang, Marente Vlekke and Micha Beekman, Martien Oosterveld, Martin De Paepe, Matt Gasnier, Matthew Green, Maximus Sandler, Michal Rudziecki, Mike Holmes, Carolina Hoyl, Nicolas Verhaeghe, Philip Duval, Rasmus Graucob, Reece Worsfold, Reuven Amitai, Rick Driessen, Rod Johnson, Roland Kurmann, Roman Flatscher, Rosemary Hopcroft, Sander Leemans, Santi Espinal, Saskia Westenberg, Scott Edwards, Sheila Miller, Shohei Takashiro, Simon Krenger, Whitney Callaghan, Will Goddard, William Koh, Yijie Hou, Yuzhou Wu and Luc Lebon.

WRITER THANKS

Damian Harper

Thanks and appreciation to everyone who helped along the way, with special gratitude to Tenzin Dolma (Kristel Ouwehand), Tashi Phuntsok, Ben Cubbage, Cheng Peng, Cheng Bing, Yin Chunye, Brice, Losang, Tsebtrim, Joanne, Sally, Jingjing, Wangden, Youyou, Qiaolei, Stanley, Patrick, Chen Hui, Father Peter, Tim, Emma and Daisy.

Jade Bremner

Xièxiè to Shanghai experts Casey Hall, Jenny Walters and Cristina Ng for their on-the-ground insider tips. Thanks to Joanna Walton for getting me my first job in this tremendous city more than a decade ago, and thanks to the Xujiahui crew and That's Shanghai team for making me fall in love with the place (plus instigating much mischief around town). Last but not least, thanks to my wonderful partner who kept our beautiful baby sleeping through the night so I could write this guide.

Stuart Butler

First and foremost I must thank my wife, Heather, and children, Jake and Grace, for their patience while I ogled pandas and trekked through remote Tibetan valleys while working on this project. In Sichuan I owe a huge debt of thanks to Gonkho of Mystic Tibet tours for all that he did and also to Namchen for showing me all the secrets of Chengdu. Thank you also to Jamin York of Himalaya Journey for the introductions and to Dawa Drolma from Khyenle.

Kate Chapman

Extremely big thanks go to Megan Eaves, for giving me a shot at writing (it's not an easy job!); to my mentor Rebecca Milner; all the supportive folks in Melbourne; Claire-who-is-learning-French and all the kind people who generously shared their time and knowledge with me while I was on the road. Final thanks go to my awesome partner for sharing the journey.

Piera Chen

Special thanks to Alvin Tse for his assistance. Gratitude also goes to Sze Pang-cheung and Clio for their love and support.

Trent Holden

First up a massive thanks to the good people from Guangxi who assisted me along the journey – offering both insightful tips and generosity with their time in answering my many questions. Also a shout out to my fellow writers, team of editors, cartographers and designers who all worked so hard to put this book together. Finally lots of love to my family and friends, particularly my beautiful fiancée, Kate.

Tess Humphrys

Thanks to Cat and Aoi for the in-China support and help, including morale-boosting chats when the road got lonely. To Jolien who ensured my WeChat wallet never ran dry and to Louisa – a constant source of information and assistance in Guizhou. Thank you to the hotel staff in Hainan who gave me a birthday to remember. And finally, my eternal gratitude to Megan for setting me on this journey and to Scott for always being there.

Stephen Lioy

So many thanks: Megan Eaves, for the trust on all these projects as well as the craft-beer meetups across Eurasia. Yereth of GoKunming, for being an excellent resource and a great guy. Jamin of Himalaya Journey, for always being full of knowledge and ready to help out whenever asked. Payton, patient while I finished this in Greece. Gulmira and Gerda, for putting up with massive absences and still coming to meet me.

Vesna Maric

Great thanks to Megan Eaves who commissioned the project and to Jade Bremner for tips and help. Thank you to Ruoqiong Zhang, for her help and company, and to Wei for showing me around some amazing eating spots.

Daniel McCrohan

A long overdue thank you to all the fabulously obliging people who work on help desks at bus stations across China; we couldn't do our job without you! And heartfelt apologies to the hundreds of hotel staff I've lied to over the years, pretending that I intended to stay at your hotels, when really I just wanted to be shown round. Massive thanks to Matt O'Brien and Chenchen for their wonderful hospitality, and to my family in Tianjin for all their love and support.

Thomas O'Malley

Xiè xiè to all my wise and wonderful Beijing peeps. Thanks to Joel Shuchat for sharing your knowledge so freely; to Lars Ulrik Thom for unbuckling Beijing's history. Thanks to Sarah Keenleyside for your venue insights, to Xi Xueqing for your film assistance, to Eric Abrahamson for your literature smarts, to William Lindsay, Paul French, Dominic Johnson-Hill, Jerimiah Jenne, Hayden Opie, Philipp Greffer, et al. Heartfelt personal shout-outs to Harold, Hubert, Yangji, Gu Yue, Liz, Carl and Beijing notables present and past. And most of all, to Ophelia (+ Almond).

Tom Spurling

Feichang xiexie to Oliver, my Sinophile sidekick who made this Dongbei adventure all the more memorable. It was a privilege to visit this strange and vital part of the world with you. Thanks to Lucy and Poppy for encouraging us to go. Thanks to the editors and writers for their support and guidance. And thank you to the typical Chinese punter who smiled and laughed and kept a couple of wayward travellers out of trouble.

Phillip Tang

感谢你 Megan Eaves for your guidance over the years and for just being a good human to talk to. Lalo (José Eduardo García Sánchez) *te debo 'la gran millonada' por tu sanidad virtual*. Thanks Wang Yu for Jinhua, Kai for yumcha and coconut in Guangzhou. *Gracias a* Ismael for misty temples in Hangzhou. Seth Glossop: Xiamen, Gulang Yu and Quanzhou wouldn't be the same without dolls in caves, weary wedding couples and hard hat man following us.

ACKNOWLEDGEMENTS

Climate map data adapted from Peel MC, Finlayson BL & McMahon TA (2007) 'Updated World Map of the Köppen-Geiger Climate Classification', *Hydrology and Earth System Sciences*, 11, 1633–44.

Cover photograph: Jiayuguan Fort, Great Wall, Blaine Harrington III/Alamy Stock Photo©

Illustrations: pp72-3 and pp290-1 by Michael Weldon.

THIS BOOK

This 16th edition of Lonely Planet's *China* guidebook was researched and written by Damian Harper, Jade Bremner, Stuart Butler, Kate Chapman, Piera Chen, Megan Eaves, Daisy Harper, Trent Holden, Tess Humphrys, Stephen Lioy, Vesna Maric, Tom Masters, Bradley Mayhew, Daniel McCrohan, Thomas O'Malley, Lorna Parkes, Christopher Pitts, Tom Spurling and Phillip Tang. This guidebook was produced by the following:

Destination Editor
Megan Eaves

Senior Product Editors
Dan Bolger, Kate Chapman, Anne Mason, Kathryn Rowan

Regional Senior Cartographer Julie Sheridan

Product Editors Paul Harding, Amy Lynch,

Book Designers Gwen Cotter, Mazzy Prinsep

Assisting Editors Peter Cruttenden, Andrea Dobbin, Bailey Freeman, Emma Gibbs, Gabrielle Innes, Anita Isalska, Kate Kiely, Ali Lemer, Lauren O'Connell, Monique Perrin, Sarah Stewart, Saralinda Turner, Simon Williamson

Assisting Cartographers
Julie Dodkins, Michael Garrett, Rachel Imeson

Assisting Book Designer
Lauren Egan

Cover Researcher Brendan Dempsey-Spencer

Thanks to Fergal Condon, Victoria Harrison, Karen Henderson, Charlotte Orr, Doug Rimington, Claire Rourke, Gabrielle Stefanos, Sam Wheeler, Amanda Williamson, Guan Yuanyuan

Index

Map Legend

Sights

- Beach
- Bird Sanctuary
- Buddhist
- Castle/Palace
- Christian
- Confucian
- Hindu
- Islamic
- Jain
- Jewish
- Monument
- Museum/Gallery/Historic Building
- Ruin
- Shinto
- Sikh
- Taoist
- Winery/Vineyard
- Zoo/Wildlife Sanctuary
- Other Sight

Activities, Courses & Tours

- Bodysurfing
- Diving
- Canoeing/Kayaking
- Course/Tour
- Sento Hot Baths/Onsen
- Skiing
- Snorkelling
- Surfing
- Swimming/Pool
- Walking
- Windsurfing
- Other Activity

Sleeping

- Sleeping
- Camping
- Hut/Shelter

Eating

- Eating

Drinking & Nightlife

- Drinking & Nightlife
- Cafe

Entertainment

- Entertainment

Shopping

- Shopping

Information

- Bank
- Embassy/Consulate
- Hospital/Medical
- Internet
- Police
- Post Office
- Telephone
- Toilet
- Tourist Information
- Other Information

Geographic

- Beach
- Gate
- Hut/Shelter
- Lighthouse
- Lookout
- Mountain/Volcano
- Oasis
- Park
- Pass
- Picnic Area
- Waterfall

Population

- Capital (National)
- Capital (State/Province)
- City/Large Town
- Town/Village

Transport

- Airport
- Border crossing
- Bus
- Cable car/Funicular
- Cycling
- Ferry
- Metro/MRT/MTR station
- Monorail
- Parking
- Petrol station
- Skytrain/Subway station
- Taxi
- Train station/Railway
- Tram
- Underground station
- Other Transport

Routes

- Tollway
- Freeway
- Primary
- Secondary
- Tertiary
- Lane
- Unsealed road
- Road under construction
- Plaza/Mall
- Steps
- Tunnel
- Pedestrian overpass
- Walking Tour
- Walking Tour detour
- Path/Walking Trail

Boundaries

- International
- State/Province
- Disputed
- Regional/Suburb
- Marine Park
- Cliff
- Wall

Hydrography

- River, Creek
- Intermittent River
- Canal
- Water
- Dry/Salt/Intermittent Lake
- Reef

Areas

- Airport/Runway
- Beach/Desert
- Cemetery (Christian)
- Cemetery (Other)
- Glacier
- Mudflat
- Park/Forest
- Sight (Building)
- Sportsground
- Swamp/Mangrove

Note: Not all symbols displayed above appear on the maps in this book

Vesna Maric
Shanghai
Vesna has been a Lonely Planet writer for nearly two decades, covering places as far and wide as Bolivia, Algeria, Sicily, Cyprus, Barcelona, London and Croatia, among others. Her latest work has been updating guidebooks to Shanghai, Florida, Greece and North Macedonia.

Daniel McCrohan
Shandong, Tianjin & Hebei, Jiangxi
Daniel is a British travel writer who specialises in China and has worked on more than 40 guidebooks on destinations across the globe. He lived in Beijing for more than a decade, during which time he developed a penchant for eating raw garlic with noodles, learned to speak Chinese with a Beijing drawl, and built up his own fleet of cycle rickshaws, much to the amusement of most of his neighbours. This is Daniel's fifth stint on the China guide. He has also co-written Lonely Planet guides to Beijing, Shanghai, Chengdu, Tibet, India, Bangladesh, Singapore and Mongolia. He tweets @danielmccrohan..

Thomas O'Malley
Beijing, Hong Kong, The Great Wall
A British writer based in Beijing, Tom is a world-leading connoisseur of hutong dives, hangovers and donkey meat sandwiches. He has contributed stories to everyone from the BBC to *Playboy*, and reviews hotels for the *Telegraph*. Tom likes the Great Wall, train travel, heritage buildings, beer and mutton. Follow him by walking behind at a distance. Or at www.tomfreelance.com.

Lorna Parkes
Hong Kong
Londoner by birth, Melburnian by palate and ex-Lonely Planet staffer in both cities, Lorna has contributed to numerous Lonely Planet books and magazines. She's discovered she writes best on planes, and is most content when researching food and booze. Wineries and the tropics (not at the same time!) are her go-to happy places, but Yorkshire will always be special to her. Follow her @Lorna_Explorer..

Christopher Pitts
Hubei, Hunan, Chongqing, Cruising the Yangzi
Born in the year of the Tiger, Chris's first expedition in life ended in failure when he tried to dig from Pennsylvania to China at the age of six. Hardened by reality but still infinitely curious about the other side of the world, he went on to study Chinese in university, living for several years in Kunming, Taiwan and Shanghai. A chance encounter in an elevator led to a Paris relocation, where he lived for over a decade before the lure of Colorado's sunny skies and outdoor adventure proved too great to resist.

Tom Spurling
Jilin, Liaoning, Heilongjiang
Tom has contributed to 10 guides for Lonely Planet, including titles on India, Central America, Japan, South Africa, Australia and Turkey. He currently lives in Perth with his wife and two little kids. There he teaches English at a posh boys school and wields a Master of International Education Policy. When on the road he is the scraggy loner in the room next door mumbling about that secondhand book shop around the corner.

Phillip Tang
Guangdong, Fujian, Zhejiang
Phillip grew up on a typically Australian diet of pho and fish'n'chips before moving to Mexico City. A degree in Chinese- and Latin-American cultures launched him into travel and then writing about it for Lonely Planet's *Canada*, *China*, *Japan*, *Korea*, *Mexico*, *Peru* and *Vietnam* guides. Writing at hellophillip.com, photos @mrtangtangtang, and tweets @philliptang.

Contributing Writers
Bradley Mayhew
Tibet

Tom Masters
Xinjiang

Piera Chen
Hong Kong, Macau, Shanxi, Ningxia

Piera is a travel writer who divides her time among Hong Kong (hometown), Taiwan and Vancouver when not on the road. She has authored over a dozen travel guides and contributed to as many travel-related titles. Piera has a BA in literature from Pomona College. Her early life was peppered with trips to Taiwan and China to visit relatives, and then to Southeast Asia where her father was working. But it was during her first trip to Europe that dawn broke. She remembers fresh off a flight, looking around her in Rome, thinking, 'I want to be doing this everyday.' And she has. Since then Piera has been to Europe, the Americas and all over Asia – solo in the past, and more recently with her young daughter in tow.

Megan Eaves
Xinjiang

Megan is a writer, Asia expert and formerly served as Lonely Planet's North and Central Asia Destination Editor. Her writing has appeared in Lonely Planet's guidebooks to China, Tibet and South Korea. Having lived everywhere from her home state of New Mexico to eastern China and Prague, she's now based in London, where she gives guided beer tours and nature excursions in between travel writing and researching gigs, and acting as a consultant. If lost, she is likely to be found stargazing in a remote desert or scarfing down dumplings on a plastic stool.

Daisy Harper
Anhui, Shaanxi

Daisy grew up in the old town of Qingdao on the Shandong coast before studying English at uni in Beijing. She moved to England in the mid-1990s and quickly developed an affection for fish and chips, *Friends* and southeast London. Daisy has also lived in Hong Kong and Singapore, but her roots are in China and she returns often in search of the finest dumplings money can buy and to explore the endless corners of her vast homeland. Her home is in Ewell, Surrey, on the leafy outskirts of the Big Smoke.

Trent Holden
Guangxi

A Geelong-based writer, located just outside Melbourne, Trent has worked for Lonely Planet since 2005. He's covered 30 plus guidebooks across Asia, Africa and Australia. With a penchant for megacities, Trent's in his element when assigned to cover a nation's capital – the more chaotic the better – to unearth cool bars, art, street food and underground subculture. On the flipside he also writes books to idyllic tropical islands across Asia, in between going on safari to national parks in Africa and the subcontinent. When not travelling, Trent works as a freelance editor, reviewer and spends all his money catching live gigs. You can catch him on Twitter @hombreholden.

Tess Humphrys
Hainan, Guizhou

Tess was born in Madrid and raised in the United Kingdom. After six years of living in China she is now back where it all began, in España. She travelled extensively while she was in China and she was a regular contributor of articles to LP.com as well as the Suzhou, Hangzhou and Nanjing 'local', working to keep LP information about the cities as up-to-date as possible. That was all good preparation for her first-ever guidebook update – working on China 2019, covering Guizhou and Hainan provinces. She's determined to tell the world how amazing China is for travelling. In between evangelising about China, she is reacquainting herself with her first love travel destination – the country of her birth.

Stephen Lioy
Yunnan, Tibet

Stephen Lioy is a photographer, writer, hiker, and travel blogger based in Central Asia. A "once in a lifetime" Eurotrip and post-university move to China set the stage for what would eventually become a semi-nomadic lifestyle based on sharing his experiences with would-be travellers and helping provide that initial push out of comfort zones and into all that the planet has to offer. Follow Stephen's travels at www.monkboughtlunch.com or see his photography at www.stephenlioy.com.

OUR STORY

A beat-up old car, a few dollars in the pocket and a sense of adventure. In 1972 that's all Tony and Maureen Wheeler needed for the trip of a lifetime – across Europe and Asia overland to Australia. It took several months, and at the end – broke but inspired – they sat at their kitchen table writing and stapling together their first travel guide, *Across Asia on the Cheap*. Within a week they'd sold 1500 copies. Lonely Planet was born.

Today, Lonely Planet has offices in Tennessee, Dublin, Beijing and Delhi, with a network of over 2000 contributors in every corner of the globe. We share Tony's belief that 'a great guidebook should do three things: inform, educate and amuse'.

OUR WRITERS

Damian Harper
Gansu, Qinghai, Inner Mongolia

Born off the Strand within earshot of Bow Bells (favourable wind permitting), Damian grew up in Notting Hill way before it was discovered by Hollywood. A one-time Shakespeare and Company bookseller and radio presenter, Damian has been authoring guidebooks for Lonely Planet since the late 1990s. He lives in South London with his wife and two kids, and frequently returns to China (his second home). Damian also wrote the Plan Your Trip, Understand and Survival chapters.

Jade Bremner
Shanghai

Jade has been a journalist for more than 15 years. She has lived in and reported on four different regions. It's no coincidence many of her favourite places have some of the best waves in the world. Jade has edited travel magazines and sections for *Time Out* and *Radio Times* and has contributed to the *Times*, CNN and the *Independent*. She feels privileged to share tales from this wonderful planet we call home and is always looking for the next adventure. @jadebremner.

Stuart Butler
Sichuan

Stuart has been writing for Lonely Planet for a decade and during this time he's come eye to eye with gorillas in the Congolese jungles, met a man with horns on his head who could lie in fire, huffed and puffed over snowbound Himalayan mountain passes, interviewed a king who could turn into a tree, and had his fortune told by a parrot. Oh, and he's met more than his fair share of self-proclaimed Gods. When not on the road for Lonely Planet he lives on the beautiful beaches of Southwest France with his wife and two young children. His website is www.stuartbutlerjournalist.com..

Kate Chapman
Jiangsu, Henan

A former senior editor at Lonely Planet, Kate loves coming back to China and is especially keen on Sichuan food, train travel, hiking and yak jerky. Kate has briefly lived in Beijing, Jerusalem and Berlin but you'll most likely find her at home in Melbourne, craving Chinese food or plotting the next home brew project with her partner.

Published by Lonely Planet Global Limited
CRN 554153
16th edition – Dec 2021
ISBN 978 1 78701 677 4
© Lonely Planet 2021   Photographs © as indicated 2021
10 9 8 7 6 5 4 3 2 1
Printed in Singapore